Hoover's Handbook of American Business

1992

Edited by Gary Hoover, Alta Campbell, and Patrick J. Spain

The
Reference
Press, Inc.

Copyright © 1991 by The Reference Press, Inc. All rights reserved. No part of this book may be reproduced or transmitted in any form or by any means, electronic or mechanical, including by photocopying, recording, or using any information storage and retrieval system, without permission in writing from The Reference Press, Inc., except that brief passages may be quoted by a reviewer in a magazine, newspaper, or broadcast review.

10 9 8 7 6 5 4 3 2 1

Publisher Cataloging-In-Publication Data

Hoover's Handbook of American Business 1992. Edited by Gary Hoover,
Alta Campbell, and Patrick J. Spain

   Includes indexes.
   1. Business enterprises — Directories. 2. Corporations — Directories.
HF3010   338.7

*Hoover's Handbook*s are available on-line on Mead Data Central, Inc.'s LEXIS/NEXIS service and in Sony Data Discman Electronic Book format.

ISBN 1-878753-01-0
ISSN 1055-7202

This book was produced by The Reference Press on Apple Macintosh computers using Aldus Corporation's PageMaker 4.01 software and Adobe System, Inc.'s fonts from the Clearface and Futura families. Graphs were created using DeltaGraph, a product of DeltaPoint, Inc. Cover design is by Hixo, Inc., of Austin, Texas. Electronic prepress was done by The Courier Connection at Westford, Massachusetts, and the book was printed by Courier Corporation at Kendallville, Indiana. Text paper is 60# Windsor offset (manufactured by Domtar) and cover paper is 10 point, coated one side, film laminated.

This book is distributed to the North American book trade exclusively by

PUBLISHERS GROUP WEST

4065 Hollis, Emeryville, California 94608 510-658-3453

*Hoover's Handbook*s are available at special discounts for bulk purchases for sales promotions,
premiums, fund-raising, or educational use. Special editions or book excerpts can also be created to
specification. For details, contact Patrick Spain at **The Reference Press, Inc.**, 6448 Highway 290 East, Suite E-104,
Austin, Texas 78723. Phone: 512-454-7778 Fax: 512-454-9401

Contents

Companies Profiled

H&R Block, Inc.	289	Mayo Foundation	364	Pitney Bowes Inc.	439
HAL, Inc.	290	Maytag Corporation	365	PNC Financial Corp	440
Halliburton Company	291	McCaw Cellular Communications, Inc.	366	Polaroid Corporation	441
Hallmark Cards, Inc.	292	McDermott International, Inc.	367	PPG Industries, Inc.	442
Harley-Davidson, Inc.	293	McDonald's Corporation	368	Premark International, Inc.	443
Harris Corporation	294	McDonnell Douglas Corporation	369	The Price Company	444
Hartmarx Corporation	295	McGraw-Hill, Inc.	370	Price Waterhouse	445
Harvard University	296	MCI Communications Corporation	371	Prime Computer, Inc.	446
Hasbro, Inc.	297	McKesson Corporation	372	Primerica Corporation	447
The Hearst Corporation	298	McKinsey & Co.	373	The Procter & Gamble Company	448
H. J. Heinz Company	299	The Mead Corporation	374	The Prudential Insurance Co. of America	449
Helmsley Enterprises Inc.	300	Mellon Bank Corporation	375	Public Service Enterprise Group Inc.	450
The Henley Group, Inc.	301	Melville Corporation	376	Publix Super Markets, Inc.	451
Hercules Inc.	302	Mercantile Stores Company, Inc.	377	The Quaker Oats Company	452
Hershey Foods Corporation	303	Merck & Co., Inc.	378	Ralston Purina Company	453
The Hertz Corporation	304	Merrill Lynch & Co., Inc.	379	Raytheon Company	454
Hewlett-Packard Company	305	Metromedia Company	380	The Reader's Digest Association, Inc.	455
Hilton Hotels Corporation	306	Metropolitan Life Insurance Company	381	Reebok International Ltd.	456
The Home Depot, Inc.	307	Microsoft Corporation	382	Reliance Electric Company	457
Honeywell Inc.	308	Midway Airlines, Inc.	383	Republican Party	458
Hospital Corporation of America	309	Milliken & Co., Inc.	384	Reynolds Metals Company	459
Household International, Inc.	310	Minnesota Mining and Manufacturing Co.	385	Riklis Family Corporation	460
Humana Inc.	311	Mobil Corporation	386	Rio Grande Industries, Inc.	461
Hyatt Corporation	312	Monsanto Company	387	Rite Aid Corporation	462
Ingersoll-Rand Company	313	Montgomery Ward Holding Corp.	388	RJR Nabisco, Inc.	463
Inland Steel Industries, Inc.	314	J.P. Morgan & Co. Inc.	389	Roadway Services, Inc.	464
Intel Corporation	315	Morgan Stanley Group Inc.	390	The Rockefeller Foundation	465
INTERCO Inc.	316	Morton International, Inc.	391	Rockwell International Corporation	466
Intergraph Corporation	317	Motorola, Inc.	392	Roman Catholic Church (US)	467
International Business Machines Corp.	318	National Geographic Society	393	Rotary International	468
International Flavors & Fragrances Inc.	319	National Medical Enterprises, Inc.	394	Rubbermaid Inc.	469
International Paper Company	320	National Organization for Women, Inc.	395	Ryder System, Inc.	470
ITT Corporation	321	National Park Service	396	Safeway Inc.	471
Jack Eckerd Corporation	322	National Semiconductor Corporation	397	Salomon Inc	472
James River Corporation	323	Navistar International Corporation	398	Santa Fe Pacific Corporation	473
John Hancock Mutual Life Insurance Co.	324	NCNB Corporation	399	Sara Lee Corporation	474
Johnson & Johnson	325	NCR Corporation	400	SCEcorp	475
S.C. Johnson & Son, Inc.	326	New York City Transit Authority	401	Schering-Plough Corporation	476
Johnson Controls, Inc.	327	New York Life Insurance Company	402	Schlumberger NV	477
Johnson Publishing Company, Inc.	328	New York Stock Exchange, Inc.	403	SCI Systems, Inc.	478
JWP Inc.	329	The New York Times Company	404	Scott Paper Company	479
Kellogg Company	330	NIKE, Inc.	405	The E.W. Scripps Company	480
Kemper Corporation	331	Nordstrom, Inc.	406	Seagate Technology, Inc.	481
Kimberly-Clark Corporation	332	Norfolk Southern Corporation	407	Sears, Roebuck & Co.	482
King Ranch, Inc.	333	Northrop Corporation	408	Security Pacific Corporation	483
Kmart Corporation	334	Northwestern Mutual	409	Service Merchandise Company, Inc.	484
Knight-Ridder, Inc.	335	Novell, Inc.	410	Sharper Image Corporation	485
Koch Industries, Inc.	336	NWA Inc.	411	The Sherwin-Williams Company	486
Kohlberg Kravis Roberts & Co.	337	NYNEX Corporation	412	Skidmore, Owings & Merrill	487
KPMG	338	Occidental Petroleum Corporation	413	Snap-on Tools Corporation	488
The Kroger Co.	339	Office Depot, Inc.	414	The Southern Company	489
L.A. Gear, Inc.	340	Ogden Corporation	415	The Southland Corporation	490
Levi Strauss Associates Inc.	341	The Ohio State University	416	Southwest Airlines Co.	491
The Limited, Inc.	342	Oracle Systems Corporation	417	Southwestern Bell Corporation	492
Litton Industries, Inc.	343	Oryx Energy Company	418	Springs Industries, Inc.	493
Liz Claiborne, Inc.	344	Outboard Marine Corporation	419	Square D Company	494
Lockheed Corporation	345	Owens-Corning Fiberglas Corporation	420	Stanford University	495
Loews Corporation	346	Owens-Illinois, Inc.	421	The Stanley Works	496
Longs Drug Stores Corporation	347	PACCAR Inc.	422	State Farm	497
Lotus Development Corporation	348	Pacific Enterprises	423	The Stop & Shop Companies, Inc.	498
Lowe's Companies, Inc.	349	Pacific Gas and Electric Company	424	Storage Technology Corporation	499
The LTV Corporation	350	Pacific Telesis Group	425	Stroh Companies Inc.	500
MacAndrews & Forbes Holdings Inc.	351	Paine Webber Group Inc.	426	Sun Company, Inc.	501
R. H. Macy & Co., Inc.	352	Pan Am Corporation	427	Sun Microsystems, Inc.	502
Manufacturers Hanover Corporation	353	Panhandle Eastern Corporation	428	SunTrust Banks, Inc.	503
Manville Corporation	354	Paramount Communications Inc.	429	Super Valu Stores, Inc.	504
Marriott Corporation	355	J. C. Penney Company, Inc.	430	Supermarkets General Holdings Corp.	505
Mars, Inc.	356	Pennzoil Company	431	Syntex Corporation	506
Marsh & McLennan Companies, Inc.	357	PepsiCo, Inc.	432	SYSCO Corporation	507
Martin Marietta Corporation	358	Peter Kiewit Sons' Inc.	433	Tandem Computers Inc.	508
Masco Corporation	359	Pfizer Inc.	434	Tandy Corporation	509
Massachusetts Mutual Life Insurance Co.	360	Phelps Dodge Corporation	435	Teachers Insurance	510
Mattel, Inc.	361	Philip Morris Companies, Inc.	436	Teamsters	511
The May Department Stores Company	362	Phillips Petroleum Company	437	Tele-Communications, Inc.	512
Mayflower Group, Inc.	363	Pinnacle West Capital Corporation	438	Teledyne, Inc.	513

ACKNOWLEDGMENTS

Publisher and Senior Editor: Gary Hoover

Editor-in-Chief: Alta Campbell

Senior Editor: Patrick J. Spain   **Senior Writer and Editor:** Alan Chai

Production Director: Holly Whitten   **Desktop Publishing and Art Director:** Marcia Jenkins

Senior Writers: Cliff Avery, Dale Ann Bean Underwood, John Mark Haney

Office Manager: Tammy Fisher

Director of Special Markets and Editor: Lawrence A. Hagemann

Editorial Board: Ray Bard, Steve Mathews

Contributing Writers
Scott A. Blech, Jim Busby, Mike Clark, Cynthia G. Dooley, Tom Linehan, Lisa C. Norman, Barbara M. Spain

Financial Editors
Maryellen Maurer, Wendy Weigant

Senior Editors
Jeff Morris, Deborah Stratton

Contributing Editors
Jill Mason, Allan L. Reagan

Senior Proofreaders and Fact Checkers
Peter A. Balderas, Britton E. Jackson, Jeanne Minnich, Jim Patterson

Proofreaders and Fact Checkers
Kathryn A. Baker, Sara Barker, Paul Beutelman, Kim L. Emery, K. C. Francis, Linda Gittins, Diane Lee, Liz Taute

Senior Desktop Publishers
Scott T. Allen, Kristin M. Jackson, Mercedes Newman

Desktop Publishers
Rita DeBellis, Monica Shomos

Indexers
Alana Cash, Linda Webster

Marketing Assistant
Lisa Treviño

Other Contributors
Andrea Avery

DEDICATION

We dedicate this book to the librarians of America and to all those volunteers and contributors who support them. While many of us make donations to trendier and more visible causes, or assume that government agencies are supporting our libraries, libraries are buying fewer books and are open fewer hours. Access to books and magazines for everyone is one of the great cornerstones of our democratic tradition; we must together ensure that this stone does not erode.

The Reference Press Mission Statement

1. To produce business and economic reference books of the highest quality, accuracy, and readability
2. To make those books widely available through mass distribution at an affordable price
3. To make sure people are aware of our product through publicity, advertising, and shelf exposure
4. To create interesting, worthwhile jobs
5. To reward our employees creatively and fairly, without prejudice
6. To allow our key people to participate in the fruits of their labor through an incentive stock option program
7. To hold to the highest ethical business standards, including complete honesty and openness in all our dealings, erring on the side of generosity when in doubt
8. To enhance the wealth of our suppliers, from distributors and printers to landlords
9. To continually expand our product line
10. To enhance the wealth of our shareholders by creating an enterprise of lasting value

ABOUT *HOOVER'S HANDBOOK* OF AMERICAN BUSINESS

Last year we at The Reference Press broke new ground with the first annual publication of *Hoover's Handbook*. This book, the first widely distributed, reasonably priced, easy-to-use annual reference book on major companies, was an immediate success. We have received many letters and cards asking us to expand our coverage of business, in particular non-US companies. In response we have moved the foreign companies to a separate volume, *Hoover's Handbook of World Business*. That book, which also contains information about the most important nations of the world, can be found at your bookstore or ordered by using the postcards at the back of this book or by calling 800-486-8666.

The book you hold in your hands is therefore limited to companies based in the United States. The only companies included in both books are the Big Six accounting firms, whose global presence is pervasive. We have used this opportunity to expand our coverage of American companies, especially the young growth companies. Additions this year include Amgen, Blockbuster, Borland, and about 30 others. We plan to continue adding companies and invite your recommendations. Of course, every one-page profile has been completely revised to bring the events and statistics up-to-date.

We believe that anyone who buys from, sells to, invests in, lends to, competes with, interviews with, or works for big companies should know about those companies. Taken together, the two *Hoover's Handbook*s represent the most complete source of basic corporate information readily available to the general public. We have gone to great effort and expense to provide you with a concise, accurate, and timely guide to business. The key items in each corporate profile are highlighted inside the front cover of the book.

This book consists of 4 components:

1. The first section, "Getting the Most Out of *Hoover's Handbook of American Business*," reviews the basic concepts of business, from principles of strategy to measures of performance. We also describe the contents of each profile in the book and recommend other sources. The section concludes with our pick of the top ten American companies for the 1990s.

2. Next we have included "A List-Lover's Compendium," which contains lists of the largest companies in the book and lists of the largest companies in various industries. This section begins with a tabulation of our Hoover's Ratings of each company in the book, a new feature this year.

3. The third and most important part of the book contains the profiles themselves — 500 one-page descriptions of major enterprises, arranged alphabetically.

4. The book concludes with three indexes: (1) the companies organized by industry groupings, (2) the companies organized by headquarters location, and (3) the main index of the book, containing the names of all brands, companies, people, and places mentioned in the profiles.

As always, we hope you find our books useful; we invite your comments: by phone, by fax, or on the postcards at the back of the book.

The Editors
Austin, Texas
October 15, 1991

Getting the Most Out of

Hoover's Handbook of
American Business

Because of the pervasive nature of business corporations, we at The Reference Press believe we can all benefit from a better understanding of these giant enterprises. Certainly, if we are thinking about buying stock, we need to know what to look for, how to predict which businesses will be successful, and how to judge and measure the performance of a company. But it is becoming equally important to judge the performance of corporations as employers, suppliers, and customers. We can no longer assume that, just because a business is big, it is permanent, or that it is a secure place to work. Most of us were born into a world where "the Big Three" meant GM, Ford, and Chrysler; within 10 years, we may find that Asia and Europe each has one of "the Big Three," perhaps all three.

Thousands of business strategists, analysts, journalists, and managers spend their lifetimes trying to figure out what's important in business, what separates the winners from the losers. Thousands of books and articles have been written on topics from management methods to marketing tactics. While *Hoover's Handbook* does not pretend to be a textbook, we believe the book will be most useful if you have a basic grasp of the key issues in business.

In the following pages, we've tried to explain concisely and clearly some of these concepts.

- First, we address the big picture — the study of why businesses do the things they do. This approach is called strategic analysis or economic analysis.

- Second, we look at financial analysis — the study of the financial performance of businesses. This section also touches on significant concepts useful to investors.

- We then describe how to use each profile and its components.

- Next we include a brief section of recommendations for further reading.

- Finally, we conclude with our selection of the ten American companies best prepared to take advantage of the opportunities of the 1990s.

THE BIG PICTURE

ENTERPRISES

The 500 organizations profiled in this book are best described as enterprises. Some are large, with bold objectives: the best example is the United States of America. Most began with more humble goals. These enterprises deliver a variety of products and services, from ketchup to hammers, from PhD degrees to surgery. To illustrate the diversity of enterprises at work in the world around us, we have included public companies and private companies, and even several nonprofit and governmental entities.

Nevertheless, all can be called enterprises. Each began in the mind of one person or a small group of people. To have made it to the size and influence required to be included in this book, they must have enlisted more people over time. To one degree or another, these people must share the same underlying goals. For an enterprise, whether private or public, for profit or not, is simply a group of people who have joined together in pursuit of a common goal.

Business Enterprises

Most of the enterprises in this book are business enterprises. These differ primarily from nonbusiness organizations in the way they are financed. Whether General Motors or the AFL-CIO, enterprises need money. Governments usually get most of their funds from taxation. Universities and religious and service organizations generally rely on the charitable instincts of people who share their interests.

By definition, business enterprises are funded by private capital. These enterprises cannot rely on taxation or on charitable solicitation. Instead, they must find investors or lenders. The most fundamental source of financing for private enterprise is equity capital (selling stock), which is further described later in this section.

In order to persuade people or financial institutions to invest their savings in a business enterprise, that enterprise must offer the promise of a financial reward, or return. While this book is full of stories of successful enterprises, others here have not been good investments.

When industry began evolving from individual craftspeople and cottage industry, requiring larger groups of people to maximize the technology of the Industrial Revolution, business was usually financed by people who already had a great deal of capital: often those who had inherited land from their feudal ancestors.

As more and more individuals, such as small merchants and skilled craftspeople, began to prosper from this revolution, there was no way for them to readily participate in large business ventures, other than by working for a paycheck. This new middle class, with modest savings, could not become part owners of a major enterprise. While they were interested in participating in the profits of these enterprises, they could not afford to take the risks involved.

The most traditional forms of business enterprise are the sole proprietorship and the partnership. In a sole proprietorship, you put everything you own at risk. If your business goes broke or gets sued successfully, you can lose your house and all your other personal property. The same is true of partners in a general partnership. Even if you put up $5 and your partner $1,000,000, people owed money by the partnership can come after you for everything you've got. This high level of risk prevented small investors from sharing in the success of great enterprises.

"An enterprise, whether private or public, for profit or not, is simply a group of people who have joined together in pursuit of a common goal."

The Corporation

It seems a natural evolution that society figured out a way around this. The idea of incorporation is that a business enterprise is an entity unto itself, that the individuals putting up the money are not personally liable for all the debts and problems of the enterprise. If you buy stock in a corporation, your risk or liability is limited to the amount you invest. In the US, we use the term *corporation*; in France, the equivalent of "anonymous society" (SA); and in the United Kingdom, *public limited company* (PLC), stressing the limited-liability aspect of the corporate entity.

When the concept of the corporation was first invented, it was considered revolutionary. Even economist Adam Smith thought the concept was a fad that would not last, one of his few obvious errors of prediction. Today, the corporation is taken for granted. Many of us who work for corporations underestimate the power of this invention.

The concept of incorporation, in whatever language, has allowed millions of people to share in the fruits of enterprise, whether their own enterprise or that of others. The corporate form of business organization has allowed massive projects to be undertaken and new ideas to be tried — ideas that would never have seen the light of day were they dependent on taxes, charity, or the willingness of sole proprietors and partners to risk everything they had.

The business corporation pervades our lives. Most of us work for one, be it large or small. Virtually everything we consume comes from one. And whether we buy stocks or bonds directly, put our money into mutual funds or pension programs, or loan it to banks or life insurance companies, much of our savings ends up financing business corporations.

THE ROLE OF DEMAND

Any understanding of a company must first start with a basic grasp of the industry in which the company competes. And that industry perspective starts with the demand for the products or services produced by the industry. In looking at any company, 3 questions must precede all others:

1. How much of the product or service do people (or other companies) buy?

2. How much of it do they buy from the enterprise under consideration, compared to what they buy from competitors (what is their market share)?

3. How easily can customers substitute some other product?

All products, from diamonds to bread, have unique characteristics, but none is as important as these 3. All companies have their own attributes, as discussed in the following pages, but none is as critical as these 3.

The nature of the soap company, whose products almost everyone uses, is different from that of the jet engine maker who sells to a few. The maker of specialized orthopedic shoes looks at the world differently than the mass producer of sneakers; he or she faces a different world. If your company has a market share leader like Kodak film or Heinz ketchup, the challenges are vastly different from those for a new, young competitor. Most business enterprises have products that are well established as well as new, experimental products. The makers of slide rules found out the hard way that their product was replaceable when the more powerful but inexpensive pocket calculator came into being.

"The corporate form of business organization has allowed massive projects to be undertaken and new ideas to be tried — ideas that would never have seen the light of day were they dependent on taxes, charity, or the willingness of sole proprietors and partners to risk everything they had."

"At one time the telegraph and the telephone were competitors; railroads and airlines fought over passengers. In each case, correctly picking the survivor paid off for investors and employees alike."

What answers should we look for to these 3 questions? While each case is unique, a company is generally in pretty good shape if everybody uses lots of the product, doesn't buy it from anybody else, and can't substitute anything for it. Aside from government-endorsed monopolies like electric utilities, we can't think of any case in this book in which a company can respond to all 3 questions with such strong answers.

That is what makes business such a challenge for the people who manage it.

Changing Demand

Of equal importance to the 3 answers is the trend in the answers: in other words, for each question, is the answer this year the same as the answer last year? Is the answer getting better or worse? A lot better or a little better? A lot worse or a little worse? To understand the direction of change over time (better or worse) and the rate of change over time (a lot or a little), we can rephrase the 3 questions:

1. Are people buying more or less of the product or service each year?

2. Is this firm's market share rising or falling?

3. Are people more often substituting other products, or is the product becoming more entrenched?

The direction of change (up or down) is the starting point here. A company with rising demand for its products, such as one that makes VCRs, has a more promising future than the maker of black-and-white TV sets. The company with a rising market share (Toyota) is headed in a better direction than the firm that's losing share (General Motors). At one time the telegraph and the telephone were competitors; railroads and airlines fought over passengers. In each case, correctly picking the survivor paid off for investors and employees alike.

Any analysis of trends must also pay attention to the rate or relative size of change. For example, suppose your company shipped 9,000 items last year and 10,000 this year and crows about the increase of 1,000 to all within earshot. But are you listening to the competitor who went from 1,000 to 2,000 in the same period of time? Next year, will they just gain 1,000 again, or will they double again, to 4,000? Any analysis of change must focus on the percentage rate of change, which was 11% (increased by 1/9) for your firm but 100% (doubled) for your smaller competitor.

The Customer

Whether we look at the absolute level (how much) or the rate of change (what percent), understanding demand is the starting point for understanding any enterprise. For those charged with the task of managing an enterprise, this means that nothing is more important than understanding the customer and the customer's needs.

We believe that the managers of the successful enterprises in this book generally follow 3 simple rules with regard to their customers:

1. These managers put themselves in the shoes of their customers and follow The Golden Rule: they treat their customers the way they would like to be treated. They use, and believe in, their own products. When Lee Iacocca starts driving a Toyota, it's time to sell your Chrysler stock.

2. They go out of their way to know the characteristics of their customers. Where do they live? How old are they? How much money do they make? How much schooling do they have? Are they single or do they have families? If customers are individuals or families, the answers to these demographic questions are discovered by conducting market research (e.g., surveys) and by studying

the census. If customers are other businesses, many of the answers are in this book.

3. These managers do everything in their power to ensure that potential customers know that the company's products and services exist, and know where to find them.

Once we understand the demand for a company's products and whether the firm is gaining or losing market share (and at what rate), we can look at the other ways in which industries and companies differ.

COMPARING INDUSTRIES

Each industry has its own unique set of characteristics that go beyond basic demand and that affect every company in the industry.

Cyclicality Versus Stability

The home-building industry goes up and down with mortgage interest rates and other factors. Stockbrokers prosper in good markets and lose customers after crashes. On the other hand, the demand for toothpaste and shoes is pretty reliable. The cyclical company must be prepared for the natural cycles it will experience; Coke is more worried about market share and Pepsi than about year-to-year swings in total soft drink demand.

Business Products and Services Versus Consumer Products and Services

The skills required by Walt Disney are vastly different from those required by Caterpillar. Selling millions of $5 movie tickets or $30 videocassettes is a radically different proposition from selling bulldozers at $500,000 apiece. Cat requires fewer but longer sales calls; Disney announces its products with ads and opens the doors. Disney doesn't even know the names of all of its customers. Some companies with expertise in selling to businesses have tried and failed to sell to individual consumers, and vice versa.

Different Price Points

There is also a big difference between selling $10,000 cars and $50,000 cars and between selling $300 washing machines and rolls of toilet paper. Marketing skills demonstrated in one area may not be successful at different price points. Higher-priced items usually require more effort per sale on the part of both buyer and seller than small, inexpensive things.

Commodities Versus Differentiated Products

When you buy gasoline, you know pretty much what you're getting. Commodities are simple products, often made in huge quantities by many firms. Usually, the most important factor in picking whom you'll buy from is price. Texaco couldn't sell gas at $5 a gallon next door to a Shell station selling it for $.50. At least Texaco wouldn't sell much. However, determining the difference between Giorgio perfume and Obsession is much trickier. Individual emotions and tastes come into play. The two products do not appear the same to the consumer. Novels by James Michener are not exact substitutes for those of Sidney Sheldon. Most companies in this book try to differentiate their products from those of the competition; some are successful and some are not.

There are many other ways that industries differ; the 4 listed above are among the most common. There is nothing inherently

> *"The skills required by Walt Disney are vastly different from those required by Caterpillar. Selling millions of $5 movie tickets or $30 videocassettes is a radically different proposition from selling bulldozers at $500,000 apiece."*

good or bad about a cyclical industry or a commodity-producing company. But a company's odds of prospering are greatest if demand is stable and growing and if that company has successfully differentiated its products or services from those of the competition.

COMPARING COMPANIES

Within any industry, each company may take any number of approaches. Which approaches it takes are what managers are paid to decide. The individual characteristics of a company include attributes relating to strategy, financing, and managing.

Strategy

Every company has a strategy, whether expressed or not. Those firms with no apparent strategy can be considered to have haphazardness as a strategy. Companies can also have the same strategy year after year or change strategies periodically, sometimes falling into haphazard phases. Perhaps more than any other aspect of a company, strategy is a direct reflection of the views of the people at the top.

Consistency

In general, the most successful companies in this book are those that have kept a clear vision in place for many years. Southwest Airlines (20 years old) sticks to its original principles: low fares, no meals, and fast, friendly service. It reduces costs by flying only Boeing 737s.

At the same time, it is pointless to stick to strategies that time has passed by. When the railroads first lost their passenger business to airlines and then most of their small

freight business to truckers, they were forced to review their status. The successful ones have emerged as huge haulers of bulky commodities such as grain and coal and of heavy products like automobiles. Many of our older industries have had to develop creative strategies to adjust to changing times, new technologies, and foreign competition.

Diversification

Probably the single most common method of shifting strategy is to diversify. While diversification generally connotes moving into whole new fields of endeavor, it can also take 3 other forms:

1. **Geographical diversification**. One of the most fundamental forms of growth is to take a good idea to new territory. Holiday Inns started in Memphis and worked outward; Wal-Mart began in Arkansas and is still in only 35 states. Coca-Cola early in its history began peddling its product in Mexico and Canada and now sells worldwide.

2. **Horizontal diversification**. This term, from economics, means to diversify by buying competitors or similar companies in other locations. The giant trusts of the late 19th and early 20th centuries (for example, U.S. Steel) were formed by combining most of the major companies in an industry. Our largest trash collectors, Browning-Ferris and Waste Management, were originally formed by buying up local and regional mom-and-pop operations.

3. **Vertical diversification, more commonly referred to as vertical integration.** This means buying up your customers and/or your suppliers. At one time, Henry Ford's River Rouge plant in Detroit made its own steel and glass, and finished Fords rolled off the other end of the production line. Integrated oil companies are those with wells, refineries, and filling stations.

"Southwest Airlines (20 years old) sticks to its original principles: low fares, no meals, and fast, friendly service. It reduces costs by flying only Boeing 737s."

Geographical, horizontal, and vertical diversification are all well-established strategies for increasing the size and competitiveness of a company. In the 1960s and 1970s, more companies began to diversify into vastly different fields.

The term *conglomerate* came into use in the 1960s to describe firms that operated in several unrelated industries. Managers of these firms came to believe that they could manage anything, that the basics of running a steel mill were no different from those of running an airline. While managers undoubtedly will continue this debate, the companies in this book indicate that prosperity is easier to achieve when an enterprise is focused, or at least sticks to fields with something in common. While Sears retail stores seem different from Allstate car insurance, the company originally sold the insurance to its retail customers. Sears's later introduction of the Discover credit card was a natural outgrowth of its experiences with its own Sears credit operation.

This book contains only 21 enterprises that were so diversified that we could not assign them to some broad industry group. While almost all the firms have diversified to one degree or another, most have remained in fields that are in some way related, such as mass-marketed consumer products. Most of the diversified companies are in two or three industries. General Electric stands out as one company that is an industry leader in several businesses that are, at best, only vaguely related.

Innovation and Technology

Each company can also take any number of roads with regard to innovation. Fred Smith at Federal Express created a whole new industry. Some companies take a good idea and apply it in a different way: Home Depot is the application of the Toys "R" Us concept of giant, low-priced specialty stores to home-improvement retailing. Other companies are based on cloning: Amdahl

was founded to make copies of IBM mainframe computers for a lower price. Costco Wholesale applied the Price Company concept in another part of the US.

While successful innovators can reap substantial rewards, they also entail substantial risk. The first successful large computer was the UNIVAC, made by a predecessor of Unisys. A late entrant to the field, IBM, made more money from the idea. The large general merchandise discount store was created by small, entrepreneurial companies. But no one executed the idea as successfully as Kmart, until the even-later entry of Wal-Mart.

While innovation often comes from small, entrepreneurial enterprises, this is not always the case. Minnesota Mining and Manufacturing (3M) is an unusual company that seems to specialize in innovation, from Scotch tape to Post-it notes. This tradition continues even as 3M grows larger and larger.

Whether we look at technology in computers, in chicken growing, or in toy stores, the management of each company must decide whether it will be a leader or a follower, which technologies to bet on, and how much to bet.

This book includes successful companies that have taken many routes with regard to innovation. The one common denominator of the successful enterprises is that they make quality products, year after year after year.

Financing

Business corporations have a number of choices as to how they finance themselves. Their first choice is whether to sell shares of stock to raise money or to borrow the money. While all companies have stock, they can have no debt, some debt, or a great deal of debt. The companies in this book range from zero indebtedness to several billion dollars of debt. This debt can take many

"The companies in this book indicate that prosperity is easier to achieve when an enterprise is focused."

"Because these documents are so revealing, smart potential investors pore over prospectuses."

forms, including bank loans and direct loans from individual or corporate investors (e.g., bonds, debentures, commercial paper, mortgages). The heavy use of debt (called leverage) can increase the returns to shareholders but also entails substantial risk. The distinctions between debt and equity and the risks of leverage are further examined in the financial analysis section, starting on page 20.

Another decision is whether to operate as a public or a private company. Most corporations are private, also called privately held or closely held corporations. Most, but not all, of the biggest corporations are public companies, or publicly held.

Private companies do not sell stock to the general public; while they may have thousands of shareholders, most are owned primarily by family members, managers, or employees. You cannot call a stockbroker and buy or sell shares. It is harder to get your money out of an investment in a private company (an illiquid investment). Private companies cannot raise money as easily as public companies, since they do not have access to the public stock markets. On the other hand, private companies are not required by law to reveal information about themselves, and some are indeed very secretive. This book includes more than 50 private companies.

Public companies, since their stock is available to anyone who calls a stockbroker, are required by the Securities and Exchange Commission (SEC) to report their sales and profits quarterly and to produce a full report to shareholders annually. When you call a broker and buy or sell stock in a public company, the transaction is normally executed in a matter of minutes; therefore, common stocks of public companies are "very liquid." Stocks can be traded on the New York Stock Exchange (NYSE, or Big Board), the

American Stock Exchange, or the Over-the-Counter (OTC) market, the most important part of which is NASDAQ (National Association of Securities Dealers Automatic Quote system). Most of the largest US companies are listed on the NYSE.

Most companies begin life as private companies; when and if they decide to sell stock, they are said to "go public" through an Initial Public Offering (IPO). At that time the SEC requires that they publish a prospectus detailing virtually every aspect of their business and management. Because these documents are so revealing, smart potential investors pore over prospectuses.

Public companies can also "go private," a practice virtually unknown 15 years ago. This recent financing strategy most commonly occurs in the form of the leveraged buyout (LBO). In an LBO a small group of investors borrows enough money to buy all the stock in a company on the stock market. This investor group usually includes an investment firm specializing in LBOs (for example, Kohlberg Kravis Roberts). The group often includes the management of the company being bought out. LBOs require huge amounts of debt — up to billions of dollars. Often the debt is in the form of "junk bonds" sold directly to the public — a concept we will return to in the financial analysis section.

Because of the rise of LBOs, there are now several companies whose stock is privately held (by the investor group) but whose bonds (debt) are publicly held. Trans World Airlines (TWA) is a good example of this. While technically not publicly held, such companies are required by the SEC to release substantial information because the public can loan money to these enterprises (that is, buy bonds issued by the companies).

Management

Perhaps the most important differences among the companies in this book are their management styles. While strategies and financing methods reflect management, there are also more direct ways to compare managers.

One of the most common ways of dividing types of management is into centralized and decentralized management. The idea here is that, prior to Alfred P. Sloan's innovations at General Motors in the 1920s, most companies were run "from the top down," with all key decisions made by very few people at headquarters, often by one person. Sloan developed the idea of passing authority and responsibility "down the line." Heads of divisions and other operating units were considered closer to the customer and were entrusted with more power. Sloan's ideas were widely copied in organizations worldwide.

Today, the distinctions have become blurred: it is not uncommon for a company to have highly centralized financial controls, while production and other decisions are decentralized. Other companies change their approach periodically, and yet others give decentralization lip service without much reality behind it. Also, such questions of management structure are not readily answered by annual reports and other company literature; you really have to talk to the people who work in the organization.

Another difference among these companies is their management style, or corporate culture. It has become very stylish to talk about corporate culture. This very broad subject can cover everything from dress (blue jeans or pinstripes) to reward systems (based on seniority or contribution to sales and profits). An enterprise's culture is usually a direct reflection of the personalities of its leaders.

An aspect of management that is less discussed is the profession of the people at the top. While, as top executives, they are defined as "management," these people worked their way up through more specific fields: finance, marketing, engineering, law, operations, production, etc. Years ago, people were classified in broad groups like doctors, lawyers, and businessmen. But to call a printer or a broadcaster or a car maker a businessman or businesswoman is not very useful. These are very different professions.

Companies that really understand their own strengths often have clear ideas about what skills are most important at the top. Pharmaceutical maker Merck is run by a man with a PhD whose strength is research; Dow Jones is run by journalists; Disney is run by an entertainment professional; and Coke is run by a lifelong Coke marketer. We believe that much of the success of these companies flows from having the right type of people in the top jobs.

COMPLETING THE PICTURE

Before descending into the mathematical details of financial analysis, we want to discuss 2 additional viewpoints that are important to a broad understanding of business: the view that each enterprise evolves over time, and the view that enterprise is a human activity. While these 2 perspectives may seem obvious, it is not uncommon for analysts to financially analyze a company "six ways to Sunday" without having completed the big picture; these 2 brief sections put the final touches on that picture.

"Pharmaceutical maker Merck is run by a man with a PhD whose strength is research; Dow Jones is run by journalists; Disney is run by an entertainment professional; and Coke is run by a lifelong Coke marketer. We believe that much of the success of these companies flows from having the right type of people in the top jobs."

The Natural Evolution of Enterprises

As can be seen from the above comments, every enterprise is unique. And yet, they do share one process: like living organisms, they grow, evolve, and mature. Each enterprise begins as an idea, usually on the part of one person or a small group of people. This idea, or invention, can be a product or a way of doing things, from service to production. In order to succeed, it should represent a better or more efficient way; it should add value. This is often described as "finding a need and filling it."

Many of the companies in this book took roundabout routes to their "destinies" — Armstrong made bottle corks before floors; Cummins Engine was based on the tinkerings of a banker's chauffeur. Other creative products were discovered by accident. Once a company "hits stride," mass-producing a commercially viable product or service, early growth is usually rapid.

As an enterprise ages, this growth slows, eventually to very low growth (no higher than the growth of the overall economy). This fast growth–medium growth–slow growth cycle is called the S-curve, based on the shape shown here.

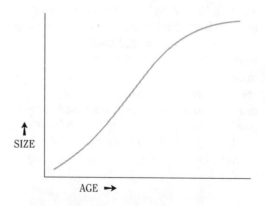

As companies evolve along this curve, they become more established, more structured, and usually more bureaucratic.

"Death comes to enterprises differently than it does to living organisms.... Companies with big bank accounts, many offices, and established reputations may rest on their laurels for many years before they are forced to admit that their time has come."

As they grow, they can become more focused on protecting their assets than on inventing new products and services. In this way they become vulnerable to the attacks of the next generation of entrepreneurs coming along, who have less to lose and more to gain through innovation.

While it has become all the vogue to praise the achievements of entrepreneurs, we often forget that managing a mature enterprise can be a very difficult challenge. At the same time that a company is at its wealthiest, with the largest number of jobs and lives depending on it, it is often also at its most vulnerable, and perhaps about to "die."

Death comes to enterprises differently than it does to living organisms. It often takes many years and is at first unrecognizable. Those closest to the company may refuse to face up to the realities. Companies with big bank accounts, many offices, and established reputations may rest on their laurels for many years before they are forced to admit that their time has come. Death, for a business enterprise, is more often a period of confusion, of selling and closing facilities, and perhaps of selling the whole company, rather than a sudden, single event. Even companies that have entered bankruptcy often re-emerge, usually in a much smaller form.

The large corporation, unlike a living organism, can be reborn. The S. S. Kresge company of 1960 was a tired chain of variety stores, 3rd in the industry after Woolworth and W. T. Grant. Sales and earnings were going nowhere. A manager named Harry Cunningham convinced top management to try a new concept: Kmart. Thirty years later, Grant is gone (fatal bankruptcy) and Woolworth is a fraction of the size of the renamed Kmart Corporation. Today, that enterprise must in turn react to relative newcomer Wal-Mart.

Sears, Roebuck was a mail-order giant selling to rural and small-town America.

If they'd stayed like that, they'd be gone today. As an encore they became a dominant retailer for America's suburbs. The icing on the cake was their successful entry into financial services, first by insuring cars. Today, Sears appears to be at another crossroads: their giant retail chain is losing market share to dozens of new competitors and struggling to find a role to play in the marketplace of the 1990s. In the last two years, Sears's retail operations have fallen from #1 in the world to the #3 position. Whether Sears will again revitalize itself is one of the many unfinished corporate life stories in this book.

No analysis of an enterprise is complete without a good grasp of whether that enterprise is a child, an adolescent, or in some later stage of life.

The Human Nature of Enterprise

It is easy to become overfocused on the strategies of businesses and on the ways we measure their performance. It is equally easy to forget that each enterprise is fundamentally a human endeavor. No computer can plan strategies, no computer can hire and fire people, and no computer can motivate people. Balance sheets and profit and loss statements do not tell the underlying story of the people in an organization. Yet, each organization really consists only of people and tools for people to use.

As a successful enterprise evolves, more people must be attracted to "the cause." In order to maintain leadership, the corporation must attract and keep talented people. These people must remain creative and responsive to their ever-changing environment.

Whether Sears survives is up to the people of Sears. Whether 3M continues to develop innovative products depends on 3M's people. Every enterprise in this book reflects the people of that enterprise: the people of the past, the present, and the future. ▲

"It is equally easy to forget that each enterprise is fundamentally a human endeavor. No computer can plan strategies, no computer can hire and fire people, and no computer can motivate people."

THE NUMBERS MADE SIMPLE

The preceding sections give us a grasp of a business — its industry, its strategies, its evolution, and its people. With this foundation in place, we can proceed to more detailed and quantitative financial analysis.

Organizations are expected to perform in a number of ways: serving customers well, creating jobs, providing secure jobs, etc. In general, the company that is performing well financially is better able to perform these other tasks well. The firm that is losing money or buried in debt is less likely to provide secure jobs or to serve customers well. Measures of financial performance are therefore key to anyone interested in the enterprise; they also tend to be more consistently applied and less subjective than most measures of product quality, job satisfaction, company reputation, etc.

If you are familiar with business accounting or have invested, you know there are a bewildering array of measures that can be used to judge the financial performance of companies. The most fundamental measure of any company's financial success, however, is return on investment (ROI).

RETURN ON INVESTMENT

"The most fundamental measure of any company's financial success... is return on investment (ROI)."

ROI is best understood if we remember that business corporations are financed by people's savings, whether those savings are invested directly by individuals or via institutions like banks, insurance companies, mutual funds, and pension funds. When you invest your savings, you should earn a return on them. The first question to ask is, "How much return?"

When you loan money to anyone, you first give up the use of the money. Even if you trust your neighbor a great deal and know that she's going to take the $1,000

you loan her for a year and put it in a safe deposit box, she should pay you interest. For the next year, you will not have the use of the money; should you have an emergency, you cannot get it back. Maybe at the end of the year you plan on buying a $1,000 stereo with it; in the meantime, you could buy the stereo now and enjoy a year's use of it. The value of the temporary sacrifice of cash is called the time value of money, and it is the first reason we need to get interest, or a return, on our money. The time value of money alone may justify only a very small rate of return — perhaps as low as 1% per year.

The next reason we need to earn a return on our money is inflation. While history has had several periods of deflation (declining prices), the economic boom times of the late 19th century and the 20th century have been characterized by inflation, usually in the 2–5% per year range. So the $1,000 stereo you want to buy may cost 5% more, or $1,050, a year from now. If you think inflation will be higher, you (as an investor or lender) need to ask for a higher rate of interest.

The next layer of determining a fair rate of return is the level of risk involved. Your neighbor may lose the $1,000 you loan her or not be able to pay the money back for other reasons. While we can get lulled into believing that big companies are all secure, cases such as W. T. Grant, Penn Central, Continental Illinois Bank, Pan Am, and Drexel Burnham Lambert teach us otherwise. Every company has some degree of risk.

In developing anticipated rates of return, we start with the "risk-free" interest rate, for which we use the rate of interest paid by the United States government for short-term loans like Treasury Bills (T-Bills). While the US government is not really risk-free, it is as close as we can come. If the government did collapse, we'd probably all have a lot more to worry about than getting our loans repaid. Normally, the rate of interest paid by the government is slightly above anticipated inflation — enough to also cover the time value of money. As of September 1991, T-Bills were paying about 5.2% a year in interest.

The "risk premium" — the amount of additional interest charged for riskier loans — varies with the risk. At the time that the government was paying 5.2%, General Motors Acceptance Corporation (GMAC), one of the biggest corporate borrowers, was paying about 5.3% when it borrowed from individual investors (through a security called commercial paper). Big corporations borrowing from banks or borrowing money for long time periods (bonds) were paying 8–9%. Start-up enterprises are much riskier than big, established ones, so the rates they pay must be higher to reflect the higher risk.

DEBT VERSUS EQUITY

Another fundamental concept in understanding corporate finance is that money can be invested in an enterprise in 2 different ways — by loaning money to a company (debt) or by buying part ownership in a company (equity). Bonds and debentures are debt; stocks represent equity. The fundamental differences between debt and equity are 3:

1. Debts are intended to be repaid. If you borrow $50,000, you are expected to repay the $50,000 principal, as well as interest on the loan. When a company sells you a $50,000 bond, it is under the same obligations. On the other hand, when you buy $50,000 worth of stock, whether from the company itself or from another

stockholder, the company does not plan ever to give you your $50,000 back. You can earn a return on stock only by selling it to someone else at a higher price or by receiving dividends from the company. Often, stockholders get both.

2. The interest payments on a debt are usually fixed and guaranteed. You know how much you'll receive and how often. Dividends on a stock, on the other hand, are strictly voluntary on the part of a company. The board of directors can reduce or delete them (or increase them) at any time. In reality a company that goes broke usually defaults on debt payments, but this occurs after they've stopped paying dividends on stock.

3. If a company is dissolved or liquidated, debt-holders (creditors) have higher priority than stockholders: the debt-holders get their money first. In a bankruptcy it is not unusual for debt-holders to get $.50 for every dollar owed them, while stockholders are wiped out. This is called "liquidation preference."

Taken together these different characteristics of debt and equity mean that equity bears more risk but can carry higher rewards. Let's say your neighbor has a great new invention and needs $10,000. You have the $10,000 to spare. He says you can loan it to him or buy half-interest in the invention. If the idea fails, you may get the loan back, but the half-interest becomes worthless. If, however, his idea becomes another Xerox or IBM, the loan will return only $10,000 plus interest — no more, no less. If you buy the half-interest, and the idea is a home run, there is no real limit on what your equity might be worth.

To use common business buzz words, debt has limited downside and limited upside. It does not share in the benefits of an enormously successful enterprise. On the other hand, equity has big downside and big upside — more to lose and more to gain.

"Money can be invested in an enterprise in 2 different ways — by loaning money to a company (debt) or by buying part ownership in a company (equity)."

FINANCIAL STATEMENTS

While most businesses pour forth a multitude of statements and reports, there are 2 that tell the financial story of an enterprise: the balance sheet and the profit and loss statement, or P&L. The balance sheet is simply a table of what a business owns and what it owes; it is calculated periodically (say monthly) and is a statement as of a certain time (e.g., midnight on December 31). The P&L, on the other hand, is a report that tells what came in and what went out and covers a time span (e.g., one minute after midnight on January 1 through midnight, January 31).

The easiest way to understand these is through an example. Perhaps the most basic business is the time-honored lemonade stand. Let's say Joey has $5 in savings from his allowance and wants to make some money for video games by running a lemonade stand one day. He borrows a pitcher from his mother but has to spend $2 on lemonade mix and $2 on paper cups. He plans to make change with the leftover $1. At the start of the day, his balance sheet is:

ASSETS	LIABILITIES
$1 Cash	$0 Debt
$2 Lemonade	
$2 Cups	**EQUITY**
	$5 Owner's Equity
$5 Total	$5 Total

Note that the total of the left side is $5, and the total of the right side is $5. A balance sheet must balance. Let's say Joey sells out of lemonade pretty fast — 20 cups at 50¢ each. His first-day P&L looks like this:

Lemonade sales	$10.00
Lemonade costs	− 2.00
Cup costs	− 2.00
Profit	$ 6.00

For this example we'll assume Joey evades his taxes. (We do not recommend you try this at home.) At the end of the day, Joey has a new balance sheet:

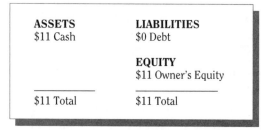

ASSETS	LIABILITIES
$11 Cash	$0 Debt
	EQUITY
	$11 Owner's Equity
$11 Total	$11 Total

The $11 cash represents his $1 change fund plus the $10 in sales he's taken in. Since Joey doesn't owe anybody anything, the $11 is all his — it is all equity. He can either pocket the money (pay himself a dividend) or leave it in the business (retained earnings) for future growth.

Joey is now so enthusiastic about more than doubling his money in one day that he gets more aggressive the second day. He borrows $15 from Mom, borrows 3 pitchers, and tells 3 kids they can have half of the sales if they run 3 lemonade stands for him. He starts day 2 with this balance sheet:

ASSETS	LIABILITIES
$10 Lemonade	$15 Borrowed from Mom
$10 Cups	
$ 6 Change	**EQUITY**
	$11 Owner's Equity
$26 Total	$26 Total

Joey has another bang-up day and sells all his lemonade; he even decides to pay Mom $1 in interest.

DAY 2 P&L	
Lemonade sales	$ 60
Commissions	− 30
Lemonade	− 10
Cups	− 10
Operating profit	10
Interest expense	− 1
Net profit	$ 9

Before Joey pays Mom her interest and principal, his balance sheet looks like this:

ASSETS	LIABILITIES
$36 Cash	$16 Owed to Mom
	EQUITY
	$20 Owner's Equity
$36 Total	$36 Total

Joey started the day with $6 in cash and added $60 in sales less $30 in commissions, ending up with $36. But he still owes Mom her $15 loan principal plus $1 in interest. After Joey pays Mom, the balance sheet looks like this:

ASSETS	LIABILITIES
$20 Cash	$0 Debt
	EQUITY
	$20 Owner's Equity
$20 Total	$20 Total

It is important to realize that the balance sheet and P&L are related: what happens to your P&L during a time period results in changes between your starting balance sheet and your ending balance sheet. Unless Joey takes out a dividend, his owner's equity is always the previous equity plus profits since then.

The left side (assets) of the balance sheet tells what the company owns — "current" assets such as cash, securities, inventories, and bills sent out but not yet paid (receivables) — as well as "fixed" assets like buildings, furniture, equipment, computers, etc. The right side of the balance sheet tells how the company is financed — how much is debt and how much is owner's equity. Debt is also broken into short-term (bills due, or payables, and loans due in the next year) and long-term (mortgages, bonds due over many years, etc.). The P&L tells whether the business is making money or not.

MEASURING RETURN ON INVESTMENT

The primary measures of return on investment are Return on Equity (ROE) and Return on Assets (ROA). ROE tells what kind of return Joey is getting on the money he has invested in the business — the return on his owner's equity. The first day, Joey put up $5 and made a profit of $6. This is an ROE of 120% (6/5). The second day, he had $11 of his money invested and made $9, for a return of 81% (9/11). For the real companies in this book, a return that is above interest rates (7–8% per year now) isn't too bad. An ROE of 15–20% is very good, and anything above that is exceptional.

Return on assets tells how a business is doing on the total amount invested — whether that investment be owner's equity or borrowed money (debt). The first day Joey made $6 on a total investment of $5 (all equity), so his ROA was the same 120% as his ROE. However, since he used debt the second day, the ROE and ROA numbers start to differ. Before paying his mother the $1 in interest, Joey made $10 the second day, but he had $26 at work to do it ($11 of his own equity and $15 borrowed from Mom). His ROA was only 38% (10/26), still a good return. As long as his ROA is above interest rates (here, he paid Mom $1 to borrow $15, a 7% rate), he can afford to borrow and put the money to work in the business. This is called "using leverage" — he is using other people's money to "leverage" his own money.

This is best illustrated if we greatly expand Joey's business with debt, as shown in the table on the next page.

"Return on assets tells how a business is doing on the total amount invested — whether that investment be owner's equity or borrowed money (debt)."

DAY 3

ASSETS	LIABILITIES
$1,000 Lemonade	$2,100 Loan from Neighbor
$1,000 Cups	
$ 120 Change fund	**EQUITY**
	$ 20 Owner's Equity
$2,120 Total	$2,120 Total

"Joey gained from 'the spread' — the difference between his profitability (ROA) and his cost of money (interest rate)."

Joey is now "highly leveraged" — 99% (2,100/2,120) of his financing is in the form of debt. Let's say the neighbor charges 10% interest for the use of the money for a day (generally called loansharking). Let's also say Joey can maintain his 38% return on assets. On $2,120 of total assets, Joey would make $806 (.38 x $2,120) before paying interest of $210 (.1 x $2,100). After interest Joey's profit would be $806 – $210 = $596, not a bad return on his $20 equity — in fact, a 2,980% return. If the lemonade stand business were really this profitable, Joey would probably have several competitors by now, unless he could get his dad, the mayor, to give him a monopoly.

As long as Joey's ROA is higher than his interest rate, he can afford to borrow money for the business. In the above example, a 38% ROA combined with an interest rate of only 10% to give Joey a phenomenal ROE of almost 3,000%. Joey gained from "the spread" — the difference between his profitability (ROA) and his cost of money (interest rate).

But leverage has its risks: say, instead of Joey making his 38% ROA on day 3 ($806 before interest), a storm comes up as soon as he starts selling lemonade. All the lemonade mix, paper cups, and money blow away. Joey is left only with $2,310 in debt and interest owed to his neighbor. If he had never gone into debt, Joey would just lose his $20 in equity. But, as things evolve, the neighbor threatens to break Dad's kneecaps, and Dad sells his golf cart to raise the $2,310 to pay off the debt. Joey decides to pursue another career.

OTHER MEASURES OF FINANCIAL PERFORMANCE

Return on Assets and Return on Equity can be used to measure any business. They can be used to compare a steel factory to an airline to a movie company, because they look only at how profitably a business puts money to work. There are many other widely used measures of business performance, but these are only meaningful when comparing similar businesses. A common example is Return on Sales (ROS), or profit as a percent of sales. This statistic would be a high percent (say 30%) for a good computer maker, but only 2% for a good supermarket. The reason is that the computer maker requires a lot more investment in assets (equipment, labs) than does a supermarket to generate the same sales. The supermarket, with a lower ROS, can have just as high an ROA, which is what really matters:

	COMPUTER MAKER	SUPERMARKET
Sales	$1,000,000	$ 1,000,000
Profits	$ 300,000	$ 20,000
ROS	30%	2%
Assets	$1,500,000	$ 100,000
ROA	20%	20%

However, within an industry or similar industries, measures like ROS can be very helpful. Other common measures include:

Current Ratio. This is the ratio of current assets to current liabilities. If a company had to pay off all its bills tomorrow, would it have enough cash and things quickly convertible into cash (such as inventory) to cover the bills? If a company's current ratio is 1, it has just enough money. If the ratio is 2, it has twice what it needs; if the ratio is .5, it has only half of what it needs. Again, this measure is most useful in comparing similar companies.

Debt Ratio. This is the percent of long-term financing that is provided by debt. Ignoring short-term liabilities, such as bills due, the ratio focuses on long-term debt (bonds, debentures, mortgages) and equity. If a company is financed by $75,000 in debt and $25,000 in equity, the debt ratio is 75% ($75,000/($75,000 + $25,000)). This is a basic measure of how leveraged a business is. A predictable business like an electric utility can generally afford to carry more debt than a risky or fluctuating enterprise. On the other hand, even 50% debt might be too much for a movie company that has hits one year and flops the next. Before his business's collapse, Joey's debt ratio was 99%.

Productivity Measures. There are many ways to measure how productive an enterprise is, such as sales per employee, factory production as a percent of capacity, etc. These are most useful when comparing similar companies.

In addition to general measures like these, each industry has its own measures of performance — for example, load factor for airlines (how many of the seats are taken), occupancy for hotels (how many of the rooms are taken), ratings for TV networks (what share of viewers are tuned in), and sales per square foot for retail stores.

TREND ANALYSIS

An important part of evaluating any business is looking at the trends. Which of these companies would you rather invest in or go to work for?

ROE BY YEAR					
	1986	1987	1988	1989	1990
Joey's Hot Dogs	50%	40%	30%	20%	15%
Alice's Restaurant	11%	12%	13%	14%	15%

Whether one is studying market share, productivity measures, profitability measures, ROA, or ROE, the direction and rate of change is very important. The stock market also usually puts a premium on consistency and predictability, because there is less risk. In the group below, the market would probably value the 3rd company the most highly, even though all 3 made the same amount of profit in the latest year.

Profits by Year						
	1985	1986	1987	1988	1989	1990
1st Co.	$100	$200	$ 50	$400	$ 0	$200
2nd Co.	$450	$400	$350	$300	$250	$200
3rd Co.	$ 25	$ 50	$ 75	$100	$150	$200

MEASURES OF SIZE

The companies in this book make it clear that big is not necessarily successful. While all of these companies must have had some good years to get to be big, big companies can go broke just like small companies. Nevertheless, in understanding the companies, it is good to know who is big and who is less big, especially when comparing companies in one industry.

By far the most universal measure of size is sales (or revenues). The total amount of money an enterprise receives from its customers is the basis for most popular rankings, like the *Fortune* 500. When we say, "It's a $3 billion company," we usually mean sales.

In some industries, like banking and insurance, it has become common practice to rank firms by assets — the total amount of money and property under the company's control.

Another interesting measure, increasingly used and the basis of the *Business*

"There are many ways to measure how productive an enterprise is, such as sales per employee, factory production as a percent of capacity, etc. These are most useful when comparing similar companies."

Week rankings included in this book, is market value or market capitalization. This is what it would cost you to buy up all the stock in a company. At this writing, the most valuable companies in the United States are IBM and Exxon.

Note that market value is often much greater than the owners' (or stockholders') equity: this is because the value of a company's reputation and the talents of its people are not fully reflected on the balance sheet. The stock market makes its own decision as to the value of Coke's internationally known trademark and values the company well above what the balance sheet shows. This valuation results from thousands of individual and corporate investors buying stock when they think it is cheap (undervalued) and selling stock when they think it is expensive (overvalued).

Less frequently, companies are ranked by other measures such as number of employees and dollars of profits. We have included several size-based lists immediately preceding the profiles in this book.

FOUR KEY CONCEPTS FOR INVESTORS

When potential investors consider buying stock in a company, they first evaluate the balance sheet and P&L, with a clear focus on trends. In addition to the basics discussed in the preceding paragraphs, investors also need to understand 4 key concepts, examined below.

Shares of Stock

A company can have any number of shares of stock that it wants to have, from one share to billions. The number of shares is simply how many pieces the ownership is

divided into. A stock split occurs when a company divides its stock into smaller pieces. Companies do this to make their price per share less, so more people can afford the shares.

3-for-1 Split		
	Before Split	**After Split**
Number of Shares	1,000,000	3,000,000
Equity	$30,000,000	$30,000,000
Equity Per Share	$30	$10
Annual Profits		
(Earnings)	$3,000,000	$3,000,000
Earnings Per Share	$3.00	$1.00
Stock Price	$60.00	$20.00
Market Value	$60,000,000	$60,000,000
Shares I Own	100	300

Many of the concepts discussed above have parallel terms on a per-share basis, because that is the way most investors look at their investments:

	Total Company	**Per-Share Basis**
Owners' Equity	Shareholders' Equity	Book Value
Profits	Net Income or Earnings	Earnings Per Share (EPS)
Market Value	Market Value or Market Capitalization	Stock Price

Earnings Per Share (EPS), or the profits of the company divided by the number of shares, is perhaps the single most important term for investors in stock.

EPS Growth Rate

This is the compound annual growth rate for the Earnings Per Share of a company. Sometimes companies sell more stock over time to raise more money for the business without going into too much debt. In these cases the number of shares increases over time and the old owners are "diluted" (their percentage of ownership of the business

> *"The stock market makes its own decision as to the value of Coke's internationally known trademark and values the company well above what the balance sheet shows."*

shrinks). Their best measure of profits is to look at their EPS. Here is a company that sold more stock but still did a good job for investors, old and new:

	1988	1989	1990
Total Net Income	$100,000	$200,000	$300,000
Shares of Stock	100,000	150,000	200,000
EPS	$1.00	$1.33	$1.50
Growth in EPS		33%	13%

Depending on whether we are in boom times or a recession, our US economy usually grows between 0% and 5% a year, excluding inflation. With inflation included the growth runs 3% to 10% a year. All business combined will grow at about that rate. If you see a business in this book with compound sales or profit growth rates of 15% or 20%, that is pretty impressive, especially if they've done it year in and year out for 5, 10, or even 25 years.

Price/Earnings Ratio (P/E)

This is how many times profits a stock sells for. Since the owner of a share of stock is entitled to all the future profits on his or her share, stocks sell for several times last year's profits per share (EPS). A company earning $1 per share per year is worth some multiple (P/E) of that $1. The statistic is quoted daily in the *Wall Street Journal* for each stock. Look at these three companies:

Annual Earnings Per Share				
	1987	1988	1989	1990
Company A	$1.00	$1.33	$1.50	$1.75
Company B	$1.00	$1.01	$1.02	$1.03
Company C	$.25	$2.50	$.65	$2.00

Company A would be considered a growth company, with consistent double-digit (over 10% a year) growth. This stock is probably worth the most money of the three. It might sell as high as 20 times earnings (P/E = 20). If so, the stock price would be $35 (20 x $1.75).

Company B is not even growing as fast as the economy as a whole. Unless it pays a big dividend (see below), its stock is not worth much, maybe 6 times earnings. This P/E of 6 would result in the stock selling for just over $6.

Company C is a cyclical company and probably the hardest to analyze. The stock market's valuation of the stock would depend on whether next year is going to be one of its good years or one of its bad years. The stock could sell for $5, or it could sell for $20 or more.

It is important to remember that there are many people trying to predict the stock market and the performance of each company. To these people, the future is much more important than the past. If Company A announces a 5-year delay in introducing its new computer, the stock will probably plummet. Past growth rates and financial performance are used more as a tool to guess the future than anything else.

To the experienced investor, the absolute price of a stock doesn't tell you whether the stock is really cheap or expensive. The P/E ratio tells you whether it is cheap or expensive.

	Cheap Stock	Expensive Stock
Last Year EPS	$ 5.00	$ .50
This Year EPS	$ 5.10	$ 1.00
Projected EPS	$ 5.20	$ 2.00
Current Stock Price	$51.00	$20.00
P/E on This Year EPS	10	20

In the example above, two stocks (in two companies) are compared. While an inexperienced investor might think the stock priced at $51 per share is "more expensive" than the one selling for $20, this is misleading. Although the $51 stock sells for about 2-½ times the price of the $20 stock, the first company's profits (This Year EPS) are over 5 times as much ($5.10 versus $1.00).

Another way of looking at this: which is a "cheap" car — a Yugo for $12,000 or a new

"To the experienced investor, the absolute price of a stock doesn't tell you whether the stock is really cheap or expensive. The P/E ratio tells you whether it is cheap or expensive."

Mercedes for $15,000? The P/E ratio is the best measure of value. In general, the higher the growth rate of a company's EPS, the higher the P/E should be, because the P/E reflects the stock market's beliefs about the future EPS of the company. As a result, a high P/E stock may still be a better long-term investment than a low P/E stock.

Dividends

Like Joey in the example above, every company has 2 options as to what to do with its profits:

1. Put them back into the business as retained earnings.

2. Pay them out to shareholders as dividends. Most young, growing companies keep most or all of their profits, believing that their stockholders will benefit most if the company plows the money into new stores or new plants or whatever. To justify retaining most earnings, a company should have a high return on investment (higher than investors could earn on their own). On the other hand, more mature or stable enterprises may have trouble finding good investments for all the profits they are generating. These companies are more likely to pay out their earnings as dividends. If management believes investors are relying on dividends, they may continue paying dividends even when the company is losing money, at least as long as they can.

Young investors tend to invest for long-term price increases in stocks and are more interested in growth than dividends. Most older investors are ready to take some of their savings out now for living expenses, and many rely on these dividends.

The 2 key measures of dividends are:

Payout. The percentage of profits that a company pays out as dividends. For many growth companies, this is 0%. Some older companies pay out 70% or more.

Yield. This is the dividend per share divided by the current market price of the share. If you pay $20 for a stock that is paying a $1 annual dividend, you get a 5% (1/20) yield. For dividend-conscious investors, this is a key number. Also of interest is the trend in dividends over time. Has the dividend been steady over the years? Has it gone up? How fast?

This section has discussed the basic concepts of financial analysis and investing. In the next section, we touch on some of the tricky things in financial analysis that can be confusing or misleading.

SOME POTHOLES ON THE ROAD TO UNDERSTANDING

Corporate Names

Companies are free to change their names at will. Often they are reflecting a new direction in their business or dropping a name they perceive to be dated. A corporate name change often does not represent any real change in the business — it has the same history, the same officers, etc.

Mergers and Acquisitions

Companies also often buy and sell one another, or acquire and divest. As strategies shift, management decides to be or not to be in any given business. While acquisitions are often referred to as mergers in the press, we have usually used that word only in the case of the true merger of equals or near-equals. In reality, one of the two companies almost always ends up "on top" — with its management in charge of the combined enterprise and with its shareholders owning most of the company. We therefore prefer

"Young investors tend to invest for long-term price increases in stocks and are more interested in growth than dividends."

the terms *acquisition* or *purchase*, rather than *merger*.

When a company sells (divests) a business, they can give its shares out to their own shareholders, or they can sell it to another corporation or to management and employees. They can also sell the business directly to the public. These divestitures are sometimes called spinoffs.

Divisions and Subsidiaries

These are legal terms for parts of a company; divisions are normally 100% owned by the parent company, whereas subsidiaries are technically separate corporations and can be partially owned. When the ownership is partial, we have pointed that out. We have treated companies as subsidiaries only when the parent company owns 51% or more.

Leveraged Buyouts (LBOs)

One way in which investors, employees, or managers can acquire a company is by a leveraged buyout. In effect, the investors put up a very small down payment (equity capital) and borrow a large amount of money to pay for the purchase. Often the borrowed money is in the form of low-quality bonds (junk bonds) sold to individual or corporate investors. These bonds are considered low quality because they carry higher risk of default than normal corporate bonds and because they often pay off after other bonds in the event the company goes broke. Because of this higher risk, junk bonds normally pay a high yield (interest rate).

In order to complete an LBO, investors and lenders must be convinced that the business will generate enough cash to meet the interest and principal obligations. While there have been a number of cases in which the investors were wrong (for example, Campeau), there are others in which the forecasts of cash flow have been right — so far.

Accounting

In order to make it easy to compare different companies, the accounting industry and government regulators have developed a set of accounting standards for use by corporations. These standards have evolved over time and become fairly complex. Things to observe:

Accounting Results vs. Real, or Economic, Results

Most people do not realize that a company's profit and loss statement can be showing profits when the company is running out of cash. This can happen for several reasons: for example, the company is investing heavily in inventories or plants, or the company cannot collect money owed to it. When companies go broke, their financial statements occasionally look fine right up until the day they go under.

The study of accounting is a field unto itself, with hundreds of textbooks available. For the purposes of this book, it is probably sufficient to realize that a company's financial statements are really just best estimates of how the company is doing. In strong, well-financed, growing companies, these estimating procedures are accurate enough, and they're certainly the best we can do. Accounting data are presented in the How Much section of each profile in this book.

Timing

The accrual system of accounting adopted by the corporate world revolves around a concept called "matching." This just means that expenses on the P&L must be shown at the same time that relevant revenues are booked. For example, if a retailer bought inventory in 1989 but did not sell it until 1990, the company could not show the expense for the inventory until 1990, even though cash had been spent the prior year.

"A company's financial statements are really just best estimates of how the company is doing."

"Each company may have its year start and end on any date; this is called its fiscal year."

Another example: your company buys a $500,000 computer that it will use for 5 years to help in the business. Under matching rules, the P&L may show an expense of $100,000 a year for each of the next 5 years, even though the company had to pay for the computer up front. There are numerous other cases like this, generally grouped under the headings "depreciation" and "amortization."

Calendars

Each company may have its year start and end on any date; this is called its fiscal year. While many companies have a fiscal year that matches the calendar year (ends on December 31), many have years that end on May 31, June 30, etc. Companies usually pick a fiscal year that reflects the seasonal nature of their business. For example, most big retailers have a fiscal year that ends on the Saturday closest to January 31. This is because they want to have a month to clean up their business after the big Christmas season (markdowns, inventory-taking, etc.), and they want to have a fiscal year that ties to their traditional Sunday-through-Saturday weekly cycle.

Investors usually look at stock price ranges on a calendar-year basis, even though the company's sales and earnings are reported on a fiscal-year basis.

Tax vs. Book

Companies also maintain one set of books for the IRS and one set for accounting and shareholder reporting purposes. This is all very legal — in fact, sometimes the accountants require a company to report data one way to shareholders, while the IRS has contradictory rules. The amount shown in financial statements for "taxes" is rarely the amount of the check the company wrote to the IRS. Big companies have numerous people devoted to the task of minimizing the taxes they pay, while staying within the law. Since tax rules change every year, and since many tax rules are subject to various interpretations, tax accounting and tax law have become big businesses in themselves.

Changing Rules

Just as tax rules are always changing, the accounting-standards setters also change their rules frequently. Sometimes a company will restate prior years' results, so that the "last year" column on a financial statement does not match the "this year" column in last year's reports. Companies can also do unusual things with businesses they are getting out of (discontinued operations) and unusual one-time expenses or profits (extraordinary items). For this book we have tried our best to adjust the information for each company so that the data is comparable. We have generally shown historical data as originally reported, not as restated. In some cases our numbers will not match those you find in other sources, including company annual reports, because of these factors. ▲

USING THE PROFILES

Selection of the Companies Profiled

The 500 enterprises profiled here include 24 governmental and nonprofit entities. These were included because they are economic entities that employ people, that have global economic importance, and that often compete with public companies. Their histories and dynamics can be as fascinating as those of profit-making corporations.

The 476 other enterprises include some mutual and co-operative organizations (owned by customers) and a number of large private corporations (like Hallmark, Mars, and Cargill). However, well over 400 of the organizations profiled are publicly held corporations.

In selecting these companies, our foremost question was, "What companies will our readers be most interested in?" Our goal was to answer as many questions as we could in one book, in effect trying to anticipate your curiosity. The approach resulted in 4 general criteria for selecting companies for inclusion in the book:

1. **Size.** The 200–300 largest American companies, measured by sales and by number of employees, are included in the book. In general, they are the ones you will have heard of and the ones you would be asking about.

2. **Growth.** We believe that relatively few readers will be going to work for, or investing in, the savings and loan industry. Therefore, only 2 S&Ls are in the book. On the other hand, we have included 23 computer and peripheral makers, and numerous other electronics and software firms.

3. **Visibility.** Most readers will have heard of Hilton Hotels, Turner Broadcasting, and William Wrigley; their consumer or service nature makes them household names, even though they are not among the corporate giants in terms of sales and employment. On the other hand, there are wholesaling, mining, and crude oil exploration companies that may have huge sales but few employees and little visibility. Such companies are less likely to appear in the book.

4. **Breadth of coverage.** To show the diversity of economic activity, we've included 2 professional sports teams, one ranch, one law firm, one architectural firm, etc. We feel that these businesses are important enough — and interesting enough — to enjoy at least "token" representation. While we might not emphasize savings and loans or wholesaling, the industry leaders are present.

We are often asked, "Is your list the *Fortune* 500?" Since the famous *Fortune* list excludes private companies and service companies (banks, airlines, retailers, etc.), it is not in any sense a list of the "500 most important companies." We have tried to create a list of "the 450 most important companies" coupled with "50 others that we can learn from."

Organization of the Profiles

The 500 profiles are presented in alphabetical order. This alphabetization is generally word by word, which means that America West Airlines precedes American Brands. We have shown the full legal name of the enterprise at the top of each page, unless it is too long, in which case you will find it above the address in the Where section of the profile. If a company name starts with a person's first name, like Arthur Andersen or Walt Disney, it will be alphabetized under the first name; if the company name starts with initials, like J. C. Penney or H. J. Heinz, look for it under the person's last name. All company names (past and present) used in the profiles are indexed in the last index in the book.

"In selecting these companies, our foremost question was, 'What companies will our readers be most interested in?' "

"We have also shown Hoover's Rating for each company."

Certain pieces of basic data are listed at the top right of each profile: where the company's stock is traded if it is public, the stock ticker symbol used by the stock exchange, and the company's fiscal year-end.

In this area of the page we have also shown Hoover's Rating for each company. The ratings for all companies, from A+ through F, are listed on pages 47–51. Each company's rating is intended to measure the overall strength of the company, primarily based on performance in the '80s and position at the end of 1990. The ratings combine specific statistical measures and our subjective conclusions based on our studies. There are 4 major determinants:

- Financial performance — sales and earnings growth, return on equity

- Financial strength — relative indebtedness

- Innovation within their industry

- Dominance/market share in their industry

Note that, while past performance is often the best indicator of future performance, this is not always the case.

The annual information contained in the profiles was current through fiscal year-end 1990 (including companies whose years ended as late as May 31, 1991). To the extent possible, we have also noted significant, more recent developments through September 1991.

Overview

In this section we have tried to give a thumbnail description of the company and what it does. We recommend that you read this section first.

When

This longer section reflects our belief that every enterprise is the sum of its

history, and that you have to know where you came from in order to know where you are going. While some companies have very little historical awareness and were unable to help us much, and other companies are just plain boring, we think the vast majority of the enterprises in the book have colorful backgrounds. When we could find information, we tried to focus on the people who made the enterprise what it is today. We have found these histories to be full of twists and ironies; they can make for some fascinating quick reading.

Who

Here we list the names of the people who run the company, insofar as space allows. In the case of public companies, we have shown the ages and pay levels of key officers. In some cases the published data are based on last year although the company has announced promotions or retirements since year-end. We have tried to show current officers, with their pay for the latest year available, often prior to a promotion. These pay data represent cash compensation, including bonuses, but exclude stock option programs.

While companies are free to structure their management titles any way they please, most modern corporations follow standard practices. The ultimate power in any corporation lies with the shareholders, who elect a board of directors, usually including officers or "insiders" as well as individuals from outside the company. The chief officer, the person on whose desk the buck stops, is usually called the chief executive officer (CEO). Normally, he or she is also the chairman of the board. As corporate management has become more complex, it is common for the CEO to have a "right-hand person" who oversees the day-to-day operations of the company, allowing the CEO plenty of time to focus on strategy and long-term issues. This right-hand person is usually designated the chief operating officer (COO) and is often the president of the company. In other cases one person is both chairman and president.

A multitude of other titles exist, including chief financial officer (CFO), chief administrative officer, and vice chairman (VC). We have always tried to include the CFO and the chief personnel or human relations officer. Our best advice is that officers' pay levels are clear indicators of who the board of directors thinks are most important on the management team.

The people named in the profiles are indexed at the back of the book.

The Who section also includes the name of the company's auditing (accounting) firm and the number of employees. This last statistic can be viewed as a measure of the complexity of managing the enterprise, since most managing is managing people.

Where

Here we include the company's headquarters street address and phone and fax numbers as available. The back of the book includes an index of companies by headquarters locations.

We have also included as much information as we could gather and fit on the geographical distribution of the company's business, including sales and profit data. Note that these profit numbers, like those in the What section below, are usually operating profits rather than net profits. Operating profits are generally those before financing costs (interest income and payments) and before taxes, which are considered costs attributable to the whole company rather than to one division or part of the world. For this reason the net income figures (in the How Much section) are usually much lower, since they are after interest and taxes. Pretax profits are after interest but before taxes.

What

This section lists as many of the company's products, services, brand names, and divisions as we could fit. We have tried to include all its major lines and all familiar brand names. The nature of this section varies by industry, company, and the amount of information available. If the company publishes sales and profit information by type of business, we have included it. The brand and division names are listed in the last index in the book, with past and present company names.

Rankings

Here we have included the rankings of the companies in the major lists published by the financial press. The best-known and oldest of these lists is the *Fortune* 500, which lists the 500 largest US publicly held industrial (manufacturing) corporations. This list does not generally include banks, retailers, foreign companies, private companies, etc.

Fortune also produces these other lists, which we have included in the Rankings section:
- 100 Largest US Banks
- 100 Largest Diversified US Service Companies
- 50 Largest Diversified US Financial Service Companies
- 50 Largest US Life Insurance Companies
- 50 Largest US Retailers
- 50 Largest US Transportation Companies
- 50 Largest US Utilities

These lists rank all companies by sales, except banks, savings and loans, financial service companies, insurance companies, and utilities, which are ranked by assets.

Forbes, a more recent participant in the "list game," ranks the 400 Largest US Private Companies, which we have also

> *"We have always tried to include the CFO and the chief personnel or human relations officer."*

included. *Forbes* also ranks companies by other measures; we have not included those rankings in this book. The magazine has made an art of estimating the wealth of rich people. While the resultant rankings are not included in our book, we recommend these lists as fascinating background reading.

We have also shown the rank of each public company in the *Business Week* 1000. This list ranks companies based on the total market value of their stock, or market capitalization.

All of the above lists are published annually by these magazines.

Key Competitors

In this section we have listed those other companies in this book and in *Hoover's Handbook of World Business* that compete with the profiled company. This feature is included as a quick way to turn to similar companies and compare them. In the case of some highly diversified or always-changing companies, we didn't have enough room to list everybody and have referred you to broad industry groupings. All the companies in the book are listed by broad industry groups in the first index at the back of the book.

How Much

Here we have tried to present as much data about each enterprise's financial performance as we could compile in the allocated space. While the information varies somewhat from industry to industry, and is less complete in the case of private companies that do not release this data, the following information is generally present. (Most of the terms used below are more fully defined in the preceding section, "The Numbers Made Simple.")

A ten-year table, with relevant nine-year (1981 through 1990) compound growth rates, covering:

- Fiscal year sales (year-end assets for most financial companies)
- Fiscal year net income (before extraordinary items)
- Fiscal year net income as a percent of sales (as a percent of assets for most financial firms)
- Fiscal year Earnings Per Share (EPS) (fully diluted unless italicized)
- Calendar year stock price high, low, and close
- Calendar year high and low Price/Earnings ratio (P/E)
- Fiscal year dividends per share
- Fiscal year-end book value (shareholders' equity per share)

For fiscal years ending between June 1, 1990, and May 31, 1991, we have called the year 1990.

Key year-end 1990 statistics that generally show the financial strength of the enterprise, including:

- Debt ratio (long-term debt as a percent of combined long-term debt and shareholders' equity)
- Return on Average Equity (average of beginning shareholders' equity and ending shareholders' equity) for the fiscal year
- Cash and marketable securities on hand at the end of fiscal 1990
- Current ratio at year-end fiscal 1990 (ratio of current assets to current liabilities)
- Total long-term debt at year-end fiscal 1990
- Number of shares of common stock outstanding at year-end fiscal 1990
- Dividend yield (fiscal year 1990 dividends per share divided by the year-end closing stock price)
- Dividend payout (fiscal year dividends divided by fiscal year Earnings Per Share for 1990)
- Market value at the end of 1990 (calendar year-end closing stock price multiplied by fiscal year-end number of shares outstanding)

> *"All the companies in the book are listed by broad industry groups in the first index at the back of the book."*

Historical per share data are adjusted for stock splits. The data for public companies (and selected others) have been provided to us by Standard & Poor's Compustat, a unit of McGraw-Hill and the nation's leading compiler of corporate share data. Compustat has gone to great lengths to make the data comparable between companies, sometimes producing numbers that will disagree with the numbers you may find in other sources. See the previous section, "Some Potholes on the Road to Understanding."

In the case of private companies, we usually did not have access to such standardized data. We have gathered estimates of sales and other statistics from numerous sources; among the most helpful were trade publications such as *Advertising Age* and *Forbes*'s estimates of the largest private companies. We have also had to become creative in deciding which statistics to use for nonprofit and governmental entities.

In the case of certain industries, we have substituted more relevant statistics for the above data. This particularly applies to insurance companies and other financial services organizations. ▲

BEYOND *HOOVER'S HANDBOOK*: FURTHER READING AND RESOURCES

The business periodical and reference publishing industry is large and growing. Because of the many ways to look at companies and the many measures used, it is often useful to compare several sources.

Basic Data

The two largest compilers of business reference books are Moody's and Standard & Poor's. These organizations produce a wide variety of books and loose-leaf binders. The annual set of *Moody's* manuals, broken into volumes covering industry groups, are the definitive sources of histories of public companies, including the many thousands too small to be included in this book. Standard & Poor's Sheets, commonly found in stock brokerage offices, contain quick two-page synopses on most public companies and are updated frequently. The *Standard & Poor's Stock Guide* is an invaluable monthly booklet with one line on each major publicly held company, primarily containing information of interest to investors.

Dun & Bradstreet is the nation's largest provider of credit information on companies, including small and private ones. A D&B report is often the only available source of information on these enterprises.

One of the best sources of information on the larger companies is the *The Value Line Investment Survey*, a black binder with quarterly updates on each of 1,700 publicly held companies. Unlike other services, Value Line gives specific stock recommendations and future performance projections. The service has established an excellent reputation among investors.

"One of the best sources of information on the larger companies is **The Value Line Investment Survey.***"*

Information from the Companies

The primary data source for this book was the companies themselves, either through their public relations departments or through their investor relations departments. Every publicly held company is required to produce quarterly and annual reports to its shareholders. While the Securities and Exchange Commission (SEC) and accounting-standards setters require certain basic data, companies often use these reports to espouse management philosophies, explain strategies, and examine product successes. Investors generally consider a company's annual report the single most important document they receive in any given year.

Companies also produce a report for investors called the 10-K, which is just a version of the annual report that meets specific SEC guidelines. These reports sometimes contain information not included in the regular annual report. Each year, each public company also holds an annual meeting of shareholders. Since most shareholders do not attend these, the company sends out a proxy statement that sets forth the issues to be voted on, including the election of the board of directors. These proxy statements include data on managers and directors, including pay data.

All of these documents are generally available free of charge from the company upon request. They are also maintained by a company named Disclosure, which makes them available in printed and electronic form.

Depending on their publicity consciousness or secrecy, most companies also produce a wealth of product information and sometimes histories and other information. Such supplementary company information can be most useful.

Analysts' Reports

Most stock brokerage firms maintain teams of securities analysts — professionals specializing in the study of one industry or a few related industries. These people are well paid to spend their full energies understanding the companies in an industry and predicting their futures. Some of the reports they write are widely circulated; others must be obtained from the brokerage firms.

Business Periodicals

The US is blessed with a strong business press. For a general understanding of business, we believe the *Wall Street Journal* is without peer. In addition to being the basic daily news source about business, the *Journal* has become recognized as one of the best-written newspapers in the nation. The *Journal* increasingly covers international developments, marketing, and other aspects of the world that are of interest to the general public.

Forbes, *Fortune*, and *Business Week* are the country's leading business magazines. Each tries to "scoop" its competitors and provide more useful information. This intense competition has, we believe, led to high quality on the part of all three magazines. Each has its fans and its detractors: we suggest you read as much as you can get your hands on. Because *Forbes* takes substantial editorial risks, we believe that this magazine is both more often right and more often wrong than its competitors. We read it religiously, with skepticism.

America's interest in business has led to the creation of many other fine periodicals, including *Investors Daily, Inc.*, and *Financial World*. Every industry also has trade publications specializing in that industry.

Advertising Age, *Chain Store Age*, and *Aviation Week* are good examples. Many of these trade publications compile annual lists comparing the companies in one industry.

We would be remiss to exclude the major national dailies: papers like the *New York Times*, the *Chicago Tribune*, the *Los Angeles Times*, and the *Dallas Morning News* are well known for their coverage of local, national, and international business developments. Most American cities also have a local business weekly or daily; this recent phenomenon has produced some very good papers.

Library References

In addition to the broad reference books discussed above, there are a multitude of business references on specific industries and topics; most of these books are fairly expensive but available at a good library. These titles include *Best's* guides to insurance companies and *Ward's* lists of companies, the latter title distributed by Gale Research, a major library supplier. There are also several books covering foreign companies, usually a separate book for each country.

It is hard to beat a good library, whether for these references or for other books and periodicals. At The Reference Press we have made extensive use of the Austin Public Library and the libraries of the Universities of Chicago, Texas, and California-Berkeley.

High-Tech Help

There are a number of new sources for business information that have become available in recent years. On-line sources are available to anyone with a computer and a modem. Dow Jones News Retrieval (call 800-522-3567 for information), LEXIS/ NEXIS (which carries *Hoover's Handbooks* on-line [call 800-227-4908 for information]), and DIALOG (call 800-334-2564 for

"For a general understanding of business, we believe the Wall Street Journal *is without peer."*

*"We think Alfred
P. Sloan Jr.'s
My Years with
General Motors
is the best
management book
ever written."*

information) are the best three. They are expensive, costing as much as several dollars per minute of use. Compuserve and Prodigy provide access to certain types of business information at a lower cost.

Compact Disc–Read Only Memory (CD–ROM) technology allows the contents of dozens of books to be stored on a single optical disk. ABI Inform allows you to scan summaries of newspapers and periodicals (going back several years) for articles of interest. Disclosure (800-843-7747), Standard & Poor's Compustat (800-525-8640), and Lotus One Source (800-343-5414) have CD–ROM products containing annual reports and financial data for thousands of companies. While costly to purchase and requiring a PC and CD–ROM drive, most of these CD–ROMs are available in libraries.

CD–ROM technology is even getting portable. In November 1991 Sony introduced its Data Discman Electronic Book Player (weighing under 2 pounds), a portable player that plays 3-inch optical disks. Among the titles published for this product are an entire encyclopedia, a 10-language translator, and *Hoover's Handbook*.

If you have access to a fax machine, still other services await you. Dow Jones's JournalFinder allows users to dial a 900 number (for a $5.00 charge) and request topical reprints or business reports using a touch-tone phone and a code published in the *Wall Street Journal*. The document is delivered in seconds by fax. Users can obtain information about this service by calling 800-345-6397. Another Dow Jones service, Facts Delivered, allows you to order company reports by calling 800-445-9454. Reports are promptly delivered by fax. Fortune Business Reports has a similar service (800-989-4636) that provides reports containing general background information on the company and up-to-the-minute news from the Reuters wire service. It is available by fax or mail.

Even if your electronic repertoire is limited to cable TV, you can watch "Wall Street Week," the "Nightly Business Report," CNBC, and other worthwhile business programming.

Other Books

There have been books written about many of the more visible companies in this book: General Motors, Coca-Cola, IBM, Walt Disney, etc. Many less well-known companies have also been documented, sometimes in histories commissioned by the companies themselves, though these books are not as widely distributed.

While there are hundreds of books on management strategies, marketing methods, etc., there are not many widely available books about the history of business in general. The one we would cite in particular is Alfred Chandler's *The Visible Hand*. This and other books by Chandler give a sweeping view of how big business evolved, and we highly recommend them. The works of Peter Drucker are also consistently insightful with regard to the world of enterprise, and we think Alfred P. Sloan Jr.'s *My Years with General Motors* is the best management book ever written.

The Real World

When we study companies, it is easy to forget that they are all around us. You probably buy products produced by, live near a plant or office of, or know someone who works for many of the enterprises in the book. Respected investor Peter Lynch has suggested that you buy stocks based on where you shop, what brands you like, what kinds of shoes your kids wear, etc. We agree: with access to our profiles, you can supplement what you already know about the businesses around you. ▲

TOP TEN AMERICAN COMPANIES FOR THE '90S

We have profiled 500 economic giants from around the US in this book. All have been included for their large and increasing role in our economy. On the following pages we focus on ten that we think are particularly exciting. These are companies that are well positioned to take maximum advantage of the opportunities of the '90s. If their managers continue to make the right moves, they should emerge stronger at the end of the decade than they were at the start. They are presented in alphabetical order.

Note that these top ten may not match the highest-scoring companies in "Hoover's Ratings," described earlier. The ratings were based on past and present performance; the following comments look to the future.

Banc One

The image of the sturdy Midwestern banker has been anything but tarnished by Banc One, and the Columbus, Ohio–based superregional is putting a sparkle into what once was called the Rust Belt.

Banc One combined high tech, good service, and canny management to make it the return-on-assets leader at the end of 1990, and the total value of its shares ranked third among banks, behind the venerable names of J.P. Morgan and BankAmerica.

As it scooped up smallish banks by the bushel — more than 100 over the years — it gave its local executives the slack to stay local and the incentive to stay profitable. A Bank One banker spends two weeks training at Bank One College and, after "graduation," can nearly double his or her salary by meeting Columbus's high expectations.

Banc One is propelled by John B. McCoy, the third generation of John McCoys at the helm. McCoy, at 47, has the skills and the vigor to continue Banc One's growth unabated for the next two decades. The company, legendary for its aggressive use of computers both early and well, combines its back-office operations with those of its acquisitions, cutting costs and making money.

Stressing loans to consumers and small businesses, the bank shied away from loans to foreign countries and to highly leveraged corporations, loans that have proved near-fatal for larger competitors. Unencumbered with those problems, Banc One is looking confidently to the future, experimenting with the concept of a "financial services market," where consumers shop for loans or travel agency services at cozy, neon-lit boutiques under a single roof.

Banc One's winning combination is spreading out of the Midwest. A favorable arrangement with federal regulators helped Banc One take over failed Texas banks; with the help of a modestly rebounding economy, it is turning them around. As the nation's banking industry pairs up and shakes out, there may be quite a few banks that will soon be saying, "Hello, Columbus."

Boeing

As the world's largest aerospace company, Boeing builds both commercial and military aircraft, avionics, and a range of defense and tactical weapons systems. It is the industry's largest employer, America's #1 exporter, and, by a wide margin, the world's leading commercial jet maker, with a 45% market share.

"[Boeing] is… America's #1 exporter, and, by a wide margin, the world's leading commercial jet maker, with a 45% market share."

"Coca-Cola is the hands-down winner globally, with a staggering 44% market share (as opposed to Pepsi's 15% share)."

Offering the broadest product line of the world's Big Three jet makers, Boeing can fill the size requirements of just about any air carrier, with planes capable of holding anywhere from 100 to 500 passengers. Its latest entry, the 777 twinjet, should start rolling off assembly lines in 1995, creating a new class of products for the 1990s. Boeing has a reputation for working with its customers — now about 160 of the world's airlines — to build the highest quality, best performing planes. Its field service is considered the best in the business and includes a 24-hour parts replacement guarantee.

Even with the airline industry (its main customer) in a financial tailspin, Boeing has enjoyed record sales for the past five years. Orders were up for the sixth consecutive year in 1990, and, so far, the company has had no cancellations. Boeing is, in fact, delivering more planes than ever and in 1991 increased production of jetliners to 38 per month — up 58% since 1988. Its 1990 backlog stood at a record $103 billion. Rival Airbus Industrie came nowhere close to that mark, with a 1990 backlog of roughly 1/3 that amount.

As the worldwide jet fleet ages, Boeing plans to capitalize on the growing replacement market, projecting a worldwide demand of 8,850 jetliners (worth $617 billion) by the year 2005. Based on its own growth projections, Boeing expects to fill about 5,400 of these orders (worth $370 billion), making it one of the decade's highest fliers.

Coca-Cola

Every day, more and more people around the world are having a Coke, and the Coca-Cola Company is smiling. Coca-Cola is the most recognized brand name in the world and is the quintessential symbol of American pop culture. After brief forays into movies (Columbia Pictures), TV ("Wheel of Fortune"), and other areas, Coca-Cola is concentrating on the business that made it famous — and what a business it is. Coke is ninth in market value among US companies and boasted a 1990 ROE of 39%.

Although competition with archrival Pepsi is still intense on the domestic front, Coca-Cola is the hands-down winner globally, with a staggering 44% market share (as opposed to Pepsi's 15% share). Coke has already gained formidable market shares in countries around the world such as Germany (42%), the Philippines (71%), and Brazil (59%). And with foreign annual per-capita consumption of Coke at about 1/5 the US level, the sky's the limit for global growth in the '90s.

Domestically Coca-Cola is also pounding Pepsi at the soda fountain. By convincing restaurant owners that Pepsi is more of a competitor than a supplier (PepsiCo owns Taco Bell, KFC, and Pizza Hut restaurants), Coke has recently landed such coveted accounts as Burger King and Wendy's, boosting its US fountain share to about 63% (compared to Pepsi's 25%). Even one Taco Bell franchisee is now serving Coke.

While consumption is maturing on the home front, Coca-Cola is still teaching the world to sing, to the tune of over $8 billion in annual soft drink sales.

Harley-Davidson

Harley-Davidson, the nation's sole remaining motorcycle manufacturer, has revved up its sales and blown past its foreign competition in the US market. In the super-heavyweight category (motorcycles with engine displacement of 850cc and higher), the company's "hogs" command a 62% market share, towering above #2 Honda and its 16% share. Despite the ups and downs of the motorcycle industry as a whole, Harley has grown steadily and impressively since going public in 1986. Demand continues to outstrip supply — at current production rates, the company has a three-year motorcycle order backlog. Harley is reluctant to risk quality problems by rapidly increasing production and does not appear to mind the resultant clamoring for its motorcycles.

Unlike the names of Harley's car- and moped-making competitors (Honda, Suzuki, Yamaha, BMW), the Harley brand is associated exclusively with heavyweight (650cc+) and super-heavyweight motorcycles and related products, enabling the company to cultivate and convey to its customers a unique and very American image. The Harley image is reinforced through distinctive styling, company-sponsored organizations such as H.O.G. (Harley Owners Group), and the company's line of motorcycle clothing.

Having sewn up a dominant position in the US, Harley is setting its sights overseas. Although its exports measured in units have surged 218% in the last six years, Harley's world market share in heavyweights is only 13%, leaving vast opportunities for growth as the company expands its distribution system. Profits are high on Harley's exports, and international demand for classic American motorcycles is strong. Sales are booming in Japan and Germany, Harley's competitors' home turf. Among heavyweight motorcycle manufacturers, Harley will be the king of the road in the 1990s.

Merck

In the lucrative pharmaceutical industry, Merck is the *crème de la crème*. Not only is Merck the largest drug company in the world (with 1990 sales of almost $8 billion), but it is also the most widely acclaimed. In 1990 *Fortune* selected Merck as its most admired company for the fifth consecutive year. Merck is admired by its stockholders as well. Under the solid guidance of CEO P. Roy Vagelos, the company maintains a flawless balance sheet and a track record of consistent growth in sales and earnings.

In an industry in which new product introductions are essential for long-term success, Merck has established itself as the master innovator. Through unparalleled R&D spending (over $850 million in 1990, 11% of sales), Merck has created a seemingly endless pipeline of blockbuster products. The company currently boasts 18 drugs in nine therapeutic categories, with annual sales of over $100 million each. Assisted by an efficient marketing and sales network, Merck has built an almost 10% US pharmaceutical market share and an over 3% global market share.

Never content to rest on previous successes, Merck expects its next blockbuster, Proscar, the first medicine for treating prostate enlargement, to hit the market in early 1992. With roughly half of the elderly men in this country suffering from this disorder and with its virtual monopoly on the market, Proscar could well become a billion-dollar-a-year drug.

Because of its financial strength, its stable of best-selling drugs, and its uncanny ability to maintain its consistent stream of lucrative new product introductions, Merck is just what the doctor ordered in the pharmaceutical industry for the '90s.

3M

What do Scotch tape, dental fillings, Post-it notes, computer diskettes, and sandpaper have in common? All are listed among the more than 50,000 products manufactured by Minnesota Mining and Manufacturing (3M). By one estimate, close to half the world's population either uses or benefits from a product made by 3M every single day.

But being big isn't what matters to this company, and 3M isn't about to rest on past achievements. It adheres to some lofty goals, including an annual earnings growth of at least 10% and a return on equity of 20%. Sometimes it misses the goal: in 1990 the recession crimped consumer spending, clipping 3M's earnings growth to only 5.5%. ROE, on the other hand, was a healthy 23%.

"Through unparalleled R&D spending (over $850 million in 1990, 11% of sales), Merck has created a seemingly endless pipeline of blockbuster products."

"Motorola challenges the Japanese at what they do best — striving for near-zero defects (99.997% defect free) in miniaturized products."

3Mers are among America's happiest employees and have been judged by some headhunters as the most difficult in corporate America to spirit away. Employees are encouraged to develop ideas, which can lead to new or improved products — the lifeblood of 3M. This company is constantly looking for ways, even small ways, of making itself useful. This can mean coming up with something brand new and revolutionary to make people's lives easier (such as the ubiquitous little yellow sticky officially known as the Post-it note) or finding a new use for an old product (3M's Scotchlite reflective materials make lots of things glow in the dark, from traffic lights to running shoes). Nearly 30% of 1990 sales came from products developed in the past five years, and the company isn't shy about pumping money into R&D. In 1990 R&D spending stood at 6.6% of sales — roughly twice that of the US industrial company average. 3M is stepping up business overseas and is in a good position to stick it to the competition in the coming decade.

Motorola

In the competitive world of electronics, where America's technological leadership is being constantly and severely challenged, Motorola stands out as a time-proven leader. Rather than accept the role of an also-ran against Japan's six high-tech giants, the company has taken them on where they live — in Japan. "Six Sigma quality" is the company's battle cry, as Motorola challenges the Japanese at what they do best — striving for near-zero defects (99.997% defect free) in miniaturized products.

Remember Star Trek communicators and Dick Tracy's wristwatch phone? Motorola recently invented them — for real — introducing both the lightweight, portable MicroTac phone and the wristwatch pager in 1989. The company started working on cellular phones back in the 1970s — over a decade before the market existed. Now, as the world's #1 cellular phone maker, it collects royalty checks from other manufacturers and is the only non-Japanese supplier to Nippon Telephone and Telegraph. Motorola is generous with R&D spending (9.2% of 1990 sales), and it has worked tirelessly to improve product quality, winning the prestigious Malcolm Baldridge National Quality Award and Japan's Nikkei Prize for manufacturing.

Motorola is America's #1 microchip maker (including the 68030 chip used in Apple's Macintosh) and recently closed a deal to codevelop the POWER PC chip with Apple and IBM. But, with its mind in the age of the Jetsons, Motorola is already working on the technology of tomorrow. Its latest project, Iridium, will surround the globe with 77 low-orbit satellites, which, in combination with ground-based switching stations, will form the first worldwide cellular phone system. Reliable, global phone service will be made available to individuals in the most remote areas, from the Arctic Sea to Australia's Outback.

Procter & Gamble

Consumer products giant Procter & Gamble has made its name by producing a wide spectrum of basic, recession-resistant products that it masterfully markets as necessities of everyday living. Indeed, one would be hard pressed to find an aisle at the grocery store that did not contain at least one P&G brand. The company's impressive product portfolio boasts #1 positions in 22 different categories.

Originally responsible for developing such now-common items as detergent, fluoride toothpaste, and combination shampoo and conditioner, P&G has a strong track record of bringing innovative new products to the mass market.

With foreign sales already at about the $10 billion mark, P&G is aiming to increase its overseas presence in the 1990s. The company seems particularly anxious to wash the hair and clothes of Eastern Europe. P&G is now the largest detergent maker in Czechoslovakia and has made significant forays into Hungary and Poland as well.

P&G's brand dominance on grocery store shelves is supported by the company's massive marketing muscle. When Clorox introduced a detergent with bleach, P&G retaliated by launching Tide with Bleach, which quickly forced Clorox out of the detergent market.

Although critics once claimed that P&G was too staid to transfer its success to the rapidly changing cosmetics industry, the company is now America's #1 cosmetics maker following the 1989 purchase of Noxell (Cover Girl, Noxzema) and the 1991 acquisition of Max Factor and Betrix (a German cosmetics line) from Revlon. The company is also expanding its presence in health care products.

With cash cows like Tide, Pert Plus, Crisco, and Pampers, which are supported by a seemingly unstoppable marketing machine; an emphasis on R&D; and a strong balance sheet, P&G promises to stay on the top shelf in the 1990s.

Turner Broadcasting

Turner Broadcasting is a long-standing leader in the cable TV revolution and the bane of network television. In 1990, when network TV viewership and advertising revenue sagged and network executives lamented the change in the economics of broadcasting, Turner's sales jumped nearly 31% and the company's 4 major services (CNN, TBS, TNT, and Headline News) scored a combined 21% gain in viewership. TBS, Turner's original cable service, has held the #1 spot among advertising-supported cable stations for 10 years. CNN is well entrenched after 11 years of broadcasting. Although only 3 years old, TNT is

already a basic cable standard. In 1990 Turner's top four services captured an astounding 40% of all cable advertising spending.

Because of founder Ted Turner's foresight, use of new technologies, and willingness to accept enormous risks, Turner has always been at the vanguard of cable TV programming. The company's TBS SuperStation (satellite TV) and CNN (24-hour news) were the first of their kind. In response to expanding demand for entertainment programming, Turner has assembled an enormous film and cartoon library, now used by TBS and TNT and syndicated to others. The company controls much of its sports entertainment programming through ownership of the Atlanta Hawks (basketball) and the resurgent Atlanta Braves (baseball) and through sponsorship of the Goodwill Games.

Turner is positioned to be a prime beneficiary of the continuing expansion of cable TV viewership in the US in the 1990s. Overseas, where national TV broadcasting systems are being privatized and cable TV is still in its infancy, the potential for Turner is enormous. Each world crisis presents CNN with a new opportunity to enhance its worldwide reputation. Although the company has launched a Latin American TNT service, the main focus of Turner's international expansion is CNN. Until 1991 CNN had no international competition.

In TV programming, it will be Turner's show in the 1990s.

Wal-Mart

Thirty years ago, even businessmen who knew Sam Walton didn't think 70,000-square-foot stores could make it in small towns. Were they ever wrong. Walton's canny mixture of cost cutting and personal charisma built an empire of discount stores that surpassed Sears in 1990 to become the

"In 1990 Turner's top four services captured an astounding 40% of all cable advertising spending."

biggest retail operation in the US. Yet Chairman Walton still flies his Cessna to two or three Wal-Marts every day, keeping personal tabs on his "associates" — the army of employees Walton credits with his success and rewards with a generous profit-sharing plan.

Wal-Mart has developed a combination of management strategies that keeps costs and expenses down, prices low, and volume high. Wal-Mart has its own supply and distribution facilities, including one of the largest over-the-road trucking fleets in the US. Cutting-edge computerized inventory systems tie it all together, reordering out-of-stock goods instantly to keep store shelves full.

Despite a sluggish retailing environment that has slowed several companies with more upscale images, $30 billion Wal-Mart continues to grow — over 30% annually during the last decade. There's no end in sight. Whole regions of the US (not to mention the rest of the world) remain for Wal-Mart to conquer, and the company's newest concept, combination grocery/discount Supercenters, looks promising in test markets.

Meanwhile, every other day the company opens a new store. Competitors see the price wars begin. Consumers see that it's time to go shopping.

"Runners Up"

Of course, there are many other outstanding companies among the hundreds in this book. Others we would particularly cite for their prospects are:

Abbott Laboratories
Automatic Data Processing
Bristol-Myers Squibb
Deluxe Corporation
Eli Lilly
Food Lion
H. J. Heinz
Home Depot
Johnson & Johnson
Kellogg
The Limited
Microsoft
NIKE
Toys "R" Us
Walt Disney
Warner-Lambert. ▲

A List-Lover's Compendium

Note: Data in these lists may not agree with data in the profiles
because of different methods of compilation.

Hoover's Ratings of the Companies Profiled in this Book

Hoover's Ratings are explained on page 32.

Company	Rating	Company	Rating
Abbott Laboratories	A+	Mayo Foundation	A
Adobe Systems, Inc.	A+	Melville Corporation	A
Amgen Inc.	A+	Office Depot, Inc.	A
Apple Computer, Inc.	A+	Pfizer Inc.	A
Automatic Data Processing, Inc.	A+	The Procter & Gamble Company	A
The Boeing Company	A+	Publix Super Markets, Inc.	A
Bristol-Myers Squibb Company	A+	Reebok International Ltd.	A
The Coca-Cola Company	A+	Schering-Plough Corporation	A
Compaq Computer Corporation	A+	Stanford University	A
Cray Research, Inc.	A+	Sun Microsystems, Inc.	A
Deluxe Corporation	A+	Syntex Corporation	A
Eli Lilly and Company	A+	United Parcel Service of America, Inc.	A
Food Lion, Inc.	A+	United States	A
The Gap, Inc.	A+	United Way of America	A
H&R Block, Inc.	A+	Walgreen Co.	A
Harley-Davidson, Inc.	A+	The Walt Disney Company	A
The Home Depot, Inc.	A+	Warner-Lambert Company	A
Intel Corporation	A+	Waste Management, Inc.	A
Intergraph Corporation	A+	Advance Publications, Inc.	A-
Johnson & Johnson	A+	American Association of Retired Persons	A-
Kellogg Company	A+	American Cancer Society	A-
The Limited, Inc.	A+	American Home Products Corporation	A-
Liz Claiborne, Inc.	A+	Anheuser-Busch Companies, Inc.	A-
McKinsey & Co.	A+	Archer-Daniels-Midland Company	A-
Merck & Co., Inc.	A+	AST Research, Inc.	A-
Microsoft Corporation	A+	Blockbuster Entertainment Corp.	A-
Minnesota Mining and Manufacturing Co.	A+	Borland International, Inc.	A-
NIKE, Inc.	A+	Brown-Forman Corporation	A-
Novell, Inc.	A+	Bruno's, Inc.	A-
The Price Company	A+	Cargill, Inc.	A-
The Reader's Digest Association, Inc.	A+	Circuit City Stores, Inc.	A-
Rubbermaid Inc.	A+	The Clorox Company	A-
Toys "R" Us, Inc.	A+	Costco Wholesale Corporation	A-
Wal-Mart Stores, Inc.	A+	Estée Lauder Inc.	A-
Wm. Wrigley Jr. Company	A+	Fleetwood Enterprises, Inc.	A-
Albertson's, Inc.	A	Gannett Co., Inc.	A-
AMP Inc.	A	Genentech, Inc.	A-
Banc One Corporation	A	General Mills, Inc.	A-
Computer Associates International, Inc.	A	Gerber Products Company	A-
Conner Peripherals, Inc.	A	Giant Food Inc.	A-
Dell Computer Corporation	A	The Goldman Sachs Group, LP	A-
The Dun & Bradstreet Corporation	A	Hallmark Cards, Inc.	A-
EG&G, Inc.	A	Kimberly-Clark Corporation	A-
Emerson Electric Co.	A	Kohlberg Kravis Roberts & Co.	A-
The Ford Foundation	A	Longs Drug Stores Corporation	A-
General Re Corporation	A	Mars, Inc.	A-
Harvard University	A	Motorola, Inc.	A-
Hasbro, Inc.	A	National Geographic Society	A-
H. J. Heinz Company	A	National Organization for Women, Inc.	A-
Hershey Foods Corporation	A	National Park Service	A-
Hewlett-Packard Company	A	NCR Corporation	A-
International Flavors & Fragrances Inc.	A	Philip Morris Companies, Inc.	A-
L.A. Gear, Inc.	A	The Prudential Insurance Co. of America	A-
Levi Strauss Associates Inc.	A	Raytheon Company	A-
Marsh & McLennan Companies, Inc.	A	The Rockefeller Foundation	A-

Hoover's Ratings of the Companies Profiled in this Book (continued)

Company	Rating	Company	Rating
Rockwell International Corporation	A-	Tyson Foods, Inc.	B+
Rotary International	A-	Vulcan Materials Company	B+
Schlumberger NV	A-	AFL-CIO	B
The Sherwin-Williams Company	A-	American Telephone & Telegraph Company	B
Snap-on Tools Corporation	A-	Arthur Andersen & Co.	B
State Farm	A-	Becton, Dickinson and Company	B
SunTrust Banks, Inc.	A-	State of California	B
Tandy Corporation	A-	ConAgra, Inc.	B
The University of Chicago	A-	Continental Grain Company	B
The University of Texas at Austin	A-	Cox Enterprises, Inc.	B
The Upjohn Company	A-	CPC International Inc.	B
The Washington Post Company	A-	Democratic Party	B
Winn-Dixie Stores, Inc.	A-	Digital Equipment Corporation	B
Woolworth Corporation	A-	Dresser Industries, Inc.	B
Amdahl Corporation	B+	E. I. du Pont de Nemours and Company	B
American International Group, Inc.	B+	Edward J. DeBartolo Corporation	B
Baker & McKenzie	B+	Exxon Corporation	B
C. R. Bard, Inc.	B+	E. & J. Gallo Winery	B
Berkshire Hathaway Inc.	B+	General Electric Company	B
Boston Celtics LP	B+	Halliburton Company	B
Capital Cities/ABC, Inc.	B+	Honeywell Inc.	B
Carlson Companies, Inc.	B+	Ingersoll-Rand Company	B
Commerce Clearing House, Inc.	B+	Johnson Publishing Company, Inc.	B
Corning Inc.	B+	JWP Inc.	B
Dillard Department Stores, Inc.	B+	KPMG	B
R. R. Donnelley & Sons Company	B+	Loews Corporation	B
Dow Jones & Company, Inc.	B+	Lowe's Companies, Inc.	B
Fluor Corporation	B+	Martin Marietta Corporation	B
GEICO Corporation	B+	Massachusetts Mutual Life Insurance Co.	B
The Gillette Company	B+	Mattel, Inc.	B
The Hearst Corporation	B+	McGraw-Hill, Inc.	B
Humana Inc.	B+	Monsanto Company	B
Hyatt Corporation	B+	National Medical Enterprises, Inc.	B
International Business Machines Corp.	B+	The New York Times Company	B
S.C. Johnson & Son, Inc.	B+	Norfolk Southern Corporation	B
King Ranch, Inc.	B+	Northwestern Mutual	B
Koch Industries, Inc.	B+	PPG Industries, Inc.	B
Lotus Development Corporation	B+	Roman Catholic Church (US)	B
McDonald's Corporation	B+	Seagate Technology, Inc.	B
Metromedia Company	B+	The Stanley Works	B
Milliken & Co., Inc.	B+	Super Valu Stores, Inc.	B
Morton International, Inc.	B+	Trammell Crow Company	B
New York Stock Exchange, Inc.	B+	Young & Rubicam	B
Nordstrom, Inc.	B+	Aluminum Company of America	B-
The Ohio State University	B+	American Cyanamid Company	B-
Oracle Systems Corporation	B+	American Financial Corporation	B-
PepsiCo, Inc.	B+	American Greetings Corporation	B-
Phelps Dodge Corporation	B+	Ameritech Corporation	B-
The Quaker Oats Company	B+	Amway Corporation	B-
Republican Party	B+	Armstrong World Industries, Inc.	B-
Roadway Services, Inc.	B+	Atlantic Richfield Company	B-
Sara Lee Corporation	B+	Avis Inc.	B-
SYSCO Corporation	B+	Baker Hughes Inc.	B-
Tandem Computers Inc.	B+	Baxter International Inc.	B-
Teachers Insurance	B+	Bechtel Group, Inc.	B-

Hoover's Ratings of the Companies Profiled in this Book (continued)

Company	Rating	Company	Rating
Bell Atlantic Corporation	B-	American Brands, Inc.	C+
BellSouth Corporation	B-	Amoco Corporation	C+
Borden, Inc.	B-	The ARA Group, Inc.	C+
Browning-Ferris Industries, Inc.	B-	Avon Products, Inc.	C+
Brunswick Corporation	B-	The Bank of New York Company, Inc.	C+
Campbell Soup Company	B-	Bankers Trust New York Corporation	C+
Chiquita Brands International, Inc.	B-	Barnett Banks, Inc.	C+
Colgate-Palmolive Company	B-	Blue Cross and Blue Shield Association	C+
Dayton Hudson Corporation	B-	Brown Group, Inc.	C+
Dole Food Company, Inc.	B-	CBS Inc.	C+
The Dow Chemical Company	B-	The Charles Schwab Corporation	C+
Ernst & Young	B-	Chevron Corporation	C+
Federal Express Corporation	B-	City of Chicago	C+
Federal National Mortgage Association	B-	CIGNA Corporation	C+
The Great Atlantic & Pacific Tea Company	B-	Cooper Industries, Inc.	C+
HAL, Inc.	B-	Coopers & Lybrand	C+
John Hancock Mutual Life Insurance Co.	B-	Cyprus Minerals Company	C+
Kmart Corporation	B-	Deere & Company	C+
Knight-Ridder, Inc.	B-	Deloitte & Touche	C+
Lockheed Corporation	B-	Delta Air Lines, Inc.	C+
Masco Corporation	B-	Duke Power Company	C+
The May Department Stores Company	B-	Eastman Kodak Company	C+
Maytag Corporation	B-	Edison Brothers	C+
MCI Communications Corporation	B-	Fleming Companies, Inc.	C+
McKesson Corporation	B-	Fred Meyer, Inc.	C+
Mercantile Stores Company, Inc.	B-	General Cinema Corporation	C+
Metropolitan Life Insurance Company	B-	Georgia-Pacific Corporation	C+
Mobil Corporation	B-	GTE Corporation	C+
J.P. Morgan & Co. Inc.	B-	Harris Corporation	C+
Morgan Stanley Group Inc.	B-	Hilton Hotels Corporation	C+
National Semiconductor Corporation	B-	International Paper Company	C+
NCNB Corporation	B-	James River Corporation	C+
New York Life Insurance Company	B-	Johnson Controls, Inc.	C+
Oryx Energy Company	B-	Kemper Corporation	C+
PACCAR Inc.	B-	Litton Industries, Inc.	C+
Pacific Telesis Group	B-	McCaw Cellular Communications, Inc.	C+
Paramount Communications Inc.	B-	McDonnell Douglas Corporation	C+
Pitney Bowes Inc.	B-	Merrill Lynch & Co., Inc.	C+
Polaroid Corporation	B-	Northrop Corporation	C+
Ralston Purina Company	B-	NYNEX Corporation	C+
Rite Aid Corporation	B-	Pacific Gas and Electric Company	C+
Southwestern Bell Corporation	B-	J. C. Penney Company, Inc.	C+
Square D Company	B-	Peter Kiewit Sons' Inc.	C+
Storage Technology Corporation	B-	Phillips Petroleum Company	C+
Teamsters	B-	Price Waterhouse	C+
Texaco Inc.	B-	Primerica Corporation	C+
Thiokol Corporation	B-	Reynolds Metals Company	C+
United Technologies Corporation	B-	SCEcorp	C+
Universal Corporation	B-	Scott Paper Company	C+
U S WEST, Inc.	B-	The E.W. Scripps Company	C+
The Vons Companies, Inc.	B-	Skidmore, Owings & Merrill	C+
Wells Fargo & Company	B-	Southwest Airlines Co.	C+
Yellow Freight System	B-	Texas Instruments Inc.	C+
Adolph Coors Company	C+	The Times Mirror Company	C+
Aetna Life & Casualty Company	C+	TLC Beatrice International Holdings, Inc	C+

Company	Rating	Company	Rating
TRW Inc.	C+	The Black & Decker Corporation	C-
Turner Broadcasting System, Inc.	C+	Burlington Northern Inc.	C-
UAL Corporation	C+	Champion International Corporation	C-
Union Pacific Corporation	C+	Chemical Banking Corporation	C-
V. F. Corporation	C+	Citicorp	C-
Wendy's International, Inc.	C+	The Coastal Corporation	C-
Whirlpool Corporation	C+	Commodore International Ltd.	C-
Alaska Air Group, Inc.	C	Commonwealth Edison Company	C-
Allied-Signal Inc.	C	CSX Corporation	C-
American Express Company	C	Cummins Engine Company, Inc.	C-
American Stores Company	C	Dana Corporation	C-
AMR Corporation	C	Data General Corporation	C-
ASARCO Inc.	C	Fieldcrest Cannon, Inc.	C-
BankAmerica Corporation	C	First Chicago Corporation	C-
The Bear Stearns Companies Inc.	C	First Fidelity Bancorporation	C-
Caterpillar Inc.	C	First Interstate Bancorp	C-
Consolidated Edison Co. of New York, Inc.	C	Fleet/Norstar Financial Group, Inc.	C-
Consolidated Rail Corporation	C	FPL Group, Inc.	C-
Eaton Corporation	C	General Motors Corporation	C-
Enron Corp.	C	W. R. Grace & Company	C-
FMC Corporation	C	Great Western Financial Corporation	C-
Ford Motor Company	C	Grumman Corporation	C-
General Dynamics Corporation	C	Helmsley Enterprises Inc.	C-
The Green Bay Packers, Inc.	C	Hospital Corporation of America	C-
Hercules Inc.	C	Inland Steel Industries, Inc.	C-
The Hertz Corporation	C	ITT Corporation	C-
Household International, Inc.	C	R. H. Macy & Co., Inc.	C-
INTERCO Inc.	C	Manufacturers Hanover Corporation	C-
MacAndrews & Forbes Holdings Inc.	C	Mellon Bank Corporation	C-
Marriott Corporation	C	NWA Inc.	C-
The Mead Corporation	C	Owens-Corning Fiberglas Corporation	C-
Montgomery Ward Holding Corp.	C	Pennzoil Company	C-
Outboard Marine Corporation	C	Prime Computer, Inc.	C-
PNC Financial Corp	C	Reliance Electric Company	C-
Premark International, Inc.	C	Sharper Image Corporation	C-
Public Service Enterprise Group Inc.	C	The Southern Company	C-
Ryder System, Inc.	C	Stroh Companies Inc.	C-
SCI Systems, Inc.	C	Tele-Communications, Inc.	C-
Sears, Roebuck & Co.	C	Teledyne, Inc.	C-
Springs Industries, Inc.	C	Textron Inc.	C-
Sun Company, Inc.	C	Time Warner Inc.	C-
Tenneco, Inc.	C	Transamerica Corporation	C-
Texas Utilities Company	C	The Travelers Corporation	C-
United Telecommunications, Inc.	C	Tribune Company	C-
Unocal Corporation	C	Union Carbide Corporation	C-
USX Corporation	C	The United States Shoe Corporation	C-
Weyerhaeuser Company	C	USF&G Corporation	C-
Xerox Corporation	C	Viacom Inc.	C-
H. F. Ahmanson & Company	C-	Westinghouse Electric Corporation	C-
AMAX Inc.	C-	Zenith Electronics Corporation	C-
American Electric Power Company, Inc.	C-	American Standard Inc.	D
American President Companies, Ltd.	C-	Atari Corporation	D
Ashland Oil, Inc.	C-	Bally Manufacturing Corporation	D
Associated Milk Producers, Inc.	C-	Bank of Boston Corporation	D
Bethlehem Steel Corporation	C-	Boise Cascade Corporation	D

Hoover's Ratings of the Companies Profiled in this Book (continued)

Company	Rating	Company	Rating
Borg-Warner Corporation	D	Occidental Petroleum Corporation	D
Burlington Holdings Inc.	D	Ogden Corporation	D
Carter Hawley Hale Stores, Inc.	D	Owens-Illinois, Inc.	D
Centel Corporation	D	Pacific Enterprises	D
The Chase Manhattan Corporation	D	Paine Webber Group Inc.	D
Chicago and North Western	D	Pan Am Corporation	D
Chrysler Corporation	D	Panhandle Eastern Corporation	D
The Circle K Corporation	D	Pinnacle West Capital Corporation	D
The Columbia Gas System, Inc.	D	Riklis Family Corporation	D
Consolidated Freightways, Inc.	D	Rio Grande Industries, Inc.	D
Continental Airlines Holdings, Inc.	D	RJR Nabisco, Inc.	D
Continental Bank Corporation	D	Safeway Inc.	D
Control Data Corporation	D	Salomon Inc	D
The Dial Corp	D	Santa Fe Pacific Corporation	D
Entergy Corporation	D	Security Pacific Corporation	D
The Equitable	D	Service Merchandise Company, Inc.	D
Farley, Inc.	D	The Southland Corporation	D
General Signal Corporation	D	The Stop & Shop Companies, Inc.	D
The Goodyear Tire & Rubber Company	D	Supermarkets General Holdings Corp.	D
Hartmarx Corporation	D	TW Holdings, Inc.	D
The Henley Group, Inc.	D	Unisys Corporation	D
Jack Eckerd Corporation	D	USAir Group, Inc.	D
The Kroger Co.	D	USG Corporation	D
The LTV Corporation	D	Wang Laboratories, Inc.	D
Manville Corporation	D	Whitman Corporation	D
Mayflower Group, Inc.	D	America West Airlines, Inc.	F
McDermott International, Inc.	D	Ames Department Stores, Inc.	F
Midway Airlines, Inc.	D	Dr Pepper/Seven-Up Companies, Inc.	F
Navistar International Corporation	D	First Executive Corporation	F
New York City Transit Authority	D	Trans World Airlines, Inc.	F

The 100 Largest Companies in *Hoover's Handbook of American Business 1992*

Rank	Company	1990 Sales ($ mil.)
1	General Motors Corporation	123,276
2	Exxon Corporation	105,519
3	Ford Motor Company	97,650
4	International Business Machines Corp.	
5	Mobil Corporation	57,819
6	General Electric Company	57,662
7	Sears, Roebuck & Co.	55,972
8	American Telephone & Telegraph Company	51,321
9	Philip Morris Companies, Inc.	44,323
10	The Prudential Insurance Co. of America	42,125
11	Cargill, Inc.	42,000
12	Texaco Inc.	40,899
13	E. I. du Pont de Nemours and Company	39,709
14	Chevron Corporation	38,607
15	Citicorp	38,385
16	Salomon Inc	35,946
17	Wal-Mart Stores, Inc.	32,602
18	Kmart Corporation	32,281
19	Chrysler Corporation	29,797
20	Amoco Corporation	28,010
21	The Boeing Company	27,595
22	Metropolitan Life Insurance Company	27,168
23	American Express Company	24,332
24	The Procter & Gamble Company	24,081
25	American Stores Company	22,156
26	Occidental Petroleum Corporation	21,694
27	United Technologies Corporation	21,550
28	ITT Corporation	20,604
29	The Kroger Co.	20,261
30	The Dow Chemical Company	19,773
31	ConAgra, Inc.	19,505
32	USX Corporation	19,326
33	Aetna Life & Casualty Company	19,021
34	Eastman Kodak Company	18,908
35	GTE Corporation	18,374
36	State Farm	18,208
37	CIGNA Corporation	18,164
38	Atlantic Richfield Company	18,008
39	PepsiCo, Inc.	17,803
40	J. C. Penney Company, Inc.	17,410
41	Koch Industries, Inc.	17,190
42	Xerox Corporation	16,951
43	McDonnell Douglas Corporation	16,246
44	American International Group, Inc.	16,214
45	Safeway Inc.	14,874
46	Continental Grain Company	14,850
47	Dayton Hudson Corporation	14,739
48	Tenneco, Inc.	14,511
49	BellSouth Corporation	14,345
50	Household International, Inc.	14,320
51	RJR Nabisco, Inc.	13,879
52	The Chase Manhattan Corporation	13,672
53	United Parcel Service of America, Inc.	13,606
54	Phillips Petroleum Company	13,603
55	NYNEX Corporation	13,585
56	Hewlett-Packard Company	13,233
57	New York Life Insurance Company	13,228
58	Enron Corp.	13,165
59	Minnesota Mining and Manufacturing Co.	13,021
60	International Paper Company	12,960
61	Digital Equipment Corporation	12,943
62	Westinghouse Electric Corporation	12,915
63	Federal National Mortgage Association	12,719
64	Georgia-Pacific Corporation	12,665
65	Rockwell International Corporation	12,379
66	Allied-Signal Inc.	12,343
67	BankAmerica Corporation	12,323
68	Bell Atlantic Corporation	12,298
69	Loews Corporation	12,281
70	Fleming Companies, Inc.	11,933
71	Sun Company, Inc.	11,812
72	AMR Corporation	11,720
73	Super Valu Stores, Inc.	11,612
74	Sara Lee Corporation	11,606
75	Time Warner Inc.	11,517
76	Caterpillar Inc.	11,436
77	The Great Atlantic & Pacific Tea Company	11,391
78	The Travelers Corporation	11,313
79	The Goodyear Tire & Rubber Company	11,273
80	Johnson & Johnson	11,232
81	Merrill Lynch & Co., Inc.	11,213
82	UAL Corporation	11,037
83	Motorola, Inc.	10,885
84	Anheuser-Busch Companies, Inc.	10,744
85	Aluminum Company of America	10,710
86	Ameritech Corporation	10,663
87	Unocal Corporation	10,645
88	J.P. Morgan & Co. Inc.	10,465
89	Security Pacific Corporation	10,327
90	Bristol-Myers Squibb Company	10,300
91	The Coca-Cola Company	10,236
92	General Dynamics Corporation	10,173
93	Unisys Corporation	10,111
94	The May Department Stores Company	10,066
95	John Hancock Mutual Life Insurance Co.	10,033
96	Lockheed Corporation	9,958
97	U S WEST, Inc.	9,957
98	Woolworth Corporation	9,789
99	Winn-Dixie Stores, Inc.	9,745
100	Pacific Telesis Group	9,716

The 100 Most Profitable Companies in *Hoover's Handbook of American Business 1992*

Rank	Company	1990 Net Income ($ mil.)	Rank	Company	1990 Net Income ($ mil.)
1	International Business Machines Corp.	6,020	51	Hewlett-Packard Company	739
2	Exxon Corporation	5,010	52	The Southern Company	719
3	General Electric Company	4,303	53	Wells Fargo & Company	712
4	Philip Morris Companies, Inc.	3,540	54	Waste Management, Inc.	709
5	American Telephone & Telegraph Company	2,735	55	Eastman Kodak Company	703
6	E. I. du Pont de Nemours and Company	2,310	56	Bankers Trust New York Corporation	665
7	Chevron Corporation	2,157	57	Intel Corporation	650
8	Mobil Corporation	1,929	58	Rockwell International Corporation	624
9	Amoco Corporation	1,913	59	Union Pacific Corporation	618
10	Merck & Co., Inc.	1,781	60	Aetna Life & Casualty Company	614
11	Bristol-Myers Squibb Company	1,748	61	General Re Corporation	614
12	Atlantic Richfield Company	1,688	62	Emerson Electric Co.	613
13	BellSouth Corporation	1,632	63	Xerox Corporation	605
14	The Procter & Gamble Company	1,602	64	United Parcel Service of America, Inc.	597
15	GTE Corporation	1,541	65	American Brands, Inc.	596
16	Texaco Inc.	1,450	66	J. C. Penney Company, Inc.	577
17	American International Group, Inc.	1,442	67	Consolidated Edison Co. of New York, Inc.	572
18	The Boeing Company	1,385	68	Public Service Enterprise Group Inc.	571
19	The Dow Chemical Company	1,384	69	Schlumberger NV	570
20	The Coca-Cola Company	1,382	70	International Paper Company	569
21	Bell Atlantic Corporation	1,313	71	H. J. Heinz Company	568
22	Minnesota Mining and Manufacturing Co.	1,308	72	Schering-Plough Corporation	565
23	Wal-Mart Stores, Inc.	1,291	73	Tenneco, Inc.	561
24	Ameritech Corporation	1,254	74	Raytheon Company	557
25	American Home Products Corporation	1,231	75	Norfolk Southern Corporation	556
26	U S WEST, Inc.	1,199	76	American Electric Power Company, Inc.	549
27	Federal National Mortgage Association	1,173	77	Monsanto Company	546
28	Johnson & Johnson	1,143	78	Entergy Corporation	541
29	Eli Lilly and Company	1,127	79	Phillips Petroleum Company	541
30	Southwestern Bell Corporation	1,101	80	Duke Power Company	538
31	PepsiCo, Inc.	1,091	81	The Dun & Bradstreet Corporation	508
32	ITT Corporation	1,056	82	Kellogg Company	503
33	Pacific Telesis Group	1,030	83	The May Department Stores Company	500
34	Pacific Gas and Electric Company	987	84	Motorola, Inc.	499
35	Texas Utilities Company	969	85	Warner-Lambert Company	485
36	Abbott Laboratories	966	86	Archer-Daniels-Midland Company	484
37	NYNEX Corporation	949	87	Capital Cities/ABC, Inc.	478
38	Sears, Roebuck & Co.	892	88	Apple Computer, Inc.	475
39	BankAmerica Corporation	877	89	PPG Industries, Inc.	475
40	Ford Motor Company	860	90	Sara Lee Corporation	470
41	Anheuser-Busch Companies, Inc.	842	91	General Mills, Inc.	464
42	SCEcorp	830	92	Allied-Signal Inc.	462
43	The Walt Disney Company	824	93	The Upjohn Company	458
44	USX Corporation	818	94	Compaq Computer Corporation	455
45	Loews Corporation	805	95	Phelps Dodge Corporation	455
46	McDonald's Corporation	802	96	First Interstate Bancorp	439
47	Pfizer Inc.	801	97	Kimberly-Clark Corporation	432
48	J.P. Morgan & Co. Inc.	775	98	Banc One Corporation	423
49	Kmart Corporation	756	99	Deere & Company	411
50	United Technologies Corporation	751	100	Dayton Hudson Corporation	410

The 100 Most Valuable Public Companies in *Hoover's Handbook of American Business 1992*

Rank	Company	1990 Market Value ($ mil.)	Rank	Company	1990 Market Value ($ mil.)
1	International Business Machines Corp.	64,567	51	Microsoft Corporation	8,556
2	Exxon Corporation	64,449	52	Federal National Mortgage Association	8,488
3	General Electric Company	50,095	53	Emerson Electric Co.	8,431
4	Philip Morris Companies, Inc.	47,932	54	American Brands, Inc.	8,315
5	Bristol-Myers Squibb Company	35,096	55	SCEcorp	8,275
6	Merck & Co., Inc.	34,781	56	Westinghouse Electric Corporation	8,268
7	Wal-Mart Stores, Inc.	34,554	57	J.P. Morgan & Co. Inc.	8,238
8	American Telephone & Telegraph Company	32,901	58	General Re Corporation	8,109
9	The Coca-Cola Company	31,073	59	General Mills, Inc.	8,090
10	The Procter & Gamble Company	29,998	60	Baxter International Inc.	7,780
11	BellSouth Corporation	26,388	61	Hewlett-Packard Company	7,780
12	Amoco Corporation	26,290	62	USX Corporation	7,763
13	Chevron Corporation	25,477	63	Capital Cities/ABC, Inc.	7,694
14	E. I. du Pont de Nemours and Company	24,617	64	Intel Corporation	7,687
15	Johnson & Johnson	23,898	65	Berkshire Hathaway Inc.	7,650
16	Mobil Corporation	23,263	66	Campbell Soup Company	7,562
17	Bell Atlantic Corporation	21,085	67	The Dun & Bradstreet Corporation	7,524
18	General Motors Corporation	20,817	68	Commonwealth Edison Company	7,377
19	PepsiCo, Inc.	20,498	69	Sara Lee Corporation	7,313
20	Atlantic Richfield Company	19,646	70	Texas Utilities Company	7,214
21	GTE Corporation	19,580	71	Union Pacific Corporation	7,072
22	Eli Lilly and Company	19,568	72	Motorola, Inc.	6,898
23	Abbott Laboratories	19,311	73	Loews Corporation	6,861
24	Minnesota Mining and Manufacturing Co.	18,851	74	Archer-Daniels-Midland Company	6,778
25	Pacific Telesis Group	18,076	75	Phillips Petroleum Company	6,759
26	Ameritech Corporation	17,644	76	Digital Equipment Corporation	6,725
27	Waste Management, Inc.	17,103	77	Kimberly-Clark Corporation	6,713
28	Southwestern Bell Corporation	16,793	78	The Upjohn Company	6,704
29	American Home Products Corporation	16,526	79	Syntex Corporation	6,656
30	American International Group, Inc.	16,309	80	Rockwell International Corporation	6,629
31	Texaco Inc.	15,619	81	Norfolk Southern Corporation	6,495
32	The Boeing Company	15,590	82	The Limited, Inc.	6,491
33	U S WEST, Inc.	15,297	83	Toys "R" Us, Inc.	6,472
34	NYNEX Corporation	14,234	84	CPC International Inc.	6,282
35	Schlumberger NV	13,781	85	Duke Power Company	6,204
36	Eastman Kodak Company	13,513	86	Unocal Corporation	6,156
37	The Walt Disney Company	13,378	87	The Gillette Company	6,100
38	Pfizer Inc.	13,334	88	Monsanto Company	6,069
39	The Dow Chemical Company	12,825	89	International Paper Company	5,869
40	Ford Motor Company	12,596	90	NCR Corporation	5,852
41	Anheuser-Busch Companies, Inc.	12,139	91	United Technologies Corporation	5,800
42	Pacific Gas and Electric Company	10,505	92	Tenneco, Inc.	5,794
43	McDonald's Corporation	10,459	93	Public Service Enterprise Group Inc.	5,762
44	Schering-Plough Corporation	9,852	94	Gannett Co., Inc.	5,744
45	American Express Company	9,580	95	Marsh & McLennan Companies, Inc.	5,735
46	Kellogg Company	9,155	96	Ralston Purina Company	5,706
47	Warner-Lambert Company	9,068	97	Kmart Corporation	5,671
48	H. J. Heinz Company	9,048	98	BankAmerica Corporation	5,654
49	The Southern Company	8,809	99	ITT Corporation	5,480
50	Sears, Roebuck & Co.	8,706	100	Occidental Petroleum Corporation	5,446

The 100 Largest Employers in *Hoover's Handbook of American Business 1992*

Rank	Company	1990 Employees	Rank	Company	1990 Employees
1	General Motors Corporation	761,400	51	BankAmerica Corporation	93,800
2	Sears, Roebuck & Co.	476,600	52	NYNEX Corporation	93,800
3	International Business Machines Corp.	373,816	53	Tenneco, Inc.	92,000
4	Kmart Corporation	373,000	54	Hewlett-Packard Company	92,000
5	Ford Motor Company	370,383	55	Federal Express Corporation	91,550
6	Wal-Mart Stores, Inc.	328,000	56	Minnesota Mining and Manufacturing Co.	89,601
7	PepsiCo, Inc.	308,000	57	The Procter & Gamble Company	89,000
8	General Electric Company	298,000	58	Borg-Warner Corporation	86,800
9	American Telephone & Telegraph Company	274,000	59	Johnson & Johnson	82,200
10	United Parcel Service of America, Inc.	246,800	60	Bell Atlantic Corporation	81,600
11	Marriott Corporation	209,000	61	H&R Block, Inc.	81,000
12	J. C. Penney Company, Inc.	196,000	62	KPMG	77,300
13	United Technologies Corporation	192,600	63	Halliburton Company	77,000
14	Roman Catholic Church (US)	182,200	64	Raytheon Company	76,700
15	McDonald's Corporation	177,000	65	R. H. Macy & Co., Inc.	76,000
16	The Kroger Co.	170,000	66	UAL Corporation	76,000
17	Philip Morris Companies, Inc.	168,000	67	Ameritech Corporation	75,780
18	American Stores Company	163,900	68	TRW Inc.	75,600
19	Dayton Hudson Corporation	161,215	69	ConAgra, Inc.	74,269
20	The Boeing Company	160,500	70	Emerson Electric Co.	73,700
21	GTE Corporation	154,000	71	Lockheed Corporation	73,000
22	E. I. du Pont de Nemours and Company	143,961	72	Woolworth Corporation	73,000
23	Blue Cross and Blue Shield Association	138,013	73	The Limited, Inc.	72,500
24	Eastman Kodak Company	134,450	74	Texas Instruments Inc.	70,138
25	The ARA Group, Inc.	134,000	75	Carlson Companies, Inc.	70,000
26	Chrysler Corporation	124,000	76	Unisys Corporation	70,000
27	McDonnell Douglas Corporation	121,190	77	International Paper Company	69,000
28	Digital Equipment Corporation	121,000	78	Mobil Corporation	67,300
29	Melville Corporation	119,000	79	Southwestern Bell Corporation	66,900
30	The May Department Stores Company	116,000	80	Publix Super Markets, Inc.	66,756
31	Westinghouse Electric Corporation	116,000	81	Montgomery Ward Holding Corp.	66,300
32	ITT Corporation	114,000	82	Pacific Telesis Group	65,800
33	Safeway Inc.	114,000	83	U S WEST, Inc.	65,469
34	Xerox Corporation	110,000	84	Ernst & Young	65,000
35	General Mills, Inc.	108,077	85	Baxter International Inc.	64,600
36	The Prudential Insurance Co. of America	107,840	86	Aluminum Company of America	63,700
37	Sara Lee Corporation	107,800	87	Georgia-Pacific Corporation	63,000
38	The Goodyear Tire & Rubber Company	107,671	88	The Dun & Bradstreet Corporation	62,900
39	American Express Company	106,836	89	Humana Inc.	62,873
40	Allied-Signal Inc.	105,800	90	The Dow Chemical Company	62,100
41	Motorola, Inc.	105,000	91	Waste Management, Inc.	62,050
42	Exxon Corporation	104,085	92	Martin Marietta Corporation	62,000
43	AMR Corporation	102,809	93	Delta Air Lines, Inc.	61,675
44	BellSouth Corporation	102,000	94	Honeywell Inc.	60,332
45	Rockwell International Corporation	101,900	95	Cargill, Inc.	60,000
46	Winn-Dixie Stores, Inc.	101,000	96	Albertson's, Inc.	58,000
47	TW Holdings, Inc.	100,000	97	Cooper Industries, Inc.	57,500
48	The Great Atlantic & Pacific Tea Company	99,300	98	Arthur Andersen & Co.	56,801
49	General Dynamics Corporation	98,100	99	Ralston Purina Company	56,127
50	Citicorp	95,000	100	Caterpillar Inc.	56,016

Companies in *Hoover's Handbook of American Business 1992* by Metropolitan Area

City Company	1990 Sales ($ mil.)
Akron, OH	
The Goodyear Tire & Rubber Company	11,273
Roadway Services, Inc.	2,971
Ashland, KY	
Ashland Oil, Inc.	8,552
Atlanta, GA	
BellSouth Corporation	14,345
Georgia-Pacific Corporation	12,665
The Coca-Cola Company	10,236
Delta Air Lines, Inc.	8,582
The Southern Company	7,975
The Home Depot, Inc.	3,815
Cox Enterprises, Inc.	2,095
Turner Broadcasting System, Inc.	1,394
American Cancer Society	NA
SunTrust Banks, Inc.	NA
Austin, TX	
Dell Computer Corporation	546
The University of Texas at Austin	NA
Baltimore, MD	
The Black & Decker Corporation	4,832
USF&G Corporation	4,181
Bartlesville, OK	
Phillips Petroleum Company	13,603
Battle Creek, MI	
Kellogg Company	5,181
Benton Harbor, MI	
Whirlpool Corporation	6,623
Bentonville, AR	
Wal-Mart Stores, Inc.	32,602
Bethlehem, PA	
Union Pacific Corporation	6,964
Bethlehem Steel Corporation	4,899
Birmingham, AL	
Bruno's, Inc.	2,395
Vulcan Materials Company	1,105
Bloomington, IL	
State Farm	18,208
Boise, ID	
Albertson's, Inc.	8,219
Boise Cascade Corporation	4,186
Boston, MA	
Digital Equipment Corporation	12,943
John Hancock Mutual Life Insurance Co.	10,033
Raytheon Company	9,268
The Stop & Shop Companies, Inc.	4,990
The Gillette Company	4,345
Wang Laboratories, Inc.	2,497
EG&G, Inc.	2,474
General Cinema Corporation	2,177
Reebok International Ltd.	2,159
Polaroid Corporation	1,972
Prime Computer, Inc.	1,589
Data General Corporation	1,216
Lotus Development Corporation	685
Boston Celtics LP	30
Bank of Boston Corporation	NA
Harvard University	NA
Charlotte, NC	
NCNB Corporation	6,682
Duke Power Company	3,681
Springs Industries, Inc.	1,878

City Company	1990 Sales ($ mil.)
Chicago, IL	
Sears, Roebuck & Co.	55,972
Amoco Corporation	28,010
Household International, Inc.	14,320
Sara Lee Corporation	11,606
UAL Corporation	11,037
Motorola, Inc.	10,885
Ameritech Corporation	10,663
Baxter International Inc.	8,100
McDonald's Corporation	6,640
Abbott Laboratories	6,159
Walgreen Co.	6,048
Waste Management, Inc.	6,034
First Chicago Corporation	5,693
Montgomery Ward Holding Corp.	5,464
Commonwealth Edison Company	5,262
The Quaker Oats Company	5,031
Arthur Andersen & Co.	4,160
Inland Steel Industries, Inc.	3,870
Navistar International Corporation	3,854
FMC Corporation	3,722
R. R. Donnelley & Sons Company	3,498
Hyatt Corporation	3,101
Continental Bank Corporation	3,070
Kemper Corporation	2,929
Premark International, Inc.	2,721
Brunswick Corporation	2,478
Tribune Company	2,353
Borg-Warner Corporation	2,340
Whitman Corporation	2,305
Santa Fe Pacific Corporation	2,297
Bally Manufacturing Corporation	1,997
USG Corporation	1,915
Square D Company	1,653
Morton International, Inc.	1,639
Farley, Inc.	1,550
Zenith Electronics Corporation	1,410
Hartmarx Corporation	1,296
Centel Corporation	1,149
Outboard Marine Corporation	1,146
Wm. Wrigley Jr. Company	1,111
Chicago and North Western	961
Commerce Clearing House, Inc.	716
Midway Airlines, Inc.	655
Baker & McKenzie	404
Johnson Publishing Company, Inc.	252
Skidmore, Owings & Merrill	53
Blue Cross and Blue Shield Association	NA
City of Chicago	NA
Rotary International	NA
The University of Chicago	NA
Cincinnati, OH	
The Procter & Gamble Company	24,081
The Kroger Co.	20,261
American Financial Corporation	7,890
Chiquita Brands International, Inc.	4,273
The United States Shoe Corporation	2,719
Mercantile Stores Company, Inc.	2,394
Cleveland, OH	
TRW Inc.	8,169
Eaton Corporation	3,639
The Sherwin-Williams Company	2,267
Reliance Electric Company	1,547
American Greetings Corporation	1,413

Companies in *Hoover's Handbook of American Business 1992* by Metropolitan Area (cont.)

City Company	1990 Sales ($ mil.)
Columbus, IN	
Cummins Engine Company, Inc.	3,462
Columbus, OH	
The Limited, Inc.	5,376
American Electric Power Company, Inc.	5,168
Banc One Corporation	3,507
Wendy's International, Inc.	1,002
The Ohio State University	NA
Corning, NY	
Corning Inc.	2,941
Dallas-Fort Worth, TX	
Exxon Corporation	105,519
J. C. Penney Company, Inc.	17,410
AMR Corporation	11,720
The Southland Corporation	7,975
Halliburton Company	6,905
Texas Instruments Inc.	6,567
Kimberly-Clark Corporation	6,407
The LTV Corporation	6,138
Burlington Northern Inc.	4,674
Texas Utilities Company	4,543
Tandy Corporation	4,500
Dresser Industries, Inc.	4,480
Oryx Energy Company	1,940
Trammell Crow Company	1,275
Southwest Airlines Co.	1,187
Dr Pepper/Seven-Up Companies, Inc.	540
Dayton, OH	
NCR Corporation	6,285
The Mead Corporation	4,772
Decatur, IL	
Archer-Daniels-Midland Company	7,751
Denver, CO	
U S WEST, Inc.	9,957
Tele-Communications, Inc.	3,625
Manville Corporation	2,245
Cyprus Minerals Company	1,866
Adolph Coors Company	1,863
Storage Technology Corporation	1,141
Rio Grande Industries, Inc.	NA
Detroit, MI	
General Motors Corporation	123,276
Ford Motor Company	97,650
Kmart Corporation	32,281
Chrysler Corporation	29,797
Masco Corporation	3,209
Stroh Companies Inc.	1,293
Fremont, MI	
Gerber Products Company	1,179
Grand Rapids, MI	
Amway Corporation	2,200
Green Bay, WI	
The Green Bay Packers, Inc.	42
Greensboro, NC	
Burlington Holdings Inc.	2,282
Fieldcrest Cannon, Inc.	1,242
Harrisburg, PA	
Rite Aid Corporation	3,447
AMP Inc.	3,044
Hershey Foods Corporation	2,716

City Company	1990 Sales ($ mil.)
Hartford, CT	
United Technologies Corporation	21550
Aetna Life & Casualty Company	19,021
The Travelers Corporation	11,313
Honolulu, HI	
HAL, Inc.	341
Houston, TX	
Tenneco, Inc.	14,511
Enron Corp.	13,165
The Coastal Corporation	9,381
SYSCO Corporation	7,591
Continental Airlines Holdings, Inc.	6,231
Cooper Industries, Inc.	6,206
Compaq Computer Corporation	3,599
Panhandle Eastern Corporation	2,988
Browning-Ferris Industries, Inc.	2,967
Baker Hughes Inc.	2,614
Pennzoil Company	2,180
King Ranch, Inc.	NA
Huntsville, AL	
SCI Systems, Inc.	1,179
Intergraph Corporation	1,045
Indianapolis, IN	
Eli Lilly and Company	5,192
Mayflower Group, Inc.	672
Jacksonville, FL	
Winn-Dixie Stores, Inc.	9,745
Barnett Banks, Inc.	3,296
Kalamazoo, MI	
The Upjohn Company	3,033
Kansas City, MO-KS	
United Telecommunications, Inc.	8,345
Hallmark Cards, Inc.	2,700
Yellow Freight System	2,302
H&R Block, Inc.	1,163
Kenosha, WI	
Snap-on Tools Corporation	985
Lakeland, FL	
Publix Super Markets, Inc.	5,758
Lancaster, PA	
Armstrong World Industries, Inc.	2,531
Little Rock, AR	
Dillard Department Stores, Inc.	3,734
Los Angeles, CA	
Occidental Petroleum Corporation	21,694
Atlantic Richfield Company	18,008
Rockwell International Corporation	12,379
Unocal Corporation	10,645
Security Pacific Corporation	10,327
Lockheed Corporation	9,958
Fluor Corporation	7,446
SCEcorp	7,199
Pacific Enterprises	6,923
First Interstate Bancorp	6,024
The Walt Disney Company	5,844
Northrop Corporation	5,490
The Vons Companies, Inc.	5,334
Litton Industries, Inc.	5,156
H. F. Ahmanson & Company	4,848

Companies in *Hoover's Handbook of American Business 1992* by Metropolitan Area (cont.)

City / Company	1990 Sales ($ mil.)
Los Angeles, CA (continued)	
Great Western Financial Corporation	4,207
National Medical Enterprises, Inc.	3,806
Teledyne, Inc.	3,446
The Times Mirror Company	3,261
Dole Food Company, Inc.	3,003
Carter Hawley Hale Stores, Inc.	2,983
Mattel, Inc.	1,471
Fleetwood Enterprises, Inc.	1,401
First Executive Corporation	1,296
Hilton Hotels Corporation	1,087
L.A. Gear, Inc.	902
AST Research, Inc.	534
Amgen Inc.	381
Louisville, KY	
Humana Inc.	4,852
Brown-Forman Corporation	1,119
Melbourne, FL	
Harris Corporation	3,053
Memphis, TN	
Federal Express Corporation	7,688
Miami, FL	
W. R. Grace & Company	6,754
Ryder System, Inc.	5,162
Knight-Ridder, Inc.	2,305
Blockbuster Entertainment Corp.	633
Office Depot, Inc.	626
Midland, MI	
The Dow Chemical Company	19,773
Milwaukee, WI	
Northwestern Mutual	6,922
Johnson Controls, Inc.	4,504
Harley-Davidson, Inc.	865
Minneapolis, MN	
Cargill, Inc.	42,000
Dayton Hudson Corporation	14,739
Minnesota Mining and Manufacturing Co.	13,021
Super Valu Stores, Inc.	11,612
Carlson Companies, Inc.	8,100
NWA Inc.	7,257
General Mills, Inc.	7,153
Honeywell Inc.	6,309
Control Data Corporation	1,691
Deluxe Corporation	1,414
Cray Research, Inc.	804
Modesto, CA	
E. & J. Gallo Winery	1,050
Moline, IL	
Deere & Company	7,759
Nashville, TN	
Hospital Corporation of America	4,631
Service Merchandise Company, Inc.	3,435
New Orleans, LA	
Entergy Corporation	3,982
McDermott International, Inc.	3,136
New York, NY/CT/NJ	
International Business Machines Corp.	69,018
General Electric Company	57,662
American Telephone & Telegraph Company	51,321
Philip Morris Companies, Inc.	44,323
The Prudential Insurance Co. of America	42,125

City / Company	1990 Sales ($ mil.)
Texaco Inc.	40,899
Citicorp	38,385
Salomon Inc	35,946
Metropolitan Life Insurance Company	27,168
American Express Company	24,332
ITT Corporation	20,604
GTE Corporation	18,374
PepsiCo, Inc.	17,803
Xerox Corporation	16,951
American International Group, Inc.	16,214
Continental Grain Company	14,850
RJR Nabisco, Inc.	13,879
The Chase Manhattan Corporation	13,672
United Parcel Service of America, Inc.	13,606
NYNEX Corporation	13,585
New York Life Insurance Company	13,228
International Paper Company	12,960
Allied-Signal Inc.	12,343
Loews Corporation	12,281
Time Warner Inc.	11,517
The Great Atlantic & Pacific Tea Company	11,391
Johnson & Johnson	11,232
Merrill Lynch & Co., Inc.	11,213
J.P. Morgan & Co. Inc.	10,465
Bristol-Myers Squibb Company	10,300
Woolworth Corporation	9,789
The Equitable	9,584
Teachers Insurance	9,360
Melville Corporation	8,687
American Brands, Inc.	8,270
Chemical Banking Corporation	7,967
Bankers Trust New York Corporation	7,919
Manufacturers Hanover Corporation	7,695
Merck & Co., Inc.	7,672
Borden, Inc.	7,633
Union Carbide Corporation	7,621
R. H. Macy & Co., Inc.	7,547
American Home Products Corporation	6,775
Pfizer Inc.	6,406
Primerica Corporation	6,190
Supermarkets General Holdings Corp.	6,126
Morgan Stanley Group Inc.	5,870
CPC International Inc.	5,781
Consolidated Edison Co. of New York, Inc.	5,739
Colgate-Palmolive Company	5,691
Toys "R" Us, Inc.	5,510
Capital Cities/ABC, Inc.	5,386
MacAndrews & Forbes Holdings Inc.	5,381
KPMG	5368
The Bank of New York Company, Inc.	5,333
Schlumberger NV	5,306
Champion International Corporation	5,090
Ernst & Young	5,006
The Dun & Bradstreet Corporation	4,818
Public Service Enterprise Group Inc.	4,800

City Company	1990 Sales ($ mil.)
New York, NY/CT/NJ (continued)	
Warner-Lambert Company	4,687
Trans World Airlines, Inc.	4,601
The Goldman Sachs Group, LP	4,600
American Cyanamid Company	4,570
Coopers & Lybrand	4,100
Grumman Corporation	3,990
Pan Am Corporation	3,917
Paramount Communications Inc.	3,869
AMAX Inc.	3,788
Deloitte & Touche	3,760
Ingersoll-Rand Company	3,738
American Standard Inc.	3,637
Avon Products, Inc.	3,454
Schering-Plough Corporation	3,323
CBS Inc.	3,261
Pitney Bowes Inc.	3,196
Ames Department Stores, Inc.	3,109
First Fidelity Bancorporation	3,082
Advance Publications, Inc.	3,040
Paine Webber Group Inc.	2,979
Price Waterhouse	2,900
JWP Inc.	2,827
Marsh & McLennan Companies, Inc.	2,723
Metromedia Company	2,530
Riklis Family Corporation	2,508
The Hertz Corporation	2,507
The Bear Stearns Companies Inc.	2,386
ASARCO Inc.	2,209
The Hearst Corporation	2,138
Estée Lauder Inc.	2,093
Becton, Dickinson and Company	2,013
The Reader's Digest Association, Inc.	2,010
The Stanley Works	1,977
McGraw-Hill, Inc.	1,939
The New York Times Company	1,777
Liz Claiborne, Inc.	1,729
Dow Jones & Company, Inc.	1,720
Automatic Data Processing, Inc.	1,714
General Signal Corporation	1,695
Viacom Inc.	1,600
Ogden Corporation	1,563
TLC Beatrice International Holdings, Inc.	1,496
Helmsley Enterprises Inc.	1,480
Computer Associates International, Inc.	1,348
Avis Inc.	1,205
Young & Rubicam Inc.	1,074
International Flavors & Fragrances Inc.	963
McKinsey & Co.	900
C. R. Bard, Inc.	785
New York Stock Exchange, Inc.	349
The Ford Foundation	NA
General Re Corporation	NA
Kohlberg Kravis Roberts & Co.	NA
New York City Transit Authority	NA
The Rockefeller Foundation	NA
Newton, IA	
Maytag Corporation	3,057
Norfolk, VA	
Norfolk Southern Corporation	4,617

City Company	1990 Sales ($ mil.)
North Wilkesboro, NC	
Lowe's Companies, Inc.	2,833
Oklahoma City, OK	
Fleming Companies, Inc.	11,933
Omaha, NE	
ConAgra, Inc.	19,505
Peter Kiewit Sons' Inc.	1,917
Berkshire Hathaway Inc.	
Peoria, IL	
Caterpillar Inc.	11,436
Philadelphia, PA	
CIGNA Corporation	18,164
Bell Atlantic Corporation	12,298
Sun Company, Inc.	11,812
Unisys Corporation	10,111
Campbell Soup Company	6,206
Scott Paper Company	5,356
The ARA Group, Inc.	4,596
Consolidated Rail Corporation	3,372
Commodore International Ltd.	887
Phoenix, AZ	
The Circle K Corporation	3,599
The Dial Corp	3,519
Phelps Dodge Corporation	2,636
Pinnacle West Capital Corporation	1,597
America West Airlines, Inc.	1,316
Pittsburgh, PA	
USX Corporation	19,326
Westinghouse Electric Corporation	12,915
Aluminum Company of America	10,710
H. J. Heinz Company	6,647
PPG Industries, Inc.	6,021
PNC Financial Corp	4,880
Mellon Bank Corporation	3,477
Portland, OR	
NIKE, Inc.	3,004
Fred Meyer, Inc.	2,476
Portsmouth, NH	
The Henley Group, Inc.	1,871
Providence, RI	
Textron Inc.	7,915
Fleet/Norstar Financial Group, Inc.	4,033
Hasbro, Inc.	1,520
Provo, UT	
Novell, Inc.	498
Racine, WI	
S.C. Johnson & Son, Inc.	3,000
Reading, PA	
V. F. Corporation	2,613
Richmond, VA	
CSX Corporation	8,205
Reynolds Metals Company	6,022
James River Corporation	3,391
Universal Corporation	2,815
Circuit City Stores, Inc.	2,367
Rochester, MN	
Mayo Foundation	1,181
Rochester, NY	
Eastman Kodak Company	18,908

City Company	1990 Sales ($ mil.)
Sacramento, CA	
State of California	NA
St. Louis, MO	
McDonnell Douglas Corporation	16,246
Anheuser-Busch Companies, Inc.	10,744
General Dynamics Corporation	10,173
The May Department Stores Company	10,066
Southwestern Bell Corporation	9,113
Monsanto Company	8,995
Emerson Electric Co.	7,573
Ralston Purina Company	7,101
Brown Group, Inc.	1,764
INTERCO Inc.	1,439
Edison Brothers	1,254
Salisbury, NC	
Food Lion, Inc.	5,584
Salt Lake City, UT	
American Stores Company	22,156
Thiokol Corporation	1,181
San Antonio, TX	
Associated Milk Producers, Inc.	3,063
San Diego, CA	
The Price Company	5,412
San Francisco, CA	
Chevron Corporation	38,607
Safeway Inc.	14,874
Hewlett-Packard Company	13,233
BankAmerica Corporation	12,323
Pacific Telesis Group	9,716
Pacific Gas and Electric Company	9,470
McKesson Corporation	8,421
Transamerica Corporation	6,703
Wells Fargo & Company	5,960
Bechtel Group, Inc.	5,631
Apple Computer, Inc.	5,558
Levi Strauss Associates Inc.	4,247
Consolidated Freightways, Inc.	4,209
Intel Corporation	3,921
Sun Microsystems, Inc.	2,466
Seagate Technology, Inc.	2,413
American President Companies, Ltd.	2,337
Longs Drug Stores Corporation	2,334
Amdahl Corporation	2,159
The Gap, Inc.	1,934
Tandem Computers Inc.	1,866
National Semiconductor Corporation	1,702
Syntex Corporation	1,521
The Clorox Company	1,484
Conner Peripherals, Inc.	1,338
Oracle Systems Corporation	1,028
The Charles Schwab Corporation	626
Genentech, Inc.	435
Atari Corporation	411
Borland International, Inc.	227
Sharper Image Corporation	181
Adobe Systems, Inc.	169
Stanford University	NA
Seattle-Tacoma, WA	
The Boeing Company	27,595
Weyerhaeuser Company	9,024
Costco Wholesale Corporation	4,133
Nordstrom, Inc.	2,894

City Company	1990 Sales ($ mil.)
PACCAR Inc.	2,778
Microsoft Corporation	1,183
Alaska Air Group, Inc.	1,047
McCaw Cellular Communications, Inc.	1,037
Spartanburg, SC	
TW Holdings, Inc.	3,682
Milliken & Co., Inc.	2,500
Springdale, AR	
Tyson Foods, Inc.	3,825
Springfield, MA	
Massachusetts Mutual Life Insurance Co.	6,700
Tampa, FL	
Jack Eckerd Corporation	3,367
Toledo, OH	
Dana Corporation	5,225
Owens-Illinois, Inc.	3,979
Owens-Corning Fiberglas Corporation	3,111
Washington, DC/MD/VA	
Mobil Corporation	57,819
Federal National Mortgage Association	12,719
Mars, Inc.	8,450
MCI Communications Corporation	7,680
Marriott Corporation	7,646
USAir Group, Inc.	6,559
Martin Marietta Corporation	6,126
Gannett Co., Inc.	3,442
Giant Food Inc.	3,350
The Washington Post Company	1,439
AFL-CIO	NA
American Association of Retired Persons	NA
Democratic Party	NA
GEICO Corporation	NA
National Geographic Society	NA
National Organization for Women, Inc.	NA
National Park Service	NA
Republican Party	NA
Roman Catholic Church (US)	NA
Teamsters	NA
United States	
United Way of America	
West Palm Beach, FL	
FPL Group, Inc.	6,289
Wilmington, DE	
E. I. du Pont de Nemours and Company	39,709
Hercules Inc.	3,200
The Columbia Gas System, Inc.	2,358
The E.W. Scripps Company	1,297
Witchita, KS	
Koch Industries, Inc.	17,190
Wooster, OH	
Rubbermaid Inc.	1,534
Youngstown, OH	
Edward J. DeBartolo Corporation	NA

30 YEARS OF CHANGE IN THE *FORTUNE* 500

25 Largest US Industrial Companies

Rank	1960	1970	1980	1990
1	General Motors	General Motors	Exxon	General Motors
2	Standard Oil (NJ)	Standard Oil (NJ)	Mobil	Exxon
3	Ford	Ford	General Motors	Ford
4	General Electric	General Electric	Texaco	IBM
5	U. S. Steel	IBM	Standard Oil of California	Mobil
6	Socony Mobil Oil	Mobil Oil	Ford	General Electric
7	Chrysler	Chrysler	Gulf Oil	Philip Morris
8	Texaco	ITT	IBM	Texaco
9	Gulf Oil	Texaco	Standard Oil (IN)	Du Pont
10	Western Electric	Western Electric	General Electric	Chevron
11	Swift	Gulf Oil	Atlantic Richfield	Chrysler
12	Bethlehem Steel	U. S. Steel	Shell Oil	Amoco
13	Du Pont	Westinghouse Electric	ITT	Boeing
14	Standard Oil (IN)	Standard Oil of California	Conoco	Shell Oil
15	General Dynamics	Ling-Temco-Vought	Du Pont	Procter & Gamble
16	Westinghouse Electric	Standard Oil (IN)	Phillips Petroleum	Occidental Petroleum
17	Shell Oil	Boeing	Tenneco	United Technologies
18	Armour	Du Pont	Sun	Dow Chemical
19	International Harvester	Shell Oil	U. S. Steel	USX
20	National Dairy Products	General Telephone & Electronics	Occidental Petroleum	Eastman Kodak
21	Standard Oil of California	RCA	United Technologies	Atlantic Richfield
22	Boeing	Goodyear Tire & Rubber	Western Electric	Xerox
23	Goodyear Tire & Rubber	Swift	Standard Oil (OH)	PepsiCo
24	Union Carbide	Union Carbide	Procter & Gamble	McDonnell Douglas
25	Radio Corp. of America	Procter & Gamble	Dow Chemical	Conagra

10 Largest US Retail Companies

Rank	1960	1970	1980	1990
1	Great Atlantic & Pacific Tea	Sears, Roebuck	Sears, Roebuck	Sears, Roebuck
2	Sears, Roebuck	Great Atlantic & Pacific Tea	Safeway	Wal-Mart
3	Safeway	Safeway	Kmart	Kmart
4	Kroger	J. C. Penney	J. C. Penney	American Stores
5	J. C. Penney	Kroger	Kroger	Kroger
6	Montgomery Ward	Marcor	F.W. Woolworth	J. C. Penney
7	F.W. Woolworth	S.S. Kresge	Great Atlantic & Pacific Tea	Safeway
8	American Stores	F.W. Woolworth	Lucky Stores	Dayton Hudson
9	National Tea	Federated Department Stores	American Stores	Great Atlantic & Pacific Tea
10	Federated Department Stores	Food Fair Stores	Federated Department Stores	May Department Stores

10 Largest US Transportation Companies

Rank	1960	1970	1980	1990
1	Pennsylvania RR	Penn Central	UAL	United Parcel Service
2	Southern Pacific	UAL	Trans World Corp.	AMR
3	New York Central RR	Southern Pacific	CSX	UAL
4	Atchison, Topeka & Santa Fe Rwy.	Trans World Airlines	United Parcel Service	Delta Air Lines
5	Union Pacific RR	American Airlines	Pan American World Airways	CSX
6	American Airlines	Pan American World Airways	Burlington Northern	NWA
7	Pan American World Airways	Norfolk & Western Rwy.	American Airlines	Union Pacific
8	Baltimore & Ohio RR	Burlington Northern	Eastern Air Lines	Federal Express
9	United Air Lines	Chesapeake & Ohio Rwy.	Santa Fe Industries	USAir Group
10	Trans World Airlines	Eastern Air Lines	Delta Air Lines	Continental Airlines

Source: *Fortune* annual list issues, 1961–91

1990 Leading Brands in the US by Category

Category	Brand	Company
Analgesics	Tylenol	Johnson & Johnson
Antacids	Maalox	Rhône-Poulenc
Apparel	Levi's, Dockers	Levi Strauss
Appliances (major)	General Electric	General Electric
Appliances (small)	Black & Decker	Black & Decker
Athletic shoes	NIKE	NIKE
Autos & trucks	Ford	Ford
Bathroom tissue	Charmin	Procter & Gamble
Beer	Budweiser	Anheuser-Busch
Cereal	Cheerios	General Mills
Cigarettes	Marlboro	Philip Morris
Chocolate candy	M&Ms	Mars
Coffee	Folgers	Procter & Gamble
Consumer electronics	Sony	Sony
Cosmetics	Cover Girl	Procter & Gamble
Coughs/colds	Hall's	Warner-Lambert
Deodorant	Secret	Procter & Gamble
Detergent	Tide	Procter & Gamble
Facial tissue	Kleenex	Kimberly-Clark
Frozen meals	Stouffer's	Nestlé
Fruit juices	Minute Maid	Coca-Cola
Hand soap	Dove	Lever Bros.
Liquor	Bacardi	Bacardi
Paper towels	Bounty	Procter & Gamble
Shampoo	Pert Plus	Procter & Gamble
Soft drinks	Coca-Cola	Coca-Cola
Toothpaste	Crest	Procter & Gamble
Wine	Sutter Home	Sutter Home Winery Inc.

Source: *Superbrands 1991, Adweek Supplement*

20 Most Advertised Brands in the US

Rank	Brand	Parent Company	1990 Ad Spending ($ mil.)
1	AT&T	AT&T	502
2	McDonald's restaurants	McDonald's	426
3	Sears stores	Sears	422
4	Kellogg's breakfast foods	Kellogg	380
5	Ford cars, trucks & vans	Ford	340
6	Toyota cars, trucks & vans	Toyota	307
7	Chevrolet cars	General Motors	306
8	Nissan cars, trucks & vans	Nissan	236
9	Kmart stores	Kmart	192
10	Kraft foods	Philip Morris	188
11	Budweiser beers	Anheuser-Busch	184
12	Miller beers	Philip Morris	181
13	Mazda cars & trucks	Mazda	181
14	Burger King restaurants	Grand Metropolitan	178
15	General Motors cars	General Motors	166
16	Coca-Cola soft drinks	Coca-Cola	160
17	Buick cars	General Motors	159
18	Pepsi beverages	PepsiCo	156
19	Chrysler cars	Chrysler	151
20	Macy's department stores	Macy	145

Source: LNA/Arbitron Multi-Media Service; *Advertising Age,* May 20, 1991, Crain Communications, Inc.

20 Largest Advertising Agencies in the US

Rank	Agency	1990 US Sales ($ mil.)
1	Young & Rubicam	451
2	Saatchi & Saatchi Advertising Worldwide	388
3	BBDO Worldwide	370
4	Ogilvy & Mather Worldwide	322
5	Backer Spielvogel Bates Worldwide	311
6	Leo Burnett Co.	299
7	DDB Needham Worldwide	298
8	Foote, Cone & Belding Communications	292
9	J. Walter Thompson Co.	285
10	D'Arcy Masius Benton & Bowles	277
11	Grey Advertising	256
12	Lintas:Worldwide	253
13	McCann-Erickson Worldwide	210
14	Bozell Inc.	156
15	Ketchum Communications	121
16	Ross Roy Group	106
17	Wells, Rich, Greene	105
18	N W Ayer	99
19	Della Femina, McNamee	94
20	Chiat/Day/Mojo	89

Source: *Advertising Age*, March 25, 1991, Crain Communications, Inc.

20 Largest Advertisers in the US

Rank	Company	1990 Ad Spending ($ mil.)
1	Procter & Gamble	2,285
2	Philip Morris	2,210
3	Sears	1,507
4	General Motors	1,503
5	Grand Metropolitan	883
6	PepsiCo	849
7	AT&T	797
8	McDonald's	764
9	Kmart	693
10	Time Warner	677
11	Eastman Kodak	665
12	Johnson & Johnson	654
13	RJR Nabisco	636
14	Nestlé	636
15	Warner-Lambert	631
16	Ford	616
17	Toyota	581
18	Kellogg	578
19	Unilever	569
20	General Mills	539

Source: *Advertising Age*, September 25, 1991, Crain Communications, Inc.

30 Largest US Media Companies

Rank	Company	1990 Media Sales ($ mil.)
1	Capital Cities/ABC	5,175
2	Time Warner	4,965
3	Gannett	3,442
4	CBS	3,261
5	General Electric	3,236
6	Advance Publications	3,040
7	TCI	2,942
8	Times Mirror	2,855
9	News Corp.	2,234
10	Hearst	2,138
11	Knight-Ridder	2,106
12	New York Times	1,777
13	Cox	1,711
14	Tribune	1,703
15	Thomson Corp.	1,404
16	Washington Post	1,356
17	Viacom	1,338
18	E.W. Scripps	1,220
19	Turner Broadcasting	1,069
20	Dow Jones	984
21	Continental Cablevision	938
22	Reed Publishing USA	804
23	Westinghouse	734
24	Reader's Digest	681
25	Advo-Systems	655
26	MediaNews Group	600
27	Comcast	592
28	McGraw-Hill	589
29	Valassis Inserts	574
30	Cablevision Systems	563

Source: *Advertising Age*, August 12, 1991, Crain Communications, Inc.

10 Largest US TV Broadcast Companies

Rank	Company	1990 TV Sales ($ mil.)
1	Capital Cities/ABC	3,610
2	General Electric	3,203
3	CBS	3,011
4	News Corp.	835
5	Westinghouse	534
6	Tribune	459
7	Gillett Holdings	389
8	Cox	320
9	Gannett	309
10	Chris-Craft Industries	278

Source: *Advertising Age*, August 12, 1991, Crain Communications, Inc.

10 Largest US Radio Broadcast Companies

Rank	Company	1990 Radio Sales ($ mil.)
1	CBS	250
2	Capital Cities/ABC	232
3	Westinghouse	200
4	Cox	99
5	Gannett	87
6	Viacom	75
7	Great American Communications	71
8	Tribune	47
9	Hearst	30
10	Park Communications	23

Source: *Advertising Age*, August 12, 1991, Crain Communications, Inc.

10 Largest US Cable Companies

Rank	Company	1990 Cable Sales ($ mil.)
1	Time Warner	3,017
2	TCI	2,942
3	Viacom	1,174
4	Turner Broadcasting	1,069
5	Continental Cablevision	938
6	Comcast	592
7	Cablevision Systems	563
8	SCI Holdings	553
9	Cox	547
10	Capital Cities/ABC	442

Source: *Advertising Age*, August 12, 1991, Crain Communications, Inc.

25 Largest Newspapers in the US

Rank	Newspaper	1990 Circulation* (thou.)	Parent Company
1	Wall Street Journal	1,857	Dow Jones
2	USA Today	1,347	Gannett
3	Los Angeles Times	1,196	Times Mirror
4	New York Times	1,108	New York Times
5	New York Daily News	1,098	Tribune
6	Washington Post	781	Washington Post
7	Chicago Tribune	721	Media General
8	Newsday (Long Island/New York)	714	Times Mirror
9	Detroit Free Press	636	Knight-Ridder
10	San Francisco Chronicle	563	Chronicle Publishing
11	Chicago Sun-Times	527	Chicago Sun Times
12	Boston Globe	521	Affiliated Publications
13	Philadelphia Inquirer	520	Knight-Ridder
14	New York Post	510	Peter Kalikow
15	Detroit News	501	Gannett
16	Star-Ledger (Newark)	476	Advance Publications
17	Houston Chronicle	442	Hearst
18	Miami Herald	429	Knight-Ridder
19	Plain Dealer (Cleveland)	428	Advance Publications
20	Minneapolis Star Tribune	407	Cowles Media
21	Dallas Morning News	385	A. H. Belo Corp.
22	St. Louis Post-Dispatch	382	Pulitzer Publishing
23	Boston Herald	359	News Corp.
24	Orange County Register	354	Freedom Newspapers
25	St. Petersburg Times	353	Times Publishing

* Circulation as of September 30, 1990

Source: *Editor and Publisher International Yearbook 1991*

25 Largest Magazines in the US

Rank	Magazine	1990 Sales ($ mil.)	1990 Paid Circulation (thou.)	Parent Company
1	TV Guide	915	15,604	News Corp.
2	People	642	3,209	Time Warner
3	Time	636	4,095	Time Warner
4	Sports Illustrated	551	3,220	Time Warner
5	Reader's Digest	436	16,265	Reader's Digest
6	Newsweek	403	3,212	Washington Post
7	Parade	355	35,092	Advance Publications
8	Business Week	284	890	McGraw-Hill
9	Better Homes & Gardens	276	8,007	Meredith
10	Good Housekeeping	260	5,153	Hearst
11	U.S. News & World Report	256	2,312	U.S. News & World Report
12	National Geographic	247	10,190	National Geographic
13	Family Circle	240	5,432	New York Times
14	PC Magazine	228	786	Ziff Communications
15	Ladies' Home Journal	213	5,002	Meredith
16	Forbes	208	744	Forbes Inc.
17	National Enquirer	206	3,804	G.P. Group
18	Cosmopolitan	205	2,601	Hearst
19	Fortune	198	673	Time Warner
20	Woman's Day	180	4,803	Hachette
21	McCall's	170	5,020	New York Times
22	Star Magazine	169	3,431	G.P. Group
23	Playboy	167	3,488	Playboy Enterprises
24	Vogue	148	1,216	Advance Publications
25	Glamour	145	2,156	Advance Publications

Source: *Advertising Age*, June 24, 1991, Crain Communications, Inc.

10 Largest US Newspaper Companies

Rank	Company	1990 Newspaper Sales ($ mil.)
1	Gannett	2,775
2	Times Mirror	2,066
3	Knight-Ridder	1,992
4	Advance Publications	1,797
5	New York Times	1,358
6	Tribune	1,197
7	Dow Jones	984
8	E.W. Scripps	785
9	Cox	745
10	Hearst	715

Source: *Advertising Age*, August 12, 1991, Crain Communications, Inc.

10 Largest US Magazine Companies

Rank	Company	1990 Magazine Sales ($ mil.)
1	Time Warner	1,948
2	Hearst	1,022
3	Advance Publications	845
4	Thomson Corp.	750
5	News Corp.	707
6	Reader's Digest	681
7	Reed Publishing USA	624
8	International Data Group	528
9	McGraw-Hill	485
10	Meredith	432

Source: *Advertising Age*, August 12, 1991, Crain Communications, Inc.

10 Largest Restaurants in the US

Rank	Restaurant	1990 Sales ($ thou.)
1	Tavern on the Green, New York, NY	27,025
2	The Rainbow Room, New York, NY	25,500
3	Smith & Wollensky, New York, NY	17,835
4	Kapok Tree, Clearwater, FL	15,170
5	Phillips Harborplace, Ocean City, MD	14,988
6	Bob Chinn's Crabhouse, Wheeling, IL	12,805
7	Zehnder's, Frankenmuth, MI	12,687
8	Spenger's Fish Grotto, Berkeley, CA	12,000
9	Frankenmuth Bavarian Inn, Frankenmuth, MI	11,703
10	The Waterfront, Covington, KY	11,000

Source: *Restaurant Hospitality*, June 1991

10 Largest Restaurant Chains in the US

Rank	Chain	1990 US Sales ($ mil.)	Parent Company
1	McDonald's	12,251	McDonald's
2	Burger King	6,100	Grand Metropolitan
3	Hardee's	4,101	Imasco
4	Pizza Hut	4,000	PepsiCo
5	KFC	3,200	PepsiCo
6	Wendy's	2,762	Wendy's International
7	Domino's Pizza	2,486	Domino's Pizza
8	Taco Bell	2,461	PepsiCo
9	Dairy Queen	1,980	American Dairy Queen
10	Denny's	1,480	TW Holdings

Source: *Nation's Restaurant News*, August 5, 1991

20 Largest Retailers in the US

Rank	Company	1990 Sales ($ mil.)
1	Wal-Mart	32,602
2	Kmart	32,070
3	Sears	31,986
4	American Stores	22,155
5	Kroger	20,261
6	J. C. Penney	16,365
7	Safeway	14,874
8	Dayton Hudson	14,739
9	Great A&P	11,391
10	May Department Stores	10,035
11	Woolworth	9,789
12	Winn-Dixie	9,744
13	Melville	8,687
14	Southland	8,348
15	Albertsons	8,219
16	Macy	7,267
17	Campeau	7,137
18	Supermarkets General	6,126
19	Walgreen	6,047
20	Publix	5,800

Source: *Chain Store Age Executive*, August 1991

Largest Soft Drink Companies in the US

Rank	Parent Company	1990 Market Share %
1	Coca-Cola	40.4
2	PepsiCo	31.8
3	Dr Pepper/7Up	9.8
4	Cadbury Schweppes	3.1
5	Royal Crown	2.6
6	A&W Brands	1.8
7	Monarch	1.7
8	Shasta Beverages	1.5
9	Faygo	0.6
10	Double Cola	0.5
	Others	6.2
	Total	**100.0**

Source: *Beverage Industry*, March 1991

Largest Beer Companies in the US

Rank	Company	1990 Market Share %
1	Anheuser-Busch	43.4
2	Miller	21.9
3	Coors	9.7
4	Stroh	8.1
5	Heileman	6.2
6	Pabst	3.4
	Others	2.7
	Imports	4.6
	Total	**100.0**

Source: *Beer Marketer's Insights*; *Wall Street Journal*, January 15, 1991

Largest Airlines in the US

Rank	Company	1990 Passenger Miles (bil.)
1	AMR	76.9
2	UAL	75.9
3	Delta	59.0
4	NWA	51.5
5	Continental Airlines	39.2
6	USAir	35.5
7	TWA	34.2
8	Pan Am	31.1
9	Eastern	16.6
10	America West	11.1
11	Southwest	10.0

Source: *Air Transport Association of America 1991 Annual Report*

1990 Car and Light Truck Sales in the US

	1990 Cars Sold (thou.)	1990 Light Trucks Sold (thou.)	1990 Cars and Trucks Total (thou.)	Market Share % 1990	Market Share % 1989
Chevrolet/Geo	1,364	1,243	2,607	18.8	18.3
Pontiac	636	30	666	4.8	4.7
Buick	537	0	537	3.9	3.7
Oldsmobile	512	26	538	3.9	4.1
Cadillac	258	0	258	1.9	1.8
GMC	0	326	326	2.4	2.4
Saturn	2	0	2	0.0	0.0
General Motors	**3,309**	**1,625**	**4,934**	**35.5**	**35.1**
Ford	1,321	1,373	2,695	19.4	20.0
Mercury	391	0	391	2.8	3.3
Lincoln	232	0	232	1.7	1.4
Ford	**1,944**	**1,373**	**3,317**	**23.9**	**24.6**
Plymouth	253	172	424	3.1	3.4
Dodge	362	466	828	6.0	6.8
Chrysler	186	3	188	1.4	1.4
Jeep	0	197	197	1.4	1.7
Eagle	61	0	61	0.4	0.5
Chrysler	**861**	**837**	**1,698**	**12.2**	**13.8**
Toyota	716	279	995	7.2	6.4
Lexus	64	0	64	0.5	0.1
Toyota	**779**	**279**	**1,058**	**7.6**	**6.5**
Honda	716	0	716	5.2	4.4
Acura	138	0	138	1.0	1.0
Honda	**855**	**0**	**855**	**6.2**	**5.4**
Nissan	422	176	598	4.3	4.5
Infiniti	24	0	24	0.2	0.0
Nissan	**446**	**176**	**622**	**4.5**	**4.6**
Volkswagen	130	7	136	1.0	0.9
Audi	21	0	21	0.2	0.1
Volkswagen	**151**	**7**	**157**	**1.1**	**1.1**
Mazda	226	124	350	2.5	2.3
Mitsubishi	150	41	191	1.4	1.0
Hyundai	137	0	137	1.0	1.3
Isuzu	6	106	112	0.8	0.8
Subaru	109	0	109	0.8	0.9
Volvo	90	0	90	0.6	0.7
Mercedes-Benz	78	0	78	0.6	0.5
BMW	64	0	64	0.5	0.4
Saab	26	0	26	0.2	0.2
Suzuki	7	14	21	0.1	0.2
Jaguar	19	0	19	0.1	0.1
Daihatsu	11	4	15	0.1	0.1
Porsche	9	0	9	0.1	0.1
Others	23	5	28	0.2	0.2
Total	**9,296**	**4,592**	**13,887**	**100.0**	**100.0**

Note: Totals may not add because of rounding.

Source: *Automotive News*, January 14, 1991

40 Largest Electronics Companies in the US

Rank	Company	1990 Electronics Sales ($ mil.)	1990 Total Sales ($ mil.)	Electronics Sales as % of Total
1	IBM	69,018	69,018	100
2	AT&T	16,832	37,285	45
3	Xerox	13,583	13,583	100
4	Hewlett-Packard	13,538	13,538	100
5	DEC	13,072	13,072	100
6	GM Hughes Electronics	11,723	11,723	100
7	Motorola	10,885	10,885	100
8	Unisys	10,111	10,111	100
9	General Electric	9,430	58,414	16
10	Texas Instruments	6,567	6,567	100
11	Honeywell	6,309	6,309	100
12	NCR	6,285	6,285	100
13	Apple	5,741	5,741	100
14	Raytheon	5,517	9,268	60
15	Rockwell	5,022	12,432	40
16	Tandy	4,648	4,648	100
17	Eastman Kodak	4,140	18,908	22
18	Intel	3,921	3,921	100
19	Lockheed	3,880	9,958	39
20	Compaq	3,599	3,599	100
21	3M	3,530	13,021	27
22	Ford	3,250	97,650	3
23	Westinghouse	3,196	12,915	25
24	Litton Industries	3,166	5,156	61
25	Harris	3,065	3,065	100
26	Martin Marietta	2,983	6,126	49
27	TRW	2,980	8,169	36
28	ITT	2,925	20,604	14
29	Allied-Signal	2,840	12,343	23
30	Sun Microsystems	2,763	2,763	100
31	Seagate	2,668	2,668	100
32	Boeing	2,600	27,595	9
33	AMP	2,587	3,044	85
34	GTE	2,500	18,374	14
35	Du Pont	2,480	40,047	6
36	Emerson	2,396	7,728	31
37	Wang	2,369	2,369	100
38	Pitney Bowes	2,283	3,196	71
39	Amdahl	2,159	2,159	100
40	McDonnell Douglas	1,915	16,255	12

Source: *Electronic Business*, July 22, 1991

20 Largest Computer Companies in North America

Rank	Company	1990 Info. Systems Sales ($ mil.)	1990 Total Sales ($ mil.)	Info. Systems Sales as % of Total
1	IBM	67,090	69,018	97
2	Digital	13,072	13,072	100
3	Unisys	9,302	10,111	92
4	Hewlett-Packard	9,300	13,233	70
5	Apple	5,740	5,740	100
6	NCR	5,617	6,179	91
7	Compaq	3,598	3,598	100
8	AT&T	2,900	37,285	8
9	EDS (General Motors)	2,870	6,109	47
10	Xerox	2,800	17,973	16
11	Sun	2,763	2,763	100
12	Seagate	2,668	2,668	100
13	Wang	2,363	2,363	100
14	Amdahl	2,159	2,159	100
15	Tandem	1,873	1,873	100
16	TRW	1,852	8,169	23
17	Andersen Consulting	1,748	1,880	93
18	ADP	1,730	1,750	99
19	Computer Sciences Corp.	1,679	1,679	100
20	Prime	1,589	1,589	100

Source: *Datamation*, June 15, 1991

20 Largest Government Contractors

Rank	Company	Fiscal 1990 Contract Awards ($ mil.)
1	McDonnell Douglas	9,791.4
2	General Electric	6,692.1
3	General Dynamics	6,613.5
4	Martin Marietta	6,451.5
5	Westinghouse Electric	5,762.8
6	Lockheed	5,036.2
7	General Motors	4,532.9
8	Rockwell International	4,388.0
9	Raytheon	4,369.5
10	United Technologies	3,336.2
11	Boeing	3,130.8
12	Grumman	2,840.7
13	AT&T	2,409.5
14	Tenneco	2,371.9
15	University of California System	2,364.4
16	Unisys	1,674.6
17	IBM	1,636.1
18	Litton Industries	1,568.7
19	Allied-Signal	1,501.8
20	EG&G	1,457.4

Source: *Government Executive*, August 1991

10 Largest Investment Institutions in the US

Rank	Company	1990 Assets ($ mil.)
1	Prudential	207,372
2	American Express	185,162
3	Equitable	124,529
4	Bankers Trust	121,501
5	Metropolitan Life	117,754
6	J.P. Morgan	113,170
7	Citicorp	104,671
8	Aetna	88,875
9	Mellon Bank	76,693
10	State Street Bank and Trust	71,950

Note: This table ranks the top ten institutions according to all assets under management as of year-end 1990, when all assets are considered — the institutions' own as well as those of their clients. The total reflects investments in the securities and real estate markets but not commercial and personal loans.

Source: *Institutional Investor*, July 1991

20 Largest Brokerage Houses in the US

Rank	Company	1990 Total Consolidated Capital ($ mil.)
1	Merrill Lynch	9,567
2	Shearson Lehman Brothers	7,499
3	Salomon	7,162
4	Goldman, Sachs	4,700
5	Morgan Stanley	3,380
6	CS First Boston	1,612
7	Prudential Securities	1,585
8	Paine Webber	1,553
9	Dean Witter Reynolds	1,405
10	Bear Stearns	1,388
11	Smith Barney, Harris Upham	1,012
12	Donaldson, Lufkin & Jenrette	919
13	Nomura	520
14	J.P. Morgan	507
15	Kidder, Peabody	503
16	BT Securities Corp.	485
17	Citicorp Securities Markets	474
18	Shelby Cullom Davis	410
19	A.G. Edwards & Sons	332
20	Charles Schwab	280

Source: *Institutional Investor*, April 1991

HOOVER'S HANDBOOK OF AMERICAN BUSINESS 1992

20 Largest Management Consulting Firms in the World

Rank	Firm	1990 Sales ($ mil.)
1	Andersen Consulting	1,875
2	Ernst & Young	1,169
3	Marsh & McLennan	910
4	McKinsey	900
5	Coopers & Lybrand	898
6	KPMG Peat Marwick	785
7	Towers Perrin	640
8	Deloitte & Touche	639
9	Price Waterhouse	634
10	Booz-Allen & Hamilton	521
11	Wyatt	430
12	CSC Consulting	370
13	Alexander Proudfoot	358
14	Hewitt Associates	297
15	PA Consulting	286
16	Arthur D. Little	242
17	Alexander Consulting Group	232
18	American Management Systems	226
18	Gemini	226
20	Hay Group	207

Source: Kennedy Publications, June 1991

10 Largest Law Firms in the US

Rank	Company	Headquarters	1990 Sales ($ mil.)
1	Skadden, Arps, Slate, Meagher & Flom	New York	503.0
2	Baker & McKenzie	Chicago	404.0
3	Jones, Day, Reavis & Pogue	Cleveland	390.0
4	Shearman & Sterling	New York	299.0
5	Gibson, Dunn & Crutcher	Los Angeles	290.0
6	Vinson & Elkins	Houston	275.5
7	Davis Polk & Wardwell	New York	250.0
8	Sullivan & Cromwell	New York	240.0
9	Latham & Watkins	Los Angeles	234.0
10	O'Melveny & Myers	Los Angeles	230.0

Source: American Lawyer Survey; New York Times, July 1, 1991

25 Largest Accounting Firms in the US

Rank	Firm	1990 Sales ($ mil.)
Big Six		
1	Arthur Andersen & Co.	2,282
2	Ernst & Young	2,239
3	Deloitte & Touche	1,921
4	KPMG Peat Marwick	1,827
5	Coopers & Lybrand	1,400
6	Price Waterhouse	1,200
7	Grant Thornton	197
8	BDO Seidman	178
9	McGladrey & Pullen	168
10	Kenneth Leventhal & Company	166
11	Pannell Kerr Forster	92
12	Baird Kurtz & Dobson	53
13	Plante & Moran	46
14	Clifton Gunderson & Co.	45
15	Crowe Chizek	43
16	Moss Adams	40
17	Altschuler Melvoin and Glasser	39
18	Cherry Bekaert & Holland	27
19	Richard A. Eisner & Company	26
20	Geo. S. Olive & Co.	26
21	Goldstein Golub Kessler	21
22	Urbach Kahn & Werlin	21
23	David Berdon & Co.	20
24	Friedman Eisenstein Raemer Schwartz	20
25	Larson Allen Weishair	19

Source: Bowman's Accounting Report

Auditors Used by Companies in this Book

Firm	No. of Companies	% of Total
Ernst & Young	96	19
Deloitte & Touche	87	17
Arthur Andersen & Co.	84	17
Price Waterhouse	77	15
KPMG	66	14
Coopers & Lybrand	57	11
Others	4	1
Inapplicable or unknown	29	6
Total	**500**	**100**

15 Companies in the Dow Jones Utility Stocks Index

American Electric Power
Arkla
Centerior Energy
Commonwealth Edison
Consolidated Edison
Consolidated Natural Gas
Detroit Edison
Houston Industries
Niagara Mohawk Power
Pacific Gas & Electric
Panhandle Eastern
Peoples Energy
Philadelphia Electric
Public Service Enterprises
SCEcorp

Source: *The Wall Street Journal*, August 2, 1991

20 Companies in the Dow Jones Transportation Stocks Index

Airborne Freight
Alaska Air
American President
AMR
Burlington Northern
Carolina Freight
Consolidated Freightways
Consolidated Rail
CSX
Delta Air Lines
Federal Express
Norfolk Southern
Roadway
Ryder
Santa Fe Pacific
Southwest Airlines
UAL
Union Pacific
USAir
Xtra Corp.

Source: *Barron's,* August 5, 1991

30 Companies in the Dow Jones Industrials Index

Alcoa
Allied-Signal
American Express
AT&T
Bethlehem Steel
Boeing
Caterpillar
Chevron
Coca-Cola
Du Pont
Exxon
General Electric
General Motors
Goodyear
IBM
International Paper
Kodak
McDonald's
Merck
3M
J.P. Morgan
Philip Morris
Procter & Gamble
Sears
Texaco
Union Carbide
United Technologies
Walt Disney
Westinghouse
Woolworth

Source: *The Wall Street Journal*, August 2, 1991

400 Companies in the Standard & Poor's Midcap Index

A & W Brands
Acuson Corp.
ADC Telecommunications
Adobe Systems
Advanced Telecommunications
Affiliated Publications
Air & Water Technologies
Airborne Freight
Alaska Air Group
Albany International
Aldus Corp.
Alexander & Baldwin
Allegheny Ludlum
Allegheny Power System
Allergan, Inc.
Altera Corp.
American Barrick Resources
American Family
American President Companies
American Waste Services
Ametek, Inc.
Anadarko Petroleum
Analog Devices
Angelica Corp.
Anthem Electronics
AON Corp.
Apache Corp.
Applied Bioscience International
Applied Materials
Arvin Industries
AST Research
Atlanta Gas Light
Atlantic Energy
Atlantic Southeast Airlines
Avnet, Inc.
Bancorp Hawaii
The Bank of New York Company
Banta Corp.
Baroid Corp.
Battle Mountain Gold
Bear Stearns Companies
Beckman Instruments
A.H. Belo Corp.
Bergen Brunswig
Betz Laboratories
Biogen Inc.
BJ Services
Black Hills Corp.
BMC Software
Bob Evans Farms
Borland International
Bowater Incorporated
Brinker International
Brooklyn Union Gas
Brush Wellman
Burlington Resources
Cadence Design Systems
Caesars World
Calgon Carbon
CalMat Co.
Cardinal Distribution
Carlisle Companies
Carpenter Technology
Carter-Wallace
Castle & Cooke
CBI Industries
Centocor, Inc.
Central Fidelity Banks
Central Louisiana Electric

Central Maine Power
Century Telephone Enterprises
Cetus Corporation
Chesapeake Corp.
Chiron Corp.
Chris-Craft Industries
Church & Dwight
Cincinnati Gas & Electric
Cintas Corp.
Circus Circus Enterprises
Cirrus Logic
Cisco Systems
City National Corp.
Claire's Stores
Clayton Homes
Cleveland-Cliffs
CMS Energy
Coca-Cola Enterprises
Colonial Companies
Comdisco, Inc.
Comerica Inc.
Communications Satellite
Conner Peripherals
Consolidated Papers
Continental Bank
Continental Medical Systems
Convex Computer
Cordis Corporation
Corona Corp.
Costco Wholesale
CPI Corporation
Cracker Barrel Old Country Store
Crestar Financial
Critical Care America
Crompton & Knowles
A.T. Cross Co.
CUC International
Cypress Semiconductor
Danaher Corporation
Datascope Corp.
Dauphin Deposit
Dean Foods
Dell Computer
Delmarva Power & Light
The Dexter Corporation
Diagnostic Products
Diamond Shamrock
Diebold, Inc.
Donaldson Company
Dreyer's Grand Ice Cream
The Dreyfus Corporation
Duriron Co.
Durr-Fillauer Medical
Duty Free International
Edison Brothers Stores
A.G. Edwards, Inc.
Ennis Business Forms
Enterra Corporation
Equifax Inc.
Exabyte Corp.
Family Dollar Stores
Federal Home Loan Mortgage
Federal-Mogul
Federal Signal
Ferro Corp.
FHP International
Fifth Third Bancorp
First Alabama Bancshares
First Bank System

First Brands
First Financial Management
First of America Bank
First Security Corp.
First Tenn National
First Virginia Banks
Flightsafety International
Florida Progress
Flowers Industries
Forest Laboratories
Franklin Resources
Freeport-McMoRan
Fruit of the Loom
H.B. Fuller
GATX Corp.
GenCorp Inc.
Genetics Institute
General Motors
Genzyme Corp.
Georgia Gulf
Gibson Greetings
Global Marine
Goulds Pumps
Great Lakes Chemical
Hancock Fabrics
M.A. Hanna Co.
HAPCO, Inc.
Harley-Davidson
Harsco Corp.
Hartford Steam Boiler Inspection
    & Insurance
Hawaiian Electric Industries
HealthCare COMPARE
HEALTHSOUTH Rehabilitation
Heilig-Meyers
Home Shopping Network
HON Industries
Houghton Mifflin
Idaho Power
Illinois Central Corp.
Illinois Power
IMC Fertilizer Group
Immunex Corp.
INB Financial Corp.
Indiana Energy
Information Resources
Intelligent Electronics
International Dairy Queen
International Game Technology
International Multifoods
International Technology
The Interpublic Group of
    Companies
Iowa-Illinois Gas & Electric
IPALCO Enterprises
Ivax Corp.
Jacobs Engineering Group
Kansas City Power & Light
Kansas City Southern Industries
Kaydon Corp.
Kelly Services
Kemper Corporation
Kennametal Inc.
KeyCorp
Keystone International
KnowledgeWare Inc.
LAC Minerals
Laidlaw Industries
Lance, Inc.

Lands' End
Lawson Products
Lawter International
LEGENT Corp.
Leggett & Platt
The Leslie Fay Companies
LG&E Energy
Liberty National Bancorp
Lincoln Telecommunications
Linear Technology
Loctite Corp.
Longview Fibre
LSI Logic
The Lubrizol Corp.
Lukens Inc.
Lyondell Petrochemical
Magma Power
MagneTek, Inc.
Manufacturers National Corp.
Marshall & Ilsley
MAXXAM Inc.
McCaw Cellular Communications
McCormick & Co.
MCN Corporation
Measurex Corp.
Medco Containment Services
Media General
Medical Care International
Mentor Graphics
Mercantile Bancorporation
Mercantile Bankshares
Meridian Bancorp
Merry-Go-Round Enterprises
Michael Foods
Micron Technology
Mid-American Waste Systems
Herman Miller
Minnesota Power & Light
MIPS Computer Systems
Mirage Resorts Inc.
MNC Financial Services
Modine Manufacturing
Molex Inc.
Montana Power
Morgan Stanley Group
Morrison Inc.
Multimedia, Inc.
Murphy Oil
Mylan Laboratories
Nabors Industries
National Fuel Gas Distribution
National Pizza
National Presto Industries
NCH Corp.
Nellcor Inc.
Network Systems
Neutrogena Corp.
Nevada Power
New England Electric System
New York State Electric & Gas
NIPSCO Industries
Noble Affilates
Nordson Corp.
Northeast Utilities
Northern Trust
NovaCare
Novell Inc.
Octel Communications
OEA Inc.

400 Companies in the Standard & Poor's Midcap Index (continued)

Office Depot
Oklahoma Gas & Electric
Olin Corp.
Omnicom Group
Oregon Steel Mills
Overseas Shipholding Group
PacifiCare Health Systems
Parametric Technology
Parker Drilling
The Penn Central Corp.
Pentair Inc.
PHH Corp.
Pic'n'Save
Pinnacle West Capital
Pioneer Hi-Bred International
Policy Management Systems
Portland General Corp.
Potomac Electric Power
Precision Castparts
Progressive Corp.
Provident Life & Accident
   Insurance
Public Service Company of
   Colorado
Public Service Company of New
   Mexico
Puget Sound Power & Light
Puritan-Bennett
Quaker State Corp.
Quantum Corp.
Questar Corp.
Ranger Oil
Reynolds & Reynolds

Rochester Telephone
Rohr Industries
Rollins, Inc.
RPM Inc.
Sanford Corp.
Savannah Foods & Industries
Sbarro, Inc.
SCANA Corp.
A. Schulman
The Charles Schwab Corp.
SciMed Life Systems
Seagate Technology
Seagull Energy
Sealed Air
Sensormatic Electronics
Sequa Corp.
Sequent Computer Systems
Service Merchandise
Shaw Industries
Sigma Aldrich
Silicon Graphics
Sizzler Restaurants International
Smith International
J.M. Smucker
Sonoco Products
Sotheby's Holdings
Southdown, Inc.
Southern New England
   Telecommunications
SouthTrust Corp.
Southwest Airlines
Southwestern Public Service
The Standard Register Company

Stanhome Inc.
State Street Boston
Sterling Chemicals
Stewart & Stevenson
Storage Technology
Stratus Computer
Structural Dynamics Research
Stryker Corp.
Sun Microsystems
Sundstrand Corp.
Surgical Care Affiliates
Symantec Corp.
Symbol Technologies
Synergen Inc.
SynOptics Communications
T2 Medical Inc.
Tambrands Inc.
TCA Cable TV
TECO Energy
Teleflex Inc.
Telephone & Data Systems
Teradyne Inc.
Thermo Electron
Thiokol Corp.
Tidewater Inc.
Tiffany & Co.
The Topps Company
Tosco Corp.
Transatlantic Holdings
Trinity Industries
Tyson Foods
U.S. HealthCare, Inc.
U.S. Shoe

United States Surgical
UJB Financial
Unifi Inc.
United Healthcare
Universal Corp.
Universal Foods
UtiliCorp United
Valero Energy
Vanguard Cellular Systems
Varco International
Varian Associates
VeriFone Inc
The Vons Companies
Waban Inc.
Wachovia Corp.
Wallace Computer Services
Washington Gas Light
Washington Post
Watts Industries
Wausau Paper Mills
Wellman, Inc.
West One Bancorp
Western Publishing
Westmark International
Willamette Industries
Wilmington Trust
Wisconsin Energy
Witco Corp.
WPL Holdings
Xilinx Inc.
XOMA Corp.

Source: Standard & Poor's, *The Wall Street Journal*, June 26, 1991

List current as of May 29, 1991.

Companies in the Standard & Poor's 500

Abbott Laboratories
ACME-Cleveland
Adolph Coors
Advanced Micro Devices
Aetna Life & Casualty
H. F. Ahmanson
Air Products & Chemicals
Alberto-Culver
Albertson's
Alcan Aluminium Ltd.
ALCO Standard
Alexander & Alexander
Allied Signal
Aluminum Company of America
ALZA
AMAX
Amdahl
Amerada Hess
American Brands
American Cyanamid
American Electric Power
American Express
American General Corp.
American Greetings
American Home Products
American International Group
American Stores
American Telephone & Telegraph
Ameritech
Amoco
AMP
AMR
Andrew
Anheuser-Busch
Apple Computer
Archer-Daniels-Midland
Arkla
Armco
Armstrong World Industries
ASARCO
Ashland Oil
Atlantic Richfield
Autodesk
Automatic Data Processing
Avery Dennison
Avon Products
Baker-Hughes
Ball
Bally Manufacturing
Baltimore Gas & Electric
Banc One
Bank of Boston
BankAmerica
Bankers Trust New York
C. R. Bard
Barnett Banks
Bassett Furniture Industries
Bausch & Lomb
Baxter International
Becton, Dickinson
Bell Atlantic
BellSouth
Bemis Company
Beneficial Corp.
Bethlehem Steel
Beverly Enterprises
Biomet
Black & Decker
H&R Block
Blockbuster Entertainment

Boatmen's Bancshares
Boeing
Boise Cascade
Borden, Inc.
Briggs & Stratton
Bristol-Myers Squibb
Brown & Sharpe Manufacturing
Brown Group
Brown-Forman
Browning-Ferris Industries
Bruno's
Brunswick Corp.
Burlington Northern
C & S Sovran Corp.
Campbell Soup
Capital Cities/ABC
Capital Holding
Carolina Power & Light
Caterpillar
CBS
Centex Corp.
Central & South West Corp.
Champion International
Charming Shoppes
Chase Manhattan
Chemical Banking Corp.
Chevron
Chrysler
Chubb
Cigna
Cincinnati Milacron
Circuit City Stores
Citicorp
Clark Equipment
Clorox
CNA Financial
Coastal Corp.
Coca-Cola
Colgate-Palmolive
Columbia Gas System
Comcast
Commonwealth Edison
Community Psychiatric Centers
Compaq Computer
Computer Associates
    International
Computer Sciences
ConAgra
Consolidated Edison of New York
Consolidated Freightways
Consolidated Natural Gas
Consolidated Rail
Continental Corp.
Control Data
Cooper Industries
Cooper Tire & Rubber
Corestates Financial
Corning
CPC International
Crane Company
Cray Research
Cross & Trecker
Crown Cork & Seal
CSX
Cummins Engine
Cyprus Minerals
Dana Corp.
Data General
Dayton Hudson
Deere

Delta Air Lines
Deluxe Corp.
Detroit Edison
Dial Corp.
Digital Equipment
Dillard Department Stores
Dominion Resources
R. R. Donnelley & Sons
Dover Corp.
Dow Chemical
Dow Jones
Dresser Industries
DSC Communications
Du Pont
Duke Power
Dun & Bradstreet
E-Systems
Eastern Enterprises
Eastman Kodak
Eaton
Echlin
Echo Bay Mines
Ecolab
EG&G
Eli Lilly
Emerson Electric
Engelhard
Enron
Ensearch
Entergy
Ethyl
Exxon
Fedders
Federal Express
Federal National Mortgage
    Association
Federal Paper Board
First Chicago
First Fidelity Bancorporation
First Interstate Bancorp
First Mississippi
First Union Corp. (NC)
Fleet/Norstar Financial Group
Fleetwood Enterprises
Fleming Companies
Fluor Corp.
FMC
Ford Motor
Foster Wheeler
FPL Group
Gannett
The Gap
General Cinema
General Dynamics
General Electric
General Mills
General Motors
General Re
General Signal
Genesco
Genuine Parts
Georgia-Pacific
Gerber Products
Giant Food
Gillette
Golden West Financial
B.F. Goodrich
Goodyear Tire & Rubber
W.R. Grace
W.W. Grainger

Great Atlantic & Pacific Tea Co.
Great Western Financial
Grumman
GTE
Halliburton
Handleman
Harcourt Brace Jovanovich
Harnischfeger Industries
Harris Corp.
Hartmarx
Hasbro
H. J. Heinz
Helmerich & Payne
Hercules Inc.
Hershey Foods
Hewlett-Packard
Hilton Hotels
Home Depot
Homestake Mining
Honeywell
Household International
Houston Industries
Humana Inc.
Illinois Tool Works
Imcera Group
Inco Ltd.
Ingersoll-Rand
Inland Steel Industries
Intel
Intergraph
Interlake
IBM
International Flavors &
    Fragrances
International Paper
ITT
James River Corp. of VA
Jefferson-Pilot
John H. Harland
Johnson & Johnson
Johnson Controls
Jostens
JWP
Kmart
Kaufman & Broad Home
Kellogg
Kerr-McGee
Kimberly-Clark
King World Productions
Knight-Ridder
Kroger
The Limited
Lincoln National
Litton Industries
Liz Claiborne
Lockheed
Longs Drug Stores
Loral
Lotus Development
Louisiana Land & Exploration
Louisiana-Pacific Corp.
Lowe's Companies
Luby's Cafeterias
M/A-Co
Manor Care
Manufacturers Hanover
Marriott
Marsh & McLennan Companies
Martin Marietta
Masco Corp.

Companies in the Standard & Poor's 500 (continued)

Mattel
Maxus Energy
May Department Stores
Maytag
McDermott International
McDonald's
McDonnell Douglas
McGraw-Hill
MCI Communications
McKesson
Mead
Medtronic
Mellon Bank
Melville
Mercantile Stores
Merck
Meredith
Merrill Lynch
Millipore
3M
Mobil
Monarch Machine Tool
Monsanto
Moore Corp. Ltd.
J.P. Morgan
Morrison Knudsen Corp.
Morton International
Motorola
Nacco Industries
Nalco Chemical
National Education Corp.
National Intergroup
National Medical Enterprises
National Semiconductor
National Service Industries
Navistar International
NBD Bancorp
NCNB
NCR
New York Times Co.
Newell Companies
Newmont Mining
Niagara Mohawk Power
Nicor
NIKE
NL Industries
Nordstrom
Norfolk Southern
Northern States Power (MN)
Northern Telecom Ltd.
Northrop
Norwest
Nucor
Nynex
Occidental Petroleum
Ogden Corp.

Ohio Edison
Oneok
Oracle Systems
Oryx Energy
Oshkosh B'Gosh
Outboard Marine
Owens-Corning Fiberglas
PACCAR
Pacific Enterprises
Pacific Gas and Electric
Pacific Telesis Group
Pacificorp
Pall
Panhandle Eastern
Paramount Communications
Parker-Hannifin
J. C. Penney
Pennzoil
Peoples Energy
Pep Boys (Manny, Moe & Jack)
PepsiCo
Perkin-Elmer
Pet
Pfizer
Phelps Dodge
Philadelphia Electric
Philip Morris Companies
Phillips Petroleum
PHM
Pitney Bowes
Pittston
Placer Dome
PNC Financial
Polaroid
Potlatch
PPG Industries
Premark International
Price Co.
Primerica
Procter & Gamble
Promus Companies
PSI Resources
Public Service Enterprise Group
Quaker Oats
Quantum Chemical
Ralston Purina
Raychem
Raytheon
Reebok International
Reynolds Metals
Rite Aid
Roadway Services
Rockwell International
Rohm & Haas
Rollins Environmental Services
Rowan Companies

Royal Dutch
Rubbermaid
Russell Corp.
Ryan's Family Steak Houses
Ryder System
Safeco
Safety-Kleen
Salomon
Santa Fe Energy Resources
Santa Fe Pacific
Sara Lee
SCEcorp
Schering-Plough
Schlumberger
Scientific-Atlanta
Scott Paper
Seagram Co. Ltd.
Sears, Roebuck
Security Pacific
Service Corporation International
Shared Medical Systems
Shawmut National
Sherwin-Williams
Shoney's
Skyline Corp.
Snap-On Tools
Sonat
Southern Company
Southwestern Bell
Springs Industries
SPX
St. Jude Medical
St. Paul Companies
Stanley Works
Stone Container
Stride Rite
Sun Company
SunTrust Banks
Super Valu Stores
Syntex
SYSCO
Tandem Computers
Tandy
Tektronix
Tele-Communications
Teledyne
Temple-Inland
Tenneco
Texas Instruments
Texas Utilities
Textron
Thomas & Betis
Time Warner
Times Mirror Co.
Timken
TJX Companies

Torchmark
Toys "R" Us
Transamerica
Transco Energy
Travelers
Tribune Company
Trinova
TRW
Tyco Laboratories
UAL
Unilever NV
Union Camp
Union Carbide
Union Pacific
Unisys
United Technologies
United Telecommunications
Unocal
Upjohn
USAir
U. S. Bancorp
USF&G
USG
USLife
UST
U S WEST
USX-Marathon Group
USX-U.S. Steel Group
Varity
V. F.
Wal-Mart Stores
Walgreen
Walt Disney
Wang Laboratories
Warner-Lambert
Waste Management
Wells Fargo
Wendy's International
Westinghouse Electric
Westmoreland Coal
Westvaco
Wetterau
Weyerhaeuser
Whirlpool
Whitman Corp.
Williams Companies
Winn-Dixie Stores
Woolworth
Worthington Industries
Wm. Wrigley Jr. Co.
Xerox
Yellow Freight System
Zenith Electronics
Zurn Industries

Source: Compustat

List current as of July 26, 1991.

The Company Profiles

ABBOTT LABORATORIES

NYSE symbol: ABT
Fiscal year ends: December 31

OVERVIEW

Abbott Labs is a major pharmaceutical company, but more than half its revenues come from nutritionals and diagnostic equipment, markets in which it has a dominant share. The company also supplies hospitals and blood banks worldwide with intravenous fluids, pumps, screening tests, anesthetics, and critical care instruments.

Having spent $567 million on R&D in 1990 (9.2% of sales), Abbott is busy preparing its next generation of pharmaceuticals, including Temafloxacin (an antibiotic) and a treatment for hypertension. Promising diagnostics products include a modern blood gas monitor and a new allergy test (Abbott Matrix).

Abbott owns 1/2 of Takeda-Abbott Pharmaceuticals, a joint venture with Japan's largest drug company, and is the major shareholder in Amgen, one of the larger biotechnology companies.

WHEN

Family physician Wallace Abbott founded the Abbott Alkaloidal Company in a Chicago suburb in 1888 to sell his improved form of the dosimetric granule (a pill that supplied uniform quantities of drugs). By 1900 sales were $125,000. The AMA criticized Dr. Abbott for his aggressive promotional style, but the doctor successfully defended himself, receiving support from much of the medical profession.

During WWI Abbott scientists discovered techniques for synthesizing anesthetics and sedatives previously available only from the more advanced German companies. In 1922 the company acquired a strong research department by buying Dermatological Research Laboratories. In 1928 Abbott acquired John T. Milliken of St. Louis, which brought to Abbott a force of well-trained salesmen.

Abbott went public in 1929 and acquired Swan-Myers of Indianapolis (glass ampuls for injectable drugs). Flamboyant salesman DeWitt Clough became president in 1933; the Abbott magazine *What's New*, prepared by his promotional staff, was considered a significant new corporate marketing tool. The company began to operate internationally as early as the mid-1930s, opening branches in England, Mexico, Brazil, Argentina, and Cuba.

Abbott was one of several drug companies that stepped up production to make the penicillin needed during WWII. After the war the company introduced new products, including different forms of penicillin. Research toward other antibiotics yielded Erythrocin

(1952), Abbott's form of the antibiotic erythromycin. After a period of slow growth in the early 1950s, sales improved as Erythrocin became more widely used. In the 1960s the company added consumer products (Selsun shampoo, Murine) and infant and nutritional formula (Similac), but drugs and hospital products remained its mainstay. The artificial sweetener Sucaryl (introduced 1950) was banned by the FDA in 1970 after tests indicated it might be carcinogenic. In 1971 millions of intravenous solutions had to be recalled following reports of contamination.

In the 1970s Abbott built its diagnostics division (early products included the Auscell hepatitis test and VP clinical analyzer) and in 1981 introduced a nutritional support service for hospitals. In the early 1980s the company obtained licenses to sell in the US pharmaceuticals developed by the Japanese. After 1979 when Robert Schoellhorn became CEO, Abbott had a steady increase in profits. Despite his successes Schoellhorn came under criticism for trying to cut R&D funds and firing several top managers and in March 1990 was himself terminated. In August 1990 the company announced it had developed a compound that inhibited AIDS in test tube experiments.

In 1990 Abbott received FDA approval to market ProSom, a new insomnia drug that will challenge Upjohn's similar Halcion. It also is defending 370 lawsuits by children of women who took a synthetic hormone (DES) in the 1950s that allegedly causes cancer.

WHO

Chairman and CEO: Duane L. Burnham, age 49, $1,161,110
President and COO: Thomas R. Hodgson, age 49, $805,779 pay
SVP Finance and CFO: Gary P. Coughlan, age 46
VP Personnel: O. Ralph Edwards, age 56
Auditors: Arthur Andersen & Co.
Employees: 43,770

WHERE

HQ: One Abbott Park Rd., Abbott Park, IL 60064-3500
Phone: 708-937-6100
Fax: 708-937-1511

The company has operations in 44 countries.

	1990 Sales		1990 Operating Income	
	$ mil.	% of total	$ mil.	% of total
US	3,914	64	1,133	76
Latin America	258	4	53	4
Europe, Mideast & Africa	1,305	21	243	16
Pacific, Far East & Canada	682	11	65	4
Adjustments	—	—	(88)	—
Total	**6,159**	**100**	**1,406**	**100**

WHAT

	1990 Sales		1990 Operating Income	
	$ mil.	% of total	$ mil.	% of total
Hospital & lab. prods.	2,998	49	583	40
Drugs & nutritional products	3,161	51	886	60
Adjustments	—	—	(63)	—
Total	**6,159**	**100**	**1,406**	**100**

Brand Names

Agricultural Products
DiPel (insecticide)
ProGibb (plant growth regulator)
VectoBac (larvacide)

Consumer Products
Faultless (rubber sundries)
Murine (eye and ear drops)
Selsun Blue (shampoo)
Tronolane (hemorrhoid medication)

Nutritional Supplements
Ensure (adult nutrition)
Glucerna (diabetic nutrition)
Osmolite (adult nutrition)
Similac (infant formula)

Prescription Drugs
Abbokinase (blood clot dissolver)
Depakote (anticonvulsant)

Erythromycin (antibiotic)
Hytrin (blood pressure drug)
Lupron (prostate cancer drug)
ProSom (sedative)
Tranxene (anxiety drug)

Hospital Products
ADD-Vantage (IV equipment)
ADx (drug testing equipment)
Aminosyn (IV nutrition)
IMx (immunoassay system)
LifeCare (pumps)
Opticath (cardiorespiratory monitor)
Pentothal (anesthetic)

RANKINGS

82nd in *Fortune* 500 Industrial Cos.
23rd in *Business Week* 1000

KEY COMPETITORS

American Home Products	Dow Chemical	Monsanto
C. R. Bard	Du Pont	Nestlé
Baxter	Hoechst	Syntex
Becton, Dickinson	Johnson & Johnson	Other drug companies

HOW MUCH

	9-Year Growth	1981	1982	1983	1984	1985	1986	1987	1988	1989	1990
Sales ($ mil.)	11.3%	2,343	2,602	2,928	3,104	3,360	3,808	4,388	4,937	5,380	6,159
Net income ($ mil.)	16.3%	247	289	348	403	465	540	633	752	860	966
Income as % of sales	—	10.6%	11.1%	11.9%	13.0%	13.8%	14.2%	14.4%	15.2%	16.0%	15.7%
Earnings per share ($)	17.8%	0.50	0.59	0.72	0.83	0.96	1.15	1.37	1.65	1.90	2.19
Stock price – high ($)	—	8.06	10.31	13.34	12.19	18.00	27.50	33.50	26.19	35.19	46.38
Stock price – low ($)	—	5.91	6.34	9.03	9.19	9.97	15.84	20.00	21.44	23.13	31.25
Stock price – close ($)	23.5%	6.75	9.69	11.31	10.44	17.09	22.81	24.13	24.06	34.00	45.00
P/E – high	—	16	17	19	15	19	24	24	16	19	21
P/E – low	—	12	11	13	11	10	14	15	13	12	14
Dividends per share ($)	18.7%	0.17	0.20	0.24	0.29	0.34	0.40	0.48	0.58	0.68	0.81
Book value per share ($)	12.1%	2.35	2.68	2.93	3.33	3.91	3.89	4.62	5.48	6.16	6.60

1990 Year-end:
Debt ratio: 4.5%
Return on equity: 34.3%
Cash (mil.): $53
Current ratio: 1.23
Long-term debt (mil.): $135
No. of shares (mil.): 429
Dividends:
　1990 average yield: 1.8%
　1990 payout: 36.8%
Market value (mil.): $19,311

Stock Price History High/Low 1981–90

ADOBE SYSTEMS, INC.

OVERVIEW

Adobe Systems has revolutionized publishing and printing for thousands of PC users. The company's PostScript software, an industry standard, allows users to integrate graphics and text to create high-quality and complex documents using a PC and laser printer. PostScript also gives users access to over 700 fonts (type styles) in Adobe's type library.

Adobe sells PostScript directly to OEMs — 38 in all, including Apple, IBM, and NEC — for use on more than 170 products. More than one million PostScript printers and typesetters have been shipped since the program was introduced in 1985. Adobe collected almost $106 million in royalties from its OEMs in 1990, and Apple, the company's largest customer, accounted for 23% of sales.

Besides PostScript, Adobe sells end-user applications, including Adobe Type Manager and the best-selling Adobe Illustrator. The company invests heavily in R&D, spending $20.2 million (about 12% of sales) in 1990.

WHEN

In the early days of laser printers, when there was no standard language for communicating the appearance of a page to a printer, John Warnock, Charles Geschke, and several other engineers left Xerox's Palo Alto Research Center to found Adobe Systems (1982, named for a creek near Warnock and Geschke's homes). Their purpose was to design a page description language capable of interpreting even the most complex page layout.

Using research started by Warnock before he joined Xerox in 1978, Adobe's founders went about the business of developing PostScript, the printer language that would eventually become an industry standard, by borrowing time on Berkeley's VAX 750 and testing their results on a printer borrowed from Digital Equipment. Apple's cofounder Steve Jobs soon heard about the project, and in 1983 Adobe signed a licensing agreement with Apple to provide printer software for the revolutionary Macintosh computer then under development. PostScript made its first appearance in Apple's LaserWriter early in 1985.

PostScript arrived just in time to help usher in the desktop publishing revolution. Quality laser printing had been made affordable by Canon, who came out with the LBP-CX desktop laser printer in 1984, the same year that the graphics-oriented Macintosh was introduced. Adobe went public in 1986 through a $5.5 million stock offering.

In 1987 Adobe introduced downloadable fonts (fonts capable of being downloaded from a computer to a laser printer) and Adobe Illustrator, its best-selling graphics application software.

In 1988 Adobe (working in partnership with Steve Jobs's new company NeXT) came out with Display PostScript, which makes images appearing on a computer workstation screen look like what will be actually printed. The company licensed the software to IBM and Digital Equipment that year.

Apple turned competitor in 1989, when it, together with Microsoft, announced its intention to develop software similar to PostScript. That same year Apple sold its 16.4% stake in Adobe. The bottom fell out of Adobe's stock temporarily, but by the end of 1990, any real threat to PostScript's market share had failed to materialize. Apple, in fact, signed a new licensing agreement with Adobe that year.

Adobe Type Manager, system software allowing users to see Adobe type on-screen and print it on non-PostScript printers, started retailing in 1989. In addition to developing new products on its own, Adobe turned acquisitive, buying Emerald City Software and BluePoint Technologies (develops ASICs) in 1990.

In 1991 Adobe announced its intention to sell hardware — a chip for laser printers that will speed up printing.

NASDAQ symbol: ADBE
Fiscal year ends: Last Friday in November

Hoover's Rating **A+**

WHO

Chairman and CEO: John E. Warnock, age 50, $378,633 pay
President and COO: Charles M. Geschke, age 51, $378,633 pay
SVP; General Manager, Systems Products: Stephen A. MacDonald, age 45, $297,933 pay
SVP New Product Development: R. Daniel Putman, age 38, $253,531 pay
VP Finance and Administration, CFO, Treasurer, and Assistant Secretary: M. Bruce Nakao, age 47
Director of Human Resources: Patty Greene
Auditors: KPMG Peat Marwick
Employees: 508

WHERE

HQ: 1585 Charleston Rd., Mountain View, CA 94039-7900
Phone: 415-961-4400
Fax: 415-961-3769

Adobe sells PostScript directly to 38 manufacturers in the US, Europe, and Japan. Other products are offered by over 3,300 dealers in the US, Canada, Europe, and Australia.

WHAT

	1990 Sales	
	$ mil.	% of total
Royalties	106	63
Product sales	55	32
Contract & other	8	5
Total	**169**	**100**

Products

Adobe Collector's Edition (predrawn illustration tools)
Adobe Illustrator (graphics software)
Adobe Photoshop (image processing and enhancement software)
Adobe Separator (utility software for creating color separations)
Adobe Streamline (graphics conversion software)
Adobe Type Library (font software)
Adobe Type Manager
Adobe Type Reunion (utility software for organizing font menus)
PostScript Cartridge and Adobe Type Cartridge (PostScript interpreter for HP LaserJet printers)
PostScript and Display PostScript (page description language and interpreter)
ReelTime (video-editing software)
Smart Art (custom headlines and graphics software)
TranScript (driver software for UNIX-based systems)
TrueForm (forms generator)

RANKINGS

509th in *Business Week* 1000

KEY COMPETITORS

Apple
Microsoft
Sun Microsystems

HOW MUCH

	5-Year Growth	1981	1982	1983	1984	1985	1986	1987	1988	1989	1990
Sales ($ mil.)	102.2%	—	—	—	—	5	16	39	83	121	169
Net income ($ mil.)	109.1%	—	—	—	—	1	4	9	21	34	40
Income as % of sales	—	—	—	—	—	10.8%	22.3%	22.8%	25.3%	27.8%	23.7%
Earnings per share ($)	127.5%	—	—	—	—	0.03	0.19	0.43	0.98	1.55	1.83
Stock price – high ($)	—	—	—	—	—	—	6.63	28.00	25.50	30.00	50.75
Stock price – low ($)	—	—	—	—	—	—	3.31	6.50	11.75	14.00	17.00
Stock price – close ($)	—	—	—	—	—	—	6.38	14.75	24.50	20.25	29.13
P/E – high	—	—	—	—	—	—	35	66	26	19	28
P/E – low	—	—	—	—	—	—	17	15	12	9	9
Dividends per share ($)	—	—	—	—	—	—	0.00	0.00	0.08	0.19	0.23
Book value per share ($)	105.6%	—	—	—	—	0.14	0.68	1.15	2.14	2.93	5.14

1990 Year-end:
Debt ratio: 0.2%
Return on equity: 45.4%
Cash (mil.): $70
Current ratio: 2.95
Long-term debt (mil.): $0
No. of shares (mil.): 21
Dividends:
   1990 average yield: 0.8%
   1990 payout: 12.6%
Market value (mil.): $610

Stock Price History High/Low 1986–90

ADOLPH COORS COMPANY

OVERVIEW

Headquartered in its Golden, Colorado, facility, Adolph Coors is the nation's 3rd largest brewer (after Anheuser-Busch and Miller), with about a 10% market share. Coors is vertically integrated, with its own packaging, labeling, transportation, distribution, and recycling operations. The company also operates businesses engaged in energy exploration, biotechnology, and ceramics.

Coors grew from a regional favorite, promoted mostly by word-of-mouth, into a major stateside player. The company gained nationwide status by entering its 50th state (Indiana) this year. In 1990 Coors Light passed Bud Light as the nation's #3 beer brand.

The company has recently launched Coors Pure Water 2000, a campaign to clean up America's rivers and lakes. The campaign was ironically hindered by Coors itself in 1991 when the company spilled 150,000 gallons of beer into Colorado's Clear Creek.

The Coors family owns 100% of Coors's voting stock and, along with management, 55% of the nonvoting stock.

WHEN

Adolph Coors landed in Baltimore in 1868, a 21-year-old stowaway fleeing Germany's military draft. He worked his way west to Denver, where he bought a bottling company in 1872 and became partners with Jacob Schueler, a local merchant, in 1873. The partners built a brewery in Golden, Colorado, a small town with many clear springs in the nearby Rocky Mountain foothills. In 1880 Coors became sole owner of the company. For most of the company's history, Coors confined sales to western states. The cost of nationwide distribution was prohibitive because Coors used a single brewery, natural brewing methods, and no preservatives; Coors beer was made, shipped, and stored under refrigeration, with a shelf life of only one month.

Coors survived Prohibition (1914–33) by making near beer and malted milk and by entering cement and porcelain chemicalware production. By this time Coors's 3 sons worked in the business, which has been run by family men to the present day. After Repeal, beer output grew steadily in Coors's 11-state market. By the 1960s Coors had achieved national popularity, as thousands of loyal customers from outside the market area packed it home.

Between 1965 and 1969 Coors jumped from 12th to 4th place in American brewing, and by 1975 Coors beer was the top seller in 10 of its 11 state markets (Coors sometimes restricted distributors in these areas to selling its beer exclusively). But Coors's meteoric rise was blunted by a fall back to 5th place in 1976 and continuing sales declines through 1978, mainly due to campaigns for new "light" and "super-premium" beers introduced by Miller and Anheuser-Busch. Coors responded by opening a marketing department and introducing light and super-premium brands. The company removed distribution restrictions and expanded its market area from 11 to 16 states.

In the late 1970s and 1980s Coors began expanding nationwide at a rate of about 2 states per year while at the same time enduring boycotts and strikes due to alleged discriminatory labor practices. After years of protests from workers and federal agencies, Coors improved its minority employment policies. During the 1970s Joe Coors, a grandson of Adolph, financed and led many ultraconservative projects, expressing the Coors family's strong opposition to student radicalism and liberal media.

In 1989 Coors agreed to purchase Stroh Brewing, then the 3rd largest US brewer (Coors surpassed them in 1990). The deal fell apart in 1990, but Coors did later buy Stroh's Memphis brewery in order to meet increasing demand for its beer.

In 1991 the company agreed to drop the "brewed with pure Rocky Mountain spring water" from its label after Anheuser-Busch complained that some of Coors's water comes from elsewhere.

NASDAQ symbol: ACCOB
Fiscal year ends: Last Sunday in December

Hoover's Rating **C+**

WHO

Chairman and President: William K. Coors, age 74
VC: Joseph Coors, age 73
Chairman, President, and CEO, Coors Brewing Company: Peter H. Coors, age 44, $729,501 pay
EVP, CFO and Secretary: Harold R. Smethills, age 43, $479,811 pay
Auditors: Price Waterhouse
Employees: 10,700

WHERE

HQ: Golden, CO 80401
Phone: 303-279-6565
Fax: 303-277-6564

Coors operates breweries in Colorado and Tennessee. Coors markets its beer in all 50 states, the District of Columbia, Bermuda, Canada, Japan, the Virgin Islands, and on US military bases worldwide.

WHAT

	1990 Sales		1990 Operating Income	
	$ mil.	% of total	$ mil.	% of total
Beer	1,477	72	71	73
Ceramics	182	9	(1)	—
Aluminum	138	7	16	17
Packaging	156	7	10	10
Other	103	5	(7)	—
Adjustments	(193)	—	(15)	—
Total	**1,863**	**100**	**74**	**100**

Coors Brewing Co.	Coors Ceramica Tecnica do
Coors	Brasil, Ltda.
Coors Cutter	Coors Ceramicon Designs,
(nonalcoholic)	Ltd.
Coors Dry	Coors Ceramics
Coors Extra Gold	Electronics, Ltd.
Coors Light	Coors Electronic Package
Coors Rocky Mountain	Co.
Sparkling Water	MicroLithics Corp.
George Killian's	Wilbanks International,
Irish Red	Inc.
Keystone	
Keystone Light	**Coors Technology Cos.**
Winterfest	Coors BioTech, Inc.
	Coors Energy Co.
Coors Ceramics Co.	Golden Aluminum Co.
Alpha Optical Systems,	Golden Technologies Co.,
Inc.	Inc.
Alumina Ceramics, Inc.	Graphic Packaging Corp.

RANKINGS

225th in *Fortune* 500 Industrial Cos.
603rd in *Business Week* 1000

KEY COMPETITORS

Allied-Lyons	Guinness
Alcoa	Heineken
Anheuser-Busch	John Labatt
Bass	Kirin
Bond	Philip Morris
BSN	San Miguel
Carlsberg	Stroh
Foster's Brewing	

HOW MUCH

	9-Year Growth	1981	1982	1983	1984	1985	1986	1987	1988	1989	1990
Sales ($ mil.)	8.0%	930	915	1,110	1,133	1,281	1,315	1,351	1,522	1,764	1,863
Net income ($ mil.)	(3.2%)	52	40	89	45	53	59	48	47	13	39
Income as % of sales	—	5.6%	4.4%	8.0%	4.0%	4.2%	4.5%	3.6%	3.1%	0.7%	2.1%
Earnings per share ($)	(3.7%)	1.48	1.15	2.55	1.28	1.52	1.65	1.32	1.28	0.36	1.05
Stock price – high ($)	—	16.50	15.00	29.13	21.63	22.25	31.63	30.00	21.00	24.38	27.38
Stock price – low ($)	—	10.13	9.88	11.88	12.00	14.50	20.38	16.25	16.88	17.38	17.13
Stock price – close ($)	7.9%	10.38	12.25	20.25	16.13	21.63	24.00	16.88	20.00	19.75	20.50
P/E – high	—	11	13	11	17	15	19	23	16	68	26
P/E – low	—	7	9	5	9	10	12	12	13	48	16
Dividends per share ($)	5.8%	0.30	0.30	0.35	0.40	0.40	0.50	0.50	0.50	0.50	0.50
Book value per share ($)	3.4%	21.52	22.37	24.57	25.45	26.46	27.41	28.19	28.96	28.75	29.20

1990 Year-end:
Debt ratio: 9.2%
Return on equity: 3.6%
Cash (mil.): $64
Current ratio: 1.63
Long-term debt (mil.): $110
No. of shares (mil.): 37
Dividends:
　1990 average yield: 2.4%
　1990 payout: 47.6%
Market value (mil.): $766

**Stock Price History
High/Low 1981–90**

ADVANCE PUBLICATIONS, INC.

OVERVIEW

Advance Publications is the holding company for the nation's 6th largest media conglomerate and #1 privately held media group. The company ranks among the leaders in all of its business segments: newspapers, magazines, books, and cable TV.

Newhouse Newspapers, the #4 US chain, publishes newspapers, including the Portland *Oregonian*, Cleveland *Plain Dealer*, Newark *Star-Ledger*, and New Orleans *Times-Picayune*; most of the company's papers have no competition in their markets. Advance's *Parade* magazine leads the US in paid circulation.

All of Advance Publications's voting stock is held in a trust managed by the founder's sons S. I. Newhouse, Jr., and Donald Newhouse. Advance chairman S. I. Newhouse, Jr., fond of frequent executive job shifts, has been shaking up management at Condé Nast and Random House. Condé Nast is #3 in US magazine publishing, with such titles as *Vogue* (the leading fashion magazine), *Glamour*, and *Vanity Fair*; it also publishes magazines in Europe. Random House is America's largest trade (excluding texts) book publisher.

Private company   Hoover's Rating **A-**

WHO

Chairman and CEO: Samuel I. ("Si") Newhouse, Jr., age 62
President: Donald E. Newhouse, age 61
Employees: 19,500

WHERE

HQ: 350 Madison Ave., New York, NY 10017
Phone: 212-880-8800
Fax: 212-880-6964

Advance Publications has 29 daily newspapers and 3 cable TV groups in the US and book and magazine operations in New York and Europe.

WHEN

Samuel I. Newhouse dropped out of school at 13 because of family poverty. He went to work for a lawyer who received the *Bayonne* (New Jersey) *Times* as payment for a debt. The lawyer put Sam, age 16, in charge of the failing newspaper in 1911; Sam turned the company around. In 1922 he bought the Staten Island *Advance*, the core of Advance Publications's holdings.

Newhouse used profits from the *Advance* to buy newspapers throughout the New York area, operating out of a briefcase rather than a headquarters suite. He purchased the *Long Island Press* (1932), the Newark *Star-Ledger* (1933), the *Long Island Star-Journal* (1938), and the *Syracuse Journal* (1939). In the 1940s he maintained this pattern with the acquisitions of the *Syracuse Herald-Standard* (1941), the *Jersey Journal* (1945), and the Harrisburg *Patriot* (1948).

In 1955 Newhouse expanded into the South by buying the *Birmingham News* and the *Huntsville Times*. Newhouse purchased Condé Nast (*Vogue*, *Bride's*, *House & Garden*) as an anniversary gift for his wife Mitzi in 1959. Newhouse acquired the New Orleans *Times-Picayune* and *New Orleans States-Item* for $42 million (1962), a record price for a newspaper transaction that held until he broke it with the purchase of the Cleveland *Plain Dealer* for $54 million (1967). By 1967 Newhouse had also established NewChannels, which owned several cable systems, with 10,000 subscribers, primarily in cities where the family owned other media holdings. As the prices of newspapers continued to rise,

Newhouse set yet another record by purchasing the Booth chain of 8 Michigan newspapers, including the *Grand Rapids Press*, for $304 million (1976).

Newhouse died in 1979, leaving his sons S. I., Jr., and Donald as trustees of the company's 10 shares of voting stock. The sons' IRS filing claimed that the estate was worth $181.9 million, taxable at $48.7 million. The IRS argued that the holdings were worth at least $1.2 billion and billed the Newhouses $658 million, plus a $305 million penalty for fraud. When the estate tax case — the largest ever — went to court in 1989, the Newhouses brought in a group of financial experts, including Rupert Murdoch (News Corporation), to testify on their behalf. In 1990 the case was decided against the IRS.

Meanwhile the sons have continued to expand the properties of Advance Publications, buying Random House (1980) and Crown Publishing (1989). Also in 1980 the company sold 5 TV stations that Newhouse had bought in earlier years to Times Mirror for $82 million. Some of the money from the sale of the stations went to buy more cable systems. The company resurrected *Vanity Fair* (1983) and bought the *New Yorker* (1985). In 1990 a decision by the Newhouses to stem the losses at Pantheon Books by cutting titles led to the resignation of senior editors and a protest by authors and publishers.

Advance launched a new book imprint, Turtle Bay, in 1990 and a new beauty magazine, *Allure*, in 1991.

Newhouse Newspapers

Birmingham, AL	*Birmingham News*
Huntsville, AL	*Huntsville News*
	The Huntsville Times
Mobile, AL	*The Mobile Press*
	The Mobile Press Register
	The Mobile Register
New Orleans, LA	*The Times-Picayune*
Springfield, MA	*Union-News & Sunday Republican*
Pascagoula, MS	*Mississippi Press*
	Mississippi Press Register
Jersey City, NJ	*Jersey Journal*
Newark, NJ	*Star-Ledger*
Trenton, NJ	*Times*
Staten Island, NY	*Advance*
Syracuse, NY	*Herald-American*
	The Post-Standard
	Syracuse Herald-Journal
Cleveland, OH	*Plain Dealer*
Portland, OR	*The Oregonian*
Harrisburg, PA	*The Evening News*
	The Patriot
	The Patriot-News

Booth Newspapers (MI)

Ann Arbor	*The Ann Arbor News*
Bay City	*Times*
Flint	*The Flint Journal*
Grand Rapids	*The Grand Rapids Press*
Jackson	*Citizen Patriot*
Kalamazoo	*Kalamazoo Gazette*
Muskegon	*The Muskegon Chronicle*
Saginaw	*The Saginaw News*

WHAT

Magazines	*Parade*	Pantheon
Allure	*Self*	Random House
Bride's	*Vanity Fair*	Turtle Bay
Condé Nast Traveler	*Vogue*	Villard
Details	*Woman*	Vintage
Glamour		
Gourmet	**Book Publishing**	**Cable Groups**
GQ	Alfred A. Knopf	MetroVision
HG (House & Garden)	Ballantine	(Atlanta)
Mademoiselle	Crown	NewChannels
The New Yorker	Modern Library	(Syracuse)
	Orion	Vision Cable (Paramus, NJ)

RANKINGS

36th in *Forbes* 400 US Private Cos.

KEY COMPETITORS

Bertelsmann	Knight-Ridder	Reed
Blockbuster	Maxwell	E.W. Scripps
Capital Cities/ABC	News Corp	TCI
Cox	New York Times	Times Mirror
Gannett	Paramount	Tribune
Hachette	Pearson	Washington Post
Hearst	Reader's Digest	

HOW MUCH

	9-Year Growth	1981	1982	1983	1984	1985	1986	1987	1988	1989	1990
Total media sales ($ mil.)	—	—	1,616	1,740	1,900	2,030	2,200	2,482	2,655	2,882	3,040
Cable TV revenues ($ mil.)	—	—	—	—	—	—	186	203	229	295	398
Cable subscribers (thou.)	10.2%	518	596	703	850	917	1,027	1,098	1,078	1,147	1,242
Newspaper revenues ($ mil.)	—	—	—	—	—	—	1,470	1,601	1,681	1,745	1,797
Newspapers	0.8%	28	27	27	26	26	27	26	36	26	30
Magazine revenues ($ mil.)	—	—	—	—	—	—	544	678	745	842	845

Total Media Sales ($ mil.) 1982–90

(bar chart with y-axis from 0 to 3,500 in increments of 500)

AETNA LIFE & CASUALTY COMPANY

NYSE symbol: AET
Fiscal year ends: December 31

Hoover's Rating **C+**

OVERVIEW

Aetna is one of the world's major providers of insurance (life, health, and property/casualty) and financial services to corporations, public and private organizations, and individuals. With assets of $89.3 billion, the company is the largest stockholder-owned insurance organization in the US and one of the 15 largest US corporations, measured by assets.

The Hartford-based company, with more than 200 US branch and marketing offices, also provides insurance and financial services in the Pacific Basin, South America, Canada, and Europe. Ninety-six percent of total revenues in 1990 were from US sources.

Aetna is the third largest US insurance company; it underwrites and administers group insurance and managed health care products and services, with 1990 premiums of $4.5 billion, and manages group pension funds. Aetna is also one of the US's largest commercial property/casualty underwriters.

In 1990 Ralph Nader's Public Citizen Group named Aetna as one of several big insurance companies likely to fail, only to withdraw its opinion days later when its analytical methods proved grossly defective. Aetna remains a strong company with a AA+ Standard & Poors rating on its debt.

WHO

Chairman and CEO: James T. Lynn, age 64, $1,066,539 pay
President: Ronald E. Compton, age 58, $737,885 pay
SVP Finance: Patrick W. Kenny, age 48
VP Corporate Human Resources: Mary Ann Champlin, age 43
SVP Marketing: John J. Martin, age 56
Auditors: KPMG Peat Marwick
Employees: 47,100

WHERE

HQ: 151 Farmington Ave., Hartford, CT 06156
Phone: 203-273-0123
Fax: 203-275-2677

Aetna operates throughout the US and in some foreign countries.

	1990 Assets		1990 Pretax Income	
	$ mil.	% of total	$ mil.	% of total
US	85,680	96	651	104
Other countries	3,621	4	(27)	(4)
Total	**89,301**	**100**	**624**	**100**

WHEN

Hartford businessman and judge Eliphalet Bulkeley started Connecticut Mutual Life Insurance Company, a mutual company owned by policyholders, in 1846. A year later he was ousted by agents who gained control of the company by obtaining proxies (votes) from policyholders.

In 1853 Bulkeley and a group of Hartford businessmen founded Aetna Life Insurance Company as a spin-off of Aetna Fire Insurance Company. Aetna's early growth is attributed to Dr. Thomas Lacey, a former Aetna medical examiner, who became known in the late 1800s as the "father" of Aetna's agency system for enlisting agents around the US to sell policies.

During the 1860s the company expanded by developing the participating life policy, which returns dividends to policyholders based on investment earnings. This policy, developed by Aetna's 2nd president, Thomas Enders, allowed the company to compete with mutual life insurance companies. In 1868 Aetna was the first company to offer renewable term life policies.

Morgan Bulkeley, son of the founder, became president in 1879 and served 43 years. Aetna began to offer multiple lines by introducing accident insurance in 1891, health insurance in 1899, worker's compensation in 1902,

and automobile and other property insurance in 1907. Bulkeley increased the company's visibility by serving as mayor of Hartford, as governor of Connecticut, and as a US senator, all while also serving as Aetna president.

By 1920 Aetna had added ocean marine and inland marine insurance and by 1922 was the largest multiple-line insurance group in the nation. Aetna's non–life-insurance companies, particularly the automobile line, expanded too fast during the 1920s, thus threatening Aetna's financial solvency. By restricting underwriting and reestablishing sufficient reserves, the company was able to withstand the Depression.

After World War II the company expanded into group life, health, and accident insurance. In 1967 the company reorganized into a holding company, Aetna Life and Casualty.

Since the 1960s the company has continued to expand its multiple lines of insurance while entering and leaving other businesses. In 1982 it bought Geosource Inc., an oil services firm, which it sold 2 years later at a loss. In 1989 Aetna sold Federated Investors (an institutional investment management firm bought in 1982) to a new company owned by Federated's management. A 1990 reorganization is expected to eliminate 2,600 positions beginning in 1991 and to result in an annual after-tax savings of about $90 million.

WHAT

	1990 Assets		1990 Pretax Income	
	$ mil.	% of total	$ mil.	% of total
Reinsurance	3,906	4	163	26
Health & life	9,371	10	422	68
Personal property/ casualty	4,629	5	(33)	(6)
Commercial property	12,313	14	116	19
International	3,621	4	(56)	(9)
Financial services	55,461	63	12	2
Total	**89,301**	**100**	**624**	**100**

Product Lines
Annuities
Life, health, and disability insurance
Managed health care
Pension plan services
Property/casualty insurance

Subsidiary
American Re-Insurance Co.

RANKINGS

4th in *Fortune* 50 Life Insurance Cos.
139th in *Business Week* 1000

KEY COMPETITORS

Allianz	Lloyd's of London
American Financial	MassMutual
AIG	MetLife
B.A.T	New York Life
Berkshire Hathaway	Northwestern Mutual
Blue Cross	Primerica
CIGNA	Prudential
Equitable	Sears
GEICO	State Farm
General Re	Teachers Insurance
Humana	Tokio Marine and Fire
ITT	Transamerica
John Hancock	Travelers
Kemper	USF&G
Loews	Xerox

HOW MUCH

	9-Year Growth	1981	1982	1983	1984	1985	1986	1987	1988	1989	1990
Assets ($ mil.)	9.4%	39,631	44,211	47,626	51,029	58,294	66,830	72,754	81,415	87,099	89,301
Net income ($ mil.)	2.5%	491	522	325	183	430	714	867	668	639	614
Income as % of assets	—	1.2%	1.2%	0.7%	0.4%	0.7%	1.1%	1.2%	0.8%	0.7%	0.7%
Earnings per share ($)	(1.1%)	6.11	5.80	3.06	1.59	3.84	6.18	7.48	5.85	5.69	5.52
Stock price – high ($)	—	47.63	48.25	43.50	39.00	53.50	66.25	68.25	52.50	62.50	58.38
Stock price – low ($)	—	30.00	32.88	32.88	27.25	36.13	52.25	43.75	39.50	46.63	29.00
Stock price – close ($)	(1.3%)	44.00	36.38	36.00	36.50	53.50	56.38	45.25	47.25	56.50	39.00
P/E – high	—	8	8	14	25	14	11	9	9	11	11
P/E – low	—	5	6	11	17	9	8	6	7	8	5
Dividends per share ($)	1.9%	2.32	2.52	2.64	2.64	1.98	2.64	2.73	2.76	2.76	2.76
Book value per share ($)	4.6%	42.90	44.04	41.40	38.74	41.52	49.14	53.56	58.11	61.94	64.23

1990 Year-end:
Equity as % of assets: 7.9%
Return on equity: 8.8%
Cash (mil.): $2,036
Long-term debt (mil.): $982
No. of shares (mil.): 110
Dividends:
   1990 average yield: 7.1%
   1990 payout: 50.0%
Market value (mil.): $4,294
Sales (mil.): $19,021

**Stock Price History
High/Low 1981–90**

AFL-CIO

Labor federation
Fiscal year ends: December 31

Hoover's Rating B

OVERVIEW

Headquartered in Washington, DC, the American Federation of Labor and Congress of Industrial Organizations is a union of unions, representing over 14 million workers (about 83% of all US union members) through 90 affiliated unions and over 60,000 locals.

The Executive Council (president, secretary-treasurer, and 33 VPs) oversees 50 state central bodies, local central bodies in 626 communities, and 9 trade and industrial departments (e.g., building trades, public employees), and sets policy between the biennial conventions. The federation's revenues are derived from regular per-capita dues paid by affiliates on behalf of their members.

The AFL-CIO encourages its affiliates' autonomy (through voluntary membership and separate officers and policies) and conducts no independent bargaining. The federation does settle jurisdictional disputes, help with organizing drives, sponsor voter registration, and present a unified labor front before legislatures. The AFL-CIO's lobbying priorities for the early 1990s include opposing a free-trade pact with Mexico and presenting an elaborate model for national health care reform.

WHO

President: Lane Kirkland, age 69
Secretary-Treasurer: Thomas R. Donahue, age 63
VP; President, International Brotherhood of Teamsters: William J. McCarthy
VP; President, American Federal, State, County & Municipal Employees: Gerald McEntee
VP; President, Service Employees International Union: John Sweeney
VP; President, United Food & Commercial Workers International Union: William Wynn
Auditors: KPMG Peat Marwick
Employees: 400

WHEN

The American Federation of Labor (AFL) formed in 1886 in Columbus, Ohio, from the merger of a small federation of 6 craft unions and a renegade craft section of the Marxist-oriented Knights of Labor. Samuel Gompers, a New York cigar factory worker who headed the AFL until his death in 1924, initiated the AFL's pragmatic focus: to work within, not to overthrow, the economic system in order to increase wages, shorten hours, improve working conditions, and abolish child labor.

Gompers's successes (the initial membership grew to 2 million by 1916) incensed employers, whose arsenal, supported by the US courts and public opinion, included court injunctions and government-backed police forces to crush strikes; "yellow dog" contracts, which pledged workers never to join a union; and the Sherman Anti-Trust Act, used to assail union monopoly powers.

WWI's production needs boosted AFL membership to 4 million by 1919. Labor clashes with management were widespread in the 1920s amidst the fear of Bolsheviks. As part of open-shop drives, employers replaced strikers with southern blacks and Mexicans.

The Great Depression brought a more acquiescent public and various pro-labor laws: the Norris-Laguardia Act eliminated legal restrictions on strikes (1932); the National Industrial Recovery Act (NIRA) allowed union organizing and collective bargaining (1933), but was declared unconstitutional. The Wagner Act (1936) restated many of NIRA's provisions and established the legal basis for unions, which remains to the present.

Union power split in 1935 when AFL coal miner John L. Lewis tried to organize the flood of unskilled mass production workers. Lewis and his allies, expelled from the AFL, formed the Congress of Industrial Organizations (CIO, 1938) and enjoyed great success in unionizing the auto, steel, textile, and other industries. The protection of the Wagner Act had swelled the AFL's membership to 9 million by 1946 and the CIO's to 5 million.

Amidst postwar public concern over rising consumer prices and Communist infiltration and corruption of the unions, Congress passed the labor-regulating Taft-Hartley Act (1947). The hostility led the AFL (headed by plumber George Meany) and the CIO (headed by autoworker Walter Reuther) to merge in 1955. The AFL-CIO soon expelled the Teamsters and other unions on charges of corruption.

During its zenith of power in the 1960s, the AFL-CIO supported equal pay for women and civil rights. Public union membership jumped after President Kennedy gave federal employees the right to unionize (1962); state, county, and municipal workers soon followed.

A decline, begun with the vast increase in imported manufactured goods in the 1970s, accelerated in the 1980s: union-heavy industries were dying from stiff foreign competition, and new technologies continued to eliminate jobs. Lane Kirkland (president since 1979) launched a reunification effort that attracted the United Auto Workers (1981), the Teamsters (1987), and the United Mine Workers (1989). In 1991 the AFL-CIO launched a push to organize hospital and health-care workers.

WHERE

HQ: American Federation of Labor and Congress of Industrial Organizations, 815 16th St. NW, Washington, DC 20006
Phone: 202-637-5010
Fax: 202-637-5058

The AFL-CIO comprises 90 unions with more than 60,000 locals in the US and Canada.

WHAT

Largest Member Unions	1989–90 Members (Thou.)	% of Total
International Brotherhood of Teamsters (IBT)	1,161	8
State, County, Municipal (AFSCME)	1,090	8
Food and Commercial Workers (UFCW)	999	7
Automobile, Aerospace, and Agriculture (UAW)	917	7
Service Employees (SEIU)	762	5
Electrical Workers (IBEW)	744	5
Carpenters (UBCJA)	613	4
Teachers (AFT)	544	4
Machinists and Aerospace (IAM)	517	4
Communications Workers (CWA)	492	3
United Steel Workers of America (USWA)	481	3
Laborers	406	3
Operating Engineers	330	2
Hotel & Restaurant Employees (HERE)	278	2
United Association of Plumbing & Pipe Fitting	220	2
Other unions	4,546	33
Total	**14,100**	**100**

Standing Committees
Civil Rights
Community Services
Economic Policy
Education
Housing
International Affairs
Legislative
Organization and Field Services
Political Education
Public Relations
Research
Safety and Occupational Health
Social Security

Trades Represented
Building and Construction Trades
Food and Allied Service Trades
Industrial Union
Maritime Trades
Metal Trades
Professional Employees
Public Employees
Transportation Trades
Union Label and Service Trades

HOW MUCH

	9-Year Growth	1981	1982	1983[2]	1984	1985	1986	1987	1988	1989	1990
Membership (mil.)[1]	0.4%	13.6	—	13.8	—	13.1	—	12.7	—	14.2	14.1
Total dues ($ mil.)	7.8%	30.1	35.9	60.9	43.5	46.9	47.1	47.0	54.0	—	59.3
All unionized workers as % of total labor force	—	—	—	20.1%	18.8%	18.0%	17.5%	17.0%	16.8%	16.4%	16.2%

All Unionized Workers as % of Total Labor Force 1983–90

[bar chart showing values declining from 25% scale: 1983 ~20%, 1984 ~19%, 1985 ~18%, 1986 ~17.5%, 1987 ~17%, 1988 ~16.8%, 1989 ~16.4%, 1990 ~16.2%]

[1] Membership figures kept only for odd years because of biennial convention periods
[2] Fiscal year switched from June 30 to December 31

H. F. AHMANSON & COMPANY

NYSE symbol: AHM
Fiscal year ends: December 31

OVERVIEW

H. F. Ahmanson, a Los Angeles–based holding company for Home Savings of America, is the largest US savings and loan organization, with over $51 billion in assets, $38 billion in deposits, and $191 million in earnings in 1990.

Home Savings, which represented 99% of Ahmanson's revenues and assets in 1990, has 386 branches in 9 states and 91 lending offices in 13 states. Ahmanson also makes loans outside California through Home Savings's Ahmanson Mortgage Company and Bowery Mortgage Company.

Of Ahmanson's $43 billion in mortgage loans outstanding at year-end 1990, 86% were monthly adjustable rate mortgages (ARMs), well above the national average of ARMs for mortgage lenders, and 92% of its portfolio is secured by residential real estate, one of the most stable plays in the thrift industry. Ahmanson takes a conservative approach; as CEO Richard Deihl puts it, "We're a high-volume, low-cost lender to low-risk home buyers." To keep overhead low, the company has cut 700 jobs in the past 2 years.

WHEN

By 1889 Walter Bonynge, 35, already had made a fortune in silver in Nevada and started a fire insurance company in San Antonio when he organized Home Investment Building and Loan, a savings and loan, in Los Angeles. In the early 1900s the company served customers from several locations in downtown Los Angeles, making Bonynge a pioneer in establishing branch banking in the US. The company changed its name to Home Building and Loan Association in 1922. Bonynge remained as secretary and director until his death in 1924.

In 1947 Howard Ahmanson, a Los Angeles insurance man, bought the company, which then became a subsidiary of H. F. Ahmanson & Company (founded 1928). In 1950 Home Building purchased Long Beach Savings and Loan, with offices in Long Beach and Huntington Park. The company changed its name to Home Savings and Loan Association in 1951 and opened a Beverly Hills branch in 1953. By the end of the 1950s, the $700 million institution led the savings industry in total assets, deposits, customer base, and mortgage lending.

In 1961 Home Savings became the first savings and loan in the US to have $1 billion in assets. That same year the company was the first savings and loan in the country to have a celebrity spokesman, Harry von Zell of the

"Burns and Allen" TV show. Ahmanson was chairman of the company until the late 1960s, and family members, as trustees of the Ahmanson Foundation, are still members of the company's board of directors.

During the 1970s Ahmanson's Home Savings grew to over 100 offices throughout California. Assets were $12 billion by 1980 compared to $2 billion in 1967. In the 1980s Home Savings pursued a long-range strategy by developing new products, including adjustable rate mortgages, interest checking, check guarantee cards, and overdraft protection.

With regulators approving expansion across state lines, Home Savings in a 4-week period in late 1981 moved into Florida, Missouri, Texas, and Illinois. The company became Home Savings of America and expanded into New York (1984), Arizona (1985), and Washington (1985). In 1988 Home Savings bought The Bowery Savings Bank, one of New York's largest and oldest savings banks.

Ahmanson maintained net income averaging over $200 million annually during the late 1980s when many savings institutions were in trouble. In a 1990 stock swap valued at $250 million, Ahmanson acquired Home Savings Bank of New York, with 13 branches and deposits of $1.5 billion. The company also added 19 San Diego branches from Coast Savings for $20 million in 1991.

WHO

Chairman and CEO: Richard H. Deihl, age 62, $1,225,000 pay
VC: Robert M. De Kruif, age 72, $428,450 pay
President and COO: Charles R. Rinehart, age 44, $696,553 pay
EVP and CFO: Jack A. Frazee, age 47, $410,438 pay
First VP Human Resources: Herschel Cardin
Auditors: KPMG Peat Marwick
Employees: 9,905

WHERE

HQ: 660 S. Figueroa St., Los Angeles, CA 90017
Phone: 213-955-4200
Fax: 213-955-4273

H. F. Ahmanson has 477 offices in 13 states.

| | 1990 Loans | |
	$ mil.	% of total
California	31,559	70
New York	3,680	8
Florida	2,501	6
Illinois	1,488	3
Texas	862	2
Washington	589	1
Ohio	417	1
Missouri	402	1
Arizona	350	1
Other states	3,094	7
Adjustments	(103)	—
Total	**44,839**	**100**

WHAT

| | 1990 Loans | |
	$ mil.	% of total
Residential		
Single family	29,481	66
Multi-family	5,595	12
Commercial	2,585	6
Non–real estate	7,178	16
Total	**44,839**	**100**

Financial Services
Consumer deposit accounts
Mortgage-backed securities
Mortgage loan servicing
Mortgage loans
Secondary mortgage loan sales

Subsidiaries
Ahmanson Mortgage Co.
Bowery Mortgage Co.
The Bowery Savings Bank
The Home Savings Bank
Home Savings of America
Savings of America

RANKINGS

1st in *Fortune* 50 Savings Institutions
328th in *Business Week* 1000

KEY COMPETITORS

Banc One	Chemical	Mellon Bank
Bank of New York	Banking	NCNB
BankAmerica	Citicorp	PNC Financial
Bankers Trust	First Chicago	SunTrust
Barnett Banks	First Interstate	Wells Fargo
Berkshire Hathaway	Fleet/Norstar	
Chase Manhattan	Great Western	

HOW MUCH

	9-Year Growth	1981	1982	1983	1984	1985	1986	1987	1988	1989	1990
Assets ($ mil.)	14.6%	15,049	16,864	20,226	24,307	27,229	27,592	30,507	40,258	44,652	51,201
Net income ($ mil.)	—	(62)	(45)	108	48	221	304	200	203	194	191
Income as % of assets	—	(0.4%)	(0.3%)	0.5%	0.2%	0.8%	1.1%	0.7%	0.5%	0.4%	0.4%
Earnings per share ($)	—	(0.86)	(0.63)	1.34	0.58	2.63	3.22	2.03	2.05	1.95	1.64
Stock price – high ($)	—	7.00	11.04	13.50	11.50	16.33	28.75	26.88	18.63	25.00	22.50
Stock price – low ($)	—	4.71	2.67	7.50	5.25	8.13	15.79	13.00	13.75	15.75	10.63
Stock price – close ($)	11.6%	5.04	9.25	10.25	8.79	16.21	21.63	16.50	16.38	19.00	13.50
P/E – high	—	—	—	10	20	6	9	13	9	13	14
P/E – low	—	—	—	6	9	3	5	6	7	8	6
Dividends per share ($)	9.2%	0.40	0.25	0.25	0.40	0.40	0.45	0.88	0.88	0.88	0.88
Book value per share ($)	7.1%	10.90	10.00	11.04	11.23	13.43	17.14	18.28	19.11	20.22	20.20

1990 Year-end:
Return on equity: 8.1%
Equity as % of assets: 4.6%
Cash (mil.): $3,036
Long-term debt (mil.): $7,551
No. of shares (mil.): 116
Dividends:
1990 average yield: 6.5%
1990 payout: 53.7%
Market value (mil.): $1,565
Sales (mil.): $4,848

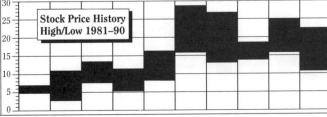

Stock Price History
High/Low 1981–90

ALASKA AIR GROUP, INC.

OVERVIEW

Alaska Air Group is a holding company for Alaska Airlines and Horizon Air Industries, 2 Seattle-based airlines serving the western US, Mexico, Canada, and the Soviet Union.

Since 1973 more passengers have flown Alaska than any other airline between the Land of the Midnight Sun and the lower 48 states. The airline (named by *Condé Nast Traveler* as the best US airline for customer service since 1989) has built a loyal clientele by putting fewer seats on each plane (adding leg room), offering free wine on every flight, and spending about $7.50 per passenger on food (compared to the industry average of $4.86). *Air Transport World* named Alaska Air

its Airline of the Year in 1990. That same year Alaska celebrated its 18th consecutive year of profitability. Much of its success is due to the leadership of former chairman Bruce Kennedy, who retired in May 1991.

Alaska offers service to 68 Alaskan communities through agreements with 5 regional airlines. The airline's link to its heritage is illustrated by the Eskimo painted on the tail of every Alaska craft.

Horizon is the largest regional commuter in the Pacific Northwest, carrying 1.8 million passengers in 1990. Service to the Canadian cities of Vancouver and Victoria accounted for 11% of the airline's passenger traffic in 1990.

WHEN

In 1932 pilot Mac McGee started McGee Airways to fly cargo between Anchorage and Bristol Bay, Alaska. He joined other local operators in 1937 to form Star Air Lines, which began air mail service between Fairbanks and Bethel in 1938. In 1944, a year after buying 3 other small airlines (including one with a mail route between Anchorage and Fairbanks), Star adopted the name Alaska Airlines.

Alaska bought 2 more local carriers and established freight service to Africa and Australia in 1950. This expansion, coupled with the seasonal nature of the airline's business, resulted in losses that continued through the early 1970s. Developer Bruce Kennedy led a boardroom revolt to gain control of the financially ailing airline in 1972 and had turned Alaska around by the end of 1973. However, the Civil Aeronautics Board forced the airline to drop service to cities in northwestern Alaska, including Nome in 1975, and by 1978 the company served only 10 Alaskan cities and Seattle.

Kennedy became CEO in 1979, shortly after congressional approval of the 1978 Airline Deregulation Act. Deregulation allowed Alaska to extend operations into new areas (such as California) and to regain routes it had lost (including Nome). By 1982 Alaska Airlines was

the largest carrier operating between the US mainland and Alaska, and in 1983, after 40 years on the ASE, Alaska was listed on the NYSE.

In 1986 Alaska bought Long Beach–based Jet America Airlines (expanding its route network eastward to Chicago, St. Louis, and Dallas) and Seattle-based Horizon Air Industries (which served 30 cities in the Northwest). When competition in the East and Midwest resulted in a 35% reduction in profits in 1987, Kennedy shut down Jet America and concentrated on Alaska's and Horizon's operations along the West Coast.

Hoping to counterbalance summer traffic to Alaska, the airline opened service to 2 Mexican resorts in 1988. International Lease Finance Corporation (aircraft financer) bought $62.5 million of convertible preferred stock in the company in 1990, and Alaska used the cash to help finance a $2.5 billion order for new planes.

High fuel prices and sluggish traffic crimped earnings for 1990. Fare discounting added to mounting costs, and Alaska posted a loss for the first quarter of 1991. The company opened service to Toronto that year and began flights to 2 cities in the Soviet Union.

NYSE symbol: ALK
Fiscal year ends: December 31

WHO

Chairman, President, and CEO; Chairman, President, and CEO, Alaska Airlines, Inc.: Raymond J. Vecci, age 48, $200,842 pay (prior to promotion)
VP Finance, CFO, and Treasurer; VP Finance and CFO, Alaska Airlines, Inc.: J. Ray Vingo, age 52, $155,935 pay
VP Human Resources, Alaska Airlines, Inc.: Charles S. Loughran
Auditors: Arthur Andersen & Co.
Employees: 6,183

WHERE

HQ: 19300 Pacific Hwy. South, Seattle, WA 98188
Phone: 206-431-7040
Fax: 206-433-3366
Reservations: 800-426-0333

Alaska flies to 37 cities in Alaska, Arizona, California, Idaho, Oregon, Washington, Mexico, Canada, and the Soviet Union. Horizon flies to 34 cities in Idaho, Montana, Oregon, Utah, Washington, and Canada.

Hub Locations

Alaska	Horizon
Anchorage, AL	Boise, ID
Portland, OR	Portland, OR
Seattle, WA	Seattle, WA
	Spokane, WA

WHAT

	1990 Sales	
	$ mil.	% of total
Passenger service	953	91
Freight & mail	69	7
Contract service & other	25	2
Total	**1,047**	**100**

Subsidiaries and Affiliates
Alaska Airlines, Inc.
Horizon Air Industries, Inc.

Flight Equipment	Number	Orders
Alaska		
Boeing 727	28	0
Boeing 737	7	20
MD-80	28	8
MD-90	0	20
	63	48
Horizon		
Fairchild Metroliner	32	0
de Havilland Dash 8	15	5
Fokker F-28	3	0
	50	5
Total	**113**	**53**

RANKINGS

26th in *Fortune* 50 Transportation Cos.

KEY COMPETITORS

America West
AMR
Continental Airlines
Delta
NWA
UAL
USAir

HOW MUCH

	9-Year Growth	1981	1982	1983	1984	1985	1986	1987	1988	1989	1990
Sales ($ mil.)	21.5%	182	235	281	362	433	468	710	814	917	1,047
Net income ($ mil.)	9.4%	8	11	16	24	26	18	13	37	43	17
Income as % of sales	—	4.2%	4.5%	5.6%	6.6%	6.0%	3.8%	1.9%	4.6%	4.7%	1.6%
Earnings per share ($)	(1.9%)	0.97	1.15	1.44	1.93	1.85	1.30	0.87	2.30	2.51	*0.82*
Stock price – high ($)	—	8.33	14.38	18.63	17.25	26.38	22.75	27.88	22.50	30.50	26.00
Stock price – low ($)	—	3.69	4.63	10.38	9.25	14.25	14.25	12.25	13.50	19.88	13.88
Stock price – close ($)	12.4%	6.13	13.25	14.13	15.13	16.13	20.00	13.50	20.00	20.63	17.50
P/E – high	—	9	13	13	9	14	18	32	10	12	32
P/E – low	—	4	4	7	5	8	11	14	6	8	17
Dividends per share ($)	—	0.00	0.12	0.09	0.14	0.15	0.16	0.16	0.16	0.20	0.20
Book value per share ($)	14.3%	6.39	6.65	8.05	10.12	13.05	14.31	17.37	19.59	22.08	21.23

1990 Year-end:
Debt ratio: 50.2%
Return on equity: 3.8%
Cash (mil.): $52
Current ratio: 0.57
Long-term debt (mil.): $282
No. of shares (mil.): 13
Dividends:
  1990 average yield: 1.1%
  1990 payout: 24.4%
Market value (mil.): $231

Stock Price History High/Low 1981–90

ALBERTSON'S, INC.

OVERVIEW

Albertson's, America's 6th largest food retailer, is extremely profitable, ranking high among its major competitors in both net earnings ($234 million in 1990) and return on equity (23.2%). Based in Boise, the company operates grocery stores in western and southern states. Last year (1990) was Albertson's 21st consecutive year of increased sales and earnings.

The company believes good retail site selection that maximizes the market area of a store is the foundation of its success. Unlike grocers who cluster stores, Albertson's operates only a few locations in each market. Another element of the company's success is having efficient, modern distribution facilities for strategic servicing of its widely dispersed stores. During 1987–90 Albertson's spent $250 million on distribution centers.

Eighty percent of the company stores' square footage is in large, food/drug combination stores or superstores. Albertson's promotes its "One Stop Shopping" advantage through having these big stores with a variety of services and maintaining its "Rock Bottom Prices" on 30,000 items every day.

The company has a commitment to provide job enrichment and motivation to its employees, 49% of whom are unionized. Unlike its more weakly performing rivals, Albertson's managed to sidestep the corporate raiders in the 1980s and is not burdened by high debt. In 1990 the company started the HOPE (Helping Our Planet's Ecology) line of environmentally safer paper products. Founder Joe Albertson and his wife, Kathryn, continue to influence the company's activities as directors.

WHEN

J. A. "Joe" Albertson left his position as district manager for Safeway in 1939 and opened his first food store, Albertson's Food Center, in Boise, Idaho. The store differed from others because it covered 10,000 square feet — 8 times the competitors' average — and had plenty of free parking, an in-store butchery, a bakery, and an ice cream shop. With these innovations, Albertson was a key developer of the "supermarket" concept in food retailing.

Albertson's refined its supermarket concept further by opening its first combination food and drug store (1951), a 60,000-square-foot superstore, and by locating stores in growing suburban areas. Jonathan Scott, who became president of Albertson's in 1955, married Joe's daughter Barbara; despite their later divorce, Scott remained president until 1975. Albertson's went public to raise expansion capital in 1959 and by 1960 had 62 stores in Idaho, Washington, Oregon, and Utah. Albertson's acquired Greater All American Markets (1964), a grocery chain based in Downey, California, and Semrau & Sons (1965) of Oakland, aiding the company's thrust into the California market.

Salt Lake City–based drugstore chain Skaggs (now part of American Stores) and Albertson's formed a partnership in 1969 to jointly operate large Skaggs Albertson's food-and-drug combination stores.

In 1973 the company built its first full-line distribution facility in Brea, California, and opened an even larger facility in Salt Lake City in 1976. Albertson's and Skaggs dissolved their partnership in 1977, with each taking 1/2 of the units in the jointly owned chain. By 1985 the company had reached $5 billion in sales, a five-fold increase over 1975. Albertson's added a distribution facility in Denver in 1982 and its first mechanized distribution center in Portland, Oregon, in 1988. Its efficient distribution centers should continue to increase operating margins.

The company expects to open 37 new stores in 1991. Present plans are to open 240 stores through 1995 at a cost of $1.5 billion. Albertson's is reworking its management information system to help it maintain its industry position.

NYSE symbol: ABS
Fiscal year ends: Thursday closest to January 31

Hoover's Rating A

WHO

Chairman and CEO: Gary G. Michael, age 50, $716,966 pay (prior to promotion)
President and COO: John B. Carley, age 57, $711,945 pay (prior to promotion)
EVP Retail Operations: Robert G. Miller, age 46, $310,645 pay
EVP Store Development: Michael F. Reuling, age 44, $277,155 pay
SVP Human Resources: Gerald R. Rudd, age 61
Auditors: Deloitte & Touche
Employees: 58,000

WHERE

HQ: PO Box 20, 250 Parkcenter Blvd., Boise, ID 83726
Phone: 208-385-6200
Fax: 208-385-6349

The company operates 535 stores in 17 western and southern states. Full-line distribution facilities are located in Brea, CA; Denver; Fort Worth; Portland, OR; and Salt Lake City.

	No. of Stores
California	124
Florida	67
Washington	61
Texas	60
Oregon	42
Colorado	39
Utah	31
Idaho	28
Nevada	21
New Mexico	15
Arizona	11
Louisiana	11
Wyoming	8
Montana	7
Nebraska	5
Kansas	4
South Dakota	1
Total	**535**

WHAT

	No. of Stores	Area (Sq. Ft. Thou.)
Combination units	148	8,581
Superstores	216	9,008
Conventional stores	136	3,800
Warehouse stores	31	1,345
Total	**531**	**22,734**

Warehouse Stores
The Canned Food Store
The Grocery Warehouse
Maxx Warehouse Food and Drug
Monte Mart

RANKINGS

14th in *Fortune* 50 Retailing Cos.
121st in *Business Week* 1000

KEY COMPETITORS

American Stores	Fred Meyer	Publix
Bruno's	Great A&P	Safeway
Costco	Kroger	Vons
Edward J. DeBartolo	Longs	Winn-Dixie
Food Lion		

HOW MUCH

	9-Year Growth	1981	1982	1983	1984	1985	1986	1987	1988	1989	1990
Sales ($ mil.)	10.0%	3,481	3,940	4,279	4,736	5,060	5,380	5,869	6,773	7,423	8,219
Net income ($ mil.)	19.1%	48	58	70	80	85	100	125	163	197	234
Income as % of sales	—	1.4%	1.5%	1.6%	1.7%	1.7%	1.9%	2.1%	2.4%	2.6%	2.8%
Earnings per share ($)	18.1%	0.39	0.48	0.54	0.61	0.64	0.75	0.94	1.22	1.47	1.75
Stock price – high ($)	—	3.70	6.19	7.56	7.38	8.31	12.38	17.00	19.38	30.13	37.75
Stock price – low ($)	—	2.44	3.02	4.94	5.63	6.59	7.63	10.13	12.00	18.31	24.38
Stock price – close ($)	30.6%	3.31	5.91	6.78	7.25	8.13	10.75	12.69	18.94	27.75	36.50
P/E – high	—	9	13	14	12	13	17	18	16	21	22
P/E – low	—	6	6	9	9	10	10	11	10	13	14
Dividends per share ($)	21.0%	0.08	0.15	0.15	0.13	0.19	0.21	0.23	0.34	0.30	0.46
Book value per share ($)	16.8%	2.01	2.61	2.98	3.44	3.90	4.45	5.01	5.98	6.94	8.13

1990 Year-end:
Debt ratio: 12.8%
Return on equity: 23.2%
Cash (mil.): $23
Current ratio: 1.16
Long-term debt (mil.): $159
No. of shares (mil.): 134
Dividends:
 1990 average yield: 1.3%
 1990 payout: 26.3%
Market value (mil.): $4,884

Stock Price History High/Low 1981–90

ALLIED-SIGNAL INC.

OVERVIEW

Allied-Signal is a diversified company operating in the aerospace, automotive, and chemical industries. Allied-Signal Aerospace manufactures components, including engines and avionics, used in commercial and military aviation. The US government accounts for 42% of the company's aerospace revenue.

Allied-Signal's automotive division produces a variety of automotive systems and components, boasting trade names such as Autolite, Bendix, Fram, and Garrett, and is a world leader in automotive braking systems. The company's chemical division leads the world in the production of hydrofluoric acid (for refrigerants). Allied also owns 39% of oil-and-gas producer Union Texas.

Board disappointment over Allied's lackluster stock and financial performance led to the appointment of former GE vice-chairman Lawrence Bossidy as the company's new CEO in 1991. Bossidy vows to improve cash flow by trimming overhead and capital spending.

WHEN

During WWI Germany controlled much of the world's chemical industry, causing shortages of such commodities as dyes and drugs. In response, *Washington Post* publisher Eugene Meyer and scientist William Nichols organized the Allied Chemical & Dye Corporation in 1920 from 5 existing companies.

In 1928 Allied opened a synthetic ammonia plant near Hopewell, Virginia, becoming the world's leading producer of ammonia. This represented the company's earliest venture into new markets. After WWII Allied began manufacturing other new products, including nylon 6 (for making everything from tires to clothes) and refrigerants. In 1958 it became Allied Chemical Corporation.

In 1962 Allied bought Union Texas Natural Gas, which owned oil and gas properties throughout the Americas. Allied regarded it mainly as a supplier of raw materials for its chemical products, but this changed in the early 1970s when CEO John Connor (former secretary of commerce under President Johnson) sold many of Allied's unprofitable businesses and invested in oil and gas exploration. By 1979, when Edward Hennessy, Jr., became CEO, Union Texas produced 80% of Allied's income.

Through purchases directed by Hennessy, Allied entered new fields, including electronics (Eltra Corporation, 1979; Bunker Ramo Corporation, 1981) and health and scientific products (Fisher Scientific Company, 1981).

Renamed the Allied Corporation (1981), the company went on to buy the Bendix Corporation, an aerospace and automotive company, in 1983. By 1984 Bendix generated 50% of Allied's income, while oil and gas generated 38%.

In 1985 Allied merged with The Signal Companies to form Allied-Signal. Founded by Sam Mosher in 1922 as The Signal Gasoline Company, Signal originally produced gasoline from natural gas. In 1928 the company changed its name to Signal Oil & Gas, entering into oil production the same year. Signal merged with the Garrett Corporation, a Los Angeles–based aerospace company, in 1964; acquired Mack Trucks in 1967 (spun off 1983); and in 1968 adopted The Signal Companies as its corporate name. Signal bought the Ampex Corporation in 1981.

The addition of Signal's Garrett division to Bendix made aerospace Allied-Signal's largest business sector. In 1985 the company sold 50% of Union Texas (by then America's largest independent oil producer) and in 1986 spun off 35 mostly unprofitable chemical and engineering businesses, collectively known as the Henley Group, to its stockholders. Hennessy sold 7 more businesses in 1987, leaving Allied-Signal in aerospace, automotive parts, and chemicals.

In 1990 Allied-Signal contributed its high-density polyethylene business to a newly formed joint venture with Exxon.

NYSE symbol: ALD
Fiscal year ends: December 31

Hoover's Rating **C**

WHO

Chairman: Edward L. Hennessy, Jr., age 62, $1,687,500 pay
CEO: Lawrence A. Bossidy, age 56
President and COO: Alan Belzer, age 58, $1,187,500 pay
SVP and CFO: John W. Barter, age 44, $510,000 pay
SVP Human Resources: Donald Redlinger, age 46
Auditors: Price Waterhouse
Employees: 105,800

WHERE

HQ: 101 Columbia Rd., PO Box 4000, Morristown, NJ 07962-4000
Phone: 201-455-2000
Fax: 201-455-4807

	1990 Sales		1990 Net Income	
	$ mil.	% of total	$ mil.	% of total
US	9,395	76	399	87
Canada	341	3	13	3
Europe	2,002	16	48	10
Other	605	5	2	—
Total	**12,343**	**100**	**462**	**100**

WHAT

	1990 Sales		1990 Operating Income	
	$ mil.	% of total	$ mil.	% of total
Aerospace	5,358	43	498	52
Automotive	4,181	34	166	18
Engineered matls.	2,786	23	287	30
Adjustments	18	—	(221)	—
Total	**12,343**	**100**	**730**	**100**

Aerospace
AiResearch (aircraft environmental control systems)
Bendix Electric Power (power generation systems)
Bendix Guidance Systems
Bendix/King (navigation systems)
Garrett Auxiliary Power
Garrett Engine

Automotive
Autolite (spark plugs)
Bendix (brakes, passenger-restraint systems)
Fram (automotive filters)

Garrett (turbochargers)
Jurid Werke (brakes)
Valeo (brakes)

Engineered Materials
Caprolactam
Circuit-board laminates
Engineered plastics
Floor-polish additives
Fluorocarbons
Hydrofluoric acid
Nylon
Plastics
Rubber and plastic additives
Sulfur hexafluoride
Textile finishes
Uranium hexafluoride

RANKINGS

36th in *Fortune* 500 Industrial Cos.
165th in *Business Week* 1000

KEY COMPETITORS

American Standard	Henley	Rockwell
BASF	Hercules	International
Borg-Warner	Hoechst	Thiokol
Dana	Honeywell	TRW
Du Pont	ITT	United
Eaton	Lockheed	Technologies
EG&G	Martin	Westinghouse
Electrolux	Marietta	Other chemical,
Formosa Plastics	Monsanto	automotive, and
General Electric	Nissan	aerospace
Grumman	Robert Bosch	companies

HOW MUCH

	9-Year Growth	1981	1982	1983	1984	1985	1986	1987	1988	1989	1990
Sales ($ mil.)	7.6%	6,407	6,167	10,022	10,734	9,115	11,794	11,116	11,909	11,942	12,343
Net income ($ mil.)	3.2%	348	272	450	487	(279)	605	515	463	528	462
Income as % of sales	—	5.4%	4.4%	4.5%	4.5%	(3.1%)	5.1%	4.6%	3.9%	4.4%	3.7%
Earnings per share ($)	(6.5%)	6.11	4.15	4.61	5.02	(3.28)	3.26	3.07	3.10	3.55	3.35
Stock price – high ($)	—	39.92	30.25	38.75	38.17	48.13	54.50	49.25	36.88	40.38	37.88
Stock price – low ($)	—	26.00	19.17	21.42	28.25	33.75	36.75	26.00	28.00	31.75	24.88
Stock price – close ($)	(0.9%)	29.25	21.58	37.17	34.50	46.75	40.13	28.25	32.50	34.88	27.00
P/E – high	—	7	7	8	8	—	17	16	12	11	11
P/E – low	—	4	5	5	6	—	11	8	9	9	7
Dividends per share ($)	1.6%	1.57	1.60	1.60	1.75	1.80	1.80	1.80	1.80	1.80	1.80
Book value per share ($)	(4.5%)	37.91	38.07	30.62	33.08	33.29	21.05	20.87	22.09	23.53	25.10

1990 Year-end:
Debt ratio: 37.8%
Return on equity: 13.8%
Cash (mil.): $382
Current ratio: 1.26
Long-term debt (mil.): $2,051
No. of shares (mil.): 135
Dividends:
1990 average yield: 6.7%
1990 payout: 53.7%
Market value (mil.): $3,637

Stock Price History High/Low 1981–90

ALUMINUM COMPANY OF AMERICA

NYSE symbol: AA
Fiscal year ends: December 31

Hoover's Rating **B-**

OVERVIEW

Now popularly known as Alcoa, the Pittsburgh-based Aluminum Company of America is the world's largest aluminum producer, serving the packaging, transportation, building, and industrial markets.

Chairman Paul O'Neill, the first CEO to come from outside the company, is shaking up Alcoa, which early on developed a reputation for being aggressive and entrepreneurial. In a 1991 restructuring marked by the departure of 4 senior executives, including President Fred Fetterolf, O'Neill shifted responsibility and incentives to Alcoa's 25 operating units around the world. A 3-person chairman's council will supervise the business units. Alcoa abandoned its organization based on 3 operating groups — metals and chemicals, aerospace and industrial products, and packaging systems.

O'Neill hopes to make the company resistant to the cyclical aluminum industry through development of such new core businesses as ceramic packaging for semiconductors. The US recession in 1990 ate into Alcoa's profits after a record 1989. US contributions to operating profit were negative in 1990, while profits in the Pacific — home of subsidiary Alcoa of Australia, the world's leading alumina producer — remained steady.

WHEN

In 1886, 2 chemists, one in France and one in the US, simultaneously discovered an inexpensive process for aluminum production. The American, Charles Martin Hall, pursued commercial applications. In 1888, with an investor group led by Captain Alfred Hunt, Hall formed the Pittsburgh Reduction Company. The first salesman, Arthur Vining Davis, secured an initial order for 2,000 cooking pots.

In 1889 the Mellon Bank loaned the company $4,000. In 1891 Alcoa recapitalized as a million-dollar corporation, with the Mellon brothers holding 12% of the stock. By the 1920s the Mellons had increased their share to 33%.

Hunt died in 1899, and Davis led the company, which remained highly centralized, until 1957, remaining on the board until his death in 1962 at age 95. Alcoa, the first industrial user of Niagara Falls (1893), introduced aluminum foil (1910) and found applications for aluminum in emerging industries (e.g., electric wire, airplanes, and automobiles). The present name was adopted in 1907.

By the end of WWI, Alcoa was integrated backward into bauxite mining and forward into end-use production. Alcoa transferred most foreign properties to Aluminium Ltd., a Canadian subsidiary, in 1928.

The government and Alcoa debated antitrust issues in court for years after the smelting patent expired in 1912. Finally, a 1946 federal ruling forced Alcoa to sell many operations built during WWII (when US smelting capacity doubled) as well as its Canadian subsidiary, today Alcan, its largest competitor.

In the more competitive aluminum industry of the 1960s, Alcoa relied on its laboratories (established 1919) and entrepreneurship. The company devised lower-cost production methods and seized market shares, especially in beverage cans. Alcoa reentered the international arena, establishing 23 locations in 13 countries between 1959 and 1965.

In the 1970s Alcoa diversified, focusing on new products such as aerospace components and lithographic sheet, and in the 1980s Alcoa doubled R&D expenditures, spent $500 million on acquisitions, and invested heavily in joint ventures and plant modernization.

CEO Paul O'Neill arrived in 1987 and shifted the company back to aluminum. Sales and earnings set records in 1988 and 1989. Use of aluminum in autos doubled between 1975 and 1990, and in 1991 Alcoa explored a venture with Audi to make the world's first aluminum car frame, replacing steel as automakers search for more fuel efficiency.

WHO

Chairman and CEO: Paul H. O'Neill, age 55, $824,847 pay
CFO: Jan H. M. Hommen, age 48
EVP Human Relations and Communications: Ronald R. Hoffman, age 57
Auditors: Coopers & Lybrand
Employees: 63,700

WHERE

HQ: 1501 Alcoa Bldg., Pittsburgh, PA 15219
Phone: 412-553-4545
Fax: 412-553-4498

Alcoa operates more than 100 plants worldwide.

	1990 Sales		1990 Operating Income	
	$ mil.	% of total	$ mil.	% of total
US	6,383	60	(147)	(13)
Other Americas	1,206	11	219	20
Pacific	2,124	20	930	85
Europe	997	9	85	8
Adjustments	—	—	399	—
Total	**10,710**	**100**	**1,486**	**100**

WHAT

	1990 Sales		1990 Operating Income	
	$ mil.	% of total	$ mil.	% of total
Alumina & chem.	1,842	17	1,319	122
Aluminum proc.	7,478	70	33	3
Nonaluminum products	1,390	13	(271)	(25)
Adjustments	—	—	405	—
Total	**10,710**	**100**	**1,486**	**100**

Operations and Products
Alumina refining
Alumina-based industrial chemicals
Aluminum foil
Aluminum and plastic bottle caps
Aluminum sheet for cans
Aluminum smelting
Bauxite mining
Can recycling
Ceramic packaging for semiconductors
Fiber optic cable
Finished aluminum products (siding, auto trim)
Gold mining
Separation, purification, and filtration systems

Major Subsidiaries and Affiliates
Alcoa Aluminio SA (74.7%, aluminum, Brazil)
Alcoa of Australia Ltd. (51%; alumina, gold)
Alcoa Composites, Inc. (transportation materials)
Alcoa Electronic Packaging, Inc. (ceramics for integrated circuits)
Alcoa Fujikura Ltd. (51%, wiring systems, Mexico)
Alcoa Mineraçao (60%, mining, Brazil)
KSL Alcoa Aluminum Company (50%, joint venture with Kobe Steel, aluminum sheet, Japan)

RANKINGS

43rd in *Fortune* 500 Industrial Cos.
109th in *Business Week* 1000

KEY COMPETITORS

Adolph Coors	Broken Hill	Norsk Hydro
Alcan	Corning	Phelps Dodge
AMAX	Cyprus Minerals	Reynolds Metals
Anglo American	FMC	RTZ
ASARCO	Inco	Thyssen

HOW MUCH

	9-Year Growth	1981	1982	1983	1984	1985	1986	1987	1988	1989	1990
Sales ($ mil.)	8.9%	4,978	4,648	5,263	5,751	5,163	4,667	7,767	9,795	10,910	10,710
Net income ($ mil.)	0.0%	296	(9)	165	256	(17)	264	224	861	945	295
Income as % of sales	—	6.0%	(0.2%)	3.1%	4.5%	(0.3%)	5.7%	2.9%	8.8%	8.7%	2.8%
Earnings per share ($)	(1.7%)	3.93	(0.15)	2.03	3.13	(0.23)	3.08	2.48	9.50	10.36	3.36
Stock price – high ($)	—	37.50	32.75	47.75	48.63	40.75	46.38	64.75	57.38	79.63	77.25
Stock price – low ($)	—	22.63	21.88	29.25	30.75	29.75	32.63	33.75	38.63	55.25	49.63
Stock price – close ($)	9.4%	25.63	31.00	44.88	37.00	38.50	33.88	46.75	56.00	75.00	57.63
P/E – high	—	10	—	24	16	—	15	26	6	8	23
P/E – low	—	6	—	14	10	—	11	14	4	5	15
Dividends per share ($)	6.0%	1.80	1.65	1.20	1.20	1.20	1.20	1.20	1.30	2.72	3.05
Book value per share ($)	4.3%	41.24	38.60	39.06	40.39	39.84	41.99	43.62	51.76	59.41	60.20

1990 Year-end:
Debt ratio: 20.1%
Return on equity: 5.6%
Cash (mil.): $636
Current ratio: 1.84
Long-term debt (mil.): $1,295
No. of shares (mil.): 85
Dividends:
  1990 average yield: 5.3%
  1990 payout: 90.8%
Market value (mil.): $4,889

Stock Price History High/Low 1981–90

AMAX INC.

OVERVIEW

AMAX, the 6th largest US metals company, oversees subsidiaries developing a wide range of natural resources. Wholly owned Alumax is the 3rd largest aluminum company in the US, after Alcoa and Reynolds, producing everything from aluminum ingot to building materials. Alumax operates more than 110 plants in 30 states, Canada, and Western Europe.

Amax Coal Industries is the 3rd largest US coal producer, with the bulk of its production in Wyoming. The company has focused on developing low-sulfur, cleaner-burning coal.

Amax Oil & Gas explores for and produces oil and natural gas in 31 states and the Gulf of Mexico. With the acquisition of Ladd Petroleum in 1990, AMAX boasted reserves of a trillion cubic feet equivalent in natural gas, positioning itself for a resurgence in demand for the environment-friendly fuel. The company also added natural gas processing plants and 650 miles of pipelines.

AMAX owns 87% of Amax Gold, which produced 354,859 ounces of gold in 1990. The open-pit Sleeper mine in Nevada leads the company's production, but Amax Gold also operates another Nevada site and a New Zealand mine and plans a California project. AMAX's Climax Metals unit is the world's largest producer of molybdenum, a metal used to harden steel.

WHEN

In 1884 Berthold Hochschild arrived in New York from Frankfurt to trade in metals for a German banking firm. The firm had expanded beyond Hanover, into London, and had hoped to profit from rich American copper deposits.

Hochschild's operation prospered and in 1887 became American Metal, Amco for short. The name proved prophetic when the company severed ties with Germany during WWI.

In 1916 Amco formed a syndicate to exploit Colorado deposits of molybdenum. Climax Molybdenum operated independently of Amco until their 1957 merger created American Metal Climax — informally known as AMAX until the company made it official in 1974.

Along with molybdenum, AMAX ventured into other mining operations, including Canadian tungsten (1961), Missouri lead (1963), and Australian iron (1963). Most important was AMAX's entry into aluminum with the purchase of Kawneer of Michigan and Apex Smelting of Chicago (1962).

AMAX added to its aluminum holdings with the purchase of California-based Hunter Engineering (1963). It sold 50% of its aluminum holdings to Mitsui (which sold 5% to Nippon Steel) in 1974. The new aluminum venture was renamed Alumax.

In 1969 AMAX acquired Ayrshire Collieries, a midwestern coal producer. In the mid-1970s the company added Wyoming mines and renewed petroleum exploration that had been begun and abandoned in the 1960s.

Ventures into copper and nickel in the early 1980s turned sour, and demand for other metals plummeted during a recession. AMAX chief Pierre Gousseland led opposition to 2 purchase offers, in 1978 and 1981, by Standard Oil of California (later Chevron). In late 1985 AMAX's board replaced Gousseland with Allen Born, grandson of a Colorado miner.

Born aggressively sold assets (phosphate and lead operations) and wrote off others (nickel and copper mining, copper refining) to return the company to record $741 million earnings (1988). He also repurchased the Japanese interest in Alumax (1986), dug into open-pit Nevada gold mining (1986), and added low-sulfur coal reserves, buying Cannelton of West Virginia (1991).

To compensate for the peaks and valleys of aluminum demand, AMAX is bolstering its energy segment. It bought Ladd Petroleum (1990) and in 1991 placed petroleum and coal subsidiaries within the new structure of Amax Energy.

NYSE symbol: AMX
Fiscal year ends: December 31

 Hoover's Rating **C-**

WHO

Chairman and CEO: Allen Born, age 57, $1,162,497 pay
President and COO.: Paul E. Drack, age 62, $1,186,500 pay (prior to promotion)
SVP and CFO: Stephen C. Knup, age 48, $387,366 pay
President and CEO, Amax Energy, Inc.: Thomas A. McKeever, age 47, $510,275 pay (prior to promotion)
Personnel Manager: Patricia Graf
Auditors: Coopers & Lybrand
Employees: 20,200

WHERE

HQ: 200 Park Ave., New York, NY 10166
Phone: 212-856-4200
Fax: 212-856-6075 (Investor Relations)

AMAX operates in the United States, Canada, Mexico, Australia, New Zealand, and Europe.

	1990 Sales		1990 Operating Income	
	$ mil.	% of total	$ mil.	% of total
US & Canada	3,529	89	345	86
Other countries	445	11	58	14
Adjustments	(186)	—	16	—
Total	**3,788**	**100**	**419**	**100**

WHAT

	1990 Sales		1990 Operating Income	
	$ mil.	% of total	$ mil.	% of total
Aluminum	2,451	65	296	61
Coal	697	18	115	23
Molybdenum	264	7	9	2
Gold	150	4	54	11
Other metals	143	4	(11)	(2)
Oil & gas	83	2	25	5
Adjustments	—	—	(69)	—
Total	**3,788**	**100**	**419**	**100**

Fabricated Aluminum
Building and construction
Consumer durables
Containers and packaging
Transportation

Other Metals
Gold
Molybdenum
Silver
Tungsten

Energy
Coal
Oil and natural gas

RANKINGS

128th in *Fortune* 500 Industrial Cos.
288th in *Business Week* 1000

KEY COMPETITORS

Alcan
Alcoa
Anglo-American
ASARCO
Broken Hill
Coastal
Cyprus Minerals
FMC

Inco
Panhandle
Eastern
Phelps Dodge
Reynolds Metals
RTZ
Oil companies
Pipeline companies

HOW MUCH

	9-Year Growth	1981	1982	1983	1984	1985	1986	1987	1988	1989	1990
Sales ($ mil.)	3.4%	2,799	2,416	2,290	2,399	1,789	1,277	3,351	3,944	3,892	3,788
Net income ($ mil.)	(0.2%)	231	(390)	(489)	(238)	(610)	(15)	77	741	360	226
Income as % of sales	—	8.2%	(16.2%)	(21.4%)	(9.9%)	(34.1%)	(1.2%)	2.3%	18.8%	9.3%	6.0%
Earnings per share ($)	(2.7%)	3.30	(6.53)	(7.74)	(3.86)	(9.18)	(0.35)	0.82	8.42	4.18	2.58
Stock price – high ($)	—	69.00	48.88	32.75	27.75	19.00	16.38	29.25	24.63	29.75	29.38
Stock price – low ($)	—	37.50	17.50	21.50	15.50	10.50	10.50	12.00	15.25	20.75	17.63
Stock price – close ($)	(8.6%)	47.25	21.75	23.75	16.25	13.63	12.13	20.00	22.63	23.00	21.13
P/E – high	—	21	—	—	—	—	—	36	3	7	11
P/E – low	—	11	—	—	—	—	—	15	2	5	7
Dividends per share ($)	(11.5%)	2.40	0.85	0.20	0.20	0.10	0.00	0.00	0.20	0.60	0.80
Book value per share ($)	(4.9%)	40.51	32.60	24.60	20.49	10.61	10.81	13.49	20.24	23.62	25.72

1990 Year-end:
Debt ratio: 38.3%
Return on equity: 10.5%
Cash (mil.): $53
Current ratio: 1.67
Long-term debt (mil.): $1,379
No. of shares (mil.): 86
Dividends:
  1990 average yield: 3.8%
  1990 payout: 31.0%
Market value (mil.): $1,822

Stock Price History High/Low 1981–90

AMDAHL CORPORATION

ASE symbol: AMH
Fiscal year ends: Last Friday in December

Hoover's Rating **B+**

OVERVIEW

Amdahl is a $2.2 billion manufacturer of IBM-compatible mainframe computers and peripherals. Based in Sunnyvale, California, 20-year-old Amdahl was the first to successfully design and build mainframes to compete head-to-head with IBM computers.

Over the years Amdahl has distinguished itself from IBM by responding to IBM's product introductions with reliable, lower-cost compatible systems, often within months of IBM's product announcement. Amdahl has pioneered new technologies, including air cooling for large-scale computers and the Multiple Domain Feature, a product that allows an Amdahl computer to run up to 4 operating systems simultaneously. Amdahl is one of the industry's heaviest R&D spenders, allocating $310 million (14.4% of revenues) in 1990 to product development, up 39% in just 2 years.

Japan's Fujitsu (computers and electronic equipment) owns 44% of Amdahl and supplies subassemblies and components.

Despite their competitive stances, IBM and Amdahl have mutual licensing agrements for substantially all system patents granted before 1992.

WHO

Chairman and CEO: John C. Lewis, age 55, $828,869 pay
President and COO: E. Joseph Zemke, age 50, $784,940 pay
VP, CFO, and Secretary: Edward F. Thompson, age 52
SVP Human Resources and Corporate Services: Anthony M. Pozos, age 50
Auditors: Arthur Andersen & Co.
Employees: 8,950

WHEN

In the 1960s Gene Amdahl was the principal architect of IBM's popular family of mainframe computers, the System 360. After his idea for a more advanced computer was rejected, Amdahl quit IBM in 1970 to start his own company, Amdahl, manufacturing IBM-compatible mainframes.

Investors were reluctant to back a company challenging IBM's market dominance in view of previous failures by others. Amdahl's strategy — to make his system faster, cheaper, with high capacity, yet compatible with IBM software and peripherals — was unique and it persuaded investors to supply enough capital to start the company. Fujitsu was one of the earliest investors. In 1975, with $47 million invested in R&D, Amdahl introduced its first computer, the 470V/6, compatible with IBM's largest 370 mainframe, the Model 168. IBM users could transfer to the less-expensive Amdahl V/6 and continue to use their existing software and peripherals.

Amdahl's strategy of building IBM clones with better performance for less money succeeded. The company went public in 1976 and, by 1978, its sales had reached $321 million. Amdahl followed its 470V/6 with the V/7 in 1977 and a V/8 model in 1978. As Amdahl prospered by outperforming and underselling IBM, Big Blue struck back by cutting prices and announcing impending technological improvements. Potential Amdahl customers delayed purchases, drying up cash flow. By 1979 Fujitsu's interest was 34% and Gene Amdahl was gone. Seeking to diversify and bolstered by funds from a 1980 stock offering, new president Eugene White bought Tran Telecommunications Corporation (data communications products, 1980) and sought to buy Memorex (1979) and Storage Technology Corporation (1980), but Fujitsu stopped both transactions.

In 1983 Amdahl Corporation's revenues shot up 68% from the previous year to $778 million following shipments of its new 5860 mainframe and diversification into disk drives. Sales flattened in 1984, however, due to bugs in the new computer. Amdahl bounced back in 1985 with its 5890 family of computers (comparable to IBM's 3090 series), which increased sales to $1.5 billion (1987), $1.8 billion (1988), and $2.1 billion (1989). In 1989 Amdahl introduced the 5995 machines and bought Key Computer Labs (computer technology).

As the US mainframe computer market matured in the 1980s, Amdahl increasingly stressed European sales, where profit derived not merely from sales but also from a declining dollar. As Europe entered the 1990–91 recession, Amdahl's sales slumped.

WHERE

HQ: 1250 E. Arques Ave., Sunnyvale, CA 94088
Phone: 408-746-6000
Fax: 408-746-6468

The company does business in 18 foreign countries and has manufacturing facilities in Northern California; Dublin, Ireland; and Ontario, Canada.

	1990 Sales		1990 Operating Income	
	$ mil.	% of total	$ mil.	% of total
US	1,124	52	34	13
Europe	756	35	218	85
Canada	143	7	(7)	(2)
Pacific Basin & other	136	6	11	4
Adjustments	—	—	3	—
Total	**2,159**	**100**	**259**	**100**

WHAT

	1990 Sales	
	$ mil.	% of total
Processors	1,358	63
Storage products	342	16
Communications products	68	3
Maintenance services	357	16
Software & education services	34	2
Total	**2,159**	**100**

Mainframe Computers
5890 series
5990 series
5995 series
7300 series

Storage Products
6100 storage processor
6110 solid-state storage system
6380 series of magnetic-disk storage units

Communications Products
4745 communications processor
Network Processor Series/2700

Systems Software
UTS

HOW MUCH

	9-Year Growth	1981	1982	1983	1984	1985	1986	1987	1988	1989	1990
Sales ($ mil.)	19.2%	443	462	778	779	862	966	1,505	1,802	2,101	2,159
Net income ($ mil.)	23.9%	27	5	43	36	24	39	142	214	153	184
Income as % of sales	—	6.0%	1.1%	5.6%	4.7%	2.8%	4.1%	9.4%	11.9%	7.3%	8.5%
Earnings per share ($)	19.8%	0.33	0.06	0.48	0.40	0.26	0.41	1.37	1.99	1.39	1.66
Stock price – high ($)	—	11.50	8.41	14.88	10.13	9.06	12.88	25.06	28.00	23.38	18.88
Stock price – low ($)	—	5.91	4.31	7.09	4.75	5.06	6.75	9.56	14.06	10.75	10.00
Stock price – close ($)	7.5%	7.38	7.44	9.19	6.69	7.31	11.69	17.63	20.25	14.38	14.13
P/E – high	—	35	140	31	25	36	32	18	14	17	11
P/E – low	—	18	72	15	12	20	17	7	7	8	6
Dividends per share ($)	0.0%	0.10	0.10	0.10	0.10	0.10	0.10	0.10	0.10	0.10	0.10
Book value per share ($)	13.9%	3.84	3.85	4.80	4.58	4.82	5.19	7.32	9.51	10.80	12.44

1990 Year-end:
Debt ratio: 1.8%
Return on equity: 14.3%
Cash (mil.): $593
Current ratio: 2.30
Long-term debt (mil.): $25
No. of shares (mil.): 110
Dividends:
1990 average yield: 0.7%
1990 payout: 6.0%
Market value (mil.): $1,556

Stock Price History
High/Low 1981–90

RANKINGS

202nd in *Fortune* 500 Industrial Cos.
384th in *Business Week* 1000

KEY COMPETITORS

Control Data	Olivetti
Hitachi	Siemens
IBM	Storage Technology
Machines Bull	Tandem
NEC	Unisys

AMERICA WEST AIRLINES, INC.

NASDAQ symbol: AWAL
Fiscal year ends: December 31

Hoover's Rating **F**

OVERVIEW

In the decade since America West started out, it has grown (somewhat spasmodically) from a niche carrier operating out of Phoenix Sky Harbor International Airport into America's 9th largest airline. Along with its route structure, the airline has built one of the industry's weakest balance sheets, with a debt-to-equity ratio of almost 97%.

Since June 1991 (after following Pan Am and Midway into bankruptcy), America West has realigned its route structure, instituted a company-wide pay freeze, and made plans to furlough some 1,500 employees. The company is also planning to reduce its fleet size by re-

turning to the manufacturer, without penalty, 9 airliners. Good news came in the form of a marketing agreement with Northwest Airlines, which, among other things, includes $20 million in financing. Northwest paid an additional $15 million for a 2-year option to buy America West's route to Nagoya, Japan.

Despite its current situation, America West boasts the industry's highest employee productivity rating and has posted an outstanding on-time record since 1987. Employees (none of whom belong to unions) now own about 35% of the company's stock.

WHEN

For years airline consultant Edward Beauvais saw the need for a Phoenix-based airline, linking cities in the Southwest to California. In 1981 he founded America West. His concept was simple: by offering low-fare flights with certain amenities (such as free cocktails and newspapers), America West would attract business commuters, creating a niche for itself in a region largely ignored by the major airlines. Starting in 1983 with 9 daily flights from Phoenix to 5 other cities, America West by 1986 served 34 cities and that year earned a modest $2 million profit.

The company doubled its operations in 1987, offering flights to Chicago, New York, and Baltimore. Beauvais established a 2nd hub at Las Vegas, but expansion-related costs and increased competition in Phoenix (with Southwest Airlines and USAir) contributed to losses of $15 million in the first half of 1987.

Industry analysts worried that America West's rapid rate of expansion would require additional capital, resulting in a larger airline absorbing the company. Beauvais and President Michael Conway (formerly of Continental) responded by selling a 20% stake in the company to Australian-based Ansett Airlines for $31.8 million. Combined with the 30% interest already owned by America West's

employees, this put 50% of the company's stock in "friendly hands." Employees were guaranteed up to 250% of their annual salaries in the event of a takeover. The company finished 1987 with a $46 million loss.

To reduce costs Beauvais and Conway sold several planes, furloughed 500 employees, and streamlined service, cutting flights 10% overall, resulting in planes filled to 58.4% capacity — nearly 2 points above breakeven (1988). The airline gained access to Washington, DC (by buying routes from bankrupt Eastern) and inaugurated service to Hawaii in 1989. By the end of 1989, America West offered 286 daily flights to 56 cities, including Honolulu, Seattle, and New York. In 1990 the airline added service to Boston, Houston, and San Francisco and agreed to buy up to 118 Airbus A320s (the first 8 were delivered early in 1991).

In 1991 America West began flying to Nagoya, Japan. However, the airline was experiencing cash-flow problems (due to expansion-related debt as well as high fuel prices and sluggish traffic resulting from the Gulf War). Management accepted a 10% to 25% pay cut early in 1991, but in June 1991 the airline was forced to suspend lease payments on 87 of its current aircraft, leaving America West no choice but to seek bankruptcy protection.

WHO

Chairman: Edward R. Beauvais, age 54, $984,050 pay
President and CEO: Michael J. Conway, age 45, $786,621 pay (prior to promotion)
SVP Finance and CFO: Alphonse E. Frei, age 52, $272,203 pay
SVP Operations: Don Monteath, age 49, $270,915 pay
SVP Administration, General Counsel, and Secretary: Martin J. Whalen, age 50
Senior Director of Recruiting, Training, Professional Development, and Human Resources: Rod Cox
Auditors: KMPG Peat Marwick
Employees: 13,704

WHERE

HQ: 51 W. 3rd St., Tempe, AZ 85281
Phone: 602-693-0800
Fax: 602-693-5546
Reservations: 800-247-5692

America West serves 49 cities in the US, Canada, and Japan.

Hub Locations
Phoenix, AZ
Las Vegas, NV

WHAT

	1990 Sales	
	$ mil.	% of total
Passenger	1,242	94
Cargo	43	3
Other	31	3
Total	**1,316**	**100**

Services
Air Cargo
America West Express small package service
AmeriWest Vacations tour packages
Careliner Shuttle
  Bus service to resort area at Scottsdale, AZ, from Phoenix Airport
Contract Services charter flights
FlightFund frequent flyer program
Las Vegas Nite Flite Service
  Late night flights to Las Vegas and 36 other destinations
The Phoenix Club airport lounges
VUSA (Visit USA Program)
  Special fares for international travelers in US

Flight Equipment	No.	Average Age in Years
Boeing 737	77	1.7
Boeing 747	4	7.7
Boeing 757	11	3.3
Other	12	19.7
Total	**104**	**7.0**

HOW MUCH

	7-Year Growth	1981	1982	1983	1984	1985	1986	1987	1988	1989	1990
Sales ($ mil.)	84.6%	—	—	18	123	241	329	575	776	993	1,316
Net income ($ mil.)	—	—	—	(10)	(15)	6	2	(46)	(12)	13	(77)
Income as % of sales	—	—	—	(54.3%)	(12.6%)	2.5%	0.5%	(7.9%)	(1.6%)	1.3%	(5.8%)
Earnings per share ($)	—	—	—	(3.07)	(3.26)	0.42	0.33	(1.35)	(0.18)	0.68	(1.57)
Stock price – high ($)	—	—	—	14.13	12.50	12.75	13.50	12.38	7.13	12.88	10.25
Stock price – low ($)	—	—	—	6.13	4.88	6.88	7.63	3.50	3.63	6.50	5.50
Stock price – close ($)	(10.0%)	—	—	11.75	7.88	10.75	9.75	3.75	6.50	10.13	5.63
P/E – high	—	—	—	—	—	30	41	—	—	19	—
P/E – low	—	—	—	—	—	16	23	—	—	10	—
Dividends per share ($)	—	—	—	0.00	0.00	0.00	0.00	0.00	0.00	0.00	0.00
Book value per share ($)	—	—	—	4.69	4.82	6.46	5.53	3.15	3.74	4.91	1.09

1990 Year-end:
Debt ratio: 96.7%
Return on equity: —
Cash (mil.): $111
Current ratio: 0.73
Long-term debt (mil.): $621
No. of shares (mil.): 19
Dividends:
  1990 average yield: —
  1990 payout: —
Market value (mil.): $109

Stock Price History High/Low 1983–90

RANKINGS

22nd in *Fortune* 50 Transportation Cos.

KEY COMPETITORS

Alaska Air	JAL	TWA
AMR	Midway	UAL
Continental Airlines	NWA	USAir
Delta	Southwest	

AMERICAN ASSOCIATION OF RETIRED PERSONS

OVERVIEW

The American Association of Retired Persons (AARP) is the nation's largest organization dedicated to protecting and increasing the rights of citizens over the age of 50. Its over 33 million members (about 40% of them still working) receive services including group insurance rates, discounted pharmaceuticals, reduced car rental and hotel rates, an investment program, a travel service, subscriptions to *Modern Maturity* magazine and *AARP Bulletin*, and AARP credit union membership, all for annual dues of only $5.

Strategically headquartered in Washington, DC, AARP acts as a political advocate for its members, focusing primarily on 4 issues: health care, older workers' equity, women's initiatives, and minority affairs. It uses its well-organized mail network to solicit new members as they turn 50, advertise its services, and promote the organization's political agenda. AARP has more than 4,000 local chapters, and its paid staff of almost 1,600 is supplemented by more than 350,000 active volunteers.

WHEN

In 1958 Ethel Andrus, a retired Los Angeles high school principal and founder of the National Retired Teachers Association (NRTA, 1947), organized the American Association of Retired Persons (AARP) to "enhance the quality of life . . . promote independence . . . lead in determining the role in society . . . and improve the image of aging" for older Americans.

Andrus offered new members the same attractive low rates for health and accident insurance that NRTA members enjoyed. Other services quickly followed, including a mail-order discount pharmacy and a travel service for older people. Andrus began publishing the organization's bimonthly magazine *Modern Maturity* in 1958, and AARP's first local chapter opened in Youngstown, Arizona in 1960.

Andrus led the organization in its increasingly influential role in legislation that concerned the elderly. She directed AARP until her death in 1967. In her honor, AARP and the University of Southern California built the Ethel Percy Andrus Gerontology Center (1973), a $4 million institute dedicated to the study of aging.

AARP (and NRTA, which eventually joined AARP in 1982) continued to expand in scope and size. Attractive new services included the popular auto club, financial services such as mutual funds and expanded insurance policies, and hotel and motel discounts. In 1983 it lowered the eligibility age from 55 to 50 and raised its annual dues from $3 to $5. AARP grew at a phenomenal rate to its 1990 membership of over 33 million. It currently adds approximately 8,000 new members a day.

AARP acts as an agent between its members and selected service providers: Prudential for health insurance; Hartford for auto and home insurance; Scudder, Stevens & Clark for mutual fund investment services; and Amoco for auto club services. *Modern Maturity* and

the *AARP Bulletin,* sent to all AARP members, have the first and 2nd largest magazine circulation totals in the US.

A new AARP credit union, which began operations in 1988 with over $66 million in deposits, is predicted to become the nation's largest credit union.

AARP's influence and organizational skills have increased as its constituency has grown. Its numerous programs and services are generally focused on 4 priorities: health care (controlling health care costs and promoting healthy lifestyles); women's initiatives (emphasizing women's contributions and addressing concerns of middle-aged and older women); worker equity (protecting rights and security of older workers through preretirement and employment planning programs and litigation); and minority affairs (encouraging changes in thinking and actions in older minorities and society at large). The association publishes a variety of promotional and informational materials and sponsors many training and educational programs.

Steadfastly nonpartisan (the membership is 40% Democratic, 40% Republican, and 20% independent), AARP directs its lobbying efforts from its main office in Washington, DC. It has garnered a reputation for being well-informed, organized, tenacious, and often successful in its political activities.

In 1988 AARP started a major planning effort to evaluate the organization's future direction. Key issues cited by the AARP for the 1990s include comprehensive health care reform, fighting age discrimination in the workplace and society, housing concerns, pension reform, and a reduction in public-sector spending. The organization also hopes to increase member participation in grassroots efforts.

Nonprofit organization
Fiscal year ends: December 31

Hoover's Rating **A−**

WHO

Executive Director: Horace B. Deets
President: Robert B. Maxwell
Director Financial Operations: James A. Maigret
Acting Director Human Resources: Insook Copes
Auditors: Price Waterhouse
Employees: 1,586

WHERE

HQ: 601 E St. NW, Washington, DC 20049
Phone: 202-434-2277
Fax: 202-434-6484

AARP has over 33 million members worldwide.

WHAT

	1990 Operating Revenues	
	$ mil.	% of total
Membership dues	102	35
Group insurance administrative allowances	75	25
Publication advertising	43	15
Income from other programs & royalties	27	9
Interest income	48	16
Other	1	—
Total	**296**	**100**

Political Advocacy
Lobbying Congress and state legislatures
Educating voters
Working to increase older citizens' representation on local boards and commissions

Periodicals
AARP Bulletin
Modern Maturity

Social Services
Educational publications and audiovisual materials
Employment planning
Legal assistance
Medicare assistance
Retirement planning
Support groups
Volunteer organizing

Insurance Plans
Automobile (Hartford)
Health/Medigap (Prudential)
Homeowners (Hartford)

Financial Services
AARP Federal Credit Union
Credit cards (Bank One)
Mutual funds (Scudder, Stevens & Clark)

Travel Services
Auto club/road service (Amoco Motor Club)
Hotel, auto rental, and airline discounts (various providers)

Affiliated Entities
AARP Foundation
AARP Andrus Foundation

HOW MUCH

	9-Year Growth	1981	1982	1983	1984	1985	1986	1987	1988	1989	1990
Membership (thou.)	10.9%	12,973	14,251	15,753	18,075	20,880	24,371	27,262	29,739	32,163	33,025

Membership (thou.) 1981–90

AMERICAN BRANDS, INC.

OVERVIEW

American Brands, the nation's 5th largest cigarette manufacturer, is a diversified consumer products company with businesses in tobacco, insurance, golf products, liquor, office supplies, optical services, and hardware. Its well-known US cigarette brands include Carlton, Tareyton, Pall Mall, and Lucky Strike. In the UK the company's Gallaher subsidiary controls a whopping 45% of the British cigarette market with such names as Benson & Hedges, Silk Cut, and Berkeley. American Brands's Jim Beam is the world's #1 bourbon.

The company's Franklin Life Insurance Company sells insurance in all 50 states and parts of Canada and the Caribbean, while its ACCO subsidiary is the world's largest producer and marketer of office products. The MasterBrand Industries unit, which produces the Master lock and other hardware, is the #2 US faucet manufacturer. American Brands also makes Titleist golf products and through its Dollond & Aitchison division is the largest optical goods and services group in Europe.

NYSE symbol: AMB
Fiscal year ends: December 31

WHO

Chairman and CEO: William J. Alley, age 61, $1,627,358 pay
President and COO: Thomas C. Hays, age 55, $945,126 pay
EVP and CFO: Arnold Henson, age 59, $795,762 pay
VP Human Resources: Steven C. Mendenhall
Auditors: Coopers & Lybrand
Employees: 51,760

WHEN

American Brands began in 1864 as W. Duke and Sons, a small tobacco company started by Washington Duke, a North Carolina farmer. James Buchanan Duke joined his father's business at age 14 (1870) and by age 25 was its president. James Duke was the first to use the Bonsack cigarette rolling machine, which produced substantially cheaper cigarettes and allowed him to undercut competitors' prices. He advertised to expanding markets; bought rival cigarette, snuff, and plug tobacco firms; and by 1904 controlled the tobacco industry. That year he merged all the competitive groups into the American Tobacco Company.

In a 1911 antitrust suit the US Supreme Court dissolved American Tobacco into its original competitive firms, ordering them to operate independently.

Duke left American Tobacco in 1912. He remained president of British American Tobacco Company (now B.A.T, which he had founded in 1902) and continued his work with Southern Power Company, a North Carolina company he had started in 1905. He later merged that company with Duke Power and Light. Duke established a $100 million trust fund, composed mainly of holdings in Duke Power and Light, for the local Trinity College, which became Duke University in 1924.

American Tobacco merely drifted under Duke's successor Percival Hill, but it found a dynamic new leader in George Washington

Hill, who succeeded his father as president in 1925. For the next 19 years until his death, Hill proved himself a consummate ad man, pushing Lucky Strikes, Pall Malls, and Tareyton cigarettes to top sales.

In 1953 research first linked cigarette smoking to lung cancer, and smokers switched to filter-tipped cigarettes in record numbers. American Tobacco, however, ignored the trend and continued to rely on its popular filterless brands until the mid-1960s.

American Tobacco remained solely in the tobacco business until 1966, when it purchased Sunshine Biscuits (sold in 1988) and Jim Beam Distillery. Later came Swingline (office supplies, 1970) and Master Lock (1970). Reflecting its increasing diversity, the company became American Brands in 1970.

Threatened by a takeover by E-II Holdings (a conglomerate of brands split from Beatrice), American Brands bought E-II for $1.1 billion in 1988. The company retained 5 of E-II's companies: Day-Timers (time management products), Aristokraft (cabinets), Waterloo (tool storage), Twentieth Century (plumbing supplies), and Vogel Peterson (office partitions), and sold the rest (Culligan and Samsonite) to Riklis Family Corporation.

Group acquisitons in 1990 included Moen (a leading US faucet maker), Whyte & Mackay (distillers), and Hetzel (office products, Germany).

WHERE

HQ: 1700 E. Putnam Ave., Old Greenwich, CT 06870-0811
Phone: 203-698-5000
Fax: 203-637-2580

	1990 Sales		1990 Operating Income	
	$ mil.	% of total	$ mil.	% of total
US	4,686	34	908	56
Europe	8,949	65	682	43
Other regions	146	1	17	1
Adjustments	(5,511)	—	(127)	—
Total	**8,270**	**100**	**1,480**	**100**

WHAT

	1990 Sales		1990 Operating Income	
	$ mil.	% of total	$ mil.	% of total
Tobacco products	8,037	58	1,103	69
Distilled spirits	1,005	7	136	8
Specialty businesses	2,276	17	61	4
Life insurance	806	6	141	9
Hardware & home imprvmt. prods.	633	5	80	5
Office products	1,025	7	88	5
Adjustments	(5,512)	—	(129)	—
Total	**8,270**	**100**	**1,480**	**100**

Representative Brand Names

Cigarettes	Distilled Spirits	Office Products
American	DeKuyper	ACCO
Benson &	Gilbey's	Day-Timers
Hedges (UK)	Jim Beam	Swingline
Berkeley (UK)	Kamchatka	Vogel Peterson
Bull Durham	Old Crow	Wilson Jones
Carlton	Old Grand-Dad	
Lucky Strike	Old Taylor	**Other Products**
Pall Mall	Vladivar	Dollond & Aitchison
Silk Cut (UK)	Whyte & Mackay	Foot-Joy
Tareyton	Windsor Canadian	Forbuoys
		Master Lock
		Titleist

Subsidiaries and Divisions

ACCO World Corp.	Gallaher Ltd. (tobacco)
Acushnet Co.	Jim Beam Brands Co.
The American Tobacco Co.	MasterBrand Industries
The Franklin Life Insurance Co.	

RANKINGS

57th in *Fortune* 500 Industrial Cos.
104th in *Forbes* Sales 500

KEY COMPETITORS

Allied-Lyons	Imasco
American Standard	Loews
B.A.T	Moore
Black & Decker	Philip Morris
Brown-Forman	RJR Nabisco
Grand Metropolitan	Seagram
Guinness	U.S. Shoe
Hanson	Life insurance companies

HOW MUCH

	9-Year Growth	1981	1982	1983	1984	1985	1986	1987	1988	1989	1990
Sales ($ mil.)	8.3%	4,039	4,026	4,436	4,475	4,692	5,261	5,036	7,236	7,265	8,270
Net income ($ mil.)	4.9%	386	381	390	414	421	365	503	541	631	596
Income as % of sales	—	9.6%	9.5%	8.8%	9.3%	9.0%	6.9%	10.0%	7.5%	8.7%	7.2%
Earnings per share ($)	6.5%	1.62	1.60	1.65	1.76	1.80	1.56	2.15	2.57	3.04	2.84
Stock price – high ($)	—	11.50	12.75	15.09	16.28	17.50	26.25	30.00	35.88	40.94	41.63
Stock price – low ($)	—	8.50	8.84	10.84	13.22	13.31	15.66	18.25	21.13	30.63	30.88
Stock price – close ($)	18.2%	9.19	11.47	14.81	16.06	16.47	21.25	22.25	32.75	35.50	41.50
P/E – high	—	7	8	9	9	10	17	14	14	13	15
P/E – low	—	5	6	7	8	7	10	9	8	10	11
Dividends per share ($)	6.4%	0.80	0.88	0.89	0.93	0.98	1.02	1.06	1.13	1.26	1.41
Book value per share ($)	9.0%	8.33	8.72	9.22	9.60	10.86	11.56	13.32	13.34	15.34	18.13

1990 Year-end:
Debt ratio: 40.0%
Return on equity: 17.0%
Cash (mil.): $154
Current ratio: —
Long-term debt (mil.): $2,434
No. of shares (mil.): 200
Dividends:
  1990 average yield: 3.4%
  1990 payout: 49.5%
Market value (mil.): $8,315

Stock Price History High/Low 1981–90

AMERICAN CANCER SOCIETY

Nonprofit organization
Fiscal year ends: August 31

Hoover's Rating **A-**

OVERVIEW

The American Cancer Society is the largest nongovernmental source of funds for cancer research in the US. The Society spends substantial amounts on public and professional education and patient and community services. The Society gave 769 research grants and awards in 1990. The Nobel Prize has been given to 25 of the Society's researchers.

Emphasis today is placed on prevention through eliminating possible environmental exposures to carcinogens and encouraging proper nutrition. The Cancer Prevention Study II, begun in 1982, has used 77,000 volunteers to collect information on 1.2 million Americans to help determine the causes of cancer.

Public education programs reach an estimated 55 million people, and the Society's 2.2 million volunteers assist over 650,000 patients. The Great American Smokeout is in its 15th year as a nationally sponsored event.

Although cancer survival rates have increased since the 1940s (40% survive 5 years versus 25% then), the incidence of new melanomas, and of breast, lung, prostate, and colorectal cancers has increased since the 1970s.

WHO

Chairman: John R. Seffrin
VC: Stanley Schmishkiss
President: Gerald D. Dodd
EVP and CEO: William M. Tipping
SVP Finance and Administration: James T. Bell
VP: Walter Lawrence, Jr.
Auditors: Arthur Andersen & Co.
Paid employees: 4,207
Volunteers: 2,208,000

WHEN

Concerned over lack of progress in detecting and treating cancer, a group of 10 physicians and 5 laymen met in New York City in 1913 to form the American Society for the Control of Cancer. Cancer in those days was a dirty word, not discussed in public. The Society's earliest goal was to educate the public about the need for early detection and reverse the notion that nothing could be done.

Early success in fund-raising and the establishment of a volunteer membership structure are credited to Elsie Mead, daughter of an ASCC founder. In its early years the Society struggled with the dilemma of how to educate the public without also raising unnecessary fears. The Society also faced the opposition of some physicians who preferred keeping knowledge of the disease from the lay public.

In the 1920s the Society started sponsoring cancer clinics and began collecting statistics on the disease. By 1923 some states could report improvements in early diagnosis and faster treatment. In 1937 the Society started its first nationwide public education program with the help of volunteers known as the Women's Field Army. President Roosevelt named April as National Cancer Control Month, a practice since followed by every president.

By 1944 some cancer rates were rising and the word cancer couldn't be mentioned on the radio. Mary Lasker, the wife of prominent advertising executive Albert Lasker, was instrumental in getting cancer messages broadcast, and, at her insistence, in 1945 the ACS (name changed in 1944) began donating at least 25% of its budget to research. The Society raised $4 million in its first major national fund-raising campaign in 1945.

With the support of board member Elmer Bobst (Hoffmann-LaRoche president), Dr. Charles Cameron, ACS medical director, used Society volunteers in the early 1950s to follow nearly 200,000 subjects in a study that first showed the link between smoking and lung cancer. That information became part of the Surgeon General's Report of 1964. In 1973 an ACS branch in Minnesota held the first Great American Smokeout, now a national event to encourage people to quit.

The ACS backed the 1971 congressional bill that inaugurated the "War on Cancer." The Society was attacked in the 1970s for emphasizing cures rather than prevention because, critics claimed, research on prevention would reveal environmental causes from industrial products made by companies with connections to ACS directors. In the 1970s and 1980s, the ACS backed tougher restrictions on tobacco and, in response to earlier criticism, directed research toward prevention as well as treatment. The Society played a major role in the 1989 airline smoking ban. Emphasis in the 1990s will be on cancer control, nutrition, and tobacco control among the underprivileged.

WHERE

National office: 1599 Clifton Rd. NE, Atlanta, GA 30329-4251
Phone: 404-320-3333
Fax: 404-325-0230
Information about cancer: 1-800-ACS-2345

The Society has 57 chartered Divisions nationwide and 3,100 local Units.

WHAT

	1990 Sources of Revenue	
	$ mil.	% of total
Public contributions	195	53
Legacies & bequests	87	24
Organization contributions	45	12
Investment income	37	11
Other	2	—
Total	**366**	**100**

	1990 Expenses	
	$ mil.	% of total
Research	88	25
Public education	65	19
Professional education	34	10
Patient services	50	15
Community services	26	7
Administration & fund-raising	85	24
Total	**348**	**100**

Research Grants and Awards

Public Education Programs
Changing the Course
Great American Food Fight Against Cancer
Great American Smokeout
I Can Cope
Smart Move (stop smoking)
"Why Charlie Brown, Why?" (TV program)

Professional Education Programs
American Cancer Society Textbook of Clinical Oncology
Cancer Staging Awareness
Cancer Topics on Tape
Clinical News
Current Concepts in Head and Neck Cancer (textbook)
Medical Affairs (newsletter)
Primary Care Newsletter
Tobacco-Free Young America (program)

Patient Services Programs
Back to School: A Handbook for Parents of Children with Cancer
Back to School: A Handbook for Teachers of Children with Cancer
CanSurmount
Look Good...Feel Better Guide for ACS Volunteers
Reach to Recovery

HOW MUCH

All amounts in $ mil.	9-Year Growth	1981	1982	1983	1984	1985	1986	1987	1988	1989	1990
Total revenue	6.9%	200	223	233	252	281	308	331	336	358	366
Public contributions	7.5%	170	183	203	221	243	271	304	301	318	327
Investment & other income	3.0%	30	40	30	31	38	37	27	35	40	39
Total expenses	7.7%	178	195	207	226	251	272	296	324	331	348
Research expenses	5.6%	54	57	58	64	69	77	83	89	89	88
Education expenses	8.6%	47	51	56	60	70	75	84	86	92	99
Patient & community svcs.	9.3%	34	39	41	46	50	54	59	63	70	76
Admin. & fund-raising exp.	8.1%	42	48	52	56	62	66	70	85	80	85
Admin. & fund-raising as % of total expenses	—	23.5%	24.6%	25.1%	24.7%	24.7%	24.2%	23.6%	26.2%	24.2%	24.4%

Total Revenue ($ mil.) 1981–90

AMERICAN CYANAMID COMPANY

OVERVIEW

American Cyanamid is a leading world supplier of biologicals (vaccines) and surgical products and a major US chemical company.

Expanding from its beginning as a chemical company, Cyanamid derived more than half of its 1990 worldwide sales from its Medical Group that includes pharmaceuticals, biologicals, and medical devices and supplies. Centrum (mulitvitamin) and Pipracil (penicillin) are leading US brands. The company has been a leading US supplier of the DPT (diphtheria-pertussis-tetanus) vaccine for US children since the 1940s.

The Chemicals Group makes chemicals, structural adhesives, and other materials for major industries, including aerospace, automobile, paint, paper, and plastics. Herbicides, particularly Pursuit and Scepter, are major products of the Agricultural Group.

After the 1990 sale of its consumer products operations, the company plans to divest about 1/3 of the Chemicals Group to concentrate on high-tech medical and agricultural products, on building-block chemicals, and on business segments keyed to proprietary research.

NYSE symbol: ACY
Fiscal year ends: December 31

 Hoover's Rating **B-**

WHO

Chairman and CEO: George J. Sella, Jr., age 62, $1,237,305 pay
VC: William A. Liffers, age 62, $539,755 pay
President: Albert J. Costello, age 55, $540,938 pay
VP and CFO: Terence D. Martin, age 47
VP Human Resources: William A. Stiller, age 39
Auditors: KPMG Peat Marwick
Employees: 32,012

WHERE

HQ: One Cyanamid Plaza, Wayne, NJ 07470
Phone: 201-831-2000
Fax: 201-831-3151

American Cyanamid produces or markets products in 135 countries.

	1990 Sales		1990 Operating Income	
	$ mil.	% of total	$ mil.	% of total
US	2,762	60	29	10
Other Western Hemisphere	439	10	14	5
Eastern Hemisphere	1,369	30	245	85
Total	**4,570**	**100**	**288**	**100**

WHEN

Frank Washburn, a civil engineer seeking new uses for hydroelectric power, learned of a German process that extracted nitrogen, lime, and carbide to make cyanamid, a basic component of fertilizer. Washburn bought the North American rights to the process and founded American Cyanamid (Maine, 1907). Washburn then began producing calcium cyanamide, the world's first synthetic fertilizer, in a process powered by a dam he built.

In 1916 the company bought Amalgamated Phosphate as a source of phosphoric acid, another ingredient in fertilizer. Washburn died in 1922 and his assistant, William Bell, became president. The company began selling cyanide to the mining industry for extracting minerals from ore. The company diversified, buying American Powder (nitrocellulose for blasting powders, 1929), Calco Chemical (dyestuffs, chemicals, 1929), Selden (sulfuric acid, 1929), Kalbfleisch (chemicals, acids, 1929), and Chemical Construction (design and construction of chemical plants, 1930).

In 1930 American Cyanamid bought Lederle Antitoxin Laboratories (antitoxins, vaccines, sulfa drugs, and veterinary products) and Davis & Geck (surgical sutures). During WWII the company supplied US troops with typhus vaccine, dried blood plasma, and surgical sutures. In 1948 Lederle became a major pharmaceutical business with its discovery of

Aureomycin, an antibiotic used to treat human infections worldwide.

In 1956 American Cyanamid diversified into consumer-related businesses, buying Formica (major part sold to Formica's management and Shearson Lehman/American Express, 1985). In 1963 the company bought John H. Breck, Inc. (shampoo) and Dumas Milner Corporation (Pine Sol cleaner). American Cyanamid's last purchase of a consumer company was Shulton (Pierre Cardin and Old Spice fragrances) in 1971.

American Cyanamid introduced Combat (roach control system) and Old Spice solid antiperspirant in 1985. In 1986 the company increased its interest in Applied Solar Energy to 75% (sold to McDonnell Douglas, 1989) and bought Acufex Microsurgical and Storz Instrument. In 1988 the company introduced Novantrone (anticancer drug) and bought Conap (adhesives, sealants). In 1989 the company bought Praxis Biologics (vaccines). American Cyanamid has decided to focus on its research-driven agricultural, medical, and chemical businesses. It left the dye business in 1989, selling its operations to BASF, and in 1990 completed sale of its consumer products business. Pine Sol (cleaner) and Combat (insecticide) were sold to Clorox, Old Spice to Procter & Gamble, and Breck hair care products to the Dial Corporation.

WHAT

	1990 Sales		1990 Operating Income	
	$ mil.	% of total	$ mil.	% of total
Medical products	2,316	51	298	103
Agric. chems.	1,109	24	133	46
Chemicals	1,145	25	(143)	(49)
Total	**4,570**	**100**	**288**	**100**

Medical
Acufex Microsurgical, Inc. (instruments)
Davis & Geck (surgical products)
Lederle Labs (pharmaceuticals)
Lederle-Praxis Biologicals (vaccines)
Praxis Biologics, Inc. (vaccines)
Storz Instrument Co. (surgical products)

Agricultural Chemicals
Feed supplements
Herbicides
Insecticides
Plant growth regulant
Veterinary medicines

Chemicals
Acrylic fibers
Adhesives
Herbicides
Insecticides
Melamine
Urethane

Joint Venture
Criterion Catalyst Company LP (with Shell Oil to sell process catalysts)

RANKINGS

108th in *Fortune* 500 Industrial Cos.
130th in *Business Week* 1000

KEY COMPETITORS

Amgen
C. R. Bard
BASF
Baxter
Bayer
Becton, Dickinson
Bristol-Myers Squibb
Dow Chemical
Du Pont
Eli Lilly
FMC
W. R. Grace

Hercules
Hoechst
Imperial Chemical
Johnson & Johnson
Kimberly-Clark
Merck
Monsanto
Pfizer
Rhône-Poulenc
Roche
Other pharmaceutical and chemical companies

HOW MUCH

	9-Year Growth	1981	1982	1983	1984	1985	1986	1987	1988	1989	1990
Sales ($ mil.)	2.5%	3,649	3,454	3,536	3,857	3,536	3,816	4,166	4,592	4,825	4,570
Net income ($ mil.)	(6.5%)	197	132	166	216	120	203	264	306	292	108
Income as % of sales	—	5.4%	3.8%	4.7%	5.6%	3.4%	5.3%	6.3%	6.7%	6.1%	2.4%
Earnings per share ($)	(6.2%)	2.06	1.37	1.71	2.21	1.25	2.18	2.89	3.41	3.12	1.15
Stock price – high ($)	—	18.25	18.75	29.50	26.56	29.63	44.94	57.00	56.00	60.38	61.50
Stock price – low ($)	—	12.25	12.19	16.81	21.06	24.00	27.13	29.00	41.88	45.63	42.00
Stock price – close ($)	15.4%	14.50	17.38	25.00	25.00	28.75	38.94	41.25	46.75	53.63	52.63
P/E – high	—	9	14	17	12	24	21	20	16	19	53
P/E – low	—	6	9	10	10	19	12	10	12	15	37
Dividends per share ($)	5.4%	0.84	0.88	0.88	0.93	0.95	0.95	1.03	1.16	1.31	1.35
Book value per share ($)	6.2%	15.94	15.91	16.37	17.13	17.53	18.71	20.85	23.02	24.30	27.43

1990 Year-end:
Debt ratio: 13.1%
Return on equity: 4.4%
Cash (mil.): $428
Current ratio: 1.45
Long-term debt (mil.): $387
No. of shares (mil.): 93
Dividends:
   1990 average yield: 2.6%
   1990 payout: 117.4%
Market value (mil.): $4,916

Stock Price History High/Low 1981–90

AMERICAN ELECTRIC POWER COMPANY, INC.

OVERVIEW

American Electric Power (AEP) is an integrated electric utility system, providing power to 7 million people in parts of 7 midwestern and Appalachian states, through 8 operating utilities. The company ranks as America's 8th largest electric utility, with over $5.1 billion in 1990 sales.

Total sales of electricity were down 0.9% to 84.4 billion kilowatt-hours in 1990, primarily as the result of mild weather conditions and refueling outages at the Cook nuclear plant. The drop in sales combined with increased operating costs and regulatory limitations to reduce AEP's 1990 earnings by over 20%.

AEP produces almost 90% of its electricity from coal and is working to develop cleaner and more efficient methods of using this resource. To this end the company, with the US Department of Energy and the State of Ohio's Coal Development Office, developed a Pressurized Fluidized Bed Combustion (PFBC) demonstration unit at AEP's Tidd Plant, near Brilliant, Ohio. PFBC uses 10% less coal to generate the same amount of electricity produced by conventional plants and removes 90% of sulfur dioxide emissions by burning crushed dolomite (a type of limestone) with the coal. AEP hopes to prove PFBC's viability for commercial use by the early years of the 21st century.

NYSE symbol: AEP
Fiscal year ends: December 31

Hoover's Rating C-

WHO

Chairman: Willis S. "Pete" White, Jr., age 64, $786,850 pay
President and CEO: Richard E. Disbrow, age 60, $539,970 pay (prior to promotion)
VP (Principal Financial Officer); EVP and CFO, AEP Service Corp.: Gerald P. Maloney, age 58
SVP Human Resources, AEP Service Corp.: Ronald A. Petti
Auditors: Deloitte & Touche
Employees: 22,798

WHERE

HQ: 1 Riverside Plaza, Columbus, OH 43215
Phone: 614-223-1000
Fax: 614-223-1823

AEP serves portions of Indiana, Kentucky, Michigan, Ohio, Tennessee, Virginia, and West Virginia.

Generating Facilities

Coal	Gas Turbine
Beckjord (OH)	Fourth Street (IN)
Big Sandy (KY)	
Breed (IN)	**Hydroelectric**
Cardinal (OH)	Berrien Springs (MI)
Clinch River (VA)	Buchanan (MI)
Conesville (OH)	Buck (VA)
Gen. James M. Gavin (OH)	Byllesby (VA)
Glen Lyn (VA)	Claytor (VA)
John E. Amos (WV)	Constantine (MI)
Kammer (WV)	Elkhart (IN)
Kanawha River (WV)	Leesville (VA)
Mitchell (WV)	London (WV)
Mountaineer (WV)	Marmet (WV)
Muskingum River (OH)	Mottville (MI)
Philip Sporn (WV)	Niagara (VA)
Picway (OH)	Racine (OH)
Rockport (IN)	Reusens (VA)
J.M. Stuart (OH)	Smith Mountain (VA)
Tanners Creek (IN)	Twin Branch (IN)
Tidd PFBC Plant (OH)	Winfield (WV)
Zimmer Plant (25.4%, OH)	**Nuclear**
	Donald C. Cook (MI)

WHEN

Late in 1906 Richard Breed, Sidney Mitchell, and Henry Doherty set up American Gas & Electric (AG&E) in New York to buy 23 utilities from Philadelphia's Electric Company of America. With properties scattered through 7 states between Illinois, New Jersey, and New York, AG&E set out to consolidate operations along geographic lines by acquiring and then merging small, sometimes competing, electric properties. The result was the creation of the predecessors of Ohio Power (1911), Kentucky Power (1919), and Appalachian Power (1926). During this period, AG&E also bought the predecessor of Indiana Michigan Power (1922).

By 1926 AG&E was serving communities in Michigan, Indiana, Kentucky, West Virginia, and Ohio. In 1935 AG&E engineer Philip Sporn, who had pioneered research on the effects of lightning on power lines (and was later known as the Henry Ford of power), introduced his high-voltage, super-fast circuit breaker. AG&E added Kingsport Power to its list of operating companies in 1938.

After becoming AG&E's president in 1947, Sporn started an ambitious building program that continued through the 1960s. During this period, plants designed by AG&E (renamed American Electric Power in 1958) were among the world's most efficient, and electric rates stayed 25-38% below the national average.

AEP bought Michigan Power in 1967— 6 years after Donald Cook succeeded Sporn as president. Cook came under fire from environmentalists concerned about the effects of acid rain in the early 1970s when he refused to attach scrubbers (devices used to decrease sulfur dioxide emissions) on the smokestacks of AEP's coal-fired plants. Coal had long been AEP's primary fuel, and Cook, who believed that scrubbers were unproven and unnecessary, chose instead to increase the height of AEP's plants' chimneys to dilute the harmful emissions. AEP's first nuclear plant (named in Cook's honor) went on-line in 1975.

AEP moved its headquarters from New York to Columbus, Ohio, in 1980, after buying what is now Columbus Southern Power. The company set up AEP Generating Company in 1982 to generate and wholesale power to its other operating units.

Conversion of AEP's 2nd nuclear plant (Zimmer) to a coal-fired plant began in 1984, after the Nuclear Regulatory Commission halted construction on the plant for failure to keep adequate construction records. The company's Tidd Plant became operational in 1990, making AEP the first North American operator of a PFBC facility. The refurbished Zimmer Plant started up early in 1991.

WHAT

	1990 Sales	
	$ mil.	% of total
Residential	1,526	30
Commercial	1,021	20
Industrial	1,432	28
Miscellaneous retail	68	1
For resale	1,055	20
Other	66	1
Total	**5,168**	**100**

Subsidiaries
AEP Generating Co.
American Electric Power Service Corp.
Appalachian Power Co.
Columbus Southern Power Co.
Indiana Michigan Power Co.
Kentucky Power Co.
Kingsport Power Co.
Michigan Power Co.
Ohio Power Co.
Wheeling Power Co.

HOW MUCH

	9-Year Growth	1981	1982	1983	1984	1985	1986	1987	1988	1989	1990
Sales ($ mil.)	2.4%	4,193	4,180	4,368	4,952	4,848	4,843	4,788	4,841	5,140	5,168
Net income ($ mil.)	2.1%	456	441	534	590	585	603	583	693	692	549
Income as % of sales	—	10.9%	10.5%	12.2%	11.9%	12.1%	12.4%	12.2%	14.3%	13.5%	10.6%
Earnings per share ($)	1.2%	2.37	2.03	2.44	2.65	2.54	2.62	2.60	3.24	3.25	2.65
Stock price – high ($)	—	18.38	19.75	20.13	21.38	24.88	31.50	31.63	29.75	33.38	33.13
Stock price – low ($)	—	15.38	15.38	16.88	15.13	19.88	22.75	23.13	25.88	25.75	26.00
Stock price – close ($)	6.2%	16.25	17.75	17.13	21.13	23.63	27.50	26.25	27.25	33.00	28.00
P/E – high	—	8	10	8	8	10	12	12	9	10	13
P/E – low	—	6	8	7	6	8	9	9	8	8	10
Dividends per share ($)	0.7%	2.26	2.26	2.26	2.34	2.26	2.26	2.34	2.34	2.36	2.40
Book value per share ($)	1.0%	20.61	20.15	20.24	20.39	20.35	20.71	20.94	21.84	22.71	22.58

1990 Year-end:
Debt ratio: 51.5%
Return on equity: 11.7%
Cash (mil.): $120
Current ratio: 1.03
Long-term debt (mil.): $5,001
No. of shares (mil.): 185
Dividends:
  1990 average yield: 8.6%
  1990 payout: 90.6%
Market value (mil.): $5,167

Stock Price History
High/Low 1981–90

RANKINGS

14th in *Fortune* 50 Utilities
128th in *Business Week* 1000

AMERICAN EXPRESS COMPANY

OVERVIEW

American Express is the largest US diversified financial services organization. The company is best known for its travel-related services, with more than 2,500 worldwide locations, and for its American Express and Optima cards and Travelers Cheques. American Express Travel Related Services currently generates 39% of company sales and includes the direct marketing of consumer products, life insurance, and investment products to 36 million American Express cardmembers.

The company's international activities include American Express Bank, with $14.5 billion in assets and 83 locations in 39 countries. American Express's securities business consists of Lehman Brothers investment banking and Shearson Lehman Brothers brokerage. The company's IDS Financial Services has more than 6,000 salespeople providing clients in the US with a wide range of savings, insurance, and investment services.

American Express's newest business, American Express Information Services, provides high-volume information processing and communications services. American Express is one of the world's largest 3rd-party processors of debit and credit card transactions, including those of VISA and MasterCard. The company also publishes several lifestyle and travel magazines.

WHEN

In 1850 Henry Wells combined his New York delivery service with his 2 main competitors to form American Express. When American Express directors refused to expand to California in 1852, Wells and VP William Fargo, while remaining at American Express, started Wells Fargo.

American Express merged with Merchants Union Express in 1868. To compete with the government's postal money order, the company developed its own money order. Fargo's difficulty in cashing letters of credit in Europe led to the introduction of Travelers Cheques in 1891. Services for US travelers overseas followed.

In WWI the US government nationalized and consolidated all express delivery services, compensating the owners. In 1919 American Express Company incorporated as an overseas freight (sold 1970) and financial services and exchange provider.

In 1958 the company introduced the American Express card (users had no credit limits and were required to pay off balances each month). In 1968 the company bought Fireman's Fund American Insurance (sold 1985 to 1989) and Equitable Securities.

James D. Robinson III (CEO 1977–present) expanded the company through acquisitions which included 1/2 of Warner Cable Communications (Warner Amex Cable, 1979, sold 1986); Shearson Loeb Rhoades (brokerage, 1981); The Boston Company (banking, 1981); Balcor (real estate, 1982); Lehman Brothers Loeb Holding Company and Investors Diversified Services (brokerage, 1984); and E.F. Hutton (brokerage, 1987). These units (excluding IDS) were combined as Shearson Lehman Brothers (SLB). In 1990 SLB lost $966 million as its operations were restructured into 2 divisions (individual investors and corporate/institutional clients), certain assets and loans were written down, and the liquidation of Balcor began.

SLB's troubles continued into 1991 with the collapse of 28%-owned First Capital Holdings (insurance, California), prompting a $144 million write-off and threats by state regulators to take action against American Express.

Another result of SLB's difficulties was the issuance of $300 million of preferred (nonvoting) stock in a private offering to Warren Buffett's Berkshire Hathaway Company.

Card profits fell 3% in the 2nd quarter of 1991 because of a decline in consumer spending in the 1990–91 recession as well as merchant protests against high fees.

NYSE symbol: AXP
Fiscal year ends: December 31

Hoover's Rating **C**

WHO

Chairman and CEO: James D. Robinson III, age 55, $1,798,077 pay
President; Chairman, IDS Financial: Harvey Golub, age 51, $1,330,769 pay
President and CEO, TRS North America: Edwin M. Cooperman, age 47, $1,271,250 pay
President and CEO, American Express International: G. Richard Thoman, age 46, $1,271,250 pay
EVP and CFO: Michael P. Monaco, age 43
SVP Human Resources: Irene C. Roberts
Auditors: Ernst & Young
Employees: 106,836

WHERE

HQ: American Express Tower, World Financial Center, New York, NY 10285
Phone: 212-640-2000
Fax: 212-619-9802

American Express has offices throughout the US and in more than 160 countries.

	1990 Sales		1990 Pretax Income	
	$ mil.	% of total	$ mil.	% of total
US	19,459	78	315	44
Europe	2,847	12	169	23
Asia/Pacific	1,417	6	177	24
All other	1,084	4	64	9
Adjustments	(475)	—	—	—
Total	**24,332**	**100**	**725**	**100**

WHAT

	1990 Sales		1990 Pretax Income	
	$ mil.	% of total	$ mil.	% of total
Investment svcs.	10,177	41	(875)	(88)
Travel-related svcs.	9,698	39	1,332	133
Financial svcs.	2,200	9	256	26
Intl. banking	1,814	7	146	15
Information svcs.	827	4	140	14
Adjustments	(384)	—	(274)	—
Total	**24,332**	**100**	**725**	**100**

Financial Services
American Express Bank
American Express cards
American Express Information Services
American Express Travelers Cheques
AMEX Life Assurance
IDS Financial Services
Lehman Brothers
Optima card
Shearson Lehman Brothers

Magazines
Departures
D Magazine
Food & Wine
L.A. Style
New York Woman
Travel & Leisure

Information Services
Cable Services Group (cable TV billing)
First Data Resources (credit card processing)
Health Systems Group (hospital billing)
Integrated Marketing Services (telemarketing)
Integrated Payment Systems (money orders and MoneyGrams)
The Shareholder Services Group (mutual fund transfer agent)

HOW MUCH

	9-Year Growth	1981	1982	1983	1984	1985	1986	1987	1988	1989	1990
Sales ($ mil.)	14.5%	7,211	8,093	9,770	12,895	12,944	16,746	17,531	22,934	25,047	24,332
Net income ($ mil.)	(4.6%)	518	581	515	610	810	1,110	533	988	1,157	338
Income as % of sales	—	7.2%	7.2%	5.3%	4.7%	6.3%	6.6%	3.0%	4.3%	4.6%	1.4%
Earnings per share ($)	(7.5%)	1.39	1.50	1.26	1.37	1.74	2.43	1.20	2.29	2.67	0.69
Stock price – high ($)	—	13.59	17.69	24.79	19.50	27.50	35.06	40.63	30.38	39.38	35.25
Stock price – low ($)	—	9.38	8.81	14.00	12.50	17.94	25.25	20.75	22.88	26.38	17.50
Stock price – close ($)	7.2%	11.03	16.06	16.31	18.81	26.50	28.31	22.88	26.63	34.88	20.63
P/E – high	—	10	12	20	14	16	14	34	13	15	51
P/E – low	—	7	6	11	9	10	10	17	10	10	25
Dividends per share ($)	10.5%	0.38	0.55	0.78	0.64	0.66	0.69	0.57	0.97	0.86	0.92
Book value per share ($)	7.0%	7.15	7.96	9.47	10.10	11.41	12.60	10.11	11.39	12.90	13.21

1990 Year-end:
Debt ratio: 60.3%
Return on equity: 5.3%
Cash (mil.): $9,956
Assets (mil.): $137,682
Long-term debt (mil.): $10,077
No. of shares (mil.): 464
Dividends:
1990 average yield: 4.5%
1990 payout: 133.3%
Market value (mil.): $9,580

Stock Price History High/Low 1981–90

RANKINGS

1st in *Fortune* 50 Diversified Financial Cos.
42nd in *Business Week* 1000

KEY COMPETITORS

Banks
Credit card issuers
Insurance companies
Investment bankers
Magazine publishers
Securities brokers
Travel services
Travelers check issuers

AMERICAN FINANCIAL CORPORATION

Private company
Fiscal year ends: December 31

Hoover's Rating **B-**

OVERVIEW

American Financial, a diversified Cincinnati-based holding company, is the nation's 8th largest private company. The company takes in large amounts of cash in the form of insurance premiums and annuity receipts, which need to be profitably invested; unlike most insurers, which invest in many companies, American Financial invests in relatively few companies and takes an active part in their management.

On the financial services side of its business, American Financial operates Hunter, one of the largest savings and loans in Ohio. Great American Insurance, suffering in recent years from a competitive rate environment, offers multiline coverage. Great American Life Insurance sells tax-sheltered annuities, primarily to schoolteachers.

Other holdings include majority ownership of Chiquita Brands International and The Charter Company (oil), and minority holdings in Penn Central, a diversified manufacturing company, and bankrupt Circle K. American Financial subsidiaries operate TV and radio stations, produce programming, and operate Kings Island amusement park.

All of American Financial's common stock is owned by the Lindner family. Carl Lindner and brothers Robert and Richard serve as directors. Carl's sons, Carl III, Craig, and Keith, run the insurance, investment, and Chiquita operations, respectively. The family has been exercising options to sell some of its shares back to the company.

WHEN

Carl Lindner, who had built his family's dairy business into the 220-unit United Dairy Farmers ice cream store chain, formed Henthy Realty (1955) and purchased 3 savings and loan companies (1959). In 1960 Lindner changed the company's name to American Financial, planning to offer diversified financial services. After going public in 1961, American Financial bought United Liberty Life Insurance Company (1963) and Cincinnati's historic Provident Bank (1966).

American Financial then diversified into several new areas. The company formed American Financial Leasing & Services Company in 1968 to lease airplanes, computers, and other equipment to corporate customers and in 1969 acquired a large Phoenix developer, Rubenstein Construction, renaming it American Continental. In 1971 American Financial bought several life, casualty, and mortgage insurance companies and entered publishing by purchasing a 95% stake in the *Cincinnati Enquirer*. In 1973 the company acquired National General, which owned the Great American Insurance Group; paperback publisher Bantam Books; and hardback publisher Grosset & Dunlap.

American Financial suffered during the mid-1970s when inflation grew faster than regulated insurance rates. In addition to selling off its book publishers (1974), the company sold the *Enquirer* (to Combined Communications, owned by Karl Eller) and American Continental (1975), leaving American Financial primarily an insurance and financial services company. The insurance companies were consolidated under the Great American Insurance Company name in 1976. American Financial spun off Provident Bank as a special dividend to shareholders in 1980.

Lindner took American Financial private in 1981 by buying all of the company's outstanding stock. That year, subsidiary American Financial Enterprises acquired a 20% interest in Penn Central, the former railroad that emerged from a 1970 bankruptcy as an industrial manufacturer. In 1984 American Financial sold convenience store chain UtoteM to Circle K for a minority interest in Circle K. The same year, the company increased its holdings in United Brands, later named Chiquita Brands International, from 29% to 45%; Lindner installed himself as CEO of United Brands and reversed the company's losses. In 1987 American Financial purchased Taft Broadcasting, renamed Great American Communications.

Since 1988 Lindner has focused his attention on American Financial's internal growth and the financial problems at Circle K, which filed for bankruptcy in 1990. Shortly afterward American Financial wrote off most of its investment in Circle K.

In 1991 American Financial merged its Hunter S&L unit with Provident Bancorp and announced its intention to increase its holdings in Penn Central to above 50%.

WHO

Chairman and CEO: Carl H. Lindner, age 72, $2,927,000 pay

President and COO: Ronald F. Walker, age 53, $2,699,000 pay

VC; President, Great American Insurance Co.: Carl H. Lindner III, age 37, $2,269,000 pay

VC; President and COO, Chiquita Brands International, Inc.: Keith E. Lindner, age 31, $2,410,000 pay

VC; SEVP, American Money Management Corporation: S. Craig Lindner, age 36, $2,269,000 pay

VC and SVP: Robert D. Lindner, age 70

VP and Treasurer: Fred J. Runk, age 48

Director of Personnel: Lawrence Otto

Auditors: Ernst & Young

Employees: 54,000

WHERE

HQ: One E. Fourth St., Cincinnati, OH 45202
Phone: 513-579-2121
Fax: 513-579-2580

American Financial operates worldwide.

	1990 Sales	
	$ mil.	% of total
US	6,575	83
Other countries	1,315	17
Total	**7,890**	**100**

WHAT

	1990 Sales		1990 Pretax Income	
	$ mil.	% of total	$ mil.	% of total
Prop./cas. ins.	1,983	25	83	—
Annuities	323	4	(39)	—
Savings & loans	119	1	15	—
Food products	4,335	54	150	—
Broadcasting & entertainment	460	6	(37)	—
Petroleum products	705	9	3	—
Other	52	1	(159)	—
Adjustments	(87)	—	(40)	—
Total	**7,890**	**100**	**55**	**—**

Subsidiaries/Affiliates
The Charter Co. (53%, petroleum marketing)
Chiquita Brands International, Inc. (53%)
Great American Communications Co. (63%; 5 TV stations and 12 FM and 6 AM radio stations)
Hanna-Barbera Productions, Inc. (animated film)
Great American Insurance Co. (personal property and casualty insurance)
Great American Life Insurance Co.
Kings Island Co. (theme park)

Other Holdings
The Circle K Corp.
The Penn Central Corp. (47%)
Spelling Entertainment Inc. (45%)
Sprague Technologies, Inc. (32%)

RANKINGS

7th in *Fortune* 100 Diversified Service Cos.
8th in *Forbes* 400 Private Cos.

KEY COMPETITORS

Banks and savings and loans
Food and tobacco companies
Food retailers
Insurance companies
Media companies
Petroleum companies

HOW MUCH

	6-Year Growth	1981	1982	1983	1984	1985	1986	1987	1988	1989	1990
Sales ($ mil.)	20.4%	—	—	—	1,959	2,310	2,791	2,588	6,814	7,177	7,890
Net income ($ mil.)	—	—	—	—	(40)	(23)	184	127	102	3	(6)
Income as % of sales	—	—	—	—	(2.0%)	(1.0%)	6.6%	4.9%	1.5%	0.0%	(0.1%)
Employees	—	—	—	—	5,500	45,800	44,300	52,800	52,000	53,000	54,000

1990 Year-end:
Debt ratio: 91.4%
Return on equity: —
Cash (mil.): $879
Assets (mil.): $12,424
Long-term debt (mil.): $2,737
No. of shares (mil.): 17

Net Income ($ mil.) 1984–90

AMERICAN GREETINGS CORPORATION

NASDAQ symbol: AGREA
Fiscal year ends: Last day in February

Hoover's Rating **B-**

OVERVIEW

American Greetings creates and sells greeting cards, gift wrap, paper party supplies, gift items, frames, stationery, and card display cabinets; licenses characters such as Ziggy, the Care Bears, and Holly Hobbie; and manufactures and sells hair care products. The company is #2 in greeting cards after Hallmark.

Along with the rest of the industry, American Greetings is benefiting from growth in "anytime" cards, while occasion (birthday, wedding) and seasonal (Christmas, Mother's Day) card sales languish. The company's "anytime" cards exploit busy lifestyles and webs of interpersonal relationships with such card series as Kid Zone (parent to child) and 78TH STREET (woman to woman). In addition, card shoppers are moving away from specialty stores to more convenient outlets where the company's presence is stronger.

American Greetings has reduced costs and production-cycle times. During the Persian Gulf crisis, the company produced "America Misses You" and "Greetings from the Gulf" cards in 3 weeks.

WHO

Chairman: Irving I. Stone, age 82, $890,600 pay
President and CEO: Morry Weiss, age 51, $990,900 pay
President, US Greeting Card Division: Edward Fruchtenbaum, age 43, $695,298 pay
SVP and CFO: Henry Lowenthal, age 59, $422,247 pay
SVP Human Resources: Harvey Levin, age 58
Auditors: Ernst & Young
Employees: 31,600

WHEN

In 1906, 22-year-old Jacob Sapirstein, nicknamed "J. S.," began a card wholesaling business in his Cleveland home. J. S.'s sons joined the company (9-year-old Irving in 1918 and Morris in 1926) to sell cards for their dad. By 1932 J. S. began producing his own cards, and the company hired its first salesperson in 1934. A 3rd son, Harry, joined the family business (1935), and the company opened its first branch office in Detroit (1936). The name American Greetings Publishers was adopted in 1938. By 1940 the company's sales had topped $1 million.

During the 1940s the company opened an Ohio production plant (1946), signed its first licensing agreement (1949), and developed new card-sorting technology. In 1952 American Greetings went public. Hi Brows, a line of funny studio cards, was introduced in 1956. In 1958 American Greetings added Carlton Cards, a Canadian subsidiary.

In 1960 Irving Stone (all 3 sons had changed their last name to Stone) was named president and J. S. became chairman. The next year the company opened a new plant in Arkansas. Employment grew to over 6,000 (1966), and new plants were opened in Kentucky (1967, 1969). In 1967 Holly Hobbie made her first appearance on greeting cards; in 1968 sales exceeded $100 million, and the next year the company opened a manufacturing subsidiary in Mexico City.

In 1972 American Greetings introduced Ziggy. In 1978 the company bought Plus Mark, a seasonal wrapping paper, boxed cards, and accessories maker; and Irving replaced his father as chairman. Morry Weiss, Irving's son-in-law, became president and COO. In 1979 American Greetings started its Amtoy subsidiary (toys, novelties, and giftware).

The licensing of Holly Hobbie prompted American Greetings to create its own licensing division, Those Characters From Cleveland (1980). The company also acquired several European cardmakers. In 1981 American Greetings began advertising on TV and in 1982 started a joint venture with Christian Publishing, a South African card company operating in European countries. American Greetings made the *Fortune* 500 list (1982) and introduced the Care Bears, licensed characters that appeared in an animated film. The company bought Drawing Board Greeting Cards in 1985 and Acme Frame Products in 1986.

In 1987 J. S. died and Morry Weiss became CEO; American Greetings bought SMD Industries, a maker of paper products and frames. In 1988 the company sold Amtoy and its Benelux subsidiaries and opened a new plant in Toronto. In 1989 the company bought Wilhold Hair Care Products.

In 1991 American Greetings launched an international pen-pal promotion in cooperation with the UN.

WHERE

HQ: 10500 American Rd., Cleveland, OH 44144
Phone: 216-252-7300
Fax: 216-252-6519 (Corporate Communications)

American Greetings has 20 offices and production facilities in the US, 6 in the UK, 3 in Canada, and one each in Mexico and France.

	1990 Sales		1990 Operating Income	
	$ mil.	% of total	$ mil.	% of total
US	1,182	83	139	86
Foreign	250	17	23	14
Adjustments	(19)	—	(19)	—
Total	**1,413**	**100**	**143**	**100**

WHAT

	1990 Sales
	% of total
Everyday greeting cards	41
Holiday greeting cards	23
Gift wrap & party goods	19
Frames, candles, etc.	10
Stationery & miscellaneous	7
Total	**100**

Licensed Characters
Care Bears
Holly Hobbie
Playground Kids
Strawberry Shortcake
Ziggy

Card Lines
American Greetings to the World
Cartoon Factory
Couples
Hi Brows
In My Thoughts...In My Heart
In Touch
Just Thinking of You
Kid Zone
78TH STREET
Soft Touch
Today...I Thought of You

Consumer Products
Acme Frame Products
Plus Mark (cards and gift wrap)
Wilhold Hair Care Products

Manufacturing
A.G. Industries (display fixtures)

HOW MUCH

Fiscal year ends February of following year	9-Year Growth	1981	1982	1983	1984	1985	1986	1987	1988	1989	1990
Sales ($ mil.)	9.9%	606	722	817	919	1,012	1,103	1,175	1,253	1,287	1,413
Net income ($ mil.)	10.8%	33	45	60	74	74	63	33	44	72	83
Income as % of sales	—	5.4%	6.2%	7.3%	8.1%	7.4%	5.7%	2.8%	3.5%	5.6%	5.8%
Earnings per share ($)	9.0%	1.20	1.54	1.91	2.35	2.32	1.97	1.04	1.38	2.25	2.61
Stock price – high ($)	—	10.38	21.63	29.25	34.25	37.50	42.00	31.63	22.38	37.13	37.38
Stock price – low ($)	—	5.31	9.00	17.31	21.50	25.75	24.00	13.00	13.38	20.38	26.63
Stock price – close ($)	14.4%	10.06	18.88	26.50	31.00	32.63	26.25	14.00	20.75	35.25	33.75
P/E – high	—	9	14	15	15	16	21	30	16	17	14
P/E – low	—	4	6	9	9	12	12	13	10	9	10
Dividends per share ($)	11.2%	0.27	0.31	0.40	0.54	0.62	0.66	0.66	0.66	0.66	0.70
Book value per share ($)	10.7%	8.31	10.18	11.62	13.35	15.01	16.55	17.02	17.55	18.89	20.77

1990 Year-end:
Debt ratio: 27.3%
Return on equity: 13.2%
Cash (mil.): $81
Current ratio: 2.90
Long-term debt (mil.): $246
No. of shares (mil.): 32
Dividends:
1990 average yield: 2.1%
1990 payout: 26.8%
Market value (mil.): $1,067

Stock Price History High/Low 1981–90

RANKINGS

294th in *Fortune* 500 Industrial Cos.
495th in *Business Week* 1000

KEY COMPETITORS

Deluxe
Hallmark
United Nations
Walt Disney

AMERICAN HOME PRODUCTS CORPORATION

NYSE symbol: AHP
Fiscal year ends: December 31

 Hoover's Rating **A-**

OVERVIEW

New York City–based American Home Products is a major pharmaceutical and consumer health care products concern. The company sells several well-known, over-the-counter consumer health care items (Advil, Chap Stick), foods (Chef Boyardee, Maypo), and household products. Most of AHP's household products (such as Black Flag and Easy-Off) were divested when the company sold its Boyle-Midway division to Reckitt & Colman PLC, a London-based consumer brands company, in 1990.

During much of the 1980s AHP's R&D expenditures lagged behind the industry average, giving the company fewer products in its pipeline. Despite another drop in R&D spending (5.4% in 1990 as opposed to 10.5% in 1989), AHP has recently released several new pharmaceutical products including Norplant (a revolutionary birth control implant) and Lodine (an anti-inflammatory drug). The company expects to file investigational applications for 12 new drugs in 1991.

WHO

Chairman and CEO: John R. Stafford, age 53, $1,275,000 pay
President: Bernard Canavan, age 55, $732,500 pay
EVP and Principal Financial Officer: Robert G. Blount, age 52, $636,000 pay
SVP Industrial Relations: Joseph R. Bock
Auditors: Arthur Andersen & Co.
Employees: 48,700

WHEN

Incorporated in 1926, American Home Products consolidated several small companies that made proprietary medicinals such as Hill's Cascara Quinine and St. Jacob's Oil. AHP's history is largely one of continuous acquisitions. One of its earliest, Wyeth Chemicals, came from Harvard University in 1932 (Stuart Wyeth, last heir to the company, had willed it to Harvard).

During the Great Depression AHP bought over 30 food and drug companies. A sunburn oil acquired in 1935 was transformed into the hemorrhoid treatment Preparation H, still a best-selling product. Other acquisitions in the 1930s included 3-in-One Oil, Anacin, Affiliated Products (Neet), and Black Flag. Chef Boyardee was added in 1946.

With the purchase of Canadian company Ayerst Laboratories in 1943 (cod liver oil; vitamins; and Premarin, estrogen from pregnant mares' urine), AHP completed the foundations of its prescription-drug business. Ayerst made penicillin for the Canadian armed forces in WWII and later introduced Antabuse (alcohol deterrent, 1951), developed in alliance with British drug company Imperial Chemical Industries (ICI). From the research alliance with ICI, Ayerst also got Inderal (1968), the first of the beta-blocker class of antihypertensives.

William F. LaPorte, who became chairman and president in 1965, introduced a highly centralized management style, unusual for

such a large company. In the early 1970s the company fought with the FTC over claims made for Preparation H, and later for Anacin, and eventually had to modify advertising copy. AHP has been a major advertiser but is virtually unknown to the average consumer, preferring to use divisional names such as Whitehall Labs (Advil, Anacin). Introduced in 1984, Advil, AHP's over-the-counter version of the analgesic ibuprofen, outsold the runner-up, Bristol-Myers's Nuprin, by more than three to one in 1989.

Recent acquisitions include Sherwood Medical Group (medical supplies, 1982) and Bristol-Myers's animal health division (1987). In 1988 AHP won a takeover battle against Rorer for A.H. Robins (Robitussin, Dimetapp), the company bankrupted by suits over the Dalkon Shield contraceptive device. AHP established a $2.3 billion fund to pay the damages and finally closed the transaction in December 1989. In the 1980s AHP sold its non–health care businesses, including Ekco (housewares, 1984), E. J. Brach (candies, 1986), Sergeant's pet care (1989), and all its South African interests (1989). In 1990 the company sold its Boyle-Midway household products subsidiary (Black Flag, Easy Off, Woolite) for $1.25 billion, and completed its integration of A.H. Robins, which strengthened AHP's line of medical, veterinary, and consumer health products.

WHERE

HQ: 685 Third Ave., New York, NY 10017-4085
Phone: 212-878-5000
Fax: 212-878-5771

The company has operations in 18 countries and sells its products in 140 countries.

	1990 Sales		1990 Pretax Income	
	$ mil.	% of total	$ mil.	% of total
US	4,608	68	1,446	79
Canada & Latin America	707	10	134	7
Europe & Africa	1,129	17	194	11
Asia & Australia	331	5	54	3
Total	**6,775**	**100**	**1,828**	**100**

WHAT

	1990 Sales		1990 Operating Income	
	$ mil.	% of total	$ mil.	% of total
Food & household	1,268	19	173	11
Health care prods.	5,507	81	1,372	89
Adjustments	—	—	(29)	—
Total	**6,775**	**100**	**1,516**	**100**

Selected Pharmaceuticals	Brand Names
Ativan (tranquilizer)	Advil
Cordarone (cardiovascular)	Anacin
Inderal (cardiovascular)	Chap Stick
Isordil (cardiovascular)	Chef Boyardee
Lodine (anti-inflammatory)	Clearblue Easy
Norplant (contraceptive)	Crunch 'n Munch
Orudis (anti-inflammatory)	Dimetapp
Premarin (estrogen replacement)	Dristan
	Gulden's
Tenex (cardiovascular)	Jiffy Pop
Triphasil (contraceptive)	Maypo
	Pam
Infant Nutrition	Preparation H
Nursoy	Primatene
S-26	Ranch Style
SMA	Robitussin

RANKINGS

70th in *Fortune* 500 Industrial Cos.
27th in *Business Week* 1000

KEY COMPETITORS

Abbott Labs	Hoechst	Siemens
Amgen	Johnson &	SmithKline
C. R. Bard	Johnson	Beecham
Baxter	Merck	Syntex
Bayer	Nestlé	Upjohn
Bristol-Myers	Pfizer	Warner-
Squibb	Procter	Lambert
Campbell Soup	& Gamble	Other food
Ciba-Geigy	Quaker Oats	products
ConAgra	Rhône-Poulenc	companies
Eastman Kodak	Roche	Other medical
Eli Lilly	Sandoz	supply
General Electric	Schering-Plough	companies
Glaxo		

HOW MUCH

	9-Year Growth	1981	1982	1983	1984	1985	1986	1987	1988	1989	1990
Sales ($ mil.)	5.7%	4,131	4,582	4,857	4,485	4,685	4,927	5,028	5,501	6,747	6,775
Net income ($ mil.)	10.6%	497	560	627	656	717	779	845	932	1,102	1,231
Income as % of sales	—	12.0%	12.2%	12.9%	14.6%	15.3%	15.8%	16.8%	16.9%	16.3%	18.2%
Earnings per share ($)	10.5%	1.59	1.80	2.00	2.13	2.35	2.59	2.87	3.19	3.54	3.92
Stock price – high ($)	—	18.63	24.00	27.13	27.88	33.44	47.44	48.38	42.44	54.69	55.13
Stock price – low ($)	—	14.06	16.63	20.88	23.38	25.06	30.63	31.00	35.19	39.88	43.00
Stock price – close ($)	12.5%	18.25	22.38	24.81	25.25	31.44	38.44	36.38	41.63	53.75	52.63
P/E – high	—	12	13	14	13	14	18	17	13	15	14
P/E – low	—	9	9	10	11	11	12	11	11	11	11
Dividends per share ($)	9.5%	0.95	1.08	1.20	1.32	1.45	1.55	1.67	1.80	1.95	2.15
Book value per share ($)	5.3%	5.33	5.91	6.57	6.87	7.59	8.03	8.71	10.18	6.30	8.52

1990 Year-end:
Debt ratio: 22.5%
Return on equity: 52.9%
Cash (mil.): $1,789
Current ratio: 3.72
Long-term debt (mil.): $777
No. of shares (mil.): 314
Dividends:
  1990 average yield: 4.1%
  1990 payout: 54.8%
Market value (mil.): $16,526

Stock Price History High/Low 1981–90

AMERICAN INTERNATIONAL GROUP, INC.

OVERVIEW

AIG is the US's largest international insurer, the only US insurer founded overseas, the US's leading commercial and industrial insurer, and the largest foreign insurer in Japan. Through subsidiaries, AIG is the largest life insurer in southeast Asia and in the Philippines. AIG's success results from strong fiscal controls, product innovation, and worldwide geographic distribution of its products.

AIG's General Insurance Underwriting provides property/casualty insurance worldwide. The Domestic General–Broker Group conducts US property/casualty operations. This group is the leading provider of pollution liability protection; has the largest share of the environmental liability insurance market; and is the nation's largest provider of directors' and officers' insurance, malpractice coverage, and risk management services (e.g., claims administration and loss control) to brokers and their customers.

AIG's Domestic General–Agency Group writes property/casualty insurance through independent agents. United Guaranty writes mortgage guaranty insurance. The Foreign General Group provides international underwriting. The Life Group (operating worldwide) has approximately 60,000 agents.

WHEN

Ice cream parlor proprietor Cornelius Starr founded casualty and property insurer C. V. Starr & Company in Shanghai in 1919. For many years, Starr merely passed business to other insurers. China remained Starr's operational base until WWII, when he relocated to the US.

In 1954 Starr began seeking multinational companies as clients. To do so, he developed an international benefits pool that provided disability, health, and life insurance, and pension plans that were transferable as employees moved from country to country. The strategy proved successful: today the company manages benefit pools for many of the *Fortune* 500.

In 1967 Starr handpicked his successor, attorney Maurice Greenberg; Starr died the following year. By 1972 CEO Greenberg had established American International Group as a holding company for the many insurance companies Starr operated worldwide. Greenberg is widely regarded as a brilliant insurance executive and the true genius behind AIG.

AIG takes risks that its competitors shun, such as insuring satellites. During the mid-1970s AIG insured offshore oil rigs when other insurers would not, charging annual premiums as high as 10% of value. Greenberg uses reinsurers around the world to help leverage otherwise risky ventures. AIG will accept larger single risks than any other insurer, making AIG the largest source of reinsurance in the US.

In 1975 the company became the first insurance company in the Western Hemisphere to be allowed to resume business operations in China. By then it was the largest foreign life insurer in Hong Kong, Japan, Malaysia, the Philippines, Singapore, and Taiwan, and the only insurer with sales and support facilities operating on a worldwide basis.

From 1979 to 1984 the property/casualty business suffered heavy price competition that cost the industry almost $21 billion in underwriting losses, but during this period AIG outperformed all rivals in terms of its combined ratio (expenses plus losses divided by premiums). In 1986 the company again leveraged its international presence by offering services to foreign manufacturers interested in the US market.

In 1990 AIG bought International Lease Finance Corporation, the world leader in leasing and remarketing of technically advanced jets to airlines, for 1.2 billion. The company also was the first US insurer licensed to operate in Poland and Hungary.

NYSE symbol: AIG
Fiscal year ends: December 31

Hoover's Rating B+

WHO

Chairman, President, and CEO: Maurice R. (Hank) Greenberg, age 65, $1,750,000 pay
VC Finance: Edward E. Matthews, age 59, $465,000 pay
VC Foreign General Insurance: Houghton Freeman, age 69, $435,700 pay
VC Domestic General Insurance: Thomas R. Tizzio, age 53, $330,000 pay
VC External Affairs: John J. Roberts, age 68, $310,000 pay
VP Human Resources: Axel I. Freudmann, age 44
Auditors: Coopers & Lybrand
Employees: 33,600

WHERE

HQ: 70 Pine St., New York, NY 10270
Phone: 212-770-7000
Fax: 212-770-7821

AIG and its member companies have 424 offices, writing policies in more than 130 jurisdictions.

	1990 Assets		1990 Pretax Income	
	$ mil.	% of total	$ mil.	% of total
US & Canada	36,049	62	940	52
Far East	10,148	17	567	31
Other regions	11,946	21	305	17
Total	**58,143**	**100**	**1,812**	**100**

WHAT

	1990 Assets		1990 Pretax Income	
	$ mil.	% of total	$ mil.	% of total
General insurance	27,994	48	1,287	68
Life insurance	16,316	28	463	25
Agency & service fee income	169	—	37	2
Financial services	14,417	24	101	5
Adjustments	(753)	—	(76)	—
Total	**58,143**	**100**	**1,812**	**100**

Affiliated Companies
AIG Capital Corp.
AIG Financial Products Corp.
AIG Trading Corp.
American Home Assurance Co.
American International Assurance Co., Ltd.
American International Reinsurance Co., Ltd.
American International Underwriters Overseas, Ltd.
American Life Insurance Co.
Delaware American Life Insurance Co.
International Lease Finance Corp.
Lexington Insurance Co.
Nan Shan Life Insurance Co., Ltd.
National Union Fire Insurance Co.
New Hampshire Insurance Co.
Pacific Union Assurance Co.
The Philippine American Life Insurance Co.
Ticino Societa d'Assicurazioni Sulla Vita
Transatlantic Holdings, Inc. (41.25%)
Uebersebank AG
United Guaranty Residential Insurance Co.

RANKINGS

7th in *Fortune* 50 Diversified Financial Cos.
25th in *Business Week* 1000

KEY COMPETITORS

Aetna	General Re	Travelers
Allianz	Lloyd's of London	USF&G
CIGNA	Tokio Marine & Fire	Other ins. cos.

HOW MUCH

	9-Year Growth	1981	1982	1983	1984	1985	1986	1987	1988	1989	1990
Assets ($ mil.)	24.7%	7,957	9,120	10,556	11,625	15,571	21,023	27,908	37,409	46,143	58,143
Net income ($ mil.)	17.2%	345	413	427	317	374	657	945	1,175	1,367	1,442
Income as % of assets	—	4.3%	4.5%	4.0%	2.7%	2.4%	3.1%	3.4%	3.1%	3.0%	2.5%
Earnings per share ($)	15.3%	1.92	2.23	2.29	1.70	1.96	3.23	4.59	5.71	6.63	6.92
Stock price – high ($)	—	22.16	26.72	31.10	29.20	44.00	57.40	67.00	55.00	89.60	84.70
Stock price – low ($)	—	15.57	17.60	20.92	20.35	26.00	41.60	42.80	39.20	53.00	57.00
Stock price – close ($)	15.7%	20.72	25.28	25.70	27.25	42.40	48.90	48.00	54.20	82.80	76.88
P/E – high	—	12	12	14	17	22	18	15	10	14	12
P/E – low	—	8	8	9	12	13	13	9	7	8	8
Dividends per share ($)	14.4%	0.12	0.15	0.17	0.18	0.18	0.18	0.21	0.28	0.35	0.41
Book value per share ($)	17.5%	10.93	12.80	14.62	15.48	19.32	23.86	28.22	34.27	41.08	46.69

1990 Year-end:
Return on equity: 15.8%
Equity as % of assets: 17.0%
Cash (mil.): $95
Long-term debt (mil.): $7,832
No. of shares (mil.): 212
Dividends:
 1990 average yield: 0.5%
 1990 payout: 6.0%
Market value (mil.): $16,309
Sales (mil.): $16,214

Stock Price History High/Low 1981–90

AMERICAN PRESIDENT COMPANIES, LTD.

NYSE symbol: APS
Fiscal year ends: Last Friday
  in December

OVERVIEW

American President offers an integrated system of ocean, rail, and truck transportation in North America, Asia, and the Middle East. With a fleet of 23 containerships and a network of feeder vessels, American President's ocean shipping line (American President Lines) serves more than 3,500 delivery points on 5 continents. Because the containers are intermodal, freight can be taken from shipboard, loaded on a truck or rail car, and then sent onward in the same container. The company is the leader in the transpacific market with a 12% market share.

Double-stack rail cars are the focus of the company's North American freight operations and accounted for 73% of domestic shipments in 1990. The company also operates a fleet of 500 trucks but is increasingly converting long-haul truck cargo to intermodal stacktrains.

American President's customers have access to information in the company's computer regarding the location of their shipments via the customers' own PCs, through a sophisticated tracking system that uses touch-tone telephones and fax machines.

WHO

Chairman and CEO: W. Bruce Seaton, age 65, $791,250 pay
President and COO: John M. Lillie, age 54
EVP, CFO, and Treasurer: Will M. Storey, age 59
SVP Human Resources: Arthur J. Reimers
Auditors: Arthur Andersen & Co.
Employees: 5,217

WHERE

HQ: 1111 Broadway, Oakland, CA 94607
Phone: 415-272-8000
Fax: 415-272-7941

American President has 159 offices in North America, Asia, the Middle East, Europe, Africa, and Australia. It serves 40 ports in the Pacific and Indian Oceans and the Persian Gulf.

	1990 Sales	
	$ mil.	% of total
US	684	29
Other countries	1,653	71
Total	**2,337**	**—**

WHEN

New York merchant William Aspinwall founded the Pacific Mail Steamship Company in 1848, planning to launch the first shipping line between Panama and California. The company's first steamers sailed from New York shipyards later that year and arrived in San Francisco Bay in 1849.

In the early 1860s Cornelius Vanderbilt (owner, Atlantic Mail Steamship Company) sent 4 ships to the Pacific, hoping to break Pacific Mail's West Coast monopoly, but sold his ships to Pacific Mail after a rate war. In 1866 Pacific Mail bought Atlantic Mail while Vanderbilt went on to take over the New York Central Railroad. In 1867 Pacific Mail pioneered trade to the Orient.

During the depression of 1873, Pacific Mail narrowly averted bankruptcy brought on by an overambitious construction program. Jay Gould gained control of the company in 1874, and by 1885 Gould's Union Pacific Railroad owned a majority share of Pacific Mail.

C. P. Huntington of the Central Pacific and Southern Pacific railroads bought Pacific Mail in 1893. Upon Huntington's death in 1900, Southern Pacific bought the company. Edward Harriman took over Southern Pacific in 1902, operating it and Pacific Mail until his death in 1909. W. R. Grace bought Pacific Mail in 1915, and then in 1926 it was acquired by the Dollar Steamship Company.

Founded by Robert Dollar, the Dollar Company had conducted transpacific trade since 1902. However, weakened by strikes, the company faced bankruptcy by the mid-1930s. In 1938 the Maritime Commission forced the Dollar family to transfer control of the company to the government, reorganizing it as American President Lines.

From 1946 to 1952 the Dollar family tried to regain the company, which, by court order, was put up for sale. A venture capitalist group led by Ralph Davies (formerly of Standard Oil) bought American President in 1952. Davies's Natomas Company (offshore oil) bought the company in 1956. Bruce Seaton (SVP Finance, Natomas) became president of American President in 1977, emphasizing transpacific trade using intermodal containers.

After buying Natomas in 1983, Diamond Shamrock spun off American President to the public. The company introduced double-stack intermodal rail cars in the US in 1984. In 1988 American President invested about $6 million in Amtech (electronic tracking of intermodal containers). However, high operating costs and interest expenses led to an 86% decline in earnings between 1988 and 1989. A $109 million restructuring charge sent the company into red ink in 1990. Seaton will retire as chairman in late 1991. President John Lillie is expected to succeed him.

WHAT

	1990 Sales		1990 Operating Income	
	$ mil.	% of total	$ mil.	% of total
Transportation	2,322	99	(64)	—
Real estate	15	1	8	—
Total	**2,337**	**100**	**(56)**	**—**

Transportation
American Consolidation Services, Ltd. (consolidation services in Asia for US importers)
American President Domestic Co., Ltd. (intermodal, freight brokerage, and time-critical cargo transportation)
American President Lines, Ltd.
American President Trucking Co., Ltd.
Amtech Corporation (10%, electronic identification of shipments)
Eagle Marine Services, Ltd. (stevedoring and terminal services)

Real Estate
American President Real Estate Co., Ltd. (owns 320 acres in California)

RANKINGS

21st in *Fortune* 50 Transportation Cos.
935th in Business Week 1000

KEY COMPETITORS

Burlington Northern
Canadian Pacific
Chicago and North Western
Consolidated Freightways
Consolidated Rail
Continental Grain
CSX
Federal Express
Norfolk Southern
Rio Grande Industries
Roadway
Santa Fe Pacific
Union Pacific
UPS
Yellow Freight

HOW MUCH

	9-Year Growth	1981	1982	1983	1984	1985	1986	1987	1988	1989	1990
Sales ($ mil.)	15.1%	659	685	806	977	1,235	1,506	1,891	2,194	2,300	2,337
Net income ($ mil.)	—	43	51	26	103	38	18	79	81	11	(60)
Income as % of sales	—	6.5%	7.5%	3.3%	10.6%	3.1%	1.2%	4.2%	3.7%	0.5%	(2.6%)
Earnings per share ($)	—	—	—	1.51	5.78	1.86	0.70	3.23	3.26	0.23	(3.46)
Stock price – high ($)	—	—	—	20.39	24.42	29.00	29.00	51.00	35.88	38.75	29.13
Stock price – low ($)	—	—	—	11.81	14.81	13.88	16.88	21.63	22.63	26.75	10.38
Stock price – close ($)	—	—	—	19.34	21.83	18.88	26.13	29.50	34.00	28.13	15.50
P/E – high	—	—	—	14	4	16	41	16	11	168	—
P/E – low	—	—	—	8	3	7	24	7	7	116	—
Dividends per share ($)	—	—	—	0.00	0.00	0.38	0.50	0.50	0.55	0.58	0.60
Book value per share ($)	—	—	—	19.21	24.54	25.87	25.96	28.87	30.52	29.73	26.47

1990 Year-end:
Debt ratio: 49.6%
Return on equity: —
Cash (mil.): $118
Current ratio: 1.25
Long-term debt (mil.): $481
No. of shares (mil.): 18
Dividends:
  1990 average yield: 3.9%
  1990 payout: —
Market value (mil.): $286

Stock Price History High/Low 1983–90

AMERICAN STANDARD INC.

OVERVIEW

American Standard is the world's largest producer of plumbing products, the 2nd largest producer of custom air-conditioning systems, and a major manufacturer of commercial refrigeration units, braking systems for heavy vehicles, and furnaces.

Roughly 1/2 of the company's sales come from its air-conditioning segment, Trane Company, which, in addition to developing customized systems, markets air conditioners through about 5,000 US dealers. Among Trane's market goals are development of air-conditioning controls, refrigerants to meet US standards, products for replacement markets, and more energy-efficient devices.

American Standard is a major supplier of plumbing fixtures in the US, Canada, and Europe and claims to be "the only manufacturer of a full line of plumbing products operating on a worldwide basis."

The company's transportation segment, the largest manufacturer of braking systems for heavy vehicles in Brazil and Europe, entered a joint marketing venture with Rockwell International Corporation in 1990.

WHEN

In 1881 American Radiator was created in Buffalo to manufacture steam and water heating equipment. J. P. Morgan acquired the company and bought out almost every other US heating-equipment company, consolidating them all under the American Radiator name in 1899.

That same year Louisville-based Ahrens & Ott joined with Pittsburgh-based Standard Manufacturing (both plumbing supply companies) to create Standard Sanitary. Standard Sanitary produced enameled cast-iron plumbing parts and developed the one-piece lavatory, built-in bathtubs, and single taps for hot and cold running water.

Both American Radiator and Standard Sanitary grew through numerous acquisitions in the early decades of the 20th century. In 1929 the 2 companies merged to form American Radiator & Standard Sanitary Corporation, headquartered in New York City. Later that year they bought CF Church (toilet seats).

During the next 3 decades the company expanded its operations across North and South America and into Europe. By the 1960s American Radiator & Standard Sanitary was the largest manufacturer of plumbing fixtures in the world.

In 1967 the company changed its name to American Standard, then diversified beyond the bathroom, acquiring a number of companies, the most important of which was Westinghouse Air Brake (WABCO, 1968).

WABCO traces its history to Union Switch and Signal, begun in 1882. In 1917 Union Switch was acquired by Westinghouse Air Brake. George Westinghouse had invented the air brake before turning his attention to electricity. Union Switch merged with its parent company and adopted the WABCO name in 1951.

During the 1970s and 1980s American Standard consolidated its operations and sold off numerous businesses that were outside its traditional product line. It purchased Clayton Dewandre (truck brake manufacturing, 1977) and Queroy (faucets and fittings, 1982). In 1984 the company purchased Trane (air conditioners).

In 1988 American Standard fought off a hostile takeover attempt by Black & Decker. The company agreed to be purchased by ASI Holding Corporation (formed by the leveraged buyout firm Kelso & Company) for $3 billion and taken private. ASI acquired 95% of common stock.

The transaction left American Standard deeply in debt. The resulting increase in interest expense led to losses in 1988 and 1989. To raise cash the company sold its Manhattan headquarters in 1988 and sold its Steelcraft division (doors and windows) to Masco for $100 million in cash in 1989.

In 1990 the company sold its railway brake products operations to a group led by Investment AB Cardo (Sweden) for $250 million. The same year American Standard opened European distribution centers and a new plant in France and entered joint ventures in Asia.

In October 1991 the company sold its Tyler Refrigeration division, a maker of commercial refrigeration equipment, to Kelso & Co.

WHO

Private company
Fiscal year ends: December 31

President and CEO: Emmanuel A. Kampouris, age 56, $975,000 pay
Chairman: William A. Marquard, age 71, $400,000 pay
SVP: H. Thompson Smith, age 53, $442,083 pay
SVP: George H. Kerchove, age 53, $377,500 pay
VP and Controller: Fred A. Allardyce, age 49
VP Human Resources: Richard I. Schultz, age 59
Auditors: Ernst & Young
Employees: 32,900

WHERE

HQ: 1114 Ave. of the Americas, New York, NY 10036
Phone: 212-703-5100
Fax: 212-703-5177 (Main Office)

The company operates in 32 countries.

	1990 Sales		1990 Operating Income	
	$ mil.	% of total	$ mil.	% of total
US	1,797	49	64	22
Europe	1,425	38	194	67
Other countries	477	13	31	11
Adjustments	(62)	—	(32)	—
Total	**3,637**	**100**	**257**	**100**

WHAT

	1990 Sales		1990 Operating Income	
	$ mil.	% of total	$ mil.	% of total
Plumbing products	1,041	29	57	20
Transportation products	686	19	91	31
Air-conditioning products	1,910	52	141	49
Adjustments	—	—	(32)	—
Total	**3,637**	**100**	**257**	**100**

Products

Plumbing	Air Conditioning
Bathtubs	Air-handling products
Fittings	Applied air-conditioning systems
Fixtures	Commercial air-conditioning products
Transportation	Gas furnaces
Braking systems	Residential air conditioners
Heavy vehicle components	

Brand Names

Plumbing	Air Conditioning
American-Standard	American-Standard
Ideal-Standard	Trane
Standard	
Transportation	
Clayton Dewandre	
WABCO	

RANKINGS

134th in *Fortune* 500 Industrial Cos.
31st in *Forbes* 400 US Private Cos.

KEY COMPETITORS

Allied-Signal	Electrolux
American Brands	Masco
Black & Decker	United Technologies
Eaton	Whitman

HOW MUCH

	9-Year Growth	1981	1982	1983	1984	1985	1986	1987	1988	1989	1990
Sales ($ mil.)	4.4%	2,471	2,125	2,182	3,215	2,912	2,998	3,400	3,716	3,334	3,637
Net income ($ mil.)	—	111	36	63	117	(3)	110	133	(26)	(34)	(97)
Income as % of sales	—	4.5%	1.7%	2.9%	3.6%	(0.1%)	3.7%	3.9%	(0.7%)	(1.0%)	(2.7%)
Employees	(2.9%)	42,700	39,200	37,900	49,500	40,000	38,900	39,300	34,100	33,300	32,900

1990 Year-end:
Debt ratio: 103.3%
Return on equity: —
Cash (mil.): $66
Current ratio: 1.46
Long-term debt (mil.): $2,143

Net Income ($ mil.) 1981–90

AMERICAN STORES COMPANY

NYSE symbol: ASC
Fiscal year ends: Saturday closest
to January 31

OVERVIEW

American Stores, a holding company based in Salt Lake City, is the largest US food retailer. It is the only company to have a major presence in both grocery and drugstore retailing.

American grew primarily through acquisitions. As a result the company operates stores throughout the country under a variety of familiar names: Acme, Jewel, Jewel Osco, Skaggs Alpha Beta, Sav-on, Lucky's, and Osco. The company is engaged in an ongoing modernization effort that included the sale or closing of 95 locations and the opening of 49 new stores in 1990.

The founding Skaggs family continues to play an important role in the development of American Stores. L. S. Skaggs, board chairman, owns 10.2% of the company's common stock. The company continues to invest in new technologies, including scanning, direct store delivery, labor scheduling, and inventory control systems.

WHEN

Leonard S. Skaggs, one of 6 sons of Safeway founder Marion Skaggs, bought Pay Less Drug Stores in Salt Lake City in 1939 with his Safeway stock proceeds. Leonard Skaggs, Jr., the current chairman, took over after his father's death in 1950. In 1965, when the business had 69 locations, it incorporated as Skaggs Drug Centers and went public. In 1969 the company formed a joint venture with Albertson's, a grocery store operator in the West, to develop food/drug combination stores under the name Skaggs Albertsons.

Skaggs merged in 1979 with a larger company, American Stores of Philadelphia. American was formed in 1917 by the combination of 5 grocers, including Acme Tea (founded 1885), and operated stores throughout the mid-Atlantic states. Skaggs then changed its name to American Stores and continued to operate as a holding company, with stores under local names. In 1977 Skaggs and Albertson's dissolved their joint venture, with each receiving 1/2 of the jointly owned locations. After acquiring American Stores, which had owned the Alpha Beta stores in Southern California since the 1940s, the company renamed its 1/2 of the joint-venture stores Skaggs Alpha Beta.

American sold Alphy's Restaurants to Denny's in 1983 and the next year sold several of its Arizona Alpha Beta food stores, Houston Sav-on drugstores, and another drug chain, Rea & Derick. Also in 1984 American acquired Chicago-based Jewel Companies. Jewel, originally the Jewel Tea Company, began in Chicago in 1899 as a route-delivery grocery operation and opened grocery stores in the 1930s. It operated stores in various parts of the US under the names of Jewel, Jewel Osco, Star Market, Buttrey's, and Osco Drug.

American bought Lucky Stores, a major California-based chain, in 1988, bringing the company's number of stores in that state to 710. A court order prevented the company from integrating the Southern California store operations of Lucky Stores and Alpha Beta, on antitrust grounds. American appealed, but the US Supreme Court ruled in 1990 against the company. Jonathan Scott, formerly president of A&P and Albertson's (and former son-in-law of Joe Albertson), became CEO of American in 1989 and president in 1990.

In 1990 the company sold its 44 Buttrey Food & Drug stores and support facilities for $179 million to Freeman Spogli and Company. In 1991 it sold 123 Alpha Beta Stores in Southern California to Food 4 Less for $241 million in cash and $10 million in assumed leases, and sold 51 Osco Drug Stores in the Rocky Mountains area to Pay Less Drug for about $60 million.

WHO

Chairman: L. S. Skaggs, age 67, $1,060,195 pay
President and CEO: Jonathan L. Scott, age 61, $1,487,206 pay
VC and CFO: Victor L. Lund, age 43, $847,794 pay
Chairman, President, and CEO, Lucky Stores: Lawrence A. Del Santo, age 57, $795,682 pay
Chairman, President, and CEO, Jewel Companies: Alan D. Stewart, age 48, $873,768 pay
SVP Benefits Administration: Scott Bergeson, age 53
Auditors: Ernst & Young
Employees: 163,900

WHERE

HQ: PO Box 27447, 709 E. South Temple, Salt Lake City, UT 84127-0447
Phone: 801-539-0112
Fax: 801-531-0768 (Shareholder Relations)

The company operates 1,848 stores in 35 states.

WHAT

	1990 Stores
Alpha Beta Company	
Alpha Beta (Los Angeles)	
California	160
American Drug Stores, Inc.	
Osco Drug (Chicago)	
26 states	503
Sav-on (Chicago)	
California, Nevada, Utah	178
Jewel Companies, Inc.	
Acme Markets (Philadelphia)	
Delaware, Maryland, New Jersey, New York, Pennsylvania	270
Jewel Food Stores (Chicago)	
Illinois, Indiana, Iowa, Michigan	213
Jewel Osco (Tampa)	
Florida	5
Skaggs Alpha Beta (Dallas)	
Arkansas, New Mexico, Oklahoma, Texas	75
Star Market (Boston)	
Massachusetts	32
Lucky Stores, Inc.	
Lucky (Oakland)	
California, Nevada	412
Total	**1,848**

RANKINGS

4th in *Fortune* 50 Retailing Cos.
247th in *Business Week* 1000

KEY COMPETITORS

Albertson's	Longs
Edward J. DeBartolo	Melville
Food Lion	Safeway
Giant Food	Stop & Shop
Great A&P	Supermarkets General
Jack Eckerd	Vons
Kroger	Walgreen

HOW MUCH

	9-Year Growth	1981	1982	1983	1984	1985	1986	1987	1988	1989	1990
Sales ($ mil.)	13.5%	7,097	7,508	7,984	12,119	13,890	14,021	14,272	18,478	22,004	22,156
Net income ($ mil.)	12.2%	65	90	118	186	154	145	154	98	118	182
Income as % of sales	—	0.9%	1.2%	1.5%	1.5%	1.1%	1.0%	1.1%	0.5%	0.5%	0.8%
Earnings per share ($)	12.5%	1.81	2.69	3.61	5.71	4.11	3.79	4.19	2.51	3.40	5.22
Stock price – high ($)	—	9.92	23.33	44.00	41.13	68.25	71.25	86.25	66.50	72.50	71.50
Stock price – low ($)	—	6.92	8.42	19.25	26.50	38.75	51.63	41.50	47.63	53.00	42.63
Stock price – close ($)	21.1%	9.83	21.67	39.63	40.00	64.75	54.38	50.50	57.88	56.50	54.88
P/E – high	—	5	9	12	7	17	19	21	27	21	14
P/E – low	—	4	3	5	5	9	14	10	19	16	8
Dividends per share ($)	17.3%	0.27	0.33	0.44	0.64	0.69	0.84	0.84	0.93	1.00	1.12
Book value per share ($)	16.6%	9.80	12.15	15.26	21.40	24.44	26.96	29.38	30.51	34.86	39.11

1990 Year-end:
Debt ratio: 69.7%
Return on equity: 14.1%
Cash (mil.): $77
Current ratio: 1.08
Long-term debt (mil.): $3,101
No. of shares (mil.): 35
Dividends:
 1990 average yield: 2.0%
 1990 payout: 21.5%
Market value (mil.): $1,895

Stock Price History High/Low 1981–90

AMERICAN TELEPHONE & TELEGRAPH COMPANY

NYSE symbol: T
Fiscal year ends: December 31

Hoover's Rating **B**

OVERVIEW

The kids may have left home, but Ma Bell is far from being an "empty nest" victim. She — AT&T — is not only the largest US telecommunications company, but also the largest US service company of any kind.

AT&T is buying Dayton, Ohio–based NCR. After losing $3 billion in the computer marketplace during the 1980s, AT&T paid $7.48 billion in stock for NCR following a prolonged and hostile fight. AT&T will fold its computer operations into NCR and cut or reassign 57% of its work force.

Most of AT&T's revenue comes from long-distance service, and AT&T retains about 70% of that market. The company is extending its telecommunications systems reach abroad with ventures in Germany, Italy, Japan, Korea, and Taiwan. In the financial services arena, the precocious AT&T Universal Card is the 4th most popular bank credit card in the US.

WHEN

"Mr. Watson. Come here. I want you."

Alexander Graham Bell's legendary summons, the first words on a telephone, came as he was perfecting his invention in 1876. As demand for the new device spread, Bell's backers, fathers of deaf students he was tutoring, organized Bell Telephone (1877) and New England Telephone (1878). The companies attracted funding from Boston financiers and were consolidated as National Bell Telephone in 1879.

After several years of litigation, National Bell barred rival Western Union from the telephone business in 1879. Western Union had tried to market Elisha Gray's competing patent, filed just hours after Bell's. By 1882 the Bell company had prospered enough to wrest control of Western Electric, the nation's largest electrical equipment manufacturer, from Western Union.

Bell's patents expired in the 1890s, and independent phone companies raced into the market. Bell struggled to compete. After changing its name to American Telephone and Telegraph and relocating the headquarters from Boston to New York in 1899, AT&T shifted focus to swallowing smaller companies. AT&T also blocked independents from access to Bell System phone lines.

Banker J. P. Morgan and his allies gained control of AT&T and installed Theodore Vail as president in 1907, and AT&T won control of Western Union in 1909. The Wilson administration threatened antitrust action against AT&T. In the 1913 Kingsbury Commitment, AT&T promised the government it would sell Western Union, buy no more independent phone companies without regulatory approval, and grant independents access to its networks.

Bell Labs, the heralded research and development unit, was formed in 1925. Bell Labs would sponsor Nobel Prize–winning research leading to invention of the transistor (1956), develop the first communications satellite (1961), and receive more than 25,000 patents.

In 1949 the Justice Department sued to force AT&T to sell Western Electric. The 1956 settlement allowed AT&T to keep Western Electric but prohibited it from entering nonregulated businesses. Federal Communications Commission rulings stripped AT&T of its monopoly on telephone equipment (1968) and permitted specialized carriers, such as MCI, to hook microwave-based communications to the phone network (1969), injecting competition into the long-distance arena.

A government suit led to the 1982 settlement that, in 1984, spun off the 7 regional Bell companies. AT&T kept the long-distance business, Western Electric, and Bell Labs. Since the breakup, CEO Robert Allen has reshuffled to compete, cut levels of management, eliminated jobs, and in 1989 divided the company into 19 units. AT&T returned to the aggressiveness of its early days, picking off Western Union's business services group (electronic mail, telex) in 1990. That same year AT&T told NCR: "Come here. I want you."

WHO

Chairman and CEO: Robert E. Allen, age 55, $2,021,000 pay
VC: Randall L. Tobias, age 48, $1,089,400 pay
Group Executive and CFO: Alex J. Mandl, age 47
SVP Human Resources: Harold W. Burlingame, age 50
Auditors: Coopers & Lybrand
Employees: 274,000

WHERE

HQ: 550 Madison Ave., New York, NY 10022
Phone: 212-605-5500
Fax: 212-308-1820 (Communications Dept.)

AT&T markets its telecommunications services and products worldwide.

WHAT

	1990 Sales	
	$ mil.	% of total
Telecommunications services	19,691	38
Access, other interconnection charges	18,692	36
Telecommunications network systems	7,303	14
Communications, computer & other products	4,898	10
Financial services and leasing	762	2
Adjustments	(25)	—
Total	**51,321**	**100**

Subsidiaries and Affiliates
AT&T American Transtech (shareholder, employee services)
AT&T Bell Labs (R&D)
AT&T Capital (leasing, financing)
AT&T EasyLink Services
AT&T International Inc. (overseas operations)
AT&T Microelectronics (electronic components)
AT&T Paradyne (data communication)
AT&T Software Japan, Ltd. (80%)
AT&T Universal Card Services (consumer credit card)
Communications Products Group (equipment)
Communications Services Group (telecommunications services)
Eaton Financial Corp. (leasing)
Federal Systems (US government)
International Group (overseas support)
NCR Corp. (computers)
Network Systems Group (switching systems)
Switching Systems (switching machines, software)
UNIX Systems Laboratories, Inc. (operating software)

RANKINGS

1st in *Fortune* 100 Diversified Service Cos.
8th in *Business Week* 1000

KEY COMPETITORS

BCE	MCI
British Telecom	Metromedia
Cable & Wireless	NEC
Centel	NTT
Ericsson	Siemens
Fujitsu	Telmex
GTE	United Telecom
Hitachi	Computer manufacturers
IBM	

HOW MUCH

	9-Year Growth	1981	1982	1983	1984	1985	1986	1987	1988	1989	1990
Sales ($ mil.)	(1.4%)	58,214	65,093	69,403	53,821	56,431	53,680	51,209	51,974	50,976	51,321
Net income ($ mil.)	(9.8%)	6,888	6,992	5,747	1,370	1,557	314	2,044	(1,669)	2,697	2,735
Income as % of sales	—	11.8%	10.7%	8.3%	2.5%	2.8%	0.6%	4.0%	(3.2%)	5.3%	5.3%
Earnings per share ($)	(12.7%)	8.55	8.06	6.00	1.25	1.37	0.21	1.88	(1.55)	2.50	2.51
Stock price – high ($)	—	61.50	64.63	70.25	20.25	27.88	27.88	35.88	30.38	47.38	46.63
Stock price – low ($)	—	47.50	49.88	59.00	14.88	19.00	20.50	22.25	24.13	28.13	29.00
Stock price – close ($)	(7.2%)	58.75	59.38	61.50	19.50	25.00	25.00	27.00	28.75	45.50	30.13
P/E – high	—	7	8	12	16	20	133	19	—	19	19
P/E – low	—	6	6	10	12	14	98	12	—	11	12
Dividends per share ($)	(14.5%)	5.40	5.40	5.85	1.20	1.20	1.20	1.20	1.20	1.20	1.32
Book value per share ($)	(16.8%)	67.52	69.07	62.92	13.26	13.68	12.64	13.46	10.68	11.84	12.90

1990 Year-end:
Debt ratio: 39.3%
Return on equity: 20.3%
Cash (mil.): $1,389
Current ratio: 1.18
Long-term debt (mil.): $9,118
No. of shares (mil.): 1,092
Dividends:
 1990 average yield: 4.4%
 1990 payout: 52.6%
Market value (mil.): $32,901

Stock Price History High/Low 1981–90

AMERITECH CORPORATION

NYSE symbol: AIT
Fiscal year ends: December 31

Hoover's Rating **B-**

OVERVIEW

AT&T spin-off Ameritech, the 7th largest US telephone holding company, provided telephone service via 16,278,000 lines at the end of 1990. Based in Chicago, Ameritech provides phone service to the Great Lake states through its Bell subsidiaries. The company has led all of the regional Bell holding companies for 7 consecutive years in ROE (now 16.3%).

Since 1989 Ameritech Information Systems has provided sales and sales support services to its regulated Bell subsidiaries for customer-owned equipment. Ameritech has more than 326,416 cellular telephone sub-

scribers through its Ameritech Mobile subsidiary, which is also the leading Midwest paging service. Ameritech Publishing provides directory advertising and publishing services. Ameritech Credit arranges financing for customers who lease telecommunications products. Ameritech Enterprise is a holding company for information service businesses, primarily voice mail and audiotex services in the US, Canada, Europe, and Japan. Newly formed Ameritech International focuses, oddly enough, on international business alliances.

WHEN

Ameritech began as an arm of AT&T. Illinois Bell, now Ameritech's largest operating company, was originally known as Chicago Telephone and operated between 1881 and 1920. From 1880 to 1885 the Bell System consolidated small, individual telephone companies such as Chicago's into larger telephone companies that, under franchise agreements, could construct long-distance lines to other Bell exchanges but not to non-Bell exchanges. Gradually the long-distance lines became AT&T Long Lines; local operations were retained by the Bell Operating Companies.

The E. T. Gilliland Company of Indianapolis, long part of Ameritech's Indiana Bell company, was vital to the Bell System in its early years. In the late 1870s Gilliland was considered Bell's most innovative manufacturer. In 1881 Gilliland sold a 61% stake in his operations to Western Electric, at that time controlled by Bell's chief rival, Western Union. The purchase could have destroyed Bell and changed the history of US telephony, but Bell regained Gilliland through an outside investor named Jay Gould, who bought shares quietly.

In 1983 AT&T spun off its local operating subsidiaries as part of its antitrust settlement. Ameritech began independent operations throughout the Great Lakes region in 1984. Ameritech received 5 of AT&T's 22 telephone subsidiaries, Ameritech Mobile Communica-

tions (cellular service provider), and a share in Bell Communications Research (Bellcore, the R&D arm shared by the Bell companies).

Since divestiture Ameritech has expanded paging services by purchasing existing operations. The company made an unsuccessful stab at the software market, purchasing Applied Data Research in 1986 and selling it in 1988 because it was unprofitable. In partnership with Bell Canada and Telenet, Ameritech started iNet (1987), an electronic mail and information services company. In 1988 the company invested in 2 companies to gain a presence in voice messaging and audiotex services. In 1990 Ameritech was chosen, along with Bell Atlantic, to purchase New Zealand's public phone system for about $2.5 billion. The New Zealand deal was the most visible of the company's overseas initiatives. It created Ameritech International in 1990 to oversee alliances in Japan, France, the Netherlands, Denmark, and Spain.

Back in the US, Ameritech in 1991 pursued development, along with a unit of Household International, of a calling credit card, a first for a regional Bell operating company. It also acquired CyberTel, one of the 2 cellular firms in St. Louis, for $512 million. The competition in the St. Louis wireless market is former Bell sister Southwestern Bell, already a competitor in the Chicago cellular market.

WHO

Chairman and CEO: William L. Weiss, age 61, $1,295,000 pay
VC: Louis J. Rutigliano, age 52
VC: Ormand J. Wade, age 51, $715,000 pay
VC: William H. Springer, age 61, $660,000 pay
VC; President, Ameritech Bell Group: Robert L. Barnett, age 49, $735,000 pay
EVP and CFO: John A. Edwardson, age 41
SVP Human Resources: Martha L. Thornton, age 55
Auditors: Arthur Andersen & Co.
Employees: 75,780

WHERE

HQ: 30 S. Wacker Dr., Chicago, IL 60606
Phone: 312-750-5000
Fax: 312-207-1601

Ameritech's telephone companies operate in Illinois, Indiana, Michigan, Ohio, and Wisconsin.

WHAT

	1990 Sales	
	$ mil.	% of total
Local service	4,789	45
Interstate access	2,009	19
Intrastate access	559	5
Long distance	1,336	13
Directory & other	1,970	18
Total	**10,663**	**100**

Telephone Companies
Illinois Bell Telephone Co.
Indiana Bell Telephone Co., Inc.
Michigan Bell Telephone Co.
The Ohio Bell Telephone Co.
Wisconsin Bell, Inc.

Major Subsidiaries/Affiliates
Ameritech Audiotex Services
Ameritech Capital Funding Corp.
Ameritech Credit Corp.
Ameritech Development Corp.
Ameritech Enterprise Holdings, Inc.
Ameritech Information Systems, Inc.
Ameritech International, Inc.
Ameritech Mobile Communications
Ameritech Properties Corp.
Ameritech Publishing, Inc.
Ameritech Services, Inc.
Bellcore (14.28%, communications research)
Telecom Corporation of New Zealand, Ltd. (34.17%)
The Tigon Corp.

RANKINGS

8th in *Fortune* 50 Utilities
29th in *Business Week* 1000

KEY COMPETITORS

AT&T	MCI
Bell Atlantic	NYNEX
BellSouth	Pacific Telesis
British Telecom	Southwestern Bell
Cable & Wireless	Telefónica
Centel	Telmex
Ericsson	United Telecom
GTE	U S West
McCaw	

HOW MUCH

	6-Year Growth	1981	1982	1983	1984	1985	1986	1987	1988	1989	1990
Sales ($ mil.)	4.2%	—	—	—	8,347	9,021	9,362	9,536	9,903	10,211	10,663
Net income ($ mil.)	4.0%	—	—	—	991	1,078	1,138	1,188	1,237	1,238	1,254
Income as % of sales	—	—	—	—	11.9%	11.9%	12.2%	12.5%	12.5%	12.1%	11.8%
Earnings per share ($)	5.7%	—	—	—	3.39	3.67	3.94	4.24	4.54	4.58	*4.73*
Stock price – high ($)	—	—	—	—	26.00	35.50	50.75	49.94	48.94	68.25	69.75
Stock price – low ($)	—	—	—	—	20.79	24.83	32.67	37.00	41.00	46.88	52.50
Stock price – close ($)	17.3%	—	—	—	25.58	35.50	44.17	42.31	47.88	68.00	66.75
P/E – high	—	—	—	—	8	10	13	12	11	15	15
P/E – low	—	—	—	—	6	7	8	9	9	10	11
Dividends per share ($)	8.3%	—	—	—	2.00	2.20	2.40	2.55	2.76	2.98	3.22
Book value per share ($)	3.3%	—	—	—	24.08	25.51	26.61	27.71	29.14	28.45	29.25

1990 Year-end:
Debt ratio: 39.6%
Return on equity: 16.4%
Cash (mil.): $119
Current ratio: 0.54
Long-term debt (mil.): $5,074
No. of shares (mil.): 264
Dividends:
 1990 average yield: 4.8%
 1990 payout: 68.1%
Market value (mil.): $17,644

Stock Price History High/Low 1984–90

AMES DEPARTMENT STORES, INC.

OVERVIEW

Ames Department Stores operates 455 Ames stores (general merchandise discount stores), down from 690 stores in January 1990, and 15 Crafts & More stores (hobby and home crafts). The company also distributes wholesale sporting goods. Traditionally located in small towns in rural areas and now also in metropolitan areas, Ames stores mainly serve middle- to lower-income customers.

Ames was reasonably profitable until it acquired money-losing Zayre in October 1988 in a controversial transaction that split the board. The turnaround effort proved too much for Ames, causing massive losses in 1989. Ames filed for Chapter 11 bankruptcy in April 1990 and has since brought in new management and aggressively lowered costs by closing stores.

Ames expects to emerge from Chapter 11 in the first half of 1992, but initial financial projections for emergence have been reduced owing to the continued recession in the Northeast and the entry of Wal-Mart into its territories.

WHEN

Ames Department Stores was started in 1958 in the former Ames Worsted Textile Company building in Southbridge, Massachusetts, by Milton and Irving Gilman, who believed that discount retail stores would succeed in small towns. Ames had $1 million in sales the first year.

The Gilmans opened additional stores in abandoned factory buildings in upstate New York and northern Vermont (1960). The company went public (1962), and by 1970 there were 23 Ames stores, with $50 million in sales.

In the 1970s and 1980s the company built new stores and bought other chains in the Northeast. As established retailers closed, Ames moved in. Acquisitions included Joseph Leavitt and K&R Warehouse (1972), Davis Wholesale (1978), Neisner Brothers' (1978), King's (1984), G.C. Murphy's (1985), and the Zayre Discount Division of Zayre Corporation (now TJX Companies), with 392 stores for $800 million (1988). Ames opened its Crafts & More stores in 1988.

After the Gilmans retired, nonfamily members assumed leadership. Peter Hollis, formerly of Zayre, became president (1986) and CEO (1987).

Although the company closed 74 Zayre stores, conversion of the remaining stores to Ames's format was costly and slow. Sales decreased at the former Zayres, which lost traditional customers when management eliminated periodic sales in favor of an "everyday low prices" policy.

The company tried to raise capital in May 1989 by selling the Zayre shoe concession to J. Baker for $60 million. In September 1989 Ames sold 130 G.C. Murphy stores and 25 Bargain World stores to the Riklis's E-II Holdings for $77.6 million. The sale of convertible bonds in October 1989 raised $155 million more.

Efforts to trim costs included corporate restructuring, consolidation of Zayre and Ames stores, and store closings (6 Office Shop Warehouse stores in December 1989). As the company's cash flow decreased, unpaid vendors refused to ship new merchandise in early 1990. In April 1990, Ames filed for Chapter 11 bankruptcy and Hollis resigned. Stephen Pistner, former chief of Dayton Hudson's Target and of Montgomery Ward, became CEO.

Since entering Chapter 11, Ames has obtained $250 million in interim financing from Chemical Bank and closed over 227 discount stores, laying off over 20,000 employees. More cuts are planned. Contributing to Ames's fiscal 1990 loss of $793 million were $374 million in costs associated with the restructuring and closing of stores and $22.5 million in miscellaneous professional and legal costs of the Chapter 11 action. Ames plans to concentrate new advertising campaigns and expanded product lines at 124 selected "high impact" stores.

NYSE symbol: ADD
Fiscal year ends: Last Saturday in January

WHO

Chairman and CEO: Stephen L. Pistner, age 59, $1,717,689 pay
President and COO: George M. Granoff, age 44, $669,902 pay
EVP and CFO: Peter Thorner, age 47, $346,385 pay
EVP Merchandising, Advertising: Gerald L. Kanter, age 56, $259,571 pay
Manager Human Resources: Lois Hobbes
Auditors: Coopers & Lybrand
Employees: 35,000

WHERE

HQ: 2418 Main St., Rocky Hill, CT 06067
Phone: 203-563-8234
Fax: 203-257-7806 (Investor and Public Relations)

Ames operates 455 Ames discount stores in 17 eastern, southern, and midwestern states and in Washington, DC; 15 Crafts & More stores in 8 states; and a wholesale sporting goods company.

State	January 1991 Ames discount stores	Crafts & More stores
Connecticut	17	1
Delaware	10	—
District of Columbia	1	—
Indiana	14	—
Kentucky	2	—
Maine	29	1
Maryland	41	1
Massachusetts	42	—
Michigan	13	—
New Hampshire	23	—
New Jersey	8	—
New York	92	—
North Carolina	—	2
Ohio	37	2
Pennsylvania	61	2
Rhode Island	7	—
South Carolina	—	2
Vermont	13	—
Virginia	29	4
West Virginia	16	—
Total Stores	**455**	**15**

WHAT

	Jan. 1991	Fall 1990	Jan. 1990
Ames stores	455	458	690
Crafts & More	15	15	15
Total Stores	**470**	**473**	**705**

Other Companies
Mathews & Boucher (wholesale sporting goods)

RANKINGS

36th in *Fortune* 50 Retailing Cos.
236th in *Forbes* Sales 500

KEY COMPETITORS

Dayton Hudson	Stop & Shop
Kmart	Wal-Mart
Price Co.	Woolworth
Riklis Family	Department and
Sears	specialty stores

HOW MUCH

	9-Year Growth	1981	1982	1983	1984	1985	1986	1987	1988	1989	1990
Sales ($ mil.)	27.4%	353	402	617	783	1,449	1,810	2,027	3,271	4,793	3,109
Net income ($ mil.)	—	10	12	20	29	40	27	33	47	(220)	(793)
Income as % of sales	—	2.8%	3.1%	3.2%	3.6%	2.8%	1.5%	1.6%	1.4%	(4.6%)	(25.5%)
Earnings per share ($)	—	0.47	0.50	0.77	1.00	1.19	0.73	0.88	1.20	(6.19)	(21.47)
Stock price – high ($)	—	3.88	6.13	13.22	15.25	26.88	34.63	29.75	18.75	20.00	10.63
Stock price – low ($)	—	2.04	3.33	5.29	8.50	12.25	19.25	7.50	10.50	8.75	0.47
Stock price – close ($)	(18.3%)	3.48	5.58	11.88	13.44	25.38	23.63	10.38	14.00	10.38	0.56
P/E – high	—	8	12	17	15	23	47	34	16	—	—
P/E – low	—	4	7	7	9	10	26	9	9	—	—
Dividends per share ($)	(10.3%)	0.07	0.07	0.07	0.10	0.10	0.10	0.10	0.10	0.10	0.03
Book value per share ($)		2.50	3.08	3.80	4.75	9.87	10.51	11.34	12.43	5.65	(15.47)

1990 Year-end:
Debt ratio: (23.8%)
Return on equity: —
Cash (mil.): $453
Current ratio: 4.92
Long-term debt (mil.): $84
No. of shares (mil.): 38
Dividends:
1990 average yield: 4.4%
1990 payout: —
Market value (mil.): $21

Stock Price History High/Low 1981–90

AMGEN INC.

NASDAQ symbol: AMGN
Fiscal year ends: December 31

Hoover's Rating A+

OVERVIEW

Headquartered near Los Angeles, Amgen is the largest independent biotechnology concern in the US and a dream come true for many stockholders. During 1990 alone profits rose 80% and revenues doubled, and the company shows little sign of slowing down.

Amgen's phenomenal success rests almost completely upon 2 products developed using recombinant DNA technology (popularly known as "gene splicing"). Epogen, which hit the market in 1989 and promises to deliver sales of over $300 million in 1991, is a red blood cell stimulator used to treat anemia in renal dialysis patients. Neupogen, which

stimulates production of infection-fighting white blood cells in chemotherapy patients, was released in 1991 and is expected to generate sales of between $150 and $250 million by the end of the year.

R&D plays a crucial role in Amgen's operations. In 1990 the company spent 22% of sales on research efforts. Nevertheless, the company has not introduced any more products that promise to live up to the standards set by Epogen and Neupogen. To remedy the problem, Amgen has started licensing promising products from other biotech companies.

WHEN

Amgen was formed as Applied Molecular Genetics in 1980 when a group of scientists and venture capitalists banded together with the common goal of developing human and animal health care products based on molecular biological technology. George Rathmann, a VP at Abbott Laboratories who was conducting research at UCLA, was recruited as the company's CEO and first employee. Under Rathmann, who decided to aim towards developing a few potentially profitable products rather than conducting general research, the company was able to raise $19 million to support Amgen's initial efforts. For its headquarters location, the company selected Thousand Oaks, California, because of its proximity to such important research centers as the California Institute of Technology, UCLA, and UC Santa Barbara.

Amgen operated dangerously close to bankruptcy until company scientist Fu-Kuen Lin cloned the human protein erythropoietin (EPO), which stimulates red blood cell production in the body, in 1983. Amgen made its first public stock offering of 2.4 million shares that same year.

On the basis of Lin's important discovery, the company was able to form a joint venture with Kirin Brewery (Japan) in 1984 to develop and market EPO. The 2 companies also col-

laborated on the development of recombinant human granulocyte colony-stimulating factor (G-CSF), another human protein that stimulates the body's immune system to combat bacterial infection.

Other marketing ventures followed. In 1985 Amgen established a marketing agreement with Ortho Pharmaceutical Corporation, a subsidiary of Johnson & Johnson (the latter filed a suit against Amgen in 1989 for breaking the agreement and was awarded $164 million in damages in 1991), and in 1988 created a tie with Roche Holdings. Company fortunes (and stock) soared in 1989 when the FDA granted Amgen a license to produce Epogen (the brand name of its EPO) to treat anemia. In 1990 the company invested $26 million in Regeneron Pharmaceuticals, a Tarrytown, New York, company involved in the development of neurotrophic (nerve cell growth) products.

In 1991 Amgen was granted approval to market Neupogen, the brand name of its G-CSF for treatment of chemotherapy patients; other uses of the drug are in clinical trials. That same year the company won a major legal victory in Federal court when rival company Genetics Institute was denied permission to market its version of EPO, effectively granting Amgen a monopoly on the lucrative product.

WHO

Chairman and CEO: Gordon M. Binder, age 55, $456,134 pay
SVP, Secretary, and General Counsel: Arthur F. Staubitz
SVP Research: Daniel Vapnek, age 52, $300,075 pay
VP Finance and CFO: Lowell E. Sears, age 40
VP Human Resources: William F. Puchlevic
Auditors: Ernst & Young
Employees: 1,179

WHERE

HQ: 1840 Dehavilland Dr., Thousand Oaks, CA 91320-1789
Phone: 805-499-5725
Fax: 805-499-9315

Amgen has offices in Belgium, Canada, France, Germany, Italy, the Netherlands, Puerto Rico, Spain, Switzerland, the UK, and the US.

WHAT

Products
Clinigen (anemia testing kit)
EGF (tissue growth factor, in clinical trials)
Epogen
Neupogen
PDGF (tissue growth factor, in clinical trials)

Research Reagents
Recombinant interleukins
Interferons
Growth factors
DNA probes
Hematopoietic factors

Key Strategic Alliances
Abbott Laboratories
Kirin Brewery Company
Roche Holdings

RANKINGS

134th in *Business Week* 1000

KEY COMPETITORS

American Cyanamid
American Home Products
Bayer
Bristol-Myers Squibb
Ciba-Geigy
Dow Chemical
Du Pont
Eli Lilly
Glaxo
Hoechst
Johnson & Johnson
Merck
Monsanto
Pfizer
Rhône-Poulenc
Sandoz
Schering-Plough
SmithKline Beecham
Syntex
Upjohn
Warner-Lambert

HOW MUCH

	9-Year Growth	1981	1982	1983	1984	1985	1986	1987	1988	1989	1990
Sales ($ mil.)	—	—	0	3	7	21	30	44	70	190	381
Net income ($ mil.)	—	—	(7)	(5)	(8)	1	1	2	(8)	19	34
Income as % of sales	—	—	—	—	—	2.6%	2.6%	3.9%	(11.6%)	10.0%	9.0%
Earnings per share ($)	—	—	(0.51)	(0.09)	(0.12)	0.01	0.01	0.02	(0.08)	0.18	0.24
Stock price – high ($)	—	—	—	2.75	1.38	2.63	4.90	7.46	6.04	10.04	21.17
Stock price – low ($)	—	—	—	0.98	0.63	0.77	2.06	2.67	4.21	5.17	7.17
Stock price – close ($)	—	—	—	1.21	0.83	2.25	3.69	5.17	5.63	8.17	20.75
P/E – high	—	—	—	—	—	315	588	448	—	56	87
P/E – low	—	—	—	—	—	93	248	160	—	29	29
Dividends per share ($)	—	—	0.00	0.00	0.00	0.00	0.00	0.00	0.00	0.00	0.00
Book value per share ($)	—	—	(0.42)	0.70	0.58	0.96	0.98	1.63	1.59	1.80	3.14

1990 Year-end:
Debt ratio: 3.1%
Return on equity: 9.9%
Cash (mil.): $157
Current ratio: 3.17
Long-term debt (mil.): $13
No. of shares (mil.): 127
Dividends:
  1990 average yield: 0.0%
  1990 payout: —
Market value (mil.): $2,628

Stock Price History High/Low 1983–90

AMOCO CORPORATION

NYSE symbol: AN
Fiscal year ends: December 31

Hoover's Rating **C+**

OVERVIEW

Chicago-based Amoco is the 2nd largest US natural gas producer, 7th largest US crude oil producer, and the western world's 9th largest petroleum company. Its 3 principal businesses are petroleum refining and marketing, oil and gas exploration and production, and chemical manufacturing. Amoco operates in more than 40 countries.

Amoco owns more North American natural gas reserves than any other company. It hopes that environmental concerns will help push the fuel as an alternative to gasoline.

The company's symbol, the familiar torch on a red, white, and blue oval background, appears with Amoco's fuel and oil brand names: American, Amoco, Standard (in the Midwest), LDO, and Permalube. The company sells batteries and tires under the Atlas name. It also manufactures chemicals used in polyester fibers, plastics, and synthetic rubber.

WHO

Chairman, President, and CEO: H. Laurance Fuller, age 52, $1,142,072 pay (prior to promotion)
VC: Richard H. Leet, age 64, $768,289 pay
EVP and CFO: Frederick S. Addy, age 59
VP Human Resources: R. Wayne Anderson, age 49
Auditors: Price Waterhouse
Employees: 54,524

WHEN

John D. Rockefeller organized the Standard Oil Trust in 1882. In 1886 he risked buying Lima (Ohio) crude oil and storing it, believing someone would develop a process to remove the sulphur from this high-sulphur crude. In 1889 Standard Oil organized Standard Oil of Indiana (Chicago) as its upper midwestern subsidiary, turning over its new Whiting, Indiana, refinery to the subsidiary. In 1887 chemist Herman Frasch patented a copper oxide process that removed sulphur from crude. Certain that the process would work on a commercial scale, Frasch persuaded the company to try it on the Lima crude, a success that assured Standard Oil (Indiana) a continued oil supply.

Standard (Indiana) built a strong retail marketing organization, including company-owned service stations, and set up a research laboratory at the refinery, both innovations in the industry.

In 1911 the Supreme Court ordered Standard Oil to split up because of antitrust violations, creating 33 new independent oil companies. The decision left Standard (Indiana) with only 2 operations, oil refining and domestic marketing, and its exclusive right to the Standard name in the Midwest. The company purchased its crude oil and transportation from ex-Standard sisters Prairie Oil & Gas and Prairie Pipe Line.

In 1917 Standard (Indiana) began buying crude oil production companies. In 1925 the company purchased a controlling interest (81% by 1929) in Pan American Petroleum and Transport, one of the world's largest crude producers, with production facilities in Mexico and Venezuela. In 1923 Pan American bought a 50% interest in American Oil, founded in 1922 by Louis Blaustein. He had introduced the first antiknock gasoline, marketed under the Amoco name. Standard (Indiana), recognizing the additional value of oil converted to chemicals, began Amoco Chemicals in 1945.

In 1956 the company purchased Utah Oil Refining, along with other refineries in the 1950s and 1960s. The supertanker *Amoco Cadiz* ran aground off the French coast in 1978, spilling 120,000 tons of oil (6 times more than the 1989 *Exxon Valdez* oil spill off the Alaskan coast), resulting in a $128 million judgment against the company in 1990. Standard (Indiana) bought Cyprus Mines (copper and industrial minerals) in 1979. The company exited the industrial minerals, metals, and coal businesses by spinning off the assets of Amoco Minerals (including Cyprus Mines) as Cyprus Minerals in 1985.

Standard (Indiana) changed its name to Amoco in 1985. In 1988 Amoco bought debt-ridden but resource-rich Dome Petroleum of Canada, making Amoco the largest private owner of North American natural gas reserves. In 1990 the company sold its life insurance operation and sold its UK refining and marketing operations to Elf Aquitaine of France. Laurance Fuller took over as CEO from retiring Richard Morrow in 1991.

WHERE

HQ: 200 E. Randolph Dr., Chicago, IL 60601
Phone: 312-856-6111
Fax: 312-856-2460

Amoco operates in more than 40 countries.

	1990 Sales		1990 Operating Income	
	$ mil.	% of total	$ mil.	% of total
US	22,816	73	1,583	40
Canada	3,207	10	413	11
Europe	2,200	7	444	11
Other foreign	3,132	10	1,488	38
Adjustments	(3,345)	—	(1,122)	—
Total	**28,010**	**100**	**2,806**	**100**

WHAT

	1990 Sales		1990 Operating Income	
	$ mil.	% of total	$ mil.	% of total
Chemicals	4,087	13	252	6
Exploration & production	4,126	13	3,220	82
Refining, mktg. & transportation	23,000	74	554	14
Other	142	—	(98)	(2)
Adjustments	(3,345)	—	(1,122)	—
Total	**28,010**	**100**	**2,806**	**100**

Lines of Business
Chemical manufacturing
Marketing of refined products and chemicals
Oil and gas exploration and production
Petroleum refining
Transportation of refined products

Other Operations
Amoco Technology Co. (lasers, solar power, biotechnology)
AmProp, Inc. (real estate)
Canmar (offshore drilling)
Oki Tedi gold and copper project (30%, Papua New Guinea)
Syncrude (3.75%, synthetic fuels)

RANKINGS

12th in *Fortune* 500 Industrial Cos.
12th in *Business Week* 1000

KEY COMPETITORS

AMAX	Imperial Oil	Pemex
Ashland	Koch	Phillips
Atlantic Richfield	Mobil	Petroleum
British	Norsk Hydro	Royal Dutch/Shell
Petroleum	Occidental	Sun
Broken Hill	Oryx	Texaco
Chevron	Pennzoil	Unocal
Coastal	Petrofina	USX
Du Pont	Petrobrás	Chemical
Elf Aquitaine	PDVSA	companies
Exxon		

HOW MUCH

	9-Year Growth	1981	1982	1983	1984	1985	1986	1987	1988	1989	1990
Sales ($ mil.)	(0.7%)	29,947	28,073	27,635	26,949	26,922	18,281	20,174	21,150	23,966	28,010
Net income ($ mil.)	(0.1%)	1,922	1,826	1,868	2,183	1,953	747	1,360	2,063	1,610	1,913
Income as % of sales	—	6.4%	6.5%	6.8%	8.1%	7.3%	4.1%	6.7%	9.8%	6.7%	6.8%
Earnings per share ($)	1.6%	3.28	3.13	3.20	3.85	3.71	1.46	2.66	4.00	3.12	3.77
Stock price – high ($)	—	40.00	28.13	27.50	30.31	35.13	36.06	45.13	40.13	55.75	60.38
Stock price – low ($)	—	23.63	16.75	19.13	24.06	25.13	26.56	28.50	33.81	36.81	49.25
Stock price – close ($)	8.1%	26.00	19.88	25.38	26.44	30.94	32.63	34.50	37.50	54.63	52.38
P/E – high	—	12	9	9	8	9	25	17	10	18	16
P/E – low	—	7	5	6	6	7	18	11	8	12	13
Dividends per share ($)	5.1%	1.30	1.40	1.40	1.50	1.65	1.65	1.65	1.75	1.90	2.04
Book value per share ($)	5.0%	18.06	19.55	21.29	23.07	22.39	22.14	23.50	25.80	26.75	28.03

1990 Year-end:
Debt ratio: 27.2%
Return on equity: 13.8%
Cash (mil.): $2,399
Current ratio: 1.21
Long-term debt (mil.): $5,249
No. of shares (mil.): 502
Dividends:
 1990 average yield: 3.9%
 1990 payout: 54.1%
Market value (mil.): $26,290

Stock Price History High/Low 1981–90

AMP INC.

OVERVIEW

AMP (pronounced "amp," not A-M-P) of Harrisburg, Pennsylvania, is the world's largest supplier of electrical and electronic connectors. It supplies more than 50,000 electrical and electronic equipment manufacturers with over 100,000 different types and sizes of terminals, splices, and connectors, as well as cable and panel assemblies, switches, and touch-screen data entry systems. Over 50% of AMP's sales and earnings come from its international operations.

AMP holds nearly 13,000 patents worldwide and adds dozens more each year. The company spends a relatively large amount on R&D (9% of sales annually), and technical staff make up over 15% of AMP's total workforce. New products (those introduced within the past 5 years) have made up between 15% and 20% of AMP's total sales for many years. AMP is also the leading connector supplier to the computer industry; IBM is the company's largest customer.

NYSE symbol: AMP
Fiscal year ends: December 31

 Hoover's Rating **A**

WHO

Chairman and CEO: Harold A. McInnes, age 63, $576,599 pay
President and COO: James E. Marley, age 55, $471,867 pay
EVP and CFO: Benjamin Savidge, age 61, $332,178 pay
VP Human Resources: Philip G. Guarneschelli, age 58
Auditors: Arthur Andersen & Co.
Employees: 24,700

WHEN

U. A. Whitaker founded Aircraft-Marine Products of Elizabeth, New Jersey, in 1941, just 2 months before the attack on Pearl Harbor. As a manufacturer of parts for aircraft, ships, and radios, AMP grew rapidly during WWII. In 1943 the company moved to Harrisburg, Pennsylvania. A preinsulated electrical terminal and a special crimping tool invented in 1943 would later become AMP's mainstay.

The company nearly failed in its transition to a peacetime economy, with profits dropping sharply in 1946. Focusing on commercial markets, primarily for its electrical terminal, the company was doing well again by the 1950s. In 1956 the company went public, shortening its name to AMP.

AMP began international expansion in the 1950s, forming 10 subsidiaries in other countries, including Canada, Japan, France, and West Germany. AMP's success is partially attributed to a policy of rapidly building plants wherever it had a market for its products and carefully adapting to foreign requirements. When Fiat needed electrical connectors for its cars, the company built a plant in Italy in 1959. AMP entered the ranks of the *Fortune* 500 in 1966 with sales of $142 million.

In the 1970s and 1980s, AMP developed new connecting devices for manufacturers of computers, telecommunications equipment, and home entertainment systems. AMP's electrical components were used in the high-speed French TGV railroad and the Washington Metro.

Expanding production in the early 1980s resulted in an excess of capacity, causing an earnings drop after the 1982 economic slowdown. The company invested in plant modernization in the mid-1980s and in the last 5 years has saved an estimated $60 million through additional quality-control measures.

AMP spent $100 million in the 1980s developing fiber-optics technology and now has several high-speed fiber-optics devices on the market. It also introduced new cable and data communication connectors, now standard on local area networks such as Ethernet and IBM's Token Ring. New products in the late 1980s were AMP's "smart" connectors and undercarpet flat cables for offices.

Expansion into the Far East continued in 1987 with the opening of plants in Taiwan, South Korea, and Singapore. AMP has avoided diversification and has grown instead by inventing new devices. The company has recently entered several new markets through acquisitions (including Matrix Science, 1988; Garry Screw Machine, 1989; Switzerland's Decolletage S.A. St-Maurice, 1989; and Kaptron, 1990) and through a joint venture with Akzo of the Netherlands (1990). In 1990 the company completed a restructuring of US operations in which its market sectors were consolidated and its R&D operation reoriented.

WHERE

HQ: PO Box 3608, Harrisburg, PA 17105-3608
Phone: 717-564-0100
Fax: 717-986-7605

AMP has 165 office, warehouse, distribution, and manufacturing facilities in 11 states, Puerto Rico, and 27 other countries, and it plans to add 11 more facilities in 1990–91.

	1990 Sales		1990 Net Income	
	$ mil.	% of total	$ mil.	% of total
US	1,237	41	133	46
Europe	1,072	35	104	36
Asia/Pacific	583	19	42	15
Americas	152	5	8	3
Total	**3,044**	**100**	**287**	**100**

WHAT

	1990 Sales
Market	**% of total**
Aerospace/military	5
Industrial/commercial	10
Communications	10
Computer/office	20
Consumer goods	10
Transportation/electrical	30
Distribution, construction, etc.	15
Total	**100**

Products
Electrical/electronic connection devices
Machines and tools for applying connectors
Printed circuit boards
Screw machines

Affiliates, Joint Ventures, and Subsidiaries
AMP Packaging Systems, Inc. (panel assemblies; Austin, TX)
AMP Products Corp. (Valley Forge, PA)
AMP-AKZO Corp. (50%; Long Island, NY)
Carroll Touch, Inc. (touch screen systems; Austin, TX)
Garry Screw Machine Corp. (small metal parts; New Brunswick, NJ)
Kaptron, Inc. (optoelectronic devices; Palo Alto, CA)
Lytel Inc. (optoelectronic devices; Somerville, NJ)
Mark Eyelet Inc. (sockets; Wolcott, CT)
Matrix Science Corp. (aerospace and military connectors; Torrance, CA)
Pamcor, Inc. (Rio Piedras, Puerto Rico)

RANKINGS

152nd in *Fortune* 500 Industrial Cos.
114th in *Business Week* 1000

KEY COMPETITORS

Hitachi   SCI Systems   Thiokol
3M   Square D

HOW MUCH

	9-Year Growth	1981	1982	1983	1984	1985	1986	1987	1988	1989	1990
Sales ($ mil.)	10.5%	1,234	1,243	1,515	1,813	1,636	1,933	2,318	2,670	2,797	3,044
Net income ($ mil.)	8.8%	135	119	163	201	108	164	250	319	281	287
Income as % of sales	—	10.9%	9.6%	10.8%	11.1%	6.6%	8.5%	10.8%	12.0%	10.0%	9.4%
Earnings per share ($)	8.9%	1.25	1.10	1.52	1.87	1.00	1.52	2.31	2.96	2.63	2.70
Stock price – high ($)	—	20.83	23.50	39.00	39.50	37.88	45.00	71.50	54.25	49.38	55.25
Stock price – low ($)	—	14.50	15.17	22.00	26.13	27.50	32.88	34.13	40.50	40.00	37.88
Stock price – close ($)	11.0%	16.96	22.71	38.13	33.38	36.00	36.13	46.75	44.50	44.50	43.50
P/E – high	—	17	21	26	21	38	30	31	18	19	20
P/E – low	—	12	14	15	14	28	22	15	14	15	14
Dividends per share ($)	14.6%	0.40	0.47	0.53	0.64	0.72	0.74	0.85	1.00	1.20	1.36
Book value per share ($)	11.9%	6.13	6.64	7.45	8.57	9.23	10.50	12.54	14.16	15.27	16.92

1990 Year-end:
Debt ratio: 3.3%
Return on equity: 16.8%
Cash (mil.): $460
Current ratio: 1.70
Long-term debt (mil.): $61
No. of shares (mil.): 106
Dividends:
  1990 average yield: 3.1%
  1990 payout: 50.4%
Market value (mil.): $4,609

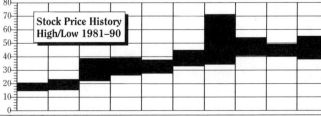

Stock Price History
High/Low 1981–90

AMR CORPORATION

OVERVIEW

NYSE symbol: AMR
Fiscal year ends: December 31

Hoover's Rating **C**

Until September 1991 (when Delta bought Pan Am's European routes), AMR's American Airlines and UAL's United were the world airline heavyweights. American still has the highest revenues of any airline and was recently rated in the Zagat Airline Survey as having the best service among US carriers.

To help maintain leadership, American is using acquisitions and marketing alliances to develop a more international route network. The airline is #1 in the US-to-Europe market, and, after buying Eastern's Latin American routes in 1990, it inaugurated flights to 20 Central and South American cities. Marketing agreements with Cathay Pacific, Air New Zealand, Qantas, and MALEV Hungarian Airlines have enhanced American's position in the Pacific and Eastern Europe. The airline now owns a 7.5% stake in Air New Zealand.

High fuel costs, a weak travel market, and a labor dispute with its pilots sent American into red ink in 1990 (along with many other US airlines). The company reached an agreement with its pilots early in 1991, but complete financial recovery may not occur until 1992.

WHO

Chairman, President, and CEO: Robert L. Crandall, age 55, $ 1,138,300 pay
EVP and CFO: Donald J. Carty, age 44, $666,667 pay
VP Employee Relations, American Airlines, Inc.: Ralph P. Craviso
Auditors: Ernst & Young
Employees: 102,809

WHERE

HQ: 4333 Amon Carter Blvd., Fort Worth, TX 76155
Phone: 817-963-1234
Fax: 817-967-9641
Reservations: 800-433-7300

American flies to 187 cities in the US and abroad.

Hub Locations

Chicago, IL	New York, NY
Dallas/Fort Worth, TX	Raleigh/Durham, NC
Miami, FL	San Jose, CA
Nashville, TN	San Juan, Puerto Rico

	1990 Sales
	% of total
US & Canada	84
Central & South America	6
Europe	9
Pacific	1
Total	**100**

WHEN

In 1929 Sherman Fairchild's Fairchild Aviation Corporation created a New York City holding company called The Aviation Corporation (AVCO). By 1930 AVCO owned about 85 small airline companies, which together formed an unconnected coast-to-coast network. Hoping to consolidate this route structure, AVCO created American Airways in 1930.

In 1934 new postal regulations forced AVCO to split up its aircraft making and transportation concerns. American Airlines was formed as a result and, through an exchange of stock, it bought American Airways.

With former AVCO manager C. R. Smith at the helm, American surpassed United as America's #1 airline in the late 1930s. The Douglas DC-3, built to Smith's specifications, was introduced into service by American in 1936 and became the first commercial airliner to pay its way on passenger revenues alone. Smith also emphasized American's safety record, directly addressing the public's fear of flying with his forthright "Afraid to Fly" advertisement in 1937.

After WWII, American bought American Export Airlines (renamed American Overseas Airlines), with flights to northern Europe, but sold this division to Pan Am in 1950. American formed Americana Hotels (a hotel subsidiary) in 1963 and introduced SABRE, the industry's first automated reservations system, in 1964.

In 1968 Smith left American to serve President Johnson as secretary of commerce.

American bought Trans Caribbean Airlines in 1971, gaining routes to the Caribbean. In 1977 Americana Hotels bought the Howard Corporation's hotel properties and by 1978 operated 21 hotels and resorts in the US, Latin America, and Korea. American had sold all of its hotels by 1987 except the Inn of the Six Flags at Arlington, Texas.

In 1979 American moved its headquarters from New York to Dallas/Fort Worth. Former CFO Bob Crandall became president in 1980 and, using SABRE to keep track of mileage, introduced the industry's first frequent flyer program (AAdvantage) in 1981. In 1982 American adopted AMR Corporation as its name. After acquiring Nashville Eagle (commuter airline) in 1987, AMR established AMR Eagle to operate commuter services, buying 4 new commuters in 1988 and 1989.

In 1989 AMR weathered an unsolicited takeover bid by Donald Trump and bought Eastern Air Lines's Latin American routes from Texas Air (now Continental Airlines Holdings). Late in 1990 the company offered $445 million for TWA's US–London routes (approved by the US and UK governments in 1991). In 1991 AMR spent $140 million to buy Continental's Seattle–Tokyo route and won DOT approval to fly to Manchester, England.

WHAT

	1990 Sales	
	$ mil.	% of total
Passengers	10,113	86
Cargo	430	4
Other	1,177	10
Total	**11,720**	**100**

Major Subsidiaries and Affiliates
American Airlines, Inc.
AMR Eagle, Inc. (commuter services)

Command Airways, Inc.	Simmons Airlines, Inc.
Executive Airlines, Inc.	West Wings Airlines, Inc.
Nashville Eagle, Inc.	

Computer Reservation System
SABRE

Flight Equipment	No.	Orders
A300	25	10
Boeing 727	164	—
Boeing 737	18	—
Boeing 747	2	—
Boeing 757	26	48
Boeing 767	45	17
DC-10	59	—
MD-80	213	47
Other	—	94
Total	**552**	**216**

RANKINGS

2nd in *Fortune* 50 Transportation Cos.
188th in *Business Week* 1000

KEY COMPETITORS

Alaska Air	KLM	Singapore
America West	Lufthansa	Airlines
British Airways	NWA	Southwest
Continental	Pan Am	TWA
Delta	Qantas	UAL
HAL	SAS	USAir
JAL		

HOW MUCH

	9-Year Growth	1981	1982	1983	1984	1985	1986	1987	1988	1989	1990
Sales ($ mil.)	12.4%	4,109	4,177	4,763	5,354	6,131	6,018	7,198	8,824	10,480	11,720
Net income ($ mil.)	—	17	(20)	228	234	346	279	198	477	455	(40)
Income as % of sales	—	0.4%	(0.5%)	4.8%	4.4%	5.6%	4.6%	2.8%	5.4%	4.3%	(0.3%)
Earnings per share ($)	—	0.26	(1.00)	4.48	4.16	5.88	4.63	3.28	7.66	7.15	(0.64)
Stock price – high ($)	—	21.63	25.75	39.13	41.25	50.75	62.13	65.50	55.00	107.50	70.25
Stock price – low ($)	—	8.63	9.00	18.50	24.25	33.50	39.25	26.75	32.63	52.13	39.75
Stock price – close ($)	17.9%	11.00	24.75	36.13	36.13	41.38	53.63	35.25	53.63	58.00	48.38
P/E – high	—	83	—	9	10	9	13	20	7	15	—
P/E – low	—	33	—	4	6	6	8	8	4	7	—
Dividends per share ($)	0.0%	0.00	0.00	0.00	0.00	0.00	0.00	0.00	0.00	0.00	0.00
Book value per share ($)	10.0%	25.42	22.45	26.87	31.23	37.17	42.30	45.58	53.54	60.54	59.83

1990 Year-end:
Debt ratio: 46.7%
Return on equity: —
Cash (mil.): $949
Current ratio: 0.55
Long-term debt (mil.): $3,272
No. of shares (mil.): 62
Dividends:
　1990 average yield: 0.0%
　1990 payout: 0.0%
Market value (mil.): $3,014

Stock Price History High/Low 1981–90

AMWAY CORPORATION

Private company
Fiscal year ends: August 31

Hoover's Rating B-

OVERVIEW

Headquartered in Ada, Michigan, a suburb of Grand Rapids, Amway is one of the world's largest direct sales organizations. The company sells its products through direct sales representatives (called distributors), who earn commissions not only on products but also on sales of new distributors they have recruited. In 1990 Amway had over one million distributorships worldwide, in more than 40 countries and territories. Amway is well known for its motivational rallies for distributors and for its near-religious devotion to free enterprise.

The company's many products include household and laundry cleaners such as Liquid Organic Cleaner (LOC); nutritional supplements such as Nutrilite vitamins; personal care products such as the Artistry cosmetics line; Queen cookware; educational books for children; and a number of services, including access to Amway's Ultimate legal network and its Motoring Plan.

Since the company's start, Amway has been environmentally conscious (LOC was biodegradable when it was introduced in 1959). Many of Amway's products are concentrated, the company does not engage in animal testing, and it sends its excess paper and plastic to recyclers.

The company also owns hotels in Michigan and the British Virgin Islands.

WHO

Chairman: Jay Van Andel, age 67
President: Richard M. DeVos, age 65
EVP and COO: William W. Nicholson
EVP Administration: Otto Stolz
VP Finance and Treasurer: James Rosloniec
VP Human Resources: Dwight Sawyer
Employees: 7,500

WHERE

HQ: 7575 East Fulton Rd., Ada, MI 49355-0001
Phone: 616-676-6000
Fax: 616-676-6177

Amway operates in the following countries and regions:

Australia	Malaysia
Canada	Mexico
The Caribbean	New Zealand
Hong Kong	Taiwan
Hungary	Thailand
Japan	US
Korea	Western Europe
Latin America	

WHEN

In the late 1950s Richard DeVos and Jay Van Andel, 2 Michigan friends who had ridden to high school together and had later jointly served in the Army Air Corps in WWII, became distributors for Nutrilite, a direct-sales vitamin company in California. Their business was so successful that they branched out into other ventures, including a health-foods bakery. In 1958, when Nutrilite's leadership was failing, DeVos and Van Andel decided to develop their own product line and founded the American Way Association (later shortened to Amway) in the basement of Van Andel's Ada, Michigan, home in 1959.

Amway's first product was a multipurpose liquid cleaner originally called Frisk and later renamed LOC (Liquid Organic Cleaner). The company began making laundry detergent, other household cleaners, and personal grooming products soon afterwards. Amway estimated its retail sales at $500,000 in 1960; by 1977 sales had reached $375 million. The company expanded its physical space as well, with 70 building projects, including factories and warehouses, between 1960 and 1978. Amway expanded to Australia in 1970, Europe in 1972, Hong Kong in 1974, Japan in 1979, and Taiwan in 1982.

In 1972 the company preserved its sales roots by purchasing Nutrilite. The following year Amway opened its Center for Free Enterprise (which included displays and an Amway museum) in Ada. The collection was later donated to Hillsdale College in Hillsdale, Michigan. In the late 1970s the company purchased the Mutual Broadcasting System, with radio stations in Chicago and New York (1977; sold in 1985 because of its lack of profitability); the Pantlind Hotel (1978, Grand Rapids), which was renovated and renamed the Amway Grand Plaza; and a resort in the Virgin Islands (1978). In 1981 Amway had estimated revenues of $1 billion.

In 1982, after several years of investigation by Canadian authorities, Van Andel and DeVos were indicted on charges of defrauding the Canadian government of $22 million in import duties. Amway pleaded guilty and paid $20 million in fines. From 1984 to 1986 the company experienced a sales slump during which revenues dropped to about $800 million from $1.2 billion in 1982, and following several suits alleging abusive sales practices, Amway brought in William Nicholson, former appointments secretary for President Gerald Ford, as an outside advisor to help the company reorganize. Amway then shifted to emphasizing sales training rather than evangelism. Company revenues rebounded to an estimated $1.5 billion in 1989.

Since beginning operations in Japan in 1979, Amway has had double-digit growth rates. In 1989 Amway, assisted by takeover specialist Irwin L. Jacobs, made a $2.1 billion buyout offer of Avon that the latter rejected. Prior to the offer Amway and Jacobs disclosed that they had bought 10.3% of Avon's stock.

In 1990 the company maintained a pace of rapid-fire international expansion, expanding its operations to Korea, Mexico, and Hungary. By the end of its 1991 fiscal year, Amway expects to sell $3 billion worth of products, which would bring it ever closer to catching its archnemesis Avon.

WHAT

Products

House care	Catalog merchandise
Air fresheners	Furniture
Bug spray	Luggage
Car-care items	Stereo systems
Dish detergents	Watches
Disinfectants	Education
Floor cleaners	Dictionaries
Furniture polish	*Encyclopedia*
Laundry products	*Americana*
Spot remover	*Grolier Atlas*
Vacuum cleaners	*Harvard Classics*
Health	Other
Diet products	Air purifiers
Vitamins	Alarm systems
Personal care	Canister sets
Cologne	Cookware
Cosmetics	Plant pots
Deodorant	Smoke detectors
Hairspray	Thermostats
Mouthwash	Water purifiers
Shampoo	
Sunscreens	**Hotels**
Toothpaste	Amway Grand Plaza Hotel
Commercial products	(Grand Rapids, MI)
Institutional laundry	Peter Island Resort (British
products	Virgin Islands)
Janitorial supplies	

RANKINGS

78th in *Forbes* 400 US Private Cos.

KEY COMPETITORS

American Home	Dow Chemical	MacAndrews
Products	Electrolux	& Forbes
Avon	Estée Lauder	Maxwell
Black & Decker	Gillette	Maytag
Brown-Forman	Johnson	Owens-Illinois
Casio	& Johnson	Procter & Gamble
Clorox	S.C. Johnson	Ricklis Family
Colgate-	Johnson	Schering-Plough
Palmolive	Publishing	Teledyne
Corning	L'Oréal	Warner-Lambert
Dial	LVMH	Unilever

HOW MUCH

	9-Year Growth	1981	1982	1983	1984	1985	1986	1987	1988	1989	1990
Estimated corporate revenues ($ mil.)	7.0%	1,000	1,200	1,130	—	1,200	800	550	1,477	1,513	1,842
Estimated retail sales ($ mil.)	6.3%	1,400	1,500	1,125	1,200	1,200	1,300	1,500	1,800	1,900	2,200

Estimated Retail Sales ($ mil.) 1981–90

ANHEUSER-BUSCH COMPANIES, INC.

NYSE symbol: BUD
Fiscal year ends: December 31

Hoover's Rating **A-**

OVERVIEW

Based in St. Louis, Anheuser-Busch is the largest brewer in the world. The company's US market share is a staggering 43.7%, and rising. Indeed, Anheuser-Busch's Budweiser brand (the world's best-selling beer) accounts for 1 out of every 3 beers sold in the US.

The driving force behind company dominance is a huge marketing effort. Hundreds of millions are spent yearly on promotions and sporting event sponsorships. The average American sees the Budweiser logo 10 times daily.

Although beer accounts for 76% of sales, Anheuser-Busch is 2nd only to Walt Disney in theme parks (Sea World, Busch Gardens) and through its Eagle Snacks subsidiary is launching an all-out assault on PepsiCo's Frito-Lay division.

Despite its domestic strength, the company exports only 3% of its beer output. Anheuser-Busch's international presence is maintained largely through licenses with such companies as Carlsberg, Suntory, and John Labatt. In 1991 the company was able to gain control of marketing and distribution of Budweiser in the UK from Grand Metropolitan. The company hopes to increase its presence in Europe by settling a long-standing trademark dispute with Czech brewer Budvar, whose own Budweiser brand has kept Anheuser-Busch out of the heart of Europe for more than 50 years.

WHEN

George Schneider founded the Bavarian Brewery in St. Louis in 1852. Unable to turn a profit, Schneider sold the brewery to Eberhard Anheuser in 1860. Anheuser's son-in-law Adolphus Busch joined the company in 1865 and in 1876 assisted restaurateur Carl Conrad in creating Budweiser, a light beer like those brewed in the Bohemian town of Budweis. The brewery's rapid growth was based in part on the popularity of Budweiser over heavier, darker beers.

In 1901 Budweiser became the 2nd American brewer to sell one million barrels annually. When Adolphus died in 1913, his son August took over the company, which was renamed Anheuser-Busch, Inc., in 1919. As beer vats lay dry during Prohibition (1920–33), August saved the company by selling yeast, refrigeration units, truck bodies, syrup, and soft drinks. When repeal came in 1933, Busch quickly resumed brewing, delivering a case of Budweiser to President Franklin Roosevelt in a carriage drawn by Clydesdale horses, which have since become the company's symbol. However, the tribulations of Prohibition had damaged August Busch's health, and he killed himself in 1934.

In 1953 Anheuser-Busch acquired the St. Louis Cardinals and 4 years later knocked Schlitz out of first place in the US brewing industry. In 1959 the company established its Busch Entertainment theme park division.

In 1970 Miller held 7th place in the industry, but tobacco giant Philip Morris acquired it and began a long, fierce challenge to Budweiser's leadership. By 1978 Miller had passed Schlitz and Pabst to take 2nd place, but Anheuser-Busch triumphed, becoming the first brewer to sell 40 million barrels a year. By 1980 the 2 foes produced over 50% of the beer sold in America, largely at the expense of smaller, independent breweries. In 1977 the company introduced Natural Light to counter the success of Miller Lite.

In 1982 Anheuser-Busch bought Campbell Taggart (baked goods) and created its Eagle snack foods unit. In 1989 the company acquired Sea World from Harcourt Brace Jovanovich.

To counter archrival Miller's successful Miller Genuine Draft (introduced in 1986), Anheuser-Busch has recently launched several new draft beers including its Michelob Golden Draft, which hit the market in 1991.

Also in 1991 August Busch IV, representing the 5th generation of Busches to work at the company, became senior brand manager for the critical Budweiser brand.

WHO

Chairman and President: August A. Busch III, age 53, $1,737,620 pay
EVP, CFO, and Chief Administrative Officer: Jerry E. Ritter, age 56, $903,062 pay
VP Human Resources: Stuart F. Meyer, age 57
Auditors: Price Waterhouse
Employees: 45,432

WHERE

HQ: One Busch Place, St. Louis, MO 63118
Phone: 314-577-3314
Fax: 314-577-2900

Anheuser-Busch has 12 breweries in the US.

WHAT

	1990 Sales		1990 Operating Income	
	$ mil.	% of total	$ mil.	% of total
Beer & beer prods.	8,151	76	1,455	91
Entertainment	625	6	58	4
Food products	1,982	18	86	5
Adjustments	(14)	—	—	—
Total	**10,744**	**100**	**1,599**	**100**

Brand Names

Beverages

Bud Light	King Cobra
Budweiser	Master Cellars Wines
Busch	Michelob
Carlsberg (imported)	Natural Light
Elephant Malt Liquor (imported)	O'Doul's (nonalcoholic)

Food and Snacks

Campbell Taggart (baked goods)	El Charrito (Mexican food)
Eagle Snacks (chips and nuts)	

Busch Entertainment Corp.

Adventure Island (water park, Tampa)
Baseball City Sports Complex (Orlando)
Busch Gardens/Sea World (theme parks)
Cypress Gardens (Winter Haven, Florida)
St. Louis Cardinals (baseball team)
Sesame Place (educational play park, Philadelphia)

Other Businesses

Anheuser-Busch International, Inc. (foreign licensing)
Anheuser-Busch Investment Capital Corporation (wholesalership investing)
Busch Agricultural Resources, Inc. (grain processing)
Busch Creative Services Corp. (communications)
Busch Properties, Inc. (real estate development; Kingsmill resort and Busch Stadium)
Container Recovery Corp. (recycling)
Manufacturers Railway Company
Metal Container Corp. (beverage containers)
Metal Label Corporation (label printing)
St. Louis Refrigerator Car Co. (railway car mfg.)

RANKINGS

44th in *Fortune* 500 Industrial Cos.
41st in *Business Week* 1000

KEY COMPETITORS

Adolph Coors	CPC	PepsiCo
Allied-Lyons	Foster's Brewing	Philip Morris
Bass	Gallo	Ralston Purina
Bond	Grand	RJR Nabisco
Borden	Metropolitan	San Miguel
Brown-Forman	Guinness	Stroh
BSN	Heineken	Tribune
Campbell Soup	Kirin	Turner
ConAgra	Mars	Broadcasting
	Matsushita	Walt Disney

HOW MUCH

	9-Year Growth	1981	1982	1983	1984	1985	1986	1987	1988	1989	1990
Sales ($ mil.)	12.1%	3,847	4,577	6,034	6,501	7,000	7,677	8,258	8,924	9,481	10,744
Net income ($ mil.)	16.3%	217	287	348	392	444	518	615	716	767	842
Income as % of sales	—	5.7%	6.3%	5.8%	6.0%	6.3%	6.7%	7.4%	8.0%	8.1%	7.8%
Earnings per share ($)	16.1%	0.77	0.98	1.08	1.23	1.42	1.69	2.04	2.45	2.68	2.95
Stock price – high ($)	—	7.35	11.79	12.83	12.40	22.88	29.06	40.13	34.38	46.00	45.25
Stock price – low ($)	—	4.60	6.44	9.75	8.96	11.81	19.75	25.75	29.00	30.63	34.00
Stock price – close ($)	22.6%	6.85	10.75	10.42	12.08	21.13	26.13	33.38	31.50	38.50	43.00
P/E – high	—	10	12	12	10	16	17	20	14	17	15
P/E – low	—	6	7	9	7	8	12	13	12	11	12
Dividends per share ($)	19.4%	0.19	0.23	0.27	0.31	0.37	0.44	0.54	0.66	0.80	0.94
Book value per share ($)	12.8%	4.42	5.27	6.08	6.91	7.84	8.61	9.87	10.95	10.95	13.03

1990 Year-end:
Debt ratio: 46.1%
Return on equity: 24.6%
Cash (mil.): $95
Current ratio: 1.01
Long-term debt (mil.): $3,147
No. of shares (mil.): 282
Dividends:
  1990 average yield: 2.2%
  1990 payout: 31.9%
Market value (mil.): $12,139

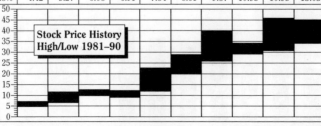

Stock Price History High/Low 1981–90

APPLE COMPUTER, INC.

OVERVIEW

Silicon Valley–based Apple Computer popularized the personal computer with the introduction of the Apple I in 1976. By 1990 Apple had become the world's 2nd largest PC maker (after IBM) with sales of $5.6 billion.

Apple's Macintosh, launched in 1984 and noted for its more intuitive graphical user interface, offered a distinct alternative to the IBM PC. In 1991 Apple shocked the computer industry by announcing a partnership with IBM to share basic technology and jointly develop new operating software.

Macintosh applications range from word processing and spreadsheets to desktop publishing and 3-D design work. Apple also develops interactive multimedia tools (text, video, animation, and sound) for instructional applications.

Education and business are Apple's principal markets. Apple hopes to reassert its dominance in the K-12 education market with its new low-cost Macintoshes. The new color Macintosh LC is targeted to replace the Apple II line, Apple's main education computer. Plans for introduction of notebook-sized computers (under joint development with Sony) and 2 high-end Macintoshes in late 1991, along with Apple's major upgrade to its operating system, System 7, should also boost its share of the business market.

WHEN

Two college dropouts, Steven Jobs and Stephen Wozniak, founded Apple in 1976 in the Santa Clara Valley. The original plan to sell circuit boards changed to selling fully assembled microcomputers after Jobs's first sales call resulted in an order for 50 units. They built the Apple I in Jobs's garage and sold it without a monitor, keyboard, or casing.

The initial demand for the Apple I made Jobs aware of the market for small computers. The choice of Apple as the company name (recalling the time Jobs spent on an Oregon farm) and the computer's "user-friendly" appearance set it apart from other companies' computers, making it appealing even to nontechnical buyers.

By 1977 Wozniak, who invented the Apple I, had substantially improved it by adding a keyboard, color monitor, and 8 slots for peripheral devices. This latter feature gave the new machine, the Apple II, considerable versatility and inspired numerous 3rd-party add-on devices and software programs.

By 1980 over 130,000 Apple II units had been sold. Revenues went from $7.8 million in 1978 to $117 million in 1980, and when Apple went public (1980), it did so with one of the largest stock offerings in recent history.

By 1983 Wozniak had left and Jobs had hired John Sculley from Pepsi to succeed Mike Markkula, the company's president. In 1985 Jobs left after a tumultuous power struggle.

Following the failure of the Apple III and Lisa computers (1983), Apple roared back in 1984 with the revolutionary Macintosh. Its introduction was preceded by an intriguing commercial, aired during the Super Bowl, that challenged chief rival IBM. Advertised as the computer "For the Rest of Us," it incorporated a graphical user interface inspired by Xerox's Alto computer. In 1986 Apple moved into the office market with the Mac Plus and the Laserwriter printer, a combination that ushered in the desktop-publishing revolution.

In 1990, citing the strategic importance of software, Apple reversed its decision to spin off its software subsidiary Claris. Following a slowdown in sales growth in 1990, Apple decided to gain market share with the introduction of 3 low-cost Macintosh computers. Shipments in the 2nd quarter of 1991 were up 85% over the same period in 1990. However, earnings were flat because of lower profit margins. To compensate, Apple cut expenses and announced a 10% staff reduction in 1991, the company's largest ever.

OTC symbol: AAPL
Fiscal year ends: Last Friday in September

WHO

Chairman and CEO: John Sculley, age 51, $2,198,866 pay
President and COO: Michael H. Spindler, age 48, $1,081,469 pay
EVP and CFO: Joseph A. Graziano, age 47, $1,292,913 pay
SVP Human Resources: Kevin J. Sullivan, age 49
EVP and Secretary: Albert A. Eisenstat, age 60
Auditors: Ernst & Young
Employees: 14,528

WHERE

HQ: 20525 Mariani Ave., Cupertino, CA 95014
Phone: 408-996-1010
Fax: 408-996-0275

The company has manufacturing facilities in California, Ireland, and Singapore. It does business in more than 120 countries and has 250 sales, distribution, and other offices worldwide.

	1990 Sales		1990 Operating Income	
	$ mil.	% of total	$ mil.	% of total
US	3,241	58	229	33
Europe	1,545	28	367	52
Other countries	772	14	104	15
Adjustments	—	—	46	—
Total	**5,558**	**100**	**746**	**100**

WHAT

Computers	Communication Products
Apple II	File servers
Macintosh II	Local and wide area
Macintosh IIsi	networks
Macintosh Classic	Modems
Macintosh LC	
Macintosh Plus	**Peripheral Products**
Macintosh Portable	Disk drives (floppy, hard,
Macintosh SE	CD-ROM)
	Monitors (monochrome
Software	and color)
A/UX	Printers (dot matrix, ink-
HyperCard	jet, and laser)
Macintosh OS	Scanner
MultiFinder	
ProDos	**Subsidiaries and Affiliates**
	Claris Corp. (software)
	General Magic Corp.

RANKINGS

95th in *Fortune* 500 Industrial Cos.
82nd in *Business Week* 1000

KEY COMPETITORS

Adobe	IBM
AT&T	Lucky-Goldstar
AST	Machines Bull
Atari	Matsushita
Canon	Microsoft
Commodore	NEC
Compaq	Oki
Daewoo	Olivetti
Dell	Prime
Data General	Sun Microsystems
DEC	Tandy
Fujitsu	Toshiba
Hewlett-Packard	Unisys
Hitachi	Wang
Hyundai	

HOW MUCH

	9-Year Growth	1981	1982	1983	1984	1985	1986	1987	1988	1989	1990
Sales ($ mil.)	36.6%	335	583	983	1,516	1,918	1,902	2,661	4,071	5,284	5,558
Net income ($ mil.)	31.9%	39	61	77	64	61	154	218	400	454	475
Income as % of sales	—	11.8%	10.5%	7.8%	4.2%	3.2%	8.1%	8.2%	9.8%	8.6%	8.5%
Earnings per share ($)	30.2%	0.35	0.53	0.64	0.53	0.50	1.20	1.65	3.08	3.53	3.77
Stock price – high ($)	—	17.25	17.44	31.63	17.19	15.56	21.94	59.75	47.75	50.38	47.75
Stock price – low ($)	—	7.13	5.38	8.63	10.88	7.13	10.88	20.06	35.50	32.50	24.25
Stock price – close ($)	16.3%	11.06	14.94	12.19	14.56	11.00	20.25	42.00	40.25	35.25	43.00
P/E – high	—	49	33	49	33	31	18	36	16	14	13
P/E – low	—	20	10	13	21	14	9	12	12	9	6
Dividends per share ($)	—	0.00	0.00	0.00	0.00	0.00	0.00	0.12	0.32	0.40	0.44
Book value per share ($)	25.7%	1.60	2.25	3.19	3.84	4.45	5.54	6.63	8.17	11.77	12.54

1990 Year-end:
Debt ratio: 0.0%
Return on equity: 31.0%
Cash (mil.): $997
Current ratio: 2.34
Long-term debt (mil.): $0
No. of shares (mil.): 115
Dividends:
 1990 average yield: 1.0%
 1990 payout: 11.7%
Market value (mil.): $4,960

Stock Price History High/Low 1981–90

THE ARA GROUP, INC.

OVERVIEW

The 1984 LBO that took ARA private is one of the most successful of the era, and ARA is now the largest food service company in the US, serving over 10 million people daily in over 400,000 locations worldwide.

The company also provides care for people of all ages, from childhood (Children's World Learning Centers) to old age (ARA Living Centers), and food services for people in all walks of life, from the top of society (Chicago's 95th Restaurant in the Hancock Building) to the bottom (Szabo Correctional Services). ARA serves people at work (ARA Environmental, janitorial services), at play (ARA Leisure), and at school (ARA Campus Dining), and provides reading material (ARA Magazine & Book Division), clothes (ARATEX uniform rental), and medical care (Spectrum Emergency Care).

Because ARA's businesses are so diverse, the potential for growth is great, and the company is taking advantage of its opportunities, especially in school catering, park concessions, and janitorial services.

WHEN

In 1959 Davidson Automatic Merchandising, owned by Davre Davidson of California, merged with a midwestern vending company owned by William Fishman. Davidson became chairman and CEO and Fishman became president of the new company, Automatic Retailers of America (changed to The ARA Group, Inc., in 1969).

ARA serviced mainly candy, beverage, and cigarette machines and by 1961 operated in 38 states and ranked first in sales among vending companies. ARA moved into food vending in the early 1960s, with clients such as the Southern Pacific Railway. Between 1959 and 1963 ARA acquired 150 local food service companies, including Slater Systems in 1961, which gave ARA a top spot in operating cafeterias at colleges, hospitals, and work sites. Davidson and Fishman eased ARA into manual vending, despite the slimmer profit margins, because it was less capital-intensive and more responsive to price changes than machines, which required nickel increases. Growth was so rapid the FTC stepped in, and ARA agreed to restrict future vending acquisitions.

ARA began diversifying into other service businesses such as publication distribution in 1967 and in 1970 expanded into janitorial and maintenance services by buying Ground Services (airline cleaning and loading services, sold 1990). In 1968 ARA provided food service at the Mexico City Olympics. Since then the company has provided service and management at 13 Olympiads.

In 1973 ARA acquired National Living Centers (now ARA Living Centers), which operates residential communities for the elderly. This acquisition also led to ARA's entry into emergency care, in which the company provides emergency room staff. A high percentage of revenues for these segments comes from Medicare and Medicaid payments. A 1976 joint venture with Mitsui & Company introduced ARA food services to Japan. ARA bought Work Wear (now ARATEX uniform rentals) in 1977 and National Child Care Centers in 1980.

In 1984 a former director, William Siegel, and 2 Texas-based partners offered chairman Joseph Neubauer $722 million for the company. Neubauer refused and, to avoid a hostile takeover, took the company private in a $1.2 billion deal. Since then ARA has repurchased shares from other investors (investment banks and employee-benefit plans) to increase management's stake to more than 90%. Stock ownership is now an incentive award for more than 900 managers. ARA has since become known for the loyalty it commands from its employees.

During the mid- to late-1980s, the company acquired Szabo (correctional food services, 1986), Cory Food Services (1986), and Children's World Learning Centers (1987). In 1990 ARA divested its airport ground handling service and won the hospitality concessions for Olympic National Park in Washington state.

In 1991 the company continued to expand by targeting smaller clients and investing in the nation's largest stadium management company — Spectacor. It also announced plans to promote, as a convention and meeting center, its concession facilities at Lake Powell National Recreation Area in Arizona and Utah.

Private company
Fiscal year ends: Friday nearest September 30

Hoover's Rating **C+**

WHO

Chairman, President, and CEO: Joseph Neubauer, age 49, $1,115,769 pay
SVP and CFO: James E. Ksansnak, age 51, $434,384 pay
VP Human Resources: Lynn McKee
Auditors: Arthur Andersen & Co.
Employees: 134,000

WHERE

HQ: 1101 Market St., Philadelphia, PA 19107
Phone: 215-238-3000
Fax: 215-238-3333

ARA operates in all 50 states and in Belgium, Canada, Germany, Japan, and the UK.

WHAT

	1990 Sales		1990 Operating Income	
	$ mil.	% of total	$ mil.	% of total
Food & leisure	2,698	59	126	45
Textile rental	689	15	73	26
Health & education	828	18	49	17
Distribution	381	8	33	12
Adjustments	—	—	(1)	—
Total	**4,596**	**100**	**280**	**100**

Food and Leisure Services
ARA Business Dining Services
ARA Campus Dining Services
ARA Healthcare Nutrition Services
ARA Leisure Services Group (park, stadium, and convention center concessions)
ARA School Nutrition Services
ARA/CORY Refreshment Services (coffee and soda services)
International Services
Parks and Fine Dining
Szabo Correctional Services (prison meals)

Textile Rental and Maintenance
ARA Environmental Services, Inc. (janitorial)
ARATEX Services, Inc. (uniform rental)
Encore Service Systems (building and grounds maintenance)
GMARA Industrial Cleaning (joint venture with GM)

Health and Education
ARA Living Centers, Inc. (nursing homes)
Children's World Learning Centers, Inc. (day care)
Correctional Medical Systems, Inc. (prison health care)
Spectrum Emergency Care, Inc. (physician staffing)

Distribution Services
ARA Magazine & Book Division, Inc.

RANKINGS

18th in *Forbes* 400 US Private Cos.

KEY COMPETITORS

Accor	Dial	Matsushita
Berkshire Hathaway	W. R. Grace	Ogden
	Marriott	TW Holdings

HOW MUCH

	9-Year Growth	1981	1982	1983	1984	1985[1]	1986	1987	1988	1989	1990
Sales ($ mil.)	5.2%	2,916	2,806	3,057	3,406	2,652	3,749	4,019	3,917	4,244	4,596
Net income ($ mil.)	1.6%	45	39	54	64	6	16	22	5	39	52
Income as % of sales	—	—	—	—	—	—	0.4%	0.5%	0.1%	0.9%	1.1%
Employees	—	—	—	—	—	—	115,000	119,000	120,000	125,000	134,000

1990 Year-end:
Debt ratio: 95.7%
Return on equity: 93.3%
Cash (mil.): $34
Current ratio: 1.09
Long-term debt (mil.): $1,111

Net Income ($ mil.) 1981–90

[1] Nine-month period due to change in fiscal year end

ARCHER-DANIELS-MIDLAND COMPANY

NYSE symbol: ADM
Fiscal year ends: June 30

Hoover's Rating A-

OVERVIEW

Based in Decatur, Illinois, Archer-Daniels-Midland (ADM) is a major processor, transporter, and marketer of agricultural products. The company is a leading processor of oilseeds in the US and ranks among the nation's largest flour millers and corn refiners. Other operations include grain storage and marketing, peanut shelling, rice milling, biochemical production, sugar refining, banking, and the production of food, feed, and malt products.

ADM's oilseed segment processes a number of seed types for the production of vegetable oil and high-grade food meals. ADM holds a trademark on textured vegetable protein (TVP) and produces a number of high-protein soy products.

The company's corn operations hold market leadership in fructose (31% share) and ethanol (corn alcohol used to make gasohol, 68%), while producing other products such as starch and sweeteners.

A friend of both Gorbachev and Yeltsin, CEO Dwayne Andreas has positioned ADM to land a commanding presence in the Soviet market. Through its 1990 purchase of 1/2 of Alfred C. Toepfer International (ACTI), ADM already handles 45% of Eastern Europe's commodities imports from the West.

The company has investments in Tate & Lyle (8%, owner of competitor A. E. Staley), International Multifoods Corp. (9.4%, specialty foods), and Arco Chemical (5%).

WHO

Chairman and CEO: Dwayne O. Andreas, age 72, $1,945,834 pay
President: James R. Randall, age 65, $916,667 pay
EVP: Michael D. Andreas, age 41, $566,667 pay
VP, Controller, and CFO: Douglas J. Schmalz, age 44
VP Employee Relations: Dale F. Benson, age 64
Auditors: Ernst & Young
Employees: 11,861

WHERE

HQ: 4666 Faries Pkwy., Box 1470, Decatur, IL 62525
Phone: 217-424-5200
Fax: 217-424-5839 (Public Relations)

	1990 Sales
	% of total
US	85
Other countries	15
Total	**100**

WHEN

In 1878 John W. Daniels started crushing flaxseed to produce linseed oil and in 1902 formed Daniels Linseed Company in Minneapolis. George A. Archer, another experienced flaxseed crusher, joined the company in 1903.

In 1923 the company bought Midland Linseed Products and adopted the name Archer-Daniels-Midland. During the 1920s the company started to conduct research (an uncommon practice at the time) on the chemical composition of linseed oil and acquired several other linseed oil companies.

ADM entered the flour milling business in 1930 with the purchase of Commander-Larabee (then the 3rd-ranking flour miller in the US). In the 1930s the company's research division discovered a method for extracting lecithin (a food additive used in candy and other products) from soybean oil.

After WWII ADM went through a period of rapid growth. By 1949 the company was the leading processor of linseed oil and soybeans in the US and was 4th in flour milling. During the early 1950s the company entered a period of foreign expansion and bought the resin division of US Industrial Chemicals (1954).

ADM encountered financial difficulty in the early 1960s due to fluctuating commodities

prices and losses in the chemical division. In 1966 the company's leadership passed to Dwayne O. Andreas, a former Cargill executive who purchased a block of Archer family stock (the Andreas family now owns some 8% of the company's stock). He sold the chemical division and bought Fleischmann Malting (malt for beer, etc.) in 1967.

Andreas, aware of the future potential of the soybean (which is about 50% protein once processed), prompted the company's effort to produce textured vegetable protein. In 1969 he established a plant in Decatur, Illinois, to produce edible soy protein.

Andreas's restructuring paved the way for productivity and expansion. In 1971 the company acquired Corn Sweeteners (glutens, high fructose syrups), which today also produces ethanol. Other acquisitions included Supreme Sugar (1973), Tabor (grain, 1975), and Columbian Peanut (1981); the latter made ADM the leading domestic sheller of peanuts.

The company continued to expand its domestic and global presence in the early 1990s through the purchases of Collingwood Grain (Kansas), and Pfizer's Citric Acid division. That same year ADM sold its White Lily Foods unit to Windmill Corporation.

WHAT

	1990 Sales
	% of total
Oilseed operations	48
Corn operations	30
Wheat flour operations	10
Other operations	12
Total	**100**

Divisions/Subsidiaries/Affiliates
ADM Biochem Products Division
ADM Corn Processing Division (corn prods. and ethanol)
ADM Europe BV
ADM Europoort BV (oilseed products)
ADM Far East Ltd.
ADM Feed Corp. (animal feeds and pet foods)
ADM Grain Co.
ADM International Ltd.
ADM Investor Services, Inc. (commodity hedging)
ADM Milling Co. (wheat, corn, rice, oats, and barley)
ADM Olmuhlen GmBH (oilseed products)
ADM Processing Division (soybean products and canola)
ADM Protein Specialties Division
ADM/GROWMARK
Agrinational Insurance Co.
Alfred C. Toepfer International (50%, trading, Germany)
American River Transportation (barges and term. facil.)
The British Arkady Co., Ltd. (vegetarian foods)
Collingwood Grain Co.
Compagnie Industrielle et Financier des Produits Amglaces SA (41.5%, agricultural processing)
Fleischmann-Kurth Malting Co., Inc. (barley malts)
Gooch Foods, Inc. (pasta)
Hickory Point Bank & Trust (banking)
Krause Milling Co.
Smoot Grain Co.
Southern Cotton Oil Co.
Supreme Sugar Co., Inc. (sugar refining)
Tabor Grain Co.

HOW MUCH

	9-Year Growth	1981	1982	1983	1984	1985	1986	1987	1988	1989	1990
Sales ($ mil.)	8.7%	3,647	3,713	4,292	4,907	4,739	5,336	5,775	6,798	7,929	7,751
Net income ($ mil.)	11.9%	176	155	110	118	164	239	265	353	425	484
Income as % of sales	—	4.8%	4.2%	2.6%	2.4%	3.5%	4.5%	4.6%	5.2%	5.4%	6.2%
Earnings per share ($)	9.3%	0.73	0.61	0.42	0.41	0.56	0.81	0.89	1.18	1.44	1.63
Stock price – high ($)	—	6.73	6.54	7.97	7.42	9.40	12.82	15.98	13.39	22.38	25.88
Stock price – low ($)	—	3.87	3.51	5.72	4.86	6.09	8.53	9.60	10.73	12.40	17.38
Stock price – close ($)	17.1%	5.52	6.47	6.32	6.34	9.05	10.08	12.24	12.62	22.02	22.75
P/E – high	—	9	11	19	18	17	16	18	11	16	16
P/E – low	—	5	6	13	12	11	10	11	9	9	11
Dividends per share ($)	10.2%	0.04	0.04	0.04	0.04	0.05	0.05	0.05	0.06	0.06	0.09
Book value per share ($)	12.4%	4.17	4.74	5.26	5.68	6.19	6.98	7.90	8.96	10.28	11.99

1990 Year-end:
Debt ratio: 17.4%
Return on equity: 14.6%
Cash (mil.): $829
Current ratio: 3.41
Long-term debt (mil.): $751
No. of shares (mil.): 298
Dividends:
1990 average yield: 0.4%
1990 payout: 5.3%
Market value (mil.): $6,778

Stock Price History High/Low 1981–90

RANKINGS

60th in *Fortune* 500 Industrial Cos.
89th in *Business Week* 1000

KEY COMPETITORS

Borden	CPC	Monsanto
Cargill	CSX	Quaker Oats
ConAgra	John Labatt	Salomon
Continental Grain	Mars	Other agribusinesses

ARMSTRONG WORLD INDUSTRIES, INC.

OVERVIEW

Armstrong World Industries is the largest domestic manufacturer and marketer of non-textile floor coverings (resilient flooring and ceramic tile) and is a leading manufacturer of other interior furnishings, including building products and furniture. The company also manufactures and markets specialty products for the automotive, textile, and other industries.

The company is divided into 4 operating segments: Floor Coverings, Building Products, Furniture, and Industry Products. Floor Coverings is the largest segment, with 1990 sales of nearly $1.1 billion. The Building Products division ($721 million) primarily produces acoustical ceiling materials and wall panels, as well as other specialty architectural products. The furniture segment ($436 million) manufactures both residential and commercial furniture through the company's Thomasville subsidiary. Industry Products ($278 million) includes pipe insulation, gasket materials, adhesives, and textile mill supplies.

Armstrong's dependence on weak domestic construction markets has dampened revenues and earnings in recent years. Overseas sales have been more encouraging, however, and management expects cost-cutting measures and new product introductions to provide stability until the US economy improves.

WHEN

Thomas Armstrong and John Glass started the Armstrong Brothers cork cutting shop in Pittsburgh in 1860. Armstrong carved the corks by hand, stamped his name on each one, and made his first deliveries in a wheelbarrow.

Concerned with fairness to his customers, Armstrong rejected the maxim of *caveat emptor* (let the buyer beware) and put a written guarantee in each of his burlap sacks of corks before shipping them. By the mid-1890s Armstrong Brothers was the largest cork company in the world. In 1895 the company changed its name to Armstrong Cork.

To compensate for the decreasing cork markets near the turn of the century (due to the invention of screw-top mason jars and spring bottle stoppers), the company found new uses for its cork in insulated corkboard and brick. In 1906 Armstrong Cork turned its attention to linoleum (which then was made with cork powder) and started building a new factory in Lancaster, Pennsylvania. Thomas Armstrong died in 1908, a year before the company's linoleum hit the market.

Armstrong continued to produce mainly flooring and insulating materials through the 1950s while establishing foreign operations (primarily in Canada, Europe, and Australia). During the 1960s the company expanded its line to include home furnishings by purchasing E & B Carpet Mills (1967) and Thomasville Furniture Industries (1968). In 1969 the company sold its packaging materials operations.

In 1980 the company dropped cork from its name and changed to Armstrong World Industries (the only cork the company still produces comes from a small Spanish plant and is mainly for champagne bottles). During the 1980s the company underwent rapid expansion with numerous acquisitions, including Applied Color Systems (computerized color systems, 1981; sold in 1989), Chemline Industries (chemicals, 1985), the W. W. Henry Company (adhesives and powder products, 1986), and American Olean (ceramic tile, 1988). In 1989 Armstrong sold its carpet operations; a hostile takeover attempt by the Canadian Belzberg family failed 11 months later.

Armstrong entered into a joint venture in 1990 with Internacional de Ceramica to manufacture ceramic tile in Mexico. In the first half of 1991 weak residential and commercial construction markets depressed earnings, while a $238 million antitrust verdict against the company (later overturned on appeal) precipitated shareholder lawsuits and a sharp drop in Armstrong stock values.

HOW MUCH

	9-Year Growth	1981	1982	1983	1984	1985	1986	1987	1988	1989	1990
Sales ($ mil.)	7.0%	1,376	1,286	1,439	1,569	1,679	1,920	2,365	2,680	2,513	2,531
Net income ($ mil.)	13.2%	47	20	63	92	101	122	150	163	154	143
Income as % of sales	—	3.4%	1.5%	4.4%	5.9%	6.0%	6.4%	6.4%	6.1%	6.1%	5.7%
Earnings per share ($)	13.4%	0.94	0.40	1.27	1.90	2.10	2.54	3.18	3.51	3.03	2.91
Stock price – high ($)	—	9.38	13.25	16.88	17.00	22.63	35.00	47.38	44.00	50.88	38.75
Stock price – low ($)	—	7.00	6.63	10.63	11.13	15.19	19.81	22.50	29.50	33.38	18.00
Stock price – close ($)	12.9%	8.38	12.38	13.81	16.81	22.31	29.88	32.25	35.00	37.25	25.00
P/E – high	—	10	34	13	9	11	14	15	13	17	13
P/E – low	—	7	17	8	6	7	8	7	8	11	6
Dividends per share ($)	8.4%	0.55	0.55	0.55	0.59	0.64	0.73	0.89	0.98	1.05	1.14
Book value per share ($)	3.9%	12.06	11.76	12.26	13.21	15.02	16.84	19.50	21.83	16.72	17.01

1990 Year-end:
Debt ratio: 35.8%
Return on equity: 17.3%
Cash (mil.): $25
Current ratio: 1.33
Long-term debt (mil.): $501
No. of shares (mil.): 37
Dividends:
1990 average yield: 4.5%
1990 payout: 39.0%
Market value (mil.): $927

Stock Price History
High/Low 1981–90

NYSE symbol: ACK
Fiscal year ends: December 31

Hoover's Rating B-

WHO

Chairman and President: William W. Adams, age 56, $622,239 pay
EVP: E. Allen Deaver, age 55, $359,837 pay
EVP: George A. Lorch, age 49, $359,497 pay
SVP Finance and Treasurer: William J. Wimer, age 56
VP Human Resources and Government Affairs: John N. Jordin
Auditors: KPMG Peat Marwick
Employees: 24,000

WHERE

HQ: PO Box 3001, Lancaster, PA 17604
Phone: 717-397-0611
Fax: 717-396-2126

The company operates 66 manufacturing facilities in the US and 17 in 10 other countries.

	1990 Sales		1990 Operating Income	
	$ mil.	% of total	$ mil.	% of total
US	1,851	73	253	75
Europe	506	20	72	21
Other countries	174	7	12	4
Adjustments	—	—	(101)	—
Total	**2,531**	**100**	**236**	**100**

WHAT

	1990 Sales		1990 Operating Income	
	$ mil.	% of total	$ mil.	% of total
Floor Coverings	1,096	43	131	39
Furniture	436	17	20	6
Industry Products	278	11	48	14
Building Products	721	29	139	41
Adjustments	—	—	(102)	—
Total	**2,531**	**100**	**236**	**100**

US Manufacturing Subsidiaries and Brand Names

American Olean Tile Company, Inc.
Homestyles
Triad

Armstrong World Industries, Inc.
Armaflex (insulation)
Cirrus (ceilings)
Components (flooring)
Fashion Tile
Glazecraft (flooring)
Solarian (flooring)
Sonotrol (wall panels)
Soundsoak (wall panels)
Taccents (wall panels)
Tubolit (insulation)

Chemline Industries, Inc.

Thomasville Furniture Industries, Inc.
Back Roads
Country Inns
Thomasville Gallery

The W. W. Henry Company

RANKINGS

177th in *Fortune* 500 Industrial Cos.
553rd in *Business Week* 1000

KEY COMPETITORS

INTERCO	3M	Premark
Masco	Owens-Corning	USG

ARTHUR ANDERSEN & CO.

OVERVIEW

Arthur Andersen & Co. is the 4th largest accounting firm in the world. The firm is increasing its international presence — its representation grew from 54 countries in 1989 to 66 in 1990 — and decreasing its reliance on the US, where it reaped 55% of its 1990 revenues, down from 59% the year before. Arthur Andersen is taking a variety of routes to international growth — mergers, acquisitions, joint ventures, and the addition of new offices. The company has begun operations throughout Eastern Europe.

The partnership is, according to *CPA Personnel Report,* the most productive of the Big 6 accounting firms. An Arthur Andersen & Co. partner generates more than $1.8 million in annual revenue.

The company is completing its first year within a new structure. Arthur Andersen & Co. is 2 distinct units: Arthur Andersen provides auditing, business advisory services, tax services, and corporate specialty services; Andersen Consulting provides systems integration and technology consulting. These units are coordinated by a Swiss entity, Arthur Andersen & Co., S.C. The new structure is designed to remove conflicts of interest between auditing and consulting.

International partnership
Fiscal year ends: August 31

Hoover's Rating **B**

WHEN

Arthur Andersen, an orphan of Norwegian parents, worked in the Chicago office of Price Waterhouse in 1907. In 1908 at 23, after becoming the youngest CPA in Illinois, he began teaching accounting at Northwestern University. Following a brief period in 1911 as controller at Schlitz Brewing, Andersen became head of the accounting department at Northwestern. In 1913 at age 28, he formed a public accounting firm, Andersen, DeLany & Company, with Clarence DeLany.

Establishment of the Federal Reserve and implementation of the federal income tax in 1913 aided the firm's early growth by increasing the demand for accounting services. The company gained large clients, including ITT, Briggs & Stratton, Colgate-Palmolive, and Parker Pen, during the period between 1913 and 1920. In 1915 it opened a branch office in Milwaukee. After DeLany's departure in 1918, the firm adopted its present name.

Andersen grew rapidly during the 1920s and added, to its list of services, financial investigations, which formed the basis for its future strength in management consulting. The firm opened 6 offices in the 1920s, including ones in New York (1921), Kansas City (1923), and Los Angeles (1926).

When Samuel Insull's empire collapsed in 1932, Andersen was appointed the bankers' representative and guarded the assets during the refinancing. During the post-Depression period, Andersen opened additional offices in Boston and Houston (1937) and in Atlanta and Minneapolis (1940).

Arthur Andersen's presence dominated the firm during his life. Upon his death in 1947, the firm found new leadership in Leonard Spacek. During Spacek's tenure, which continued until 1963, the firm opened 18 new US offices and began a period of foreign expansion with the establishment of a Mexico City office, followed by 25 more in other countries. Over the same period (1947–63) revenues increased from $6.5 million to $51 million.

Andersen has been an innovator among the major accounting firms. The company opened Andersen University, its Center for Professional Education, in the early 1970s on a campus in St. Charles, Illinois, and provided the first worldwide annual report in 1973. To broaden its scope, it transferred its headquarters to Geneva in 1977.

During the 1970s Andersen increased its consulting business, which accounted for 21% of revenues by 1979; by 1988 consulting fees made up 40% of revenues, making Andersen the world's largest consulting firm. Tension between the consultants and the auditors eventually forced a 1989 restructuring, which established Arthur Andersen and Andersen Consulting as distinct entities.

A rash of megamergers among the then–Big 8 accounting firms led Andersen and Price Waterhouse to flirt briefly with a merger (1989), but discussions broke down over legal and stylistic issues. In 1990 revenues per partner from the consulting operations were nearly $2.6 million, compared to $1.4 million for the tax and auditing arm.

WHO

Chairman: Gerard Van Kemmel
Managing Partner and Chief Executive:
   Lawrence A. Weinbach, age 51
Managing Partner, Arthur Andersen: Richard L. Measelle
Managing Partner, Andersen Consulting: George T. Shaheen
CFO: John D. Lewis
Human Resources: Paul C. Wilson
Employees: 56,801

WHERE

HQ: Arthur Andersen & Co., Société Coopérative, 18, quai Général-Guisan, 1211 Geneva 3, Switzerland
Phone: 011-41-22-214444
Fax: 011-41-22-214418
US HQ: 59 W. Washington St., Chicago, IL 60602-3094
US Phone: 312-580-0069
US Fax: 312-507-6748

Arthur Andersen & Co. maintains 299 offices in 66 countries.

	1990 Revenues	
	$ mil.	% of total
US	2,282	55
Europe, India, Africa & Middle East	1,359	33
Asia/Pacific	309	7
Other Americas	210	5
Total	**4,160**	**100**

WHAT

	1990 Revenues	
	$ mil.	% of total
Arthur Andersen	2,284	55
Andersen Consulting	1,876	45
Total	**4,160**	**100**

Major Services and Operating Units

Arthur Andersen
Auditing and business advisory
Corporate specialty services
Tax services

Andersen Consulting
Application software products
Change management services
Integration services
Strategic services
Technology services

Center for Professional Education
Client services training
In-house technical training
Management training

Representative Clients

Bond
Cadbury Schweppes
Electrolux
Fiat
Hachette
John Labatt
Olivetti

HOW MUCH

	9-Year Growth	1981	1982	1983	1984	1985	1986	1987	1988	1989	1990
Revenues ($ mil.)	17.5%	973	1,124	1,238	1,388	1,574	1,924	2,316	2,820	3,382	4,160
No. of countries	4.9%	43	42	45	45	49	50	49	49	54	66
No. of offices	7.5%	156	157	168	176	215	219	226	231	243	299
No. of partners	6.7%	1,274	1,388	1,477	1,528	1,630	1,847	1,957	2,016	2,134	2,292
No. of employees	11.7%	20,157	22,397	22,815	24,852	28,172	34,270	37,688	43,902	49,280	54,509

1990 revenues per partner: $1,815,000

Revenues ($ mil.) 1981–90

KEY COMPETITORS

Coopers & Lybrand
Deloitte & Touche
Ernst & Young
General Motors
H&R Block
IBM
KPMG
Marsh & McLennan
McKinsey & Co.
Price Waterhouse

ASARCO INC.

OVERVIEW

NYSE symbol: AR
Fiscal year ends: December 31

New York–based ASARCO (formerly American Smelting and Refining Company) is one of the largest copper producers, the largest silver producer, and the 2nd largest lead miner in the US. ASARCO's primary businesses are mining, smelting, and refining metals (from its own mines and those of other companies) and manufacturing chemicals for finishing and processing metals. Its metals businesses include nonferrous (copper, lead, and zinc) and precious (silver and gold) metals.

ASARCO expanded its specialty chemicals business in the late 1980s to offset the fluctuations of the nonferrous metals market. The company has spent the last 4 years cutting costs and acquiring mines in an effort to become an integrated metal producer that can be profitable even at the bottom of the metal market price cycle.

ASARCO's largest shareholder is M.I.M. Holdings (Australia), which owns 25.2% of the company. ASARCO in turn owns 18.9% of M.I.M. ASARCO also owns 52.3% of Southern Peru Copper (copper, silver, molybdenum) and 34% of Mexico Desarrollo Industrial Minero (copper, lead, zinc, and other metals).

WHO

Chairman, President, and CEO: Richard de J. Osborne, age 57, $1,106,687 pay
EVP: Thomas C. Osborne, age 64, $421,071 pay
EVP: George W. Anderson, age 57, $410,667 pay
VP Finance and Administration: Francis R. McAllister, age 49, $500,384 pay
VP Industrial Relations and Personnel: John R. Corbett, age 63
Auditors: Coopers & Lybrand
Employees: 9,300

WHEN

Henry Rogers, who had helped form Standard Oil Trust in 1882, joined with Leonard and Adolph Lewisohn (copper mine owners) and others in 1899 to consolidate the US lead and silver smelting (melting and then separating ores) and refining (purifying metals) industry. The major holdouts to the enterprise, M. Guggenheim's Sons, the smelting and refining business of the Guggenheim family of Colorado (later benefactors of Mount Sinai Hospital and the Guggenheim Museum in New York), rejected the $11 million offered for their US and Mexico lead and silver smelters and their US copper refinery.

The newly formed American Smelting and Refining Company (officially renamed ASARCO in 1975) began with 16 smelters, 18 refineries, and some mines. Strong competition from the Guggenheims along with labor strikes against ASARCO resulted in immediate financial troubles. In 1901 M. Guggenheim's Sons merged with ASARCO for $45.2 million in ASARCO stock. The Guggenheims and their allies accounted for 51% of the stock. Daniel Guggenheim became chairman (president in 1905), and 4 of his brothers sat on the board. After the panic of 1907, the Guggenheims sold all but 10% of their ASARCO stock to the public.

The company expanded, buying 5 mines in Mexico (1901), Federal Mining and Smelting in Idaho (1903), and a controlling interest in US Zinc (1903). Next ASARCO bought copper mining properties in the Silver Bell district of Arizona in 1910. It began the company's first open-pit copper mine there in 1954. The company entered manufacturing with an interest in Michigan Copper and Brass (later Revere Copper and Brass, makers of Revere Ware) in 1928 (sold 1982).

The company started mining in Peru in 1921. In 1930 ASARCO invested in Mount Isa Mines (now M.I.M. Holdings), an Australian silver, lead, zinc, and copper mining company. ASARCO expanded into specialty chemicals in 1957 with the purchase of Enthone and began asbestos mining in Quebec in 1958. The company added coal to its mining operations in 1970 with the purchase of 4 mines in Illinois (sold 1990).

ASARCO bought chemical companies OMI International (1988) and IMASA Group (1989) to augment its chemical subsidiary, Enthone. ASARCO exited asbestos mining in 1989.

By 1992 the company hopes to mine all the copper it needs for its smelting and refining. When its drive to become a fully integrated producer began in 1985, it supplied less than 25% of its copper and 5% of its lead needs. After spending $793 million on expansion, acquisitions, and modernization, the figures grew to 70% and 50%, respectively.

WHERE

HQ: 180 Maiden Ln., New York, NY 10038
Phone: 212-510-2000
Fax: 212-510-2271

ASARCO's principal US mines are located in Arizona, Colorado, Idaho, Missouri, Montana, and Tennessee. Major foreign mines are located in Australia, Canada, Mexico, and Peru.

	1990 Sales	
	$ mil.	% of total
US	1,778	80
Other countries	431	20
Total	**2,209**	**100**

WHAT

	1990 Sales		1990 Operating Income	
	$ mil.	% of total	$ mil.	% of total
Minerals	36	2	5	4
Metals	1,797	81	165	135
Specialty chemicals	272	12	5	4
Other	104	5	(53)	(43)
Total	**2,209**	**100**	**122**	**100**

Mining and Smelting
Copper
Gold
Lead
Molybdenum
Platinum
Silver
Zinc

Major Subsidiaries and Affiliates
American Limestone Co., Inc. (building materials)
Capco Pipe Co. (PVC pipe)
Encycle, Inc. (recycling)
Enthone–OMI, Inc. (chemicals)
IMASA Group (chemicals)
Mexico Desarrollo Industrial Minero, SA de CV (MEDIMSA, 34%, mining)
M.I.M. Holdings Ltd. (18.9%, mining, Australia)
Southern Peru Copper Corp. (52.3%)

HOW MUCH

	9-Year Growth	1981	1982	1983	1984	1985	1986	1987	1988	1989	1990
Sales ($ mil.)	4.2%	1,532	1,351	1,512	1,325	1,167	1,057	1,355	1,988	2,211	2,209
Net income ($ mil.)	12.9%	50	(39)	58	(306)	(62)	9	208	207	231	149
Income as % of sales	—	3.3%	(2.9%)	3.9%	(23.1%)	(5.3%)	0.9%	15.4%	10.4%	10.5%	6.8%
Earnings per share ($)	9.9%	1.54	(2.40)	1.54	(12.56)	(2.87)	(0.05)	4.88	4.78	5.40	3.60
Stock price – high ($)	—	48.50	31.00	44.25	34.50	27.75	22.88	34.25	29.50	35.88	33.00
Stock price – low ($)	—	24.75	17.25	25.63	18.50	15.75	10.00	14.88	19.38	26.13	22.25
Stock price – close ($)	0.6%	25.75	29.13	30.00	19.00	18.38	14.88	28.50	27.38	29.88	27.13
P/E – high	—	32	—	29	—	—	—	7	6	7	9
P/E – low	—	16	—	17	—	—	—	3	4	5	6
Dividends per share ($)	1.5%	1.40	0.50	0.40	0.30	0.00	0.00	0.10	0.70	1.50	1.60
Book value per share ($)	(1.6%)	42.46	38.77	39.63	26.73	23.33	23.09	28.49	31.67	34.56	36.78

1990 Year-end:
Debt ratio: 25.7%
Return on equity: 10.1%
Cash (mil.): $35
Current ratio: 1.86
Long-term debt (mil.): $523
No. of shares (mil.): 41
Dividends:
1990 average yield: 5.9%
1990 payout: 44.4%
Market value (mil.): $1,114

**Stock Price History
High/Low 1981–90**

RANKINGS

199th in *Fortune* 500 Industrial Cos.
476th in *Business Week* 1000

KEY COMPETITORS

Alcoa	FMC	Reynolds Metals
AMAX	Inco	RTZ
Anglo American	Manville	Vulcan
Broken Hill	Phelps Dodge	Chemical companies
Cyprus Minerals		

ASHLAND OIL, INC.

OVERVIEW

NYSE symbol: ASH
Fiscal year ends: September 30

Hoover's Rating C-

Although its headquarters are tucked away in a small town in Kentucky (Russell, not Ashland), Ashland Oil is one of the largest US independent petroleum refiners and marketers, and its operations extend around the world.

Ashland Exploration drills in the US (concentrating on natural gas) and in Nigeria (crude oil). Ashland Petroleum's 3 refineries sell much of their gasoline output to independent marketers. Ashland refineries also provide gasoline to the company's 746 SuperAmerica convenience stores in 18 states.

Ashland owns Valvoline, which includes the well-known motor oil and other automotive products. Ashland Chemical is the leading US distributor of petrochemicals needed for fiberglass-reinforced plastics. Other products include resins, foundry chemicals, water-treatment chemicals, and chemicals for semiconductor production. Ashland Coal (46% owned) operates mines in West Virginia and Kentucky.

APAC, the company's construction group, operates a network of 161 asphalt plants and is a major supplier of construction services and materials. APAC also builds highways and other major projects in 15 Sunbelt states. Ashland has sold most of its troubled engineering consulting segment, but retains 42% of Los Angeles–based AECOM Technology.

WHO

Chairman and CEO: John R. Hall, age 58, $1,099,427 pay
President and COO: Charles J. Luellen, age 61, $813,038 pay
SVP and CFO: Paul W. Chellgren, age 47, $562,392 pay
SVP Human Resources and Law: Richard W. Spears, age 54, $548,785 pay
SVP; Group Operating Officer, Ashland Chemical: John A. Brothers, age 50
Auditors: Ernst & Young
Employees: 33,400

WHERE

HQ: 1000 Ashland Dr., Russell, KY 41169
Phone: 606-329-3333
Fax: 606-329-5274

Ashland businesses operate worldwide.

WHAT

	1990 Sales		1990 Operating Income	
	$ mil.	% of total	$ mil.	% of total
Exploration	399	4	40	9
Chemical	2,245	21	70	16
Petroleum	3,949	37	206	49
SuperAmerica	1,998	19	46	11
Valvoline	701	6	37	9
Construction	1,083	10	53	13
Engineering	348	3	(28)	(7)
Adjustments	(2,171)	—	(93)	—
Total	**8,552**	**100**	**331**	**100**

Businesses
AECOM Technology Corp. (42%, engineering)
APAC (construction)
Arch Mineral Corp. (50%, coal)
Ashland Branded Marketing, Inc. (retailing)
Ashland Chemical, Inc. (chemicals)
Ashland Coal, Inc. (46%, coal)
Ashland Exploration, Inc. (oil and gas production)
Ashland Petroleum (refining, transportation)
Ecogard, Inc. (oil recycling)
LOOP INC. (18.6%, offshore oil terminal, Louisiana)
Mac's Oil & Chemicals (automotive products)
Scurlock Permian Corp. (crude oil gathering)
SuperAmerica Group, Inc. (retailing)
Valvoline, Inc. (automotive products)

Brand Names

Ashland	Payless	Save More
Bi-Lo	Pyroil	SoLo
Hi-Fy	Red Head	SuperAmerica
IG-LO	Rich Oil	TECTYL
Mac's	Save Mart	Valvoline

RANKINGS

56th in *Fortune* 500 Industrial Cos.
341st in *Business Week* 1000

KEY COMPETITORS

Amax	Fluor	Petrobrás
Amoco	Halliburton	PDVSA
Atlantic Richfield	Koch	Pemex
Bechtel	McDermott	Royal Dutch/Shell
British Petroleum	Mobil	Salomon
Broken Hill	Norsk Hydro	Southland
Chevron	Occidental	Sun
Circle K	Oryx	Texaco
Coastal	Pennzoil	Unocal
Du Pont	Phillips	USX
Elf Aquitaine	Petroleum	Other chemical
Exxon	Petrofina	companies

WHEN

J. Fred Miles sold his Oklahoma oil drilling company in 1917 to wheel and deal in Kentucky. He attracted Chicago backers and prominent Kentuckians to invest in his Swiss Oil Company drilling venture.

In 1924 Swiss bought a troubled refinery in Catlettsburg, then a rough river town near sedate Ashland, and created the Ashland Refining subsidiary. Miles battled Swiss directors for control, lost, and resigned in 1927.

Swiss expanded by buying Tri-State Refining (1930) and Cumberland Pipeline's eastern Kentucky network (1931). Swiss changed its name to Ashland Oil and Refining in 1936.

Following WWII, CEO Paul Blazer spurred Ashland to acquire small independent oil firms (Allied Oil in 1948, Aetna Oil in 1950). When Ashland bought Freedom-Valvoline in 1950, it acquired the venerable Valvoline name. Ashland purchased Frontier Oil of Buffalo and National Refining of Cleveland in 1950.

Blazer passed the torch to Orin Atkins in 1965. Ashland formed its Ashland Chemical subsidiary in 1967 after acquiring Anderson-Prichard Oil (1958), United Carbon (1963), and ADM Chemical (1967). The company added its SuperAmerica retail marketing chain (1970) and began exploring Nigeria for oil (1973).

In 1975 Atkins admitted ordering Ashland executives to make illegal contributions to the Nixon campaign. Atkins was deposed in 1981 after Ashland made questionable payments to highly placed "consultants" with connections to oil-rich Middle Eastern governments. In one such payment, Ashland had bankrolled a consultant's scheme to manufacture reusable sausage casings.

Atkins was arrested in 1988 for attempting to fence purloined documents regarding litigation between Ashland and the National Iranian Oil Company. Ashland, which launched the federal investigation that led to Atkins's arrest, settled with NIOC for $325 million in 1989. Atkins pleaded guilty to charges related to the documents and, after cooperating in other proceedings, received a probated sentence.

Even without Atkins as a lightning rod, Ashland faced challenges. Chairman John Hall had to fend off a hostile takeover by the Belzberg family of Canada (1986) by expanding an employee stock ownership plan. In 1990 banking firm J.P. Morgan took a 5.1% stake in Ashland for a "passive" investment.

Ashland bought Permian Corporation (crude oil gathering and marketing) in 1991 and merged it into its Scurlock Oil. The combination sells 400,000 barrels of crude a day.

HOW MUCH

	9-Year Growth	1981	1982	1983	1984	1985	1986	1987	1988	1989	1990
Sales ($ mil.)	(0.9%)	9,262	8,865	7,852	8,330	7,945	7,083	6,993	7,826	8,062	8,552
Net income ($ mil.)	8.1%	90	181	97	(172)	147	209	133	184	86	182
Income as % of sales	—	1.0%	2.0%	1.2%	(2.1%)	1.8%	2.9%	1.9%	2.3%	1.1%	2.1%
Earnings per share ($)	12.5%	1.11	2.64	1.11	(4.46)	2.06	3.08	2.14	3.13	1.55	3.20
Stock price – high ($)	—	20.88	17.50	19.00	14.75	19.69	32.13	35.88	38.13	43.00	40.13
Stock price – low ($)	—	13.50	10.25	12.38	10.38	12.00	17.75	23.25	26.38	33.13	26.38
Stock price – close ($)	6.4%	15.63	14.50	14.25	12.00	18.69	28.00	28.88	33.50	40.00	27.25
P/E – high	—	19	7	17	—	10	10	17	12	28	13
P/E – low	—	12	4	11	—	6	6	11	8	21	8
Dividends per share ($)	(2.0%)	1.20	1.20	1.10	0.80	0.80	0.85	0.90	0.95	1.00	1.00
Book value per share ($)	2.1%	18.29	19.70	19.63	15.10	16.37	14.92	17.17	19.06	19.62	22.14

1990 Year-end:
Debt ratio: 49.1%
Return on equity: 15.3%
Cash (mil.): $81
Current ratio: 1.19
Long-term debt (mil.): $1,235
No. of shares (mil.): 58
Dividends:
 1990 average yield: 3.7%
 1990 payout: 31.3%
Market value (mil.): $1,575

Stock Price History High/Low 1981–90

ASSOCIATED MILK PRODUCERS, INC.

OVERVIEW

San Antonio–based Associated Milk Producers, Inc. (AMPI), is the largest milk cooperative in the US, accounting for 12% of the country's milk supply. The association has about 18,000 members in 20 states, down from 23,500 in 1986 due to the attrition of dairy farms.

The 3 operating regions of AMPI differ in their market focus. The North Central Region processes most of its milk production into cheese, nonfat dry milk, and canned sauces under the name State Brand. The Morning Glory Farms Region supplies milk to the Chicago market and manufactures cheese, sour cream, and frozen yogurt. The Southern Region concentrates on supplying Grade A milk to several markets but also operates 10 manufacturing plants, with an 11th to open in 1992.

Modern farm cooperatives are the descendants of thousands of cooperatives formed in the 1870s by an organization called the Grange. Originally established to aid farmers with purchasing, storage, and marketing needs, these cooperatives have consolidated over the past century. Extended services offered to members include credit, life insurance, and retirement programs.

Through C-TAPE, one of the largest agricultural PACs in the US, AMPI contributed $1 million to political campaigns in 1990. Despite the contributions, AMPI was disappointed with the 1990 Farm Bill, complaining it did little to restore price stability to milk. When milk prices plummeted 25% in 1990, AMPI posted its first-ever loss, and General Manager Ira Rutherford resigned.

WHEN

In 1969, faced with declining dairy income and milk consumption by the public, about 100 dairy cooperatives in the Midwest and the South merged to form Associated Milk Producers, Inc. (AMPI). The membership elected John Butterbrodt, from a Wisconsin cooperative, as the first president and established headquarters in San Antonio, home of the largest of the predecessor cooperatives, Milk Producers Association. Cooperatives throughout the central US clamored to join, making AMPI the largest US dairy cooperative within 2 years of its formation.

Almost from the beginning, AMPI became embroiled in the 2 main controversies involving dairy cooperatives: monopolistic practices and political contributions. In 1972 consumer advocate Ralph Nader alleged that the 3 main dairy cooperatives — AMPI, Dairymen, and Mid-America Dairymen — had illegally contributed $422,000 to President Nixon's re-election campaign in an attempt to obtain higher price supports (enacted in 1971) and an agreement that the administration would drop antitrust suits against the cooperatives. Watergate investigators subpoenaed Nixon's tapes, and AMPI was accused of bribery, destruction of evidence, and attempting to achieve "complete market dominance." In 1974 AMPI pleaded guilty to making illegal political contributions in 1968, 1970, and 1972. By 1975, 3 former AMPI employees had

been convicted of various charges and Butterbrodt had resigned.

AMPI spent the last half of the 1970s quietly reorganizing, including establishing its current regional management structure. In 1982 a suit for monopolistic practices, originally filed in 1971 by the National Farmers' Organization (NFO), finally reached the federal courts. The case was decided in favor of AMPI and 2 other large cooperatives, but before the year was out an appeals court reversed the decision, saying AMPI and its codefendants had conspired to eliminate competitive sellers of milk. In 1983 Congress rejected a bill to cut price supports for dairy farmers and instead adopted a program to pay farmers not to produce milk. Industry critics charged that the 3 major milk cooperatives had bought the legislation through large political contributions.

AMPI extended its dominance of the industry in 1985 by merging its central region, then called the Mid-States Region, with 2,200 members of Shawano, Wisconsin–based Morning Glory Farms Cooperative. In 1989 the US Supreme Court upheld the appeals court ruling in the NFO antitrust case.

In 1990 business soured for AMPI: it posted a $27 million loss. In 1991 dissatisfied Arkansas farmers threatened to bolt AMPI. Southern Regional manager Noble Anderson replaced Ira Rutherford as general manager.

Mutual company
Fiscal year ends: December 31

Hoover's Rating C-

WHO

President: Irvin J. Elkin
General Manager: Noble Anderson, age 47
Controller and CFO: Harry Pickens
Auditors: Deloitte & Touche
Employees: 4,500

WHERE

HQ: 6609 Blanco Rd., PO Box 790287, San Antonio, TX 78279
Phone: 512-340-9100
Fax: 512-340-9158

AMPI is divided into 3 regions. The North Central Region (7,899 farms) encompasses parts of Iowa, Minnesota, Missouri, Nebraska, and South Dakota. The Morning Glory Farms Region (6,590 farms) includes parts of Illinois, Indiana, Michigan, Ohio, and Wisconsin. The Southern Region (3,989 farms) serves Arkansas, New Mexico, Oklahoma, Texas, and parts of Colorado, Kansas, Kentucky, Louisiana, Mississippi, Missouri, Nebraska, and Tennessee.

	1990 Sales	
	$ mil.	% of total
Southern Region	1,082	37
North Central Region	966	33
Morning Glory Farms Region	885	30
Adjustments	130	—
Total	**3,063**	**100**

WHAT

	1990 Production
	Pounds mil.
Milk	17,700
Cheese	615
Butter	138
Nonfat dry milk	194
Dried whey	239

Dairy Activities
Grade A milk production
Production and packaging of dairy products, canned cheese sauces, and other milk-based goods under the New Holstein, Morning Glory, and other labels

Subsidiaries and Affiliates
Farm Credit System Banks
Land O'Lakes, Inc.
Northland Foods Cooperative (86%)
Prairie Farms Dairy, Inc.

Membership Services
AMPI Investment Corp.
Investment subsidiary of the Southern Region
Women and Young Cooperator programs, retirement plans, and member insurance

Political Activities
Committee for Thorough Agricultural Political Education (C-TAPE)
Texans for Thorough Agricultural Political Education (TEX-TAPE)

RANKINGS

36th in *Fortune* 100 Diversified Service Cos.

KEY COMPETITORS

| Borden | General Mills | Philip Morris |
| BSN | Kellogg | RJR Nabisco |

HOW MUCH

	9-Year Growth	1981	1982	1983	1984	1985	1986	1987	1988	1989	1990
Sales ($ mil.)	1.9%	2,593	2,592	2,654	2,485	2,416	2,489	2,710	2,777	2,987	3,063
Net margin ($ mil.)	—	18	21	4	6	—	—	7	4	12	(27)
Member farms	(4.0%)	26,500	26,400	25,400	24,600	23,300	23,500	22,400	20,800	19,400	18,478
Milk deliveries (mil. lbs.)	1.4%	15,560	15,730	16,400	15,050	15,700	15,900	17,200	17,700	17,300	17,700

1990 Year-end
Debt ratio: 59.1%
Cash (mil.): $10
Current ratio: 1.53
Long-term debt (mil.): $184
Members' equity (mil.): $127

Sales ($ mil.) 1981–90

AST RESEARCH, INC.

OVERVIEW

Business is booming at AST Research. Since 1986 the company has evolved from a maker of enhancement boards to a full-fledged PC producer. PC systems sales now represent 88% of sales. Reasonable prices and quality products (marketed under the Premium [high end] and Bravo [low end] brand names) have made the company a strong competitor in the crowded PC market.

AST uses multiple distribution channels, including independent authorized resellers, major retail computer chains (ComputerLand, Sears Business Centers), federal resellers, and major distributors (Ingram Micro D). Texas Instruments, Tandem, Sharp, and 16 other OEMs sell AST PCs under their own labels.

AST also offers enhancement products for improving computer memory and graphics capability, as well as data communications products that allow PCs to double as terminals for mainframes and minicomputers.

The company is expanding internationally, especially in developing countries. AST is the first non-Japanese computer maker to directly challenge NEC in Japan by producing and selling an NEC clone that also runs IBM-compatible software.

AST stock was the best-performing NASDAQ stock of 1990, with a price appreciation of 259%. By 1991 AST had clearly established itself as one of the players likely to survive in the rough-and-tumble PC industry.

WHEN

In 1979 friends Albert Wong, Safi Qureshey, and Tom Yuen started off to be high-tech consultants, drawing lots to see who would be president. They called themselves AST Associates after the initials of their first names. In 1980 they incorporated as AST Research, Inc. and the 3 Asian-born engineers, working from Yuen's garage, set out to make computer enhancement and peripheral products.

Their timing couldn't have been better. Only 4 months after IBM came out with its PC in 1981, AST had a memory enhancer. In 1983 sales reached $12 million. The following year AST went public, raising over $13 million to help finance future growth.

As PCs became more sophisticated, with more software features built in, demand for enhancement products matured. AST responded by introducing its own PC, the Premium/286 (based on Intel's 286 chip), in 1986. But the company fell behind in introducing a machine based on the more powerful 386 chip in 1987.

In 1988, after Wong left AST to start his own competing company, Qureshey and Yuen reorganized the company, selling divisions that made enhancement boards for Apple and Digital Equipment and cutting staff by 6%.

AST was in trouble: its former marketing complacency had led to financial woes, and the company reported its first annual loss in fiscal 1989. But by mid-1989, AST was back on track with two 386 computers.

Qureshey and Yuen forged ahead. In 1989 AST introduced a line of PCs that put the microprocessor on a separate board, allowing users to upgrade easily without having to buy a complete new motherboard. This enabled the company to be one of the first to have a PC operating on the 486 processor. AST also began emphasizing overseas business, establishing subsidiaries in Europe and the Far East.

In 1990 AST introduced 12 new computers, including a notebook-sized PC priced 30% to 50% lower than its competitors. The company also unveiled the first PC to run both NEC 9801 (the de facto standard in Japan) and MS-DOS operating systems, making it a potential contender in the hard-to-crack Japanese market. AST hopes to sell 20,000 of the machines per year despite having no existing brand name recognition in Japan.

Fiscal 1991 closed with $689 million in sales (up 29% from the year earlier) and $65 million in profits, almost double the 1990 level.

NASDAQ symbol: ASTA
Fiscal year ends: June 30

Hoover's Rating **A-**

WHO

Co-Chairman, President, and CEO: Safi U. Qureshey, age 39, $762,200 pay
Co-Chairman and COO: Thomas C. K. Yuen, age 39, $750,900 pay
SVP Finance and CFO: Bruce C. Edwards, age 36, $265,800 pay
SVP Worldwide Marketing: James W. Ashbrook, age 48, $216,000 pay
Director Human Resources: Howard Derman
Auditors: Ernst & Young
Employees: 2,312

WHERE

HQ: 16215 Alton Pkwy., PO Box 19658, Irvine, CA 92713-9658
Phone: 714-727-4141
Fax: 714-727-9355

AST has plants in the US, Hong Kong, Taiwan, and the UK, and sales offices in 12 countries. Its products are sold in 89 countries.

	1990 Sales		1990 Net Income	
	$ mil.	% of total	$ mil.	% of total
North America	350	66	(3)	(8)
Europe	97	18	(1)	(3)
Pacific	87	16	39	111
Total	**534**	**100**	**35**	**100**

WHAT

	1990 Sales	
	$ mil.	% of total
Systems sales	470	88
OEM & government sales	41	8
Other	23	4
Total	**534**	**100**

Computer Products	Enhancement Products
PCs	Graphics adapters
AST Dual	AST-VGA and AST-VGA
Bravo Series	Plus
Premium Series	Memory and multifunction
Portable	products
Premium Exec	RampagePlus
(notebook family)	SixPak Plus

Data Communications Products
Local area network products
Micro-to-AT-compatible minicomputer emulation products
Micro-to-mainframe emulation products
Multi-port products

RANKINGS

639th in *Business Week* 1000

KEY COMPETITORS

AT&T	Intel
Apple	IBM
Atari	Lucky-Goldstar
Canon	Machines Bull
Commodore	Matsushita
Compaq	NEC
Daewoo	Olivetti
Data General	Prime
Dell	SCI Systems
DEC	Sun Microsystems
Fujitsu	Tandy
Hewlett-Packard	Toshiba
Hitachi	Unisys
Hyundai	

HOW MUCH

	6-Year Growth	1981	1982	1983	1984	1985	1986	1987	1988	1989	1990
Sales ($ mil.)	42.5%	—	—	—	64	139	172	206	413	457	534
Net income ($ mil.)	34.2%	—	—	—	6	19	27	13	15	(7)	35
Income as % of sales	—	—	—	—	9.0%	13.7%	15.8%	6.3%	3.7%	(1.6%)	6.6%
Earnings per share ($)	23.0%	—	—	—	0.35	0.99	1.17	0.57	0.64	(0.32)	1.21
Stock price – high ($)	—	—	—	—	4.56	16.38	15.75	11.38	8.69	5.69	18.88
Stock price – low ($)	—	—	—	—	3.50	4.25	5.31	3.13	3.63	3.31	5.19
Stock price – close ($)	26.4%	—	—	—	4.56	15.38	6.44	3.69	3.94	5.19	18.63
P/E – high	—	—	—	—	13	17	13	20	14	—	16
P/E – low	—	—	—	—	10	4	5	6	6	—	4
Dividends per share ($)	—	—	—	—	0.00	0.00	0.00	0.00	0.00	0.00	0.00
Book value per share ($)	50.3%	—	—	—	0.55	2.54	3.79	4.35	5.01	4.68	6.34

1990 Year-end:
Debt ratio: 13.5%
Return on equity: 21.9%
Cash (mil.): $92
Current ratio: 3.41
Long-term debt (mil.): $30
No. of shares (mil.): 31
Dividends:
 1990 average yield: —
 1990 payout: —
Market value (mil.): $568

Stock Price History High/Low 1984–90

ATARI CORPORATION

OVERVIEW

Atari Corporation, once America's premier video game producer, today is a major manufacturer of personal computers. The Sunnyvale, California, company continues to manufacture and develop game systems, but personal computers, ranging from laptops to powerful PC-compatibles to the Atari ST and TT series, are Atari's primary product line (79% of net sales). Europe accounted for 83% of Atari's 1990 sales.

Atari's Portfolio "palmtop" computer, introduced in 1989, weighs under a pound and is small enough to fit in a coat pocket. Atari responded to sluggish sales of the portable PC with a lower retail price in 1990 and promises of new software titles in 1991. The company

introduced a 2-pound notebook computer in 1991 and the Atari STylus portable, which uses an electronic pen for entering information.

Atari was counting on the Lynx, introduced in 1989, to revive its games segment. Initial sales of the full-color, hand-held video game, however, were disappointing. To counter, Atari lowered Lynx's retail price in 1990 and announced plans for additional game titles. Nintendo continues to dominate the hand-held electronic game market with its Game Boy. Sega of America and NEC Technologies recently introduced competitive products.

Atari's chairman, Jack Tramiel, is former CEO of competitor Commodore. His son Sam is Atari's president and CEO.

WHEN

Atari was established in Sunnyvale, California, in 1972 by Nolan Bushnell, an engineer, who produced his first video arcade game while tinkering with microcomputers at home. The game, Computer Space, developed in 1971, was a commercial flop, but Bushnell's 2nd game, Pong, became an overwhelming success. Atari sold 10,000 of its units in 1973 and 150,000 home versions in 1975.

Atari's success lured others into the industry, including Magnavox, Bally, Coleco, and RCA. With the added competition, prices dropped and the demand for new games increased. By 1976 the enthusiasm for home video games had waned, and Atari was in need of an infusion of capital. That year Bushnell sold Atari to Warner Communications for $28 million, of which Bushnell received $15 million. Bushnell left Atari 2 years later and went on to start Chuck E. Cheese pizza parlors, among other things.

In 1979 Atari sales picked up because of the popularity of its Video Computer System, a cartridge-loaded color graphics console that sold for $200 (introduced in 1977), and the success of its newer, more advanced video arcade games (Asteroids and Missile Command). In 1980 Atari sales reached

$415 million, representing 1/3 of Warner's sales.

Atari introduced its first line of personal computers in 1980. Initial sales were disappointing, however, and the company took a loss of $10 million in computer sales its first year.

By 1982 the interest in video games had diminished. In 1983 Atari's competitors began dropping out of the market, and Atari lost $533 million. In 1984 Warner sold Atari to Jack Tramiel, former CEO of Commodore — Atari's prime competitor in home computers.

By 1986 Tramiel had Atari in the black, with net income of $25 million on revenues of $258 million. Contributing to the turnaround was Atari's successive introductions of low-cost personal computers (Atari ST line).

In 1988 Atari took a loss of $84.8 million due largely to discontinuation of certain operations of its electronics retail chain, Federated Group (acquired by Atari in 1987). In 1989 Atari placed Federated up for sale and in 1990 succeeded in selling 26 of its California stores to Silo and closed the rest. Atari's revenues declined in 1990 for the 3rd consecutive year—$411 million compared to $424 million in 1989 and $452 million in 1988.

ASE symbol: ATC
Fiscal year ends: Saturday closest to December 31

Hoover's Rating **D**

WHO

Chairman: Jack Tramiel, age 62, $179,850 pay
President and CEO: Sam Tramiel, age 41, $195,779 pay
VP and CFO: August J. Liguori, age 39
EVP Sales and Marketing: Alwin Stumpf, age 41
Auditors: Deloitte & Touche
Employees: 1,260

WHERE

HQ: 1196 Borregas Ave., Sunnyvale, CA 94089
Phone: 408-745-2000
Fax: 408-745-8800

The company has offices in the US and 19 foreign countries, R&D facilities in the US, UK, Japan, and Taiwan, and a manufacturing facility in Taiwan.

	1990 Sales		1990 Operating Income	
	$ mil.	% of total	$ mil.	% of total
North America*	57	14	(34)	—
Europe	342	83	7	—
Other regions	12	3	2	—
Total	**411**	**100**	**(25)**	**—**

*includes $11 million of export sales

WHAT

Portable Personal Computers
Atari Portfolio
Atari ST Notebook
Atari STylus

Laptop
Stacy

Personal Computers
ABC286
ABC386
Atari 65XE
Atari 130XE
Atari 386SX PC
Atari 1040STE
Atari MegaSTE
Atari PC4
Atari ST
Atari TT030
AtariPC 5

Printers
SLM605 Laser Printer

Game Products
Atari 2600
Atari 7800
Atari Lynx
Video games

KEY COMPETITORS

Apple	Mattel
AST	NEC
Avon	Nintendo
Commodore	Premark
Dell	Tandy
Hasbro	

Makers of IBM-compatible personal computers

HOW MUCH

	5-Year Growth	1981	1982	1983	1984	1985	1986	1987	1988	1989	1990
Sales ($ mil.)	23.7%	—	—	—	—	142	258	493	452	424	411
Net income ($ mil.)	—	—	—	—	—	(14)	25	44	39	4	(21)
Income as % of sales	—	—	—	—	—	(10.1%)	9.7%	9.0%	8.7%	0.9%	(5.1%)
Earnings per share ($)	—	—	—	—	—	(0.31)	0.53	0.74	0.67	0.07	(0.36)
Stock price – high ($)	—	—	—	—	—	—	7.63	16.19	9.13	12.75	9.75
Stock price – low ($)	—	—	—	—	—	—	5.63	4.88	4.88	4.75	1.50
Stock price – close ($)	—	—	—	—	—	—	7.06	7.50	5.63	8.63	1.75
P/E – high	—	—	—	—	—	—	14	22	14	182	—
P/E – low	—	—	—	—	—	—	11	7	7	68	—
Dividends per share ($)	—	—	—	—	—	0.00	0.00	0.00	0.00	0.00	0.00
Book value per share ($)	—	—	—	—	—	(0.60)	1.82	2.91	1.44	1.49	1.75

1990 Year-end:
Debt ratio: 32.6%
Return on equity: —
Cash (mil.): $37
Current ratio: 2.08
Long-term debt (mil.): $49
No. of shares (mil.): 58
Dividends:
　1990 average yield: 0.0%
　1990 payout: 0.0%
Market value (mil.): $101

Stock Price History
High/Low 1986–90

ATLANTIC RICHFIELD COMPANY

NYSE symbol: ARC
Fiscal year ends: December 31

Hoover's Rating **B-**

OVERVIEW

Los Angeles–based Atlantic Richfield (ARCO) is the 8th largest US petroleum refiner and the leader in gasoline sales on the West Coast, the largest US market. Because it cut overhead and sells aggressively, its gas sales per outlet are twice the industry average. By some calculations, its 29.3% ROE in 1990 made it the most profitable oil company.

ARCO operates its am/pm minimarkets (with and without accompanying gasoline pumps) on the West Coast and has licensed minimarkets in Japan and Taiwan. The company sells $500 million in food a year and is the world's biggest vendor of Reese's Peanut Butter Cups.

ARCO produces 90% of its oil from US assets, including 65% from its huge Alaska holdings. Anticipating declines in its domestic reserves, it is exploring in politically sensitive areas such as the Congo, Syria, and Yemen.

WHEN

In 1866 Charles Lockhart and other pioneers in the Pennsylvania oil industry formed Atlantic Petroleum Storage. In 1870 the company changed its name to Atlantic Refining after it bought a small refinery. Atlantic Refining, a secret affiliate of Standard Oil, was spun off after the Supreme Court dissolved Standard Oil in 1911.

In the 1920s Atlantic Refining explored for oil in Iraq and in the 1930s designed the first all-welded ship. Through the 1950s and 1960s Atlantic Refining bought oil and plastic companies. In 1963 it bought Hondo Oil & Gas (New Mexico) from independent oilman Robert Anderson. Anderson became the company's largest shareholder and was elected chairman in 1965.

Under Anderson, Atlantic Refining grew from a small East Coast oil refiner to a large West Coast integrated oil leader. In 1966 Atlantic Refining purchased Richfield Oil, which had been founded as Rio Grande (California, 1905), and adopted Atlantic Richfield (ARCO) as its name. Richfield's assets included an exploration program on Alaska's North Slope (at Prudhoe Bay).

In 1968 ARCO, exploring on the North Slope in partnership with Humble Oil (later Exxon), drilled into the largest oil deposit in North America. To transport the oil to the lower 48 states, 8 oil companies formed the Trans Alaska Pipeline System (TAPS). ARCO owned 21% of TAPS. In 1977 the oil field began production, and the completed pipeline began transporting oil from Prudhoe Bay to the ice-free coastal waters of Valdez, 800 miles away.

In 1969 ARCO bought Sinclair Oil, a midwestern integrated oil company. ARCO moved its headquarters to Los Angeles in 1972. To diversify, ARCO bought Anaconda (1977), a Montana copper and uranium mining company. In 1986 Anderson retired, and Lodwrick M. Cook, a Louisianan who started out pumping gas at a family general store, took the helm.

In 1985 ARCO authorized the repurchase of up to $4 billion of its stock to make itself a less appealing takeover target. The company sold or closed its weak, noncore businesses, including Anaconda operations, and buttressed its energy and chemical businesses. In 1989 ARCO spun off 50.1% of Houston-based Lyondell Petrochemical, a subsidiary created in 1988, and notched a $634 million pretax gain. To stem the decline of reserves, ARCO bought oil and gas properties in California (from Tenneco, 1988; Oryx, 1990) and Oklahoma (USX's TXO Production, 1990).

Cook kept ARCO in a favorable public relations light by freezing pump prices after the 1990 invasion of Kuwait and by announcing in 1991 that ARCO had developed a gasoline formula that could cut pollutants by a third. ARCO said the cost of marketing the fuel was prohibitive unless government standards forced competitors to market the formula as well.

WHO

Chairman and CEO: Lodwrick M. Cook, age 62, $2,264,672 pay
President and COO: Robert E. Wycoff, age 60, $1,525,197 pay
EVP and CFO: James S. Morrison, age 61, $1,237,505 pay
EVP: James A. Middleton, age 55, $1,236,625 pay
EVP: Ronald J. Arnault, age 47, $1,194,094 pay
VP Human Resources: Donald A. Murray
Auditors: Coopers & Lybrand
Employees: 27,300

WHERE

HQ: 515 S. Flower St., Los Angeles, CA 90071
Phone: 213-486-3511
Fax: 213-486-2063

ARCO explores for oil and gas in the US and the North Sea. It has 2 US refineries and chemical plants in 5 countries. It sells gasoline at 1,550 ARCO service stations in 5 western states and mines coal in Colorado, Utah, Wyoming, and Australia.

	1990 Sales	
	$ mil.	% of total
US	14,080	78
Other countries	3,928	22
Total	**18,008**	**100**

WHAT

	1990 Sales		1990 Operating Income	
	$ mil.	% of total	$ mil.	% of total
Oil & gas	6,114	32	2,147	63
Coal	541	3	130	3
Refining & mktg.	8,624	46	806	24
Transportation	596	3	436	13
Intermediate chemicals & specialty prods.	2,926	16	439	13
Other	7	—	(553)	(16)
Adjustments	(800)	—	(838)	—
Total	**18,008**	**100**	**2,567**	**100**

Major Operations
Chemical manufacturing
Coal mining
Convenience stores (am/pm minimarkets)
Oil and gas exploration and production
Petroleum refining
Service station operations (ARCO)
Smog checking services (SMOGPROS)
Transportation of crude and refined products

RANKINGS

21st in *Fortune* 500 Industrial Cos.
21st in *Business Week* 1000

KEY COMPETITORS

AMAX	Koch	Phillips
Amoco	Mobil	Petroleum
Ashland	Norsk Hydro	Royal Dutch/
British Petroleum	Occidental	Shell
Broken Hill	Oryx	Southland
Chevron	Pennzoil	Sun
Circle K	Petrofina	Texaco
Coastal	Petrobrás	Unocal
Du Pont	PDVSA	USX
Elf Aquitaine	Pemex	Coal companies
Exxon		Chemical cos.

HOW MUCH

	9-Year Growth	1981	1982	1983	1984	1985	1986	1987	1988	1989	1990
Sales ($ mil.)	(4.7%)	27,797	26,462	25,147	23,768	21,723	14,487	16,282	17,626	15,351	18,008
Net income ($ mil.)	0.1%	1,671	1,676	1,548	1,129	333	615	1,224	1,583	1,953	1,688
Income as % of sales	—	6.0%	6.3%	6.2%	4.8%	1.5%	4.2%	7.5%	9.0%	12.7%	9.4%
Earnings per share ($)	4.9%	6.66	6.61	6.03	4.41	1.55	3.38	6.68	8.78	11.26	10.20
Stock price – high ($)	—	66.50	50.00	52.75	52.50	67.88	64.38	99.13	90.88	114.38	142.25
Stock price – low ($)	—	38.25	32.25	37.00	40.63	42.00	45.25	58.75	67.50	80.38	105.50
Stock price – close ($)	11.4%	46.88	42.00	43.25	44.13	63.75	60.00	69.00	80.63	111.38	123.63
P/E – high	—	10	8	9	12	44	19	15	10	10	14
P/E – low	—	6	5	6	9	27	13	9	8	7	10
Dividends per share ($)	9.6%	2.20	2.40	2.40	3.00	3.75	4.00	4.00	4.00	4.50	5.00
Book value per share ($)	2.6%	35.77	39.88	43.44	42.02	30.62	29.62	33.07	36.32	39.96	44.98

1990 Year-end:
Debt ratio: 45.6%
Return on equity: 24.0%
Cash (mil.): $3,031
Current ratio: 1.42
Long-term debt (mil.): $5,997
No. of shares (mil.): 159
Dividends:
 1990 average yield: 4.0%
 1990 payout: 49.0%
Market value (mil.): $19,646

Stock Price History High/Low 1981–90

AUTOMATIC DATA PROCESSING, INC.

OVERVIEW

Automatic Data Processing (ADP) is the largest independent information processing company in the US and sells payroll services to over 200,000 employers that pay 11 million workers. Services include payroll-tax calculation, check processing, and human resource record keeping. Employer Services provides 55% of the company's revenues, with processing centers located in the US, Canada, Brazil, and Western Europe.

The company offers on-line stock and commodity trading, quotation, and information services to stockbrokers in the US, Europe, and Hong Kong through 68,000 terminals.

ADP also processes and distributes corporate documents to stockholders.

ADP sells information services, including parts catalogs on computer disks, to over 6,500 vehicle and heavy-equipment dealers in the US. ADP recently introduced its new hand-held computer for insurance adjusters to use in outlying locations.

ADP also produces on-site accounting and inventory systems for manufacturers, distributors, and wholesalers and provides financing for its systems. The company ended 1990 with increases in earnings per share for the 29th consecutive year.

WHEN

Twenty-two-year-old Henry Taub started Automatic Payrolls, a manual payroll preparation service, in 1949 in Paterson, New Jersey. Taub's business had 8 accounts that created gross revenues of around $2,000 in 1949. In 1952 Taub's brother Joe joined the company, as did a childhood friend, Frank R. Lautenberg, who took a pay cut to become the company's first salesman. During the 1950s the company continued selling its payroll services to new clients and grew steadily.

In 1961 the company went public and changed its name to Automatic Data Processing (ADP). The next year ADP offered back-office services to brokerage houses and bought its first computer, beginning the automation of the company's manual accounting business. In 1962 ADP's revenues reached $1 million.

During the 1970s ADP bought more than 30 companies in the US, Brazil, and the UK, all involved in data and payroll processing, shareholder services, computer networks, inventory control, or automated banking. ADP stock began trading on the NYSE (1970), revenues reached $50 million (1971), and the company started data centers in Florida (1972) and Connecticut (1973). In 1975 Lautenberg became CEO.

ADP bought over 25 more businesses during the 1980s in the US, Canada, and Germany, mainly in data and information services. ADP's purchases of stock information provider GTE Telenet (1983) and Bunker Ramo's information system business (1986) brought the company 45,000 stock quote terminals in brokerages such as E.F. Hutton, Dean Witter, and Prudential-Bache. When Frank Lautenberg resigned as CEO to become one of New Jersey's US senators in 1983, Josh Weston, who had joined ADP as VP of planning in 1970, replaced him.

By 1984 ADP revenues had climbed to $1 billion. Soon after, founder Henry Taub retired as chairman. In 1986 the company sold the German data processing firm it had bought in 1981, as well as the US banking operations ADP had bought earlier in 1986 as part of Bunker Ramo. ADP installed 15,000 computer workstations at brokerages in 1986 and in 1989 began installing more than 38,000 new integrated workstations at Merrill Lynch and Shearson Lehman, which ADP claimed made it the leading stock quote provider in the US. ADP shed its automated teller, Canadian stock quote, terminal maintenance, and Brazilian businesses in 1989 and 1990 and bought Chicago-based Robert White payroll service in 1991.

WHO

Chairman and CEO: Josh S. Weston, age 62, $780,070 pay
Group President: Robert J. Casale, age 52, $402,678 pay
Group President: Robert J. Levenson, age 50, $349,775 pay
Group President: Glenn W. Marschel, age 45, $354,775 pay
SVP Administration and Finance: Arthur F. Weinbach, age 48, $394,333 pay
VP Human Resources: Richard C. Berke, age 46
Auditors: Deloitte & Touche
Employees: 19,000

NYSE symbol: AUD
Fiscal year ends: June 30

Hoover's Rating **A+**

WHERE

HQ: One ADP Blvd., Roseland, NJ 07068
Phone: 201-994-5000
Fax: 201-994-5387

The company has 71 regional processing centers in the US, Canada, and Western Europe, and back- and front-office brokerage service centers in New Jersey.

WHAT

	1990 Approximate % of Sales
Employer services	55
Brokerage services	20
Dealer services	10
Automotive claims services	5
Other	10
Total	**100**

Employer Services
Payroll processing and tax filing
Personnel record keeping and reporting
Unemployment compensation management

Brokerage Services
Trade processing
On-line inquiry and data collection
Order matching and on-line trading
Portfolio reporting and stock loan accounting
Proxy mailing and tabulation

Dealer Services
Computer systems sales and maintenance
Software licensing and support

Automotive Claims Service
Collision repair estimates
Vehicle replacement values
Parts exchange and pricing

Other
Leasing and financing services
Timeshared and interactive computing services

RANKINGS

61st in *Fortune* 100 Diversified Service Cos.
148th in *Business Week* 1000

KEY COMPETITORS

BankAmerica
Citicorp
Control Data
Dow Jones
H&R Block
JWP
Knight-Ridder
Mead
Reuters

Banks offering payroll services

HOW MUCH

	9-Year Growth	1981	1982	1983	1984	1985	1986	1987	1988	1989	1990
Sales ($ mil.)	13.3%	558	669	753	889	1,030	1,204	1,384	1,549	1,678	1,714
Net income ($ mil.)	18.1%	47	58	65	75	88	106	132	170	188	212
Income as % of sales	—	8.5%	8.6%	8.6%	8.5%	8.5%	8.8%	9.5%	11.0%	11.2%	12.4%
Earnings per share ($)	16.0%	0.76	0.86	0.93	1.07	1.24	1.40	1.68	2.14	2.46	2.88
Stock price – high ($)	—	15.88	19.00	22.25	20.13	30.00	38.75	54.50	47.25	50.75	60.25
Stock price – low ($)	—	11.69	10.31	16.44	14.75	17.63	28.00	27.75	34.63	35.75	45.25
Stock price – close ($)	17.5%	12.56	18.50	17.75	19.50	29.50	35.25	44.88	38.75	49.00	53.63
P/E – high	—	21	22	24	19	24	28	32	22	21	21
P/E – low	—	15	12	18	14	14	20	17	16	15	16
Dividends per share ($)	13.7%	0.20	0.23	0.26	0.29	0.32	0.35	0.40	0.46	0.54	0.63
Book value per share ($)	14.0%	4.67	5.33	6.02	6.75	7.77	9.05	11.29	12.71	13.05	15.27

1990 Year-end:
Debt ratio: 4.5%
Return on equity: 20.3%
Cash (mil.): $396
Current ratio: 1.92
Long-term debt (mil.): $53
No. of shares (mil.): 74
Dividends:
1990 average yield: 1.2%
1990 payout: 21.7%
Market value (mil.): $3,959

Stock Price History
High/Low 1981–90

AVIS INC.

OVERVIEW

After years of being passed from company to company like so much corporate chattel, Avis seems settled under employee ownership. Since going private through an Employee Stock Ownership Plan (ESOP) in 1987, the company has been named best in the car rental category by *Financial World* (1990) and appeared in *Fortune* magazine's list of what American business does best (1991). Avis is on the heels of industry leader Hertz, with 20.4% of the world market compared to Hertz's 22.6%. The company has been more profitable than Hertz since 1984, and Avis Europe (8.8% owned by Avis) is already the established market leader in Europe, with a 31% share.

Most of Avis's international operations are handled through joint ventures and licensee operations in 68 countries. The company's Wizard System, the industry's oldest and largest computer reservation system, now operates in 25 countries. Wizard System technology is also available to the hotel industry through Avis's WizCom International subsidiary.

WHEN

In the mid-1940s a young Detroit car dealer by the name of Warren Avis noticed that although there were plenty of car rental agencies around, none — including Hertz — had airport operations. A former army pilot, Avis firmly believed that air travel was the way of the future. In 1946 he invested his Air Corps savings along with $75,000 of borrowed funds to open car rental outlets at Detroit's Willow Run Airport and Miami International Airport. Avis's idea was a success, and in 1948 his company, Avis Rent-A-Car System, opened intercity locations to serve hotels and office buildings.

By 1954 Avis had expanded to Mexico, Canada, and Europe. That year Warren Avis sold the company to Richard Robie, a Boston-based car rental agent, for $8 million. Robie had big plans for the company, including a nationwide system of one-way car rentals and a company charge card, but he ran out of money and sold Avis to a group of Boston investors in 1956.

After forming a holding company (Avis, Inc.) with Avis Rent A Car System as its main operating subsidiary, the new owners moved the company into car leasing. In 1962 they sold it to investment bankers Lazard Frères, who named Robert Townsend (author of *Up the Organization: How to Stop the Organization from Stifling People and Strangling Profits*) as president and moved Avis's headquarters from Boston to Garden City, New York. That was the year Avis first used the slogan "We're only No. 2. We try harder."

ITT bought Avis in 1965. Winston V. Morrow, Jr., replaced Townsend as CEO and focused the company on overseas expansion. A headquarters serving Europe, Africa, and the Middle East (now Avis Europe) was established in the UK. In 1972 Avis pioneered use of a computer rental and reservation system (Wizard System). That year, as part of an antitrust settlement, ITT sold 48% of the company to the public; the rest was held by a court-appointed trustee. Within 5 years Avis once again had become privately owned; Norton Simon bought it for $174 million in 1977. In 1979 Avis's fleet started to feature GM cars.

Avis got a new president in 1982 — former Hertz executive Joseph Vittoria. Vittoria, who had been demoted twice during his tenure at Hertz, took 15 people with him when he went to Avis. Soon after taking office, Vittoria renewed the company's "We Try Harder" slogan and introduced express rental services for airport customers.

Over the next 4 years Avis was passed from owner to owner: Esmark bought Norton Simon in 1983 and, in turn, was bought by Beatrice in 1984. Kohlberg Kravis Roberts took Beatrice private through an LBO in 1985 and sold Avis to William Simon's Wesray Capital Corporation (an investment partnership) in 1986. That year Avis sold its leasing operations (which continues to use the Avis name) to PHH Group. Also that year most of Avis Europe was sold to the public (on the London Exchange).

While under Wesray ownership, Avis made a brief foray into the quick lube business in 1987. Later that year Avis's employees, led by Vittoria, established an ESOP and bought the company for $1.75 billion. Also in 1987 Avis established WizCom International, a subsidiary to sell the Wizard System to other industries. Avis then joined General Motors and Lease International to form Cilva Holdings, which bought Avis Europe in 1989. By March 1991 the company had reduced its ESOP acquisition debt (originally $785 million) by 65% to $272.2 million.

Private company
Fiscal year ends: Last day of February

Hoover's Rating **B-**

WHO

Chairman and CEO: Joseph V. Vittoria
EVP and CFO: Lawrence Ferezy
SVP and General Manager: F. Robert Salerno
SVP Human Resources: Donald Korn
Auditors: Price Waterhouse
Employees: 14,350

WHERE

HQ: 900 Old Country Rd., Garden City, NY 11530
Phone: 516-222-3000
Fax: 516-222-4381
Reservations: 800-331-1212

Avis operates through 4,900 locations in 138 countries.

WHAT

	1990 Sales
	% of total
US Rent A Car	83
International	16
Other	1
Total	**100**

Major Subsidiaries and Affiliates
Avis Europe (8.8%)
Avis Rent A Car System, Inc.
  International Division
  US Rent A Car Division
WizCom International, Ltd.
  HotelLink credit card authorization
  ResAccess and FastAccess links between hotels and airline computer reservations systems

Services
Wizard System
  Preferred Express rental check-outs
  Roving Rapid Return procedures
  Wizard Number customer profiles
Worldwide Reservation Center (Tulsa, OK)

RANKINGS

126th in *Forbes* 400 US Private Cos.

KEY COMPETITORS

Accor
Chrysler
Ford
Hertz
Sears
Volvo

HOW MUCH

Fiscal year ends February of following year	5-Year Growth	1981	1982	1983	1984	1985	1986	1987	1988	1989	1990
Sales ($ mil.)	5.6%	—	—	—	—	916	813	1,060	1,117	1,159	1,205
Employees	6.4%	—	—	—	—	10,500	10,500	14,000	14,000	13,000	14,350

1990 Year-end:
Long-term debt (mil.): $272

Sales ($ mil.) 1985–90

AVON PRODUCTS, INC.

OVERVIEW

Headquartered in New York City, Avon is a leading US cosmetics and direct-sales company. The company achieved household-word status in the US through its door-to-door sales method and advertising campaign "Avon calling." The company's many products include toiletries and cosmetics, costume jewelry, gift items, fashions, preschool educational toys, and fitness videos.

Avon's newest beauty products include Undeniable (perfume), and Renewable Color Lipstick and Blush. Avon's Giorgio Beverly Hills makes prestige fragrances Giorgio and Red, the nation's top-selling fragrance in 1990.

The company credits direct selling for its initial success in the US and current top sales status in foreign countries. At the end of 1990, Avon's 1.5 million active representatives (including 445,000 in the US) sold products at their workplaces, as part-time jobs, and through personal contacts. The company has recently entered markets that were previously off-limits, such as Eastern Europe (including a 1991 foray into Czechoslovakia) and China, where Avon is working around the clock to keep up with consumer demand.

NYSE symbol: AVP
Fiscal year ends: December 31

WHO

Chairman, President, and CEO: James E. Preston, age 57, $1,188,068 pay
EVP and CFO: Edward J. Robinson, age 50, $566,079 pay
SVP Human Resources: Marcia L. Worthing, age 48
Auditors: Coopers & Lybrand
Employees: 30,000

WHEN

During the 1880s, book salesman David McConnell gave small bottles of perfume to New York housewives who listened to his sales pitch. The perfume was more popular than the books, so in 1886 McConnell created the California Perfume Company (renamed Avon in 1950 after the Avon River in England) and hired women to sell door-to-door. From the 1960s until the mid-1980s, Avon was the world's largest cosmetic company, known for its appeal to middle-class homemakers, an image reinforced by pictures of impeccably made-up housewives.

Avon hit hard times in 1974, when recession made many of its products unaffordable for blue-collar customers. At the same time, women were leaving home to enter the work force, making door-to-door sales less viable, and Avon's traditional products had little appeal for younger women. In response to these trends, President David Mitchell directed Avon's attempts to diversify and overhaul its product line, introducing the Colorworks line for teenagers with the slogan "It's not your mother's makeup" and ads picturing active young women.

In 1979 Avon acquired the Tiffany jewelry company to help improve the company's image, sold it in 1984, and decided to expand into the health care field. Acquisitions included

Mallinckrodt, Inc. (hospital supply and chemical company, 1982), Foster Medical (1984), and 60 other medical suppliers. The health care field soon proved unprofitable due to stricter reimbursement policies set by Medicare. In 1986 Avon sold Mallinckrodt and continued to sell off remaining health care companies through 1990.

To boost profits Avon entered the retail prestige fragrances business by launching a joint venture with Liz Claiborne (1985) and buying Giorgio (1987). When Avon bought Parfums Stern, a Claiborne competitor, in 1987 (sold in 1990), Claiborne dissolved the joint venture. That same year Avon sold 40% of Avon Japan (started in 1969) to the Japanese public for $218 million.

Avon introduced Avon Color cosmetics in 1988 and sleepwear, preschool toys, and videos in 1989. That same year Amway and Irwin Jacobs made an unsuccessful attempt to buy Avon. In 1990 the company expanded into Eastern Europe and China and in 1991 branched into direct mail. Also in 1991 Avon reached a peaceful settlement with Chartwell Associates, ending an 18-month attempt by Chartwell to gain control of Avon. Under the agreement, Chartwell may not increase its Avon holdings beyond 4.9% (it currently owns 3.5%).

WHERE

HQ: 9 W. 57th St., New York, NY 10019
Phone: 212-546-6015
Fax: 212-546-6136

Avon has 3 manufacturing plants in the US, 5 in Europe, 6 elsewhere in the Americas, and 4 in the Pacific. It has 5 US distribution centers, 6 in Europe, 12 elsewhere in the Americas, and 9 in the Pacific.

	1990 Sales		1990 Operating Income	
	$ mil.	% of total	$ mil.	% of total
US	1,521	44	218	41
Europe	655	19	43	8
Other Americas	824	24	198	37
Pacific	454	13	73	14
Adjustments	—	—	(89)	—
Total	**3,454**	**100**	**443**	**100**

WHAT

	1990 Sales		1990 Operating Income	
	$ mil.	% of total	$ mil.	% of total
Direct selling	3,292	95	498	94
Retail sales	162	5	33	6
Adjustments	—	—	(88)	—
Total	**3,454**	**100**	**443**	**100**

Direct Sales	Retail Sales
Costume jewelry	Giorgio
Fashions	Red by Giorgio
Fragrances	
Gift items	
Makeup lines	
Preschool educational toys	
Skin care products	
Videos	

RANKINGS

138th in *Fortune* 500 Industrial Cos.
270th in *Business Week* 1000

KEY COMPETITORS

American Home Products	L'Oréal
Amway	LVMH
Colgate-Palmolive	MacAndrews & Forbes
Estée Lauder	Mattel
Gerber	Pfizer
Hasbro	Premark
Johnson & Johnson	Procter & Gamble
S. C. Johnson	Rubbermaid
Johnson Publishing	Toys "R" Us
	Unilever

HOW MUCH

	9-Year Growth	1981	1982	1983	1984	1985	1986	1987	1988	1989	1990
Sales ($ mil.)	3.1%	2,614	3,001	3,000	3,141	2,470	2,883	2,763	3,063	3,300	3,454
Net income ($ mil.)	(1.3%)	220	197	164	182	128	159	238	121	152	195
Income as % of sales	—	8.4%	6.6%	5.5%	5.8%	5.2%	5.5%	8.6%	4.0%	4.6%	5.7%
Earnings per share ($)	(3.7%)	3.66	2.75	2.21	2.16	1.60	2.18	3.35	1.70	2.11	2.60
Stock price – high ($)	—	42.38	30.50	36.88	26.00	29.00	36.38	38.63	28.38	41.25	38.13
Stock price – low ($)	—	29.13	19.38	21.25	19.25	17.88	25.00	19.25	18.63	19.50	22.75
Stock price – close ($)	(0.2%)	30.00	26.75	25.13	21.88	27.63	27.00	25.75	19.50	36.88	29.38
P/E – high	—	12	11	17	12	18	17	12	17	20	15
P/E – low	—	8	7	10	9	11	11	6	11	9	9
Dividends per share ($)	(11.5%)	3.00	2.50	2.00	2.00	2.00	2.00	2.00	1.50	1.00	1.00
Book value per share ($)	(9.1%)	15.51	16.40	16.16	14.47	11.69	9.76	10.66	4.11	3.72	6.60

1990 Year-end:
Debt ratio: 46.0%
Return on equity: 50.4%
Cash (mil.): $380
Current ratio: 1.07
Long-term debt (mil.): $335
No. of shares (mil.): 57
Dividends:
   1990 average yield: 3.4%
   1990 payout: 38.5%
Market value (mil.): $1,671

Stock Price History
High/Low 1981–90

BAKER & MCKENZIE

OVERVIEW

Chicago-based Baker & McKenzie is the largest law firm in the world (though 2nd in terms of billings, to New York's Skadden, Arps, Slate, Meagher & Flom). Its practice includes virtually every field of law in the domestic and international arenas. As of June 1991 it had 1,575 lawyers in 49 offices in 30 countries. Over 50% of its lawyers are not US citizens. Baker & McKenzie is a prime example of the new generation of "megafirms" intended to meet the complete legal needs of their clients.

Its far-flung operations, growth through occasional acquisition of other law firms, and practice of employing local lawyers rather than Americans in its overseas offices have led some to call the firm a franchise and to compare it with fast food chains. While separate partnerships exist in many countries to comply with local requirements, Baker & McKenzie operates as a single firm (an Illinois partnership) in which the governing principle is one vote per partner. Although a complex profit-sharing formula favors the offices and lawyers originating revenue, the firm is managed as a single business.

The firm seems likely to continue its growth and commitment to the international practice of law. It was one of the first US firms to begin practice in China and now has 3 offices there. In 1991 Baker & McKenzie opened an office in Stockholm. In 1991 its Moscow office (opened 1989) was retained to advise on the privatization of the USSR's largest auto producer, Volga Automobile Associated Works.

Private company
Fiscal year ends: June 30

Hoover's Rating **B+**

WHO

Chairman of the Executive Committee:
Robert Cox
CFO: Charles W. Kessler
Director of Hiring: Peter J. Mone
Auditors: Arthur Andersen & Co.
Lawyers: 1,575

WHERE

HQ: One Prudential Plaza, 130 E. Randolph Dr., Chicago, IL 60601
Phone: 312-861-8000
Fax: 312-861-2898

Other Offices

Amsterdam	Juárez	San Diego
Bangkok	London	San Francisco
Barcelona	Los Angeles	São Paulo
Beijing	Madrid	Seoul
Bogotá	Manila	Shanghai
Brussels	Melbourne	Singapore
Budapest	Mexico City	Stockholm
Buenos Aires	Miami	Sydney
Cairo	Milan	Taipei
Caracas	Moscow	Tijuana
Dallas	New York	Tokyo
Frankfurt	Palo Alto	Toronto
Geneva	Paris	Valencia
Guangzhou	Rio de Janeiro	Vienna
Hong Kong	Riyadh	Washington, DC
Jakarta	Rome	Zurich

WHEN

Russell Baker arrived in Chicago from his native New Mexico on a railroad freight car to attend law school. Upon graduation in 1925, he began the practice of law with his classmate Dana Simpson as the firm of Simpson & Baker. Inspired by Chicago's role as a manufacturing and agricultural center for the world and influenced by the strong international focus of his alma mater, the University of Chicago, Baker dreamed of developing an international law practice headquartered in Chicago.

In his first cases Baker represented members of Chicago's growing Mexican-American community in a variety of minor criminal and civil matters. Since he frequently dealt with Mexican lawyers and issues involving multiple jurisdictions and legal systems, Baker developed an expertise in international law, which brought in other clients. In 1934 Abbott Laboratories retained him to handle its worldwide legal affairs, and Baker was on his way to fulfilling his dream.

In 1949 Baker joined forces with Chicago litigator John McKenzie to form the law firm that bears their names. In 1955 Baker opened the firm's first foreign office in Caracas to meet the needs of his expanding US client base. During the next 10 years the firm opened offices in Amsterdam, Brussels, Zurich, São Paulo, Mexico City, London, Frankfurt, Milan, Tokyo, Toronto, Paris, Manila, Sydney, and Madrid. Growth continued with another 23 offices added in Europe, Asia, and the Americas between 1965 and 1990. Baker's death in 1979 did not slow the firm's growth nor change its international character.

To manage what had become the world's largest law firm, in 1984 Baker & McKenzie created the new position of chairman of the executive committee. Robert Cox has held this office since its creation. He has forsaken, for a time, the practice of law in order to guide the firm — a rare situation in large firms, where income is usually tied to the number of hours billed to clients. Cox's mandate is to maintain Baker & McKenzie as the strongest full-line international law firm in the world.

In 1990 the firm recruited former SEC chairman David Ruder and agreed to meet the needs of any client he brings in.

Baker & McKenzie's position during the 1990s will be based in part on its adaptation to the new technology of the legal field. The firm is making strenuous efforts to update its information systems, automating its library facilities and taking greater advantage of its international resources.

While growth slowed in 1991, Baker & McKenzie has avoided the layoffs forced on many large law firms by the depressed financial services and real estate industries.

WHAT

Areas of Practice

Admiralty	Corporate	Litigation
Antitrust	Criminal	Municipal
Banking	Employment	Patent
Bankruptcy	Environmental	Real estate
Civil rights	Estates	Securities
Commodities	Insurance	Taxation
Computer	International	Trademark
Copyright	Labor	

Representative Clients

Amdahl	Kellogg
BASF	NCR
Brunswick	Tandem
R. R. Donnelley	Tyson Foods
Ford	

Journals and Bulletins

Banking Law Reporter	*European Legal*
Canadian Legal Report	*Developments*
China Law Quarterly	*Bulletin*
Colombian Newsletter	*US Employment Law*
Computer & Software	*Update*
Update	*Hazardous Waste*
EEC Competition Law	*Update*
Newsletter	*Newsletter from Spain*
Employee Benefits	*Pacific Basin Legal*
Update	*Developments*
European Benefits	*Bulletin*
Update	*Taiwan Newsletter*

HOW MUCH

	9-Year Growth	1981	1982	1983	1984	1985	1986	1987	1988	1989	1990
Revenues	—	—	—	—	—	—	—	196	261	341	404
Total lawyers	11.3%	583	613	658	704	755	908	946	1,179	1,339	1,522
No. of partners	8.9%	222	236	256	276	287	333	338	404	432	478
No. of associates	12.5%	361	377	402	428	468	575	608	775	907	1,044
Associates per partner	—	1.63	1.60	1.57	1.55	1.63	1.73	1.80	1.92	2.10	2.18
No. of offices	7.3%	26	27	28	29	30	31	35	41	48	49

Starting Salaries for First Year Associates:
1980 — $32,000
1984 — $47,000
1986 — $65,000
1990 — $70,000

Total No. of Lawyers 1981–90

BAKER HUGHES INC.

OVERVIEW

Baker Hughes provides products and services for the oil well and mining industries. The company has 27 divisions organized in 3 major operating groups — Drilling Equipment, Production Tools, and Process Technologies — and is a world leader in each of its industry segments. Baker Hughes is 6% owned by Borg-Warner Corporation.

The Drilling Equipment group (1990 operating income $57 million) produces drill bits and other equipment used in the oil and gas well drilling process. The Production Tools group (1990 operating income $98 million) produces equipment and provides services involved in the completion and rehabilitation of oil and gas wells. With its 1990 acquisition of ChemLink, it became the largest US oilfield chemicals company. The Process Technologies group (1990 operating income $60 million) provides equipment and instruments used in various industries, ranging from mining to wastewater treatment. The company completed its spinoff of BJ Services (pumping services) to the public in the spring of 1991.

WHEN

Howard R. Hughes, Sr., developed the first oil well drill bit for rock in 1909. Hughes and partner Walter Sharp opened a plant in Houston, and Sharp & Hughes soon had a near monopoly on rock bits. When Sharp died in 1912, Hughes bought his half of the company, incorporating as Hughes Tool. Hughes held 73 patents when he died in 1924 and the company passed to Howard R. Hughes, Jr.

It is estimated that the tool company, which has had a 45% market share for most of its life, provided Hughes, Jr., with $745 million in pretax profits between 1924 and 1972, which he used to diversify into movies (RKO), airlines (TWA), and Las Vegas casinos. In 1972 Hughes sold the tool division of Hughes Tool to the public for $150 million. After 1972 the company expanded into aboveground oil production tools.

In 1913 oil well drilling contractor Carl Baker organized the Baker Casing Shoe Company in California to collect royalties on his 3 oil tool inventions. In 1918 Baker began to manufacture his own products. During the 1920s, Baker expanded nationwide, began international sales and formed Baker Oil Tools in 1928. Sales increased sixfold between 1933 and 1941. In the late 1940s and the 1950s, Baker grew as oil drilling boomed.

During the 1960s Baker prospered despite fewer US well completions. Foreign sales increased from 19% to 33% of total revenues. The company bought Kobe (oil field pumping equipment) in 1963. Baker diversified into mining equipment with the purchase of Galigher (1969) and Ramsey Engineering (1974). The company bought Reed Tool (oil well drill bits) in 1975. In 1979 revenues topped $1 billion for the first time.

Between 1982 and 1986 US expenditures for oil services fell from $40 billion to $9 billion. In 1987, when both Baker and Hughes faced declining revenues and Hughes had large debts from expansion, the 2 companies merged to form Baker Hughes. By closing plants and combining operations, the company cut annual expenses by $80 million and was profitable by the end of fiscal 1988. The company made several small acquisitions in 1989, including Bird Machine (process centrifuges) and EDECO Petroleum Services (pumps). In 1990 the company bought Eastman Christensen (world leader in directional and horizontal drilling equipment) and added the instrumentation unit of Tracor Holdings to its Process Technologies group.

Expecting brisk business as Kuwaiti oilfields rebuild and drilling picks up worldwide, the company launched a new Integrated Engineering Services group in 1991 to coordinate its diverse products and services for drilling customers.

NYSE symbol: BHI
Fiscal year ends: September 30

WHO

Chairman, President, and CEO: James D. Woods, age 59, $1,253,479 pay
SVP; President, Baker Hughes Drilling Equipment: Joel V. Staff, age 46, $603,116 pay
SVP; President, Baker Hughes Production Tools: Max L. Lukens, age 42, $492,386 pay
SVP; President, Baker Hughes Process Technologies: Stephen T. Harcrow, age 44, $424,655 pay
VP Human Resources: Phillip A. Rice, age 55
Controller: George S. Finley, age 39
VP and Treasurer: Eric L. Mattson, age 39
Auditors: Deloitte & Touche
Employees: 20,900

WHERE

HQ: 3900 Essex Ln., Houston, TX 77027
Phone: 713-439-8600
Fax: 713-439-8699

Baker Hughes has 117 plants worldwide.

	1990 Sales		1990 Operating Income	
	$ mil.	% of total	$ mil.	% of total
US	1,471	53	66	23
Other Western Hemisphere	361	13	58	20
Europe	528	19	84	29
Other Eastern Hemisphere	420	15	81	28
Adjustments	(166)	—	—	—
Total	**2,614**	**100**	**289**	**100**

WHAT

	1990 Sales		1990 Operating Income	
	$ mil.	% of total	$ mil.	% of total
Drilling	973	42	57	26
Production	756	33	98	46
Process	580	25	60	28
Adjustments	305	—	74	—
Total	**2,614**	**100**	**289**	**100**

Business Operations
Downhole drilling motors
Drilling fluids
Fracturing materials
Liquids processing equipment
Mining drill bits
Oil production tools
Oil well drilling equipment
Surface and downhole data collection instruments

RANKINGS

173rd in *Fortune* 500 Industrial Cos.
173rd in *Business Week* 1000

KEY COMPETITORS

Bechtel	Ingersoll-Rand
Cooper Industries	LTV
Dresser	McDermott
Fluor	Pearson
FMC	Schlumberger
Halliburton	

HOW MUCH

	9-Year Growth	1981	1982	1983	1984	1985	1986	1987	1988	1989	1990
Sales ($ mil.)	2.2%	2,140	2,535	1,838	1,834	1,904	1,557	1,924	2,316	2,328	2,614
Net income ($ mil.)	(5.0%)	225	249	(64)	71	88	(362)	(255)	59	83	142
Income as % of sales	—	10.5%	9.8%	(3.5%)	3.9%	4.6%	(23.2%)	(13.2%)	2.6%	3.6%	5.4%
Earnings per share ($)	(12.0%)	3.36	3.60	(0.91)	1.00	1.25	(5.15)	(2.22)	0.45	0.64	1.06
Stock price – high ($)	—	49.38	38.88	26.63	23.50	18.88	17.88	27.38	19.88	27.63	34.75
Stock price – low ($)	—	31.75	17.63	16.00	15.00	14.13	8.88	11.13	12.13	13.63	21.75
Stock price – close ($)	(4.3%)	38.00	22.50	19.25	16.63	17.88	11.88	13.63	14.00	25.50	25.63
P/E – high	—	15	11	—	24	15	—	—	44	43	33
P/E – low	—	9	5	—	15	11	—	—	27	21	21
Dividends per share ($)	(0.9%)	0.50	0.76	0.92	0.92	0.92	0.81	0.46	0.46	0.46	0.46
Book value per share ($)	(3.3%)	14.03	16.98	14.78	14.34	14.43	9.67	7.78	8.10	8.31	10.36

1990 Year-end:
Debt ratio: 30.0%
Return on equity: 11.4%
Cash (mil.): $125
Current ratio: 2.07
Long-term debt (mil.): $612
No. of shares (mil.): 137
Dividends:
 1990 average yield: 1.8%
 1990 payout: 43.4%
Market value (mil.): $3,522

Stock Price History High/Low 1981–90

Note: 1981–86 figures for Baker International Corporation only

BALLY MANUFACTURING CORPORATION

NYSE symbol: BLY
Fiscal year ends: December 31

Hoover's Rating **D**

OVERVIEW

Bally is the world's largest operator of casino hotels, the largest operator of fitness centers in the US, and a leading manufacturer of slot machines and other gaming equipment.

Finding itself $1.86 billion in debt (and in default on $1.1 billion) and spiraling toward bankruptcy, Bally initiated a plan in 1990 to restructure the company from the top down. Chairman and CEO Robert Mullane retired suddenly and was replaced by Arthur Goldberg.

The company, which used junk bonds to finance expansion in the 1980s, has reduced debt by $535 million and plans to raise more cash through asset sales, including its manufacturing subsidiaries Life Fitness (for $62.5 million) and Scientific Games (for an undisclosed amount). Through a recent agreement with bondholders, Bally will surrender equity in its 2 Nevada casinos.

WHO

Chairman and CEO: Arthur M. Goldberg, age 49
President and COO: Richard Gillman, age 59, $3,850,000 pay
VP, Treasurer, and Acting CFO: William E. Chandler
Director of Personnel and Administration: Lois Balodis
Auditors: Ernst & Young
Employees: 33,250

WHEN

Bally's predecessor, Lion Manufacturing of Chicago, was founded in 1931 by Roy Moloney, Joel Linehan, and Charles Weldt. Lion produced the Ballyhoo, the first pinball machine, in 1932 and its first slot machine in 1938. During WWII the company shifted production to detonator fuses and gun-sights for bombers but after the war went back to making games. Lion produced soft drink and coffee dispensers in the 1950s, selling the coffee machine business to jukebox maker Seeburg in 1960.

The death of Roy Moloney in 1957 sent the company into a state of confusion until 1963, when sales manager William O'Donnell and his partners bought the company. The market for slot machines grew worldwide during the 1960s, and Lion, with its new Money Honey slot machine and computerized control system (Slot Data System) became the industry leader. The company was renamed Bally in 1968 in honor of its first pinball game and went public in 1969.

Throughout the 1970s O'Donnell led the company through a series of acquisitions, including Midway Manufacturing (arcade games, 1969), Gunter Wulff Appartebau (amusement games, Germany, 1972), and American Amusements (amusement arcades, renamed Aladdin's Castle, 1974). The company launched its first casino hotel in 1977. But before the New Jersey Gaming Commission would issue a license to Bally, it required

O'Donnell to resign and place his company stock in a blind trust. Apparently, part of the money he had used to buy the company in 1963 had come from persons connected with organized crime. O'Donnell admitted that accepting the money had been a mistake but asserted that the company had no connection with organized crime. Robert Mullane replaced him as chairman.

At Aladdin's Castle business boomed in the early 1980s when Bally introduced a new generation of video arcade games, including Space Invaders (1979), Pac-Man (1980), and Ms. Pac-Man (1982). The company continued to diversify, buying Six Flags Corporation (1982), Health and Tennis Corporation of America (1983), Great America Theme Park (from Marriott, 1984), Lifecycle (1984), MGM Grand Hotels in Las Vegas and Reno (1986), and the Golden Nugget Casino in Atlantic City (1987). The company successfully fended off a takeover attempt by Donald Trump in 1987, funding the battle by selling its theme park business. Bally then sold most of its amusement-game manufacturing business in 1988 and Aladdin's Castle in 1989, completing its evolution from the amusement-game business.

In 1990 the company missed an $18.4 million interest payment on its Nevada casinos and, with its financial problems in the public eye, pulled out of a deal to buy London's Clermont casino.

WHERE

HQ: 8700 W. Bryn Mawr Ave., Chicago, IL 60631
Phone: 312-399-1300
Fax: 312-693-2982

The company operates 2 casino hotels in New Jersey, 2 casino hotels in Nevada, and 310 fitness centers throughout the US.

WHAT

	1990 Sales		1990 Operating Income	
	$ mil.	% of total	$ mil.	% of total
Casino hotels	915	44	119	93
Fitness centers	815	39	3	2
Products & services	363	17	6	5
Adjustments	(96)	—	(75)	—
Total	**1,997**	**100**	**53**	**100**

Casino Hotels
Bally's Grand (Atlantic City)
Bally's Las Vegas
Bally's Park Place (Atlantic City)
Bally's Reno

Fitness Centers
Chicago Health Clubs
Health and Racquet Clubs
Holiday Fitness and Racquet Clubs
Holiday Health
Holiday Spa
Jack LaLanne
Manhattan Sports Clubs
President's First Lady
Scandinavian
The Vertical Clubs
Vic Tanny

Products and Services
Bally Gaming, Inc.
    Bally/Wulff German wall machines
    Slot machines
Bally Systems
    Computerized cash monitoring and security systems

RANKINGS

51st in *Fortune* 100 Diversified Service Cos.

KEY COMPETITORS

Bass
Control Data
Hanson
Hilton
Premark

HOW MUCH

	9-Year Growth	1981	1982	1983	1984	1985	1986	1987	1988	1989	1990
Sales ($ mil.)	9.7%	866	1,254	1,148	1,309	1,295	1,209	1,676	1,867	1,990	1,997
Net income ($ mil.)	—	82	91	5	(100)	26	17	(6)	38	26	(292)
Income as % of sales	—	9.4%	7.3%	0.5%	(7.7%)	2.0%	1.4%	(0.4%)	2.0%	1.3%	(14.6%)
Earnings per share ($)	—	3.03	3.20	0.20	(3.86)	0.95	0.60	(0.60)	1.12	0.66	(10.57)
Stock price – high ($)	—	32.25	32.38	28.13	23.13	18.63	24.13	27.75	25.25	29.75	15.63
Stock price – low ($)	—	17.13	22.50	19.38	11.63	11.13	14.63	10.50	12.88	13.50	2.13
Stock price – close ($)	(25.0%)	29.13	23.38	19.63	11.63	16.50	19.75	12.88	22.13	15.13	2.13
P/E – high	—	11	10	141	—	20	40	—	23	45	—
P/E – low	—	6	7	97	—	12	24	—	12	20	—
Dividends per share ($)	9.4%	0.10	0.15	0.20	0.20	0.20	0.20	0.20	0.22	0.29	0.23
Book value per share ($)	(3.9%)	15.26	18.62	18.49	14.16	15.15	15.91	21.17	21.63	21.25	10.68

1990 Year-end:
Debt ratio: 69.1%
Return on equity: —
Cash (mil.): $72
Current ratio: 0.46
Long-term debt (mil.): $744
No. of shares (mil.): 31
Dividends:
    1990 average yield: 10.6%
    1990 payout: —
Market value (mil.): $66

Stock Price History High/Low 1981–90

BANC ONE CORPORATION

NYSE symbol: ONE
Fiscal year ends: December 31

Hoover's Rating **A**

OVERVIEW

Columbus, Ohio–based Banc One is a bank holding company with 54 banks and 858 branches in 7 states: Ohio, Indiana, Wisconsin, Michigan, Kentucky, Texas, and, with 2 acquisitions in 1991, Illinois. Through its conservative approach to lending and expansion, Banc One avoided the problems of most banks in recent years, delivering increases in earnings for 22 straight years.

Its $30.3 billion in assets ranks 22nd among US banks. Its Texas holdings — failed MCorp banks and Bright Banc thrifts seized by federal regulators — are being purchased over time from the government. If its Texas assets were figured in (accounting rules forbid that until Banc One buys more equity), Banc One would rank 16th in the US in assets. It ranks #1 in return on assets among US banks.

Banc One grew in the Midwest by adding smaller banks, consolidating some back-office operations, and mixing local control with regional marketing clout. Banc One stresses retail banking — loans for small- to medium-sized-businesses and for consumers.

Banc One is known for early adoption of cutting-edge technology such as ATMs and computer-based home banking experiments.

WHO

Chairman: John B. McCoy, age 47, $1,247,602 pay
Chairman, Bonnet Resources Corp.: Robert H. Potts, age 66, $607,384 pay
Chairman, Banc One Ohio Corp.: Donald L. McWhorter, age 55, $478,505 pay
SVP and CFO: John W. Westman, age 49
Senior Executive, Personnel Division: Michael Hager
Auditors: Coopers & Lybrand
Employees: 19,300

WHEN

Banc One began in 1868 when F. C. Session opened a banking house in Columbus, Ohio. He later combined his operations with those of J. A. Jeffrey and Orange Johnson to form Commercial Bank, later Commercial National.

In 1929 Commercial National and City National Bank of Commerce combined to form City National Bank and Trust. In 1935 John H. McCoy became the bank's president, beginning a dynasty that would eventually oversee a multistate bank holding company stretching from the Great Lakes to the Gulf of Mexico.

John G. McCoy succeeded his father in 1958, and in the 1960s City National began to break from tradition. The bank hired a housewife-turned-comedienne from Lima, Ohio, for radio and TV commercials. Both Phyllis Diller and City National were on their way.

In 1966 the upstart bank introduced the first VISA (then BankAmericard) credit card service outside California. McCoy formed the First Banc Group of Ohio in 1967, folding in City National. In its first foray outside Columbus, the company bought Farmers Savings and Trust of Mansfield, Ohio (1968), the first of 44 Ohio banks it would add by 1985.

While it grew through acquisitions, First Banc Group scored a coup in 1977 when Merrill Lynch hired it to handle its Cash Management Account. The breakthrough financial service package combined a retail brokerage account with a checking account and debit card.

In 1979 First Banc Group changed its name to Banc One, and all affiliated banks included Bank One — with a "k" — in their names. The holding company uses a "c" in its name because Ohio law restricts use of the term "bank." John B. McCoy, the 3rd generation of bankers, succeeded his father as CEO in 1984 as barriers to interstate banking were falling. Banc One expanded rapidly into Indiana (buying Indiana's 2nd largest bank, American Fletcher, in 1986), Kentucky, Michigan, and Wisconsin. In 1989 Banc One announced it was acquiring, with a large dose of federal aid, 20 failed MCorp banks in beleaguered Texas. Banc One paid $34 million for $11 billion in assets, including $2.5 billion in problem loans managed by Banc One but guaranteed by the government. Banc One, to convert the big Texas operation to its brand of retail banking, added failed Dallas-based Bright Banc Savings to its Texas holdings in 1990.

In 1991 Banc One added Illinois banks, acquiring Springfield-based Marine Corporation ($1.2 billion in assets) and First Illinois ($1.6 billion) in suburbs of Chicago.

WHERE

HQ: 100 E. Broad St., Columbus, OH 43271
Phone: 614-248-5944
Fax: 614-248-5624

Banc One operates retail banks in 7 states.

WHAT

	1990 Assets	
	$ mil.	% of total
Cash & due from banks	1,881	6
Deposits in other banks	23	—
Short-term investments	606	2
Securities	5,272	18
Net loans & leases	20,043	66
Notes receivable from FDIC	416	1
Investment in Bank One Texas, NA	352	1
Other	1,743	6
Total	**30,336**	**100**

Loans	Affiliates
Commercial loans	Banc One Indiana Corp.
Credit card loans	Banc One Ohio Corp.
Installment loans	(Kentucky, Michigan,
Leases	Ohio)
Real estate loans	Banc One Wisconsin Corp.
Tax-exempt loans	Bank One, Texas, NA

Deposit Accounts	Nonbank Affiliates
Demand deposits	Banc One Capital Corp.
Money market accounts	Banc One Services Corp.
Savings deposits	Bonnet Resources Corp.
Time deposits	

Financial Services	Banc One Diversified Services Corp.
Consumer finance	Banc One Credit Corp.
Credit life insurance	Banc One Financial Services
Discount brokerage	Inc.
Equipment leasing	Banc One Leasing Corp.
Mortgage banking	Banc One Insurance Group
Trust services	Banc One Mortgage Corp.
	Banc One Securities Corp.
	Banc One Travel Corp.
	Bank One Ohio
	Trust Co., NA

HOW MUCH

	9-Year Growth	1981	1982	1983	1984	1985	1986	1987	1988	1989	1990
Assets ($ mil.)	26.6%	3,639	5,029	7,270	9,106	10,824	17,372	18,730	25,274	26,552	30,336
Net income ($ mil.)	30.5%	39	58	83	108	130	200	209	340	348	423
Income as % of assets	—	1.1%	1.1%	1.1%	1.2%	1.2%	1.2%	1.1%	1.3%	1.3%	1.4%
Earnings per share ($)	11.9%	1.00	1.09	1.28	1.44	1.65	1.75	1.79	2.35	*2.41*	*2.76*
Stock price – high ($)	—	7.45	12.14	14.17	13.15	20.94	27.38	24.38	25.11	33.64	33.13
Stock price – low ($)	—	5.89	7.04	10.02	10.39	12.52	17.66	14.67	19.42	20.23	19.00
Stock price – close ($)	16.2%	7.18	11.69	11.73	12.84	19.35	18.91	19.83	20.23	29.43	27.75
P/E – high	—	7	11	11	9	13	16	14	11	14	12
P/E – low	—	6	6	8	7	8	10	8	8	8	7
Dividends per share ($)	13.6%	0.33	0.36	0.43	0.49	0.58	0.68	0.74	0.84	0.95	1.04
Book value per share ($)	13.2%	5.92	6.46	7.42	8.55	10.02	11.40	12.52	14.18	15.66	18.11

1990 Year-end:
Return on equity: 16.3%
Equity as % of assets: 9.4%
Cash (mil.): $1,904
Long-term debt (mil.): $525
No. of shares (mil.): 159
Dividends:
  1990 average yield: 3.7%
  1990 payout: 37.7%
Market value (mil.): $4,408
Sales (mil.): $3,507

Stock Price History High/Low 1981–90

RANKINGS

22nd in *Fortune* 100 Commercial Banking Cos.
127th in *Business Week* 1000

KEY COMPETITORS

H. F. Ahmanson	First Interstate
American Financial	NCNB
Chase Manhattan	PNC Financial
Chemical Banking	Other multistate bank
Citicorp	holding companies
First Chicago	

BANK OF BOSTON CORPORATION

NYSE symbol: BKB
Fiscal year ends: December 31

Hoover's Rating **D**

OVERVIEW

Bank of Boston, the 18th largest US banking organization, with $32.5 billion in assets at the end of 1990, owns First National Bank of Boston, New England's largest bank, and banks in Connecticut, Maine, Rhode Island, and Vermont.

About 85% of the company's total loans at the end of 1990 were to US borrowers and the balance to borrowers overseas. Of the domestic loans, the majority were made in New England, through 265 branches.

Bank of Boston's National Banking Group provides credit, operating, investment, and merchant banking services outside New England to large and middle-market corporations, as well as to specialized industries, including high technology, transportation, energy, and media and entertainment.

The company's Global Banking Group serves US multinational customers in Europe and elsewhere. Other groups are the Technology and Operations Group, Finance and Control Group, and the Corporate Center (corporate services).

Bank of Boston hopes to slow its decline after a $438 million loss in 1990. Its problems stem from real estate loans gone sour in New England's recessionary economy.

WHO

Chairman and CEO: Ira Stepanian, age 54, $650,000 pay
President: Charles K. Gifford, age 48, $450,000 pay
EVP: Peter C. Read, age 54, $318,750 pay
EVP: Michael Simmons, age 51, $316,667 pay
EVP: Kevin J. Mulvaney, age 42, $233,750 pay
EVP and CFO: Peter J. Manning, age 52
Director of Human Resources: W. Grant Chandler, age 62
Auditors: Coopers & Lybrand
Employees: 17,400

WHEN

William Phillips and 5 other leading Boston merchants founded the Massachusetts Bank in 1784. Profitable from the beginning, the bank was known as very conservative, with strict credit requirements, a policy that both made enemies and encouraged competing banks to open. In 1865 the bank became Massachusetts National Bank, joining the National Bank System after other Boston banks.

Deposits of the bank grew from $1 million to over $6 million between 1900 and 1903, under President John Weeks. In 1903 Weeks and others purchased First National Bank of Boston (founded in 1859) and then combined it with Massachusetts National, adopting the purchased bank's name. Weeks selected Dan Wing, 32, as president of First National.

Under Wing the bank grew to become the 8th largest US bank in deposits in 1932. The bank expanded internationally, opening branches in Argentina (1917) and Cuba (1923). By 1927 the bank also had representative offices in Europe and was a leading US bank in financing foreign trade, serving New England companies.

In 1929 the bank acquired Old Colony Trust Company, a major Boston banking and trust organization. In 1934 the bank, complying with the Banking Act of 1933, spun off its investment banking business into a new corporation, The First Boston Corporation.

In 1945 the bank got approval to open a branch in Brazil. In the late 1940s Bank of Boston became the first US bank to offer a full factoring service (loans on accounts receivable). In the early 1960s the bank started international factoring.

In 1970 the bank reorganized as a subsidiary of First National Boston Corporation, which changed its name to Bank of Boston Corporation in 1983. In the 1970s and 1980s the bank became the largest in New England, purchasing banks in Massachusetts, Maine, Connecticut, Vermont, and Rhode Island. In 1989 Bank of Boston Corporation earned a net income of $70 million despite a $722 million provision for possible real estate and foreign loan losses to less developed countries.

Continued real estate loan problems led to a loss in 1990. Despite the problems, Bank of Boston bid (unsuccessfully) for seized rival Bank of New England. Bank of Boston suspended its second quarter dividend in 1991, the first such curtailment since 1936. The dividend curtailment helped shore up capital, and regulators allowed Bank of Boston to take control of the failed, 17-branch First Mutual Bank for Savings in Boston.

WHERE

HQ: 100 Federal St., Boston, MA 02110
Phone: 617-434-2200
Fax: 617-575-2232 (Shareholder Services)

Bank of Boston has operations in 20 states in the US and 25 foreign countries.

	1990 Average Assets	
	$ mil.	% of total
US	30,350	83
Latin America	2,392	6
Europe	2,097	6
Asia/Pacific	1,337	4
Other	315	1
Total	**36,491**	**100**

WHAT

	1990 Assets	
	$ mil.	% of total
Cash & due from banks	1,961	6
Deposits in other banks	1,226	4
Federal funds sold & securities purchased to resell	1,139	4
Trading account securities	172	—
Mortgages for sale	294	1
Investment securities	3,526	11
Net loans & lease financing	20,971	64
Premises & equipment	492	2
Other	2,748	8
Total	**32,529**	**100**

Financial Services
Corporate lending
Correspondent banking
International banking
Investment banking
Leasing
Mortgage services
Real estate lending
Retail banking
Securities and payments services
Trust services

Major Bank Subsidiaries
Bank of Boston Connecticut
Bank of Vermont
Casco Northern Bank, NA (Maine)
First National Bank of Boston
Rhode Island Hospital Trust National Bank

HOW MUCH

	9-Year Growth	1981	1982	1983	1984	1985	1986	1987	1988	1989	1990
Assets ($ mil.)	7.6%	16,809	18,267	19,538	22,079	28,296	34,045	34,117	36,061	39,178	32,529
Net income ($ mil.)	—	119	124	136	164	174	233	20	322	70	(438)
Income as % of assets	—	0.7%	0.7%	0.7%	0.7%	0.6%	0.7%	0.1%	0.9%	0.2%	(1.3%)
Earnings per share ($)	—	2.08	2.22	2.47	2.78	2.82	3.49	0.10	4.43	0.80	(6.21)
Stock price – high ($)	—	10.64	13.21	15.88	14.63	20.83	29.92	38.00	30.00	30.63	20.00
Stock price – low ($)	—	7.53	7.13	10.88	9.67	13.21	19.29	17.88	20.88	15.75	6.00
Stock price – close ($)	(5.0%)	10.14	11.25	13.50	13.25	20.83	26.58	22.50	23.63	19.00	6.38
P/E – high	—	5	6	6	5	7	9	380	7	38	—
P/E – low	—	4	3	4	3	5	6	179	5	20	—
Dividends per share ($)	4.0%	0.58	0.66	0.72	0.78	0.82	0.91	1.02	1.12	1.24	0.82
Book value per share ($)	3.6%	14.34	16.23	17.75	19.58	21.53	24.47	23.62	27.02	26.51	19.67

1990 Year-end:
Return on equity: —
Equity as % of assets: 5.1%
Cash (mil.): $3,386
Long-term debt (mil.): $1,182
No. of shares (mil.): 74
Dividends:
  1990 average yield: 12.9%
  1990 payout: —
Market value (mil.): $469
Sales (mil.): $5,658

Stock Price History High/Low 1981–90

RANKINGS

18th in *Fortune* 100 Commercial Banking Cos.
781st in *Business Week* 1000

KEY COMPETITORS

Fleet/Norstar
Major money-center banks
Mutual savings banks
Savings and loans

THE BANK OF NEW YORK COMPANY, INC.

NYSE symbol: BK
Fiscal year ends: December 31

Hoover's Rating C+

OVERVIEW

The Bank of New York, the 15th largest bank holding company in the US, focuses on 5 businesses: corporate banking, retail banking, securities processing, trust and investment management, and financial market services.

The bank serves the international banking needs of US companies in foreign trade financing as one of the industry's largest participants in issuance of letters of credit and international funds transfer systems. The bank currently has the largest network of branches (222) in the suburbs of New York City. It provides custom banking at 19 locations in New York City for corporations, retail customers, and wealthy individuals. Bank of New York has the 4th largest portfolio of highly leveraged transactions (HLTs), but executives are quick to point out that 1/3 of its HLTs are to the media industry, where the bank has a solid record and, therefore, reduced exposure.

As the leading provider of securities processing services in the US, Bank of New York is custodian for $700 billion in securities. Its personal trust business is ranked 8th largest in the US in personal assets under management.

WHO

Chairman and CEO: J. Carter Bacot, age 58, $1,006,516 pay
President; VC, The Bank of New York: Peter Herrick, age 64, $687,081 pay
SEVP; SEVP and CFO, The Bank of New York: Deno D. Papageorge, age 52, $510,382 pay
SVP Personnel, The Bank of New York: Frank L. Peterson
Auditors: Deloitte & Touche
Employees: 13,847

WHEN

Alexander Hamilton and a group of influential New York merchants and lawyers founded New York City's first bank, the Bank of New York, in 1784. Attorney Hamilton at age 27 recognized the need to grant credit for the new nation's economy and to return credibility to the monetary system.

For 15 years the bank was the only commercial lending firm in the city. The Bank of New York, with the Bank of North America (created by the US Congress), became the depository for the first foreign loans granted by the US. The bank has paid dividends continuously since 1785.

Hamilton became US Secretary of the Treasury in 1789. He soon negotiated the new US government's first loan, issued by the Bank of New York for $200,000. The bank also assisted in financing the War of 1812 by offering subscription books for $16 million, and the Civil War by loaning the government $150 million. In 1878 the bank became a US Treasury depository for the sale of 4% government bonds.

Bank of New York emphasized commercial banking to select customers, and, because it did not compete for size with other banks, the bank was no longer one of the largest in the US by 1904. In 1922 the bank merged with New York Life Insurance and Trust Company to form Bank of New York and Trust Company. The bank began to develop trust and investment services, investing trust assets in common stocks, including IBM, after the 1929 Crash. In 1938 the bank changed its name to Bank of New York.

In 1948 Bank of New York acquired the Fifth Avenue Bank to get a mid-Manhattan location and expand trust services. In 1966 the bank acquired Empire Trust Company, which specialized in lending to developing industries. The Bank of New York Company, Inc., a new holding company created in 1968, expanded statewide by acquiring banks in White Plains, Endicott-Binghamton, Albany, Olean, Syracuse, and Buffalo. In 1980 the bank bought Empire National Bank (Newburgh), with 38 branches, the 2nd largest branch network in the state outside New York City.

The company acquired New York competitor Irving Bank in a 1988 hostile takeover for $1.4 billion in cash and equity securities to make it the 10th largest US banking company at the time. The bank acquired the credit card portfolio of First City Bancorporation of Texas and of Dreyfus Consumer Bank's Gold MasterCard in 1990.

Problems with highly leveraged transactions led to a loss in early 1991, and the bank cut its dividend. The bank announced it would sell its profitable factoring operations, Bank of New York Financial, to improve its finances.

WHERE

HQ: 48 Wall St., New York, NY 10286
Phone: 212-495-1784
Fax: 212-495-1239 (Public Relations)

Bank of New York has offices or affiliates in 45 states and overseas.

WHAT

	1990 Assets	
	$ mil.	% of total
Cash & due from banks	2,860	6
Interest-bearing deposits in banks	853	2
Investment securities	3,287	7
Trading assets	219	1
Federal funds sold & securites purchased under resale agreements	1,590	4
Loans	34,131	75
Less allowance for loan losses	(2,159)	(5)
Other	4,609	10
Total	**45,390**	**100**

Banking Services

Corporate Banking	Retail banking
Asset-based lending	Credit cards
Cash management	Mortgage loans
Foreign trade financing	
Funds transfer	
Letters of credit	
Merger and acquisition services	

Securities Processing
Mutual fund servicing
Securities custody
Securities lending
Stock transfer services

Trust and Investment Management

Financial Market Services

RANKINGS

15th in *Fortune* 100 Commercial Banking Cos.
329th in *Business Week* 1000

HOW MUCH

	9-Year Growth	1981	1982	1983	1984	1985	1986	1987	1988	1989	1990
Assets ($ mil.)	16.5%	11,463	12,724	12,797	15,157	18,486	20,709	23,065	47,388	48,857	45,390
Net income ($ mil.)	20.4%	58	73	91	108	130	155	103	213	51	308
Income as % of assets	—	0.5%	0.6%	0.7%	0.7%	0.7%	0.8%	0.4%	0.5%	0.1%	0.7%
Earnings per share ($)	5.1%	2.54	2.77	3.15	3.57	4.02	4.54	2.81	5.21	0.27	3.98
Stock price – high ($)	—	15.79	18.58	22.08	24.50	34.92	46.75	45.88	37.25	55.00	41.75
Stock price – low ($)	—	10.96	12.04	15.75	17.50	23.25	32.83	24.50	25.88	36.75	13.25
Stock price – close ($)	2.4%	14.29	16.58	21.83	23.67	34.25	38.88	25.75	37.00	40.25	17.75
P/E – high	—	6	7	7	7	9	10	16	7	204	10
P/E – low	—	4	4	5	5	6	7	9	5	136	3
Dividends per share ($)	8.5%	1.02	1.08	1.16	1.26	1.40	1.56	1.71	1.83	1.97	2.12
Book value per share ($)	6.1%	21.10	23.05	25.39	27.88	28.38	31.76	33.65	37.34	34.87	35.92

1990 Year-end:
Return on equity: 11.2%
Equity as % of assets: 6.4%
Cash (mil.): $3,713
Long-term debt (mil.): $865
No. of shares (mil.): 69
Dividends:
  1990 average yield: 11.9%
  1990 payout: 53.3%
Market value (mil.): $1,231
Sales (mil.): $5,333

Stock Price History High/Low 1981–90

KEY COMPETITORS

American Express
BankAmerica
Bankers Trust
Barclays
Canadian Imperial
Chase Manhattan
Chemical Banking
Citicorp
Crédit Lyonnais
Deutsche Bank
First Chicago
Fleet/Norstar
HSBC
J.P. Morgan
Royal Bank
Other money-center banks

BANKAMERICA CORPORATION

NYSE symbol: BAC
Fiscal year ends: December 31

OVERVIEW

Every cloud has a silver lining, and once the clouds of its foray into foreign lending lifted, BankAmerica was lining its pockets with troubled thrifts, on the way to becoming the nation's 2nd largest banking institution (Citicorp leads in assets).

BankAmerica, sidelined by high expenses and problem loans to less-developed countries (LDCs) in the mid-1980s, sat out much of the frenzy of domestic real estate lending and highly leveraged transactions. When those businesses battered competitors, BankAmerica was recovering and re-establishing itself as the dominant consumer bank in the western US.

Its 1990 acquisitions in Arizona, Nevada, and Washington built its "core capital" and positioned BankAmerica for the largest deal in banking history — the 1991 purchase of Security Pacific, forming the largest US bank in terms of market capitalization, equity capital, core earnings, domestic assets, and branch networks.

BankAmerica is expected to use the additional clout acquired from Security Pacific to continue to expand throughout the US. With consumer banking in 10 states, BankAmerica may be a suitor for New England's Shawmut or other East Coast banks.

WHEN

Amadeo Giannini, son of Italian immigrants, founded the Bank of Italy in San Francisco in 1904. Two years later he saved the cash, gold, and notes from the bank before it was destroyed by the fire caused by the 1906 earthquake. Giannini opened for business in a temporary location on a pier and loaned money to finance the reconstruction.

Giannini circumvented a 1921 federal ruling prohibiting branching by acquiring the Bank of America of Los Angeles, which had 21 branches. In 1928 Giannini formed a holding company, Transamerica Corporation, to manage his banks and other businesses. By 1930 Bank of Italy and Bank of America were operating as Bank of America.

By the end of 1945 Bank of America had passed Chase Manhattan to become the largest US bank. The Bank Holding Company Act of 1956 forced the 1958 separation of Bank of America from the insurance and other services of Transamerica. Also in 1958 Bank of America introduced BankAmericard, the bank credit card that became VISA in 1977.

In the 1950s and 1960s the bank expanded internationally, and by 1970 it was one of the largest international lenders in the US. The bank became the subsidiary of BankAmerica Corporation, a bank holding company formed in 1968.

A. W. Clausen became CEO in 1970, and the bank rapidly expanded in real estate and foreign loans. Earnings and assets quadrupled during the 1970s but decreased steadily in the early 1980s when the bank suffered loan losses. At the end of 1980, Citicorp had replaced BankAmerica as the largest US bank.

In 1981 Clausen became head of the World Bank and was replaced by Samuel Armacost. In 1983 the company acquired Seafirst (Seattle–First National Bank) and Charles Schwab (discount brokerage, sold back to Schwab in 1987). By 1985 loan losses had forced Armacost to lay off employees for the first time in company history. In 1986 Armacost resigned under fire, and the board reappointed Clausen as CEO.

After reducing costs and domestic problem loans, the bank became profitable again in 1988 after 3 years of losses. In 1990 Clausen retired, and President Richard M. Rosenberg, a 22-year Wells Fargo veteran, became CEO. The company began 1990 with banking operations in 3 states and ended the year represented in 7, through 8 acquisitions of troubled thrifts. A 1991 bid for Bank of New England failed, but BankAmerica bought Security Pacific, the nation's 5th largest bank, in a $4.5 billion stock swap that solidified its domination of the California and Washington markets.

WHO

Chairman and CEO: Richard M. Rosenberg, age 60, $1,600,000 pay (prior to merger)
VC and CFO: Frank N. Newman, age 48, $975,000 pay
EVP and Personnel Relations Officer: Robert N. Beck, age 50
Auditors: Ernst & Young
Employees: 93,800

WHERE

HQ: Bank of America Center, San Francisco, CA 94104
Phone: 415-622-2091
Fax: 415-622-7915 (Corporate Secretary)

BankAmerica provides banking services in 10 western states and has offices worldwide.

	1990 Assets	
	$ mil.	% of total
US	88,351	80
Europe, Middle East & Africa	7,702	7
Asia	8,243	7
Latin America & the Caribbean	5,007	5
Canada	1,425	1
Total	**110,728**	**100**

WHAT

	1990 Assets	
	$ mil.	% of total
Cash and due from banks	7,845	7
Interest-bearing deposits with banks	3,183	3
Federal funds sold	760	1
Securities purchased for resale	871	1
Trading account assets	843	1
Investment securities	6,910	6
Loans	85,765	78
Allowance for credit losses	(2,912)	(3)
Premises and equipment, net	2,510	2
Other	4,953	4
Total	**110,728**	**100**

Financial Services
Bank credit cards
Capital market services
Consumer and
  real estate loans
Corporate lending
Credit-related insurance
Depository services
Employee benefit trusts
Investment banking
Money transfer services
Mortgage banking
Payment services

Travelers checks

Selected Other Holdings
KorAm Bank (31.2%, Korea)
Managistics (payroll services)

Major Subsidiaries
Bank of America Arizona
Bank of America Idaho
Bank of America Nevada
Bank of America Oregon
Bank of America State Bank
Seattle-First National Bank

RANKINGS

2nd in *Fortune* 100 Commercial Banking Cos.
85th in *Business Week* 1000

HOW MUCH

	9-Year Growth	1981	1982	1983	1984	1985	1986	1987	1988	1989	1990
Assets ($ mil.)	(1.0%)	121,158	122,221	121,176	117,680	118,541	104,189	92,833	94,647	98,764	110,728
Net income ($ mil.)	7.8%	445	390	390	346	(337)	(518)	(955)	547	820	877
Income as % of assets	—	0.4%	0.3%	0.3%	0.3%	(0.3%)	(0.5%)	(1.0%)	0.6%	0.8%	0.8%
Earnings per share ($)	2.7%	3.02	2.61	2.18	1.77	(2.68)	(3.74)	(6.43)	2.77	3.74	3.84
Stock price – high ($)	—	30.75	26.25	25.50	23.13	22.75	18.75	15.38	19.13	36.38	33.50
Stock price – low ($)	—	20.63	15.63	18.00	14.50	12.88	9.50	5.25	6.75	17.00	17.50
Stock price – close ($)	2.5%	21.25	20.13	20.88	18.13	15.63	14.63	6.88	17.63	26.75	26.50
P/E – high	—	10	10	12	13	—	—	—	7	10	9
P/E – low	—	7	6	8	8	—	—	—	2	5	5
Dividends per share ($)	(4.4%)	1.50	1.52	1.52	1.52	1.16	0.00	0.00	0.00	0.60	1.00
Book value per share ($)	(0.2%)	27.72	28.96	29.43	29.10	25.11	21.49	15.12	18.43	23.32	27.21

1990 Year-end:
Return on equity: 15.2%
Equity as % of assets: 5.8%
Cash (mil.): $11,028
Long-term debt (mil.): $3,931
No. of shares (mil.): 213
Dividends:
  1990 average yield: 3.8%
  1990 payout: 26.0%
Market value (mil.): $5,654
Sales (mil.): $12,323

Stock Price History High/Low 1981–90

KEY COMPETITORS

H. F. Ahmanson
American Express
ADP
Banc One
Bank of Boston
Bank of New York
Canadian Imperial
Chase Manhattan
Chemical Banking
Citicorp
Crédit Lyonnais
CS Holdings
Dai-Ichi Kangyo
First Interstate
Fleet/Norstar
Great Western
HSBC
J.P. Morgan
Royal Bank
Union Bank of Switzerland
Wells Fargo
Other multistate bank holding companies

BANKERS TRUST NEW YORK CORPORATION

OVERVIEW

Bankers Trust New York Corporation owns Bankers Trust, one of the largest US banks, and provides corporate finance, money and securities market trading, and trust services. Bankers Trust is known for pioneering the use of derivates (designer options and futures). Its focus is on addressing the challenges of the globalization and deregulation of financial markets.

Having sold its consumer banking business to become a merchant bank on a global scale, Bankers operates nationally and internationally. Problem loans to less-developed countries led to a loss of nearly $1 billion in 1989.

Bankers rebounded to record net income

and return on equity in 1990, but recession whittled away at the company, and it announced staff reductions in early 1991.

The company operates 2 core businesses, Financial Services and PROFITCo. Financial Services embraces merchant banking for corporations and international clients. The PROFITCo division conducts trust and custodial services and securities processing.

Subsidiaries include Bankers Trust Company, the big commerical bank; BT Securities, an underwriter and dealer in US Treasury and agency securities, municipal bonds, and other debt securities; and Bankers Trust (Delaware), a state bank.

NYSE symbol: BT
Fiscal year ends: December 31

Hoover's Rating **C+**

WHO

Chairman: Charles S. Sanford, Jr., age 54, $1,500,000 pay
EVP and CFO: Timothy T. Yates, age 43
EVP Human Resources: Mark Bieler
Auditors: Ernst & Young
Employees: 13,522

WHERE

HQ: 280 Park Ave., New York, NY 10017
Phone: 212-250-2500
Fax: 212-454-1704 (Public Relations)

Bankers Trust operates worldwide.

	1990 Assets	
	$ mil.	% of total
US	39,271	49
Other Western Hemisphere	14,710	18
Asia & the Pacific	9,190	12
UK	8,686	11
Other Europe	7,024	9
Middle East & Africa	677	1
Adjustments	(15,962)	—
Total	**63,596**	**100**

WHEN

Henry Davison, a 35-year-old New York banker, and his young banker friends founded Bankers Trust Company in 1903 to handle trust business referred by commercial banks. The company raised capital with the sale of 10,000 shares of stock totaling $20 million in subscriptions.

In 1908 the company started a foreign department to handle transactions with correspondent banks abroad. Bankers Trust bought Mercantile Trust (1911), Manhattan Trust (1912), and Astor Trust (1917). Under the Federal Reserve Act of 1913, banks were allowed to offer trust services, eliminating Bankers Trust's competitive advantage. To be able to offer broader banking services, Bankers Trust became a member of the Federal Reserve System in 1917.

The bank's securities department, started in 1916, expanded in 1919 to include underwriting and distributing securities and in 1928 became a subsidiary; in 1931 it closed to comply with the Glass-Steagall Act (which required separation of investment banking from commercial banking).

In 1945 Bankers Trust opened a metropolitan division and for the first time offered savings accounts, checking accounts without minimum balances, home improvement loans,

automobile loans, and unsecured business loans.

In 1950 the company bought Lawyers Trust, Title Guaranty & Trust's banking division, and Flushing National Bank. The company also added Commercial National (1951), Bayside National (1953), and Public National (1955). From 1955 through 1965 the company added 22 branches and bought South Shore Bank (Staten Island) and First National Bank (Long Island).

In 1965 Bankers Trust formed a holding company to own Bankers Trust Company and 3 other banks in upstate New York. By 1967 the holding company had 89 offices in New York and 2 in London. In the next 8 years the company grew to more than 200 offices. The company's international operations expanded in the 1970s to more than 30 countries, with a correspondent network of more than 1,200 banks in 123 countries.

In the early 1980s the company sold its consumer banking business to various financial institutions in order to focus on corporate services, particularly commercial and merchant banking in international markets. The company formed an investment banking venture in Poland (1990) and advised Czechoslovakia on industry privatization (1991).

WHAT

	1990 Assets	
	$ mil.	% of total
Cash & due from banks	4,149	7
Interest-bearing deposits with banks	4,593	7
Securities purchased for resale	4,645	7
Trading account assets	17,228	27
Investment securities	7,030	11
Loans	21,474	34
Allowance for credit losses	(2,169)	(3)
Premises & equipment, net	706	1
Other	5,940	9
Total	**63,596**	**100**

Financial Services
Commercial banking services
Corporate finance
Fiduciary and securities services
Global operating and information services
International merchant banking
Investment management

RANKINGS

8th in *Fortune* 100 Commercial Banking Cos.
182nd in *Business Week* 1000

KEY COMPETITORS

Bank of New York	First Chicago
BankAmerica	Goldman Sachs
Barclays	HSBC
Bear Stearns	Industrial Bank of
Canadian Imperial	Japan
Chase Manhattan	Merrill Lynch
Chemical Banking	J.P. Morgan
Citicorp	Morgan Stanley
Continental Bank	Royal Bank
Crédit Lyonnais	Salomon
CS Holding	Union Bank of
Dai-Ichi Kangyo	Switzerland
Deutsche Bank	

HOW MUCH

	9-Year Growth	1981	1982	1983	1984	1985	1986	1987	1988	1989	1990
Assets ($ mil.)	7.1%	34,213	40,427	40,003	45,208	50,581	56,420	56,521	57,942	55,658	63,596
Net income ($ mil.)	15.1%	188	223	257	307	371	428	1	648	(980)	665
Income as % of assets	—	0.6%	0.6%	0.6%	0.7%	0.7%	0.8%	0.0%	1.1%	(1.8%)	1.0%
Earnings per share ($)	9.5%	3.45	3.88	4.20	4.76	5.29	5.97	0.02	8.01	(12.10)	7.80
Stock price – high ($)	—	18.94	22.75	24.75	29.13	37.81	52.50	55.25	41.25	58.25	46.75
Stock price – low ($)	—	13.44	12.63	17.81	18.88	26.81	32.88	26.25	29.63	34.50	28.50
Stock price – close ($)	11.0%	16.94	18.56	22.56	27.38	36.75	45.25	31.75	35.00	41.38	43.38
P/E – high	—	6	6	6	6	7	9	2,763	5	—	6
P/E – low	—	4	3	4	4	5	6	1,313	4	—	4
Dividends per share ($)	10.8%	0.95	1.05	1.15	1.26	1.38	1.53	1.71	1.92	2.14	2.38
Book value per share ($)	3.7%	22.54	24.93	27.65	30.51	34.32	38.78	37.39	43.14	26.29	31.19

1990 Year-end:
Return on equity: 27.1%
Equity as % of assets: 4.8%
Cash (mil.): $8,742
Long-term debt (mil.): $2,650
No. of shares (mil.): 81
Dividends:
1990 average yield: 5.5%
1990 payout: 30.5%
Market value (mil.): $3,510
Sales (mil.): $7,919

Stock Price History High/Low 1981–90

C. R. BARD, INC.

NYSE symbol: BCR
Fiscal year ends: December 31

OVERVIEW

Headquartered in Murray Hill, New Jersey, Bard is a major producer of medical and health care products. Known traditionally in the urological field for its Foley catheter, the company is also a leader in cardiovascular and surgical products. Bard sells about 90% of its products to hospitals, doctors, and nursing homes.

Bard had a net income decrease of 38% in 1990, caused primarily by the company's recall of the New Probe angioplasty catheter from the US market in 1989 at the direction of the FDA. This was followed by a voluntary withdrawal of the Sprint and Solo angioplasty catheters in March 1990 after a company investigation revealed improper labeling. Both of these recalls resulted in Bard's temporary withdrawal from the US balloon angioplasty market, although the company reentered the market with its Probe III catheter in 1991.

Promising new products in Bard's future include Contigen, a urinary incontinence implant for which the company hopes to gain approval by the end of 1991, an umbrella catheter for the covering of arterial holes, and a clamshell catheter used for heart defects.

WHEN

When visiting Europe at the turn of the century, silk importer Charles Russell Bard discovered that Gomenol, a mixture of olive oil with an extract distilled from eucalyptus, gave him relief from urinary problems caused by tuberculosis. He brought the "medicine" to America and began distributing it.

In 1907 Bard began selling a ureteral catheter developed by J. Eynard, a French firm. Bard incorporated in 1923 under the company's present name. In 1926, because of failing health, Charles Bard sold the company to John F. Willits, his sales manager, and Edson L. Outwin, his accountant. He stayed on as a consultant until 1932 and died in 1934. That year the company became the sole agent for Davol Rubber's newly developed Foley catheter. By 1948 sales had topped $1 million.

From 1950 to 1959 sales increased over 400% to $9 million. The company introduced its first presterilized packaged product in 1958 and began to expand its product line with disposable drainage tubes and an intravenous feeding device.

In 1963 Bard formed 2 joint ventures with Davol to manufacture and distribute hospital and surgical supplies internationally. The company began manufacturing plastic tubing in 1964 and by 1969 was manufacturing over 75% of the 6,000 products it distributed.

During this period Bard acquired United States Catheter and Instrument (1966). Net sales had increased to $51 million by 1969.

The company bought over a dozen companies during the 1970s, diversifying into the cardiovascular, respiratory therapy, home-care product, and kidney dialysis fields. By 1976 Bard was offering 13,000 products.

In 1979 Bard introduced the first angioplasty catheter, a nonsurgical device to clear blocked arteries. Bard bought Automated Screening Devices (producers of a high-tech blood pressure monitor) in 1980. Also that year the company purchased Davol for $48 million, assuring Bard's supply of its #1-selling Foley catheters and more than doubling sales of surgical implants.

Bard increased its R&D budget throughout the 1980s, spending $36.2 million in 1989, but that year breakage problems caused the company to recall an angioplasty catheter. Net income dropped from $79 million in 1988 to $65 million in 1989. In March of 1990 Bard recalled its angioplasty catheters from the US market because of improper labeling.

In 1990 Bard sold its Shield Healthcare Centers and greatly increased its presence in the Australasia market by purchasing the 50% that it did not already own of Bard Bio-Spectrum (Australia).

WHO

Chairman and CEO: George T. Maloney, age 58, $458,500 pay (prior to promotion)
EVP and COO: William H. Longfield, age 52, $330,000 pay
EVP and CFO: George A. Davis, age 63, $228,700 pay
VP Personnel: Eugene B. Schultz, age 62
Auditors: Arthur Andersen & Co.
Employees: 8,750

WHERE

HQ: 730 Central Ave., Murray Hill, NJ 07974
Phone: 908-277-8000
Fax: 908-277-8240

Bard has operations in 17 countries.

	1990 Sales		1990 Operating Income	
	$ mil.	% of total	$ mil.	% of total
US	572	73	41	53
Foreign	213	27	36	47
Adjustments	—	—	(10)	—
Total	**785**	**100**	**67**	**100**

WHAT

	1990 Sales	
	$ mil.	% of total
Cardiovascular products	334	42
Urological products	185	24
Surgical products	245	31
General health products & services	21	3
Total	**785**	**100**

Products
Ambulatory pumps
Angiographic catheters
Blood oxygenators
Cardiopulmonary support systems
Cardiotomy reservoirs
Cardiovascular recanalization devices (balloon angioplasty catheters, laser devices)
Diagnostic catheter systems
Disposable obstetrical instruments
Drug infusion pumps
Electrophysiology products (pacing, diagnostic, and therapeutic electrodes; cardiac mapping)
Hemo-concentrators
Medical fabrics and mesh
Ostomy devices
Surgical products (wound drainage devices, vascular access catheters and ports)
Urological products (catheters, trays, collection systems)
Wound management and skin care products

RANKINGS

400th in *Fortune* 500 Industrial Cos.
485th in *Business Week* 1000

KEY COMPETITORS

Abbott Labs
American Cyanamid
American Home Products
Baxter
Becton, Dickinson
Eli Lilly
Hewlett-Packard
Johnson & Johnson
Pfizer

HOW MUCH

	9-Year Growth	1981	1982	1983	1984	1985	1986	1987	1988	1989	1990
Sales ($ mil.)	10.1%	330	343	397	417	465	548	641	758	778	785
Net income ($ mil.)	6.7%	23	27	33	35	42	51	62	79	65	40
Income as % of sales	—	6.8%	7.9%	8.4%	8.5%	9.0%	9.3%	9.7%	10.4%	8.4%	5.1%
Earnings per share ($)	7.9%	0.38	0.46	0.56	0.58	0.70	0.86	1.07	1.38	1.18	0.76
Stock price – high ($)	—	5.48	8.75	11.69	9.44	11.00	20.19	25.13	24.63	26.50	22.50
Stock price – low ($)	—	3.29	4.58	6.88	4.75	5.41	9.38	12.50	16.88	18.75	12.88
Stock price – close ($)	14.5%	5.04	7.56	8.63	5.63	11.00	18.13	17.25	23.00	22.13	17.00
P/E – high	—	14	19	21	16	16	23	23	18	22	30
P/E – low	—	9	10	12	8	8	11	12	12	16	17
Dividends per share ($)	20.8%	0.08	0.09	0.10	0.11	0.13	0.17	0.22	0.28	0.36	0.42
Book value per share ($)	11.4%	2.45	2.81	3.22	3.66	4.25	4.56	5.23	5.83	6.12	6.45

1990 Year-end:
Debt ratio: 16.9%
Return on equity: 12.1%
Cash (mil.): $20
Current ratio: 2.00
Long-term debt (mil.): $70
No. of shares (mil.): 53
Dividends:
  1990 average yield: 2.5%
  1990 payout: 55.3%
Market value (mil.): $902

Stock Price History High/Low 1981–90

BARNETT BANKS, INC.

NYSE symbol: BBI
Fiscal year ends: December 31

Hoover's Rating **C+**

OVERVIEW

Jacksonville-based Barnett is Florida's largest financial institution, with 23.9% of the state's deposits, and is Georgia's 9th largest bank. Barnett was the 20th largest banking organization in the US before the recent round of bank mergers, which included the proposed combination of Barnett rivals C&S/Sovran and NCNB.

Real estate loans account for 49% of Barnett's loan portfolio. Although the bank enjoyed years of uninterrupted expansion, recent declines in in-migration, economic weakness and a slow real estate market in Florida put a halt to Barnett's growth in 1990, when the bank began experiencing weaker demand for loans while booking higher provisions for bad debt. Commercial real estate loans have been a weak spot.

Barnett is cutting costs by trimming the payroll and consolidating back-office operations into regional centers. The bank is investing in automation, including a check processing system that uses digitized check images stored on computers.

Additional branch services and territorial expansion are in Barnett's future plans. The bank recently called off merger talks with troubled Southeast Banking. Barnett and Southeast have engaged in periodic merger discussions since 1985.

WHEN

William Barnett, a Kansas banker, and his family moved to Jacksonville, Florida, in 1877 for his wife's health. The same year he started a family-owned company, The National Bank of Jacksonville.

In 1930 the Barnetts formed Barnett National Securities Corporation, a bank holding company, which soon acquired and reopened 3 banks that had failed after the 1929 stock market crash (in Cocoa, DeLand, and St. Augustine). The day before President Franklin Roosevelt's bank holiday during the Great Depression in 1933, Barnett opened every teller window and had tellers slowly count money for withdrawals using nothing larger than a $20 bill; the strategy prevented a run on the bank because many people in line were reassured and went home.

Jacksonville attorney Guy W. Botts, who joined the bank as president in 1963, wanted the bank to become a statewide banking institution and a leader in every market. In 1966 Barnett acquired First National Bank of Winter Park, and by 1969 the holding company had purchased 7 other banks throughout Florida. To clarify its identity, the company in 1969 changed its name to Barnett Banks of Florida (changed to Barnett Banks, Inc. in 1987).

During the 1970s Barnett established Florida's first credit card franchise, which resulted in Barnett's becoming a leader among the state's banks in the use of computers. Barnett also was the first southeastern bank holding company to be listed on the New York Stock Exchange.

The company survived the Florida real estate crash of the mid-1970s and, when state law changed to allow banks to open branch office operations, opened 4 branches in 1977 and 9 more the following year. By the end of the decade, the company had purchased 29 more banks.

Barnett continued to acquire banks (over 32) and add branches (267) in the 1980s. Following Florida's approval of regional interstate banking, Barnett moved into Georgia by acquiring First National Bank of Cobb County (1986). Barnett bought several small Georgia and Florida financial institutions in 1989 and 1990.

After completing a review performed in connection with Barnett's 1991 stock offering, the SEC forced a downward mid-year revision of the bank's 1990 earnings, disputing Barnett's handling of certain tax and securities valuation issues.

WHO

Chairman and CEO: Charles E. Rice, age 55, $925,000 pay
President and COO: Allen L. Lastinger, Jr., age 48, $480,000 pay (prior to promotion)
SEVP and CFO: Stephen A. Hansel, age 43, $355,000 pay
Chief Human Resources Executive: Paul T. Kerins, age 47
Auditors: Price Waterhouse
Employees: 17,905

WHERE

HQ: 100 Laura St., PO Box 40789, Jacksonville, FL 32203-0789
Phone: 904-791-7720
Fax: 904-791-7166

Barnett Banks has 553 offices in Florida and 42 in Georgia.

WHAT

	1990 Assets	
	$ mil.	% of total
Cash & due from banks	1,884	6
Securities	4,315	13
Loans	25,139	78
Reserve for loan loss	(411)	(1)
Unearned income	(889)	(3)
Other	2,160	7
Total	**32,198**	**100**

Nonbanking Subsidiaries

Barnett Banks Insurance, Inc. (reinsurance of credit insurance written against affiliates' loans)
Barnett Banks Trust Co., NA
Barnett Brokerage Service, Inc.
Barnett Card Services Corp.
Barnett Mortgage Co. (mortgage servicing)
Barnett Recovery Corp. (loan collection services)
CreditQuick, Inc. and CreditQuick Finance Co. (consumer finance)

RANKINGS

20th in *Fortune* 100 Commercial Banking Cos.

KEY COMPETITORS

H. F. Ahmanson
Citicorp
Great Western
NCNB
SunTrust

HOW MUCH

	9-Year Growth	1981	1982	1983	1984	1985	1986	1987	1988	1989	1990
Assets ($ mil.)	21.7%	5,504	6,932	9,397	12,501	14,829	20,229	23,451	25,748	29,007	32,198
Net income ($ mil.)	10.5%	41	57	82	103	128	162	196	226	257	101
Income as % of assets	—	0.7%	0.8%	0.9%	0.8%	0.9%	0.8%	0.8%	0.9%	0.9%	0.3%
Earnings per share ($)	(2.7%)	1.35	1.48	1.92	2.20	2.57	2.96	3.25	3.75	4.07	1.06
Stock price – high ($)	—	13.19	15.50	18.89	19.56	30.00	40.88	41.75	37.38	40.00	37.75
Stock price – low ($)	—	8.22	8.33	11.56	14.44	18.67	25.67	27.13	29.00	32.25	14.13
Stock price – close ($)	7.2%	10.11	12.00	17.33	19.50	29.83	31.25	28.38	34.00	36.13	18.88
P/E – high	—	10	11	10	9	12	14	13	10	10	36
P/E – low	—	6	6	6	7	7	9	8	8	8	13
Dividends per share ($)	13.6%	0.41	0.47	0.52	0.59	0.67	0.77	0.89	1.01	1.16	1.29
Book value per share ($)	11.4%	9.37	10.53	12.60	14.60	16.34	19.07	21.97	24.37	26.79	24.84

1990 Year-end:
Return on equity: 4.1%
Equity as % of assets: 4.9%
Cash (mil.): $1,884
Long-term debt (mil.): $495
No. of shares (mil.): 63
Dividends:
 1990 average yield: 6.8%
 1990 payout: —
Market value (mil.): $1,194
Sales (mil.): $3,296

Stock Price History High/Low 1981–90

BAXTER INTERNATIONAL INC.

OVERVIEW

Headquartered in Deerfield, Illinois, Baxter International is the world's largest producer and marketer of health care products, systems, and services. The company's 120,000 products include intravenous systems, heart valves, diagnostic devices, and surgical instruments.

The company's operations are geared for efficiency, offering services and savings to hospitals aimed at reducing costs while improving the quality of patient care. To this end Baxter recently released its InterLink Access System,

a needle-less syringe that promises to prevent involuntary needle-stick accidents common with hypodermic needles. The new system will be marketed through an agreement with Becton, Dickinson.

Baxter is in the midst of a cost-cutting restructuring (for which it took a $566 million charge in 1990) in which some plants will be closed, the work force reduced, and management decentralized.

NYSE symbol: BAX
Fiscal year ends: December 31

 Hoover's Rating **B-**

WHO

Chairman and CEO: Vernon R. Loucks, Jr., age 56, $1,748,674 pay
President: Wilbur H. Gantz, age 53, $1,034,685 pay
SVP and CFO: Robert J. Lambrix, age 51, $541,263 pay
SVP Human Resources: Anthony J. Rucci, age 40
Auditors: Price Waterhouse
Employees: 64,600

WHEN

Dr. Ralph Falk, an Idaho surgeon, his brother Harry, and Dr. Donald Baxter, a California physician, formed The Don Baxter Intravenous Products Corporation in 1931 to distribute intravenous (IV) solutions manufactured by Dr. Baxter in Los Angeles. Two years later the company opened its first manufacturing plant in Glenview, Illinois. Dr. Falk bought Dr. Baxter's interest in the company in 1935 and began in-house R&D efforts that led to the introduction of the first sterilized vacuum-type blood collection device (1939), which could store blood for 21 days instead of a few hours. Demand for medical supplies and growing acceptance of IV products during WWII spurred growth to more than $1.5 million in sales by 1945.

In 1949 the company created Travenol Laboratories to make and sell drugs. Baxter went public in 1951 and began an acquisition program the following year. Failing health caused both Falks in 1953 to turn over control of the company to William Graham, manager since 1945. Graham continued the acquisition program that absorbed 5 US companies, including Hyland Laboratories (1952), Wallerstein Company (1957), Fenwal Laboratories and Flint, Eaton (1959), and Dayton Flexible Products (1967).

In 1975 Baxter moved its headquarters to Deerfield, Illinois. The company achieved $1 billion in sales in 1978, the same year it introduced the first portable dialysis machine.

In 1985 Baxter acquired American Hospital Supply, a company founded by Foster McGaw in 1922 that had been a Baxter distributor from 1932 until 1962. American had 65% more sales than Baxter but had been more a distributor of lower-margin products than Baxter, which manufactured most of its own items. The merger made Baxter the world's largest hospital supply company.

Offering more than 120,000 products and an electronic order-entry system (ASAP) that connects customers with over 1,500 vendors, Baxter captured nearly 25% of the US hospital supply market in 1988. That same year the company changed its name from Baxter Travenol to Baxter International.

In recent years Baxter has begun to form alliances with other large companies such as Waste Management and Kraft to provide hospitals with computerized services relating to medical-waste disposal and food services. It also has joint ventures with Nestlé and IBM to sell nutrition products and computer services to hospitals.

In 1991 Baxter came under fire from pro-Jewish groups when it allegedly closed a plant in Israel to remove itself from the Arab blacklist of companies engaged in business in Israel. As a result the company is being investigated by the US Justice Department for possible violation of the 1977 antiboycott law. Because of the controversy, Baxter scrapped plans to build a factory in Syria in 1991.

WHERE

HQ: One Baxter Pkwy., Deerfield, IL 60015-4625
Phone: 708-948-2000
Fax: 708-948-3948

Baxter has manufacturing facilities in 21 countries and sells products in about 100 countries. The company also maintains 17 R&D centers worldwide.

	1990 Sales		1990 Operating Income	
	$ mil.	% of total	$ mil.	% of total
US	6,245	77	592	56
Europe	983	12	201	19
Other countries	872	11	261	25
Adjustments	—	—	(126)	—
Total	**8,100**	**100**	**928**	**100**

WHAT

	1990 Sales		1990 Operating Income	
	$ mil.	% of total	$ mil.	% of total
Hospital products & services	4,071	50	409	39
Medical systems & specialties	1,729	21	202	20
Alternate site prods. & services	1,820	23	356	34
Industrial products	480	6	70	7
Adjustments	—	—	(109)	—
Total	**8,100**	**100**	**928**	**100**

Products
Artificial heart valves
Blood-handling equipment
Cardiac monitoring and bypass systems
Diagnostic systems
Gowns, gloves, and drapes
Intravenous therapy products
Laboratory apparatus and supplies
Mail-order prescriptions
Procedure trays and kits
Respiratory and anesthesia products
Surgical instruments and supplies
Veterinary supplies

RANKINGS

59th in *Fortune* 500 Industrial Cos.
58th in *Business Week* 1000

KEY COMPETITORS

Abbott Labs
American Cyanamid
American Home Products
C. R. Bard
Bayer
Ciba-Geigy
Eli Lilly
Henley
Johnson & Johnson
Pfizer
Roche

HOW MUCH

	9-Year Growth	1981	1982	1983	1984	1985	1986	1987	1988	1989	1990
Sales ($ mil.)	20.6%	1,504	1,671	1,843	1,800	2,355	5,543	6,223	6,861	7,399	8,100
Net income ($ mil.)	(13.7%)	151	187	218	29	137	181	323	388	446	40
Income as % of sales	—	10.0%	11.2%	11.8%	1.6%	5.8%	3.3%	5.2%	5.7%	6.0%	0.5%
Earnings per share ($)	—	0.99	1.22	1.45	0.20	0.83	0.64	1.09	1.30	1.49	(0.05)
Stock price – high ($)	—	16.88	25.50	31.31	24.88	16.88	21.25	29.25	26.13	25.88	29.50
Stock price – low ($)	—	12.00	15.19	20.00	11.75	12.38	15.13	15.50	16.25	17.50	20.50
Stock price – close ($)	5.8%	16.75	24.19	23.25	13.13	15.75	19.25	22.75	17.63	25.00	27.88
P/E – high	—	17	21	22	124	20	33	27	20	17	—
P/E – low	—	12	12	14	59	15	24	14	13	12	—
Dividends per share ($)	14.4%	0.19	0.23	0.28	0.33	0.37	0.40	0.44	0.50	0.56	0.64
Book value per share ($)	7.6%	6.94	7.52	8.17	7.83	9.86	11.51	11.79	12.61	13.49	13.45

1990 Year-end:
Debt ratio: 29.7%
Return on equity: —
Cash (mil.): $40
Current ratio: 1.48
Long-term debt (mil.): $1,729
No. of shares (mil.): 279
Dividends:
 1990 average yield: 2.3%
 1990 payout: —
Market value (mil.): $7,780

Stock Price History High/Low 1981–90

THE BEAR STEARNS COMPANIES INC.

OVERVIEW

Bear Stearns is the holding company that presides over principal subsidiary Bear, Stearns & Company, a leading investment banking, securities trading, and brokerage firm. In average ROE for 5 years, it is second in the investment banking/brokerage industry only to Morgan Stanley. Known as "The Bear" in financial circles, its reputation is that of an aggressive, bare-knuckles firm, a reflection of CEO Alan "Ace" Greenberg.

Its securities trading includes US government obligations, corporate securities and mortgage-related products, arbitrage, and foreign exchange. A UK subsidiary introduced fixed-rate mortgage-backed securities to that country.

A major operation of the company clears trades for other financial service firms and earns interest from the "float" in those transactions. Interest also comes to the company through its lucrative margin accounts. The company also operates Custodial Trust, a New Jersey financial institution, with more than $10 billion in assets held in trust.

NYSE symbol: BSC
Fiscal year ends: June 30

Hoover's Rating C

WHO

Chairman and CEO: Alan C. Greenberg, age 63, $4,211,810 pay
President: James E. Cayne, age 56, $3,634,201 pay
EVP and COO: Alvin H. Einbender, age 61
SVP Finance and CFO: William J. Montgoris, age 43
Director of Personnel: Stephen Lacoff
Auditors: Deloitte & Touche
Employees: 5,732

WHEN

As the 1920s roared onto Wall Street, a fledgling brokerage firm opened in 1923 with $500,000 capital. The partners were Joseph Ainslee Bear, Robert B. Stearns, and Harold C. Mayer. They named their firm Bear, Stearns & Co.

The firm grew rapidly and weathered the 1929 stock market crash with no layoffs. During the New Deal, Bear Stearns aggressively promoted government bonds. Its Arbitrage Department, created in 1938, dealt in the securities of New York City transit systems.

In 1940 Bear Stearns opened its first branch office in Chicago. The company's International Department was created in 1948, and in 1955 Bear Stearns opened its first overseas office in Amsterdam. Other branches followed in Geneva (1963), San Francisco (1965), Paris (1967), and Los Angeles (1968).

Bear Stearns was guided in the 1950s and 1960s by colorful trader Salim "Cy" Lewis. Lewis began his career as a runner for Salomon Brothers. At Bear Stearns, he climbed the ladder to chairman, becoming a Wall Street legend as the hard-charging, Scotch-drinking taskmaster of "The Bear," as the firm came to be known. During the 1950s Lewis originated block (large-scale) trading.

In 1973, after Bear Stearns moved to new headquarters, it found itself with additional space. It recruited brokers for the space and gave them free rent if they would use the company for clearing — matching stock trades for others. Clearing grew to be a major contributor to the company's bottom line.

When Lewis died in 1978, Alan Greenberg took the CEO post and not only maintained his predecessor's reputation for aggressive trading but surpassed it. Greenberg, Kansas-born and Oklahoma-reared, came to Wall Street from the University of Missouri and grappled to the top of Bear Stearns, handling the risk arbitrage desk at a tender 25.

Greenberg charted the firm's emergence as a full-blown investment bank. The company formed a Government Securities Department (1979), a Mortgage-Backed Securities Department (1981), and Bear Stearns Asset Management (1984). Also in 1984 the company created Custodial Trust, a New Jersey bank and trust company.

In 1985, to raise capital, Bear Stearns formed a holding company called the Bear Stearns Companies Inc. and took the company public. In the late 1980s Bear Stearns moved into investment banking with hopes of becoming one of the leading US firms. The firm announced in 1991 that it would create a separate unit to clear trades for more than 900 Bear Stearns customers.

WHERE

HQ: 245 Park Ave., New York, NY 10167
Phone: 212-272-2000
Fax: 212-272-3105

Bear Stearns operates in the US and in Amsterdam, Geneva, Hong Kong, London, Paris, and Tokyo.

WHAT

	1990 Sales	
	$ mil.	% of total
Commissions	339	14
Principal transactions	429	18
Investment banking	222	9
Interest & dividends	1,384	58
Other income	12	1
Total	**2,386**	**100**

Services
Securities trading
Arbitrage
Block trading
Commodities arbitrage
Corporate fixed income securities
Foreign exchange
Government obligations
Mortage-related securities
Municipal securities
Options and indexes
Over-the-counter equity securities
Specialist activities

Brokerage
Commodities
Individual investing
Institutional investing
International services
Option and index products

Investment Banking
Asset-based financings
Corporate recapitalizations
Corporate reorganizations
LBOs
Mergers and acquisitions
Private placement of debt and equity securities
Public offerings of debt and equity securities
Real estate
Underwriting

Interest
Customer financing for securities transactions
Securities lending

Other activities
Asset management
Fiduciary services
Insurance
Securities clearance
Securities research
Trust services

RANKINGS

16th in *Fortune* 50 Diversified Financial Cos.
433rd in *Business Week* 1000

HOW MUCH

	5-Year Growth	1981	1982	1983	1984	1985	1986	1987	1988[1]	1989	1990
Sales ($ mil.)	5.8%	—	—	—	1,804	2,164	1,774	1,888	—	2,365	2,386
Net income ($ mil.)	(6.8%)	—	—	—	169	182	176	143	—	172	119
Income as % of sales	—	—	—	—	9.4%	8.4%	9.9%	7.6%	—	7.3%	5.0%
Earnings per share ($)	—	—	—	—	—	—	1.54	1.16	—	1.47	1.05
Stock price – high ($)	—	—	—	—	—	11.17	18.95	16.26	11.47	14.40	13.15
Stock price – low ($)	—	—	—	—	—	8.69	10.10	5.97	7.84	9.23	7.14
Stock price – close ($)	(1.6%)	—	—	—	—	10.43	11.73	7.74	9.42	11.00	9.64
P/E – high	—	—	—	—	—	—	12	14	—	10	13
P/E – low	—	—	—	—	—	—	7	5	—	6	7
Dividends per share ($)	—	—	—	—	0.00	0.14	0.32	0.36	0.37	0.36	0.46
Book value per share ($)	—	—	—	—	—	5.55	6.88	7.78	—	8.80	9.30
Employees	5.8%	—	—	—	4,316	5,013	5,700	6,060	—	6,000	5,732

1990 Year-end:
Debt ratio: 26.3%
Return on equity: 11.6%
Cash (mil.): $2,640
Current ratio: —
Long-term debt (mil.): $384
No. of shares (mil.): 108
Dividends:
1990 average yield: 4.8%
1990 payout: 43.8%
Market value (mil.): $1,038

Stock Price History
High/Low 1985–90

[1] Fiscal year change

KEY COMPETITORS

American Express
Canadian Imperial
Charles Schwab
CS Holding
Dai-Ichi Kangyo
Deutsche Bank
Equitable
Goldman Sachs
Industrial Bank of Japan
Kemper
Merrill Lynch
Morgan Stanley
Nomura
Paine Webber
Prudential
Royal Bank
Salomon
Sears
Travelers
Union Bank of Switzerland

BECHTEL GROUP, INC.

OVERVIEW

Private company
Fiscal year ends: December 31

Hoover's Rating **B-**

Privately owned, family-controlled Bechtel is one of the world's largest companies devoted solely to engineering and construction (E&C) and ranks 2nd in the US E&C field, after Fluor. Bechtel has worked on more than 15,000 projects in over 135 countries on all 7 continents.

Company projects include electric-power generation (nuclear, fossil, solar, hydro), environmental cleanups, oil and gas pipelines, chemical plants, transportation systems, mining, telecommunications, and buildings. The company's Bechtel Power Corp. subsidiary performs 60% of the maintenance work for the US nuclear power industry.

Before the Gulf War, Bechtel was building a chemical plant for Iraq. After the war, the company won a lucrative commission from Kuwait to manage the rebuilding of the country's oil sector.

Bechtel's public reputation is that of a powerful force in the halls of governments around the world. George Schultz (secretary of the treasury under Nixon and secretary of state under Reagan) and Caspar Weinberger (secretary of defense under Reagan) were high-level Bechtel employees before their public service. Schultz returned to Bechtel's board of directors in 1989.

WHO

Chairman Emeritus: Stephen D. Bechtel, Jr., age 67
President and CEO: Riley P. Bechtel, age 39
EVP: Cordell W. Hull, age 59
EVP: John Neerhout, Jr., age 60
VP and Controller: Paul Unruh
SVP and Manager of Human Resources: Chuck Collyer
Auditors: Coopers & Lybrand
Employees: 32,500

WHERE

HQ: Fifty Beale St., San Francisco, CA 94105
Phone: 415-768-1234
Fax: 415-768-9038

Bechtel operates worldwide with 4 regional offices in the US (Gaithersburg, MD; Houston; Los Angeles; and San Francisco) and a regional office in London.

	1990 New Work Booked
	% of total
US	64
Foreign	36
Total	**100**

WHEN

In 1898 26-year-old Warren Bechtel left his Kansas farm to grade railroads in the Oklahoma Indian territories, where he soon founded his namesake. After Bechtel settled in Oakland, California, his engineering and management skills led to large projects such as the Northern California Highway and Bowman Dam. By the time of its incorporation in 1925, Bechtel was the West's largest construction company.

Stephen Bechtel (president after his father's death in 1933) weathered the Great Depression with massive projects such as the Hoover Dam (where Bechtel supervised 8 companies, including industrialist Henry Kaiser's) and the Oakland Bay Bridge. WWII meant full recovery, the many contracts including the construction of 570 ships in Bechtel-built yards in California.

In the postwar years Bechtel grew along with America's global presence, building pipelines (TransArabian, 1947; Canada's TransMountain, 1954; Australia's first, 1964) and numerous power projects, including one that doubled South Korea's energy output (1948). By the time Stephen Bechtel, Jr., became CEO in 1960 (when his father moved to chairman), the company was operating on 6 continents.

Bechtel built many nuclear power plants in the next 2 decades, including the world's first large one to be privately financed (Dresden, Illinois, opened 1960) and Canada's first (1962). Large transportation projects included San Francisco's Bay Area Rapid Transit system (BART, 1961–74) and Washington, DC's subway system (early 1970s). Bechtel's Jubail project, begun in 1976, will raise from the Arabian desert a city of 275,000 (projected completion date 1996). Work on Canada's James Bay hydroelectric project was begun in 1972 (completed mid-1980s, supplying energy to 8 million people).

With the attractions of nuclear power fading in the wake of Three Mile Island (which Bechtel won the right to clean up, starting in 1979 and still ongoing), Bechtel concentrated on less controversial markets such as mining in New Guinea (gold and copper, 1981–84) and China (coal, 1984).

Bechtel reeled under the general recession and rising Third World debt of the early 1980s. The company cut its work force by 22,000 (almost 1/2 the total) and stemmed the losses by taking on plant modernizations and other small projects.

Under 4th generation Riley Bechtel (CEO in 1990), the resurgent Bechtel (beginning the 1990s with 50% more clients than a decade earlier) has won numerous contracts, including a $16 billion deal with Hong Kong for a new airport and transit system (by 1997), project management of the channel tunnel between Britain and France (1993), and a giant technology center outside Moscow. In 1991 it won a contract to oversee a $3 billion expansion of the Dallas–Fort Worth Airport and another to assess damage from Lebanon's civil war.

WHAT

Engineering, Construction, and Management
Civil projects
  Airports
  Buildings and infrastructure
  Public transit systems, highways, tunnels, bridges, and ports
  Waste-to-energy plants
Food-processing plants
Microelectronics plants
Mining and metals plants
Missile launch complexes
Petroleum and chemical plants
Pipelines
Power plants
  Fossil-fired plants
  Hydroelectric plants
  Nuclear plants
Pulp and paper mills
Weapons storage and security systems

Environmental
Environmental assessment
Hazardous waste cleanups (EPA Superfund sites, pesticide plants)
Regulatory compliance
Wastewater treatment

Operating Units
Bechtel Civil Co.
Bechtel Construction Co.
Bechtel Ltd.
Bechtel National, Inc.
Bechtel Petroleum, Chemical & Industrial Co.
Bechtel Power Corp.
Becon Construction Co., Inc.

Operations
Nuclear and fossil fuel plants
Strategic oil reserves
Utilities

Major Projects Under Way
1992 Olympics (Barcelona)
Central Artery Harbor & Tunnel (Boston)
Disney-MGM Studio Tour (Florida)
Eurotunnel (England/France)
International airport (Hong Kong)
Jubail (Saudi industrial city)
SEMASS (waste-to-energy project, Massachusetts)
Three Mile Island (nuclear reactor decontamination)

HOW MUCH

	9-Year Growth	1981	1982	1983	1984	1985	1986	1987	1988	1989	1990
Sales ($ mil.)	(7.5%)	11,400	13,600	14,100	8,600	6,891	6,679	4,501	4,472	5,036	5,631
New work booked ($ mil.)	(8.5%)	10,600	5,700	13,000	5,000	4,982	3,675	3,537	4,486	5,427	4,787
Number of clients	5.6%	550	—	—	—	750	—	800	900	950	900
Number of active projects	6.7%	950	—	—	—	1,300	—	1,350	1,450	1,600	1,700

Sales ($ mil.) 1981–90

[Bar chart showing Sales ($ mil.) from 1981 to 1990, y-axis from 0 to 16,000]

RANKINGS

15th in *Forbes* 400 US Private Cos.

KEY COMPETITORS

ABB
Ashland
Baker Hughes
Consolidated Rail
Dresser
Duke Power
Fluor

W. R. Grace
Halliburton
Hanson
McDermott
Peter Kiewit Sons'

Raytheon
TRW
Union Pacific
Waste Management
Westinghouse

BECTON, DICKINSON AND COMPANY

OVERVIEW

New Jersey–based Becton, Dickinson manufactures and sells a broad line of health care products worldwide to hospitals, doctors, laboratories, pharmaceutical companies, medical schools, and the general public. The company operates 2 business sectors: Medical (57% of 1990 revenues) and Diagnostic (43%). Leading the world in single-use medical devices, the company manufactures hypodermic needles and syringes, gloves, IV catheters, and insulin syringes. Becton, Dickinson produces more syringes than any other company in the world

and has well over 50% of the US market. The company also produces thermometers, elastic support and suction products, and surgical blades.

The company has met the challenge of a changing health care industry by providing cost-effective products, appealing to newly formed hospital buying groups, selling aggressively overseas, and developing new areas of technology (it is the world leader in microbiology, cellular analysis, and blood collection).

NYSE symbol: BDX
Fiscal year ends: September 30

Hoover's Rating **B**

WHO

Chairman: Wesley J. Howe, age 69
President and CEO: Raymond V. Gilmartin, age 49, $729,067 pay
VP Finance: Robert A. Reynolds, age 58, $269,067
VP Human Resources: James R. Wessel
Auditors: Ernst & Young
Employees: 18,500

WHEN

Maxwell Becton and Fairleigh Dickinson established a medical supply firm in New York in 1897. In 1907 the company moved into a new factory in East Rutherford, New Jersey, and became one of the first in the US to manufacture hypodermic needles.

During WWI Becton, Dickinson manufactured all-glass syringes and introduced a new product, the all-cotton elastic (ACE) bandage. After the war, researchers Andrew Fleischer and Oscar Schwidetzky joined the firm. Fleischer designed an improved stethoscope, while Schwidetzky created specialized hypodermic needles.

During WWII the company received an award for excellence in medical equipment supplied to the armed forces, and Becton and Dickinson helped establish Fairleigh Dickinson Junior College (now Fairleigh Dickinson University). Becton, Dickinson continued to develop new products such as the VACUTAINER blood collection apparatus, the company's first medical laboratory aid.

After the deaths of Dickinson (1948) and Becton (1951), their sons Fairleigh Dickinson, Jr., and Henry Becton took over the company. Disposable hypodermic syringes developed by the company (1961) virtually replaced reusable syringes domestically, with disposables capturing almost the entire US syringe market by 1987. The company offered stock to the public (1963) to raise money for manufacturing,

packaging, and distribution facilities for the new syringes. Becton, Dickinson opened a plant in Canada (1963) followed by plants in France, Ireland, and Brazil, and diversified into nonmedical businesses with purchases such as Edmont (industrial gloves, 1966) and Spear (computer systems, 1968).

Wesley J. Howe, successor to Dickinson, expanded the company's foreign sales from 19% of its 1974 volume to 40% by 1989. From 1976 to 1980 the company added new medical products through internal research and purchases such as Johnston Laboratories (automated bacteriology, 1979).

In 1978 the company thwarted a takeover bid by the Sun Company, which had purchased 32.5% of the company's stock. Howe began to sell the company's nonmedical businesses in 1983, ending with the 1989 sale of Edmont. The company acquired Deseret Medical (IV catheters, surgical gloves and masks) for $230 million in 1986.

Price competition from Japanese syringe maker Terumo (which aims to boost its market share from 5% in 1989 to 20% in 1992) threatens to erode the company's share of the US market, but the company has so far maintained its share and opened plants in Japan and Singapore.

In 1991 the company signed an agreement to manufacture and market Baxter's new InterLink needle-less injection system.

WHERE

HQ: One Becton Dr., Franklin Lakes, NJ 07417-1880
Phone: 201-848-6800
Fax: 201-848-6475

The company has facilities in 23 countries. Its principal markets are the US, Canada, Europe, Brazil, Mexico, and Japan.

	1990 Sales		1990 Operating Income	
	$ mil.	% of total	$ mil.	% of total
US	1,178	58	267	75
Europe	539	27	57	16
Other countries	296	15	34	9
Adjustments	—	—	(84)	—
Total	**2,013**	**100**	**274**	**100**

WHAT

	1990 Sales		1990 Operating Income	
	$ mil.	% of total	$ mil.	% of total
Medical	1,155	57	243	68
Diagnostic	858	43	115	32
Adjustments	—	—	(84)	—
Total	**2,013**	**100**	**274**	**100**

Medical
Disposable hypodermic products
Elastic support products
Examination gloves
Intravenous and cardiovascular catheters
Operating room products
Suction products
Surgical blades
Thermometers

Diagnostic
Blood collection products
Cellular analysis equipment
Hematology instruments
Laboratory ware and supplies
Microbiology products
Other diagnostic systems

RANKINGS

212th in *Fortune* 500 Industrial Cos.
240th in *Business Week* 1000

KEY COMPETITORS

Abbott Labs	Eli Lilly
American Cyanamid	Henley
American Home Products	Hewlett-Packard
C. R. Bard	Johnson & Johnson
Baxter	Pfizer
EG&G	

HOW MUCH

	9-Year Growth	1981	1982	1983	1984	1985	1986	1987	1988	1989	1990
Sales ($ mil.)	7.3%	1,066	1,114	1,120	1,127	1,144	1,312	1,582	1,709	1,811	2,013
Net income ($ mil.)	10.2%	76	77	36	63	88	112	142	149	158	182
Income as % of sales	—	7.1%	6.9%	3.2%	5.6%	7.7%	8.5%	9.0%	8.7%	8.7%	9.1%
Earnings per share ($)	10.9%	1.81	1.82	0.86	1.52	2.10	2.62	3.42	3.69	4.00	4.58
Stock price – high ($)	—	27.25	25.19	26.75	20.63	33.00	61.25	69.00	62.13	62.25	76.75
Stock price – low ($)	—	18.56	18.00	17.00	15.38	19.75	30.94	42.25	46.50	48.38	55.75
Stock price – close ($)	13.5%	23.88	21.25	18.38	19.81	31.00	50.00	51.00	52.00	61.88	74.50
P/E – high	—	15	14	31	14	16	23	20	17	16	17
P/E – low	—	10	10	20	10	9	12	12	13	12	12
Dividends per share ($)	8.9%	0.50	0.55	0.58	0.58	0.60	0.66	0.74	0.86	1.00	1.08
Book value per share ($)	9.3%	14.01	14.21	14.40	15.03	16.82	19.62	21.62	24.33	27.99	31.35

1990 Year-end:
Debt ratio: 34.5%
Return on equity: 15.4%
Cash (mil.): $73
Current ratio: 1.68
Long-term debt (mil.): $649
No. of shares (mil.): 38
Dividends:
  1990 average yield: 1.5%
  1990 payout: 23.6%
Market value (mil.): $2,804

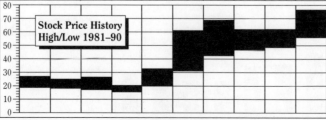

Stock Price History High/Low 1981–90

BELL ATLANTIC CORPORATION

NYSE symbol: BEL
Fiscal year ends: December 31

Hoover's Rating **B-**

OVERVIEW

Bell Atlantic is the nation's 3rd largest provider (after GTE and BellSouth) of local telephone services (with approximately 17 million lines), offered under the Bell name in New Jersey, Pennsylvania, Delaware, the District of Columbia, Maryland, Virginia, and West Virginia. The company is pinning its hopes for leadership on its network services, wireless services, and business systems.

Bell Atlantic pioneered some of the special calling features sweeping the industry. One such feature, Caller ID, displays the number of the calling party. Another allows use of residential phone extensions as intercoms. These features could add up to $500 million of sales by 1996.

Bell Atlantic provides cellular and paging services through Bell Atlantic Mobile Systems. Mobile Systems operates in 5 of the largest 15 markets. Bell Atlantic is on the leading edge of researching wireless communication, opening its Wireless Technology Laboratory in 1990.

Bell Atlantic Business Systems, formerly Sorbus, is the leader in independent maintenance of DEC and IBM hardware. Other activities of the company include equipment leasing (US, Canada, and Europe); directory publishing; telecommunications and computer hardware sales to businesses and consumers; and worldwide telecommunications consulting through Bell Atlantic International.

WHO

Chairman and CEO: Raymond W. Smith, age 53, $1,283,800 pay
President: Anton J. Campanella, age 59, $714,500 pay
VP and CFO: William O. Albertini, age 47
VP Human Resources: Charles W. Crist, age 48
Auditors: Coopers & Lybrand
Employees: 81,600

WHERE

HQ: 1600 Market St., Philadelphia, PA 19103
Phone: 215-963-6000
Fax: 215-963-6470 (Investor Relations)

Bell Atlantic provides local telephone operations in 6 eastern states and Washington, DC. The company operates overseas in 16 countries.

WHEN

Bell Atlantic's mid-Atlantic telephone companies were rooted in the AT&T/Bell System, which began in the 1870s. For example, Bell Telephone of Pennsylvania was originally incorporated under the name Bell Telephone of Philadelphia in 1879. Local telephone traffic and service quality continued to grow from 1900 until the Depression. Since WWII, telephone traffic has steadily increased, and local telephone service is now a mature market, growing less than 4% annually.

In 1983 Bell Atlantic was split from AT&T in a now-historic antitrust settlement. Bell Atlantic was incorporated that year and began operations in 1984. The settlement gave Bell Atlantic local phone service rights in parts of 6 states and Washington, DC; Bell Atlantic Mobile Systems (cellular service); and 1/7 of an R&D arm, Bell Communications Research, shared by the Bell companies, formerly called the Central Services Organization.

Given the maturity of local telephone services, Bell Atlantic must look for growth in nonregulated services such as its cellular/paging operations, equipment leasing, electronic mail and other on-line services, voice messaging, directory publishing, and sales of computer and office supplies via catalog.

Bell Atlantic has invested heavily in data transport markets to supplement existing voice services. The company introduced a data network known as PDN (1986); began testing integrated voice/data network services known as ISDN (1987); acquired (1985) and divested (1988) CompuShop, a chain of retail computer stores; acquired 3 computer-maintenance vendors (by 1987); acquired ESS (1986), a computer parts sales-and-repair organization; and purchased computer parts distributor Camex (1987). Yet Bell Atlantic is not ignoring its mainstream revenue base. It introduced new custom-calling features to residences (1987) and plans to install optical fiber to residences. The company began a test of services available through fiber optics in Virginia (1990).

The company is reaching out internationally; it helped modernize Spain's telephone network (1988 contract). In 1990 Bell Atlantic was chosen, along with Ameritech, to purchase New Zealand's public phone system for about $2.5 billion. It also agreed with the Korean Telecommunications Authority to explore cooperation and, along with U S WEST, won the right to offer wireless communications and a packet-switching network in Czechoslovakia.

WHAT

	1990 Sales		1990 Operating Income	
	$ mil.	% of total	$ mil.	% of total
Communications	11,525	94	2,606	98
Financial & real estate services	773	6	58	2
Adjustments	—	—	165	—
Total	**12,298**	**100**	**2,829**	**100**

Local Telephone Subsidiaries
The Bell Telephone Co. of Pennsylvania
The Chesapeake and Potomac Telephone Co. (Washington, DC)
The Chesapeake and Potomac Telephone Co. of Maryland
The Chesapeake and Potomac Telephone Co. of Virginia
The Chesapeake and Potomac Telephone Co. of West Virginia
The Diamond State Telephone Co.
New Jersey Bell Telephone Co.

Other Major Subsidiaries and Affiliates
Bell Atlantic Business Systems, Inc. (computer maintenance, support)
Bell Atlantic Capital Corp. (leasing and financing)
Bell Atlantic Computer Technology Services (computer repair)
Bell Atlantic Directory Graphics, Inc. (joint venture with R.R. Donnelley to provide photocomposition service)
Bell Atlantic Healthcare Systems, Inc. (systems integration for hospitals)
Bell Atlantic International (worldwide consulting)
Bell Atlantic Mobile Systems (cellular operations)
Bell Atlantic Paging
Bell Atlantic Properties (real estate investment)
Bell Atlantic Software Systems
Bell Atlantic Systems Integration Corp. (joint venture with American Management Systems to provide information)
Bell Atlanticom Systems, Inc. (installation and maintenance)
Telecom Corporation of New Zealand (34.2%)

RANKINGS

3rd in *Fortune* 50 Utilities
26th in *Business Week* 1000

KEY COMPETITORS

AT&T	GTE	Southwestern Bell
Ameritech	McCaw	United Telecom
BCE	MCI	U S West
BellSouth	NYNEX	Xerox
Centel	Pacific Telesis	Other telephone cos.

HOW MUCH

	6-Year Growth	1981	1982	1983	1984	1985	1986	1987	1988	1989	1990
Sales ($ mil.)	7.2%	—	—	—	8,090	9,084	9,921	10,298	10,880	11,449	12,298
Net income ($ mil.)	5.1%	—	—	—	973	1,093	1,167	1,240	1,317	1,075	1,313
Income as % of sales	—	—	—	—	12.0%	12.0%	11.8%	12.0%	12.1%	9.4%	10.7%
Earnings per share ($)	5.2%	—	—	—	2.49	2.74	2.93	3.12	3.33	2.72	3.38
Stock price – high ($)	—	—	—	—	20.75	26.84	38.50	39.88	37.25	56.13	57.13
Stock price – low ($)	—	—	—	—	16.41	19.44	25.00	30.25	31.13	34.69	39.50
Stock price – close ($)	17.8%	—	—	—	20.09	26.63	33.75	32.50	35.56	55.63	53.63
P/E – high	—	—	—	—	8	10	13	13	11	21	17
P/E – low	—	—	—	—	7	7	9	10	9	13	12
Dividends per share ($)	6.4%	—	—	—	1.60	1.70	1.80	1.92	2.04	1.65	2.32
Book value per share ($)	3.2%	—	—	—	18.84	19.83	20.91	22.07	23.29	21.78	22.71

1990 Year-end:
Debt ratio: 47.8%
Return on equity: 15.2%
Cash (mil.): $110
Current ratio: 0.64
Long-term debt (mil.): $8,171
No. of shares (mil.): 393
Dividends:
  1990 average yield: 4.3%
  1990 payout: 68.6%
Market value (mil.): $21,085

Stock Price History High/Low 1984–90

BELLSOUTH CORPORATION

OVERVIEW

BellSouth is the largest of 7 regional holding companies created in the AT&T breakup. It is the 2nd largest US utility, behind GTE, and in 1990 it became the largest US local exchange telephone company.

Chairman John Clendenin and BellSouth have aggressively pursued new technologies. BellSouth is among the largest cellular telephone operators in the nation and exports cellular service to Argentina. It operates an extensive mobile paging network and runs an electronic "gateway" to give computer users access to databanks.

The company has persuaded regulators in 6 of the 9 states where it operates to permit incentive-based phone rates that, the company argues, would spur it to be even more profitable (it already makes more money than any other former Bell regional company) and more efficient. Incentive-based rates covered 40% of its network at the end of 1988, 73% at the beginning of 1991.

NYSE symbol: BLS
Fiscal year ends: December 31

Hoover's Rating **B-**

WHO

Chairman, President, and CEO: John L. Clendenin, age 56, $1,272,500 pay
VC Finance and Administration: Harvey R. Holding, age 56, $413,000 pay (prior to promotion)
EVP Governmental Affairs: Raymond L. McGuire, age 58, $432,500 pay
EVP and General Counsel: Walter H. Alford, age 52, $412,500 pay
SVP Corporate Human Resources: Roy B. Howard, age 62
Auditors: Coopers & Lybrand
Employees: 102,000

WHEN

Executives of Boston-based National Bell struggled at first as they tried to market Alexander Graham Bell's telephone throughout the nation. In 1878 general manager Theodore Vail recruited agent James Merrill Ormes, a former Union soldier, to head South.

Ormes created Bell exchanges throughout the region, but growth was hampered by competition with Western Union, then dominant in telecommunications. In 1879 Ormes, with approval of National Bell, hammered out an agreement with Western Union that ended telephone competition in the South and created Southern Bell Telephone and Telegraph. Western Union dropped its own telephone enterprise in exchange for a controlling interest in Southern Bell, and National Bell granted a license for the use of telephones. The agreement was the forerunner of a nationwide truce between National Bell and Western Union.

In the 1890s, after the Bell organization had acquired controlling interest in Southern Bell, another challenge arose. Bell's original telephone patents expired, and a slew of competitors entered the business. Southern Bell president Edward Hall forced his company to upgrade quality, undercut competition, and, when necessary, buy out rivals. Southern Bell had bought 23 of 52 competing telephone exchanges by 1909.

In 1912 the Atlanta-based company relinquished its Virginia and West Virginia territory, and AT&T arranged Southern Bell's merger with Cumberland Telephone and Telegraph, which served Kentucky, Louisiana, Mississippi, Tennessee, and parts of Illinois and Indiana. Illinois and Indiana franchises were later redistributed within the Bell system. Southern Bell hooked up its millionth customer in 1929, but revenues plummeted during the Depression. In the post-WWII boom, growth resumed.

In 1957 Southern Bell was structured into 2 divisions, a prelude to the 1968 split of the company into Birmingham-based South Central Bell (Alabama, Kentucky, Louisiana, Mississippi, and Tennessee) and Atlanta-based Southern Bell (Florida, Georgia, North Carolina, and South Carolina).

The division was short-lived. The 1982 settlement in the landmark antitrust case required AT&T to spin off 7 regional holding companies. BellSouth, reuniting Southern Bell and South Central Bell, was the largest.

BellSouth bought L. M. Berry, a directory publisher (1986), and MCCA, a paging and mobile communications firm (1989). In 1990 it agreed to purchase Graphic Scanning Corp. (cellular, paging). Its bid for LIN Broadcasting, with extensive cellular telephone holdings, was thwarted by McCaw Cellular in 1989, but BellSouth bought 18 midwest cellular systems from struggling McCaw in 1991. In a 1991 reshuffling, BellSouth combined its telephone operations in one unit and its cellular in another.

WHERE

HQ: 1155 Peachtree St. NE, Atlanta, GA 30367-6000
Phone: 404-249-2000
Fax: 404-249-5599

BellSouth operates local phone service in 9 states through 2 subsidiaries. Directory and cellular firms operate throughout the US and overseas.

WHAT

	1990 Sales	
	$ mil.	% of total
Local service	5,707	40
Interstate access	2,842	20
Intrastate access	912	6
Toll	1,565	11
Other	3,319	23
Total	**14,345**	**100**

BellSouth Telephone Operations
Marketing
Network and Technology
Regulatory and External Affairs
Services (staff support for regulated businesses)
South Central Bell (local phone service in Alabama, Kentucky, Louisiana, Mississippi, and Tennessee)
Southern Bell (local phone service in Florida, Georgia, North Carolina, and South Carolina)

BellSouth Enterprises
BellSouth Advertising and Publishing (directories)
BellSouth Cellular (mobile communications)
BellSouth International (overseas operations)

Bell Communications Research, Inc. (14.3%)
Research and development
US government telecommunications

RANKINGS

2nd in Fortune 50 Utilities
17th in *Business Week* 1000

HOW MUCH

	6-Year Growth	1981	1982	1983	1984	1985	1986	1987	1988	1989	1990
Sales ($ mil.)	7.1%	—	—	—	9,519	10,664	11,444	12,269	13,597	13,996	14,345
Net income ($ mil.)	4.5%	—	—	—	1,257	1,418	1,589	1,665	1,666	1,695	1,632
Income as % of sales	—	—	—	—	13.2%	13.3%	13.9%	13.6%	12.3%	12.1%	11.4%
Earnings per share ($)	2.9%	—	—	—	2.85	3.13	3.38	3.46	3.51	3.55	3.38
Stock price – high ($)	—	—	—	—	23.92	32.83	46.00	44.25	43.88	58.13	59.25
Stock price – low ($)	—	—	—	—	18.17	21.58	30.00	28.75	35.75	39.00	49.00
Stock price – close ($)	15.8%	—	—	—	22.67	32.67	38.50	36.38	39.88	57.88	54.75
P/E – high	—	—	—	—	8	11	14	13	13	16	18
P/E – low	—	—	—	—	6	7	9	8	10	11	15
Dividends per share ($)	7.3%	—	—	—	1.73	1.40	1.99	2.16	2.32	2.48	2.64
Book value per share ($)	3.8%	—	—	—	20.98	22.27	23.61	24.89	25.51	27.21	26.28

1990 Year-end:
Debt ratio: 38.1%
Return on equity: 12.6%
Cash (mil.): $469
Current ratio: 0.85
Long-term debt (mil.): $7,781
No. of shares (mil.): 482
Dividends:
　1990 average yield: 4.8%
　1990 payout: 78.1%
Market value (mil.): $26,388

Stock Price History High/Low 1984–90

KEY COMPETITORS

AT&T
Ameritech
BCE
Bell Atlantic
Centel
R. R. Donnelley
Ericsson
GTE
McCaw
MCI
NYNEX
Pacific Telesis
Southwestern Bell
United Telecom
U S West
Other telephone cos.

BERKSHIRE HATHAWAY INC.

NYSE symbol: BRK
Fiscal year ends: December 31

Hoover's Rating **B+**

OVERVIEW

Berkshire Hathaway is a holding company managed by 42%-owner Warren E. Buffett, a highly regarded investor and, according to Forbes, the 2nd richest man in the US after John Kluge of Metromedia. Buffett refrains from interfering with management of operating units and takes a long-term view toward investing.

Berkshire's operating units include several insurers, publishers (*World Book, Buffalo News*), a candy maker (See's Candies), and a vacuum cleaner manufacturer (Kirby). Berkshire also owns large stakes in other companies, directly and through its insurance subsidiaries. Capital Cities/ABC, Coca-Cola, GEICO, and Washington Post are core holdings.

Buffett's strong investment track record is underscored by the 23.2% annual growth in the book value of Berkshire shares over the last 26 years. Berkshire pays no dividends and shuns stock splits to attract only loyal, long-term stockholders.

Believing that the insurance industry is underpricing its services, Berkshire insurance units are de-emphasizing new policies. Instead, they are engaging in reinsurance, deemed more profitable over the long run.

In 1991 Buffett took the post of interim chairman at Salomon Bros., a Berkshire holding, after Salomon's top brass stepped down in a bond-dealing scandal.

WHEN

Warren Buffett began his career at age 11 by purchasing 3 shares of Cities Service. In the 1950s Buffett attended Columbia to study under famed value investor Benjamin Graham. Buffett absorbed the master's teachings: use strictly quantitative analysis to discover companies whose intrinsic worth (what a rational investor would pay) exceeds their stock prices; popularity is irrelevant; and the market will eventually vindicate the patient investor.

In 1956 Buffett, then 25, founded Buffett Partnership, Ltd. The $105,000 in initial assets grew quickly, making possible bargain purchases like Berkshire Hathaway (textiles, 1965) and National Indemnity (insurance, 1967). Feeling that stocks were overvalued, Buffett dissolved the partnership (1969); the initial value per share had grown thirtyfold and net assets were over $100 million.

Buffett had become disenchanted with businesses with intrinsically poor economics (like textile albatross Berkshire Hathaway, closed in 1985). He adopted the Berkshire name for his new investment firm and began searching for solid businesses with strong management. In 1972 Berkshire bought See's Candies; between 1976 and 1981 Berkshire invested $45 million in GEICO (worth more than $1 billion by the end of 1990).

Buffett liked media-based companies that capital-intensive industries (e.g., car or chemical manufacturers) needed as advertising conduits. During the stock market slump of 1973 and 1974, Buffett bought stakes in advertising agencies (Interpublic, Ogilvy & Mather) and newspapers (*Washington Post, Boston Globe*), followed by the *Buffalo News* (fully owned, 1977) and Capital Cities/ABC (1985).

In the 1980s Berkshire bought majority interests in Nebraska Furniture Mart (1983) and Fechheimer Brothers (uniform makers, 1986) and full ownership of Scott Fetzer (*World Book* encyclopedias and Kirby vacuum cleaners, 1986). Berkshire sold the *Boston Globe* in 1986. The company provided a haven for takeover targets, spending billions on high-yield convertible preferreds of businesses with strong franchises: Salomon (investment banking, 1987), Gillette (1989), USAir Group (1989), Champion International (forest products, 1990), and American Express (1991).

Berkshire bought RJR Nabisco junk bonds (1989–90) and stakes in Coca-Cola (1988–89), Borsheim's jewelry store (1989), and Wells Fargo (1989–91). In 1991 Berkshire received Federal Reserve clearance to buy up to 22% of Wells Fargo.

WHO

Chairman and CEO: Warren E. Buffett, age 60, $100,000 pay
VC; Chairman, Wesco: Charles T. Munger, age 67, $100,000 pay
VP, CFO, and Secretary: J. Verne McKenzie, age 62, $252,500 pay
Treasurer and Personnel Officer: Marc Hamburg
Auditors: Deloitte & Touche
Employees: 20,000

WHERE

HQ: 1440 Kiewit Plaza, Omaha, NE 68131
Phone: 402-346-1400
Fax: 402-536-3030

Berkshire Hathaway's main plants are located in California, New York, Ohio, Texas, Arkansas, Kentucky, and Tennessee. The company operates 225 See's Candies in 12 western and midwestern states.

WHAT

	1990 Sales		1990 Operating Income	
	$ mil.	% of total	$ mil.	% of total
Insurance	943	36	316	61
Candy	196	7	38	8
Newspaper	135	5	43	8
Home furnishings — retail	164	6	17	3
Encyclopedias & reference materials	343	13	32	6
Home cleaning sys.	188	7	28	6
Uniform mfg. & distribution	95	4	12	2
Other	595	22	30	6
Total	**2,659**	**100**	**516**	**100**

Insurance
Columbia Insurance Co.
National Indemnity Co.

Noninsurance
Borsheim's (80%, jewelry retailing)
Buffalo News (daily newspaper)
Fechheimer Brothers Co. (85%, uniform manufacturing and distribution)
Kirby (home cleaning systems)
Nebraska Furniture Mart (80%)
Scott Fetzer Co. (diverse manufacturing)
See's Candies

Wesco Financial Corp. (80.1%, includes Mutual Savings and Loan, CA)
World Book encyclopedias

Major Equity Investments
American Express (2.6%)
Capital Cities/ABC (18%)
Champion International (8%)
Coca-Cola (7%)
Federal Home Loan Mortgage Corp. (4%)
GEICO (48%)
Gillette (11%)
Salomon (14%)
USAir Group (12%)
Washington Post Co. (14%)
Wells Fargo (10%)

RANKINGS

170th in *Fortune* 500 Industrial Cos.
60th in *Business Week* 1000

KEY COMPETITORS

H. F. Ahmanson	KKR
ARA	Mars
Cadbury Schweppes	Maxwell
Campbell Soup	Maytag
Electrolux	Nestlé
Fred Meyer	V. F.
Great Western	Insurance companies
Hachette	Investment funds
Hershey	

HOW MUCH

	9-Year Growth	1981	1982	1983	1984	1985	1986	1987	1988	1989	1990
Sales ($ mil.)	22.7%	422	421	534	640	826	2,049	2,158	2,317	2,483	2,659
Net income ($ mil.)	29.0%	40	32	68	70	93	131	215	313	447	394
Income as % of sales	—	9.4%	7.5%	12.8%	11.0%	11.3%	6.4%	10.0%	13.5%	18.0%	14.8%
Earnings per share ($)	26.9%	40.27	31.93	63.93	61.21	81.04	114.62	187.24	273.37	390.01	344.00
Stock price – high ($)	—	590	775	1,385	1,360	2,730	3,250	4,270	5,000	8,875	8,675
Stock price – low ($)	—	425	430	755	1,220	1,275	2,220	2,635	3,000	4,625	5,550
Stock price – close ($)	31.7%	560	775	1,310	1,275	2,430	2,820	2,950	4,700	8,675	6,675
P/E – high	—	15	24	22	22	34	28	23	18	23	25
P/E – low	—	11	13	12	20	16	19	14	11	12	16
Dividends per share ($)	0.0%	0.00	0.00	0.00	0.00	0.00	0.00	0.00	0.00	0.00	0.00
Book value per share ($)	27.2%	526	738	976	1,109	1,644	2,073	2,477	2,976	4,298	4,614

1990 Year-end:
Debt ratio: 18.6%
Return on equity: 7.7%
Cash (mil.): $8,994
Long-term debt (mil.): $1,209
No. of shares (mil.): 1
Dividends:
 1990 average yield: 0.0%
 1990 payout: 0.0%
Market value (mil.): $7,650
Sales (mil.): $10,670

Stock Price History
High/Low 1981–90

BETHLEHEM STEEL CORPORATION

NYSE symbol: BS
Fiscal year ends: December 31

Hoover's Rating C-

OVERVIEW

Bethlehem, Pennsylvania, is home to Bethlehem Steel, the 2nd largest US steel producer (after USX). Bethlehem is a leader in the US in production of steel plates, structural shapes, and piling. It is the nation's largest supplier to the construction industry. The company produces 80% of its steel at 2 of its 5 steelmaking plants: Burns Harbor, Indiana, and Sparrows Point, Maryland.

In response to strong foreign steel competition in the 1980s, USX diversified, LTV filed for Chapter 11, and Bethlehem Steel sold many of its nonsteel assets to concentrate on basic steelmaking. To lower costs, Bethlehem has spent $4 billion since 1980 to modernize its steel plants. Burns Harbor and Sparrows Point are 2 of the world's most efficient steel mills.

Bethelehem's strategy is still unfolding as it faces the challenge of domestic mini-mills — small, high-efficiency steel operations. The company has turned its gaze on its 3 Pennsylvania plants for reorganization and has agreed to sell its Freight Car Division.

WHO

Chairman and CEO: Walter F. Williams, age 62, $679,000 pay
SVP, General Counsel, and Secretary: Curtis H. Barnette, age 56, $391,000 pay
SVP and CFO: Gary L. Millenbruch, age 53, $351,000 pay
SVP Human Resources: John A. Jordan, Jr., age 55
Auditors: Price Waterhouse
Employees: 29,600

WHEN

Bethlehem Steel began as Saucona Iron in South Bethlehem, Pennsylvania, in 1857, rolling iron railroad rails. In 1859 the company changed its name to Bethlehem Rolling Mills & Iron, then again in 1861 to Bethlehem Iron. In 1886 the US government urged Bethlehem to make armor plate and military items. The company settled on the name Bethlehem Steel in 1899.

The president of United States Steel, Charles Schwab, personally bought (1901), sold (1902), and again bought (1902) Bethlehem Steel. He then transferred Bethlehem to a new venture, United States Shipbuilding. This venture failed in 1903, spinning off Bethlehem Steel in 1904 with Schwab as president. Bethlehem's assets then included the steel plant in South Bethlehem, shipbuilding yards on both US coasts, and iron ore mines in Cuba.

Schwab saw the potential in Henry Grey's one-piece, wide-flange steel beams for building construction. Schwab built a structural mill at Saucon, Pennsylvania, and bought Grey's patents, and the resulting, successful Bethlehem section (1908) found a commercial market in the construction industry.

In 1912 Schwab bought the Tofo Iron Mines in Chile, a cheap source of superior-grade iron ore. Bethlehem grew with the purchases of Pennsylvania Steel and Maryland Steel in 1916. With shipbuilding facilities, steel manufacturing plants, and good sources of ore and coal, Bethlehem was well prepared for the steel and shipbuilding needs of WWI.

In 1930 the company bought Pacific Coast Steel and Southern California Iron & Steel. With the purchase of the fabricating business of McClintic-Marshall Construction (1931), Bethlehem entered bridge and building construction. Bethlehem made the steelwork for structures such as the Golden Gate bridge, Rockefeller Center, and the US Supreme Court building. During WWII Bethlehem built 1,121 ships.

In the 1960s Bethlehem built research laboratories and developed products such as tin-free steel for cans. In the 1970s and 1980s the US imported increased amounts of low-cost steel (26% of the US steel market in 1984 from less than 1% in the 1950s). To face the import challenge, Bethlehem reduced production and sold some steel plants, shipyards, and mines. In 1981 the company initiated a major modernization of its steel plants, and in 1986 Bethlehem focused on steel and began building new facilities. In 1989 Bethlehem bought an interest in Walbridge Coatings (electro-galvanized, corrosion-resistant steel sheets).

A slimmer Bethlehem faced an industry-wide slump in demand and the recession of 1990–91. The company took a $550 million charge in 1990 to prepare for restructuring its structural and rail facilities into a joint venture with British Steel, proposed in early 1991.

WHERE

HQ: 701 E. 3rd St., Bethlehem, PA 18016-7699
Phone: 215-694-2424
Fax: 215-694-1509

Major Plants

Bethlehem, PA	Structural steel shapes, piling, foundry products
Burns Harbor, IN	Steel plate and sheet
Johnstown, PA	Steel bars, rods, wire
Sparrows Point, MD	Steel plate and sheet, tinplate, Galvalume sheet
Steelton, PA	Rail products, pipe

	1990 Pretax Income	
	$ mil.	% of total
US	(474)	—
Foreign	17	—
Total	**(457)**	**—**

WHAT

	1990 Sales		1990 Operating Income	
	$ mil.	% of total	$ mil.	% of total
Basic steel operns.	4,440	91	(425)	—
Steel-related operns.	459	9	(18)	—
Total	**4,899**	**100**	**(443)**	**—**

Products
Carbon and alloy bars
Coal mining and processing
Iron ore
Piling
Plates
Railroad rails, tie plates, joint bars, special trackwork
Rods, wire, pipe
Semifinished steel
Sheet and strip products
Structural shapes
Tin products

Major Markets
Appliance makers
Automotive industry
Construction industry
Container industry
Defense industry
Machinery industry
Oil and gas industry
Railroads
Service centers

HOW MUCH

	9-Year Growth	1981	1982	1983	1984	1985	1986	1987	1988	1989	1990
Sales ($ mil.)	(4.3%)	7,298	5,260	4,898	5,392	5,118	4,333	4,621	5,489	5,251	4,899
Net income ($ mil.)	—	211	(1,470)	(314)	(132)	(196)	(153)	104	392	246	(464)
Income as % of sales	—	2.9%	(27.9%)	(6.4%)	(2.4%)	(3.8%)	(3.5%)	2.2%	7.1%	4.7%	(9.5%)
Earnings per share ($)	—	4.83	(33.64)	(6.42)	(3.32)	(4.37)	(3.37)	1.48	4.77	2.86	(6.45)
Stock price – high ($)	—	32.00	23.50	28.50	29.50	21.13	22.00	19.75	25.50	28.50	21.13
Stock price – low ($)	—	19.75	14.50	19.00	14.25	12.50	4.63	6.38	15.25	15.25	10.63
Stock price – close ($)	(4.9%)	23.25	19.25	28.50	17.50	15.63	6.25	16.75	23.25	18.50	14.75
P/E – high	—	7	—	—	—	—	—	13	5	10	—
P/E – low	—	4	—	—	—	—	—	4	3	5	—
Dividends per share ($)	(14.3%)	1.60	1.30	0.60	0.60	0.30	0.00	0.00	0.00	0.20	0.40
Book value per share ($)	(14.4%)	63.26	28.31	23.53	20.02	15.13	11.98	14.74	19.59	22.37	15.56

1990 Year-end:
Debt ratio: 28.4%
Return on equity: —
Cash (mil.): $274
Current ratio: 1.45
Long-term debt (mil.): $590
No. of shares (mil.): 76
Dividends:
 1990 average yield: 2.7%
 1990 payout: —
Market value (mil.): $1,119

Stock Price History High/Low 1981–90

RANKINGS

106th in *Fortune* 500 Industrial Cos.
508th in *Business Week* 1000

KEY COMPETITORS

Broken Hill	Inland Steel	Nippon Steel
Cargill	IRI	Thyssen
Friedrich Krupp	LTV	USX
Hyundai	Mitsubishi	

THE BLACK & DECKER CORPORATION

NYSE symbol: BDK
Fiscal year ends: December 31

Hoover's Rating **C-**

OVERVIEW

Black & Decker, the world's largest power-tool and home-improvement products company, has built its reputation on convenient, innovative tools and appliances. The 7th most powerful brand name in the US and 19th in Europe, Black & Decker manufactures, distributes, sells, and services its products to an international market. The company's active product development leads to continual introduction of new products (200 new or redesigned products in 1990).

The purchase of Emhart Corporation (formerly American Hardware, 1989) broadened Black & Decker's product line for the do-it-yourself customer (with locks and faucets) and the commercial contractor (with Molly bolts, POP rivets, and other mechanical fasteners). The purchase also burdened Black & Decker with $2.6 billion in debt. The company streamlined its operations, but sales of nonstrategic Emhart businesses were slowed by the 1990–91 economic downturn.

WHEN

In 1910 when S. Duncan Black and Alonzo G. Decker opened the Black & Decker Manufacturing Company in Baltimore with a $1,200 investment, they began a partnership that would last over 40 years. Starting with milk-bottle-cap machines and candy dippers, the partners introduced their first major tool in 1916 — a portable 1/2" electric drill with patented pistol grip and trigger switch.

The company built its first manufacturing plant, which would become the company headquarters, in 1917 in rural Towson, Maryland. Sales passed $1 million in 1919 and the company added a 20,000-square-foot factory. Black & Decker quickly established itself in international markets. It had sales representatives in Russia, Japan, and Australia in 1918, and in 1922 Black & Decker Ltd., a Canadian subsidiary, opened as its first facility outside the US.

Black & Decker produced tools that defined the power-tool industry — the first portable screwdriver (1922), the 1/2" BB special drill (1923), the first electric hammer (1936), portable electric drills for the do-it-yourself home consumer (1946), finishing sanders and jigsaws (1953), and the Dustbuster hand-held vacuum (1979). The original founders led Black & Decker until their deaths — Black in 1951 and Decker in 1956.

In 1984 Black & Decker acquired the General Electric housewares operations, replacing the storied GE brand with the Black & Decker

hexagonal trademark on such items as toaster ovens, can openers, and irons.

While the company's brand maintained its strong reputation, by the mid-1980s it was rapidly losing market share. Administrative and production costs were high and product quality was suffering. Black & Decker's worldwide manufacturing network was inefficient, its management was fat, and customer service was faltering. In 1985 Black & Decker showed a $158 million loss on $1.7 billion in sales.

Nolan Archibald, the 3rd CEO in the company's history who is not part of the Black or Decker family, joined the company in 1985, and the company began a major restructuring. Black & Decker closed 5 plants, streamlined distribution systems, consolidated overseas facilities, and cut payroll 10%. By 1987 the company's net earnings showed a 100% increase over 1986. Its 1989 earnings ($30 million) were down from the year before because of the expensive Emhart purchase, and to service its debt, Black & Decker sold off pieces of its acquisition.

By 1991 it had sold 6 Emhart businesses, among them Bostik adhesives, Arcotronics capacitors, True Temper Hardware, the Medic division of PRC information systems, GardenAmerica lawn products, and North American Mallory Controls. The company also put "For Sale" signs on its Brazilian operations, on the remainder of PRC, and on its Dynapert printed circuit boards unit.

WHO

Chairman, President, and CEO: Nolan D. Archibald, age 47, $1,292,006 pay
EVP and CFO: Stephen F. Page, age 51
VP Human Resources: Leonard A. Strom, age 45
Auditors: Ernst & Young
Employees: 43,400

WHERE

HQ: 701 E. Joppa Rd., Towson, MD 21204
Phone: 301-583-3900
Fax: 301-583-2933

Black & Decker operates 63 manufacturing facilities, including 30 in 14 foreign countries.

	1990 Sales		1990 Operating Income	
	$ mil.	% of total	$ mil.	% of total
US	2,786	58	256	56
Europe	1,371	28	158	34
Other countries	675	14	45	10
Adjustments	—	—	27	—
Total	**4,832**	**100**	**486**	**100**

WHAT

	1990 Sales	
	$ mil.	% of total
Power tools	1,118	23
Household products	782	16
Accessories	307	6
Security hardware	453	10
Outdoor products	448	10
Plumbing	156	3
Product service	162	3
Fastening systems	388	8
Other commercial and industrial	499	10
Information systems	519	11
Total	**4,832**	**100**

Brand Names

Power Tools
Alligator (saws)
Black & Decker
DeWalt (stationary tools)
Kodiak (drills, screwdrivers)
Quattro (hammer drill)
ThunderVolt (cordless tools)
Univolt (charging system)
Wildcat (sander/grinder)
Workmate (work bench)

Appliances
Dustbuster (hand vacuum)
Spacemaker (under-the-cabinet appliances)
Toast-R-Oven

Outdoor
SweepStick (cordless broom)
True Temper (lawn tools, golf club shafts)
YardCleaner (blowers)

Hardware
Corbin (locks)
Kwikset (locks)
Molly (bolts)
POP (rivets)
Price Pfister (faucets)

HOW MUCH

	9-Year Growth	1981	1982	1983	1984	1985	1986	1987	1988	1989	1990
Sales ($ mil.)	14.5%	1,431	1,160	1,168	1,533	1,732	1,791	1,935	2,281	3,190	4,832
Net income ($ mil.)	(2.7%)	66	41	28	95	(158)	28	56	97	30	51
Income as % of sales	—	4.6%	3.5%	2.4%	6.2%	(9.1%)	1.5%	2.9%	4.3%	0.9%	1.1%
Earnings per share ($)	(6.6%)	1.56	0.97	0.65	1.95	(3.11)	0.49	0.95	1.65	0.51	0.84
Stock price – high ($)	—	21.88	19.50	27.25	28.63	26.88	25.25	26.50	24.75	25.25	20.13
Stock price – low ($)	—	14.25	12.00	17.88	17.25	17.25	14.50	13.00	17.13	18.13	8.00
Stock price – close ($)	(5.2%)	15.13	18.13	26.38	23.50	21.50	16.25	18.88	23.13	19.50	9.38
P/E – high	—	14	20	42	15	—	52	28	15	50	24
P/E – low	—	9	12	28	9	—	30	14	10	36	10
Dividends per share ($)	(6.9%)	0.76	0.76	0.52	0.58	0.64	0.58	0.40	0.40	0.40	0.40
Book value per share ($)	0.4%	14.44	10.70	11.79	13.58	9.94	10.61	11.12	12.38	12.24	14.94

1990 Year-end:
Debt ratio: 75.0%
Return on equity: 6.2%
Cash (mil.): $84
Current ratio: 1.13
Long-term debt (mil.): $2,756
No. of shares (mil.): 62
Dividends:
　1990 average yield: 4.3%
　1990 payout: 47.6%
Market value (mil.): $578

Stock Price History High/Low 1981–90

RANKINGS

107th in *Fortune* 500 Industrial Cos.
587th in *Business Week* 1000

KEY COMPETITORS

American Brands
American Standard
Amway
Cooper Industries
Electrolux
Emerson
Gillette
Honda
Ingersoll-Rand
Masco
Matsushita
Philips
Premark
Robert Bosch
Sears
Snap-on Tools
Stanley Works
Textron

BLOCKBUSTER ENTERTAINMENT CORP.

OVERVIEW

Ft. Lauderdale–based Blockbuster Entertainment is the undisputed leader in the video rental industry. With revenues that surpass the combined total of its 99 largest competitors, it holds an 11% market share. The company's 1,964 stores (about 1/2 of which are franchised) cater to a consumer network of over 20 million Blockbuster cardmembers, who rent more than 1 million of the company's videos daily. Founder Wayne Huizenga owns about 12% of the company and still sits on the board.

Blockbuster revolutionized the video rental industry by consolidating smaller chains and the numerous mom-and-pop video rental stores into a formidable national network of stores that offer efficiency, variety, and convenient hours. The company's stores provide a family-oriented atmosphere with an extensive selection of children's videos and no X-rated titles.

Despite its stellar growth since it opened its first store in 1985, Blockbuster is haunted by numerous Wall Street naysayers who believe the video rental industry is doomed. Already in a mature market, the company is facing the threat of cable companies who offer interactive video capabilities (allowing consumers to call up movies from their phones). Determined to prove the doomsday prophets wrong, Blockbuster is opening a new store every 17 hours.

WHEN

In 1982 David P. Cook founded Cook Data Services in Dallas to sell software and computing services to the oil and gas industries. The company went public in 1982. When the energy industry slowed in the mid-1980s, Cook sold these businesses and shifted direction in favor of flashy, computerized video rental stores. The company opened its first store in 1985 and changed its name to Blockbuster Entertainment the following year.

Blockbuster might never have hit the big time had it not attracted the attention of Wayne Huizenga, the recently retired brainchild behind Waste Management's remarkable growth. Looking for an investment in video rental, Huizenga invested $18 million in Blockbuster in 1987 and had bought out the founders by the end of the year. That same year Huizenga bought Southern Video Partnership and Movies to Go, increasing the number of Blockbuster stores to 130 by year's end.

Rapid expansion continued in 1988, when the company bought the California-based Video Library chain. By the end of the year, Blockbuster had increased its video chain to 415 stores (stock appreciation was so rapid during 1988 that the company declared two 2-for-1 stock splits in the space of 20 weeks).

During 1989 Blockbuster continued to gobble up its competitors, including Major Video (a 175-store chain based in Las Vegas) and Video Superstore MLP (its biggest franchise owner). Also in 1989 the company opened a store in London and began trading on the New York Stock Exchange.

In 1990 Blockbuster added several more chains to its growing list of acquisitions, including Applause Video (Omaha), Video Express (Kansas City, Missouri), Movie Emporium (Orlando), as well as units in Arizona, California, and Texas, bringing the store total past the 1,500 mark. The company also established a store in Puerto Rico and signed agreements for outlets in Japan, Mexico, and Australia. The first Blockbuster Bowl, which featured a football game between Florida State and Penn State, was played that same year. An avid sports fan, Huizenga is the driving force behind the push to get a pro baseball team in Miami.

In 1990 Cox Enterprises, Blockbuster's 3rd largest franchisee, announced that it would sell its stores. Video rentals fell sharply during the Gulf War in 1991. Nevertheless, the company bought Virginia-based Erol's, the nation's 3rd largest video chain, and bought out its Tampa franchisee that same year.

NYSE symbol: BV
Fiscal year ends: December 31

Hoover's Rating **A-**

WHO

Chairman and CEO: H. Wayne Huizenga, age 53, $398,077 pay
VC and CFO: Steven R. Berrard, age 36, $286,418 pay
VC: Scott A. Beck, age 32, $240,193 pay
President and COO: Joseph R. Baczko, age 45
VP Human Resources: Frederick W. Ley
Auditors: Arthur Andersen & Co.
Employees: 12,500

WHERE

HQ: 901 E. Las Olas Blvd., Ft. Lauderdale, FL 33301-2320
Phone: 305-524-8200
Fax: 305-462-4139

Blockbuster has stores in Australia, Canada, Chile, Guam, Japan, Mexico, Puerto Rico, Venezuela, the UK, and the US.

Location	No. of Stores	Location	No. of Stores
Alabama	17	Nebraska	17
Alaska	3	Nevada	18
Arizona	31	New Hampshire	4
Arkansas	9	New Jersey	34
California	215	New Mexico	12
Colorado	33	New York	102
Connecticut	27	North Carolina	58
Delaware	2	Ohio	73
Florida	128	Oklahoma	20
Georgia	69	Oregon	10
Hawaii	13	Pennsylvania	77
Idaho	4	Rhode Island	27
Illinois	100	South Carolina	37
Indiana	17	Tennessee	30
Iowa	6	Texas	168
Kansas	16	Utah	15
Kentucky	7	Virginia	137
Louisiana	17	Washington	15
Maryland	110	Washington, DC	13
Massachusetts	42	West Virginia	1
Michigan	64	Wisconsin	21
Minnesota	6	Wyoming	1
Mississippi	8	Foreign	87
Missouri	43		
		Total	**1,964**

HOW MUCH

	8-Year Growth	1981	1982	1983	1984	1985	1986	1987	1988	1989	1990
Sales ($ mil.)	79.0%	—	6	6	5	0	8	43	137	403	633
Net income ($ mil.)	69.8%	—	1	0	0	(1)	(3)	4	16	44	69
Income as % of sales	—	—	15.2%	—	—	—	(35.9%)	9.5%	11.3%	11.0%	10.9%
Earnings per share ($)	—	—	0.05	0.01	0.01	(0.03)	(0.08)	0.07	0.14	0.29	0.42
Stock price – high ($)	—	—	—	1.30	0.38	0.39	1.06	2.61	6.25	10.81	13.38
Stock price – low ($)	—	—	—	0.36	0.18	0.19	0.35	0.73	1.06	4.91	6.81
Stock price – close ($)	—	—	—	0.38	0.23	0.35	0.73	1.08	4.97	8.50	12.94
P/E – high	—	—	—	259	26	—	—	37	44	38	32
P/E – low	—	—	—	72	13	—	—	11	7	17	16
Dividends per share ($)	—	—	0.00	0.00	0.00	0.00	0.00	0.00	0.00	0.00	0.00
Book value per share ($)	70.2%	—	0.03	0.29	0.29	0.27	0.25	0.58	0.99	1.45	2.11

1990 Year-end:
Debt ratio: 35.0%
Return on equity: 23.6%
Cash (mil.): $49
Current ratio: 1.05
Long-term debt (mil.): $169
No. of shares (mil.): 149
Dividends:
  1990 average yield: 0.0%
  1990 payout: 0.0%
Market value (mil.): $1,930

Stock Price History High/Low 1983–90

WHAT

	1990 Sales	
	$ mil.	% of total
Rental revenues	468	74
Product sales	129	20
Royalties & other	36	6
Total	**633**	**100**

RANKINGS

314th in *Business Week* 1000

KEY COMPETITORS

Advance Publications	Paramount
Capital Cities/ABC	Philips
CBS	E.W. Scripps
Cox	Sony
General Cinema	TCI
General Electric	Time Warner
Hearst	Times Mirror
Knight-Ridder	Turner Broadcasting
Matsushita	Viacom
New York Times	Walt Disney
News Corp.	Washington Post

BLUE CROSS AND BLUE SHIELD ASSOCIATION

Nonprofit organization
Fiscal year ends: December 31

Hoover's Rating **C+**

OVERVIEW

The Blue Cross and Blue Shield Association is the national coordinating organization for the 73 autonomous Blue Cross and Blue Shield prepaid health care plans operating throughout the US. The "Blues," as they are called in the industry, are the US's oldest and largest health insurers and provide insurance plans for about 70% of the US's largest industrial firms. If the association were eligible for the *Fortune* 500, it would be #5, with over $62 billion of premium revenues.

Rising health care costs and competition from private insurers have resulted in declining enrollment for the plans and substantial losses. New Jersey, Vermont, Rhode Island, New Hampshire, and Blue Shield of Western New York plans have a negative net worth.

The Blues' original policy of determining plan rates based solely on community claims experience has enabled competing insurers to "cherry pick" the Blues' healthier clients by offering them lower premiums. To survive, some plans have abandoned original precepts such as guaranteed enrollment; others have given up their nonprofit status to become mutual insurance companies.

WHO

President and CEO: Bernard R. Tresnowski
SVP Legal and Corporate: Roger G. Wilson
SVP Business Support and Strategy: Preston Jordan
SVP Federal Programs: Harry P. Cain II
SVP National Marketing: Leonard Wood
SVP External Affairs: Douglas S. Peters
SVP Finance and Management Services: Frederick C. Cue
Executive Director Human Resources and Administration: Phil Petrilli
Auditors: Coopers & Lybrand
Employees: 138,013 (all plans, including subsidiaries)

WHEN

Blue Cross prepaid hospital plans were developed to provide working people with a means of paying for private hospitalization and to ensure that hospitals were paid for their services. The first plans were sponsored by hospitals in Texas, Iowa, and Illinois. The Dallas plan, begun in 1929, cost schoolteachers 50¢ per month and achieved 75% voluntary participation in the first year. Fundamental to the Blue Cross concept was its community rating system, in which premiums were calculated based on the claims experience of the subscriber's community, rather than on the individual subscriber's health or on the age, sex, or occupational makeup of the subscriber's group.

These early experiments were followed by larger plans in New Jersey, Cleveland, Chicago, and St. Paul, the last of which developed the Blue Cross name and symbol in 1934. By 1935 there were 15 Blue Cross plans in 11 states. In the late 1930s many states adopted legislation exempting plans from regulation and solidifying their nonprofit status. In 1936 the American Hospital Association formed the Committee on Hospital Service (renamed the Blue Cross Association, 1948) as an umbrella for the plans.

Simultaneously with the rise of Blue Cross, state medical societies began to sponsor prepaid medical plans to cover physicians' fees. In 1946 they loosely banded together under the guidance of the AMA as the Associated Medical Care Plans (renamed Association of Blue Shield Plans).

In 1945 Blue Cross enrollment was 19 million, while that of Blue Shield stood at 3 million in 1946. To coordinate their efforts, in 1948 the Blues decided to merge, but last-minute opposition from the AMA killed the proposal. Blue Cross decided to form a nonprofit stock corporation to coordinate the activities of its various plans, as did Blue Shield. Despite the failure of formal union, the Blues cooperated on public policy matters while competing vigorously for members.

The Blues enjoyed large enrollment gains in the late 1940s and 1950s, although their growth rate slowed due to increased competition from private insurers. In 1960 Blue Cross boasted almost 1/3 of the nation's population as members (56 million). The Blues became involved in administering federal health benefits (e.g., Medicare) during the 1960s. Half of Blue Cross's 1970 premiums of $10 billion came from these government sources.

Rapidly rising medical costs in the 1970s required the Blues to adopt such cost control measures as utilization review of hospital admissions to stem increasing premiums; many plans even abandoned the community rating system. In the 1980s spiraling health costs and harsh regulatory environments in some states began to undermine the financial health of some of the Blues, which had finally joined forces in 1982. The Blues suffered combined losses of approximately $3 billion in 1987 and 1988. In 1990 some policyholders were left with unpaid medical bills when Blue Cross & Blue Shield of West Virginia collapsed.

In 1991, in a break with traditional emphasis on treatment over prevention, Blue Cross issued guidelines for preventive care coverage.

WHERE

HQ: 676 N. St. Clair St., Chicago, IL 60611
Phone: 312-440-6000
Fax: 312-440-6609

The association has offices in Chicago and Washington, DC; 73 licensees operating in 50 states, Canada, Jamaica, and the UK; and over 100 million private and Medicare subscribers.

WHAT

	1990 Enrollment
	% of total
Group subscribers	87
Individual subscribers	13
Total	**100**

	1990 Enrollment
	No. of subscribers (mil.)
Private	70
Medicare	30
Total	**100**

Policies and Programs
Group major medical insurance
Health maintenance programs (HMO–USA)
Individual major medical insurance
Medicare administration
Preferred-provider organizations

Organization Goals
Attainment of wide public acceptance of the principle of voluntary, nonprofit prepayment of health services
Betterment of public health
Cooperation with federal, state, and local governments for provision of health services
Development and maintenance of membership standards
Protection of Blue Cross and Blue Shield service marks

Publications
Inquiry (scholarly journal)
Your Healthy Best (health booklets)

KEY COMPETITORS

Aetna
CIGNA
Humana
John Hancock
MassMutual
MetLife
New York Life
Prudential
Travelers

HOW MUCH

	9-Year Growth	1981	1982	1983	1984	1985	1986	1987	1988	1989	1990
Net subscriptions revenue ($ mil.)	—	—	—	—	—	—	—	—	51,249	56,040	62,566
Pvt. subscribers (mil.)	(2.1%)	85	80	80	80	78	77	76	74	73	70
Employees of plans (thou.)	—	—	—	89	89	98	110	118	125	129	133
HQ budget ($ mil.)	—	—	71	71	85	87	98	95	97	104	108

Private Subscribers (mil.) 1981–90

THE BOEING COMPANY

OVERVIEW

Seattle-based Boeing is a diversified aerospace company that designs and manufactures commercial and military aircraft, missiles, helicopters, spare parts, and related products. America's largest exporter (58% of 1990 revenues were derived from exports), Boeing is also the world's largest commercial aircraft maker — and has been since the 707 launched the jet age in 1958.

Boeing's record $103 million backlog both assures leadership into the 1990s and presents its biggest customer problem. For the first time in 20 years, the company has been delivering planes behind schedule, which some analysts believe might have benefited rival Airbus Industrie. However, Boeing has stepped up production to help meet demand. The new 777 will fill a size gap in its line of commercial jets (between the jumbo 747 and the economical 767) and will compete directly with the Airbus 330. Boeing is also studying next-generation supersonic transport jointly with Germany's Deutsche Airbus.

The company is also considering the sale of turboprop maker de Havilland to Alenia (Italy) or Aerospatiale (France).

WHEN

Bill Boeing built his first airplane in 1916 with the help of navy officer Conrad Westervelt. His Seattle factory, at first called Pacific Aero Products Company, changed its name to Boeing Airplane Company the following year.

During WWI Boeing built training planes for the US Navy and afterward, when military sales evaporated, began the first international airmail service, between Seattle and Victoria (British Columbia), using the newly designed B-1 flying boat. Another key airmail route (from San Francisco to Chicago) followed in 1927, and Boeing established an airline subsidiary, Boeing Air Transport.

The airline's success was helped along by Boeing's Model 40A, the first plane using Frederick Rentschler's new air-cooled engine, the Wasp. (Rentschler went on to become the head of engine-maker Pratt & Whitney.) In 1927 Boeing bought Pacific Air Transport and in 1928 formed a holding company, Boeing Airplane and Transport Corporation, for its manufacturing and transportation concerns. In 1929 Rentschler and Boeing combined their companies as United Aircraft and Transport. United soon owned a number of aviation-related businesses, including Sikorsky Aviation, Stout Air Services, and Clement Keys' National Air Transport.

The company introduced the first all-metal airliner in 1933. But in 1934 new airmail regulations forced United to sell the airline (the predecessor of today's UAL Corporation), leaving Boeing Airplane (as it was known until 1961) with the manufacturing concerns.

Between 1935 and 1965 Boeing built many successful planes, including the Model 314 Clipper (flying boats) used by Pan Am; the Model 307 Stratoliner (the first aircraft with a pressurized cabin); the B-17, B-29, and B-52 bombers; and 707 and 727 jetliners.

In the 1960s Boeing built the first stage of the rockets used in the Apollo space program. It delivered the first of the best-selling 737s in 1967; the 747 (the first of jumbo jets) also went into production in the late 1960s.

World fuel shortages and concern over aircraft noise prompted Boeing to design the efficient and quiet 757 and 767 late in the 1970s. Meanwhile, the company expanded its information services and aerospace capabilities by establishing Boeing Computer Services (data communications services, 1970). It bought an equity interest in Carnegie Group (artificial intelligence, 1984) and ARGOSystems (defense electronics, 1987). Boeing also bought De Havilland Aircraft, a Canadian turboprop commuter aircraft maker, in 1986.

In 1990 Boeing launched its first new commercial aircraft in 11 years — the 2-engine, wide-body 777. Delivery is scheduled for 1995.

NYSE symbol: BA
Fiscal year ends: December 31

WHO

Chairman and CEO: Frank A. Shrontz, age 59, $1,094,542 pay
SVP and CFO: B. E. Givan, age 54, $314,821 pay
SVP Operations: D. D. Cruze, age 60
VP Human Resources: L. G. McKean, age 55
Auditors: Deloitte & Touche
Employees: 160,500

WHERE

HQ: 7755 E. Marginal Way South, Seattle, WA 98108
Phone: 206-655-2121
Fax: 206-655-7004

Boeing has worldwide operations. Its plants are located in 7 US states and 2 Canadian provinces.

	1990 Sales	
	$ mil.	% of total
US	11,502	42
Europe	7,762	28
Asia & Oceania	6,760	24
Other countries	1,571	6
Total	**27,595**	**100**

WHAT

	1990 Sales		1990 Operating Income	
	$ mil.	% of total	$ mil.	% of total
Commercial transport	21,230	77	2,189	128
Military transport	4,123	15	(299)	(17)
Missiles & space	1,739	6	(119)	(7)
Other industries	503	2	(66)	(4)
Total	**27,595**	**100**	**1,705**	**100**

Commercial Transport
737
747
757
767
777
de Havilland Dash 8
Triton

Military Transport
Aircraft electronic systems
B-2 bomber
B-52 bomber
CH-47D Chinook transport helicopter
Wings for A-6 attack aircraft

Missiles and Space
Airborne Warning and Control System (AWACS)
Inertial Upper Stage (IUS) booster rockets
Living, laboratory, and support modules for Space Station *Freedom*
Short Range Attack Missile (SRAM II)
TACAMO submarine-communication aircraft

RANKINGS

13th in *Fortune* 500 Industrial Cos.
30th in *Business Week* 1000

KEY COMPETITORS

Airbus	Martin Marietta
Daimler-Benz	McDonnell Douglas
General Dynamics	Raytheon
Grumman	Rockwell
Lockheed	Textron
LTV	Thomson SA

HOW MUCH

	9-Year Growth	1981	1982	1983	1984	1985	1986	1987	1988	1989	1990
Sales ($ mil.)	12.2%	9,788	9,035	11,129	10,354	13,636	16,341	15,355	16,962	20,276	27,595
Net income ($ mil.)	12.7%	473	292	355	787	566	665	480	614	675	1,385
Income as % of sales	—	4.8%	3.2%	3.2%	7.6%	4.2%	4.1%	3.1%	3.6%	3.3%	5.0%
Earnings per share ($)	12.0%	1.45	0.89	1.09	2.29	1.64	1.90	1.38	1.79	1.96	4.01
Stock price – high ($)	—	13.11	10.52	14.30	17.63	23.44	28.83	24.33	30.06	41.25	61.88
Stock price – low ($)	—	6.52	4.44	9.44	10.56	16.07	20.33	15.11	16.61	25.72	37.75
Stock price – close ($)	23.8%	6.67	10.04	12.96	16.78	23.22	22.72	16.44	26.94	39.58	45.38
P/E – high	—	9	12	13	8	14	15	18	17	21	15
P/E – low	—	4	5	9	5	10	11	11	9	13	9
Dividends per share ($)	9.6%	0.41	0.41	0.41	0.41	0.46	0.53	0.62	0.69	0.78	0.95
Book value per share ($)	10.7%	8.15	8.63	9.28	11.26	12.50	13.83	14.56	15.67	17.73	20.30

1990 Year-end:
Debt ratio: 4.3%
Return on equity: 21.1%
Cash (mil.): $3,326
Current ratio: 1.23
Long-term debt (mil.): $311
No. of shares (mil.): 344
Dividends:
  1990 average yield: 2.1%
  1990 payout: 23.7%
Market value (mil.): $15,590

Stock Price History High/Low 1981–90

BOISE CASCADE CORPORATION

NYSE symbol: BCC
Fiscal year ends: December 31

Hoover's Rating **D**

OVERVIEW

Boise Cascade is a major producer of paper, paper products, and wood building supplies and a leading distributor of office supplies, furniture, and paper.

Like others in the forest products industry, the company faces the challenges of a sluggish economy and soft market for pulp and paper products. But Boise Cascade seems especially affected; earnings dropped 72% in 1990, and, so far, 1991 has been even worse. The company lost $49.4 million in the first half and still must contend with a glut in many of its main paper products (including uncoated freesheet paper, linerboard, and newsprint), which has caused prices to drop sharply. In response, the company is planning to reduce production of newsprint and to focus on white papers, which offer more potential return. Investment will continue in the office-product and building-product sectors.

Conservationist efforts have limited the supply of publicly owned timber now available for sale to companies. This poses the threat of shortages to Boise Cascade, which depends on outside sources for almost 50% of its raw timber.

WHEN

Boise Cascade got its start in 1957 with the merger of 2 small lumber companies — Boise Payette Lumber Company (Boise, Idaho) and Cascade Lumber Company (Yakima, Washington). The company diversified in the 1960s under the leadership of Robert Hansberger, moving into office-products distribution in 1964. A number of acquisitions followed, including Ebasco Industries, which had started out as a holding company (Electric Bond & Share) and, over time, had expanded into a consulting, engineering, and construction firm (1969). By 1970 Boise Cascade had used more than 30 acquisitions to diversify into building materials, paper products, real estate, recreational vehicles, and publishing. Hansberger gave managers much individual discretion, making the company an attractive place for young college graduates to work.

Meanwhile, Boise Cascade had continued to rely on its access to public timberlands instead of investing in a strong reforestation program, which led to a timber shortage in the early 1970s. Concurrent plans to develop recreational communities in Hawaii, Washington, and California met opposition from environmentally conscious residents, causing the company to scrap all but 6 of the 29 projects. Costs related to the remaining projects were higher than originally planned, and by 1972

Boise Cascade was $1 billion in debt; it recorded a loss of $171 million that year.

John Fery, who replaced Hansberger as president in 1972, responded to the crisis by centralizing authority and selling most of Hansberger's acquisitions not directly related to the company's core forest-products operations. Among those sold were the recreational-vehicle businesses (1972), the engineering and construction businesses (Chemical Construction Corporation, 1973), and the publishing companies (Communications/Research/Machines and George Macy Companies, 1973). Boise Cascade sold Ebasco in 1973 and its Latin American bonds in 1976. The company bought 348,000 acres of New England timberland in 1980 and now owns 46% of the timberland it uses.

Boise Cascade's focus during the last 5 years has been on manufacturing forest products and distributing building materials and office supplies. In 1989 the company invested $602 million to upgrade 10 papermaking facilities in the US and Canada; capital investment reached a record level of $824 million in 1990.

Also in 1990, Jon Miller, who had succeeded Fery as president in 1978, stepped down to pursue other interests. Miller's duties were assumed by chairman Fery.

WHO

Chairman and CEO: John B. Fery, age 61, $756,351 pay
SVP and CFO: Rex L. Dorman, age 57
SVP Human Resources and General Counsel: John E. Clute, age 56, $349,864 pay
Auditors: Arthur Andersen & Co.
Employees: 19,810

WHERE

HQ: One Jefferson Sq., PO Box 50, Boise, ID 83728-0001
Phone: 208-384-6161
Fax: 208-384-7298

Owned or Leased Timberland	Acres Thou.
Washington, Oregon & Idaho	1,361
Maine & New Hampshire	673
Alabama, Louisiana & Texas	797
Canada (including leases)	3,354
Total	**6,185**

	1990 Sales		1990 Operating Income	
	$ mil.	% of total	$ mil.	% of total
US	3,848	92	240	81
Canada	318	8	55	19
Adjustments	20	—	(60)	—
Total	**4,186**	**100**	**235**	**100**

WHAT

	1990 Sales		1990 Operating Income	
	$ mil.	% of total	$ mil.	% of total
Paper & paper products	2,207	53	187	63
Office products	1,077	26	58	20
Building products	889	21	42	14
Other	12	—	8	3
Adjustments	—	—	(60)	—
Total	**4,185**	**100**	**235**	**100**

Paper Products
Coated paper
Copy paper
Corrugated containers
Envelopes
Labels
Laser-printer paper
Linerboard
Market pulp
Newsprint
Offset-printing papers

Building Products
Doors
Engineered wood products
Fiberboard siding

Gypsum board
Lumber
Metal products
Molding
Particleboard
Plywood
Roofing
Windows

Office Products Distribution
Copy paper
Office and computer supplies
Office furniture

RANKINGS

118th in *Fortune* 500 Industrial Cos.
542nd in *Business Week* 1000

KEY COMPETITORS

Bridgestone
Canadian Pacific
Champion International
Fletcher Challenge
Georgia-Pacific
Goodyear
International Paper
James River
Kimberly-Clark

Manville
Mead
3M
Nobel
Owens-Corning
Scott
USG
Weyerhaeuser

HOW MUCH

	9-Year Growth	1981	1982	1983	1984	1985	1986	1987	1988	1989	1990
Sales ($ mil.)	3.4%	3,107	2,912	3,451	3,817	3,737	3,740	3,821	4,095	4,338	4,186
Net income ($ mil.)	(5.1%)	120	7	60	70	104	102	183	289	268	75
Income as % of sales	—	3.9%	0.2%	1.8%	1.8%	2.8%	2.7%	4.8%	7.1%	6.2%	1.8%
Earnings per share ($)	(5.5%)	2.70	0.16	1.25	1.44	2.11	2.02	3.64	6.15	5.70	1.62
Stock price – high ($)	—	28.95	24.15	28.42	27.00	30.60	38.92	52.12	50.00	48.00	46.25
Stock price – low ($)	—	16.95	11.85	20.70	19.50	22.35	26.70	28.80	36.00	39.75	19.75
Stock price – close ($)	2.6%	20.55	23.40	26.25	24.37	28.20	35.85	40.80	41.25	44.38	26.00
P/E – high	—	11	155	23	19	14	19	14	8	8	29
P/E – low	—	6	76	17	14	11	13	8	6	7	12
Dividends per share ($)	3.2%	1.14	1.14	1.14	1.14	1.14	1.14	1.16	1.35	1.43	1.52
Book value per share ($)	1.2%	30.09	29.15	29.10	28.92	29.90	30.34	32.41	37.34	33.52	33.54

1990 Year-end:
Debt ratio: 55.1%
Return on equity: 4.8%
Cash (mil.): $26
Current ratio: 1.32
Long-term debt (mil.): $1,935
No. of shares (mil.): 38
Dividends:
  1990 average yield: 5.8%
  1990 payout: 93.8%
Market value (mil.): $987

Stock Price History High/Low 1981–90

BORDEN, INC.

OVERVIEW

Based in New York City, Borden is a leading diversified food company. Borden's dairy unit (its traditional business, popularized by Elsie the Cow) is the nation's largest, producing milk, ice cream, frozen desserts, cottage cheese, yogurt, and sour cream. The company is also the largest worldwide pasta producer (its US market share is about 34%) with such names as Creamette and Catelli. Borden is the 2nd largest salty snacks maker in North America (after PepsiCo's Frito-Lay division) and the leading producer of sweet baked snacks in West Germany.

The company holds #1 or #2 positions in 27 niche grocery markets with such products as caramel corn (Cracker Jack), bouillon (Wyler's), jellies (Bama), and coffee creamer (Cremora). Aside from producing Elmer's Glue, Borden's nonfood group is the world's largest wallpaper producer and the global leader in vinyl foodwraps and wood adhesives.

Borden has just completed a 2-year restructuring in which it streamlined operations and reshuffled assets to reduce production costs.

WHEN

Galveston resident Gail Borden, Jr., founded one of Texas's first newspapers (*Telegraph and Texas Register*) and in it headlined the phrase "Remember the Alamo." Over the years his inventions included a portable bathhouse, oar-driven steamboat, and nonperishable meat biscuit, created about 1850.

His meat biscuit led to the process for which he became famous. Returning from London (1851) after accepting an award for the biscuit, Borden witnessed infant deaths from putrefied milk and decided to make nonperishable milk. His process required condensation in a vacuum to preserve the milk. It took 4 efforts (1856) and a personal commendation from Sam Houston before the patent was approved.

In 1857 Borden located in Burrville, Connecticut, as Gail Borden, Jr., and Company; his first big break came with the Civil War when the US Army placed an order for 500 pounds of condensed milk. Condensed milk was later carried on Peary's North Pole and Annapurna expeditions. By the time of his death (1874), Borden was the leading milk condenser in the US. Renamed New York Condensed Milk, the company sold condensed milk door-to-door in New York City and soon added fresh milk.

The company incorporated in 1899, gaining capital from 66 initial stockholders. Between 1928 and 1929 Borden doubled in

size through the purchase of more than 90 companies, gaining operations in ice cream, cheese, and powdered milk. By 1929 Borden was one of the nation's largest food companies and had diversified into chemicals through the purchase of glue maker Casein.

By 1937 the company had expanded internationally and branched into synthetic adhesives. By the end of WWII, Borden was well positioned internationally and in the chemicals market. However, until 1956 upper management was still focused upon dairy operations. As part of a plan to reduce dependency upon dairy revenues, Augustine Marusi, as chemical division head and later president, expanded chemical operations by buying Columbus Coated Fabrics (1961) and Smith-Douglass (1964).

Expansion into salted snacks began in 1964 with the purchase of Wise Foods and Cracker Jack. In 1979 Borden bought Buckeye and Guy's Food potato chip manufacturers.

The company launched a major expansion effort beginning in 1986 in which it made 88 acquisitions including Meadow Gold (dairies, 1986) and Moore's (snack foods, 1989). Borden is selling off 1/3 of its dairy operations but continues expansion in groceries. The company's most recent acquisitions include Catelli (pasta, 1989) and Weissenfelser Backwaren (a German bakery, 1991).

HOW MUCH

	9-Year Growth	1981	1982	1983	1984	1985	1986	1987	1988	1989	1990
Sales ($ mil.)	6.3%	4,415	4,111	4,265	4,568	4,716	5,002	6,514	7,244	7,593	7,633
Net income ($ mil.)	9.6%	160	166	189	191	194	223	267	312	(61)	364
Income as % of sales	—	3.6%	4.0%	4.4%	4.2%	4.1%	4.5%	4.1%	4.3%	(0.8%)	4.8%
Earnings per share ($)	12.3%	0.87	0.94	1.08	1.19	1.25	1.50	1.81	2.11	(0.41)	2.46
Stock price – high ($)	—	5.00	8.75	10.17	10.83	17.83	26.25	31.94	30.56	38.63	37.88
Stock price – low ($)	—	4.17	4.48	7.54	8.31	10.54	15.88	15.00	23.56	27.69	27.00
Stock price – close ($)	22.9%	4.67	7.94	9.42	10.79	17.21	23.44	24.75	29.63	34.38	29.88
P/E – high	—	6	9	9	9	14	18	18	14	—	15
P/E – low	—	5	5	7	7	8	11	8	11	—	11
Dividends per share ($)	13.3%	0.34	0.36	0.40	0.44	0.49	0.55	0.62	0.75	0.90	1.04
Book value per share ($)	5.8%	7.50	7.84	8.28	8.77	9.14	9.77	11.26	12.51	11.12	12.50

1990 Year-end:
Debt ratio: 42.1%
Return on equity: 20.8%
Cash (mil.): $162
Current ratio: 1.10
Long-term debt (mil.): $1,340
No. of shares (mil.): 147
Dividends:
 1990 average yield: 3.5%
 1990 payout: 42.1%
Market value (mil.): $4,400

Stock Price History High/Low 1981–90

NYSE symbol: BN
Fiscal year ends: December 31

Hoover's Rating B-

WHO

Chairman: R. J. Ventres, age 66, $1,618,700 pay
President, CEO, and COO: Anthony S. D'Amato, age 60, $833,734 pay (prior to promotion)
SVP and CFO: Lawrence O. Doza, age 52, $547,131 pay
SVP and Chief Administrative Officer: Allan L. Miller, age 58
Auditors: Price Waterhouse
Employees: 46,300

WHERE

HQ: 277 Park Ave., New York, NY 10172
Phone: 212-573-4000
Fax: 212-371-2659

The company has 105 US and 47 foreign plants.

	1990 Sales	
	$ mil.	% of total
US	5,468	72
Foreign	2,165	28
Total	**7,633**	**100**

WHAT

	1990 Sales		1990 Operating Income	
	$ mil.	% of total	$ mil.	% of total
Grocery & specialty prods.	2,035	27	354	45
Snacks & int'l consumer prods.	2,013	26	190	24
Dairy	1,761	23	76	10
Packaging & industrial prods.	1,824	24	170	21
Adjustments	—	—	(48)	—
Total	**7,633**	**100**	**742**	**100**

Dairy	Cheez Doodles	Hilton's
Borden	Guy's	Kava
Eagle Brand	Humpty Dumpty	MBT
Lady Borden	Jays	None Such
Lite-line	Krunchers!	Ocean Fresh
Meadow Gold	La Famous	Orleans
Viva	Moore's	ReaLemon
	Snacktime	ReaLime
Pasta	Wise	Snow's
Catelli		Soup Starter
Creamette	**Niche Grocery**	Steero
DeCecco	American Original	Wyler's
Gioia	Aunt Millie's	
Lancia	Bama	**Nonfoods**
Luxury	Bennett's	Elmer's
Pennsylvania	Campfire	Fill 'N Finish
Dutch	Classico	Krazy Glue
Prince	Cracker Jack	Stix-All
Red Cross	Cremora	Sunworthy
R•F	Doxsee	Wall-Tex
	Fisher	Wonder Bond
Snacks	Harris	
Bravos		

RANKINGS

64th in *Fortune* 500 Industrial Cos.
135th in *Business Week* 1000

KEY COMPETITORS

Anheuser-Busch	Georgia-Pacific	PepsiCo
Associated Milk	Grand Metropolitan	Philip Morris
Producers	Hershey	Procter &
BSN	John Labatt	Gamble
ConAgra	Kellogg	RJR Nabisco
CPC	Nestlé	USG
General Mills		

BORG-WARNER CORPORATION

OVERVIEW

Chicago-based Borg-Warner is a privately owned manufacurer of automobile parts and the leading provider of protective and security services. Merrill Lynch Capital Partners, a subsidiary of Merrill Lynch, now controls the company, having acquired 89% of Borg-Warner's stock in a 1987 LBO.

The company's automotive segment is a leading supplier of powertrain components (transmissions, drive trains, engine timing systems, transfer cases). Since its inception, Borg-Warner has produced over 50 million automatic and manual transmissions and overdrives. About 27% of the company's 1990 sales were to Ford and General Motors.

Engineering, the heart of Borg-Warner's automotive operations, keeps the company at the forefront of technology. The company has been a sponsor of the Indianapolis 500 since 1936 and annually awards the coveted Borg-Warner trophy, a symbol of automotive excellence.

Borg-Warner's protective services subsidiary, Baker Industries (60% of sales — up from 57% in 1989), provides armored transportation, alarm systems, courier services, and fire detection systems under the Wells Fargo, Burns, and Pony Express service marks.

WHEN

Borg-Warner was formed in 1928 when 4 major auto parts companies (Borg & Beck, clutches; Warner Gear, transmissions; Mechanics Universal Joint; and Marvel Carburetor) merged in Chicago. In 1929 Borg-Warner acquired numerous other companies, including Ingersoll Steel & Disc (agricultural blades and discs) and Norge (refrigerators).

The Great Depression struck shortly after Borg-Warner's formation. The company weathered the crisis largely through the contributions of its Norge and Ingersoll divisions. In the late 1930s Borg-Warner purchased several companies including Calumet Steel (1935) and US Pressed Steel (1937).

In the early 1940s the company geared up for wartime production and manufactured parts for planes, trucks, and tanks and in 1941 received a navy contract to build amphibious tanks for use in the Pacific. Between 1942 and 1945 Borg-Warner produced more than 1.6 million automotive transmissions, leaving the company in a good position to manufacture transmissions for the growing automobile industry at the end of WWII. Borg-Warner's 1948 contract from Ford to build 1/2 of its transmissions resulted in massive growth for the company.

In 1950 Roy Ingersoll, president of the Ingersoll Steel & Disc division, assumed leadership of Borg-Warner and embarked on a major diversification program. In 1953 the company developed Cycolac, a thermoplastic resin with numerous consumer applications (including telephone casings, car interiors, aircraft fittings, and sporting goods). In 1956

Borg-Warner purchased several companies including York (air conditioning and refrigeration), Humphreys Manufacturing, Industrial Crane & Hoist, Dittmer Gear, and the Chemical Process Company.

Diversification continued into the 1960s and 1970s with several acquisitions that took Borg-Warner into foreign markets. In 1968 James Beré became president and continued to expand the company away from its core businesses. Key acquisitions during this time included Recold Corporation (refrigeration, 1966), Owens Plastics (1966), Precision Automotive Components (1966), E.W. Twitchell (fiber and paper products, 1967), H. Robert Industries (institutional products and furniture, 1970), and Unit Parts (auto parts, 1972).

In 1978 the company bought Baker (firefighting equipment and protective services) for $123 million. Norge, which had added washers and dryers, was sold to Fedders Corporation for $20 million in 1968, and in 1980 the company sold its Ingersoll Products division to a group of investors led by Jack Maxwell.

In 1987 Borg-Warner was threatened by a takeover from Irwin Jacobs and Samuel Heyman until Merrill Lynch Capital Partners organized an LBO and took the company private, assuming $4.5 billion in debt. To help pay the debt, Borg-Warner sold its chemical group to General Electric for $2.3 billion (1988) and its credit unit, Chilton, to TRW for $330 million (1989). Slow auto sales in 1990 and 1991 led Borg-Warner to strengthen its protective services unit, acquiring Globe Security (guard services) for $40 million (1990).

Private company
Fiscal year ends: December 31

WHO

Chairman and CEO: James F. Beré, age 68, $1,400,000 pay
VP and COO: Donald C. Trauscht, age 57, $650,000 pay
VP and CFO: Neal F. Farrell, age 56, $509,000 pay
VP Human Resources: John D. O'Brien, age 48, $436,000 pay
Auditors: Deloitte & Touche
Employees: 86,800

WHERE

HQ: 200 S. Michigan Ave., Chicago, IL 60604
Phone: 312-322-8500
Fax: 312-322-8849 (main office)

The company's automotive segment operates 17 manufacturing facilities in the US, Canada, Italy, Japan, Korea, Wales, and Germany. The protective services group operates in North and South America.

	1990 Sales		1990 Operating Income	
	$ mil.	% of total	$ mil.	% of total
US	2,063	88	142	80
Canada	77	3	9	5
Europe	162	7	17	10
Other foreign	38	2	3	2
Divested operations	—	—	7	4
Total	**2,340**	**100**	**178**	**100**

WHAT

	1990 Sales		1990 Operating Income	
	$ mil.	% of total	$ mil.	% of total
Automotive	926	40	74	42
Protective services	1,414	60	97	54
Divested operations	—	—	7	4
Total	**2,340**	**100**	**178**	**100**

Automotive Products
Automatic transmissions
Automatic transmission
  components
  Actuators
  Bands
  Dampers
  Electronic sensors
  Engine control devices
  Engine timing systems
  Friction plates
  Solenoids
  Torque converters
  Transfer cases for
  4-wheel drive vehicles
Drive chains

Industrial transmissions
Manual transmissions
Marine transmissions

Protective Services
Burns
  Investigative services
  Security guards
Pony Express
  Courier services
Wells Fargo
  Alarm services
  Armored transport
  Investigative services
  Security guards
  Security systems

RANKINGS

53rd in *Forbes* 400 US Private Cos.

KEY COMPETITORS

Allied-Signal
Cooper Industries
Dana
Eaton
FMC
Johnson Controls
JWP

HOW MUCH

	9-Year Growth	1981	1982	1983	1984	1985	1986	1987	1988	1989	1990
Sales ($ mil.)	(1.8%)	2,761	3,195	3,542	3,916	3,330	3,379	2,957	2,145	2,216	2,340
Net income ($ mil.)	(25.6%)	172	167	183	206	180	155	2	(3)	36	12
Income as % of sales	—	6.2%	5.2%	5.2%	5.3%	5.4%	4.6%	0.1%	(0.2%)	1.6%	0.5%
Employees	4.9%	56,300	75,100	79,700	85,700	82,000	78,000	72,800	70,200	75,300	86,800

1990 Year-end:
Debt ratio: 56.5%
Return on equity: —
Cash (mil.): $21
Current ratio: 0.78
Long-term debt (mil.): $855

Net Income
1981–90

BORLAND INTERNATIONAL, INC.

NASDAQ symbol: BORL
Fiscal year ends: March 31

Hoover's Rating **A-**

OVERVIEW

After buying Ashton-Tate in 1991, Borland International became the world's 3rd largest maker of PC software (after Microsoft and Lotus) and the #1 maker of database software.

Borland's Paradox software is fast becoming the database management software of choice for corporations, with 35% of the market. The company's award-winning high-end spreadsheet program Quattro Pro is giving Lotus 1-2-3 a run for its money. Borland plans to come out with Windows versions of Paradox and Quattro Pro but has not yet announced a timetable for their introduction.

Borland's products are sold through dealers, independent distributors, and OEMs, as well as directly to customers in corporate, educational, and governmental sectors. Overseas sales accounted for about 38% of revenues in fiscal 1991.

Founder Philippe Kahn, whose antics have earned him a reputation as a prankster, owns 10% of Borland's stock. Kahn likes to refer to Borland's casual corporate culture as "barbarian" and has been known to greet visitors wearing a Hawaiian shirt, shorts, and tennis shoes.

WHO

Chairman, President, and CEO: Philippe Kahn, age 39, $1,629,821 pay
SVP Worldwide Sales: Douglas R. Antone, age 38, $368,321 pay
SVP Finance and Operations and CFO: Alan Hendricks, age 40, $289,873 pay
VP Human Resources: Douglas R. Cuenin, age 40
Auditors: Price Waterhouse
Employees: 986

WHEN

In 1982 Philippe Kahn, a mathematician and self-taught computer programmer, left his native France for America, hoping to land a job in the high-tech mecca of Silicon Valley. After an offer from Hewlett-Packard petered out (the company discovered that he had no green card or work permit), the determined Kahn and a few American friends completed work on Turbo Pascal, an advanced computer language Kahn had been tinkering with while still in France, and to market it launched Borland International (Kahn thought the name had a multinational ring to it). Kahn persuaded *BYTE* magazine to run the company's first advertisement on credit, and by the end of the first month Borland had received 100,000 orders.

The company continued as a relatively small concern, known mostly for its languages, until the mid-1980s, when Kahn started acquiring other software makers to augment Borland's product line. He bought Analytica International, the maker of Reflex database management software, in 1985 and followed with Ansa Software, which had developed the database management system Paradox, in 1987. It was Borland's version of Paradox (introduced 2 years later) that eventually helped to alter the company's direction and image in the software industry.

But first Borland had to work through financial difficulties. In 1988 Kahn reported an unexpected 2nd quarter loss, followed by an annual loss of $3 million. Although Kahn attributed the loss (at least in part) to sluggish European sales, he also regarded it as a personal failure and responded by strengthening financial controls, reducing the work force by 25%, and replacing 2 high-level European managers. In 1989 Borland was back in the black, reporting a profit of $12 million. Kahn took the company public that year in a $11.9 million offering.

In 1989 Borland came out with a new version of Paradox and with Quattro Pro, a high-end spreadsheet program. In 1990 the company introduced the Turbo C++ programming language. Later that year Lotus filed suit against Borland, claiming that user interfaces for Quattro and Quattro Pro violated copyrights for Lotus 1-2-3. Borland introduced a number of new products in 1991, including ObjectVision, a business application program for use with Microsoft Windows. ObjectVision provides programming tools to people without programming knowledge, enabling them to easily create tailored business software applications.

Borland effectively doubled its size in 1991 by buying longtime rival Ashton-Tate through a $439 million stock swap.

WHERE

HQ: 1800 Green Hills Rd., Scotts Valley, CA 95066
Phone: 408-438-8400
Fax: 408-438-3623

Borland has offices in the US, Canada, Europe, and Australia. Its products are sold worldwide.

	1990 Sales		1990 Operating Income	
	$ mil.	% of total	$ mil.	% of total
US	141	62	32	82
Europe	67	30	7	18
Other countries	19	8	—	—
Total	**227**	**100**	**39**	**100**

WHAT

Database Products
ObjectVision
Paradox
Paradox Engine Q
Paradox SQL Link

Spreadsheet Products
Quattro Pro

Language Products
Borland C++
Turbo C++
Turbo Pascal
Turbo Pascal for Windows

Other Products
Reflex (flat-file database)
Sidekick (desktop organizing)
Sprint (word processing)
SuperKey (macro)

RANKINGS

673rd in *Business Week* 1000

KEY COMPETITORS

Computer Associates
IBM
Lotus
Microsoft
Novell
Oracle
Wang

HOW MUCH

Fiscal year ends March of following year	4-Year Growth	1981	1982	1983	1984	1985	1986	1987	1988	1989	1990
Sales ($ mil.)	67.3%	—	—	—	—	—	29	82	91	113	227
Net income ($ mil.)	73.2%	—	—	—	—	—	3	2	(3)	12	27
Income as % of sales		—	—	—	—	—	10.7%	2.1%	(3.1%)	10.4%	11.8%
Earnings per share ($)		—	—	—	—	—	0.30	0.15	(0.25)	0.90	1.81
Stock price – high ($)		—	—	—	—	—	—	—	—	—	32.00
Stock price – low ($)		—	—	—	—	—	—	—	—	—	9.88
Stock price – close ($)		—	—	—	—	—	—	—	—	—	31.75
P/E – high		—	—	—	—	—	—	—	—	—	18
P/E – low		—	—	—	—	—	—	—	—	—	5
Dividends per share ($)		—	—	—	—	—	0.00	0.00	0.00	0.00	0.00
Book value per share ($)	28.8%	—	—	—	—	—	2.21	2.75	2.47	4.03	6.09

1990 Year-end:
Debt ratio: 10.5%
Return on equity: 35.8%
Cash (mil.): $43
Current ratio: 2.09
Long-term debt (mil.): $10
No. of shares (mil.): 14
Dividends:
  1990 average yield: 0.0%
  1990 payout: 0.0%
Market value (mil.): $442

Net Income ($ mil.) 1986–90

BOSTON CELTICS LP

NYSE symbol: BOS
Fiscal year ends: June 30

Hoover's Rating **B+**

OVERVIEW

Boston Celtics Limited Partnership operates what its fans hail as the most successful sports franchise ever. The team boasts 16 National Basketball Association titles, 17 Hall-of-Famers, and 15 Most Valuable Players.

Don Gaston, Alan Cohen, and Paul Dupee, Jr., own a corporation that serves as the general partner. Approximately 80,000 other investors, 50,000 of whom own 1 share each, own about 49% of the partnership units.

The team generates its revenues through home-game ticket sales; licensing of TV, cable, and radio rights; and the merchandising of the Celtics' name. The Celtics play most of their home games in the historic 14,890-seat Boston Garden and fans have bought an average of 12,934 season tickets each year for the last 5 years. The Celtics earn approximately $.15 per partnership unit for each playoff round the team enters. After winning their conference title with a 56-26 won-lost record, the Celtics were eliminated in the 2nd round of the 1991 playoffs.

New COO David Gavitt will have to contend with rising player-salary demands while staying under the NBA salary cap and will soon have to replace aging veteran stars Larry Bird, Kevin McHale, and Robert Parish.

WHO

Chairman: Don F. Gaston, age 56
President: Arnold "Red" Auerbach, age 73, $275,000 pay
SVP and COO: David R. Gavitt, age 52, $550,000 pay
EVP and General Manager: Jan Volk, age 44, $246,000 pay
VP Finance: Joseph G. DiLorenzo, age 35, $112,000 pay
Head Coach: Chris Ford, age 42
Auditors: Ernst & Young
Employees: 43

WHEN

Walter Brown founded the Boston Celtics basketball team (so-named partially because of Brown's Irish background) in 1946. After 4 initial losing seasons, Brown hired Arnold "Red" Auerbach as head coach in 1950.

Auerbach quickly turned the Celtics into a competitive organization by acquiring such players as Bob Cousy, Chuck Cooper (the first black player in the NBA), Bill Sharman, and Frank Ramsey. Although the Celtics improved tremendously during Auerbach's first 6 years as head coach, the team was unable to win an NBA title.

The turning point came in 1956, when Auerbach traded 2 players to the St. Louis Hawks for a first-round draft pick that turned out to be Bill Russell. Around Russell's gifted play, Auerbach created the greatest dynasty in basketball history, winning 9 NBA championships (8 in a row) between 1956 and 1966. Auerbach stepped down as coach to become the team's general manager in 1966. Russell assumed coaching responsibilities (the first black NBA coach) and led the team to 2 additional titles in 1968 and 1969.

During the early 1970s, under new coach Tom Heinsohn, the team restructured and, with the talents of players like John Havlicek, Don Nelson, Jo Jo White, and Dave Cowens, took NBA titles in 1974 and 1976. By the late 1970s, however, the team had slipped into last place, and Brown sold his interest to Harry Mangurian.

During the 1979–80 season the team registered another major turnaround, due largely to the efforts of 1978 draft choice Larry Bird. With the assistance of players like Kevin McHale and Robert Parish, the Celtics won their 14th title in 1981.

In 1983 Mangurian sold control of the team to a triumvirate consisting of Don Gaston, Paul Dupee, Jr., and Alan Cohen. K. C. Jones became head coach in 1983 and led the team to titles in 1984 and 1986.

In late 1986 the 3 owners established a limited partnership and offered units to the public (a first for a pro franchise).The offering yielded gains of over $44 million for the 3 principal shareholders.

In 1989 the Celtics purchased WFXT-TV and WEEI-AM, Boston-area broadcasters with rights to Celtics games. In 1990, after a disappointing season, the Celtics fired coach Jim Rodgers and replaced him with his former assistant, Chris Ford. In the same year the Celtics spun off WFXT-TV and WEEI-AM to unit holders in a rights offering.

WHERE

HQ: 151 Merrimac St., Boston, MA 02114
Phone: 617-523-6050
Fax: 617-523-5949

The team plays the majority of its 41 regular-season home games at the Boston Garden arena in downtown Boston but also plays some games at the civic center in nearby Hartford, Connecticut.

WHAT

	1990 Sales	
	$ mil.	% of total
Regular season		
Ticket sales	15	50
Television, cable & radio	11	36
Advertising, other	2	7
Playoffs	2	7
Total	**30**	**100**

Scoring 1990–1991			
	Made	Attempted	%
Field goals	3,695	7,214	.512
3-point field goals	109	346	.315
Free throws	1,646	1,997	.824

Rebounds (1990–91)
Offensive rebounds (1,088)
Defensive rebounds (2,697)
Total rebounds (3,785)

Roster
John Bagley (#5, Guard)
Larry Bird (#33, Forward, Captain)
Dee Brown (#7, Guard)
Rick Fox (#44, Guard/Forward)
Kevin Gamble (#34,Guard/Forward)
Anderson Hunt (#8, Guard)
Joe Kleine (#53, Center)
Reggie Lewis (#35, Guard/Forward)
Kevin McHale (#32, Forward/Center)
Robert Parish (#00, Center)
Ed Pinckney (#54, Forward)
Dave Popson (#42, Forward)
Brian Shaw (#20, Guard)
Derek Smith (#43, Guard/Forward)
Michael Smith (#11, Forward)
Stojko Vrankovic (#52, Center)
A. J. Wynder (#12, Guard)

HOW MUCH

	4-Year Growth	1981	1982	1983	1984	1985	1986	1987	1988	1989	1990
Sales ($ mil.)	8.1%	—	—	—	—	—	22	27	28	27	30
Net income ($ mil.)	12.5%	—	—	—	—	—	5	7	10	12	8
Income as % of sales	—	—	—	—	—	—	21.7%	26.6%	36.4%	44.6%	26.9%
Earnings per share ($)	—	—	—	—	—	—	—	1.59	1.88	1.23
Stock price – high ($)	—	—	—	—	—	—	18.38	16.13	15.75	19.50	19.13
Stock price – low ($)	—	—	—	—	—	—	15.25	10.38	11.63	13.50	14.50
Stock price – close ($)	3.2%	—	—	—	—	—	15.75	11.50	13.75	18.13	17.88
P/E – high	—	—	—	—	—	—	—	—	10	10	16
P/E – low	—	—	—	—	—	—	—	—	7	7	12
Dividends per share ($)	—	—	—	—	—	—	0.00	0.70	1.60	1.60	1.35
Book value per share ($)	—	—	—	—	—	—	58.11	—	—	—	—

1990 Year-end:
Debt ratio: 0.0%
Return on equity: —
Cash (mil.): $0
Current ratio: 1.93
Long-term debt (mil.): $0
No. of shares (mil.): 6
Dividends:
  1990 average yield: 7.6%
  1990 payout: 109.8%
Market value (mil.): $115

Stock Price History High/Low 1986–90

RANKINGS

1st in Eastern Conference, Atlantic Division

KEY COMPETITORS

Paramount
Turner Broadcasting

BRISTOL-MYERS SQUIBB COMPANY

OVERVIEW

New York City–based Bristol-Myers Squibb is a major drug and consumer-products company, boasting an impressive 22 products that bring in over $100 million each in annual sales. The company is the global leader in anticancer drugs, orthopedic implants, and treatments for high blood pressure (its blood pressure drug Capoten is the US's 6th best-selling drug). Other well-known company products include Enfamil (the #2 infant formula in the US), Nice 'n Easy (the #1 US hair coloring), and Bufferin (the #1 painkiller in Japan).

Bristol-Myers Squibb spent 8.6% of sales on R&D in 1990. New drugs in the company's future include Pravachol (an anticholesterol medicine), and Videx (an antiviral drug used to treat AIDS). The company has recently reached an agreement with the US government that gives it exclusive rights to harvest from federal land the rare yew trees that are used to develop the cancer-fighting compound Taxol. Bristol-Myers is also developing new treatments for hypertension, infections, anxiety, depression, and skin diseases.

WHEN

Competitors for many years, Bristol-Myers and Squibb both have origins in the 19th century. Squibb is one of the oldest American drug firms, founded by Edward Squibb in New York City in 1858. A navy doctor who developed his own techniques for making pure ether and chloroform, Squibb headed the business most of his life, turning it over to his sons in 1891. Theodore Weicker, one of Merck's founders, bought a major interest in Squibb in 1905.

Sales of $414,000 in 1904 grew to $13 million by 1928. Squibb was a major supplier of penicillin and morphine during WWII. In 1952 the company was bought by Mathieson Chemical, and then by Olin Industries in 1953 to form Olin Mathieson Chemical.

In 1968 Squibb was spun off to shareholders, then merged with Beech-Nut (baby food, Life Savers candy); Squibb Beech-Nut bought Lanvin–Charles of the Ritz (cosmetics) in 1971 and changed its name to the Squibb Corporation. By 1975 sales had reached $1 billion. Capoten and Corgard, 2 major cardiovascular drugs, were introduced in the late 1970s. Capoten was the first drug developed by the method of "rational design" (i.e., to attack a specific disease-causing mechanism) rather than by the traditional method of trial and error. In a restructuring, the company sold Lanvin–Charles of the Ritz to Yves Saint Laurent and LifeSavers to Standard Brands in the 1980s. Squibb formed a joint venture with Denmark's Novo in 1982 to sell insulin.

Bristol-Myers originated as Clinton Pharmaceutical of Clinton, New York, founded by William Bristol and John Myers in 1887 (renamed Bristol-Myers in 1900). The company sold bulk pharmaceuticals to doctors and druggists. Bristol-Myers made antibiotics after the 1943 purchase of Cheplin Biological Labs.

The company began overseas expansion in the 1950s with the purchase of English and German drug and chemical companies. In 1959 Bristol-Myers bought Clairol. Subsequent acquisitions included Drackett (Windex, Drano, 1965), Mead Johnson (drugs, infant and nutritional formula, 1967), and Zimmer (orthopedic implants, 1972). Bristol-Myers introduced new drugs for treating cancer (Platinol, 1978) and a new type of antianxiety drug (BuSpar, 1986). In 1986 the company acquired the biotech companies Oncogen and Genetic Systems. Bristol-Myers bought Squibb in 1989 for $12.7 billion.

In 1990 the company bought Concept (arthroscopy products, US), Orthoplant (implants, Germany), and a minority interest in Rueil-Malmaison (drugs, France). In 1991 an FDA committee took the extraordinary action of recommending that the company's anti-AIDS drug DDI be approved for sale before clinical trials were completed.

NYSE symbol: BMY
Fiscal year ends: December 31

Hoover's Rating **A+**

WHO

Chairman and CEO: Richard L. Gelb, age 66, $2,102,400 pay
President: Richard M. Furlaud, age 67, $1,695,600 pay
EVP and CFO: Michael E. Autera, age 52
SVP Human Resources: William Flatley, age 49
Auditors: Price Waterhouse
Employees: 52,900

WHERE

HQ: 345 Park Ave., New York, NY 10154-0037
Phone: 212-546-4000
Fax: 212-546-4020

Bristol-Myers Squibb has facilities in 17 countries.

	1990 Sales		1990 Operating Income	
	$ mil.	% of total	$ mil.	% of total
US	7,017	61	1,747	66
Other Americas	906	8	198	7
Pacific	833	7	80	3
Other countries	2,682	24	633	24
Adjustments	(1,138)	—	(269)	—
Total	**10,300**	**100**	**2,389**	**100**

WHAT

	1990 Sales		1990 Operating Income	
	$ mil.	% of total	$ mil.	% of total
Prescription drugs	5,261	51	1,548	59
Medical devices	1,436	14	346	13
Cons. health prods.	1,773	17	390	15
Household prods.	1,830	18	326	13
Adjustments	—	—	(221)	—
Total	**10,300**	**100**	**2,389**	**100**

Pharmaceuticals
Azactam (antibiotic)
BuSpar (anti-anxiety drug)
Capoten (cardiovascular)
CardioTec (diagnostic)
Corgard (cardiovascular)
Exelderm (dermatological)
Monopril (cardiovascular)
Paraplatin (cancer drug)
Platinol (cancer drug)
Questran (cardiovascular)
Stadol (analgesic)
VePesid (cancer drug)

Medical Devices
Breast implants
Prosthetic devices
Surgical instruments

Consumer Products
Drano
Endust
Final Net
Miss Clairol
Nice 'n Easy
Renuzit
Theragran-M
Vanish
Vitalis
Windex

Nonprescription Drugs
Bufferin
Excedrin
Nuprin

Nutritionals
Enfamil
Isocal

HOW MUCH

	9-Year Growth	1981	1982	1983	1984	1985	1986	1987	1988	1989	1990
Sales ($ mil.)	12.8%	3,497	3,600	3,917	4,189	4,444	4,836	5,401	5,973	9,189	10,300
Net income ($ mil.)	21.4%	306	349	408	472	531	590	710	829	747	1,748
Income as % of sales	—	8.7%	9.7%	10.4%	11.3%	12.0%	12.2%	13.1%	13.9%	8.1%	17.0%
Earnings per share ($)	12.8%	1.12	1.27	1.48	1.70	1.90	2.03	2.43	2.85	1.41	3.33
Stock price – high ($)	—	14.69	18.50	23.94	26.31	34.25	44.25	55.81	46.50	58.00	68.00
Stock price – low ($)	—	11.44	12.69	15.59	20.50	24.50	30.13	28.25	38.13	44.00	50.50
Stock price – close ($)	19.7%	13.28	16.81	21.13	26.19	33.13	41.31	41.63	45.25	56.00	67.00
P/E – high	—	13	15	16	16	18	22	23	16	41	20
P/E – low	—	10	10	11	12	13	15	12	13	31	15
Dividends per share ($)	19.4%	0.45	0.51	0.73	0.80	0.94	1.18	1.05	2.18	2.03	2.19
Book value per share ($)	6.5%	5.88	6.34	7.00	7.82	8.88	9.91	11.23	12.33	9.68	10.34

1990 Year-end:
Debt ratio: 4.1%
Return on equity: 33.3%
Cash (mil.): $1,958
Current ratio: 2.01
Long-term debt (mil.): $231
No. of shares (mil.): 524
Dividends:
  1990 average yield: 3.3%
  1990 payout: 65.8%
Market value (mil.): $35,096

Stock Price History High/Low 1981–90

RANKINGS

46th in *Fortune* 500 Industrial Cos.
7th in *Business Week* 1000

KEY COMPETITORS

American Cyanamid
American Home Products
Amgen
Bayer
Ciba-Geigy
Clorox
Dow Chemical
Du Pont
Eastman Kodak

Eli Lilly
Glaxo
Hoechst
Johnson & Johnson
S. C. Johnson
L'Oréal
MacAndrews & Forbes
Merck
Monsanto

Pfizer
Procter & Gamble
Rhône-Poulenc
Roche
Sandoz
Schering-Plough
SmithKline Beecham
Syntex
Upjohn
Warner-Lambert

BROWN GROUP, INC.

NYSE symbol: BG
Fiscal year ends: Saturday nearest January 31

Hoover's Rating **C+**

OVERVIEW

Although almost 100 years old, Buster Brown, the comic-strip-character-turned-trademark, is still selling shoes for the St. Louis–based Brown Group, the largest domestic shoe manufacturer and a leading shoe retailer. Altogether Brown produces about 12% of the non-rubber shoes and about 1/3 of the women's shoes manufactured in the US. Aside from its venerable Buster Brown name, the company's branded shoe lines include Connie, Naturalizer, Life Stride, and FootGear. Women's shoes represented almost 3/4 of 1990

sales in Brown's footwear segment. In addition to operating 22 manufacturing facilities in North America, Brown imports over 60 million pairs of shoes annually.

The company's 1,824 retail shoe stores include Buster Brown, Famous Footwear, Naturalizer, and Regal Shoes. Brown also commands a major presence in North American department stores, where its Wohl Division operates 635 leased shoe departments. Brown also operates the 316-unit Cloth World chain of retail fabric stores.

WHEN

In 1878 salesman George Warren Brown conceived the idea of mass-producing women's shoes in St. Louis, an unheard-of notion at a time when the shoe industry was firmly entrenched in New England. With the financial backing of partners Alvin Bryan and Jerome Desnoyers, Brown hired 5 shoemakers and opened Bryan, Brown and Company. The company's fashionable first shoes, which were a pleasant contrast to the staid, black shoes typical of New England, were an instant success, with first-year sales of $110,000.

The enterprise grew rapidly, and in 1893, Brown, who was by then the sole remaining partner, renamed the operation the Brown Shoe Company. By 1900 sales had reached $4 million.

In 1902 company executive John Bush decided to use comic strip character Buster Brown (created by famous cartoonist Richard Outcault) as a trademark for Brown's children's shoes, using it for the first time at the St. Louis World's Fair. Although Bush acquired the rights to the character, he failed to purchase the exclusive rights, and Buster Brown became the trademark for scores of products, even cigars and whiskey. Nevertheless, Buster Brown became a famous trademark for the company. Bush eventually hired midgets to dress as Buster Brown and crisscross the country selling Brown shoes, always with the catchy jingle, "I'm Buster Brown; I

live in a shoe. (WOOF! WOOF!) That's my dog Tige: he lives there too."

During the Great Depression, company VP Clark Gamble developed the concept, now commonplace, of having salesmen sell only specific branded shoe lines instead of traveling with samples of all the company's shoes.

During the 1950s Brown modernized its operations and entered the retailing business by purchasing Wohl Shoe (1951), Regal Shoe (1954), and G. R. Kinney (1956, sold in 1963 to Woolworth because of antitrust litigation). The company also launched a national advertising push through major magazines and children's TV shows.

Brown diversified in the 1970s, buying Cloth World stores (1970), Eagle Rubber (toys and sporting goods, 1971), Hedstrom (bicycles and equipment, 1971), Meis Brothers (department stores, 1972), and Outdoor Sports Industries (1979), among others. Acquisitions continued in the 1980s as the company added several shoe and specialty retailers. In 1985 Brown sold its recreational products segment, and in 1989 announced a restructuring in which it shed all of its specialty retailers except Cloth World and sold or closed many of its unprofitable shoe units.

In 1991 another restructuring led to realignment of Brown's children's shoes unit, termination of 1,400 employees, and closing of 4 plants.

WHO

Chairman, President, and CEO: B. A. Bridgewater, Jr., age 57, $800,000 pay
EVP and CFO: Harry E. Rich, age 51, $363,000 pay
Auditors: Ernst & Young
Employees: 27,500

WHERE

HQ: 8400 Maryland Ave., PO Box 29, St. Louis, MO 63166
Phone: 314-854-4000
Fax: 314-854-4274

The company's shoes are sold by approximately 7,500 retailers throughout the US and Canada.

	1990 Sales		1990 Pretax Income	
	$ mil.	% of total	$ mil.	% of total
US	1,469	82	38	78
Foreign	321	18	11	22
Adjustments	(26)	—	—	—
Total	**1,764**	**100**	**49**	**100**

WHAT

	1990 Sales		1990 Operating Income	
	$ mil.	% of total	$ mil.	% of total
Footwear	1,552	88	76	101
Fabric stores	212	12	(1)	(1)
Adjustments	—	—	(12)	—
Total	**1,764**	**100**	**63**	**100**

	No. of Stores
Naturalizer	866
Connie/Fanfares	266
Famous Footwear	304
Buster Brown (licensed independent)	286
Life Stride (licensed independent)	13
Regal/Castleby	89
Family Footwear (independent)	1,154
Wohl Shoe (leased departments)	635
Cloth World	316
Total	**3,929**

Children's Shoes
Barbie's Fashion Footwear (license)
Brittania (license)
Buster Brown
FootGear
Jordache (license)
Mickey Mouse and Friends (license)
Playskool (license)
The Little Mermaid (license)
Wildcats

Men's Shoes
Brittania (license)
Donnay (license)

Jean Pier Clementé
Jeep (license)
Levi's Shoes and Boots (license)
Paragon
Regal
Roblee

Women's Shoes
Air Step
Brittania (license)
Connie
DeLiso
Jordache (license)
Life Stride
Naturalizer
NaturalSport

HOW MUCH

	9-Year Growth	1981	1982	1983	1984	1985	1986	1987	1988	1989	1990
Sales ($ mil.)	3.1%	1,338	1,397	1,501	1,572	1,400	1,400	1,678	1,707	1,821	1,764
Net income ($ mil.)	(5.9%)	55	60	67	54	49	40	47	30	31	32
Income as % of sales	—	4.1%	4.3%	4.5%	3.4%	3.5%	2.9%	2.8%	1.8%	1.7%	1.8%
Earnings per share ($)	(3.4%)	2.52	2.74	3.15	2.62	2.45	2.15	2.60	1.73	1.77	1.85
Stock price – high ($)	—	15.50	30.75	39.88	33.00	36.75	43.38	44.25	38.50	35.50	30.00
Stock price – low ($)	—	10.00	13.13	25.50	22.75	25.00	31.00	26.63	31.00	26.75	19.75
Stock price – close ($)	5.1%	14.19	28.00	31.88	27.38	33.75	34.50	32.75	31.38	27.13	22.13
P/E – high	—	6	11	13	13	15	20	17	22	20	16
P/E – low	—	4	5	8	9	10	14	10	18	15	11
Dividends per share ($)	8.8%	0.75	0.88	1.04	1.28	1.36	1.46	1.52	1.56	1.60	1.60
Book value per share ($)	2.6%	15.50	17.28	18.81	19.81	19.72	19.25	20.33	19.10	19.39	19.47

1990 Year-end:
Debt ratio: 27.7%
Return on equity: 9.5%
Cash (mil.): $16
Current ratio: 2.14
Long-term debt (mil.): $129
No. of shares (mil.): 17
Dividends:
 1990 average yield: 7.2%
 1990 payout: 86.5%
Market value (mil.): $382

Stock Price History High/Low 1981–90

RANKINGS

860th in *Business Week* 1000

KEY COMPETITORS

Carter Hawley Hale	L.A. Gear	Reebok
Edison Brothers	May	U.S. Shoe
General Cinema	Melville	Wal-Mart
Hanson	NIKE	Woolworth
INTERCO	Nordstrom	

BROWN-FORMAN CORPORATION

OVERVIEW

NYSE symbol: BFB
Fiscal year ends: April 30

Hoover's Rating **A-**

Based in the whiskey-rich state of Kentucky, Brown-Forman is a leading producer of spirits, wine, glassware, and luggage, including such names as Jack Daniel's Tennessee Whiskey, Early Times Kentucky Whiskey, California Cooler, Southern Comfort liqueur, Korbel California Champagnes, Hartmann luggage, and Lenox china, crystal, and giftware.

Brown-Forman's Wines and Spirits segment provides the lion's share (75%) of company sales. Operations include producing, bottling, importing, exporting, and marketing beverages.

Jack Daniel's ranks as the #1 premium spirits brand in the US; Southern Comfort ranks as the #1 domestic proprietary liqueur; Korbel is the largest-selling premium champagne; and Bolla is the leading premium imported table wine. Jack Daniel's and Southern Comfort are Brown-Forman's leading exports and are sold through an international network of distributors.

Brown-Forman's Consumer Durables segment is the largest domestic producer and marketer of fine china dinnerware and lead crystal stemware, as well as a leading producer of luggage. The company also operates retail and outlet stores through which it sells its products.

WHO

Chairman and CEO: W. L. Lyons Brown, Jr., age 54, $1,004,550 pay
VC: Owsley Brown Frazier, age 55, $525,237 pay
VC: William M. Street, age 52, $677,025 pay
President: Owsley Brown II, age 48, $835,847 pay
SVP and Executive Director of Financial Operations: Clifford G. Rompf, Jr., age 60
SVP and Executive Director of Human Resources: Russell C. Buzby, age 57
Auditors: Coopers & Lybrand
Employees: 5,600

WHEN

In 1870 George G. Brown and John Forman opened the Brown-Forman Distillery in Louisville, Kentucky, to produce Old Forester brand bourbon. Old Forester sold well through the end of the century due in part to the company's innovative packaging of the product (safety seals and quality guarantees on the bottles). Forman sold his interest in the company to the Brown family (who still control Brown-Forman today) in 1902.

Old Forester continued to be successful under the Brown family. In 1923 the company bought Early Times, its first purchase. The company went public just before Prohibition and obtained government approval to keep the distillery open to produce alcohol for medicinal purposes. The company reestablished the Old Forester image as an alcoholic beverage after Prohibition.

During WWII the government greatly curtailed alcoholic beverage production (alcohol was needed for the war effort). The company compensated by providing alcohol for wartime rubber and gunpowder production. In 1941 Brown-Forman correctly predicted that the war would be over by 1945 and started the 4-year aging process for its bourbon. As a result Early Times dominated the bourbon market after the war.

In 1956 Brown-Forman expanded beyond Old Forester by purchasing Lynchburg, Tennessee–based Jack Daniel's (sour mash whiskey). The company retained the simple, black Jack Daniel's label and promoted the image of a small, Tennessee distillery. Today the brand sells 4 million cases a year and is known worldwide (Japanese executives pay upwards of $60 per bottle for it).

Brown-Forman continued to expand its alcohol line during the 1960s and 1970s, acquiring Korbel (champagne and brandy, 1965), Quality Importers (Ambassador Scotch, Ambassador Gin, and Old Bushmills Irish Whiskey; 1967), Bolla and Cella (wines, 1968), and Canadian Mist (blended whiskey, 1971). In 1979 Brown-Forman purchased Southern Comfort (a top-selling liqueur).

Brown-Forman acquired Lenox (the largest American producer of fine china, as well as crystal, gifts, and Hartmann luggage) in 1983 and California Cooler (wine coolers) in 1985. In 1989 Brown-Forman introduced Icy (Icelandic vodka).

In 1990 the company bought Kirk-Stieff, a producer of silver and pewter, and in 1991 purchased Dansk International Designs, a producer of china, crystal, and silver including the high-quality Gorham line.

WHERE

HQ: PO Box 1080, Louisville, KY 40201-1080
Phone: 502-585-1100
Fax: 502-774-7164 (Public Relations)

The Wines and Spirits segment operates 10 facilities in the Tennessee-Kentucky area, 2 in Ontario, 2 in the US Virgin Islands, and one in Ireland. Consumer Durables operates 17 facilities in the US, one in El Salvador, and 13 domestic retail stores.

WHAT

	1990 Sales		1990 Operating Income	
	$ mil.	% of total	$ mil.	% of total
Wines & Spirits	1,018	74	215	89
Consumer Durables	363	26	34	14
Other	7	—	(8)	(3)
Adjustments	(269)	—	(17)	—
Total	**1,119**	**100**	**223**	**100**

Brand Names

Spirits	Wines
Black Bush	Bolla
Bushmills	Brolio Wines
Canadian Mist	California Cooler
Crystal Comfort	Fontana Candida
Earl Grey	Korbel Brandy
Early Times	Korbel Champagnes
Gentleman Jack	Noilly Prat
Icy Vodka	
Jack Daniel's	**Consumer Durables**
Old Forester	Athalon (luggage)
Pepe Lopez	Dansk (china and crystal)
Sempé Armagnac	Gorham (china and silver)
Southern Comfort	Hartmann (luggage)
Usher's Scotch	Kirk-Stieff (silver and pewter)
	Lenox (china and crystal)

RANKINGS

342nd in *Fortune* 500 Industrial Cos.
319th in *Business Week* 1000

HOW MUCH

Fiscal year ends April 30 of following year	9-Year Growth	1981	1982	1983	1984	1985	1986	1987	1988	1989	1990
Sales ($ mil.)	7.6%	578	605	864	928	995	1,098	1,067	1,006	1,017	1,119
Net income ($ mil.)	5.9%	87	95	74	82	86	90	103	145	81	145
Income as % of sales	—	15.0%	15.7%	8.5%	8.8%	8.7%	8.2%	9.7%	14.4%	8.0%	13.0%
Earnings per share ($)	9.6%	2.29	2.51	1.93	2.29	2.68	2.78	3.25	5.15	2.88	5.21
Stock price – high ($)	—	24.08	30.08	26.00	21.92	32.00	43.00	55.38	58.00	88.25	91.75
Stock price – low ($)	—	17.33	18.75	18.33	15.50	20.42	29.83	26.63	33.88	56.25	56.00
Stock price – close ($)	12.5%	24.08	23.92	21.67	20.67	31.00	40.42	35.25	57.63	88.25	69.75
P/E – high	—	11	12	13	10	12	15	17	11	31	18
P/E – low	—	8	7	9	7	8	11	8	7	20	11
Dividends per share ($)	17.5%	0.51	0.59	0.59	0.59	0.67	0.90	1.24	1.52	1.88	2.16
Book value per share ($)	9.7%	10.20	12.07	13.42	14.11	16.10	18.01	15.82	19.44	20.86	23.47

1990 Year-end:
Debt ratio: 14.5%
Return on equity: 23.5%
Cash (mil.): $108
Current ratio: 3.27
Long-term debt (mil.): $112
No. of shares (mil.): 28
Dividends:
 1990 average yield: 3.1%
 1990 payout: 41.5%
Market value (mil.): $1,928

Stock Price History High/Low 1981–90

KEY COMPETITORS

Allied-Lyons	Guinness
American Brands	LVMH
Amway	Nestlé
Anheuser-Busch	Owens-Illinois
Carlsberg	Pearson
Colgate-Palmolive	Riklis Family
Corning	Sara Lee
Gallo	Seagram
Grand Metropolitan	

BROWNING-FERRIS INDUSTRIES, INC.

OVERVIEW

Houston-based Browning-Ferris Industries is the 2nd largest waste services company in the US (after Waste Management). Headed by William D. Ruckelshaus, former EPA director, the 24-year-old, $2.97 billion company collects, treats, and disposes of commercial, residential, and municipal solid waste. In 1990 the company discontinued its hazardous waste operations after 18 years of operation.

BFI, which started as a one-truck garbage collection business, today operates worldwide, with 454 locations. The company has gone from a period of growth through acquisitions to one of expansion through internal growth and movement into foreign markets.

Public concerns about the environment have translated into business opportunities for BFI. In addition to solid-waste collection, the company handles medical waste, engages in asbestos abatement, and operates recycling programs. BFI's joint venture operation, American Ref-Fuel Co., started up its 2nd waste-to-energy plant in New Jersey in 1991, which has the capability of generating 67,000 kilowatts of electricity. Five more plants are in various stages of development.

NYSE symbol: BFI
Fiscal year ends: September 30

Hoover's Rating **B-**

WHO

Chairman and CEO: William D. Ruckelshaus, age 58, $806,100 pay
VC and Chief Marketing Officer: Norman A. Myers, age 55, $418,100 pay
EVP Solid Waste Operations: Bruce E. Ranck, age 42, $371,100 pay
Acting CFO: David R. Hopkins, age 47
VP Human Resources: Robert R. Schuldt, age 60
Auditors: Arthur Andersen & Co.
Employees: 25,200

WHEN

Accountant Tom Fatjo and Harvard MBA Louis Waters founded American Refuse Systems in 1967 with a single truck, providing garbage collection to a Houston neighborhood. They saw that the 1960s clean air laws created opportunities for large garbage businesses with the resources to comply with changing environmental regulations. In 1969 the company bought construction equipment distributor Browning-Ferris Machinery and changed its name to Browning-Ferris Industries. Subsequently BFI bought numerous waste disposal firms, acquiring a total of 157 by 1973.

Revenues fell 18% in 1975, and earnings dropped from $18 million to just under $5.3 million, partly because of decreased demand for waste paper, which had previously provided nearly 1/2 of revenues. BFI spun off its waste-paper subsidiary (Consolidated Fibres) in 1976. In late 1976 and again in 1977 BFI succeeded in hiking prices across its entire operation 5% to 5.5%, resulting in a 37% rise in earnings in 1977. That year Harry Phillips, who had joined BFI in 1970 when BFI acquired his 5 companies, became CEO, replacing Louis Waters, who became BFI's chairman. Tom Fatjo had left BFI in 1976 to run an investment company.

By 1980, with revenues of $553 million, BFI had become the 2nd largest US waste disposal company. Phillips continued to expand BFI, acquiring 508 companies from 1981 to 1988. BFI bought hazardous-waste disposer CECOS International (1983), formed a joint venture to market trash-burning power plants (1984), and entered the medical-waste field by buying 2 small firms (1986).

BFI paid fines of $1.35 million after pleading guilty to price fixing in 1987, and $2.5 million in 1988 and $1.55 million in 1990 to settle suits arising from environmental violations at Louisiana hazardous-waste sites. The company also settled a 3-year-old class action lawsuit brought against it for price fixing. Some of BFI's legal problems were the result of the actions of BFI's regional management and Phillips's "hands off" approach to managing its subsidiaries. To clean up its image BFI brought in former EPA administrator William Ruckelshaus as CEO in 1988.

After the EPA denied BFI permits to recommence operation of hazardous-waste facilities in Ohio and New York in 1990, the company discontinued hazardous-waste operations altogether. BFI subsequently took a $295 million write-down associated with that discontinuation. A recession in the Northeast and on the Atlantic Seaboard are blamed for BFI's lower 1990 earnings.

In 1991 BFI fired its CFO and general counsel for selling stock in the company just prior to the release of a negative earnings projection.

WHERE

HQ: PO Box 3151, 757 N. Eldridge, Houston, TX 77253
Phone: 713-870-8100
Fax: 713-870-7844

BFI operates in 454 locations in the US (including Puerto Rico) and in Australia, Canada, Hong Kong, Italy, the Netherlands, New Zealand, Spain, the UK, and Venezuela.

	1990 Sales		1990 Operating Income	
	$ mil.	% of total	$ mil.	% of total
US	2,514	85	450	92
Foreign	453	15	40	8
Adjustments	—	—	68	—
Total	**2,967**	**100**	**558**	**100**

WHAT

	1990 Sales
	% of total
Commercial & industrial collection	58
Residential collection	17
Processing & disposal	16
Special services	9
Total	**100**

Solid-Waste Operations
Collection
Transportation
Treatment
Disposal (landfills)
Recycling
Asbestos abatement
Medical-waste services (using incineration or autoclaving)
Portable restroom services
Street and parking-lot sweeping

Chemical-Waste Services
Chemical-waste treatment and processing
Wastewater processing

Subsidiaries and Affiliates
American Ref-Fuel Co. (50%, joint venture with Air Products and Chemicals, Inc.)
BFI Services Group Inc.
Browning-Ferris Industries, Europe Inc.
Browning-Ferris Overseas, Inc.
Congress Development Company (50%)
Swire BFI Waste Services Ltd. (50%, joint venture with Swire Pacific)

HOW MUCH

	9-Year Growth	1981	1982	1983	1984	1985	1986	1987	1988	1989	1990
Sales ($ mil.)	18.2%	661	715	844	1,001	1,145	1,328	1,657	2,067	2,551	2,967
Net income ($ mil.)	20.4%	48	63	80	89	112	137	172	227	263	257
Income as % of sales	—	7.3%	8.8%	9.4%	8.9%	9.8%	10.3%	10.4%	11.0%	10.3%	8.7%
Earnings per share ($)	16.9%	0.41	0.52	0.60	0.65	0.80	0.95	1.15	1.51	1.74	1.68
Stock price – high ($)	—	6.23	9.21	11.91	11.13	16.00	23.69	35.75	29.25	42.75	49.25
Stock price – low ($)	—	3.81	4.08	8.19	6.63	9.16	15.13	17.50	20.88	26.88	20.75
Stock price – close ($)	17.1%	5.35	8.90	10.75	9.25	16.00	22.38	28.00	27.38	38.75	22.25
P/E – high	—	15	18	20	17	20	25	31	19	25	29
P/E – low	—	9	8	14	10	11	16	15	14	15	12
Dividends per share ($)	18.4%	0.14	0.17	0.20	0.24	0.27	0.32	0.40	0.48	0.56	0.64
Book value per share ($)	13.8%	2.37	1.82	2.99	3.39	3.95	5.11	5.93	7.05	8.33	7.61

1990 Year-end:
Debt ratio: 50.7%
Return on equity: 21.1%
Cash (mil.): $139
Current ratio: 1.03
Long-term debt (mil.): $1,193
No. of shares (mil.): 153
Dividends:
  1990 average yield: 2.9%
  1990 payout: 38.1%
Market value (mil.): $3,398

Stock Price History High/Low 1981–90

RANKINGS

38th in *Fortune* 100 Diversified Service Cos.
158th in *Business Week* 1000

KEY COMPETITORS

Consolidated Rail
Ogden
TRW
Union Pacific
Waste Management

BRUNO'S, INC.

NASDAQ symbol: BRNO
Fiscal year ends: Saturday nearest June 30

Hoover's Rating **A-**

OVERVIEW

Bruno's is a large supermarket chain in the Southeast with sales of almost $2.4 billion in 1990, up more than 12% from 1989 sales of just over $2.1 billion. Headquartered in Birmingham, the company operates 240 stores in Alabama, Florida, Georgia, Mississippi, Tennessee, and South Carolina under several names — Food World, Food Fair, Food Max, Bruno's Food and Pharmacy, Piggly Wiggly (through its subsidiary PWS Holding), Bruno's Finer Foods, and Vincent's Market. Its 3 American Fare hypermarkets are a joint venture (49% owned by Bruno's) with Kmart.

With an almost 25% market share in Alabama, Bruno's tailors store size, decor, and merchandise to a targeted clientele, allowing the company to operate several stores in the same market area. The company tightly controls operating costs by buying large quantities of merchandise, often more than currently needed, at low prices. Bruno's competitive pricing and company growth has increased earnings more than 23% and sales more than 19% annually over the past 10 years.

The company owns 39 of its stores and 6 shopping centers and has interests in 14 of its Piggly Wiggly store leases through PM Associates, a 50% joint venture with Metropolitan Life Insurance Company. The founding Bruno family still owns 26% of the company.

WHEN

Bruno's was founded in 1932 in Birmingham by brothers Joseph and Sam Bruno with $600 of their mother's savings. The 800-square-foot food store was run by their father, Vincent, a former steelworker, and their mother, Theresa, with the 8 children helping after school. A 2nd store opened in 1935.

Brothers Joseph, Sam, Lee, and Angelo Bruno incorporated as Bruno's, Inc., with 10 stores (1959). Bruno's opened Big B Discount Drug Stores in 1968 and later spun off the 70-store subsidiary in a stock distribution (1981). By 1970 there were 29 Bruno's Food Stores in Alabama. The company went public to develop discount food stores (1971) and began the Food World chain, opening large 40,000- to 48,000-square-foot discount supermarkets (1972).

The earlier Bruno's Food Stores were remodeled as Bruno's Food & Pharmacy (1983), combination supermarket and drug stores (52,000 to 60,000 square feet) located in suburban markets and featuring more extensive meat and seafood, produce, bakery, and delicatessen departments than conventional supermarkets. Bruno's Finer Foods (1983) are also combination stores. The Food Fair stores (1985) are small supermarkets (17,000 to 32,000 square feet) offering competitive pricing in areas unable to support a high-volume warehouse like Food World.

The company acquired the Megamarket stores in Birmingham (1985) and converted them to Food Max stores, large warehouse supermarkets (48,000 to 65,000 square feet). Vincent's Market in Birmingham (1988) offers gourmet foods and wines, an in-house chef, a 40-seat cafe, catering services, and home delivery.

In the 1970s Bruno's expanded into adjacent states. Recent acquisitions include Steven's Supermarket (Nashville, 1987), Piggly Wiggly (central and southern Georgia, 1988), and 7 BI-LO supermarkets (Macon, Georgia; 1988). The company plans to open 30 new stores in 1991 and to continue its trend toward larger stores.

In 1989, as a joint venture, Bruno's and Kmart opened American Fare, a 240,000-square-foot hypermarket, in Atlanta; Bruno's operates the supermarket section, while Kmart operates the general merchandise areas. American Fare stores also opened in Charlotte, North Carolina, and Jackson, Mississippi (1990). In 1991 Bruno's was added to the Standard & Poor's 500 index.

WHO

Chairman Emeritus: Joseph S. Bruno, age 77, $250,000 pay
Chairman: Angelo J. Bruno, age 66, $325,000 pay
VC and SVP: Lee J. Bruno, age 70
President and CEO: Ronald G. Bruno, age 39, $310,000 pay
EVP Operations: Paul F. Garrison, age 61, $265,000 pay
EVP and CFO: Glenn J. Griffin, age 52, $225,000 pay
VP Personnel: R. Randolph Page, Jr.
Auditors: Arthur Andersen & Co.
Employees: 8,399 full time and 11,988 part time

WHERE

HQ: PO Box 2486, 800 Lakeshore Pkwy., Birmingham, AL 35201-2486
Phone: 205-940-9400
Fax: 205-940-9534 (CFO)

Bruno's operates 240 supermarkets and combination food and drug stores in 6 southern states (Alabama, Florida, Georgia, Mississippi, Tennessee, and South Carolina.)

Distribution Centers	Area (sq. ft.)
Birmingham, AL	1,341,000
Vidalia, GA	706,000
Total	**2,047,000**

WHAT

Stores	No. of Stores
Food World (supermarkets)	76
Food Fair (supermarkets)	30
Food Max (warehouse supermarkets)	40
Bruno's Food and Pharmacy (combination stores)	12
Piggly Wiggly (supermarkets)	69
Other formats	13
Total	**240**

Subsidiaries
PWS Holding Corporation
  Piggly Wiggly Southern, Inc.

Joint Ventures
American Fare hypermarkets (49%, joint venture with Kmart)
PM Associates (50%, joint venture between PWS and Metropolitan Life Insurance Co.)

RANKINGS

404th in *Business Week* 1000

KEY COMPETITORS

Albertson's
Food Lion
Great A&P
Kroger
Winn-Dixie

HOW MUCH

	9-Year Growth	1981	1982	1983	1984	1985	1986	1987	1988	1989	1990
Sales ($ mil.)	19.3%	488	549	605	716	887	1,018	1,143	1,982	2,134	2,395
Net income ($ mil.)	23.4%	9	12	15	19	25	30	31	43	48	60
Income as % of sales	—	1.9%	2.3%	2.5%	2.6%	2.8%	3.0%	2.7%	2.2%	2.2%	2.5%
Earnings per share ($)	20.9%	0.13	0.19	0.23	0.27	0.35	0.39	0.40	0.53	0.59	0.74
Stock price – high ($)	—	3.05	3.70	5.25	5.16	9.00	11.88	12.63	12.88	15.13	16.75
Stock price – low ($)	—	1.27	1.33	3.38	3.19	5.09	7.38	7.56	9.63	10.13	12.88
Stock price – close ($)	31.8%	1.28	3.48	3.69	5.13	8.75	7.56	10.38	10.25	14.75	15.38
P/E – high	—	23	20	23	19	26	31	32	24	26	23
P/E – low	—	9	7	15	12	15	19	19	18	17	17
Dividends per share ($)	15.8%	0.04	0.04	0.05	0.06	0.07	0.08	0.09	0.10	0.12	0.14
Book value per share ($)	27.3%	0.47	0.62	0.98	1.18	1.94	2.25	2.55	3.06	3.56	4.13

1990 Year-end:
Debt ratio: 34.8%
Return on equity: 19.2%
Cash (mil.): $41
Current ratio: 1.75
Long-term debt (mil.): $180
No. of shares (mil.): 82
Dividends:
  1990 average yield: 0.9%
  1990 payout: 18.9%
Market value (mil.): $1,254

Stock Price History High/Low 1981–90

BRUNSWICK CORPORATION

OVERVIEW

Brunswick is the world's #1 recreational marine engine and pleasure boat manufacturer, with such brands as Mercury, Mariner, Force, Bayliner, and Sea Ray. Brunswick is also involved in bowling, billiards, fishing, and golf. The company operates one of North America's largest bowling chains and is a US leader in the manufacture of bowling equipment (Brunswick) and fishing reels (Zebco).

After the 1990 sale of its aerospace and industrial products businesses, Brunswick's last remaining nonrecreation operation is its Defense Division, a manufacturer of composite structures for aircraft and weapons.

Brunswick's boating business slumped since 1988. Restructuring caused a loss in 1989, but resulted in a lower cost structure that enabled Brunswick to post a profit in 1990.

NYSE symbol: BC
Fiscal year ends: December 31

Hoover's Rating **B-**

WHO

Chairman, President, and CEO: Jack F. Reichert, age 60, $1,118,887 pay
EVP: John M. Charvat, age 60, $579,893 pay
VP Finance: William R. McManaman, age 43
Director Human Resources: Patrick J. Gannon
Auditors: Arthur Andersen & Co.
Employees: 20,500

WHEN

Swiss immigrant woodworker John Brunswick built his first billiard table in 1845 in Cincinnati. In 1874 Brunswick formed a partnership with Julius Balke, and 10 years later they teamed with H. W. Collender, forming the Brunswick-Balke-Collender Company.

Following Brunswick's death, son-in-law Moses Bensinger became president and diversified into bowling equipment in the 1880s. His son B. E. followed as president (1904) and led the company into wood and rubber products, phonographs, and records. (Al Jolson recorded "Sonny Boy" on a Brunswick label.) Brunswick went public after WWI.

By 1930 Brunswick had sold many businesses to concentrate on bowling and billiards, sports that had acquired bad reputations during Prohibition and the Great Depression. When B. E. died in 1935, his son Bob became CEO and launched a massive promotional campaign, redesigned bowling alleys, and upgraded equipment lines to make the sports more respectable.

Bob Bensinger moved to chairman in 1954 and his brother Ted succeeded him as CEO. Rival A.M.F. introduced the first automatic pinsetter in 1952, and Brunswick followed in 1956. By 1958 Brunswick had captured the industry lead, as bowling equipment sales rose 650% between 1956 and 1961. Under Ted, Brunswick diversified, adding MacGregor (sporting goods, 1958), Aloe (medical supplies, 1959), Mercury (marine products, 1961), and Zebco (fishing equipment, 1961). The company adopted its present name in 1960.

By 1963 bowling sales had dropped drastically, and in 1965 Brunswick lost $76.9 million. The company sold many unprofitable enterprises, intensified research on an automatic scorer and metal fiber technology (for industrial and defense applications), and emphasized health products through subsidiary Sherwood Medical Industries.

After discontinuing many of its recreation lines, in 1978 Brunswick added Oxford Laboratories (medical diagnostics, $10 million) and the Vapor Corporation (energy and transportation products, $92 million). To foil a takeover by Whittaker Corporation in 1982, Brunswick sold Sherwood to American Home Products. CEO Jack Reichert, a former pin boy who became chairman in 1983, cut corporate staff 59% and promoted the marine business.

In 1986 Brunswick sparked an industry-wide consolidation trend by spending $774 million to buy boat builders Bayliner and Ray Industries. Marine sales increased from 42% of 1982 total sales to 67% in 1990.

A 1989 marine industry slump led to a $71 million loss. Brunswick has laid off employees, closed plants, cut inventories, and offered dealer rebates in response to continuing weakness in marine product sales.

In 1990 Brunswick bought Kiekhaefer Aeromarine, a maker of propulsion engines for marine use. The next year Brunswick and Chrysler announced they would jointly develop a 2-stroke automobile engine.

WHERE

HQ: One Brunswick Plaza, Skokie, IL 60077
Phone: 708-470-4700
Fax: 708-470-4765

Brunswick operates approximately 40 US and 5 foreign plants, and 125 bowling centers in the US, Canada, and Europe.

	1990 Sales		1990 Operating Income	
	$ mil.	% of total	$ mil.	% of total
US	2,113	85	70	66
Foreign	365	15	37	34
Adjustments	—	—	(19)	—
Total	**2,478**	**100**	**88**	**100**

WHAT

	1990 Sales		1990 Operating Income	
	$ mil.	% of total	$ mil.	% of total
Marine	1,652	67	28	26
Recreation	455	18	58	54
Technical	371	15	21	20
Adjustments	—	—	(19)	—
Total	**2,478**	**100**	**88**	**100**

Brand Names

Boats	Boat Motors
Arriva	Force
Astro	L-Drive
Bayliner	Mariner
Cobra	MerCruiser
Escort (trailers)	Mercury
Fisher	Quicksilver
Laguna	U.S. Marine Power
Maxum	
MonArk	**Sporting Goods**
Procraft	Brunswick Billiards
Quantum	Brunswick Golf
Sea Ray	Brunswick (bowling)
Spectrum	Quantum (fishing)
Starcraft	Zebco (fishing)
Trophy	
	Bowling/Recreation Centers
	Brunswick Recreation Centers
	Leiserv, Inc.

RANKINGS

183rd in *Fortune* 500 Industrial Cos.
463rd in *Business Week* 1000

KEY COMPETITORS

Harley-Davidson	Suzuki
Honda	Volvo
S. C. Johnson	Yamaha
Outboard Marine	Defense contractors
Reebok	

HOW MUCH

	9-Year Growth	1981	1982	1983	1984	1985	1986	1987	1988	1989	1990
Sales ($ mil.)	9.6%	1,085	1,068	1,216	1,468	1,539	1,717	3,086	3,282	2,826	2,478
Net income ($ mil.)	5.8%	43	(20)	66	94	100	110	169	193	(71)	71
Income as % of sales	—	3.9%	(1.9%)	5.4%	6.4%	6.5%	6.4%	5.5%	5.9%	(2.5%)	2.9%
Earnings per share ($)	15.0%	0.23	(0.17)	0.73	1.10	1.17	1.32	1.90	2.20	(0.81)	0.80
Stock price – high ($)	—	2.81	3.50	7.47	9.06	11.38	19.69	30.25	24.13	21.50	16.13
Stock price – low ($)	—	1.63	1.77	3.08	5.94	7.75	10.81	10.75	14.50	13.00	6.38
Stock price – close ($)	16.2%	2.33	3.13	7.22	8.47	10.91	16.94	14.75	16.88	14.13	9.00
P/E – high	—	12	—	10	8	10	15	16	11	—	20
P/E – low	—	7	—	4	5	7	8	6	7	—	8
Dividends per share ($)	16.4%	0.11	0.13	0.13	0.18	0.25	0.28	0.30	0.40	0.44	0.44
Book value per share ($)	13.2%	3.05	3.92	4.45	5.38	6.23	7.80	9.52	10.97	8.83	9.33

1990 Year-end:
Debt ratio: 26.8%
Return on equity: 8.8%
Cash (mil.): $85
Current ratio: 1.53
Long-term debt (mil.): $302
No. of shares (mil.): 88
Dividends:
  1990 average yield: 4.9%
  1990 payout: 55.0%
Market value (mil.): $795

Stock Price History
High/Low 1981–90

BURLINGTON HOLDINGS INC.

OVERVIEW

Burlington Holdings is the parent company of Burlington Industries, one of the world's largest textile manufacturing concerns. The company is a leading producer of finished textiles for the apparel industry, producing yarns; cotton and cotton/polyester knitted fabrics; and worsted, denim, polyester, and various blends of woven fabrics. Major customers of the 5 apparel divisions include Levi Strauss and retailers who sell the products under their private labels.

Burlington Industries also makes decorative fabrics and prints for the home and is a major producer of rugs and carpets. The 6 divisions that form this product group manufacture draperies, sheers, shades, and window top treatments; bedspreads and mattress tickings; upholstery fabrics; and carpets and bath and area rugs. Brand names include Burlington House, Lees Carpets, and Monticello Carpets. Retail stores form the primary customer base for this group's products.

Since taking the company private in an LBO in 1987, management continues to sell businesses not related to core product lines. Management blames weak retail sales and excess inventories for Burlington's less-than-stellar performance in 1990, but the company remains weighted with more than $1.6 million of debt (most related to its 1987 LBO) and has recently considered bankruptcy proceedings as a release from mounting interest expenses.

All of the company's stock is controlled by its officers, key employees, and its ESOP.

WHEN

J. Spencer Love, who had entered the milling business after WWI, moved his North Carolina cotton mill from Gastonia to Burlington in 1923. In order to finance the new mill, he convinced the citizens of Burlington to help him sell stock in a new company, Burlington Mills. A year later, when the mill was struggling as the demand for its cotton products waned, Love switched from cotton milling to a new, increasingly popular product, rayon.

When textile prices dropped during the Great Depression, many mills went out of business, especially in the North, where labor was more expensive. Burlington continued to grow rapidly and bought several of these failed businesses. Corporate headquarters moved to Greensboro in 1935, and by 1936 the company had 22 plants in 9 towns. In 1940 Burlington started producing hosiery. It continued to expand through acquisitions, buying Pacific Mills and Klopman Mills in the 1950s, and changed its name to Burlington Industries in 1955.

Burlington further diversified into consumer products with the acquisitions of Charm Tred Mills, a scatter-rug manufacturer (1959), and Philadelphia carpet producer James Lees & Company (1960). The company bought Globe Furniture, based in High Point, North Carolina, in 1966 and made several other acquisitions in the furniture business through the 1970s. William Klopman, son of Klopman Mills's founder, became CEO in 1976 and focused on the renovation of plant facilities and the company's move into consumer products and clothing fabrics in response to increasing foreign competition in its traditional textiles markets.

By 1980 Burlington was by far the largest textile producer in the world; however, most of the company's profits came from consumer products sold under private labels and Burlington's brand names: Anne Klein and Oleg Cassini (home products), Lees (carpets), and Monticello (linen). The company's inability to move beyond the commodity textiles business led to several years of poor profits and a takeover attempt by Montreal-based Dominion Textile, a former Burlington partner in the rayon business. Chairman Frank Greenberg, whose father had owned Charm Tred, led management in an LBO (financed primarily by Morgan Stanley), taking the company private in 1987. Since the buyout, Burlington has sold off all of its foreign operations except those in North America and is focusing on repaying its acquisition debt. In 1989 the company placed 16% of its stock in an ESOP, and in 1990 Morgan Stanley transferred its remaining shares (about 77% of the company) to the company's managers and key employees.

Burlington sold its automotive interior carpet and trim manufacturing subsidiary (C. H. Masland & Sons) to Masland's management and other investors in 1991.

Private company
Fiscal year ends: Saturday closest to September 30

Hoover's Rating **D**

WHO

Chairman and President: Frank S. Greenberg
VC and CFO: Donald R. Hughes
VP Personnel and Public Relations: J. Kenneth Lesley
Auditors: Ernst & Young
Employees: 24,000

WHERE

HQ: 3330 W. Friendly Ave., Greensboro, NC 27420
Phone: 919-379-2000
Fax: 919-379-4504

Burlington operates 41 plants in 7 states and 3 in Mexico.

WHAT

	1990 Sales		1990 Operating Income	
	$ mil.	% of total	$ mil.	% of total
Apparel products	1,041	45	117	70
Home products	813	36	23	14
Other products	428	19	26	16
Adjustments	—	—	(14)	—
Total	**2,282**	**100**	**152**	**100**

Apparel Products

Products
Knitted fabrics
Woven fabrics

Divisions
Burlington Denim
Burlington Knitted Fabrics
Burlington Madison Yarn Co.
Burlington Menswear
Klopman Fabrics

Home Furnishings Products

Products
Area rugs
Bedspreads
Carpets
Draperies
Shades
Upholstery and mattress tickings

Divisions
Burlington Decorative Prints
Burlington House Area Rugs
Burlington House Decorative Fabrics
Burlington House Draperies
Lees Commercial Carpets
Lees Residential Carpets

RANKINGS

57th in *Forbes* 400 US Private Cos.

KEY COMPETITORS

Du Pont
Farley
Fieldcrest Cannon
Milliken
Springs Industries

HOW MUCH

	9-Year Growth	1981	1982	1983	1984	1985	1986	1987	1988	1989	1990
Sales ($ mil.)	(3.9%)	3,263	2,876	2,990	3,169	2,802	2,778	3,279	2,452	2,181	2,282
Net income ($ mil.)	—	115	52	88	62	13	57	22	(33)	(23)	(95)
Income as % of sales	—	3.5%	1.8%	3.0%	2.0%	0.4%	2.0%	0.7%	(1.3%)	(1.1%)	(4.2%)
Employees	(9.1%)	64,000	53,000	53,000	53,000	45,000	43,000	44,000	28,000	27,500	27,000

1990 Year-end:
Debt ratio: 105.7%
Return on equity: —
Cash (mil.): $42
Current ratio: 2.19
Long-term debt (mil.): $1,647

Net Income ($ mil.) 1981-90

BURLINGTON NORTHERN INC.

OVERVIEW

Burlington Northern (BN) operates the largest rail network in America, a 25,329-mile system spanning 25 states and 2 Canadian provinces. Having sold its trucking and natural resource operations in 1988, BN is strictly a railroading company. Subsidiary BN Leasing acquires rail cars and other equipment.

With track stretching from Pensacola to Vancouver, Fort Worth–based BN controls a far-flung empire. The company hauls forest products from the Pacific Northwest, Midwest, and South; grain from the Midwest and Great Plains; and coal from Montana and Wyoming. BN also carries automotive, industrial, food, and consumer products, and offers doublestack intermodal (truck-to-train) services through its BN AMERICA program.

Coal transportation accounted for 33% of BN's revenues in 1990, with 92% of the coal coming from the Powder River Basin of Montana and Wyoming and the rest coming from mines in the South and Midwest. Most of the company's coal traffic terminated at electric generating plants in the North Central, South Central, Mountain, and Pacific regions of the US.

NYSE symbol: BNI
Fiscal year ends: December 31

Hoover's Rating C-

WHEN

Burlington Northern is largely the creation of James J. Hill, who began his railroad empire in 1878 by acquiring the St. Paul & Pacific Railroad in Minnesota. By 1893 Hill had completed the Great Northern Railway, which extended from St. Paul to Seattle. The following year he gained control of Northern Pacific (chartered in 1864), which had been constructed between Duluth, Minnesota, and Tacoma, Washington, with extensions to Portland, Oregon, and St. Paul. With the help of J. P. Morgan, in 1901 Hill acquired the Chicago, Burlington & Quincy (Burlington), whose routes included Chicago-St. Paul, Chicago-Denver, Omaha-Billings, and Billings-Denver-Fort Worth-Houston. To give Great Northern an entrance to Oregon, Hill in 1905 created the Spokane, Portland & Seattle Railway (SP&S), completed in 1908.

Hill intended to merge Great Northern, Northern Pacific, SP&S, and Burlington under his Morgan-backed Northern Securities Company, but in 1904 the Supreme Court found that Northern Securities had violated the Sherman Anti-Trust Act. Although the Court dissolved the holding company, Hill kept control of the individual railroads, remaining a director of Great Northern until his death in 1916.

Meanwhile, Jim Hill's railroads produced some of America's best-known passenger trains. Great Northern's Empire Builder began service between Chicago and Seattle in 1929; it is operated today by Amtrak. The 1934 Burlington Zephyr was the nation's first streamlined passenger diesel.

After several years of deliberation by the Interstate Commerce Commission, Great Northern and Northern Pacific were allowed to merge in 1970 along with jointly owned subsidiaries Burlington and SP&S. The new company, Burlington Northern (BN), acquired the St. Louis–San Francisco Railway (Frisco) in 1980. The Frisco, with lines stretching from St. Louis to such cities as Dallas, Oklahoma City, Kansas City, and Pensacola, added more than 4,650 miles to the BN rail network.

The company formed Burlington Motor Carriers (BMC) in 1985 to manage 5 trucking companies it had acquired. Later (in 1988), as part of its decision to focus only on railroads, BN sold BMC and spun off Burlington Resources, an independent holding company for its nonrailroad businesses (primarily natural gas, oil, minerals, construction, and forest products, including 1.8 million acres of land), leaving Burlington Northern Railroad and BN Leasing as its principal subsidiaries.

In 1990 BN committed $567 million to upgrade its physical properties, including track repair and the purchase of 50 new locomotives and 1,000 grain hoppers.

WHO

Chairman, President, and CEO; Chairman, President, and CEO, Burlington Northern Railroad Co.: Gerald Grinstein, age 58, $1,286,667 pay
EVP and CFO; EVP and CFO, Burlington Northern Railroad Co.: David C. Anderson, age 50
COO, Burlington Northern Railroad Co.: William E. Greenwood, age 52, $658,125 pay
VP Human Resources, Burlington Northern Railroad Co.: Donald W. Scott, age 45
Auditors: Coopers & Lybrand
Employees: 32,900

WHERE

HQ: 3800 Continental Plaza, 777 Main St., Fort Worth, TX 76102-5384
Phone: 817-878-2000
Fax: 817-878-2377

Principal Cities Served

Billings, MT	Minneapolis-
Birmingham, AL	St. Paul, MN
Cheyenne, WY	Mobile, AL
Chicago, IL	Omaha, NE
Dallas, TX	Pensacola, FL
Denver, CO	Portland, OR
Des Moines, IA	Seattle, WA
Fargo-Moorhead, SD	Spokane, WA
Fort Worth, TX	Springfield, MO
Galveston, TX	St. Louis, MO
Houston, TX	Tulsa, OK
Kansas City, MO	Vancouver, BC
Lincoln, NE	Wichita, KS
Memphis, TN	Winnipeg, MB

WHAT

	1990 Sales	
Items transported	$ mil.	% of total
Coal	1,585	33
Agricultural commodities	758	16
Industrial products	720	15
Intermodal	690	14
Forest products	480	10
Food & consumer products	428	9
Automotive products	148	3
Other	9	—
Adjustments	(144)	—
Total	**4,674**	**100**

Subsidiaries
BN Leasing Corp.
Burlington Northern Railroad Co.

RANKINGS

12th in *Fortune* 50 Transportation Cos.
287th in *Business Week* 1000

KEY COMPETITORS

American President	Rio Grande
Canadian Pacific	Industries
Chicago and	Roadway
North Western	Santa Fe Pacific
Consolidated Freightways	Union Pacific
Consolidated Rail	Yellow Freight
Norfolk Southern	

HOW MUCH

	9-Year Growth	1981	1982	1983	1984	1985	1986	1987	1988	1989	1990
Sales ($ mil.)	(0.6%)	4,936	4,198	4,508	9,156	8,651	6,941	6,621	4,700	4,606	4,674
Net income ($ mil.)	(2.2%)	272	178	413	579	633	(529)	367	207	243	222
Income as % of sales	—	5.5%	4.2%	9.2%	6.3%	7.3%	(7.6%)	5.5%	4.4%	5.3%	4.8%
Earnings per share ($)	(2.1%)	3.51	2.28	5.39	7.15	7.96	(7.53)	4.91	2.76	3.18	2.89
Stock price – high ($)	—	36.38	31.25	54.75	50.00	72.63	82.38	84.25	80.38	32.38	39.25
Stock price – low ($)	—	18.50	17.13	25.50	35.00	46.25	46.50	35.00	56.00	21.38	22.25
Stock price – close ($)	0.8%	26.81	26.56	49.50	47.00	68.25	53.25	62.75	79.00	31.50	28.75
P/E – high	—	10	14	10	7	9	—	17	29	10	14
P/E – low	—	5	8	5	5	6	—	7	20	7	8
Dividends per share ($)	5.1%	0.77	0.76	0.87	1.00	1.40	1.70	2.05	2.20	1.20	1.20
Book value per share ($)	(8.2%)	35.37	38.33	50.76	56.98	63.13	47.90	50.80	12.31	14.33	16.29

1990 Year-end:
Debt ratio: 62.7%
Return on equity: 18.9%
Cash (mil.): $56
Current ratio: 0.53
Long-term debt (mil.): $2,083
No. of shares (mil.): 76
Dividends:
1990 average yield: 4.2%
1990 payout: 41.5%
Market value (mil.): $2,190

Stock Price History High/Low 1981–90

STATE OF CALIFORNIA

OVERVIEW

California's diverse, $700 billion economy would be one of the world's 10 largest if it were a separate country. The state leads the US in microelectronics, biotechnology, aerospace, agriculture (50% of US produce), entertainment, and foreign trade. The state boasts high-tech meccas (such as Silicon Valley) and exceptional universities and draws much new foreign investment in the US.

The state's government has executive, legislative, and judicial branches but also includes a unique proposition process that allows voters to act directly on issues.

After a decade of growth (population up 25%, GSP up over 100%) fueled by booming real estate and defense industries, California seemed immune to the recession that gripped the rest of the US. But the state succumbed in late 1990. After Senator Pete Wilson became governor in 1990, housing starts dropped and an outbreak of peace clobbered defense. As Wilson's estimate of the deficit rose to $13 billion (by the end of FY 1992), the legacy of 5 years of drought (expected to cost $3 billion in 1991), combined with 2 popularly legislated propositions, 13 (property tax rollback, 1978) and 98 (which assigned 40% of revenues to education, 1988), became apparent. Both cost cuts and higher taxes have been proposed.

Official name: State of California
Admitted as state: September 9, 1850
State capital: Sacramento
Motto: "Eureka"
Fiscal year ends: June 30

Hoover's Rating **B**

WHO

Governor: Pete Wilson (R), age 58, $120,000 pay
Lieutenant Governor: Leo T. McCarthy (D), age 61, $90,000 pay
Secretary of State: March Fong Eu (D), age 67, $90,000 pay
Attorney General: Dan Lungren (R), age 45, $102,000 pay
Controller: Gray Davis (D), age 48, $90,000 pay
Treasurer: Kathleen Brown, age 46, $90,000 pay
Senators: Alan Cranston (D), John Seymour (R)

WHEN

Though both the Spanish and the English claimed parts of California in the 1500s, the coast remained largely inaccessible until 1769, when King Charles III of Spain extended his New Spain (Mexican) empire northward. Father Junípero Serra and his Franciscan missionaries established 21 missions that became centers of economic activity.

When Mexico gained independence in 1821, it made California a province. Americans, like Swiss-born John A. Sutter, slowly filtered westward and in 1846 revolted against Mexican rule. After the Mexican-American War (1846–48), the US annexed the territory.

Immigration following the discovery of gold at Sutter's Mill (1848) pushed California's non-native population from 13,000 to 112,000 by 1850, the year that California became a state. Paper, flour, lumber, and textile mills, and iron works, shipyards, and banks sprouted. Supply centers San Francisco, Sacramento, and Stockton grew rapidly.

California's gold transformed the world economy and was the impetus for the first transcontinental railroad (1869). Railways opened huge new markets for crops and citrus fruits, launching a food processing industry and Los Angeles's first real estate boom (1887). L.A.'s population expanded from 12,000 to 350,000 between 1880 and 1910. In 1906 San Francisco was destroyed by an earthquake and 3-day fire.

California's climate drew filmmakers west; by 1913 Hollywood was the world's film center, but the county remained the country's largest source of produce through the 1920s. Shipbuilding, oil refining, and many new industries flourished during WWI.

The 1920s saw large oil discoveries and aviation pioneers (Donald Douglas, John Northrop, et al.) founding namesake firms. During the Great Depression the Golden Gate and Oakland Bay bridges were built, and Dust Bowl refugees flooded the state.

WWII and the Korean and Vietnamese wars led to a heavy concentration of defense industries in California in the 1940s, 1950s, and 1960s. The invention of personal computers and microprocessors in the 1970s led to the replacement in the 1980s of the old, heavy industries by new service and technical businesses (Silicon Valley).

Buoyed by a migration that fueled construction and job expansions, the economy exploded. By 1987 the state coffers were in surplus. In 1988 Proposition 98 (40% of revenues earmarked for education) passed. (In 1978, Prop. 13 had rolled back property taxes.) Another 30% of the budget went to social spending. These measures made the state especially vulnerable to any decrease in revenue, and when the state went into recession in 1990 and 1991, California's budget went deeply into the red.

WHERE

HQ: Office of the Governor, State Capitol, 1st Floor, Sacramento, CA 95814
Phone: 916-445-2841
Fax: 916-445-4633

California is the US's 3rd largest state in area, approximately the same size as Japan. The state has 58 counties. Total state land area is 158,692 square miles.

Largest Metropolitan Areas	1990 Population (Thou.)
Los Angeles–Long Beach	8,989
Riverside–San Bernardino	2,696
San Diego	2,549
Anaheim–Santa Ana	2,453
San Francisco–Oakland	1,103
Sacramento	1,067
San Jose	1,513
Oxnard-Ventura	678
Fresno	687

WHAT

	1986 GSP Distribution	
	$ mil.	% of total
Service	103,397	19
Manufacturing	97,680	18
Trade (wholesale & retail)	93,927	18
Finance, insurance & real estate	93,790	18
Government	62,029	12
Transportation & public utilities	41,928	8
Construction	23,855	4
Farms, forestry & fishing	11,282	2
Mining	5,927	1
Total	**533,815**	**100**

Imports
Clothing
Computers
Home entertainment goods
Office machines
Passenger cars
Semiconductors
Sporting goods
Toys
Trucks

Exports
Agricultural products
Aircraft
Computers
Electronic components
Office machine components
Semiconductors

HOW MUCH

	9-Year Growth	1981	1982	1983	1984	1985	1986	1987*	1988*	1989*	1990*
Population (mil.)	2.5%	24.27	24.79	25.31	25.78	26.36	27.00	27.65	28.20	29.06	30.35
Gross state product (GSP) ($ bil.)	8.4%	354.9	372.5	408.2	456.9	496.8	533.8	580.0	638.2	680.0	735
GSP per capita (const. $)	1.9%	15,575	15,450	15,448	16,330	16,844	17,222	17,902	18,440	18,582	18,451
GSP ($ bil., const. $)	4.5%	378	383	391	421	444	465	495	520	540	560
State revenues ($ bil.)	8.1%	23.4	24.2	27.6	31.6	33.5	37.6	38.2	42.3	46.0	47.2
State expenditures ($ bil.)	8.0%	24.8	24.9	26.4	30.4	34.0	37.1	39.6	43.5	46.1	49.6

GSP Per Capita ($ mil.) 1981–90

(Bar chart showing values ranging 0 to 20,000)

RANKINGS

1st in US agricultural output and exports
1st in US manufacturing output and exports
1st in US population

* Estimated

CAMPBELL SOUP COMPANY

NYSE symbol: CPB
Fiscal year ends: Sunday
nearest August 1

Hoover's Rating **B-**

OVERVIEW

Based in Camden, New Jersey, Campbell Soup is the largest US maker of canned soups and a major producer of other food products, including such recognized names as Pepperidge Farm (cookies and crackers), Godiva (chocolates), Swanson (frozen dinners), and Vlasic (pickles). Campbell's familiar red-and-white soup cans command about 2/3 of the US soup market.

While many companies are scrambling for market share in the emerging European market, Campbell has focused the greater part of its attention closer to home by integrating its US, Canadian, and Mexican operations under a single entity (Campbell North America). The new division puts Campbell in a position to exploit an anticipated North American common market, which would consist of over 400 million people by the year 2000.

Following years of lackluster performance, the company was in danger of being sold by the Dorrance family (heirs of the founder who control close to 60% of Campbell's stock) until former Gerber executive David Johnson came in and launched a top-to-bottom restructuring in which management was trimmed and unprofitable segments were divested.

WHO

Chairman: Robert J. Vlasic, age 64
President and CEO: David W. Johnson, age 58, $585,221 pay
VP and Controller: Leo J. Greaney, age 56
VP Human Resources: Stephen R. Armstrong, age 43
Auditors: Price Waterhouse
Employees: 49,941

WHERE

HQ: Campbell Place, Camden, NJ 08103-1799
Phone: 609-342-4800
Fax: 609-342-3878

Campbell has operations in 13 countries.

	1990 Sales		1990 Operating Income	
	$ mil.	% of total	$ mil.	% of total
US	4,527	72	428	146
Europe	1,101	17	(179)	(61)
Other foreign	674	11	45	15
Adjustments	(96)	—	312	—
Total	**6,206**	**100**	**606**	**100**

WHEN

Campbell Soup Company began in Camden, New Jersey, in 1869 as a canning and preserving business. The company's founders, icebox maker Abram Anderson and fruit merchant Joseph Campbell, quickly established Campbell's enduring reputation for quality. Anderson left in 1876, and Arthur Dorrance took his place. Campbell retired in 1894, and the Dorrance family assumed control.

Arthur Dorrance's nephew, John Dorrance, joined Campbell in 1897. The talented chemist soon found a way to condense soup by removing most of its water, a discovery crucial to Campbell's subsequent success. Without the heavy bulk of water-filled cans, Campbell rapidly gained much wider, less costly distribution than its 2 major competitors, and its products spread nationally.

In 1904 the company introduced its Campbell Kids to help sell soup. Entering the California market in 1911, Campbell became one of the first American companies to achieve national distribution of a food brand. The company bought Franco-American, the first American soupmaker, in 1915.

Campbell's ubiquity in American kitchens made the Campbell soup can an American pop culture icon, as emphasized by Andy Warhol's 1960s print, and brought great wealth and social prestige to the Dorrance family. When Dorrance died in 1930 after 16 years as company president, he left the 3rd largest estate recorded at that time, $115 million. His son John, Jr., became chairman in 1962.

Campbell built a reputation as a conservatively managed concern, more focused on food quality, operational efficiency, and production skills than on marketing hype. Campbell was similarly cautious in diversifying beyond soups. Campbell acquired V8 juice (1948), Swanson (1955), Vlasic pickles (1978), and Mrs. Paul's seafood (1982), and formed Godiva Chocolatier (1966) to sell chocolates in the US. It introduced Prego spaghetti sauce and Le Menu frozen dinners in the early 1980s.

In 1989 chairman Robert Vlasic touched off a family feud with "Project Toad," a bid to merge with Quaker Oats. The deal was scuttled, but 3 disenchanted Dorrance heirs, who control 17.4% of the company's stock, pressed for sale of the company. In 1990 the dissidents suspended their demands for a sale while new CEO David Johnson restructured the company for more profits. Johnson's impressive performance thus far has earned him increasing support from the Dorrance family.

In 1991 Campbell was forced to change its advertising when the FTC ruled that its ads deceptively claimed that Campbell's soups reduced the risk of heart disease while neglecting to mention their high sodium content.

WHAT

	1990 Sales		1990 Operating Income	
	$ mil.	% of total	$ mil.	% of total
Campbell USA	3,634	58	341	116
Campbell Int'l	1,775	28	(134)	(46)
Pepperidge Farm	582	9	57	19
Campbell Enterprises	311	5	30	11
Adjustments	(96)	—	312	—
Total	**6,206**	**100**	**606**	**100**

Brand Names

Beeck	Logro
Bounty	Lutti
Budget Breakfasts	Marie's
Campbell's	Mrs. Giles
Country Style	Mrs. Kinser's
Delacre	Mrs. Paul's
Early California	Open Pit
Franco-American	Pepperidge Farm
Freshbake	Prego
Godiva	Produce Partners
Great Starts	Swanson
Hearty Slices	Swift
Home Cookin'	TeddyOs
Lacroix	V8
Lamy	Vlasic
Le Menu	Win Schuler's
Light Style	

RANKINGS

80th in *Fortune* 500 Industrial Cos.
61st in *Business Week* 1000

HOW MUCH

	9-Year Growth	1981	1982	1983	1984	1985	1986	1987	1988	1989	1990
Sales ($ mil.)	9.3%	2,798	2,945	3,292	3,657	3,989	4,379	4,490	4,869	5,672	6,206
Net income ($ mil.)	(31.3%)	130	150	165	191	198	223	247	242	13	4
Income as % of sales	—	4.6%	5.1%	5.0%	5.2%	5.0%	5.1%	5.5%	5.0%	0.2%	0.1%
Earnings per share ($)	(32.3%)	1.00	1.16	1.28	1.48	1.53	1.73	1.91	1.87	0.10	0.03
Stock price – high ($)	—	8.47	12.44	16.03	18.03	29.06	34.25	35.38	35.25	60.63	62.00
Stock price – low ($)	—	6.56	7.00	10.69	13.56	15.09	22.00	22.75	23.88	30.50	43.75
Stock price – close ($)	26.3%	7.16	12.09	15.25	17.38	24.69	28.50	27.88	31.50	58.63	58.50
P/E – high	—	8	11	13	12	19	20	19	19	—	—
P/E – low	—	7	6	8	9	10	13	12	13	—	—
Dividends per share ($)	—	0.51	0.53	0.54	0.57	0.61	0.65	0.71	0.81	0.90	0.98
Book value per share ($)	6.0%	7.76	8.19	8.91	9.76	10.69	11.86	13.35	14.69	13.72	13.09

1990 Year-end:
Debt ratio: 32.3%
Return on equity: 0.2%
Cash (mil.): $103
Current ratio: 1.28
Long-term debt (mil.): $806
No. of shares (mil.): 129
Dividends:
1990 average yield: 1.7%
1990 payout: —
Market value (mil.): $7,562

Stock Price History High/Low 1981–90

KEY COMPETITORS

Allied-Lyons	Heinz
American Home Products	Hershey
Anheuser-Busch	Kellogg
Berkshire Hathaway	Mars
BSN	Nestlé
Cadbury Schweppes	Procter & Gamble
ConAgra	Ralston Purina
CPC	RJR Nabisco
Dial	Sara Lee
General Mills	Tyson Foods
Grand Metropolitan	Unilever

CAPITAL CITIES/ABC, INC.

OVERVIEW

Capital Cities/ABC is a media giant and operates the ABC TV network, sandwiched between leading NBC and #3 CBS in a tight ratings race. ABC broadcasts through 227 television affiliates and 8 owned TV stations. ABC leads among younger viewers, the demographic segment most popular with advertisers, but as a whole continues to lose market share to cable. ABC Radio Networks broadcast through 21 owned stations and 3,050 affiliates. The company owns important interests in ESPN, The Arts & Entertainment network, and other cable TV programmers.

Cap Cities publishes daily and weekly newspapers, special-interest magazines, and trade publications including *Los Angeles*, *Institutional Investor*, and the *Kansas City Star*.

Tightfisted CEO Daniel Burke is cutting costs in response to weak advertising revenues. Company management is highly regarded by Warren Buffett, whose Berkshire Hathaway holding company owns 18% of Cap Cities stock.

WHEN

Capital Cities/ABC resulted from the 1986 acquisition of the American Broadcasting Companies by the much smaller Capital Cities Communications. ABC had begun as a spinoff from RCA's Blue Network in 1943 and was sold in that year to LifeSavers candy promoter Edward J. Noble.

In the late 1940s and early 1950s, ABC was in 3rd place, with 5 TV stations and no daytime programming. Attempts to buy ABC by CBS and 20th Century Fox failed, but in 1953 the struggling network merged with United Paramount Theatres. United Paramount's Leonard Goldenson hired Disney Studios to produce a series for ABC's 1954–55 season. Soon other movie studios, including Warner Brothers, were producing programming ("Ozzie and Harriet," "Wyatt Earp," "Cheyenne," 1955) for ABC.

About the same time (1954) Hudson Valley Broadcasting, owner of a struggling TV station in Albany, New York, hired Thomas Murphy to bail out the station. In 1957 Hudson Valley went public, becoming Capital Cities Television Corporation. While Cap Cities founder Frank Smith bought and sold TV and radio stations and publications, Murphy ran the company's operations. Smith died in 1966, and in 1968 Cap Cities, under Murphy, bought Fairchild Publications, publisher of *Women's Wear Daily*, and continued throughout the 1970s buying and selling media companies.

Still in 3rd place in the 1960s, ABC fended off takeover attempts by Norton Simon, General Electric, and Howard Hughes. Programming whiz Fred Silverman defected from CBS, joining ABC in 1975. The next year ABC was the #1 network, and, with hits like "Love Boat" and "Happy Days," ABC stayed on top until 1979, the year after Silverman went to NBC. In 1979 ABC sold its records division and bought Chilton, a specialty publisher.

In the 1980s Cap Cities bought cable systems; ABC produced programming for cable and bought ESPN in 1984. In 1986 Cap Cities, backed by Warren Buffett's Berkshire Hathaway, bought ABC for $3.5 billion, at the time the largest purchase in media history. With the purchase, Murphy became chairman and CEO of the new company. In 1986 and 1987 Cap Cities/ABC sold its 53 cable systems to the Washington Post Company, formed a joint venture home video company, and bought radio stations.

In 1990 Cap Cities/ABC sold *Compute!* magazine and several other small publishing operations and entered into video programming ventures in Japan, France, and Spain. Murphy remained as chairman but was replaced as CEO by Daniel Burke, formerly president of Cap Cities.

In 1991 the company joined with 2 French companies to purchase WH Smith's European TV operations.

HOW MUCH

	9-Year Growth	1981	1982	1983	1984	1985	1986	1987	1988	1989	1990
Sales ($ mil.)	28.2%	574	664	762	940	1,021	4,124	4,440	4,773	4,957	5,386
Net income ($ mil.)	21.9%	81	96	115	135	142	182	279	387	486	478
Income as % of sales	—	14.0%	14.5%	15.0%	14.4%	13.9%	4.4%	6.3%	8.1%	9.8%	8.9%
Earnings per share ($)	18.3%	6.12	7.25	8.53	10.40	10.87	11.20	16.46	22.31	27.25	27.71
Stock price – high ($)	—	80.50	136.75	157.50	174.50	229.00	279.75	450.00	369.75	568.00	633.00
Stock price – low ($)	—	56.50	64.38	114.75	123.50	152.25	208.25	268.00	297.00	353.00	380.00
Stock price – close ($)	22.5%	73.75	119.63	144.00	164.63	224.50	268.12	345.00	362.25	564.12	459.12
P/E – high	—	13	19	18	17	21	25	27	17	21	23
P/E – low	—	9	9	13	12	14	19	16	13	13	14
Dividends per share ($)	0.0%	0.20	0.20	0.20	0.20	0.20	0.20	0.20	0.20	0.20	0.20
Book value per share ($)	21.8%	34.07	41.30	47.72	57.08	68.42	120.84	137.40	168.09	187.74	200.96

1990 Year-end:
Debt ratio: 35.5%
Return on equity: 14.3%
Cash (mil.): $1,360
Current ratio: 3.14
Long-term debt (mil.): $1,851
No. of shares (mil.): 17
Dividends:
 1990 average yield: 0.0%
 1990 payout: 0.7%
Market value (mil.): $7,694

Stock Price History High/Low 1981–90

WHO

Chairman: Thomas S. Murphy, age 65, $891,000 pay
President, CEO, and COO: Daniel B. Burke, age 62, $907,100 pay
SVP and CFO: Ronald J. Doerfler, age 49, $748,600 pay
VP Human Resources: John E. Frisoli
Auditors: Ernst & Young
Employees: 20,100

WHERE

HQ: 77 W. 66th St., New York, NY 10023-6298
Phone: 212-456-7777
Fax: 212-456-6850 (Public Relations)

Capital Cities/ABC conducts business throughout the US. Principal network broadcast facilities are located in New York and Los Angeles.

WHAT

	1990 Sales		1990 Operating Income	
	$ mil.	% of total	$ mil.	% of total
Publishing	1,102	20	132	14
Broadcasting	4,284	80	830	86
Adjustments	—	—	(39)	—
Total	**5,386**	**100**	**923**	**100**

ABC Television Network Group
ABC Early Morning and Late Night Entertainment
ABC Entertainment
ABC News
ABC Productions
ABC Sports, Daytime and Children's Entertainment
ABC Television Network

Broadcast Group
ABC Radio Networks
Radio stations
Television stations
 KABC-TV, Los Angeles
 KFSN-TV, Fresno
 KGO-TV, San Francisco
 KTRK-TV, Houston
 WABC-TV, New York
 WLS-TV, Chicago
 WPVI-TV, Philadelphia
 WTVD-TV, Durham-Raleigh
Video Enterprises
 Arts & Entertainment Network (38%)
 ESPN (80%)
 Lifetime (33 1/3%)
 Video Enterprises International

Publishing Group
Diversified Publishing Group
Agricultural Publishing Group
 Farm Futures
 Prairie Farmer
The Chilton Co.
 Automobile guides
 Electronic News
 Motor Age
Los Angeles Magazine
NILS Publishing Co. (insurance law database)
Word, Inc. (religious books, music, and films)
Fairchild Fashion and Merchandising Group
 M inc.
 W
 Women's Wear Daily
Financial Services and Medical Group
 Institutional Investor
 Internal Medicine News
Newspapers
 Fort Worth Star-Telegram
 The Kansas City Star

RANKINGS

19th in *Fortune* 100 Diversified Service Cos.
73rd in *Business Week* 1000

KEY COMPETITORS

Advance Publications	Hearst	Tribune
Bertelsmann	Knight-Ridder	Turner
Blockbuster	News Corp.	Broadcasting
CBS	Reed	Viacom
Cox	TCI	Other media
General Electric	Thomson Corp.	companies
Hachette	Time Warner	

CARGILL, INC.

Private company
Fiscal year ends: May 31

Hoover's Rating A-

OVERVIEW

With estimated revenues of $42 billion for 1990, Cargill is the largest privately owned company in the nation and ranks 8th among all US companies in terms of revenues. This 126-year-old food industry giant employs about 60,000 people and has operations that span the globe.

Cargill's success has been the trading of a variety of commodities: grains and seed, sugar, coffee, orange juice, rubber, cocoa, molasses, precious and scrap metals, and petroleum products. The company buys, produces, transports, processes, and packages these goods and hedges its commodity prices through extensive futures trading. Cargill is thought to be the world's largest grain trader. Cargill conducts its grain trading activity through Tradax International, a Panamanian company operating from Geneva, Switzerland.

Cargill also produces and trades high-quality steel products (it operates the largest steel "minimill" in the US), animal feeds (Nutrena), and salt (Leslie). The company is one of the country's 3 largest meatpackers.

The Cargill and MacMillan families still control 85% of Cargill's stock. In 1991 family members considered selling 4% of company stock (worth about $300 million) to an employee stock ownership plan. If the plan goes through, it would be the first time since the early 1900s that stock would be non-family owned. Both of the families and the company avoid publicity and are not well known even in Minneapolis, where Cargill is based.

WHO

Chairman and CEO: Whitney MacMillan
VC: William R. Pearce, age 63
President and COO: Heinz F. Hutter
CFO: Robert Lumpkins, age 45
SVP Human Resources: Peter S. Price
Auditors: KPMG Peat Marwick
Employees: 60,000

WHERE

HQ: PO Box 9300, 15407 McGinty Rd., Minnetonka, MN 55440-9300
Phone: 612-475-7575
Fax: 612-475-6208

Cargill, its subsidiaries, and its affiliates have about 800 plants, 500 US offices, and 300 foreign offices in 54 countries. Its largest foreign operations are in Canada, Brazil, Argentina, and Europe.

	1990 Employees	
	No.	% of total
US	33,500	56
Other countries	26,500	44
Total	**60,000**	**100**

WHEN

William Cargill, the son of a Scottish immigrant farmer, bought his first grain elevator in Conover, Iowa, shortly after the Civil War. He and his brother Sam bought grain elevators all along the Southern Minnesota Railroad in 1870, a time when Minnesota was becoming an important shipping route for grain. Sam and another brother, James, expanded the elevator operations while William worked with the railroads to monopolize grain transport to markets and coal transport back to the farmers.

Around the turn of the century, Cargill's son, also named William, invested in a Montana irrigation project and other ill-fated ventures. Cargill Sr. went to Montana to find that his name had been used to finance these undertakings and shortly afterward died of pneumonia. Cargill's creditors grew worried and started pressing for repayment, which threatened to bankrupt the company. John MacMillan, who had married William Sr.'s daughter Edna, wrested control after the founder's death and rebuilt Cargill. By the time the company recovered in 1916, it had been stripped of timber holdings and land in Mexico and Canada that William Sr. had collected. MacMillan opened offices in New York (1922) and Argentina (1929), expanding Cargill's grain trading and transport operations nationally and internationally.

During the Depression Cargill expanded, building the river barges necessary to transport its products. When the grain fields turned into the Dust Bowl, Cargill bought up all the corn futures on the Chicago exchange, prompting the Board to kick Cargill's broker off the floor. During WWII Cargill built ships for the navy, using its barge-building facilities.

After WWII North American wheat became an increasingly important product because of the ravages of war and a growing world population. In 1945 Cargill bought animal feed producer Nutrena Mills and also entered soybean processing; corn processing began a few years later and has grown along with the demand for corn sweeteners. In 1954 the US began lending money to Third World countries to buy American grain, and Cargill was one of the main beneficiaries of the policy. The company's subsidiary Tradax, established in 1955, quickly became one of the largest grain traders in Europe. In 1965 Cargill entered sugar trading by buying sugar and molasses in the Philippines and selling it abroad.

As a requirement for an unsuccessful takeover bid of Missouri Portland Cement, Cargill made its finances public in 1973, revealing it as one of America's largest companies ($5.2 billion in sales). In the 1970s the company expanded into coal, steel, and waste disposal, and throughout the 1980s developed these areas; it also became a major force in metals processing, beef, and salt production. In 1991 the company agreed to buy Milwaukee-based Ladish Malting, making Cargill the world's largest maltster. Cargill recently entered the competitive area of selling meats and packaged foods directly to supermarkets.

WHAT

Commodities Trading and Transport	Financial Operations
Barges and vessels (Cargo Carriers, Inc.)	Equipment leasing
Coffee and cocoa	Futures trading and foreign exchange
Cotton (Hohenberg Bros.)	Life insurance
Fertilizers	Risk management
Grain and oilseeds	
Iron and finished steel	**Food Production and Processing**
Juice and fruit concentrates	Animal byproducts
Molasses and sugar	Beef, pork, and chicken processing and packaging
Oceangoing vessels	Bulk commodities
Petroleum products and petrochemicals	Corn syrup
Rubber	Flour and corn milling
Tallow	Salt

Industrial Products	Agricultural Products
Industrial chemicals	Animal feeds
Scrap steel yards (Magnimet)	Feed supplements
Steel and wire	Seed and fertilizer
Steel minimills (North Star)	Technical services

RANKINGS

1st in *Forbes* 400 US Private Cos.

KEY COMPETITORS

American President	Morton
ADM	Nippon Steel
Bethlehem Steel	Occidental
Chiquita Brands	Philip Morris
ConAgra	Ralston Purina
Continental Grain	Salomon
CSX	Sara Lee
Dial	Thyssen
Friedrich Krupp	Tyson Foods
General Mills	Universal Corp.
W. R. Grace	USX
Inland Steel	Waste Management
IRI	Chemical and food
LTV	companies

HOW MUCH

Fiscal year ends May of following year	9-Year Growth	1981	1982	1983	1984	1985	1986	1987	1988	1989	1990
Estimated sales ($ mil.)	—	—	—	—	30,000	32,000	32,400	38,200	43,000	42,000	42,000
Net income ($ mil.)	—	—	—	—	—	—	—	—	—	372	—
Income as % of sales	—	—	—	—	—	—	—	—	—	0.8%	—
Total employees	4.8%	39,094	37,954	40,202	41,738	46,351	51,600	55,020	53,710	55,200	60,000

Estimated Sales ($ mil.) 1984–90

(bar chart with y-axis values: 45,000; 40,000; 35,000; 30,000; 25,000; 20,000; 15,000; 10,000; 5,000; 0)

CARLSON COMPANIES, INC.

Private company
Fiscal year ends: December 31

Hoover's Rating **B+**

OVERVIEW

Curtis L. Carlson, the founder and chairman of Carlson Companies, has personally built his Minneapolis-based travel/hotel/marketing services company. Most of the company's revenues come from the Carlson Travel Group, the largest travel organization in North America. The group includes Carlson Travel Network — formerly Ask Mr. Foster — America's oldest and largest travel agency, and P. Lawson, the largest travel agency in Canada. The group expanded into Europe in 1990 and now operates 2,103 travel agencies worldwide.

Carlson Hospitality Group operates and franchises 250 Radisson Hotels worldwide and 70 Colony Hotels & Resorts. The group also oversees TGI Friday's restaurants and Country Kitchens.

Carlson Marketing Group is the largest motivation company in the world, providing sales and event promotion services and employee sales training and incentives programs. K-Promotions is the country's largest supplier of logo-identified promotional merchandise.

The company is a founding member of the Minnesota Keystone Club, whose members donate 5% of profits to charitable causes. The University of Minnesota renamed its business school in honor of Curtis Carlson after he had donated $25 million in 1986.

Carlson operates its companies by outlining 5-year plans and using employee motivation programs to ensure performance. The current plan, announced in 1987, calls for expanding the company's hospitality and travel-related businesses, including the new Country Inn roadside motel chain, and reaching $9.2 billion in sales in 1992.

WHO

Chairman: Curtis L. Carlson, age 77
President and CEO: Edwin C. Gage, age 50
VP and Controller: Bruce Paulsen
VP Human Resources: Terry Butorac
Auditors: Arthur Andersen & Co.
Employees: 70,000

WHERE

HQ: Carlson Pkwy., PO Box 59159, Minneapolis, MN 55459-8202
Phone: 612-540-5000
Fax: 612-540-5832
Reservations (Radisson Hotels International): 800-333-3333

Carlson Marketing Group operates in 32 US cities and in over 21 countries. The Travel Group has 2,100 offices throughout the US, Canada, and UK.

WHEN

Curtis Carlson, the son of Swedish immigrants, graduated from the University of Minnesota in 1937 and went to work as a Procter & Gamble soap salesman in the Minneapolis/ St. Paul area. In 1938 he borrowed $50 and formed Gold Bond Stamp Company to sell trading stamps to grocery stores in his spare time. His wife, Arleen, dressed as a drum majorette and twirled a baton to promote the concept. By 1941 the company had 200 accounts. In 1952 a large local chain, Super Valu, started using the stamps, boosting Gold Bond's sales to $2.4 million. By 1960 the trading stamps were generating so much cash that Carlson began investing in other enterprises: Ardan catalog and jewelry showrooms, travel agencies, and business promotion and employee motivation programs.

In 1962 Carlson bought the original Radisson Hotel in Minneapolis. He followed with 7 more hotels throughout the state and in 1970 expanded the Radisson chain outside Minnesota, buying the future Radisson Denver from Hyatt. By 1976 the majority of Radisson rooms were outside Minnesota. Carlson diversified into restaurants with the purchase of the 11-unit TGI (Thank God It's) Friday's, a dining and singles bar chain. In 1977 he bought Country Kitchen International, a family-style restaurant chain.

Radisson, which by 1978 already had 19 hotel properties, including one in the West Indies, expanded into major markets that year with the addition of the Radisson Chicago and the reopening of Detroit's Cadillac Hotel as a Radisson. Many of the Radissons were older hotels remodeled by Contract Services Associates, another Carlson company. Radisson fought the image of look-alike hotel chains with its ad campaign, "A Collection, Not a Chain," introduced in 1978. In 1979 Carlson added to his hotel operations with Colony Resorts, a hotel/ condominium management company operating mainly in Hawaii, which he purchased from its founder, baseball commissioner Peter Ueberroth.

Carlson Companies slowed the pace of its acquisitions in the 1980s, focusing instead on internal growth. Carlson took TGI Friday's public in 1983 (retaining 76% of the stock) to fund expansion of the chain, but reacquired all outstanding shares in 1990 for approximately $50 million. In 1990 and 1991 Carlson expanded into the UK travel market by buying 2 major travel agencies, A.T. Mays and Smith Travel. Another acquisition (Pickfords Travel) is now in the works, which, if successful, will make Carlson the UK's #1 travel group.

WHAT

	1990 Sales	
	$ mil.	% of total
Marketing group	900	11
Hospitality group	2,100	26
Travel group	5,100	63
Total	**8,100**	**100**

Carlson Marketing Group
Carlson International Division
  Carlson Marketing Group International (includes joint venture operating Kentucky Fried Chicken franchises in Japan)
  Carlson Marketing Group Ltd. (Canada)
Carlson Motivation Division
  Carlson Learning Co.
  E.F. MacDonald Motivation
Carlson Promotion Division
  Jason/Empire (sports optics and leisure products)
  K-Promotions

Carlson Hospitality Group
Colony Hotels & Resorts
Country Hospitality
  Country Inn
  Country Kitchen
Radisson Hotels International
TGI Friday's, Inc.

Carlson Travel Group
Carlson Travel Network (commercial and retail travel agents)
P. Lawson Travel (Canada)
A.T. Mays Group (76%)
Neiman Marcus Travel
Supercities and Great Escapes (vacation packages)

Carlson Investment Group
Carlson Center (Minneapolis)
Plaza VII (Minneapolis)
Office buildings, hotels, and shopping centers

RANKINGS

82nd in *Forbes* 400 US Private Cos.

KEY COMPETITORS

Accor	Helmsley	Nestlé
American Express	Hilton	Rank
Bass	Hyatt	Saatchi & Saatchi
Canadian Pacific	ITT	Thomson Corp.
Dial	Loews	Trammell Crow
Edward J. DeBartolo	Marriott	Young &
General Mills	Metromedia	Rubicam

HOW MUCH

	9-Year Growth	1981	1982	1983	1984	1985	1986	1987	1988	1989	1990
Estimated sales ($ mil.)	22.5%	1,600	2,000	2,300	2,600	3,100	3,600	4,300	5,300	6,200	8,100
Owned hotels & motels	31.7%	23	25	39	55	75	135	160	195	225	250
Hotel rooms	25.6%	7,100	7,500	9,200	14,000	20,000	32,000	38,000	47,000	50,000	60,000
Employees	14.9%	22,000	38,000	38,000	45,000	48,000	50,000	50,000	53,000	61,000	70,000

Hotel Rooms 1981–90

(bar chart showing hotel rooms rising from about 7,000 in 1981 to 60,000 in 1990; y-axis 0 to 60,000)

CARTER HAWLEY HALE STORES, INC.

NYSE symbol: CHH
Fiscal year ends: Saturday closest to January 31

Hoover's Rating **D**

OVERVIEW

Los Angeles–based Carter Hawley Hale (CHH) was the largest department store retailer (89 stores) in the western US in 1990, with 90% of its sales attributed to California. CHH's department stores — Broadway, Emporium, and Weinstocks — sell merchandise ranging from apparel and accessories to home furnishings and electronics.

In 1991 CHH filed for protection under Chapter 11 of the federal bankruptcy code. The company had amassed a large debt in the process of fending off a 1987 takeover bid. Its debt reduction efforts were thwarted by the 1989 San Francisco area earthquake, which took 12 of its 22 Emporium stores out of operation for varying lengths of time, and by a slump in retail sales — particularly 1990 holiday sales. To raise cash, CHH sold Thalhimers, one of its better-performing department stores, in 1990 to the May Company for $317 million.

CHH's performance deteriorated in 1991, reflecting the continued slump in consumer spending. Employees own 43.9% of CHH stock through their profit-sharing plan.

WHO

Chairman and CEO: Philip M. Hawley, age 65, $375,000 pay
President: H. Michael Hecht, age 51, $250,000 pay (prior to promotion)
EVP and CFO: John M. Gailys, age 49, $217,500 pay
SVP Human Resource Development: Theodore J. Cotti
Auditors: Price Waterhouse
Employees: 24,000

WHEN

Arthur Letts opened the first Broadway Department Store on the corner of Fourth and Broadway in Los Angeles in 1896. Letts, an English immigrant, had failed with his first store in Seattle and started the Broadway on the site of another failed store.

The company opened stores in Hollywood (1931) and Pasadena (1940) but continued as a small, local retailer until 1947 when Edward Carter, a 34-year-old Harvard graduate, became president. Carter expanded into the Los Angeles suburbs and in 1951, after merging with Hale Brothers Stores of San Francisco, operator of Weinstocks department stores, renamed the company Broadway-Hale.

In 1956 the company acquired Dohrmann Commercial Company, a Northern California hotel-supply business that owned 24% of Emporium Capwell Company. The Emporium, itself the result of an 1897 merger with San Francisco's even larger Golden Rule Bazaar, had acquired H. C. Capwell, an Oakland retailer, in 1927 and had grown to become the largest department store chain in the Bay Area. Broadway-Hale sold Dohrmann Commercial (1962) and continued to buy Emporium stock, merging the 2 companies in 1970.

Broadway-Hale acquired interests in Coulter's department store (1960, Los Angeles), Marston (1961, San Diego), Korrick's (1962, Arizona), mail-order house Sunset House (1969), and Walden Book Company (1969, renamed Waldenbooks; sold 1984 to Kmart). Also in 1969 it acquired Texas-based Neiman-Marcus. In 1970 CHH joined with Ogden Development to build Broadway Plaza in downtown Los Angeles, consisting of the flagship Broadway store, a shopping center, a hotel, and 32 floors of office space. Broadway-Hale bought Bergdorf Goodman, the exclusive New York store, in 1972.

The company changed its name to Carter Hawley Hale in 1974 to incorporate the names of Carter and his heir apparent, Philip Hawley. The company purchased John Wanamaker (1978; sold 1986), the department store chain founded in Philadelphia in 1861; Thalhimer Brothers (1978), founded in Richmond, Virginia, in 1842; and specialty retailer Contempo Casuals (1979).

Facing a takeover bid by The Limited in 1987, CHH restructured, piling up $1.3 billion in debt and spinning off specialty retailers Contempo Casuals, Bergdorf Goodman, and Neiman-Marcus. In 1991 CHH filed for protection under Chapter 11 of the bankruptcy code. Other department stores are said to be interested in buying some of CHH's stores, and Chicago investor Sam Zell reached an agreement to buy out bondholders' claims, which when converted to stock will give him control of CCH.

WHERE

HQ: 444 S. Flower St., Los Angeles, CA 90071
Phone: 213-620-0150
Fax: 213-620-0555

Carter Hawley Hale operates 89 department stores in 6 states.

Stores	No.	% of total	Sq. ft.(thou.)	% of total
			Area	Area
California	73	83	14,069	84
Arizona	8	9	1,321	8
Nevada	3	3	459	3
Utah	3	3	444	3
New Mexico	1	1	162	1
Colorado	1	1	135	1
Total	**89**	**100**	**16,590**	**100**

WHAT

Store Divisions	Sq. ft. (thou.)	% of total
	Area	Area
The Broadway — Southern California (Los Angeles) Southern California (43 stores)	7,483	45
The Broadway — Southwest (Phoenix) Arizona, Colorado, Nevada, & New Mexico (12 stores)	1,928	11
Emporium (San Francisco) Bay Area (22 stores)	5,244	32
Weinstocks (Sacramento) Northern California, Nevada & Utah (12 stores)	1,935	12
Total	**16,590**	**100**

RANKINGS

41st in *Fortune* 50 Retailing Cos.

KEY COMPETITORS

Brown Group	Macy
Dayton Hudson	May
Dillard	Melville
Edison Brothers	Mercantile Stores
The Gap	Montgomery Ward
General Cinema	Nordstrom
Hartmarx	J. C. Penney
INTERCO	Sears
Kmart	U.S. Shoe
The Limited	Wal-Mart

HOW MUCH

	9-Year Growth	1981	1982	1983	1984	1985	1986	1987[1]	1988	1989	1990
Sales ($ mil.)	0.1%	2,948	3,149	3,730	3,834	4,105	4,194	1,198	2,683	2,882	2,983
Net income ($ mil.)	—	45	49	67	27	48	48	—	9	7	(9)
Income as % of sales	—	1.5%	1.6%	1.8%	0.7%	1.2%	1.1%	—	0.3%	0.3%	(0.3%)
Earnings per share ($)	—	1.51	1.53	1.90	0.83	1.50	1.45	—	0.33	0.34	(0.37)
Stock price – high ($)	—	20.88	17.25	24.75	32.25	31.25	57.50	78.00	12.50	14.63	8.13
Stock price – low ($)	—	14.25	10.50	15.13	18.25	22.63	26.50	6.50	7.75	7.00	1.88
Stock price – close ($)	(15.3%)	15.00	15.63	23.50	23.63	28.63	48.00	8.50	8.38	8.25	3.38
P/E – high	—	14	11	13	39	21	40	—	38	43	—
P/E – low	—	9	7	8	22	15	18	—	23	21	—
Dividends per share ($)	(100%)	1.21	1.22	1.22	1.22	1.22	1.22	1.22	17.00	0.00	0.00
Book value per share ($)	—	22.22	21.60	22.07	18.26	18.37	16.18	7.16	(10.19)	(9.18)	(6.49)

1990 Year-end:
Debt ratio: 113.6%
Return on equity: 4.7%
Cash (mil.): $14
Current ratio: 2.71
Long-term debt (mil.): $1,618
No. of shares (mil.): 30
Dividends:
　1990 average yield: 0.0%
　1990 payout: 0.0%
Market value (mil.): $101

Stock Price History High/Low 1981–90

[1] 1987 fiscal year was only 26 weeks, ending August 1, 1987

CATERPILLAR INC.

OVERVIEW

Based in Peoria, Illinois, Caterpillar is the world's #1 producer of earthmoving equipment and a leading producer of engines. Caterpillar is known for the high quality and performance of its products. Earthmoving, construction, and materials-handling machinery account for the bulk of sales; the remainder comes from the manufacture of engines and electric power generation systems.

Company products sell under the Caterpillar, Cat, and Solar nameplates through more than 1,000 outlets. Caterpillar counts itself as one of the US's largest net exporters and figures that its $3.44 billion in exports accounted for 18,500 US jobs in 1990.

The company rebounded from losses of $953 million between 1982 and 1984 to post 1989 profits of $497 million. Caterpillar beat back heavy competition from Japanese rival Komatsu by beginning the "Plant with a Future" (PWAF) program in 1985 to reduce costs, improve efficiency, and increase divisional responsibility.

Caterpillar's profits are currently under pressure from recession-related weakness in construction spending in the US and other countries, especially Brazil. Nevertheless, the company is continuing to spend heavily on modernization of its plants.

CEO Donald Fites is trying to reorganize Caterpillar along product lines, dispensing with the functionally oriented organization of the past. The change is intended to push decision-making down the organization and make the company more responsive to customers.

WHO

Chairman, President, and CEO: Donald V. Fites, age 56, $536,577 pay
VC and EVP: James W. Wogsland, age 59, $391,335 pay
Group President: Glen A. Barton, age 51
Group President: Gerald S. Flaherty, age 52
VP Human Resources: Wayne M. Zimmerman
VP and CFO: Charles E. Rager, age 62
Auditors: Price Waterhouse
Employees: 56,016

WHERE

HQ: 100 NE Adams St., Peoria, IL 61629-7310
Phone: 309-675-1000
Fax: 309-675-5948

Caterpillar operates 20 US and 16 foreign plants.

	1990 Sales*		1990 Operating Income	
	$ mil.	% of total	$ mil.	% of total
US	8,020	72	624	97
Europe	1,998	18	12	2
Other countries	1,085	10	10	1
Adjustments	333	—	(104)	—
Total	**11,436**	**100**	**542**	**100**

*Based on location of manufacturing operations.

WHAT

	1990 Sales		1990 Operating Income	
	$ mil.	% of total	$ mil.	% of total
Machinery	8,735	76	494	60
Engines	2,368	21	152	19
Financial services	333	3	173	21
Adjustments	—	—	(277)	—
Total	**11,436**	**100**	**542**	**100**

Products
Backhoe loaders
Diesel engines
Dump trucks
Excavators
Industrial engines
Lift trucks
Log skidders
Materials-handling vehicles
Motor graders
Paving products
Pipelayers
Power generation systems
Spark-ignited engines
Tractors
Turbine engines

Brand Names
Cat
Caterpillar
Solar

WHEN

In 1904 in Stockton, California, combine-maker Benjamin Holt modified the farming tractor by substituting a gas engine for steam and replacing iron wheels with crawler tracks. This improved the tractor's mobility over dirt by making it lighter and distributing its weight more evenly.

In 1915 the British adapted the "caterpillar" (Holt's nickname for the tractor) design to the armored tank. Following WWI the US Army donated tanks to local governments for construction work. The caterpillar's efficiency surprised Holt and spurred the development of earthmoving and construction equipment.

Holt merged with another California company, Best Tractor, in 1925. In 1928 the new organization, named Caterpillar, moved to its present Peoria, Illinois, headquarters.

In the 1930s Cat expanded into foreign markets, forming a worldwide dealer network, and phased out combine production to concentrate on construction and road equipment.

Sales volume more than tripled during WWII when Cat supplied the military with earthmoving equipment. Returning servicemen touted Cat's durability and quality, and the company enjoyed continued high demand during the postwar reconstruction effort. Cat emerged in solid first place in the industry, far ahead of 2nd-place International Harvester.

In 1951 Cat established its first overseas plant, in England. In 1963 the company entered one of the first 50-50 joint ventures in Japan, with Mitsubishi.

Sales increased steadily, reaching almost $8.6 billion by 1980. Diesel engine sales to outside customers nearly doubled between 1977 and 1980, accounting for 25% of total sales. In 1981 Cat purchased Solar Turbines (gasoline engines) for $505 million. However, 50 consecutive years of profits ended when Cat ran up 3 consecutive loss years (1982–84) as equipment demand fell and competition from foreign firms, Komatsu in particular, intensified.

Cat doubled its product line between 1984 and 1989. The PWAF program, introduced in 1985, shifted production toward smaller equipment, cut the work force by 33%, and enabled Cat to recoup lost market share. Labor negotiations will take place in 1991 with the Caterpillar UAW members for a new globally competitive contract.

RANKINGS

39th in *Fortune* 500 Industrial Cos.
117th in *Business Week* 1000

KEY COMPETITORS

Cummins Engine	Ford	Navistar
Daimler-Benz	Hitachi	Peugeot
Deere	Hyundai	Rolls-Royce
Dresser	Ingersoll-Rand	Tenneco
Fiat	Isuzu	Volvo
FMC	Mitsubishi	

HOW MUCH

	9-Year Growth	1981	1982	1983	1984	1985	1986	1987	1988	1989	1990
Sales ($ mil.)	2.5%	9,155	6,469	5,424	6,576	6,725	7,321	8,180	10,435	11,126	11,436
Net income ($ mil.)	(10.7%)	579	(180)	(345)	(428)	198	76	319	616	497	210
Income as % of sales	—	6.3%	(2.8%)	(6.4%)	(6.5%)	2.9%	1.0%	3.9%	5.9%	4.5%	1.8%
Earnings per share ($)	(11.8%)	6.44	(2.04)	(3.74)	(4.47)	2.00	0.76	3.20	6.04	4.88	2.07
Stock price – high ($)	—	73.25	55.25	49.50	52.75	43.13	55.63	74.75	68.50	69.00	68.50
Stock price – low ($)	—	49.63	33.13	37.38	28.38	29.00	36.63	39.88	53.88	52.88	38.13
Stock price – close ($)	(1.8%)	55.50	40.13	47.25	31.00	42.00	40.13	62.00	63.63	57.88	47.00
P/E – high	—	11	—	—	—	22	73	23	11	14	33
P/E – low	—	8	—	—	—	15	48	12	9	11	18
Dividends per share ($)	(7.4%)	2.40	2.40	1.50	1.25	0.50	0.50	0.50	0.75	1.20	1.20
Book value per share ($)	0.2%	44.03	39.61	35.07	29.46	31.19	31.86	35.15	40.56	44.11	44.99

1990 Year-end:
Debt ratio: 38.9%
Return on equity: 4.6%
Cash (mil.): $110
Current ratio: 1.39
Long-term debt (mil.): $2,890
No. of shares (mil.): 101
Dividends:
  1990 average yield: 2.6%
  1990 payout: 58.0%
Market value (mil.): $4,743

Stock Price History High/Low 1981–90

CBS INC.

OVERVIEW

Buyout rumors continue to swirl around CBS, the #3 US television network. Saddled with an expensive baseball broadcast contract and with what CEO Laurence Tisch calls a fundamental change in the economics of network TV (more competition and higher programming costs), the company's earnings are under pressure. Tisch-controlled Loews owns 22.9% of CBS.

CBS produces and distributes news, public affairs, sports, and entertainment programming and feature films to 212 affiliate and 5 owned and operated TV stations. The company provides programming services to 1,300 radio affiliates and 19 CBS-owned stations. CBS also owns 50% of CBS/Fox, a videocassette-rights partnership, and CBS/MTM, a film studio.

NYSE symbol: CBS
Fiscal year ends: December 31

WHO

Chairman, President, and CEO: Laurence A. Tisch, age 68, $1,457,489 pay
VP; President, CBS Broadcast Group: Howard Stringer, age 49, $896,627 pay
SVP Finance: Peter W. Keegan, age 46
SVP Administration: Edward Grebow, age 41
SVP: Jay L. Kriegel, age 50
SVP, General Counsel, and Secretary: George Vradenburg III, age 47
VP Personnel: Joan Showalter
Auditors: Coopers & Lybrand
Employees: 6,650

WHEN

Young William Paley (23) was an early radio advertiser (1925) on behalf of his father's Philadelphia-based La Palina cigars. Sensing a great opportunity, Paley in 1928 bought control of the fledgling Columbia Broadcasting System radio network, which had been incorporated in 1927 by radio pioneer Major J. Andrew White, concert master Arthur Judson, and promoter George Coats.

Paley changed the face of broadcasting and created industry standards. He promoted daytime dramas; attracted stars from NBC such as George Burns, Gracie Allen, and Jack Benny for evening programming; developed a strong news organization; and gave this programming package to local affiliates, which grew from 22 in 1928 to 97 in 1935. Edward R. Murrow, who served at CBS from 1930 to 1960, broke new ground in broadcasting news and was well known for his denunciation of Senator Joseph McCarthy.

In 1938 CBS bought American Recording, which became CBS Records in 1939. To develop emerging technology, CBS hired scientist Peter Carl Goldmark (1936), who invented the long-playing record in 1948 and worked on a color TV system into the 1950s. To CBS's disappointment, the FCC approved RCA/NBC's color system in 1953.

From 1955 to 1968 CBS was #1 in the entertainment ratings. CBS lost ratings and revenues in the early 1970s due to bans on cigarette advertising, a national economic downturn, and lack of programming geared to younger viewers. From the 1960s to the 1980s, CBS bought and sold such famous

names as the New York Yankees, Fender guitars, Steinway pianos, *Family Weekly* and *Cuisine* magazines, and the Holt, Rinehart and Winston publishing company.

CBS purchased cable companies in the 1960s, only to be forced to divest them in 1970 (forming Viacom) due to new FCC regulations prohibiting major networks from owning cable companies. In 1982 CBS and Twentieth Century Fox-Video formed CBS/Fox, and in 1983 CBS, HBO, and CPI Film Holdings formed Tri-Star Pictures (sold in 1985).

During the mid-1980s costly takeover attempts by Ted Turner and by Ivan Boesky, an ideological battle with Senator Jesse Helms, and falling ratings following the retirement of popular anchor Walter Cronkite weakened CBS's finances. Paley's inability to pick a successor left the company without strong leadership between 1971 and 1986. In 1985 Loews Corporation, led by billionaire Laurence Tisch, began buying CBS stock with the blessing of CBS, and Tisch joined its board that year. In 1986 CBS sold off 2 jets, Fawcett Books, and its St. Louis TV station and laid off 1,200 employees. CBS rejected an approach from Coca-Cola in 1986 and in 1987 elected Tisch CEO and Paley chairman.

Tisch sold CBS's remaining book and magazine businesses in 1986 and 1987, respectively. Sony bought CBS Records in 1988. In 1989 CBS bought WCIX-TV in Miami. William Paley died in 1990.

Also in 1990 CBS cut by 20% its fees paid to affiliates for airing network shows. The next year CBS bought back 44% of its stock.

WHERE

HQ: 51 W. 52nd St., New York, NY 10019
Phone: 212-975-4321
Fax: 212-975-7133

CBS manages facilities in major metropolitan areas nationwide.

WHAT

	1990 Sales		1990 Operating Income	
	$ mil.	% of total	$ mil.	% of total
Broadcasting	3,261	100	(74)	—
Other	—	—	24	—
Total	**3,261**	**100**	**(50)**	**100**

CBS/Broadcast Group Divisions	
CBS Affiliate Relations	WCBS (AM/FM), New York
CBS Enterprises	WLTT (FM), Washington, DC
CBS Broadcast International	WODS (FM), Boston
CBS Video	WSUN (AM)/WYNF (FM), Tampa
CBS Entertainment	WWJ (AM)/WJOI (FM), Detroit
CBS Marketing	
CBS News	
CBS Radio	CBS Sports
KCBS (AM)/KRQR (FM), San Francisco	CBS Television Stations
KLTR (FM), Houston	KCBS-TV, Los Angeles
KMOX (AM)/KLOU (FM), St. Louis	WBBM-TV, Chicago
KNX (AM)/KODJ (FM), Los Angeles	WCAU-TV, Philadelphia
KTXQ (FM), Dallas	WCBS-TV, New York
WBBM (AM/FM), Chicago	WCIX-TV, Miami
WCAU (AM)/WOGL (FM), Philadelphia	**Other**
	The CBS/Fox Co. (50%)
	The CBS/MTM Co. (50%)

RANKINGS

31st in *Fortune* 100 Diversified Service Cos.
276th in *Business Week* 1000

KEY COMPETITORS

Blockbuster	Sony
Capital Cities/ABC	TCI
Cox	Time Warner
General Cinema	Tribune
General Electric	Turner Broadcasting
Hearst	Viacom
Matsushita	Walt Disney
News Corp.	Washington Post
Paramount	

HOW MUCH

	9-Year Growth	1981	1982	1983	1984	1985	1986	1987	1988	1989	1990
Sales ($ mil.)	(2.3%)	4,027	4,052	4,458	4,831	4,677	4,646	2,762	2,778	2,962	3,261
Net income ($ mil.)	(7.8%)	190	150	187	245	203	190	136	283	297	92
Income as % of sales	—	4.7%	3.7%	4.2%	5.1%	4.3%	4.1%	4.9%	10.2%	10.0%	2.8%
Earnings per share ($)	(7.0%)	6.82	5.35	6.31	8.24	7.27	7.54	5.53	11.14	11.65	3.55
Stock price – high ($)	—	61.25	67.00	81.75	87.75	126.25	151.50	226.25	182.75	221.00	206.25
Stock price – low ($)	—	46.00	33.38	55.00	61.50	70.88	110.00	127.50	146.00	166.00	151.50
Stock price – close ($)	15.5%	47.38	59.75	66.25	72.38	115.88	127.00	157.00	170.50	188.00	172.63
P/E – high	—	9	13	13	11	17	20	41	16	19	58
P/E – low	—	7	6	9	7	10	15	23	13	14	43
Dividends per share ($)	5.2%	2.80	2.80	2.80	2.85	3.00	3.00	3.00	3.35	4.40	4.40
Book value per share ($)	9.5%	44.62	45.02	48.54	52.25	20.53	34.28	50.83	93.54	101.22	101.02

1990 Year-end:
Debt ratio: 22.9%
Return on equity: 3.5%
Cash (mil.): $2,599
Current ratio: 4.33
Long-term debt (mil.): $712
No. of shares (mil.): 24
Dividends:
 1990 average yield: 2.5%
 1990 payout: 123.9%
Market value (mil.): $4,089

**Stock Price History
High/Low 1981–90**

CENTEL CORPORATION

NYSE symbol: CNT
Fiscal year ends: December 31

Hoover's Rating **D**

OVERVIEW

Centel is a leading supplier of telephone and cellular services. Since fending off a 1988 takeover bid, the company has shed businesses (electric utilities, business telephone systems, cable television) to focus on telephone operations.

Its local telephone services include 1.6 million lines in 9 states, and its largest franchises are in Las Vegas, Nevada; Tallahassee, Florida; and Des Plaines, Illinois, a Chicago suburb. In early 1991 Centel traded its local operations in Minnesota and Iowa to Rochester Telephone in exchange for a 9.1% stake in New York–based Rochester and rights to Rochester's cellular franchises.

Having acquired United Telecom's cellular holdings in 1988, Centel owns a majority stake and operates cellular phone service in 45 metropolitan service areas (MSAs), including Las Vegas; Norfolk–Newport News, Virginia; and Toledo–Lima, Ohio. Minority interests put it in New York, Chicago, and Houston. Its also owns pieces of 33 rural service areas (RSAs).

WHO

Chairman and CEO: John P. Frazee, Jr., age 46, $930,236 pay
President: J. Stephen Vanderwoude, age 47, $579,536 pay
EVP and CFO: Eugene H. Irminger, age 62, $379,300 pay
SVP Planning and Technology: A. Allan Kurtze, age 46
SVP Human Resources: Janet A. Lang, age 45
Auditors: Arthur Andersen & Co.
Employees: 12,317

WHEN

Centel began in a 17-year-old boy's workshop in Sioux City, Iowa. Max McGraw began his career as an electrician in 1900. Two years later he began manufacturing electrical materials. In 1907 he began manufacturing equipment for the electric power and telephone industries, and he accepted equity in his customer's business in lieu of cash.

In 1922 McGraw Electric won control of Central Telephone & Electric, a St. Louis company that owned midwestern utilities. After more acquisitions, McGraw spun off more than 20 electric and telephone utilities into Central West Public Service Company. McGraw Electric later merged with the Thomas Edison Company to form McGraw-Edison, and McGraw served as chairman of both companies. McGraw-Edison was purchased by Cooper Industries in 1985.

After adding telephone companies in the Midwest (Illinois, Iowa, Minnesota, and North Dakota, 1929) and South (Virginia, West Virginia, North Carolina, 1930), Central West became Central Electric & Telephone in 1935, and then Central Electric & Gas in 1944. That same year, it shifted all its telephone holdings to a new, wholly owned subsidiary, Central Telephone Company.

During the 1950s Central Telephone added small telephone companies in rural America — for example, Fort Dodge, Iowa, and Lexington, Virginia. One exception was the addition of Southern Nevada Telephone, including the glittery resort of Las Vegas (1961).

The company changed its name again to Central Telephone & Utilities and became listed on the New York Stock Exchange in 1968. The stock's newspaper listing — which was to stick with the company over the years — was Cen Tel. In 1972 Robert Reuss came to the company from AT&T and began diversification. Along with adding Texas telephone operations (1975) and moving corporate offices from Lincoln, Nebraska, to Chicago (1976), the company bought 2 telephone equipment distributors and acquired its first cable television franchise in suburban Chicago (1978). During his tenure, Reuss added cable franchises from Florida to Michigan, created the Videopath microwave network to connect Chicago-area cable systems, and dipped the company's toes in electronic publishing (KEYCOM, folded in 1986). Most importantly, Centel, which adopted its present name in 1982, entered cellular telephony with a minority stake in one of 2 Chicago franchises (1982).

Reuss retired in 1988, and young chairman Jack Frazee faced a proxy fight from raiders Asher Edelman and George Lindemann, who hoped to break up the company. Frazee and his board survived but ended up selling Centel's cable systems (to Warner, $750 million, 1989) and its electric utilities (to UtiliCorp United, $345 million, 1990).

WHERE

HQ: O'Hare Plaza, 8725 Higgins Rd., Chicago, IL 60631
Phone: 312-399-2500
Fax: 312-399-4795 (Corporate Communications)

Centel provides local telephone exchange service in 9 states and cellular communications in 15 states and Mexico.

WHAT

	1990 Sales		1990 Operating Income	
	$ mil.	% of total	$ mil.	% of total
Telephone	964	84	227	119
Cellular	182	16	(14)	(7)
Other	3	—	(23)	(12)
Total	**1,149**	**100**	**190**	**100**

Local Telephone
Las Vegas, Nevada (432,905 lines)
Tallahassee, Florida (139,557 lines)
Des Plaines, Illinois (70,309 lines)
Charlottesville, Virginia (58,111 lines)
Park Ridge, Illinois (40,250 lines)
Lorain, Ohio (36,473 lines)
Hickory, North Carolina (35,263 lines)
Fort Walton Beach, Florida (35,174 lines)
Killeen, Texas (33,565 lines)

Cellular
Chicago (5%)
Greensboro, North Carolina
Harrisburg-York-Lancaster, Pennsylvania
Houston (8%)
Las Vegas, Nevada
New York (10%)
Norfolk–Newport News, Virginia
Raleigh-Durham-Burlington, North Carolina
Richmond (27%)
Toledo-Lima, Ohio

RANKINGS

231st in *Business Week* 1000

KEY COMPETITORS

Ameritech
Bell Atlantic
BellSouth
GTE
McCaw
MCI
NYNEX
Pacific Telesis
Southwestern Bell
Telmex
US West
Other cellular telephone firms

HOW MUCH

	9-Year Growth	1981	1982	1983	1984	1985	1986	1987	1988	1989	1990
Sales ($ mil.)	1.3%	1,020	1,156	1,272	1,375	1,326	1,370	1,199	1,095	1,188	1,149
Net income ($ mil.)	(8.5%)	105	108	113	123	129	109	155	110	11	47
Income as % of sales	—	10.2%	9.4%	8.9%	9.0%	9.7%	8.0%	13.0%	10.0%	0.9%	4.1%
Earnings per share ($)	(8.0%)	1.14	1.17	1.22	1.31	1.36	1.15	*1.58*	1.16	0.11	0.54
Stock price – high ($)	—	10.59	11.19	11.96	11.41	14.00	19.30	22.37	23.22	45.00	43.83
Stock price – low ($)	—	6.85	8.11	9.70	9.07	10.81	13.33	14.56	15.22	21.94	22.75
Stock price – close ($)	13.1%	9.81	11.07	10.41	11.15	14.00	16.59	15.78	22.33	43.00	29.75
P/E – high	—	9	10	10	9	10	17	14	20	397	81
P/E – low	—	6	7	8	7	8	12	9	13	194	42
Dividends per share ($)	3.4%	0.63	0.49	0.67	0.69	0.71	0.72	0.75	0.76	1.49	0.85
Book value per share ($)	7.2%	6.73	7.19	7.80	8.42	9.06	9.76	10.58	10.97	13.91	12.59

1990 Year-end:
Debt ratio: 56.9%
Return on equity: 4.1%
Cash (mil.): $21
Current ratio: 0.43
Long-term debt (mil.): $1,420
No. of shares (mil.): 84
Dividends:
 1990 average yield: 2.9%
 1990 payout: 158.0%
Market value (mil.): $2,511

Stock Price History High/Low 1981–90

CHAMPION INTERNATIONAL CORPORATION

NYSE symbol: CHA
Fiscal year ends: December 31

Hoover's Rating: C-

OVERVIEW

Champion International, America's 8th largest forest products company, is a major manufacturer of paper for business communications, printing, publication, and newspaper applications. In addition, the company maintains sizable plywood and lumber operations.

With the market weak for many of Champion's products, the company has put expansion plans for its Brazilian subsidiary Papel e Celulose on hold. Coping with the worldwide glut of pulp, linerboard, and kraft paper remains a key issue for the company, as does finding ways of dealing with soft newsprint, lumber, and plywood markets in a generally weakened economy. The company faced higher tax rates at Papel e Celulose in 1990 and a significant drop in earnings at its 84.6%-owned Canadian wood products and pulp subsidiary Weldwood.

Overall, Champion's earnings dropped 48% in 1990 and continued to decline in the first half of 1991. In response, the company has cut capital spending by nearly $1 billion. Champion has also settled several labor disputes that had a negative impact on 1990 mill production levels. Currently, 66% of the company's employees belong to unions.

WHO

Chairman and CEO: Andrew C. Sigler, age 59, $1,240,000 pay
VC: Kenwood C. Nichols, age 51, $590,000 pay
President and COO: L. C. Heist, age 59, $790,000 pay
SVP Finance and Principal Financial Officer: Gerald J. Beiser, age 60
SVP Organizational Development and Human Resources: Richard L. Porterfield, age 44
Auditors: Arthur Andersen & Co.
Employees: 28,500

WHEN

Champion International was formed by the 1967 merger of US Plywood and Champion Paper & Fibre. US Plywood, founded in New York by Lawrence Ottinger in 1919, started out selling glue and WWI surplus plywood. By 1932 the company had started manufacturing its own products and consolidated operations with Aircraft Plywood in 1937.

Champion Paper & Fibre, the other party in the merger, was created when Reuben Robertson, who founded Champion Fibre in Ohio in 1906, married the daughter of the founder of similarly named Champion Coated Paper, incorporated in Ohio in 1893.

The first years for US Plywood–Champion Paper, the name of the company resulting from the 1967 merger, were marked by internal quarrels between the paper and plywood divisions over such issues as allocation of the company's timber resources. During that same period the company diversified, buying Drexel Enterprises (furniture, 1968, sold in 1977), Trend Industries (carpet, 1969, sold in 1978), Path Fork Harlan Coal (to power the company's pulp and paper mills, 1970), and AW Securities (carpets, 1974, sold in 1980), and in 1972 adopted its present name.

In 1974 director Karl Bendetson, who disapproved of plans to diversify the company into chemicals, persuaded the board to fire CEO Thomas Willers. Andrew Sigler replaced Willers and quickly turned the company's focus back to forest products by selling more than a dozen nonforest businesses.

In 1977 Champion International bought Hoerner Waldorf, the 4th largest American producer of paper packaging products such as grocery bags and cardboard boxes. Hoerner Waldorf traces its roots back to the 1966 merger of Hoerner Boxes (formed in Keokuk, Iowa, in 1920) and Waldorf Paper (originated in St. Paul as part of Baker-Collins in 1886).

In 1984 Champion bought St. Regis for $1.8 billion. With the St. Regis acquisition, Champion narrowed its focus to pulp and paper production. The company sold its office products businesses in 1984; 39 corrugated container plants, 13 packaging plants, and 3 paperboard mills in 1986; its Pasadena, Texas, mill in 1987; and its McKinney, Texas, coating and finishing plant and Columbus, Ohio, specialty paper plant in 1988.

In 1989 Champion sold 300,000 shares of new stock to Berkshire Hathaway (an investment firm controlled by Warren Buffett) in an attempt to discourage hostile takeovers. Another investment firm, Loews, began buying the company's shares in 1990 and now owns a 12.2% stake.

WHERE

HQ: One Champion Plaza, Stamford, CT 06921
Phone: 203-358-7000
Fax: 203-358-2975

	1990 Sales		1990 Operating Income	
	$ mil.	% of total	$ mil.	% of total
US	4,220	83	379	71
Canada	525	10	27	5
Brazil	345	7	126	24
Adjustments	—	—	1	—
Total	**5,090**	**100**	**533**	**100**

Owned or Leased Timberland	Acres (Thou.)
California, Montana, Oregon & Washington	1,562
Northern Alabama, eastern Florida, Georgia, Mississippi, North Carolina, South Carolina, Tennessee & Virginia	1,675
Southern Alabama, western Florida & Texas	1,539
Maine, Michigan, New Hampshire, New York & Vermont	1,621
Total	**6,397**

WHAT

	1990 Sales		1990 Operating Income	
	$ mil.	% of total	$ mil.	% of total
Paper products	4,103	81	512	96
Wood products	987	19	19	4
Adjustments	—	—	2	—
Total	**5,090**	**100**	**533**	**100**

Paper Products
Bleached hardwood kraft pulp
Bleached paperboard
Bleached softwood kraft pulp
Directory paper
Linerboard
Milk and juice cartons
Newsprint
Ovenable packaging
Printing paper
Publication papers
Pulp
Writing paper
Xerographic paper

Wood Products
Hardboard
Logs
Lumber
Plywood
Sidings

RANKINGS

104th in *Fortune* 500 Industrial Cos.
267th in *Business Week* 1000

KEY COMPETITORS

Boise Cascade
Canadian Pacific
Fletcher Challenge
Georgia-Pacific
International Paper
James River
Kimberly-Clark
Nobel
Mead
Scott
Weyerhaeuser

HOW MUCH

	9-Year Growth	1981	1982	1983	1984	1985	1986	1987	1988	1989	1990
Sales ($ mil.)	2.7%	4,004	3,737	4,264	5,121	5,770	4,388	4,615	5,129	5,163	5,090
Net income ($ mil.)	7.1%	120	40	82	(6)	163	201	382	456	432	223
Income as % of sales	—	3.0%	1.1%	1.9%	(0.1%)	2.8%	4.6%	8.3%	8.9%	8.4%	4.4%
Earnings per share ($)	1.1%	1.88	0.45	1.22	(0.36)	1.59	2.05	3.92	4.65	4.43	2.08
Stock price – high ($)	—	30.25	24.88	28.88	28.88	25.38	34.00	44.63	38.13	37.75	33.75
Stock price – low ($)	—	17.38	11.75	21.75	16.88	20.00	22.50	23.25	29.50	28.88	23.13
Stock price – close ($)	2.9%	19.75	23.75	28.88	22.25	24.88	30.75	34.50	32.13	32.00	25.63
P/E – high	—	16	55	24	—	16	17	11	8	9	16
P/E – low	—	9	26	18	—	13	11	6	6	7	11
Dividends per share ($)	(3.2%)	1.48	0.67	0.40	0.40	0.46	0.52	0.72	0.95	1.10	1.10
Book value per share ($)	3.4%	29.17	28.85	29.65	25.27	26.34	27.52	30.82	35.06	38.60	39.58

1990 Year-end:
Debt ratio: 42.2%
Return on equity: 5.3%
Cash (mil.): $103
Current ratio: 1.38
Long-term debt (mil.): $2,689
No. of shares (mil.): 93
Dividends:
　1990 average yield: 4.3%
　1990 payout: 52.9%
Market value (mil.): $2,382

Stock Price History
High/Low 1981–90

THE CHARLES SCHWAB CORPORATION

OVERVIEW

Charles Schwab, called by some the Wal-Mart of brokerage houses, with a market share of 45% of the discount market, is the nation's largest discount brokerage house, and the most expensive. In the first quarter of 1991, the average daily transaction volume was nearly 19,000.

Schwab's 1.4 million clients (with $30.6 billion in assets in Schwab accounts) take the responsibility of directing their own investments in return for significant savings on brokers' commissions. Though Schwab offers services nationwide, 46% of business comes from just 3 states (California, 31%; New York, 8%; and Texas, 7%).

In addition to its core business of executing client transactions, Schwab has diversified into money-market and mutual funds, and IRA/Keogh accounts, from which it earns considerable income in management fees. It also offers market research and analysis separate from its trading services.

The company is one of the most aggressive advertisers in the business, with 1990 expenditures of $19.9 million, up 44% since 1988. Schwab is also one of the most technologically up-to-date brokers, offering an array of computerized and telephone services, including an automated touch-tone trading system that reduces commissions still more.

WHEN

After his graduation from Stanford, Charles Schwab managed personal investment portfolios, started a mutual fund, and published a newsletter in the 1960s for his California investment firm, named the First Commander Corporation. The firm became Charles Schwab & Company, Inc., in 1971.

Initially a full-service broker, Schwab put his idea for a discount brokerage service into effect in May 1975 following the repeal of rules requiring fixed commissions in the industry. While most brokers raised commissions, Schwab cut its rates to about 1/2 of what most charged.

From 1977 to 1983, Schwab's client list increased 30-fold while revenues grew from $4.6 million to $126.5 million, enabling the firm to automate its operations and develop cash-management account systems.

To gain capital for expansion, Schwab agreed to be bought by BankAmerica Corporation Holdings for $55 million, effective in 1983. Schwab grew, but expansion into mutual funds and services like telephone trading was prevented by federal regulations prohibiting banks from acting as brokerages.

In 1987 Charles Schwab repurchased his company in a $280-million leveraged buyout and took it public. When the stock market crashed later in the year, trading volume fell by nearly half, from 17,900 per day. Revenues dropped from $465 million in 1987 to $392 million in 1988. Schwab rebounded in 1989.

Stung by the stock crash, Schwab increased its efforts to diversify, offering new services and accounts to increase income from other sources. Since 1987, commission contributions to revenues have fallen steadily, from 64% to 42% in 1989 and 39% in 1990.

The company has spent heavily on communications and computer systems, including the opening in 1990 of a communications center in Indianapolis that can handle 3 million calls per day. Technological innovation has reduced the company's break-even volume to 10,000 trades per day.

Schwab has begun acquiring other companies, including Rose & Company (discount brokerage, 1989) and Bank of New England's brokerage service operations (1990), and entered the over-the-counter market with Mayer & Schweitzer (OTC stock wholesaler, 1991).

Recent rulings involving Schwab clients have concluded that discount brokers are responsible for protecting unqualified clients from the results of bad trading and may adversely affect the discount industry.

NYSE symbol: SCH
Fiscal year ends: December 31

 Hoover's Rating C+

WHO

Chairman and CEO: Charles R. Schwab, age 53, $1,867,900 pay
President and COO: Lawrence J. Stupski, age 45, $871,389 pay
EVP and CFO: A. John Gambs, age 45
SVP Human Resources: James F. Wiggett
Auditors: Deloitte & Touche
Employees: 2,900

WHERE

HQ: 101 Montgomery St., San Francisco, CA 94104
Phone: 415-627-7000
Fax: 415-627-8538 (Corporate Communications)

The firm has 129 branch offices throughout the US.

WHAT

	1990 Sales	
	$ mil.	% of total
Commission revenue	244	39
Interest revenue	310	50
Mutual fund service fees	46	7
Other revenue	26	4
Total	**626**	**100**

Accounts & Services
Charles Schwab Select Card (VISA and MasterCard)
Financial Advisors Service (management for fee-based investment advisors)
Option Finance Service (stock options)
Schwab Brokerage Account
Schwab IRA/Keogh Accounts
Schwab MoneyLink Transfer Service (automatic funds transfer)
Schwab One Asset Management Account
Schwab 144 Stock Service (sale of restricted stock)
Schwab TeleBroker Service (trading and information by telephone)

Investment Choices
Charles Schwab CD Service
Equities and Options
Fixed Income Investments
Money Market Funds
Mutual Fund Marketplace

Investor Information
The Equalizer (personal investment system software)
Investor Seminars
InvestorSource (catalog of investment products and information guides)
PC Broker software (on-line trading via modem)

RANKINGS

854th in *Business Week* 1000

KEY COMPETITORS

American Express	Paine Webber
Equitable	Primerica
Kemper	Prudential
Merrill Lynch	Sears

HOW MUCH

	9-Year Growth	1981	1982	1983	1984	1985	1986	1987	1988	1989	1990
Sales ($ mil.)	35.4%	41	67	126	148	203	308	465	392	553	626
Net income ($ mil.)	—	—	5	11	1	11	32	26	7	19	17
Income as % of sales	—	—	7.5%	8.7%	0.7%	5.4%	10.4%	5.5%	1.9%	3.4%	2.7%
Earnings per share ($)	—	—	—	—	—	—	—	1.12	0.27	0.68	0.62
Stock price – high ($)	—	—	—	—	—	—	—	17.00	9.63	17.00	17.88
Stock price – low ($)	—	—	—	—	—	—	—	5.75	5.88	6.75	10.63
Stock price – close ($)	—	—	—	—	—	—	—	6.00	6.75	13.88	11.38
P/E – high	—	—	—	—	—	—	—	15	36	25	29
P/E – low	—	—	—	—	—	—	—	5	22	10	17
Dividends per share ($)	—	—	—	—	—	—	—	0.00	0.00	0.09	0.13
Book value per share ($)	—	—	—	—	—	—	—	5.89	6.26	6.78	6.31

1990 Year-end:
Debt ratio: 43.8%
Return on equity: 9.5%
Cash (mil.): $3,141
Assets (mil.): $4,188
Long-term debt (mil.): $120
No. of shares (mil.): 24
Dividends:
   1990 average yield: 1.1%
   1990 payout: 21.0%
Market value (mil.): $278

Stock Price History High/Low 1987–90

THE CHASE MANHATTAN CORPORATION

NYSE symbol: CMB
Fiscal year ends: December 31

OVERVIEW

Chase Manhattan, at the end of 1990, was the 3rd largest US commercial banking concern, after Citicorp and BankAmerica. That ranking is bound to change as competitors — Chemical and Manufacturers Hanover, for example — combine.

Chase, under new CEO Thomas Labrecque, is scrambling to recover from losses on real estate loans in Arizona and on loans to less-developed countries (LDCs). As part of the restructuring, Labrecque is concentrating on

6 lines of business in 2 areas, individual and wholesale banking. In individual banking, Chase focuses on credit cards, mortgage services, and finance for the well-to-do. Chase is the 2nd largest US issuer of credit cards, with balances of about $10 billion.

In wholesale banking, Chase concentrates on global corporate finance, risk management, and information services. Chase is the largest global custodian of financial assets and the world's largest dollar-clearing bank.

WHEN

Chase Manhattan traces its roots to a water utility founded in 1799. The Manhattan Company was created by the New York legislature to bring pure water to the city, but investor Aaron Burr, later US vice president and the man who killed Alexander Hamilton in a duel, lobbied to allow the company to use surplus funds for other services. The Bank of the Manhattan Company was the result, and, after the water company was sold to the city in 1808, it survived as the Bank of Manhattan.

On the other side of the family tree, John Thompson formed Chase National Bank (1877), named in honor of Abraham Lincoln's secretary of the treasury, Salmon P. Chase. Chase National grew to prominence under Albert Wiggin, who became president in 1911.

Wiggin engineered Chase's merger with John D. Rockefeller, Jr.'s, Equitable Trust (1930), and Chase became the world's largest bank in assets. After retiring in 1932, Wiggin was implicated in a scandal involving speculation with bank funds.

In 1932 Rockefeller's brother-in-law, Winthrop Aldrich, stepped in to lead the bank. Aldrich secured international beachheads for Chase, including postwar Germany and Japan, and he recruited his eventual successor — nephew David Rockefeller. In 1955 Chase merged with the Bank of Manhattan, which had expanded to branches in all 5 boroughs.

David Rockefeller, the last Rockefeller to command center stage in business, became

co–chief executive in 1960 and chairman in 1969. His globe-trotting brought prestige and controversy to the bank. Critics accused Rockefeller of tilting US foreign policy, most notably in Vietnam and Iran.

Rockefeller retired in 1981, leaving Willard Butcher to face (in 1982) assumption of liabilities from the failed Drysdale Government Securities and the collapse of Penn Square Bank, an Oklahoma City bank bloated by bad oil loans. Chase eventually charged off $161 million in Penn Square loans.

Chase formed a Delaware subsidiary in 1982 to market consumer credit instruments across state lines. In 1984 Chase purchased Lincoln First, with 135 bank branches in upstate New York. The bank also bought thrifts in Ohio, created a subsidiary in Maryland, and purchased a Phoenix bank.

In 1989, along with many other large US banks, Chase was forced to absorb special charges for Third-World and other loans totalling almost $1.3 billion. In the 2nd quarter of 1990, past-due real estate loans and foreclosed properties rose 52%. As the situation worsened, Butcher retired, and Thomas Labrecque became CEO.

Labrecque cut 5,000 from the payroll, raised capital with infusions from Saudi interests and by selling $6 billion in assets, and bought 2 Connecticut banks for deposit strength. Chase posted a $117 million profit in the first quarter of 1991.

WHO

Chairman and CEO: Thomas G. Labrecque, age 52, $628,000 pay
President and COO: Arthur F. Ryan, age 48, $520,000 pay
EVP and CFO: Michael P. Esposito, Jr., age 51
EVP Human Resources: Charles A. Smith, age 47
Auditors: Price Waterhouse
Employees: 39,480

WHERE

HQ: 1 Chase Manhattan Plaza, New York, NY 10081
Phone: 212-552-2222
Fax: 212-552-5005

Chase has operations in more than 50 countries.

	1990 Assets	
	$ mil.	% of total
US	72,131	74
Other Western Hemisphere	8,909	9
Asia	6,173	6
Other countries	10,851	11
Total	**98,064**	**100**

WHAT

	1990 Assets	
	$ mil.	% of total
Cash and due from banks	5,295	5
Interest-bearing deposits	2,539	3
Securities	7,234	8
Trading account assets	2,169	2
Loans	74,727	76
Credit loss reserve	(2,837)	(3)
Other	8,937	9
Total	**98,064**	**100**

Services

Individual Banking
Automobile loans
Consumer loans
Credit cards
Residential mortgages

Wholesale Banking
Cash management
Commercial real estate loans
Corporate finance activities
Custodial services
Foreign exchange services
Institutional trust services
Investment banking
Lease and commodities financing

RANKINGS

3rd in *Fortune* 100 Commercial Banking Cos.
327th in *Business Week* 1000

KEY COMPETITORS

H. F. Ahmanson	CS Holding
American Express	Dai-Ichi Kangyo
Banc One	Deutsche Bank
Bank of New York	First Chicago
BankAmerica	First Interstate
Bankers Trust	Fleet/Norstar
Barclays	HSBC
Canadian Imperial	Industrial Bank of Japan
Chemical Banking	J.P. Morgan
Citicorp	Royal Bank
Crédit Lyonnais	Union Bank of Switzerland

HOW MUCH

	9-Year Growth	1981	1982	1983	1984	1985	1986	1987	1988	1989	1990
Assets ($ mil.)	2.6%	77,839	80,863	81,921	86,883	87,685	94,766	99,133	97,455	107,369	98,064
Net income ($ mil.)	—	412	307	430	406	565	585	(895)	1,059	(665)	(334)
Income as % of assets	—	0.5%	0.4%	0.5%	0.5%	0.6%	0.6%	(0.9%)	1.1%	(0.6%)	(0.3%)
Earnings per share ($)	—	5.37	3.65	5.22	4.33	6.15	6.50	(11.56)	11.48	(7.94)	(3.31)
Stock price – high ($)	—	29.94	30.19	31.13	26.38	36.63	49.50	46.25	30.75	44.88	35.75
Stock price – low ($)	—	20.50	15.63	20.56	17.81	23.25	34.00	19.38	20.88	28.00	9.75
Stock price – close ($)	(9.9%)	26.94	24.50	22.75	23.88	36.31	35.63	22.13	28.63	34.75	10.50
P/E – high	—	6	8	6	6	6	8	—	3	—	—
P/E – low	—	4	4	4	4	4	5	—	2	—	—
Dividends per share ($)	3.8%	1.55	1.70	1.75	1.83	1.90	2.05	2.16	2.16	2.36	2.16
Book value per share ($)	(3.1%)	39.18	40.71	43.91	45.81	49.19	52.95	38.70	47.19	36.40	29.54

1990 Year-end:
Equity as % of assets: 4.8%
Return on equity: —
Cash (mil.): $7,834
Long-term debt (mil.): $6,349
No. of shares (mil.): 132
Dividends:
   1990 average yield: 20.6%
   1990 payout: —
Market value (mil.): $1,383
Sales (mil.): $13,672

Stock Price History
High/Low 1981–90

CHEMICAL BANKING CORPORATION

NYSE symbol: CHI
Fiscal year ends: December 31

Hoover's Rating C-

OVERVIEW

In a move that seemed to spark a series of big bank mergers, Chemical agreed to merge with Manufacturers Hanover in 1991. The "merger of equals" calls for Chemical chairman Walter Shipley to act as president and COO of the new entity until 1994, when he will become CEO. Managements of both banks expect to reap huge savings by closing approximately 70 branches and eliminating 6,200 jobs. The new bank would be a New York–based giant and 3rd largest in the US behind Citicorp and the proposed Bank of America/Security Pacific combination.

Before the merger craze, Chemical had been the nation's 6th largest banking organization, with a leading position in 3 states: Chemical Bank in New York, Texas Commerce Bancshares, and Chemical Bank New Jersey (formerly Horizon Bancorp). Chemical dominates the New York middle market, doing business with 36% of the mid-sized companies in the region.

Although Chemical posted improved results over 1989, the bank remained weakened by bad loans. Additions to loan loss reserves were lower in 1990 but remained substantial as the bank reported a 42% surge in nonperforming commercial real estate loans, mostly in Texas and New Jersey.

WHO

Chairman and CEO: Walter V. Shipley, age 55, $738,167 pay
President: Robert J. Callander, age 60, $659,500 pay
CFO: Joseph G. Sponholz, age 47
Auditors: Price Waterhouse
Employees: 26,689

WHERE

HQ: 277 Park Ave., New York, NY 10172
Phone: 212-310-6161
Fax: 212-593-2194

	1990 Assets	
	$ mil.	% of total
US	62,523	86
Europe	3,718	5
Other international	6,778	9
Total	**73,019**	**100**

WHEN

Balthazar P. Melick founded Chemical Bank as part of the New York Chemical Manufacturing Company in 1824. The bank was run by a small group of New York businessmen and operated separately from the manufacturing company. In 1844 the bank's directors liquidated the chemical firm and obtained a charter to operate only in banking.

The bank was a founding member (1853) of the New York Clearing House, an association formed to expedite the exchange and settlement of funds among New York City banks. In 1865 the bank took a national charter and started issuing national bank notes backed by government bonds. Building on a strong correspondent banking business (acting as agent for other banks), Chemical grew to be one of the largest and strongest US banks by 1900.

In 1920 the bank acquired Citizens National Bank in the first of several mergers with New York institutions. Chemical opened its first branch in 1923 and its first foreign office in London in 1929. The same year, Chemical converted to a state charter in order to gain trust powers and to facilitate a merger with United States Mortgage & Trust.

The bank acquired another dozen banks in New York state, including, in 1954, Corn Exchange Bank Trust Company, a major branching system. Other acquisitions were New York Trust, a wholesale banking (corporate and institutional clients) and trust operation (1959), and Security National Bank (1975), with a Long Island branch system.

To allow acquisition of related businesses outside traditional banking, Chemical formed a bank holding company (1968). The bank acquired companies handling consumer loans, mortgage banking, and factoring. The 1960s also saw a vast expansion of Chemical's international business.

Chemical is known as a technological innovator. The bank introduced BankLink (1977), a computerized cash management system with more than 10,000 business customers, and Pronto, the first electronic home banking service in the US (1982).

Chemical's growth through mergers increased in the 1980s with the acquisition of Texas Commerce Bancshares (1987), one of the largest banks in Texas, and Horizon Bancorp (1989), the 5th largest New Jersey bank. Chemical's losses in 1987 and 1989 were due largely to nonperforming Third World loans.

In 1990 Chemical sold its stake in Florida National Banks. Manufacturers Hanover and Chemical agreed to merge in 1991.

WHAT

	1990 Assets	
	$ mil.	% of total
Cash & due from banks	5,194	7
Deposits in other banks	1,101	1
Federal funds sold	4,591	6
Investment securities	10,686	15
Loans	45,131	62
Loan loss allowance	(2,090)	(3)
Other	8,406	12
Total	**73,019**	**100**

Major Subsidiaries
Chemical Bank
Chemical Financial Services
  Chemical Card Services Corp.
  Chemical Student Services Corp.
Chemical First State Corp.
  Chemical Bank Delaware
  Chemical Connecticut Corp.
Chemical New Jersey, NA Holding Inc.
  Chemical Bank New Jersey, NA
  Chemical Pennsylvania Corp.
  Princeton Bank and Trust Co. (fund management)
Chemical Securities, Inc.
Chemical Technologies Corp.
  BankLink, Inc. (electronic banking)
Chemical Venture Capital Associates (80%)
The Portfolio Group, Inc. (fund management)
Texas Commerce Bancshares, Inc.

RANKINGS

6th in *Fortune* 100 Commercial Banking Cos.
384th in *Business Week* 1000

HOW MUCH

	9-Year Growth	1981	1982	1983	1984	1985	1986	1987	1988	1989	1990
Assets ($ mil.)	5.5%	44,917	48,275	51,165	52,236	56,990	60,564	78,189	67,349	71,513	73,019
Net income ($ mil.)	4.0%	205	241	306	341	390	402	(854)	754	(482)	291
Income as % of assets	—	0.5%	0.5%	0.6%	0.7%	0.7%	0.7%	(1.1%)	1.1%	0.7%	0.4%
Earnings per share ($)	(7.7%)	4.88	5.12	6.02	6.26	7.15	7.42	(16.68)	12.02	(8.29)	2.38
Stock price – high ($)	—	28.00	31.58	37.50	35.88	46.25	56.25	49.50	33.88	41.13	31.38
Stock price – low ($)	—	18.67	17.67	25.67	23.50	33.13	40.75	20.25	20.00	28.50	9.63
Stock price – close ($)	(8.6%)	24.22	27.00	29.33	34.50	45.38	42.25	21.38	31.00	29.88	10.75
P/E – high	—	6	6	6	6	6	8	—	3	—	13
P/E – low	—	4	3	4	4	5	6	—	2	—	4
Dividends per share ($)	3.3%	1.71	1.92	2.16	2.36	2.48	2.60	2.72	2.72	2.72	2.29
Book value per share ($)	(1.9%)	38.98	41.70	43.74	46.86	51.17	56.14	41.14	47.19	34.09	32.94

1990 Year-end:
Return on equity: 7.1%
Equity as % of assets: 4.9%
Cash (mil.): $6,295
Long-term debt (mil.): $3,233
No. of shares (mil.): 91
Dividends:
  1990 average yield: 21.3%
  1990 payout: 96.2%
Market value (mil.): $983
Sales (mil.): $7,967

Stock Price History High/Low 1981–90

KEY COMPETITORS

H. F. Ahmanson
American Express
Banc One
Bank of New York
BankAmerica
Bankers Trust
Barclays
Canadian Imperial
Chase Manhattan
Citicorp
Crédit Lyonnais
CS Holding
Dai-Ichi Kangyo
Deutsche Bank
First Chicago
First Fidelity
First Interstate
Fleet/Norstar
Great Western
HSBC
Industrial Bank of Japan
J.P. Morgan
NCNB
Royal Bank
Union Bank of Switzerland
Other money center banks

CHEVRON CORPORATION

NYSE symbol: CHV
Fiscal year ends: December 31

Hoover's Rating **C+**

OVERVIEW

Chevron, the 10th largest industrial company in the US, is the largest combined oil and gas producer in the lower 48 states. Pennzoil owns 9.4% of Chevron, but fears of a takeover try have subsided.

Chevron is a vertically integrated oil company (doing business from wellhead to filling station). It looks for and produces petroleum in the US, Canada, Africa, and the North Sea; refines and produces petrochemicals, primarily in the US, Japan, Brazil, Ecuador, and France; and markets its products in more than 11,300 outlets worldwide (not including half-owned Caltex outlets in the Far East). Chevron has interests in 513 companies worldwide.

Chevron has more than a passing interest in the shifting political fortunes of the USSR. After months of negotiating, Chevron is on the brink of launching a joint venture with the Soviets to develop a multi-billion-barrel oilfield in Kazakhstan, in the Caspian Sea area.

WHEN

Thirty years after the California Gold Rush, a small company started selling a different product from the ground — oil. The crude came from wildcatter Frederick Taylor's well north of Los Angeles. In 1879 Taylor and other oil marketers in the area formed Pacific Coast Oil.

Pacific Coast's debut wasn't as earthshaking as Sutter's Mill's, but in time it attracted the attention of John D. Rockefeller's Standard Oil in California. Standard and Pacific Coast competed fiercely until Standard bought Pacific Coast in 1900.

When the Supreme Court ordered the breakup of Standard Oil in 1911, West Coast operations became the stand-alone Standard Oil Company (California), the only former subsidiary considered a truly integrated petroleum company — with production, refining, pipelines, and marketing. All its former Standard stablemates were running on fewer than those 4 legs.

The San Francisco–based company, nicknamed Socal and marketing products under the Chevron name, found itself at a different kind of golden gate when it won drilling concessions on the island of Bahrain and in Saudi Arabia in the 1930s.

The desert oil trove proved so vast that Socal summoned Texaco to help market the crude. They formed Caltex — the California Texas Oil Company — as equal partners. In 1948 Jersey Standard (later Exxon) and Socony (later Mobil) bought 40% of Caltex's Saudi operations, and the Saudi arm became Aramco (Arabian American Oil Company).

Socal exploration pushed into Louisiana and into the Gulf of Mexico in the 1940s. In 1961 Socal bought Standard Oil Company of Kentucky — Kyso — to acquire southern service stations.

Caltex suffered nationalization of some Arab holdings in the OPEC-spawned upheaval of the 1970s, and in 1980 Aramco became an arm of the Saudi Arabian government.

In 1984 Socal renamed itself Chevron, assuming its brand name. Also in 1984 Chevron purchased Gulf for a record $13.3 billion, serving as a white knight to ward off corporate raider T. Boone Pickens's overtures.

Gulf began in the 1901 Spindletop gusher in Texas as J.M. Guffey Petroleum, bankrolled by the Mellon family of Pittsburgh. Founder Guffey was unseated by William Larimer Mellon in 1902, and the company's name was changed to Gulf in 1907. Gulf, spurred by strikes in Louisiana and Oklahoma, became an oil power developing Kuwaiti concessions. In the 1970s OPEC-inspired oil cutbacks in Kuwait and revelations of payoffs to officials at home and abroad hobbled Gulf. The Gulf deal almost doubled Chevron's oil and gas reserves.

In 1988 Chevron spent $2.5 billion for Tenneco wells in the Gulf of Mexico. To focus on large, high-percentage fields, Chevron discarded marginal prospects, more than 400 in 1990.

WHO

Chairman and CEO: Kenneth T. Derr, age 54, $1,102,488 pay
VC: J. Dennis Bonney, age 60, $712,200 pay
VC: James N. Sullivan, age 53, $563,859 pay
VP Finance: Martin R. Klitten, age 46
VP Human Resources: Louis Fernandez, Jr.
Auditors: Price Waterhouse
Employees: 54,208

WHERE

HQ: 225 Bush St., San Francisco, CA 94104
Phone: 415-894-7700
Fax: 415-894-0593

Chevron conducts integrated petroleum operations in the US and 102 other countries.

	1990 Sales		1990 Operating Income	
	$ mil.	% of total	$ mil.	% of total
US	29,994	78	1,896	41
Canada	1,396	4	289	6
Other foreign	7,196	18	2,462	53
Adjustments	21	—	(836)	—
Total	**38,607**	**100**	**3,811**	**100**

WHAT

	1990 Sales		1990 Operating Income	
	$ mil.	% of total	$ mil.	% of total
Petroleum	34,818	90	4,584	109
Chemicals	3,325	9	44	1
Minerals	443	1	19	—
Other	21	—	(434)	(10)
Adjustments	—	—	(402)	—
Total	**38,607**	**100**	**3,811**	**100**

Selected Major Subsidiaries and Affiliates
Caltex (50%, refining and marketing)
Chevron Canada Ltd.
Chevron Chemical (industrial chemicals, consumer products)
Chevron International Oil Co. Inc. (trading and marketing)
Chevron Overseas Petroleum Inc.
Chevron Pipe Line (petroleum products transportation)
Chevron Shipping (marine management)
Chevron Transport (marine transportation)
Chevron USA, Inc. (integrated petroleum)
Gulf Oil (Great Britain) Ltd.
Huntington Beach Co.
Insco Ltd.
Pittsburg & Midway Coal Mining Co.

RANKINGS

10th in *Fortune* 500 Industrial Cos.
13th in *Business Week* 1000

KEY COMPETITORS

AMAX	Koch	Sun
Amoco	Mobil	Texaco
Ashland	Norsk Hydro	Unocal
Atlantic	Occidental	USX
Richfield	Oryx	California real
British	Pennzoil	estate
Petroleum	Petrofina	companies
Broken Hill	Petrobrás	Chemical
Coastal	PDVSA	companies
Du Pont	Pemex	Coal mining
Elf Aquitaine	Phillips Petroleum	companies
Exxon	Royal Dutch/Shell	

HOW MUCH

	9-Year Growth	1981	1982	1983	1984	1985	1986	1987	1988	1989	1990
Sales ($ mil.)	(1.5%)	44,224	34,362	27,342	26,798	41,742	24,351	26,015	25,196	29,443	38,607
Net income ($ mil.)	(1.1%)	2,380	1,377	1,590	1,534	1,547	715	1,007	1,768	251	2,157
Income as % of sales	—	5.4%	4.0%	5.8%	5.7%	3.7%	2.9%	3.9%	7.0%	0.9%	5.6%
Earnings per share ($)	(1.5%)	6.96	4.03	4.65	4.48	4.52	2.09	2.94	5.17	0.73	6.10
Stock price – high ($)	—	51.75	42.88	40.88	40.25	40.75	48.13	64.63	52.00	73.50	81.63
Stock price – low ($)	—	35.13	23.50	30.88	30.00	29.25	34.00	32.00	39.00	45.38	63.13
Stock price – close ($)	6.0%	42.88	32.00	34.63	31.25	38.13	45.38	39.63	45.75	67.75	72.63
P/E – high	—	7	11	9	9	9	23	22	10	101	13
P/E – low	—	5	6	7	7	6	16	11	8	62	10
Dividends per share ($)	3.3%	2.20	2.40	2.40	2.40	2.40	2.40	2.40	2.55	2.80	2.95
Book value per share ($)	1.5%	37.13	38.72	41.23	43.15	45.47	45.29	46.13	43.23	39.38	42.29

1990 Year-end:
Debt ratio: 31.1%
Return on equity: 14.9%
Cash (mil.): $1,684
Current ratio: 1.12
Long-term debt (mil.): $6,710
No. of shares (mil.): 351
Dividends:
  1990 average yield: 4.1%
  1990 payout: 48.4%
Market value (mil.): $25,477

Stock Price History High/Low 1981–90

CITY OF CHICAGO

Form of government: Mayor/Council
Fiscal year ends: December 31
Motto: Urbs in Horto (City in a Garden)

Hoover's Rating C+

OVERVIEW

The "Second City" is the 3rd largest city in the US (after New York and Los Angeles). Its name, first recorded as Che-cau-gou in 1680, is American Indian in origin and has been variously translated as "strong," "powerful," "skunk cabbage," and "wild onion." Chicago is situated along 26 miles of the southwestern shoreline of Lake Michigan. The downtown and North Side are vibrant, bustling commercial areas surrounded by ethnic neighborhoods of varying economic vitality. Its South and West Sides are among the nation's worst examples of urban blight. The city remains the Midwest's commercial, financial, shipping, and industrial center, and the nation's rail, truck,

and air hub. It is, however, no longer Hog Butcher for the World, the slaughterhouses having moved to more bucolic locations.

Plagued by an early reputation for vice, its gangster legacy, and its "second city" status, Chicago has spent much of its civic effort overcompensating. It claims the first skyscraper (Home Insurance Building); the world's tallest building (Sears Tower), busiest airport (O'Hare), largest commercial building (Merchandise Mart), and largest stock options and futures exchanges (Chicago Board Options Exchange and Chicago Board of Trade); and the self-proclaimed "world's greatest newspaper" (*Chicago Tribune*).

WHEN

Chicago was visited by French explorers Louis Joliet and Father Jacques Marquette in 1673. The city's first permanent settler was Jean Baptiste Point du Sable, a fur trader of African-French descent who arrived in 1779. In 1803 the US built Fort Dearborn, most of whose inhabitants were slain by Indians in 1812. The fort was rebuilt in 1816 and was occupied until the 1830s. In 1830, 48 blocks of what was to become Chicago were first platted. In 1833 its 200 inhabitants incorporated as a town, and in 1837 it incorporated as a city of 4,170.

From the 1830s to 1870 the city became a port for Great Lakes shipping and a terminus for more than 20 railroad lines. By 1865 its population was over 300,000, and by 1870 it had become the largest city in the Midwest.

In 1871 the Great Chicago Fire killed 250 people and leveled 17,450 buildings. Rising from the ashes, the city rebuilt rapidly and gloriously. Within 3 years virtually all traces of the fire were gone and by 1880 Chicago's population had ballooned to half a million.

The 1880s and 1890s found Chicago the focus of labor unrest. The Haymarket Riot of 1886, prompted by labor's demand for an 8-hour day, resulted in the deaths of 7 policemen and the probably wrongful execution of

4 anarchists. In 1894 Eugene Debs led the Pullman strike, halting national rail traffic.

The Columbian Exposition of 1892–93, costing about $40 million, allowed the city to flaunt its prosperity. During the 1890s and early 20th century, the city was home to such great architects as Dankmar Adler, Daniel Burnham, Louis Sullivan, and Frank Lloyd Wright. During the 1920s and 1930s it was also home to such infamous gangsters as Al Capone and John Dillinger.

Fueled by immigration from Europe (particularly Ireland and Poland) and migration of southern blacks, the city's population reached 3.4 million by 1940. Following WWII, urban decay and flight to the suburbs sapped the city's strength. Not until the election of Mayor Richard J. Daley in 1955 did the city's fortunes change. Daley ruled a coalition of labor and business for 21 years, backed by the awesome power of the last big-city political machine. His efforts and those of his successors (including the current mayor, his son Richard M. Daley, now in his second term), and the continued migration to the city of those seeking better lives (particularly Hispanic and Asian immigrants), have kept Chicago a vital center of commerce and cultural activity.

WHO

Mayor: Richard M. Daley, $80,000 pay
City Treasurer: Walter S. Kozubowski, $60,000 pay
City Clerk: Miriam Santos, $60,000 pay
City Comptroller: Walter K. Knorr, $92,664 pay
Commissioner of Personnel: Glenn Carr, $87,216 pay
Auditors: Deloitte & Touche
Employees: 38,500

WHERE

HQ: 121 N. LaSalle St., Chicago, IL 60602
Phone: 312-744-4000
Fax: 312-744-9538 (Mayor's office)
County: Cook
Altitude: 623 feet above sea level

WHAT

	1989 Revenues	
	$ mil.	% of total
Property tax	627	24
Utility tax	277	10
Sales tax	284	11
Transportation tax	208	8
State income tax	195	7
Other taxes	212	8
Internal service	149	6
Licenses/permits	35	1
Fines	33	1
Interest	62	2
Charges — services	52	2
Government grants	491	19
Miscellaneous	37	1
Total	**2,662**	**100**

Vital Statistics

Airports	3
Beaches	31
Colleges	95
Firefighters	4,311
Libraries	83
Manholes	146,000
Parks	563
Police officers	11,818
Population	3,026,857
Public school students	408,442
Square miles	228.5
TV stations	9

Sights and Institutions

Adler Planetarium
Art Institute
Chicago Historical Society
Chicago Symphony Orchestra
Comiskey Park
Field Museum of Natural History

Lincoln Park Zoo
Museum of Science & Industry
Newbery Library
Oriental Institute
Robie House
Shedd Aquarium
Soldier Field
University of Chicago
Wrigley Field

RANKINGS

3rd largest city in US
10th best US travel destination — *Traveler* magazine
18th best place to live in America — *Places Rated Almanac*
110th best place to live — *Money* magazine

KEY COMPETITORS

None

HOW MUCH

	9-Year Growth	1980	1981	1982	1983	1984	1985	1986	1987	1988	1989
Population (mil.)	0.1%	3.00	3.00	3.00	2.99	2.99	3.01	3.01	3.02	3.02	3.03
Households (mil.)	0.1%	1.14	1.09	1.09	1.10	1.10	1.12	1.13	1.14	1.15	1.15
Employment (mil.)	0.9%	1.24	1.19	1.12	1.08	1.14	1.18	1.20	1.25	1.24	1.34
Per capita income ($)	6.3%	7,160	7,297	7,612	7,994	8,956	9,788	10,315	11,092	11,619	12,379
Market value of real estate ($ bil.)	4.9%	45	47	47	48	50	51	58	60	67	69
New construction costs ($ mil.)	8.7%	555	507	544	484	322	617	519	644	817	1,172
Retail sales ($ bil.)	3.1%	12.2	12.5	12.4	12.6	14.4	14.5	14.7	14.8	14.6	16.1
City revenue ($ mil.)	5.5%	1,645	—	1,999	2,035	2,051	2,076	2,126	2,388	2,366	2,662

Mkt. Value of Real Estate ($ bil.) 1980–89

CHICAGO AND NORTH WESTERN

OVERVIEW

Private company
Fiscal year ends: December 31

Chicago and North Western Holdings is a private holding company formed in the 1989 LBO of CNW Corporation by Blackstone Capital Partners LP, which is composed partly of CNW managers and the Union Pacific Railroad.

CNW operates a 5,800-mile railroad, Chicago and North Western Transportation Company (the North Western), whose main east-west line lies between Chicago and terminals in Council Bluffs, Iowa, and Fremont, Nebraska. This line forms a central link between the Union Pacific and major railroads serving the East. The company transports coal, grain, automotive and steel products, bulk and consumer products, and intermodal (truck-to-train) freight. The North Western also operates a commuter rail system in Chicago and its suburbs through a contract with a regional transportation authority.

CNW's most profitable subsidiary, Western Railroad Properties, hauls low-sulfur coal from Wyoming's Powder River Basin to electric generating plants, primarily in the Midwest and Southwest. WRPI is the smaller of 2 railroads serving the Powder River area (the other is Burlington Northern), but long-term contracts generate about 80% of its revenues.

Interest payments on the debt created by the Blackstone Capital Partners buyout have impacted CNW's earnings for the last 2 years. Long-term debt ($558 million in 1988) now exceeds $1.2 billion. To help meet its obligations, CNW has sold rolling stock and some real estate, but the company's future depends upon improved performance in an industry now characterized by fierce competition and weak traffic.

WHO

Chairman, President, and CEO: Robert Schmiege, age 49, $554,167 pay
SVP Operations, Chicago and North Western Transportation Co.: Robert A. Jahnke, age 47, $315,000 pay
SVP Finance and Accounting, Chicago and North Western Transportation Co.: Thomas A. Tingleff, age 44
VP Human Resources, Chicago and North Western Transportation Co.: R. F. Ard
Auditors: Arthur Andersen & Co.
Employees: 6,939

WHERE

HQ: Chicago and North Western Holdings Corp., One North Western Center, Chicago, IL 60606
Phone: 312-559-7000
Fax: 312-559-7072

Principal Cities Served

Casper, WY	Green Bay, WI
Cedar Rapids, IA	Iron Mountain, WI
Chicago, IL	Kansas City, MO
Clinton, IA	Madison, WI
Council Bluffs, IA	Milwaukee, WI
Des Moines, IA	Peoria, IL
Duluth, MN	Rapid City, SD
Eau Claire, WI	Sioux City, IA
Fremont, NE	St. Louis, MO

WHEN

Chicago's first mayor, William Butler Ogden, founded the Galena & Chicago Union Railroad in 1836 but did not begin its construction until 1848. The road eventually operated between the Chicago area and Fulton, Illinois. In 1864 it was consolidated with the Chicago & North Western Railway (founded in 1855 as the Chicago, St. Paul & Fond du Lac Railroad to link Cary, Illinois; St. Paul, Minnesota; and Wisconsin's iron and copper mines). By 1925, when the North Western (as the line was known) acquired the Chicago, St. Paul, Minneapolis & Omaha, it had trackage in Illinois, Missouri, Iowa, Nebraska, Wyoming, South Dakota, Minnesota, and Wisconsin.

Ben Heineman became president of the North Western in 1956 and promptly became famous for, among other things, making the railroad's Chicago commuter trains run on time. The North Western gained a route into St. Louis with the 1958 merger of the Litchfield & Madison and also acquired the 1,500-mile Minneapolis & St. Louis (1960). Heineman intended to create a large midwestern railroad by acquiring 3 rival lines: the Chicago, Rock Island & Pacific (Rock Island); the Chicago, Milwaukee, St. Paul & Pacific (the Milwaukee Road); and the Chicago Great Western. He succeeded in buying only the Chicago Great Western (1968) and, in the meantime, turned his attention to diversifying the company. In 1967 Heineman led the

creation of Northwest Industries, a holding company for the railroad and its diversified interests, including Velsicol Chemical (acquired in 1965).

The North Western's unstable earnings record, labor problems, and other handicaps led Heineman to put the railroad up for sale in 1969. The following year he offered the North Western to former acquisition target Milwaukee Railroad, which refused the deal. A group of North Western employees led by President Larry S. Provo expressed an interest, however, and in 1972 bought the railroad, making it the first employee-owned major American railroad. In 1976 the company and Burlington Northern (BN) started building a 103-mile rail line serving Wyoming's Powder River Basin, a rich source of low-sulfur coal. The North Western dropped out of the project in 1979 because of a cash shortage, but it won a court battle with BN to reacquire a 1/2 interest in the line for $76 million in 1983. The railroad created a new holding company, CNW Corporation, in 1985.

In 1988 CNW began selling certain noncore assets, such as snowplow manufacturer Douglas Dynamics (acquired 1986), to lower its debt. In 1989, after Japonica Partners made a hostile takeover bid for CNW, Blackstone Capital Partners bought the company for $1.6 billion, thereby ensuring Union Pacific's continued direct access to Chicago.

WHAT

	1990 Sales	
	$ mil.	% of total
Railroad freight	850	88
Commuter & other	111	12
Total	**961**	**100**

	1990 Sales	
	$ mil.	% of total
Coal	255	24
Grain	193	18
Automotive & steel	157	15
Intermodal	99	10
Bulk & consumer products	232	22
Commuter & other	111	11
Adjustments	(86)	—
Total	**961**	**100**

Operating Subsidiaries
Chicago and North Western Transportation Co.
Western Railroad Properties, Inc.

RANKINGS

27th in *Fortune* 50 Transportation Cos.
180th in *Forbes* 400 US Private Cos.

KEY COMPETITORS

American President
Burlington Northern
Canadian Pacific
Consolidated Freightways
Roadway
Yellow Freight

HOW MUCH

	9-Year Growth	1981	1982	1983	1984	1985	1986	1987	1988	1989	1990
Sales ($ mil.)	0.2%	982	804	860	882	898	959	957	995	955	961
Net income ($ mil.)	—	45	(19)	34	21	(31)	43	30	69	(21)	(58)
Income as % of sales	—	4.6%	(2.4%)	3.9%	2.4%	(3.4%)	4.5%	3.1%	7.0%	(2.2%)	(6.1%)
Employees	(6.5%)	12,717	10,409	10,929	11,123	10,255	9,800	8,850	8,194	7,562	6,939

1990 Year-end:
Debt ratio: 99.6%
Cash (mil.): $167
Current ratio: .88
Long-term debt (mil.): $1,213
Assets (mil.): $1,905

Net Income ($ mil.) 1981–90

CHIQUITA BRANDS INTERNATIONAL, INC.

OVERVIEW

Based in Cincinnati, Chiquita Brands is the world's #2 marketer of fresh fruits and vegetables (after Dole Food). Chiquita Bananas, the company's flagship brand and the #1 banana in the world, is one of the great global product names. In 1990 alone the company sold over 14 billion bananas.

Chiquita Brands is divided into 2 segments: Fresh Foods and Prepared Foods. The Fresh Foods segment, which accounts for 48% of total sales, includes bananas, vegetables, and various types of citrus and tropical fruits. The

Prepared Foods segment, with 52% of total sales, produces fruit juices, purees, margarine, shortening, and various processed meats marketed under the John Morrell, Rath Black Hawk, and numerous regional brand names.

Chiquita continues to expand its global presence. In 1990 the company entered new markets in Australia, New Zealand, Korea, and Turkey. In 1991 Chiquita expressed interest in acquiring Polly Peck International's (Del Monte) fruit plantations, a purchase that would increase its international presence.

NYSE symbol: CQB
Fiscal year ends: December 31

Hoover's Rating **B-**

WHO

Chairman and CEO: Carl H. Lindner, age 71, $400,000 pay
President and COO: Keith E. Lindner, age 31, $1,225,000 pay
VP and CFO: Fred J. Runk, age 48
VP Human Resources: Peter P. Fay
Auditors: Ernst & Young
Employees: 46,000

WHERE

HQ: 250 E. 5th St., Cincinnati, OH 45202
Phone: 513-784-8011
Fax: 513-784-8030

The company sells its products in Europe, North America, and the Far East.

	1990 Sales		1990 Operating Income	
	$ mil.	% of total	$ mil.	% of total
North America	2,973	70	31	16
Central & South America	163	4	11	6
Europe	1,137	26	145	78
Adjustments	—	—	(13)	—
Total	**4,273**	**100**	**174**	**100**

WHAT

	1990 Sales		1990 Operating Income	
	$ mil.	% of total	$ mil.	% of total
Fresh foods	2,049	48	170	91
Prepared foods	2,224	52	16	9
Adjustments	—	—	(12)	—
Total	**4,273**	**100**	**174**	**100**

Brand Names

Bananas
Amigo
Bananos
Chico
Chiquita
Consul
Petite 150

Other Fruits and Vegetables
Chiquita
Classic
Frupac
Pascual
Premium

Meats
Bob Ostrow
Dinner Bell
Hunter
John Morrell
Kretschmar
Krey
Liguria
Mosey's

Nathan's Famous
Partridge
Peyton's
Rath Black Hawk
Rodeo
Scott Petersen
Solar AquaFarms
Tobin's First Prize

Prepared Foods
Chiquita Processed Foods (fruit juices)
Chiquita Caribbean Splash
Chiquita Orange Banana Juice
Chiquita Tropical Squeeze
Numar Processed Foods (vegetable oils)
Clover
Maravilla
Numar

WHEN

In 1870 Lorenzo Baker sailed into Jersey City with 160 bunches of Jamaican bananas. Finding the new fruit profitable, Baker arranged to sell bananas through Boston produce agent Andrew Preston. With the support of Preston's partners, the 2 men formed the Boston Fruit Company in 1885. In 1899 Boston Fruit merged with 3 other banana companies that had been importing produce and incorporated as United Fruit Company. Soon the company was importing bananas from numerous Central American plantations for expanded distribution in the US.

The company entered the Cuban sugar trade (Fidel Castro worked on a United Fruit sugar plantation) with the purchase of Nipe Bay (1907) and Saetia Sugar (1912). In 1930 the company bought Samuel Zemurray's Cuyamel Fruit Company, leaving Zemurray as the largest shareholder. Zemurray, who had masterminded the overthrow of the Honduran government in 1905 to establish a government favorable to his business, forcibly established himself as United Fruit's president in 1933. Because of its broad influence throughout Honduran politics and society, Hondurans came to call the company "Octopus."

In 1954, when leftist Guatemalan leader Jacobo Arbenz threatened to seize United Fruit holdings, the company convinced Congress and the American public that Arbenz was a Communist threat and provided its own ships

to transport CIA-backed troops and ammunition for his ultimate overthrow. In 1961 United Fruit provided 2 ships for the unsuccessful Bay of Pigs invasion of Cuba. The term "banana republic" originates from United Fruit's involvement in establishing Central American regimes friendly to its operations.

During the 1950s the company introduced its catchy calypso-style Chiquita Banana ad campaign and in the 1960s diversified, buying A&W (restaurants and root beer, 1966) and Baskin-Robbins (ice cream, 1967).

Eli Black, founder of AMK (which included the Morrell meat company), bought United Fruit in 1970 and changed its name to United Brands. After Hurricane Fifi destroyed much of the Honduran banana crop and the news leaked that he had bribed the Honduran president, Black committed suicide in 1975.

During the 1970s and 1980s, United Brands sold many of its previous acquisitions including Baskin-Robbins (1973), Foster Grant (sunglasses, 1974), and A&W (restaurants, 1982; soft drinks, 1987). Financier Carl Lindner's American Financial took over the controlling interest in United Brands in 1987 (it now owns over 52%).

In 1990 the company changed its name to Chiquita Brands International. It also acquired interests in more than 10 food-related businesses, including Chilean fruit-and-vegetable concern Frupac.

RANKINGS

114th in *Fortune* 500 Industrial Cos.
372nd in *Business Week* 1000

KEY COMPETITORS

Cadbury Schweppes	CPC	Sara Lee
Cargill	Dole	Seagram
Coca-Cola	Philip Morris	TLC Beatrice
ConAgra	Procter & Gamble	Tyson Foods
Continental Grain		

HOW MUCH

	9-Year Growth	1981	1982	1983	1984	1985	1986	1987	1988	1989	1990
Sales ($ mil.)	0.6%	4,058	2,406	3,360	3,220	2,288	3,307	3,268	3,503	3,823	4,273
Net income ($ mil.)	13.8%	29	(167)	46	21	23	54	61	60	68	94
Income as % of sales	—	0.7%	(7.0%)	1.4%	0.7%	1.0%	1.6%	1.9%	1.7%	1.8%	2.2%
Earnings per share ($)	12.6%	0.76	(4.61)	1.05	0.46	0.46	1.09	1.30	1.45	1.67	2.20
Stock price – high ($)	—	5.79	3.88	9.04	7.25	9.29	12.33	16.67	19.88	17.63	32.13
Stock price – low ($)	—	3.13	2.17	2.58	3.42	3.50	7.38	9.33	13.75	12.88	16.00
Stock price – close ($)	26.0%	4.00	2.83	5.17	3.58	9.25	11.08	15.21	16.38	17.38	32.00
P/E – high	—	8	—	9	16	20	11	13	14	11	15
P/E – low	—	4	—	2	7	8	7	7	9	7	7
Dividends per share ($)	8.6%	0.17	0.05	0.00	0.00	0.02	0.02	0.15	0.20	0.20	0.35
Book value per share ($)	(1.2%)	16.97	5.09	6.90	7.21	7.70	8.82	9.69	10.38	11.94	15.21

1990 Year-end:
Debt ratio: 43.1%
Return on equity: 16.2%
Cash (mil.): 349
Current ratio: 1.63
Long-term debt (mil.): $522
No. of shares (mil.): 45
Dividends:
 1990 average yield: 1.1%
 1990 payout: 15.9%
Market value (mil.): $1,447

Stock Price History
High/Low 1981–90

CHRYSLER CORPORATION

NYSE symbol: C
Fiscal year ends: December 31

OVERVIEW

In 1990 Chrysler was the #3 US carmaker (after GM and Ford), but Honda was close behind and gaining quickly. Chrysler is #9 in world vehicle sales, producing cars and trucks under the Chrysler, Dodge, Plymouth, Jeep/Eagle, and Lamborghini nameplates. The company owns the Dollar, Snappy, Thrifty, and General car rental agencies. Chrysler Financial is the US's 4th largest nonbank finance company.

Led by Lee Iacocca, scheduled to retire in late 1992, Chrysler is betting the ranch ($16.6 billion over 5 years) on product development. The company desperately needs a new design to replace its outdated K-car platform. Chrysler is trying to survive until its new LH vehicles, slated for release in late 1992, generate hoped-for profits. In the meantime the company's market share is declining in a weak market, causing losses and a steadily worsening cash shortage. Further complicating the outlook is corporate raider Kirk Kerkorian, who bought 9.8% of Chrysler in 1990.

Chrysler has cut costs company-wide and has asked for and received 2,291 cost-reducing suggestions from its suppliers. Virtually everything except its core auto business is up for sale. Mitsubishi Motors, a possible merger partner, recently received FTC clearance to buy Chrysler's share of the companies' joint venture, Diamond-Star Motors. Chrysler owns 12% of Mitsubishi Motors and sells Mitsubishi cars under its own nameplates.

WHO

Chairman and CEO: Lee A. Iacocca, age 66, $918,182 pay
President: Robert A. Lutz, age 59, $562,574 pay
EVP and CFO: Jerome B. York, age 52
VP Employee Relations: Anthony P. St. John, age 54
Auditors: Deloitte & Touche
Employees: 124,000

WHERE

HQ: 12000 Chrysler Dr., Highland Park, MI 48288
Phone: 313-956-5741
Fax: 313-956-3747

	1990 Sales		1990 Pretax Income	
	$ mil.	% of total	$ mil.	% of total
US	26,887	88	(84)	(57)
Canada	2,674	9	66	45
Other countries	1,059	3	165	112
Adjustments	(823)	—	—	—
Total	**29,797**	**100**	**147**	**100**

WHAT

	1990 Sales		1990 Operating Income	
	$ mil.	% of total	$ mil.	% of total
Cars & trucks	27,009	88	344	42
Financial services	3,774	12	476	58
Adjustments	(986)	—	861	—
Total	**29,797**	**100**	**1,681**	**100**

Chrysler	Shadow	**Lamborghini**
Imperial	Spirit	Diablo
LeBaron	Stealth	
New Yorker		**Plymouth**
Town & Country	**Eagle**	Acclaim
	Premier	Colt
Dodge	Summit	Laser
Caravan	Talon	Sundance
Colt		Voyager
Dakota	**Jeep**	
Daytona	Cherokee	
Dynasty	Comanche	
Monaco	Grand Wagoneer	
Ram	Wrangler	

Major Subsidiaries
Chrysler Canada Ltd.
Chrysler de Mexico SA
Chrysler Financial Corp.
Chrysler Technologies Airborne Systems, Inc.
Dollar Rent A Car Inc.
Electrospace Systems, Inc. (defense electronics)
General Rent-A-Car, Inc.
Snappy Car Rental, Inc.
Thrifty Rent-A-Car Systems, Inc.

WHEN

When the Maxwell Motor Car Company entered receivership in 1920, a bankers' syndicate hired Walter Chrysler, former Buick president and GM VP, to reorganize it. Chrysler became president in 1923.

In 1924 he introduced his own car, the Chrysler. Offering the attractions of a high-performance model (e.g., top speed 50 mph) at a mid-range price, the Chrysler borrowed from WWI aircraft in the design of its 6-cylinder engine. In 1925 Chrysler took over Maxwell and renamed it after himself.

In 1928 Chrysler acquired Dodge and introduced the low-priced Plymouth and the luxurious DeSoto. The Chrysler R&D budget never decreased during the Great Depression, and innovations included overdrive and a 3-point engine suspension on rubber mountings. In 1933 Chrysler's sales surpassed Ford's. In 1935 Walter Chrysler retired.

To minimize costs Chrysler kept the same car models from 1942 until 1953, while other manufacturers were making yearly style modifications. Consequently, Chrysler lost market share and slipped to 3rd place by 1950.

Chrysler misjudged customer demands in the 1960s when it introduced small cars and in the 1970s when it maintained production of large cars. Steadily declining market share led to losses of over $1 billion in 1979 and 1980.

Lee Iacocca, former Ford president, became CEO in 1978. Iacocca became one of the most visible CEOs ever, appearing in TV commercials, publishing his autobiography, and making an issue of Japanese trading practices.

Iacocca consolidated advertising under one agency; announced the 30-day money-back guarantee; and persuaded the government to cosign $1.5 billion in loans. Chrysler cut production costs by using the K-car chassis for several models and repaid all guaranteed loans by 1983, 7 years ahead of schedule. Chrysler's minivan (1984) created a new market.

Chrysler purchased Gulfstream Aerospace (corporate jets, sold in 1990), E.F. Hutton Credit, and Finance America in 1985 for a total of $1.2 billion. In 1986 Chrysler began a joint venture with Mitsubishi (Diamond-Star) and in 1987 purchased American Motors. Between 1989 and 1991 Chrysler bought Thrifty, Snappy, Dollar, and General car rental agencies.

In 1991 Chrysler announced a stock issue that would dilute shareholdings by 20%. New shares valued at $300 million would be contributed to Chrysler's pension fund (underfunded by $3.6 billion at the end of 1990).

RANKINGS

11th in *Fortune* 500 Industrial Cos.
207th in *Business Week* 1000

KEY COMPETITORS

Avis	Isuzu
BMW	Mazda
Daimler-Benz	Nissan
Fiat	Saab-Scania
Ford	Sears
General Motors	Suzuki
Hertz	Toyota
Honda	Volkswagen
Hyundai	Volvo

HOW MUCH

	9-Year Growth	1981	1982	1983	1984	1985	1986	1987	1988	1989	1990
Sales ($ mil.)	11.9%	10,822	10,045	13,240	19,573	21,256	22,586	26,277	35,473	34,922	29,797
Net income ($ mil.)	—	(476)	(69)	302	1,496	1,635	1,404	1,290	1,050	315	68
Income as % of sales	—	(4.4%)	0.7%	2.3%	7.6%	7.7%	6.2%	4.9%	3.0%	0.9%	0.2%
Earnings per share ($)	—	(3.19)	(0.57)	1.04	5.19	6.22	6.29	5.89	4.65	1.35	0.30
Stock price – high ($)	—	3.39	8.28	15.83	15.00	20.89	31.42	48.00	27.88	29.63	20.38
Stock price – low ($)	—	1.33	1.56	6.22	9.28	13.28	18.11	19.63	20.50	18.13	9.13
Stock price – close ($)	26.7%	1.50	7.89	12.28	14.22	20.72	24.67	22.13	25.75	19.00	12.63
P/E – high	—	—	—	15	3	3	5	8	6	22	68
P/E – low	—	—	—	6	2	2	3	3	4	13	30
Dividends per share ($)	—	0.00	0.00	0.00	0.38	0.44	0.80	1.00	1.00	1.20	1.20
Book value per share ($)	—	(3.28)	(1.84)	4.17	12.10	18.50	24.67	29.39	32.53	32.42	30.47

1990 Year-end:
Debt ratio: 65.1%
Return on equity: 1.0%
Cash (mil.): $1,572
Current ratio: —
Long-term debt (mil.): $12,750
No. of shares (mil.): 225
Dividends:
　1990 average yield: 9.5%
　1990 payout: 400.0%
Market value (mil.): $2,838

Stock Price History High/Low 1981–90

CIGNA CORPORATION

NYSE symbol: CI
Fiscal year ends: December 31

Hoover's Rating C+

OVERVIEW

Based on 1990 assets, CIGNA is the 4th largest US insurance company. Focused on commercial markets since 1988, the Philadelphia-based company, through Connecticut General and Insurance Company of North America (INA) subsidiaries, provides services in 4 areas: employee life and health, employee retirement and savings, property and casualty, and individual financial services. Individual financial services, which CIGNA may divest, include life and disability insurance and investment products for small-business owners and affluent individuals.

CIGNA's group retirement programs provide pension and profit-sharing services to middle-sized companies, with plans from $500,000 to $50 million. CIGNA is one of the largest US providers of group life, health, and long-term disability insurance. With its 1990 acquisition of EQUICOR-Equitable HCA Corporation, CIGNA became the dominant stock insurance company in managed health care services. The property and casualty division provides commercial property and casualty insurance through independent agents and brokers. Property and casualty insurance accounted for 41% of 1990 revenues.

WHEN

In 1982 Connecticut General and INA merged to form CIGNA Corporation. INA, the older of the 2, formed as Insurance Company of North America by a group of Philadelphia businessmen in 1792, was the first stock insurance company as well as the first marine insurance company in the US. It insured the ship *America* and its cargo on a trip from Philadelphia.

In 1794 INA issued its first life insurance policy, became the first US issuer of fire insurance outside city limits, and was the first to insure building contents against fire. In 1808 INA appointed independent agents in 5 states, thus originating the American Agency System. In the late 1800s INA grew internationally, appointing an agent for marine insurance in Canada (1873) and adding agents in London and Vienna (1887) and in Shanghai (1897); INA was the first US company to write insurance in China.

In 1942 INA's Indemnity Insurance company wrote accident and health insurance for the US Army's 30 men working on the Manhattan Project, the effort to develop the atom bomb. In 1950 INA introduced the homeowner's policy, the first homeowner coverage with broad availability. In 1978 INA bought HMO International, the largest publicly owned prepaid health care provider in the US.

In 1865 Dr. Guy Phelps, one of the founders of Connecticut Mutual, helped organize Connecticut General as a life insurance company. In 1912 Connecticut General formed an accident department to offer health insurance. The company in 1913 wrote its first group insurance for the *Hartford Courant* newspaper. In 1926 Connecticut General wrote the first individual regular accident coverage for airline passengers.

In the late 1930s Connecticut General was an industry leader in developing group medical and surgical insurance. Connecticut General in 1952 offered the first group medical coverage for general use and in 1964 introduced group dental insurance.

After the merger of INA and Connecticut General in 1982, CIGNA purchased Crusader Insurance (UK, 1983) and AFIA (1984). CIGNA sold its individual insurance products division to InterContinental Life (Jackson, Mississippi; 1988) and its Horace Mann Companies (individual financial services) to an investor group (1989) in order to focus on commercial business. In 1990 CIGNA bought EQUICOR, a group insurance and managed health care organization with $2.5 million in 1989 revenues, and began withdrawing from the personal auto insurance business to focus on small and medium-sized commercial clients.

WHO

Chairman and CEO: Wilson H. Taylor, age 47, $1,283,000 pay

EVP and CFO: James G. Stewart, age 48, $766,000 pay

EVP; President, Investments Division: George R. Trumbull, age 46, $721,000 pay

EVP; President, Employee Benefits Division: G. Robert O'Brien, age 54, $709,000 pay

EVP; President, Property and Domestic Casualty Division: Caleb L. Fowler, age 48, $619,000 pay

EVP Human Resources and Services: Donald M. Levinson, age 45

Auditors: Price Waterhouse

Employees: 53,542

WHERE

HQ: One Liberty Place, Philadelphia, PA 19192-1550

Phone: 215-761-1000

Fax: 215-761-5515

CIGNA serves customers in 69 countries through more than 160 offices.

	1990 Sales		1990 Pretax Income	
	$ mil.	% of total	$ mil.	% of total
US	15,646	86	479	136
Other countries	2,518	14	(127)	(36)
Total	**18,164**	**100**	**352**	**100**

WHAT

	1990 Sales		1990 Pretax Income	
	$ mil.	% of total	$ mil.	% of total
Employee retirement & savings	2,131	12	232	66
Property & casualty	7,516	41	(294)	(84)
Life & health	7,334	40	425	121
Indiv. fin. svcs.	1,037	6	100	28
Other	146	1	(111)	(31)
Total	**18,164**	**100**	**352**	**100**

Financial Services
Group life, health, accident, and disability insurance
Health care services
Individual life and health insurance
Investment management
Pension and retirement services
Property and casualty insurance

Principal Subsidiaries
Connecticut General Life Insurance Co.
Insurance Company of North America

RANKINGS

7th in *Fortune* 50 Life Insurance Cos.
197th in *Business Week* 1000

KEY COMPETITORS

Aetna	Humana	Primerica
Allianz	ITT	Prudential
American Financial	John Hancock	Sears
	Kemper	State Farm
AIG	Lloyd's of London	Teachers
B.A.T	Loews	Insurance
Berkshire Hathaway	MassMutual	Tokio Marine & Fire
Blue Cross	MetLife	Transamerica
Equitable	New York Life	Travelers
GEICO	Northwestern Mutual	USF&G
General Re		Xerox

HOW MUCH

	9-Year Growth	1981	1982	1983	1984	1985	1986	1987	1988	1989	1990
Assets ($ mil.)	15.1%	18,034	31,395	35,117	39,035	44,736	50,016	53,495	55,825	57,779	63,691
Net income ($ mil.)	(1.3%)	357	490	401	39	(855)	535	617	410	458	318
Income as % of assets	—	2.0%	1.6%	1.1%	0.1%	(1.9%)	1.1%	1.2%	0.7%	0.8%	0.5%
Earnings per share ($)	(7.7%)	8.65	6.38	5.22	0.11	(12.46)	6.26	7.14	4.88	5.58	4.20
Stock price – high ($)	—	58.25	55.38	51.50	45.50	64.25	77.25	69.50	55.38	66.75	60.63
Stock price – low ($)	—	41.75	31.00	37.63	27.00	43.50	51.13	41.25	42.75	45.88	33.25
Stock price – close ($)	(2.2%)	50.00	44.25	43.75	44.38	64.25	55.00	43.88	47.13	59.50	40.88
P/E – high	—	7	9	10	414	—	12	10	11	12	14
P/E – low	—	5	5	7	245	—	8	6	9	8	8
Dividends per share ($)	6.3%	1.76	2.24	2.48	2.60	2.60	2.60	2.80	2.96	2.96	3.04
Book value per share ($)	2.2%	60.41	62.71	66.74	62.79	51.84	58.83	63.52	66.64	70.59	73.51

1990 Year-end:
Return on equity: 5.8%
Equity as % of assets: 8.2%
Cash (mil.): $1,148
Long-term debt (mil.): $832
No. of shares (mil.): 71
Dividends:
  1990 average yield: 7.4%
  1990 payout: 72.4%
Market value (mil.): $2,915
Sales (mil.): $18,164

Stock Price History High/Low 1981–90

THE CIRCLE K CORPORATION

OVERVIEW

Phoenix-based Circle K is the 2nd largest convenience store operator in the country after Southland (7-Eleven). It also operates about 64 stores under the Charter name. The company's stores sell over 4,200 consumer items, primarily national brands, including fast food, tobacco products, both alcoholic and nonalcoholic beverages, groceries, magazines, health and beauty aids, and other nonfood items (including gasoline). The stores often offer such services as movie rental, money orders, and lottery tickets. Circle K stores generally have about 2,600 square feet of retail space. Most are open 7 days a week, 24 hours a day.

After increasing sales sixfold in the course of a decade, Circle K sought the protection of bankruptcy in May 1990. In September 1991 it remained under bankruptcy protection. Compounding the uncertainty of Circle K's future is increased competition from national grocery and gasoline chains, supermarkets, and drug stores. This competition may be exacerbated by what some analysts see as a shrinking customer base for convenience stores, primarily due to the aging of the baby-boomers. Another factor likely to affect sales is that the bankruptcy procedures have restricted the company's ability to build new and modernize current stores.

WHEN

Circle K Corporation was formed in Texas in 1951 by Fred Hervey, a 2-term mayor of El Paso. Hervey bought the 3 locations of Kay's Food Stores in El Paso that year and soon extended the chain to 10 locations. In 1957 he expanded into Arizona, changed the stores' name to Circle K, and adopted the distinctive, western-style logo. Circle K went public in 1963. During the 1960s and 1970s, the company expanded into New Mexico, California, Colorado, Montana, Idaho, and Oregon. In 1979 Circle K licensed UNY of Japan to operate Circle K stores there. UNY currently operates 1,087 Circle K stores in Japan and Hong Kong.

The corporation became a holding company in 1980, with its Circle K chain as a subsidiary, and began an expansion phase through acquisitions. That year the company bought 13% of Nucorp Energy, an oil and gas development company. Nucorp filed for bankruptcy in 1982, and Circle K sold its remaining interest in 1983 at a large loss. Also in 1983 Circle K nearly doubled its size by acquiring the 960-store UtoteM chain from American Financial, headed by Cincinnati financier Carl Lindner. Hervey's and Lindner's friend Karl Eller became chairman and CEO.

Eller committed Circle K to an aggressive growth plan aimed at increasing the number of stores almost 400% by 1990. Through acquisitions Circle K grew from 1,221 stores in 1983 to 5,751 at the end of 1989, increasing its long-term debt from $40.5 million to $1.1 billion.

Circle K began having financial problems in 1989, due in part to $96 million in annual interest payments. It put itself up for sale, but no buyers emerged. Lindner (whose American Financial owned 15% of Circle K's common stock and was a major creditor) brought in Robert Dearth from his Chiquita Brands as Circle K's president and COO in 1990. Shortly afterward, Eller left the company "to pursue personal business opportunities." In early 1990 prices were made more competitive and store managers were given more authority to purchase products desired by their customers, but it was too late; in May Circle K filed for bankruptcy protection.

The company's deadline for reorganization has been extended a number of times, the last time to January 15, 1992. In June 1991 Dearth resigned. A net income loss of $307 million for 1990, large amounts of acquisition debt, and management shake-ups continue to place Circle K's future in doubt.

NYSE symbol: CKP
Fiscal year ends: April 30

WHO

Chairman and CEO: Bart A. Brown, Jr., age 59
President and COO: John F. Antioco, age 41
SVP Finance and CFO: Larry J. Zine, age 36, $389,333 pay
Acting VP Human Resources: Terry Broekemeir
Auditors: Arthur Andersen & Co.
Employees: 27,377

WHERE

HQ: PO Box 52084, 1601 N. 7th St., Phoenix, AZ 85072
Phone: 602-253-9600
Fax: 602-257-4468

Circle K operates 3,859 convenience stores in 32 states, primarily in the Sunbelt, and 1,650 stores in 16 foreign countries.

	Convenience Store Locations	
	No. of stores	% of total
Florida	708	13
Arizona	648	12
Texas	615	11
California	414	8
Louisiana	264	5
Georgia	184	3
Other US	1,026	18
Total US	**3,859**	**70**
Japan (licensed)	1,016	18
UK (joint-venture)	220	4
Canada (licensed)	152	3
Other foreign	262	5
Total	**5,509**	**100**

WHAT

	1990 Revenues	
	$ mil.	% of total
Merchandise sales	1,698	47
Gasoline sales	1,852	52
Other revenues	49	1
Total	**3,599**	**100**

	1990 Percentage of US Sales
	% of total
Food items	31
Non-food items	17
Gasoline	52
Total	**100**

RANKINGS

31st in *Fortune* 50 Retailers

KEY COMPETITORS

Atlantic Richfield
British Petroleum
Chevron
Coastal
Exxon
Kroger
Mobil
Royal Dutch/Shell
Southland
Texaco
Gasoline and grocery retailers

HOW MUCH

Fiscal year ends April of following year	9-Year Growth	1981	1982	1983	1984	1985	1986	1987	1988	1989	1990
Sales ($ mil.)	19.3%	733	754	1,035	1,694	2,129	2,317	2,657	3,495	3,737	3,599
Net income ($ mil.)	—	(15)	15	22	33	40	49	55	15	(773)	(307)
Income as % of sales	—	(2.1%)	2.0%	2.1%	2.0%	1.9%	2.1%	2.1%	0.4%	(20.7%)	(8.5%)
Earnings per share ($)	—	(0.47)	0.44	0.57	0.71	0.75	0.85	0.96	0.20	(17.91)	(7.09)
Stock price – high ($)	—	5.83	5.63	9.08	11.25	12.33	18.63	18.63	16.38	16.63	3.88
Stock price – low ($)	—	3.54	2.67	4.50	6.92	9.56	9.69	7.00	10.50	3.25	0.28
Stock price – close ($)	(25.4%)	3.92	4.79	8.50	10.54	10.31	16.13	10.63	11.38	3.38	0.28
P/E – high	—	—	13	16	16	16	22	19	82	—	—
P/E – low	—	—	6	8	10	13	11	7	53	—	—
Dividends per share ($)	(100.0%)	0.24	0.25	0.25	0.25	0.25	0.28	0.28	0.28	0.07	0.00
Book value per share ($)	—	1.84	2.05	2.63	3.38	4.62	6.23	6.56	6.44	(11.51)	(17.51)

1990 Year-end:
Debt ratio: —
Return on equity: —
Cash (mil.): $149
Current ratio: 1.46
Long-term debt (mil.): $86
No. of shares (mil.): 45
Dividends:
  1990 average yield: 0.0%
  1990 payout: 0.0%
Market value (mil): $13

Stock Price History High/Low 1981–90

CIRCUIT CITY STORES, INC.

OVERVIEW

Headquartered in Richmond, Virginia, Circuit City is the largest specialty electronics and appliance retailer in the US. As of early 1991 its operations consisted of 14 Circuit City stores (between 4,000 and 15,000 square feet), 157 Circuit City Superstores (the backbone of the company, with units between 15,000 and 47,000 square feet), and 14 Impulse stores (mall-based retailers between 2,000 and 4,000 square feet), most of which are concentrated in the south, central, and western United States.

At a time when many electronics retailers are running for the bankruptcy courts, Circuit City is flying high, although its recent earnings have dropped in the wake of reduced consumer spending. The secret of the company's success is a mixture of heavy advertising, a superefficient computerized distribution system, and bargain prices. Indeed, if a shopper can find a lower price elsewhere, Circuit City will refund 110% of the difference.

The company is continuing to expand rapidly in the early 1990s through a strategy of regional concentration and domination of each market in which it operates. Circuit City always opts for local market saturation over geographic breadth. In 1990 alone the company opened 34 new superstores.

NYSE symbol: CC
Fiscal year ends: Last day of February

Hoover's Rating **A-**

WHO

Chairman: Alan L. Wurtzel, age 57
President and CEO: Richard L. Sharp, age 44, $656,479 pay
SVP and CFO: Michael T. Chalifoux, age 44
SVP Human Resources: William E. Zierden, age 52, $312,167 pay
Auditors: KPMG Peat Marwick
Employees: 14,982

WHERE

HQ: 9950 Mayland Drive, Richmond, VA 23233-1464
Phone: 804-527-4000
Fax: 804-527-4164

The company's 185 stores are concentrated primarily in the southern, central, and western regions of the US. Circuit City also has 59 stores under development.

State	No. of Stores
Alabama	5
Arizona	4
California	49
Delaware	1
Florida	26
Georgia	11
Illinois	1
Indiana	1
Kentucky	5
Maryland	16
Massachusetts	4
Missouri	5
Nevada	3
New Jersey	3
North Carolina	9
Ohio	2
Pennsylvania	5
South Carolina	5
Tennessee	9
Texas	1
Virginia	18
West Virginia	2
Total	**185**

WHEN

While on vacation in Richmond, Virginia, in 1949, Samuel S. Wurtzel learned from a local barber that the first TV station in the South was about to go on the air. Wurtzel immediately decided to launch a southern TV retailing operation, and founded Wards Company (an acronym for family names Wurtzel, Alan, Ruth, David, and Samuel) in Richmond that same year. The company gradually diversified into small appliances and went public in 1961.

Throughout the 1960s and early 1970s, Wards expanded by acquiring several appliance retailers including Murmic (Delaware, 1965), Custom Electronics (Washington, DC; 1969), Certified TV & Appliance (Virginia, 1969), and Woodville Appliances (Ohio, 1970). Samuel's son Alan joined the business in 1966, at a time when the store was focused on selling stereos. Predicting the end of the stereo boom, Alan Wurtzel converted the stores into full-line electronic specialty retailers.

The company took its boldest step in 1975 when it spent half of its net worth to open an electronics superstore in Richmond. The store was an immediate success, and in 1981 Wurtzel made the fateful decision to branch into the New York market with the purchase of Lafayette Radio Electronics. In New York the company found itself unable to compete with exuberant competitors like Crazy Eddie and abandoned the market. From its experiences in New York, Wurtzel developed the strategy of concentrating the stores in southern and western markets. In 1984 the company changed its name to Circuit City.

In 1986 Wurtzel stepped down to spend more time with his family, and company leadership passed to Richard Sharp, an ex–computer consultant who had designed Circuit City's advanced computerized sales system. Sharp made it a company priority to maintain one of the most efficient distribution and records systems in the industry.

Earnings slipped 18% in 1990 as consumer spending dropped and the electronics industry was slow to introduce new blockbuster products. During this time Circuit City expanded its operations to mall settings by opening the first of its mall-based Impulse stores.

In 1991 the company became the first superstore retailer to offer the IBM PS/1 computer. That same year Circuit City took its first steps into the Texas market, beginning construction on stores in Dallas, Houston, and Austin.

WHAT

Product Category	% of Sales
TV	24
VCR	22
Audio	22
Other electronics	14
Appliances	18
Total	**100**

	No. of Stores
Superstore	157
Circuit City	14
Impulse	14
Total	**185**

RANKINGS

373rd in *Forbes* Sales 500
629th in *Business Week* 1000

KEY COMPETITORS

Costco	Price Co.
Dayton Hudson	Sears
Dillard	Service Merchandise
Kmart	Sharper Image
Montgomery Ward	Tandy
J. C. Penney	Wal-Mart

HOW MUCH

Fiscal year ends February of following year	9-Year Growth	1981	1982	1983	1984	1985	1986	1987	1988	1989	1990
Sales ($ mil.)	33.5%	176	246	357	519	705	1,011	1,350	1,722	2,097	2,367
Net income ($ mil.)	45.5%	2	4	12	20	22	35	50	69	78	57
Income as % of sales	—	1.1%	1.8%	3.4%	3.9%	3.1%	3.5%	3.7%	4.0%	3.7%	2.4%
Earnings per share ($)	40.5%	0.06	0.12	0.31	0.48	0.49	0.79	1.13	1.53	1.70	1.22
Stock price – high ($)	—	0.74	1.03	4.49	7.38	7.75	17.13	20.81	22.63	27.00	29.00
Stock price – low ($)	—	0.33	0.36	0.85	2.91	4.66	5.88	8.50	9.31	17.69	9.00
Stock price – close ($)	46.2%	0.42	0.90	4.06	5.34	6.22	15.31	9.19	17.69	21.75	12.75
P/E – high	—	13	9	15	15	16	22	19	15	16	24
P/E – low	—	6	3	3	6	9	7	8	6	10	7
Dividends per share ($)	35.6%	0.01	0.01	0.01	0.02	0.02	0.03	0.04	0.06	0.08	0.10
Book value per share ($)	33.5%	0.59	0.72	1.21	2.04	2.54	3.36	4.50	6.05	7.83	7.92

1990 Year-end:
Debt ratio: 20.5%
Return on equity: 15.5%
Cash (mil.): $25
Current ratio: 1.73
Long-term debt (mil.): $94
No. of shares (mil.): 46
Dividends:
  1990 average yield: 0.7%
  1990 payout: 7.8%
Market value (mil.): $591

Stock Price History High/Low 1981–90

CITICORP

NYSE symbol: CCI
Fiscal year ends: December 31

Hoover's Rating C-

OVERVIEW

New York–based Citicorp, with its primary operating company, Citibank, is the largest banking enterprise in the US, and a major force in international banking. The bank is one of the largest residential mortgage lenders and remains the leading issuer of credit cards in the US. Citicorp has invested heavily in technology and owns Quotron, a major on-line financial information distributor.

After years of rapid expansion, Citicorp is changing its hard-charging ways. Capital adequacy concerns and the prospect of

substantial increases in provisions for bad real estate and Third-World loans have refocused the bank on quickly raising equity and cutting costs.

Citicorp slashed its dividend in early 1991. Chairman John Reed and president Richard Braddock have personally taken control of problem-ridden US real estate lending and Australian corporate banking units. The bank's problems have left it on the sidelines during the recent wave of bank mergers.

WHO

Chairman: John S. Reed, age 52, $1,201,242 pay
President: Richard S. Braddock, age 49, $825,826 pay
Controller and Principal Financial Officer: Roger W. Trupin, age 49
Director Human Resources: Gerald Lieberman
Auditors: KPMG Peat Marwick
Employees: 95,000

WHERE

HQ: 399 Park Ave., New York, NY 10043
Phone: 212-559-1000
Fax: 212-527-3277

Citicorp operates in 90 countries.

	1990 Average Total Assets	
	$ mil.	% of total
US	132,781	57
North America	4,949	2
Caribbean, Central & South America	15,726	7
Europe, Middle East & Africa	48,224	21
Asia/Pacific	30,108	13
Total	**231,788**	**100**

WHAT

	1990 Assets	
	$ mil.	% of total
Cash & due from banks	7,098	3
Deposits	7,546	3
Investment securities	14,075	7
Trading account assets	7,518	3
Federal funds sold & securities purchased under resale agreements	4,071	2
Loans	156,308	72
Credit loss allowance	(4,451)	(2)
Customer acceptance liability	2,165	1
Other	22,656	11
Total	**216,986**	**100**

Services

Global Consumer	Global Finance
Checking and savings	Cash management
Consumer loans	Corporate banking
Credit cards	Corporate finance
Electronic banking	Foreign exchange
Investment accounts	Investment banking
	Securities trading

WHEN

Colonel Samuel Osgood, first commissioner of the US Treasury, founded City Bank of New York in 1812. City Bank initially served cotton, sugar, metal, and coal merchants. During the Civil War the bank changed its name to National City Bank of New York.

In the early 1900s the bank opened its first foreign (London, 1902) and Latin American (Buenos Aires, 1914) branches. The bank expanded into retail (consumer) banking in the 1920s, opening branches for individuals (1921) and becoming the first commercial bank to make personal loans (1928). During the 1920s and 1930s, the bank's international operations grew (to 100 foreign offices by 1939).

James Stillman Rockefeller, who expanded the bank's retail banking in the late 1940s and early 1950s, became president in 1952. In 1955 the bank merged with First National (New York) to become First National City Bank. In 1961 the bank, under VP Walter Wriston, invented the certificate of deposit (CD), paying a higher interest rate on funds deposited for specified time periods. With CDs the bank could compete for funds with US government securities. Wriston served as president from 1967 to 1970 and chairman from 1970 to 1984, leading the bank to international prominence.

In 1968 the bank formed a bank holding company, First National City Corporation (renamed Citicorp in 1974) to offer

nonbanking financial services. Other major banks soon formed holding companies. At the end of 1968, Citibank replaced Chase Manhattan as the largest New York City bank, with $19.4 billion in assets.

Citibank became a major issuer of VISA and MasterCard in the 1970s and acquired Carte Blanche (1978) and Diners Club (1981). In 1977 Citibank was the first bank to introduce automated teller machines (ATMs) on a large scale, installing 500 in the New York City area alone. John Reed, who developed the ATM and consumer banking markets, became chairman when Wriston retired (1984).

At the end of 1980, the bank passed BankAmerica to become the largest US bank, with $114.9 billion in assets. In the 1980s Citibank's acquisitions included Fidelity Savings (California, 1982), First Federal of Chicago (1984), Biscayne Federal (Miami, 1984), and National Permanent Savings (Washington, DC; 1986).

The bank's loans to foreign countries became a problem in the late 1980s. Citicorp surprised competitors by reserving $3 billion in 1987 and $1 billion in 1989 against possible foreign losses.

In 1990 Citicorp raised $1.2 billion in fresh capital, nearly 1/2 of it from a Saudi prince, and sold 50.3% of Ambac, its profitable municipal bond insurance operation.

RANKINGS

1st in *Fortune* 100 Commercial Banking Cos.
132nd in *Business Week* 1000

KEY COMPETITORS

H. F. Ahmanson	Dai-Ichi Kangyo	Knight-Ridder
American Express	Deutsche Bank	Mead
ADP	Dow Jones	Mellon Bank
Bank of New York	Dun & Bradstreet	J.P. Morgan
BankAmerica	First Chicago	PNC Financial
Banc One	First Fidelity	Reuters
Bankers Trust	First Interstate	Royal Bank
Barnett Banks	Fleet/Norstar	SunTrust
Canadian Imperial	Great Western	Union Bank of
Chase Manhattan	H&R Block	Switzerland
Chemical Banking	HSBC	Wells Fargo
Crédit Lyonnais	Industrial Bank	
CS Holding	of Japan	

HOW MUCH

	9-Year Growth	1981	1982	1983	1984	1985	1986	1987	1988	1989	1990
Assets ($ mil.)	6.9%	119,232	129,997	134,655	150,586	173,597	196,124	203,607	207,666	230,643	216,986
Net income ($ mil.)	(5.5%)	531	723	860	890	998	1,058	(1,138)	1,698	498	318
Income as % of assets	—	0.4%	0.6%	0.6%	0.6%	0.6%	0.5%	(0.6%)	0.8%	0.2%	0.1%
Earnings per share ($)	(13.1%)	2.01	2.67	3.08	3.18	3.56	3.57	(4.26)	4.87	1.16	0.57
Stock price – high ($)	—	15.19	20.00	23.06	20.25	25.88	31.88	34.19	27.00	29.63	29.63
Stock price – low ($)	—	10.44	10.75	15.25	13.69	18.44	23.44	15.88	18.00	24.63	10.75
Stock price – close ($)	0.0%	12.63	16.25	18.56	19.38	24.69	26.50	18.63	25.88	28.88	12.63
P/E – high	—	8	8	8	6	7	9	—	6	31	52
P/E – low	—	5	4	5	4	5	7	—	4	21	19
Dividends per share ($)	9.3%	0.78	0.86	0.94	1.03	1.13	0.92	1.32	1.45	1.59	1.74
Book value per share ($)	4.0%	17.08	18.92	21.00	22.91	25.31	27.96	22.83	25.93	25.36	24.34

1990 Year-end:
Return on equity: 2.3%
Equity as % of assets: 4.5%
Cash (mil.): $14,644
Long-term debt (mil.): $23,187
No. of shares (mil.): 337
Dividends:
  1990 average yield: 13.8%
  1990 payout: 305.3%
Market value (mil.): $4,248
Sales (mil.): $38,385

Stock Price History High/Low 1981–90

THE CLOROX COMPANY

OVERVIEW

Based in Oakland, Clorox is the #1 bleach producer in the US, with over 50% of the domestic market. The company also owns dominant brands in several other categories including household cleanser (Pine Sol), charcoal (Kingsford, Match Light), salad dressing (Hidden Valley), drain opener (Liquid-plumr), and barbecue sauce (K.C. Masterpiece). Clorox also sells bottled water under the Deer Park and Deep Rock labels and through its Moore's division provides food to the food service industry.

In 1991 Clorox pulled out of the laundry detergent business (it entered the business in 1988) after it was battered by heavyweights Procter & Gamble and Unilever. Clorox had hoped to carve out about a 5% market share by introducing a detergent with bleach. The plan backfired when P&G retaliated by introducing Tide With Bleach, which it supported with massive advertising muscle. While Clorox was licking its wounds, P&G's brand stung the company further by stealing a chunk of its bleach market share.

Foreign sales account for less than 10% of total sales.

WHEN

Known in its first few years as the Electro-Alkaline Company, Clorox was founded in 1913 by 5 Oakland investors to make bleach using water from salt ponds around San Francisco Bay. The next year the company registered the brand name Clorox and its diamond-shaped trademark; the name is believed to come from the product's 2 main ingredients, chlorine and sodium hydroxide. At first Clorox sold only industrial strength bleach, but in 1916 the company formulated a less concentrated household solution.

With the establishment of a Philadelphia distributor in 1921, Clorox began a national expansion. The company went public in 1928. In the late 1930s Clorox built 2 more plants, in Chicago and New Jersey; in the late 1940s and early 1950s it opened 9 more plants throughout the country. In 1957 Procter & Gamble (P&G) bought Clorox. Antitrust questions were raised by the FTC, and litigation ensued over the next decade. P&G was ordered to divest Clorox, and in 1969 Clorox again became an independent company.

Following its split with P&G, Clorox implemented plans to add new products, mostly household consumer goods and foods, acquiring the brands Liquid-plumr (drain opener, 1969), Formula 409 (spray cleaner, 1970), Litter Green (cat litter, 1971), and Hidden Valley Ranch (salad dressings, 1972). In 1970 the company introduced Clorox 2, a non-chlorine bleach to compete with new enzymatic cleaners. Clorox entered the specialty food products business by buying Grocery Store Products (Kitchen Bouquet, 1971), Martin-Brower (food products and restaurant equipment for the food service industry, 1972), and Kingsford (charcoal briquets, 1973). Sales of $412 million in 1973 put Clorox into the *Fortune* 500 for the first time.

In 1974 Henkel, a large West German maker of cleansers and detergents, purchased 15% of Clorox stock as part of an agreement to share research, later expanded to include joint manufacturing and marketing. Beginning in 1977 Clorox sold off Country Kitchen Foods (1979) and other subsidiaries and brands to focus on household products, particularly those sold through grocery stores. Also in 1977 Clorox introduced Soft Scrub, the first liquid cleanser in the US.

During the 1980s the company launched a variety of new products including Match Light (instant-lighting charcoal, 1980), Tilex (stain remover, 1981), and Fresh Step (cat litter, 1984). In 1990 the company bought American Cyanamid's household products group, which included Pine Sol cleanser and Combat insecticide, for $465 million. Clorox is currently testing the waters with a foray into the frozen dinner market under the Hidden Valley name.

HOW MUCH

	9-Year Growth	1981	1982	1983	1984	1985	1986	1987	1988	1989	1990
Sales ($ mil.)	8.5%	714	867	914	975	1,055	1,089	1,126	1,260	1,356	1,484
Net income ($ mil.)	16.8%	38	45	66	80	86	96	105	133	146	154
Income as % of sales	—	5.3%	5.2%	7.2%	8.2%	8.2%	8.8%	9.3%	10.5%	10.7%	10.4%
Earnings per share ($)	14.5%	0.83	0.93	1.32	1.51	1.59	1.75	1.90	2.40	2.63	2.80
Stock price – high ($)	—	7.06	14.00	18.25	15.50	25.25	30.19	36.00	33.75	44.50	45.38
Stock price – low ($)	—	4.88	5.31	10.25	11.25	13.75	22.00	23.50	26.13	30.13	32.13
Stock price – close ($)	23.6%	5.63	12.38	13.25	14.38	23.81	25.31	27.75	31.00	42.00	37.75
P/E – high	—	9	15	14	10	16	17	19	14	17	16
P/E – low	—	6	6	8	7	9	13	12	11	11	11
Dividends per share ($)	13.7%	0.41	0.43	0.48	0.54	0.62	0.70	0.79	0.92	1.09	1.29
Book value per share ($)	11.9%	5.45	5.88	6.74	8.20	9.18	10.31	11.51	13.19	14.19	15.00

1990 Year-end:
Debt ratio: 0.9%
Return on equity: 19.2%
Cash (mil.): $125
Current ratio: 1.86
Long-term debt (mil.): $8
No. of shares (mil.): 54
Dividends:
  1990 average yield: 3.4%
  1990 payout: 46.1%
Market value (mil.): $2,040

Stock Price History High/Low 1981–90

NYSE symbol: CLX
Fiscal year ends: June 30

Hoover's Rating A-

WHO

Chairman and CEO: Charles R. Weaver, age 61, $1,127,321 pay
President and COO: Robert A. Bolingbroke, age 52, $452,662 pay
EVP Technology: Sheldon N. Lewis, age 56, $579,145 pay
VP and CFO: William F. Ausfahl, age 50
VP Human Resources: John J. Calderini, age 54
Auditors: Deloitte & Touche
Employees: 5,500

WHERE

HQ: 1221 Broadway, Oakland, CA 94612-1888
Phone: 415-271-7000
Fax: 415-465-8875

Clorox sells products in 73 countries and produces them in more than 40 plants in the US and abroad.

WHAT

Domestic Brands
BBQ Bag (single-use briquets)
Brita (water filter systems)
Clorox (liquid bleach)
Clorox Clean-Up (household cleaner)
Clorox Pre-Wash (stain remover)
Clorox 2 (color-safe bleach)
Combat (insecticide)
Control (cat litter)
Deep Rock (bottled water)
Deer Park (bottled water)
Formula 409 (spray cleaner)
Fresh Step (cat litter)
Hidden Valley Ranch (salad dressings)
K.C. Masterpiece (barbecue sauce)
Kingsford (charcoal briquets and lighter)
Kitchen Bouquet (seasoning sauce)
Liquid-plumr (drain opener)
Litter Green (cat litter)
Match Light (instant-lighting briquets)
Moore's (food-service onion rings)
Pine Sol (cleaner)
Salad Crispins (minicroutons)
Soft Scrub (liquid cleanser)
Spruce Ups (moistened household wipes)
Tackle (household cleaner/disinfectant)
Take Heart (low-fat salad dressing)
Tilex (mildew stain remover)

International Brands
Ayudin (liquid chlorine bleach)
Cloro Plus (household cleaner)
Clorogar (bleach)
Sonic (bleach)

RANKINGS

262nd in *Fortune* 500 Industrial Cos.
304th in *Business Week* 1000

KEY COMPETITORS

Amway
Bayer
Bristol-Myers Squibb
BSN
Colgate-Palmolive
Dial
Eastman Kodak

Heinz
S.C. Johnson
Procter & Gamble
Source Perrier
Teledyne
Unilever

THE COASTAL CORPORATION

NYSE symbol: CGP
Fiscal year ends: December 31

 Hoover's Rating C-

OVERVIEW

Houston-based Coastal is the 12th largest energy company in the US. Its natural gas pipeline network stretches more than 19,500 miles, and the company handles nearly 13% of the natural gas consumed in the US. Coastal's pipeline systems purchase gas from producers, transport it, and sell it to end-users, utilities, and large industries.

Chairman and founder Oscar Wyatt — even though he has stepped down from the CEO job — is extending Coastal into the lucrative northeastern US with stakes in the Iriquois and Empire State pipelines. Expansion into California has been put on hold.

Coastal subsidiaries operate 6 US refineries, a fleet of tugs, tankers, and barges, and 808 C-Mart convenience/gas stores. Coastal subsidiaries are involved in compressed natural gas (CNG) service stations in Denver and Wisconsin. The company also mines coal in West Virginia, Kentucky, Virginia, and Utah. It drills for oil and gas in 15 states and in the Gulf of Mexico, and owns power generation plants in the eastern US.

WHO

Chairman: Oscar S. Wyatt, Jr., age 66, $1,202,606 pay
President and CEO: James R. Paul, age 56, $917,935 pay
EVP and CFO: David A. Arledge, age 46, $514,085
VP Corporate Communications and Employee Relations: E. C. Simpson
Auditors: Deloitte & Touche
Employees: 13,900

WHEN

After boyhood summers working in the oil fields, a stint as a bomber pilot in WWII, and earning a mechanical engineering degree from Texas A&M, Oscar Wyatt started a small natural gas gathering business in Corpus Christi, Texas. It was 1951.

In 1955 the company became Coastal States Gas Producing Company. It collected and distributed natural gas from South Texas oil fields. In 1962 Coastal purchased Sinclair Oil's Corpus Christi refinery and pipeline network. Also in the early 1960s a Coastal subsidiary, Lo-Vaca Gathering, supplied natural gas to Texas cities and utilities. During the energy crisis of the early 1970s, Lo-Vaca curtailed its natural gas supplies and then raised prices. Unhappy customers sued Coastal, and regulators in 1977 ordered Lo-Vaca to refund $1.6 billion. To finance the settlement, Coastal spun off Lo-Vaca as Valero Energy.

Meanwhile, the combative Wyatt, who would earn a reputation as one of the swashbuckling corporate raiders of the 1980s, had been expanding Coastal through a series of deals. Coastal won Rio Grande Valley Gas, a small South Texas pipeline (1968), and then in 1973 mounted a successful $182 million hostile bid for Colorado Interstate Gas and changed its name to Coastal States Gas Corporation. With aggressive acquisitions, Coastal moved into low-sulfur Utah coal (Southern Utah Fuel, 1973), New England pipelines

(Union Petroleum, 1973), California refining (Pacific Refining, 1976), and Florida petroleum marketing and transportation (Belcher Oil, 1977; renamed in 1990). In 1980 Coastal adopted its present name.

Wyatt tried to snare Texas Gas Resources (1983) and Houston Natural Gas (1984). The bids were thwarted, but when the companies bought back stock owned by Coastal to defend themselves, Coastal made money. Wyatt, a tenacious opponent, led the company in the courtroom as well as the boardroom. Among the lawsuits fought during his tenure was a libel action against a Houston newspaper that compared him to J. R. Ewing of TV's "Dallas." (The litigants settled out of court.)

In 1985 Coastal purchased Detroit-based American Natural Resources in a $2.45 billion hostile takeover. In 1989, just before Wyatt stepped down as CEO, Coastal bid $2.6 billion for Texas Eastern, but Texas Eastern sold to "white knight" Panhandle Eastern.

Before the 1991 Gulf War, Wyatt flirted with the Iraqis in an effort to exchange refining and marketing assets for a steady supply of crude (Coastal and Libya share ownership in a German refinery). Wyatt and Coastal director John B. Connally, the former secretary of the treasury, met with Saddam Hussein and flew hostages out of Baghdad, but Wyatt's statements against Operation Desert Storm drew harsh criticism in the US.

WHERE

HQ: Nine Greenway Plaza, Houston, TX 77046
Phone: 713-877-1400
Fax: 713-877-6754

Coastal operates in the US, Canada, Europe, and Aruba.

WHAT

	1990 Sales		1990 Operating Income	
	$ mil.	% of total	$ mil.	% of total
Natural gas	2,206	24	394	51
Refining & marketing	6,484	69	243	31
Oil & gas	248	3	61	8
Coal	443	4	77	10
Adjustments	—	—	(56)	—
Total	**9,381**	**100**	**719**	**100**

Subsidiaries/Divisions

Exploration and Production
ANR Production Co.
CIG Exploration, Inc.
Javelina Co. (40%)
Coastal Limited Ventures, Inc.
Coastal Oil & Gas Corp.

Natural Gas
ANR Pipeline Co.
ANR Storage Co.
Coastal Gas Marketing Co.
Colorado Interstate Gas Co.
Great Lakes Gas Transmission Co. (50%)
High Island Offshore System (40%)
U-T Offshore System (33.3%)
Wyoming Interstate Co. Ltd.

Chemicals
Coastal Biotechnology
Coastal Chem, Inc.

Refining, Marketing, and Distribution
Coastal Aruba Refining Co. NV
Coastal Derby Refining Co.
Coastal Eagle Point Oil Co.
Coastal Fuels Marketing, Inc.
Coastal Mart, Inc. (C-Mart)
Coastal Mobile Refining Co.
Coastal Oil New England, Inc.
Coastal Oil New York, Inc.
Coastal Refining & Marketing, Inc.
Holborn Europa Raffinerie GmbH (33.3%)
Pacific Refining Co. (50%)

Coal
ANR Coal Co.
Coastal Coal Sales, Inc.
Coastal Power Production Co.
Coastal Remediation Co.
Coastal States Energy Co.
Skyline Coal Co.
Southern Utah Fuel Co.

HOW MUCH

	9-Year Growth	1981	1982	1983	1984	1985	1986	1987	1988	1989	1990
Sales ($ mil.)	5.3%	5,910	5,799	5,963	6,260	7,275	6,668	7,429	8,187	8,271	9,381
Net income ($ mil.)	—	(20)	66	94	102	142	72	113	157	178	226
Income as % of sales	—	(0.3%)	1.1%	1.6%	1.6%	2.0%	1.1%	1.5%	1.9%	2.2%	2.4%
Earnings per share ($)	—	(0.37)	0.71	1.07	1.31	1.56	0.56	1.39	1.79	1.89	2.15
Stock price – high ($)	—	16.03	10.03	9.76	10.57	17.44	17.78	26.92	23.67	33.08	39.63
Stock price – low ($)	—	6.80	3.80	4.95	6.96	8.19	10.44	14.00	17.58	22.00	29.25
Stock price – close ($)	14.5%	9.53	5.29	9.02	8.37	17.39	15.56	17.33	22.83	33.08	32.25
P/E – high	—	—	14	9	8	11	32	19	13	17	18
P/E – low	—	—	5	5	5	5	19	10	10	12	14
Dividends per share ($)	15.4%	0.11	0.11	0.11	0.22	0.16	0.18	0.24	0.27	0.30	0.40
Book value per share ($)	13.9%	5.92	6.53	7.43	8.45	11.40	11.58	12.67	14.24	17.36	19.12

1990 Year-end:
Debt ratio: 63.4%
Return on equity: 11.8%
Cash (mil.): $71
Current ratio: 1.09
Long-term debt (mil.): $3,436
No. of shares (mil.): 104
Dividends:
  1990 average yield: 1.2%
  1990 payout: 18.6%
Market value (mil.): $3,341

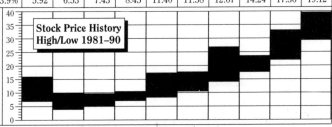

Stock Price History High/Low 1981–90

RANKINGS

51st in *Fortune* 500 Industrial Cos.
203rd in *Business Week* 1000

KEY COMPETITORS

Amoco	Exxon	Phillips
Ashland	Koch	Petroleum
Atlantic Richfield	Mobil	Sun
Chevron	Oryx	Tenneco
Columbia Gas	Pennzoil	Texaco
Du Pont	Panhandle	Unocal
Enron	Eastern	USX

THE COCA-COLA COMPANY

NYSE symbol: KO
Fiscal year ends: December 31

Hoover's Rating **A+**

OVERVIEW

Atlanta-based Coca-Cola is the world's largest soft drink producer. The Coke and Coca-Cola trademarks are the world's best known.

One of the South's great enterprises, Coke has also emerged as one of America's foremost global marketers. Despite aggressive advertising by Pepsi, Coke has maintained or expanded market share.

Although the mature US market consumes 292 servings per person per year and the overseas market only 59, the overseas average is rising rapidly. Foreign operations currently generate 60% of sales and 80% of profits. Coke's market share of the global soft drink business is now 44%.

Coca-Cola uses a franchise system for distribution, with local bottlers purchasing syrup or concentrate from Coke. The largest US bottler is a $4 billion public company, Coca-Cola Enterprises.

Coke is also a leading citrus products maker (Minute Maid). Coke and Nestlé are jointly marketing canned coffee in Korea.

Coca-Cola has a long record of profitable growth and financial strength. It has also been an influential citizen of Atlanta: early leader Asa Candler gave land to Emory University and later chief Robert Woodruff gave Emory over $200 million.

WHEN

Atlanta pharmacist John S. Pemberton invented Coke in 1886. His bookkeeper Frank Robinson named the product after 2 ingredients, kola nuts and coca leaves (later cleaned of narcotics), and wrote the name in the now-familiar script. By 1891 Atlanta druggist Asa Candler had bought the company for $2,300. By 1895 the soda fountain drink was available in all states, entering Canada and Mexico by 1898.

Candler sold most US bottling rights in 1899 to Benjamin Thomas and John Whitehead of Chattanooga for $1.00. With the backing of John Lupton, these men developed the regional franchise bottling system, creating over 1,000 bottlers within 20 years. The bottlers used the contoured bottle designed by the C. J. Root Glass Company (Terre Haute, Indiana) in 1916.

In 1916 Candler retired to become Atlanta's mayor; his family sold the company to Atlanta banker Ernest Woodruff for $25 million in 1919, the same year Coca-Cola went public. In 1923 Woodruff appointed his son Robert president. Robert continued as chairman until 1942 and remained influential until his death in 1985 at age 95.

Robert Woodruff's contributions were in advertising and overseas expansion. He introduced "The Pause that Refreshes" (1929) and "It's the Real Thing" (1941), adding to the

"Delicious and Refreshing" slogan used in the early days. During WWII Woodruff decreed that every soldier would have access to a 5-cent bottle of Coke. With government assistance Coca-Cola built 64 overseas bottling plants during WWII. Also during this period (1941) the company accepted "Coke" as an official name.

Coca-Cola bought Minute Maid in 1960 and introduced Sprite (now the world's #1 lemon-lime soft drink) in 1961, TAB in 1963, and Diet Coke in 1982. New Coke, introduced in 1985, was widely rejected, and the original formula soon returned as Coca-Cola Classic.

The company has entered and left several industries. The largest of these diversifications was the acquisition of Columbia Pictures in 1982, followed by other entertainment purchases (e.g., Merv Griffin Enterprises), all sold to Sony in 1989.

In 1986 the company consolidated the US bottling operations it owned into Coca-Cola Enterprises (CCE) and sold 51% of the new company, the largest US soft drink bottler, to the public. US price wars have led to weak earnings for CCE, which in 1991 announced plans to buy #2 bottler Johnston Coca-Cola. The 2 bottlers produce 55% of US Coke.

WHO

Chairman and CEO: Robert Goizueta, age 59, $2,962,000 pay
President and COO: Donald Keough, age 64, $2,102,500 pay
SVP and CFO: Jack L. Stahl, age 37
Director of Strategic Communications: Linda Peek
VP Human Resources: Michael Walters
Auditors: Ernst & Young
Employees: 24,000

WHERE

HQ: One Coca-Cola Plaza, NW, Atlanta, GA 30313
Phone: 404-676-2121
Fax: 404-676-6792

Soft drink products are sold in over 160 countries; syrup and/or concentrates are made at 44 plants worldwide.

	1990 Sales		1990 Operating Income	
	$ mil.	% of total	$ mil.	% of total
US	3,931	39	440	19
Latin America	813	8	300	13
European Community	2,805	28	667	30
Pacific & Canada	2,080	20	672	30
NE Europe & Africa	563	5	174	8
Adjustments	44	—	(301)	—
Total	**10,236**	**100**	**1,952**	**100**

WHAT

	1990 Sales		1990 Operating Income	
	$ mil.	% of total	$ mil.	% of total
US soft drinks	2,461	24	358	16
Int'l. soft drinks	6,125	60	1,801	80
Foods	1,605	16	94	4
Adjustments	45	—	(301)	—
Total	**10,236**	**100**	**1,952**	**100**

Brand Names

Soft Drinks	
Caffeine-free Coca-Cola	Minute Maid
Caffeine-free Diet Coke	Mr. PiBB
Caffeine-free TAB	PowerAde
Cherry Coke	Ramblin' Root Beer
Coca-Cola	Santiba
Coca-Cola Classic	Sprite
Coke	TAB
Diet Cherry Coke	
Diet Coke	**Juices and Foods**
Diet Minute Maid	Bacardi Tropical Fruit
Diet Sprite	Mixers
Fanta	Belmont Springs Water
Fresca	Bright & Early
Hi-C	Five Alive
Mello Yello	Hi-C
	Minute Maid

RANKINGS

47th in *Fortune* 500 Industrial Cos.
9th in *Business Week* 1000

KEY COMPETITORS

Bass	Kirin
BSN	Nestlé
Cadbury Schweppes	PepsiCo
Chiquita Brands	Procter & Gamble
Dole	Seagram
Dr Pepper/7Up	Source Perrier
Heineken	Whitman

HOW MUCH

	9-Year Growth	1981	1982	1983	1984	1985	1986	1987	1988	1989	1990
Sales ($ mil.)	6.3%	5,889	6,250	6,829	7,364	7,904	8,669	7,658	8,338	8,966	10,236
Net income ($ mil.)	13.4%	447	512	558	629	678	934	916	1,045	1,193	1,382
Income as % of sales	—	7.6%	8.2%	8.2%	8.5%	8.6%	10.8%	12.0%	12.5%	13.3%	13.5%
Earnings per share ($)	14.5%	0.60	0.66	0.68	0.79	0.86	1.21	1.22	1.43	1.70	2.04
Stock price – high ($)	—	6.71	8.94	9.58	11.00	14.71	22.44	26.56	22.63	40.50	49.00
Stock price – low ($)	—	5.08	4.96	7.58	8.17	9.92	12.79	14.00	17.50	21.69	32.63
Stock price – close ($)	26.0%	5.79	8.67	8.92	10.40	14.08	18.88	19.06	22.31	38.63	46.50
P/E – high	—	11	14	14	14	17	19	22	16	24	24
P/E – low	—	8	8	11	10	12	11	12	12	13	16
Dividends per share ($)	8.4%	0.39	0.41	0.45	0.46	0.49	0.52	0.56	0.60	0.68	0.80
Book value per share ($)	7.0%	3.06	3.41	3.57	3.54	3.86	4.56	4.33	4.29	4.73	5.65

1990 Year-end:
Debt ratio: 12.2%
Return on equity: 39.3%
Cash (mil.): $1,492
Current ratio: 0.96
Long-term debt (mil.): $536
No. of shares (mil.): 668
Dividends:
　1990 average yield: 1.7%
　1990 payout: 39.2%
Market value (mil.): $31,073

Stock Price History High/Low 1981–90

COLGATE-PALMOLIVE COMPANY

OVERVIEW

Although headquartered in New York, Colgate-Palmolive is a true multinational, deriving 67% of its sales from outside the US. The company ranks 2nd in household consumer products (after Procter & Gamble), selling such brands as Ajax (cleanser), Fab (detergent), Irish Spring (soap), and Hill's (pet food).

Marketed in more than 160 countries, the Colgate brand is the world's best-selling toothpaste with over 40% of the global market. The company hopes to begin producing toothpaste in the Soviet Union in 1991.

Colgate's Ajax brand is the world's #1 brand in household cleaning, while the company's hand dishwashing products dominate 22 of the 39 countries in which they are sold. Colgate is also the largest marketer of bleach outside the US, distributing bleach throughout Asia and Mexico through a joint venture with Clorox.

The company plans to sustain its growth by entering new product categories, expanding its already formidable overseas presence, and introducing new products. In 1990 alone Colgate launched more than 200 new products.

WHEN

In 1806 William Colgate founded The Colgate Company in Manhattan to produce soap, candles, and starch. The company moved to Jersey City in 1847. William Colgate died 10 years later, and the company passed to his son Samuel, who renamed it Colgate and Company. In 1877 the company introduced Colgate Dental Cream, which it began selling in a tube in 1890. By 1906 Colgate was making 160 kinds of soap, 625 perfumes, and 2,000 other products. The company went public in 1908.

In 1898 a Milwaukee soap maker, B. J. Johnson Soap Company (founded in 1864), introduced Palmolive, a soap made of palm and olive oils. The product became so popular that the firm changed its name to the Palmolive company in 1917. In 1927 Palmolive merged with fine soap maker Peet Brothers, a Kansas City company founded in 1872. Palmolive-Peet merged with Colgate in 1928, forming Colgate-Palmolive-Peet (shortened to Colgate-Palmolive in 1953). The stock market crash of 1929 prevented a planned merger of the company with Hershey and Kraft.

During the 1930s the company purchased French and German soap makers and opened branches in Europe. After WWII the Ajax, Colgate, and Palmolive brands were outselling competitors in European markets. The company expanded its operations to the Far East by opening several new plants in the 1950s. By 1961 foreign sales were 52% of the total.

Colgate-Palmolive introduced several new products in the 1960s including Cold Power detergent (1965), Palmolive dishwashing liquid (1966), Ultra Brite toothpaste (1968), and Colgate with MFP (1968). During the 1960s and 1970s the company diversified by buying approximately 70 other companies including Helena Rubenstein (1973), Ram Golf (1974), and Maui Divers (1977). The strategy failed, however, and most were sold in the 1980s.

In the late 1980s the company, under CEO Reuben Mark, launched a reorganization to focus on building Colgate-Palmolive's core businesses: personal care and household products. In 1987 the company took a $145 million charge against earnings to cover reorganization and asset disposition costs.

Products introduced during the 1980s include Palmolive automatic dishwasher detergent (1986), Colgate Tartar Control toothpaste (1986), and Fab 1-Shot laundry detergent (1987). The company strengthened its hold on the global bleach market through its purchases of Cotelle (France, 1988), Klorin (Scandinavia, 1988), Unisol (Portugal, 1990), and Javex (Canada's #1 bleach producer, 1990). Other recent Colgate-Palmolive acquisitions include McKesson's veterinary distribution business (1989), Vipont Pharmaceutical (1990), OraPharm (dental products, Australia, 1990), and the dental therapeutics unit of Scherer Laboratories (1990).

NYSE symbol: CL
Fiscal year ends: December 31

 Hoover's Rating **B-**

WHO

Chairman, President, and CEO: Reuben Mark, age 52, $1,554,148 pay
SEVP and COO: William S. Shanahan, age 50, $764,629 pay
SEVP: Roderick L. Turner, age 59, $601,833 pay
EVP and CFO: Robert M. Agate, age 55, $413,500 pay
SVP Human Resources: Douglas M. Reid, age 56
Auditors: Arthur Andersen & Co.
Employees: 24,800

WHERE

HQ: 300 Park Ave., New York, NY 10022-7499
Phone: 212-310-2000
Fax: 212-310-3284

Colgate-Palmolive operates 76 facilities in the US and 123 located in 41 foreign countries.

	1990 Sales		1990 Operating Income	
	$ mil.	% of total	$ mil.	% of total
US	1,899	33	209	36
Western Hemisphere	1,130	20	149	26
Europe	1,923	34	153	26
Far East & Africa	739	13	73	12
Adjustments	—	—	(47)	—
Total	**5,691**	**100**	**537**	**100**

WHAT

	1990 Sales		1990 Operating Income	
	$ mil.	% of total	$ mil.	% of total
Household & personal care	4,968	87	477	82
Specialty marketing	723	13	107	18
Adjustments	—	—	(47)	—
Total	**5,691**	**100**	**537**	**100**

Household Care
Ajax
Dermassage
HandiWipes
Palmolive
Stretch 'N Dust
Wash 'N Dri

Housewares & Gifts
Nouveau Cookware
Princess House Products (crystal and china)
Sterno (cooking products)

Laundry Care
Ajax
Axion
Cold Power
Dynamo 2
Fab
Fresh Start

Personal Care
Cleopatra (soap, Europe)
Colgate
Dermassage (lotion)
Irish Spring (soap)
Palmolive
Respons (hair care, Europe)
Sesame Street (children's products)
Softsoap
Ultra Brite
Vel Beauty Bar
Village (bath products)
Wildroot (hair care)

Pet Care
Fresh Feliners (cat box liners)
Hill's (pet food)

HOW MUCH

	9-Year Growth	1981	1982	1983	1984	1985	1986	1987	1988	1989	1990
Sales ($ mil.)	0.9%	5,261	4,888	4,865	4,910	4,524	4,985	4,366	4,734	5,039	5,691
Net income ($ mil.)	4.9%	208	197	198	54	168	177	1	153	280	321
Income as % of sales	—	4.0%	4.0%	4.1%	1.1%	3.7%	3.6%	0.0%	3.2%	5.6%	5.6%
Earnings per share ($)	5.8%	2.55	2.41	2.42	0.64	2.11	2.50	0.01	2.21	3.80	4.24
Stock price – high ($)	—	18.38	22.63	25.38	26.50	33.38	47.00	52.63	49.50	64.88	75.50
Stock price – low ($)	—	13.88	16.00	19.00	20.50	22.63	30.38	28.00	38.50	44.13	52.75
Stock price – close ($)	17.9%	16.75	19.63	21.50	24.88	32.75	40.88	39.25	47.00	63.50	73.75
P/E – high	—	7	9	10	41	16	19	5,263	22	17	18
P/E – low	—	5	7	8	32	11	12	2,800	17	12	12
Dividends per share ($)	5.2%	1.14	1.20	1.26	1.28	1.30	1.36	1.39	1.58	1.56	1.80
Book value per share ($)	(1.2%)	15.69	15.97	16.21	14.69	12.66	13.81	13.54	16.48	10.59	14.13

1990 Year-end:
Debt ratio: 43.9%
Return on equity: 34.3%
Cash (mil.): $276
Current ratio: 1.40
Long-term debt (mil.): $1,068
No. of shares (mil.): 67
Dividends:
1990 average yield: 2.4%
1990 payout: 42.5%
Market value (mil.): $4,912

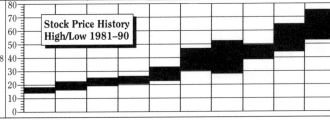
Stock Price History High/Low 1981–90

RANKINGS

94th in *Fortune* 500 Industrial Cos.
140th in *Business Week* 1000

KEY COMPETITORS

Amway
ADM
Avon
Brown-Forman
Carlsberg
Clorox
Corning

Dial
Gillette
Heinz
S. C. Johnson
L'Oréal
Mars

Nestlé
Pearson
Procter & Gamble
Quaker Oats
Ralston Purina
Unilever

THE COLUMBIA GAS SYSTEM, INC.

OVERVIEW

Columbia Gas, one of America's largest integrated gas systems, operates 23,000 miles of natural gas pipeline linking producing fields in the Gulf of Mexico, Texas, Louisiana, Appalachia, and Canada (a total of 3.1 million acres) with distributors in 14 states and the District of Columbia. Columbia's TriStar Ventures subsidiary develops gas-fired cogeneration facilities (producing both steam and electricity) throughout the US.

Columbia has been burdened by fixed-price supply contracts since the early 1980s. Originally intended to assure the company an uninterrupted supply of natural gas, the contracts have served only to drag down Columbia whenever the market price of gas falls below that owed to its suppliers. In the summer of 1991 efforts to renegotiate the contracts failed; Columbia defaulted on $39 million in short-term debt and then entered bankruptcy. Columbia has convinced a federal judge to nullify 4,100 of the fixed-price contracts, freeing the company from an estimated $1 billion in related losses over the next decade.

WHEN

In 1906, 4 eastern and midwestern businessmen founded Columbia Gas & Electric. Based in Huntington, West Virginia, Columbia managed about 232,000 acres of oil and gas fields in Kentucky and West Virginia and by 1909 operated a 180-mile natural gas pipeline serving 4 cities in Kentucky and Ohio. In 1926 Columbia merged with George Crawford's Ohio Fuel, which provided natural gas to parts of Ohio, Pennsylvania, and West Virginia. With Crawford as chairman, the new Columbia moved its headquarters to Wilmington, Delaware, and was listed on the NYSE in 1926. Purchases over the next 40 years expanded Columbia's service area to the District of Columbia, Maryland, and New York state.

In 1931 Columbia completed a 460-mile pipeline linking Washington to gas fields in Kentucky. After adopting its current name in 1948, the company bought Gulf Interstate Gas in 1958. Gulf operated an 845-mile pipeline linking Louisiana's gas fields to eastern Kentucky, where the gas was distributed. By 1972 Columbia was supplying about 10% of America's gas customers.

With fuel shortages predicted as early as 1970, Columbia explored for gas in Canada (1971) and arranged for delivery of gas from Alaska's North Slope (1974). Still, supplies ran short, forcing schools and factories to close throughout Columbia's territory during the winter of 1976–77.

Hoping to assure future supplies, Columbia (with Consolidated System LNG) built a liquid natural gas plant at Cove Point, Maryland, in 1978. The plant closed in 1980 over price disputes with Algerian suppliers, and in 1988 Columbia sold 50% interest in the plant to Shell Oil. In 1981 Columbia bought Commonwealth Natural Resources, expanding its service area to central and eastern Virginia.

In another effort to secure future gas supplies, Columbia entered into several take-or-pay contracts between 1982 and 1984, agreeing to buy large amounts of gas at the seller's price. These contracts required Columbia to pay for the gas whether or not the company could resell it. Gas supplies rose in the mid-1980s while demand fell, and Columbia faced bankruptcy by 1985, mostly as a result of the take-or-pay contracts. CEO John Croom renegotiated the contracts (1985), and by 1989 Columbia was operating with some of the lowest costs and most competitive rates in the industry.

In 1990 the company agreed to sell its New York distribution subsidiary to New York State Electric & Gas for $39 million. Mild winter weather (1990–91) impacted 1990 earnings, which were lower than management anticipated. The price of gas fell below the company's supply costs and ultimately caused Columbia to enter bankruptcy in 1991.

NYSE symbol: CG
Fiscal year ends: December 31

WHO

Chairman, President, and CEO: John H. Croom, age 58, $688,000 pay
EVP and CFO: Robert A. Oswald, age 45, $335,200 pay
VP Human Resources: Dennis P. Geran
Auditors: Arthur Andersen & Co.
Employees: 10,829

WHERE

HQ: 20 Montchanin Rd., Wilmington, DE 19807-0020
Phone: 302-429-5000
Fax: 302-429-5461

Columbia Gas operates a 23,000-mile gas pipeline system extending from the Gulf of Mexico to the Northeast. The company explores for oil and gas in the US and Canada.

WHAT

	1990 Sales		1990 Operating Income	
	$ mil.	% of total	$ mil.	% of total
Oil & gas	195	8	43	16
Transmission	627	27	128	47
Distribution	1,425	60	97	35
Other	111	5	6	2
Adjustments	—	—	(12)	—
Total	**2,358**	**100**	**262**	**100**

Oil and Gas Exploration
Columbia Gas Development Corp.
Columbia Gas Development of Canada Ltd.
Columbia Natural Resources, Inc.

Transmission Companies (Gas Pipeline)
Columbia Gas Transmission Corp. (18,800 miles through 14 states)
Columbia Gulf Transmission Co. (4,300 miles from Louisiana to Kentucky)
Columbia LNG Corp. (liquid natural gas terminal at Cove Point, MD)

Distribution Companies
Columbia Gas of Kentucky, Inc.
Columbia Gas of Maryland, Inc.
Columbia Gas of New York, Inc.
Columbia Gas of Pennsylvania, Inc.
Commonwealth Gas Services, Inc.

Other Energy Companies
Columbia Atlantic Trading Corp.
Columbia Coal Gasification Corp. (coal reserves)
Columbia Propane Corp.
Commonwealth Propane, Inc.
The Inland Gas Co., Inc.
TriStar Capital Corp.
TriStar Ventures Corp. (cogeneration plants)

RANKINGS

39th in *Fortune* 50 Utilities
312th in *Business Week* 1000

KEY COMPETITORS

Coastal
Enron
Occidental
Panhandle Eastern
Tenneco

HOW MUCH

	9-Year Growth	1981	1982	1983	1984	1985	1986	1987	1988	1989	1990
Sales ($ mil.)	(6.8%)	4,426	5,071	5,078	4,593	4,053	3,370	2,798	3,129	3,204	2,358
Net income ($ mil.)	(6.7%)	196	185	191	180	(94)	99	111	119	146	105
Income as % of sales	—	4.4%	3.6%	3.8%	3.9%	(2.3%)	3.0%	4.0%	3.8%	4.6%	4.4%
Earnings per share ($)	(9.6%)	5.50	5.10	4.87	4.22	(2.67)	2.12	2.29	2.46	3.19	*2.21*
Stock price – high ($)	—	41.50	33.88	35.50	37.50	40.00	46.00	56.50	44.75	52.75	54.75
Stock price – low ($)	—	27.88	26.88	27.88	27.00	26.75	34.75	35.50	26.88	33.75	41.50
Stock price – close ($)	4.3%	32.13	28.88	35.25	34.00	39.50	45.25	40.25	34.50	52.00	46.88
P/E – high	—	8	7	7	9	—	22	25	18	17	25
P/E – low	—	5	5	6	6	—	16	16	11	11	19
Dividends per share ($)	(2.3%)	2.70	2.86	3.02	3.18	3.18	3.18	3.18	2.30	2.00	2.20
Book value per share ($)	(1.1%)	38.50	40.73	41.16	41.22	35.10	34.06	34.08	34.18	35.50	34.83

1990 Year-end:
Debt ratio: 44.8%
Return on equity: 6.3%
Cash (mil.): $8
Current ratio: 0.76
Long-term debt (mil.): $1,429
No. of shares (mil.): 50
Dividends:
  1990 average yield: 4.7%
  1990 payout: 99.5%
Market value (mil.): $2,366

Stock Price History High/Low 1981–90

COMMERCE CLEARING HOUSE, INC.

OVERVIEW

Commerce Clearing House (CCH) publishes reports and books on tax and business law, provides state-required legal representation and other services to corporations, and processes income tax returns by computer. Legal reports are published in the US, Australia, Canada, the UK, New Zealand, Singapore, and Japan. The company also publishes Facts on File news-related reference materials and the "pink sheets," listings of daily over-the-counter stock quotations and dealer information.

CCH's finances remain strong but earnings are under pressure. Technological change has forced CCH to spend heavily to create CCH ACCESS, an on-line system designed to give automated access to the information contained in the company's legal publications. Most of the company's legal reports have been published in loose-leaf form. CCH has developed a tax system for PCs in response to new tax return processing competition from PC software companies.

The 1991 issuance of nonvoting Class B shares was intended to allow continued voting control of CCH by the Thorne family, owner of 56% of the company's stock.

WHEN

The Corporation Trust Company was formed in 1892 and began providing state-required legal representation to early customers such as U.S. Steel, AT&T, and Prudential. When the Tariff Act of 1913 was introduced, the company began publishing *The Income Tax Reporter*, providing information on this first federal income tax law, including the law's text, related administrative decisions, and other documents. The company began publications covering the new Federal Trade Commission and Federal Reserve Board in 1914, and subscriptions to the *Reporter* grew as tax laws were amended in 1916 and 1917.

By the late 1910s William KixMiller had started publishing import/export and income tax guides as Commerce Clearing House in Chicago. Both companies grew in the 1920s, reporting on the myriad new state, local, corporate, and inheritance tax laws. The 2 companies merged in 1927 as Commerce Clearing House (CCH), headquartered in Chicago.

CCH began buying independent state tax publications and utility and industrial indices and digests. In 1933 KixMiller sold his interest, and in the 1930s the company started new publications covering New Deal regulations and agencies. Tax increases brought on by WWII and reporting on war and labor law expanded CCH's publication list, and in 1945 CCH created a Canadian subsidiary.

The company published reports on the Defense Production Act (1950) after the outbreak of war in Korea, followed in the late 1950s by the *Corporation Law Guide* and the *New York Stock Exchange Guide*. CCH went public in 1961.

During the 1960s CCH started publications covering the European Common Market, taxes on interest and dividends, employment practices and accounting, British and Puerto Rican tax law, and education and environmental regulation. In 1965 CCH bought a Mexican tax and business law publisher and Facts on File and formed Computax, a joint venture.

In the late 1960s CCH published reports on consumer credit, mutual funds, Medicare, and personnel issues. New publications in the early 1970s dealt with the Tax Reform Act of 1969, the IRS, and workplace and product safety regulations. CCH bought companies, including the Washington Service Bureau (1979), a software operation (1980), and Trademark Research Corporation (1983). CCH bought 4 companies involved in tax processing in 1988 and 1989 and 2 microcomputer software companies in 1990. In 1989 CCH's Facts on File unit paid over $100,000 to settle a software piracy lawsuit.

In 1990 CCH announced plans for a CD-ROM-based federal tax product scheduled to be available in 1991.

NASDAQ symbol: CCLR
Fiscal year ends: December 31

Hoover's Rating **B+**

WHO

Chairman: Oakleigh B. Thorne, age 58, $303,938 pay
President and CEO: Edward L. Massie, age 61, $383,335 pay (prior to promotion)
VP, Treasurer, and CFO: Bernard Elafros, age 64
Group President: Oakleigh Thorne, age 33
Director of Personnel: Darde Gaertner
Auditors: Deloitte & Touche
Employees: 7,613

WHERE

HQ: 2700 Lake Cook Rd., Riverwoods, IL 60015
Phone: 708-940-4600
Fax: 708-940-0113

CCH operates in 50 states and 6 foreign countries.

	1990 Sales		1990 Operating Income	
	$ mil.	% of total	$ mil.	% of total
US	616	86	45	87
Other countries	100	14	7	13
Total	**716**	**100**	**52**	**100**

WHAT

	1990 Sales		1990 Operating Income	
	$ mil.	% of total	$ mil.	% of total
Publishing	398	56	40	76
Computer processing services	224	31	4	9
Legal info. services	94	13	8	15
Total	**716**	**100**	**52**	**100**

Publishing
CCH Asia Ltd.
CCH Australia Ltd.
CCH Canadian Ltd.
CCH Editions Ltd.
CCH Japan Ltd.
CCH New Zealand Ltd.
Commerce Clearing House, Inc.
Facts on File, Inc. (reference materials)
Les Publications CCH/FM Ltée
LYF, SA de CV (49%, Spanish language publications)
National Quotation Bureau, Inc. ("pink sheets")
State Capital Information Service, Inc. (government information services)

Computer Processing Services
Accutax Systems, Inc.
CCH Computax, Inc.
Taxx, Inc.
TLS Co.

Legal Information Services
CT Corporation System (representation)
McCord Co. (document distribution)
Trademark Research Corp. (trademark research)
Washington Service Bureau (government documents)

HOW MUCH

	9-Year Growth	1981	1982	1983	1984	1985	1986	1987	1988	1989	1990
Sales ($ mil.)	9.6%	313	350	379	414	454	505	552	612	677	716
Net income ($ mil.)	3.9%	29	32	25	40	45	48	53	49	34	41
Income as % of sales	—	9.2%	9.0%	6.6%	9.7%	9.9%	9.4%	9.6%	8.1%	5.1%	5.7%
Earnings per share ($)	4.1%	1.60	1.75	1.39	2.24	2.49	2.64	2.93	2.75	1.92	2.29
Stock price – high ($)	—	28.63	32.25	38.75	35.00	50.75	65.50	71.00	65.00	65.50	53.50
Stock price – low ($)	—	13.63	22.63	26.00	25.00	33.25	47.50	48.38	46.50	42.50	38.00
Stock price – close ($)	5.0%	28.63	31.00	30.00	33.25	49.25	61.00	61.50	47.50	43.00	44.50
P/E – high	—	18	18	28	16	20	25	24	24	34	23
P/E – low	—	9	13	19	11	13	18	17	17	22	17
Dividends per share ($)	9.5%	0.62	0.78	0.86	0.91	1.06	1.20	0.96	1.72	1.40	1.40
Book value per share ($)	15.8%	3.36	4.31	4.82	6.13	7.46	8.89	10.47	11.99	12.11	12.61

1990 Year-end:
Debt ratio: 6.2%
Return on equity: 18.5%
Cash (mil.): $117
Current ratio: 3.90
Long-term debt (mil.): $15
No. of shares (mil.): 18
Dividends:
    1990 average yield: 3.1%
    1990 payout: 61.1%
Market value (mil.): $784

Stock Price History
High/Low 1981–90

RANKINGS

410th in *Fortune* 500 Industrial Cos.
578th in *Business Week* 1000

KEY COMPETITORS

Dow Jones
Dun & Bradstreet
Knight-Ridder
Maxwell
McGraw-Hill
Mead
Reed
Thomson Corp.

COMMODORE INTERNATIONAL LTD.

NYSE symbol: CBU
Fiscal year ends: June 30

 Hoover's Rating C-

OVERVIEW

Commodore International, based in West Chester, Pennsylvania, is a leading manufacturer of PCs for the home market (estimated at 22% of the installed base) and is fast becoming a contender in the office PC market.

While sales of the entry-level Commodore 64 computer, introduced in 1982, have dropped to $160 million in 1990 from approximately $711 million in 1986, Commodore still sold over 700,000 units in 1990.

The Amiga 2000 and 3000 series (high-end graphic computers with multimedia capabilities), MS-DOS PC-compatible, and UNIX-based computers make up Commodore's professional PC line. For the 3rd year in a row,

Commodore's entry-level Amiga 500 was named "Home Computer of the Year" by European journalists.

The European market accounted for 75% of Commodore's 1990 revenues. Commodore is the #2 seller of PCs in Europe (IBM is #1). Total 1990 sales ran slightly behind 1989 but bounced back in 1991, with the first 3 quarters of revenues up 21% over the year-ago period.

In 1991, beating such formidable competitors as Sony and Microsoft to market, Commodore launched CDTV, a compact-disc-based interactive multimedia product targeted for the home entertainment market.

WHO

Chairman and CEO: Irving Gould, age 72, $1,750,000 pay
President: Mehdi R. Ali, age 46, $2,015,949 pay
EVP and COO: Henri Rubin, age 64, $435,511 pay
Director of Human Resources: Patricia Reikard
Auditors: Arthur Andersen & Co.
Employees: 3,000

WHERE

HQ: 1200 Wilson Dr., West Chester, PA 19380
Phone: 215-431-9100
Fax: 215-431-9156

Commodore markets its products through 17 sales offices in North America, Western Europe, Australia, and New Zealand and has manufacturing facilities in North America, Germany, and Hong Kong.

	1990 Sales		1990 Operating Income	
	$ mil.	% of total	$ mil.	% of total
North America	163	18	18	75
Europe	663	75	4	17
Asia/Australia	61	7	2	8
Adjustments	—	—	(6)	—
Total	**887**	**100**	**18**	**100**

WHEN

Commodore, founded by Jack Tramiel, started as Commodore Portable Typewriter, a typewriter repair shop, in the Bronx in 1954. Tramiel relocated the business to Toronto in 1956 and, with financing from a Canadian company, Atlantic Acceptance, expanded into selling adding machines and typewriters.

Tramiel turned to another Canadian financier, Irving Gould, following the bankruptcy of Atlantic in 1965. Gould loaned Commodore $400,000, acquired controlling interest, and became chairman. In 1969 Commodore began producing low-priced pocket calculators and eventually became a major player in the business. In 1975 Texas Instruments, Commodore's microprocessor supplier, put Commodore out of the calculator business by introducing a pocket calculator priced at $49 — $1 cheaper than the microprocessor it sold to Commodore. That year Commodore lost $5 million on sales of $50 million.

Tramiel countered by buying one of its suppliers, MOS Technology, in 1976 for $800,000. MOS manufactured the 6502 chip, which Commodore sold to computer companies (Apple and Atari) and later used in its own computers.

In 1977 Commodore introduced its first computer, the PET. It quickly became a

success, particularly in Europe, where there was less competition with Apple and Tandy's Radio Shack. Commodore followed with the VIC-20 and Commodore 64 computers, both introduced in 1982. Sales of the 2 computers took Commodore's revenues over the $1 billion mark in 1984.

In 1984, after a falling out with Commodore chairman Gould, Tramiel resigned and resurfaced in 1985 as owner and CEO of Atari, Commodore's primary competitor.

From 1984 to 1987 Commodore's sales dropped 36%, from $1.27 billion to $807 million. In 1985 Commodore introduced the Amiga — a high-end home computer with superior color graphics — anticipating its sales would revive the company. But the Amiga was expensive for the home market and lacked the software and standard DOS operating system used in IBM PCs and compatibles for the business market. Commodore has since added a DOS PC-compatible to its Amiga line as well as a UNIX-based model. In 1990 the company introduced a DOS-based notebook-size computer. Atari founder Nolan Bushnell joined Commodore in 1990 to assist in developing and launching the company's CDTV, a compact disc home entertainment player that hooks up to a TV and stereo.

WHAT

Commodore Amiga Series	64C/128D Computers
Amiga 500	Commodore 64C
Amiga 2000	Commodore 128D
Amiga 2500	
Amiga 3000	**Peripherals**
	Add-on memory boards
MS-DOS PC-Compatible Computers	Application boards
	Disk drives
Commodore PC Colt	Monitors
Commodore PC 10 Series III	Printers
Commodore PC 20 Series III	**Semiconductor Integrated Circuits**
Commodore PC 30 Series III	Custom CMOS and NMOS Large Scale Integrated Circuit semiconductors
Commodore PC 40 Series III	
Commodore PC 60	Logic circuits
C286-LT (laptop)	Microprocessors
Slimline 386SX	Read-Only Memory (ROM) chips
Compact Interactive Disc Player	
CDTV	

RANKINGS

780th in *Business Week* 1000

KEY COMPETITORS

Apple	Hitachi	Oki
AST	Hyundai	Olivetti
Atari	IBM	Philips
Canon	Machines Bull	Sharp
Casio	Matsushita	Siemens
Compaq	Microsoft	Sony
Dell	NEC	Tandy
Fujitsu	Nintendo	Toshiba

HOW MUCH

	9-Year Growth	1981	1982	1983	1984	1985	1986	1987	1988	1989	1990
Sales ($ mil.)	18.9%	187	305	681	1,267	883	889	807	871	940	887
Net income ($ mil.)	(26.8%)	25	41	88	144	(114)	(128)	23	48	50	2
Income as % of sales	—	13.4%	13.3%	12.9%	11.3%	(12.9%)	(14.4%)	2.8%	5.5%	5.3%	0.2%
Earnings per share ($)	(26.6%)	0.81	1.32	2.86	4.66	(3.66)	(4.08)	0.71	1.51	1.55	0.05
Stock price – high ($)	—	17.25	42.56	60.63	49.38	18.13	11.38	15.00	14.13	19.75	11.88
Stock price – low ($)	—	8.00	11.63	29.25	16.25	8.25	4.75	6.25	6.75	7.13	4.50
Stock price – close ($)	(2.9%)	15.33	33.13	41.50	16.38	10.63	8.88	7.50	14.00	10.75	11.75
P/E – high	—	21	32	21	11	—	—	21	9	13	238
P/E – low	—	10	9	10	3	—	—	9	4	5	90
Dividends per share ($)	0.0%	0.00	0.00	0.00	0.00	0.00	0.00	0.00	0.00	0.00	0.00
Book value per share ($)	16.1%	2.03	3.50	6.23	10.56	7.12	3.31	4.58	6.32	7.57	7.81

1990 Year-end:
Debt ratio: 38.2%
Return on equity: 0.7%
Cash (mil.): $78
Current ratio: 2.33
Long-term debt (mil.): $157
No. of shares (mil.): 32
Dividends:
  1990 average yield: 0.0%
  1990 payout: 0.0%
Market value (mil.): $380

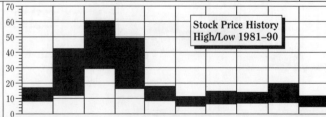
Stock Price History
High/Low 1981–90

COMMONWEALTH EDISON COMPANY

NYSE symbol: CWE
Fiscal year ends: December 31

Hoover's Rating **C-**

OVERVIEW

With a service area covering 11,525 square miles in 25 Illinois counties, Commonwealth Edison (Comm Ed) provides electricity to about 8 million people — approximately 70% of the state's population. The company owns and operates the largest network of nuclear power plants in the US, with almost 79% of the electricity generated in 1990 coming from nuclear sources.

Comm Ed is still experiencing the fallout from a $480 million 2-step rate increase, approved by the Illinois Commerce Commission (ICC) in 1988 and overturned by the Illinois Supreme Court in 1990. Since the court ruling, the ICC has remanded some $461 million (which Comm Ed wrote off in 1990) in costs related to the construction of Unit 1 of the company's Byron nuclear plant. As the ICC investigation continues, Comm Ed may have to write off even more construction costs (related to Byron 2 and Braidwood Units 1 and 2) in 1991. The commission did approve a 3-year, $750 million rate increase in 1991, which should bring Comm Ed some relief, if approved by the state supreme court.

WHO

Chairman: James J. O'Conner, age 54, $606,591 pay
President: Bide L. Thomas, age 55, $336,817 pay
SVP: Cordell Reed, age 53, $208,540 pay
SVP and Principal Financial Officer: Ernest M. Roth, age 64, $210,702 pay
VP (Personnel): J. Patrick Sanders, age 53
Auditors: Arthur Andersen & Co.
Employees: 19,000

WHEN

A group of Chicago businessmen formed Western Edison Light in 1882. It was reorganized as Chicago Edison by its 39 shareholders in 1887 and, under the leadership of Samuel Insull, bought its main competitor, Chicago Arc Light & Power, in 1893. In 1898 the company created a holding company, Commonwealth Electric to buy other power companies in the Chicago area. Commonwealth and Chicago Edison merged in 1907 to form Commonwealth Edison.

Comm Ed finished its Northwest Station in 1912, the largest steam generator built to date, and followed with the even more powerful Crawford Station in 1924. Comm Ed also continued to buy other utilities and by 1933 consisted of 77 separate companies.

Comm Ed bought the Public Service Company of Northern Illinois (1937) and Chicago District Electric Generating Corporation (1939), which, combined with Western United Gas & Electric and Illinois Northern Utility (both bought in 1950), created one unit providing power in northern Illinois (outside Chicago). Comm Ed consolidated its position in Chicago through other purchases, including Produce Terminal Corporation (1956) and Central Illinois Electric and Gas (1966).

In 1960 Comm Ed opened the world's first full-scale, privately owned nuclear facility (Dresden Station) and by 1974 had built 7 nuclear plants. That year the company bought the Cotter Corporation, a Colorado uranium mining company, to provide low-cost fuel for its nuclear plants. In 1976 Comm Ed bought mining rights to 8,200 coal-rich acres in Wyoming and in 1979 formed Edison Development Canada to explore for uranium deposits in Newfoundland.

In 1984 and 1985, 2 nuclear plants went on-line, but when construction costs skyrocketed in 1986, the ICC threatened to revoke licenses for 2 other nuclear plants (Byron 2 and Braidwood 1 & 2) still under construction. These went into service in 1987 and 1988. A decrease in tax credits related to the Byron and Braidwood construction, combined with higher operational and maintenance costs, contributed to a 36% decline in earnings from 1987 to 1989.

Even so, Comm Ed was touted as one of America's best-run nuclear utilities during the mid-1980s. In recent years, however, the company has drawn criticism from environmental and consumer groups for its heavy investment in nuclear construction, resulting in some of the highest utility bills in the US.

Comm Ed is still negotiating a long-term franchise agreement with the City of Chicago. Its current agreement with the city expires December 31, 1991.

WHERE

HQ: 37th Floor, One First National Plaza, PO Box 767, Chicago, IL 60690-0767
Phone: 312-294-4321
Fax: 312-294-3110

Generating Facilities

Fossil Fuels
Collins (near Morris, IL)
Crawford (Chicago, IL)
Fisk (Chicago, IL)
Joliet 6, 7, and 8 (near Joliet, IL)
Kincaid (near Taylorville, IL)
Powerton (near Pekin, IL)
State Line (Hammond, IN)
Waukegan (Waukegan, IL)
Will County (near Lockport, IL)

Nuclear
Braidwood (near Braidwood, IL)
Byron (near Byron, IL)
Dresden (near Morris, IL)
LaSalle County (near Seneca, IL)
Quad-Cities (75%, near Cordova, IL)
Zion (Zion, IL)

WHAT

	1990 Sales	
	$ mil.	% of total
Residential	2,113	40
Commercial & industrial	3,096	59
Public authorities	433	8
Electric railroads	27	—
Sales for resale	82	2
Other	47	1
Provisions for refunds	(536)	(10)
Total	**5,262**	**100**

	1990 Fuel Sources
	% of total
Nuclear	79
Coal	20
Natural gas	1
Oil	—
Total	**100**

RANKINGS

12th in *Fortune* 50 Utilities
69th in *Business Week* 1000

HOW MUCH

	9-Year Growth	1981	1982	1983	1984	1985	1986	1987	1988	1989	1990
Sales ($ mil.)	3.9%	3,737	4,130	4,634	4,930	4,964	5,479	5,674	5,613	5,751	5,262
Net income ($ mil.)	(13.0%)	450	607	802	875	956	1,050	1,086	738	694	128
Income as % of sales	—	12.0%	14.7%	17.3%	17.8%	19.3%	19.2%	19.1%	13.1%	12.1%	2.4%
Earnings per share ($)	(25.4%)	3.06	3.75	4.39	4.43	4.45	4.69	4.73	3.01	2.83	0.22
Stock price – high ($)	—	22.38	25.88	29.25	28.88	32.88	35.75	38.00	33.38	40.75	37.88
Stock price – low ($)	—	17.75	19.25	24.50	20.00	27.00	28.63	25.25	22.75	32.13	27.25
Stock price – close($)	6.4%	19.88	25.25	26.00	27.88	29.38	33.88	27.50	33.00	37.63	34.75
P/E – high	—	7	7	7	7	7	8	8	11	14	172
P/E – low	—	6	5	6	5	6	6	5	8	11	124
Dividends per share ($)	1.2%	2.70	2.85	3.00	3.00	3.00	3.00	3.00	3.00	3.00	3.00
Book value per share ($)	1.4%	26.26	26.25	27.54	28.71	29.96	31.60	33.27	32.86	32.68	29.89

1990 Year-end:
Debt ratio: 51.8%
Return on equity: 0.7%
Cash (mil.): $576
Current ratio: 0.94
Long term debt (mil.): $7,306
No. of shares (mil.): 212
Dividends:
  1990 average yield: 8.6%
  1990 payout: 1,363.6%
Market value (mil.): $7,377

Stock Price History High/Low 1981–90

COMPAQ COMPUTER CORPORATION

NYSE symbol: CPQ
Fiscal year ends: December 31

Hoover's Rating **A+**

OVERVIEW

Houston's Compaq, the #1 maker of IBM-compatible computers, reached $1 billion in annual sales within 5 years of founding. Unlike other IBM clone makers, the 9-year-old Compaq conducts its own R&D and engineers many of its products. Compaq has a long list of innovations. It was first to develop a fully IBM-compatible portable, first to successfully integrate a hard disk drive into a portable, and first with a monitor that displays both graphics and high-resolution text. In 1990, according to Dataquest, Compaq ranked #1 in US sales of notebook computers.

Compaq owns approximately 21% of hard disk manufacturer Conner Peripherals, from which it bought $255 million worth of products in 1990. In 1990 Compaq's investment in Conner had a market value of $275 million.

In 1990 Compaq delivered its first computer (DESKPRO 486/25) based on the Extended Industry Standard Architecture (EISA) championed by Compaq, an alternative to IBM's microchannel-based computers introduced in the PS/2 line. To protect its estimated 7.4% share of the world PC market from other clone makers, Compaq cut prices in late 1990 and early 1991 by as much as 34%. The reduction, along with the strong dollar overseas, was blamed in part for the sharp drop in earnings in the first 2 quarters of 1991, raising concern about Compaq's ability to sustain its earnings growth at the lower prices.

WHO

Chairman: Benjamin M. Rosen, age 58
President and CEO: Joseph R. Canion, age 46, $2,327,160 pay
EVP and COO: Eckhard Pfeiffer, age 49, $1,335,612 pay (prior to promotion)
SVP Finance and CFO: Daryl J. White, age 43
VP Human Resources: Jerry G. Welch, age 52
Auditors: Price Waterhouse
Employees: 11,600

WHEN

Joseph R. (Rod) Canion and 2 other ex–Texas Instruments managers started Compaq in Houston in 1982 to manufacture and sell portable IBM-compatible computers. Compaq's first portable was developed from a prototype the 3 sketched on a paper place mat when they first discussed the product idea.

Compaq shipped its first computer in 1982 and in 1983 recorded sales of $111 million — unprecedented growth for a computer startup. The company went public in 1983. Sales continued to skyrocket in the following years, climbing to $329 million in 1984 and to $504 million in 1985. Compaq's success was due in part to its ability to hit the market with the right machine at the right time. In 1983 Compaq introduced a portable computer 18 months before IBM, and in 1986 it was first to market with a computer based on Intel's 386 chip.

However, introducing a product at the right time has not always meant being first to market. Compaq delayed introduction of its laptop until the prototype's display and battery technologies were satisfactorily developed. Although introduced late (1988), Compaq's SLT/286 laptop with its crisp display screen became an immediate success.

To sell its products, Compaq capitalized on the extensive base of dealers and suppliers built up around the IBM PC. Rather than establish a large sales force, Compaq gave exclusive rights to dealers for sales and service of its products and by 1990 had a network of 3,800 retailers in 152 countries. The dealer channel has proven effective. In 1988 Compaq sales reached almost $2.1 billion, making the company the first to exceed the $2 billion mark in only 6 years from its first product introduction (1982–88). Sales in 1989 climbed to $2.9 billion.

In 1989 the company dropped Businessland, its 2nd largest reseller (after ComputerLand), as an authorized dealer after Businessland demanded preferential discounts. Compaq reauthorized Businessland as a dealer in 1990 after it agreed to abide by Compaq's policies. In 1991 Compaq purchased a 13% interest in engineering workstation-maker Silicon Graphics and paid $50 million for access to its graphics technology. Compaq also took a lead role in creating a 21-company alliance, Advanced Computer Environment, set up to establish a standard for Reduced Instruction Set Computing (RISC) computers to compete with those of Sun and IBM.

WHERE

HQ: 20555 SH 249, Houston, TX 77070
Phone: 713-370-0670
Fax: 713-374-1740

The company does business in 66 countries and has manufacturing facilities in Houston, Scotland, and Singapore.

	1990 Sales		1990 Operating Income	
	$ mil.	% of total	$ mil.	% of total
US & Canada	1,658	46	414	59
Europe	1,807	50	169	24
Other countries	134	4	122	17
Adjustments	—	—	(56)	—
Total	**3,599**	**100**	**649**	**100**

WHAT

Laptops
COMPAQ LTE
COMPAQ LTE/286
COMPAQ SLT/286
COMPAQ LTE 386s/20
COMPAQ SLT 386s/20

Portables
COMPAQ PORTABLE II
COMPAQ PORTABLE III
COMPAQ PORTABLE 386

Desktop PCs
COMPAQ DESKPRO 286N
COMPAQ DESKPRO 386/25e
COMPAQ DESKPRO 386/33L
COMPAQ DESKPRO 386N
COMPAQ DESKPRO 386s/20
COMPAQ DESKPRO 486/33L

PC Systems
COMPAQ SYSTEMPRO
COMPAQ SYSTEMPRO Model 486

Investments
Conner Peripherals, Inc. (21%, hard drive maker)
Silicon Graphics, Inc. (13%, workstation maker)

RANKINGS

136th in *Fortune* 500 Industrial Cos.
103rd in *Business Week* 1000

HOW MUCH

	7-Year Growth	1981	1982	1983	1984	1985	1986	1987	1988	1989	1990
Sales ($ mil.)	64.4%	—	—	111	329	504	625	1,224	2,066	2,876	3,599
Net income ($ mil.)	104.9%	—	—	3	13	27	43	136	255	333	455
Income as % of sales	—	—	—	2.3%	3.9%	5.3%	6.9%	11.1%	12.4%	11.6%	12.6%
Earnings per share ($)	61.1%	—	—	0.07	0.24	0.45	0.67	1.79	3.14	3.88	5.12
Stock price – high ($)	—	—	—	6.25	7.31	7.13	10.81	39.25	32.88	56.25	67.88
Stock price – low ($)	—	—	—	5.50	1.75	3.06	5.81	9.63	21.00	29.63	35.50
Stock price – close ($)	27.7%	—	—	6.25	3.31	6.63	9.63	27.69	29.81	39.75	56.38
P/E – high	—	—	—	96	31	16	16	22	10	15	13
P/E – low	—	—	—	85	7	7	9	5	7	8	7
Dividends per share ($)	—	—	—	0.00	0.00	0.00	0.00	0.00	0.00	0.00	0.00
Book value per share ($)	31.9%	—	—	1.79	2.08	2.58	3.39	5.85	10.57	14.92	21.59

1990 Year-end:
Debt ratio: 3.8%
Return on equity: 28.0%
Cash (mil.): $435
Current ratio: 2.62
Long-term debt (mil.): $73
No. of shares (mil.): 86
Dividends:
 1990 average yield: 0.0%
 1990 payout: 0.0%
Market value (mil.): $4,853

Stock Price History High/Low 1983–90

KEY COMPETITORS

AT&T
Apple
AST
Atari
Canon
Casio
Commodore
Data General
Dell
DEC
Fujitsu
Hewlett-Packard
Hitachi
Hyundai
IBM
Machines Bull
Matsushita
NEC
NCR
Oki
Prime
Sharp
Siemens
Sun Microsystems
Tandy
Toshiba
Unisys
Wang

COMPUTER ASSOCIATES INTERNATIONAL, INC.

NYSE symbol: CA
Fiscal year ends: March 31

Hoover's Rating **A**

OVERVIEW

Computer Associates is the world's largest firm engaged solely in the design and development of application computer software. The company is run by founder and chairman Charles Wang and his brother Anthony.

CA has supplied mainframe computer software (systems, database management, and applications) to 80% of the approximately 40,000 mainframe sites worldwide. The company is also a leader in PC software (spreadsheets, accounting, graphics) and software for DEC's VAX minicomputers. CA's more than 250 products are used by over 85% of the *Fortune* 500.

Computer Associates's rapid growth in the 1980s (annual average of 65% between 1982 and 1989) is attributed to its more than 26 acquisitions. But when acquisition activity slowed after 1989, CA's revenue growth dipped before spurting again with the 1991 acquisitions of On-Line and Pansophic.

In 1990 CA announced its CA90s strategy designed to integrate CA's software with that of its acquired companies by developing a common software architecture of screens, menus, and interfaces for over 250 applications.

WHO

Chairman and CEO: Charles B. Wang, age 46, $2,150,373 pay
President and COO: Anthony W. Wang, age 48, $1,877,377 pay
EVP Sales: Arnold S. Mazur, age 48, $476,208 pay
EVP Research and Development: Russell M. Artzt, age 44, $586,281 pay
SVP Finance and CFO: Peter A. Schwartz, age 47
VP Human Resources: Lisa Mars
Auditors: Ernst & Young
Employees: 6,700

WHEN

Young Charles Wang and his family fled Communist China in 1952. After graduating from Queens College (New York), Wang in 1976 opened a US subsidiary of Swiss-owned Computer Associates (CA) in Manhattan. Wang started with 4 employees and one product, a file organizer for IBM storage systems (CA-SORT); it was a great success.

Wang soon realized that a penetrating distribution and service network, fed by an ever-increasing number of products, would be the key to the software kingdom; acquiring existing software (and its customers) would reduce the risk of in-house development and move products to market sooner. CA's purchasing flurry (of mostly struggling software firms) produced the first independent software company to reach $1 billion in sales (1989); sales 5 years earlier had been $85 million.

Wang moved beyond mainframe utilities into microcomputer software, buying the popular SuperCalc spreadsheet (from Sorcim, 1984) and BPI (accounting software, 1987); data security software, including the Top Secret program (1985); and a string of applications vendors, including Software International (financial, 1986) and Integrated Software Systems (graphics, 1986).

CA's 1987 purchase of chief utilities rival UCCEL made CA the world's largest independent software supplier — and gave Swiss billionaire Walter Haefner 20% of CA. CA then had 64% of the tape/disk-management software market and strong presences in banking applications and data security.

CA entered the mainframe database software market in 1988 with the purchase of Applied Data Research (ADR) from Ameritech. In 1989, with the $300 million acquisition of Cullinet, CA added the IDMS database line, software for VAX computers, and banking applications to its product line. But the incompatibility of Cullinet's IDMS software with that of ADR left customers guessing which one CA would ultimately support. This uncertainty and other problems in assimilating Cullinet caused product sales and net income to drop in 1990. Posting flat product sales again in 1991, CA cited the Gulf War and recession.

In 1991 CA converted several programs to run on VAX machines and announced a collaboration with Hewlett-Packard to develop UNIX applications. Also in 1991 it made its first major acquisition in several years, buying New Jersey–based On-Line Software, a maker of mainframe debugging software, for $120 million. This acquisition was followed quickly by the $290 million purchase of Pansophic Systems, maker of database and CASE software applications.

WHERE

HQ: 711 Stewart Ave., Garden City, NY 11530
Phone: 516-227-3300
Fax: 516-227-3937

CA operates in 27 countries.

	1990 Sales		1990 Net Income	
	$ mil.	% of total	$ mil.	% of total
US	837	55	150	94
Other countries	698	45	9	6
Adjustments	(187)	—	—	—
Total	**1,348**	**100**	**159**	**100**

WHAT

	1990 Sales	
	$ mil.	% of total
Products	888	66
Maintenance	460	34
Total	**1,348**	**100**

Systems Management Software
Automated production control (CA-APCDOC)
Data center administration
Data center automation (CA-UNIPACK)
Performance measurement and accounting (CA-JARS)
Project estimation and planning
Resource accounting and chargeback system (CA-PMA/ChargeBack)
Security, control, and auditing (CA-TOP SECRET)
Storage and resource management

Information Management Software
Applications development
Information distribution
Programmer productivity (CA-LIBRARIAN)
Project management
Relational database management
Visual information systems

Applications Software
Banking and thrift institutions
Business decision software (CA-SuperCalc spreadsheet)
Financial management (Masterpiece)
Specialized accounting

Microcomputer Software
Accounting
Decision support (SuperCalc5 spreadsheet)
Micro-mainframe links
Database management (CA-DATACOM/PC; CA-IDMS/PC)

HOW MUCH

Fiscal year ends March of following year	9-Year Growth	1981	1982	1983	1984	1985	1986	1987	1988	1989	1990
Sales ($ mil.)	53.6%	28	58	85	129	191	309	709	1,030	1,296	1,348
Net income ($ mil.)	58.0%	3	6	10	13	19	37	102	164	158	159
Income as % of sales	—	9.1%	9.7%	11.2%	10.3%	9.7%	11.8%	14.4%	15.9%	12.2%	11.8%
Earnings per share ($)	35.2%	0.06	0.08	0.11	0.15	0.21	0.37	0.63	0.98	0.85	0.86
Stock price – high ($)	—	0.89	2.34	4.41	3.69	4.38	7.72	18.63	16.44	22.13	16.88
Stock price – low ($)	—	0.80	0.72	2.11	1.84	2.28	4.06	6.84	11.94	10.50	4.38
Stock price – close ($)	27.2%	0.89	2.23	3.00	2.42	4.38	6.88	16.00	15.94	12.50	7.75
P/E – high	—	16	29	40	25	21	21	30	17	26	20
P/E – low	—	14	9	19	12	11	11	11	12	12	5
Dividends per share ($)	—	0.00	0.00	0.00	0.00	0.00	0.00	0.00	0.00	0.00	0.10
Book value per share ($)	49.1%	0.16	0.42	1.08	1.21	1.77	2.21	3.15	4.46	5.31	5.99

1990 Year-end:
Debt ratio: 2.2%
Return on equity: 15.2%
Cash (mil.): $248
Current ratio: 2.46
Long-term debt (mil.): $25
No. of shares (mil.): 182
Dividends:
  1990 average yield: 1.3%
  1990 payout: 11.6%
Market value (mil.): $1,411

Stock Price History High/Low 1981–90

RANKINGS

82nd in *Fortune* 100 Diversified Service Cos.
366th in *Business Week* 1000

KEY COMPETITORS

Borland	H&R Block	Novell
Data General	IBM	Oracle
DEC	Lotus	Wang
Dun & Bradstreet	Microsoft	

CONAGRA, INC.

OVERVIEW

Headquartered in Omaha, Nebraska, ConAgra is a major diversified food company. Since its 1990 purchase of Beatrice, the company has vaulted to the #2 spot in the US food industry (after Philip Morris's Kraft group).

ConAgra's operations are divided into 3 segments: Agri-Products, Trading and Processing, and Prepared Foods. The Agri-Products division produces crop protection chemicals, feed and feed additives, and fertilizer. The Trading and Processing segment trades grain and other food items worldwide. The company also operates 91 Country General Stores and 89 Northwest Fabrics & Crafts stores.

ConAgra has traditionally maintained a strong line of meat products including Monfort, Armour, and Country Pride. The Beatrice acquisition strengthened its position not only in meat (Butterball, Eckrich) but in other areas of the grocery store as well, with such respected names as Wesson, Hunt's, and Swiss Miss. Already #1 in the nation in frozen foods (Banquet, Chun King), the company's new Healthy Choice frozen dinner line, which hit the market in 1989, is giving the competition ulcers, and now holds the #1 spot in the premium frozen dinner market.

WHEN

In 1919, 4 flour mills joined to form Nebraska Consolidated Mills and established headquarters in Omaha. The company did not expand to other states until the 1940s.

In the 1950s the company developed Duncan Hines cake mix (later sold to Procter & Gamble) and in 1957 established a flour and feed mill in Puerto Rico. The company entered the poultry processing business in the 1960s while continuing to buy flour mills nationwide.

By 1970 the company had opened poultry processing plants in Alabama, Georgia, and Louisiana. In 1971 the company changed its name to ConAgra (which means "in partnership with the land" in Latin). During the 1970s the company expanded into the fertilizer, catfish, and pet accessory businesses.

Bad investments and commodity speculation caused ConAgra severe financial problems until 1974 when Charles M. "Mike" Harper, a former Pillsbury executive, took charge. Harper sold nonessential properties to reduce debt and had the company back on its feet by 1976. In 1977 ConAgra established large-scale grain and feed merchandising operations and in 1978 bought United Agri Products (agricultural chemicals).

In 1980 the company bought Banquet (frozen food) from RCA and within 6 years had introduced almost 90 new products under the Banquet label. With the purchases of Singleton Seafood and Sea-Alaska products, ConAgra achieved $1 billion in sales for the first time in 1981. ConAgra bought Peavey (milling and specialty retailing) and Country Pride (chicken) in 1982 and in 1983 acquired Armour Food Company (meats, dairy products, and frozen food).

In 1986 ConAgra bought RJR Nabisco's frozen food business, which included the Chun King, Morton, and Patio brands. The company became a major factor in the red meat market with the 1987 purchases of E. A. Miller (boxed beef), Monfort (beef and lamb), and Swift Independent Packing. Further acquisitions included O'Donnell-Usen (seafood, 1987) and Blue Star (frozen food, 1988).

In 1990 ConAgra swallowed its biggest fish by buying Beatrice. Beatrice was formed as a dairy company in 1894 and grew by acquiring such companies as La Choy (1943), Rosarita Mexican Foods (1961), Peter Eckrich & Sons (1972), Martha White Foods (baking products, (1975), and Esmark (originally Swift Brothers, 1984) before going private in a 1986 LBO. With Beatrice, Conagra got the US's #1 popcorn (Orville Redenbacher's) and #1 tomato sauce (Hunt's). In 1991 ConAgra bought Golden Valley Microwave Foods.

NYSE symbol: CAG
Fiscal year ends: Last Sunday in May

Hoover's Rating **B**

WHO

Chairman and CEO: Charles M. Harper, age 62, $1,619,825 pay
President and COO: Philip B. Fletcher, age 57, $650,738 pay
SVP Finance and Corporate Secretary: L. B. "Red" Thomas, age 54
SVP Human Resources: Gerald B. Vernon
Auditors: Deloitte & Touche
Employees: 74,269

WHERE

HQ: ConAgra Center, One Central Park Plaza, Omaha, NE 68102
Phone: 402-978-4000
Fax: 402-595-4000 (Public Relations)

ConAgra operates trading offices in 26 countries.

WHAT

	1990 Sales		1990 Operating Income	
	$ mil.	% of total	$ mil.	% of total
Prepared Foods	15,045	77	663	76
Agri-Products	2,444	12	94	11
Trading	1,862	10	100	12
Finance companies	154	1	13	1
Adjustments	—	—	(80)	—
Total	**19,505**	**100**	**790**	**100**

Agri-Products
Animal feeds
Crop protection chemicals
Feed additives
Fertilizer
Livestock health care

Trading and Processing
Corn meal and mixes
Feed ingredient merchandising
Global commodity trading
Grain milling

Selected Food Brands
Armour
Banquet
Butterball
Chun King
Cook Family Food
Country Pride
Country Skillet
Decker
Eckrich
Gebhardt
Healthy Choice
Home Brand

Hunt's
La Choy
Longmont
Manwich
Monfort
Morton
Orville Redenbacher's
Patio
Peter Pan
Reddi–Wip
Rosarita
Sizzlean
Swift Premium
Swiss Miss
Taste O'Sea
Ultra Slim-Fast
Wesson
World's Fare

Other Operations
Commodity futures brokerage
Country General Stores
Livestock financing
Northwest Fabrics & Crafts
Truck financing

RANKINGS

25th in *Fortune* 500 Industrial Cos.
108th in *Business Week* 1000

KEY COMPETITORS

Anheuser-Busch
ADM
Borden
BSN
Campbell Soup
Cargill
Chiquita Brands
Continental Grain
CPC
Dial
General Mills
W. R. Grace

Grand Metropolitan
Heinz
Nestlé
Philip Morris
Procter & Gamble
Quaker Oats
RJR Nabisco
Salomon
Sara Lee
Sandoz
Tyson Foods
Unilever

HOW MUCH

Fiscal year ends May of following year	9-Year Growth	1981	1982	1983	1984	1985	1986	1987	1988	1989	1990
Sales ($ mil.)	31.1%	1,705	2,320	3,302	5,498	5,911	9,002	9,475	11,340	15,501	19,505
Net income ($ mil.)	28.4%	33	48	65	92	105	149	155	198	232	311
Income as % of sales	—	1.9%	2.1%	2.0%	1.7%	1.8%	1.7%	1.6%	1.7%	1.5%	1.6%
Earnings per share ($)	16.1%	0.56	0.57	0.68	0.87	1.00	1.22	1.28	1.62	1.86	2.13
Stock price – high ($)	—	5.17	6.56	8.00	9.19	15.75	21.42	25.33	22.67	30.25	38.25
Stock price – low ($)	—	3.56	3.72	5.72	6.58	8.67	12.96	13.92	15.83	19.33	22.75
Stock price – close ($)	28.5%	3.86	6.22	7.61	9.13	14.17	19.08	16.92	19.33	28.50	37.00
P/E – high	—	9	12	12	11	16	18	20	14	16	18
P/E – low	—	6	7	8	8	9	11	11	10	10	11
Dividends per share ($)	15.3%	0.19	0.21	0.25	0.28	0.32	0.37	0.43	0.50	0.58	0.67
Book value per share ($)	19.3%	2.65	3.30	4.08	4.61	5.14	6.17	6.96	7.87	8.93	13.01

1990 Year-end:
Debt ratio: 53.5%
Return on equity: 19.4%
Cash (mil.): $967
Current ratio: 1.06
Long-term debt (mil.): $2,093
No. of shares (mil.): 140
Dividends:
  1990 average yield: 1.8%
  1990 payout: 31.4%
Market value (mil.): $5,168

Stock Price History High/Low 1981–90

CONNER PERIPHERALS, INC.

NYSE symbol: CNR
Fiscal year ends: December 31

Hoover's Rating **A**

OVERVIEW

Conner Peripherals is a leading manufacturer of 3-1/2" and 2-1/2" hard disk drives used in microcomputers and is the dominant supplier to the rapidly growing laptop and notebook computer segments. The company has employed design advantages and close ties to customers to become in 1989 the fastest-growing US startup manufacturer in history, reaching the *Fortune* 500 in only its 3rd full year. Compaq owns 20.5% of Conner and is the company's largest customer (19% of sales).

Software instructions imbedded in chips accompanying Conner's disk drives have enabled the company to use fewer parts, increasing speed and durability while reducing costs. Conner subcontracts component production to outside vendors, avoiding plant costs but exposing the company to periodic parts shortages.

Conner's software allows quick customization of products for computer makers. By working closely with customers before designing and producing, the company feels it presells its products, breaking with the traditional sequence of producing products and then selling them.

Since its inception Conner has tried to exploit ignored market niches and preempt competitors with new technology. With earnings under pressure as competition, particularly from Seagate, intensifies in the 3-1/2" drive business, Conner is working on 1.8" drives and high-end products for workstations.

WHEN

Having cofounded and left computer disk drive manufacturers Shugart Associates and Seagate Technologies, Finis Conner created Conner Peripherals in 1985 as a vehicle for yet another disk drive venture. In 1986 he merged his new company with Co-Data Memory, a newly established company owned by John Squires, a disk drive designer and co-founder of Miniscribe, a disk drive manufacturer that had filed for bankruptcy. Conner's search for capital led him to his old friend Rod Canion, the president of Compaq, a company interested in small hard disk drives for its portable microcomputers. Conner sold Canion on Squires's 3-1/2" drive designs (5-1/4" drives were standard at the time) and talked him into arranging for Compaq to sink $6 million into his start-up company. Another $6 million injection followed months later.

In 1987, with 90% of its output sold to Compaq, Conner Peripherals's first full year sales of $113 million eclipsed the previous record — held by Compaq. With a dominant position in high-capacity 3-1/2" drives and with a design edge that made its drives more reliable and power efficient than its competitors', Conner began selling to other computer makers, particularly those involved in the emerging laptop computer market.

By 1988 Conner had established its pattern of designing its products in Colorado, beginning pilot production in San Jose and then transferring volume production to low-cost countries, initially Singapore. In 1988 Conner went public and bought 49% control of a money-losing Olivetti disk drive subsidiary in Italy, renamed Conner Peripherals Europe. Olivetti soon became a major customer.

In 1989 Conner raised its stake in Conner Peripherals Europe to 51% and shipped its first 2-1/2" disk drives, beating its competition to the market by a year. Compaq, Olivetti, and Toshiba accounted for 29%, 12%, and 10% of 1989 sales, respectively.

In a modest contradiction of its subcontracting policy, Conner bought Domain Technologies's disk coating operations in 1990. Conner began building new offshore plants in Malaysia and Scotland, and Conner Peripherals Europe turned profitable in 1990. Sales soared to well over $1 billion as laptop and notebook computer makers snapped up the company's products as fast as it could make them.

WHO

Chairman and CEO: Finis F. Conner, age 47, $1,405,158 pay
President and COO: William J. Almon, age 58, $1,277,591 pay
SVP and CFO: Carl W. Neun, age 47, $756,761 pay
VP Human Resources: Harvey Kroll
Auditors: Price Waterhouse
Employees: 9,576

WHERE

HQ: 3081 Zanker Rd., San Jose, CA 95134-2128
Phone: 408-456-4500
Fax: 408-456-4501

Conner maintains R&D facilities in Colorado and plants in California, Singapore, Italy, Malaysia, and Scotland.

	1990 Sales		1990 Operating Income	
	$ mil.	% of total	$ mil.	% of total
US	910	68	12	7
Asia	363	27	151	87
Europe	65	5	10	6
Total	**1,338**	**100**	**173**	**100**

WHAT

Product Lines
Cougar (3-1/2", workstation)
CP-3040 (3-1/2", laptop)
CP-3200F (3-1/2", workstation)
Hopi (3-1/2", desktop/laptop)
Jaguar (3-1/2", desktop)
Kato (2-1/2", notebook/noncomputer)
Pancho (2-1/2", notebook)
Stubby (3-1/2", notebook/laptop)
Summit (3-1/2", workstation)

RANKINGS

286th in *Fortune* 500 US Industrial Cos.
397th in *Business Week* 1000

KEY COMPETITORS

Fujitsu
Hitachi
IBM
Matsushita
NEC
Seagate
Sony
Toshiba

HOW MUCH

	3-Year Growth	1981	1982	1983	1984	1985	1986	1987	1988	1989	1990
Sales ($ mil.)	127.9%	—	—	—	—	—	—	113	257	705	1,338
Net income ($ mil.)	127.8%	—	—	—	—	—	—	11	20	41	130
Income as % of sales	—	—	—	—	—	—	—	10.0%	7.7%	5.9%	9.7%
Earnings per share ($)	—	—	—	—	—	—	—	0.43	0.58	1.00	2.41
Stock price – high ($)	—	—	—	—	—	—	—	—	10.13	15.50	31.25
Stock price – low ($)	—	—	—	—	—	—	—	—	6.88	6.50	12.25
Stock price – close ($)	—	—	—	—	—	—	—	—	7.88	13.13	23.63
P/E – high	—	—	—	—	—	—	—	—	17	16	13
P/E – low	—	—	—	—	—	—	—	—	12	7	5
Dividends per share ($)	—	—	—	—	—	—	—	0.00	0.00	0.00	0.00
Book value per share ($)	87.7%	—	—	—	—	—	—	1.61	3.08	5.04	10.64

1990 Year-end:
Debt ratio: 5.7%
Return on equity: 30.8%
Cash (mil.): $237
Current ratio: 3.94
Long-term debt (mil.): $37
No. of shares (mil.): 57
Dividends:
  1990 average yield: 0.0%
  1990 payout: —
Market value (mil.): $1,341

Stock Price History
High/Low 1988–90

CONSOLIDATED EDISON CO. OF NEW YORK, INC.

OVERVIEW

Consolidated Edison (Con Ed), in business since 1823, provides electric, gas, and steam power to about 4 million customers in a service area covering 660 square miles of New York City and Westchester County. Con Ed generated more than $5.7 billion in revenues in 1990, making it America's 5th largest electric utility.

Although oil remains one of Con Ed's biggest fuel sources, the company has successfully diversified its fuel mix, reducing its oil dependence by 50% since the mid-1970s. At the same time, nuclear power and natural gas have grown in importance to Con Ed. Together oil, natural gas, and nuclear sources generate 85% of the company's power needs.

Since 1971, when it introduced the Save-A-Watt program, Con Ed has been a leader in conservation, promoting energy savings through programs designed to cut back usage during summer peak periods and to teach the public ways to save on energy costs. Business customers can receive rebates for installing efficient heating and cooling systems.

NYSE symbol: ED
Fiscal year ends: December 31

WHO

Chairman, President and CEO: Eugene R. McGrath, age 49, $633,850 pay (prior to promotion)
EVP and CFO: Raymond J. McCann, age 56, $401,258 pay
SVP (Personnel): Thomas J. Galvin, age 52
Auditors: Price Waterhouse
Employees: 19,483

WHERE

HQ: 4 Irving Place, New York, NY 10003
Phone: 212-460-4600
Fax: 212-982-7816

Generating Facilities

Electric – Fossil-Fueled
Arthur Kill (Staten Island)
Astoria (Queens)
Bowline Point (Haverstraw, 66.6%)
East River (Manhattan)
Hudson Avenue (Brooklyn)
Ravenswood (Queens)
Roseton (Newburgh, 40%)
Waterside (Manhattan)
59th Street (Manhattan)
74th Street (Manhattan)

Electric – Gas Turbines
Gowanus (Brooklyn)
Indian Point (Buchanan)
Narrows (Brooklyn)

Electric – Nuclear
Indian Point (Buchanan)

Steam
East River (Manhattan)
Hudson Avenue (Brooklyn)
Ravenswood (Queens)
Waterside (Manhattan)
59th Street (Manhattan)
E. 60th Street (Manhattan)
74th Street (Manhattan)

WHEN

A group of New York professionals, led by Timothy Dewey, founded The New York Gas Light Company in 1823 to provide utility service to a limited area of Manhattan. Various companies served other areas of New York City, and in 1884, 5 of these joined with New York Gas Light to form the Consolidated Gas Company of New York.

This unification occurred on the heels of the introduction of Thomas Edison's incandescent lamp (1879). The Edison Electric Illuminating Company of New York was formed in 1880 to build the world's first commercial electric power station with the financial support of a group led by J. P. Morgan. Edison supervised this project, known as the Pearl Street Station, and in 1882 New York became the first major city to experience electric lighting.

Realizing that electric lighting would most certainly replace gas, Consolidated Gas started buying New York's electric companies, including Anthony Brady's New York Gas and Electric Light, Heat and Power Company (1900), which consolidated with Edison's Illuminating Company in 1901 to form the New York Edison Company. More than 170 other purchases followed, including the 1930 acquisition of The New York Steam Company (founded in 1882) to provide a cheap source of steam for the company's electric turbines. In 1936 this amalgamation of utilities unified as the Consolidated Edison Company of New York, furnishing power to all of New York City and Westchester County.

In 1962 Con Ed opened its first nuclear station at Indian Point. Environmentalists worried that Con Ed's proposed Cornwall pumped-storage plant, to be built at the foot of Storm King Mountain, would damage the local ecosystem and managed to delay construction throughout the 1960s and early 1970s. A federal court ordered Con Ed to cease construction of the plant in 1974. In the meantime Con Ed had trouble supplying enough power to meet demand. Inflation and the Arab oil embargo drove up the price of oil (Con Ed's main energy source), and in 1974 the company skipped a dividend for the first time since 1885. The New York State Power Authority bought 2 of Con Ed's unfinished power plants, saving the company about $200 million.

Con Ed started buying power from various suppliers, including Hydro-Quebec, and in 1984 agreed to a 2-year rate freeze, a boon to New Yorkers, whose electric bills were nearly twice as high as those of most other big city residents. Con Ed continues to contract for additional power and in 1990 agreed to buy up to 1,600 megawatts (780 from Hydro-Quebec) to be delivered during its peak demand period (April through October). New gas supplies from Canada should be available to the company starting in November 1991.

WHAT

	1990 Sales	
	$ mil.	% of total
Residential	1,829	32
Commercial & industrial	3,178	55
Sales to other utilities	54	1
Other	675	12
Adjustments	3	—
Total	**5,739**	**100**

	1990 Sales		1990 Operating Income	
	$ mil.	% of total	$ mil.	% of total
Electric	4,745	83	964	88
Gas	698	12	115	11
Steam	296	5	11	1
Total	**5,739**	**100**	**1,090**	**100**

	1990 Fuel Sources
	% of total
Natural gas	29
Nuclear	28
Oil	28
Coal	8
Hydroelectric	6
Refuse	1
Total	**100**

HOW MUCH

	9-Year Growth	1981	1982	1983	1984	1985	1986	1987	1988	1989	1990
Sales ($ mil.)	1.9%	4,866	5,067	5,516	5,729	5,498	5,198	5,094	5,109	5,551	5,739
Net income ($ mil.)	2.7%	448	493	576	620	564	546	550	599	606	572
Income as % of sales	—	9.2%	9.7%	10.4%	10.8%	10.3%	10.5%	10.8%	11.7%	10.9%	10.0%
Earnings per share ($)	4.2%	1.61	1.78	2.08	2.24	2.13	2.13	2.21	2.47	2.49	2.34
Stock price – high ($)	—	8.41	10.56	12.94	15.63	19.81	26.44	26.00	23.75	29.88	29.25
Stock price – low ($)	—	5.66	7.72	9.50	11.31	14.69	18.81	18.75	20.44	22.19	19.75
Stock price – close ($)	12.6%	8.13	10.25	12.44	15.38	19.75	23.56	20.88	23.25	29.13	23.63
P/E – high	—	5	6	6	7	9	12	12	10	12	13
P/E – low	—	4	4	5	5	7	9	8	8	9	8
Dividends per share ($)	10.5%	0.74	0.84	0.94	1.06	1.20	1.34	1.48	1.60	1.72	1.82
Book value per share ($)	5.4%	12.28	13.16	14.27	15.44	16.35	17.03	17.59	18.44	19.21	19.73

1990 Year-end:
Debt ratio: 39.8%
Return on equity: 12%
Cash (mil.): $353
Current ratio: 1.35
Long-term debt (mil.): $3,371
No. of shares (mil.): 228
Dividends:
  1990 average yield: 7.7%
  1990 payout: 77.8%
Market value (mil.): $5,392

Stock Price History High/Low 1981–90

RANKINGS

24th in *Fortune* 50 Utilities
124th in *Business Week* 1000

CONSOLIDATED FREIGHTWAYS, INC.

NYSE symbol: CNF
Fiscal year ends: December 31

Hoover's Rating: D

OVERVIEW

Consolidated Freightways (CF) is a full-service transportation company capable of delivering freight or packages to almost any address in the world by road, rail, sea, or air. Its trucking division, one of America's largest, operates 4 long-haul trucking companies, specializing in less-than-truckload (LTL) shipments, those weighing less than 10,000 pounds. Its regional trucking division (Con-Way) offers overnight deliveries to cities in 28 states and Mexico. Con-Way's intermodal operations (freight shipped by truck, train, or ship in the same container) serve almost 200 ports. Its Emery Worldwide division is the world's #1 heavy freight air carrier.

Since buying Emery in 1989, CF's earnings have decayed from a $113 million profit in 1988 to a $28 million loss in 1990. Volatile fuel prices and the recession are partly to blame; however, Emery seems to be the main culprit, with losses totaling $128 million in 1990.

CF has moved to improve its financial position by renegotiating bank financing agreements and implementing strict cost controls. President Lary Scott resigned under pressure in mid-1990; his replacement, financial wizard Donald E. Moffitt, came out of retirement to help turn the company around.

WHO

Chairman: Raymond F. O'Brien, age 68, $315,005 pay
VC: J. Frank Leach, age 70
President and CEO: Donald E. Moffitt, age 58, $263,429 pay (prior to promotion)
EVP Operations; President, Consolidated Freightways Corp. of Delaware: Robert H. Lawrence, age 53, $326,994 pay
SVP and CFO: Gregory L. Quensel, age 42
VP Personnel and Safety, CF Motor Freight: William F. McCann
Auditors: Arthur Andersen & Co.
Employees: 41,300

WHEN

Leland James, co-owner of a Portland, Oregon, bus company, founded Consolidated Truck Lines in 1929. The company offered heavy hauling, moving, and other transportation services in the Pacific Northwest. Operations extended to San Francisco and Idaho by 1934 and North Dakota by 1936. The company adopted its present name in 1939.

James formed Freightways Manufacturing that year, making CF the only trucking company to design and build its own trucks (Freightliners). Between 1940 and 1950 CF used acquisitions to extend service to Chicago, Minneapolis, and Los Angeles.

After going public in 1951, CF moved its headquarters to Menlo Park, California, in 1956. More acquisitions (52 between 1955 and 1960) extended operations throughout the US and Canada. When an attempt to coordinate intermodal services with railroads and shipping lines failed, contributing to a loss of $2.7 million in 1960, William White (formerly of the Delaware Lackawanna and Western Railroad) became president. White terminated intermodal operations and decided to focus trucking operations on LTL shipments.

In 1969 CF bought Pacific Far East Lines, a San Francisco shipping line founded in 1946. This company still operates as part of Con-Way

Intermodal, which serves Europe, Australia, and the Pacific Rim. In 1970 CF formed CF AirFreight to offer air cargo services in the US and Canada. CF used the proceeds from the 1981 sale of Freightways Manufacturing to establish regional trucking operations called Con-Way Transportation Services (1983).

In 1989 CF bought Emery Air Freight, an international air cargo service, planning to operate it with CF AirFreight as Emery Worldwide. Founded in 1946 by ex–naval officer John Emery, Emery Air Freight expanded across the US (and overseas, 1956) by using extra cargo space on scheduled airlines. The company chartered aircraft in the early 1970s and bought its first plane in 1979. Emery established hubs at Dayton, Ohio (1981), and Maastricht, Holland (1985). After buying Purolator Courier in 1987, Emery had trouble merging Purolator's envelope delivery and its own air cargo businesses. It was further plagued by a 1988 takeover attempt by former Federal Express president Arthur Bass, resulting in losses of almost $100 million.

CF brought in Bass as Emery's president in 1990, hoping he could turn it around. But early in 1991, as Emery's losses dragged CF into red ink, Bass resigned. W. Roger Curry, his replacement, has been with CF since 1969.

WHERE

HQ: 175 Linfield Dr., Menlo Park, CA 94025-3799
Phone: 415-326-1700
Fax: 415-321-1741

CF has trucking operations in the US, Canada, Mexico, Puerto Rico, and the Caribbean through a network of 709 terminals and offers air freight services in 90 countries. CF operates 55,010 trucks, tractors, trailers, and vans, and 90 aircraft.

	1990 Sales		1990 Operating Income	
	$ mil.	% of total	$ mil.	% of total
US	3,640	86	16	—
Other countries	569	14	(10)	—
Adjustments	—	—	11	—
Total	**4,209**	**100**	**17**	**—**

WHAT

	1990 Sales		1990 Operating Income	
	$ mil.	% of total	$ mil.	% of total
Air freight	1,385	33	(128)	—
Long-haul trucking	2,185	52	108	—
Regional trucking	639	15	26	—
Adjustments	—	—	11	—
Total	**4,209**	**100**	**17**	**—**

Consolidated Freightways Corp. of Delaware
Canadian Freightways
CF Motor Freight
Menlo Logistics
Milne & Craighead Customs Brokers
Road Systems, Inc. (trailer manufacturer)
Willamette Sales Co. (equipment distributor)

Con-Way Transportation Services, Inc.
Con-Way (regional trucking companies)
Con-Way Intermodal, Inc. (intermodal)

Emery Worldwide
EMCON (telecommunications)
Emery Worldwide Customs Brokers
Emery Worldwide Airlines, Inc.

RANKINGS

14th in *Fortune* 50 Transportation Cos.
760th in *Business Week* 1000

KEY COMPETITORS

American President	Norfolk Southern
Burlington Northern	Rio Grande Industries
Canadian Pacific	Roadway
Chicago and North Western	Santa Fe Pacific
Consolidated Rail	Union Pacific
CSX	UPS
Federal Express	Yellow Freight
Lufthansa	Other airlines

HOW MUCH

	9-Year Growth	1981	1982	1983	1984	1985	1986	1987	1988	1989	1990
Sales ($ mil.)	15.6%	1,144	1,204	1,355	1,705	1,882	2,124	2,297	2,689	3,760	4,209
Net income ($ mil.)	—	64	55	65	74	79	89	75	113	9	(28)
Income as % of sales	—	5.6%	4.6%	4.8%	4.4%	4.2%	4.2%	3.2%	4.2%	0.2%	(0.7%)
Earnings per share ($)	—	1.60	1.36	1.62	1.87	2.07	2.31	1.93	3.00	0.02	(1.16)
Stock price – high ($)	—	15.00	18.42	20.42	20.00	27.50	36.50	41.25	34.75	37.75	26.88
Stock price – low ($)	—	8.17	10.67	16.00	13.42	18.67	23.67	22.75	25.25	25.25	10.75
Stock price – close ($)	(1.3%)	13.17	16.67	20.08	19.17	26.50	30.00	27.50	33.00	26.50	11.75
P/E – high	—	9	14	13	11	13	16	21	12	1,888	—
P/E – low	—	5	8	10	7	9	10	12	8	1,263	—
Dividends per share ($)	0.7%	0.50	0.53	0.58	0.65	0.72	0.80	0.88	0.96	1.04	0.53
Book value per share ($)	4.1%	11.60	12.32	13.33	14.42	15.69	17.22	18.16	20.32	18.01	16.63

1990 Year-end:
Debt ratio: 53.6%
Return on equity: —
Cash (mil.): $218
Current ratio: 1.10
Long-term debt (mil.): $674
No. of shares (mil.): 35
Dividends:
  1990 average yield: 4.5%
  1990 payout: —
Market value (mil.): $411

Stock Price History High/Low 1981–90

CONSOLIDATED RAIL CORPORATION

OVERVIEW

Philadelphia-based Consolidated Railroad Corporation (Conrail), the corporate successor of the bankrupt Penn Central railroad, is the dominant railroad in the populous and highly industrialized Northeast. Its 12,828-mile rail network stretches from Massachusetts to Missouri, across 13 northeastern and midwestern states and Quebec, with connections to the West Coast, Texas, and the South.

For the past 5 years Conrail has been a leading transporter of intermodal (truck-to-train) cargo. Specialized intermodal services (including door-to-door delivery) are handled by its subsidiary Conrail Mercury. Automotive parts and vehicle traffic (another important source of revenue) was down 11.4% in 1990, reflecting the sluggish state of the US economy; chemical products remained stable; and coal traffic improved by 7.4%, primarily as the result of Conrail's 1990 acquisition of the Monongahela Railway Company.

Conrail is a partner in Concord Resource Group, an operator of solid and hazardous waste facilities. Since 1989 it has been a limited partner in Union Energy Partnership, which develops electric cogeneration projects.

NYSE symbol: CRR
Fiscal year ends: December 31

Hoover's Rating C

WHO

Chairman, President, and CEO: James A. Hagen, age 59, $799,893 pay
SVP Finance: H. William Brown, age 52, $340,889 pay
SVP Operations: Donald A. Swanson, age 60, $296,422 pay
VP (Human) Resource Development: Richard C. Sullivan, age 62
Auditors: Coopers & Lybrand
Employees: 27,787

WHEN

Conrail's earliest predecessor, the Mohawk & Hudson, opened a line between Albany and Schenectady, New York, in 1831. It merged with 9 other railroads to form the New York Central (NYC) in 1853. Cornelius Vanderbilt acquired NYC in 1867 and merged it with other railroads 2 years later. By 1914 the railroad stretched from New York to Chicago. Alfred E. Perlman (appointed president by chairman Robert R. Young) shifted the railroad's emphasis from passenger traffic to freight operations in the 1950s. He led the company to merge with the rival Pennsylvania Railroad (the Pennsy) in 1968.

The Pennsy (chartered in 1846 to run from Harrisburg to Philadelphia) for many years led the industry in revenues and tonnage hauled and had an unequaled history of dividend payment until 1946. After WWII the company was burdened by an overbuilt system and declining traffic. Pennsy chairman James M. Symes began planning a merger with NYC in 1957; the merger was completed 11 years later under his successor, Stuart T. Saunders. The new company was named Penn Central Transportation Company.

Penn Central, hurt by mismanagement and still-dwindling traffic, endured heavy losses for 2 years before declaring bankruptcy (one of the nation's largest) in 1970. After studying the chaotic state of the eastern rail system, in 1976 the US government created Conrail to assume the operations of Penn Central and 5 other failed railroads: Central of New Jersey, Erie Lackawanna, Lehigh & Hudson River, Lehigh Valley, and Reading (Penn Central survives as a diversified holding company). With federal financing of $2.1 billion, Conrail sold its intercity passenger operations to Amtrak and rebuilt its physical plant.

Conrail had lost $1.5 billion by 1981, when former Southern Railway chairman L. Stanley Crane became CEO. Crane, with the help of labor concessions and favorable federal legislation, engineered a dramatic turnaround that culminated in a 1984 profit of $472 million. The government sold its 85% stake in Conrail to the public for $1.59 billion in 1987, with the remaining 15% going to the railroad's employees. After Crane's retirement in 1988, Conrail continued as a profitable railroad.

The company took its first step outside the railroad business in 1989 by forming a joint venture with OHM Corporation (Concord Resource Group) to operate a network of solid and hazardous waste handling facilities. That same year Conrail formed a subsidiary to handle door-to-door intermodal deliveries (Conrail Mercury). In 1990 Conrail bought the remaining 2/3 of coal-hauling Monongahela Railway Company and sold its Pennsylvania Truck Lines subsidiary.

WHERE

HQ: Six Penn Center Plaza, Philadelphia, PA 19103-2959
Phone: 215-977-4000
Fax: 215-977-5567

Principal Cities Served

Albany, NY	Indianapolis, IN
Baltimore, MD	Louisville, KY
Boston, MA	Montreal, Quebec
Buffalo, NY	New York, NY
Charleston, WV	Newark, NJ
Chicago, IL	Philadelphia, PA
Cincinnati, OH	Pittsburgh, PA
Cleveland, OH	Streator, IL
Columbus, OH	Syracuse, NY
Detroit, MI	Toledo, OH
East St. Louis, IL	Washington, DC
Hagerstown, MD	Wilmington, DE
Harrisburg, PA	

WHAT

	1990 Sales	
Items transported	$ mil.	% of total
Chemical products	578	17
Intermodal	554	16
Automotive	481	14
Coal	520	15
Metal products	402	12
Food & grain products	324	10
Forest products	295	9
Other	218	7
Total	**3,372**	**100**

Subsidiaries and Affiliates
Concord Resources Group (50%, hazardous waste handling joint venture with OHM Corporation)
Conrail Mercury (customized intermodal service)
Trailer Train Company (21.8%, rail-car leasing)

RANKINGS

16th in *Fortune* 50 Transportation Cos.
335th in *Business Week* 1000

KEY COMPETITORS

American President	Ogden
Bechtel	Roadway
Browning-Ferris	Ryder
Canadian Pacific	TRW
Consolidated	Union Pacific
Freightways	Waste
CSX	Management
JWP	Yellow Freight
Norfolk Southern	

HOW MUCH

	9-Year Growth	1981	1982	1983	1984	1985	1986	1987	1988	1989	1990
Sales ($ mil.)	(2.4%)	4,201	3,617	3,076	3,379	3,208	3,144	3,247	3,490	3,411	3,372
Net income ($ mil.)	22.7%	39	174	298	472	361	316	267	306	148	247
Income as % of sales	—	0.9%	4.8%	9.7%	14.0%	11.3%	10.1%	8.2%	8.8%	4.3%	7.3%
Earnings per share ($)	25.5%	0.62	2.80	4.75	7.43	5.55	4.75	3.88	4.44	2.17	4.78
Stock price – high ($)	—	—	—	—	—	—	—	40.88	35.38	49.38	51.38
Stock price – low ($)	—	—	—	—	—	—	—	19.88	26.38	32.00	32.38
Stock price – close ($)	—	—	—	—	—	—	—	27.63	33.75	47.88	40.25
P/E – high	—	—	—	—	—	—	—	11	8	23	11
P/E – low	—	—	—	—	—	—	—	5	6	15	7
Dividends per share ($)	—	—	—	—	—	—	—	0.50	1.10	1.30	1.50
Book value per share ($)	43.8%	2.46	5.38	10.65	18.56	25.99	26.54	55.52	59.00	60.24	64.99

1990 Year-end:
Debt ratio: 36.5%
Return on equity: 7.6%
Cash (mil.): $153
Current ratio: 0.80
Long-term debt (mil.): $1,680
No. of shares (mil.): 41
Dividends:
  1990 average yield: 3.7%
  1990 payout: 31.4%
Market value (mil.): $1,636

Stock Price History
High/Low 1987–90

CONTINENTAL AIRLINES HOLDINGS, INC.

ASE symbol: CTA
Fiscal year ends: December 31

Hoover's Rating **D**

OVERVIEW

Continental Airlines Holdings is primarily made up of Continental Airlines but also operates the Chelsea catering service and, through a partnership with Electronic Data Systems (EDS) Corporation (a GM subsidiary), the System One computer reservations system.

Despite its 1990 bankruptcy proceedings, Continental remains the dominant carrier at its Houston and Newark hubs. Route expansion has continued, and in 1991 Continental added many of its defunct Eastern Air Lines unit's Florida routes and service to Frankfurt.

Without Eastern as a drain on cash flow, Continental seems to be in a good position to improve its balance sheet. In mid-1991 the company negotiated $120 million in financing from Chase Manhattan Bank. It is considering a possible merger with Northwest Airlines (America's 4th largest airline). Continental is talking to H. Ross Perot, Jr., (son of EDS founder) about a possible investment. Other interested investors include USAir Group and Marvin Davis. SAS currently owns a 16.8% stake in Continental.

WHEN

Trans Texas Airways, a Houston-based, local-service airline, began serving Texas communities in 1947. The company changed its name to Texas International in 1968 and was serving the West Coast and Mexico by 1970. However, the company was unable to compete with major airlines on interstate routes and commuter airlines in Texas and faced bankruptcy by 1972, when Frank Lorenzo's Jet Capital Corporation gained control. With Lorenzo at the helm, Texas International had netted over $3 million by 1976. In 1980 Lorenzo formed Texas Air, a holding company for Texas International and a newly created New York–to–Washington, DC, shuttle, New York Air.

In 1981 Texas Air bought 50% of Continental Airlines (founded as Varney Speed Lines in 1934), which operated in the western US, Mexico, and the Pacific. Continental's employees tried to block the takeover, but Texas Air bought the rest of the company in 1982. Continental had lost over $500 million between 1978 and 1983, and in 1983 Lorenzo's efforts to wrest wage concessions from the airline's unions resulted in a strike. Lorenzo then maneuvered the airline into Chapter 11, thereby canceling all union contracts. Continental emerged from bankruptcy in 1986 as a nonunion, low-fare carrier with the industry's lowest labor costs.

That year Texas Air bought Eastern Air Lines (founded as Pitcairn Aviation in 1927).

WWI ace Eddie Rickenbacker ran Eastern from 1935 until his retirement in 1963, but losses throughout the 1960s and 1970s, compounded by union disputes, forced CEO Frank Borman (ex-astronaut) to sell it in 1986. Texas Air also bought People Express Airlines and Frontier Airlines in 1986, making it the #1 US airline in terms of passenger miles flown.

In 1988 Lorenzo sold Eastern's Air Shuttle to Donald Trump, but in 1989 mounting losses and a machinists' strike forced Eastern into bankruptcy. In 1990 the bankruptcy court removed Texas Air from Eastern's management, appointing Martin Shugrue as trustee. Texas Air then changed its name to Continental Airlines Holdings. Lorenzo resigned as chairman, president, and CEO after selling his stake in the company to SAS for a substantial premium plus $19.7 million in salary and severance pay. Following Lorenzo's resignation, Hollis L. Harris, former president of Delta Air Lines, was named CEO.

With fuel prices skyrocketing and traffic down, Continental followed Eastern into bankruptcy late in 1990. Eastern held on until January 1991, when mounting losses forced it to liquidate. Harris, who opposed new cost-cutting efforts (which included flight and employee cutbacks and the deferral of $315 million in debt payments), left Continental in 1991 and was replaced by former CFO Robert Ferguson III.

WHO

Chairman: Carl R. Pohlad, age 75
President and CEO; VC and CEO, Continental Airlines, Inc.: Robert R. Ferguson III, age 42
EVP and COO; EVP Corporate Affairs, Continental Airlines, Inc.: Charles T. Goolsbee, age 56
VP Finance and CFO, Continental Airlines, Inc.: Richard H. Shuyler, age 44
SVP Human Resources, Continental Airlines, Inc.: Robert Allen, age 44
Auditors: Arthur Andersen & Co.
Employees: 34,800

WHERE

HQ: 2929 Allen Pkwy., Suite 2010, Houston, TX 77019
Phone: 713-834-2950
Fax: 713-834-2087
Reservations: 800-525-0280

Continental flies to 161 cities in the US and 55 foreign countries.

Hub Locations
Cleveland
Denver
Honolulu
Houston
Newark

WHAT

| | 1990 Sales | |
	$ mil.	% of total
Passengers	5,166	83
Cargo, mail & other	1,065	17
Total	**6,231**	**100**

Major Subsidiaries and Affiliates
Continental Airlines, Inc.
System One Holdings, Inc. (computer reservation system)
Chelsea Catering Corp. (airline catering services)

Flight Equipment	No.	Average Age in Years
Boeing 747	9	19.4
DC-10	17	16.2
Boeing 727	103	17.4
MD-80	65	6.0
DC-9	35	19.9
Boeing 737	94	11.7
A300	17	9.6
Total	**340**	**13.5**

RANKINGS

10th in *Fortune* 50 Transportation Cos.

KEY COMPETITORS

Alaska Air	KLM	Singapore
America West	Lufthansa	Airlines
AMR	Midway	Southwest
British Airways	NWA	Swire Pacific
Delta	Pan Am	TWA
HAL	Qantas	UAL
JAL	SAS	USAir

HOW MUCH

	9-Year Growth	1981	1982	1983	1984	1985	1986	1987	1988	1989	1990
Sales ($ mil.)	—	719	1,516	1,246	1,372	1,944	4,407	8,475	8,573	6,685	6,231
Net income ($ mil.)	—	(47)	(49)	(180)	28	49	42	(466)	(719)	(886)	(2,403)
Income as % of sales	—	(6.6%)	(3.2%)	(14.4%)	2.0%	2.5%	1.0%	(5.5%)	(8.4%)	(13.2%)	(38.6%)
Earnings per share ($)	—	(8.11)	(7.27)	(14.74)	1.20	1.81	0.68	(12.58)	(18.88)	(22.71)	(58.96)
Stock price – high ($)	—	15.25	13.88	12.38	9.88	20.00	40.88	51.50	17.13	23.38	12.13
Stock price – low ($)	—	5.13	4.00	4.75	5.63	8.88	14.13	9.00	8.88	11.13	1.00
Stock price – close ($)	(12.2%)	5.63	10.75	6.63	9.13	15.00	33.75	10.88	11.88	11.50	1.75
P/E – high	—	—	—	—	8	11	60	—	—	—	—
P/E – low	—	—	—	—	5	5	21	—	—	—	—
Dividends per share ($)	(100%)	0.16	0.16	0.08	0.00	0.00	0.00	0.00	0.00	0.00	0.00
Book value per share ($)	—	7.30	4.90	(8.88)	(5.24)	5.48	22.00	12.53	(5.47)	(26.80)	(80.18)

1990 Year-end:
Debt ratio: 0.0%
Return on equity: —
Cash (mil.): $198
Current ratio: 0.95
Long-term debt (mil.): $0
No. of shares (mil.): 43
Dividends:
  1990 average yield: 0.0%
  1990 payout: 0.0%
Market value (mil.): $75

Stock Price History High/Low 1981–90

CONTINENTAL BANK CORPORATION

OVERVIEW

When Continental stumbled in 1984, it was the biggest banking collapse in US history: Continental was larger than all the banks that failed during the Great Depression combined.

Even now Continental is the 26th largest bank holding company in the nation. Its primary holding is the bank, Chicago's 2nd largest (after First Chicago), all but indistinguishable from the corporate parent. After a round of layoffs, all but 53 of Continental's more than 6,402 employees work for the bank.

In 1991 Continental, free of government ownership for the first time, is recovering with a new "business bank" orientation, the latest in a string of strategies since 1984. The bank is trying to woo corporate clients with services ranging from cash management to merger and acquisition arrangement. The bank offers private banking services to well-to-do individuals.

NYSE symbol: CBK
Fiscal year ends: December 31

 Hoover's Rating **D**

WHO

Chairman and CEO: Thomas C. Theobald, age 53, $890,000 pay
CFO: Hollis W. Rademacher, age 55, $450,000 pay
Chief Human Resources Officer: Joseph V. Thompson, age 48
Auditors: Price Waterhouse
Employees: 6,402

WHEN

Continental Bank, still struggling to climb out of its 1984 collapse and federal bailout, traces its modern history to another government rescue during the Great Depression.

In the 1920s Continental emerged from a series of Chicago bank mergers. Merchants' Loan and Trust, Illinois Trust and Savings, and Corn Exchange National Bank became Illinois Merchants' Trust in 1924. Illinois Merchants' Trust in turn joined with Continental and Commercial Banks in 1928 to become Continental Illinois Bank and Trust.

In 1932 the New Deal's Reconstruction Finance Corporation loaned $50 million to Depression-battered Continental. Walter Cummings, an official of the newly created FDIC, became chairman of the bank. His conservative leadership — investing in low-risk government securities and loaning to the most creditworthy of customers — retired the bank's debt to the government in 1939.

In 1959 Cummings retired, and successor David Kennedy, later to serve as Richard Nixon's first secretary of the treasury, loosened the purse strings for more aggressive lending. In the 1970s Continental surpassed archrival First Chicago, hobbled by loan problems of its own, as Chicago's largest bank. Continental eschewed gathering traditional deposits in favor of riskier, short-term transactions to raise money to lend.

Much of Continental's growth came from energy loans, some purchased from Penn Square, an oil-boom bank headquartered in an

Oklahoma City shopping center. Penn Square's failure in 1982 left Continental with $1 billion in bad loans. That snowballed into a 1984 run on the bank by large depositors.

Federal officials and major banks shored up Continental with $4.5 billion in guarantees. The FDIC in effect nationalized the bank, taking 80% ownership. Federal officials recruited John Swearingen, Amoco's former chairman, to lead the bank. Continental bought 3 small suburban banks (1986) to boost retail deposits and purchased First Options, the nation's largest clearing firm for option traders (1986).

When Swearingen retired in 1987, Continental replaced him with Citicorp executive Thomas Theobald. Theobald sold Continental's suburban holdings (1988) and First Options (1991) to reposition Continental to serve corporate customers. In 1988 Continental formally dropped "Illinois" from its name to stress its nationwide focus. Continental sold all retail accounts to First Chicago and lowered its exposure to bad international loans, but retooling to a business bank hasn't been easy. In 1990 the company cut 900 jobs from its trading and distribution payroll, an area it had beefed up only 2 years before.

The Tisch family bought more than 7% of Continental stock, and the government sold off the last of its bailout stake in 1991. Also that year the bank quit its role as a primary US securities dealer; it cut jobs and closed offices as it increased reserves against potentially damaging California real estate loans.

WHERE

HQ: 231 S. LaSalle St., Chicago, IL 60697
Phone: 312-828-7450
Fax: 312-828-7150

Chicago-based Continental operates in 9 other US cities and 11 foreign countries.

	1990 Assets	
	$ mil.	% of total
US	20,262	75
Continental Europe	1,468	5
Latin America/Caribbean	1,885	7
Asia/Pacific	1,345	5
UK	1,885	7
Other countries	317	1
LDC reserve	(19)	—
Total	**27,143**	**100**

WHAT

	1990 Assets	
	$ mil.	% of total
Cash and noninterest deposits	2,176	8
Interest-bearing deposits	2,266	8
Federal funds sold	704	3
Securities purchased to resell	2,105	7
Trading account assets	1,518	6
Investment securities	1,458	5
Loans	15,330	57
Reserve for credit losses	(288)	(1)
Customers' liability on acceptances	268	1
Interest and fees receivable	196	1
Properties and equipment	231	1
Other assets	1,179	4
Total	**27,143**	**100**

Corporate Finance
Distribution of loans
Loans to corporations
Syndication of loans

Market Making/Risk Management
Foreign exchange trading
Trading accounts
Venture capital

Specialized Financial Services
Cash-management services
Personal trust services
Private banking services
Securities and clearing services

HOW MUCH

	9-Year Growth	1981	1982	1983	1984	1985	1986	1987	1988	1989	1990
Assets ($ mil.)	(5.9%)	46,972	42,899	42,097	30,413	30,528	32,809	32,391	30,578	29,549	27,143
Net income ($ mil.)	(11.1%)	255	78	101	(1,087)	134	99	(610)	316	286	88
Income as % of assets	—	0.5%	0.2%	0.2%	(3.6%)	0.4%	0.3%	(1.9%)	1.0%	1.0%	0.3%
Earnings per share ($)	(30.7%)	25.76	7.80	9.84	(107.96)	1.68	1.16	(24.28)	5.19	4.64	0.95
Stock price – high ($)	—	171.00	146.00	103.50	91.00	40.50	41.00	24.50	23.50	26.63	21.50
Stock price – low ($)	—	123.50	60.50	74.00	11.00	23.00	20.00	9.00	11.00	18.50	7.13
Stock price – close ($)	(25.9%)	132.50	81.50	87.50	23.00	39.50	21.50	12.00	20.75	19.88	8.88
P/E – high	—	7	19	11	—	24	35	—	5	6	23
P/E – low	—	5	8	8	—	14	17	—	2	4	8
Dividends per share ($)	(20.2%)	7.60	8.00	8.00	2.00	0.00	0.08	0.32	0.44	0.85	1.00
Book value per share ($)	(19.6%)	172.79	171.23	172.55	56.41	64.06	42.92	17.48	23.60	24.51	24.21

1990 Year-end:
Return on equity: 3.9%
Equity as % of assets: 6.1%
Cash (mil.): $4,442
Long-term debt (mil.): $917
No. of shares (mil.): 50
Dividends:
  1990 average yield: 11.3%
  1990 payout: 105.3%
Market value (mil.): $441
Sales (mil.): $3,070

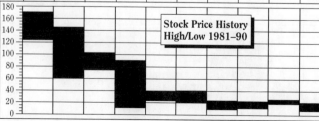

Stock Price History High/Low 1981–90

RANKINGS

26th in *Fortune* 100 Commercial Banking Cos.
722nd in *Business Week* 1000

KEY COMPETITORS

Bankers Trust
First Chicago
J.P. Morgan
Other money-center and international banks

CONTINENTAL GRAIN COMPANY

OVERVIEW

From its headquarters in New York City, privately owned Continental Grain oversees the world's 2nd largest grain and related commodities empire (Cargill is #1). With estimated sales of almost $15 billion, Continental is the nation's 3rd largest private company (after Cargill and Koch Industries) and handles roughly 1/5 of the grain and oilseeds exported from the US. The company has additional operations in livestock, shipping, chemicals, food processing, and financial services.

Through its various commodities groups, Continental buys and sells commodities in more than 58 countries throughout the world. Each year the company stores, handles, and ships billions of bushels of wheat, soybeans, oilseeds, rice, feed grains, cotton, and other agricultural products. Continental stores and transports its goods through an international network of grain elevators, railroad cars, and ships.

The company's livestock operations annually process billions of pounds of beef, pork, chicken, shrimp, and fish. The chemicals unit distributes and trades liquefied petroleum gases (LPG) and fertilizers. Continental's Financial Services Group provides a range of services including government securities trading and trade financing.

Today ownership of the company rests primarily in the hands of Michel Fribourg, great-great-grandson of Continental's founder, who is said to own about 90% of the company's stock (Fribourg's share of the company is estimated to be worth almost $1 billion).

Private company
Fiscal year ends: March 31

Hoover's Rating **B**

WHO

Chairman: Michel Fribourg, age 77
CEO and President: Donald L. Staheli, age 59
EVP and CFO: James J. Bigham
SVP: Paul Fribourg, age 37
Director of Human Resources: Dwight Coffin
Employees: 14,500

WHERE

HQ: 277 Park Ave., New York, NY 10172-0178
Phone: 212-207-5100
Fax: 212-207-5181

Continental Grain has operations in 58 countries.

WHEN

In 1813 Simon Fribourg founded a commodity trading business in Belgium. The company operated primarily as a domestic concern until 1848 when a severe drought in Belgium caused the company to buy large stocks in Russian wheat.

As the Industrial Revolution swept across Europe and populations shifted towards the cities, countries became more dependent upon traded grain. In the midst of such rapid changes, the company prospered.

After WWI, Russia, which had previously been Europe's primary grain supplier, ceased to be a significant player in the trading game, and the countries of the Western Hemisphere picked up the slack. Sensing the shift, Jules and René Fribourg reorganized the business as Continental Grain and opened the company's first US office in Chicago in 1921. Seven years later Continental leased a grain elevator in St. Louis. During the Depression, the company directed its US agents to buy grain elevators wherever they could find them, often at depressed prices. In 1930 Continental leased a Galveston terminal from the Southern Pacific Railroad. Through its rapid purchases, the company built an elaborate North American grain network including such important locations as Kansas City, Nashville, and Toledo.

Meanwhile, in Europe the Fribourgs were forced to weather constant political and economic upheaval, often profiting from it (the Fribourgs supplied food to the Republican forces during the Spanish Civil War). When the Nazis invaded Belgium in 1940, the Fribourgs were forced to flee but reorganized the business in New York City after the war.

During the postwar years, Continental constructed a lucrative grain trade with the Soviets and expanded its international presence. During the 1960s and 1970s, the company went on a buying spree beginning with Allied Mills (flour milling, 1965), rapidly absorbing several agricultural and transport businesses, including feedlots in Texas, an English soybean producer, and a bakery. In 1970 Continental bought Quaker Oat's agricultural products unit.

In 1979 the company found itself uncomfortably caught between US diplomacy and business when it tried to collect $80 million from Toprak Mahsulleri Ofisi, a state-owned Turkish grain company that had reneged on a contract to buy 385,000 tons of wheat from Continental.

During the 1980s the company decided to trim its fat and sold its baking units (Oroweat and Arnold) as well as its commodities brokerage house. Michel Fribourg stepped down as CEO in 1988, passing the title to Donald Staheli, the first non–family member to hold the position. However, it is entirely possible that a 6th generation of Fribourgs will lead the company — Michel's son Paul is a senior vice president.

In 1991 the company announced a joint venture with Scoular Co. to form a grain-handling and -merchandising business.

WHAT

World Grain Group
Arabfin (Middle Eastern trading unit, Geneva)
ContiCarriers & Terminals (transport, Chicago)
Finagrain (European trading unit, Geneva)
North American Grain (Chicago)
World Grain Merchandising and Marketing (New York)

World Oilseeds and Merchandising Group
ContiLatin (Latin American trading unit, New York)
ContiQuincy Export (soybean merchandising partnership with Quincy Soybean)
World Oilseeds Processing Division (New York)

General Commodities Group
ContiChem (liquefied petroleum gases, New York)
ContiChem Fertilizer (Tampa, Florida)
ContiCotton (cotton merchandising, Fresno)
Continental Grain (Canada)
Rice Division (rice trading, New York)

World Milling Industries Group
Asian Agri Industries (China)
Baronet Corporation (women's accessories; Secaucus, New Jersey)
ContiMilling (New York)
Wayne Feed (Chicago)

World Meat Industries Group
Cattle Feeding Division (Chicago)
Dutch Quality House (poultry, Georgia)
Loveland Foods (pork, Colorado)
Southern Foods (pork, Georgia)
Wayne Poultry (Georgia)

Financial Services Group
ContiFinancial Services (New York)
ContiTrade Services (New York)
Foreign Exchange Trading Division (New York)
Government Securities Trading Division (New York)

RANKINGS

3rd in *Forbes* 400 US Private Cos.

KEY COMPETITORS

American President	CSX
ADM	W. R. Grace
Cargill	Salomon
Chiquita Brands	Tyson Foods
ConAgra	Universal Corp.
CPC	

HOW MUCH

	4-Year Growth	1981	1982	1983	1984	1985	1986	1987	1988	1989	1990
Estimated sales ($ mil.)	1.5%	—	—	—	—	—	14,000	13,500	13,000	13,500	14,850
Employees	4.8%	—	—	—	—	—	12,000	12,000	12,000	12,000	14,500

Estimated Sales ($ mil.) 1986–90

(bar chart, y-axis 0 to 16,000 in increments of 2,000)

CONTROL DATA CORPORATION

NYSE symbol: CDA
Fiscal year ends: December 31

Hoover's Rating **D**

OVERVIEW

Minneapolis-based Control Data Corporation (CDC) is a computer manufacturer and information systems services company.

CDC has organized its businesses into 2 groups: computer systems and information services. Computer systems include high-performance mainframes (CYBER 930, 960, and 2000 models) and workstations (CYBER and Control Data 4000 series) for engineering and scientific markets. This group also supplies electronics (avionics, parallel processing, and space computers) to the DOD and NASA.

CDC's services group includes the US's largest audience measurement service (Arbitron), computer systems for managing electric utilities (Empros), credit card authorization services (TeleMoney), and on-line computer systems for lotteries (Automated Wagering). CDC's Business Management Services is the 2nd largest payroll processing service. After the company sold off its disk drives, supercomputers, semiconductors, and trading room systems, CDC's 1990 revenues were 34% of peak 1984 levels, dropping 42% from 1989.

WHEN

In 1957 William Norris founded Minneapolis-based Control Data Corporation (CDC) to challenge IBM in mainframe computers for scientific applications, the giant's weak side. Norris drew fellow engineers from Sperry Rand, where he had managed the UNIVAC computer division. The gifted designer Seymour Cray helped create a stream of computers popular with the scientific community, starting with the 1604 mainframe (1958); Cray's genius also produced the advanced 6600 supercomputer (1963).

Booming computer sales allowed Norris to sponsor dearly loved social projects such as computer-based education (PLATO). CDC also diversified, buying Commercial Credit Company (1968) to provide financing for its customers' leasing needs. The company also entered joint ventures for tape and disk drive peripherals with several companies (including NCR, 1972, and Honeywell, 1975). CDC later formed the Imprimis peripherals division.

CDC's greatest coup was its settlement in 1973 of an antitrust suit against IBM, which allowed the company to purchase IBM's service bureau for far below market value. That service was the forerunner of several currently successful CDC businesses, including payroll processing and tax filing services.

In the early 1980s CDC plunged into costly supercomputers (ETA Systems, discontinued in 1989) and semiconductors (VTC division,

sold in 1990), which drained cash while remaining unprofitable. Meanwhile, CDC's Cyber mainframes and peripherals were suffering under intense Japanese competition. Losses in 1985 and 1986 totaling $800 million prompted Norris protégé Robert Price in 1986 to spin off Commercial Credit to its shareholders and sell PLATO to various buyers.

By the end of 1990, CDC had sold Imprimis (to Seagate), its 3rd-party maintenance service, the rest of the education businesses, its semiconductor operations, and its Micrognosis trading room systems. CDC's sales in 1990 dropped $1.2 billion. Employment was down to 14,500 from 18,000 in 1989 and 33,500 in 1988.

Since the hiring of new CEO Lawrence Perlman (1990), CDC has focused on a new strategic direction, which includes a commitment to open systems, systems integration, and cooperative arrangements with other computer vendors. These partnerships have included Silicon Graphics (OEM agreement for its graphics workstations), MIPS Computer Systems (development of the Control Data 4000), and Volkswagen (development of integrated computer-assisted engineering and manufacturing [ICEM] software). In spite of progress made in controlling costs, CDC's sales and earnings remained weak in 1991 due to recession in the US and Europe.

WHO

President and CEO: Lawrence Perlman, age 52, $900,000 pay

EVP and President, Computer Products: James E. Ousley, age 45, $499,598 pay

EVP and President, Information Services: William J. Miller, age 45, $314,488 pay

EVP Organization Resources (Personnel): Glenn W. Jeffrey, age 44

VP and Corporate Controller: John R. Eickhoff, age 50

Auditors: KPMG Peat Marwick

Employees: 14,500

WHERE

HQ: 8100 34th Ave. South, Box 0, Minneapolis, MN 55440
Phone: 612-853-8100
Fax: 612-853-7173

CDC's principal non-US offices are located in Canada, England, France, and Germany.

	1990 Sales		1990 Pretax Income	
	$ mil.	% of total	$ mil.	% of total
US	1,150	68	(1)	(11)
Other countries	541	32	10	111
Adjustments	—	—	7	—
Total	**1,691**	**100**	**16**	**100**

WHAT

	1990 Sales	
	$ mil.	% of total
Sales & rentals	724	43
Services	967	57
Total	**1,691**	**100**

Businesses

The Arbitron Co. (radio and TV audience measurement, product tracking)

Automated Wagering (on-line lottery systems)

Business Management Services (payroll processing, payroll tax filing, accounting)

Computer Products (mainframes, minicomputers, workstations, networking software)

Empros Systems International (electric utility management)

Government Systems (computer systems for DOD, NASA)

RANKINGS

239th in *Fortune* 500 Industrial Cos.
803rd in *Business Week* 1000

KEY COMPETITORS

Amdahl	IBM
AT&T	Machines Bull
ADP	NEC
Bally	Prime
Data General	Siemens
DEC	Storage Technology
Dun & Bradstreet	Sun Microsystems
Fujitsu	Tandem
Hewlett-Packard	Unisys
Hitachi	Wang
Intergraph	

HOW MUCH

	9-Year Growth	1981	1982	1983	1984	1985	1986	1987	1988	1989	1990
Sales ($ mil.)	(6.5%)	3,101	4,292	4,583	5,027	3,680	3,347	3,367	3,628	2,935	1,691
Net income ($ mil.)	(36.9%)	170	155	162	5	(531)	(269)	25	2	(680)	3
Income as % of sales	—	5.5%	3.6%	3.5%	0.1%	(14.4%)	(8.0%)	0.7%	0.0%	(23.2%)	0.2%
Earnings per share ($)	(39.3%)	4.46	4.04	4.19	0.12	(13.65)	(6.58)	0.59	0.03	(16.11)	0.05
Stock price – high ($)	—	42.13	42.75	64.38	48.50	38.75	28.75	38.25	30.50	24.00	21.63
Stock price – low ($)	—	29.81	21.13	35.50	24.38	15.13	18.75	17.63	16.38	16.25	7.63
Stock price – close ($)	(14.2%)	35.25	37.13	45.25	35.25	20.75	26.38	21.63	19.63	18.13	8.88
P/E – high	—	9	11	15	404	—	—	65	1,017	—	433
P/E – low	—	7	5	8	203	—	—	30	546	—	153
Dividends per share ($)	(100.0%)	0.48	0.55	0.60	0.66	0.54	0.00	0.00	0.00	0.00	0.00
Book value per share ($)	(14.3%)	42.20	46.10	47.59	45.63	29.21	23.72	24.84	24.97	9.43	10.48

1990 Year-end:
Debt ratio: 29.7%
Return on equity: 0.5%
Cash (mil.): $351
Current ratio: 1.52
Long-term debt (mil.): $193
No. of shares (mil.): 43
Dividends:
  1990 average yield: 0.0%
  1990 payout: 0.0%
Market value (mil.): $377

Stock Price History
High/Low 1981–90

COOPER INDUSTRIES, INC.

NYSE symbol: CBE
Fiscal year ends: December 31

Hoover's Rating: C+

OVERVIEW

Cooper is over 150 years old, but today's $6.2-billion diversified global manufacturer bears little resemblance to the Cooper of 2 decades ago. The company's original engine business now accounts for a small fraction of its sales, with the rest coming from electrical and oil-drilling equipment, household and industrial tools, and automotive products — mostly from companies acquired over the last 20 years.

Cooper's most famous consumer brand, Champion Spark Plug (acquired in 1989) anchors its auto segment, which also manufactures headlamps, windshield wipers, and brakes. Other consumer lines include Crescent wrenches, Xcelite screwdrivers, and Kirsch window treatments, all within Cooper's "tool basket."

Other 1980s acquisitions, such as McGraw-Edison and Cameron Iron Works, have given Cooper a significant presence in industrial and electrical equipment. The company's electrical products range from massive power transformers to tiny fuses used on circuit boards. Cooper's engines and compressors now serve the oil and gas industry, and the Cooper-Bessemer engine division forms half of a joint venture with Rolls-Royce. Cooper's purchases have more than tripled the company's size since 1983, generating an annualized average growth rate of 20% for the period.

WHEN

In 1833 Charles Cooper sold a horse for $50 and borrowed money to open a foundry with his brother Elias in Mount Vernon, Ohio. Known as C. & E. Cooper, the company made plows, hog troughs, maple syrup kettles, stoves, and wagon boxes.

In the 1840s Cooper began making steam engines for use in mills and on farms and later adapted the engines for wood-burning locomotives. In 1868 the company built its first Corliss steam engine, a significant improvement over earlier designs, and in 1875 introduced the first steam-powered farm tractor. By 1900 Cooper's steam engines were widely used and sold in the US and overseas. In 1909 Cooper introduced an internal combustion engine-compressor for natural-gas pipelines; the company's last steam engine was shipped to Japan in 1920.

In the 1920s Cooper became the biggest seller of compression engines for oil and gas pipeline transmission. A 1929 merger with Bessemer (a maker of smaller gas and diesel engines) created Cooper-Bessemer, whose diesel engines powered marine vessels. The company was hurt badly by the Depression; sales dropped 90% in 1931. The success of a new turbocharged diesel to power locomotives revived revenues.

Diversification began in the late 1950s with the purchase of Rotor Tools (1959). The company adopted its current name in 1965 and moved its headquarters to Houston in 1967. Cooper went on to acquire 20 other companies, including its "tool basket": Lufkin Rule (measuring tapes, 1967), Crescent (wrenches, 1968), and Weller (soldering tools, 1970).

The purchase of Gardner-Denver in 1979 gave Cooper a strong position in oil-drilling and mining equipment, and the 1981 acquisition of Crouse-Hinds was a significant diversification into electrical materials. Another 1981 purchase was Kirsch, maker of drapery hardware.

The dramatic decline in oil prices in the early 1980s caused sales to drop over 35% between 1981 and 1983, but the company remained profitable (though less so) because of its diversification into tools and electrical products.

The electrical segment expanded further with the 1985 purchase of McGraw-Edison, manufacturer of both consumer products (Buss fuses) and heavy transmission gear for electrical utilities. Cooper added electrical equipment maker RTE in 1988 and in 1989 bought Champion Spark Plug and Cameron Iron Works (oil-drilling equipment). In 1990 Cooper made no major purchases but spent $273 million "digesting" Champion and Cameron.

WHO

Chairman, President, and CEO: Robert Cizik, age 59, $1,342,447 pay
SVP Administration: Alan E. Riedel, age 60, $707,438 pay
SVP Finance: Dewain K. Cross, age 53, $455,541 pay
VP Personnel: Laurence H. Polsky, age 48
Auditors: Ernst & Young
Employees: 57,500

WHERE

HQ: PO Box 4446, First City Tower, 1001 Fannin St., Suite 4000, Houston, TX 77002
Phone: 713-739-5400
Fax: 713-739-5555

Cooper operates 185 plants in 24 countries.

	1990 Sales		1990 Operating Income	
	$ mil.	% of total	$ mil.	% of total
US	4,900	75	671	75
Europe	903	14	116	13
Canada	397	6	50	6
Other regions	294	5	58	6
Adjustments	(288)	—	(68)	—
Total	**6,206**	**100**	**827**	**100**

WHAT

	1990 Sales		1990 Operating Income	
	$ mil.	% of total	$ mil.	% of total
Petroleum & industrial equip.	1,857	30	242	27
Electrical products	1,611	26	289	32
Electrical power equipment	681	11	82	9
Tools & hardware	906	15	128	15
Automotive prods.	1,151	18	154	17
Adjustments	—	—	(68)	—
Total	**6,206**	**100**	**827**	**100**

Electrical Products
Belden electronic wire and cable
Buss fuses
Crouse-Hinds industrial lighting
Halo lighting

Electrical Power Equipment
McGraw-Edison transformers
RTE power system components

Tools and Hardware
Crescent wrenches
Gardner-Denver pneumatic tools

Kirsch drapery hardware
Wiss scissors and shears
Xcelite screwdrivers

Automotive Products
Anco windshield wipers
Belden wire and cable
Champion spark plugs
Wagner brakes and lights

Industrial Equipment
Ajax engine-compressors
Cameron oilfield equipment
Coberra turbines (50%, joint venture with Rolls-Royce)
Cooper-Bessemer engines and turbines
Gardner-Denver drilling equipment

RANKINGS

81st in *Fortune* 500 Industrial Cos.
120th in *Business Week* 1000

KEY COMPETITORS

ABB
Baker Hughes
Black & Decker
Borg-Warner
Dana
Dresser
Eaton

Emerson
General Electric
General Signal
Ingersoll-Rand
Masco
PACCAR

Robert Bosch
Siemens
Snap-on Tools
Square D
Stanley Works
Westinghouse

HOW MUCH

	9-Year Growth	1981	1982	1983	1984	1985	1986	1987	1988	1989	1990
Sales ($ mil.)	9.0%	2,861	2,395	1,842	2,028	3,062	3,421	3,575	4,250	5,115	6,206
Net income ($ mil.)	4.6%	241	135	71	107	135	148	174	224	268	361
Income as % of sales	—	8.4%	5.6%	3.9%	5.3%	4.4%	4.3%	4.9%	5.3%	5.2%	5.8%
Earnings per share ($)	1.7%	2.41	1.38	0.64	1.06	1.39	1.52	1.73	2.20	2.49	2.81
Stock price – high ($)	—	27.88	26.13	19.00	18.94	21.19	25.75	37.25	31.38	40.00	46.00
Stock price – low ($)	—	21.00	9.63	13.50	13.00	14.00	17.81	19.50	25.06	26.88	31.25
Stock price – close ($)	5.3%	25.75	14.31	17.38	14.19	21.00	20.69	27.75	27.00	40.00	41.13
P/E – high	—	12	19	30	18	15	17	22	14	16	16
P/E – low	—	9	7	21	12	10	12	11	11	11	11
Dividends per share ($)	6.4%	0.62	0.76	0.76	0.76	0.76	0.80	0.84	0.90	1.00	1.08
Book value per share ($)	7.4%	14.55	14.74	14.49	14.65	14.58	14.66	15.91	17.47	24.75	27.66

1990 Year-end:
Debt ratio: 35.5%
Return on equity: 10.7%
Cash (mil.): $14
Current ratio: 1.56
Long-term debt (mil.): $1,684
No. of shares (mil.): 110
Dividends:
 1990 average yield: 2.6%
 1990 payout: 38.4%
Market value (mil.): $4,512

Stock Price History High/Low 1981–90

COOPERS & LYBRAND

OVERVIEW

Coopers & Lybrand is the 5th largest of the Big 6 accounting firms. CEO Peter Scanlon has stepped down, unable to complete another term before reaching the firm's retirement age. Successor Eugene Freedman will reach retirement after a 3-year term.

While Coopers & Lybrand sat out the accounting mergers of the 1980s, it has become the unexpected beneficiary as the refuge for partners defecting from other international mergers. Since the 1989 merger of Deloitte Haskins & Sells and Touche Ross & Company, Coopers & Lybrand units have attracted disaffected DH&S partnerships in the Netherlands, Austria, and Belgium. In the UK, Coopers & Lybrand (leader in management consulting) joined with the former UK branch of Deloitte Haskins & Sells (the leader in international tax advice and corporate finance) to form Coopers & Lybrand Deloitte, the largest accounting firm in that nation.

The company aggressively uses technology, including expert systems (sophisticated computer programs that use large, specialized databases to analyze client problems). Coopers has joined IBM to offer computer consulting targeted to consumer goods companies, health care firms, and pharmaceutical concerns.

International association of partnerships

Fiscal year ends: September 30

WHO

Chairman and CEO: Peter R. Scanlon, age 60; Eugene M. Freedman, age 59 (effective Oct. 1, 1991)
Deputy Chairman for Operations: Stephen W. McKessy
CFO: Frank Scalia
Director of Personnel Management: Robert McDowell
Employees: 16,145

WHERE

HQ: 1251 Ave. of the Americas, New York, NY 10020
Phone: 212-536-2000
Fax: 212-642-7328

Coopers & Lybrand operates more than 95 offices in the US and 600 offices in 104 countries.

	1990 Revenues	
	$ mil.	% of total
US	1,400	34
Foreign	2,700	66
Total	**4,100**	**100**

WHEN

Coopers & Lybrand, the product of a 1957 trans-Atlantic merger, literally wrote the book on auditing. Lybrand, Ross Bros. & Montgomery, as the US ancestor was known, had been formed in 1898 by 4 partners — William M. Lybrand, T. Edward Ross, Adam A. Ross, and Robert H. Montgomery. In 1912 Montgomery wrote *Montgomery's Auditing*, termed by many as the "Bible" of the accounting profession. The book is now in its 11th edition.

In the early years the accounting firm grew slowly, and the Ross brothers' sister served as secretary, typist, and bookkeeper. In 1902 the company opened a New York office at 25 Broad Street. Other offices across the country followed — Pittsburgh (1908), Chicago (1909), and Boston (1915). WWI focused attention on Washington, DC, and the Lybrand firm opened an office there (1919) and then branched out to the new auto capital of Detroit (1920), to Seattle (1920), and to Baltimore (1924). A merger with the firm of Klink, Bean & Company gave the firm a window on California (1924), and another merger drove the firm into Dallas (1930), with an offshoot office in Houston a year later.

In Europe the Lybrand firm established offices in Berlin (1924, closed in 1938 as WWII loomed), Paris (1926), and London (1929). During the same period the UK firm of Cooper Brothers was also expanding in Europe.

Cooper Brothers had begun in 1854 when William Cooper, the oldest son of a Quaker banker, formed his accountancy at 13 George Street in London. He was quickly joined by his brothers, Arthur, Francis, and Ernest. The firm's name of Cooper Brothers & Company was adopted in 1861. After WWI Cooper Brothers branched out to Liverpool (1920), Brussels (1921), New York (1926), and Paris (1930). After WWII Cooper Brothers acquired 3 venerable firms — Alfred Tongue & Company; Aspell Dunn & Company; and Rattray Brothers, Alexander & France.

In 1957 Coopers & Lybrand was formed by the amalgamation of the international accounting firms, and by 1973 the affiliated partnerships had gravitated toward the Coopers & Lybrand name. In the 1960s the company branched out to employee benefits consulting and introduced a new auditing method that included evaluating clients' systems of internal control. During the 1970s Coopers focused on integrating computer technology into the auditing process.

While some of its sisters in the then–Big 8 were pairing off in the 1980s, Coopers & Lybrand sat out the mergers. As a result it dropped from the top of the Big 8 to 5th in the Big 6. That was the least of its problems, though, as it faced charges from federal regulators relating to its 1986 audit of failed Silverado Banking, Savings & Loan, the Denver-based thrift made famous by its association with presidential son Neil Bush.

In the first such action against a Big 6 firm, the Office of Thrift Supervision accused Coopers & Lybrand of understating potential losses. In 1990 Coopers & Lybrand, without admitting to guilt, agreed to accept penalties that included banning one partner from audits of banks or thrifts.

WHAT

Services

Accounting and Auditing
Computer audit services
Corporate financial planning
Financial audits, reviews, and compilations
Internal audit assistance
Management accounting systems
SEC services

Actuarial, Benefits, and Compensation Consulting
Defined benefit programs
Executive compensation
Group health and welfare services
Insurance/risk management

Business Investigation
Business reorganization
Litigation and claims

Government Contracting
Negotiations consulting
Standards compliance

International Trade
Business planning
Regulations compliance

Management Consulting
Business planning
Information systems
Productivity

Mergers and Acquisitions
Business planning
Corporate finance advice
Target identification
Valuation

Tax
International taxation
Financial planning
State and local tax services

Representative Clients

B.A.T	Johnson & Johnson
British Telecom	Maxwell
Cadbury Schweppes	Pearson
Fletcher Challenge	Peugeot
Glaxo	RTZ
Humana	Telmex
Ito-Yokado	Unilever

HOW MUCH

	9-Year Growth	1981	1982	1983	1984	1985	1986	1987	1988	1989	1990
Worldwide revenues ($ mil.)	12.8%	998	1,066	1,100	1,250	1,375	1,695	1,998	2,398	3,000	4,100
No. of offices[1]	—	—	—	93	94	95	96	99	100	100	99
No. of partners	—	—	—	890	915	987	1,054	1,110	1,270	1,333	1,301
No. of employees	—	—	—	10,673	11,586	9,530	13,409	14,270	15,400	16,625	16,145

1990 revenues per partner: $1,076,095

Worldwide Revenues ($ mil.) 1981–90

KEY COMPETITORS

Arthur Andersen	KPMG
Deloitte & Touche	Marsh & McLennan
Ernst & Young	McKinsey & Co.
H&R Block	Price Waterhouse

CORNING INC.

OVERVIEW

Corning, best known for its Pyrex and Corning kitchenware, also holds leading shares in such high-tech markets as optical fibers and auto emission-control substrates. The company's Laboratory Services group has become a leader in clinical and environmental testing and life-science research. Yet Corning remains headquartered in a small town in upstate New York, and members of the founding Houghton family still manage the company and own 15% of its stock.

Since 1908 Corning's laboratories have generated a steady flow of innovations. The company now makes about 60,000 products—many in cooperation with 19 joint-venture partners worldwide — in 3 fields: Specialty Materials, Communications, and Consumer Products. Aggressive acquisitions in the Laboratory Services segment and ever-growing demand for fiber-optic communications have kept profits and stock values high, while lagging US auto demand has slowed sales growth for Corning's emission-control systems. CEO James Houghton plans to maintain Corning's focus on health care and environmental products.

WHEN

Amory Houghton started the Houghton Glass Company in Massachusetts in 1851 and moved to Corning, New York, in 1868. By 1876 the company, renamed Corning Glass Works, was already manufacturing several types of technical and pharmaceutical glass. In 1880 Corning supplied the glass for Thomas Edison's first light bulb.

Houghton's son, Amory, Jr., enlisted the help of a Cornell University physicist in 1877 to develop improved lenses for railroad signals. By using red, yellow, and green lenses, the company contributed to the development of the current traffic-signal color system.

In 1912 Corning improved the brakeman's lantern by using borosilicate glass (able to withstand sudden temperature changes), which was also used in 1915 to make Pyrex oven and laboratory ware.

Joint ventures have been crucial to Corning's success. The early ones included Pittsburgh Corning (Pittsburgh Plate Glass, 1937, glass construction blocks), Owens-Corning (Owens-Illinois, 1938, fiberglass), and Dow Corning (Dow Chemical, 1943, silicones).

By 1945 Corning's laboratories (established 1908) had made the company the undisputed leader in the manufacture of specialty glass (i.e., not flat glass or containers). Among the applications for Corning's glass technology were the first mass-produced TV tubes, freezer-to-oven ceramic cookware (Pyroceram, Corning Ware), and car headlights.

After WWII Corning emphasized consumer-product sales, which climbed from 12% of total sales in 1953 to 25% in 1963. Corning next expanded globally, nearly tripling foreign sales between 1966 and 1970. In the 1970s the company pioneered the development of optical fiber and auto emission technology, now two of Corning's principal products.

Recognizing maturing markets for such established products as light bulbs and TV tubes, Corning began to buy companies in the higher-growth laboratory services industry (MetPath, 1982; Hazleton, 1987; Enseco, 1989; G.H. Besselaar, 1989). High-tech joint ventures with European and Asian partners (e.g., Siemens, Mitsubishi, Samsung) enhanced Corning's already solid leadership positions in specialty materials and video glass. Reflecting its broadened orientation, Corning in 1989 dropped Glass Works from its name. In 1988 the company bought Revere Ware (cookware).

In 1990 Corning established a joint venture with Samtel to manufacture glassware in Italy. The following year the company created a joint venture with Mexican glassmaker Vitro SA in which Corning exchanged 49% of its consumer product assets for $130 million and 49% of Vitro's business.

NYSE symbol: GLW
Fiscal year ends: Sunday nearest December 31

Hoover's Rating **B+**

WHO

Chairman and CEO: James R. Houghton, age 54, $915,715 pay
President and COO: Roger G. Ackerman, age 52, $508,503 pay
VC; Group President, Consumer Housewares: Richard Dulude, age 57, $510,519
VC (Principal Financial Officer): Van C. Campbell, age 52, $502,985
VC: David A. Duke, age 55
SVP Human Resources: Richard C. Marks, age 53
Auditors: Price Waterhouse
Employees: 28,600

WHERE

HQ: Houghton Park, Corning, NY 14831
Phone: 607-974-9000
Fax: 607-974-8551

Corning operates 48 plants in 8 countries.

	1990 Sales		1990 Pretax Income	
	$ mil.	% of total	$ mil.	% of total
US	2,390	81	282	81
Europe	378	13	47	13
Other countries	173	6	19	6
Adjustments	—	—	(40)	—
Total	**2,941**	**100**	**308**	**100**

WHAT

	1990 Sales		1990 Pretax Income	
	$ mil.	% of total	$ mil.	% of total
Consumer Products	727	25	83	18
Communications	783	26	144	31
Specialty Materials	700	24	119	25
Laboratory Services	731	25	125	26
Adjustments	—	—	(163)	—
Total	**2,941**	**100**	**308**	**100**

Consumer Products
Corelle (dinnerware)
Corning Ware (cookware)
Micro Dur (cookware)
Pyrex (glassware)
Revere Ware (cookware)
Serengeti (sunglasses)
Steuben (crystal)
Visions (cookware)

Communications
Flat-panel displays
Optical fiber

Laboratory Services
G. H. Besselaar Associates (pharmaceutical testing)
Enseco Inc. (environmental testing)
Hazleton Corp. (life-science lab services)

MetPath Inc. (clinical testing)

Specialty Materials
Auto emission-control substrates

Major Joint-Venture Partners
Asahi Glass (Corning Asahi)
Dow Chemical (Dow Corning)
IBM (PCO)
Mitsubishi (Cormetech)
PPG (Pittsburgh Corning)
Samsung (Samsung-Corning)
Samtel
Siemens (Siecor)
Vitro

HOW MUCH

	9-Year Growth	1981	1982	1983	1984	1985	1986	1987	1988	1989	1990
Sales ($ mil.)	7.0%	1,599	1,579	1,589	1,733	1,691	1,856	2,084	2,122	2,439	2,941
Net income ($ mil.)	12.9%	97	75	92	89	108	162	189	292	259	289
Income as % of sales	—	6.1%	4.7%	5.8%	5.1%	6.4%	8.7%	9.1%	13.8%	10.6%	9.8%
Earnings per share ($)	9.7%	1.33	0.88	1.10	1.06	1.27	1.85	2.05	3.25	2.79	3.07
Stock price – high ($)	—	18.81	17.00	22.56	18.56	31.44	40.75	38.50	34.94	43.38	51.75
Stock price – low ($)	—	12.50	9.81	16.25	14.88	17.06	23.31	17.38	22.38	32.00	34.75
Stock price – close ($)	14.8%	12.97	16.47	17.44	17.25	30.88	27.44	23.38	34.69	43.00	44.88
P/E – high	—	14	19	21	18	25	22	19	11	16	17
P/E – low	—	9	11	15	14	13	13	8	7	11	11
Dividends per share ($)	5.3%	0.58	0.58	0.58	0.60	0.66	0.70	0.71	0.96	1.05	0.93
Book value per share ($)	4.8%	13.21	11.99	12.25	12.60	13.82	15.20	17.05	17.56	18.16	20.14

1990 Year-end:
Debt ratio: 24.8%
Return on equity: 16.0%
Cash (mil.): $133
Current ratio: 1.72
Long-term debt (mil.): $611
No. of shares (mil.): 92
Dividends:
  1990 average yield: 2.1%
  1990 payout: 30.1%
Market value (mil.): $4,122

Stock Price History High/Low 1981–90

RANKINGS

154th in *Fortune* 500 Industrial Cos.
119th in *Business Week* 1000

KEY COMPETITORS

Alcoa
Amway
Brown-Forman
Carlsberg
Colgate-Palmolive
Hanson
Ogden
Owens-Illinois
Pearson

COSTCO WHOLESALE CORPORATION

OVERVIEW

Costco Wholesale is the 3rd largest membership wholesale club in the US (after Sam's, a division of Wal-Mart, and Price Company), with revenues of over $4 billion in 1990 (about 20% of the $24 billion market).

As of mid-1991 the company operated 69 stores in 10 states and in 3 Canadian provinces. These 110,000- to 125,000-square-foot stores contain a limited variety (3,600 items in contrast to most discount stores' 40,000 to 60,000) of low-priced, brand-name merchandise, including housewares, appliances, apparel, jewelry, office supplies and furniture, automotive supplies, consumer electronics, and even grand pianos and cars, at some stores. New and remodeled stores have pharmacies, optical stores, photo processing, and fresh food departments.

Costco chooses markets where its stores can effectively achieve high turnover rates and sales volumes. The company sharply undercuts competitors by shipping merchandise directly to stores and paying vendors early, in exchange for favorable discounts. Small merchandise is usually sold by the case or carton or in multiple packages. Costco maintains low overhead costs in sparsely decorated, self-service warehouse stores by limiting hours, employees, and advertising.

Costco's 2.5 million members, paying annual fees of $25 (business members) or $30 (individual members), include small businesses, nonprofit organizations, and employees of selected businesses and public institutions.

WHEN

Costco Wholesale started in 1983 as Cost Club, of Seattle, founded by Jeffrey Brotman and James Sinegal, a former EVP of Price Company, the format's pioneer. The company soon incorporated as Costco Wholesale and opened the first warehouse stores in Seattle, Portland, and Spokane.

The company went public in 1985 and expanded into Canada. Brotman's and Sinegal's creativity with the warehouse format led in 1986 to the introduction of fresh foods, including meat and baked goods prepared on site. Though this increased labor costs, the gamble paid off with increased sales. Costco entered the Midwest with 3 stores in Minnesota and Wisconsin in 1986 and 1987 but found the market uncongenial and closed these stores in 1988, while jumping across the Pacific to open a unit in Honolulu, Hawaii, that same year.

Costco added 4 more stores in 1988, the year it reached $2 billion in sales. The company has consistently shown a willingness to take a loss by closing underperforming stores, most recently closing 3 units in Florida (1990). Though much of the company's expansion is financed by bank borrowings paid out of operating revenues, Costco has also raised money with stock offerings in 1989 and 1991. Carrefour, a French hypermarket chain, was an early investor through its subsidiary, Carrefour Nederland BV, and now owns 20% of the company.

In 1990 the company expanded its merchandise to include do-it-yourself home improvement items. While its 600 items are not expected to challenge the large home center warehouse stores, which typically carry 25,000 to 30,000 items, this is an increasingly important retail segment. The company also opened 2 stores in Massachusetts and, despite the depressed economic condition of the Northeastern region, expects to open more in 1991 and 1992.

Despite the retail recession of 1990 and 1991, Costco's sales increased by 38%, as membership increased 25% and selling costs remained steady at about 8%, thanks to management's strict control of costs, refusal to accept credit cards, and no-frills mentality. In 1991 the company declared a 2 for 1 stock split.

NASDAQ symbol: COST
Fiscal year ends: Sunday nearest August 31

Hoover's Rating **A-**

WHO

Chairman: Jeffrey H. Brotman, age 48, $416,429 pay
President, CEO, and COO: James D. Sinegal, age 54, $415,560 pay
EVP Operations: Richard D. DiCerchio, age 47, $279,050 pay
SVP, CFO, and Treasurer: Richard A. Galanti, age 34, $208,288 pay
VP Personnel and Administration: Michael D. Anderton
Auditors: Arthur Andersen & Co.
Employees: 12,400

WHERE

HQ: 10809 120th Ave. NE, Kirkland, WA 98033
Phone: 206-828-8100
Fax: 206-828-8103

Costco operates 69 warehouse clubs in the western, northwestern, and southeastern US and in Canada.

State/Province	Warehouses (12/90)
Alaska	1
California	29
Florida	9
Hawaii	1
Idaho	1
Massachusetts	2
Nevada	2
Oregon	5
Utah	1
Washington	10
Alberta, British Columbia, Manitoba	8
Total	**69**

WHAT

	1990 Sales	
	$ mil.	% of total
Net sales	4,060	98
Membership fees	73	2
Total	**4,133**	**100**

1990 Sales by Product Line	% of Total
Food	31
Dry, fresh, and packaged foods	
Sundries	32
Snack foods, health and beauty aids, tobacco, soft drinks, cleaning supplies	
Hardlines	23
Appliances, electronics, tools, office supplies, automotive supplies	
Softlines	13
Apparel, linens, cameras, jewelry, housewares, books	
Other	1
Pharmacy, optical, tire shop	
Total	**100**

HOW MUCH

	5-Year Growth	1981	1982	1983	1984	1985	1986	1987	1988	1989	1990
Sales ($ mil.)	62.0%	—	—	—	—	371	762	1,401	2,030	3,000	4,133
Net income ($ mil.)	—	—	—	—	—	(6)	3	4	12	27	49
Income as % of sales	—	—	—	—	—	(1.5%)	0.5%	0.3%	0.6%	0.9%	1.2%
Earnings per share ($)	—	—	—	—	—	(0.51)	0.15	0.14	0.46	0.95	1.40
Stock price – high ($)	—	—	—	—	—	12.88	19.50	15.25	16.25	35.63	49.00
Stock price – low ($)	—	—	—	—	—	10.63	8.50	5.63	8.38	15.75	30.00
Stock price – close ($)	32.7%	—	—	—	—	11.75	13.38	8.25	15.88	35.25	48.25
P/E – high	—	—	—	—	—	—	130	109	35	38	35
P/E – low	—	—	—	—	—	—	57	40	18	17	21
Dividends per share ($)	—	—	—	—	—	0.00	0.00	0.00	0.00	0.00	0.00
Book value per share ($)	38.8%	—	—	—	—	2.20	3.41	3.65	4.32	7.82	11.32

1990 Year-end:
Debt ratio: 16.2%
Return on equity: 14.6%
Cash (mil.): $14
Current ratio: 1.08
Long-term debt (mil.): $76
No. of shares (mil.): 35
Dividends:
　1990 average yield: 0.0%
　1990 payout: —
Market value (mil.): $1,672

Stock Price History
High/Low 1985–90

RANKINGS

29th in *Fortune* 50 Retailing Cos.
255th in *Business Week* 1000

KEY COMPETITORS

Circuit City	Pacific Enterprise	Tandy
Fred Meyer	Price Co.	Walgreen
Home Depot	Sears	Wal-Mart
Kmart	Service	Food retailers
Montgomery Ward	Merchandise	

COX ENTERPRISES, INC.

OVERVIEW

Privately held Atlanta-based Cox Enterprises is a diversified publisher and broadcaster owned by the descendants of founder and one-time presidential candidate James M. Cox. Since 1980 the combined annual revenues of Cox Enterprises and its formerly public sister company, Cox Communications, have tripled.

Cox Newspapers is the 9th largest newspaper publisher in the nation and publishes 17 daily newspapers, 10 weekly "shopper" publications, and one magazine. In 1990 Cox's *Atlanta Journal* and *Constitution* were the fastest-growing major newspapers in the US.

Cox Cable is among the US's largest cable operators; its San Diego system is # 3 in the nation. Cox owns part of The Discovery Channel (25%), Viewer's Choice (17%), and Movietime (11%). STOFA, a 50% joint venture, is Denmark's largest private cable operator. Cox Cable has announced plans to sell its 82 franchised Blockbuster Video stores.

Cox Broadcasting's Atlanta, Charlotte, Dayton, and Orlando TV stations and its Charlotte and Los Angeles FM radio stations are #1 in their markets. Manheim Auctions is the US's largest auto auction operator.

WHEN

James Middleton Cox dropped out of school at 16 and worked as a teacher, reporter, and congressional secretary before buying the *Dayton Daily News* in 1898 at the age of 28. He acquired the nearby *Springfield Press-Republican* in 1905 and soon took an interest in politics. Cox served 2 terms in the US Congress (1909–13) and 3 terms as governor of Ohio (1913–15; 1917–21). In 1920 Cox became the Democratic candidate for president, with Franklin D. Roosevelt as his running mate, but lost to rival Ohio publisher Warren G. Harding. Afterward Cox bought the *Miami Daily News* (1923) and formed WHIO-AM, Dayton's first radio station. In 1939 Cox bought Atlanta's WSB-AM, the South's first radio station, which he expanded in 1948 by starting WSB-FM and WSB-TV, the South's first FM-radio and TV stations. The following year Cox started WHIO-FM and WHIO-TV, the first FM-radio and TV broadcasters in Dayton. The *Atlanta Constitution*, now the company's flagship paper, joined Cox's collection in 1950. When Cox died in 1957, his company owned 7 newspapers, 3 TV stations, and several radio stations.

Cox Enterprises expanded its broadcasting interests with the acquisitions of WSOC-AM/FM/TV (Charlotte, 1959) and KTVU-TV (San Francisco–Oakland, 1963). The company became one of the first major broadcasting companies to enter cable TV when it purchased a small system in Lewistown, Pennsylvania (1962). In 1964 the company created publicly held Cox Broadcasting to consolidate the family's broadcasting interests, but the newspapers continued as privately held Cox Enterprises. Cox Broadcasting's cable holdings were split off as publicly held Cox Cable Communications in 1968, with 83,450 subscribers, and by 1969 the company was the 2nd largest cable operator in the US. The broadcasting arm diversified by buying Manheim Services, the nation's largest auto auction operator (1968), and Kansas City Automobile Auction (1969).

Cox Broadcasting acquired TeleRep, a TV industry advertising sales representation firm (1972), and Christal, which performs the same services for radio (1973). Cox Cable was in 9 states and had 500,000 subscribers by 1977, when it merged back into Cox Broadcasting. The broadcasting company changed its name to Cox Communications in 1982; the increasing value of its holdings, especially its cable interests, led the family to take the company private in 1985, combining it with Cox Enterprises. James Kennedy, grandson of the founder, became head of Cox in 1987.

In 1990 Cox bought 2 radio stations, sold 2 newspapers, launched the *Gilbert Tribune* (Phoenix), and sold its one million shares of Blockbuster at a profit. In 1991 Cox merged its Manheim unit with the auto auction businesses of Ford Motor Credit and GE Capital.

Also in 1991 the company began experimenting with personal communications systems (small wireless phones that compete with cellular phones) and bought a 12.5% stake in Merrill Lynch's Teleport Communications Group, a fiber optics company. These moves into telecommunications would appear to hasten the day when Cox and other cable operators move into direct competition with local phone companies.

HOW MUCH

	9-Year Growth	1981	1982	1983	1984	1985	1986	1987	1988	1989	1990
Sales ($ mil.)	11.0%	820	968	1,132	1,347	1,472	1,569	1,666	1,816	1,974	2,095
Cable subscribers (thou.)	5.2%	1,020	1,132	1,348	1,494	1,511	1,372	1,442	1,442	1,555	1,616
Daily newspapers	(0.6%)	18	17	18	19	19	20	20	20	18	17
Daily circulation (thou.)	1.1%	1,195	1,169	1,196	1,236	1,210	1,250	1,275	1,310	1,306	1,320

1990 Year-end:
Sales (mil.): $2,095
Capital expenditures:
  Existing businesses
  (mil.): $192
New businesses
  (mil.): $21

Sales ($ mil.) 1981–90

Note: Figures prior to 1985 are for the combined operations of the predecessor companies, Cox Enterprises and Cox Communications.

Private company
Fiscal year ends: December 31

Hoover's Rating **B**

WHO

Chairman and CEO: James C. Kennedy
SVP and CFO: John R. Dillon
VP Human Resources: Timothy W. Hughes
Auditors: Deloitte & Touche
Employees: 27,000

WHERE

HQ: 1400 Lake Hearn Dr., Atlanta, GA 30319
Phone: 404-843-5000
Fax: 404-843-5142

Cox Enterprises operates businesses in 34 states.

WHAT

	1990 Sales	
	$ mil.	% of total
Newspapers	745	36
Broadcasting	419	20
Cable	547	26
Auctions & other	384	18
Total	**2,095**	**100**

Cox Newpapers
Major newspapers
  The Atlanta Constitution
  The Atlanta Journal
  Arizona Pennysaver (weekly)
  Austin American-Statesman
  Dayton Daily News
  Florida Pennysaver (weekly)
  The Palm Beach Post and *Daily News*
Cox Target Media (direct-mail and in-store advertising)

Cox Broadcasting
Radio stations
  KFI (AM) and KOST (FM), Los Angeles
  KLRX (FM), Dallas
  WCKG (FM), Chicago
  WHIO (AM) and WHKO (FM), Dayton
  WIOD (AM) and WFLC (FM), Miami
  WSB (AM/FM), Atlanta
  WSOC (AM/FM), Charlotte
  WSUN (AM) and WWRM (FM), Tampa/St. Petersburg
  TeleRep (sales representation)
Television stations

KTVU-TV, San Francisco	WPXI-TV, Pittsburgh
WFTV-TV, Orlando	WSB-TV, Atlanta
WHIO-TV, Dayton	WSOC-TV, Charlotte
WKBD-TV, Detroit	

Cox Cable

Top 5 systems	Movietime (11%)
San Diego (CA)	STOFA (50%, Danish
Hampton Roads area (VA)	cable systems)
Jefferson Parish (LA)	Viewer's Choice (17%)
Oklahoma City (OK)	Manheim Auctions
New Orleans (LA)	(majority-owned)
The Discovery Channel (25%)	46 auto auctions in
	the US and Canada

Other
Southeast Paper
  Manufacturing (33 1/3%)

RANKINGS

69th in *Forbes* 400 US Private Cos.

KEY COMPETITORS

Advance	Knight-Ridder	Tribune
Publications	New York Times	Turner
Blockbuster	News Corp.	Broadcasting
CBS	Reader's Digest	Viacom
Dow Jones	E.W. Scripps	Washington
Gannett	TCI	Post
Hearst	Time Warner	

CPC INTERNATIONAL INC.

NYSE symbol: CPC
Fiscal year ends: December 31

Hoover's Rating: B

OVERVIEW

Beginning as a corn refinery, modern-day CPC, headquartered in Englewood Cliffs, New Jersey, generates 81% of its sales from consumer products and is among the largest US food processors. CPC garnered 60% of its 1990 revenues outside the US, a higher percentage than any other US-based food processor.

The company boasts over 1,300 trademarks for such products as sauces, soups, corn oils, peanut butters, margarines, jellies, pastas, cheeses, seasonings, syrups, starches, and bakery products.

While many companies are mobilizing to enter foreign markets, CPC has been there for years. The company already sells its products in all of the EC countries and has facilities in most of them. CPC's foreign presence and its established brand recognition give it a great advantage over companies that are going overseas for the first time.

WHEN

In 1842 Thomas Kingsford developed a technique for separating starch from corn, and by 1890 the corn refining industry had emerged. Severe competition forced a group of 20 cornstarch and syrup manufacturers to band together as National Starch Manufacturing. The group established production quotas and gained 70% of the cornstarch market, but their pool broke down and ruinous pricing competition resumed.

This pattern of collusion was typical of the highly unstable corn refining industry for the next decade. By 1906 price competition had forced Edward Bedford's New York Glucose to merge with Glucose Sugar Refining Company, of which National Starch was by then a part, forming Corn Products Refining Company. CPRC became the first stable corn refining company by improving refinery equipment and processes. That year CPRC controlled 64% of starch and 100% of glucose output in the US.

Between 1910 and 1916 CPRC dominated corn refining and faced antitrust action. In 1916 Judge Learned Hand forced CPRC's eventual sale of portions of its business.

In 1922 CPRC faced antitrust charges in connection with Karo syrup. CPRC guaranteed buyers that Karo's price would not decline; the charges were later dismissed. Between 1940 and 1942 the FTC filed antitrust charges against CPRC for "phantom freight" prices; CPRC, to control prices, charged for shipping from places other than actual point of origin. Removing phantom freight (1945) reduced industry concentration; by 1954 CPRC had only a 46% share of corn-grinding capacity.

Although the company produced some branded products (Mazola, Karo, Argo, and Kingsford's), CPRC remained largely a corn refinery until 1958. That year the company merged with Best Foods, producers of Hellmann's, Best Foods, Skippy, and Rit brands, and bought C. H. Knorr (soups). During the 1960s CPRC bought 4 educational companies — the best known of these (MIND) made remedial training systems to improve workers' skills — but sold them all by 1980.

In 1969 the company was renamed CPC International to place emphasis upon international expansion. CPC bought S. B. Thomas (English muffins, 1969), C.F. Mueller (pasta, 1983), and Arnold Foods (crackers, 1986).

In 1986 CPC successfully defended itself against a takeover attempt by financier Ronald Perelman (MacAndrews & Forbes). The ensuing restructuring cost over 7,000 people their jobs and caused the company to withdraw from much of the Asian market. CPC also sold its Bosco brand chocolate syrup.

Since 1986 CPC has acquired 28 consumer food businesses. The company's 10 1990 acquisitions include Ambrosia (desserts, UK), Conimex (oriental foods, Netherlands), and Milwaukee Seasonings (US).

In 1991 CPC settled a lawsuit with McKesson, in which CPC charged that McKesson inflated performance projections during the sale of its C.F. Mueller pasta unit.

WHO

Chairman, President, and CEO: Charles R. Shoemate, age 51, $758,334 pay (prior to promotion)
VC: Richard W. Siebrasse, age 64, $666,667 pay
SVP and General Counsel: Clifford B. Storms, age 58, $410,000 pay
SVP Finance: Konrad Schlatter, age 55
VP Human Resources: Richard P. Bergeman, age 52
Auditors: KPMG Peat Marwick
Employees: 35,000

WHERE

HQ: International Plaza, PO Box 8000, International Plaza, Englewood Cliffs, NJ 07632-9976
Phone: 201-894-4000
Fax: 201-894-0297

CPC has 115 manufacturing plants in 47 countries.

	1990 Sales		1990 Operating Income	
	$ mil.	% of total	$ mil.	% of total
US	2,322	40	336	44
Europe	2,116	37	232	30
Latin America	905	16	123	16
Canada	248	4	36	5
Asia	190	3	37	5
Adjustments	—	—	(29)	—
Total	**5,781**	**100**	**735**	**100**

WHAT

	1990 Sales		1990 Operating Income	
	$ mil.	% of total	$ mil.	% of total
Consumer foods	4,695	81	581	76
Corn refining	1,086	19	182	24
Adjustments	—	—	(28)	—
Total	**5,781**	**100**	**735**	**100**

Major US Brand Names

Mayonnaise	Margarines	Corn Syrups
Best Foods	Holiday	Crown
Goodall's	Mazola	Golden Griddle
Hellmann's	Royal	Karo
Lady's Choice		
	Baked Goods	**Laundry Starches**
Corn Oil	Arnold	Argo
Lady's Choice	Old London	Niagara
Mazola	Thomas'	
		Pastas
Soups, Spices	**Cornstarches**	Mueller's
Goodall's	Argo	Royal
Knorr	Kingsford	
		Dyes
Peanut Butter		Rit
Skippy		

RANKINGS

91st in *Fortune* 500 Industrial Cos.
100th in *Business Week* 1000

KEY COMPETITORS

Allied-Lyons	ConAgra	Monsanto
Anheuser-Busch	Continental Grain	Nestlé
ADM	General Mills	Philip Morris
Borden	Grand Metropolitan	RJR Nabisco
BSN	Heinz	Sara Lee
Campbell Soup	Hershey	TLC Beatrice
Cargill	John Labatt	Unilever
Chiquita Brands		

HOW MUCH

	9-Year Growth	1981	1982	1983	1984	1985	1986	1987	1988	1989	1990
Sales ($ mil.)	3.2%	4,343	4,092	4,011	4,373	4,210	4,549	4,903	4,700	5,103	5,781
Net income ($ mil.)	6.2%	218	232	136	193	142	219	355	289	328	374
Income as % of sales	—	5.0%	5.7%	3.4%	4.4%	3.4%	4.8%	7.2%	6.2%	6.4%	6.5%
Earnings per share ($)	8.7%	2.29	2.40	1.41	1.99	1.45	2.30	4.31	3.66	4.20	4.83
Stock price – high ($)	—	17.88	21.00	22.44	20.94	26.63	44.25	58.50	58.38	73.75	84.75
Stock price – low ($)	—	13.88	14.69	16.81	17.13	19.13	23.25	26.00	39.50	49.38	62.00
Stock price – close ($)	18.7%	17.75	20.81	19.25	20.00	25.50	39.63	40.50	51.88	73.75	83.25
P/E – high	—	8	9	16	11	18	19	14	16	18	18
P/E – low	—	6	6	12	9	13	10	6	11	12	13
Dividends per share ($)	8.5%	0.96	1.05	1.10	1.10	1.10	1.14	1.29	1.52	1.75	2.00
Book value per share ($)	2.8%	12.93	13.48	13.46	13.63	14.10	11.58	13.61	15.25	13.46	16.61

1990 Year-end:
Debt ratio: 40.5%
Return on equity: 32.1%
Cash (mil.): $48
Current ratio: 1.10
Long-term debt (mil.): $990
No. of shares (mil.): 75
Dividends:
  1990 average yield: 2.4%
  1990 payout: 41.4%
Market value (mil.): $6,282

Stock Price History High/Low 1981–90

CRAY RESEARCH, INC.

OVERVIEW

Eagan, Minnesota–based Cray Research, the company that invented supercomputers, is the largest manufacturer of supercomputers in the world, with 66% of the market. Cray's supercomputers can process in one minute what it takes an ordinary mainframe 3 hours to do.

Cray's computers are used predominantly by scientists and engineers for modeling physical events. These computationally intensive simulations include weather forecasting, seismic analysis, and molecular modeling. While government (60% of 1990 orders) and universities constitute the majority of Cray's installed base, commercial sales are on the rise. Aerospace (18% of 1990 orders) and automobile manufacturers (12% of 1990 orders) shorten product-development cycles by simulating the designs on a Cray. The petroleum industry (7% of 1990 orders) uses the supercomputers to model oil reservoir conditions.

The company devotes 15% of revenues to R&D. Cray's creation of an Entry Level Systems (ELS) division and introduction of 2 entry-level minisupercomputers in 1990, the Y-MP2E and the CRAY XMS, demonstrate its commitment to this fast-growing segment.

WHEN

Cray Research was started in 1972 in Chippewa Falls, Wisconsin, by Seymour Cray after he left Control Data Corporation (CDC). While at CDC, Cray had developed the CDC 1604 computer in 1959 (one of the first to use transistors), the CDC 6600 in 1963 (fastest computer on the market), and the CDC 7600 in 1968. When Cray's planned 8600 was put on hold in 1972, he left CDC and set up Cray Research. Four years later (1976) Cray introduced the first supercomputer, the Cray-1, and took the company public.

The Cray-1, with its unusual design (from above, it looks like a "C"), was faster than any other mainframe (10 times faster than the CDC 7600). Cray recovered the $8.6 million investment in the Cray-1 with his first sale to the National Center for Atmospheric Research.

By 1980 Cray Research's annual revenues had grown to $61 million. In 1981 Seymour Cray turned over leadership of the company to John Rollwagen, freeing Cray to work on the Cray-2. In 1982 Cray introduced the highly successful X-MP computer line, a project headed by Taiwanese computer whiz Steve Chen. The X-MP was 3 times faster than the Cray-1. The Cray-2 — 10 times faster than the Cray-1 — was introduced in 1985, and the current top-of-the-line Y-MP machine was released in 1987.

Cray Research began work on a 64-processor MP under the direction of Chen in 1986. However, in 1987, after realizing it would require double the $50 million originally budgeted and breakthroughs in 5 technologies, Rollwagen pulled the plug on the MP. Chen quit and started Supercomputer Systems, which, with backing from IBM, is developing a computer targeted to be 100 times faster than existing Crays (due in 1995).

In 1989 Cray Research spun off Cray Computer Corporation (CCC, headed by 65-year-old Seymour Cray). In order to focus on the C-90, a follow-on project to the Y-MP, Cray Research retained 10% interest in CCC.

Cray Research expanded into the low-end supercomputer market in 1990 by acquiring Supertek Computers, a manufacturer of small, less-expensive Cray-compatible supercomputers. Growing competition from Japanese computer makers NEC, Fujitsu, and Hitachi has challenged the company to deliver more powerful machines. Cray's advantages, however, are its installed base and large software library. The company plans to deliver a 16-processor Y-MP in 1992 that will have 3 to 5 times the computing power of its Y-MP8. Its goal is to build a Teraflops computer by the mid-1990s that can perform one trillion calculations per second.

NYSE symbol: CYR
Fiscal year ends: December 31

WHO

Chairman and CEO: John A. Rollwagen, age 50, $526,797 pay
President and COO: John F. Carlson, age 52, $337,268 pay (prior to promotion)
VC and Counsel: Andrew Scott, age 62, $272,389 pay
CFO: Michael J. Lindseth, age 38
VP Human Resources: Deborah E. Barber
Auditors: KPMG Peat Marwick
Employees: 4,857

WHERE

HQ: 655-A Lone Oak Dr., Eagan, MN 55121
Phone: 612-683-7100
Fax: 612-683-7299 (Investor Relations)

The company has 2 manufacturing facilities; one software development, marketing, and administrative facility; and 30 sales and support offices in the US. It operates 17 subsidiary operations abroad.

	1990 Sales		1990 Operating Income	
	$ mil.	% of total	$ mil.	% of total
US	477	59	239	63
Western Europe	232	29	101	27
Other countries	95	12	38	10
Adjustments	—	—	(216)	—
Total	**804**	**100**	**162**	**100**

WHAT

	1990 Sales	
	$ mil.	% of total
Sales (products)	556	69
Leased systems	80	10
Service fees	168	21
Total	**804**	**100**

Supercomputers
CRAY X-MP series
CRAY XMS
CRAY Y-MP8 (8-processor models)
CRAY Y-MP4 (4-processor models)
CRAY Y-MP2 (2-processor models)
CRAY-2 series

Storage Devices
DD-60
DD-61
SSD-3I
SSD-5I
SSD-5
SSD-6
SSD-7

Systems Software
COS
UNICOS (UNIX-based operating system)

HOW MUCH

	9-Year Growth	1981	1982	1983	1984	1985	1986	1987	1988	1989	1990
Sales ($ mil.)	25.8%	102	141	170	229	380	597	687	756	785	804
Net income ($ mil.)	22.5%	18	19	26	45	76	125	147	157	89	113
Income as % of sales	—	17.9%	13.5%	15.4%	19.8%	19.9%	20.9%	21.4%	20.7%	11.3%	14.0%
Earnings per share ($)	22.2%	0.66	0.69	0.89	1.53	2.47	3.99	4.65	4.99	3.02	4.02
Stock price – high ($)	—	24.19	22.88	28.56	29.69	70.75	99.63	135.75	88.50	65.88	51.25
Stock price – low ($)	—	14.00	10.00	18.19	19.25	24.94	57.25	47.00	52.63	30.50	20.00
Stock price – close ($)	5.7%	18.25	19.31	27.81	26.25	65.50	80.88	70.75	60.75	39.00	30.00
P/E – high	—	37	33	32	19	29	25	29	18	22	13
P/E – low	—	21	15	21	13	10	14	10	11	10	5
Dividends per share ($)	0.0%	0.00	0.00	0.00	0.00	0.00	0.00	0.00	0.00	0.00	0.00
Book value per share ($)	24.0%	3.48	4.98	5.91	7.51	10.23	14.59	19.85	23.14	21.11	24.05

1990 Year-end:
Debt ratio: 14.4%
Return on equity: 17.8%
Cash (mil.): $67
Current ratio: 1.89
Long-term debt (mil.): $105
No. of shares (mil.): 26
Dividends:
  1990 average yield: 0.0%
  1990 payout: 0.0%
Market value (mil.): $785

Stock Price History High/Low 1981–90

RANKINGS

389th in *Fortune* 500 Industrial Cos.
514th in *Business Week* 1000

KEY COMPETITORS

Fujitsu	IBM
Hitachi	NEC
Intel	

CSX CORPORATION

OVERVIEW

CSX Corporation provides a wide array of transportation services, engaging in rail, intermodal (ship-to-truck-to-train), and ocean container shipping; trucking; inland barging; warehousing; and distribution. The company also operates resorts (Greenbriar Resort Management), develops real estate (CSX Realty), and runs several communications and information processing services (CSX Technology).

The striking blue and yellow locomotives of America's #1 coal-hauling railroad roll over a 19,054-mile rail system concentrated in the East, Midwest, and South. Rail operations accounted for 62% of sales and 78% of operating income in 1990. CSX also operates the nation's largest inland barge line, American Commercial Lines (which owns the WATERCOM marine phone system) and the largest US-flag container-shipping company, Sea-Land Service. Sea-Land, with lucrative transatlantic and transpacific shipping routes to Europe, Asia, and the Middle East, recently agreed to coordinate services between North America and Asia with Denmark's A.P. Moller-Maersk Line.

NYSE symbol: CSX
Fiscal year ends: December 31

 Hoover's Rating **C-**

WHO

Chairman, President, and CEO: John W. Snow, age 51, $966,738 pay (prior to promotion)
SVP Finance: James Ermer, age 48
SVP (Human Resources): Donald D. Davis
Auditors: Ernst & Young
Employees: 51,437

WHERE

HQ: One James Center, 901 E. Cary St., Richmond, VA 23219
Phone: 804-782-1400
Fax: 804-782-1409

CSX's 19,054-mile rail system links 20 states in the East, Midwest, and South, DC, and Ontario, Canada.

WHEN

CSX Corporation was formed in 1980, when Chessie System and Seaboard Coast Line merged in an effort to reduce costs and improve the efficiency of their railroads.

Chessie was a holding company for several railroads in the Northeast and Midwest. The oldest of these, the Baltimore & Ohio (B&O), was chartered in 1827 to help the port of Baltimore compete against New York and Philadelphia for freight traffic. By the late 1800s the railroad served DC, New York, Cincinnati, Chicago, and St. Louis. Under president Daniel Willard (1910–41), B&O modernized its tracks and equipment and gained a reputation for courteous service. Chesapeake & Ohio (C&O) acquired it in 1962.

C&O originated in Virginia with the Louisa Railroad in 1836. It gained access to Chicago, Cincinnati, and Washington, and by the mid-1900s C&O had become a major coal carrier. After B&O and C&O acquired joint control of Baltimore-based Western Maryland Railway (1967), the 3 railroads became subsidiaries of newly formed Chessie System (1973).

Among the predecessors of Seaboard Coast Line, Seaboard Air Line Railroad (SAL) had its beginnings in the Virginia-based Portsmouth & Roanoke Rail Road of 1832. By 1875 the line was controlled by John M. Robinson, who gave the system its name. SAL eventually acquired routes in Georgia, Florida, and Alabama.

Atlantic Coast Line Railroad (ACL) took shape between 1869 and 1893 as William T. Walters acquired a number of southern railroads. In 1902 ACL acquired the Plant System (several railroads in Georgia, Florida, and other southern states) and the Louisville & Nashville (a major north-south line connecting New Orleans, Nashville, St. Louis, Cincinnati, and Chicago), giving ACL the basic form it retained until 1967, when it merged with SAL to form Seaboard Coast Line (SCL). The merger enabled the railroads to eliminate their duplicate routes.

CSX inherited from Chessie System and SCL a combined rail network of over 27,000 route miles. The company bought Texas Gas Resources (gas pipeline, 1983), American Commercial Lines (Texas Gas's river barge subsidiary, 1984), and Sea-Land Corporation (ocean container shipping, 1986). In an effort to improve its market value, CSX sold most of its oil and gas properties, its communications holdings (LightNet), and most of its resort properties (Rockresorts) in 1988 and 1989. In 1990 CSX focused on employee safety, improving its safety record by 38% (from one of the industry's worst to one of the best). In 1991 the company sold its remaining natural gas unit (CSX Energy) to Enron Corp. and earmarked about $550 million for equipment and roadbed improvements.

WHAT

	1990 Sales		1990 Operating Income	
	$ mil.	% of total	$ mil.	% of total
Transportation	7,947	97	767	87
Properties	225	3	116	13
Technology	33	—	—	—
Adjustments	—	—	(68)	—
Total	**8,205**	**100**	**815**	**100**

Major Subsidiaries and Affiliates
American Commercial Lines Inc. (inland barges)
CSX Realty Inc. (real estate development)
CSX Technology Inc. (electronic data interchange)
CSX Transportation Inc. (rail service)
Grand Teton Lodge Co. (resort, Moran, WY)
The Greenbrier (resort, White Sulphur Springs, WV)
The Greenbrier Resort Management Co. (manages Carambola Beach Resort and Golf Club, St. Croix, Virgin Islands)
Jeffboat (barge and towboat manufacturing)
Sea-Land Service Inc. (container shipping)
Waterway Communications System Inc. (WATERCOM, marine telephone service)

	1990 Sales	
	$ mil.	% of total
Rail commodities		
Automotive	341	4
Chemicals	587	7
Minerals	324	4
Food & consumer products	193	2
Agricultural products	299	3
Metals	222	3
Forest products	462	5
Phosphates & fertilizer	274	3
Coal	1,647	20
Intermodal	638	8
Other	136	2
Container shipping	2,664	32
Barge	369	4
Nontransportation	258	3
Adjustments	(209)	—
Total	**8,205**	**100**

RANKINGS

5th in *Fortune* 50 Transportation Cos.
191st in *Business Week* 1000

KEY COMPETITORS

American President	Consolidated Rail	Santa Fe
ADM	Continental Grain	Pacific
Canadian Pacific	Norfolk Southern	Union Pacific
Consolidated	Roadway	UPS
Freightways	Ryder	Yellow Freight

HOW MUCH

	9-Year Growth	1981	1982	1983	1984	1985	1986	1987	1988	1989	1990
Sales ($ mil.)	4.7%	5,432	4,909	5,787	7,934	7,320	6,345	8,043	7,592	7,745	8,205
Net income ($ mil.)	(0.1%)	368	338	272	465	(118)	418	432	(38)	427	365
Income as % of sales	—	6.8%	6.9%	4.7%	5.9%	(1.6%)	6.6%	5.4%	(0.5%)	5.5%	4.4%
Earnings per share ($)	2.2%	2.97	2.70	2.07	3.15	(0.78)	2.73	2.78	(0.33)	4.09	3.63
Stock price – high ($)	—	20.17	19.75	27.50	26.25	31.88	37.50	41.75	32.50	38.63	38.13
Stock price – low ($)	—	13.67	12.08	15.42	18.38	22.38	25.63	22.13	24.38	29.75	26.00
Stock price – close ($)	5.7%	19.33	17.04	24.75	24.00	30.25	29.13	29.13	31.75	35.88	31.75
P/E – high	—	7	7	13	8	—	14	15	—	9	11
P/E – low	—	5	4	7	6	—	9	8	—	7	7
Dividends per share ($)	5.0%	0.90	0.95	0.99	1.04	1.13	1.16	1.18	1.29	1.28	1.40
Book value per share ($)	4.0%	25.31	26.83	31.00	32.82	30.15	31.64	31.25	30.39	33.24	35.93

1990 Year-end:
Debt ratio: 46.1%
Return on equity: 10.5%
Cash (mil.): $609
Current ratio: 0.75
Long-term debt (mil.): $3,025
No. of shares (mil.): 99
Dividends:
  1990 average yield: 4.4%
  1990 payout: 38.6%
Market value (mil.): $3,129

Stock Price History High/Low 1981–90

CUMMINS ENGINE COMPANY, INC.

NYSE symbol: CUM
Fiscal year ends: December 31

Hoover's Rating **C-**

OVERVIEW

Cummins is the world's largest diesel engine maker. The company sells primarily to heavy-duty truck manufacturers but also to construction, mining, agricultural, and other industrial equipment makers. Cummins also produces a range of engine-related parts (21% of sales) and power systems (14% of sales).

Cummins's share of the heavy-duty engine market has declined from over 50% in 1989 to 41% in the first half of 1991. The drop is attributed to stronger competition from Detroit Diesel (owned 80% by Penske and 20% by GM) and Caterpillar — a competition made worse by problematic engines produced by Cummins in 1988.

The Gulf War and the recession are blamed for Cummins's 1990 loss of $165 million (its highest ever). Continued losses in 1991 caused Cummins to reduce its quarterly dividend from 55¢ per share to 5¢. Having twice repelled unwelcome foreign suitors in 1989, Cummins sold 27% of its stock, collectively, to Ford, Tenneco, and Japanese tractor maker Kubota for $250 million in 1990, a move that gave Cummins much-needed cash and offers protection against future takeover bids.

WHEN

Chauffeur Clessie Cummins believed that Rudolph Diesel's cumbersome and smoky engine could be improved for use in transportation. Borrowing money and work space from his employer — Columbus, Indiana, banker W. G. Irwin — Cummins founded Cummins Engine in 1919.

Irwin eventually invested over $2.5 million in the business, and in the mid-1920s Cummins produced a fairly dependable mobile diesel engine. Truck manufacturers were reluctant to make the switch from gas to diesel, so Cummins used publicity stunts (including racing in the Indianapolis 500 and driving from New York to Los Angeles) to advertise his engine, and Irwin installed the engines in his California Purity Stores delivery truck fleet. The company earned its first profit in 1937, the year Irwin's grandnephew, J. Irwin Miller, began a 40-year term as company leader. During WWII the engine was used in trucks transporting large, heavy shipments.

Heavy postwar demand caused sales to jump from $20 million in 1946 to over $100 million by 1956. In the 1950s Cummins pioneered a line of 4-stroke diesel engines, started its first overseas plant in Scotland (1956), and purchased Atlas Crankshafts (1958). By 1967 Cummins had 50% of the diesel engine market. Two years later General Motors agreed to offer Cummins engines.

In 1970 Cummins acquired businesses not related to diesel engine production, including the K2 Ski Company (fiberglass skis) and Coot Industries (all-terrain vehicles), but sold them by 1976. In 1979 Cummins introduced a 10-liter engine to accompany its 14-liter model, long the company mainstay.

After touring Japanese factories Henry Schacht, CEO since 1973, began a program to modernize company plants. When he learned that some of his customers were testing engines from Japanese firms (e.g., Komatsu and Nissan), he lowered Cummins prices 20% to 40%.

In the early 1980s Cummins introduced a line of midrange engines developed in a joint venture with Tenneco subsidiary J. I. Case. To remain competitive in manufacturing, Cummins cut costs 22%, which doubled productivity in its US and UK plants, and spent $1.8 billion to update factories.

The strategy yielded mixed results. Profits have been erratic. Restructuring prevented Cummins from taking advantage of an industry boom between 1987 and 1988. Though the Gulf War gave its defense sales a boost, overall engine orders continued to decline in 1991, due in part to the recession. Cummins reported a 2nd quarter loss in 1991 of $17.2 million compared to a profit of $6.1 million in the comparable 1990 period.

WHO

Chairman and CEO: Henry B. Schacht, age 56, $441,750 pay
President and COO: James A. Henderson, age 56, $392,667 pay
VP and CFO: Peter B. Hamilton, age 44, $244,033 pay
VP Human Resources: Mark E. Chesnut, age 44
Auditors: Arthur Andersen & Co.
Employees: 24,900

WHERE

HQ: 500 Jackson St., Columbus, IN 47202-3005
Phone: 812-377-5000
Fax: 812-377-3334

The company's principal US manufacturing facilities are located in Indiana, New York, and North Carolina. Other operations are located in Australia, Brazil, Canada, France, Mexico, Scotland, Spain, and the UK.

	1990 Sales		1990 Operating Income	
	$ mil.	% of total	$ mil.	% of total
US	2,282	66	(128)	—
UK/Europe	764	22	49	—
Other countries	416	12	(11)	—
Adjustments	—	—	63	—
Total	**3,462**	**100**	**(27)**	**—**

WHAT

	1990 Sales	
	$ mil.	% of total
Engines	2,389	65
Components	796	21
Power systems	519	14
Adjustments	(242)	—
Total	**3,462**	**100**

Products

Engines (COMMAND, L10, B and C series, 6BT)
Engine components (crankshafts, gears, flywheels, camshafts, remanufactured engines and replacement parts, filters, turbochargers, air compressors, vibration dampers and couplings)
Power systems (components and systems for electrical power generation, emissions aftertreatment, electronic controls, and heat transfer)

RANKINGS

140th in *Fortune* 500 Industrial Cos.
889th in *Business Week* 1000

KEY COMPETITORS

Caterpillar	Isuzu
Daimler-Benz	Mitsubishi
Dana	Navistar
Fiat	Renault
General Motors	Saab-Scania
Hitachi	Volvo

HOW MUCH

	9-Year Growth	1981	1982	1983	1984	1985	1986	1987	1988	1989	1990
Sales ($ mil.)	6.5%	1,962	1,587	1,605	2,326	2,146	2,304	2,767	3,310	3,511	3,462
Net income ($ mil.)	—	100	8	5	188	50	(107)	14	(63)	(6)	(165)
Income as % of sales	—	5.1%	0.5%	0.3%	8.1%	2.3%	(4.7%)	0.5%	(1.9%)	(0.2%)	(4.8%)
Earnings per share ($)	—	11.16	0.21	0.36	19.38	5.22	(10.18)	1.14	(3.84)	0.68	(14.47)
Stock price – high ($)	—	58.75	49.25	81.50	88.25	88.50	78.75	94.75	68.00	72.25	55.50
Stock price – low ($)	—	30.00	26.00	47.63	61.25	58.25	51.25	40.75	43.13	48.00	31.13
Stock price – close ($)	0.5%	35.50	48.75	80.50	77.63	72.00	67.13	47.25	64.25	50.75	37.25
P/E – high	—	5	235	226	5	17	—	83	—	106	—
P/E – low	—	3	124	132	3	11	—	36	—	71	—
Dividends per share ($)	1.9%	1.85	2.00	2.00	2.05	2.20	2.20	2.20	2.20	2.20	2.20
Book value per share ($)	(6.0%)	65.31	58.18	53.38	68.62	74.29	61.89	64.99	55.03	39.78	37.37

1990 Year-end:
Debt ratio: 38.1%
Return on equity: —
Cash (mil.): $80
Current ratio: 1.36
Long-term debt (mil.): $411
No. of shares (mil.): 15
Dividends:
  1990 average yield: 5.9%
  1990 payout: —
Market value (mil.): $553

Stock Price History High/Low 1981–90

CYPRUS MINERALS COMPANY

NYSE symbol: CYM
Fiscal year ends: December 31

Hoover's Rating C+

OVERVIEW

Cyprus Minerals is a diversified mining company that is the 2nd largest US copper producer (after Phelps Dodge), the largest US talc producer, and one of the 15 largest coal companies in the US. The company is the world's leading producer of lithium and a leader in mining molybdenum, an ore used in steelmaking.

Copper, molybdenum, and gold accounted for 65% of sales and 93% of company operating income in 1990. Since being spun off by Amoco in 1985, Cyprus has sought to insulate itself from price swings in its 3 core

minerals — copper, coal, and lithium. It has broadened its mining operations and increased sales volume with more than 20 acquisitions.

CEO Kenneth Barr retired in 1991, and his successor, Chester Stone, began re-evaluation of the company's businesses. Stone has called for increased productivity at company mines, lowering costs through such measures as building cogeneration plants.

Cyprus has shuttered a troubled Nevada molybdenum mine and may axe other laggards. The company hopes to diversify into other minerals.

WHO

Chairman: Calvin A. Campbell, Jr., age 56
President and CEO: Chester B. Stone, Jr., age 55, $443,031 pay (prior to promotion)
President, Cyprus Copper Co.: F. Stephen Mooney, age 56
President, Cyprus Coal Co.: Donald P. Brown, age 45
SVP Industrial Minerals and Specialty Metals; President, Cyprus Industrial Minerals; President, Cyprus Foote Mineral Co.: Philip C. Wolf, age 43, $227,914 pay
SVP and CFO: Gerald J. Malys, age 46, $263,783 pay
VP Human Resources: Gerard H. Peppard, age 47
Auditors: Price Waterhouse
Employees: 8,400

WHEN

In 1912 prospector Charles Gunther persuaded Philip Wiseman and Seeley Mudd, both veteran managers of western copper mines, to back his exploration for mineral deposits, especially copper, in the countries along the Mediterranean Sea. In 1914 he found ores with as much as 5% copper (first grade) on Cyprus. Wiseman and Mudd, with offices in Los Angeles, formally founded Cyprus Mines in 1916.

The company encountered problems mining ore in Cyprus in the years that followed, including shortfalls of capital, the military and political turmoil of WWI, and the remote location. In the winter of 1919 the miners discovered "devil's mud," a slimy, corrosive material that contained gold and silver, which the company began to mine in 1932.

During the 1920s and 1930s the company continued exploring for minerals on Cyprus and eventually operated 6 mines there. Cyprus Mines produced strategic minerals (copper and zinc) to help the US war effort in WWII.

In 1951 the company began diversifying, with interests in oil in Kansas, Texas, and Louisiana. Cyprus Mines entered joint ventures with Utah Construction in 1952 to mine iron ore on the Marcona Plateau in Peru and in 1954 to mine copper near Tucson, because the mines on Cyprus by then were nearing depletion. During the 1950s, 1960s, and 1970s,

the company added other mining operations in the US, including zinc and talc.

In 1979 Amoco Minerals (subsidiary of Amoco, an integrated petroleum company) bought Cyprus Mines. Amoco Minerals grew through additional purchases to include mining for coal and molybdenum. In 1985 Amoco spun off its unprofitable Amoco Minerals as a publicly traded company, Cyprus Minerals.

Cyprus Minerals went on a buying spree, purchasing coal mines in Utah (Plateau, 1985), Colorado (Yampa and Twentymile, 1985), and Wyoming (Shoshone, 1987) and copper mines in Arizona (Sierrita, 1986; Casa Grande, 1987) and New Mexico (Pinos Altos, 1987). Also in 1987 Cyprus Minerals began to mine for gold, both in Arizona (Copperstone) and in Australia (Gidgee).

Cyprus Minerals continued its rapid growth, buying Foote Mineral (lithium, 1988), Windsor Minerals (talc division of Johnson & Johnson, 1989), Sociedad Chilena (lithium, fully acquired 1989), Reserve Mining (iron ore, 1989), and Warrenton Refining (copper ingot, 1989). The company purchased MCR (copper rod, Chicago, 1990).

In 1991 Cyprus awaited the outcome of bankruptcy court proceedings related to LTV, once Cyprus's biggest coal customer. Cyprus is claiming $505 million from LTV for lost profits and unpaid receivables.

WHERE

HQ: 9100 E. Mineral Circle, Englewood, CO 80112
Phone: 303-643-5000
Fax: 303-643-5049

Cyprus has major operations in 24 states and 7 foreign countries.

Mines

Copper	Iron Ore	Talc
Arizona	Minnesota	Alabama
Illinois		California
Missouri	**Molybdenum**	Montana
New Mexico	Arizona	Spain
	Idaho	Vermont
Coal		
Colorado	**Lithium**	**Zinc**
Kentucky	Chile	Mexico
Pennsylvania	Nevada	New Mexico
Utah	North Carolina	
West Virginia	Pennsylvania	
Wyoming	Tennesee	
	Virginia	
Gold		
Arizona		
Australia		

HOW MUCH

	5-Year Growth	1981	1982	1983	1984	1985	1986	1987	1988	1989	1990
Sales ($ mil.)	21.5%	—	—	—	—	706	811	795	1,289	1,790	1,866
Net income ($ mil.)	—	—	—	—	—	(429)	21	26	170	250	111
Income as % of sales	—	—	—	—	—	(60.8%)	2.6%	3.3%	13.2%	14.0%	5.9%
Earnings per share ($)	—	—	—	—	—	—	0.54	0.68	3.98	5.30	2.29
Stock price – high ($)	—	—	—	—	—	11.75	16.58	20.00	24.00	33.00	28.50
Stock price – low ($)	—	—	—	—	—	7.33	9.58	9.33	13.17	21.33	13.88
Stock price – close ($)	10.8%	—	—	—	—	11.08	10.83	16.17	21.67	26.50	18.50
P/E – high	—	—	—	—	—	—	31	29	6	6	12
P/E – low	—	—	—	—	—	—	18	14	3	4	6
Dividends per share ($)	—	—	—	—	—	0.00	0.00	0.00	0.13	0.63	0.80
Book value per share ($)	6.4%	—	—	—	—	20.49	21.34	21.95	25.62	30.92	27.94

1990 Year-end:
Debt ratio: 16.1%
Return on equity: 7.8%
Cash (mil.): $39
Current ratio: 2.47
Long-term debt (mil.): $246
No. of shares (mil.): 39
Dividends:
 1990 average yield: 4.3%
 1990 payout: 34.9%
Market value (mil.): $720

Stock Price History High/Low 1985–90

WHAT

	1990 Sales		1990 Operating Income	
	$ mil.	% of total	$ mil.	% of total
Coal/iron ore	480	26	(4)	(2)
Copper/gold/ molybdenum	1,222	65	178	93
Lithium/talc	164	9	18	9
Adjustments	—	—	47	—
Total	**1,866**	**100**	**239**	**100**

RANKINGS

223rd in *Fortune* 500 Industrial Cos.
595th in *Business Week* 1000

KEY COMPETITORS

Alcoa	Fluor
AMAX	FMC
Anglo American	Phelps Dodge
ASARCO	RTZ
Broken Hill	Coal mining companies

DANA CORPORATION

OVERVIEW

Toledo-based Dana Corporation is a leading world manufacturer and distributor of vehicle components for truck, industrial, and off-highway markets. Dana's products include drivetrain components, engine parts, chassis products, fluid power systems, and industrial power transmissions, which are sold to OEMs and distributors around the world. The company's largest customer is the Ford Motor Company, which accounted for 16.4% of 1990 sales. Dana's Vehicular segment contributed 73% of the company's sales and its Industrial

segment 22%. Dana's Financial Services segment (Diamond S&L, leasing, and real estate companies) accounted for 5% of 1990 revenues. Dana agreed to sell Diamond S&L to Banc One Ohio in 1991.

To counter its dependence on cyclical OEM markets, Dana is concentrating on growing its more profitable distribution business (currently 39% of total sales). It is also working harder to expand international sales, which rose 10% in 1990, accounting for 36% of total sales.

WHEN

Clarence Spicer began developing a universal joint and driveshaft for automobiles while studying at Cornell University. Leaving Cornell in 1904, he patented his design and founded Spicer Manufacturing in Plainfield, New Jersey. Spicer marketed the product himself, signing Mack Trucks in 1906 and International Harvester in 1914. Both have been continuous customers.

The company encountered financial trouble in 1913, and in 1914 New York attorney Charles Dana joined, advancing Spicer money to refinance.

Acquisitions after WWI strengthened Spicer's position in the growing truck industry: Chadwick Engine Works (U-joints), Parish Pressed Steel (vehicle frames), Brown-Lipe Gear Company (truck transmissions), Salisbury (axles), and Sheldon (axles).

The company moved to Toledo in 1929 to be nearer the emerging Detroit automotive center. Sales increased 18.4% annually from 1930 to 1940, rising to $19 million. In 1946 the company was renamed in honor of Charles Dana, who became chairman 2 years later. In the 1950s sales topped $150 million.

In the 1960s Dana adopted a strategy of market penetration and product development, targeting the heavy truck and service industries. Dana entered a new market by purchasing 2 replacement-parts makers in 1963,

Perfect Circle and Aluminum Industries. In 1966 Dana added Victor Manufacturing and Gasket. Dana also decentralized, giving divisional managers more responsibility. Charles Dana retired in 1966, after 50 years of service.

Dana continued to grow throughout the 1970s, adding the Weatherhead Company (1977; hoses, fittings, and couplings), the Wix Corporation (1979, filters), and Tyrone Hydraulics (1980, pumps and motors). By 1980 sales had exceeded $2.5 billion. In 1981 Dana purchased General Ohio S&L for $23 million.

Dana polished its production and sourcing methods during the 1980s. As a result, sales rose to $4.9 billion by 1989, while employment remained about even. Overall dependence on automotive original equipment decreased from nearly 60% of total sales to 50%. The company emerged as a leader in mobile fluid power (e.g., pumps, motors, and hoses) and mechanical and electrical industrial equipment.

In 1989 Dana introduced a 9-speed, heavy-duty truck transmission (developed jointly with Navistar), the first all-new design of its type in over 25 years. A sluggish truck market in the 2nd half of 1989 extending into 1990, along with losses in the company's financial segment, reduced 1990 earnings 42%. Sales and earnings continued their slide into 1991.

NYSE symbol: DCN
Fiscal year ends: December 31

WHO

Chairman, CEO, President, and COO: Southwood J. Morcott, age 52, $749,083 pay
EVP; President, Dana Europe: Borge R. Reimer, age 60, $507,393 pay
CFO, VP Finance, and Treasurer: James E. Ayers, age 58
Auditors: Price Waterhouse
Employees: 36,500

WHERE

HQ: 4500 Dorr St., Toledo, OH 43697
Phone: 419-535-4500
Fax: 419-535-4643

Dana operates 140 manufacturing plants in North America and 78 overseas.

	1990 Sales $ mil.	1990 Sales % of total	1990 Operating Income $ mil.	1990 Operating Income % of total
US	3,765	72	198	59
Europe	682	13	43	13
Other countries	761	15	95	28
Adjustments	17	—	122	—
Total	**5,225**	**100**	**458**	**100**

WHAT

	1990 Sales $ mil.	1990 Sales % of total	1990 Operating Income $ mil.	1990 Operating Income % of total
Vehicular prods.	3,804	73	309	92
Industrial prods.	1,143	22	73	22
Financial services	261	5	(46)	(14)
Adjustments	17	—	122	—
Total	**5,225**	**100**	**458**	**100**

Drivetrain Systems
Chelsea
Spicer

Engine Parts
Perfect Circle
Speedostat
Victor
Wix

Chassis Products
C&M
Parish
Perfect Circle
Spicer
Victor

Fluid Power Systems
Boston
Chelsea
Everflex
Gresen
Hyco
Tyrone
Weatherhead

Industrial Power Transmission Products
Boston
Formsprag
Gerbing
Seco
Warner Electric
Wichita

Financial Services Subsidiaries
Dana Commercial Credit

RANKINGS

101st in *Fortune* 500 Industrial Cos.
477th in *Business Week* 1000

KEY COMPETITORS

Allied-Signal
Borg-Warner
Cummins Engine
Cooper Industries
Eaton
Emerson
General Electric

Litton Industries
Reliance Electric
Robert Bosch
Rockwell
Siemens
Textron
Thyssen

HOW MUCH

	9-Year Growth	1981	1982	1983	1984	1985	1986	1987	1988	1989	1990
Sales ($ mil.)	7.6%	2,711	2,423	2,865	3,575	3,754	3,695	4,142	5,190	5,157	5,225
Net income ($ mil.)	(4.6%)	116	52	109	191	165	86	141	162	132	76
Income as % of sales	—	4.3%	2.1%	3.8%	5.4%	4.4%	2.3%	3.4%	3.1%	2.6%	1.4%
Earnings per share ($)	(1.7%)	2.17	0.95	1.97	3.40	2.95	1.68	3.21	3.79	3.10	1.85
Stock price – high ($)	—	22.33	23.67	33.33	31.13	30.38	36.50	54.25	40.50	42.88	38.13
Stock price – low ($)	—	14.17	14.58	20.58	21.13	22.25	25.50	27.50	32.50	33.00	19.88
Stock price – close ($)	4.8%	19.67	23.17	28.00	26.63	27.25	34.88	34.13	38.88	34.63	29.88
P/E – high	—	10	25	17	9	10	22	17	11	14	21
P/E – low	—	7	15	10	6	8	15	9	9	11	11
Dividends per share ($)	4.6%	1.07	1.07	1.08	1.20	1.28	1.28	1.40	1.54	1.60	1.60
Book value per share ($)	3.5%	18.82	18.67	19.80	21.73	22.73	21.40	21.63	23.61	24.93	25.57

1990 Year-end:
Debt ratio: 52.4%
Return on equity: 7.3%
Cash (mil.): $42
Current ratio: —
Long-term debt (mil.): $1,152
No. of shares (mil.): 41
Dividends:
 1990 average yield: 5.4%
 1990 payout: 86.5%
Market value (mil.): $1,225

Stock Price History High/Low 1981–90

DATA GENERAL CORPORATION

OVERVIEW

Data General (DG), based in Westboro, Massachusetts, is a 23-year-old minicomputer manufacturer. The $1.2 billion company has an installed base of approximately 300,000 computers worldwide.

Responding to a 4-year trend of declining earnings, DG adopted a strategy in 1988 to decrease its reliance on its proprietary ECLIPSE/MV minicomputer series by developing an open-system computer (the AViiON) and communications products to connect with other vendors' computers.

DG's AViiON, introduced in 1989, is a family of computers based on Motorola's 88000 RISC microprocessor that runs the widely used UNIX operating system. The introductory entry-level $7,950 AViiON, priced the same as DG's first NOVA minicomputer (1969), was 170 times faster, with 1,000 times the memory capacity. While DG continues to support and enhance its core ECLIPSE/MV series (an MV/30000 series was introduced in 1990), revenues from AViiON sales in its first full year of shipment exceeded $100 million. The success of the AViiON is largely credited with returning DG to profitability in 1991. Following 5 years of losses, DG reported a profit for the first 2 quarters of 1991.

WHEN

Edson de Castro and 2 other engineers left Digital Equipment Corporation (DEC) in 1968 to form Data General in Westboro, Massachusetts. Starting with $800,000, the company developed a minicomputer targeted at distributors who would add customized software and sell it to specialized markets such as manufacturers and hospitals.

Data General's first computer, the 16-bit NOVA minicomputer, quickly became a success by filling a gap in DEC's product line. The NOVA's simple design made use of the latest advances in chips and incorporated large-sized printed circuit boards that reduced the computer's costs. With low overhead, an aggressive pricing strategy, and a brash marketing campaign, DG soon became a major contender in the minicomputer market. DG later began making computers ranging from microcomputers to its $600,000 ECLIPSE, all based on the NOVA architecture. In 10 years (1969–79) DG sold over 70,000 computers. It made the *Fortune* 500 list in 1978.

By 1979, however, DG was slipping. Many of its rivals had already introduced 32-bit superminicomputers. In response DG introduced its version, called the MV8000, in 1980. The crash project to build the supermini was chronicled in Tracy Kidder's 1981 bestseller, *The Soul of a New Machine.*

Between 1980 and 1984, DG's sales climbed following the introduction of new machines and the highly rated Comprehensive Electronic Office (CEO) software, an office automation product that included word processing, electronic mail, and a filing system. In 1984 gross revenues were up 40% from 1983.

Like that of its rivals in the minicomputer industry, however, DG's growth slowed after 1985 due to increased competition from the less expensive but powerful PCs. In response, between 1985 and the end of 1989, DG reduced its work force from 16,535 to 12,000 and closed several plants. Nevertheless, DG's net income continued to drop.

In 1989 founder Edson de Castro stepped down as CEO and assumed the position of chairman. He left DG altogether in 1990. Ronald Skates, DG's CEO, continued to pare operations in 1990, reducing employment by 1,400 to 10,600 and terminating some of its development projects. With over 20 models now available and encouraging sales, DG's open-system AViiON series holds the greatest promise. In 1991 DG introduced a new AViiON workstation rated 2 times faster than its existing models. Also in 1991 DG began delivery of AViiONs to the US Geological Survey as part of its $127 million procurement award.

NYSE symbol: DGN
Fiscal year ends: September 30

Hoover's Rating **C-**

WHO

President and CEO: Ronald L. Skates, age 49, $464,000
SVP: J. Thomas West, age 51, $282,000
VP and CFO: Michael B. Evans, age 46
VP Information Management: James J. Ryan
Auditors: Price Waterhouse
Employees: 10,600

WHERE

HQ: 4400 Computer Dr., Westboro, MA 01580
Phone: 508-366-8911
Fax: 508-366-1319

The company has 27 subsidiaries and more than 250 sales and service offices in 60 countries.

	1990 Sales		1990 Operating Income	
	$ mil.	% of total	$ mil.	% of total
US	623	51	(65)	—
Europe	399	33	(37)	—
Far East	80	7	(9)	—
Other international	114	9	(21)	—
Adjustments	—	—	(1)	—
Total	**1,216**	**100**	**(133)**	**—**

WHAT

	1990 Sales	
	$ mil.	% of total
Products	784	64
Services	432	36
Total	**1,216**	**100**

Computers
AViiON (workstations and multiuser systems)
DASHER (personal computers)
DATA GENERAL/One (laptops)
ECLIPSE/MV series
NOVA (16-bit computer systems)

Software
CEO (integrated office automation)
CEO Connection (communications)
CEO Object Office (PC graphics interface)
CEOwrite (word processing)

Peripheral Equipment	**Operating Systems**
Communication	AOS/VS
controllers	AOS/VSII
Graphics workstations	DG/RDOS
Magnetic disc memories	DG/UX
Video display terminals	MV/UX

RANKINGS

302nd in *Fortune* 500 Industrial Cos.

KEY COMPETITORS

AT&T	Matsushita
AST	NEC
Apple	Oki
Computer Associates	Prime
Compaq	Sharp
Control Data	Siemens
DEC	Sony
Dell	Sun Microsystems
Fujitsu	Tandem
Hewlett-Packard	Tandy
Hitachi	Toshiba
Intergraph	Unisys
IBM	Wang

HOW MUCH

	9-Year Growth	1981	1982	1983	1984	1985	1986	1987	1988	1989	1990
Sales ($ mil.)	5.7%	737	806	829	1,161	1,239	1,268	1,274	1,365	1,314	1,216
Net income ($ mil.)	—	41	20	23	80	24	6	(83)	(16)	(120)	(140)
Income as % of sales	—	5.5%	2.5%	2.8%	6.9%	2.0%	0.5%	(6.5%)	(1.1%)	(9.1%)	(11.5%)
Earnings per share ($)	—	1.93	0.92	0.94	3.07	0.92	0.21	(3.07)	(0.55)	(4.10)	(4.65)
Stock price – high ($)	—	34.19	27.31	41.38	59.75	76.00	48.50	38.75	28.13	19.50	13.25
Stock price – low ($)	—	20.25	10.13	19.19	38.00	31.00	25.00	16.00	16.75	11.75	3.50
Stock price – close ($)	(18.0%)	26.88	19.88	37.25	58.75	45.38	29.63	23.63	18.50	12.50	4.50
P/E – high	—	18	30	44	19	83	231	—	—	—	—
P/E – low	—	11	11	20	12	34	119	—	—	—	—
Dividends per share ($)	0.0%	0.00	0.00	0.00	0.00	0.00	0.00	0.00	0.00	0.00	0.00
Book value per share ($)	(3.5%)	18.21	19.56	20.71	24.32	25.84	25.76	21.32	21.51	17.68	13.21

1990 Year-end:
Debt ratio: 12.3%
Return on equity: —
Cash (mil.): $75
Current ratio: 1.34
Long-term debt (mil.): $57
No. of shares (mil.): 31
Dividends:
　1990 average yield: 0.0%
　1990 payout: 0.0%
Market value (mil.): $138

Stock Price History
High/Low 1981–90

DAYTON HUDSON CORPORATION

OVERVIEW

Dayton Hudson, a combination of 2 local department stores, is a department store and discount retailer. The 61 Dayton's, Hudson's, and Marshall Field's department stores dominate the markets in Minneapolis, Detroit, and Chicago, respectively. The company's 227 Mervyn's discount soft-goods stores and 420 Target general-merchandise discount stores generated 83% of Dayton Hudson's 1990 sales.

Target remains well behind discount leaders Wal-Mart and Kmart. Ambitious expansion plans (300 new Targets by 1995) will bring the 3 discounters into direct competition in 40% (currently 15%) of their territories by 1995. Facing heavy competition in 1991, Dayton

Hudson switched Target's marketing emphasis from its up-market selection to low-price. However, the 1990 purchase of Chicago-based Marshall Field's for $1.05 billion indicates that Dayton Hudson has not abandoned the high-margin high-end market.

Dayton Hudson is a leader in retailing technology, having spent nearly $500 million on computerized systems for check-out, inventory control and reorders, and shipping. It has continued to expand and improve these systems in 1991.

Dayton Hudson has a long history of corporate philanthropy, for years giving 5% of its pretax earnings to charity.

NYSE symbol: DH
Fiscal year ends: Saturday nearest January 31

Hoover's Rating **B-**

WHO

Chairman and CEO: Kenneth A. Macke, age 52, $1,636,219 pay
President: Stephen E. Watson, age 46, $808,425 pay
Chairman and CEO, Target: Robert J. Ulrich, age 47, $832,764 pay
Chairman and CEO, Department Stores: Marvin W. Goldstein, age 47, $496,061 pay
Chairman and CEO, Mervyn's: Walter T. Rossi, age 48, $711,437 pay
SVP and CFO: Willard C. Shull III, age 50
SVP Personnel: Edwin H. Wingate, age 58
Auditors: Ernst & Young
Employees: 161,215

WHEN

The Panic of 1873 left Joseph Hudson bankrupt. After he paid his debts at 60 cents on the dollar he saved enough to open a men's clothing store in Detroit in 1881. Among Hudson's innovations were merchandise return privileges and price marking in place of bargaining. By 1891 Hudson's was the largest retailer of men's clothing in America. Hudson repaid his creditors from 1873 in full with interest.

When Hudson died in 1912, 4 nephews took over and expanded the business. In 1928 Hudson's built a new building in downtown Detroit that became the 2nd largest retail store building in the US, eventually growing to 25 stories with 49 acres of floor space.

In 1902 former banker George Dayton established a dry-goods store in Minneapolis on the spot where he found the highest foot traffic. Like Hudson, Dayton offered return privileges as well as liberal credit. His store grew to a full-line department store 12 stories high.

After WWII both companies saw that the future lay in the suburbs. In 1954 Hudson's built Northland in Detroit, then the largest US shopping center. Dayton's built the world's first fully enclosed shopping mall, Southdale, in Minneapolis (1956), opened its first Target discount store (1962) and its first B. Dalton bookstore (1962; sold 1986).

In 1966 Dayton's went public and in 1969 bought the still-family-owned Hudson's for stock, forming Dayton Hudson Corporation. The corporation increased its ownership of malls and invested in such specialty stores as consumer electronics (Team Central, Minneapolis, 1970; sold 1979) and hard goods (Lechmere, Boston, 1969; sold 1989).

In 1977 Target became the company's top money maker. The company then bought California-based Mervyn's and began selling other operations. In the late 1970s and 1980s, it sold 9 regional malls and several other businesses.

In the late 1980s Dayton Hudson took Target to Los Angeles and the Northwest and in 1991 started to move Mervyn's into Florida.

In 1990 the company bought Marshall Field's department store. Marshall Field's grew out of a dry-goods store started in Chicago in 1852 by Potter Palmer. Marshall Field bought into the store in 1865, building it into one of Chicago's biggest retailers. His motto, "Give the lady what she wants," became the hallmark of customer-oriented modern retailing.

The 1991 stock market recovery and end of the Gulf War failed to lift retailing out of the doldrums, and Dayton Hudson's sales stayed flat.

WHERE

HQ: 777 Nicollet Mall, Minneapolis, MN 55402
Phone: 612-370-6948
Fax: 612-370-5502

Dayton Hudson operates 708 stores in the US.

Major Markets	No. of Targets	No. of Mervyn's
Atlanta	14	6
Dallas/Ft. Worth	15	13
Denver	12	6
Detroit	15	9
Houston	15	9
Indianapolis	10	—
Los Angeles	56	39
Minneapolis/St. Paul	20	—
Phoenix	11	8
Sacramento	—	6
Salt Lake City	—	6
San Diego	12	10
San Francisco	14	21
Seattle-Tacoma	—	6
Other locations	226	88
Total	**420**	**227**

Location	No. of Dayton's	No. of Hudson's	No. of Marshall Field's
Illinois	—	—	15
Michigan	—	17	—
Minnesota	12	—	—
North Datoka	3	—	—
Texas	—	—	4
Wisconsin	—	—	4
Other states	2	3	1
Total	**17**	**20**	**24**

WHAT

	1990 Sales		1990 Operating Income	
	$ mil.	% of total	$ mil.	% of total
Target	8,175	55	466	46
Mervyn's	4,055	28	366	36
Department stores	2,509	17	183	18
Adjustments	—	—	(32)	—
Total	**14,739**	**100**	**983**	**100**

RANKINGS

8th in *Fortune* 50 Retailing Cos.
143rd in *Business Week* 1000

KEY COMPETITORS

Ames	Kmart	Nordstrom
Carter Hawley	The Limited	J. C. Penney
Hale	Macy	Price Co.
Costco	May	Sears
Dillard	Mercantile Stores	Wal-Mart
The Gap	Montgomery Ward	Other retailers

HOW MUCH

	9-Year Growth	1981	1982	1983	1984	1985	1986	1987	1988	1989	1990
Sales ($ mil.)	12.9%	4,943	5,661	6,963	8,009	8,793	9,259	10,677	12,204	13,644	14,739
Net income ($ mil.)	11.1%	160	198	243	259	284	255	228	287	410	410
Income as % of sales	—	3.2%	3.5%	3.5%	3.2%	3.2%	2.8%	2.1%	2.4%	3.0%	2.8%
Earnings per share ($)	13.4%	1.67	2.06	2.50	2.67	2.91	2.61	2.40	3.44	5.35	5.17
Stock price – high ($)	—	15.69	32.13	40.63	37.25	48.75	58.50	63.00	45.50	67.00	79.50
Stock price – low ($)	—	10.88	13.19	25.00	26.13	29.38	40.00	21.50	28.25	38.75	46.25
Stock price – close ($)	16.0%	15.00	27.56	31.13	31.50	45.88	42.50	27.63	39.63	63.63	57.25
P/E – high	—	9	16	16	14	17	22	26	13	13	15
P/E – low	—	7	6	10	10	10	15	9	8	7	9
Dividends per share ($)	11.1%	0.51	0.56	0.61	0.67	0.76	0.84	0.92	1.02	1.12	1.32
Book value per share ($)	9.8%	12.42	13.98	15.91	17.90	20.04	22.38	23.15	23.97	24.73	28.82

1990 Year-end:
Debt ratio: 64.3%
Return on equity: 19.3%
Cash (mil.): $92
Current ratio: 1.51
Long-term debt (mil.): $3,682
No. of shares (mil.): 71
Dividends:
 1990 average yield: 2.3%
 1990 payout: 25.5%
Market value (mil.): $4,068

Stock Price History High/Low 1981–90

DEERE & COMPANY

OVERVIEW

Deere is the largest manufacturer of farm equipment in the world. Deere is also a leading manufacturer of industrial equipment, primarily for the construction and forestry industries, and lawn care equipment for the consumer. Deere's insurance and finance businesses are important contributors.

Deere's major businesses are highly cyclical. Agricultural equipment sales are directly tied to farmers' financial health, and construction equipment demand parallels fluctuations in general economic activity. As a result, after enjoying record-breaking sales and profits in 1990, Deere is experiencing weakness in both sectors. Farm equipment profits are eroding further as Tenneco's troubled J. I. Case unit engages in price-cutting to reduce its agricultural equipment inventory. Deere is cutting back in an effort to keep its own inventory under control.

Deere wants to maintain its reputation for quality while engaging in relentless cost reduction. Taking a cue from Japanese auto makers, the company has begun trimming production costs with just-in-time inventory management techniques.

WHEN

Vermont-born John Deere moved westward to Grand Detour, Illinois, in 1836 and set up a blacksmith shop. Deere and other pioneers had trouble with the black midwestern soil sticking to the iron plows designed for sandy eastern soils, and in 1837 Deere used a circular steel saw blade to fashion a self-scouring plow. Deere sold only 3 in 1838 but was making 25 a week by 1842.

Deere moved to Moline, Illinois, in 1847. His son Charles joined the firm in 1853, beginning a tradition of family management. All 5 presidents prior to 1982 were related by blood or marriage. Charles Deere set up a system of distribution to independent dealerships and expanded the product line to include wagons, buggies, and corn planters.

Under Charles Deere's son-in-law William Butterworth (1907–28), the company bought other agricultural equipment manufacturers and developed harvesting equipment and tractors with internal combustion engines. Butterworth's nephew Charles Wiman, who became president in 1928, extended credit to farmers throughout the Great Depression, a policy that won long-term customer loyalty. In 1931 Deere opened its first foreign plant, in Canada.

William Hewitt, Wiman's son-in-law, became CEO in 1955. In 1958 Deere passed International Harvester to become the largest US producer of agricultural equipment, and by 1963 it had become the largest in the world. Operations abroad expanded to include Mexico, Argentina, France, and Spain; today 20% of revenues come from sales in 110 foreign countries and 7 foreign plants.

Deere used joint ventures (Yanmar, small tractors, 1977; Hitachi, excavators, 1983) and internal research to diversify.

Despite an industry-wide sales slump culminating in losses totaling $328 million in 1986 and 1987, Deere was the only major agricultural equipment maker to neither change ownership nor close factories during the 1980s. Deere cut its work force 44% and improved efficiency, lowering the manufacturing break-even point from 70% to 35% of capacity.

Robert Hanson became the first nonfamily CEO in 1982. He poured $2 billion into R&D during the 1980s, and in 1989 Deere introduced its largest new product offering, including the 9000 series of combines, which had taken 15 years to develop. Deere acquired Funk Manufacturing, a powertrain components manufacturer, for $87 million in 1989.

In recent years Deere has rapidly expanded its lawn care equipment business, particularly in Europe. In 1991 the company announced it would acquire SABO Maschinenfabrik, a German manufacturer of commercial lawn mowers.

NYSE symbol: DE
Fiscal year ends: October 31

Hoover's Rating **C+**

WHO

Chairman and CEO: Hans W. Becherer, age 55, $1,025,705 pay
President and COO: David H. Stowe, Jr., age 54, $652,076 pay
SVP Accounting-Control: Joseph W. England, age 50
SVP Engineering, Technology, and Human Resources: Michael S. Plunkett, age 53
Auditors: Deloitte & Touche
Employees: 38,500

WHERE

HQ: John Deere Rd., Moline, IL 61265-8098
Phone: 309-765-8000
Fax: 309-765-5772

The company sells its products through a network of dealers and distributors in over 110 countries. Deere operates 14 factories in the US and Canada and additional plants in Germany, Spain, Argentina, Australia, France, and South Africa.

	1990 Sales		1990 Operating Income	
	$ mil.	% of total	$ mil.	% of total
US & Canada	6,205	80	727	89
Overseas	1,554	20	89	11
Adjustments	—	—	85	—
Total	**7,759**	**100**	**901**	**100**

WHAT

	1990 Sales		1990 Operating Income	
	$ mil.	% of total	$ mil.	% of total
Farm equip.	5,431	70	578	71
Industrial equip.	1,348	17	63	8
Credit	510	7	120	15
Insurance & health care	470	6	55	6
Adjustments	—	—	85	—
Total	**7,759**	**100**	**901**	**100**

Agricultural Equipment	Crawler dozers
Balers	Elevating scrapers
Combines	Excavators
Planters	Loaders
Tillage tools	Log skidders
Tractors	Motor graders
	Powertrain components
Lawn Care	
Equipment	**Financial Services**
Riding mowers	Customer credit
Small tractors	Property and life insurance
Walk-behind mowers	
	Health Care Services
Industrial Equipment	Heritage National
Backhoe loaders	Healthplan Services (HMO)

RANKINGS

62nd in *Fortune* 500 Industrial Cos.
169th in *Business Week* 1000

KEY COMPETITORS

Black & Decker	Ford	Navistar
Caterpillar	Hitachi	Tenneco
Daewoo	Honda	Volvo
Dresser	Hyundai	Finance and
Fiat	Ingersoll-Rand	insurance
FMC	Mitsubishi	companies

HOW MUCH

	9-Year Growth	1981	1982	1983	1984	1985	1986	1987	1988	1989	1990
Sales ($ mil.)	4.0%	5,447	4,608	3,968	4,399	4,061	3,516	4,135	5,365	7,113	7,759
Net income ($ mil.)	5.6%	251	53	23	105	31	(229)	(99)	287	380	411
Income as % of sales	—	4.6%	1.1%	0.6%	2.4%	0.8%	(6.5%)	(2.4%)	5.3%	5.3%	5.3%
Earnings per share ($)	4.2%	3.74	0.78	0.34	1.55	0.45	(3.38)	(1.46)	3.90	5.06	5.42
Stock price – high ($)	—	48.00	36.88	42.38	40.38	33.13	35.13	43.00	50.50	64.25	78.38
Stock price – low ($)	—	32.13	22.00	28.88	24.63	24.25	21.50	22.50	33.38	44.00	37.63
Stock price – close ($)	3.1%	35.50	29.50	38.50	29.75	28.75	22.88	34.75	48.00	61.50	46.88
P/E – high	—	13	47	125	26	74	—	—	13	13	14
P/E – low	—	9	28	85	16	54	—	—	9	9	7
Dividends per share ($)	0.3%	1.95	2.00	1.00	1.00	1.00	0.75	0.25	0.65	1.30	2.00
Book value per share ($)	1.0%	36.29	35.29	33.60	33.78	33.29	29.46	28.23	32.92	36.76	39.52

1990 Year-end:
Debt ratio: 37.4%
Return on equity: 14.2%
Cash (mil.): $986
Current ratio: —
Long-term debt (mil.): $1,799
No. of shares (mil.): 76
Dividends:
  1990 average yield: 4.3%
  1990 payout: 36.9%
Market value (mil.): $3,568

Stock Price History High/Low 1981–90

DELL COMPUTER CORPORATION

OVERVIEW

Dell Computer, one of America's fastest growing PC makers, is also one of the most respected. In 1991 J. D. Power named Dell the overall leader in its first-ever PC customer-satisfaction survey.

The Austin, Texas–based company owes much of its success to the marketing genius of 26-year-old founder-chairman Michael Dell, who pioneered the direct-mail approach to PC marketing in 1984. Highly trained sales representatives take direct phone orders from end-users over the company's toll-free lines 24 hours daily. Dell's list of customers has grown from its initial base of individuals and small businesses to include major accounts (including the RTC and World Bank) and value-added remarketers (including Anderson Consulting and Electronic Data Systems). Repeat customers make up about 70% of the company's business.

The company uses databases to track customer orders and service calls. According to Michael Dell, 91% of customer problems are handled over the phone, but the company also offers on-site service through agreements with Xerox Corporation and Sorbus.

WHEN

At the age of 13, Michael Dell was already a successful businessman. From his parents' home in Houston, Dell ran a mail-order stamp trading business that, within a few months, grossed over $2,000. At 16 he sold subscriptions to the *Houston Post* and at 17 bought his first BMW. Little wonder that when he enrolled at the University of Texas in 1983 he was thoroughly bitten by the business bug.

Although Dell started off as a pre-med student, on the side he sold RAM chips and disk drives for IBM PCs. Dell bought his products at cost from IBM dealers, who, at the time, were required to order large monthly quotas of PCs from IBM, which frequently exceeded demand. Dell resold his stock through ads in local papers (and later through national computer magazines) at 10% to 15% below retail.

By April 1984 Dell's dorm room computer components business was grossing about $80,000 a month — enough to convince Michael Dell to drop out of college. At about that time he started making and selling his own IBM-compatible PCs under the brand name PC's Limited. Drawing on his previous sales experience, Dell sold his machines directly to end-users rather than through retail computer outlets, as most manufacturers did. By eliminating the customary retail markup, Dell was able to sell his machines at about 40% of the price of an IBM.

The company (renamed Dell Computer) expanded its customer base by adding international sales offices in 1987. Dell was plagued by management changes during the mid-1980s. In 1988 it started selling to government agencies and added a sales force to serve larger customers. That year Dell took his company public in a $34.2 million offering.

Dell tripped in 1989, reporting a 64% drop in profits. Sales were growing — but so were costs, mostly because of the company's expensive efforts to design a PC using proprietary components and RISC chips; the project has since been largely abandoned. Also, the company's warehouses were greatly oversupplied. But within a year the company turned itself around by cutting inventories and coming out with 8 new products (including its first notebook PCs).

In 1990 Dell moved into the retail arena by allowing Soft Warehouse Superstores (a Texas-based discount computer chain, now CompUSA) to sell its machines at mail-order prices. In 1991 the company struck a similar deal with Staples, an office supply chain. Dell also introduced its new processor upgradable systems, which allow users to replace slower processors with faster ones as they come out. Potential growth in its European operations prompted Dell to open a new plant in Limerick, Ireland, early in 1991.

NASDAQ symbol: DELL
Fiscal year ends: Around January 31 (52/53 week year)

Hoover's Rating **A**

WHO

Chairman and CEO: Michael S. Dell, age 26, $479,913 pay
SVP Product Group: G. Glenn Henry, age 48, $396,363 pay
SVP Marketing and International: Andrew R. Harris, age 36, $369,897 pay
SVP US Sales and Operations: Joel J. Kocher, age 34, $381,604 pay
CFO and Treasurer: James R. Daniel, age 43, $244,311 pay
VP Human Resources: Savino R. Ferrales, age 40
Auditors: Price Waterhouse
Employees: 2,400

WHERE

HQ: 9505 Arboretum Blvd., Austin, TX 78759-7299
Phone: 512-338-4400
Fax: 512-338-8700

Dell has operations in the US, Canada, the UK, France, Germany, Italy, Japan, Sweden, Finland, Spain, and the Netherlands. It has manufacturing plants in the US and Ireland.

	1990 Sales	
	$ mil.	% of total
US & Canada	397	73
Other countries	149	27
Total	**546**	**100**

WHAT

	1990 Sales
	% of total
Major accounts	48
Small/medium businesses and individuals	40
Value-added remarketers	12
Total	**100**

	1990 Sales
	% of total
486 products	5
386 products	69
286 products	12
Other products/services	14
Total	**100**

Products
Dell Stations graphics workstations
Dell System deskside computers
Dell System desktop computers
Dell System laptop computers
Dell System notebook computers

KEY COMPETITORS

AT&T	IBM
Apple	Machines Bull
AST	Matsushita
Atari	NEC
Canon	Oki
Commodore	Olivetti
Compaq	Philips
Data General	Sharp
DEC	Siemens
Fujitsu	Sony
Hewlett-Packard	Sun Microsystems
Hitachi	Tandy
Honeywell	Toshiba
Intel	

HOW MUCH

	5-Year Growth	1981	1982	1983	1984	1985	1986	1987	1988	1989	1990
Sales ($ mil.)	74.2%	—	—	—	—	34	70	159	258	389	546
Net income ($ mil.)	93.3%	—	—	—	—	1	2	9	14	5	27
Income as % of sales	—	—	—	—	—	2.3%	3.1%	5.9%	5.6%	1.3%	5.0%
Earnings per share ($)	—	—	—	—	—	—	—	0.72	0.80	0.27	1.36
Stock price – high ($)	—	—	—	—	—	—	—	—	12.63	10.63	18.88
Stock price – low ($)	—	—	—	—	—	—	—	—	7.75	5.00	4.63
Stock price – close ($)	—	—	—	—	—	—	—	—	10.00	5.50	18.50
P/E – high	—	—	—	—	—	—	—	—	16	39	14
P/E – low	—	—	—	—	—	—	—	—	10	19	3
Dividends per share ($)	—	—	—	—	—	—	—	0.00	0.00	0.00	0.00
Book value per share ($)	—	—	—	—	—	—	—	0.86	4.03	4.25	5.79

1990 Year-end:
Debt ratio: 3.6%
Return on equity: 27.1%
Cash (mil.): $37
Current ratio: 1.67
Long-term debt (mil.): $4
No. of shares (mil.): 19
Dividends:
  1990 average yield: 0.0%
  1990 payout: 0.0%
Market value (mil.): $358

Stock Price History High/Low 1988–90

DELOITTE & TOUCHE

OVERVIEW

Deloitte & Touche is #3 of the Big 6 accounting firms. A year after the 1989 merger of Deloitte Haskins & Sells with Touche Ross & Company, Deloitte & Touche proclaimed itself the #1 auditor of US- and Canadian-based companies with sales of more than $500 million.

The company specializes in retail (Macy's, Toys "R" Us), utilities (13 of the 36 electric and gas companies included in the *Fortune* 50 Utilities), health care (Mayo Clinic), brokerage (Bear Stearns), insurance (Metropolitan Life), and manufacturing (General Motors). As with its 5 major competitors, Deloitte & Touche offers a range of services, including auditing, management consulting, tax advice, and mergers-and-acquisitions support.

Its overseas operations — handled under the umbrella of DRT International — are positioning the company for expansion in the Pacific Rim, in a unified Western Europe, and in a newly market-driven Eastern Europe. DRT stands for "Deloitte Ross Tohmatsu." Tohmatsu & Company, Japan's largest auditor, came under the DRT banner as a part of Touche Ross. In the Soviet Union, DRT has a joint venture with Inaudit, the state-run accounting and auditing group.

WHEN

In 1845 — 3 years after the UK initiated an income tax — William Welch Deloitte opened his accounting office in London. Deloitte was the grandson of a Count de Loitte, who fled France during the Reign of Terror (1793–94), abandoned his title, and made a living as a French teacher.

In the early years of his accountancy, William Deloitte, a former staff member of the Official Assignee in Bankruptcy of the City of London, solicited business from bankrupts. During the 1850s and 1860s, Parliament established general rules for forming limited liability companies, and the rules required companies to hire accountants. Deloitte performed accounting for the Great Western Railway and, later, for telegraph companies.

As the firm grew, Deloitte added partners, among them John Griffiths (1869). Griffiths visited the US in 1888, and in 1890 the Deloitte firm opened a branch on Wall Street. Branches followed in Cincinnati (1905), Chicago (1912), Montreal (1912), Boston (1930), and Los Angeles (1945). In 1952, the Deloitte firm formed an alliance with the accounting firm of Haskins & Sells. Haskins & Sells operated 34 US offices.

Deloitte developed a reputation as a thorough, and therefore expensive, firm. By the late 1970s a partner proclaimed to *Fortune*, "We want to be the Cadillac, not the Ford, of the profession." But Deloitte Haskins & Sells, as it had become known, began to lose its conservatism as competition for auditing contracts and for management consulting clients became more intense. When government regulators nudged the profession to drop restrictions on advertising, Deloitte Haskins & Sells was the first Big 8 firm with aggressive ads extolling its virtues as an advisor.

In 1984, in a move that foreshadowed the merger mania to come, Deloitte Haskins & Sells tried to merge with Price Waterhouse. British partners in Price Waterhouse objected to the deal, and it was dropped.

The Big 8 accounting firms became the Big 6 in 1989. Ernst & Whinney merged with Arthur Young to become Ernst & Young, and Deloitte Haskins & Sells teamed up with Touche Ross & Company to form Deloitte & Touche. Touche Ross had been founded in New York in 1947. Premerger Touche Ross earned a reputation as the hard-charging, bare-knuckled bad boy of the Big 8. Touche Ross had run into controversy for its role in junk-bond deals that turned sour during the 1980s.

In 1990 DRT International was formed as an umbrella for the Deloitte & Touche organization around the world. That same year the UK arm of Spicer and Oppenheim was merged into the DRT organization. Faced with reduced business during the 1990 economic downturn, Deloitte announced that it was cutting its number of partners by 5%.

HOW MUCH

	9-Year Growth	1981	1982	1983	1984	1985	1986	1987	1988	1989	1990
Worldwide revenues ($ mil.)											
Deloitte Haskins & Sells	10.7%	800	852	894	940	953	1,188	1,500	1,920	3,700	3,760
Touche Ross	10.7%	704	800	845	904	973	1,151	1,450	1,840		
No. of offices [1,2]	—	—	—	183	185	192	205	195	196	—	110
No. of partners[1]	—	—	—	1,585	1,614	1,619	1,600	1,590	1,600	—	1,670
No. of employees[1]	—	—	—	14,463	16,009	17,253	17,521	18,252	19,276	—	18,800

1990 revenues per partner: $2,514,970

Worldwide Revenues ($ mil.) 1981–90

[1] Combined Deloitte Haskins & Sells, Touche Ross   [2] US offices

International partnership
Fiscal year ends: First Saturday in June

WHO

Chairman and CEO: J. Michael Cook
Managing Partner: Edward A. Kangas
CFO: Jerry W. Kolb
Recruitment/College Relations: Lester M. Sussman
Employees: 18,800

WHERE

HQ: 10 Westport Rd., PO Box 820, Wilton, CT 06897-0820
Phone: 203-761-3179
Fax: 203-834-2231

Deloitte & Touche operates 110 offices in the US and has offices in 100 countries.

WHAT

	1990 Revenues
	% of total
Accounting & auditing	56
Tax	24
Management consulting	20
Total	**100**

Services
Accounting and auditing
Management consulting
Mergers and acquisitions consulting
Tax advice and planning

Representative Clients

Bank of New York	Merrill Lynch
BASF	MetLife
Bayer USA	Mitsubishi
Bear Stearns	Mitsui
Boeing	Monsanto
Bridgestone	New York Times
Chrysler	Nissan Motor (USA)
Dow Chemical	PPG
Equitable	Procter & Gamble
General Motors	Prudential
Great A&P	Macy
Honeywell	Rockwell
KKR	Sears
Litton Industries	Sumitomo Corp. of America
Loews	Toshiba America
Mayo Clinic	Toys "R" Us

Affiliated Firms
Actuarial, Benefits, and Compensation Group (consultation on employee pay and benefits)
Braxton Associates (strategic planning)
Deloitte & Touche Valuation Group (business valuations)
Douglass Group of Deloitte & Touche (health care facility planning and strategy)
DRT Eastern Europe
DRT International
DRT Systems Ltd. (computer consulting)
Garr Consulting Group (consulting to retail and wholesale industries)
Polaris Consulting Services (database, systems development)
Tohmatsu & Co. (auditing, Japan)

KEY COMPETITORS

Arthur Andersen	KPMG
Coopers & Lybrand	Marsh & McLennan
Ernst & Young	McKinsey & Co.
H&R Block	Price Waterhouse

DELTA AIR LINES, INC.

NYSE symbol: DAL
Fiscal year ends: June 30

Hoover's Rating **C+**

OVERVIEW

From humble southern beginnings Delta has emerged as one of the world's largest airlines. The company operates 90% of the flights from its home base at Hartsfield Atlanta Airport (America's 3rd largest), up from 65% before Eastern Air Lines's shutdown in January 1991. Delta and Eastern are, in fact, credited with inventing the popular hub-and-spoke system at Atlanta in the 1970s. Independent commuter airlines (Delta Connection) feed Delta's route network, flying passengers to one of 7 US hubs to make connecting flights.

A relative newcomer to the international arena, Delta added flights to Copenhagen, Berlin, Tokyo, and Hong Kong in 1991 and has petitioned the DOT for approval to start flying to Rio de Janeiro in 1992. The company is also investigating the possibility of establishing a hub in Taipei as a gateway to the Pacific Rim.

Delta is considered one of America's best employers, with a generous employee benefits package and a nonlayoff policy. About 13% of Delta's employees belong to unions. The company is known for being fiscally conservative and has maintained the industry's lowest customer complaint record for 17 consecutive years.

WHEN

Delta was founded in Macon, Georgia, in 1924 as the world's first crop-dusting service, Huff-Daland Dusters, to combat a boll weevil infestation of southern cotton fields. After moving to Monroe, Louisiana, in 1925, the company was bought by field manager C. E. Woolman and 2 partners and renamed Delta Air Service (alluding to the Mississippi Delta region served by the airline) in 1928.

In 1929 Delta pioneered passenger service from Dallas to Jackson, Mississippi, operating without benefit of a government mail subsidy until 1934, when the US Postal Service awarded the airline a mail contract from Fort Worth to Charleston, South Carolina, via Atlanta. Delta moved to Atlanta in 1941. Woolman (president of Delta since 1945) ran the airline until his death in 1966.

Delta added flights to Cincinnati and New Orleans in 1943 and from Chicago to Miami in 1945. Its 1952 purchase of Chicago and Southern Airlines added a direct route from Chicago to New Orleans, making Delta the 5th largest US airline, with service to cities in the South, the Midwest, Texas, and the Caribbean.

Delta offered its first transcontinental flight in 1961. In 1972 the airline bought Northeast Airlines, thereby expanding service to New England and Canada, and then crossed the Atlantic in 1978 with service to London.

In 1982 Delta's employees pledged $30 million to buy a Boeing 767 jet. Christened *The Spirit of Delta*, this aircraft was a token of appreciation to the company from its employees. In fiscal 1983 Delta succumbed to the weak US economy, posting its first loss in 36 years ($87 million). Earnings rebounded to $259 million in 1985, and Delta bought Los Angeles–based Western Air Lines in 1986.

Delta established service to the Far East in 1987. By 1989 international routes provided 11% of the company's passenger revenues. In 1989 Delta signed agreements with Swissair and Singapore Airlines, allowing the 3 airlines to buy stakes of up to 5% in one another. In 1990 Delta joined TWA and Northwest to form WORLDSPAN, a computer reservation service. Fare discounts and higher fuel and labor costs reduced earnings by 34% in 1990, despite a 6% growth in sales.

In 1991 Delta bought gates, planes, and 3 Canadian routes from Eastern for $243 million. Its 1991 purchase of Pan Am's New York-to-Boston shuttle, European routes, and Frankfurt hub (for $621 million in cash and $668 million in debt assumption) pushed Delta past American and United as the world's largest airline in terms of cities served and profitability. The deal also gave Delta a 45% stake in Pan Am.

WHO

Chairman and CEO: Ronald W. Allen, age 48, $751,812 pay
President and COO: W. Whitley Hawkins, age 59, $358,234 pay (prior to promotion)
EVP Technical Operations: Russell H. Heil, age 48
SVP Finance and CFO: Thomas J. Roeck, Jr., age 46, $355,284 pay
SVP Personnel: Maurice W. Worth
Auditors: Arthur Andersen & Co.
Employees: 61,675

WHERE

HQ: Hartsfield Atlanta International Airport, Atlanta, GA 30320
Phone: 404-765-2600
Fax: 404-765-2233
Reservations: 800-221-1212

Delta serves 187 cities in 45 states and 15 foreign countries.

Hub Locations
Atlanta, GA	Frankfurt, Germany
Boston, MA	Los Angeles, CA
Cincinnati, OH	Orlando, FL
Dallas/Fort Worth, TX	Salt Lake City, UT

WHAT

	1990 Sales	
	$ mil.	% of total
Passengers	8,042	94
Freight	301	4
Mail	115	1
Other	124	1
Total	**8,582**	**100**

Major Subsidiaries and Affiliates
The Delta Connection (commuter airlines)
Atlantic Southeast Airlines
Business Express
Comair
SkyWest Airlines

Computer Reservation System
WORLDSPAN (38%)

Flight Equipment	No.	Orders
Boeing 727	129	—
Boeing 737	72	57
Boeing 757	67	17
Boeing 767	42	15
DC-9	33	—
L-1011	41	9
MD-90	—	50
MD-88	75	36
MD-11	2	13
Total	**461**	**197**

RANKINGS

4th in *Fortune* 50 Transportation Cos.
210th in *Business Week* 1000

KEY COMPETITORS

Alaska Air	KLM	SAS
America West	Lufthansa	Southwest
AMR	Midway	Swire Pacific
British Airways	NWA	TWA
Continental Airlines	Pan Am	UAL
HAL	Qantas	USAir
JAL		

HOW MUCH

	9-Year Growth	1981	1982	1983	1984	1985	1986	1987	1988	1989	1990
Sales ($ mil.)	10.4%	3,533	3,618	3,616	4,264	4,684	4,460	5,318	6,915	8,089	8,582
Net income ($ mil.)	8.4%	146	21	(87)	176	259	47	264	307	461	303
Income as % of sales	—	4.1%	0.6%	(2.4%)	4.1%	5.5%	1.1%	5.0%	4.4%	5.7%	3.5%
Earnings per share ($)	4.1%	3.69	0.52	(2.18)	4.42	6.50	1.18	5.90	6.27	9.34	5.28
Stock price – high ($)	—	41.38	47.00	51.00	45.88	52.75	51.88	67.13	55.13	85.75	80.88
Stock price – low ($)	—	23.69	22.63	29.00	27.00	36.13	37.75	32.00	36.00	48.75	52.50
Stock price – close ($)	9.6%	24.50	44.25	39.75	43.63	39.00	48.13	37.13	50.13	68.25	55.75
P/E – high	—	11	90	—	10	8	44	11	9	9	15
P/E – low	—	6	44	—	6	6	32	5	6	5	10
Dividends per share ($)	10.4%	0.70	0.95	1.00	0.60	0.70	1.00	1.00	1.20	1.20	1.70
Book value per share ($)	8.9%	26.17	25.75	22.56	26.38	32.21	32.45	39.84	44.99	53.17	56.32

1990 Year-end:
Debt ratio: 33.6%
Return on equity: 9.6%
Cash (mil.): $68
Current ratio: 0.56
Long-term debt (mil.): $1,315
No. of shares (mil.): 46
Dividends:
1990 average yield: 3.1%
1990 payout: 32.2%
Market value (mil.): $2,569

Stock Price History High/Low 1981–90

DELUXE CORPORATION

OVERVIEW

St. Paul–based Deluxe Corporation is the nation's #1 check printer with 53% of the market. Other printing operations, including gift wrap, greeting cards, stationery, and computer and business forms, represent a smaller proportion of sales.

There was a widespread prediction in the early 1980s that check-writing would succumb to electronic, PC-based bill paying. The prediction failed to materialize within the decade, giving Deluxe time to sell more checks and position itself to profit from the increasing automation of transactions. Through acquisitions the company became the US leader in

3rd-party electronic transaction processing (through ATM networks and point-of-sale systems), retail check authorization, and new-account verification for banks. Deluxe can also handle automated government benefit payments. Benefiting from heavy R&D spending, this segment of Deluxe is growing much faster than the mature check-printing business.

Oddly, financial trouble at banks, Deluxe's biggest check customers, will help the company to sell more checks. As banks merge, customers of acquired banks will need to buy new checks.

NYSE symbol: DLX
Fiscal year ends: December 31

Hoover's Rating A+

WHO

Chairman: Eugene R. Olson, age 64
President and CEO: Harold V. Haverty, age 60, $716,764 pay
EVP: Jerry K. Twogood, age 50, $464,196 pay
SVP: William R. Phillips, age 57, $318,021 pay
SVP: Arnold A. Angeloni, age 50, $273,444 pay
SVP: Kenneth J. Chupita, age 49
SVP and CFO: Charles M. Osborne, age 37, $296,575 pay
VP Human Resources: Terry Quigley
Auditors: Deloitte & Touche
Employees: 17,000

WHEN

The 75-year history of Deluxe Corporation is characterized by challenge, determination, opportunity, and pioneering. From the company's beginnings in 1915, newspaper-publisher-turned-chicken-farmer William R. Hotchkiss was determined to produce one product better, faster, and more economically than anyone else.

From his office in St. Paul, Minnesota, Hotchkiss set out to provide the banks of the Federal Reserve Ninth District with business checks, offering 48-hour delivery. Sales reached $4,173 at the end of 1916, tripled the next year, rose to $18,961 in 1918, and increased 106% to $39,163 in 1919. Deluxe became even more prosperous in the 1920s when Hotchkiss introduced the most successful product in Deluxe's history, the Long Handy, a small pocket check.

Because Deluxe Check Printing was a private company, it avoided some effects of the 1929 stock market crash, but the company suffered along with other businesses during the Great Depression. Although Deluxe cut employee hours and pay during this period, not a single employee lost his job.

George McSweeney, sales manager, became a driving force for the company. He created the Personalized Check Program in 1939. McSweeney was elected president in 1941.

During WWII he persuaded Washington to release its grip on Deluxe's paper supply and stabilized the company by printing ration forms for banks.

In the 1950s Deluxe entered the new era of automation as one of the first to implement the government's magnetic-ink character-recognition program. Because of its leadership, by 1960 Deluxe was selling its printing services to 99% of the nation's commercial banks.

Deluxe introduced its new Fashion Chec covers in 1965, and brought out its Distinctive line of checks, featuring American scenic designs, in 1969.

Deluxe bought Chex Systems (new-account verification service) in 1984, Colwell Systems (business forms for medical markets) and John A. Pratt and Associates (renamed Deluxe Sales Development) in 1985, A. O. Smith Data Systems (ATM and electronic funds-transfer software) in 1986, and Current (mail-order greeting cards and specialty products) in 1987.

In 1990 Deluxe bought ACH Systems (systems for paperless funds transfers between financial institutions) and Electronic Transaction Corp. (retail check authorization), and formed an electronic funds-transfer system alliance with Scicon, the UK's largest computer services company.

WHERE

HQ: 1080 W. County Rd. F, St. Paul, MN 55126
Phone: 612-483-7111
Fax: 612-483-7821

Deluxe Corporation operates 81 facilities located in 34 states.

WHAT

	1990 Sales		1990 Operating Income	
	$ mil.	% of total	$ mil.	% of total
Consumer specialty products	217	15	24	9
Payment & business systems	1,197	85	251	91
Total	**1,414**	**100**	**275**	**100**

Divisions and Subsidiaries

Consumer Specialty Division
Current, Inc. (mail-order gift wrap, greeting cards, and stationery)

Payment Systems Division
Chex Systems, Inc. (account verification)
Deluxe Check Printers
Deluxe Data Systems, Inc. (electronic funds transfers)
Deluxe Sales Development Systems, Inc. (sales training)
Electronic Transaction Corp. (check authorization)

Business Systems Division
Colwell Systems, Inc. (health care forms)

RANKINGS

273rd in *Fortune* 500 Industrial Cos.
212th in *Business Week* 1000

KEY COMPETITORS

American Greetings
AT&T
Carlson
Hallmark
Moore
United Nations

HOW MUCH

	9-Year Growth	1981	1982	1983	1984	1985	1986	1987	1988	1989	1990
Sales ($ mil.)	12.1%	504	550	620	683	764	867	948	1,196	1,316	1,414
Net income ($ mil.)	13.9%	53	65	77	88	104	121	149	143	153	172
Income as % of sales	—	10.6%	11.8%	12.4%	12.9%	13.6%	14.0%	15.7%	12.0%	11.6%	12.2%
Earnings per share ($)	14.9%	0.58	0.71	0.84	1.01	1.22	1.42	1.74	1.68	1.79	2.03
Stock price – high ($)	—	7.88	10.13	11.94	14.50	24.81	38.00	42.25	28.38	35.75	35.88
Stock price – low ($)	—	6.00	4.63	8.69	8.88	13.63	21.56	20.00	21.00	24.00	26.63
Stock price – close ($)	19.5%	7.03	10.06	9.97	14.25	23.38	35.25	24.38	25.00	34.38	35.00
P/E – high	—	14	14	14	14	20	27	24	17	20	18
P/E – low	—	10	7	10	9	11	15	12	13	13	13
Dividends per share ($)	19.4%	0.22	0.27	0.31	0.39	0.49	0.58	0.76	0.86	0.98	1.10
Book value per share ($)	14.5%	2.38	2.81	3.18	3.48	4.14	4.85	5.77	6.65	7.40	8.04

1990 Year-end:
Debt ratio: 1.7%
Return on equity: 26.3%
Cash (mil.): $114
Current ratio: 1.73
Long-term debt (mil.): $12
No. of shares (mil.): 84
Dividends:
   1990 average yield: 3.1%
   1990 payout: 54.2%
Market value (mil.): $2,943

Stock Price History High/Low 1981–90

DEMOCRATIC PARTY

Political party
Party symbol: donkey

Hoover's Rating **B**

OVERVIEW

One of the oldest surviving political organizations in existence, the Democratic party is the majority party in America. Known as an "everyone party," the Democrats' support base is more diverse than that of the Republican party; traditionally, urban dwellers, blacks, labor, immigrants, and southern whites have constituted the core of the party. The party's donkey symbol traces its origin to the Jacksonian era.

Although the party strengthened its lead in Congress following the 1988 election (it now holds 56 Senate and 267 House seats), it has lost 7 of the last 10 presidential elections and is losing the allegiance of many of its previous supporters.

Gearing up for the 1992 elections, the Democrats are a somnolent party. Reluctant to face the popularity of George Bush, promising Democratic candidates are dropping out of the presidential race. Struggling to find a rallying cry, the Democrats have pushed the national health care crisis and extension of benefits to those left unemployed for long periods by the economic recession (which the Democrats blame on Ronald Reagan's budget-busting deficits) to the forefront of their assault on Bush.

WHO

Chairman: Ronald H. Brown
Vice Chairmen: Lynn Cutler, Jack Otero, Carmen Perez, James Ruvolo, Lottie Shackelford
Secretary: Kathleen M. Vick
Treasurer: Robert Farmer

WHERE

HQ: 430 S. Capitol St., Washington, DC 20003
Phone: 202-863-8000
Fax: 202-863-8028

WHEN

During the 1790s Antifederalists supporting popular government united their support behind Thomas Jefferson and took the name Republicans, creating a 2-party system: the Federalists and the Jeffersonian Republicans. In 1800 Jefferson narrowly won the presidential election over John Adams.

During the early 1800s the party broke into numerous factions and virtually collapsed. In the election of 1828, 3 major factions came together and carried Andrew Jackson into the White House. The Jacksonians reaffirmed the ideals of the Jeffersonians and, at the convention of 1840, adopted the name Democratic party.

Following Jackson's retirement in 1837, the Democrats dominated presidential contests for the next 2 decades with the elections of Martin Van Buren (1836), James Polk (1844), Franklin Pierce (1852), and James Buchanan (1856). During this time the party began to divide over the issues of slavery and westward expansion. The growing schism proved disastrous at the Charleston convention of 1860, when the northern and southern Democrats nominated separate candidates. The split allowed the newly formed Republicans to elect Lincoln, who would lead the nation during the Civil War.

After the Civil War, white Southerners (who associated the Republicans with the harsh Radical Reconstruction movement) became strongly Democratic (the "Solid South"), and the party became agrarian and conservative. Between 1860 and 1900 the Democrats held the White House for only 8 years, during the 2 terms of Grover Cleveland (1884, 1892).

The Democrats did not regain the presidency until 1912, when a split in the Republican party allowed them to elect Woodrow Wilson. Wilson was reelected in 1916, but the party lost control of Congress, a situation that would prove fatal to Wilson's League of Nations.

During the 1920s the Democrats again broke into factions, allowing the Republicans to dominate the decade. When the Great Depression hit, the nation turned to Democratic candidate Franklin D. Roosevelt, whose New Deal changed the party's direction and united a new generation of Democrats that included farmers, organized labor, minorities, and liberals. The Democrats regained control of Congress and kept the presidency until 1952, with Roosevelt (who was elected to a record 4 terms before his death in 1945) and Harry S Truman.

During the 1960s John F. Kennedy's "New Frontier" and Lyndon B. Johnson's "Great Society" were extensions of New Deal politics. Kennedy (assassinated in 1963) and Johnson, who actively supported civil rights and desegregation, lost the support of many southern Democrats. The war in Vietnam split the party further, and the Democrats' 1968 Chicago convention was marred by riots and internal strife. The Democratic candidate, Hubert Humphrey, was defeated by Richard Nixon, as was George McGovern in the 1972 election.

Jimmy Carter, the last Democratic president to date, lost his reelection to the Reagan-Bush ticket in a landslide in 1980. In 1984 the Democrats nominated the first female candidate from a major party (Geraldine Ferraro) to run for vice-president, but nevertheless suffered landslide defeats both in 1984 and 1988. In recent years some Democrats (e.g., Governor Buddy Roemer of Louisiana in 1991) have switched to the Republican party as part of the continuing restructuring of Franklin Roosevelt's coalition.

WHAT

Sources of Receipts 1990 Election Cycle

	$ mil.	% of total
Contributions from individuals	56	64
Contributions from political action committees	12	14
Transfers from other party committees	7	8
Other receipts	12	14
Total	**87**	**100**

Party Presidential Voting 1860–1988

Year	Democratic candidate	Popular votes (mil.)	Electoral votes	Won/ lost
1988	Michael S. Dukakis	41.8	111	L
1984	Walter F. Mondale	37.6	13	L
1980	Jimmy Carter	35.5	49	L
1976	Jimmy Carter	40.8	297	W
1972	George S. McGovern	29.2	17	L
1968	Hubert H. Humphrey	31.3	191	L
1964	Lyndon B. Johnson	43.1	486	W
1960	John F. Kennedy	34.2	303	W
1956	Adlai E. Stevenson	26.0	73	L
1952	Adlai E. Stevenson	27.3	89	L
1948	Harry S Truman	24.2	303	W
1944	Franklin D. Roosevelt	25.6	432	W
1940	Franklin D. Roosevelt	27.3	449	W
1936	Franklin D. Roosevelt	27.8	523	W
1932	Franklin D. Roosevelt	22.8	472	W
1928	Alfred E. Smith	15.0	87	L
1924	John W. Davis	8.4	136	L
1920	James M. Cox	9.1	127	L
1916	Woodrow Wilson	9.1	227	W
1912	Woodrow Wilson	6.3	435	W
1908	William J. Bryan	6.4	162	L
1904	Alton B. Parker	5.1	140	L
1900	William J. Bryan	6.4	155	L
1896	William J. Bryan	6.5	176	L
1892	Grover Cleveland	5.6	277	W
1888	Grover Cleveland	5.5	168	L
1884	Grover Cleveland	4.9	219	W
1880	Winfield S. Handcock	4.4	155	L
1876	Samuel J. Tilden	4.3	184	L
1872	Horace Greeley	2.8	—	L
1868	Horatio Seymour	2.7	80	L
1864	George McClellan	1.8	21	L
1860	Stephen A. Douglas (N)	1.4	12	
	John C. Breckenridge (S)	.8	72	L

KEY COMPETITORS

Republican party

HOW MUCH

	10-Year Growth	1979–1980	1981–1982	1983–1984	1985–1986	1987–1988	1989–1990
Money raised ($ mil.)	8.9%	37	39	99	65	128	87
Money spent ($ mil.)	—	35	40	97	66	122	—

Money Raised ($ mil.) 1979–90

THE DIAL CORP

OVERVIEW

In 2 steps in 1990 and 1991, Greyhound changed its name to Dial Corporation, reflecting the company's steady withdrawal from bus transportation services. Dial produces personal care products including the leading deodorant and liquid soap brand in the US and Breck hair care products; household products, including Brillo, Purex, and 20 Mule Team Borax; such food items as Armour Star canned meats and highly successful Lunch Bucket microwave meals; and buses.

Dial prepares food for companies, airports, and airlines; provides aircraft ground services; operates drug, gift, and duty-free shops; and runs resorts. The company also provides services to conventions and trade shows, has a temporary technical personnel service, sells money orders, and provides commercial financing in the US and abroad. Dial operates cruise ships and still owns 69% of Greyhound Lines of Canada.

NYSE symbol: DL
Fiscal year ends: December 31

Hoover's Rating **D**

WHO

Chairman, President, and CEO: John W. Teets, age 57, $2,035,307 pay
President and COO, The Dial Corporation: Andrew S. Patti, age 50, $556,980 pay
VP and General Counsel: L. Gene Lemon, age 50, $527,660 pay
President and CEO, Greyhound Financial Corp.: Samuel L. Eichenfield, age 54, $502,165 pay
VP Finance: F. Edward Lake, age 56
VP Human Resource Management: Joan F. Ingalls
Auditors: Deloitte & Touche
Employees: 36,200

WHEN

In 1914 Swedish immigrant Carl Eric Wickman used a 7-passenger car to run miners between Hibbing, Minnesota, and a nearby town with a saloon. Wickman's bus operations expanded and became Northland Transportation (1925). In 1928 Northland sold 80% of its stock for $240,000 to Great Northern Railroad. With the infusion of capital, Northland kept buying more bus lines, as many as 60 in 6 weeks, including some using Greyhound in their names. In 1930 Northland renamed itself The Greyhound Corporation and settled into new headquarters in Chicago.

During the Great Depression General Motors helped bail out its customer Greyhound by assuming $1 million of its debt. Another boon came when Clark Gable courted Claudette Colbert on a Greyhound bus in the 1934 film *It Happened One Night*. The company's business soared.

During WWII the company's crowded buses transported draftees to training centers under a military contract. In the postwar years it bought control in bus lines throughout the country. In the 1950s the company adopted its "Go Greyhound — and leave the driving to us" slogan. Greyhound became synonymous in America with bus.

In the 1960s Greyhound began to diversify away from buses. It bought an equipment leasing company (Boothe Leasing, 1962), a food service company (Prophet Company, 1964),

and a money order business (Travelers Express, 1965).

In 1970 Greyhound stretched to purchase Armour & Company for $355 million. Armour, the meat-packing company begun in 1863, was annually selling $2.5 billion of products, from Dial soap to meat products. Greyhound, a new force in consumer products, moved its headquarters from Chicago to Phoenix (1971).

Airline and bus deregulation hurt Greyhound in the early 1980s. When Greyhound cut wages to stem losses, 12,700 workers staged a 7-week strike in 1983. Greyhound sold the meatpacking and frozen foods parts of Armour to ConAgra (1983) and established a cruise line (1984).

In 1987 it sold control of its US intercity bus business to a group of Dallas investors for $257 million. Greyhound, effectively removed from the US bus business that made it famous, purchased Dobbs Houses, an airport and in-flight concessions company and GM's bus manufacturing division in 1987.

The company changed its name to Greyhound Dial in 1990 and to Dial in 1991. The company acquired Breck from American Cyanamid and wrote off $100 million related to its 22.5% minority stake in the bankrupt Greyhound bus business in 1990.

In 1991 Carnival Cruise Lines backed out of a deal to buy Dial's Premier Cruise Lines and bought UK travel company Crystal Holidays.

WHERE

HQ: Greyhound Tower, Phoenix, AZ 85077
Phone: 602-248-4000
Fax: 602-248-5473

Dial operates 26 plants in the US and 2 in Canada. The company also has 81 duty-free shops and 391 food service facilities, principally in the US.

	1990 Sales		1990 Operating Income	
	$ mil.	% of total	$ mil.	% of total
US	3,023	86	255	81
Other countries	496	14	59	19
Total	**3,519**	**100**	**314**	**100**

WHAT

	1990 Sales		1990 Operating Income	
	$ mil.	% of total	$ mil.	% of total
Consumer products	979	28	97	31
Services	1,729	49	143	45
Transportation manufacturing	533	15	31	10
Financial	278	8	43	14
Total	**3,519**	**100**	**314**	**100**

Consumer Brands

Armour Star	Dial	Purex
Borateem	Fleecy	Sno Bol
Boraxo	Light Balance	Tone
Breck	Lunch Bucket	Treet
Brillo	Pure & Natural	20 Mule Team Borax

Services
Carson International, Inc. (airport concessions)
Dobbs Houses, Inc. (airport concessions)
Dobbs International Services, Inc. (in-flight catering)
Greyhound Exposition Services, Inc.
Greyhound Financial Corp.
Greyhound Leisure Services, Inc. (duty-free shops)
Greyhound Lines of Canada, Ltd. (69%)
Motor Coach Industries Companies
Premier Cruise Lines, Ltd.
Travelers Express Co., Inc. (money orders)

HOW MUCH

	9-Year Growth	1981	1982	1983	1984	1985	1986	1987	1988	1989	1990
Sales ($ mil.)	(3.2%)	4,699	4,526	2,131	2,201	2,562	2,584	2,259	3,305	3,537	3,519
Net income ($ mil.)	(1.9%)	138	106	70	125	120	94	83	93	109	116
Income as % of sales	—	2.9%	2.3%	3.3%	5.7%	4.7%	3.7%	3.7%	2.8%	3.1%	3.3%
Earnings per share ($)	0.0%	2.89	2.29	1.43	2.52	2.44	2.07	2.09	2.41	2.74	2.90
Stock price – high ($)	—	20.25	19.00	28.00	26.25	34.50	38.00	46.00	36.88	37.75	32.25
Stock price – low ($)	—	13.25	12.63	17.13	18.63	23.88	27.13	19.25	25.38	28.75	19.00
Stock price – close ($)	5.3%	15.50	17.25	25.38	24.25	32.38	31.00	25.50	30.00	32.00	24.63
P/E – high	—	7	8	20	10	14	18	22	15	14	11
P/E – low	—	5	6	12	7	10	13	9	11	11	7
Dividends per share ($)	1.4%	1.20	1.20	1.20	1.20	1.26	1.32	1.32	1.32	1.32	1.36
Book value per share ($)	2.5%	20.90	22.06	22.86	24.07	24.99	26.72	24.80	26.32	27.00	26.17

1990 Year-end:
Debt ratio: 65.4%
Return on equity: 10.9%
Cash (mil.): $824
Current ratio: —
Long-term debt (mil.): $1,939
No. of shares (mil.): 39
Dividends:
 1990 average yield: 5.5%
 1990 payout: 46.9%
Market value (mil.): $967

Stock Price History High/Low 1981–90

RANKINGS

30th in *Fortune* 100 Diversified Service Cos.
489th in *Business Week* 1000

KEY COMPETITORS

Accor	Clorox	Hyatt
American Express	Colgate-Palmolive	S.C. Johnson
Amway	ConAgra	L'Oréal
ARA	Daimler-Benz	Marriott
Barclays	Dentsu	Procter & Gamble
Campbell Soup	Dow Chemical	TW Holdings
Carlson	Gillette	Unilever

DIGITAL EQUIPMENT CORPORATION

OVERVIEW

Maynard, Massachusetts–based Digital is the 2nd largest information systems supplier in the world (after IBM), a leader in networking and systems integration, and the world's 3rd largest workstation manufacturer (after Sun and Hewlett-Packard).

Cofounder Kenneth H. Olsen has been hailed as America's greatest entrepreneur (*Fortune*, 1986). DEC derives 55% of its revenue from abroad. Innovation remains sacred, with fiscal 1990 R&D exceeding $1.6 billion, or 12.5% of sales — 5th highest in the US.

Although DEC has had many years of success designing its own hardware and software, it is also a major player in the industry move to open systems, aggressively developing its Network Applications Support (NAS) software that allows computers of various vendors to share applications. DEC is expected to introduce a line of RISC-based VAX computers that will be compatible with software running under many operating systems including its own VMS. DEC stumbled in 1990 and 1991, seeing profits drop 93% in 1990 and suffering a $617 million loss in 1991 due to a $1.1 billion restructuring charge.

WHEN

Two young MIT engineers, Kenneth Olsen and Harlan Anderson, founded DEC in 1957 to pioneer beyond mainframes into smaller, less-expensive computers that were interactive. DEC's converted woolen mill near Boston soon produced innovations popular with engineers and scientists, including the PDP-1 (the first interactive computer, 1960) and the PDP-5 (dubbed the minicomputer, 1963). The PDP-8 (1965) and later the PDP-11 (1970) provided major number-crunching breakthroughs.

Olsen began minicomputer sales in the mid-1960s using the matrix management model (with individuals answerable to both functional and line managers) and sales to OEMs; revenue and profit growth averaged 30% per year for almost 2 decades.

DEC began its networking tradition in 1974, introducing the Digital network architecture (DNA) to link its PDP-11s to local- and wide-area networks (LANs and WANs); the result was DECnet Phase I. DEC engineering whiz Gordon Bell conceived of the VAX line of computers, which allowed easy upgrades from PDPs and virtually unlimited memory; the VAX-11/780 appeared in 1977.

In 1979 Olsen pledged billions to an expanded VAX generation using all DEC-made components. Olsen dispensed with the matrix model and instituted unified marketing during

the arduous 5-year undertaking. The company refocused the new VAXes (like the VAX 6000 mini, 1984) on the larger commercial market and extended its DECnet umbrella to provide global company/client/supplier connections. During the VAX glory days, between 1984 and 1988, sales doubled and earnings nearly quadrupled ($329 million to $1.3 billion).

By 1988 DEC was embracing open systems and entering alliances to connect PCs to VAXes (Apple, Compaq), to translate VAX software to ULTRIX (DEC's version of UNIX), and to bring popular software to the VAX line (Lotus 1-2-3, dBase). DEC also took a 5% stake in MIPS Computer (which provides the RISC chip for the RISC-based DECstation) and joined the ACE consortium, a 61-company alliance established to set hardware and software standards for desktop computers.

DEC reported its first quarterly loss ever in 1990 and a $617 million annual operating loss for fiscal 1991. Contributing to its poor performance was sluggish sales of its recently introduced VAX 9000 mainframe (1990). In response, DEC restructured and reduced its work force. Further employee cuts were made in fiscal 1991. In 1991 DEC announced plans to make its largest acquisition ever, purchasing the $1 billion computer business of Holland's Philips.

NYSE symbol: DEC
Fiscal year ends: Saturday nearest June 30

Hoover's Rating **B**

WHO

President: Kenneth H. Olsen, age 65, $982,452 pay
SVP Operations: John F. Smith, age 56, $555,858 pay
SVP: Winston R. Hindle, Jr., age 61, $455,813 pay
VP Finance: James M. Osterhoff, age 55, $387,188 pay
VP, Strategic Resources (Personnel): John L. Sims
Auditors: Coopers & Lybrand
Employees: 121,000

WHERE

HQ: 146 Main St., Maynard, MA 01754-2571
Phone: 508-493-5111
Fax: 508-493-8780

Digital does business in more than 81 countries.

	1990 Sales		1990 Operating Income	
	$ mil.	% of total	$ mil.	% of total
US	5,824	45	(381)	—
Europe	5,243	41	478	—
Canada/Far East/ Americas	1,876	14	255	—
Adjustments	—	—	211	—
Total	**12,943**	**100**	**563**	**—**

WHAT

	1990 Sales	
	$ mil.	% of total
Products	8,146	63
Services & other	4,797	37
Total	**12,943**	**100**

Computers
Mainframes
  VAX 9000
  VAXclusters
Minicomputers
  VAX 6000 series
  VAX 4000 systems and servers
  VAXft 3000 fault-tolerant systems
Personal computers
  DECpc series
Workstations and servers
  DECstation 2100, 3100, 5000
  DECsystem 3100, 5400, 5800
  VAXstation

Software
ALL-IN-1 (office automation)
Business, engineering, and productivity applications
DECnet (networking)
PATHWORKS (PC networking)
ULTRIX (UNIX version)
VMS (VAX operating system)

Peripherals
Disk storage devices
Displays
Magnetic tape transports
Printers
Tape cassette devices
Terminals

RANKINGS

30th in *Fortune* 500 Industrial Cos.
54th in *Business Week* 1000

KEY COMPETITORS

AT&T	Fujitsu	Oracle
Apple	Hewlett-Packard	Prime
AST	Hitachi	Sharp
Compaq	Intergraph	Siemens
Computer	IBM	Sony
Associates	Machines Bull	Sun
Control Data	Matsushita	Microsystems
Data General	NCR	Tandem
Dell	NEC	Toshiba
Dun & Bradstreet	Oki	

HOW MUCH

	9-Year Growth	1981	1982	1983	1984	1985	1986	1987	1988	1989	1990
Sales ($ mil.)	16.8%	3,198	3,881	4,272	5,584	6,686	7,590	9,389	11,475	12,742	12,943
Net income ($ mil.)	(15.6%)	343	417	284	329	447	617	1,137	1,306	1,073	74
Income as % of sales	—	10.7%	10.8%	6.6%	5.9%	6.7%	8.1%	12.1%	11.4%	8.4%	0.6%
Earnings per share ($)	(17.5%)	3.35	3.77	2.50	2.87	3.71	4.81	8.53	9.90	8.45	0.59
Stock price – high ($)	—	56.63	57.50	66.06	55.63	68.38	109.00	199.50	144.75	122.38	95.13
Stock price – low ($)	—	40.13	30.88	32.00	35.19	42.63	65.81	104.50	86.38	79.75	45.50
Stock price – close ($)	2.7%	43.25	49.75	36.00	55.38	66.25	104.75	135.00	98.38	82.00	54.88
P/E – high	—	17	15	26	19	18	23	23	15	14	161
P/E – low	—	12	8	13	12	11	14	12	9	9	77
Dividends per share ($)	0.0%	0.00	0.00	0.00	0.00	0.00	0.00	0.00	0.00	0.00	0.00
Book value per share ($)	11.7%	24.65	28.65	31.42	34.42	38.43	44.54	49.87	59.47	66.12	66.76

1990 Year-end:
Debt ratio: 1.8%
Return on equity: 0.9%
Cash (mil.): $2,009
Current ratio: 2.32
Long-term debt (mil.): $150
No. of shares (mil.): 123
Dividends:
  1990 average yield: 0.0%
  1990 payout: 0.0%
Market value (mil.): $6,725

Stock Price History High/Low 1981–90

DILLARD DEPARTMENT STORES, INC.

OVERVIEW

Little Rock–based Dillard's is one of the largest department store chains in the US, operating 186 Dillard's stores and 12 Higbee's stores in 19 states from Arizona to Florida totaling over 15 million square feet of space. In 1990 and 1991, amid a retailing recession, Dillard's has prospered (and has continued to add stores) with a strategy of selling mid-priced, nationally recognized brand names in family apparel and home furnishings in 2nd-tier markets.

With 1990 sales of over $3.7 billion and a 17.6% compound annual growth rate in the past 5 years, the company has grown as a result of shrewd family management (the Dillards own 99% of class B voting stock and control the board). Dillard's purchases under-performing department store companies carrying similar merchandise and catering to similar customers. Dillard's is rapidly assimilating stores and making them profitable.

During the 1980s Dillard's remained profitable in spite of the depressed economy of the Southwest. To boost customer loyalty the company keeps prices down and eschews sales events and private-label merchandise. A computerized information system, with its hourly departmental inventory tracking and automatic reordering, allows close monitoring of sales in each store.

WHEN

At age 12 William Dillard began working in his father's general store in Mineral Springs, Arkansas. After graduation from Columbia University (1937), the 3rd-generation retailer spent 7 months in the Sears, Roebuck manager training program in Tulsa.

With $8,000 borrowed from his father, Dillard opened his first department store in Nashville, Arkansas, in 1938. He sold the store in 1948 to finance a partnership in Wooten's Department Store in Texarkana, Arkansas, later buying out Wooten and establishing Dillard's, Inc., in 1949.

During the 1950s and 1960s, the company became a strong regional retailer developing its strategy of buying well-established downtown stores in small cities — Mayer & Schmidt (Tyler, Texas; 1956), Brown-Dunkin (Tulsa, 1960), Joseph Pfeifer (Little Rock, 1963), and Gus Blass (Little Rock, 1964). Dillard's moved its headquarters to Little Rock after buying Pfeifer. When Dillard's went public in 1969, the chain had 15 stores in 3 states, with sales of $65.2 million.

During the early 1960s E. Ray Kemp, now vice-chairman, began computerizing operations to streamline inventory and information management. In 1970 the company added computerized cash registers, which gave management hourly sales figures.

Dillard's acquisitions during the 1970s included 5 Fedways (Southwest, 1971), 5 Leonard's (Dallas–Fort Worth, 1974), and Alden's (Texarkana, 1978).

Acquisitions in the 1980s included 12 Stix, Baer & Fuller stores; 12 Diamond's and 5 John A. Brown stores; 12 Macy stores; 27 Joske's; 4 Cain-Sloan stores; and 17 D. H. Holmes stores. In a 1988 joint venture with Edward J. DeBartolo, Dillard's bought a 50% interest in the 12 Higbee's stores in Ohio. In the 1990s Dillard's acquired 23 J. B. Ivey stores in South Carolina, North Carolina, and Florida, and agreed to buy 7 stores from Maison Blanche Department Stores.

In 1991 Vendamerica BV, a subsidiary of Vendex International NV and the only major nonfamily holder of the company's stock, sold its 8.9 million shares of Class A stock (25% of the class) in an underwritten public offering in April 1991. The sale appears to reflect more of Vendex's need to raise money to shore up its own troubled retail operations than any lack of confidence by Vendex in Dillard or its management. In August 1991 the company made a $75 million cash offer for 12 of Campeau's Jordan Marsh stores in Florida.

NYSE symbol: DDS
Fiscal year ends: Saturday nearest January 31

Hoover's Rating **B+**

WHO

Chairman and CEO: William Dillard, age 76, $1,637,995 pay
VC: E. Ray Kemp, age 66, $450,000 pay
President and COO: William Dillard II, age 46, $1,300,000 pay
EVP: Alex Dillard, age 41, $1,210,000 pay
EVP: Mike Dillard, age 39, $935,000 pay
VP and CFO: James I. Freeman, age 41
Head of Personnel: Cecilia Glymp
Auditors: Deloitte & Touche
Employees: 31,786

WHERE

HQ: 1600 Cantrell Rd., Little Rock, AR 72201
Phone: 501-376-5200
Fax: 501-376-5917

As of June 1991, Dillard's operates 198 department stores in 19 midwestern and Sunbelt states.

	No. of Stores	% of Total
Alabama	1	1
Arizona	13	6
Arkansas	7	3
Florida	11	5
Illinois	1	1
Iowa	1	1
Kansas	8	4
Louisiana	19	10
Mississippi	2	1
Missouri	19	10
Nebraska	3	1
Nevada	3	1
New Mexico	4	2
North Carolina	10	5
Ohio (Higbee's)	12	7
Oklahoma	16	8
South Carolina	2	1
Tennessee	7	4
Texas	59	29
Total	**198**	**100**

Included above are 12 Higbee's stores in Ohio (50% interest with Edward J. DeBartolo, not including 1991 openings).

WHAT

	1990 Sales
	% of total
Cosmetics	12
Women's clothing	25
Lingerie & accessories	11
Juniors' clothing	5
Children's clothing	7
Men's clothing & accessories	17
Shoes	6
Decorative home fashion	6
Housewares, furniture & appliances	8
Jewelry, other	3
Total	**100**

HOW MUCH

	9-Year Growth	1981	1982	1983	1984	1985	1986	1987	1988	1989	1990
Sales ($ mil.)	22.7%	593	711	847	1,277	1,601	1,851	2,206	2,655	3,160	3,734
Net income ($ mil.)	30.8%	16	22	34	50	67	74	91	114	148	183
Income as % of sales	—	2.7%	3.1%	4.0%	3.9%	4.2%	4.0%	4.1%	4.3%	4.7%	4.9%
Earnings per share ($)	24.6%	0.69	0.93	1.38	1.82	2.29	2.35	2.83	3.53	4.36	5.01
Stock price – high ($)	—	3.11	6.95	15.69	20.94	38.50	45.75	57.50	46.50	74.25	96.00
Stock price – low ($)	—	1.58	2.75	5.66	10.81	18.13	32.00	24.00	25.13	41.00	61.75
Stock price – close ($)	45.4%	3.00	6.58	14.00	19.13	37.50	37.88	24.63	42.38	71.00	87.38
P/E – high	—	5	7	11	12	17	19	20	13	17	19
P/E – low	—	2	3	4	6	8	14	8	7	9	12
Dividends per share ($)	16.7%	0.05	0.05	0.08	0.09	0.11	0.12	0.14	0.16	0.18	0.20
Book value per share ($)	25.0%	4.94	5.81	7.36	10.24	12.42	17.31	20.00	23.39	30.68	36.92

1990 Year-end:
Debt ratio: 39.0%
Return on equity: 14.8%
Cash (mil.): $38
Current ratio: 2.80
Long-term debt (mil.): $871
No. of shares (mil.): 37
Dividends:
  1990 average yield: 0.2%
  1990 payout: 4.0%
Market value (mil.): $3,229

Stock Price History High/Low 1981–90

RANKINGS

32nd in *Fortune* 50 Retailing Cos.
174th in *Business Week* 1000

KEY COMPETITORS

Circuit City	Montgomery Ward
Dayton Hudson	J. C. Penney
Macy	Sears
May	Apparel retailers
Mercantile Stores	Other department stores

DOLE FOOD COMPANY, INC.

OVERVIEW

Formerly Castle & Cooke, Dole Food is the world's largest producer and marketer of fresh fruits and vegetables, with additional operations in real estate development. Food, the company's lifeblood, contributed 93% of sales in 1990.

Although Dole is headquartered in Los Angeles, the company's roots are in Hawaii. Dole owns 98% of the Hawaiian island of Lanai, the 6th largest of the Hawaiian archipelago, making it the 3rd largest private landowner in the state. The company's pineapples, bananas, and other major products are produced in 14 countries around the world. Dole distributes fresh produce with its 30 refrigerated vessels, including 2 of the world's largest refrigerated container ships. Through a joint venture with Snow Brand Milk Products, the company is Japan's #1 producer of 100% fruit juices.

Dole's real estate business, Castle & Cooke Properties (formerly Oceanic Properties), develops commercial and residential property in Hawaii, California, and Arizona. Landholdings in California and Arizona are 10,500 and 9,135 acres respectively.

WHEN

Samuel Castle and Amos Cooke, missionaries to Hawaii, formed a partnership, Castle & Cooke, in 1851 to manage their church's failing depository, which supplied outlying mission posts with staple goods. Within a year they had added a store in Honolulu, selling goods to the general public.

In 1858 they entered the sugar business and within 10 years served as agents for several Hawaiian sugar plantations and the ships that carried their cargoes.

In 1907 C&C became agent and part owner of Matson Navigation, the largest shipping company operating between Hawaii and the mainland. C&C entered another Hawaiian industry in 1932, buying 1/5 of the Hawaiian Pineapple Company, founded by James Dole in 1901. Extensive advertising made Dole pineapples a major product by 1936.

After WWII, labor unions successfully organized and wages improved, almost doubling payrolls at C&C's sugar plantations. The sugar and pineapple industries responded by increasing mechanization in their operations.

In the late 1950s and early 1960s, C&C began the transition to a food and land business. It bought an Oregon seafood company (Bumble Bee brand, 1959) and completed the purchase of Dole Pineapple (including thousands of acres of Hawaiian land, 1961). In

1964 C&C became a banana importer with the purchase of Standard Fruit of New Orleans and sold its 24% stake in Matson Navigation. The company started pineapple and banana farms in the Philippines in the 1960s to supply the Far East markets.

In the early 1980s the company was heavily in debt and earnings were down. In 1985, following 2 takeover attempts, C&C agreed to merge with Flexi-Van, a container-leasing company headed by David Murdock, who became a 23% owner of C&C stock and took over operations. He brought in management talent and capital as well as Flexi-Van's fleet of ships to transport Dole produce. Murdock trimmed operations, selling off Bumble Bee (1986) and Flexi-Van's container-leasing business (1987), leaving C&C with its fruit and real estate operations. In 1987 C&C bought the agricultural operations of Apache Corporation and Tenneco West and in 1988 the raisin operations of Bonner Packing.

In 1991 the company changed its name to Dole Food Company. That same year CEO David Murdock shocked Hawaiians when he announced that Dole would end its pineapple operations on Lanai by 1993 to concentrate on building the tourist industry there. With its Lodge at Koele (1990) and Manele Bay (1991), Dole is already drawing tourists to Lanai.

NYSE symbol: DOL
Fiscal year ends: Saturday nearest December 31

WHO

Chairman and CEO: David H. Murdock, age 68, $1,305,000 pay
EVP; President, Dole Food: David A. DeLorenzo, age 44, $778,846 pay
VP Finance: William J. Hain, Jr., age 55
VP Human Resources: George R. Horne, age 54
Auditors: Arthur Andersen & Co.
Employees: 51,000

WHERE

HQ: 10900 Wilshire Blvd., Los Angeles, CA 90024
Phone: 213-824-1500
Fax: 213-824-9505

The company conducts business in 50 countries and has 36 selling offices in North America, Western Europe, and the Far East.

	1990 Sales		1990 Operating Income	
	$ mil.	% of total	$ mil.	% of total
North America	2,165	72	109	42
Latin America	165	5	68	27
Far East	320	11	60	23
Europe	353	12	21	8
Adjustments	—	—	(29)	—
Total	**3,003**	**100**	**229**	**100**

WHAT

	1990 Sales		1990 Operating Income	
	$ mil.	% of total	$ mil.	% of total
Food products	2,792	93	234	91
Real estate	211	7	24	9
Adjustments	—	—	(29)	—
Total	**3,003**	**100**	**229**	**100**

Food and Other Products

DOLE dried fruits and nuts	Peaches
	Pears
DOLE fresh and prepared vegetables	Pineapples
	Tangerines
DOLE fresh fruit	DOLE juices
Apples	DOLEWHIP
Apricots	Fresh Lites
Bananas	Fruit'N Juice bars
Cantaloupe	Pure & Light juices
Coconuts	SunTops
Grapefruit	**Real Estate**
Grapes	Commercial
Kiwi	Industrial
Lemons	Residential
Mangos	Resorts
Oranges	

RANKINGS

37th in *Fortune* 100 Diversified Service Cos.
321st in *Business Week* 1000

KEY COMPETITORS

Cadbury Schweppes	ITT
Chiquita Brands	Kirin
Coca-Cola	San Miguel
Hilton	Seagram
Hyatt	TLC Beatrice

HOW MUCH

	9-Year Growth	1981	1982	1983	1984	1985	1986	1987	1988	1989	1990
Sales ($ mil.)	5.6%	1,845	1,823	1,552	1,520	1,601	1,738	1,749	2,469	2,718	3,003
Net income ($ mil.)	12.4%	42	10	(39)	1	(10)	76	89	112	95	120
Income as % of sales	—	2.3%	0.5%	(2.5%)	0.1%	(0.6%)	4.4%	5.1%	4.5%	3.5%	4.0%
Earnings per share ($)	—	—	0.17	(1.52)	(0.30)	(0.71)	1.21	1.49	1.90	1.60	2.03
Stock price – high ($)	—	13.37	9.91	17.93	19.02	15.87	20.25	26.63	29.38	45.25	38.63
Stock price – low ($)	—	8.30	6.62	8.36	8.84	9.57	13.00	12.00	17.25	25.38	26.25
Stock price – close ($)	13.4%	9.45	8.60	17.20	12.48	13.00	19.25	18.50	28.25	34.75	29.38
P/E – high	—	—	58	—	—	—	17	18	15	28	19
P/E – low	—	—	39	—	—	—	11	8	9	16	13
Dividends per share ($)	(19.9%)	0.74	0.55	0.00	0.00	0.00	0.00	0.00	0.00	0.00	0.10
Book value per share ($)	(0.2%)	15.98	15.53	13.51	9.36	8.35	9.97	11.22	12.53	14.11	15.67

1990 Year-end:
Debt ratio: 36.9%
Return on equity: 13.6%
Cash (mil.): $27
Current ratio: 1.42
Long-term debt (mil.): $543
No. of shares (mil.): 59
Dividends:
  1990 average yield: 0.3%
  1990 payout: 4.9%
Market value (mil.): $1,741

Stock Price History High/Low 1981–90

R. R. DONNELLEY & SONS COMPANY

NYSE symbol: DNY
Fiscal year ends: December 31

Hoover's Rating **B+**

OVERVIEW

Chicago-based R. R. Donnelley & Sons is the world's largest printer, churning out books, magazines, computer documentation, catalogs, financial documents, and telephone and business directories for more than 3,000 customers. Magazines printed include *TV Guide*, *Time*, and *Newsweek*. With a 27.8% interest in AlphaGraphics, the company is involved in quick-printing services as well.

Donnelley's Metromail unit manages databases (mailing lists and related information) for direct mail marketers. Other services Donnelley provides to its printing customers include prepress operations, directory distribution, book fulfillment and distribution,

computer software documentation packaging, and computer disk replication.

Donnelley invests heavily in technology and has developed Selectronic Services, a system enabling a magazine or catalog publisher to personalize each copy. In partnership with McGraw-Hill, the company is creating on-demand college texts composed of articles in the publisher's database.

The Meredith/Burda acquisition diluted Donnelley's earnings per share. Earnings progress is also being hampered by lower advertising spending, which is reducing magazine page-counts and inhibiting direct mail and newspaper advertising insert business.

WHEN

R. R. Donnelley & Sons began in 1864 when printer Richard Robert Donnelley joined publishers Edward Goodman and Leroy Church of Chicago. Their partnership became Lakeside Publishing and Printing in 1870. The company was a major midwestern publishing house, producing a variety of periodicals and some of the first inexpensive paperback books. The Chicago Fire of 1871 destroyed the Lakeside building, but by 1873 the company was back in operation.

By 1877 Lakeside had fallen on hard times and closed its doors, but its paperback subsidiary survived as Donnelley, Loyd & Company. Richard R. Donnelley bought out his partners in 1879 and separated the firm's printing component (reorganized as R. R. Donnelley & Sons in 1882) from its publishing arm (Chicago Directory Company). Chicago Directory emerged as the Reuben H. Donnelley Corporation (1916), named for one of Richard Donnelley's sons. Reuben H. Donnelley Corporation was bought by Dun & Bradstreet in 1961.

Before the turn of the century, R. R. Donnelley & Sons printed telephone books and the Montgomery Ward catalog. In 1910 it began printing the *Encyclopædia Britannica*. Capture of the printing contract for *Time* in

1927 propelled the company into the big leagues of printing. Donnelley's innovation in high-speed printing was a major factor in the decision to launch *Life* in 1936.

Donnelley has been a family business during most of its history. Donnelley descendants served as chairmen and as several of the company's presidents. An in-law, Charles Haffner, was chairman from 1952 to 1964, during which time the company's stock went public (1956). The first chairman from outside the family circle was Charles Lake in 1975.

During the late 1970s and the 1980s Donnelley expanded worldwide, acquiring printing companies in the UK (Ben Johnson, 1978; Index Press and Thompson Photo Litho, 1985), Japan (Dowa Insatsu, 1988), and Ireland (Irish Printers, 1989). In 1987 it bought Metromail, the largest US mailing list business.

Also during the 1980s Donnelley developed the Selectronic binding process that can tailor editions of magazines and catalogs to small target audiences. Donnelley bought 25% of AlphaGraphics, the retail quick-print chain, in 1989 and in 1990 acquired Meredith/Burda, a high-quality printer, and Business Mail Data Services, a UK company similar to Metromail.

WHO

Chairman and CEO: John R. Walter, age 44, $767,773 pay
President: Carl K. Doty, age 59, $389,018 pay (prior to promotion)
EVP Finance and CFO: Frank R. Jarc, age 48, $336,445 pay
VP Human Resources: J. E. Treadway
Auditors: Arthur Andersen & Co.
Employees: 30,400

WHERE

HQ: 2223 Martin Luther King Dr., Chicago, IL 60616
Phone: 312-326-8000
Fax: 312-326-8543

The company operates over 100 facilities worldwide.

WHAT

	1990 Sales
	% of total
Catalogs	37
Magazines	18
Directories	17
Books	11
Documentation services	7
Other	10
Total	**100**

Groups

Books
Hardcover and softcover books
Fulfillment and distribution

Catalogs
Catalogs, tabloids, and newspaper inserts
Direct mail services

Documentation Services
Software distribution
Software documentation
Software replication

Financial Printing Services

Information Services
Database management
Electronic publishing

International
Far East operations
UK operations

Magazines
Magazines and Sunday supplements
Mailing and distribution services

Metromail
Mailing list management
Mailing services

Telecommunications
Telephone and business directories

HOW MUCH

	9-Year Growth	1981	1982	1983	1984	1985	1986	1987	1988	1989	1990
Sales ($ mil.)	12.2%	1,244	1,404	1,546	1,814	2,038	2,234	2,483	2,878	3,122	3,498
Net income ($ mil.)	12.4%	79	91	114	134	148	158	218	205	222	226
Income as % of sales	—	6.4%	6.5%	7.4%	7.4%	7.3%	7.1%	8.8%	7.1%	7.1%	6.5%
Earnings per share ($)	12.0%	1.05	1.20	1.50	1.75	1.94	2.03	2.80	2.64	2.85	2.91
Stock price – high ($)	—	10.75	16.84	24.00	24.63	32.19	40.00	45.38	38.75	51.25	52.63
Stock price – low ($)	—	7.53	8.94	14.59	16.00	23.00	29.44	25.50	29.88	34.25	34.13
Stock price – close ($)	17.3%	9.44	14.88	19.25	24.50	31.81	30.63	32.63	34.63	51.25	39.75
P/E – high	—	10	14	16	14	17	20	16	15	18	18
P/E – low	—	7	7	10	9	12	15	9	11	12	12
Dividends per share ($)	13.0%	0.32	0.36	0.41	0.50	0.58	0.64	0.70	0.78	0.88	0.96
Book value per share ($)	12.0%	7.42	8.21	9.25	10.44	11.73	12.90	14.91	16.69	18.56	20.60

1990 Year-end:
Debt ratio: 28.9%
Return on equity: 14.9%
Cash (mil.): $123
Current ratio: —
Long-term debt (mil.): $647
No. of shares (mil.): 77
Dividends:
　1990 average yield: 2.4%
　1990 payout: 33.0%
Market value (mil.): $3,079

Stock Price History High/Low 1981–90

RANKINGS

139th in *Fortune* 500 Industrial Cos.
178th in *Business Week* 1000

KEY COMPETITORS

Bertelsmann
Maxwell
Moore

Southwestern Bell
United Telecom
U S West

THE DOW CHEMICAL COMPANY

NYSE symbol: DOW
Fiscal year ends: December 31

Hoover's Rating **B-**

OVERVIEW

Dow, America's 2nd largest chemical company (after Du Pont), produces chemicals used as raw materials for manufacturing in the food processing, personal care products, pharmaceuticals, pulp and paper, utilities, and other industries. More than half of Dow's business is conducted overseas through subsidiaries located in nearly every industrialized nation.

Dow found a silver lining in the economic downturn of 1990–91 when its consumer specialties business shored up sales with record results. That, executives said, was evidence that the company's diversification had freed itself from the cyclical fortunes of basic chemicals and plastics.

Dow's plastics are used in several markets, including automotive, electronics, packaging, and recreation. The company also makes several well-known consumer brands, including Dow bathroom cleaner. Through Marion Merrell Dow (68.9% owned), it produces prescription drugs and over-the-counter health care items such as Cepacol mouthwash and Novahistine antihistamine. Dow owns 60% of DowElanco, which produces agricultural chemicals.

WHEN

Herbert Dow founded Dow Chemical in 1897 after developing a process that used electricity to extract bromides and chlorides from underground brine deposits around Midland, Michigan. The company's first product was chlorine bleach. Dow sold his products on the world market and eventually overcame British and German monopolies on bleach, bromides, and other chemicals.

In the mid-1920s the company rejected an attempt at takeover by the chemical giant Du Pont. By 1930, the year of Herbert Dow's death, sales had reached $15 million. Dow began building new plants around the country in the late 1930s. The Freeport, Texas, plant, completed in 1941 to supply magnesium and other products for the military, was the beginning of today's Texas Gulf Coast petrochemical complex.

Dow research yielded new plastics in the 1940s that became leaders in the industry by the 1950s. Saran Wrap (introduced 1953) was the company's first major consumer product. By 1957 plastics accounted for 32% of Dow's sales, compared to 2% in 1940.

Plastics and silicone products helped boost sales through the 1950s and propelled Dow into the top ranks of US companies. In 1964 sales passed $1 billion. With the 1960 purchase of Allied Labs, Dow entered the pharmaceutical field.

Although Dow had exported chemicals for years (the diamond trademark on its indigo dyes was known in China before 1920), the company built its first plant outside North America in partnership with the Japanese in 1952 (Asahi-Dow) to make plastic nets for their fishing industry.

Despite increasing sales ($10.6 billion by 1980) Dow suffered earnings drops in the recession years of 1981 to 1983 because of drops in chemical prices. To limit the cyclical effect of chemicals on profits, Dow has continued to expand other business segments, notably pharmaceuticals (Merrell Drug, 1981) and consumer goods (Texize, household cleaners, 1984). Bulk chemicals accounted for less than 40% of sales in 1989, compared to 64% in 1982. In 1989 the company merged its pharmaceutical division, Merrell Dow, with the pharmaceutical company Marion Labs, creating Marion Merrell Dow (combined sales $2.3 billion). In a joint venture with Eli Lilly in 1989, Dow formed DowElanco, the 5th largest agricultural chemicals firm in the world.

In 1991 Dow spun off 27.7% of its Destec Energy, the largest US producer of cogenerated power. Also in 1991 Dow announced it would reduce its dependence on hydrocarbons and energy as it focused on 3 market sectors — basic chemicals, industrial specialties, and consumer specialties.

WHO

Chairman: Paul F. Oreffice, age 63
President and CEO: Frank P. Popoff, age 55, $933,127 pay
EVP and CFO: Enrique C. Falla, age 51, $436,428 pay
VP Human Resources: Gerald Hornsby
Auditors: Deloitte & Touche
Employees: 62,100

WHERE

HQ: 2030 Willard H. Dow Center, Midland, MI 48674
Phone: 517-636-1000
Fax: 517-636-0922

Dow has 63 manufacturing plants in 23 states and 118 plants in 31 foreign countries.

	1990 Sales		1990 Operating Income	
	$ mil.	% of total	$ mil.	% of total
US	9,494	48	1,622	58
Europe	6,278	32	692	24
Other countries	4,001	20	504	18
Adjustments	—	—	(65)	—
Total	**19,773**	**100**	**2,753**	**100**

WHAT

	1990 Sales		1990 Operating Income	
	$ mil.	% of total	$ mil.	% of total
Consumer specialties	5,053	26	832	30
Chemicals & performance prods.	5,088	26	779	28
Plastic products	7,392	37	990	35
Hydrocarbons & energy	2,210	11	156	5
Other	30	—	61	2
Adjustments	—	—	(65)	—
Total	**19,773**	**100**	**2,753**	**100**

Chemicals and Performance Products
Calcium chloride
Caustic soda
Chlorinated solvents
Chlorines
Ion exchange resins (Dowex)
Latex coatings
Membrane systems (Filmtec)

Plastic Products
Fabricated (Styrofoam)
Epoxies (Quatrex)
Polymers
Polystyrenes (Stryon)

Consumer Products
Cepacol
Fantastik
Gaviscon (antacid)
Handi-Wrap
Nicorette
Perma Soft (hair care)
Saran Wrap
Spiffits
Spray 'n Wash
Treflan (herbicide)
Ziploc (storage bags)

RANKINGS

18th in *Fortune* 500 Industrial Cos.
40th in *Business Week* 1000

KEY COMPETITORS

Abbott Labs	Dial	Mobil
American Cyanamid	Du Pont	Monsanto
Amgen	Eastman Kodak	Nobel
Amway	Formosa Plastics	Phillips Petroleum
BASF	W. R. Grace	Rhône-Poulenc
Bayer	Hoechst	Union Carbide
Clorox	Hercules	Warner-Lambert
	Imperial Chemical	

HOW MUCH

	9-Year Growth	1981	1982	1983	1984	1985	1986	1987	1988	1989	1990
Sales ($ mil.)	5.8%	11,873	10,618	10,951	11,418	11,537	11,113	13,377	16,682	17,600	19,773
Net income ($ mil.)	10.5%	564	342	293	549	58	741	1,245	2,410	2,487	1,384
Income as % of sales	—	4.8%	3.2%	2.7%	4.8%	0.5%	6.7%	9.3%	14.4%	14.1%	7.0%
Earnings per share ($)	11.0%	1.18	1.01	1.89	0.21	2.58	4.33	8.55	9.20	5.10
Stock price – high ($)	—	26.00	19.25	25.58	23.00	27.92	41.17	73.08	62.67	72.25	75.75
Stock price – low ($)	—	15.58	13.08	16.67	17.17	18.00	26.58	39.17	51.17	55.50	37.00
Stock price – close ($)	11.7%	17.50	17.25	22.25	18.33	27.33	39.00	60.00	58.50	71.38	47.50
P/E – high	—	13	16	25	12	135	16	17	7	8	15
P/E – low	—	8	11	17	9	87	10	9	6	6	7
Dividends per share ($)	9.0%	1.20	1.20	1.20	1.20	1.20	1.27	1.43	1.73	2.37	2.60
Book value per share ($)	7.2%	17.22	17.30	17.18	17.75	16.80	18.01	20.31	26.35	29.55	32.33

1990 Year-end:
Debt ratio: 37.4%
Return on equity: 16.5%
Cash (mil.): $299
Current ratio: 1.39
Long-term debt (mil.): $5,209
No. of shares (mil.): 270
Dividends:
  1990 average yield: 5.5%
  1990 payout: 51.0%
Market value (mil.): $12,825

Stock Price History High/Low 1981–90

DOW JONES & COMPANY, INC.

OVERVIEW

New York–based Dow Jones (DJ) is the leading provider of business and financial news in the US. The company is best known as publisher of the *Wall Street Journal*, the country's largest newspaper (1.92 million circulation). DJ also produces Asian and European editions of the *Journal*, bringing worldwide circulation of the daily to over 2 million.

While DJ's business publication segment (the *Wall Street Journal, Barron's, Far Eastern Economic Review, National Business Employment Weekly*, etc.) is what DJ is best known for, it represents less than 1/2 of DJ's $1.72 billion in revenues. DJ's 2 other segments — Information Services and Community Newspapers — accounted for $971 million in 1990 revenues. Of that, DJ's wholly owned Telerate, an international supplier of real-time market data, accounted for $544 million. Telerate's revenue growth slowed to 7.5% in 1990 compared to 14.9% in 1989 and 31.2% in 1988. Also included in DJ's Information segment is Dow Jones News/Retrieval, an on-line business and financial news service, and recently introduced The Trading Service (TTS), an electronic foreign exchange system used by currency traders for negotiating and executing deals.

Two thirds of DJ's voting stock is controlled by heirs of Clarence Barron.

WHEN

Charles Dow, Edward Jones, and Charles Bergstresser, 3 financial reporters, left their employer, The Kiernan News Agency, and began Dow Jones & Company (DJ) in 1882 working out of a humble office on Wall Street next door to the NYSE. The company sold handwritten bulletins with stock and bond trade information delivered to subscribers in New York's financial districts. In 1883 DJ printed the day's summary in the *Customers' Afternoon Letter* (annual subscription cost: $18.00), which evolved into the *Wall Street Journal* (1889). DJ offered more timely summary reports through its stock ticker service, acquired in 1897 from ex-employer Kiernan.

Jones sold out to his partners in 1899; in 1902 Dow and Bergstresser sold DJ to Clarence Barron, the company's Boston correspondent and owner of 2 other dailies. Dow died later in 1902. Circulation of the *Journal* grew from 7,000 in 1902 to over 50,000 in 1928, the year Barron died.

Until 1940 the *Journal* was primarily a financial newspaper. In 1941 the new managing editor, Bernard Kilgore, broadened its coverage to include summaries of major news events and more in-depth business articles. Kilgore became president of DJ in 1945. His leadership is credited with DJ's steady growth.

By 1966, when Kilgore retired, the *Journal* had a circulation of 1 million. In 1962 DJ started the *National Observer*, a weekly general-interest newspaper; however, production of the *Observer* was stopped in 1977 due to accumulated losses of $16.2 million.

In 1975 DJ began to transmit the *Journal* via satellite to its regional plants around the country, enabling it to offer same-day service to all of its US readers.

By the end of 1989, DJ consisted of several financial and business news publications and an array of electronic news retrieval services, including Telerate, which DJ had acquired through a series of stock purchases (1985–90) totalling $1.6 billion.

Since the October 1987 stock market crash, ad sales have declined, as have subscriptions. Circulation of the *Journal* and *Barron's* (a weekly first published in 1921) declined slightly in 1990, while the Asian and European editions of the *Journal* rose 7% and 9% respectively. Overall DJ's earnings dropped 30% in 1990 because of costs associated with assimilating Telerate and a recession in the financial industry and the economy as a whole. The newsstand price of the *Journal* in 1990 was increased to $.75 from $.50 — the first increase since 1984.

NYSE symbol: DJ
Fiscal year ends: December 31

Hoover's Rating B+

WHO

Chairman and CEO: Peter R. Kann, age 48, $535,000 pay (prior to promotion)
President and COO: Kenneth L. Burenga, age 46, $385,000 pay
VP Finance and CFO: Kevin J. Roche, age 56
VP Employee Relations: Donald L. Miller, age 58
Auditors: Coopers & Lybrand
Employees: 9,679

WHERE

HQ: World Financial Center, 200 Liberty St., New York, NY 10281
Phone: 212-416-2000
Fax: 212-416-3299

Dow Jones publications are circulated worldwide.

	1990 Sales		1990 Operating Income	
	$ mil.	% of total	$ mil.	% of total
US	1,303	76	180	74
Other countries	417	24	64	26
Adjustments	—	—	(15)	—
Total	**1,720**	**100**	**229**	**100**

WHAT

	1990 Sales		1990 Operating Income	
	$ mil.	% of total	$ mil.	% of total
Business publications	749	43	84	34
Information services	736	43	129	53
Community papers	235	14	31	13
Adjustments	—	—	(15)	—
Total	**1,720**	**100**	**229**	**100**

Information Services
AP-Dow Jones
Capital Markets Report
Dow Jones News Service (Broadtape)
Dow Jones News/Retrieval
Dow Jones Report (FM radio)
DowPhone
DowVision
JournalFax
JournalFinder
JournalPhone
Professional Investor Report
Telerate
The Trading Service

"The Wall Street Journal Report" (AM radio & TV shows)

Business Publications
American Demographics
Asian Wall Street Journal
Barron's
Far Eastern Economic Review
National Business Employment Weekly
The Wall Street Journal
The Wall Street Journal/Europe

Major Subsidiaries and Affiliates
AmericaEconomia (50%, Chile)
Automated Call Processing Corp.
DataTimes
Eurexpansion (19.7%)
Federal Filings, Inc.
FX Development Group, Inc.
Global Transactions Services
Groupe Expansion SA (11.2%, France)
Mediatex Communications Corp. (*Texas Monthly* mag.)
Nation Publishing Group (Thailand)
Ottaway Newspapers, Inc. (23 daily community papers)

HOW MUCH

	9-Year Growth	1981	1982	1983	1984	1985	1986	1987	1988	1989	1990
Sales ($ mil.)	11.6%	641	731	866	966	1,039	1,135	1,314	1,603	1,688	1,720
Net income ($ mil.)	4.6%	71	88	114	129	139	183	203	228	317	107
Income as % of sales	—	11.1%	12.1%	13.2%	13.4%	13.3%	16.2%	15.4%	14.2%	18.8%	6.2%
Earnings per share ($)	3.9%	0.75	0.92	1.19	1.34	1.43	1.88	2.09	2.35	3.14	1.06
Stock price – high ($)	—	18.42	23.50	37.50	34.25	33.33	42.13	56.25	36.50	42.50	33.75
Stock price – low ($)	—	9.85	11.92	21.33	23.42	24.50	28.08	28.00	26.75	29.25	18.13
Stock price – close ($)	4.3%	16.50	21.92	32.42	27.83	31.50	39.00	29.88	29.50	33.25	24.00
P/E – high	—	24	26	32	26	23	22	27	16	14	32
P/E – low	—	13	13	18	17	17	15	13	11	9	17
Dividends per share ($)	10.6%	0.31	0.36	0.40	0.48	0.52	0.55	0.64	0.68	0.72	0.76
Book value per share ($)	19.5%	2.86	3.49	4.34	5.24	6.21	7.52	8.80	11.51	13.94	14.23

1990 Year-end:
Debt ratio: 29.7%
Return on equity: 7.5%
Cash (mil.): $18
Current ratio: 0.61
Long-term debt (mil.): $608
No. of shares (mil.): 101
Dividends:
  1990 average yield: 3.2%
  1990 payout: 71.7%
Market value (mil.): $2,421

Stock Price History High/Low 1981–90

RANKINGS

240th in *Fortune* 500 Industrial Cos.
250th in *Business Week* 1000

KEY COMPETITORS

ADP	Knight-Ridder	Pearson
Citicorp	Maxwell	Reed
Dun & Bradstreet	McGraw-Hill	Reuters
Gannett	Mead	Time Warner
H&R Block	New York Times	Washington Post

DR PEPPER/SEVEN-UP COMPANIES, INC.

Private company
Fiscal year ends: December 31

Hoover's Rating **F**

OVERVIEW

A privately held, Dallas-based holding company, Dr Pepper/Seven-Up Companies is the nation's 3rd largest soft drink manufacturer (after Coca-Cola and PepsiCo). The company manufactures and markets syrup for international Dr Pepper sales and Seven-Up sales in the US. The 2 subsidiaries are jointly managed but operate separate sales and marketing divisions within the parent company. The company's St. Louis facility manufactures more than 200 brands of soft drink concentrate, many for contract customers.

The Dr Pepper brand, unique in its flavor category, is the nation's #5 soft drink (behind the regular and diet versions of Coke and Pepsi), with a 4.8% market share. It is also the fastest growing non-cola soft drink in the US, with sales up 8.9% in 1990.

Seven-Up, the #8 US soft drink with a 2.9% market share, continued to slip in 1990 as competition from Coca-Cola's Sprite remained particularly strong. The largest drop among the Seven-Up family was Cherry 7-Up, whose sales dropped 25%.

WHO

President and CEO: John Albers, age 59
EVP and CFO: Ira M. Rosenstein, age 51
SVP; EVP and COO, Dr Pepper: True Knowles, age 53
SVP; EVP and COO, Seven-Up: Dale Schaufel, age 48
Auditors: KPMG Peat Marwick
Employees: 842

WHERE

HQ: PO Box 655086, Dallas, TX 75265
Phone: 214-360-7000
Fax: 214-360-7981

Dr Pepper/Seven-Up Companies sell the 7-Up brands in the US only and the Dr Pepper brands throughout the US and in 15 countries.

	1990 Sales	
	$ mil.	% of total
US	537	99
Foreign	3	1
Total	**540**	**100**

WHEN

The Dr Pepper brand was first sold in 1885 in Waco, Texas, at Morrison's Old Corner Drug Store. The pharmacist, Charles Alderton, concocted the unique syrup, and the store's owner, Wade Morrison, named the new drink after an acquaintance in his home state of Virginia. A Waco bottler, Robert Lazenby, began producing the syrup and bottling the drink at his Circle "A" Ginger Ale Bottling Works. Lazenby and Morrison formed a new company, the Artesian Manufacturing and Bottling Company, and in 1923 they moved its headquarters to Dallas. In 1924 the name was changed to the Dr Pepper Company. The drink's popularity continued to grow, and in 1946 the company's stock was listed on the NYSE. Dr Pepper remained a public company until 1984, when its shareholders voted to accept a $22-per-share bid by Forstmann Little & Company, which privatized the company.

Dr Pepper is distinguished by its non-cola flavor and its memorable advertising slogans, including the 1930s motto "10, 2 and 4" (the times of day to drink Dr Pepper); the 1960s description as the most "misunderstood" soft drink; the "Be a Pepper" campaign in the 1980s; and the current "Just what the Dr ordered."

The 7-Up soft drink began in 1929 when C. L. Grigg, owner of The Howdy Company in St. Louis (home of Howdy Orange drink), introduced his new lemon-lime soda. The drink's success prompted Grigg to change his company's name to The Seven-Up Company in 1936, and by the late 1940s 7-Up was the world's 3rd best-selling soft drink. The company remained in family hands until it went public in 1967. Sales increased with the "Uncola" marketing campaign and the introduction of Diet 7-Up.

Philip Morris bought Seven-Up in 1978, but profits began to slide. By 1986 Philip Morris was negotiating to sell Seven-Up to PepsiCo. About the same time Coca-Cola was reaching an agreement to buy Dr Pepper. The FTC ruled that the sales were anticompetitive, and Hicks and Haas, a Dallas investment firm, stepped in to buy both companies in 1986. Dr Pepper sold for $416 million and Seven-Up sold for $240 million.

Hicks and Haas merged the 2 companies in 1988 to form Dr Pepper/Seven-Up Companies, Inc. The new company managers (many of them from Dr Pepper) consolidated plant operations at Seven-Up's St. Louis facility, selling other property and trimming Seven-Up staff. While sales for the Dr Pepper unit have grown since the company's merger, 7-Up sales have diminished, falling 7.2% in 1989 to $246.9 million.

In 1991 Dr Pepper began test-marketing Nautilus, a low-calorie sports drink that the company hopes will steal some of the market from Quaker Oats's Gatorade brand. The Dr Pepper/Seven-Up parent company is currently calling on its Dr Pepper unit for assistance in handling its debts, although Dr Pepper, by previous agreement, has strict limits on the dividend it can pay to the parent.

WHAT

	1990 Sales		1990 Operating Income	
	$ mil.	% of total	$ mil.	% of total
Dr Pepper	310	57	86	70
Seven-Up	230	43	37	30
Total	**540**	**100**	**123**	**100**

Brand Names
Dr Pepper
  Caffeine-Free Diet Dr Pepper
  Caffeine-Free Dr Pepper
  Diet Dr Pepper
  Dr Pepper
  Welch's (soft drinks only)
Seven-Up
  7-Up
  7-Up Gold
  Cherry 7-Up
  Diet 7-Up
  Like

Contract Services
Beverage analysis
Concentrate production
Flavor formulation
Technical assistance for soft drink packaging, plant design, quality control, and marketing

RANKINGS

362nd in *Forbes* 400 US Private Cos.

KEY COMPETITORS

Bass
Cadbury Schweppes
Coca-Cola
Heineken
PepsiCo
Source Perrier
Whitman

HOW MUCH

	9-Year Growth	1981	1982	1983	1984	1985	1986	1987	1988	1989	1990
Sales ($ mil.)	—	—	—	—	—	—	—	—	510	514	540
Net income ($ mil.)	—	—	—	—	—	—	—	—	(68)	(42)	(33)
Dr Pepper sales ($ mil.)	—	—	—	149	166	174	181	207	244	267	310
7-Up sales ($ mil.)	—	—	—	275	301	291	272	297	266	247	230
Dr Pepper cases sold (mil.)	4.9%	298.6	288.4	284.4	301.5	320.5	323.6	355.6	399.5	416.8	460.4
Dr Pepper % of market	—	5.6	5.2	4.9	4.9	4.9	4.8	5.0	5.3	5.4	5.8
7-Up cases sold (mil.)	(0.1%)	319.2	369.3	412.4	417.3	383.8	340.7	374.9	350.5	318.8	315.5
7-Up % of market	—	5.9	6.7	7.2	6.8	5.9	5.0	5.2	4.7	4.1	4.0
Total cases sold (mil.)	2.6%	617.8	657.7	696.8	718.8	704.3	664.3	730.5	750.0	735.6	775.9

1990 Year-end:
Debt ratio: —
Return on equity: —
Cash (mil.): $8
Current ratio: 0.80
Long-term debt (mil.): $1,032

Total Cases Sold (mil.) 1981–90

DRESSER INDUSTRIES, INC.

OVERVIEW

Dallas-based Dresser Industries is a major world industrial equipment manufacturer. Since 1983 Dresser, under CEO Jack Murphy, has refocused its efforts on equipment for the petroleum industry.

Dresser's strategy is to manufacture equipment necessary all along the path, from wellhead to gas pump, reasoning that while one segment of the oil business suffers, another will thrive. After the Iraqi invasion of Kuwait in 1990 spiked crude oil prices, Dresser's "upstream" operations (exploration and production) were revitalized while demand for "downstream" products (refining and marketing) sagged.

Serving the upstream, Dresser's M-I Drilling Fluids (64% owned) is the industry leader in drilling fluids and is a joint effort with Halliburton. Dresser owns 30% of Western Atlas International (Litton owns the rest). Western Atlas is the leading firm offering seismic exploration and data processing services and core and fluid analysis.

Downstream, Dresser's engineering services unit — notably M. W. Kellogg — has grown rapidly. Dresser-Rand, a joint venture with Ingersoll-Rand, makes compressors and turbines. Dresser and Ingersoll-Rand plan to merge their pump operations as well.

Dresser continues to manufacture equipment for industries other than the petroleum business. Its Komatsu Dresser joint venture is a leader in heavy construction equipment.

NYSE symbol: DI
Fiscal year ends: October 31

Hoover's Rating **B**

WHO

Chairman, President, and CEO: John J. Murphy, age 59, $1,108,260 pay
EVP Administration: Bill D. St. John, age 59, $615,355 pay
SVP Accounting and Tax: James J. Corboy, age 61
VP and General Counsel: M. Scott Nickson, Jr., age 56, $297,395 pay
VP Human Resources: Richard E. Hauslein, age 60
Auditors: Price Waterhouse
Employees: 33,100

WHEN

Solomon Dresser arrived in the oil boom town of Bradford, Pennsylvania, in 1878 with a consumptive wife and 4 children. He eked out a living in oil field jobs. He also tinkered with an invention, and in 1880 Dresser was granted a patent for a cap packer, a device that prevents crude oil from mixing with other fluids in a well. In the 1880s and 1890s he perfected a coupling that used fitted rubber to prevent leaks in pipeline connections.

As the natural gas industry grew, so did demand for the reliable Dresser coupling. The family firm prospered even after Solomon's death in 1911, but his heirs, anxious to pursue other interests, sold the company to W. A. Harriman & Company in 1928, and the investment banker took Dresser public.

Soon after, 3 Harriman executives — including Roland Harriman, son of the founder, and Prescott Bush, father of future US president George Bush — were discussing the vacant Dresser presidency. Just then, an old Yale friend, Neil Mallon, dropped by the office, and Harriman tapped Mallon for the top post.

During Mallon's 41-year career with Dresser, the company grew to an oil field conglomerate. Bryant Heating and Manufacturing was the first acquisition (bought in 1933 and sold in 1949). As Dresser tried to develop a high-speed compressor for gas pipelines, it purchased Clark Brothers (1937). It later abandoned its compressor research, but Olean, New York–based Clark became a company cornerstone.

The company moved its headquarters to Cleveland in 1945, then to Dallas in 1950. Dresser acquisitions ranged from Magnet Cove (drilling "mud" lubricant for oil well holes, 1949) to Symington-Wayne (gasoline pumps, 1968).

In 1983, after an oil services boom had peaked, CEO Jack Murphy began refocusing on the petroleum business, balancing upstream and downstream services and products. Dresser bought M. W. Kellogg Company (refinery engineering, 1988) just in time for a petrochemical boom but withdrew a 1989 bid for drill-bit maker Smith International in the face of antitrust problems. In 1990 Dresser bought the diamond drill-bit product line of rival Baker Hughes. Also that year Dresser bought 2 European businesses, Mono Group (pumps) and Peabody (blowers and combustion equipment).

WHERE

HQ: 1600 Pacific Bldg., Dallas, TX 75201
Phone: 214-740-6000
Fax: 214-740-6584

Dresser operates in the US and in 63 foreign countries.

	1990 Sales		1990 Operating Income	
	$ mil.	% of total	$ mil.	% of total
US	2,432	54	184	59
Canada	129	3	17	5
Europe	973	22	68	22
Other countries	946	21	45	14
Adjustments	—	—	(114)	—
Total	**4,480**	**100**	**200**	**100**

WHAT

	1990 Sales		1990 Operating Income	
	$ mil.	% of total	$ mil.	% of total
Mining & construction equip.	311	7	18	6
Oil field products & services	589	13	59	19
Energy processing & conversion equip.	1,587	35	142	46
Engineering services	1,576	35	31	10
General industry	426	10	60	19
Adjustments	(9)	—	(110)	—
Total	**4,480**	**100**	**200**	**100**

Oil Field Products and Services
Drill bits
Drilling fluid systems
Exploration services
Production tools
Rigs and equipment

Industrial Operations
Mining, construction equipment
Pneumatic tools

Refractory products
Specialty products

Energy Processing Products
Compressors and turbines
Control products
Engineering services
Marketing systems (Wayne gas pumps)
Power systems
Pumps

RANKINGS

111th in *Fortune* 500 Industrial Cos.
193rd in *Business Week* 1000

KEY COMPETITORS

ABB	Deere	LTV
Baker Hughes	Fluor	McDermott
Bechtel	FMC	Peter Kiewit Sons'
Caterpillar	Ingersoll-Rand	Schlumberger
Cooper Industries		

HOW MUCH

	9-Year Growth	1981	1982	1983	1984	1985	1986	1987	1988	1989	1990
Sales ($ mil.)	(0.3%)	4,615	4,161	3,473	3,732	4,111	3,661	3,120	3,942	3,956	4,480
Net income ($ mil.)	(6.4%)	317	172	5	97	(196)	1	16	123	163	174
Income as % of sales	—	6.9%	4.1%	0.1%	2.6%	(4.8%)	0.0%	0.5%	3.1%	4.1%	3.9%
Earnings per share ($)	(4.9%)	2.02	1.10	0.03	0.62	(1.29)	0.01	0.11	0.89	1.21	1.29
Stock price – high ($)	—	27.44	16.75	12.75	11.69	12.13	10.19	17.81	17.81	24.00	28.13
Stock price – low ($)	—	15.44	6.13	7.50	7.63	8.38	7.00	8.81	11.25	14.50	16.50
Stock price – close ($)	2.6%	16.63	9.88	10.38	9.13	9.06	9.69	13.13	14.69	22.44	20.88
P/E – high	—	14	15	425	19	—	—	162	20	20	22
P/E – low	—	8	6	250	12	—	—	80	13	12	13
Dividends per share ($)	5.8%	0.33	0.39	0.40	0.40	0.40	0.35	0.20	0.28	0.45	0.55
Book value per share ($)	0.7%	12.25	12.79	12.31	12.45	10.80	10.67	10.76	11.19	11.88	13.01

1990 Year-end:
Debt ratio: 11.6%
Return on equity: 10.4%
Cash (mil.): $361
Current ratio: 1.60
Long-term debt (mil.): $232
No. of shares (mil.): 136
Dividends:
  1990 average yield: 2.6%
  1990 payout: 42.6%
Market value (mil.): $2,830

Stock Price History High/Low 1981–90

E. I. DU PONT DE NEMOURS AND COMPANY

OVERVIEW

Du Pont is the largest chemical producer in the US. The Wilmington, Delaware–based company's products, however, go beyond chemicals, ranging from fibers to oil to firearms. With $40 billion in sales, 43% of which comes from overseas, Du Pont is the 7th largest exporter in the US.

Du Pont has 6 principal business segments — chemicals (chemicals, pigments, and petrochemicals); fibers (Dacron, Lycra, Nomex, etc.); polymers (nylon resins, acetyl resins, Teflon, etc.); petroleum (Conoco); coal (Consolidation Coal Company); and diversified businesses (agricultural products, electronics, imaging systems, pharmaceuticals, and sporting goods). Du Pont is the 11th largest natural gas producer in the world and the 2nd largest US coal producer, after Hanson's Peabody. It is also one of the world's largest producers of crop-protection products.

In 1990 Du Pont spent over $1.4 billion on research, making it one of the largest R&D spenders in the US. In 1991 Du Pont introduced a line of refrigerants to substitute for ozone-depleting chlorofluorocarbons (CFCs). Du Pont has committed to phase out CFC production by 2000.

Seagrams owns 24.5% of the company's stock, which it acquired in 1981 in exchange for its Conoco holdings.

NYSE symbol: DD
Fiscal year ends: December 31

Hoover's Rating: B°

WHO

Chairman and CEO: Edgar S. Woolard, Jr., age 57, $1,338,925 pay
VC: Elwood P. Blanchard, Jr., age 59, $965,325 pay
SVP and CFO: John J. Quindlen, age 58
SVP Human Resources: Jerald A. Blumberg, age 51
Auditors: Price Waterhouse
Employees: 143,961

WHEN

Eleuthère Irénée du Pont de Nemours, a Frenchman who had studied gunpowder manufacture under chemist Antoine Lavoisier, fled to America in 1800 after the French Revolution. In 1802 with the help of French capital, he founded E. I. du Pont de Nemours and Company and set up a gunpowder plant on Delaware's Brandywine Creek.

Within a decade the plant grew to be the largest of its kind in the US and benefited greatly from government contracts in the War of 1812. After Irénée's death in 1834, his sons Alfred and Henry took over, buying out the other partners to ensure du Pont family control. Under their leadership the company profited from selling gunpowder to the US government in the Mexican-American War (1840s) and to both sides in the Crimean War (1850s). Du Pont added dynamite and nitroglycerine (1880) and introduced guncotton (1892) and smokeless powder (1894).

In 1902 du Pont cousins Pierre, Alfred, and Coleman bought Du Pont and in 1903 instituted a centralized structure with functionally organized departments, an innovation that big business widely adopted. By 1906 Du Pont controlled 70% of the American explosives market. A 1912 antitrust decision forced Du Pont to dispose of part of the powder business, but the outbreak of WWI in 1914 generated Du Pont $89 million in earnings to use in diversifying into paints, plastics, and dyes.

In 1917 Du Pont acquired an interest in General Motors that had increased to 37% by 1922. In 1962, after 13 years of litigation, the US Supreme Court ordered the Du Pont–GM connection broken for antitrust violations; Du Pont distributed its GM shares to Du Pont shareholders. In the 1920s Du Pont bought and improved French cellophane technology and began production of rayon. Du Pont's list of inventions includes neoprene synthetic rubber (1931), Lucite (1937), nylon and Teflon (1938), Orlon, Dacron, and many others.

The last du Pont to head the company resigned as chairman in 1972, but the du Pont family still controls about 22% of common stock.

In 1981 Du Pont acquired Conoco, formerly Continental Oil, for $7.6 billion — one of the largest US acquisitions as of that date. In 1990 Conoco was the major contributor to Du Pont's earnings. Du Pont sold 50% of its coal subsidiary, Consolidation Coal Co., in 1991 to German coal company Rheinbraum. Du Pont and Merck began a joint venture in 1991 to create an independent drug company focusing on non-US markets.

WHERE

HQ: 1007 Market St., Wilmington, DE 19898
Phone: 302-774-1000
Fax: 302-774-7322

Du Pont conducts operations in 40 countries.

	1990 Sales		1990 Net Income	
	$ mil.	% of total	$ mil.	% of total
US	22,634	57	1,442	52
Europe	13,119	33	1,215	43
Other countries	4,294	10	138	5
Adjustments	(338)	—	(485)	—
Total	**39,709**	**100**	**2,310**	**100**

WHAT

	1990 Sales		1990 Operating Income	
	$ mil.	% of total	$ mil.	% of total
Coal	1,803	4	213	7
Chemicals	3,677	9	464	17
Fibers	6,085	15	430	15
Polymers	5,809	15	409	15
Petroleum	15,976	40	1,078	39
Other businesses	6,697	17	201	7
Adjustments	(338)	—	(485)	—
Total	**39,709**	**100**	**2,310**	**100**

Energy Subsidiaries
Conoco (crude oil, natural gas production, Conoco, Jet, and Seca brands)
Consolidation Coal Co. (50%, coal mining)

Consumer Product Materials and Brands
Antron	Lucite	Stainmasters
Corian	Lycra	Teflon
Dacron	Mylar	Tyvek
Kevlar	Sontara	

Other Products
Agricultural herbicides and insecticides
Firearms (Remington)
Fishing line (High Impact, Magnathin, Magnum, Prime Plus, and Stren brands)
Imaging systems
Industrial chemicals (e.g., titanium)
Medical products
Pharmaceuticals

HOW MUCH

	9-Year Growth	1981	1982	1983	1984	1985	1986	1987	1988	1989	1990
Sales ($ mil.)	6.4%	22,790	33,223	35,247	35,764	29,314	26,988	30,300	32,657	35,209	39,709
Net income ($ mil.)	8.8%	1,081	894	1,127	1,431	1,118	1,538	1,786	2,190	2,480	2,310
Income as % of sales	—	4.7%	2.7%	3.2%	4.0%	3.8%	5.7%	5.9%	6.7%	7.0%	5.8%
Earnings per share ($)	6.5%	1.93	1.25	1.56	1.98	1.53	2.11	2.46	3.04	3.53	3.40
Stock price – high ($)	—	18.67	14.79	18.92	18.38	23.13	30.83	43.67	30.96	42.17	42.38
Stock price – low ($)	—	11.92	10.00	11.71	14.13	15.88	19.83	25.00	25.25	28.71	31.38
Stock price – close ($)	12.8%	12.42	11.96	17.33	16.50	22.63	28.00	29.13	29.42	41.00	36.75
P/E – high	—	10	12	12	9	15	15	18	10	12	12
P/E – low	—	6	8	7	7	10	9	10	8	8	9
Dividends per share ($)	6.5%	0.92	0.80	0.83	0.97	1.00	1.02	1.10	1.23	1.45	1.62
Book value per share ($)	5.8%	14.53	14.96	15.68	16.69	17.21	18.25	19.55	21.36	22.71	24.16

1990 Year-end:
Debt ratio: 25.6%
Return on equity: 14.5%
Cash (mil.): $611
Current ratio: 1.22
Long-term debt (mil.): $5,663
No. of shares (mil.): 670
Dividends:
1990 average yield: 4.4%
1990 payout: 47.6%
Market value (mil.): $24,617

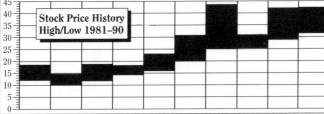

Stock Price History High/Low 1981–90

RANKINGS

9th in *Fortune* 500 Industrial Cos.
16th in *Business Week* 1000

KEY COMPETITORS

Allied-Signal	Farley	Monsanto
American Cyanamid	Fieldcrest Cannon	Nobel
BASF	FMC	Occidental
Bayer	Formosa Plastics	PPG
Burlington Holdings	W. R. Grace	Rhône Poulenc
Ciba-Geigy	Hercules	Sherwin-Williams
Clorox	Hoechst	Union Carbide
Dow Chemical	Imperial Chemical	Petroleum and drug
Eastman Kodak	S. C. Johnson	companies

DUKE POWER COMPANY

OVERVIEW

Duke Power is widely viewed as one of the best-run utilities in the industry. Its coal-fired plants have been ranked as the nation's most efficient by *Electric Light & Power* magazine for the last 16 years. Duke Power provides electric service to more than 1.6 million customers in a 20,000-square-mile service area covering 56 counties of North and South Carolina. Electric revenues (down slightly in 1990) totaled $3.68 billion (70% from North Carolina, 30% from South Carolina). Lower 1990 earnings reflect higher maintenance costs and increased employee retirement benefits.

Nantahala Power & Light (a subsidiary) provides electricity to 47,000 customers in 5 North Carolina counties. Other subsidiaries support Duke Power's core utility business by providing engineering and technical expertise (Duke Engineering & Services) and designing and building power plants (Duke Energy Corp.). Duke/Fluor Daniel (a partnership with Fluor Corporation) designs, builds, and manages coal-fired plants nationwide. Duke Power also owns 270,000 acres of Carolina timberland and engages in real estate development through subsidiary Crescent Resources, Inc.

NYSE symbol: DUK
Fiscal year ends: December 31

Hoover's Rating **C+**

WHO

Chairman and President: William S. Lee, age 61, $519,727 pay
EVP Power Group: Warren H. Owen, age 64, $313,238 pay
EVP Customer Group: William H. Grigg, age 58, $288,059 pay
VP Finance: Richard J. Osborne, age 39
VP Human Resources: James R. Bavis, age 51
Auditors: Deloitte & Touche
Employees: 19,900

WHEN

In 1899 engineer-turned-surgeon Dr. W. Gill Wylie founded the Catawba Power Company and hired engineer W. S. Lee to design the company's first hydroelectric power plant near Fort Mill, South Carolina. Operational by 1904, this plant set the standard for the company's future plants — each one was designed by company engineers and after 1924 built by company construction teams.

In 1905 the Southern Power Company was formed out of the American Development Company, which had acquired all of Catawba Power's stock. Wylie was installed as president and Lee as chief engineer. James "Buck" Duke (founder of the American Tobacco Company and the W. Duke and Sons tobacco empire), who was instrumental in the formation of the power companies, became president in 1910 and organized Mill-Power Supply to sell heavy electric equipment to the region's textile mills. Duke formed The Southern Public Utility Company (SPUC) in 1913 to buy various Piedmont utilities (gas, water, and electric). By 1933 SPUC provided power to 195 North and South Carolina communities.

In 1917 Duke established Wateree Electric. Wateree was renamed Duke Power Company in 1924 and owned all of the properties formerly held by Southern Power by 1935. When Buck Duke died in 1925, about 85% of Duke Power's stock was held by the Duke family, Doris Duke Trust, and Duke Endowment (a trust created in 1924 for Piedmont area colleges, including Trinity College, which was renamed Duke University in 1924 in Buck Duke's honor). When the company's stock was first traded publicly (Curb Exchange, 1950), the Duke family, Endowment, and Trust still owned 67%. This was diluted to about 15% after the company was listed on the NYSE in 1961.

In 1970 Duke Power bought 3 Kentucky coal mining companies to provide fuel for its steam generators. Oconee, the company's first nuclear plant (designed by Lee's grandson, W. S. Lee III) was operational by 1974. The company bought the electrical systems at Duke University in 1975 and at the University of North Carolina at Chapel Hill in 1976. Its McGuire nuclear plant was operational by 1984, and a 3rd nuclear plant (Catawba) went on-line in 1986.

Duke had begun offering its engineering expertise to outside firms in 1982 and formed a related subsidiary, Duke Engineering and Services, in 1987. In 1988 the company organized the Duke Energy Corporation to develop and finance power projects outside the Piedmont area and bought Nantahala Power and Light. Because it no longer related to the company's long-term strategy, Mill-Power Supply was sold in 1990.

WHERE

HQ: 422 S. Church St., Charlotte, NC 28242-0001
Phone: 704-373-4011
Fax: 704-373-8038

Generating Facilities

Hydroelectric	
Bad Creek (SC)	Saluda (SC)
Bridgewater (NC)	Turner (NC)
Buzzard Roost (SC)	Tuxedo (NC)
Cedar Creek (SC)	Wateree (SC)
Cowans Ford (NC)	Wylie (SC)
Dearborn (SC)	**Nuclear**
Fishing Creek (SC)	Catawba (12.5%, NC)
Gaston Shoals (SC)	McGuire (NC)
Great Falls (SC)	Oconee (SC)
Holliday's Bridge (SC)	
Jocassee (SC)	**Steam**
Keowee (SC)	Allen (NC)
Lookout Shoals (NC)	Belews Creek (NC)
Mountain Island (NC)	Buck (NC)
Ninety-Nine Islands (SC)	Cliffside (NC)
Oxford (NC)	Dan River (NC)
Rhodhiss (NC)	Lee (SC)
Rocky Creek (SC)	Marshall (NC)
	Riverbend (NC)

WHAT

	1990 Sales	
	$ mil.	% of total
Residential	1,217	33
General service	886	24
Textile industry	476	13
Other industries	655	18
Wholesale & other energy sales	368	10
Other revenues	79	2
Total	**3,681**	**100**

	1990 Fuel Sources
	% of total
Coal	43
Nuclear	43
Hydroelectric	10
Oil & gas	4
Total	**100**

Major Subsidiaries and Affiliates
Church Street Capital Corp.
Crescent Resources, Inc. (real estate)
Duke Energy Corp. (plant construction)
Duke Engineering & Services, Inc.
Duke/Fluor Daniel (partnership with Fluor Corp.)
Kaleidoscope Consultant Group (technical training, planning, and consulting)
Nantahala Power and Light Co.

RANKINGS

26th in *Fortune* 50 Utilities
122nd in *Business Week* 1000

HOW MUCH

	9-Year Growth	1981	1982	1983	1984	1985	1986	1987	1988	1989	1990
Sales ($ mil.)	7.5%	1,913	2,250	2,426	2,717	2,906	3,409	3,714	3,636	3,648	3,681
Net income ($ mil.)	5.4%	336	350	431	461	438	468	500	448	572	538
Income as % of sales	—	17.6%	15.6%	17.8%	17.0%	15.1%	13.7%	13.5%	12.3%	15.7%	14.6%
Earnings per share ($)	4.7%	1.59	1.54	1.88	1.99	1.86	2.02	2.20	*1.95*	2.56	*2.40*
Stock price – high ($)	—	11.25	12.00	13.19	15.06	18.44	26.00	25.88	24.50	28.25	32.38
Stock price – low ($)	—	7.94	10.13	10.88	11.13	14.25	17.44	19.69	21.13	21.38	25.50
Stock price – close ($)	12.9%	10.31	11.63	12.56	14.50	17.69	22.63	21.44	23.13	28.06	30.63
P/E – high	—	7	8	7	8	10	13	12	13	11	13
P/E – low	—	5	7	6	6	8	9	9	11	8	11
Dividends per share ($)	4.9%	1.04	1.12	1.16	1.21	1.27	1.32	1.37	1.44	1.52	1.60
Book value per share ($)	5.2%	11.92	12.45	13.13	13.90	14.49	15.17	15.98	17.01	18.05	18.84

1990 Year-end:
Debt ratio: 41.8%
Return on equity: 13.0%
Cash (mil.): $63
Current ratio: 1.20
Long-term debt (mil.): $3,103
No. of shares (mil.): 203
Dividends:
  1990 average yield: 5.2%
  1990 payout: 66.7%
Market value (mil.): $6,204

Stock Price History High/Low 1981–90

THE DUN & BRADSTREET CORPORATION

NYSE symbol: DNB
Fiscal year ends: December 31

Hoover's Rating **A**

OVERVIEW

Dun & Bradstreet (D&B) supplies marketing and business information. A.C. Nielsen measures television audiences and performs marketing research; it derives about 70% of its revenues from overseas. R. H. Donnelley is the largest publisher of Yellow Pages telephone directories. D&B operates the world's largest credit reporting agency, selling credit information on more than 17 million businesses worldwide; adverse publicity about the unit's selling practices hurt its sales in 1990. Moody's Investors Service issues widely followed credit ratings on debt securities and is a respected publisher of financial information.

Dun & Bradstreet Software (DBS) claims that 65% of the world's IBM mainframe installations run DBS software. DBS is having trouble meshing the operations of its McCormack & Dodge unit and newly acquired Management Science America. The companies had been bitter rivals in mainframe business-applications software.

Other divisions provide market information to health care, financial services, and high-technology industries and sell services related to health insurance.

WHO

Chairman and CEO: Charles W. Moritz, age 54, $1,465,104 pay
President and COO: Robert W. Weissman, age 50, $1,018,084 pay
EVP Finance and CFO: Edwin A. Bescherer, Jr., age 57, $619,431 pay
SVP Human Resources: John J. Fitzpatrick
Auditors: Coopers & Lybrand
Employees: 62,900

WHERE

HQ: 299 Park Ave., New York, NY 10171
Phone: 212-593-6800
Fax: 212-593-4143

Dun & Bradstreet sells services in over 60 countries.

	1990 Sales		1990 Operating Income	
	$ mil.	% of total	$ mil.	% of total
US	3,075	64	566	73
Europe	1,274	26	135	18
Other countries	469	10	70	9
Total	**4,818**	**100**	**771**	**100**

WHEN

Dun & Bradstreet's origins were in Lewis Tappan's Mercantile Agency, established in 1841 in New York City. The Mercantile Agency was one of the first commercial credit reporting agencies created to supply wholesalers and importers with information on their customers. Tappan's credit reporters, who prepared written reports on companies, included 4 men who became US presidents (Lincoln, Grant, Cleveland, and McKinley). In the 1840s Tappan opened offices in Boston, Philadelphia, and Baltimore and in 1857 established offices in Montreal and London. Two years later Robert Dun took over the agency, changing its name to R.G. Dun & Company. The first edition of Dun's Reference Book (1859) contained information on 20,268 businesses; by 1886 the number had risen to over one million. By 1869 Dun had a branch office in San Francisco. John M. Bradstreet, a rival company founded in Cincinnati in 1849, merged with Dun in 1933; the company adopted the Dun & Bradstreet name in 1939.

In 1961 Dun & Bradstreet bought Reuben H. Donnelley Corporation, publisher of the Yellow Pages (first published in 1886), 10 trade magazines, and a direct-mail advertising business. The following year Moody's Investors Service (founded 1900) and Official

Airline Guide (guides first published in 1929) became part of D&B.

D&B's records were first computerized in the 1960s and eventually became the largest private database in the world (2nd only to the government's). By 1975 D&B had a national electronic network with a centralized database. Able to create new products by repackaging information from its vast database (such as Dun's Financial Profiles in 1979), the company doubled sales in 5 years to $1.4 billion by 1980.

Since the late 1970s the company has purchased National CSS (computer services company, 1979), McCormack & Dodge (software, 1983), and Technical Publishing (trade and professional publications, 1978). The addition of A.C. Nielsen (includes Nielsen TV ratings, 1984) and IMS International (pharmaceutical sales data, 1988) made D&B the largest marketing research company in the world. In 1988 D&B sold Official Airline Guide to Maxwell Communications for $750 million. D&B bought Management Science America in 1989.

In 1990 D&B unloaded noncore businesses, including Zytron and Neodata. The next year the company sold Donnelley Marketing, a direct marketing company and owner of a database containing detailed consumer information on 85 million households, to a group including publisher Peter Diamandis.

WHAT

	1990 Sales		1990 Operating Income	
	$ mil.	% of total	$ mil.	% of total
Risk-mgmt. info. svcs.	956	20	113	13
Directory info. svcs.	450	10	178	20
Marketing info. svcs.	1,937	40	316	36
Software services	539	11	17	2
Financial info. svcs.	345	7	106	12
Business services	591	12	145	17
Adjustments	—	—	(104)	—
Total	**4,818**	**100**	**771**	**100**

Risk-Management Information Services
Dun & Bradstreet Information Services (credit information and insurance, receivables management)

Directory Information Services
The Reuben H. Donnelley Corp. (*Yellow Pages*)

Marketing Information Services
A.C. Nielsen Co. (marketing and media research)
IMS International Inc. (health care market research)

Software Services
Dun & Bradstreet Software Services, Inc. (business applications software)
Sales Technologies (field sales systems)

Financial Information Services
Datastream International Ltd. (investment information)
Interactive Data Corp. (stock price data)
Moody's Investors Service, Inc. (fin. info., bond rating)

Business Services
Dataquest Inc. (high-technology market research)
Dun & Bradstreet Business Marketing Services
Dun & Bradstreet Plan Services (health insurance administration and marketing)
NCH Promotional Services (coupon processing)

RANKINGS

23rd in *Fortune* 100 Diversified Service Cos.
71st in *Business Week* 1000

HOW MUCH

	9-Year Growth	1981	1982	1983	1984	1985	1986	1987	1988	1989	1990
Sales ($ mil.)	15.4%	1,331	1,462	1,510	2,397	2,772	3,114	3,359	4,267	4,322	4,818
Net income ($ mil.)	17.2%	121	142	142	253	295	340	393	499	586	508
Income as % of sales	—	9.1%	9.7%	9.4%	10.5%	10.6%	10.9%	11.7%	11.7%	13.6%	10.5%
Earnings per share ($)	11.2%	1.08	1.26	1.25	1.66	1.93	2.23	2.57	2.66	3.14	2.80
Stock price – high ($)	—	17.56	26.00	35.00	33.75	43.94	60.19	71.75	57.50	60.25	48.63
Stock price – low ($)	—	13.31	14.63	24.44	25.56	31.38	40.38	44.50	45.88	41.25	36.13
Stock price – close ($)	11.6%	15.75	24.63	31.00	32.81	41.88	52.63	54.75	53.63	46.00	42.13
P/E – high	—	16	21	28	20	23	27	28	22	19	17
P/E – low	—	12	12	20	15	16	18	17	17	13	13
Dividends per share ($)	15.5%	0.57	0.67	0.77	0.91	1.06	1.24	1.45	1.68	1.94	2.09
Book value per share ($)	12.9%	3.89	4.48	5.15	8.06	8.92	9.80	10.95	11.18	11.80	11.65

1990 Year-end:
Debt ratio: 0.0%
Return on equity: 23.9%
Cash (mil.): $338
Current ratio: 1.07
Long-term debt (mil.): $0
No. of shares (mil.): 179
Dividends:
 1990 average yield: 5.0%
 1990 payout: 74.6%
Market value (mil.): $7,524

Stock Price History High/Low 1981–90

KEY COMPETITORS

Citicorp	DEC	Oracle
Commerce Clearing House	Dow Jones	Reed
	H&R Block	Reuters
Computer Associates	Knight-Ridder	Thomson Corp.
Control Data	McGraw-Hill	TRW

EASTMAN KODAK COMPANY

NYSE symbol: EK
Fiscal year ends: December 31

Hoover's Rating **C+**

OVERVIEW

Although the Rochester, New York–based Eastman Kodak Company is best known as the market leader in the amateur photography business, the bulk of Kodak's revenues are generated from its information systems, chemicals, and health and household products segments. In 1990, revenues from Kodak's imaging segment (photographic films and papers and cameras) accounted for $7.1 billion in sales; the information, chemical, and health segments generated $12 billion.

In 1990 the familiar bright red-and-yellow Kodak logo found all over the world on the company's film and cameras adorned Kodak's newest product introduction, the Photo CD system, which stores photos on compact discs. With the discs, photographers can view the photos on a TV or load them into a computer for editing.

Having spent $1.3 billion on R&D in 1990, Kodak was among the US's largest R&D spenders. And with 43% of its revenues attributed to international sales, it was also among the largest US exporters in 1990.

Kodak was ordered to pay $873.2 million to Polaroid in 1990, a record award resulting from a 14-year suit brought against Kodak following its 1976 introduction of instant cameras.

WHEN

George Eastman, after developing a method for dry-plate photography, established The Eastman Dry Plate and Film Company in 1884 in Rochester, New York. The company went through a succession of name changes, settling on Kodak in 1892, after Eastman tried many combinations of letters starting and ending with "K," which he thought was a "strong, incisive sort of letter."

In 1888 the company introduced its first camera, a small, easy-to-use device that sold for $25, loaded with enough film for 100 pictures. To develop the film, owners mailed the camera to Kodak, which returned it with the pictures and more film. The very successful Brownie followed in 1900. In 1923 Kodak introduced a home-movie camera, projector, and film.

Ailing and concluding his work was done, Eastman shot and killed himself at the age of 77 (1932). Kodak continued to dominate the photography industry with the introduction of color film (Kodachrome, 1935) and the Brownie hand-held movie camera (1951). Kodak established manufacturing facilities in Tennessee (1920) and Texas (1950) to produce the chemicals, plastics, and fibers used in its film production.

The Instamatic, introduced in 1963, became Kodak's biggest success. The camera, with the film in a foolproof cartridge, eliminated the need for loading in the dark. By 1976 Kodak had sold an estimated 60 million Instamatics, 50 million more cameras than all its competitors combined. Subsequent introductions have included the Kodak instant camera (which caused Polaroid to wage a successful legal suit for patent infringement against the company) and the disc camera. Both products have since been discontinued, the instant camera because of the Polaroid suit and the disc camera because of inferior photo quality (too grainy).

In 1983, responding to lagging sales and growing competition, Kodak streamlined operations and began diversifying into electronic publishing, batteries, floppy disks (Verbatim, 1985, sold 1990), and, more recently, pharmaceuticals. In 1988 Kodak acquired Sterling Drug (Bayer aspirin and Lysol) for $5.1 billion, its largest acquisition ever. Paying off the debt for Sterling continues to burden Kodak, partly because of the sluggish performance of Sterling's product development efforts. In 1991 the Sterling unit entered into a joint venture agreement with French oil giant Elf Aquitaine's subsidiary, Sanofi, Europe's 12th largest pharmaceutical company. The partnership will open new markets for Kodak and boost product development efforts.

WHO

Chairman, President, and CEO: Kay R. Whitmore, age 58, $871,711 pay
SVP Finance and Administration: Paul L. Smith, age 55
SVP and Director Corporate Relations: John R. McCarthy
Auditors: Price Waterhouse
Employees: 134,450

WHERE

HQ: 343 State St., Rochester, NY 14650
Phone: 716-724-4000
Fax: 716-724-0663

Eastman Kodak sells its products in 150 countries and has offices around the world.

	1990 Sales		1990 Operating Income	
	$ mil.	% of total	$ mil.	% of total
US	10,663	57	1,698	60
Canada & Latin America	1,388	7	290	10
Europe	5,165	27	675	24
Other countries	1,692	9	184	6
Total	**18,908**	**100**	**2,844**	**100**

WHAT

	1990 Sales		1990 Operating Income	
	$ mil.	% of total	$ mil.	% of total
Chemicals	3,297	17	602	21
Imaging	7,122	38	1,611	58
Health prods.	4,349	23	626	22
Info. systems	4,140	22	5	(1)
Total	**18,908**	**100**	**2,844**	**100**

Chemicals
Kodel polyester
Plastics and adhesives
Polymers and resins

Imaging
Batteries
Cameras
Film and papers (Ektachrome and Kodachrome)

Information Systems
Atex (publishing)
Diconix printers
Optical disks
Photo CD
Photocopiers

Health and Other Products
Bayer aspirin
Blood analyzers
Campho-Phenique
Cling
d-Con
Diaperene
Lysol
Midol
Minwax
Mop & Glo
Neo-Synephrine
pHiso Hex
Red Devil
Resolve
Stridex
X-ray films

HOW MUCH

	9-Year Growth	1981	1982	1983	1984	1985	1986	1987	1988	1989	1990
Sales ($ mil.)	6.9%	10,337	10,815	10,170	10,600	10,631	11,550	13,305	17,034	18,398	18,908
Net income ($ mil.)	(6.1%)	1,239	1,162	565	923	332	374	1,178	1,397	529	703
Income as % of sales	—	12.0%	10.7%	5.6%	8.7%	3.1%	3.2%	8.9%	8.2%	2.9%	3.7%
Earnings per share ($)	(4.9%)	3.40	3.16	1.52	2.54	0.99	1.12	3.48	4.26	1.63	2.16
Stock price – high ($)	—	37.94	43.61	40.78	34.67	35.58	46.67	70.67	53.25	52.38	43.88
Stock price – low ($)	—	26.94	29.06	28.50	26.78	27.33	30.58	41.92	39.13	40.00	33.75
Stock price – close ($)	3.1%	31.61	38.22	33.83	31.94	33.75	45.75	49.00	45.13	41.13	41.63
P/E – high	—	11	14	27	14	36	42	20	13	32	20
P/E – low	—	8	9	19	11	28	27	12	9	25	16
Dividends per share ($)	2.8%	1.56	1.58	1.58	1.60	1.62	1.63	1.71	1.90	2.00	2.00
Book value per share ($)	1.3%	18.52	20.25	20.18	20.37	19.37	18.84	18.54	20.90	20.46	20.75

1990 Year-end:
Debt ratio: 50.9%
Return on equity: 10.5%
Cash (mil.): $916
Current ratio: 1.20
Long-term debt (mil.): $6,989
No. of shares (mil.): 325
Dividends:
 1990 average yield: 4.8%
 1990 payout: 92.6%
Market value (mil.): $13,513

Stock Price History High/Low 1981–90

RANKINGS

20th in *Fortune* 500 Industrial Cos.
39th in *Business Week* 1000

KEY COMPETITORS

American Home Products
Bayer
Bristol-Myers Squibb
Canon
Clorox
Dow Chemical
Du Pont
Fuji Photo
General Electric
Harris
International Paper
Johnson & Johnson
S. C. Johnson
3M
Minolta
Philips
Polaroid
Procter & Gamble
Siemens
Xerox
Chemical, pharmaceutical, photo, and household products companies

EATON CORPORATION

NYSE symbol: ETN
Fiscal year ends: December 31

Hoover's Rating: C

OVERVIEW

Eaton, headquartered in Cleveland, is a leading manufacturer of automobile and truck components. The company manufactures more than 5,000 products, principally truck transmissions, axles, engine components, electrical equipment, and controls (for industrial, military, and appliance/automotive uses). Eaton's 2 groups, Vehicle Components and Electrical and Electronic Controls, serve the transportation, industrial, aerospace, and military markets.

Eaton's largest customer is Ford, whose purchases amounted to 20% of 1990 net sales.

The recession, which has continued into 1991, hurt Eaton's 1990 earnings (down $46 million, or 20%, from 1989), leading the company to take cost-control measures that included work force reductions. Eaton took a first quarter pretax restructuring charge in 1991 of $39 million.

Eaton's strategy includes continuing to invest in new product development; sticking with businesses in which it has a competitive advantage; and restructuring as necessary to become more cost efficient.

WHEN

In 1911 Joseph Eaton and Viggo Torbensen started the Torbensen Gear and Axle Company to manufacture an internal-gear rear axle for trucks patented by Torbensen in 1902. The company moved from Newark, New Jersey, to Cleveland in 1914. In 1917 Republic Motor Truck purchased Torbensen.

Eaton formed the Eaton Axle Company in 1919, repurchased Torbensen in 1922, and by 1931 had bought 11 more automotive parts companies (making bumpers, springs, heaters, gasoline tank caps, and engine parts). In 1932 the company became Eaton Manufacturing.

The Great Depression reduced demand for automobiles, and profits plummeted. Researchers produced the first heavy-duty, 2-speed axle in 1934. In 1937 Eaton opened its first foreign plant in Ontario. Heavy wartime demand helped Eaton recover, and in 1946 the company acquired Dynamatic (eddy-current drives). Joseph Eaton died in 1949.

The company built or renovated 11 plants during the 1950s. Attempting to diversify, Eaton acquired Fuller Manufacturing (truck transmissions, 1958), Cleveland Worm & Gear (worm gearing, 1959), Dole Valve (controls, valves, and beverage dispensers; 1963), and Yale & Towne Manufacturing (locks and fork-lift trucks, 1963). In 1966 the company changed its name to Eaton Yale & Towne.

The acquisitions augmented Eaton's international business, and foreign sales increased from virtually zero in 1961 to 20% of total sales by 1966. In 1971 Eaton adopted its present name.

In 1978 Eaton sold the lock and security business to Scovill Manufacturing and acquired Cutler-Hammer (industrial controls and defense electronics), Kenway (automated storage and retrieval systems), and Samuel Moore (plastics technology and fluid power). By 1980 Eaton was supplying the space shuttle's landing and communications system and traffic control systems for the air and waterways. In 1981 the US government awarded Eaton the $3 billion B-1B bomber defense avionics (radar-jamming) contract.

Downturns in the truck and automobile industries forced Eaton to close 30 plants and trim 23,000 employees between 1979 and 1983. In 1982 the company reported its first loss in 50 years, but a restructuring plan called "Operation Shrink" led Eaton to record profits and sales by 1984.

In 1987 Eaton announced plans to sell its defense electronics businesses (partially completed). Vehicle components and controls now make up the core of Eaton's businesses. The downturn in the economy in 1990 and 1991 resulted in reduced demand in most of the company's markets and lower earnings.

In 1991 Eaton restructured into 6 smaller operating groups in an effort to make the company more responsive to market conditions.

WHO

Chairman: James R. Stover, age 64, $1,053,109 pay
CEO: William E. Butler, age 60, $673,144 pay (prior to promotion)
President and COO: John S. Rodewig, age 57
VC and Chief Financial and Administrative Officer: Stephen R. Hardis, age 55, $610,945 pay (prior to promotion)
EVP: Gerald L. Gherlein, age 53
VP Human Resources: John D. Evans, age 60
Auditors: Ernst & Young
Employees: 40,058

WHERE

HQ: Eaton Center, Cleveland, OH 44114-2584
Phone: 216-523-5000
Fax: 216-523-4787

Eaton has 130 facilities in 20 countries.

	1990 Sales		1990 Operating Income	
	$ mil.	% of total	$ mil.	% of total
US	2,716	71	247	82
Canada	188	5	16	6
Europe	698	18	25	8
Other countries	213	6	13	4
Adjustments	(176)	—	(8)	—
Total	3,639	100	293	100

WHAT

	1990 Sales		1990 Operating Income	
	$ mil.	% of total	$ mil.	% of total
Vehicle components	2,015	55	179	59
Electrical & electronic controls	1,624	45	122	41
Adjustments	—	—	(8)	—
Total	3,639	100	293	100

Vehicle Components
Axles
Brakes
Clutches
Engine valves
Fan drives
Hydraulic and hydrostatic equipment
Transmissions

Electrical and Electronic Controls
Controllers
Distribution equipment
Electric drives
Materials-handling systems
Sensors
Starters
Switches
Timers

RANKINGS

120th in *Fortune* 500 Industrial Cos.
324th in *Business Week* 1000

KEY COMPETITORS

Allied-Signal
American Standard
Borg-Warner
Cooper Industries
Dana
Ingersoll-Rand
Litton Industries
Motorola
Raytheon
Reliance Electric
Robert Bosch
Rockwell
Siemens
Square D
Tenneco
Textron
Thyssen
Westinghouse
Vehicle manufacturers

HOW MUCH

	9-Year Growth	1981	1982	1983	1984	1985	1986	1987	1988	1989	1990
Sales ($ mil.)	1.6%	3,165	2,453	2,674	3,510	3,675	3,812	3,138	3,469	3,671	3,639
Net income ($ mil.)	8.3%	82	(71)	93	254	231	138	206	228	210	169
Income as % of sales	—	2.6%	(2.9%)	3.5%	7.2%	6.3%	3.6%	6.6%	6.6%	5.7%	4.6%
Earnings per share ($)	10.5%	1.95	(1.60)	1.97	5.00	4.48	2.78	4.79	6.11	5.59	4.77
Stock price – high ($)	—	27.67	23.92	37.00	37.67	43.25	53.25	71.83	57.33	67.50	64.38
Stock price – low ($)	—	17.67	15.17	19.08	25.17	33.00	42.00	37.00	44.67	53.00	40.75
Stock price – close ($)	9.9%	21.25	21.33	36.83	35.42	42.75	49.17	52.83	55.75	57.00	49.88
P/E – high	—	14	—	19	8	10	19	15	9	12	14
P/E – low	—	9	—	10	5	7	15	8	7	9	9
Dividends per share ($)	7.0%	1.15	1.15	0.53	0.73	0.90	1.07	1.27	1.67	2.00	2.10
Book value per share ($)	3.5%	24.77	18.57	20.55	24.58	28.33	28.63	28.51	31.24	31.01	33.63

1990 Year-end:
Debt ratio: 39.8%
Return on equity: 14.8%
Cash (mil.): $217
Current ratio: 2.05
Long-term debt (mil.): $755
No. of shares (mil.): 34
Dividends:
 1990 average yield: 4.2%
 1990 payout: 44.0%
Market value (mil.): $1,691

Stock Price History High/Low 1981–90

EDISON BROTHERS

OVERVIEW

St. Louis–based Edison Brothers is a specialty retailer with a major market presence in both shoes and apparel. Although its stores were considered conservative and out of date as recently as the mid-1980s, the company has blossomed under the guidance of President Martin Sneider and Chairman Andrew Newman, who transformed the ailing stores into some of the trendiest boutiques in the industry. The Edison family still controls about 27% of the company.

The company's shoe operations, once the cornerstone of the business, include such store names as Bakers and Leeds (affordable women's footwear), The Wild Pair (young women's shoes), Velocity (an experimental Wild Pair men's shoe store), and Sacha London (fine European footwear). Edison Brothers also operates shoe departments in several department stores.

Edison Brothers claims to be the largest US retailer of men's fashion apparel, with such stores as J. Riggings, Oaktree, Jeans West, Coda, and Repp Ltd. Women's retail units include 5-7-9 Shops (stores for small teenage girls), Spirale (an experimental 5-7-9 preteen shop), and Joan Bari.

Since 1990 the company has also operated amusement centers (arcades, etc.), primarily in malls.

WHEN

In 1922 Harry, Irving, Mark, Sam, and Simon Edison established Edison Brothers in St. Louis to sell shoes. Unlike Brown Group, its crosstown competitor that produced its own shoes, Edison Brothers remained exclusively a retailer, selling women's shoes under the Chandler Boot Shops and Baker's Shoe Stores names. The company had achieved sales of over $1 million by 1926 and went public 3 years later. For the next several decades Edison Brothers remained a closely knit, family operated shoe merchant. By the mid-1950s sales had approached the $100 million mark.

The company took its first step outside shoe retailing in 1969 with the purchase of the Handyman Home Improvement Centers chain. The following year it entered the apparel business by acquiring 5-7-9 Shops, clothing stores that catered to petite teenage girls. Further purchases in the 1970s included the 48-store Jeans West chain and the 126-outlet Fashion Conspiracy chain.

In 1984 Edison Brothers bought Gussini, a low-cost footwear store, and in 1985 spun off its Handyman division to stockholders. Around this time, the company discovered that it had allowed its stores to become outdated and stagnant. To spark some life back into its operations, Edison Brothers brought in some new managerial blood, naming Andrew Newman (who had married into the family) as chairman and Martin Sneider as president (the first outsider to hold the position).

The new leaders shifted the company's emphasis increasingly away from shoes and toward young men's fashions, buying the 209-store J. Riggings chain in 1987. They also pared some unprofitable operations, phasing out the Fashion Conspiracy in 1987 and selling 169 Gussini stores in 1988. Finally, the 2 men converted many of the company's prime locations to trendy, fashion-conscious boutiques aimed at younger shoppers (e.g., The Wild Pair, a shoe store where music videos are aired over ubiquitous monitors).

The numerous changes resulted in a drastic financial turnaround for Edison Brothers, which suddenly found itself as popular with Wall Street as its clothes were with trendy teens. In 1990 the company bought Foxmoor (women's apparel) and Zeidler & Zeidler (menswear). That same year the company created an entertainment division (video arcades, etc.) with the purchase of Adventure Properties, Consolidated Amusement Company, and Time-Out Family Amusement Centers.

NYSE symbol: EBS
Fiscal year ends: Saturday closest to January 31

Hoover's Rating **C+**

WHO

Chairman: Andrew E. Newman, age 46, $784,168 pay
President: Martin Sneider, age 48, $784,168 pay
VP Finance and Treasurer: Lee G. Weeks, age 57, $304,172 pay
VP Human Resources: Eric A. Freesmeier, age 38
Auditors: Ernst & Young
Employees: 21,100

WHERE

HQ: 501 N. Broadway, St. Louis, MO 63102-2196
Phone: 314-331-6000
Fax: 314-331-7200

Edison Brothers operates 2,733 stores in all 50 states and Puerto Rico.

WHAT

	1990 Sales		1990 Operating Income	
	$ mil.	% of total	$ mil.	% of total
Footwear	461	37	28	26
Apparel	754	60	84	76
Other	39	3	(4)	(2)
Total	**1,254**	**100**	**108**	**100**

Men's Apparel	No. of stores
Big & Tall	12
Coda	51
J. Riggings	322
Jeans West	477
Oaktree	290
Webster	123
Total	**1,275**

Women's Apparel	No. of stores
5-7-9 Shops	391
Joan Bari/Cabaret	60
Total	**451**

Footwear	No. of stores
Bakers/Leeds	578
Sacha London	23
The Wild Pair/Velocity	262
Leased departments	11
Total	**874**

Entertainment	No. of stores
Dave & Buster's	2
Mall entertainment	131
Total	**133**

RANKINGS

711th in *Business Week* 1000

KEY COMPETITORS

Brown Group	Marks & Spencer
Carter Hawley Hale	May
Dayton Hudson	Melville
General Cinema	Nordstrom
Hartmarx	U.S. Shoe
INTERCO	Wal-Mart
Kmart	Other department stores
The Limited	

HOW MUCH

	9-Year Growth	1981	1982	1983	1984	1985	1986	1987	1988	1989	1990
Sales ($ mil.)	3.1%	951	916	1,022	1,055	808	904	931	919	1,074	1,254
Net income ($ mil.)	3.4%	44	23	49	33	22	34	(21)	36	61	59
Income as % of sales	—	4.6%	2.5%	4.8%	3.1%	2.7%	3.8%	(2.2%)	4.0%	5.7%	4.7%
Earnings per share ($)	3.9%	1.92	1.04	2.23	1.58	1.06	1.66	(1.05)	1.79	2.95	2.71
Stock price – high ($)	—	15.63	14.75	23.38	21.50	19.13	21.88	22.00	17.25	35.13	48.88
Stock price – low ($)	—	11.88	10.13	12.88	16.25	15.50	16.25	10.94	12.31	16.00	17.50
Stock price – close ($)	6.8%	12.50	13.69	20.88	16.75	17.31	16.94	12.75	16.13	31.75	22.63
P/E – high	—	8	14	11	14	18	13	—	10	12	18
P/E – low	—	6	10	6	10	15	10	—	7	5	6
Dividends per share ($)	4.7%	0.69	0.72	0.74	0.80	0.80	0.80	0.90	0.90	0.94	1.04
Book value per share ($)	3.6%	11.64	11.98	13.41	13.94	10.63	11.31	9.75	10.62	12.01	16.06

1990 Year-end:
Debt ratio: 29.7%
Return on equity: 19.3%
Cash (mil.): $49
Current ratio: 1.75
Long-term debt (mil.): $145
No. of shares (mil.): 21
Dividends:
  1990 average yield: 4.6%
  1990 payout: 38.4%
Market value (mil.): $484

Stock Price History High/Low 1981–90

EDWARD J. DEBARTOLO CORPORATION

Private company

OVERVIEW

Edward J. DeBartolo Corporation, based in the founder's hometown of Youngstown, Ohio, is a leading builder and operator of enclosed shopping malls in the US. It placed 3rd among retail developers in 1990 growth, with over 3 million square feet completed and nearly 17 million square feet in new construction starts. The company's 76 million square feet of mall space makes up nearly 10% of all mall space in the country and is visited by approximately 40 million customers each week.

Although some of the malls are managed for others or operated as joint ventures, most of the sites are owned directly by the company. Recently built urban malls, such as New Orleans Centre and The Rivercenter in San Antonio, ride the trend toward downtown "urban centers."

DeBartolo also owns and manages 18 smaller strip shopping centers, with more planned or under construction.

The company uses promotions and gimmicks to increase business in its malls. These include mall credit cards, frequent shopper prizes, shopper magazines, and an exercise program promoted by Richard Simmons.

DeBartolo also owns 50% of Cleveland's Higbee's department stores, in a joint venture with Dillard's. In addition, the company develops and operates office buildings, office parks, and hotels. DeBartolo's sports holdings include the San Francisco 49ers (the most successful football team of the 1980s), the Pittsburgh Penguins hockey team, and horse tracks in Ohio, Louisiana, and Oklahoma.

WHO

Chairman and CEO: Edward J. DeBartolo, age 81
President and COO: Edward J. DeBartolo, Jr., age 44
EVP Personnel and Public Relations: Marie Denise DeBartolo York, age 39
SVP Corporate Planning and Finance and CFO: Anthony Liberati
Asst. VP Human Resources: Irving M. Kravitz
Auditors: Deloitte & Touche
Employees: 15,000

WHERE

HQ: 7620 Market St., PO Box 3287, Youngstown, OH 44513-6085
Phone: 216-758-7292
Fax: 216-758-3598

DeBartolo maintains and operates 76 million square feet of mall space across the US. Regional branches are in Pittsburgh, Miami, Orlando, Dallas, Indianapolis, Cleveland, and Seattle.

WHEN

Edward J. DeBartolo left his stepfather's paving business in 1948 to establish the company that bears his name. He built subsidized housing in Boardman, Ohio (near Youngstown) for young WWII veterans who were anxious to move to the suburbs. DeBartolo's foresight of the growth of the suburbs led him to build one of the first strip-style malls outside California in Boardman in 1950. Over the next 15 years the company built 45 more strip centers throughout the US.

DeBartolo also anticipated the real estate boom in Florida and bought large tracts of land there in the 1960s. Although the market developed later than DeBartolo had expected, the company had 1/3 of its holdings there when the boom did hit. Also in the 1960s DeBartolo became one of the first to develop large, covered regional malls in many parts of the nation.

DeBartolo opened Louisiana Downs, the first of his racetracks, in 1974; the track closed after 50 days of racing because it could not meet its payroll on time. With better economic times in the late 1970s, the track prospered. DeBartolo expanded his sports interests when he bought the San Francisco 49ers in 1977. The Pittsburgh Penguins came under DeBartolo ownership in 1978 when he received them as repayment for a debt.

In 1986 the management of Allied Stores asked DeBartolo to help fend off a bid by Campeau. DeBartolo, recognizing that control of Allied's department store chains would

complement his mall development activities by providing anchor stores, instead loaned Campeau $150 million for the takeover. In 1988 he stepped in with a $480 million loan to Campeau for its acquisition of Federated Department Stores. In 1990 DeBartolo acquired a 60.3% stake in Ralphs Grocery Co., a successful Southern California supermarket owned by Campeau, in exchange for forgiveness of the Federated debt.

Meanwhile, DeBartolo has continued to expand his other interests, opening the newest of his racetracks, Remington Park, in Oklahoma City in 1988. The $94 million racetrack's location was chosen because the company's research indicated that Oklahoma City had the highest number of horses per capita in the US (one horse for every 14 people); the location was a success, with 11,000 people going to the track each race day.

The Rivercenter (San Antonio) and Lakeland Square (Florida) malls also opened in 1988, with over one million square feet apiece; Chesapeake Square (Virginia) and Port Charlotte Town Center (Florida) opened in 1989. DeBartolo in 1991 opened malls in Texas, Virginia, Tennessee, and Illinois.

DeBartolo's son Edward Jr. serves as owner of the 49ers as well as president and COO of the company. DeBartolo's daughter Marie Denise York is credited with developing employee programs that have become models for the industry.

WHAT

Retail Stores
Higbee's, Cleveland (50%, department store)
Ralphs Grocery Co., Los Angeles (60.3%, supermarket)

Major Malls
Aventura Mall, Miami
Castleton Square, Indianapolis
Century III Mall, Pittsburgh
CoolSprings Galleria, Nashville
Dadeland Mall, Miami
The Florida Mall, Orlando
Great Lakes Mall, Cleveland
Illinois Centre, Marion, IL
Lafayette Square, Indianapolis
Mall of the Mainland, Texas City, TX
Northshore Shopping Center, Peabody, MA
Randall Park Mall, Cleveland
Rivercenter, San Antonio, TX
Sherman Oaks Galleria, Los Angeles
Virginia Center Commons, Richmond

Office Projects and Hotels
Brickell Bay Office Tower, Miami
CNG Tower, New Orleans
DeBartolo Square, Pittsburgh (under development)
Sheraton Plaza Hotel at The Florida Mall, Orlando

Sports Enterprises and Complexes
Civic Arena, Pittsburgh
Remington Park, Oklahoma City (racetrack)
San Francisco 49ers (football)
Louisiana Downs, Shreveport (racetrack)
Thistle Downs, Cleveland (racetrack)

RANKINGS

103rd in *Forbes* 400 US Private Cos.

KEY COMPETITORS

Albertson's	Helmsley	Sears
American Stores	Longs	Trammell Crow
Campeau	Paramount	Vons
Green Bay Packers		

Other real estate development companies

HOW MUCH

	4-Year Growth	1981	1982	1983	1984	1985	1986	1987	1988	1989	1990
Revenues ($ mil.)	28.2%	—	—	—	—	—	500	650	1,066	1,189	1,350
No. of employees	8.1%	—	—	—	—	—	11,000	12,000	12,000	15,000	15,000
Total sq. ft. under construction (thou.)	—	—	—	—	—	—	—	—	—	12,377	11,541

Revenues ($ mil.) 1986–90

[Bar chart showing Revenues ($ mil.) from 1986 to 1990, y-axis from 0 to 1,400 in increments of 200]

EG&G, INC.

OVERVIEW

Wellesley, Massachusetts–based EG&G is composed of more than 50 companies providing thousands of technologically advanced products and services to both government and commercial entities.

Under government contracts the company is active in engineering, developmental, and site-management programs related to national defense and security, physics and space research, and nuclear and non-nuclear energy research and development. EG&G's largest business segment provides direct support for the Department of Energy through 6 management contracts related to nuclear weapons testing and other energy research.

In the commercial sector EG&G provides technical and management services to the auto industry and the NSF. The company manufactures components for aircraft (including the Stealth Fighter and Boeing's 737 and 767 commercial jets) and launch systems for space vehicles. While continuing a strategy of diversification into new markets, EG&G currently provides components and instruments for radiation detection, security systems, optoelectronics, and industrial measurement.

Its latest DOE contract — providing support at the Rocky Flats nuclear weapons components facility — helped to boost EG&G's earnings by 50% in 1990.

NYSE symbol: EGG
Fiscal year ends: December 31

Hoover's Rating **A**

WHO

Chairman and CEO: John M. Kucharski, age 55, $505,356 pay
President: Donald M. Kerr, age 51, $379,869 pay
SVP and CFO: John R. Dolan, age 64
VP Human Resources: Richard F. Murphy, age 54
Auditors: Arthur Andersen & Co.
Employees: 32,000

WHERE

HQ: 45 William St., Wellesley, MA 02181
Phone: 617-237-5100
Fax: 617-431-4115

EG&G has operations in 29 states and 16 foreign countries.

	1990 Sales		1990 Operating Income	
	$ mil.	% of total	$ mil.	% of total
US	2,300	93	113	86
Other countries	174	7	18	14
Adjustments	—	—	(23)	—
Total	**2,474**	**100**	**108**	**100**

WHAT

	1990 Sales		1990 Operating Income	
	$ mil.	% of total	$ mil.	% of total
Instruments	208	8	6	5
Components	241	10	26	20
Technical services	311	13	28	20
Aerospace	131	5	6	5
Defense	246	10	21	16
DOE support	1,337	54	44	34
Adjustments	—	—	(23)	—
Total	**2,474**	**100**	**108**	**100**

Instruments
Analyzer systems
Digital delay generators
Flow calibrators
Measurement systems
Multichannel analyzers
Plasma monitors
Radiation detectors
Sonar systems
Spectrometers
Surface barrier detectors
X-ray screening equipment

Components
"Atomic" clocks
Electromechanical products
Flashtubes
Laser systems
Light detectors
Photodiodes
Seals

Technical Services
Automotive precision testing
Chemical decontamination training

Institutional, technical, and maintenance support at Kennedy Space Center
Nuclear technical and engineering support

Aerospace
Aircraft exhaust components
Military aircraft, missile, and spacecraft subassemblies and components
Static metal seals
Turbine engine valves

Defense
Chemical weapons disposal services
Technical and operational support to the DOD

DOE Support Services
Nuclear weapons technical and nontechnical support

WHEN

MIT professor Harold Edgerton invented the strobe light in 1931 while researching the operation of electric motors. After failing to sell the new device to General Electric, he and former student Kenneth Germeshausen formed a consulting business using the strobe light and high-speed photography to help manufacturers solve industrial problems. As business picked up, they brought in another former student, Herbert Grier, and in 1947 formed Edgerton, Germeshausen and Grier. Their first contract (which continues to the present day) was to use high-speed photographic techniques to record the explosions of nuclear weapons being tested by the government. The company went public in 1959.

After changing its name to EG&G in 1966, the company started to move away from being a one-contract firm through a program of expansion and diversification involving internal growth and acquisitions of existing companies. Over the past 25 years EG&G has bought over 70 companies involved in electronic instruments and components, biomedical services, energy research and development (nuclear, geothermal, coal, oil, and gas), nuclear weapons research and development, manufacture of seals and gaskets, automotive testing, and various aspects of the aerospace industry. Key

acquisitions included Reynolds Electrical & Engineering (1967), which provides support services for the DOE and DOD, including the nuclear weapons testing program; Sealol (1968), a worldwide manufacturer of seals for industrial applications; and Automotive Research Associates (1973).

EG&G started providing institutional management and technical support at the Kennedy Space Center in Florida in 1983. In 1988 the company secured 2 important DOE contracts: first, to manage and operate the DOE's Mound facility in Miamisburg, Ohio, which is involved in R&D and production in the fields of components for nuclear weapons and nuclear electric generators for use in spacecraft; and 2nd, to support Universities Research Association in the development of the DOE's Superconducting Super Collider project in Texas. In 1990 EG&G took over operation of the DOE's Rocky Flats nuclear weapons components production facility near Golden, Colorado. That year founder Harold Edgerton died at age 86.

Recently, EG&G bought the optoelectronics businesses of General Electric Canada (1990) and agreed to buy control of Heimann, a German manufacturer of optoelectronic devices, from Siemens (1991).

RANKINGS

182nd in *Fortune* 500 Industrial Cos.
502nd in *Business Week* 1000

KEY COMPETITORS

Allied-Signal	Hewlett-Packard	Texas
Becton, Dickinson	Martin Marietta	Instruments
General Signal	Nissan	Thiokol
	Raytheon	Thomson SA

HOW MUCH

	9-Year Growth	1981	1982	1983	1984	1985	1986	1987	1988	1989	1990
Sales ($ mil.)	15.0%	704	801	904	1,072	1,155	1,145	1,236	1,406	1,650	2,474
Net income ($ mil.)	9.0%	34	40	47	54	56	45	55	69	70	74
Income as % of sales	—	4.8%	5.0%	5.2%	5.0%	4.8%	3.9%	4.5%	4.9%	4.2%	3.0%
Earnings per share ($)	9.3%	1.17	1.33	1.53	1.85	2.07	1.65	2.00	2.30	2.40	2.60
Stock price – high ($)	—	22.00	30.63	38.13	36.13	43.00	43.00	45.13	39.00	36.50	41.00
Stock price – low ($)	—	16.19	14.50	26.00	26.13	31.25	27.63	27.00	26.63	28.38	28.00
Stock price – close ($)	5.1%	19.75	28.25	32.50	31.63	38.38	28.25	33.25	28.75	34.00	31.00
P/E – high	—	19	23	25	20	21	26	23	17	15	16
P/E – low	—	14	11	17	14	15	17	14	12	12	11
Dividends per share ($)	13.2%	0.25	0.32	0.36	0.40	0.48	0.52	0.56	0.60	0.68	0.76
Book value per share ($)	11.7%	4.86	5.93	7.13	5.59	7.47	8.62	9.79	11.07	12.04	13.16

1990 Year-end:
Debt ratio: 1.9%
Return on equity: 20.6%
Cash (mil.): $34
Current ratio: 1.58
Long-term debt (mil.): $7
No. of shares (mil.): 28
Dividends:
  1990 average yield: 2.5%
  1990 payout: 29.2%
Market value (mil.): $871

**Stock Price History
High/Low 1981–90**

ELI LILLY AND COMPANY

NYSE symbol: LLY
Fiscal year ends: December 31

Hoover's Rating A+

OVERVIEW

Indianapolis-based drug company Eli Lilly is a major supplier of several important antibiotics and has been known for decades to diabetics for its life-saving insulin. The company's primary products include the antidepressant Prozac, the antibiotic Ceclor, and Humulin insulin. Lilly has an impressive 10 drugs that bring in over $100 million annually. The company also makes medical devices (including monitors and pacemakers), diagnostic products, and animal health products.

Lilly's R&D expenditures (13.5% of sales) are among the highest in the industry. Major targets of its research include new antibiotics, anticancer agents, and drugs to control such disorders as schizophrenia, epilepsy, and Alzheimer's disease.

In 1991 Lilly fell victim to a smear campaign launched by the Church of Scientology. The group, which traditionally has harbored a loathing for psychiatrists and psychiatric drugs, claimed that Prozac triggered psychotic and suicidal reactions in its users. The claims were unsubstantiated but nevertheless cut Prozac's antidepressant market share from 25% to 21%.

WHO

Chairman, President, and CEO: Vaughn D. Bryson, age 53, $914,218 pay (prior to promotion)
VP Finance and CFO: James M. Cornelius, age 47
VP Human Resources: Stephen A. Stitle
Auditors: Ernst & Young
Employees: 29,900

WHERE

HQ: Lilly Corporate Center, Indianapolis, IN 46285
Phone: 317-276-2000
Fax: 317-276-2095

The company sells its products in over 120 countries.

	1990 Sales		1990 Pretax Income	
	$ mil.	% of total	$ mil.	% of total
US	3,315	64	1,135	71
Japan, Middle East & Europe	1,442	28	381	24
Other countries	435	8	87	5
Adjustments	—	—	(4)	—
Total	**5,192**	**100**	**1,599**	**100**

WHEN

Colonel Eli Lilly, pharmacist and Union officer in the Civil War, opened Eli Lilly & Company in Indianapolis in 1876 with $1,300. By 1881 sales had reached $81,637. Colonel Lilly developed a process in 1879 for coating pills with gelatin, and later the company made gelatin capsules, which it continues to sell today. After Lilly died in 1898, his son and 2 grandsons successively headed the company until 1953.

Following an intensive research effort, Lilly introduced insulin in 1923. To extract one ounce of the substance in those days, the pancreas glands of 6,000 cattle or 24,000 hogs had to be processed. Other Lilly products created in the 1920s and 1930s included liver extracts (for pernicious anemia), digitalis preparations (for heart disease), Merthiolate (an antiseptic), and Seconal (a powerful sedative). Sales went from $13 million in 1932 to $72 million by the end of WWII. In 1952 Lilly researchers isolated the antibiotic erythromycin from a species of mold found in the Philippines. In the 1950s Lilly produced more than 60% of Salk vaccine supplies. In the 1950s and 1960s the company opened manufacturing plants overseas.

Diversification began in the 1970s with the purchase of Elizabeth Arden (cosmetics, 1971) and IVAC (medical instruments, 1977). Lilly's Darvon captured 80% of the prescription analgesic market. Increases in R&D spending resulted in new antibiotics, including Ceclor (1979). In the 1980s antibiotics accounted for about 1/3 of Lilly's sales.

Not all Lilly products have been wonder drugs. Since 1974 the company has been involved in litigation over DES (diethylstilbestrol; widely used until 1971, it may have caused cancer and other problems in children whose mothers took the drug) and lost a $6 million lawsuit in 1983 over a death caused by the arthritis drug Oraflex. The company halted distribution at one of its plants in 1989 for quality-control problems after an FDA investigation.

In 1982 Lilly became the first company to market a biotechnology product when it introduced Humulin (licensed from Genentech), a genetically engineered insulin identical to human insulin. In 1986 Lilly acquired Hybritech, a biotechnology company, for more than $300 million. In 1987 the company sold Elizabeth Arden to a subsidiary of Riklis Family Corporation.

In 1988 Lilly introduced Axid (antiulcer drug) and Prozac. Amidst the controversy surrounding Prozac, the company in 1991 offered to pay for the legal representation of any doctor who is sued after prescribing the drug.

WHAT

	1990 Sales	
	$ mil.	% of total
Anti-infectives	1,604	31
Medical devices & diagnostics	1,013	19
Central nervous system products	1,006	19
Diabetic care	552	11
Animal health products	351	7
Other products	666	13
Total	**5,192**	**100**

Selected Pharmaceuticals
Axid (antiulcer drug)
Ceclor (antibiotic)
Darvon (analgesic)
Dobutrex (cardiovascular)
Humatrope (hormones)
Humulin (diabetic care)
Prozac (antidepressant)
Tazidime (antibiotic)
Vancocin (antibiotic)

Subsidiaries
Advanced Cardiovascular Systems, Inc. (balloon catheter systems)
Cardiac Pacemakers, Inc.

Devices for Vascular Intervention, Inc. (catheter systems)
Elanco Products Co. (animal health products)
Elco Diagnostics Co. (diagnostic products)
Hybritech, Inc. (immunodiagnostic products)
IVAC Corp. (patient-monitoring systems)
Physio-Control Corp. (cardiac monitors)

RANKINGS

103rd in *Fortune* 500 Industrial Cos.
19th in *Business Week* 1000

KEY COMPETITORS

Abbott Labs
American Cyanamid
American Home Products
Amgen
C. R. Bard
Baxter
Bayer
Becton, Dickinson

Bristol-Myers Squibb
Ciba-Geigy
Dow Chemical
Du Pont
Genentech
Glaxo
Hoechst
Johnson & Johnson
Merck
Monsanto

Pfizer
Rhône-Poulenc
Roche
Sandoz
Schering-Plough
SmithKline Beecham
Syntex
Upjohn
Warner-Lambert

HOW MUCH

	9-Year Growth	1981	1982	1983	1984	1985	1986	1987	1988	1989	1990
Sales ($ mil.)	7.2%	2,773	2,963	3,034	3,109	3,271	3,720	3,644	4,070	4,176	5,192
Net income ($ mil.)	13.0%	374	412	457	490	518	558	411	761	940	1,127
Income as % of sales	—	13.5%	13.9%	15.1%	15.8%	15.8%	15.0%	11.3%	18.7%	22.5%	21.7%
Earnings per share ($)	13.7%	1.23	1.35	1.52	1.67	1.81	1.95	1.42	2.67	3.20	3.90
Stock price – high ($)	—	17.19	16.31	17.09	16.91	27.97	41.75	53.88	45.88	68.50	90.38
Stock price – low ($)	—	11.31	11.28	14.13	13.25	16.09	25.13	28.88	35.38	42.38	58.75
Stock price – close ($)	20.2%	14.00	14.38	14.47	16.50	27.88	37.13	39.00	42.75	68.50	73.25
P/E – high	—	14	12	11	10	15	21	38	17	21	23
P/E – low	—	9	8	9	8	9	13	20	13	13	15
Dividends per share ($)	12.0%	0.59	0.65	0.69	0.74	0.80	0.90	1.00	1.15	1.35	1.64
Book value per share ($)	8.5%	6.21	6.78	7.22	7.76	8.56	9.85	10.92	11.76	13.48	12.98

1990 Year-end:
Debt ratio: 7.4%
Return on equity: 29.5%
Cash (mil.): $751
Current ratio: 0.89
Long-term debt (mil.): $277
No. of shares (mil.): 267
Dividends:
  1990 average yield: 2.2%
  1990 payout: 42.1%
Market value (mil.): $19,568

Stock Price History High/Low 1981–90

EMERSON ELECTRIC CO.

OVERVIEW

Emerson, the 7th largest maker of electrical and electronic products in the US, had its 33rd straight year of higher earnings in 1990.

Emerson's 40 companies supply industrial, commercial, and individual users. Products include electric motors (world's largest manufacturer); uninterruptable power supplies for computers; meters and instrumentation; switches and valves; compressors; and heating, ventilating, and air conditioning equipment. Consumer products include saws, drills, and sanders.

Emerson has a first- or 2nd-ranked product in 86% of its markets (up from 78% in 1980);

some of the leaders include In-Sink-Erator kitchen waste disposers and Ridgid commercial hand and power tools. Throughout the 1980s Emerson strove to be a "best cost producer" and maintain its earnings growth by moving thousands of jobs overseas and to non-union US plants.

Expanding international sales accounted for 30% of Emerson's business in 1990, and the company has acquired several firms in Europe and Asia. Emerson has joint ventures in 15 countries, with total sales of $1.5 billion.

NYSE symbol: EMR
Fiscal year ends: September 30

Hoover's Rating **A**

WHO

Chairman and CEO: Charles F. Knight, age 54, $1,774,288 pay
President and COO: A. E. Suter, age 55, $650,000 pay
VC and Chief Administrative Officer: R. W. Staley, age 55, $475,000 pay
SVP Finance and Controller: W. J. Galvin, age 44
SVP Industrial Relations: J. C. Rohrbaugh
Auditors: KPMG Peat Marwick
Employees: 73,700

WHERE

HQ: 8000 W. Florissant Ave., PO Box 4100, St. Louis, MO 63136
Phone: 314-553-2000
Fax: 314-553-3527

Emerson has 197 plants in 16 countries.

	1990 Sales		1990 Pretax Income	
	$ mil.	% of total	$ mil.	% of total
US	5,308	70	719	73
Europe	1,797	24	187	19
Other foreign	468	6	82	8
Adjustments	—	—	1	—
Total	**7,573**	**100**	**989**	**100**

WHAT

	1990 Sales		1990 Pretax Income	
	$ mil.	% of total	$ mil.	% of total
Commercial & industrial prods.	5,810	77	830	77
Consumer products	1,154	15	221	20
Government & defense products	609	8	28	3
Adjustments	—	—	(90)	—
Total	**7,573**	**100**	**989**	**100**

Major Business Units
ASCO/Joucomatic (pneumatic and solenoid valves)
Astec (47%, power supplies)
Branson (ultrasound equipment)
CESET (appliance motors)
Copeland (HVAC compressors)
Emerson Motors
In-Sink-Erator (waste disposers)
Leroy-Somer (industrial motors)
Liebert (power supplies)
Louisville Ladder
McGill (power transmission equipment)
Ridge Tool (Ridgid commercial hand and power tools)
Rosemount (process control systems)
Skil (power tools)
Vermont American (power and hand tools, 50% joint venture with Robert Bosch)
Western Forge (Sears Craftsman hand tools)
White-Rodgers (thermostats and gas controls)

WHEN

Emerson was cofounded in St. Louis in 1890 by Alexander and Charles Meston, inventors of an alternating-current electric motor based on the pioneering work of Nikola Tesla. The inventors were backed by venture capitalist (and former judge and US marshal) John Emerson. Their most widely recognized product was an adaptation of the electric motor — the electric fan, first introduced in 1892. The company also put its motors to use in player pianos, hair dryers, sewing machines, and water pumps. In the 1910s the company played a part in developing the first forced-air circulating systems.

The Great Depression and labor problems in the 1930s nearly forced Emerson into bankruptcy. New developments, including a hermetic motor for refrigerators, pulled the company back from the brink, and Emerson's electric motors were adapted to new uses during WWII, particularly in aircraft. Emerson also made the gun turret for the B-24 bomber.

The company, having grown dependent on defense business, suffered again in postwar years. Former football coach Wallace Persons took over as president in 1954 and began turning Emerson into a major manufacturer of electrical products.

Beginning in the early 1960s, Persons bought a number of smaller companies: White-Rodgers (1962, thermostats and gas controls),

Ridge (1966, Ridgid tools), In-Sink-Erator (1968), Browning (1969, power transmission products), Harris (1973, welding and cutting tools), and Louisville Ladder (1973). Persons retired in 1974, having boosted sales from $56 million in 1954 to $800 million in 1973.

Former college footballer Chuck Knight, who was only 37 when he became CEO in 1974, changed the company's character again, taking Emerson into high-tech and expanding its hardware segment. Acquisitions included Varec (1975, chemical and petroleum measurement systems), Rosemount (1976, industrial measurement and control systems), Weed Eater (1977, Skil (1979, power tools), Western Forge (1981, Sears Craftsman hand tools), Beckman Industrial (1984, analytical and electrical instruments), Hazeltine (1986, defense electronics), and Liebert (1987, computer support systems).

With defense spending expected to decline, Emerson spun off Hazeltine and other businesses in 1990 as ESCO Electronics. Emerson also bought European motor-makers Leroy-Somer (France) and CESET (Italy) and a 47% stake in Hong Kong–based Astec (power supplies), thus increasing its international positions. The company also bought 50% of toolmaker Vermont American in a joint venture with Robert Bosch.

RANKINGS

66th in *Fortune* 500 Industrial Cos.
56th in *Business Week* 1000

KEY COMPETITORS

ABB	Honeywell
Black & Decker	Reliance Electric
Cooper Industries	Snap-on Tools
Dana	Square D
General Electric	Stanley Works
General Signal	

HOW MUCH

	9-Year Growth	1981	1982	1983	1984	1985	1986	1987	1988	1989	1990
Sales ($ mil.)	9.2%	3,429	3,502	3,476	4,179	4,649	4,953	6,170	6,652	7,071	7,573
Net income ($ mil.)	9.4%	273	300	303	349	401	409	467	529	588	613
Income as % of sales	—	8.0%	8.6%	8.7%	8.4%	8.6%	8.3%	7.6%	8.0%	8.3%	8.1%
Earnings per share ($)	7.6%	1.42	1.46	1.47	1.70	1.81	1.87	2.00	2.31	2.63	2.75
Stock price – high ($)	—	16.58	21.33	22.96	23.92	27.50	30.88	41.92	36.00	39.88	44.38
Stock price – low ($)	—	12.00	13.29	18.29	19.38	22.25	26.04	26.75	27.25	29.50	30.75
Stock price – close ($)	10.7%	15.13	20.17	22.17	23.17	27.08	27.92	34.63	30.38	39.00	37.75
P/E – high	—	12	15	16	14	15	16	21	16	15	16
P/E – low	—	8	9	12	11	12	14	13	12	11	11
Dividends per share ($)	8.9%	0.59	0.67	0.70	0.77	0.87	0.92	0.97	1.00	1.12	1.26
Book value per share ($)	7.1%	7.23	7.58	8.28	9.09	10.03	10.90	11.68	12.51	13.79	13.39

1990 Year-end:
Debt ratio: 14.2%
Return on equity: 20.2%
Cash (mil.): $98
Current ratio: 1.34
Long-term debt (mil.): $496
No. of shares (mil.): 223
Dividends:
 1990 average yield: 3.3%
 1990 payout: 45.8%
Market value (mil.): $8,431

Stock Price History High/Low 1981–90

ENRON CORP.

NYSE symbol: ENE
Fiscal year ends: December 31

Hoover's Rating **C**

OVERVIEW

Houston-based Enron, America's leading integrated natural gas company, touts natural gas as the clean-burning fuel of the future that will finally reduce the nation's dependence on foreign oil. The core of its operation is a 38,000-mile natural gas pipeline system — the nation's largest — which in 1990 delivered 8.2 billion cubic feet of gas daily (about 18% of America's natural gas consumption). Enron is America's 5th largest natural gas processor and a leading worldwide marketer of natural gas liquids (selling 3.3 billion gallons of gas liquids in 1990). It owns 84% of Enron Oil & Gas, one of America's largest nonintegrated oil and gas companies.

An active participant in the development of new gas technologies, Enron is building a cogeneration plant (a gas-fired facility that simultaneously produces steam and electricity) on the northeast coast of Scotland. This plant, which will be the world's largest cogeneration plant, is expected to go on line in 1993. The company is also developing a "gas bank" by pooling supply commitments from various producers to create long-term contracts for industrial users.

WHO

Chairman and CEO: Kenneth L. Lay, age 48, $1,536,393 pay
President and COO: Richard D. Kinder, age 46, $1,026,346 pay
SVP and CFO: Jack I. Tompkins, age 45, $436,660 pay
VP Human Resources: James E. Street
Auditors: Arthur Andersen & Co.
Employees: 6,962

WHERE

HQ: 1400 Smith St., Houston, TX 77002-7369
Phone: 713-853-6161
Fax: 713-853-3129

Enron operates a 38,000-mile network of gas pipelines serving California, Texas, Florida, and the Midwest. The company explores for oil and gas primarily in the US and Canada. It builds cogeneration facilties in the US and the UK.

	1990 Pretax Income	
	$ mil.	% of total
US	232	89
Other countries	28	11
Total	**260**	**100**

WHEN

Enron traces its history through 2 well-established natural gas companies — InterNorth and Houston Natural Gas (HNG).

InterNorth started out in 1930 as Northern Natural Gas, an Omaha, Nebraska, gas pipeline company. By 1950 Northern had doubled its capacity and in 1960 started processing and transporting natural gas liquids. The company changed its name to InterNorth in 1980. In 1983 it spent $768 million to buy Belco Petroleum, adding 821 billion cubic feet of natural gas and 67 million barrels of oil to its reserves. At the same time, the company (with 4 partners) was building the Northern Border Pipeline to link Canadian producing fields with US markets.

HNG, formed in 1925 as a South Texas natural gas distributor, served more than 55,000 customers by the early 1940s. It started developing producing oil and gas properties in 1953 and bought Houston Pipe Line Company in 1956. Other major acquisitions included Valley Gas Production, a South Texas natural gas company (1963), and Houston's Bammel Gas Storage Field (1965). In the 1970s the company started developing offshore fields in the Gulf of Mexico, and in 1976 it sold its original gas distribution properties to Entex. In 1984 HNG, faced with a hostile takeover attempt by Coastal Corporation, brought in former Exxon executive Kenneth Lay as CEO.

Lay refocused the company on its natural gas businesses by selling $632 million worth of unrelated assets. The company added Transwestern Pipeline (California) and Florida Gas Transmission to its system and operated the only transcontinental gas pipeline by 1985.

In 1985 InterNorth ($7.5 billion in 1984 sales) bought HNG ($2.0 billion in 1984 sales) for $2.4 billion, creating America's largest natural gas pipeline system (37,000 miles). Soon after the sale, Kenneth Lay became chairman and CEO of the new company, named Enron in 1986. That year Enron moved its headquarters from Omaha to Houston.

Laden with $3.3 billion of debt (most related to the HNG acquisition), Enron raised cash by selling 50% of Citrus Corportation (operates Florida Gas Transmssion, 1986), 50% of Enron Cogeneration (1988), and 16% of Enron Oil & Gas (1989). In the meantime the company paid $31 million for Tesoro Petroleum's gathering and transporation businesses in 1988.

In 1990 the company bought CSX Energy's Louisiana production facilities, which helped to increase Enron's production of natural gas liquids by nearly 33%. Enron also benefited from higher oil prices that year, which combined with increased production volumes to produce a 25% growth in revenues.

WHAT

	1990 Sales		1990 Operating Income	
	$ mil.	% of total	$ mil.	% of total
Natural gas	3,278	25	227	52
Oil & gas	196	1	42	10
Liquid fuel	9,691	74	165	38
Adjustments	—	—	(3)	—
Total	**13,165**	**100**	**431**	**100**

Natural Gas
Enron Gas Services Group (natural gas services)
Enron Power Corp. (cogeneration facilities)
Major pipelines companies
  Florida Gas Transmission Co. (50%, 4,400-mile pipeline from South Texas to Florida)
  Houston Pipe Line Co. (5,500-mile pipeline in Texas)
  Northern Border Pipeline Co. (35%, 822-mile pipeline from the US-Canadian border to Iowa)
  Northern Natural Gas Co. (23,500-mile pipeline from Texas to the Minnesota-Canadian border)
  Transwestern Pipeline Co. (4,500-mile pipeline from West Texas and southern Oklahoma to California)

Exploration and Production
Enron Exploration Co.
Enron Oil & Gas Co. (84%)
Enron Oil Canada, Ltd.

Liquid Fuels
Enron Americas, Inc.
Enron Gas Liquids, Inc.
Enron Gas Processing Co.
Enron Liquids Pipeline Co.
Enron Oil Trading & Transportation Co.

RANKINGS

2nd in *Fortune* 100 Diversified Service Cos.
238th in *Business Week* 1000

HOW MUCH

	9-Year Growth	1981	1982	1983	1984	1985	1986	1987	1988	1989	1990
Sales ($ mil.)	15.3%	3,655	4,159	4,997	7,510	10,253	7,453	5,916	5,708	9,836	13,165
Net income ($ mil.)	(2.0%)	243	181	255	297	125	(108)	54	130	226	202
Income as % of sales	—	6.7%	4.4%	5.1%	4.0%	1.2%	(1.4%)	0.9%	2.3%	2.3%	1.5%
Earnings per share ($)	(4.9%)	5.43	4.06	5.11	5.19	1.74	(3.53)	0.63	2.13	3.85	3.44
Stock price – high ($)	—	43.50	32.00	41.00	42.50	54.63	50.63	53.50	43.00	61.00	62.75
Stock price – low ($)	—	27.50	21.00	24.13	32.75	39.00	33.75	31.00	34.88	35.50	50.25
Stock price – close ($)	6.4%	31.25	26.75	39.50	42.25	45.00	39.50	39.13	36.63	57.63	54.75
P/E – high	—	8	8	8	8	31	—	85	20	16	18
P/E – low	—	5	5	5	6	22	—	49	16	9	15
Dividends per share ($)	2.7%	1.96	2.12	2.22	2.40	2.48	2.48	2.48	2.48	2.48	2.48
Book value per share ($)	0.8%	29.91	30.80	33.28	35.60	28.03	21.68	29.33	29.54	30.76	32.09

1990 Year-end:
Debt ratio: 61.6%
Return on equity: 10.9%
Cash (mil.): $214
Current ratio: 0.88
Long-term debt (mil.): $2,983
No. of shares (mil.): 50
Dividends:
  1990 average yield: 4.5%
  1990 payout: 72.1%
Market value (mil.): $2,762

Stock Price History
High/Low 1981–90

KEY COMPETITORS

Coastal
Columbia Gas
Koch
Occidental
Panhandle Eastern
Public Service Enterprise
Tenneco

ENTERGY CORPORATION

NYSE symbol: ETR
Fiscal year ends: December 31

OVERVIEW

Entergy provides electricity to more than 1.7 million customers in Arkansas, Louisiana, Mississippi, and southeastern Missouri through 4 operating utilities: Arkansas Power & Light (AP&L), Louisiana Power & Light (LP&L), Mississippi Power & Light (MP&L), and New Orleans Public Service, Inc. (NOPSI).

In a cost-cutting effort, Entergy is streamlining operations along functional lines. This strategy has proven to be successful in the company's new nuclear subsidiary (Entergy Operations), where costs remained under budget in 1990 despite unexpected expenses at Arkansas Nuclear One. The company also

launched an employee incentive program ("pay for performance") that helped to save Entergy some $17 million in operations and maintenance costs in 1990. To foster future growth, Entergy is investigating possible investments or acquisitions to expand its service area.

Electec (another Entergy subsidiary) is involved in several joint agreements; one, with Coopers & Lybrand, will market Customer Information System software. Electec is also working to develop a telecommunications system for Costa Rica (with First Pacific Networks of California).

WHO

Chairman and CEO: Edwin Lupberger, age 54, $756,568 pay
VC: James M. Cain, age 57, $554,672 pay (prior to promotion)
SVP and System Executive Operations: Jack L. King, age 51
SVP and CFO: Gerald D. McInvale
Auditors: Deloitte & Touche
Employees: 13,379

WHEN

Little Rock–based AP&L, founded in 1913, consolidated operations with Arkansas Central Power, Arkansas Light & Power, and Pine Company in 1926. That year NOPSI (founded in New Orleans in 1922) merged with 2 of the city's other electric companies (Citizens Light & Power, Consumers Electric Light & Power). LP&P, another New Orleans–based utility, was founded in 1927 to acquire the assets of 6 Louisiana electric companies. MP&L was also formed in 1927, through the consolidation of 3 Mississippi power companies.

AP&L, LP&L, MP&L, NOPSI, and several other utilities were consolidated under a Maine holding company, Electric Power and Light (formed in 1925). Electric Power and Light was dissolved in 1949, and a new holding company, Middle South Utilities, emerged to take over the assets of AP&L, LP&L, MP&L, and NOPSI.

Floyd Lewis joined the Middle South's legal staff in 1949. He rose through the ranks to become president in 1970. In 1971 the company bought Arkansas-Missouri Power Company and its affiliate, Associated Natural Gas (both were consolidated with AP&L in 1981). In 1974 Middle South brought its first nuclear plant (near Russellville, Arkansas) on-line and formed Middle South Energy (later System

Energy Resources) to finance and construct units 1 and 2 of another nuclear facility (Grand Gulf). Unfortunately, Grand Gulf 1 was completed 6 years behind schedule (in 1985) at a cost of $3.8 billion. When Middle South tried to pass costs related to the plant's construction on to its customers, rate disputes with state regulators and lawsuits ensued. Construction of Grand Gulf 2 was halted, and, as the controversy raged, Lewis retired in 1985. Only 2 years after his replacement CFO Edwin Lupberger took over, losses related to the unsettled rate issues took Middle South to the brink of bankruptcy.

With Lupberger's guidance, the company moved to settle the disputes by absorbing a $900 million loss on its $926 million investment in Grand Gulf 2 in 1989. Then, to distance itself from the controversy, it adopted the name Entergy Corporation.

Entergy formed 2 new subsidiaries in 1990: Entergy Operations (to streamline operation of the company's nuclear plants) and Entergy Power (to take advantage of the wholesale electricity market). In 1991 the US Supreme Court agreed to hear litigation between NOPSI and the City of New Orleans related to rate increases stemming from NOPSI's $135 million Grand Gulf 1 costs.

WHERE

HQ: 225 Baronne St., New Orleans, LA 70112
Phone: 504-529-5262
Fax: 504-569-4265

Generating Facilities

Coal
Independence (57%)
White Bluff (57%)

Hydroelectric
Carpenter (AP&L)
Remmel (AP&L)

Natural Gas and Oil
A. B. Paterson (NOPSI)
Baxter Wilson (MP&L)
Blytheville (AP&L)
Buras (LP&L)
Cecil Lynch (AP&L)
Delta (MP&L)
Gerald Andrus (MP&L)
Hamilton Moses (AP&L)
Harvey Couch (AP&L)
Lake Catherine (AP&L)

Little Gypsy (LP&L)
Lynch (AP&L)
Mabelvale (AP&L)
Market Street (NOPSI)
Michoud (NOPSI)
Natchez (MP&L)
Ninemile Point (LP&L)
Rex Brown (MP&L)
Richie (AP&L)
Robert E. Ritchie (AP&L)
Sterlington (LP&L)

Nuclear
Arkansas Nuclear One (AP&L)
Grand Gulf (System Energy Resources)
Waterford (LP&L)

WHAT

	1990 Sales	
	$ mil.	% of total
Electricity		
Residential	1,449	37
Commercial	988	25
Industrial	1,052	26
Governmental	125	3
Sales for resale	213	5
Other	67	2
Natural gas	88	2
Total	**3,982**	**100**

Utility Companies
Arkansas Power & Light Co.
Louisiana Power & Light Co.
Mississippi Power & Light Co.
New Orleans Public Service, Inc.

Other Subsidiaries
Electec, Inc. (nonutility operations)
Entergy Operations, Inc. (nuclear plant management)
Entergy Power, Inc. (produces and wholesales electricity)
Entergy Services, Inc. (technical support)
System Energy Resources, Inc. (owns 90% Grand Gulf Nuclear Station)
System Fuels, Inc.

HOW MUCH

	9-Year Growth	1981	1982	1983	1984	1985	1986	1987	1988	1989	1990
Sales ($ mil.)	4.1%	2,772	2,902	2,910	3,146	3,238	3,486	3,455	3,565	3,724	3,982
Net income ($ mil.)	5.2%	342	379	458	575	492	542	449	498	(397)	541
Income as % of sales	—	12.3%	13.1%	15.7%	18.3%	15.2%	15.5%	13.0%	14.0%	(10.7%)	13.6%
Earnings per share ($)	0.0%	2.44	2.33	2.46	2.76	2.01	2.21	1.74	2.01	(2.31)	2.44
Stock price – high ($)	—	13.88	15.75	16.75	14.75	15.25	15.00	16.25	16.13	23.25	23.63
Stock price – low ($)	—	11.00	12.25	13.13	9.25	8.13	10.50	7.75	8.50	15.50	18.00
Stock price – close ($)	6.6%	12.63	14.88	13.38	13.75	10.63	13.13	8.25	16.00	23.25	22.38
P/E – high	—	6	7	7	5	8	7	9	8	—	10
P/E – low	—	5	5	5	3	4	5	4	4	—	7
Dividends per share ($)	(4.8%)	1.63	1.67	1.71	1.75	0.89	0.00	0.00	0.20	0.90	1.05
Book value per share ($)	2.6%	17.64	17.75	18.00	18.28	19.03	21.20	22.06	23.87	20.62	22.19

1990 Year-end:
Debt ratio: 57.7%
Return on equity: 11.4%
Cash (mil.): $1,049
Current ratio: 1.15
Long-term debt (mil.): $6,072
No. of shares (mil.): 185
Dividends:
  1990 average yield: 4.7%
  1990 payout: 43.0%
Market value (mil.): $4,145

Stock Price History High/Low 1981–90

RANKINGS

14th in *Fortune* 50 Utilities
152nd in *Business Week* 1000

THE EQUITABLE

OVERVIEW

Mutual company
Fiscal year ends: December 31

The Equitable Life Assurance Company was the 4th largest life insurance company in the US in 1990, down from 3rd in 1989 owing to losses arising from real estate and junk bond investments, and the issuance in the 1970s and 1980s of fixed-return pension instruments called guaranteed investment contracts.

In addition to providing traditional life insurance policies, The Equitable has functioned in the past 15 years as a financial services company offering annuities, investment and advisory services, investment banking, pension fund management, agribusiness financing, and real estate investment management.

In the 1970s and 1980s The Equitable added to its core business investment bankers Donaldson, Lufkin & Jenrette (founded by current Equitable CEO Richard Jenrette); mutual and other funds, managed through Alliance Capital Management (over $50 billion in assets under management); and real estate investments (1990 revenues declined 11%).

Under Jenrette, the company has restructured from 3 holding companies to one and has cut 12% of its staff and over $150 million in annual expenses. In 1990 the company announced plans to recapitalize by converting from a mutual to a stock company. As a first step, in July 1991 it announced that the French insurance company Axa would invest $1 billion in exchange for a percentage of stock to be determined later.

WHO

Chairman and CEO: Richard H. Jenrette, age 62
President and COO: Joseph J. Melone
VC: Harry D. Garber, age 63
CFO: Thomas M. Kirwan
SVP Human Resources: Thomas F. Mann
Auditors: Deloitte & Touche
Employees: 12,000

WHERE

HQ: The Equitable Life Assurance Society of the United States, 787 Seventh Ave., New York, NY 10019
Phone: 212-554-1234
Fax: 212-554-2320

The company is licensed in all 50 states; Puerto Rico; Washington, DC; and the US Virgin Islands.

WHEN

As a student in Catskill, New York, Henry Hyde was advised by his teacher, General John Johnston (who formed Northwestern Mutual Life Insurance Company in 1857), to pursue life insurance as a career. Hyde joined Mutual Life of New York and left in 1859 at the age of 25 to found The Equitable Life Assurance Society in New York as a joint stock company named after the 18th-century Equitable Life Assurance Society of London. He chose fellow Presbyterian church member William Alexander as president.

Business boomed as the Civil War raged. The company flourished and soon opened offices in Asia, Europe, South America, and the Middle East. Equitable grew faster than the insurance industry overall and by 1899 was the first company in the world to have $1 billion of life insurance in force.

Beginning in 1905 a series of revelations about the company's financial condition led to the resignation of management, and, in 1917, conversion to a mutual company. Equitable was the first company to write group insurance (Montgomery Ward, 1911), and it developed a system to determine how to apportion dividends within a particular group, which was adopted by others in the industry.

After the boom of the 1920s, Equitable weathered the Depression and WWII. In the 1960s the company continued to grow and became known for its social conscience, with job training and housing rehabilitation programs.

The 1970s saw the beginning of diversification into computers (Informatics, 1973), mining (Peabody coal, 1976), and real estate. The company also pioneered a new product, guaranteed investment contracts (GICs), which guaranteed principal and returns of up to 18% and allowed contributions for the life of the contract. This obligated the company to pay inflationary rates even after interest rates fell in the 1980s. To cover the difference, the company invested in increasingly risky high-yield junk bonds and real estate. It continued diversifying, acquiring Donaldson, Lufkin & Jenrette, and even formed an HMO (Equicor, with Hospital Corporation of America; 1986; sold 1990). When the boom faded in the late 1980s, the company was left with $15 billion in GIC obligations.

In a total management change in May 1990, Richard Jenrette became CEO and began cutting costs and seeking new capital.

By the end of 1990, GIC obligations were down to $10 billion. In 1990 and 1991 rumors of the company's demise brought a run of policy redemptions, further increasing the need for cash. Equitable also invested in new areas. In 1990 the company formed COMPASS (property leasing and management), acquired an interest in Europolis (European property markets), and expanded Capital Management Corporation overseas, opening offices in London and Tokyo.

WHAT

	1990 Sales	
	$ mil.	% of total
Premiums	5,980	57
Net investment income	3,917	37
Other income	680	6
Adjustments	(993)	—
Total	**9,584**	**100**

	1990 Assets	
	$ mil.	% of total
Bonds	18,459	31
Stocks	6,319	10
Investments	2,340	4
Loans	16,546	27
Real estate	10,286	17
Other assets	6,572	11
Total	**60,522**	**100**

Major Operations and Subsidiaries

Insurance Companies
Equico Securities, Inc.
The Equitable of Colorado, Inc.
Equitable Seimei Hoken
Equitable Variable Life Insurance Co.
Pension Financial Management Group
TRAEBCO

Equitable Investment Corp.
Alliance Capital Management Corp.
Donaldson, Lufkin & Jenrette, Inc.
Equico Capital Corp.
Equitable Agri-Business, Inc.
Equitable Capital Management Corp.
Equitable Real Estate Investment Management, Inc.

RANKINGS

4th in *Fortune* 50 Life Insurance Cos.

KEY COMPETITORS

Aetna	New York Life
AIG	Northwestern Mutual
American Express	Paine Webber
Bear Stearns	Primerica
CIGNA	Prudential
CS Holding	Salomon
First Executive	Sears
John Hancock	State Farm
Kemper	Teachers Insurance
MassMutual	Transamerica
Merrill Lynch	Travelers
MetLife	USF&G
Morgan Stanley	

HOW MUCH

	9-Year Growth	1981	1982	1983	1984	1985	1986	1987	1988	1989	1990
Assets ($ mil.)	5.6%	37,219	41,090	44,445	46,418	51,168	54,577	56,794	58,028	61,684	60,522
Change in surplus ($ mil.)	—	135	74	(106)	56	24	61	(57)	63	15	(204)
Change as % of assets	—	0.4%	0.2%	(0.2%)	(0.1%)	0.0%	0.1%	(0.1%)	0.1%	0.0%	(0.3%)

1990 Year-end:
Equity as % of assets: 1.9%
Return on equity: —
Cash (mil.): $71
Sales (mil.): $9,584

Assets ($ mil.) 1981–90

70,000
60,000
50,000
40,000
30,000
20,000
10,000
0

ERNST & YOUNG

OVERVIEW

With annual revenues exceeding $5 billion worldwide, Ernst & Young is 2nd in US accounting firm revenues, after Arthur Andersen, and 2nd in the world, after KPMG.

Ernst & Young apparently subscribes to the theory that 2 heads are better than one, because it has 2 CEOs — William Gladstone and Ray Groves — a legacy of the 1989 merger of Ernst & Whinney and Arthur Young. Says Groves, "We concluded that, at least in the early going, it's a 2-person job."

Accounting firm pairings are the logical result of the mergers and consolidations conducted in other industries during the 1980s; big accounting firms compete for fewer big clients. As accounting firms use auditing services to attract more lucrative consulting jobs, critics contend that auditing quality suffers, and several big firms — including Ernst & Young — are being called to account by angry regulators and shareholders of clients in the troubled thrift industry.

International partnership
Fiscal year ends: September 30

Hoover's Rating **B-**

WHO

Co-CEO: William L. Gladstone
Co-CEO: Ray J. Groves
Chief Financial Partner: Stephen Key
VC Human Resources: Paul Ostling
Employees: 65,000

WHERE

HQ: 277 Park Ave., 32nd Fl., New York, NY 10127
Phone: 212-773-3000
Fax: 212-773-2821

Ernst & Young operates in more than 100 countries.

	1990 Revenues	
	$ mil.	% of total
US	2,239	45
Foreign	2,767	55
Total	**5,006**	**100**

WHAT

	1990 Revenues
	% of total
Accounting & auditing	53
Tax	25
Management consulting	22
Total	**100**

Services
Accounting and auditing
  Compliance services
  Financial statement examination
  Management assistance
Tax planning
  Compensation planning
  Compliance assistance
  Corporate tax planning
  International tax planning
  Merger and acquisition assistance
  Personal financial planning
  Return preparation
Management consulting
  Financial management
  Human resources consulting
  Information systems
  Operations enhancement
  Strategic planning

WHEN

While the 1494 publication in Venice of Luca Pacioli's *Summa di Arithmetica* — the first published work dealing with double-entry bookkeeping — boosted the accounting profession, it really wasn't until the Industrial Revolution in the UK that accountants developed their craft.

Frederick Whinney joined the UK firm of Harding & Pullein in 1849. R. P. Harding reputedly had been a hatmaker whose business ended up in court. The ledgers he produced were so well kept that an official advised him to take up accounting.

Whinney's name was added to the firm in 1859, and later his sons also became partners. The firm's name changed to Whinney, Smith & Whinney (1894). The name became the longest-lived of the firm's many incarnations, not yielding until 1965.

After WWII, Whinney, Smith & Whinney formed an alliance with the American firm of Ernst & Ernst. Ernst & Ernst had been founded in Cleveland in 1903 by brothers Alwin and Theodore Ernst. The alliance, which recognized that the accountants' business clients were getting larger and more international in orientation, provided that each firm would operate in the other's behalf within their respective markets.

In 1965 the Whinney firm merged with Brown, Fleming & Murray to become Whinney Murray. The merger also included the fledgling computer department — the harbinger of electronic accounting systems — set up by Brown, Fleming & Murray to serve British Petroleum. Whinney Murray also formed joint ventures with other accounting firms to provide consulting services.

In 1979 Whinney Murray and Turquands Barton Mayhew — itself the product of a merger that began with a cricket match — united with Ernst & Ernst to form Ernst & Whinney, a firm with an international scope.

Ernst & Whinney, a merger melting pot, was by no means finished with its combinations. Having grown to the world's 4th largest accounting firm by 1989, it merged with the 5th largest, Arthur Young. Arthur Young had taken its name from the Scottish immigrant who had founded a partnership with C. U. Stuart in Chicago in 1894. When Stuart withdrew, Young took brother Stanley as a partner. Arthur Young — the firm — was long known as the "old reliable" of the accounting giants. In 1984 the spotlight shone on it as then–vice-presidential candidate Geraldine Ferraro chose the firm to sort out her tax troubles.

The new firm of Ernst & Young, for a time the world's largest accounting company, faced a rocky start, though. At the end of 1990, it was forced to defend itself from rumors of collapse, just as 2nd-tier firms Laventhol & Horwath and Spicer and Oppenheim filed for bankruptcy and disbanded, respectively. In 1991 Ernst & Young planned to cut 150 partners from the rolls, either through retirement or dismissal. The firm also faced legal problems. A suit against Ernst & Young by the FDIC sought $841 million on 6 separate claims. The claims arose out of audits performed by its predecessor firms on troubled savings and loans. Ernst & Young steadfastly denied the FDIC allegations. The firm was also under fire in California, where it eventually settled with a state agency that had threatened to revoke its license (1990).

Representative Clients

American Airlines	LVMH
American Express	Martin Marietta
Apple Computer	McDonald's
BankAmerica	Mobil
British Airways	Pirelli
British Petroleum	Renault
Coca-Cola	Thorn EMI
Eli Lilly	Time Warner
Hanson	Unisys
Lloyd's of London	

KEY COMPETITORS

Arthur Andersen
Coopers & Lybrand
Deloitte & Touche
General Motors
KPMG
Marsh & McLennan
McKinsey & Co.
Price Waterhouse

HOW MUCH

	9-Year Growth	1981	1982	1983	1984	1985	1986	1987	1988	1989	1990
Worldwide revenues ($ mil.)											
Arthur Young	12.8%	880	955	1,003	1,060	1,160	1,427	1,702	2,053	4,300	5,006
Ernst & Whinney	12.8%	807	887	972	1,028	1,185	1,492	1,778	2,191		
No. of offices[1,2]	—	—	—	200	203	206	265	212	210	124	125
No. of partners	—	—	—	1,650	1,735	2,139	1,925	2,039	2,109	2,000	2,025
No. of employees[1]	—	—	—	17,912	19,335	20,657	21,837	21,864	25,440	—	22,702

1990 revenues per partner: $2,472,099

Worldwide Revenues ($ mil.) 1981–90

[1] Combined Ernst & Whinney, Arthur Young   [2] US offices

ESTÉE LAUDER INC.

Private company
Fiscal year ends: December 31

Hoover's Rating **A-**

OVERVIEW

New York–based Estée Lauder is the leading brand of cosmetics sold in department stores. Privately held by the Lauder family, the group of companies includes Aramis, Clinique Laboratories, Estée Lauder, Origins Natural Resources, Prescriptives, and Estée Lauder International. Each company has its own marketing and sales department.

Estée Lauder has cultivated an image of aloof elegance. Although it recently restricted its products to upscale department stores, the company is planning the rollout of a nationwide retail store chain. In 1991 Estée Lauder opened its first Origins (its new natural skin care line) boutique in the Boston area.

None of the major cosmetics companies in the US (Revlon, Elizabeth Arden, Max Factor) remained independent after the death or retirement of the founder. CEO Leonard Lauder, son of Estée Lauder's founder, hopes the family's company will prove the exception.

WHO

Chairman: Estée Lauder, age 83
President and CEO: Leonard A. Lauder, age 59
CEO, Estée Lauder USA: Robin Burns, age 38
SVP: Evelyn H. Lauder
SVP and CFO: Robert Aquilina
SVP Human Resources: Ed Callahan
Employees: 10,000

WHERE

HQ: 767 5th Ave., New York, NY 10153
Phone: 212-572-4600
Fax: 212-572-3941

Estée Lauder's products are sold worldwide, exclusively in department stores.

Manufacturing Plants

Australia	England	Switzerland
Belgium	Mexico	US
Canada	Spain	Venezuela

WHEN

Estée Lauder (then Josephine Esther Mentzer) started her beauty career by selling skin care products formulated by a Hungarian uncle, John Schotz, during the 1930s. Eventually she packaged and peddled her own variations of her uncle's formulas, which included an all-purpose face cream and a cleansing oil.

With the help of her husband, Joseph Lauder, she set up her first office in New York City in 1944 and added lipstick, eye shadow, and face powder to her line. Joseph oversaw production, and Estée sold her wares to beauty salons and department stores, using samples and gifts to convince customers to buy her products. At one Manhattan beauty salon, Estée Lauder asked the owner about her blouse: Where had she bought it? The owner looked down her nose at the cosmetics saleswoman and scoffed that she didn't need to know, because she would never be able to afford it. Lauder has been driven ever since. Throughout the 1950s Lauder traveled cross-country, first to sell her line to high-profile department stores like Neiman-Marcus, I. Magnin, and Saks, later to train saleswomen in the same stores.

Estée Lauder created her first fragrance, a bath oil called Youth Dew, in 1953. In the late 1950s many of the large cosmetics houses in the US introduced "European" skin care lines, products that had scientific-sounding names and supposedly advanced skin repair properties. Estée Lauder's contribution was Re-Nutriv cream. It sold for $115 a pound in 1960, the same year the company hit the million-dollar profit mark. Re-Nutriv was expensive for the Lauder line, which has always been sold exclusively in department stores. The advertising campaign for the cream established the "Lauder look": aristocratic, sophisticated, and tastefully wealthy, an image that Estée Lauder herself cultivated.

In 1964 the company introduced Aramis, a fragrance for men, and in 1968, with the help of a *Vogue* editor, launched Clinique, one of the first hypoallergenic skin care lines. In 1972 Estée Lauder's son Leonard became president, although Estée remained CEO.

Much of her work has been as a living symbol of the confident sophisticate, sharing meals with the rich and with royalty. When Princess Diana was to be fêted at a White House dinner, she commanded the presence of Bruce Springsteen, Robert Redford, and Estée Lauder.

By 1978 the Aramis line consisted of 40 products; Aramis cologne and aftershave accounted for 50-80% of men's fragrance sales in some department stores. Also in 1978 the company put out 2 fragrances for women, White Linen and Cinnabar. In 1979 Estée Lauder introduced Prescriptives, a skin care and makeup line targeted at young professional women.

Under Leonard Lauder, between 1978 and 1983, the R&D budget for skin care products was increased, resulting in Night Repair, one of the company's largest-selling formulas. The company also expanded international marketing. Leonard Lauder was named CEO in 1983. By 1988 Estée Lauder had captured 33% of the US market in prestige cosmetics.

During the early 1990s Estée Lauder unveiled its new Origins lines of environmentally safe cosmetics. In 1990 the company recruited ex–Calvin Klein executive Robin Burns to head its domestic branch. Burns quickly made her mark at Estée Lauder by breathing life back into the company's traditionally conservative advertising (Burns promoted Estée Lauder's new Spellbound fragrance by wrapping a 2-minute videocassette commercial in a plastic bag with *Elle* magazine in 1991).

WHAT

Subsidiaries and Affiliates

Aramis Inc.
Toiletries (first product for women introduced 1990)
Aramis Classic
Aramis 900
Lab Series
New West for Him
New West Skinscent for Her
Tuscany

Clinique Laboratories Inc.
Hypoallergenic skin care and makeup
Clinique skin care
Precision makeup
Skin Supplies for Men

Estée Lauder Inc.
Makeup and fragrances
Beautiful
Cinnabar
Lauder for Men
Spellbound
White Linen

Estée Lauder International Inc.
Marketing and sales abroad for Lauder companies

Estée Lauder Realty Corp.
Properties in Long Island, New York

Len-Ron Manufacturing Co., Inc.
Cosmetics manufacturing

Origins Natural Resources Inc.
Environmentally safe, natural skin care products

Prescriptives, Inc.
Makeup and skin care for professional women
Calyx (fragrance)
Custom-blended powder and foundation

RANKINGS

60th in *Forbes* 400 US Private Cos.

KEY COMPETITORS

Amway
Avon
Colgate-Palmolive
S.C. Johnson
L'Oréal
LVMH
MacAndrews & Forbes
Procter & Gamble
Unilever

HOW MUCH

	5-Year Growth	1981	1982	1983	1984	1985	1986	1987	1988	1989	1990
Estimated sales ($ mil.)	11.8%	—	—	—	—	1,200	1,200	1,350	1,600	1,900	2,093
Employees	0.0%	—	—	—	—	10,000	10,000	10,000	10,000	10,000	10,000

Estimated Sales ($ mil.) 1985–90

EXXON CORPORATION

NYSE symbol: XON
Fiscal year ends: December 31

Hoover's Rating: B

OVERVIEW

Now headquartered in the Dallas–Fort Worth area (it moved from New York City in 1990), Exxon is the world's 3rd largest industrial company, after General Motors and the Royal Dutch/Shell group. The company has extensive holdings of oil and gas properties throughout the world and leads US oil companies in proven reserves. Major production projects are underway in the North Sea and Malaysia. Exxon owns 70% of Canadian oil giant Imperial Oil.

Exploration and production activities are balanced by downstream (refining and marketing) operations. Refining margins shot up in early 1991 as a result of heavy demand from allied forces stationed in Saudi Arabia.

Exxon also manufactures and sells petrochemicals, explores for and mines coal and other minerals, and owns 60% of Castle Peak station in Hong Kong, the largest coal-fired electric generating plant in Asia.

Despite expenditures of more than $2 billion to clean up the Alaska coast, the *Valdez* oil spill remains a public relations and legal nightmare for Exxon, threatening its ability to gain rights to drill in other US coastal areas.

WHEN

John D. Rockefeller, a commodity trader, started his first oil refinery in 1863 in Cleveland. Realizing that the price of oil at the well would shrink with each new strike, Rockefeller chose to monopolize oil refining and transportation. He raised $1 million in loans and investments and in 1870 formed the Standard Oil Company. In 1882 Rockefeller and his associates created the Standard Oil Trust, which allowed Rockefeller and 8 others to dissolve existing Standard Oil affiliates and set up new, ostensibly independent companies in different states, including the Standard Oil Company of New Jersey (Jersey Standard).

Initially capitalized at $70 million, the Standard Oil Trust controlled 90% of the petroleum industry. In 1911, after 2 decades of political and legal wrangling, the Supreme Court disbanded the Trust into 34 companies, the largest of which was Jersey Standard. In this year John D. Archbold took over as president of Jersey Standard and commenced more active exploration efforts.

Walter Teagle took over the presidency in 1917, secretly bought half of Humble Oil of Texas (1919), and expanded into South America. In 1928 Jersey Standard joined in the Red Line Agreement, which reserved most Middle East oil for a handful of companies. Congressional investigation of a prewar research pact giving Farben of Germany patents for a lead essential to the development of aviation fuel in exchange for a formula for synthetic rubber (never received) led to Teagle's resignation in 1942.

The 1948 purchase of a 30% interest in Arabian American Oil Company for $74 million, combined with a 7% share of Iranian production acquired in 1954, made Jersey Standard the world's largest oil company.

Other US companies still using the Standard Oil name objected to Jersey Standard marketing in their territories as Esso (derived from the initials S.O. for Standard Oil). To end the confusion, Jersey Standard became Exxon in 1972. The name change cost $100 million.

In the 1970s nationalization of oil assets by producing countries reduced Exxon's access to oil. Despite increased exploration in the 1970s and 1980s, Exxon's reserves shrank faster than new reserves could be found.

The oil tanker *Exxon Valdez* spilled nearly 11 million gallons of oil into Alaska's Prince William Sound in 1989. In early 1991 Exxon and officials representing the US and Alaska agreed to a $1 billion plea bargain over the spill. Exxon withdrew its guilty pleas when a federal judge rejected the criminal fines as inadequate. In late 1991 a $1.15 billion settlement was reached but must be approved by the court.

WHO

Chairman and CEO: Lawrence G. Rawl, age 62, $1,551,300 pay
President: Lee R. Raymond, age 52, $1,093,314 pay
SVP: Jack G. Clarke, age 63, $917,572 pay
SVP: Donald K. McIvor, age 62, $859,824 pay
SVP: Charles R. Sitter, age 60, $836,087 pay
VP and Treasurer (Principal Financial Officer): E. A. Robinson, age 57
VP Human Resources: M. E. Gillis, age 60
Auditors: Price Waterhouse
Employees: 104,085

WHERE

HQ: 225 E. John W. Carpenter Freeway, Irving, TX 75062-2298
Phone: 214-444-1000
Fax: 214-444-1505

Exxon conducts operations in the US and 79 foreign countries.

	1990 Sales		1990 Net Income	
	$ mil.	% of total	$ mil.	% of total
US	26,295	23	1,691	29
Other Western Hemisphere	19,862	18	344	6
Eastern Hemisphere	67,536	59	3,840	65
Adjustments	(8,174)	—	(865)	—
Total	**105,519**	**100**	**5,010**	**100**

WHAT

	1990 Sales		1990 Operating Income	
	$ mil.	% of total	$ mil.	% of total
Chemicals	9,591	8	737	8
Petroleum	104,102	92	8,052	92
Adjustments	(8,174)	—	(183)	—
Total	**105,519**	**100**	**8,606**	**100**

Petroleum
Upstream operations
  Oil and gas exploration
  Oil and gas production
Downstream operations
  Convenience stores
  Refining
  Service stations
  Transportation
Other
  Coal mining
  Power generation
  Mineral mining

Chemicals
Basic chemicals
Performance products
  (vinyl intermediates,
  chemicals for oil
  field operations)
Polymers

RANKINGS

2nd in *Fortune* 500 US Industrial Cos.
2nd in *Business Week* 1000

COMPETITION

Amoco	Koch	Pemex
Ashland	Mobil	Phillips Petroleum
Atlantic Richfield	Norsk Hydro	Royal Dutch/Shell
Broken Hill	Occidental	Sun
British Petroleum	Oryx	Texaco
Chevron	Pennzoil	Unocal
Coastal	Petrofina	USX
Du Pont	Petrobrás	Other chemical and
Elf Aquitaine	PDVSA	mining companies

HOW MUCH

	9-Year Growth	1981	1982	1983	1984	1985	1986	1987	1988	1989	1990
Sales ($ mil.)	(0.3%)	108,107	97,173	88,561	90,854	86,673	69,888	76,416	79,557	86,656	105,519
Net income ($ mil.)	(1.2%)	5,567	4,186	4,978	5,528	4,870	5,360	4,840	5,260	2,975	5,010
Income as % of sales	—	5.2%	4.3%	5.6%	6.1%	5.6%	7.7%	6.3%	6.6%	3.4%	4.7%
Earnings per share ($)	2.3%	3.22	2.41	2.89	3.39	3.23	3.71	3.43	3.95	2.32	3.96
Stock price – high ($)	—	20.50	16.13	19.88	22.75	27.94	37.06	50.38	47.75	51.63	55.13
Stock price – low ($)	—	14.75	12.44	14.25	18.06	22.06	24.19	30.88	32.00	40.50	44.88
Stock price – close ($)	14.2%	15.63	14.88	18.69	22.50	27.56	35.06	38.13	44.00	50.00	51.75
P/E – high	—	6	7	7	7	9	10	15	12	22	14
P/E – low	—	5	5	5	5	7	7	9	8	17	11
Dividends per share ($)	5.7%	1.50	1.50	1.55	1.68	1.73	1.80	1.90	2.15	2.30	2.47
Book value per share ($)	5.1%	16.42	16.42	17.40	18.42	19.91	22.30	24.38	24.65	23.39	25.78

1990 Year-end:
Debt ratio: 18.9%
Return on equity: 16.1%
Cash (mil.): $1,379
Current ratio: 0.76
Long-term debt (mil.): $7,687
No. of shares (mil.): 1,245
Dividends:
  1990 average yield: 4.8%
  1990 payout: 62.4%
Market value (mil.): $64,449

Stock Price History
High/Low 1981–90

FARLEY, INC.

Private company
Fiscal year ends: December 31

Hoover's Rating **D**

OVERVIEW

Now laden with debt from a series of highly leveraged acquisitions made in the 1980s, Farley once boasted controlling interests in Fruit of the Loom and West Point–Pepperell. But since mid-1991 William Farley's Chicago-based holding company has seen its voting power in Fruit of the Loom slip from 43% to 33% and its 95% stake in West Point–Pepperell dwindle to less than 5%.

Farley recently reached an accord with the bondholders of West Point Acquisition (the unit he set up to buy sheet and towel maker West Point–Pepperell in 1989), surrendering to them about 90% of Pepperell and leaving himself a 5% stake. With its debt reduced by nearly 58% (from $1.9 billion) West Point Acquisition, which is controlled by Farley, Inc., most likely will file bankruptcy proceedings.

Farley, Inc., which entered bankruptcy in September 1991, will cede about 3 million Fruit of the Loom shares and a 9.2% stake in Doehler-Jarvis LP (owned by a group that includes William Farley) to bondholders in exchange for $172 million of debt. Farley still owns western boot maker Acme Boots and railroad ball bearings maker Magnus. Fruit of the Loom is America's leading maker of men's and boys' underwear, with a 40% market share.

WHEN

In 1976 William Farley, a 33-year-old former door-to-door encyclopedia salesman, started building his industrial empire by buying Anaheim Citrus Products, a California citrus-processing plant. Farley bought the company for $1.7 million through an LBO, investing only $25,000 of his own money. In 1977 he formed Farley Industries (now Farley, Inc.), a Chicago-based holding company that by the mid-1980s would be one of America's largest privately owned industrial corporations.

Between 1977 and 1984 Farley made several acquisitions, including Baumfolder (paper folders) and Condec (defense and electrical equipment), but none compared to the $1.4 billion LBO of Ben Heineman's Northwest Industries in 1985, completed with the aid of LBO specialists Drexel Burnham Lambert.

Northwest (originally akin to the Chicago and North Western Railway) included Union Underwear Company, which marketed Fruit of the Loom brand men's and boys' briefs; Acme Boots, the world's leading manufacturer of western-style boots; General Battery Corporation; and Velsicol Chemical. Farley spun off Northwest's Lone Star Steel company in 1985 and, to offset acquisition debt, sold Northwest's stake in 2 other businesses. Farley then changed Northwest's name, to Farley/Northwest Industries in 1985 and in 1987 to Fruit of the Loom, selling, in the meantime, Velsicol's agrichemical division (1986) and General Battery (1987). In 1987 Farley, Inc., made a 27-million-share offering of its Fruit of the Loom stock but retained control of the company. Meanwhile, William Farley toyed with the idea of running for president of the US in 1988.

In 1989 Drexel financed Farley's $1.56 billion LBO of West Point–Pepperell. Fresh from acquiring J. P. Stevens & Company in 1988, Georgia-based Pepperell also owned Cluett, Peabody & Company, makers of Arrow shirts and Gold Toe socks. Farley bought 95% of Pepperell in 1989, but his hopes of raising the $83 million necessary to buy the remaining 5% by floating bonds through Drexel were dashed by the collapse of the junk bond market in 1990. Farley sold Cluett's Arrow, Gold Toe, and Schoeneman divisions to the US subsidiary of Bidermann in 1990 but, without full Pepperell ownership, could not use the $410 million proceeds to reduce Farley's debt ($2.4 billion of which was related to the Pepperell acquisition).

Beleaguered by massive LBO debt and pretax losses of about $40 million (1989), Farley raised cash by selling Doehler-Jarvis (aluminum die-casting business) to a group of partners that included himself.

West Point Acquisition defaulted on $1.5 billion in bond payments and a $796 million bank loan early in 1990. Later that year Farley sold $43 million of Fruit of the Loom stock to Land Free Investment, a group headed by ex-Drexel banker Leon Black, presumably to help pay off some of Farley, Inc.'s LBO debt. Farley bought back the shares in 1991 and combined them with some of his own in a public stock offering.

In 1991 Farley, Inc., defaulted on $20 million in interest payments to its bondholders. The company reached an agreement with creditors to reorganize under a prepackaged bankruptcy plan in September 1991.

WHO

Chairman and CEO: William F. Farley, age 49
SEVP Corporate Development: Richard M. Cion, age 48
EVP and CFO: Paul M. O'Hara
Director Human Resources: Susan VanderHorn
Auditors: Ernst & Young
Employees: 54,000

WHERE

HQ: 233 S. Wacker Dr., 5000 Sears Tower, Chicago, IL 60606
Phone: 312-876-1724
Fax: 312-993-1783

WHAT

Apparel

Fruit of the Loom, Inc. (33%)
Union Underwear (20%)
  Socks
  Sweats
  T-shirts
  Underwear

Major Brands
BVD
Fruit of the Loom
Munsingwear
Screen Stars

Automotive Parts and Accessories

Tool and Engineering
Prototype automotive body parts

Footwear

Acme Boot Co., Inc.	Major Brands
Lucchese Boot Co.	Acme
Nonathletic footwear	Dan Post
Western boots	Dingo
	Lucchese

Metal Parts and Fasteners

Magnus
Railroad ball bearings

Textiles

West Point–Pepperell, Inc. (5%)
J. P. Stevens & Co., Inc. (5%)
  Blankets
  Sheets
  Towels
  Other bed and bath accessories

Major Brands
Lady Pepperell
Martex
Vellux

RANKINGS

85th in *Forbes* 400 US Private Cos.

KEY COMPETITORS

Burlington Holdings	INTERCO
Fieldcrest Cannon	Milliken
W. R. Grace	Springs Industries
Ingersoll-Rand	U. S. Shoe

HOW MUCH

	6-Year Growth	1981	1982	1983	1984	1985	1986	1987	1988	1989	1990
Sales ($ mil.)	14.2%	—	—	—	700	962	1,110	1,318	1,517	2,865	1,550
Net income ($ mil.)	—	—	—	—	50	(73)	(17)	44	(29)	—	—
Income as % of sales	—	—	—	—	7.1%	(7.6%)	(1.5%)	3.3%	(1.9%)	—	—
Employees	37.5%	—	—	—	8,000	28,500	22,000	22,000	25,000	46,500	54,000

Net Income ($ mil.) 1984–88

FEDERAL EXPRESS CORPORATION

OVERVIEW

Federal Express, still run by founder Fred Smith (who owns 8.2% of the company), has become a $7.7 billion company in just 20 years, making it one of the greatest entrepreneurial success stories of our era.

Operating the world's largest expedited delivery service, FedEx ships an average of 1.3 million express packages daily. With its 1989 purchase of Tiger International, the company also runs the world's largest full-service, all-cargo airline. Unfortunately, international expansion has proven costly. Despite strong earnings on domestic operations, losses on international operations have accelerated and, combined with restructuring charges and recession, have depressed fiscal 1991 earnings.

FedEx remains employee-oriented, offering Guaranteed Fair Treatment, minority recruitment, and no-layoff policies and has high employee morale. It was officially recognized for its devotion to quality service in 1990 when the Department of Commerce awarded it the prestigous Malcolm Baldridge Quality Award.

WHEN

FedEx was the inspiration of Fred Smith, who recognized in the late 1960s that the US was becoming a service-oriented economy with a need for reliable, overnight delivery services. Smith presented FedEx's business concept in a Yale term paper — his grade, a "C," now seems ironic. Between 1969 and 1971 Smith found investors willing to contribute $40 million, used $8 million of family money, and eventually received sufficient bank financing to total $90 million, making FedEx the largest start-up ever funded by venture capital. Services to 22 US cities started in 1973 and included overnight and 2nd-day delivery and a $5-per-package Courier Pak envelope for expediting documents. Offering virtually the same services today, FedEx has spread to include delivery to any domestic destination and 129 countries.

Several factors contributed to the company's success. Air passenger traffic was growing rapidly so that parcel service became less important to commercial airlines; United Parcel Service union workers went on strike in 1974, disrupting customer service; and, finally, competitor REA Express went bankrupt. By fiscal year-end 1975 FedEx had lost $29.3 million; by 1976, only 3 years after beginning operations, FedEx was profitable — but owed creditors $49 million. It went public in 1978 and has had a steady history of strong earnings since that time.

FedEx has had one fiasco. Believing hard-copy delivery services could be severely eroded by the burgeoning electronic mail market, the company invested heavily in ZapMail, a satellite-based network that provided 2-hour document delivery service. Failing to anticipate the impact of low-cost fax machines, FedEx lost over $300 million in 1986 on the now-disbanded ZapMail. Despite heavy ZapMail losses, FedEx remained profitable.

FedEx is now focusing on international expansion. The company bought Island Courier Companies and Cansica Inc. (1987), SAMIMA (Italy, 1988), and 3 Japanese freight carriers (1988). In 1989, as part of an effort to increase its share of larger cargo services, the company bought Tiger International (Flying Tigers cargo airline) for $880 million. With the Tiger acquisition, FedEx more than doubled overseas revenues, becoming the world's #1 air cargo company. It also inherited Tiger's losses in international markets and has yet to make a profit on operations abroad.

A new challenge presented itself in 1990 when UPS started offering guaranteed 10:30 a.m. delivery services in the US. In 1991 Fed Ex introduced EXPRESSfreighter, a new international air-express cargo service. Also in 1991 the company began to explore diversifying into such aviation services as aircraft maintenance and pilot training through a new unit, FEDEX Aeronautics Corporation.

NYSE symbol: FDX
Fiscal year ends: May 31

Hoover's Rating **B-**

WHO

Chairman, President, and CEO: Frederick W. Smith, age 47, $662,491 pay
EVP and COO: James L. Barksdale, age 48, $531,576 pay
VP and Controller: Graham R. Smith, age 43
SVP and Chief Personnel Officer: James A. Perkins, age 47
Auditors: Arthur Andersen & Co.
Employees: 91,550

WHERE

HQ: 2005 Corporate Ave., Memphis, TN 38132
Phone: 901-369-3600
Fax: 901-795-1027

FedEx offers package delivery services in the US and 129 foreign countries. The company operates about 33,700 automotive delivery vehicles.

Hub Locations

Brussels, Belgium	Newark, NJ
Indianapolis, IN	Oakland, CA
Memphis, TN	

	1990 Sales		1990 Operating Income	
	$ mil.	% of total	$ mil.	% of total
US	5,058	66	671	—
Other countries	2,630	34	(391)	—
Total	**7,688**	**100**	**280**	**—**

WHAT

	1990 Sales	
Services	$ mil.	% of total
Priority overnight	3,571	46
Standard overnight	545	7
Economy 2-day	724	9
Domestic freight	38	1
International priority	839	11
International freight	809	11
Charter	372	5
Other	790	10
Total	**7,688**	**100**

Flight Equipment	No.	Orders
MD-11	2	16
DC-10	27	—
Boeing 747	15	—
Boeing 727	151	—
Other	226	—
A300	—	25
Total	**421**	**41**

RANKINGS

8th in *Fortune* 50 Transportation Cos.
302nd in *Business Week* 1000

KEY COMPETITORS

Consolidated Freightways
Ryder
UPS

HOW MUCH

Fiscal year ends May of following year	9-Year Growth	1981	1982	1983	1984	1985	1986	1987	1988	1989	1990
Sales ($ mil.)	28.5%	804	1,008	1,436	2,031	2,606	3,178	3,883	5,167	7,015	7,688
Net income ($ mil.)	(25.0%)	78	89	115	76	132	167	188	166	116	6
Income as % of sales	—	9.8%	8.8%	8.0%	3.7%	5.1%	5.3%	4.8%	3.2%	1.7%	0.1%
Earnings per share ($)	(26.9%)	1.85	2.04	2.52	1.61	2.64	3.21	3.56	3.18	2.18	0.11
Stock price – high ($)	—	36.13	39.38	48.50	47.00	61.00	73.75	75.50	51.00	57.88	58.00
Stock price – low ($)	—	20.25	20.75	32.56	27.75	31.38	51.00	35.25	35.38	42.13	29.50
Stock price – close ($)	0.9%	31.25	37.13	46.25	34.50	60.63	63.13	39.88	50.63	45.75	33.88
P/E – high	—	20	19	19	29	23	23	21	16	27	527
P/E – low	—	11	10	13	17	12	16	10	11	19	268
Dividends per share ($)	0.0%	0.00	0.00	0.00	0.00	0.00	0.00	0.00	0.00	0.00	0.00
Book value per share ($)	15.6%	8.44	11.47	15.47	17.27	21.49	20.90	25.17	28.59	31.03	31.11

1990 Year-end:
Debt ratio: 52.3%
Return on equity: 0.4%
Cash (mil.): $118
Current ratio: 0.86
Long-term debt (mil.): $1,827
No. of shares (mil.): 54
Dividends:
   1990 average yield: 0.0%
   1990 payout: 0.0%
Market value (mil.): $1,817

Stock Price History High/Low 1981–90

FEDERAL NATIONAL MORTGAGE ASSOCIATION

OVERVIEW

The Federal National Mortgage Association (FNMA), better known as Fannie Mae, was created by the federal government to ensure a source of credit for low- and moderate-income homebuyers. Fannie Mae dominates the national secondary real estate market, buying mortgages from loan originators (e.g., banks, S&Ls) with money borrowed at favorable rates because of its government backing.

FNMA is a publicly owned, private corporation. It operates for profit, pays federal corporate income taxes, and pays dividends to its stockholders. It is one of the largest corporations in the US, with assets of over $133 billion. Fannie Mae is also the largest borrower in the country, 2nd only to the US Treasury.

Fannie Mae is exempt from state and local taxes and from the SEC's registration requirements. FNMA derives its income from the difference between the mortgage payments it receives and the cost of borrowing money, and from securities related fees. If, as in 1981, income from mortgage payments is less than the cost of borrowing, Fannie Mae loses money.

With Fannie Mae's $1 trillion in borrowings, there is some fear, as yet groundless, that in the event of large-scale defaults, the US government might be forced by an implicit guaranty to fund the debt. Yet FNMA must walk a fine line between responsible credit underwriting and cutting off the flow of credit to those who need it most.

WHEN

Fannie Mae was created in 1938 by President Franklin Roosevelt as part of the government-owned Reconstruction Finance Corporation to buy FHA (Federal Housing Administration) loans. Fannie Mae began buying VA (Veterans Administration) mortgages in 1948. In 1954 it was rechartered as a partly private, partly governmental "mixed ownership corporation." The Housing Act of 1968 divided the corporation into 2 entities: the Government National Mortgage Association (Ginnie Mae, which, as part of Housing and Urban Development, retained explicit US backing) and Fannie Mae, which went public. Fannie Mae retained its "treasury backstop authority," whereby the Secretary of the Treasury can purchase up to $2.24 billion of the company's obligations.

Fannie Mae introduced nationwide uniform conventional loan mortgage documents in 1970; began to purchase conventional, in addition to VA and FHA, mortgages in 1972; and started buying condominium and planned unit development mortgages in 1974. By 1976 Fannie Mae was purchasing more conventional loans than FHA and VA loans.

As interest rates rose in the 1970s, FNMA's profits declined; by 1981 Fannie Mae was losing money at the rate of more than $1 million a day. In that year the company began to offer mortgage-backed securities (MBSs) and introduced adjustable rate mortgages (ARMs) nationally. The company began to issue securities based on ARMs in 1982 and funded 14% of US home mortgages.

In 1984 Fannie Mae began borrowing money overseas as well as buying conventional multi-family and co-op housing loans. In 1985 the FNMA tightened its credit rules and started to issue securities aimed at foreign investors, becoming the first US corporation to issue a yen-denominated security in the domestic market. The company issued its first real estate mortgage investment conduit (REMIC) securities (shares in mortgage pools of specific maturities and risk classes) and introduced a program to allow small lenders to pool loans with other lenders to create MBSs in 1987.

In 1991 chairman and CEO David Maxwell retired with a reported $27 million pension package, which on top of his 1990 pay of over $1.3 million made him one of the 30 highest paid executives in the US. This outraged members of Congress. Lawrence Small, formerly of Citibank, replaced Roger Birk as president and COO in September 1991.

NYSE symbol: FNM
Fiscal year ends: December 31

Hoover's Rating **B-**

WHO

Chairman and CEO: James A. Johnson, age 47, $715,141 pay (prior to promotion)
VC: Franklin D. Raines, age 42
President and COO: Lawrence M. Small, age 49
EVP and Chief Credit Officer: Michael A. Smilow, age 53, $402,406 pay
EVP, Secretary, and General Counsel: Caryl S. Bernstein, age 57
EVP and CFO: J. Timothy Howard, age 42
EVP Marketing: Robert J. Levin, age 35
VP Human Resource: Patricia Singletary
Auditors: KPMG Peat Marwick
Employees: 1,899

WHERE

HQ: 3900 Wisconsin Ave. NW, Washington, DC 20016
Phone: 202-752-7000
Fax: 202-752-6099

Fannie Mae operates throughout the US with 5 regional offices.

	1990 Mortgage Portfolio
	% of total
California	23
New York	7
Texas	7
Florida	5
Illinois	4
Other states	54
Total	**100**

WHAT

	1990 Assets	
	$ mil.	% of total
Mortgage portfolio, net	113,875	85
Investments	9,868	8
Cash & cash equivalents	4,178	3
Accrued interest receivable	1,032	1
Receivable from currency swaps	2,376	2
Acquired property & foreclosure claims, net	370	—
Other assets	1,414	1
Total	**133,113**	**100**

	1990 Mortgage Portfolio	
	$ mil.	% of total
Single-family mortgages		
First mortgages		
Government insured or guaranteed	11,204	9
Conventional fixed-rate	72,290	62
Conventional adjustable-rate	20,736	18
Second mortgages	1,851	2
Multifamily mortgages		
Government insured	4,243	4
Conventional	6,304	5
Adjustments	(2,753)	—
Total	**113,875**	**100**

RANKINGS

2nd in *Fortune* 50 Diversified Financial Cos.
48th in *Business Week* 1000

KEY COMPETITORS

Other financial institutions in the secondary mortgage market

HOW MUCH

	9-Year Growth	1981	1982	1983	1984	1985	1986	1987	1988	1989	1990
Assets ($ mil.)	8.8%	62,096	73,467	78,918	88,359	99,087	100,400	103,459	112,258	124,315	133,113
Net income ($ mil.)	—	(190)	(134)	76	(57)	37	183	376	507	807	1,173
Income as % of assets	—	(0.3%)	(0.2%)	0.1%	(0.1%)	0.0%	0.2%	0.4%	0.5%	0.7%	0.9%
Earnings per share ($)	—	(1.07)	(0.73)	0.38	(0.29)	0.17	0.82	1.54	2.11	3.10	4.49
Stock price – high ($)	—	4.04	9.08	10.04	8.42	9.88	14.00	16.13	17.54	46.08	44.63
Stock price – low ($)	—	2.13	2.38	6.58	3.63	4.67	7.58	8.33	9.67	16.71	24.88
Stock price – close ($)	32.5%	2.83	8.17	7.67	5.13	8.63	13.58	10.17	16.92	33.88	35.63
P/E – high	—	—	—	27	—	57	17	10	8	15	10
P/E – low	—	—	—	17	—	27	9	5	5	5	6
Dividends per share ($)	21.0%	0.13	0.05	0.05	0.05	0.05	0.07	0.12	0.24	0.43	0.72
Book value per share ($)	10.0%	7.01	6.13	6.46	6.12	6.14	7.20	7.67	9.58	12.52	16.54

1990 Year-end:
Debt ratio: 95.6%
Return on equity: 30.9%
Cash (mil.): $14,046
Long-term debt (mil.): $84,950
No. of shares (mil.): 238
Dividends:
  1990 average yield: 2.0%
  1990 payout: 16.0%
Market value (mil.): $8,488
Sales (mil.): $12,719

Stock Price History High/Low 1981–90

FIELDCREST CANNON, INC.

NYSE symbol: FLD
Fiscal year ends: December 31

Hoover's Rating **C-**

OVERVIEW

Headquartered in Greensboro, North Carolina, Fieldcrest Cannon is the 6th largest textile manufacturer in the US. The company designs and produces a broad spectrum of home textiles, including sheets, blankets, towels, and woven and tufted carpets. Fieldcrest Cannon has an almost 50% share of the US towel market and 20% of the sheet market.

Major corporate restructuring, plant modernization, and product redirection brought profits back in 1988 and 1989 after a brief period of operating losses. In 1989 the company made $23.4 million in profits on sales of nearly $1.4 billion. But the continued retail recession in 1990 and 1991 brought a decline in home textile products, and the real estate slump brought a decline in commercial orders for carpets. These factors, plus charges associated with continued restructuring and discontinuing electric-blanket production in 1991, led to a loss of $38 million in fiscal 1990.

Fieldcrest Cannon is controlled by Amoskeag Company, which holds 83.5% of the voting power. Amoskeag itself is 49% owned by the Dumaine trust (F. C. Dumaine, a director, is former president and CEO of Amoskeag).

WHEN

Fieldcrest's founder, industrialist Benjamin Franklin Mebane, built 6 mills between 1898 and 1905 in Eden, North Carolina. When Mebane was unable to repay loans from Marshall Field & Company, the Thread Mills Company, a subsidiary of the Chicago retailer, took over in 1910.

Thread Mills built the communities of Fieldale and Fieldale Mill (1916, the latter renamed Dumaine Mill in 1989), and began making huck and terry towels in 1919. Royal Velvet towels (1954) are still manufactured in Dumaine. The company also introduced Karastan, an oriental-design carpet in 1928.

In 1935 Marshall Field organized mills in North Carolina and Virginia as the Manufacturing Division to sell textile goods nationwide. In 1947, to enhance brand identity, Thread Mills's name was changed to Fieldcrest Mills. In 1953 Marshall Field sold Fieldcrest Mills to Amoskeag Company, a Boston investment trust, to finance department store expansion in shopping centers. Fieldcrest went public in 1962.

Acquisitions since then have included Muscogee Manufacturing (1963); North Carolina Finishing (1964); Winchester Spinning (1966, merged 1970); Morgan Carpet Mills Division (1967); Foremost Screen Print (merged 1969); and Swift Spinning Mills (1973, sold 1989 to Masaru Tsuzuki of Kitaura Spinning, Japan).

In January 1986 Fieldcrest paid $250 million to entrepreneur David Murdock for rival Cannon Mills's name and its sheet, towel, and rug plants. Murdock had paid $413 million in 1982 for the ailing Cannon Mills of Kannapolis, North Carolina, founded by James Cannon in 1888 to produce cotton fabric and, later, huck towels and terry towels (1898). The 2 companies merged as Fieldcrest Cannon, Inc. (June 1986), and quickly bought Bigelow-Sanford, a South Carolina carpet company.

The company restructured in 1988, establishing Fieldcrest, Cannon, and Karastan Bigelow as 3 divisions with separate corporate managements and sales forces to respond quickly to customer needs and changing markets, but with shared manufacturing facilities to lower production costs. Closing inefficient plants and shifting more automated plants to 24-hour operations, the company began a 5-year $250 million capital investment program to modernize towel manufacturing plants in 1989.

In 1990 to further reduce debt from the 1986 acquisitions, the company closed one plant and consolidated operations (at a loss of 1,700 jobs), discontinuing electric-blanket production (1989 market share was 48%) and concentrating on further restructuring, equipment upgrades, and reduction of excess inventory.

WHO

Chairman and CEO: James M. Fitzgibbons, age 56
President and COO: Charles G. Horn, age 51, $500,000 pay
SVP and CFO: K. William Fraser, Jr., age 53, $245,000 pay
VP Human Resources: Izzie Raines
Auditors: Ernst & Young
Employees: 18,723

WHERE

HQ: 725 North Regional Rd., Greensboro, NC 27409
Phone: 919-665-4300
Fax: 919-665-4314 (Human Resources)

Fieldcrest Cannon manufactures home furnishing textiles, does custom finishing in 32 plants (primarily in the Southeast), and has 24 distribution facilities.

	No. of Manufacturing Plants
Alabama	2
Georgia	3
North Carolina	20
Pennsylvania	1
South Carolina	5
Virginia	1
Total	**32**

WHAT

	1990 Sales	
	$ mil.	% of total
Bed & bath products	927	75
Carpets & rugs	315	25
Total	**1,242**	**100**

	1990 Sales
Home Furnishings	% of total
Brand names	92
Private labels	8
Total	**100**

Brand Names
Bed and bath products
  Cannon
  Charisma
  Court of Versailles
  Fieldcrest
  Monticello
  Royal Family
  Royal Velvet
  St. Mary's
  Sequences
  Suite 250
  Supreme Touch
Carpets and rugs
  Bigelow
  Karastan

Private Labels
Bed and bath products
  Common Sense
    (Wal-Mart)
  Martha Stewart
    (Kmart)
  Whisper (Burdine's)

Subsidiaries
Cannon Mills
  International, Ltd. (UK)
Delaware Valley Wool
  Scouring Co.
Encee, Inc.
Fieldcrest Mills
  International, Inc.
St. Marys, Inc.

HOW MUCH

	9-Year Growth	1981	1982	1983	1984	1985	1986	1987	1988	1989	1990
Sales ($ mil.)	10.0%	526	492	551	573	586	1,083	1,400	1,338	1,362	1,242
Net income ($ mil.)	—	10	10	15	4	13	17	(4)	11	23	(38)
Income as % of sales	—	1.8%	2.1%	2.7%	0.7%	2.2%	1.6%	(0.3%)	0.8%	1.7%	(3.0%)
Earnings per share ($)	—	1.21	1.32	1.88	0.54	1.64	2.11	(0.36)	1.10	2.14	(3.64)
Stock price – high ($)	—	18.13	15.38	19.50	19.50	17.63	43.00	41.00	24.75	30.25	23.75
Stock price – low ($)	—	9.81	8.56	14.00	12.63	12.88	17.31	13.25	14.25	18.63	5.75
Stock price – close ($)	(5.7%)	11.19	14.50	18.38	15.50	17.44	33.50	14.38	19.88	22.50	6.63
P/E – high	—	15	12	10	36	11	20	—	23	14	—
P/E – low	—	8	6	7	24	8	8	—	13	9	—
Dividends per share ($)	(7.4%)	1.00	1.00	1.00	1.00	0.63	0.57	0.68	0.68	0.77	0.50
Book value per share ($)	0.7%	21.54	21.93	22.66	22.25	23.22	26.37	25.36	25.73	27.24	23.01

1990 Year-end:
Debt ratio: 62.8%
Return on equity: —
Cash (mil.): $13
Current ratio: 2.83
Long-term debt (mil.): $404
No. of shares (mil.): 10
Dividends:
  1990 average yield: 7.5%
  1990 payout: —
Market value (mil.): $69

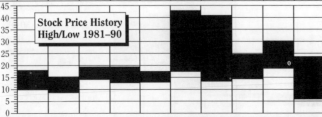

Stock Price History High/Low 1981–90

KEY COMPETITORS

Burlington Holdings
Du Pont
Farley
W. R. Grace
Milliken
Springs Industries

FIRST CHICAGO CORPORATION

OVERVIEW

At the end of 1990, before the recent round of bank mergers, First Chicago was the 13th largest bank holding company in the US. The company's assets include First National Bank of Chicago, American National Corporation, and several other smaller banking operations in the Chicago area. First Chicago oversees its subsidiaries from its distinctive 60-story building downtown.

The company's banking operations are divided into 2 major "bank" groups. The Global Corporate Bank provides commercial and investment banking services to large international corporations, governments, and institutions. The Superregional Bank provides banking services to individuals and, through American National, middle-market businesses; operates the nation's 4th largest bankcard business; and engages in local community retail banking.

Experiencing problems with commercial real estate loans, First Chicago is cutting costs and jobs and is shifting its focus toward fee-based businesses and consumer banking.

NYSE symbol: FNB
Fiscal year ends: December 31

Hoover's Rating **C-**

WHEN

In 1863 the US Comptroller of the Currency granted Charter #8 to the First National Bank of Chicago. First National, from its first office nestled on LaSalle Street, grew rapidly after the Civil War. When the Chicago Fire leveled much of the city, First National's "fireproof" building burned too. A cashier named Lyman Gage, later to become president of the bank and McKinley's secretary of the treasury, discovered that the bank's documents and money had survived in a vault, and the bank resumed operations quickly as the city rebuilt.

First National bought the Union National Bank in 1900 and Metropolitan National Bank in 1902, almost doubling in size in 2 years. First National launched a subsidiary called First Trust and Savings Bank in 1903, renamed First Union Trust and Savings Bank after the 1929 merger with Union Trust.

As the Great Depression settled in, First National took over troubled Foreman State Banks (1931), weathered a run on the bank for $50 million (1933), and folded First Union Trust back into First National (1933). WWII spurred the bank's growth again, and in 1959 it stretched into the international marketplace, opening an office in London. It added a Tokyo office in 1962. A 1969 reorganization created First Chicago as the bank's holding corporation.

First Chicago grew rapidly — some said too rapidly — in the early 1970s under Chairman Gaylord Freeman. After Deputy Chairman Robert Abboud took over in 1975, the bank wrestled with $2 billion in problem loans, particularly in real estate, and with the threat of a shutdown by federal regulators. Abboud tempered the bank's growth and drew criticism from and, eventually, dismissal by the bank's board of directors in 1980.

Barry Sullivan replaced Abboud and resumed the bank's growth. First Chicago acquired credit card accounts from Bankers Trust New York (1982), Beneficial National Bank of Delaware (1987), and Society for Savings Bancorp (1989) to make it the 3rd largest credit card issuer in the nation.

Chief competitor Continental of Illinois stumbled in 1984 and required a federal bailout. First Chicago surged ahead of its rival, acquiring the $3 billion American National Corporation, holding company for American National Bank and Trust, Chicago's 5th largest bank. In the late 1980s First Chicago added more Chicagoland banking concerns — First United Financial Services (1987), Gary-Wheaton (1988), Bank of Ravenswood (1989), and Winnetka Bank (1989). It even bought 95,000 personal and small business accounts from beleaguered old foe Continental Bank.

First Chicago added Great American Savings and Loan in 1990 and 11 Horizon Savings Bank branches in 1991.

WHO

Chairman: Barry F. Sullivan, age 60, $735,632 pay
President: Richard L. Thomas, age 60, $524,904 pay
EVP and CFO: W. G. Jurgensen, age 39
SVP Human Resources: M. James Alef, Jr.
Auditors: Arthur Andersen & Co.
Employees: 17,500

WHERE

HQ: One First National Plaza, Chicago, IL 60670
Phone: 312-732-4000
Fax: 312-732-5976 (Corporate Affairs)

	1990 Assets	
	$ mil.	% of total
US	41,320	82
Europe, Middle East, Africa	4,178	8
Latin America	697	1
North America, Caribbean	1,315	3
Asia/Pacific	3,269	6
Total	**50,779**	**100**

WHAT

	1990 Assets	
	$ mil.	% of total
Cash & due from banks	8,956	18
Securities	9,029	18
Loans	27,706	54
Reserve for loan loss	(994)	(2)
Other assets	6,082	12
Total	**50,779**	**100**

Global Corporate Bank

Superregional Bank
American National Corp.
Bankcard Group
Community Banking

Other
First Capital Corp. of Chicago
First Chicago Financial Corp.

RANKINGS

13th in *Fortune* 100 Commercial Banking Cos.
392nd in *Business Week* 1000

KEY COMPETITORS

H. F. Ahmanson	Crédit Lyonnais
American Express	CS Holding
Banc One	Dai-Ichi Kangyo
Bank of New York	Deutsche Bank
BankAmerica	HSBC
Bankers Trust	Industrial Bank
Barclays	of Japan
Canadian Imperial	J.P. Morgan
Chase Manhattan	NCNB
Chemical Banking	Royal Bank
Citicorp	Union Bank
Continental Bank	of Switzerland

HOW MUCH

	9-Year Growth	1981	1982	1983	1984	1985	1986	1987	1988	1989	1990
Assets ($ mil.)	4.7%	33,562	35,876	36,323	39,846	38,893	39,148	44,209	44,432	47,907	50,779
Net income ($ mil.)	8.6%	119	137	184	86	169	276	(571)	513	359	249
Income as % of assets	—	0.4%	0.4%	0.5%	0.2%	0.4%	0.7%	(1.3%)	1.2%	0.7%	0.5%
Earnings per share ($)	1.2%	2.98	3.33	3.92	1.19	2.84	4.70	(10.71)	7.92	4.99	3.32
Stock price – high ($)	—	20.75	23.13	28.00	27.00	30.13	34.88	34.00	35.25	49.63	38.25
Stock price – low ($)	—	15.13	13.50	17.13	18.63	20.13	26.38	16.63	18.75	29.25	13.13
Stock price – close ($)	(1.7%)	19.25	18.13	25.38	21.38	29.50	28.63	18.88	29.63	37.13	16.50
P/E – high	—	7	7	7	23	11	7	—	4	10	12
P/E – low	—	5	4	4	16	7	6	—	2	6	4
Dividends per share ($)	5.8%	1.20	1.20	1.26	1.32	1.32	1.32	1.50	1.50	1.80	2.00
Book value per share ($)	1.4%	31.87	33.55	35.80	34.12	34.10	36.91	24.21	31.29	34.82	36.25

1990 Year-end:
Debt ratio: 46.7%
Return on equity: 9.3%
Cash (mil.): $8,956
Sales (mil.): $5,693
Long-term debt (mil.): $2,463
No. of shares (mil.): 66
Dividends:
 1990 average yield: 12.1%
 1990 payout: 60.2%
Market value (mil.): $1,089

Stock Price History High/Low 1981–90

FIRST EXECUTIVE CORPORATION

OVERVIEW

In May 1991 First Executive Corporation filed for Chapter 11 bankruptcy. It was the holding company for a group of insurance companies that included Executive Life (seized by California regulators in April 1991), Executive Life–New York (placed under supervision in March), First Delaware and First Stratford in Delaware, and Lincoln Life and Lincoln Indemnity (Nebraska). By May 1991 all of these companies were enjoined from transferring cash or assets to one another or the parent, leaving First Executive unable to service its 9 issues of debt and riddled with losses from its junk bond (it was the largest buyer of Drexel Burnham Lambert junk bonds) and real estate portfolios.

After California seized Executive Life, regulators stopped bond payments while continuing death benefit and selected hardship annuity payments at face value and reducing other annuity benefits by 30%. The state also took over ongoing discussions with other companies for recapitalization and restructuring, and in August 1991 announced a preliminary agreement for liquidation of Executive Life in which the 360,000 individual policies would be sold to a French group headed by Mutuelle Assurance Artisanale de France, while the subsidiary's junk bond portfolio would be sold at a 58% discount to a group including Altus France (68% owned by Crédit Lyonnais) and Leon Black, formerly of Drexel Burnham. But in October 1991, before final approval was granted, new bidders appeared. The fate of the other subsidiaries is as yet undecided and the parent company, assetless, faces numerous lawsuits.

WHEN

Incorporated in 1969, First Executive was an obscure insurance company until 1974, when Fred Carr, a high-flying mutual fund manager during the 1960s, became CEO. He transformed First Executive from a $15-million-a-year company to a $1.6-billion-a-year company by 1982.

Recognizing that First Executive was too small to compete in the life insurance market, which required large cash reserves, he marketed a single-premium, tax-deferred annuity in which a prepaid lump sum earned tax-deferred interest. This provided working capital, which Carr invested for high returns.

The annuities market took a turn for the worse in 1983, wiping out industry leaders Baldwin-United and Charter, leaving First Executive the largest annuities seller. In the 1980s First Executive diversified, buying Bay Colony Life (1982, renamed First Delaware Life) and Lincoln Liberty (1984).

The company also offered guaranteed investment contracts (GICs), which promised high returns, primarily to pension funds. The need to provide these returns led to heavy investments in high-yield, risky ventures, including junk bonds and real estate partnerships. The near simultaneous collapse of these 2 markets brought regulatory scrutiny, and a 1987 order by New York regulators to refrain from risky new investments led to an attempt to transfer existing investments into dummy partnerships, which was disallowed. The result was that the New York company was required to set aside loss reserves based on the full value of its portfolio.

In 1990 First Executive hemorrhaged money; its asset values fell as 71 of its bond issuers defaulted and business declined, and turned negative as policyholders rushed to cash in their policies. The company took to issuing convertible stock in lieu of payment for services.

In early 1991 the company tried to restructure, but time had run out. In April California and New York placed their respective subsidiaries under supervision, and in May First Executive filed Chapter 11 bankruptcy. The parent company hoped to rebuild its business around its other subsidiaries. But Lincoln Indemnity's and First Stratford's business consisted of reinsurance agreements within the First Executive family in which they supplied capital or assumed loss reserves in return for relatively small payments. First Executive's plans were stymied by supervisory orders in Delaware and Nebraska as well. After the subsidiaries were placed under supervision by their respective states, First Executive's management team was terminated from Executive Life in California (except for newcomer Alan Snyder, who became interim CEO), and California began liquidating the subsidiary. Many suits over California's actions, including one by the IRS relating to Executive Life's 1981–83 taxes, were pending in mid-1991.

NASDAQ symbol: FEXC
Fiscal year ends: December 31

Hoover's Rating **F**

WHO

Chairman and CEO: Fred Carr, age 59, $612,683 pay
VP, General Counsel, and Secretary: William J. Adams, age 61, $270,083 pay
VP, CFO, and Treasurer: William L. Sanders, age 44, $244,918 pay
Auditors: Deloitte & Touche
Employees: 1,070 (before conservatorships)

WHERE

HQ: 11444 W. Olympic Blvd., Los Angeles, CA 90064
Phone: 213-312-1000
Fax: 213-477-3279

First Executive served customers through independent agents in all 50 states; Washington, DC; Puerto Rico; Guam; and the US Virgin Islands.

WHAT

	1990 Sales	
	$ mil.	% of total
Premiums	332	26
Net investment income	1,624	125
Gains (losses) on investments	(660)	(51)
Total	**1,296**	**100**

	1990 Assets	
	$ mil.	% of total
Investments	13,505	89
Cash	20	—
Investment income accrued	299	2
Deferred policy acquisition costs	1,218	8
Other assets	151	1
Total	**15,193**	**100**

Life Insurance Companies
Executive Life Insurance Co.
Executive Life Insurance Co. of New York
First Delaware Life Insurance Co.
Lincoln Liberty Life Insurance Co.

Other Services
Annuities
Guaranteed investment contracts

RANKINGS

27th in *Fortune* 50 Life Insurance Cos. (Executive Life)

KEY COMPETITORS

Equitable
John Hancock
MassMutual
New York Life
Prudential
Teachers Insurance
Transamerica
Travelers

HOW MUCH

	9-Year Growth	1981	1982	1983	1984	1985	1986	1987	1988	1989	1990
Assets ($ mil.)	26.2%	1,876	3,451	4,810	6,547	9,040	14,716	16,903	18,782	19,256	15,193
Net income ($ mil.)	—	17	27	44	73	93	104	125	175	(776)	(366)
Income as % of assets	—	0.9%	0.8%	0.9%	1.1%	1.0%	0.7%	0.7%	0.9%	(4.0%)	(2.4%)
Employees	—	—	—	—	—	—	—	—	—	1,050	1,070

1990 Year-end:
Equity as % of assets: 2.5%
Return on equity: —
Cash (mil.): $20
Sales (mil.): $1,296

Net Income ($ mil.) 1981–90

FIRST FIDELITY BANCORPORATION

NYSE symbol: FFB
Fiscal year ends: December 31

Hoover's Rating C-

OVERVIEW

Lawrenceville, New Jersey–based First Fidelity is a major banking force in New Jersey and Pennsylvania and, before the recent flurry of bank mergers, was the 24th largest bank in the US. The holding company's principal affiliates are 4 First Fidelity banks and Morris Savings Bank in New Jersey, and Fidelity Bank and 2 Merchants Banks in Pennsylvania.

A weak real estate market and problem loan write-offs led to a loss in 1990. However, under Chairman Anthony Terracciano, First Fidelity has put itself in a position to buy weaker banks in its territory by cutting costs, selling nonbank subsidiaries, and raising new capital. Already controlling the state's largest branch system, First Fidelity is rapidly acquiring branches of failed New Jersey banks from the government.

Banco de Santander, Spain's 2nd largest bank, has agreed to buy 13.3% of First Fidelity for $220 million, further improving finances.

WHO

Chairman, President, and CEO: Anthony P. Terracciano, age 52, $826,164 pay
VC and Chief Credit Officer: Peter C. Palmieri, age 56, $489,315 pay
VC and CFO: Wolfgang Schoellkopf, age 58, $490,384 pay
SEVP: Leslie E. Goodman, age 47, $451,342 pay
EVP Human Resources: William A. Karmen, age 49
Auditors: KPMG Peat Marwick
Employees: 10,500

WHEN

The New Jersey legislature established the State Bank of Newark in 1812 with $400,000 in authorized stock, 1/2 of which was reserved for the state. Within a year the bank bought the state's rights to the stock and paid a dividend, the first in an uninterrupted series of regular dividend payments that continues today.

In 1865 the bank got a national charter and became the National State Bank of Newark. The bank grew to about $3.5 million in assets by 1900. As a result of business and industry growth in the Newark area, the bank's assets totaled $7 million in 1920. National State Bank got through the Great Depression on the strength of its 1920s growth. By 1940 the bank's assets were about $38 million.

In 1949 National State bought Merchants and Newark Trust Company. The following year the bank purchased Orange (New Jersey) First National Bank, giving it a presence in Newark's suburbs, and United States Trust Company ($40 million in assets). The bank continued expanding by opening an office at the Newark airport (1953) and by acquiring Newark-based Lincoln National Bank (1955) and Federal Trust Company in Newark (1958). The bank's total assets were more than $418 million after these acquisitions.

Having expanded outside Newark, the bank changed its name to First National State Bank of New Jersey in 1965. The bank formed First National State Bancorporation in 1969 and continued its expansion throughout New Jersey by purchasing another 15 banks during the 1970s.

In 1984 First National State, by then New Jersey's largest banking organization, acquired Fidelity Union Bancorporation, the #3 bank organization in the state, to form First Fidelity Bancorporation, a $10 billion banking organization. The acquisition brought together First National's corporate banking and financial services and Fidelity Union's personal banking services, resulting in a new organization with 288 offices in 21 New Jersey counties.

First Fidelity became a major regional bank in 1988 when it merged with Fidelcor, a $13 billion organization with 190 banking offices in eastern Pennsylvania. Fidelcor, founded in 1866 as a safe-deposit company, was a major banking institution centered on its largest bank, Fidelity Bank of Philadelphia. Fidelcor's loan-quality problem depressed 1988 earnings.

In 1990 Anthony Terracciano, former president of Mellon Bank, became CEO of First Fidelity. Later that year the bank sold its mortgage banking business and bought 9 branches of City Savings Bank (New Jersey) from the RTC. In 1991 First Fidelity bought 48 more City Savings branches and, with federal assistance, First National Bank of Toms River (New Jersey), while selling its Fidelcor Business Credit (commercial finance) unit.

WHERE

HQ: 1009 Lenox Dr., Lawrenceville, NJ 08648-0980
Phone: 609-895-6800
Fax: 609-895-6863 (Investor Relations)

First Fidelity operates 550 banking offices in New Jersey and eastern Pennsylvania.

WHAT

	1990 Assets	
	$ mil.	% of total
Cash & due from banks	2,244	8
Interest bearing deposits	519	2
Securities	6,812	23
Federal funds sold	132	1
Loans	18,530	63
Credit loss reserve	(556)	(2)
Other	1,429	5
Total	**29,110**	**100**

Banking Subsidiaries
Fidelity Bank, N. A.
  Fidelity Bank London
  Fidelity International Bank
First Fidelity Bank, N. A., New Jersey
First Fidelity Bank, N. A., North Jersey
First Fidelity Bank, N. A., South Jersey
First Fidelity Bank, Princeton
Merchants Bank, N. A.
Merchants Bank (North)
Morris Savings Bank

Nonbank Subsidiaries
Broad & Lombardy Associates, Inc. (insurance brokerage)
First Fidelity Brokers, Inc. (stock brokerage)
First Fidelity Community Development Corp.
First Fidelity Leasing Group, Inc.

RANKINGS

24th in *Fortune* 100 Commercial Banking Cos.
438th in *Business Week* 1000

KEY COMPETITORS

Chemical Banking
Citicorp
Mellon Bank
PNC Financial

HOW MUCH

	9-Year Growth	1981	1982	1983	1984	1985	1986	1987	1988	1989	1990
Assets ($ mil.)	24.3%	4,105	4,868	6,417	10,680	12,620	15,170	28,850	29,777	30,728	29,110
Net income ($ mil.)	—	30	35	47	82	94	120	86	34	160	(6)
Income as % of assets	—	0.7%	0.7%	0.7%	0.8%	0.7%	0.8%	0.3%	0.1%	0.5%	0.0%
Earnings per share ($)	—	2.83	3.30	3.48	3.18	3.42	3.95	1.37	0.50	2.52	(0.14)
Stock price – high ($)	—	12.14	17.00	21.13	23.44	31.81	42.50	46.50	40.88	34.00	24.25
Stock price – low ($)	—	9.52	10.69	14.06	15.63	22.75	28.38	27.00	25.25	21.38	11.63
Stock price – close ($)	5.9%	10.50	15.63	20.69	23.44	30.81	35.00	29.88	26.88	23.25	17.63
P/E – high	—	4	5	6	7	9	11	34	82	14	—
P/E – low	—	3	3	4	5	7	7	20	51	8	—
Dividends per share ($)	0.4%	1.06	1.15	1.26	1.38	1.50	1.62	1.76	1.92	2.00	1.10
Book value per share ($)	1.4%	19.60	21.11	23.32	24.59	26.42	29.31	25.80	23.52	24.07	22.22

1990 Year-end:
Return on equity: —
Equity as % of assets: 5.1%
Cash (mil.): $2,764
Long-term debt (mil.): $1,117
No. of shares (mil.): 60
Dividends:
  1990 average yield: 6.2%
  1990 payout: —
Market value (mil.): $1,051
Sales (mil.): $3,082

Stock Price History High/Low 1981–90

FIRST INTERSTATE BANCORP

OVERVIEW

At the end of 1990, First Interstate ranked 11th among US banking organizations. The holding company's separately chartered subsidiary banks in 14 states give First Interstate a large branch network. Franchisees operate 31 banks under the First Interstate banner.

Although progress has been made in lowering costs and in dealing with bad loans, First Interstate keeps delivering negative surprises to shareholders. In mid-1991 bank chairman Edward Carson announced a dividend cut and writeoffs associated with First Interstate's

Nevada and Oregon units. The bank is still suffering from problem real estate loans in Texas and Arizona.

Institutional shareholders own a signifcant proportion of First Interstate stock (Sanford C. Bernstein, 9.6%; Kohlberg Kravis Roberts, 9.9%; Windsor Fund 5%) and some have suggested that a merger with a stronger partner may be in order. In the resultant buyout rumors, Wells Fargo is most often mentioned as a possible acquirer.

WHEN

First Interstate began as a gleam in the eye of Amadeo Peter Giannini, the son of an Italian immigrant. Giannini made enough money in his stepfather's produce firm to retire at age 31. Instead he began dabbling in real estate and banking. He launched the San Francisco–based Bank of Italy in a remodeled tavern in 1904.

Giannini dreamed of a nationwide bank chain and formed Transamerica in 1928 as the umbrella company over Bank of Italy and Bank of America. In 1930 Transamerica bought an Oregon bank and, over the next several years, acquired other non-California banks.

Under the mandates of the Bank Holding Company Act of 1956, Transamerica spun off 2 new entities — Bank of America, comprised of California banks, and Firstamerica, with 23 banks in 11 other western states. The 2 former siblings were destined to become arch-competitors.

Firstamerica bought California Bank (1959) and First Western Bank and Trust (1961). The 2 merged to become United California Bank, with 122 branches in 30 counties. In 1961 Firstamerica changed its name to Western Bancorporation.

In 1978 Joseph Pinola became chairman and CEO of Western. Pinola had spent 25 years rising through the ranks of Bank of America after answering a help-wanted ad when he was

discharged from the navy. At Western the fiery Pinola centralized policymaking and launched an ambitious acquisition program, including an unsuccessful bid to purchase Bank of America and its parent company for $3.4 billion (1986).

In 1981 Western changed its name to First Interstate Bancorp. First Interstate began franchising its name, advertising, products, and services to locally owned banks (1982). In 1985 it divided the California banking operations into 2 sections, retail and wholesale (banking to other corporations). The wholesale arm used a London merchant bank bought from Continental Illinois.

First Interstate acquired retail banks in Denver (1983) and Oklahoma (1986). Even Pinola acknowledged the mistake in First Interstate's purchase of Texas's troubled Allied Bancshares for $160 million (1988).

In 1989 First Interstate acquired Alex Brown Financial Group. In the same year the bank announced it wanted to sell $400 million more stock to cover Texas and Arizona real estate loan losses. Stockholders lambasted the move, and Pinola stepped down under fire in 1990. First Interstate scaled down the offering to $276 million in 1990 and sold 40% of the new stock to Kohlberg Kravis Roberts.

First Interstate sold its consumer lending unit, NOVA Financial Services, in 1990 and 3 New Mexico banks in 1991.

NYSE symbol: I
Fiscal year ends: December 31

Hoover's Rating C-

WHO

Chairman and CEO: Edward M. Carson, age 61, $909,007 pay
President: William E. B. Siart, age 44, $729,270 pay
EVP and CFO: Thomas P. Marrie, age 52
SVP Human Resources: Lillian R. Gorman, age 37
Auditor: Ernst & Young
Employees: 35,471

WHERE

HQ: 633 W. Fifth St., Los Angeles, CA 90071
Phone: 213-614-3001
Fax: 213-614-3741

Subsidiary banks operate in 14 states and 19 foreign countries.

	1990 Average Assets	
	$ mil.	% of total
First Interstate Bank of:		
California	19,999	32
Texas	5,826	9
Arizona	6,682	11
Oregon	6,022	10
Washington	3,639	6
Nevada	3,811	6
Rocky Mountain & other banks	7,142	11
Nonbank subsidiaries	2,217	4
Parent corporation	6,558	11
Eliminations	(7,691)	—
Total	**54,205**	**100**

WHAT

	1990 Assets	
	$ mil.	% of total
Cash & due from banks	5,171	10
Time deposits	336	1
Investment securities	6,667	13
Securities held for sale	308	1
Trading acct. securities	625	1
Securities purchased to resell	891	2
Loans	33,007	64
Credit loss allowance	(1,011)	(2)
Loans held for sale	1,166	2
Other	4,197	8
Total	**51,357**	**100**

Loans	Services
Commercial, agricultural, and financial	Bank credit cards
Installment	Checking and NOW accounts
Real estate construction	Savings accounts
Real estate mortgages	

RANKINGS

11th in *Fortune* 100 Commercial Banking Cos.
299th in *Business Week* 1000

KEY COMPETITORS

H. F. Ahmanson	Great Western
Banc One	NCNB
BankAmerica	Sumitomo
Chase Manhattan	Wells Fargo
Chemical Banking	Other multistate bank
Citicorp	holding companies

HOW MUCH

	9-year Growth	1981	1982	1983	1984	1985	1986	1987	1988	1989	1990
Assets ($ mil.)	3.7%	36,982	40,884	44,423	45,544	48,991	55,422	50,927	58,194	59,051	51,357
Net income ($ mil.)	7.1%	236	221	247	276	313	338	(556)	102	(152)	439
Income as % of assets	—	0.6%	0.5%	0.6%	0.6%	0.6%	0.6%	(1.1%)	0.2%	(0.3%)	0.9%
Earnings per share ($)	1.7%	5.83	5.35	5.72	6.01	6.64	7.13	(11.99)	2.03	(3.89)	6.79
Stock price – high ($)	—	44.88	38.00	47.00	45.25	55.38	67.38	62.75	53.50	70.38	45.88
Stock price – low ($)	—	32.75	21.63	29.25	30.25	41.50	50.75	35.00	39.13	40.75	15.63
Stock price – close ($)	(4.6%)	35.75	31.38	41.63	43.00	52.88	52.00	39.25	43.38	41.88	23.50
P/E – high	—	8	7	8	8	8	9	—	26	—	7
P/E – low	—	6	4	5	5	6	7	—	19	—	2
Dividends per share ($)	4.7%	1.99	2.12	2.22	2.32	2.46	2.62	2.77	2.89	2.98	3.00
Book value per share ($)	(0.4%)	41.24	43.85	47.42	51.29	55.02	58.65	44.39	42.56	36.77	39.77

1990 Year-end:
Return on equity: 17.7%
Equity as % of assets: 5.6%
Cash (mil.): $5,506
Long-term debt (mil.): $3,178
No. of shares (mil.): 62
Dividends:
 1990 average yield: 12.8%
 1990 payout: 44.2%
Market value (mil.): $1,461
Sales (mil.): $6,024

Stock Price History
High/Low 1981–90

FLEET/NORSTAR FINANCIAL GROUP, INC.

NYSE symbol: FNG
Fiscal year ends: December 31

Hoover's Rating **C-**

OVERVIEW

Rhode Island–based Fleet/Norstar in 1991 became the largest banking organization in New England. With the assistance of Kohlberg Kravis Roberts, it catapulted past hobbled Bank of Boston with the 1991 acquisition of the government-seized assets of the failed Bank of New England (BNE).

The BNE purchase added 320 branches and $15 billion in assets to Fleet/Norstar at a price of only $625 million. Fleet emerged from relative obscurity after the deal, but even before the spotlight turned, the company was a major, if unknown, player. Now, after years of aggressive acquisitions and diversifications under Chairman Terrence Murray, Fleet is the 2nd largest mortgage banker in the US (after Citicorp) and the largest 3rd-party student loan processor. Its Atlanta-based consumer finance company, Fleet Finance, boasts $1.5 billion in assets and 151 offices in 26 states.

Despite strong 1990 performance by Fleet's nonbanking subsidiaries ($126 million in net income) and by the Norstar banks in New York ($78 million), bad real estate loans in recession-battered New England led to a $74 million loss.

WHO

Chairman, President, and CEO: J. Terrence Murray, age 51, $755,846 pay
VC: Charles W. Carey, $377,923 pay
VC and CFO: John W. Flynn, $377,923 pay
VP Human Resources: Edward Devin
Auditors: KPMG Peat Marwick
Employees: 18,200

WHERE

HQ: 50 Kennedy Plaza, Providence, RI 02903
Phone: 401-278-5800
Fax: 401-278-5801

Fleet/Norstar has banking operations in New England and New York and financial services units operating nationwide.

WHEN

Fleet/Norstar began celebrating its bicentennial in 1991. Like all good New Englanders, it can trace its roots back to early America — the 1791 founding of The Providence Bank.

The Providence Bank evolved into Fleet National Bank, and in 1968 Fleet became the wholly owned subsidiary of Industrial Bancorp, one of the first bank holding companies permitted as regulatory laws changed. The holding company changed its name in 1970 to Industrial National Corporation. The bank's specialty was lending to the jewelry industry in the Northeast. In the 1970s the bank began to branch out, opening foreign offices and expanding beyond its traditional US market and beyond traditional banking, into consumer finance in Atlanta (Southern Discount, 1973) and mortgage banking in Milwaukee (Mortgage Associates, Inc. 1974).

Terrence Murray, media-described as a bold and brash banker who didn't act like one, became CEO in 1982, the year that Industrial National Corporation changed its name to Fleet Financial Group. Murray was born of a working-class Rhode Island family and played football and baseball while earning a Harvard education. The young CEO continued the bank's diversification, acquiring Credico of New Jersey (consumer lending, 1983) and folding it into Atlanta-based Fleet Finance.

Fleet also crossed the banking borders once Rhode Island permitted reciprocal interstate banking in New England in 1984.

During the 1980s Fleet acquired 46 companies as it grew from assets of $4.2 billion in 1980 to $32.5 billion in 1990. Even its failed acquisitions were successes. Fleet was outbid for Massachusetts-based Conifer Group in 1986, but Conifer quickly proved to be saddled with bad real estate loans. The "winner" was the doomed Bank of New England.

In 1988 Fleet completed acquisition of New York–based Norstar in a $1.3 billion deal. Norstar began in 1971 as Union Bank Corporation of New York and in short order acquired banks in Albany and Buffalo. By the time Fleet bought Norstar, it included 7 banking subsidiaries and 12 financial service companies. Fleet shoehorned back-office computer operations of the 2 banks into a single data center and cut staff 25%.

The FDIC selected Fleet to take over assets of the failed, larger Bank of New England in 1991. The decision doubled Fleet's number of branches, thwarted Fleet competitors BankAmerica and Bank of Boston, and broke new ground with the inclusion of out-of-industry Kohlberg Kravis Roberts in the bid mix. KKR bought $283 million in a new issue of Fleet stock to help Fleet pay for BNE.

WHAT

	1990 Assets	
	$ mil.	% of total
Cash & due from banks	1,794	5
Interest-bearing deposits	106	1
Portfolio securities	5,270	16
Securities for resale	1,882	6
Federal funds sold	240	1
Loans and leases (banking subsidiaries)	16,293	50
Loan loss reserve	(620)	(2)
Loans and leases (nonbank subsidiaries)	4,171	13
Loan loss reserve	(79)	(1)
Mortgages held for resale	978	3
Other	2,472	8
Total	**32,507**	**100**

Banking Subsidiaries
Fleet Bank - Rhode Island
Fleet Bank - New Hampshire
Fleet Bank of Connecticut
Fleet Bank of Maine
Norstar Bank of Central New York
Norstar Bank of Upstate New York
Norstar Bank, NA (Buffalo, NY)

Major Nonbank Subsidiaries
AFSA Data Corp. (student loan processing, California)
Fleet Associates (investment banking)
Fleet Credit Corp. (finance/leasing)
Fleet Factors Corp. (factoring, New York)
Fleet Finance, Inc. (consumer lending, Atlanta)
Fleet Mortgage Group, Inc. (mortgage banking)
Fleet/Norstar Employee Benefit Services, Inc. (pension, administrative services)
Fleet/Norstar Investment Advisors
Fleet/Norstar Trust Group
Fleet/Norstar Securities, Inc. (municipal securities dealer)
Fleet/Norstar Services Corp. (data processing)
Norstar Brokerage Corp. (discount brokerage, New York)

RANKINGS

19th in *Fortune* 100 Commercial Banking Cos.
336th in *Business Week* 1000

KEY COMPETITORS

H. F. Ahmanson	Bankers Trust	First Chicago
Banc One	Charles Schwab	First Interstate
Bank of Boston	Chase Manhattan	First Fidelity
Bank of New York	Chemical Banking	Mellon Bank
BankAmerica	Citicorp	Wells Fargo

HOW MUCH

	9-Year Growth	1981	1982	1983	1984	1985	1986	1987	1988	1989	1990
Assets ($ mil.)	25.5%	4,223	4,536	5,736	5,747	7,122	11,690	24,531	29,052	33,441	32,507
Net income ($ mil.)	—	33	39	52	65	82	137	185	336	371	(74)
Income as % of assets	—	0.8%	0.9%	0.9%	1.1%	1.2%	1.2%	0.8%	1.2%	1.1%	(0.2%)
Earnings per share ($)	—	1.30	1.51	1.59	1.82	2.17	2.50	1.82	3.01	3.30	(0.75)
Stock price – high ($)	—	6.78	9.88	12.69	14.44	21.50	28.06	30.63	27.88	30.88	27.63
Stock price – low ($)	—	4.84	5.13	8.47	10.13	14.25	18.63	17.00	22.38	23.75	8.88
Stock price – close ($)	5.6%	6.72	8.63	11.94	14.28	20.31	23.25	22.75	25.50	26.13	11.00
P/E – high	—	5	7	8	8	10	11	17	9	9	—
P/E – low	—	4	3	5	6	7	7	9	7	7	—
Dividends per share ($)	11.9%	0.46	0.51	0.56	0.62	0.68	0.74	0.88	1.20	1.31	1.25
Book value per share ($)	8.9%	8.18	9.20	10.48	11.86	13.28	14.01	16.00	17.84	19.87	17.65

1990 Year-end:
Return on equity: —
Equity as % of assets: 6.4%
Cash (mil.): $1,900
Long-term debt (mil.): $2,314
No. of shares (mil.): 110
Dividends:
  1990 average yield: 11.4%
  1990 payout: —
Market value (mil.): $1,212
Sales (mil.): $4,033

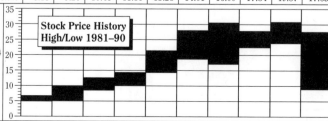

Stock Price History High/Low 1981–90

FLEETWOOD ENTERPRISES, INC.

OVERVIEW

Headquartered in Riverside, California, Fleetwood Enterprises is the nation's largest producer of recreational vehicles (motor homes and travel trailers) and manufactured housing. Fleetwood holds 30.9% of the 1990 motor home market. Many similar products are sold under several brand names, including Jamboree, Pace Arrow, Southwind, Tioga, and Cambria. Fleetwood also controls 28.4% of the travel trailer market and produces Coleman folding trailers, the leader in their niche.

Fleetwood is #1 in manufactured housing, with an 18.4% share, and the nation's largest homebuilder. The company also owns a credit operation (which finances customer recreational vehicle purchases — unique in the industry) and supply operations providing lumber, aluminum windows, fiberglass, and cabinet doors for its own operations and to other companies.

Recession and the Persian Gulf crisis has inhibited demand for RVs and manufactured housing since 1990, even hurting tight-fisted Fleetwood. Signs of recovery emerged in the middle of 1991.

Fleetwood is looking forward to the aging of the baby-boom generation — typical RV buyers are in their 50s.

WHEN

In 1950 John Crean started a business in California to assemble and sell venetian blinds to the motor home manufacturing industry. This small enterprise was the forerunner of Fleetwood, Crean's 1957 entry into the manufactured housing industry, headquartered in Riverside.

Fleetwood entered the recreational vehicle market in 1964 with the purchase of a small plant producing the Terry travel trailer. The following year Fleetwood went public; Crean currently holds 17.7% of the outstanding stock.

In 1969 Fleetwood acquired Pace Arrow, a motor home producer, expanding Fleetwood's offerings in the rapidly growing recreational vehicle market. Between 1968 and 1973 Fleetwood's sales grew at a nearly 55% annual rate.

An industry-wide recession caused by the 1970s oil shock and subsequent credit crunch dropped Fleetwood's stock from a 1972 high of $49.50 to $3.50 in 1974. Intensive cost cutting helped position Fleetwood for the eventual upturn, and in 1976 the company purchased Avion Coach Corporation, a manufacturer of luxury-class travel trailers and motor homes.

COO Glenn Kummer succeeded Crean as president in 1982, but Crean remains chairman and CEO. Strong recreational vehicle sales helped pull Fleetwood out of a mild recession in the mid-1980s, when the company's stock plummeted again, from a 1983 high of $42 to $14 in 1985.

In 1987 the company opened its first credit office in Southern California to finance customer purchases of recreational vehicles, avoiding riskier loans to manufactured housing buyers. Fleetwood Credit Corporation now has offices in California, Oregon, Indiana, Georgia, Massachusetts, and Texas.

Fleetwood added to its existing supply operations (fiberglass and lumber) with the purchase of a cabinet door manufacturer (1988) and an aluminum window maker (1989).

In 1989 Fleetwood became the first company to surpass the $1 billion annual sales mark in recreational vehicles, increasing market share during an industry slump. Total sales increased 15% to a company record $1.6 billion, while Fleetwood continued to steer clear of any long-term debt. The company added 2 new motor home models to its recreational vehicle line: the lower-priced Flair and the curved-wall Cambria.

In 1989 Fleetwood improved its product offering by acquiring Coleman's folding trailer business, the largest in the industry. The company received a Saudi Arabian order for 2,000 manufactured homes in 1990.

NYSE symbol: FLE
Fiscal year ends: Last Sunday in April

Hoover's Rating **A-**

WHO

Chairman and CEO: John C. Crean, age 66, $479,268 pay
President and COO: Glenn F. Kummer, age 57, $421,234 pay
Financial VP: Paul M. Bingham, age 49, $234,307 pay
VP Administration and Human Resources: Robert W. Graham, age 54
Auditors: Arthur Andersen & Co.
Employees: 11,000

WHERE

HQ: 3125 Myers St., Riverside, CA 92503
Phone: 714-351-3500
Fax: 714-351-3690

Fleetwood operates 40 manufacturing plants in the US and one in Canada. The company sells its products through independent dealers in 3,500 locations in 49 states and Canada.

WHAT

	1990 Sales		1990 Operating Income	
	$ mil.	% of total	$ mil.	% of total
Manufactured housing	567	40	24	69
Supply operations	11	1	(3)	(9)
Recreational vehicles	797	56	15	43
Finance operations	30	2	5	14
Corporate & other	8	1	(6)	(17)
Adjustments	(12)	—	14	—
Total	**1,401**	**100**	**49**	**100**

Recreational Vehicles

American Eagle	Coleman	Pace Arrow
Avion	(folding trailers)	Prowler
Bounder	Coronado	Southwind
Cambria	Flair	Terry
Caribou	Jamboree	Tioga
	Limited	Wilderness

Subsidiaries
Buckingham Development Co.
C. V. Aluminum, Inc.
Continental Lumber Products, Inc.
FLE Corp.
Fleetwood Credit Corp.
Fleetwood Credit Receivables Corp.
Fleetwood Foreign Sales Corp.
Fleetwood Holidays, Inc.
Fleetwood Insurance Services, Inc.
Fleetwood International, Inc.
Flordevco, Inc.
Gibraltar Insurance Co., Ltd.
Gold Shield Fiberglass, Inc.
Gold Shield Fiberglass of Indiana, Inc.
GSF Installation Co.
Hauser Lake Lumber Operation, Inc.
Housing Supply, Inc.

RANKINGS

257th in *Fortune* 500 Industrial Cos.
772nd in *Business Week* 1000

KEY COMPETITORS

Harley-Davidson
MacAndrews & Forbes

HOW MUCH

Fiscal year ends April of following year	9-Year Growth	1981	1982	1983	1984	1985	1986	1987	1988	1989	1990
Sales ($ mil.)	10.3%	581	858	1,420	1,277	1,218	1,259	1,406	1,619	1,549	1,401
Net income ($ mil.)	14.3%	9	30	64	54	39	40	48	70	55	30
Income as % of sales	—	1.6%	3.5%	4.5%	4.2%	3.2%	3.2%	3.4%	4.4%	3.6%	2.2%
Earnings per share ($)	14.3%	0.41	1.33	2.71	2.29	1.69	1.70	2.08	3.06	2.42	1.37
Stock price – high ($)	—	7.38	20.63	41.88	30.75	28.75	33.50	32.00	26.63	30.63	29.13
Stock price – low ($)	—	4.06	5.31	18.00	14.13	17.50	20.75	14.00	17.00	22.00	15.75
Stock price – close ($)	14.6%	6.44	20.44	26.63	26.38	24.38	25.38	17.38	25.13	24.00	21.88
P/E – high	—	18	16	15	13	17	20	15	9	13	21
P/E – low	—	10	4	7	6	10	12	7	6	9	12
Dividends per share ($)	13.9%	0.26	0.27	0.30	0.36	0.44	0.52	0.60	0.64	0.76	0.84
Book value per share ($)	16.7%	4.87	6.85	9.25	11.10	12.37	13.56	15.02	17.49	19.02	19.55

1990 Year-end:
Debt ratio: 0.0%
Return on equity: 7.1%
Cash (mil.): $15
Current ratio: —
Long-term debt (mil.): 0
No. of shares (mil.): 22
Dividends:
  1990 average yield: 3.8%
  1990 payout: 61.3%
Market value (mil.): $479

Stock Price History High/Low 1981–90

FLEMING COMPANIES, INC.

OVERVIEW

Fleming Companies of Oklahoma City is the US's largest wholesale food distributor and in 1990 celebrated its 75th year. With 1990 sales of almost $12 billion, the company serves nearly one out of every 10 supermarkets in the US. The company services over 4,800 retail food stores in 36 states, with 30 distribution centers carrying a variety of groceries, produce, meats, dairy products, frozen foods, and general merchandise. Independent retailers represent 64% of sales volume, with corporate chains providing the balance.

The company also operates 117 retail food stores in 16 midwestern and southern states under the names of Piggly Wiggly, Food 4 Less, Thriftway, and Sentry. Also, the company provides support services to food retailers, including accounting, financing, data processing, advertising, insurance, and store design and engineering.

Sales of perishable foods in 1990 increased to 39% of product mix, nearing a corporate objective of 40%.

NYSE symbol: FLM
Fiscal year ends: Last Saturday in December

Hoover's Rating **C+**

WHO

Chairman and CEO: E. Dean Werries, age 61, $683,149 pay
President and COO: John E. Moll, age 56, $647,833 pay
VP; President, Godfrey Division: James H. DeWees, age 57, $411,770 pay
EVP and CFO: R. Randolph Devening, age 49, $394,211 pay
SVP Human Resources: Larry A. Wagner, age 44
Auditors: Deloitte & Touche
Employees: 22,900

WHEN

Fleming Companies was incorporated in 1915 as Lux Mercantile, a Topeka, Kansas, wholesale grocery founded by O. A. Fleming, Gene Wilson, and Sam Lux. In 1918 the company became Fleming-Wilson Mercantile.

Facing stiff competition from chain stores, independent wholesalers and grocers formed the "voluntary group," to provide competitive mass merchandising, advertising, and efficient store operations. Fleming's son Ned helped establish the company as the first voluntary wholesaler west of the Mississippi (1927). The company was renamed The Fleming Company, Inc. (1941), and Ned Fleming was president (1945–64) and later chairman and CEO (1964–81). The company went public in 1959, adopted its present name in 1972, and was reincorporated in Oklahoma in 1981.

Since the 1930s the company has grown steadily by acquisitions, primarily of midwestern wholesale food distributors and supermarkets. Acquisitions in the 1930s and 1940s included Hutchinson Wholesale Grocery (1935), Carroll, Brough & Robinson (1941), Ryley-Wilson Grocery (1949), and Golden Wedding Coffee (1948; renamed Certified Brands, 1949). In the 1950s and 1960s Fleming bought Ruston Bakery (1953, renamed Certified Bakers), Topeka Wholesale Drug (1958, renamed Drug Distributors), Grainger Brothers (1962, renamed The Fleming Company of Nebraska), Inter-State

Grocer (1964), and Nelson Davis (1964). The only acquisition from the 1970s that the company still has is Benson-Dixieland, with 44 supermarkets in the Southeast (bought in 1974). More recent acquisitions the company still has include American-Strevell (1983); an Alpha Beta distribution center (1985); Associated Grocers of Arizona (1985); a wholesale distribution center of Foodland Super Markets (1986); and Godfrey, with 32 Sentry supermarkets and 4 Sun warehouse markets (1987).

The $600 million purchase of Tennessee-based Malone & Hyde (1988), the 6th largest wholesale food distributor in the US, made Fleming the largest food distributor in the US. In 1988 the company sold the 99-store retail drug subsidiary (M&A Drugs) of Malone & Hyde for $55 million, and White Swan (bought in 1982) for $217 million.

When Albertson's completed its own warehouse and Alpha Beta merged with Lucky, Fleming lost them as customers and had to close the Fremont, California, distribution center (1990). The company has worked to make up for losing Albertson's and Alpha Beta's business. Recent customers represent wholesale volumes of over $600 million annually.

In January 1991 Fleming agreed to buy the warehouse and transportation assets of Furr's. It is expected that this will increase western Texas and New Mexico sales by $650 million.

WHERE

HQ: PO Box 26647, 6301 Waterford Blvd., Oklahoma City, OK 73126
Phone: 405-840-7200
Fax: 405-841-8149

Fleming operates 30 wholesale food and general merchandise distribution centers totaling 20 million square feet and serving more than 4,800 stores in 36 states. It has 36 divisions divided in 5 geographic regions.

	1990 Sales
	% of total
Malone & Hyde subsidiary	26
Western US	25
Central US	20
Southern US	19
Eastern US	10
Total	**100**

WHAT

	1990 Sales
Product mix	% of total
Groceries	56
Perishables	39
General merchandise	5
Total	**100**

Volume by customer type	% of total
Independents	
Voluntary groups	45
Nonfranchised	19
Company owned	7
Corporate chains	29
Total	**100**

Volume by store format	% of total
Conventional supermarkets	55
Combination stores	14
Superstores	15
Price impact stores	16
Total	**100**

RANKINGS

3rd in *Fortune* 100 Diversified Service Cos.
517th in *Business Week* 1000

KEY COMPETITORS

McKesson
Super Valu

HOW MUCH

	9-Year Growth	1981	1982	1983	1984	1985	1986	1987	1988	1989	1990
Sales ($ mil.)	15.0%	3,399	3,688	4,898	5,512	7,095	7,653	8,608	10,467	12,045	11,933
Net income ($ mil.)	15.8%	26	29	42	50	60	36	49	65	80	97
Income as % of sales	—	0.8%	0.8%	0.9%	0.9%	0.8%	0.5%	0.6%	0.6%	0.7%	0.8%
Earnings per share ($)	5.7%	1.78	1.98	2.27	2.57	2.79	1.67	1.86	2.43	2.54	2.93
Stock price – high ($)	—	16.13	23.31	31.13	35.38	41.88	44.88	45.88	35.50	40.00	37.63
Stock price – low ($)	—	11.56	11.31	22.25	22.25	32.00	31.00	22.00	26.50	27.50	28.00
Stock price – close ($)	11.7%	13.00	22.75	28.88	34.13	38.88	34.63	27.25	35.00	30.13	35.25
P/E – high	—	9	12	14	14	15	27	25	15	16	13
P/E – low	—	7	6	10	9	11	19	12	11	11	10
Dividends per share ($)	6.4%	0.59	0.64	0.71	0.84	0.97	1.00	1.00	1.00	1.00	1.03
Book value per share ($)	10.2%	10.44	13.09	14.73	17.72	20.56	21.33	19.58	21.79	22.95	25.02

1990 Year-end:
Debt ratio: 54.7%
Return on equity: 12.2%
Cash (mil.): $21
Current ratio: 1.45
Long-term debt (mil.): $981
No. of shares (mil.): 31
Dividends:
1990 average yield: 2.9%
1990 payout: 35.2%
Market value (mil.): $1,077

Stock Price History High/Low 1981–90

FLUOR CORPORATION

OVERVIEW

Irvine, California–based Fluor is the world's largest engineering and construction (E&C) firm. Its E&C activities, conducted under the Fluor Daniel umbrella, are organized into 5 major sectors: Hydrocarbon, Government, Industrial, Process, and Power.

Well along the road to recovery from its financial troubles of the mid-1980s caused by over-reliance on energy megaprojects, Fluor boasts a balanced backlog — a barometer of an engineering firm's health — of $10 billion.

Among its major innovations, Fluor has developed its alliance concept, in which its engineers work not on a single project for a client but become long-term adjuncts to the client's organization. Clients have included Du Pont and Duke Power.

Fluor also runs subsidiaries in coal (A.T. Massey Coal) and lead (The Doe Run Company). Doe Run is the largest lead producer in North America, but Fluor has said it would consider selling the unit.

NYSE symbol: FLR
Fiscal year ends: October 31

Hoover's Rating B+

WHO

Chairman and CEO: Leslie G. McCraw, age 56, $898,906 pay (prior to promotion)
President and COO: Vincent L. Kontny, age 53, $711,529 pay (prior to promotion)
SVP and CFO: Robert L. Guyett, age 54
VP Human Resources and Administration: Charles J. Bradley
Auditors: Ernst & Young
Employees: 22,188

WHEN

The world's largest engineering and construction firm began with a Swiss immigrant carpenter in Santa Ana, California. Si Fluor launched a modest, family-run construction firm in 1912. In 1922 Fluor's company won a contract to build a 10,000-gallon-a-day refinery for Richfield Oil, and in 1930 it won work on a midwestern pipeline.

After WWII the company entered the world of the international petrochemical industry with a contract in Saudi Arabia. During the early 1960s, when Si Fluor's grandson Bob began running the company, Fluor continued to emphasize oil and gas work, acquiring drilling companies to establish a contract-drilling unit.

Despite a slump in the early 1970s, Fluor didn't cut staff, and when the Arab oil embargo of 1973 touched off oil and gas price increases, Fluor was ready. In 1977 the company won a $3 billion contract for a Saudi Arabian petrochemical plant. Also that year, in what would prove to be a masterstroke, Fluor bought Daniel International, a South Carolina–based engineering and construction firm with more than $1 billion in annual revenues.

Daniel International had begun in 1934 when Charlie Daniel quit his lumber company job and opened a contracting firm. The non-union firm moved to Greenville, South Carolina, in 1942 and became heavily involved in construction for the textile industry. Daniel later branched out to serve clients in the chemical, pharmaceutical, pulp and paper, metals, food, and power industries.

In the 1980s Bob Fluor's company was flush with cash and a backlog of huge petroleum industry projects. In 1981 Fluor spent an at-the-time-eye-popping $2.2 billion to buy St. Joe Minerals. In a *Forbes* article that year, analysts projected "a 25% annual revenue and earnings gain for the company throughout the decade."

Wrong.

A drop in oil prices in the early 1980s killed demand for the big projects that had become Fluor's bread and butter. St. Joe didn't help the bottom line because, along with servicing debt to buy the minerals concern, Fluor also faced declining metals prices. And then Bob Fluor died of lung cancer in 1984.

David Tappan stepped in as CEO and faced a $573 million loss his first year on the job. The white-haired son of missionaries to China, Tappan became known as "the Ice Man" as he dumped subsidiaries and cut the payroll in half. In 1986 Tappan merged Daniel into Fluor's engineering subsidiary to form Fluor Daniel and give the company a fresh orientation, from petroleum megaprojects to smaller jobs. Leslie McCraw succeeded Tappan as chairman and CEO in 1991, as analysts salivated at Fluor's prospects for rebuilding war-ravaged Kuwait. McCraw, a Daniel veteran, recalled petroleum-fired exuberance of a decade earlier and downplayed Fluor's role.

WHERE

HQ: 3333 Michelson Dr., Irvine, CA 92730
Phone: 714-975-2000
Fax: 714-975-5271

Fluor operates major facilities in 12 US states, Puerto Rico, and 16 foreign countries.

	1990 Sales		1990 Operating Income	
	$ mil.	% of total	$ mil.	% of total
US	6,244	84	209	90
Europe	595	8	14	6
Canada	388	5	6	3
Mid East	24	1	1	—
Other countries	195	2	2	1
Adjustments	—	—	(64)	—
Total	**7,446**	**100**	**168**	**100**

WHAT

	1990 Sales		1990 Operating Income	
	$ mil.	% of total	$ mil.	% of total
Engineering & Construction	6,383	86	135	58
Coal	866	11	60	26
Lead	197	3	36	16
Adjustments	—	—	(63)	—
Total	**7,446**	**100**	**168**	**100**

Engineering and Construction
Hydrocarbon Sector
Government Sector
Industrial Sector
Process Sector
Power Sector

Fluor Constructors International
Unionized construction service

Natural Resource Investments
Coal (99.5%, A.T. Massey Coal)
Lead (The Doe Run Co.)

RANKINGS

13th in *Fortune* 100 Diversified Service Cos.
161st in *Business Week* 1000

KEY COMPETITORS

ABB
Ashland
Baker Hughes
Bechtel
Dresser
Halliburton
McDermott
Mitsubishi
Peter Kiewit Sons'
Coal and lead mining companies

HOW MUCH

	9-Year Growth	1981	1982	1983	1984	1985	1986	1987	1988	1989	1990
Sales ($ mil.)	2.3%	6,073	7,336	5,300	4,401	4,168	4,660	3,924	5,132	6,278	7,446
Net income ($ mil.)	(1.5%)	159	153	81	1	(573)	(28)	(75)	56	108	139
Income as % of sales	—	2.6%	2.1%	1.5%	0.0%	(13.8%)	(0.6%)	(1.9%)	1.1%	1.7%	1.9%
Earnings per share ($)	(5.4%)	2.83	1.94	1.02	0.01	(7.25)	(0.35)	(0.95)	0.71	1.35	1.71
Stock price – high ($)	—	61.88	30.50	25.38	23.38	20.13	19.25	21.63	23.88	37.75	49.25
Stock price – low ($)	—	26.00	11.88	16.13	14.50	13.75	11.13	11.00	12.75	21.63	29.00
Stock price – close ($)	2.3%	30.00	19.50	17.25	14.75	15.50	11.50	13.75	23.38	36.75	36.75
P/E – high	—	22	16	25	2,338	—	—	—	34	28	29
P/E – low	—	9	6	16	1,450	—	—	—	18	16	17
Dividends per share ($)	(12.5%)	0.80	0.80	0.80	0.60	0.40	0.40	0.10	0.02	0.14	0.24
Book value per share ($)	(7.3%)	21.36	22.68	22.19	21.49	13.06	11.99	6.74	7.61	9.03	10.75

1990 Year-end:
Debt ratio: 7.7%
Return on equity: 17.3%
Cash (mil.): $271
Current ratio: 1.24
Long-term debt (mil.): $72
No. of shares (mil.): 80
Dividends:
  1990 average yield: 0.7%
  1990 payout: 14.0%
Market value (mil.): $2,954

Stock Price History High/Low 1981–90

FMC CORPORATION

OVERVIEW

Chicago-based FMC has attained a degree of earnings stability through diversification, as weakness in one sector tends to be offset by strength in another. The company's main businesses are industrial and performance (agricultural, pharmaceutical, specialty) chemicals, defense systems, and machinery and equipment. The company produces gold and silver through 79%-owned FMC Gold. Employees, directors, and officers own 29% of FMC.

FMC leads the world in the production of natural soda ash (used in chemicals and glass),

phosphorous chemicals (used in detergents), and lithium-based products. The company's Bradley tanks were used heavily by the US Army in the Gulf War. Under pressure from the EPA, FMC has agreed to slowly reduce US sales of the granular form of its popular insecticide Furadan.

Responding to economic uncertainty, FMC has cut capital spending but left R&D budgets intact. Much of the company's new plant R&D spending is focused on its industrial chemical business. Foreign expansion plans continue.

NYSE symbol: FMC
Fiscal year ends: December 31

WHO

Chairman, President, and CEO: Robert N. Burt, age 53, $488,149 pay (prior to promotion)
EVP: Larry D. Brady, age 48, $393,093 pay
VP Finance: Arthur D. Lyons, age 54
VP Human Resources: Lawrence P. Holleran, age 60
Auditors: KPMG Peat Marwick
Employees: 23,882

WHERE

HQ: 200 E. Randolph Dr., Chicago, IL 60601
Phone: 312-861-6000
Fax: 312-861-6176

FMC operates 92 plants and mines in 24 states and 16 foreign countries.

	1990 Sales		1990 Pretax Income	
	$ mil.	% of total	$ mil.	% of total
US	3,059	80	353	84
Latin America, Canada	145	4	5	1
Europe	591	15	62	15
Other countries	42	1	2	—
Adjustments	(115)	—	(115)	—
Total	**3,722**	**100**	**307**	**100**

WHAT

	1990 Sales		1990 Pretax Income	
	$ mil.	% of total	$ mil.	% of total
Defense systems	1,067	29	97	23
Performance chem.	594	16	85	20
Machinery & equip.	846	23	52	12
Industrial chem.	1,030	27	107	26
Precious metals	188	5	81	19
Adjustments	(3)	—	(115)	—
Total	**3,722**	**100**	**307**	**100**

Industrial Chemicals
Hydrogen peroxide
Lithium-based products
Pesticides
Phosphates
Soda ash

Machinery
Automotive equipment
Food processing and packaging equipment
Material handling equipment
Oil field machinery
Street sweepers

Precious Metals
Gold
Silver

Performance Chemicals
Food additives
Insecticides
Pharmaceutical ingredients

Defense Systems
Armored tanks and personnel carriers
Naval weapons

WHEN

After retiring to California, inventor John Bean developed a pump to deliver a continuous spray of insecticide (1884). This invention led to the Bean Spray Pump Company (1904). In 1928 Bean Spray Pump went public and bought Anderson-Barngrover (food growing and processing equipment). The new company name, John Bean Manufacturing, gave way to Food Machinery Corporation in 1929. The company bought Peerless Pump (agricultural and industrial pumps) in 1933.

During WWII the company started manufacturing military equipment and entered the agricultural chemical field with the purchase of Niagara Sprayer & Chemical (1943). After the war, it bought Westvaco Chemical (industrial chemicals, 1948) and changed its name to Food Machinery & Chemical. The company extended its product line, buying such companies as Oil Center Tool (wellhead equipment, 1957), Sunland Industries (fertilizer, insecticides, and seeds; 1959), and Barrett Equipment (automotive brake equipment, 1961). The Bean family ran the company until 1956, when John Crummey, grandson of John Bean, retired as chairman.

In light of its growing diversification, the company changed its name to FMC in 1961. FMC's major purchases in the 1960s were American Viscose (rayon and cellophane, 1963) and Link-Belt (equipment for power

transmission and for bulk-material handling, 1967).

To be centrally located, FMC moved its headquarters from San Jose to Chicago in 1972. In 1976 it sold its pump division, its fiber division, and its 50% interest in Ketchikan Pulp (part of the American Viscose purchase). FMC continued to sell its slow-growing businesses, including the semiconductor division (1979), the industrial packaging division (1980), the Niagara Seed Operation (1980), and the Power Transmission Group (1981).

In 1979 FMC entered mining in a joint venture (30/70) with Freeport Minerals to continue developing a gold mine in Jerritt Canyon, Nevada (discovered 1973, mine in operation 1982). In the 1980s FMC found more gold near Gabbs, Nevada (Paradise Peak) and entered the lithium business with the purchase of Lithium Corporation of America (integrated lithium producer, 1985). In a 1986 anti-takeover move, FMC financed a $2 billion recapitalization, paying shareholders $80 per share and giving employees a larger stake in the company. In 1989 FMC bought the French company Mather et Platt (harvesters, food processing equipment). The next year FMC Gold bought Meridian Gold from Burlington Resources. FMC received a $1.1 billion US Army contract for Bradley tanks and rocket system carriers in 1991.

RANKINGS

131st in *Fortune* 500 Industrial Cos.
461st in *Business Week* 1000

KEY COMPETITORS

Alcoa	Cyprus Minerals	Hoechst
American Cyanamid	Deere	Ingersoll-Rand
Anglo American	Dow Chemical	LTV
AMAX	Dresser	Monsanto
ASARCO	Du Pont	Morton
Baker Hughes	General Dynamics	Pearson
BASF	Halliburton	Phelps Dodge
Borg-Warner	Hanson	Vulcan
Caterpillar	Hercules	

HOW MUCH

	9-Year Growth	1981	1982	1983	1984	1985	1986	1987	1988	1989	1990
Sales ($ mil.)	1.1%	3,367	3,499	3,498	3,338	3,261	3,003	3,139	3,287	3,415	3,722
Net income ($ mil.)	(1.4%)	177	152	169	226	197	153	191	129	157	155
Income as % of sales	—	5.2%	4.4%	4.8%	6.8%	6.0%	5.1%	6.1%	3.9%	4.6%	4.2%
Earnings per share ($)	19.6%	0.86	0.75	0.83	1.27	1.30	1.62	4.52	3.60	4.34	4.30
Stock price – high ($)	—	6.31	6.18	8.60	10.94	12.71	26.38	60.38	39.13	49.00	38.75
Stock price – low ($)	—	4.28	4.08	5.56	7.32	9.48	11.50	24.00	24.38	31.63	25.38
Stock price – close ($)	24.2%	4.52	5.69	8.14	9.95	11.56	25.75	33.75	32.00	35.25	31.88
P/E – high	—	7	8	10	9	10	16	13	11	11	9
P/E – low	—	5	5	7	6	7	7	5	7	7	6
Dividends per share ($)	—	0.28	0.29	0.32	0.34	0.39	0.10	0.00	0.00	0.00	0.00
Book value per share ($)	(5.2%)	6.97	7.32	7.65	6.65	7.69	(11.25)	(10.12)	(6.53)	(2.05)	4.30

1990 Year-end:
Debt ratio: 88.6%
Return on equity: —
Cash (mil.): $93
Current ratio: 1.03
Long-term debt (mil.): $1,159
No. of shares (mil.): 35
Dividends:
 1990 average yield: 0.0%
 1990 payout: 0.0%
Market value (mil.): $1,108

Stock Price History High/Low 1981–90

FOOD LION, INC.

OVERVIEW

Salisbury, North Carolina–based Food Lion is one of the strongest grocery chains in the US. 1990 was a record year, with earnings up 23.5%. Same-store sales increased by 4.5%, lower than historical gains of 5% to 6%. Earnings for 1990 had a net margin of 3%, triple the industry norm.

The company centralizes buying and pricing food. All 778 stores have essentially the same layout. Food Lion follows an "ink blot" approach to expansion in which the company builds many relatively small stores carrying only food items and fast-moving nongrocery items (average size 24,700 square feet, costing only about 1/3 of that to build a superstore) in a new market. Such an approach allows

increased distibution-center efficiency by serving as many locations as possible. This saturation policy, along with a nonunionized work force and an obsession with operating efficiencies, enables the company to sell at extremely low prices. New retail strategies emphasize more healthful foods and foods that can be quickly prepared.

Ralph Ketner, one of the 3 founders, resigned as chairman in May 1990; Tom Smith, president and CEO, subsequently added the duties of chairman to his other responsibilities. Delhaize "Le Lion," Belgium's 3rd largest public company, and its American subsidiary, Delhaize The Lion America, Inc., own 50.3% of the company's voting stock.

NASDAQ symbols: FDLNA and FDLNB

Fiscal year ends: Saturday nearest to December 31

Hoover's Rating **A+**

WHO

Chairman, President, and CEO: Tom E. Smith, age 49, $795,370 pay
SVP and COO: Jerry W. Helms, age 50, $370,124 pay
VP Finance: Dan A. Boone, age 38
Director of Employee Benefits and Services: Ronnie Smith
Auditors: Coopers & Lybrand
Employees: 47,276

WHERE

HQ: PO Box 1330, 2110 Executive Dr., Salisbury, NC 28145-1330
Phone: 704-633-8250
Fax: 704-636-5024

Food Lion operates 778 general food supermarkets in 11 states, primarily in the Southeast and mid-Atlantic regions.

	1990 Store Locations	
	No. of stores	% of total
North Carolina	312	40
Virginia	173	22
South Carolina	86	11
Florida	83	11
Tennessee	63	8
Other states	61	8
Total	**778**	**100**

	1990 Warehouse Space	
	Sq. ft. thou.	% of total
Dunn, NC	1,225	20
Prince George County, VA	1,125	18
Elloree, SC	1,093	17
Salisbury, NC	1,336	21
Green Cove Springs, FL	732	12
Clinton, TN	726	12
Total	**6,237**	**100**

WHEN

Food Lion was formed in 1957 in Salisbury, North Carolina, by 3 former Winn-Dixie employees — Wilson Smith, Ralph Ketner, and Ralph's brother Brown Ketner. They named the market Food Town and peddled stock in the new company at $10 per share to anyone in Salisbury who would buy. Two of the store's first employees were bagger Tom Smith (now chairman and CEO) and produce manager Jerry Helms (now COO).

The company struggled through its first 10 years of operation; by the end of 1967 (after opening 16 stores and closing 9), it was foundering. Trading stamps, contests, and drawings failed to attract customers. That year Ralph Ketner pored over 6 months of store receipts and determined that if Food Town lowered the prices on all 3,000 items and sales increased 50%, the company would survive. The strategy paid off, and the company was reborn as a resolute cost-cutter. The company's slogan, LFPINC (Lowest Food Prices in North Carolina), soon appeared on bumper stickers.

In 1974 a Belgian grocery company, Etablissements Delhaize Freres et Cie, "Le Lion," which used a lion as its symbol, began investing in Food Town. By 1989 it owned

50.3% of the voting stock. Food Town changed its name in 1983 to avoid confusion with another Food Town store in its market area. Ketner adopted the name Food Lion not only because of the lion symbol of Delhaize Freres, but also because he could save money by replacing only the *t* and the *w* at the company's stores.

In the 1980s Food Lion increased its number of stores from 106 to 663, always following the company's low-price, cost-cutting formula, and built 3 distribution centers.

Food Lion maintained its high growth rate in 1990 by having a net increase of 115 new stores. By the end of 1991 Food Lion expects to have about 40 new stores in the Dallas–Ft. Worth area with "Texas Sized Savings." Entering the Texas market changes the company's expansion strategy of moving into contiguous states. The company also expects to open 3 distribution centers; one will be in Texas.

Food Lion has made its 100+ original shareholders very rich; its phenomenal growth, from $5.8 million in 1967 to $5.58 billion in 1990, is reflected by the fact that a single share of stock bought for $10 in 1957 would have split into 12,960 shares, worth nearly $200,000 today.

WHAT

	1990 Sales	
	$ mil.	% of total
Existing stores	5,281	95
New stores	303	5
Total	**5,584**	**100**

	1990 Stores	
	No. of stores	% of total
Existing stores	657	84
New stores	121	16
Total	**778**	**100**

RANKINGS

21st in *Fortune* 50 Retailing Cos.
123rd in *Business Week* 1000

KEY COMPETITORS

Albertson's	Publix
American Stores	Safeway
Bruno's	Super Valu
Great A&P	Winn-Dixie
Kroger	

HOW MUCH

	9-Year Growth	1981	1982	1983	1984	1985	1986	1987	1988	1989	1990
Sales ($ mil.)	26.6%	667	947	1,172	1,470	1,866	2,407	2,954	3,815	4,717	5,584
Net income ($ mil.)	27.5%	19	22	28	37	48	62	86	113	140	173
Income as % of sales	—	2.9%	2.3%	2.4%	2.5%	2.6%	2.6%	2.9%	3.0%	3.0%	3.1%
Earnings per share ($)	27.1%	0.06	0.07	0.09	0.12	0.15	0.20	0.27	0.35	0.43	0.54
Stock price – high ($)	—	1.08	2.27	2.48	2.42	3.71	7.31	13.69	12.88	12.50	15.50
Stock price – low ($)	—	0.62	0.86	1.67	1.42	2.21	3.33	5.50	9.00	9.00	10.38
Stock price – close ($)	32.3%	1.06	2.19	1.71	2.42	3.63	5.56	12.00	9.38	10.88	13.13
P/E – high	—	17	32	28	20	25	38	51	37	29	29
P/E – low	—	10	12	19	12	15	17	20	26	21	19
Dividends per share ($)	43.3%	0.01	0.01	0.01	0.01	0.01	0.02	0.05	0.07	0.10	0.13
Book value per share ($)	26.5%	0.25	0.31	0.39	0.51	0.65	0.83	1.05	1.34	1.67	2.07

1990 Year-end:
Debt ratio: 27.4%
Return on equity: 28.8%
Cash (mil.): $10
Current ratio: 1.27
Long-term debt (mil.): $252
No. of shares (mil.): 322
Dividends:
  1990 average yield: 1.0%
  1990 payout: 25.0%
Market value (mil.): $4,229

Stock Price History
High/Low 1981–90

THE FORD FOUNDATION

OVERVIEW

The Ford Foundation is the largest philanthropic foundation in the US. Through 1990 the foundation has granted over $7 billion to more than 9,000 organizations in all 50 states and more than 80 foreign countries.

Educational, research, and development grants (mainly to organizations) focus on urban and rural poverty, human rights, public policy, education, the creative and performing arts, and international affairs. Overseas grants target developing countries, which receive about 35% of the overall program budget.

A board of trustees sets broad policies and grants objectives while the program staff identifies and recommends worthy recipients. The foundation's headquarters, completed in 1967, is in New York and is noted for its award-winning architectural design.

The foundation no longer has stock in Ford Motor Company or ties to the Ford family. Funds are derived solely from an internal stock and bond portfolio, which the 1980s bull market pushed to a record $5.6 billion in 1989, although it has fallen to $5.2 billion in 1990.

Nonprofit organization
Fiscal year ends: September 30

Hoover's Rating **A**

WHEN

Henry Ford and his son Edsel established the Ford Foundation in Michigan in 1936 with an initial gift of $25,000, followed the next year by 250,000 shares of nonvoting stock in the Ford Motor Company. The foundation's activities were limited mainly to Michigan until the deaths of Edsel (1943) and Henry (1947) made the foundation the owner of 90% of the automaker's nonvoting stock (catapulting the endowment to $474 million, the US's largest).

In 1951 under a new mandate and president (Paul Hoffman, formerly head of the Marshall Plan), the foundation announced broad commitments to world peace, strengthening of democracy, and improved education. Early education program grants overseen by University of Chicago chancellor Robert Maynard Hutchins ($100 million in 1951–53 alone) helped establish major international programs (e.g., Harvard's Center for International Legal Studies) and the National Merit Scholarships.

Under McCarthyite criticism for its experimental education grants, the foundation in 1956 granted $550 million (after selling 22% of its Ford shares to the public) to non-controversial recipients: 600 liberal arts colleges, 3,500 nonprofit hospitals, and 44 private medical schools. Ford money set up the Radio and Television Workshop (1951). Public TV support (totaling some $293 million by 1977) became a foundation trademark.

Overseas work, begun in Asia and the Middle East (1950) and extended to Africa (1958) and Latin America (1959), focused on education and rural development; the foundation also supported the Population Council and research in high-yield agriculture with the Rockefeller Foundation. Other grants supported the arts and the upgrading of US engineering schools.

An emerging activism in the early 1960s (as the foundation spent $300 million a year and exceeded its income) targeted innovative approaches to employment, race relations, and minority voting rights. Grants to the arts included $80 million to numerous symphony orchestras. Assets were $3.7 billion by 1968.

McGeorge Bundy (1966, formerly President Kennedy's national security advisor) increased the activist trend with grants for direct voter registration; the NAACP and the Urban League; public interest law centers serving consumer, environmental, and minority causes; and housing for the poor.

The early 1970s saw support for black colleges and scholarships ($100 million) and women (child care, job training), but by 1974 inflation, weak stock prices, and overspending had seriously eroded assets. Programs, including support for public-interest law and public TV, were cut.

Under lawyer Franklin Thomas (president in 1979) the foundation has kept expenditures in line with income. The resurgent assets in the 1980s have allowed the foundation to help the homeless and, in cooperation with companies and local charities, to revitalize poor neighborhoods. A new reorganization along program (rather than geographical) lines permits greater sharing of solutions within fields and between countries to address concerns such as global warming.

In 1990 the Foundation renewed its resolve to promote cultural diversity and ethnic harmony throughout the world.

WHO

Chairman: Edson W. Spencer, age 65
President: Franklin A. Thomas
VP Program Division: Susan V. Berresford
VP and Chief Investment Officer: John W. English
VP, Secretary, and General Counsel: Barron M. Tenny
Treasurer and Director of Financial Services: John J. Koprowski
Director, Office of Human Resources: Margaret B. Lowe
Auditors: Price Waterhouse
Employees: 350 (New York)

WHERE

HQ: 320 E. 43rd St., New York, NY 10017
Phone: 212-573-5000
Fax: 212-599-4584

The foundation has field offices and suboffices in Asia, Latin America, the Middle East, and Africa.

	1990 Program Expenditures	
	$ mil.	% of total
US & international affairs programs	165	61
Developing country programs	73	27
Other	33	12
Total	**271**	**100**

WHAT

	1990 Program Expenditures	
	$ mil.	% of total
Urban Poverty	46	17
Rural Poverty and Resources	39	14
Human Rights and Social Justice	32	12
Governance and Public Policy	29	11
Education and Culture	49	18
International Affairs	32	12
Other programs	11	4
Other	33	12
Total	**271**	**100**

Representative Programs

Urban Poverty
Child and family services
Community revitalization
Research on poverty

Rural Poverty and Resources
Agricultural productivity
Employment generation
Natural resource management

Human Rights and Social Justice
Access to social justice and legal services
Refugees' and migrants' rights
Women's rights and opportunities

Governance and Public Policy
Government structures and functions
Local initiatives
Minority public affairs and public policy

Education and Culture
Artistic creativity and resources
Cultural preservation
Curriculum development

International Affairs
International economics and development
International organizations and law
International peace, security, and arms control
International relations
International studies

HOW MUCH

	9-Year Growth	1981	1982	1983	1984	1985	1986	1987	1988	1989	1990
Year-end fund balance ($ mil.)	9.6%	2,401	2,701	3,388	3,322	3,748	4,535	5,225	4,856	5,582	5,201
Dividend and interest income ($ mil.)	5.3%	197	226	203	218	246	253	252	289	307	314
Program expenditures ($ mil.)	10.3%	112	122	121	154	139	205	229	242	245	271

Assets ($ mil.) 1981–90

[bar chart showing assets from 1981 to 1990, vertical axis from 0 to 6,000]

FORD MOTOR COMPANY

OVERVIEW

Ford is #2 in the US and world automobile sales (after General Motors). Its principal business is the manufacture and sale of cars, trucks, and related parts and accessories. Ford manufactures models under the Ford, Lincoln, Mercury, and Jaguar nameplates. It also provides financial services through 5 subsidiaries. Ford owns 23.9% of Mazda Motor. Each of the 2 companies manufactures vehicles for the other.

Recession is battering Ford's US sales and the automaker is losing US market share as well. Business is no better in Europe, where production problems and disappointing reviews marred the launch of the new Escort. Production inefficiencies at newly acquired Jaguar have proven more intractable than anticipated. Making matters worse, bad commercial real estate loans are hurting First Nationwide Financial.

Stock buybacks and acquisitions depleted Ford's cash reserves just before its troubles began. Facing a potential cash crisis, Ford cut its dividend in early 1991 and slashed payroll and expense in order to maintain heavy spending on product development.

WHEN

Henry Ford began the Ford Motor Company in 1903 in Dearborn, Michigan, hoping to design a simple, inexpensive car he could mass-produce. In 1908 Ford introduced the Model T, and in 1909 he dropped all other models.

His business manager, James Couzens, recommended he lower the selling price to $600, so Ford perfected the moving assembly line. Couzens and William Knudsen (later GM president) also created the first branch assembly plant system and a national dealer network. By 1916 the cars cost $360; by 1920 60% of all vehicles on the road were Fords.

In 1916 Ford omitted its customary extra dividend in order to retain earnings for reinvestment. Stockholders sued for payment, and in 1919 Ford purchased all outstanding shares for $100 million. It was 1956 before the Fords again allowed outside ownership, and the family still retains 40% voting power.

Ford purchased Lincoln in 1922 and discontinued the Model T in 1927. Its replacement, the Model A (1932), was the first low-priced car with a V-8 engine, triple the horsepower of the Model T's engine.

With Henry Ford's health deteriorating, his son Edsel became president in 1932. Despite the introduction of the Mercury (1938), market share slipped behind GM and Chrysler.

Following Edsel's sudden death in 1943, the navy released his son, Henry II, to run the company. Henry the elder stepped in until 1945; he died in 1947. Henry II decentralized the company — then losing $10 million a month — following the GM model. In 1950 Ford recaptured 2nd place from Chrysler.

In the 1950s Ford expanded international operations (begun in England, 1911), created the Aerospace Division (1956), and introduced the Edsel (1958). In 1964 Ford launched the popular Mustang, created by Ford president Lee Iacocca. In 1979 Henry II retired.

Ford cut its work force by 33% and closed 15 manufacturing facilities during the 1980s. In 1986 Ford earned higher profits than GM (on 33% less revenue) for the first time since 1924. With the acquisition of New Holland (1986) and Versatile (1987), Ford became the world's 3rd largest agricultural equipment maker. Ford purchased First Nationwide in 1986. The 1988 introduction of the Taurus and Sable (both the inspiration of then-CEO Donald Petersen) spurred Ford to its largest US car market share (21.7%) in 10 years, surpassed in 1989 by a 22.3% share. In 1989 Ford bought The Associates from Paramount Communications ($3.35 billion) and Jaguar ($2.5 billion).

In 1990 Harold "Red" Poling succeeded Petersen as CEO and the company sold Ford Aerospace to Loral. Ford merged its New Holland unit with a Fiat subsidiary in 1991.

NYSE symbol: F
Fiscal year ends: December 31

Hoover's Rating **C**

WHO

Chairman and CEO: Harold A. Poling, age 65, $1,221,339 pay
President and COO: Philip E. Benton, Jr., age 62, $788,392 pay
EVP and CFO: Stanley A. Seneker, age 59
VP Employee Relations: J. Craig Hausman
Auditors: Coopers & Lybrand
Employees: 370,383

WHERE

HQ: The American Rd., Dearborn, MI 48121
Phone: 313-322-3000
Fax: 313-322-7896

	1990 Sales		1990 Net Income	
	$ mil.	% of total	$ mil.	% of total
US	61,771	63	628	73
Europe	25,398	26	263	30
Canada	3,716	4	67	8
Other countries	6,765	7	(98)	(11)
Total	**97,650**	**100**	**860**	**100**

WHAT

	1990 Sales		1990 Pretax Income	
	$ mil.	% of total	$ mil.	% of total
Automotive mfg.	81,844	84	274	18
Financial services	15,806	16	1,221	82
Total	**97,650**	**100**	**1,495**	**100**

Ford		Lincoln
Aerostar	Mustang	Continental
Bronco	Probe	Mark VII
Crown Victoria	Ranger	Town Car
Econoline	Taurus	
Escort	Tempo	**Mercury**
Explorer	Thunderbird	Capri
F-Series	**Jaguar**	Cougar
Festiva	XJ-6	Grand Marquis
	XJ-12	Sable
		Topaz
		Tracer

Financial Subsidiaries
The American Road Insurance Co.
Associates First Capital Corp.
First Nationwide Financial Corp.
Ford Motor Credit Co.
United States Leasing International, Inc.

Other Holdings
Autolatina (49%, South American joint venture with Volkswagen)
Mazda Motor Corp. (23.9%)

RANKINGS

3rd in *Fortune* 500 Industrial Cos.
35th in *Business Week* 1000

KEY COMPETITORS

Avis	Navistar
BMW	Nissan
Caterpillar	PACCAR
Chrysler	Peugeot
Daimler-Benz	Renault
Deere	Saab-Scania
Fiat	Suzuki
General Motors	Toyota
Honda	Volkswagen
Hyundai	Volvo
Isuzu	Banks
Mazda	Finance companies
Mitsubishi	Savings and loans

HOW MUCH

	9-Year Growth	1981	1982	1983	1984	1985	1986	1987	1988	1989	1990
Sales ($ mil.)	11.0%	38,247	37,067	44,455	52,366	52,774	62,716	71,643	92,446	96,146	97,650
Net income ($ mil.)	—	(1,060)	(658)	1,867	2,907	2,515	3,285	4,625	5,300	3,835	860
Income as % of sales	—	(2.8%)	(1.8%)	4.2%	5.6%	4.8%	5.2%	6.5%	5.7%	4.0%	0.9%
Earnings per share ($)	—	(1.96)	(1.21)	3.21	4.97	4.41	6.06	8.92	10.80	8.12	1.84
Stock price – high ($)	—	5.78	9.25	15.58	17.13	19.71	31.75	56.31	55.00	56.63	49.13
Stock price – low ($)	—	3.50	3.69	7.61	11.00	13.38	17.92	28.44	38.06	41.38	25.00
Stock price – close ($)	24.5%	3.72	8.64	14.13	15.21	19.33	28.13	37.69	50.50	43.63	26.63
P/E – high	—	—	—	5	3	4	5	6	5	7	27
P/E – low	—	—	—	2	2	3	3	3	4	5	14
Dividends per share ($)	30.7%	0.27	0.00	0.17	0.67	0.80	1.11	1.58	2.30	3.00	3.00
Book value per share ($)	15.4%	13.57	11.20	13.74	17.62	21.97	27.68	36.44	43.87	48.07	49.12

1990 Year-end:
Debt ratio: 66.1%
Return on equity: 3.8%
Cash (mil.): $8,247
Current ratio: —
Long-term debt (mil.): $45,332
No. of shares (mil.): 473
Dividends:
 1990 average yield: 11.3%
 1990 payout: 163.0%
Market value (mil.): $12,596

Stock Price History
High/Low 1981–90

FPL GROUP, INC.

OVERVIEW

FPL Group, through Florida Power & Light Company, provides electricity to 3.2 million customers (nearly 90% of which are residential) on Florida's east and lower west coasts — a 35-county area that includes 5 of the 6 fastest-growing metropolitan areas in the US. It is America's 4th largest electric utility, with almost $6.3 million in 1990 sales.

After an unsuccessful foray into the insurance business, FPL has found a buyer for its ailing Colonial Penn unit. New York's Leucadia National Corporation agreed to pay $150 million for Colonial Penn in 1991. FPL is also leaving the real estate, Florida citrus, and cable TV businesses in an effort to refocus its energies on utility-related operations. FPL plans to limit nonutility activities to the development of alternate energy sources through ESI Energy (including solar and geothermal power, wind power, and energy from municipal waste) and to providing quality consulting services through Qualtec.

NYSE symbol: FPL
Fiscal year ends: December 31

Hoover's Rating **C-**

WHO

Chairman, President, and CEO: James L. Broadhead, age 55, $866,627 pay
President and COO, Florida Power and Light: Stephen E. Frank, age 49, $374,432 pay
VP and CFO: Joe L. Howard, age 49, $338,560 pay
VP Human Resources and Administration: Lawrence J. Kelleher, age 43
Auditors: Deloitte & Touche
Employees: 19,138

WHERE

HQ: 700 Universe Blvd., Juno Beach, FL 33408
Phone: 407-694-4646
Fax: 407-694-6385

Generating Facilities

Coal
St. Johns River Power Park (20%, Jacksonville, FL)

Oil and Gas
Cape Canaveral (Cocoa, FL)
Cutler (Miami, FL)
Fort Myers (Fort Myers, FL)
Lauderdale (Dania, FL)
Manatee (Parrish, FL)
Martin (Indiantown, FL)
Port Everglades (Port Everglades, FL)
Putnam (Palatka, FL)
Riviera (Riviera Beach, FL)
Sanford (Lake Monroe, FL)
Turkey Point (Florida City, FL)

Nuclear
St. Lucie (85.1%, Hutchinson Island, FL)
Turkey Point (Florida City, FL)

WHEN

In 1923 Florida experienced a land boom. New homes and businesses were built at an impressive rate. But electric utilities were few and far between, and no transmission lines linked one system to another. In 1925 American Power & Light Company (AP&L), a holding company already operating utilities throughout the Americas, set up Florida Power and Light (FPL) to buy and consolidate Florida's electric properties. AP&L built transmission lines from Miami to Stuart on the Atlantic Coast and from Arcadia to Punta Gorda on the Gulf Coast, linking 58 communities in the FPL power system. Besides electric generating and transmission facilities, FPL's holdings included ice, water, and cold storage companies; streetcar and telephone companies; a steam laundry; and a limestone quarry.

More purchases in 1926 and 1927 nearly doubled FPL's electric properties. In 1927 the company used an electric pump to demonstrate how swamp lands could be drained and cultivated. In the 1940s and 1950s FPL sold its nonelectric properties. AP&L ceased operations in 1950 and, as part of its dissolution plan, spun off FPL to its stockholders. FPL was listed on the NYSE in 1950.

Marshall McDonald became president of FPL in 1971. FPL's first nuclear plant (Turkey Point), located on the mud flats south of Miami, went on-line in 1972. While the plant was under construction (1965–72), FPL established youth camps, nature trails, shrimp ponds, and a US Air Force Sea Survival School at Turkey Point to illustrate the company's concern for the area's ecological balance.

In the 1970s and 1980s the company diversified by forming Fuel Supply Service (1973, oil and uranium acquisition, later renamed Qualtec), W. Flagler Investment (1981, real estate development, later renamed Alandco), and ESI Energy (1985, nonutility fuel sources). FPL bought Telesat Cablevision (1985, cable television operator), Colonial Penn Group (1985, insurance), and Turner Foods Corporation (1988, citrus grower). FPL sold Praxis Group, a Colonial Penn subsidiary providing information services, in 1988.

In 1981 McDonald, then chairman, began a quality improvement program (QIP), using teams of employees and statistical methods to track and solve company problems. Received with little enthusiasm at first, McDonald's QIP eventually caught on with impressive results. In 1989 FPL became the first non-Japanese company to win the Deming Prize, Japan's prestigious international award for quality.

In 1990 FPL took a $752 million charge (related to its decision to get out of insurance, cable TV, real estate, and citrus growing) that greatly contributed to its $347 million loss. That year the company also agreed to buy a 76% stake in Georgia Power's Scherer Unit 4 — its first out-of-state plant (the sale is pending regulatory approval).

WHAT

	1990 Sales		1990 Operating Income	
	$ mil.	% of total	$ mil.	% of total
Utility operations	4,988	79	885	—
Insurance & financial services	1,301	21	(836)	—
Adjustments	—	—	(43)	—
Total	**6,289**	**100**	**6**	**—**

	1990 Fuel Sources
	% of total
Coal	3
Natural gas	17
Nuclear	24
Oil	23
Purchased power	33
Total	**100**

Florida Power & Light Co.

FPL Group Capital, Inc.
Bay Loan and Investment Bank (financial services)
ESI Energy, Inc. (energy projects)
Qualtec, Inc. (quality services)

RANKINGS

17th in *Fortune* 50 Utilities
145th in *Business Week* 1000

HOW MUCH

	9-Year Growth	1981	1982	1983	1984	1985	1986	1987	1988	1989	1990
Sales ($ mil.)	8.2%	3,089	2,941	3,353	3,941	4,349	4,092	4,439	5,854	6,180	6,289
Net income ($ mil.)	—	224	267	314	349	419	413	451	493	454	(347)
Income as % of sales	—	7.3%	9.1%	9.4%	8.9%	9.6%	10.1%	10.2%	8.4%	7.4%	(5.5%)
Earnings per share ($)	—	2.13	2.39	2.51	2.62	3.11	2.90	3.10	3.42	3.12	(2.86)
Stock price – high ($)	—	16.00	18.81	21.13	22.81	29.00	38.00	34.88	32.50	36.75	36.50
Stock price – low ($)	—	11.94	14.06	17.50	17.63	20.50	26.38	24.38	27.75	29.00	26.13
Stock price – close ($)	7.9%	14.69	18.13	20.13	22.38	28.25	31.63	28.63	31.13	36.38	29.00
P/E – high	—	8	8	8	9	9	13	11	10	12	—
P/E – low	—	6	6	7	7	7	9	8	8	9	—
Dividends per share ($)	5.2%	1.48	1.64	1.77	1.86	1.94	2.02	2.10	2.18	2.26	2.34
Book value per share ($)	1.0%	17.95	18.80	19.47	20.14	21.38	22.99	23.82	24.90	25.89	19.63

1990 Year-end:
Debt ratio: 52.4%
Return on equity: —
Cash (mil.): $731
Current ratio: —
Long-term debt (mil.): $3,863
No. of shares (mil.): 161
Dividends:
  1990 average yield: 8.1%
  1990 payout: —
Market value (mil.): $4,671

Stock Price History High/Low 1981–90

FRED MEYER, INC.

OVERVIEW

OTC symbol: MEYR
Fiscal year ends: Saturday nearest January 31

Hoover's Rating **C+**

Portland-based Fred Meyer, Inc., is a $2.5 billion retail chain of 122 stores in 7 western states, primarily Oregon and Washington. Its 94 "multidepartment" stores, having up to 200,000 square feet under one roof, feature as many as 225,000 items in 9 departments. The 28 specialty mall stores are smaller (15,000 to 39,000 square feet) and carry one type of product. The company's policy of distribution center centralization allows deliveries to be frequent, thus maximizing retail space because in-store storage is kept to a minimum.

The company is the 47th largest retailer in the US and the largest private employer in Oregon. The Northwest's expected increased population, income, and employment in the 1990s should bode well for the chain's growth and profit outlook .

Fred Meyer believes its customers are increasingly time poor and, thus, the appeal of its "One Stop Shopping" is likely to grow. In 1990 the company reorganized into 3 merchandising divisions (Food, General, and Home Electronics and Jewelry) to reflect shopping patterns; the stores' layout also reflect this pattern.

Fred Meyer is known for environmental achievement. Its efforts to provide certification for products with environmental claims led to a national certification system. The company sponsors a volunteer council to coordinate employees' volunteer efforts. Employees, 74% of whom belong to unions, may take classes to learn more about company products and computers. They may also be on an employee team to improve company performance.

WHO

Chairman and CEO: Robert G. Miller, age 47
VC: Jerome Kohlberg, Jr., age 64
President and COO: Cyril K. Green, age 59, $305,771 pay
SVP, CFO, and Secretary: Kenneth Thrasher, age 41
SVP Personnel: Gary L. Baker, age 51
Auditors: Deloitte & Touche
Employees: 22,000

WHERE

HQ: PO Box 42121, 3800 SE 22nd Ave., Portland, OR 97202
Phone: 503-232-8844
Fax: 503-233-4535 (Public Affairs)

Fred Meyer operates 94 multidepartment retail stores and 28 specialty stores in 7 western states.

State	No. of Stores 1990
Alaska	8
California	3
Idaho	8
Montana	2
Oregon	49
Utah	13
Washington	39
Total	**122**

WHEN

Founder Fred G. Meyer peddled coffee, tea, and spices door-to-door in Portland, Oregon (1909), and opened his first grocery and variety store in downtown Portland (1922). Meyer opened a branch in Hollywood, a Portland suburb, after police banned downtown parking because of traffic problems (1931).

During the next 3 decades, the Fred Meyer Stores spread through Oregon and southern Washington state. Fred Meyer's innovations included free parking, prepackaged goods, cash-and-carry pricing, self-service, and one-stop shopping with separate departments under one roof.

In 1960 the 18-store chain went public, posting sales of $56 million. The company added prepared entrees and frozen foods (1968) and home improvement and garden centers (late 1960s). During the 1960s and 1970s the company expanded into Idaho, Alaska, and western Montana.

KKR (Kohlberg Kravis Roberts) took the company private in a $420 million management LBO (1981). The company bought the 30-store Grand Central chain, retaining 21

stores in Utah and Idaho (1984). KKR took the company public (1986), selling a 35% stake and raising $63 million to reduce debt. During its 5 years as a private company, sales increased 53%, from $1.1 billion to $1.7 billion, and net income increased 340%, from $5.1 million to $22.5 million. KKR controls 65% of the voting stock.

In April 1988 the company hired Frederick Stevens to modernize the aging chain. Stevens's remodeling and replacing of older stores and moving to a computer system that improved inventory tracking and information management contributed to Fred Meyer's 1989 loss of $6.8 million. Strikes at the Seattle stores and a distribution center also negatively affected income. Stevens's abrupt departure in January 1991 led to speculation that KKR was preparing to restructure the chain or planning to sell it. There are concerns for future earnings because of increased competition from wholesale clubs and from Wal-Mart, which reportedly plans to open 25 stores in Oregon.

WHAT

	1990 Sales	
	$ mil.	% of total
Nonfood sales	1,585	64
Food sales	891	36
Total	**2,476**	**100**

Store Types	No. of Stores 1990
Multidepartment stores	
With food	68
Without food	26
Specialty stores	
Grocery	2
Fine jewelry	18
Apparel and shoes	3
Nutrition	3
General merchandise	2
Total	**122**

RANKINGS

47th in *Fortune* 50 Retailing Cos.
991st in *Business Week* 1000

KEY COMPETITORS

Albertson's
Berkshire Hathaway
Costco
J.C. Penney
Kmart
Longs
Price Co.
Safeway
Walgreen
Wal-Mart

HOW MUCH

	9-Year Growth	1981	1982	1983	1984	1985	1986	1987	1988	1989	1990
Sales ($ mil.)	10.2%	1,035	1,103	1,214	1,449	1,584	1,688	1,848	2,074	2,285	2,476
Net income ($ mil.)	9.0%	16	5	15	13	19	24	32	37	(7)	34
Income as % of sales	—	1.5%	0.5%	1.2%	0.9%	1.2%	1.4%	1.7%	1.8%	(0.3%)	1.4%
Earnings per share ($)	—	—	—	—	—	1.06	1.15	1.31	1.50	(0.28)	1.37
Stock price – high ($)	—	—	—	—	—	—	14.63	17.88	17.25	23.00	18.75
Stock price – low ($)	—	—	—	—	—	—	12.63	9.50	10.75	15.75	10.00
Stock price – close ($)	—	—	—	—	—	—	13.13	10.63	16.13	18.50	12.50
P/E – high	—	—	—	—	—	—	13	14	12	—	14
P/E – low	—	—	—	—	—	—	11	7	7	—	7
Dividends per share ($)	—	—	—	—	—	—	0.00	0.00	0.00	0.00	0.00
Book value per share ($)	—	—	2.90	3.79	4.72	5.87	8.61	9.88	11.53	11.18	12.64

1990 Year-end:
Debt ratio: 46.8%
Return on equity: 11.5%
Cash (mil.): $29
Current ratio: 1.52
Long-term debt (mil.): $251
No. of shares (mil.): 23
Dividends:
  1990 average yield: 0.0%
  1990 payout: 0.0%
Market value (mil.): $282

Stock Price History
High/Low 1986–90

E. & J. GALLO WINERY

OVERVIEW

Based in Modesto, California, privately owned Gallo is the world's largest winemaker, with a daily production of about 250,000 cases and annual sales of over $1 billion. Leading brands include Gallo, Andre, Bartles & Jaymes, and Carlo Rossi. Gallo dominates every wine category in which it competes (including dessert wines, ports, sherries, varietals, and wine coolers) and holds about 25% of the US market.

Full ownership of the company still rests firmly in the hands of the Gallo family. The company's success is due to the unique partnership between brothers Ernest and Julio Gallo, who now rank among the world's billionaires, with a combined estimated net worth of about $1.4 billion. Ernest is the marketing genius while Julio runs the winery, applying scientific principles to the art of

winemaking. Three generations of Gallos now work for the company.

Gallo grows less than 5% of the grapes it uses. Most of its wines are made in stainless steel tanks (except the premium wines, which are aged in barrels of Yugoslavian oak). The company's storage tanks can hold about 300 million gallons of wine.

Gallo is the largest vineyard owner in the wine-rich Sonoma area of California, holding over 2,000 acres of land.

Although Gallo's Andre champagne is the leading US sparkling wine, its sales have dropped 18% since 1987 as consumer tastes have shifted in favor of more expensive brands (e.g., Cook's). Riding the trend, Gallo is expected to unveil its new Eden Roc brand, a mid-priced sparkling wine, in late 1991.

WHEN

At the end of Prohibition in 1933, the Gallo brothers, Ernest and Julio, began making wine with a $200 grape crusher and redwood casks in a rented warehouse in Modesto, California. Ernest sold their first product, 6,000 gallons of table wine, to Pacific Wine Company (a Chicago distributor), which bottled the wine under several labels. The Gallos reported making a $34,000 profit their first year.

In the early 1940s the brothers began producing wine under the Gallo label from bottling plants in Los Angeles and New Orleans. In 1942 the Gallos got their first trademark, "Jolly Old Gallo." In the late 1940s Julio began experimenting with over 100 grape varieties to find those best for the Northern California climate. The company later led the industry in applying new technologies to the art of making wine. In the 1950s Gallo built its own bottle-making plant, becoming the first winery to do so. Thunderbird, a juice-flavored fortified wine introduced in 1957, was one of the company's first big successes, selling 2.5 million bottles in one year.

By the 1960s most small California vintners had folded or had been absorbed by larger wineries. Gallo, on the other hand, continued to grow as its wine gained in popularity. The company also spurred growth by spending large amounts on advertising (nearly half that spent by the entire wine industry in 1963) and keeping prices low. In 1964 Gallo introduced Hearty Burgundy, leading a trend in dry Cali-

fornia jug wines. Even in the face of increasing European imports, Gallo was the #1 winemaker in the US at the end of the decade, annually producing 66 million gallons of wine.

Gallo introduced the carbonated, fruit-flavored Boone's Farm Apple Wine in 1969, creating an interest in "pop" wines that lasted for a few years. In 1974 the company introduced its first premium varietal wines (an area in which Gallo leads today).

In the mid-1970s Gallo field workers switched unions, dropping the United Farm Workers in favor of the Teamsters. Repercussions included protests and boycotts, but sales were largely unaffected. From 1976 to 1982 Gallo was placed under an FTC order limiting its control over wholesalers. The order was lifted after heavyweight rivals (like Coca-Cola, who briefly experimented with wine) entered the industry and changed the competitive balance. Gallo has, however, remained the country's top winemaker. Its latest money maker has been the wine cooler Bartles & Jaymes (introduced 1985), promoted by "Ed and Frank" in humorous TV ads. In 1988 Gallo began bottling Hearty Burgundy with a cork rather than a screw cap and started labeling all of its varietal wines with a vintage date.

Gallo is currently preparing to enter the super premium wine market (the only wine sector in which it is not a major player) by releasing 2,000 cases each of $60 Cabernet and $30 Chardonnay.

Private company
Fiscal year ends: December 31

Hoover's Rating **B**

WHO

Chairman: Ernest Gallo, age 82
President: Julio Gallo, age 81
VP Finance: Louis Freedman
President, Gallo Sales Co.: Joseph E. Gallo
President, Gallo Glass Co. and Fairbanks Trucking Inc.: Robert J. Gallo
President, Midcal Aluminum Inc.: James E. Coleman
Employees: 3,000

WHERE

HQ: PO Box 1130, Modesto, CA 95353
Phone: 209-579-3111
Fax: 209-579-4361 (Public Relations)

Vineyards in California (counties)
Fresno
Merced
Sonoma
Stanislaus

WHAT

Label Names
Andre
Ballatore
Bartles & Jaymes
Boone's
Carlo Rossi
E & J Brandy
Eden Roc
Ernest & Julio Gallo
Gallo
Livingston Cellars
The Reserve Cellars of Ernest & Julio Gallo
Tott's
Wm. Wycliffe

Subsidiaries
E & J Gallo Winery Europe (wholesale distributor in Europe)
Fairbanks Trucking Inc. (long-distance trucking)
Frei Bros. Winery (Sonoma winery and vineyards)
Gallo Glass Co. (glass wine bottles)
Gallo Sales Co. (wholesale wine distributor)
Midcal Aluminum Inc. (metal bottle closures)
Mountain Wine Distributing Co. (Gallo wines distributor in Colorado)
Northwest Wine Co. (wholesale distributor of Gallo wines in Southern California and Pacific Northwest)
San Joaquin Valley Express (partnership, agricultural trucking)
United Packing Co. (partnership, importer of wine bottle corks)
US Intermodal Services (partnership, freight brokerage)

RANKINGS

151st in *Forbes* 400 US Private Cos.

KEY COMPETITORS

Allied-Lyons	LVMH
Anheuser-Busch	Nestlé
Bass	San Miguel
Brown-Forman	Seagram
Grand Metropolitan	Stroh
Heineken	

HOW MUCH

	9-Year Growth	1981	1982	1983	1984	1985	1986	1987	1988	1989	1990
Estimated sales ($ mil.)	—	—	—	—	—	—	—	1,000	1,000	1,000	1,050
Wine shipments (gallons mil.)	3.7%	131.4	137.3	146.1	143.6	154.3	169.2	166.0	165.4	169.2	156.8
Employees								—	3,000	3,000	2,950	3,000

Wine Shipments (gallons mil.) 1981–90

GANNETT CO., INC.

OVERVIEW

Gannett is the largest newspaper group in the US. Headquartered in Arlington, Virginia, Gannett owns and operates 82 daily and 66 nondaily newspapers and is best known as publisher of *USA TODAY*. From the time Gannett went public in 1967 until 1990 it recorded 89 consecutive quarters of earnings gains. This uninterrupted streak — one of the longest in corporate history — was broken in the 2nd quarter of 1990. Gannett earnings remained depressed in 1991, reflecting a recession-induced drop in advertising revenues.

USA TODAY, the colorful national daily with a circulation of 1.8 million (2nd only to the *Wall Street Journal*), is in its 9th year of publication. It has yet to turn an annual profit.

Gannett owns 10 TV stations, 15 radio stations, and the largest outdoor advertising company in North America. Other ventures include Gannett News Services and the Louis Harris & Associates international opinion research company.

In 1991 Gannett purchased the 10% stake in the company held by the charitable Gannett Foundation. The foundation was set up in 1935 by founder Frank Gannett, who died in 1957. The purchase, worth $670 million, will eliminate the possibility of the holdings being bought up by a hostile bidder.

NYSE symbol: GCI
Fiscal year ends: Last Sunday of the calendar year

Hoover's Rating **A-**

WHO

Chairman, President, and CEO: John J. Curley, age 52, $1,300,000 pay
VC and CFO: Douglas H. McCorkindale, age 51, $1,030,000
SVP Personnel: Madelyn P. Jennings, age 56
Auditors: Price Waterhouse
Employees: 36,600

WHERE

HQ: 1100 Wilson Blvd., Arlington, VA 22234
Phone: 703-284-6000
Fax: 703-558-4697

Gannett has facilities in 41 states, the District of Columbia, and 6 foreign countries.

	1990 Sales	
	$ mil.	% of total
US	3,339	97
Foreign	103	3
Total	**3,442**	**100**

WHEN

The Gannett Company started in 1906 in Elmira, New York, when Frank Gannett and his associates purchased a half-interest in the *Elmira Gazette*. The small company expanded slowly, purchasing 2 additional small newspapers by 1912. In 1918 the company moved to Rochester, where it acquired 2 more newspapers, and in 1923 Frank Gannett, having bought out his associates' interests, formed the Gannett Company. In 1929 Frank Gannett co-invented the teletypesetter. Gannett continued to buy up small and medium-sized dailies in the Northeast, and by 1947 the company operated 21 newspapers and 7 radio stations. At the time of his death in 1957, Frank Gannett had accumulated 30 newspapers.

During the 1960s Gannett continued its acquisition of local newspapers, expanding beyond a regional focus to become a national newspaper chain. It was not until 1966, however, that Gannett started its own newspaper, *TODAY*, in Cocoa Beach, Florida. Gannett went public in 1967.

Gannett went through its greatest expansion during the 1970s and 1980s under the direction of Allen Neuharth, who became CEO in 1973 and chairman in 1979. Gannett captured national attention in 1979 when it merged with Phoenix-based Combined

Communications Corporation (CCC), another media conglomerate whose holdings included TV and radio stations, an outdoor advertising business (2nd largest in the US), the Louis Harris polling business, and the *Cincinnati Enquirer* and *Oakland Tribune*. Gannett's revenues passed the $1 billion mark in 1979.

In 1982 Gannett started *USA TODAY*, a national newspaper whose splashy format and short articles made it an industry novelty. By 1990 circulation of *USA TODAY* had grown to 1.8 million, making it 2nd only to the *Wall Street Journal* in daily circulation.

Gannett's largest acquisition came in 1986 when it bought the Evening News Association for $717 million, giving Gannett 5 more newspapers, including the *Detroit News*, and 2 TV stations. In 1988 Gannett started the "USA Today on TV" program (cancelled in 1990 due to poor ratings and consistent losses).

Neuharth retired as chairman of Gannett in 1989. During his 16-year tenure as the company's leader, the outspoken Neuharth spent approximately $1.5 billion on acquisitions and increased the combined circulation of Gannett's newspapers to 6.3 million.

In 1991 Gannett launched *USA TODAY Baseball Weekly*, a tabloid with statistics, schedules, and TV previews.

WHAT

	1990 Sales		1990 Operating Income	
	$ mil.	% of total	$ mil.	% of total
Newspaper publishing	2,774	81	616	83
Broadcasting	397	11	87	12
Outdoor advertising	271	8	37	5
Adjustments	—	—	(61)	—
Total	**3,442**	**100**	**679**	**100**

Major Newspapers
Arkansas Gazette
Cincinnati Enquirer
Courier-Journal (Louisville, KY)
Des Moines Register
Detroit News
USA TODAY/USA WEEKEND

TV Stations
10 stations in 9 states and the District of Columbia

Radio Stations
15 FM and AM stations in 5 states

Other Businesses
Gannett Direct Marketing Services, Inc.
Gannett News Services
Gannett Outdoor (billboards)
Gannett TeleMarketing, Inc.
Louis Harris & Associates (opinion research)
USA TODAY Update (electronic information)

RANKINGS

141st in *Fortune* 500 Industrial Cos.
96th in *Business Week* 1000

KEY COMPETITORS

Advance Publications
Cox
Dow Jones
Hearst
Knight-Ridder
Maxwell
New York Times
News Corp.
Reuters
E. W. Scripps
Thomson Corp.
Times Mirror
Tribune
Washington Post

HOW MUCH

	9-Year Growth	1981	1982	1983	1984	1985	1986	1987	1988	1989	1990
Sales ($ mil.)	10.8%	1,367	1,520	1,704	1,960	2,209	2,802	3,079	3,314	3,518	3,442
Net income ($ mil.)	9.1%	173	181	192	224	253	276	319	364	398	377
Income as % of sales	—	12.6%	11.9%	11.3%	11.4%	11.5%	9.9%	10.4%	11.0%	11.3%	11.0%
Earnings per share ($)	9.3%	1.06	1.13	1.20	1.40	1.58	1.71	1.98	2.26	2.47	2.36
Stock price – high ($)	—	15.33	22.00	24.00	25.38	33.06	43.56	56.25	39.88	49.88	44.50
Stock price – low ($)	—	11.17	9.83	17.13	16.69	23.50	29.63	26.00	29.25	34.50	29.50
Stock price – close ($)	13.0%	12.04	21.13	19.67	23.50	30.63	36.06	39.13	35.63	43.50	36.13
P/E – high	—	15	19	20	18	21	25	28	18	20	19
P/E – low	—	11	9	14	12	15	17	13	13	14	13
Dividends per share ($)	9.8%	0.52	0.58	0.61	0.67	0.77	0.86	0.94	1.02	1.11	1.21
Book value per share ($)	10.6%	5.26	5.82	6.39	7.12	7.94	8.88	9.94	11.09	12.40	12.98

1990 Year-end:
Debt ratio: 29.1%
Return on equity: 18.6%
Cash (mil.): $56
Current ratio: 1.34
Long-term debt (mil.): $849
No. of shares (mil.): 159
Dividends:
 1990 average yield: 3.4%
 1990 payout: 51.3%
Market value (mil.): $5,744

Stock Price History
High/Low 1981–90

THE GAP, INC.

OVERVIEW

Headquartered in San Francisco, The Gap is a leading clothing retailer. The company's 1,092 (as of early 1991) stores include The Gap (moderately priced yet trendy casual clothing aimed at 20- to 45-year-old customers), GapKids (children's clothing stores, more than 50 of which include babyGap infant departments), and Banana Republic (travel and safari clothing). About 50% of the company is still owned by founder Don Fisher and his family.

Unlike many clothing retailers who include numerous brand names, The Gap sells only 2: its own Gap brand (sold under the Banana Republic label in its Banana Republic stores), and Levi's, which the company has been selling since opening in 1969 but which it will no longer sell after 1991. Today Levi's accounts for about 7% of merchandise. The company believes that its Gap brand is the 2nd best-selling clothing line in the US (after Levi Strauss).

The Gap is currently involved in a partnership with Carpenter & Company and Nomura Securities to build the first of potentially many anchorless malls (The Gap's stores would replace large department stores as the mall anchors) in a suburb of Chicago.

NYSE symbol: GPS
Fiscal year ends: First Saturday in February

Hoover's Rating **A+**

WHO

Chairman and CEO: Donald G. Fisher, age 62, $1,876,064 pay
President: Millard ("Mickey") S. Drexler, age 46, $1,875,778 pay
EVP and COO: James V. O'Donnell, age 50, $1,017,800 pay
SVP and CFO: David M. DeMattei, age 34
VP Human Resources: Daniel E. Walker
Auditors: Deloitte & Touche
Employees: 26,000

WHEN

In 1969 Donald Fisher and his wife Doris opened a small store near San Francisco State College. The couple named their store The Gap (after "the generation gap") and concentrated on selling Levi's jeans. In the beginning Fisher catered almost exclusively to teenagers but in the 1970s expanded into active wear that would appeal to a larger spectrum of customers. Nevertheless, by the early 1980s The Gap was still dependent upon its largely teenage customer base.

In a 1983 effort to revamp the company's image, Fisher hired Mickey Drexler, the former president of Ann Taylor who had a spotless track record in the apparel industry, as The Gap's new president. Drexler immediately overhauled the motley clothing lines to concentrate on sturdy, brightly colored cotton clothing. He also consolidated the store's many private clothing labels into The Gap brand. As a final touch, Drexler ripped out the stores' circular clothing racks and installed white shelving upon which the clothes could be neatly stacked and displayed.

Also in 1983 the company bought Banana Republic, a unique chain of stores that sold safari clothing in a jungle decor. The company expanded the chain, which enjoyed tremendous success in the mid-1980s; however, after the novelty of the stores wore off in the late 1980s, sales went into a slump. Drexler responded by introducing a broader range of clothes (including higher-priced leather items) and playing down the jungle image. By 1990 Banana Republic was again profitable.

In 1985 the company opened its first GapKids after Drexler could not find clothing that he liked for his son. Five years later he introduced baby clothing into GapKids stores under the babyGap brand name. In 1987 the company opened its experimental Hemisphere chain to sell European-style clothing, but the stores were discontinued in 1989.

Also in 1987 The Gap shareholders filed 5 civil class action lawsuits against the company, claiming that it had misrepresented the strength of its financial condition. The charges were dismissed by the courts in 1989.

During the late 1980s and early 1990s, The Gap continued to grow rapidly, opening 152 new stores in 1990 alone. It also opened its first stores in Canada and the UK and is looking to expand to continental Europe soon.

Despite a sluggish economy, The Gap posted strong results in early 1991, opening 38 new stores and increasing sales by 22% for the first quarter over the year-ago period. In July 1991 the company announced that it would stop selling Levi's at the end of the year. Levi's, which once represented 100% of The Gap jeans sales, had fallen to only 2% of Gap jean sales.

WHERE

HQ: One Harrison, San Francisco, CA 94105
Phone: 415-952-4400
Fax: 415-896-0322

The Gap has stores in the 50 largest metropolitan areas in the US.

Location	No. of Stores
US	1,046
Canada	24
UK	22
Total	**1,092**

	1990 Pretax Profits	
	$ mil.	% of total
US	214	90
Other countries	23	10
Total	**237**	**100**

WHAT

	No. of Stores
The Gap	795
GapKids	168
Banana Republic	129
Total	**1,092**

Stores
The Gap
   Casual and active clothing
GapKids
   Gap clothing for children
babyGap
   Infant clothing boutiques within GapKids stores
Banana Republic
   Safari and travel fashions

RANKINGS

198th in *Business Week* 1000

KEY COMPETITORS

Edison Brothers
General Cinema
Hartmarx
L.A. Gear
Levi Strauss
The Limited
Liz Claiborne
Melville
NIKE
Nordstrom
Reebok
U.S. Shoe
V.F.
Department and discount stores

HOW MUCH

	9-Year Growth	1981	1982	1983	1984	1985	1986	1987	1988	1989	1990
Sales ($ mil.)	18.6%	417	445	481	534	647	848	1,062	1,252	1,587	1,934
Net income ($ mil.)	32.1%	12	18	22	12	34	68	70	74	98	145
Income as % of sales	—	2.8%	4.1%	4.5%	2.3%	5.3%	8.0%	6.6%	5.9%	6.2%	7.5%
Earnings per share ($)	29.9%	0.19	0.29	0.32	0.18	*0.51*	0.97	0.98	1.02	1.38	2.04
Stock price – high ($)	—	1.91	2.40	5.66	2.95	7.94	22.94	38.94	21.19	30.75	36.25
Stock price – low ($)	—	0.84	0.79	2.02	2.19	2.56	7.75	8.00	9.25	17.63	19.50
Stock price – close ($)	46.2%	1.08	2.03	2.63	2.58	7.84	17.88	10.13	20.88	25.69	33.13
P/E – high	—	10	8	18	16	16	24	40	21	22	18
P/E – low	—	4	3	6	12	5	8	8	9	13	10
Dividends per share ($)	31.8%	0.04	0.04	0.05	0.06	0.07	0.16	0.25	0.26	0.34	0.44
Book value per share ($)	21.8%	1.11	1.37	1.78	1.87	2.16	2.98	3.80	3.93	4.81	6.59

1990 Year-end:
Debt ratio: 1.1%
Return on equity: 35.8%
Cash (mil.): $67
Current ratio: 1.39
Long-term debt (mil.): $5
No. of shares (mil.): 71
Dividends:
   1990 average yield: 1.3%
   1990 payout: 21.6%
Market value (mil.): $2,340

Stock Price History High/Low 1981–90

GEICO CORPORATION

OVERVIEW

GEICO is the holding company for Government Employees Insurance Company, which provides auto, homeowners, and other property and casualty insurance products to traditionally low-risk demographic groups.

It keeps its costs, and therefore premiums, low by marketing its insurance products primarily to preferred-risk government and military employees and drivers age 50 and over via direct mail and by word of mouth. This saves the expense of commissioned agents. Almost 59% of new auto insurance comes from customer referrals. In addition, the company concentrates on retention of current policyholders; in 1990 more than 91% of auto policyholders who were offered renewals accepted.

GEICO enters the 1990s as a company known for strict underwriting guidelines. The company is a vigorous lobbyist for car safety, especially air bags (its 1990 Annual Report lists 1991 car models with airbags). The corporation is 45% owned by Warren Buffett's Berkshire Hathaway.

WHO

Chairman and CEO: William B. Snyder, age 61, $992,308 pay
VC: Louis A. Simpson, age 54, $494,231 pay
President: Edward H. Utley, age 61, $244,035 pay
President, Government Employees Insurance: Olza M. Nicely, age 47, $249,539 pay
SVP: W. Alvon Sparks, Jr., age 55, $180,522 pay
SVP and General Counsel: Donald K. Smith, age 58
VP Human Resources: Donn Knight
Treasurer: Charles G. Schara
Auditors: Coopers & Lybrand
Employees: 6,851

WHEN

Leo Goodwin, an accountant for a San Antonio insurer, believed he could start an auto insurance company during the Depression by selling direct to targeted customers without an agent. In 1936, at age 50, Goodwin founded Government Employees Insurance Company in Fort Worth with $25,000, plus $75,000 from Fort Worth banker Cleaves Rhea.

At first Leo and his wife Lillian worked 12 hours a day for a combined income of $250 a month. They targeted government employees (mature people with steady incomes in a time of financial uncertainty). In 1937 the company moved to Washington, DC, where the most government workers were.

GEICO had $15,000 net income in 1940, the first of 35 consecutive profitable years. In 1941, after a major hailstorm damaged cars in the Washington area, Goodwin engaged auto repair shops to work 24 hours a day solely for GEICO. Goodwin's policyholders told friends about the service and business grew by word of mouth. GEICO participated in the post-WWII boom by insuring the new homes and autos of veterans. GEICO's new premium income reached $2.5 million in 1946, a 50% increase over 1945.

In 1948 the Rhea family sold its 75% interest to the Graham-Newman Corporation which, later that year, distributed its shares to its stockholders, and the company became publicly owned. In 1949 GEICO profits exceeded $1 million and the company diversified into life insurance and financial services.

The company targeted state, county, and municipal employees in 1952 and non-governmental professional, technical, and managerial employees in 1958. Goodwin retired in 1958.

In the 1970s GEICO was shaken by federal wage and price controls and no-fault insurance. By 1975 these factors, as well as poor management decisions, resulted in an $85 million loss. As GEICO neared insolvency, new management was installed. John Byrne, the new CEO, increased rates, cut costs, reunderwrote all policies, and retained Salomon Brothers to underwrite a $76 million stock offering. One of the new investors was Warren Buffett's Berkshire Hathaway Company. The plan worked and GEICO returned to profitability in 1977.

After expanding into financial services and life insurance in the 1980s, GEICO management decided in 1988 to concentrate again on property, casualty, and auto lines, but as yet has found no buyers for its noncore businesses. In 1990 GEICO agreed to buy Southern Heritage Insurance Company, operating in the Southeast. Because of state limits on auto insurance premiums, the company is allowing its business in Pennsylvania to shrink, and is awaiting the outcome of court challenges to California's Proposition 103, which rolled back insurance rates across the state.

WHERE

HQ: GEICO Plaza, Washington, DC 20076-0001
Phone: 301-986-3000
Fax: 301-986-2113

GEICO operates in all 50 states and Washington, DC.

WHAT

	1990 Assets		1990 Operating Income	
	$ mil.	% of total	$ mil.	% of total
Property & casualty insurance	3,082	88	235	102
Reinsurance	66	2	(4)	(1)
Life & health insurance	142	4	5	2
Finance	177	5	1	—
Other	39	1	(6)	(3)
Adjustments	70	—	(8)	—
Total	**3,576**	**100**	**223**	**100**

Insurance Services
Auto insurance
Homeowners and renters insurance
Life and health insurance
Personal liability insurance

Subsidiaries
Criterion Casualty
Garden State Life Insurance Co.
GEICO Annuity and Insurance
GEICO Financial Services, GmbH (auto insurance to military in Europe)
GEICO General Insurance Co.
GEICO Indemnity Co.
GEICO Philanthropic Foundation
Government Employees Financial Corp. (consumer and business lending)
Maryland Ventures, Inc. (real estate)
Plaza Resources Co. (investment)
Resolute Reinsurance Co.
Safe Driver Motor Club, Inc. (motor club)

HOW MUCH

	9-Year Growth	1981	1982	1983	1984	1985	1986	1987	1988	1989	1990
Assets ($ mil.)	11.3%	1,362	1,564	1,776	1,907	2,378	2,715	2,846	3,061	3,434	3,576
Net income ($ mil.)	13.9%	64	77	95	100	78	119	150	134	213	208
Income as % of assets	—	4.7%	5.0%	5.3%	5.3%	3.3%	4.4%	5.3%	4.4%	6.2%	5.8%
Earnings per share ($)	18.4%	2.98	3.67	4.48	5.11	4.21	6.91	9.01	8.48	13.74	13.64
Stock price – high ($)	—	29.38	45.75	64.00	65.63	88.00	105.50	136.75	132.00	156.00	169.50
Stock price – low ($)	—	14.38	21.00	41.00	48.88	57.13	77.75	90.13	101.50	122.75	125.75
Stock price – close ($)	21.7%	27.75	43.00	58.13	58.00	87.00	98.50	110.50	124.00	152.50	162.13
P/E – high	—	10	12	14	13	21	15	15	16	11	12
P/E – low	—	5	6	9	10	14	11	10	12	9	9
Dividends per share ($)	17.2%	0.48	0.56	0.72	0.88	1.00	1.08	1.36	1.64	1.80	2.00
Book value per share ($)	21.0%	11.76	16.85	19.88	22.40	29.14	37.33	39.18	45.82	59.18	65.32

1990 Year-end:
Return on equity: 21.9%
Equity as % of assets: 27.1%
Cash (mil.): $36
Long-term debt (mil.): $212
No. of shares (mil.): 15
Dividends:
  1990 average yield: 1.2%
  1990 payout: 14.7%
Market value (mil.): $2,408
Sales (mil.): $1,932

Stock Price History High/Low 1981–90

RANKINGS

39th in *Fortune* 50 Diversified Financial Cos.
245th in *Business Week* 1000

KEY COMPETITORS

Aetna	Prudential
B.A.T	Sears
CIGNA	State Farm
ITT	Travelers
Kemper	USF&G
Loews	Xerox
MetLife	

GENENTECH, INC.

NYSE symbol: GNE
Fiscal year ends: December 31
Hoover's Rating A-

OVERVIEW

Headquartered in San Francisco, Genentech is one of the world's largest and most profitable biotechnology companies. Since 1990 Swiss pharmaceutical giant Roche has controlled 60% of Genentech and has an option to buy the remainder of the company through 1995. Although it has the largest product pipeline in the industry, Genentech has only 3 products currently on the market.

The company sells its products primarily to hospital specialists in the US and Canada. Sales outside the US are made through foreign drug companies (such as Mitsubishi in Japan and Boehringer Ingelheim in Europe) who pay royalties to Genentech. The company has a subsidiary in Canada and a small research unit in Japan.

Genentech's R&D expenditures run at a staggering 40% of sales, allowing the company to further develop such promising drugs as relaxin (a drug that facilitates childbirth), gp120 (a possible vaccine against AIDS), and HER-2 (a treatment for breast and ovarian cancer). In 1990 the company received FDA approval to sell Actimmune (which treats a rare disease of the immune system).

WHO

Chairman: Robert A. Swanson, age 43, $700,000 pay
President and CEO: G. Kirk Raab, age 55, $675,000 pay
SVP: William D. Young, age 46, $340,000 pay
VP and CFO: Louis J. Lavigne, Jr., age 42, $316,461 pay
VP Human Resources: Larry Setren, age 39
Auditors: Ernst & Young
Employees: 1,923

WHEN

Venture capitalist Robert Swanson and molecular biologist Herbert Boyer founded Genentech in South San Francisco in 1976 to commercialize products of the new science of genetic engineering. Boyer held a patent on techniques for splicing genes into microorganisms that could then be used as "microfactories" to produce large amounts of specific therapeutic substances. Genentech's first product was a bioengineered human form of insulin. Before any product reached the market, however, Genentech achieved fame when company stock went public in 1980. Its market value doubled on the first day of trading to $668 million but fell back closer to its issue level within a month. Boyer's initial investment of a few hundred dollars was briefly worth $80 million.

In 1982 Genentech's insulin became the first biotech product to be approved by the FDA. The company licensed it to Eli Lilly, who sold it by the trade name Humulin. Selling marketing rights to major firms in exchange for royalties allowed the company to focus on research, which could cost over $100 million per product. The company next developed the human immune system protein alpha interferon and licensed it to Hoffmann-La Roche, who sold it as Roferon-A (cancer treatment). The first product to bear the Genentech name was its human growth hormone, Protropin, approved by the FDA in 1985. An accounting charge for R&D expenses resulted in a significant drop in profits and the recording of a loss in 1986.

Genentech achieved the largest first-year sales of any new drug ($180 million in 1988) with Activase, a natural clot-dissolving substance (also known as t-PA) used to treat heart attacks, which was approved by the FDA in 1987. In 1988 and 1989 half of Genentech's sales came from Activase.

Genentech has fought competitors in court to protect its exclusive right to make and sell Activase as well as other genetically engineered products. In April 1990 it won a federal suit against 2 other makers of t-PA and may get exclusive marketing rights in the US. UK courts have invalidated Genentech's t-PA patent. Development of Activase required $200 million and 5 years. The company anticipated sales of $1 billion by 1990, but expectations have dropped since a March 1990 announcement that heart attack survival rates are no greater with Activase than with its rival, streptokinase, which costs 1/10 as much.

In 1990 Genentech sold a 60% interest to Roche Holding for $2.1 billion. The transaction resulted in a special charge of $168 million, causing a 1990 loss of $98 million for Genentech, but guaranteed a steady supply of funds for continued research.

WHERE

HQ: 460 Point San Bruno Blvd., South San Francisco, CA 94080
Phone: 415-266-1000
Fax: 415-588-3255

Genentech sells products in the US and Canada and licenses its products internationally.

	1990 Sales	
	$ mil.	% of total
US	402	92
Europe	18	4
Asia	6	2
Canada	9	2
Total	**435**	**100**

WHAT

	1990 Sales	
	$ mil.	% of total
Activase	210	48
Protropin	157	36
Royalties	48	11
Contract & other	20	5
Total	**435**	**100**

On the Market
Actimmune (treatment of a rare immune disorder)
Activase (for dissolving clots in heart and lung vessels)
Protropin (human growth hormone)

Royalty-producing Products
Hepatitis B vaccine (licensed to Merck)
Humulin (recomb. human insulin licensed to Eli Lilly)
Roferon-A (cancer treatment, licensed to Hoffmann–La Roche)

Under Development
Activin/Inhibin (for sickle-cell anemia)
Argatroban (anticoagulant)
CD4-IgG (AIDS treatment)
DNase (mucus-dissolving enzyme)
gp120 (potential basis for an HIV vaccine)
HER-2 monoclonal antibody (cancer)
IGF-1 (nutritional support and wound healing)
Relaxin (to ease childbirth and reduce cesareans)

RANKINGS

371st in *Business Week* 1000
603rd in *Business Week* Global 1000

HOW MUCH

	9-Year Growth	1981	1982	1983	1984	1985	1986	1987	1988	1989	1990
Sales ($ mil.)	45.1%	15	29	42	66	82	127	219	323	383	435
Net income ($ mil.)	—	0	1	1	3	6	(352)	42	21	44	(98)
Income as % of sales	—	2.0%	2.2%	2.7%	4.1%	6.9%	—	19.3%	6.4%	11.5%	(22.5%)
Earnings per share ($)	—	0.01	0.01	0.02	0.05	0.09	—	0.50	0.24	0.51	(1.05)
Stock price – high ($)	—	7.96	8.17	12.44	10.56	18.81	49.38	65.25	47.50	23.38	30.88
Stock price – low ($)	—	4.33	4.33	6.47	7.19	8.56	16.44	26.00	14.38	16.00	20.13
Stock price – close ($)	15.7%	6.04	6.96	8.63	8.56	17.44	42.50	42.00	16.00	20.75	22.50
P/E – high	—	1,194	613	622	222	209	—	131	198	46	—
P/E – low	—	650	325	323	151	95	—	52	60	31	—
Dividends per share ($)	—	0.00	0.00	0.00	0.00	0.00	0.00	0.00	0.00	0.00	18.00
Book value per share ($)	24.9%	1.09	1.46	1.60	1.71	2.98	3.69	4.35	4.82	5.57	8.08

1990 Year-end:
Debt ratio: 14.7%
Return on equity: —
Cash (mil.): $691
Current ratio: 7.85
Long-term debt (mil.): $154
No. of shares (mil.): 111
Dividends:
1990 average yield: 80.0%
1990 payout: —
Market value (mil.): $2,489

Stock Price History High/Low 1981–90

KEY COMPETITORS

Abbott Labs
American Cyanamid
American Home Products
Amgen
Bayer
Bristol-Myers Squibb
Ciba-Geigy
Dow Chemical
Du Pont
Glaxo
Hoechst
Johnson & Johnson
Monsanto
Pfizer
Rhône-Poulenc
Sandoz
Schering-Plough
SmithKline Beecham
Syntex
Upjohn
Warner-Lambert

GENERAL CINEMA CORPORATION

NYSE symbol: GCN
Fiscal year ends: October 31

Hoover's Rating C+

OVERVIEW

General Cinema manages the 4th largest theater circuit in the US, with 1,467 movie screens in 299 theaters across the country. The company's strategy of operating multi-screen theaters and locating them in or near major shopping centers reduces the risk of losses associated with any one film. Nearly 80 million people attended movies at General Cinema theaters in 1990.

Less well known is the fact that less than 1/4 of General Cinema's 1990 sales came from its theaters. The company owns 62% of the Dallas–based Neiman Marcus Group, which operates 241 Contempo Casuals stores in 31 states as well as the tony Neiman Marcus and Bergdorf Goodman department stores. Despite a $20 million loss in 1990 at NMG's Horchow Mail Order subsidiary, NMG generated all of General Cinema's profits.

After a 2-year search for strategic acquisitions, General Cinema entered the publishing industry in 1991 with the purchase of financially troubled, Orlando-based Harcourt Brace Jovanovich.

WHO

Chairman and CEO: Richard A. Smith, age 66, $1,232,500 pay
President and COO: Robert J. Tarr, Jr., age 47, $1,166,900 pay
VC and CFO: J. Atwood Ives, age 54, $860,000 pay
SVP, General Counsel, and Secretary: Samuel Frankenheim, age 58, $688,000 pay
Auditors: Deloitte & Touche
Employees: 25,500

WHEN

Philip Smith, a former salesman for Pathe films, started to put together a chain of movie theaters in the 1920s. Before WWII he pioneered in building drive-in theaters and in 1950 founded a chain of drive-ins called Mid-West Drive-In Theaters. In 1951 Mid-West built the first theater located in a shopping center. In 1960, when the Boston-based company went public, it owned 20 outdoor theaters and 19 indoor theaters in several eastern and midwestern states under the corporate name General Drive-In Corporation.

When Smith died in 1961, his son Richard took over the company. General Drive-In opened its first 2-screen theater in 1963. By that time the company operated 72 theaters. It adopted its present name in 1964.

General Cinema entered the soft drink bottling business by acquiring Ohio and Florida Pepsi-Cola bottling plants in 1968. By the mid-1970s it also owned 7-Up and Dr Pepper bottlers. The Justice Department charged that the company's 1970 purchase of 15 Minneapolis theaters eliminated competition in the Minneapolis–St. Paul area among exhibitors bidding for films, and the company was ordered to sell 9 of its 21 area theaters. General Cinema entered broadcasting in 1972, buying control of a Miami TV station, and subsequently bought radio stations in Chicago (1973) and Boston (1979). The company sold all of its stations between 1982 and 1986.

In 1973 General Cinema was the largest movie theater operator in the country, with 501 theaters and $118 million in sales. However, the rising costs of suburban land led to a phaseout of drive-ins, and by 1978 the company operated only 10 outdoor theaters.

The company's soft drink bottling division continued to grow. By 1981 General Cinema had become America's largest independent soft drink bottler. The company, which had introduced Sunkist Orange Soda in 1979, sold its Sunkist operations to R. J. Reynolds in 1984. Also in 1984 General Cinema bought 39% of Carter Hawley Hale, operator of the Broadway, Emporium, Bergdorf Goodman, and Neiman Marcus retail stores, increasing its stake in CHH to 49% in 1986. When CHH spun off its specialty stores as The Neiman Marcus Group in 1987, General Cinema exchanged its stake in CHH for 60% of the new company (increased to 62% in 1991).

In 1989 General Cinema sold its soft drink bottling operations to PepsiCo for $1.77 billion. The company, facing increasingly competitive conditions in the exhibition industry, began looking for acquisitions. It had bought significant shares in British candy and soft drink maker Cadbury Schweppes in 1987 and 1988 but sold most of its holdings in 1990. Finally General Cinema agreed to buy textbook publisher Harcourt Brace Jovanovich for $1.5 billion in 1991.

WHERE

HQ: 27 Boylston St., Chestnut Hill, MA 02167
Phone: 617-232-8200
Fax: 617-738-4007 (Investor Relations)

Location	No. of Stores	
	Neiman Marcus	Bergdorf Goodman
Texas	6	—
California	5	—
Illinois	3	—
Florida	2	—
DC	1	—
Virginia	1	—
Massachusetts	1	—
Colorado	1	—
Georgia	1	—
Missouri	1	—
Nevada	1	—
New York	1	2
Total	**24**	**2**

WHAT

	1990 Sales		1990 Operating Income	
	$ mil.	% of total	$ mil.	% of total
Theaters	461	21	(11)	(13)
Specialty retailing	1,689	79	99	113
Adjustments	27	—	(27)	—
Total	**2,177**	**100**	**61**	**100**

Motion Picture Theaters

Specialty Retailing (62% interest in Neiman Marcus Group, Inc.)
Bergdorf Goodman
Contempo Casuals
Horchow Mail Order
Neiman Marcus
Pastille

Publishing
Harcourt Brace Jovanovich, Inc.

RANKINGS

50th in *Fortune* 50 Retailing Cos.
379th in *Business Week* 1000

KEY COMPETITORS

Advance Publications
Blockbuster
Brown Group
Campeau
Carter Hawley Hale
CBS
Dayton Hudson
Dillard
Edison Brothers
The Gap
The Limited
Macy

Matsushita
Maxwell
May
McGraw-Hill
Melville
Nordstrom
Paramount
Sony
TCI
Time Warner
U.S. Shoe
Woolworth

HOW MUCH

	9-Year Growth	1981	1982	1983	1984	1985	1986	1987	1988	1989	1990
Sales ($ mil.)	11.4%	824	886	929	916	967	998	1,040	2,346	1,937	2,177
Net income ($ mil.)	10.8%	44	48	99	74	88	90	87	83	106	111
Income as % of sales	—	5.4%	5.4%	10.6%	8.0%	9.1%	9.0%	8.3%	3.5%	5.5%	5.1%
Earnings per share ($)	13.1%	0.50	0.60	1.31	0.98	1.17	1.23	1.18	1.12	1.43	1.51
Stock price – high ($)	—	5.06	7.63	11.44	14.00	21.13	29.50	31.75	25.75	28.50	27.00
Stock price – low ($)	—	3.13	3.72	6.84	8.38	12.13	18.31	13.75	15.75	23.13	16.50
Stock price – close ($)	17.5%	4.56	7.28	11.25	13.38	19.31	22.13	19.38	25.50	25.75	19.50
P/E – high	—	10	13	9	14	18	24	27	23	20	18
P/E – low	—	6	6	5	9	10	15	12	14	16	11
Dividends per share ($)	17.6%	0.11	0.12	0.14	0.17	0.21	0.26	0.32	0.37	0.41	0.45
Book value per share ($)	29.1%	2.34	2.15	5.60	7.13	5.77	7.25	—	8.75	22.28	23.35

1990 Year-end:
Debt ratio: 31.4%
Return on equity: 6.6%
Cash (mil.): $1,634
Current ratio: 3.78
Long-term debt (mil.): $747
No. of shares (mil.): 70
Dividends:
1990 average yield: 2.3%
1990 payout: 29.8%
Market value (mil.): $1,357

Stock Price History High/Low 1981–90

GENERAL DYNAMICS CORPORATION

NYSE symbol: GD
Fiscal year ends: December 31

OVERVIEW

General Dynamics, the nation's 2nd largest defense contractor after McDonnell Douglas, produces a wide range of major weapons systems for all branches of the armed forces.

One of the hardest hit by recent cutbacks in defense spending (the company took a $700 million write-off related to the cancellation of the A-12 in 1990), General Dynamics is implementing cost control measures designed to return it to profitability. On the heels of Chairman Stanley Pace's retirement in 1991, William Anders (his replacement) announced the elimination of 27,000 jobs over the next 4 years, and, pending shareholder approval, proposed making the company's remaining employees stockholders.

Anders is also considering moving the company into commercial markets (its subsidiary Cessna Aircraft is already one of the world's top makers of business jets, with about 60% of the market) to reduce its dependence on government contracts. In the meantime General Dynamics is changing its address from St. Louis to a Virginia suburb of Washington, DC, where it will be closer to its primary customer, the US government, which accounted for 84% of sales in 1990. The move should be complete in March 1992.

WHEN

The history of General Dynamics begins with the Electric Boat Company, a New Jersey ship and submarine builder founded by John Holland in 1899. Electric Boat produced large numbers of submarines, ships, and PT boats during WWII. Faced with dwindling orders after the war, the company, under the direction of John Jay Hopkins, began to diversify with the 1947 purchase of Canadian aircraft builder Canadair. Hopkins formed General Dynamics in 1952, merging Electric Boat and Canadair into the new company, and bought California-based Consolidated Vultee Aircraft (Convair), a major producer of military and civilian aircraft, in 1954.

Electric Boat launched the first nuclear submarine, the Nautilus, in 1955; the following year, at the urging of Howard Hughes, Convair began designing its first commercial jetliners, the Convair 880 and 990. While nuclear subs became a mainstay for General Dynamics, the company gave up on its jetliners after losses on the aircraft reached $425 million (1961). Meanwhile, weakened by the cost of producing the 880 and 990, General Dynamics in 1959 merged with profitable Chicago building-materials supplier Material Service Corporation, whose owner, Colonel Henry Crown, received a 20% stake in General Dynamics.

During the 1960s General Dynamics developed the controversial F-111 fighter. Despite numerous problems, the aircraft proved financially and militarily successful (F-111s participated in the 1986 US bombing raid on Libya).

Backed by Crown (the company's largest stockholder), David Lewis became CEO in 1970. Under Lewis, General Dynamics won contracts for the navy's 688 class attack submarine (1971), liquefied natural gas tankers for Burmah Oil Company (1972), the Trident ballistic missile submarine (1974), and the F-16 lightweight fighter aircraft (1975). The company sold Canadair (1976) and bought Chrysler Defense, which had a contract to build the army's new M1 tank, in 1982. Lewis made General Dynamics profitable but retired in 1985 amid federal investigations of overcharges to the government.

CEO Stanley Pace instituted tough ethics rules and cut costs. The company bought Cessna Aircraft in 1986 and sold its Quincy shipyard in 1987. In 1989 General Dynamics received orders (along with Tenneco subsidiary Newport News Shipbuilding) for the Seawolf attack submarine. The company was on the team chosen to build the new Advanced Tactical Fighter for the air force in 1991.

The Crown family still owns 22% of the company.

Hoover's Rating: C

WHO

Chairman and CEO: William A. Anders, age 57, $1,050,000 pay (prior to promotion)
VC: Herbert F. Rogers, age 65, $576,922 pay (prior to promotion)
President and COO: James R. Mellor, age 60, $685,731 pay (prior to promotion)
SVP and CFO: James J. Cunnane, age 52
SVP Human Resources: Arch H. Rambeau, age 55
Auditors: Arthur Andersen & Co.
Employees: 98,100

WHERE

HQ: Pierre Laclede Center, St. Louis, MO 63105-1861
Phone: 314-889-8200
Fax: 314-889-8839
New HQ: 3190 Fairview Park, Falls Church, VA 22042

	1990 Sales	
	$ mil.	% of total
US	8,549	84
Foreign (through US govt.)	1,083	11
Foreign (direct)	541	5
Total	**10,173**	**100**

WHAT

	1990 Sales		1990 Operating Income	
	$ mil.	% of total	$ mil.	% of total
Govt. aerospace	5,817	57	(758)	—
Submarines	1,731	17	85	—
Land systems	1,008	10	65	—
General aviation	716	7	106	—
Material service & resources	408	4	25	—
Other	493	5	(334)	—
Total	**10,173**	**100**	**(811)**	**—**

Principal Operating Units
Government aerospace
   Electronic systems (SINCGARS, avionics)
   Military aircraft (F-16)
   Missile systems (Tomahawk, Advanced Cruise Missile, Sparrow, Stinger)
   Space systems (Atlas launch vehicle, Centaur)
Submarines (SSN 688, Trident, Seawolf)
Land systems (M1 tank)
General aviation (Cessna Citation, Caravan)
Material service and resources (sand, gravel, lime, coal)

RANKINGS

48th in *Fortune* 500 Industrial Cos.
559th in *Business Week* 1000

KEY COMPETITORS

Boeing	Northrop
Daimler-Benz	Raytheon
FMC	Rockwell
General Electric	Siemens
General Motors	Tenneco
Grumman	Textron
Litton Industries	Thiokol
Lockheed	Thomson SA
Martin Marietta	Thorn EMI
McDonnell Douglas	United Technologies
Nobel	Vulcan

HOW MUCH

	9-Year Growth	1981	1982	1983	1984	1985	1986	1987	1988	1989	1990
Sales ($ mil.)	8.1%	5,063	6,155	7,146	7,839	8,164	8,892	9,344	9,551	10,043	10,173
Net income ($ mil.)	—	124	161	287	382	373	(63)	437	379	293	(639)
Income as % of sales	—	2.5%	2.6%	4.0%	4.9%	4.6%	(0.7%)	4.7%	4.0%	2.9%	(6.3%)
Earnings per share ($)	—	2.25	2.90	5.29	8.07	8.80	(1.46)	10.25	9.03	7.01	(15.34)
Stock price – high ($)	—	43.00	36.63	61.75	69.75	84.00	89.25	79.00	59.00	60.50	46.13
Stock price – low ($)	—	21.00	18.75	30.63	42.00	62.00	64.25	42.63	46.75	42.50	19.00
Stock price – close ($)	0.3%	24.50	33.00	58.13	69.50	68.75	67.75	48.75	50.75	44.88	25.25
P/E – high	—	19	13	12	9	10	—	8	7	9	—
P/E – low	—	9	6	6	5	7	—	4	5	6	—
Dividends per share ($)	3.7%	0.72	0.72	0.93	1.00	1.00	1.00	1.00	1.00	1.00	1.00
Book value per share ($)	6.8%	19.99	21.56	23.91	24.58	31.46	29.45	38.19	46.10	51.12	36.24

1990 Year-end:
Debt ratio: 37.3%
Return on equity: —
Cash (mil.): $115
Current ratio: 1.35
Long-term debt (mil.): $900
No. of shares (mil.): 42
Dividends:
   1990 average yield: 4.0%
   1990 payout: —
Market value (mil.): $1,052

Stock Price History High/Low 1981–90

GENERAL ELECTRIC COMPANY

OVERVIEW

General Electric is a $57.7 billion conglomerate with roots to Thomas Edison's 1879 invention of the light bulb. Based on sales GE is the 6th largest US company and the 10th largest in the world. GE's business segments range from financial services (GE Financial Services) to aircraft engines to broadcasting (National Broadcasting Company) to plastics.

GE's strategy for the 1980s was to retain only those businesses with the potential to become first or 2nd in the world market. GE entered the 1990s with a leading market position in each of its business segments and an overall ranking of 3rd most profitable public company in the US in 1990. GE's top producer

is GEFS (financing, insurance, brokerage [Kidder, Peabody], equipment leasing), with 1990 revenues of $14.8 billion. If it were a bank, GEFS would be the 8th largest (ranked by assets) in the US.

GE's management training institute in Crotonville, New York, has long been a model for US businesses. GE continues to apply its innovative 2-year-old "Work-Out" program as a way to bring together employees from different levels and functions to identify and work out inefficiencies. GE also seeks out innovative practices of other companies that can be adapted to its operations.

NYSE symbol: GE
Fiscal year ends: December 31

Hoover's Rating **B**

WHO

Chairman and CEO: John F. Welch, Jr., age 55, $2,982,873 pay
VC and Executive Officer: Edward E. Hood, Jr., age 60, $1,609,555 pay
SVP: Dennis D. Dammerman, age 45
SVP Human Resources: Jack O. Peiffer, age 57
Auditors: KPMG Peat Marwick
Employees: 298,000

WHERE

HQ: 3135 Easton Turnpike, Fairfield, CT 06431
Phone: 203-373-2211
Fax: 203-373-3131

GE is a large, diversified company with operations all over the world.

	1990 Sales		1990 Operating Income	
	$ mil.	% of total	$ mil.	% of total
US	50,142	86	6,862	89
Foreign	8,272	14	883	11
Adjustments	(752)	—	5,124	—
Total	**57,662**	**100**	**12,869**	**100**

WHEN

General Electric was established in 1892 in New York, the result of a merger between the Thomson-Houston Company and the Edison General Electric Company, with combined sales of $14 million. Charles Coffin was GE's first president and Thomas Edison one of its directors. Edison left the company in 1894.

GE's financial strength (backed by the Morgan banking house) and focus on research (it started one of the first corporate research laboratories in 1900) led to the company's success. Products included elevators (1885), trolleys, motors, toasters (1905) and other appliances under both the GE and Hotpoint labels, and the light bulb. In the 1920s GE joined Westinghouse and AT&T in a joint venture, Radio Corporation of America (RCA), a radio broadcasting company. GE sold off its RCA holdings (1930) because of an antitrust ruling (one of 65 antitrust actions against GE between 1911 and 1967).

By 1940 GE had grown to a company of 86,000 employees and $456 million in sales. From 1940 to 1952 annual sales increased six-fold to $2.6 billion. GE entered the computer industry in 1956 (ranked 5th in computer sales by 1965) but sold the business in 1970 to Honeywell because of operating losses.By 1980 GE's revenues had reached $25 billion from

sales of plastics, consumer electronics, nuclear reactors, and jet engines.

In the 1980s GE's strategy was to pursue only high-performance ventures. Between 1980 and 1989, GE sold operations that comprised 25% of its 1980 sales and focused on medical equipment, financial services, and high-performance plastics and ceramics. GE shed its air conditioning (1982), housewares (1984), mining (1984), and semiconductor (1988) businesses. It acquired Employers Reinsurance in 1984 ($1.1 billion); RCA, including the National Broadcasting Company, in 1986 ($6.4 billion); the investment banking firm of Kidder, Peabody (completed in 1990); and CGR medical equipment from Thomson of France in 1987 as part of an exchange for GE's consumer electronics division.

GE entered Eastern Europe in 1990, taking a majority interest in the Hungarian lighting company Tungsram. In 1991 GE acquired an interest in THORN Light Source in the UK. The 2 purchases increased GE's European share of the lamp market from 2% to 20%. GE's subsidiary and the #1 rated network, NBC, reported a 21% operating loss in 1990. In response, NBC closed 2 of its 9 US news bureaus in 1991.

WHAT

	1990 Sales		1990 Operating Income	
	$ mil.	% of total	$ mil.	% of total
Aircraft engines	7,488	13	1,263	16
Major appliances	5,706	10	467	6
Materials	5,113	9	1,017	13
Aerospace	5,545	9	648	8
Technical products & services	4,565	8	595	8
Broadcasting	3,236	5	477	6
Financing	9,000	15	1,267	17
Insurance, securities & other	6,049	10	329	4
Power systems	5,644	10	739	10
Industrial products	6,449	11	884	12
Adjustments	(1,133)	—	5,183	—
Total	**57,662**	**100**	**12,869**	**100**

Products and Services

Aircraft engines	Locomotives
Appliances	Medical imaging
Broadcasting	equipment
Electrical and electronic	Military vehicles
equipment	Plastics
Electronics	Radar
Finance and insurance	Satellites
Generators	Spacecraft
Information services	Transformers
Lighting products	Turbines

HOW MUCH

	9-Year Growth	1981	1982	1983	1984	1985	1986	1987	1988	1989	1990
Sales ($ mil.)	8.7%	27,240	26,500	26,797	27,947	28,285	35,211	39,315	49,414	53,884	57,662
Net income ($ mil.)	11.2%	1,652	1,817	2,024	2,280	2,336	2,492	2,119	3,386	3,939	4,303
Income as % of sales	—	6.1%	6.9%	7.6%	8.2%	8.3%	7.1%	5.4%	6.9%	7.3%	7.5%
Earnings per share ($)	11.5%	1.82	2.00	2.23	2.52	2.57	2.73	2.33	3.73	4.32	4.85
Stock price – high ($)	—	17.47	25.00	29.44	29.69	36.94	44.38	66.38	47.88	64.75	75.50
Stock price – low ($)	—	12.78	13.75	22.69	24.13	27.81	33.25	38.75	38.38	43.50	50.00
Stock price – close ($)	16.7%	14.34	23.72	29.31	28.31	36.38	43.00	44.13	44.75	64.50	57.38
P/E – high	—	10	13	13	12	14	16	28	13	15	16
P/E – low	—	7	7	10	10	11	12	17	10	10	10
Dividends per share ($)	10.4%	0.79	0.84	0.94	1.03	1.12	1.19	1.33	1.46	1.70	1.92
Book value per share ($)	10.6%	10.02	11.19	12.39	13.82	15.25	16.57	18.25	20.47	23.09	24.83

1990 Year-end:
Debt ratio: 49.3%
Return on equity: 20.2%
Cash (mil.): $1,975
Current ratio: —
Long-term debt (mil.) $21,043
No. of shares (mil.): 873
Dividends:
 1990 average yield: 3.3%
 1990 payout: 39.6%
Market value (mil.): $50,095

Stock Price History High/Low 1981–90

RANKINGS

6th in *Fortune* 500 Industrial Cos.
4th in *Business Week* 1000

KEY COMPETITORS

ABB	Hitachi	Time Warner
Capital Cities/ABC	Maytag	Turner
CBS	Philips	Broadcasting
Electrolux	Reliance Electric	United
Friedrich Krupp	Rolls-Royce	Technologies
General Motors	Siemens	Westinghouse
GTE	Square D	Whirlpool

GE also competes with dozens of other companies, from finance companies to broadcasters.

GENERAL MILLS, INC.

OVERVIEW

With a 27% US market share, Minneapolis-based General Mills is the 2nd largest producer of breakfast cereals (after Kellogg) and holds the #1 or #2 position in several other food categories, including dessert mixes (Betty Crocker, #1), flour and dry mixes (#1), yogurt (Yoplait, #2), frozen seafood (Gorton's, #2), ready-to-make dinners (Hamburger and Tuna Helper, #1), fruit snacks (#1), and microwave popcorn (Pop Secret, #2). The company's Cheerios brand is the nation's best-selling cereal.

General Mills's restaurant division, its fastest growing segment, operates the highly successful Red Lobster and Olive Garden chains in the US and Canada and is currently test-marketing a 3rd restaurant called China Coast. The company has also opened 46 Red Lobsters in Japan through a joint venture with JUSCO.

General Mills has gained a reputation for generous philanthropy and in 1990 donated almost 3% of its income ($20 million) to charity. *Fortune* has named General Mills America's most-admired food company.

NYSE symbol: GIS
Fiscal year ends: Last Sunday in May

Hoover's Rating **A-**

WHO

Chairman and CEO: H. Brewster Atwater, Jr., age 60, $1,431,382 pay
VC and Chief Financial and Administrative Officer: F. Caleb Blodgett, age 64, $1,069,402 pay
President and COO: Mark H. Willes, age 50, $997,290 pay
VP Human Resources: Joseph R. Mucha
Auditors: KPMG Peat Marwick
Employees: 108,077

WHERE

HQ: 1 General Mills Blvd., PO Box 1113, Minneapolis, MN 55440
Phone: 612-540-2311
Fax: 612-540-4925

General Mills exports its products worldwide. Its 2 restaurant chains operate 840 locations throughout the US and Canada.

WHEN

In 1866 Cadwallader Washburn founded the Washburn Crosby Company. After winning a gold medal for flour at an 1880 exhibition, the company introduced the Gold Medal Flour trademark. In 1921 advertising manager Sam Gale created fictional spokeswoman Betty Crocker so that correspondence to housewives could go out with her signature. The company introduced Wheaties ready-to-eat cereal in 1924. James F. Bell, made president of Washburn Crosby in 1925, consolidated the company with other mills around the country (including Red Star, Rocky Mountain Elevator, and Kalispell Flour) to form General Mills, the world's largest miller. Although the companies operated independently of one another, a corporate headquarters coordinated advertising and merchandising.

General Mills introduced convenience foods such as Bisquick (1930s) and Cheerios (1941) and supported these brands with radio and, later, television advertising. Along with flour these products generated sufficient sales to permit General Mills to keep paying dividends throughout the 1930s and 1940s. During WWII the company produced goods needed for the war, such as ordnance equipment, and developed chemical and electronics divisions.

When Edwin Rawlings became CEO in 1961, he closed down half the flour mills and divested such unprofitable lines as electronics.

This cost $200 million in annual sales but freed resources for such acquisitions as the Tom Huston Peanut Company (snack foods, 1966), Kenner Products (toys, 1967), and Parker Brothers (board games, 1968). The Kenner and Parker purchases made General Mills the world's largest toy company. Other acquisitions included Gorton's (frozen seafood, 1968), Monet (jewelry, 1968), David Crystal (Izod sportswear, 1969), Red Lobster (restaurants,1970), Eddie Bauer (outerwear, 1971), and Talbots (women's clothing, 1973).

In 1977 the company sold the chemical division and bought Ship 'n Shore (blouses), Wallpapers to Go (interior decorating supplies), and the rights to Yoplait yogurt. The restaurant division started The Olive Garden restaurants in 1983.

When toy and fashion division profits fell more than 30% in 1984, the company spun off these groups as Kenner Parker Toys and Crystal Brands (1985). Reemphasizing food, General Mills sold Wallpapers to Go (1986); Eddie Bauer and Talbots (1989); and O-Cel-O (sponges, 1990). In 1991 the company sold its Lancia Brava division (pasta, Canada).

In 1989 General Mills masterminded a *blitzkrieg* into the European cereal market, which has traditionally been dominated by Kellogg, by forming the CPW (Cereal Partners Worldwide) joint venture with Nestlé. The partnership commenced operations in 1991.

WHAT

	1990 Sales		1990 Operating Income	
	$ mil.	% of total	$ mil.	% of total
Consumer foods	4,940	69	690	80
Restaurants	2,213	31	172	20
Adjustments	—	—	(35)	—
Total	**7,153**	**100**	**827**	**100**

Brand Names

Cereals	Other Foods
Basic 4	Bac*Os
Cheerios	Betty Crocker
Cinnamon Toast Crunch	Bisquick
Clusters	Bugles
Cocoa Puffs	Creamy Deluxe
Crispy Wheats 'N Raisins	Fruit Roll-Ups
Fiber One	Fruit Wrinkles
Golden Grahams	Gold Medal
Kix	Gorton's
Lucky Charms	Hamburger Helper
Oatmeal Raisin Crisp	MicroRave (popcorn)
Oatmeal Swirlers	Nature Valley
Raisin Nut Bran	Oriental Classics
Total	Pop Secret
Total Raisin Bran	Potato Buds
Triples	Suddenly Salad
Trix	Tuna Helper
Wheaties	Yoplait

Restaurants
The Olive Garden
Red Lobster

RANKINGS

77th in *Fortune* 500 Industrial Cos.
62nd in *Business Week* 1000

KEY COMPETITORS

Associated Milk Producers	Kellogg
Borden	McDonald's
BSN	Metromedia
Campbell Soup	Nestlé
Cargill	PepsiCo
ConAgra	Philip Morris
CPC	Quaker Oats
Grand Metropolitan	Ralston Purina
Heinz	RJR Nabisco
Imasco	TW Holdings
John Labatt	Wendy's

HOW MUCH

Fiscal year ends May of following year	9-Year Growth	1981	1982	1983	1984	1985	1986	1987	1988	1989	1990
Sales ($ mil.)	3.4%	5,312	5,551	5,601	4,285	4,587	5,189	5,179	5,621	6,448	7,153
Net income ($ mil.)	8.4%	226	245	233	115	184	222	265	315	374	464
Income as % of sales	—	4.2%	4.4%	4.2%	2.7%	4.0%	4.3%	5.1%	5.6%	5.8%	6.5%
Earnings per share ($)	10.9%	1.12	1.22	1.25	0.65	1.03	1.25	1.53	1.93	2.28	2.82
Stock price – high ($)	—	9.88	13.69	14.44	15.00	17.31	23.69	31.06	29.00	38.44	52.00
Stock price – low ($)	—	6.69	8.22	11.06	10.41	11.94	14.13	20.38	21.56	25.19	31.38
Stock price – close ($)	20.8%	8.97	12.19	13.06	12.72	15.28	21.56	24.81	25.94	36.19	49.00
P/E – high	—	9	11	12	23	17	19	20	15	17	18
P/E – low	—	6	7	9	16	12	11	13	11	11	11
Dividends per share ($)	13.5%	0.41	0.46	0.51	0.56	0.57	0.63	0.80	0.94	1.10	1.28
Book value per share ($)	(1.1%)	6.13	6.42	6.76	5.76	3.81	4.14	3.88	4.54	4.96	6.74

1990 Year-end:
Debt ratio: 44.1%
Return on equity: 48.2%
Cash (mil.): $40
Current ratio: 0.85
Long-term debt (mil.): $879
No. of shares (mil.): 165
Dividends:
1990 average yield: 2.6%
1990 payout: 45.4%
Market value (mil.): $8,090

Stock Price History High/Low 1981–90

GENERAL MOTORS CORPORATION

NYSE symbol: GM
Fiscal year ends: December 31

 Hoover's Rating **C-**

OVERVIEW

Detroit-based General Motors is the world's largest company and the largest auto maker. GM produces cars and trucks under the Chevrolet, Buick, Cadillac, Pontiac, Oldsmobile, Saturn, and GMC nameplates in the US and led the domestic automobile market with a 35.5% share in 1990. The auto maker's modest gain in US market share in 1990 resulted from large cash incentives to buyers. GM produces cars and trucks in Europe under the Vauxhall, Opel, and Holden nameplates and resells autos made by Suzuki and Isuzu.

GM also provides financial and insurance services and, through its Electronic Data Systems and Hughes Aircraft units, manages information systems and manufactures weapon systems, locomotives, and commercial satellites.

Despite strong sales in Europe, especially in Germany, losses continue as a result of a weak US automobile market. Further compounding GM's difficulties is the problem-ridden launch of the new Saturn line of cars. Production glitches have prevented the new GM unit from ramping up output to planned levels.

WHEN

In its early years the automobile industry consisted of hundreds of firms, each producing a few models. William Durant, who bought and reorganized a failing Buick Motors in 1904, reasoned that if several makers united, each would be protected in an off year. After attempts to join with Ford and Maxwell failed, Durant formed the General Motors Company in Flint, Michigan, in 1908.

Durant had bought 17 companies (including Oldsmobile, Cadillac, and Pontiac) by 1910, the year a bankers' syndicate gained control and forced him to step down. In a 1915 stock swap, Durant regained control of GM through Chevrolet, a company he had formed in 1911 with race car driver Louis Chevrolet. In 1919 GM acquired Fisher Body and Frigidaire (sold 1979) and created the GM Acceptance Corporation (auto financing).

Du Pont, looking to invest company profits, began purchasing GM stock in 1917. Durant resigned in 1920 and sold his stock to Du Pont, bringing its total stake to 23%. Du Pont kept this share until a 1957 Supreme Court antitrust ruling forced it to divest.

Alfred Sloan, president from 1923 to 1937, implemented a decentralized management system, now emulated worldwide. Sloan remained chairman until 1956, and his 1963 book, *My Years with General Motors*, is considered a management classic.

GM competed by offering models ranging from luxury to economy, colors besides black, and yearly style modifications. By 1927 GM had become the industry leader. Later improvements included independent front-wheel suspension and automatic transmissions.

The first US company to downsize its cars (1977) in response to Japanese imports, GM introduced a line of front-wheel-drive compacts in 1979. A $70 billion, 10-year capital investment program initiated in 1979 included company-wide restructuring and cost-cutting. Under Roger Smith, CEO from 1981 to 1990, GM laid off tens of thousands of workers, whose plight was depicted in the award-winning 1989 film *Roger and Me*.

GM bought H. Ross Perot's Electronic Data Systems (1984) and Hughes Aircraft (1986) and entered into more than 50 joint ventures in the 1980s. Since 1985 GM has redesigned over 84% of its cars, and in 1988 Chevrolet launched the Geo line of compacts. Still, intense competition from imports and Ford dropped GM's market share from 47% in 1979 to 35% by 1989. GM bought 50% of Saab Automobile in 1989.

In 1990 GM launched Saturn, its first new nameplate since 1926, and wrote off $2.1 billion to cover plant closings. The next year GM announced plans to build electric cars in Lansing and released redesigned Cadillacs aimed at younger car buyers.

WHO

Chairman and CEO: Robert C. Stempel, age 57, $869,000 pay
President: Lloyd E. Reuss, age 54, $652,000 pay
EVP and CFO: Robert T. O'Connell, age 52
VP Personnel Administration and Development: Gerald Knechtel
Auditors: Deloitte & Touche
Employees: 761,400

WHERE

HQ: 3044 W. Grand Blvd., Detroit, MI 48202
Phone: 313-556-5000
Fax: 313-556-5108

GM has manufacturing and other facilities at 254 US locations and in 36 other countries.

	1990 Sales		1990 Net Income	
	$ mil.	% of total	$ mil.	% of total
US	86,967	70	(4,570)	—
Canada	6,824	6	169	—
Europe	23,922	19	1,914	—
Latin America	4,047	3	245	—
Other countries	2,945	2	256	—
Adjustments	(1,429)	—	—	—
Total	**123,276**	**100**	**(1,986)**	**—**

WHAT

	1990 Sales		1990 Operating Income	
	$ mil.	% of total	$ mil.	% of total
Automotive prods.	96,906	79	(3,446)	—
Financing & insurance	11,812	10	—	—
Other products	13,303	11	1,017	—
Adjustments	1,255	—	—	—
Total	**123,276**	**100**	**(2,429)**	**—**

Cars and Trucks

Buick	Holden	Pontiac
Cadillac	Lotus	Saturn
Chevrolet	Oldsmobile	Vauxhall
GMC	Opel	

Major Divisions and Subsidiaries
Allison Gas Turbine Division
Allison Transmission Division
Delco Electronics Corp.
Electro-Motive Division (locomotives)
Electronic Data Systems Corp.
General Motors Acceptance Corp. (GMAC)
GM Hughes Electronics Corp.
GMAC Mortgage Corp.
GMFanuc Robotics Corp.
Hughes Aircraft Co.
Motors Insurance Corp.
Power Products and Defense Operations
Saab Automobile AB (50%)

RANKINGS

1st in *Fortune* 500 Industrial Cos.
18th in *Business Week* 1000

KEY COMPETITORS

Arthur Andersen	Hyundai	Toyota
Chrysler	IBM	Volkswagen
Cummins Engine	Mitsubishi	Volvo
Daimler-Benz	Navistar	Defense
Ernst & Young	Nissan	contractors
Fiat	PACCAR	Electronics
Ford	Renault	companies
Honda	Saab-Scania	Other automakers

HOW MUCH

	9-Year Growth	1981	1982	1983	1984	1985	1986	1987	1988	1989	1990
Sales ($ mil.)	7.8%	62,699	60,026	74,582	83,890	96,372	102,813	101,781	121,816	124,993	123,276
Net income ($ mil.)	—	333	963	3,730	4,517	3,999	2,945	3,551	4,632	4,224	(1,986)
Income as % of sales	—	0.5%	1.6%	5.0%	5.4%	4.2%	2.9%	3.5%	3.8%	3.4%	(1.6%)
Earnings per share ($)	—	0.54	1.55	5.92	7.11	6.14	4.11	5.03	*6.82*	6.17	(4.09)
Stock price – high ($)	—	29.00	32.25	40.00	41.38	42.50	44.31	47.06	44.06	50.50	50.50
Stock price – low ($)	—	16.94	17.00	28.00	30.50	32.13	32.94	25.00	30.00	39.13	33.13
Stock price – close ($)	6.7%	19.25	31.19	37.19	39.19	35.19	33.00	30.69	41.75	42.25	34.38
P/E – high	—	54	21	7	6	7	11	9	6	8	—
P/E – low	—	32	11	5	4	5	8	5	4	6	—
Dividends per share ($)	10.7%	1.20	1.20	1.40	2.38	2.50	2.50	2.50	2.50	3.00	3.00
Book value per share ($)	6.2%	28.72	28.87	32.52	37.97	46.29	47.99	53.13	57.81	57.37	49.23

1990 Year-end:
Debt ratio: 56.2%
Return on equity: —
Cash (mil.): $3,689
Current ratio: —
Long-term debt (mil.): $38,510
No. of shares (mil.): 606
Dividends:
 1990 average yield: 8.7%
 1990 payout: —
Market value (mil.): $20,817

Stock Price History High/Low 1981–90

GENERAL RE CORPORATION

OVERVIEW

General Re, through subsidiary General Reinsurance, is the nation's largest reinsurer (it sells insurance for part or all of the risk of other insurance companies) and is estimated to be the world's 3rd largest reinsurer. Most of its business is written on an excess-of-loss basis, meaning that the company pays after a primary insurer's losses exceed a specific sum.

The company provides property/casualty reinsurance in the US primarily through its General Reinsurance unit. General Re is consistently profitable: even after 1989's catastrophic losses (nearly $8 billion) from the California earthquake and Hurricane Hugo,

General Re's domestic property/casualty operations showed a profit.

General Re had a good year in 1990. There were few disasters, and demand for reinsurance grew as primary insurers, shaken by investment and real estate downturns, sought to cushion their losses with reinsurance. The company may also benefit from Lloyd's of London's problems. Expansions included acquisition of the Royal Insurance Group's excess and surplus lines, the opening of an office in Argentina, and the formation of General Re Financial Products to engage in interest rate and currency swaps and related products.

NYSE symbol: GRN
Fiscal year ends: December 31

WHO

Chairman, President, and CEO: Ronald E. Ferguson, age 49, $1,253,100 pay
VC: John C. Etling, age 55, $1,038,000 pay
VP, General Counsel, and Secretary: Edmond F. Rondepierre, age 61, $480,600 pay
VP Investments: Ernest C. Frohboese, age 50
VP Finance: Ronald G. Anderson, age 42, $451,500 pay
SVP Human Resources: Theron S. Hoffman, Jr.
Auditors: Coopers & Lybrand
Employees: 2,496

WHEN

In 1921, when Duncan A. Reid became president of the newly organized General Casualty and Surety Reinsurance Corporation of New York, the field of reinsurance was virtually nonexistent in the US. By 1923 the company's name had changed to General Reinsurance Corporation; Carl Hansen, an underwriting expert, became VP and general manager. By 1925 Hansen and 2 partners controlled the company, and General Reinsurance began providing property and casualty reinsurance — its domain to this day.

Reinsurance was a small market, and business grew slowly. It began to take off when, in 1945, the Mellon family united its privately owned Mellon Indemnity with General Re and took over operations. Edward Lowry, Jr., was brought in to head the company in 1946. Reinsurers then paid claims on losses but provided no other services. Lowry, recognizing that reinsurers were the first to know when a branch of the industry was at risk, began offering management consulting services, which remain important to General Re in customer retention.

After the merger General Re held a near monopoly on reinsurance. From 1945 to 1980, General Re's policy was to charge the highest premiums in the business. The company was consistently the most profitable US reinsurer.

Lowry retired in 1960. Successor James Cathcart began international expansion in 1962, starting Zurich-based International Reinsurance and buying Stockholm's Swedish Atlas Reinsurance and an interest in Reinsurance Company of Australasia. During the late 1960s and early 1970s General Re expanded its facultative group (companies that insure against specific risks), started in 1954. Beginning from a small revenue base, the group contributed 1/2 of General Re's premium income by 1978. In the mid-1970s the company also began reinsuring against medical malpractice and equipment leasing losses.

By 1978 General Re had suffered stiff price competition from smaller start-ups; concurrently, about a dozen of the company's senior managers left, some to form competitor Trenwick Re.

In 1980 General Re formed a holding company for its operations and began investing in other insurers such as British-based Trident Insurance Group (sold in 1985) and Monarch Insurance Company of Ohio (1985).

General Re did not join the 1980s stampede into risky investments. Non-investment-grade securities and real estate each comprise less than 0.5% of investments. Consequently, the company and its subsidiaries remain strongly capitalized.

WHERE

HQ: 695 E. Main St., Stamford, CT 06904-2351
Phone: 203-328-5000
Fax: 203-328-5329

General Re conducts business in the US and Canada and through 11 offices in Australia, Egypt, England, Switzerland, Japan, Spain, and New Zealand.

	1990 Sales		1990 Pretax Income	
	$ mil.	% of total	$ mil.	% of total
US/Canada	2,842	95	712	96
Foreign	151	5	26	4
Total	**2,993**	**100**	**738**	**100**

WHAT

Domestic Operations
General Reinsurance Corp.
General Re Financial Products
General Re Services Corp.
General Star Indemnity Co.
General Star Management Co.
General Star National Insurance Co.
Genesis Underwriting Management Co.
Herbert Clough, Inc. (reinsurance intermediary)
North Star Reinsurance Corp.
United States Aviation Underwriters, Inc.

International Operations
General Re Correduría de Reaseguros, SA (Spain)
General Reinsurance Corp. (Europe)
General Reinsurance Ltd. (England)
Reinsurance Company of Australasia Ltd. (Australia/New Zealand)

RANKINGS

28th in *Fortune* 50 Diversified Financial Cos.
68th in *Business Week* 1000

KEY COMPETITORS

Aetna
Allianz
AIG
CIGNA
Kemper
Lloyd's of London
MetLife
Prudential
Tokio Marine and Fire
USF&G

HOW MUCH

	9-Year Growth	1981	1982	1983	1984	1985	1986	1987	1988	1989	1990
Assets ($ mil.)	11.4%	4,168	4,741	5,440	6,053	6,689	8,677	9,438	9,394	10,390	11,033
Net income ($ mil.)	14.8%	178	207	192	72	159	279	486	513	599	614
Income as % of assets	—	4.3%	4.4%	3.5%	1.2%	2.4%	3.2%	5.2%	5.5%	5.8%	5.6%
Earnings per share ($)	14.5%	2.03	2.33	2.13	0.80	1.69	2.74	4.79	5.39	6.52	6.89
Stock price – high ($)	—	21.88	32.25	36.50	34.13	53.13	69.50	68.88	59.38	96.25	93.25
Stock price – low ($)	—	12.84	16.94	26.00	23.13	30.19	49.25	46.00	45.50	54.38	69.00
Stock price – close ($)	18.5%	20.19	31.88	34.25	31.88	50.06	55.50	55.88	55.50	87.13	93.00
P/E – high	—	11	14	17	43	31	25	14	11	15	14
P/E – low	—	6	7	12	29	18	18	10	8	8	10
Dividends per share ($)	14.8%	0.44	0.54	0.64	0.72	0.78	0.88	1.00	1.20	1.36	1.52
Book value per share ($)	13.9%	11.11	12.64	14.60	15.16	18.50	23.47	26.21	29.04	34.31	35.78

1990 Year-end:
Debt ratio: 7.8%
Return on equity: 19.7%
Cash (mil.): $28
Sales (mil.): $2,993
Long-term debt (mil.): $277
No. of shares (mil.): 87
Dividends:
  1990 average yield: 1.6%
  1990 payout: 22.1%
Market value (mil.): $8,109

Stock Price History High/Low 1981–90

GENERAL SIGNAL CORPORATION

OVERVIEW

General Signal, based in Stamford, Connecticut, is a leading supplier of equipment for the electrical, semiconductor, and process control industries. It is a diversified conglomerate with $1.7 billion in sales and products ranging from industrial valves to advanced photolithography products for the semiconductor manufacturing industry.

Of General Signal's 3 primary business segments (process controls, industrial technology, electrical controls), process controls is its largest. This segment supplies mixing equipment, industrial valves and pumps, and control systems predominantly to the chemical, pulp and paper, electric utility, and water and wastewater treatment industries.

General Signal's industrial technology segment is working with the SEMATECH consortium to develop the next-generation manufacturing process for the semiconductor industry. GS's electrical controls segment includes power protection equipment, uninterruptible power system products, broadcast transmission equipment, and alarm systems.

After earnings dropped precipitously during the 1980s, GS began in 1988 to "reposition" itself as a profitable market leader in its segments. The company sold the bulk of its transportation segment — including its original business, General Railway Signal — and several semiconductor businesses in 1990. GS has consolidated its 44 units into 22 and cut 1,109 jobs since 1987; special charges related to this restructuring led the company to report a loss in 1990.

WHEN

General Railway Signal Company, incorporated in 1904, set up in Rochester, New York, to manufacture railway safety equipment (railroad signals, crossing gates, automatic train controls, etc.) and grew to become the largest supplier in the US, with 50% of the market in 1930. Sales grew from $8.7 million in 1930 to $15.9 million in 1954 to $21.7 million in 1959.

There was little change in General Railway Signal's product line until 1960, when it acquired Regina (vacuum cleaners). Two years later, following the hiring of Nathan Owen as CEO, the company launched an aggressive diversification effort. Its present name was adopted in 1963.

GS's early acquisitions were specialty electronics and electrical equipment companies. Owen's strategy to become a small General Electric changed with the acquisition of New York Air Brake (1967), a maker of air brakes and pneumatic and hydraulic control systems. The acquisition doubled the size of GS and put it on the *Fortune* 500 list in 1967. It also gave GS a foothold in the water treatment business. By 1972 GS had acquired 5 more pollution-control-related companies.

GS entered the energy control business by acquiring Sola Basic Industries (specialty products for utilities, 1977) and Leeds & Northrup (temperature and pressure controls, 1978).

Between 1980 and 1985 GS ventured into the semiconductor and telecommunications equipment businesses. Acquisitions included Xynetics (semiconductor fabrication systems), Kayex (silicon-crystal-growing furnaces), and Telecommunications Technology (electronic testing equipment). GS sold Regina in 1984.

GS's earnings dropped from $109 million in 1984 to $49 million in 1985, caused in part by a slowdown in the semiconductor capital equipment market. Since hiring chairman Edmund Carpenter (1988), GS has pared operations, sold off units and sold assets to lower debt resulting from the company's buyback of 30% of its stock. At the same time, GS bought 12 new businesses, mostly product lines complementing successful GS units.

In 1990 GS announced the sale of General Railway Signal and New York Air Brake for $100 million; the company retained the latter's lucrative electronic farebox business.

PSE and NYSE symbol: GSX
Fiscal year ends: December 31

Hoover's Rating **D**

WHO

Chairman and CEO: Edmund M. Carpenter, age 49, $758,000 pay
SVP Finance and CFO: Stephen W. Nagy, age 50, $280,500 pay
VP Human Resources: George Falconer, age 58
Auditors: KPMG Peat Marwick
Employees: 14,992

WHERE

HQ: 1 High Ridge Park, PO Box 10010, Stamford, CT 06904
Phone: 203-357-8800
Fax: 203-329-4159

The company does business worldwide. It has 86 plants in the US and 12 foreign countries.

	1990 Sales		1990 Operating Income	
	$ mil.	% of total	$ mil.	% of total
US	1,449	82	129	92
Foreign	323	18	12	8
Adjustments	(77)	—	(15)	—
Total	**1,695**	**100**	**126**	**100**

WHAT

	1990 Sales		1990 Operating Income	
	$ mil.	% of total	$ mil.	% of total
Electrical controls	503	30	47	32
Process controls	728	43	74	50
Industrial technology	451	27	28	18
Dispositions	13	—	(8)	—
Adjustments	—	—	(15)	—
Total	**1,695**	**100**	**126**	**100**

Process Controls
Centrifugal and wastewater pumps
Electronic feeders and scales
Electronic measurement and control instrumentation
Heat processing equipment
High-vacuum pumps
Industrial aerators
Industrial valves (deZurik)
Mechanical mixers (Labmaster)

Electrical Controls
Broadcast transmission equipment and TV/radio antennas
Electric motors
Electrical fittings
Emergency lighting systems

Fire alarm systems
Power conditioning equipment
Power transmission
Signaling devices
Specialty fittings
Transformers

Industrial Technology
Communications transmission equipment
Crystal-growing furnaces
Electronic fareboxes and turnstiles
Photolithography wafer steppers
Plasma etching/stripping systems
Telecommunications test equipment
Wafer saws

RANKINGS

233rd in *Fortune* 500 Industrial Cos.
617th in *Business Week* 1000

KEY COMPETITORS

Cooper Industries
Eaton
EG&G
Emerson
General Electric
Harris
Hewlett-Packard
Hitachi

Honda
Honeywell
Ingersoll-Rand
Oki
Siemens
Square D
Thorn EMI
Westinghouse

HOW MUCH

	9-Year Growth	1981	1982	1983	1984	1985	1986	1987	1988	1989	1990
Sales ($ mil.)	(0.1%)	1,702	1,622	1,575	1,787	1,801	1,583	1,603	1,760	1,918	1,695
Net income ($ mil.)	—	117	108	90	109	49	75	69	25	78	(13)
Income as % of sales	—	6.9%	6.6%	5.7%	6.1%	2.7%	4.7%	4.3%	1.4%	4.1%	(0.8%)
Earnings per share ($)	—	4.18	3.81	3.12	3.75	1.71	2.58	2.45	0.91	4.09	(0.69)
Stock price – high ($)	—	51.38	47.00	52.38	54.00	53.88	54.25	61.25	56.50	57.88	59.38
Stock price – low ($)	—	33.38	28.00	40.50	39.63	37.00	39.25	33.25	40.00	45.75	31.38
Stock price – close ($)	(0.2%)	38.63	44.88	50.75	47.00	46.38	44.25	47.00	47.50	48.25	37.88
P/E – high	—	12	12	17	14	32	21	25	62	14	—
P/E – low	—	8	7	13	11	22	15	14	44	11	—
Dividends per share ($)	2.0%	1.51	1.62	1.68	1.74	1.80	1.80	1.80	1.80	1.80	1.80
Book value per share ($)	(1.7%)	27.17	28.66	29.66	31.53	31.47	32.33	33.02	24.19	26.50	23.38

1990 Year-end:
Debt ratio: 46.9%
Return on equity: —
Cash (mil.): $8
Current ratio: 1.77
Long-term debt (mil.): $398
No. of shares (mil.): 19
Dividends:
  1990 average yield: 4.8%
  1990 payout: —
Market value (mil.): $730

Stock Price History High/Low 1981–90

GEORGIA-PACIFIC CORPORATION

NYSE symbol: GP
Fiscal year ends: December 31

Hoover's Rating **C+**

OVERVIEW

Based in Atlanta, Georgia-Pacific is the world's 2nd largest forest products company after International Paper. It is the world's largest producer of market pulp and 2nd largest producer of containerboard. In the US the company leads in the manufacture and distribution of building materials. It is the #2 American maker of printing and writing papers and #5 tissue maker. Major brand names include Spectrum business papers, Angel Soft tissue, and Delta paper towels.

Georgia-Pacific has taken steps toward reducing its debt (after taking on an additional $5.4 billion with the 1990 hostile takeover of Great Northern Nekoosa) through a $1 billion sale of nonstrategic assets completed early in 1991, but interest on the debt is high (about $600 million per year). The company also sold 49,000 acres of Washington timberland in 1991, raising an additional $29 million. Even so, earnings declined 45% in 1990, mostly as a result of acquisition-related costs and a weak economy.

WHO

Chairman and CEO: T. Marshall Hahn, Jr., age 64, $1,569,807 pay
VC: Harold L. Airington, age 63, $2,149,723 pay
President and COO: Ronald P. Hogan, age 50, $687,009 pay
EVP Finance and CFO: James C. Van Meter, age 52
SVP Human Resources and Administration: David W. Reynolds
Auditors: Arthur Andersen & Co.
Employees: 63,000

WHEN

Owen Cheatham founded the Georgia Hardwood Lumber Company in Augusta, Georgia, in 1927 to wholesale hardwood lumber (which he bought from others). By 1938 the company was operating 5 southern sawmills and during WWII became the largest lumber supplier to the US armed forces.

In 1947 the company bought a plywood mill in Bellingham, Washington. Recognizing the potential of plywood (which was gaining rapid acceptance in the construction field), Cheatham acquired several more plywood mills in the late 1940s.

In 1951 Cheatham began an aggressive land-buying spree that would give the company its first timberlands. The company moved its headquarters to Oregon in 1954 and 3 years later adopted its present name. In 1957 Georgia-Pacific entered the pulp and paper business by establishing a new mill at Toledo, Oregon, and embarked on a period of explosive growth. By 1960 the company had one million acres of timberland.

During the 1960s the company acquired several competitors and built new facilities that allowed it to diversify into containers, paperboard, tissue, and chemicals, producing its own chemicals for paper, resin, plywood glue, and other products. By 1968 the company had reached $1 billion in sales.

In 1972 the FTC forced Georgia-Pacific to sell 20% of its assets to reduce its size (the spinoff became Louisiana-Pacific). The following year, the company bought Boise Cascade's wood-products operations at Fort Bragg, California, and in 1975 acquired Exchange Oil and Gas.

In 1976 Chairman Robert Flowerree continued the diversification into chemicals and cautiously introduced cheaper substitutes for plywood, like waferboard. Under Flowerree the company acquired timberland in the South and modernized existing paper mills. In 1979 Georgia-Pacific bought Hudson Pulp and Paper and reached $5 billion in sales.

The company returned to Georgia in 1982, and in 1984 decided to sell most chemical operations unrelated to forest products. During the 1980s, because of a slump in the home-building industry, the company emphasized selling materials for home remodeling rather than home building.

In 1988 Georgia-Pacific bought Brunswick Pulp and Paper in Georgia, greatly increasing its southern timber holdings. The 1990 acquisition of Great Northern Nekoosa increased Georgia-Pacific's dependence on pulp and paper. To help pay off some of the debt related to the takeover of Nekoosa, Georgia-Pacific sold some $1 billion in assets in 1990, including 19 corrugated container plants, 4 UK paper mills, a French containerboard mill, and 540,000 acres of timberland.

WHERE

HQ: 133 Peachtree St. NE, Atlanta, GA 30303
Phone: 404-521-4000
Fax: 404-521-4422

Georgia-Pacific has over 265 manufacturing facilities in the US, Mexico, and Canada.

Owned Timberland	Acres
Geographic area	Thou.
Northeast	3,000
South	3,900
Pacific Northwest	637
Appalachia	666
Total	**8,203**

WHAT

	1990 Sales		1990 Operating Income	
	$ mil.	% of total	$ mil.	% of total
Building products	5,923	47	423	30
Pulp & paper prods.	6,702	53	979	69
Other	40	—	17	1
Adjustments	—	—	(142)	—
Total	**12,665**	**100**	**1,277**	**100**

Building Products	
Adhesives	Containers
Building product–related chemicals	Envelopes
Doors	Market pulp
Fiberboard	Packaging materials
Gypsum	Paperboard
Hardboard	Printing paper
Insulation	Tissue
Lumber	Writing paper
Metal construction products	**Paper Products Brand Names**
Particleboard	Angel Soft
Roofing	Big 'n Pretty
Siding	Big 'n Soft
Specialty products	Big 'n Thirsty
Structural wood panels	Coronet
Pulp and Paper Products	Delta
Computer paper	MD
	Sparkle

RANKINGS

34th in *Fortune* 500 Industrial Cos.
176th in *Business Week* 1000

KEY COMPETITORS

Boise Cascade	Kimberly-Clark
Borden	Manville
Canadian Pacific	Mead
Champion International	Nobel
Fletcher Challenge	Owens-Corning
Goodyear	Scott
International Paper	USG
James River	Weyerhaeuser

HOW MUCH

	9-Year Growth	1981	1982	1983	1984	1985	1986	1987	1988	1989	1990
Sales ($ mil.)	9.9%	5,414	5,402	6,469	6,682	6,716	7,223	8,603	9,509	10,171	12,665
Net income ($ mil.)	9.6%	160	52	105	253	207	296	458	467	661	365
Income as % of sales	—	3.0%	1.0%	1.6%	3.8%	3.1%	4.1%	5.3%	4.9%	6.5%	2.9%
Earnings per share ($)	12.4%	1.49	0.50	0.96	2.24	1.80	2.64	4.21	4.75	7.37	4.28
Stock price – high ($)	—	32.38	27.25	31.88	25.75	27.38	41.25	52.75	42.88	62.00	52.13
Stock price – low ($)	—	17.75	13.25	22.38	18.00	20.50	24.75	22.75	30.75	36.63	25.38
Stock price – close ($)	7.1%	20.13	26.25	24.75	25.00	26.50	37.00	34.50	36.88	48.50	37.25
P/E – high	—	22	55	33	12	15	16	13	9	8	12
P/E – low	—	12	27	23	8	11	9	5	6	5	6
Dividends per share ($)	3.2%	1.20	1.05	0.60	0.70	0.80	0.85	1.05	1.25	1.45	1.60
Book value per share ($)	6.5%	19.47	19.63	19.83	19.85	20.80	22.84	25.59	27.79	31.35	34.31

1990 Year-end:
Debt ratio: 63.7%
Return on equity: 13.0%
Cash (mil.): $58
Current ratio: 0.70
Long-term debt (mil.): $5,218
No. of shares (mil.): 87
Dividends:
 1990 average yield: 4.3%
 1990 payout: 37.4%
Market value (mil.): $3,230

Stock Price History High/Low 1981–90

GERBER PRODUCTS COMPANY

OVERVIEW

Gerber Products, based in Fremont, Michigan, is the world's leading producer of processed baby foods. The company's US baby food market share is now about 70%. Gerber's other operations include infant and children's apparel, child-care products (nursers, toys, and infant-care items), and life insurance.

The company's many varieties of baby and toddler food (which include First Foods fruits and vegetables, strained foods, junior and toddler wet products, dry cereals, juice, bakery products, and Gerber Graduates microwaveable meals) account for 53.6% of the company's sales, with the balance coming from its merchandise and service sectors.

Gerber's Apparel Group is divided into 2 subsidiaries: Buster Brown Apparel and Gerber Childrenswear. Gerber Life Insurance sells insurance via mail and agents nationwide.

Gerber's strategy is to establish the Gerber name as a highly recognizable children's products trademark — a SUPERBRAND in Gerber parlance.

Gerber recently introduced its Diaper Starter Kit, which familiarizes parents with cloth diapers, another Gerber product.

WHEN

In 1901 Frank Gerber helped found and became president of the Fremont Canning Company, a small company established to provide a market for local produce in Fremont, Michigan. In 1920 Gerber's son Daniel joined the company and became assistant general manager in 1926.

By 1928 Daniel Gerber was married with a baby. At that time parents had to strain all of their babies' food by hand, and Daniel's wife Dorothy asked if he could do the straining at the cannery. This gave Daniel Gerber the idea for a line of commercially prepared baby food. Frank Gerber approved, and a series of marketing tests predicted success.

In late 1928 the company released its first line of Gerber strained baby foods (peas, carrots, spinach, prunes, and vegetable soup), which sold for 15¢ a can. The Gerbers began using a charcoal sketch of a baby by artist Dorothy Hope Smith in advertisements, putting it on baby food labels in 1932. The Gerber baby became a successful trademark, and today Gerber keeps the original sketch under glass in the company vault.

Sales increased during the 1930s, which led the company to introduce new varieties. At the same time Gerber began issuing consumer information on such topics as nutrition, child care, and home economics.

In 1941 the company changed its name to the Gerber Products Company and 2 years later dropped all of its adult foods. Consumer demand led Gerber to open new plants in Oakland, California (1943); Rochester, New York (1950); and Niagara, Ontario (1950). Frank Gerber died in 1952.

During the 1960s Gerber expanded into a number of foreign countries while diversifying its product line to include toys, lotions, bibs, and vinyl baby pants (the last would become part of the Gerber Babywear line). The company began producing its own metal cans in 1962. In 1968 it organized Gerber Life Insurance and in 1970 entered the child-care business by acquiring Jack & Jill School of Villa Park (a national chain), which it changed to Gerber Children's Centers (sold in 1990).

By 1973 Gerber was the world's largest supplier of baby foods. In 1982 the company created a children's furniture division (sold in 1988) and in 1986 introduced its First Foods line of baby food (single-serving fruits and vegetables). That same year the company's market share dropped from around 69% to 52% when a rumor started of broken glass in its baby food jars. Gerber reestablished its reputation and in 1989 entered into a joint baby formula venture with Bristol-Myers. In 1990 the company discontinued its money-losing Weather Tamer apparel unit.

NYSE symbol: GEB
Fiscal year ends: March 31

Hoover's Rating **A-**

WHO

Chairman, President, and CEO: Alfred A. Piergallini, age 44, $916,000 pay
VC: Robert L. Johnston, age 59, $378,517 pay
EVP and CFO: Fred K. Schomer, age 51, $630,732 pay
EVP and President, Gerber Products Division: James T. Smith, age 43, $183,750 pay
VP Human Resources: E. Curtis Mairs
Auditors: Ernst & Young
Employees: 12,025

WHERE

HQ: 445 State St., Fremont, MI 49413
Phone: 616-928-2000
Fax: 616-928-2723 (Public Relations)

The company owns baby food plants in Fremont, MI; Fort Smith, AR; and Asheville, NC. Baby products are sold through over 40,000 retailers in the US. The company's products are available in 58 countries.

WHAT

	1990 Sales		1990 Pretax Income	
	$ mil.	% of total	$ mil.	% of total
Gerber Products Division	707	60	179	87
Apparel Group	371	31	16	8
Other	101	9	11	5
Total	**1,179**	**100**	**206**	**100**

Baby Food
Baby formula
Dry cereals
Fruits and vegetables
Juices

General Merchandise
Bedding
Bottles and eating utensils
Diapers
Nursers
Safety items
Toys

Apparel
Beatrix Potter's Peter Rabbit and Friends
Buster Brown
Crayon Crowd
Kaboom!
Snoopy
Peanuts
Tige's Pals

Life Insurance
Gerber Life
Grow-up (life insurance for children)
Young People's (life insurance for children)

RANKINGS

313th in *Fortune* 500 Industrial Cos.
306th in *Business Week* 1000

KEY COMPETITORS

Avon	Premark
BSN	Procter & Gamble
Hallmark	Ralston Purina
Hasbro	Rubbermaid
Heinz	Scott
Kimberly-Clark	Weyerhaeuser
Mattel	

HOW MUCH

Fiscal year ends March of following year	9-Year Growth	1981	1982	1983	1984	1985	1986	1987	1988	1989	1990
Sales ($ mil.)	5.9%	703	719	805	929	968	917	943	1,068	1,136	1,179
Net income ($ mil.)	12.5%	39	39	50	56	46	37	53	85	95	113
Income as % of sales	—	5.6%	5.4%	6.2%	6.1%	4.7%	4.1%	5.6%	8.0%	8.3%	9.6%
Earnings per share ($)	13.3%	0.98	0.97	1.24	1.39	1.12	0.93	1.33	2.17	2.50	3.00
Stock price – high ($)	—	7.44	9.42	14.58	16.00	21.50	28.81	31.50	30.81	52.25	61.75
Stock price – low ($)	—	5.78	5.33	7.42	10.25	12.19	17.88	11.25	17.13	28.81	38.38
Stock price – close ($)	27.1%	6.36	8.21	14.17	12.38	21.19	20.69	17.25	29.31	47.50	55.00
P/E – high	—	8	10	12	12	19	31	24	14	21	21
P/E – low	—	6	5	6	7	11	19	8	8	12	13
Dividends per share ($)	12.3%	0.42	0.45	0.49	0.58	0.66	0.66	0.66	0.74	0.92	1.19
Book value per share ($)	5.5%	6.51	7.04	7.86	8.62	9.10	8.35	8.24	8.68	9.33	10.55

1990 Year-end:
Debt ratio: 29.4%
Return on equity: 30.2%
Cash (mil.): $129
Current ratio: 2.30
Long-term debt (mil.): $165
No. of shares (mil.): 37
Dividends:
1990 average yield: 2.2%
1990 payout: 39.7%
Market value (mil.): $2,057

Stock Price History High/Low 1981–90

GIANT FOOD INC.

AMSE symbol: GFSA
Fiscal year ends: Last Saturday
in February

Hoover's Rating **A-**

OVERVIEW

Landover, Maryland–based Giant Food operates 152 stores in the Baltimore/Washington area. It is the #1 grocer in the Washington, DC, market (where it has a 45% share) and is strong in Baltimore (where it has a 25% share). Most of the stores are located in shopping centers, 12 of which the company owns.

Giant Food differs from other retailers by its extraordinary degree of vertical integration. Company subsidiaries perform site analysis, buy real estate, design and construct stores, and produce advertisements. The company also produces many of its own products and offers some of its services to other companies.

Giant Food's high concentration of stores in a relatively small area allows it to exploit efficiencies in the manufacture and distribution of food and in advertising. The company is financially sound and has avoided mergers and LBOs. The company relies on state-of-the-art scanning and ordering systems and highly automated warehouses to reduce costs. Although Giant Food is a public company, all voting stock and about 16% of the common stock is held by Israel Cohen and other descendants of the founding partners. Cohen has said he won't retire until age 90.

WHEN

Nehemiah Cohen, who owned 3 groceries in Lancaster, Pennsylvania, and Jac Lehrman, a wholesale grocer in Harrisburg, formed Giant Food Shopping Center in 1935. The pair opened their first store in Washington, DC, the following year. A second store, opened in 1937, was noted for its design and beauty. Giant Food was the first to operate self-service grocery stores in Washington and was an early builder of supermarkets on the East Coast.

Giant Food adopted its current name in 1957 and sold stock to the public 2 years later. The company grew slowly, adding locations through internal growth rather than acquisitions, and keeping an eye on service. Giant's policy of developing the services it needs in-house when possible led it to form Giant Construction in 1967 and its own advertising agency in 1972.

By the mid-1970s the company was 2nd in the Washington market and 4th in Baltimore. Also during the mid-1970s Giant Food diversified into other retailing ventures: discount department stores, optical stores, and apparel outlets. The last of these enterprises, The Pants Corral, was divested in 1985.

Cohen retired in 1979, at age 90, leaving his son Israel in charge. Israel, who had helped in his father's butcher shop since he was 12, has run the company since 1964 and became president in 1977. In 1979 Giant Food became the first food chain in the world to install laser scanners in all its stores, demonstrating the company's habit of quickly adapting new technologies to enhance its operations. The company opened a gourmet store, Someplace Special, in 1983, emphasizing service departments and specialty items such as llama steaks and triple cream cheese. Giant Construction built 22 stores between 1986 and 1989; during the same period the company closed 9 stores, in order to maintain modern, efficient locations.

In 1987 the company developed a consumer information program with the National Cancer Institute called Eat for Health, which provides nutritional information to consumers. SUPERdeals, a merchandising program initiated in 1990 offering large-size and multi-pack items at steep discounts, continues to be successful. Giant opened 4 new stores in 1990 and expects to open 6 more in 1991. In June 1991 the company announced that it is considering going into the deep-discount drug business. Giant's Apples for the Students program has provided 30,000 free Apple computers to 2,500 participating schools in the last 2 years in exchange for cash register tapes.

WHO

Chairman, President, and CEO: Israel Cohen, age 78, $1,286,900 pay
SVP Finance: David B. Sykes, age 72, $580,520 pay
SVP Operations: Alvin Dobbin, age 59, $370,520 pay
SVP and General Counsel: David W. Rutstein, age 46, $368,100 pay
SVP Food Operations: Pete L. Manos, age 54, $368,100 pay
SVP Labor Relations and Personnel: Roger D. Olsen, age 46
Auditors: Price Waterhouse
Employees: 25,700

WHERE

HQ: 6300 Sheriff Rd., Landover, MD 20785
Phone: 301-341-4100
Fax: 301-341-4804

Giant Food operates 152 stores, principally in Washington, DC; Maryland; and Virginia. The company maintains distribution and manufacturing facilities in Landover, Jessup, and Silver Spring, Maryland.

	1990 Grocery Store Locations	
	No. of stores	% of total
Washington, DC, metro area	105	69
Baltimore metro area	40	26
Other Maryland & Virginia	7	5
Total	**152**	**100**

WHAT

	1990 Store Formats	
	No. of stores	% of total
Supermarkets	152	98
Drugstores	2	1
Gourmet store	1	1
Total	**155**	**100**

	1990 Sources of Sales by %
Grocery & nonfood	66
Meat, seafood, dairy & deli	25
Fresh produce	9
Total	**100**

Food Processing
Baked goods
Bottled water
Dairy products
Ice cubes
Orange juice
Soft drinks

Other Operations
Automated teller machines
Construction
Import-export
In-house advertising agency
Pharmaceuticals
Shopping centers
Trucking brokerage
Wholesale produce
Wholesale tobacco

Affiliate
Shaw Community Supermarket (85%)

RANKINGS

37th in *Fortune* 50 Retailing Cos.
365th in *Business Week* 1000

KEY COMPETITORS

American Stores
Great A&P
Safeway

HOW MUCH

Fiscal year ends February of following year	9-Year Growth	1981	1982	1983	1984	1985	1986	1987	1988	1989	1990
Sales ($ mil.)	7.9%	1,684	1,852	1,957	2,139	2,247	2,529	2,721	2,987	3,249	3,350
Net income ($ mil.)	24.3%	17	37	41	45	57	46	76	98	108	119
Income as % of sales	—	1.0%	2.0%	2.1%	2.1%	2.5%	1.8%	2.8%	3.3%	3.3%	3.6%
Earnings per share ($)	24.3%	0.28	0.63	0.68	0.75	0.94	0.76	1.24	1.60	1.78	2.01
Stock price – high ($)	—	1.83	4.54	6.25	7.50	13.44	16.81	21.19	25.88	36.25	29.88
Stock price – low ($)	—	1.39	1.52	4.23	4.81	6.78	11.88	12.06	16.06	22.13	21.13
Stock price – close ($)	37.5%	1.63	4.22	5.66	7.13	13.25	12.50	17.44	24.25	28.50	28.50
P/E – high	—	6	7	9	10	14	22	17	16	20	15
P/E – low	—	5	2	6	6	7	16	10	10	12	11
Dividends per share ($)	22.0%	0.10	0.12	0.15	0.20	0.25	0.30	0.33	0.40	0.50	0.60
Book value per share ($)	17.2%	2.25	2.76	3.30	3.84	4.53	4.99	5.91	7.11	8.25	9.42

1990 Year-end:
Debt ratio: 30.6%
Return on equity: 22.7%
Cash (mil.): $168
Current ratio: 1.42
Long-term debt (mil.): $245
No. of shares (mil.): 59
Dividends:
  1990 average yield: 2.1%
  1990 payout: 29.9%
Market value (mil.): $1,681

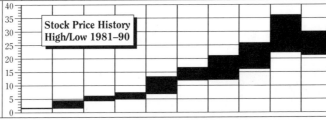
Stock Price History High/Low 1981–90

THE GILLETTE COMPANY

OVERVIEW

Boston-based Gillette is a leading producer of personal products, with profitable lines in razors and blades, writing implements, toiletries, electric shavers and small appliances (Braun), and dental products (Oral-B).

Gillette's razor and blades division (Sensor, Trac II, Atra, Good News), which accounts for 36% of net sales, leads the market in North America as well as in most other areas of the world. Since its introduction in 1990, Sensor, the company's newest razor and the most successful product launch in Gillette's history,

has already grabbed a 9% US market share, and has helped Gillette to shift its emphasis away from low-margin disposable razors.

The toiletries division holds a strong international position with such well-known names as Right Guard, Foamy, and Dry Idea. Gillette's stationery products division (Paper Mate, Waterman, Liquid Paper) is the world's leading seller of writing instruments and correction fluids, and its Oral-B division is the #1 seller of toothbrushes in the US.

NYSE symbol: GS
Fiscal year ends: December 31

 Hoover's Rating **B+**

WHO

Chairman and CEO: Alfred M. Zeien, age 61, $785,000 pay (prior to promotion)
VC: Joseph E. Mullaney, age 57
SVP Finance: Thomas F. Skelly, age 57
SVP Administration: William J. McMorrow, age 59
Auditors: KPMG Peat Marwick
Employees: 30,400

WHEN

In 1895 King C. Gillette, a salesman for the Baltimore Seal Company, originated the idea of a disposable razor blade while shaving with a dull straight razor at his home in Brookline, Massachusetts. For the next 6 years Gillette developed his idea, yet could find neither investors nor toolmakers to back him. Finally in 1901 MIT machinist William Nickerson joined with Gillette and perfected the safety razor. With the financial support of some wealthy friends, the 2 men formed the American Safety Razor Company in Boston.

Gillette put his first safety razor on the market in 1903, selling only 51 razor sets the first year. Word of the new product spread quickly, and Gillette sold 90,844 sets the following year. In 1905 Gillette established his first overseas operation in London and 3 years later adopted the Gillette diamond trademark.

Gillette sold most of his interest in the business in 1910 (although he remained president of the company until 1931) to pursue his utopian corporate theories, which he had first published in his 1894 book *The Human Drift*.

During WWI the company sold 3.5 million Service Set shaving kits to the US government. In the 1920s the company distributed free razors through such diverse mediums as banks (via the "Shave and Save" plan) and boxes of Wrigley's gum. The sales tactic brought millions of new customers, who depended on Gillette for the blades.

During the difficult years of the 1930s, Gillette began its program of sponsoring major sporting events such as bowl games and the World Series. The many sporting events that the company sponsored became known as Gillette's "Cavalcade of Sports" and carried its advertising worldwide.

In 1948 the company took its first step toward diversifying its product line by purchasing Toni (home permanent kits), which was renamed the Personal Care Division in 1971. During the 1950s Gillette adopted its present name, introduced Foamy (1953), and purchased Paper Mate (pens, 1955).

During the 1960s and 1970s the company expanded its product line further by introducing Right Guard (deodorant, 1960), Trac II (twin-blade razors, 1971), Cricket (disposable lighters, 1972), Good News (disposable razors, 1975), and Eraser Mate (erasable pens, 1979), and acquiring Braun (electric shavers and appliances, 1967) and Liquid Paper (correction fluid, 1979). In 1984 Gillette branched into dental products with the purchase of Oral-B.

The 1989–90 purchase of Swedish Match (maker of Wilkinson Sword razors) has been problematic with US, UK, and other EC governments opposing the high market shares it gave Gillette. In 1991 Gillette was ordered to divest the UK portion of Swedish Match. Gillette sold its European skin and hair care business to Nobel in 1990.

WHERE

HQ: Prudential Tower Bldg., Boston, MA 02199
Phone: 617-421-7000
Fax: 617-421-7123

Gillette sells its products in over 200 countries and manufactures at 48 locations in 25 countries.

	1990 Sales		1990 Operating Income	
	$ mil.	% of total	$ mil.	% of total
US	1,433	33	262	32
Europe	1,828	42	329	41
Latin America	508	12	152	19
Other	576	13	69	8
Adjustments	—	—	(39)	—
Total	**4,345**	**100**	**773**	**100**

WHAT

	1990 Sales		1990 Operating Income	
	$ mil.	% of total	$ mil.	% of total
Blades & razors	1,571	36	487	60
Toiletries & cosmetics	941	22	108	13
Stationery products	469	11	66	8
Appliances	1,098	25	119	15
Oral care	263	6	32	4
Other	3	—	—	—
Adjustments	—	—	(39)	—
Total	**4,345**	**100**	**773**	**100**

Major US Brand Names

Dental Products	Paper Mate (pens)
Oral-B	Waterman (pens)

Razors and Blades
Atra Plus
Braun (shavers)
Daisy Plus
Good News
Sensor
Trac II

Small Appliances
Braun

Toiletries and Cosmetics
Dry Idea (antiperspirant)
Epic Waves (home permanents)
Foamy (shave cream)
Jafra (skin care)
Lustrasilk (ethnic hair care)
Right Guard (deodorant)
Soft & Dri (deodorant)
White Rain (styling spritz)

Stationery Products
Eraser Mate (erasable pens)
Flair (pens)
Flexgrip (flexible ballpoint pen)
Liquid Paper (correction fluid)

RANKINGS

113th in *Fortune* 500 Industrial Cos.
80th in *Business Week* 1000

KEY COMPETITORS

Amway
Black & Decker
Colgate-Palmolive
Dial
Hallmark
Johnson & Johnson
S.C. Johnson

Johnson Publishing
L'Oréal
Philips
Procter & Gamble
Unilever
Warner-Lambert

HOW MUCH

	9-Year Growth	1981	1982	1983	1984	1985	1986	1987	1988	1989	1990
Sales ($ mil.)	7.1%	2,334	2,239	2,183	2,289	2,400	2,818	3,167	3,581	3,819	4,345
Net income ($ mil.)	12.8%	124	135	146	159	160	16	230	269	285	368
Income as % of sales	—	5.3%	6.0%	6.7%	7.0%	6.7%	0.6%	7.3%	7.5%	7.5%	8.5%
Earnings per share ($)	13.8%	1.00	1.08	1.15	1.24	1.23	0.13	1.97	2.44	2.68	3.20
Stock price – high ($)	—	8.91	12.25	12.88	14.63	18.00	34.44	45.88	49.00	49.75	65.25
Stock price – low ($)	—	6.75	7.66	10.22	10.66	13.28	17.19	17.63	29.13	33.00	43.50
Stock price – close ($)	25.0%	8.44	11.25	12.16	14.16	17.38	24.63	28.38	33.25	49.13	62.75
P/E – high	—	9	11	11	12	15	276	23	20	19	20
P/E – low	—	7	7	9	9	11	138	9	12	12	14
Dividends per share ($)	8.6%	0.50	0.55	0.58	0.61	0.65	0.67	0.74	0.86	0.94	1.05
Book value per share ($)	(13.0%)	5.95	5.93	6.16	6.42	7.26	4.01	5.20	(0.88)	0.72	1.70

1990 Year-end:
Debt ratio: 79.8%
Return on equity: 264.0%
Cash (mil.): $81
Current ratio: 1.60
Long-term debt (mil.): $1,046
No. of shares (mil.): 97
Dividends:
   1990 average yield: 1.7%
   1990 payout: 32.8%
Market value (mil.): $6,100

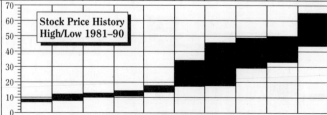

Stock Price History High/Low 1981–90

THE GOLDMAN SACHS GROUP, LP

OVERVIEW

Goldman Sachs is the largest private US financial services company, based on total assets (over $60 billion), and is the only private partnership among the major Wall Street investment bankers. Its strength is underwriting. In 1990 it was the #2 underwriter after Merrill Lynch.

Goldman Sachs provides worldwide investment and financial services to 1,600 institutional investors and wealthy individuals, rather than to the mass markets. In an investment banking industry often characterized by changes in ownership, strategy, and names,

Goldman Sachs is distinguished by its stability. Goldman Sachs has a reputation for refusing to represent parties attempting hostile takeovers.

The company has become somewhat more aggressive, increasingly trading with its own money (which has raised conflict of interest issues among its clients) and starting an indexed commodities fund that it advertises as a safe, yield-bearing investment.

Despite record 1990 earnings of approximately $600 million, Goldman is cutting costs and jobs.

WHEN

Philadelphia retailer Marcus Goldman moved to New York in 1869 and began to purchase customers' promissory notes from jewelry merchants and resell them to commercial banks. The business, renamed M. Goldman and Sachs in 1882 when Samuel Sachs, Goldman's son-in-law, joined the firm, became Goldman, Sachs & Company in 1885.

In 1887 Goldman Sachs, through Kleinwort Sons, a British merchant banking firm, offered its clients foreign exchange and currency arbitrage between the New York and London markets. To serve clients such as Sears, Roebuck, the firm expanded New York commercial paper operations to Chicago and St. Louis. In 1896 Goldman Sachs joined the NYSE.

In the late 1890s and early 1900s, Sachs established contacts in major European cities. Henry Goldman concentrated on making the firm a major source of financing for US industry. In 1906 Goldman Sachs co-managed its first public offering, $4.5 million for United Cigar Manufacturers (later General Cigar). By 1920 the firm had arranged for initial offerings of Sears, May Department Stores, Brown Shoe, Continental Can, Jewel Tea, B.F. Goodrich, and Merck.

Sidney Weinberg became a partner in 1927 at age 35 and was a leading force in the firm until he died in 1969. In the 1930s Goldman Sachs started an active securities dealer (rather than agent) operation and sales departments. Since WWII the firm has become a leader in investment banking. In the 1950s

Goldman Sachs advised the Ford family on taking the auto company public and co-managed its first public offering (1956).

In the 1970s the firm was the first to buy big blocks of stock for resale. Under John L. Weinberg (retired 1991), Goldman Sachs expanded its international operations, became a leader in mergers and acquisitions (M&A), and acquired J. Aran Co. (1981, commodities) and First Dallas, Ltd. (1982, landed merchant banking). By 1982 Goldman was the largest M&A lead manager, with $24.7 billion in mergers, including U.S. Steel–Marathon Oil, Occidental Petroleum–Cities Service, and Connecticut General–INA. As the 1980s boom faded, Goldman sought new capital, raising $275 million from an insurance company consortium and over $500 million for a non participatory 12.5% interest by Sumitomo.

After the 1980s investment frenzy died down, Goldman sought to cut costs by trimming staff (10% in 1991 alone) and seeking new opportunities. One option was a vulture fund named Water Street. The aim of this fund was to buy enough junk bonds in a company to gain a voice in corporate restructures. Companies whose bonds the fund bought included Federated Department Stores, JP Stevens, INTERCO, USG, Southland, and Carter Hawley Hale. But because of the firm's involvement in some of these bond offerings, conflict of interest accusations led to the fund's phaseout. Despite somewhat hard times, Goldman Sachs is estimated to have made over $600 million in 1990, more than 13% of revenues.

HOW MUCH

	9 Yr. Growth	1981	1982	1983	1984	1985	1986	1987	1988	1989	1990
Assets ($ mil.)	21.4%	10,564	12,224	17,167	21,065	33,989	38,794	46,898	51,300	61,298	60,365
Partners' capital ($ mil.)	27.8%	272	363	502	585	868	1,104	1,656	1,876	2,145	2,477
Capital as % of assets	—	2.6%	3.0%	2.9%	2.8%	2.6%	2.8%	3.5%	3.7%	3.5%	4.1%
Employees	9.7%	2,527	3,145	3,251	3,903	4,516	6,049	6,087	6,500	6,400	5,800

1990 Year-end:
Equity as % of assets: 4.1%
Long-term debt (mil.): $2,223
Cash (mil.): $2,182
Sales (mil.): $4,600

Partners' Capital ($ mil.) 1981–90

Private company
Fiscal year ends: Last Friday in November

WHO

Senior Partner and Co-Chairman of the Management Committee: Stephen Friedman, age 53
Senior Partner and Co-Chairman of the Management Committee: Robert E. Rubin, age 52
Partner, Personnel: Jonathan L. Cohen
Partner, Financial Division: Angelo DeCaro
Auditors: Coopers & Lybrand
Employees: 5,800

WHERE

HQ: 85 Broad St., New York, NY 10004
Phone: 212-902-1000
Fax: 212-902-3925

Goldman Sachs has 11 offices in the US and 11 overseas.

WHAT

	1990 Net Value of Placements Led	1990 Total Issues
	$ mil.	No.
Corporate underwriting	40,743	474
Municipal securities	13,860	210
Private placements	16,056	197
Debt issues	37,596	441
Total	**108,255**	**1,322**

Services

Commodity trading
Debt financing
Equity financing
Foreign exchange
Information technology
Investment banking
Investment research
Investment services
Mergers, acquisitions, and restructurings
Municipal finance
Real estate
Underwriting

Subsidiaries

Goldman Sachs International Ltd. (UK)
Goldman Sachs (Japan) Corp.
Goldman Sachs (Asia) Ltd.
Goldman Sachs (Singapore) Pte. Ltd.
Goldman, Sachs & Co. (Zurich)
Goldman, Sachs & Co. Finanz GmbH (Frankfurt)
Goldman Sachs (Australia) Ltd.

RANKINGS

19th in *Forbes* 400 US Private Cos.

KEY COMPETITORS

American Express
Bear Stearns
CS Holding
Deutsche Bank
Equitable
General Electric
KKR
Merrill Lynch
Morgan Stanley
Nomura
Paine Webber
Primerica
Prudential
Salomon
Sears
Travelers

THE GOODYEAR TIRE & RUBBER COMPANY

NYSE symbol: GT
Fiscal year ends: December 31

Hoover's Rating **D**

OVERVIEW

Goodyear, headquartered in Akron, is the largest rubber producer in the world. The last major American tire business, Goodyear leads the US tire market and is #2 in the world (after Michelin). Its distinctive blimps are among the best-known advertising symbols in the US.

Goodyear sells tires directly to auto makers and to car owners through its extensive dealer network. Most of the tires made by the company's Kelly-Springfield unit are sold under other companies' brand names. Nontire activities include production of rubber and related synthetic materials and products.

A sense of crisis has engulfed Goodyear since 1990, when recession, overcapacity, and price cutting led to hard times for tire makers worldwide. The company's problems have been worsened by heavy interest payments (over $1 million per day) on debt incurred in its 1986 hostile takeover defense and by continuing losses at All American Pipeline, the underused Texas-California oil transport unit.

In 1991 Goodyear's board tapped former Rubbermaid chairman and son of one of Rubbermaid's founders, Stan Gault, to take the reins of the troubled company. Gault has pledged to continue cost cutting through layoffs, plant closures, and capital spending reductions, and plans to lower debt by selling nontire businesses.

WHO

Chairman and CEO: Stanley C. Gault, age 65
President and COO: Hoyt M. Wells, age 64, $323,990 pay (prior to promotion)
EVP and CFO: Oren G. Shaffer, age 48, $366,490 pay (prior to promotion)
EVP Human Resources and Total Quality Culture: Frank R. Tully
Auditors: Price Waterhouse
Employees: 107,671

WHERE

HQ: 1144 E. Market St., Akron, OH 44316
Phone: 216-796-2121
Fax: 216-796-2222

Goodyear operates 43 US plants in 21 states and 43 plants in 25 foreign countries. In addition, the company operates 1,363 retail outlets in the US and 442 overseas.

	1990 Sales		1990 Operating Income	
	$ mil.	% of total	$ mil.	% of total
US	6,460	58	327	53
Europe	2,301	20	36	6
Latin America	1,352	12	195	32
Canada	567	5	(21)	(3)
Asia & Africa	593	5	75	12
Adjustments	—	—	(144)	—
Total	**11,273**	**100**	**468**	**100**

WHEN

In 1898 in Akron, Frank and Charles Seiberling founded a tire and rubber company, naming it after Charles Goodyear (inventor of the vulcanization process, 1839). Initially producing bicycle and carriage tires, Goodyear soon targeted the fledgling automotive industry. The introduction of the Quick Detachable tire and the Universal Rim (1903) made Goodyear the world's largest tire manufacturer by 1916, the year it introduced the pneumatic truck tire.

The company is known for its marketing tactics. Frank Seiberling created the winged-foot emblem in 1900. In 1924 Goodyear acquired rights to manufacture zeppelins, and by the 1930s Goodyear blimps served as advertisements nationwide.

Goodyear began foreign manufacturing in Canada in 1910 and greatly expanded during the 1920s and 1930s (Australia, Argentina, Indonesia). The company established a sales office in England (1912) and began its own rubber plantations in Sumatra (1916). By 1926 Goodyear led the world in rubber production.

Financial troubles led to reorganization in 1921, and investment bankers Dillon, Read & Company forced out the Seiberlings. Succeeding a caretaker management team, Paul Litchfield began 3 decades as CEO (1926).

Goodyear opened company stores during the 1930s, acquired Kelly-Springfield in 1935, and began producing synthetic rubber tires in 1937. Following WWII the tire market boomed, and Goodyear led in implementing technological developments such as polyester tire cord (1962) and the bias-belted tire (1967). In 1971 Goodyear provided the tires used on the Apollo 14 lunar landing mission.

Michelin introduced the radial tire in the US in 1966. By 1976 radials accounted for 45% of tire sales and, with the introduction of the all-weather Tiempo and the Arriva (1980), Goodyear led the US market. Goodyear also introduced the popular Eagle tire in 1980.

Fending off Sir James Goldsmith's takeover attempt in 1986, CEO Robert Mercer raised $1.7 billion by selling nontire businesses (Motor Wheel, Goodyear Aerospace, and Celeron Oil) and by borrowing heavily, accumulating $4.7 billion of debt in a 47% stock buyback. Goodyear sold its South African operations in 1989 for $41 million. After posting a loss in 1990, Goodyear replaced its top 2 executives in 1991 and slashed its dividend. The dividend cut was Goodyear's first since the Great Depression.

WHAT

	1990 Sales		1990 Operating Income	
	$ mil.	% of total	$ mil.	% of total
Tires & related	9,216	82	463	77
General products	2,027	18	194	32
Oil transportation	30	—	(53)	(9)
Adjustments			(136)	
Total	**11,273**	**100**	**468**	**100**

Products
Chemical products
Film products
Industrial rubber products
Polyester products
Roofing products
Shoe products
Tires
Vehicle components

US Tire Brands
All-American
Arriva
Concorde
Corsa
Eagle
Invicta
Tiempo

Ultra Grip
Wrangler

Major Subsidiaries
Brad Ragan, Inc. (74.5%, tire sales and service chain)
Celeron Corp. (oil pipelines)
All American Pipeline Co.
Celeron Gathering Corp.
Celeron Trading & Transportation Co.
Goodyear Rubber Plantations Company
The Kelly-Springfield Tire Co.
Lee Tire & Rubber Co.
Reneer Films Corp. (vinyl laminates and films)
Wingfoot Corp. (stretch and shrink films for packaging and other uses)

HOW MUCH

	9-Year Growth	1981	1982	1983	1984	1985	1986	1987	1988	1989	1990
Sales ($ mil.)	2.3%	9,153	8,689	9,736	10,241	9,585	9,103	9,905	10,810	10,869	11,273
Net income ($ mil.)	—	244	248	270	411	301	101	514	350	189	(38)
Income as % of sales	—	2.7%	2.9%	2.8%	4.0%	3.1%	1.1%	5.2%	3.2%	1.7%	(0.3%)
Earnings per share ($)	—	3.36	3.35	2.71	3.87	2.81	0.94	8.49	6.05	3.28	(0.66)
Stock price – high ($)	—	20.25	36.88	36.38	31.50	31.25	50.00	76.50	67.88	59.75	46.38
Stock price – low ($)	—	15.88	17.88	27.00	23.00	25.13	29.00	35.00	47.00	42.13	12.88
Stock price – close ($)	(0.1%)	19.00	35.00	30.38	26.00	31.25	41.88	60.00	51.13	43.50	18.88
P/E – high	—	6	11	13	8	11	53	9	11	18	—
P/E – low	—	5	5	10	6	9	31	4	8	13	—
Dividends per share ($)	3.7%	1.30	1.40	1.40	1.50	1.60	1.60	1.60	1.70	1.80	1.80
Book value per share ($)	0.9%	32.96	33.14	28.61	29.78	32.44	30.93	32.19	35.30	37.09	35.88

1990 Year-end:
Debt ratio: 61.0%
Return on equity: —
Cash (mil.): $277
Current ratio: 1.45
Long-term debt (mil.): $3,286
No. of shares (mil.): 58
Dividends:
1990 average yield: 9.5%
1990 payout: —
Market value (mil.): $1,104

Stock Price History High/Low 1981–90

RANKINGS

40th in *Fortune* 500 Industrial Cos.
422nd in *Business Week* 1000

KEY COMPETITORS

Bayer
Boise Cascade
Bridgestone
Corning
Georgia-Pacific
Hercules
Manville
Michelin
Owens-Corning
Pirelli
Sears
Sumitomo

W. R. GRACE & COMPANY

OVERVIEW

With businesses ranging from artificial insemination to cocoa to drilling rigs, W. R. Grace is amazingly diverse. After relocating its headquarters from New York to Florida, though, Grace is holding a moving sale, restructuring under new president J. P. Bolduc.

The Specialty Chemicals Division accounts for 53% of company sales. The company's specialty businesses include Grace Cocoa, a world leader in supplying cocoa and chocolate to the baking, candy, and dairy industries; and Baker & Taylor Books, the nation's leading supplier of books and audiocassettes to retailers and libraries.

Grace's Health Care Group includes National Medical Care, US leader in kidney dialysis services, and biotechnology research in diabetes and blood cholesterol.

Grace owns 83.4% of publicly traded Grace Energy, the largest US land-based contractor of drilling rigs, with 190 at year-end 1990. Grace Energy conducts oil and gas exploration, mines coal, and sells specialized services to the petroleum industry. The company has announced it will sell its energy services business as the company restructures. "We're in too many businesses," President Bolduc said to the *Wall Street Journal* in early 1991.

WHEN

W. R. Grace & Company grew from the Peruvian business activities of Irishman William R. Grace. Grace, who had left Ireland because of the potato famine, was in Peru in 1854 chartering ships to trade guano (bird dung), a natural fertilizer. In 1866 he moved his headquarters to New York and established 3-way shipping routes from New York to South America to Europe, trading fertilizer, agricultural products, and US manufactured goods.

W. R. Grace, who served as mayor of New York City in the 1880s, died in 1904. His brother Michael took over until 1907, when W. R.'s son Joseph became president. Under Joseph's direction the shipping business grew, powered first by sail, then by steam, and became known as the Grace Line. Joseph expanded the company's investments in South America, eventually owning cotton mills, sugar plantations, and sugar refineries in Peru and nitrate production facilities in Chile. In 1916 he established the W. R. Grace & Company's Bank (later the Grace National Bank). The company entered aviation in 1928 in a joint venture with Pan American Airlines, forming Pan American–Grace Airways, called Panagra, which served Latin America.

In 1945 J. Peter Grace, Joseph's son, took the helm at the age of 32. To capitalize his planned diversification of W. R. Grace, Peter

took the company public in 1953. In 1954 Grace expanded into chemicals with the purchases of Davison Chemical (industrial and agricultural chemicals, silica gels) and Dewey & Almy Chemical (can sealants, batteries). Peter also sold Grace National Bank (1965), Panagra (to Braniff, 1967), and the Grace Line (1969), 3 of the company's oldest businesses.

Purchases during the 1960s and 1970s further illustrated the changing nature of the company: American Breeders Service (1967); consumer goods retailers such as Herman's (sporting goods, 56% interest, 1970) and Sheplers (western wear, 1976); El Torito–La Fiesta Restaurants (1976); and 2 home improvement stores, Handy City (1976) and Channel (1977). The company bought Baker & Taylor book wholesalers (1970). Peru nationalized Grace's paper and chemical outfits (1974).

In 1986 Grace sold virtually all of its full-service restaurants, Sheplers, and its 56% interest in Herman's Sporting Goods. In 1988 Grace sold its agricultural and fertilizer businesses. In 1990 the company added 3 European water treatment businesses to its holdings.

Grace chalked up 1991 as a restructuring year as executives worked to develop a strategic plan. President Bolduc wants to focus Grace on its best-performing businesses — specialty chemicals, cocoa, and health care.

NYSE symbol: GRA
Fiscal year ends: December 31

 Hoover's Rating **C-**

WHO

Chairman and CEO: J. Peter Grace, age 77, $1,585,000 pay
President and COO: J. P. Bolduc, age 51, $957,917 pay
EVP and CFO: Brian J. Smith, age 46
VP Human Resources: William L. Monroe
Auditors: Price Waterhouse
Employees: 52,000

WHERE

HQ: One Town Center, Boca Raton, FL 33486
Phone: 407-362-2000
Fax: 407-362-2193

Grace sells its products in over 45 countries.

	1990 Sales		1990 Operating Income	
	$ mil.	% of total	$ mil.	% of total
US & Canada	4,406	65	371	56
Europe	1,919	29	184	28
Other countries	429	6	109	16
Adjustments	—	—	(190)	—
Total	**6,754**	**100**	**474**	**100**

WHAT

	1990 Sales		1990 Operating Income	
	$ mil.	% of total	$ mil.	% of total
Energy	480	7	41	6
Specialty chemicals	3,570	53	431	65
Specialty businesses	1,829	27	80	12
Health care	875	13	112	17
Adjustments	—	—	(190)	—
Total	**6,754**	**100**	**474**	**100**

Energy
Coal mining
Oil and gas exploration and production
Petroleum drilling services and equipment

Specialty Chemicals
90 product lines for construction, energy, water treatment, transportation, packaging, electronics, and graphic arts industries

Specialty Businesses
Agriculture (bull semen, livestock feed)
Book, videocassette, and software distribution
Cocoa and chocolate production
Textiles (mattress ticking, upholstery, fabrics)

Health Care
Home infusion therapy and kidney dialysis

Other
Canonie Environmental Services Corp. (45.5%, hazardous waste remediation)
Grace Ventures Corp. (venture capital)

RANKINGS

71st in *Fortune* 500 Industrial Cos.
252nd in *Business Week* 1000

KEY COMPETITORS

American Cyanamid	Dow	Milliken
ARA	Chemical	Monsanto
BASF	Du Pont	Morton
Bayer	Farley	National Medical
Bechtel	Fieldcrest	Rhône-Poulenc
Burlington	Cannon	Springs Industries
Holdings	Hercules	TRW
Cargill	Hoechst	Union Carbide
ConAgra	Humana	Union Pacific
Consolidated Rail	Imperial	Waste
Continental Grain	Chemical	Management

HOW MUCH

	9-Year Growth	1981	1982	1983	1984	1985	1986	1987	1988	1989	1990
Sales ($ mil.)	0.4%	6,521	6,128	6,220	6,728	5,193	3,726	4,515	5,786	6,115	6,754
Net income ($ mil.)	(6.2%)	361	320	160	196	128	(375)	142	192	257	203
Income as % of sales	—	5.5%	5.2%	2.6%	2.9%	2.5%	(10.1%)	3.1%	3.3%	4.2%	3.0%
Earnings per share ($)	(4.9%)	3.72	3.27	1.63	2.01	1.23	(4.47)	1.67	2.19	2.86	2.36
Stock price – high ($)	—	29.81	23.13	25.19	23.44	24.75	30.38	37.31	29.88	39.13	33.63
Stock price – low ($)	—	19.25	14.25	19.13	18.25	17.75	22.63	19.13	23.50	25.13	17.00
Stock price – close ($)	0.5%	22.88	19.19	22.63	19.88	23.94	24.19	24.00	26.00	32.75	23.88
P/E – high	—	8	7	15	12	20	—	22	14	14	14
P/E – low	—	5	4	12	9	14	—	11	11	9	7
Dividends per share ($)	1.5%	1.23	1.35	1.40	1.40	1.40	1.40	1.40	1.40	1.40	1.40
Book value per share ($)	0.3%	21.51	22.71	22.40	22.53	21.70	15.41	17.31	18.18	20.16	22.14

1990 Year-end:
Debt ratio: 50.7%
Return on equity: 11.2%
Cash (mil.): $116
Current ratio: 1.42
Long-term debt (mil.): $1,964
No. of shares (mil.): 86
Dividends:
  1990 average yield: 5.9%
  1990 payout: 59.3%
Market value (mil.): $2,055

Stock Price History
High/Low 1981–90

THE GREAT ATLANTIC & PACIFIC TEA COMPANY

OVERVIEW

Montvale, New Jersey–based A&P, after struggling through the 1960s and 1970s, is on the rebound. The company is the 4th largest food retailer in the US.

While most of its competitors have spent recent years fighting off takeover attempts and absorbing huge amounts of debt, A&P has slowly renovated its stores and bought strong regional chains. Since 1982 A&P has acquired 530 supermarkets and superstores and remodeled or expanded hundreds more, spending over $2 billion.

This strategy has helped A&P increase its market presence. The company is now ranked first or 2nd in nearly all of its markets. It has kept the #1 position in New York City, where it operates A&P, Waldbaum's, and Food Emporium stores. Its A&P and Dominion stores in Ontario also make it the market leader there. The company's new central purchasing operation, which purchases national-brand groceries for the whole company at headquarters, will lower total costs of goods significantly and provide the flexibility to emphasize market share growth and still maintain strong margins and profitability.

A&P is 53% owned by Tenglemann, a German retailer, and itself owns 19.9% of Isosceles, which operates Gateway, the 3rd largest grocer in the UK. Profits have increased from a $232 million loss in 1981 to $151 million net income in 1990.

WHEN

George Gilman and George H. Hartford, both of Augusta, Maine, set up shop in 1859 on New York City's docks to sell tea at a 50% discount by eliminating middlemen. The company, The Great American Tea Company, advertised by drawing a red wagon through the city's streets. By 1869 the company, renamed The Great Atlantic & Pacific Tea Company, had 11 stores offering discounted items.

Gilman retired in 1878; Hartford brought in his sons George and John. In 1912, when the company had 400 stores, John opened a store on a low-price, cash-and-carry format, without customer credit or premiums. The format proved popular. When the company passed to the sons in 1916, A&P had over 1,000 cash-and-carry stores with identical layouts and a strategy of having "a store on every corner."

During the 1920s and 1930s, when the company grew to over 15,000 stores throughout the US, there was a move by small retailers to restrict chain stores in general and A&P in particular. John Hartford initiated innovative marketing and customer service policies to improve the company's image. A&P grew in the 1940s by converting its stores to supermarkets. However, an antitrust suit in 1949 and the company's reluctance to carry more nonfood items pushed the company into decline. To maintain operations, management shut stores in California and Washington to shore up the Northeastern stores.

In 1975, after a prolonged period of poor sales and failed discount format attempts, the board chose a new CEO: Jonathan Scott, former president of Albertson's (now CEO of American Stores). Scott cut costs by closing stores and reducing the work force. Scott's efforts to resuscitate the "Grandma" of grocery stores proved ineffective. The company's 1978 sales increases failed to keep ahead of inflation, and it posted a $52 million loss.

The Hartford Foundation sold its A&P holdings to the Tengelmann Group (1979), a German retailer, who appointed English-born James Wood as CEO (1980). A&P has since sold or remodeled most of its old stores and has acquired Super Fresh (1982), Kohl's (1983), Pantry Pride (1984), and Borman's (1989).

In 1990 the company acquired the 70 stores of Miracle Food Mart, further increasing A&P Canada's leading market share in Ontario.

NYSE symbol: GAP
Fiscal year ends: Last Saturday in February

Hoover's Rating **B−**

WHO

Chairman, President, and CEO: James Wood, age 61, $3,617,771 pay
VC: James W. Rowe, age 67, $559,616 pay
EVP, CFO, and Treasurer: Fred Corrado, age 50, $447,693 pay (prior to promotion)
EVP: Michael J. Larkin, $363,755 pay
EVP: Aaron Malinsky, $450,780 pay
VP Human Resources: H. Nelson Lewis
Auditors: Deloitte & Touche
Employees: 99,300

WHERE

HQ: 2 Paragon Dr., Montvale, NJ 07645
Phone: 201-573-9700
Fax: 201-930-8106 (Investor Relations)

A&P operates 1,275 locations in 23 states, the District of Columbia, and the Canadian province of Ontario. The company also owns 3 bakeries, 2 coffee plants, 2 delicatessen food kitchens, and an ice cream plant.

	1990 Sales		1990 Pretax Income	
	$ mil.	% of total	$ mil.	% of total
US	9,196	81	201	77
Canada	2,195	19	61	23
Total	**11,391**	**100**	**262**	**100**

1990 Store Locations		
	No. of stores	% of total
Mid-Atlantic	469	37
Ontario	265	21
South	235	18
Midwest	190	15
New England	116	9
Total	**1,275**	**100**

WHAT

Store and Trade Names
A&P
Compass Foods
Dominion
Family Mart
Farmer Jack
Food Bazaar
Food Emporium
Food Mart
Futurestore
Kohl's
Miracle Food Mart
Sav-A-Center
Sun
Super Fresh
Waldbaum's

RANKINGS

9th in *Fortune* 50 Retailing Cos.
316th in *Business Week* 1000

KEY COMPETITORS

Albertson's	Kroger
American Stores	Safeway
Bruno's	Stop & Shop
Food Lion	Supermarkets General
Giant Food	Winn-Dixie

HOW MUCH

Fiscal year ends February of following year	9-Year Growth	1981	1982	1983	1984	1985	1986	1987	1988	1989	1990
Sales ($ mil.)	6.9%	6,227	4,608	5,222	5,878	6,615	7,835	9,532	10,068	11,148	11,391
Net income ($ mil.)	—	(232)	21	31	51	56	69	103	128	147	151
Income as % of sales	—	(3.7%)	0.5%	0.6%	0.9%	0.8%	0.9%	1.1%	1.3%	1.3%	1.3%
Earnings per share ($)	—	(6.19)	0.57	0.84	1.35	1.48	1.82	2.71	3.34	3.84	3.95
Stock price – high ($)	—	6.63	9.38	14.25	18.00	22.00	27.75	46.88	48.13	65.38	61.75
Stock price – low ($)	—	3.50	3.75	8.00	11.63	14.38	19.25	23.63	31.88	44.25	37.75
Stock price – close ($)	31.0%	3.88	8.25	12.25	16.00	21.88	23.50	37.50	44.63	58.88	44.13
P/E – high	—	—	16	17	13	15	15	17	14	17	16
P/E – low	—	—	7	10	9	10	11	9	10	12	10
Dividends per share ($)	—	0.00	0.00	0.00	0.00	0.10	0.40	0.48	0.58	0.68	0.78
Book value per share ($)	16.5%	8.08	8.81	10.02	15.48	17.63	19.85	22.32	25.42	28.59	31.96

1990 Year-end:
Debt ratio: 38.2%
Return on equity: 13.0%
Cash (mil.): $29
Current ratio: 1.11
Long-term debt (mil.): $753
No. of shares (mil.): 38
Dividends:
 1990 average yield: 1.8%
 1990 payout: 19.6%
Market value (mil.): $1,686

Stock Price History High/Low 1981–90

GREAT WESTERN FINANCIAL CORPORATION

NYSE symbol: GWF
Fiscal year ends: December 31

OVERVIEW

Great Western is the holding company of the 2nd largest (after H. F. Ahmanson) US thrift institution, Great Western Bank, with nearly $40 billion in assets. In 1990 Beverly Hills–based Great Western Corporation had about $10.7 billion in new mortgage loans for the year, compared to Citicorp and H. F. Ahmanson, each of which had about $13 billion.

About 93% of the company's $29.2 billion real estate loan portfolio is home mortgages. The company became the first savings institution to offer its own group of mutual funds (Sierra) in 1989.

Great Western Bank, a federal savings bank, has more than 346 retail banking branches located statewide in California and in Arizona, Florida, and Washington. With its 1990 purchases in Florida, the company became the 6th largest financial institution in the state, with 118 branches and about $6 billion in deposits. The company's ability to expand into Florida was due in part to its strict adherence to capital standards.

WHEN

Great Western began operations in California as a state-licensed savings and loan in 1919.

In 1955 Great Western became part of Great Western Financial Corporation, the holding company it formed. Within 5 years of its creation, Great Western Financial acquired Santa Ana Savings (1956), West Coast Savings (Sacramento, 1957), Guaranty Savings (San Jose, 1958), Central Savings (San Luis Obispo, 1959), and First Savings (Oakland, 1959). The company later bought Santa Rosa Savings (1968) and Safety Savings (Los Angeles, 1969).

In 1970 and 1971 Great Western continued expanding in California by purchasing Belmont Savings, Citizen Savings (Santa Barbara), Victory Savings (North Hollywood), and Sentinel Savings (San Diego). In 1972 Great Western Financial combined its acquired subsidiary savings associations into Great Western Savings.

In 1974 the company was the first to offer variable-rate mortgages (interest rate changes according to lender's cost of funds), which by 1979 were 60% of the company's mortgage loans and accounted for about $20 million in annual revenues.

The company entered the 1980s with $9 billion in assets and began offering only adjustable-rate mortgages (ARMs) — tied to an index rate outside the lender's control — as soon as they were authorized by federal regulators in 1981. Under James F. Montgomery, CEO since 1979, the company has grown and diversified while building a strong capital position. Great Western expanded its consumer finance business in 1983 by buying Aristar and its Blazer Financial Services subsidiary. That year Great Western began mortgage lending in Florida by opening a real estate loan office in Boca Raton.

In 1984 the company became the first US savings institution to issue floating-rate notes in Europe. By 1987, 75% of the company's fixed-rate and variable-rate mortgage loans were converted to ARMs. The company expanded its operations to Washington and Arizona and purchased City Finance (consumer finance, 1987).

By 1989 Great Western was focusing on single-family mortgages and consumer loans. At year's end the company added about $200 million to its loan reserves for commercial and multifamily real estate loans, resulting in net earnings of $100 million in 1989, compared to $248 million in 1988.

In 1990 Great Western purchased 71 CenTrust Savings Bank branches, 18 Gibraltar Savings Bank branches, 13 Carteret Savings branches, and 27 City Savings branches in Florida from the Resolution Trust Corporation.

WHO

Chairman and CEO: James F. Montgomery, age 56, $1,350,933 pay
President and COO: John F. Maher, age 47, $924,849 pay
EVP and CFO: Carl F. Geuther, age 45
President, Consumer Finance: Michael M. Pappas, age 58, $462,986 pay
VP Human Resources: Toby Lombardi
Auditors: Price Waterhouse
Employees: 14,000

WHERE

HQ: 8484 Wilshire Blvd., Beverly Hills, CA 90211
Phone: 213-852-3411
Fax: 213-852-3799 (Corporate Communications)

Great Western has 346 retail banking offices in 4 states; 197 real estate lending offices in 21 states; and 470 consumer finance offices in 23 states.

WHAT

	1990 Assets	
	$ mil.	% of total
Cash & securities	1,820	5
Mortgage-backed securities	3,945	10
Loans	31,107	79
Loan loss provision	(285)	(1)
Real estate	961	2
Interest receivable	373	1
Other	1,485	4
Total	**39,406**	**100**

Financial Services
Adjustable rate mortgages
Installment loans
Real estate lending and investing
Retail banking
Securities brokerage

Subsidiaries and Affiliates
Blazer Financial Services
California Reconveyance Company
City Finance Company
Great Western Bank, a Federal Savings Bank
Great Western Bank, a Savings Bank
Great Western Financial Insurance Company
Great Western Financial Services
Great Western Investment Management Corporation
Great Western Mortgage Corporation

RANKINGS

300th in *Business Week* 1000

KEY COMPETITORS

H. F. Ahmanson	Household International
BankAmerica	ITT
Barnett Banks	NCNB
Citicorp	Primerica
First Interstate	SunTrust
Ford	Wells Fargo
General Electric	Other major banks

HOW MUCH

	9-Year Growth	1981	1982	1983	1984	1985	1986	1987	1988	1989	1990
Assets ($ mil.)	15.7%	10,646	12,675	18,639	23,555	25,471	27,630	28,631	32,815	37,176	39,406
Net income ($ mil.)	—	(28)	(75)	74	94	202	301	210	248	100	193
Income as % of assets	—	(0.3%)	(0.6%)	0.4%	0.4%	0.8%	1.1%	0.7%	0.8%	0.3%	0.5%
Earnings per share ($)	—	(0.50)	(1.07)	0.82	1.00	1.78	2.51	1.64	1.95	0.78	1.50
Stock price – high ($)	—	7.65	11.95	12.60	10.55	13.90	19.30	24.38	17.38	25.13	21.13
Stock price – low ($)	—	4.80	3.80	7.45	6.60	9.00	13.25	12.00	12.63	14.63	8.50
Stock price – close ($)	8.7%	5.80	10.95	8.80	10.15	13.85	18.60	15.25	15.00	17.50	12.25
P/E – high	—	—	—	15	11	8	8	15	9	32	14
P/E – low	—	—	—	9	7	5	5	7	6	19	6
Dividends per share ($)	10.0%	0.35	0.21	0.21	0.35	0.38	0.46	0.66	0.75	0.79	0.83
Book value per share ($)	4.3%	11.05	9.26	9.68	10.31	11.93	14.19	14.87	15.48	15.48	16.15

1990 Year-end:
Return on equity: 9.5%
Equity as % of assets: 5.3%
Cash (mil.): $1,820
Long-term debt (mil.): $3,995
No. of shares (mil.): 129
Dividends:
 1990 average yield: 6.8%
 1990 payout: 55.3%
Market value (mil.): $1,575
Sales (mil.): $4,207

Stock Price History High/Low 1981–90

THE GREEN BAY PACKERS, INC.

OVERVIEW

Eat your heart out, George Steinbrenner.

While some pro team owner-moguls grab the headlines, owners of the Green Bay Packers still remember the fans, mostly because they *are* the fans — 1,856 of them, at least.

That's how many shareholders own the 4,627 shares of The Green Bay Packers, Inc., a private, nonprofit corporation. Of course, a National Football League team can turn a buck or 2, between tickets and TV, but the Packers corporation pays no dividends. If the team is ever liquidated, proceeds will go to build a war memorial in Green Bay.

The Green Bay Packers, Inc., is governed by 45 directors and a 7-person executive committee. The Packers have had 11 coaches — 1989 NFL Coach of the Year Lindy Infante is the latest — but they didn't get a full-time CEO until 1982. President Robert Harlan took the helm in 1989.

WHEN

In 1919 Curly Lambeau and George Calhoun met in the newsroom of the *Green Bay Press-Gazette* to organize a football team. The pair later talked Lambeau's employer — Indian Packing — into buying equipment for the team; to honor the sponsor, the team became known as the Packers.

Fans passed the hat at games. Heartened by early gridiron successes, Lambeau and 2 businessmen in 1921 obtained a franchise from the National Football League. Packer receipts didn't cover expenses, and the franchise had to be forfeited at the end of the season.

Lambeau and other backers bought the franchise again in 1922, but the Packers ran afoul of bad weather. A game was rained out, and the team's insurance company wouldn't pay off on its rain-out policy because the rainfall was 1/100-inch less than the policy required. Later that year, a storm threatened to cancel another game and ruin the team's fiscal health. A. B. Turnbull, an executive of the *Press-Gazette*, convinced merchants in Green Bay to underwrite the team, and the Packers became a corporation.

In 1934 a fan fell from the stands and successfully sued the Packers for $5,000. The club's insurance company went out of business, and the Packers were forced into receivership. Green Bay merchants raised $15,000 to revive the corporation.

With Lambeau as coach, Green Bay developed a reputation for hard-nosed football. Spurred by end Don Hutson, the Packers racked up championships in 1936, 1939, and 1944.

Even though pro football grew in popularity after WWII, Green Bay continued to suffer financially. A 1949 intrasquad game raised $50,000 to keep the team afloat, and a 1950 stock drive in the community raised another $118,000.

Lambeau resigned from the Packers in 1950. Packer football fortunes dipped in the 1950s, until Coach Vince Lombardi arrived in 1959. The team immediately returned to winning, and Lombardi teams dominated the game, winning back-to-back Super Bowls (1967, 1968). Green Bay still boasts the most league championships (11).

Lombardi left coaching for the Packer front office in 1968, and the team struggled to regain its luster during dismal seasons in the 1970s and 1980s.

In 1982 Robert Parins became the team's first full-time CEO. Parins spurred the corporation to a record $3 million profit (1986). Parins assumed the chairmanship in 1989, and Robert Harlan, a former sports publicist, became president and CEO. Harlan supervised additions of club seats and private boxes to Lambeau field.

In a front office version of cross training, Bud Selig of the Milwaukee Brewers baseball team was named to the Packer board of directors in 1990. Another executive addition was Michael Reinfeldt, a former Houston Oiler and Los Angeles Raider, as CFO.

Private company
Fiscal year ends: March 30

Hoover's Rating **C**

WHO

Honorary Chairman: Judge Robert J. Parins, age 73
President and CEO: Robert E. Harlan, age 54
CFO: Michael R. Reinfeldt, age 38
Controller: Richard Blasczyk, age 57
EVP Football Operations: Tom Braatz, age 58
Head Coach: Lindy Infante, age 51
Auditors: Wipfli, Ullrich, & Bertelson
Employees: 112

WHERE

HQ: 1265 Lombardi Ave., Green Bay, WI 54304
Phone: 414-496-5700
Fax: 414-496-5712

The Green Bay Packers, Inc., fields a football team. In the 1991–92 season the Packers are scheduled to play 5 games in Green Bay, 3 in Milwaukee, and 1 each in (in order of occurrence) Detroit, Miami, Los Angeles, Tampa Bay, New York, Atlanta, Chicago, and Minneapolis.

	1990 Sales	
	$ mil.	% of total
Home games	5.7	14
Out-of-town games	4.0	9
Other	32.6	77
Total	**42.3**	**100**

WHAT

	1990 Sales	
	$ mil.	% of total
Regular season		
Net receipts from home games	5.7	14
Out-of-town games	4.0	9
TV, radio & programs	26.5	63
Preseason	2.3	5
Miscellaneous		
Private box income	1.1	3
NFL properties	.9	2
Other	1.8	4
Total	**42.3**	**100**

Touchdowns (1990)
Passing (20)
Returns (4)
Rushing (5)

Defense (1990)
Interceptions (16)
Quarterback sacks (27)
Yards allowed
　Rushing (2,059)
　Passing (3,383)

RANKINGS

1990
2nd in NFC Central Division (4-way tie)
23rd in NFL in points scored
18th in NFL in points allowed
27th in NFL in sacks for
28th in NFL in sacks against

KEY COMPETITORS

Edward J. DeBartolo

HOW MUCH

Fiscal year ends March of following year	9 Yr. Growth	1981	1982[1]	1983	1984	1985	1986	1987[1]	1988	1989	1990
Sales ($ mil.)	11.5%	11.7	12.3	20.2	22.8	24.4	27.4	23.7	28.0	30.1	42.3
Net income ($ mil.)	—	.9	(1.7)	1.9	1.5	2.0	3.1	2.8	1.3	0.4	1.9
Attendance (thou.)	—	919	460	847	874	821	865	697	811	876	906
Games won	—	8	5	8	8	8	4	5	4	10	6
Games lost	—	8	3	8	8	8	12	9	12	6	10
Games tied	—	0	1	0	0	0	0	1	0	0	—
Points for	—	324	226	429	390	337	254	255	240	362	271
Points against	—	361	169	439	309	355	418	300	315	356	347
Division finish	—	2	1	2	2	2	4	3	5	2	2
Winning percentage	—	50.0%	55.6%	50.0%	50.0%	50.0%	25.0%	33.3%	25.0%	62.5%	37.5%

Winning Percentage 1981–90

[Bar chart showing winning percentage from 1981 to 1990, with y-axis from 0% to 70%]

Note: All figures for regular season   [1]Strike-shortened season

GRUMMAN CORPORATION

OVERVIEW

Founded on the heels of the stock market crash of 1929, Grumman Corporation grew when other aircraft builders were shrinking. Now Grumman is shrinking, and some analysts wonder if the company will survive.

Sales to the US government (including foreign military contracts) make up a big part of Grumman's business (81% in 1990), and the company's future hinges, in part, on its ability to win new DOD contracts in a time of defense cutbacks. The success of Grumman's Joint STARS (Joint Surveillance Target Attack Radar System) air-to-ground radar system and the 20-year-old F-14 Tomcat fighter in the

Persian Gulf War resulted in new DOD orders at a time when the Long Island–based company really needed them. Grumman also has a contract to upgrade the F-14, but production of new F-14s (which account for 20% of sales) will end in 1992.

In response to its crisis Grumman has announced staff cuts (1,900 workers in 1991) to match reductions in workload and has reorganized into 4 business units — aerospace, electronics systems, information and other services, and special-purpose vehicles. As part of this reorganization, the company sold its historic boat division in 1990.

WHEN

In 1929, when Loening Aircraft Engineering Company was sold, employees Roy Grumman, Jake Swirbul, and Bill Schwendler decided to start their own aircraft company (Grumman Aircraft Engineering Corporation). Within 3 months they had a contract to design a navy fighter, which resulted in the FF-1, a plane so durable that it earned the Grumman plant the nickname "The Iron Works."

In 1937, a year before going public, Grumman completed its first commercial aircraft (the Grumman Goose) and moved into its Bethpage, New York, headquarters. That year the first of the Wildcat fighters took flight; the Hellcat followed in 1942. Both planes were used by the US during WWII, fueling Grumman's explosive wartime growth.

Roy Grumman, foreseeing hard times if his company continued to rely only on military contracts, had moved into the production of aluminum truck bodies in 1930 and of aluminum canoes (later boats, yachts, and hydrofoils) in 1944. The company's first corporate jet (Gulfstream) took to the air in 1958. Grumman started work on the Lunar Module for the Apollo space program in 1963 and adopted its present name in 1969.

That year Grumman signed a contract with the navy to build the F-14 Tomcat fighter. Payment was calculated in advance and did

not take into account higher inflation rates or the cost of working out design flaws (which inevitably occurred). By 1972 Grumman was nearly bankrupt. It ended up writing off about $1 million for each of the 134 F-14s delivered.

John Bierwirth became CEO in 1974. His legal and financial background allowed him to negotiate a new F-14 contract financed by the navy. When Congress unexpectedly called in the navy loans, Grumman turned to the Shah of Iran, who loaned the company $75 million. Bierwirth also tried to develop new commercial businesses for Grumman, chiefly through acquisitions. Many failed, including Grumman's foray into refrigerated storage containers (Dormavac, dissolved in 1982) and bus manufacturing (Flxible, assets sold in 1983). Grumman also sold the division that produced the Gulfstream (Grumman American Aviation) in 1978.

Grumman rebuilt its military business in the 1980s, achieving its greatest success in electronic systems. In 1985 the company won a contract to develop Joint STARS, which was used extensively by the Allied forces in the 1991 Persian Gulf War. That year, as the F-14 program was extended with 12 upgrade orders, the company proposed a new navy bomber, the A-X. If accepted, the plane will go into production at the end of the decade.

NYSE symbol: GQ
Fiscal year ends: December 31

WHO

Chairman and CEO: Renso L. Caporali, age 57, $435,000 pay
VC and CFO: Robert Anderson, age 54
President and COO: Robert J. Myers, age 56, $260,000 pay (prior to promotion)
VP Human Resources and Administration and Secretary: Robert W. Bradshaw, age 61
Auditors: Arthur Andersen & Co.
Employees: 26,100

WHERE

HQ: 1111 Stewart Ave., Bethpage, NY 11714-3580
Phone: 516-575-0574
Fax: 516-575-1411

Grumman has worldwide operations.

	1990 Sales	
	$ mil.	% of total
US government	3,618	81
Other	830	19
Adjustments	(458)	—
Total	**3,990**	**100**

WHAT

	1990 Sales		1990 Operating Income	
	$ mil.	% of total	$ mil.	% of total
Aerospace	2,922	66	157	68
Electronic systems	493	11	13	6
Info. & other serv.	642	14	34	15
Special purpose vehicles	391	9	25	11
Adjustments	(458)	—	(53)	—
Total	**3,990**	**100**	**176**	**100**

Aerospace
A-6 Intruder attack aircraft
C-2A Greyhound carrier on-board delivery system
Center wing section (Boeing 767)
E-2C Hawkeye early warning aircraft
EA-6B Prowler tactical jamming system
F-14 Tomcat fighter
Nacelles and thrust reversers (Gulfstream IV, Fokker)

Electronic Systems
Automatic test equipment
Joint Surveillance Target Attack Radar System

Information and Other Services
Computer systems design, development, and operation
Real estate and insurance services
Space shuttle instrumentation, measurement, and calibration
Space station information and control systems

Special Purpose Vehicles
Aluminum truck bodies
Fire trucks
Long Life Vehicles (LLVs)

HOW MUCH

	9-Year Growth	1981	1982	1983	1984	1985	1986	1987	1988	1989	1990
Sales ($ mil.)	8.5%	1,916	2,003	2,220	2,558	3,049	3,440	3,325	3,591	3,506	3,990
Net income ($ mil.)	17.2%	20	90	111	108	82	79	27	86	67	86
Income as % of sales	—	1.1%	4.5%	5.0%	4.2%	2.7%	2.3%	0.8%	2.4%	1.9%	2.1%
Earnings per share ($)	14.9%	0.71	3.29	3.81	3.59	2.60	2.29	0.67	2.48	1.91	2.46
Stock price – high ($)		19.88	25.38	33.63	29.63	36.38	33.13	32.63	26.00	23.00	21.13
Stock price – low ($)		10.88	10.50	23.06	21.75	24.88	23.00	17.13	17.63	14.75	12.63
Stock price – close ($)	3.9%	13.88	24.13	24.25	27.13	31.63	24.50	17.25	19.75	15.38	19.63
P/E – high	—	28	8	9	8	14	14	49	10	12	9
P/E – low	—	15	3	6	6	10	10	26	7	8	5
Dividends per share ($)	4.0%	0.70	0.73	0.85	0.93	1.00	1.00	1.00	1.00	1.00	1.00
Book value per share ($)	8.1%	13.09	13.62	16.07	19.00	20.70	22.14	22.27	23.90	24.80	26.45

1990 Year-end:
Debt ratio: 46.4%
Return on equity: 9.6%
Cash (mil.): $75
Current ratio: 3.13
Long-term debt (mil.): $752
No. of shares (mil.): 33
Dividends:
  1990 average yield: 5.1%
  1990 payout: 40.7%
Market value (mil.): $644

Stock Price History High/Low 1981–90

RANKINGS

122nd in *Fortune* 500 Industrial Cos.
828th in *Business Week* 1000

KEY COMPETITORS

Allied-Signal	Harris	Rockwell
Boeing	Lockheed	Siemens
EG&G	Martin Marietta	Textron
GEC	McDonnell	Thorn EMI
General	Douglas	Thiokol
Dynamics	Nobel	Thomson SA
General Electric	Northrop	United
Harley-Davidson	Raytheon	Technologies

GTE CORPORATION

NYSE symbol: GTE
Fiscal year ends: December 31

Hoover's Rating C+

OVERVIEW

GTE is swallowing Contel. Under a merger consummated in 1991, GTE has become the largest US-based local telephone utility, with more lines than any of the Bell regional companies. Post-merger GTE, with more than 650,000 customers, is also the nation's 2nd largest cellular telephone provider, after McCaw Cellular.

The Contel merger is part of GTE's strategy of stressing its core telephone business, now providing service through 18.5 million lines in the US, Canada, and the Dominican Republic. GTE also produces phone directories (the most titles in the US) and makes more than 6,000 types of Sylvania lamps and bulbs.

Other services are more unconventional. GTE's Airfone provides ground-to-air phone service to over 1,400 airliners. Spacenet provides satellite-based communications. In California GTE is testing the "network of the future": fiber-optic-delivered telephone and 2-way television service to homes.

WHEN

Two former staff members of the Wisconsin Railroad Commission — Sigurd Odegard and John O'Connell — formed Richland Center Telephone in Wisconsin dairy country in 1918.

On a vacation to California, Odegard came upon an independent telephone company for sale in Long Beach. With backing from a utilities executive and a Paine Webber partner, Odegard and O'Connell created Associated Telephone Utilities in 1926 to buy the Long Beach company. Associated Telephone grew rapidly, but the company ran afoul of the Great Depression. Lenders took control in 1932 and moved headquarters from Chicago to New York. Still beset by problems, Associated was forced into bankruptcy and emerged as General Telephone in 1935.

Attorney David Power, named CEO in 1951, guided post-WWII growth as General Telephone acquired Theodore Gary and Company (1955) and Sylvania (1959). The Gary acquisition included phone companies in Canada and the Dominican Republic, but the crown jewel was Automatic Electric, a manufacturer of telephone switching equipment. Automatic Electric traced its heritage to the 1889 invention of an automatic switch by Kansas City undertaker Almon Strowger. Strowger was convinced that he was losing business when the telephone company operators didn't handle calls properly.

The 1959 Sylvania purchase changed General Telephone's complexion and its name.

It became a manufacturer and developer of lighting and electronics, and it became General Telephone and Electronics. Sylvania had begun in 1901 when Frank Poor invested in a Massachusetts company that refilled burned-out light bulbs.

The company, long the largest phone company independent of the Bell group, continued expansion with the purchase of phone companies in Florida (1957), the Southwest (1964), and Hawaii (1967). GTE sold its US consumer electronics to North American Philips in 1981, and GTE Mobilnet was formed in 1982 to provide cellular telephone service.

GTE spent the 1980s organizing its varied activities, from military hardware to phone books. Under Chairman James (Rocky) Johnson, it sold most of its US Sprint long-distance service, purchased in 1983 from Southern Pacific, to partner United Telecom in 1989. Concentrating again on its lucrative local phone businesses, GTE jettisoned Automatic Electric — as AG Communication Systems — creating a joint venture to be owned gradually by AT&T. In 1990 GTE announced plans to merge with Contel, in one of the largest telecommunications deals in history. Atlanta-based Contel had begun in 1960, formed by Charles Wohlstetter and 2 partners. By the time of the merger Contel had grown to $3 billion in annual sales. In 1991 GTE announced that it would pare 4,900 jobs from the combined GTE-Contel payroll over 4 years.

WHO

Chairman and CEO: James L. Johnson, age 63, $1,741,612 pay
President and COO: Charles R. Lee, age 51, $1,164,916 pay
SVP External Affairs and General Counsel: Edward C. Schmults, age 60, $686,846 pay
SVP Finance: Nicholas L. Trivisonno, age 43, $668,564 pay
SVP Human Resources and Administration: Bruce Carswell, age 61, $671,913 pay
Auditors: Arthur Andersen & Co.
Employees: 154,000

WHERE

HQ: One Stamford Forum, Stamford, CT 06904
Phone: 203-965-2000
Fax: 203-965-2277

GTE operates worldwide.

	1990 Sales		1990 Net Income	
	$ mil.	% of total	$ mil.	% of total
US	15,330	83	1,287	84
Foreign	3,044	17	244	16
Total	**18,374**	**100**	**1,541**	**100**

WHAT

	1990 Sales		1990 Operating Income	
	$ mil.	% of total	$ mil.	% of total
Telephone operns.	12,762	69	3,059	89
Electrical products	2,276	12	238	7
Telecommunications	3,390	19	155	4
Adjustments	(54)	—	(163)	—
Total	**18,374**	**100**	**3,289**	**100**

Major Operations

GTE Telephone Operations

GTE Telecommunications
GTE Airfone
GTE Government Systems
GTE Information Services
GTE Mobile Communications
GTE Spacenet

GTE Electrical Products
GTE Lighting Business
GTE Precision Materials

GTE Laboratories

Selected Subsidiaries and Affiliates
AG Communication Systems (51%)
British Columbia Telephone Co.
Compania Dominicana de Telefonos, C. por A
Quebec Telephone
US Sprint (19.9%)

RANKINGS

1st in *Fortune* 50 Utilities
20th in *Business Week* 1000

KEY COMPETITORS

AT&T	Ericsson	NYNEX
Ameritech	General Electric	Pacific Telesis
BCE	IBM	Philips
Bell Atlantic	ITT	Siemens
BellSouth	McCaw	Southwestern Bell
British Telecom	MCI	United Telecom
Cable & Wireless	Metromedia	U S West

HOW MUCH

	9-Year Growth	1981	1982	1983	1984	1985	1986	1987	1988	1989	1990
Sales ($ mil.)	5.8%	11,026	12,066	12,944	14,547	15,732	15,112	15,421	16,460	17,424	18,374
Net income ($ mil.)	8.8%	722	836	978	1,080	(161)	1,184	1,119	1,225	1,417	1,541
Income as % of sales	—	6.5%	6.9%	7.6%	7.4%	(1.0%)	7.8%	7.3%	7.4%	8.1%	8.4%
Earnings per share ($)	5.6%	1.37	1.51	1.65	1.72	(0.32)	1.72	1.61	1.77	2.06	2.24
Stock price – high ($)	—	11.42	15.21	16.13	14.63	15.46	21.29	22.38	22.94	35.56	36.00
Stock price – low ($)	—	8.17	8.79	12.88	11.63	12.71	15.08	14.69	16.88	21.44	23.50
Stock price – close ($)	11.9%	10.67	13.83	14.58	13.54	15.33	19.46	17.69	22.25	35.00	29.25
P/E – high	—	8	10	10	8	—	12	14	13	17	16
P/E – low	—	6	6	8	7	—	9	9	10	10	11
Dividends per share ($)	5.7%	0.93	0.96	0.99	1.01	1.04	1.10	1.24	1.30	1.40	1.52
Book value per share ($)	2.9%	9.94	10.50	11.30	12.03	10.75	11.64	11.92	12.45	12.01	12.90

1990 Year-end:
Debt ratio: 56.8%
Return on equity: 18.0%
Cash (mil.): $431
Current ratio: 1.03
Long-term debt (mil.): $11,974
No. of shares (mil.): 669
Dividends:
  1990 average yield: 5.2%
  1990 payout: 67.9%
Market value (mil.): $19,580

Stock Price History High/Low 1981–90

H&R BLOCK, INC.

OVERVIEW

H&R Block is America's largest tax preparer, filling out about one of every 9 returns that the IRS sees. The company serves 15 million taxpayers and operates about 9,000 offices (company-owned and franchised) in the US, Canada, Europe, Australia, and New Zealand.

The company has enjoyed a renaissance in the maturing tax business with its Rapid Refund program. Using the IRS's new electronic filing program, H&R Block files a client's return and sends it to a participating bank. The bank issues the Block customer a loan equal to the return (less small fees for the bank and Block), and the IRS sends the refund to the

bank. Demand for the service soared from 724,000 in 1989 to more than 4 million in 1991.

H&R Block owns Columbus-based CompuServe, the #1 on-line service for personal computer users, with over 800,000 subscribers. CompuServe also operates a data communications network and markets software. Block's Personnel Pool of America provides personnel agency services for home health care, industrial, and office workers.

Founder Henry Bloch and his son Thomas (who became president in 1989) own about 6.5% of the company.

NYSE symbol: HRB
Fiscal year ends: April 30

Hoover's Rating A+

WHO

Chairman and CEO: Henry W. Bloch, age 68, $790,447 pay
President and COO: Thomas M. Bloch, age 37, $422,264 pay
VC: Jerome B. Grossman, age 71, $417,277 pay
VP Finance and Treasurer: Donald W. Ayers, age 57
Assistant VP and Director of Human Resources: Ruth H. Gustin
Auditors: Deloitte & Touche
Employees: 81,000

WHEN

Brothers Henry and Richard (they called each other "Hank" and "Dick") Bloch opened the United Business Company in Kansas City in 1946. They provided bookkeeping, collection, management, and income tax services to small businesses in the area.

The tax preparation end of the business monopolized the brothers' time, and they planned to turn away their clients, but one, an advertising salesman for a Kansas City newspaper, suggested they instead concentrate only on preparing taxes. The Blochs bought 2 ads from the salesman. The first ad filled their office with customers.

In 1955 United Business changed its focus to tax preparation and became H&R Block (the brothers Bloch didn't want customers to read the name as "blotch"). Block charged not on the client's income or time to prepare a return, but on the number and complexity of forms. That meant low fees and a mass market.

The first tax season was a success, and the brothers tested their formula in New York City (1956), where it was similarly successful, but neither Hank nor Dick wanted to move to New York. Instead, they worked out a franchise-like agreement with local CPAs, the first step toward a nationwide chain.

The Blochs returned to the Midwest and opened offices in Columbia, Missouri, and

Topeka, Kansas, in 1957, adding offices in Des Moines, Little Rock, and Oklahoma City in 1958. To assure consistency from office to office, Block began training preparers at H&R Block Income Tax Schools. By 1969, H&R Block boasted more than 3,000 offices in the US and Canada. That same year Richard Bloch retired from the company.

In the 1970s Hank Bloch appeared in commercials to offer "17 reasons why H&R Block should prepare your taxes." Bloch's avuncular, midwestern-Rotarian steadiness reassured millions of Americans they wouldn't have to wend through the maze of tax forms alone.

Fearing market saturation, Henry Bloch pushed the company into new areas. It purchased Personnel Pool of America in 1978, and in 1980 Block bought 80% of Hyatt Legal Services, a pioneer in chains of law offices. The synergies between the tax operations and the legal clinics never developed, and Block sold its stake in 1987 back to a group headed by founder Joel Hyatt. Block also flirted with the management seminar business, buying Path Management (1985, sold 1990).

Block purchased CompuServe in 1980. In 1990 CompuServe acquired longtime on-line competitor The Source and bought MicroSolutions, a vendor of computer connectivity products.

WHERE

HQ: 4410 Main St., Kansas City, MO 64111
Phone: 816-753-6900
Fax: 816-753-5346

H&R Block operates 8,955 offices in the US, Canada, Australia, New Zealand, and Europe.

	1990 Pretax Income	
	$ mil.	% of total
US	207	92
Other countries	19	8
Total	**226**	**100**

WHAT

	1990 Sales		1990 Operating Income	
	$ mil.	% of total	$ mil.	% of total
Tax operations	632	54	165	73
Computer services	252	21	49	22
Temporary services	266	22	16	7
Other	34	3	(4)	(2)
Adjustments	(21)	—	(9)	—
Total	**1,163**	**100**	**217**	**100**

Major Subsidiaries and Affiliates
AB Personnel Pool Ltd.
Applied Computing
BWA Advertising, Inc.
Collier-Jackson, Inc. (software marketing)
CompuPlex, Inc.
CompuServe Data Technologies (database management software)
CompuServe Inc.
H&R Block Canada, Inc.
H&R Block International, Inc.
H&R Block (NYC), Inc.
H&R Block Personnel Services, Inc.
Interim Systems Corp. (temporary personnel services)
Medical Personnel Pool, Inc.
MicroSolutions, Inc. (LAN reseller)
Personnel Pool of America, Inc.
PNB Home Health Services, Inc.
SEARA Information Strategy Corp. (LAN products)
Source Telecomputing Corp.
Victor Temporary Services, Inc.

HOW MUCH

Fiscal year ends April of following year.	9-Year Growth	1981	1982	1983	1984	1985	1986	1987	1988	1989	1990
Sales ($ mil.)	16.5%	293	310	400	476	591	687	778	877	1,028	1,163
Net income ($ mil.)	15.5%	38	41	48	55	60	73	88	100	124	140
Income as % of sales	—	13.1%	13.2%	12.0%	11.7%	10.2%	10.7%	11.3%	11.4%	12.0%	12.1%
Earnings per share ($)	14.2%	0.79	0.79	0.84	0.97	1.13	1.21	1.43	1.71	1.90	2.31
Stock price – high ($)	—	9.75	10.94	12.28	12.50	19.81	26.44	33.31	34.38	37.38	45.50
Stock price – low ($)	—	7.19	6.31	8.88	9.25	11.03	17.88	20.00	22.75	26.13	30.00
Stock price – close ($)	18.3%	9.50	10.44	12.13	11.13	19.25	22.50	31.00	28.38	36.00	43.25
P/E – high	—	12	13	13	11	16	18	19	18	16	17
P/E – low	—	9	8	9	8	9	13	12	12	11	11
Dividends per share ($)	13.7%	0.47	0.48	0.51	0.58	0.66	0.73	0.85	1.00	1.22	1.49
Book value per share ($)	12.2%	3.82	4.19	4.77	5.08	5.86	6.82	7.37	8.49	9.53	10.77

1990 Year-end:
Debt ratio: 0.0%
Return on equity: 25.8%
Cash (mil.): $228
Current ratio: 1.48
Long-term debt (mil.): $0
No. of shares (mil.): 53
Dividends:
　1990 average yield: 3.4%
　1990 payout: 56.9%
Market value (mil.): $2,303

Stock Price History High/Low 1981–90

RANKINGS

96th in *Fortune* 100 Diversified Service Cos.
251st in *Business Week* 1000

KEY COMPETITORS

ARA	Deloitte	Knight-Ridder
Arthur Andersen	& Touche	KPMG
ADP	Dow Jones	Mead
Citicorp	Dun & Bradstreet	Novell
Computer	General Electric	Oracle
Associates	IBM	Price
Coopers & Lybrand	JWP	Waterhouse

HAL, INC.

OVERVIEW

HAL is the parent company of Hawaiian Airlines and the West Maui Airport, an airport facility located at Mahinahina, Maui.

Although Honolulu-based Hawaiian is Hawaii's largest airline, it has lost money for 4 of the past 5 years. It has also been losing passengers, and in 1990 it was surpassed by key rival Aloha for the largest share of inter-island traffic for the first time. Aloha, with a 54.3% share of the market compared to Hawaiian's 44.9% share, has a reputation for better service.

HAL has responded to its financial crisis by putting West Maui Airport up for sale (no buyers have appeared). Both staff and flight service have been pared, and in 1990 the company sold 3 South Pacific routes to NWA (parent of Northwest Airlines). As part of their agreement, NWA leased HAL the aircraft and crews necessary for it to open a route from Honolulu to Fukuoka, Japan, in 1991. NWA also bought a 25% stake in the ailing Hawaiian carrier, joining Japan Airlines (which owns 17% of HAL) as a minority shareholder.

WHO

Chairman and CEO: John A. Ueberroth, age 46, $132,562 pay (prior to promotion)
President and COO: H. Mitchell O'Olier
SVP Finance and CFO: Glen L. Stewart, age 48, $114,058 pay
VP, Secretary, and General Counsel; VP Administration (Personnel): Stephen R. Thompkins, age 46
Auditors: KPMG Peat Marwick
Employees: 2,640

WHEN

In 1929 former WWI naval pilot Stanley Kennedy, then general manager of the Inter-Island Steam Navigation Company, persuaded the Inter-Island board to put up 76% equity financing to establish Inter-Island Airways, Ltd., a passenger line linking Honolulu (Oahu) with the islands of Hawaii, Maui, Kauai, Molokai, and Lanai. The company started airmail service from Honolulu to Hilo and Kauai in 1934.

The company changed its name to Hawaiian Airlines in 1941. TWA bought 20% of the company in 1944 but sold it 4 years later. In 1946 the creation of Trans-Pacific Airlines (later Aloha Airlines) ended Hawaiian's 17-year service monopoly in Hawaii.

Hawaiian and Aloha operated almost identical routes, creating intense competition. Each struggled for technological superiority: Hawaiian introduced the Douglas DC-9 in 1966, and Aloha, the Boeing 737 in 1969. Rising costs were not matched by increased sales, however, and the airlines agreed to merge in 1970, with John Magoon, who had bought control of Hawaiian in 1964, as president. However, negotiations failed and merger plans were abandoned in 1971.

With the 1978 Airline Deregulation Act, Hawaiian, like other intrastate carriers, gained access to new markets. The company adopted HAL as its corporate name in 1982 and had expanded service to the West Coast (Los Angeles, San Francisco, Las Vegas, and Seattle) and the South Pacific (American Samoa and Tonga) by 1985. While the airline was able to fill its planes to 65.2% capacity (the industry's highest), its yields per passenger were among the lowest because of fare discounts sparked by competition with United and Continental to the West Coast.

HAL built the $8.5 million West Maui Airport in 1987 but had to contend with increasing aircraft maintenance costs (up to $70 million in 1988 from $35 million in 1986) due to the corrosive salt air and stress from frequent short flights. Magoon decided to sell a 46.5% stake in the airline to a group of investors, which included long-time friend and ex–baseball commissioner Peter Ueberroth. The group, headed by Jet America Airlines's founder J. Thomas Talbot, bought control of HAL in 1989 for $37 million. Magoon stayed on as a director of HAL, and Talbot took over as chairman and CEO.

Late in 1990 NWA bought a 25% minority stake in HAL and 3 of its South Pacific routes (Honolulu-Sydney, Guam-Saipan, and Nagoya-Fukuoka) for $20 million. HAL's president John Ueberroth (younger brother of Peter Ueberroth and former president of Carlson Travel Group) replaced Talbot as chairman in 1991. Talbot continues to serve on the company's board.

WHERE

HQ: 1164 Bishop St., PO Box 30008, Honolulu, HI 96820
Phone: 808-835-3001
Fax: 808-835-3015

HAL flies to 6 Hawaiian islands, the West Coast, and the South Pacific.

Hawaiian Destinations
Hilo and Kona, Hawaii
Honolulu, Oahu
Hoolehua, Molokai
Kahului and Kapalua, Maui
Lanai, Lanai
Lihue, Kauai

South Pacific Destinations
Apia, Western Samoa
Fukuoka, Japan
Nuku' alofa, Tonga
Pago Pago, American Samoa
Papeete, Tahiti
Rarotonga, Cook Islands

Mainland Destinations
Los Angeles and San Francisco, CA
Seattle, WA

	1990 Sales	
	$ mil.	% of total
US	275	81
Other countries	66	19
Total	**341**	**100**

	1990 Sales	
	$ mil.	% of total
Inter-island	132	39
Transpacific	143	42
Overseas charters	66	19
Total	**341**	**100**

WHAT

	1990 Sales	
	$ mil.	% of total
Passengers	249	73
Charters	68	20
Cargo	15	4
Other	9	3
Total	**341**	**100**

Subsidiaries
Hawaiian Airlines, Inc.
West Maui Airport, Inc.

Flight Equipment	No.
DC-8	7
DC-9	14
L-1011	6
Other	9
Total	**36**

RANKINGS

45th in *Fortune* 50 Transportation Cos.

KEY COMPETITORS

America West	Delta	TWA
AMR	JAL	UAL
Continental Airlines		

HOW MUCH

	9-Year Growth	1981	1982	1983	1984	1985	1986	1987	1988	1989	1990
Sales ($ mil.)	14.8%	99	101	94	128	160	225	299	354	349	341
Net income ($ mil.)	—	5	(17)	(6)	6	0	3	(9)	(9)	(47)	(118)
Income as % of sales	—	5.4%	(16.7%)	(6.1%)	4.5%	(0.1%)	1.5%	(2.9%)	(2.5%)	(13.5%)	(34.7%)
Earnings per share ($)	—	2.75	(8.79)	(3.01)	3.04	(0.10)	1.83	(4.57)	(4.48)	(24.00)	(54.51)
Stock price – high ($)	—	9.00	7.00	5.63	10.38	10.13	21.75	48.00	34.00	40.25	23.38
Stock price – low ($)	—	3.63	3.63	3.75	4.13	7.13	8.13	17.00	17.25	20.13	5.00
Stock price – close ($)	7.5%	4.25	4.88	4.63	7.50	9.00	21.75	17.75	23.25	20.63	8.13
P/E – high	—	3	—	—	3	—	12	—	—	—	—
P/E – low	—	1	—	—	1	—	4	—	—	—	—
Dividends per share ($)	0.0%	0.00	0.00	0.00	0.00	0.10	0.00	0.15	0.00	0.00	0.00
Book value per share ($)	—	7.14	(1.65)	7.04	10.07	9.91	11.61	6.79	2.31	3.07	(50.15)

1990 Year-end:
Debt ratio: 0.0%
Return on equity: —
Cash (mil.): $18
Current ratio: 0.21
Long-term debt (mil.): $0
No. of shares (mil.): 2
Dividends:
  1990 average yield: 0.0%
  1990 payout: 0.0%
Market value (mil.): $18

Stock Price History High/Low 1981–90

HALLIBURTON COMPANY

NYSE symbol: HAL
Fiscal year ends: December 31

Hoover's Rating **B**

OVERVIEW

Halliburton is one of the world's leading oil field engineering and construction services companies. It is divided into 3 segments: the Oil Field Services Group, Engineering and Construction Services, and Insurance Services. Halliburton expects increased business from the Kuwait cleanup and from industry coping with the Clean Air Act of 1990.

Its Oil Field Services Group performs a wide range of activities, from measurement-while-drilling (MWD) services to selling software for the energy industry. The group spent over $100 million in 1990 R&D and was awarded 100 patents. In the Engineering and Construction Services Group, its Brown & Root division, a leader in erecting offshore drilling platforms and laying underwater pipelines, builds many of the US's nuclear, chemical, and petrochemical plants. Halliburton's NUS subsidiary provides environmental engineering, and Halliburton Environmental Technologies handles hazardous waste issues.

Halliburton provides property, casualty, and marine insurance, and health care cost-management services through Highlands Insurance and Health Economics companies.

WHO

Chairman and CEO: Thomas H. Cruikshank, age 59, $750,000 pay
President: Dale P. Jones, age 54, $437,500 pay
President and CEO, Brown & Root, Inc.: W. Bernard Pieper, age 59, $400,417 pay
President, Oil Field Services Group: Alan A. Baker, age 58, $361,250 pay
EVP Finance and Corporate Development: Lester L. Coleman, age 48, $310,000 pay
VP Administration (Personnel): Karen S. Stuart
Auditors: Arthur Andersen & Co.
Employees: 77,000

WHEN

Erle Halliburton began his oil career in 1916, when he went to work for Perkins Oil Well Cementing. Discharged for suggesting too many new ideas, Halliburton left for Burkburnett, Texas, in 1919 and started his Better Method Oil Well Cementing Company. Halliburton used cement to hold a steel pipe in a well, which kept oil out of the water table; although his contribution is widely recognized today, it was considered nonessential then. In 1921, the same year he moved to Duncan, Oklahoma, he recorded his first profit — of $.50. In 1924 he incorporated as Halliburton Oil Well Cementing Company.

Between the 1950s and 1970s Halliburton built up its present-day, Dallas-based oil service business by buying companies with expertise throughout the oil and gas market. Halliburton acquired Welex, a well-logging company (1957), and Houston-based Brown & Root industrial/marine construction company (1966), which had expertise in offshore platforms. Halliburton bought Ebasco Services, an electric utility engineering company with expertise in nuclear plants (1973), but the Justice Department forced its sale (1976), fearing Halliburton's share of the utility engineering market (20%) would limit market competition.

The investments in Welex and Brown & Root left Halliburton well positioned to benefit from the oil exploration boom of the 1970s. Later that decade, as drilling costs surged, Halliburton shifted focus and quickly became the leader in stimulating old and abandoned wells by developing new techniques for fracturing deep formations.

When the oil industry slumped in 1982, Halliburton steered clear of further oil- and gas-related investments, instead cutting employment by more than half, while rivals Schlumberger and Dresser were buying up distressed companies at bargain prices. Other Halliburton businesses were not faring well either. In 1985 Halliburton's largest division, Brown & Root, already suffering a scarcity of new construction projects, settled out of court for $750 million for mismanagement of the South Texas Nuclear Project.

In 1988 Halliburton began reinvesting in the oil and gas services market by buying 60% of Texas Instrument's Geophysical Services (GSI), the 2nd largest seismic service company in the US, and Geosource, another provider of geophysical services. That year Halliburton also purchased wireline services provider Gearhart Industries and merged it with Welex to form Halliburton Logging Services, and announced plans with Du Pont to enter the hazardous waste cleanup business. In 1991 Halliburton purchased TI's remaining interest in GSI.

WHERE

HQ: 3600 Lincoln Plaza, Dallas, TX 75201
Phone: 214-978-2600
Fax: 214-978-2611

Halliburton conducts business in the US and in 119 foreign countries.

	1990 Sales		1990 Operating Income	
	$ mil.	% of total	$ mil.	% of total
US	4,815	70	231	65
Europe	1,001	14	41	11
Other countries	1,110	16	84	24
Adjustments	(21)	—	(40)	—
Total	**6,905**	**100**	**316**	**100**

WHAT

	1990 Sales		1990 Operating Income	
	$ mil.	% of total	$ mil.	% of total
Oil field services	2,916	42	283	80
Insurance services	356	5	2	—
Engineering & construction	3,654	53	71	20
Adjustments	(21)	—	(40)	—
Total	**6,905**	**100**	**316**	**100**

Oil Field Services
Cementing and well stimulation
Jet perforating services
Logging equipment sales
Gas equipment leasing
Measurement-while-drilling (MWD)
Sales of seismic equipment
Sand and water control
Seismic data collection and data processing
Software
Tubing-conveyed well completion systems
Wireline and mineral logging services

Engineering and Construction Services
Design and construction of utilities, chemical plants, mills, highways, and bridges
Environmental/waste management services
Marine services

Insurance Services
Health care cost containment
Property and casualty insurance

RANKINGS

14th in *Fortune* 100 Diversified Service Cos.
113th in *Business Week* 1000

KEY COMPETITORS

ABB
Ashland
Baker Hughes
Bechtel
CSX
Duke Power
Fluor
FMC
General Electric
Litton Industries
McDermott
Ogden
Peter Kiewit Sons'
Schlumberger
Siemens
Union Pacific
Waste Management
Westinghouse

HOW MUCH

	9-Year Growth	1981	1982	1983	1984	1985	1986	1987	1988	1989	1990
Sales ($ mil.)	(2.2%)	8,435	7,282	5,511	5,428	4,781	3,527	3,836	4,826	5,660	6,905
Net income ($ mil.)	(12.8%)	674	497	315	330	29	(515)	48	85	134	197
Income as % of sales	—	8.0%	6.8%	5.7%	6.1%	0.6%	(14.6%)	1.3%	1.8%	2.4%	2.9%
Earnings per share ($)	(11.8%)	5.72	4.21	2.66	2.87	0.27	(4.85)	0.45	0.81	1.26	1.85
Stock price – high ($)	—	84.50	52.75	47.25	44.00	33.88	28.00	43.13	36.50	44.50	58.75
Stock price – low ($)	—	44.13	21.00	29.25	27.13	24.50	17.38	20.13	24.38	27.50	38.75
Stock price – close ($)	(1.5%)	52.13	35.38	40.38	28.50	27.50	24.38	24.75	28.00	42.75	45.63
P/E – high	—	15	13	18	15	125	—	96	45	35	32
P/E – low	—	8	5	11	9	91	—	45	30	22	21
Dividends per share ($)	(2.9%)	1.30	1.60	1.65	1.80	1.80	1.20	1.00	1.00	1.00	1.00
Book value per share ($)	(2.7%)	26.85	29.49	30.18	31.19	26.30	20.30	19.76	19.80	19.90	21.04

1990 Year-end:
Debt ratio: 7.8%
Return on equity: 9.0%
Cash (mil.): $168
Current ratio: —
Long-term debt (mil.): $190
No. of shares (mil.): 107
Dividends:
1990 average yield: 2.2%
1990 payout: 54.1%
Market value (mil.): $4,873

Stock Price History High/Low 1981–90

HALLMARK CARDS, INC.

Private company
Fiscal year ends: December 31

Hoover's Rating **A-**

OVERVIEW

Privately owned, Kansas City–based Hallmark is the #1 producer of greeting cards and a leading producer of ribbons and bows, gift wrap, crayons, candles, jigsaw puzzles, Christmas ornaments, wedding products, party goods, plush toys, and related gift items. Hallmark has the world's largest creative staff, and its name is known by 99 out of 100 consumers. Hallmark has a reputation for philanthropy, with over 900 charitable grants in 1990.

Hallmark and its Ambassador division lead the US in greeting card sales. Cards are published in over 20 languages and sold in over 100 countries. Nonoccasion cards, many designed to help tongue-tied correspondents with conflict resolution, are a new growth avenue for the company. But retail trends are working against the 11,000 independently owned and about 200 company-owned specialty shops carrying Hallmark cards. Consumers are increasingly shifting their card purchases to mass-market and convenience outlets, where competition is greater.

In 1991 Hallmark plunged into the cable industry in a big way, buying a controlling interest in St. Louis–based Cencom Cable in a transaction valued at about $1 billion.

WHO

Chairman: Donald J. Hall, age 63
President and CEO: Irvine O. Hockaday, Jr., age 55
EVP and CFO: Henry F. Frigon, age 57
VP Personnel and Services: Lowell J. Mayone
Auditors: KPMG Peat Marwick
Employees: 34,000

WHERE

HQ: 2501 McGee, PO Box 419580, Kansas City, MO 64141-6580
Phone: 816-274-5111
Fax: 816-274-8513

Hallmark has production facilities in 4 cities in Kansas (Lawrence, Leavenworth, Osage City, and Topeka) and in Kansas City, Missouri. It also has distribution centers in Enfield, Connecticut, and Liberty, Missouri. Products are distributed in over 100 countries.

WHEN

Eighteen-year-old Joyce C. Hall started selling postcards from a rented room at the Kansas City, Missouri, YMCA in 1910. Hall's brother Rollie joined him in 1911, and the 2 added greeting cards (which were made by another company) to their product line in 1912. By the mid-teens the brothers had established Hall Brothers, a store that sold postcards, gifts, books, and stationery. After a 1915 fire destroyed their entire inventory (just before Valentine's Day), the brothers quickly regrouped, got a loan, bought an engraving company, and produced their first original greeting cards in time for Christmas. The company's first humorous greeting card depicted a small cartoon dog with the caption: "Not little like this tiny pup/But big just like a dog grown up! I'm wishing you a DOG-GONE MERRY CHRISTMAS."

During the 1920s a 3rd brother, William, joined the firm, and the company started stamping the back of its cards with the phrase "A Hallmark Card." By 1922 Hall Brothers had salesmen in all 48 states and for the first time expanded beyond greeting cards with the introduction of gift wrap. Joyce Hall placed the company's first national ad in the *Ladies Home Journal* in 1928.

In 1936 Hall Brothers introduced a display case fixture for greeting cards (which had previously been kept haphazardly under store counters) and sold it to retailers across the country. The company aired its first radio ad in 1938 and in 1944 adopted the slogan, "When You Care Enough to Send the Very Best," written by employee Ed Goodman. In 1942 Hall Brothers introduced a friendship card that showed a cart filled with flowers. The card would become the company's all-time bestseller and is still sold today.

After WWII Hall Brothers grew tremendously as Joyce Hall strove to give his company's products a reputation for high quality. In 1950 the company opened its first greeting card retail store and in 1951 broadcast the first "Hallmark Hall of Fame" television production (a color version of *Amahl and the Night Visitors*). The critically acclaimed "Hallmark Hall of Fame" (with 61 Emmy awards to date) would become the longest-running dramatic television series in history. Hall Brothers changed its name to Hallmark in 1954 and 3 years later went international. In 1959 the company opened its Ambassador Cards unit.

Hallmark introduced a line of paper party products and started putting "Peanuts" characters (Charlie Brown, Snoopy) on its cards in 1960. In 1968 the company started construction on Crown Center (a $500 million complex of offices, shops, and residences), which surrounds the company headquarters in Kansas City. Tragedy struck the complex in 1981 when a walkway collapsed at the Crown Hyatt Regency, killing 114. During the 1970s, Hallmark added Christmas ornaments to its product line.

In 1982 Joyce Hall died, and his son Donald became chairman of the board in 1983. The company acquired Binney & Smith (Crayola Crayons, Magic Marker) in 1984 and Univision (Spanish-language TV network) in 1987. Hallmark celebrated its 75th anniversary in 1985 and opened its Hallmark Visitors Center, a museum that traces its history. In 1990 Hallmark's agreement to buy Dakin (plush toys) fell through, but it did acquire Willitts Designs (collectibles).

WHAT

Products
Albums
Art supplies and crayons
Baby products
Calendars
Candles
Christmas ornaments and collectibles
Gifts, gift wrap, ribbons, and bows
Greeting cards
Home decorations
Jigsaw puzzles
Party goods
Wedding products
Writing papers and pens

Brand Names
Ambassador
Crayola (crayons)
Hallmark
Liquitex (art supplies)
Magic Marker
Shoebox Greetings
Springbok (jigsaw puzzles)
Willitts Designs

Subsidiaries
Binney & Smith (crayons and art materials)
Crown Center Redevelopment Corp. (Kansas City real estate complex)
Crown Media, Inc. (cable TV systems)
Graphics International Trading Co. (overseas supplies)
Hallmark Marketing (sales)
Halls Merchandising, Inc. (clothing stores)
Litho-Krome Co. (lithography)
Univision Holdings, Inc. (Spanish-language TV)

RANKINGS

46th in *Forbes* 400 US Private Cos.

KEY COMPETITORS

American Greetings
Deluxe
Gerber
Gillette
United Nations
TCI
Other cable companies

HOW MUCH

	9-Year Growth	1981	1982	1983	1984	1985	1986	1987	1988	1989	1990
Sales ($ mil.)	—	—	—	—	—	1,500	1,680	2,000	2,250	2,500	2,700
Domestic employees[1]	3.1%	16,101	15,736	16,187	17,968	17,971	17,495	18,121	19,075	20,850	23,880

Sales
1985–90

3,000
2,500
2,000
1,500
1,000
500
0

[1]Excludes Evenson's, Binney & Smith, and Univision, acquired in 1980, 1984, and 1987, respectively.

HARLEY-DAVIDSON, INC.

NYSE symbol: HDI
Fiscal year ends: December 31

Hoover's Rating **A+**

OVERVIEW

After 7 consecutive years of increasing market share, Harley-Davidson has 62.3% of the US "superheavyweight" (850cc or larger engines) motorcycle market. The only US motorcycle maker today (its last competitor folded in 1953), H-D nearly went under itself trying to compete against the Japanese. Its comeback in the mid-1980s is one of the greatest US business success stories of recent years. Today 134,000 members of H.O.G. (Harley Owners Group) receive the company's newsletter.

H-D's sales are capacity-constrained. Management prefers to keep dealers and customers hungry for "hogs" rather than sacrifice quality

in production. A new paint facility is expected to allow the company to increase output. H-D is progressing well overseas, particularly in Japan, Germany, and the UK and, with a 13% world market share in "heavyweight" (650cc and over) motorcycles, has plenty of room to grow.

H-D also makes motor homes, travel trailers, and specialized commercial vehicles, as well as bomb casings and rocket, snow thrower, and marine engines.

The Harley "look" is the creation of the vice president of styling, Willie G. Davidson, grandson of a company founder.

WHEN

William Harley and the Davidson brothers (Walter, William, and Arthur) of Milwaukee sold their first motorcycles in 1903. Essentially motor-assisted bicycles that required pedaling going uphill, they had 25-cubic-inch, 3-HP engines. Demand was high, and most sold before they left the factory. In 1909 the company introduced a 2-cylinder, V-twin engine (an H-D trademark) and by 1914 introduced a step starter.

WWI put British cycle makers out of the consumer cycle business and created a demand for US motorcycles overseas that made H-D's foreign sales important. In the 1920s H-D introduced new models with the "teardrop" gas tank that became part of the H-D look.

The Great Depression did in several H-D competitors (over 300 US motorcycle makers have existed at various times). Exports and sales to the police and military helped H-D survive. To improve sales, H-D added styling features like art deco decals and 3-tone paint. The 1936 EL model with its "knucklehead" engine (so called because of its odd appearance) was a forerunner of today's models.

War again brought prosperity to H-D, with production elevated to record levels (90,000 cycles were built for the military). After WWII the company introduced new motorcycles: the

K-model (1952), Sportster (1957), and Duo-Glide (1958). In 1960 H-D opened a plant in Italy and a branch in Switzerland. The company began making golf carts in the early 1960s.

In 1965 the company went public and in 1969 merged with American Machine and Foundry (AMF). By the late 1970s, certain that H-D would lose to Japanese bikes flooding the market, AMF put the company up for sale. Vaughn L. Beals and others from AMF's H-D division bought the company in 1981. Faced with decreased demand for big power bikes and competition from a Japanese product that was not only cheaper but also better, Beals fought back, updating manufacturing methods, improving quality, and expanding the model line. By 1987 H-D had gained 25% of the US "heavyweight" motorcycle market, up from 16% in 1985. H-D was doing well enough that in 1987 it asked for removal of a 5-year tariff on Japanese bikes a year ahead of schedule. H-D returned to public ownership in 1986 and by that year had also recovered enough to buy Holiday Rambler (recreational vehicles).

The company opened its first retail mall outlet, to sell Motor Clothes, in Kansas City in 1990. In early 1991 a strike reduced H-D's motorcycle output, and the Persian Gulf crisis trimmed demand for RVs.

WHO

Chairman: Vaughn L. Beals, Jr., age 63
President and CEO: Richard F. Treelink, age 54, $646,595 pay
VP Continuous Improvement: Thomas A. Gelb, $324,125 pay
President and COO, Motorcycle Division: James H. Paterson, $403,910 pay
VP and CFO: James L. Ziemer
VP Human Resources: C. William Gray
Auditors: Ernst & Young
Employees: 5,000

WHERE

HQ: 3700 W. Juneau Ave., PO Box 653, Milwaukee, WI 53208
Phone: 414-342-4680
Fax: 414-935-4977

Harley-Davidson owns 7 manufacturing facilities in Wisconsin, Pennsylvania, Indiana, and California.

	1990 Sales	
	$ mil.	% of total
US	782	90
Foreign	83	10
Total	**865**	**100**

WHAT

	1990 Sales		1990 Operating Income	
	$ mil.	% of total	$ mil.	% of total
Motorcycles & related prods.	595	69	88	96
Defense & other	29	3	2	3
Transportation vehicles	241	28	1	1
Adjustments	—	—	(6)	—
Total	**865**	**100**	**85**	**100**

Motorcycles and Related Products
Eagle Iron (parts and accessories)
883cc Sportster
Fat Boy
FLTC and FLHTC Ultra Classics
FXDB Sturgis
FXR Super Glide
FXSTS Springer Softail
Harley-Davidson Motor Clothes
Leathers by Willie G.

Transportation Vehicles
Holiday Rambler Corp. (recreational)
    Aluma-Lite Free Spirit
    Imperial
    Limited Crown Imperial
Utilimaster Corporation
    Aeromate (walk-in van)
    Parcel delivery vans

Defense (DOD) Products
Metal bomb casings and suspension systems
Rocket, snow thrower, and marine engines

HOW MUCH

	5-Year Growth	1981	1982	1983	1984	1985	1986	1987	1988	1989	1990
Sales ($ mil.)	24.7%	—	—	—	—	287	295	685	757	791	865
Net income ($ mil.)	66.2%	—	—	—	—	3	4	18	27	33	38
Income as % of sales	—	—	—	—	—	0.9%	1.5%	2.6%	3.6%	4.1%	4.4%
Earnings per share ($)	—	—	—	—	—	0.36	0.41	1.36	1.71	1.89	2.15
Stock price – high ($)	—	—	—	—	—	—	6.94	13.25	14.94	21.50	34.38
Stock price – low ($)	—	—	—	—	—	—	3.63	4.63	5.94	12.19	13.38
Stock price – close ($)	—	—	—	—	—	—	5.25	6.50	12.69	19.63	19.25
P/E – high	—	—	—	—	—	—	17	10	9	11	16
P/E – low	—	—	—	—	—	—	9	3	3	6	6
Dividends per share ($)	—	—	—	—	—	0.00	0.00	0.00	0.00	0.00	0.00
Book value per share ($)	77.8%	—	—	—	—	0.63	2.30	4.55	7.04	8.97	11.19

1990 Year-end:
Debt ratio: 19.6%
Return on equity: 21.3%
Cash (mil.): $14
Current ratio: 1.34
Long-term debt (mil.): $48
No. of shares (mil.): 18
Dividends:
    1990 average yield: 0.0%
    1990 payout: 0.0%
Market value (mil.): $342

Stock Price History High/Low 1986–90

RANKINGS

375th in *Fortune* 500 Industrial Cos.
821st in *Business Week* 1000

KEY COMPETITORS

BMW	Grumman	Suzuki
Brunswick	Honda	Thiokol
Fleetwood	Outboard Marine	Yamaha

HARRIS CORPORATION

OVERVIEW

Harris, formerly a leading maker of printing presses, is now a leader in electronics. Harris is one of the largest industrial companies headquartered in Florida.

The Electronic Systems Sector (30% of total sales) provides a variety of avionics, command/control, communications, and intelligence systems to DOD, the FAA, and NASA. The sector also provides private communications networks, management systems for utilities, and newspaper composition systems.

The Semiconductor Sector (26% of sales) focuses on chips designed for harsh environments, such as in automotive electronics, and satellites. The acquisition of GE Solid State in 1988 doubled the sector's size. Harris is the largest chip supplier to the US government.

The Communications Sector (14% of sales) sells broadcasting equipment, 2-way radios, and telecommunications systems worldwide. Harris has captured 65% of the US VHF television market and is North America's largest maker of low- and medium-capacity microwave communication systems.

The 4th sector, Lanier Worldwide (30% of sales), markets its copiers, fax machines, dictation equipment, and office supplies in more than 50 countries. Lanier recently introduced its first plain-paper fax machine to use LED array printing.

In 1991 Harris was awarded the avionics subcontract on the DOD's Advanced Technical Fighter project, the largest US weapons project of all time. However, the recession contributed to a substantial drop in Harris's earnings in fiscal 1991.

US government contracts were 36.3% of Harris's 1990 sales (down from 55.4% in 1988).

WHEN

Harris was founded in Niles, Ohio, in 1895 by 2 brothers, Alfred and Charles Harris, both jewelers and inventors. Among their inventions was a printing press that became Harris Automatic Press Company's flagship product.

Harris remained a small, family-run company until 1944, when engineer George Diveley was hired as general manager. Under Dively, Harris began manufacturing bindery, typesetting, and paper-converting equipment while remaining a leading supplier of printing presses. In 1957 Harris merged with Intertype, a typesetter manufacturer, and became known as Harris-Intertype Corporation.

Harris-Intertype continued to expand its business through several acquisitions in the 1960s. In 1967 Harris-Intertype bought electronics and data-processing-equipment manufacturer Radiation, a $50 million company heavily dependent upon government contracts, and relocated to Radiation's headquarters in Melbourne, Florida. The company also bought RF Communications (2-way radios, 1969), General Electric's broadcast equipment line (1972), and UCC-Communications Systems (data-processing equipment, 1972).

The company changed its name to Harris Corporation in 1974. In 1980 Harris bought Farinon, manufacturer of microwave radio systems, and Lanier Business Products, the leading maker of dictating equipment. In 1983 Harris sold its printing equipment business. In 1986 Harris formed a joint venture with 3M called Harris/3M Document Products to market copiers and fax machines and in 1989 acquired the entire operation, which became Lanier Worldwide. Other late-80s acquisitions included Scientific Calculations (1986), a computer-aided design (CAD) software developer. In 1988 the company purchased General Electric's Solid State group. Harris also sold off its PC, information systems, and data communications businesses in 1989 and 1990.

In 1991 Harris won a $1 billion contract for avionics systems for the new Army Light Helicopter.

A soft semiconductor market led Harris to lay off 2,000 employees in September of 1991.

NYSE symbol: HRS
Fiscal year ends: June 30

 Hoover's Rating **C+**

WHO

Chairman, President, and CEO: John T. Hartley, age 61, $1,109,578 pay
EVP; President, Semiconductor Sector: Philip W. Farmer, age 53, $407,354 pay (prior to promotion)
President and CEO, Lanier Worldwide: Wesley E. Cantrell, age 56, $976,076 pay
President, Electronic Systems Sector: Allen S. Henry, age 52
President, Communications Sector: Guy W. Numann, age 59, $367,315 pay
SVP Finance: Bryan R. Roub, age 50
VP Human Resources: Nick E. Heldreth, age 49
Auditors: Ernst & Young
Employees: 28,000

WHERE

HQ: 1025 W. NASA Blvd., Melbourne, FL 32919
Phone: 407-727-9100
Fax: 407-727-5118

Harris has 46 manufacturing and 513 other facilities worldwide.

	1990 Sales		1990 Pretax Income	
	$ mil.	% of total	$ mil.	% of total
US	2,376	78	146	77
Other countries	677	22	44	23
Total	**3,053**	**100**	**190**	**100**

WHAT

	1990 Sales		1990 Operating Income	
	$ mil.	% of total	$ mil.	% of total
Semiconductors	784	26	66	22
Communications	454	14	45	15
Electronic systems	907	30	85	29
Lanier office equipment	908	30	101	34
Adjustments	—	—	(107)	—
Total	**3,053**	**100**	**190**	**100**

Products and Services
Broadcast radio and television systems
Control systems for electric utilities and railroads
Digital telephone switches
Ground-based data collection systems
Information systems for aircraft and spacecraft
Land-based and satellite communications systems
Microwave and 2-way radios
Office equipment distribution
Semiconductors
Standard, semicustom, and custom integrated circuits
Video teleconferencing systems
Wide- and local-area networks

RANKINGS

149th in *Fortune* 500 Industrial Cos.
538th in *Business Week* 1000

KEY COMPETITORS

Canon	Minolta	Sharp
Eastman Kodak	Motorola	Siemens
Fujitsu	National	Sony
GEC	Semiconductor	Sun Microsystems
General Signal	NEC	Thomson Corp.
Grumman	Pitney Bowes	Xerox
Hitachi	Raytheon	Other electronics
Hyundai	Rockwell	and defense
Intel	Samsung	companies

HOW MUCH

	9-Year Growth	1981	1982	1983	1984	1985	1986	1987	1988	1989	1990
Sales ($ mil.)	7.8%	1,552	1,719	1,424	1,996	2,281	2,217	2,079	2,063	2,214	3,053
Net income ($ mil.)	2.6%	104	76	50	80	80	60	85	65	116	131
Income as % of sales	—	6.7%	4.4%	3.5%	4.0%	3.5%	2.7%	4.1%	3.2%	5.2%	4.3%
Earnings per share ($)	(0.2%)	3.33	2.40	1.58	2.01	1.99	1.47	2.03	1.63	2.97	3.28
Stock price – high ($)	—	60.25	41.13	51.88	42.63	35.00	36.88	42.75	33.25	39.50	36.13
Stock price – low ($)	—	37.50	20.38	33.25	22.75	22.25	25.50	22.00	24.25	26.38	13.75
Stock price – close ($)	(7.8%)	41.13	37.00	40.13	27.13	27.25	29.75	26.00	27.00	33.13	19.88
P/E – high	—	18	17	33	21	18	25	21	20	13	11
P/E – low	—	11	8	21	11	11	17	11	15	9	4
Dividends per share ($)	2.0%	0.80	0.88	0.88	0.88	0.88	0.88	0.88	0.88	0.88	0.96
Book value per share ($)	4.7%	17.81	19.05	20.12	20.48	21.56	22.37	23.64	24.94	24.45	27.02

1990 Year-end:
Debt ratio: 21.7%
Return on equity: 12.7%
Cash (mil.): $138
Current ratio: 1.33
Long-term debt (mil.): $301
No. of shares (mil.): 40
Dividends:
  1990 average yield: 4.8%
  1990 payout: 29.3%
Market value (mil.): $797

Stock Price History High/Low 1981–90

HARTMARX CORPORATION

NYSE symbol: HMX
Fiscal year ends: November 30

Hoover's Rating **D**

OVERVIEW

Hartmarx Corporation manufactures and sells such well-known men's and women's clothing as Hart Schaffner & Marx and Hickey-Freeman, Country Miss, and Kuppenheimer. Sales of these brands to unaffiliated retailers accounted for 45% of Hartmarx's 1990 sales ($580 million, down from $598 million in 1989).

Hartmarx's 485 retail apparel stores, which sell primarily Hartmarx clothes, include Wallach's on the East Coast, Silverwood's in California and Nevada, and Jas. K. Wilson in Texas. The company's retail stores produced 55% ($716 million, up from $699 million) of 1990 sales.

The company's performance has been hit by the retail recession of 1990 and 1991 and an expensive corporate restructuring that closed 4 factories and up to 65 retail outlets. Though the company had begun to rebound from the effects of increased prices for wool (driving men's suit prices up by 30%), it may be adversely affected by changes in the US work environment, which include more casual office wear and an increase in at-home workers.

WHEN

Harry Hart (21) and his brother Max (18), of Chicago, opened a men's clothing store, Harry Hart and Brother, in 1872. After Marcus Marx and Joseph Schaffner joined, the company became Hart Schaffner & Marx in 1887.

The young clothiers contracted with independent tailors to produce suits for their new store. Recognizing the potential of the whole-sale garment industry, they began selling to other merchants. In 1897 Hart Schaffner & Marx launched a national ad campaign in leading magazines and newspapers.

In 1910 a walkout by 17 young women protesting low wages and poor working conditions in one of the company's 48 tailoring shops sparked a citywide garment workers' strike. Schaffner and Harry Hart negotiated a settlement (not honored by the other major Chicago companies) in January 1911, and their employees returned to work.

In 1935 Hart Schaffner & Marx began adding to its domain with the purchase of Wallach Brothers, a New York men's clothing chain. Other purchases, including Hastings, a California clothier (1952); Hanny's in Arizona (1962); Hickey-Freeman, with stores in Chicago, New York, and Detroit (1964); and Field Brothers in New York, (1968), led to a 1970 antitrust decree ordering Hart Schaffner & Marx to sell 30 of its 238 men's clothing stores and, for 10 years, refrain from further purchases without court approval. Despite this restriction, the company made approved purchases, including 49% of Roberts SA, a Mexican clothing-store chain (sold in 1990). In 1982 it bought Kuppenheimer's, founded in 1876.

In 1983 Hart Schaffner & Marx became Hartmarx Corporation. A costly 1986 reorganization of the retail stores to automate; centralize buying; and consolidate credit, accounting, and distribution resulted in the termination of 800 employees. Earnings that year fell 42%. Later acquisitions included the Raleigh clothing stores (Washington, DC; 1988) and Biltwell (clothing manufacturer, Missouri, 1989) from ailing Interco.

After a brief recovery in 1987 and 1988, 1989 earnings declined to $17.4 million, a 54% drop from 1988. Hartmarx undertook further restructuring (costing $51 million) in 1990 to close unprofitable stores and other operations, reorganize its women's lines into a new marketing concept under the name Barrie Pace, and experiment with siting Kuppenheimer stores in Sears stores. In 1991 Hartmarx updated its upper-market men's lines by concluding agreements with Krizia (Italy) and Karl Lagerfeld (who also designs for Chanel) to design more fashionable clothes.

WHO

Chairman and CEO: Harvey A. Weinberg, age 53, $565,000 pay
President and COO: Elbert O. Hand, age 51, $494,000 pay
EVP and CFO: Jerome Dorf, age 54, $262,000 pay
VP, Secretary, and General Counsel: Carey M. Stein, age 43, $201,000 pay
VP Human Resources: Sherman D. Rosen, $197,000 pay
Auditors: Price Waterhouse
Employees: 22,000

WHERE

HQ: 101 N. Wacker Dr., Chicago, IL 60606
Phone: 312-372-6300
Fax: 312-444-2710

Hartmarx has manufacturing facilities in 16 states. Its 485 clothing stores, operating under 41 different names, are located throughout the US.

WHAT

	1990 Sales		1990 Operating Income	
	$ mil.	% of total	$ mil.	% of total
Wholesale apparel	580	45	28	—
Retail apparel	716	55	(72)	—
Adjustments	—	—	41	—
Total	**1,296**	**100**	**(3)**	**—**

Brand Names

Men's Clothing
Allyn St. George
Austin Reed of Regent Street
Bannister & Beale
Bobby Jones
Briar
Christian Dior Monsieur
Confezioni Riserva Luciano Franzoni
Escadrille
Gieves & Hawkes
Gleneagles
Graham and Gunn
Hart Schaffner & Marx
Henry Grethel
Hickey-Freeman
J. G. Hook
Jack Nicklaus
John Alexander
Johnny Carson
Kuppenheimer
Nino Cerruti Rue Royale
Pierre Cardin
Racquet Club–Wimbledon
Sansabelt
Society Brand, Ltd.

Women's Clothing
Country Suburbans
Lady Sansabelt
Sterling & Hunt Womenswear
Weathervane

RANKINGS

293rd in *Fortune* 500 Industrial Cos.

KEY COMPETITORS

Brown Group
Edison Brothers
The Gap
The Limited
Marks and Spencer
Liz Claiborne
Levi Strauss
V. F.
Department stores

HOW MUCH

	9-Year Growth	1981	1982	1983	1984	1985	1986	1987	1988	1989	1990
Sales ($ mil.)	5.3%	816	863	962	1,071	1,110	1,063	1,080	1,174	1,297	1,296
Net income ($ mil.)	—	27	32	38	42	43	25	41	38	17	(62)
Income as % of sales	—	3.4%	3.7%	3.9%	3.9%	3.8%	2.3%	3.8%	3.2%	1.3%	(4.8%)
Earnings per share ($)	—	1.40	1.68	1.91	2.09	2.10	1.20	2.01	2.03	0.89	(3.11)
Stock price – high ($)	—	10.72	18.11	24.17	21.83	26.42	32.00	34.75	29.75	28.13	19.88
Stock price – low ($)	—	6.22	8.06	14.56	15.67	18.67	23.50	18.25	20.75	18.75	5.50
Stock price – close ($)	(1.7%)	10.22	16.44	21.58	19.00	26.33	27.00	23.50	24.25	19.75	8.75
P/E – high	—	8	11	13	10	13	27	17	15	32	—
P/E – low	—	4	5	8	7	9	20	9	10	21	—
Dividends per share ($)	7.1%	0.48	0.54	0.61	0.75	0.85	0.90	0.98	1.08	1.18	0.90
Book value per share ($)	1.5%	12.72	13.51	14.80	16.24	17.60	17.59	18.26	19.21	18.37	14.60

1990 Year-end:
Debt ratio: 43.7%
Return on equity: —
Cash (mil.): $3
Current ratio: 2.38
Long-term debt (mil.): $227
No. of shares (mil.): 20
Dividends:
1990 average yield: 10.3%
1990 payout: —
Market value (mil.): $175

Stock Price History High/Low 1981–90

HARVARD UNIVERSITY

OVERVIEW

Harvard University is the oldest and one of the most prestigious institutions of higher education in the US. The private, coeducational school, located across the Charles River from Boston, consists of Harvard College (the men's undergraduate college), Radcliffe (the women's undergraduate college), and 10 graduate schools. Harvard's endowment of $4.7 billion is the nation's largest.

Only about 18% of freshmen applicants to Harvard are accepted. Beginning in the sophomore year, all students live in one of 13 campus houses, each a self-sufficient community.

Harvard's outstanding campus resources include a computer center with 200 computers; the university museums; and a library system (led by the Widener Library) with 11 million bound volumes, 3 million microforms, and 100,000 periodical subscriptions.

Harvard's alumni list reads like a *Who's Who of American History*, including such notable figures as John Adams, John Quincy Adams, T. S. Eliot, Ralph Waldo Emerson, John Hancock, Rutherford B. Hayes, Oliver Wendell Holmes, Helen Keller, John F. Kennedy, Increase Mather, Franklin D. Roosevelt, Theodore Roosevelt, and Gertrude Stein. Additionally, 33 Nobel laureates (2 in 1990) and 30 Pulitzer Prize winners have been associated with the university.

WHEN

In 1636 the General Court of Massachusetts appropriated £400 for the establishment of a college. The first building (Old College) was completed at Cambridge in 1639 and was named for John Harvard, who had willed his collection of about 400 books and half of his land to the school. Henry Dunster, a master of Old Testament languages, became the school's first president (and faculty) in 1640. The first freshman class consisted of 4 students.

During its first 150 years, Harvard adhered to the educational standards of European schools, with emphasis on classical literature and languages, logic, philosophy, and mathematics. Theology was studied only by graduate students (about half of Harvard's early graduates became ministers). The president and a small group of tutors (usually men who had just earned their BAs) taught all of the subjects. Harvard's early presidents included Increase Mather and John Leverett.

In 1721 Harvard established its first professorship (the Hollis Divinity Professorship), which was quickly followed by professorships in mathematics and natural philosophy. In 1780 Harvard became a university and in 1783 appointed its first professor of medicine.

Harvard went through a period of reform in the early 1800s after Edward Everett (a Greek literature professor) returned from studying abroad with reports of the modern teaching methods practiced at German universities. The school initiated an investigation and updated its curriculum. Harvard established a Divinity School in 1816, a Law School in 1817, and 2 schools of science in the 1840s.

In 1869 Charles W. Eliot became president of Harvard and engineered a period of growth that included the development of graduate programs in arts and sciences, engineering, and architecture. Eliot also raised the standards of the schools of medicine and law and laid the groundwork for the graduate School of Business Administration (there is no undergraduate business instruction at Harvard) and the School of Public Health. In addition, Eliot expanded the elective system to allow students to better design their own courses of study.

During the 20th century, Harvard's enrollment, faculty, and endowment grew tremendously. The Graduate School of Education opened in 1920 and, in 1930, the first undergraduate residential house. In the 1930s and 1940s the school established a scholarship program as well as a General Education curriculum for undergraduates.

Since then the school has continued to grow, with new buildings, expanded programs, and a concerted effort to increase library holdings. In 1979 Harvard introduced its new core curriculum. Neil Rudenstine took Derek Bok's place as Harvard's president in 1991 and will lead the school in its $2 billion fund drive.

Also in 1991 Harvard resolved a $135 million lawsuit against Merrill Lynch, who allegedly sold Harvard short-term securities without alerting the school to the risk of the investment. That same year a group of Harvard professors and Soviet economists jointly drafted a plan by which the Soviet Union could be converted to a market economy.

Private university
Fiscal year ends: June 30

WHO

President: Neil L. Rudenstine, age 56
VP Finance: Robert H. Scott
Treasurer: D. Robert Daniel

WHERE

HQ: 1350 Massachusetts Ave., Cambridge, MA 02138
Phone: 617-495-1000
Fax: 617-495-0754

Harvard University is located on more than 380 acres in Cambridge, Massachusetts.

Geographic Distribution of Freshman Class	% of total
Mid-Atlantic	29
New England	21
Pacific	14
South	15
Middle Western	9
Mountain	3
Central	2
Foreign	7
Total	**100**

WHAT

	1990 Revenues ($1,026 mil.)
	% of total
Tuition & fees	31
Research	25
Endowment	20
Gifts	11
Other	13
Total	**100**

Academic Unit	1990 Enrollment	% of Total
Harvard/Radcliffe	6,622	36
Graduate School of Arts and Sciences	3,237	18
Divinity School	484	3
Medical School	670	4
Dental School	158	1
School of Public Health	554	3
Law School	1,755	9
School of Design	482	2
School of Education	1,233	7
Kennedy School of Govt.	717	4
Business School	1,654	9
Extension	717	4
Adjustments	(104)	—
Total	**18,179**	**100**

Affiliated Institutions
Arnold Arboretum
Beth Israel Hospital
Center for Hellenic Studies
Children's Hospital
Dana-Farber Cancer Institute
Dumbarton Oaks Research Library
Harvard Art Museums
Harvard College Observatory
Harvard Forest
Harvard University Museums of Natural History
Harvard-Yenching Institute
John F. Kennedy School of Government
Joslin Diabetes Center
Loeb Drama Center
Semitic Museum
Villa I Tatti (Florence, Italy)

KEY COMPETITORS

Ohio State
Stanford
University of Chicago
University of Texas

HOW MUCH

	9-Year Growth	1981	1982	1983	1984	1985	1986	1987	1988	1989	1990
Enrollment	1.4%	16,053	16,027	16,566	16,781	16,871	17,298	17,419	17,454	17,762	18,179
Tuition ($)	10.3%	6,000	6,930	8,195	9,035	9,800	10,590	11,390	12,015	12,715	14,450
Endowment market value ($ mil.)	13.5%	1,491	1,622	1,617	2,037	2,187	2,694	3,435	4,018	4,155	4,651

Annual Tuition ($) 1981–90

HASBRO, INC.

OVERVIEW

Hasbro is the largest and most profitable toy company in the world. The company produces a wide array of toys, games, puzzles, and infant products under such recognized names as Hasbro, Milton Bradley, Tonka, and Playskool. Toys "R" Us was the company's largest customer with 14% of sales.

Hasbro's toy line includes G.I. Joe (14% of 1989 sales), My Little Pony, and Cabbage Patch Kids. Despite the strength of its existing toy line, the company continually emphasizes new product development. In 1990 Hasbro spent 4% of revenue on R&D.

The company's Milton Bradley division produces a broad line of board games, including Scrabble, Scattergories, and Battleship. Playskool's toy line produces toys for preschool children, including such childhood standards as Lincoln Logs, Mr. Potato Head, and Raggedy Ann and Andy. The Playskool Baby line produces pacifiers, infant health care products, toys, and infant apparel.

The Hassenfeld family still controls about 10% of Hasbro, while an additional 17.7% is controlled by Time Warner. Through the Hasbro Charitable Trust and the Hasbro Children's Foundation, the company maintains a generous policy of philanthropy aimed primarily at children.

WHEN

In 1923 Henry and Hillel Hassenfeld formed Hassenfeld Brothers in Pawtucket, Rhode Island, to distribute fabric remnants. By 1926 the company was manufacturing fabric-covered pencil boxes and shortly thereafter was making the pencils themselves.

Hassenfeld Brothers branched into the toy industry during the 1940s by introducing toy nurse and doctor kits. The company's toy division was the first to use TV to promote a toy product (Mr. Potato Head) in 1952.

The company continued to expand both its toy and pencil businesses. In the mid-1960s the company introduced G.I. Joe (an action doll for boys), which quickly became its primary toy line. Hassenfeld Brothers went public in 1968 and changed its name to Hasbro Industries. In 1969 Hasbro bought Romper Room (TV productions).

During the 1970s the toy and pencil divisions, managed by different members of the family, were in conflict over the company's finances, future direction, and leadership. The dispute caused the company (and the shareholders) to split in 1980. The toy division continued to operate under the Hasbro name; the pencil division (Empire Pencil Corporation in Shelbyville, Tennessee), led by Harold Hassenfeld, became a separate corporation.

Hasbro expanded rapidly in the 1980s under new CEO Stephen Hassenfeld, one of the 3rd generation of family members to run the company. Hassenfeld reduced the number of products by 1/3 to concentrate on developing a stable line of toys aimed at specific markets.

During the 1980s Hasbro released a number of successful toys, including G.I. Joe (a newer and smaller version of the original, 1982), My Little Pony (a horse with brushable hair, 1983), and Transformers (small vehicles that "transform" into robots, 1984).

In 1983 Hasbro acquired from Warner Bros. much of the inventory of Knickerbocker (plush toys). In 1984 the company bought Milton Bradley, a major producer of board games (Chutes and Ladders, Candy Land), puzzles, and preschool toys (Playskool). By the mid-1980s Hasbro had passed Mattel as the world's #1 toymaker. In 1989 the company acquired certain items from Coleco (which went bankrupt in 1988), including Cabbage Patch Kids, Scrabble, and Parcheesi (board games). After Stephen Hassenfeld died in 1989, his brother Alan became CEO.

In 1991 Hasbro purchased financially ailing Tonka for $486 million. The acquisition brought the company such famous toy names as Play-Doh, Monopoly, and Nerf.

ASE symbol: HAS
Fiscal year ends: Last Sunday in December

Hoover's Rating **A**

WHO

Chairman, President, and CEO: Alan G. Hassenfeld, age 42, $1,147,500 pay
COO Domestic Toy Operations: Alfred J. Verrecchia, Jr., age 48, $518,519 pay
COO Games and International: George R. Ditomassi, Jr., age 56, $475,000 pay
VC: Barry J. Alperin, age 50, $478,952 pay
EVP and CFO: John T. O'Neill, age 46, $387,112 pay
SVP Human Resources: Christopher P. Dona, age 40
Auditors: KPMG Peat Marwick
Employees: 7,700

WHERE

HQ: 1027 Newport Ave., Pawtucket, RI 02862-1059
Phone: 401-431-8697
Fax: 401-727-5433

Hasbro has operations in 15 countries.

	1990 Sales		1990 Operating Income	
	$ mil.	% of total	$ mil.	% of total
US	939	62	63	40
Foreign	581	38	97	60
Total	**1,520**	**100**	**160**	**100**

WHAT

Brand Names

Toys	Games
Baby Uh-Oh	Battleship
Baby Wanna Walk	Candy Land
Big Ben puzzles	Chutes and Ladders
Busy Beads	Connect Four
Busy Toddler Playhouse	Crocodile Dentist
Cabbage Patch Kids	Guesstures
Dolly Surprise	HeroQuest
G.I. Joe	Hungry Hungry Hippos
Gloworm	Life
Go Go My Walking Pup	Monopoly
Go-Go Gears	Mousetrap
Lincoln Logs	Nintendo games
Lite Bright	Operation
Little Walker	Parcheesi
Mr. Potato Head	A Question of Scruples
Musical Dream Screen	Scattergories
My Buddy	Scrabble
My Little Pony	Taboo
Nerf	Trouble
New Kids on the Block dolls	Twister
Play-Doh	Win, Lose or Draw
Pretty Mermaids dolls	Yahtzee
Raggedy Ann and Andy	
Record Breakers	**Infant Products**
Scribble Stix	Hugger
Sounds Around	Pur
Tiny Toons plush dolls	Scooties
Tonka Trucks	Tommee Tippee
Transformers	
WWF Action Figures	

RANKINGS

260th in *Fortune* 500 Industrial Cos.
443rd in *Business Week* 1000

KEY COMPETITORS

Atari	Mattel	Rubbermaid
Avon	Premark	Nintendo
Gerber		

HOW MUCH

	9-Year Growth	1981	1982	1983	1984	1985	1986	1987	1988	1989	1990
Sales ($ mil.)	34.5%	106	136	224	719	1,233	1,345	1,345	1,358	1,410	1,520
Net income ($ mil.)	39.7%	4	7	15	52	99	99	48	72	92	89
Income as % of sales	—	4.2%	5.2%	6.8%	7.3%	8.0%	7.4%	3.6%	5.3%	6.5%	5.9%
Earnings per share ($)	27.1%	0.18	0.28	0.48	1.27	1.78	1.70	0.82	1.24	1.56	1.54
Stock price – high ($)	—	1.01	2.76	5.63	12.45	19.75	30.88	26.50	17.00	24.38	21.50
Stock price – low ($)	—	0.46	0.76	2.12	4.60	10.93	16.56	10.00	12.00	15.25	11.25
Stock price – close ($)	38.4%	0.84	2.16	5.40	10.85	17.38	19.50	13.25	15.63	18.75	15.63
P/E – high	—	6	10	12	10	11	18	32	14	16	14
P/E – low	—	3	3	4	4	6	10	12	10	10	7
Dividends per share ($)	36.8%	0.01	0.02	0.04	0.05	0.08	0.08	0.09	0.11	0.15	0.19
Book value per share ($)	33.7%	1.12	1.37	2.27	6.21	8.59	10.95	12.07	13.19	13.67	15.36

1990 Year-end:
Debt ratio: 6.2%
Return on equity: 10.6%
Cash (mil.): $289
Current ratio: 2.41
Long-term debt (mil.): $57
No. of shares (mil.): 57
Dividends:
  1990 average yield: 1.2%
  1990 payout: 12.3%
Market value (mil.): $883

Stock Price History High/Low 1981–90

THE HEARST CORPORATION

OVERVIEW

The privately held Hearst Corporation (100% owned by the William Randolph Hearst Trust) is a diversified media company engaged in publishing, broadcasting, and cable TV programming activities. With such titles as *Good Housekeeping* and *Cosmopolitan*, Hearst ranks 2nd to Time Warner in US magazine revenue. Hearst Magazines president D. Claeys Bahrenburg recently presided over an editorial staff shakeup intended to enliven the unit's publications. The company is considering copublishing a monthly business magazine with Dow Jones.

Hearst's newspapers, including the *San Francisco Examiner* and the *Houston*

Chronicle, place it 10th in US newspaper revenue. Hearst's King Features Syndicate provides newspapers with such comic strips as "Blondie" and "Wizard of Id," as well as regular columns. Books are published under imprints including Avon and William Morrow.

Broadcast and entertainment properties include 6 network affiliate TV stations, 7 radio stations, and minority stakes in the Arts & Entertainment, Lifetime, and ESPN cable TV networks. Hearst is the leading producer of made-for-TV movies. The company is increasing its emphasis on international expansion of its video programming business as well as its magazine and book publishing activities.

Private company
Fiscal year ends: December 31

WHO

Chairman: Randolph A. Hearst, age 76
Chairman, Executive Committee: William R. Hearst, Jr., age 83
President and CEO: Frank A. Bennack, Jr., age 58
EVP and COO: Gilbert C. Maurer, age 63
VP: George R. Hearst, Jr., age 64
VP and Controller: Peter J. DeMaria, age 52
VP and Treasurer: Edwin A. Lewis, age 49
VP and Director Human Resources: Kenneth A. Feldman
Employees: 14,000

WHERE

HQ: 959 Eighth Ave., New York, NY 10019
Phone: 212-649-2000
Fax: 212-765-3528 (Corporate Communications)

Hearst products are available throughout the US and in more than 80 countries.

WHEN

William Randolph Hearst, son of a wealthy California mining magnate, began his career when he became editor of the family-owned *San Francisco Examiner* in 1887. The sensationalist style Hearst brought to the paper transformed it into a financial success. In 1895 he bought the *New York Morning Journal* and competed against the *New York World*, owned by Joseph Pulitzer, Hearst's first employer (Hearst worked as a reporter after being expelled from Harvard for playing jokes on his professors in 1884). The "yellow journalism" resulting from the rivalry of the 2 papers characterized American journalism at the turn of the century. Hearst was accused by some of causing the Spanish-American War in 1896 when he reportedly cabled artist Frederic Remington in Cuba, saying, "You furnish the pictures, and I'll furnish the war."

The growth of the Hearst empire continued with the establishment of 7 more daily papers by 1920. Hearst editorials initially supported public education, public ownership of utilities, and labor unions, but later became known for communist-baiting and ultranationalism. In 1935 Hearst was at its peak with nearly 14% of total US daily and 24% of Sunday circulation, with newspapers in 19 cities; the largest syndicate (King Features); international news and photo services; 13 magazines; 8 radio stations; and 2 motion picture companies. Two years later the company began selling movie compa-

nies, radio stations, and magazines to lessen its large debt.

When Hearst died in 1951, 1/3 of the company and all of the voting rights were left in trust for his heirs, and the rest was left to charity. Hearst had lived in style in San Simeon, his California estate, and had bought, among many other things, Tibetan yaks, Egyptian mummies, a Spanish abbey, and a castle in Wales. The controversial businessman inspired the famous 1941 Orson Welles film, *Citizen Kane*.

During the 1950s and early 1960s, Richard Berlin, in charge of the company since 1940, sold many failing papers and merged others to improve finances. Hearst's major magazines included *Good Housekeeping*, *Cosmopolitan*, and *Popular Mechanics*.

Hearst has undergone a period of growth under Frank Bennack, Jr., president and CEO since 1979. Additions have included several publishing companies, notably William Morrow (1981); new magazines, including *Country Living* (1978), *Redbook* (1982), and *Esquire* (1986); TV stations KMBC in Kansas City (1982) and WCVB in Boston (1986); and 20% of cable sports network ESPN (1990). In the 1980s Hearst partnerships launched the Lifetime and Arts & Entertainment cable channels. Hearst closed the Los Angeles *Herald Examiner* in 1989 and sold its cable TV systems in 1990.

WHAT

	1990 Sales	
	$ mil.	% of total
Newspapers	715	33
Magazines	1,022	48
Broadcasting	290	14
Other	111	5
Total	**2,138**	**100**

Major US Magazines
Connoisseur
Cosmopolitan
Country Living
Esquire
Good Housekeeping
Harper's Bazaar
House Beautiful
Popular Mechanics
Redbook
Town & Country

Major Newspapers
Houston Chronicle
San Antonio Light
San Francisco Examiner
Seattle Post-Intelligencer

Broadcasting
KMBC-TV, Kansas City, MO
WAPA (AM), San Juan, PR
WBAL (AM), Baltimore
WBAL-TV, Baltimore
WCVB-TV, Boston
WDTN-TV, Dayton, OH
WHTX (FM), Pittsburgh
WISN (AM), Milwaukee
WISN-TV, Milwaukee
WIYY (FM), Baltimore
WLTQ (FM), Milwaukee
WTAE (AM), Pittsburgh
WTAE-TV, Pittsburgh

Book Publishing
Avon Books
Hearst
William Morrow

Business Publishing
American Druggist
Black Book series (auto guides)
Motor Magazine

Entertainment/ Syndication
Arts & Entertainment Cable Network (38%)
Cowles Syndicate
ESPN (20%)
Hearst Entertainment Productions
King Features Syndicate
Lifetime Television (33 1/3%)
North America Syndicate

Other
Down East Timberlands
First DataBank (drug database)
Eastern News Distributors
Hearst Realties
Sunical Land & Livestock Division

HOW MUCH

	9-Year Growth	1981	1982	1983	1984	1985	1986	1987	1988	1989	1990
Sales ($ mil.)	6.6%	1,200	1,300	1,116	1,400	1,540	1,529	1,886	1,986	2,094	2,138
Newspaper revenue ($ mil.)	—	—	—	—	—	—	390	650	689	700	715
Magazine revenue ($ mil.)	—	—	—	—	—	—	780	873	919	992	1,022
Broadcast revenue ($ mil.)	—	—	—	—	—	—	280	262	263	270	290
Cable TV revenue ($ mil.)	—	—	—	—	—	—	9	11	15	21	—
Other media revenue ($ mil.)	—	—	—	—	—	—	70	90	100	111	111

Total Sales ($ mil.) 1981–90

RANKINGS

59th in *Forbes* 400 US Private Cos.

KEY COMPETITORS

Advance Publications	Hachette	Reed
Bertelsmann	Knight-Ridder	E.W. Scripps
Blockbuster	McGraw-Hill	TCI
Capital Cities/ABC	New York Times	Time Warner
CBS	News Corp.	Times Mirror
Cox	Paramount	Tribune
Gannett	Reader's Digest	Washington Post

H. J. HEINZ COMPANY

OVERVIEW

With over 3,000 products, Pittsburgh-based H. J. Heinz is one of the world's leading food processing companies. Heinz's products include ketchup, tuna, pet food, baby food, frozen potato products, soup, low-calorie frozen meals, beans, sauces and condiments, pickles, vinegar, rice cakes, and corn derivatives. Fifty-six percent of Heinz's global sales comes from products that hold the #1 brand position in their respective markets.

Heinz ketchup (the company's flagship brand) holds more than 50% of the US market. The company is the market leader in frozen entrees (Weight Watchers), canned cat food (9-Lives), and relish. Other market leaders include frozen potatoes (Ore-Ida) and "dolphin safe" tuna (Star-Kist; now has 36% market share).

In addition to domestic leadership, Heinz's products command a strong presence overseas and are sold in over 200 countries. About 42% of Heinz's sales come from foreign operations.

The company (a significant portion of which is still owned by the Heinz family) has successfully maintained a reputation for high-quality products, good management, and generous social philanthropy. In 1990 Heinz CEO Anthony O'Reilly was named *Chief Executive* magazine's CEO of the Year.

NYSE symbol: HNZ
Fiscal year ends: Wednesday nearest April 30

Hoover's Rating **A**

WHO

Chairman, President, and CEO: Anthony J. F. O'Reilly, age 55, $2,756,545 pay
VC and SVP; Chairman, Star-Kist: Joseph J. Bogdanovich, age 79, $1,169,411 pay
SVP Corporate Development and CFO: R. Derek Finlay, age 59, $964,616 pay
VP Organization Development and Administration: George C. Greer
Auditors: Coopers & Lybrand
Employees: 37,300

WHERE

HQ: 600 Grant St., Pittsburgh, PA 15219
Phone: 412-456-5700
Fax: 412-237-5377 (Public Relations)

Heinz operates 75 food processing plants in 17 countries.

	1990 Sales		1990 Operating Income	
	$ mil.	% of total	$ mil.	% of total
US	3,863	58	542	52
UK	939	14	187	18
Continental Europe	976	15	183	18
Canada and other	869	13	125	12
Total	**6,647**	**100**	**1,037**	**100**

WHAT

Brand Names

Sauces and Condiments
57 Sauce
Heinz barbecue sauce
Heinz ketchup
Heinz pickles
Heinz relish
Heinz tartar sauce
Heinz vinegar
HomeStyle Gravy

Ore-Ida
Orlando (tomato products)
Petit Navire (fish)
Plasmon (baby food)
Scaramellini (candy)
Sperlari (candy)
Star-Kist
Steak-umm
Weight Watchers

Food and Beverages
Alba (beverage mixes)
Chico-San (rice cakes)
Dieterba (baby food)
Guloso (tomato products)
Heinz baby food
Heinz soups
Marie Elisabeth (sardines)
Misura (dietetic products)
Near East (flavored rice)
Nipiol (baby food)

Pet Food
Amore
Jerky Treats
Kozy Kitten
Meaty Bones
9-Lives
Recipe
Reward
Skippy Premium
Vets

WHEN

In 1852 8-year-old Henry J. Heinz started selling produce from the family garden to his neighbors in Sharpsburg, Pennsylvania. In 1869 Heinz formed a partnership with his friend L. C. Noble to bottle horseradish sauce. The business went bankrupt in 1875.

With the help of his brother John and his cousin Frederick, Heinz created F. & J. Heinz the following year. At his new company Heinz developed tomato ketchup (1876) and sweet pickles (1880). He gained financial control of the firm in 1888 and changed the name to the H. J. Heinz Company.

Heinz developed a reputation as an advertising and marketing genius. At the 1893 World's Fair in Chicago, he had the largest exhibit. Three years later he coined his "57 Varieties" slogan. In 1900 Heinz raised New York City's first large electric sign (a 40-foot green pickle) as an advertising gimmick.

By 1905 Heinz was manufacturing his food products in England. In America his Pittsburgh plants (complete with an indoor gym, swimming pool, hospital, and 3-story stable) became known as a "utopia for working men." While most of the food industry was opposed to the Pure Food Act in 1906, Heinz sent his son to Washington to campaign for the legislation. During the entire time that Heinz controlled his company, there was never a strike at his plants. Following the death of H. J. Heinz in 1919, the company, under the direction of Heinz's son and later his grandson (whose son, H. J. Heinz III, was a US senator until his tragic death in a plane crash in 1991), continued to rely on its traditional product line for the next 4 decades. In 1969 R. Burt Gookin became CEO of the company (the first person not a member of the Heinz family to hold the position).

During the 1960s the company started a program of acquisition that would eventually include Star-Kist (1963), Ore-Ida (1965), Tuffy's (pet food, 1971), Weight Watchers (weight reduction programs and products, 1978), and Chico-San (rice cakes, 1984).

Irishman Anthony J. F. O'Reilly became CEO in 1979 and focused the company's strategy around international expansion, particularly in Europe. Heinz also established facilities in such developing countries as Zimbabwe, China, and Thailand.

In 1991 the company sold its Hubinger (corn milling) unit to French company Roquette Freres and bought Greek tomato processor Copais Canning. That same year Heinz acquired the JL Foods division of Canadian brewer John Labatt for $500 million.

RANKINGS

87th in *Fortune* 500 Industrial Cos.
55th in *Business Week* 1000

KEY COMPETITORS

Allied-Lyons
BSN
Campbell Soup
Clorox
Colgate-Palmolive
CPC
General Mills
Gerber
Grand Metropolitan

Hershey
Kellogg
Mars
Nestlé
Philip Morris
Quaker Oats
Ralston Purina
RJR Nabisco
Sandoz

HOW MUCH

Fiscal year ends April of following year	9-Year Growth	1981	1982	1983	1984	1985	1986	1987	1988	1989	1990
Sales ($ mil.)	6.8%	3,689	3,738	3,954	4,048	4,366	4,639	5,244	5,801	6,086	6,647
Net income ($ mil.)	12.8%	193	214	238	266	302	339	386	440	504	568
Income as % of sales	—	5.2%	5.7%	6.0%	6.6%	6.9%	7.3%	7.4%	7.6%	8.3%	8.5%
Earnings per share ($)	13.8%	0.67	0.74	0.83	0.96	1.09	1.23	1.45	1.65	1.88	2.13
Stock price – high ($)	—	4.96	6.92	9.50	11.25	17.13	24.13	25.88	25.00	35.88	37.00
Stock price – low ($)	—	3.81	4.17	6.00	8.00	10.25	14.63	16.75	18.75	22.50	27.50
Stock price – close ($)	25.0%	4.67	6.73	9.50	10.75	16.19	20.25	20.19	23.38	35.00	34.88
P/E – high	—	7	9	11	12	16	20	18	15	19	17
P/E – low	—	6	6	7	8	9	12	12	11	12	13
Dividends per share ($)	16.6%	0.23	0.27	0.34	0.39	0.44	0.50	0.61	0.70	0.81	0.93
Book value per share ($)	10.3%	3.62	3.97	4.11	4.50	5.09	5.41	6.24	6.91	7.44	8.77

1990 Year-end:
Debt ratio: 24.0%
Return on equity: 26.3%
Cash (mil.): $314
Current ratio: 1.48
Long-term debt (mil.): $717
No. of shares (mil.): 259
Dividends:
 1990 average yield: 2.7%
 1990 payout: 43.7%
Market value (mil.): $9,048

Stock Price History High/Low 1981–90

HELMSLEY ENTERPRISES INC.

OVERVIEW

Helmsley is a holding company for real estate, hotel, shopping center, and related enterprises, valued at $5 billion. The privately held company is owned by Harry and Leona Helmsley. Most of its properties are located in Manhattan; the Helmsley-Spear commercial brokerage is the largest in New York City. Harry owns the deeds to 40 acres of Manhattan land.

In addition to owning properties, Helmsley-Spear and Helmsley-Noyes manage over 600 office and apartment buildings in New York, Florida, Texas, California, and elsewhere, in most of which Harry Helmsley has an interest. Of these, the best known is the Empire State Building. Helmsley's holdings are estimated at more than $4 billion.

Helmsley Hotels operates 6 luxury hotels, including the Helmsley Palace, in New York City, and the Harley Hotels. Although some Harleys have been sold recently, the chain still operates 17 hotels in 10 states. Subsidiaries include Deco Purchasing, the purchasing arm for Helmsley Hotels, and Owners Maintenance, a cleaning services company that holds contracts with many Helmsley properties.

Declining property values in the recession-plagued New York City property market and the notoriety stemming from Leona Helmsley's conviction on income tax evasion charges in 1989 have not helped the company in recent years.

WHEN

Harry Helmsley began his career as a Manhattan rent collector in 1925. Rent collecting, then handled in person, gave Harry contact with building owners and an ability to evaluate a building. When the real estate market crashed in 1929, Harry obtained property at bargain prices. He paid $1,000 down for a building with a $100,000 mortgage and has quipped that he did so to provide employment for his father, whom he hired as superintendent. In 1946 he sold the building for $165,000.

In 1949 Harry teamed up with his lawyer Lawrence Wien. Helmsley located property; Wien found financing. The deal they made on the Empire State Building, purchased in 1961 after 3 years of negotiation, is typical of their tactics. They bought the building for $65 million and sold it to Prudential for $29 million, obtaining a 114-year leaseback. A public offering for the newly created Empire State Building Company made up the difference, and both men received stock for their efforts.

During the 1950s Harry bought into many noteworthy office buildings, including the Flatiron (1951), Berkeley (1953), and Equitable (1957). He bought the property management firm of Leon Spear in 1955. In the mid-1960s he began developing properties, beginning with a 52-story office tower on Broadway. By 1967 Harry was investing in shopping centers. In 1969 he bought the trust of Furman and Wolfson, which held about 30 buildings nationwide, for $165 million. To finance the trust, Harry borrowed $78 million in cash on his reputation — the largest unsecured signature loan ever.

Harry's association with Spear precipitated a meeting with successful real estate broker Leona Roberts, from whom Spear had purchased an apartment. Spear arranged for them to meet (1969); Helmsley hired Leona, promoted her to SVP, and later divorced his wife to marry her (1971).

Harry became interested in hotels in the 1970s, although the Manhattan market for luxury hotels was considered saturated. In 1974 he leased a historical building (now called the Helmsley Palace) from the Catholic church and began renovation; the Palace opened in 1980. Leona's extravagance cost Harry millions on the venture. Beginning in 1979 Harry invested in Florida, first building Miami Palace and, in a later project that went bankrupt, Helmsley Center.

During the 1980s Harry's empire began to crumble as Leona gained control. Numerous lawsuits, lackadaisical bookkeeping, shoddy building maintenance (a ceiling collapsed at the Helmsley Windsor, killing a guest), and extravagant spending culminated in indictments for tax evasion. Harry was declared mentally incompetent to stand trial, but in August 1989 Leona was convicted, fined $7.1 million, and sentenced to 4 years in jail.

In 1990 the Helmsleys sold their Helmsley-Greenfield subsidiary and also put the Brown, Harris, Stevens brokerage — where Leona is still listed as a broker — up for sale. In 1991 the limited partners of the Helmsley Palace filed suit to remove the Helmsleys from control of the hotel.

Private company

WHO

President: Harry Helmsley, age 81
President, Helmsley Hotels: Leona Helmsley, age 71
SVP: William Lubliner
VP and Assistant Secretary: Alvin Schwartz, age 70
VP and Assistant Secretary: Irving Schneider, age 72
Treasurer: Martin S. Stone
Employees: 13,000

WHERE

HQ: 60 E. 42nd St., New York, NY 10165
Phone: 212-687-6400
Fax: 212-687-6437

Helmsley operates primarily in Manhattan but has holdings elsewhere in New York and in California, Florida, Illinois, and Texas.

WHAT

Real Estate Management and Sales
Basic Estates Inc.
Brown, Harris, Stevens, Inc.
California Jewelry Mart Realty Corp.
Charles F. Noyes Co. Inc.
Fifth-Central Park Corp.
Garden Bay Manor Associates
H 33 Manor Corp.
H 321 Cloister Corp.
Helmsley-Noyes Co., Inc.
Helmsley-Spear Conversion Sales
Helmsley Spear Hospitality Services
Helmsley-Spear, Inc.
Investment Properties Associates
John J. Reynolds, Inc.
National Realty Corp.
Parkmerced Corp.
77 Park Inc.
6th & 55th Corp.
36 Central Park South Corp.
Willoughby Properties Inc.
York East Realty Corp.
York East Willoughby Properties Inc.

Hotels
Boardwalk & Missouri Corp.
Carlton House Hotel
Harley Hotels, Inc.
Helmsley Hotels, Inc. (The Helmsley Palace)
Hospitality Motor Inns (96.8%)
Moritz Inc. (Hotel St. Moritz)
Park Lane Hotel, Inc.

Other
Deco Purchasing Co. (purchasing agent)
Owners Maintenance Corp. (janitorial services)
Supervisory Management Corp. (management and public relations)

RANKINGS

92nd in *Forbes* 400 US Private Cos.

KEY COMPETITORS

Accor	Hilton	Metromedia
Bass	Hyatt	Nestlé
Canadian Pacific	ITT	Rank
Carlson	Loews	Trammell
Edward	Marriott	Crow
J. DeBartolo		

HOW MUCH

	5 Yr. Growth	1981	1982	1983	1984	1985	1986	1987	1988	1989	1990
Estimated sales ($ mil.)	8.2%	—	—	—	—	1,000	1,000	1,700	1,430	1,400	1,480
Employees	5.4%	—	—	—	—	10,000	13,000	13,000	13,000	13,000	13,000

Est. Sales ($ mil.) 1985–90

THE HENLEY GROUP, INC.

NYSE symbol: HENG
Fiscal year ends: December 31

OVERVIEW

Originally established as a vehicle for CEO Michael Dingman to make money for shareholders through "perpetual liquidation" of purchased assets, Henley has altered its strategy, cancelling plans for spinoffs. Instead the company has focused on operating its principal units, Fisher Scientific and Pneumo Abex.

Henley plans to raise cash through a public offering of Fisher, a growing laboratory instrument manufacturer. Henley has used the proceeds from recent asset sales to lower debt, sometimes by buying Pneumo Abex bonds at prices far below face value. Sales are declining

at debt-laden Pneumo Abex, a manufacturer of aerospace components and braking materials.

Relics of past deals remain on Henley's balance sheet. The company owns a small stake in New Zealand's Fletcher Challenge, received when it sold Cape Horn Methanol in 1991, as well as warrants and payment-in-kind debentures issued by Henley Properties. Itel has an option to buy Henley's holdings of Itel shares. Libra Invest & Trade, a Swiss firm controlled by Lebanese interests with ties to Dingman, owns 30.1% of Henley.

WHEN

In 1986 Allied-Signal spun off The Henley Group, a collection of 35 companies dubbed "Dingman's dogs" after the Allied-Signal president who quit to run the new company. Henley's initial public stock offering of $1.28 billion was the largest in US history. Soon after the stock was issued, Henley completed the purchase of Imed (medical supplies) for $163 million. Henley has been an active trader in companies ever since.

Henley's 1986 asset sales included its 10% of Mack Truck and 49% of its Wyoming soda ash unit. During that year Henley arranged a $3 billion revolving credit agreement with a consortium of 21 banks and bought Allied-Signal's remaining 15.6% share in Henley.

During 1987 Henley pursued Santa Fe Southern Pacific, offering almost $10 billion. Henley purchased 16.9% of Santa Fe stock before giving up in 1988 and selling its interests in Santa Fe, along with its wholly owned Signal Capital and Equilease (railcars), to Itel for cash and 18.7 million shares (40%) of Itel common stock. Also in 1987 Henley sold M. W. Kellogg Company (oil industry construction) to Dresser Industries, sold 17% of Wheelabrator Technologies stock to the public, and spun off Henley Manufacturing in a stock distribution to shareholders, with Henley retaining 55% ownership.

In 1988 the company was divided into The Wheelabrator Group, which owned 60% of Wheelabrator Technologies, and The Henley Group in a spinoff of 19 million shares of new stock. The old Henley Group was renamed The Wheelabrator Group, and stock in the newly formed Henley Group was distributed to owners of old Henley. The new Henley Group owned 12% of The Wheelabrator Group, 81% of Fisher Group (medical and laboratory supplies), 100% of Signal Landmark Holdings (real estate), 82% of Cape Horn Methanol, 40% of Itel, and 50% of PA Holdings. PA Holdings, jointly owned by Henley and Wasserstein Perella, bought Pneumo Abex (aerospace and defense) for $1.3 billion.

In 1989 Henley bought the rest of Pneumo Abex and Fisher Group; the company's 55% interest in Henley Manufacturing was sold to New Hampshire Oak, a company owned by Henley CEO Michael Dingman and president Paul Montrone; and Henley spun off Henley Properties (real estate) to its stockholders. In 1990 Henley sold its Wheelabrator stake and began selling its Itel shares back to Itel. In 1991 Libra Invest & Trade offered $22 per share for Henley. Calling the bid inadequate, Henley looked, unsuccessfully, for higher offers. Later in the year Henley found buyers for its Instrument Labs (part of the Fisher Group) and Cape Horn Methanol units.

WHO

Chairman and CEO: Michael D. Dingman, age 59, $850,000 pay
President: Paul M. Montrone, age 49, $400,000 pay
CFO: Paul M. Meister, age 38
Director of Compensation and Benefits: William E. Coffey
Auditors: Deloitte & Touche
Employees: 10,300

WHERE

HQ: Liberty Ln., Hampton, NH 03842
Phone: 603-926-5911
Fax: 603-926-5661

At the end of 1990 Henley had 16 US and 4 foreign manufacturing facilities.

	1990 Sales		1990 Net Income	
	$ mil.	% of total	$ mil.	% of total
North America	1,531	80	(134)	—
Europe & other	385	20	33	—
Adjustments	(45)	—	—	—
Total	**1,871**	**100**	**(101)**	**—**

WHAT

	1990 Sales		1990 Operating Income	
	$ mil.	% of total	$ mil.	% of total
Laboratory & medical prods.	947	51	9	—
Aerospace	598	32	(72)	—
Industrial products	326	17	(43)	—
Adjustments	—	—	201	—
Total	**1,871**	**100**	**95**	**—**

Operating Units
Fisher Scientific
  Analytical instruments
  Educational materials
  Laboratory equipment and furniture
  Laboratory glassware and supplies
  Reagent solutions and chemicals
Pneumo Abex
  Abex Aerospace (pumps and motors)
  Abex Friction Products (brake products)
  Cleveland Pneumatic (landing gear)
  Jetway Systems (aircraft boarding bridges)
  NWL Control Systems (flight control systems)

Investments
Fletcher Challenge (2%)
Henley Properties (6.3%, debentures and warrants)
Itel (9%)

RANKINGS

224th in *Fortune* 500 Industrial Cos.
986th in *Business Week* 1000

KEY COMPETITORS

Allied-Signal	Robert Bosch
Baxter	Rockwell
Becton, Dickinson	Teledyne
Eaton	Thomson SA
Ingersoll-Rand	United Technologies
Litton Industries	

HOW MUCH

	5-Year Growth	1981	1982	1983	1984	1985	1986	1987	1988	1989	1990
Sales ($ mil.)	0.3%	—	—	—	—	1,845	3,172	3,516	1,036	1,566	1,871
Net income ($ mil.)	—	—	—	—	—	(65)	(426)	(278)	(271)	(207)	(101)
Income as % of sales	—	—	—	—	—	(3.5%)	(13.4%)	(7.9%)	(26.2%)	(13.2%)	(5.4%)
Earnings per share ($)	—	—	—	—	—	—	(23.69)	(12.76)	(14.76)	(10.45)	(5.13)
Stock price – high ($)	—	—	—	—	—	—	112.22	136.67	116.11	74.25	47.50
Stock price – low ($)	—	—	—	—	—	—	76.67	80.00	83.33	50.50	14.50
Stock price – close ($)	—	—	—	—	—	—	100.56	86.11	96.11	54.25	16.00
P/E – high	—	—	—	—	—	—	—	—	—	—	—
P/E – low	—	—	—	—	—	—	—	—	—	—	—
Dividends per share ($)	—	—	—	—	—	0.00	0.00	0.00	0.00	0.00	0.00
Book value per share ($)	—	—	—	—	—	—	119.71	89.35	77.43	55.64	56.69

1990 Year-end:
Debt ratio: 54.6%
Return on equity: —
Cash (mil.): $407
Current ratio: 2.39
Long-term debt (mil.): $1,346
No. of shares (mil.): 20
Dividends:
  1990 average yield: 0.0%
  1990 payout: 0.0%
Market value (mil.): $316

Stock Price History High/Low 1986–90

HERCULES INC.

OVERVIEW

Hercules is a worldwide supplier of specialty chemicals and engineered polymers (absorbent and textile products and packaging films). The Chemical Specialties segment is the company's sales leader, with 52% of sales. Hercules also makes resins used in rubber and plastics fabrication worldwide and markets fragrances and food gums. The company is a global leader in supplying chemicals to the papermaking industry.

Hercules manufactures polypropylene film, used in packaging consumer products. In the decorative fabrics and textiles market, Hercules is known for its Herculon olefin fiber.

The Aqualon Group manufactures water-soluble polymers, additives to foods and fluids. Hercules's Aerospace Group makes solid rocket motor systems for Trident II missiles and Titan IV and Delta II launch systems.

New CEO Thomas Gossage is stressing Hercules's core businesses, expecting improvement from 2 — Packaging Films and Resins — or they may be sold. In 1990 Hercules labored to divest itself of noncore businesses, ranging from a Minnesota yeast business to aircraft electronics. Gossage also wants to reduce Aerospace's role to 20% of the company's portfolio.

WHEN

A 1912 federal court decision forced Du Pont, which controlled 2/3 of US explosives production, to spin off 1/2 the business into 2 companies, Hercules Powder and Atlas Powder.

Hercules began operating explosives plants across the US in 1913. Russell Dunham, Hercules's first president, had expanded the company's operations by 1915 into Utah and Missouri. During WWI the company became the largest US producer of TNT, making 71 million pounds for the US military.

After WWI Hercules diversified into nonexplosive products, such as nitrocellulose for the manufacture of plastics, lacquers, and films. The 1920 purchase of Yaryan Rosin and Turpentine made Hercules the world's largest steam-distilled rosin and turpentine producer.

By the late 1920s the company's core business had changed from powders to chemicals, which would be its focus for the next 3 decades. Hercules expanded the marketing of its rosin products to dozens of industries, including the paper industry, the largest user. Hercules also became the largest US producer of nitrocellulose in 1930. In the 1940s the company developed water-soluble polymers.

In the early 1950s Hercules developed a new process for making phenol, used in plastics, paints, and pharmaceuticals. The company's explosives department made

important contributions in rocketry, developing propellants for Nike rockets and making motors for Minuteman and Polaris missiles.

By the late 1950s Hercules was making chemical propellants, petrochemical plastics, synthetic fibers, agricultural and paper chemicals, and food additives. In the 1960s and early 1970s the company, renamed Hercules Inc., in 1966, increased plastic resin and fabricated plastic production, opening 5 new plants.

Hercules also developed foreign markets, doubling export sales between 1962 and 1972. Following the energy crisis of the 1970s, CEO Alexander F. Giacco decided to reduce dependence on commodity petrochemicals and increase specialty chemical and defense-related rocket propulsion businesses. In 1987 it sold its interest in the polypropylene resins business (HIMONT) and in 1989 took full ownership of The Aqualon Group, which since 1987 had been a 50–50 joint venture with Henkel KGaA of West Germany.

In 1989 Hercules had a $96 million loss, taking a $323 million charge to cover cost overruns on Titan IV, Delta II, and SRAM missile contracts. Problems continued with the 1991 explosion of a Titan IV at its first test firing. Hercules stock plummeted, and the company took a $68 million pretax charge.

NYSE symbol: HPC
Fiscal year ends: December 31

Hoover's Rating **C**

WHO

Chairman and CEO: Thomas L. Gossage, age 56, $460,843 pay (prior to promotion)
President and COO: Fred L. Buckner, age 58, $497,562 pay
VP and Controller: George MacKenzie, age 41
VP Human Resources: Thomas V. McCarthy, age 46
Auditors: Coopers & Lybrand
Employees: 19,867

WHERE

HQ: Hercules Plaza, 1313 N. Market St., Wilmington, DE 19894
Phone: 302-594-5000
Fax: 302-594-5400

Hercules has nearly 100 production facilities worldwide, including subsidiaries and affiliates.

	1990 Sales		1990 Operating Income	
	$ mil.	% of total	$ mil.	% of total
US	2,310	72	69	36
Europe	710	22	106	55
Other countries	180	6	18	9
Adjustments	—	—	49	—
Total	**3,200**	**100**	**242**	**100**

WHAT

	1990 Sales		1990 Operating Income	
	$ mil.	% of total	$ mil.	% of total
Chemical Specialties	1,647	52	154	80
Aerospace	996	31	60	31
Materials	546	17	(24)	(12)
Other	11	—	3	1
Adjustments	—	—	49	—
Total	**3,200**	**100**	**242**	**100**

Chemical Specialties
Aroma chemicals
Citrus specialties
Coatings
Crosslinkers
Flavors and fragrances
Food gums
Paper chemicals
Resins
Water-soluble polymers

Materials
Carbon fiber
Composite structures
Electronics chemicals
Liquid molding resins
Photoresists
Polypropylene fibers
Polypropylene film
Printing plates

Aerospace
Electronic equipment
Smokeless powders
Solid propellant rocket motors

RANKINGS

147th in *Fortune* 500 Industrial Cos.
332nd in *Business Week* 1000

KEY COMPETITORS

Allied-Signal
American Cyanamid
BASF
Bayer
Dow Chemical
Du Pont
Elf Aquitaine
FMC
W. R. Grace
Hoechst
Imperial Chemical
IFF
Monsanto
Rhône-Poulenc
Roche
Thiokol
Union Carbide
Vulcan
Wrigley
Petrochemical companies

HOW MUCH

	9-Year Growth	1981	1982	1983	1984	1985	1986	1987	1988	1989	1990
Sales ($ mil.)	1.8%	2,718	2,469	2,629	2,571	2,587	2,615	2,693	2,802	3,092	3,200
Net income ($ mil.)	(3.8%)	136	87	174	197	133	227	821	120	(96)	96
Income as % of sales	—	5.0%	3.5%	6.6%	7.7%	5.1%	8.7%	30.5%	4.3%	(3.1%)	3.0%
Earnings per share ($)	(4.5%)	3.09	1.97	3.17	3.54	2.40	4.02	14.18	2.54	(2.09)	2.04
Stock price – high ($)	—	26.38	28.75	43.13	38.00	40.75	60.00	73.50	54.00	52.25	41.50
Stock price – low ($)	—	18.75	16.88	27.25	27.25	31.13	37.00	40.00	42.63	38.38	25.63
Stock price – close ($)	4.5%	22.63	27.63	35.75	33.88	39.38	50.63	47.00	44.50	39.00	33.63
P/E – high	—	9	15	14	11	17	15	5	21	—	20
P/E – low	—	6	9	9	8	13	9	3	17	—	13
Dividends per share ($)	6.6%	1.26	1.32	1.38	1.48	1.60	1.72	1.84	2.00	2.24	2.24
Book value per share ($)	5.9%	24.73	24.18	24.33	25.57	27.13	31.11	44.88	44.58	40.77	41.35

1990 Year-end:
Debt ratio: 23.6%
Return on equity: 5.0%
Cash (mil.): $225
Current ratio: 1.76
Long-term debt (mil.): $601
No. of shares (mil.): 47
Dividends:
1990 average yield: 6.7%
1990 payout: 109.8%
Market value (mil.): $1,579

Stock Price History
High/Low 1981–90

HERSHEY FOODS CORPORATION

NYSE symbol: HSY
Fiscal year ends: December 31

Hoover's Rating **A**

OVERVIEW

Based in the Pennsylvania town that shares its name, Hershey Foods is the #1 confectioner in North America (with a 36% market share) and the #2 pasta producer (after Borden).

The Hershey Chocolate U.S.A. division, the nation's largest chocolatier, makes more than 55 brands of confectionery products. This division also produces cocoa, chocolate chips, baking bars, syrup, and flavored drink mixes. The company's chocolate milk is produced by about 30 independent dairies in the US.

Hershey Pasta Group produces several regional pasta brands under such names as American Beauty, San Giorgio, Skinner, and Ronzoni.

Hershey Refrigerated Products sells ready-to-eat puddings in 4 candy bar flavors, the first product line to emerge from the company's effort to move into new areas.

Through its Hershey International division and numerous international joint ventures and licensing agreements, the company sells its products throughout the Far East and Latin America. The 1991 purchase of Gubor Schokoladen provided Hershey with its first European manufacturing facility.

WHO

Chairman and CEO: Richard A. Zimmerman, age 58, $770,000 pay
President and COO: Kenneth L. Wolfe, age 52, $620,000 pay
President, Hershey Chocolate U.S.A.: Joseph P. Viviano, age 52, $439,735 pay
SVP and CFO: Michael F. Pasquale, age 43, $324,744 pay
VP Human Resources: Sharon A. Lambly, age 50
Auditors: Arthur Andersen & Co.
Employees: 12,700

WHEN

Hershey is the legacy of Milton Hershey of Pennsylvania Dutch origin. Apprenticed in 1872 at age 15 to a candy maker, Hershey was a confectioner all his adult life and started Lancaster Caramel Company at age 30. During an 1893 visit to the Chicago Exposition, he noticed a new chocolate-making machine and, immediately interested, sold the caramel operations for $1 million in 1900 to start a chocolate factory.

The factory was completed in 1905 in Derry Church, Pennsylvania, renamed Hershey in 1906. In 1909 he founded the Milton Hershey School, an orphanage; in 1918 the company was donated to a trust and for years existed solely to fund the school. Although the company is now publicly traded, the school still retains majority stock control; former chairman William Dearden (1976–84) was a graduate, as are many Hershey employees.

Hershey pioneered mass-production techniques for chocolates and developed much of the machinery for making and packaging its products. At one time the company supplied its own sugar cane from Cuba and enlarged the world's almond supply 6 times over through nut farm ownership. The Hershey bar has become Americana and is so universally recognized that it was used overseas during WWII as currency.

Concerned more with benevolence than profits, Hershey put people to work during the Great Depression building a hotel, golf courses, a library, theaters, a museum, a stadium, and other facilities in Hershey.

One of Hershey's peculiarities was that he refused to advertise, believing quality would speak for itself. Even after his death in 1945, the company continued his policy. Then, in 1970, facing a sluggish candy market after failing to recognize a more diet-conscious public, Hershey lost share to Mars, and management relented.

In the 1970s Hershey embarked on a diversification path to stabilize the effects of changing commodity prices. It brought out Big Block (large-sized) bars (1980), bought the Friendly Ice Cream chain (1979, sold in 1988), and ventured into pasta. The company continued to expand candy operations with the purchase of Cadbury's US candy business (Peter Paul, Cadbury, Caramello; 1988).

In 1990 Hershey formed a joint venture with Fujiya (Tokyo) to distribute Hershey confections and other products in Japan. The company purchased Ronzoni's pasta, cheese, and sauce operations in 1990, and the following year made a bid for American Italian Pasta, but the acquistion was blocked by the Justice Department.

WHERE

HQ: 100 Mansion Rd. East, Hershey, PA 17033
Phone: 717-534-4001
Fax: 717-534-4078

Hershey Foods manufactures its products in the US and Canada and internationally through joint ventures or licensing arrangements.

	1990 Sales		1990 Operating Income	
	$ mil.	% of total	$ mil.	% of total
US	2,509	92	344	98
Foreign	207	8	7	2
Total	**2,716**	**100**	**351**	**100**

WHAT

Confections	Rolo
Almond Joy	RSVP
Bar None	Skor
Big Block	Special Dark
Cadbury's	Symphony
Caramello	Twizzlers
Golden Almond	Whatchamacallit
Helps	York
Hershey's Kisses	5th Avenue
Hershey's Miniatures	
Kit Kat	**Pasta**
Krackel	American Beauty
Luden's	Delmonico
Mello Mint	Light 'N Fluffy
Mounds	P&R
Mr. Goodbar	Pastamania!
Y&S Nibs	Perfection
Oh Henry!	Ronzoni
Queen Anne	San Giorgio
Reese's	Skinner

RANKINGS

164th in *Fortune* 500 Industrial Cos.
192nd in *Business Week* 1000

KEY COMPETITORS

Berkshire Hathaway
Borden
Cadbury Schweppes
Campbell Soup
CPC
Heinz
Mars
Nestlé
Philip Morris

HOW MUCH

	9-Year Growth	1981	1982	1983	1984	1985	1986	1987	1988	1989	1990
Sales ($ mil.)	7.2%	1,451	1,566	1,706	1,893	1,996	2,170	2,434	2,168	2,421	2,716
Net income ($ mil.)	11.6%	80	94	100	109	121	133	148	145	171	216
Income as % of sales	—	5.5%	6.0%	5.9%	5.7%	6.0%	6.1%	6.1%	6.7%	7.1%	8.0%
Earnings per share ($)	11.0%	0.94	1.00	1.07	1.16	1.28	1.42	1.64	1.60	1.90	2.39
Stock price – high ($)	—	6.83	9.92	11.67	13.75	18.33	29.92	37.75	28.63	36.88	39.63
Stock price – low ($)	—	3.85	5.40	8.13	9.42	11.67	15.50	20.75	21.88	24.75	28.25
Stock price – close ($)	22.6%	6.00	9.40	10.54	12.88	17.17	24.63	24.50	26.00	35.88	37.50
P/E – high	—	7	10	11	12	14	21	23	18	19	17
P/E – low	—	4	5	8	8	9	11	13	14	13	12
Dividends per share ($)	14.5%	0.29	0.33	0.37	0.41	0.48	0.52	0.58	0.66	0.74	0.99
Book value per share ($)	11.9%	5.00	5.66	6.34	7.03	7.74	8.07	9.23	11.15	12.39	13.79

1990 Year-end:
Debt ratio: 18.0%
Return on equity: 18.3%
Cash (mil.): $27
Current ratio: 1.94
Long-term debt (mil.): $273
No. of shares (mil.): 90
Dividends:
   1990 average yield: 2.6%
   1990 payout: 41.4%
Market value (mil.): $3,382

Stock Price History High/Low 1981–90

THE HERTZ CORPORATION

OVERVIEW

Hertz invented the car rental business in 1918 and since then has remained the industry leader. But these days employee-owned Avis isn't far behind, with a 20.4% world market share compared to Hertz's leading 22.6% share (down from 37% in 1982). Still, Hertz remains the #1 renter of construction and industrial equipment in the US and has car leasing operations in Australia, New Zealand, and the UK.

Hertz maintains a fleet of 270,000 vehicles (about 160,000 in the US alone). It is the world's largest private customer of new vehicles, buying over $2.6 billion worth annually. Of the 216,000 new vehicles Hertz bought in 1990, about 75% were Fords. Hertz is Ford's largest customer. Unlike some of its smaller competitors, which depend primarily on the leisure market, Hertz derives 60% of its car rental revenue from the business market (down from 85% in 1985) and is, therefore, somewhat insulated from the periodic adverse effects of recession and high air fares on the leisure market.

Hertz is owned by Park Ridge Corporation, which is in turn owned by Ford (49%), Volvo North America (26%), a Hertz management partnership (20%), and Commerzbank (5%). Hertz CEO Frank Olson is the sole voting member of the management partnership.

WHEN

In 1918, 22-year-old John Jacobs opened a car rental business in Chicago with 12 Model T Fords that he repaired himself. By 1923, when John Hertz (president of both Yellow Cab and Yellow Truck and Coach Manufacturing Company) bought Jacobs's business, it was generating annual revenues of about $1 million. Jacobs continued as top operating and administrative executive of the company, renamed Hertz Drive-Ur-Self System. In 1925 General Motors acquired the rental business when it bought Yellow Truck from John Hertz and completed the company's coast-to-coast rental network. Hertz introduced the first car rental charge card in 1926 and the first one-way (rent-it-here/leave-it-there) plan in 1933.

Omnibus bought Hertz from General Motors in 1953, sold its bus interests, and concentrated on car and truck leasing and renting. In 1954 Omnibus changed its name to The Hertz Corporation and was listed on the NYSE. John Jacobs remained as president until he retired in 1960.

In 1965 Hertz formed its Hertz Equipment Rental subsidiary to rent construction equipment worldwide. Hertz was bought by RCA in 1967 but maintained its own board of directors and management. In 1972 the company introduced the first frequent-traveler's club, the #1 Club, which allowed the rental location to prepare a rental agreement before the customer arrived at the counter. Hertz introduced nationwide emergency road service in 1978.

Hertz introduced the industry's first express rental service in 1980. In 1985 United Airlines bought Hertz from RCA as part of UAL's strategy to form a global travel service company. In 1987 UAL changed its plans and sold Hertz for $1.3 billion to Park Ridge, which had been formed by Hertz management and Ford specifically to acquire Hertz, Ford's largest customer. The company moved to new corporate headquarters in Park Ridge, New Jersey, in 1988. In the same year, Ford, which held 80% of Park Ridge, sold 20% to Volvo North America for $100 million.

Also in 1988 Hertz pleaded guilty to overcharging more than 100,000 customers between 1978 and 1985 for repairs on damaged rental vehicles. The company was fined $6.85 million (the largest criminal consumer fraud fine ever imposed on a corporation) and ordered to pay $13.7 million in restitution, mostly to insurance companies. Hertz had already returned $3 million voluntarily and fired 20 employees who had acted without authorization.

Later in 1988 Ford sold more Park Ridge shares to Volvo, reducing its stake to 49% and upping Volvo's to 26%. Hertz sold its stock in the Hertz Penske truck leasing joint venture for $85.5 million and issued Penske a license to use the Hertz name.

In 1989 Hertz increased its share of Axus (car leasing; Belgium, Luxembourg, Holland, France, Italy, and Spain) from 25% to 79%, and introduced "#1 Club Gold Service," which allows members (who pay an annual fee) to rent a car without a counter rental transaction. The service, available at 30 major airports, was expanded to more than 130 locations in 1991 through the Hertz Gold Key Service.

Private company
Fiscal year ends: December 31

WHO

Chairman, CEO, and COO: Frank A. Olson, age 58, $916,192 pay
EVP and CFO: William Sider, age 57, $386,880 pay
SVP Employee Relations: Donald F. Steele, age 52
Auditors: Arthur Andersen & Co.
Employees: 18,700

WHERE

HQ: 225 Brae Blvd., Park Ridge, NJ 07656-0713
Phone: 201-307-2000
Fax: 201-307-2644
Reservations: 800-654-3131

Hertz rents 270,000 vehicles at its more than 5,100 locations in the US and more than 120 countries worldwide.

	1990 Sales		1990 Pretax Income	
	$ mil.	% of total	$ mil.	% of total
US	1,656	62	71	71
Other countries	1,010	38	29	29
Adjustments	(159)	—	—	—
Total	**2,507**	**100**	**100**	**100**

WHAT

	1990 Sales		1990 Operating Income	
	$ mil.	% of total	$ mil.	% of total
Car rental & leasing	2,274	91	285	84
Construction equip. rental & sales	233	9	54	16
Adjustments	—	—	(159)	—
Total	**2,507**	**100**	**180**	**100**

Services
Hertz Gold Key Service
The Hertz #1 Club
Hertz #1 Club Gold Service
Rent it Here-Leave it There program

Subsidiaries
Axus, SA (78.8%, vehicle leasing in Europe)
Bierly & Associates, Inc. (worker's compensation claims service)
HCM Claim Management Corp. (3rd party casualty and injury claim administration service)
Hertz Equipment Rental Corp. (construction equipment leasing)
Hertz International, Ltd. (vehicle leasing)
Hertz System, Inc. (franchise licensing)
Transportation Reinsurance (Barbados) Ltd. (reinsurance business)

RANKINGS

41st in *Fortune* 100 Diversified Service Cos.
54th in *Forbes* 400 Private Cos.

KEY COMPETITORS

Avis
Chrysler
Sears
Automakers' leasing units

HOW MUCH

	9-Year Growth	1981	1982	1983	1984	1985	1986	1987	1988	1989	1990
Sales ($ mil.)	6.6%	1,409	1,531	1,346	1,420	1,499	1,577	1,836	1,967	2,181	2,507
Net income ($ mil.)	18.7%	19	40	41	50	31	48	54	80	65	89
Income as % of sales	—	1.4%	2.6%	3.1%	3.5%	2.0%	3.0%	3.0%	4.1%	3.0%	3.6%
Employees	—							15,600	16,600	18,000	18,700

1990 Year-end:
Debt ratio: 66.6%
Return on equity: —
Cash (mil.): $122
Current ratio: —
Long-term debt (mil.): $1,485

Net Income ($ mil.) 1981–90

HEWLETT-PACKARD COMPANY

NYSE symbol: HWP
Fiscal year ends: October 31

OVERVIEW

Palo Alto–based Hewlett-Packard is the world's largest and most diversified manufacturer of electronic measurement and testing equipment and the world's 2nd largest computer workstation manufacturer (after Sun Microsystems), with 21% of the market.

HP has over 12,000 products including reduced-instruction-set computing (RISC) minicomputers and computer workstations, networking products, medical electronic equipment, testing and measurement systems, calculators, and chemical analysis systems. Seven years after introducing the LaserJet, its best-selling product ever, HP continues to dominate sales of PC laser printers with over 60% of the estimated $3.6 billion market.

HP labs is one of the world's leading electronic research centers. R&D expenses rank among the highest in the US; at $1.4 billion they amount to 10.3% of HP's sales. More than half of HP's orders in 1990 were for products introduced in the last 3 years.

HP has often been ranked by business leaders as one of America's most admired companies. However, in 1990, in response to declining earnings and delays in the introduction of a new workstation line, HP reorganized to simplify its structure and streamline its committee-oriented decision-making. HP's 1991 6-month earnings were up 22% over the same period a year ago.

WHO

Chairman: David Packard, age 79
President and CEO: John A. Young, age 59, $1,483,473 pay
EVP and COO: Dean O. Morton, age 59, $947,841 pay
SVP and CFO: Robert P. Wayman, age 46
Director of Human Resources: Pete Peterson
Auditors: Price Waterhouse
Employees: 92,000

WHERE

HQ: 3000 Hanover St., Palo Alto, CA 94304
Phone: 415-857-1501
Fax: 415-857-7299

The company operates worldwide.

	1990 Sales		1990 Operating Income	
	$ mil.	% of total	$ mil.	% of total
US	6,025	46	1,069	62
Europe	4,764	36	363	21
Other regions	2,444	18	281	17
Adjustments	—	—	(551)	—
Total	**13,233**	**100**	**1,162**	**100**

WHEN

In 1938, 2 Stanford engineers, encouraged by their professor, Frederick Terman (considered the founder of Silicon Valley), started Hewlett-Packard out of a garage in Palo Alto, California, with $538. Their first product was an audio oscillator. One of HP's first major customers was Walt Disney Studios, which bought 8 oscillators to use in the making of *Fantasia*.

Demand for HP's electronic testing equipment during WWII spurred revenue growth from $34,000 (1940) to near $1 million (1943). HP expanded 50% to 100% per year during the 1950s and opened up European subsidiaries. In 1961 HP entered the medical field by acquiring Sanborn Company, and the analytical instrumentation business with the acquisition of F&M Scientific in 1965.

In 1972 HP pioneered personal computing with the world's first hand-held scientific calculator (HP-35) and introduced the HP 3000 for business computing. By the late 1970s computers accounted for 1/2 of HP's revenues.

Under the leadership of John Young, the founders' chosen successor (president in 1977, CEO in 1978), HP introduced the first desktop mainframe (HP 9000, 1982), personal computers (HP-85, 1980; HP Vectra PC, 1985), and the LaserJet printer.

Young's 5-year, $250 million open-systems effort (starting in the early 1980s) produced a high-performance RISC-based Spectrum line in 1986 able to run the UNIX operating system. HP licensed its RISC chip to Hitachi and Samsung to increase the availability of Spectrum applications.

HP became a leader in the workstation market with the 1989 purchase of workstation pioneer Apollo Computers for $500 million. Difference in technologies, however, caused problems with integrating the 2 product lines and delayed HP's new workstation development. The company's recent introductions include NewWave software (the subject of litigation with Apple) to boost office productivity; the HP LaserJet III laser printer; the advanced HP 3000 line, which launched HP into mainframe power; and the HP 95LX palmtop PC — a $699 computer the size of a checkbook — that has Lotus 1-2-3 built in and that connects to a PC via an infrared optical link and will have a wireless pager.

In 1991 HP introduced its powerful Model 700 family of workstations, which moved the company out in front of its competitors in the workstation price-performance race.

WHAT

	1990 Sales	
	$ mil.	% of total
Measurement, design, information, & manufacturing equipment	4,856	37
Peripherals & network products	3,975	30
Service for equipment & systems	2,653	20
Medical electronics	875	7
Analytical instrumentation & service	572	4
Electronic components	302	2
Total	**13,233**	**100**

Computer Products
Apollo (workstations)
HP 1000 (factory automation computers)
HP 3000 (commercial computers)
HP 9000 (UNIX-based workstations and multiuser computers)
HP 95LX palmtop PC
HP Vectra (PCs)
HP VUE (software interface for UNIX workstations)
LaserJet (laser printers)
OpenView (network management products)
ThinkJet, DeskJet, DeskWriter (ink-jet printers)

Other Products
Electronic components
Hand-held calculators
Medical electronic equipment
Test and measurement systems

RANKINGS

29th in *Fortune* 500 Industrial Cos.
44th in *Business Week* 1000

KEY COMPETITORS

Apple	IBM	Tandem
C. R. Bard	Intel	Texas
Becton, Dickinson	NEC	Instruments
Casio	NCR	Unisys
Compaq	Oki	Wang
Control Data	Prime	Electronic
Data General	Sharp	instrument
DEC	Sony	manufacturers
EG&G	Sun	
General Signal	Microsystems	

HOW MUCH

	9-Year Growth	1981	1982	1983	1984	1985	1986	1987	1988	1989	1990
Sales ($ mil.)	15.6%	3,578	4,254	4,710	6,044	6,505	7,102	8,090	9,831	11,899	13,233
Net income ($ mil.)	10.1%	312	383	432	665	489	516	644	816	829	739
Income as % of sales	—	8.7%	9.0%	9.2%	11.0%	7.5%	7.3%	8.0%	8.3%	7.0%	5.6%
Earnings per share ($)	10.2%	1.28	1.53	1.69	2.59	1.91	2.02	2.50	3.36	3.52	3.06
Stock price – high ($)	—	26.94	41.25	48.25	45.50	38.88	49.63	73.63	65.50	61.50	50.38
Stock price – low ($)	—	19.19	18.00	34.25	31.13	28.75	35.75	35.75	43.75	40.25	24.88
Stock price – close ($)	5.4%	19.81	36.50	42.38	33.88	36.75	41.88	58.25	53.25	47.25	31.88
P/E – high	—	21	27	29	18	20	25	29	20	17	16
P/E – low	—	15	12	20	12	15	18	14	13	11	8
Dividends per share ($)	16.1%	0.11	0.12	0.16	0.19	0.22	0.22	0.23	0.28	0.36	0.42
Book value per share ($)	14.3%	7.83	9.37	11.33	13.82	15.50	17.08	19.52	19.35	22.92	26.07

1990 Year-end:
Debt ratio: 2.1%
Return on equity: 12.5%
Cash (mil.): $1,077
Current ratio: 1.47
Long-term debt (mil.): $139
No. of shares (mil.): 244
Dividends:
  1990 average yield: 1.3%
  1990 payout: 13.7%
Market value (mil.): $7,780

Stock Price History High/Low 1981–90

HILTON HOTELS CORPORATION

OVERVIEW

Hilton is one of America's largest hotel operators and has interests in approximately 96,000 rooms worldwide. The company owns or manages 45 US properties (including the historic Waldorf-Astoria) and manages 5 international hotels under the Hotel Conrad name in Dublin, Monte Carlo, the French West Indies, Hong Kong, and London. In addition, the company franchises 210 hotels, which are owned and operated by others under the Hilton or CrestHil by Hilton names.

Hilton has 4 hotel/casinos in Nevada and an equity interest in a 5th in Australia and has received regulatory approval to buy another in Atlantic City (Donald Trump rejected a $165 million offer from the company for his troubled Trump Castle in July 1991). Hilton is also thinking about buying riverboat casinos operating in Iowa. Revenue from hotel/casinos accounted for 52% of earnings in 1990.

Hotel design and furnishing services are provided through subsidiary Hilton Equipment. Hilton and Budget Rent-a-Car each own 50% of Compass Computer, a computerized hotel reservation system managed by a subsidiary of AMR Corporation.

WHEN

Conrad Hilton got his start in hotel management by renting rooms in his family's New Mexico home. He served as a state legislator and started a bank before leaving for Texas in 1919 with hopes of making his fortune in banking. There Hilton combined his $5,000 savings with a $20,000 loan and $15,000 from partners to buy his first hotel — in Cisco, Texas. Over the next decade he bought 7 more Texas hotels. The Great Depression took a heavy toll on his business, and by 1934 he had only 5 hotels, but his business was saved, in part because he had leased land for his hotels instead of borrowing to buy it.

He began buying hotels again, moving into California (1938), New Mexico (1939), and Mexico (1942). In 1942 he met and married Zsa Zsa Gabor, whom he later divorced. He founded Hilton International to manage his foreign business (1948) and realized his ambition to run New York's Waldorf-Astoria (1949), which he called "the greatest of them all." Hilton's first European hotel opened in Madrid in 1953. He paid $111 million for the 10-hotel Statler chain in 1954 in the biggest transaction in hotel history to that date.

The company began franchising in 1965 to capitalize on the best-known name in the hotel business and by 1987 had franchised 225 hotels. Conrad Hilton's son Barron became president in 1966. Barron persuaded his father to sell the 38-chain Hilton International to TWA in 1967 in exchange for TWA stock. In 1970 Barron bought 2 hotels in Las Vegas, creating a gaming division.

Upon Conrad's death in 1979, Barron became chairman. He re-entered the overseas hotel business with Conrad International Hotels in 1982 and opened a gaming hotel in Australia in 1985. The company spent $1.2 billion to refurbish and expand its 12 most glamorous hotels in the 1980s, including the Waldorf-Astoria and its 2 Las Vegas hotels (making them the 2 largest hotels in the world).

Settlement of his father's will in 1988 gave Barron Hilton control of 25% of Hilton's stock. He put the company up for sale in 1989, after high offers were made by foreign investors for other US hotels, but took it off the market after 9 months because bids did not meet his expectations. Meanwhile, the company opened the first Hilton Suites, hotels that provide only suites, and CrestHil, a chain of country inns that provides moderately priced lodging for the middle-market segment.

The travel market suffered early in 1991 owing to the combined effects of the Gulf War and a sluggish US economy. In the first quarter hotel occupancy dropped to 59% (from 66% in 1990); Hilton's earnings showed a 51% decline in the same period.

NYSE symbol: HLT
Fiscal year ends: December 31

Hoover's Rating C+

WHO

Chairman, President, and CEO: Barron Hilton, age 63, $1,050,000 pay
EVP Nevada Gaming Operations; President, Hilton Nevada Corp.: John V. Giovenco, age 54, $707,979 pay
EVP Operations; President, Hilton Hotels Division: Carl T. Mottek, age 62, $656,417 pay
SVP Finance: Maurice J. Scanlon, age 56, $361,579 pay
SVP Human Resources, Hilton Hotels Division: William R. McDonald
Auditors: Arthur Andersen & Co.
Employees: 38,000

WHERE

HQ: 9336 Civic Center Dr., Beverly Hills, CA 90209-5567
Phone: 213-278-4321
Fax: 213-205-4599
Reservations: 800-445-8667

Hilton owns 18 hotels, manages 37 hotels, and franchises 210 hotels in 44 US states, Australia, Hong Kong, the West Indies, Ireland, the UK, and Monaco.

WHAT

	1990 Sales	
	$ mil.	% of total
Rooms	373	33
Food & beverage	237	21
Casino	386	34
Management & franchise fees	78	7
Other	62	5
Adjustments	(49)	—
Total	**1,087**	**100**

Owned Hotels and Casinos
Atlanta Airport Hilton
Flamingo Hilton–Las Vegas (hotel/casino)
Flamingo Hilton–Laughlin (hotel/casino, Laughlin, NV)
Flamingo Hilton–Reno (hotel/casino)
Hilton Suites (Brentwood, TN)
Hilton Suites (Orange, CA)
Hilton Suites (Phoenix, AZ)
Hotel Conrad & Jupiters Casino (10%; Queensland, Australia)
Hotel Conrad Hong Kong (30%)
Las Vegas Hilton (hotel/casino)
New Orleans Airport Hilton
O'Sheas (Irish theme casino, Las Vegas)
Paco's (Mexican theme casino, Reno)
Palmer House (Chicago)
Portland Hilton (Portland, OR)
Waldorf-Astoria (New York)

Leased Hotels
Logan Airport Hilton (Boston)
Oakland Airport Hilton
Pittsburgh Hilton & Towers
San Diego Hilton Beach & Tennis Resort
San Francisco Airport Hilton
Seattle Airport Hilton

HOW MUCH

	9-Year Growth	1981	1982	1983	1984	1985	1986	1987	1988	1989	1990
Sales ($ mil.)	7.4%	571	600	649	647	684	719	815	915	954	1,087
Net income ($ mil.)	0.0%	113	83	113	114	100	98	140	131	110	113
Income as % of sales	—	19.7%	13.9%	17.3%	17.6%	14.6%	13.6%	17.2%	14.3%	11.5%	10.3%
Earnings per share ($)	1.2%	2.11	1.56	2.10	2.17	2.02	1.96	2.80	2.72	2.27	2.34
Stock price – high ($)	—	26.13	26.00	30.13	29.00	36.75	40.13	45.88	55.25	115.50	84.38
Stock price – low ($)	—	16.63	13.81	20.06	22.75	27.88	30.25	27.50	34.00	48.38	26.38
Stock price – close ($)	7.8%	19.00	22.38	28.50	28.81	32.44	33.63	35.50	53.38	82.50	37.25
P/E – high	—	12	17	14	13	18	20	16	20	51	36
P/E – low	—	8	9	10	11	14	15	10	13	21	11
Dividends per share ($)	3.8%	0.83	0.90	0.90	0.90	0.90	0.90	0.90	0.98	1.00	1.15
Book value per share ($)	7.7%	9.99	10.65	11.87	12.00	13.14	14.23	15.79	17.03	18.40	19.44

1990 Year-end:
Debt ratio: 36.3%
Return on equity: 12.4%
Cash (mil.): $100
Current ratio: 1.18
Long-term debt (mil.): $527
No. of shares (mil.): 48
Dividends:
 1990 average yield: 3.1%
 1990 payout: 49.1%
Market value (mil.): $1,769

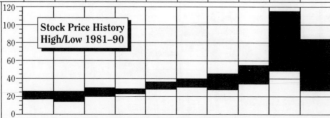
Stock Price History
High/Low 1981–90

RANKINGS

87th in *Fortune* 100 Diversified Service Cos.
301st in *Business Week* 1000

KEY COMPETITORS

Accor	Dole	Marriott
Bally	Helmsley	Nestlé
Bass	Hyatt	Rank
Canadian Pacific	ITT	Trammell Crow
Carlson	Loews	

THE HOME DEPOT, INC.

NYSE symbol: HD
Fiscal year ends: Sunday nearest January 31

Hoover's Rating **A+**

OVERVIEW

Headquartered in Atlanta, Home Depot is the largest operator of home improvement supply centers in the US, with 145 warehouse stores in 12 states and sales of $3.8 billion in 1990 (up 38% over 1989), a slow year for retailers.

Home Depot's strategy of targeting the do-it-yourself market by offering a wide variety of home improvement supplies paid off during the 1990–91 housing slump, when people unable to buy new houses improved their existing quarters.

The company's specialized customer service is an innovation in the industry. Employees called "Homers," many of them professional craftsmen, not only help customers with their purchases, but also educate them through in-store clinics, thereby broadening the do-it-yourself customer base. In an industry that relies mainly on minimum wage part-timers, 95% of Home Depot's employees work full time.

Home Depot locates stores in suburbs in or near metropolitan areas of the Sunbelt and the Northeast where, despite a deep recession, they continue to prosper. Many of its new stores are sited to draw customers from older, smaller stores. In 1990 Home Depot added decoration assistance to its list of services.

WHEN

Home Depot was founded in 1978 after Bernard Marcus and Arthur Blank lost their executive jobs with Handy Dan Home Improvement Centers in a corporate buyout. They joined Handy Dan coworker Ronald Brill to launch a new and improved home center for the do-it-yourselfer. In 1979 they opened 3 stores in the Atlanta area, soon expanding to 4 stores (1980).

In 1981 Home Depot went public, raising more than $4 million, opening 4 stores in southern Florida, and posting sales of $50 million. After opening 2 more Florida stores and making sales of $100 million in 1982, the company was named Retailer of the Year in the home building supply industry.

The chain next entered Louisiana and Arizona, opening 5 stores there, plus 4 more in Florida in 1983. That year sales were more than $250 million. The company also began shifting from manual to computerized information management, installing computerized checkout systems. In 1984 inventory reordering was computerized.

Also in 1984 Home Depot's stock was listed on the NYSE, and the company acquired 9 Bowater Home Centers in Texas, Louisiana, and Alabama. The company then entered Southern California, Handy Dan's home turf, opening 6 stores and finishing 1985 with 50 stores and sales of $700 million. The Bowater acquisition and rapid internal expansion caused Home Depot to falter in 1985 and experience the only dip in earnings in its history.

Back on track in 1986, Home Depot opened 10 more stores (5 in California), and sales exceeded $1 billion in the 60 stores. The company initiated the current policy of "low day-in day-out pricing" in 1987, achieving Marcus's dream of eliminating sales events. It also began installing bar code scanning systems, completing the job within 2 years.

With sales over $2 billion in 96 stores (1988), Home Depot was included in the S&P 500. Entering the competitive Northeast market, the company bought 3 Modell's Shoppers World stores on Long Island.

In 1989 the company added 22 stores, primarily in California, Florida, and New England, and installed a satellite communication network to enhance its continual-training policy.

Home Depot's sales rose during the 1990–91 recession. The company opened 25 new stores in 1990. Though Home Depot is the leader of its retail category, its 4% market share leaves room for further expansion.

WHO

Chairman, CEO, and Secretary: Bernard Marcus, age 61, $1,586,633 pay
President and COO: Arthur M. Blank, age 48, $1,377,842 pay
EVP Merchandising: James W. Inglis, $409,131 pay
SVP and CFO: Ronald M. Brill, age 47, $415,058 pay
SVP Corporate Development: William E. Harris, $396,786 pay
SVP Merchandising: Bruce Berg
VP Human Resources: Donald P. McKenna
Auditors: KPMG Peat Marwick
Employees: 21,500

WHERE

HQ: 2727 Paces Ferry Rd., Atlanta, GA 30339
Phone: 404-433-8211
Fax: 404-431-2707

The Home Depot sells home improvement and building materials in 145 warehouse stores in the Sunbelt and Northeast.

	No. of Stores	% of Total
Alabama	2	1
Arizona	10	7
California	41	28
Connecticut	3	2
Florida	37	26
Georgia	14	10
Louisiana	5	3
New Jersey	4	3
New York	5	3
South Carolina	2	1
Tennessee	5	3
Texas	17	13
Total	**145**	**100**

WHAT

	1990 Sales
	% of total
Plumbing, heating & electrical supplies	29
Building materials, lumber, floor & wall coverings	32
Hardware & tools	12
Seasonal & specialty items	15
Paint & other	12
Total	**100**

RANKINGS

30th in *Fortune* 50 Retailing Cos.
105th in *Business Week* 1000

KEY COMPETITORS

Kmart
Lowe's
Montgomery Ward
Sears
Sherwin-Williams
Supermarkets General
Wal-Mart

HOW MUCH

	9-Year Growth	1981	1982	1983	1984	1985	1986	1987	1988	1989	1990
Sales ($ mil.)	61.3%	52	118	256	433	701	1,011	1,454	2,000	2,759	3,815
Net income ($ mil.)	72.5%	1	5	10	14	8	24	54	77	112	163
Income as % of sales	—	2.4%	4.5%	4.0%	3.3%	1.2%	2.4%	3.7%	3.8%	4.1%	4.3%
Earnings per share ($)	62.4%	0.02	0.07	0.12	0.17	0.10	0.27	0.50	0.66	0.94	1.35
Stock price – high ($)	—	0.76	4.26	9.41	8.26	6.04	6.44	12.48	14.22	25.58	43.50
Stock price – low ($)	—	0.47	0.73	3.57	3.56	3.11	3.19	5.30	7.72	12.78	23.00
Stock price – close ($)	55.4%	0.73	3.63	7.78	5.26	3.70	5.30	8.33	14.06	24.42	38.63
P/E – high	—	44	60	77	50	62	24	25	21	27	32
P/E – low	—	28	10	29	21	32	12	11	12	14	17
Dividends per share ($)	—	0.00	0.00	0.00	0.00	0.00	0.00	0.02	0.05	0.07	0.11
Book value per share ($)	61.5%	0.08	0.24	0.78	0.95	1.05	1.70	2.88	3.39	4.45	5.79

1990 Year-end:
Debt ratio: 43.7%
Return on equity: 26.4%
Cash (mil.): $137
Current ratio: 1.73
Long-term debt (mil.): $531
No. of shares (mil.): 118
Dividends:
 1990 average yield: 0.3%
 1990 payout: 8.1%
Market value (mil.): $4,560

Stock Price History High/Low 1981–90

HONEYWELL INC.

OVERVIEW

Honeywell is the world's leading producer of industrial control systems and avionics equipment and a major producer of environment controls (e.g., thermostats) for homes and buildings. The company produces a broad range of products, including a variety of sensors, security and fire alarm systems, and navigation systems. Honeywell is a major player in foreign markets, which are responsible for about 32% of its sales, and the company continues its efforts to expand internationally.

The company's space and aviation segment, for example, generated 40% of its revenues from overseas, and foreign sales bolstered its homes and buildings business in the face of slumping US housing starts. With help from Asia and Europe, Honeywell managed to increase its 1990 homes and buildings operating profit to $237 million, a 5% increase over 1989.

Honeywell's homes and buildings segment accounts for 35% of sales; its industrial market represents 26% of sales.

In the past few years, Honeywell has concentrated on its fundamental mission — producing control and sensing systems — and has completed a 5-year plan to return to the basics that made it a worldwide business.

WHEN

An invention patented by Al Butz in 1885, the Damper Flapper, led to the building regulation equipment that Honeywell still provides. The Damper Flapper, forerunner of the thermostat, opened furnace vents automatically. Butz formed the Butz Thermo-Electric Regulator Company to market the product but sold patent rights to investor William Sweatt in 1893. Sweatt led the company for 4 decades. The company eventually began producing a burner-control system for fire protection on oil and gas furnaces. Sweatt persuaded manufacturers to redesign furnaces to accommodate controls, establishing a new market.

In 1927 the company's primary competitor was the Mark Honeywell Heating Specialties Company (of Indiana). The companies merged that year as Minneapolis-Honeywell Regulator Company based in Minneapolis. In 1964 the company adopted its present name.

Honeywell developed expertise in precision optics during WWII, when the US military sought Honeywell's assistance in developing instrumentation and control systems for long-range bombers, including B-17s and B-29s.

In the 1950s Honeywell used computers in control and guidance systems. It formed Datamatic Corporation (1955) with Raytheon to develop and market data processors. In 1970 Honeywell purchased GE's computer division, receiving with it 66% interest in a French company, Machines Bull. Honeywell then bought Xerox's computer business in 1976. The same year it merged its Machines Bull unit with a computer company owned by the French government, which purchased Honeywell's entire interest (after threatening to nationalize it) in 1982. In 1987 Honeywell renewed its ties with Bull, creating Honeywell Bull Inc. (now Bull HN Information Systems), owned 42.5% by Honeywell, 42.5% by Bull, and 15% by NEC. This unit was Honeywell's only remaining involvement in the computer business.

In 1990 Honeywell decided to sell its US defense segment in order to concentrate on systems for commercial aircraft traffic alert, collision avoidance, and wind-shear detection.

Also in 1990 Boeing selected Honeywell to be a major supplier for the new Boeing 777, a move that could increase Honeywell's revenues by $2 billion over the next several years. Honeywell also was selected by Lockheed Missiles and Space Co. to develop parts for the US space station. And under a $13.4 million air force contract, Honeywell will upgrade the navigation system for the F-16.

In 1991 Honeywell decided to sell the rest of Bull HN Information Systems in order to concentrate on its core controls business.

NYSE symbol: HON
Fiscal year ends: December 31

Hoover's Rating **B**

WHO

Chairman and CEO: James J. Renier, age 61, $1,469,323 pay
EVP and CFO: Christopher J. Steffen, age 49, $794,445 pay
EVP; COO, Industrial, and Space and Aviation: D. Larry Moore, age 54, $678,837 pay
EVP; COO, International, and Homes and Buildings: Michael R. Bonsignore, age 49, $631,521 pay
SVP International: Joseph E. Chenoweth, age 55, $658,511 pay
VP Human Resources: Fosten A. Boyle
Auditors: Deloitte & Touche
Employees: 60,332

WHERE

HQ: Honeywell Plaza, Minneapolis, MN 55408
Phone: 612-870-5200
Fax: 612-870-5780

Honeywell has a presence in 90 countries and operates facilities in the US, Australia, Belgium, Canada, France, Germany, Hong Kong, Italy, the Netherlands, Singapore, Switzerland, Taiwan, and the UK.

	1990 Sales		1990 Operating Income	
	$ mil.	% of total	$ mil.	% of total
US	4,302	68	436	64
Europe	1,392	22	193	29
Other countries	615	10	47	7
Adjustments	—	—	(125)	—
Total	**6,309**	**100**	**551**	**100**

WHAT

	1990 Sales		1990 Operating Income	
	$ mil.	% of total	$ mil.	% of total
Homes & buildings	2,197	35	237	35
Industrial	1,653	26	220	32
Space & aviation	2,071	33	200	30
Other	388	6	19	3
Adjustments	—	—	(125)	—
Total	**6,309**	**100**	**551**	**100**

Products
Commercial avionics
Environmental controls
Industrial controls
Security systems

Joint Venture
Yamatake-Honeywell Co. Ltd. (24.2%)

RANKINGS

69th in *Fortune* 500 Industrial Cos.
154th in *Business Week* 1000

KEY COMPETITORS

Allied-Signal
Emerson
General Signal
Johnson Controls
Rockwell
Thomson SA
Other defense electronics companies

HOW MUCH

	9-Year Growth	1981	1982	1983	1984	1985	1986	1987	1988	1989	1990
Sales ($ mil.)	1.8%	5,351	5,490	5,753	6,074	6,625	5,378	6,679	7,148	6,059	6,309
Net income ($ mil.)	4.2%	256	271	231	335	275	13	254	(435)	550	372
Income as % of sales	—	4.8%	4.9%	4.0%	5.5%	4.2%	0.2%	3.8%	(6.1%)	9.1%	5.9%
Earnings per share ($)	6.7%	2.74	2.95	2.46	3.50	2.95	0.14	2.85	(5.11)	6.37	*4.90*
Stock price – high ($)	—	28.63	26.44	34.88	33.75	43.38	42.13	45.25	38.13	45.88	56.19
Stock price – low ($)	—	17.25	14.88	20.75	23.19	27.13	29.13	24.50	27.13	29.75	35.31
Stock price – close ($)	10.9%	17.47	21.34	32.50	31.63	37.06	29.56	26.94	29.88	43.38	44.50
P/E – high	—	10	9	14	10	15	301	16	—	7	11
P/E – low	—	6	5	8	7	9	208	9	—	5	7
Dividends per share ($)	6.5%	0.80	0.88	0.90	0.95	0.98	1.00	1.01	1.05	1.13	1.41
Book value per share ($)	0.6%	22.63	23.58	24.68	25.48	28.04	24.34	26.40	20.07	23.98	23.97

1990 Year-end:
Debt ratio: 26.6%
Return on equity: 20.4%
Cash (mil.): $368
Current ratio: 1.19
Long-term debt (mil.): $616
No. of shares (mil.): 71
Dividends:
  1990 average yield: 3.2%
  1990 payout: 28.7%
Market value (mil.): $3,150

Stock Price History High/Low 1981–90

HOSPITAL CORPORATION OF AMERICA

Private company
Fiscal year ends: December 31

Hoover's Rating **C-**

OVERVIEW

Privately owned Hospital Corporation of America was the 2nd largest for-profit owner and operator of medical/surgical and psychiatric hospitals in the US in 1990 after Humana. The company also operates 75 medical/surgical and 53 psychiatric hospitals in the US and owns part of one medical/surgical hospital in Italy.

Since its 1989 LBO, the company has been selling assets to repay a $1.3 billion bridge loan (due in 1991). Operations sold include Allied Clinical Laboratories, HCA Management Company, and the company's UK, Australian, and Brazilian operations.

Since the largest portion of HCA's medical hospital profits derive from room and board charges, company income has fallen as admissions have declined in the cost-conscious 1980s (40% since 1986). In addition, Medicare, Medicaid (from which it derives over 30% of its billings), and many insurors pay procedural bills on a fixed schedule. Though outpatient procedures have increased, they are less expensive. However, HCA's psychiatric hospitals, which are still largely inpatient and reimbursed on a billings basis, have seen admissions rise by 55% in the same period, making HCA's psychiatric beds somewhat more profitable than its medical beds.

WHO

Chairman, President, and CEO: Thomas F. Frist, Jr., age 52, $1,006,260 pay
EVP and CFO: Roger E. Mick, age 44, $505,000 pay
VP Human Resources: Phil Patton
Auditors: Ernst & Young
Employees: 53,900

WHERE

HQ: One Park Plaza, Nashville, TN 37203
Phone: 615-327-9551
Fax: 615-320-2222 (Human Resources)

Location	No. of Medical/ Surgical Hospitals	No. of Psychiatric Hospitals
Arizona	—	1
Arkansas	1	—
California	2	4
Colorado	—	1
Delaware	—	1
Florida	18	6
Georgia	8	1
Illinois	—	3
Kansas	1	—
Kentucky	2	—
Louisiana	2	5
Missouri	—	1
Nevada	—	3
New Hampshire	2	1
New Mexico	2	1
North Carolina	2	1
Oklahoma	2	—
South Carolina	3	—
Tennessee	8	5
Texas	14	13
Utah	1	—
Virginia	5	4
West Virginia	2	1
Wisconsin	—	1
US subtotal	**75**	**53**
Italy (50%)	1	—
Total	**76**	**53**

WHEN

Jack Massey, a former hospital supplier and druggist who spent 12 years building the Baptist Hospital in Nashville into one of the US's largest medical centers (he also made a fortune with Kentucky Fried Chicken Corporation, which he founded), cofounded Hospital Corporation of America in 1968 with Dr. Thomas Frist and Frist's son, Dr. Thomas Frist, Jr. From a single 150-bed hospital in Nashville, they built HCA into the largest for-profit hospital company in the world.

In 1973 the company ran 50 hospitals with 14 under construction, all concentrated in the Southeast. As an economy measure HCA built all its hospitals, regardless of size, to look alike. In that year revenues reached $174 million with profits of $10 million. By 1977 the company owned 88 hospitals, which had increased to 148 in 1979. In 1981 the company acquired Hospital Affiliates International's 133 hospitals, increasing the number of its facilities by 65%. By 1983 HCA owned and managed 376 hospitals (51,000 beds) in the US and 7 foreign countries. The next year the company earned $297 million on sales of $3.5 billion, but expansion expenses led to debt amounting to 51% of capital.

Hoping to acquire capital for further expansion, HCA attempted in 1985 to merge with American Hospital Supply, the largest medical supply company in the country. The resulting company would have had combined revenues of over $7.6 billion (1984 figures). The companies publicly announced the merger on March 31, 1985, but it fell through,

and Baxter International bought AHS in July of that year.

Hospital occupancy rates began falling in 1983, when the Health Care Financing Administration began reimbursing Medicare claims on a fixed schedule rather than on percentages of billing. Occupany rates and admissions were also reduced by the introduction of HMOs, which encourage preventive health care. By 1985 hospital occupancy reached a 40-year low, causing declining profits for for-profit hospital chains. To offset this slump, HCA launched its own HMO, Equicor, in 1986 (a venture with Equitable Life Assurance). In 1987 the company sold 104 of its rural hospitals to employees for $2.1 billion through a stock ownership plan. The resulting company, Healthtrust, has prospered. In 1989 Thomas Frist, Jr., now HCA's chairman, led a $4.5 billion LBO with an equity group that included the Rockefeller family, Goldman Sachs, Morgan Guaranty, and Texas financier Richard Rainwater.

The company went private in March 1989. To pay down debt from the LBO, Frist attempted to sell the company's psychiatric hospitals through a $1.4 billion employee buy-out plan, but the deal collapsed. In 1990 Equicor was sold to CIGNA Corporation for $777 million. In August 1990 the psychiatric division borrowed $515 million and transferred $500 million of it to the parent company to reduce the unpaid balance of its bridge loan to about $140 million. Since then sales of 2 facilities have further reduced debt.

WHAT

	1990 Sales	
	$ mil.	% of total
US medical/surgical hospitals	4,000	86
US psychiatric hospitals	590	13
Other	41	1
Total	**4,631**	**100**

	1990 Licensed Beds	
	No. of beds	% of total
US medical/surgical hospitals	17,712	75
US psychiatric hospitals	5,684	24
Foreign hospital	163	1
Total	**23,559**	**100**

RANKINGS

24th in *Fortune* 100 Diversified Service Cos.
22nd in *Forbes* 400 US Private Cos.

KEY COMPETITORS

Humana
Mayo Foundation
National Medical

HOW MUCH

	9-Year Growth	1981	1982	1983	1984	1985	1986	1987	1988	1989	1990
Sales ($ mil.)	9.4%	2,064	2,977	3,203	3,499	4,352	4,931	4,676	4,111	4,274	4,631
Net income ($ mil.)	(6.3%)	111	173	243	297	284	175	(58)	259	83	62
Income as % of sales	—	5.4%	5.8%	7.6%	8.5%	6.5%	3.5%	(1.2%)	6.3%	1.9%	1.3%
Employees	(0.8%)	75,000	76,000	71,000	79,000	89,500	89,000	63,000	65,000	68,000	70,000

1990 Year-end:
Assets (mil.): $6,300
Book value (mil.): $673
Debt ratio: 93.4%
Return on equity: 25.9%
Cash (mil.): $47
Current ratio: 1.11
Long-term debt (mil.): $3,715

Net Income ($ mil.) 1981–90

HOUSEHOLD INTERNATIONAL, INC.

NYSE symbol: HI
Fiscal year ends: December 31

 Hoover's Rating **C**

OVERVIEW

Household International, the 17th largest diversified financial services company in the US, is expanding aggressively. Its goal, articulated in 1989, is to double its assets in 5 years.

One avenue of growth for the parent company is its consumer bank, called Household Bank. Household hopes to expand by buying banks and thrifts in the area from Illinois to the East Coast. Household Bank targets customers who are more affluent than those served by Household Finance Corporation (HFC), the company's cornerstone. HFC, with more than 1.1 million accounts, provides consumer loans. The company is shifting HFC's back office operations to regional centers so it can focus on sales at its branch offices.

Household International, through its Household Retail Services subsidiary, handles credit card accounts for other businesses. It is the 2nd largest issuer of private-label retail credit cards in the US, after GE Capital, with 1.4 million cardholders and $1.9 billion in receivables. The Alexander Hamilton Life Insurance subsidiary sells policies in all states through 9,000 independent agents and through its own sister companies.

Household Bank's performance and the parent company's loan portfolio prompted Moody's to downgrade HFC's credit rating in 1991. However, confidence in the company remained high, and the stock price doubled between October 1990 and April 1991.

WHO

Chairman and CEO: Donald C. Clark, age 59, $1,160,000 pay
President and COO: Edwin P. Hoffman, age 48, $1,006,500 pay
Group VP and Chief Accounting Officer: Gaylen N. Larson, age 51
VP Human Resources: Colin P. Kelly, age 48
Auditors: Arthur Andersen & Co.
Employees: 14,400

WHERE

HQ: 2700 Sanders Rd., Prospect Heights, IL 60070
Phone: 708-564-5000
Fax: 708-205-7452

Household Bank has 124 branches in 7 states. HFC Bank PLC has 166 branches in the UK. The company's consumer finance subsidiaries have 589 offices in the US, 109 in Canada, and 34 in Australia.

	1990 Sales		1990 Pretax Income	
	$ mil.	% of total	$ mil.	% of total
US	3,389	78	331	94
Canada	394	9	51	15
UK	433	10	(19)	(5)
Australia	104	3	(14)	(4)
Total	**4,320**	**100**	**349**	**100**

WHAT

	1990 Sales		1990 Pretax Income	
	$ mil.	% of total	$ mil.	% of total
Consumer financial services	3,320	77	346	86
Commercial financial services	578	13	30	7
Individual life insurance	422	10	27	7
Adjustments	—	—	(54)	—
Total	**4,320**	**100**	**349**	**100**

Major US Subsidiaries
Alexander Hamilton Life Insurance Co. of America
Household Bank, f.s.b. (full-service consumer banking)
Household Bank, NA (MasterCard and Visa accounts)
Household Commercial Financial Services, Inc.
Household Finance Corp. (consumer credit, home equity loans)
Household Mortgage Services (mortgage lending via Household Bank, f.s.b., and 4 loan origination offices)
Household Retail Services, Inc. (revolving credit administration for retailers)

WHEN

"Never borrow money needlessly..."
That radio jingle of the 1950s cheerfully admonished consumers about financial responsibility, a Household Finance theme since its start in Minneapolis in 1878, when Frank Mackey opened a finance company to loan cash to workers between paychecks.

In 1925 more than 30 such companies across the country, controlled by Mackey and operating under a variety of names, consolidated as Chicago-based Household Finance Corporation. That year the company paid the first of 262 consecutive quarterly dividends. The company went public in 1928.

In 1930 HFC set up the Money Management Institute to teach people how to handle credit. One pamphlet showed a family of 5 how to live on $150 a month. In 1931 HFC's banks froze the company's credit, making it unable to lend, but the freeze was lifted in 1932 and the company weathered the Depression. After WWII the unleashed US demand for goods propelled HFC into the suburbs, and by 1960 it boasted 1,000 branch offices.

In the conglomerate-crazed 1960s, Household, viewing itself broadly as a retailer of money, began to diversify into other kinds of retailing — hardware stores (Coast-to-Coast,

1961), variety chains (Ben Franklin and TG&Y, 1965), vacuum jugs (King-Seeley Thermos, 1968), and car rental (National, 1969). Household also purchased a savings and loan, 4 banks, and Alexander Hamilton Life (1977).

The company adopted Household International as its corporate name in 1981. Later in the 1980s, as Wall Street turned sour on bric-a-brac conglomerates, Chairman Donald Clark refocused the company on financial services, particularly consumer banking. In 1984 Clark thwarted an $8 billion takeover by dissident shareholders by adopting a "poison pill" that, after a takeover, would have permitted stockholders to buy stock in the resulting company for 1/2 price.

Household sold its merchandising operations for more than $700 million in 1985 (to Foxmeyer; Donaldson, Lufkin & Jenrette Securities; and former managers); National Car Rental in 1986; and most other nonfinancial operations. In 1989 Household spun off 3 manufacturing units (Eljer Industries, Schwitzer, and Scotsman Industries).

In 1991 Household announced a new stock offering and increased its assets by acquiring portions of S&Ls in Illinois and California.

RANKINGS

17th in *Fortune* 50 Diversified Financial Cos.
374th in *Business Week* 1000

KEY COMPETITORS

H. F. Ahmanson
Ford
General Electric
Great Western
ITT
Primerica

Textron
Transamerica
Banks
Life insurance companies
Savings and loan associations

HOW MUCH

	9-Year Growth	1981	1982	1983	1984	1985	1986	1987	1988	1989	1990
Assets ($ mil.)	15.0%	8,397	8,235	8,446	10,041	11,929	13,207	16,986	21,032	26,163	29,455
Net income ($ mil.)	5.8%	142	125	206	234	168	138	222	184	218	235
Income as % of assets	—	1.7%	1.5%	2.4%	2.3%	1.4%	1.0%	1.3%	0.9%	0.8%	0.8%
Earnings per share ($)	9.4%	2.56	2.01	3.50	3.95	2.82	2.85	5.32	4.78	5.60	5.75
Stock price – high ($)	—	19.25	26.13	34.00	34.38	43.38	52.50	62.50	61.00	65.50	53.25
Stock price – low ($)	—	14.25	14.75	19.00	24.00	32.25	39.13	32.50	39.50	46.38	19.38
Stock price – close ($)	8.9%	15.25	23.00	30.75	32.75	42.25	47.75	39.88	56.88	51.88	32.88
P/E – high	—	8	13	10	9	15	18	12	13	12	9
P/E – low	—	6	7	5	6	11	14	6	8	8	3
Dividends per share ($)	3.3%	1.63	1.65	1.68	1.73	1.78	1.84	1.93	2.07	2.14	2.17
Book value per share ($)	3.3%	28.08	27.59	28.92	30.28	31.70	28.57	28.96	33.59	33.82	37.54

1990 Year-end:
Debt ratio: 83.4%
Return on equity: 16.1%
Cash (mil.): $5,248
Long-term debt (mil.): $7,751
No. of shares (mil.): 36
Dividends:
  1990 average yield: 6.6%
  1990 payout: 37.7%
Market value (mil.): $1,177
Sales (mil.): $4,320

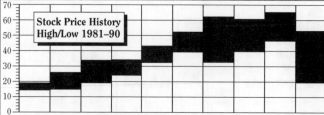
Stock Price History
High/Low 1981–90

HUMANA INC.

NYSE symbol: HUM
Fiscal year ends: August 31

Hoover's Rating **B+**

OVERVIEW

Louisville-based Humana, which passed Hospital Corporation of America in 1990 to become the largest US hospital chain, oversees a vertically integrated system of 85 hospitals (more than 17,000 beds) in 19 states, the UK, and Switzerland and health benefit plans (health maintenance organizations, preferred provider organizations, and indemnity plans) servicing more than one million people. Three of the hospitals specialize in care for women; the others provide general medical and surgical care.

Over the past 5 years, about 1/3 of the company's revenues came from Medicare and Medicaid sources. But despite intense federal pressures to slow the rise of health care costs, Humana established an average sales growth rate of more than 15% over the past 10 years. In 1990 Humana reported a 19% increase in revenues over 1989, from $4.1 billion to $4.9 billion. Likewise, 1989 revenues increased by 19% over 1988 revenues. The company intends to increase volume in both its hospital and health-plan segments, thus minimizing pricing pressures and increasing margins.

Humana also espouses an aggressive capital strategy, with plans to spend $500 million on building and equipment modernization.

WHEN

In 1961 David Jones and Wendell Cherry, 2 Louisville lawyers, bought a nursing home as a real estate investment. Within 6 years their company, Extendicare, was the largest nursing-care chain in the US, with 8 homes.

Noticing that hospitals received nearly 7 times more money per patient per day than nursing homes and faced with a glutted market of over 80 nursing chains, the partners took their company public in 1968 to finance the buying of hospitals (one per month from 1968 to 1971). Wishing to concentrate on hospitals, the company sold its 40 nursing homes. Sales leaped from $7.7 million in 1968 to $106 million at the end of 1973, when the company decided to change its name to Humana.

Between 1972 and 1975 Humana constructed 27 hospitals in the South and Southwest. In 1978 Humana, then the 3rd largest for-profit hospital operator in the country, bought #2-ranked American Medicorp for $304 million, making the company the 2nd largest in America.

In marketing, operation, and location of its hospitals, Humana targeted young, privately insured patients because short hospital stays made the most money. The company kept its charity cases and bad-debt expenses to just 2.5% of revenues in 1980.

In 1982 the University of Louisville, unable to continue absorbing a $4 million annual loss at its public University Hospital, decided to close the facility. Humana stepped in and within a year was generating profits while still meeting the community's indigent care needs.

Humana experienced several problems between 1983 and 1987. In 1983 the government began reimbursing Medicare payments (40% of company revenues) on fixed rates rather than a percentage of full costs. Occupancy in hospitals dropped. Health insurance write-offs and several closed clinics amounted to a total of $130 million. The company's net income fell 75%, from $216 million in 1985 to $54 million in 1986.

The company solved its profitability problems by offering health insurance at low premiums to attract employers; policyholders paid no deductibles to use Humana hospitals. In 1990 Humana acquired Chicago's Michael Reese Hospital (1,008 beds) and an associated health plan. That move has set the stage for intense price competition with Blue Cross and Blue Shield in Chicago.

Humana founding partner Wendell Cherry died in 1991, leaving behind a $4.9 billion enterprise started just 30 years ago with a $6,000 investment.

WHO

Chairman and CEO: David A. Jones, age 59, $1,141,691 pay
President and COO: Carl F. Pollard, age 52, $623,385 pay (prior to promotion)
EVP and General Counsel: Thomas J. Flynn, age 53
EVP Finance and Administration: William C. Ballard, Jr., age 50, $519,244 pay
VP Human Resources: Steven L. Durbin, age 41
Auditors: Coopers & Lybrand
Employees: 62,873

WHERE

HQ: PO Box 1438, 500 W. Main St., Louisville, KY 40202-1438
Phone: 502-580-1000
Fax: 502-580-3694 (Public Affairs Department)

	No. of Hospitals
Alabama	7
Arizona	2
California	5
Colorado	2
Florida	19
Georgia	4
Kansas	2
Kentucky	7
Louisiana	8
Tennessee	3
Texas	12
Virginia	3
West Virginia	2
Other states	6
Switzerland	1
UK	2
Total	**85**

WHAT

	1990 Sales		1990 Operating Income	
	$ mil.	% of total	$ mil.	% of total
Hospitals	3,358	69	637	93
Health plans	1,494	31	49	7
Adjustments	—	—	(152)	—
Total	**4,852**	**100**	**534**	**100**

	1990 Licensed Beds	
	No. of beds	% of total
Health Care Division	8,020	45
Hospital Division	9,335	52
Foreign Hospitals	483	3
Total	**17,838**	**100**

Businesses
Health maintenance organizations
Hospitals
Indemnity insurance plans
Preferred provider organizations

HOW MUCH

	9-Year Growth	1981	1982	1983	1984	1985	1986	1987	1988	1989	1990
Sales ($ mil.)	15.3%	1,343	1,516	1,765	1,961	2,188	2,601	2,832	3,435	4,088	4,852
Net income ($ mil.)	14.6%	93	127	161	193	216	54	183	227	256	318
Income as % of sales	—	6.9%	8.4%	9.1%	9.9%	9.9%	2.1%	6.5%	6.6%	6.3%	6.6%
Earnings per share ($)	13.7%	0.97	1.34	1.63	1.96	2.19	0.56	1.86	2.30	2.56	3.08
Stock price – high ($)	—	19.32	28.75	33.33	33.00	36.75	33.88	29.50	28.63	44.00	50.88
Stock price – low ($)	—	12.08	12.58	19.58	21.50	21.88	19.13	16.13	19.00	24.38	35.25
Stock price – close ($)	12.5%	14.58	28.13	21.88	23.50	31.25	19.13	19.25	25.38	44.00	42.13
P/E – high	—	20	22	20	17	17	61	16	12	17	17
P/E – low	—	12	9	12	11	10	34	9	8	10	11
Dividends per share ($)	18.9%	0.23	0.34	0.47	0.58	0.66	0.74	0.77	0.83	0.95	1.08
Book value per share ($)	19.6%	3.34	4.25	6.35	7.67	9.28	9.20	10.36	11.80	13.48	16.77

1990 Year-end:
Debt ratio: 29.1%
Return on equity: 20.4%
Cash (mil.): $155
Current ratio: 1.08
Long-term debt (mil.): $717
No. of shares (mil.): 104
Dividends:
 1990 average yield: 2.6%
 1990 payout: 35.1%
Market value (mil.): $4,394

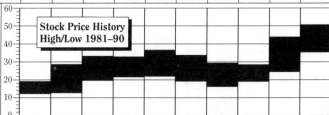
Stock Price History High/Low 1981–90

RANKINGS

22nd in *Fortune* 100 Diversified Service Cos.
138th in *Business Week* 1000

KEY COMPETITORS

Aetna	Mayo Foundation
Blue Cross	MetLife
CIGNA	National Medical
Hospital Corp.	New York Life
John Hancock	Prudential
MassMutual	Other insurers

HYATT CORPORATION

Private company
Fiscal year ends: December 31

Hoover's Rating **B+**

OVERVIEW

Hyatt Corporation, part of H Group Holdings, is the best known operation of Chicago's publicity-shy Pritzker family. Hyatt is a sister to the Pritzkers' mammoth Marmon Group, composed of some 60 industrial companies. Many of the firms are nuts-and-bolts concerns (railroad tank cars, casters), but with the Pritzker touch, they often make up in profits what they lack in glamour.

Hyatt owns about 40% of the hotels it manages. The chain is known for its superla-

tive service, and many of the amenities it introduced (complimentary shampoo, restricted-access floors) have been copied by other chains. These days Hyatt is emphasizing overseas expansion and plans to open its first South American hotels early in 1992. The company already operates hotels throughout the Pacific region, including China, and other deals may put Hyatt hotels in Warsaw and Prague. Overseas revenues grew by 22% in 1990, compared to 4% domestic gains.

WHEN

Nicholas Pritzker came to Chicago from Kiev in 1881 to begin his family's ascent to a fortune now worth more than $4 billion.

Nicholas's son, A. N., left the family law practice in the 1930s and began investing in a variety of businesses. He turned one $25,000 investment (Cory Corporation) in 1942 into $23 million by 1967.

After WWII, A. N.'s son Jay followed in his father's wheeling-and-dealing footsteps. In 1953, with the help of his father's banking connections, Jay purchased Colson Company and recruited brother Bob, an industrial engineer, to restructure a company that made tricycles and navy rockets. By 1990 Jay and Bob had added 60 industrial companies, with annual sales exceeding $3 billion, to the entity they called the Marmon Group.

In 1957 Jay bought a hotel called Hyatt House, located near the Los Angeles airport, from Hyatt von Dehn. Jay had added 5 locations by 1961 and brought his gregarious youngest brother, Donald, to California to manage the company.

In 1967 the Pritzkers took the company public, but the move that opened new vistas for the hotel chain was the purchase of an 800-room hotel in Atlanta that both Hilton and Marriott had turned down. John Portman's innovative design, incorporating a 21-story atrium, a large fountain, and a revolving rooftop restaurant, became a Hyatt trademark. The Pritzkers formed Hyatt International in 1969 to operate hotels overseas, and the company grew rapidly during the 1970s in the US and abroad. Donald Pritzker died in 1972 and his successor ran up some questionable expenses. This prompted the family to

move corporate offices to Chicago in 1977 and to take the company and subsidiaries private in 1979. In 1980 Hyatt introduced its first Park Hyatt, a European-style super-luxury hotel, near the Water Tower in Chicago. The Park Hyatt concept expanded slowly, and the company waited 6 years before it opened its next Park Hyatt, in Washington, DC.

Much of the company's growth in the 1970s came from contracts to manage, under the Hyatt banner, hotels built by other investors. In the 1980s Hyatt's cut on those contracts diminished, and it launched its own hotel and resort developments under Nick Pritzker, a cousin to Jay and Bob. In 1988, with US and Japanese partners, it built the $360 million Hyatt Regency Waikoloa on Hawaii's Big Island. The resort was, according to *Fortune*, the most expensive hotel ever built.

Through Hyatt subsidiaries, the Pritzkers bought bedraggled Braniff Airlines in 1983 as it emerged from bankruptcy court. Braniff had been the carrier with many-colored planes but had fallen victim to airline deregulation. Hoping to strengthen Braniff through a merger, the Pritzkers made a bid for Pan Am in 1987, but Pan Am's unions refused wage concessions, and the deal fell apart. The Pritzkers sold Braniff in 1988 but kept some of its maintenance operations under the Dalfort name.

Using the real estate and hospitality skills from the Hyatt operations, the Pritzkers have branched out beyond innkeeping. In 1989 Hyatt launched Classic Residence by Hyatt, an upscale retirement community. Jay Pritzker made another attempt to buy bankrupt Pan Am in 1991 but lost out to Delta.

WHO

Chairman and CEO: Jay Pritzker, age 69
President; Chairman, Hyatt Hotels Corp.: Thomas V. Pritzker, age 41
SVP and CFO: Ken Posner
VP Marketing: Jim Evans
VP Human Resources: Myrna Hellerman
President, Hyatt Hotels Corp.: Darryl Hartley-Leonard
President, Classic Residence: Penny S. Pritzker, age 32
President, Marmon Group: Robert Pritzker, age 65
Auditors: KPMG Peat Marwick
Employees: 55,195

WHERE

HQ: 200 W. Madison, Chicago, IL 60606
Phone: 312-750-1234
Fax: 312-750-8550
Reservations: 800-233-1234

	1990 Estimated Sales	
	$ mil.	% of total
US	2,300	74
Other countries	801	26
Total	**3,101**	**100**

	1990 Hotels	
	No. of hotels	% of total
US, Canada & Caribbean	105	66
Other countries	53	34
Total	**158**	**100**

WHAT

Subsidiaries
Hyatt Hotels Corp.
  Hyatt Hotels International
  Classic Residence by Hyatt (upscale retirement communities)
  Grand Hyatt
  Hyatt
  Hyatt Regency
  Park Hyatt
Spectacor Management Group (50%, arena mgmt.)
Related Pritzker Businesses
American Medical International (hospitals)
Conwood Co. (tobacco products)
Dalfort Corp. (aircraft maintenance)
Hawthorn Suites (lodging)
Itel Corp. (7.8%, railroad cars)
Marmon Group (60 industrial companies)
Royal Caribbean Cruises Ltd. (cruise line, 50%)
Tampa Bay Hockey Group (applicant for National Hockey League franchise)
Ticketmaster (event ticket sales)

RANKINGS

40th in *Forbes* 400 US Private Cos.

KEY COMPETITORS

Accor	Dole	Marriott
American Express	Helmsley	Metromedia
Bass	Hilton	Nestlé
Canadian Pacific	ITT	Ogden
Carlson	Loews	Rank
Dial		

HOW MUCH

	9-Year Growth	1981	1982	1983	1984	1985	1986	1987	1988	1989	1990
Estimated sales ($ mil.)	—	—	—	—	—	—	2,000	2,300	2,330	2,400	3,101
Total hotels	12.7%	54	60	64	68	72	79	85	91	101	158
New hotels	9.0%	7	6	4	4	4	7	6	6	10	57
Total rooms	6.5%	32,407	35,289	37,054	39,081	40,715	44,409	47,124	50,396	54,127	57,137
New rooms	(1.2%)	3,369	2,882	1,765	2,027	1,634	3,694	2,715	3,272	3,731	3,010
Employees	—	—	—	—	—	—	30,000	30,000	40,000	40,000	55,195

Total Rooms 1981–90

[Bar chart showing Total Rooms from 1981 to 1990, ranging from about 32,000 to 60,000, vertical axis from 0 to 60,000]

INGERSOLL-RAND COMPANY

OVERVIEW

Ingersoll-Rand is a major international producer of industrial machinery and equipment. Global operations are divided into 3 segments: Standard Machinery; Engineered Equipment; and Bearings, Locks, and Tools.

The Standard Machinery segment (39% of sales) produces air compressors for industrial and home use, construction equipment, and mining machinery.

The Engineered Equipment segment (14% of sales) manufactures pumps and industrial process machinery (pulp and paper processing machinery, filters, aerators, etc.).

The Bearings, Locks, and Tools segment (47% of sales) produces bearings and components (sold primarily to the auto and aerospace industries), production equipment (air-powered equipment, waterjet cutting systems), and door hardware. The company is the largest domestic producer of a broad line of bearings.

Ingersoll-Rand's products are used worldwide, from drills in Soviet mines to pipeline pumps in Saudi Arabia to air compressors in the English Channel tunnel construction project. Customers outside of the US account for 36% of company sales.

NYSE symbol: IR
Fiscal year ends: December 31

Hoover's Rating **B**

WHO

Chairman, President, and CEO: Theodore H. Black, age 62, $1,197,417 pay
VC and CFO: Clyde H. Folley, age 63, $792,750 pay
VP Human Resources: Robert G. Ripston, age 62
Auditors: Price Waterhouse
Employees: 33,700

WHERE

HQ: 200 Chestnut Ridge Rd., Woodcliff Lake, NJ 07675
Phone: 201-573-0123
Fax: 201-573-3448

The company owns 81 plants worldwide.

	1990 Sales		1990 Operating Income	
	$ mil.	% of total	$ mil.	% of total
US	2,400	64	217	56
Europe	881	24	111	28
Other countries	457	12	61	16
Adjustments	—		(32)	—
Total	**3,738**	**100**	**357**	**100**

WHAT

	1990 Sales		1990 Operating Income	
	$ mil.	% of total	$ mil.	% of total
Standard machinery	1,445	39	144	37
Engineered equip.	511	14	47	12
Bearings, locks & tools	1,783	47	197	51
Adjustments	—	—	(31)	—
Total	**3,738**	**100**	**357**	**100**

Products and Services

Agricultural pumps	Generator sets
Air compressors	Hoists
Air motors	Industrial pumps
Air tools	Lubrication equipment
Aircraft support equipment	Material-handling equipment
Asphalt-paving equipment	Mining machinery
Automated production systems	Needle bearings
Automotive components	Paving equipment
Ball bearings	Pneumatic valves
Breathing air systems	Pulp-processing machinery
Construction equipment	Road-building machinery
Door hardware	Rock drills
Electronic security systems	Roller bearings
Engine-starting systems	Roller mills
Fluid-handling equipment	Rotary drills
Food-processing equipment	Rough-terrain forklifts
	Soil compactors
	Spray coating systems
	Waterjet cutting systems
	Winches

WHEN

Simon Ingersoll invented the steam-driven rock drill in New York City in 1871. In 1874 he sold the patent to José Francisco de Navarro, who quickly financed the organization of the Ingersoll Rock Drill Company. Three years later the company merged with Sergeant Drill, a company formed by Navarro's former foreman, Henry Clark Sergeant.

In 1871, at the same time Ingersoll was inventing his drill, Albert, Jasper, and Addison Rand were forming the Rand Drill Company. Both companies continued to make drills and other equipment through the turn of the century. In 1905 they merged to become Ingersoll-Rand.

During the next several years Ingersoll-Rand started producing air compressors in addition to its basic line of rock drills. In 1912 the company added centrifugal compressors and turbo blowers to its product line. Further diversification occurred with the purchase of A. S. Cameron Steam Pump Works and Imperial Pneumatic Tool Company (portable air tools). For several decades the company continued to grow as a major manufacturer of compressed-air tools, sold mostly to the mining industry.

After WWII Ingersoll-Rand expanded its operations to Canada, Europe, South America, and Africa. During the 1960s the company diversified into new specialized machinery. Acquisitions during this period included Aldrich Pump (high-pressure plunger pumps, 1961), Pendleton Tool (mechanics' service tools, 1964), and Torrington (antifriction bearings and textile machine needles, 1969).

Diversification continued during the 1970s and 1980s with the acquisitions of DAMCO (truck-mounted drilling rigs, 1973); Schlage Lock (lock and door hardware, 1974); California Pellet (1974); Western Land Roller (vertical water pumps, 1977); and Fafnir Bearings, which made Ingersoll-Rand the largest US bearing manufacturer (1986).

During this time the company developed several new products, including small air compressors, high-speed pumps, hydraulic turbines for moderate-flow areas, and waterjet systems capable of cutting steel and concrete. In 1986 Ingersoll-Rand formed a partnership with Dresser Industries (Dresser-Rand) to produce gas turbines, compressors, and similar equipment. In 1990 Ingersoll-Rand bought Aro (air-powered tools, from Todd Shipyards) and ABG, a German paving-equipment maker.

Ingersoll-Rand and Dresser announced in 1991 that they were combining their pump businesses into another joint venture. The combined operations had $800 million in 1990 sales.

RANKINGS

132nd in *Fortune* 500 Industrial Cos.
244th in *Business Week* 1000

KEY COMPETITORS

Anglo American	Farley	Litton Industries
Baker Hughes	Fiat	Masco
Black & Decker	FMC	Rolls-Royce
Borg-Warner	Friedrich Krupp	Robert Bosch
Caterpillar	General Signal	Stanley Works
Cooper Industries	Henley	Teledyne
Deere	Honda	Texas
Dresser	ITT	Instruments
Eaton	JWP	

HOW MUCH

	9-Year Growth	1981	1982	1983	1984	1985	1986	1987	1988	1989	1990
Sales ($ mil.)	1.1%	3,378	2,775	2,274	2,478	2,637	2,799	2,648	3,021	3,447	3,738
Net income ($ mil.)	(0.5%)	193	52	(112)	59	80	101	108	162	202	185
Income as % of sales	—	5.7%	1.9%	(4.9%)	2.4%	3.0%	3.6%	4.1%	5.3%	5.9%	5.0%
Earnings per share ($)	(0.4%)	3.70	0.94	(2.38)	1.08	1.51	1.90	1.94	2.99	3.76	3.55
Stock price – high ($)	—	32.00	23.30	23.10	22.30	22.70	27.55	45.75	44.63	50.25	60.50
Stock price – low ($)	—	21.10	14.20	15.50	14.20	17.70	20.35	22.50	31.00	33.63	28.50
Stock price – close ($)	5.7%	22.60	15.80	20.95	18.20	21.40	22.30	35.50	34.25	50.25	37.25
P/E – high	—	9	25	—	21	15	15	24	15	13	17
P/E – low	—	6	15	—	13	12	11	12	10	9	8
Dividends per share ($)	(0.8%)	1.36	1.33	1.04	1.04	1.04	1.04	1.04	1.04	1.16	1.26
Book value per share ($)	1.7%	25.93	24.63	20.88	20.44	21.22	22.09	21.96	24.26	26.73	30.09

1990 Year-end:
Debt ratio: 14.6%
Return on equity: 12.5%
Cash (mil.): $52
Current ratio: 1.76
Long-term debt (mil.): $265
No. of shares (mil.): 52
Dividends:
1990 average yield: 3.4%
1990 payout: 35.5%
Market value (mil.): $1,927

Stock Price History High/Low 1981–90

INLAND STEEL INDUSTRIES, INC.

NYSE symbol: IAD
Fiscal year ends: December 31

OVERVIEW

Inland Steel Industries, which ranks 4th in sales among US steel producers, is a fully integrated producer of steel, about 99% of which is carbon and high-strength, low-alloy steel. The company is divided into 2 segments: Integrated Steel and Steel Service Centers (customized steel products).

Integrated Steel Operations consists of Inland Steel Flat Products (steel strip and sheet) and Inland Steel Bar (steel bar and plate), both located at the company's Indiana Harbor Works. Total 1990 steel production was 5.3 million tons — 5.5% of US output.

The Steel Service Center segment sells metal products to manufacturers and fabricators. Inland's operations are comprised of Joseph T. Ryerson & Son (the largest steel service center organization in the US) and J. M. Tull Metals (one of the largest metal distributors in the southeastern US).

Inland is pinning its hopes for the future on high-end flat-rolled and bar steel for industrial customers such as automakers and appliance manufacturers. Inland abandoned the structural steel business in 1990, citing pressure from high efficiency minimills.

WHO

Chairman and CEO: Frank W. Luerssen, age 63, $492,157 pay
President and COO: Robert J. Darnall, age 52, $379,937 pay
VP Corporate Planning: David B. Anderson, age 48, $247,318 pay
CFO: Earl L. Mason, age 43
VP Human Resources: Judd R. Cool, age 55
Auditors: Price Waterhouse
Employees: 20,200

WHERE

HQ: 30 W. Monroe St., Chicago, IL 60603
Phone: 312-346-0300
Fax: 312-899-3672

The company produces all of its raw steel products at Indiana Harbor Works in East Chicago, IL. Through its Ryerson and Tull segments, the company operates 57 Steel Service Centers nationwide. In addition, the company operates a Great Lakes fleet of 3 ships, a fleet of 410 railroad hopper cars, and 3 iron ore mines.

WHEN

In 1893 8 partners purchased 40 freight cars of used steel-making machinery from the bankrupt Chicago Steel Company and established Inland Steel in the Chicago Heights area. By 1894 the company was producing agricultural implements (plows, etc.).

In 1901 the Lake Michigan Land Company offered 50 acres of land at Indiana Harbor to any company that would spend $1 million to develop the land by building an open-hearth steel mill. Inland raised the money and built Indiana Harbor Works. In 1906 the company bought the Laura Ore iron mine in Minnesota.

Inland saw steady growth through the mid-teens. In 1916 the company began a program of rapid expansion to meet the need for steel caused by WWI. By 1920 Inland was producing 2% of the steel in the US. The company converted its mills back to peacetime production and in 1922 started producing rails.

During the difficult Great Depression years, Inland turned its production emphasis from heavy steel to the lighter steel (tinplate, sheets) needed for consumer goods. In 1931 the company, under Chairman L. E. Block, started construction on facilities to produce strip, sheet, and plate steel. Inland acquired Joseph T. Ryerson & Son (steel warehousing) in 1935 and Wilson & Bennett Manufacturing (later renamed Inland Steel Containers) in

1939. The company introduced Ledloy (a steel/lead alloy machining metal) in 1938.

Inland's attention was turned to wartime production again in the early 1940s. In 1947 the company expanded the capacity of its rolling mills. Inland introduced its line of galvanized steel sheets (marketed under the TI-CO trade name) in 1951. In 1957 the company built its new skyscraper headquarters (one of the first to use external columns and stainless steel in its construction) in Chicago.

In 1966 Inland became a billion-dollar company. The 1970s brought a steel boom. When the boom ended in the 1980s, Inland suffered big losses.

In 1986 Inland acquired J. M. Tull Metals from Bethlehem Steel. During the late 1980s Inland increasingly turned its attention to the production of custom work (such as painted steel for appliances). In 1987 and 1989 Inland entered into 2 joint ventures with Nippon Steel to build and operate cold rolling (I/N Tek, 60%-owned) and coating (I/N Kote, 50%) facilities.

The I/N Tek plant has been plagued by glitches in its high-tech operations, and the company was hit by a slump in demand during the 1990–91 recession. Inland posted a loss in 1990 and continued to take a beating in early 1991.

WHAT

	1990 Sales		1990 Operating Income	
	$ mil.	% of total	$ mil.	% of total
Integrated Steel	2,055	53	1	5
Steel Service Centers	1,815	47	18	95
Total	**3,870**	**100**	**19**	**100**

Integrated Steel
Inland Steel Co.

Products
Bar steel
Coil
Expanded metal
Grating
Pipe
Plate
Raw steel
Rod
Semifinished products
Sheet
Strip
Tubing
Wire

Joint Ventures
I/N Kote (50%)
I/N Tek (60%)

Service Centers
Joseph T. Ryerson & Son, Inc.
J. M. Tull Metals Co., Inc.
AFCO Metals, Inc.

RANKINGS

125th in *Fortune* 500 Industrial Cos.
644th in *Business Week* 1000

KEY COMPETITORS

Bethlehem Steel
Broken Hill
Cargill
Friedrich Krupp
Hyundai
IRI
LTV
Thyssen
USX

HOW MUCH

	9-Year Growth	1981	1982	1983	1984	1985	1986	1987	1988	1989	1990
Sales ($ mil.)	0.3%	3,755	2,808	3,046	3,325	2,999	3,173	3,453	4,068	4,147	3,870
Net income ($ mil.)	—	57	(133)	(111)	(40)	(147)	35	112	249	120	(21)
Income as % of sales	—	1.5%	(4.7%)	(3.6%)	(1.2%)	(4.9%)	1.1%	3.2%	6.1%	2.9%	(0.5%)
Earnings per share ($)	—	2.69	(6.27)	(4.51)	(1.93)	(6.14)	0.95	3.04	6.36	3.06	(1.41)
Stock price – high ($)	—	36.00	26.75	35.00	32.75	26.00	28.38	35.25	42.63	48.50	36.38
Stock price – low ($)	—	22.25	18.13	24.75	19.88	19.50	14.50	17.00	27.50	31.38	20.50
Stock price – close ($)	0.6%	23.38	26.00	31.00	23.25	22.63	18.88	30.38	41.50	33.75	24.75
P/E – high	—	13	—	—	—	—	30	12	7	16	—
P/E – low	—	8	—	—	—	—	15	6	4	10	—
Dividends per share ($)	(3.9%)	2.00	1.13	0.50	0.50	0.38	0.00	0.00	0.75	1.40	1.40
Book value per share ($)	(4.4%)	62.29	52.90	45.41	42.64	34.68	35.73	41.68	45.75	43.04	41.63

1990 Year-end:
Debt ratio: 34.9%
Return on equity: —
Cash (mil.): $58
Current ratio: 1.76
Long-term debt (mil.): $692
No. of shares (mil.): 31
Dividends:
  1990 average yield: 5.7%
  1990 payout: —
Market value (mil.): $764

Stock Price History High/Low 1981–90

INTEL CORPORATION

OVERVIEW

Intel is only the 3rd largest US semiconductor manufacturer (after Motorola and Texas Instruments), but the company's x86 series (286, 386, 486) chip designs supply the brains for 80% of all existing desktop computers (PCs and workstations). This near-monopoly, resulting from Intel chips' use in the IBM PC, began to disappear in 1990 as competitors won the right to make their own versions of the popular microprocessors.

In addition, Intel has also been threatened by the industry's shift to RISC chips for workstations. However, new operating systems for PCs have increased demand for Intel's 486 series of chips — a product that Intel has begun to advertise directly to end users.

Intel also makes chips that control robots, run printers and communications systems, and store data in memory. Intel also produces computer systems (including PCs), sold under other manufacturers' names (e.g., AT&T) against products that use Intel chips. Systems accounted for about 25% of 1990 sales.

Intel maintains leadership in transistor density, recently announcing a new version of its i860 chip that contains 2.55 million transistors. R&D remains high at $517 million, or 13% of sales.

NASDAQ symbol: INTC
Fiscal year ends: Last Saturday in December

Hoover's Rating **A+**

WHO

President and CEO: Andrew S. Grove, age 54, $860,300 pay
Chairman: Gordon E. Moore, age 62, $709,700 pay
EVP: Craig R. Barrett, age 51, $593,000 pay
SVP and CFO: Robert W. Reed, age 44
VP and Director Human Resources: Carlene M. Ellis, age 44
Auditors: Ernst & Young
Employees: 23,900

WHEN

In 1968, 3 PhD engineers from Fairchild Semiconductor created Intel in Mountain View, California, to realize the potential of large-scale integration (LSI) technology for silicon-based chips. Robert Noyce (co-inventor of the integrated circuit, 1957) and Gordon Moore handled long-range planning while current CEO Andrew Grove oversaw manufacturing.

Intel started with 12 employees and first-year sales of $2,672 but soon mushroomed as a supplier of semiconductor memory for large computers (DRAM chips, which replaced magnetic core memory storage, 1970; and EPROM chips, which allowed memory to be erased and reused, 1971).

This success funded Intel's microprocessor designs (the 4004 in 1971 and its descendants the 8008, 8080, and 8088), which revolutionized the electronics industry by putting vast amounts of power on silicon chips. When IBM chose the 8088 chip for its PC in 1981, Intel secured its place as the microcomputer standards supplier.

Noyce stepped down from top management in 1979, serving as a director and deputy chairman of the company's board, as well as a founder of the SEMATECH manufacturing consortium, until his death in June 1990. In 1991 Intel established Robert Noyce Fellowships at the University of California at Berkeley, MIT, and the University of Texas.

Cutthroat pricing of DRAMs by Japanese competitors forced Grove (who succeeded Noyce as president and CEO) to close plants, cut the work force by 30%, and withdraw from the DRAM market; 1984's $198 million profit became a $183 million loss by 1986.

To recoup, Grove focused on proprietary PC chips. Intel had allowed competitors like AMD to make their own versions of its 80286 chip (1982), only to see AMD capture 52% of the 286 market by 1990. In response, Intel fiercely protected the technology of the successor 386 chip (1985). However, in 1990 an arbitrator ruled against Intel in a case brought by AMD 3 years earlier, thus validating the 1982 technology exchange agreement. AMD later announced that it had successfully reverse-engineered the 386. Faced with this competition, Intel announced it would sue any manufacturer who used the "386" trademark.

The new Intel 80486 chip (1989) can give PCs the power of mainframe computers, and their success made Intel one of the most profitable electronics companies in 1990, with one of the fastest sales growths. In 1991 Intel demonstrated a new 100 MHz microprocessor — twice as powerful as anything currently on the market.

WHERE

HQ: 3065 Bowers Ave., Santa Clara, CA 95052
Phone: 408-765-8080
Fax: 408-765-1402

Intel has 79 sales offices in 21 nations and sells through distributors in 34 countries; manufacturing plants are in the US, Ireland, Israel, Malaysia, the Philippines, Puerto Rico, and Singapore.

	1990 Sales		1990 Operating Income	
	$ mil.	% of total	$ mil.	% of total
US	2,116	54	788	68
Europe	866	22	112	10
Japan	400	10	29	3
Asia, Pacific & other	539	14	222	19
Adjustments	—	—	(293)	—
Total	**3,921**	**100**	**858**	**100**

WHAT

Microprocessors		
16-bit	8086	
	8088	
	80286	
32-bit	386 DX	
	386 SX	
	i486	
64-bit	i860	

Application-Specific Integrated Circuits (ASICs)
Board-level products
Microprocessor peripheral components

Memories
DRAM (reseller)
EPROM
Flash memories
SRAM

Computer Systems
ActionMedia 750 (Digital Video Interactive)

Microcomputers
Model 303
Model 302-20
Model 300-SX
Personal computer enhancement (add-in boards)
Networking products
Supercomputers
iPSC 860

Software
Developmental tools
High-level network systems
Microcomputer operating systems

Embedded Control Products	
8-bit	8048, 8051
16-bit	8096, 80C196
32-bit	i960

RANKINGS

119th in *Fortune* 500 Industrial Cos.
52nd in *Business Week* 1000

KEY COMPETITORS

Apple	Hitachi	SCI Systems
AST	Hyundai	Sharp
Canon	IBM	Siemens
Cray Research	Lucky-Goldstar	Sun
Data General	Motorola	Microsystems
Dell	National	Texas
DEC	Semiconductor	Instruments
Fujitsu	NEC	Toshiba
Harris	Oki	Unisys
Hewlett-Packard	Samsung	

HOW MUCH

	9-Year Growth	1981	1982	1983	1984	1985	1986	1987	1988	1989	1990
Sales ($ mil.)	19.5%	789	900	1,122	1,629	1,365	1,265	1,907	2,875	3,127	3,921
Net income ($ mil.)	42.2%	27	30	116	198	2	(183)	176	453	391	650
Income as % of sales	—	3.5%	3.3%	10.4%	12.2%	0.1%	(14.5%)	9.2%	15.8%	12.5%	16.6%
Earnings per share ($)	35.8%	0.20	0.22	0.70	1.13	0.01	(1.05)	0.98	2.51	2.06	3.20
Stock price – high ($)	—	13.92	13.83	33.00	29.00	21.67	21.50	41.83	37.25	36.00	52.00
Stock price – low ($)	—	7.50	6.92	12.33	16.50	13.83	10.92	13.83	19.25	22.88	28.00
Stock price – close ($)	19.9%	7.50	12.92	28.00	18.67	19.50	14.00	26.50	23.75	34.50	38.50
P/E – high	—	68	64	47	26	3,250	—	43	15	17	16
P/E – low	—	37	32	18	15	2,075	—	14	8	11	9
Dividends per share ($)	0.0%	0.00	0.00	0.00	0.00	0.00	0.00	0.00	0.00	0.00	0.00
Book value per share ($)	19.1%	3.72	4.06	6.69	7.97	8.16	7.22	7.76	11.52	13.81	17.99

1990 Year-end:
Debt ratio: 8.8%
Return on equity: 20.1%
Cash (mil.): $1,785
Current ratio: 2.37
Long-term debt (mil.): $345
No. of shares (mil.): 200
Dividends:
  1990 average yield: 0.0%
  1990 payout: 0.0%
Market value (mil.): $7,687

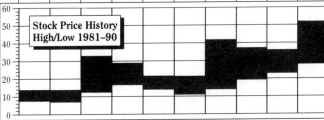

Stock Price History High/Low 1981–90

INTERCO INC.

OVERVIEW

INTERCO, a major producer of furniture and footwear, is a casualty of the 1980s LBO craze. Though its 4 core companies (Broyhill, Lane, Florsheim, and Converse) are all profitable, the company is so loaded with debt from fighting off a hostile takeover that it was forced into Chapter 11 bankruptcy in January 1991 after defaulting on bond interest payments in 1990.

INTERCO's furniture segment (Broyhill, Lane) generates 55% of sales. Broyhill, one of the industry's largest and best-known furniture companies, with a 3% market share, produces primarily wood, upholstered, and occasional furniture. Lane makes furniture and offers more than 5,000 items.

The company's shoe segment consists of Florsheim and Converse. Florsheim is the largest producer of men's quality footwear, with a 20% market share. Florsheim shoes are sold through approximately 490 company-owned Florsheim retail outlets (that now sell only Florsheim shoes) and through approximately 5,000 independent dealers. Converse is a major producer of athletic footwear. Converse's strongest and most popular product line is its men's basketball shoes, which generates 32% of its revenues.

WHEN

In 1911 the Roberts, Johnson and Rand Shoe Company (founded 1898) and Peters Shoe Company (founded 1836) formed the International Shoe Company in St. Louis. After 4 successful decades, in 1953 International Shoe purchased Florsheim (a manufacturer and retailer of men's shoes) for $20.8 million, starting a long history of acquisitions.

Despite its name, the company did not become "international" until 1954 when it purchased Savage Shoes of Canada. By 1962 when the company acquired a majority interest in Marlow Holding (men's shoes) in Melbourne, Australia, it had major difficulties with its retail shoe operations. In that year, Maurice Chambers, a former shoe salesman, became president of International Shoe and began modernizing operations and trimming unprofitable stores and inventory. During Chambers's first decade as president, the company tripled its sales. In 1966 the company changed its name to INTERCO.

Chambers diversified widely during the 1960s and 1970s with such disparate purchases as Central Hardware Stores (1966), Campus Sweater & Sportswear (name changed to Megastar Apparel, 1968), Biltwell (men's pants, 1970), Golde's Department Stores (1971), Big Yank (leisure and work clothes, 1972), Devon Apparel (women's sportswear,

1974), Londontown (rainwear, 1976), and Stuffed Shirt/Stuffed Jeans (1976, the year Chambers stepped down as CEO). In 1986 INTERCO bought Converse (athletic shoes), for which William Loynd worked.

During the 1980s the company became a major force in the furniture industry with the purchases of Ethan Allen, Broyhill, Highland House, and Lane.

In 1988, under a takeover threat by S. Rales and M. Rales, INTERCO retained the investment banking firm of Wasserstein Perella, which advised payment of a $76 special dividend, for which INTERCO borrowed $1.8 billion. When INTERCO began selling off assets to repay the debt, the assets yielded lower prices than projected or lacked buyers. Units sold included Londontown, Biltwell, Central Hardware, and Ethan Allen. There were no buyers for Sky City, Megastar, and Schrader, which were liquidated.

Following a shareholder suit against the company that was settled in 1990 for $18.5 million, INTERCO went into Chapter 11 to gain time to reorganize and filed a malpractice suit against Wasserstein Perella (which received $5.5 million in fees). Since reorganization, fees paid to other bankers include $3 million to J.P. Morgan and up to $2 million per month to Smith Barney and others.

NYSE symbol: ISS
Fiscal year ends: Last Saturday in February

WHO

Chairman, President, and CEO: Richard B. Loynd, age 63, $682,084 pay
VP; Chairman, Lane Company: R. Stuart Moore, age 67, $455,949 pay
VP; President, Florsheim: Ronald J. Mueller, age 56, $357,048 pay
EVP and CFO: Eugene F. Smith, age 58, $261,788 pay
Operations Director (Personnel): Robert Haas
Auditors: KPMG Peat Marwick
Employees: 22,100

WHERE

HQ: 101 S. Hanley Rd., St. Louis, MO 63105
Phone: 314-863-1100
Fax: 314-863-5306

The company's major plants, offices, and warehouses include 19 Broyhill, 5 Converse, 9 Florsheim, and 17 Lane facilities distributed throughout the US. Florsheim has 530 stores (65 outside the US) and operates subsidiaries in Australia and Canada. Converse products are sold in more than 90 countries.

WHAT

	1990 Sales		1990 Operating Income	
	$ mil.	% of total	$ mil.	% of total
Footware	653	45	9	11
Furniture	786	55	75	89
Total	**1,439**	**100**	**84**	**100**

Brand Names

Furniture	Shoes
Broyhill	Converse
Contract	All-Star
Highland House	American Sports Casuals
Premier	Chick Taylor
Showcase Gallery	Conasaurs
Timbertown	Cons
Lane	EnergyWave
Hickory Chair	EVOLO
James River	Jack Purcell
Collection	Magic
Mark Hampton	Skip Grid
Collection	Small Star
Weathermaster	Florsheim
	ComforTech
Stores	Designer Collection
Florsheim	Idlers
Florsheim Thayer	Imperial
McNeil	Outdoorsman
	Pro Action
	Ramblers
	Royal Imperial
	Sea Tracs
	Signature

RANKINGS

201st in *Fortune* 500 Industrial Cos.

KEY COMPETITORS

Armstrong World	Melville
Brown Group	NIKE
Edison Brothers	Reebok
Hanson	U.S. Shoe
L.A. Gear	Wal-Mart
Masco	Other discount and
May	department stores

HOW MUCH

Fiscal year ends February of following year	9-Year Growth	1981	1982	1983	1984	1985	1986	1987	1988	1989	1990
Sales ($ mil.)	(6.7%)	2,674	2,567	2,679	2,626	2,511	2,614	3,341	2,012	1,656	1,439
Net income ($ mil.)	—	119	86	116	72	92	99	145	(4)	(51)	(151)
Income as % of sales	—	4.4%	3.3%	4.3%	2.7%	3.7%	3.8%	4.3%	(0.2%)	(3.1%)	(10.5%)
Earnings per share ($)	—	3.62	2.61	3.51	2.23	2.92	3.13	3.50	(0.42)	(3.37)	(6.38)
Stock price – high ($)	—	28.63	30.88	42.50	34.00	36.81	47.63	54.00	73.63	3.88	0.81
Stock price – low ($)	—	22.75	17.75	29.00	27.50	29.63	33.50	29.50	3.13	0.19	0.07
Stock price – close ($)	(46.1%)	23.63	30.50	33.25	29.88	35.44	36.88	32.25	3.63	0.56	0.09
P/E – high	—	8	12	12	15	13	15	15	—	—	—
P/E – low	—	6	7	8	12	10	11	8	—	—	—
Dividends per share ($)	(100%)	1.44	1.44	1.44	1.52	1.54	1.57	1.60	39.49	0.00	0.00
Book value per share ($)	—	31.18	32.32	34.41	35.22	36.52	38.06	33.01	(26.70)	(25.08)	(29.43)

1990 Year-end:
Debt ratio: 0.0%
Return on equity: —
Cash (mil.): $97
Current ratio: 7.43
Long-term debt (mil.): $0
No. of shares (mil.): 39
Dividends:
  1990 average yield: 0.0%
  1990 payout: 0.0%
Market value (mil.): $3

Stock Price History High/Low 1981–90

INTERGRAPH CORPORATION

NASDAQ symbol: INGR
Fiscal year ends: December 31

Hoover's Rating **A+**

OVERVIEW

Huntsville, Alabama–based Intergraph is the #2 supplier (behind IBM) of computer-aided design, manufacturing, and engineering (CAD/CAM/CAE) systems in the world. The company ranks #1 in architecture, engineering, and construction (A/E/C) design software and mapping applications, and is the #4 manufacturer of computer workstations (estimated 6.8% world market share). Intergraph is also a leading supplier of computer graphics systems to the US government (16% of 1990 sales).

The company is one of the few vendors in the industry offering a turnkey system, selling its hardware and application software as an integrated package. Intergraph's workstations are built around its proprietary RISC microprocessor, called CLIPPER. The company has made its file formats public, enabling 3rd parties to port their software to Intergraph's machines.

For the 3rd year in a row, Intergraph ranked #1 in customer satisfaction in a survey of computer vendors conducted by Daratech market research. Intergraph is supplying contractors involved in rebuilding Kuwait with the Kuwaiti Municipal Database, a geographic information system containing detailed maps of the city's streets and utilities.

WHEN

James Meadlock, his wife Nancy, Terry Schantzman, and several other former IBM coworkers, all software developers for Saturn rockets at IBM's Federal Systems Division in Huntsville, Alabama, founded M&S Computing in 1969. The company's initial focus was consulting work. The first contract, a guidance system for the US Army Missile Command in Huntsville, used the real-time applications that later grew into Intergraph's core computer graphics business.

The first commercial graphics systems sale was for mapping applications (1973). Penetration of the architectural, engineering, and construction (A/E/C) markets followed, with the introduction of a single graphics product, the Interactive Graphics Design System (IGDS). Meadlock packaged the graphics software with industry-accepted hardware such as DEC's PDP-11, while competitors stuck to more restricted proprietary versions.

In the late 1970s the company began making its own computers to produce customized solutions, compatibility across product lines, and larger profit margins. The company name was changed to Intergraph in 1980; the newly public Intergraph (1981) grew 40-60% yearly during the graphics boom of the early 1980s. In 1984 Intergraph introduced the competitive InterPro 32 workstation, followed by the first dual-screen workstation, Interact.

Intergraph supported open (freely communicating) systems by adopting the industry-standard UNIX operating system and networking Intergraph workstations on the Ethernet standard. The company powered the workstations with its speedy RISC microprocessor and anticipated demand for generic workstations unbundled from applications graphics software (introduced in 1987).

Intergraph also absorbed key technologies, buying its CLIPPER supplier (1987), scanning and plotting hardware (Optotronics, 1986; AnaTech, 1987), computer software (Tangent Systems, 50%, 1984; 82%, 1988), and software development tools (Quintus, 1989). Intergraph bought a 50% stake in Bentley Systems (creator of Intergraph's MicroStation software, 1987) and acquired Daisy Cadnetix (1990), making it a leading supplier to the electronic design automation (EDA) industry.

A 2nd-generation CLIPPER chip (the C300) fueled the 3000 workstation series (1988) and the successor 6000 series (1990). In 1989 Intergraph moved into the dispatch management system and technical information management (TIM) markets. Intergraph introduced the Series 2000 in 1990, a workstation for the low-end market.

WHO

Chairman and CEO: James W. Meadlock, age 57, $300,000 pay
President: Eliott D. James, age 50, $341,430 pay
EVP: Nancy B. Meadlock, age 52
EVP and CFO: Larry J. Laster, age 39
VP Corporate Human Resources: Milford B. French
Auditors: Ernst & Young
Employees: 9,600

WHERE

HQ: Huntsville, AL 35894-0001
Phone: 205-730-2000
Fax: 205-730-2164 (Investor Relations)

Intergraph sells its systems in 41 countries.

	1990 Sales		1990 Operating Income	
	$ mil.	% of total	$ mil.	% of total
US	592	57	81	88
Europe	343	33	8	9
Other foreign	110	10	3	3
Adjustments	—	—	2	—
Total	**1,045**	**100**	**94**	**100**

WHAT

	1990 Sales	
	$ mil.	% of total
Systems	770	74
Service	275	26
Total	**1,045**	**100**

Intergraph Systems
Peripherals (disk and tape drives, line printers, scanning hardware)
Servers
  2000 series (CLIPPER-based)
  6000 series (CLIPPER-based)
UNIX- and VAX-based software
Workstations
  380 (VAX-based)
  2000 series (CLIPPER-based)
  6000 series (CLIPPER-based)
  ImageStation 6187

Intergraph Systems Software
Data Management and Retrieval System (VAX-based)
Interactive Graphics Design System
MicroStation (for workstations, PCs)

Intergraph Applications
Architectural and engineering design
Civil engineering
Dispatch management
Electrical design and engineering
Electronics design automation
Electronic publishing
Energy exploration and development
Geographic information systems
Mapping
Mechanical design, engineering, and manufacturing
Scanning and document management
Utilities (gas and water)

RANKINGS

339th in *Fortune* 500 Industrial Cos.
488th in *Business Week* 1000

KEY COMPETITORS

AT&T
Control Data
Data General
DEC
Fujitsu
Hewlett-Packard
Hitachi
IBM
NEC
Prime
Schlumberger
Sun Microsystems
Tandem
Unisys
Wang

HOW MUCH

	9-Year Growth	1981	1982	1983	1984	1985	1986	1987	1988	1989	1990
Sales ($ mil.)	31.1%	91	156	252	404	526	606	641	800	860	1,045
Net income ($ mil.)	25.2%	8	13	29	63	68	70	70	88	80	63
Income as % of sales	—	9.1%	8.4%	11.6%	15.6%	12.9%	11.6%	10.9%	11.0%	9.2%	6.0%
Earnings per share ($)	23.8%	0.19	0.28	0.58	1.22	1.25	1.26	1.23	1.55	1.48	1.28
Stock price – high ($)	—	8.22	12.69	25.69	28.88	38.00	40.50	30.50	32.50	22.75	23.50
Stock price – low ($)	—	4.50	3.94	11.28	16.38	21.00	15.25	16.50	19.25	13.75	10.50
Stock price – close ($)	9.2%	6.25	11.94	19.25	27.50	36.75	17.00	24.75	21.00	17.25	13.75
P/E – high	—	44	45	44	24	30	32	25	21	15	18
P/E – low	—	24	14	19	13	17	12	13	12	9	8
Dividends per share ($)	—	0.00	0.00	0.00	0.00	0.00	0.00	0.00	0.00	0.00	0.00
Book value per share ($)	33.1%	1.10	1.41	3.17	4.52	7.28	8.80	10.06	11.72	12.58	14.35

1990 Year-end:
Debt ratio: 2.4%
Return on equity: 9.5%
Cash (mil.): $90
Current ratio: 3.25
Long-term debt (mil.): $17
No. of shares (mil.): 48
Dividends:
  1990 average yield: 0.0%
  1990 payout: 0.0%
Market value (mil.): $654

Stock Price History
High/Low 1981–90

INTERNATIONAL BUSINESS MACHINES CORP.

OVERVIEW

Armonk, New York–based IBM is the largest computer maker in the world. The company's $69 billion in revenues exceeds the combined revenues of its top 10 US competitors. IBM's leadership position extends beyond computers to include disk drives, software, support services, and semiconductors.

An exemplary multinational, IBM employs virtually all-native work forces in over 130 host countries; Europe alone has over 100,000 IBMers. Foreign sales made up 61% of total sales in 1990, compared to 43% in 1985, and accounted for 76% of 1990 profits.

Faced with eroding marketshare, IBM has become more assertive in the marketplace, announcing partnership agreements with 2 of its longstanding rivals in 1991: Apple Computer and Wang Laboratories. Big Blue (as IBM is commonly referred to) has over 10,000 patents. R&D expenses topped $6.6 billion in 1990 (2nd highest in the US, after GM).

Once-mighty IBM now must face the challenges of intensifying competition in the computer industry. IBM's strategy, called Systems Application Architecture, is to provide connectivity solutions across multiple computers.

WHEN

In 1914 National Cash Register's star salesman, 40-year-old Thomas J. Watson, left to rescue the flagging Computing-Tabulating-Recording Company. Watson aggressively marketed C-T-R's Hollerith machine (a punch card tabulator) and supplied tabulators to the US government during WWI, tripling C-T-R's revenues to almost $15 million by 1920.

Watson then expanded operations to Europe, Latin America, and the Far East and in 1924 changed the company name to International Business Machines. IBM soon dominated the market for tabulators, time clocks, and electric typewriters (introduced in 1935), becoming the US's largest office machinery firm by 1940, with sales approaching $50 million. IBM supplied accounting machines during WWII, producing a further tripling in size.

IBM perfected electromechanical calculation (the Harvard Mark I, 1944) but initially dismissed the potential of computers. When Remington Rand's commercial computer (UNIVAC, 1951) began replacing IBM machines, IBM quickly recouped, using its superior R&D and marketing to build a market share near 80% in the 1960s and 1970s; competitors scattered to niches on the periphery.

Triumphs achieved under Thomas J. Watson, Jr., (president in 1952) included IBM's first computer (the 701, 1952), the STRETCH systems (which eliminated vacuum

tubes, 1960), and the first compatible family of computers (System/360, 1964; System/370, 1970). Accompanying innovations included the FORTRAN programming language (1957) and floppy disk storage (1971).

IBM later moved into mid-range systems (System/38, 1978; AS/400, 1988). The IBM PC (1981) spawned whole new PC-related industries. PC Jr. (1983) failed; the PC AT (1984) and PS/2 (1987) succeeded.

The shift to open, smaller systems along with greater competition in all of its segments has caused wrenching change. Between 1986 and 1990 IBM reduced its US employment by 33,000 through attrition and early retirement inducements, with 14,000 more job cuts planned for 1991. IBM also sold many noncomputer businesses, like ROLM telecommunications (to Siemens, 1988); the copier division (to Kodak, 1988); and its typewriter, keyboard, personal printer, and supplies business (to Clayton & Dubilier, 1991).

IBM's systems integration focus for the 1990s includes numerous key strategic alliances; the most notable of late include Sears (Prodigy electronic information service), Wang, and Apple. The company's sales and earnings were down sharply in the first half of 1991, attributed to the recession, anticipation of new product introductions, and stiffer competitive pricing.

NYSE symbol: IBM
Fiscal year ends: December 31

 Hoover's Rating **B+**

WHO

Chairman: John F. Akers, age 56, $2,028,400 pay
President: Jack D. Kuehler, age 58, $1,307,760 pay
SVP; Chairman, IBM World Trade: C. Michael Armstrong, age 52, $929,100 pay
SVP; General Manager, IBM US: Terry R. Lautenbach, age 52, $929,100 pay
SVP Finance and Planning: Frank A. Metz, Jr., age 57, $970,607 pay
SVP Personnel: Walton E. Burdick, age 58
Auditors: Price Waterhouse
Employees: 373,816

WHERE

HQ: Old Orchard Rd., Armonk, NY 10504
Phone: 914-765-1900
Fax: 914-765-4190

	1990 Sales		1990 Net Income	
	$ mil.	% of total	$ mil.	% of total
US	27,132	39	1,459	24
Europe & other	27,234	40	2,977	50
Asia/Pacific	9,564	14	1,151	19
Americas	5,088	7	420	7
Adjustments	—	—	13	—
Total	**69,018**	**100**	**6,020**	**100**

WHAT

	1990 Sales	
	$ mil.	% of total
Processors	16,433	24
Personal system workstations	9,644	14
Other workstations	4,312	6
Peripherals	13,190	19
Software	9,952	14
Maintenance services	7,768	11
Other information technology	5,791	9
Federal systems	1,928	3
Total	**69,018**	**100**

Brand Names (Current Offerings)

Application System/400	Personal System/2
Disk Operating System 4.0	Personal System/2 L40
DisplayWrite 5	SX Laptop
Enterprise System/3090	Portable 70
ES 9000	Proprinter
LaserPrinter	Quietwriter
Micro Channel	RISC System/6000
Operating System/2	Storyboard
Personal System/1	System/390

HOW MUCH

	9-Year Growth	1981	1982	1983	1984	1985	1986	1987	1988	1989	1990
Sales ($ mil.)	10.1%	29,070	34,364	40,180	45,937	50,056	51,250	54,217	59,681	62,710	69,018
Net income ($ mil.)	6.9%	3,308	4,409	5,485	6,582	6,555	4,789	5,258	5,491	3,758	6,020
Income as % of sales	—	11.4%	12.8%	13.7%	14.3%	13.1%	9.3%	9.7%	9.2%	6.0%	8.7%
Earnings per share ($)	7.2%	5.62	7.33	8.98	10.69	10.54	7.76	8.66	9.27	6.47	10.51
Stock price – high ($)	—	71.50	98.00	134.25	128.50	158.75	161.88	175.88	129.50	130.88	123.13
Stock price – low ($)	—	48.38	55.63	92.25	99.00	117.38	119.25	102.00	104.25	93.38	94.50
Stock price – close ($)	7.9%	56.88	96.25	122.00	123.13	155.50	120.00	115.50	121.88	94.13	113.00
P/E – high	—	13	13	15	12	15	21	20	14	20	12
P/E – low	—	9	8	10	9	11	15	12	11	14	9
Dividends per share ($)	3.9%	3.44	3.44	3.71	4.10	4.40	4.40	4.40	4.40	4.73	4.84
Book value per share ($)	10.4%	30.66	33.13	38.02	43.23	51.98	56.73	64.09	66.99	67.01	74.96

1990 Year-end:
Debt ratio: 21.8%
Return on equity: 14.8%
Cash (mil.): $4,551
Current ratio: 1.54
Long-term debt (mil.): $11,943
No. of shares (mil.): 571
Dividends:
  1990 average yield: 4.3%
  1990 payout: 46.1%
Market value (mil.): $64,567

Stock Price History High/Low 1981–90

RANKINGS

4th in *Fortune* 500 Industrial Cos.
1st in *Business Week* 1000

KEY COMPETITORS

Amdahl	Dun & Bradstreet	SCI Systems
AT&T	Fujitsu	Siemens
Apple	General Motors	Storage
Arthur Andersen	H&R Block	Technology
AST	Hewlett-Packard	Sun
Atari	Hitachi	Microsystems
Canon	Hyundai	Tandem
Commodore	Intergraph	Tandy
Compaq	Lucky-Goldstar	Unisys
Computer Associates	Machines Bull	Semiconductor
Conner Peripherals	Matsushita	makers
Control Data	Microsoft	Other computer-
Cray Research	NEC	related
Data General	Olivetti	companies
Dell	Oracle	
DEC	Prime	

INTERNATIONAL FLAVORS & FRAGRANCES INC.

NYSE symbol: IFF
Fiscal year ends: December 31

Hoover's Rating **A**

OVERVIEW

New York–based International Flavors & Fragrances is the world's leading independent producer of synthetic tastes and smells. By one estimate IFF holds 13% of the world's market. The company states that it has over 80,000 recipes on file.

Most of IFF's fragrances are sold to makers of perfume, cosmetics, and household cleaners; famous clients include Procter & Gamble, Estée Lauder, Calvin Klein, and Halston. Most of the company's flavors are used in food, drugs, tobacco, and pet food.

With 70% of its sales coming from overseas, IFF is in a strong position to take advantage of the increasingly globalized economy. The company has recently established new facilities in China, Korea, Argentina, and Spain. IFF's highest growth area is the Pacific Rim, where the company is building a growing network of customers. In Europe, where IFF conducts about 45% of its business, the company hopes to expand into the former Communist bloc countries in the 1990s.

IFF spent a record $54 million on R&D in 1990. It researched olfactory neurons with Johns Hopkins Medical School and looked for ways to enhance flavor in microwaveable foods.

WHO

Chairman and President: Eugene P. Grisanti, age 61, $712,500 pay
SVP; President, IFF Flavors: Hendrik C. van Baaren, age 51, $445,015 pay
SVP; President, IFF Fragrances: Hugh R. Kirkpatrick, age 54
VP Finance and Treasurer: John P. Winandy, age 64, $412,936 pay
VP and Corporate Director Employee Relations: William Myers, Jr.
Secretary and General Attorney: Wallace G. Dempsey, age 65
Controller: Thomas H. Hoppel, age 60
Auditors: Price Waterhouse
Employees: 4,180

WHEN

International Flavors & Fragrances began in 1909 when a Dutch immigrant and perfumer, A. L. van Ameringen, and William Haebler formed a fragrance company, van Ameringen-Haebler, in New York.

In 1953 the company produced the fragrance for Youth Dew, Estée Lauder's first big cosmetics hit. One biographer of Estée Lauder linked her romantically with van Ameringen after her 1939 divorce (she later remarried ex-husband Joseph Lauder). The business association with van Ameringen's company endured, and by the late 1980s IFF had produced an estimated 90% of Lauder's fragrances.

In 1958 van Ameringen-Haebler bought Polak & Schwartz, a Dutch firm, and changed the name of the combined companies to International Flavors & Fragrances. The US market for fragrances grew as consumers bought items such as air fresheners and as manufacturers began adding fragrances to household items such as laundry detergent. IFF was a major supplier of scents.

In 1963 Henry Walter, the company's counsel, became CEO when van Ameringen retired. Walter expanded IFF's presence overseas, with highest sales in Europe and Latin America. Walter, once pictured in a national magazine riding his bicycle through Manhattan to work, boasted, "Most of the great soap fragrances have been ours," and so have many famous French perfumes. However, because most perfume companies wanted to retain product mystique, IFF often couldn't take credit for its scents.

While most of IFF's products were made for consumer goods manufacturers, under Walter's direction in the 1970s, IFF's R&D personnel experimented to find scents for museum exhibits and even participated in Masters & Johnson research on the connection between sex and smell. Said Walter, "Our business is sex and hunger."

During the early 1980s IFF conducted research into fragrances for relieving stress, lowering blood pressure, and alleviating depression. In 1982 IFF researchers developed a way to bind odors to plastic, a process that has been used by manufacturers of garbage bags and toys.

In 1985 Walter retired, and Eugene Grisanti became CEO. Grisanti reorganized the company's management structure, eliminating the COO position and giving the vice presidents more decision-making power. After a 3-year creative slump, IFF created fragrances for several prestige perfumes, such as Eternity (Calvin Klein) and Halston in 1988.

Expansion continued in 1991 with new operations in Turkey and Argentina.

WHERE

HQ: 521 W. 57th St., New York, NY 10019
Phone: 212-765-5500
Fax: 212-708-7132

The company operates 26 flavor and fragrance laboratories in 21 countries and maintains 48 sales offices in 33 countries.

	1990 Sales		1990 Operating Income	
	$ mil.	% of total	$ mil.	% of total
US	288	30	61	25
Western Europe	447	46	134	55
Other countries	228	24	49	20
Adjustments	—	—	(5)	—
Total	**963**	**100**	**239**	**100**

WHAT

	1990 Sales
	% of total
Fragrances	61
Flavors	39
Total	**100**

Flavors	Fragrances
Baked goods	After-shave lotions
Beverages	Air fresheners
Candy	Cosmetic creams
Convenience foods	Deodorants
Dairy products	Detergents
Dental hygiene products	Hair preparations
Desserts	Household cleaners
Diet foods	Laundry soap
Drink powders	Lipsticks
Pet foods	Lotions and powders
Pharmaceuticals	Perfumes
Tobacco	Plastics
	Soaps

HOW MUCH

	9-Year Growth	1981	1982	1983	1984	1985	1986	1987	1988	1989	1990
Sales ($ mil.)	8.8%	451	448	461	477	501	621	746	840	870	963
Net income ($ mil.)	10.1%	66	63	68	69	70	86	107	129	139	157
Income as % of sales	—	14.7%	14.1%	14.8%	14.5%	13.9%	13.8%	14.3%	15.3%	15.9%	16.3%
Earnings per share ($)	9.5%	1.81	1.73	1.87	1.89	1.89	2.29	2.83	3.40	3.65	4.11
Stock price – high ($)	—	23.00	30.00	35.75	29.25	40.00	48.88	58.00	54.50	77.50	75.13
Stock price – low ($)	—	17.88	17.38	23.75	22.88	26.00	34.50	37.25	43.13	48.50	54.63
Stock price – close ($)	16.1%	19.50	27.63	27.25	28.00	40.00	37.25	44.38	49.38	67.75	74.50
P/E – high	—	13	17	19	15	21	21	21	16	21	18
P/E – low	—	10	10	13	12	14	15	13	13	13	13
Dividends per share ($)	9.8%	0.96	1.02	1.05	1.09	1.13	1.18	1.33	1.68	1.98	2.22
Book value per share ($)	11.2%	9.02	9.19	9.39	9.56	11.52	13.87	17.45	18.34	20.09	23.53

1990 Year-end:
Debt ratio: 0.0%
Return on equity: 18.8%
Cash (mil.): $376
Current ratio: 5.40
Long-term debt (mil.): $0
No. of shares (mil.): 38
Dividends:
    1990 average yield: 3.0%
    1990 payout: 54.0%
Market value (mil.): $2,843

Stock Price History High/Low 1981–90

RANKINGS

350th in *Fortune* 500 Industrial Cos.
209th in *Business Week* 1000

KEY COMPETITORS

Bayer
Hercules
MacAndrews & Forbes
Roche
Wrigley

INTERNATIONAL PAPER COMPANY

NYSE symbol: IP
Fiscal year ends: December 31

Hoover's Rating C+

OVERVIEW

International Paper is the world's leading integrated paper manufacturer. Already the #1 producer of bleached board (for milk and food packaging), the company plans to increase production by recycling used juice and milk cartons. It is a leading producer of uncoated free-sheet paper (including Hammermill and Springhill white and colored business papers), America's #3 containerboard producer, and a major supplier of corrugated containers in the US and Europe. Other products include coated (magazine) papers, Strathmore and Beckett stationery and art papers, and Veratac nonwoven products (used to make disposable diapers and fabric softener sheets). The company owns more than 6 million acres of timberland in the US.

In recent years International Paper has used acquisitions to increase production and strengthen its position in the world marketplace. Sales have been strong since 1986; earnings nearly tripled between 1986 and 1989 but fell in 1990, primarily as a result of the sluggish US economy.

WHEN

In 1898, 18 northeastern pulp and paper companies consolidated to lower operating costs. The resulting International Paper Company started with 20 mills in Maine, New Hampshire, Vermont, Massachusetts, and New York (including one at Ticonderoga, known for its Ticonderoga paper).

These mills depended on the forests of the northeastern US and those in neighboring Canada for wood pulp. However, Canadian provinces were enacting legislation to prevent the export of pulpwood, wanting instead to export finished products. Thus in 1919 International Paper formed Canadian International Paper, which bought Riordon (a Canadian paper company) in 1925.

In the 1920s International Paper built a hydroelectric plant on the Hudson River, and between 1928 and 1941 the company called itself International Paper & Power. The company entered the *kraft* (German for strength) paper market (e.g., paper sacks) in 1925 with the purchase of the Bastrop Pulp & Paper kraft paper mill (Louisiana). Mass production of paper was made possible by the Fourdrinier paper machine, which could make paper in a continuous sheet (patented by Henry and Sealy Fourdrinier in England about 1807). International Paper first mass-produced kraft containerboard in 1931 using the Fourdrinier process at its mill in Panama City, Florida. (The mill was sold in 1979.)

During the 1940s and 1950s, International Paper bought Agar Manufacturing (shipping containers, 1940), Single Service Containers (Pure-Pak milk containers, 1946), and Lord Baltimore Press (folding cartons, 1958). The company diversified in the 1960s and 1970s, buying Davol (hospital products, 1968, sold to C.R. Bard in 1980), American Central (land development, 1968, assets sold to developers in 1974), and General Crude Oil (gas and oil, 1975, sold to Mobil Oil in 1979).

In the 1980s International Paper modernized its plants to change its business mix to less cyclical products and became the industry's low-cost producer. After selling Canadian International Paper in 1981, the company embarked on a buying spree, starting with Hammermill Paper (office paper, 1986), Arvey (paper manufacturer and distributor, 1987), and Masonite (composite wood products, 1988). In 1989 International Paper bought Aussedat Rey (paper, France), Ilford Group (photographic film and paper, UK), and Zanders (paper, West Germany). The company's 1990 acquisitions included Dixon Paper (paper and graphic arts supply distributor), Nevamar (laminates), and the UK's Cookson Group (printing plates and chemicals).

In 1991 International Paper enhanced its midwestern, southeastern, and southwestern distribution networks by buying Dillard Paper and Leslie Paper.

WHO

Chairman and CEO: John A. Georges, age 60, $1,440,303 pay
SVP and CFO: Robert C. Butler, Jr., age 60
SVP Human Resources: Robert M. Byrnes, age 53
Auditors: Arthur Andersen & Co.
Employees: 69,000

WHERE

HQ: Two Manhattanville Rd., Purchase, NY 10577
Phone: 914-397-1500
Fax: 914-397-1596

International Paper manufactures its products in 24 countries and sells them in more than 120 countries.

	1990 Sales		1990 Operating Income	
	$ mil.	% of total	$ mil.	% of total
US	10,119	77	1,139	85
Europe	2,730	21	177	13
Other countries	314	2	29	2
Adjustments	(203)	—	90	—
Total	**12,960**	**100**	**1,435**	**100**

WHAT

	1990 Sales		1990 Operating Income	
	$ mil.	% of total	$ mil.	% of total
Pulp & paper	4,665	34	657	49
Paperboard & packaging	3,460	26	426	32
Distribution businesses	2,485	18	7	—
Specialty products	1,765	13	225	17
Wood products & timber	1,160	9	30	2
Adjustments	(575)	—	90	—
Total	**12,960**	**100**	**1,435**	**100**

Pulp and Paper
Coated and uncoated papers (Aussedat Rey, Beckett, Hammermill, Liberty Web, Springhill, Strathmore, Ward, Zanders)
Market pulp

Paperboard and Packaging
Containers (Barrier-Pak, ClassicPak Anvilbox)
Folding carton boards (Barrier-Plus, Val-U-Coat)
Food and paper packaging (Nicolet, Thilmany)
Kraft packaging papers
Preprinted linerboards (Pipeliner, ColorBrite)
Silicone-coated papers (Akrosil)

Specialty Products
Chemicals (Arizona Chemical, Bergvik Kemi)
Oil and natural gas exploration and production (GCO Minerals)
Photographic films, papers, and chemicals (Ilford, Anitec)
Specialty panels (Masonite, Craftmaster, SureWood)

Wood Products and Timber
Hardboard siding and paneling (Masonite, Colorlok)
Real estate development (IP Realty)

RANKINGS

32nd in *Fortune* 500 Industrial Cos.
90th in *Business Week* 1000

KEY COMPETITORS

Bayer
Boise Cascade
Canadian Pacific
Champion International
Eastman Kodak
Fletcher Challenge
Fuji Photo
Georgia-Pacific
James River
Kimberly-Clark
Manville
Mead
Nobel
Scott
Weyerhaeuser

HOW MUCH

	9-Year Growth	1981	1982	1983	1984	1985	1986	1987	1988	1989	1990
Sales ($ mil.)	11.2%	4,983	4,015	4,357	4,716	4,502	5,500	7,763	9,533	11,378	12,960
Net income ($ mil.)	0.9%	525	161	255	120	131	305	407	754	864	569
Income as % of sales	—	10.5%	4.0%	5.9%	2.5%	2.9%	5.5%	5.2%	7.9%	7.6%	4.4%
Earnings per share ($)	0.4%	5.04	1.36	2.31	0.94	1.07	2.90	3.68	6.57	7.52	5.21
Stock price – high ($)	—	25.75	25.81	30.00	29.94	28.88	40.06	57.81	49.38	58.75	59.75
Stock price – low ($)	—	18.56	16.38	23.00	23.00	22.13	24.19	27.00	36.50	45.13	42.75
Stock price – close ($)	11.8%	19.56	24.19	29.50	26.94	25.38	37.56	42.25	46.38	56.50	53.50
P/E – high	—	5	19	13	32	27	14	16	8	8	11
P/E – low	—	4	12	10	24	21	8	7	6	6	8
Dividends per share ($)	3.8%	1.20	1.20	1.20	1.20	1.20	1.20	1.23	1.28	1.53	1.68
Book value per share ($)	5.3%	32.20	32.47	33.38	33.02	33.34	35.05	36.35	41.14	47.35	51.34

1990 Year-end:
Debt ratio: 35.5%
Return on equity: 10.6%
Cash (mil.): $256
Current ratio: 1.25
Long-term debt (mil.): $3,096
No. of shares (mil.): 110
Dividends:
    1990 average yield: 3.1%
    1990 payout: 32.2%
Market value (mil.): $5,869

Stock Price History
High/Low 1981–90

ITT CORPORATION

NYSE symbol: ITT
Fiscal year ends: December 31

OVERVIEW

Despite 12 years of restructuring, ITT remains a broadly diversified conglomerate. The company has identified 9 principal businesses in which to operate and owns 30% of Alcatel NV, a telecommunications joint venture with France's Alcatel Alsthom.

ITT Hartford, the company's top-rated insurance unit, is performing well. ITT's automotive business (auto components and ITT Teves antilock braking systems) and ITT Rayonier forest products subsidiary are suffering from the US recession. The company's Sheraton hotel chain is recovering from a 1990 slowdown in international travel brought on by the crisis in the Persian Gulf. Sales are

off at ITT's defense electronics unit, and its consumer and commercial lending business has been weak. Other ITT businesses include electronic component and pump manufacturing, and ITT World Directories, the leader in non-US Yellow Pages production.

ITT Chairman and CEO Rand Araskog has come under fire from shareholders questioning whether the company's financial and stockmarket performance warranted the more than 100% annual increase in his total compensation (cash, incentives, and perquisites) to $11.4 million in 1990. Nearly 21% of 1990 net income came from the sales of assets.

WHO

Chairman, President, and CEO: Rand V. Araskog, age 59, $3,888,040 pay
VC and CFO: M. Cabell Woodward, Jr., age 62, $1,201,869 pay
EVP and General Counsel: Howard J. Aibel, age 61, $1,042,480 pay
Director Affirmative Action and Headquarters Personnel: Lynda Sussman
Auditors: Arthur Andersen & Co.
Employees: 114,000

WHEN

Colonel Sosthenes Behn founded the International Telephone and Telegraph Corporation in 1920. The company initially managed Cuban and Puerto Rican telephone companies. By 1925 Behn had purchased 3 small Spanish telephone companies to form Compañía Telefónica Nacional de España (CTNE), co-managed with a government board.

In 1925 ITT purchased International Western Electric (renamed International Standard Electric) from AT&T, making ITT a major international phone equipment manufacturer. In the late 1920s the company bought United River Plate Telephone of Buenos Aires, the Mackay Companies (parent of Postal Telegraph and Commercial Cable), and Societatea Anonima Romana de Telefoane, from the Romanian government.

In the 1940s ITT sold Romana de Telefoane (1941), CTNE (1945), and River Plate (1946) to concentrate on equipment manufacturing rather than utilities. During the 1950s the company relied on its overseas operations for growth and financial strength. In 1959 Harold Geneen became CEO.

Geneen doubled company revenues and profits; 1962 revenues passed $1 billion for the first time. In 1964 the company formed ITT Financial Services by purchasing Aetna

Finance, Kellogg Credit, and a 50% interest in Great International Life Insurance and by starting ITT Credit. This began a major shift by ITT to financial and consumer services.

The company added Avis car rental and a dozen other firms in 1965 and 1966. In 1968 ITT bought Continental Baking (Hostess and Wonder brands), Levitt & Sons (home construction), Sheraton hotels, and Rayonier (wood products). In 1969 it purchased Canteen Corporation (vending machines), Hartford Insurance, and Grinnell (fire-protection sprinkler systems).

In the early 1970s Geneen sold Avis, Levitt, and Canteen. But by 1979, ITT was only marginally profitable, posting earnings of just $382 million on sales of $22 billion.

After the Geneen era, Rand Araskog, CEO since 1979, sold all or part of 100 companies. Between 1984 and 1987 the company's work force was slashed by about 2/3. In 1986 ITT spun off its European telecommunications operation into Alcatel NV, a joint venture managed by Compagnie Générale d'Electricité (now known as Alcatel Alsthom).

ITT sold 7% of Alcatel in 1990, the same year in which Iraqis took over ITT's Sheraton hotels in Baghdad and Basra.

WHERE

HQ: 1330 Ave. of the Americas, New York, NY 10019-5490
Phone: 212-258-1000
Fax: 212-258-1037

ITT operates worldwide.

	1990 Sales		1990 Operating Income	
	$ mil.	% of total	$ mil.	% of total
US	14,106	69	514	47
Western Europe	5,606	27	443	40
Canada & other	892	4	138	13
Adjustments	—	—	673	—
Total	**20,604**	**100**	**1,768**	**100**

WHAT

	1990 Sales		1990 Operating Income	
	$ mil.	% of total	$ mil.	% of total
Defense Technology	1,612	8	103	9
Hotels	832	4	39	4
Communication-Information Ser.	973	5	131	12
Automotive	2,916	14	207	19
Electronic Components	1,110	5	(6)	(1)
Fluid Technology	1,057	5	102	9
Forest Products	1,118	6	214	20
Dispositions	254	1	(17)	(2)
Insurance	8,836	43	283	26
Finance	1,896	9	39	4
Adjustments	—	—	673	—
Total	**20,604**	**100**	**1,768**	**100**

Major Subsidiaries and Affiliates
Alcatel NV (30%)
Hartford Fire Insurance Company
International Standard Electric Corporation
ITT Rayonier Incorporated
ITT Sheraton Corporation

RANKINGS

10th in *Fortune* 50 Diversified Financial Cos.
94th in *Business Week* 1000

KEY COMPETITORS

Automobile brake manufacturers
Communications equipment companies
Defense communications manufacturers
Electronic component manufacturers
Finance companies
Hotels
Insurance companies
Pulp and wood products companies
Pump manufacturers

HOW MUCH

	9-Year Growth	1981	1982	1983	1984	1985	1986	1987	1988	1989	1990
Sales ($ mil.)	2.0%	17,306	15,958	14,155	12,701	11,871	7,596	8,551	19,355	20,054	20,604
Net income ($ mil.)	4.8%	695	703	675	303	286	528	1,085	858	922	1,056
Income as % of sales	—	4.0%	4.4%	4.8%	2.4%	2.4%	7.0%	12.7%	4.4%	4.6%	5.1%
Earnings per share ($)	5.6%	4.63	4.68	4.44	2.00	1.83	3.45	7.13	5.97	6.30	7.57
Stock price – high ($)	—	35.63	34.38	47.75	47.38	38.88	59.50	66.38	54.88	64.50	60.88
Stock price – low ($)	—	25.13	22.38	30.00	20.63	28.38	35.38	41.75	43.25	49.75	40.25
Stock price – close ($)	5.5%	29.75	31.25	44.75	29.38	38.00	53.38	44.50	50.38	58.88	48.00
P/E – high	—	8	7	11	24	21	17	9	9	10	8
P/E – low	—	5	5	7	10	16	10	6	7	8	5
Dividends per share ($)	(5.1%)	2.62	2.70	2.76	1.88	1.00	1.00	1.06	1.31	1.51	1.63
Book value per share ($)	4.9%	43.16	42.67	41.81	40.87	43.75	48.28	55.52	58.05	57.67	66.33

1990 Year-end:
Debt ratio: 45.9%
Return on equity: 12.2%
Cash (mil.): $3,017
Current ratio: —
Long-term debt (mil.): $7,245
No. of shares (mil.): 114
Dividends:
 1990 average yield: 3.4%
 1990 payout: 21.5%
Market value (mil.): $5,480

Stock Price History High/Low 1981–90

JACK ECKERD CORPORATION

OVERVIEW

Jack Eckerd, based in Clearwater, Florida, is the 3rd largest drugstore chain in the country (after Walgreen and Rite Aid) with 1,673 stores in 13 East Coast and southern states. The company has been privately held since management led a $1.2 billion LBO in 1986.

Eckerd drugstores rely heavily upon prescription sales. In 1990 over 70 million prescriptions valued at $1.4 billion accounted for 42% of total sales. OTC medication sales accounted for an additional $450 million.

In 1989 the company acquired Insta-Care Pharmacy Services, a provider of prescription services to nursing homes and institutions in 6 states. Through this purchase and Eckerd's own store labs, the company has become one of the nation's largest institutional providers.

Jack Eckerd operates traditional drugstores as well as Eckerd Express Photo film-processing stores and 2 optical store chains: Eckerd Optical, which provides traditional optical services; and Visionworks, which offers a "superstore" format with large selection, an on-site optometrist, and one-hour service.

Eckerd is 58% owned by Merrill Lynch and affiliated entities, which handled the LBO.

WHEN

In 1898 Jack Eckerd's father, J. Milton Eckerd, started one of the first drugstore chains, in Erie, Pennsylvania. Jack worked for his father's company during the Great Depression but left to start his own chain of stores in Florida by buying 3 locations in Tampa and Clearwater in 1952. In a case that he won in the Supreme Court of Florida, he challenged "fair" trade laws that imposed price restrictions to prevent him from underselling competitors.

Eckerd took the company public, as Eckerd Drugs of Florida, in 1961 and began buying other companies, beginning with Old Dominion Candies in 1966 (sold 1972). In 1968 the company bought Jackson's/Byrons, renamed J. Byrons, a Miami junior department store chain. The company further expanded in 1969 with its purchases of Gray Security Service and food-service supplier Kurman Company, both sold in 1976.

Jack Eckerd ran unsuccessful campaigns for the governorship of Florida in 1970 and for US Senator from Florida in 1974 but joined the Ford administration in 1975 as head of the General Services Administration. He donated $10 million to Florida Presbyterian College, renamed Eckerd College, in 1971.

Meanwhile, the company continued to expand its drugstores, buying Brown's Thrift City Wholesale Drugs and Mading-Dugan Drugs in 1970, then Ward Cut-Rate Drug and Eckerd Drugs Eastern in 1973. Finally, in 1977 Jack Eckerd Drugs bought Eckerd Drugs of Charlotte from Edward O'Herron, Jr., son-in-law of Milton Eckerd, bringing all the Eckerd stores under its control. Eckerd built up its Texas operations with the purchase of Abilene-based Sav-X drugstores (1980) and 40 Sommers Drug Stores from Malone & Hyde (1981). The company bought American Home Video (Video Concepts stores) in 1981, selling it and J. Byrons in 1985.

Eckerd's management turned to Merrill Lynch Capital Partners to handle a $1.2 billion leveraged buyout of the company in 1986, for which the firm received $14.5 million in fees. That year Eckerd closed 45 stores because of poor performance or potential, sold 11 stores in Tulsa, bought 32 Shoppers Drug Mart stores in Florida, and started 50 new stores. The company began remodeling stores, completing 250–300 units per year since the buyout at an annual cost of $20 million.

Between 1987 and 1989, Jack Eckerd expanded its optical services with 23 Visionworks stores, and its photofinishing business with 79 Express Photo locations. In 1990, the company acquired 220 stores from the bankrupt Revco, of Ohio.

The company continues to streamline and restructure, adding stores through openings or acquisition and divesting others, and has made good progress in reducing senior debt from the original LBO level of $800 million to $511 million in 1989 and $476 million at the end of 1990. Jack Eckerd has done reasonably well during the 1990 and 1991 retail recession, thanks to its reliance on pharmacy sales. Without the cost of the LBO, net earnings for 1990 would have been $195 million.

In September 1991 the company offered to buy all of the Revco drugstore chain for $970 million. As part of that transaction Eckerd would take the combined company public.

Private company
Fiscal year ends: Saturday closest to January 31

Hoover's Rating **D**

WHO

Chairman, President, and CEO: Stewart Turley, age 56, $1,021,420 pay
SVP; President, Eckerd Drug Company: Harry W. Lambert, age 57, $594,174 pay
SVP; EVP, Eckerd Drug Company: Ronald D. Peterson, age 52, $459,440 pay
SVP Finance and Administration: John W. Boyle, age 62, $528,771 pay
VP Human Resources: Wayne A. Saunders, age 56
Auditors: KPMG Peat Marwick
Employees: 40,800

WHERE

HQ: 8333 Bryan Dairy Rd., Largo, FL 34647
PO Box 4689, Clearwater, FL 34618
Phone: 813-397-7461
Fax: 813-398-8369 (Public Affairs)

Jack Eckerd operates 1,673 drugstores in 13 states, with the highest concentration in Florida and Texas. The company also operates 345 optical and photofinishing stores in 8 states.

	1990 Drugstores	
	No. of locations	% of total
Florida	529	32
Texas	456	27
North Carolina	184	11
Georgia	166	10
Louisiana	113	7
South Carolina	82	5
Other	143	8
Total	**1,673**	**100**

WHAT

	1990 Store Formats	
	No. of locations	% of total
Drugstores	1,673	83
Optical centers	43	2
Visionworks	44	2
Express Photo	258	13
Total	**2,018**	**100**

Drugstores
Cosmetics
Health-care advice
Over-the-counter drugs
Prescription drugs

One-hour service
Prescription lenses

Express Photo
One-hour minilabs
Photo finishing

Optical Centers

Visionworks
Contact lenses
Frames

Insta-Care Pharmacy Services Corp.
Services to nursing homes

RANKINGS

32nd in *Forbes* 400 US Private Cos.

KEY COMPETITORS

American Stores
Grand Metropolitan
Kmart
Kroger
Lowe's

Melville
Rite Aid
U.S. Shoe
Walgreen

HOW MUCH

	9-Year Growth	1981	1982	1983	1984	1985	1986	1987	1988	1989	1990
Sales ($ mil.)	7.5%	1,753	2,080	2,325	2,622	2,509	1,912	2,727	2,876	3,171	3,367
Net income ($ mil.)	—	79	71	72	85	58	(146)	(137)	(1)	(8)	(33)
Income as % of sales	—	4.5%	3.4%	3.1%	3.3%	2.3%	(7.6%)	(5.0%)	0.0%	(0.3%)	(1.0%)
Employees	—	27,900	30,600	32,000	36,300	32,400	—	35,400	36,400	40,000	40,800

1990 Year-end:
Debt ratio: —
Return on equity: —
Cash (mil.): $6
Current ratio: 1.79
Long-term debt (mil.): $1,063
No. of shares (mil.): 31
Dividends:
1990 average yield: —
1990 payout: —
Market value (mil.): —

Net Income ($ mil.) 1981–90

JAMES RIVER CORPORATION

NYSE symbol: JR
Fiscal year ends: Last Sunday
in December

Hoover's
Rating **C+**

OVERVIEW

Richmond-based James River is a young company (founded 1969) and yet it is already a leader in the worldwide paper industry. The buying fever of founders Brenton Halsey and Robert Williams accounts for the company's tremendous growth, from assets of $2.7 million in 1970 to $5.7 billion in 1990.

James River is a leading US manufacturer of paper towel and tissue products, under the Northern, Brawny, and Gala brand names. It is also a major producer of of paperboard and plastic beverage and food service products, including the familiar Dixie brand plates and cups. Quilt Rap sandwich wraps, a new James River product, offer fast food restaurants an alternative to traditional foam containers.

In 1990 the company restructured into 3 business units — Consumer Products, Food and Consumer Packaging, and Communication Papers — incurring a one-time $144 million charge. Unrelated businesses were sold, including the coated and specialty papers divisions.

WHEN

In 1969, when Ethyl Corporation (Richmond, Virginia) wanted to sell Albemarle Paper Company's Hollywood Mill, its small (100 employees), unprofitable paper manufacturing company, Ethyl executives Brenton Halsey and Robert Williams, some Albemarle employees, and a few investors joined forces to buy the mill, which was located on the James River in Richmond. Halsey became chairman and CEO, and Williams became president and COO of the resulting company, James River Paper. The company initially focused on new, special paper products, developing a new grade of oil filter paper for AC Spark Plug (division of General Motors) that same year. In 1973 the company went public and changed its name to James River Corporation of Virginia.

Rather than establishing new pulp and paper enterprises, James River bought existing ones from other companies. These included 80% of Pepperell Paper (packaging papers, 1971), Peninsular Paper (1974), and Weyerhaeuser Massachusetts (specialty papers, 1975). In 1977 James River bought Curtis Paper, Rochester Paper, and Riegel Products (packaging and electrical papers).

James River entered the industrial film products market in 1978, buying Scott Graphics from Scott Paper, and the wood pulp business in 1980, buying Brown Paper from Gulf & Western. *Fortune* magazine first ranked James River in its top 500 companies in 1981, at 447.

The company became the maker of Dixie cups, Northern towels and tissues, and Marathon folding cartons in 1982 when it bought Dixie/Northern paper and forest properties from American Can Company for $455 million. A year later James River bought the pulp and papermaking facilities of Diamond International (Vanity Fair products).

James River expanded into Europe in 1984 (GB Papers, Scotland). In 1986 the company bought the pulp, papermaking, flexible packaging, and distribution businesses of Crown Zellerbach for $1.6 billion, then sold Crown's distribution concern for $250 million. Crown Zellerbach (San Francisco), founded about 1870, was one of the world's largest integrated paper companies, operating primarily in the western US. Its brand names included Nice'n Soft, Zee, and Spill Mate.

James River bought 50% of Kaysersberg, France's leading manufacturer of paper towel and tissue products, in 1987. The company sold its Nonwovens Group in 1990, and, as part of its 1990 restructuring plan, James River sold its specialty paper business to AEA Investors in 1991. Concurrently, the company formed a joint venture (JA/MONT, of which it owns 42%) with Italy's Gruppo Feruzzi and Finland's Nokia Corporation to gain a foothold in the European tissue market.

WHO

Chairman: Brenton S. Halsey, age 63, $697,692 pay
President and CEO: Robert C. Williams, age 61, $598,462 pay (prior to promotion)
SVP and CFO: David J. McKittrick, age 45
SVP Human Resources: Malcolm E. Shaw, age 64
Auditors: Coopers & Lybrand
Employees: 38,000

WHERE

HQ: James River Corporation of Virginia, 120 Tredegar St., Richmond, VA 23219
Phone: 804-644-5411
Fax: 804-649-4428

James River operates 212 pulp and papermaking facilities in 11 countries: 139 are located in the US, 1 in Canada, 2 in Mexico, 68 in Western Europe, and 2 in Turkey.

WHAT

	1990* Sales		1990* Operating Income	
	$ mil.	% of total	$ mil.	% of total
Consumer products	1,584	45	179	49
Food & consumer packaging	1,086	30	100	27
Communication papers	603	17	89	24
Operations divested or held for sale	283	8	(194)	—
Adjustments	(165)	—	—	—
Total	**3,391**	**100**	**174**	**100**

*35-week period from April 30, 1990 to December 30, 1990

Product Lines

Baby wipes (Natural Touch)	Laminated foam plates and bowls
Baking cups	Magazine paper (Monterey)
Bathroom tissue (Northern, Nice'n Soft, Aurora, Lotus)	Offset printing paper
Coated films and imaging materials	Paper cups and plates (Dixie)
Coffee filters	Paper napkins (Northern, Vanity Fair, Zee)
Computer paper	Paper towels (Brawny, Gala, Spill Mate)
Copy paper	Paperboard cartons
Facial tissue (Zee, Lotus)	Party goods (Gala, Deeko)
Feminine hygiene products (Vania)	Plastic cups, plates, and utensils (Paper Maid)
Flexible multilayer packaging	Plastic pouches
Food wrap (Quilt Rap)	Specialty industrial papers
High-volume forms bond	Specialty packaging papers
Institutional hygienic paper products (Dixie, Marathon, Handi-Kup, Canada Cup)	Textured and colored printing media

RANKINGS

97th in *Fortune* 500 Industrial Cos.
296th in *Business Week* 1000

KEY COMPETITORS

Boise Cascade	Mead
Canadian Pacific	Mobil
Champion International	Moore
Fletcher Challenge	Nobel
Georgia-Pacific	Procter & Gamble
International Paper	Reynolds Metals
Kimberly-Clark	Scott
	Weyerhaeuser

HOW MUCH

	9-Year Growth	1981	1982	1983	1984	1985	1986	1987	1988	1989	1990[1]
Sales ($ mil.)	—	773	1,656	2,301	2,492	2,607	4,479	5,098	5,872	5,950	3,391
Net income ($ mil.)	—	22	55	98	101	95	170	209	255	222	153
Income as % of sales	—	2.9%	3.3%	4.3%	4.1%	3.7%	3.8%	4.1%	4.3%	3.7%	4.5%
Earnings per share ($)	—	0.85	1.48	1.97	1.93	1.73	2.03	2.36	2.87	2.45	1.67
Stock price – high ($)	—	10.37	16.94	28.17	23.92	26.42	35.00	43.75	29.75	34.38	29.25
Stock price – low ($)	—	6.56	5.89	15.44	15.67	15.83	22.00	18.50	21.13	25.75	18.50
Stock price – close ($)	12.9%	8.78	16.83	23.58	19.17	26.42	33.88	23.75	28.63	28.38	26.25
P/E – high	—	12	11	14	12	15	17	19	10	14	18
P/E – low	—	8	4	8	8	9	11	8	7	11	11
Dividends per share ($)	14.3%	0.18	0.18	0.27	0.37	0.37	0.40	0.40	0.48	0.60	0.60[2]
Book value per share ($)	18.3%	6.01	9.32	11.75	13.35	14.40	21.22	23.12	25.24	27.14	27.21

1990 Year-end:
Debt ratio: 41.3%
Return on equity: 8.8%
Cash (mil.): $32
Current ratio: 2.42
Long-term debt (mil.): $1,802
No. of shares (mil.): 81
Dividends:
  1990 average yield: 2.3%
  1990 payout: 36.0%
Market value (mil.): $2,134

Stock Price History High/Low 1981–90

[1] 35-week period from April 30, 1990 to December 30, 1990   [2] 35 weeks annualized

JOHN HANCOCK MUTUAL LIFE INSURANCE CO.

Mutual company
Fiscal year ends: December 31

Hoover's Rating **B-**

OVERVIEW

Boston-based John Hancock is the 8th largest life insurance and 5th largest mutual life insurance company in the US, with $35.3 billion in assets at the end of 1990.

The company is a strong advocate of deregulation that would allow insurance companies to operate freely in banking, securities and finance. Yet it is prevented by its mutual company status from full participation in these fields.

However, the company has diversified as far as possible into brokerage and limited banking services (First Signature Bank, New Hampshire, credit cards, 1985) and venture capital and other investment funds, especially in nontraditional areas: real estate syndicates and asset management. It has also invested in foreign insurance companies in Indonesia, Malaysia, Singapore and Thailand.

In 1990, despite a bad year for insurers, the company remained profitable and even increased sales of controversial Guaranteed Investment Contracts (GICs), a fixed-rate pension investment product.

John Hancock is an innovative employer, sponsoring on-site day care, and is a major sponsor of such sports events as the Boston Marathon and the John Hancock Bowl.

WHO

Chairman and CEO: E. James Morton, age 65
VC, President, and COO: Stephen L. Brown, age 54
CFO: William L. Boyan, age 54
General Counsel: Richard S. Scipione, age 54
VP Human Resources: David L. Murphy, Jr.
Auditors: Ernst & Young
Employees: 26,000

WHERE

HQ: PO Box 111, Boston, MA 02117
Phone: 617-572-6000
Fax: 617-572-1899

John Hancock is licensed in all 50 states and the District of Columbia. It is also authorized in Puerto Rico, the US Virgin Islands, and Canada.

WHEN

In 1862 Albert Murdock and other Boston businessmen founded John Hancock Mutual Life Insurance Company, named after the signer of the Declaration of Independence. Murdock became the company's first agent in Boston. In 1865 the company added agents in Pennsylvania, Illinois, Connecticut, and Missouri.

In 1866 the company began making annual distributions (instead of every 5 years) of surplus to paid-up policyholders. In 1879 John Hancock became the first US mutual life insurance company to offer industrial insurance (weekly premium life insurance in small amounts). The company was also a pioneer in granting dividends and cash surrender values (the amount returned to the policyholder when a policy is cancelled) with industrial insurance. In 1902 the company's weekly premium agencies began to sell annual premium insurance. By 1912, the company had more than $600 million of insurance in force.

John Hancock began offering annuities in 1922, group insurance in 1924, and individual health insurance in 1957. In 1968 the company formed John Hancock Advisers (mutual funds) and John Hancock International Group Program (group health and life insurance overseas). In 1969 the company bought Maritime Life Assurance (Canada). In the early 1970s the company started property and casualty insurance operations in partnership with Sentry Insurance.

Despite these forays into new areas, John Hancock's mainstay was still whole life insurance, which was traditionally seen as a safe investment. In the late 1970s, as interest rates soared toward 20%, policyholders borrowed on their policies at low rates to invest at higher rates, draining company funds. Though interest rates declined, the company was convinced that it had to diversify into new areas in order to survive and prosper.

Acquisitions included Tucker Anthony & R.L. Day (securities brokerage, Boston, 1982); Gabriele, Hueglin & Cashman (fixed-income securities, New York, 1985); and Sutro & Co. (investments, California, 1986). New product offerings included equipment leasing (1980), universal life (1983), and credit cards (1985).

Despite the proliferation of products, Hancock's position in the industry declined from 5th in 1978 to 9th in 1989 as its policy base eroded and other insurers and investments captured the market.

In the late 1980s Hancock became known for unusual investment vehicles. By 1990, of the $2.9 billion in nontraditional assets it managed for institutional investors, 31% was in timber funds, 31% in venture capital funds, and the remainder in power, real estate and agriculture. Because of its relatively large investment in real estate during the 1980s, the company has established a $168 million loss reserve to protect against the possibility of defaults.

Insurers have generally found asset management a successful diversification and John Hancock is aiming to become a major player in mutual funds, but, otherwise, in 1990 the company began to shift back to pure insurance. It acquired Costcare, a medical review company, as well as interests in insurers in Singapore and Thailand.

WHAT

	1990 Assets *	
	$ mil.	% of total
Bonds	12,320	35
Mortgage loans	11,523	33
Assets in separate accounts	5,246	15
Policyowner loans	2,017	6
Other assets	4,226	11
Total	**35,332**	**100**

	1990 Income (Before Expenses) *	
	$ mil.	% of total
Premiums	7,171	72
Net investment income	2,774	27
Other income	88	1
Total	**10,033**	**100**

* Life insurance only

Financial Services
Group life, accident, and health insurance
Group retirement funds
Guaranteed investment contracts
John Hancock's First Signature Bank & Trust's credit cards
Life insurance and annuities
Long-term care insurance
Mortgage loans
Mutual funds
Property and casualty insurance
Securities brokerage and investment banking

RANKINGS

8th in *Fortune* 50 Life Insurance Cos.

KEY COMPETITORS

Aetna	Prudential
American Express	Sears
AIG	State Farm
Blue Cross	Teachers Insurance
CIGNA	Transamerica
Equitable	Travelers
Humana	USF&G
Kemper	Mortage lenders
MassMutual	Other life insurance
MetLife	companies
New York Life	Securities brokerage
Northwestern Mutual	and investment
Primerica	banking firms

HOW MUCH

Life insurance only	9-Year Growth	1981	1982	1983	1984	1985	1986	1987	1988	1989	1990
Assets ($ mil.)	6.6%	19,942	21,723	23,540	24,840	26,594	27,818	28,211	29,461	32,344	35,332
Net income ($ mil.)	8.1%	111	169	31	158	105	134	132	171	232	224
Net income as % of assets	1.5%	0.6%	0.8%	0.1%	0.6%	0.4%	0.5%	0.5%	0.6%	0.7%	0.6%

1990 Year-end:
Equity as % of assets: 4.0%
Return on equity: 8.4%
Cash (mil.): $58
Sales (mil.): $10,033

Assets ($ mil.)
1981–90

JOHNSON & JOHNSON

OVERVIEW

Headquartered in New Brunswick, New Jersey, Johnson & Johnson is a giant in the consumer and pharmaceutical industries. Although it produces some of the most recognized pharmaceutical names, more than 1/2 of its business is in health products other than drugs, such as diagnostic equipment, orthopedic implants, infusion devices, monitors, and other medical equipment. The company's extensive line of consumer products includes such well-known names as Band-Aid and Tylenol.

J&J maintains a roster of joint ventures with leading companies like Merck and the biotech concern Chiron, with which J&J developed the first screening test for hepatitis C in 1990. About 43% of J&J's profit comes from Europe through subsidiaries like Cilag and Janssen.

Spending 7.4% of sales on R&D, the company has recently released several new drugs including Floxin (antibacterial), Vascor (cardiovascular), and Duragesic (analgesic patches to relieve severe chronic pain).

NYSE symbol: JNJ
Fiscal year ends: Sunday nearest the end of December

Hoover's Rating **A+**

WHO

Chairman and CEO: Ralph S. Larsen, age 52, $1,270,000 pay
VC: Robert E. Campbell, age 57, $969,200 pay
VC: Robert N. Wilson, age 50, $958,700 pay
VP Finance: Clark H. Johnson, age 55
VP Administration: Roger S. Fine, age 48
Auditors: Coopers & Lybrand
Employees: 82,200

WHERE

HQ: One Johnson & Johnson Plaza, New Brunswick, NJ 08933
Phone: 908-524-0400
Fax: 908-214-0332

The company has 196 plants worldwide.

	1990 Sales		1990 Operating Income	
	$ mil.	% of total	$ mil.	% of total
US	5,427	48	904	44
Europe	3,418	30	875	43
Other Americas	1,314	12	168	8
Africa, Asia, Pacific	1,073	10	106	5
Adjustments	—	—	(61)	—
Total	**11,232**	**100**	**1,992**	**100**

WHAT

	1990 Sales		1990 Operating Income	
	$ mil.	% of total	$ mil.	% of total
Consumer prods.	4,212	38	440	22
Professional prods.	3,717	33	517	25
Pharmaceuticals	3,303	29	1,096	53
Adjustments	—	—	(61)	—
Total	**11,232**	**100**	**1,992**	**100**

Consumer Products
Acuvue (contact lens)
Baby Oil
Baby Shampoo
Band-Aid
Glucoscan (blood monitor)
Imodium A-D (antidiarrheal)
Medipren (analgesic)
Modess (sanitary napkin)
Mylanta (antacid)
Piz Buin (sunscreen)
Reach (toothbrush)
Sesame Street (vitamins)
Sine-Aid (decongestant)
Stayfree (sanitary napkin)
Tylenol (pain reliever)

Pharmaceuticals
Duragesic (pain-killer)
Eprex (blood cell stimulant)

Ergamisol (cancer treatment)
Floxin (antibiotic)
Hismanal (antihistamine)
Imodium (antidiarrheal)
Monistat (antifungal)
Orthoclone OKT3 (organ transplant antibody)
Ortho-Novum (birth control)
Prepulsid (digestive aid)
Retin-A (skin treatment)
Tolectin (antiarthritic)
Vascor (cardiovascular)

Professional Products
Implants
IV devices
Surgical instruments
Surgical products

WHEN

Brothers James Johnson and Edward Mead Johnson founded the medical-products company that bears the family name in 1885 in New Brunswick, New Jersey. In 1886 Robert Johnson joined with his brothers to manufacture and sell an antiseptic surgical dressing he had developed after being inspired by surgeon Joseph Lister.

In 1897 Edward Mead Johnson left to found the drug company Mead Johnson (now a part of Bristol-Myers Squibb). In 1916 J&J bought gauze-maker Chicopee Manufacturing. A byproduct of Johnson's dressing, the Band-Aid, was introduced in 1921 along with Johnson's Baby Cream.

In 1932 Robert Johnson, Jr., became chairman and served until 1963. General Johnson (Army general in WWII) believed in decentralization; managers were given substantial freedom, a principle still in use today. Early product lines formed into business units like Ortho (birth-control products) and Ethicon (sutures) in the 1940s. In the mid-1950s the company began to acquire other businesses, creating the divisions that today make up J&J. In 1959 J&J bought McNeil Labs, which introduced Tylenol (acetaminophen) as an over-the-counter drug in 1960. Foreign acquisitions included Cilag-Chemie of Switzerland (1959) and Janssen of Belgium (1961).

J&J bought Iolab Corporation, a leader in the development of intraocular lenses used in cataract surgery (1980), and Lifescan, a maker of blood glucose monitoring systems for diabetics (1986). J&J's sales had grown to nearly $5 billion by 1980. But there have since been problems: the new drug Zomax (for arthritis pain) was linked to 5 deaths and had to be pulled in 1983; J&J quit selling disposable diapers in the US in 1981 after losing much of its market share to Procter & Gamble and Kimberly-Clark. When someone laced Tylenol capsules with cyanide in 1982, killing 8 people, it cost J&J $240 million in recalls, advertising, and repackaging, and cut Tylenol's profits by nearly 50%. J&J's immediate recall of 31 million bottles and its openness in dealing with the problem saved the Tylenol brand. Now sold as tablets and caplets to prevent tampering, Tylenol has maintained its lead in the over-the-counter analgesic market.

New products in the 1980s included Acuvue (a disposable contact lens), Retin-A (skin treatment), and Eprex (a bioengineered treatment for specific forms of anemia). In 1989 J&J bought L'Oréal's sanitary protection business in France and formed a joint venture with Merck to sell Mylanta and other drugs bought from ICI Americas. In 1990 the company penetrated the Eastern European market by establishing facilities in Hungary, Poland, and Yugoslavia, as well as its first administrative office in Moscow.

HOW MUCH

	9-Year Growth	1981	1982	1983	1984	1985	1986	1987	1988	1989	1990
Sales ($ mil.)	8.5%	5,399	5,761	5,973	6,125	6,421	7,003	8,012	9,000	9,757	11,232
Net income ($ mil.)	10.4%	468	523	489	515	614	330	833	974	1,082	1,143
Income as % of sales	—	8.7%	9.1%	8.2%	8.4%	9.6%	4.7%	10.4%	10.8%	11.1%	10.2%
Earnings per share ($)	12.1%	1.23	1.40	1.26	1.36	1.64	0.90	2.37	2.82	3.19	3.43
Stock price – high ($)	—	19.69	25.63	25.75	21.44	27.63	37.13	52.69	44.06	59.50	74.13
Stock price – low ($)	—	14.13	16.25	19.50	14.00	17.56	22.88	27.50	34.63	41.50	51.13
Stock price – close ($)	16.2%	18.56	24.81	20.44	18.06	26.31	32.81	37.44	42.56	59.38	71.75
P/E – high	—	16	18	20	16	17	41	22	16	19	22
P/E – low	—	11	12	15	10	11	25	12	12	13	15
Dividends per share ($)	13.3%	0.43	0.49	0.54	0.59	0.64	0.69	0.81	0.96	1.12	1.31
Book value per share ($)	9.0%	6.76	7.40	7.91	8.02	9.16	8.17	10.13	10.52	12.45	14.71

1990 Year-end:
Debt ratio: 21.2%
Return on equity: 25.3%
Cash (mil.): $931
Current ratio: 1.78
Long-term debt (mil.): $1,316
No. of shares (mil.): 333
Dividends:
  1990 average yield: 1.8%
  1990 payout: 38.2%
Market value (mil.): $23,898

Stock Price History High/Low 1981–90

RANKINGS

41st in *Fortune* 500 Industrial Cos.
11th in *Business Week* 1000

KEY COMPETITORS

Abbott Labs
American Cyanamid
American Home Products
Amgen
Amway
Avon
C. R. Bard
Baxter
Bayer
Becton, Dickinson
Bristol-Myers Squibb
Ciba-Geigy
Clorox
Dow Chemical
Eastman Kodak
Eli Lilly
James River
S.C. Johnson
3M
Pfizer
Procter & Gamble
Sandoz
Syntex
Unilever
Upjohn
Other drug cos.

S.C. JOHNSON & SON, INC.

OVERVIEW

Headquartered in its Frank Lloyd Wright–designed building in Racine, Wisconsin, S.C. Johnson & Son is one of the largest private consumer-products companies in the US.

With estimated 1990 sales of $3 billion, the company is a leader and innovator in insect control (Raid and Off!), cleaning products (Pledge), and personal care products (Agree). Johnson Wax, as the company is called both within and outside its walls because of its well-known floor wax products, also has interests in real estate, recreational products, sanitation services, and venture capital financing.

The 5th generation of Johnsons is now working at this paternalistic, employee-oriented, community-minded company, which operates a charitable foundation and is known for philanthropic civic contributions. The company gives 5% of pretax profits to charity — one of the highest rates of any US company. It has never had a layoff or a strike and offers one of the most generous employee benefits packages in this or any other industry. Its employee turnover rate (less than 2% annually) is one of the lowest of any company.

A recent joint venture in China and its 40% equity interest in Modern Home Care Products, an Indian company test-marketing floor cleaners, exemplify Johnson's belief that the future is in the international marketplace.

WHEN

S.C. Johnson & Son was founded in Racine, Wisconsin, in 1886 by Samuel C. Johnson, a carpenter whose customers were as interested in his floor wax product as in his parquet floors. Forsaking carpentry, Johnson began to manufacture floor care products. By the time his son and successor, Herbert Fiske Johnson, died in 1928, annual revenues were $5 million. A dispute over Herbert's estate was settled after 10 years, with his son Herbert Jr. and his daughter Henrietta Louis receiving 60% and 40%, respectively, of the company.

In 1954, when annual sales were $45 million, Herbert Jr.'s son Samuel Curtis Johnson joined the company. As new products director, Samuel turned his attention in 1955 to insect control. In 1956 the company introduced Raid, the first indoor/outdoor insecticide and soon thereafter an insect repellent, Off!, each of which now holds about 50% of its market. The 1950s and 1960s saw unsuccessful diversification efforts into the paint, chemical, and lawn care businesses. Home care products, however, prospered with the introduction of Pledge aerosol furniture polish and Glade aerosol air freshener.

Herbert Jr. suffered a stroke in 1965 and Samuel became president. Sales were $200 million that year. Herbert Jr. lived 13 more years, spending much of them ensuring continued family ownership of the business. Samuel, also determined to maintain family ownership, decided in 1965 to develop a recreational products business that could eventually be sold to pay estate taxes. This company acquired boating, fishing, and camping gear companies and a manufacturer of ink stamping equipment. When the company went public in 1987 as Johnson Worldwide Associates, Inc., the family retained a large ownership interest and effective voting control. Worldwide had 1990 sales of $266 million and earnings of $15.6 million.

In the 1970s successful product launches included Edge shaving gel and Agree hair products. The company also moved into real estate through Johnson Wax Development. In 1989 with a portfolio worth $600 million, Johnson announced that it would wind down Development and sell its portfolio.

S. Curtis Johnson, Samuel's son, joined Johnson in 1983 (all 4 of the chairman's children work there) and was instrumental in the company's investment in Wind Point Partners I, a $36 million venture capital fund, and, later, Wind Point Partners II. In 1986 Johnson acquired Bugs Burger Bug Killers, to learn about commercial pest control.

In 1990 the company entered into an agreement with Mycogen Corporation for Mycogen to develop biological pesticides for household pests. Also in 1990 the company began marketing a new line of children's shampoos under the Fisher-Price (toy maker recently spun off by Quaker Oats) label.

In 1991 Johnson became the target of a boycott launched by Christian Leaders for Responsible Television (CLear-TV) for advertising during TV programs that the group deemed offensive. That same year the company introduced Off! Skintastic (insect repellent) and Halsa styling gels and hair sprays.

Private company
Fiscal year ends: Friday nearest June 30

WHO

Chairman: Samuel C. Johnson, age 63
President and CEO: Richard M. Carpenter
President and COO, Worldwide Consumer Products: William D. George, Jr.
SVP and CFO: Larry K. Switzer
SVP Human Resources and Corporate Public Affairs: M. Garvin Shankster
Auditors: Coopers & Lybrand
Employees: 13,600

Stockholder	Approx. % of Total Shares Held
S. C. Johnson and immediate family	60
Henrietta Louis and immediate family	30
S. C. Johnson employees and directors	10
Total	**100**

WHERE

HQ: 1525 Howe St., Racine, WI 53403-5011
Phone: 414-631-2000
Fax: 414-631-2133

S.C. Johnson has operations in 48 countries and distributors in over 20 countries.

	No. of Employees	% of Total
US	3,300	24
Other countries	10,300	76
Total	**13,600**	**100**

WHAT

Principal US Subsidiaries and Affiliates
Johnson Venture Capital, Inc. (Racine, WI; major limited partner in venture capital fund Wind Point Partners LP)
Johnson Worldwide Associates, Inc. (42% equity/72% voting; diversified manufacturer)
Micro-Gen Equipment Corp. (San Antonio, TX; pest control equipment and chemicals)
PRISM (Miami, FL; sanitation services for restaurants and hotels)

Principal US Brand Names

Home Care	Personal Care
Brite	Agree (hair care)
Clean 'n Clear	Aveeno (bath products)
Duster Plus	Curél (lotion)
Favor	Edge (shaving products)
Fine Wood	Fisher-Price (children's
Future	toiletries)
Glade	Hälsa (hair care)
Glo-Coat	Soft Sense (lotion)
Glory	
Jubilee	**Insect Control**
Klean 'n Shine	Off!
Klear	Raid
Pledge	
Shout	
Step Saver	

RANKINGS

33rd in *Forbes* 400 US Private Cos.

KEY COMPETITORS

Amway	Gerber
Avon	Gillette
Bayer	Johnson & Johnson
Bristol-Myers Squibb	L'Oréal
Clorox	Nobel
Colgate-Palmolive	Pfizer
Dial	Procter & Gamble
Du Pont	Unilever
Eastman Kodak	

HOW MUCH

	9-Year Growth	1981	1982	1983	1984	1985	1986	1987	1988	1989	1990
Estimated sales ($ mil.)	—	—	—	—	—	2,000	2,000	2,000	2,400	2,500	3,000
Advertising expenditures ($ mil.)	10.0%	67	75	87	90	146	145	96	112	160	158
Employees	—	—	—	—	—	12,000	11,000	11,000	11,500	13,000	13,600

Advertising Expenditures ($ mil.) 1981–90

JOHNSON CONTROLS, INC.

NYSE symbol: JCI
Fiscal year ends: September 30

Hoover's Rating **C+**

OVERVIEW

Long a leading manufacturer of devices to control temperature, lighting, and energy in nonresidential buildings, Milwaukee-based Johnson Controls has added 3 major new lines of business in the last 13 years. The company is now the leading independent automobile seat manufacturer in North America, the #1 US automobile battery producer, and the country's largest plastic soft drink bottle maker.

With 80% of its sales derived from service and building retrofits, the controls business has been hurt but not devastated by the current construction slowdown. However, Johnson's Automotive segment, which also manufactures window regulators, latches, and locks, is suffering from weak automobile sales. Johnson is diversifying its plastics business beyond soft drink packaging and is aggressively expanding in Europe.

Johnson is considering the sale or merger of its low-margin auto battery business. The company sells 85% of its batteries in the replacement market and makes the new batteries featuring back-up units sold by Sears, Wal-Mart, and others under their own brand names.

WHEN

Professor Warren Johnson developed the electric tele-thermoscope in 1880 so janitors at Whitewater, Wisconsin's State Normal School could regulate room temperature without disturbing classrooms. Johnson's device used mercury to move a heat element that opened and shut a circuit. Milwaukee hotelier William Plankinton, a believer in Johnson's invention, invested $150,000 to begin production.

The men formed Johnson Electric Service Company in 1885; sold off marketing, installation, and service rights to the thermostat; and concentrated on manufacturing. Johnson kept inventing other devices; in the 1890s he worked on the invention for which he is best remembered: tower clocks. Johnson also experimented with the telegraph, forming American Wireless Telegraph in 1900; this venture was abandoned when Johnson became intrigued with the automobile.

Johnson put his factory into steam-powered car production. He won the Post Office's first automotive delivery contract but never gained support for the steamers within his own company and continued to look elsewhere for financing until his death in 1911.

In 1912 the renamed Johnson Services regained full rights to its thermostats, and newly elected president Harry Ellis sold all other businesses. During the Great Depression the company brought out economy systems, which automatically lowered building temperature during off-peak periods. During WWII Johnson Services diversified to aid the war effort — building devices to gather weather data, inspect barrage balloons, and test radar sets.

Beginning in 1960 Johnson Services established an international division and focused upon military and research facilities requiring highly reliable control systems. Meanwhile, Johnson Services acquired Penn Controls (1968), a maker of water pump pressure controls. In the 1960s Johnson Services began to develop centralized control systems, first introduced in 1967, for temperature, fire alarm, lighting, and security regulation.

In 1978 Johnson Controls (renamed in 1974) acquired automotive battery manufacturer Globe-Union. In 1985 the company bought auto seat and plastics manufacturer Hoover Universal. It continued expansion in the controls business through purchase of ITT's European controls group (1982) and Pan Am World Services (1989), a provider of facilities management to the government.

In 1991, in a major sex discrimination case, the US Supreme Court ruled against Johnson and its fetal protection policy that excluded pregnant women from holding jobs posing health risks to unborn children.

WHO

President and CEO: James H. Keyes, age 50, $709,267 pay
VP Controls Group: Joseph W. Lewis, age 55, $333,745 pay
VP Battery Group: J. William Horton, age 52, $361,242 pay
VP Plastics Technology and Automotive Systems Groups: John M. Barth, age 44, $320,028 pay
VP and CFO: James M. Wade, age 47, $273,121 pay
VP Human Resources: Walter M. Oliver, age 45
Auditors: Price Waterhouse
Employees: 43,500

WHERE

HQ: 5757 N. Green Bay Ave., PO Box 591, Milwaukee, WI 53201
Phone: 414-228-1200
Fax: 414-228-2302

Johnson Controls has 93 manufacturing plants in the US, Canada, Belgium, Italy, Mexico, the Netherlands, the UK, and Germany.

	1990 Sales		1990 Operating Income	
	$ mil.	% of total	$ mil.	% of total
US	3,731	83	199	88
Foreign	773	17	26	12
Adjustments	—	—	3	—
Total	**4,504**	**100**	**228**	**100**

WHAT

	1990 Sales		1990 Operating Income	
	$ mil.	% of total	$ mil.	% of total
Automotive	1,405	31	56	25
Batteries	728	16	46	20
Controls	1,702	38	70	30
Plastics	669	15	56	25
Total	**4,504**	**100**	**228**	**100**

Automotive Systems Group Products
Latches
Locks
Seats and components
Window regulators

Battery Group Products
Automotive and boat batteries
Rechargeable batteries

Controls Group Products
Building controls
Industrial automation equipment

Plastics Technology Group Products
Automotive components
Blowmolding machinery
Containers

RANKINGS

112th in *Fortune* 500 US Industrial Cos.
511th in *Business Week* 1000

KEY COMPETITORS

Borg-Warner
Bridgestone
Eaton
General Motors
Hitachi
Honeywell
JWP
Owens-Illinois
Reynolds Metals
Tenneco
United Technologies

HOW MUCH

	9-Year Growth	1981	1982	1983	1984	1985	1986	1987	1988	1989	1990
Sales ($ mil.)	16.6%	1,128	1,252	1,323	1,425	1,787	2,639	2,677	3,100	3,684	4,504
Net income ($ mil.)	7.5%	48	54	59	67	78	96	90	104	98	92
Income as % of sales	—	4.3%	4.3%	4.5%	4.7%	4.4%	3.6%	3.3%	3.3%	2.6%	2.1%
Earnings per share ($)	2.0%	1.72	1.92	2.09	2.36	2.40	2.36	2.20	2.71	2.42	2.05
Stock price – high ($)	—	17.13	19.38	24.38	24.69	25.31	36.00	40.00	38.50	46.75	32.25
Stock price – low ($)	—	11.13	8.75	17.00	18.75	19.44	23.88	20.50	24.75	27.88	17.13
Stock price – close ($)	8.2%	12.25	17.69	24.19	20.69	24.50	28.63	25.63	36.63	32.25	25.00
P/E – high	—	10	10	12	10	11	15	18	14	19	16
P/E – low	—	6	5	8	8	8	10	9	9	12	8
Dividends per share ($)	7.1%	0.65	0.70	0.75	0.83	0.93	1.00	1.06	1.10	1.16	1.20
Book value per share ($)	5.4%	13.64	14.53	15.75	16.32	20.41	21.89	20.88	23.42	20.38	21.86

1990 Year-end:
Debt ratio: 31.8%
Return on equity: 9.7%
Cash (mil.): $54
Current ratio: 1.17
Long-term debt (mil.): $483
No. of shares (mil.): 39
Dividends:
  1990 average yield: 4.8%
  1990 payout: 58.5%
Market value (mil.): $985

Stock Price History High/Low 1981–90

JOHNSON PUBLISHING COMPANY, INC.

OVERVIEW

Wholly owned by black business pioneer John Johnson, Chicago-based Johnson Publishing is America's 2nd largest black-owned business after TLC Beatrice. Johnson is the leading US publisher of black-oriented magazines. *Ebony*, with circulation of nearly 1.9 million, and *Jet*, with circulation approaching 1 million, dominate the market. Johnson also publishes *EM*, a men's magazine; produces the syndicated TV series "Ebony/Jet Showcase," and owns 3 radio stations. The company's book division features black authors. Although Johnson is currently suffering from a slowdown in advertising spending, it is said to be consistently profitable.

Johnson's Fashion Fair cosmetics line, currently accounting for approximately 35% of the company's sales, is expected to eventually grow to 50% of sales. Johnson also makes Duke and Raveen hair care products.

In 1987 *Black Enterprise* magazine selected Johnson as Entrepreneur of the Decade. Johnson has served on the advisory board of the Harvard Business School and is a major contributor to the United Negro College Fund and other black-oriented causes.

John Johnson has no intention of retiring, but has named his daughter and COO, Linda Johnson Rice, as his successor. He remains in total control, still signing all company checks.

Private company
Fiscal year ends: December 31

Hoover's Rating **B**

WHO

Chairman and CEO: John H. Johnson, age 73
President and COO: Linda Johnson Rice, age 33
Secretary / Treasurer: Eunice W. Johnson, age 70
Director Personnel: LaDoris Foster
Employees: 2,382

WHERE

HQ: 820 S. Michigan Ave., Chicago, IL 60605
Phone: 312-322-9200
Fax: 312-322-0918

WHEN

John Johnson launched his publishing business in 1942 while still attending college in Chicago. The idea for a magazine oriented to blacks came to him while working part-time for a life insurance company where one of his jobs was to summarize news about the black community from magazines and newspapers. With $500 his mother raised by mortgaging family furniture, Johnson mailed a $2 charter subscription offer to potential subscribers. He got 3,000 replies and with that $6,000 printed the first issue of *Negro Digest*, a black-oriented magazine patterned after *Reader's Digest*. It was such a hit that within a year circulation had reached 50,000.

In 1945 Johnson started *Ebony* magazine, an immediate hit in the black community and still Johnson Publishing's premier publication. *Ebony* (similar to *Life*, but focusing on black culture and achievements) and *Jet* magazine (a shorter, celebrity-oriented magazine started in 1951) were the only black-oriented publications in the US for the next 20 years.

In the early days of *Ebony*, Johnson was unable to obtain advertising because of discrimination, so he formed his own mail-order business called Beauty Star and advertised its products (dresses, wigs, hair care products, and vitamins) through his magazines. Even so, he realized he could not publish a magazine without outside advertisers and, through persistence, won his first major account, Zenith Radio, by 1947.

By the 1960s Johnson had become one of the most prominent black men in America. In 1963 he posed with John F. Kennedy to publicize a special issue of *Ebony* celebrating the Emancipation Proclamation. *Negro Digest*, renamed *Black World*, became an important information source for blacks, carrying some of the more provocative articles of the times. However, circulation dwindled from its peak of 100,000 to 15,000, and Johnson stopped publishing the magazine in 1975. In the meantime, in 1972 US magazine publishers named Johnson Publisher of the Year — the magazine world's equivalent of the "Oscar."

Unable to find the proper makeup for his black *Ebony* models, Johnson founded his own cosmetics business, Fashion Fair Cosmetics, in 1973. Fashion Fair competed successfully against Revlon (who later introduced cosmetic lines for blacks) and another black cosmetics company, Johnson Products (unrelated) of Chicago. In 1982 sales for the Fashion Fair division alone were over $30 million. Customers bought Fashion Fair makeup not only in the US, Canada, and Great Britain, but also in the West Indies and Africa.

In 1973 Johnson also launched *Ebony Jr!*, a magazine for black preteens, the purpose of which, like many of Johnson Publishing's ventures, was to provide "positive black images." Johnson bought radio stations WJPC (Chicago's first black-owned station) and WLOU (Louisville, Kentucky) in 1974 and WLNR (Lansing, Illinois) in the mid-1980s. In 1984 Johnson Publishing passed Motown Industries to become the largest black-owned business in America. Since 1987 it has been 2nd after TLC Beatrice.

In 1991 Johnson and Spiegel announced that they would jointly develop black women's fashions and an associated mail order catalog business. The catalog, to be called *E Style*, is scheduled to begin publication in 1993.

WHAT

Beauty Aids
Fashion Fair Cosmetics
Supreme Beauty Products Co.
  Duke (hair care for men)
  Raveen (hair care for women)

Books
Johnson Publishing Co. Book Division

Fashion
E Style (women's fashion catalog)
Ebony Fashion Fair

Magazines
Ebony
EM (Ebony Man)
Jet

Radio Stations
WJPC (AM), Chicago
WLNR (FM), Lansing, IL
WLOU (AM), Louisville

Television Productions
"American Black Achievement Awards"
"Ebony/Jet Showcase"

Travel Agency
Mahogany Travel Service, Inc.

KEY COMPETITORS

Advance Publications
Amway
Avon
Capital Cities/ABC
Colgate-Palmolive
Estée Lauder
Gillette
Hachette
S.C. Johnson
L'Oréal
MacAndrews & Forbes
Procter & Gamble
Time Warner
Unilever
Washington Post
Other publishers

HOW MUCH

	9-Year Growth	1981	1982	1983	1984	1985	1986	1987	1988	1989	1990
Sales ($ mil.)	13.4%	81	103	118	139	155	174	202	217	241	252
Employees	5.3%	1,500	1,586	1,690	1,786	1,802	1,828	1,903	2,364	2,370	2,382

Sales ($ mil.) 1981–90

JWP INC.

OVERVIEW

JWP describes itself as the world's premier technical services company specializing in information and facility systems. The company is the largest specialty contractor in the US and, with its 1991 acquisition of Businessland, has become the largest company-owned computer reseller. It also runs the largest investor-owned water utility in New York state.

JWP designs, integrates, installs, and maintains complex electrical, electronic, computer, communication, mechanical, environmental, and energy systems in North America and, to a lesser extent, Europe (through its Drake & Scull unit).

A growing player in the environmental and energy systems markets, JWP is active in fluidized bed combustion for the waste-to-energy market and in the sludge recycling and disposal industry. Its water utility (currently subject to condemnation proceedings by New York City, which seeks to acquire it) generates only 2% of sales but 10% of profits.

JWP's phenomenal growth through acquisitions (sales have grown 60% annually in the last decade) has made it one of the fastest-growing companies in the US. In 1989 it entered the *Fortune* Diversified Service 100 at #55 and was added to the S&P 500 in 1990.

NYSE symbol: JWP
Fiscal year ends: December 31

Hoover's Rating B

WHO

Chairman and President: Andrew T. Dwyer, age 42, $1,574,000 pay
EVP and CFO: Ernest W. Grendi, age 45, $1,387,166 pay
EVP and General Counsel: Sheldon I. Cammaker, age 51, $341,000 pay
EVP: William D. King, age 49, $252,750 pay
SVP Finance: John K. McQuade, age 49, $259,006 pay
SVP Human Resources: Susan B. Garelli
Auditors: Ernst & Young
Employees: 20,000

WHEN

Jamaica Water Supply Company was incorporated in 1887 to supply water to some residents of Queens and Nassau counties in New York. In 1902 it made its first acquisition, absorbing the Jamaica Township Water Company. By 1906 it was generating $93,084 of revenue and making a healthy net operating profit of $25,158 (27%). By 1932 revenue reached $1,624,861, on which it made $324,594 net operating profit (20%). During the next 35 years the company grew as the population of its service area grew.

In 1966 the company was acquired by Jamaica Water and Utilities, a newly incorporated company, through an exchange of shares. That year it purchased Sea Cliff Water Company in another exchange of shares. In 1969 and 1970 the company acquired Welsbach (electrical contractors) and A to Z Equipment (construction trailer suppliers) and in 1974 briefly changed its name to Welsbach Corporation before becoming Jamaica Water Properties, Inc., in 1976. Diversification proved unprofitable. In 1976 the company lost almost $2.5 million, and by 1979 it had lost $3.2 million on revenues of just over $40 million. In 1977 a major investor in the company, Martin Dwyer, and his son Andrew, a 29-year-old recent law school graduate, took over management control of the struggling company. By 1980 it was profitable. In 1983 the Dwyers began to diversify again.

Between 1983 and 1990 the Dwyers acquired more than 30 companies in the electrical and mechanical contracting, security systems, telecommunications, computer, and energy/environmental businesses. The company's revenues of $55 million (most of it from the water utility) rose to over $2.8 billion. In 1985 Andrew Dwyer became president and in 1986 the company changed its name to JWP Inc.

Between 1986 and 1990 JWP acquired over a dozen companies, including Extel Corporation (1986, telecommunications), Gibson Electric (1987, electrical contracting), Dynalectric (1988, specialty contracting), Drake & Scull (1989, British electrical contractor), NEECO, Inc. and Compumat (1990, computer resellers), and Comstock Canada (1990, Canada's largest electrical and mechanical contractor). It left the electronic data interchange business.

In 1991 JWP capped its strategy of buying up US computer systems resellers by acquiring troubled Businessland ($1.3 billion in sales in 1990) for $32 million plus assumption of $43 million of debt. JWP then purchased French microelectronics distributor SIVEA (1990 revenue $125 million).

WHERE

HQ: 2975 Westchester Ave., Purchase, NY 10577
Phone: 914-935-4000
Fax: 914-694-1215

The company operates 120 offices throughout the US and in the UK.

	1990 Sales		1990 Net Income	
	$ mil.	% of total	$ mil.	% of total
US	2,481	88	126	94
Europe	346	12	9	6
Total	**2,827**	**100**	**135**	**100**

WHAT

	1990 Sales		1990 Operating Income	
	$ mil.	% of total	$ mil.	% of total
Supply of water	59	2	14	10
Facility Systems	1,920	68	92	62
Information Systems	848	30	42	28
Adjustments	—	—	(13)	—
Total	**2,827**	**100**	**135**	**100**

Facility Systems
Bridge and tunnel lighting
Electrical cogeneration systems
Electrical contracting services
Electrical power distribution systems
Fluidized bed combustion and gasification systems to process solid wastes
HVAC installation and maintenance
Piping and plumbing systems
Regenerative fume oxidation systems
Sludge management
Street lighting and traffic signal systems
Trailer leasing and manufacturing

Information Systems
Building control systems
Cable and fiber-optic installation
Local area networks
Network consulting services
Personal computer systems
Tempest computer manufacturing
Water and sewer control systems

Supply of Water
Water supply to several Long Island, NY, communities

RANKINGS

40th in *Fortune* 100 Diversified Service Cos.
622nd in *Business Week* 1000

HOW MUCH

	9-Year Growth	1981	1982	1983	1984	1985	1986	1987	1988	1989	1990
Sales ($ mil.)	59.7%	42	51	55	90	132	379	637	925	1,742	2,827
Net income ($ mil.)	48.0%	2	2	3	3	5	14	22	28	39	59
Income as % of sales	—	4.2%	4.6%	4.7%	3.8%	4.0%	3.6%	3.5%	3.0%	2.2%	2.1%
Earnings per share ($)	31.2%	0.14	0.16	0.17	0.18	0.24	0.53	0.80	0.99	1.27	1.56
Stock price – high ($)	—	2.06	3.11	5.50	6.17	5.61	12.22	14.67	12.00	21.00	29.83
Stock price – low ($)	—	0.94	1.50	2.56	2.83	3.44	4.50	5.22	6.17	10.78	13.25
Stock price – close ($)	25.1%	2.06	2.67	4.00	3.61	5.39	7.72	6.28	11.67	20.00	15.38
P/E – high	—	15	19	33	35	23	23	18	12	17	19
P/E – low	—	7	9	15	16	14	8	7	6	9	9
Dividends per share ($)	0.0%	0.00	0.00	0.00	0.00	0.00	0.00	0.00	0.00	0.00	0.00
Book value per share ($)	64.8%	0.11	0.47	0.95	1.40	1.92	3.35	4.16	5.15	7.56	10.00

1990 Year-end:
Debt ratio: 50.4%
Return on equity: 17.8%
Cash (mil.): $57
Current ratio: 1.58
Long-term debt (mil.): $386
No. of shares (mil.): 38
Dividends:
  1990 average yield: 0.0%
  1990 payout: 0.0%
Market value (mil.): $584

Stock Price History High/Low 1981–90

KEY COMPETITORS

Borg-Warner
Consolidated Rail
Dell
H&R Block
Ingersoll-Rand
Ogden
Tandy
Building control systems makers
Companies involved in cogeneration

KELLOGG COMPANY

NYSE symbol: K
Fiscal year ends: December 31

OVERVIEW

Located in Battle Creek, Michigan, Kellogg is the world's #1 producer of ready-to-eat cereals. The company commands 38% of the US cereal market and 51% of the world market through the strength of such brands as All-Bran, Cocoa Krispies, Corn Flakes, Frosted Flakes, Rice Krispies, and Special K. Retail products under the Kellogg's brand name include croutons, granola bars, non-dairy creamers, toaster pastries, and stuffings.

Through its subsidiary Mrs. Smith, Kellogg makes Eggo waffles and has the largest share of the US frozen dessert-pie market. Kellogg owns Salada Foods (tea and drink mixes),

Fearn International (Fearn and LeGout brand soups, gelatins, pie fillings, and entrees for the wholesale market), and Whitney's Foods and LeShake (yogurts).

Recent product emphasis has been on high-fiber and oat-bran products for older and health-conscious adults, including Müeslix, Common Sense, and Balance cereals.

Although Kellogg controls roughly 1/2 of the European market, it is girding for battle against a powerful cereal alliance between Nestlé and General Mills, which promises to challenge Kellogg's European dominance.

WHO

Chairman and CEO: William E. LaMothe, age 64, $1,567,650 pay
President and COO: Arnold G. Langbo, age 53, $648,840 pay
EVP; President, US Food Products Division: Gary E. Costley, age 47, $501,920 pay
EVP Administration and CFO: Charles W. Elliott, age 59, $480,000 pay
VP Employee Relations: Robert L. Creviston
Auditors: Price Waterhouse
Employees: 17,239

WHEN

William Kellogg first discovered wheat flakes in 1894 while working for his brother, Dr. John Kellogg, at Battle Creek's famed homeopathic sanitarium. An experiment with grains (for patients' diets) was disrupted; by the time the men returned to the dough, the dough had absorbed water. They rolled it anyway, then toasted the result, and accidentally created the first flaked cereal.

Dr. Kellogg sold the flakes via mail-order to former patients (1899) in a partnership that William managed. In 1906 William started his own firm to produce corn flakes. As head of the Battle Creek Toasted Corn Flake Company, William competed against 42 cereal companies in Battle Creek (one run by ex-patient C. W. Post) and became the leader because of his innovative marketing ideas. A 1906 *Ladies Home Journal* ad helped to increase demand from 33 cases a day earlier that year to 2,900 a day by year-end. In 1907 he formed campaigns around his cereal's main ingredient, corn grit, termed "The Sweetheart of the Corn." Another ad, then considered risqué, offered a free box of cereal to every woman who winked at her grocer. In 1912 he used the world's largest sign (in Times Square) to advertise his logo. Kellogg was the first to use full-color magazine ads, test markets, and widespread consumer sampling.

William continued to introduce new products, such as Bran Flakes (1915), All-Bran (1916), and Rice Krispies (1928). Another innovation was the Waxtite inner lining to keep cereal fresh (1914). International expansion began in the same period and included Canada (1914), Australia (1924), and England (1938).

Concerned with nutrition, Kellogg pioneered nutrient labeling in the 1930s, produced the first combination grain product (1943) and first high-protein cereal (Special K, 1955), and became the first cereal company to label sugar (1977) and salt (1979) content.

Kellogg has diversified little beyond cereal and other breakfast products, but purchased Eggo waffles and Mrs. Smith's pies in the 1970s and developed Whitney's Foods, a yogurt maker, in 1982. In 1983 Kellogg's US market share hit a low of 36.7% due to aggressive competition by rival General Mills and others. The company targeted new cereals toward health-conscious adults and chose international growth over diversification, aggressively pursuing the fastest-growing food category in Europe.

New cereals introduced in 1990 and 1991 include Kenmei, Bigg Mixx, and Cinnamon Mini Buns. In voluntary compliance with the FDA, Kellogg changed the name of its Heartwise cereal to Fiberwise in 1991.

WHERE

HQ: One Kellogg Square, Battle Creek, MI 49016-3599
Phone: 616-961-2000
Fax: 616-961-2871

Kellogg manufactures its products in 16 countries and distributes them in 130 countries.

	1990 Sales		1990 Net Income	
	$ mil.	% of total	$ mil.	% of total
US	3,044	59	326	65
Europe	1,321	25	108	21
Other countries	816	16	69	14
Total	**5,181**	**100**	**503**	**100**

WHAT

Kellogg's Brand (Cereals)	
All-Bran	Nut & Honey Crunch
Apple Jacks	Nutri-Grain
Apple Raisin Crisp	Oatbake
Balance	Pops
Bigg Mixx	Product 19
Bran Buds	Rice Krispies
Cinnamon Mini Buns	Smacks
Cocoa Krispies	Special K
Common Sense	
Cracklin' Oat Bran	**Other Brands**
Crispix	Croutettes (stuffing mix)
Fiberwise	Culinary Classics (soups)
Froot Loops	Eggo (frozen waffles)
Frosted Krispies	Fearn (soups)
Frosted Mini-Wheats	Gourmet Edge (bases)
Fruitful Bran	LeGout (gravies,
Fruity Marshmallow	puddings, sauces)
Krispies	LeShake (yogurt)
Just Right	Mrs. Smith's (frozen
Kellogg's Bran Flakes	desserts)
Kellogg's Corn Flakes	Nutri-Grain Cereal Bars
Kellogg's Frosted Flakes	Pop-Tarts (toaster
Kellogg's Raisin Bran	pastries)
Kellogg's Squares	Salada (tea and drink
Kenmei	mixes)
Müeslix	Smart Start (cereal bars)
	Whitney's Foods
	(yogurt)

RANKINGS

102nd in *Fortune* 500 Industrial Cos.
53rd in *Business Week* 1000

KEY COMPETITORS

Associated Milk Producers	Mars
Borden	Nestlé
BSN	Philip Morris
Cadbury Schweppes	Quaker Oats
Campbell Soup	Ralston Purina
General Mills	RJR Nabisco
Grand Metropolitan	Sara Lee
Heinz	

HOW MUCH

	9-Year Growth	1981	1982	1983	1984	1985	1986	1987	1988	1989	1990
Sales ($ mil.)	9.3%	2,321	2,367	2,381	2,602	2,930	3,341	3,793	4,349	4,652	5,181
Net income ($ mil.)	10.5%	205	228	243	251	281	319	396	480	422	503
Income as % of sales	—	8.8%	9.6%	10.2%	9.6%	9.6%	9.5%	10.4%	11.0%	9.1%	9.7%
Earnings per share ($)	13.4%	1.35	1.49	1.59	1.68	2.28	2.58	3.20	3.90	3.46	4.16
Stock price – high ($)	—	12.50	15.56	16.50	21.38	36.00	58.75	68.75	68.50	81.63	77.50
Stock price – low ($)	—	8.69	10.88	12.56	13.50	19.25	31.50	37.88	49.00	57.75	58.75
Stock price – close ($)	23.6%	11.25	13.31	16.19	20.00	34.75	51.75	52.38	64.25	67.63	75.88
P/E – high	—	9	10	10	13	16	23	21	18	24	19
P/E – low	—	6	7	8	8	8	12	12	13	17	14
Dividends per share ($)	11.6%	0.71	0.76	0.81	0.85	0.90	1.02	1.29	1.52	1.72	1.92
Book value per share ($)	12.9%	5.30	5.79	6.39	3.96	5.54	7.27	9.82	12.07	13.41	15.76

1990 Year-end:
Debt ratio: 13.5%
Return on equity: 28.5%
Cash (mil.): $101
Current ratio: 0.94
Long-term debt (mil.): $296
No. of shares (mil.): 121
Dividends:
 1990 average yield: 2.5%
 1990 payout: 46.2%
Market value (mil.): $9,155

Stock Price History High/Low 1981–90

KEMPER CORPORATION

NYSE symbol: KEM
Fiscal year ends: December 31

Hoover's Rating **C+**

OVERVIEW

Kemper Corporation, based near Chicago, is a financial services holding company offering products and services in life insurance, property/casualty insurance, reinsurance, asset management, and securities brokerage.

The Insurance Services Group includes life insurance (Federated Kemper Life and Kemper Investors Life), which accounted for 27% of company revenue in 1990. Property/casualty (Economy Fire and Federal Kemper) represented 18% of revenues, and reinsurance operations added 15% of revenues.

Kemper's Investment Services Group accounts for 37% of corporate revenues. In 1990 losses from non-investment grade securities and real estate (together constituting about 40% of total investments) dragged down segment earnings. That year, Illinois limited the amount of such investments permissible, and the company suspended purchases until it is in compliance. Kemper manages one of the 10 largest money market funds in the US.

Lumbermens Mutual Casualty company owns 39.9% of Kemper common stock.

WHEN

James Kemper founded Lumbermens, the predecessor of Kemper Corporation, in Illinois in 1912 to provide workers' compensation insurance for lumberyard owners. Within a few months the company was one of the first in the US to sell automobile insurance.

In 1913 Kemper started National Underwriters to provide additional fire insurance for lumber dealers. Lumbermens, with $1 million in assets in 1919, opened new offices in Philadelphia, Boston, and Syracuse. By 1921 the company had established its home office in Chicago, where a receptionist is believed to have begun answering the phone by saying "Kemper Insurance."

In 1926 Kemper founded American Motorists Insurance Company (AMICO) to write personal and commercial insurance. During the early 1930s Kemper assumed management of Glen Cove Mutual Insurance and added boiler and machinery, surety bond, and inland marine insurance.

Kemper and his brother Hathaway in 1936 helped found the Northwestern University Traffic Institute to promote safe driving and to provide scholarships for police officers. Following WWII Kemper founded the James S. Kemper Foundation to provide college students with scholarships and business experience. Kemper died in 1981 at the age of 94.

In 1957 Lumbermens began offering ocean marine coverage and began advertising on national television, sponsoring sports events. The Kemper Group of companies added Federal Kemper Life Assurance in 1961 and American Protection Insurance in 1962. In 1964 the company introduced Highly Protected Risk commercial insurance coverage.

Lumbermens formed Kemperco, Inc., a publicly owned holding company now called Kemper Corporation, in 1967 to acquire 5 of the Kemper Group companies. The company's advertising program included the Kemper Open (golf), started in 1968.

In the 1980s Kemper bought stockbrokers Loewi (1982), Prescott, Ball & Turben (1982), and Boettcher (1985).

In 1989 Lumbermens purchased AMICO from Kemper Corporation for 9.6 million shares of Kemper stock and then authorized a reorganization of Kemper (approved by the stockholders in 1990) into Kemper Corporation and Kemper National Insurance Companies. Kemper Corporation now includes all the stockholder-owned companies, and Kemper National Insurance has all the mutual companies of the Kemper Group. Reduced 1990 earnings were due primarily to the poor performance of the brokerage business, exacerbated by weather-related losses in the property/casualty group. In 1990 Kemper moved many regional brokerage functions to the Chicago area and decided in 1991 to focus its attention on retail brokerage services.

WHO

Chairman and CEO: Joseph E. Luecke, age 64, $730,975 pay
President and COO: David B. Mathis, age 53, $553,224 pay
SVP and CFO: John H. Fitzpatrick, age 34, $283,260 pay
VP Human Resources: Antony Catania
Auditors: KPMG Peat Marwick
Employees: 9,500

WHERE

HQ: Long Grove, IL 60049
Phone: 708-540-2000
Fax: 708-540-2494

Kemper provides financial services worldwide.

WHAT

	1990 Assets		1990 Pretax Income	
	$ mil.	% of total	$ mil.	% of total
Property/casualty insurance	852	6	29	—
Reinsurance	1,282	9	45	—
Life insurance	8,886	65	91	—
Investment services	2,542	19	(148)	—
Other	178	1	23	—
Adjustments	(152)	—	—	—
Total	**13,588**	**100**	**40**	**—**

Financial Services
Investment management and advisory services
Life insurance
Mutual funds
Property and casualty insurance
Reinsurance
Securities brokerage

Securities Brokerage Subsidiaries
Bateman Eichler, Hill Richards, Inc. (Los Angeles)
Blunt Ellis & Loewi, Inc. (Milwaukee)
Boettcher & Company, Inc. (Denver)
INVEST Financial Corp. (Tampa)
Kemper Capital Markets, Inc. (Chicago)
Kemper Clearing Corp. (Milwaukee)
Lovett Underwood Neuhaus & Webb, Inc. (Houston)
Prescott, Ball & Turben, Inc. (Cleveland)

RANKINGS

24th in *Fortune* 50 Diversified Financial Cos.
299th in *Business Week* 1000

KEY COMPETITORS

Aetna	Loews
Allianz	MassMutual
American Express	Merrill Lynch
American Financial	MetLife
AIG	Morgan Stanley
B.A.T	New York Life
Bear Stearns	Northwestern Mutual
Berkshire Hathaway	Paine Webber
Charles Schwab	Primerica
CIGNA	Prudential
Equitable	Sears
General Re	Tokio Marine & Fire
Imasco	Travelers
ITT	USF&G
John Hancock	Xerox
Lloyd's of London	Other insurers

HOW MUCH

	9-Year Growth	1981	1982	1983	1984	1985	1986	1987	1988	1989	1990
Assets ($ mil.)	15.2%	3,789	6,174	6,838	7,085	9,264	9,735	10,742	12,078	12,696	13,588
Net income ($ mil.)	(19.1%)	80	75	68	25	76	148	195	198	230	12
Income as % of assets	—	2.1%	1.2%	1.0%	0.3%	0.8%	1.5%	1.8%	1.6%	1.8%	0.1%
Earnings per share ($)	(20.8%)	2.03	1.77	1.56	0.57	1.54	2.51	3.19	3.37	4.44	0.25
Stock price – high ($)	—	12.50	14.67	17.21	15.42	24.33	35.50	38.75	27.50	51.88	51.00
Stock price – low ($)	—	10.00	7.67	12.04	9.75	14.67	23.00	19.25	20.75	22.75	17.13
Stock price – close ($)	9.0%	10.92	12.58	13.29	14.67	24.33	25.00	20.50	24.00	47.00	23.75
P/E – high	—	6	8	11	27	16	14	12	8	12	204
P/E – low	—	5	4	8	17	10	9	6	6	5	69
Dividends per share ($)	6.2%	0.53	0.60	0.60	0.60	0.60	0.60	0.60	0.72	0.81	0.92
Book value per share ($)	9.6%	15.02	16.27	18.32	17.51	19.18	23.48	26.50	29.97	35.25	34.20

1990 Year-end:
Return on equity: 0.7%
Equity as % of assets: 12.0%
Cash (mil.): $197
Long-term debt (mil.): $235
No. of shares (mil.): 48
Dividends:
 1990 average yield: 3.9%
 1990 payout: 368.0%
Market value (mil.): $1,128
Sales (mil.): $2,929

Stock Price History High/Low 1981–90

KIMBERLY-CLARK CORPORATION

OVERVIEW

Kimberly-Clark makes paper and fiber products for personal care, health care, and industrial use. In the US it is best known for its Kleenex and Kotex brand consumer products, controlling about 45% of the facial tissue market and 33% of the feminine pad market in 1990. Kimberly-Clark dominates the incontinence care market, with a 49% market share, and is a major producer of disposable diapers (Huggies), with a 32% market share. The company views foreign markets as the key to continued growth in the 1990s.

Commercial products include barber towels, business paper, envelopes, cigarette and tea bag papers, and newsprint.

Kimberly-Clark's pioneering work in the development of nonwoven fabrics (with compressed rather than woven fibers) led to the manufacture of disposable surgical gowns, masks, and related products.

K-C Aviation operates the company's Milwaukee-based commercial airline, Midwest Express, and aircraft maintenance facilities in Dallas and Milwaukee. Midwest Express provides wide, leather-upholstered seats, gourmet food, and fresh-baked cookies for its passengers (about 5% of whom are Kimberly-Clark employees), earning it Consumer Reports Travel Letter's designation as the best overall US airline in 1990.

WHEN

In 1872 John Kimberly, Charles Clark, Havilah Babcock, and Frank Shattuck founded Kimberly, Clark & Company in Neenah, Wisconsin, to manufacture newsprint from rags. After incorporating as Kimberly & Clark Company (1880), the company built a pulp- and paper-making plant on the Fox River (1889). The community of Kimberly, Wisconsin, formed as a result of the plant and was named in John Kimberly's honor.

In 1914 the company developed cellucotton, a cotton substitute used by the US army as surgical cotton during WWI. Army nurses began using cellucotton pads as disposable sanitary napkins, and in 1920 the company introduced Kotex, the first disposable feminine hygiene product. Kleenex, the first throw-away handkerchief, followed in 1924, and soon many Americans were referring to all sanitary napkins and facial tissues as Kotex and Kleenex. In 1926, the company joined with the New York Times Company to build a newsprint mill (now Spruce Falls Power and Paper) in Ontario. In 1928 the company adopted its present name and was listed on the NYSE.

Kimberly-Clark opened plants in Mexico, Germany, and the UK in the 1950s and expanded operations to 17 more foreign locations in the 1960s.

Before his retirement in 1971, Guy Minard (CEO since 1968) sold the 4 paper mills that handled Kimberly-Clark's unprofitable coated-paper business and entered the paper towel and disposable diaper markets. Minard's successor, Darwin Smith, introduced Kimbies diapers in 1968, but they leaked and were temporarily withdrawn from the market. An improved version of Kimbies came out in 1976 and was followed closely by the introduction of Huggies, a premium-priced diaper with elastic leg bands, in 1978.

From its corporate flight department, the company formed Midwest Express Airlines in 1984. Initially offering daily flights from Milwaukee to Boston and Dallas, Midwest Express served 18 cities by the end of 1990.

Smith moved Kimberly-Clark's headquarters from Neenah to Dallas in 1985. From 1988 to 1989 he served as chairman and president of the King Ranch while still acting as chief executive of Kimberly-Clark.

Kimberly-Clark introduced Huggies Pull-Ups (disposable training pants for toddlers, 1989) and His/Hers Huggies (separate diapers for boys and girls, 1990). The company (along with New York Times) decided to sell Spruce Falls Power and Paper in 1990.

NYSE symbol: KMB
Fiscal year ends: December 31

Hoover's Rating **A-**

WHO

Chairman and CEO: Darwin E. Smith, age 64, $1,368,000 pay
President and COO: Wayne R. Sanders, age 43, $702,300 pay
SVP and Principal Financial Officer: Brendan M. O'Neill, age 52
Director of Human Resources: Barbara Kimps
Auditors: Deloitte & Touche
Employees: 39,954

WHERE

HQ: PO Box 619100, DFW Airport Station, Dallas, TX 75261-9100
Phone: 214-830-1200
Fax: 214-830-1289

Kimberly-Clark has manufacturing plants in 19 US states and 17 foreign countries.

	1990 Sales		1990 Operating Income	
	$ mil.	% of total	$ mil.	% of total
US	4,656	70	594	77
Canada	711	11	50	6
Europe	888	13	69	9
Other countries	398	6	59	8
Adjustments	(246)	—	(18)	—
Total	**6,407**	**100**	**754**	**100**

WHAT

	1990 Sales		1990 Operating Income	
	$ mil.	% of total	$ mil.	% of total
Consumer & service products	5,101	79	613	79
Newsprint & paper	1,104	17	141	19
Air transportation	259	4	18	2
Adjustments	(57)	—	(18)	—
Total	**6,407**	**100**	**754**	**100**

Consumer and Service Products
Baby wipes (Kleenex, Huggies)
Bathroom tissue (Delsey, Kleenex)
Commercial wipes (Kimwipes)
Disposable diapers and training pants (Huggies, Pull-Ups)
Disposable surgical gowns and accessories (Kimguard)
Facial tissue (Kleenex)
Feminine hygiene products (Kotex, New Freedom, Lightdays, Anyday, Profile)
Incontinence products (Depend)
Paper napkins (Kleenex)
Paper towels (Hi-Dry)
Physical therapy equipment (Spenco)
Pulp

Newsprint and Paper
Business and writing papers (Neenah)
Newsprint
Printing papers
Technical papers
Tobacco industry papers

Air Transportation
Midwest Express Airlines

HOW MUCH

	9-Year Growth	1981	1982	1983	1984	1985	1986	1987	1988	1989	1990
Sales ($ mil.)	9.3%	2,886	2,946	3,274	3,616	4,073	4,303	4,885	5,394	5,734	6,407
Net income ($ mil.)	8.7%	205	197	189	218	267	269	325	379	424	432
Income as % of sales	—	7.1%	6.7%	5.8%	6.0%	6.6%	6.3%	6.7%	7.0%	7.4%	6.7%
Earnings per share ($)	10.1%	2.28	2.20	2.09	2.38	2.91	2.94	3.73	4.71	5.26	5.40
Stock price – high ($)	—	18.31	20.19	24.75	24.38	35.00	46.31	63.25	65.75	75.38	85.75
Stock price – low ($)	—	13.34	14.19	16.44	19.69	22.50	31.69	39.38	46.13	57.38	61.50
Stock price – close ($)	19.9%	16.44	18.47	23.00	23.81	33.50	39.94	50.00	58.25	73.50	84.00
P/E – high	—	8	9	12	10	12	16	17	14	14	16
P/E – low	—	6	6	8	8	8	11	11	10	11	11
Dividends per share ($)	13.1%	0.90	1.00	1.05	1.10	1.16	1.24	1.44	1.60	2.60	2.72
Book value per share ($)	7.3%	15.03	15.74	16.41	17.20	19.03	20.89	19.61	23.17	25.85	28.28

1990 Year-end:
Debt ratio: 24.4%
Return on equity: 20.0%
Cash (mil.): $60
Current ratio: 0.95
Long-term debt (mil.): $729
No. of shares (mil.): 80
Dividends:
  1990 average yield: 3.2%
  1990 payout: 50.4%
Market value (mil.): $6,713

Stock Price History High/Low 1981–90

RANKINGS

78th in *Fortune* 500 Industrial Cos.
87th in *Business Week* 1000

KEY COMPETITORS

American Cyanamid
Boise Cascade
Champion International
Fletcher Challenge
Georgia-Pacific
Gerber
International Paper
James River
Johnson & Johnson
Mead
Midway
Nobel
Procter & Gamble
Scott
Southwest
Weyerhaeuser

KING RANCH, INC.

Private company
Fiscal year ends: December 31

Hoover's Rating **B+**

OVERVIEW

The King Ranch is the epitome of the Great Texas Ranching Empire. It inspired Edna Ferber's *Giant* and the Rock Hudson–Elizabeth Taylor–James Dean film that followed.

King Ranch's 825,000-acre expanse, larger than Rhode Island, sprawls across the southern tip of Texas. The ranch has, throughout its history, been the domain of one family — the heirs of the founder, Capt. Richard King.

The ranch operates an oil-and-gas subsidiary that handles royalties — more than $1 billion since WWII — and explores for oil and gas on its own. The ranch runs 60,000 head of Santa Gertrudis cattle, the breed that it developed. The ranch also breeds quarter horses and thoroughbreds. King Ranch owns overseas real estate and cultivates grain sorghum and cotton in Texas and sugarcane, sweet corn, and wildflowers in Florida.

WHO

Chairman: Leroy G. Denman, Jr.
President and CEO: Roger L. Jarvis, age 36
VP: Stephen J. "Tio" Kleberg, age 45
VP, Controller, and Assistant Secretary: James E. Savage
VP Audit: James B. Spear
Personnel Manager: Rickey Blackman
Director: Thomas W. Keesee, Jr.
Director: Abraham Zaleznik
Director: John H. Duncan
Employees: 500

WHEN

Just as Texas was joining the Union in 1845, steamboat pilot Richard King arrived at the Rio Grande to ferry goods. After he had traveled through the vast plain between the river and Corpus Christi, he and a Texas Ranger friend began running cattle around Santa Gertrudis Creek in 1853.

The Ranger was later killed by a jealous husband, but King continued to build the ranch in the Wild Horse Desert, an area known for the mustangs that roamed free. In 1858 King and his wife, Henrietta, built their homestead at a site recommended by friend Robert E. Lee.

King relocated the residents of an entire drought-ravaged Mexican village to the ranch and employed them as ranch hands, known ever since as *Kineños* ("King's men"). King Ranch endured attacks from Union guerrillas during the Civil War and from Mexican bandits after the war. In 1867 the ranch used its famed Running W brand for the first time.

After King's death in 1885, a Corpus Christi attorney named Robert Kleberg married King's daughter Alice and managed the ranch for his mother-in-law.

Henrietta King died in 1925, and the Klebergs assembled land through inheritance or purchase from other heirs. Before his death in 1932, Kleberg passed control of the ranch to his sons, Richard Kleberg, Sr., and Bob Kleberg. In 1933 Bob Kleberg negotiated an exclusive and lucrative oil and gas lease through the year 2013 with Humble Oil, later part of Exxon. The ranch was incorporated in 1935.

While Richard Kleberg, Sr., served in Congress, Bob Kleberg intensified crossbreeding of cattle. British breeds, imported to flesh out the stringy native longhorns, were not

suited to dry, hot South Texas. From crossbreeding Indian Brahman cattle, the King Ranch developed the Santa Gertrudis breed, recognized by the US government in 1940 as the first beef breed ever created in America.

Bob Kleberg also made King Ranch a leader in breeding quarter horses, the stock used to work cattle. In thoroughbred breeding, Bob Kleberg bought Kentucky Derby winner Bold Venture (1938) and Idle Hour Stable, a noted Kentucky breeding farm (1946). In 1946 a King Ranch horse, Assault, won racing's Triple Crown.

Richard Kleberg, Sr., died in 1955, and with Bob's death in 1974 the family asked James Clement, husband of one of the founder's great-granddaughters, to become CEO. The corporation formed King Ranch Oil and Gas in 1980 to explore for and produce oil and gas in 5 states and the Gulf of Mexico. King Ranch Oil and Gas sold Louisiana and Oklahoma properties to Presidio Oil for more than $40 million in cash and stock (1988).

When Clement retired in 1988, Darwin Smith became the first CEO not related by blood or marriage to founder Richard King. Smith doubled as CEO for Dallas-based Kimberly-Clark, and he returned full-time to Kimberly-Clark after only a year. The reins passed to Roger Jarvis, head of the Houston-based oil and gas operation, and corporate headquarters moved to Houston. The company sold its Australian operations in 1989.

In 1991 King Ranch began irrigated cotton farming on 17,700 leased acres in Arizona. Vice President Tio Kleberg, son of Richard Kleberg, Jr., remained in charge of the South Texas giant that his great-great-grandfather had carved out of the Wild Horse Desert.

WHERE

HQ: Two Greenspoint Plaza, 16825 Northchase, Suite 1450, Houston, TX 77060
Phone: 713-872-5566
Fax: 713-872-7209

King Ranch operates ranching and farming interests in South Texas, Arizona, Kentucky, Florida, and Brazil.

US Agricultural Operations
Encino Ranch (Encino, TX)
Eslabon Feedyard (Kingsville, TX)
King Ranch — Arizona (Phoenix)
King Ranch Farm (Lexington, KY)
King Ranch Farms — Florida (Belle Glade, FL)
Laureles Ranch (Kingsville, TX)
Main Ranch (Kingsville, TX)
Norias Ranch (Kingsville, TX)

WHAT

	1990 Production (King Ranch Oil and Gas)*
	Barrels of oil equivalent
Oil (Texas)	2,997
Natural gas condensate (Louisiana)	4,079
Natural gas (Louisiana)	59,614
Total	**66,690**

*King Ranch Oil and Gas–operated wells only; does not include minority participation with other companies.

Ranching Animals

Cattle	Thoroughbred Horses
Monkey	Assault (1946 Triple
(foundation sire of the	Crown winner)
Santa Gertrudis breed)	Bold Venture
Running W "A" herd	Chicaro
Quarter Horses	Gallant Bloom
Mr San Peppy	High Gun
Old Sorrel	Middleground
Peppy	
Peppy San Badger	
Wimpy	

Farming

Cotton	Sweet corn
Sod	Wheat
Sugar cane	Wildflowers

Subsidiaries
King Ranch Oil and Gas, Inc.
King Ranch Properties, Inc.
King Ranch Properties of Texas, Inc.
King Ranch Texas, Inc.
Kingsville Lumber (retail building material)
Kingsville Publishing Co. (newspaper)
Robstown Hardware (farm equipment)

KEY COMPETITORS

Agricultural, ranching, and oil companies

HOW MUCH

	9-Year Growth	1981	1982	1983	1984	1985	1986	1987	1988	1989	1990
Taxable value ($ mil.)											
Santa Gertrudis ISD	(16.8%)	1,133	1,086	1,070	997	1,078	593	336	243	197	216
Laureles ISD	(10.6%)	369	421	460	485	480	305	219	168	133	135
Total ($ mil.)	(14.9%)	1,502	1,507	1,530	1,482	1,558	898	555	411	330	351

Taxable Value of King Ranch Land ($ mil.) 1981–90

[Bar chart showing values from 1,600 down to 0, with bars approximately: 1981–1985 around 1,500–1,600, 1986 around 900, 1987 around 560, 1988 around 400, 1989 around 330, 1990 around 350]

Note: The King Ranch comprises more than 90% of the property in 2 Texas school districts, Santa Gertrudis Independent School District (197 sq. mi.) and Laureles Independent School District (360 sq. mi.)

KMART CORPORATION

OVERVIEW

Troy, Michigan–based Kmart is the 2nd largest retailer in the US after Wal-Mart, and a pioneer of the discount concept.

Kmart's discount department stores face stiff competition, not only from rival discounters but also from membership warehouses including its own PACE club.

Kmart is one year into an aggressive 6-year, $2.3-billion modernization effort and has streamlined operations by reducing its structure from 5 regions to 3. Newly installed point-of-sale scanning and satellite systems that capture sales information are expected to improve productivity and inventory control, but Kmart is far behind Wal-Mart and Dayton Hudson's Target stores in this area.

Kmart owns Pay Less pharmacies, Waldenbooks (the nation's largest bookstore chain), Builders Square, and Sports Authority. In addition, Kmart holds 22% of Coles Myer, the largest retailer in Australia, and 21.6% of OfficeMax, a discount office-supply chain.

WHEN

Sebastian S. Kresge and John McCrory opened five-and-dime stores in Memphis and Detroit in 1897. When the partners split in 1899, Kresge got Detroit, and McCrory took Memphis.

By the time Kresge incorporated as the S. S. Kresge Company in 1912, the company had grown into the 2nd largest dime store chain in the country. Kresge expanded rapidly during the next several decades, forming S. S. Kresge, Ltd., in 1929 to operate stores in Canada. During the late 1920s and 1930s, the company began opening stores in suburban shopping centers. By the 1950s Kresge had grown to become one of the largest general merchandise retailers in the nation.

In 1958 a marketing study on discounting prompted management to enter discount retailing. Three unprofitable locations were transformed into Jupiter Discount stores in 1961. The company judged this a success and opened the first Kmart discount store in Detroit in 1962. Kresge formed a joint venture with G. J. Coles & Coy Ltd. (later Coles Myer Ltd., Australia's largest retailer) to operate Kmart stores in Australia (1968).

The company built up the Kmart format swiftly during the 1970s and adopted Kmart for its corporate name in 1977. Diversifications initiated in 1980 led to the purchase of Furr's Cafeterias (1980) and Bishop Buffets (1983, both sold in 1986). In 1984 Kmart acquired Walden Book Company and Builders Square, formerly Texas-based Home Centers of America.

In 1985 the company acquired Oregon-based Pay Less Drug Stores Northwest and Bargain Harold's Discount Outlets, a Canadian retailer (sold in 1990), and in 1987 sold most of its remaining Kresge and Jupiter locations in the US to McCrory's, the chain started by Sebastian Kresge's former partner.

The company also entered the warehouse club business in 1988 with Makro (which it merged with Colorado-based PACE Club) and in 1990 with the 17 Price Savers clubs and the Sports Authority. Also in 1988 Kmart opened American Fare, its first hypermarket — a combination food and general merchandise store — in partnership with Alabama food retailer Bruno's.

While Kmart passed Sears in retail revenue in 1990, both were overtaken by rapidly growing Wal-Mart. By 1991 Kmart trailed Wal-Mart in sales and market share. Most of its stores were older and smaller (though frequently better sited than its later-arriving rivals) and often perceived by patrons as less attractive.

To remain competitive, Kmart will improve its technology, renovate existing stores, and add new locations. It will also add more name brand and upscale merchandise and drop prices. However, its high expenses (22% of sales versus Wal-Mart's 15%) may make price cuts difficult.

NYSE symbol: KM
Fiscal year ends: Last Wednesday in January

Hoover's Rating **B-**

WHO

Chairman, President, and CEO: Joseph E. Antonini, age 49, $992,625 pay
VP and CFO: Thomas F. Murasky, age 45
VP Human Resources: Thomas M. Nielsen, age 47
Auditors: Price Waterhouse
Employees: 373,000

WHERE

HQ: 3100 W. Big Beaver Rd., Troy, MI 48084
Phone: 313-643-1000
Fax: 313-643-5249

Kmart operates 4,180 retail stores in all 50 states, Puerto Rico, and all provinces of Canada.

	1990 Sales		1990 Pretax Income	
	$ mil.	% of total	$ mil.	% of total
US	30,984	97	1,057	92
Canada	1,099	3	89	8
Adjustments	198	—	—	—
Total	**32,281**	**100**	**1,146**	**100**

WHAT

	1990 Sales		1990 Operating Income	
	$ mil.	% of total	$ mil.	% of total
Specialty retail	7,192	22	167	11
Gen. mrchndisg.	25,157	78	1,307	89
Adjustments	(68)	—	(100)	—
Total	**32,281**	**100**	**1,374**	**100**

General Merchandise Operations
American Fare (51%; 49% owned by Bruno's)
  2 food/general merchandise hypermarkets
Kmart
  2,205 Kmart discount department stores in the US and Puerto Rico and 143 Kmart, Kresge, and Jupiter stores in Canada
PACE
  78 PACE discount warehouse stores

Specialty Retail Operations
Builders Square
  144 warehouse home-improvement stores
Pay Less Drug Stores Northwest
  321 super drugstores in 9 western states
The Sports Authority and Sports Giant
  19 warehouse sporting-goods stores
Walden Book Co.
  1,268 Waldenbooks stores

Other
Coles Myer Ltd. (22%)
  1,652 stores in Australia and New Zealand
Meldisco (49%)
  Operates footwear departments in Kmarts (51% owned by Melville)
OfficeMax (21.6%)
  46 discount office-supply stores

RANKINGS

2nd in *Fortune* 50 Retailing Cos.
74th in *Business Week* 1000

KEY COMPETITORS

Ames	Pacific	Stop & Shop
Circuit City	Enterprises	Vendex
Costco	Price Co.	Walgreens
Dayton Hudson	Riklis Family	Wal-Mart
Fred Meyer	Rite Aid	Drug and other
Home Depot	Sears	specialty
Lowe's	Service Merchandise	retailers
Office Depot		

HOW MUCH

	9-Year Growth	1981	1982	1983	1984	1985	1986	1987	1988	1989	1990
Sales ($ mil.)	7.6%	16,679	16,942	18,789	21,303	22,645	24,046	25,864	27,550	29,793	32,281
Net income ($ mil.)	14.7%	220	262	492	499	471	570	692	803	323	756
Income as % of sales	—	1.3%	1.5%	2.6%	2.3%	2.1%	2.4%	2.7%	2.9%	1.1%	2.3%
Earnings per share ($)	14.0%	1.17	1.37	2.53	2.56	2.42	2.84	3.40	4.00	1.61	3.78
Stock price – high ($)	—	15.92	18.17	26.17	25.08	27.67	38.25	48.38	39.75	44.88	37.25
Stock price – low ($)	—	10.25	10.33	14.50	17.83	20.42	22.42	21.63	29.00	32.50	23.38
Stock price – close ($)	11.7%	10.50	14.67	22.17	23.50	23.58	29.25	29.75	35.13	35.00	28.38
P/E – high	—	14	13	10	10	11	13	14	10	28	10
P/E – low	—	9	8	6	7	8	8	6	7	20	6
Dividends per share ($)	11.6%	0.63	0.66	0.71	0.80	0.91	0.97	1.12	1.28	1.56	1.70
Book value per share ($)	8.2%	13.20	13.93	15.57	17.24	17.32	19.66	22.08	25.12	24.90	26.94

1990 Year-end:
Debt ratio: 38.0%
Return on equity: 14.6%
Cash (mil.): $278
Current ratio: 1.80
Long-term debt (mil.): $3,299
No. of shares (mil.): 200
Dividends:
  1990 average yield: 6.0%
  1990 payout: 45.0%
Market value (mil.): $5,671

Stock Price History High/Low 1981–90

KNIGHT-RIDDER, INC.

NYSE symbol: KRI
Fiscal year ends: December 31

Hoover's Rating **B-**

OVERVIEW

Miami-based Knight-Ridder is an international newspaper publishing and information services company. Knight-Ridder publishes 29 daily newspapers and the *Journal of Commerce*, an international business newspaper focusing on trade and transportation. The *Philadelphia Inquirer, Philadelphia Daily News, Miami Herald, San Jose Mercury News*, and *Detroit Free Press* generate 50% of the company's sales. Advertising revenues have been sliding since 1990, prompting Knight-Ridder to intensify its cost cutting. Simultaneously the company is experimenting with the *Boca Raton News* in an effort to develop a format that will induce TV-bound baby boomers to read newspapers. Lessons learned in Boca Raton will be used in reformatting other newspapers.

Knight-Ridder is looking to business information services for growth. The centerpiece of its electronic publishing business is DIALOG, a major information retrieval service offering access to a diverse set of databases. Other services provide on-line access to information including financial news and market data.

Knight-Ridder owns minority positions in 2 newsprint mills and TKR Cable, a cable TV system operator.

WHEN

Knight-Ridder began as a 1974 merger between Knight Newspapers, the 2nd largest newspaper group by circulation, with 16 dailies, and Ridder Publications, the 3rd largest, with 19 dailies. Knight Newspapers swapped stock worth nearly $160 million for 77,000 shares of Ridder and dominated the new company's board of directors.

Knight Newspapers began in 1903 when Charles L. Knight, a lawyer turned editor, purchased the *Akron Beacon Journal* and became a publisher. Knight died in 1933, leaving the paper to his sons, Jack and Jim. With their guidance the company grew to include 16 metropolitan dailies, including the *Miami Herald* (1937), the *Detroit Free Press* (1940), and the *Philadelphia Inquirer* (1969). The company went public in 1969.

Ridder Publications began in 1892 when Herman Ridder bought a New York German-language newspaper, the *Staats-Zeitung*. He expanded in 1926 with the purchase of the *Journal of Commerce*, a New York shipping daily that is still operated by the company today. Over the next 5 decades the company grew to 19 dailies and 8 weeklies, mostly in the West. In 1969 Ridder became publicly owned. After the merger in 1974, Knight's Lee Hills became chairman and CEO, and Ridder's Bernard H. Ridder, Jr., became vice-chairman.

Knight's president, Alvah H. Chapman, became president of the new company until his promotion to CEO in 1976.

During the 1970s and 1980s, Knight-Ridder expanded into television, radio, and book publishing. In 1978 the company purchased VHF stations in Rhode Island, Michigan, and New York. The company bought HP Books in 1979 and formed TKR Cable Company with Tele-Communications in 1981. A year later Knight-Ridder launched VU/TEXT, an on-line library retrieval system, followed in 1983 with Viewtron, America's first consumer videotex system. In 1988 the company bought DIALOG, the world's largest on-line, full-text information system, from Lockheed for $353 million. Broadcast properties were sold in 1989.

During the 1980s Knight-Ridder lost more than $90 million in Detroit because of fierce competition between the *Detroit News* (owned by Gannett Company) and the *Detroit Free Press*. After a 43-month court battle, the 2 newspapers in 1989 signed a joint operating agreement.

In 1990 Knight-Ridder launched a Boca Raton newspaper redesigned to appeal to the baby-boom generation, and DIALOG extended its reach by linking up with WESTLAW, a legal information service with 100,000 subscribers.

WHO

Chairman and CEO: James K. Batten, age 55, $636,225 pay
President: P. Anthony Ridder, age 50, $457,740 pay
SVP Finance: Robert F. Singleton, age 60, $376,566 pay
VP Human Resources: Mary Jean Connors, age 38
Auditors: Ernst & Young
Employees: 21,000

WHERE

HQ: One Herald Plaza, Miami, FL 33132
Phone: 305-376-3800
Fax: 305-376-3828

Knight-Ridder prints and publishes newspapers in 26 cities in 16 states and maintains business information service facilities worldwide.

WHAT

	1990 Sales		1990 Operating Income	
	$ mil.	% of total	$ mil.	% of total
Newspapers	1,992	86	324	95
Business information svcs.	313	14	17	5
Adjustments	—	—	(40)	—
Total	**2,305**	**100**	**301**	**100**

Major Newspapers	Daily Circulation (Average)
Charlotte Observer	234,264
Detroit Free Press	638,083
Miami Herald	427,536
Philadelphia Daily News	233,978
Philadelphia Inquirer	513,462
St. Paul Pioneer Press Dispatch	198,881
San Jose Mercury News	280,023

Other Newspaper Interests
Fort Wayne Newspapers, Inc. (55%)
Newspapers First (33 1/3%, advertising sales)
Seattle Times Co. (49.5% voting interest)

Business Information Services
DIALOG (business, chemical, patent, and general information databases)
Journal of Commerce (transportation and trade newspaper)
Knight-Ridder Financial News
MoneyCenter (real-time price quotations)
Tradecenter (financial instrument price database)
VU/TEXT (full-text newspaper database)

Other
Ponderay Newsprint Co. (13.5%)
SCI Holdings, Inc. (15%, cable TV systems)
Southeast Paper Manufacturing Co. (33 1/3%)
TKR Cable Co. (50%)

HOW MUCH

	9-Year Growth	1981	1982	1983	1984	1985	1986	1987	1988	1989	1990
Sales ($ mil.)	7.2%	1,237	1,328	1,473	1,665	1,730	1,911	2,073	2,083	2,268	2,305
Net income ($ mil.)	4.5%	100	103	119	141	133	140	155	147	180	149
Income as % of sales	—	8.1%	7.8%	8.1%	8.5%	7.7%	7.3%	7.5%	7.0%	7.9%	6.5%
Earnings per share ($)	7.5%	1.54	1.55	1.79	2.14	2.18	2.40	2.65	2.58	3.40	2.94
Stock price – high ($)	—	20.88	25.75	30.44	31.00	41.38	57.88	61.25	47.75	58.38	58.00
Stock price – low ($)	—	13.38	13.63	22.13	21.25	28.00	37.50	33.25	35.75	42.88	37.00
Stock price – close ($)	13.1%	15.13	24.75	26.50	29.25	39.88	46.88	40.13	45.38	58.38	45.75
P/E – high	—	14	17	17	14	19	24	23	19	17	20
P/E – low	—	9	9	12	10	13	16	13	14	13	13
Dividends per share ($)	13.5%	0.43	0.46	0.58	0.67	0.79	0.91	1.03	1.15	1.25	1.34
Book value per share ($)	6.2%	10.55	11.71	12.59	14.17	12.38	14.28	15.85	15.47	17.83	18.09

1990 Year-end:
Debt ratio: 47.3%
Return on equity: 16.4%
Cash (mil.): $26
Current ratio: 1.24
Long-term debt (mil.): $804
No. of shares (mil.): 49
Dividends:
  1990 average yield: 2.9%
  1990 payout: 45.6%
Market value (mil.): $2,263

Stock Price History High/Low 1981–90

RANKINGS

194th in *Fortune* 500 Industrial Cos.
266th in *Business Week* 1000

KEY COMPETITORS

Advance Publications	Cox	Mead
ADP	Dow Jones	New York
Blockbuster	Dun & Bradstreet	Times
Capital Cities/ABC	Gannett	Reuters
Citicorp	H&R Block	Thomson
Commerce Clearing House	Hearst	Corp.
	McGraw-Hill	Times Mirror

KOCH INDUSTRIES, INC.

OVERVIEW

Koch (pronounced "coke") Industries is the hidden giant of the oil patch. Its estimated sales of $17.2 billion make it the #2 privately held company in the US, after Cargill. If it were a *Fortune* 500 company, it would be in the top 25, ahead of Phillips Petroleum.

With its headquarters hidden away in Wichita, Kansas, Koch Industries trades, produces, and refines petroleum products nationwide. It has 20,000 miles of liquid pipeline and 20 oil and gas liquid storage terminals. It is the largest purchaser of Oklahoma-produced crude oil and one of the main refiners in Minnesota. It owns interests in wells from the Beaufort Sea above Alaska to the Gulf of Mexico. Its subsidiaries mine coal and make cooling systems for the proposed supercollider. Koch operates 60 grain and fertilizer elevators and farm service centers in the Midwest and runs cattle on 400,000 acres, mainly in Montana, Texas, and Kansas.

Koch is 80% controlled by 2 brothers, Charles and David Koch, survivors of a decade-long — and still lingering — feud with exiled brother William. Oldest brother Frederick no longer concerns himself with the family business and patronizes the arts in New York City. The remainder is held by directors and executives. The Marshall family in Texas owns 16% of Koch Industries stock; J. Howard Marshall, a former Ashland Oil president, was an old ally of the founding father, Fred Koch.

Koch Industries shares its presiding family's passion for privacy but, with its size, the effort has been described as "trying to hide an elephant behind a telephone pole."

WHEN

The history of Koch Industries is littered with bitter lawsuits, fringe politics, and family squabbles.

In 1928 Fred Koch developed a process to refine more gasoline from crude oil, but when he tried to market his invention, he was sued by the major oil companies for patent infringement. Koch, unable to attract many customers at home, took his process abroad, to the USSR in the 1930s. Appalled by Stalin's brand of communism, he returned to the US and helped found the stridently anticommunist John Birch Society.

Koch launched Wood River Oil & Refining in Illinois (1940) and bought the Rock Island refinery in Duncan, Oklahoma (1946). Koch would later sell the refineries, but he folded the remaining purchasing and gathering network into Rock Island Oil & Refining.

After Koch's death in 1967, his 32-year-old son Charles, armed with 3 MIT degrees and 6 years' experience with the company, took the helm and renamed the company Koch Industries. With the help of his father's confidant, Sterling Varner, Koch embarked on an ambitious acquisition program that included buying, with Wichita businessman George Ablah, Chrysler's real estate subsidiary. The company even considered buying Checker Motors, the taxicab makers (1979).

In 1980 Koch Industries was thrust into various arenas, legal and political. The Carter Administration's anti-inflation council criticized Koch Industries. The company and 3 non-family executives pleaded guilty to federal charges of fraudulent leasing practices. At Charles's urging, brother David, also a Koch Industries executive, ran for vice-president on the Libertarian ticket in 1980.

Most jarring of all, the other 2 Koch brothers, Frederick and William, launched a proxy fight for the company. Charles, with the help of David, William's twin, retained control, and William was fired from his vice-president's job. The brothers traded lawsuits, and in a 1983 "settlement" Charles and David bought out the dissident family members, reportedly for $1.5 billion. William, though, continued to challenge his brothers in court, claiming he had been shorted in the deal. One 1987 suit listed his mother as a defendant.

Despite the legal wrangling by the founding family, Koch Industries continued to expand in the 1980s. It purchased Sun's Corpus Christi, Texas, refinery for $265 million (1981). Its Massachusetts-based Koch Process Systems subsidiary purchased Helix Process Systems (1981), and it added pipeline mileage to its already large system with the acquisition of Bigheart Pipe Line in Oklahoma (1986) and 2 systems from Santa Fe Southern Pacific (1988). In 1989 its Koch Engineering subsidiary purchased Tulsa-based John Zink Co., an international manufacturer of burners for the refining and chemical industries. But the family feud was never far away; in 1991 William, as he competed for the America's Cup, contested his mother's $10 million will.

Private company
Fiscal year ends: December 31

 Hoover's Rating **B+**

WHO

Chairman and CEO: Charles Koch, age 55
President and COO: W. W. Hanna
EVP and CFO: F. Lynn Markel
EVP Legal/Corporate Affairs: Donald L. Cordes
EVP, Refined Products: Joe W. Moeller
EVP, Chemical Technology: David H. Koch, age 51
Director Employee Relations: Dale Ballew
Auditors: KPMG Peat Marwick
Employees: 9,300

WHERE

HQ: PO Box 2256, Wichita, KS 67201
Phone: 316-832-5500
Fax: 316-832-5739 (Public Affairs)

Koch explores for oil and gas in 13 states and Canada. It operates 2 refineries, in Corpus Christi, TX, and St. Paul, MN.

WHAT

Activities

Oil and Gas
Exploration and production
Marketing
Natural gas (gathering, trading, storage, pipeline transportation, and truck transportation)
Processing (petrochemicals)
Refining (gasoline, fuels)

Chemicals
Specialty chemicals

Minerals
Carbon products
Iron ore
Lime

Agriculture
Grain and fertilizer elevators
Ranching

Manufacturing
Automobile sealants
Burners and flares (John Zink Co.)
Specialized equipment for oil and gas industry (distillation and gas absorption towers, tower packings)

RANKINGS

2nd in *Forbes* 400 US Private Cos.

KEY COMPETITORS

Amoco	Imperial Oil	PPG
Ashland	Mobil	Royal Dutch/
Atlantic Richfield	Norsk Hydro	Shell
British Petroleum	Occidental	Sun
Broken Hill	Oryx	Tenneco
Chevron	Pennzoil	Texaco
Coastal	Petrofina	Unocal
Du Pont	Petrobrás	USX
Elf Aquitaine	PDVSA	Other chemical
Enron	Pemex	companies
Exxon	Phillips Petroleum	

HOW MUCH

	5-Year Growth	1981	1982	1983	1984	1985	1986	1987	1988	1989	1990
Estimated sales ($ mil.)	7.5%	—	—	—	—	12,000	16,000	13,000	16,000	16,000	17,190
Employees	7.4%	—	—	—	—	6,500	6,500	7,000	7,500	8,000	9,300

Est. Sales ($ mil.) 1985–90

18,000
16,000
14,000
12,000
10,000
8,000
6,000
4,000
2,000
0

KOHLBERG KRAVIS ROBERTS & CO.

Private partnership

OVERVIEW

Jerome Kohlberg, Jr., envisioned KKR as a means of improving businesses by helping managements to buy their own companies and profit directly from improved efficiency and productivity. KKR assembled investors, added a large stake of its own, and shared the risk in return for the eventual gain when the companies turned profitable.

The vehicle for this was a "blind pool" of money from pension funds, insurance companies, and banks, which was used to help secure bank loans for up to 90% of the deal's cost. In the early 1980s return on equity reached 40%.

In 1985 KKR turned hostile, forcing the sale of Beatrice ($6.2 billion) against management's wishes and servicing the resulting debt by dismembering the company. Deals kept getting larger until 1988, when KKR engineered the $29.6 billion RJR Nabisco LBO.

As the size of deals increased, the firm's actual investments (and therefore risk) have remained low, an average of just 2% of each of the 5 pools raised since 1980, while profits from up-front fees (1.5% annual management fee, transaction fees, 1% investment banking fee, monitoring and consulting fees) have grown enormously.

The "cash is king" early 1990s saw KKR trying to keep some of its LBOs afloat, trying to raise still more money from investors increasingly repelled by the firm's fee structure, and shifting its strategy to the "growing" of companies and the acquisition of minority interests in promising companies.

WHEN

In 1976 Jerome Kohlberg left investment banker Bear Stearns, where he had been assisting corporate managements with leveraged buyouts for over a decade, to form his own firm. He brought with him Henry Kravis and Kravis's cousin, George Roberts. Together the 3 formed Kohlberg Kravis Roberts & Co. (KKR).

KKR originally put together friendly buyouts using equity contributed by a group of investors and a large amount of debt. The company assisted in the 1977 buyouts of brake-drum maker A. J. Industries ($23 million) and oilfield equipment manufacturer L. B. Foster ($106 million). In 1979 KKR made the first buyout of a major NYSE company, Houdaille Industries, a machine tool manufacturer, for $335 million.

In the purchase of the American Forest Products division of Bendix in 1981, KKR lost all $93 million it had invested. By 1984 KKR had raised its 4th LBO fund and made the first $1 billion buyout, of Wometco Enterprises, following it with Pace Industries (air conditioning, $1.6 billion).

In 1985 KKR raised its 5th LBO fund and turned raider, engineering the record-setting buyout of Beatrice ($6.2 billion), which depended heavily upon junk bond financing provided by Michael Milken of Drexel Burnham Lambert. This fund also financed the acquisitions of Safeway Stores ($5.7 billion) and Owens-Illinois ($3.6 billion) in 1986. KKR bought out Jim Walter Homes (now Hillsborough Holdings, $2.4 billion) in 1987 and Stop & Shop ($1.2 billion) in 1988.

In 1987 Kohlberg, unhappy with the firm's hostile image, left to form Kohlberg & Company. He later sued KKR over alleged undervaluing of companies in relation to his departure settlement. The suit was settled for an undisclosed amount.

The Beatrice LBO had triggered a rash of LBOs as brokerages and investment bankers sought fat fees. The frenzy culminated in the 1988 RJR Nabisco buyout.

After 1989, as the US slid into recession, LBO activities died out, and KKR turned to managing its LBOs. Some of these have turned troublesome. Seaman Furniture (1988) and RJR Nabisco have required new cash infusions. Investment of an additional $1.7 billion in RJR has doubled KKR's investors' equity stakes, halved return on equity, and necessitated the investment of over 50% of the 1987 investment pool in a single company. At the end of 1989, Hillsborough Holdings went into Chapter 11 bankruptcy after profitable operations were sold to service debt and the remaining operations were hit by a rash of asbestos claims.

In 1991, as stock trading revived, KKR responded by selling off some shares in its companies: Duracell shares rose from their offering price of $15 to $20 in the first day of trading, and RJR stock rose 140% (from $5 to $12) in 2 months. The company went into banking by buying, with banking group Fleet/Norstar, the Bank of New England from the RTC and expanded its K-III publishing company with the purchase of Rupert Murdoch's US magazine holdings.

WHO

Founding Partner: Henry R. Kravis, age 47
Founding Partner: George R. Roberts, age 47
Employees: 20

WHERE

HQ: 9 W. 57th St., Suite 4200, New York, NY 10019
Phone: 212-750-8300
Fax: 212-593-2430 (public relations firm)

The companies controlled by KKR operate nationally and globally.

WHAT

Largest LBO Deals	$ bil.
RJR Nabisco	29.6
Beatrice	6.2
Safeway	5.7
Owens-Illinois	3.6

Investment Holdings

Auto Zone automotive parts retailer (61%)
Duracell (61%)
First Interstate (10%)
Fred Meyer (65%)
Hillsborough Holdings (92%, in Chapter 11)
IDEX Corp.
K-III
KKR Funds
Marley
Owens-Illinois (89%)
PacTrust (Pacific Realty trust)
RJR Nabisco (98%)
Safeway (82%)
SCI Television
Seaman Furniture
The Stop & Shop Cos.
Union Texas Petroleum (39%)
World Color Press

Investors in KKR Partnerships

Insurance companies
  Equitable
  John Hancock
  Metropolitan
Nonprofit organizations
  Harvard
  MIT
  Salvation Army
State pension funds
  Michigan
  Montana
  New York
  Oregon
  Washington
Bank venture capital firms
  BankAmerica
  Bankers Trust
  Continental Bank
  First Chicago
  Security Pacific

HOW MUCH

	9-Year Growth	1981	1982	1983	1984	1985	1986	1987	1988	1989	1990
Value of major investments ($ mil.)	—	1,145	—	350	3,907	10,800	9,290	2,400	32,930	405	0
No. of major investments	—	5	—	1	5	3	2	1	4	2	0

Value of Major Investments ($ mil.) 1981–90

KEY COMPETITORS

Other firms active in buyouts include:

American Express	Goldman Sachs	Morgan Stanley
American Financial	Hanson	Nomura
Bear Stearns	Loews	Prudential
Berkshire Hathaway	MacAndrews &	Riklis Family
CS Holdings	Forbes	Salomon
General Electric	Merrill Lynch	Vons

KPMG

OVERVIEW

Klynveld Peat Marwick Goerdeler (KPMG) is the largest of the Big 6 accounting firms. KPMG is owned by its 6,300 partners.

The firm has focused recently on increased international coverage, major quality service initiatives, and development of industry specializations. In 1989 KPMG participated in successful mergers in Sweden (Bohlins Revisionsbyrå) and Germany (the Treuverkehr AG with affiliate Deutsche Treuhand), and the firm grew 30% in Europe. In 1990 European revenues (47% of total) surpassed those in the US (44%).

In the US new KPMG Peat Marwick chairman Jon Madonna (described by the *New York Times* as "a raven-haired man with an incandescent smile") came to office in 1990 with a mandate to increase partner pay, reportedly $25,000 to $50,000 a year below competitors'. After only a 3% increase in US revenues in 1990, Madonna announced that 265 partners would be cut from the payroll and that the firm would take an inter-disciplinary approach to the industries it served, rather than divide its services along traditional audit, tax, and consulting lines.

WHEN

KPMG was formed in 1987 when Peat, Marwick, Mitchell, & Copartners joined KMG, an international federation of accounting firms. The combined firms immediately jumped into first place in worldwide revenues.

Peat Marwick traces its roots back to 1911. In that year William Peat, who had established a respected accounting practice in London, met James Marwick on a westbound crossing of the Atlantic. Marwick and fellow University of Glasgow alumnus S. Roger Mitchell had formed Marwick, Mitchell & Company in New York in 1897. Peat and Marwick agreed to join their firms, first under an agreement that terminated in 1919, and again in 1925 through a permanent merger to form Peat, Marwick, Mitchell, & Copartners.

In 1947 a partner named William Black became the senior partner, a position he held until 1965. Black guided the firm's 1950 merger with Barrow, Wade, Guthrie, the oldest and most prestigious US firm. Black also built up the firm's management consulting practice. Peat Marwick restructured its international practice as PMM&Co. (International) in 1972 and reformed as Peat Marwick International in 1978.

In 1979 a group of European accounting firms led by the Netherlands' top-ranked Klynveld Kraayenhoff and Germany's 2nd-ranked Deutsche Treuhand discussed the formation of an international federation of accounting firms to aid in serving multinational companies. At that time 2 American firms that had been founded around the turn of the century, Main Lafrentz and Hurdman Cranstoun, agreed to merge in order to combat the growing reach of the Big 8. The Europeans needed an American member for their federation to succeed and had encouraged the formation of the new firm, Main Hurdman & Cranstoun. By the end of 1979, Main Hurdman had joined the Europeans to form Klynveld Main Goerdeler (KMG), named after 2 of the member firms and the chairman of Deutsche Treuhand, Dr. Reinhard Goerdeler. Other members of the federation included C. Jespersen (Denmark), Thorne Riddel (Canada), Thomson McLintok (UK), and Fides Revision (Switzerland). KMG immediately became the one of the world's largest accounting firms, muscling into the ranks of the Anglo-American firms.

In 1987 Peat Marwick, then the 2nd largest firm, merged with KMG to form Klynveld Peat Marwick Goerdeler (KPMG). Through the merger KPMG lost 10% of its business due to the departure of competing companies that had formerly been clients of Peat Marwick or KMG; but the firm nevertheless jumped into the #1 position worldwide, exceeding 2nd-ranked Arthur Andersen in total revenues in 1987.

Larry Horner, chairman of the keystone US operation, stepped down in 1990 after younger partners, vexed by what they saw as top-heavy management, jockeyed for higher pay and more say in the firm. The partners turned to 47-year-old Jon Madonna, head of the firm's San Francisco office.

International association of partnerships

Fiscal year ends: September 30

WHO

Chairman: P. Jim Butler
Chairman, KPMG Peat Marwick: Jon C. Madonna, age 47
Administration and Finance Partner, KPMG Peat Marwick: Daniel Brennan, age 48
Human Resources Partner, KPMG Peat Marwick: Bernie Milano
Personnel: 77,300

WHERE

HQ: Klynveld Peat Marwick Goerdeler, PO Box 74111, 1070 BC Amsterdam, The Netherlands
Phone: 011-31-20-656-6700
Fax: 011-31-20-656-6777
US HQ: KPMG Peat Marwick, 767 Fifth Ave., New York, NY 10153-0002
US Phone: 212-909-5000
US Fax: 212-909-5088 (Communications)

	1990 Revenues	
	$ mil.	% of total
North & Latin America	2,373	44
Europe	2,503	47
Asia/Pacific	424	8
Other regions	68	1
Total	**5,368**	**100**

WHAT

	1990 Revenues	
	$ mil.	% of total
Auditing & accounting	2,707	50
Tax	1,032	19
Management consulting	786	15
Other	843	16
Total	**5,368**	**100**

Areas of Specialization

Banking and financial services	Manufacturing
Food and agribusiness	Merchandising
Health care	Petroleum
High technology	Real estate
Insurance	Transportation

Representative Clients

Aetna	PepsiCo
Apple Computer	Polaroid
BMW	Rolls-Royce
State of California	Saatchi & Saatchi
Citicorp	Siemens
Daimler-Benz	Texaco
Deutsche Bank	Thyssen
Grand Metropolitan	Union Carbide
Heineken	United Nations
Imperial Chemical	Volvo
Motorola	Xerox
Paine Webber	

Affiliated Firms
Berger, Block, Kirschen, Schellekens & Co. (Belgium)
Century Audit Corp. (Japan)
KPMG Deutsche Treuhand (Germany)
KPMG Klynveld Kraayenhoff (Netherlands)
KPMG Peat Marwick (US)
KPMG Peat Marwick (UK)
KPMG Peat Marwick Thorne (Canada)

KEY COMPETITORS

Arthur Andersen	Marsh & McLennan
Coopers & Lybrand	McKinsey & Co.
Deloitte & Touche	Price Waterhouse
Ernst & Young	Other consulting firms
H&R Block	

HOW MUCH

	9-Year Growth	1981	1982	1983	1984	1985	1986	1987	1988	1989	1990
Revenues ($ mil.)	20.8%	979	1,146	1,232	1,340	1,446	1,672	3,250	3,900	4,300	5,368
No. of countries	7.2%	66	71	79	82	89	88	115	94	117	123
No. of offices	—	—	—	—	328	335	342	620	637	700	800
No. of partners	14.0%	1,931	2,015	2,242	2,326	2,507	2,726	5,150	5,050	5,300	6,300
No. of employees	14.3%	23,149	25,492	27,033	27,746	29,864	32,183	60,000	63,700	68,000	77,300

1990 revenues per partner: $852,063

Revenues ($ mil.) 1981–90

Note: Figures prior to 1987 are Peat Marwick only; 1987 through 1990 are total figures for post-merger KPMG Peat Marwick.

THE KROGER CO.

NYSE symbol: KR
Fiscal year ends: Saturday closest to December 31

Hoover's Rating **D**

OVERVIEW

Cincinnati-based Kroger is the 2nd largest grocery chain in the US, behind American Stores. Company sales reached over $20 billion for the first time in 1990. The company borrowed $4.1 billion to deflect unwelcome takeover overtures in 1988 and was forced to sell off about $333 million in assets. Kroger lost $16 million in 1989, but, by cost-cutting and repackaging its debt, it was able to have a net income of $83 million in 1990.

At the end of 1990, the company operated 1,255 food stores, and it plans to add 40 new stores and remodel 100 each year into the mid-1990s. Kroger promotes its one-stop shopping approach through its combination food-and-drug stores, which offer about 30,000 items and have service-oriented specialty departments. The combination store's average size is 48,745 square feet. Kroger is the 4th largest operator of convenience stores in the US, with 959 convenience stores (1990 sales: $863 million) under various names.

Kroger makes many of the groceries it sells; it has about 4,000 private-label items. The company operates 37 food-processing plants including dairies and bakeries.

WHO

Chairman and CEO: Joseph A. Pichler, age 51, $763,450 pay
President and COO: Richard L. Bere, age 59, $429,794 pay
EVP and CFO: William J. Sinkula, $457,440 pay
EVP: David B. Dillon, $408,248 pay
Auditors: Coopers & Lybrand
Employees: 170,000

WHERE

HQ: 1014 Vine St., Cincinnati, OH 45202-1100
Phone: 513-762-4000
Fax: 513-762-4454

Kroger operates 1,255 supermarkets in 24 midwestern and southern states. Of these, 230 are operated under other names in 9 states. The company also operates 959 convenience stores under various names in 16 states.

WHEN

Bernard Kroger was only 22 when he began the Great Western Tea Company in 1883 in Cincinnati. The son of German immigrant shopkeepers quickly turned a profit and added new stores. Kroger was the first grocer to use newspaper advertising and to have bakeries in grocery stores.

In 1902 the company became Kroger Grocery and Baking Company, with 40 stores in Cincinnati and northern Kentucky. Two years later, Kroger became the first company to offer in-store butcher shops. Mr. Kroger had a reputation as a demanding boss and a tough competitor, keeping overhead low and discounting prices. The company spread to St. Louis in 1912. Kroger sold his holdings in the company for $28 million in 1928, just before the stock market crash, and retired to Florida.

In the late 1920s the Kroger company bought Piggly-Wiggly stores in Ohio, Tennessee, Michigan, Kentucky, Missouri, and Oklahoma and acquired most of the stock of Piggly-Wiggly Corporation, which it held until the early 1940s.

In 1930 Kroger manager Michael Cullen suggested the idea of the supermarket, but Kroger executives demurred. Cullen left Kroger and began King Kullen supermarkets, still a chain in the Northeast.

During the 1950s Kroger acquired companies, including stores in Texas, Georgia, and Washington, DC. Its 1960 purchase of Sav-on drugstores of New Jersey and its 1961 opening of the first SupeRx drugstore in Ohio, Kroger broadened its sales. In 1983 Kroger bought Kansas-based Dillon Food Stores and acquired Kwik Shop convenience stores.

In 1987 Kroger sold most of its interests in the Hook and SupeRx drug chains and focused on its combination food-and-drug stores. In 1988 Kroger faced takeover bids from the Herbert Haft family and from KKR (Kohlberg Kravis Roberts). Chairman and CEO Lyle Everingham and President Joseph Pichler warded off the raiders. They, in effect, launched an internal LBO; they borrowed $4.1 billion to pay a hefty dividend to shareholders and to purchase shares for an employee stock plan. Pichler was named chairman and CEO in 1990; Everingham retired.

To reduce debt Kroger sold assets (most of its equity in Price Saver Membership Wholesale Clubs, 95 food stores, 29 liquor stores, and its Fry's California stores). The company put up for sale 12 food processing plants. In 1990 it made its first major acquisition since the 1988 restructuring by buying 29 Great Scott! supermarkets in Michigan. Through stock purchases and company benefit plans, employees own about 36% of Kroger common stock.

WHAT

	1990 Sales	
	$ mil.	% of total
Food stores	18,485	91
Convenience stores	863	4
Other sales	913	5
Total	**20,261**	**100**

Grocery Stores
City Market (CO, NM, UT, and WY)
Dillon Food Stores (KS)
Fry's Food Stores (AZ)
Gerbes Supermarkets (MO, OK, AR, and KS)
King Soopers (CO)
Kroger (Midwest and South)
Sav-mor

Convenience Stores
Kwik Shop (KS, OK, IA, NE, and IL)
Loaf 'N Jug (CO, NM, and OK)
Mini Mart (CO, MT, ND, SD, WY, and NE)
Quik Stop Market (CA)
Time Savers Stores (LA)
Tom Thumb Food Stores (FL and AL)
Turkey Hill Minit Market (PA)

RANKINGS

5th in *Fortune* 50 Retailing Cos.
349th in *Business Week* 1000

KEY COMPETITORS

Albertson's	Longs
American Stores	Melville
Ashland	Mobil
Atlantic Richfield	Publix
Bruno's	Rite Aid
Circle K	Safeway
Coastal	Southland
Food Lion	Texaco
Great A&P	Walgreen
Jack Eckerd	Winn-Dixie

HOW MUCH

	9-Year Growth	1981	1982	1983	1984	1985	1986	1987	1988	1989	1990
Sales ($ mil.)	6.7%	11,267	11,902	15,236	15,923	17,124	17,123	17,660	19,053	19,104	20,261
Net income ($ mil.)	(4.8%)	129	144	127	157	181	56	183	35	(16)	83
Income as % of sales	—	1.2%	1.2%	0.8%	1.0%	1.1%	0.3%	1.0%	0.2%	(0.1%)	0.4%
Earnings per share ($)	(9.0%)	2.22	2.32	1.38	1.73	2.03	0.60	2.18	0.23	(0.23)	0.95
Stock price – high ($)	—	13.94	23.63	21.44	19.75	30.81	35.00	41.50	59.00	19.75	17.00
Stock price – low ($)	—	9.63	11.69	16.88	14.56	18.94	21.38	23.38	8.38	8.38	10.63
Stock price – close ($)	1.0%	13.00	19.69	18.50	19.63	23.94	29.88	24.75	8.88	14.75	14.25
P/E – high	—	6	10	16	11	15	58	19	257	—	18
P/E – low	—	4	5	12	8	9	36	11	36	—	11
Dividends per share ($)	(100%)	0.79	0.88	0.96	1.00	1.00	1.03	1.05	40.82	0.00	0.00
Book value per share ($)	—	13.53	14.66	11.99	12.74	13.61	12.25	12.84	(36.20)	(35.42)	(33.42)

1990 Year-end:
Debt ratio: —
Return on equity: —
Cash (mil.): $55
Current ratio: 0.95
Long-term debt (mil.): $4,558
No. of shares (mil.): 86
Dividends:
  1990 average yield: 0.0%
  1990 payout: 0.0%
Market value (mil.): $1,219

Stock Price History High/Low 1981–90

L.A. GEAR, INC.

OVERVIEW

L.A. Gear, America's 3rd largest producer of athletic shoes (after NIKE and Reebok), is known for stylish, flashy sneakers that appeal particularly to affluent young women. In an effort to capture a bigger share of the men's performance shoe market, the company has come out with the Catapult line of shock-absorbing basketball shoes and the Regulator, which features inflatable air cushions. L.A. Gear also makes a line of sportswear and casual apparel. Its products are backed by a $71.2 million advertising budget (8% of 1990 sales) and a stable of celebrity endorsers that includes Paula Abdul and Karl Malone.

A darling of Wall Street throughout the late 1980s, L.A. Gear has performed poorly since late in 1990. Unprepared for the retailing slump, the company overstocked its warehouses and ended up posting a 4th quarter loss. Continued losses in early 1991 led Trefoil Capital Investors — a limited partnership established to bail out troubled companies, spearheaded by Roy Disney (the late Walt Disney's nephew) — to infuse the company with much needed capital in 1991 by buying 34% of L.A. Gear's stock. Trefoil now displaces founder Robert Greenberg (who owns 18%) as L.A. Gear's largest stockholder.

NYSE symbol: LA
Fiscal year ends: November 30

Hoover's Rating **A**

WHO

Chairman and CEO: Robert Y. Greenberg, age 51, $3,467,014 pay
VC: Gil N. Schwartzberg, age 49, $1,695,192 pay (prior to promotion)
President and COO: Mark R. Goldston, age 36
CFO: William L. Benford, age 49
VP Human Resources: Paul Johnson
Auditors: KPMG Peat Marwick
Employees: 1,502

WHERE

HQ: 4221 Redwood Ave., Los Angeles, CA 90066
Phone: 213-822-1995
Fax: 213-822-0843

L.A. Gear sells its products in more than 100 countries. The company's shoes are manufactured primarily at plants in South Korea and Taiwan; L.A. Gear brand apparel is made in the US, Latin America, and Asia.

	1990 Sales	
	$ mil.	% of total
US	741	82
Other North America	39	4
Europe	72	8
Asia	26	3
Other countries	24	3
Total	**902**	**100**

WHAT

	1990 Sales	
	$ mil.	% of total
Footwear	819	91
Apparel & other products	83	9
Total	**902**	**100**

Footwear
Catapult (basketball)
Street Hiker (casual)
Regulator (air-cushioned athletic)

Apparel
Hats
Jackets
Jeans
Shorts
Sports bags
Sweatshirts
T-shirts
Watches

KEY COMPETITORS

Brown Group
Edison Brothers
The Gap
INTERCO
The Limited
Liz Claiborne
NIKE
Reebok
U.S. Shoe

WHEN

By the time Robert Greenberg started L.A. Gear in 1983, he had been a hairdresser and, on different occasions, a salesman of wigs, roller skates, and E. T. shoelaces. He opened L.A. Gear as a women's clothing store on Melrose Avenue in Los Angeles. In addition to name brands, Greenberg's shop sold its own line of casual apparel and footwear. L.A. Gear's trendy, glitzy shoes were practically an overnight success, and in 1984 Greenberg hired ad man Sandy Saemann to market them nationwide. The company expanded into women's athletic shoes in 1985, introducing the canvas Workout, which has been a company mainstay ever since. Monthly sales exploded from $200,000 at the first of the year to $1.8 million at mid-year.

The company went public in 1986. Proceeds of the stock offering ($16.5 million) were used to develop new products and to beef up the company's advertising campaign. More new lines of footwear followed, including shoes for infants, children, and men in 1986. The company introduced a line of activewear for men and young women in 1987 and a line of young women's jeans in 1988. By the end of 1989 L.A. Gear had surpassed INTERCO's Converse as America's 3rd largest athletic shoe maker. Its stock continued as a strong performer on Wall Street, but there were rumblings of trouble ahead as 7 top executives began unloading their shares.

In 1989 Saemann unveiled the award-winning campaign "Unstoppable," featuring basketball celebrity Akeem Olajuwon. In 1990 other "Unstoppable" ads featuring basketball legend Kareem Abdul-Jabbar and 49ers quarterback Joe Montana were released, and the company signed Michael Jackson to a separate $20 million promotional deal. The Jackson deal failed to produce results, and the company, which maintained huge inventories of shoes ready to ship as orders arrived, wound up with a stockpile of unwanted merchandise. The retailing slump hit, and, to clear out inventories, the company sold its high-priced shoes at a sizeable discount, which contributed to L.A. Gear's first quarterly loss since going public ($7.1 million in the 4th quarter of 1990). In December 1990 the company received more bad publicity when one of its high-tops (worn by a Marquette University basketball player) collapsed during a game.

Facing continued financial troubles, the company received fresh capital in 1991 in the form of a $100 million investment from Trefoil Capital Investors. Within 2 weeks of the Trefoil investment, Saemann left L.A. Gear to "pursue other business interests." He will continue as an L.A. Gear consultant until 1994.

HOW MUCH

	5-Year Growth	1981	1982	1983	1984	1985	1986	1987	1988	1989	1990
Sales ($ mil.)	141.4%	—	—	—	—	11	36	71	224	617	902
Net income ($ mil.)	—	—	—	—	—	—	2	4	22	55	31
Income as % of sales	—	—	—	—	—	2.2%	4.8%	6.2%	9.8%	8.9%	3.5%
Earnings per share ($)	139%	—	—	—	—	0.02	0.14	0.27	1.29	3.01	1.56
Stock price – high ($)	—	—	—	—	—	—	6.19	3.47	11.88	46.75	50.38
Stock price – low ($)	—	—	—	—	—	—	1.94	1.63	2.31	10.75	9.75
Stock price – close ($)	—	—	—	—	—	—	2.06	2.34	10.94	31.13	13.38
P/E – high	—	—	—	—	—	—	44	13	9	16	32
P/E – low	—	—	—	—	—	—	14	6	2	4	6
Dividends per share ($)	—	—	—	—	—	0.00	0.00	0.00	0.00	0.00	0.00
Book value per share ($)	250.8%	—	—	—	—	0.02	1.09	1.36	2.52	8.80	10.62

1990 Year-end:
Debt ratio: 0.0%
Return on equity: 16.1%
Cash (mil.): $3
Current ratio: 2.14
Long-term debt (mil.): $0
No. of shares (mil.): 19
Dividends:
 1990 average yield: 0.0%
 1990 payout: 0.0%
Market value (mil.): $259

Stock Price History High/Low 1986–90

LEVI STRAUSS ASSOCIATES INC.

Private company
Fiscal year ends: Last Sunday in November

Hoover's Rating **A**

OVERVIEW

With sales of $4.2 billion, privately owned Levi Strauss is the world's largest apparel manufacturer and the 2nd largest jeans maker in the US after V.F. Corporation (Wrangler and Lee), and has the world's most recognized apparel trademark. Aided by strong global demand and innovative advertising, Levi Strauss has sold over 2.5 billion pairs of jeans.

Levi's domestic operations consist of 6 marketing units: Men's Jeans, Youthwear, Womenswear, Menswear, Shirts, and Brittania Sportswear, marketed through over 40,000 domestic retail outlets.

The company's International division, encompassing Europe, Canada, Latin America, and Asia/Pacific, sells Levi's products in over 70 countries. Levi Strauss grants licenses to make and sell its products in countries where the company does not have manufacturing facilities.

Since its LBO in 1985, the company has jettisoned unprofitable or non-core lines and greatly streamlined production. Levi Strauss's new computer network (LeviLink) will connect the company with its fabric suppliers and will allow retailers to order and pay for new inventory electronically.

The company is committed to a program of social responsibility that includes innovative personnel policies, a worldwide code of ethics, and generous charitable contributions. Descendants of founder Levi Strauss own over 90% of the company, and employees own the rest.

WHO

Honorary Chairman of the Board: Walter A. Haas, Jr., age 75
Chairman of the Executive Committee of the Board: Peter E. Haas, age 72
Chairman and CEO: Robert D. Haas, age 48, $1,382,539 pay
SVP; President of Levi Strauss International: Lee C. Smith, age 48, $589,698 pay
SVP Operations: Peter L. Thigpen, age 51, $572,621 pay
SVP and Chief Information Officer: R. William Eaton, Jr., age 47
President and COO: Thomas W. Tusher, age 49, $1,017,841 pay
SVP and CFO: George B. James, age 53, $592,652 pay
SVP Personnel: Donna J. Goya, age 43
Auditors: Arthur Andersen & Co.
Employees: 31,323

WHEN

Levi Strauss arrived in New York City from Bavaria in 1847 to join his 2 brothers' dry goods business. In 1853 Strauss moved to San Francisco to sell dry goods (particularly tent canvas) to the gold rush miners.

Shortly after Strauss arrived, a prospector told him of miners' problems in finding sufficiently sturdy pants. Strauss made a pair out of canvas for the prospector, and word of the sturdy pants spread quickly.

Strauss made a few more pairs of canvas pants before switching to a durable French fabric called serge de Nimes, soon known as denim. Strauss began coloring the fabric with indigo dye and adopted the idea of Nevada tailor Jacob Davis of reinforcing the pants with copper rivets. In 1873 Strauss and Davis produced their first pair of Levi's Patent Riveted 501 (501 was the lot number) Waist High Overalls. The pants, which soon became the standard attire of lumberjacks, cowboys, railroad workers, oil drillers, and farmers, are the same today as they were in 1873 (minus the rivets on the crotch and back pockets). The 2-horse patch (on the back of every pair) was introduced in 1886.

Strauss continued to build his lucrative pants and wholesaling business until his death in 1902, when the company passed to his 4 nephews, who continued to produce their uncle's bluejeans (the term jeans traces its roots to the cotton trousers worn by ancient Genoese sailors) while maintaining the company's reputation for philanthropy.

After WWII Walter Haas, Jr., and Peter Haas (the 4th generation of the family) assumed leadership and in 1948 discontinued the wholesale segment (then most of the company) to concentrate solely on Levi's clothing.

Levi's bluejeans gained widespread popularity during the 1950s and were soon the uniform of young people everywhere. In the 1960s the company introduced divisions for women's clothing and international sales.

In 1971 Levi Strauss went public and diversified, buying Koret sportswear, bringing out a women's career line, and making a licensing agreement with Perry Ellis. By the mid-1980s profits had declined and the firm was losing its family business tradition. The Haas family engineered a $1.65 billion LBO and took the company private in 1985.

In 1987 the company acquired Brittania and in 1988 restructured operations. In 1989 Levi Strauss publicly offered shares of Levi Strauss Japan (its subsidiary in Tokyo).

Levi's, under Robert Haas (great-great-grandnephew of Strauss), is an innovator in employee-management relations, instituting flex time and telecommuting. Despite a decline in the basic jeans business as the population ages (370 million pairs sold in 1990 compared to over 500 million 10 years ago), the Dockers lines and overseas sales growth (37% in 1990) have brought sufficient income for Levi Strauss to repurchase $84.4 million in subordinated debt and $450 million in common stock.

WHERE

HQ: 1155 Battery St., San Francisco, CA 94111
Phone: 415-544-6000
Fax: 415-544-3939

The company operates 34 production and 5 distribution facilities in the US. Foreign operations consist of 19 distribution and 15 production facilities.

	1990 Operating Income	
	$ mil.	% of total
US	313	42
Europe	296	40
Other countries	136	18
Adjustments	(72)	—
Total	**673**	**100**

WHAT

	1990 Sales
	% of total
Men's Jeans	49
Menswear	18
Youthwear	16
Womenswear	9
Britannia	4
Shirts	4
Total	**100**

Products	Brittsport
Jackets	Dockers
Jeans	501 jeans
Shirts	Levi's Action
Slacks	Levi's for Men
Sportswear	Levi's 900 Series
Tops	Little Levi's
	Silver Label
Brand Names	Sutter Creek
Bend Over	
Brittania	**Subsidiaries and Affiliates**
Brittgear	Levi Strauss Japan (85%)

RANKINGS

28th in *Forbes* 400 US Private Cos.

KEY COMPETITORS

The Gap	Liz Claiborne
Hartmarx	V. F.
The Limited	

HOW MUCH

	9-Year Growth	1981	1982	1983	1984	1985	1986	1987	1988	1989	1990
Sales ($ mil.)	4.5%	2,851	2,572	2,731	2,514	2,584	2,762	2,867	3,117	3,628	4,247
Net income ($ mil.)	4.9%	172	127	195	41	(19)	49	116	85	272	265
Income as % of sales	—	6.0%	4.9%	7.1%	1.6%	(0.7%)	1.8%	4.0%	2.7%	7.5%	6.2%
Employees	(4.7%)	48,000	45,000	44,000	37,000	35,000	32,000	32,000	32,000	31,000	31,000

1990 Year-end:
Debt ratio: 19.8%
Return on equity: 36.0%
Cash (mil.): $166
Current ratio: 1.37
Long-term debt (mil.): $159

Net Income ($ mil.) 1981–90

THE LIMITED, INC.

OVERVIEW

The Limited is one of the great success stories of modern retailing. From a single store in 1963, the company has grown to 3,864 stores, with 1990 sales of almost $5.4 billion.

Its 17 retail clothing store divisions include The Limited, Express (fashionable clothes for women and men), Victoria's Secret (the world leader in intimate apparel), Lerner (the largest US women's specialty apparel chain), and Lane Bryant (large-size fashions). The Limited also owns 4 large catalog operations.

The Limited produces its goods, mostly private-label pseudo-designer names like Forenza, Outback Red (now discontinued), and the recently failed Paul et Duffier line, through its contract manufacturing subsidiary, Mast Industries. The company also operates a bank that issues credit cards and grants credit for each of the company's divisions.

In 1990 poor performance by the flagship Limited stores led to the 1991 resignation of division president Verna Gibson and her replacement by Howard Gross. Throughout 1991, insiders, including chairman Wexner (owner of 27.6% of shares), sold off large numbers of shares.

NYSE symbol: LTD
Fiscal year ends: Saturday closest to January 31

Hoover's Rating **A+**

WHO

Chairman and President: Leslie H. Wexner, age 53, $1,829,473 pay
VC: Thomas G. Hopkins, age 58, $837,827 pay
President, Mast Industries: Martin Trust, age 56, $1,035,588 pay
EVP and CFO: Kenneth B. Gilman, age 44, $837,827 pay
President, Store Planning: Charles W. Hinson, age 54, $569,926 pay
VP Personnel, Limited Stores: Ron Lucas
Auditors: Coopers & Lybrand
Employees: 72,500

WHEN

In 1963, after a disagreement with his father over operations of the family store (Leslie's), Leslie Wexner, then 26, opened the first Limited store in Columbus, Ohio, with $5,000 borrowed from his aunt. The store sold moderately-priced fashions to teenagers and young women. When The Limited went public in 1969, it had only 5 stores, but the rapid development of large, covered malls spurred growth to 100 stores by 1976. The Limited acquired Mast Industries, an international apparel purchasing and importing company, in 1978. Two years later Wexner created Express, with a trendier format aimed at younger girls; it has since widened its product line.

In 1982 The Limited began an acquisitions program, beginning with Lane Bryant, founded in 1900, which specializes in "fashions for larger women." The Brylane fashion catalog division was formed when the company acquired Roaman's, a catalog merchandiser, that same year. Also in 1982 The Limited acquired Victoria's Secret, a chain of 4 stores and a catalog specializing in women's lingerie. The division has since surpassed Maidenform and Vanity Fair as the leading seller of lingerie in the US. Meanwhile, new decor and the introduction of the company's Forenza and Outback Red lines helped increase The Limited's sales.

Beginning in 1984 Wexner made unsuccessful takeover bids for Carter Hawley Hale, Federated Department Stores, and R.H. Macy. But now the synergy of the clusters of The Limited's stores within malls has created the pulling power of a department store.

The Limited acquired Lerner Stores and Henri Bendel in 1985. Since 1987 the company has introduced several new shops including Cacique (French lingerie), Limited Too (children's fashions), Structure (men's clothes), and Victoria's Secret Bath Shops. The Limited bought Abercrombie & Fitch, founded in 1892, in 1988 and Penhaligon's, a London-based perfume shop founded in 1870, in 1990. In 1989 it sold its Lerner Woman division to a new company (United Retail Group, Inc.) in which it took a 1/3 interest.

In 1990 and 1991 organizational problems caused late delivery of new season merchandise to some Limited stores. The failure of the Paul et Duffier line and the retail downturn depressed profit growth and reduced same-store sales for 8 consecutive months. In an effort to boost sagging profits at the budget-priced Lerner stores, the company introduced the popular Forenza line, which had previously been offered exclusively at The Limited. In addition, new divisions Limited Too, Cacique, Structure, and Bath & Body Works were restructured. Even Victoria's Secret, previously the corporate growth leader, slowed.

WHERE

HQ: Two Limited Pkwy., PO Box 16000, Columbus, OH 43216
Phone: 614-479-7000
Fax: 614-479-7080

The Limited operates 3,864 stores nationwide and in Europe. Distribution centers are located in Columbus and Indianapolis.

WHAT

	No. of Stores	Total Selling Sq. Ft. (thou.)
Lerner	858	5,721
Limited stores	778	3,526
Lane Bryant	752	3,295
Express	549	2,151
Victoria's Secret stores	442	1,210
Structure	152	355
Victoria's Secret Bath Shops	109	76
Limited Too	108	268
Cacique	51	115
Abercrombie & Fitch	27	192
Bath & Body Works	27	24
Penhaligon's	7	3
Henri Bendel	4	72
Total	**3,864**	**17,008**

Other Operations
Brylane Catalog
Mast Industries, Inc.
Victoria's Secret Catalog
World Financial Network National Bank

RANKINGS

25th in *Fortune* 50 Retailing Cos.
59th in *Business Week* 1000

KEY COMPETITORS

Carter Hawley Hale
Dayton Hudson
Dillard
The Gap
General Cinema
Hartmarx
Levi Strauss
Marks and Spencer
May
Melville
Mercantile Stores
Montgomery Ward
Nordstrom
J. C. Penney
Sears
U.S. Shoe
Other department stores

HOW MUCH

	9-Year Growth	1981	1982	1983	1984	1985	1986	1987	1988	1989	1990
Sales ($ mil.)	34.8%	365	721	1,086	1,363	2,426	3,224	3,616	4,155	4,750	5,376
Net income ($ mil.)	37.7%	22	34	71	93	145	228	235	245	347	398
Income as % of sales	—	6.1%	4.7%	6.5%	6.8%	6.0%	7.1%	6.5%	5.9%	7.3%	7.4%
Earnings per share ($)	36.5%	0.07	0.10	0.20	0.26	0.40	0.61	0.63	0.68	0.96	1.10
Stock price – high ($)	—	0.70	2.04	5.17	4.67	10.63	17.25	26.44	13.94	19.94	25.56
Stock price – low ($)	—	0.45	0.57	1.89	2.54	4.33	10.25	7.94	8.19	12.63	11.75
Stock price – close ($)	46.1%	0.59	2.00	4.08	4.50	10.42	15.88	8.63	13.63	17.50	18.00
P/E – high	—	10	21	26	18	27	29	42	21	21	23
P/E – low	—	7	6	10	10	11	17	13	12	13	11
Dividends per share ($)	50.0%	0.01	0.01	0.02	0.04	0.05	0.08	0.12	0.12	0.16	0.24
Book value per share ($)	37.1%	0.25	0.35	0.54	0.77	1.12	2.07	2.04	2.64	3.45	4.33

1990 Year-end:
Debt ratio: 25.7%
Return on equity: 28.3%
Cash (mil.): $13
Current ratio: 2.84
Long-term debt (mil.): $540
No. of shares (mil.): 361
Dividends:
1990 average yield: 1.3%
1990 payout: 21.8%
Market value (mil.): $6,491

Stock Price History High/Low 1981–90

LITTON INDUSTRIES, INC.

OVERVIEW

Litton manages 4 businesses — industrial automation, resource exploration, advanced electronics, and marine engineering — operating in different business cycles. In 1991 the industrial automation segment (manufacturing systems, automated material-handling systems, document management systems) wrote off $100 million in connection with the closing of a division. Western Atlas, Litton's 70%-owned oil services subsidiary (Dresser owns the rest) and leader in seismic exploration, is expanding rapidly internationally and profiting from reconstruction in the Persian Gulf. Litton's defense electronics business is suffering from a slowdown in defense spending. The company's shipbuilding unit, although completely dependent on Defense Department contracts, is working off a 4-year backlog. In 1990 45% of Litton's sales were to the US government.

Litton has boosted earnings per share by buying back 7.6 million shares since 1986. Teledyne and an affiliate own 29.3% of Litton.

NYSE symbol: LIT
Fiscal year ends: July 31

 Hoover's Rating C+

WHO

Chairman and CEO: Orion L. Hoch, age 61, $1,336,099 pay
President and COO: Alton J. Brann, age 48
VC and CFO: Joseph T. Casey, age 59, $852,670 pay
VP Industrial Relations: Mathias J. Diederich
Auditors: Deloitte & Touche
Employees: 50,600

WHERE

HQ: 360 N. Crescent Dr., Beverly Hills, CA 90210-4867
Phone: 213-859-5000
Fax: 213-859-5940

Litton maintains offices and plants at 51 locations in 24 states in the US, and in Canada and Western Europe.

US Plant and Office Space

California	19%	Illinois	5%
Mississippi	16%	Michigan	5%
Texas	14%	Massachusetts	3%
Pennsylvania	8%	Maryland	3%
Kentucky	6%	Other states	16%
Connecticut	5%		

	1990 Sales		1990 Operating Income	
	$ mil.	% of total	$ mil.	% of total
US	3,787	73	341	75
Foreign	1,368	27	114	25
Adjustments	1	—	(60)	—
Total	**5,156**	**100**	**395**	**100**

WHAT

	1990 Sales		1990 Operating Income	
	$ mil.	% of total	$ mil.	% of total
Advanced Electronics	2,074	40	180	39
Industrial Systems & Services	1,960	38	139	30
Marine Engineering	1,125	22	140	31
Adjustments	(3)	—	(64)	—
Total	**5,156**	**100**	**395**	**100**

Advanced Electronics
Litton Holdings, Inc.
  Litton Technology Corporation Ltd.
Litton Systems, Inc.

Industrial Systems and Services
Intermec Corp. (industrial barcode systems)
Litton Industrial Automation Systems, Inc.
WG of America Holdings, Inc.
  Western Atlas International, Inc. (69%, oil services)

Marine Engineering and Production
Ingalls Shipbuilding, Inc.

RANKINGS

100th in *Fortune* 500 Industrial Cos.
364th in *Business Week* 1000

KEY COMPETITORS

Eaton	Raytheon
General Dynamics	Schlumberger
General Electric	Siemens
General Motors	Teledyne
Halliburton	Tenneco
Henley	Thomson SA
Honeywell	Westinghouse
Ingersoll-Rand	Other defense companies
Motorola	

WHEN

Charles "Tex" Thornton, head of the Statistical Control Department of the Army Air Force during WWII, was responsible for predicting manufacturing needs in the war effort. He foresaw a growing demand for new, technologically advanced military products in the postwar years. In 1953, after working for Ford and for Howard Hughes, he organized a company of his own (Electro Dynamics) to reap the benefits of this new market. Thornton began by borrowing $1.5 million and buying Litton Industries, which produced microwave tubes for the Navy. Thornton added 8 more smaller firms by the end of his company's first 9 months. Litton stock went public in 1954, and the cash generated was invested in R&D and expansion, which were to be the hallmarks of Litton for nearly 2 decades. In 1958 Litton bought privately owned Monroe Calculating Machine. Sales topped $100 million that year.

After 1959 Litton continued to expand both internally and by acquisition, buying over 50 companies during the next decade. These purchases included Svenska Dataregister AB (Sweden, cash registers, 1959), Western Geophysical (seismic oil exploration, 1960), Ingalls Shipbuilding (1961), Cole Steel Equipment (office furniture, 1961), Winchester Electronics (1963), and Fitchburg Paper (1964). With the acquisition of Royal McBee (typewriters) and Hewitt-Robbins (office equipment) in 1965, Litton's annual sales topped $1 billion. Litton continued to expand worldwide, acquiring Kester Solder, Rust Engineering, Business Equipment Holdings (Australia), Stouffer Foods, and Eureka X-Ray Tube in 1967; Landis Tool in 1968; and Triumph Werke Nürmburg (Germany, typewriters) in 1969. Litton's annual sales passed the $2 billion mark in 1968, but that year also saw the first quarterly decline in earnings in the company's history. Litton stock quickly dropped from over $120 to around $60.

During the 1970s and 1980s Litton management restructured the company. Although acquisitions continued, they were more strategic and were coupled with consolidations and major divestitures, including Rust Engineering (1972), Stouffer Foods food divisions (1973), and Triumph Werke Nürmburg (1980). During the 1970s Litton's sales and net earnings fluctuated as the company reorganized.

In the 1980s the company concentrated on its 4 core business segments, selling its unrelated and unprofitable businesses. The Defense Department temporarily suspended business with Litton after the company admitted to 300 counts of fraud.

In 1991 Litton bought Intermec, an industrial automatic identification (barcode) systems specialist, and General Instrument's defense electronics business.

HOW MUCH

	9-Year Growth	1981	1982	1983	1984	1985	1986	1987	1988	1989	1990
Sales ($ mil.)	0.5%	4,936	4,933	4,720	4,601	4,585	4,521	4,420	4,864	5,023	5,156
Net income ($ mil.)	(6.0%)	312	315	232	277	299	71	138	167	178	179
Income as % of sales	—	6.3%	6.4%	4.9%	6.0%	6.5%	1.6%	3.1%	3.4%	3.6%	3.5%
Earnings per share ($)	0.0%	7.27	7.37	5.39	6.44	7.24	2.52	5.12	6.32	6.99	7.26
Stock price – high ($)	—	86.69	58.33	71.45	80.00	93.50	92.25	108.25	87.25	98.00	81.38
Stock price – low ($)	—	46.14	34.60	47.55	56.25	64.38	71.75	64.00	67.50	71.50	68.88
Stock price – close ($)	4.1%	54.19	49.14	70.63	64.88	83.75	74.00	72.13	71.88	77.25	77.50
P/E – high	—	12	8	13	12	13	37	21	14	14	11
P/E – low	—	6	5	9	9	9	28	13	11	10	9
Dividends per share ($)	(100%)	1.17	1.39	1.61	1.84	2.00	0.00	0.00	0.00	0.00	0.00
Book value per share ($)	6.2%	33.71	39.68	43.47	47.94	34.47	37.39	40.60	46.15	51.98	58.00

1990 Year-end:
Debt ratio: 52.8%
Return on equity: 13.2%
Cash (mil.): $1,244
Current ratio: 1.99
Long-term debt (mil.): $1,452
No. of shares (mil.): 22
Dividends:
  1990 average yield: 0.0%
  1990 payout: 0.0%
Market value (mil.): $1,734

Stock Price History High/Low 1981–90

LIZ CLAIBORNE, INC.

OVERVIEW

Liz Claiborne, Inc., with 1990 sales of $1.7 billion, is the largest US producer of clothing and accessories for the working woman. The company designs and markets popular sportswear; stylish professional suits, dresses, and tailored slacks; matched accessories; and fragrances for women under the labels Liz Claiborne, Elisabeth, Liz & Co., and Dana Buchman. It also produces a line of men's sportswear under the Claiborne label. The company introduced a new line of fragrances for men (1989) and its first collection of costume jewelry (1990).

Although Liz Claiborne products are considered "designer" items, prices tend to fall in the "better" apparel range ($80 to $175).

The company markets its products in the US and Canada, in department stores, specialty shops, and 74 company-owned stores. It owns 14 shops that carry exclusively Liz Claiborne (women's) and Claiborne (men's) products, 24 Liz Claiborne outlet stores, and 36 First Issue specialty stores. In 1991 the company expanded into the UK at 6 locations, including Harrod's.

WHEN

It was 1975. Liz Claiborne, a dress designer in Jonathan Logan's Youth Guild division, had a vision of stylish, sporty, and affordable clothes for America's working woman. Unable to sell the concept to her employer, Claiborne left the company and joined her husband Arthur Ortenberg and 2 other partners, Jerome Chazen and Leonard Boxer, to found Liz Claiborne, Inc., in 1976. With a starting investment of $250,000, the company was an immediate success. It showed a profit its first year and became the fastest growing, most profitable US apparel company in the 1980s.

In 1981 Liz Claiborne went public at $19 per share, raising $6.1 million. In 1986, after only 10 years, the company was on *Fortune*'s list of the top 500 industrial companies. Revenues that year were over $800 million.

The company is noted for its well-organized management, distribution, and sales teams. Until her retirement Ms. Claiborne maintained close control over the design side of the business, overseeing and "editing" the work of the designers. The company's emphasis on detail, quality, and attention to consumer preferences has created a loyal customer base. It produces 6 new collections a year (Holiday, Pre-Spring, Spring I, Spring II, Summer, and Fall), which provide consumers with new styles every 2 months. These short cycles allow more frequent

updates of new styles and put clothes on the racks in the appropriate season. An automated inventory network that gives each week's sales trends allows quick response to market demand.

Liz Claiborne expanded into men's clothing (Claiborne, 1985), cosmetics (Liz Claiborne, a 1986 joint venture with Avon; in 1988 the company regained full rights to the line), a clothing line for larger women (Elisabeth, 1989), and a line of knit sportswear (Liz & Co., 1989). A new label of higher-priced sportswear by in-house designer Dana Buchman was introduced in 1987. A 1984 foray into girls' clothes failed by 1987.

The company moved into the retail apparel business in 1988 when it opened its first retail stores, offering the First Issue brand of casual sportswear. It expanded with Liz Claiborne and Claiborne stores in 1989. Liz Claiborne's "store-within-a-store" concept offers department store shoppers the recognizable Liz Claiborne image in a space of about 7,000 square feet. These areas are jointly managed by the stores and Liz Claiborne's staff.

Liz Claiborne and Arthur Ortenberg retired from management in 1989 and from the board in 1990. In 1990 the company established a separate shoe division and began to explore the possibility of entering the performance shoe market.

WHO

Chairman: Jerome A. Chazen, age 64, $1,226,000 pay
VC and President: Harvey L. Falk, age 56, $1,226,000 pay
VC; President, Women's Sportswear Group: Jay Margolis, age 42, $1,226,000 pay
SVP Finance: Samuel M. Miller, age 53
President, Human Resources: Kathryn D. Connors
Auditors: Arthur Andersen & Co.
Employees: 6,000

WHERE

HQ: 1441 Broadway, New York, NY 10018
Phone: 212-354-4900
Fax: 212-719-9049

About 115 of Liz Claiborne's 380 independent suppliers are located in the US; the remainder are located principally in Hong Kong, South Korea, Taiwan, the Philippines, China, and Brazil. The company's products are sold by approximately 9,400 stores throughout North America, and at 6 locations in the UK.

WHAT

	1990 Sales	
	$ mil.	% of total
Misses' sportswear	756	42
Petite women's sportswear	213	12
Dresses	160	9
Accessories	155	9
Men's sportswear	114	6
Cosmetics	72	4
Outlet stores	62	3
Liz & Co. label	59	3
Retail specialty stores	59	3
Elisabeth label	53	3
Canada	41	2
Dana Buchman label	17	1
Shoes	13	1
Jewelry	9	1
Men's furnishings	7	1
Licensing	4	—
Adjustments	(65)	—
Total	**1,729**	**100**

Brand Names

Women's Apparel and Cosmetics

Collection	Liz & Co.
Dana Buchman	Liz Claiborne
Elisabeth	Lizsport
First Issue	Lizwear
Limited Edition	Realities

Men's Clothing
Claiborne

RANKINGS

237th in *Fortune* 500 Industrial Cos.
172nd in *Business Week* 1000

KEY COMPETITORS

The Gap	The Limited	NIKE
Hartmarx	L'Oréal	Reebok
L.A. Gear	LVMH	U.S. Shoe
Levi Strauss	Marks & Spencer	V. F.

HOW MUCH

	9-Year Growth	1981	1982	1983	1984	1985	1986	1987	1988	1989	1990
Sales ($ mil.)	34.9%	117	166	229	391	557	814	1,053	1,184	1,411	1,729
Net income ($ mil.)	39.7%	10	14	22	42	61	86	114	110	165	206
Income as % of sales	—	8.7%	8.5%	9.8%	10.7%	10.9%	10.6%	10.9%	9.3%	11.7%	11.9%
Earnings per share ($)	38.4%	0.13	0.17	0.27	0.50	0.71	1.00	1.32	1.26	1.87	2.37
Stock price – high ($)	—	1.29	2.56	4.69	6.63	12.38	24.25	39.13	20.00	27.75	35.00
Stock price – low ($)	—	0.86	0.99	2.00	3.09	5.88	11.88	12.25	12.75	16.50	20.25
Stock price – close ($)	42.6%	1.22	2.33	4.25	6.38	12.13	21.38	16.50	17.25	24.00	29.75
P/E – high	—	10	15	18	13	17	24	30	16	15	15
P/E – low	—	7	6	8	6	8	12	9	10	9	9
Dividends per share ($)	—	0.00	0.00	0.00	0.05	0.08	0.12	0.16	0.17	0.19	0.24
Book value per share ($)	43.7%	0.32	0.49	0.77	1.23	1.90	2.86	4.10	5.22	6.94	8.40

1990 Year-End:
Debt ratio: 2.1%
Return on equity: 30.9%
Cash (mil.): $432
Current ratio: 3.49
Long-term debt (mil.): $15
No. of shares (mil.): 85
Dividends:
  1990 average yield: 0.8%
  1990 payout: 10.0%
Market value (mil.): $2,527

Stock Price History High/Low 1981–90

LOCKHEED CORPORATION

NYSE: LK
Fiscal year ends: Sunday nearest December 31

Hoover's Rating **B-**

OVERVIEW

Lockheed Corporation is the 6th largest defense contractor and the largest defense R&D contractor in the US.

Lockheed is developing Milstar, a military communications satellite network, as well as the Trident II submarine-launched ballistic missile and systems for NASA's Space Station *Freedom*. The company is also developing (with Aerojet General) new space shuttle solid rocket motors. Lockheed also offers services such as space shuttle processing, aircraft modification and maintenance, and data processing.

Chief Executive Daniel Tellep has pulled the company through some hard times lately, including 2 highly publicized battles for control with investor Harold Simmons. Since 1990 Tellep has moved decisively toward making Lockheed a leaner, more cost-conscious company by reducing capital spending by 15%, cutting 9,500 jobs, and transferring operations to lower cost areas. The company is enjoying favorable publicity related to the success of its F-117A Stealth fighter during the Persian Gulf War and in 1991 became the prime contractor to build the US Air Force's new Advanced Tactical Fighter.

WHO

Chairman and CEO: Daniel M. Tellep, age 59, $1,011,250 pay
VC and Chief Financial and Admininstrative Officer: Vincent N. Marafino, age 60, $899,635 pay
VP Human Resources: Louis J. Bernard, age 58
VP Operations: E. Allan Thompson, age 64
Auditors: Ernst & Young
Employees: 73,000

WHERE

HQ: 4500 Park Granada Blvd., Calabasas, CA 91399
Phone: 818-712-2000
Fax: 818-712-2329

Lockheed has approximately 40 manufacturing plants and R&D facilities throughout the US.

WHEN

Brothers Allan and Malcolm Loughead (pronounced "Lockheed") formed 2 unsuccessful California-based aircraft manufacturing companies before teaming with Fred Keeler in 1926 to form Lockheed Aircraft. John Northrop (later to found Northrop Corporation) designed Lockheed's first airplane, the famous Vega (flown by such pilots as Wiley Post and Amelia Earhart). Detroit Aircraft Company bought Lockheed in 1929 but went bankrupt in 1931.

Robert Gross, Carl Squier, and Lloyd Stearman bought Lockheed in 1932. With designer Clarence "Kelly" Johnson, the company produced a long series of successes, including the Electra transport (1934), the P-38 Lightning fighter of WWII, the P-80 Shooting Star jet fighter (1944), the Constellation airliner (1945), the U-2 spyplane (1955), and the SR-71 Blackbird. The company also produced submarine-launched ballistic missiles, beginning with the Polaris (1958); military transports such as the C-5 Galaxy (1968); and the L-1011 TriStar airliner (1970).

In the late 1960s and early 1970s the company suffered the cancellation of its Cheyenne attack helicopter, the C-5A cost-overrun scandal, and financial problems with the L-1011. Government-sponsored loans saved the company from bankruptcy in 1971.

In the 1970s and 1980s, Lockheed developed the space shuttle's thermal insulation system, the Hubble Space Telescope, and the F-117A stealth fighter. The company bought electronics maker Sanders Associates (1986), sold its DIALOG computer information system to Knight-Ridder (1988), and sold 2 other computer service companies, CADAM and Lockheed DataPlan (1989). In 1989 Lockheed wrote off $491 million in program losses on fixed-price contracts, primarily related to development of the navy's P-7A patrol aircraft and to subcontract work for the air force's C-17 transport.

In 1990 the main aircraft plant in Burbank, California was closed, eliminating 5,500 jobs. Disappointing post-launch performance of the Hubble telescope added to the company's woes. Also in 1990 Dallas billionaire Harold Simmons rallied investors who wanted to stop the company's expansion into nondefense operations, spearheading 2 proxy battles (in 1990 and 1991) aimed at gaining control of the company. Lockheed emerged intact, and Simmons sold most of his 19.8% stake in the company at a $42 million loss. In 1991 Lockheed's F-22 was chosen as the next generation air force advanced fighter, which could mean up to $60 billion in sales for the company over the life of the program.

	1990 Sales		1990 Operating Income	
	$ mil.	% of total	$ mil.	% of total
US	9,701	97	535	95
Other countries	257	3	26	5
Total	**9,958**	**100**	**561**	**100**

WHAT

	1990 Sales		1990 Operating Income	
	$ mil.	% of total	$ mil.	% of total
Missiles & space systems	5,116	51	379	68
Aeronautical systems	2,329	23	96	17
Technology services	1,550	16	58	10
Electronic systems	963	10	28	5
Total	**9,958**	**100**	**561**	**100**

	1990 Sales	
	$ mil.	% of total
US government	8,663	87
Other governments	539	5
Commercial	756	8
Total	**9,958**	**100**

Principal Operating Units
Aeronautical Systems (F-117A, F-22 Advanced Tactical Fighter, C-130)
Electronic Systems (ALQ-126B electronic warfare system)
Lockheed Missiles & Space (Hubble Space Telescope, Trident II submarine-launched ballistic missile, systems for Space Station *Freedom*, Milstar communications satellite)
Technology Services (space shuttle processing; International Airport, Toronto, Canada)

HOW MUCH

	9-Year Growth	1981	1982	1983	1984	1985	1986	1987	1988	1989	1990
Sales ($ mil.)	7.5%	5,176	5,613	6,490	8,113	9,535	10,273	11,321	10,590	9,891	9,958
Net income ($ mil.)	9.0%	155	207	263	344	401	408	436	442	6	335
Income as % of sales	—	3.0%	3.7%	4.1%	4.2%	4.2%	4.0%	3.9%	4.2%	0.1%	3.4%
Earnings per share ($)	6.7%	2.96	3.59	4.14	5.26	6.09	6.17	6.63	7.34	0.10	5.30
Stock price – high ($)	—	16.67	28.17	47.50	48.75	58.00	60.25	61.50	48.00	54.75	41.50
Stock price – low ($)	—	8.50	14.46	24.17	30.13	40.75	43.00	28.75	34.75	35.75	24.75
Stock price – close ($)	8.9%	15.58	24.42	40.00	44.00	49.13	50.13	34.38	41.25	39.00	33.63
P/E – high	—	6	8	11	9	10	10	9	7	548	8
P/E – low	—	3	4	6	6	7	7	4	5	358	5
Dividends per share ($)	—	0.00	0.00	0.00	0.45	0.75	0.95	1.30	1.55	1.75	1.80
Book value per share ($)	32.5%	2.89	7.76	13.08	17.81	23.17	28.44	33.31	41.73	32.63	36.54

1990 Year-end:
Debt ratio: 45.5%
Return on equity: 15.3%
Cash (mil.): $372
Current ratio: 1.36
Long-term debt (mil.): $1,929
No. of shares (mil.): 63
Dividends:
  1990 average yield: 5.4%
  1990 payout: 34.0%
Market value (mil.): $2,125

Stock Price History High/Low 1981–90

RANKINGS

50th in *Fortune* 500 Industrial Cos.
256th in *Business Week* 1000

KEY COMPETITORS

Allied-Signal	Grumman	Siemens
Boeing	Martin Marietta	Textron
General Dynamics	McDonnell Douglas	Thiokol
General Electric	Northrop	Thomson SA
GEC	Raytheon	Thorn EMI
General Motors	Rockwell	

LOEWS CORPORATION

NYSE symbol: LTR
Fiscal year ends: December 31

Hoover's Rating **B**

OVERVIEW

Loews Corporation is a holding company managed by the Tisch family. Larry Tisch, the company's chairman and co-CEO, is also CEO of CBS. He and Bob Tisch, Loews's co-CEO and president, together own more than 27% of the company.

CNA Financial, an 83%-owned subsidiary, is Loews's main revenue source and a leading US life and property/casualty insurer. Despite a $1 billion junk bond portfolio, CNA retains an A+ performance rating from A.M. Best. Loews's profit leader is its Lorillard cigarette company. Newport, the #5 cigarette brand in the US, and Kent account for 61% and 24% of Lorillard sales, respectively. As a result of price increases, cigarette sales and earnings rose in 1990 despite a drop in unit shipments.

Bucking the industry trend, Loews Hotels is still expanding rapidly. When the Coronado Bay Resort is opened, Loews will be operating 15 first-class hotels. Other Loews holdings include 97% of Bulova, a watch maker and defense contractor; Diamond M, an oil rig operator; 22.9% of CBS; and 49% of tanker-fleet operator Hellespont. CNA also has substantial investments in several large banks.

WHEN

In 1946 Larry Tisch, who had received an NYU business degree at age 18, dropped out of Harvard Law and with his younger brother Bob bought a Lakewood, New Jersey, resort hotel, with help from their parents.

Tisch Hotels, the new entity, purchased Atlantic City's Traymore and Ambassador Hotels in the early 1950s and 10 others by 1955. In the early 1960s the brothers erected 6 hotels simultaneously in New York City.

Moving beyond hotels, the brothers bought money-losing companies saddled with poor management; discarding the management along with underperforming divisions, they quickly tightened operational control and eliminated frills such as fancy offices, company planes, and even memos.

In 1960 Tisch Hotels gained control of MGM's ailing Loew's Theaters division following a 1959 antitrust ruling, and sold the prime real estate underneath many of the elegant one-screen theaters to developers. The company name became Loews in 1971; Loews sold its remaining theater operations in 1985.

In 1968 the company bought Lorillard, shed pet food and candy operations, and regained its slipping tobacco market share by introducing low-tar brands (Kent III, True). CNA Financial (purchased in 1974) was next: the Tisch method turned losses of $208 million in 1974 to $110 million in profits the next year.

Bulova Watch (1979), guided by Larry's son Andrew, combated a nagging image problem with sleek new watch styles; profitability returned in 1984.

In 1985 Loews helped CBS fend off a takeover attempt by Ted Turner, and ended up with almost 25% of the company and Larry as president of CBS.

Loews's deep pockets allowed the purchase of 6 used tankers for $5.5 million apiece (average construction cost: $60 million) during a period of depressed prices for supertankers in the early 1980s. In 1990 Loews sold 3 of the Majestic supertankers for $133 million and exchanged the other 3 for 49% interest in the purchasing entity (Hellespont), for a pretax gain of $105 million. Loews bought offshore drilling rig operator Diamond M in 1989.

Loews's caution during the hotel overexpansion of the 1980s later enabled the company to purchase some bargains (e.g., Loews Giorgio, Denver; 1989).

In 1989 Loews also entered a joint venture with Covia, a United Airlines affiliate, to create a new computer reservation service for hotels. Loews bought back over 5 million of its shares in 1990. In the same year, experiencing a decline in market share, Lorillard introduced Heritage, its first reduced-priced cigarette brand.

WHO

Chairman and Co-CEO: Laurence A. Tisch, age 68, $1,682,757 pay
President and Co-CEO: Preston Robert (Bob) Tisch, age 64, $1,245,280 pay
EVP: James S. Tisch, age 38, $367,334 pay
Chairman and CEO, Lorillard Tobacco Co.: Andrew H. Tisch, age 41
SVP and CFO: Roy E. Posner, age 57, $415,064 pay
VP: Jonathan M. Tisch, age 37
VP Personnel: Kenneth Abrams, age 57
Auditors: Deloitte & Touche
Employees: 26,600

WHERE

HQ: 667 Madison Ave., New York, NY 10021-8087
Phone: 212-545-2000
Fax: 212-545-2498

Loews operates in the US, Monaco, and Canada.

WHAT

	1990 Sales		1990 Net Income	
	$ mil.	% of total	$ mil.	% of total
Hotels	240	2	29	3
Cigarettes	1,582	13	758	75
Prop. cas. ins.	7,517	62	54	5
Life insurance	2,425	20	72	7
Watches & timing	182	2	6	1
Shipping	125	1	111	11
Offshore drilling	41	—	(18)	(2)
Adjustments	169	—	(31)	—
Total	**12,281**	**100**	**981**	**100**

Major Holdings

CNA Financial (83%)
Continental Assurance
Continental Casualty

Lorillard, Inc.
Heritage
Kent
Newport
Old Gold
Triumph
True

Loews Hotels
Howard Johnson Hotel (NYC)
Loews Anatole (Dallas)
Loews Annapolis
Loews Coronado Bay Resort (San Diego)
Loews Giorgio (Denver)
Loews Glenpointe (Teaneck, NJ)
Loews Le Concorde (Quebec City)
Loews L'Enfant Plaza (DC)

Loews Monte Carlo
Loews Santa Monica Beach
Loews Summit (NYC)
Loews Vanderbilt Plaza (Nashville)
Loews Ventana Canyon Resort (Tucson)
Ramada Hotel (NYC)
Regency (NYC)

Bulova Corporation (97%)
Clocks
Mechanical time fuses
Ultimé gold jewelry
Watches

Diamond M Corporation
Drilling rigs

Hellespont (49%)
Crude oil tankers

CBS Inc. (22.9%)

RANKINGS

13th in *Fortune* 50 Diversified Financial Cos.
77th in *Business Week* 1000

KEY COMPETITORS

Accor	Casio	Imasco
American Brands	CSX	ITT
B.A.T	Edward J. DeBartolo	Marriott
Bass	Helmsley	Philip Morris
Canadian Pacific	Hilton	Rank
Carlson	Hyatt	RJR Nabisco
		Ins. cos.

HOW MUCH

	9-Year Growth	1981	1982	1983	1984	1985	1986	1987	1988	1989	1990
Sales ($ mil.)	11.7%	4,534	4,606	4,808	5,274	6,333	8,248	8,965	10,424	11,098	12,281
Net income ($ mil.)	13.5%	257	216	266	329	503	546	656	890	907	805
Income as % of sales	—	5.7%	4.7%	5.5%	6.2%	7.9%	6.6%	7.3%	8.5%	8.2%	6.6%
Earnings per share ($)	16.8%	2.67	2.40	3.16	4.03	6.17	6.69	8.41	11.70	12.02	10.82
Stock price – high ($)	—	14.38	21.27	25.07	35.50	56.25	72.38	96.25	83.13	135.00	126.88
Stock price – low ($)	—	9.73	10.57	17.67	23.50	33.00	53.75	58.00	62.00	77.00	75.00
Stock price – close ($)	26.5%	11.87	19.13	24.87	35.00	54.50	58.25	66.63	78.88	124.25	98.13
P/E – high	—	5	9	8	9	9	11	11	7	11	12
P/E – low	—	4	4	6	6	5	8	7	5	6	7
Dividends per share ($)	22.6%	0.16	0.16	0.16	0.29	3.00	1.00	1.00	1.00	1.00	1.00
Book value per share ($)	19.6%	14.40	16.92	20.71	24.63	29.97	36.07	42.56	53.20	64.09	72.10

1990 Year-end:
Debt ratio: 24.4%
Return on equity: 15.9%
Cash (mil.): $3,609
Current ratio: —
Long-term debt (mil.): $1,623
No. of shares (mil.): 70
Dividends:
  1990 average yield: 1.0%
  1990 payout: 9.2%
Market value (mil.): $6,861

Stock Price History High/Low 1981–90

LONGS DRUG STORES CORPORATION

OVERVIEW

Walnut Creek, California–based Longs Drug Stores operates 261 drugstores in 6 western states, 86% of which are in California, where Longs holds a 20% market share.

Two things distinguish Longs from its competitors. First, the company gives store managers extraordinary independence in running their stores and ties managers' salaries to each location's performance. Consequently, store managers can tailor their stores to local preferences and are highly motivated to do so. This practice breeds management loyalty, which is further strengthened by the company's policy of promoting from within.

Second, the company's stores (ranging from 15,000 to 40,000 square feet) are larger than the industry average. This allows each location to offer a greater selection of high-margin general merchandise. These 2 factors have allowed Longs to achieve high sales per employee and per store with the lowest expense ratio of any public drug chain (21.2%).

Longs is conservatively managed and employee-oriented, adding locations steadily and maintaining high profitability. Stock repurchases in recent years have left a smaller share of ownership in public hands: 47% of common stock is held either by the Long family or by employee benefit plans. A relatively high percentage of nonpharmacy sales (80%), traditionally an advantage, leaves Longs dependent on the highly competitive general merchandise market at the same time that Wal-Mart is moving into Long's California territories.

NYSE symbol: LDG
Fiscal year ends: Last Thursday in January

WHO

Chairman and CEO: Robert M. Long, age 52, $440,314 pay
President: S. D. Roath, age 50, $332,905 pay
SVP Development: Ronald A. Plomgren, age 57, $258,115 pay
SVP Properties and Secretary: O. D. Jones, age 52, $204,057 pay
SVP Marketing: D. R. Wilson, age 49, $185,582 pay
SVP: G. A. Duey, age 58
VP Administration and Treasurer: W. G. Combs, age 60
VP and Controller: Grover L. White, age 50
VP Personnel, Longs Drug Stores California, Inc.: L. C. Anderson
Auditors: Deloitte & Touche
Employees: 15,100

WHEN

Joseph Long, son-in-law of Safeway founder Marion Skaggs, and Long's brother Thomas opened their first store, Longs Self-Service Drug Store, in Oakland, California, in 1938 and their 2nd store in nearby Alameda in 1939. The Oakland store (which is still operating today) was the first to introduce the then-new retailing idea of self-service to drug stores. The brothers believed that the manager of each store should make the decisions regarding its operation. The stores offered the lowest prices in their neighborhoods.

By 1950 the company had 6 stores in the Oakland area and one in Fresno. Longs opened 10 more stores during the 1950s in California and Hawaii. In 1969 the chain went public. In the late 1970s it expanded into Oregon, Alaska, Arizona, and Nevada.

Longs continued its decentralized philosophy in the late 1980s despite its growing number of locations. Unlike most chain stores, where stocking and operations decisions are made at headquarters, Robert Long, president since his father, Joseph, became chairman in 1975, has given each store manager extraordinary freedom in price setting, inventory selection, and sales promotion.

In 1987 the company departed from its habit of growing through new openings by acquiring one Osco Drug store in Denver and 11 in California from American Stores, increasing its market share in California to 20%. At the same time it sold all 15 Longs locations in Arizona to Osco.

The company is also trying to position itself for the growth in the industry that it foresees as the elderly population increases. Part of this strategy has been to offer free blood pressure and cholesterol screenings and to promote its pharmacists as health care advisors through informational advertising. The company plans to continue its slow-growth pattern, opening 10 to 15 stores per year.

The pharmacy of each store remains the core of Longs. In late 1989 a pharmacy distribution center was opened in Southern California. And to speed up prescription dispensing, some high-volume stores have been upgraded to "super pharmacy" status.

Joseph Long died in 1990 and was succeeded as chairman by Robert Long. Longs is currently upgrading its checkout, inventory, and ordering systems; by the end of 1991 installation will be complete in over 100 stores.

WHERE

HQ: 141 N. Civic Dr., Walnut Creek, CA 94596
Phone: 415-937-1170
Fax: 415-944-6657

Longs operates drugstores in 6 western states, primarily in California. The company also operates a pharmacy distribution center in Southern California.

	No. of Stores	% of Total
California	223	86
Hawaii	22	8
Nevada	6	2
Colorado	6	2
Arizona	2	1
Alaska	2	1
Total	**264**	**100**

WHAT

Estimated Product Mix	% of Total
Prescription drugs	18
Cosmetics	10
Housewares & appliances	9
Candy	7
Liquor, wine & beer	7
Nonprescription drugs	6
Food	6
Household supplies	6
Photofinishing & equipment	6
Stationery & greeting cards	5
Related drug items	4
Sporting goods & toys	3
Toiletries	2
Tobacco & magazines	2
Miscellaneous	9
Total	**100**

HOW MUCH

	9-Year Growth	1981	1982	1983	1984	1985	1986	1987	1988	1989	1990
Sales ($ mil.)	9.8%	1,005	1,123	1,214	1,376	1,481	1,635	1,772	1,925	2,111	2,334
Net income ($ mil.)	7.8%	30	31	36	40	38	39	49	56	61	60
Income as % of sales	—	3.0%	2.8%	3.0%	2.9%	2.5%	2.4%	2.8%	2.9%	2.9%	2.6%
Earnings per share ($)	8.4%	1.43	1.45	1.70	1.86	1.72	1.76	2.31	2.75	3.01	2.94
Stock price – high ($)	—	18.44	23.50	25.06	24.88	31.75	38.75	41.00	37.38	48.50	44.88
Stock price – low ($)	—	12.75	12.38	16.88	17.00	21.63	26.63	25.13	29.38	34.50	33.25
Stock price – close ($)	11.1%	14.44	17.81	24.31	22.13	30.63	29.50	30.38	35.50	44.63	37.38
P/E – high	—	13	16	15	13	18	22	18	14	16	15
P/E – low	—	9	9	10	9	13	15	11	11	11	11
Dividends per share ($)	9.5%	0.45	0.51	0.55	0.62	0.70	0.75	0.79	0.86	0.94	1.02
Book value per share ($)	9.3%	8.42	9.38	10.57	12.23	13.33	13.74	14.59	15.46	16.68	18.80

1990 Year-end:
Debt ratio: 5.1%
Return on equity: 16.6%
Cash (mil.): $10
Current ratio: 1.58
Long-term debt (mil.): $21
No. of shares (mil.): 20
Dividends:
　1990 average yield: 2.7%
　1990 payout: 34.7%
Market value (mil.): $754

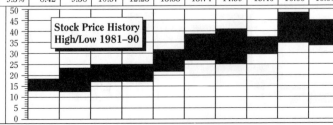

Stock Price History
High/Low 1981–90

RANKINGS

49th in *Fortune* 50 Retailing Cos.
655th in *Business Week* 1000

KEY COMPETITORS

Albertson's
American Stores
Edward J. DeBartolo
Fred Meyer
Kmart
Kroger
Melville
Walgreen
Wal-Mart
Other supermarket companies

LOTUS DEVELOPMENT CORPORATION

OTC symbol: LOTS
Fiscal year ends: December 31

Hoover's Rating **B+**

OVERVIEW

Cambridge, Massachusetts–based Lotus is the leading spreadsheet maker for IBM-compatible PCs, with 64% of the market, and is the 2nd largest independent PC software company (after Microsoft). Lotus 1-2-3 is the de facto spreadsheet standard for PCs. Translated into 17 languages, including a top-selling Japanese version, it has sold over 8 million copies.

Lotus continues to port 1-2-3 to other computer platforms with versions available on Sun workstations, DEC minicomputers, IBM mainframes, NeXT computers, and Apple Macintoshes. Other products include CD-ROM–based financial information prod-

ucts (Lotus One Source); groupware (Notes), which allows PC users to exchange information on a network; a personal information manager (Agenda); a hard disk utility (Magellan); a presentation graphics product (Freelance Plus); and a word processor (Samna's Ami and Ami Pro).

Lotus's 1990s strategy is to focus on key application markets including spreadsheet, wordprocessing (bought Samna, 1990), graphics, and electronic mail software (acquired cc: Mail, 1991). Its 1990 profits were hurt by a $53 million one-time charge, associated with the Samna acquisition.

WHEN

When the IBM PC was introduced in 1981, Mitch Kapor quickly saw the light and designed an electronic spreadsheet for it. He called it Lotus 1-2-3 (after the Hindu symbol of enlightenment), and soon the former Transcendental Meditation teacher saw his Cambridge-based company blossom. One year after the 1982 founding, sales were $53 million; by 1985, $226 million.

Kapor brought to Lotus the values of his late 1960s Yale undergraduate days; consensus, jeans, and t-shirts were staples. Unwieldy growth, however, prompted the structure-shy Kapor to boost star marketer Jim Manzi to president in 1984. Manzi transformed Lotus into a market-driven company and injected a management team drawn from mainframe vendor ranks after Kapor left in 1986.

When the highly touted Symphony spreadsheet and Jazz (for Macintosh computers) drew muted responses, Manzi focused on 1-2-3. Lotus acquired a number of smaller companies offering 1-2-3 enhancements and developed foreign language versions for Europe, the Middle East, and Japan. In 1985 and 1986 Manzi began broadening beyond 1-2-3, purchasing Dataspeed, Inc. (Signal and Quotrek stock-quote services), ISYS Corp. (developer of the One Source CD/ROM), and Graphics Communications (graphics software).

When competing spreadsheets threatened market share, Lotus undertook an arduous 3-year development of 1-2-3 Release 3.0, which doubled the work force and brought order to programming chaos with progress reports and shared standards. Release 3.0 (featuring 3-D graphics) and, for less powerful PCs, Release 2.2 (with spreadsheet publishing strength) finally appeared in 1989; customers seeking the attributes of both had to wait for Release 3.1 (1990).

In 1989 the company took a 15% equity position in Sybase, Inc., a database management software developer. In 1990 it agreed to acquire networking software leader Novell, but the deal collapsed before it was completed.

The new decade saw Lotus emerge leaner (stock-quote services Signal and Quotrek were shed in 1989) and focused on broadening 1-2-3's scope, releasing 1-2-3 for a number of hardware platforms. Lotus underestimated the success of Microsoft's graphics interface software Windows 3.0, and its delay in developing a version of 1-2-3 for Windows (finally released in mid-1991) allowed competitors, Microsoft (Excel) and Borland (Quatro Pro) to cash in. In 1991 Lotus abandoned sales of its CD-ROM direct marketing database, Lotus Marketplace, after thousands complained the product was an invasion of privacy.

WHO

Chairman, President, and CEO: Jim P. Manzi, age 39, $867,545 pay
SVP Finance and Operations and CFO: Robert P. Schechter, age 42, $442,125 pay
VP Human Resources: Russell J. Campanello
Auditors: Coopers & Lybrand
Employees: 3,500

WHERE

HQ: 55 Cambridge Pkwy., Cambridge, MA 02142
Phone: 617-577-8500
Fax: 617-693-1299

Lotus Development has locations in 32 foreign countries and conducts manufacturing and distribution operations in the US, Puerto Rico, Singapore, and Ireland.

	1990 Sales		1990 Operating Income	
	$ mil.	% of total	$ mil.	% of total
North America	396	58	20	17
Other countries	293	42	94	83
Adjustments	(4)	—	(13)	—
Total	**685**	**100**	**101**	**100**

WHAT

Spreadsheets
Lotus Improv (NeXT computer)
Lotus 1-2-3 for Windows
Lotus Spreadsheet for DeskMate
1-2-3 enhancement products
  Datalens Developer Toolkit
  Add-in Toolkit
1-2-3 Release 2.2
1-2-3 Release 3.0
1-2-3 Release 3.1
1-2-3 versions for Apple Macintosh, DEC, IBM, Sun, UNIX System V
1-2-3/G (graphical user interface)
Symphony
Symphony 2.0 Plus
Symphony 2.2

Consulting Services

Database Management
Lotus/DBMS
LotusWorks
Symphony

Graphics
Allways
Freelance Graphics for OS/2
Freelance Release 3J

Freelance Plus Release 3.01
Graphwriter II

Information Management
cc: Mail
Lotus Agenda
Lotus Magellan
Lotus Notes

Information Services
Lotus One Source
  CD/Banking
  CD/Banking:Branches
  CD/Corporate
  CD/Corporate:European M&A
  CD/Corporate:U.K. Private+
  CD/Corporate:U.K. Public Companies
  CD/International
  CD/Investment
  CD/M&A
  CD/Marketplace
  CD/Networker
  CD/Private+

Investments
Sybase, Inc. (15%, relational database management)

Wordprocessing
Ami
Ami Professional

RANKINGS

510th in *Business Week* 1000

KEY COMPETITORS

Apple
Borland
Computer Associates
IBM
Microsoft
Oracle
Wang

HOW MUCH

	7-Year Growth	1981	1982	1983	1984	1985	1986	1987	1988	1989	1990
Sales ($ mil.)	44.1%	—	—	53	157	226	283	396	469	556	685
Net income ($ mil.)	7.3%	—	—	14	36	38	48	72	59	68	23
Income as % of sales	—	—	—	25.9%	23.0%	16.9%	17.1%	18.2%	12.6%	12.2%	3.4%
Earnings per share ($)	7.3%	—	—	0.33	0.75	0.77	1.03	1.57	1.29	1.58	0.54
Stock price – high ($)	—	—	—	10.33	13.25	11.25	19.33	38.50	34.25	33.50	39.25
Stock price – low ($)	—	—	—	7.42	5.08	5.08	6.71	16.33	14.75	18.00	12.50
Stock price – close ($)	—	—	—	10.33	8.00	8.33	17.25	30.75	18.25	31.00	20.00
P/E – high	—	—	—	32	18	15	19	25	27	21	73
P/E – low	—	—	—	23	7	7	7	10	11	11	23
Dividends per share ($)	—	—	—	0.00	0.00	0.00	0.00	0.00	0.00	0.00	0.00
Book value per share ($)	28.7%	—	—	1.25	2.02	2.85	2.72	4.60	5.57	6.69	7.33

1990 Year-end:
Debt ratio: 34.1%
Return on equity: 7.7%
Cash (mil.): $245
Current ratio: 2.32
Long-term debt (mil.): $160
No. of shares (mil.): 42
Dividends:
  1990 average yield: 0.0%
  1990 payout: 0.0%
Market value (mil.): $844

Stock Price History High/Low 1983–90

LOWE'S COMPANIES, INC.

OVERVIEW

Lowe's Companies, based in North Wilkesboro, North Carolina, sells hardware and building supplies, home decoration materials, major appliances, and consumer electronics through over 300 stores in 20 states. Most of the stores are located in small cities where the company can avoid the level of competition found in large urban centers. The company is #2 in its industry after Home Depot. It is the 6th largest appliance dealer in the US and the only home center chain to offer appliances and electronics products.

Since 1984 Lowe's has followed Home Depot's lead in shifting away from the highly cyclical building market toward the home improvement do-it-yourself market. To this end the company has enlarged and relocated its stores to better accommodate retail customers and plans to continue this long term. Sales to do-it-yourselfers are up from 52% in 1984 to 66% in 1990.

About 8% of Lowe's stock is owned by its officers and directors. Lowe's Companies Employee Stock Ownership Trust owns 23%. Chiefly because of its generous employee stock ownership plan, Lowe's has been honored as one of the 100 best companies to work for in the US.

WHEN

Lowe's was founded in 1921 as Mr. I. S. Lowe's North Wilkesboro Hardware in North Wilkesboro, North Carolina. A family operation by 1945, Mr. Lowe's store was run by his son Jim and son-in-law Carl Buchan. Jim and Buchan opened a 2nd store in Sparta, North Carolina (about 40 miles from North Wilkesboro) in 1949. Buchan bought Jim Lowe's share in the company in 1952. Incorporating as Lowe's North Wilkesboro Hardware, Buchan kept Lowe's as part of the company name because he liked the slogan "Lowe's Low Prices." Sales in 1952 were $4 million. By 1960 Buchan had 15 stores in North Carolina, Virginia, Tennessee, and South Carolina and sales of $31 million.

Buchan had planned to create a profit-sharing plan for Lowe's employees, but he died of a heart attack in 1960. In 1961 Lowe's management and the executors of Buchan's estate established the Lowe's Employees Profit Sharing and Trust, which bought Buchan's 89% of the company (later renamed Lowe's Companies). They financed the transaction through a public offering in 1961, which diluted the employees' stock. Lowe's was listed on the NYSE in 1979.

Harvard MBA Robert Strickland, who joined the company directly out of business school in 1957, became chairman in 1978.

Revenues increased from $170 million in 1971 to more than $900 million, with net income of $25 million, in 1979. Traditionally, over 1/2 of Lowe's business was in sales to professional home builders, but in 1980 housing starts fell to 1.3 million and Lowe's net income dropped 24%. Concurrently, Home Depot introduced its low-price warehouse concept, which Strickland initially rejected. Instead, he reorganized his stores' layouts and by 1982 had redesigned 1/2 of the 229 stores to be more oriented toward do-it-yourself consumers. The new designs featured softer lighting and displays of entire room layouts to appeal to women, who made up over 1/2 of all do-it-yourself customers. In 1982 Lowe's made more than 50% of its sales to consumers for the first time in its history.

In 1984 Lowe's got on the warehouse bandwagon, announcing that it would increase its total store floor space from 2.5 million square feet to 5 million square feet by 1988 through new store construction and relocation.

By 1989, however, Home Depot overtook Lowe's, which had continued to target contractors as well as do-it-yourselfers so that, despite an increase in retail sales, 1/3 of earnings remained vulnerable to the vagaries of the construction market, which in 1990 and 1991 was in a slump.

NYSE symbol: LOW
Fiscal year ends: January 31

WHO

Chairman: Robert L. Strickland, age 60, $550,916 pay
President and CEO: Leonard G. Herring, age 63, $577,916 pay
EVP Sales/Store Operations: Wendell R. Emerine, age 52, $358,120 pay
SVP, Treasurer, and CFO: Harry Underwood II, age 48, $218,107 pay
Auditors: Deloitte & Touche
Employees: 16,000

WHERE

HQ: PO Box 1111, North Wilkesboro, NC 28656
Phone: 919-651-4000
Fax: 919-651-4766

	No. of Stores
Alabama	14
Arkansas	7
Delaware	3
Florida	19
Georgia	22
Illinois	1
Indiana	4
Kentucky	18
Louisiana	13
Maryland	9
Mississippi	7
Missouri	1
North Carolina	71
Ohio	6
Pennsylvania	7
South Carolina	23
Tennessee	27
Texas	8
Virginia	34
West Virginia	15
Total	**309**

WHAT

	1990 Sales	
	$ mil.	% of total
Building commodities, lumber	1,235	43
Home decorating, lighting	419	15
Yard, patio & garden products	293	10
Kitchen, bathroom & laundry products	272	10
Other products	614	22
Total	**2,833**	**100**

Principal Sales Segments
Building commodities
Consumer electronics
Heating, cooling, and water systems
Home decorating and lighting products
Home entertainment products
Kitchen, bathroom, and laundry fixtures
Major appliances
Tools
Yard, patio, and garden products

HOW MUCH

	9-Year Growth	1981	1982	1983	1984	1985	1986	1987	1988	1989	1990
Sales ($ mil.)	13.8%	888	1,034	1,431	1,689	2,073	2,283	2,442	2,517	2,651	2,833
Net income ($ mil.)	16.6%	18	25	51	61	60	55	56	71	75	71
Income as % of sales	—	2.0%	2.4%	3.5%	3.6%	2.9%	2.4%	2.3%	2.8%	2.8%	2.5%
Earnings per share ($)	14.9%	0.55	0.76	1.40	1.70	1.64	1.41	1.41	1.83	2.01	1.91
Stock price – high ($)	—	11.35	22.35	32.75	25.13	31.13	41.50	32.75	24.38	32.13	49.63
Stock price – low ($)	—	6.30	7.13	17.33	16.25	20.75	22.50	15.25	16.25	20.75	18.38
Stock price – close ($)	13.8%	7.65	20.78	22.38	24.75	25.88	26.00	16.13	21.00	29.50	24.50
P/E – high	—	21	30	23	15	19	29	23	13	16	26
P/E – low	—	12	9	12	10	13	16	11	9	10	10
Dividends per share ($)	6.8%	0.29	0.29	0.32	0.32	0.36	0.40	0.43	0.46	0.49	0.52
Book value per share ($)	14.7%	5.45	5.96	8.04	9.42	10.99	13.64	14.75	15.80	17.33	18.72

1990 Year-end:
Debt ratio: 18.9%
Return on equity: 10.6%
Cash (mil.): $50
Current ratio: 1.83
Long-term debt (mil.): $159
No. of shares (mil.): 36
Dividends:
  1990 average yield: 2.1%
  1990 payout: 27%
Market value (mil.): $893

Stock Price History
High/Low 1981–90

Hoover's Rating B

RANKINGS

42nd in *Fortune* 50 Retailing Cos.
503rd in *Business Week* 1000

KEY COMPETITORS

Circuit City	Sears
Home Depot	Sherwin-Williams
Kmart	Tandy
Montgomery Ward	Wal-Mart

THE LTV CORPORATION

OVERVIEW

In 1991 Dallas-based LTV Corporation moved forward on settling its more than $6 billion in debts by submitting its long overdue reorganization plan to the federal bankruptcy court. Nevertheless, the steel, aerospace/defense, and energy company continues to struggle for its financial health. LTV ended 1990 with a 73% drop in earnings, from $265 million in 1989 to $71 million in 1990. Further complicating matters is a 1990 Supreme Court ruling requiring LTV to take back its underfunded pension from the federal Pension Benefit Guaranty Corp. (PBGC) — a $3.1 billion

liability. To raise the cash to fund its pension liabilities, LTV placed its aerospace and defense businesses up for sale.

LTV is the 3rd largest US steel manufacturer after USX and Bethlehem. The company's aerospace and defense segments are major subcontractors on the military C-17 cargo aircraft, the B-2 stealth bomber, and Boeing's commercial aircraft. In addition, LTV is a major missile supplier to the Defense Department. Its energy segment manufactures and sells oil and gas drilling and production equipment.

NYSE symbol: LTV
Fiscal year ends: December 31

Hoover's Rating **D**

WHO

Chairman, President and CEO: David H. Hoag, age 51, $590,051 pay (prior to promotion)
SVP and CFO: Jay E. Hawley
VP Human Resources: Jack W. Johnson
Auditors: Ernst & Young
Employees: 35,300

WHERE

HQ: PO Box 655003, 2001 Ross Ave., Dallas, TX 75265
Phone: 214-979-7711
Fax: 214-979-7946

LTV offices and facilities are in the US and Canada.

WHEN

LTV was established in Dallas in 1961, the result of a series of mergers and acquisitions orchestrated by James Ling. Ling had taken his company (Ling Electric) public in 1955, aggressively marketing his stock, even distributing its prospectus at the Texas State Fair. LTV's formation began with the acquisition of L. M. Electronics by Ling Electric in 1956. The company acquired Altec Electronics in 1959 and in 1960 merged with Temco (an electronics and missile company). In 1961 Ling-Temco acquired Dallas-based Chance Vought — a well-known manufacturer of Navy planes — to become Ling-Temco-Vought (LTV).

In 1964 Ling was able to increase the value of LTV's assets by making it a holding company and breaking out its operations into 3 public companies: LTV Aerospace, LTV Ling Altec, and LTV Electrosystems. LTV maintained majority interest in all 3. This "redeployment" strategy drove up the price of each subsidiary's stock and subsequently raised the value of LTV's assets. LTV then used its shares in the 3 companies as collateral for further acquisitions.

With borrowed funds LTV continued its acquisition campaign — applying the redeployment strategy where profitable — beginning with Okonite (1965), a copper wire and cable manufacturer; Wilson (1967), the

nation's 3rd largest meatpacker, with divisions in sporting goods and pharmaceuticals; Greatamerica (1968), parent company of Braniff Airlines and National Car Rental; and Jones & Laughlin Steel (1968).

In 1969 LTV's financial health began to deteriorate, made worse by a declining stock market. That year LTV reported a net loss of $38.1 million and was forced to sell off divisions to pay its debt. In 1970 the LTV board demoted Ling to president. He quit 6 weeks later at the age of 47. In 1971 LTV sold Okonite and Braniff as part of an antitrust settlement. The antitrust suit was a consequence of LTV's numerous acquisitions.

In 1977 LTV purchased Lykes, a petroleum equipment company, and Youngstown Sheet & Tube (steel). LTV sold off Wilson in 1981 and was left with LTV Steel, LTV Aerospace & Defense, and LTV Energy Products. In 1984, in an attempt to strengthen its position in steel, LTV acquired Republic Steel for $770 million. But by 1986, with steel and petroleum prices low and with 5 years of losses, LTV was forced into Chapter 11 bankruptcy — the largest industrial filing as of that date. Since LTV's bankruptcy filing, the company has closed down numerous plants, modernized others, and reduced its work force from 48,300 in 1986 to 35,300 in 1990.

WHAT

	1990 Sales		1990 Operating Income	
	$ mil.	% of total	$ mil.	% of total
Steel	3,860	63	56	120
Energy products	317	5	8	17
Aircraft products	780	13	(19)	(41)
Missiles & electronics	1,181	19	2	4
Adjustments	—	—	(30)	—
Total	**6,138**	**100**	**17**	**100**

LTV Steel
Galvanized products   Tin mill products
Rolled sheet   Tubular products

Aircraft Products
Production of military and commercial aircraft components; modernization and support programs
  A-7 aircraft program
  Advanced Technology Bomber (B-2) program
  Boeing 747 program
  Boeing 757 program
  Boeing 767 program
  Canadair program
  McDonnell Douglas C-17A program
  McDonnell Douglas DC-10 program

Missiles and Electronics
Antiradiation missile decoy systems
Army Tactical Missiles System
Computerized flight inspection systems
Military wheeled vehicles (the Hummer)
Multiple Launch Rocket System
Stationkeeping equipment
VT-1 Missile

Energy Products
Drilling, production, and other equipment
Oilfield supplies
Tubular products (casing, tubing, and drill pipe)

RANKINGS

84th in *Fortune* 500 Industrial Cos.

KEY COMPETITORS

Baker Hughes	IRI
Bethlehem Steel	Mitsubishi
Broken Hill	Nippon Steel
Cargill	Northrop
Dresser	Pearson
FMC	Raytheon
Friedrich Krupp	Schlumberger
General Dynamics	Thyssen
Halliburton	USX
Inland Steel	Other aerospace and defense companies

HOW MUCH

	9-Year Growth	1981	1982	1983	1984	1985	1986	1987	1988	1989	1990
Sales ($ mil.)	(2.2%)	7,511	4,777	4,578	7,046	8,199	7,271	7,582	7,325	6,362	6,138
Net income ($ mil.)	(17.6%)	405	(163)	(238)	(378)	(772)	(3,252)	503	(891)	265	71
Income as % of sales	—	5.4%	(3.4%)	(5.2%)	(5.4%)	(9.4%)	(44.7%)	6.6%	(12.2%)	4.2%	1.2%
Earnings per share ($)	(29.6%)	7.97	(3.36)	(4.79)	(5.84)	(9.50)	(35.41)	3.67	(8.97)	1.82	0.34
Stock price – high ($)	—	26.13	17.75	19.13	19.88	13.25	9.88	5.88	3.88	2.50	1.63
Stock price – low ($)	—	12.63	8.13	11.63	8.88	5.25	1.13	1.50	2.13	1.13	0.31
Stock price – close ($)	(32.1%)	16.38	11.38	18.38	9.88	6.75	1.63	2.50	2.25	1.13	0.50
P/E – high	—	3	—	—	—	—	—	2	—	1	5
P/E – low	—	2	—	—	—	—	—	0	—	1	1
Dividends per share ($)	0.0%	0.00	0.44	0.25	0.19	0.00	0.00	0.00	0.00	0.00	0.00
Book value per share ($)	—	26.12	22.38	20.50	16.21	7.19	(26.99)	(20.37)	(49.59)	(45.38)	(42.39)

1990 Year-end:
Debt ratio: —
Return on equity: —
Cash (mil.): $1,082
Current ratio: 2.78
Long-term debt (mil.): $13
No. of shares (mil.): 115
Dividends:
  1990 average yield: 0.0%
  1990 payout: 0.0%
Market value (mil.): $57

Stock Price History High/Low 1981–90

MACANDREWS & FORBES HOLDINGS INC.

Private company
Fiscal year ends: December 31

OVERVIEW

Ronald Perelman's MacAndrews & Forbes Holdings is an eclectic group of businesses in industries ranging from beauty products to banking, including MacAndrews & Forbes, a maker of licorice extract used in flavorings; Coleman Company, a maker of camping and recreational products; and First Gibraltar, a Texas S&L group. MacAndrews & Forbes Holdings also owns Beverly Hills–based Andrews Group, a company that controls Marvel Entertainment Group, the leading comic book company and publisher of Spider-Man comics; and New World Entertainment, which produces such television shows as "The Wonder Years."

Perelman, who assembled MacAndrews & Forbes by acquiring companies, is now selling off pieces of his empire. Revlon remains the conglomerate's crown jewel, but the need to lower the company's debt has forced the financier to part with Revlon's Max Factor and Betrix cosmetics units. Revlon was not generating enough cash to cover the debt service on the high-yield bonds issued when MacAndrews & Forbes first bought control of the cosmetics giant in 1985. Perelman has also raised cash through a public offering of Marvel Entertainment.

More sales are waiting in the wings. Perelman has announced his intention to sell 40% of MacAndrews & Forbes's 82% holding in National Health Laboratories. More sales of Revlon units, including Almay, are possible, as is a public offering of the cosmetics company.

WHO

Chairman and CEO: Ronald O. Perelman, age 48
VC: Howard Gittis, age 57
VC: Donald G. Drapkin, age 42
President: Bruce Slovin, age 56
EVP: Meyer Laskin
EVP and CFO: Fred L. Tepperman
Auditors: KPMG Peat Marwick
Employees: 44,000

WHERE

HQ: 36 E. 63rd St., New York, NY 10021
Phone: 212-572-5980
Fax: 212-572-5022

WHEN

Ron Perelman grew up in his father's Philadelphia-based conglomerate, Belmont Industries, but left it behind at the age of 35 to seek his fortune in New York. In 1978 he bought 40% of jewelry store operator Cohen-Hatfield Industries. Cohen-Hatfield bought a minority interest in MacAndrews & Forbes (licorice flavoring, 1979), acquired the rest of the company (1980), and subsequently adopted MacAndrews & Forbes Group as its corporate name.

In 1982 the company bought an 82% stake in Technicolor, a motion picture processor (sold in 1988). Perelman took MacAndrews & Forbes Group private in 1983. The company subsequently acquired control of video production company Compact Video (1983).

In 1984 MacAndrews & Forbes Group became a unit of new holding company, MacAndrews & Forbes Holdings. In effect, the Group owned MacAndrews & Forbes (licorice maker) and Technicolor, while the holding company (which was owned by Perelman) owned the Group. That same year MacAndrews & Forbes Holdings bought 80% of cigar maker Consolidated Cigar Holdings (sold in 1988).

MacAndrews & Forbes Holdings acquired control of Pantry Pride, a Florida-based supermarket chain, in 1985. Later that year Pantry Pride (by that time a corporate shell manipulated by Perelman) announced a $1.8 billion hostile takeover bid for Revlon.

Revlon was #1 in US cosmetics until 1975, when founder Charles Revson died. His successor, Michel Bergerac, cut R&D spending on cosmetics and used beauty division earnings to buy health care and pharmaceutical companies. Perelman sold Revlon's health care businesses, except for National Health Laboratories, and during the late 1980s bought several cosmetics companies (Max Factor, Germaine Monteil, Yves Saint Laurent's fragrance and cosmetic lines). MacAndrews & Forbes took Revlon private in 1987.

In 1988, encouraged by generous tax credits, MacAndrews & Forbes Holdings agreed to invest $315 million in 5 failing Texas S&Ls, which Perelman combined and named First Gibraltar. The company also bought the Coleman Company (camping equipment) in 1989 for $545 million. Coleman makes 90% of all camping stoves and lanterns in the US.

The company's latest venture, the Andrews Group, started out as Compact Video, which was a dumping ground for Perelman's less profitable businesses for several years. Andrews Group, 100% owned since 1990, owns television and movie producer Four Star International (and other entertainment companies) and bought controlling interest in Marvel Entertainment Group (publishers of *The Amazing Spider-Man* and *The Incredible Hulk*) from New World Entertainment in 1988, agreeing to buy the rest of New World in 1989. In 1988 and 1990 MacAndrews & Forbes sold 18% of National Health Laboratories.

In 1991 Perelman sold Revlon's Max Factor and Betrix units to Procter & Gamble for over $1 billion, sold New World Entertainment's theatrical film division back to its founders, and took Marvel Entertainment public.

WHAT

	Estimated Market Value	
	$ mil.	% of total
Almay Cosmetics	225	5
Borghese	250	5
Real estate	175	3
Beauty products	2,225	43
National Health Labs (82%)	1,500	29
Coleman	350	7
New World Productions	160	3
Marvel Entertainment	215	4
Licorice	63	1
Total	**5,163**	**100**

Groups

Entertainment and Publishing
Andrews Group, Inc.
    Marvel Entertainment Group (60%, comic book
      publishing)
    New World Entertainment, Ltd. (television
      production)

Industrial and Consumer Products
Coleman Co., Inc. (camping equipment, power tools,
  recreational vehicle accessories)
MacAndrews & Forbes Group, Inc.
Revlon Group, Inc.
    Almay, Inc. (cosmetics)
    Charles of the Ritz Group Ltd. (cosmetics and
      fragrances)
    Germaine Monteil Cosmetiques (cosmetics)
    MacAndrews & Forbes Co. (flavorings)
    National Health Laboratories (82%, medical testing
      services)
    The Princess Marcella Borghese, Inc. (cosmetics)
    Revlon, Inc. (cosmetics and fragrances)

Financial Services Group
First Gibraltar Bank
Plano Savings & Loan
San Antonio Savings
Sooner Federal

RANKINGS

13th in *Forbes* 400 US Private Cos.

KEY COMPETITORS

Amway	LVMH
Avon	NCNB
Bayer	Procter & Gamble
Bristol-Myers Squibb	Roche
Chemical Bank	Rubbermaid
Colgate-Palmolive	Sony
Estée Lauder	Time Warner
Fleetwood	Unilever
IFF	Other entertainment
Johnson Publishing	companies
L'Oréal	Texas savings & loans

HOW MUCH

	3-Year Growth	1981	1982	1983	1984	1985	1986	1987	1988	1989	1990
Sales ($ mil.)	30.2%	—	—	—	—	—	—	2,440	2,500	5,325	5,381
Employees	16.3%	—	—	—	—	—	—	28,000	24,582	44,000	44,000

Sales ($ mil.) 1987–90

R. H. MACY & CO., INC.

OVERVIEW

New York City–based R. H. Macy is one of the world's most recognized names in retailing. Since going private in 1986, Macy's has faced huge losses, and its suppliers have been increasingly nervous. Sales have grown since the buyout at an average annual rate in excess of 12% (1990 sales were $7.5 billion).

The company's flagship store is the Macy's in Herald Square in midtown Manhattan. At 2.15 million square feet, it is rightly billed as "the world's largest store," and since 1924 it has been associated with some of New York's grandest traditions: Macy's Thanksgiving Day Parade, Santaland, and 4th of July fireworks. The store draws tourists to its wide selection

of merchandise and claims, "If you haven't seen Macy's, you haven't seen New York!"

Edward S. Finkelstein and other Macy executives hold 63% of the company's stock, with the balance held by other investors. A general weakening of retail climate coupled with the company's hefty $4.5 billion debt load (from both the LBO and Macy's 1988 acquisition of Bullock's and I. Magnin) has caused vendors and investors increasing concern over Macy's financial health, which grew worse after Macy reported a record loss of $101 million in its fiscal 1991 3rd quarter. In 1991 Macy's announced it would reorganize into 2 divisons, Macy's East and West.

Private company
Fiscal year ends: Saturday
nearest July 31

Hoover's Rating **C-**

WHO

Chairman and CEO: Edward S. Finkelstein, age 65, $1,134,149 pay
President and COO: Mark S. Handler, age 57, $864,707 pay
EVP: Myron E. Ullman III, age 43, $519,886 pay
Chairman, Macy's Northeast: Arthur E. Reiner, age 50, $574,312 pay
Chairman, Macy's South/Bullock's: Harold D. Kahn, age 45, $603,729 pay
Chairman, Macy's California: Daniel B. Finkelstein, age 35
SVP Finance: Diane P. Baker, age 36
SVP Personnel and Labor Relations: A. David Brown, age 48
Auditors: Deloitte & Touche
Employees: 76,000

WHEN

Rowland H. Macy, a Nantucket Quaker and whaling captain, opened a small store under his name in Manhattan in 1858. His policies of selling for cash only, setting fixed prices, advertising heavily, and underselling the competition were uncommon at the time and quickly gained him customers. He added new lines constantly and gained a reputation for selling everything the housewife might need.

Macy hired a woman, Margaret La Forge, as the store's superintendent in 1866, a first in the industry. La Forge, who was Macy's distant relative, had started as his bookkeeper in 1860. Upon Macy's death in Paris in 1877, La Forge and her husband Abiel became co-owners of the store with Robert Macy Valentine, the founder's nephew. After the death of Abiel La Forge, Valentine bought Margaret out and brought in a new partner, Charles Webster. Valentine died shortly thereafter. His widow married Webster, who invited Isidor and Nathan Straus to become partners with him in 1887. The Straus family, New York china merchants, ran Macy's in partnership with Webster and finally bought him out in 1896. Macy's outgrew its site at 6th Avenue and 14th Street and moved to the Herald Square location at 34th and Broadway in 1902, becoming the world's largest department store.

The Strauses expanded the company outside New York by buying Lasalle & Koch, a Toledo retailer (1923) and Davison-Paxon-Stokes of Atlanta (1925). In 1929 the company bought New Jersey–based L. Bamberger and in 1945 O'Connor, Moffatt & Company, a San

Francisco department store, which became the company's first West Coast location.

Meanwhile, the company continued to build its reputation as a New York institution. Macy's sponsored the first Thanksgiving Day Parade (1924), which has since announced the arrival of Santa Claus to Herald Square each year. Customers were encouraged to work around Macy's no-credit policy by depositing money with the company, against which they could charge purchases, and the company set up Macy's Bank in 1939 to manage these funds. In 1961 the company formed Macy's Credit in response to customers' growing needs to finance larger purchases.

The Straus family continued to run Macy's into the 3rd and 4th generations. By 1986 the only Straus still in Macy's management was board member Kenneth Straus, a retired chairman of the Buying Division. That year Chairman Edward Finkelstein and senior management led a buyout of the company. Macy's made a bid for Federated Department Stores in 1988, which it lost to Campeau, but was able to purchase the California-based I. Magnin and Bullock's units of Federated.

Despite its mounting losses, Macy's has cut its debt, buying back $300 million of its bonds in 1991 for less than 1/2 of their face value. The company also has sold stock to outside investors, including $50 million to Hong Kong moviemaker Sir Run Run Shaw; Chairman Finkelstein's son Mitchell (Macy's head buyer) is married to an actress who starred in many of Shaw's popular kung fu movies.

WHERE

HQ: 151 W. 34th St., New York, NY 10001-2101
Phone: 212-695-4400
Fax: 212-629-6814

Macy operates 147 Macy's, Bullock's, and I. Magnin department stores in 18 states, and 105 Aeropostale, Charter Club, and Fantasies by Morgan Taylor specialty stores in suburban malls throughout the US.

WHAT

Store Divisions	Area	
	Sq. ft. thou.	% of total
Macy's Northeast		
46 Macy's in Connecticut, Delaware, Maryland, New Jersey, New York, Pennsylvania & Virginia	14,724	45
Macy's South/Bullock's		
26 Macy's in Alabama, Florida, Georgia, Louisiana, South Carolina & Texas	5,739	17
22 Bullock's in Arizona, California & Nevada	4,395	13
Macy's California		
25 Macy's in California	5,841	18
I. Magnin		
28 I. Magnins in Arizona, California, Illinois, Maryland & Washington	2,166	7
Total	32,865	100

RANKINGS

16th in *Fortune* 50 Retailing Cos.
9th in *Forbes* 400 US Private Cos.

KEY COMPETITORS

Carter Hawley Hale
Dayton Hudson
Dillard
General Cinema
The Limited
Liz Claiborne
May
Melville
Montgomery Ward
Nordstrom
J. C. Penney
Discount and specialty stores

HOW MUCH

	9-Year Growth	1981	1982	1983	1984	1985	1986	1987	1988	1989	1990
Sales ($ mil.)	12.3%	2,657	2,979	3,628	4,260	4,595	4,890	5,449	5,972	7,225	7,547
Net income ($ mil.)	—	120	136	187	222	189	221	(14)	(134)	(63)	(215)
Income as % of sales	—	4.5%	4.6%	5.1%	5.2%	4.1%	4.5%	(0.3%)	(2.2%)	(0.9%)	(2.9%)
Employees	5.7%	46,000	49,000	49,000	54,000	57,000	55,000	56,000	70,000	78,000	76,000

1990 Year-end:
Debt ratio: —
Return on equity: 8.2%
Cash (mil.): $120
Current ratio: 1.71
Long-term debt (mil.): $4,530

Net Income ($ mil.) 1981–90

MANUFACTURERS HANOVER CORPORATION

NYSE symbol: MHC
Fiscal year ends: December 31

Hoover's Rating C-

OVERVIEW

The Manufacturers Hanover name appears set to vanish with the planned merger with Chemical Bank. The new Chemical Bank will be a New York powerhouse, #1 in New York City consumer deposits and the regional leader in the lucrative middle market (borrowers with sales under $100 million). The new bank will rank 3rd in the US after Citicorp and the planned combination of Bank of America and Security Pacific. The new Chemical plans to reap savings from the merger by cutting staffing levels and closing branches.

Before merger-mania gripped the US banking community, Manufacturers Hanover had ranked 9th among US banks. The bank operates globally and owns 40% of CIT Group, a company offering asset-based financing.

Manufacturers Hanover has been eliminating jobs and strengthening its capital base as problems with loans in the areas of real estate and highly leveraged transactions joined nonperfoming Latin American debt on the bank's list of headaches.

WHO

Chairman and CEO: John F. McGillicuddy, age 60, $1,081,922 pay
VC: Edward D. Miller, age 50, $533,059 pay
President: Thomas S. Johnson, age 50, $846,705 pay
EVP and Chief Credit Officer: William C. Langley, age 52, $413,313 pay
SVP Personnel: Martin H. Zuckerman
Auditors: KPMG Peat Marwick
Employees: 19,177

WHEN

Manufacturers Hanover Corporation is the result of the 1961 merger of Manufacturers Trust Company and Hanover Bank, 2 banks started in the 1800s.

Manufacturers Trust Company started in Brooklyn in 1853 as Manufacturers National Bank and grew by purchasing 13 more banks by 1930. In 1931 Harvey Gibson and a group of associates bought enough Manufacturers stock to make Gibson president. Within a year Manufacturers bought Chatham and Phenix National Bank of New York. Manufacturers continued to purchase banks, the largest being Brooklyn Trust Company (1950), with 26 branches.

The Hanover Bank opened in 1851 in Hanover Square, center of New York City's wholesale dry-goods trade. In 1876 James Woodward began a 34-year term as president of Hanover. During his presidency the bank sought the business of country banks, which was the beginning of the bank's extensive correspondent banking business today. In 1901 Hanover made its first purchase, Continental Bank (Manhattan). Hanover merged with Central Union Trust in 1929 to form Central Hanover Bank and Trust. Central Union Trust already had opened 5 overseas offices in the 1920s. In 1938 Central Hanover opened its first full-service foreign branch. Central Hanover changed its name back to Hanover Bank in 1951.

Less than 2 hours after the 1961 merger to form Manufacturers Hanover, the US Department of Justice filed an antitrust injunction, which left the new bank's fate in doubt for 5 years. The merger was regarded as an excellent combination of Manufacturers' large retail branch system and Hanover's wholesale, trust, and correspondent banking. In late 1965 the US Congress amended the Banking Act of 1960, freeing this merger and many others from antitrust claims. In 1969 the bank formed Manufacturers Hanover Corporation, a holding company. That same year the company became the first US bank to start a merchant bank in London.

In the early 1970s the bank diversified, acquiring mortgage and consumer finance businesses and forming a leasing company. Manufacturers bought CIT Financial from RCA for $1.51 billion (1984) and then sold 60% of CIT to Dai-Ichi Kangyo Bank for $1.28 billion (1989). That year Manufacturers also issued $750 million in common stock to increase capital. The bank incurred losses in 1987 and 1989, after increasing reserves against Latin American loans.

In 1989 and 1990 Manufacturers agreed to buy 24 New York branches of Goldome, a savings bank. Manufacturers announced plans to merge with Chemical Bank in 1991.

WHERE

HQ: 270 Park Ave., New York, NY 10017
Phone: 212-270-6000
Fax: 212-682-3761 (Communications)

Manufacturers Hanover maintains 219 branches in the New York region and offices around the world.

	1990 Assets	
	$ mil.	% of total
US	38,609	62
Europe	11,140	18
Latin America, the Caribbean	6,131	10
Asia/Pacific	4,010	7
Canada	577	1
Middle East	1,063	2
Total	**61,530**	**100**

WHAT

	1990 Assets	
	$ mil.	% of total
Cash & due from banks	2,222	3
Interest-bearing deposits	1,696	3
Securities	9,966	16
Trading accounts	3,211	5
Loans	40,554	66
Credit loss reserve	(2,139)	(3)
Other	6,020	10
Total	**61,530**	**100**

Developing Markets Group
Corporate finance
Correspondent banking
Country debt refinancing
Credit
Debt/equity swaps
Foreign exchange
Trade financing

Global Banking
Credit
Financial advisory services

Risk management
Securities finance
Venture capital

Regional Banking
Consumer deposit services
Consumer leases and loans
Credit cards
Middle market banking
Real estate financing

Geoserve
Information processing
Transaction processing

RANKINGS

9th in *Fortune* 100 Commercial Banking Cos.
612th in *Business Week* 1000

KEY COMPETITORS

Following their merger Manufacturers Hanover will compete with all Key Competitors of Chemical Bank.

HOW MUCH

	9-Year Growth	1981	1982	1983	1984	1985	1986	1987	1988	1989	1990
Assets ($ mil.)	0.4%	59,109	64,041	64,332	75,714	76,526	74,397	73,348	66,710	60,479	61,530
Net income ($ mil.)	(6.4%)	252	295	337	353	407	411	(1,140)	752	(588)	139
Income as % of assets	—	0.4%	0.5%	0.5%	0.5%	0.5%	0.6%	(1.6%)	1.1%	(1.0%)	0.2%
Earnings per share ($)	(17.9%)	7.48	7.78	8.37	7.12	8.38	8.80	(27.02)	14.24	(11.49)	1.27
Stock price – high ($)	—	40.25	45.00	51.00	41.50	47.38	57.75	49.13	31.63	44.75	38.25
Stock price – low ($)	—	30.50	26.00	34.75	22.50	33.88	41.13	21.13	18.75	27.75	15.00
Stock price – close ($)	(5.6%)	35.63	41.63	38.00	36.63	47.13	45.13	21.50	28.38	33.13	21.13
P/E – high	—	5	6	6	6	6	7	—	2	—	30
P/E – low	—	4	3	4	3	4	5	—	1	—	12
Dividends per share ($)	1.9%	2.77	2.95	3.07	3.17	3.21	3.25	3.28	3.28	3.28	3.28
Book value per share ($)	—	55.02	59.34	64.27	64.94	70.08	74.32	42.01	55.88	41.50	38.94

1990 Year-end:
Return on equity: 3.2%
Equity as % of assets: 5.6%
Cash (mil.): $3,918
Long-term debt (mil.): $2,531
No. of shares (mil.): 73
Dividends:
  1990 average yield: 15.5%
  1990 payout: 258.3%
Market value (mil.): $1,546
Sales (mil.): $7,695

Stock Price History
High/Low 1981–90

MANVILLE CORPORATION

OVERVIEW

Headquartered in Denver, Manville produces forest products (e.g., lumber, beverage containers, folding cartons, and plywood) and owns over 765,000 acres of timberland and 6 mines (producing diatomite, perlite, palladium, and platinum).

Manville was in Chapter 11 bankruptcy from 1982 until 1988, seeking protection from the large number of claims filed in asbestos-related cases.

Since its Chapter 11 reorganization, a controlling interest in Manville has been held by a trust benefiting asbestos victims. Previously Manville was barred from paying common stock dividends through at least 1996, but through an agreement with the trust, the company can now pay as much as $650 million over a 7-year period.

Beginning in 1992, 20% of Manville's net 1991 earnings will go to the trust. Plagued with such problems, Manville plans to cut costs, partly through layoffs.

Although Manville reported record earnings in 1989 (up 94% over 1988), its leadership expects soft markets, especially in its construction-related segments.

NYSE symbol: MVL
Fiscal year ends: December 31

Hoover's Rating **D**

WHO

Chairman, President, and CEO: W. Thomas Stephens, age 48, $866,583 pay
SVP; President, Manvillle Forest Products Corporation: Thomas H. Johnson, age 41, $660,538 pay
EVP; President, Manville Sales Corporation: John D. C. Roach, age 47, $377,161 pay
Senior Director Human Resources: Pam Hamilton
Auditors: Coopers & Lybrand
Employees: 18,000

WHEN

In 1858 H. W. Johns founded a roofing materials business in Brooklyn. In 1868 he patented a line of products containing asbestos, a substance that would cost the company dearly more than a century later. In 1901 the company merged with Manville Covering Company (begun 1886 in Milwaukee to produce pipe coverings and insulation materials).

Thomas Manville headed the new company, named Johns-Manville, until his death in 1925. His brother Hiram purchased most of the stock and in 1927 sold 53% of the company to J.P. Morgan & Company for about $20 million. Under Morgan the company focused on building materials, moving away from earlier diversification ventures such as automobile horns, fire extinguishers, and spark plugs.

Johns-Manville had moved to Colorado by 1973 and in 1979 acquired Olinkraft, a paper producer. The company adopted its present name in 1981.

In 1974, 448 WWII shipyard workers filed the first major asbestos health suit against Manville. By 1982 Manville had settled more than 4,100 suits yet faced a backlog of nearly 17,000. Bankruptcy followed.

While in Chapter 11, Manville closed its plastic pipe and residential roofing operations and terminated all activities related to asbestos. In 1985 the company acquired Eastex Packaging (forest products).

The reorganization plan finalized in 1988 created a trust fund designed to bar any party from taking future asbestos-related action directly against Manville. The personal injury trust, which has faced liquidity problems since 1989, owns 50% of the company's common stock, with options to increase it to 80%. In 1991 Manville began paying this trust $75 million annually for 24 years, and beginning in 1992 the company will transfer 20% of its annual earnings to the trust.

Manville emerged from bankruptcy focusing on forest products, fiberglass, and mining. In 1989 the company sold its Holophane lighting business for $125 million and purchased oil and gas reserves for $70 million.

In 1990 the company purchased DRG Cartons, the 3rd largest British folding carton company; Visypack Pty., Ltd., the leading carton manufacturer in Australia; and Fiskeby Board AB, a Swedish producer of recycled paperboard. Acquisitions and capital improvements cost Manville $373 million (almost 17% of sales) in 1990.

By the end of 1990, the personal injury trust had received 164,900 claims, 27,508 of which had been settled for $1.2 billion.

WHERE

HQ: 717 17th St., PO Box 5108, Denver, CO 80217-5108
Phone: 303-978-2000
Fax: 303-978-2363

Manville has 61 plants in the US and 10 foreign countries; mines in California, Montana, New Mexico, France, and Spain; and timberlands in Arkansas, Louisiana, Texas, and Brazil.

	1990 Sales		1990 Operating Income	
	$ mil.	% of total	$ mil.	% of total
US	1,752	77	177	67
Other countries	514	23	88	33
Adjustments	(21)	—	(23)	—
Total	**2,245**	**100**	**242**	**100**

WHAT

	1990 Sales		1990 Operating Income	
	$ mil.	% of total	$ mil.	% of total
Building products	610	27	49	21
Forest products	892	40	145	63
Engineered products	616	27	22	9
Mining & minerals	127	6	15	7
Adjustments	—	—	11	—
Total	**2,245**	**100**	**242**	**100**

Building products
Insulation
Perlite products
Roofing products

Forest products
Beverage carriers
Cartons
Containers
Lumber
Paper
Paperboard
Plywood

Engineered products
Air duct materials and filters
Automotive parts
Insulation

Mining and minerals
Diatomite
Palladium
Perlite
Platinum

RANKINGS

197th in *Fortune* 500 Industrial Cos.

KEY COMPETITORS

Anglo American
ASARCO
Boise Cascade
Bridgestone
Champion International
Fletcher Challenge
Georgia-Pacific
Goodyear
International Paper
James River
Mead
Nobel
Owens-Corning
PPG
Weyerhaeuser
Other natural resource companies

HOW MUCH

	9-Year Growth	1981	1982	1983	1984	1985	1986	1987	1988	1989	1990
Sales ($ mil.)	0.3%	2,186	1,772	1,729	1,814	1,880	1,920	2,063	2,062	2,192	2,245
Net income ($ mil.)	6.3%	60	(88)	60	77	(45)	81	164	89	173	104
Income as % of sales	—	2.8%	(4.9%)	3.5%	4.3%	(2.4%)	4.2%	8.0%	4.3%	7.9%	4.6%
Earnings per share ($)	(7.8%)	1.53	(4.73)	1.47	2.18	(2.92)	2.34	5.79	0.73	1.21	0.74
Stock price – high ($)	—	26.50	16.50	16.63	13.63	8.63	8.88	5.38	8.00	10.50	9.38
Stock price – low ($)	—	13.75	4.25	9.88	5.63	5.13	1.63	1.75	1.25	6.88	4.38
Stock price – close ($)	(12.2%)	14.88	10.25	11.00	5.88	6.00	1.88	2.25	7.13	9.13	4.63
P/E – high	—	17	—	11	6	—	4	1	11	9	13
P/E – low	—	9	—	7	3	—	1	0	2	6	6
Dividends per share ($)	(100.0%)	1.92	0.68	0.00	0.00	0.00	0.00	0.00	0.00	0.00	0.00
Book value per share ($)	(11.6%)	38.36	31.90	34.62	37.33	36.59	40.58	44.59	7.39	9.87	12.57

1990 Year-end:
Debt ratio: 43.3%
Return on equity: 6.6%
Cash (mil.): $124
Current ratio: 1.45
Long-term debt (mil.): $870
No. of shares (mil.): 48
Dividends:
1990 average yield: 0.0%
1990 payout: 0.0%
Market value (mil.): $222

Stock Price History
High/Low 1981–90

MARRIOTT CORPORATION

OVERVIEW

Marriott, one of the world's leading hoteliers, operated 639 hotels (including franchises) in 1990, with 57 more scheduled to open in 1991. It is also the #1 American provider of food and services management to the business, health care, and education industries, providing food, beverages, and merchandise to airport and highway travelers through Host and Travel Plaza, as well as under license agreements with Pizza Hut, Dunkin Donuts, TCBY Yogurt, and others. The company is positioning itself for leadership in the US senior-living services market and also has an interest in an employer-sponsored day care chain.

It has diversified into golf course management (1990) and is also relying on joint ventures with foreign partners to take advantage of market potential overseas.

One of the 1980s' highest fliers, Marriott used tax loopholes and investments in new hotel construction to become an extremely profitable developer. But with the onslaught of recession, earnings plunged 74% in 1990. Marriott halted its construction program and has laid off 1,300 workers. Through asset sales the company raised over $1 billion in 1990 and in the first half of 1991. The Marriott family owns 27% of the company.

WHEN

In 1927 John Marriott and his wife, Alice, left the Mormon settlement of Marriott, Utah (founded by John's grandparents), to open a root beer stand in Washington, DC. In order to attract wintertime customers, the Marriotts converted the stand into a Hot Shoppe, selling tamales and chili con carne, and over the next 10 years built it into a regional chain.

The company entered the airline food service business with a contract from Eastern Air Lines in 1937 and opened its first hotel in Arlington, Virginia, in 1957. When Marriott's son Bill became president (1964), the company had sales of $85 million from 4 hotels, 45 Hot Shoppes, and airline catering.

From 1964 to 1971 Marriott added 10 hotels, expanded in-flight services into Europe and South America (1964), bought Bob's Big Boy chain (coffee shops, 1967), started Roy Rogers (roast beef restaurants, 1968), bought an Athens cruise line (Oceanic) and a 45% interest in another (Sun, 1971), and acquired Farrell's (ice cream parlors, 1972).

After Bill Marriott became CEO (1972), the company opened 2 Great America theme parks near Chicago and San Francisco at a cost of $155 million (1976). When the parks failed to make enough money, the company sold one and discontinued the other (1984).

By 1977 sales had topped $1 billion, and Marriott operated 1,335 restaurants, 34 full-service hotels, and 14 franchised inns. As part of a plan to manage rather than own, Marriott sold 8 hotels to Equitable Life Assurance for $92 million (1978). The company originated moderately priced (then $49- to $72-a-night) Courtyard hotels (1983), which numbered 140 by 1989. In 1985 Marriott bought competitor Howard Johnson for $531 million (sold manufacturing operations in 1986) and in 1986 bought Saga (contract food service and restaurants) for $694 million.

In 1987 Marriott sold its cruise ships and entered 3 new market segments: full-service suites (Marriott Suites), moderately priced suites (Residence Inn, acquired for $260 million), and $30- to $40-a-night economy hotels (Fairfield Inns). In 1988 Marriott began developing "life-care" communities, which provide apartments, meals, and limited nursing care to the elderly. In 1989 Marriott sold its airline catering businesses to management because of the lack of sufficient long-term growth potential. It also decided to leave the fast food and family restaurant businesses, selling Roy Rogers to Hardee's in 1990 and agreeing to sell another 230 family restaurants (representing most of its remaining restaurant holdings) in 1991.

NYSE symbol: MHS
Fiscal year ends: Friday nearest December 31

 Hoover's Rating **C**

WHO

Chairman, President, and CEO: J. W. "Bill" Marriott, Jr., age 58, $725,000 pay
VC and EVP: Richard E. Marriott, age 51
EVP and CFO: William J. Shaw, age 45, $575,000 pay
SVP Human Resources: Clifford J. Ehrlich, age 52
Auditors: Arthur Andersen & Co.
Employees: 209,000

WHERE

HQ: 10400 Fernwood Rd., Bethesda, MD 20058
Phone: 301-380-9000
Fax: 301-897-9014 (Public Relations)
Reservations: 800-228-9290

Marriott owns 223 hotels in 41 states, the District of Columbia, and 16 foreign countries. The company operates concessions at 45 airports in the US and New Zealand and Marriott Travel Plazas in 12 states. Its 13 retirement communities are located in 9 states.

	1990 Sales	
	$ mil.	% of total
US	7,329	96
Other countries	317	4
Total	**7,646**	**100**

WHAT

	1990 Sales		1990 Operating Income	
	$ mil.	% of total	$ mil.	% of total
Lodging	3,942	52	239	68
Contract services	3,704	48	114	32
Adjustments	—	—	16	—
Total	**7,646**	**100**	**369**	**100**

Hotels and Resorts
Courtyard by Marriott
Fairfield Inn
Marriott hotels and resorts
Marriott Suites
Residence Inn

Retirement Communities
Brighton Gardens
Stratford Court

Contract Services
Host (airport concessions)
Marriott Distribution Services (US purchasing, warehousing, and distribution)
Marriott Food and Services Management (catering and food service operations)
Marriott Golf Management Services
Marriott Travel Plazas

RANKINGS

10th in *Fortune* 100 Diversified Service Cos.
370th in *Business Week* 1000

KEY COMPETITORS

Accor	Edward J.	Loews
ARA	DeBartolo	Nestlé
Bass	Helmsley	Ogden
Canadian Pacific	Hilton	Owens-Illinois
Carlson	Hyatt	Rank
Dial	ITT	TW Holdings

HOW MUCH

	9-Year Growth	1981	1982	1983	1984	1985	1986	1987	1988	1989	1990
Sales ($ mil.)	16.1%	2,000	2,541	3,037	3,525	4,242	5,267	6,522	7,370	7,536	7,646
Net income ($ mil.)	(6.5%)	86	94	115	135	167	192	223	232	181	47
Income as % of sales	—	4.3%	3.7%	3.8%	3.8%	3.9%	3.6%	3.4%	3.1%	2.4%	0.6%
Earnings per share ($)	(3.6%)	0.64	0.69	0.83	1.00	1.24	1.40	1.67	1.95	1.62	0.46
Stock price – high ($)	—	9.40	12.38	16.20	16.05	23.30	38.20	43.75	33.38	41.25	33.63
Stock price – low ($)	—	5.95	6.40	10.05	11.70	14.68	20.63	24.00	26.25	29.75	8.38
Stock price – close ($)	4.3%	7.18	11.70	14.25	15.15	21.80	29.00	30.00	31.63	33.38	10.50
P/E – high	—	15	18	20	16	19	27	26	17	25	73
P/E – low	—	9	9	12	12	12	15	14	13	18	18
Dividends per share ($)	20.8%	0.05	0.06	0.08	0.09	0.11	0.14	0.17	0.21	0.25	0.28
Book value per share ($)	3.4%	3.22	3.89	4.67	5.24	6.48	7.59	6.83	6.53	6.11	4.35

1990 Year-end:
Debt ratio: 89.7%
Return on equity: 8.8%
Cash (mil.): $283
Current ratio: 0.87
Long-term debt (mil.): $3,553
No. of shares (mil.): 94
Dividends:
 1990 average yield: 2.7%
 1990 payout: 60.9%
Market value (mil.): $983

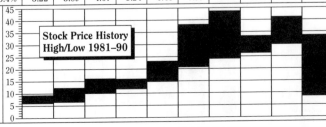
Stock Price History
High/Low 1981–90

MARS, INC.

Private company

OVERVIEW

Based in McLean, Virginia, privately held Mars is the world's 2nd largest candy maker (after Hershey) and a major producer of pet food and rice products.

The company is fully owned by the secretive Mars family (one of the US's wealthiest, with net worth estimated at $12.5 billion) and the Mars Foundation. The family desires privacy to such an extent that very little is known about the company's history or operations. Executives are forbidden to be photographed or interviewed; publicity-shy Mars even refused to allow M&Ms to appear in the very successful movie *E.T. The Extra-Terrestrial* — an opportunity from which rival Hershey's Reese's Pieces benefited.

In 1990 Mars boasted 4 of the US's top 10 candies: Snickers (the nation's #1 candy bar), M&M Peanut, M&M Plain, and Milky Way. The company's pet food brands include Kal Kan, Pedigree, and Whiskas. Other major brands include Dove (ice cream bars), Uncle Ben's (rice), Snackmaster (salty snacks), and Kudos (granola bars).

Since losing the #1 candymaker honors to Hershey in 1988, Mars has forsaken its previously standoffish attitude toward joint promotions, recently proposing everything from a "Fill-er-up, get a free Snickers" campaign with Getty gas stations to a joint ice cream bar marketing effort with Hardee's restaurants.

WHEN

Frank Mars, inventor of the Milky Way candy bar (1923), hired his son Forrest after the latter's Yale graduation to work at his candy operation. After arguments between the 2 men, Forrest moved to England and started his own Mars company in the 1930s. Forrest also began making pet food and at one point controlled 55% of the British pet food market.

During WWII Forrest returned to the US and introduced Uncle Ben's rice and M&Ms. The idea for M&Ms was borrowed from British Smarties, for which Mars obtained rights (from Rowntree Mackintosh) by relinquishing similar rights for its Snickers bar in some foreign markets. The ad slogan "Melts in your mouth, not in your hand" elevated Mars to industry leader.

Little is known about Mars between the mid-1940s and 1964, when Forrest merged his operations with his deceased father's company after bitter family quarrels. In 1968 Mars bought Kal Kan and followed with Puppy Palace pet shops in 1969 (sold in 1976). During the 1970s Mars produced 5 of the country's top 10 candy bars.

Mars refuses to discuss whether Forrest (born 1904) is alive; likened to the late Howard Hughes, he may be living as a recluse in Las Vegas, having delegated responsibility to his sons, Forrest E. and John F. Mars, in 1973. The men share the presidency and allegedly are engaged in a power struggle to control the company.

By 1978 the brothers, looking for snacks to replace dwindling candy revenues from a more diet-conscious America, brought out Twix, a chocolate-covered cookie. In 1987 they bought Dove Bar International, an ice cream bar manufacturer that had been started by Greek immigrant Leo Stefanos in his Chicago candy store in 1939 (to keep his children from buying ice cream bars from the passing ice cream trucks) and had grown to production of 40,000 per day by 1985.

Around 1988 Forrest and John Mars purchased Ethel M Chocolates, producer of liqueur-flavored chocolates, a business their father began in his retirement. Ethel M Chocolates are made in Henderson, Nevada, 13 miles southeast of Las Vegas. Unlike the other secretive Mars plants, Ethel M is open to the public for conducted tours of its facilities.

Mars attempted to purchase Dutch candy maker Tonnema in 1988, but withdrew temporarily after dissent within the family-owned Tonnema erupted in lawsuits, and was eventually outbid by a European concern. Hershey's passed Mars as the US's largest candy maker in 1988 when it acquired Cadbury Schweppes US division (Mounds and Almond Joy). In 1989 Mars introduced Bounty Bars, PB Max, and Suissande Fine Chocolates.

In response to the success of Hershey's Symphony Bar, Mars introduced a new dark chocolate candy bar under the Dove name in 1991 (the company also uses the Dove division to produce ice cream bar versions of its candy bars). Other new offerings include peanut butter, mint, and almond M&Ms, Milky Way Dark, and Peanut Butter Snickers. Also in 1991 Mars denied a rumor that it had engaged in merger talks with Nestlé.

WHO

Chairman, CEO, and Co-President: Forrest E. Mars, Jr., age 60
Co-President: John F. Mars, age 55
President, M&M/Mars: William B. Hellegas
Employees: 22,000

WHERE

HQ: 6885 Elm St., McLean, VA 22101
Phone: 703-821-4900
Fax: 703-448-9678

Mars owns candy plants in Hackettstown, NJ; Chicago, IL; Albany, GA; Waco, TX; Henderson, NV; and Cleveland, TN. It owns a pet food plant in Vernon, CA, and a rice plant in Houston, TX.

Products are sold in more than 25 countries.

WHAT

Brand Names

Candy	Ice Cream Products
Almond M&Ms	Dove
Balisto	Milky Way
Bounty	Rondos
M&Ms Peanut	Snickers
M&Ms Plain	3 Musketeers
Mars	
Milky Way	**Other**
Milky Way Dark	Kudos
Mint M&Ms	Snackmaster
PB Max	Twix
Peanut Butter M&Ms	
Peanut Butter Snickers	**Rice**
Skittles	Uncle Ben's
Snickers	Uncle Ben's
Starburst	Aromatica
Suissande Fine Chocolates	Uncle Ben's
3 Musketeers	Country Inn

Pet Food	Electronic Products
Crave	Coin changers
Kal Kan	Hand-held scanning
Mealtime	devices
Pedigree	
Sheba	**Major Subsidiaries**
Whiskas	Dove International, Inc.
	Kal Kan Foods, Inc.
	Uncle Ben's, Inc.

RANKINGS

7th in *Forbes* 400 US Private Cos.

KEY COMPETITORS

Anheuser-Busch
ADM
Berkshire Hathaway
Cadbury Schweppes
Campbell Soup
Colgate-Palmolive
Grand Metropolitan
Heinz
Hershey
Nestlé
PepsiCo
Philip Morris
Quaker Oats
Ralston Purina
Reynolds Metals
RJR Nabisco

HOW MUCH

	9-Year Growth	1981	1982	1983	1984	1985	1986	1987	1988	1989	1990
Sales ($ mil.)	8.7%	4,000	—	—	—	5,300	7,000	7,700	8,000	8,541	8,450
Estimated ad spending ($ mil.)	14.9%	78	120	120	139	276	313	379	340	293	272

Sales ($ mil.) 1981–90

MARSH & McLENNAN COMPANIES, INC.

NYSE symbol: MMC
Fiscal year ends: December 31

Hoover's Rating **A**

OVERVIEW

Marsh & McLennan is the world's largest insurance broker. The New York–based company had $2.7 billion in 1990 revenues from its 3 principal services: insurance (56%), consulting (33%), and investment management (10%). The company provides its services worldwide. Its Guy Carpenter & Company and C. T. Bowring Reinsurance provide reinsurance (insurance to cover other insurers' losses), advice, and services.

The company's consulting services, its fastest growing segment, include William M. Mercer (employee benefits consulting) and Temple, Barker & Sloane/Strategic Planning Associates, an international general management consulting firm, as well as other consulting subsidiaries.

Marsh & McLennan's Putnam Companies manages 62 mutual funds and 157 pension funds totaling $42 billion in assets.

In 1991 the company moved to strengthen its European presence, in anticipation of 1992 EC unification, by selling its interest in a Dutch consulting firm, Hudig Langeveldt, to open its own office in the Netherlands. It also opened a subsidiary in Hungary.

WHO

Chairman and CEO: Frank J. Tasco, age 63, $1,559,168 pay
President: A. J. C. Smith, age 56, $1,249,089 pay
Chairman, Marsh & McLennan, Inc.: Robert Clements, age 58, $855,715 pay
SVP and CFO: Frank J. Borelli, age 55
SVP Human Resources: Francis N. Bonsignore, age 44
Auditors: Deloitte & Touche
Employees: 24,400

WHEN

Marsh & McLennan evolved from 3 turn-of-the-century midwestern firms: Marsh Ullmann & Co. (led by Henry Marsh, who pioneered insurance broking and in 1901 set up U.S. Steel's self-insurance program), Manley-McLennan of Duluth (specialists in railroad insurance), and D.W. Burrows (a small Chicago-based railroad insurance firm with which Marsh was contemplating a merger).

In 1904, after discovering that they both had been promised the Burlington Northern Railroad account, Donald McLennan and Marsh joined forces with Daniel Burrows to become the world's largest insurance brokerage, with $3 million in premiums.

In 1906 the firm became Marsh & McLennan, with Marsh as the chief rainmaker, McLennan overseeing the railroad business and midwestern client relations, and a new partner, Charles Seabury, handling the company's technical and support services.

In the early 20th century, Marsh won AT&T's business by arranging to meet the company's president on an Atlantic crossing; McLennan acquired Armour Meat Packing Company as an account by riding on the same commuter train to Chicago as P.D. Armour and talking with him.

In 1923 Marsh & McLennan became a closely held corporation. As the business became more technical and professional,

Henry Marsh lost interest in it and sold out to McLennan in 1935. The company weathered the Depression without major layoffs by cutting pay and branching into life insurance and employee benefits consulting after the Social Security Act (1937).

Until the late 1930s the company did not bill for consulting services, as they were expected to lead to insurance placements. This changed when the president of American Can insisted on paying for time. In 1946 the company won Ford Motor Company's business.

In the 1950s, as the company grew through acquisitions, rivalries developed between the offices. In 1962 the company went public and in 1969 organized a holding company that became Marsh & McLennan Companies. In the 1970s the company began to diversify with the acquisition of The Putnam Companies (investment management).

In 1975 Marsh & McLennan set up its employee benefits consulting business as a separate subsidiary, William M. Mercer, and in 1980 acquired a foothold in the UK with C. T. Bowring.

As the insurance business stagnated in the 1980s, the financial and consulting fields grew. In 1989 consulting grew by 19%, and by 1990 the company had its eyes on displacing McKinsey as the top consultant in the US.

WHERE

HQ: 1166 Ave. of the Americas, New York, NY 10036
Phone: 212-345-3000
Fax: 212-345-4838 (Public Affairs)

Marsh & McLennan operates in 80 countries.

	1990 Sales		1990 Operating Income	
	$ mil.	% of total	$ mil.	% of total
US	1,831	67	383	68
Europe	620	23	133	23
Canada	188	7	37	7
Other countries	84	3	13	2
Adjustments	—	—	(39)	—
Total	**2,723**	**100**	**527**	**100**

WHAT

	1990 Sales		1990 Operating Income	
	$ mil.	% of total	$ mil.	% of total
Insurance services	1,537	56	359	63
Investment mgmt.	276	10	77	14
Consulting	910	34	130	23
Adjustments	—	—	(39)	—
Total	**2,723**	**100**	**527**	**100**

Selected Subsidiaries
Bowring U.K. Ltd. (insurance brokerage)
Clayton Environmental Consultants, Inc. (business research)
Guy Carpenter & Co., Inc., and C. T. Bowring Reinsurance Ltd. (reinsurance)
Lippincott & Margulies, Inc. (corporate identity consulting)
Marsh & McLennan Group Associates, Inc. (program management)
Marsh & McLennan, Inc. (insurance brokerage)
National Economic Research Associates, Inc. (business and public policy research)
Seabury & Smith, Inc. (insurance products)
The Putnam Cos., Inc. (investment management)
Temple, Barker & Sloane, Inc./Strategic Planning Associates, Inc. (management consulting)
William M. Mercer Cos., Inc. (employee benefits consulting)

RANKINGS

47th in *Fortune* 50 Diversified Financial Cos.
106th in *Business Week* 1000

KEY COMPETITORS

American Express	General Re	USF&G
AIG	KPMG	Other insurance
Arthur Andersen	McKinsey & Co.	firms
Coopers & Lybrand	Merrill Lynch	Other money
Deloitte & Touche	Price Waterhouse	management
Ernst & Young	Prudential	firms

HOW MUCH

	9-Year Growth	1981	1982	1983	1984	1985	1986	1987	1988	1989	1990
Sales ($ mil.)	13.9%	847	924	960	1,101	1,368	1,804	2,147	2,272	2,428	2,723
Net income ($ mil.)	10.9%	120	120	94	59	163	243	302	296	295	304
Income as % of sales	—	14.2%	13.0%	9.8%	5.3%	11.9%	13.5%	14.1%	13.0%	12.1%	11.2%
Earnings per share ($)	10.9%	1.64	1.68	1.33	0.81	2.23	3.30	4.06	4.09	4.10	4.15
Stock price – high ($)	—	21.25	22.25	25.38	29.69	41.75	76.75	72.00	59.75	89.75	81.00
Stock price – low ($)	—	14.81	14.81	18.31	17.88	28.25	40.63	43.75	45.25	55.13	59.75
Stock price – close ($)	18.8%	16.50	20.63	24.88	29.50	40.75	60.75	49.50	56.25	78.00	78.00
P/E – high	—	13	13	19	37	19	23	18	15	22	20
P/E – low	—	9	9	14	22	13	12	11	11	13	14
Dividends per share ($)	11.0%	1.00	1.05	1.10	1.43	1.28	1.70	1.68	2.43	2.50	2.55
Book value per share ($)	7.6%	7.66	6.54	6.33	5.10	7.02	8.65	10.72	10.56	12.05	14.76

1990 Year-end:
Debt ratio: 22.8%
Return on equity: 31.0%
Cash (mil.): $305
Current ratio: 1.44
Long-term debt (mil.): $320
No. of shares (mil.): 74
Dividends:
  1990 average yield: 3.3%
  1990 payout: 61.4%
Market value (mil.): $5,735

Stock Price History High/Low 1981–90

MARTIN MARIETTA CORPORATION

OVERVIEW

Martin Marietta's diverse operations include aerospace, information technologies, construction materials, and specialty chemical products. It has more than 1,000 contracts ranging from the Titan family of expendable launch vehicles to mail sorting machines.

As America's 8th largest defense company, Martin Marietta is a leading contractor for the Peacekeeper (MX) missile and a number of other military systems, including the LANTIRN airborne night vision system and the ADATS mobile air defense system. The company also develops computer systems for air traffic control, data processing, military applications, and advanced computer simulations. The Materials Group supplies construction aggregates (crushed stone, sand, and gravel), magnesium products (used in producing steel), and, through a joint venture with NKK Corporation of Japan, light metal components for aircraft. Its Energy Systems subsidiary manages the DOE research facility at Oak Ridge, Tennessee.

The company's diversity and fiscal conservatism have made it a Wall Street favorite, and in 1990 Martin Marietta was named the best in its field by *Aviation Week & Space Technology*.

NYSE symbol: ML
Fiscal year ends: December 31

Hoover's Rating **B**

WHO

Chairman and CEO: Norman R. Augustine, age 55, $1,121,691 pay
President and COO: A. Thomas Young, age 52, $697,402 pay
SVP and CFO: Marcus C. Bennett, age 55, $466,698 pay
VP Human Resources: Bobby F. Leonard, age 58
Auditors: Ernst & Young
Employees: 62,000

WHERE

HQ: 6801 Rockledge Dr., Bethesda, MD 20817
Phone: 301-897-6000
Fax: 301-897-6704

Martin Marietta has major facilities and operations in 11 states.

	1990 Sales	
	$ mil.	% of total
US government	5,300	87
Other	826	13
Total	**6,126**	**100**

WHEN

In 1917 Glenn Martin, a barnstormer and aircraft designer, founded the Glenn L. Martin Company in Cleveland. The company moved to Baltimore in 1929. Martin produced the first US-built bombers (Donald Douglas, a founder of McDonnell Douglas, was chief designer until 1920) as well as military and commercial flying boats, including M-130, the famous Pan Am "Clipper" that made transpacific air service practical (1935). Martin also designed the WWII-era B-26 Marauder bomber.

After the war Martin made an unsuccessful attempt to enter the commercial transport market with the M-202 airliner. Development costs of the aircraft finally resulted in a 1951 loss of $22 million, after which George Bunker replaced Glenn Martin as chairman. Under Bunker the company began reducing aircraft production in favor of missiles, electronics, and nuclear systems. In 1953 the company began designing the Titan, an ICBM that later evolved into a versatile space launch vehicle. Martin produced its last airplane in 1960.

In 1961 Bunker consolidated Martin with the American-Marietta Company, a supplier of construction materials and chemical products. Formed in 1913 as American Asphalt Paint Company, American-Marietta had made dozens of acquisitions over the years to become a $368 million corporation with over 360 plants in the US and Canada. Bunker, now president of Martin Marietta Corporation, sold off many of the company's less profitable holdings during the 1960s but made an important acquisition in 1968 with the purchase of Harvey Aluminum.

With a mix of aerospace, chemicals, electronics, building materials, and aluminum production, Martin Marietta began a period of growth in the 1970s. The company received government contracts for the Viking Mars lander (1969), the space shuttle's external fuel tank (1973), and the MX missile (1979).

Martin Marietta defeated a hostile takeover bid by Bendix in 1982. To reduce the $1.34 billion debt incurred during the takeover battle, the company, led by CEO Thomas Pownall, sold many of its businesses, including cement, chemical, and aluminum operations. By 1989 a brisk defense electronics business and accelerating orders for Titan launchers, space shuttle external tanks, and other space vehicles had helped push the company's sales to a record $5.8 billion.

The company-built *Magellan* spacecraft, launched in early 1989, began mapping the surface of Venus in 1990. In 1991 Martin Marietta (with TRW) won a $659 million contract to develop Brilliant Pebbles space-based missile interceptors.

WHAT

	1990 Sales		1990 Operating Income	
	$ mil.	% of total	$ mil.	% of total
Astronautics	3,229	52	249	46
Electronics, Info. & Missiles	2,596	41	168	31
Materials	398	6	82	15
Other	50	1	42	8
Adjustments	(147)	—	—	—
Total	**6,126**	**100**	**541**	**100**

Astronautics
Brilliant Pebbles
Commercial Titan
Flight Telerobotic Servicer
Magellan spacecraft
Peacekeeper/MX
Small ICBM
Space Shuttle External Tank
Titan II, III, and IV

Electronics, Information, and Missiles
ADATS air defense
Air traffic control systems
LANTIRN airborne night vision system
Mail sorting machines
MK 41 Vertical Launching System
Optimized Hellfire missiles
Patriot missile launcher
Target Acquisition and Designation Sight/Pilot Night Vision Sensor

Materials
Crushed stone
Fabricated metal components
Gravel
Magnesium oxide products
Sand

Other
Government facility management
Real estate (50%, Peabody Orlando Hotel)
Verdix (17%, software and secure computer systems)

RANKINGS

83rd in *Fortune* 500 Industrial Cos.
277th in *Business Week* 1000

KEY COMPETITORS

Allied-Signal	Lockheed	Textron
ASARCO	McDonnell	Thiokol
Boeing	Douglas	Thomson SA
General Dynamics	Nissan	TRW
General Electric	Northrop	United
General Motors	Raytheon	Technologies
Grumman	Rockwell	Vulcan
Inco	Siemens	Westinghouse

HOW MUCH

	9-Year Growth	1981	1982	1983	1984	1985	1986	1987	1988	1989	1990
Sales ($ mil.)	7.1%	3,294	3,527	3,899	3,920	4,410	4,753	5,165	5,727	5,796	6,126
Net income ($ mil.)	5.6%	200	92	141	176	249	202	231	320	307	328
Income as % of sales	—	6.1%	2.6%	3.6%	4.5%	5.7%	4.3%	4.5%	5.6%	5.3%	5.3%
Earnings per share ($)	11.8%	2.40	1.30	2.70	3.02	4.36	3.67	4.25	6.02	5.82	6.52
Stock price – high ($)	—	22.74	20.94	28.78	30.92	44.38	48.50	56.50	48.25	53.50	48.13
Stock price – low ($)	—	12.63	9.89	16.72	20.17	27.42	32.25	35.00	38.25	37.75	34.25
Stock price – close ($)	11.9%	16.00	19.44	23.83	29.67	35.50	38.63	42.00	40.50	44.38	44.00
P/E – high	—	10	16	11	10	10	13	13	8	9	7
P/E – low	—	5	8	6	7	6	9	8	6	6	5
Dividends per share ($)	6.3%	0.80	0.85	0.86	0.89	0.97	1.00	1.05	1.10	1.23	1.39
Book value per share ($)	8.8%	14.71	8.45	14.17	9.64	12.83	15.35	17.16	22.73	26.67	31.53

1990 Year-end:
Debt ratio: 23.1%
Return on equity: 22.4%
Cash (mil.): $87
Current ratio: 1.41
Long-term debt (mil.): $463
No. of shares (mil.): 49
Dividends:
  1990 average yield: 3.2%
  1990 payout: 21.3%
Market value (mil.): $2,150

Stock Price History High/Low 1981–90

MASCO CORPORATION

NYSE symbol: MAS
Fiscal year ends: December 31

Hoover's Rating **B-**

OVERVIEW

The Masco Corporation is the world's largest producer of faucets, with a 35% market share in the US. It is also a leading US producer of home furnishings (8% of the market), plumbing supplies, home improvement products, and cabinets for the kitchen and bath (10% of the market). In 1990 most of Masco's $3.2 billion sales were generated by leading brands such as Delta (faucets); Henredon, Drexel Heritage, and Lexington (furniture); Merillat (cabinets); and Brass-Craft (plumbing fixtures).

Under the leadership of the founding Manoogian family, Masco owns or has partial ownership in more than 50 subsidiaries. The Masco Group has approximately 315 manufacturing plants around the world.

Despite being buffeted by the 1990–91 recession, Masco's sales rose, allowing it to increase its market share at the expense of its competitors, many of whom were in dire financial straits.

WHEN

Alex Manoogian, Masco's founder, came to the US in 1920, when he was 19. A series of jobs in Detroit machine shops gave him enough experience to start the Masco Screw Products Company, with 2 partners and less than $5,000, a mere 8 days before the crash of 1929. The 2 other partners withdrew from the company within the year.

Largely dependent on Detroit's auto industry, Masco grew slowly during the Depression, producing custom parts for Chrysler, Ford, Hudson Motor Company, and Spicer Manufacturing. By 1937, with sales of over $200,000, it offered shares to the public and was listed on the Detroit Stock Exchange. During WWII Masco devoted its production to defense, and in 1942 sales topped $1 million. A new manufacturing plant, opened in 1948 in Dearborn, Michigan, expanded production space to nearly 100,000 square feet. Masco resumed peacetime business, primarily with the auto industry, although the Korean War prompted a return to defense production.

In 1954 Masco began producing and marketing Manoogian's version of a single-handle kitchen faucet, under the Delta brand. The faucet was efficient and popular. Delta sales had exceeded $1 million by 1958, and Masco opened a new faucet plant in Greensburg, Indiana.

Under the leadership of Alex Manoogian's son, Richard, the company (renamed Masco Corporation in 1961) diversified its product line and began buying other companies. In 1962 it was listed on the ASE.

Since 1964 Masco has acquired more than 50 companies, concentrating on tool and metal casting, energy exploration, and other industrial products such as pumping equipment and air compressors. The company continued to focus on both industrial and consumer products until 1984, when it underwent a major corporate restructuring that split it into 2 entities. Masco Corporation pursued the course set by its successful faucet sales, expanding its interests in home improvement and home furnishings companies. The company spun off its industrial products business into a separate public corporation, Masco Industries, of which it owns 49%.

Masco Corporation became the nation's largest furniture manufacturer in the mid-1980s by purchasing several leading North Carolina furniture makers, including Henredon and Drexel Heritage (1986), Hickorycraft and Lexington Furniture (1987), and Universal Furniture (1989).

Despite the 1990–91 recession, Masco continued to consolidate its position by expanding sales and market share (though profits declined). In 1990 Masco acquired KraftMaid cabinets (in exchange for stock), repurchased 9 million of its shares, launched a new furniture line (Lineage), and opened 3 new wood products plants in China.

WHO

Chairman and CEO: Richard A. Manoogian, age 54, $1,099,500 pay
President and COO: Wayne B. Lyon, age 58, $825,000 pay
SVP Finance: Richard G. Mosteller, age 58, $549,800 pay
VP Human Resources: David G. Wesenberg, age 60
Auditors: Coopers & Lybrand
Employees: 41,300

WHERE

HQ: 21001 Van Born Rd., Taylor, MI 48180
Phone: 313-274-7400
Fax: 313-374-6666 (Public Relations)

Masco Corporation has approximately 158 manufacturing plants in 22 states and 19 countries.

	1990 Sales		1990 Operating Income	
	$ mil.	% of total	$ mil.	% of total
US	2,717	85	348	83
Foreign	492	15	73	17
Adjustments	—	—	(58)	—
Total	**3,209**	**100**	**363**	**100**

WHAT

	1990 Sales		1990 Operating Income	
	$ mil.	% of total	$ mil.	% of total
Building & home improvement products	1,734	54	303	72
Home furnishings & specialty prods.	1,475	46	118	28
Adjustments	—	—	(58)	—
Total	**3,209**	**100**	**363**	**100**

Furniture
Dixie
Drexel Heritage
Frederick Edward
Henredon
Henry Link
Hickorycraft
La Barge
Lexington
Link-Taylor
Maitland-Smith
Marbro
Marge Carson
Robert Allen
Universal
Young-Hinkle

Plumbing Products
Alsons
American Bath
Aqua Glass
Artistic Brass
Brass-Craft
Damixa
Delex

Delta
Epic
Hot Spring Spa
Hueppe Duscha
Jung
Mariani
Peerless
Plumb Shop
The Plumber's Faucet
Sherle Wagner

Cabinets
Fieldstone
Merillat
StarMark

Hardware
Baldwin
Gibraltar
Saflok
Weiser

Appliances
Thermador
WasteKing

RANKINGS

146th in *Fortune* 500 Industrial Cos.
201st in *Business Week* 1000

KEY COMPETITORS

American Standard
Armstrong World
Black & Decker
Cooper Industries
Electrolux
General Electric
Hanson
Ingersoll-Rand
INTERCO
Stanley Works

HOW MUCH

	9-Year Growth	1981	1982	1983	1984	1985	1986	1987	1988	1989	1990
Sales ($ mil.)	15.5%	877	856	1,059	1,020	1,154	1,452	2,023	2,439	3,151	3,209
Net income ($ mil.)	5.2%	88	78	107	116	164	203	219	288	221	139
Income as % of sales	—	10.1%	9.1%	10.1%	11.4%	14.3%	14.0%	10.8%	11.8%	7.0%	4.3%
Earnings per share ($)	0.7%	0.87	0.75	0.96	1.00	1.26	1.54	1.61	2.06	1.41	0.92
Stock price – high ($)	—	10.56	14.25	18.50	16.94	21.19	34.50	40.88	30.38	31.13	26.75
Stock price – low ($)	—	7.00	6.72	12.38	11.25	13.00	19.50	18.75	22.00	23.75	14.25
Stock price – close ($)	7.1%	9.25	14.19	16.88	14.00	20.13	29.00	21.63	25.38	24.38	17.13
P/E – high	—	12	19	19	17	17	22	25	15	22	29
P/E – low	—	8	9	13	11	10	13	12	11	17	15
Dividends per share ($)	13.0%	0.18	0.20	0.22	0.25	0.29	0.34	0.38	0.44	0.50	0.54
Book value per share ($)	10.5%	4.89	5.49	6.47	6.60	7.60	8.84	10.34	11.30	11.94	12.01

1990 Year-end:
Debt ratio: 42.9%
Return on equity: 7.7%
Cash (mil.): $69
Current ratio: 2.47
Long-term debt (mil.): $1,334
No. of shares (mil.): 148
Dividends:
 1990 average yield: 3.2%
 1990 payout: 58.7%
Market value (mil.): $2,530

Stock Price History High/Low 1981–90

HOOVER'S HANDBOOK OF AMERICAN BUSINESS 1992

359

MASSACHUSETTS MUTUAL LIFE INSURANCE CO.

OVERVIEW

MassMutual, headquartered in Springfield, Massachusetts, is one of the nation's largest insurance companies, with over $118 billion in policies in force at the end of 1990 and over $6.5 billion in annual revenues. MassMutual's Insurance and Financial Management division is among the nation's largest life insurers, with over $587 million in insurance sales and $339 million in investment products in 1990 and the industry's lowest policy lapse rates.

The Life and Health Benefits Management division provides health coverage and managed care and case review services in over 100 major markets, with 1990 sales of $355 million and $1.7 billion in policies in force.

MassMutual's Pension Management group prospered in 1990, despite difficulties in the pension industry. This segment manages over $13.5 billion in assets.

The Investment Management group manages income from the company and outside clients. While many other insurance companies found themselves hampered by poor investments in the 1980s, MassMutual's conservative strategy left it able to participate in over $2.3 billion of new high-quality investments. In 1990 it pared its real estate portfolio.

WHEN

Springfield-based Massachusetts Mutual was formed by George Rice, an insurance agent, in 1851. The company started as a stock company but in 1867 repurchased the stock and became a mutual (owned by the policyholders). By 1868 MassMutual had opened an office in San Francisco. For its first 50 years the company sold only individual life but after 1900 branched out, offering annuities (1917) and disability (1918).

Though WWI brought a deluge of claims and forced the company to adopt higher premiums on new policies, the 1918 flu epidemic was more costly. In the Great Depression MassMutual lost money through policy terminations and loans, but endured, offering new products such as income insurance, and weathered the Depression and WWII. In 1946 MassMutual wrote its first group policy for Brown-Forman Distillers (Louisville), makers of Jack Daniel's. By 1950 the company had over 200 employees in its group insurance sector and had diversified into medical insurance.

MassMutual began investing in stocks in the 1950s, switching over from reliance upon fixed-return bonds and mortgages to receive a higher return. It also decentralized its operations and bought its first computer. It began automating operations in 1961. By 1970 MassMutual had a computer network linking independent agents. During this period of low inflation, whole life remained the dominant product. MassMutual was also responsive to social needs, investing in and anchoring commercial development that helped Springfield's city redevelopment.

After the interest rate increases of the late 1970s, many insurers began to diversify, offering high-yield products funded by high-risk investments. MassMutual resisted for a while, sticking to traditional whole life, but as interest rates soared to 20% the company experienced a rash of policy loans, which led to a cash crunch. In 1981, with its policy growth rate trailing the rest of the industry, it sought new products. Fearing that a rush into universal life would hurt agents' earnings, the company instead developed UPDATE, which offered whole life holders much higher dividends in return for adjustable interest on policy loans. Over 750,000 policyholders converted to UPDATE. It also expanded its pension business to $1.5 billion by 1989. Yet, though the competition began diversifying into financial services, MassMutual stuck to its core business and refrained from risky investments.

MassMutual conservatively moved the bulk of its investments from stocks to bonds and other products, and by 1987 only 5% of total investments were in stocks. As a result, the company emerged virtually unscathed from the stock market crash of 1987. The company was not as lucky with real estate (though not as troubled as other insurers). The collapse of the real estate market in 1990 and 1991 has left the company with some unsalable assets. But MassMutual has continually received the highest ratings possible from A. M. Best, Standard & Poor's, and Moody's Investor Service.

In 1991 MassMutual bought a controlling interest in mutual fund manager Oppenheimer Management.

Mutual company
Fiscal year ends: December 31

Hoover's Rating **B**

WHO

President and CEO: Thomas B. Wheeler
EVP and Chief Investment Officer: Richard G. Dooley
EVP Insurance and Financial Management: Kenneth L. Fry, Jr.
EVP and General Counsel: Warren W. Wise
EVP Corporate Human Resources: John J. Pajak
EVP and CFO: James L. Wertheimer
Auditors: Coopers & Lybrand
Employees: 11,000

WHERE

HQ: 1295 State St., Springfield, MA 01111-0001
Phone: 413-788-8411
Fax: 413-744-6003

Massachusetts Mutual writes approximately 40% of its premiums in New York, California, Texas, Massachusetts, and Illinois, and the remaining 60% in other states and in Puerto Rico and Canada.

WHAT

	1990 Sales	
	$ mil.	% of total
Individual policies	927	14
Life & health	355	5
Pension	1,610	24
Other premiums	1,661	25
Net investment income	2,147	32
Total	**6,700**	**100**

	1990 Assets	
	$ mil.	% of total
Bonds	11,664	42
Stocks	290	1
Mortgage loans	7,160	26
Policy loans	2,122	8
Real estate	719	3
Investments	703	3
Separate account assets	2,520	9
Other	2,329	8
Total	**27,507**	**100**

Services
Disability income protection
Health insurance
Investment management
Life insurance
Pension management

Subsidiaries
Mass Life Insurance Co. of New York
MML Bay State Life Insurance Co.
MML Life Insurance Co.
MML Pension Insurance Co.

RANKINGS

12th in *Fortune* 50 Life Insurance Cos.

KEY COMPETITORS

Aetna	Primerica
AIG	Prudential
Blue Cross	Sears
CIGNA	State Farm
Equitable	Teachers Insurance
Humana	Transamerica
John Hancock	Travelers
Kemper	USF&G
MetLife	Other insurance
New York Life	companies
Northwestern Mutual	

HOW MUCH

	9-Year Growth	1981	1982	1983	1984	1985	1986	1987	1988	1989	1990
Assets ($ mil.)	11.9%	10,022	11,152	12,173	13,449	15,716	18,182	20,042	22,589	25,062	27,507
Income ($ mil.)	—	—	—	—	—	75	288	51	50	142	101
Income as % of assets	—	—	—	—	—	0.5%	1.6%	0.3%	0.2%	0.6%	0.4%
Employees	—	—	—	—	—	—	—	—	—	11,500	11,000

1990 Year-end:
Equity as % of assets: 4.3%
Return on equity: 8.7%
Cash (mil.) $1,449
Sales (mil.): $6,700

Income ($ mil.) 1985–90

MATTEL, INC.

NYSE symbol: MAT
Fiscal year ends: Last Saturday in December

Hoover's Rating **B**

OVERVIEW

California-based Mattel is the 2nd largest US toymaker, after Hasbro. Its popular products include the Barbie doll, Hot Wheels, a line of Disney toys, and its large dolls (e.g., Li'l Miss and P.J. Sparkles). The company also distributes Nintendo products in Australia, Canada, and Italy.

Following a slump in the mid-1980s, new management redirected Mattel to focus on proven winners. The company's increased promotion of its most popular toy, the Barbie doll (adding a selection of military uniforms to her wardrobe), has proven particularly successful. In 1990 the doll's sales were $740 million, and

Mattel estimates that 90% of young American girls own at least one Barbie.

Mattel is by far the most successful US seller of toys abroad. In 1990 it opened offices in Berlin, Budapest, and Prague. Mattel also expanded its presence in the Japanese toy market (the largest after the US) by establishing a Japanese subsidiary and in 1991 purchased Auritel, a Mexican toy company of which Mattel already controlled 40%. Auritel will be converted to a Mattel subsidiary and will strengthen the company's impressive 50% share of the Mexican market. Mattel is also the leading toymaker in Australia.

WHEN

In 1945 Mattel, Inc., began as a small California toy manufacturer operating out of a converted garage and producing toy furniture. Harold Matson and Elliot Handler named their new company Mattel, using letters from their last and first names. Matson soon sold his share to Handler and his wife, Ruth, who incorporated the business in 1948 with headquarters in Culver City, California.

By 1952 the company's toy line had expanded to include burp guns and musical toys, and sales exceeded $5 million. Sponsorship of Walt Disney's Mickey Mouse Club (1955), a first in toy advertising, was a shrewd marketing step for Mattel, providing direct, year-round access to millions of young potential customers.

In 1959 Mattel introduced the Barbie doll, named after the Handlers' daughter, Barbara, and later introduced Ken, named after their son. The doll, with her fashionable wardrobe and extensive accessories, was an immediate hit, and in the past 30 years it has become the most successful brand-name toy ever sold.

Mattel became a public company in 1960, with sales of $25 million, and within 2 years sales had jumped to $75 million. The company began its purchases of smaller toy companies and nontoy businesses, such as the Dee & Cee Toy Company (1962), the A&A Die Casting

Company (1968), Western Printing (1979), and the Ringling Brothers–Barnum & Bailey Combined Shows circus (1979).

The Handlers were ousted from management in 1974 after an investigation by the SEC found irregularities in their reporting of the company's profits. The company was ordered to restructure its board and the Handlers, with 29% of the company's stock, could no longer direct Mattel's activities.

By the 1980s Mattel was a high-volume business with heavy overhead expenses and high development costs. In an effort to recapitalize, Mattel sold all its nontoy assets by 1983. In 1987 sales were over $1 billion, but Mattel showed a $93 million net loss. In that year John Amerman, the newly appointed board chairman, closed down 40% of Mattel's manufacturing capacity, fired 22% of the headquarters staff, and reduced by 25% the number of toys produced. The results were positive. The next year Mattel posted a $36 million net income and in 1989 it showed an $80 million profit. That same year it bought UK toy car maker Corgi.

In 1990 the company introduced Shani, a line of Afro-American dolls, and in 1991 bought Aviva Sport, a San Francisco–based producer of toys and sports equipment.

WHO

Chairman and CEO: John W. Amerman, age 59, $1,220,846 pay
EVP and CFO: James A. Eskridge, age 48, $509,923 pay
SVP Human Resources: Robert A. K. Welch
Auditors: Price Waterhouse
Employees: 12,500

WHERE

HQ: 333 Continental Blvd., El Segundo, CA 90245-5012
Phone: 213-524-4600
Fax: 213-524-3861

Mattel has operations in more than 20 countries and sells its toys in more than 100 countries.

	1990 Sales		1990 Operating Income	
	$ mil.	% of total	$ mil.	% of total
US	678	46	100	45
Canada & Europe	660	45	79	35
Far East & Latin America	133	9	44	20
Adjustments	—	—	(40)	—
Total	**1,471**	**100**	**183**	**100**

WHAT

	1990 Sales	
	$ mil.	% of total
Barbie	740	50
Large dolls	200	14
Disney toys	135	9
Hotwheels & Corgi	100	7
Other toys	296	20
Total	**1,471**	**100**

Brand Names

Infant/Preschool Toys	P.J. Sparkles
Disney Action Blocks	Shani
Disney Dreamtime Carousel	**Action Toys**
Disney Ride-On Mickey	Convertables
See 'N Say	Corgi
	He-Man
Dolls	Hot Wheels
Barbie	Light-Speeders
First Surprise	Skeletor
Ken	
Li'l Miss Dress Up	**Video Games/ Accessories**
Li'l Miss Magic Hair	Computer Warriors
Li'l Miss Makeup	Power Glove
Magic Nursery	Super Glove Ball
Nia	

RANKINGS

265th in *Fortune* 500 Industrial Cos.
500th in *Business Week* 1000

KEY COMPETITORS

Atari
Avon
Commodore
Gerber
Hasbro
Premark
Rubbermaid

HOW MUCH

	9-Year Growth	1981	1982	1983	1984	1985	1986	1987	1988	1989	1990
Sales ($ mil.)	2.9%	1,134	1,342	633	881	1,051	1,059	1,020	990	1,237	1,471
Net income ($ mil.)	9.9%	39	42	17	45	58	(1)	(93)	36	80	91
Income as % of sales	—	3.4%	3.2%	2.7%	5.1%	5.5%	(0.1%)	(9.1%)	3.6%	6.4%	6.2%
Earnings per share ($)	1.7%	1.55	1.66	*0.57*	1.17	1.00	(0.20)	(2.26)	0.75	1.60	1.80
Stock price – high ($)	—	12.50	31.50	16.88	13.63	17.13	15.50	15.88	10.75	20.88	26.38
Stock price – low ($)	—	6.00	10.13	4.88	4.88	9.88	7.75	6.38	6.13	9.38	15.50
Stock price – close ($)	6.9%	11.00	16.63	5.00	10.25	12.25	8.25	6.88	9.50	19.75	20.13
P/E – high	—	8	19	30	12	17	—	—	14	13	15
P/E – low	—	4	6	9	4	10	—	—	8	6	9
Dividends per share ($)	(12.5%)	0.30	0.30	0.15	0.00	0.00	0.00	0.00	0.00	0.00	0.09
Book value per share ($)	(8.0%)	14.12	14.86	(7.55)	4.12	5.59	3.98	2.19	2.73	4.41	6.68

1990 Year-end:
Debt ratio: 33.9%
Return on equity: 32.5%
Cash (mil.): $198
Current ratio: 1.89
Long-term debt (mil.): $168
No. of shares (mil.): 49
Dividends:
 1990 average yield: 0.4%
 1990 payout: 5.0%
Market value (mil.): $988

Stock Price History
High/Low 1981–90

THE MAY DEPARTMENT STORES COMPANY

OVERVIEW

The May Department Stores Company, based in St. Louis, is the US's largest "conventional" department store operator. Each division maintains a separate identity (e.g., Lord & Taylor or May Company) and has separate management (including merchandise buying).

In an industry characterized in the 1980s by slower expansion and heavy debt (R.H. Macy, Campeau), May has maintained its independence and financial strength. Despite recession, 1990 brought May its 16th consecutive year of record sales and earnings per share. This strength has allowed May to acquire good operations from other companies.

May ventured into upscale discount stores (Venture) but has since left this field and has reduced its role in shopping mall development and management. The company does remain the largest factor in discount shoe selling.

The company ranks 10th in *Fortune*'s top retailers list and has developed a reputation as an excellent training ground for merchants. The company has paid a dividend every quarter since December 1911.

NYSE symbol: MA
Fiscal year ends: Saturday nearest January 31

Hoover's Rating **B-**

WHO

Chairman and CEO: David C. Farrell, age 57, $1,505,304 pay
President: Thomas A. Hays, age 58, $1,140,121 pay
VC: Richard L. Battram, age 55, $784,986 pay
VC and CFO: Jerome T. Loeb, age 50, $782,761 pay
VC: Lawrence E. Honig, age 43, $724,819 pay
SVP Human Resources: Douglas J. Giles
Auditors: Arthur Andersen & Co.
Employees: 116,000

WHEN

David May, age 15, arrived in New York from his native Germany in 1863. After several jobs in the Midwest, he tried (unsuccessfully) mining in Colorado. He finally tried retailing, opening a clothing store in Leadville in 1877 and expanding to Denver in 1888. In 1892 he and 3 brothers-in-law (the Schoenbergs) bought the Famous in St. Louis, and in 1898 they bought a Cleveland store.

Having moved headquarters to St. Louis in 1905, the partners bought competitor Barr's in 1911 when that store's owners ran out of money trying to build the Railway Exchange Building. The building still serves as May's headquarters and is the site of the flagship Famous-Barr store.

The company continued to buy others throughout the 20th century, including O'Neil's (Akron, 1912), Hamburger & Sons (Los Angeles, 1923), Bernheimer-Leader (Baltimore, 1927), Kaufmann's (Pittsburgh, 1946), Daniels & Fischer (Denver, 1957), Hecht's (Washington, 1959), G. Fox (Hartford, 1965), and Meier & Frank (Portland, Oregon, 1966).

Meanwhile, 2 other companies, the Associated Merchants Company and the United Dry Goods Companies, had reorganized in 1916 to form Associated Dry Goods. Their core businesses were Lord & Taylor in New York, Hahne's in Newark, and Hengerer's in Buffalo. This company also bought out numerous family-owned stores: J. W. Robinson (Los Angeles, 1955), Sibley's (Rochester, 1957), Pogue's (Cincinnati, 1961), Goldwater's (Phoenix, 1962), Stix, Baer (St. Louis, 1963), Denver Dry Goods (1965), Horne's (Pittsburgh, 1966), and Ayres (Indianapolis, 1972). Associated also created Robinson's of Florida in the 1970s.

Like other department store companies, both companies entered the discount store business, May with Venture Stores and Associated with Loehmann's and Caldor. May became heavily involved in the development and management of regional mall shopping centers (now joint-ventured with Melvin Simon and Prudential Insurance) and in 1979 acquired the Volume Shoe Corporation (now Payless ShoeSource), the nation's largest operator of discount shoe stores.

The corporate restructuring that swept America in the 1980s affected the big retailers as well; in late 1986 May bought Associated for 70 million shares of stock. In 1988 May also bought Foley's (Houston) and Filene's (Boston) for $1.5 billion from Federated Department Stores (as it was being acquired by Campeau). Since then May has consolidated some operations, closed others, and sold or spun off others (Caldor and Venture are now public companies). In late 1990 May picked up Thalhimers from Carter Hawley Hale for $317 million. Five-year plans call for spending $3.5 billion to add 88 department stores and 1,325 shoe stores.

WHERE

HQ: 611 Olive St., St. Louis, MO 63101
Phone: 314-342-6300
Fax: 314-342-6584

May operates 14 department store divisions with stores in 31 states and Washington, DC. Payless ShoeSource has stores in 46 states and Washington, DC. May Merchandising Corporation, based in New York, maintains 14 overseas buying offices.

WHAT

Division, HQ	1990 Sales $ mil.	No. of Stores
Foley's, Houston	1,150	36
Lord & Taylor, New York	1,147	46
May Company, Los Angeles	987	37
Hecht's, Washington, DC	940	27
Kaufmann's, Pittsburgh	768	25
Robinson's, Los Angeles	734	28
Famous-Barr, St. Louis	507	17
Filene's, Boston	488	19
Thalhimers, Richmond, VA	156	26
May Company, Cleveland	441	16
G. Fox, Hartford	436	12
L.S. Ayres, Indianapolis	345	15
May D&F, Denver	286	12
Meier & Frank, Portland, OR	284	8
Adjustments	31	—
Total department stores	8,700	324
Payless ShoeSource, Topeka	1,366	2,967
Total	**10,066**	**3,291**

Thalhimers sales included from date of acquisition (11/4/90); full year sales $455 million.

RANKINGS

10th in *Fortune* 50 Retailing Cos.
93rd in *Business Week* 1000

KEY COMPETITORS

Ames	Mercantile Stores
Brown Group	Montgomery Ward
Campeau	Nordstrom
Carter Hawley Hale	Pacific Enterprises
Dayton Hudson	J. C. Penney
Dillard	Riklis Family
Edison Brothers	Sears
The Gap	U.S. Shoe
INTERCO	Wal-Mart
Kmart	Woolworth
The Limited	Specialty and discount
Macy	retailers
Melville	

HOW MUCH

Fiscal year ends following January	9-Year Growth	1981	1982	1983	1984	1985	1986	1987	1988	1989	1990
Sales ($ mil.)	12.8%	3,413	3,670	4,229	4,762	5,080	10,376	10,581	11,742	9,602	10,066
Net income ($ mil.)	16.5%	126	142	187	214	235	381	444	503	515	500
Income as % of sales	—	3.7%	3.9%	4.4%	4.5%	4.6%	3.7%	4.2%	4.3%	5.4%	5.0%
Earnings per share ($)	11.2%	1.44	1.62	2.16	2.48	2.69	2.44	2.90	3.41	3.64	3.74
Stock price – high ($)	—	10.67	16.42	21.00	21.56	32.50	44.13	50.88	40.00	52.63	59.13
Stock price – low ($)	—	7.75	7.67	13.33	15.17	19.06	30.00	22.25	28.75	34.63	37.63
Stock price – close ($)	19.9%	8.33	15.71	17.92	19.06	31.25	35.50	29.13	36.25	47.88	42.75
P/E – high	—	7	10	10	9	12	18	18	12	14	16
P/E – low	—	5	5	6	6	7	12	8	8	10	10
Dividends per share ($)	12.0%	0.55	0.60	0.65	0.78	0.92	1.02	1.12	1.25	1.39	1.54
Book value per share ($)	6.9%	10.97	11.94	13.39	14.99	16.58	17.01	18.26	20.45	18.65	20.07

1990 Year-end:
Debt ratio: 59.1%
Return on equity: 19.3%
Cash (mil.): $80
Current ratio: 2.51
Long-term debt (mil.): $3,565
No. of shares (mil.): 123
Dividends:
  1990 average yield: 3.6%
  1990 payout: 41.2%
Market value (mil.): $5,254

Stock Price History High/Low 1981–90

MAYFLOWER GROUP, INC.

Private company
Fiscal year ends: December 31

Hoover's Rating **D**

OVERVIEW

Since going private in 1986 through a $351 million LBO, Mayflower has lost money — but not because business is bad. The company, named for the ship that ferried the Pilgrims across the Atlantic to Plymouth Rock, is burdened by high interest debt and is now moving toward a major restructuring plan that could permanently split up its international moving (Mayflower Transit) and public transportation (Contract Services) businesses.

CEO Michael Smith hopes to reorganize the 2 divisions of Mayflower Group under separate holding companies. According to Smith, the split would divide debt payment responsibilities equally between the new holding companies, lower Mayflower's outstanding debt, and require smaller payments from the 2 new entities.

Mayflower offers an array of relocation services, as well as contract busing services to schools, corporations, and cities. Chairman John Smith (no relation to Michael Smith), his family, and the Mayflower's managers own 49% of the company; New York investment bankers Smith Barney and other investors own 40%; the rest is in reserve for other bondholders who helped finance the LBO.

WHO

Chairman: John B. Smith, age 59
President and CEO: Michael L. Smith, age 42
SVP and CFO: Patrick F. Carr, age 39
SVP, Secretary, and General Counsel: Robert H. Irvin, age 39
Auditors: Ernst & Young
Employees: 10,900

WHERE

HQ: 9998 N. Michigan Rd., Carmel, IN 46032
Phone: 317-875-1000
Fax: 317-875-2214

Mayflower Transit offers international moving services through 750 agents. Contract Services operates 8,000 buses in the US.

WHEN

In 1927 Indiana truck drivers Conrad Gentry and Don Kenworthy founded Mayflower Transit Company (renamed Aero Mayflower Transit Company, 1928), a household moving company, in Indianapolis. Within 3 years the company had appointed independent agents to operate Aero Mayflower moving vans and storage facilities in key metropolitan areas.

The company established America's first school for professional movers in 1934. Aero Mayflower was first to receive Interstate Commerce Commission approval to operate nationwide household moving services in 1940; it expanded to Mexico and Canada in 1948 and to Europe in 1956.

Aero Mayflower improved customer service by equipping its vans with Air-Ride suspension to provide a smoother ride (1960) and installing a computerized management system in its dispatch facilities to more efficiently track equipment and orders (1967). The Mayflower Corporation was formed in 1973 and, through an exchange of stock, it acquired Aero Mayflower. The company opened a new headquarters facility in Carmel, Indiana, in 1973 and made its first public stock offering in 1976.

Planning to expand service beyond household moving, Mayflower established Air Mayflower, an air freight forwarder, in 1976. Unable to compete effectively with established air freight forwarders such as Emery and Airborne Express, Air Mayflower had ceased operations by 1983. In 1979 Mayflower formed the Gentry Insurance Agency to provide limited insurance to its operators and agents. In 1981 Mayflower bought a 90% stake in ADI Appliances, a Midwest wholesaler of household appliances (Whirlpool and Litton) and home video equipment (RCA). By the end of 1981, Mayflower also offered Atari and Texas Instruments brand products through its ADI (Consumer Products) division. It sold this division in 1987.

In 1984 the company started offering school bus transportation services by purchasing R. W. Harmon & Sons, a school bus company, and 3 more school bus companies the following year. Mayflower's fleet of 4,500 buses was one of America's largest, 2nd only to Canada's Laidlaw Transportation. In 1986 Laidlaw offered $29.25 per share to gain control of Mayflower. Mayflower's managers, led by CEO John B. Smith, responded by taking the company private in a $351 million LBO, financed by several New York investment firms, including Smith Barney.

Over the next 2 years, Mayflower's LBO-related debt contributed to losses totaling $15 million. In 1989 an attempted buyout led by former Mayflower Transit president Richard Russell failed when managers were unable to secure financing. Smith, who had backed the buyout plan, stepped down as chief executive but continues to serve as chairman.

In April 1990 CEO Michael Smith announced that, in an effort to reduce its $213 million long-term debt, Mayflower would split its 2 operating units into separate companies. Later that year Transit's managers considered buying their division. Smith indicated that Contract Services might be spun off to the public, but no definitive action had been taken by October 1991.

WHAT

	1990* Sales		1990* Operating Income	
	$ mil.	% of total	$ mil.	% of total
Transit	360	71	10	77
Contract Services	146	29	3	23
Adjustments	—	—	(1)	—
Total	**506**	**100**	**12**	**100**

*9 months ended September 30

Mayflower Transit, Inc.
Electronic and Trade Show (special handling and other services)
Household Goods (household moving services)
International (freight forwarding)
Moving and Storage (company-owned agencies)
Other transportation operations
   Group insurance agency
   Moving supplies and equipment sales
   Road equipment maintenance
   Tractor and trailer sales

Mayflower Contract Services, Inc.
Allied Bus Sales, Inc.
Public transportation (city bus operations)
Student transportation (school bus operations)

RANKINGS

33rd in *Fortune* 50 Transportation Cos.
271st in *Forbes* 400 US Private Cos.

KEY COMPETITORS

American President
Burlington Northern
Chicago and North Western
Consolidated Freightways
Consolidated Rail
CSX
Norfolk Southern
Roadway
Ryder
Union Pacific
Yellow Freight

HOW MUCH

	9-Year Growth	1981	1982	1983	1984	1985	1986	1987	1988	1989	1990
Sales ($ mil.)	8.2%	330	341	379	481	619	706	585	612	676	672
Net income ($ mil.)	—	4	4	8	14	15	4	(6)	(9)	(4)	(10)
Income as % of sales	—	1.3%	1.3%	2.0%	2.9%	2.4%	0.5%	(1.1%)	(1.5%)	(0.5%)	(1.5%)
Employees	26.0%	1,357	1,236	1,378	2,129	2,485	6,947	6,800	9,600	11,400	10,900

Net Income ($ mil.)
1981–90

MAYO FOUNDATION

OVERVIEW

The Mayo Foundation is the governing body for the largest private medical center in the world (the Mayo Clinic in Rochester, Minnesota), with additional outpatient facilities in Jacksonville, Florida, and Scottsdale, Arizona. The Mayo Clinic in Rochester works in association with its 2 local hospitals (Saint Marys and Rochester Methodist).

Intertwined with the clinical practice are extensive programs in medical education and research. Since the clinic started keeping records in 1907, it has served over 4 million patients from more than 150 countries. Medical education is conducted by the Mayo Graduate School of Medicine (one of the largest medical programs in the country), Mayo Medical School, and the Mayo School of Health-Related Sciences.

The Mayo Clinic is known for its integrated approach to health care. The clinic's team of more than 900 physicians and scientists work together to provide some of the most comprehensive health care possible.

The foundation also runs a number of enterprises complementary to its medical operations, including its *Health Letter*, Mayo Medical Ventures to commercialize its research, and a testing laboratory. Through a subsidiary, Mayo runs the Rochester airport, 40% of whose passengers are connected to the clinic.

WHEN

William W. Mayo emigrated to the US from England in 1845. After studying medicine at Indiana Medical College, Mayo practiced medicine in Indiana and Minnesota until finally settling in Rochester, Minnesota, in 1863. Twenty years later a tornado struck the town, and Mayo was assigned to take charge of a makeshift hospital. Following the disaster, the Sisters of St. Francis (a Roman Catholic order) arranged for the construction of a permanent hospital and asked Mayo to assume leadership of the medical staff. Mayo reluctantly agreed (at that time hospitals were associated with the poor and the insane) and took charge when Saint Marys Hospital opened in 1889.

Mayo's 2 sons, William and Charles, had already joined their father's practice when Saint Marys opened, and they served with their father as the hospital's medical staff. After the elder Mayo retired, the sons ran the hospital by themselves, assisted only by a small group of Catholic sisters. The brothers accepted all medical cases, regardless of the patient's ability to pay, yet they were still able to make the hospital self-sufficient. Under the brothers' direction, Saint Marys was the first hospital in the US to implement the antiseptic surgical techniques developed by Joseph Lister.

By the turn of the century, the Mayos' expanding practice had helped thousands of patients. Physicians were added to the staff and a new wing was opened in 1905, at about the same time the present name was adopted

(Saint Marys would remain one of the facilities under the Mayo umbrella). In 1915 the brothers established the Mayo Graduate School of Medicine in affiliation with the University of Minnesota. During WWI the brothers served as the head surgical consultants to the US Army.

In 1919 the brothers organized the Mayo Properties Association, a self-perpetuating charity, to assume ownership of the clinic. Ten years later a new clinic building, with modern waiting rooms, laboratories, a library, and administrative offices, was opened. In 1933 the Clinic established the first blood bank in the US and in 1938 saw its millionth patient. Both of the brothers died in 1939.

In 1950 scientists at the clinic won a Nobel Prize for their development of the drug cortisone. The clinic grew during the 1960s when it moved Rochester Methodist Hospital to a new building (1966) and completed a 10-story addition to the Mayo Building (1969).

In 1972 the Mayo Medical School (its 2nd medical school) was opened. The clinic's reputation for medical research and practice continued to grow, and it established satellite facilities in Jacksonville, Florida (1986), and Scottsdale, Arizona (1987). The Clinic started its liver transplant program in 1985 and 3 years later performed its first coronary atherectomy (a new procedure to open clogged arteries). In 1990 the Foundation initiated an 8-month planning process to define its goals and direction for the next several years.

Nonprofit organization
Fiscal year ends: December 31

Hoover's Rating **A**

WHO

Chairman, Board of Trustees: Edson W. Spencer, age 65
President and CEO: Robert R. Waller
Treasurer and CFO: John H. Herrell
Director for Education; Dean, Mayo Medical School: Franklyn G. Knox
Chairman, Department of Personnel Services: Sharon Duneman
Auditors: Deloitte & Touche
Employees: 17,836

WHERE

HQ: Mayo Clinic, Rochester, MN 55905
Phone: 507-284-2511
Fax: 507-284-8713 (Communications)

The Mayo Foundation is based in Rochester, Minnesota. Mayo Clinic outpatient facilities exist in Rochester; Jacksonville, Florida; and Scottsdale, Arizona. Foundation hospitals are Saint Marys in Rochester, Rochester Methodist Hospital, and St. Luke's Hospital in Jacksonville.

	1990 Revenues
	% of total
Mayo Clinic, Rochester	47
Rochester hospitals	23
St. Luke's Hospital	7
Research	4
Reference laboratories	5
Mayo Clinic, Scottsdale	4
Mayo Clinic, Jacksonville	4
Other	6
Total	**100**

WHAT

	Sources of Gifts	
	$ thou.	% of total
Estates	21,328	51
Individuals	10,616	26
Personal/family foundations	3,005	7
Corporations	2,267	6
Philanthropic foundations	2,158	5
Alumni	879	2
Memorials	487	1
Other	698	2
Total	**41,438**	**100**

	1990 Allocation of Gift Money	
	$ thou.	% of total
Medical education & research	12,397	30
Facilities	17,055	41
Research	5,656	14
Education	2,286	5
Hospitals	1,626	4
Charity & other	1,608	4
Private grants	810	2
Total	**41,438**	**100**

Mayo Services 1990

Clinic patient registrations	343,291
Diagnostic X-ray procedures	1,125,134
Laboratory tests	8,013,351
Total surgical cases	67,645
Hospital beds licensed	2,240
Hospital occupancy (%)	57
Hospital admissions	60,822
Hospital days of patient care	466,165

KEY COMPETITORS

Hospital Corp. Humana National Medical

HOW MUCH

	9-Year Growth	1981	1982	1983	1984	1985[1]	1986	1987	1988	1989	1990
Revenues ($ mil.)	15.8%	316	342	395	418	658	761	836	965	1,058	1,181
Net operating inc. ($ mil.)	—	—	—	—	—	49	65	26	38	42	42
Net op. inc. as % of rev.	—	—	—	—	—	7.4%	8.5%	3.1%	3.9%	4.0%	3.6%
Patient regs. (thou.)	9.6%	273	272	277	280	282	283	303	320	328	343
Donations ($ mil.)	2.6%	18	12	15	15	18	25	27	32	31	41
Employees	—	—	—	—	—	—	—	—	16,524	17,165	17,836

Revenues ($ mil.) 1981–90

[Bar chart showing revenues from 1981 to 1990, scale 0–1,200]

[1] Rochester Methodist and St. Marys Hospitals excluded prior to 1985

MAYTAG CORPORATION

NYSE symbol: MYG
Fiscal year ends: December 31

Hoover's Rating B-

OVERVIEW

Maytag is the 4th largest appliance manufacturer in the US, after Whirlpool, General Electric, and White Consolidated Industries (Electrolux), and is the #1 soft drink vending machine producer. Maytag has built its reputation on the quality and durability of its products, and its Maytag and Jenn-Air brands are the US leaders in high-end appliances. The company has maintained emphasis on quality by manufacturing a high percentage of its own parts and by testing every machine it makes. In 1989 Maytag redesigned its washing machine transmission for the first time in 35 years in order to make it even more reliable.

Facing a saturated home market, Maytag is looking abroad for growth. The company's recently acquired Hoover unit manufactures a full line of home appliances overseas in addition to vacuum cleaners and has given the company increased access to markets in Europe and Australia. The economic environment in Maytag's foreign markets has been weak, as it has in the US. The company has responded by cutting employment, inventory, and its dividend.

WHEN

In 1893 F. L. Maytag and 3 associates formed the Parsons Bandcutter and Self Feeder Company in Newton, Iowa, to manufacture feeder attachments for grain threshing machines. In 1903 the firm changed its name to the Maytag Company. In 1907 Maytag produced its first washing machine, a hand-cranked wooden tub model. At about the same time F. L. Maytag became sole owner of the firm. The company introduced a washer with an electric motor in 1911, brought out a gasoline-powered washer in 1914, and in 1919 cast the first aluminum washer tub. L. B. Maytag, son of F. L. and president of the company from 1920 to 1926, along with Howard Snyder, head of Maytag's development department, designed and produced the first vaned agitator washer in 1922. The agitator washer was very successful, and Maytag concentrated on washing machine production, producing one million by 1927.

In 1925 the company's stock began trading on the NYSE. In 1929 Maytag's earnings reached a prewar high of $6.8 million on sales of $25.6 million. The company survived the Great Depression without a loss. During the war years, 1941 to 1945, Maytag suspended production of washers and made components for military airplanes. In 1949 the company built a 2nd plant to produce a new line of automatic washing machines. During the Korean War, Maytag built tank parts and other military hardware while continuing production of washers. Clothes dryers went into production in 1953. In the late 1950s Maytag began to make products for the commercial laundry field. In 1966 the company entered the kitchen appliance field, introducing a line of dishwashers and, in 1968, food waste disposers.

Maytag began growing by acquisition in 1981, entering the field of cooking appliances with the purchase of Hardwick Stove and Jenn-Air. In 1986 Maytag more than doubled its size by buying the Magic Chef group of companies, including Magic Chef, Toastmaster, and Admiral. The company sold Toastmaster in 1987 and in 1988 consolidated Admiral into the company's other divisions. Maytag sold Magic Chef air conditioning in 1988 and in 1989 bought Chicago Pacific (furniture manufacturing and Hoover appliances) for $960 million, doubling Maytag's debt. The company sold Chicago Pacific's 6 furniture manufacturing companies to Ladd Furniture for $213.4 million in 1989, retaining the Hoover unit. In 1989 the company introduced its first line of Maytag brand refrigerators.

In 1991 Maytag licensed its Admiral brand to Montgomery Ward, allowing the retailer to place the Admiral label on independently made audio and video equipment.

WHO

Chairman and CEO: Daniel J. Krumm, age 64, $925,531 pay
EVP and COO: Leonard A. Hadley, age 56, $481,457 pay
EVP and CFO: Jerry A. Schiller, age 58, $417,993 pay
SVP Human Resources: William R. Foust, age 48, $209,785 pay
Auditors: Ernst & Young
Employees: 24,273

WHERE

HQ: 403 W. Fourth St. North, Newton, IA 50208
Phone: 515-792-8000
Fax: 515-791-8395

Maytag has 22 plants in 7 countries.

	1990 Sales		1990 Operating Income	
	$ mil.	% of total	$ mil.	% of total
North America	2,404	79	263	106
Europe	497	16	(23)	(9)
Other countries	156	5	9	3
Adjustments	—	—	(18)	—
Total	**3,057**	**100**	**231**	**100**

WHAT

	1990 Sales		1990 Operating Income	
	$ mil.	% of total	$ mil.	% of total
Home appliances	2,866	94	224	90
Vending equipment	191	6	25	10
Adjustments	—	—	(18)	—
Total	**3,057**	**100**	**231**	**100**

Appliance Group
Admiral Co.
Jenn-Air Co.
Magic Chef Co.
Maycor Appliance Parts and Service Co.
Maytag Co.

Hoover Group
Domicor, Inc. (international marketing)
Hoover Australia
Hoover Company
Hoover Ltd.
Hoover Trading Company

Dixie-Narco Group
Dixie-Narco, Inc. (vending machines)

Other
Maytag Financial Services

Appliance Brand Names
Admiral
Hardwick
Hoover
Jenn-Air
Magic Chef
Maytag
Norge

RANKINGS

151st in *Fortune* 500 Industrial Cos.
410th in *Business Week* 1000

KEY COMPETITORS

Amway
Berkshire Hathaway
Electrolux
GEC
General Electric
Hitachi
Masco
Raytheon
Robert Bosch
Sharp
Siemens
Thomson SA
Toshiba
Whirlpool

HOW MUCH

	9-Year Growth	1981	1982	1983	1984	1985	1986	1987	1988	1989	1990
Sales ($ mil.)	25.1%	409	441	597	643	684	1,724	1,909	1,886	3,089	3,057
Net income ($ mil.)	11.4%	37	37	61	63	72	119	153	136	131	99
Income as % of sales	—	9.2%	8.4%	10.2%	9.8%	10.5%	6.9%	8.0%	7.2%	4.3%	3.2%
Earnings per share ($)	4.0%	0.66	0.67	1.09	1.16	1.33	1.38	1.91	1.77	1.27	0.94
Stock price – high ($)	—	7.50	9.75	14.19	13.75	19.94	27.44	32.31	27.63	26.75	20.63
Stock price – low ($)	—	5.97	5.56	9.16	9.06	10.88	18.00	17.00	18.88	18.88	9.88
Stock price – close ($)	5.8%	6.38	9.41	12.81	11.19	19.47	23.63	22.38	19.38	19.50	10.63
P/E – high	—	11	15	13	12	15	20	17	16	21	22
P/E – low	—	9	8	8	8	8	13	9	11	15	11
Dividends per share ($)	6.5%	0.54	0.54	0.68	0.75	0.83	0.85	0.95	0.98	0.95	0.95
Book value per share ($)	12.1%	3.43	3.58	4.00	4.22	4.72	6.53	5.43	6.55	8.89	9.60

1990 Year-end:
Debt ratio: 45.8%
Return on equity: 10.2%
Cash (mil.): $70
Current ratio: 2.10
Long-term debt (mil.): $858
No. of shares (mil.): 106
Dividends:
1990 average yield: 8.9%
1990 payout: 101.1%
Market value (mil.): $1,123

Stock Price History High/Low 1981–90

MCCAW CELLULAR COMMUNICATIONS, INC.

OVERVIEW

McCaw Cellular is the largest cellular telephone company in the US, based on the number of subscribers and the number of potential users (about 73 million). McCaw owns about 52% of LIN Broadcasting, which includes 7 television stations and cellular operations in 5 of the top 10 markets.

Nationwide in scope, McCaw organizes its holdings in 3 super-regions: the East Coast, Midwest-to-Northwest, and California/Nevada.

McCaw aims to create a single, seamless nationwide cellular network that would yield royalties to the company on every call made. In McCaw's vision, callers would dial for people, not places, and be able to reach a McCaw subscriber with one number anywhere in the nation. McCaw is the chief operator under the Cellular One trademark and, in a venture with Southwestern Bell's cellular subsidiary, is promoting the Cellular One brand and establishing quality standards.

McCaw is also the 5th largest radio common carrier (including radio paging) in the US, with more than 294,000 subscribers. With the help of Swedish equipment-maker Ericsson, McCaw hopes to test wireless personal miniphones for office workers in 9 US cities.

WHEN

Seattle's radio-and-TV pioneer John Elroy McCaw started Centralia, Washington's first radio station (1937), was one of the first cable television operators (1952), and was among the first to air rock 'n' roll (New York City's WINS, 1950s). After Elroy's sudden death in 1969, his widow and 4 sons were forced to winnow the scattered, debt-ridden empire back to a sole, small cable system in Centralia.

While a student at Stanford, Elroy's son Craig took over McCaw Communications and adopted his father's strategy of securing loans against the Centralia business to buy cable companies; he then slashed costs, improved programming, and raised subscription rates. McCaw also moved into radio common carrier services (1974) and formed a partnership in 1981 with Affiliated Publications (owners of the *Boston Globe*) to purchase cable systems before their prices skyrocketed. Affiliated's $12 million stake was eventually raised to $85 million (or 43% of McCaw).

But cellular technology soon attracted McCaw, who in the early 1980s got several of the first FCC-granted franchises. As late as 1984, McCaw paid a mere $5 per potential subscriber; by 1989 McCaw would ante up $350. Sagging under cable debt, McCaw wavered briefly in the face of uncertain demand (with phones costing over $2,000 apiece) but soon, with Affiliated's nod, began devouring licenses using junk-bond financing.

McCaw tempered the rocketing debt in 1987 by selling the cable business (to Jack Kent Cooke) and offering to the public 12% of McCaw Cellular (into which the old McCaw Communications was merged). A subsequent buying spree included stakes in Metro Mobile CTS and Graphics Scanning and the purchase of Washington Post's Florida licenses.

In 1989 Affiliated spun off the stake in McCaw (then worth about $1.5 billion) to its shareholders. In 1989, as its $1.8 billion debt approached 87% of capital, McCaw sold a 22% stake to British Telecom PLC and announced sale of its southeastern cellular systems to Contel (later merged with rival GTE).

McCaw's 1990 purchase of a 51.9% stake in LIN Broadcasting for $3.4 billion added major markets such as New York, Los Angeles, and Dallas. The alliance was seen as crucial in weaving a nationwide blanket from McCaw's scattered properties.

In 1991 McCaw grappled with the debt it incurred buying cellular operations. The company offered a debt-for-equity swap to reduce debt. It sold cellular interests in 18 midwest markets to BellSouth. The deal was valued at $410 million, and McCaw came away owning 100% of a Milwaukee mobile phone system.

NASDAQ symbol: MCAWA
Fiscal year ends: December 31

 Hoover's Rating **C+**

WHO

Chairman and CEO: Craig O. McCaw, age 41, $209,199 pay
VC: Wayne M. Perry, age 41, $208,030 pay
President: Harold S. Eastman, age 52, $366,453 pay
EVP Acquisitions: John E. McCaw, Jr., age 40, $193,012 pay
SVP and CFO: Peter L. S. Currie, age 34
VP People Development: Kerry Larson
Auditors: Arthur Andersen & Co.
Employees: 6,200

WHERE

HQ: 5400 Carillon Point, Kirkland, WA 98033
Phone: 206-827-4500
Fax: 206-828-8616

McCaw Cellular operates in more than 100 markets in 13 states, and its services are available to about 48% of the US population. McCaw has more than 294,000 pagers in service.

WHAT

	1990 Sales		1990 Operating Income	
	$ mil.	% of total	$ mil.	% of total
Cellular telephone service	830	80	29	41
Radio paging service	90	9	(13)	(18)
Broadcasting	117	11	55	77
Adjustments	—	—	(23)	—
Total	**1,037**	**100**	**48**	**100**

Cellular Operations
Cellular One telephone service
Cellular telephone sales and service
  Car-mounted
  Fully portable
  Transportable

Radio Common Carrier Operations
Paging services
Telephone answering
2-way mobile phone service

LIN Broadcasting (51.9%)
Cellular telephone systems
Specialty publishing (GuestInformant)
TV stations
  KXAN, Austin, TX
  KXAS, Dallas/Fort Worth, TX
  WAND, Champaign, IL
  WANE, Fort Wayne, IN
  WAVY, Norfolk, VA
  WISH, Indianapolis, IN
  WOTV, Grand Rapids, MI

RANKINGS

156th in *Business Week* 1000

KEY COMPETITORS

Ameritech	NYNEX
Bell Atlantic	Pacific Telesis
BellSouth	Southwestern Bell
Cable & Wireless	Telmex
Centel	U S West
GTE	

HOW MUCH

	4-Year Growth	1981	1982	1983	1984	1985	1986	1987	1988	1989	1990
Sales ($ mil.)	175.5%	—	—	—	—	—	18	150	311	504	1,037
Net income ($ mil.)	—	—	—	—	—	—	(39)	(134)	(297)	(287)	371
Income as % of sales	—	—	—	—	—	—	(215.9%)	(89.3%)	(95.6%)	(57.2%)	35.8%
Earnings per share ($)	—	—	—	—	—	—	(0.40)	(1.31)	(2.39)	(1.95)	1.92
Stock price – high ($)	—	—	—	—	—	—	—	26.00	28.13	47.25	38.50
Stock price – low ($)	—	—	—	—	—	—	—	11.00	16.25	25.75	11.00
Stock price – close ($)	—	—	—	—	—	—	—	16.13	27.00	38.25	17.25
P/E – high	—	—	—	—	—	—	—	—	—	—	20
P/E – low	—	—	—	—	—	—	—	—	—	—	6
Dividends per share ($)	—	—	—	—	—	—	0.00	0.00	0.00	0.00	0.00
Book value per share ($)	—	—	—	—	—	—	(0.66)	1.04	(0.08)	6.13	11.41

1990 Year-end:
Debt ratio: 71.9%
Return on equity: 21.9%
Cash (mil.): $411
Current ratio: 1.80
Long-term debt (mil.): $5,225
No. of shares (mil.): 179
Dividends:
  1990 average yield: 0.0%
  1990 payout: 0.0%
Market value (mil.): $3,091

Stock Price History
High/Low 1987–90

MCDERMOTT INTERNATIONAL, INC.

NYSE symbol: MDR
Fiscal year ends: March 31

OVERVIEW

McDermott International has 2 specialities: marine construction services and power generation systems and equipment. The marine construction segment provides technical services to the oil and gas industry, including engineering, fabrication, and installation of offshore platforms and pipelines.

The Power Generation Group, headed by Babcock and Wilcox, constructs power-generating facilities for the utility industry and industrial boilers (US market leader), and provides construction services, pollution control systems, and other equipment and services to the pulp and paper industry and to fossil and nuclear power plants internationally.

McDermott has suffered from lack of growth in the energy industry and may be the target of asbestos litigation relating to portions of B&W now discontinued. However, the company expects an improvement in the wake of the Gulf War, the effects of which may spur new exploration, as well as sales opportunities for replacement of destroyed oil equipment. In 1991 the company became the prime contractor for Amoco's USSR development contract in the Caspian Sea.

WHO

Chairman and CEO: Robert E. Howson, age 59, $675,809 pay
President and COO: John P. Eckert, age 57, $317,383 pay
EVP; Group Executive, Power Generation Group: Joe J. Stewart, age 53, $277,115 pay
EVP; Group Executive, Domestic and Southeast Asia Group: William L. Higgins III, age 48, $248,720 pay
SVP and CFO: Brock A. Hattox
Director of Human Resources: L. J. Sannino
Auditors: Ernst & Young
Employees: 34,000

WHEN

In 1923 when R. Thomas McDermott won a contract to supply drilling rigs to a Texas wildcatter, he started a new company, J. Ray McDermott & Co., named after his father, who supervised construction. During the 1930s the oil industry expanded to Louisiana and the McDermotts followed, making New Orleans their headquarters. When the company incorporated in 1946, it supplied services for marshland oil and natural gas production.

After WWII McDermott became a pioneer in the construction of offshore drilling platforms. Spurred by increased demand for oil in the 1960s and by the price rises of the 1970s, McDermott's offshore business boomed. The company also supplied the US Navy, salvage, and subsea markets.

By 1978, when 86% of revenues were from marine construction, McDermott had diversified into other energy areas with the acquisition of Babcock and Wilcox, which manufactured energy generation equipment and provided maintenance, repair, and other services. In 1980 the company became McDermott Inc., and in 1983, McDermott International.

B&W had begun as a boiler maker in 1867 when Stephen Wilcox and his partner, George Babcock, patented an improved boiler. B&W built the boilers for the nation's first 2 electrical stations. They incorporated in 1881. In 1889 B&W began building marine boilers and began a relationship with the US Navy. During WWII B&W supplied 75% of major US military vessels' boilers. After WWII the company focused on nuclear energy and built the reactor for the first nuclear-powered merchant ship. During the 1950s B&W made significant contributions to the navy's nuclear program; today it supplies fuel and services to nuclear power plants as well as waste-disposal and emission-control systems.

In 1978 the combination of the 2 companies seemed ideal: oil and gas exploration, as well as electrical generation, including nuclear. Then came the oil gluts of the 1980s, which led to the price collapse of 1986 and curtailed demand for exploration equipment. The marine construction group went into the red in 1987 and stayed. B&W remained profitable, though the backlash against nuclear power ended construction of new plants and reduced B&W's nuclear segment to providing only repair services and parts replacement to other companies and supplies to the navy's nuclear shipbuilding program. Between 1988 and 1990 the company sold its insulating, controls, trading, and seamless tube production operations.

In 1991 the company announced it would sell certain cogeneration and marine equipment assets and issue more stock to raise money.

WHERE

HQ: 1010 Common St., New Orleans, LA 70112-2401
Phone: 504-587-5400
Fax: 504-587-6433

McDermott's power generation equipment is sold throughout the US; marine services are provided worldwide.

	1990 Sales		1990 Operating Income	
	$ mil.	% of total	$ mil.	% of total
US	2,028	65	69	—
Europe & West Africa	488	15	(1)	—
Other foreign	620	20	(32)	—
Adjustments	—	—	(47)	—
Total	**3,136**	**100**	**(11)**	**—**

WHAT

	1990 Sales		1990 Operating Income	
	$ mil.	% of total	$ mil.	% of total
Marine construction services	1,390	44	(52)	—
Power generation systems & equipment	1,746	56	88	—
Adjustments	—	—	(47)	—
Total	**3,136**	**100**	**(11)**	**—**

Marine Construction Services
Construction of petrochemical plants
Engineering services
Marine pipelines
Offshore platforms
Shipyard operation
Vessel chartering operations

Power Generation Systems and Equipment
Air-cooled heat exchangers
Pollution control systems
Process recovery boilers
Utility plant repair and construction

HOW MUCH

Fiscal year ends March of following year	9-Year Growth	1981	1982	1983	1984	1985	1986	1987	1988	1989	1990
Sales ($ mil.)	(4.7%)	4,843	3,708	3,089	3,234	3,257	3,289	2,352	2,423	2,645	3,136
Net income ($ mil.)	—	213	51	121	19	56	87	(231)	(115)	(101)	(86)
Income as % of sales	—	4.4%	1.4%	3.9%	0.6%	1.7%	2.7%	(9.8%)	(4.7%)	(3.8%)	(2.8%)
Earnings per share ($)	—	4.56	1.37	2.95	0.51	1.52	2.31	(6.23)	(3.09)	(2.68)	(1.97)
Stock price – high ($)	—	41.88	38.13	26.38	31.63	30.13	23.38	33.13	21.50	26.25	34.50
Stock price – low ($)	—	27.13	14.75	17.13	23.75	16.38	13.63	13.00	13.75	14.63	21.63
Stock price – close ($)	(4.7%)	38.00	20.50	24.88	24.38	18.25	21.75	14.75	14.75	23.13	24.63
P/E – high	—	9	28	9	62	20	10	—	—	—	—
P/E – low	—	6	11	6	47	11	6	—	—	—	—
Dividends per share ($)	(5.4%)	1.65	1.80	1.80	1.80	1.80	1.80	1.80	1.40	1.00	1.00
Book value per share ($)	(9.6%)	31.92	33.13	33.92	32.57	32.57	27.94	19.95	16.00	15.24	12.88

1990 Year-end:
Debt ratio: 53.0%
Return on equity: —
Cash (mil.): $204
Current ratio: 0.81
Long-term debt (mil.): $640
No. of shares (mil.): 44
Dividends:
  1990 average yield: 4.1%
  1990 payout: —
Market value (mil.): $1,085

Stock Price History High/Low 1981–90

RANKINGS

193rd in *Fortune* 500 Industrial Cos.
494th in *Business Week* 1000

KEY COMPETITORS

ABB
Alcatel Alsthom
Ashland
Baker Hughes
Bechtel
Dresser
Duke Power
Fluor
General Electric
Halliburton
Rolls-Royce
Schlumberger
Siemens
Westinghouse
Other power equipment companies

MCDONALD'S CORPORATION

OVERVIEW

McDonald's Corporation, inventor of the fast-food restaurant, is the world's largest food service organization. Its golden arches trademark is one of the world's most recognized and, with an annual advertising budget exceeding $1 billion, McDonald's is one of the most advertised brands in the world.

Every day more than 20 million people visit McDonald's restaurants. The company has built its reputation through the uniformity (and availability) of its products. Every 18 hours, McDonald's opens a new restaurant. The company owns 60% of its restaurant sites and holds leases on virtually all the rest.

McDonald's is the largest US employer of minority youth. About 65% of franchisees who trained to become owner/operators in 1990 were minorities or women as the result of an affirmative-action program. McDonald's has the largest stock-option program in the history of US business and has a generous profit-sharing program.

In response to public awareness regarding nutrition and good health, McDonald's has stopped frying in beef fat and added low-fat selections to its menu. The company is also taking steps to become more environmentally responsible by phasing out foam packaging.

WHEN

The first McDonald's opened in 1948 in San Bernardino, California. In 1954 its owners, brothers Dick and Mac McDonald, signed a franchise agreement with 52-year-old Ray Kroc (a malt machine salesman). A year later Kroc opened his first restaurant in Des Plaines, Illinois. By 1957 Kroc operated 14 McDonald's restaurants in Illinois, Indiana, and California. The company sold its 100 millionth hamburger in 1958 and opened its 100th restaurant in 1959. Kroc bought out the McDonald brothers for $2.7 million in 1961.

In 1962 McDonald's adopted the golden arches as its company trademark. The company served its 1 billionth hamburger live on the "Art Linkletter Show" in 1963. Ronald McDonald made his debut that year, as did the company's first new menu item — the Filet-O-Fish sandwich. In 1965 McDonald's went public, and Kroc, aware of the value of well-placed advertising, ran McDonald's first TV ads. In 1967 the company opened its first international stores, in Canada and Puerto Rico.

In 1968 McDonald's added the Big Mac to its menu and opened its 1,000th restaurant. The company's advertising began featuring the slogan "You deserve a break today — so get up and get away to McDonald's" in 1970.

During the 1970s McDonald's grew at the rate of about 500 restaurants per year. New menu items included the Quarter Pounder (1972), the Egg McMuffin (pioneering breakfast fast food, 1973), and Happy Meals (1979). The first Ronald McDonald House (residence for families of hospitalized children) opened in 1974. That year Fred Turner, longtime operations chief and Kroc protegé, was named CEO. (Turner became chairman in 1977, with Kroc staying on as senior chairman until his death in 1984). In 1975, the year the drive-thru appeared, McDonald's formed the National Operators Advisory Board in response to a group of operators unhappy with the franchising system. (NOAB gave some power back to franchisees). By 1978 McDonald's had more than 5,000 restaurants, with sales of over $3 billion.

During the 1980s (and into the 1990s) McDonald's faced growing competition in the domestic market as its US sales growth slowed from over 20% per year in the 1970s to just over 10% in the 1980s. International sales continued to grow at over 20% per year. After introducing Chicken McNuggets in 1983, McDonald's became the first fast-food chain to provide customers a list of its products' ingredients (1986). In 1987 it started serving ready-to-eat salads. McDonald's served its 75 billionth hamburger in 1989. The McLean Deluxe, a low-fat hamburger, made its debut in 1991.

HOW MUCH

	9-Year Growth	1981	1982	1983	1984	1985	1986	1987	1988	1989	1990
Sales ($ mil.)	11.6%	2,477	2,715	3,001	3,366	3,695	4,144	4,853	5,521	6,065	6,640
Net income ($ mil.)	13.1%	265	301	343	389	433	480	549	646	727	802
Income as % of sales	—	10.7%	11.1%	11.4%	11.6%	11.7%	11.6%	11.3%	11.7%	12.0%	12.1%
Earnings per share ($)	14.2%	0.65	0.74	0.85	0.98	1.09	1.23	1.42	1.70	1.91	2.14
Stock price – high ($)	—	7.20	9.72	11.04	12.42	18.17	25.58	30.56	25.50	34.88	38.50
Stock price – low ($)	—	4.78	5.73	8.13	9.07	11.36	16.22	15.69	20.38	23.00	25.00
Stock price – close ($)	18.2%	6.46	8.94	10.44	11.47	17.97	20.29	22.00	24.06	34.50	29.13
P/E – high	—	11	13	13	13	17	21	22	15	18	18
P/E – low	—	7	8	10	9	10	13	11	12	12	12
Dividends per share ($)	15.1%	0.09	0.12	0.14	0.17	0.20	0.22	0.24	0.28	0.30	0.33
Book value per share ($)	14.2%	3.37	3.78	4.38	4.94	5.67	6.45	7.72	9.09	9.25	11.09

1990 Year-end:
Debt ratio: 51.4%
Return on equity: 21.0%
Cash (mil.): $143
Current ratio: 0.46
Long-term debt (mil.): $4,429
No. of shares (mil.): 359
Dividends:
  1990 average yield: 1.1%
  1990 payout: 15.5%
Market value (mil.): $10,459

Stock Price History High/Low 1981–90

NYSE symbol: MCD
Fiscal year ends: December 31

Hoover's Rating **B+**

WHO

Senior Chairman: Fred L. Turner, age 58, $1,175,000 pay
Chairman and CEO: Michael R. Quinlan, age 47, $1,250,000 pay
COO; President and COO, McDonald's USA: Edward H. Rensi, age 47, $850,000 pay
SEVP and CFO: Jack M. Greenberg, age 49, $621,842 pay
SVP (Personnel): Stanley R. Stein
Auditors: Ernst & Young
Employees: 177,000

WHERE

HQ: McDonald's Plaza, Oak Brook, IL 60521
Phone: 708-575-3000
Fax: 708-575-5211 (Stockholder Relations)

McDonald's has restaurants in 53 countries.

	No. of Restaurants
US	8,576
Canada	626
UK	356
Germany	349
France	150
Australia	269
Japan	776
Other countries	701
Total	**11,803**

	1990 Sales		1990 Operating Income	
	$ mil.	% of total	$ mil.	% of total
US	3,871	58	986	62
Canada	651	10	130	8
Europe	1,636	25	325	20
Pacific	340	5	121	8
Latin America	142	2	34	2
Adjustments	—	—	(95)	—
Total	**6,640**	**100**	**1,501**	**100**

WHAT

	Restaurants	
	No.	% of total
Operated by the company	2,643	22
Operated by franchisees	8,131	69
Operated by affiliates	1,029	9
Total	**11,803**	**100**

	1990 Sales	
	$ mil.	% of total
Company restaurants	5,019	76
Fees from franchised restaurants	1,621	24
Total	**6,640**	**100**

Major Products
Big Breakfast	Happy Meal
Big Mac	McChicken Sandwich
Biscuits	McD.L.T.
Chicken McNuggets	McLean Deluxe
Egg McMuffin	McRib Sandwich
Filet-O-Fish	Quarter Pounder
French fries	Salads

RANKINGS

17th in *Fortune* 50 Retailing Cos.
43rd in *Business Week* 1000

KEY COMPETITORS

Accor
Quaison
General Mills
Grand Metropolitan
Imasco
Metromedia
PepsiCo
TW Holdings
Wendy's

MCDONNELL DOUGLAS CORPORATION

NYSE symbol: MD
Fiscal year ends: December 31

Hoover's Rating **C+**

OVERVIEW

McDonnell Douglas Corporation (MDC) is the largest US defense contractor, the West's leading builder of combat aircraft, and the 3rd largest maker of commercial airplanes (after Boeing and Airbus Industrie).

McDonnell Douglas has maintained a 14% share of the world airliner market since 1989, but its market share has been eroded by Airbus and stands at less than 1/2 of what it was 10 years ago. Its military programs are also on shaky ground as the company faces the end of

major programs (F-15 and Harrier fighters, Apache helicopter) in 1991. The C-17 cargo transport is over budget and behind schedule — problems that resulted in the 1991 cancellation of the A-12 fighter program.

McDonnell Douglas has implemented a strict cost-control program and plans to sell its finance subsidiary (which could raise more than $400 million). But new bank borrowings ($373 million) have brought its debt ratio up to nearly 50%.

WHO

Chairman and CEO: John F. McDonnell, age 52, $577,791 pay
President: Gerald A. Johnston, age 59, $376,039 pay
SVP Finance: Herbert J. Lanese, age 45, $526,762 pay
VP Human Resources: Michael R. Becker
Auditors: Ernst & Young
Employees: 121,190

WHEN

Donald Douglas started the Davis-Douglas Company in the back of a Los Angeles barbershop in 1920 to build the Cloudster biplane for David Davis, who planned to fly it in the first nonstop transcontinental flight in 1921. When the attempt failed, Davis left the firm, which then became the Douglas Company. Many records were set in Douglas airplanes, including the first round-the-world flight (completed in 1924 by the US Army). The company was renamed Douglas Aircraft in 1928.

In 1935 Douglas introduced the twin-engined DC-3 airliner. Fast, rugged, and economical, the legendary DC-3 revolutionized air travel, and the company built over 10,000 as military transports during WWII. Douglas also built attack aircraft, such as the Dauntless dive bomber.

The DC-3 and its descendants enabled Douglas to dominate the airliner market until the advent of the Boeing 707 jetliner in the late 1950s. The DC-8 (1958) proved unable to compete with the 707, but the smaller DC-9 (1965) became Douglas's best seller and one of the world's most popular airliners.

Despite its success, the DC-9's development costs and slow sales of the DC-8 resulted in losses in 1966, leading Douglas to invite merger proposals from financially healthier companies. McDonnell Aircraft made the winning offer of $68.7 million in 1967.

James McDonnell had started his St. Louis–based company in 1939 mainly as a

supplier of aircraft parts. A series of fighters included the navy's first jet, the FH-1 (1945), and culminated in the famous F-4 Phantom II (1958). Like Douglas, which produced an upper stage for the Saturn moon rocket (1961) as well as the Delta expendable launch vehicle (1960), McDonnell also built missiles and spacecraft, including the Mercury and Gemini capsules of the early 1960s.

After the merger, the new McDonnell Douglas Corporation produced the DC-10 widebody airliner (1970), the Skylab space station (1973), and several fighter/attack aircraft (F-15, 1972; F/A-18, 1978; AV-8B, 1978). With the 1984 purchase of Hughes Helicopter, the company inherited production of the AH-64 Apache attack helicopter.

Although orders for airliners reached record levels in 1988 and 1989, the transport segment of McDonnell Douglas endured a $222 million operating loss in 1989 due to a reorganization and a production buildup for the MD-80 and the MD-11. The company experienced more disappointment in 1991 when the government cancelled the A-12 stealth program, costing McDonnell Douglas $350 million in pretax writeoffs for the 4th quarter of 1990. Additional losses related to the program could reach $850 million if the company fails to win its lawsuit against the government (filed along with partner General Dynamics in 1991), which challenges the government's aircraft procurement practices.

WHERE

HQ: PO Box 516, St. Louis, MO 63166-0516
Phone: 314-232-0232
Fax: 314-777-1739 (Personnel)

	1990 Sales	
	$ mil.	% of total
US government	6,723	41
Foreign (through US govt.)	3,538	22
Other	5,985	37
Total	**16,246**	**100**

WHAT

	1990 Sales		1990 Operating Income	
	$ mil.	% of total	$ mil.	% of total
Combat aircraft	5,830	36	46	25
Transport aircraft	5,812	36	(177)	(96)
Missiles, space & electronic systems	3,188	19	167	90
Financial services	619	4	100	54
Other	797	5	49	27
Adjustments	—	—	221	—
Total	**16,246**	**100**	**406**	**100**

Principal Operating Units
Douglas Aircraft Co. (MD-80, MD-90, MD-11 commercial transports, C-17 military transport)
McDonnell Aircraft Co. (F-15 Eagle, F/A-18 Hornet, AV-8B Harrier II fighters, T-45 Goshawk military trainer)
McDonnell Douglas Electronics Systems Co. (defense electronics, simulators, lasers)
McDonnell Douglas Helicopter Co. (AH-64 Apache attack helicopter)
McDonnell Douglas Missile Systems Co. (Harpoon antiship missile, Standoff Land Attack Missile, Tomahawk cruise missile)
McDonnell Douglas Space Systems Co. (Delta II launch vehicle, Payload Assist Module, systems for Space Station *Freedom*)

RANKINGS

24th in *Fortune* 500 Industrial Cos.
396th in *Business Week* 1000

KEY COMPETITORS

Airbus	Martin Marietta
Allied-Signal	Nissan
Boeing	Northrop
Daimler-Benz	Raytheon
General Dynamics	Rockwell
General Electric	Siemens
General Motors	Textron
Grumman	Thomson SA
Harris	Thorn EMI
Koor	United Technologies
Lockheed	

HOW MUCH

	9-Year Growth	1981	1982	1983	1984	1985	1986	1987	1988	1989	1990
Sales ($ mil.)	9.0%	7,454	7,412	8,242	9,819	11,618	12,772	13,289	15,069	14,581	16,246
Net income ($ mil.)	5.0%	177	215	275	325	346	278	313	350	(37)	275
Income as % of sales	—	2.4%	2.9%	3.3%	3.3%	3.0%	2.2%	2.4%	2.3%	(0.3%)	1.7%
Earnings per share ($)	5.5%	4.44	5.44	6.91	8.07	8.60	6.86	7.75	9.13	(0.97)	7.18
Stock price – high ($)	—	49.63	44.50	62.75	73.75	87.00	91.13	87.50	79.38	94.50	63.63
Stock price – low ($)	—	22.50	28.63	39.75	47.63	64.25	71.00	54.50	59.00	59.63	34.00
Stock price – close ($)	3.0%	29.75	42.00	59.25	72.25	74.25	71.25	59.50	75.25	61.25	38.88
P/E – high	—	11	8	9	9	10	13	11	9	—	9
P/E – low	—	5	5	6	6	7	10	7	6	—	5
Dividends per share ($)	11.5%	1.06	1.24	1.42	1.62	1.84	2.08	2.32	2.56	2.82	2.82
Book value per share ($)	8.8%	42.93	47.24	52.39	58.55	65.34	70.12	76.71	83.40	85.82	91.75

1990 Year-end:
Debt ratio: 49.7%
Return on equity: 8.1%
Cash (mil.): $226
Current ratio: —
Long-term debt (mil.): $3,466
No. of shares (mil.): 38
Dividends:
　1990 average yield: 7.3%
　1990 payout: 39.3%
Market value (mil.): $1,489

Stock Price History High/Low 1981–90

MCGRAW-HILL, INC.

OVERVIEW

New York–based McGraw-Hill is a diversified multimedia publishing and information services company. Services provided by the $1.9 billion company range from textbook and magazine publishing (*Business Week*, *BYTE*, etc.) to financial services (Standard & Poor's Ratings) to TV broadcasting.

The company's 61-year-old *Business Week* magazine, for the 16th year in a row, carried more ad pages in 1990 than any other in the US. The company's joint venture company, the Macmillan/McGraw-Hill School Publishing Company, is the largest US textbook publisher for the K-12 markets.

McGraw-Hill prides itself on using the latest in technology to disseminate information.

It was the first to produce compact discs with financial data on 12,000 public companies. It also produced (in partnership with Kodak and R. R. Donnelley) the first computerized college textbook that allows instructors to customize textbooks, a product that earned McGraw-Hill the 1990 "Innovator of the Year" award from XPLOR International (electronic printing association). Through its Compustat division, McGraw-Hill maintains an in-depth database of company financial information. (Many of the financial tables in this book were provided by Compustat.)

The McGraw family still owns over 5% of the company; members of it sit on the board and are active in management.

WHEN

Magazine publishers James McGraw (*Street Railway Journal*) and John Hill (*American Machinist* and *Locomotive Engineer*) formed the McGraw-Hill Book Company in 1909 in New York to publish scientific and technical books. Initially the 2 kept their magazines apart, but following Hill's death in 1916 the magazine segments were merged with McGraw-Hill. The company started its first year with a list of 200 titles; by 1919 it had grown to over 1,000, with McGraw-Hill well established in the higher-education market.

In the 1920s McGraw-Hill expanded its offerings beyond purely technical books and pioneered the risky but successful "send-no-money" plan, giving customers a free 10-day examination of its books. In 1929, 2 months before the stock market crash, McGraw-Hill started *Business Week* magazine, in which it expressed concerns about the economy's health — a view contrary to general opinion.

During the 1930s and 1940s McGraw-Hill continued to expand as a publisher of trade journals and college textbooks. It entered the trade publishing business in 1930 under the Whittlesey House name (changed to McGraw-Hill in 1950), but it was not until the 1950s that the trade division earned some distinc-

tion. Its biggest commercial success was *Betty Crocker's Picture Cook Book* (1947), which sold 2.3 million copies the first 2 years.

McGraw-Hill continued to grow in the 1960s and 1970s, acquiring Standard & Poor's, a business investment information service (1966); 4 TV stations from Time (1972); Datapro Research Corporation, a product information service (1976); and Data Resources Inc. (DRI), an economic forecasting service (1979). In 1979 McGraw-Hill successfully fended off a hotly contested $830 million takeover attempt by American Express.

In the 1980s McGraw-Hill focused on expansion of its electronic information services and acquisition of small, industry-specific publishing and information service companies. McGraw-Hill sold its 59-year-old trade books division in 1989. In 1989 S & P downgraded its parent company's common stock rating to A- after McGraw-Hill took a $152 million restructuring charge associated with its reorganization. In 1990 the company bought J.J. Kenny, a provider of municipal securities information. While the streamlining process resulted in higher profits in 1990, it could not counter the impact of the recession on 1991 revenues, which were down the first half of the year.

NYSE symbol: MHP
Fiscal year ends: December 31

Hoover's Rating **B**

WHO

Chairman, President, and CEO: Joseph L. Dionne, age 57, $1,028,644 pay
EVP Operations: Harold W. McGraw III, age 42, $510,587 pay
EVP Operations: Walter D. Serwatka, age 53, $510,587 pay
EVP and CFO: Robert J. Bahash, age 45, $390,661 pay
SVP Corporate Human Resources: Patrick M. Pavelski
Auditors: Ernst & Young
Employees: 13,868

WHERE

HQ: 1221 Ave. of the Americas, New York, NY 10020
Phone: 212-512-2000
Fax: 212-512-4871

WHAT

	1990 Sales		1990 Operating Income	
	$ mil.	% of total	$ mil.	% of total
Info. & pub. svcs.	747	39	127	35
Ed. & prof. pub.	551	28	78	22
Financial services	537	28	122	34
Broadcasting	104	5	34	9
Adjustments	—	—	(36)	—
Total	**1,939**	**100**	**325**	**100**

Information and Publication Services
Aviation Week Group (*Aviation Week & Space Technology* and Aviation/Aerospace Online)
Business Week Group (*Business Week*, Management Information Center, Executive Programs)
Computers and Communications Group (*BYTE*, Datapro)
Construction Information Group (F.W. Dodge Group)
Science and Technology Group (*Chemical Engineering* and *Modern Plastics*)

Educational and Professional Publishing
Education Group (college textbooks)
Legal Information Group (Shepard's)
Professional Publishing Group (international, medical, and health care books, magazines and book clubs)

Financial Services
DRI/McGraw-Hill (business and information services)
Kenny S&P (municipal securities market information)
S&P Information Group (S&P Equity Services, Compustat)
S&P Ratings Group
Tower Group (customs brokers and freight forwarding)

Broadcasting
KERO-TV (Bakersfield, CA)   KMGH-TV (Denver)
KGTV (San Diego)   WRTV (Indianapolis)

Joint Ventures
Macmillan/McGraw-Hill Publishing Co. (50%, joint venture with Maxwell Communications)
Rock-McGraw, Inc. (45%, owns company HQ with Rockefeller Group, Inc.)

HOW MUCH

	9-Year Growth	1981	1982	1983	1984	1985	1986	1987	1988	1989	1990
Sales ($ mil.)	6.4%	1,110	1,194	1,295	1,402	1,491	1,577	1,751	1,818	1,789	1,939
Net income ($ mil.)	6.5%	98	110	126	144	147	154	165	186	40	172
Income as % of sales	—	8.8%	9.2%	9.8%	10.3%	9.9%	9.8%	9.4%	10.2%	2.2%	8.9%
Earnings per share ($)	6.7%	1.97	2.20	2.52	2.86	2.92	3.04	3.27	3.83	0.82	3.53
Stock price – high ($)	—	28.00	40.50	53.88	48.75	52.00	64.00	84.50	76.00	86.13	61.13
Stock price – low ($)	—	19.69	22.44	35.00	34.00	39.75	46.50	43.00	46.75	53.50	39.88
Stock price – close ($)	8.2%	25.88	37.63	42.25	42.75	48.00	54.63	48.25	62.25	56.75	52.63
P/E – high	—	14	18	21	17	18	21	26	20	105	17
P/E – low	—	10	10	14	12	14	15	13	12	65	11
Dividends per share ($)	11.1%	0.84	0.94	1.08	1.24	1.40	1.52	1.68	1.84	2.05	2.16
Book value per share ($)	7.7%	9.97	10.86	12.29	13.87	15.40	17.04	17.11	19.01	18.08	19.50

1990 Year-end:
Debt ratio: 34.7%
Return on equity: 18.8%
Cash (mil.): $21
Current ratio: 1.14
Long-term debt (mil.): $508
No. of shares (mil.): 49
Dividends:
  1990 average yield: 4.1%
  1990 payout: 61.2%
Market value (mil.): $2,575

Stock Price History
High/Low 1981–90

RANKINGS

218th in *Fortune* 500 Industrial Cos.
224th in *Business Week* 1000

KEY COMPETITORS

Bertelsmann	Hearst	Paramount
Commerce	Knight-Ridder	Pearson
Clearing House	Lloyd's of London	Reed
Dow Jones	Maxwell	Reuters
Dun & Bradstreet	Mead	Thomson Corp.
H&R Block	News Corp.	Time Warner

MCI COMMUNICATIONS CORPORATION

NYSE symbol: MCIC
Fiscal year ends: December 31

OVERVIEW

MCI, headquartered in the nation's capital, is the US's 2nd largest long-distance telephone company after AT&T, providing long-distance telephone service within the US and from the US to more than 180 countries. The company also offers long-distance telephone service for overseas callers. Although MCI provides fax and electronic mail services, more than 90% of the company's revenue is generated by long-distance telephone calls. The company expects to have a 100% digital communications network by the end of 1991.

MCI is continuing its constant barrage of new niche service introductions in an effort to differentiate itself from its competitors. Aggressive promotion has enabled the company to garner a 15% US market share in a rapidly growing business. Competition remains intense as AT&T fights to maintain its dominant share of the long-distance business. Competition and recession have combined to inhibit earnings progress.

MCI's indefatigable chairman is William McGowan, who returned from a 1987 heart transplant operation to manage the company.

WHEN

MCI's history is tied to a series of legal actions against AT&T. In 1963 John Goeken submitted a request to construct a microwave radio system between St. Louis and Chicago on behalf of his mobile radio company, Microwave Communications, Inc. At that time AT&T was acting as a monopoly. The monopoly had not been explicitly granted, but FCC authorization was required for MCI to compete with AT&T. Further, MCI would have to win the right to connect to AT&T's Bell companies.

In 1966 the FCC ruled that MCI was qualified to provide services. William McGowan, a consultant looking for new business opportunities, obtained new financing for the company in 1968. He served as chairman of newly named MCI Communications while Goeken independently went on to found Airfone, which provides air-to-ground service. In 1969 the FCC ruled that MCI could operate, with no assurances that it could expand its network or obtain interconnection to the Bell companies. After appealing, AT&T withdrew its arguments, and MCI began service in 1972.

By 1973 MCI's network reached more than 40 cities but could not provide switched services, which required connection to the Bell system. MCI instead provided dedicated services between user-owned switches. In 1973 MCI won interconnection rights at AT&T facilities, prompting a new MCI switched service

known as Execunet. Finally, in 1976, MCI won interconnection rights at its own facilities.

In response to Execunet, AT&T filed interconnection tariffs, which eliminated the cost savings MCI had provided to its customers. In 1978 MCI was forced to fight AT&T on antitrust grounds. This battle continued until 1983, when the US Court of Appeals overturned a $1.8 billion settlement in MCI's favor, concluding that AT&T had not engaged in predatory pricing.

MCI has been the 2nd largest long-distance provider since it began offering service and has continually introduced services that compete directly with AT&T. Major acquisitions include Western Union International (1982), a telex provider; Satellite Business Systems (1986), a satellite-based long-distance carrier; and RCA Global Communications (1988), a data communications service provider.

Beginning in 1986, as its price advantage over AT&T shriveled, MCI invested heavily in digital upgrades to its network and back-office computer systems. The latter enabled MCI to get a jump on the competition in customized billing and calling plans. In 1990 the company purchased Telecom*USA, which had slightly more than 1% of the long-distance market, and agreed to build a transatlantic fiber optic cable with British Telecom.

WHO

Chairman and CEO: William G. McGowan, age 63, $1,443,899 pay
President and COO: Bert C. Roberts, Jr., age 48, $1,112,457 pay
EVP and CFO: O. Gene Gabbard, age 50, $415,425 pay
EVP: Richard T. Liebhaber, age 55, $523,023 pay
EVP: Eugene Eidenberg, age 51
EVP: Daniel F. Akerson, age 42, $490,452 pay
SVP Human Resources: John H. Zimmerman
Auditors: Price Waterhouse
Employees: 24,509

WHERE

HQ: 1133 Nineteenth St. NW, Washington DC 20036
Phone: 202-872-1600
Fax: 202-887-2154

MCI operates throughout the US and through offices in 50 other countries.

WHAT

Long Distance Services
Call Canada, Call Europe, Call Mexico, Call Pacific (discount plans)
Dial 1 access
Friends & Family (flexible consumer call plan)
MCI 800 Service (inbound WATS-like service)
MCI 900 Service (caller paid service)
MCI CALL USA (MCI operator-assisted, US inbound call service)
MCI Global Communications Service
MCI Mail (electronic mail)
MCI Preferred (small-business package)
MCI PRISM (WATS-like service)
MCI Vision (comprehensive business service package)
MCI Vnet (private line service)
MCI WATS

Messaging Services
MCI fax (fax transmission and management)
MCI mail (electronic mail, telex services)

RANKINGS

9th in *Fortune* 100 Diversified Service Cos.
86th in *Business Week* 1000

KEY COMPETITORS

AT&T
British Telecom
Cable & Wireless
GTE
Metromedia
United Telecom

HOW MUCH

	9-Year Growth	1981	1982	1983	1984	1985	1986	1987	1988	1989	1990
Sales ($ mil.)	35.3%	506	1,073	1,665	1,959	2,542	3,592	3,939	5,137	6,471	7,680
Net income ($ mil.)	14.8%	86	171	156	59	140	(431)	85	356	603	299
Income as % of sales	—	17.1%	15.9%	9.4%	3.0%	5.5%	(12.0%)	2.2%	6.9%	9.3%	3.9%
Earnings per share ($)	10.5%	0.43	0.82	0.67	0.25	0.59	(1.57)	0.30	1.26	2.26	1.06
Stock price – high ($)	—	9.03	22.88	28.44	16.25	11.38	13.25	12.13	24.50	48.50	44.88
Stock price – low ($)	—	2.72	6.53	12.63	6.00	7.38	6.00	5.00	9.38	21.63	18.50
Stock price – close ($)	9.7%	8.50	18.19	14.38	7.50	11.25	6.25	9.38	22.63	44.00	19.63
P/E – high	—	21	28	42	65	19	—	40	19	21	42
P/E – low	—	6	8	19	24	13	—	17	7	10	17
Dividends per share ($)	—	0.00	0.00	0.00	0.00	0.00	0.00	0.00	0.00	0.00	0.10
Book value per share ($)	24.8%	1.25	3.31	4.87	5.11	5.59	4.43	4.73	5.59	7.98	9.21

1990 Year-end:
Debt ratio: 57.4%
Return on equity: 12.3%
Cash (mil.): $231
Current ratio: 0.75
Long-term debt (mil.): $3,147
No. of shares (mil.): 254
Dividends:
　1990 average yield: 0.5%
　1990 payout: 9.4%
Market value (mil.): $4,985

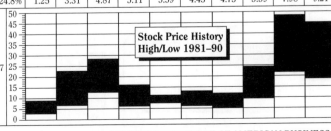

Stock Price History High/Low 1981–90

MCKESSON CORPORATION

OVERVIEW

San Francisco–based McKesson Corporation is the nation's largest distributor of drugs, with a 27% market share, and a leading distributor of wholesale health and beauty aid products. The drug distribution segment generated 84% of the company's total revenues in 1990. The service merchandise segment distributes health and beauty aids and general products and has an equity investment in an office products distribution company. Through its 50% interest in Medis, the company distributes drugs and health and beauty products throughout Canada.

The water segment processes, delivers, and sells bottled drinking water through stores and vending machines in the sunbelt and western states. Armor All Products Corporation, a majority owned subsidiary, sells automotive and household appearance-protection products. The PCS segment provides prescription drug claims processing and drug benefit plan design services.

Employees, through the employee stock ownership plan, own 20.4% of the company's common stock.

NYSE symbol: MCK
Fiscal year ends: March 31

Hoover's Rating **B-**

WHO

Chairman and CEO: Alan Seelenfreund, age 54, $826,733 pay
President and COO: Rex R. Malson, age 59, $826,733 pay
VP Finance: Garret A. Scholz, age 51
VP Personnel: Ronald C. Pohls, age 55
Auditors: Deloitte & Touche
Employees: 13,300

WHERE

HQ: McKesson Plaza, One Post St., San Francisco, CA 94104
Phone: 415-983-8300
Fax: 415-983-7160

McKesson and its subsidiaries operate throughout the US. Medis distributes drugs throughout Canada.

WHEN

In Manhattan in 1833, John McKesson formed a company that in 1853 he renamed McKesson-Robbins to recognize assistant Daniel Robbins's contributions. Having initially opened a drugstore, he expanded into chemicals and drug manufacturing. Because of differences between the descendants of McKesson and Robbins, the company was sold to F. Donald Coster in 1926.

Coster was actually twice-convicted felon Philip Musica, who purchased McKesson-Robbins with fraudulently obtained bank loans. For over a decade his real identity was a secret — from all but a single blackmailer. By 1930 McKesson-Robbins had wholesale drug operations in 33 states serving over 15,000 retail druggists and employing over 6,000 people. The company appeared to be growing, but a treasurer discovered a Musica-orchestrated accounting scam and a cash shortfall of $3 million. Faced with certain exposure, Musica committed suicide in 1939; bankruptcy followed.

McKesson & Robbins emerged from bankruptcy in 1941. By the early 1960s it was acquiring drug suppliers. In a 1967 hostile takeover, San Francisco–based Foremost Dairies bought McKesson & Robbins to form Foremost-McKesson. Over the next 20 years, the company bought wholesalers in the liquor, chemical, and software industries and several

bottled water companies; entered and exited homebuilding; and sold Foremost Dairies (1983) in order to focus on distribution businesses.

The company, renamed McKesson in 1984, continued to build its drug wholesaling business through acquisitions. By 1985 McKesson was the US's largest distributor of drug and medical equipment, wine and liquor, bottled water, and car waxes and polishes. A 1988 antitrust action blocked McKesson's acquisition of drug and consumer goods wholesaler Alco Health Services, which claimed that the combined companies would control 90% of drug distribution in some states.

After becoming CEO in 1986, Thomas Field sold McKesson's liquor and chemical distributors to narrow the company's focus. After Field resigned in 1989, McKesson created a 2-man Office of the Chief Executive and named Alan Seelenfreund and Rex Malson to replace Field.

The drug distribution business grew even stronger in 1989 when McKesson won the contract to supply the nearly 1,000 Wal-Mart stores and in 1990 when it acquired 50% of Medis, a leading Canadian drug distributor, buying the remaining 50% in 1991. Also in 1991, to improve efficiency, the company restructured all 5 segments and created the McKesson Distribution Group linking the drug segment, the service merchandise segment, and Medis.

WHAT

	1990 Sales		1990 Operating Income	
	$ mil.	% of total	$ mil.	% of total
Drug distribution	7,104	84	162	65
Service merchandisng	841	10	24	10
Water	237	3	24	10
Appearance-protection products	134	2	13	5
Prescription claims processing	96	1	25	10
Adjustments	9	—	(23)	—
Total	**8,421**	**100**	**225**	**100**

Major Brand Names and Service Marks

Drug Distribution
Econolink (hospital on-line ordering system)
Economost (inventory management and ordering system)
Great Valu$ (special promotions)
MajoRx (cost management program)
Medalist (health and beauty aids)
QUANTUM Alert (drug utilization review program)
SunMark (home health care products)
3 PM (pharmacy computer systems)
Valu-Rite Pharmacies (cooperative marketing)
Zee Medical (first-aid supplies to industry)

Service Merchandising
Bright Idea (kitchenware)
Valu-Star (health and beauty aids)

Water
Alhambra   Crystal   Wallaroo
Aqua-Vend   Sparkletts

Appearance-Protection Products
Armor All (83%; car cleaner, wax, and protectant)
No. 7 (engine appearance and maintenance)
Rain Dance (car wax)
Rally (car wax)

Prescription Claims Processing
Recap (electronic drug claims processing system)

RANKINGS

8th in *Fortune* 100 Diversified Service Cos.
457th in *Business Week* 1000

KEY COMPETITORS

Abbott Labs	Coca-Cola	Source
Amway	Fleming	Perrier
Avon	Johnson &	Super Valu
Baxter	Johnson	Teledyne
BSN	Premark	

HOW MUCH

Fiscal year ends March of following year	9-Year Growth	1981	1982	1983	1984	1985	1986	1987	1988	1989	1990
Sales ($ mil.)	7.2%	4,493	4,054	4,260	4,887	6,264	6,672	7,283	7,046	7,791	8,421
Net income ($ mil.)	4.9%	69	63	63	64	78	94	95	94	99	105
Income as % of sales	—	1.5%	1.6%	1.5%	1.3%	1.2%	1.4%	1.3%	1.3%	1.3%	1.3%
Earnings per share ($)	2.0%	1.94	1.72	1.63	1.67	1.85	2.04	2.14	2.14	2.10	2.31
Stock price – high ($)	—	20.19	22.63	25.50	22.13	26.75	35.25	40.13	35.88	39.75	38.38
Stock price – low ($)	—	15.69	14.50	18.75	16.19	18.50	24.75	23.25	25.75	29.63	26.88
Stock price – close ($)	7.1%	18.38	20.13	19.94	19.13	26.19	31.75	26.50	31.13	35.63	34.00
P/E – high	—	10	13	16	13	15	17	19	17	19	17
P/E – low	—	8	8	12	10	10	12	11	12	14	12
Dividends per share ($)	4.0%	1.12	1.20	1.20	1.20	1.20	1.26	1.28	1.44	1.44	1.60
Book value per share ($)	(0.2%)	14.50	14.85	15.13	15.20	16.74	17.73	16.75	17.01	14.05	14.27

1990 Year-end:
Debt ratio: 44.2%
Return on equity: 16.3%
Cash (mil.): $146
Current ratio: 1.25
Long-term debt (mil.): $534
No. of shares (mil.): 38
Dividends:
    1990 average yield: 4.7%
    1990 payout: 69.3%
Market value (mil.): $1,298

Stock Price History High/Low 1981–90

MCKINSEY & CO.

OVERVIEW

According to one partner of the world's largest independent management consulting firm, "There are only three great institutions left in the world: the Marines, the Catholic Church and McKinsey."

McKinsey & Co. practically invented the profession of management consulting (now a $22 billion business) and is the US's oldest consulting firm. Its meticulous approach to information gathering, its discretion, and its cultivated mystique have given it a reputation as the ultimate source of reliable, objective advice.

It has worked for over 150 of the largest 500 companies in America, and its 2,300 alumni are woven into the fabric of American business life. Tom Peters, author of *In Search of Excellence*, was with McKinsey until 1981. The new head of American Express, Harvey

Golub, and his predecessor are also alumni. The head of its Tokyo office, Kenichi Ohmae, is one of the best-known and most widely published commentators on world economic and business trends. McKinsey also has a reputation for generosity in its *pro bono* work, which reaps added benefits in the form of low-key marketing and relationship building.

One of the earliest consulting firms to recognize the globalization of the economy, McKinsey has survived challenges to its dominance (several of the consulting arms of the Big 6 accounting firms generate higher revenues) to retain its claim as the consummate management consulting firm.

The company is managed by a team elected by the firm's associates, who make up the majority of McKinsey's consulting staff.

WHEN

McKinsey & Co. was founded in Chicago in 1926 by University of Chicago accounting professor James O. McKinsey as a vehicle for his management consulting practice. The firm developed a reputation for collecting and analyzing data to provide its clients with advice on the overall structure and operation of their companies. After McKinsey's death in the 1930s, the firm moved to New York.

In 1950, with billings at $2 million, Marvin Bower became managing partner. He was to revolutionize the firm and the consulting industry by emphasizing the "big picture" rather than specific operating problems. He began hiring staff straight out of the nation's most prestigious business schools, a recruiting model still followed today by McKinsey and other consulting firms. Bower also implemented the "up or out" policy that requires employees who are not continuously promoted to leave the firm. Although fewer than one in 11 of all starting consultants become partners, the system has created a vast network of alumni who send business to the firm.

By 1959 Bower had expanded the firm to 5 US offices and opened the first overseas office in London, soon followed by others in Europe staffed by locals. When Bower retired as managing partner in 1967, firm sales had reached $20 million, and McKinsey was the preeminent management consulting firm. During the late 1960s and 1970s the firm continued to expand internationally. In 1976 Ronald Daniel became managing director and

immediately faced the task of fighting off several rapidly growing competitors that had begun attracting McKinsey's clients and potential staff members. Daniel created specialty practices to complement the firm's traditional emphasis on business generalism and used McKinsey's presence overseas to expand its foreign revenue base. He also changed the firm's secretive attitude about its work and encouraged publications by staff members. The firm rode the consulting wave of the 1980s, as the total value of the market rose from just $3 billion in 1980 to $22 billion in 1990. When Daniel retired in 1988, McKinsey's consulting staff was 1,800, revenues were $620 million, and 50% of billings came from overseas offices (which outnumbered US offices 2 to one).

In 1988 Frederick W. Gluck, a graduate of Manhattan College and New York University with 2 engineering degrees (and no MBA), became managing director.

While the 1980 recession had provided the impetus for consulting's boom during the 1980s, the recession of 1990 and 1991 hit the consultants hard. As the demands of clients shift from mere analysis into implementation, McKinsey has responded by upgrading its technical side through acquisition of the Information Consulting Group of Washington, DC. It has also begun to emphasize its large store of consulting information through use of its internal database, PDNet.

Private company
Fiscal year ends: December 31

WHO

Managing Director: Frederick W. Gluck, age 55
CFO: James Rogers
Partner in charge of human resources: Jerome Vascellaro
Employees: 4,500

WHERE

HQ: 55 E. 52nd St., New York, NY 10022
Phone: 212-446-7000
Fax: 212-446-8575

McKinsey has 48 offices in 25 countries.

	1990 Estimated Sales	
	$ mil.	% of total
US	330	37
Foreign	570	63
Total	**900**	**100**

WHAT

Areas of Practice
Cost reduction and profit improvement
Electronic data processing
Management controls
Manufacturing and operations management
Marketing
Operations research
Organizational change
Strategic planning

Representative Clients
Alcoa
American Express
AT&T
Citicorp
Deutsche Bank
First Interstate Bank
Ford
General Electric
General Motors
Hewlett-Packard
Levi Strauss
Merrill Lynch
Mobil
New York City Transit Authority
Nissan
Pacific Gas & Electric
PepsiCo
Royal Dutch/Shell
Wells Fargo Bank

***Pro Bono* Clients**
Golden Gate National Park Association
Greater Cleveland Regional Transit Authority
San Francisco Symphony

RANKINGS

291st in *Forbes* 400 US Private Cos.

KEY COMPETITORS

Arthur Andersen	General Motors
Coopers & Lybrand	KPMG
Deloitte & Touche	Marsh & McLennan
Ernst & Young	Price Waterhouse

HOW MUCH

	8-Year Growth	1981	1982	1983	1984	1985	1986	1987	1988	1989	1990
Estimated sales ($ mil.)	25.6%	—	145	—	—	350	400	510	620	635	900
Employees		—	—	—	—	—	—	—	—	4,000	4,500

Estimated Sales ($ mil.) 1982–90

THE MEAD CORPORATION

OVERVIEW

Mead, America's 9th largest forest products company, leads in the production of paper-based school and office supplies under the brand names Mead, Cambridge, Gilbert, and Ampad. About 17% of the company's raw materials are supplied by its 1.38 million acres of US timberland.

Mead is also a leading electronic publisher through its Mead Data Central division, which developed the legal database LEXIS and its companion news database NEXIS, on which *Hoover's Handbook*s are available. Both are widely used by lawyers and other professionals for full-text, on-line research. Sales of this segment rose from $308 million in 1988 to $440 million in 1990.

Mead's Cycolor products are used in color copiers and slide printers of leading manufacturers. Because growth in this sector was much slower than expected, in 1990 Mead wrote down its investment in color imaging. This, and writedowns of other nonproductive assets (totaling $88.5 million), combined with the soft demand for pulp and paper products in 1990 to produce a 51% decline in earnings for that year. Mead reduced capital spending by 29% in 1991 and postponed plans to build a new major pulp and papermaking facility. The company also implemented a voluntary early retirement program to help control costs.

NYSE symbol: MEA
Fiscal year ends: December 31

 Hoover's Rating C

WHO

Chairman and CEO: Burnell R. Roberts, age 63, $694,779 pay
VC: Steven C. Mason, age 54, $504,004 pay (prior to promotion)
President and COO: Samuel S. Benedict
SVP and CFO: William A. Enouen, age 62, $290,572 pay
VP Human Resources: Charles J. Mazza, age 48
Auditors: Deloitte & Touche
Employees: 21,600

WHERE

HQ: Mead World Headquarters, Courthouse Plaza NE, Dayton, OH 45463
Phone: 513-495-6323
Fax: 513-461-2424

WHEN

Daniel Mead established Mead Paper in 1882 when he became the sole owner of a small Dayton, Ohio, paper mill. The company faltered after his death in 1891 until a grandson, George Mead, took over in 1905. The company raised cash by going public in 1906 and was operating in the black by 1915. Over the next 40 years Mead expanded by buying and building pulp and paper mills in the East and the South.

After WWII Mead continued to grow by acquiring other paper companies and packaging firms in both the US and Europe. Jackson Box of Cincinnati (1955) was the beginning of Mead's container division; Atlanta Paper (1957) began the packaging division, which originated the 6-pack carrier. Mead began diversifying in the 1960s, eventually buying coal, furniture, fabric, and steel and rubber products companies. The 1966 purchase of Westab of Dayton, Ohio, began the school and office supply division. In 1968 Mead bought a small data processing company, Data Corporation, which became the company's electronic publishing division (Mead Data Central). In the mid-1970s Mead Data Central introduced LEXIS, the largest legal research database, and NEXIS, the largest full-text database of news and business information.

After a protracted public battle for control, Mead managed to avoid a takeover attempt by Occidental Petroleum in the late 1970s. In the early 1980s the recession caused a slump in demand for paper products, and Mead lost $62 million in 1982 — its first loss in 44 years. In 1982 and 1983 Mead shed many divisions to better focus on forest products and electronic publishing. Mead school products were top sellers in the 1980s, those marked with the Smurfs and Garfield the Cat accounting for about 30% of the division's earnings in 1983. Recent acquisitions include Micromedex (medical database, 1985), Ampad (office supplies, 1986), Dataline (financial information, 1987), Zellerbach (paper distribution, 1988), and Michie (legal publishing, 1989). In 1988 Mead introduced Cycolor, a copier paper that reproduces color by an inexpensive technique and has entered joint ventures with others, including Seiko of Japan, to produce color copiers and printers.

The company added a new line of recycled school and office products (Green Cycle) in 1989. In 1990 Mead's newly expanded Coated Natural Kraft (laminated paperboard) machine was started up. It represented a $580 million investment — the company's largest ever.

WHAT

	1990 Sales		1990 Operating Income	
	$ mil.	% of total	$ mil.	% of total
Pkg. & paperboard	970	20	97	32
Distrib. & school & office prods.	2,184	46	(2)	(1)
Electronic pub.	440	9	28	9
Paper	1,178	25	185	60
Adjustments	—	—	(4)	—
Total	**4,772**	**100**	**304**	**100**

Packaging and Paperboard
Coated Natural Kraft packaging board
Corrugated shipping containers

Distribution and School and Office Products
Ampad and Cambridge office products
Filler paper
Wirebound notebooks
Looseleaf binders
Portfolios
Zellerbach (distributor of papers, packaging)

Electronic Publishing
Jurisoft (legal computer software)
LEXIS/NEXIS (on-line databases)
The Michie Co. (legal references)

Paper
Carbonless paper
Coated and uncoated printing papers

Decorative laminating papers
Offset printing paper
Premium text and cover paper (Gilbert)
Technical and specialty papers (Gilbert)

Forest Products Affiliates
Northwood Forest Industries Ltd. (50%, pulp manufacturing joint venture with Noranda Forest Inc.)
Northwood Panelboard Co. (50%, waferboard manufacturing joint venture with Noranda Forest Inc.)

Other Activities
Cycolor desktop copier and slide printer

HOW MUCH

	9-Year Growth	1981	1982	1983	1984	1985	1986	1987	1988	1989	1990
Sales ($ mil.)	5.7%	2,900	2,667	2,367	2,720	2,740	3,218	4,209	4,464	4,612	4,772
Net income ($ mil.)	(0.1%)	107	(62)	30	139	94	109	218	364	216	106
Income as % of sales	—	3.7%	(2.3%)	1.3%	5.1%	3.4%	3.4%	5.2%	8.2%	4.7%	2.2%
Earnings per share ($)	(1.5%)	1.96	(1.19)	0.52	2.27	1.51	1.75	3.47	5.54	3.33	1.71
Stock price – high ($)	—	16.38	11.63	21.00	20.63	22.44	30.44	48.38	49.50	46.63	39.50
Stock price – low ($)	—	10.50	6.75	9.38	13.56	16.81	21.25	21.00	29.00	34.25	19.50
Stock price – close ($)	9.4%	11.50	9.38	19.38	17.13	22.19	27.31	33.88	39.00	36.75	25.75
P/E – high	—	8	—	41	9	15	17	14	9	14	23
P/E – low	—	5	—	18	6	11	12	6	5	10	11
Dividends per share ($)	0.1%	0.96	0.88	0.50	0.53	0.60	0.60	0.65	0.74	0.85	0.97
Book value per share ($)	5.1%	16.84	14.15	14.30	15.72	16.63	16.91	19.85	23.95	26.55	26.28

1990 Year-end:
Debt ratio: 45.1%
Return on equity: 6.5%
Cash (mil.): $21
Current ratio: 1.42
Long-term debt (mil.): $1,257
No. of shares (mil.): 58
Dividends:
 1990 average yield: 3.8%
 1990 payout: 56.7%
Market value (mil.): $1,501

Stock Price History High/Low 1981–90

RANKINGS

109th in *Fortune* 500 Industrial Cos.
369th in *Business Week* 1000

KEY COMPETITORS

ADP
Boise Cascade
Champion International
Citicorp
Commerce Clearing House
Dow Jones
Fletcher Challenge

Georgia-Pacific
H&R Block
International Paper
James River
Kimberly-Clark
Knight-Ridder
Maxwell

McGraw-Hill
Nobel
Paramount
Reed
Reuters
Scott
Thomson Corp.
Weyerhaeuser

MELLON BANK CORPORATION

NYSE symbol: MEL
Fiscal year ends: December 31

Hoover's Rating **C-**

OVERVIEW

Mellon Bank is the 25th largest US commercial banking organization, with assets of $28.8 billion. Mellon has 388 domestic banking branches. It strives for balance in 3 basic lines of business: retail banking, wholesale and middle-market banking, and service products.

Retail banking added $119 million to 1990 net income. Geographically, Mellon is the largest commercial banking organization in Pennsylvania since taking over 54 PSFS branches in the Philadelphia area in the largest acquisition in Mellon history. By 1992 the company hopes to add branches in 22 Pennsylvania supermarkets. Its retail and middle-market business is also strong in Delaware and Maryland.

Wholesale and middle-market banking, with $109 million in 1990 profits, provides financing to large corporations, midsized companies in the Central Atlantic region, and governments. The bank says that after years of struggle with losses, it has eliminated the drag on earnings caused by loans to developing nations. However, back home, the company lost $253 million on real estate loans in 1990.

Mellon's 3rd sector, service products, contributed $140 million to 1990 net income and includes trust and investment services, cash management, and data processing.

WHO

Chairman, President, and CEO: Frank V. Cahouet, age 58, $1,116,500 pay
EVP and CFO: Steven G. Elliott, age 44
EVP Human Resources: D. Michael Roark
Auditors: KPMG Peat Marwick
Employees: 16,400

WHERE

HQ: One Mellon Bank Center, Pittsburgh, PA 15258-0001
Phone: 412-234-5000
Fax: 412-234-6265

Mellon has operations in 15 states and 6 foreign countries.

	1990 Assets	
	$ mil.	% of total
US	26,497	92
Europe	628	2
North America	861	3
Asia-Pacific	726	3
Latin America	70	—
Middle East & Africa	37	—
Adjustments	(57)	—
Total	**28,762**	**100**

WHEN

Judge Thomas Mellon founded T. Mellon and Sons in 1869. In 1882 at age 69, the judge turned over control of the bank to his son, Andrew, who 5 years later gave half of it to his brother Richard B. In 1902 T. Mellon and Sons became a national bank named Mellon National Bank.

Under Andrew Mellon the bank was instrumental in financing Pittsburgh businesses. Mellon investments by Andrew and Richard included Alcoa, Westinghouse, Bethlehem Steel, Pullman, Pittsburgh Coal, Pittsburgh Plate Glass, Koppers, and Carborundum. The bank's most successful investment was in an oil company that became Gulf Oil.

In 1921 Andrew went to Washington to serve as Secretary of Treasury under Presidents Harding, Coolidge, and Hoover. Richard B. assumed the presidency of Mellon National Bank. About a year before Andrew left, Richard B.'s son Richard K. Mellon had joined the bank as a messenger.

In anticipation of branch banking becoming federal law, Richard B. in 1929 formed Mellbank, a holding company of various banks in which the Mellons had a stake. Richard K. was assigned to manage Mellbank.

Richard B. died at the age of 75, and a few months later in 1934 Richard K. was elected president of Mellon National Bank. In 1946 Mellon merged with Union Trust Company to form Mellon National Bank & Trust. In 1967 Richard K. became honorary chairman, ending the Mellon family's near-century-long management of the bank. In 1972 the bank created a holding company, Mellon National Corporation (current name adopted 1984).

In 1983 under CEO J. David Barnes, the bank acquired Girard Bank and renamed the Philadelphia bank Mellon Bank East. Mellon, set back by loans to oil companies, the Third World, and real estate developers, reported the first loss in its history, $60 million for the first quarter of 1987, and cut dividends. The board and the Mellon family forced Barnes to resign, and Frank V. Cahouet became CEO.

Cahouet is credited with turning the bank around. He froze wages and increased loan-loss reserves. In 1990 Mellon Bank completed acquisition of 54 branches of PSFS, a Philadelphia-area savings institution. The company in 1990 bailed out of its consumer finance business in Chicago, concentrating its retail efforts on the Central Atlantic region.

Under a new Pennsylvania law permitting branch banking, in 1991 the company plans to consolidate its Keystone State branches into its main subsidiary, Mellon Bank, N.A.

WHAT

	1990 Assets	
	$ mil.	% of total
Cash & due from banks	2,594	9
Interest-bearing deposits	425	1
Securites for resale & federal funds sold	423	1
Trading account securities	99	1
Investment securities	4,614	16
Loans	18,738	65
Credit loss reserve	(525)	(2)
Customer acceptance liability	160	1
Other	2,234	8
Total	**28,762**	**100**

Financial Services
Capital markets products
Corporate banking
Credit cards
Data processing services
Deposit accounts
Leasing
Money market accounts
Money transfer
Real estate loans
Trust and investment management

RANKINGS

25th in *Fortune* 100 Commercial Banking Cos.
506th in *Business Week* 1000

HOW MUCH

	9-Year Growth	1981	1982	1983	1984	1985	1986	1987	1988	1989	1990
Assets ($ mil.)	5.1%	18,448	20,294	26,433	30,603	33,406	34,499	30,525	31,153	31,467	28,762
Net income ($ mil.)	4.7%	116	134	184	159	202	183	(844)	(65)	181	174
Income as % of assets	—	0.6%	0.7%	0.7%	0.5%	0.6%	0.5%	(2.8%)	(0.2%)	0.6%	0.6%
Earnings per share ($)	(7.8%)	5.88	6.83	7.44	5.64	7.13	6.14	(31.19)	(3.65)	3.33	2.83
Stock price – high ($)	—	40.00	44.75	56.50	52.00	56.50	72.50	58.00	33.25	38.13	30.00
Stock price – low ($)	—	30.88	27.50	36.75	33.50	44.50	51.88	25.13	22.75	25.00	17.63
Stock price – close ($)	(4.7%)	36.75	37.88	51.00	46.75	52.13	55.38	27.00	25.00	28.63	23.75
P/E – high	—	7	7	8	9	8	12	—	—	11	11
P/E – low	—	5	4	5	6	6	8	—	—	8	6
Dividends per share ($)	(4.4%)	2.09	2.24	2.44	2.60	2.68	2.76	1.74	1.40	1.40	1.40
Book value per share ($)	(5.6%)	49.69	54.19	53.62	56.21	60.39	63.68	30.57	30.14	33.47	29.43

1990 Year-end:
Return on equity: 9.0%
Equity as % of assets: 5.8%
Cash (mil.): $3,019
Long-term debt (mil.): $1,420
No. of shares (mil.): 44
Dividends:
    1990 average yield: 5.9%
    1990 payout: 49.5%
Market value (mil.): $1,044
Sales (mil.): $3,477

Stock Price History
High/Low 1981–90

KEY COMPETITORS

H.F. Ahmanson	Citicorp
Banc One	Continental Bank
Bank of Boston	First Chicago
Bank of New York	First Fidelity
BankAmerica	Fleet/Norstar
Bankers Trust	Household International
Canadian Imperial	J.P. Morgan
Chase Manhattan	PNC Financial
Chemical Banking	Other money-center banks

MELVILLE CORPORATION

OVERVIEW

The Melville Corporation, comprising 14 different store chains, is America's largest specialty store retailer (after Woolworth) and one of the few to succeed in diverse product lines, including apparel, footwear, prescription drugs, toys, and household furnishings. The company has started new chains from scratch and bought small chains with national potential, usually keeping and supporting acquired management talent. Melville leases its 42 million square feet of store space primarily in regional malls and strip shopping centers. The

company manufactures men's shoes in one factory and furniture in 5 factories.

Melville has a compounded annual growth rate of 16% in sales over the past 25 years. Unlike the growth of other retailers, Melville's growth has come without great debt (17.6% debt ratio). Dividends have been declared for 75 consecutive years. Melville adopted an employee stock ownership plan in 1989, which has put over 6% of the company's stock into the hands of its employees.

NYSE symbol: MES
Fiscal year ends: December 31

Hoover's Rating **A**

WHO

Chairman, President, and CEO: Stanley P. Goldstein, age 56, $1,214,800 pay
EVP: Michael A. Friedheim, age 47, $751,900 pay
EVP and CFO: Robert D. Huth, age 45, $674,100 pay
Group VP: Jerald S. Politzer, age 45, $608,400 pay
VP Human Resources: Frederick A. Postelle, age 45
Auditors: KPMG Peat Marwick
Employees: 119,000

WHEN

In 1892 shoe supplier Frank Melville took over 3 New York shoe stores when their owner left town owing him money, forming Melville Shoe. During WWI Ward Melville, Frank's son and vice-president of the firm, served in the Quartermaster Corps's shoe and leather division under shoe manufacturer J. Frank McElwain. The 2 men devised the merchandising scheme of mass-producing shoes for distribution through a chain of low-price stores. Melville opened the first of its Thom McAn (from the name of a Scottish professional golfer) stores, for which McElwain provided the shoes, in New York in 1922. There were 370 stores in the chain by 1927.

By 1931 Melville operated 476 shoe stores under the names John Ward, Thom McAn, Rival, and Courdaye and had income of $1.2 million on sales of over $26 million. In 1939 Melville bought the McElwain factory, consolidating production and distribution into one corporation. By 1958 Melville was operating 1,034 stores, 796 of them Thom McAn stores, but profits were declining because of changes in customer tastes and shifting populations.

Melville met the challenge of change, moving stores from urban areas to the suburbs and adding more fashionable merchandise to existing lines. The company's Meldisco division began leasing space for shoe sales operations in S. S. Kresge's Kmart discount department stores in 1961. In 1968 the company launched

its Chess King (young men's apparel) and Foxwood (young women's apparel) stores. Melville bought the Consumer Value Stores chain (CVS, drugstores) in 1969.

In 1975 S.S. Kresge demanded a 49% equity interest in all Meldisco subsidiaries operating in Kmart stores. Melville accepted the terms of the new agreement rather than lose one of its largest divisions. The company purchased Marshalls (discount department stores, 1976), Mack Drug (1977), Kay-Bee Toy and Hobby Shops (1981), Wilsons House of Suede (1982), Freddy's (deep-discount drugstores, 1984), Prints Plus (1985), This End Up Furniture (1985), and Accessory Lady (1987), and sold Foxmoor (1985).

Chairman and CEO Francis Rooney was succeeded by Stanley Goldstein in 1987. Shortly thereafter the Meldisco division signed an agreement (1988) to operate shoe outlets in Pay Less Drug Stores.

In 1990 Melville added 823 stores by buying Bob's Stores (apparel and footwear "superstores"), People's Drug Stores (merged with CVS), and Circus World toys (merged with Kay-Bee). The acquisitions made Melville the 5th largest drugstore operator in the US and one of the largest toy retailers. Despite the dismal retail climate in 1990 and 1991, the company again achieved substantial sales growth, aided by its 1990 purchases and the strong performance of CVS and Marshalls.

WHERE

HQ: One Theall Rd., Rye, NY 10580
Phone: 914-925-4000
Fax: 914-925-4026

Melville has stores in 50 states, DC, Canada, Puerto Rico, and the US Virgin Islands.

WHAT

	1990 Sales		1990 Operating Income	
	$ mil.	% of total	$ mil.	% of total
Footwear	1,714	20	145	21
Drugstores	2,679	31	183	26
Apparel	3,036	35	231	34
Toys & household furnishings	1,258	14	127	19
Adjustments	—	—	(31)	—
Total	**8,687**	**100**	**655**	**100**

	No. of Stores	1990 Sales ($ mil.)
Apparel		
Accessory Lady	94	61
Bob's Stores	7	83
Chess King	541	259
Marshalls	386	2,183
Wilsons	524	450
Drugstores		
CVS/People's	1,196	2,485
Freddy's	29	194
Footwear		
Fan Club	88	65
Meldisco	2,464	1,153
Thom McAn	835	496
Toys & Household Furnishings		
Kay-Bee/Circus World	1,116	927
Linens 'n Things	141	202
Prints Plus	86	38
This End Up	247	91
Total	**7,754**	**8,687**

RANKINGS

13th in *Fortune* 50 Retailing Cos.
129th in *Business Week* 1000

KEY COMPETITORS

American Stores	Kmart	Toys "R" Us
Brown Group	L.A. Gear	U.S. Shoe
Carter Hawley Hale	The Limited	V. F.
Dayton Hudson	Liz Claiborne	Walgreen
Edison Brothers	Longs	Wal-Mart
The Gap	May	Woolworth
General Cinema	NIKE	Discount and
INTERCO	Reebok	department
Jack Eckerd	Rite Aid	stores

HOW MUCH

	9-Year Growth	1981	1982	1983	1984	1985	1986	1987	1988	1989	1990
Sales ($ mil.)	13.6%	2,761	3,262	3,923	4,423	4,775	5,262	5,930	6,780	7,554	8,687
Net income ($ mil.)	12.3%	136	142	176	190	220	238	285	355	398	385
Income as % of sales	—	4.9%	4.4%	4.5%	4.3%	4.6%	4.5%	4.8%	5.2%	5.3%	4.4%
Earnings per share ($)	11.5%	1.32	1.37	1.68	1.80	2.04	2.20	2.63	3.26	3.52	3.49
Stock price – high ($)	—	12.00	19.13	23.81	22.75	26.44	36.88	42.00	38.31	53.63	57.75
Stock price – low ($)	—	8.78	9.22	15.19	15.38	17.63	24.63	22.13	26.63	36.88	32.75
Stock price – close ($)	18.0%	9.44	17.69	17.44	18.63	25.25	27.00	26.50	37.19	44.63	42.00
P/E – high	—	9	14	14	13	13	17	16	12	15	17
P/E – low	—	7	7	9	9	9	11	8	8	10	9
Dividends per share ($)	13.6%	0.45	0.51	0.55	0.66	0.72	0.78	0.88	1.05	1.30	1.42
Book value per share ($)	10.6%	5.87	6.73	7.89	9.03	10.20	11.64	13.41	15.65	12.28	14.52

1990 Year-end:
Debt ratio: 17.6%
Return on equity: 26.0%
Cash (mil.): $111
Current ratio: 1.76
Long-term debt (mil.): $395
No. of shares (mil.): 103
Dividends:
　1990 average yield: 3.4%
　1990 payout: 40.7%
Market value (mil.): $4,323

Stock Price History
High/Low 1981–90

MERCANTILE STORES COMPANY, INC.

NYSE symbol: MST
Fiscal year ends: January 31

Hoover's Rating **B-**

OVERVIEW

With annual sales of over $2 billion, Mercantile Stores is one of the nation's most consistently profitable and least-known major retailers. The company operates 12 regional department store chains from its headquarters outside Cincinnati, recently relocated from New York. The best-known and largest of these chains include McAlpin's in Cincinnati, The Jones Store in Kansas City, Joslin's in Denver, and Gayfer's in the South. Most of the company's other stores are in smaller cities.

While other major department store organizations have either gone on acquisition sprees (May Department Stores, Dillard's) or been burdened by heavy debt (Campeau, Macy's), Mercantile has not made an acquisition since 1955 and operates with very little debt.

The company has prospered as the result of a unique merchandising strategy and extremely stable management and control. It has been effectively controlled by South Carolina's textile-producing Milliken family since after WWI; today, they control almost 44% of the stock. They have supported a stable management, encouraged by bonuses and stock options.

Mercantile enters the 1990s with its strategies well established, seemingly oblivious to the turmoil in the retail industry. The company plans to continue to build 2 to 3 new stores and remodel 4 to 5 old ones each year.

WHO

Chairman and CEO: David R. Huhn, age 53, $647,092 pay
VC: James C. Lovell, age 64, $715,000 pay
President and COO: Roger D. Ciskie, age 50, $399,615 pay
VP, Treasurer, and CFO: David L. Nichols, age 49, $326,923 pay
Corporate Director of Human Resources: Louis L. Ripley
Auditors: Arthur Andersen & Co.
Employees: 21,000

WHEN

H. B. Claflin Company, a large New York dry goods wholesaler, expanded into retailing around the turn of the century with the acquisitions of such major names as Lord & Taylor of New York and Hahne's of Newark. In 1914 the company collapsed into bankruptcy and eventually emerged as 2 creditor-controlled firms: Associated Dry Goods got Lord & Taylor and other premier, primarily northeastern names, while Mercantile Stores got the smaller and less attractive names. Mercantile's lead creditor was Milliken & Company, the textile giant. While Associated became part of May Department Stores Company in 1986, Mercantile has remained an independent public company under Milliken control.

With weak positions in their markets, the company's divisions barely survived the Great Depression. The chief executive ordered them to sell off inventory to raise cash but did it in person because he didn't trust the telephone. After WWII, management adopted a 2-part merchandising strategy. First, local buyers selected fashion merchandise to remain in tune with local markets, as did other department stores. Second, centralized buyers in New York bought commodity items such as sheets and socks to minimize costs and passed savings on to the customer (a strategy similar to that of Sears and J. C. Penney). The company also established a tradition of excellent expense control. These traditions remain in place at Mercantile today.

Mercantile acquired the Glass Block in Duluth (1944) and de Lendrecie's in Fargo (1955), the company's most recent acquisitions.

In the 1980s Mercantile's sales doubled and earnings tripled. The company has consistently been in or near the top of the industry in sales per square foot and profit margin. In conjunction with Milliken, Mercantile is experimenting with quick-response inventory replenishment, in which sales data are sent immediately and directly to manufacturers.

The company prides itself on employee longevity; few key people are lost to competitors and even fewer are hired from outside the company. Mercantile has recently witnessed intensified competition from Dillard's, which seems to buy Mercantile's competitors after Mercantile has taken away much of their business. Nevertheless, nothing in the company's past indicates that Mercantile will depart from one of the most consistent long-term strategies in retailing.

WHERE

HQ: 9450 Seward Rd., Fairfield, OH 45014
Phone: 513-860-8000
Fax: 513-860-8689

Mercantile operates 81 department stores and one specialty store under 12 different chain names and maintains a central buying office in New York City.

WHAT

Department Store Chains and Headquarters
Bacons
  Louisville
Castner Knott
  Nashville
de Lendrecies
  Fargo, ND
Gayfers
  Mobile and Montgomery, AL
Glass Block
  Duluth, MN
Hennessys
  Billings, MT
J.B. White
  Augusta, GA
The Jones Store Co.
  Kansas City, MO
Joslins
  Denver
Lion
  Toledo, OH
McAlpin's
  Lexington, KY and Cincinnati
Root's
  Terre Haute, IN

Mercantile also operates 13 freestanding beauty salons.

RANKINGS

435th in *Business Week* 1000

KEY COMPETITORS

Campeau
Carter Hawley Hale
Dayton Hudson
Dillard
May
J. C. Penney
Discount and specialty stores

HOW MUCH

	9-Year Growth	1981	1982	1983	1984	1985	1986	1987	1988	1989	1990
Sales ($ mil.)	7.2%	1,276	1,434	1,628	1,711	1,883	2,032	2,175	2,286	2,337	2,394
Net income ($ mil.)	8.8%	58	70	83	85	102	111	130	144	130	124
Income as % of sales	—	4.5%	4.9%	5.1%	5.0%	5.4%	5.5%	6.0%	6.3%	5.6%	5.2%
Earnings per share ($)	8.8%	1.57	1.90	2.26	2.30	2.78	3.02	3.52	3.92	3.54	3.36
Stock price – high ($)	—	9.12	19.52	30.20	23.60	31.25	46.80	53.38	46.50	50.50	45.38
Stock price – low ($)	—	5.48	8.56	15.84	16.10	21.80	29.10	30.63	34.75	37.50	24.25
Stock price – close ($)	14.4%	8.94	18.52	22.00	22.60	31.25	38.30	37.00	42.75	39.13	30.00
P/E – high	—	6	10	13	10	11	16	15	12	14	14
P/E – low	—	3	5	7	7	8	10	9	9	11	7
Dividends per share ($)	17.2%	0.23	0.32	0.40	0.46	0.51	0.58	0.68	0.78	0.89	0.96
Book value per share ($)	12.8%	10.77	12.43	14.29	16.13	18.40	20.84	23.68	26.62	29.24	31.87

1990 Year-end:
Debt ratio: 15.0%
Return on equity: 11.0%
Cash (mil.): $45
Current ratio: 6.13
Long-term debt (mil.): $208
No. of shares (mil.): 37
Dividends:
  1990 average yield: 3.2%
  1990 payout: 28.5%
Market value (mil.): $1,105

Stock Price History High/Low 1981–90

MERCK & CO., INC.

OVERVIEW

New Jersey–based Merck is the world's largest pharmaceutical company, controlling 9.3% of the US market and 3.4% of the global market. The company has a phenomenal 18 drugs that annually generate over $100 million each. Merck also makes pesticides, specialty chemicals, and animal health products including its best-selling Ivomec.

To maintain its reputation as a constant innovator, Merck spent $854 million on R&D in 1990 (11% of sales). The company's efforts account for 5% of global pharmaceutical research. Merck's pipeline includes Varivax (a chicken pox vaccine), Trusopt (a treatment for glaucoma), and its soon-to-be-released Proscar (a drug to treat prostate enlargement).

Merck maintains joint ventures with some of the biggest names in the industry, including Johnson & Johnson and Du Pont. Recent ventures include work on an AIDS vaccine with biotech firm Repligen and a vaccine venture with Institut Merieux (France).

In 1990 Merck was named *Fortune* magazine's most admired company for the 5th year in a row.

NYSE symbol: MRK
Fiscal year ends: December 31

Hoover's Rating **A+**

WHO

Chairman, President, and CEO: P. Roy Vagelos, age 61, $2,091,667 pay
VC: John Lyons, age 64, $1,132,919 pay
VP Finance and CFO: Judy C. Lewent, age 42
VP Human Resources: Steven M. Darien, age 48
Auditors: Arthur Andersen & Co.
Employees: 36,900

WHERE

HQ: PO Box 2000, Rahway, NJ 07065-0909
Phone: 908-594-4000
Fax: 908-594-4662

Merck has manufacturing plants in 17 countries.

	1990 Sales		1990 Pretax Income	
	$ mil.	% of total	$ mil.	% of total
US	4,039	53	1,833	68
OECD	3,451	45	823	31
Other foreign	182	2	21	1
Adjustments	—	—	(26)	—
Total	**7,672**	**100**	**2,651**	**100**

WHAT

	1990 Sales		1990 Pretax Income	
	$ mil.	% of total	$ mil.	% of total
Health products	7,121	93	2,570	97
Specialty chemicals	551	7	68	3
Adjustments	—	—	13	—
Total	**7,672**	**100**	**2,651**	**100**

	1990 Sales	
	$ mil.	% of total
Antihypertensives & cardiovasculars	3,140	41
Antibiotics	856	11
Anti-ulcerants	600	8
Anti-inflammatories/ analgesics	594	8
Ophthalmologicals	404	5
Vaccines/biologicals	353	5
Other	1,725	22
Total	**7,672**	**100**

Selected Pharmaceuticals

Aldomet (cardiovascular)	Pepcid (anti-ulcer)
Clinoril (anti-arthritis)	Prilosec (gastrointestinal)
Dolobid (analgesic)	Primaxin (antibiotic)
Indocin (anti-arthritis)	Prinivil (cardiovascular)
M-M-R II (vaccine)	Sinemet (anti-Parkinson)
Mefoxin (antibiotic)	Timoptic (anti-glaucoma)
Mevacor (cardiovascular)	Vaseretic (cardiovascular)
Moduretic (cardiovascular)	Vasotec (cardiovascular)
Noroxin (antibiotic)	Zocor (cardiovascular)

RANKINGS

63rd in *Fortune* 500 Industrial Cos.
5th in *Business Week* 1000

KEY COMPETITORS

Abbott Labs	Eli Lilly	Rhône-Poulenc
American Cyanamid	Genentech	Roche
American Home Products	Glaxo	Sandoz
Amgen	Hoechst	Schering-Plough
Bayer	Johnson & Johnson	SmithKline Beecham
Bristol-Myers Squibb	Monsanto	Syntex
Ciba-Geigy	Pfizer	Upjohn
Dow Chemical	Procter & Gamble	Warner-Lambert

WHEN

Merck was started in 1887 when chemist Theodore Weicker came to the US from Germany to set up an American branch of E. Merck AG of Germany. George Merck (grandson of the German company's founder) came in 1891 and entered into a partnership with Weicker. At first the firm imported and sold drugs and chemicals from Germany, but in 1903 it opened a plant in Rahway, New Jersey, to manufacture alkaloids. Weicker sold out to Merck in 1904 and bought a controlling interest in competitor Squibb. During WWI Merck gave the US government the 80% of company stock owned by family in Germany (George kept his shares). After the war the stock was sold to the public.

The company merged in 1927 with Powers-Weightman-Rosengarten of Philadelphia (a producer of the antimalarial quinine). At its first research laboratory, established in 1933, Merck scientists did pioneering work on vitamin B-12 and developed the first steroid (cortisone, 1944). Five Merck scientists received Nobel prizes in the 1940s and 1950s. Unfortunately the company was also a major producer of DES (diethylstilbestrol, widely used until 1971, suspected of causing cancer in children of women who used it during pregnancy) and is still involved in lawsuits over the drug. In 1953 Merck merged with Sharp & Dohme of Philadelphia, bringing together complementary lines of pharmaceuticals and Sharp & Dohme's strong sales force.

Merck introduced Diuril (antihypertensive) in 1958 and other drugs in the early 1960s (Indocin, Aldomet), but for nearly 10 years there were few new drugs. John Horan, who took over in 1976, accelerated R&D in an effort to create new products. By the late 1970s the company had produced Clinoril (antiarthritic), Flexeril (muscle relaxant), and Timoptic (for glaucoma).

Biochemist Roy Vagelos, current chairman, who joined Merck in 1976 as head of research and became CEO in 1985, has continued the commitment to R&D. The company introduced 10 major new drugs in the 1980s, including Mevacor for treating high cholesterol and Vasotec for high blood pressure. In 1983 Merck bought half of the Japanese drug company Banyu.

In 1990 Merck bought the nonprescription drug segment of ICI Americas (includes Mylanta), whose drugs it markets through a joint venture with Johnson & Johnson. Merck and Du Pont formed a joint venture in 1991 to market drugs in the US and Europe.

Also in 1991 the company received FDA approval to market Prilosec as an ulcer remedy and announced its intentions to gain a stronger foothold in Europe by buying assets of Woelm Pharma (Germany).

HOW MUCH

	9-Year Growth	1981	1982	1983	1984	1985	1986	1987	1988	1989	1990
Sales ($ mil.)	11.3%	2,929	3,063	3,246	3,560	3,548	4,129	5,061	5,940	6,551	7,672
Net income ($ mil.)	18.1%	398	415	451	493	540	676	906	1,207	1,495	1,781
Income as % of sales	—	13.6%	13.6%	13.9%	13.8%	15.2%	16.4%	17.9%	20.3%	22.8%	23.2%
Earnings per share ($)	19.9%	0.89	0.94	1.02	1.12	1.26	1.62	2.19	3.02	3.74	4.56
Stock price – high ($)	—	17.17	14.71	17.44	16.25	22.96	43.17	74.33	59.63	80.75	91.13
Stock price – low ($)	—	12.71	10.67	13.63	13.04	15.04	22.38	40.67	48.00	56.25	67.00
Stock price – close ($)	22.8%	14.13	14.10	15.06	15.67	22.83	41.29	52.83	57.75	77.50	89.88
P/E – high	—	19	16	17	15	18	27	34	20	22	20
P/E – low	—	14	11	13	12	12	14	19	16	15	15
Dividends per share ($)	18.4%	0.44	0.47	0.48	0.51	0.55	0.67	0.90	1.38	1.72	2.02
Book value per share ($)	9.1%	4.51	4.97	5.49	5.88	6.26	6.28	5.37	7.20	8.90	9.91

1990 Year-end:
Debt ratio: 3.1%
Return on equity: 48.5%
Cash (mil.): $1,197
Current ratio: 1.33
Long-term debt (mil.): $124
No. of shares (mil.): 387
Dividends:
 1990 average yield: 2.2%
 1990 payout: 44.3%
Market value (mil.): $34,781

Stock Price History
High/Low 1981–90

MERRILL LYNCH & CO., INC.

NYSE symbol: MER
Fiscal year ends: Last Friday in December

Hoover's Rating **C+**

OVERVIEW

Merrill Lynch & Co., Inc., is the holding company for the world's largest securities brokerage firm, Merrill Lynch, Pierce, Fenner & Smith, with more than 11,000 brokers. Merrill's 460 branch offices had more than 7.9 million customer accounts with $356 billion in client assets at the end of 1990.

In keeping with founder Charles Merrill's aim of becoming a department store of finance, Merrill Lynch offers a wide array of services including investment, banking, and credit services; asset management; insurance; investment banking; and debt and equity offerings (#1 market share worldwide —11%) to individuals, corporations, and governments in the US and abroad.

Despite a 20% downsizing since 1987 (from 47,900 employees to 38,500), and losses of $217 million in 1989, Merrill Lynch rebounded in 1990, returning to profitability after an extensive restructuring. The company is now responding to the refinancing needs of some of the 1980s' most famous LBOs, including the $1.5 billion recapitalization of RJR Nabisco, which Merrill Lynch supervised in 1986. Merrill Lynch is set to maintain and expand its market shares in a new atmosphere emphasizing caution and cash.

WHEN

Wall Street bond salesman Charles Merrill opened an underwriting firm in 1914 and within 6 months took on his friend, Edmund Lynch, as partner. In the 1920s the new firm pursued nontraditional investors by stressing personal service and advice, and took a lead in financing the new supermarkets that sprang up in the 1920s.

In 1930 the company sold its retail business — branches, employees, and all — to Wall Street's largest brokerage firm, E. A. Pierce and survived the Depression as an investment banking firm. Merrill Lynch reacquired the retail business in a 1940 merger with Pierce and in 1941 the company merged with Fenner and Beane. Winthrop Smith, an employee transferred to Pierce in 1930, became a partner in 1958.

Company expansion continued through pursuit of new investor groups (women) and through public information and advertising campaigns aimed at the small investor. Merrill Lynch was the first NYSE member to incorporate (1959) and go public (1971). In the 1960s it diversified into government securities, real estate financing (and sales in the 1970s), and asset management and consulting. In the 1970s under the chairmanship of Donald Regan (secretary of the treasury and chief of staff under President Reagan), the company introduced the patented Cash Management Account, and built up its investment banking, insurance, and foreign operations.

In the 1980s, Merrill Lynch's underwriting business boomed because of the M&A fever. It became the global leader in offerings and advised on the largest of them all, Kohlberg Kravis Roberts' LBO of RJR Nabisco.

Since the 1987 crash, Merrill Lynch has retrenched and reorganized, jettisoning or trimming less profitable segments (merchant banking, real estate, and Family Life Insurance Company's mortgage insurance business) and closing some overseas offices. In addition to trying to increase the proportion of earnings from management and other fees (11%), and reduce dependence on commissions (28%), Merrill Lynch moved to reduce its holdings of junk bonds and curtail its granting of bridge loans to ailing companies. In 1990, to reduce staff turnover (14% to 15% of its 10,500 member professional staff annually), the company introduced new training and pay procedures to reward long service and reduce dependency of inexperienced staff members on commission earnings.

Merrill Lynch is a member of many of the world's most important stock exchanges; in 1991 it received permission to buy a seat on the Seoul (South Korea) exchange.

WHO

Chairman and CEO: William A. Schreyer, age 63, $1,550,000 pay
President and COO: Daniel P. Tully, age 59, $1,315,000 pay
President Human Resources: Patrick J. Walsh
EVP Finance and Administration: Herbert M. Allison, Jr., age 47
Auditors: Deloitte & Touche
Employees: 38,500

WHERE

HQ: World Financial Center, North Tower, 250 Vesey St., New York, NY 10281
Phone: 212-236-4376
Fax: 212-236-4384

Merrill Lynch operates in the US and in 27 foreign countries.

	1990 Sales		1990 Pretax Income	
	$ mil.	% of total	$ mil.	% of total
US	9,742	87	308	109
Foreign	1,471	13	(25)	(9)
Total	**11,213**	**100**	**283**	**100**

WHAT

	1990 Sales		1990 Pretax Income	
	$ mil.	% of total	$ mil.	% of total
Insurance	925	8	89	31
Investment & financing svcs.	10,288	92	194	69
Total	**11,213**	**100**	**283**	**100**

	1990 Sales	
	$ mil.	% of total
Commissions	1,699	15
Interest & dividends	5,166	46
Principal transactions	1,441	13
Investment banking	796	7
Insurance	925	8
Asset management & custodial fees	674	6
Other	512	5
Total	**11,213**	**100**

Financial Services
Capital builder accounts
Cash management accounts
Commodity futures
Government and municipal securities
Investment banking and underwriting
Mutual funds
Securities and economic research
Securities brokerage

RANKINGS

5th in *Fortune* 50 Diversified Financial Cos.
215th in *Business Week* 1000

KEY COMPETITORS

American Express	Nomura
Bear Stearns	Paine Webber
Charles Schwab	Primerica
CS Holding	Prudential
Deutsche Bank	Salomon
Equitable	Sears
Goldman Sachs	Travelers
Kemper	Other ins. and financial
Morgan Stanley	svcs. cos.

HOW MUCH

	9-Year Growth	1981	1982	1983	1984	1985	1986	1987	1988	1989	1990
Sales ($ mil.)	12.0%	4,038	5,026	5,687	5,911	7,117	9,475	11,036	10,547	11,335	11,213
Net income ($ mil.)	(0.6%)	203	309	230	95	224	469	391	463	(217)	192
Income as % of sales	—	5.0%	6.1%	4.0%	1.6%	3.2%	5.0%	3.5%	4.4%	(1.9%)	1.7%
Earnings per share ($)	(5.2%)	2.57	3.74	2.59	1.03	2.21	4.28	3.51	4.21	(2.35)	1.59
Stock price – high ($)	—	22.13	35.63	56.50	36.38	36.75	43.75	46.75	28.38	36.75	27.25
Stock price – low ($)	—	14.31	10.50	27.50	22.00	25.50	32.38	19.50	22.13	23.50	16.13
Stock price – close ($)	2.5%	16.56	30.00	32.00	27.00	34.38	36.50	22.38	24.00	26.25	20.75
P/E – high	—	9	10	22	35	17	10	13	7	—	17
P/E – low	—	6	3	11	21	12	8	6	5	—	10
Dividends per share ($)	5.8%	0.60	0.66	0.78	0.80	0.80	0.80	0.95	1.00	1.00	1.00
Book value per share ($)	7.9%	15.04	18.36	21.09	21.64	22.98	26.56	32.54	35.31	27.83	29.77

1990 Year-end:
Debt ratio: 51.8%
Return on equity: 5.5%
Cash (mil.): $5,829
Current ratio: —
Long-term debt (mil.): $3,461
No. of shares (mil.): 100
Dividends:
  1990 average yield: 4.8%
  1990 payout: 62.9%
Market value (mil.): $2,072

Stock Price History High/Low 1981–90

METROMEDIA COMPANY

Private partnership
Fiscal year ends: December 31

Hoover's Rating **B+**

OVERVIEW

Metromedia is one of the largest private partnerships in the nation and, in many ways, a symbol of the Deal Decade, the 1980s.

It rode high on the glamour of its television holdings as the decade began and delved into that heady combination of telephony and computers called cellular. Metromedia went private in a 1984 LBO. Once it was private, Metromedia's guiding genius John Kluge turned to junk bond king Michael Milken to refinance its debt. Then it began to sell off assets — so well that some would criticize Kluge for undervaluing the company. During the 1980s it meandered meaningfully —

television, cellular, the Harlem Globetrotters, the Ice Capades, computerized billboards. All but the billboards are now sold.

Now, as multibillionaire Kluge approaches 80, the company's main activities are Metromedia Communications, the 4th largest long-distance carrier in the US, and its restaurant chains — Ponderosa Steakhouses (some of the Bonanza steakhouses it acquired also adopted the Ponderosa brand), Steak'n'Ale, and Bennigan's. The company also owns 66.6% of Orion Pictures, the company that scored a major victory from the jaws of defeat with *Dances With Wolves*.

WHEN

Metromedia began when German immigrant John Kluge (pronounced kloo-gy), fresh from a stint with US Army intelligence during WWII, bought WGAY radio station in Silver Spring, Maryland, in 1946. Kluge, born in 1914, came to Detroit at age 8 with his mother and stepfather. At Columbia on scholarship, he studied economics and, to the chagrin of college administrators, poker. At graduation he had built a tidy sum with his winnings. After the army he bought and sold small radio stations and dabbled in other enterprises.

A chance meeting on a Washington, DC, street led Kluge to investigate the possibility of buying independent television stations, stations not affiliated with any of the major networks. In 1959 he purchased control of Metropolitan Broadcasting, including TV stations in New York and Washington. The company was later renamed Metromedia, Inc.

Metromedia added independent stations — to the ceiling of 7 permitted by law — in other major markets, paying relatively little compared to what network affiliates could command. The stations struggled through years of Ginzu steak knife commercials, but thrived in the late 1970s and early 1980s. Metromedia's stock price rose from $4.50 in 1974 to more than $500 in 1983. The company also acquired radio stations, the Harlem Globetrotters exhibition basketball team, and the Ice Capades.

In a 1983 purchase that would cement Kluge's reputation as a visionary, Kluge spurred Metromedia to pay $300 million for cellular telephone and paging licenses across the US, but the payback on cellular would have to wait: in 1984 Kluge took Metromedia private in a $1.6 billion buyout. A year later the company began to sell off its assets. It sold a

TV station in Boston to Hearst and sold the other 6 to controversial press magnate Rupert Murdoch. The stations fetched $2 billion.

The sell-off continued in 1986 with transactions involving Metromedia's outdoor advertising (sold for $710 million), 9 of 11 radio stations ($285 million), and the Globetrotters and Ice Capades ($30 million). Kluge also began the withdrawal from cellular telephone, surprising industry analysts with the sale of much of the company's properties to Southwestern Bell for $1.65 billion. Metromedia sold its New York cellular operations to LIN Broadcasting (later to be controlled by McCaw) in 1989 for $275 million. Metromedia's Philadelphia operations were sold to Comcast Corporation for $1.1 billion in 1991.

Kluge, even though he was in his 70s and was arguably the richest man in America, continued to use Metromedia as a vehicle for an assortment of enterprises. In 1988 Kluge and Metromedia executives formed an LBO firm — Kluge Subotnick Perkowski (dissolved 1990). Metromedia took a stake in steak, buying the Ponderosa Steakhouse chain in 1988 from Asher Edelman. Metromedia later added Dallas-based USA Cafes (Bonanza steakhouses) and S & A Restaurant Corp. (Steak'n'Ale, Bennigan's). On another front, Metromedia integrated ITT's long-distance service into its operations in 1989.

In 1988 Kluge went to the rescue of friend Arthur Krim, whose Orion Pictures was threatened by Sumner Redstone's Viacom. Metromedia paid $78 million for control of the filmmaker. While it has hinted that it would sell its Orion stake, Metromedia in 1991 strengthened its presence in Orion operations, and Krim retired.

WHO

General Partner, Chairman, President, and CEO: John W. Kluge, age 77
General Partner and EVP: Stuart Subotnick, age 49
SVP, Secretary, and General Counsel: Arnold L. Wadler, age 48
VP and Controller: David Gassler
Director Human Resources: Beverly Scoggins
Auditors: KPMG Peat Marwick
Employees: 18,732

WHERE

HQ: 1 Meadowlands Plaza, East Rutherford, NJ 07073
Phone: 201-804-6400
Fax: 201-804-6540

Metromedia subsidiaries operate nationwide with headquarters in Dallas (S & A Restaurants); Vandalia, OH (Metromedia Steakhouses, Inc.); Los Angeles (Metromedia Technologies); and New York (Orion Pictures, Empire Hotel).

WHAT

Major Deals of the 1980s
1984: LBO of Metromedia, Inc., $1.6 billion
1985: Sale of 7 TV stations, $2 billion
1986: Sale of outdoor advertising business, $710 million
1986: Sale of radio stations, $285 million
1986: Sale of cellular holdings, $1.65 billion
1988: Acquired majority of Orion Pictures, $78 million
1988: Purchased Ponderosa Steakhouses
1989: Purchased control of Steak'n'Ale and Bennigan's restaurants
1989: Sold New York cellular to LIN Broadcasting, $275 million

Subsidiaries
Empire Hotel (New York)
ESI Meats, Inc. (meat processing)
Make Systems (software development, Mountain View, CA)
Metbenale (holding company for Steak'n'Ale and Bennigan's restaurant operations)
Metromedia Communications (long-distance services)
Metromedia Steakhouses, Inc. (Ponderosa and Bonanza family restaurants)
Metromedia Technologies (robotic painting)
Orion Pictures (68%, motion pictures)
Stanadyne Automotive Corp. (automotive equipment, Windsor, CT)

RANKINGS

44th in *Forbes* 400 US Private Cos.

KEY COMPETITORS

AT&T	Helmsley	PepsiCo
Cable	Hyatt	Sony
& Wireless	Imasco	Time Warner
Carlson	Loews	TW Holdings
Dial	Matsushita	Tyson Foods
General Mills	McDonald's	United Telecom
Grand	MCI	Walt Disney
Metropolitan	Paramount	Wendy's
GTE		

HOW MUCH

	5-Year Growth	1981	1982	1983	1984	1985	1986	1987	1988	1989	1990
Sales ($ mil.)	34.0%	—	—	—	—	585	—	—	620	2,060	2,530
Employees	27.8%	—	—	—	—	5,500	—	—	3,000	18,732	18,732

Sales ($ mil.) 1985–90

(bar chart, vertical axis 0 to 3,000)

METROPOLITAN LIFE INSURANCE COMPANY

Mutual company
Fiscal year ends: December 31
 Hoover's Rating **B-**

OVERVIEW

Metropolitan Life is the #2 insurance company in the US (after Prudential) based on assets, and offers a variety of life and other insurance products. But Metropolitan is more than an insurance company. Its Century 21 subsidiary is the largest real estate franchise sales organization in the world. It operates real estate leasing, appraising, and mortgage banking subsidiaries and franchises and, until recently, developed hotels (the Doubletree and Compri chains, which formed MetHotels; 80% was sold to Canadian Pacific in 1990).

Other subsidiaries, led by State Street Research & Management, offer financing and investment services. Because of its conservative investment strategies (with only 4.4% of its real estate investments in default), it is well placed to capitalize on the problems of more daring companies such as Executive Life and Mutual Benefit Life. It has taken over management of Mutual Benefit Life, hired the company's remaining 400 agents, and may ultimately buy portions of the Mutual Benefit business.

WHEN

Though Metropolitan Life's ads feature Snoopy as a WWI flying ace, the company's origin goes back to an earlier conflict, the Civil War.

Simeon Draper, a New York merchant, tried to form National Union Life and Limb Insurance to cover Yankee soldiers, but investors were scared off by heavy battlefield losses. After a series of reorganizations and name changes, the company emerged in 1868 as Metropolitan Life Insurance.

Sustained at first by business from mutual assistance societies for German immigrants, Metropolitan went into industrial insurance with workers' burial policies. Until much-needed reform in 1900, if a worker missed a payment, the company kept all premiums and owed the policyholder nothing.

Aggressive sales became a Metropolitan hallmark. The company became known for importing polished British salesmen if no American could be found. The company's success was measured by the growth of the landmark New York City headquarters. The tower at One Madison Avenue was completed in 1909, and its beacon became an advertising symbol: "The Light That Never Fails."

Metropolitan became a mutual company, owned by policyholders, in 1915, and in 1917 offered group insurance. Metropolitan expanded to Canada in 1924.

Led by the conservative Eckers, Frederick Sr. and Jr., from 1929 to 1963, Metropolitan began to change, dropping industrial insurance in 1964 after both men died. In 1974 Metropolitan began offering automobile and homeowner insurance.

Under President and CEO John Creedon, Metropolitan began to diversify in the 1980s (along with most insurers after interest rates began to rise). It bought Manhattan's Pan Am Building (1981), State Street Research & Management (founder of the first US mutual fund, 1983), Century 21 Real Estate (1985), London-based Albany Life Assurance (1985), and Allstate's group life and health business (1988). In 1987 Metropolitan took over the annuities segment of the failed Baldwin United Company and expanded with a joint venture in Spain and a branch in Taiwan in 1988.

In 1989 the company bought J.C. Penney's casualty insurance portfolio, United Resources Insurance Services (retirement and financial programs), and Texas Life Insurance. The company also launched a "Family Reunion" program to contact holders of several million of the old industrial insurance policies still in force.

In 1989 Chairman Robert Schwartz became CEO. In the changed climate of the 1990s, Metropolitan began to cut costs by trimming 1,000 jobs and transferring several thousand others from its New York offices. It has also begun to re-emphasize its core insurance products and add new ones, such as long-term care insurance, which are expected to become more important as the population ages. As insurance solvency became a worry in 1991, the company continued to use the beloved Peanuts characters to convey its simple message: "Get Met. It pays."

WHO

Chairman, President, and CEO: Robert G. Schwartz, age 63
VC: Philip Briggs, age 63
SEVP Insurance: Stewart G. Nagler, age 47
SEVP Investments: Robert E. Chappell, Jr., age 53
SVP and Controller: Fred P. Hauser, age 54
EVP Administration and Human Resources: Catherine A. Rein
Auditors: Deloitte & Touche
Employees: 45,342

WHERE

HQ: One Madison Ave., New York, NY 10010
Phone: 212-578-2211
Fax: 212-685-1224 (Human Resources)

Metropolitan Life and its affiliated companies operate in the US, Canada, Europe, Australia, New Zealand, and Asia.

WHAT

	1990 Assets	
	$ mil.	% of total
Bonds	47,415	46
Stocks	2,383	2
Real estate	31,927	31
Policy loans	2,466	2
Cash	3,996	4
Other	15,041	15
Total	**103,228**	**100**

US Affiliates

Insurance
MetLife Security Insurance Cos.
Metropolitan Insurance and Annuity Co.
Metropolitan Property and Casualty Insurance Co.
Metropolitan Reinsurance Co.
Metropolitan Tower Life Insurance Co.
Texas Life Insurance Co.

Financing and Investment
MetLife Capital Corp.
MetLife Capital Credit Corp.
MetLife Funding, Inc.
MetLife Securities, Inc.
MetLife-State Street Investment Services, Inc.
State Street Research & Management Co.

Real Estate
Century 21 Real Estate Corp.
Cross & Brown Co.
Farmers National Co.
Metmor Financial, Inc.

Health Care
Corporate Health Strategies, Inc.
MetLife HealthCare Management Corp.

RANKINGS

2nd in *Fortune* 50 Life Insurance Cos.

KEY COMPETITORS

Aetna	Northwestern Mutual
Blue Cross	Prudential
GEICO	Sears
General RE	State Farm
Humana	Tokio Marine and Fire
John Hancock	Travelers
Kemper	Other insurance companies
Lloyd's of London	Other investment
MassMutual	management companies
New York Life	Real estate companies

HOW MUCH

	9-Year Growth	1981	1982	1983	1984	1985	1986	1987	1988	1989	1990
Assets ($ mil.)	8.0%	51,757	55,731	60,599	67,354	73,803	78,773	88,140	94,232	98,740	103,228
Income ($ mil.)	—	—	—	—	—	—	—	809	836	494	360
Income as % of assets	—	—	—	—	—	—	—	0.9%	0.9%	0.5%	0.3%
Employees	0.3%	44,081	42,000	40,000	36,000	35,000	33,000	33,000	37,000	42,464	45,342

1990 Year-end:
Equity as % of assets: 4.2%
Return on equity: 8.9%
Cash (mil.): $3,996
Sales (mil.): $ 27,168

Assets ($ mil.)
1981–90

MICROSOFT CORPORATION

OTC symbol: MSFT
Fiscal year ends: June 30

Hoover's Rating A+

OVERVIEW

Microsoft is the leading developer of PC systems and applications software in the world. Based in Redmond, Washington, the 16-year-old company is headed by William Gates III, who, at age 19, cofounded the company.

Microsoft's operating system software, MS-DOS, introduced for the IBM PC in 1981, today runs on over 60 million IBM PC and compatible computers. The company's relationship with IBM in recent years, however, has turned competitive. Microsoft was excluded from IBM's and Apple's 1991 partnership, one that may result in a new line of computers and a whole new operating system.

Microsoft's offerings include systems software (MS-DOS, Microsoft OS/2, and XENIX), operating environment software (Windows), applications software (word processing, spreadsheet, presentation graphics), computer-related books (Microsoft Press), and CD-ROM products.

In 1990 Microsoft launched Windows 3.0 with great fanfare. Windows is an easy-to-use (Macintosh-like) interface for PCs that also allows more than one application to run simultaneously. Since introduction, the company has shipped more than 4 million copies.

WHO

Chairman and CEO: William H. Gates III, age 35, $261,242 pay
President and COO: Michael R. Hallman, age 46, $1,169,393 pay
SVP Finance and Administration: Francis J. Gaudette, age 55
Auditors: Deloitte & Touche
Employees: 5,635

WHERE

HQ: One Microsoft Way, Redmond, WA 98052
Phone: 206-882-8080
Fax: 206-883-8101

The company has plants in the US and Ireland and subsidiaries in 21 countries.

	1990 Sales		1990 Operating Income	
	$ mil.	% of total	$ mil.	% of total
US	718	60	269	62
Europe	363	31	149	34
Other countries	102	9	17	4
Adjustments	—	—	(48)	—
Total	**1,183**	**100**	**387**	**100**

WHEN

Microsoft started in 1975 after 19-year-old William Gates dropped out of Harvard and teamed up with high school friend Paul Allen to sell a condensed version of the programming language BASIC. While Gates was at Harvard, the pair had written the language for the Altair, the first commercially available microcomputer (sold by MITS, an Albuquerque-based maker of electronic kits). Gates and Allen moved to Albuquerque and set up Microsoft in a hotel room to produce the program for MITS. Although MITS folded in 1979, Microsoft continued to grow by modifying its BASIC program for other computers.

Microsoft moved to the Seattle area (Bellevue) in 1977, where it developed software that enabled others to write programs for PCs. Microsoft's big break came in 1980 when it was chosen by IBM to write the critical operating system (software that controls the computer's basic functions and runs applications software such as word processing) for IBM's new PC. Given the complexity of the task and the time constraints, Microsoft bought the rights to an operating system for $50,000 from a Seattle programmer, Tim Paterson, and converted it to Microsoft Disk Operating System (MS-DOS).

The popularity of IBM's PC made MS-DOS a huge success. And because other PC makers wanted to be compatible with IBM, MS-DOS was licensed to over 100 companies, making it the standard PC operating system in the 1980s. By 1984 Microsoft sales had exceeded $100 million. Microsoft went on to develop software for IBM, Apple, and Radio Shack computers.

In the meantime, Paul Allen, ill from Hodgkin's disease, left Microsoft in 1983. He later started his own software company, Asymetrix. Today, Allen owns 15% of Microsoft's stock and serves on its board.

Microsoft went public in 1986. Gates retained 45% of the shares, making him the PC industry's first billionaire in 1987. In 1990 his paper value surpassed $2 billion.

Most recently Microsoft has focused on developing graphic user interfaces (GUIs) for its operating systems. The company makes 2 GUIs for IBM-compatible PCs: Windows (MS-DOS) and Presentation Manager (OS/2), for the IBM PS/2. Windows's popularity has boosted sales of Microsoft's business software developed for Windows, a market which Microsoft dominates. In addition to enhanced networking software, Microsoft is developing a PC electronic stylus used for entering commands, a database program, and a new operating system (Windows NT).

WHAT

Product groups	1990 Net Revenues % of total
Systems software	39
Applications software	48
Hardware, books, other	13
Total	**100**

Channels of distribution	1990 Net Revenues % of total
Domestic OEM	13
Domestic retail	30
International OEM	13
International finished goods	42
Press and other	2
Total	**100**

Operating Systems
Microsoft LAN Manager
Microsoft OS/2
Microsoft XENIX
MS-DOS

Business Application Software
Microsoft Mail
Microsoft Multiplan
The Microsoft Office
Microsoft PowerPoint
Microsoft Project
Microsoft Word
Microsoft Works
Microsoft Write

Systems/Languages Software
Microsoft BASIC
Microsoft C
Microsoft COBOL
Microsoft FORTRAN

Microsoft Macro Assembler
Microsoft Pascal
Microsoft Quick BASIC
Microsoft QuickC Compiler
   with QuickAssembler
Microsoft QuickPascal
Microsoft Windows/286
Microsoft Windows/386

Hardware, Recreation & CD-ROM
Microsoft Bookshelf
   (CD-ROM)
Microsoft Flight Simulator
Microsoft Mouse
Microsoft Programmer's
   Library (CD-ROM)
Microsoft Small Business
   Consultant (CD-ROM)
Microsoft Stat Pack
   (CD-ROM)

Microsoft Press Books

HOW MUCH

	5-Year Growth	1981	1982	1983	1984	1985	1986	1987	1988	1989	1990
Sales ($ mil.)	53.2%	—	—	—	—	140	198	346	591	804	1,183
Net income ($ mil.)	14.8%	—	—	—	—	24	39	72	124	171	279
Income as % of sales	—	—	—	—	—	17.2%	19.9%	20.8%	21.0%	21.2%	23.6%
Earnings per share ($)	—	—	—	—	—	0.26	0.39	0.65	1.11	1.52	2.34
Stock price – high ($)	—	—	—	—	—	—	12.81	39.63	35.25	44.63	80.75
Stock price – low ($)	—	—	—	—	—	—	5.25	11.88	22.63	22.88	42.00
Stock price – close ($)	—	—	—	—	—	—	12.06	27.13	26.63	43.50	75.25
P/E – high	—	—	—	—	—	—	33	61	32	29	35
P/E – low	—	—	—	—	—	—	13	18	20	15	18
Dividends per share ($)	—	—	—	—	—	0.00	0.00	0.00	0.00	0.00	0.00
Book value per share ($)	66.6%	—	—	—	—	0.63	1.37	2.27	3.50	5.15	8.08

1990 Year-end:
Debt ratio: 0.0%
Return on equity: 35.4%
Cash (mil.): $449
Current ratio: 3.85
Long-term debt (mil.): $0
No. of shares (mil.): 114
Dividends:
   1990 average yield: 0.0%
   1990 payout: 0.0%
Market value (mil.): $8,556

Stock Price History High/Low 1986–90

RANKINGS

45th in *Business Week* 1000

KEY COMPETITORS

Adobe	Borland	Lotus
AT&T	Computer Associates	Novell
Apple	IBM	Oracle

MIDWAY AIRLINES, INC.

NYSE symbol: MDW
Fiscal year ends: December 31

Hoover's Rating **D**

OVERVIEW

The original idea behind Midway Airlines — similar to the one behind Herb Kelleher's Southwest Airlines — was to offer air travelers a low-fare, less-congested alternative to the airlines serving Chicago's O'Hare International Airport. Midway continues as the leading airline at its home base, Chicago's Midway, boarding about 72% of the passengers flying out of the airport in 1990.

An ill-timed attempt to establish a 2nd hub, in Philadelphia, created pressures that left Midway bankrupt in 1991. The home base of USAir (ranked 7th in the world), Philadelphia became a hotbed of competition between Midway, USAir, and Eastern (which had slashed fares trying to save its own skin) in 1990. When fuel prices skyrocketed and passenger traffic fell, Midway defaulted on aircraft leases and other loan agreements, leaving it no option other than bankruptcy protection.

Northwest Airlines recently announced a plan to buy Midway's facilities at Midway Airport for $20 million. The deal, struck in September 1991, hinges upon bankruptcy court approval. Northwest is also negotiating to buy Midway's remaining assets.

WHO

Chairman and CEO: David R. Hinson, age 58, $350,000 pay
President and COO: Thomas E. Schick, age 49
SVP Finance and CFO: Alfred S. Altschul, age 51, $153,600 pay
VP Human Resources: Daniel W. Shea, age 55, $184,839 pay
Auditors: Ernst & Young
Employees: 5,352

WHEN

In 1976 Irv Tague left his position as COO of Hughes Airwest to establish an airline at Chicago's Midway Airport. Once the world's busiest airport, Midway was practically abandoned when most airline traffic was diverted to O'Hare in 1962, but Tague saw opportunity in the empty terminals. Planning to operate a no-frills, low-fare, low-cost airline, he raised $5.7 million from venture capitalists and in 1979 offered flights from Midway to Kansas City, Cleveland, and Detroit. By 1981 Midway Airlines (named after its home port) had added 7 more cities to its route network and reported its first profit.

But in 1982 the airline was caught in fare wars with United, American, and Northwest, causing it to barely break even. Tague left the company that year, and Arthur Bass, former president of Federal Express, became CEO.

Recognizing that Midway served important eastern and midwestern commercial centers, Bass upgraded the airline to appeal to business travelers by creating new business-class (Metrolink) flights featuring complimentary cocktails and gourmet snacks. Midway introduced Metrolink service between Chicago and New York in 1983. But when the service failed to catch on, the airline incurred losses of $23 million in 1984. Bass resigned the following year, and David Hinson (an original investor) took over as CEO.

That year Midway bought Miami-based Air Florida and began operating it as a regional airline called Midway Express. Hinson streamlined Express operations, retaining service within Florida and to the Virgin Islands, and phased out Metrolink flights. By the end of 1986, Midway had experienced an 82% increase in passenger traffic and posted its first profit in 4 years.

Midway served 26 cities by 1987 and offered flights to 8 additional cities in 1988. But traffic overflows at O'Hare had brought competitors to Midway Airport (including archrival Southwest). With increased competition at its home port, Midway's profits fell nearly 64% in 1988.

The airline established a 2nd hub at Philadelphia in 1989 by purchasing boarding facilities at the Philadelphia Airport from Eastern Airlines. This transaction, which, among other assets, included Eastern's routes to Montreal and Toronto, cost Midway about $213 million — explaining (at least in part) the airline's 1989 loss of $21 million. High fuel prices and sluggish traffic resulting from the Persian Gulf crisis led to more serious losses in 1990. Midway was forced to sell its Philadelphia assets and Canadian routes to USAir for $64.5 million late in 1990 and filed bankruptcy proceedings in March 1991.

WHERE

HQ: 5959 S. Cicero Ave., Chicago, IL 60638
Phone: 312-838-0001
Fax: 312-284-6439

Midway provides scheduled air service to 54 cities in 21 states, the District of Columbia, and the Bahamas. It also provides charter service in the US and between the US and Canada.

Hub Location
Chicago

WHAT

	1990 Sales	
	$ mil.	% of total
Passenger service	626	96
Other	29	4
Total	**655**	**100**

Flight Equipment	No.
Boeing 737	3
DC-9	40
MD-80 derivatives	15
Others	26
Total	**84**

Subsidiaries
Midway Aircraft Engineering, Inc. (aircraft inspection and maintenance)
Midway Airlines, Inc. (regional air service under tradename Midway Commuter)

RANKINGS

35th in *Fortune* 50 Transportation Cos.

KEY COMPETITORS

America West
AMR
Continental Airlines
Delta
Kimberly-Clark
NWA
Pan Am
Southwest
TWA
UAL
USAir

HOW MUCH

	9-Year Growth	1981	1982	1983	1984	1985	1986	1987	1988	1989	1990
Sales ($ mil.)	27.4%	74	95	104	149	181	261	347	412	494	655
Net income ($ mil.)	—	4	0	(15)	(23)	(4)	5	11	4	(21)	(139)
Income as % of sales	—	5.9%	0.4%	(14.4%)	(15.5%)	(2.0%)	1.8%	3.3%	1.0%	(4.2%)	(21.2%)
Earnings per share ($)	—	1.18	0.09	(2.52)	(3.15)	(0.50)	0.33	*0.99*	0.36	(2.15)	(14.11)
Stock price – high ($)	—	22.63	17.88	22.38	12.25	9.75	14.88	18.13	17.00	21.75	13.63
Stock price – low ($)	—	8.38	7.38	10.75	3.38	3.00	6.25	8.75	9.25	12.13	3.13
Stock price – close ($)	(12.7%)	12.25	16.75	11.75	4.00	6.88	13.13	11.00	12.25	12.50	3.63
P/E – high	—	19	199	—	—	—	45	18	47	—	—
P/E – low	—	7	82	—	—	—	19	9	26	—	—
Dividends per share ($)	—	0.00	0.00	0.00	0.00	0.00	0.00	0.00	0.00	0.00	0.00
Book value per share ($)	—	6.61	7.21	6.34	3.46	5.91	7.17	7.32	7.95	5.41	(11.06)

1990 Year-end:
Debt ratio: —
Return on equity: —
Cash (mil.): $27
Current ratio: .54
Long-term debt (mil.): —
No. of shares (mil.): 11
Dividends:
  1990 average yield: —
  1990 payout: —
Market value (mil.): $41

Stock Price History
High/Low 1981–90

MILLIKEN & CO., INC.

Private company
Fiscal year ends: November 30

Hoover's Rating **B+**

OVERVIEW

Privately owned Milliken is America's #1 textile company. With 1990 sales estimated at $2.5 billion, Milliken keeps up with the latest in mill technology and produces finished fabrics that are used in a wide array of products. Milliken makes the cloth that becomes uniforms for McDonald's, Burger King, and other companies. Its stretch fabrics are used for swimsuits and sportswear. Milliken even provides braided polyester cords that become Michelin tires. Among its patents (numbering more than 1,200) is the one for Visa, a stain-resistant finish.

Although Milliken has about 200 shareholders (most from the ranks of the Milliken family), Roger Milliken, along with brother Gerrish and cousin Minot, control more than 50% of the company's stock. Roger Milliken supports conservative political causes and has lobbied vigorously for legislation to protect the US textile industry from international trade. With his eye on the company's future, Milliken has attempted to change the company's certificate of incorporation to require 80% shareholder approval of any change in ownership.

WHO

Chairman: Roger Milliken, age 75
President and COO: Thomas J. Malone
VP and CFO: Minot K. Milliken
Director Human Resources: Tommy Hodge
Auditors: Arthur Andersen & Co.
Employees: 14,000

WHERE

HQ: 920 Milliken Rd., Spartanburg, SC 29303-9301
Phone: 803-573-2020
Fax: 803-573-2100

Milliken operates 47 manufacturing plants in the US and 8 plants in France, Belgium, and the UK. The company's 28 businesses produce more than 48,000 products.

WHEN

Seth Milliken and William Deering formed a company in 1865 to become selling agents for textile mills in New England and the South. Deering left the partnership and in 1869, founded Deering Harvester (later folded into International Harvester, now Navistar).

Milliken moved his operations to New York before the turn of the century, began buying the accounts receivable of cash-short textile mill operators, and invested in some of the companies. He also allied himself with leaders in the Spartanburg, South Carolina, area. Milliken and a Spartanburg associate tried to stem the power of the white labor unions by experimenting with black labor at the Vesta Cotton Mill. The venture failed in 1901 after Milliken withdrew his support.

In his position as agent and financier, Milliken was able to spot failing mills. He bought out the distressed owners at a discount and soon became a major mill owner himself. In 1905 Milliken and allies waged a bitter proxy fight and court case to win control of 2 mills, earning Milliken a fearsome reputation.

H. B. Claflin Co., a New York dry goods wholesaler who began operating retail stores, owed money to Milliken. After Claflin went bankrupt in 1914, Milliken won stores in the settlement. They became Mercantile Stores, and the Milliken family retains about 44% of the stock of the department store chain.

Roger Milliken, grandson of the founder, became the president of the company in 1947 and ruled with a firm hand. He fired his brother-in-law W. B. Dixon Stroud in 1955, and none of Milliken's children, nephews, or nieces have ever been allowed to work for the company. In 1956 the workers at Milliken's Darlington, South Carolina, mill voted to

unionize. The next day Milliken closed the plant. That began 24 years of litigation that ended at the US Supreme Court. Milliken settled with the workers for $5 million.

In the 1960s the company introduced Visa, a fabric finish for easy-care fabrics. Milliken launched its Pursuit of Excellence program in 1981. The program stressed self-managed teams of employees and has since eliminated 700 management positions. Roger Milliken also emphasized research, training, and new technology. The company adapted quickly to automation, sometimes buying all the latest equipment a manufacturer could make, and competitors were left out in the cold. The company's quality record — some clients are so confident about Milliken goods they don't even inspect for defects — earned a highly coveted Malcolm Baldrige National Quality Award in 1989.

Away from that limelight, Milliken has always been a secretive, closely held business. In 1989 that secrecy and family control were threatened when members of the Stroud branch of the family sold stock to a group that included Erwin Maddrey and Bettis Rainsford, executives of Milliken competitor Delta Woodside. The Strouds have announced that they plan to sell all their Milliken stock, about 17% of the company. Maddrey and Rainsford hope to buy more Stroud stock and sued Milliken to win the right to inspect its records and share the information with potential backers. A Delaware court sided with the 2 in 1990.

In 1991 Milliken introduced Fashion Effects, a new process that allowed it to customize drapery designs and textures. Also in that year the company tried unsuccessfully to convince the US government to levy countervailing tariffs on shop towels from Bangladesh.

WHAT

	1990 Estimated Sales
	$ mil.
Cotton broadwoven fabrics	2,000
Synthetic broadwoven fabrics	35
Weft knit fabric	12
Synthetic finishing	14
Other	439
Total	**2,500**

Textiles
Apparel fabrics
Area rugs
Automotive upholstery
Carpet and carpet tiles
Lining fabrics
Shop towels
Stretch fabrics
Textured yarns
Uniform fabrics

Industrial Chemicals
The company makes chemicals that are used in several industries:
  Oil industry
  Paint industry
  Paper industry
  Plastics industry
  Textile industry

RANKINGS

47th in *Forbes* 400 US Private Cos.

KEY COMPETITORS

Burlington Holdings
Du Pont
Farley
Fieldcrest Cannon
W. R. Grace
Rhône Poulenc
Samsung
Springs Industries
Other chemical companies

HOW MUCH

	5-Year Growth	1981	1982	1983	1984	1985	1986	1987	1988	1989	1990
Estimated sales ($ mil.)	4.6%	—	—	—	—	2,000	2,200	2,400	2,400	2,900	2,500
Employees	(20.8%)	—	—	—	—	45,000	45,000	20,000	20,000	20,000	14,000

Estimated Sales ($ mil.) 1985–90

MINNESOTA MINING AND MANUFACTURING CO.

NYSE symbol: MMM
Fiscal year ends: December 31

Hoover's Rating **A+**

OVERVIEW

From its stumbling start as a corundum supplier and sandpaper producer, 3M has extended its reach worldwide, leading in markets that include pressure-sensitive tapes, fluorochemical products (e.g., carpet and fabric protectors), magnetic storage media (e.g., floppy disks), reflective sheetings for advertising and highway safety signs, and films, as well as sandpaper. The company offers a vast array of products (50,000 by one estimate) and takes pride in its heavy R&D investment (6.6% of sales in 1990), reflected in the fact that nearly 1/3 of its 1990 sales came from products introduced in the previous 5 years.

Since 1985 the company has slashed its manufacturing cycle time by 21% and spent $4.9 billion on capital investments. Tough goals continue to be part of the 3M strategy, which calls for cuts by 1995 in manufacturing costs (10%), waste (35%), and energy use (20%). The company plans to reduce its air emissions by 70% by 1993 and hopes to halve the time it takes for R&D projects to reach market.

Other plans call for increased penetration of overseas markets, which accounted for about 1/2 of 3M's sales in 1990.

WHEN

In 1902 3M was started by 5 businessmen in Two Harbors, Minnesota, to sell corundum to manufacturers for grinding wheels. When they made only one sale, one of the founders, John Dwan, asked his friend Edgar Ober for working capital in exchange for 60% of 3M's stock. Convinced of the need for a company to make sandpaper and abrasive wheels, Ober persuaded Lucius Ordway, vice-president of a plumbing company, to underwrite 3M. At the 3rd annual meeting (May 1905), Ober and Ordway took over the company.

They moved 3M to Duluth and converted an old flour mill to a sandpaper factory. Orders began coming in by January 1906, but expenses exceeded sales, and Ordway's investment reached $200,000. In 1910 the plant moved to St. Paul to escape Duluth's high humidity.

In 2 years sales doubled, and the board of directors declared a dividend to stockholders in the last quarter of 1916. The company has not missed a quarterly dividend since.

The next 2 products 3M developed — Scotch brand masking tape (1925) and Scotch brand cellophane tape (1930) — assured 3M's future. In 1947 3M introduced the first commercially acceptable magnetic recording tape. In 1950, after a decade of work and $1 million, 3M employee Carl Miller invented Thermo-Fax copying machines.

The copying machine was the beginning of 3M's Duplicating Division, a group that produced image-related products such as microfilm, overhead-projection transparencies, carbonless papers, and facsimile and word processing equipment.

The company developed Post-it notes (1980) when a 3M scientist wanted to attach page markers to his church hymnal. Recalling that a colleague had developed an adhesive that wasn't very sticky, he brushed some on paper and began a product line that alone had sales of $500 million in 1990.

In 1990 3M increased by 15% its sales to overseas markets, which it considers prime territory for growth. The company also bought O-Cel-O, a sponge manufacturer, opened a tape and telecommunication products plant in India, and purchased Australia's largest "out-of-home" advertising company.

In keeping with its own tradition, the company introduced a wide variety of products, including medical imaging devices (e.g., Laser Imager XL); a cartridge holding 1.35 gigabytes of computer data; a completely automated color proofing system (Digital Matchprint); reflective sheeting (Scotchlite Diamond Grade); and a medical device that allows patients to inhale a precise amount of medication.

WHO

Chairman and CEO: L. D. DeSimone, age 54, $657,161 pay (prior to promotion)
SVP Finance: Giulio Agostini, age 56
SVP Human Resources: Christopher J. Wheeler, age 59
Auditors: Coopers & Lybrand
Employees: 89,601

WHERE

HQ: 3M Center, St. Paul, MN 55144-1000
Phone: 612-733-1110
Fax: 612-736-8261

3M has 88 plants in 28 US states and 41 foreign countries. It sells its products worldwide.

	1990 Sales		1990 Operating Income	
	$ mil.	% of total	$ mil.	% of total
US	6,802	52	1,268	58
Europe	3,705	29	463	21
Asia/Pacific & Canada	1,883	14	304	14
Other areas	631	5	156	7
Total	**13,021**	**100**	**2,191**	**100**

WHAT

	1990 Sales		1990 Operating Income	
	$ mil.	% of total	$ mil.	% of total
Industrial & Electronic	4,611	35	781	35
Information & Imaging	3,582	28	448	20
Life Sciences	2,873	22	593	27
Commercial & Consumer	1,916	15	398	18
Adjustments	39	—	(29)	—
Total	**13,021**	**100**	**2,191**	**100**

Industrial and Electronic Products
Abrasives
Adhesives
Coatings
Connectors
Emblems
Fabric protectors
Fasteners
Fluorochemicals
Polyester films
Roofing granules
Shielding
Tape

Life Sciences
Tapes, dressings, bandages
Diagnostic products
Surgical drapes, masks

Information and Imaging Technologies
Computer tapes
Digital imaging systems
Lithographic plates
Photographic film (Scotch)
Video and audio tape (Scotch)
X-ray films and screens

Commercial and Consumer Products
Carbonless papers
Masking tape
Self-stick notes (Post-it)
Tape (Scotch)
Cleaning pads (Scotch-Brite)

HOW MUCH

	9-Year Growth	1981	1982	1983	1984	1985	1986	1987	1988	1989	1990
Sales ($ mil.)	8.0%	6,508	6,601	7,039	7,705	7,846	8,602	9,429	10,581	11,990	13,021
Net income ($ mil.)	7.7%	673	631	667	733	664	779	918	1,154	1,244	1,308
Income as % of sales	—	10.3%	9.6%	9.5%	9.5%	8.5%	9.1%	9.7%	10.9%	10.4%	10.0%
Earnings per share ($)	8.4%	2.87	2.69	2.84	3.14	2.89	3.40	4.02	5.06	5.55	5.91
Stock price – high ($)	—	32.50	39.69	45.25	42.75	45.81	59.44	83.50	67.50	81.88	91.38
Stock price – low ($)	—	24.00	24.38	36.31	34.63	36.81	43.00	45.00	55.25	60.13	73.63
Stock price – close ($)	13.6%	27.25	37.50	41.25	39.31	44.88	58.31	64.38	62.00	79.63	85.75
P/E – high	—	11	15	16	14	16	17	21	13	15	15
P/E – low	—	8	9	13	11	13	13	11	11	11	12
Dividends per share ($)	7.7%	1.50	1.60	1.65	1.70	1.75	1.80	1.86	2.12	2.60	2.92
Book value per share ($)	7.3%	14.68	15.05	15.77	16.40	17.49	19.53	22.24	24.58	24.15	27.79

1990 Year-end:
Debt ratio: 11.1%
Return on equity: 22.8%
Cash (mil.): $591
Current ratio: 1.72
Long-term debt (mil.): $760
No. of shares (mil.): 220
Dividends:
1990 average yield: 3.4%
1990 payout: 49.4%
Market value (mil.): $18,851

Stock Price History High/Low 1981–90

RANKINGS

31st in *Fortune* 500 Industrial Cos.
24th in *Business Week* 1000

KEY COMPETITORS

BASF
Bayer
Boise Cascade
Eastman Kodak
Fuji Photo
General Electric
Hitachi
Johnson & Johnson
Polaroid
PPG
Siemens
Sony
USG
Xerox

MOBIL CORPORATION

OVERVIEW

Mobil is the 4th largest petroleum company in the world and one of the most active US companies in overseas trade.

It explores for and produces oil and natural gas in 20 countries, with major foreign operations in Canada, the North Sea, Nigeria, and Indonesia. The company owns all or part of 25 refineries worldwide, owns 34 oil tankers, and markets its petroleum products in more than 100 countries.

At the end of 1990, Mobil had 20,302 retail outlets, 56% outside the US. That figure includes 226 service stations purchased along with refinery support from Exxon's Australian subsidiary.

Mobil Chemical makes Hefty brand garbage bags, Baggies, and other plastic items. It added to its consumer brands with the 1990 purchase of Tucker Housewares, manufacturer of molded plastic items. Through its mining subsidiary, Mobil is a leading producer of phosphates. Mobil also develops real estate in Arizona, California, Colorado, Florida, Georgia, Texas, and Virginia.

WHEN

Mobil is yet another of the companies flung into orbit after the Big Bang breakup of John D. Rockefeller's Standard Oil universe. The pieces that would eventually form Mobil's cosmos were Rochester, New York–based Vacuum Oil and Standard Oil of New York. Vacuum, under founders Hiram Bond Everest and Matthew Ewing, had developed a way to make kerosene by distilling crude oil in a vacuum. Rockefeller bought 75% of Vacuum in 1879. The Standard Oil Company of New York was founded in 1882 and nicknamed Socony. Vacuum and Socony were 2 of the 33 subsidiaries cut loose when the US Supreme Court ordered the Standard Oil of New Jersey holding company dissolved in 1911.

After the breakup, Socony, which had depended on its sisters in the Standard Oil household for oil to sell in New York, New England, and overseas, quickly cast about for supplies of its own. The company bought control of Texas-based Magnolia Petroleum (1918) and acquired California-based General Petroleum (1926).

Vacuum, which had grown to 1,500 service stations in the Midwest, and Socony reunited in 1931 as Socony-Vacuum. Shortly after the new company emerged, it adopted the Flying Red Horse (Pegasus) as a trademark. The symbol (representing speed and power) was first used by company operations in South Africa and colored red by operations in Japan.

Socony-Vacuum still needed crude and, in a deal patterned after Caltex (the partnership of Standard Oil of California and Texaco in the Middle East), joined with Standard Oil (New Jersey) to form Stanvac in 1933 for drilling in the Far East. Socony-Vacuum added crude supplies, buying a 10% stake in Aramco (Arabian American Oil Company) in 1948.

The company changed its name to Socony Mobil Oil, adopting its trade name, in 1955. That was shortened to Mobil Oil in 1966.

In 1974 it gained control of Marcor, Chicago-based parent of retail chain Montgomery Ward & Company, and of Container Corporation of America, the giant maker of paper packaging. While it dropped "oil" from its name in 1976, Mobil continued as an outspoken defender of the petroleum industry, purchasing editorial-type ads in major publications.

In 1984 Mobil bought Superior Oil, at the time the largest independent producer of crude and natural gas, for $5.7 billion. To reduce debt from the Superior deal and to refocus on energy, Mobil has sold $7 billion in assets, including Container Corporation of America (1986) and Montgomery Ward (1988).

Mobil upgraded its refinery operations in the early 1990s with a $300 million project at its Beaumont, Texas, facility and, as exploration boomed in Australia and possibly Vietnam, a $100 million effort in Singapore.

NYSE symbol: MOB
Fiscal year ends: December 31

Hoover's Rating **B-**

WHO

Chairman, President, and CEO: Allen E. Murray, age 61, $1,865,000 pay
SVP: Robert G. Weeks, age 54
VP and CFO: Lucio A. Noto, age 52
VP Administration: Rex D. Adams, age 50
Auditors: Ernst & Young
Employees: 67,300

WHERE

HQ: 3225 Gallows Rd., Fairfax, VA 22037
Phone: 703-849-3000
Fax: 703-846-4669

Mobil explores for and produces oil in 20 countries.

	1990 Sales		1990 Net Income	
	$ mil.	% of total	$ mil.	% of total
US	21,006	33	415	17
Canada	1,133	2	113	4
Other foreign	41,660	65	2,019	79
Adjustments	(5,980)	—	(618)	—
Total	**57,819**	**100**	**1,929**	**100**

WHAT

	1990 Sales		1990 Operating Income	
	$ mil.	% of total	$ mil.	% of total
Chemical	4,084	6	397	8
Exploration & production	5,833	9	3,840	74
Marketing & refining	53,882	85	957	18
Adjustments	(5,980)	—	(1,001)	—
Total	**57,819**	**100**	**4,193**	**100**

Principal Products and Activities
Coal mining
Crude oil and natural gas production
Petrochemicals and plastics
Petroleum pipelining, refining, and marketing
Phosphate rock mining
Plastic film and other packaging materials
Real estate development
Specialty and synthetic lubricants

Brand Names
Baggies (plastic food-storage bags)
Hefty (plastic bags, housewares)
Kordite (plastic garbage bags)
Mobil 1
Mobilgrease
Mobilheat
Mobiloil
Tucker (molded household plastics)

RANKINGS

5th in *Fortune* 500 Industrial Cos.
14th in *Business Week* Global 1000

KEY COMPETITORS

Amoco	Imperial Oil	Premark
Ashland	Koch	Reynolds Metals
Atlantic Richfield	Norsk Hydro	Royal Dutch/Shell
British Petroleum	Occidental	Rubbermaid
	Oryx	Sun
Broken Hill	Pennzoil	Texaco
Chevron	Petrofina	Unocal
Coastal	Petrobrás	USX
Dow Chemical	PDVSA	Chemical and
Du Pont	Pemex	mining
Elf Aquitaine	Phillips	companies
Exxon	Petroleum	

HOW MUCH

	9-Year Growth	1981	1982	1983	1984	1985	1986	1987	1988	1989	1990
Sales ($ mil.)	(1.2%)	64,488	59,946	54,607	56,047	55,960	44,866	51,223	48,198	50,220	57,819
Net income ($ mil.)	(2.5%)	2,433	1,380	1,503	1,268	1,040	1,407	1,258	2,031	1,809	1,929
Income as % of sales	—	3.8%	2.3%	2.8%	2.3%	1.9%	3.1%	2.5%	4.2%	3.6%	3.3%
Earnings per share ($)	(2.4%)	5.72	3.31	3.70	3.11	2.55	3.45	3.06	4.93	4.40	4.60
Stock price – high ($)	—	41.19	28.63	34.63	32.13	34.38	40.88	55.00	49.13	63.25	69.50
Stock price – low ($)	—	24.13	19.50	24.25	23.13	25.50	26.25	32.00	38.63	45.25	55.88
Stock price – close ($)	10.2%	24.13	25.13	28.75	27.13	30.25	40.13	39.13	45.50	62.63	58.00
P/E – high	—	7	9	9	10	13	12	18	10	14	15
P/E – low	—	4	6	7	7	10	8	10	8	10	12
Dividends per share ($)	3.9%	2.00	2.00	2.00	2.20	2.20	2.20	2.20	2.35	2.55	2.83
Book value per share ($)	1.8%	34.45	36.30	34.30	33.42	34.50	37.28	40.80	38.19	37.88	40.57

1990 Year-end:
Debt ratio: 20.1%
Return on equity: 11.7%
Cash (mil.): $1,138
Current ratio: 0.97
Long-term debt (mil.): $4,298
No. of shares (mil.): 401
Dividends:
1990 average yield: 4.9%
1990 payout: 61.4%
Market value (mil.): $23,263

Stock Price History High/Low 1981–90

MONSANTO COMPANY

NYSE symbol: MTC
Fiscal year ends: December 31

Hoover's Rating **B**

OVERVIEW

St. Louis–based Monsanto, the 3rd largest US chemical company (after Du Pont and Dow), operates worldwide.

Monsanto's chemicals unit (45% of sales) makes nylon carpet fiber, Saflex (plastic interlayer), high-performance plastics, detergents, and other chemicals. Monsanto continues to position itself away from the commodity chemical market and toward the pharmaceutical and biotechnology market.

Crop chemicals include Roundup — the company's most profitable product — and Lasso herbicides. In 1990 Monsanto harvested a field of its new genetically engineered, bug-resistant cotton. Monsanto's Searle makes Calan SR, an antihypertensive drug that is one of the top 15 in US pharmaceutical sales.

A majority of Monsanto's NutraSweet sweetener sales are to the carbonated diet beverage market. The NutrsaSweet subsidiary was the first company to introduce a fat substitute, Simplesse, in an ice cream–like product, and it is testing Desserve, reduced-calorie treats distributed with the help of cookie maven Mrs. Fields.

The company's Fisher Controls unit is a leading worldwide manufacturer of process control gear, including valves and regulators.

WHEN

John Queeny, buyer for a St. Louis drug company, had only one source for saccharin in 1900: Germany. He believed that this sweetener (derived from coal tar) had a growing market in the US. Thus in 1901 in St. Louis, with $5,000 and using his wife's maiden name of Monsanto, Queeny founded Monsanto Chemical Works to manufacture saccharin. The German competition cut prices to drive Monsanto from the marketplace but failed. Monsanto soon diversified with caffeine (1904), vanillin (1905), phenol (antiseptic used in WWI, 1916), and aspirin, when Bayer's German patent expired (1917). Monsanto Chemical went public in 1927.

In 1928 Edgar Monsanto Queeny, only son of the founder, became president. Edgar recognized the potential of rubber additives, buying Rubber Service Laboratories (Akron, Ohio; 1929), and plastics, buying Fiberloid (Springfield, Massachusetts; 1938). In 1943 Monsanto began production of styrene monomer (used in synthetic rubber) for the army's first synthetic tire in WWII.

Monsanto entered the synthetic fiber market (1949) in a joint venture with American Viscose, forming Chemstrand (bought the whole company, 1961); it developed Acrilan fibers (1952) and the synthetic surface AstroTurf (first used commercially in the Houston Astrodome, 1966). In 1952 Monsanto marketed "all" (detergent) but in 1957 abandoned consumer products and sold "all" to Unilever. In 1954 Monsanto and Bayer (Germany) entered into a joint venture (Mobay Chemical) for the R&D of urethane foams. Bayer bought Mobay in 1967.

In 1960 Edgar resigned as chairman. In 1964 the company changed its name to Monsanto Company to emphasize its diversity. Monsanto introduced new products, including the herbicides Lasso (1969) and Roundup (1973). In 1969 Monsanto bought 67% of Fisher Governor (valves and control systems; Marshalltown, Iowa), changing its name to Fisher Controls (bought remaining 33%, 1983). In 1972 Monsanto abandoned saccharin because of competition from Japan.

In 1985 Monsanto acquired G. D. Searle (pharmaceuticals, founded 1868) and, consequently, the lawsuits resulting from Searle's Copper-7 intrauterine contraceptive device (introduced in 1974). Through Searle, Monsanto also bought the licensing rights to manufacture NutraSweet (artificial sweetener) and formed a subsidiary to promote Nutra-Sweet before its patent expires in late 1992.

In 1991 Monsanto sold its animal feed business to 2 Japanese companies, Mitsui and Nippon Soda.

WHO

Chairman and CEO: Richard J. Mahoney, age 57, $1,220,000 pay
President and COO: Earle H. Harbison, Jr., age 62, $855,000 pay
SVP and CFO: Francis A. Stroble, age 60
VP Human Resources: Barry Blitstein
Auditors: Deloitte & Touche
Employees: 41,000

WHERE

HQ: 800 N. Lindbergh Blvd., St. Louis, MO 63167
Phone: 314-694-1000
Fax: 314-694-7625

Monsanto produces and sells its products throughout the US and worldwide.

	1990 Sales		1990 Operating Income	
	$ mil.	% of total	$ mil.	% of total
US	5,685	63	639	66
Europe & Africa	1,995	22	235	24
Canada	413	5	32	3
Latin America	341	4	17	2
Asia/Pacific	561	6	42	5
Adjustments	—	—	(56)	—
Total	**8,995**	**100**	**909**	**100**

WHAT

	1990 Sales		1990 Operating Income	
	$ mil.	% of total	$ mil.	% of total
Chemicals	4,035	45	297	32
Process controls	927	10	95	10
Pharmaceuticals	1,424	16	93	10
Low-calorie sweetener	933	10	183	19
Agri. products	1,676	19	327	35
Biotechnology R&D	—	—	(52)	(6)
Adjustments	—	—	(34)	—
Total	**8,995**	**100**	**909**	**100**

Major Products
Herbicides
Industrial chemicals
Industrial process control equipment
Low-calorie sweeteners (NutraSweet, Equal)
Fat substitute products (Simplesse, Simple Pleasures)
Synthetic fibers and plastics
Prescription pharmaceuticals

RANKINGS

53rd in *Fortune* 500 Industrial Cos.
78th in *Business Week* 1000

HOW MUCH

	9-Year Growth	1981	1982	1983	1984	1985	1986	1987	1988	1989	1990
Sales ($ mil.)	2.9%	6,948	6,325	6,299	6,691	6,747	6,879	7,639	8,293	8,681	8,995
Net income ($ mil.)	2.3%	445	329	369	439	(128)	433	436	591	679	546
Income as % of sales	—	6.4%	5.2%	5.9%	6.6%	(1.9%)	6.3%	5.7%	7.1%	7.8%	6.1%
Earnings per share ($)	4.5%	2.86	2.05	2.24	2.71	(0.84)	2.78	2.82	4.14	5.02	4.23
Stock price – high ($)	—	21.88	22.25	29.09	26.94	27.69	40.75	50.13	46.19	62.13	60.13
Stock price – low ($)	—	14.88	14.16	18.56	20.31	20.31	22.38	28.50	36.75	40.25	38.75
Stock price – close ($)	11.9%	17.53	19.06	26.31	22.00	23.88	38.25	41.50	40.88	57.69	48.25
P/E – high	—	8	11	13	10	—	15	18	11	12	14
P/E – low	—	5	7	8	8	—	8	10	9	8	9
Dividends per share ($)	8.2%	0.94	0.99	1.04	1.13	1.23	1.29	1.38	1.48	1.65	1.91
Book value per share ($)	4.9%	21.09	21.49	22.40	23.21	22.19	24.34	26.32	27.60	29.79	32.51

1990 Year-end:
Debt ratio: 28.8%
Return on equity: 13.6%
Cash (mil.): $204
Current ratio: 1.60
Long-term debt (mil.): $1,652
No. of shares (mil.): 126
Dividends:
1990 average yield: 3.9%
1990 payout: 45.0%
Market value (mil.): $6,069

Stock Price History High/Low 1981–90

KEY COMPETITORS

Abbott Labs	CPC	Imperial
Allied-Signal	Dow Chemical	Chemical
American	Du Pont	ITT
Cyanamid	Elf Aquitaine	Occidental
Amgen	Eli Lilly	Pfizer
ADM	FMC	Procter
BASF	General Signal	& Gamble
Bayer	W. R. Grace	Rhône-Poulenc
Bristol-Myers	Hercules	Union Carbide
Squibb	Hoechst	Other drug
Cargill	Honeywell	companies

MONTGOMERY WARD HOLDING CORP.

OVERVIEW

For most of the 20th century, Montgomery Ward has suffered from sluggish sales growth, weak management, and a dowdy image. Following a 1988 management-led buyout from former owner Mobil Corporation, Chairman Bernard F. Brennan has refocused Montgomery Ward, the 9th largest US retailer and 2nd largest privately held retailer (after R.H. Macy).

Brennan's strategy for rebuilding the 346-store chain included shifting the company from private-label to name-brand merchandising; in 1990 Ward was a leading retailer of General Electric, Sony, Maytag, Panasonic, and Michelin products. The brand-name approach has since been adopted by Sears, whose chairman is Brennan's older brother Edward.

Another part of the company's strategy is the remodeling of each location into 4 distinct "specialty stores," often with separate entrances. These divisions represent the focus of Montgomery Ward's remaining product lines.

Montgomery Ward has now had 5 years of record earnings and has reduced its debt to under $700 million. The LBO actually reduced the company's absolute level of debt.

WHEN

Aaron Montgomery Ward started the company that bears his name in Chicago in 1872. The company was the world's first general merchandise mail-order concern. Prior to this time farmers purchased goods from the general store or peddlers. Ward provided them with an inexpensive way to shop, by mail-order catalog. In 1873 Ward took as a partner brother-in-law George Thorne. In 1875 the company pioneered the "Satisfaction Guaranteed or Your Money Back" policy.

In 1893 Thorne bought a controlling interest in the company. By 1900 Ward's sales had fallen behind flamboyant Chicago rival Sears (founded in 1893). In 1904 Ward introduced its first employee magazine, which is believed to be the first company magazine edited by employees without policy dictated by the company. Profits surpassed $1 million for the first time in 1909, and the following year George Thorne retired, leaving son Charles and 4 other sons in control of the company. In 1913 Ward died and Charles Thorne became president. Three years later Charles Thorne became chairman and his brother Robert became president. In 1919 Ward became a public corporation and General Robert Wood became general merchandise manager. The following year Ward suffered its first loss despite over $100 million in sales.

From 1920 to 1924 Ward's sales grew by 47.5%, compared to Sears's 15.9% decrease. Because Wood wanted Ward to develop retail stores and the company wanted to remain in the mail-order business, Wood left Ward in 1924 and went to work for Sears. Two years later Ward opened its first retail store in Plymouth, Indiana. By the end of 1928 the company had 244 retail stores.

In 1931 Sewell Avery became CEO, and under his leadership Ward ended 4 years of losses and was profitable in 1934. Avery refused to turn over the company to federal control during a WWII labor dispute, and President Franklin Roosevelt had National Guardsmen carry Avery out of his office. Avery, who had correctly predicted the Great Depression, also was convinced there would be a recession after WWII and canceled expansion plans, missing out on the postwar boom.

After Avery's departure (1955), Ward started a new expansion program, which included new stores in Alaska and the company's first major distribution center (1958). In 1968 the company merged with Container Corporation of America to form Marcor. In 1974 Mobil Oil acquired 54% control of Ward and completed the acquisition of the entire company in 1976. Mobil made huge loans to the company in hopes of Ward's becoming profitable.

In 1985 Mobil, declaring that it had had enough, put Ward up for sale and brought in Bernard Brennan — who had left Sears in 1976, joined Ward in 1982, and quit after disputes with then-CEO Stephen Pistner in 1983 — to lead the company. After jettisoning money-losing operations — including the catalog operations that Aaron Montgomery Ward had founded — Brennan and other senior management led an investor group that bought Ward in a $3.8 billion LBO in 1988. Brennan sold Ward's credit card business to General Electric Capital for about $1 billion in cash and assumption of $1.7 billion in debt.

In 1990 Ward announced the expansion of its revived catalog operations, which now serve the new specialty formats. Wards plans to open 15 more stores by the end of 1991.

Private company
Fiscal year ends: Last Saturday in December

WHO

Chairman, President, and CEO: Bernard F. Brennan, age 52
VC and COO: Daniel H. Levy, age 47
EVP; President Marketing: William J. McCarthy, age 54
EVP; President Store Operations: Richard M. Bergel, age 55
SVP Finance and CFO: Edwin G. "Buck" Pohlmann, age 43
SVP Human Resources and Customer Satisfaction: Robert A. Kasenter, age 44
Auditors: Arthur Andersen & Co.
Employees: 66,300

WHERE

HQ: One Montgomery Ward Plaza, Chicago, IL 60671-0042
Phone: 312-467-2000
Fax: 312-467-7158

Montgomery Ward operates 346 retail stores in 39 states. In addition, the company operates 22 liquidation stores, 24 distribution facilities, and 138 product service centers. Foreign purchasing offices are maintained in Italy, Hong Kong, Taiwan, Japan, and Korea.

WHAT

	1990 Sales		1990 Operating Income	
	$ mil.	% of total	$ mil.	% of total
Retail merchandising	5,128	94	194	72
Direct marketing	312	6	77	28
Adjustments	24	—	(73)	—
Total	**5,464**	**100**	**198**	**100**

Retail Specialties
The Apparel Store
Includes Kids Store and Gold 'N Gems fine jewelry
Auto Express
Tires, batteries, parts and service
Electric Avenue
Electronics and major appliances
Home Ideas
Home furnishings and accessories

Subsidiaries
Signature Financial/Marketing, Inc.
Montgomery Ward Auto Club, insurance, and direct-mail marketing
Standard T Chemical
Paints and detergents

RANKINGS

14th in *Forbes* 400 US Private Cos.

KEY COMPETITORS

Ames	Home Depot	J. C. Penney
Circuit City	Kmart	Price Co.
Costco	The Limited	Sears
Dayton Hudson	Liz Claiborne	Tandy
Dillard	Lowe's	Toys "R" Us
The Gap	Melville	Wal-Mart
General Cinema	Mercantile Stores	Woolworth

HOW MUCH

	9-Year Growth	1981	1982	1983	1984	1985	1986	1987	1988	1989	1990
Sales ($ mil.)	(0.6%)	5,742	5,570	6,003	6,486	5,388	4,870	5,024	5,403	5,349	5,464
Net income ($ mil.)	—	(124)	(75)	54	68	(298)	110	130	139	151	153
Income as % of sales	—	(2.2%)	(1.3%)	0.9%	1.0%	(5.5%)	2.3%	2.6%	2.6%	2.8%	2.8%

1990 Year-end:
Debt ratio: 61.4%
Return on equity: 38.3%
Cash (mil.): $674
Current ratio: —
Long-term debt (mil.): $669

Net Income ($ mil.) 1981–90

J.P. MORGAN & CO. INC.

OVERVIEW

J.P. Morgan is a holding company that traditionally specialized in "relationship banking" — arrangement of large-scale financing to governments, large corporations, and wealthy individuals. Its primary subsidiary is Morgan Guaranty Trust, the 5th largest US bank (after the Chemical–Manufacturers Hanover merger). The company operates one of the largest trust departments in the US.

Morgan is a major dealer in government securities, foreign currencies, and precious metals. The company operates a clearance system for internationally traded securities, handling $4.1 trillion in 1990 transactions.

Morgan's non-US sales were 45% of its $10.5 billion total in 1990. After a 1989 loss — its first in 49 years — J.P. Morgan rebounded with a $775 million profit in 1990. With top-notch assets, by mid-1991 it was the only New York bank that had managed to retain its triple-A credit rating.

Morgan has returned to its glory days as a dealmaker since the Federal Reserve Board approved the company's reentry into stock underwriting.

NYSE symbol: JPM
Fiscal year ends: December 31

WHO

Chairman and CEO: Dennis Weatherstone, age 60, $1,583,000 pay
President and COO: Douglas A. Warner III, age 44, $1,329,667 pay
CFO: James T. Flynn, age 51
SVP Human Resources: Herbert Hefke
Auditors: Price Waterhouse
Employees: 12,968

WHERE

HQ: 60 Wall St., New York, NY 10260
Phone: 212-483-2323
Fax: 212-235-4945

J.P. Morgan oversees offices in 7 US cities and in 27 other cities around the world.

	1990 Assets	
	$ mil.	% of total
US	52,693	57
Other Western Hemisphere	4,571	5
Europe, Middle East & Africa	31,778	34
Asia & Pacific	4,061	4
Total	**93,103**	**100**

WHAT

	1990 Assets	
	$ mil.	% of total
Cash & due from banks	2,200	2
Interest-earning deposits	8,382	9
Investment securities	18,541	20
Trading account	15,653	17
Securities purchased to resell, borrowed; federal funds sold	8,705	9
Loans	27,562	30
Allowance for credit losses	(1,850)	(2)
Customers' acceptance of liability	1,098	1
Other	12,812	14
Total	**93,103**	**100**

Services to Clients
Financing
Investments
Long-term advisory relationships
Risk management
Strategic advice

WHEN

J.P. Morgan & Co. was born into international capitalism and has lived there ever since. Junius Spencer Morgan became, in 1854, a partner in London-based financier George Peabody's banking house. Morgan assumed control and renamed the firm J. S. Morgan and Company when Peabody retired in the early 1860s.

Morgan's son began his own firm, J. Pierpont Morgan and Company, in New York in 1862. Connections on both sides of the Atlantic led to profits and power as the firm funneled European capital into the US. Early in its career, the Morgan firm came to the rescue of the US government. In 1877, when Congress bickered over the Hayes-Tilden election and didn't get around to paying the army, a Morgan affiliate came up with the funds until Congress reconvened.

After Junius's death in 1890, his son reorganized his businesses in London and New York as J.P. Morgan & Co. The firm had already financed and restructured much of the American railroad network, and J. P. Morgan, who became the personification of Wall Street, helped devise the deals that created U.S. Steel, General Electric, and International Harvester.

In 1907 J.P. Morgan served as the country's *de facto* central bank when it led a group of bankers who rallied to stop a financial panic. The firm's influence was pervasive. In 1912 a congressional panel investigating collusion in big business discovered that Morgan partners held 72 directorships in 47 corporations with total resources of $10 billion.

Morgan's son, J. P. Morgan, Jr., became senior partner of the firm upon his father's death in 1913. Morgan yielded day-to-day control to partner Thomas Lamont, who tried in 1929, just as J. P., Sr., had in 1907, to stem national financial collapse; however, the stock crash overwhelmed the effort.

In 1933, following Glass-Steagall Act reform of American banking, the company split its activities. Morgan remained a commercial banking firm, and a spinoff entity — Morgan Stanley — became the underwriter for securities.

In 1959 Morgan merged with Morgan Guaranty Trust and in 1969 became a bank holding company. In the 1960s the company became the most active trader in government securities and intensified its international efforts. After a 1987 restructuring, Morgan pushed into merger-and-acquisitions services.

In 1991 an arm of the Morgan organization, J.P. Morgan Securities, served as underwriter for a $56 million equity issue for Amsco, a health products manufacturer. The event was historic — the first time since the Glass-Steagall Act that an affiliate of a commercial bank was permitted to underwrite.

RANKINGS

4th in *Fortune* 100 Commercial Banking Cos.
70th in *Business Week* 1000

KEY COMPETITORS

American Express	First Chicago
Bank of New York	HSBC
BankAmerica	Industrial Bank of Japan
Bankers Trust	Merrill Lynch
Barclays	MetLife
Bear Stearns	Morgan Stanley
Canadian Imperial	Paine Webber
Chase Manhattan	Royal Bank
Chemical Banking	Salomon
Citicorp	Sears
Continental Bank	Travelers
Crédit Lyonnais	Union Bank of Switzerland
CS Holding	Other money-center banks
Dai-Ichi Kangyo	Investment banking firms
Deutsche Bank	Securities brokerage firms

HOW MUCH

	9-Year Growth	1981	1982	1983	1984	1985	1986	1987	1988	1989	1990
Assets ($ mil.)	6.3%	53,522	58,597	58,023	64,126	69,375	76,039	75,414	83,923	88,964	93,103
Net income ($ mil.)	9.3%	348	394	460	538	705	873	83	1,002	(1,275)	775
Income as % of assets	—	0.7%	0.7%	0.8%	0.8%	1.0%	1.1%	0.1%	1.2%	(1.4%)	0.8%
Earnings per share ($)	7.3%	2.11	2.38	2.63	3.04	3.91	4.74	0.39	5.38	(7.04)	3.99
Stock price – high ($)	—	15.97	18.00	21.56	20.19	33.00	48.00	53.63	40.25	48.13	47.25
Stock price – low ($)	—	12.28	11.38	15.63	14.13	19.13	29.50	27.00	30.75	34.00	29.63
Stock price – close ($)	14.2%	13.44	16.88	16.84	19.63	32.06	41.25	36.25	34.88	44.00	44.38
P/E – high	—	8	8	8	7	8	10	138	7	—	12
P/E – low	—	6	5	6	5	5	6	69	6	—	7
Dividends per share ($)	9.9%	0.79	0.87	0.94	1.03	1.13	1.26	1.40	1.54	1.70	1.86
Book value per share ($)	5.6%	15.52	17.11	18.85	21.03	23.70	27.42	26.57	30.52	21.78	25.29

1990 Year-end:
Return on equity: 17.0%
Equity as % of assets: 5.3%
Cash (mil.): $10,582
Sales (mil.): $10,465
Long-term debt (mil.): $4,723
No. of shares (mil.): 186
Dividends:
1990 average yield: 4.2%
1990 payout: 46.6%
Market value (mil.): $8,238

Stock Price History High/Low 1981–90

MORGAN STANLEY GROUP INC.

OVERVIEW

Morgan Stanley, with $53.5 billion in assets, is a major international securities firm serving institutional and individual clients through offices in the US, Canada, Europe, Hong Kong, Japan, Australia, and Singapore.

The firm is a leading underwriter of common and preferred stock and taxable fixed-income securities in the US, and taxable-fixed income and equity securities internationally. Morgan Stanley provides sales, trading and research services and is recognized for its planning. The firm became an industry pioneer in 1980 by designing a common database to be used to trade and settle securities transactions in any market in the world.

Although Morgan Stanley remained more profitable than most Wall Street firms in 1990, with a 19% increase in trading, asset management, and commission revenues, it suffered a 12% decline in net revenues due to a 31% decline in investment banking results and a whopping 99% decline in the firm's own investment income. In addition, the firm is mired in numerous lawsuits arising from investor dissatisfaction with Morgan Stanley's M&A and LBO activities in the 1980s.

In 1990 the firm began considering moving its offices from New York City. Such a move, made possible by the development of electronic trading, would cut overhead.

NYSE symbol: MS
Fiscal year ends: December 31

 Hoover's Rating **B-**

WHO

Chairman: Richard B. Fisher, age 54, $2,150,000 pay
President: Robert F. Greenhill, age 54, $2,150,000 pay
Director Human Resources: William Higgins
Auditors: Ernst & Young
Employees: 7,100

WHERE

HQ: 1251 Ave. of the Americas, New York, NY 10020
Phone: 212-703-4000
Fax: 212-703-6503

Morgan Stanley operates from its headquarters, 4 US regional offices, and 11 foreign offices.

	1990 Net Sales	
	$ mil.	% of total
North America	1,206	56
Europe	673	31
Asia	280	13
Total	**2,159**	**100**

WHEN

Morgan Stanley split from the J.P. Morgan banking company after the 1934 Glass-Steagall Act required banks to separate commercial banking (deposit taking and lending) from investment banking activities (issuing and trading securities).

In 1935 Henry Morgan, Harold Stanley, and others resigned and established Morgan Stanley as an investment banking firm. Capitalizing on its old ties to major corporations, the company handled $1 billion in issues during its first year.

By the time Morgan Stanley became a partnership in 1941, so it could join the New York Stock Exchange, it had managed 25% of all bond issues underwritten since the Glass-Steagall Act.

In the 1950s Morgan Stanley was known as a well-managed firm that handled issues by itself and rarely participated with other firms. Despite having only $3 million in capital, the partnership was the investment bank for such major US corporations as General Motors, U.S. Steel, General Electric, and Du Pont.

Morgan Stanley chose not to help finance the merger wave of the 1960s (when conglomerates purchased unrelated companies), since Morgan Stanley's blue-chip clients were not involved. In the early 1970s it entered the mergers and acquisitions world, forming Wall Street's first M&A department. In 1974 Morgan Stanley handled its first hostile takeover, International Nickel's takeover of ESB, the world's largest battery manufacturer. Competing investment banking firms then became involved in hostile takeovers.

In 1986 Morgan Stanley became a publicly owned corporation, with its managing directors and principals retaining 81% of the stock. It amassed a $1.6 billion investment pool and joined the LBO fray, acquiring Burlington Industries for $46.3 million and $2.2 billion in debt (1987). Since then, Burlington's best assets have been sold off to service the debt, and Morgan Stanley has received over $176 million in fees and dividends.

The 1987 crash sent the financial world into a tailspin, curtailing most trading activities, though securities offerings continued strongly until 1989, and then declined as well. Foreign operations, however, especially in Japan (where the firm has one of the strongest presences of any US securities firm), remained strong, contributing 44% of net sales in 1990. As the stock market revived in 1991, Morgan Stanley's trading operations strengthened.

WHAT

	1990 Sales	
	$ mil.	% of total
Investment banking	652	11
Trading, as principal	902	15
Investments, as principal	2	—
Commissions	275	5
Interest & dividends	3,894	66
Asset management	131	2
Other	14	1
Total	**5,870**	**100**

Financial Services
Asset management
Corporate finance
Futures, options, foreign exchange, and commodities trading
Merchant banking
Securities custody, clearance, and lending
Securities distribution and trading
Securities underwriting
Stock brokerage and research

RANKINGS

9th in *Fortune* 50 Diversified Financial Cos.
232nd in *Business Week* 1000

KEY COMPETITORS

American Express	Nomura
Bear Stearns	Paine Webber
CS Holding	Primerica
Deutsche Bank	Prudential
Equitable	Salomon
Goldman Sachs	Travelers
Kemper	Major investment
Merrill Lynch	managers

HOW MUCH

	5-Year Growth	1981	1982	1983	1984	1985	1986	1987	1988	1989	1990
Sales ($ mil.)	26.7%	—	—	—	—	1,795	2,463	3,148	4,109	5,831	5,870
Net income ($ mil.)	20.6%	—	—	—	—	106	201	231	395	443	270
Income as % of sales	—	—	—	—	—	5.9%	8.2%	7.3%	9.6%	7.6%	4.6%
Earnings per share ($)	—	—	—	—	—	—	5.57	5.95	10.12	11.21	6.75
Stock price – high ($)	—	—	—	—	—	—	54.67	57.25	56.58	79.50	75.50
Stock price – low ($)	—	—	—	—	—	—	40.92	25.50	31.17	54.83	47.13
Stock price – close ($)	—	—	—	—	—	—	43.25	34.17	55.33	64.63	54.38
P/E – high	—	—	—	—	—	—	10	10	6	7	11
P/E – low	—	—	—	—	—	—	7	4	3	5	7
Dividends per share ($)	—	—	—	—	—	0.00	0.23	0.53	0.63	1.00	1.50
Book value per share ($)	36.8%	—	—	—	—	10.22	21.05	26.96	38.17	47.85	48.97

1990 Year-end:
Debt ratio: 35.8%
Return on equity: 13.9%
Cash (mil.): $2,275
Assets (mil.): $53,526
Long-term debt (mil.): $1,209
No. of shares (mil.): 36
Dividends:
  1990 average yield: 2.8%
  1990 payout: 22.2%
Market value (mil.): $1,978

**Stock Price History
High/Low 1986–90**

MORTON INTERNATIONAL, INC.

OVERVIEW

Morton International is a Chicago-based manufacturer of specialty chemicals, salt, and automobile air bags.

Specialty chemicals account for 62% of Morton's sales and include adhesives and coatings for food packaging and liquid plastic coatings for automobiles. Morton also makes electronic materials used in printed circuit boards and semiconductor wafers and is a leading provider of dyes used for leak detection and for coloring petroleum products, plastics, food, and cosmetics.

Morton salt, accounting for 28% of sales, has 50% of the US market, and Morton's Windsor Salt leads in Canada. About 8% of Morton's revenues come from ice control. The symbol of Morton salt — the little umbrella girl — is one of the 10 most memorable consumer symbols in America.

Morton's air bag business (inflators and driver modules) accounts for 10% of sales but is growing fast, with 55% of the worldwide market. Morton expects the product line to grow to 30% of sales by 1995.

NYSE symbol: MII
Fiscal year ends: June 30

Hoover's Rating **B+**

WHEN

Alonzo Richmond started Richmond & Company, agents for Onondaga Salt, in Chicago in 1848. During the first year Richmond received 36,656 barrels of salt for packing from Onondaga Lake near Syracuse.

In 1867 the company became Haskins, Martin & Wheeler, and the salt supply came by boat from lumber towns in northern Michigan. In 1886 Joy Morton became the controlling owner of Haskins, Martin & Wheeler (renamed Joy Morton & Company). The company remained a sales agency until 1890, when it built its first salt evaporation plant in Wyandotte, Michigan.

In 1910 the company was renamed Morton Salt Company. In 1914, after 3 years of advertisements featuring the Morton Salt girl holding an umbrella, the company added its well-known slogan: "When it rains it pours."

Morton expanded nationwide with 8 production centers in the 1940s. It also bought a Louisiana salt plant (1947) for salt cake (paper making) and muriatic acid (steel production).

In 1951 the company purchased Edwal Laboratories, an Illinois manufacturer of photographic chemicals, and introduced Morton Pellets, salt for recharging home water softeners. In 1954 Morton purchased The Canadian Salt Company Ltd.

In the 1960s Morton diversified by purchasing Adcote Chemicals (1964, commercial adhesives), Simoniz (1965, waxes), and

Williams Hounslow (1967, food and cosmetic dyes). In 1969 privately owned Morton merged with Norwich Pharmacal, maker of drugs (Pepto-Bismol, Chloraseptic) and household cleaners (Fantastik, Spray 'n Wash), to form Morton-Norwich Products, Inc.

During the 1970s, CEO John W. Simmons organized the company into 4 divisions: salts, pharmaceuticals, household products, and specialty chemicals. In 1982 the company sold its Norwich-Eaton Pharmaceuticals division to Procter & Gamble for $371 million. Later that year Morton-Norwich bought Thiokol, Inc., a rocket and chemical manufacturer, to form Morton Thiokol, Inc.

The company successfully applied Thiokol's propulsion knowledge to develop automobile air bags (used by Mercedes, Chrysler, and Saab). However, CEO Charles Locke was concerned that aerospace represented about 45% of sales but only 28% of profits in 1987. By 1989 salt and specialty chemicals outperformed aerospace by an even wider margin, and the company spun off aerospace into a new company, Thiokol Corporation. Morton International retained the salt, chemical, and air bag businesses.

In 1990 the company bought Whittaker Corporation (coatings, adhesives). A 1991 joint venture with Germany's Robert Bosch will propel Morton into the European market for air bags.

WHO

Chairman and CEO: Charles S. Locke, age 61, $1,073,333 pay
President and COO: S. Jay Stewart, age 51, $610,312 pay
Group VP, Salt: William E. Johnston, Jr., age 49, $434,169 pay
Group VP, Specialty Chemicals: Robert B. Covalt, age 58, $343,942 pay
SVP and CFO: John R. Bowen, age 56, $341,264 pay
VP Human Resources: John C. Hedley, age 60
Auditors: Ernst & Young
Employees: 9,700

WHERE

HQ: 110 N. Wacker Dr., Chicago, IL 60606-1560
Phone: 312-807-2000
Fax: 312-807-2241

Morton has operations throughout the US and in 11 foreign countries.

	1990 Sales		1990 Operating Income	
	$ mil.	% of total	$ mil.	% of total
US	1,141	70	159	66
Canada & Bahamas	180	11	37	15
Europe	297	18	45	19
Other countries	21	1	—	—
Adjustments	—	—	(41)	—
Total	**1,639**	**100**	**200**	**100**

WHAT

	1990 Sales		1990 Operating Income	
	$ mil.	% of total	$ mil.	% of total
Specialty chemicals	1,022	62	140	58
Salt	454	28	86	36
Inflatable restraint systems	163	10	15	6
Adjustments	—	—	(41)	—
Total	**1,639**	**100**	**200**	**100**

Products
Auto air bag systems
Salt
  Morton and Windsor table salts
  Nature's Seasons and Lite Salt brands
  Private label table salts
  Salt for ice melting
  Salt pellets (water conditioning)
Specialty chemicals
  Adhesives and coatings
  Dry film photoresists (for circuit boards)
  Specialty dyes and colors
  Specialty polymers

RANKINGS

248th in *Fortune* 500 Industrial Cos.
284th in *Business Week* 1000

HOW MUCH

	2-Year Growth	1981	1982	1983	1984	1985	1986	1987	1988	1989	1990
Sales ($ mil.)	14.6%	—	—	—	—	—	—	—	1,248	1,407	1,639
Net income ($ mil.)	7.9%	—	—	—	—	—	—	—	116	97	135
Income as % of sales	—	—	—	—	—	—	—	—	9.3%	6.9%	8.2%
Earnings per share ($)	7.3%	—	—	—	—	—	—	—	2.43	2.03	2.80
Stock price – high ($)	—	—	—	—	—	—	—	—	—	41.88	47.50
Stock price – low ($)	—	—	—	—	—	—	—	—	—	31.50	33.50
Stock price – close ($)	—	—	—	—	—	—	—	—	—	35.88	45.63
P/E – high	—	—	—	—	—	—	—	—	—	21	17
P/E – low	—	—	—	—	—	—	—	—	—	16	12
Dividends per share ($)	—	—	—	—	—	—	—	—	0.00	0.00	0.86
Book value per share ($)	—	—	—	—	—	—	—	—	—	18.80	21.00

1990 Year-end:
Debt ratio: 20.6%
Return on equity: 14.1%
Cash (mil.): $87
Current ratio: 1.80
Long-term debt (mil.): $261
No. of shares (mil.): 48
Dividends:
  1990 average yield: 1.9%
  1990 payout: 30.7%
Market value (mil.): $2,190

Stock Price History High/Low 1989–90

KEY COMPETITORS

American	FMC	Mobil
Cyanamid	W. R. Grace	PPG
Atlantic Richfield	Hercules	Rhône-Poulenc
Bayer	Hitachi	Sherwin Williams
BASF	Hoechst	TRW
Cargill	Imperial	Union Carbide
Ciba-Geigy	Chemical	Specialty
Dow Chemical	S.C. Johnson	chemical
Du Pont	3M	manufacturers

MOTOROLA, INC.

OVERVIEW

Former car-radio maker Motorola is now the leading US supplier of semiconductors (#4 in the world) and the world's leading supplier of mobile radios, cellular telephone systems, and pagers. The $10.8 billion electronics giant spent over $1 billion on R&D in 1990. Motorola controls 4,066 US and 2,286 foreign patents, including 407 awarded in 1990.

Motorola's communications products include the best-selling MicroTAC mobile phone, which weighs under one pound. Motorola has aggressively pursued business overseas and is the only non-Japanese supplier of car telephones and pagers to Nippon Telegraph & Telephone. In 1990 Motorola announced plans to develop the Iridium system, a chain of 77 satellites to bring cellular telephone service anywhere on the globe.

Since 1979, the company's semiconductor sector has sold more than 30 million microprocessors. It is the only manufacturer of the 68030 chip used in the Apple Macintosh and Hewlett-Packard microcomputers, although this business was clouded when Motorola lost customers by delaying shipments of faster chips.

Motorola's Information Systems Group produces data communications hardware; the Government Electronics Group pursues defense contracts; and the Automotive and Industrial Electronics Group makes instrumentation and sensors for automobiles. The company has also formed a "New Enterprises" group to explore additional lines of business.

WHEN

Two individuals share primary responsibility for shaping Motorola. The first, Paul Galvin, founded Galvin Manufacturing in 1928. Based in Chicago, Galvin began producing car radio receivers in 1929 and began speculating whether he could make a mobile radio for police. He met Daniel Noble, a professor working on mobile design, and persuaded him to join the company.

In 1947 Galvin renamed the company Motorola, after its car radios. That same year Noble established an Arizona research laboratory for the pursuit of defense contracts for radio communications. Radios and TVs required vacuum tubes, which Motorola purchased from key competitor RCA. Noble persuaded Galvin to invest R&D dollars in solid-state devices, and in the late 1950s the company turned to semiconductor development. Since then Motorola has manufactured integrated circuits and microprocessors; each allowed the company to market outside its mainstay, the automotive industry. In 1959 Galvin died and his son Robert became CEO. Noble continued as chairman of the science committee.

Motorola changed focus in the 1970s, selling its TV business to Matsushita (Japan, 1974) and investing in the data communications market for hardware such as modems, through acquisition of Codex (1977) and Universal Data Systems (1978). Motorola has recently invested more heavily in data communications.

In 1990 Motorola announced a settlement of an ongoing patent dispute with Hitachi over the 68030 chip. The company's semiconductor business for microcomputers has been running into trouble, with delays in shipping the 68040 successor chip leading to Motorola's being passed over by firms such as Tandem and Sony, as well as by the IBM/Apple joint venture to make RISC-based workstations. However, Motorola has received a major order for under-the-hood chips from Ford.

Galvin's chosen successor, George Fisher, took over in 1990; his son, Christopher Galvin, is widely expected to become Fisher's successor. In 1990, Robert Galvin was elected chairman of the SEMATECH manufacturing consortium.

NYSE symbol: MOT
Fiscal year ends: December 31

Hoover's Rating A-

WHO

Chairman and CEO: George M. C. Fisher, age 50, $931,347 pay
VC: John F. Mitchell, age 62, $763,942 pay
President and COO: Gary L. Tooker, age 51, $763,224 pay
SEVP and Assistant COO: Christopher B. Galvin, age 40
EVP and CFO: Donald R. Jones, age 60
EVP; Director, Personnel: James Donnelly, age 51
Auditors: KPMG Peat Marwick
Employees: 105,000

WHERE

HQ: 1303 E. Algonquin Rd., Schaumburg, IL 60196
Phone: 708-576-5000
Fax: 708-576-8003

Motorola has major facilities in 10 states, Puerto Rico, Asia, Australia, Canada, Mexico, Central America, Europe, and the Middle East.

	1990 Sales		1990 Operating Income	
	$ mil.	% of total	$ mil.	% of total
US	8,759	59	682	68
Other nations	5,896	41	308	32
Adjustments	(3,770)	—	(39)	—
Total	**10,885**	**100**	**951**	**100**

WHAT

	1990 Sales		1990 Operating Income	
	$ mil.	% of total	$ mil.	% of total
Government electronics	685	6	60	6
Communications	3,560	32	225	23
Information systems	599	5	(1)	—
Semiconductors	3,433	30	314	34
General systems	2,648	23	352	37
Other	436	4	—	—
Adjustments	(476)	—	1	—
Total	**10,885**	**100**	**951**	**100**

Products
Automotive electronics
Cellular telephone systems and telephones
Computers and workstations
Local area networks
Modems
Paging systems and pagers
Radar, avionics and navigation systems
Semiconductors
Transistors
Two-way radios

Data Communications Hardware Brands
Codex
Universal Data Systems

RANKINGS

42nd in *Fortune* 500 Industrial Cos.
66th in *Business Week* 1000

KEY COMPETITORS

BCE
Eaton
Fujitsu
Harris
Hitachi
Hyundai
Intel
IBM
Litton Industries
Lucky-Goldstar
Matsushita
Mitsubishi
National Semiconductor
NEC
Philips
Pioneer
Oki
Robert Bosch
Samsung
Siemens
Texas Instruments
Thomson SA
Toshiba
Westinghouse

HOW MUCH

	9-Year Growth	1981	1982	1983	1984	1985	1986	1987	1988	1989	1990
Sales ($ mil.)	14.0%	3,336	3,786	4,328	5,534	5,443	5,888	6,707	8,250	9,620	10,885
Net income ($ mil.)	12.3%	175	170	244	387	72	194	308	445	498	499
Income as % of sales	—	5.2%	4.5%	5.6%	7.0%	1.3%	3.3%	4.6%	5.4%	5.2%	4.6%
Earnings per share ($)	8.3%	1.85	1.55	2.09	3.27	0.61	1.53	2.39	3.43	3.83	3.80
Stock price – high ($)	—	30.17	31.17	50.00	46.92	40.75	50.00	74.00	54.63	62.50	88.38
Stock price – low ($)	—	18.58	16.42	27.33	29.25	29.13	33.63	34.50	35.88	39.50	49.13
Stock price – close ($)	11.8%	19.25	29.00	45.42	33.75	38.88	35.63	49.75	42.00	58.38	52.38
P/E – high	—	16	20	24	14	67	33	31	16	16	23
P/E – low	—	10	11	13	9	48	22	14	10	10	13
Dividends per share ($)	4.0%	0.53	0.53	0.53	0.61	0.64	0.64	0.64	0.67	0.76	0.76
Book value per share ($)	10.1%	13.60	14.80	16.49	19.18	19.15	21.48	23.26	26.02	29.16	32.32

1990 Year-end:
Debt ratio: 15.7%
Return on equity: 12.4%
Cash (mil.): $577
Current ratio: 1.46
Long-term debt (mil.): $792
No. of shares (mil.): 132
Dividends:
 1990 average yield: 1.5%
 1990 payout: 20.0%
Market value (mil.): $6,898

Stock Price History High/Low 1981–90

NATIONAL GEOGRAPHIC SOCIETY

OVERVIEW

The National Geographic Society defines its primary purpose as "the increase and diffusion of geographic knowledge." Recent articles in the Society's monthly journal, *National Geographic*, have covered the war's environmental effects on the Persian Gulf; culture in Austin, Texas; and African-American folkways.

Since 1890 the Society has supported over 4,000 exploration and research projects ranging from Robert E. Peary's expedition to the North Pole to the exploration of the sunken *Titanic*. It now has 10 million members and an estimated 40 million readers of its publications.

The Society also publishes maps, atlases, and books and makes its popular TV documentaries available on videotape.

Concerned with geographic illiteracy in the US, the Society has launched several educational efforts such as its interactive, multimedia computer system (released in 1990 under a grant from the California Department of Education) and its geographic training of 1,300 teachers in the 1990–91 school year (these teachers in turn reached an additional 60,000 through workshops).

Nonprofit organization
Fiscal year ends: December 31

WHO

President and Chairman: Gilbert M. Grosvenor, age 60
Editor: William Graves, age 64
SVP and COO: John T. Howard, age 44
SVP, Treasurer, and CFO: Alfred J. Hayre
VP Human Resources: H. Lance Barclay
Employees: 2,358

WHERE

HQ: 1600 M St. NW, Washington, DC 20036
Phone: 202-857-7000
Fax: 202-828-6679

The Society has 10.2 million members worldwide.

WHAT

	1990 Sales	
	$ mil.	% of total
Membership dues & magazine subscriptions	231	53
Journal subscriptions	28	6
Advertising sales	37	9
Publication sales	104	24
TV and audiovisual receipts	35	8
Other	2	—
Total	**437**	**100**

Publications

The Adventure of Archaeology
Images of the World
Inside the Vatican
Journey into China
Living Tribes
Lost Empires
National Geographic Atlas of the World
National Geographic Magazine
National Geographic Research
National Geographic Traveler
National Geographic World
Peoples and Places of the Past
We Americans

TV Documentaries (1991–92 season)

"Braving Alaska"
"Eternal Enemies: Lions and Hyenas"
"Hawaii: Strangers in Paradise"
"The Mexicans: Through Their Eyes"

Educational Programs

Geography Education Program
GTV
National Geographic Kids Network
National Geography Bee
The Jason Project
The Weather Machine software

People Supported by the Society

Dr. Robert D. Ballard (discovery of the *Titanic*)
Dr. George F. Bass (underwater archaeology)
Jacques-Yves Cousteau (oceanography)
Drs. John and Frank Craighead (bioecology)
Dr. Harold E. Edgerton (strobe photography)
Dr. Kenan T. Erim (archaeology-Aphrodisias)
Dr. Jane Goodall (primatology)
Sir Edmund Hillary (Everest mountaineer)
Drs. Richard and Mary Leakey (anthropology)
Thayer Soule (travel lectures)
Barbara and Bradford Washburn (cartography)

WHEN

On January 13, 1888, a group of prominent scientists and explorers gathered at Washington, DC's Cosmos Club, across from the White House, to form the National Geographic Society. Gardiner Hubbard was elected as its first president. The Society mailed the first edition of its magazine, dated October 1888, to 165 members. The magazine was clothed in a dull terra-cotta cover and contained a few esoteric articles (such as "The Classification of Geographic Forms by Genesis"). Regular monthly issues didn't appear until after the January 1896 issue, which was sold on newsstands in an attempt to boost sales.

In 1898, following Hubbard's death, his son-in-law, inventor Alexander Graham Bell, became president. Bell wanted to make the magazine as popular as *Harper's Weekly* and *McClure's*. To do the job, he hired Gilbert Grosvenor, who started as assistant editor in 1899 and became managing editor in 1900. Grosvenor later married Bell's daughter. Grosvenor turned the magazine from a dry, technical publication to one of more general interest. It was Bell's idea to send the magazine to "members only," a unique marketing concept still in use today.

Grosvenor accepted only accurate, first-hand accounts for Society magazine articles. The magazine pioneered the use of photography, including the first hand-tinted colored photographs in a 1910 edition. Rare photographs of remote Tibet were published in 1905, and the first bare-breasted woman appeared in a photograph of "a Zulu bride and bridegroom" in the November 1896 issue. The Society sponsored Robert Peary's conquest of the North Pole in 1909 and Hiram Bingham's 1912 exploration of Machu Picchu in Peru. Members raised $100,000 in 1915 to save what is now Sequoia National Park in California.

The 1900 circulation of 2,200 had risen to 1.2 million by 1930. Grosvenor's policy of printing only "what is of a kindly nature . . . about any country or people" resulted in 2 articles that were sharply criticized for their kindly portrayal of prewar Nazi Germany (one picture showed children with the caption, "Green as Goslings now, but practice makes the goose step perfect"). That policy eased over the years, and in 1961 an article by Peter White and Wilbur E. Garrett was one of the first to describe the growing US involvement in Vietnam.

Gilbert Grosvenor retired in 1954 after serving the society for 55 years. His son, Melville Bell Grosvenor, who ran the magazine until 1967, accelerated book publishing (over 50 titles since 1957) and created a film and TV department that broadcast its first documentary, "Americans on Everest," in 1965.

A 3rd generation Grosvenor, Gilbert Melville, took over in 1970 (editor from 1970 to 1980, president since 1980). Since that time the magazine has increasingly covered important social and political events as well as scientific and environmental subjects, and has continued its tradition of photographic innovation, printing a hologram in 1984. The Society faces several challenges in the 1990s such as declining membership amidst rising costs. In 1990 editor Wilbur E. Garrett resigned after a dispute with Gil Grosvenor over the direction of the magazine.

HOW MUCH

	9-Year Growth	1981	1982	1983	1984	1985	1986	1987	1988	1989	1990
Cumulative no. of projects supported	—	2,000	2,200	2,350	2,600	2,800	3,100	3,300	3,400	3,700	4,000
Magazine circulation (thou.)	(0.7%)	10,861	10,614	10,626	10,393	10,549	10,765	10,499	10,575	10,891	10,190
Employees	1.3%	2,253	2,248	2,258	2,275	2,340	2,459	2,522	2,649	2,628	2,526

Cumulative Number of Exploration and Research Projects Supported 1981–90

NATIONAL MEDICAL ENTERPRISES, INC.

OVERVIEW

National Medical Enterprises, headquartered in Santa Monica, is one of the nation's largest health-care providers. Just over 22 years old, the company owns or operates facilities for treatment of psychiatric illness, drug abuse, and physical rehabilitation. NME also operates general hospitals in the US and Singapore.

Since 1986 NME has decreased its average number of licensed general hospital beds by 18%. During the same period it increased the licensed psychiatric and drug abuse hospital beds by 105%. The number of licensed beds in rehabilitation hospitals has increased by 128%.

The company's strategy calls for continued growth in its specialty and general hospital segments and new foreign markets. NME continues to watch for specific health-care niches, such as women's care. The hospital group alone plans to spend about $200 million annually for capital improvements.

But the company is also capable of dramatic retreats, such as the spinoff of Hillhaven Corporation. In 1989 NME claimed $1.1 billion in net revenues from long-term facilities. Just 2 years later it reported none.

WHEN

Hospital attorney and financial consultant Richard Eamer founded National Medical Enterprises in 1969. With $23 million from the sale of public stock in May 1969, the company bought 4 general hospitals, 3 nursing homes, an office building, and 3 potential hospital sites, all in California. Within 6 years the company owned, operated, and managed 23 hospitals, owned a home health care business, sold medical equipment, provided training for vocational nurses, and distributed bottled oxygen.

The company bought Stolte, a hospital construction company (1977), and Medfield's 5 Florida hospitals (1979). In 1980 the company expanded into long-term care with the acquisition of The Hillhaven Corporation, expanding services to 33 states.

NME signed a 5-year, billion-dollar health care contract with Saudi Arabia in 1980 and by 1981 had become the 3rd largest health care company in the US, owning or managing 193 hospitals and nursing homes (24,000 beds). Total revenues exceeded $1 billion for the first time in 1982.

During the first half of the 1980s, NME continued to expand, buying National Health Enterprises's 66 long-term homes (1982); Psychiatric Institutes of America (PIA), operator of 21 mental health centers (1983); and Rehabilitation Hospital Services Corporation

(RHSC), which owned 5 specialized facilities (1985). In 1983 the company formed Recovery Centers of America (RCA), opening 8 substance abuse treatment programs (by 1989 this had grown to 48). By 1985 the company had become the 2nd largest publicly owned health care company. Before the end of the 1980s, NME's Specialty Hospital Group (PIA, RCA, and RHSC) was bringing in more than 50% of the company's net operating revenues.

In January 1990 NME spun off most of its long-term care businesses (including 345 long-term care facilities, 120 Medi-$ave Pharmacies, and 24 retirement homes) to its shareholders as The Hillhaven Corporation. NME kept 14% of the Hillhaven stock and about 1/3 of the nursing home real estate, which it leases to Hillhaven. NME kept the 19 long-term care facilities operated in the UK by its Westminster Health Care Limited subsidiary.

Despite stiff competition and cost-reduction pressures in the health-care industry, NME has prospered. In 1991 its Hospital Group operating profit increased by 15% over 1990 operating profit. Operating profits increased by 16% during the same period in the company's Specialty Hospital Group.

In May 1991 NME opened a 275-bed teaching hospital at the University of Southern California medical school, representing the largest capital project in the company's history.

NYSE symbol: NME
Fiscal year ends: May 31

Hoover's Rating **B**

WHO

Chairman and CEO: Richard K. Eamer, age 63, $1,979,347 pay
President and COO: Leonard Cohen, age 66, $1,458,420 pay
SEVP: John C. Bedrosian, age 56, $982,445 pay
SEVP and Director of Operations: Michael H. Focht, Sr., age 48, $777,769 pay (prior to promotion)
EVP and CFO: Taylor R. Jenson, age 52
SVP Human Resources: Alan R. Ewalt, age 47
Auditors: KPMG Peat Marwick
Employees: 48,500

WHERE

HQ: 2700 Colorado Ave., PO Box 4074, Santa Monica, CA 90404-4070
Phone: 213-315-8000
Fax: 213-315-8329

Location	Specialty Hospitals	General Hospitals
California	15	17
Florida	16	5
Louisiana	5	4
Maryland	6	—
Missouri	2	2
Pennsylvania	9	—
Tennessee	1	3
Texas	21	4
Virginia	5	—
Alabama, Arkansas, Connecticut, District of Columbia, Kansas, Michigan, Minnesota, New Mexico, Oklahoma, South Carolina, Washington (one each)	11	—
Illinois, New Hampshire, North Carolina, Utah (2 each)	8	—
Arizona, Colorado, Georgia, Indiana, New Jersey, Wisconsin (3 each)	18	—
Total	**117**	**35**

WHAT

	1990 Sales		1990 Operating Income	
	$ mil.	% of total	$ mil.	% of total
Specialty hospitals	1,744	46	320	55
General hospitals	1,908	50	216	38
Lease and other	154	4	41	7
Adjustments	—	—	(8)	—
Total	**3,806**	**100**	**569**	**100**

1990 Licensed Beds	No. of Beds	% of Total
Specialty hospitals	9,427	59
General hospitals	6,591	41
Total	**16,018**	**100**

HOW MUCH

Fiscal year ends May of following year	9-Year Growth	1981	1982	1983	1984	1985	1986	1987	1988	1989	1990
Sales ($ mil.)	14.4%	1,139	1,747	2,065	2,530	2,947	2,870	3,199	3,679	3,935	3,806
Net income ($ mil.)	15.6%	75	93	121	149	118	140	170	192	242	277
Income as % of sales	—	6.6%	5.3%	5.9%	5.9%	4.0%	4.9%	5.3%	5.2%	6.2%	7.3%
Earnings per share ($)	10.2%	1.28	1.47	1.74	1.98	1.48	1.68	2.09	2.32	2.67	3.08
Stock price – high ($)	—	23.00	23.80	32.38	25.63	32.88	26.75	30.88	24.75	39.00	40.25
Stock price – low ($)	—	12.50	9.80	20.13	17.63	18.75	19.25	16.13	17.63	21.38	29.25
Stock price – close ($)	11.7%	13.90	23.20	23.00	23.38	22.38	22.50	18.88	21.50	38.75	37.50
P/E – high	—	18	16	19	13	22	16	15	11	15	13
P/E – low	—	10	7	12	9	13	11	8	8	8	10
Dividends per share ($)	11.0%	0.31	0.38	0.43	0.50	0.55	0.59	0.63	0.68	0.72	0.80
Book value per share ($)	11.3%	7.70	9.95	11.03	12.36	12.83	12.47	13.11	14.80	15.93	20.16

1990 Year-end:
Debt ratio: 39.3%
Return on equity: 17.1%
Cash (mil.): $197
Current ratio: 1.58
Long-term debt (mil.): $1,140
No. of shares (mil.): 87
Dividends:
  1990 average yield: 2.1%
  1990 payout: 26.0%
Market value (mil.): $3,277

Stock Price History High/Low 1981–90

RANKINGS

29th in *Fortune* 100 Diversified Service Cos.
189th in *Business Week* 1000

KEY COMPETITORS

Hospital Corp.
Humana
Mayo Foundation

NATIONAL ORGANIZATION FOR WOMEN, INC.

OVERVIEW

Nonprofit organization
Fiscal year ends: December 31

Hoover's Rating **A-**

Headquartered in Washington, DC, the National Organization for Women (NOW) is the nation's largest women's rights group, with over 250,000 female and male members. The organization's broad goal is equality for women in American society. Specific activities include lobbying, litigation, educational programs, and political organizing.

NOW is governed by 4 salaried national officers and a board of directors and has several national issues committees. Local chapters of 10 or more members and state chapters (which help coordinate local chapters and lobby in state legislatures) are chartered by the national organization; each chapter belongs to one of 9 regions.

Despite its success in championing women's issues, NOW has drawn criticism from other activist groups (such as the National Abortion Rights Action League) which claim that NOW's militant style of feminism often alienates more moderate individuals who may share the group's political goals but not its approach.

WHO

President: Patricia Ireland
VP Action: Rosemary Dempsey
Secretary: Kim Gandy
Press Secretary: Jeanne Clark

NOW membership is available to women and men who support the organization's goals.

WHERE

HQ: 1000 16th St. NW, Suite 700, Washington, DC 20036
Phone: 202-331-0066
Fax: 202-785-8576

Regions	Areas Served
Northeast	Maine, New Hampshire, Vermont, New York, Rhode Island, Massachusetts, Connecticut
Mid-Atlantic	New Jersey, Pennsylvania, West Virginia, Virginia, Delaware, District of Columbia, Maryland
Southeast	North Carolina, South Carolina, Georgia, Florida, Puerto Rico, Virgin Islands
Mid-South	Tennessee, Alabama, Mississippi, Louisiana, Arkansas
South Central	Texas, Oklahoma, New Mexico, Kansas, Colorado
Great Lakes	Michigan, Wisconsin, Ohio, Indiana, Illinois, Kentucky
Prairie States	Minnesota, Missouri, Iowa, North Dakota, South Dakota, Nebraska
Northwest	Washington, Alaska, Oregon, Montana, Idaho, Wyoming
Southwest	California, Nevada, Utah, Arizona, Hawaii, Guam, American Samoa, Trust Territory of the Pacific Islands

WHEN

NOW, the National Organization for Women, began in June 1966 at a Washington, DC, conference on the status of women. The founding group of 28 feminists, headed by author Betty Friedan (*The Feminine Mystique*), held its first national conference, with more than 300 delegates, in October of that year.

Officially incorporated in 1967, NOW addressed a wide range of inequities toward American women in employment, the law, the media, education, and economics. Its strategies to achieve its goal of bringing "women into full participation in the mainstream of American society" included mass mailings, lobbying, lectures, and demonstrations. From its beginning NOW promoted the development of local chapters, viewing their grassroots activities as the "focus of feminist action."

Conflict within NOW between various factions marked its development. In 1968 its early support of the Equal Rights Amendment (ERA) caused a split with members of the UAW union, an important group within the ranks of the newly founded NOW. The union reversed its position and supported the ERA in 1970. Disagreements among members concerning a woman's right to abortion and support for lesbian rights, differences between radical and moderate factions, and conflicting views of NOW's focus all resulted in a heady mix of impassioned arguments, changes, and compromises for the young organization. NOW activists broke off to form other more narrowly focused groups, such as the National Women's Political Caucus (NWPC), the Women's Equity Action League (WEAL), and the Older Women's League (OWL).

The feminist movement expanded rapidly during the early 1970s. A NOW-sponsored demonstration, the Women's Strike for Equality, on August 26, 1970, brought 10,000 women and men to New York City in a visible show of support. In 1972 Congress approved the ERA (a major part of NOW's social agenda), sending it to state legislatures for ratification. More traditional groups such as the League of Women Voters and the Young Women's Christian Association (YWCA) gave their support to many of NOW's causes. In 1975 NOW stated that endorsement of national and local candidates would be part of its official agenda, and in 1977 it focused its work on ratification of the ERA.

By June 30, 1982, even with a 3-year extension and the public support of over 75% of the population, only 35 of the required 38 states had ratified the ERA, and the amendment failed. The ERA was reintroduced on July 14, 1982, and ratification remains one of NOW's top priorities.

While membership declined from 1983 to 1985, it resurged with the massive East Coast/West Coast Abortion Rights demonstration in 1986 and then mushroomed in 1989 with the Supreme Court's decision in the *Webster* case. A 1989 march and rally for abortion rights organized by NOW drew 600,000 to Washington, DC. At its 1989 national conference, NOW, under the leadership of President Molly Yard, decided to explore the establishment of a new national political party. By 1990 NOW's paid membership had risen to 250,000.

After suffering a stroke in 1991, Molly Yard passed leadership of NOW to Patricia Ireland, a flight-attendant-turned-lawyer whose political role model is George Wallace (she admires his methods, not his message). Among Ireland's priorities are efforts to attract a younger membership and the continuation of Molly Yard's call for the formation of a 3rd political party.

WHAT

Political Advocacy
Campus organizing
Educational programs and materials
Litigation
Lobbying
National and regional conferences
Public demonstrations

Insurance Plans
NOW Medicare supplement
NOWlife term life
NOWmed comprehensive medical

Periodicals
NOW Times
State and chapter publications

Targeted Areas for Activity
Early childhood education
Economic rights for women
Education discrimination
Eliminating racism
Equal Rights Amendment
Homemakers' rights
Lesbian/gay rights
Older women's rights
Reproductive rights
Violence against women

HOW MUCH

	9-Year Growth	1981	1982	1983	1984	1985	1986	1987	1988	1989	1990
Membership (thou.)	5.0%	162	199	176	141	115	127	139	135	205	252

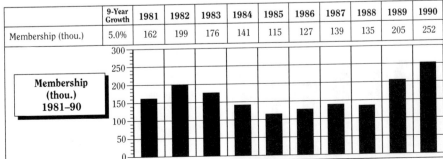

Membership (thou.) 1981–90

NATIONAL PARK SERVICE

OVERVIEW

Celebrating its 75th anniversary in 1991, the National Park Service (part of the Interior Department) manages 360 national parks, monuments, historic sites, and recreation areas in the US, Puerto Rico, the Virgin Islands, and Guam. With almost 80 million total acres, America's national park system is the world's largest public land holding and includes areas of spectacular beauty as well as points of scientific and historical interest.

The Park Service classifies areas by size and number of resources preserved; for instance, a national park is characterized by large water or land areas and a variety of flora, fauna, and topography (e.g., Grand Canyon National Park), while a national monument is usually smaller and preserves at least one significant resource (e.g., Statue of Liberty). Wrangell–St. Elias National Park and Preserve, the Park Service's largest area, encompasses more than 13 million acres in Alaska. The smallest area, Philadelphia's Thaddeus Kosciuszko National Memorial, covers less than 1,000 square feet.

The Park Service offers tours, films, and other guidance to over 250 million visitors annually.

In the 1990s the Service faces issues relating to concession contracts and overuse of facilities.

Government agency
Fiscal year ends: September 30

Hoover's Rating **A-**

WHO

Secretary of Interior: Manuel Lujan, Jr., age 63, $138,900 pay
Director National Park Service: James M. Ridenour, age 49, $108,300 pay
Associate Director Budget and Administration: Edward L. Davis, age 58, $104,400 pay
Employees: 12,614 full-time; 3,306 part-time, temporary, or seasonal; 53,600 volunteers

WHERE

HQ: 1800 C St. NW, Washington, DC 20240
Phone: 202-208-4990
Fax: 202-208-5977

The National Park Service administers 360 parks and national monuments in the District of Columbia, Puerto Rico, the Virgin Islands, Saipan, American Samoa, Guam, and every state except Delaware.

Classification	Federal Acreage	No.
International Historic Site	22	1
National Battlefield	11,211	11
National Battlefield Park	8,725	3
National Battlefield Site	1	1
National Capital Park	6,469	1
National Historic Park	140,436	31
National Historic Site	18,274	69
National Lakeshore	227,263	4
National Mall	146	1
National Memorial	7,949	26
National Military Park	34,031	9
National Monument	5,302,748	78
National Park	56,376,732	50
National Parkway	168,600	4
National Preserve	9,899,725	13
National Recreation Area	3,507,443	18
National River	317,341	6
National Scenic Trail	3,172,203	3
National Seashore	596,663	10
National Wild and Scenic River and Riverway	279,322	9
Park (other)	38,519	11
White House	18	1
Total	**80,113,841**	**360**

WHEN

Yellowstone, the world's first national park, was created by an Act of Congress in 1872. Signed into law by President Grant, the act provided for the protection and preservation of the area "for the benefit and enjoyment of the people." Management of Yellowstone was entrusted to the secretary of the interior.

When the Lacey Antiquities Act of 1906 gave the president authority to establish national monuments, Teddy Roosevelt proclaimed Devil's Tower, a Wyoming stone formation, the first such monument. In 1910, with parks proliferating, President Taft urged Congress to create a national park bureau.

Secretary of the Interior Franklin Lane, with Steven Mather and attorney Horace Albright as his assistants, promoted the legislation that created the National Park Service in 1916, "to conserve...and provide for the enjoyment of" the scenery, historic objects, and wildlife. Mather became the Service's first director, followed by Albright in 1929. When Albright resigned in 1933, the Park Service managed 128 units, compared to only 39 when it was established. Mather's and Albright's legacy includes park recreational facilities and the educational programs provided by rangers to teach visitors about each area's geology, history, and wildlife.

Between 1940 and 1955 the Park Service gained only 20 new areas, but visitors increased fourfold to 56 million per year. The Park Service grew rapidly under the directorship of George Hartzog (1964–72), gaining about 100 new areas for a total of 297 by 1972. By 1985, when William Penn Mott took over as director and outlined his 12-point plan to protect the parks' natural resources, the number of visitors to the nation's 337 parks and monuments had grown to 263 million annually. The Park Service gained 3 new areas in 1989.

Smokey the Bear, the symbol for fire prevention, went into semiretirement in 1972 when the Park Service began its current policy of allowing naturally caused fires (regarded as a part of the forest ecocycle) to burn as long as there is no danger to people or private property. Human-caused fires are extinguished. This policy came under public scrutiny in 1988 when fires threatened millions of acres in Yellowstone Park, but the Park Service has been vindicated by the public's fascination with the regeneration of the burned areas.

Balancing the tension between preservation of pristine wilderness and animal habitats and the recreational and safety needs of the public is becoming increasingly difficult. In 1990 and 1991 questions were raised about concession award procedures after the acquisition of the Yosemite concession by Matsushita. There have also been protests about concessionaires overcommercializing the parks and reaping profits vastly exceeding the value of their concession contracts.

WHAT

	1990 Sources of Revenues	
	$ mil.	% of total
Appropriations	769	94
Revenues from operations	50	6
Total	**819**	**100**

Selected National Park Service Facilities
Antietam National Battlefield (Maryland)
Custer Battlefield (Montana)
Big Bend National Park (Texas)
Death Valley National Monument (California)
Everglades National Park (Florida)
Fire Island (New York)
Gettysburg National Park (Pennsylvania)
Glacier National Park (Montana)
Grand Canyon National Park (Arizona)
Lincoln Memorial (Washington, DC)
Mammoth Cave (Kentucky)
Manassas National Battlefield (Virginia)
Mount Rushmore National Memorial (South Dakota)
Point Reyes (California)
Rock Creek Park (Washington, DC)
Thomas Jefferson Memorial (Washington, DC)
Washington Monument (Washington, DC)
Yellowstone National Park (Wyoming)
Yosemite National Park (California)

HOW MUCH

	9-Year Growth	1981	1982	1983	1984	1985	1986	1987	1988	1989	1990
Total appropriations ($ mil.)	5.5%	475	522	605	616	636	611	704	754	792	769
Number of areas	0.8%	334	334	335	334	337	338	343	354	355	360
Land (thou. acres)	0.9%	73,665	74,800	74,846	74,913	75,749	75,863	75,970	76,176	80,105	80,114
Visits (mil.)	0.9%	239	244	244	249	263	281	287	283	269	259
Appropriations per visit ($)	4.5%	1.99	2.14	2.48	2.47	2.42	2.17	2.45	2.66	2.94	2.96
Overnight stays (mil.)	1.3%	16	16	16	16	16	16	17	17	17	18

Visits (mil.) 1981–90

NATIONAL SEMICONDUCTOR CORPORATION

NYSE symbol: NSM
Fiscal year ends: Last Sunday in May

Hoover's Rating **B-**

OVERVIEW

Once the largest semiconductor maker, National Semiconductor has slipped to 4th place among US makers and has the 2nd lowest sales-per-employee ratio in the *Fortune* 500. It is the world leader, however, in certain specialty chips, such as Ethernet chips for local area networks.

National offers more than 5,000 different semiconductor products. Most have been high-volume standard products, such as linear (analog) chips for audio equipment. However, after years of substantial losses in the 1980s,

National has shifted emphasis to application-specific integrated circuits (ASICs) for computer peripherals and aerospace, among other niche markets. The company's 1990 restructuring is intended to highlight innovative products and "foster an entrepreneurial environment" at National.

National assembles most of its products offshore; non-US employees account for 63% of the total. R&D expenditure remains exceptionally high at 15% of revenues.

WHO

Chairman: Peter J. Sprague, age 52
President and CEO: Dr. Gilbert F. Amelio, age 48
President, Communications and Computing Group: Raymond J. Farnham, age 44, $195,368 pay (prior to promotion)
Co-President, Standard Products Group: Kirk P. Pond, age 47, $255,412 pay (prior to promotion)
Co-President, Standard Products Group: R. Thomas Odell, age 42
EVP; President, Innovative Products Division: Charles P. Carinalli
SVP; President, Military/Aerospace Division: Edgar R. Parker, age 51, $220,071 pay (prior to promotion)
VP Finance (Acting): John G. Webb, age 47
VP Human Resources: Michael E. Hawkins, age 52
Auditors: KPMG Peat Marwick
Employees: 32,700

WHEN

National, a transistor company founded in 1959 in Danbury, Connecticut, was by 1967 struggling on only $7 million in sales. Peter Sprague, heir to the Sprague electric fortune, took over as chairman and in February of 1967 hired manufacturing expert Charles Sporck from Fairchild Semiconductor.

Sporck transferred operations to Silicon Valley, halved the transistor work force, and plowed the savings into developing linear and digital logic chips. During the 1970s, National's successful mass manufacturing of low-cost chips made the company the leading semiconductor maker in America for a time, while its no-frills management approach led to its employees being dubbed "the animals of Silicon Valley."

The chip successes pushed National by 1981 to over $1 billion in sales. It then purchased National Advanced Systems (a distributor/servicer of Hitachi mainframes, 1979) and Data Terminal Systems (point-of-sale terminals, 1983, which became Datachecker).

When Japanese manufacturers dumped digital memory chips on the market in 1984 and 1985, National pulled out of the memory business. Its logic chips also suffered price squeezes, and in 1986 the company lost $148 million.

Sporck's new strategy was to transform his low-cost commodity chipmaker into a higher-margin supplier of niche products. National

bought most assets of troubled Fairchild Semiconductor for a mere 24% of its annual revenues (1987) to obtain superior logic chip designs and custom linear circuits for the US military.

Sluggish mainframe demand, coupled with mounting mainframe competition from IBM and Amdahl, prompted National in 1989 to sell NAS for $386 million (to a Hitachi/Electronic Data Systems joint venture) and Datachecker for $126 million (to ICL, Inc.), consolidate plants, and lay off 5% of its work force.

As National's sales continued to decline, Sporck implemented a restructuring plan in 1989 that grouped the company into 3 market-based divisions to better respond to customer needs. The changes failed to improve results, and in early 1991 Sporck retired after 24 years as National's president.

With some executives feeling a fresh perspective was needed at National, Gilbert Amelio from Rockwell International's communications group was hired as National's new president. Amelio implemented a new restructuring plan in 1991 that divided National into 2 groups, Standard Products (responsible for commodity chips, including re-introduced memory chips) and Communications and Computing (responsible for niche devices). National also formed its Innovative Products division to focus on R&D and on developing new businesses.

WHERE

HQ: 2900 Semiconductor Dr., PO Box 58090, Santa Clara, CA 95052-8090
Phone: 408-721-5000
Fax: 408-739-9803

Wafer fabrication plants are located in the US, Israel, and Scotland; assembly plants are in Brazil, Hong Kong, Malaysia, the Philippines, Singapore, Thailand, Scotland, and the US. Sales regions are Europe, Japan, Southeast Asia, and North America.

	1990 Sales	
	$ mil.	% of total
Americas	829	49
Europe	386	23
Asia	488	28
Total	**1,702**	**100**

WHAT

Integrated Circuits (ICs)
Application-specific integrated circuits (ASICs)
Customized ICs for computation, telecommunications, and military applications
Digital
  Memory
  Microprocessors
  Standard logic

Linear (analog)
  Audio amplifiers
  Automotive circuits
  Comparators
  Timers
  Voltage regulators
Digital-to-analog converters
ICs for floppy and hard disks, laser printers, and computer terminals

Discrete devices
Transistors

RANKINGS

244th in *Fortune* 500 Industrial Cos.
636th in *Business Week* 1000

HOW MUCH

Fiscal year ends May of following year	9-Year Growth	1981	1982	1983	1984	1985	1986	1987	1988	1989	1990
Sales ($ mil.)	4.9%	1,104	1,211	1,655	1,788	1,478	1,868	2,470	1,648	1,675	1,702
Net income ($ mil.)	—	(11)	(14)	56	34	(148)	(29)	63	(206)	(29)	(150)
Income as % of sales	—	(1.0%)	(1.2%)	3.4%	1.9%	(10.0%)	(1.5%)	2.5%	(12.5%)	(1.8%)	(8.8%)
Earnings per share ($)	—	(0.16)	(0.20)	0.66	0.38	(1.73)	(0.42)	0.53	(1.83)	(0.17)	(1.55)
Stock price – high ($)	—	13.96	8.75	20.00	19.25	15.13	15.63	22.25	15.00	10.00	8.88
Stock price – low ($)	—	5.83	4.38	7.17	9.50	10.13	8.25	9.75	8.13	6.38	3.00
Stock price – close ($)	(4.1%)	6.38	7.33	15.63	11.88	12.50	10.63	12.00	9.75	7.25	4.38
P/E – high	—	—	—	30	51	—	—	42	—	—	—
P/E – low	—	—	—	11	25	—	—	18	—	—	—
Dividends per share ($)	0.0%	0.00	0.00	0.00	0.00	0.00	0.00	0.00	0.00	0.00	0.00
Book value per share ($)	3.1%	4.83	4.68	7.12	7.64	7.91	8.69	9.41	8.28	7.91	6.34

1990 Year-end:
Debt ratio: 2.9%
Return on equity: —
Cash (mil.): $193
Current ratio: 1.47
Long-term debt (mil.): $20
No. of shares (mil.): 104
Dividends:
  1990 average yield: 0.0%
  1990 payout: 0.0%
Market value (mil.): $454

Stock Price History High/Low 1981–90

KEY COMPETITORS

Fujitsu	IBM	Philips
General Signal	Lucky-Goldstar	Pioneer
Harris	Mitsubishi	Samsung
Hitachi	Motorola	Siemens
Hyundai	NEC	Texas Instruments
Intel	OKI	Toshiba

NAVISTAR INTERNATIONAL CORPORATION

NYSE symbol: NAV
Fiscal year ends: October 31

Hoover's Rating: D

OVERVIEW

Chicago-based Navistar, formerly International Harvester, is the leading US producer of medium and heavy-duty trucks (27.9% of the market in 1990), and the largest supplier of medium diesel engines (130–270 horsepower). Over 14% ($558 million) of Navistar's revenues are from parts sales. The company receives 5% of its revenues from its financial services (truck sales and lease financing). With 899 dealers, Navistar has the largest truck dealer network in North Amerca.

The recession has hurt the industrial sector, causing weak truck sales. North American deliveries of Navistar's trucks dropped 15% in 1990 (281,800 compared to 331,500). On the bright side, Navistar announced agreements in 1990 with Perkins Group of England to market Navistar products worldwide through its 4,000 distributors in 160 countries, and with DINA Camiones, a leading Mexican truck manufacturer, to use its engines.

WHEN

Cyrus McCormick, the Virginia-born inventor who perfected the reaper in 1831, moved west and set up his first factory in Chicago in 1846. To compete with other manufacturers, McCormick offered such innovations as the installment plan, a written guarantee, and factory-trained repairmen. In 1886 a strike at the Chicago works in favor of the 8-hour workday led to the infamous Haymarket Square riot. In 1902, with the backing of J. P. Morgan, McCormick merged with Deering and several smaller firms to form International Harvester (IH). The new enterprise controlled 85% of US harvester production.

IH set up its first overseas factory in 1905 in Sweden. In 1906 Harvester entered the tractor industry and in 1907 began production of the Auto Buggy, forerunner of the truck. By 1910 the firm was annually producing 1,300 trucks and 1,400 tractors and had reached over $100 million in sales.

In 1913 Cyrus Jr. (Sr. had died in 1884) borrowed $5 million from John D. Rockefeller and gained control of the company. The new general manager, Alexander Legge (also president from 1922 to 1929) introduced the Farmall, the first all-purpose tractor, in 1924. In 1928 IH began production of a heavy truck with a 4-cylinder engine and by 1937 was the top US producer of medium and heavy trucks.

In the post-WWII industry boom, IH's neglect of product development and capital improvement, combined with the effects of overdiversification, caused market share to decline for most of its products. The company sold more trucks than agricultural equipment for the first time in 1955. IH lost its lead in agricultural equipment to John Deere in 1958. During the 1960s, IH lost its medium industry sales leadership to Ford, and the company's construction equipment business, although buoyed by the 1952 acquisition of the Payloader, consistently lost market share.

The 1980s recession, combined with a 6-month strike by the UAW (1980), sent IH to the edge of bankruptcy. Between 1980 and 1982 the company lost $2.3 billion. Restructuring, IH sold the construction equipment division to Dresser Industries in 1982. In 1985 Tenneco bought the agricultural equipment business and the International Harvester name. By 1986 the number of employees had dropped 85%, and plants had decreased from 48 worldwide to 6 in North America.

Renamed Navistar in 1986, the company has redesigned 85% of its truck line since 1987. In 1989 Navistar introduced 27 new truck models, plus a 9-speed heavy truck transmission (developed jointly with Dana), the first all-new design in more than 25 years. Navistar also introduced the Smokeless Diesel engine, which meets stricter emissions standards. In response to a loss in 1990 earnings, Navistar entered 1991 with plans to reduce costs by $167 million for the year, including elimination of 525 white-collar jobs.

WHO

Chairman and CEO: James C. Cotting, age 57, $450,000 pay
President and COO: John R. Horne, age 52, $270,000 pay
Group VP Marketing, Sales, and Distribution: Gary E. Dewel, $220,000 pay
EVP and CFO: Robert C. Lannert, age 50
SVP Employee Relations and Administration: John M. Sheahin, $190,000 pay
Auditors: Deloitte & Touche
Employees: 14,071

WHERE

HQ: 455 N. Cityfront Plaza Dr., Chicago, IL 60611
Phone: 312-836-2000
Fax: 312-836-2192

Navistar has 7 manufacturing and assembly plants in the US and one in Canada. The company sells its products through 899 dealers in North America.

	1990 Sales	
	$ mil.	% of total
US	3,511	91
Canada	343	9
Total	**3,854**	**100**

WHAT

	1990 Sales		1990 Pretax Income	
	$ mil.	% of total	$ mil.	% of total
Manufacturing	3,643	95	(68)	—
Financial services	211	5	61	—
Total	**3,854**	**100**	**(7)**	**—**

Transportation Products	1990 Sales
	% of total
Heavy trucks	41
Medium trucks	33
Replacement parts	15
Engines	11
Total	**100**

Products and Services
Customer financing
Diesel engines
International diesel trucks
Replacement parts
School buses
Used truck sales

RANKINGS

126th in *Fortune* 500 Industrial Cos.
554th in *Business Week* 1000

KEY COMPETITORS

Caterpillar
Cummins Engine
Fiat
Ford
General Motors
Mitsubishi
PACCAR

HOW MUCH

	9-Year Growth	1981	1982	1983	1984	1985	1986	1987	1988	1989	1990
Sales ($ mil.)	(6.5%)	7,041	4,292	3,601	4,802	3,508	3,357	3,530	4,080	4,241	3,854
Net income ($ mil.)	—	(636)	(1,266)	(533)	(61)	113	(2)	146	259	87	(11)
Income as % of sales	—	(9.0%)	(29.5%)	(14.8%)	(1.3%)	3.2%	(0.1%)	4.1%	6.3%	2.1%	(0.3%)
Earnings per share ($)	—	(17.70)	(34.36)	(9.42)	(0.50)	0.85	0.02	0.60	0.98	0.33	(0.04)
Stock price – high ($)	—	26.13	8.50	14.75	13.63	11.25	11.63	8.75	7.38	7.00	4.63
Stock price – low ($)	—	6.25	2.75	4.00	5.13	6.38	4.13	3.50	3.13	3.25	2.00
Stock price – close ($)	(12.0%)	7.13	4.25	11.50	8.13	8.50	4.75	4.25	5.38	3.88	2.25
P/E – high	—	—	—	—	—	13	581	15	8	21	—
P/E – low	—	—	—	—	—	8	206	6	3	10	—
Dividends per share ($)	—	0.30	0.00	0.00	0.00	0.00	0.00	0.00	0.00	0.00	0.00
Book value per share ($)	(27.2%)	39.76	—	—	(10.76)	(13.81)	(2.78)	1.50	2.41	2.64	2.28

1990 Year-end:
Debt ratio: 45.6%
Return on equity: —
Cash (mil.): $588
Current ratio: —
Long-term debt (mil.): $682
No. of shares (mil.): 250
Dividends:
  1990 average yield: 0.0%
  1990 payout: 0.0%
Market value (mil.): $563

Stock Price History High/Low 1981–90

NCNB CORPORATION

NYSE symbol: NCB
Fiscal year ends: December 31

Hoover's Rating **B-**

OVERVIEW

After the proposed acquisition of C&S/Sovran, NCNB will become NationsBank, the 4th largest banking organization in the US. With 1,900 offices, NationsBank will operate the country's largest branch network and dominate banking in the southeast US. The new bank will rank #1 in North and South Carolina, Georgia, Texas, and Virginia.

NCNB management plans to cut costs and eliminate jobs at the new bank. Management faces a challenge heading off a potential culture clash as it attempts to blend NCNB's aggressive style with C&S/Sovran's more conservative ways.

On its own NCNB had been the #7 US bank, prior to the wave of consolidation sweeping the banking industry. The bank has been grabbing market share, both by acquiring companies and by employing aggressive lending practices. Some of the loans, most notably commercial real estate and HLTs (highly leveraged transactions) have turned into problems.

WHEN

NCNB was formed from 3 North Carolina banks. In 1874 several prominent citizens of Charlotte organized Commercial National Bank, and in 1901 George Stephens and Word Wood of Charlotte started Southern States Trust Company, which was renamed American Trust Company in 1907.

In 1957 Commercial National and American Trust merged to become American Commercial Bank and 2 years later merged with First National of Raleigh to begin forming a statewide banking system. In 1960 American Commercial merged with Security National (founded Greensboro, 1933) to form North Carolina National Bank, with 40 offices in 20 North Carolina cities.

In the 1960s the bank expanded by buying 9 banks and formed NCNB Corporation, a holding company, in 1968. By 1970 NCNB had 91 offices in 27 North Carolina cities. In 1979 mergers with the Bank of Asheville and Carolina First (Lincolnton) helped make NCNB the largest bank in North Carolina.

In 1982 NCNB became the first non-Florida bank to expand its retail banking into Florida by buying First National Bank of Lake City. From 1982 to 1984 the company bought banks in Boca Raton, Tampa, Miami, and Bradenton. In 1985 NCNB bought Pan American, a $2 billion Miami bank with 51 offices. By 1988 NCNB was the 4th largest bank in Florida, with 200 offices.

NCNB entered 2 more states by purchasing Southern National Bankshares, Inc., of Atlanta (1985) and Bankers Trust of South Carolina (122 branches statewide, 1986). It added Prince William Bank of Dumfries, Virginia (1986), to become the first banking organization in the South to operate in 5 states. In 1987 it bought CentraBank of Baltimore, adding a 6th state.

The company, under Hugh L. McColl, Jr., chairman since 1983, nearly doubled its assets in 1988, when the FDIC chose NCNB to manage the restructured banks of First RepublicBank Corporation (closed by the FDIC earlier in 1988), the largest Texas bank. NCNB bought 20% in 1988 and the remainder in 1989. First RepublicBank had been formed in 1987 by the merger of InterFirst and Republic, 2 large, struggling banking organizations. NCNB also bought University Federal Savings in Texas in 1989 and Florida-based Freedom Savings and Loan Association from the Resolution Trust Corporation in 1989.

In 1990 NCNB bought 9 banks from National Bancshares (San Antonio) and the next year received a contract to manage the problem loans and real estate of Bright Banc Savings (Texas). NCNB agreed to take over C&S/Sovran, the product of a 1990 merger between Georgia-based Citizens & Southern and Virginia-based Sovran, in a $4.26 billion deal in 1991.

WHO

Chairman and CEO: Hugh L. McColl, Jr., age 55, $700,000 pay
VC: Timothy P. Hartman, age 51, $450,000 pay
VC: James W. Thompson, age 51, $450,000 pay
EVP and CFO: James H. Hance, Jr., age 46
EVP Personnel Group: Charles J. Cooley, age 55
Auditors: Price Waterhouse
Employees: 28,393

WHERE

HQ: One NCNB Plaza, Charlotte, NC 28255
Phone: 704-374-5000
Fax: 704-339-6655

WHAT

	1990 Assets	
	$ mil.	% of total
Cash	4,045	6
Deposits	790	1
Securities	16,144	25
Loans	36,715	56
Leases	391	1
Allowance for credit losses	(670)	(1)
Other	7,870	12
Total	**65,285**	**100**

US Banking Subsidiaries
NationsBank NA (bank cards)
NCNB National Bank (Georgia)
NCNB National Bank of Florida
NCNB National Bank of Maryland
NCNB National Bank of North Carolina
NCNB National Bank of South Carolina
NCNB Texas National Bank
NCNB Virginia

RANKINGS

7th in *Fortune* 100 Commercial Banking Cos.
218th in *Business Week* 1000

KEY COMPETITORS

H. F. Ahmanson
Banc One
Bank of New York
BankAmerica
Bankers Trust
Barnett Banks
Chase Manhattan
Chemical Banking
Citicorp
First Chicago
First Interstate
Great Western
J.P. Morgan
SunTrust
Other banks operating in the southeast US

HOW MUCH

	9-Year Growth	1981	1982	1983	1984	1985	1986	1987	1988	1989	1990
Assets ($ mil.)	26.8%	7,724	11,560	12,808	15,679	19,754	27,472	28,915	29,848	66,191	65,285
Net income ($ mil.)	23.4%	55	76	92	119	164	199	167	252	447	366
Income as % of assets	—	0.7%	0.7%	0.7%	0.8%	0.8%	0.7%	0.6%	0.8%	0.7%	0.6%
Earnings per share ($)	10.8%	1.33	1.59	1.84	2.04	2.28	2.51	2.01	2.87	4.44	3.34
Stock price – high ($)	—	9.00	10.31	14.94	18.25	23.56	27.75	29.13	29.13	55.00	47.25
Stock price – low ($)	—	6.50	5.88	9.25	11.50	16.94	20.00	15.50	17.50	27.00	16.88
Stock price – close ($)	13.3%	7.44	9.38	13.69	17.94	22.63	21.50	17.25	27.25	46.25	22.88
P/E – high	—	7	6	8	9	10	11	15	10	12	14
P/E – low	—	5	4	5	6	7	8	8	6	6	5
Dividends per share ($)	14.8%	0.41	0.46	0.52	0.59	0.69	0.78	0.86	0.94	1.10	1.42
Book value per share ($)	12.6%	9.90	10.98	11.78	13.13	14.23	16.42	17.87	22.43	29.21	28.75

1990 Year-end:
Return on equity: 11.5%
Equity as % of assets: 4.9%
Cash (mil.): $4,835
Long-term debt (mil.): $1,697
No. of shares (mil.): 103
Dividends:
   1990 average yield: 6.2%
   1990 payout: 42.5%
Market value (mil.): $2,353
Sales (mil.): $6,682

Stock Price History High/Low 1981–90

NCR CORPORATION

OVERVIEW

Dayton, Ohio–based NCR, the 2nd largest manufacturer of ATMs in the US (after Diebold) and the 5th largest computer manufacturer, acquiesced to a 1991 hostile takeover by AT&T. The $7.4 billion purchase gives AT&T needed computer expertise and a strong market presence in finance and retail, 2 industries reliant on the integration of computers and communications.

An early implementer of AT&T Bell Laboratories' UNIX operating system, NCR is committed to an open-system strategy that allows users of its machines to choose from a wealth of non–vendor-specific software. NCR is currently developing (in partnership with Teradata) large-scale, general-purpose computers based on parallel processing technology. In addition to computers and ATMs, NCR produces business forms, semiconductors, and components, and is a worldwide provider of 3rd-party computer maintenance services for over 120 computer manufacturers. NCR's overall strategy has been to build products using as few parts as possible, adopt industry standards, and emphasize integration.

NYSE symbol: NCR
Fiscal year ends: December 31

 Hoover's Rating **A-**

WHO

Chairman and CEO: Charles E. Exley, Jr., age 61, $1,194,995 pay
President: Gilbert P. Williamson, age 53, $672,667 pay
EVP: R. Elton White, age 48, $396,244 pay
SVP Finance and Administration and CFO: J. L. Giering, age 46
VP Personnel and Education: J. E. McElwain, age 56
Auditors: Price Waterhouse
Employees: 55,000

WHEN

John Patterson founded National Cash Register in 1882, after buying control of a Dayton cash register factory. By 1910 Patterson had created a market for cash registers. He rapidly gained a 90% share, drawing Justice Department attention. In 1913 he was fined for anticompetitive violations — which included tampering with products, spying, and bribing competitors — and sentenced to jail. A heavy flood hit Dayton that year; Patterson turned NCR's energies to rescue operations. Dayton officials commended his actions, and he stayed out of jail.

In 1899 Colonel Edward Deeds, later chairman, joined NCR. In 1904 he hired Dayton inventor Charles Kettering to develop an electric cash register. The 2 men also developed an electric automobile ignition system and left to start Delco (purchased by General Motors in 1929).

Accounting machines, which prepared vouchers and audit sheets, were introduced in the early 1920s and became almost as important as cash registers to NCR. Patterson did not live to see business plunge in 1929 and NCR's stock drop from $154 to $6.87. By 1936 the company had recovered fully.

During the postwar period NCR faced competition from data processing. The company focused R&D efforts on computing (1945); acquired Computer Research for computer development (1952); opened data processing centers and introduced mainframes (1960); established microelectronics research facilities (1963); and introduced disk-based computers (1968). Yet NCR failed to anticipate how rapidly computers were evolving and their impact upon its products — still primarily cash registers and accounting machines; in 1969 the company had record profits of $50 million, but by 1971 they had plunged to $2 million.

In 1972 William Anderson became president and is credited with saving the company. Anderson reduced NCR's Dayton work force by 75%, reorganized, established NCR's presence in computing with retail scanners and ATMs, and, in 1974, gave the company its current name. By 1981 NCR again faced potential obsolescence due to the proprietary technology of its products in the face of a market moving toward standardization. To counter, NCR adopted widely used Unix and IBM-endorsed MS-DOS operating systems. Anderson retired in 1984.

Now chaired by Charles Exley, NCR has become a market leader in ATMs and retail checkout scanners. In keeping with its Open, Cooperative Computing strategy, announced in 1990, NCR continues to build on an entire line (System 3000) of Intel X86–based computers ranging from PCs to mainframes. Exley is expected to retire following the consummation of the AT&T merger.

WHERE

HQ: 1700 S. Patterson Blvd., Dayton, OH 45479
Phone: 513-445-5000
Fax: 513-445-1238

NCR's products are sold in the US, Europe, Australia, the Far East, Canada, Latin and South America, the Middle East, and Africa. The company maintains numerous domestic and international facilities.

	1990 Sales		1990 Operating Income	
	$ mil.	% of total	$ mil.	% of total
US	2,393	38	241	36
Europe	2,212	35	242	36
Asia, Pacific, Australia & Canada	1,341	21	174	27
Africa, Middle East, S. America & Mexico	339	6	9	1
Adjustments	—	—	(13)	—
Total	**6,285**	**100**	**653**	**100**

WHAT

	1990 Sales	
	$ mil.	% of total
Equipment & software	3,353	54
Media & business forms	522	8
Semiconductors & components	146	2
Services	2,264	36
Total	**6,285**	**100**

Products

Automated teller machines	Networking hardware and software
Bank automation products	Personal computers
Business forms and supplies	Point-of-sale terminals and systems
Data collection terminals	Retailing and banking software
Disk storage subsystems	
Microchips	Self-service terminals
Minicomputers	Workstations

RANKINGS

79th in *Fortune* 500 Industrial Cos.
97th in *Business Week* 1000

KEY COMPETITORS

NCR competes with all Key Competitors of AT&T.

HOW MUCH

	9-Year Growth	1981	1982	1983	1984	1985	1986	1987	1988	1989	1990
Sales ($ mil.)	7.0%	3,433	3,526	3,731	4,074	4,317	4,882	5,641	5,990	5,956	6,285
Net income ($ mil.)	6.6%	208	234	288	343	315	337	419	439	412	369
Income as % of sales	—	6.1%	6.6%	7.7%	8.4%	7.3%	6.9%	7.4%	7.3%	6.9%	5.9%
Earnings per share ($)	12.2%	1.93	2.17	2.64	3.30	3.15	3.42	4.51	5.33	5.38	5.43
Stock price – high ($)	—	18.88	24.34	34.19	33.03	42.50	57.00	87.25	69.88	66.63	92.88
Stock price – low ($)	—	9.81	9.69	20.50	20.63	24.88	38.63	44.13	51.38	52.50	44.50
Stock price – close ($)	26.5%	10.91	21.50	32.00	26.63	40.25	44.13	63.25	53.38	58.88	90.75
P/E – high	—	10	11	13	10	14	17	19	13	12	17
P/E – low	—	5	4	8	6	8	11	10	10	10	8
Dividends per share ($)	10.8%	0.55	0.60	0.65	0.80	0.88	0.92	1.00	0.93	1.30	1.38
Book value per share ($)	5.3%	17.41	18.10	19.34	20.84	23.68	25.50	25.73	28.20	28.12	27.76

1990 Year-end:
Debt ratio: 11.6%
Return on equity: 19.4%
Cash (mil.): $731
Current ratio: 1.32
Long-term debt (mil.): $236
No. of shares (mil.): 64
Dividends:
  1990 average yield: 1.5%
  1990 payout: 25.4%
Market value (mil.): $5,852

Stock Price History High/Low 1981–90

NEW YORK CITY TRANSIT AUTHORITY

OVERVIEW

The New York City Transit Authority (NYCTA) operates subways in 4 New York City boroughs and buses in all 5 boroughs. It is the largest subway-bus system in the world. The NYCTA is part of the Metropolitan Transportation Authority, which is responsible for all public transit in the New York City metropolitan area. NYCTA carried almost 1.5 billion passengers in 1990, down 60 million from 1989.

Plagued by crime, vandalism, panhandlers, and the homeless, the system has a reputation for being unpleasant and unsafe. Massive infusions of capital, a concerted fight against graffiti and crime, and changes in union work rules undertaken by former chairman David Gunn improved NYCTA's operations. During the 1980s, ridership, which had been declining for 40 years, began to increase. In 1990 ridership again began to decline partly because of the loss of 100,000 jobs in the city's financial sector. In 1991 the system's deficit grew to $212 million, and NYCTA began issuing revenue anticipation notes.

Government agency
Fiscal year ends: December 31

Hoover's Rating **D**

WHO

President: Alan F. Kiepper, age 62, $149,500 pay
EVP: David Winfield, age 46, $125,000 pay
SVP Operations: Thomas F. Prendergast
VP and CFO: Edward G. Towle, $107,000 pay
VP and General Counsel: Albert Cosenza, $109,500 pay
VP Administration and Personnel: Liz Lowe
Auditors: Ernst & Young
Employees: 48,810

WHERE

HQ: 370 Jay St., Brooklyn, NY 11201
Phone: 718-330-3000
Fax: 718-852-6858

The NYCTA operates buses and subways in the Manhattan, Brooklyn, Bronx, Queens, and Staten Island boroughs of New York City.

	1990 Ridership	
	No. (mil.)	% of total
Bronx and Manhattan	847	57
Brooklyn	350	23
Queens	208	14
Staten Island	26	2
Unallocated	65	4
Total	**1,496**	**100**

WHAT

	1990 Avg. Weekday Ridership	
	No. (mil.)	% of total
Buses	1.3	28
Subways	3.3	72
Total	**4.6**	**100**

	1990 Train Route Miles	
	No.	% of total
Subway	137	59
Elevated	95	41
Total	**232**	**100**

	1990 Employees	
	No.	% of total
Operations	43,066	88
Police	4,463	9
Other	1,281	3
Total	**48,810**	**100**

Affiliates
Manhattan and Bronx Surface Transit Operating Authority
South Brooklyn Railroad
Staten Island Rapid Transit Operating Authority
Transit Authority Citizen's Advisory Council

WHEN

Mass passenger transit in New York City is said to have originated in 1746, when ox carts began carrying customers up Broadway from the Battery. Early in the 19th century, a number of private companies running omnibuses (horse-drawn multipassenger carriages) proliferated. By 1832 a horse-drawn car set on rails began operating on Fourth Avenue. Several years later this line was converted to steam power, but horse-drawn rail cars continued to prosper.

In 1864 local papers reported that cars and buses were overcrowded and drivers were intolerably rude to passengers. In 1868 the legislature authorized an underground pneumatic subway in which a 22-passenger vehicle was shot through a 312-foot-long tube under Broadway. While novel when it was opened to the public in 1870, it was never more than an amusement. Companies were granted authority to build elevated train lines into the city during the next several years, but no progress was made in building a subway system.

In 1894 legislation was finally passed authorizing construction of underground rail lines and vesting ownership with public rather than private interests. Construction of the first line was completed in 1904. It was operated for the city by the Interborough Rapid Transit Company (IRT), which had the previous year leased the primary elevated train line for 999 years and enjoyed effective operating control of most of the rail transit in Manhattan and the Bronx. In 1905 the IRT merged with the Metropolitan Street Railway, which controlled almost all surface rail operations in Manhattan, giving the combined company almost absolute control of rapid transit in the city. Public outrage over this private monopoly of public transit caused the city to grant licenses to operate rail lines to the Brooklyn Rapid Transit Company (later to be called the BMT), creating the Dual System. The 2 rail companies quickly covered most of the city.

By the 1920s the transit system was again in crisis, largely because the 2 lines were unable to raise the 5-cent fare, which they had agreed to maintain for the 49-year life of their contract with the city. In 1932 both the IRT and the BMT were in receivership; the city decided not only to own but also to operate a part of the rail system and organized the Independent (IND) rail line. Pressure for public ownership and operation of the transit system resulted in the city's purchase of all assets of the IRT and BMT in 1940 for $326 million. The 3 lines were overseen by the Transit Commission of the New York State Department of Public Service.

In 1953 the legislature created the New York City Transit Authority (NYCTA), to which the city leased all transit facilities, creating the first truly unified system. During the 1950s ridership and revenue declined as people moved to the suburbs. The Metropolitan Transportation Authority (MTA) was created in 1968 to coordinate NYCTA's activities with other commuter services.

The 1970s and 1980s saw the NYCTA's infrastructure, service, and sanitary conditions deteriorate and crime, accidents, graffiti, and fares rise. In 1990 Alan Kiepper succeeded David Gunn as head of the NYCTA. Under his direction, plans were made for the installation of new automatic fare turnstiles (at a cost of $675 million), which were expected to recoup about $40 million lost annually to fare evaders. But in 1991 the system was faced with a $212 million dollar deficit, which was expected to require a fare increase to $1.50.

HOW MUCH

	9-Year Growth	1981	1982	1983	1984	1985	1986	1987	1988	1989	1990
Revenues ($ mil.)	5.5%	949	1,034	1,056	1,231	1,228	1,372	1,401	1,411	1,401	1,532
Ridership (mil.)	(0.2%)	1,525	1,501	1,529	1,488	1,512	1,524	1,547	1,568	1,559	1,496
Fare ($)	7.5%	0.60	0.75	0.75	0.90	0.90	1.00	1.00	1.00	1.00	1.15

Ridership (mil.) 1981–90

NEW YORK LIFE INSURANCE COMPANY

OVERVIEW

New York Life is the 6th largest life insurance company in the US, with assets of over $50 billion and life insurance in force topping $300 billion. It was one of the first mutual life insurance companies in the US and has insured the lives of 11 US presidents, George A. Custer, and Susan B. Anthony.

New York Life offers life, health, and disability insurance; annuities; MainStay mutual funds and other investments; and health care management services to clients throughout the US, Puerto Rico, Canada, and Hong Kong.

The company emphasizes its commitment to AIDS research through a total investment of $28 million in 2 biomedical firms (Biogen and IDEC) and through its $1 million in donations to AIDS patient services. However, it opposes antitesting legislation on underwriting grounds.

In 1990 and 1991, despite a recession and fears about the insurance industry, New York Life retained its premium ratings from Moody's, Standard & Poor's, and Best Insurance Reports.

WHEN

In 1841 actuary Pliny Freeman and 56 New York businessmen invested $50,000 to found Nautilus Insurance Company, the 3rd mutual (owned by its policyholders) in the US. The company began operating in 1845 and became New York Life in 1849.

In 1846 New York Life had the first life insurance agent west of the Mississippi River, in Little Rock, Arkansas. Although cut off from its southern business during the Civil War, New York Life honored all its obligations and renewed former policies afterwards. By 1865 the company had assets of about $4 million, and by 1887 it had developed the branch office system that the whole industry adopted.

By 1900 the company had established the Nylic Plan for compensating agents, which features a lifetime income after 20 years of active service; it is still in use today. New York Life expanded through Europe in the late 1800s, but after WWI withdrew because of over-regulation.

Much of the company's growth and product development has occurred since WWII. In the early 1950s the company simplified insurance policy forms, slashed premium rates, and replaced mortality rates of the 1860s with a current rate table. These actions resulted in new company sales records and were widely copied by competitors. In 1956 the company was the first life insurance firm to use large-scale data processing equipment.

In 1968 New York Life was instrumental in developing variable life insurance, a new product with variable benefits and level premiums. Also that year the company began offering variable annuities. The company continued its steady growth until the late 1970s, when high

interest rates led to heavy policyholder borrowing. Jarred by the outflow of money, the company sought to make its products more competitive as investments.

In 1981 the company offered single- and flexible-premium deferred annuities, and in 1982, universal life product. New York Life also formed New York Life and Health Insurance Company in 1982 and New York Life Insurance Company of Canada in 1984.

To diversify its operations further, the company in 1984 acquired MacKay-Shields Financial Corporation, which oversees its MainStay mutual funds. NYLIFE Realty, another wholly owned subsidiary, offered the company's first pure investment product, real estate limited partnerships, that year.

Donald K. Ross, president (1981–90), continued the company's expansion in 1987 by purchasing control of Hillhouse Associates Insurance, a 3rd party administrator of insurance plans, and Madison Benefits Administrators, which administers group insurance programs. In 1987 New York Life acquired Sanus Corporation Health Systems, the largest privately held manager of health care programs in the United States. A recent technological advancement is the New York Life Television Network, a satellite network started in 1988 to communicate to agency offices. Also that year the company returned to Europe with an office in Ireland.

With the "The Company You Keep" advertising campaign, New York Life entered the 1990s guided by its 1986 mission statement — to use trained field representatives and new technologies to gain profitable, prudent growth.

Mutual company
Fiscal year ends: December 31

Hoover's Rating **B-**

WHO

Chairman and CEO: Harry G. Hohn, age 59
President: George A. W. Bundschuh, age 58
VP and Treasurer: Bruce J. Davey
VP Human Resources: George Trapp
Auditors: Price Waterhouse
Employees: 18,200

WHERE

HQ: 51 Madison Ave., New York, NY 10010
Phone: 212-576-7000
Fax: 212-576-6794

Operations are conducted in all 50 states, the District of Columbia, Puerto Rico, all 10 provinces of Canada, and Hong Kong.

WHAT

	1990 Sales	
	$ mil.	% of total
Premiums	8,782	66
Net investment income	4,072	31
Funds left with the company	259	2
Other income	115	1
Total	**13,228**	**100**

	12/31/90 Assets	
	$ mil.	% of total
Bonds	30,861	62
Stocks	498	1
Real estate & mortgage loans	7,902	16
Policyowner loans	5,161	10
Other assets	5,704	11
Total	**50,126**	**100**

Product Lines

New York Life Insurance Co.
Disability income insurance
Group life and health insurance
Guaranteed investment contracts
Pension fund investment accounts
Target life insurance
Term life insurance
Whole life insurance

New York Life Insurance and Annuity Co.
Deferred annuities
Immediate annuities
Variable annuities

MainStay (mutual funds)

New York Life (real estate, oil and gas limited partnerships)

RANKINGS

6th in *Fortune* 50 Life Insurance Cos.

KEY COMPETITORS

Aetna
Blue Cross
CIGNA
Equitable
First Executive
Humana
John Hancock
Kemper
MassMutual
MetLife
Northwestern Mutual
Primerica
Prudential
Sears
State Farm
Teachers Insurance
Transamerica
Travelers
USF&G
Other insurance companies

HOW MUCH

Life Insurance Only	9-Year Growth	1981	1982	1983	1984	1985	1986	1987	1988	1989	1990
Assets ($ mil.)	10.0%	21,193	23,116	25,441	28,060	31,740	35,087	38,877	43,417	46,648	50,126
Change in surplus ($ mil.)	9.4%	130	55	76	171	32	194	92	204	57	291
Change as % of assets	—	0.6%	0.2%	0.3%	0.6%	0.1%	0.6%	0.2%	0.5%	0.1%	0.6%
Employees	—	—	—	—	—	—	—	—	—	19,438	18,200

1990 Year-end:
Equity as % of assets: 4.8%
Return on equity: —
Cash (mil.): $1,107
Sales (mil.): $13,228

Assets ($ mil.) 1981–90

[bar chart with y-axis from 0 to 60,000]

NEW YORK STOCK EXCHANGE, INC.

Not-for-profit corporation
Fiscal year ends: December 31

Hoover's Rating **B+**

OVERVIEW

The New York Stock Exchange (NYSE) is the oldest and largest stock exchange in the US, with 1,366 seats held by 516 member firms and 1,744 listed companies. Among investors, it also is known as the Big Board.

The Big Board, which is an organized market for trading securities, had 39.6 billion shares traded in 1990. Initial public stock offerings (IPO) on the NYSE in 1990 raised $8.8 billion for US companies (80% of all the money raised in IPOs). Trades are executed by NYSE-assigned dealers and communicated to the participating parties within seconds by a computerized system.

Participants in the NYSE market include listed companies, individual and institutional investors, and securities firms and dealers. NYSE board of directors includes members of the public and NYSE-member organizations.

The NYSE operates under SEC regulation. In the 1990s the NYSE faces great challenges. Trading volume and market share have fallen (daily volume is down by 17% since 1987; market share is now only 48%) due to a less-active market and the increase of off-exchange and electronic trading. An attempt in 1991 to recapture market share by extending hours failed when members (particularly those on the US West Coast, who must rise early for the 9:30 opening) protested. Off-exchange trading saves fees and reduces the effectiveness of SEC supervision.

WHEN

To prevent a monopoly on sales by securities auctioneers, 24 New York stockbrokers and businessmen agreed in 1792 to avoid "public auctions," to charge a commission on sales of stock, and to "give preference to each other" in their transactions. The historic Buttonwood Agreement, named after a tree on Wall Street under which they met, established the first organized stock market in New York.

In 1817 the brokers created the New York Stock & Exchange Board, a stock market with regular meeting times. In 1853 the NYS&EB began to require companies to qualify for trading (listing) by furnishing statements of capital and number of shares. In 1863 the Board became the New York Stock Exchange.

Stock tickers replaced messenger boys in recording securities trades in 1867. Two years later the Exchange consolidated with its strongest competitors, the Open Board of Brokers and the Government Bond Department.

During the 1920s the Exchange installed a centralized stock quotation service. In the October 29, 1929, crash more than 16 million shares were traded. The Exchange registered with the SEC as a national securities exchange in 1934. After a period of increased regulation of the securities industry, the NYSE in 1938 reorganized with a board of directors representing member firms, nonmember broker firms, and the public, and hired its first full-time president, William McChesney Martin, Jr., a member of the Exchange.

In the 1960s NYSE introduced electronic trading. In 1968 the Exchange finally broke the 1929 one-day record.

In 1971 the Exchange became a not-for-profit corporation, and members began listing their stocks on the Exchange. The Exchange began in 1979 to upgrade capabilities to handle high-volume trading days and sustained periods of high volume. In 1982 149 million shares were traded in one day and one billion shares were traded in a 2-week period. Even before the 600-million-share days of the October 1987 crash, the NYSE had begun to invest in new technology to further expand trading capacity.

In 1991 Chairman John Phelan, Jr., retired with a pension package reported at $10 million. Yet, 350 jobs have been cut since 1989. The staff cuts cost $10.6 million, which, along with provisions for taxes, reduced net income from $3.6 million to a loss of $3 million. In this climate the cost of a seat has declined by 70% from $1.15 million in 1988 to $350,000.

WHO

Chairman and CEO: William H. Donaldson, age 60
EVC, President, and COO: Richard A. Grasso, age 45
EVP Equity Marketing and NYFE: Lewis J. Horowitz
EVP Equities and Audit: Catherine R. Kinney
EVP Regulation: Edward Kwalwasser
EVP Fixed Income, Options, and Administration: Donald J. Solodar
EVP New Listings and Corporate Liaison and CFO: David L. Domijan
EVP and General Counsel: Henry P. Poole
SVP Human Resources: Joseph P. Johnson
Auditors: Price Waterhouse
Employees: 1,850

WHERE

HQ: 11 Wall St., New York, NY 10005
Phone: 212-656-3000
Fax: 212-269-4830 (Communications)

The New York Stock Exchange has market operations in New York City. It has a service office in London to assist European companies.

1990 US Stock Trades	% of Total
NYSE	48
Other exchanges	52
Total	**100**

WHAT

	1990 Sales	
	$ mil.	% of total
Listing fees	119	34
Trading fees	68	20
Market data fees	53	15
Regulatory fees	42	12
Facility & equipment fees	37	11
Membership fees	7	2
Investment & other income	23	6
Total	**349**	**100**

Services
Market regulation
Member regulation
Securities clearing
Securities depository
Securities information
Securities trading

Subsidiaries and Affiliates
Depository Trust Company (33.7%)
National Securities Clearing Corporation (33%)
New York Futures Exchange, Inc. (NYFE)
Options Clearing Corporation (minority)
Securities Industry Automation Corporation (66.7%, owned with American Stock Exchange)

RANKINGS

Largest stock exchange in US
Largest centralized bond market of any exchange

KEY COMPETITORS

Reuters

HOW MUCH

	9-Year Growth	1981	1982	1983	1984	1985	1986	1987	1988	1989	1990
Sales ($ mil.)	9.6%	153	169	217	223	258	296	349	324	349	349
Net income ($ mil.)	—	6	9	17	10	18	22	34	10	6	(3)
Income as % of sales	—	3.9%	5.3%	7.8%	4.9%	7.0%	7.4%	9.7%	3.1%	1.7%	(0.9%)
Reported share volume (mil.)	14.4%	11,854	16,458	21,590	23,071	27,511	35,680	47,801	40,849	41,699	39,644
Daily average share volume (mil.)	14.4%	46.9	65.1	85.3	91.2	109.2	141.0	188.9	161.5	165.5	156.8
No. of member organizations	(1.7%)	604	617	639	628	599	611	596	555	535	516
No. of listed companies	1.4%	1,565	1,526	1,550	1,543	1,541	1,575	1,647	1,681	1,720	1,774
Total shares listed (mil.)	10.1%	38,298	39,516	45,118	49,092	52,427	59,620	71,802	76,175	82,972	90,732

Daily Average Share Volume (mil.) 1981–90

THE NEW YORK TIMES COMPANY

OVERVIEW

The New York Times Company publishes newspapers and magazines, operates broadcast and information service businesses, and owns interests in Canadian newsprint mills.

With an average daily circulation of 1.2 million and Sunday circulation topping 1.7 million, the *New York Times* is the nation's #1 Sunday newspaper and #2 on weekdays. Although circulation is increasing, earnings are off at the *Times,* as a soft economy in the New York region continues to depress advertising spending.

In addition to the *Times* the company publishes 32 smaller-city newspapers, principally in the South, and owns a 50% interest in the *International Herald Tribune*, an international English language newspaper, in partnership with the Washington Post Company.

The New York Times publishes women's and sports-oriented magazines including *McCall's, Family Circle, Golf Digest, Golf World,* and *Tennis.* Broadcasting properties include 2 classical radio stations in New York City and 5 network-affiliated TV stations in 5 states. The company also sells news and syndication services to other newspaper and magazine publishers.

The start-up of a new highly automated production and distribution facility in New Jersey, ready to open since 1990, has been delayed until completion of negotiations with labor unions.

WHEN

The *New York Times* was founded in 1851 by George Jones and Henry J. Raymond, 2 former staffers on the *New York Tribune*, one of the first penny papers. The *Times* began a long tradition of political coverage during the Civil War and investigative reporting with the Tammany Hall scandals, but by the late 1800s it had lost popularity to the yellow journalism style of the Hearst and Pulitzer papers.

In 1896 Adolph Ochs, a newspaperman from Chattanooga, bought the *Times.* Choosing to continue covering hard news and business stories, Ochs added the slogan that still molds the paper's news content today, "All the news that's fit to print." Ochs's son-in-law Arthur Sulzberger and Sulzberger's son-in-law Orvil Dryfoos ran the paper from 1935 to 1963, when Dryfoos died, leaving Adolph's grandson, Arthur "Punch" Ochs Sulzberger, in charge.

In the 1960s declining ad revenues from Manhattan stores and a newspaper strike (1962–63) sent the company into the red. To regain strength Punch began building what became the largest news-gathering staff of any newspaper. The *Times*'s coverage of the Vietnam War changed public sentiment, and the newspaper won a Pulitzer Prize in 1972 for publishing the Pentagon Papers.

Punch began turning the company into a diverse media corporation in the 1970s. It bought magazines (*Golf Digest*, 1969; *Family Circle*, 1971; *Child*, 1987), publishing houses, television stations, smaller newspapers, and cable television systems and began co-publishing the *International Herald Tribune.* It also published a wide range of books and educational materials, such as the *New York Times Index*. The *Times* started a wire service that is today received by more than 600 news organizations worldwide.

To contain costs the company bought interests in several pulp and paper companies in Canada and Maine.

In the 1980s the *Times* added feature sections on subjects from home decorating to science to compete with suburban papers. The company bought *Golf World* in 1988. In 1989 the company bought *McCall's* magazine and sold its cable television systems.

In 1990 the *Times* won its 61st Pulitzer Prize, an award that it has won more often than any other news organization. The next year the New York Times and Washington Post each increased their ownership of the *International Herald Tribune* to 50% by buying out Whitcom Investment Company's interest.

HOW MUCH

	9-Year Growth	1981	1982	1983	1984	1985	1986	1987	1988	1989	1990
Sales ($ mil.)	8.7%	840	925	1,091	1,230	1,394	1,565	1,690	1,700	1,769	1,777
Net income ($ mil.)	2.9%	50	54	79	100	116	132	160	161	68	65
Income as % of sales	—	6.0%	5.9%	7.2%	8.1%	8.3%	8.5%	9.5%	9.5%	3.9%	3.7%
Earnings per share ($)	2.7%	0.67	0.72	1.01	1.27	1.45	1.63	1.96	2.00	0.87	0.85
Stock price – high ($)	—	6.42	9.54	15.29	19.50	25.44	42.00	49.63	32.75	34.75	27.50
Stock price – low ($)	—	4.42	5.48	9.00	10.94	17.50	23.31	24.75	24.38	24.50	16.88
Stock price – close ($)	13.9%	6.42	9.54	14.00	19.19	24.50	35.50	31.00	26.88	26.50	20.63
P/E – high	—	10	13	15	15	18	26	25	16	40	32
P/E – low	—	7	8	9	9	12	14	13	12	28	20
Dividends per share ($)	13.3%	0.18	0.19	0.22	0.25	0.29	0.33	0.40	0.46	0.50	0.54
Book value per share ($)	14.9%	3.91	4.38	5.17	6.09	7.24	8.59	10.04	11.02	13.63	13.68

1990 Year-end:
Debt ratio: 23.2%
Return on equity: 6.2%
Cash (mil.): $32
Current ratio: 0.79
Long-term debt (mil.): $319
No. of shares (mil.): 77
Dividends:
  1990 average yield: 2.6%
  1990 payout: 63.5%
Market value (mil.): $1,592

Stock Price History High/Low 1981–90

NYSE symbol: NYTA
Fiscal year ends: December 31

Hoover's Rating **B**

WHO

Chairman and CEO: Arthur Ochs Sulzberger, age 65, $487,636 pay
President and COO: Walter E. Mattson, age 58, $389,833 pay
SVP: Michael E. Ryan, age 52, $327,091 pay
SVP, CFO, and Treasurer: David L. Gorham, age 58, $311,613 pay
VP Human Resources and Director of Corporate Personnel: Leslie Mardenborough, age 42
Auditors: Deloitte & Touche
Employees: 10,400

WHERE

HQ: 229 W. 43rd St., New York, NY 10036
Phone: 212-556-1234
Fax: 212-556-4607

The *New York Times* is sold throughout the US and in 70 foreign countries. The company maintains the *New York Times* publishing facilities in New York and New Jersey.

WHAT

	1990 Sales		1990 Operating Income	
	$ mil.	% of total	$ mil.	% of total
Magazines	340	19	(12)	(8)
Newspapers	1,358	77	140	98
Broadcasting/ information svcs.	79	4	15	10
Adjustments	—	—	(13)	—
Total	**1,777**	**100**	**130**	**100**

Magazines
Child
Cruising World
Decorating Remodeling
Family Circle
Golf Digest
Golf Illustrated Weekly
Golf Shop Operations
Golf World
Golf World Industry News
McCall's
Sailing World
Snow Country
Tennis
Tennis Buyer's Guide

Newspapers
International Herald Tribune (50%)
New York Times
24 daily newspapers
8 nondaily newspapers

Broadcasting
KFSM-TV, Fort Smith, AR
WHNT-TV, Huntsville, AL

WNEP-TV, Wilkes-Barre, PA
WQAD-TV, Moline, IL
WQXR (AM/FM), New York
WREG-TV, Memphis, TN

Information Services
New York Times Index
New York Times News Service
Special Features (supplemental news and graphics)
TimesFax

Forest Products
Donahue Malbaie, Inc. (49%)
Gaspesia Pulp & Paper Co. Ltd. (49%)
Northern SC Paper Corporation (80%)
Spruce Falls Power and Paper Company, Ltd. (49.5%)

RANKINGS

234th in *Fortune* 500 Industrial Cos.
367th in *Business Week* 1000

KEY COMPETITORS

Advance Publications
Blockbuster
Cox
Dow Jones
Gannett
Hachette
Hearst

Knight-Ridder
Maxwell
E.W. Scripps
Time Warner
Times Mirror
Tribune
Washington Post

NIKE, INC.

OVERVIEW

NIKE, still 35% owned by founder Phil Knight, is a major designer, producer, and international distributor of athletic and leisure footwear. In addition to its basketball, fitness, and running shoes, NIKE offers fitness and sporting wear, athletic bags, and accessories. NIKE leads the domestic athletic shoe market with a 29% market share. Domestic sales account for 71% of company revenues. The company is #2 in the $5-billion-a-year Western European market, after Adidas.

NIKE maintains an aggressive commitment to researching and developing high-tech footwear, publishing articles in sports medicine and other professional journals and vigorously defending its patents.

NIKE produces almost all of its shoes and about 50% of its apparel overseas through independent contractors in South Korea, Taiwan and elsewhere.

Though foreign sales are only 22% of sales, it is the fastest growing segment. In 1990 and 1991, the company began preparing for 1992 EC unification by establishing a new European headquarters in Amsterdam. NIKE expects foreign sales to exceed US sales by the year 2000.

WHEN

In 1958 Phil Knight, an undergraduate business student at the University of Oregon and a good miler, often spoke with his coach Bill Bowerman about the lack of a good American running shoe. Bowerman, resolving to create a better shoe, sent an original design to several leading sporting goods companies. Turned down by all of them, Bowerman made the shoes himself.

In 1964 Knight and Bowerman formed their own athletic shoe company, Blue Ribbon Sports, each putting up $300 for the first order of 300 pairs of shoes, manufactured by Onitsuka Tiger, a Japanese shoe manufacturer. They stored the shoes in the basement of Knight's father's house and sold them out of cars at track meets.

In 1968 the 2 men formed NIKE, Inc., named for the Greek goddess of Victory, said to have been invoked by the legendary runner from Marathon. The NIKE "swoosh" logo was designed by a graduate student named Carolyn Davidson, who was paid $35. In 1972 they broke with Onitsuka in a dispute over distribution rights.

At the 1972 Olympic Trials in Eugene, Oregon, Knight and Bowerman persuaded some of the marathoners to wear NIKE shoes. When some of these runners placed, the 2 men quickly advertised that NIKEs were worn by "four of the top seven finishers."

In 1975 Bowerman had an idea for a new sole, which he tested by stuffing a piece of rubber into a waffle iron. The result was the waffle sole, which NIKE added to its running shoes. When running became popular in the 1970s, NIKE improved its line of running shoes to appeal to the new market. By 1982 annual sales had reached almost $700 million.

When enthusiasm for running faded, rival Reebok forged ahead with its aerobic lines, and NIKE responded with shoes for other sports such as basketball, football, baseball, volleyball, hiking, wrestling, and soccer. NIKE introduced Air Jordan (a popular basketball shoe named for Chicago Bulls star Michael Jordan) in 1985, the Cross Trainer in 1987, the "Just Do It" slogan in 1988, Air Pressure (basketball shoes with inflatable soles) in 1989, and Aqua Sock (water shoes) in 1990. In the meantime NIKE bought Cole Haan (dress shoes, 1988).

In 1990 and 1991, despite the US recession, a boycott by civil rights organization PUSH, and a maturing US athletic shoe market, NIKE's market share increased. But the company expects its greatest future growth overseas, where sales have risen almost 200% in 2 years. NIKE reorganized its European sales force (and will do so in other world regions) and increased its 1991 European ad budget by 44% to $39 million, with the aim of becoming #1 in Europe by the year 2000.

NYSE symbol: NIKE
Fiscal year ends: May 31

Hoover's Rating A+

WHO

Chairman and CEO: Philip H. Knight, age 53, $653,584 pay
President and COO: Richard K. Donahue, age 64, $497,500 pay
Deputy Chairman and SVP: William J. Bowerman, age 80
EVP: Delbert J. Hayes, age 56
VP Finance: George E. Porter, age 60
Auditors: Price Waterhouse
Employees: 5,500

WHERE

HQ: One Bowerman Dr., Beaverton, OR 97005-6453
Phone: 503-671-6453
Fax: 503-626-7252 (Public Relations)

The company sells its products in over 99 countries and maintains administrative offices in the US, Europe, Asia, and Canada.

	1990 Sales		1990 Operating Income	
	$ mil.	% of total	$ mil.	% of total
US	2,142	71	325	64
Europe	665	22	134	26
Other countries	197	7	52	10
Adjustments	—	—	(30)	—
Total	**3,004**	**100**	**481**	**100**

WHAT

	1990 US Sales	
	$ mil.	% of total
Domestic footwear	1,676	78
Domestic apparel	326	15
Other brands	140	7
Total	**2,142**	**100**

Aerobics Shoes
Elite

Basketball Shoes
Air Jordan
Air Pressure
Flight
Force

Cross-Training Shoes
Air Trainer
All Conditions Gear

Running Shoes
Air Flow
Air Max
Light
Air Pegasus
Air Stab
NIKE International
Socks

Tennis Shoes
Air Challenge Court
Air Tech Challenge
Challenge Court

Water Sports Shoes
Aqua Sock

Dress Shoes
Cole Haan

Apparel Products
Accessories
Athletic bags
Bicycling clothing
Fitness wear
Running clothes
Shirts
Shorts

RANKINGS

48th in *Fortune* 100 Diversified Service Cos.
168th in *Business Week* 1000

KEY COMPETITORS

Brown Group
Edison Brothers
The Gap
Hartmarx
INTERCO
L.A. Gear
Levi Strauss
The Limited
Melville
Reebok
V. F.
U.S. Shoe

HOW MUCH

Fiscal year ends May of following year	9-Year Growth	1981	1982	1983	1984	1985	1986	1987	1988	1989	1990
Sales ($ mil.)	17.7%	694	867	920	946	1,069	877	1,203	1,711	2,235	3,004
Net income ($ mil.)	21.7%	49	57	41	10	59	36	102	167	243	287
Income as % of sales	—	7.1%	6.6%	4.4%	1.1%	5.5%	4.1%	8.5%	9.8%	10.9%	9.6%
Earnings per share ($)	20.9%	0.69	0.77	0.54	0.14	0.78	0.47	1.35	2.23	3.21	3.77
Stock price – high ($)	—	7.13	14.00	11.88	8.19	7.38	10.25	12.38	17.19	34.63	47.94
Stock price – low ($)	—	4.31	6.22	7.19	3.31	3.94	5.19	5.75	8.63	12.63	24.00
Stock price – close ($)	21.3%	7.06	11.28	7.25	3.94	7.06	5.88	9.75	13.25	26.63	40.25
P/E – high	—	10	18	22	61	10	22	9	8	11	13
P/E – low	—	6	8	13	25	5	11	4	4	4	6
Dividends per share ($)	—	0.00	0.00	0.10	0.20	0.20	0.15	0.20	0.25	0.35	0.48
Book value per share ($)	24.7%	1.88	3.23	3.68	3.63	4.19	4.45	5.55	7.53	10.46	13.72

1990 Year-end:
Debt ratio: 2.8%
Return on equity: 31.2%
Cash (mil.): $120
Current ratio: 2.04
Long-term debt (mil.): $30
No. of shares (mil.): 75
Dividends:
    1990 average yield: 1.2%
    1990 payout: 12.7%
Market value (mil.): $3,031

Stock Price History High/Low 1981–90

NORDSTROM, INC.

NASDAQ symbol: NOBE
Fiscal year ends: January 31

 Hoover's Rating **B+**

OVERVIEW

High-end specialty clothier Nordstrom has achieved great success in a turbulent retail economy. The Seattle-based company, 40%-owned by the Nordstrom family, has tripled its store count and increased sales by nearly 600% since 1980 but now faces challenges that threaten its uniqueness.

What has set the company apart from other retailers is the personal service provided to customers by commissioned salespeople. Stories of employees warming up customers' cars in winter, delivering packages, and writing thank you notes have enhanced Nordstrom's reputation as a special place to shop.

Recently, Nordstrom's competitors have taken notice, placing their sales clerks on commission and even redesigning their stores in what has been called the "Nordstromization" of retailing. A more serious challenge is the state of Washington's 1990 decision that Nordstrom's after-hours requirements of its employees violate labor laws. Class-action lawsuits now pending as a result of the decision could cost the company over $15 million in back wages. In addition, the labor claims spawned litigation by Nordstrom shareholders that led in 1991 to a $7.5 million settlement.

Nordstrom has aggressively countered its bad press by touting its company-wide recycling program, its high number of women in management (including 1 of 4 co-presidents), and its frequent use of minorities in its advertising (1/3 of all models). Nordstrom also highlighted the contributions of its sales force in its 1991 annual report, dubbing itself "a company of entrepreneurs."

WHEN

In 1901 John W. Nordstrom, a gold miner and lumberjack from Sweden, opened Wallin & Nordstrom shoe store in Seattle with shoemaker Carl F. Wallin. Nordstrom retired in 1928, selling his 1/2 of the business, which by then had opened a 2nd store, to his sons Everett and Elmer. Wallin sold out to the Nordstroms in 1929, and a 3rd Nordstrom son, Lloyd, joined in 1933. The shoe chain thrived and incorporated in 1946 as Nordstrom's, Inc.

By 1963 Nordstrom's was the largest independent shoe chain in the country. The company decided to expand into apparel retailing and that year acquired Best Apparel, which had a store in Seattle and another in Portland. In 1966 Nordstrom's bought Portland's Nicholas Ungar, a fashion retailer that it merged with a Portland Nordstrom's shoe store under the name Nordstrom Best.

The company, also renamed Nordstrom Best in 1966, went public in 1971; in 1973 the name changed simply to Nordstrom, Inc. Lloyd Nordstrom organized a group of investors to found the Seattle Seahawks for $16 million in 1975. The family considered selling its 51% interest when the team's players' union representative was cut in 1984, causing many Seattleites to destroy their Nordstrom credit cards. The family later bought out the remaining investors and sold the franchise.

Meanwhile, the company continued to expand the retail stores. In 1976 Nordstrom started Place Two, featuring apparel and shoes in smaller stores than the traditional Nordstrom. Expansion into Southern California began with the opening of a store in Orange County (1978). Nordstrom also had stores in Washington, Oregon, Alaska, and Utah when in 1988 the company opened its first store on the East Coast in an affluent Virginia suburb. This opening had the highest first-day sales in the company's history — $1 million — until a San Francisco opening later in the year eclipsed it with $1.7 million.

Nordstrom has since opened more stores in Northern California and Virginia, and broke into metropolitan New York in 1990 and Chicago in 1991. The company built a large distribution center in Maryland, and new stores are being built or have been announced for Baltimore, New York, Indianapolis, Denver, and Minneapolis.

WHO

Co-Chairman: Bruce A. Nordstrom, age 57, $300,000 pay
Co-Chairman: John N. Nordstrom, age 54, $300,000 pay
Co-Chairman: James F. Nordstrom , age 51, $300,000 pay
Co-Chairman: John A. McMillan, age 59, $300,000 pay (prior to promotion)
VC: Robert E. Bender, age 55, $265,000 pay (prior to promotion)
Co-President: Darrel J. Hume, age 43
Co-President: Galen Jefferson, age 41
Co-President: Raymond A. Johnson, age 49
Co-President: John J. Whitacre, age 38
EVP and Treasurer: John Goesling, age 45
VP Human Resources: Charles Dudley
Auditors: Deloitte & Touche
Employees: 29,000

WHERE

HQ: 1501 Fifth Ave., Seattle, WA 98101
Phone: 206-628-2111
Fax: 206-628-1289

Nordstrom operates 64 stores in 8 states, with 3 more planned for 1992 opening.

	Retail Locations	
	Sq. ft. thou.	% of total
Southern California	2,535	30
Northern California	1,921	22
Washington	1,393	16
Oregon	759	9
DC area	750	9
New Jersey	538	6
Utah	317	4
Illinois	249	3
Alaska	97	1
Total	**8,559**	**100**

WHAT

	1990 Retail Sales
	% of total
Women's apparel	39
Women's accessories	20
Shoes	19
Men's apparel & furnishings	16
Children's apparel & other	6
Total	**100**

Nordstrom
47 large stores in 8 states, selling apparel, shoes, and accessories
Nordstrom Rack
12 discount/clearance stores in 4 states
Place Two
5 small specialty stores in the Northwest
Other
11 shoe departments in Hawaii department stores

RANKINGS

40th in *Fortune* 50 Retailing Cos.
237th in *Business Week* 1000

KEY COMPETITORS

Brown Group	General Cinema	May
Carter Hawley Hale	Hartmarx	Melville
Dayton Hudson	INTERCO	J. C. Penney
Edison Brothers	The Limited	U.S. Shoe
The Gap	Macy	

HOW MUCH

	9-Year Growth	1981	1982	1983	1984	1985	1986	1987	1988	1989	1990
Sales ($ mil.)	21.0%	522	613	788	981	1,302	1,630	1,920	2,328	2,671	2,894
Net income ($ mil.)	18.7%	25	27	40	41	50	73	93	123	115	116
Income as % of sales	—	4.7%	4.4%	5.1%	4.1%	3.8%	4.5%	4.8%	5.3%	4.3%	4.0%
Earnings per share ($)	16.8%	0.35	0.38	0.54	0.55	0.65	0.91	1.13	1.51	1.41	1.42
Stock price – high ($)	—	4.72	6.31	11.56	9.63	13.19	25.63	40.75	34.00	42.50	39.25
Stock price – low ($)	—	2.47	3.34	5.75	6.63	7.06	11.88	15.75	19.75	29.75	17.25
Stock price – close ($)	21.2%	3.94	6.06	8.94	7.75	11.94	20.88	19.75	30.25	37.25	22.25
P/E – high	—	13	17	22	18	20	28	36	23	30	28
P/E – low	—	7	9	11	12	11	13	14	13	21	12
Dividends per share ($)	20.7%	0.06	0.06	0.07	0.10	0.11	0.13	0.18	0.22	0.28	0.30
Book value per share ($)	18.1%	2.27	2.73	3.21	3.65	4.22	5.57	6.55	7.86	8.99	10.11

1990 Year-end:
Debt ratio: 36.7%
Return on equity: 14.9%
Cash (mil.): $25
Current ratio: 1.98
Long-term debt (mil.): $479
No. of shares (mil.): 82
Dividends:
1990 average yield: 1.3%
1990 payout: 21.1%
Market value (mil.): $1,819

**Stock Price History
High/Low 1981–90**

NORFOLK SOUTHERN CORPORATION

NYSE symbol: NSC
Fiscal year ends: December 31

Hoover's Rating B

OVERVIEW

Virginia-based Norfolk Southern Corporation is a holding company controlling a major freight railway (Norfolk Southern Railway) and motor carrier (North American Van Lines). The company also conducts a growing business in international trade, principally coal exports. Pocahontas Land Corporation (a subsidiary) owns substantial coal-producing properties in the Appalachian Mountains, with almost 2 billion tons of coal reserves.

With 14,842 miles of track in the Midwest, Southeast, and Ontario (Canada), Norfolk Southern Railway hauls coal, coke, iron ore, chemicals, automobiles, and many other commodities. In recent years Norfolk Southern has launched several intermodal programs (freight transported in the same container by train, truck, or ship), including Triple Crown Services, which employs Roadrailers, freight containers that can be converted quickly from railcars (with undercarriages) to trailers (with truck wheels).

North American (purchased in 1985) moves household goods, general merchandise, and specialized shipments by truck and forwards international freight traffic by sea and air.

WHO

Chairman and CEO: Arnold B. McKinnon, age 63, $1,631,457 pay
President: David R. Goode, age 50
VC: Joseph R. Neikirk, age 62
EVP Finance: John R. Turbyfill, age 59, $767,400 pay
EVP Operations: Paul R. Rudder, age 58
EVP Administration: Thomas C. Sheller, age 60
Auditors: KPMG Peat Marwick
Employees: 31,968

WHEN

Norfolk Southern Corporation is the result of the 1982 merger of 2 major US railroads: Norfolk & Western Railway Company (N&W) and Southern Railway Company.

N&W dates to 1838, when a single track first connected Petersburg, Virginia, to City Point (now Hopewell). This 8-mile stretch became part of the Atlantic, Mississippi & Ohio (AM&O), which was created by the consolidation of 3 Virginia railways in 1870. In 1881 the Philadelphia banking firm of E. W. Clark and Company bought the AM&O, renamed it the Norfolk & Western, and established headquarters at Roanoke, Virginia. N&W rolled into Ohio by purchasing 2 other railroads (1892, 1901) and took over the Virginian Railway, a coal carrier with trackage paralleling much of its own (1959). In 1964 N&W acquired the New York, Chicago & St. Louis Railroad (a fast freight line nicknamed the Nickel Plate Road); the Akron, Canton & Youngstown; and Pennsylvania Railroad's line between Columbus and Sandusky, Ohio. Also in 1964 N&W leased the Wabash Railroad, gaining lines from Detroit and Chicago to Kansas City and St. Louis.

The Southern Railway can be traced back to the South Carolina Canal & Rail Road, a 9-mile line chartered in 1827 and built by Horatio Allen to win trade for the port of Charleston. It became the longest railway in the world when it opened a 136-mile line to Hamburg, South Carolina (1833). Soon other railroads sprang up throughout the South, including the Richmond & Danville (Virginia, 1847) and the East Tennessee, Virginia & Georgia (1869), which were combined to form the Southern Railway System in 1894. Southern eventually gained control of more than 100 railroads, forging a system that extended from Washington, DC, to St. Louis and New Orleans.

The 1982 merger of Southern and N&W created an extensive rail system operating throughout the East, South, and Midwest. Norfolk Southern (a holding company created for the 2 railroads) bought North American Van Lines in 1985 and attempted (unsuccessfully) to buy Consolidated Rail in 1986. Triple Crown Services, the company's intermodal subsidiary, began operations in 1986. The company attempted to take over Piedmont Aviation in 1987 but sold its 17% stake when Piedmont agreed to merge with USAir. In 1988 under Arnold McKinnon (chairman and CEO since 1987), the company continued a cost-cutting program and reported record earnings of $635 million. A slow economy and higher costs (particularly fuel costs) resulted in slightly lower earnings for 1989 and 1990.

WHERE

HQ: Three Commercial Place, Norfolk, VA 23510
Phone: 804-629-2680
Fax: 804-629-2777

Norfolk Southern operates a 14,842-mile rail system in 20 states, mainly in the Southeast and Midwest, and in Ontario, Canada. North American Van Lines offers moving and other trucking services through 742 agents in the US, 190 agents in Canada, and 280 agents in the UK, Germany, and Panama.

WHAT

	1990 Sales	
	$ mil.	% of total
Railway operations		
Coal, coke & iron ore	1,409	30
Chemicals	442	10
Paper	406	9
Automotive	352	8
Intermodal	351	8
Agriculture	224	5
Construction	215	5
Metals	145	3
Food	64	1
Household	12	—
Other commodities	43	1
Other sales	123	2
Motor carrier operations	831	18
Total	**4,617**	**100**

Major Subsidiaries and Affiliates
Norfolk Southern Railway Co. (railroad)
Norfolk and Western Railway Co. (railroad)
North American Van Lines, Inc. (motor carrier)
Pocahontas Land Corp. (coal mines and other energy-related properties)
Triple Crown Services, Inc. (intermodal services)
Wheelersburg Coal Terminal Co. (coal storage and blending)

RANKINGS

11th in *Fortune* 50 Transportation Cos.
88th in *Business Week* 1000

KEY COMPETITORS

American President
Canadian Pacific
Consolidated Freightways
Consolidated Rail
CSX
Mayflower
Roadway
Ryder
Union Pacific
Yellow Freight

HOW MUCH

	9-Year Growth	1981	1982	1983	1984	1985	1986	1987	1988	1989	1990
Sales ($ mil.)	11.0%	1,802	3,359	3,148	3,525	3,825	4,076	4,113	4,462	4,536	4,617
Net income ($ mil.)	7.5%	291	411	356	482	500	519	172	635	606	556
Income as % of sales	—	16.2%	12.2%	11.3%	13.7%	13.1%	12.7%	4.2%	14.2%	13.4%	12.0%
Earnings per share ($)	1.9%	2.90	2.19	1.89	2.55	2.65	2.74	0.91	3.51	4.49	3.43
Stock price – high ($)	—	18.42	21.67	23.54	21.42	27.08	33.08	38.25	32.88	41.25	47.25
Stock price – low ($)	—	13.13	13.42	17.13	16.17	19.25	24.63	21.00	24.50	30.25	35.00
Stock price – close ($)	10.3%	17.29	18.25	21.04	19.54	27.08	28.17	26.25	31.38	40.50	41.75
P/E – high	—	6	10	12	8	10	12	42	9	9	14
P/E – low	—	5	6	9	6	7	9	23	7	7	10
Dividends per share ($)	6.4%	0.87	0.90	0.93	1.07	1.13	1.13	1.20	1.26	1.38	1.52
Book value per share ($)	6.1%	18.46	18.48	22.11	23.69	25.20	26.78	26.48	28.74	30.44	31.57

1990 Year-end:
Debt ratio: 17.3%
Return on equity: 11.1%
Cash (mil.): $625
Current ratio: 1.27
Long-term debt (mil.): $1,030
No. of shares (mil.): 156
Dividends:
  1990 average yield: 3.6%
  1990 payout: 44.3%
Market value (mil.): $6,495

Stock Price History High/Low 1981–90

NORTHROP CORPORATION

OVERVIEW

Northrop is one of America's largest aerospace manufacturers. Its principal product is the B-2 Stealth bomber, one of the most sophisticated aircraft ever produced. The B-2 accounts for more than 1/2 of Northrop's revenues.

Northrop also builds fuselage sections for the Boeing 747 jetliner and 40% of the airframe for the F/A-18 fighter. It produces advanced electronic systems (including the guidance system for the MX missile) and unmanned vehicles such as target drones. With sales to the US government accounting for 90% of its business, Northrop faces an uncertain future as diminished East-West tensions decrease demand for its products. In 1990 Congress cut the B-2 program from 132 to 75 aircraft, and in 1991 Northrop (and partner McDonnell Douglas) lost the competition to build the air force's Advanced Tactical Fighter after investing some $250 million to develop the project.

On the brighter side, the navy has asked Northrop to participate in a $1.4 billion upgrade of the F/A-18. The company is also faring better financially than in recent years; in 1990 Northrop reduced debt and cut capital spending by 33%. The company plans to pay off all existing debt by the mid-1990s.

WHEN

John K. "Jack" Northrop, cofounder of Lockheed Aircraft (1927) and designer of that company's record-setting Vega monoplane, founded Northrop Aircraft Corporation in California in 1939. Northrop had previously established 2 other companies, Avion Corporation (formed in 1928 and bought by United Aircraft and Transportation) and Northrop Corporation (formed in 1932 in cooperation with Douglas Aircraft, which absorbed it in 1938).

During WWII Northrop produced the P-61 fighter. It also built the famous Flying Wing bombers, which advanced the state of aeronautical engineering but failed to win a production contract.

In the 1950s Northrop's income depended heavily on the F-89 fighter and the Snark missile, items which made the company sensitive to fluctuations in government funding. When Thomas Jones succeeded Jack Northrop as president in 1959, he moved the company away from risky prime contracts in favor of numerous subcontracts and bought Page Communications Engineers (telecommunications, 1959) and Hallicrafters (electronics, 1966) to help reduce Northrop's dependence on government contracts. Jones also promoted the company's inexpensive F-5 fighter for export to developing countries. F-5 production continued until 1989, when the 3,806th aircraft was completed.

In the meantime Northrop was hit with a bribery scandal and the disclosure of illegal payments to Richard Nixon's 1972 campaign fund. The company lost an air force fighter competition to General Dynamics's F-16 in 1975, but the navy ordered a modified version of Northrop's aircraft (the F-18 Hornet). McDonnell Douglas won the role of prime contractor for the F-18, with Northrop getting 40% of the work.

Another major Northrop project initiated in the 1970s was the F-20 fighter. Jones championed the F-20 overseas, but none were sold. Northrop ceased marketing the airplane in 1986, but federal investigations into questionable payments to South Korean officials continued into 1990. In 1981 Northrop won the contract to develop the B-2 Stealth bomber.

After 30 years as CEO, Jones, 70, retired in 1990. That year, under the leadership of Kent Kresna, the company pleaded guilty to 34 counts related to falsifying test results on some government projects and paid a $17 million fine. In a related shareholder's suit, Northrop agreed to pay $18 million in damages in 1991. It also won a $2.2 billion contract to develop a new missile (Brilliant Anti-Tank) for the army that same year.

NYSE symbol: NOC
Fiscal year ends: December 31

WHO

Chairman, President, and CEO: Kent Kresa, age 52, $1,125,000 pay
EVP Operations: F. J. Manzella, age 60, $655,000 pay
SVP Finance: John B. Campbell, age 67, $601,467 pay
SVP Human Resources: Arthur F. Dauer, age 54
Auditors: Deloitte & Touche
Employees: 38,200

WHERE

HQ: 1840 Century Park East, Los Angeles, CA 90067
Phone: 213-553-6262
Fax: 213-553-2076

Northrop operates 5 US regional offices and has facilities in 7 states.

WHAT

	1990 Sales		1990 Operating Income	
	$ mil.	% of total	$ mil.	% of total
Aircraft	4,929	75	262	75
Electronics	791	15	56	16
Missiles & unmanned vehicle systems	455	8	24	7
Services	117	2	5	2
Adjustments	—	—	(55)	—
Total	**5,490**	**100**	**292**	**100**

	1990 Sales	
	$ mil.	% of total
US government	4,929	90
Other customers	561	10
Total	**5,490**	**100**

Aircraft
B-2 Stealth bomber
F-23 Advanced Tactical Fighter prototype
F/A-18 Hornet strike fighter subassemblies
Boeing 747 subassemblies

Electronic Systems
Accelerometers
Automated test equipment
Electronic sensor and tracking systems
Gyroscopes
Inertial guidance and control systems
Military electronic countermeasure systems (ECM, radar jamming)
Strategic guidance and navigation

Northrop Research and Technology Center
Technology research programs

RANKINGS

96th in *Fortune* 500 Industrial Cos.
474th in *Business Week* 1000

KEY COMPETITORS

Allied-Signal	Martin Marietta
Daimler-Benz	McDonnell Douglas
General Dynamics	Rockwell
General Electric	Siemens
General Motors	Textron
Grumman	Thomson SA
Lockheed	Thorn EMI
LTV	United Technologies

HOW MUCH

	9-Year Growth	1981	1982	1983	1984	1985	1986	1987	1988	1989	1990
Sales ($ mil.)	11.9%	1,991	2,473	3,261	3,688	5,057	5,608	6,053	5,797	5,248	5,490
Net income ($ mil.)	17.9%	48	5	101	167	214	41	94	(31)	(81)	210
Income as % of sales	—	2.4%	0.2%	3.1%	4.5%	4.2%	0.7%	1.6%	(0.5%)	(1.5%)	3.8%
Earnings per share ($)	16.8%	1.10	0.12	2.21	3.63	4.63	0.89	2.01	(0.65)	(1.71)	4.48
Stock price – high ($)	—	21.00	25.92	32.75	39.50	56.63	51.63	52.63	35.88	29.75	20.25
Stock price – low ($)	—	11.00	13.08	21.92	23.67	31.63	36.88	24.75	25.13	16.00	13.75
Stock price – close ($)	(0.1%)	17.46	25.13	28.75	35.25	44.13	39.25	25.50	27.75	17.50	17.38
P/E – high	—	19	216	15	11	12	58	26	—	—	5
P/E – low	—	10	109	10	7	7	41	12	—	—	3
Dividends per share ($)	8.0%	0.60	0.60	0.60	0.90	1.20	1.20	1.20	1.20	1.20	1.20
Book value per share ($)	7.6%	11.32	10.87	12.64	15.72	19.42	19.29	20.23	21.40	18.65	22.00

1990 Year-end:
Debt ratio: 40.1%
Return on equity: 22.0%
Cash (mil.): $173
Current ratio: 1.47
Long-term debt (mil.): $691
No. of shares (mil.): 47
Dividends:
  1990 average yield: 6.9%
  1990 payout: 26.8%
Market value (mil.): $816

Stock Price History High/Low 1981–90

NORTHWESTERN MUTUAL

OVERVIEW

Northwestern Mutual is the 10th largest life insurance company in the US, with assets of $31.4 billion. The Milwaukee-based company has more than 2 million policyholders of life and disability insurance and annuities. Northwestern has 4.1 million policies, with over $224 billion of insurance in force. Northwestern's policies have exceptional renewal rates; average life policy longevity is over 40 years.

Northwestern markets its services through a nationwide network of 7,200 exclusive agents. *Fortune* has ranked the company as "the most admired" among the 10 largest life insurance companies for 9 years running. In the last 50 years Northwestern has been the industry's low-cost provider more times than any other company.

Northwestern resisted the 1980s urge to diversify and to invest in risky, high-yield areas, and thus remains well capitalized on the basis of a diversified, high-quality portfolio (the company's bond default and delinquency rates declined by 85% from 1986 to 1990). The company also continues to reduce expenses and control costs to keep premiums low.

WHEN

In 1854 John Johnston, a successful New York insurance agent, moved to Wisconsin at age 72 to become a farmer. Three years later Johnston returned to the insurance business when he and 36 leading Wisconsin citizens founded Mutual Life Insurance Company.

The company changed its name to Northwestern Mutual Life Insurance Company in 1865. By then it was already the 14th largest company in total amount of insurance in force. By the 1880s the company had made clear its goal to be first in benefits to policyholders rather than first in size.

In 1907 Northwestern appointed policyholders to evaluate the entire company's operations. This 5-person committee, whose members change every year, still operates, and a summary of their report is published in the company's annual report.

The company continued to offer level-premium life insurance in the 1920s while competitors offered new types of products. As a result of its conservatism, the company's rank by insurance in force fell from 6th in 1918 to 8th in 1946.

The company began to develop the industry's most comprehensive computer system in the late 1950s. One result was the 1962 introduction of the Insurance Service Account (ISA), in which all policies owned by a family or business could be combined into one premium with monthly payments by preauthorized checks. The ISA set the standard for the industry.

Northwestern was one of the first major companies, beginning in 1959, to give women a lower premium rate than men because of economic and health gains by females.

Northwestern in 1968 introduced Extra Ordinary Life (EOL), which combined whole life with term insurance, using dividends to convert term to paid-up whole life each year. In less than a year, EOL became the company's most popular policy.

Northwestern became a major advertiser in 1972 by spending $1.4 million on ABC's coverage of the summer Olympics to introduce "The Quiet Company" campaign. The result was a jump from 34th to 3rd place in public awareness of Northwestern.

In the 1980s Northwestern began financing leveraged buyouts. In return Northwestern gained an ownership share and stock options in addition to loan payments. The company and other insurers bought a 2/3 interest in Congoleum, a flooring manufacturer, and a majority interest in Robert W. Baird, a Milwaukee securities firm (1982), and in Mortgage Guaranty Insurance (1985).

Despite these modest purchases, the company remained largely immune to the 1980s mania for fast money and high-risk diversification. Only 10% of Northwestern Mutual's investments are in below-investment-grade securities, and its real estate investment delinquency rate is below industry average. The company has prospered by sticking to its core business, individual life and annuity sales.

In 1990 the 3 major insurance rating services continued to give Northwestern their highest ratings.

Mutual company
Fiscal year ends: December 31

Hoover's Rating **B**

WHO

Chairman and CEO: Donald J. Schuenke, age 62
COO: James D. Ericson, age 56
EVP Agencies and Marketing: Robert E. Carlson
SVP Human Resources and Administration: James W. Ehrenstrom, age 55
SVP Insurance Operations: Peter W. Bruce, age 46
SVP Investments: Edward J. Zore, age 46
SVP Planning and Finance: Walt J. Wojcik, age 51
Auditors: Price Waterhouse
Employees: 3,050

WHERE

HQ: The Northwestern Mutual Life Insurance Co., 720 E. Wisconsin Ave., Milwaukee, WI 53202
Phone: 414-271-1444
Fax: 414-299-7022

Northwestern Mutual operates in all 50 US states and the District of Columbia, with more than 100 general agency offices.

WHAT

	1990 Sales	
	$ mil.	% of total
Premiums	4,589	66
Net investment income	2,333	34
Total	**6,922**	**100**

	12/31/90 Assets	
	$ mil.	% of total
Bonds	13,285	42
Stocks	925	3
Mortgage loans	5,597	18
Real estate	1,304	4
Policyowner loans	5,321	17
Other assets	4,957	16
Total	**31,389**	**100**

Insurance Products
Annuities
Disability insurance
Mortgage insurance
Permanent and term life insurance
Securities brokerage

RANKINGS

10th in *Fortune* 50 Life Insurance Cos.

KEY COMPETITORS

Aetna
American Express
AIG
CIGNA
Equitable
John Hancock
Kemper
KKR
MassMutual
Merrill Lynch
MetLife
Morgan Stanley
New York Life
Primerica
Prudential
Sears
State Farm
Transamerica
Travelers
Other individual life insurance companies
Other securities brokerage firms
Mortgage insurance companies

HOW MUCH

	9 Yr. Growth	1981	1982	1983	1984	1985	1986	1987	1988	1989	1990
Assets ($ mil.)	11.1%	12,154	13,253	14,620	16,055	18,087	20,196	22,613	25,362	28,515	31,389
Income ($ mil.)	3.8%	102	60	49	61	13	18	40	118	372	143
Income as % of assets	—	0.8%	0.4%	0.3%	0.4%	0.1%	0.1%	0.2%	0.5%	1.3%	0.5%
Employees	3.1%	2,313	2,385	2,371	2,357	2,432	2,468	2,761	2,840	2,970	3,050

1990 Year-end:
Equity as % of assets: —
Return on equity: —
Cash (mil.): $714
Sales (mil.): $6,922

Income ($ mil.)
1981–90

NOVELL, INC.

NASDAQ symbol: NOVL
Fiscal year ends: Last Saturday
in October

OVERVIEW

From its headquarters in Provo, Utah (and not in Silicon Valley), Novell specializes in local area networks (LANs) for PCs, based on its own proprietary NetWare Operating System. LANs enable individual PCs to share hard disk storage, printers, and other peripherals and to communicate with other PCs and mainframes on the same network.

NetWare is the industry standard, with 57% of the LAN market. It is compatible with most common operating systems, including MS-DOS, OS/2, and Macintosh. Novell is currently developing NetWare systems to support UNIX and other large computer systems. Software products generated about 78% of Novell's 1990 sales, and the company is continuing to phase out its networking hardware business (such as the manufacture of add-on circuit boards, which Novell now farms out).

The influence of CEO Raymond Noorda, now 66, has been a major factor in Novell's success in creating NetWare's market niche. Noorda, who owns a 17.5% stake in the company, took over Novell in 1983 and has managed to instill a real sense of old-fashioned loyalty in his employees.

WHEN

Novell Data Systems started out in 1980 as a Provo, Utah–based maker of PC peripherals. In 1981 Safeguard Scientifics, a high-tech venture capital firm, bought a 55% stake in Novell (raised to 88% in 1982). Novell, which had gone through 8 presidents, was nearly defunct by 1983. Safeguard provided 51% of the capital needed to revive the company and brought in turn-around artist Raymond Noorda as CEO. Noorda invested $125,000 of his own money in the new Novell (then equal to a 33% stake).

By the time Noorda took over, Novell was already working on solutions to PC networking. Noorda approached the challenge by designating one machine in the network as a file server to manage the network and to control access to shared devices, such as disk drives and printers. As a result of Noorda's vision, Novell introduced NetWare, the first LAN software based on file server technology, in 1983.

After going public in 1985, Novell kept up with growing demand for LAN systems by introducing new and upgraded NetWare products and by buying other manufacturers to enhance and expand its product line. In 1987 Novell bought Santa Clara Systems (microcomputer workstations), CXI (computer products), and SoftCraft (programming tools). The company bought 60% of Indisy Software (electronic messaging systems, 1988), Excelan (networking software and related equipment,

1989), a minority stake in Gupta Technologies (database servers, 1990), and the remaining 40% of Indisy (1990). At the end of fiscal 1988 Novell announced it would drop production of most hardware products (46% of 1988 sales). In 1989 hardware represented 33% of sales.

In 1990 Lotus, at Noorda's instigation, announced it would acquire Novell for $1.5 billion in Lotus stock. Had the deal gone through, the combined Lotus-Novell would have surpassed Microsoft as the #1 software maker; as it happened, Novell's directors nixed the deal in May. Originally, the company had accepted 3 seats to Lotus's 4 on a 7-member board. At the last minute Novell demanded equal representaion. Lotus refused. Novell in 1990 joined Canon, Fujitsu, NEC, Sony, Toshiba, and SOFTBANK Corporation in forming Novell Japan in Tokyo to develop NetWare for the Japanese market.

Novell lost a longtime rival in 1991 when 3Com dropped out of the LAN market. But Microsoft picked up where 3Com left off, taking over development for LAN Manager, formerly a joint 3Com-Microsoft product. Novell then bought Digital Research, a DOS clone maker, for $81 million in 1991. Based in Monterey, California, Digital created the first PC operating system (CP/M), which lost out to Bill Gates's MS-DOS when IBM needed an operating system for its original PC.

WHO

Chairman, President, and CEO: Raymond J.
Noorda, age 66
SVP and CFO: James R. Tolonen, age 41,
$212,491 pay
SVP Human Resources: Ernest J. Harris
Auditors: Ernst & Young
Employees: 2,557

WHERE

HQ: 122 E. 1700 S., Provo, UT 84606
Phone: 801-429-7000
Fax: 801-429-5775

Novell has 33 sales offices in the US and 11 sales offices overseas.

	1990 Sales		1990 Pretax Income	
	$ mil.	% of total	$ mil.	% of total
US	301	60	141	97
Other countries	197	40	4	3
Total	**498**	**100**	**145**	**100**

WHAT

	1990 Sales
	% of total
Software	78
Hardware	22
Total	**100**

Network Operating Systems
Advanced NetWare
ELS NetWare Levels 1 and 2
NetWare 386
NetWare for Macintosh
NetWare for VMS
Portable NetWare
SFT NetWare

Communications and Connectivity Products
Host connectivity gateways
MultiNet (TCP/IP networking)
Remote PC access to LAN products
Wide area networking products

Database Products
NetWare Btrieve (record manager)
NetWare SQL (database engine)

Store-and-Forward Products
NetWare MHS (message handling service)

RANKINGS

185th in *Business Week* 1000

KEY COMPETITORS

Borland
Computer Associates
H&R Block
Lotus
Microsoft
Oracle
Wang

HOW MUCH

	5-Year Growth	1981	1982	1983	1984	1985	1986	1987	1988	1989	1990
Sales ($ mil.)	71.1%	—	—	—	—	34	82	183	281	422	498
Net income ($ mil.)	88.0%	—	—	—	—	4	10	20	30	49	94
Income as % of sales	—	—	—	—	—	12.4%	12.4%	11.1%	10.8%	11.5%	19.0%
Earnings per share ($)	—	—	—	—	—	0.10	0.23	0.39	0.55	0.73	1.36
Stock price – high ($)	—	—	—	—	—	5.00	6.63	14.88	16.31	19.13	34.00
Stock price – low ($)	—	—	—	—	—	1.13	3.50	5.75	8.75	11.88	13.75
Stock price – close ($)	47.2%	—	—	—	—	4.78	6.44	12.00	15.00	15.50	33.00
P/E – high	—	—	—	—	—	49	29	38	30	26	25
P/E – low	—	—	—	—	—	11	16	15	16	16	10
Dividends per share ($)	—	—	—	—	—	0.00	0.00	0.00	0.00	0.00	0.00
Book value per share ($)	109.6%	—	—	—	—	0.14	0.80	1.89	2.49	3.57	5.66

1990 Year-end:
Debt ratio: 0.6%
Return on equity: 29.5%
Cash (mil.): $255
Current ratio: 4.29
Long-term debt (mil.): $2
No. of shares (mil.): 70
Dividends:
  1990 average yield: 0.0%
  1990 payout: 0.0%
Market value (mil.): $2,324

**Stock Price History
High/Low 1985–90**

NWA INC.

Private company
Fiscal year ends: December 31

Hoover's Rating C-

OVERVIEW

1991 has been a busy year for NWA. The Minneapolis-based parent of Northwest Airlines started the year off buying Eastern Airlines's Washington, DC, landing slots. It then arranged $20 million in debtor-in-possession financing for America West, gaining the option to buy the ailing Phoenix-based carrier's route from Honolulu to Nagoya, Japan. In July NWA reached an agreement to operate the Washington–New York–Boston Trump Shuttle for the next decade. The company has expressed an interest in buying a stake in Qantas when the Australian government takes it public and is talking to Continental about a possible merger. In September 1991 the company agreed to pay

$20 million for Midway Airlines's gates and other facilities at Chicago's Midway Airport. NWA is already linked with KLM Royal Dutch Airlines, which currently owns 20% of the company.

All this activity is part of NWA's strategy to build Northwest (now America's 4th largest airline after Delta, AMR, and UAL) into a world leader. NWA posted its first loss since deregulation in 1990 and must address the additional challenge of about $3.5 billion in debt. In May 1991 the company received $740 million in financial support from the state of Minnesota, most of which will be used to finance new aircraft and build maintenance facilities.

WHO

Co-Chairman: Alfred A. Checchi, age 42
Co-Chairman: Gary Wilson
VC: Fred Malek
President and CEO: John Dasburg
EVP Customer Service: Joe Leonard
EVP Operations: Bill Slattery
SVP Finance and Treasurer: Joseph Francht
SVP Finance and Controller: Herb Ihle
SVP Human Resources: Bruce Rismiller
Auditors: Ernst & Young
Employees: 40,000

WHEN

A group of Detroit, Minneapolis, and St. Paul businessmen led by Colonel Louis Brittin founded Northwest Airways in 1926 to provide air mail service between Minneapolis and Chicago. In 1928 Northwest became the first US airline to offer coordinated airline and railroad service.

In 1934 the company changed its name to Northwest Airlines. Its air routes expanded west to Seattle in 1934, and service to New York completed the airline's transcontinental route in 1945. Northwest started flying to the Far East in 1947, pioneering a Great Circle route (over Alaska and the Aleutians) to the Orient. Flights from Seattle to Honolulu commenced in 1948.

Former Civil Aeronautics Board chairman Donald Nyrop became Northwest's president in 1954. Famous for his thrift, Nyrop held debt to 10% of capital, the lowest proportion in the airline industry. When Nyrop retired in 1978, his successor, Joseph Lapensky, continued Nyrop's fiscal policies, keeping Northwest profitable throughout his tenure.

In 1984 the company formed NWA, a holding company. In 1986 NWA bought Republic Airlines, making Northwest America's 5th largest airline. Steve Rothmeier (former financial VP) became NWA's chairman and CEO that year. Rothmeier bought Mainline Travel, a national travel service, to help generate

passengers and negotiated agreements with 4 regional airlines, providing commuter service to feed Northwest's routes. In 1986 Northwest bought a 50% interest in PARS (TWA's computer reservation system, which merged with Delta's DATAS II system in 1990, forming WORLDSPAN).

Unfortunately, Rothmeier's failure to reach an agreement with Northwest's unions after the Republic acquisition led to low employee morale. Northwest's pilots still had no contract in 1989 when Wings Holdings — an investment group that included KLM and was led by ex-Marriott executive Alfred Checchi — took NWA private through a $3.65 billion LBO. Rothmeier resigned soon after the Wings buyout, and Checchi became chairman.

In 1990 NWA spent $20 million for a 25% stake in Hawaiian Airlines's parent, HAL. As part of the deal NWA gained 3 South Pacific routes, including authority to fly from Honolulu to Sydney, Australia. The high fuel prices that accompanied Iraq's invasion of Kuwait in 1990 produced huge 4th quarter losses for NWA and resulted in a $10.4 million loss for the year. Losses (mostly related to discount fares and a weak travel market) continued into 1991. That year Northwest announced service to China and offered the first flights by a US airline to Ho Chi Minh City (formerly Saigon) since the Vietnam War.

WHERE

HQ: Minneapolis/St. Paul International Airport, St. Paul, MN 55111-3075
Phone: 612-726-2111
Fax: 612-726-3942
Reservations: 800-225-2525

Northwest Airlines flies to 129 cities in 21 countries. It serves 41 states in the US.

Hub Locations
Detroit, MI
Memphis, TN
Minneapolis/St. Paul, MN
Washington, DC
Toyko, Japan

WHAT

Major Subsidiaries and Affiliates
Northwest Airlines, Inc.
Northwest Airlink (commuter services)
MLT Vacations, Inc. (wholesale travel and tour programs)
Northwest Aerospace Training Corp. (pilot training)
Northwest Aircraft, Inc. (acquires new and markets used aircraft)

Computer Reservation System
WORLDSPAN (32%, joint venture with Delta, TWA, and Abacus)

Flight Equipment	No.	Orders
Boeing 727	71	—
DC-10	20	7
A320	11	89
Boeing 747	50	6
Boeing 757	33	40
MD-80	8	—
DC-9	139	11
A330	—	16
A340	—	20
Total	**332**	**189**

HOW MUCH

	9-Year Growth	1981	1982	1983	1984	1985	1986	1987	1988	1989	1990
Sales ($ mil.)	16.4%	1,854	1,878	2,196	2,445	2,655	3,589	5,142	5,650	6,554	7,257
Net income ($ mil.)	—	11	5	50	56	73	77	103	135	355	(10)
Income as % of sales	—	0.6%	0.3%	2.3%	2.3%	2.7%	2.1%	2.0%	2.4%	5.4%	(0.1%)
Available seat miles (mil.)	13.6%	24,815	26,257	29,511	32,664	37,149	48,408	61,421	61,275	70,213	78,050
Revenue passenger miles (mil.)	15.5%	14,252	15,675	17,712	19,772	22,341	28,815	39,550	40,148	45,663	52,150
Passenger load factor	—	57.4%	59.7%	60.0%	60.5%	60.1%	58.5%	64.4%	65.5%	65.0%	66.8%
Size of operating fleet	12.9%	111	113	117	120	130	312	316	321	324	332
Employees	13.2%	13,096	13,754	14,187	15,185	16,864	33,427	33,724	35,532	39,323	40,000

1990 Year-end:
Assets (mil.): $5,374
Stockholders' equity (mil.): $2,453

Net Income ($ mil.) 1981–90

RANKINGS

6th in *Fortune* 50 Transportation Cos.
11th in *Forbes* 400 US Private Cos.

KEY COMPETITORS

Alaska Air	Qantas
America West	SAS
AMR	Singapore Airlines
Continental Airlines	Southwest
Delta	Swire Pacific
JAL	TWA
Midway	UAL
Pan Am	USAir

NYNEX CORPORATION

OVERVIEW

NYNEX, the 4th largest of the old Bell companies, serves 7 northeastern states through subsidiaries New York Telephone and New England Telephone. Telephone sales accounted for 82% of 1990 revenues.

A 1990 restructuring created 2 groups — Telecommunications (including the 2 phone companies) and Worldwide Services.

Worldwide Services includes NYNEX Mobile Communications, one of the 10 largest cellular companies in the US, with service to 259,000 customers. NYNEX Mobile plans to be the first cellular company to install digital technology in the US. NYNEX Information Resources publishes Yellow Pages in New England, New York, and Los Angeles, distributing more than 30 million copies in 1990 and generating sales of $854 million.

NYNEX subsidiaries (AGS, Stockholder Systems) also make the company the largest US provider of applications software to the financial services industry. Other operations include NYNEX Network Systems and NYNEX Venture Company, both formed in 1990. NYNEX Network Systems includes 11 UK cable television franchises, and NYNEX Venture works on long-term projects (security systems, electronic imaging) with companies in Ireland and Germany.

NYNEX owns 1/7 of Bellcore, the shared research arm of the Bell operating companies, as well as its own R&D facilities.

NYSE symbol: NYN
Fiscal year ends: December 31

Hoover's Rating **C+**

WHO

Chairman and CEO: William C. Ferguson, age 60, $1,045,000 pay
VC: Robert J. Eckenrode, age 60, $622,000 pay
VC; President, Worldwide Services: Frederic V. Salerno, age 47
VC Telecommunications: Ivan G. Seidenberg, age 44, $384,400 pay
VP Finance and Treasurer: Jeffrey S. Rubin, age 47
VP Human Resources: Donald B. Reed, age 46
Auditors: Coopers & Lybrand
Employees: 93,800

WHERE

HQ: 335 Madison Ave., New York, NY 10017
Phone: 212-370-7400
Fax: 212-682-1324 (Investor Relations)

NYNEX offers telecommunications services in Maine, Massachusetts, New Hampshire, Rhode Island, Vermont, New York, and Connecticut and mobile services in 22 metropolitan areas in the same territory. The company has overseas offices in Geneva, London, and Hong Kong.

WHEN

NYNEX's 2 telephone divisions, New York Telephone and New England Telephone, began as arms of AT&T. The larger of the 2, New York Telephone, was incorporated in 1896 and grew out of 2 small, independent telephone companies, Metropolitan Telephone & Telegraph and Westchester Telephone. Gardiner Hubbard, Alexander Bell's father-in-law, formed New England Telephone Company in 1878 with a plan to offer switching hardware. Half interest was later sold to a group that included Colonel William Forbes, who merged New England Telephone into the Bell system.

In 1983 AT&T and the Bell companies were split up as part of the AT&T antitrust suit settlement. NYNEX incorporated that same year and began separate operations in 1984. NYNEX also received cellular service operations for the same New York/New England territory (now under the auspices of NYNEX Mobile Communications) and a 1/7 share in Bell Communications Research (Bellcore).

In 1986 NYNEX purchased IBM's computer retailing operations. It also invested in software development for banks and financial institutions through acquisition of Business Intelligence Services Limited (1987) and AGS Computers Inc. (1988). The company attempted to enter the market for international long-distance service between 1986 and 1988 but failed to receive the necessary approvals. NYNEX continues to form alliances with overseas telecommunications entities; it is developing a telemarketing center for France Télécom and a network management system for British Telecom.

NYNEX has suffered setbacks recently. Over 60,000 union workers went on strike in 1989. The company's central purchasing subsidiary, NYNEX Material Enterprises Company (MECO) came in for intense scrutiny from regulators in 1990. While a Commonwealth of Massachusetts audit found no improprieties, an FCC inquiry led to NYNEX agreeing to rebate interstate customers $35.5 million and paying $1.4 million to the government. NYNEX merged MECO with another subsidiary to form Telesector Resources to support the NYNEX telephone companies.

NYNEX sold its 77 computer retail stores to ComputerLand in 1991, retreating from one of the boldest moves by a former Bell operating company to broaden its scope beyond telephone service.

WHAT

	1990 Sales		1990 Operating Income	
	$ mil.	% of total	$ mil.	% of total
Telecommunications	11,076	82	2,407	105
Cellular	314	2	60	3
Publishing	851	6	118	5
Financial/real estate	84	1	76	3
Other	1,260	9	(374)	(16)
Adjustments	—	—	(272)	—
Total	**13,585**	**100**	**2,015**	**100**

Telecommunications
New England Telephone Co.
New York Telephone Co.
Telesector Resources Group, Inc.

Cellular
NYNEX Mobile Communications Co.

Publishing
NYNEX Information Resources Co.
United Publishers Corp.

Financial/Real Estate
NYNEX Capital Funding Co.
NYNEX Credit Co.
NYNEX Properties Co.

Other Diversified Operations
AGS Computers, Inc.
The BIS Group Ltd.
NYNEX Development Co.
NYNEX International Co.
NYNEX Network Systems Co.
NYNEX Venture Co.

HOW MUCH

	6-Year Growth	1981	1982	1983	1984	1985	1986	1987	1988	1989	1990
Sales ($ mil.)	6.1%	—	—	—	9,507	10,314	11,342	12,084	12,661	13,211	13,585
Net income ($ mil.)	(0.64%)	—	—	—	986	1,095	1,215	1,277	1,315	808	949
Income as % of sales	—	—	—	—	10.4%	10.6%	10.7%	10.6%	10.4%	6.1%	7.0%
Earnings per share ($)	(0.91%)	—	—	—	5.05	5.43	6.00	6.25	6.63	4.10	4.78
Stock price – high ($)	—	—	—	—	37.94	49.25	73.25	78.38	70.88	92.00	91.00
Stock price – low ($)	—	—	—	—	29.31	36.44	46.44	58.00	60.88	65.25	67.13
Stock price – close ($)	11.4%	—	—	—	37.13	48.88	64.13	64.25	66.00	91.38	71.13
P/E – high	—	—	—	—	8	9	12	13	11	22	19
P/E – low	—	—	—	—	6	7	8	9	9	16	14
Dividends per share ($)	7.2%	—	—	—	3.00	3.20	3.48	3.80	4.04	4.36	4.56
Book value per share ($)	2.7%	—	—	—	39.08	41.29	43.75	45.65	47.83	47.55	45.72

1990 Year-end:
Debt ratio: 43.2%
Return on equity: 10.3%
Cash (mil.): $122
Current ratio: 0.71
Long-term debt (mil.): $6,945
No. of shares (mil.): 200
Dividends:
1990 average yield: 6.4%
1990 payout: 95.4%
Market value (mil.): $14,234

Stock Price History
High/Low 1984–90

RANKINGS

5th in *Fortune* 50 Utilities
37th in *Business Week* 1000

KEY COMPETITORS

British Telecom
Cable & Wireless
Centel
Ericsson
GTE
McCaw
United
Telecom
Regional Bell operating companies

OCCIDENTAL PETROLEUM CORPORATION

OVERVIEW

Occidental Petroleum ("Oxy") is entering a new era after the death of the charismatic Armand Hammer at age 92 in 1990. Like a dutiful executor, Hammer's successor, Ray Irani, has been untangling affairs, separating Oxy from Hammer's presence.

The company, ranked 16th in the 1990 *Fortune* 500, is selling off some of the eclectic collection of companies Hammer assembled. Irani wants to whittle down debt by $3 billion by 1993 and return Oxy to its core businesses of petroleum and chemicals.

The company explores for, develops, and markets crude oil worldwide. It is known as a finder of oil at the lowest cost. The company's MidCon Corp. operates a large natural gas transmission system. The highly integrated chemical operation Occidental Chemical is a domestic leader in polyvinyl chloride (PVC) and chloralkali.

As part of its post-Hammer restructuring, Oxy took a $2 billion charge in 1990, cut its dividend from $2.50 to $1 per share, and plans to cut 2,300 jobs by the end of 1991.

NYSE symbol: OXY
Fiscal year ends: December 31

 Hoover's Rating **D**

WHO

Chairman, CEO, and President: Ray R. Irani, age 56, $2,095,584 pay (prior to promotion)
EVP and CFO: Anthony R. Leach, age 51
EVP Human Resources: Ronald H. Asquith, age 58
Auditors: Arthur Andersen & Co.
Employees: 55,000

WHERE

HQ: 10889 Wilshire Blvd., Los Angeles, CA 90024
Phone: 213-208-8800
Fax: 213-824-2372

Occidental operates worldwide.

	1990 Sales		1990 Operating Income	
	$ mil.	% of total	$ mil.	% of total
US	20,508	93	(241)	—
Europe	287	1	43	—
Other countries	1,356	6	(39)	—
Adjustments	(457)	—	(763)	—
Total	**21,694**	**100**	**(1,000)**	**—**

WHAT

	1990 Sales		1990 Net Income	
	$ mil.	% of total	$ mil.	% of total
Coal	672	3	(280)	—
Chemicals	5,040	23	(212)	—
Agribusiness	10,187	47	95	—
Oil & gas	3,727	17	(185)	—
Pipelining	2,310	10	281	—
Adjustments	(242)	—	(1,387)	—
Total	**21,694**	**100**	**(1,688)**	**—**

Subsidiaries and Affiliates
Canadian Occidental Petroleum Ltd. (CanadianOxy, 48%, exploration and production)
Island Creek Corp. (coal; Lexington, KY)
MidCon Corp. (interstate and intrastate pipeline transmission systems; Lombard, IL)
Natural Gas Pipeline Co. of America (interstate and intrastate pipeline transmission systems)
Occidental Chemical Corp. (OxyChem; Dallas, TX)
Occidental Oil and Gas Corp. (exploration and production; Tulsa, OK)
OXY Oil and Gas USA, Inc. (exploration and production; Tulsa, OK)
United Texas Transmission Co. (UTTCO, intrastate pipeline transmission systems)

WHEN

The Occidental Petroleum Corporation was founded in 1920 but remained small until 1956, when Dr. Hammer, seeking a tax shelter, sank $100,000 into the company (whose net worth was $34,000). Both wells drilled with the investment came in. Hammer acquired more stock and, eventually, control of Oxy.

Oxy's discovery of California's 2nd largest gas field (1959) was followed by the company's biggest coup: a concession from Libya's King Idris (1966) and the discovery of a billion-barrel Libyan oil field. In 1968 Oxy purchased Signal Oil's European refining and marketing organization as an outlet for the Libyan crude, and diversified, buying Island Creek Coal and Hooker Chemical. Through Hooker, Oxy inherited the notorious Niagara Falls Love Canal, a toxic waste disposal site.

In 1969 Oxy sold — under duress — 51% of its Libyan production to the Libyan government (after Colonel Qaddafi ousted Idris). Oxy started oil exploration in Latin America (1971) and the North Sea (1972–73) — where it discovered the lucrative Piper field. Other projects included a 20-year fertilizer-for-ammonia deal with the USSR (1974) and a coal joint venture with China (1985).

In the 1980s Oxy opted for safer domestic shores by purchasing Cities Service for almost $4 billion (US oil and gas exploration, 1982; sold Citgo refining and marketing unit to Southland, 1983) and MidCon for $2.6 billion

(US natural gas pipelines, 1986) and selling portions of its foreign oil operations (1984 and 1985). Oxy also bought Iowa Beef Processors (IBP) for stock worth $750 million (1981); the company spun off 49% of IBP in 1987 for $960 million.

In 1983 Hammer hired Ray Irani to revive Oxy's ailing chemical business (losses that year: $38 million). Irani integrated operations to ensure high margins during industry downturns, purchasing Diamond Shamrock Chemicals for $850 million (1986), Shell's vinyl chloride monomer unit (1987), a Du Pont chloralkali facility (1987), and Cain Chemical (1988). Oxychem's profits reached $1.05 billion by 1989.

The colorful Hammer died at the end of 1990, and Irani took the CEO post. In 1991, to reduce debt, Oxy exited the Chinese coal business, sold North Sea oil properties to France's Elf Aquitaine (for $1.5 billion), and sold half its US natural gas liquids business into its joint venture with Dallas investment firm Hicks, Muse & Co. ($700 million).

Unable to find a buyer for its 51% stake in IBP, the largest US red meat producer, Oxy spun it off to its shareholders (reducing debt $760 million). In a symbolic move, Irani even sold Oxy's 5.4% interest in Church & Dwight, a company Hammer had courted because of its chief product — Arm & Hammer baking soda.

RANKINGS

16th in *Fortune* 500 Industrial Cos.
107th in *Business Week* 1000

KEY COMPETITORS

Amoco	Imperial Oil	Sun
Ashland	Koch	Tenneco
Atlantic Richfield	Mobil	Texaco
Chevron	Monsanto	Unocal
Coastal	Oryx	USX
Dow Chemical	Pennzoil	Other chemical
Du Pont	Phillips	and oil cos.
Enron	Petroleum	Pipeline and
Exxon	Royal Dutch/	mining cos.
Hoechst	Shell	

HOW MUCH

	9-Year Growth	1981	1982	1983	1984	1985	1986	1987	1988	1989	1990
Sales ($ mil.)	4.4%	14,708	18,212	19,116	15,586	14,534	15,344	17,096	19,417	20,068	21,694
Net income ($ mil.)	—	722	156	480	569	455	172	184	313	256	(1,688)
Income as % of sales	—	4.9%	0.9%	2.5%	3.6%	3.1%	1.1%	1.1%	1.6%	1.3%	(7.8%)
Earnings per share ($)	—	7.55	0.70	1.15	3.05	2.20	0.66	0.78	1.26	0.92	(5.80)
Stock price – high ($)	—	34.88	24.75	27.00	35.75	36.75	31.25	39.63	29.00	31.00	30.25
Stock price – low ($)	—	21.63	17.00	18.00	24.38	23.13	22.63	22.25	23.50	25.13	17.75
Stock price – close ($)	(2.9%)	24.00	19.75	24.88	28.00	31.00	27.50	24.38	25.38	29.63	18.38
P/E – high	—	5	35	23	12	17	47	51	23	34	—
P/E – low	—	3	24	16	8	11	34	29	19	27	—
Dividends per share ($)	0.3%	2.43	2.50	2.50	2.50	2.50	2.50	2.50	2.50	2.50	2.50
Book value per share ($)	(8.1%)	29.41	27.50	26.90	26.77	26.59	24.14	23.98	23.08	21.68	13.74

1990 Year-end:
Debt ratio: 66.0%
Return on equity: —
Cash (mil.): $364
Current ratio: 1.03
Long-term debt (mil.): $7,992
No. of shares (mil.): 296
Dividends:
  1990 average yield: 13.6%
  1990 payout: —
Market value (mil.): $5,446

Stock Price History High/Low 1981–90

OFFICE DEPOT, INC.

NASDAQ symbol: ODEP
Fiscal year ends: Last Saturday in December

Hoover's Rating **A**

OVERVIEW

Headquartered in Boca Raton, Florida, Office Depot is the largest chain of office supply superstores in the US. As of mid-1991 the company operated 128 stores in the southeast and midwest under the Office Depot name, and, since its 1991 acquisition of Office Club, 58 stores in western states under that name. These numbers won't last for long — the company has slated 35–45 new Office Depots and 20–25 new Office Clubs for 1991 alone.

Office Depot (like competitors Staples and BizMart) owes its success to bringing the superstore concept (started by Toys "R" Us) to the retail office supplies industry. The company's unpretentious warehouse-style stores average 21,000 square feet of selling space and its merchandise is displayed on basic steel shelving with additional stock stacked above and below the display items. By purchasing in tremendous volume directly from the manufacturer, Office Depot is able to offer the customer prices that average 40% to 60% below the suggested retail price.

The company's extensive selection includes everything from basic office products (papers, clips, and pens) to office furniture to electronic business machines (fax machines, telephones, and even computers).

WHEN

In 1986 Pat Scher, Stephen Dougherty, and Jack Kopkin opened the first Office Depot, one of the first office supply superstores, in Lauderdale Lakes, Florida. Scher was selected as chairman, and the company spent its early months searching for new markets, raising money, hiring personnel, and creating an efficient management information system. By the end of the year, 2 additional stores were opened in Miami and West Palm Beach.

Office Depot opened just one more store (in Georgia) in the first half of 1987 as it continued to organize but in the latter half of the year launched an aggressive expansion program in which it opened 6 more Georgia and Florida stores. When Scher died that same year, the company recruited David Fuente, the former head of the Sherwin-Williams paint store chain, as his successor.

Under Fuente Office Depot continued its pace of rapid expansion. In 1988 the company opened 16 stores and broke into new markets in Texas, North Carolina, Tennessee, and Kentucky. Office Depot made its initial public offering that same year. Young rivals Staples, BizMart, and Office Club also became public companies.

The company stepped up its pace in 1989 by adding 41 new stores and breaking into Alabama, Missouri, North Carolina, Indiana, Louisiana, Oklahoma, and South Carolina.

Fifty-five new stores followed in 1990 including units in Kansas, Maryland, Mississippi, Nebraska, Ohio, Pennsylvania, and Wisconsin. Also in 1990 Office Depot introduced computers and peripherals into its product line and opened its first delivery center to coordinate shipments to customers of its busy southern Florida stores.

In 1991 the company expanded its presence into the western states almost overnight through the acquisition of former rival Office Club, another warehouse-type office supply chain of 58 stores. Like Office Depot, Office Club was formed in 1986 and in 1987 opened its first warehouse store in California. Later that year Office Club opened 5 additional stores in northern California. Over the next few years, Office Club opened stores in Arizona, Colorado, Hawaii, Oregon, Nevada, New Mexico, Texas, and Washington. The stores in Colorado and further west retained the Office Club name following the acquisition, and former Office Club CEO Mark Begelman became President and COO of Office Depot.

WHO

Chairman and CEO: David I. Fuente, age 45, $478,250 pay
President and COO: Mark D. Begelman, age 43, $272,650 pay
EVP Finance, CFO, and Secretary: Barry J. Goldstein, age 48, $223,000 pay (prior to promotion)
VP Human Resources: John D. Banville
Auditors: Deloitte & Touche
Employees: 5,600

WHERE

HQ: 851 Broken Sound Parkway, NW
  Boca Raton, Florida 33487
Phone: 407-994-2131
Fax: 407-994-2131, ext. 236

The company operates 128 Office Depots primarily in the South and Midwest, and 58 Office Club stores in Colorado and states west of the Rockies.

State	No. of Stores
Alabama	5
Arkansas	1
Florida	36
Georgia	10
Indiana	7
Kansas	1
Kentucky	3
Louisiana	5
Maryland	2
Mississippi	1
Missouri	8
Nebraska	2
North Carolina	4
Ohio	2
Oklahoma	5
Pennsylvania	3
South Carolina	3
Tennessee	4
Texas	22
Wisconsin	4
Western states (Office Club)	58
Total	**186**

WHAT

	1990 Sales % of total
General office supplies	44
Business machines, business supplies, computers & computer accessories	30
Office furniture	16
Other	10
Total	**100**

RANKINGS

919th in *Business Week* 1000

KEY COMPETITORS

Costco
Kmart
Price Co.
Tandy
Wal-Mart

HOW MUCH

	2-Year Growth	1981	1982	1983	1984	1985	1986	1987	1988	1989	1990
Sales ($ mil.)	117.8%	—	—	—	—	—	—	—	132	315	626
Net income ($ mil.)	82.6%	—	—	—	—	—	—	—	3	6	10
Income as % of sales	—	—	—	—	—	—	—	—	2.4%	1.9%	1.5%
Earnings per share ($)	43.8%	—	—	—	—	—	—	—	0.29	0.40	0.60
Stock price – high ($)	—	—	—	—	—	—	—	—	12.17	27.25	21.50
Stock price – low ($)	—	—	—	—	—	—	—	—	8.42	10.67	11.00
Stock price – close ($)	21.0%	—	—	—	—	—	—	—	10.67	18.00	15.63
P/E – high	—	—	—	—	—	—	—	—	42	68	36
P/E – low	—	—	—	—	—	—	—	—	29	27	18
Dividends per share ($)	0.0%	—	—	—	—	—	—	—	0.00	0.00	0.00
Book value per share ($)	67.6%	—	—	—	—	—	—	—	2.56	6.58	7.19

1990 Year-end:
Debt ratio: 11.5%
Return on equity: 8.7%
Cash (mil.) $8
Current ratio: 1.41
Long-term debt (mil.): $14
No. of shares (mil.): 15
Dividends:
  1990 average yield: 0.0%
  1990 payout: 0.0%
Market value (mil.): $242

Stock Price History
High/Low 1988–90

OGDEN CORPORATION

OVERVIEW

Ogden Corporation is the holding company for a true conglomerate, a diverse collection of businesses functioning together to produce $1.6 billion in sales in 1990.

The company is divided into 2 main segments, Ogden Services and Ogden Projects. Ogden Services (100% owned) provides building housekeeping and management services for such buildings as the World Trade Center; management, concessions, and promotion services for entertainment and sports facilities such as the Target Center of Minneapolis; asbestos abatement services; consulting engineering services in environment, energy, space, and defense; and aviation ground services at over 60 airports.

Ogden Projects, Inc., a separate public company 85% owned by Ogden, specializes in recycling, waste-disposal and waste-to-energy facilities, and toxic site remediation.

NYSE symbol: OG
Fiscal year ends: December 31

Hoover's Rating **D**

WHO

Chairman: Ralph E. Ablon, age 74, $1,868,544 pay
President and CEO: R. Richard Ablon, age 41, $1,384,656 pay
EVP: Constantine G. Caras, age 52, $771,536 pay
SVP and CFO: Philip G. Husby, age 44
VP Human Resources: David Belka
Auditors: Deloitte & Touche
Employees: 45,000

WHERE

HQ: Two Pennsylvania Plaza, New York, NY 10121
Phone: 212-868-6100
Fax: 212-868-4578

Ogden performs services for clients located throughout the US, in Canada, and at 12 European airports.

WHEN

Ogden Corporation has reinvented itself several times since its founding in 1939 as a holding company for a failing public utilities company. The new company liquidated most of the utility's assets and was about to dissolve when Allen & Co. bought 80% of the stock between 1949 and 1951. Allen transformed it into a nondiversified investment company, buying and then selling companies such as Syntex (1956, sold 1958).

Some companies remained part of the organization. One was Luria Brothers (scrap metal dealer, 1955), whose president, Ralph E. Ablon, has guided Ogden since 1962. Under Ablon, the company became a collection of industrial companies, whose centerpiece was Luria's scrap metal operation. Further industrial acquisitions included Better Built Machinery in 1965. The company also invested heavily in Avondale shipyard (Louisiana, 1959) and shipping services, such as International Terminal Operating (cargo handling, 1962). But, in the late 1960s, scrap prices declined, and Ablon added food services with the purchase of Tillie Lewis Foods (1966), Wilson Foods (1967), International Products (1967), and Chef's Orchid (airline catering, 1968). Expansion in the food industry continued in 1969 with Doggie Diner restaurants (Oakland) and Schreibers Catering (Cleveland).

The company grew at an annually compounded rate of more than 60% in Allen's first 10 years. In the 1970s Ogden consolidated the 3 areas of scrap metal, shipping services, and food, and divested businesses that did not fit in, including a number of race tracks. The company weathered the uncertainties of the 1970s with continued steady growth and emerged ready to take a new turn in the 1980s — into services.

In 1982 the company bought Allied Maintenance (janitorial services). In 1984 it obtained the US rights to a waste-to-energy process developed by Martin GmbH of Germany and established Ogden Projects, the waste disposal group. Throughout the decade, the company divested most of its industrial and shipping interests, selling its shipbuilding and industrial companies to a new employee-owned company, Avondale Industries, in 1985 and its food services to IC Industries in 1986.

In an effort to concentrate on its core businesses, Ogden left the financial services and child-care businesses in 1990. In 1990 and 1991 Ogden suffered from the recession and the decrease in air traffic related to the Gulf War. It received new contracts with airports in the UK and New Zealand and continued to acquire waste-disposal and waste-to-energy companies (Catalyst New Martinsville Hydroelectric Inc., Blount Energy Resource, and Qualtec). In 1991 Ogden became one of 2 US companies qualified to apply a new technique for immobilizing waste in a cement-like substance, which reduces the danger of groundwater contamination. Also in 1991 executive pay was decreased following shareholder complaints about compensation levels.

WHAT

	1990 Sales		1990 Operating Income	
	$ mil.	% of total	$ mil.	% of total
Operating services	1,194	76	59	57
Project services	369	24	44	43
Adjustments			30	
Total	**1,563**	**100**	**133**	**100**

Operating Services (Ogden Services Corp.)
Asbestos clean-up
Building maintenance (HVAC, electrical, plumbing)
Catering and other support services for oil-drilling, mining, and construction workers
Contract services for airlines (e.g., fueling, security, in-flight catering)
ERC International (61.2%, environmental and energy services)
Industrial services (e.g., warehousing and trucking)
International Terminal Operating Co., Inc. (50%, stevedoring services)
Logistical and operating services for federal agencies (e.g., NASA flight centers)
Manufacturing plant designs
Office building janitorial services
Sports and entertainment promotion
Stadium management and concession services

Project Services (Ogden Projects, Inc., 85%)
Ogden Martin Systems, Inc., waste-to-energy facilities for mass-burning solid waste to produce steam and electricity

RANKINGS

68th in *Fortune* 100 Diversified Service Cos.
589th in *Business Week* 1000

KEY COMPETITORS

Accor	Hyatt
ARA	JWP
Browning-Ferris	Matsushita
Consolidated Rail	TW Holdings
Corning	Union Pacific
Dial	Waste Management
Halliburton	

HOW MUCH

	9-Year Growth	1981	1982	1983	1984	1985	1986	1987	1988	1989	1990
Sales ($ mil.)	(4.3%)	2,324	2,202	1,728	2,137	1,026	800	858	1,088	1,369	1,563
Net income ($ mil.)	(1.7%)	65	58	52	40	21	39	54	58	67	56
Income as % of sales	—	2.8%	2.7%	3.0%	1.9%	2.1%	4.8%	6.3%	5.3%	4.9%	3.6%
Earnings per share ($)	(6.0%)	2.25	1.51	1.32	1.00	0.54	0.97	1.32	1.41	1.66	1.29
Stock price – high ($)	—	19.94	14.38	17.19	15.25	17.31	24.00	44.63	32.38	34.75	32.88
Stock price – low ($)	—	12.38	8.75	12.63	12.06	13.25	13.75	17.50	25.13	25.50	15.00
Stock price – close ($)	4.1%	13.06	14.00	15.06	14.13	16.56	20.00	27.75	29.38	31.88	18.75
P/E – high	—	9	10	13	15	32	25	34	23	21	25
P/E – low	—	6	6	10	12	25	14	13	18	15	12
Dividends per share ($)	4.4%	0.85	0.90	0.90	0.90	0.90	0.90	1.00	1.10	1.25	1.25
Book value per share ($)	(4.3%)	16.84	14.28	9.43	9.48	8.00	10.25	10.63	10.74	11.00	11.30

1990 Year-end:
Debt ratio: 77.6%
Return on equity: 11.6%
Cash (mil.): $127
Current ratio: —
Long-term debt (mil.): $1,682
No. of shares (mil.): 43
Dividends:
  1990 average yield: 6.7%
  1990 payout: 96.9%
Market value (mil.): $804

Stock Price History
High/Low 1981–90

THE OHIO STATE UNIVERSITY

OVERVIEW

With 54,094 students, Ohio State University in Columbus is the largest university in the country. The state school's 3,297-acre red-brick campus is a city within itself, with 380 buildings, a 500-acre airport, an 18-hole golf course, and housing for 9,610 students (about 500 of whom live in the football stadium).

OSU offers a staggering 8,500 courses with 219 programs leading to a bachelor's degree, 125 programs leading to a master's, and 94 leading to a doctorate. Students come to OSU from every state and over 100 foreign countries.

The school's modern library system consists of the William Oxley Thompson main library and 28 other libraries with 4.2 million volumes, 3.1 million microforms, and 32,000 periodical subscriptions. The university also houses the only collection of medieval Slavic manuscripts in the nation.

OSU's 31 varsity teams make its athletic program the largest in the Big 10. A traditional powerhouse, OSU's football team (the Buckeyes) has produced 5 Heisman Trophy winners and 105 All-Americans and has captured 4 national championships.

Public university
Fiscal year ends: June 30

Hoover's Rating **B+**

WHO

Chief Executive: Edward Jennings
VP Business and Administration: Richard Jackson
Director of Admissions: James J. Mager
University Registrar: R. Eugene Schuster
Employees: 29,706

WHERE

HQ: 1800 Cannon Dr., Columbus, OH 43210
Phone: 614-292-6446
Fax: 614-292-5903

Ohio State's 3,297-acre main campus is located in the state capital city of Columbus. The Ohio State system maintains additional campuses at Lima, Mansfield, Marion, Newark, and Wooster.

Geographic Distribution of Students	% of Total
Ohio	84
Other US	11
Foreign	5
Total	**100**

WHEN

In 1870 the Ohio legislature, prompted by Governor Rutherford B. Hayes, agreed to establish the Ohio Agricultural and Mechanical College in Columbus as the state's land-grant college on property provided by the Morrill Act of 1862 (which provided land to states and territories for the establishment of colleges). The college opened in 1873 and admitted its first class of 24 students under president Edward Orton. Two years later the school appointed its first woman faculty member and in 1879 graduated its first female student. The school changed its name to Ohio State University in 1878.

Under the administration of President William H. Scott (1883–95), Ohio State grew dramatically, adding schools of veterinary medicine (1885), pharmacy (1885), law (1891), and dairy (1895). OSU awarded its first MA in 1886.

The university continued to grow in the early 20th century under President William Oxley Thompson. Enrollment surpassed 3,000 for the first time in 1908 and by 1923 had reached 10,000. New schools were added in education (1907), medicine and dentistry (1913), and commerce and journalism (1923). During WWI Ohio State designated part of its campus as training grounds and established the only college schools in the nation for airplane and balloon squadrons. OSU's stadium was dedicated in 1922.

In 1930 the university established departments of phonetics, medical and surgical research, photography, and adult education. During the difficult Great Depression years, Ohio State was forced to cut back salaries and course offerings. In the 1940s (under President Howard L. Bevis) the school geared for war once again by establishing radiation and war research laboratories as well as special programs and services for students who were drafted. OSU captured its first national football championship in 1942.

The 1950s ushered in the era of now-legendary OSU football coach Woody Hayes. Hayes led his beloved Buckeyes to 3 national championships and 9 Rose Bowl appearances before he was discharged for striking a Clemson player in 1978. Hayes died in 1987.

Novice G. Fawcett assumed leadership of the university in 1956 and began to restructure its various schools. During Fawcett's presidency OSU established 4 regional campuses.

In the early 1960s the university was engaged in internal free-speech battles. By the end of the 1960s enrollment had surpassed 50,000. In 1970 the school library implemented a computerized control system to keep track of its extensive holdings. OSU opened its School of Social Work in 1976.

In 1986 OSU and hated rival Michigan shared the Big 10 football conference title (OSU's most recent). Enrollment at OSU topped 54,000 in 1990, making that year's class the largest the school had seen in a decade.

WHAT

Academic unit	1990 Enrollment (Columbus campus)	% of total
Agriculture	1,299	2
Allied Medical Professions	606	1
Architecture	479	1
Arts and Sciences	10,220	19
Business	3,219	6
Continuing Education	1,938	4
Dental Hygiene	95	—
Education	1,371	3
Engineering	3,869	7
Human Ecology	1,179	2
Natural Resources	311	1
Nursing	510	1
Pharmacy	456	1
Social Work	174	—
University College	15,435	28
Postbaccalaureate Professional	2,705	5
Graduate	10,228	19
Total	**54,094**	**100**

Affiliated Institutions
Bio-Medical Engineering Center
Center for Human Resources Research
Center for Medieval and Renaissance Studies
Comprehensive Cancer Research Center
ERIC Information Analysis Center
Institute for Polar Studies
Institute for Research in Vision
Lake Erie Area Research Center
Mershon Center for Public Policy
National Center for Research in Vocational Education
National Regulatory Research Institute
Nisonger Center for Mental Retardation

KEY COMPETITORS

Harvard
Stanford
University of Chicago
University of Texas

HOW MUCH

	9-Year Growth	1981	1982	1983	1984	1985	1986	1987	1988	1989	1990
Enrollment (Columbus campus)	0.3%	52,682	53,438	53,757	52,434	53,199	53,880	53,115	53,669	52,895	54,094
Tuition per quarter – resident undergrad ($)	7.1%	460	486	519	547	568	568	630	680	730	856
Tuition per quarter – nonresident undergrad ($)	9.0%	1,170	1,242	1,328	1,417	1,472	1,472	1,660	1,876	2,093	2,536
Endowment market value ($ mil.)	17.4%	85	94	122	121	167	207	242	248	287	360

Resident Undergraduate Tuition per Quarter 1981–90

ORACLE SYSTEMS CORPORATION

NASDAQ symbol: ORCL
Fiscal year ends: May 31

Hoover's Rating **B+**

OVERVIEW

Oracle Systems, a leading maker of database management systems (DBMS), developed the first commercially available relational database, ORACLE DBMS. Prior to ORACLE's introduction in 1979, database users had to tell their machines what information to find and exactly how to find it. ORACLE made it possible for the machine to do the work of locating information for the user. Oracle's databases work on many types of computers, from PCs to mainframes, and on most operating systems, including MS-DOS and OS/2. The company also offers tools and applications software to support its database systems.

In fiscal 1990 earnings collapsed after years of breakneck growth under lax financial controls. The outlook for fiscal 1991 is better. Founder-chairman Lawrence Ellison, who owns 25.1% of the company's stock and is known for his single-minded devotion to growth, has shaken up top management and plans a new line of products, including a major upgrade of ORACLE DBMS, which is due out in May 1992. In 1991 Nippon Steel agreed to buy 49% of Oracle's Japanese subsidiary for $200 million. The 2 companies plan to sell Oracle's products in the Japanese market.

WHEN

Lawrence Ellison, Robert Miner, and Edward Oates founded Oracle in 1977 to create a relational database management system (DBMS) for minicomputers according to specifications published by IBM. Ellison, who was part of the team at Amdahl that developed the first IBM-compatible mainframe, was named president and CEO. Miner, a programmer with more than 14 years of experience, was mostly responsible for developing ORACLE DBMS, introduced in 1979. One of the company's early advantages was its ability to tailor its products to run on many brands of computers of all sizes — from PCs to mainframes.

Oracle went public in 1986 and grew at an average rate of 82.3% per year between 1986 and 1989. The company's databases started making inroads in government circles in 1986, and within 2 years Oracle had a healthy 36% share of the government PC database market. The company also added new types of software to its product line, including financial management programs, graphics programs, and human resource management packages. In 1989 Oracle moved its headquarters from Belmont, California, to its present location in Redwood City.

After releasing 3rd quarter reports in 1990, red-faced Oracle announced that its sales figure ($236 million) was $15 million short

because a couple of big sales had fallen through. Oracle's stock price took a 29% plunge, and angry investors, accusing the company of securities fraud, filed legal actions. Some analysts pointed out that Oracle's fall was inevitable. The company's growth-at-all-costs strategy had led to bug-ridden products and left customers in the cold once sales were complete. Oracle also capitalized R&D expenditures (rather than writing them off as a cost of doing business) and counted outstanding receivables ($468 million in 1990, compared to Microsoft's $181 million) as money in the bank.

As Oracle's troubles continued, the company reported its first-ever quarterly loss ($28.7 million) in September 1990. Ellison, who had made it a personal goal to push the company past the $1 billion revenue mark by the end of fiscal 1990, laid off about 400 employees, including 4 high-ranking executives, and realigned growth expectations to a more reasonable 25% annual rate. Longtime CFO Jeffrey Walker, who had little financial background, was bumped as CFO and left the company in May 1991. More layoffs followed early in 1991, but cost controls failed to stay an annual loss of $12 million for the fiscal year ended May 31, 1991.

WHO

Chairman, President, and CEO: Lawrence J. Ellison, age 47, $900,000 pay
SVP: Robert Miner, age 49, $262,000 pay
EVP and President of Worldwide Distribution Operations: Geoffrey W. Squire, age 44, $432,336 pay
EVP and CFO: Jeffrey O. Henley, age 46
VP Human Resources: Rand Weston
VP Desktop Products: Edward Oates
Auditors: Arthur Andersen & Co.
Employees: 7,466

WHERE

HQ: 500 Oracle Parkway, Redwood City, CA 94065
Phone: 415-506-7000
Fax: 415-506-7150

Oracle has operations in 46 US cities and 92 foreign countries.

	1990 Sales		1990 Operating Income	
	$ mil.	% of total	$ mil.	% of total
US	426	42	(5)	(28)
Europe	487	47	31	172
Other countries	115	11	(8)	(44)
Adjustments	—	—	9	—
Total	**1,028**	**100**	**27**	**100**

WHAT

	1990 Sales
	% of total
Licenses	63
Maintenance	15
Consulting, training & other services	22
Total	**100**

Database Management Systems
Networkstation ORACLE
ORACLE for Macintosh
ORACLE relational DBMS

Application Development Tools
CASE*Designer
CASE*Dictionary
CASE*Generator
CASE*Method
Oracle Graphics
ORACLE Precompilers
SQL* Forms
SQL* Menu
SQL* Plus
SQL* ReportWriter
SQL* TextRetrieval

Applications Software
Oracle Financials
Oracle Government Financials

Network Products
SQL*Net

Connect Products
SQL*Connect

RANKINGS

486th in *Business Week* 1000

KEY COMPETITORS

Borland	H&R Block	Novell
Computer Associates	IBM	Prime
DEC	Lotus	Wang
Dun & Bradstreet	Microsoft	

HOW MUCH

Fiscal year ends May of following year	6-Year Growth	1981	1982	1983	1984	1985	1986	1987	1988	1989	1990
Sales ($ mil.)	88.4%	—	—	—	23	55	131	282	584	971	1,028
Net income ($ mil.)	—	—	—	—	2	6	16	43	82	117	(12)
Income as % of sales	—	—	—	—	6.7%	10.6%	11.9%	15.2%	14.0%	12.1%	(1.2%)
Earnings per share ($)	—	—	—	—	0.02	0.05	0.13	0.33	0.61	0.86	(0.09)
Stock price – high ($)	—	—	—	—	—	—	3.61	9.50	11.13	26.00	28.38
Stock price – low ($)	—	—	—	—	—	—	1.63	2.53	5.69	9.38	4.88
Stock price – close ($)	—	—	—	—	—	—	2.59	7.25	9.75	23.38	7.88
P/E – high	—	—	—	—	—	67	76	34	43	33	—
P/E – low	—	—	—	—	—	30	20	18	15	6	—
Dividends per share ($)	—	—	—	—	0.00	0.00	0.00	0.00	0.00	0.00	0.00
Book value per share ($)	92.3%	—	—	—	0.05	0.27	0.72	1.12	1.82	2.96	2.53

1990 Year-end:
Debt ratio: 5.0%
Return on equity: —
Cash (mil.): $101
Current ratio: 1.22
Long-term debt (mil.): $18
No. of shares (mil.): 136
Dividends:
1990 average yield: 0.0%
1990 payout: 0.0%
Market value (mil.): $1,073

Stock Price History
High/Low 1986–90

ORYX ENERGY COMPANY

OVERVIEW

NYSE symbol: ORX
Fiscal year ends: December 31

Dallas-based Oryx Energy is the largest independent oil and gas producer in the world. It boasts reserves of more than one billion barrels of oil equivalent (BOE).

The company, renowned for its entrepreneurship since it was spun off from Sun Oil in 1988, has developed a 3-prong strategy: use advanced technology, focus on natural gas, and expand international production.

Oryx plans to use advanced technology, including 3-dimensional seismic search techniques and horizontal drilling, to develop its properties worldwide. Oryx drew widespread acclaim for reviving the Austin Chalk formation in Texas using horizontal drilling.

Domestically, it is concentrating on natural gas as the fuel of the future because it is more abundant than crude in the US, lower priced, and more environmentally sound. Now independent, Oryx no longer has to think first about supplying Sun refineries with crude oil. Domestic exploration and production is conducted through Sun Energy Partners, a 98%-owned limited partnership.

Oryx also wants to exploit its new foreign holdings, acquired from British Petroleum at the beginning of 1990. The bulk of its oil and gas production still comes from its US properties, which it inherited from Sun (Sun kept the international properties). But it hopes, through the use of horizontal drilling in the UK North Sea and other areas, that international holdings will constitute 1/2 its reserves later in the decade.

WHEN

In the early 1960s Canada's Bronfman family branched out beyond distilleries (they run the Seagram Company) and acquired Texas Pacific Oil and oil and gas properties in the southwest. In the 1970s the Sun Company, long a leading independent oil refiner and marketer under the Sunoco banner, branched out beyond oil and gas into medical equipment and other nonpetroleum ventures. In 1980 Seagram and Sun ended their branching out. Sun bought Seagram's Texas Pacific assets for $2.39 billion.

Oil prices collapsed in 1986, and in 1988 Sun spun off its domestic oil and gas exploration assets as Sun Exploration and Production. Sun's president, Robert Hauptfuhrer, elected to jump to the new, Dallas-based company.

Sun E&P chairman Hauptfuhrer and president James McCormick led a brisk makeover of the company. The number of managerial reports was slashed 28%, and the levels of management between thinking about doing something and doing something were decreased. Management also tackled rifts between exploration and production divisions.

Within a year of its creation, Sun E&P slashed the cost of finding the average barrel of oil equivalent from $9.27 in 1987 to an astounding $4.37 in 1990. The same company that replaced only 42% of its reserves in 1986 replaced 311% in 1990.

In 1989 Sun Exploration and Production changed its name to Oryx Energy. Like the antelope in its logo, Oryx was leaping, first into the Austin Chalk formation of Texas and then into international exploration.

Oryx modified offshore drilling techniques and brought them into play in the all-but-abandoned Austin Chalk's Pearsall Fields. Many oil companies had left the area because wells averaged only 5 barrels of oil a day. With the new technology of horizontal drilling (in which the drilling veers parallel to the surface), an Oryx well in the summer of 1989 produced 1,300 barrels a day.

In a purchase completed in 1990, Oryx paid $1.1 billion for British Petroleum properties in the UK North Sea, Ecuador, Gabon, Indonesia, and Italy. In late 1990 it repurchased 25 million of its shares held by the Glenmede, the trust for Sun's founding family, the Pews. To whittle debt from those deals, Oryx sold California oil and gas properties to ARCO and Unocal (1990).

WHO

Chairman and CEO: Robert P. Hauptfuhrer, age 59, $983,574 pay
President and COO: James E. McCormick, age 63, $619,464 pay
VP Finance and CFO: Edward W. Moneypenny, age 49, $302,421 pay
VP Human Resources and Administration: Harold R. Ashby, age 50
Auditors: Coopers & Lybrand
Employees: 2,700

WHERE

HQ: 13155 Noel Rd., Dallas, TX 75240-5067
Phone: 214-715-4000
Fax: 214-715-3798 (Investor Relations)

Oryx produces oil and gas from 12,807 wells in the US and 450 wells overseas.

	1990 Sales		1990 Operating Income	
	$ mil.	% of total	$ mil.	% of total
US	1,295	67	548	78
UK	468	24	109	16
Other countries	177	9	42	6
Adjustments	—	—	(328)	—
Total	**1,940**	**100**	**371**	**100**

WHAT

	1990 Wells Drilled			
	Exploratory		Developmental	
	No.	% of total	No.	% of total
Oil	11	27	117	70
Gas	5	12	44	27
Dry	25	61	5	3
Total	**41**	**100**	**166**	**100**

Major Producing Formations
Arkoma Basin (Arkansas, Oklahoma)
Austin Chalk (Texas)
Bakken (North Dakota)
California offshore
Delaware Basin (New Mexico)
Ellengburger (Texas)
Gulf of Mexico offshore
Mississippi Salt Basin
Niobrara (Colorado, Wyoming)
Saratoga (Texas, Louisiana)
UK North Sea
Williston Basin (North Dakota)

RANKINGS

211th in *Fortune* 500 Industrial Cos.
214th in *Business Week* 1000

KEY COMPETITORS

Ashland	Occidental
Atlantic Richfield	Oryx
British Petroleum	Pennzoil
Broken Hill	Petrofina
Chevron	Petrobrás
Coastal	PDVSA
Du Pont	Pemex
Elf Aquitaine	Phillips Petroleum
Exxon	Royal Dutch/Shell
Imperial Oil	Sun
Koch	Texaco
Mobil	Unocal
Norsk Hydro	USX

HOW MUCH

	3-Year Growth	1981	1982	1983	1984	1985	1986	1987	1988	1989	1990
Sales ($ mil.)	9.8%	—	—	—	—	—	—	1,465	1,070	1,140	1,940
Net income ($ mil.)	12.5%	—	—	—	—	—	—	158	(305)	54	225
Income as % of sales	—	—	—	—	—	—	—	10.8%	(28.5%)	4.7%	11.6%
Earnings per share ($)	—	—	—	—	—	—	—	—	0.51	2.19	
Stock price – high ($)	—	—	—	—	—	—	—	—	28.00	46.25	54.88
Stock price – low ($)	—	—	—	—	—	—	—	—	23.13	25.50	34.75
Stock price – close ($)	—	—	—	—	—	—	—	—	25.88	44.38	36.13
P/E – high	—	—	—	—	—	—	—	—	—	91	25
P/E – low	—	—	—	—	—	—	—	—	—	50	16
Dividends per share ($)	—	—	—	—	—	—	—	0.00	0.30	1.20	1.20
Book value per share ($)	—	—	—	—	—	—	—	—	15.24	14.17	7.72

1990 Year-end:
Debt ratio: 78.5%
Return on equity: 20.0%
Cash (mil.): $81
Current ratio: 0.95
Long-term debt (mil.): $2,267
No. of shares (mil.): 80
Dividends:
  1990 average yield: 3.3%
  1990 payout: 54.8%
Market value (mil.): $2,878

Stock Price History
High/Low 1988–90

OUTBOARD MARINE CORPORATION

NYSE symbol: OM
Fiscal year ends: September 30

Hoover's Rating: C

OVERVIEW

Outboard Marine Corporation (OMC), the world's largest producer of outboard motors, makes the well-known Evinrude and Johnson brands. The company is also the world's 2nd largest manufacturer of stern-drive engines. OMC's motors range in size from 1.5 to 300 horsepower.

The company is the #2 publicly held recreational powerboats manufacturer in the US (after Brunswick) with Chris-Craft, Donzi, Four Winns, Topaz, and several other boat brands. The company's boats range in size from the 10-foot Sea Nymph to 50-foot Chris-Craft cruisers. OMC distributes through the world's largest marine products network, and its Club Nautico centers rent OMC boats. OMC has been snapping up boat manufacturers in response to an industry trend toward selling engines and boats together as a package.

Although OMC is faring better than the boating industry as a whole, sales remain dismal. In 1990 US sales fell 29% from the previous year, reflecting consumer unwillingness to buy big-ticket products in a weak US economy. The company is continuing plant closures and layoffs and is consolidating its boat-building operations.

WHO

Chairman: Charles D. Strang, age 69
President and CEO: James C. Chapman, age 59, $421,139 pay
SVP Administration: Thomas J. Beeler, age 57, $245,820 pay
VP; Chairman, Four Winns, Inc.: John A. Winn, age 43, $222,922 pay
VP Finance: Samuel J. Winett, age 56
VP Employee Relations: F. James Short, age 63
Auditors: Arthur Andersen & Co.
Employees: 8,000

WHEN

In 1903 Ole Evinrude helped design Harley-Davidson's first carburetor. His outboard-motor design provided the basis for his own company, Evinrude Motor Company, formed in Milwaukee in 1907. Evinrude sold the company to Chris Meyer (1914) and in 1921 formed ELTO Outboard Motor Company, producing a motor 33% lighter than the Evinrude.

In 1926 gasoline-engine pioneer Briggs & Stratton purchased Evinrude Motor but sold it in 1929 to Briggs's cofounder Stephen Briggs, who formed a syndicate with Ole Evinrude called the Outboard Motors Corporation. OMC introduced electric-starting outboards in 1930 and fully enclosed engines (for greater safety and noise reduction) in 1934. In 1935 OMC purchased Johnson Motors, makers of Sea Horse outboards.

After WWII OMC discontinued the ELTO line. In 1952 OMC purchased RPM Manufacturing of Lamar, Missouri, makers of power mowers. OMC renamed the mowers Lawn-Boy, and by 1957 Lawn-Boy led the nation in power-mower sales.

Foreign sales, an important revenue source from early on, tripled between 1949 and 1956, the year the company adopted its present name. Between 1956 and 1958 OMC purchased Industrial Engineering, Canada's largest chain-saw manufacturer (renamed Pioneer Chain Saw, sold to Electrolux in 1977); acquired Cushman Motor Works, makers of lightweight vehicles such as golf carts; and introduced the first mass-produced, die-cast, aluminum V-engine (a V-4).

In the 1960s OMC entered new product fields, most importantly stern-drive marine engines. In 1967 the company introduced an all-electronic outboard ignition, now the industry standard. Additionally, OMC acquired Trade Winds (marine products) and Ryan Equipment (turf care equipment).

OMC expanded its marine business in the 1980s. In 1985 the company introduced the first V-8 outboard engine. Between 1986 and 1989 OMC spent approximately $230 million acquiring 10 boat manufacturers (including Chris-Craft and Donzi). In 1989 OMC sold both Cushman (to Ransomes America, $150 million) and Lawn-Boy (to Toro, $85 million). The boating industry boomed between 1982 and June 1989, carrying OMC to record profits in 1988.

In 1990 OMC continued to buy boat makers, acquiring the assets of Grumman's aluminum boat operations, of Topaz Marine, and of 3 other boat builders located in Canada and Australia.

WHERE

HQ: 100 Sea-Horse Dr., Waukegan, IL 60085
Phone: 708-689-6200
Fax: 708-689-5555

Outboard Marine operates 16 US plants and 10 plants in Canada, Mexico, Belgium, Australia, Hong Kong, Sweden, and Brazil.

	1990 Sales		1990 Operating Income	
	$ mil.	% of total	$ mil.	% of total
US	793	69	(81)	—
Europe	165	15	(4)	—
Other countries	188	16	17	—
Adjustments	—	—	(7)	—
Total	**1,146**	**100**	**(75)**	**—**

WHAT

Brand Names

Boats	
Chris-Craft	Seaswirl
Donzi	Stacer
Four Winns	Stratos
Grumman	Sunbird
Haines Hunter	Suncruiser
Hydra-Sports	Topaz
Javelin	
Lowe	**Marine Power Systems**
Princecraft/Springbok	Evinrude
Ryds	Johnson
Sea Nymph	OMC Cobra
SeaBird	
	Boat Rentals
	Club Nautico

Principal US Subsidiaries
Adventurent, Inc.
Carl A. Lowe Industries, Inc.
Donzi Marine Corp.
Four Winns, Inc.
Hydra-Sports, Inc.
OMCCC Inc. (Chris-Craft)
OMCGB Inc. (Grumman)
Sea Nymph, Inc.
Seaswirl Boats, Inc.
Stratos Boats, Inc.
Sunbird Boat Co., Inc.

RANKINGS

314th in *Fortune* 500 Industrial Cos.

KEY COMPETITORS

Brunswick
Harley-Davidson
Honda
Reebok
Suzuki
Volvo
Yamaha

HOW MUCH

	9-Year Growth	1981	1982	1983	1984	1985	1986	1987	1988	1989	1990
Sales ($ mil.)	4.1%	796	778	789	922	880	972	1,289	1,605	1,464	1,146
Net income ($ mil.)	—	27	34	39	53	29	11	47	72	21	(77)
Income as % of sales	—	3.4%	4.4%	5.0%	5.7%	3.3%	1.1%	3.6%	4.5%	1.4%	(6.7%)
Earnings per share ($)	—	1.61	2.02	2.26	3.02	1.74	0.66	2.56	3.74	1.09	(3.98)
Stock price – high ($)	—	11.25	16.06	26.00	29.63	31.50	38.50	38.00	35.50	46.00	28.25
Stock price – low ($)	—	5.94	9.31	13.50	18.38	19.63	23.88	16.25	21.88	25.00	9.00
Stock price – close ($)	3.4%	10.00	14.44	24.88	28.50	28.00	27.00	21.88	31.00	26.00	13.50
P/E – high	—	7	8	12	10	18	58	15	10	42	—
P/E – low	—	4	5	6	6	11	36	6	6	23	—
Dividends per share ($)	9.2%	0.36	0.41	0.47	0.58	0.64	0.64	0.64	0.70	0.80	0.80
Book value per share ($)	5.6%	17.57	18.23	19.71	21.79	22.77	23.06	26.67	30.09	33.30	28.63

1990 Year-end:
Debt ratio: 22.0%
Return on equity: —
Cash (mil.): $15
Current ratio: 2.05
Long-term debt (mil.): $158
No. of shares (mil.): 20
Dividends:
  1990 average yield: 5.9%
  1990 payout: —
Market value (mil.): $263

Stock Price History High/Low 1981–90

OWENS-CORNING FIBERGLAS CORPORATION

OVERVIEW

Toledo-based Owens-Corning, the world's largest fiber glass materials producer and an important source of polyester resins, manufactures construction and industrial products, including thermal and acoustical insulation, roofing materials, and underground storage tanks. The company also produces reinforcements, yarns, and resins that offer alternatives to materials such as steel and wood.

Faced with sluggish construction starts, the company plans to streamline operations by flattening its organizational chart, reducing staff size, and "reducing capacity." Owens-Corning predicts that this belt-tightening will result in annual cost reductions of about $40 million. In 1990 alone the company spent

$146 million (4.7% of sales) for capital improvements to enhance product quality and manufacturing efficiency.

By the end of 1990, the company reported that it faced 84,500 personal-injury claims stemming from alleged asbestos-related injuries and that another 56,400 personal-injury claims had been resolved. Now Owens-Corning has sued some of its insurance carriers over their proposed methods for calculating insurance deductibles. Should the company fail to convince the courts, it could face $230 million in deductibles over the next several years. Regardless of the outcome, however, the company reports that its unexhausted insurance coverage is "substantial."

WHEN

In the 1930s Corning Glass Works and Owens-Illinois Glass Company independently discovered that glass has special resilience and strength. Optimistic that a large market would result, they formed Owens-Corning Fiberglas Corporation in 1938 as a joint venture. The company rapidly expanded in the 1940s and 1950s, establishing several US plants and one in Ontario. Products included fine fibers, thermal wool, textiles, and continuous filaments.

In 1949 a US antitrust decree denied the 2 founding firms any control over Owens-Corning or claim to its earnings. Soon after (1952), Owens-Corning went public and the 2 founding companies retained 1/3 ownership each, which they later reduced.

During the 1950s the company developed new uses for glass fibers in automobile bodies, roofing shingles, and insulation. The company expanded overseas in the 1960s. Uses for glass fibers continued to multiply, as applications developed in aerospace, tires, and noncorrosive underground storage tanks.

In 1977 Owens-Corning bought Lloyd Fry (roofing and asphalt) for $108 million. By 1980 Owens-Corning had invested over $700 million in acquisitions and internal development to strengthen the company's position in roofing

materials and had introduced the Pink Panther in its ad campaigns. Owens-Corning had introduced a rolled insulation in 1982.

A takeover attempt by Wickes Companies in 1986 was successfully fended off, but the effort necessitated a $2.6 billion debt burden and forced Owens-Corning to redirect its strategy. It sold 10 noncore businesses, halved its research budget, laid off or lost to divestitures 46% of its total work force, and mothballed 14% of productive capacity by 1987.

Debt reduction was ahead of schedule in 1989, and Owens-Corning completed full purchase of Fiberglas Canada, Canada's largest manufacturer of glass fiber insulation, for $195 million.

The company's major markets fell to a 9-year low in 1990, but despite slowing construction, the company expects the demand per unit to increase. To extend global reach a variety of alliances were created in 1990 with BASF (Germany), Lucky-Goldstar (Korea), and Siam Cement (Thailand).

Max O. Weber took over as chairman and CEO in 1990 following the retirement of William W. Boeschenstein, a 40-year veteran of the company.

NYSE symbol: OCF
Fiscal year ends: December 31

Hoover's Rating **C-**

WHO

Chairman and CEO: Max O. Weber, age 61, $633,826 pay
SVP (Principal Financial Officer): Paul V. Daverio, age 52, $330,000 pay
SVP Law: William W. Colville, age 56, $318,667 pay
SVP; President, Industrial Materials Group: Charles H. Dana, age 51
SVP; President, Construction Products Group: Larry T. Solari, age 48, $310,000 pay
SVP Human Resources: Robert D. Heddens, age 52
Auditors: Arthur Andersen & Co.
Employees: 16,800

WHERE

HQ: Fiberglas Tower, Toledo, OH 43659
Phone: 419-248-8000
Fax: 419-248-5337 (Public Relations)

Owens-Corning operates manufacturing plants at 32 US and 16 foreign locations.

	1990 Sales		1990 Operating Income	
	$ mil.	% of total	$ mil.	% of total
US	2,204	71	238	72
Canada	319	10	(27)	(8)
Other countries	588	19	118	36
Adjustments	—	—	29	
Total	**3,111**	**100**	**358**	**100**

WHAT

	1990 Sales		1990 Operating Income	
	$ mil.	% of total	$ mil.	% of total
Construction prods.	2,036	65	116	35
Industrial materials	1,075	35	213	65
Adjustments	—	—	29	—
Total	**3,111**	**100**	**358**	**100**

Construction Products
Asphalt materials for roofing, industrial uses, and paving
Built-up roofing products
Calcium silicate insulation
Glass fiber roofing shingles
Glass-fiber–reinforced underground fuel storage tanks
Insulated windows
Modified bitumen roofing membranes
Thermal and acoustical insulation for constructed and manufactured buildings, appliances, and air-handling duct systems

Industrial Materials
Glass fiber reinforcements for auto body panels
Glass fiber textile yarns (for, e.g., reinforcements in paper and tape products, printed circuit boards)
Polyester resins

RANKINGS

148th in *Fortune* 500 Industrial Cos.
546th in *Business Week* 1000

KEY COMPETITORS

Boise Cascade	Goodyear
Bridgestone	Manville
Georgia-Pacific	PPG

HOW MUCH

	9-Year Growth	1981	1982	1983	1984	1985	1986	1987	1988	1989	1990
Sales ($ mil.)	3.0%	2,375	2,373	2,753	3,021	3,305	3,644	2,891	2,831	3,000	3,111
Net income ($ mil.)	4.6%	50	30	80	114	131	16	220	197	172	75
Income as % of sales	—	2.1%	1.3%	2.9%	3.8%	4.0%	0.4%	7.6%	7.0%	5.7%	2.4%
Earnings per share ($)	1.0%	1.63	0.98	2.77	3.87	4.42	0.49	5.30	4.71	4.08	1.78
Stock price – high ($)	—	31.00	37.88	46.88	38.88	38.75	82.50	32.38	26.50	36.88	26.50
Stock price – low ($)	—	21.50	15.38	30.25	25.13	30.50	8.88	9.00	15.88	22.25	13.63
Stock price – close ($)	(3.7%)	22.50	37.50	36.50	32.00	37.50	13.75	16.38	22.25	25.13	16.00
P/E – high	—	19	39	17	10	9	168	6	6	9	15
P/E – low	—	13	16	11	7	7	18	2	3	5	8
Dividends per share ($)	(100.0%)	1.20	1.20	1.20	1.30	1.40	53.05	0.00	0.00	0.00	0.00
Book value per share ($)	—	25.24	23.67	26.09	28.48	31.70	(25.93)	(20.23)	(15.18)	(10.78)	(8.62)

1990 Year-end:
Debt ratio: —
Return on equity: —
Cash (mil.): $7
Current ratio: 1.09
Long-term debt (mil.): $1,086
No. of shares (mil.): 41
Dividends:
  1990 average yield: 0.0%
  1990 payout: 0.0%
Market value (mil.): $649

Stock Price History High/Low 1981–90

OWENS-ILLINOIS, INC.

Private company
Fiscal year ends: December 31

Hoover's Rating **D**

OVERVIEW

Along with its affiliates and licensees, Owens-Illinois is thought to be the producer of almost 1/2 of the glass containers made worldwide. The Toledo-based company makes 40% of all glass containers used in the US (up from 25% in 1985). The company also is among the leading manufacturers of plastic packaging items (18% of sales) such as labels, container safety seals, bottle and can carriers, and containers for drinks, medicines, and cosmetics. Through OI-NEG TV Products (a joint venture with Nippon Electric Glass) Owens produces glass parts for televisions.

Owens-Illinois also is the 6th largest operator of investor-owned US nursing and retirement homes (134 homes with 17,500

licensed beds), which net 8% of the company's sales.

The company's glass container segment (its oldest) accounts for more than 60% of its sales. Among the primary customers of the glass-container division are brewers, soft-drink bottlers, and food producers. Libbey Glass, one of the world's largest producers of stemware and tumblers, and Kimble Glass are part of the glass segment.

Kohlberg Kravis Roberts (KKR) owns 89% of the company as the result of a 1987 LBO. Current and former senior managers own the balance. The company has announced that it will go public again in late 1991, after which KKR's ownership will fall to 36%.

WHEN

The Owens Bottle Machine Corporation was incorporated in Toledo in 1907 as the successor to a New Jersey company of the same name established in 1903. During the next 2 decades, the company grew by acquiring several other small glass companies. In 1929 Owens bought The Illinois Glass Company (medical and pharmaceutical glass) and renamed itself Owens-Illinois Glass.

During the 1930s the company purchased Libbey-Glass (tableware, 1935) and started conducting research into the uses of glass fibers. In 1938 Owens-Illinois and Corning Glass, which had been conducting similar research, established a joint venture (Owens-Corning Fiberglas). With a clear lead in fiberglass technology, Owens-Corning gained a virtual monopoly on the industry and now ranks 149th on the *Fortune* 500.

After WWII Owens-Illinois started to diversify beyond glass. In 1956 the company bought National Container, then the 3rd largest producer of cardboard boxes. During the 1950s Owens-Illinois also turned its attention to plastic and created a semirigid plastic container that was adopted by several bleach and laundry detergent companies in 1958.

The introduction of the nonreturnable bottle in the 1960s gave new life to the glass industry. The new, thinner bottles gave the company fresh fuel for the struggle against aluminum cans. During the late 1960s Owens-Illinois bought Lily Tulip Cups (paper products, 1968; sold to KKR in 1981) and entered

such diverse ventures as Bahamas sugar cane farming and Florida phosphate mining. In the 1970s the company modernized its production facilities and started producing specialty optical and TV glass.

While much of the glass industry was floundering at the beginning of the 1980s, under pressure from the increased use of alternate packaging materials, Owens-Illinois invested over $600 million to realign and modernize its glass operations. In 1981 the company entered the health care field with a minority interest in Health Group, Inc. Three years later Owens-Illinois purchased the Health Care and Retirement Corporation.

In 1986 KKR offered to purchase the company. Owens-Illinois initially refused but was forced to deal when the offer was raised to $60 per share. In 1987 KKR acquired the company for $4.6 billion and took it private. Total debt after the LBO was a whopping $4.4 billion. The following year the company acquired Brockway (glass and plastic containers).

Since the LBO, the company has sold its forest products and mortgage banking businesses and since 1990 has been trying to sell its nursing home facilities. Despite these sales Owens-Illinois has remained unprofitable since the LBO largely because of high interest payments on its still massive debt.

Owens-Illinois continues to deal with about 90,000 lawsuits resulting from the company's production and sale of asbestos-containing insulation between 1948 and 1958.

WHO

President and CEO: Joseph H. Lemieux, age 59, $1,023,334 pay
SVP and CFO: Lee A. Wesselmann, age 54, $389,681 pay
VP and General Manager Specialty Glass Operations: Terry L. Wilkison, age 49, $345,503 pay
VP and General Manager Glass Container Operations: Robert S. Coakley, age 59, $373,323 pay
Director Personnel: John Frechette
Auditors: Ernst & Young
Employees: 47,000

WHERE

HQ: One SeaGate, Toledo, OH 43666
Phone: 419-247-5000
Fax: 419-247-2839 (Main Office)

The company has over 60 plants in the US and operations in 13 foreign countries. In addition, the company operates 134 long-term health care facilities in 18 states.

	1990 Sales		1990 Operating Income	
	$ mil.	% of total	$ mil.	% of total
US	3,363	85	448	81
Other Western Hemisphere & Europe	616	15	103	19
Adjustments	—	—	7	—
Total	**3,979**	**100**	**558**	**100**

WHAT

	1990 Sales		1990 Operating Income	
	$ mil.	% of total	$ mil.	% of total
Glass containers	2,485	63	303	55
Health care	332	8	27	5
Plastics & closures	720	18	132	24
Specialized glass	441	11	91	16
Adjustments	1	—	5	—
Total	**3,979**	**100**	**558**	**100**

Glass Containers
Glass bottles and jars

Health Care
Assisted-living facilities
Nursing homes
Retirement centers

Plastics and Closures
Carriers (for beverage containers)
Closures
Containers
Plastic foam labels
Prescription medicine containers

Specialized Glass
Laboratory ware (beakers, flasks, tubes)
Pharmaceutical products (ampuls, vials, syringes)
Tableware (tumblers, stemware, decorative glass)
Television parts

RANKINGS

29th in *Forbes* 400 US Private Cos.

KEY COMPETITORS

Amway
Brown-Forman
Carlsberg
Corning
Henley

Johnson Controls
Marriott
Reynolds Metals
Tenneco

HOW MUCH

	9-Year Growth	1981	1982	1983	1984	1985	1986	1987	1988	1989	1990
Sales ($ mil.)	0.1%	3,943	3,553	3,422	3,510	3,674	3,642	3,098	3,572	3,605	3,979
Net income ($ mil.)	—	154	40	69	136	156	179	(39)	(59)	(68)	(56)
Income as % of sales	—	3.9%	1.1%	2.0%	3.9%	4.3%	4.9%	(1.3%)	(1.7%)	(1.9%)	(1.4%)
Employees	(0.9%)	50,954	46,684	43,854	46,093	44,048	45,000	31,900	46,500	47,000	47,000

1990 Year-end:
Debt ratio: —
Return on equity: —
Cash (mil.): $116
Current ratio: 1.42
Long-term debt (mil.): $3,928

Net Income ($ mil.) 1981–90

PACCAR INC.

OVERVIEW

Headquartered in Bellevue, Washington, PACCAR derives 81% of all revenues from the sale of trucks manufactured under the Peterbilt, Kenworth, and Foden (UK) nameplates. PACCAR is the industry heavy truck (minimum gross vehicle weight of 33,000 pounds) leader in the US with 23% of the market.

PACCAR also provides financing and leasing services to support truck sales and markets medium-sized trucks made in Brazil by Volkswagen. In addition, the company manufactures oilfield extraction pumps and industrial winches (it is the world's largest full-line

manufacturer) and sells automotive components through its 139 Al's Auto Supply and Grand Auto retailers.

PACCAR assembles major components (purchased mostly from outside suppliers); its trucks are customized products with a high-quality reputation. The company markets its trucks through 314 independent dealers.

Overall, total truck sales in the US were down 17% in 1990. The weak truck market continued into 1991, with the exception of Mexico where PACCAR's 49% joint venture facility, VILPAC, continues to generate income for the company.

WHEN

William Pigott founded the Seattle Car Manufacturing Company in 1905 to produce railroad cars for timber transport. Meeting with immediate success, Pigott expanded production to other rail cars in 1906. The Seattle plant burned in 1907, and the company moved to near Renton, Washington. In 1911 Pigott renamed the company Seattle Car & Foundry.

Seattle Car merged in 1917 with the Twohy Brothers of Portland, and the new company, Pacific Car & Foundry, was sold to American Car & Foundry in 1924. Under the new owners Pacific Car diversified into bus manufacturing, structural steel fabrications, and metal technology. A company metallurgist developed a strong, lightweight steel called Carcometal that was used in new designs for tractor equipment and winches.

When Pacific Car was in decline in 1934, the founder's son Paul Pigott purchased it, and the company has remained under family management since. Pigott added Hofius Steel and Equipment, and Tricoach, a bus manufacturer, in 1936.

The company entered the growing truck manufacturing industry with the 1945 purchase of Seattle-based Kenworth. In the 1950s Pacific Car became the industry leader in mechanical refrigerator car production; began producing off-road, heavy trucks; and acquired

Peterbilt Trucks of Oakland (1958). To augment its winch business, Pacific Car purchased Gearmatic, a Canadian company, in 1963.

The company moved its headquarters to Bellevue in 1969 and changed its name to PACCAR in 1971. Acquisitions in the 1970s included Wagner Mining Equipment (1973); the largest US caboose producer, International Car (1975); and Braden Winch (1977). In 1980 PACCAR acquired Foden trucks of Britain.

A shift in customer demand toward smaller trucks caused industry heavy truck sales to decline 35% between 1979 and 1986, leading PACCAR to close 2 factories, the first closures in 41 years. In 1987 PACCAR introduced its first medium truck, bought Trico Industries (oil drilling equipment), and entered the auto parts sales market.

In 1989 PACCAR surpassed Navistar as the industry leader in heavy truck sales, with 24.5% of the market. While PACCAR kept its market lead in 1990, truck demand hit a 9-year low. PACCAR responded by cutting jobs by 11% in 1990 and withdrawing from the auto parts wholesale market.

CEO Charles Pigott, SVP Mark Pigott, and board member James Pigott are direct descendents of PACCAR's founder. Family members own over 12% of PACCAR's stock.

NASDAQ symbol: PCAR
Fiscal year ends: December 31

 Hoover's Rating **B-**

WHO

Chairman and CEO: Charles M. Pigott, age 61, $2,286,047 pay
President: Joseph M. Dunn, age 64, $1,237,222 pay
EVP: David J. Hovind, age 50, $829,620 pay
EVP and CFO: William E. Boisvert, age 48
VP Employee Relations: Laurie Baker
Auditors: Ernst & Young
Employees: 11,586

WHERE

HQ: 777 106th Ave. NE, Bellevue, WA 98004
Phone: 206-455-7400
Fax: 206-453-4900

PACCAR has manufacturing plants in 7 US states, Canada, Australia, Mexico, and the UK. Its 2 auto supply houses operate in 139 locations in the Pacific Northwest, California, and Nevada.

	1990 Sales		1990 Pretax Income	
	$ mil.	% of total	$ mil.	% of total
US	2,345	84	78	82
Canada	257	9	4	4
Other countries	189	7	13	14
Adjustments	(13)	—	(1)	—
Total	**2,778**	**100**	**94**	**100**

WHAT

	1990 Sales		1990 Pretax Income	
	$ mil.	% of total	$ mil.	% of total
Trucks	2,268	81	101	107
Auto parts	226	8	(18)	(19)
Financial services	191	7	10	10
Other	106	4	2	2
Adjustments	(13)	—	(1)	—
Total	**2,778**	**100**	**94**	**100**

Product lines
Auto supply retailing
  Al's Auto Supply
  Grand Auto
Financing and leasing programs for trucks
Heavy trucks
  Foden
  Kenworth
  Peterbilt
Industrial winches
Medium trucks
Oilfield extraction pumps
Truck parts

RANKINGS

161st in *Fortune* 500 Industrial Cos.
440th in *Business Week* 1000

KEY COMPETITORS

Baker Hughes	General Motors
Cooper Industries	McDermott
Daimler-Benz	Navistar
Dresser	Renault
Fiat	Sears
Ford	Volvo

HOW MUCH

	9-Year Growth	1981	1982	1983	1984	1985	1986	1987	1988	1989	1990
Sales ($ mil.)	5.4%	1,735	1,230	1,412	2,249	1,893	1,796	2,424	3,267	3,523	2,778
Net income ($ mil.)	(3.2%)	85	37	37	125	73	54	112	176	242	64
Income as % of sales	—	4.9%	3.0%	2.7%	5.6%	3.9%	3.0%	4.6%	5.4%	6.9%	2.3%
Earnings per share ($)	(2.7%)	2.35	1.03	1.04	3.46	2.01	1.51	3.13	4.90	6.90	1.83
Stock price – high ($)	—	19.83	22.38	29.50	29.75	26.63	29.13	39.13	44.00	52.50	45.75
Stock price – low ($)	—	13.58	13.13	20.25	19.25	19.88	20.50	21.75	27.00	37.75	26.75
Stock price – close ($)	6.4%	18.41	20.56	28.88	22.31	23.25	23.38	28.50	41.00	42.75	32.25
P/E – high	—	8	22	29	9	13	19	13	9	8	25
P/E – low	—	6	13	20	6	10	14	7	6	5	15
Dividends per share ($)	4.7%	0.66	0.50	0.53	1.10	1.10	0.70	1.60	2.40	2.50	1.00
Book value per share ($)	6.9%	16.58	16.11	16.66	18.88	19.70	20.27	22.33	25.18	28.87	30.15

1990 Year-end:
Debt ratio: 24.2%
Return on equity: 6.2%
Cash (mil.): $478
Current ratio: —
Long-term debt (mil.): $325
No. of shares (mil.): 34
Dividends:
  1990 average yield: 3.1%
  1990 payout: 54.6%
Market value (mil.): $1,090

Stock Price History High/Low 1981–90

PACIFIC ENTERPRISES

NYSE symbol: PET
Fiscal year ends: December 31

OVERVIEW

Los Angeles–based Pacific Enterprises owns Southern California Gas Company (SoCalGas), America's largest natural gas utility, and Thrifty Corporation, a western and midwestern retailer. The company also explores for and produces oil and gas through its subsidiary Pacific Enterprises Oil Company (PEOC).

In 1990 SoCalGas delivered about 2.8 billion cubic feet of gas daily to more than 4.6 million customers in a 23,000-square-mile region of southern and central California. Thrifty Corporation specializes in combination discount drug and variety stores, offering a wide array of merchandise, from cosmetics and drugs to televisions and housewares. Store names vary from state to state: Thrifty Drug Stores are in most western states; Pay'n Saves are in California, Washington, Idaho, Alaska, and Hawaii; and Bi-Marts are in Washington and Oregon. Thrifty also operates the Big 5, MC, and Gart Bros. sporting goods chains.

Thrifty has experienced poor sales and continued losses since Pacific Enterprises bought it in 1986. One time write-downs at Thrifty and at PEOC resulted in charges of $275 million, contributing to Pacific Enterprises's $35 million loss in 1990. The company has instituted a hiring freeze and reduced its dividend and plans to sell some oil and gas assets to help reduce costs and raise cash.

WHO

Chairman and CEO: James R. Ukropina, age 53, $790,000 pay
President: Willis B. Wood, Jr., age 56, $556,000 pay
EVP and CFO: Lloyd A. Levitin, age 58, $371,000 pay
VP and Chief Administrative Officer, Human Resources: Charles F. Weiss, age 51
Auditors: Deloitte & Touche
Employees: 42,400

WHERE

HQ: 633 W. Fifth St., Los Angeles, CA 90017-2006
Phone: 213-895-5000
Fax: 213-629-1225

Pacific Enterprises conducts utility operations in southern and central California. Its retail stores operate in 19 western and midwestern states.

WHEN

In 1886 Walter Cline and C. O. G. Miller started Pacific Lighting Company, a San Francisco gas lamp rental business. Competition from the increasingly popular electric lamp led them to expand into gas distribution. In 1889 they bought 3 Los Angeles gas and electric utilities, including Los Angeles Gas Company, and in 1890 added Los Angeles Electric Company to Pacific Lighting's growing list of utility properties. Cline then opened an office in Los Angeles to manage the company's activities in southern California, while Miller remained in San Francisco.

Pacific Lighting consolidated in the 1920s, buying Southern Counties Gas and Industrial Fuel Supply in 1925, Santa Maria Gas in 1928, and a majority stake in Southern California Gas in 1929. In 1937 the company sold its Los Angeles electric properties to the city of Los Angeles in exchange for a long-term gas utility franchise agreement.

During WWII Pacific Lighting converted idle gas plants to the manufacture of butadiene, an essential ingredient in the production of synthetic rubber. Population growth in southern California doubled the company's size to almost 3 million gas customers between 1950 and 1965. Miller's son Robert served as the company's CEO during this period and was succeeded by his son Paul in 1968.

The company diversified into oil and gas exploration and development in 1960. It later moved its headquarters to Los Angeles (1967) and bought Blackfield Hawaii Corporation, marking its move into land development (1969). Pacific Lighting's gas properties were merged in 1970, forming SoCalGas.

In the 1970s the company got in and out of fruit growing and agriculture management. It then bought Terra Resources (1983), greatly increasing its participation in oil and gas exploration, and more than doubled its land development operations by buying the Presley Companies (1984). Oil and gas prices fell, resulting in a $227 million charge in 1986. The company sold its land development businesses in 1987.

Pacific Lighting spent $900 million to buy Thrifty Corporation (1986) and $700 million to buy oil and gas producer Sabine Corporation (1988). In 1988 the company changed its name to Pacific Enterprises and spent $234 million to add Pay'n Save and Bi-Mart drugstores to Thrifty's assets. Paul Miller retired in 1989 and was succeeded by James Ukropina, the first person outside the Miller family to serve as Pacific Enterprises's chairman.

WHAT

	1990 Sales		1990 Operating Income	
	$ mil.	% of total	$ mil.	% of total
Utility	3,204	46	438	67
Oil & gas	338	5	138	21
Retailing	3,193	46	48	7
Other	188	3	32	5
Adjustments	—	—	(455)	—
Total	**6,923**	**100**	**201**	**100**

	1990 Gas Sales	
	$ mil.	% of total
Residential	1,548	53
Commercial & industrial	906	31
Utility electric generation	181	6
Wholesale	130	4
Other	181	6
Total	**2,946**	**100**

	No. of Retail Stores
Drug & discount	
Thrifty	554
Thrifty Jr.	71
Pay'n Save	124
Bi-Mart	43
Sporting goods	
Big 5	129
MC Sporting Goods	65
Gart Bros.	72
Total	**1,058**

Major Subsidiaries
Pacific Energy (power plants and facilities)
Pacific Enterprises Leasing Company
Pacific Enterprises Oil Company
Pacific Interstate Company (natural gas transmission)
Southern California Gas Company
Thrifty Corporation

RANKINGS

15th in *Fortune* 100 Diversified Service Cos.
221st in *Business Week* 1000

KEY COMPETITORS

Albertson's	Kmart	Riklis Family
American Stores	Kroger	Walgreen
Costco	Long's	Wal-Mart
Jack Eckerd	Melville	

HOW MUCH

	9-Year Growth	1981	1982	1983	1984	1985	1986	1987	1988	1989	1990
Sales ($ mil.)	8.4%	3,357	4,359	4,586	4,781	5,083	5,324	5,339	5,932	6,762	6,923
Net income ($ mil.)	—	124	130	159	146	163	91	232	229	218	(35)
Income as % of sales	—	3.7%	3.0%	3.5%	3.1%	3.2%	1.7%	4.3%	3.9%	3.2%	(0.5%)
Earnings per share ($)	—	4.52	4.57	5.02	3.56	3.80	1.34	3.69	3.51	3.05	(0.86)
Stock price – high ($)	—	29.88	31.00	36.38	41.88	48.75	57.50	61.25	52.88	53.75	52.00
Stock price – low ($)	—	19.88	22.50	28.00	30.88	39.00	45.00	45.75	35.63	37.13	34.25
Stock price – close ($)	4.0%	27.25	28.38	36.25	41.63	48.50	49.00	49.75	37.50	50.50	38.88
P/E – high	—	7	7	7	12	13	43	17	15	18	—
P/E – low	—	4	5	6	9	10	34	12	10	12	—
Dividends per share ($)	3.3%	2.60	2.82	3.04	3.20	3.36	3.48	3.48	3.48	3.48	3.48
Book value per share ($)	(3.1%)	31.65	33.20	34.73	34.85	35.52	26.25	27.11	28.40	27.55	23.76

1990 Year-end:
Debt ratio: 49.0%
Return on equity: —
Cash (mil.): $187
Current ratio: 0.99
Long-term debt (mil.): $1,998
No. of shares (mil.): 71
Dividends:
　1990 average yield: 9.0%
　1990 payout: —
Market value (mil.): $2,748

Stock Price History High/Low 1981–90

PACIFIC GAS AND ELECTRIC COMPANY

NYSE symbol: PCG
Fiscal year ends: December 31

Hoover's Rating **C+**

OVERVIEW

Pacific Gas and Electric (PG&E), America's largest electric and natural gas utility, serves approximately 7.6 million customers in northern and central California. In 1990 its Diablo Canyon Nuclear Power Plant generated 16.3 billion kilowatt-hours of electricity and $1.5 billion in revenues — about 16% of PG&E's revenues for that year.

PG&E Enterprises, a subsidiary, manages nonutility projects, including ownership and operation of independent power plants (PG&E-Bechtel Generating Company). PG&E Properties, the company's real estate development subsidiary, has completed 5 projects in California.

In an effort to help reduce air pollution, PG&E is investigating the potential of electric-powered and compressed natural gas (CNG)–powered vehicles. The company operates several natural gas vehicle fueling stations and plans to open 5 more in 1991.

The company plans to invest up to $1.75 billion in its utility business between 1991 and 1996. PG&E will also spend another $1.5 billion to expand a pipeline bringing gas to its service area from Canadian gas fields.

WHEN

Peter Donahue founded the first gas company in the western US, San Francisco Gas, in 1852. This company became San Francisco Gas & Electric (SFG&E) in 1896 after merging with Edison Light & Power.

In the meantime in San Francisco, money broker George Roe and other investors founded California Electric Light (1879), the first electric utility in the US, predating Edison's New York Pearl Street Station by 3 years. California Electric and SFG&E consolidated in 1905 to form Pacific Gas and Electric (PG&E).

In 1928 PG&E discovered natural gas reserves in California's Kings County and, in 1930, began converting more than 2.5 million appliances to burn this fuel — the largest conversion in history. The company began exploring for out-of-state gas supplies in the 1950s, first in Texas and New Mexico and then in western Canada.

PG&E operated the world's first private atomic power plant (Vallecitos) in 1957, and developed the first geothermal plant (The Geysers) to operate in North America in 1960. PG&E's Humboldt Bay facility (completed in 1963) was one of the world's first nuclear plants to produce electricity at a cost commensurable to conventional steam plants.

From its inception through the late 1970s, PG&E bought about 500 utilities (water, gas, and electric) and by 1978 was serving about 9 million customers. The company sold the last of its water systems by 1985, the same year Unit 1 of the Diablo Canyon nuclear facility went on line. Diablo Canyon, begun in 1968, had been plagued by delays and cost overruns (a design problem discovered in 1981 resulted in a 15-month review of construction plans and methods). Unit 2 was in operation by 1986. In 1988, instead of utilizing traditional rate structures, PG&E started basing revenues chiefly on how much electricity Diablo Canyon generates, creating a direct relationship between the plant's performance and the company's earnings. Settlement of the Diablo Canyon rate issues in 1988 and an unscheduled refueling outage resulted in negative earnings for that year.

Under natural gas deregulation, customers began to bypass PG&E in the mid-1980s (finding it cheaper to generate their own electricity or buy gas directly from suppliers). The company responded by eliminating about 2,500 jobs in 1987 and announced a 3-year phase-out of about 300 management positions in 1990.

The company added Corpus Christi Exploration Company (oil and gas exploration in the Gulf of Mexico) to its nonutility business group in 1990.

WHO

Chairman and CEO: Richard A. Clarke, age 60, $1,099,517 pay
VC and Principal Financial Officer: Stanley T. Skinner, age 53, $695,293
President: George A. Maneatis, age 64, $685,229 pay
VP Human Resources: Russell H. Cunningham
Auditors: Arthur Andersen & Co.
Employees: 26,200

WHERE

HQ: 77 Beale St., San Francisco, CA 94106
Phone: 415-973-7000
Fax: 415-543-7813

Generating Facilities

Fossil Fueled
Contra Costa (Contra Costa County)
Humboldt Bay (Humboldt County)
Hunters Point (San Francisco County)
Kern (Kern County)
Morro Bay (San Luis Obispo County)
Moss Landing (Monterey County)
Oakland (Alameda County)
Pittsburg (Contra Costa County)
Potrero (San Francisco County)

Geothermal
The Geysers (Sonoma and Lake Counties)

Hydroelectric
Helms Pumped Storage Plant (Fresno County)

Nuclear
Diablo Canyon (San Luis Obispo County)

WHAT

	1990 Sales	
	$ mil.	% of total
Electric	7,036	74
Gas	2,434	26
Total	**9,470**	**100**

	1990 Fuel Sources
	% of total
Hydroelectric	8
Fossil fuels	27
Geothermal	8
Nuclear	18
Other	39
Total	**100**

Natural Gas Transmission & Supply
Pacific Gas Transmission Co.
Alberta and Southern Gas Co. Ltd. (Canadian-based gas supplier)
Pacific Energy Fuels Co. (finances the purchase of nuclear fuels)

PG&E Enterprises
PG&E Operating Services Co. (technical support)
PG&E Properties (real estate development)
PG&E Resources Co. (natural gas and oil exploration and development)
PG&E-Bechtel Generating Co. (joint venture with Bechtel)

RANKINGS

7th in *Fortune* 50 Utilities
51st in *Business Week* 1000

HOW MUCH

	9-Year Growth	1981	1982	1983	1984	1985	1986	1987	1988	1989	1990
Sales ($ mil.)	4.8%	6,195	6,785	6,647	7,830	8,431	7,817	7,186	7,646	8,588	9,470
Net income ($ mil.)	6.4%	565	810	788	975	1,031	1,081	597	62	901	987
Income as % of sales	—	9.1%	11.9%	11.9%	12.5%	12.2%	13.8%	8.3%	0.8%	10.5%	10.4%
Earnings per share ($)	2.3%	1.71	2.46	2.15	2.62	2.65	2.60	1.29	(0.10)	1.90	2.10
Stock price – high ($)	—	12.06	14.38	16.75	17.25	20.38	27.50	27.88	18.38	22.00	25.63
Stock price – low ($)	—	9.75	10.13	13.94	12.00	16.00	18.75	15.00	14.00	17.25	20.00
Stock price – close ($)	10.1%	10.50	14.06	14.88	16.38	20.00	24.25	16.25	17.50	22.00	25.00
P/E – high	—	7	6	8	7	8	11	22	—	12	12
P/E – low	—	6	4	6	5	6	7	12	—	9	10
Dividends per share ($)	1.2%	1.36	1.47	1.58	1.69	1.81	1.90	1.92	1.66	1.40	1.52
Book value per share ($)	1.8%	15.15	15.87	16.39	17.18	18.05	19.06	18.68	16.79	17.38	17.86

1990 Year-end:
Debt ratio: 47.8%
Return on equity: 11.9%
Cash (mil.): $101
Current ratio: 1.06
Long-term debt (mil.): $7,786
No. of shares (mil.): 420
Dividends:
1990 average yield: 6.1%
1990 payout: 72.4%
Market value (mil.): $10,505

Stock Price History High/Low 1981–90

PACIFIC TELESIS GROUP

NYSE symbol: PAC
Fiscal year ends: December 31

Hoover's Rating **B-**

OVERVIEW

Pacific Telesis is the 8th largest US telephone company. The company provides local telephone service and access to long-distance services for about 14.3 million lines in California and Nevada. Investors who bought $100 of stock at its 1983 initial offering would have had stock worth $443 in mid-1991, more than for any other former Bell company.

Subsidiary PacTel Cellular provides cellular phone service to 587,000 customers in 33 markets (owning majority interests in 5 of the US's top 20 markets). Through Pacific Telesis International, it owns 26% of Mannesmann Mobilfunk, which is building the world's largest cellular system in Germany. Overseas interests include Thai paging and Korean credit clearing.

Pacific Telesis owns one of the US's largest paging companies, PacTel Paging, serving some 474,000 units in more than 17 markets. After negotiating to buy an option to purchase control of Chicago's cable TV service, Pacific Telesis is primed if US District Judge Harold Greene, supervising the court-dismantled Bell empire, opens the doors to previously restricted information services such as cable. PacTel Cable already has interests in UK cable systems, outside the court's jurisdiction.

WHEN

The Pacific and Nevada Bell companies owned by Pacific Telesis were formerly 2 of AT&T's 22 operating companies. California's first exchange was opened in 1878 in San Francisco, the city that in 1915 was one end (with New York) of the first coast-to-coast telephone call.

By 1980 AT&T was rumored to be considering Pacific Bell's sale. Pacific Bell's battles with the California Public Utilities Commission (CPUC) had soured relations with AT&T to the point that it claimed AT&T had denied it equity capital. But during 1980 and 1981, instead of selling, AT&T hired a new management team for the company. Donald Guinn, CEO of Pacific Bell (and chairman and CEO of Pacific Telesis from 1984 to 1988), and new CFO John Hulse took steps to cut spending and improve relations with the CPUC.

Pacific Bell was folded into parent Pacific Telesis Group in 1984, after divestiture from AT&T. Pacific Telesis gained California and Nevada phone territories, 1/7 interest in Bell Communications Research (R&D arm shared by the Bell companies), and PacTel Cellular.

In 1986 the CPUC ordered Pacific Bell to refund subscribers for fees derived from deceptive marketing practices (combining optional features with basic service and charging for both) and ordered a rate refund instead of the requested hike. But unregulated enterprises began to fuel Pacific Telesis's growth. The 1986 purchase of Communications Industries made Pacific Telesis a top player in cellular radio and paging, giving it 5 cellular and 14 paging operations outside of its territory. In 1988 Guinn retired.

In 1989 Pacific Telesis purchased a minority interest (8.5%) in International Digital Communications, formed with several Japanese companies that are constructing a transpacific fiber-optic cable. Pacific Telesis owns 26% of a group licensed in 1989 to supply Germany with its first privately owned cellular phone system, designed to be the world's largest digital system.

The company agreed to buy an option for 75% of a Chicago cable TV franchise (if the former Bell companies win court approval to compete in cable) and ventured into the UK cable market, winning licenses to serve more than a million homes by 1990. In 1990 the company agreed to combine its Ohio and Michigan cellular units with those of Cellular Communications (CCI), gaining the option to acquire CCI over several years.

Pacific Telesis sold its interest in UK's Microtel to British Aerospace in 1991. The company said the field to offer a pocket-phone network was too crowded.

WHO

Chairman, President, and CEO: Sam Ginn, age 53, $963,683 pay
VC and CFO: John E. Hulse, age 57, $615,458 pay
Group President, PacTel Companies: C. Lee Cox, age 49, $561,875 pay
Group President, Bell Operating Companies: Philip J. Quigley, age 48, $561,667 pay
EVP Human Resources: Jim R. Moberg, age 55
Auditors: Coopers & Lybrand
Employees: 65,800

WHERE

HQ: 130 Kearny St., San Francisco, CA 94108
Phone: 415-394-3000
Fax: 415-362-2913 (External Affairs)

Pacific Telesis provides telephone service and publishes directories in California and Nevada and has unregulated operations throughout the US and in Germany, Japan, South Korea, Thailand, and the UK.

WHAT

	1990 Sales	
	$ mil.	% of total
Local service	3,153	32
Network access — interstate	1,536	16
Network access — intrastate	704	7
Toll service	2,211	23
Other (includes cellular)	2,112	22
Total	**9,716**	**100**

Telephone Companies
Nevada Bell
Pacific Bell

Unregulated Operations
Bell Communications Research (14.28%)
Pacific Bell Directory (directory publishing)
Pacific Telesis International (international operations)
PacTel Business Systems (communications equipment sales, service, and financing)
PacTel Cable (UK cable operations)
PacTel Cellular (cellular telephone service)
PacTel Paging (paging service)
PacTel Properties (real estate development)
PacTel Teletrac (vehicle radiolocation services)

RANKINGS

9th in *Fortune* 50 Largest Utilities
31st in *Business Week* 1000

KEY COMPETITORS

Ameritech	GTE
Bell Atlantic	McCaw
BellSouth	NYNEX
British Telecom	Southwestern Bell
Cable & Wireless	Telmex
Centel	United Telecom
Ericsson	U S West

HOW MUCH

	6-Year Growth	1981	1982	1983	1984	1985	1986	1987	1988	1989	1990
Sales ($ mil.)	3.7%	—	—	—	7,824	8,499	8,977	9,131	9,483	9,593	9,716
Net income ($ mil.)	3.7%	—	—	—	829	929	1,079	950	1,188	1,242	1,030
Income as % of sales	—	—	—	—	10.6%	10.9%	12.0%	10.4%	12.5%	12.9%	10.6%
Earnings per share ($)	—	—	—	—	2.12	2.27	2.51	2.20	2.80	3.00	2.59
Stock price – high ($)	—	—	—	—	17.78	21.47	31.13	34.50	32.50	51.13	51.50
Stock price – low ($)	—	—	—	—	13.13	16.66	19.38	22.50	24.88	30.38	36.25
Stock price – close ($)	17.5%	—	—	—	17.22	21.16	26.63	26.63	30.88	50.38	45.25
P/E – high	—	—	—	—	8	9	12	16	12	17	20
P/E – low	—	—	—	—	6	7	8	10	9	10	14
Dividends per share ($)	7.0%	—	—	—	1.35	1.43	1.52	1.64	1.76	1.88	2.02
Book value per share ($)	2.3%	—	—	—	16.20	17.04	18.01	18.47	19.30	18.92	18.53

1990 Year-end:
Debt ratio: 43.1%
Return on equity: 13.8%
Cash (mil.): $110
Current ratio: 0.70
Long-term debt (mil.): $5,611
No. of shares (mil.): 399
Dividends:
  1990 average yield: 4.5%
  1990 payout: 78.0%
Market value (mil.): $18,076

Stock Price History High/Low 1984–90

PAINE WEBBER GROUP INC.

OVERVIEW

Paine Webber Group is the holding company that embraces the nation's 4th largest brokerage firm, PaineWebber Inc. The company is rebounding from a record loss in 1990, caused by one-time charges for layoffs and bad investments associated with mergers and acquisitions and LBOs. In early 1991 it posted healthy results, a testament to years of cost cutting and restructuring.

The group divides itself into 4 major business segments — Retail Sales, Asset Management, Institutional Sales and Trading, and Banking. Along with brokerage fees, the Retail Sales unit makes money on the interest from loans it makes to clients who buy on margin.

More than 40% of its revenues comes from retail (individual investor) activity.

Its asset management activities are conducted mainly by subsidiaries Mitchell Hutchins Asset Management and Mitchell Hutchins Institutional Investors. A joint venture with Yasuda, a Japanese financial services company that owns 20% of Paine Webber voting stock, offers asset management in London.

The Institutional Sales and Trading division serves large institutions and corporations. Paine Webber's banking operations include investment banking and management of tax-exempt securities.

WHEN

Two former clerks at the Blackstone National Bank in Boston opened a brokerage house in 1880. They were William Paine and Wallace Webber. The firm joined the New York Stock Exchange (1890) and bought seats on the Chicago Board of Trade (1909) and Chicago Stock Exchange (1916).

The company opened its first branch in 1899, in Houghton, Michigan, the headquarters of copper companies Paine Webber had helped underwrite. During WWI the company added branches, including one in New York, and expanded rapidly as the stock market bulled through the 1920s. During the Depression the firm eliminated offices.

In 1942 Paine Webber merged with another Boston brokerage house, Jackson and Curtis. Jackson and Curtis had begun when Charles Cabot Jackson and Laurence Curtis formed their partnership in 1879. Paine, Webber, Jackson & Curtis moved its offices from Boston to New York in 1963 and broadened its national scope by buying Kansas City brokerage Barret Fitch North (1967) and Richmond, Virginia–based Abbott, Proctor & Paine (no relation, 1970). The firm also launched overseas offices in London and Tokyo (1973).

Paine Webber, which had converted from a partnership to a corporation in 1970, went

public in 1972. The company created a holding company for its operations — Paine Webber Incorporated. The company added Mitchell Hutchins (equity research, 1977) and Blyth Eastman Dillon (investment banking, 1979). Blyth executives defected and took customers with them, and Paine Webber was late bringing its new investment bank into play during the mergers-and-acquisitions craze of the 1980s.

Donald Marron, named CEO in 1980, continued to expand the company, buying Houston-based Rotan Mosle and First Mid America, a Nebraska company. After the 1987 stock market crash, Marron, who began his career running his own investment bank at age 25, aggressively restructured and sold operations including PaineWebber's commercial paper business (1987) and its venture capital unit (1988). Japanese insurance company Yasuda injected capital for an equity stake in Paine Webber in 1987, one that grew to 20% by 1990. A 1988 bridge loan to financially beleaguered Federated Department Stores dogged Paine Webber into 1990, when the company curtailed merchant banking and increased reserves against bad loans by $71 million. Paine Webber posted its worst loss as a publicly traded corporation that year.

NYSE symbol: PWJ
Fiscal year ends: December 31

Hoover's Rating D

WHO

Chairman and CEO: Donald B. Marron, age 56, $950,000 pay
President, PaineWebber Inc.: Paul B. Guenther, age 51, $700,000 pay
EVP, PaineWebber Inc.: James C. Treadway, Jr., age 47, $450,000 pay
CFO: Robert H. Silver
EVP and Director of Human Resources: Ronald M. Schwartz, age 55, $448,750 pay
Auditors: Ernst & Young
Employees: 12,700

WHERE

HQ: 1285 Ave. of the Americas, New York, NY 10019
Phone: 212-713-2000
Fax: 212-713-4924 (Investor Relations)

Paine Webber Group operates 267 offices in the US, Japan, Switzerland, France, Hong Kong, and the UK.

WHAT

	1990 Sales	
	$ mil.	% of total
Commissions	652	22
Interest	1,395	47
Principal transactions	472	16
Investment banking	236	8
Asset management	177	6
Other	47	1
Total	**2,979**	**100**

Services

Retail Sales	Asset Management
Commodities and financial futures	Investment advice
Direct investments	Mutual funds
Insurance	Portfolio management
Listed securities	
Margin lending	**Banking**
Mutual funds	Investment banking
Options	Municipal securities offerings
OTC securities	

Institutional Sales and Trading
Fixed Income Sales and Trading
  Corporate bonds
  Federal government and agency securities (primary dealer)
  Mortgage securities
  Municipal and state securities
  Options and futures contracts
Global Equity Sales and Research

RANKINGS

20th in *Fortune* 50 Diversified Financial Cos.
820th in *Business Week* 1000

KEY COMPETITORS

American Express	Kemper
Bank of Boston	Merrill Lynch
Bear Stearns	Morgan Stanley
Canadian Imperial	Nomura
Charles Schwab	Primerica
CS Holding	Prudential
Dai-Ichi Kangyo	Royal Bank
Deutsche Bank	Salomon
Equitable	Sears
General Electric	Transamerica
Goldman Sachs	Travelers
Industrial Bank of Japan	Union Bank of Switzerland

HOW MUCH

	9-Year Growth	1981	1982	1983	1984	1985	1986	1987	1988	1989	1990
Sales ($ mil.)	12.6%	1,027	1,100	1,541	1,553	1,885	2,385	2,437	2,512	2,926	2,979
Net income ($ mil.)	—	16	35	91	13	34	72	75	42	52	(57)
Income as % of sales	—	1.5%	3.2%	5.9%	0.8%	1.8%	3.0%	3.1%	1.7%	1.8%	(1.9%)
Earnings per share ($)	—	0.93	2.02	4.33	0.62	1.36	2.46	2.25	0.58	1.05	(3.23)
Stock price – high ($)	—	16.73	33.60	49.10	31.10	34.50	39.13	39.13	18.88	23.63	20.63
Stock price – low ($)	—	7.35	8.25	24.30	18.90	20.20	25.40	13.13	14.38	15.63	11.50
Stock price – close ($)	(1.1%)	15.15	31.60	28.00	22.00	28.00	31.50	14.38	16.13	16.88	13.75
P/E – high	—	18	17	11	50	25	16	17	33	23	—
P/E – low	—	8	4	6	31	15	10	6	25	15	—
Dividends per share ($)	7.8%	0.26	0.29	0.42	0.48	0.48	0.49	0.52	0.52	0.52	0.52
Book value per share ($)	12.5%	7.85	9.62	15.82	15.83	16.82	20.60	23.90	24.87	26.09	22.61

1990 Year-end:
Debt ratio: 45.3%
Return on equity: —
Cash (mil.): $1,194
Current ratio: —
Long-term debt (mil.): $742
No. of shares (mil.): 25
Dividends:
  1990 average yield: 3.8%
  1990 payout: —
Market value (mil.): $339

Stock Price History
High/Low 1981–90

PAN AM CORPORATION

NYSE symbol: PN
Fiscal year ends: December 31

OVERVIEW

In its heyday Pan Am was America's airline to the world. Even as late as 1990 it was the leading US airline to Europe — but no more. Since its bankruptcy filing in January 1991, Pan Am has sold its London routes to United and its Frankfurt hub, New York–to–Europe routes, and northeastern shuttle to Delta. What remains is a single hub in Miami and routes to Paris and Latin America. Pan Am Express, the airline's regional airline service (formerly Ransome Airlines), continues to serve cities in the US and the Bahamas.

Pan Am's unsecured creditors have proposed relocating the airline's headquarters to Miami, which will be the base for its planned Latin American expansion. Bondholders also want to reissue the company's stock, with them owning 55% and Delta (which will invest $50 million in Pan Am and loan it $155 million) owning 45%. Thomas Plaskett, who was under fire for his weak handling of Pan Am's financial crisis, resigned as president and CEO in September 1991. Plaskett received $1.25 million in severance pay and continues temporarily as Pan Am's chairman. Former McDonnell Douglas executive Russell Ray replaced Plaskett at the helm.

WHO

Chairman: Thomas G. Plaskett, age 47, $500,000 pay
President and CEO: Russell L. Ray, age 56
SVP Human Resources: Kenneth Meyer, age 48
VP and CFO: Rolf S. Andresen, age 56
Auditors: Ernst & Young
Employees: 24,600

WHERE

HQ: Pan Am Building, 200 Park Ave., New York, NY 10166
Phone: 212-880-1234
Fax: 212-880-1782
Reservations: 800-221-1111

Hub Locations
Miami

Pan Am flies to cities in the Caribbean, Mexico, Central America, and South America, and between Miami and Paris.

	1990 Sales		1990 Net Income	
	$ mil.	% of total	$ mil.	% of total
US	745	21	(296)	—
Atlantic	2,079	57	(277)	—
Latin America	810	22	87	—
Other countries	—	—	(167)	—
Adjustments	283	—	(10)	—
Total	**3,917**	**100**	**(663)**	**—**

WHEN

Army captain J. K. Montgomery founded Pan American Airways in 1927 to fly mail from Key West to Havana. Short of cash and equipment, the airline merged with Florida Airways and Juan Trippe's Aviation Company of America in 1927. Within 2 years Trippe had spearheaded Pan Am's expansion throughout the Caribbean and Central America. In 1929 Pan Am joined W. R. Grace and Company (shipping company) to form Pan American–Grace Airways to operate along the South American west coast and by 1930 had added operations on South America's east coast. In 1935 Pan Am's *China Clipper* pioneered transpacific air service from Honolulu to Manila.

Pan Am opened its chain of Intercontinental Hotels in 1946, bought American Airlines's European routes in 1950, and offered the first transatlantic jet service in 1958. But, along the way, the airline had been losing passengers to competitors as more countries developed their own airlines and TWA and Northwest began flying overseas. In 1969 (a year after Trippe retired) TWA temporarily replaced Pan Am as America's #1 airline to Europe.

With its finances deteriorating, Pan Am asked the Shah of Iran for a $300 million loan in 1975. Rebuffed, the airline pared its routes, sold some planes, and in 1977 reported a profit. But federal airline deregulation (1978)

created new problems by allowing Pan Am's domestic competitors easier access to foreign routes. These airlines, with their extensive US route networks, had a built-in system for funneling passengers into international routes, but Pan Am had no domestic routes. To remedy this the company bought Miami-based National Airlines (1980), gaining connections along the East Coast and to the West Coast, but in a bidding war with Texas Air (now Continental Airlines Holdings) paid a hefty price.

To offset losses Pan Am sold its hotels to Grand Metropolitan (1981) and its Pacific routes to United (1986). In 1986 Pan Am bought Philadelphia's Ransome Airlines (now Pan Am Express) and New York Air's northeastern shuttle from Texas Air. The 1988 terrorist bombing of Flight 103 over Lockerbie, Scotland, dramatically reduced transatlantic revenues, contributing heavily to Pan Am's $452 million loss in 1989.

Thomas Plaskett, who took over as chairman in 1988, tried to strengthen Pan Am's finances by launching an unsuccessful and expensive takeover bid for Northwest in 1989. In 1990 Plaskett agreed to sell Pan Am's London routes to United for $400 million. But high fuel prices and weak traffic related to the Gulf crisis brought on more losses in 1990, and Pan Am entered bankruptcy in 1991.

WHAT

	1990 Sales	
	$ mil.	% of total
Passenger	3,175	87
Freight & mail	249	7
Charter & other	210	6
Adjustments	283	—
Total	**3,917**	**100**

Major Subsidiaries and Affiliates
Pan American World Airways, Inc.
Pan Am Express, Inc. (regional services)

Flight Equipment	No.	Average Age in Years
Boeing 747	22	19.5
Boeing 727	88	18.0
A300	13	6.0
A310	21	3.7
Total	**144**	**14.9**

RANKINGS

15th in *Fortune* 50 Transportation Cos.

KEY COMPETITORS

AMR
Continental Airlines
Delta
TWA
UAL
USAir

HOW MUCH

	9-Year Growth	1981	1982	1983	1984	1985	1986	1987	1988	1989	1990
Sales ($ mil.)	(0.3%)	3,797	3,716	3,789	3,685	3,484	3,039	3,593	3,569	3,561	3,917
Net income ($ mil.)	—	(260)	(485)	(60)	(207)	49	(463)	(265)	(97)	(452)	(663)
Income as % of sales	—	(6.8%)	(13.1%)	(1.6%)	(5.6%)	1.4%	(15.2%)	(7.4%)	(2.7%)	(12.7%)	(16.9%)
Earnings per share ($)	—	(2.53)	(4.61)	(0.68)	(1.06)	0.42	(2.45)	(1.28)	(0.33)	(2.32)	(3.38)
Stock price – high ($)	—	6.00	4.25	9.00	9.25	9.00	9.50	6.38	3.38	5.13	4.00
Stock price – low ($)	—	2.38	2.50	3.50	4.00	4.00	4.00	2.63	2.25	2.25	1.00
Stock price – close ($)	(9.5%)	2.75	3.63	8.13	4.63	7.75	4.25	2.75	2.25	2.63	1.13
P/E – high	—	—	—	—	—	21	—	—	—	—	—
P/E – low	—	—	—	—	—	10	—	—	—	—	—
Dividends per share ($)	0.0%	0.00	0.00	0.00	0.00	0.00	0.00	0.00	0.00	0.00	0.00
Book value per share ($)	—	11.05	4.11	4.19	2.17	3.36	0.06	(1.75)	(2.12)	(4.26)	(7.97)

1990 Year-end:
Debt ratio: 0.0%
Return on equity: —
Cash (mil.): $90
Current ratio: 0.21
Long-term debt (mil.): $0
No. of shares (mil.): 160
Dividends:
1990 average yield: 0.0%
1990 payout: 0.0%
Market value (mil.): $180

Stock Price History High/Low 1981–90

PANHANDLE EASTERN CORPORATION

OVERVIEW

Houston-based Panhandle Eastern operates one of America's largest integrated natural gas pipelines. Its 4 transmission subsidiaries delivered 2.19 trillion cubic feet of natural gas in 1990 (roughly 12% of America's gas consumption). The company also imports and regasifies Algerian liquefied natural gas for sale in the US through its subsidiary Trunkline LNG and, through another subsidiary, owns a 14.3% interest in Midland Cogeneration Venture LP, which utilizes natural gas to produce both electricity and industrial process steam.

Continued mild weather through the winters of 1990 and 1991 has adversely affected Panhandle Eastern's bottom line. The company is also facing some $218.6 million in cleanup costs related to polychlorinated biphenyl (PCB) contamination of sites near pipelines acquired from Texas Eastern in 1989. To raise cash, the company recently offered 12 million shares of common stock (80% in the US and 20% in international markets) and will use the proceeds from the offering to reduce debt.

WHEN

Panhandle Eastern first appeared in 1929 as Interstate Pipe Line Company. Renamed Panhandle Eastern Pipe Line Company in 1930, it completed its first pipeline in 1931, which extended 2,100 miles from the Texas Panhandle to eastern Illinois by the end of 1939.

In 1951 the company started building its 2nd major pipeline system (Trunkline Gas Company), linking the Gulf Coast to Panhandle Eastern's system in Illinois.

In 1959 Panhandle Eastern bought Anadarko Production Company, an oil-and-gas exploration firm. The company then joined National Distillers and Chemical to form National Helium in 1961, which built a helium extraction plant near Liberal, Kansas, in 1963.

Trunkline extended its system to the Indiana-Michigan border through 2 more pipelines, and by the end of 1969 the combined Panhandle-Trunkline system supplied natural gas to 12 states and Canada.

Panhandle Eastern entered a 20-year contract for liquefied natural gas (LNG) with Algerian supplier Sonatrach in 1975, hoping to reduce the effects of gas shortages. It also bought a coal-mining firm (Youghiogheny and Ohio Coal, 1976) and an oil-drilling firm (Dixilyn Corporation, 1977), which owned 1/3 of an offshore contractor, Dixilyn Godager Company (renamed Dixilyn-Field Godager, 1979). Panhandle Eastern completed its acquisition of Dixilyn-Field in 1980.

The company adopted the name Panhandle Eastern Corporation in 1981 and, in response to falling gas prices, suspended its Algerian LNG contract in 1983. Sonatrach subsequently filed for international arbitration.

In 1986, after rejecting a takeover bid from Wagner and Brown (a Midland, Texas–based oil and gas firm), Panhandle Eastern spun off Anadarko to its stockholders. In 1987 the company charged $460 million against earnings as part of its settlement with Sonatrach and shut down Dixilyn-Field and Youghiogheny and Ohio Coal (both were sold in 1990).

In 1989, when Texas Eastern Corporation (another Houston-based pipeline company) faced a hostile takeover by Coastal Corporation, Panhandle Eastern agreed to buy the company for $3.2 billion. Founded in 1947, Texas Eastern operated a gas pipeline extending from the Gulf Coast to the Eastern Seaboard. Panhandle Eastern took on $2.6 billion of debt to finance the Texas Eastern acquisition ($1.7 billion was retired that year through the sale of Texas Eastern's non-pipeline assets).

In 1990 the company finished the Lebanon Lateral, a pipeline linking Panhandle Eastern's midwestern and northeastern systems. Nonrecurring charges ($280 million), mostly related to the writedown of certain LNG facilities, contributed to the company's $233 million loss in 1990.

NYSE symbol: PEL
Fiscal year ends: December 31

WHO

Chairman, President, and CEO: Dennis R. Hendrix, age 51
SVP and CFO: James B. Hipple, age 57, $219,179 pay
VP Human Resources: Dan Hennig
Auditors: KPMG Peat Marwick
Employees: 6,000

WHERE

HQ: 5400 Westheimer Ct., PO Box 1642, Houston, TX 77251-1642
Phone: 713-627-5400
Fax: 713-627-4145

Panhandle Eastern operates a 27,500-mile natural gas pipeline system between producing regions in the Southwest and Canada and markets throughout the Northeast and Midwest.

WHAT

	1990 Sales	
	$ mil.	% of total
Natural gas sales	2,159	72
Natural gas transmission	550	18
Petroleum products	26	1
Natural gas liquids	89	3
Other	164	6
Total	**2,988**	**100**

Gas Transmission
Algonquin Gas Transmission Co.
Northern Border Pipeline Co. (22.75%)
Panhandle Eastern Pipeline Co.
Texas Eastern Transmission Corp.
Trunkline Gas Co.

Other Activities
Centana Energy Corp. (gas gathering system in Kansas)
National Helium Corp. (extraction and marketing of liquid petroleum products)
National Methanol Co. (25%)
Panhandle Trading Co. (nonregulated natural gas sales)
Source Midland LP
  Midland Cogeneration Venture LP (14.3%)
TEPPCO Partners (transportation and storage of petroleum products)
Trunkline LNG Co. (storage and regasification terminal for liquefied natural gas)

RANKINGS

40th in *Fortune* 50 Utilities
448th in *Business Week* 1000

KEY COMPETITORS

AMAX
Coastal
Columbia Gas
Enron
Occidental
Tenneco

HOW MUCH

	9-Year Growth	1981	1982	1983	1984	1985	1986	1987	1988	1989	1990
Sales ($ mil.)	(1.0%)	3,266	3,391	3,405	3,212	2,889	2,250	1,563	1,262	2,781	2,988
Net income ($ mil.)	—	262	220	152	166	125	(404)	110	(172)	70	(233)
Income as % of sales	—	8.0%	6.5%	4.5%	5.2%	4.3%	(17.9%)	7.0%	(13.6%)	2.5%	(7.8%)
Earnings per share ($)	—	6.52	5.36	3.64	3.88	2.83	(8.23)	2.07	(3.13)	0.97	(2.63)
Stock price – high ($)	—	46.75	37.00	39.00	40.00	41.50	50.25	34.75	27.38	30.75	29.75
Stock price – low ($)	—	30.38	20.50	23.88	31.00	32.38	24.25	18.25	21.00	20.50	10.38
Stock price – close ($)	(11.3%)	36.75	26.25	36.13	37.25	38.00	27.75	20.75	25.63	29.88	12.50
P/E – high	—	7	7	11	10	15	—	17	—	32	—
P/E – low	—	5	4	7	8	11	—	9	—	21	—
Dividends per share ($)	(3.9%)	2.00	2.30	2.30	2.30	2.30	2.23	2.00	2.00	2.00	1.40
Book value per share ($)	(9.8%)	31.85	34.80	36.04	37.53	37.89	18.92	19.15	14.06	16.21	12.53

1990 Year-end:
Debt ratio: 68.6%
Return on equity: —
Cash (mil.): $48
Current ratio: 0.71
Long-term debt (mil.): $2,484
No. of shares (mil.): 91
Dividends:
  1990 average yield: 11.2%
  1990 payout: —
Market value (mil.): $1,135

Stock Price History
High/Low 1981–90

PARAMOUNT COMMUNICATIONS INC.

OVERVIEW

Paramount is an entertainment and publishing giant in flux. After recent movie flops and a drop in the moviemaker's share of US box office revenue to 14.9% in 1990 from 22.2% in 1986, Paramount's tough CEO Martin Davis has shaken up the company's top management. Paramount Pictures, the company's film and TV production unit, is cutting costs and is working on lower-budget movies. A long-expected major media acquisition, to be financed by Paramount's large cash hoard, has not materialized, adding to uncertainty over the direction of entertainment operations.

In addition to making movies, Paramount's entertainment division operates movie theaters and TV stations, produces and distributes TV programs and videocassettes, and owns Madison Square Garden, the New York Knicks (basketball), the New York Rangers (hockey), and 50% of USA Network, a cable channel.

Paramount's Simon & Schuster unit, the nation's largest educational publisher, is emphasizing higher-margin educational and professional publishing (at the expense of its more volatile trade book business) and is investing in computerization of its internal operations and its educational products.

NYSE symbol: PCI
Fiscal year ends: October 31

 Hoover's Rating **B-**

WHO

Chairman and CEO: Martin S. Davis, age 63, $950,000 pay
President and COO: Stanley R. Jaffe, age 50
Chairman Paramount Pictures: Brandon Tartikoff, age 42
EVP and CFO: Ronald L. Nelson, age 38, $475,000 pay
Director Human Resources: Betty Panarella
Auditors: Ernst & Young
Employees: 12,100

WHERE

HQ: 15 Columbus Cir., New York, NY 10023-7780
Phone: 212-373-8000
Fax: 212-373-8558 (Corporate Communications)

Paramount operates worldwide and maintains its principal facilities in the US.

WHAT

	1990 Sales		1990 Operating Income	
	$ mil.	% of total	$ mil.	% of total
Entertainment	2,447	63	213	58
Publishing	1,422	37	156	42
Adjustments	—	—	(65)	—
Total	**3,869**	**100**	**304**	**100**

Entertainment
Paramount Pictures
  Home video distribution
  Movie production and distribution
  Television programming and distribution
  USA Network (50%)
Motion Picture Exhibition
  Cinamerica (50%)
  Cinema International Corporation (51%)
  Famous Players (Canada)
  United Cinemas International (25%)
TVX Broadcast Group Inc (83%)
  KRRT-TV, San Antonio
  KXTA-TV, Dallas
  KXTH-TV, Houston
  WDCA-TV, Washington, DC
  WLFL-TV, Raleigh/Durham
  WTXF-TV, Philadelphia
Madison Square Garden
  Arena
  NY Knickerbockers Basketball Club
  NY Rangers Hockey Club
  SRO/Pace Motor Sports (65%; Miss Universe pageant, auto thrill shows)

Publishing
Computer Curriculum Corp.   Poseidon Press
Linden Press   Simon & Schuster
Pocket Books   Zebra

WHEN

Paramount Communications (formerly Gulf+Western) was founded by Charles G. Bluhdorn, an Austrian who had escaped the Nazi invasion of Austria and the London Blitz and arrived in the US at age 16 in 1942.

Bluhdorn started his first job at $15 a week and then spent some time in the import-export business. In 1956 he bought Michigan Plating and Stamping Co. (which made the rear bumper for the Studebaker) for about $1 million. Two years later he merged the company with Beard & Stone Electric Co. (a Houston auto parts warehouse) with the idea of supplying auto replacement parts for the growing automobile industry. A year later, after buying another warehouse in El Paso, the company adopted the name Gulf+Western Industries.

By 1965 Gulf+Western had 27 regional warehouses and had reached $182 million in sales. Within the next 3 years the company acquired such companies as New Jersey Zinc, South Puerto Rico Sugar, E. W. Bliss (industrial products), Consolidated Cigar, Universal American (industrial equipment), Brown Company (paper and building products), and Associates Investment (auto loans). In 1966 Gulf+Western bought struggling Paramount Pictures because Bluhdorn saw an opportunity to turn it around.

Paramount had started in 1912 when Adolph Zukor bought the US rights to a French film starring Sarah Bernhardt. Zukor's company became Paramount Pictures after merging with a company formed by Jesse L. Lasky, Samuel Goldwyn, and Cecil B. DeMille. In the 1940s the government forced Paramount to divest its theater holdings. All efforts to fight the emerging television industry failed to keep movie attendance from slipping in the 1950s. Gulf+Western bought Simon & Schuster in 1975 and Madison Square Garden in 1977. Bluhdorn died in 1983 and his successor, Martin Davis, sold every business except Associates Investment, Paramount, and Simon & Schuster. In 1984 the company bought publisher Prentice-Hall (absorbed by Simon & Schuster, 1991).

The company developed its motion picture, television, and home video production business in the 1980s. In 1989 it sold Associates Investment to Ford for $3.35 billion and changed the company name to Paramount Communications. In the same year the company made an unsuccessful $200-per-share bid for Time.

Paramount bought computer-based learning systems company Computer Curriculum Corp. and a controlling interest in TV station operator TVX in 1990.

RANKINGS

28th in *Fortune* 100 Diversified Service Cos.
137th in *Business Week* 1000

KEY COMPETITORS

Advance Publications	Matsushita	Time Warner
Bertelsmann	Maxwell	Turner Broadcasting
Blockbuster	McGraw-Hill	Viacom
Boston Celtics	Metromedia	Walt Disney
CBS	News Corp.	Other entertainment
General Cinema	Pearson	and publishing
Hachette	Sony	companies
Hearst	TCI	

HOW MUCH

	9-Year Growth	1981	1982	1983	1984	1985	1986	1987	1988	1989	1990
Sales ($ mil.)	(4.2%)	5,702	5,331	3,993	4,182	1,677	2,094	2,904	3,056	3,392	3,869
Net income ($ mil.)	(1.3%)	291	199	260	263	130	229	356	385	12	259
Income as % of sales	—	5.1%	3.7%	6.5%	6.3%	7.7%	10.9%	12.3%	12.6%	0.3%	6.7%
Earnings per share ($)	2.5%	1.74	1.22	1.63	1.80	0.92	1.83	2.88	3.21	0.09	2.16
Stock price – high ($)	—	11.06	9.38	15.75	17.50	25.44	36.25	46.75	45.75	66.38	52.88
Stock price – low ($)	—	7.00	5.63	8.00	12.56	13.88	23.88	29.81	34.06	39.50	31.50
Stock price – close ($)	20.0%	7.94	8.38	15.06	14.19	24.88	31.69	35.56	40.63	50.50	40.88
P/E – high	—	6	8	10	10	28	20	16	14	738	24
P/E – low	—	4	5	5	7	15	13	10	11	439	15
Dividends per share ($)	7.2%	0.38	0.38	0.38	0.45	0.45	0.45	0.56	0.68	0.70	0.70
Book value per share ($)	9.5%	14.35	14.67	12.26	13.11	14.57	15.42	17.52	19.50	30.98	32.63

1990 Year-end:
Debt ratio: 15.7%
Return on equity: 6.8%
Cash (mil.): $1,666
Current ratio: 2.64
Long-term debt (mil.): $712
No. of shares (mil.): 117
Dividends:
  1990 average yield: 1.7%
  1990 payout: 32.4%
Market value (mil.): $4,797

Stock Price History High/Low 1981–90

J. C. PENNEY COMPANY, INC.

OVERVIEW

J. C. Penney, the largest clothing retailer in the US, operates more than 2,400 JCPenney department stores, catalog stores, and drugstores (Thrift Drug and Treasury Drug) throughout all 50 states and Puerto Rico. The $17.4 billion company has changed its historical image as a discount dime store and targeted upper-middle-class consumers by adding brand-name soft goods and dropping hard goods from the in-store product mix. The store has also remodeled 15 million square feet of floor space.

The JCPenney catalogs, which produced 18% of 1990 sales, still carry hard goods. Penney is the nation's 2nd largest catalog retailer and also the fastest, with 90% of orders reaching the customer within 2 days.

Penney has based its changes on extensive research, including customer surveys via satellite television. Noting that women make over 70% of the purchases in JCPenney stores, the company has formed a group to enhance the role of women in management and has strongly emphasized quality.

Penney also operates an insurance company and issues major credit cards through its JCPenney National Bank. In addition, it sells its telemarketing and credit processing services to other companies.

WHEN

In 1902 James C. Penney (1875–1971) and 2 former employers opened The Golden Rule, a dry goods store, in Kemmerer, Wyoming. Buying out his partners (1907), Penney opened stores in small communities and sold high-demand soft goods. He based customer service policy on his Baptist heritage, holding employees, called "associates," to a high moral code. Managers, usually former salesclerks, were offered 1/3 partnerships in the stores.

The company incorporated in Utah (1913) as the J. C. Penney Company, with headquarters in Salt Lake City, but moved to New York City (1914) to aid buying and financial operations. During the 1920s the company expanded to nearly 1,400 stores and publicly offered stock in 1929. By 1951 sales had surpassed $1 billion in more than 1,600 stores. A company study of consumer trends led the chain to introduce credit plans (1958; in all stores, 1962) and hard goods (1963; appliances, furniture, and automotive products).

Through the purchase of General Merchandise Company (1962, Milwaukee, mail order catalog and Treasure Island discount stores, renamed The Treasury; sold 1981), the company established a catalog service (1963). JCPenney Insurance started from companies bought in the mid-1960s. The company bought Thrift Drug in 1969 and in the 1970s operated food stores and expanded overseas, buying Sarma, a retail and supermarket chain in Belgium (1968, sold 1987).

The company bought First National Bank (Harrington, Delaware; 1983), renamed JCPenney National Bank (1984), to issue MasterCard and VISA cards. In the 1980s Penney discontinued automotive services and hard goods in stores and closed many downtown locations or moved them to suburban malls. Stores were classified as metropolitan or geographic (outside metropolitan areas).

The company entered the cable television shopping market (1987) through Telaction, an interactive home shopping program (discontinued in 1989). Penney also established a joint venture with Shop Television Network (1987; purchased and renamed JCPenney Television Network, 1989; sold 1991). In 1988 JCPenney Telemarketing was started to take catalog phone orders and provide telemarketing services for other companies; the network is the largest privately owned telemarketing system in the US.

To cut expenses the company sold its 45-story headquarters in New York City for $350 million and moved to Dallas (1988).

HOW MUCH

	9-Year Growth	1981	1982	1983	1984	1985	1986	1987	1988	1989	1990
Sales ($ mil.)	4.0%	12,271	11,942	12,647	14,038	14,418	15,443	16,008	15,938	17,045	17,410
Net income ($ mil.)	4.5%	387	430	467	435	397	530	608	807	802	577
Income as % of sales	—	3.2%	3.6%	3.7%	3.1%	2.8%	3.4%	3.8%	5.1%	4.7%	3.3%
Earnings per share ($)	5.2%	2.75	2.94	3.13	2.91	2.66	3.53	4.11	5.92	5.86	4.33
Stock price – high ($)	—	18.25	29.00	33.94	28.56	28.88	44.19	66.00	55.75	73.25	75.63
Stock price – low ($)	—	10.75	13.63	20.88	23.00	22.31	26.31	35.63	38.00	50.38	37.38
Stock price – close ($)	13.4%	14.31	24.19	28.31	23.19	27.75	36.13	43.38	50.63	72.75	44.25
P/E – high	—	7	10	11	10	11	13	16	9	13	17
P/E – low	—	4	5	7	8	8	7	9	6	9	9
Dividends per share ($)	12.9%	0.92	1.00	1.08	1.18	1.18	1.24	1.48	2.00	2.24	2.74
Book value per share ($)	5.0%	20.41	21.97	23.97	25.63	27.16	29.00	30.15	26.47	30.32	31.72

1990 Year-end:
Debt ratio: 41.6%
Return on equity: 14.0%
Cash (mil.): $137
Current ratio: 2.55
Long-term debt (mil.): $3,135
No. of shares (mil.): 117
Dividends:
  1990 average yield: 6.2%
  1990 payout: 63.3%
Market value (mil.): $5,158

Stock Price History High/Low 1981–90

NYSE symbol: JCP
Fiscal year ends: Last Saturday in January

Hoover's Rating C+

WHO

Chairman and CEO: William R. Howell, age 55, $1,323,981 pay
VC; COO, JCPenney Stores and Catalog Division: Robert B. Gill, age 59, $884,194 pay
EVP; Director, JCPenney Stores: James E. Oesterreicher, age 49
EVP and CFO: Robert E. Northam, age 60, $517,130 pay
EVP; Director, Corporate Personnel and Administration: Richard T. Erickson, age 59, $380,875 pay
President, Catalog Division: Rodney M. Birkins, age 60
Auditors: KPMG Peat Marwick
Employees: 196,000

WHERE

HQ: 14841 N. Dallas Pkwy., Dallas, TX 75240-6760
Phone: 214-591-1000
Fax: 214-591-1315

J. C. Penney operates 1,312 JCPenney retail stores, 487 Thrift and Treasury drugstores, 626 free-standing catalog sales centers, and 6 catalog distribution centers throughout the US.

WHAT

	1990 Sales	
	$ mil.	% of total
Stores & catalogs	15,268	88
Drugstores	1,097	6
Finance charges	674	4
Other	371	2
Total	**17,410**	**100**

	No. of Stores	% of Total
Metropolitan market stores	697	29
Geographic market stores (outside large metropolitan areas)	615	25
Drugstores	487	20
Catalog stores	626	26
Total	**2,425**	**100**

Subsidiaries and Operations
J. C. Penney Funding Corp.
JCPenney Insurance (life, health, and credit insurance)
JCPenney National Bank (VISA and MasterCard)
JCP Realty, Inc. (shopping center ventures)
Thrift Drug
Treasury Drug

RANKINGS

6th in *Fortune* 50 Retailing Cos.
95th in *Business Week* 1000

KEY COMPETITORS

Carter Hawley Hale	May
Circuit City	Mercantile Stores
Dayton Hudson	Montgomery Ward
Dillard	Nordstrom
Fred Meyer	Sears
General Cinema	Discount and specialty retailers
Macy	Drugstore chains

PENNZOIL COMPANY

NYSE symbol: PZL
Fiscal year ends: December 31

Hoover's Rating **C-**

OVERVIEW

Pennzoil, best known for its yellow-packaged motor oil, is the 19th largest US oil company, an umbrella for 4 wholly owned subsidiaries in the petroleum and minerals businesses.

Pennzoil Exploration and Production (PEPCO) searches for oil in more than 14 states, the Gulf of Mexico, Canada, the UK North Sea, Papua New Guinea, and Indonesia.

Pennzoil Products manufactures the nation's best-selling motor oil, with about 20% of the market. Golfer Arnold Palmer is the longtime spokesman in the company's commercials. The company sells Pennzoil-brand gasoline in 450 outlets in 8 states.

Pennzoil Sulphur extracts sulphur in far West Texas. Richland Development oversees real estate and mineral rights, including a Borneo gold and silver deposit.

Pennzoil is buying the last piece (17.6%) of Jiffy Lube International, the largest franchiser of quick-lube operations, to make it a wholly owned subsidiary. Pennzoil has decided to keep Purolator (auto products) after changing management and restoring profitability.

WHEN

The post-WWII oil boom in West Texas attracted brothers J. Hugh and Bill Liedtke and a Connecticut scion named George Bush. Anxious to make their fortunes, they formed Zapata Petroleum. Zapata hit big, with more than 120 producing wells in the Jameson Field in Coke County.

Zapata expanded with a subsidiary that drilled in the Gulf of Mexico. In 1959 Bush bought out the subsidiary and moved to Houston, where he later embarked on a political career that continues in the White House. The Liedtkes set their sights on South Penn Oil of Oil City, Pennsylvania — a rusty relic from the 1911 dissolution of Standard Oil. Enlisting the support of oilman J. Paul Getty, the Liedtkes took control of South Penn in 1963, merged it with Zapata, renamed it Pennzoil in honor of the lubricant it sold, and moved the headquarters to Houston.

In 1965 J. Hugh Liedtke engineered the historic takeover of Shreveport-based United Gas Pipeline, 5 times the size of Pennzoil. Though blessed with a large pipeline system and vast mineral interests, United Gas was hampered by lethargic management.

Using a takeover tactic that would break ground for a generation of corporate raiding, Liedtke launched a hostile cash tender offer. Pennzoil invited United Gas shareholders to sell their shares at a price higher than the market price.

Shareholders tendered 5 times the number of shares that Pennzoil wanted to buy. Undaunted, the Liedtkes raised the additional funds to buy 42% of United Gas stock. Pennzoil spun off a scaled-down United in 1974.

In the late 1960s Pennzoil pioneered financing of oil exploration with the use of subsidiaries (with colorful acronyms like POGO and PLATO) that raised money for speculative drilling by selling stock directly to the public. Shareholders in the subsidiaries were given some security with rights to Pennzoil stock if the risky drilling proved unsuccessful.

In 1983 J. Hugh Liedtke hoped to purchase Getty Oil, the company begun by his old benefactor, and thought he had a deal. Texaco bought Getty instead. Pennzoil sued, and in 1985 a Texas jury awarded a record $10.53 billion in damages. Texaco sought refuge in bankruptcy court, emerging only after settling with Pennzoil for $3 billion.

Liedtke stepped down as CEO in 1988 but remained chairman as Pennzoil determined how to spend its booty. In 1989 Pennzoil spent $2.1 billion for 8.8% of Chevron, but Liedtke denied that his company had a takeover in mind. With Liedtke's swashbuckling history at Pennzoil, Chevron wasn't convinced and filed suit in 1989 to keep him at bay. Much of the suit was dismissed in 1990, and by year's end Pennzoil had increased its stake to 9.4%, just under Chevron's poison pill threshold.

WHO

Chairman: J. Hugh Liedtke, age 69
President and CEO: James L. Pate, age 55, $660,900 pay
Group VP, Oil and Gas: William H. Schell, age 64, $400,100 pay
Group VP, Sulphur: John Davis
SVP Finance and Treasurer: David P. Alderson II, age 41
VP Human Resources: Harry C. Mitchell
Auditors: Arthur Andersen & Co.
Employees: 11,600

WHERE

HQ: Pennzoil Place, PO Box 2967, Houston, TX 77252-2967
Phone: 713-546-4000
Fax: 713-546-7591

Exploration and Production: Drilling in 13 states and offshore, and in 4 foreign countries.

Products: 3 refineries — Oil City, PA; Shreveport, LA; and Roosevelt, UT. Pennzoil motor oil sold internationally.

Sulphur: Mining in Culberson County, TX; processing in Galveston, TX; and in Antwerp, Belgium.

Richland Development: Acreage in Colorado and New Mexico; gold and silver deposits in Borneo.

WHAT

	1990 Sales		1990 Operating Income	
	$ mil.	% of total	$ mil.	% of total
Oil & gas	332	14	122	31
Automotive prods.	1,536	65	62	15
Sulphur	239	10	60	15
Franchise ops.	108	5	3	1
Other	152	6	149	38
Adjustments	(187)	—	(235)	—
Total	**2,180**	**100**	**161**	**100**

Brand Names
Gumout carburetor cleaner and automotive products
Jiffy Lube quick lubrication shops
Pennzoil gasoline (East Coast and upper Midwest)
Pennzoil motor oils, lubricants
Purolator filters and related products
Wolf's Head lubricants and related products

RANKINGS

190th in *Fortune* 500 Industrial Cos.
228th in *Business Week* 1000

KEY COMPETITORS

Amoco	Occidental
Ashland	Oryx
Atlantic Richfield	Petrofina
British Petroleum	Petrobrás
Broken Hill	PDVSA
Chevron	Pemex
Coastal	Pennzoil
Du Pont	Phillips Petroleum
Elf Aquitaine	Royal Dutch/Shell
Exxon	Sun
Koch	Texaco
Mobil	Unocal
Norsk Hydro	USX

HOW MUCH

	9-Year Growth	1981	1982	1983	1984	1985	1986	1987	1988	1989	1990
Sales ($ mil.)	(2.3%)	2,682	2,269	2,317	2,349	2,239	1,908	1,809	2,124	1,985	2,180
Net income ($ mil.)	(9.1%)	222	189	164	214	188	69	46	(187)	236	94
Income as % of sales	—	8.3%	8.3%	7.1%	9.1%	8.4%	3.6%	2.5%	(8.8%)	11.9%	4.3%
Earnings per share ($)	(6.2%)	4.23	3.60	3.03	3.89	3.96	1.28	0.72	(5.22)	6.06	2.37
Stock price – high ($)	—	58.25	50.25	42.50	45.38	72.00	91.00	95.00	79.13	88.88	89.50
Stock price – low ($)	—	35.25	23.63	31.25	30.75	40.50	48.13	38.50	65.25	71.63	61.75
Stock price – close ($)	3.6%	48.00	35.13	34.00	44.50	64.00	67.00	71.00	71.75	88.63	66.00
P/E – high	—	14	14	14	12	18	71	132	—	15	38
P/E – low	—	8	7	10	8	10	38	53	—	12	26
Dividends per share ($)	3.5%	2.20	2.20	2.20	2.20	2.20	2.20	2.20	2.60	3.00	3.00
Book value per share ($)	4.2%	21.55	22.99	23.88	21.38	18.23	16.79	7.67	35.67	35.23	31.10

1990 Year-end:
Debt ratio: 64.5%
Return on equity: 7.1%
Cash (mil.): $266
Current ratio: 1.18
Long-term debt (mil.): $2,275
No. of shares (mil.): 40
Dividends:
 1990 average yield: 4.5%
 1990 payout: 126.6%
Market value (mil.): $2,656

Stock Price History High/Low 1981–90

PEPSICO, INC.

OVERVIEW

Headquartered in Purchase, New York, PepsiCo is a major force in 3 different markets: soft drinks, fast-food restaurants, and snack foods. The company's respected and internationally known products generate annual retail sales of $44 billion. Eight of the company's brands generate $1 billion or more each in annual retail sales.

PepsiCo's soft drink segment, which boasts such names as Pepsi, Diet Pepsi, Mountain Dew, and Slice, commands approximately 33% of the US market and 15% of the international market.

PepsiCo's restaurant segment has more units (14,921 in the US alone) than any other restaurant system in the world. The segment consists of Pizza Hut (the world's #1 pizza chain), KFC (the world's #1 chicken chain), and Taco Bell (the #1 US Mexican-food chain).

PepsiCo's very profitable snack food segment (Frito-Lay) accounts for almost 13% of the total US snack market, with such dominant names as Fritos, Lay's, Ruffles, and Doritos. Its hefty brands account for 8 of the top 10 US snack chips.

Internationally, where the company lags behind archrival Coca-Cola, PepsiCo has increased its presence everywhere from Eastern Europe to Mexico, where its 1990 purchase of almost 80% of Empresas Gamesa, Mexico's #1 cookie maker, makes PepsiCo that country's largest consumer products company.

WHEN

In New Bern, North Carolina, pharmacist Caleb D. Bradham invented Pepsi in 1898. Bradham named his new drink Pepsi-Cola (he claimed it cured dyspepsia) and registered his trademark in 1903.

Following Coca-Cola's example, Bradham developed a system of bottling franchises. By WWI 300 bottlers had signed agreements with Pepsi-Cola. After the war Bradham stockpiled sugar as a safeguard against rising costs. The price of sugar plunged in 1920, and Bradham was forced to sell the company in 1923.

Pepsi existed on the brink of ruin under various owners for the next decade, until the Loft candy company bought Pepsi in 1931. The company's fortunes took a turn for the better in 1934 when, in the midst of the Depression, it doubled the size of its bottles to 12 ounces without raising the 5¢ price. In 1939 Pepsi introduced the world's first radio jingle. In 1941 Loft merged with its Pepsi subsidiary and became the Pepsi-Cola Company.

Pepsi started to produce drinks in cans in 1948. Two years later former Coca-Cola executive Alfred N. Steele became president. Steele introduced the slogan "Be Sociable, Have a Pepsi" and in 1954 put his wife, actress Joan Crawford, to work as a Pepsi spokesperson.

Donald M. Kendall, who became president of Pepsi in 1963, persuaded Soviet premier Nikita Khrushchev to down a Pepsi for the cameras at the Moscow Trade Fair and turned Pepsi's attention to young people ("The Pepsi Generation").

In 1965 Pepsi acquired Frito-Lay and became PepsiCo. Dallas-based Frito-Lay was created when Elmer Doolin (who had discovered Fritos at a cafe near the Mexican border in 1932) and Herman Lay (HW Lay & Company) joined efforts in 1960.

During the early 1970s Kendall broke into the Soviet market by agreeing to distribute Stolichnaya vodka in the US in exchange for Pepsi in the USSR. With the purchase of Pizza Hut (1977), Taco Bell (1978), and Kentucky Fried Chicken (1986), PepsiCo built a system of over 18,000 restaurants, the world's largest group and a major new market for Pepsi-Cola.

When Coca-Cola changed its formula in 1985, Pepsi stepped up the competition with its longtime archrival, claiming victory in the cola wars.

In 1991 the company jumped into the burger business by purchasing Hot 'n Now, a 77-unit Midwestern drive-through chain.

HOW MUCH

	9-Year Growth	1981	1982	1983	1984	1985	1986	1987	1988	1989	1990
Sales ($ mil.)	10.9%	7,027	7,499	7,896	7,699	8,057	9,291	11,485	13,007	15,242	17,803
Net income ($ mil.)	14.1%	333	224	284	207	420	458	605	762	901	1,091
Income as % of sales	—	4.7%	3.0%	3.6%	2.7%	5.2%	4.9%	5.3%	5.9%	5.9%	6.1%
Earnings per share ($)	14.7%	0.40	0.27	0.33	0.24	0.50	0.58	0.77	0.96	1.13	1.37
Stock price – high ($)	—	4.36	5.56	4.47	5.08	8.38	11.88	14.08	14.54	21.96	27.88
Stock price – low ($)	—	3.00	3.46	3.63	3.83	4.51	7.33	8.50	10.00	12.58	18.00
Stock price – close ($)	23.0%	4.04	3.97	4.25	4.76	8.08	8.67	11.13	13.17	21.33	26.00
P/E – high	—	11	21	13	21	17	20	18	15	19	20
P/E – low	—	8	13	11	16	9	13	11	10	11	13
Dividends per share ($)	10.4%	0.16	0.18	0.18	0.19	0.20	0.21	0.22	0.27	0.32	0.38
Book value per share ($)	13.5%	1.99	1.96	2.13	2.19	2.33	2.64	3.21	4.01	4.92	6.22

1990 Year-end:
Debt ratio: 54.6%
Return on equity: 24.6%
Cash (mil.): $1,816
Current ratio: 0.86
Long-term debt (mil.): $5,900
No. of shares (mil.): 788
Dividends:
  1990 average yield: 1.5%
  1990 payout: 28.0%
Market value (mil.): $20,498

Stock Price History High/Low 1981–90

NYSE symbol: PEP
Fiscal year ends: Last Saturday in December

Hoover's Rating **B+**

WHO

Chairman and CEO: D. Wayne Calloway, age 55, $1,900,210 pay
Chairman, Frito-Lay, Inc.: Roger A. Enrico, age 46, $953,358 pay
EVP and CFO: Robert G. Dettmer, age 59, $686,711 pay
SVP Personnel: J. Roger King, age 50
Auditors: KPMG Peat Marwick
Employees: 308,000

WHERE

HQ: Purchase, NY 10577
Phone: 914-253-2000
Fax: 914-253-2070

PespiCo's soft drinks are sold worldwide.

	1990 Sales		1990 Operating Income	
	$ mil.	% of total	$ mil.	% of total
US	14,047	79	1,853	83
Europe	1,345	8	109	5
Canada, Mexico	1,089	6	164	7
Other countries	1,322	7	98	5
Total	**17,803**	**100**	**2,224**	**100**

WHAT

	1990 Sales		1990 Operating Income	
	$ mil.	% of total	$ mil.	% of total
Soft drinks	6,523	37	768	35
Snack foods	5,054	28	934	42
Pizza Hut	2,950	17	246	11
Taco Bell	1,746	10	149	6
KFC	1,530	8	127	6
Total	**17,803**	**100**	**2,224**	**100**

				Restaurants
	Owned	Franchised	JV	Total
Pizza Hut	3,952	3,810	278	8,040
Taco Bell	1,879	1,394	—	3,273
KFC	1,807	5,964	416	8,187
Total	**7,638**	**11,168**	**694**	**19,500**

Brand Names

Soft Drinks	Snack Foods	
Diet Mountain Dew	Chee•Tos	Smiths
Diet Mug	Doritos	Sun Chips
Diet Pepsi	Fritos	Tostitos
Diet Slice	Grandma's	Walkers
Miranda	Lay's	
Mountain Dew	Rold Gold	**Restaurants**
Mountain Dew Sport	Ruffles	Hot 'n Now
Mug	Sabritas	KFC
Pepsi-Cola	Santitas	Pizza Hut
7UP (outside US)	Smartfood	Taco Bell
Slice		

RANKINGS

23rd in *Fortune* 500 Industrial Cos.
15th in *Business Week* 1000

KEY COMPETITORS

Anheuser-Busch	Grand Metropolitan	Seagram
Borden	Imasco	Source Perrier
BSN	Mars	TLC Beatrice
Cadbury Schweppes	McDonald's	TW Holdings
Coca-Cola	Metromedia	Wendy's
Dr Pepper/7Up	Procter & Gamble	
General Mills	RJR Nabisco	

PETER KIEWIT SONS' INC.

OVERVIEW

Omaha-based Peter Kiewit Sons' is one of the largest heavy-construction contractors in the US. Since the death of the founder's son Peter Kiewit in 1979, the low-profile company has been owned by its employees.

Kiewit Construction, the company's original business, acts as general contractor on many projects, 73% of them for the public sector. Projects include roads, tunnels, dams, and water treatment plants.

Kiewit also mines coal, largely through 50% interests in Montana, Texas, and Wyoming mines. The company jointly owns Black Butte Coal Co. with Union Pacific.

Metropolitan Fiber Systems (80% owned by Kiewit) builds and operates digital telecommunications networks allowing central business district customers to bypass local Bell monopolies. Kiewit also owns an interest in a California geothermal energy developer.

CEO Walter Scott wants to focus Peter Kiewit on construction and has sold the Continental Can businesses purchased in 1984. The last Continental Can units, including the world's largest manufacturer of closures for food containers (White Cap) and a plastic container production business, were sold in 1991.

Private company
Fiscal year ends: Last Saturday in December

Hoover's Rating C+

WHO

Chairman, President, and CEO: Walter Scott, Jr., age 59, $871,250 pay
VC: Donald L. Sturm, age 59, $724,173 pay
VC: William L. Grewcock, age 65, $542,720 pay
VP and CFO: Robert E. Julian, age 51
VP Human Resources: J. Brad Chapman
Auditors: Coopers & Lybrand
Employees: 23,000

WHERE

HQ: 1000 Kiewit Plaza, Omaha, NE 68131
Phone: 402-342-2052
Fax: 402-271-2829

Kiewit Construction performs work in the US, Canada, and Denmark. Mining is carried out in Montana, Texas, and Wyoming.

	1990 Sales		1990 Operating Income	
	$ mil.	% of total	$ mil.	% of total
US	1,683	88	175	101
Canada	210	11	6	—
Other countries	24	1	(8)	(1)
Adjustments	—	—	(88)	—
Total	**1,917**	**100**	**85**	**100**

WHAT

	1990 Sales		1990 Operating Income	
	$ mil.	% of total	$ mil.	% of total
Construction	1,684	88	78	45
Coal mining	219	11	95	55
Other countries	14	1	—	—
Adjustments	—	—	(88)	—
Total	**1,917**	**100**	**85**	**100**

Subsidiaries

Kiewit Construction Group, Inc.
Buildings
Dams and reservoirs
Government facilities
Power
Residential
Sewer and waste disposal
Transportation
Water supply systems

Kiewit Mining Group, Inc.
Big Horn Mine (closed)
Black Butte Coal Co. (50%)
Decker Coal Co. (50%)
Rosebud Mine (closed)
Walnut Creek Mining Company (50%)

Kiewit Holdings Group, Inc.
California Energy Company (13.8%, geothermal energy development)
Metropolitan Fiber Systems, Inc. (80%, private, fiber-optic telecommunications networks)

WHEN

Peter Kiewit, the son of Dutch immigrants, founded a masonry business in 1884 in Omaha, Nebraska. By 1912 several of the founder's 6 children were working at the company, and the name was changed to Peter Kiewit & Sons. One of the sons, Peter, started working at the company as a bricklayer at 19. He went to Dartmouth for a year but grew bored and came back to work at the company full-time. He changed the company name to Peter Kiewit Sons' in honor of his father in 1931, after the rest of the family had left.

During the Depression, Peter Kiewit Sons' worked on huge public works projects initiated by the Roosevelt administration to put unemployed people back to work. In the 1940s the company focused on defense wartime emergency projects, including 1,500 buildings at Fort Lewis (built in 90 days) and the Martin Bomber Plant in Omaha (built in 6 months in 1941).

One of the company's most difficult projects was the construction of Thule Air Force Base in Greenland, above the Arctic Circle, where 5,000 men worked 12 hours a day and 7 days a week for more than 2 years beginning in 1951. During the 1950s and 1960s Kiewit took on bigger projects. The company was a contractor for the interstate highway system and in 1952 was awarded the largest contract ever in the US, a $1.2 billion gas diffusion plant in Portsmouth, Ohio.

In the 1970s the company faced charges of overruns and bid-rigging and was fined $5 million for rigging bids on Army Corps of Engineers projects in 1970 and 1976.

Peter Kiewit died in 1979, leaving instructions that the company, which was already largely employee-owned, should remain under employee control and that no one employee could own more than 10% of the company. Kiewit's stock, when contributed back to the company, increased the value of all the other employees' holdings, making many of them millionaires.

Under Walter Scott, who became chairman, president, and CEO in 1979, Peter Kiewit has continued to grow. In 1984 British takeover artist Sir James Goldsmith made a bid for the Continental Group, a diversified company that made cans and boxes, ran timber operations, and owned gas and oil operations. Peter Kiewit Sons' intervened to purchase the company with the help of developer David Murdoch, whom Kiewit later bought out.

In 1990 Kiewit decided to dispose of many of Continental's packaging operations, including its US and Canadian food and beverage metal can divisions, sold to Crown Cork & Seal. In the same year Kiewit agreed to pay $415 million to settle a lawsuit alleging that the company used a secret computer program to identify and selectively lay off workers just before they fulfilled time-in-service requirements to qualify for pensions.

In 1991 Kiewit bought 13.8% of geothermal energy developer California Energy and agreed to sell Continental Can Europe, Kiewit's remaining packaging operations, to Viag, a German firm. A 1990 deal to sell the European unit to Ball Corporation had foundered on financing problems.

RANKINGS

21st in *Forbes* 400 US Private Cos.

KEY COMPETITORS

Bechtel	Halliburton
Dresser	Rolls-Royce
Fluor	Other coal mining companies

HOW MUCH

	6-Year Growth	1981	1982	1983	1984	1985	1986	1987	1988	1989	1990
Sales ($ mil.)	(0.1%)	—	—	—	1,926	4,377	4,661	4,682	4,820	5,058	1,917
Net income ($ mil.)	(4.6%)	—	—	—	143	101	156	124	240	140	108
Income as % of sales	—	—	—	—	7.4%	2.3%	3.3%	2.6%	5.0%	2.8%	5.6%
Employees	—	—	—	—	—	—	33,300	32,000	28,000	28,000	23,000

1990 Year-end:
Debt ratio: 18.5%
Return on equity: 9.6%
Cash (mil.): $679
Current ratio: 1.65
Long-term debt (mil.): $269

Net Income ($ mil.) 1984–90

PFIZER INC.

OVERVIEW

New York City–based Pfizer is a major drug producer with additional operations in medical products (heart valves, catheters, and blood oxygenators), veterinary drugs, specialty chemicals (such as the bulking agent polydextrose, used in dietetic foods), consumer products (Visine, Ben Gay), and specialty minerals (primarily for the iron, glass, steel, and paper industries).

Although not noted in the past for new product introduction, Pfizer has recently unleashed a plethora of new drugs, which contributed 30% of pharmaceutical sales in 1990. New company powerhouses include Diflucan (the #1 global antifungal drug), Norvask (for hypertension), and Procardia XL (a longer-acting version of Procardia, the most widely prescribed cardiovascular medicine in the US).

Pfizer hopes to sustain its growth by increasing R&D spending from its current 10% of sales to about 12% by 1995. Future drugs include the antidepressant Zoloft, the antihistamine Reactine, and the antibiotic Zithromax.

NYSE symbol: PFE
Fiscal year ends: December 31

Hoover's Rating **A**

WHEN

Charles Pfizer and his cousin, confectioner Charles Erhart, started to manufacture chemicals in Brooklyn in 1849. For the next 90 years Pfizer's products included camphor, citric acid (business sold in 1990), and santonin (an early antiparasitic). The company was incorporated in 1900 as Chas. Pfizer & Co. Pfizer was propelled into the modern drug business when the company was asked in 1941 to adapt its fermentation technology to mass-produce penicillin for the war effort.

After WWII Pfizer continued to make penicillin as well as streptomycin, most of which it sold to other pharmaceutical houses. Pfizer researchers discovered Terramycin, which the company introduced in 1950 and sold through a small but aggressive sales force. The sales campaign also relied upon expensive ads in medical journals.

Pfizer bought the drug firm Roerig in 1953, its first major acquisition. In the early 1950s the company opened its first overseas branches (Canada, Mexico, Cuba, the UK, and Belgium) and began manufacturing in Europe, Japan, and South America. By the mid-1960s Pfizer had worldwide sales of over $200 million in 100 countries.

Beginning in the late 1950s, Pfizer made Salk and Sabin polio vaccines and began adding new pharmaceuticals, including Diabinese (antidiabetic, 1958) and Vibramycin (antibiotic, 1967). Pfizer acquired 14 other companies in the early 1960s, including makers of specialty metals, consumer products (Ben-Gay, Desitin), and cosmetics (Coty). The company bought its first hospital products company, Howmedica, in 1972 and heart-valve maker Shiley in 1979. Failures of Shiley valves have subjected Pfizer to continuing lawsuits.

Growth slowed during the 1970s, although sales had reached $2 billion by 1977. A new chairman, Edmund Pratt, increased R&D expenditures, resulting in the development of several new drugs, including Minipress (antihypertensive, 1975), Feldene (arthritis pain reliever, 1982), and Glucotrol (antidiabetic, 1984). Licensing agreements with foreign drug companies allowed Pfizer to sell Procardia (for angina and hypertension, developed by Bayer in Germany) and Cefobid (antibiotic, from Japan). In the 1980s Pfizer expanded its hospital products division, buying 18 product lines or companies. The company bought Plax (mouthwash) in 1988 and in 1990 sold its citric acid business to Archer-Daniels-Midland. That same year Pfizer acquired the license to market the anti-cancer drug D-99, being developed by the Liposome Company.

In 1991 Pfizer established a joint venture with Hungarian drug company Biogal to market and distribute drugs in Europe.

WHO

Chairman: Edmund T. Pratt, Jr., age 64, $1,573,200 pay
President and CEO: William C. Steere, Jr., age 54, $716,413 pay (prior to promotion)
VP Finance: Henry A. McKinnell, age 48
VP Personnel: Bruce R. Ellig, age 54
Auditors: KPMG Peat Marwick
Employees: 42,500

WHERE

HQ: 235 E. 42nd St., New York, NY 10017
Phone: 212-573-2323
Fax: 212-573-7851

	1990 Sales		1990 Operating Income	
	$ mil.	% of total	$ mil.	% of total
US	3,473	54	736	66
Europe	1,503	23	252	22
Asia	873	14	61	5
Other countries	557	9	74	7
Adjustments	—	—	38	—
Total	**6,406**	**100**	**1,161**	**100**

WHAT

	1990 Sales		1990 Operating Income	
	$ mil.	% of total	$ mil.	% of total
Health care	4,336	68	952	82
Animal health	510	8	95	8
Specialty chemicals	548	9	29	2
Consumer products	668	10	45	4
Specialty minerals	344	5	40	4
Total	**6,406**	**100**	**1,161**	**100**

Selected Drugs
Cardura (cardiovascular)
Cefobid (antibiotic)
Diflucan (antifungal)
Feldene (antiarthritic)
Glucotrol (antidiabetic)
Minipress (antihypertensive)
Norvas (cardiovascular)
Procardia XL (cardiovascular)
Unasyn (antibiotic)

Infusaid
Schneider
Shiley
Valleylab

Consumer Products
Barbasol
Ben-Gay
Coty
Desitin
Plax
Unisom
Visine

Medical Devices
American Medical Systems
Deknatel
Howmedica

RANKINGS

73rd in *Fortune* 500 Industrial Cos.
28th in *Business Week* 1000

KEY COMPETITORS

Abbott Labs
American Cyanamid
American Home Products
Amgen
Amway
Avon
C. R. Bard
Baxter
Bayer
Becton, Dickinson
Bristol-Myers Squibb
Ciba-Geigy
Colgate-Palmolive
Dow Chemical
Du Pont
Eastman Kodak
Eli Lilly
Estée Lauder

Glaxo
Hoechst
Johnson & Johnson
L'Oréal
LVMH
MacAndrews & Forbes
Merck
Monsanto
Procter & Gamble
Rhône-Poulenc
Roche
Sandoz
Schering-Plough
SmithKline Beecham
Syntex
Unilever
Upjohn
Warner-Lambert

HOW MUCH

	9-Year Growth	1981	1982	1983	1984	1985	1986	1987	1988	1989	1990
Sales ($ mil.)	7.8%	3,250	3,454	3,750	3,855	4,025	4,476	4,920	5,385	5,672	6,406
Net income ($ mil.)	12.7%	274	333	447	508	580	660	690	690	681	801
Income as % of sales	—	8.4%	9.6%	11.9%	13.2%	14.4%	14.7%	14.0%	14.7%	12.0%	12.5%
Earnings per share ($)	11.5%	0.89	1.06	1.36	1.54	1.72	1.95	2.04	2.35	2.02	2.39
Stock price – high ($)	—	13.72	20.16	22.38	21.19	28.13	36.44	38.50	30.13	37.88	40.88
Stock price – low ($)	—	10.00	12.47	16.78	14.69	18.81	23.13	20.63	23.69	27.00	27.25
Stock price – close ($)	13.1%	13.31	17.22	17.88	21.13	25.31	30.50	23.31	29.00	34.75	40.38
P/E – high	—	15	19	16	14	16	19	19	13	19	17
P/E – low	—	11	12	12	10	11	12	10	10	13	11
Dividends per share ($)	13.0%	0.40	0.46	0.58	0.66	0.74	0.82	0.90	1.00	1.10	1.20
Book value per share ($)	11.8%	5.66	6.41	6.83	7.73	8.93	10.35	11.80	13.00	13.72	15.42

1990 Year-end:
Debt ratio: 3.7%
Return on equity: 16.4%
Cash (mil.): $1,068
Current ratio: 1.42
Long-term debt (mil.): $193
No. of shares (mil.): 330
Dividends:
  1990 average yield: 3.0%
  1990 payout: 50.3%
Market value (mil.): $13,334

Stock Price History High/Low 1981–90

PHELPS DODGE CORPORATION

NYSE symbol: PD
Fiscal year ends: December 31

Hoover's Rating **B+**

OVERVIEW

Phoenix-based Phelps Dodge, the largest copper producer in North America (2nd largest worldwide after Chile's Codelco), reported a record production for the 6th year in a row of 1.1 billion pounds of copper in 1990. The company leads the world in the production of copper rod (used for electrical wire and cable) and is a major supplier of sulfuric acid, and copper in concentrate form. In addition, Phelps produces gold, silver, molybdenum, fluorspar, lead, and zinc from its mines in 23 countries.

During the past few years, the company has made an effort to reduce its production costs. In 1990 Phelps produced about 32% of its copper by the solvent extraction/electrowinning "SX/EW" process, which is substantially less expensive than the traditional mining techniques.

In the late 1980s Phelps added less cyclical businesses to its core mining business. Its resulting Industries segment includes Accuride, North America's largest steel rim and wheel manufacturer; Columbian Chemicals, the world's 2nd largest producer of carbon black (used to strengthen rubber); and Hudson Conductors, the world's leading specialty high-temperature conductors and alloys manufacturer.

WHO

Chairman and CEO: Douglas C. Yearley, age 55, $1,304,771 pay
President and COO: Leonard R. Judd, age 52, $1,062,394 pay
SVP and CFO: Thomas M. St. Clair, $418,684 pay
VP Human Resources: John C. Replogle
Auditors: Price Waterhouse
Employees: 14,066

WHERE

HQ: 2600 N. Central Ave., Phoenix, AZ 85004-3014
Phone: 602-234-8100
Fax: 602-234-8337

Phelps Dodge operates mines and manufacturing plants in 23 countries.

	1990 Sales	
	$ mil.	% of total
US	2,112	80
Foreign	524	20
Total	**2,636**	**100**

WHEN

In 1821 Anson Greene Phelps established a trading business between New York and England, exporting cotton and importing metals (particularly tin). In 1834 Phelps formed a partnership with sons-in-law William Dodge and Daniel James (James took charge of the England office), founding the firm Phelps Dodge & Company. In the 1830s Phelps Dodge invested in coal, iron, and timber in Pennsylvania. It established 2 metal manufacturing companies in Connecticut in the early 1840s: Ansonia Brass & Battery and Ansonia Manufacturing. Their products included the soft copper wire used for the first transcontinental telegraph (1861). Anson Phelps died in 1853.

Although principally an East Coast mercantile business, Phelps Dodge bought 2 copper mines near Bisbee, Arizona: the Atlanta (1881) and the Copper Queen (1885). The company expanded its mining operations into the northern Sonora region of Mexico (founding Moctezuma Copper, 1895), the Morenci area of eastern Arizona (purchasing Detroit Copper Mining, 1897), and the Dawson, New Mexico, area (buying coal miner Stag Canon Fuel).

In 1901 Phelps Dodge built a copper smelter near Bisbee, and the town of Douglas (named for a company geologist) grew up around the site. The company also built railroad connections to transport its copper, including the El Paso and Southwestern (1903). Copper mining was so successful that Phelps Dodge closed its original East Coast businesses in 1906.

In 1921 the company purchased Arizona Copper and in 1930 bought Nichols Copper, which had a modern refinery in El Paso. To increase its ore reserves, the company purchased Calumet & Arizona Mining (with properties in Bisbee and Ajo, Arizona, 1931) and mines in the Rio Verde Valley near Jerome, Arizona. In the 1950s the company expanded into other countries. In 1971 Phelps Dodge bought Western Nuclear (uranium mining) and a 40% share in Consolidated Aluminum.

After suffering losses due to a depressed metals market between 1982 and 1984, Phelps Dodge moved its headquarters from New York to Phoenix to reduce costs. The company also diversified, purchasing Columbian Chemicals (carbon black, 1986), Accuride (truck wheels and rims, 1988), and Hudson International Conductors (specialty wire and cable conductors, 1989). Primarily because of high copper prices and record copper production, Phelps Dodge reported record earnings in 1990 of $455 million on revenues of $2.6 billion.

WHAT

	1990 Sales		1990 Operating Income	
	$ mil.	% of total	$ mil.	% of total
Primary metal	1,448	55	590	81
Manufacturing & chemicals	1,188	45	139	19
Adjustments	—	—	(31)	—
Total	**2,636**	**100**	**698**	**100**

Phelps Dodge Mining Company
Copper mining, smelting, and refining
Copper rod production
Exploration for metals and minerals
Fluorspar, gold, silver, lead, zinc, and copper (from foreign mines)
Silver, gold, molybdenum, and sulfuric acid (as byproducts of copper operations)

Phelps Dodge Industries
Accuride Corp.
  Truck wheels and rims
Columbian Chemicals Company
  Carbon black
  Synthetic iron oxide
Hudson International Conductors
  Alloy, silver, nickel, and tin-plated copper conductors
Phelps Dodge International Corporation
  Interests in foreign wire and cable producers
Phelps Dodge Magnet Wire Company
  Copper and aluminum wire

RANKINGS

168th in *Fortune* 500 Industrial Cos.
279th in *Business Week* 1000

KEY COMPETITORS

ABB	Broken Hill
Alcoa	Cyprus Minerals
AMAX	FMC
Anglo American	RTZ
ASARCO	

HOW MUCH

	9-Year Growth	1981	1982	1983	1984	1985	1986	1987	1988	1989	1990
Sales ($ mil.)	7.0%	1,439	958	977	910	887	846	1,612	2,320	2,700	2,636
Net income ($ mil.)	25.6%	59	(74)	(64)	(207)	19	42	151	420	267	455
Income as % of sales	—	4.1%	(7.8%)	(6.5%)	(22.8%)	2.1%	4.9%	9.3%	18.1%	9.9%	17.3%
Earnings per share ($)	19.7%	2.61	(3.59)	(2.76)	(8.81)	0.21	1.06	4.17	11.28	7.46	13.12
Stock price – high ($)	—	48.50	34.00	34.00	27.88	24.00	32.50	56.00	53.75	78.63	71.63
Stock price – low ($)	—	31.13	18.25	22.50	12.88	13.50	16.00	20.63	32.50	51.38	46.13
Stock price – close ($)	6.0%	33.63	28.13	25.25	13.88	23.00	20.75	47.00	53.00	59.13	56.63
P/E – high	—	19	—	—	—	114	31	13	5	11	5
P/E – low	—	12	—	—	—	64	15	5	3	7	4
Dividends per share ($)	7.2%	1.60	0.30	0.00	0.00	0.00	0.00	0.15	0.95	12.85	3.00
Book value per share ($)	(0.3%)	50.09	44.94	39.81	29.16	28.78	30.36	35.37	47.10	39.00	48.86

1990 Year-end:
Debt ratio: 19.3%
Return on equity: 29.9%
Cash (mil.): $162
Current ratio: 1.71
Long-term debt (mil.): $404
No. of shares (mil.): 34
Dividends:
  1990 average yield: 5.3%
  1990 payout: 22.9%
Market value (mil.): $1,950

Stock Price History High/Low 1981–90

PHILIP MORRIS COMPANIES, INC.

NYSE symbol: MO
Fiscal year ends: December 31

OVERVIEW

Headquartered in New York City, Philip Morris is the largest consumer packaged-goods company in the world, controlling such dominant names as Kraft, General Foods, Oscar Mayer, and Miller Brewing. Its combined operations make Philip Morris the largest cigarette company in the world, the 2nd largest global beer company, and the largest US food company. Other operations include financial services and real estate.

Tobacco remains the company's primary business, with 41% of revenues and 68% of operating profit. Marlboro, the company's flagship brand, is the world's best-selling consumer packaged product.

Kraft General Foods produces a prolific line of packaged products and is the largest coffee and cheese processor and marketer in the US. Miller trails only Anheuser-Busch in world beer production and currently holds 22% of the US market. Miller Lite is the leading US low-calorie beer.

Philip Morris continues to increase its presence in the EC where it is #1 in tobacco and #3 in food. The company has recently followed its 1990 purchase of Swiss candymaker Jacobs Suchard with the acquisition of a German cigarette company and a joint venture with Hungarian coffeemaker BEV, among others.

WHO

Chairman and CEO: Michael A. Miles, age 51, $1,315,810 pay (prior to promotion)
President: John A. Murphy, age 61, $1,342,750 pay
SVP and CFO: Hans G. Storr, age 59
SVP Human Resources and Administration: John J. Tucker, age 50
Auditors: Coopers & Lybrand
Employees: 168,000

WHERE

HQ: 120 Park Ave., New York, NY 10017
Phone: 212-880-5000
Fax: 212-878-2165

	1990 Sales		1990 Operating Income	
	$ mil.	% of total	$ mil.	% of total
US	36,014	70	6,715	81
Europe	12,474	25	1,173	14
Other countries	2,681	5	394	5
Adjustments	(6,846)	—	(336)	—
Total	**44,323**	**100**	**7,946**	**100**

WHAT

	1990 Sales		1990 Operating Income	
	$ mil.	% of total	$ mil.	% of total
Beer	3,534	7	285	3
Tobacco	21,090	41	5,596	68
Food	26,085	51	2,205	27
Finance/real estate	460	1	196	2
Adjustments	(6,846)	—	(336)	—
Total	**44,323**	**100**	**7,946**	**100**

Philip Morris	Miracle Whip	Vegemite
Alpine	Parkay	**Oscar Mayer Foods**
Benson & Hedges	Philadelphia	Claussen
Cambridge	Sealtest	Louis Kemp
Chesterfield	Seven Seas	Louis Rich
Lark	Tombstone	Lunchables
Marlboro	Velveeta	Oscar Mayer
Merit		Zappetites
Parliament	**General Foods**	
Virginia Slims	Brim	**Miller**
	Country Time	Lite
Kraft	Dream Whip	Löwenbräu
Breakstone's	Entenmann's	Meister Bräu
Breyers	Jell-O	Miller Genuine Draft
Budget Gourmet	Kool-Aid	Milwaukee's Best
Bull's-Eye	Log Cabin	Sharp's
Cheez Whiz	Maxwell House	
Chiffon	Post	**Jacobs Suchard**
Cool Whip	Sanka	Milka
Cracker Barrel	Shake 'n Bake	Toblerone
Frusen Glädjé	Stove Top	
Light n' Lively	Tang	

WHEN

In 1847 Philip Morris opened a London tobacco store. By 1854 he was making his own cigarettes. When Morris died in 1873, the company passed to his brother and widow, who sold it to William Thomson just before the turn of the century. In 1902 Thomson introduced his company's cigarettes to the United States. American investors purchased the rights to the Philip Morris Cambridge, Oxford Blues, English Ovals, Marlboro, and Players brands in 1919 and 10 years later began manufacturing cigarettes in Richmond, Virginia.

When the original members of the old Tobacco Trust (broken up by the federal government in 1911) raised their prices in 1930, Philip Morris countered by introducing the Philip Morris economy brand cigarette. The success of the inexpensive cigarettes, popular with Depression-weary consumers, was further guaranteed by a popular ad campaign in 1933 featuring bellhop Johnny Roventini chanting the slogan, "Call for Philip Morris."

In 1954 Philip Morris acquired Benson & Hedges and its president Joseph Cullman III. Cullman, assigned to market the filtered Marlboro brand, enlisted the help of advertiser Leo Burnett, who created a simple red-and-white box, the slogan, "flavor, filter, fliptop box," and the hugely successful Marlboro Man. In 1968 the company introduced Virginia Slims, a cigarette designed for women. Under Cullman, Philip Morris experienced tremendous overseas expansion.

In 1970 Philip Morris purchased Miller Brewing Company (formed in 1855 by Frederic Miller), with aggressive marketing vaulting it from the #7 world position in beer to the #2 position by 1980.

In 1985 Philip Morris spent $5.6 billion to purchase food and coffee giant General Foods, which traces its origins to cereal developer C. W. Post. In 1925 Post's cereal company started a series of acquisitions that would become General Foods by 1929: Jell-O (1925), Birds Eye (frozen food, 1929), Kool-Aid (1953), and Oscar Mayer (meats, 1981), to name a few.

In 1988 Philip Morris spent $12.9 billion to purchase Kraft, which was created in 1930 when Thomas McInnerney's National Dairy Products bought Kraft-Phenix (formed in 1903 by cheese wholesaler James Kraft). With the 2 major acquisitions, Philip Morris is increasingly turning its attention to food. In 1991 Hamish Maxwell retired and Kraft executive Michael Miles became chairman, the first non-tobacco man to fill the post.

RANKINGS

7th in *Fortune* 500 Industrials Cos.
3rd in *Business Week* 1000

KEY COMPETITORS

Adolph Coors	Heineken	Quaker Oats
Allied-Lyons	Heinz	RJR Nabisco
American Brands	Hershey	Sara Lee
Anheuser-Busch	Imasco	Stroh
B.A.T	John Labatt	Unilever
Bond	Kellogg	Other food, beer, and
CPC	Nestlé	tobacco companies
General Mills	Procter & Gamble	

HOW MUCH

	9-Year Growth	1981	1982	1983	1984	1985	1986	1987	1988	1989	1990
Sales ($ mil.)	20.4%	8,307	9,102	9,466	10,138	12,149	20,681	22,279	25,860	39,011	44,323
Net income ($ mil.)	20.2%	676	782	904	889	1,255	1,478	1,842	2,064	2,946	3,540
Income as % of sales	—	8.1%	8.6%	9.5%	8.8%	10.3%	7.1%	8.3%	8.0%	7.6%	8.0%
Earnings per share ($)	21.2%	0.68	0.78	0.90	0.91	1.31	1.55	1.94	2.22	3.18	3.83
Stock price – high ($)	—	6.89	8.47	9.05	10.41	11.89	19.50	31.13	25.50	45.75	52.00
Stock price – low ($)	—	5.25	5.52	6.75	7.77	9.00	10.98	18.16	20.13	25.00	36.00
Stock price – close ($)	26.8%	6.09	7.50	8.97	10.08	11.05	17.97	21.34	25.47	41.63	51.75
P/E – high	—	10	11	10	12	9	13	16	12	14	14
P/E – low	—	8	7	8	9	7	7	9	9	8	9
Dividends per share ($)	22.5%	0.25	0.30	0.36	0.43	0.50	0.62	0.79	1.01	1.25	1.55
Book value per share ($)	16.4%	3.29	3.64	4.03	4.21	4.96	5.94	7.21	8.31	10.31	12.90

1990 Year-end:
Debt ratio: 57.4%
Return on equity: 33.0%
Cash (mil.): $146
Current ratio: —
Long-term debt (mil.): $16,108
No. of shares (mil.): 926
Dividends:
  1990 average yield: 3.0%
  1990 payout: 40.4%
Market value (mil.): $47,932

Stock Price History High/Low 1981–90

PHILLIPS PETROLEUM COMPANY

NYSE symbol: P
Fiscal year ends: December 31

Hoover's Rating: C+

OVERVIEW

Phillips Petroleum is the 9th largest integrated petroleum company in the US.

The company's Exploration and Production group produced an average of 218,300 barrels of crude oil, 154,000 barrels of natural gas liquids, and 1.3 billion cubic feet of natural gas each day in 1990.

Its Gas and Gas Liquids group owns interests in 44 US plants that remove gas liquids — ethane, propane, butanes, and pentanes — from natural gas for further processing. Phillips is the largest US producer of natural gas liquids.

Its Downstream group runs 3 US refineries and can use 80% of its refining capacity on high-sulfur crude. Its Phillips 66 banner flies over 9,300 service stations. Phillips is racing to rebuild its Chemicals segment's polyethylene capacity after a 1989 explosion at the company's Houston complex.

Phillips's emphasis on chemicals and plastics relies heavily on research. It holds 4,026 active US patents. The company accomplishes this from its headquarters in Bartlesville, Oklahoma, a city of 35,000 located 50 miles north of Tulsa.

WHEN

Frank Phillips was a prosperous Iowa barber who, after marrying a banker's daughter in 1897, turned to selling bonds. He met a Methodist missionary assigned to Indians in Oklahoma, and the missionary regaled him with stories of opportunities in the oil patch.

Phillips migrated to Bartlesville, Oklahoma, and established Anchor Oil (1903). Anchor's first 2 wells were dry holes, but the next one — the Anna Anderson No. 1 — began a string of 81 producing wells. Phillips and his brother, L. E., who doubled as bankers in Bartlesville, transformed Anchor into Phillips Petroleum (1917).

With continued success, particularly on Indian lands in Oklahoma, Phillips branched out to refining and marketing. In 1927 the company opened its first filling station in Wichita, Kansas. The Phillips 66 name for the company's gasoline was a salute to Route 66 (hence the highway-sign shape of the company's logo) and to the speed reached during a test drive using the gasoline.

Frank Phillips retired after WWII and was succeeded as chairman by William Keeler, a Cherokee called Tsula Westa Nehi (worker who doesn't sit down) by his tribesmen.

In 1951, 2 Phillips chemists stumbled onto a petrochemical compound. The chemical, eventually marketed as Marlex, became the building block for many modern plastic products. The hula hoop fad of the 1950s spurred demand for Marlex, saving the new substance from a rocky debut and earning a place for the toy in the Phillips president's office.

In the 1970s Phillips was rocked by disclosure of illegal campaign contributions. Settlement of the resulting stockholder-initiated suit required appointment of 6 new directors from outside the cloistered executive suite.

Phillips was besieged by corporate raiders T. Boone Pickens (1984) and Carl Icahn (1985) in separate takeover attempts. Phillips ran its debt up to $9 billion to repurchase stock and fend off the raiders. At one point it spent more on interest than it did on exploring for oil. The company beefed up the employee stock ownership plan, cut 8,300 employees from the payroll, and sold billions of dollars of assets.

Leaner after the takeover tries, the company saw its stock price and profits rebound but suffered another blow when its Houston Chemical Complex exploded and burned in 1989, killing 23 people and shutting down domestic polyethylene production.

In 1990 Phillips won rights to explore 700,000 acres of offshore Australia as it pressed to replace reserves in low-cost areas. Also the company began to consider sale of one of its 3 refineries, representing 8% of US capacity.

WHO

Chairman and CEO: C. J. Silas, age 58, $1,161,000 pay
President and COO: Glenn A. Cox, age 61, $812,500 pay
VP, Treasurer, and CFO: James J. Mulva, age 44
VP Human Resources and Services: Lavele L. Frantz, age 49
Auditors: Ernst & Young
Employees: 22,411

WHERE

HQ: Phillips Bldg., Bartlesville, OK 74004
Phone: 918-661-6600
Fax: 918-661-7636

Phillips owns properties for oil and gas exploration in Africa, Australia, the Norwegian North Sea, the Netherlands, New Guinea, Pakistan, the UK's North Sea, and the US.

	1990 Sales		1990 Operating Income	
	$ mil.	% of total	$ mil.	% of total
US	11,195	82	1,078	51
UK	1,020	8	141	7
Other Europe	796	6	660	31
Africa & other areas	592	4	220	11
Adjustments	—	—	(664)	
Total	**13,603**	**100**	**1,435**	**100**

WHAT

	1990 Sales		1990 Operating Income	
	$ mil.	% of total	$ mil.	% of total
Exploration & production	1,440	10	1,226	58
Gas & gas liquids	771	6	202	10
Petroleum prods.	9,253	68	220	11
Chemicals	2,120	16	448	21
Corporate	19	—	3	—
Adjustments	—	—	(664)	—
Total	**13,603**	**100**	**1,435**	**100**

Operating Groups
Exploration and Production
Gas and Gas Liquids
Downstream Operations (petroleum products and chemicals)

RANKINGS

27th in *Fortune* 500 Industrial Cos.
83rd in *Business Week* 1000

KEY COMPETITORS

Amoco	Norsk Hydro
Ashland	Occidental
Atlantic Richfield	Oryx
British Petroleum	Pennzoil
Broken Hill	Petrofina
Chevron	Petrobrás
Coastal	PDVSA
Dow Chemical	Phillips Petroleum
Du Pont	Royal Dutch/Shell
Elf Aquitaine	Sun
Exxon	Texaco
Imperial Oil	Unocal
Koch	USX
Mobil	Chemical companies

HOW MUCH

	9-Year Growth	1981	1982	1983	1984	1985	1986	1987	1988	1989	1990
Sales ($ mil.)	(1.8%)	15,966	15,698	15,249	15,537	15,636	9,786	10,721	11,304	12,384	13,603
Net income ($ mil.)	(5.3%)	879	646	721	810	596	234	35	650	219	541
Income as % of sales	—	5.5%	4.1%	4.7%	5.2%	3.8%	2.4%	0.3%	5.8%	1.8%	4.0%
Earnings per share ($)	1.4%	1.93	1.41	1.57	1.75	2.07	0.91	0.06	2.72	0.90	2.18
Stock price – high ($)	—	19.83	13.58	12.96	18.75	17.17	12.75	10.00	12.13	30.13	31.13
Stock price – low ($)	—	11.33	7.83	9.79	11.13	11.00	8.25	10.00	12.13	19.13	22.50
Stock price – close ($)	7.6%	13.50	10.88	11.50	14.92	12.13	11.75	14.00	19.50	25.25	26.13
P/E – high	—	10	10	8	11	8	14	313	8	33	14
P/E – low	—	6	6	6	6	5	9	167	4	21	10
Dividends per share ($)	3.8%	0.73	0.73	0.73	0.78	0.95	0.70	0.60	0.66	1.02	1.03
Book value per share ($)	(1.5%)	12.01	12.57	13.38	14.28	7.24	7.55	7.08	8.69	8.74	10.51

1990 Year-end:
Debt ratio: 58.5%
Return on equity: 22.6%
Cash (mil.): $670
Current ratio: 1.14
Long-term debt (mil.): $3,839
No. of shares (mil.): 259
Dividends:
  1990 average yield: 3.9%
  1990 payout: 47.2%
Market value (mil.): $6,759

Stock Price History High/Low 1981–90

PINNACLE WEST CAPITAL CORPORATION

NYSE symbol: PNW
Fiscal year ends: December 31

Hoover's Rating **D**

OVERVIEW

Pinnacle West, through its Arizona Public Service (APS) subsidiary, operates the largest electric utility in Arizona, providing electric service to about 1.7 million people in 11 of Arizona's 15 counties. APS generated about 94% of Pinnacle West's revenues in 1990.

SunCor, Pinnacle West's real estate development company, owns undeveloped properties in Tempe, northeast Phoenix, Glendale, and the Litchfield Park resort area. Through El Dorado, a venture capital firm, Pinnacle West has invested about $40 million in more than 60 companies.

Pinnacle West has moved decisively toward putting the failure of its former S&L unit (MeraBank) behind it. In 1990 the company repaid $265 million of debt and plans to eliminate another $355 million over the next 3 years. APS has adopted an aggressive cost-control program, which includes an early retirement program that should save the company about $50 million per year; construction expenditures have been cut by $770 million. If recovery measures are successful, Pinnacle West hopes to reinstitute its dividend in 1993.

WHO

Chairman, President, and CEO, Pinnacle West; Chairman, Arizona Public Service: Richard Snell, age 60, $468,846 pay
EVP and CFO: Henry B. Sargent, age 56, $389,647 pay
VP Corporate Planning and Development: Arlyn J. Larson, age 56, $135,176 pay
VP and Controller: Kevin S. Steele, age 35, $105,714 pay
VP Corporate Relations and Administration and Secretary: Faye Widenmann, age 42, $102,873 pay
Auditors: Deloitte & Touche
Employees: 7,800

WHEN

In 1906, 3 Phoenix businessmen organized the Pacific Gas & Electric Company (PG&E, no relationship to the California utility), which served the city's electric power needs until 1920 when Central Arizona Light & Power Company (Calapco) was formed to assume its operations. In 1924 Calapco became a subsidiary of American Power & Light and by 1926 had expanded westward to Buckeye. When Phoenix businessmen expressed interest in buying Calapco's stock, American Power & Light offered it to the public in 1945.

In 1949 Calapco expanded into northern Arizona by purchasing Northern Arizona Light & Power, which was founded as Prescott Gas & Electric in the late 1890s. In 1951 Calapco merged with Arizona Edison (formed in the 1920s by the consolidation of several central and south Arizona utilities) to form Arizona Public Service Company (APS).

In the 1950s, when Arizona began experiencing unprecedented population growth, the demand for power was greater than ever. Between 1955 and 1960, APS built 3 gas-fired plants, and then decided to develop coal as its major fuel. The Cholla Power Plant, completed in 1962, was the company's first coal-burning power station.

Under CEO Keith Turley, APS was reorganized as a subsidiary of AZP Group, a holding company, in 1985. This signaled the beginning

of a diversification plan, which included the purchase of a Phoenix-based S&L (MeraBank), an investment in real estate (Suncor), and the purchase of Mobil Oil's Wyoming uranium mines, all in 1986. AZP also invested $115 million in venture capital. In 1987 AZP adopted the name Pinnacle West Capital Corporation.

MeraBank bought 3 Texas S&Ls in 1988 to loosen Pinnacle West's financial dependence on Arizona, which was experiencing an economic downturn. Early in 1989 Pinnacle West had to cover about $100 million worth of bad real estate loans made by MeraBank. The thrift was taken over by federal regulators in January 1990. Pinnacle West was released from further obligation in the S&L's failure in March, after a $450 million capital infusion.

Turley, who had suspended dividends in 1989, retired in 1990 and was replaced by former Ramada executive Richard Snell. That year Pinnacle West sold its uranium mining firm (Malapai Resources) for $38 million in cash. In the meantime the company had rejected a series of takeover bids from PacifiCorp, an Oregon-based utility. In 1990 the 2 companies reached an agreement that included much-needed seasonal power sharing. In addition, PacifiCorp will buy Pinnacle West's Cholla 4 unit for $222 million; Pinnacle West plans to use the proceeds to reduce debt.

WHERE

HQ: 400 E. Van Buren St., Suite 700, Phoenix, AZ 85004
Phone: 602-379-2500
Fax: 602-379-2640

Major Generating Facilities

Coal
Cholla (Joseph City, AZ)
Four Corners, Units 1, 2, and 3 (near Farmington, NM)
Four Corners, Units 4 and 5 (15%, near Farmington, NM)
Navajo (14%, near Page, AZ)

Oil and Gas
Ocotillo (Tempe, AZ)
Yucca (near Yuma, AZ)

Nuclear
Palo Verde (29.1%, west of Phoenix, AZ)

WHAT

	1990 Sales	
	$ mil.	% of total
Electricity	1,508	94
Real estate	89	6
Total	**1,597**	**100**

Subsidiaries
Arizona Public Service Co.
El Dorado Investment Co.
SunCor Development Co.

	1990 Fuel Sources
	% of total
Coal	66
Natural gas	3
Nuclear	31
Total	**100**

RANKINGS

34th in *Fortune* 50 Utilities
550th in *Business Week* 1000

HOW MUCH

	9-Year Growth	1981	1982	1983	1984	1985	1986	1987	1988	1989	1990
Sales ($ mil.)	6.8%	882	1,064	1,074	995	1,175	1,250	1,313	1,442	1,508	1,597
Net income ($ mil.)	(7.2%)	197	231	265	298	324	273	301	38	157	101
Income as % of sales	—	22.4%	21.7%	24.7%	29.9%	27.6%	21.9%	22.9%	2.6%	10.4%	6.3%
Earnings per share ($)	(14.3%)	3.26	3.30	3.46	3.65	3.88	3.04	*3.21*	*0.05*	*1.44*	*0.81*
Stock price – high ($)	—	19.63	25.13	26.50	22.63	28.13	32.00	32.75	29.75	16.38	18.63
Stock price – low ($)	—	15.13	18.00	17.75	14.50	20.63	26.00	26.38	15.00	5.00	9.38
Stock price – close ($)	(7.1%)	19.38	24.38	19.38	22.00	27.25	28.38	27.75	15.75	11.13	10.00
P/E – high	—	6	8	8	6	7	11	10	595	11	23
P/E – low	—	5	5	5	4	5	9	8	300	3	12
Dividends per share ($)	(100%)	2.20	2.40	2.56	2.60	2.69	2.72	2.78	2.80	1.20	0.00
Book value per share ($)	(2.6%)	22.13	22.94	23.78	24.18	25.36	25.84	26.62	23.46	16.31	17.40

1990 Year-end:
Debt ratio: 65.7%
Return on equity: 4.8%
Cash (mil.): $59
Current ratio: 0.62
Long-term debt (mil.): $3,218
No. of shares (mil.): 87
Dividends:
1990 average yield: 0.0%
1990 payout: 0.0%
Market value (mil.): $869

Stock Price History
High/Low 1981–90

PITNEY BOWES INC.

OVERVIEW

NYSE symbol: PBI
Fiscal year ends: December 31

Hoover's Rating **B-**

Pitney Bowes, headquartered in Stamford, Connecticut, is a leading manufacturer and marketer of business equipment, including copiers, facsimile machines, and voice-processing devices (through Dictaphone). Pitney Bowes also sells mailing equipment and devices for product marking (for pricing and merchandise tracking).

Other company services include repro-graphic and mailroom management services, lease financing for its products, and other financial services.

The company, which plans to speed up its new product introductions in the next 3 years, increased research and development spending by 25% over 1989's R&D budget and opened a new technology center, moves that reflect its commitment to new electronic technology and software development.

Late in 1989 Pitney Bowes began a number of changes intended to improve its efficiency. Among changes made since then are a decreased work force, consolidation of its distribution centers, and retraining of some personnel.

WHEN

In 1912 English-born addressing-machine salesman Walter Bowes obtained control of the Universal Stamping Machine Company (Stamford, Connecticut), which became a major producer of post office stamp-cancelling machines. In 1920 Bowes formed a partnership with Arthur Pitney, who had been developing a postage-metering machine for 14 years. In 1921 Pitney received his final patent, congressional legislation authorizing the use of his invention was passed, and the Pitney-Bowes Postage Meter Company began leasing its new machines to customers.

In 1929 Pitney-Bowes expanded to overseas markets and by 1932 had revenues of almost $1.5 million. In 1945 the company adopted its current name. It continued to grow in the postage-meter and letter-handling business throughout the 1940s and 1950s.

In the 1960s Pitney Bowes focused on accelerated growth and diversification. In 1967 the company began to market a new line of internally produced copiers. In 1968 Pitney Bowes bought Monarch Marking Systems (price-marking and inventory-control products) and Malco Plastics (credit and ID cards).

In 1973 the company wrote off its 4-year-old point-of-sale terminal joint venture with Alpex, for its first loss in 54 years. Despite this setback Pitney Bowes continued to grow during the 1970s. In 1979 the company bought Dictaphone Corporation, including subsidiar-ies Data Documents (computer supplies) and Grayarc (office supplies), for $124 million.

The company bought The Drawing Board (office supply catalog) in 1980 and in 1981 consolidated The Drawing Board and Grayarc into a new entity, The Wheeler Group. In 1982 Pitney Bowes entered the facsimile market, selling products provided by outside suppliers. The company sold Data Documents and bought Baldwin Cooke (calendars) in 1988. In 1989 the company took a $110 million charge to earnings in transition costs related to employee reduction, establishment of a dedicated copier division, and administrative streamlining.

In 1990 Pitney Bowes decided to sell its Wheeler Group. The company also purchased VOCAM, which produces logistics management software.

Also in 1990 Pitney Bowes stopped remanufacturing old copiers and started selling new copiers to larger businesses, a move that helped cut expenses and increase margins.

Products introduced in 1990 included a desktop folder/inserter (3280 Letter-Perfect), a new bar-coding system (PostEdge), a meter resetting system(Premier Postage by Phone), and plain-paper facsimile machines (models 9250 and 9100). Pitney Bowes also introduced digital voice-processing products (ExpressTalk and the 6600 Digital On-Line Recorder).

WHO

Chairman, President, and CEO: George B. Harvey, age 59, $774,756 pay
President, Pitney Bowes Office Systems: Marc C. Breslawsky, age 48, $603,454 pay
President, Pitney Bowes Mailing Systems: Hiro R. Hiranandani, age 53, $563,137 pay
President, Pitney Bowes Financial Services: John J. Canning, age 49
President, Pitney Bowes Logistics Systems and Business Services: Carole F. St. Mark, age 48, $454,457 pay
VP Finance and Administration and Treasurer: Carmine F. Adimando, age 46, $418,012 pay
VP, Secretary, General Counsel, and Chief Personnel Officer: Michael J. Critelli, age 42
Auditors: Price Waterhouse
Employees: 29,942

WHERE

HQ: Pitney Bowes Inc., Stamford, CT 06926-0700
Phone: 203-356-5000
Fax: 203-351-6303 (Public Relations)

Pitney Bowes products are sold in 120 countries.

Manufacturing Facilities

US	Mexico	Switzerland
Australia	Singapore	UK
Canada		

	1990 Sales		1990 Operating Income	
	$ mil.	% of total	$ mil.	% of total
US	2,448	77	334	78
Europe	419	13	48	11
Canada, other	329	10	47	11
Adjustments	—	—	238	—
Total	**3,196**	**100**	**667**	**100**

WHAT

	1990 Sales		1990 Operating Income	
	$ mil.	% of total	$ mil.	% of total
Business equip.	2,283	71	231	54
Business supplies & services	365	12	34	8
Financial services	548	17	160	38
Adjustments	—	—	242	—
Total	**3,196**	**100**	**667**	**100**

Products and Services
Business equipment
Business supplies and services
Copying systems
Facsimile systems
Financial services
Mailing systems
Mailroom and reprographics services
Merchandise identification equipment
Voice-processing systems

RANKINGS

145th in *Fortune* 500 Industrial Cos.
164th in *Business Week* 1000

KEY COMPETITORS

Alcatel Alsthom	Harris	Moore
Canon	Hitachi	NEC
Eastman Kodak	IBM	Sharp
Fuji Photo	Matsushita	Xerox
GEC	Minolta	

HOW MUCH

	9-Year Growth	1981	1982	1983	1984	1985	1986	1987	1988	1989	1990
Sales ($ mil.)	9.5%	1,414	1,455	1,606	1,732	1,832	1,987	2,251	2,650	2,876	3,196
Net income ($ mil.)	12.9%	70	83	118	138	145	166	199	237	180	207
Income as % of sales	—	4.9%	5.7%	7.3%	8.0%	7.9%	8.4%	8.9%	8.9%	6.3%	6.5%
Earnings per share ($)	12.0%	0.94	1.08	1.50	1.76	1.83	2.10	2.52	3.00	2.27	2.60
Stock price – high ($)	—	8.78	12.06	18.25	18.13	24.94	38.25	50.25	47.50	54.75	53.50
Stock price – low ($)	—	5.50	5.38	10.50	13.25	16.81	22.75	29.63	33.75	40.88	27.00
Stock price – close ($)	22.8%	6.25	11.44	16.31	17.75	24.25	36.63	38.25	42.75	47.50	39.75
P/E – high	—	9	11	12	10	14	18	20	16	24	21
P/E – low	—	6	5	7	8	9	11	12	11	18	10
Dividends per share ($)	13.0%	0.40	0.40	0.45	0.52	0.60	0.66	0.76	0.92	1.04	1.20
Book value per share ($)	13.3%	6.55	7.19	7.86	9.05	10.35	11.70	13.47	16.16	18.15	20.13

1990 Year-end:
Debt ratio: 41.7%
Return on equity: 13.6%
Cash (mil.): $80
Current ratio: 0.62
Long-term debt (mil.): $1,136
No. of shares (mil.): 79
Dividends:
  1990 average yield: 3.0%
  1990 payout: 46.2%
Market value (mil.): $3,128

Stock Price History High/Low 1981–90

PNC FINANCIAL CORP

OVERVIEW

Prior to recent banking industry consolidation, PNC ranked 14th among US banks and was the nation's 6th largest investment manager. PNC's centerpiece is the consistently profitable Pittsburgh National Bank. Since 1983 PNC has, through mergers and acquisitions, expanded beyond its Pennsylvania base and today has significant banking operations in Ohio, Kentucky, and Delaware.

PNC has had its share of problem real estate loans, particularly in eastern Pennsylvania. Reserves against such loans caused a sharp drop in earnings in 1990. Already known for its lean cost structure and low salaries, PNC is continuing its belt-tightening. The bank is centralizing its back-office operations and has expressed its readiness to jettison its distant French and Italian units. Despite the recession, PNC's fee-based trust operations remain highly profitable and are growing rapidly.

WHEN

In 1863 First National Bank of Pittsburgh, chartered under the National Bank Act, began its operations. Ten years later it had $2 million in deposits.

First National and Second National Bank of Pittsburgh, chartered in 1864, consolidated their operations as First-Second National in 1913. The bank changed its name to First National in Pittsburgh in 1918 and, 3 years later, bought Peoples National (Pittsburgh).

In the 1940s First National purchased Peoples–Pittsburgh Trust (1946), Sewickley Valley Trust (1947), and Monongahela Trust (1947). The bank acquired 12 other Pennsylvania banks during the 1950s, including Fidelity Trust (1959). First National then changed its name to Pittsburgh National.

Pittsburgh National entered the bank credit card business in 1965 and joined the BankAmericard program 4 years later. The bank formed Pittsburgh National Corporation, a holding company, in 1968.

In the 1970s Pittsburgh National Corporation diversified by establishing new operations in commercial paper financing (Pittsburgh National Discount, 1972); insurance on consumer loans (PINACO, 1972); lease financing (Pittsburgh National Leasing, 1979); and credit life, health, and accident reinsurance (Pittsburgh National Life, 1979).

In 1983 Pittsburgh National merged with Provident National of Philadelphia to form PNC Corporation. Provident was a holding company that owned Provident National Bank, which had started as Provident Life & Trust in 1865. The merger, made possible by the easing of Pennsylvania's banking rules in 1982, combined Pittsburgh National's corporate lending strength with Provident's expertise in money management and trust operations.

The PNC network expanded by buying banks across Pennsylvania, including Marine (1984), Northeastern (1985), and Hershey (1986). Much of this growth and the interstate expansion that followed were directed by Thomas H. O'Brien, CEO since 1985. PNC purchased Citizen's Fidelity of Louisville (1987) and Central Bancorporation (Cincinnati, 1988). In 1987 PNC, with $37 billion in assets, passed Mellon as Pennsylvania's largest bank. That year PNC led the 15 largest US banking companies in return on assets and return on equity.

PNC continued to expand in 1988 by starting PNC National of Cherry Hill (New Jersey). In 1989 PNC moved into Delaware with the acquisition of Bank of Delaware.

In 1991 PNC bought First Federal Savings and Loan Association of Pittsburgh and its 64 branches in western Pennsylvania from the RTC. In the same year, in what has been viewed as a reversal of the holding company's Ohio expansion strategy, PNC's Central Bancorporation sold 4 of its banks to Banc One.

NYSE symbol: PNC
Fiscal year ends: December 31

Hoover's Rating **C**

WHO

Chairman, President, and CEO: Thomas H. O'Brien, age 54, $740,834 pay
VC: Daniel C. Ulmer, Jr., age 58, $325,000 pay
VC: Robert E. Chappell, age 46, $300,000 pay
VC: James E. Rohr, age 42, $316,367 pay
VC: Edward P. Junker III, age 54
EVP Finance and Administration: Walter E. Gregg, Jr., age 49, $277,574 pay
SVP Human Resources: Daniel F. Gillis, age 50
Auditors: Ernst & Young
Employees: 18,000

WHERE

HQ: 5th Ave. and Wood St., Pittsburgh, PA 15222
Phone: 412-762-2666
Fax: 412-762-6238

PNC operates 535 banking offices and conducts business in 15 states.

	1990 Assets	
	$ bil.	% of total
Pittsburgh Nat'l Bank	16.4	36
Provident Nat'l Bank (Philadelphia)	8.9	20
Citizens Fidelity (Louisville)	5.7	13
Central Trust (Cincinnati)	3.6	8
Northeastern Bank (Scranton)	2.4	5
Bank of Delaware	2.2	5
Marine Bank (Erie)	1.8	4
Other	4.5	9
Total	**45.5**	**100**

WHAT

	1990 Assets	
	$ mil.	% of total
Cash & due from banks	2,561	6
Interest-earning deposits	598	1
Resale agreements & federal funds sold	1,167	3
Securities	12,259	27
Loans	27,634	60
Credit loss reserve	(785)	(2)
Other	2,100	5
Total	**45,534**	**100**

Major Non-Banking Affiliates
Advanced Investment Management
PNC Merchant Banking Company
PNC Mortgage Servicing Company
PNC Securities (investment banking and brokerage)
PNC Trust Company of Florida, N.A.
PNC Trust Company of New York
PNC Venture Corp.

RANKINGS

14th in *Fortune* 100 Commercial Banking Cos.
225th in *Business Week* 1000

KEY COMPETITORS

Banc One
First Fidelity
Mellon Bank
Other money center banks

HOW MUCH

	9-Year Growth	1981	1982	1983	1984	1985	1986	1987	1988	1989	1990
Assets ($ mil.)	23.3%	6,935	7,622	12,245	14,870	18,778	26,936	36,504	40,811	45,661	45,534
Net income ($ mil.)	2.4%	57	62	117	143	188	286	256	443	377	71
Income as % of assets	—	0.8%	0.8%	1.0%	1.0%	1.0%	1.1%	0.7%	1.1%	0.8%	0.2%
Earnings per share ($)	(12.0%)	2.32	2.49	2.75	3.10	3.64	4.19	2.93	4.95	3.91	0.73
Stock price – high ($)	—	14.13	18.88	23.13	23.44	35.63	51.00	51.00	46.50	49.00	44.13
Stock price – low ($)	—	11.06	11.44	15.75	18.06	22.81	34.88	33.25	36.50	38.50	15.75
Stock price – close ($)	5.3%	13.63	16.00	21.44	23.13	35.00	41.25	37.25	39.75	41.63	21.63
P/E – high	—	6	8	8	8	10	12	17	9	13	60
P/E – low	—	5	5	6	6	6	8	11	7	10	22
Dividends per share ($)	11.4%	0.81	0.91	1.01	1.11	1.28	1.47	1.64	1.83	2.06	2.12
Book value per share ($)	6.3%	15.69	17.26	18.45	21.22	24.47	25.68	25.60	28.83	30.16	27.20

1990 Year-end:
Return on equity: 2.5%
Equity as % of assets: 5.7%
Cash (mil.): $3,158
Long-term debt (mil.): $1,319
No. of shares (mil.): 96
Dividends:
　1990 average yield: 9.8%
　1990 payout: 290.4%
Market value (mil.): $2,066
Sales (mil.): $4,880

Stock Price History
High/Low 1981–90

POLAROID CORPORATION

OVERVIEW

Polaroid, the leading producer of instant cameras and second only to Eastman Kodak in sales of photographic products, has turned an eye to the future through corporate reorganization and development of international markets. The company also continues its substantial investment in research and development (7.5% of sales in 1990). Reorganization of the Cambridge-based corporation in 1990 created three primary divisions responsible for instant imaging in home, business, and technical and industrial applications. A fourth division focuses on electronic imaging, an area that promises intense competition in the years to come.

Eastern Europe markets have increased with the demand for personal documentation, such as passports, and because of sales in Germany, the company in 1990 saw its first rise in consumer camera sales since 1986. Polaroid products are now sold in a Moscow retail store, and in 1990 the company opened film manufacturing, film packaging, and marketing operations in India and China. As a result of such growth, almost 1/2 of Polaroid's revenues come from foreign markets.

Polaroid continued its patent-infringement litigation filed against Eastman Kodak in 1976 by appealing as insufficient the $873 million award it won early in 1991.

WHO

Chairman, President, and CEO: I. MacAllister Booth, age 59, $701,067 pay
VC: Sheldon A. Buckler, age 59, $422,638 pay
SVP: Milton S. Dietz, age 59
SVP: Peter O. Kliem, age 52, $357,861 pay
VP Human Resources: Owen Gaffney
Group VP and CFO: William J. O'Neill, Jr., age 48, $351,690 pay
Auditors: KPMG Peat Marwick
Employees: 11,768

WHEN

In the late 1920s Harvard University undergraduate Edwin Land began the research that led to his development of the world's first synthetic light-polarizing material, which he named Polaroid. In 1932, just months before he would have graduated, Land left Harvard to establish a company exploiting the new material. He was 23 years old.

During the 1930s the company licensed the use of the new material, using the resulting cash to fund further research and development. Polaroid prospered during WWII, developing a number of military uses for its basic product. The company's sales rose from $1 million in 1941 to over $15 million by 1945. Although sales dropped back to about $1.5 million in 1947, Land unveiled his instant-picture camera that year, and the course of the company was set.

Polaroid introduced the $14 Swinger in 1965; by 1968 it had sold 7 million of the cameras. But its SX-70 camera, introduced in 1972, sold sluggishly, and Polaroid's net income foundered until 1975, when the company introduced the inexpensive Pronto, which set an annual sales record of 6 million cameras.

Introduction of the new, high-quality Spectra camera and film in 1986 revived sales after 6 years of decline, but Polaroid spent most of

the 1980s streamlining operations in pursuit of profits and in the face of a hostile takeover bid (1988–89) by Shamrock Holdings. Polaroid introduced conventional film in 1989.

In 1990 Polaroid released a number of new products and announced progress on others. The company plans to release a more versatile, higher-resolution instant color film in 1992, and its ID-2000, an electronic system for access to high-security areas. A new instant photo system (code-named "Joshua") is undergoing marketing evaluation before its scheduled introduction in 1992.

Polaroid also is scheduled to begin sales of Helios, an instant-imaging system involving no chemical processing or toxic fluids, for recording diagnostic images, such as sonograms.

In 1991, Polaroid won an $873 million award in its 15-year-old patent infringement suit against Eastman Kodak. Unhappy with the award, Polaroid appealed. The suit followed Kodak's 1975 introduction of its own line of instant cameras. Change continued in other ways at Polaroid, with the appointment of I. MacAllister Booth to replace retiring chairman William J. McCune, Jr. The end of an era also came in 1991, with the death of Polaroid founder Edwin Land, who had retired in 1982. He was 81 years old.

WHERE

HQ: 549 Technology Sq., Cambridge, MA 02139
Phone: 617-577-2000
Fax: 617-577-5618

Polaroid sells its products in 118 countries.

Polaroid owns or leases 57 buildings, primarily in eastern Massachusetts, which are used for manufacturing, office, research, and warehouse space.

	1990 Sales		1990 Operating Income	
	$ mil.	% of total	$ mil.	% of total
US	1,058	54	180	60
Europe	599	30	98	32
Other countries	315	16	24	8
Adjustments	—	—	(18)	—
Total	**1,972**	**100**	**284**	**100**

WHAT

Products
Camera backs
Film holders
Instant and conventional films
Instant cameras
  Auto Focus Spectra 2
  Neon Cool Cam
  OneStep Flash
  600 Business Edition
  Spectra
  Studio Express (document cameras)
  SX-70
Instruments
Medical imaging systems
Overhead enlargers
Photo identification systems
Slide makers
Specialized photographic equipment
Videotapes

HOW MUCH

	9-Year Growth	1981	1982	1983	1984	1985	1986	1987	1988	1989	1990
Sales ($ mil.)	3.7%	1,420	1,294	1,255	1,272	1,295	1,629	1,764	1,863	1,905	1,972
Net income ($ mil.)	19.2%	31	24	50	37	104	116	(23)	145	151	
Income as % of sales	—	2.2%	1.8%	4.0%	2.0%	2.8%	6.4%	6.6%	(1.2%)	7.6%	7.7%
Earnings per share ($)	18.6%	0.48	0.37	0.81	0.42	0.60	1.67	1.88	(0.34)	2.23	2.20
Stock price – high ($)	—	16.75	14.50	18.63	17.38	22.63	37.38	42.75	44.13	50.38	48.25
Stock price – low ($)	—	9.50	8.38	12.38	12.69	12.13	21.13	16.50	21.50	35.13	20.25
Stock price – close ($)	9.6%	10.25	12.63	16.75	13.88	21.63	33.25	23.63	36.88	45.75	23.38
P/E – high	—	35	40	23	42	38	22	23	—	23	22
P/E – low	—	20	23	15	31	20	13	9	—	16	9
Dividends per share ($)	2.0%	0.50	0.50	0.50	0.50	0.50	0.50	0.60	0.60	0.60	0.60
Book value per share ($)	(13.0%)	14.58	14.58	14.88	14.80	14.89	16.06	17.34	14.12	2.86	4.15

1990 Year-end:
Debt ratio: 71.2%
Return on equity: 62.8%
Cash (mil.): $198
Current ratio: 1.97
Long-term debt (mil.): $514
No. of shares (mil.): 50
Dividends:
  1990 average yield: 2.6%
  1990 payout: 27.3%
Market value (mil.): $1,170

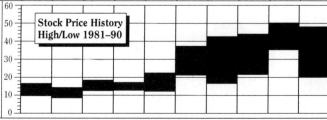

Stock Price History High/Low 1981–90

RANKINGS

213th in *Fortune* 500 Industrial Cos.
446th in *Business Week* 1000

KEY COMPETITORS

BASF
Bayer
Canon
Eastman Kodak
Fuji Photo
General Electric
Hitachi
3M
Minolta
Mitsubishi
Siemens
Sony
Xerox

PPG INDUSTRIES, INC.

NYSE symbol: PPG
Fiscal year ends: December 31

Hoover's Rating B

OVERVIEW

Pittsburgh-based PPG is the world's largest automotive and industrial finishes supplier and a leading producer of optical resins. PPG is the 2nd largest producer of fiber glass, 3rd in chlorine and caustic soda, and 3rd in flat glass.

Major markets for glass products include automotive, commercial construction, furniture and mirror, and aircraft industries. Construction and industrial markets account for much of the company's coatings and resins segment. Chemicals and biomedical systems make up the remaining parts of PPG's business.

PPG attributes record 1990 earnings and sales to its long-term strategy, which emphasizes expansion of foreign markets. The company already makes 1/3 of its sales overseas. Despite the company's optimism early in 1990, sales and earnings fell in the first half of 1991 because of the weak US and European economies. Corporate strategy also includes heavy spending in research and development and capital expansion.

In 1990 PPG, which owned 1/3 of Dutch fiber glass producer Silenka BV, purchased the remaining 2/3 of the company.

WHEN

After the failure of 2 previous plants, John Ford persuaded former railroad superintendent John Pitcairn to invest $200,000 in a 3rd plate glass factory in 1883 in Creighton, Pennsylvania. Named Pittsburgh Plate Glass, the enterprise became the first commercially successful US plate glass factory.

Ford left in 1896 when Pitcairn pushed through a plan to set up a company distribution system, replacing glass jobbers. Ford went on to found a predecessor of competitor Libbey-Owens-Ford, now owned by Pilkington (UK). Expanding the existing business, Pitcairn built a soda ash plant in 1899, bought a Milwaukee paint company in 1900, and began producing window glass in 1908.

Strong automobile and construction markets in the early part of the century increased demand for the company's products. Pitcairn died in 1916 and left his stock (31% of the total) to his sons. In 1924 PPG revolutionized the glass production process with the introduction of a straight-line conveyor manufacturing method. In the 1930s and 1940s PPG successfully promoted structural glass for use in the commercial construction industry.

PPG was listed on the NYSE in 1945. In 1952 PPG began making fiber glass. In 1968 the company adopted its present name.

Vincent Sarni, CEO since 1984, recognized that PPG's markets (85% of sales were to the construction and automobile industries) were maturing. Sarni wrote a document, entitled *Blueprint for the Decade, 1985-1994*, which spelled out his vision for the company. Principal among the goals were global expansion and an ROE of 18%.

In 1986 PPG spent $154 million on acquisitions, the most important of which were the worldwide medical electronics units of Litton Industries and Honeywell, which gave PPG its first entry into the high-technology instrumentation business. PPG acquired the medical technology business of Allegheny International in 1987 for $100 million.

At its halfway point, Sarni judges the *Blueprint* a success. ROE has met the targeted 18% mark. In 1989 the company purchased Casco Nobel, a coatings distributor, and the Olympic and Lucite paint lines from Clorox for $134 million. PPG also received the Philip Crosby Quality Fanatic Award.

PPG's 1990 acquisition of Silenka BV and the purchase or expansion of facilities in England, Taiwan, and Venezuela are in part responsible for PPG's 50% increase in fiber glass production capacity since 1985.

In 1990 PPG also formed a joint venture to manufacture lenses with Essilor International, a French prescription lens maker.

WHO

Chairman and CEO: Vincent A. Sarni, age 62, $1,145,000 pay
Group VP, Coatings and Resins: Eugene B. Mosier, age 51, $527,000 pay
Group VP, Glass: Robert D. Duncan, age 51, $481,400 pay
Group VP, Chemicals: Richard M. Rompala, age 44, $454,005 pay
VP Finance: Raymond W. LeBoeuf, age 44, $373,300 pay
VP Human Resources: Russell L. Crane
Auditors: Deloitte & Touche
Employees: 35,100

WHERE

HQ: One PPG Place, Pittsburgh, PA 15272
Phone: 412-434-3131
Fax: 412-434-2448

PPG has 78 plants in the US, Canada, Mexico, France, Italy, the Netherlands, Spain, Taiwan, the UK, and Germany.

	1990 Sales		1990 Operating Income	
	$ mil.	% of total	$ mil.	% of total
US	3,958	66	639	70
Canada	418	7	36	4
Europe	1,527	25	204	22
Other countries	118	2	35	4
Adjustments	—	—	(10)	—
Total	**6,021**	**100**	**904**	**100**

WHAT

	1990 Sales		1990 Operating Income	
	$ mil.	% of total	$ mil.	% of total
Chemicals	1,150	19	231	25
Coatings & resins	2,292	38	346	38
Glass	2,380	40	332	36
Other	199	3	5	1
Adjustments	—	—	(10)	—
Total	**6,021**	**100**	**904**	**100**

Chemicals	**Glass**
Flame retardants	Automotive glass
Industrial	Eyeglass lenses
Optical resins	Fiber glass
Pool treatment	Flat glass
Silica products	
Surfactants	**Biomedical Products**
Water treatment	Diagnostic machinery
	Patient data management
Coatings and Resins	systems
Adhesives	Patient monitoring
Architectural finishes	equipment
Automotive coatings	
Industrial coatings	
Sealants	

HOW MUCH

	9-Year Growth	1981	1982	1983	1984	1985	1986	1987	1988	1989	1990
Sales ($ mil.)	6.7%	3,354	3,296	3,682	4,242	4,346	4,687	5,183	5,617	5,734	6,021
Net income ($ mil.)	9.4%	211	155	233	303	303	316	377	468	465	475
Income as % of sales	—	6.3%	4.7%	6.3%	7.1%	7.0%	6.8%	7.3%	8.3%	8.1%	7.9%
Earnings per share ($)	12.2%	1.56	1.13	1.67	2.16	2.26	2.65	3.17	4.24	4.16	4.41
Stock price – high ($)	—	14.56	13.41	18.63	19.00	25.69	38.81	53.50	46.88	46.00	55.25
Stock price – low ($)	—	8.88	7.25	12.56	12.38	16.44	22.50	27.50	31.25	37.00	34.50
Stock price – close ($)	19.5%	9.44	12.94	17.44	16.44	25.50	36.44	33.13	40.38	39.75	47.00
P/E – high	—	9	12	11	9	11	15	17	11	11	13
P/E – low	—	6	6	8	6	7	9	9	7	9	8
Dividends per share ($)	12.3%	0.58	0.59	0.62	0.70	0.82	0.94	1.11	1.33	1.48	1.64
Book value per share ($)	8.0%	11.97	12.27	13.21	14.40	14.39	16.56	18.43	20.48	20.98	24.01

1990 Year-end:
Debt ratio: 31.8%
Return on equity: 19.6%
Cash (mil.): $59
Current ratio: 1.51
Long-term debt (mil.): $1,186
No. of shares (mil.): 106
Dividends:
 1990 average yield: 3.5%
 1990 payout: 37.2%
Market value (mil.): $4,984

Stock Price History High/Low 1981–90

RANKINGS

86th in *Fortune* 500 Industrial Cos.
118th in *Business Week* 1000

KEY COMPETITORS

C.R. Bard	Manville
BASF	Owens-Corning
Baxter	Sherwin-Williams
Du Pont	USG
Hewlett-Packard	Other chemical companies
Hoechst	and medical electronics
Imperial Chemical	companies

PREMARK INTERNATIONAL, INC.

NYSE symbol: PMI
Fiscal year ends: Last Saturday of December

Hoover's Rating: **C**

OVERVIEW

Premark, a Deerfield, Illinois–based spinoff of the former Dart & Kraft, holds 2/3 of the US market and is the worldwide leader for plastic storage and serving containers.

Premark's Tupperware Group (just over $1 billion of sales in 1990) makes over 200 products, including plastic toys, plastic personal care items, and home products. Approximately 70% of group sales are generated outside the US.

Premark's Food Equipment Group ($999 million sales) is a leading manufacturer of food preparation, cooking, storage, and cleaning equipment for restaurants and commercial food preparation facilities.

The Consumer and Decorative Products Group ($703 million sales) has more than 45% of the US market for decorative laminates, which are used on cabinetry, countertops, vanities, store fixtures, and furniture. It is also a leader in prefinished hardwood flooring through its Tibbals Flooring subsidiary. It manufactures small electric appliances such as woks, electric skillets, corn poppers, and slow cookers in 12 countries under 14 brand names, including West Bend, and makes Precor fitness equipment, sold through fitness specialty shops.

WHO

Chairman and CEO: Warren L. Batts, age 58, $943,500 pay
EVP: James M. Ringler, age 45, $729,872 pay
VP and Treasurer: David S. Simon, age 50
VP Human Resources: Wallace J. Nichols, age 51
Auditors: Price Waterhouse
Employees: 25,400

WHERE

HQ: 1717 Deerfield Rd., Deerfield, IL 60015
Phone: 708-405-6000
Fax: 708-405-6013

Premark manufactures and markets products in more than 100 countries.

	1990 Sales		1990 Operating Income	
	$ mil.	% of total	$ mil.	% of total
US	1,564	57	25	16
Europe	749	28	95	60
Pacific	210	8	23	14
Latin America & Canada	198	7	16	10
Adjustments	—	—	(5)	—
Total	**2,721**	**100**	**164**	**100**

WHAT

	1990 Sales		1990 Operating Income	
	$ mil.	% of total	$ mil.	% of total
Tupperware	1,019	37	65	41
Food Equipment	999	37	27	17
Other	703	26	66	42
Adjustments	—	—	6	—
Total	**2,721**	**100**	**164**	**100**

Principal Subsidiaries

Dart Industries Inc. (Tupperware)
Florida Tile Industries, Inc.
Hobart Corp.
Precor Inc.
Ralph Wilson Plastics Co.
Tibbals Flooring Co.
The West Bend Co.

Consumer Products
Precor (fitness equipment)
Tupperware (plastic products)
West Bend (appliances)

Commercial Food Equipment
Adamatic
Hobart
Regethermic
Stero
Vulcan
Wolf

Decorative Products
Florida Tile (decorative tile)
Hartco (flooring installation and care products)
Tibbals (flooring)
Wilsonart (laminates)

WHEN

The story of Premark begins with Justin Dart. A native of Illinois, Dart played football for Northwestern University in the 1920s and was elected president of his senior class. After college, he married (and subsequently divorced) the daughter of Walgreen Company's founder Charles Walgreen. When Walgreen died in 1939, Dart became general manager of Walgreens but left in 1941 to join United Drugs, a Boston-based drug company started in 1903. Dart took control of United Drugs in 1943, moving its headquarters from Boston to Los Angeles in 1945.

Boasting Rexall as a major brand, the company adopted the name Rexall Drug in 1947. Dart led Rexall through a series of acquisitions, including Tupper Corporation, former Du Pont chemist Earl Tupper's plastic container company (Tupperware, 1958); Ralph Wilson Plastics, a decorative laminated plastics manufacturer (Wilsonart, 1966); and West Bend, a cookware maker (1968). The company adopted the name Dart Industries in 1969.

Dart sold its Rexall division, the last vestige of the original drug company, in 1977 and bought P. R. Mallory and Company, maker of Duracell batteries, in 1978.

In 1980 the company merged with Kraft, the Chicago food conglomerate, to form Dart & Kraft. Founded in 1903 by cheese wholesaler James Kraft, Kraft merged with rival cheesemaker Phenix Cheese in 1928 to form Kraft-Phenix. In 1930 the company was acquired by National Dairy Products Corporation, which adopted the name Kraftco (1969) and then Kraft, Inc. (1976) to take advantage of the name value of its best-known products. After the Dart-Kraft merger, John Richman, chief executive of Kraft since 1979, became chairman and CEO of Dart & Kraft. Justin Dart acted as an advisor to the company until his death in 1984.

Warren Batts, former CEO of Mead, became president and COO of Dart & Kraft in 1981. That year the company bought Hobart Corporation, maker of commercial kitchen equipment, including KitchenAid appliances (sold in 1986). Other purchases included Precor (fitness equipment, 1984) and Vulcan-Hart (gas stoves, 1986).

In 1986 the company decided to split its food and nonfood divisions. As a result, Tupperware, Hobart, Vulcan-Hart, Ralph Wilson Plastics, and West Bend were spun off into Premark International, a new company headed by Batts. Kraft kept all of its pre-1980 assets and Duracell batteries. Premark has since acquired several businesses, including oak flooring maker Tibbals (1988) and Florida Tile (decorative tiles, 1990).

RANKINGS

163rd in *Fortune* 500 Industrial Cos.
690th in *Business Week* 1000

KEY COMPETITORS

Armstrong World	Gerber
Atari	Hanson
Avon	Hasbro
Bally	Mattel
Black & Decker	Mobil
Electrolux	Rubbermaid

HOW MUCH

	5-Year Growth	1981	1982	1983	1984	1985	1986	1987	1988	1989	1990
Sales ($ mil.)	9.1%	—	—	—	—	1,763	1,959	2,197	2,397	2,592	2,721
Net income ($ mil.)	(5.8%)	—	—	—	—	70	(98)	72	121	78	52
Income as % of sales	—	—	—	—	—	4.0%	(5.0%)	3.3%	5.1%	3.0%	1.9%
Earnings per share ($)	—	—	—	—	—	—	(2.87)	2.08	3.50	2.24	1.64
Stock price – high ($)	—	—	—	—	—	—	21.50	31.75	36.25	42.00	31.00
Stock price – low ($)	—	—	—	—	—	—	17.50	18.50	22.13	29.38	12.75
Stock price – close ($)	—	—	—	—	—	—	19.63	22.38	31.50	30.75	17.38
P/E – high	—	—	—	—	—	—	—	15	10	19	19
P/E – low	—	—	—	—	—	—	—	9	6	13	8
Dividends per share ($)	—	—	—	—	—	—	0.00	0.05	0.29	0.53	0.78	0.84
Book value per share ($)	—	—	—	—	—	—	16.84	19.68	22.27	23.53	24.67

1990 Year-end:
Debt ratio: 39.6%
Return on equity: 6.8%
Cash (mil.): $41
Current ratio: 1.56
Long-term debt (mil.): $496
No. of shares (mil.): 31
Dividends:
  1990 average yield: 4.8%
  1990 payout: 51.2%
Market value (mil.): $534

**Stock Price History
High/Low 1986–90**

THE PRICE COMPANY

OVERVIEW

The Price Company, based in San Diego, operates 67 Price Clubs, mostly along the Atlantic and Pacific coasts of the US and Canada. Price Club members, who pay a $25 fee to join, spend more than $125 per visit, a figure well above the average at most other general merchandise stores. The company's strict membership controls are designed to keep the per-visit sales figures high. Price Club's large warehouse-style discount stores average nearly $100 million in annual sales per location.

The company has 6 million cardholders, mainly small businesses, union members, and government employees. In addition to grocer-

ies and appliances, the company offers in-store photo-processing and optical labs, pharmacies, and furniture departments. Price owns almost all of its locations outright and has developed many shopping centers around its properties; the company in 1991 formed a real estate investment trust to control its nonwarehouse property.

As the first developer of large discount clubs, Price earned a reputation for efficiency and profitability, but imitators like Costco and Sam's Wholesale Clubs (operated by Wal-Mart) are gaining momentum through aggressive expansion.

WHEN

Sol Price, who from 1954 to 1974 built Fedmart into a $300 million chain selling general merchandise at a discount to government employees, sold that company to West German Hugo Mann in 1975. With son Robert, Rick Libenson, and Giles Bateman, Price opened the first Price Club warehouse in San Diego in 1976 to sell in volume to small businesses at steep discounts. Former Fedmart employees who joined the company added $500,000 to Sol's $800,000 to help get the venture going.

The company posted a large loss its first year, prompting the decision to expand membership to include government, utility, and hospital employees, as well as credit union members. In 1978 Price Club opened a 2nd store, in Phoenix. Laurence Price, Sol's other son, who had declined to join the startup company, started a chain of tire-mounting stores with the help of his father. The stores, located adjacent to Price Club locations on land leased from the company, mounted tires sold by the Price Clubs.

Price Company went public in 1980 with 4 stores in California and Arizona (Sol Price, chairman emeritus, currently owns about 10% of the stock). Price Clubs expanded into Albuquerque and Richmond, Virginia, the first East Coast location (1984), and Glen Burnie, Maryland (1985). Steinberg, a Canadian retailer,

and Price formed a joint venture in 1986 to operate stores in Canada. The first Canadian warehouse opened that year in Montreal.

In 1986 a quarrel between Sol and Laurence led Price Company to cancel the leases for the son's business. Laurence won a $3.7 million arbitration award and has since hired famed divorce lawyer Marvin Mitchelson to sue Price Company for $100 million in damages. In 1987 the company added stores in the New York area.

Price acquired A. M. Lewis, a wholesale grocery distributor operating in Southern California and Arizona (1988), for Lewis's real estate. The company started a delivery service in 1989 to better serve its 1 million small business customers and opened Price Club Furnishings, a home and office furniture extension of the company's discount format, at 2 locations. In 1990 Price bought out Steinberg's interest in the Canadian locations and announced a joint venture to create Price Club de Mexico. The same year Price added stores in existing California and East Coast markets as well as in Colorado and British Columbia; it plans to open 11 new stores in calendar 1991. Bateman left the company in 1990 to pursue other interests, and Robert Price relinquished the post of president.

NASDAQ symbol: PCLB
Fiscal year ends: Sunday closest to August 31

Hoover's Rating A+

WHO

Chairman and CEO: Robert E. Price, age 48, $240,385 pay
President: Mitchell G. Lynn, age 41
EVP; COO, East Coast: Theodore Wallace, age 42, $245,538 pay
EVP; COO, West Coast: Dennis R. Zook, age 41, $194,827 pay
CFO: Robert Hunt
Human Resource Manager: John Matthews
Auditors: Ernst & Young
Employees: 13,336

WHERE

HQ: 4649 Morena Blvd., San Diego, CA 92117-3650
Phone: 619-581-4600
Fax: 619-581-4773

The Price Company operates 67 Price Clubs in 9 states and 3 Canadian provinces and has entered into a joint venture to open locations in Mexico.

	Stores	% of Total
California	31	46
Arizona	7	11
Virginia	6	9
Maryland	5	7
New Mexico	1	2
New York	2	3
New Jersey	2	3
Connecticut	1	2
Colorado	2	3
Ontario	3	4
Quebec	5	7
British Columbia	2	3
Total	**67**	**100**

WHAT

	1990 Sales	
	$ mil.	% of total
Net sales	5,286	98
Membership fees	115	2
Real estate	11	—
Total	**5,412**	**100**

Price Club	1990 Merchandise Sales
	% of total
Housewares	21
Food	27
Hardlines	9
Liquor	4
Soft goods	6
Sundries	33
Total	**100**

Other Operations

Automotive centers	Price Club Optical
Club distribution	Price Club Packaging
Meat processing	Price Club Pharmacy
Photo processing	Price Company REIT
Price Club Furnishings	

HOW MUCH

	9-Year Growth	1981	1982	1983	1984	1985	1986	1987	1988	1989	1990
Sales ($ mil.)	42.0%	230	370	641	1,158	1,871	2,649	3,306	4,140	5,012	5,412
Net income ($ mil.)	42.6%	5	8	15	29	46	59	73	95	117	125
Income as % of sales	—	2.2%	2.1%	2.3%	2.5%	2.5%	2.2%	2.2%	2.3%	2.3%	2.3%
Earnings per share ($)	38.7%	0.13	0.20	0.34	0.64	1.02	1.25	1.50	1.93	2.30	2.47
Stock price – high ($)	—	—	12.00	20.69	24.38	36.13	55.75	52.50	42.25	49.50	48.25
Stock price – low ($)	—	—	3.06	9.56	11.88	20.38	28.25	23.50	31.00	34.75	26.50
Stock price – close ($)	—	—	12.00	16.19	20.88	35.00	32.75	32.75	37.50	46.25	39.25
P/E – high	—	—	61	61	38	36	45	35	22	22	20
P/E – low	—	—	16	28	19	20	23	16	16	15	11
Dividends per share ($)	0.0%	0.00	0.00	0.00	0.00	0.00	0.00	0.00	0.00	1.50	0.00
Book value per share ($)	51.5%	0.30	0.51	1.55	2.25	3.53	6.18	7.74	9.73	10.75	12.68

1990 Year-end:
Debt ratio: 23.9%
Return on equity: 21.1%
Cash (mil.): $51
Current ratio: 0.97
Long-term debt (mil.): $194
No. of shares (mil.): 49
Dividends:
  1990 average yield: 0.0%
  1990 payout: 0.0%
Market value (mil.): $1,907

Stock Price History High/Low 1982–90

RANKINGS

23rd in *Fortune* 50 Retailing Cos.
313th in *Business Week* 1000

KEY COMPETITORS

Circuit City	Wal-Mart
Costco	Food, general merchandise, and
Fred Meyer	specialty retailers
Kmart	

PRICE WATERHOUSE

OVERVIEW

For decades London-based Price Waterhouse was one of the top 3 accounting firms in the US and the world. The firm earned a reputation as the "Rolls-Royce" of auditors, primarily because of its impressive list of blue-chip clients, but slow growth and recent mergers among accounting firms have placed Price Waterhouse last among the US Big 6.

Price Waterhouse has responded to these changes by developing a 3-part strategy. First, the firm is focusing on improving its client service. The 2nd part of the strategy is to improve the recruitment and training of young college graduates. The final part of the strategy is to concentrate on selected types of clients; Price Waterhouse is focusing on multinational companies, financial institutions, and information technology services.

As Price Waterhouse grapples with growth issues, it also finds itself ensnared in the BCCI banking collapse. Regulators around the world are investigating fraud at BCCI, already convicted of money laundering and revealed as the owner of Washington's largest bank. BCCI may be missing billions. Price Waterhouse's British unit gave the intrigue-laden international bank a favorable audit report in 1990 while privately apprising the bank of irregularities. Price Waterhouse defended its actions, saying its report conformed to British standards.

International association of partnerships
Fiscal year ends: June 30

Hoover's Rating **C+**

WHO

Chairman – Europe: Ian Brindle
Chairman – US: Shaun F. O'Malley
CFO: Thomas H. Chamberlain
National Director, Human Resources: Richard P. Kearns
Employees: 46,406

WHERE

HQ: Southwark Towers, 32 London Bridge St., London SE1 9SY, UK
Phone: 011-44-71-939-3000
Fax: 011-44-71-378-0647
US HQ: 1251 Ave. of the Americas, New York, NY 10020
US Phone: 212-819-5000
US Fax: 212-790-6620

Price Waterhouse maintains 450 offices in 110 countries.

	1990 Revenues	
	$ mil.	% of total
US	1,200	41
Foreign	1,700	59
Total	**2,900**	**100**

WHEN

In 1860 S. H. Price and Edwin Waterhouse, both chartered accountants, founded Price Waterhouse in England. The firm quickly attracted several important accounts and a group of prestigious partners that included 4 Knights of the British Empire. Aided by the explosive industrial growth of Britain and the rest of the world, Price Waterhouse expanded rapidly (as did the accounting industry as a whole) and by the late 1900s had established itself as the most prestigious accounting firm, providing its services in accounting, auditing, and business consulting.

By the 1890s the firm's dealings in America had grown sufficiently to warrant permanent representation, so Lewis Jones and William Caesar were sent to open offices in New York City and Chicago. In 1902 United States Steel chose the firm as its auditors.

Through the next several decades, Price Waterhouse's London office initiated tremendous expansion into other countries. By the 1930s, 57 Price Waterhouse offices boasting 2,500 employees operated globally. The growth of Price Waterhouse in New York was largely due to the Herculean efforts of partner Joseph Sterrett, and Price Waterhouse, along with other accounting firms, benefited from SEC audit requirements. The firm's reputation was enhanced further in 1935 when it was chosen to handle the Academy Awards balloting (which it still does today), and its prestige attracted several important clients, notably large oil and steel interests.

During WWII Price Waterhouse recruited women with college experience to fill its depleted ranks for the duration; some remained with the firm after the end of the hostilities.

While Price Waterhouse tried to coordinate and expand its international offices after the war, the firm lost its dominance in the 1960s, although by 1970 it still retained 100 of the *Fortune* 500 as clients. The company came to be viewed as the most traditional and formal of the major firms. Price Waterhouse tried to show more aggressiveness in the 1980s.

In 1989 the firm announced plans to merge with Arthur Andersen, but the 2 managements were unable to agree on terms and style and the merger was called off. When the deal fell through, the firm expanded internationally, merging with Swiss firm Revisuisse and opening a Budapest office (1989).

As the 1990s began, legal wrangling vexed Price Waterhouse. In addition to the BCCI affair, an ex-employee sued, claiming the firm had unfairly denied her a partnership. When the then-employee had asked how to earn a promotion, a male supervisor suggested she dress "more femininely," wear makeup, and get her hair done. Price Waterhouse denied discrimination, but a court ordered that the ex-employee be made a partner and receive back pay.

WHAT

	1990 Revenues
	% of total
Auditing & accounting	52
Tax	24
Management consulting	22
Total	**100**

Services

Audit and Business Advisory Services	Litigation and Reorganization Consulting
Employee Benefits Services	Management Consulting Services
Government Services	
Industry Services	
International Business Development Services	Merger and Acquisition Services
International Trade Services	Partnership Services
Inventory Services	Personal Financial Services
Investment Management and Securities Operations Consulting	Tax Services
	Valuation Services

Representative Clients

Anheuser-Busch	W. R. Grace
Barclays	Guinness
Barnett Banks	Imperial Oil
Baxter	IBM
Campbell Soup	Kmart
Canadian Pacific	NEC
Chase Manhattan	NIKE
Chemical Banking	NTT
CIGNA	Nomura
Compaq	Phelps Dodge
Du Pont	Scott
Ericsson	Shell
Exxon	Telefónica
Fuji Photo	Warner-Lambert
Gannett	Washington Post

KEY COMPETITORS

Arthur Andersen	KPMG
Coopers & Lybrand	Marsh & McLennan
Deloitte & Touche	McKinsey & Co.
Ernst & Young	Other consulting firms
H&R Block	

HOW MUCH

	9-Year Growth	1981	1982	1983	1984	1985	1986	1987	1988	1989	1990
Worldwide revenues ($ mil.)	14.6%	850	946	1,013	1,082	1,170	1,411	1,691	2,097	2,468	2,900
US revenues ($ mil.)	13.2%	392	458	502	568	645	742	848	960	1,098	1,200
No. of offices[1]	—	—	—	84	90	99	111	112	115	—	115
No. of partners	—	—	—	587	623	662	704	805	870	900	920
No. of employees	—	—	—	8,499	9,018	10,374	10,937	—	12,150	13,000	13,000

1990 revenues per partner: $3,152,174

Worldwide Revenues ($ mil.) 1981–90

3,000
2,500
2,000
1,500
1,000
500
0

[1] US offices

PRIME COMPUTER, INC.

OVERVIEW

Boston area–based Prime Computer is the world's #3 supplier of computer-aided design and computer-aided manufacturing (CAD/CAM) software (after IBM and Intergraph); a leader in the automotive, industrial equipment, and aerospace design software markets; and a major manufacturer of minicomputers. The company derived 40% of its revenues from CAD/CAM products in 1990 and 19% from computer sales (down from 26% in 1989). Non-US sales accounted for 59% of Prime's sales.

The company reorganized in 1990 into 5 business units: Computervision (CAD/CAM products), Computer Systems (computers), PrimeService (customer service and support),

Systems Integration (consulting and project management), and International.

A 1989 hostile takeover attempt forced Prime to turn to investment firm J.H. Whitney, which formed DR Holdings along with Shearson Lehman and Prudential Insurance to purchase Prime. Because of this as well as a sluggish computer industry and the company's late arrival into open systems, Prime is struggling to maintain its position as a contender in the midrange computer market. The company is shifting its focus to software and related services for continued sales growth. Prime reported a $320 million loss in the first half of 1991.

WHEN

Seven ex-Honeywell engineers founded Prime Computer in Natick, Massachusetts, in 1972 to develop powerful 32-bit superminicomputers. Older manufacturers were loath to supersede their profitable 16-bit lines; unencumbered by such ties, Prime introduced its 200 model. It was an instant success.

The company designed fully compatible product lines (such as the 50 series of minis, 1979) and networking software (PRIMENET, RINGNET). Sales jumped from $11 million in 1975 to $365 million in 1981; in 1978 Prime became the youngest-ever company to be listed in the NYSE.

IBM alumnus Joe Henson (president in 1982) centralized planning, expanded to the Far East, and began a growth-by-acquisition strategy that by 1988 had catapulted Prime to revenues of $1.6 billion.

Henson targeted CAD/CAM software companies, buying Compeda (1982), VersaCAD (1987), and Computervision (1988); Computervision alone raised Prime's CAD/CAM market share from 3.5% to 17%. Prime purchased the CALMA mechanical design product from GE in 1988.

Prime also moved beyond superminis to provide platforms for its burgeoning CAD/CAM

line. New computer platforms included supermicros (the EXL Series, 1987) and, from a series of joint ventures, workstations (the CADDStation and WS3600, with Sun Microsystems, 1987), mainframes (the EXL 1200 series, with Sequent Computers, 1989), and minisupers (the MXCL 5, with Cydrome, 1989). All use the open UNIX operating system. In 1990 Prime introduced a RISC-based EXL 7000 series — the result of a partnership with MIPS Computer Systems. Prime developed PRIMELINK (for PC communications, 1986) and linked its PRIMENET with communications standards Ethernet and X.25.

In 1989 defense against a hostile takeover contributed to a $278 million loss. After J.H. Whitney, a New York investment firm, purchased Prime (January 1990), the company laid off 20% of its staff and decentralized into 5 new product-based divisions. Another 800 employees were let go in 1991.

Also in 1991 Prime introduced a complete rewrite of its popular CADDS 5 design software. Plans include placing greater emphasis on Prime software products, including offering the company's CAD/CAM software as a separate package and making it available through independent resellers.

HOW MUCH

	9-Year Growth	1981	1982	1983	1984	1985	1986	1987	1988	1989	1990
Sales ($ mil.)	17.8%	365	436	517	643	770	860	961	1,595	1,518	1,589
Net income ($ mil.)	—	38	45	33	60	58	47	65	13	(278)	(135)
Income as % of sales	—	10.3%	10.3%	6.3%	9.3%	7.5%	5.5%	6.7%	0.8%	(18.3%)	(8.5%)
Earnings per share ($)	—	0.83	0.99	0.68	1.25	1.20	0.97	1.23	0.27	—	(2.41)
Stock price – high ($)	—	32.83	25.83	30.25	21.50	23.88	28.00	31.00	18.75	21.00	7.25
Stock price – low ($)	—	11.50	10.42	13.25	11.75	14.50	15.63	12.13	11.88	6.00	4.25
Stock price – close ($)	(12.5%)	15.75	23.08	17.63	18.00	21.63	16.38	15.50	17.50	6.38	4.75
P/E – high	—	39	26	44	17	20	29	25	69	—	—
P/E – low	—	14	11	19	9	12	16	10	44	—	—
Dividends per share ($)	0.0%	0.00	0.00	0.00	0.00	0.00	0.00	0.00	0.00	0.00	0.00
Book value per share ($)	—	3.20	4.86	5.63	6.80	8.06	9.08	10.54	11.06	(5.07)	(7.50)

1990 Year-end:
Debt ratio: —
Return on equity: —
Cash (mil.): $68
Current ratio: 1.11
Long-term debt (mil.): $1,239
No. of shares (mil.): 36
Dividends:
  1990 average yield: 0.0%
  1990 payout: 0.0%
Market value (mil.): $173

Stock Price History High/Low 1981–90

WHO

Chairman: Russell E. Planitzer, age 47
VC: James F. McDonald, age 51, $2,000,000 pay
President and CEO: John J. Shields, age 52, $761,077 pay
VP Finance and CFO: Harvey A. Wagner, age 50, $302,928 pay
VP Human Resources: Lawrence M. Bornstein, age 48
Auditors: Arthur Andersen & Co.
Employees: 7,900

WHERE

HQ: Prime Park, Natick, MA 01760
Phone: 508-655-8000
Fax: 508-655-8000, ext. 5090

Prime has 2 plants in the US.

	1990 Sales		1990 Operating Income	
	$ mil.	% of total	$ mil.	% of total
US	875	41	42	100
Europe	1,094	51	14	33
Other countries	188	8	(14)	(33)
Adjustments	(568)	—	40	—
Total	**1,589**	**100**	**82**	**100**

WHAT

	1990 Sales	
	$ mil.	% of total
Products	934	59
Service & other	655	41
Total	**1,589**	**100**

	1990 Sales	% of Total
CAD-CAM products		40
General purpose computer systems		19
Service & other revenue		41
Total		**100**

Computervision
Workstations
  CADDstation
Design software
  CADDS
  CALMA
  MEDUSA
  Personal Designer
  VersaCAD
Geographic information
  systems
SYSTEM 9

Computer Systems
50 series (minicomputers)
PRIME EXL series
  (supermicrocomputers
  to mainframes)
Prime INFORMATION
  (database management
  software)

PRIMELINK, PRIMENET
  (communications
  software)

PrimeService
Worldwide field service,
  customer education,
  and support

Systems Integration
Worldwide consulting,
  project management,
  facilities management,
  product modification
  and development

International
Coordination of product
  and services marketing
  internationally

RANKINGS

86th in *Forbes* 400 US Private Cos.

KEY COMPETITORS

AT&T	Hewlett-Packard	Schlumberger
Apple	IBM	Siemens
Computer Associates	Intergraph	Sun Microsystems
Control Data	Machines Bull	Tandem
Data General	Matsushita	Toshiba
DEC	NEC	Unisys
Fujitsu	Oracle	Wang

PRIMERICA CORPORATION

NYSE symbol: PA
Fiscal year ends: December 31

Hoover's Rating **C+**

OVERVIEW

Primerica is a leading US diversified financial services firm, offering consumer lending, insurance, and investment and specialty retail services.

The consumer services group (36% of sales) includes secured and unsecured consumer lending via Commercial Credit Corporation and the newly acquired BarclaysAmerican/Financial and Landmark Financial; also included are Primerica Bank's lucrative credit card operation and Fingerhut and C.O.M.B. catalog sales.

The insurance group (37% of sales) encompasses Primerica Financial Services (formerly A. L. Williams insurance) and various specialty lines. This division is plagued by legal and regulatory investigations relating to marketing and commercial espionage, and has sold or discontinued some unprofitable lines.

Investment services (27% of sales) is dominated by Smith Barney, with a 1.2% share of the brokerage market. Also included are American Capital Management (mutual funds) and asset management services.

WHO

Chairman and CEO: Sanford I. Weill, age 58, $1,846,154 pay
VC: Frank Zarb, $1,593,351 pay (prior to promotion)
VC: Robert I. Lipp, age 52, $1,007,345 pay (prior to promotion)
President and CFO: James Dimon, age 35, $903,459 pay (prior to promotion)
VP Human Resources: Barry L. Mannes, age 52
Auditors: KPMG Peat Marwick
Employees: 23,600

WHEN

Primerica is a combination of the former American Can Company and Commercial Credit Company.

American Can started in 1901 in New Jersey as an amalgam of 123 small canning and can manufacturing firms and became an industry leader in the 1920s and 1930s.

Commercial Credit, started in 1912 by Alexander Duncan and others, initially bought acceptances (negotiable bank time drafts) and receivables from manufacturers and financed motor vehicles and equipment.

From the 1950s to the 1970s, as the can/container business underwent drastic changes, American Can diversified into tin and aluminum can recycling and Dixie Paper's forest products division as well as into record wholesaling and retailing (Musicland, 1977) and catalog sales (Fingerhut, 1977).

In 1981 American Can bought Associated Madison, a life insurance company headed by Gerald Tsai, Jr., who became American Can's largest individual stockholder (3.4%) and was named EVP for financial services. In 1986 American Can sold most of its container business and became primarily a financial services and specialty retail company. In 1987 it changed its name to Primerica and bought Smith Barney, Inc. (securities) for $750 million, and then A. L. Williams insurance. A. L. Williams, the company's flamboyant founder,

had built a 190,000-person sales force to sell primarily term life insurance.

In 1986 Sanford I. Weill, former American Express president, engineered a buyout of Commercial Credit from its owner, Control Data, and became the new public company's chairman and CEO.

Weill, who had sold Shearson Loeb Rhoades to American Express in 1981, sought to assemble a diversified financial company like American Express. In 1988 Commercial Credit bought the much larger Primerica. Tsai became a director and Weill became chairman and CEO of the new Primerica.

To gain cash and focus the company on finance, Weill sought to divest non-core segments including Musicland and the remainder of its interest in containers. Fingerhut proved less attractive to potential purchasers and, instead of selling it off, Primerica has decreased its ownership through public offerings in 1990 and a projected offering in 1991. The A. L. Williams insurance operation (renamed Primerica Financial Services — PFS) has proven troublesome due to the commission expenses of its huge (150,000) sales force. There have also been allegations in Florida of spying on competitors. Since Mr. Williams has left the company (1990), employee morale has declined, and its sales force is increasingly being used to sell both credit and investment products.

WHERE

HQ: 65 E. 55th St., New York, NY 10022
Phone: 212-891-8900
Fax: 212-891-8910 (Corporate Communications)

Primerica and its subsidiaries operate in 38 states, the Virgin Islands, and 10 other nations.

WHAT

	1990 Sales		1990 Pretax Income	
	$ mil.	% of total	$ mil.	% of total
Consumer services	2,199	36	311	38
Insurance svcs.	2,263	37	388	48
Investment svcs.	1,698	27	111	14
Adjustments	30	—	(208)	—
Total	**6,190**	**100**	**602**	**100**

Consumer Services
American Health & Life (credit-related insurance)
BarclaysAmerican/Financial (consumer loans)
Commercial Credit (consumer loans)
Fingerhut (direct marketing)
Primerica Bank (credit cards)

Insurance Services
Gulf (property and casualty)
Milico (life)
Primerica Financial Services (formerly A. L. Williams, life)

Investment Services
American Capital Management & Research (mutual funds)
Margaretten (home mortgages)
RCM Capital (investment management)
Smith Barney (securities brokerage and investment banking)

RANKINGS

19th in *Fortune* 50 Diversified Financial Cos.
199th in *Business Week* 1000

HOW MUCH

	9-Year Growth	1981	1982	1983	1984	1985	1986	1987	1988	1989	1990
Assets ($ mil.)	15.9%	5,231	5,185	6,892	7,373	6,322	4,864	4,306	14,435	17,955	19,689
Net income ($ mil.)	25.0%	50	42	30	66	32	38	102	162	289	373
Income as % of assets	—	1.0%	0.8%	0.4%	0.9%	0.5%	0.8%	2.4%	1.1%	1.6%	1.9%
Earnings per share ($)	—	—	—	—	—	—	0.95	2.00	3.61	2.87	3.27
Stock price – high ($)	—	—	—	—	—	—	22.75	34.63	29.00	30.00	37.75
Stock price – low ($)	—	—	—	—	—	—	19.75	17.00	20.50	20.25	16.88
Stock price – close ($)	—	—	—	—	—	—	20.50	22.38	21.75	28.50	22.88
P/E – high	—	—	—	—	—	—	24	17	8	10	12
P/E – low	—	—	—	—	—	—	21	9	6	7	5
Dividends per share ($)	—	—	—	—	—	—	0.06	0.24	0.27	0.29	0.36
Book value per share ($)	—	—	—	—	—	—	18.38	15.33	20.28	23.52	26.40

1990 Year-end:
Debt ratio: 55.9%
Equity as % of assets: 14.5%
Return on equity: 13.1%
Long-term debt (mil.): $3,628
No. of shares (mil.): 108
Dividends:
  1990 average yield: 1.6%
  1990 payout: 11.0%
Market value (mil.): $2,477
Sales (mil.): $6,190

Stock Price History High/Low 1986–90

KEY COMPETITORS

Aetna
H. F. Ahmanson
American Express
BankAmerica
Bear Stearns
Charles Schwab
CIGNA
Citicorp
Dai-Ichi Kangyo
Dial
Equitable
Ford
General Electric
Goldman Sachs
Great Western
Household International
ITT
John Hancock

Kemper
MassMutual
Merrill Lynch
MetLife
Morgan Stanley
New York Life
Northwestern Mutual
Paine Webber
J. C. Penney
Prudential
Salomon
Sears
Transamerica
Travelers
USF&G
Other insurance companies
Other commercial banks

THE PROCTER & GAMBLE COMPANY

OVERVIEW

Cincinnati-based Procter & Gamble sells many of the most recognized brand names found on grocery store shelves in America and throughout the world. P&G's 160+ products include cleansers for home and laundry, personal care items, foods and beverages, and a growing list of beauty and health care products.

The company's products lead its competitors' in the US and are near the top in several foreign markets. P&G has a #1 item in 22 of 40 product categories. Among these are Crisco, Tide, Bounty, Charmin, Ultra Pampers, NyQuil, Metamucil, and Oil of Olay.

The company's primary strategy for the 1990s is to increase its global presence. P&G took a firm step in that direction in 1991 by purchasing Rakona, the largest detergent producer in Czechoslovakia.

During the last year, the company has had several run-ins with the FDA, which has forced P&G to remove the "no cholesterol" claims on many of its products and the "fresh" on its Citrus Hill orange juice. Nevertheless, the company hopes to win the FDA's favor for its caprenin, a lower-calorie substitute for cocoa butter that can be used in candy.

NYSE symbol: PG
Fiscal year ends: June 30

Hoover's Rating **A**

WHO

Chairman and CEO: Edwin L. Artzt, age 60, $1,436,359 pay
President: John E. Pepper, age 52, $1,250,218 pay
SVP and CFO: James W. Nethercott, age 62
VP Personnel: Samuel H. Pruett, age 57
Auditors: Deloitte & Touche
Employees: 89,000

WHERE

HQ: One Procter & Gamble Plaza, Cincinnati, OH 45202
Phone: 513-983-1100
Fax: 513-562-2062

	1990 Sales		1990 Net Income	
	$ mil.	% of total	$ mil.	% of total
US	14,962	61	1,304	74
Foreign	9,618	39	467	26
Adjustments	(499)	—	(169)	—
Total	**24,081**	**100**	**1,602**	**100**

WHEN

Procter & Gamble came into existence in 1837 in Cincinnati when candlemaker William Procter and soapmaker James Gamble merged their small businesses. By 1859 they had become one of the largest companies in Cincinnati, with sales of $1 million. In 1879 the company introduced Ivory, a floating soap. The campaign for the product, a forerunner of P&G's advertising of later years, was one of the first to advertise directly to the consumer. P&G introduced its next major product, Crisco shortening, in 1911.

Family members headed the company until 1930, when William Deupree became president. In the 29 years that Deupree served as president and then chairman, P&G became the largest seller of packaged consumer goods in the US. P&G advertising innovations included sponsorship of daytime dramas, the first being "The Puddle Family," a 1932 radio show. P&G introduced Tide detergent in 1947 after years of research to determine how to make a cleanser work well in hard water.

Acquisitions over the years included Spic and Span (1945), Duncan Hines (1956), Charmin Paper Mills (1957), Clorox (1957), and Folgers Coffee (1963). Following an antitrust action, P&G sold Clorox in 1968. Introduced in 1955, Crest was the first toothpaste with fluoride that was endorsed by the American Dental Association. In 1961 the company rolled out Pampers disposable diapers and Head & Shoulders shampoo.

A few brands haven't fared so well: P&G bought Crush soft drinks in 1980 and sold it in 1989; Duncan Hines lost out to Nabisco in the "cookie wars" of the early 1980s; Rely tampons had to be removed from the market in 1980 when investigators linked them to toxic shock syndrome. Several P&G products had lost market share by the mid-1980s.

In 1985 the company suffered its first decline in profits in 33 years. Under CEO John Smale, P&G improved existing products to make them more competitive and introduced new ones. The improved Ultra Pampers is now the #1 disposable diaper in markets worldwide. In 1990 Edwin Artzt was appointed CEO.

Acquisitions in the 1980s included moves into health care: Norwich-Eaton (1982, pharmaceuticals); the nonprescription drug division of G. D. Searle (1985, Metamucil); and Richardson-Vicks (1985, NyQuil, Formula 44). In 1990 P&G bought the rights from Rorer to sell Maalox. The 1989 acquisition of Noxell (Cover Girl, Noxzema) made P&G the biggest cosmetics company in America, a position which P&G strengthened in 1991 by buying Max Factor and Betrix from Revlon.

P&G is currently cutting costs by trimming jobs and unprofitable brands.

WHAT

	1990 Sales		1990 Operating Income	
	$ mil.	% of total	$ mil.	% of total
Laundry & cleaning prod.	7,942	33	781	29
Personal care prod.	11,767	49	1,314	49
Food & beverage	3,318	14	304	11
Pulp & chemicals	1,054	4	307	11
Adjustments	—	—	(404)	—
Total	**24,081**	**100**	**2,302**	**100**

Brand Names

Laundry and Cleaning	Personal Care	
Bold	Bain de Soleil	Pepto-Bismol
Bounce	Camay	Puffs
Bounty	Charmin	Safeguard
Cascade	Clearasil	Secret
Cheer	Coast	Scope
Comet	Cover Girl	VapoRub
Dawn	Crest	Vidal Sassoon
Downy	Dramamine	Zest
Joy	Fixodent	
Lestoil	Formula 44	**Food and Beverage**
Mr. Clean	Head & Shoulders	Citrus Hill
Oxydol	Ivory	Crisco
Spic and Span	Lava	Duncan Hines
Tide	Metamucil	Folgers
	Noxzema	Hawaiian Punch
	NyQuil	Jif
	Oil of Olay	Maryland Club
	Old Spice	Pringles
	Pampers	

HOW MUCH

	9-Year Growth	1981	1982	1983	1984	1985	1986	1987	1988	1989	1990
Sales ($ mil.)	8.6%	11,416	11,994	12,452	12,946	13,552	15,439	17,000	19,336	21,398	24,081
Net income ($ mil.)	10.2%	668	777	866	890	635	709	327	1,020	1,206	1,602
Income as % of sales	—	5.9%	6.5%	7.0%	6.9%	4.7%	4.6%	1.9%	5.3%	5.6%	6.7%
Earnings per share ($)	8.7%	2.02	2.35	2.61	2.67	1.89	2.08	0.93	2.96	3.47	4.27
Stock price – high ($)	—	20.22	30.75	31.63	29.94	35.88	41.25	51.75	44.00	70.38	91.25
Stock price – low ($)	—	16.28	19.44	25.25	22.81	25.19	31.88	30.00	35.38	42.13	61.75
Stock price – close ($)	17.6%	20.09	29.56	28.44	28.50	34.88	38.19	42.69	43.50	70.25	86.63
P/E – high	—	10	13	12	11	19	20	56	15	20	21
P/E – low	—	8	8	10	9	13	15	32	12	12	14
Dividends per share ($)	7.0%	0.95	1.03	1.13	1.20	1.30	1.31	1.35	1.38	1.50	1.75
Book value per share ($)	5.4%	11.67	12.59	13.88	15.21	15.74	16.95	16.98	18.71	16.10	18.82

1990 Year-end:
Debt ratio: 32.3%
Return on equity: 24.5%
Cash (mil.): $1,407
Current ratio: 1.41
Long-term debt (mil.): $3,588
No. of shares (mil.): 346
Dividends:
  1990 average yield: 2.0%
  1990 payout: 41.0%
Market value (mil.): $29,998

Stock Price History High/Low 1981–90

RANKINGS

15th in *Fortune* 500 Industrial Cos.
10th in *Business Week* 1000

KEY COMPETITORS

American Home Products	Coca-Cola	L'Oréal
Amway	Colgate-Palmolive	LVMH
Avon	Dial	Monsanto
Bristol-Myers Squibb	Eastman Kodak	Scott
Chiquita Brands	Gerber	Seagram
Clorox	James River	Unilever
	S. C. Johnson	Warner-Lambert
	Kimberly-Clark	Weyerhaeuser

THE PRUDENTIAL INSURANCE CO. OF AMERICA

Mutual company
Fiscal year ends: December 31

Hoover's Rating **A-**

OVERVIEW

Prudential is the largest insurance company in the US. The Prudential "rock" is one of the most widely recognized corporate symbols.

A mutual insurance company owned by its policyholders, Prudential sold over $4 billion in individual life insurance in North America in 1990, a 27% increase over 1989. The company's 1990 revenues of $42 billion were primarily from investment income (27%) and premiums and annuities (65%).

Prudential is a huge investor, with over $247 billion in assets under management. This figure includes nearly $100 billion Prudential manages for others.

Prudential is the largest commercial health insurer in the US, offering PruCare HMO and PruCare plus, among other products. The American Association of Retired Persons is its largest group-health client. In 1990 Prudential had $1.7 billion in new group life and health insurance sales.

In 1991 persistent losses in the company's securities firm, Prudential-Bache, led to the resignation of Pru-Bache's president, George Ball, and eventual replacement by Hardwick Simmons, formerly of Shearson Lehman. In an effort to staunch the losses and restore morale in the 4th largest securities sales force, the company has restructured its securities company, closed its arbitrage department, and renamed the group Prudential Securities.

WHO

Chairman and CEO: Robert C. Winters, age 59
President: Ron D. Barbaro
SVP and Comptroller: Eugene M. O'Hara, age 54
SVP Human Resources: Donald C. Mann
Auditors: Deloitte & Touche
Employees: 107,840

WHERE

HQ: 751 Broad St., Newark, NJ 07102-3777
Phone: 201-802-6000
Fax: 201-802-6092 (Human Resources)

Prudential operates in all 50 states, the District of Columbia, the US Virgin Islands, Puerto Rico, Guam, Canada, Hong Kong, Taiwan, Korea, Japan, Spain, and Italy.

WHEN

In 1873 John Fairfield Dryden founded the Widows and Orphans Friendly Society in New Jersey to sell workers industrial insurance (life insurance with small face values and premiums paid weekly). In 1875 he changed the name to the Prudential Friendly Society, naming it after the successful Prudential Assurance Company of England. The following year Dryden visited the English company and copied some of its methods, such as recruiting agents from neighborhoods where insurance was to be sold. In 1877 the company adopted its current name.

In 1886 the company began issuing ordinary life insurance (term or whole life) in addition to industrial insurance, and by the end of 1890 it was selling more than 2,000 ordinary life policies a year. By this time the company had 3,000 field agents in 8 states. In 1896 Dryden commissioned the J. Walter Thompson advertising agency to design a company trademark, the Rock of Gibraltar.

In 1928 Prudential introduced 3 new insurance policies. An Intermediate Monthly Premium Plan combined some features of the industrial and ordinary life policies. The Modified 3 policy was a whole-life policy with a rate change after 3 years. The Accidental Death Benefit feature was added to weekly premium policies, resulting in beneficiaries receiving an extra $3 million in the next year alone.

In the late 1920s the company was the first to establish procedures in which an employer as client of the insurance company kept the records for group life insurance, instead of Prudential. Prudential issued its first group life insurance policy in 1916, and it became a leading group carrier in the mid-1940s.

In 1943 the company became a mutual insurance company owned by the policyholders. In the 1940s President Carroll Shanks implemented a program to decentralize the company's operations by establishing 7 regional home offices. Other companies copied Prudential after the system proved successful. The company introduced a Property Investment Separate Account (PRISA), which gave pension plans a real estate investment option. In 1974 the company, group pension leader in the life insurance industry, reported that 20 of the country's largest 100 corporations were PRISA contract holders.

In 1981 Prudential acquired the Bache Group, Inc. (now called Prudential Securities), a securities brokerage firm, for $385 million. Bache's forte was retail investments, which was expected to blend well with Prudential's insurance business. However, under George Ball, the company caught the 1980s investment fever and attempted to become a powerhouse investment banker, in which it failed. In 1991, after over $250 million in losses and expensive lawsuits stemming from sales of real estate limited partnerships (in which some of the Pru-Bache traders had personal interests), Ball resigned. Despite these problems, however, the parent company remains strong. In 1990 Prudential introduced a Living Needs program that allows prepayment of death benefits to medically impoverished policyholders to use for current expenses.

WHAT

	1990 Sales	
	$ mil.	% of total
Premiums & annuities	27,776	65
Broker-dealer revenue	3,612	8
Investments	11,485	27
Adjustments	(748)	—
Total	**42,125**	**100**

	12/31/90 Assets	
	$ mil.	% of total
Fixed maturities	65,145	38
Mortgage loans	28,919	17
Separate account assets	28,582	17
Trading account securities	6,324	4
Other	40,076	24
Total	**169,046**	**100**

Product Lines
Annuities
Asset management
Credit card services
Deposit accounts
Estate and financial planning
Life, health, and property insurance
Reinsurance
Residential real estate services

Major Subsidiaries
The Prudential Asset Management Co., Inc.
Prudential Capital and Investment Services, Inc.
Prudential Capital Management Group
The Prudential Investment Corp.
Prudential Property and Casualty Insurance Co.
The Prudential Realty Group
Prudential Reinsurance Co.
Prudential Relocation Management
Prudential Securities, Inc.
Prudential Venture Capital Management, Inc.

RANKINGS

1st in *Fortune* 50 Life Insurance Cos.

KEY COMPETITORS

Aetna
Allianz
American Express
Bear Stearns
Blue Cross
CIGNA
Equitable
First Executive
General Electric
Humana
John Hancock
Kemper
MassMutual

MetLife
New York Life
Northwestern Mutual
Paine Webber
Sears
State Farm
Teachers Insurance
Travelers
Investment bankers
Real estate brokers
Stockbrokers
Other insurance companies

HOW MUCH

	9-Year Growth	1981	1982	1983	1984	1985	1986	1987	1988	1989	1990
Assets ($ bil.)	11.7%	62.5	66.7	72.2	78.9	115.7	134.5	140.9	153.0	164.0	169.0
Income ($ mil.)	—	—	—	—	—	—	—	967	829	743	113
Income as % of assets	—	—	—	—	—	—	—	0.7%	0.5%	0.5%	0.1%

1990 Year-end:
Equity as % of assets: 3.2%
Return on equity: 2.2%
Cash (mil.): $1,289
Sales (mil.): $42,125

Income ($ mil.)
1987–90

(bar chart values: 1,000, 900, 800, 700, 600, 500, 400, 300, 200, 100, 0)

PUBLIC SERVICE ENTERPRISE GROUP INC.

OVERVIEW

Public Service Enterprise Group is the parent company of Public Service Electric and Gas Company (PSE&G), America's 8th largest electric and natural gas utility in 1990. With a service area covering the northeast and central regions of New Jersey, PSE&G served 3.4 million customers in 1990, representing about 70% of the state's population.

About 47% of the company's electric power is generated by its nuclear facilities, located in New Jersey and Pennsylvania. Units 2 and 3 of the Peach Bottom plant, shut down by the Nuclear Regulatory Commission in 1987 for safety violations, are back on-line. A lawsuit filed by PSE&G against the plant's operator (Philadelphia Electric) is pending.

To help offset slow growth in the utility sector, PSE Group is planning to spend about $2.3 billion on its nonutility businesses (Enterprise Diversified Holdings) over the next 5 years. Current nonutility activities include oil and gas exploration, joint cogeneration (production of steam and electricity) projects, small power plants, and commercial real estate development in New Jersey, Maryland, Pennsylvania, Virginia, and Florida.

WHEN

Newark, New Jersey, was the scene of a tragedy in 1903 when a trolley full of high school students collided with a Delaware, Lackawanna and Western train. While investigating the accident, state attorney general Thomas McCarter discovered the underlying financial weakness of the trolley company and many of New Jersey's other transportation, gas, and electric companies. Planning to buy and consolidate these companies, McCarter resigned as attorney general. He and several colleagues then established the Public Service Corporation (1903).

The company originally formed separate divisions for gas utilities, trolley and other transportation companies, and electric utilities. Management spent most of its energies on the trolley company, rationalizing that these operations would be most profitable. Indeed, during its first full year of operation, the trolley company generated almost half of Public Service's total sales.

In 1924 the gas and electric companies consolidated as Public Service Electric and Gas (PSE&G). A new company formed to operate buses that year and merged with the trolley company in 1928 to form Public Service Coordinated Transport (later Transport of New Jersey).

PSE&G signed interconnection agreements with 2 Pennsylvania electric companies in 1928 to form the world's first integrated power pool — later known as the Pennsylvania–New Jersey–Maryland (PJM) Interconnection when Baltimore Gas & Electric joined in 1956. Four more companies joined in 1965.

PSE&G began exploring new gas fields in Texas and Louisiana in response to the 1972 Arab oil embargo and formed a research subsidiary in 1977 to develop solar and other non–fossil fuel energy sources.

The state of New Jersey, which had been subsidizing Transport of New Jersey, bought it from PSE&G in 1980. Public Service Enterprise Group (PSE Group), a holding company, was formed in 1985 to allow PSE&G to diversify into nonutility enterprises. A new subsidiary, Enterprise Diversified Holdings, was formed in 1989 to handle these activities, which include commercial real estate development (Enterprise Group Development) and 94 oil- and gas-producing properties in West Texas and the Gulf of Mexico (Energy Development Corporation). In 1989 Energy Development paid Houston-based Southdown $320 million for Pelto Oil Company (oil and gas exploration).

PSE&G plans to file for a gas rate increase in 1991 (its first since 1987) to help offset inflation-related costs and the effects of a softening economy.

NYSE symbol: PEG
Fiscal year ends: December 31

Hoover's Rating C

WHO

Chairman, President, and CEO: E. James Ferland, age 49, $527,971 pay
VP (Principal Financial Officer): Everett L. Morris, age 62, $323,756 pay
VP Human Resources, PSE&G: Gregory M. Thomson, age 43
Auditors: Deloitte & Touche
Employees: 13,128

WHERE

HQ: 80 Park Plaza, PO Box 1171, Newark, NJ 07101-1171
Phone: 201-430-7000
Fax: 201-430-5983

The company's service area includes Camden, Newark, and Trenton, NJ.

Generating Facilities

Fossil Fuels	Nuclear
Bayonne (NJ)	Hope Creek (95.0%, NJ)
Bergen (NJ)	Peach Bottom (42.5%, PA)
Burlington (NJ)	Salem (42.6%, NJ)
Conemaugh (22.5%, PA)	
Edison (NJ)	**Pumped Storage**
Essex (NJ)	Yard Creek (50.0%, NJ)
Hudson (NJ)	
Kearny (NJ)	**Steam**
Keystone (22.8%, PA)	Bergen (NJ)
Linden (NJ)	Burlington (NJ)
Mercer (NJ)	Conemaugh (22.5%, PA)
National Park (NJ)	Hudson (NJ)
Salem (42.6%, NJ)	Kearny (NJ)
Sewaren (NJ)	Keystone (22.8%, PA)
	Linden (NJ)
	Mercer (NJ)
	Sewaren (NJ)

WHAT

	1990 Sales	
	$ mil.	% of total
Utility activities		
Electric	3,332	69
Gas	1,237	26
Nonutility activities	231	5
Total	**4,800**	**100**

	1990 Fuel Sources
	% of total
Nuclear	47
Coal	26
Natural gas	8
Residual oil	2
Interchange & 2-party purchases	17
Total	**100**

Public Service Electric and Gas Co.

Enterprise Diversified Holdings, Inc.
Community Energy Alternatives, Inc. (22 cogeneration and small power plants)
Energy Development Corp. (oil and gas exploration, development, and production)
Enterprise Capital Funding Corp. (financing for nonutility operations)
Enterprise Group Development Corp. (commercial real estate development)
PSEG Capital Corp. (financing for nonutility operations)
Public Service Resources Corp. (outside investments)

RANKINGS

15th in *Fortune* 50 Utilities
112th in *Business Week* 1000

HOW MUCH

	9-Year Growth	1981	1982	1983	1984	1985	1986	1987	1988	1989	1990
Sales ($ mil.)	3.7%	3,472	3,874	3,963	4,196	4,409	4,498	4,211	4,395	4,805	4,800
Net income ($ mil.)	9.0%	264	343	390	490	545	430	559	560	571	571
Income as % of sales	—	7.6%	8.9%	9.8%	11.7%	12.4%	9.6%	13.3%	12.7%	11.9%	11.9%
Earnings per share ($)	4.3%	1.75	2.16	2.27	2.63	2.64	1.89	2.55	2.57	2.62	2.56
Stock price – high ($)	—	13.42	15.83	17.67	18.08	22.08	32.17	30.58	26.88	29.38	29.75
Stock price – low ($)	—	11.00	11.83	14.17	13.42	16.92	20.50	20.00	22.00	23.00	22.50
Stock price – close ($)	9.1%	12.00	15.50	15.17	17.83	21.08	26.83	23.88	24.50	29.25	26.38
P/E – high	—	8	7	8	7	8	17	12	10	11	12
P/E – low	—	6	5	6	5	6	11	8	9	9	9
Dividends per share ($)	2.8%	1.63	1.69	1.75	1.80	1.87	1.95	1.99	2.01	2.05	2.09
Book value per share ($)	1.6%	17.64	17.75	18.04	18.54	19.08	17.92	18.54	19.11	19.85	20.44

1990 Year-end:
Debt ratio: 49.1%
Return on equity: 12.7%
Cash (mil.): $61
Current ratio: 0.63
Long-term debt (mil.): $4,722
No. of shares (mil.): 218
Dividends:
 1990 average yield: 7.9%
 1990 payout: 81.6%
Market value (mil.): $5,762

Stock Price History High/Low 1981–90

PUBLIX SUPER MARKETS, INC.

Private company
Fiscal year ends: Last Saturday
in December

Hoover's Rating **A**

OVERVIEW

Lakeland, Florida–based Publix is the largest grocery chain in that state and the 8th largest grocery chain in the US. The company is one of the largest employee-owned companies in the US; the stock is controlled by current employees, directors, and members of the founding Jenkins family.

Founder George Jenkins's philosophy is that Publix stores should be places "where customers find it a pleasure to shop and employees find it a pleasure to work." Jenkins also believes that "no sale is complete until the meal is eaten and enjoyed." The company added "Singles Nights" to woo younger shoppers. And, as the labor pool has grown smaller, the company has recruited about 5,000 senior citizens.

Publix, under the direction of the founder's son Howard, will soon be expanding into Georgia with its new prototype store. Howard Jenkins expects Publix to expand throughout the Southeast. In the meantime, current Publix stores face tough competition in the 1990s. Competitors such as American Stores and Pueblo International (the leading chain in Puerto Rico and the Virgin Islands) are making inroads in Florida.

WHO

Chairman of the Executive Committee of the Board: Charles H. Jenkins, Jr., $300,221 pay
Chairman: Howard M. Jenkins, age 40, $387,221 pay
President: Mark C. Hollis, age 56, $382,221 pay
EVP: Hoyt R. Barnett, age 47
VP Finance and Treasurer: William H. Vass, age 41
VP Personnel: Edward H. Ruth, age 59
Auditors: KPMG Peat Marwick
Employees: 66,756

WHEN

In 1930 George Jenkins, age 20, left his manager position at the Piggly Wiggly grocery store in Winter Haven, Florida. He took the money he had saved to buy a car and opened his own grocery store, the first Publix, next door to his old employer. Despite the Depression the small store prospered, and in 1935 Jenkins opened another Publix in Winter Haven.

In 1940 after the supermarket format became popular, he closed his 2 smaller locations and opened a new Publix Market, a modern marble, tile, and stucco edifice. It boasted pastel colors and electric-eye doors and was the first store in the US to feature air conditioning.

In 1944 Publix purchased the All-American chain based in Lakeland, Florida (19 stores). Corporate headquarters also moved to Lakeland, and Publix built a warehouse there (1950). Publix began offering S&H Green Stamps (1953) and replaced its original Winter Haven supermarket with a mall featuring an enlarged Publix, a Green Stamp redemption center, and other retailers (1956). The company expanded to populous southeastern Florida, first opening a Publix in Miami and then buying and converting 7 former Grand Union stores (1959).

As Florida's population grew, Publix continued to expand and opened its 100th store in 1964. In 1970 the company launched a discount chain — Food World — but sold it in the mid-1980s.

Publix was the first grocery chain in Florida to use bar code scanners and all stores had scanners by the end of 1980. The company beat Florida banks in installing ATMs, and during the 1980s began using debit card stations.

Publix continued to grow throughout the 1980s, unthreatened by the takeover activity because Publix has always been owned by employee-stockholders. In 1988 the company purchased stores from takeover-refugee Kroger. That same year Publix installed the first automated checkout systems in South Florida, affording customers a checkout lane that is always open.

The company completed its withdrawal from offering Green Stamps in 1989, and most of the $19 million decrease in Publix advertising expenditures was attributed to the end of the 36-year promotion. Also in 1989, after almost 60 years, "Mr. George" — as visionary founder Jenkins is known — stepped down as chairman in favor of his son Howard.

In 1990 Publix announced it would open 3 stores in Georgia. Howard Jenkins expects Publix to become a major player all over the Southeast. The company's latest vehicle toward this end is a new store prototype that takes "celebrating food" to a new height. The store's first aisle tempts shoppers with freshly made ready-to-eat offerings including fresh pasta, breads, pizzas, and Chinese food. There is also a sit-down cafe. Activities such as meat cutting, baking, and salad chopping, which are usually kept out of sight, are on display. Produce is piled high.

Because of Publix's current low debt, it is in a good expansion position.

WHERE

HQ: PO Box 407, 1936 George Jenkins Blvd., Lakeland, FL 33802-0407
Phone: 813-688-1188
Fax: 813-680-5257 (Public Relations)

Publix Super Markets operates 378 grocery stores, all located in Florida. Three stores are currently planned for Georgia. The company also operates dairy processing plants at Deerfield Beach and Lakeland, a bakery at Lakeland, and distribution centers in Boynton Beach, Deerfield Beach, Jacksonville, Lakeland, North Miami, and Sarasota.

	1990 Store Locations	
	No. of locations	% of total
Broward County	50	13
Dade County	42	11
Palm Beach County	39	11
Pinellas County	31	8
Other counties	216	57
Total	**378**	**100**

WHAT

	1990 Sales	
	$ mil.	% of total
Existing stores	5,608	97
New/closed stores	150	3
Total	**5,758**	**100**

Lines of Business
Food/drug supermarkets
Food processing plants
  Dairy
  Baking (Danish Bakery brand)
  Bottling
  Delicatessen
Supermarkets

Private Label Goods
Publix (outside manufacturers)

RANKINGS

20th in *Fortune* 50 Retailing Cos.
12th in *Forbes* 400 US Private Cos.

KEY COMPETITORS

Albertson's
American Stores
Food Lion
Kroger
Walgreen
Winn-Dixie

HOW MUCH

	9-Year Growth	1981	1982	1983	1984	1985	1986	1987	1988	1989	1990
Sales ($ mil.)	10.3%	2,376	2,507	2,835	3,206	3,446	3,760	4,152	4,804	5,331	5,758
Net income ($ mil.)	15.7%	40	47	57	76	72	84	87	102	128	149
Income as % of sales	—	1.7%	1.9%	2.0%	2.4%	2.1%	2.2%	2.1%	2.1%	2.4%	2.6%
Employees	9.3%	29,997	30,137	33,607	37,042	40,098	44,813	50,123	57,791	64,037	66,756

1990 Year-end:
Debt ratio: 1.3%
Return on equity: 16.8%
Cash (mil.): $206
Current ratio: 1.43
Long-term debt (mil.): $13

Net Income ($ mil.) 1981–90

THE QUAKER OATS COMPANY

OVERVIEW

Best known for its cereal products, Chicago-based Quaker Oats is a diverse international food and pet food company. Since its 1990 decision to spin off its Fisher-Price toy division, the company has returned to selling only food for the first time in 22 years. In North America almost 80% of Quaker's brands hold the #1 or #2 spots in their respective markets. Top-selling names include Quaker Oats (61% market share), Aunt Jemima syrup (23% market share), and Van Camp's beans. Gatorade is Quaker's largest-selling brand.

The company achieved its competitive position in the food industry largely through acquisitions and new product introductions during the last decade. Quaker has particularly focused product development on cereals, pet foods, convenience foods, and microwave items. New items on the company's horizon include Rice-a-Roni Lunch-for-One meals, Tiny Toons cereal, Quaker Ovenstuffs (microwaveable sandwiches), and frisbee-shaped throwable dog treats.

WHEN

The familiar, friendly Quaker Man of the Quaker Oats Company was first used as a trademark in 1877 by Henry P. Crowell at his Quaker Mill in Ravenna, Ohio. Crowell was one of 7 prominent millers who formed the American Cereal Company of Chicago in 1891. This powerful consolidation (some called it the "oatmeal trust") changed its name to the Quaker Oats Company in 1901 and adopted Crowell's Quaker Man as its logo.

The company was an immediate success. Crowell's creative marketing practices and powerful sales staff covered the nation with the innovative image. The Quaker Man was everywhere — on billboards, in magazines, in newspapers, on cards on subways and streetcars, and in coupon promotions and miniature samples left on doorsteps — extolling the healthful virtues of oatmeal. Crowell spent nearly $500,000 on advertising in 1899, an enormous outlay for the time.

Robert Stuart, another founder, served as the company's first secretary-treasurer from 1891 to 1897. Stuart consolidated mill operations to 2 locations — a large mill in Akron, Ohio, and his Cedar Rapids mill, which he modernized and expanded. With streamlined facilities and the attraction of oatmeal as a cheap, nutritious food, Quaker Oats prospered during the difficult 1890s.

By 1911 the company was diversifying its product line with such purchases as animal feed and grocery items. Sales reached $123 million in 1918. In 1925 Quaker Oats bought Aunt Jemima pancake flour, one of its most successful brands. In 1969 Fisher-Price toys, then the world's largest maker of toys for preschool children, became a major addition to Quaker Oats.

Since 1981 the company has purchased companies with top-selling products. It bought Stokely-Van Camp in 1983 for $238 million and kept its top brands of canned beans and Gatorade beverage. In 1986 Quaker Oats paid $801 million for Anderson, Clayton & Company, a Houston food products company with such brands as Seven Seas salad dressings, Chiffon margarine, Igloo ice chests, and Gaines dog food (purchased from General Foods in 1984). Quaker subsequently sold all Anderson Clayton businesses except Gaines. In 1990 Quaker Oats announced that it would spin off its Fisher-Price toy company to its shareholders. In 1991 Fisher-Price became an independent public company and moved its headquarters to New York.

Following a down year in 1990, Quaker reinforced its back-to-basics food strategy by increasing its advertising budget, reformulating its dog food brands, and launching an array of new products.

NYSE symbol: OAT
Fiscal year ends: June 30

WHO

Chairman and CEO: William D. Smithburg, age 52, $1,077,110 pay
President and COO: Frank J. Morgan, age 65, $748,379 pay
SVP Finance and CFO: Terry G. Westbrook, age 44
SVP Human Resources: Lawrence M. Baytos
Auditors: Arthur Andersen & Co.
Employees: 28,200

WHERE

HQ: Quaker Tower, PO Box 9001, 321 N. Clark St., Chicago, IL 60604-9001
Phone: 312-222-7111
Fax: 312-222-8304

	1990 Sales		1990 Operating Income	
	$ mil.	% of total	$ mil.	% of total
US	3,378	67	345	64
Canada	232	5	18	3
Europe	1,085	21	89	16
Other countries	336	7	93	17
Adjustments	—	—	(52)	—
Total	**5,031**	**100**	**493**	**100**

WHAT

	US 1990 Sales	
	$ mil.	% of total
Grocery specialties	765	23
Pet foods	518	15
Food service	460	14
Ready-to-eat cereals	441	13
Hot cereals	369	11
Aunt Jemima	236	7
Celeste	196	6
Snacks	110	3
Other	283	8
Total	**3,378**	**100**

Brand Names

Cereals
Cap'n Crunch
Instant Quaker Oatmeal
Life
Oh!s
Quaker 100% Natural
Quaker Oat Bran
Quaker Oat Squares
Quaker Oats

Quaker Chewy granola bars
Quaker Butter Popped Corn Cakes
Quaker Rice Cakes
Rice-A-Roni
Van Camp's (pork & beans)
Wolf (chili)

Other Food Products
Ardmore Farms (citrus juice)
Aunt Jemima
Celeste (pizza)
Continental Coffee
Gatorade
Granola Dipps
Noodle Roni

Pet Food
Gaines Cycle
Gravy Train
Ken-L-Ration
Kibbles 'n Bits
King Kuts
Pounce
Puss 'n Boots

HOW MUCH

	9-Year Growth	1981	1982	1983	1984	1985	1986	1987	1988	1989	1990
Sales ($ mil.)	7.6%	2,600	2,712	2,611	3,344	3,520	3,671	4,421	5,330	5,724	5,031
Net income ($ mil.)	9.0%	105	121	119	139	157	174	186	256	203	229
Income as % of sales	—	4.0%	4.4%	4.6%	4.1%	4.4%	4.7%	4.2%	4.8%	3.5%	4.6%
Earnings per share ($)	9.9%	1.25	1.50	1.46	1.68	1.88	2.18	2.36	3.20	2.56	2.93
Stock price – high ($)	—	9.44	12.16	15.97	19.06	31.50	44.88	57.63	61.50	59.50	59.50
Stock price – low ($)	—	7.50	8.00	10.19	13.66	16.50	27.38	31.75	38.50	49.63	41.00
Stock price – close ($)	21.8%	8.94	10.72	14.75	19.06	28.63	40.00	41.63	53.13	57.75	52.88
P/E – high	—	8	8	11	11	17	21	24	19	27	20
P/E – low	—	6	5	7	8	9	13	13	12	19	14
Dividends per share ($)	14.9%	0.40	0.45	0.50	0.55	0.62	0.70	0.80	1.00	1.20	1.40
Book value per share ($)	6.0%	8.00	8.04	8.02	8.89	9.76	10.65	13.68	15.76	14.44	13.46

1990 Year-end:
Debt ratio: 42.1%
Return on equity: 21.0%
Cash (mil.): $18
Current ratio: 1.30
Long-term debt (mil.): $740
No. of shares (mil.): 76
Dividends:
1990 average yield: 2.6%
1990 payout: 47.8%
Market value (mil.): $3,997

Stock Price History High/Low 1981–90

RANKINGS

93rd in *Fortune* 500 Industrial Cos.
155th in *Business Week* 1000

KEY COMPETITORS

American Home Products
Cadbury Schweppes
Coca-Cola
Colgate-Palmolive
ConAgra
General Mills
Grand Metropolitan
Heinz
Kellogg
Mars
Nestlé
Philip Morris
Ralston Purina
RJR Nabisco
Seagram

RALSTON PURINA COMPANY

NYSE symbol: RAL
Fiscal year ends: September 30

Hoover's Rating **B-**

OVERVIEW

Internationally recognized by its checkerboard packages, St. Louis–based Ralston Purina is the world-leading producer of dry dog foods (Purina Dog Chow), dry and moist cat foods (Alley Cat, Tender Vittles), and dry-cell battery products (Eveready, Energizer). The company also owns the US's largest wholesale baker (Continental Baking Company, with Wonder Bread and Hostess baked goods), and its Beech-Nut baby food business is the 2nd largest brand (after Gerber) in the US.

During the 1980s, Ralston Purina sold its interests in fast-food restaurants (Jack-in-the-Box), seafood (Chicken of the Sea brand tuna), and domestic livestock feeds, the core of the original enterprise, to concentrate on consumer products such as cereals, baked goods, and pet foods.

The company hopes to increase its international presence during the 1990s by building upon its international leadership in pet foods, batteries, and formula feeds.

WHEN

In 1894 William Danforth founded the Robinson-Danforth Commission Company, a small St. Louis feed producer. The company's slogan, "Where Purity is Paramount," inspired Danforth to name a new whole-wheat cereal product Purina (1898). The popularity of Danforth's cereal was enhanced by the endorsement of Everett Ralston, a well-known advocate of whole-grain foods. In return, Ralston's name was included and the cereal became Ralston health breakfast food. Trading on the cereal's popularity, Danforth renamed his company Ralston Purina in 1902.

Danforth proved to be a skillful marketer, introducing slogans, trademarks, and logos that would support Ralston Purina's image and products for many years. In 1900 he introduced the distinctive checkerboard design used on Ralston packages, grain elevators, and delivery trucks. The pattern was based on his childhood memory of a neighboring family who dressed in red-and-white checks. He changed the word "feed" to "chow" in the company's brands after returning from the front lines of WWI, where he noted the soldiers' eager response to each evening's "chow call." Ralston's animal foods have used the word "chow" ever since.

Danforth retired in 1932 and devoted his next 20 years to a variety of philanthropic activities. His book, *I Dare You*, sets forth his life philosophy of enthusiasm, hard work, and optimism.

During the 1950s the company decided to apply its knowledge of animal feeds to producing a domestic dog food. Purina Dog Chow, introduced in 1957, quickly became the nation's leading brand of dry dog food.

In 1962 the company experienced the worst disaster in its history when a dust explosion and fire demolished its St. Louis mill. Nevertheless, Ralston Purina embarked on a major diversification program in the 1960s, buying the Van Camp Seafood Company, with its Chicken of the Sea brands (1963, sold in 1988) and Foodmaker (1968), which included Jack-in-the-Box hamburger restaurants (sold in 1985).

The company became the nation's largest baker following the 1984 purchase of Continental Baking Company (Wonder Bread and Hostess Twinkies, Cupcakes, and Ding Dongs) from ITT for approximately $475 million. Two years later it became the #1 battery producer in the world, with the acquisition of the Eveready and Energizer brands from Union Carbide.

In 1986 Ralston sold its domestic livestock feed business (Purina Mills) to British Petroleum, but kept its international feed business intact. In 1989 the company bought Beech-Nut baby foods from Nestlé.

In 1990 Ralston entered the East European market through a joint venture (Purina-Hage Industrial and Trading Company) to produce animal feeds in Hungary.

WHO

Chairman, CEO, and President: William P. Stiritz, age 56, $1,161,425 pay
VP; Chairman and CEO, Continental Baking: Jay W. Brown, age 45, $405,148 pay
VP; President and CEO, Grocery Products Group: William H. Lacey, age 50, $403,459 pay
VP and CFO: James R. Elsesser, age 46
Chairman, Human Resources Committee: Theodore A. Burtis
Auditors: Price Waterhouse
Employees: 56,127

WHERE

HQ: Checkerboard Sq., St. Louis, MO 63164
Phone: 314-982-1000
Fax: 314-982-1211

	1990 Sales		1990 Operating Income	
	$ mil.	% of total	$ mil.	% of total
US	5,084	72	716	82
Europe	764	11	56	6
South & Central America	515	7	33	4
Asia Pacific & other	738	10	74	8
Adjustments	—	—	1	—
Total	**7,101**	**100**	**880**	**100**

WHAT

	1990 Sales		1990 Operating Income	
	$ mil.	% of total	$ mil.	% of total
Human & pet foods	4,382	62	611	70
Batteries, other	1,812	25	220	25
Agricultural prods.	907	13	47	5
Adjustments	—	—	2	—
Total	**7,101**	**100**	**880**	**100**

Brand Names

Pet Foods	Pet Treats	Baked Products
Alley Cat	Beggin' Strips	Home Pride
Cat Chow Mature	Bonz	Hostess Ding
Cat Menu	Hearty Chews	Dongs
Chuck Wagon	Purina Biscuits	Hostess Ho Hos
Deli-Cat	Whisker Lickin's	Hostess Mini
Fit & Trim		Muffins
Lucky Dog	**Cereals**	Hostess Sno
Meow Mix	Almond Delight	Balls
Purina Cat Chow	Batman	Hostess Suzy Q's
Purina Dog Chow	Breakfast With	Hostess Twinkies
Purina Pro Plan	Barbie	Rykrisp
Tender Vittles	Chex	Wonder
Thrive	Cookie Crisp	
	Oat Bran	**Baby Food**
Batteries	Options	Beech-Nut
Energizer	Sun Flakes	
Eveready	Teenage Mutant	
UCAR	Ninja Turtles	

RANKINGS

67th in *Fortune* 500 Industrial Cos.
104th in *Business Week* 1000

KEY COMPETITORS

Anheuser-Busch	Eastman Kodak	Kellogg
British	General Mills	Mars
Petroleum	Gerber	Nestlé
Campbell Soup	Grand	Philip Morris
Colgate-	Metropolitan	Quaker Oats
Palmolive	Heinz	RJR Nabisco

HOW MUCH

	9-Year Growth	1981	1982	1983	1984	1985	1986	1987	1988	1989	1990
Sales ($ mil.)	3.5%	5,225	4,803	4,872	4,980	5,864	5,515	5,868	5,876	6,658	7,101
Net income ($ mil.)	8.9%	184	91	256	243	256	264	526	363	351	396
Income as % of sales	—	3.5%	1.9%	5.3%	4.9%	4.4%	4.8%	9.0%	6.2%	5.3%	5.6%
Earnings per share ($)	15.7%	0.82	0.42	1.26	1.31	1.54	1.69	3.58	2.61	2.52	3.03
Stock price – high ($)	—	7.31	9.44	15.00	18.06	25.31	38.50	47.00	44.19	50.75	54.19
Stock price – low ($)	—	5.00	5.44	8.56	12.50	16.88	21.88	28.81	31.88	39.38	38.88
Stock price – close ($)	26.9%	6.00	8.75	13.88	17.88	23.50	35.38	31.94	40.94	41.50	51.25
P/E – high	—	9	22	12	14	16	23	13	17	20	18
P/E – low	—	6	13	7	10	11	13	8	12	16	13
Dividends per share ($)	11.1%	0.35	0.38	0.41	0.45	0.49	0.54	0.60	0.72	0.81	0.90
Book value per share ($)	(0.9%)	5.70	5.42	5.80	5.77	5.76	6.55	6.85	7.88	6.75	5.26

1990 Year-end:
Debt ratio: 77.0%
Return on equity: 50.5%
Cash (mil.): $112
Current ratio: 1.18
Long-term debt (mil.): $1,961
No. of shares (mil.): 111
Dividends:
  1990 average yield: 1.8%
  1990 payout: 29.7%
Market value (mil.): $5,706

**Stock Price History
High/Low 1981–90**

RAYTHEON COMPANY

OVERVIEW

These days (at least since the Gulf War) Raytheon is known as the maker of the Patriot missile. The anti-Scud Patriot is the company's biggest program (representing $1.2 billion of 1990 sales). In 1990 nearly 55% of Raytheon's total sales were to the US government, making it America's 5th largest defense contractor.

Raytheon's better-known commercial products include Amana, Caloric, and Speed Queen appliances, as well as Beech turboprop and light jet aircraft. The company engages in geophysical exploration for the petrochemical industry (Seismograph) and builds chemical and power plants (Badger, United Engineers).

Through D.C. Heath, Raytheon publishes school and college textbooks. Because of the Patriot's recent success and growth in Raytheon's commercial businesses (especially Badger and Beech), the company seems to be better shielded from potential defense cutbacks and cancellations than other big defense contractors.

Tom Phillips, who presided over Raytheon's diversification into commercial markets in the 1960s and 1970s, retired as chairman in 1991 after 43 years with the company. His tenure at Raytheon concluded with record sales and earnings for the 5th consecutive year. He is succeeded by former president Dennis Picard.

NYSE symbol: RTN
Fiscal year ends: December 31

Hoover's Rating **A-**

WHO

Chairman and CEO: Dennis J. Picard, age 58, $925,002 pay (prior to promotion)
President: Max E. Bleck, age 63, $605,004 pay (prior to promotion)
SVP and Treasurer: Herbert Deitcher, age 57
SVP Human Resources: E. Leonard Kane, age 61
VP Public and Financial Relations: Robert A. Skelly, age 48
Auditors: Coopers & Lybrand
Employees: 76,700

WHERE

HQ: 141 Spring St., Lexington, MA 02173
Phone: 617-862-6600
Fax: 617-860-2172

Raytheon has facilities in 23 states and 6 foreign countries.

	1990 Sales		1990 Net Income	
	$ mil.	% of total	$ mil.	% of total
US	8,699	94	531	95
Other countries	569	6	26	5
Total	**9,268**	**100**	**557**	**100**

WHEN

When Laurence Marshall joined several others to start the American Appliance Company in 1922, he planned to manufacture C. G. Smith's new home refrigerator. Smith's invention worked on paper, but, unfortunately, it failed in practice. Marshall then turned to producing radio tubes under the brand name Raytheon, which in 1925 became the company's name.

Raytheon bought the radio division of Chicago's Q. R. S. Company in 1928 and formed the Raytheon Production Company with National Carbon Company (the makers of the Eveready battery) to market Eveready Raytheon tubes in 1929. National Carbon withdrew from the venture in 1933.

While enjoying a period of unprecedented growth during WWII, Raytheon became the first company to produce magnetrons (tubes used in both radar and microwave ovens). Wartime sales peaked at $173 million but had dwindled to $66 million by 1947. With rumors of bankruptcy in the air, Charles Adams (still a director in 1991) became president. Adams sold Raytheon's unprofitable radio and TV business to Admiral Corporation in 1956.

Military orders stemming from the Korean conflict boosted sales in the mid-1950s. In 1964 Adams (then chairman) named missile engineer Thomas Phillips president. Phillips presided over a series of acquisitions designed to equalize Raytheon's commercial and military earnings, beginning with Amana Refrigeration in 1965. Raytheon added D.C. Heath and Company (textbook publishing, 1966), the Caloric Corporation (stoves, 1967), and 3 companies involved in petrochemical construction and exploration (1966, 1968, 1969). In the meantime Raytheon built the on-board computers for the Apollo command and landing spacecraft.

Raytheon started making computer terminals in 1971 but could not compete with the likes of IBM and got out of the business in 1984. In 1980 the company bought Grumman's Beech Aircraft division and began manufacturing single- and twin-engine planes.

But in spite of its diversification efforts, Raytheon still depended on missiles, radar, and communications systems for 90% of its earnings in 1987. A 1990 government investigation revealed that Raytheon and other defense contractors had been trading in Pentagon secrets. After pleading guilty, Raytheon agreed to pay a $1 million fine. In 1991 the company joined Deutsche Aerospace (Germany) to jointly develop programs related to Hawk, Patriot, and other missile projects.

WHAT

	1990 Sales		1990 Operating Income	
	$ mil.	% of total	$ mil.	% of total
Electronics	5,517	59	793	77
Aircraft products	1,074	12	113	11
Energy services	993	11	60	6
Appliances	1,041	11	4	—
Other	643	7	59	6
Total	**9,268**	**100**	**1,029**	**100**

Electronics
Air traffic control
  Terminal Doppler
  Weather Radar
Military computers
Shipboard systems
  Aegis radar and fire
  control equipment,
  Trident missile
  guidance systems
Submarine systems
Surveillance radars
Tactical missiles
  Patriot, Hawk air-
  defense systems, Tacit
  Rainbow

Other
Cedarapids (road paving equipment)
D.C. Heath (textbook publisher)
Raytheon Service Co. (technical services)

Energy Services
The Badger Co. (process industry engineering and construction)
GeoQuest Systems (geophysical and geological software)
Seismograph Service Corp.
Seis-Pro & Consultants (seismic data processing)
United Engineers & Constructors International

Appliances
Amana
Caloric
Speed Queen

Aircraft Products
Beech 1300 and 1900
Beech Bonanza
Beechjet 400A
King Air
Starship I

HOW MUCH

	9-Year Growth	1981	1982	1983	1984	1985	1986	1987	1988	1989	1990
Sales ($ mil.)	5.7%	5,636	5,513	5,937	5,996	6,409	7,308	7,659	8,192	8,796	9,268
Net income ($ mil.)	6.2%	324	319	300	340	376	393	445	490	529	557
Income as % of sales	—	5.8%	5.8%	5.1%	5.7%	5.9%	5.4%	5.8%	6.0%	6.0%	6.0%
Earnings per share ($)	9.2%	3.84	3.77	3.53	4.02	4.57	5.06	6.06	7.31	7.96	8.49
Stock price – high ($)	—	54.88	49.88	57.50	48.88	55.63	71.75	84.88	73.88	85.00	71.25
Stock price – low ($)	—	34.00	28.25	41.38	34.75	39.38	52.38	57.25	61.00	64.63	57.75
Stock price – close ($)	7.2%	37.38	44.75	43.13	40.13	53.63	67.25	66.63	67.00	69.50	70.13
P/E – high	—	14	13	16	12	12	14	14	10	11	8
P/E – low	—	9	8	12	9	9	10	9	8	8	7
Dividends per share ($)	8.0%	1.20	1.40	1.75	1.05	1.60	1.70	1.80	2.50	2.20	2.40
Book value per share ($)	10.1%	18.25	20.28	22.30	23.46	24.84	26.39	27.31	31.96	36.97	43.55

1990 Year-end:
Debt ratio: 1.6%
Return on equity: 21.1%
Cash (mil.): $138
Current ratio: 1.15
Long-term debt (mil.): $46
No. of shares (mil.): 65
Dividends:
  1990 average yield: 3.4%
  1990 payout: 28.3%
Market value (mil.): $4,583

Stock Price History
High/Low 1981–90

RANKINGS

133rd in *Business Week* 1000

KEY COMPETITORS

Allied-Signal
Bechtel
Boeing
Eaton
EG&G
Electrolux
General Dynamics
General Electric

GEC
General Motors
Grumman
Harris
Litton Industries
Martin Marietta
Maytag
Rockwell

Siemens
Texas Instruments
Textron
Thomson SA
Thorn EMI
Whirlpool

THE READER'S DIGEST ASSOCIATION, INC.

NYSE symbol: RDA
Fiscal year ends: June 30

OVERVIEW

Reader's Digest is a highly profitable publisher of books, magazines, recorded music, and videocassettes. *Reader's Digest*, the "world's most widely read magazine," according to its cover, has an estimated readership of 100 million. Worldwide circulation is about 28 million; US paid circulation tops 16 million — the 3rd highest, after *Parade* (newspaper insert) and AARP's *Modern Maturity*. The magazine sports a 69% renewal rate and, generating 70% of revenue from circulation, is insulated from downturns in advertising spending. *Reader's Digest* is published in 15 languages and the company is in talks to begin a Russian edition.

Reader's Digest has built a database of 100 million households, about half in the US, which it uses to carry out direct mail campaigns for all its products. Books (nearly 50% of total sales) include reference, how-to, and condensed books, as well as multiple-volume series in various subject areas. The company is also building a special-interest magazine business. The QSP subsidiary assists schools and youth groups in fundraising.

Charities own 53% of Reader's Digest non-voting stock, and foundations established by the founding Wallace family own 98% of voting control.

WHEN

The first edition of DeWitt and Lila Wallace's monthly *Reader's Digest* appeared in 1922 and was an immediate success. Within 3 years circulation had almost quintupled, and the Wallaces moved from New York City to Pleasantville, New York. The idea of condensing material from other magazines into a compact, readable form proved to be popular, and the magazine grew enormously in the 1920s and 1930s, reaching a circulation of one million by 1935. In 1939 the company moved to Chappaqua, New York, but kept Pleasantville, the company's home since 1924, as a mailing address.

In the 1940s the *Digest* expanded internationally (the first overseas edition started in England in 1938), opening offices on 5 continents and providing foreign-language translations. Circulation rose from almost 3 million in 1939 to 9 million in 1946. During the 1940s DeWitt Wallace began to write his own articles (partly because some magazines had stopped allowing him reprint rights), giving the *Digest* the conservative, optimistic style that has since characterized it.

In 1950 the company published the first of the Reader's Digest Condensed Books series. In 1955 the *Digest* accepted its first advertising but did not carry liquor ads until 1978 and has never carried cigarette ads. The *Digest* published articles in the mid-1950s examining the link between smoking and cancer.

The company added the Recorded Music Division in 1959 and the General Books Division in 1963. The company was the first to use direct mail advertising with "personalized"

letters to promote these products. Its huge mailing list was later used for promotions such as the *Reader's Digest* Sweepstakes.

The Wallaces continued to manage the company until 1973. DeWitt died at age 91 in 1981; Lila died at age 94 three years later. Since the Wallaces had no children, their voting stock in the company passed to The DeWitt and Lila Wallace Trust, and about 6 million nonvoting shares were divided among 10 charities, including the Metropolitan Museum of Art, Lincoln Center, the New York Zoological Society, Macalester College, and the Sloan-Kettering Cancer Center.

Ex-marine George Grune took over as chairman and CEO in 1984. He cut costs by reducing staff by 20% and disposing of unprofitable subsidiaries, which ushered in an era of increased profitability for the company. Reader's Digest added a line of specialty magazines by purchasing *Travel-Holiday* in 1986 (the company's first acquisition of another US magazine), *Family Handyman* in 1988, *50 Plus* (renamed *New Choices for the Best Years*) in 1988, and *American Health* magazine in 1990. The company bought 50% of British publisher Dorling Kindersley in 1987.

Following the 1990 public offering, as Reader's Digest made its transition from nearly a public trust to a profit-oriented company, it lost several top executives, including its president, general counsel, and CFO. The next year, citing disappointing circulation figures, the company shut down *Budgets Famille*, a French family finance magazine it had launched in 1990.

WHO

Chairman and CEO: George V. Grune, age 61, $1,192,809 pay
President and COO: James P. Schadt, age 53
VP and Editor-in-Chief: Kenneth O. Gilmore, age 59, $542,219 pay
VP and CFO: Anthony W. Ruggiero, age 49
VP Human Resources: Joseph M. Grecky, age 51
Auditors: KPMG Peat Marwick
Employees: 7,400

WHERE

HQ: Pleasantville, NY 10570
Phone: 914-238-1000
Fax: 914-238-4559

Reader's Digest's principal operating facilities are located in Westchester County, NY. Operations outside the US are located in Australia, Canada, France, Germany, Italy, and the UK.

	1990 Sales		1990 Operating Income	
	$ mil.	% of total	$ mil.	% of total
US	928	46	151	51
Europe	791	39	100	33
Other countries	291	15	48	16
Adjustments	—	—	(59)	—
Total	**2,010**	**100**	**240**	**100**

WHAT

	1990 Sales		1990 Operating Income	
	$ mil.	% of total	$ mil.	% of total
Reader's Digest	624	31	75	25
Books, records, videos	1,220	61	229	77
Special-interest magazines	58	3	(26)	(9)
Other	108	5	21	7
Adjustments	—	—	(59)	—
Total	**2,010**	**100**	**240**	**100**

Products and Services

Magazines
American Health	*Reader's Digest*
The Family Handyman	*Travel-Holiday*
Moneywise (UK)	
New Choices for the Best Years	

Books, Records, Videos
Anthology series (e.g., *World's Best Reading*)
General/reference books
Reader's Digest Condensed Books
Recorded music packages
Videocassette packages

Other Operations
Direct mail services
Fundraising products and services for school and community groups (QSP, Inc.)

RANKINGS

209th in *Fortune* 500 Industrial Cos.
167th in *Business Week* 1000

KEY COMPETITORS

Advance Publications	News Corp.
Bertelsmann	Paramount
Cox	Reed
Hachette	Thomson Corp.
Hearst	Time Warner
New York Times	

HOW MUCH

	6-Year Growth	1981	1982	1983	1984	1985	1986	1987	1988	1989	1990
Sales ($ mil.)	7.5%	—	—	—	1,304	1,217	1,255	1,420	1,712	1,832	2,010
Net income ($ mil.)	42.5%	—	—	—	21	52	73	95	142	151	176
Income as % of sales	—	—	—	—	1.6%	4.3%	5.8%	6.7%	8.3%	8.3%	8.8%
Employees	—	—	—	—	—	—	—	—	—	7,400	7,400

1990 Year-end:
Debt ratio: 1.8%
Return on equity: 34.3%
Cash (mil.): $319
Current ratio: 2.15
Long-term debt (mil.): $12
No. of shares (mil.): 119
Dividends:
  1990 average yield: 0.4%
  1990 payout: 8.1%
Market value (mil.): $3,522

Net Income ($ mil.) 1984–90

REEBOK INTERNATIONAL LTD.

NYSE symbol: RBK
Fiscal year ends: December 31

Hoover's Rating A

OVERVIEW

With a 24% market share, Reebok is the 2nd largest domestic producer of athletic shoes (after NIKE). The company's well-known shoe brand names include Reebok, Weebok, AVIA, Rockport, and Ellesse. Reebok also produces sports apparel, and its Boston Whaler Division is a leading producer of recreational boats.

The company is a leader in athletic shoe technology, with such innovations as THE PUMP, Energy Return System (ERS), Hexalite, and Energaire, and with AVIA's cantilever sole, subject of a 1991 patent infringement suit against NIKE.

CEO Paul Fireman, owner of 18% of Reebok stock, has been one of the most highly paid US executives, with compensation exceeding $13 million annually for the past 5 years. In 1991 his salary will be capped at $1 million annually with a bonus of up to $1 million more.

In 1991 Reebok expanded its line with new styles for outdoor walking, hiking, and training, and casual wear, but stirred controversy by including in its annual report a foldout of a strategically shadowed male clad only in a pair of Reeboks.

WHO

Chairman, President, and CEO: Paul B. Fireman, age 47, $14,822,331 pay
EVP and CFO: Paul R. Duncan, age 50, $637,021 pay
Director Human Services: Larry Stone
SVP; President Reebok Division: John H. Duerden, age 50, $596,561 pay
Auditors: Ernst & Young
Employees: 3,800

WHERE

HQ: 100 Technology Center Dr., Stoughton, MA 02072
Phone: 617-341-5000
Fax: 617-341-5087

The company sells its products in 75 countries.

	1990 Sales		1990 Net Income	
	$ mil.	% of total	$ mil.	% of total
US	1,655	77	92	52
Europe	385	18	83	47
Other countries	119	5	2	1
Total	**2,159**	**100**	**177**	**100**

WHEN

English runner Joseph W. Foster invented a spiked running shoe in 1894. Other runners liked the shoe so much that Foster started his own shoe company (JW Foster and Sons). In 1924 Foster supplied the shoes for the British Olympic team (of *Chariots of Fire* fame). Two of Foster's grandsons formed a companion company, Reebok (named for a speedy African antelope), in 1958 that eventually absorbed JW Foster and Sons.

Reebok remained a small British shoe company until 1979, when Paul Fireman, a distributor of fishing and camping supplies, noticed the shoes at a Chicago international trade show. Fireman quickly acquired the exclusive North American license to sell Reebok shoes. Pentland Industries, another British company, agreed to finance Fireman for 55.5% ownership of Reebok USA. Fireman acquired 40% of the new venture, with the remainder going to a group of US investors. Reebok established its headquarters in Massachusetts, and started production in Korea.

Sales executives at Reebok USA realized the difficulty the company would have competing with the running shoes of established competitors NIKE and Adidas; therefore, they looked to the aerobic shoe market. In 1982 Reebok introduced Freestyle, a women's oxford-style sneaker, following with a line of

men's fitness shoes in 1983. Reebok's new aerobic shoe lines coincided with a rise in the popularity of aerobics, and the Freestyle became the largest-selling shoe in history. Sales went from $3.5 million in 1982 to $800 million in 1986, giving Reebok the lead over NIKE in the athletic shoe industry.

In 1985 Reebok USA acquired the original British Reebok company. Later that year Reebok went public, acquiring Rockport (walking and casual shoes, 1986), AVIA (athletic shoes, 1987), Frye (boots, 1987, sold 1989), and Boston Whaler (recreational boats, 1989). The hot-selling PUMP (inflatable basketball shoe) was introduced in 1989.

Facing a mature US market (flat growth in 1990), Reebok turned its emphasis to Europe, where it is 3rd behind Adidas and NIKE, and where it gained almost all its 1990 sales increases. In 1990 Reebok bought out its European distributor and reorganized its US and international operations into a single division. It also ended agency sales to deal directly with retailers (Foot Locker, its largest customer, accounts for 11.5% of sales) and opened outlet and "concept" stores. In 1991 Reebok also squelched the danger of a takeover by buying back stock to reduce Pentland's interest from 31.5% to 13%.

WHAT

	1990 Sales	
	$ mil.	% of total
Reebok (US and International)	1,647	76
Rockport	232	11
AVIA	154	7
Apparel	42	2
Ellesse	47	2
Boston Whaler	37	2
Total	**2,159**	**100**

Shoes	Apparel
AVIA	Aerobics outfits
Ellesse	Golf wear
Reebok	Running clothes
AXT	Shirts
CXT	Shorts
Dance Reebok	Socks
ERS	Tennis wear
Freestyle	
Metaphors	**Recreational Boats**
SXT	Boston Whaler
THE PUMP	
Weebok	
Rockport	
Boating shoes	
DresSports	
RocSports	
Signature Line	
THE WALKING PUMP	

HOW MUCH

	6-Year Growth	1981	1982	1983	1984	1985	1986	1987	1988	1989	1990
Sales ($ mil.)	78.8%	—	—	—	66	307	919	1,389	1,786	1,822	2,159
Net income ($ mil.)	75.8%	—	—	—	6	39	132	165	137	175	177
Income as % of sales	—	—	—	—	9.3%	12.7%	14.4%	11.9%	7.7%	9.6%	8.2%
Earnings per share ($)	63.7%	—	—	—	0.08	0.45	1.28	1.49	1.20	1.53	1.54
Stock price – high ($)	—	—	—	—	—	4.96	17.63	25.19	18.38	19.63	20.00
Stock price – low ($)	—	—	—	—	—	3.29	4.19	7.00	9.50	11.13	8.13
Stock price – close ($)	—	—	—	—	—	4.67	11.69	10.63	12.25	19.00	11.50
P/E – high	—	—	—	—	—	11	14	17	15	13	13
P/E – low	—	—	—	—	—	7	3	5	8	7	5
Dividends per share ($)	—	—	—	—	0.00	0.00	0.00	0.20	0.30	0.30	0.30
Book value per share ($)	114.3%	—	—	—	0.09	0.93	2.82	5.20	6.12	7.42	8.71

1990 Year-end:
Debt ratio: 9.6%
Return on equity: 19.1%
Cash (mil.): $227
Current ratio: 3.50
Long-term debt (mil.): $106
No. of shares (mil.): 114
Dividends:
  1990 average yield: 2.6%
  1990 payout: 19.5%
Market value (mil.): $1,316

Stock Price History
High/Low 1985–90

RANKINGS

395th in *Forbes* Sales 500
239th in *Business Week* 1000

KEY COMPETITORS

Brown Group	MacAndrews & Forbes
Brunswick	Melville
Edison Brothers	NIKE
The Gap	Outboard Marine
INTERCO	U.S. Shoe
L.A. Gear	V. F.
Levi Strauss	Other apparel manufacturers

RELIANCE ELECTRIC COMPANY

Private company
Fiscal year ends: December 31

OVERVIEW

Former Exxon subsidiary Reliance Electric is a leading manufacturer of both industrial and telecommunications equipment. The company's products can be used to provide complete plant automation for manufacturers.

Reliance's industrial equipment group manufactures both electrical and mechanical devices. The latter include mounted bearings, speed reducers, conveyor belt components, transmissions, brakes and clutches, and other products used in material handling, food processing, and other applications.

Electrical products include motors and motor controls, distributed control equipment, and power transformers. Both electrical and industrial products are sold to a variety of other businesses worldwide.

Reliance's telecommunications business, Comm/Tec, manufactures and markets transmission, protection, and connection devices; power supplies; and related equipment for all US telephone companies.

The 87-year-old company regained its independence from Exxon in a 1987 LBO and is now owned primarily by company management, Citicorp, and Prudential-Bache. Reliance's management team has an average of 23 years' service to the company.

WHEN

Reliance Electric was founded in Cleveland in 1904, as Lincoln Motor Works, by inventor John C. Lincoln and investor Peter Hitchcock. Lincoln had invented the first variable-speed D-C motor, which became the first product of the company (renamed Reliance in 1909). It and subsequent refinements established the company as a supplier of high-quality motors.

Reliance continued to make high-quality products but eventually lost touch with the demands of its marketplace. In the late 1950s Reliance designed a futuristic motor control unit that used a complex series of vacuum tubes. But customers found the drive too complicated and delicate, and it was a commercial failure. By the mid-1960s Reliance's annual growth rate was down to around 4% per year, far below more innovative competitors such as General Electric.

In 1967, the company began to reorganize at the corporate level and to diversify in order to bring its production in line with market demands. Reliance focused on production of industrial automation systems; the company bought Dodge Manufacturing (mechanical power transmission products, 1967), Toledo Scale (weighing equipment, bulk material handling equipment, and elevators, 1967), and Applied Dynamics (analog computers, 1969). By 1970 the company was in a position to sell a full line of automation equipment, which provided over 80% of sales in that year.

Reliance entered the telecommunications field in the 1970s with the purchases of Lorain (power supplies, 1973), a unit of Continental Telephone (local transmission equipment,

1976), and Reliable Electric (wire and splicing equipment, 1977). Reliance also expanded overseas during this period, with international profits quadrupling between 1970 and 1974.

In 1979 Reliance bought Federal Pacific Electric (FPE, circuit breakers) for $345 million. Shortly after that acquisition, FPE revealed that it had cheated on Underwriters' Laboratories tests for its equipment; Reliance went to court in an attempt to reverse its acquisition of FPE. At the same time, Exxon, seeking to diversify into electrical equipment, agreed to acquire Reliance for $1.2 billion, paying $72 per share for stock that had recently traded at $34. The acquisition, one of the largest in history, was widely criticized and spawned antitrust litigation.

Exxon's stated reason for buying Reliance was to manufacture a new A-C motor control that Exxon executives believed would revolutionize the industry. The device turned out to be similar to existing products (including one made by Reliance) and impractical to produce. Reliance limped on until 1987, when Reliance's top management, Citicorp, and Prudential-Bache paid $1.35 billion for the company in an LBO.

In 1989 Reliance sold Toledo Scale to a subsidiary of Ciba-Geigy of Switzerland for $210 million. The company used proceeds from the sale, as well as from earnings, to reduce its long-term debt. In 1991 Reliance began issuing junior preferred debentures on the American Stock Exchange.

WHO

Chairman: H. Virgil Sherrill, age 70
President and CEO: John C. Morley, age 59, $750,000 pay
EVP: Leon J. Hendrix, Jr., age 49, $400,000 pay
CFO, VP, Controller, and Treasurer: Keith C. Moore, Jr., age 53, $361,000 pay
VP Human Resources and Community Affairs: E. Scott Dalton, age 50
VP, General Counsel, and Secretary: John H. Portwood, age 62
Auditors: Price Waterhouse
Employees: 14,000

WHERE

HQ: 6065 Parkland Blvd., Cleveland, OH 44124-8020
Phone: 216-266-5800
Fax: 216-266-7666

Reliance operates 42 factories in Australia, Brazil, Canada, Germany, Japan, Mexico, Switzerland, the UK, and the US and has 176 sales and service offices worldwide.

	1990 Sales		1990 Operating Income	
	$ mil.	% of total	$ mil.	% of total
US	1,358	86	177	86
Foreign	218	14	28	14
Adjustments	(29)	—	(7)	—
Total	**1,547**	**100**	**198**	**100**

WHAT

	1990 Sales		1990 Operating Income	
	$ mil.	% of total	$ mil.	% of total
Industrial products	1,142	73	181	88
Telecommunications	412	27	24	12
Adjustments	(7)	—	(7)	—
Total	**1,547**	**100**	**198**	**100**

Trademarks

Electrical Products
A-C motors, generators, alternators, and drives
Low voltage D-C motors
Power utility transformers
Programmable process controllers

Mechanical Products
Adjustable speed drives
Bushings
English and metric bearings and mountings
Shaft mounted gear reducers
Transmissions

Telecommunications
Digital Subscriber Carrier Systems
Fiber-optic monitoring test equipment
Uninterruptible power supplies

RANKINGS

258th in *Fortune* 500 Industrial Cos.
93rd in *Forbes* 400 US Private Cos.

KEY COMPETITORS

ABB	Emerson
AT&T	General Electric
BCE	General Signal
Borg-Warner	Honeywell
Cooper Industries	Siemens
Dana	Square D
Eaton	Westinghouse

HOW MUCH

	3-Year Growth	1981	1982	1983	1984	1985	1986	1987	1988	1989	1990
Sales ($ mil.)	3.2%	—	—	—	—	—	—	1,408	1,303	1,411	1,547
Net income ($ mil.)	—	—	—	—	—	—	—	(5)	27	33	49
Income as % of sales	—	—	—	—	—	—	—	(0.4%)	2.1%	2.3%	3.2%
Employees	(6.3%)	—	—	—	—	—	—	17,000	13,000	13,000	14,000

1990 Year-end:
Debt ratio: 92.2%
Return on equity: —
Cash (mil.): $40
Current ratio: 2.33
Long-term debt (mil.): $605
No. of shares (mil.): 13

Net Income ($ mil.)
1987–90

REPUBLICAN PARTY

OVERVIEW

The Republican party, often called the "Grand Old Party" (GOP), is the minority of the 2 major American political parties. More conservative than that of the Democratic party, Republican support consists largely of corporate, financial, and farming interests. Politically the party favors free enterprise, laissez faire (government noninterference), and opposition to the welfare state. The party's symbol (the elephant) was invented by political cartoonist Thomas Nast.

The Republican party has launched a major effort to regain majority party status by the year 2000. It hopes to broaden its support base by attracting groups (primarily minorities) that have historically voted for Democratic candidates.

In addition, the party hopes to regain control of the House and Senate, where it is outnumbered by the Democrats 267 to 166 and 56 to 44, respectively. Gaining a congressional majority may prove to be a tall order, considering the shortfalls of the party at the state and local levels.

Political party
Party symbol: Elephant

Hoover's Rating **B+**

WHO

Chairman: Clayton Yeutter
Co-Chairman: Jeanie Austin
Vice Chairmen: Bernard M. Shanley, Jack Londen, Martha Moore, Nelda Barton, Ernest Angelo, Jr., Kay Riddle, Elsie Vartanian, Duane Acklie
Secretary: Kit Mehrtens
Treasurer: William J. McManus

WHERE

HQ: 310 First St., SE, Washington, DC 20003
Phone: 202-863-8500
Fax: 202-863-8820

WHEN

In 1854 widespread opposition to the Kansas-Nebraska Act (which opened both territories to slavery) resulted in the formation of a new political party, named Republican after the Democratic-Republican party formed by Thomas Jefferson. The party grew quickly, absorbing many Whigs, Free Soilers, and Northern Democrats. After overcoming the rival American (Know-Nothing) party, the Republicans became the political power of the North.

The election of Abraham Lincoln (the first Republican president) in 1860 set the solidly Democratic South on the road toward secession, giving the Republicans control of the federal government. During the ensuing Civil War, the Republican party split into Conservative and Radical factions. Following Lincoln's assassination in 1865, the Radical faction gained the upper hand in the Reconstruction process and passed the Fourteenth Amendment (civil rights) in 1868.

With the war over and the slaves freed, the Republicans lacked a central doctrine. Nevertheless, the Republican party dominated presidential elections for the next 2 decades with the victories of Ulysses S. Grant (1868, 1872), Rutherford B. Hayes (1876), James A. Garfield (1880, assassinated in 1881), and Benjamin Harrison (1888).

In 1896 the Republicans committed themselves to the gold standard and, after defeating opposing candidate William Jennings Bryan, put William McKinley in the White House. The election was a turning point for the party because it gave the Republicans control of both houses of Congress and established them as the majority party (at which time they adopted the GOP nickname). McKinley was reelected in 1900, followed by Republicans Theodore Roosevelt (1904) and William H. Taft (1908).

The Republican party was divided in 1912 between Taft and Roosevelt (who split off the Bull Moose party) when both men sought the nomination for the presidential race. Roosevelt switched to the Progressive party and the divided Republicans lost the election to Woodrow Wilson.

The Republicans regained the White House with the elections of Warren G. Harding (1920), during whose administration the infamous Teapot Dome scandal occurred; Calvin Coolidge (1924); and Herbert Hoover (who was president when the stock market collapsed in 1929). The Great Depression crumbled Republican fortunes, and both its majority party position and control of Congress passed to the Democrats.

The Republicans would not elect another president until 1952, when WWII general Dwight D. Eisenhower took office. During his presidency the Republicans were caught up in the Communist witch hunt concocted by Senator Joseph McCarthy (R-WI).

After Eisenhower the Republican party continued its movement to the political right, represented by such figures as Barry Goldwater (whose landslide presidential defeat in 1964 was the party's worst since 1932), Richard Nixon (lost the 1960 election; elected president 1968, 1972; resigned in 1974 following the Watergate scandal), Gerald Ford (who took Nixon's place in 1974 but lost the election in 1976), Ronald Reagan (1980, 1984), and George Bush (1988).

Following the death of the controversial Lee Atwater (instigator of the infamous "Willie Horton" ads, which badly hurt Michael Dukakis in the 1988 presidential race) in 1991, Clayton Yeutter became chairman of the Republican National Committee.

WHAT

Sources of Receipts 1990 Election Cycle

	$ mil.	% of total
Contributions from individuals	180	87
Contributions from political action committees	3	2
Transfers from other party committees	9	4
Other receipts	15	7
Total	**207**	**100**

Party Presidential Voting 1860-1988

Year	Republican candidate	Popular votes (mil.)	Electoral votes	Won/ lost
1988	George Bush	48.9	426	W
1984	Ronald Reagan	54.3	525	W
1980	Ronald Reagan	43.9	489	W
1976	Gerald R. Ford	39.1	240	L
1972	Richard M. Nixon	47.2	520	W
1968	Richard M. Nixon	31.8	301	W
1964	Barry M. Goldwater	27.2	52	L
1960	Richard M. Nixon	34.1	219	L
1956	Dwight D. Eisenhower	35.6	457	W
1952	Dwight D. Eisenhower	33.9	442	W
1948	Thomas E. Dewey	22.0	189	L
1944	Thomas E. Dewey	22.0	99	L
1940	Wendell Willkie	22.3	82	L
1936	Alfred M. Landon	16.7	8	L
1932	Herbert C. Hoover	15.8	59	L
1928	Herbert C. Hoover	21.4	444	W
1924	Calvin Coolidge	15.7	382	W
1920	Warren G. Harding	16.2	404	W
1916	Charles E. Hughes	8.5	254	L
1912	William H. Taft	3.5	8	L
1908	William H. Taft	7.7	321	W
1904	Theodore Roosevelt	7.6	336	W
1900	William McKinley	7.2	292	W
1896	William McKinley	7.0	271	W
1892	Benjamin Harrison	5.2	145	L
1888	Benjamin Harrison	5.4	233	W
1884	James G. Blaine	4.8	182	L
1880	James A. Garfield	4.4	214	W
1876	Rutherford B. Hayes	4.0	185	W
1872	Ulysses S. Grant	3.6	286	W
1868	Ulysses S. Grant	3.0	214	W
1864	Abraham Lincoln	2.2	212	W
1860	Abraham Lincoln	1.9	180	W

KEY COMPETITORS

Democratic party

HOW MUCH

	10-Year Growth	1979–1980	1981–1982	1983–1984	1985–1986	1987–1988	1989–1990
Money raised ($ mil.)	2.0%	170	215	298	255	263	207
Money spent ($ mil.)	—	162	214	301	259	257	—

Money Raised ($ mil.) 1979–90

REYNOLDS METALS COMPANY

NYSE symbol: RLM
Fiscal year ends: December 31

Hoover's Rating **C+**

OVERVIEW

Richmond-based Reynolds Metals is the 2nd largest US producer of aluminum (after Alcoa) and a major manufacturer of aluminum cans. It leads the world in the manufacture of aluminum foil and makes the #1 US household foil: Reynolds Wrap.

Reynolds is a mining company and a plastics and aluminum products manufacturer, distributor, and recycler. Its foreign endeavors include mining gold in Australia and marketing its aluminum cans in Europe, South America, and Japan. The company, with its focus on consumer goods and gold, enjoyed 4 consecutive years of increasing profits until the combination of recession and lower aluminum prices hit in 1990.

Anticipating slow growth in US demand, Reynolds has expanded internationally with a can plant in Austria, mills in Spain and Canada, and a proposed plant in Russia.

WHO

Chairman and CEO: William O. Bourke, age 63, $1,441,250 pay
President and COO: Richard G. Holder, age 59, $941,250 pay
EVP and CFO: R. Bern Crowl, age 59, $775,000 pay
VP Human Resources: John R. McGill, age 55
Auditors: Ernst & Young
Employees: 30,800

WHEN

Richard S. Reynolds began his business career in the tutelage of his uncle R. J. Reynolds, of tobacco industry fame and fortune. In 1912 Richard Reynolds returned to Bristol, Tennessee, to run his father's Reynolds Company (silica-based cleansers). Near the end of WWI, the company changed from producing cleansers to manufacturing waterproof gunpowder canisters (from tin, asphalt, and asphalt felt paper) for the military.

After WWI, the company needed a peacetime product. In 1919 Reynolds entered a joint venture with R.J. Reynolds Tobacco, forming United States Foil Company to roll tinfoil for cigarette packaging. Reynolds Tobacco sold its shares of US Foil to outsiders in 1924. US Foil then bought the company that made Eskimo Pies, the ice cream product wrapped in foil.

During 1928 Reynolds bought Robertshaw Thermostat, Fulton Sylphon, and part of Beechnut Foil. He added these companies to US Foil to form Reynolds Metals (1928). By the late 1920s Reynolds Metals was using both tin and the lighter-weight aluminum in its metal business. In the late 1930s Reynolds foresaw that the US need for aluminum would dramatically increase if it became involved in WWII. In 1940 the company began mining bauxite (aluminum ore) in Arkansas. In early 1941 Reynolds Metals built its first aluminum plant (near Sheffield, Alabama). The company quickly built other plants in Alabama and Washington.

In 1946 the US government forced Alcoa (ruled a monopoly by the Supreme Court in 1945) to give the government the patent rights to its process of obtaining aluminum from bauxite. Thus Reynolds Metals received this process gratis when it bought 6 surplus government aluminum plants (which used Alcoa's patented process) after WWII. Reynolds Metals developed many of the innovative uses of aluminum, including siding (1945) and Reynolds Wrap foil (1947). The company began to search for bauxite in Jamaica (1949) and British Guyana (1952, mines nationalized 1975). In 1959 the company bought British Aluminum jointly with Tube Investments (sold to Tube, 1978). Reynolds Metals developed the aluminum beverage can (1963) and began the recycling of it (1968). The company bought Industrial Metals (1969) and May Aluminum (1971).

In 1982 the company introduced Reynolds Plastic Wrap. In 1986 the company began mining gold in Australia, and made a major strike in 1987. In 1988 it bought Presto Products (plastic bags, food wrap). David Reynolds (son of the founder) retired as chairman in 1988. David (now chairman emeritus) and his nephew Randolph (an EVP) own a total of only 3.5% of the company's stock.

To structure for retirement of CEO William Bourke, the company in 1990 created 3 new EVP posts, reporting to Bourke's likely successor, Richard Holder.

WHERE

HQ: 6601 W. Broad St., PO Box 27003, Richmond, VA 23261
Phone: 804-281-2000
Fax: 804-281-4160 (Public Relations)

Reynolds has operations in 20 countries.

	1990 Sales		1990 Operating Income	
	$ mil.	% of total	$ mil.	% of total
US	4,648	77	378	61
Canada	232	4	32	5
Other foreign	1,142	19	209	34
Adjustments	—	—	(4)	—
Total	**6,022**	**100**	**615**	**100**

WHAT

	1990 Sales		1990 Operating Income	
	$ mil.	% of total	$ mil.	% of total
Aluminum production & processing	3,509	58	461	73
Finished products & other	2,513	42	170	27
Adjustments	—	—	(16)	—
Total	**6,022**	**100**	**615**	**100**

Major Products
Aluminum cans and containers
Aluminum foil (Reynolds Wrap)
Aluminum wire and cable
Baking cups (Baker's Choice)
Building products
Flat rolled aluminum
Ice cream bars (84%, Eskimo Pie)
Microwave wrap
Plastic bags (Sure Seal)
Plastic containers and lids
Plastic film (Reynolds Plastic Wrap)
Semifinished aluminum
Utility bags (Qwik-Seal)
Wax paper (Cut-Rite)

Gold Mines
Boddington (40%, Australia)
Mt. Gibson (50%, Australia)

RANKINGS

88th in *Fortune* 500 Industrial Cos.
179th in *Business Week* 1000

HOW MUCH

	9-Year Growth	1981	1982	1983	1984	1985	1986	1987	1988	1989	1990
Sales ($ mil.)	6.3%	3,481	2,981	3,341	3,728	3,416	3,639	4,284	5,567	6,143	6,022
Net income ($ mil.)	14.6%	87	(24)	(91)	131	(298)	102	201	482	533	297
Income as % of sales	—	2.5%	(0.8%)	(2.7%)	3.5%	(8.7%)	2.8%	4.7%	8.7%	8.7%	4.9%
Earnings per share ($)	10.5%	2.04	(0.49)	(1.93)	2.85	(6.05)	1.94	3.67	8.35	9.06	5.01
Stock price – high ($)	—	19.88	13.69	20.69	20.81	20.63	26.38	61.75	58.00	62.75	70.00
Stock price – low ($)	—	11.56	9.38	12.44	13.00	15.13	18.19	20.19	34.00	49.00	48.50
Stock price – close ($)	18.9%	12.00	12.69	19.75	16.75	18.88	20.00	47.63	53.75	53.63	57.00
P/E – high	—	10	—	—	7	—	14	17	7	7	14
P/E – low	—	6	—	—	5	—	9	6	4	5	10
Dividends per share ($)	4.6%	1.20	0.88	0.50	0.50	0.50	0.50	0.58	0.90	1.70	1.80
Book value per share ($)	4.1%	34.38	33.11	28.09	30.45	22.92	27.05	29.69	37.77	45.24	49.22

1990 Year-end:
Debt ratio: 37.3%
Return on equity: 10.6%
Cash (mil.): $90
Current ratio: 1.86
Long-term debt (mil.): $1,742
No. of shares (mil.): 60
Dividends:
 1990 average yield: 3.2%
 1990 payout: 35.9%
Market value (mil.): $3,391

Stock Price History High/Low 1981–90

KEY COMPETITORS

Alcan
Alcoa
AMAX
ASARCO
Broken Hill
Dow Chemical
Grand Metropolitan
James River
Johnson Controls
Mars
Norsk Hydro
Owens-Illinois
Peter Kiewit Sons'
Thyssen

RIKLIS FAMILY CORPORATION

OVERVIEW

Its major business is operating dime stores, but Riklis Family Corporation is best known for its deals, controversial business practices, and shaky financial state. New York City–based Riklis Family Corporation is the holding company for Meshulam Riklis's diversified and highly leveraged interests.

After the dust settled in 1988 on the Riklis Family Corporation's acquisition of Beatrice spinoff E-II from American Brands, the company included Riklis's McCrory retail store chains (Bargain Time, J. J. Newberry, McCrory, S. H. Kress, T. G. & Y., and others), McGregor (apparel), Samsonite (luggage), and Culligan (water treatment). Meshulam Riklis sold Fabergé to Unilever, made McCrory an E-II subsidiary, transferred more than $600 million of E-II's assets to McCrory, and then resigned from E-II in 1990 while simultaneously buying McCrory back from E-II with a $250 million, non–interest-bearing, non-recourse note and no money down.

Riklis and his wife, actress-turned-singer Pia Zadora, own Pickfair, the Los Angeles mansion once owned by Douglas Fairbanks, Jr., and Mary Pickford.

WHEN

Meshulam Riklis emigrated from Tel Aviv in 1947, graduated from Ohio State University with a degree in mathematics in 1950, and began working at the Minneapolis brokerage house of Piper, Jaffray, and Hopwood in 1951. With a pool of funds he coaxed from clients, he bought control of Rapid-American, an office machine and greeting card company, in 1957.

In the late 1950s Riklis used high-yield bonds and stock swaps to gain control of several firms, including clothing makers and packaging firms. In 1960 Rapid bought McCrory's, a chain of variety stores. But poor earnings forced Riklis to sell all his holdings except a majority stake in the chain by 1963.

Riklis rebuilt Rapid, which bought Glen Alden Corporation and, with it, liquor distributor Schenley Industries (1972). But, squeezed by recession and tight credit, Rapid sold off holdings again in 1974. The companies sold included Lerner Shops, the women's clothing retailer, and undergarment companies Playtex and BVD; proceeds were used to reduce debt. Riklis took Rapid private in 1981. At this time, Rapid consisted of the McCrory chain, Family Bargain Centers, Schenley, and McGregor.

Rapid bought Fabergé and Elizabeth Arden in 1984. In 1986 Riklis transferred the assets of Fabergé to his Riklis Family Corporation (RFC), leaving Rapid's bondholders with non-voting Fabergé preferred stock.

Riklis drew criticism for his role in the 1986 Guinness takeover of liquor producer Distillers Company. Riklis, Ivan Boesky, and others bought Guinness stock, raising the price, just as it was being used to acquire Distillers. Riklis's Schenley unit depended on continued US distribution rights of Dewar's, a Distillers brand, after the takeover. Amid the ensuing stock manipulation lawsuits, Guinness chief Ernest Saunders resigned, but Riklis escaped legal entanglement after selling Schenley to Guinness in 1987 at a loss.

RFC bought E-II Holdings (Samsonite, Culligan, Lowrey's Meat Specialties) in 1988. The day after the acquisition, Riklis drained $925 million in cash from E-II by selling it Fabergé. E-II bondholders sued over the transaction. The complaint was dismissed when E-II sold Fabergé/Elizabeth Arden to Unilever for $1.55 billion in 1989. E-II then paid Riklis $25 million not to compete with Unilever.

E-II sold Lowrey's in 1988 and Riklis transferred all the assets of Rapid to E-II in 1989. Other transactions in 1989 included the sale of Samsonite Furniture to Ditri Associates, the sale of Culligan's Arrowhead Industrial Water subsidiary to B.F. Goodrich, and the purchase of 130 GC Murphy stores and 25 Bargain World stores from Ames Department Stores. In December of 1990 Riklis severed his ties with E-II and simultaneously bought back McCrory.

During Riklis's tenure as chairman, E-II's bond prices plummeted to between 12% and 24% of face value; meanwhile, McCrory's 1990 annual report admitted that certain transactions with Riklis and his companies were not agreed upon at arm's length. These transactions, along with the millions poured by E-II into McCrory (which lost over $100 million during E-II's "ownership"), have led to lawsuits by bondholders and downgradings of the company's bond rating.

Private company
Fiscal year ends: December 31

WHO

Chairman: Meshulam Riklis, age 67, $2,900,000 pay
Employees: 39,600

WHERE

HQ: 725 Fifth Avenue, New York, NY 10022
Phone: 212-735-9500
Fax: 212-735-9450

The company's McCrory Corp. unit operates 1,056 variety stores and 5 fast food restaurants in 40 states and the District of Columbia, and one manufacturing/distribution facility in Canada.

WHAT

Riklis Family Holdings Corp.
McCrory Corp. (90%)
  Distribution (Gault Brothers)
  Real estate (Mack Realty)
  Variety stores (McCrory, McLellan, H. L. Green, T. G. & Y., J. J. Newberry, S. H. Kress, GC Murphy)
McGregor Holding Corp. (has voting trust agreement with SG Corp.)
Rapid-American Corp. (owns SCH Holdings securities)
Riklis Holding Corp.
  McCrory Parent Corp. (owns 10% of McCrory Corp.)
SCH Holdings (sold Schenley to Guinness)

SG Corp. (controls assets through voting trust agreement with McGregor Holding)
McGregor Acquisition Corp.
  E-II Holdings Inc.
    Apparel (MacGregor)
    Luggage (Samsonite)
    Water treatment (Culligan)

RANKINGS

45th in *Forbes* 400 US Private Cos.

KEY COMPETITORS

Ames
Amway
Brown-Forman
Costco
Dayton Hudson
The Gap
Kmart
KKR
Levi Strauss
Pacific Enterprises
Sara Lee
Stop & Shop
V.F.
Wal-Mart
Woolworth

HOW MUCH

	5-Year Growth	1981	1982	1983	1984	1985	1986	1987	1988	1989	1990
Sales ($ mil.)	6.7%	—	—	—	—	1,816	1,898	1,894	2,931	2,500	2,508
Employees	8.8%	—	—	—	—	26,000	56,500	40,100	44,200	30,000	39,600

Sales ($ mil.) 1985–90

RIO GRANDE INDUSTRIES, INC.

OVERVIEW

Rio Grande Industries (RGI) operates an integrated transportation system through 3 railroad subsidiaries: the Denver and Rio Grande Western Railroad (Rio Grande), Southern Pacific Transportation Company, and SPCSL.

The Rio Grande is mainly a coal-hauling road but also handles other commodities, including transportation equipment and lumber products, over a central corridor route in the western US. Southern Pacific operates freight rail and intermodal (truck-to-train) services in 14 states and trucking services nationwide.

The company owns real estate in several major cities and plans to sell those holdings not related to its core transportation activities. SPCSL operates an integrated rail line with Southern Pacific and Rio Grande between the Gulf Coast and Chicago.

RGI is a private company, 71.25% owned by the Anschutz Corporation, a Denver-based holding company owned by billionaire Philip Anschutz. Anschutz is an extremely private individual with a personal fortune of about $1.7 billion, according to *Forbes*.

Private company
Fiscal year ends: December 31

Hoover's Rating **D**

WHO

Chairman, President, and CEO: Philip F. Anschutz, age 51
VC and VP: D. L. Polson, age 48
VP Finance and Treasurer: L. C. Yarberry, age 48
VP Human Resources, Southern Pacific Transportation Co. and Denver and Rio Grande Western Railroad Co.: T. J. Matthews, age 50
Auditors: KPMG Peat Marwick
Employees: 23,814

WHEN

Southern Pacific dates back to 1861, when 4 Sacramento merchants, later known as the Big Four, founded the Central Pacific Railroad. Construction began in Sacramento in 1863. Six years later the Central Pacific reached Promontory, Utah, where its rails were spiked to those of the Union Pacific (which had built westward from Omaha, Nebraska), thus completing the first transcontinental railway.

The Central Pacific expanded throughout California (1884) and to Texas (1881) and Oregon (1887) by building new track and buying other railroads, including the Southern Pacific (1868), a San Francisco–to–San Jose line founded in 1865. A joint Central Pacific/ Southern Pacific headquarters was established in San Francisco in 1873. The 2 railroads were officially merged in 1885 under a holding company called Southern Pacific Company.

Union Pacific bought control of Southern Pacific in 1901 but was ordered by the Supreme Court to sell its stake on antitrust grounds in 1913. In 1932 Southern Pacific bought control of the St. Louis Southwestern Railway (Cotton Belt), gaining an entrance to St. Louis.

Facing intense competition from Union Pacific and Burlington Northern (both of which had merged with other railroads to create enormous systems), Southern Pacific merged with competitor Atchison, Topeka &

Santa Fe Railway in 1983 to form Santa Fe Southern Pacific Corporation. In 1987 the ICC deemed the merger anticompetitive, and in 1988 Santa Fe Southern Pacific sold Southern Pacific to RGI — a holding company for the Rio Grande railroad — which was controlled by Anschutz Corporation.

The Rio Grande was founded as the Denver and Rio Grande in 1871 by General William Jackson Palmer to build a line from Denver to Mexico City. The company entered Salt Lake City in 1882, but an attempt to build on to San Francisco resulted in bankruptcy. Renamed the Denver and Rio Grande Western, the railroad emerged from receivership in 1924. It opened the Dotsero Cutoff in 1934, finally placing Denver on a transcontinental main line. Anschutz bought the Rio Grande in 1984.

The combined Southern Pacific and Rio Grande gained access to Chicago in 1989, when SPCSL Corporation (a new subsidiary of RGI) bought 282 miles of track between East St. Louis and Chicago from the trustees of bankrupt Chicago, Missouri & Western Railway Company. In 1990 Anschutz sold 5% of RGI to Nippon Yusen, a Japanese shipping firm. That year the company entered into an agreement with Burlington Northern granting RGI track rights between Chicago and Kansas City.

WHERE

Southern Pacific Transportation Co.: Southern Pacific Bldg., One Market Plaza, San Francisco, CA 94105
Phone: 415-541-1000
Fax: 415-541-1256
Rio Grande Holding, Inc.: 1515 Arapahoe St., Denver, CO 80202
Phone: 303-595-2254
Fax: 303-595-2195

Southern Pacific operates 20,240 miles of track in 14 western and southwestern states. Rio Grande operates 3,414 miles of track in 4 western states. SPCSL operates 748 miles of track between Chicago and East St. Louis and between Chicago and Kansas City.

WHAT

	1990 Sales	
	$ mil.	% of total
Railroad	2,781	99
Other	38	1
Total	**2,819**	**100**

SPTC Holding, Inc.
Southern Pacific Transportation Co.
  Northwestern Pacific Railroad Co.
  St. Louis Southwestern Railway Co. (99.9%)
  Southern Pacific Telecommunications Co.
  Southern Pacific Trucking Co.
  SPT Real Estate

Rio Grande Holding, Inc.
Denver and Rio Grande Western Railroad Co.

SPCSL Corp.

Items Transported	% of Total
Southern Pacific Transportation Co.	
Intermodal	24
Lumber products	15
Chemicals	15
Metals & ores	9
Energy & hazardous materials	7
Food & grain products	12
Automotive	9
Other	9
Total	**100**
Denver and Rio Grande Western Railroad Co.	
Coal	29
Transportation equipment	19
Lumber products	8
Food products	9
Steel	6
Other	29
Total	**100**

HOW MUCH

	9-Year Growth	1981	1982	1983	1984	1985	1986	1987	1988	1989	1990
Rio Grande Industries											
Sales ($ mil.)	—	—	—	—	—	—	—	—	—	2,702	2,819
Net income ($ mil.)	—	—	—	—	—	—	—	—	—	14	30
Income as % of sales	—	—	—	—	—	—	—	—	—	0.5%	1.1%
Southern Pacific Trans.											
Sales ($ mil.)	(1.5%)	2,832	2,482	2,430	2,714	2,546	2,362	2,395	2,412	2,372	2,470
Net income ($ mil.)	(10.8%)	81	9	32	141	118	(253)	143	219	98	29
Income as % of sales		2.9%	0.4%	1.3%	5.2%	4.6%	(10.7%)	6.0%	9.1%	4.1%	1.2%
Rio Grande Holding											
Sales ($ mil.)	—	363	304	314	313[1]	252[2]	309	257	276	456[3]	331
Net income ($ mil.)	—	46	30	33	67[1]	2[2]	10	19	(4)	12[3]	12
Income as % of sales	—	12.7%	9.9%	10.5%	21.4%	0.8%	3.2%	7.4%	(1.4%)	26.0%	3.6%

1990 Year-end
Debt ratio: 85.4%
Return on equity: 12.1%
Cash (mil.): $89
Current ratio: 0.43
Long-term debt (mil.): $1,500

Southern Pacific Transportation Company
Net Income ($ mil.) 1981–90

[1] 10 months ended 10/31/84 [2] 9 months ended 7/31/85 [3] 17 months ended 12/31/89

KEY COMPETITORS

American President
Burlington Northern
Consolidated Freightways
Roadway
Santa Fe Pacific
Union Pacific
Yellow Freight

RITE AID CORPORATION

OVERVIEW

Rite Aid has more discount drugstores (2,420) than any other chain in the US, although the corporation claims only about 1/2 the annual sales of top competitor Walgreen's. Rite Aid plans for continued growth by emphasizing low prices, a wide choice of products, and careful selection of location and by eliminating unprofitable stores.

Rite Aid also holds 79 ADAP and Auto Palace auto parts stores, 62 Encore Books stores, 172 Concord Custom dry-cleaning establishments, and 27 Sera-Tec Biologicals plasma collection centers, but drugstore sales account for 95% of revenues. Almost 1/2 the drugstore sales, in turn, come from pharmacy sales, the

fastest growing income source. And almost 1/2 of the pharmacy sales come from 3rd-party payers, which are especially vulnerable to cost-cutting pressures in light of rising health-care costs. Increasing sales of generic prescription drugs have helped Rite Aid cut these costs while increasing profits.

Rite Aid's "Rite Buy" program, an example of the corporation's aggressive pricing strategy, passes manufacturers' discounts along to customers. The corporation also claims the nation's largest private label line, which sells at discounts of 30–50% of national brand prices.

WHEN

In 1958 wholesale grocer Alex Grass incorporated Pennsylvania-based Rack Rite Distributors to provide health and beauty aids and other nonfood products to grocery stores. Grass offered these same products at his first discount drugstore, Thrif D Discount Center, opened in 1962 in Scranton, Pennsylvania. By 1966, when the company opened its first pharmacy, it had 36 drugstores.

Rite Aid adopted its current name and went public in 1968 and in 1969 bought Daw Drug (47 stores), Blue Ridge Nursing Homes, and plasma suppliers Immuno Serums and Sero Genics.

In 1971 the company bought Sera-Tec Biologicals of New Jersey (blood plasma); the 40 stores of Cohen Drug of Charleston, West Virginia; and 50% of Superdrug Stores, Ltd., a UK-based chain. Rite Aid filled over 5 million prescriptions that year. In 1973 the company bought 2 Philadelphia-area chains, 50-store Warner and 49-store Thomas Holmes, and, in 1976, the 52-store Keystone Centers. In 1977 it bought the Read chain, adding 99 Baltimore drugstores, and sold its nursing homes in 1978.

By 1981 acquisitions had made Rite Aid the 3rd largest drugstore chain, and sales had

exceeded $1 billion. In 1983 the company began to install point-of-sale and pharmacy computer systems in its stores. Diversifying, Rite Aid bought American Discount Auto Parts's 32-store chain and Encore Books's 19-store discount chain in 1984. In the same year the company spun off its wholesale grocery operation as Super Rite, retaining a 47% interest.

In 1987 Rite Aid bought 113 SupeRx drugstores in Florida, Georgia, and Alabama and 94 Gray Drug Fair stores and sold its share in Superdrug to Woolworth Holdings, netting about $68 million. The company bought the rest of the 356-store Gray Drug Fair operation in 1988. The costs associated with rapid expansion eroded Rite Aid's profit margins from 4.4% in 1986 to 2.6% in 1989.

In 1989 the company sold its Super Rite interest to an investment group headed by CEO Alex Grass and finished equipping all its stores with computers.

Rite Aid revenues increased by 8.6% in 1990, a year that included the addition of 68 drugstores and the purchase of prescription records from 65 drugstores in Washington, D.C. Plans call for the addition of 125 drugstores and elimination of 40. Rite Aid filled 67.3 million prescriptions in 1990.

NYSE symbol: RAD
Fiscal year ends: Saturday nearest February 29 or March 1

Hoover's Rating B-

WHO

Chairman and CEO: Alex Grass, age 63, $925,000 pay
President and COO: Martin L. Grass, age 37, $550,000 pay
SVP and Chief Accounting and Financial Officer: Frank M. Bergonzi, age 45
SVP Personnel: Robert R. Souder
Auditors: KPMG Peat Marwick
Employees: 29,900

WHERE

HQ: 431 Railroad Ave., Shiremanstown, PA 17011
Phone: 717-761-2633
Fax: 717-975-5871

Rite Aid operates in 22 eastern states and the District of Columbia.

State	No. of Drugstores
Alabama	4
Connecticut	44
Delaware	21
District of Columbia	6
Florida	209
Georgia	53
Indiana	7
Kentucky	92
Maryland	183
Massachusetts	41
Michigan	90
New Hampshire	12
New Jersey	163
New York	258
North Carolina	119
Ohio	358
Pennsylvania	342
Rhode Island	13
South Carolina	82
Tennessee	33
Vermont	7
Virginia	175
West Virginia	108
Total	**2,420**

WHAT

	1990 Sales		1990 Operating Income	
	$ mil.	% of total	$ mil.	% of total
Retail drug	3,259	95	213	94
Specialty retailing	140	4	8	4
Medical services	48	1	6	2
Total	**3,447**	**100**	**227**	**100**

Operating Units
ADAP (auto parts stores)
Auto Palace (auto parts stores)
Concord Custom Cleaners
Encore Books
Rite Aid (drugstores)
Sera-Tec Biologicals (plasma laboratories)

RANKINGS

38th in *Fortune* 50 Retailing Cos.
357th in *Business Week* 1000

KEY COMPETITORS

Jack Eckerd
Kmart
Melville
J. C. Penney
Supermarkets General
Vendex
Walgreen

HOW MUCH

Fiscal year ends February of following year	9-Year Growth	1981	1982	1983	1984	1985	1986	1987	1988	1989	1990
Sales ($ mil.)	13.9%	1,066	1,295	1,223	1,446	1,564	1,757	2,486	2,868	3,173	3,447
Net income ($ mil.)	11.6%	40	55	74	70	68	78	94	94	82	107
Income as % of sales	—	3.7%	4.2%	6.1%	4.8%	4.3%	4.4%	3.8%	3.3%	2.6%	3.1%
Earnings per share ($)	11.8%	0.95	1.31	1.76	1.69	1.65	1.89	2.27	2.30	1.97	2.59
Stock price – high ($)	—	12.08	17.83	23.44	27.25	33.50	35.50	46.25	40.88	41.13	38.63
Stock price – low ($)	—	7.75	9.00	14.08	17.50	21.50	24.25	28.50	29.13	29.50	29.50
Stock price – close ($)	16.2%	9.54	15.42	22.25	25.38	25.88	29.50	36.00	32.63	33.38	36.88
P/E – high	—	13	14	13	16	20	19	20	18	21	15
P/E – low	—	8	7	8	10	13	13	13	13	15	11
Dividends per share ($)	16.6%	0.23	0.28	0.34	0.43	0.52	0.60	0.68	0.76	0.84	0.93
Book value per share ($)	15.3%	5.17	6.19	7.68	8.58	9.65	10.96	13.81	15.35	16.98	18.64

1990 Year-end:
Debt ratio: 43.1%
Return on equity: 14.5%
Cash (mil.): $26
Current ratio: 3.98
Long-term debt (mil.): $585
No. of shares (mil.): 42
Dividends:
　1990 average yield: 2.5%
　1990 payout: 35.7%
Market value (mil.): $1,531

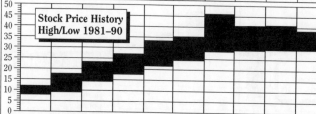
Stock Price History High/Low 1981–90

RJR NABISCO, INC.

NYSE symbol: RN
Fiscal year ends: December 31

OVERVIEW

Headquartered in New York City, RJR Nabisco is one of the largest tobacco and food operations in the world, with a portfolio of strong brand names. R.J. Reynolds, the company's tobacco division, is the 2nd largest producer of cigarettes in the US (after Philip Morris), with such popular brands as Camel, Winston, and Salem. The company's share of the US cigarette market is about 31%. Tobacco International, the company's global division, sells more than 55 brands of cigarettes in the international market.

RJR Nabisco's food operations consist primarily of Nabisco (the largest US producer of cookies and crackers, with a 44% market share) and Planters LifeSavers (the leader in packaged nuts and roll candy). Brand names that command the #1 positions in their respective US markets include Ritz crackers, Oreo cookies, and Milk-Bone dog biscuits.

Since its $29.6 billion LBO in 1989 (the largest in history), the company has regained the image of a no-nonsense, focused enterprise. In 1991 the company returned to the NYSE with a sale of 100 million common shares, which put about 25% of the company back in public hands. Buyout specialists KKR still own most of the remaining shares.

WHO

Chairman, President, and CEO: Louis V. Gerstner, Jr., age 49, $3,020,229 pay
EVP and CFO: Karl M. von der Heyden, age 54, $801,793 pay
EVP Human Resources and Administration: Eugene R. Croisant, age 53
Auditors: Deloitte & Touche
Employees: 55,000

WHERE

HQ: 1301 Ave. of the Americas, New York, NY 10019
Phone: 212-258-5600
Fax: 212-969-9173

The company sells its products in more than 160 countries.

	1990 Sales		1990 Operating Income	
	$ mil.	% of total	$ mil.	% of total
US	11,939	86	2,696	92
Canada	881	7	111	4
Europe	875	6	86	3
Other foreign	184	1	30	1
Adjustments	—	—	(122)	—
Total	**13,879**	**100**	**2,801**	**100**

WHEN

In 1875 R. J. Reynolds formed the R.J. Reynolds Tobacco Company in Winston, North Carolina, to produce chewing tobacco. During the late 1890s Reynolds was forced to sell his company to James Duke of the American Tobacco trust for $3 million (Duke threatened to break Reynolds with his Battle Ax brand cigarette if he did not sell). Reynolds regained his company in 1911 (after the Supreme Court dismantled the trust), turned his attention to cigarettes, and in 1913 introduced Camel, which became the company's best-selling cigarette. After Reynolds's death in 1918, company leadership passed to Bowman Gray, whose family would successfully run the company for the next 50 years.

With the success of Camel, R.J. Reynolds became the largest domestic cigarette company. During the 1930s and 1940s Camel was locked in a seesawing struggle for the #1 cigarette position with American Tobacco's Lucky Strike brand.

In response to growing health concerns in the 1950s, the company introduced its filtered Winston (1954) and Salem (1956) brands.

Antismoking sentiment led the company to embark on a diversification program during the 1960s and 1970s that included Chun King (Chinese food, 1966), Patio Foods (1967), American Independent Oil (1970, sold in 1984), and Del Monte (fruits and other foods, 1979). In 1970 the company changed its name to R.J. Reynolds Industries.

Heublein, Inc., was acquired in 1982. Its Kentucky Fried Chicken chain was sold to PepsiCo in 1986. Grand Metropolitan bought the Heublein liquor business in 1987.

In 1985 the company bought Nabisco Brands for $4.9 billion. The National Biscuit Company was formed by the 1898 consolidation of several baking companies. Adolphus Green (Nabisco's first president) transformed the company from a loose network of regional bakeries to a uniform system producing the same powerhouse products (including Fig Newtons, Oreo, and Premium Saltines). Nabisco acquired Shredded Wheat (1929), Milk-Bone (1931), Dromedary (1954), Cream of Wheat (1961), James Welch (candy, 1963), and Standard Brands (Planters nuts, Blue Bonnet margarine, beer, wine; 1981). Standard Brands's CEO Ross Johnson emerged as CEO of Nabisco after the acquisition and later landed the top spot when R.J. Reynolds bought Nabisco.

In 1987 Johnson tried to take advantage of falling stock prices by organizing an LBO. The plan backfired when Kohlberg Kravis Roberts (KKR) outbid Johnson to acquire the company for $29.6 billion and took it private in 1989. Johnson was replaced by former American Express president Louis Gerstner.

To reduce the tremendous debt incurred from the LBO, the company has sold many of its holdings, including Nabisco's European food business (1989), Chun King (1989), Del Monte's processed-food operations (1990), and Curtiss Confections (1990). Through divestitures and stock and bond offerings, the company shrank its debt to $18.7 billion in 1990 (down from its original debt of $29 billion).

WHAT

	1990 Sales	
	$ mil.	% of total
Tobacco	8,053	58
Food	5,826	42
Total	**13,879**	**100**

Brand Names

Cigarettes	Nabisco Cookies, Crackers, and Cereals	Suddenly S'Mores
Camel	Barnums Animals	Teddy Grahams
Century	Chips Ahoy!	Triscuit
Doral	Cream of Wheat	Waverly
Magna	Devil's Food Cakes	Wheat Thins
More	Doo Dads	
NOW	Fig Newtons	**Other Brands**
Salem	Giggles	A.1.
Sterling	Honey Maid	Blue Bonnet
Vantage	Mallomars	Brer Rabbit
Winston	Mister Salty	Fleischmann's
	Mystic	Fruit Wheats
Candy and Gum	Nilla	Grey Poupon
Beech-Nut	Nutter Butter	Milk-Bone
Breath Savers	Oreo	My*T*Fine
Bubble Yum	Planters	Ortega
Care*Free	Premium Saltines	Planters
Fruit Stripe Gum	Ritz	Regina
LifeSavers	Shredded Wheat	Royal
LifeSavers Holes	Sociables	Toastettes
		Vermont Maid

RANKINGS

28th in *Fortune* 500 Industrial Cos.
428th in *Business Week* 1000

HOW MUCH

	9-Year Growth	1981	1982	1983	1984	1985	1986	1987	1988	1989	1990
Sales ($ mil.)	4.0%	9,766	10,906	10,371	9,915	13,533	15,978	15,766	16,956	12,764	13,879
Net income ($ mil.)	—	768	870	835	843	1,001	1,080	1,081	1,393	(1,172)	(462)
Income as % of sales	—	7.9%	8.0%	8.1%	8.5%	7.4%	6.8%	6.9%	8.2%	(9.2%)	(3.3%)
No. of employees	(4.8%)	85,776	99,869	96,228	97,551	147,513	124,617	120,334	116,881	48,000	55,000

1990 Year-end:
Debt ratio: 87.2%
Return on equity: —
Cash (mil.): $323
Current ratio: 0.79
Long-term debt (mil.): $16,955

Net Income ($ mil.) 1981–90

KEY COMPETITORS

Allied-Lyons	Campbell Soup	Loews
American Brands	ConAgra	Mars
Anheuser-Busch	CPC	Philip Morris
Associated Milk Producers	General Mills	Procter & Gamble
B.A.T	Heinz	Quaker Oats
Borden	Hershey	Ralston Purina
BSN	Imasco	Unilever
	Kellogg	Wrigley

ROADWAY SERVICES, INC.

OVERVIEW

Roadway Services is a holding company specializing in the transportation of freight and packages on a regional and national scale. Roadway Express, the company's main operating subsidiary (accounting for almost 2/3 of sales), specializes in less-than-truckload (LTL) shipments (those weighing less than 10,000 pounds). Other subsidiaries include Spartan, which provides LTL service in southern and central US; Viking Freight, the leading regional carrier in the West; and Roberts Express, which offers expedited delivery of fragile, high-security, and hazardous shipments in North America and Europe. Roberts also recently began offering air charter services.

Roadway Package System (RPS) offers small-package pickup and delivery to businesses in 43 states. Only 5 years old, RPS has exceeded management's expectations in both sales and earnings and in 1990 added service to Hawaii and Canada. A portable computerized tracking system (STAR SYSTEM), introduced in 1990, makes it possible for RPS customer service agents to track shipments instantly and relay information to customers via telephone.

WHEN

Brothers Galen and Carroll Roush founded Roadway Express in 1930. Based in Akron, Ohio, the company started with 10 owner-operated trucks and terminals in Chicago, Houston, and Kansas City. By 1935 Roadway was moving freight over an extensive network in 20 eastern states.

In 1945 the company began converting from owner-operators to a company-owned fleet. This process, completed in 1956, coincided with the Roushes' decision (1950) to specialize in LTL shipments. Although LTLs cost more to operate than full truckloads (one truck carrying multiple shipments to and from various destinations), rates were proportionately higher. By 1956 Roadway Express had 60 terminals to support its LTL route network.

In 1956 Carroll Roush sold his half of the company to the public and went on to buy ONC Fast Freight (later part of ROCOR). Galen Roush remained Roadway's chairman until his retirement in 1974. By 1975 Roadway was operating 300 terminals in 40 states, with coast-to-coast operations by 1977.

During the recession of the mid-1970s, Roadway fared better than most trucking companies by cutting labor costs (which accounted for 60% of its operating expenses), thereby sustaining profits even though tonnage dropped 15% between 1974 and 1975. The company was also (and remains) debt free.

In the early 1980s Roadway expanded its network in the West, concentrating on the Pacific Northwest (traditionally dominated by Consolidated Freightways), and established service to Alaska, Hawaii, Canada, Mexico, and Puerto Rico. In 1984 Roadway bought Roberts Express, which specialized in direct (from shipper to consignee) express delivery. The company also bought 2 regional trucking companies to consolidate its transcontinental network: Spartan Express, based in Greer, South Carolina, which enhanced operations in the South (1984); and San Jose, California–based Viking Freight, which served 10 western states and Guam (1988).

However, increased competition in the LTL market made diversification necessary. In 1985 Roadway Express fell from its position as America's #1 freight carrier, to #3 (behind Yellow Freight and Consolidated Freightways). The company entered the small-package shipping market in 1985 by establishing Roadway Package System (RPS), which utilized owner-operated trucks to deliver packages weighing up to 100 pounds. In 1989 Roadway formed Roadway Logistics Systems to design transportation and distribution systems based on customer needs.

Roadway expanded LTL service to include Mexico City in 1990 and added export services to Europe in 1991.

NASDAQ symbol: ROAD
Fiscal year ends: December 31

 Hoover's Rating **B+**

WHO

Chairman, President, and CEO: Joseph M. Clapp, age 54, $707,717 pay
VP Finance and Secretary: D. A. Wilson, age 46, $365,248 pay
Director Human Resources: Jack White
Auditors: Ernst & Young
Employees: 36,000

WHERE

HQ: 1077 Gorge Blvd., PO Box 88, Akron, OH 44309-0088
Phone: 216-384-8184
Fax: 216-258-6042

Roadway operates in the US, Canada, Mexico, and Europe through 606 terminals.

WHAT

	1990 Freight	
	Tons	% of total
Less-than-truckload	7,967	76
Truckload	2,532	24
Total	**10,499**	**100**

Roadway Express Inc. (Akron, OH)
606 terminals in US, Canada, Mexico, and Puerto Rico
Roadway Bodegas y Consolidación (Mexico)
E•Z Bill (computerized billing)
E•Z Link (on-line shipment information)
E•Z Rate (simplified rate system)
QUIKTRAK (shipment tracking)
Roadway Services (Canada) Ltd.

Roadway Package System (Pittsburgh, PA)
167 terminals in 43 states (small-package shipping)

Roberts Transportation Services, Inc. (Akron, OH)
CarVan (automotive components)
MediQuik Express (deliveries to hospitals)
Pivot Systems (automotive components)
Roberts Express (guaranteed on-time delivery; US, Canada, and Europe)
Customer Link (satellite communications)
"White Glove" (special handling)

Viking Freight, Inc. (San Jose, CA)
Viking Freight System, Inc.
42 terminals in 10 western states
Spartan Express, Inc.
52 service centers in 16 south-central states

Roadway Logistics Systems (Akron, OH)
Integrated logistics support

RANKINGS

17th in *Fortune* 50 Transportation Cos.
361st in *Business Week* 1000

KEY COMPETITORS

American President	Federal Express
Burlington Northern	Norfolk Southern
Canadian Pacific	Rio Grande Industries
Chicago and North	Ryder
Western	Santa Fe Pacific
Consolidated Freightways	Union Pacific
Consolidated Rail	UPS
CSX	Yellow Freight

HOW MUCH

	9-Year Growth	1981	1982	1983	1984	1985	1986	1987	1988	1989	1990
Sales ($ mil.)	11.3%	1,130	1,147	1,253	1,462	1,580	1,718	1,909	2,185	2,661	2,971
Net income ($ mil.)	5.8%	72	76	99	100	76	76	51	80	96	119
Income as % of sales	—	6.4%	6.6%	7.9%	6.8%	4.8%	4.5%	2.6%	3.7%	3.6%	4.0%
Earnings per share ($)	5.9%	1.82	1.92	2.47	2.49	1.90	1.91	1.26	2.00	2.44	3.05
Stock price – high ($)	—	25.13	31.50	37.38	35.25	35.75	45.75	43.00	35.00	43.25	43.00
Stock price – low ($)	—	16.38	15.25	28.50	23.50	24.75	30.75	23.25	26.75	27.75	27.25
Stock price – close ($)	8.1%	19.13	28.63	34.38	30.50	34.75	34.50	32.00	30.75	42.25	38.50
P/E – high	—	14	16	15	14	19	24	34	18	18	14
P/E – low	—	9	8	12	9	13	16	18	13	11	9
Dividends per share ($)	6.5%	0.63	0.70	0.83	0.98	1.00	1.10	1.10	1.10	1.10	1.10
Book value per share ($)	8.0%	10.10	11.37	13.12	14.49	15.37	16.28	16.45	17.06	18.35	20.15

1990 Year-end:
Debt ratio: 0.0%
Return on equity: 15.8%
Cash (mil.): $145
Current ratio: 1.05
Long-term debt (mil.): $0
No. of shares (mil.): 39
Dividends:
1990 average yield: 2.9%
1990 payout: 36.1%
Market value (mil.): $1,486

Stock Price History High/Low 1981–90

THE ROCKEFELLER FOUNDATION

Nonprofit organization
Fiscal year ends: December 31

Hoover's Rating **A-**

OVERVIEW

Headquartered in New York City, the Rockefeller Foundation is one of the US's oldest and largest philanthropic organizations. Although it provides grants for a diverse range of causes, the foundation has targeted 3 primary areas: the arts and humanities, international science-based development, and equal opportunities for minorities in the US.

Unlike many of its US peers who concentrate almost exclusively on domestic issues, the Rockefeller Foundation devotes over half of its grants to international causes, emphasizing the agricultural, population, and health sciences.

The foundation's scientific approach combats human suffering at its sources, supporting basic research and teaching/training programs. Once a strong research organization in its own right, the foundation is credited with discovering the cure for numerous diseases, including yellow fever.

Today the foundation maintains no ties to the Rockefeller family and holds no original Rockefeller oil stock. An independent board of trustees sets guidelines and approves expenditures. Three of the foundation's presidents (John Foster Dulles, Dean Rusk, and Cyrus Vance) later became US secretaries of state.

WHO

Chairman: John R. Evans
President: Peter C. Goldmark, Jr.
SVP: Kenneth Prewitt
Treasurer and Chief Investment Officer: David A. White
Manager Personnel Office: Lynne C. Burkhart
Auditors: Ernst & Young
Employees: 151

WHERE

HQ: 1133 Ave. of the Americas, New York, NY 10036
Phone: 212-869-8500
Fax: 212-764-3468

The foundation has field offices in India, Kenya, Malawi, and the Philippines and maintains the Bellagio Study and Conference Center in Italy.

WHEN

Oil baron John D. Rockefeller, one of America's most criticized capitalists, was also one of its pioneer philanthropists. Before founding the Rockefeller Foundation in 1913, he funded the creation of the University of Chicago (with $36 million over a quarter century) and formed organizations for medical research (1901), the education of southern blacks (1903), and hookworm eradication in the southern US.

Rockefeller's faith in science's ability to cure all human ills was reflected in the foundation's early global campaigns to combat hookworm, malaria, and yellow fever (using his initial $35 million endowment); hookworm control alone was used in 62 countries on 6 continents. To ensure lasting effects on public health, Rockefeller gave another $50 million (1919) to strengthen medical schools in Europe, Canada, and Southeast Asia.

In the mid-1920s the foundation started conducting basic medical research. In 1928 the foundation absorbed several other Rockefeller philanthropies, thus adding programs in the natural and social sciences and the arts and humanities.

During the 1930s the foundation developed the first effective yellow fever vaccine (1935), continued its worldwide battles against disease, and supported pioneering research in the field of biology. Other grants supported the performing arts in the US and social science research at various US research institutes.

During WWII the foundation supplied major funding for nuclear science, created new research tools (spectroscopy, X-ray diffraction), and fought typhus epidemics.

In 1951, when an increasing number of large public ventures modeled after the foundation (e.g., the UN's World Health Organization) were taking over its traditional physical/natural sciences territory, the foundation dissolved its famed biology division.

Emphasis swung to agricultural studies under chairman John D. Rockefeller III (1952). The foundation took wheat seeds developed at its Mexican food project (begun in 1942) to Colombia (1950), Chile (1955), and India (1956); a rice institute in the Philippines followed in 1960. The resulting Green Revolution sprouted 12 more world institutes.

In the 1960s the foundation began dispatching expertise to Third World universities in an effort to raise the level of training at those institutions. The long bear market of the 1970s caused the foundation's assets to drop to a low of $732 million (1977).

President Peter Goldmark is allocating $50 million over 5 years to global environmental issues and education reform efforts targeting poor children in the US.

In 1990 the foundation established the Energy Foundation, a joint effort with the MacArthur Foundation and the Pew Charitable Trusts, to explore alternate energy sources and promote energy efficiency.

WHAT

	1990 Program Expenditures	
	$ mil.	% of total
Agricultural sciences	13	14
Arts & humanities	14	15
Equal opportunity	14	15
Health sciences	14	15
Population sciences	11	11
Global environment	3	3
Special programming	5	5
School reform	3	3
International security	1	1
Special interests & explorations	3	3
Other	4	4
Interprogram	11	11
Total	**96**	**100**

Representative Programs

Agricultural Sciences
Disease control (Beijing University, China)
Genetically improved foodstuffs (International Rice Research Institute; Manila, the Philippines)
Improved food production systems in Africa (maize research, Malawi)

Health Sciences
Disease prevention through vaccinology and pharmacology (World Health Organization [WHO]; Geneva, Switzerland)
Population-based health care (International Clinical Epidemiology Network — INCLEN)

Population Sciences
Human reproductive biology studies in Mexico (Instituto Nacional de la Nutricion Salvador Zubiran; Mexico City, Mexico)
Training of nurse/midwives in Africa (Women for Women's Health)

Global Environmental Program
Facilitating compliance from nongovernmental bodies

in formulating accord on climatic change (Environmental Defense Fund, New York)

Special Programming
Maintaining a science camp for high school students in Tanzania (University of Dar es Salaam, Tanzania)

Arts & Humanities
Cross-culture artistic experimentation (Dance Theatre Workshop, New York Shakespeare Festival; New York, NY)

Equal Opportunity
Combating urban poverty (Children's Defense Fund; Washington, DC)

School Reform
Rural education in arts and humanities (South Carolina Committee for the Humanities, Columbia)

International Security
Establishment of multinational research network on weapons proliferation (Institut Français des Relations Internationales; Paris, France)

HOW MUCH

	9-Year Growth	1981	1982	1983	1984	1985	1986	1987	1988	1989	1990
Assets ($ mil.)	9.3%	883	1,014	1,119	1,109	1,354	1,615	1,676	1,845	2,152	1,972
Net investment income ($ mil.)[1]	—	67	64	51	59	206	367	288	157	305	33
Program expenditures ($ mil.)	9.3%	43	40	37	38	43	48	71	65	75	96

Assets ($ mil.) 1981–90

[1] Includes realized gains on sale of securities of $149 mil. (1985); $304 mil. (1986); $205 mil. (1987); $67 mil. (1988); and $216 mil. (1989).

ROCKWELL INTERNATIONAL CORPORATION

OVERVIEW

Most people think of the space shuttle and the B-1B bomber when they think of Rockwell International, but the company is also a major producer of electronics, automotive parts, and printing presses.

Rockwell rolled out the new shuttle, *Endeavour*, in 1991 and is building the power system for Space Station *Freedom*. It has been NASA's #1 contractor for the last 17 years, and space systems generated 23% of the company's revenues in 1990.

But with the *Endeavour* now complete and defense-related sales on the decline, Rockwell is shifting its emphasis toward commercial and international markets. The company builds 65% of the modems used in fax machines (most are shipped to the Far East). Rockwell's Graphics division is the world's #1 maker of web offset press equipment for commercial and newspaper printing. The company also holds a leading market share in the field of avionics (aircraft electronic systems) and supplies a broad international market with axles, clutches, transmissions, and other components for vehicles ranging from small cars to heavy-duty trucks.

WHEN

Rockwell International is the legacy of 2 early 20th-century entrepreneurs: Willard Rockwell and Clement Melville Keys.

Willard Rockwell gained control of Wisconsin Parts Company, an Oshkosh maker of automotive axles, in 1919. He went on to acquire a number of industrial manufacturers, merging them in 1953 to create Rockwell Spring & Axle. Renamed Rockwell-Standard (1958), by 1967 this company led the world in the production of mechanical automotive parts.

In 1928 Keys founded North American Aviation (NAA) as a holding company for his aviation interests. General Motors bought North American in 1934 and installed James Kindelberger as its president. In 1935 the company moved from Dundalk, Maryland, to Inglewood, California, where it built military training planes. North American built over 15,000 AT-6 trainers during WWII and produced the B-25 bomber (1940) and the P-51 fighter (1940). By the end of WWII the company had built nearly 43,000 aircraft, more than any other US manufacturer. Sales peaked at $700 million in 1944.

North American's sales plunged at the end of WWII. In 1948 GM took its subsidiary public; Kindelberger revitalized the company, opening new factories in Downey, California (1948), and Columbus, Ohio (1950). Major products included the F-86 (1948), a highly successful jet fighter of the Korean War, and its successor the F-100 (1953), America's first production supersonic aircraft. The company also produced the X-15 rocket plane (1959) and the XB-70 bomber (1964).

In the 1960s North American built rocket engines and spacecraft for the Apollo program. In 1967 the company merged with Rockwell Standard, creating North American Rockwell (which became Rockwell International in 1973).

Rockwell won the prime contracts for the B-1 bomber (1970) and the space shuttle orbiter (1972). In 1973 Rockwell bought Collins Radio, which would form the backbone of its avionics segment. The company ventured into consumer goods briefly, buying Admiral in 1974 and selling it in 1979.

Rockwell invested its B-1 proceeds in industrial electronics, acquiring Allen-Bradley for $1.7 billion in 1985. Facing decline in defense-related revenues as B-1 production ended, CEO Don Beall funneled billions into plant modernization and R&D for Rockwell's electronics and graphics segments. In 1989 Rockwell sold its Measurement & Flow Control Division and bought Baker Perkins, a UK-based printing machinery company. The company sold its fiber optic transmission equipment unit to French telecommunications giant Alcatel in 1991.

NYSE symbol: ROK
Fiscal year ends: September 30

Hoover's Rating **A-**

WHO

Chairman and CEO: Donald R. Beall, age 52, $1,492,102 pay
VC: Robert A. dePalma, age 55, $594,083 pay (prior to promotion)
EVP and COO: Kent M. Black, age 51, $754,706 pay
EVP and COO: Sam F. Iacobellis, age 61, $725,777 pay
SVP Finance and Planning and CFO: William M. Barnes, age 48
SVP Organization and Human Resources: Robert H. Murphy, age 52
Auditors: Deloitte & Touche
Employees: 101,900

WHERE

HQ: 2230 E. Imperial Hwy., El Segundo, CA 90245
Phone: 213-647-5000
Fax: 213-647-5524

Rockwell operates in the US and 24 other nations.

	1990 Sales		1990 Operating Income	
	$ mil.	% of total	$ mil.	% of total
US	9,966	81	1,032	82
Europe	1,392	11	112	9
Canada	387	3	55	4
South America	273	2	45	3
Other	361	3	20	2
Adjustments	—	—	(151)	—
Total	**12,379**	**100**	**1,113**	**100**

WHAT

	1990 Sales		1990 Operating Income	
	$ mil.	% of total	$ mil.	% of total
Electronics	5,003	40	563	45
Aerospace	3,781	31	447	35
Automotive	2,560	21	136	11
Graphics	1,035	8	118	9
Adjustments	—	—	(151)	—
Total	**12,379**	**100**	**1,113**	**100**

Electronics
Allen-Bradley industrial automation
Avionics
Defense electronics
Telecommunications

Aerospace
B-1B support
NAVSTAR satellites
Rocketdyne rocket engines
Space shuttle orbiter

Automotive
Heavy vehicles systems/ components
Light vehicles systems/ components

Graphics
Baker Perkins printing equipment
Goss newspaper and commercial presses

RANKINGS

35th in *Fortune* 500 Industrial Cos.
91st in *Business Week* 1000

KEY COMPETITORS

Allied-Signal
Boeing
Dana
Eaton
General Dynamics
Grumman
Harris
Henley
Hitachi
Honeywell
Lockheed
Martin Marietta
McDonnell Douglas
Northrop
Raytheon
Square D
Texas Instruments
Textron
United Technologies
Westinghouse
Other electronics and aerospace companies

HOW MUCH

	9-Year Growth	1981	1982	1983	1984	1985	1986	1987	1988	1989	1990
Sales ($ mil.)	6.5%	7,040	7,395	8,098	9,322	11,338	12,296	12,123	11,946	12,518	12,379
Net income ($ mil.)	8.8%	292	332	389	497	595	611	635	812	735	624
Income as % of sales	—	4.1%	4.5%	4.8%	5.3%	5.3%	5.0%	5.2%	6.8%	5.9%	5.0%
Earnings per share ($)	11.8%	0.93	1.06	1.23	1.60	1.96	2.03	2.23	3.01	2.84	2.53
Stock price – high ($)	—	11.19	11.75	17.75	16.81	20.88	24.44	30.94	23.50	27.13	28.75
Stock price – low ($)	—	5.91	6.28	10.56	11.50	14.94	15.69	14.25	16.13	19.75	20.50
Stock price – close ($)	14.5%	8.19	10.63	16.50	15.19	17.88	22.69	19.00	21.75	23.75	27.75
P/E – high	—	12	11	14	11	11	12	14	8	10	11
P/E – low	—	6	6	9	7	8	8	6	5	7	8
Dividends per share ($)	9.3%	0.36	0.39	0.42	0.47	0.53	0.58	0.65	0.71	0.75	0.80
Book value per share ($)	11.9%	6.38	6.85	7.65	8.47	9.87	10.98	12.04	14.14	15.91	17.51

1990 Year-end:
Debt ratio: 11.7%
Return on equity: 15.1%
Cash (mil.): $411
Current ratio: 1.24
Long-term debt (mil.): $553
No. of shares (mil.): 239
Dividends:
  1990 average yield: 2.9%
  1990 payout: 31.6%
Market value (mil.): $6,629

Stock Price History High/Low 1981–90

ROMAN CATHOLIC CHURCH (US)

Religious denomination
Fiscal year ends: December 31

Hoover's Rating B

OVERVIEW

With over 20% of the population, the Roman Catholic Church is the largest religious denomination in the US. One of its principal achievements is the creation and operation of the largest private educational system in the world. Roman Catholics were traditionally lower- and middle-class, urban-dwelling immigrants who voted Democratic, but are becoming geographically, economically, and politically indistinguishable from American society as a whole.

The church is a supporter of separation of church and state. However, like many religious organizations in the US, it has involved itself in the political arena in a number of instances, e.g., support for federal aid to parochial schools and opposition to abortion. It supports missionary work and since WWII has been a leader in the struggle for social and economic justice for the underprivileged.

One of the greatest challenges facing the US Catholic church today is the decline in the number of clergy, which has left many parishes without a resident priest. In the void, priestly duties (except for officiating at Mass) are being taken over by laymen and women.

WHO

His Holiness the Pope, Bishop of Rome, Vicar of Jesus Christ, Supreme Pontiff of the Catholic Church: Pope John Paul II (Karol Wojtyla), age 71
Apostolic Pro-Nuncio to the US: Archbishop Agostino Cacciavillan
President, National Conference of Catholic Bishops: Archbishop Daniel Pilarczyk
Treasurer, National Conference of Bishops: Archbishop Daniel Kucera
Auditors: Coopers & Lybrand
Employees: 182,200

WHEN

Tracing its foundation to AD 33 in Jerusalem by Jesus of Nazareth, Catholicism probably first came to North America with Norse traders in the 12th and 13th centuries. The next Catholics came in 1492 — Christopher Columbus and his crew.

The first Catholic settlement in what is now the US was the Spanish colony of St. Augustine, founded in 1565. The Spanish sent missionaries to New Mexico in 1582 and California in 1601, and French missionaries arrived in 1613 in the northern and central US.

Catholic history in the British colonies began in 1634 when George Calvert founded the Maryland colony. Catholicism in the colonies was confined to Maryland and tolerant Quaker Pennsylvania until after the Revolutionary War. The US's first diocese was in Baltimore (1789) and encompassed the entire country. John Carroll, the first bishop, had 25 priests and 25,000 to 35,000 members, less than 1% of the US population.

The first US Catholic school was probably set up by monks at St. Augustine in 1606. Attempts to start schools in New York and Maryland failed due to civil opposition. The Church's first permanent schools, Georgetown Visitation (1799; Washington, DC) and one in Emmitsburg, Maryland (1810), were soon followed by many others.

Immigration from Germany and Ireland and the annexation of French and Spanish territories increased the Catholic population in the US to 200,000 in 1820 and 3 million in 1860, making it the largest Christian denomination in the US. By 1908 the Pope had removed the American Catholic church's mission status. Heavy immigration from southern Europe, especially Italy, helped the Catholic population to rise from 10 million in 1890 to over 20 million by 1929. Catholics began to take a more active role in political life; Alfred Smith was elected governor of New York, though anti-Catholic sentiment contributed to his defeat in the 1928 presidential election. In 1960, however, John F. Kennedy was elected president.

The American delegation was the 2nd largest at the Second Vatican Council of 1962. The Americans were instrumental in updating liturgical practice (e.g., by eliminating Latin as its primary language), giving lay persons (nonpriests) a greater voice in church affairs, and opening doctrinal matters to discussion.

In the 1980s the US Catholic church experienced several heated internal debates involving collisions between modern lifestyles and church doctrines (e.g., use of birth control, acceptance of homosexuality).

Though church membership is rising, many dioceses are burdened with aging churches to maintain, aging religious communities to support, and fewer priests and nuns. These expenses are made worse by the decline in donations, possibly linked to church positions on political and social issues. In response to these pressures, many dioceses are unwilling to increase their contributions to the $34 million budget of the national bishop's conference.

WHERE

HQ: 3211 4th St. NE, Washington, DC 20017
Phone: 202-541-3000
Fax: 202-541-3322

The church operates worldwide, serving its nearly 900 million members through 212,636 parishes and almost 2.3 million clerical and lay personnel. The US church operates through its 399 bishops, 185 dioceses, and 19,620 parishes in all 50 states.

	Members		Priests	
	Mil.	% of total	No.	% of total
New England	5.5	10	5,589	11
Mid-Atlantic	14.0	25	13,074	25
South Atlantic	3.4	6	4,366	8
Midwest	10.3	19	10,708	21
South Central	0.7	1	1,268	2
North Central	3.4	6	5,225	10
Southwest	5.0	9	3,575	7
Mountain	2.0	4	1,972	4
Pacific	8.1	15	5,272	10
Other regions	0.5	1	689	1
Military	1.6	4	797	1
Total	**54.5**	**100**	**52,535**	**100**

WHAT

Official Units
Campaign for Human Development
Canon Law Society of America
Catholic Charities
Catholic Relief Services
Conference of Major Religious Superiors of Men
Leadership Conference of Women Religious
National Catholic Education Association
National Conference of Catholic Bishops
National Council of Catholic Laity
National Council of Catholic Women
National Office for Black Catholics
The United States Catholic Conference
US Catholic Bishops' Advisory Council
Word of God Institute

Other Influential Organizations
Catholic Youth Organization
Confraternity of Christian Doctrine
Knights of Columbus
Opus Dei
Society of Jesus (Jesuits)
Sovereign Military Order (Knights) of Malta

HOW MUCH

	9-Year Growth	1981	1982	1983	1984	1985	1986	1987	1988	1989	1990
Members (mil.)	0.9%	50.5	51.2	52.1	52.4	52.3	52.7	52.9	53.5	55.0	54.5
Priests	(1.2%)	58,398	58,085	57,870	57,891	57,317	57,183	53,382	53,522	52,948	52,535
Deacons	7.9%	4,725	5,471	6,066	6,702	7,204	7,562	7,981	8,512	9,065	9,356
Brothers	(1.9%)	7,966	7,880	7,658	7,596	7,544	7,429	7,418	7,069	6,977	6,721
Sisters	(2.0%)	122,653	121,370	120,699	118,027	115,386	113,658	112,489	106,912	104,419	102,504
Parishes	0.5%	18,829	18,903	19,039	19,118	19,244	19,313	19,546	19,596	19,705	19,620

Membership (mil.) 1981–90

(Bar chart showing membership values from 1981 to 1990, ranging approximately 50–55 million)

ROTARY INTERNATIONAL

OVERVIEW

Rotary International is the oldest and most international service organization in the world. It has more than one million members forming more than 25,000 clubs in 172 countries. Many other service clubs, including the Kiwanis and Lions clubs, have patterned themselves after the Rotary.

The organization's motto, "Service Above Self," exemplifies the organization's dedication to its "four avenues" of club, vocational, community, and international service. The organization is devoted to promoting high ethical standards in business and international

understanding, goodwill, and peace. Rotary's scholarship, immunization, and nutritional programs have helped millions of people throughout the world. It operates the world's largest privately sponsored scholarship program through The Rotary Foundation.

Rotary International has raised almost $250 million toward its goal of eradicating polio by the end of the century. Its Interact and Rotaract clubs for teens and young adults and its Youth Exchange program promote Rotarian values to young people.

Service organization
Fiscal year ends: June 30

Hoover's Rating **A-**

WHO

General Secretary: Spencer Robinson, Jr.
President: Rajendra K. Saboo (1991–92 year)
President-Elect: Clifford L. Dochterman
Finance Officer: James Fallen
Auditors: Coopers & Lybrand
Employees: 532

WHERE

HQ: One Rotary Center, 1560 Sherman Ave., Evanston, IL 60201
Phone: 708-866-3000
Fax: 708-328-8554

Rotary International has 25,462 clubs in 172 countries.

WHEN

Created on the night of February 23, 1905, at Madame Galli's restaurant in Chicago by a shy, 37-year-old bachelor attorney, Paul Percy Harris, and 3 business acquaintances, the Conspirators, as the club was first called, was to be an organization dedicated to fellowship and the mutual business advantage of its members (no 2 of whom were to be from the same profession or business). The club very early on assumed the additional objective of service, which has come to dominate its activities.

Rotary's first foray into community service occurred when it waged a successful 2-year campaign to bring the first public lavatory to Chicago in the face of opposition from tavern and department store owners who used their facilities to draw customers. The name Rotary was derived from the organization's early propensity to meet at different hotels and offices.

Initially Harris assumed no office in the Rotary Club of Chicago, the organization's first official name, waiting until 1907 to serve as its president. At this time, as its name suggested, the club still focused its activities on the Chicago area. Harris, wanting to spread the organization's ideals more widely, opened the 2nd club in San Francisco in 1908. Once started, expansion occurred rapidly. By 1910 there were 16 clubs (including the first international club in Winnipeg) and 1,500 Rotarians, and, to reflect its broader geographic base, the organization changed its name to the National Association of Rotary Clubs. By 1912 there were 50 clubs, including 3 outside the US, prompting yet another name change, to the International Association of Rotary Clubs.

Chesley Perry became Rotary's first general secretary in 1910, holding that position for the

next 32 years. Under him the Rotary continued to expand its membership and refine its concept of service. It adopted its present name in 1922.

The Rotary Foundation was established in 1917 to advance the cause of international understanding. The Foundation has since provided millions of dollars for scholarships, the prevention of polio, and other worthy causes. During WWI and WWII the Rotary was instrumental in assisting the victims of war and played an important role in founding UNESCO in 1945. Rotary lost a number of clubs in Eastern Europe during and after WWII.

Growth continued, with membership rising to 682,183 in 1970 and 875,949 by 1980. In 1986 Rotary established the Village Corps to promote self-help community service projects among members. With the admission of women to the US clubs in May 1987, following a US Supreme Court decision upholding a California law prohibiting Rotary's ban of women members (extended worldwide in July 1989), membership again grew. In 1988 Rotary established the Peace Forum in an effort to enhance and formalize its well-known peacemaking efforts.

In 1989 the new political order in Eastern Europe prompted Rotarians to reestablish clubs abolished after WWII in Warsaw and Budapest and to begin discussions to establish clubs in the USSR, which culminated in the 1990 inauguration of a Moscow club. In 1991 then Rotary president Paulo Costa challenged Rotarians to take advantage of world change and increase membership to 2 million by the end of the decade.

WHAT

1990 Organization/Program	Membership
Rotary	1,125,050
Interact	152,878
Rotaract	120,359
Village Corps	3,683
Youth Exchange	7,800
Total	**1,409,770**

1990 Sources of Revenue	$ mil.	% of total
Dues	26	65
Magazine	6	15
Tenant revenue	3	8
Convention	2	5
Publication sales	2	5
License fees	1	2
Total	**40**	**100**

1990 Foundation Expenses	$ mil.	% of total
Scholarships	18	29
Group Study Exchange	3	5
Health, Hunger & Humanity	4	6
Matching Grants	3	5
PolioPlus	22	35
Other programs	12	20
Total	**62**	**100**

Prominent Members

US Presidents
Dwight Eisenhower
Warren Harding
Herbert Hoover
John Kennedy
Richard Nixon
Franklin Roosevelt
Harry Truman
Woodrow Wilson

Politicians
Winston Churchill
J. William Fulbright
Mark Hatfield
Wayne Morse
Adlai Stevenson
Earl Warren

Literary Figures
Thomas Mann
Norman Vincent Peale
James Whitcomb Riley
Albert Schweitzer

Business Leaders
Wally "Famous" Amos
Frank Borman
Raymond Firestone
Connie Mack
Charles Walgreen

Royalty
King Baudouin I (Belgium)
Prince Bernhard (Netherlands)
King Carl VI Gustav (Sweden)
King Hassan II (Morocco)
Prince Philip (England)
Prince Rainier (Monaco)

Others
Neil Armstrong
Admiral Richard Byrd
Gordon Cooper
Alan Shepard
Orville Wright

HOW MUCH

	9-Year Growth	1981	1982	1983	1984	1985	1986	1987	1988	1989	1990
Revenues ($ mil.)	—	—	—	—	—	—	—	—	—	35	40
Membership (thou.)	2.6%	896	908	926	961	991	1,013	1,039	1,057	1,077	1,125
Clubs	3.1%	19,339	19,786	20,187	20,838	21,662	22,365	23,095	23,679	24,408	25,462
Countries	1.1%	156	157	157	159	159	160	160	162	167	172

Membership (thou.) 1981–90

(bar chart showing membership values 1981–1990, vertical scale from 0 to 1,200)

RUBBERMAID INC.

NYSE symbol: RBD
Fiscal year ends: December 31

OVERVIEW

Rubbermaid Incorporated is a major producer of rubber and plastic products for the consumer and institutional markets. The company primarily manufactures housewares, decorative coverings, toys, industrial maintenance goods, and products for leisure, office, and garden.

The company consists of several key operating divisions, including Housewares (the largest unit), Specialty Products, Little Tikes (toys), Commercial Products, and Office Products. Rubbermaid also maintains joint ventures with French company Allibert (Rubbermaid-Allibert) and the Curver group of the Dutch conglomerate DSM (Curver Rubbermaid Group), which makes the company the largest housewares operation in the EC and related markets.

Much of Rubbermaid's success stems from its ability to successfully predict and develop products for new markets. In the last 5 years, the company has introduced more than 1,000 new products. Rubbermaid was listed in the top 10 of *Fortune*'s America's Most Admired Corporations for the 6th consecutive year, ranking 2nd in 1990.

WHEN

In 1920, 5 local businessmen formed The Wooster Rubber Company in a rented building in Wooster, Ohio, to manufacture the Sunshine brand toy balloon. Horatio Ebert and Errett Grable purchased the company in the mid-1920s.

In the early 1930s, while at a department store, Ebert noticed a line of housewares products that had been developed by James Caldwell. Caldwell's product line (which he named Rubbermaid) included rubber dustpans, drainboard mats, soap dishes, and sink stoppers. Ebert contacted Caldwell, and the 2 men agreed to join their businesses. In 1934 Wooster Rubber began producing Rubbermaid brand products.

In 1942 the government froze civilian use of rubber due to WWII. The Wooster Rubber Company was forced to halt its production of housewares but was able to survive the war by producing self-sealing fuel tanks, life jackets, and tourniquets for the government.

At the end of WWII, Wooster Rubber resumed production of housewares products. In 1950 the company established a Canadian manufacturing facility. During the mid-1950s the company produced its first plastic product (a dishpan) and introduced a line of commercial goods for hotels, motels, restaurants, and institutions. In 1955 the company made its first public stock offering and 2 years later changed its name to Rubbermaid. Caldwell stepped down as president in 1958, and Donald Noble became CEO in 1959.

When Noble retired in 1980, Rubbermaid recruited General Electric executive Stanley Gault, the son of one of the 5 founders, as its new chairman and CEO. Gault immediately restructured the company and led Rubbermaid through a decade of phenomenal growth in which sales more than quadrupled from just over $300 million to over $1.5 billion.

Rubbermaid acquired Con-Tact (decorative coverings, 1981), Little Tikes (plastic toys, 1984), Gott (leisure and recreational products, 1985), SECO (floor products, 1986), MicroComputer Accessories (1986), and Viking Brush (cleaning supplies, 1987).

In 1989 Rubbermaid entered a joint venture with French company Allibert to produce resin furniture and the following year established a joint venture with the Curver group of the Dutch chemical company DSM to market housewares in Europe, North Africa, and the Middle East. Also in 1990 the company purchased EWU AG (floor care supplies, Switzerland) and Eldon Industries (office accessories).

In 1991 Stanley Gault retired from Rubbermaid and after only a 5-week rest became CEO of Goodyear.

WHO

Chairman and CEO: Walter W. Williams, age 56, $726,290 pay (prior to promotion)
President and COO: Wolfgang R. Schmitt, age 47, $496,111 pay (prior to promotion)
SVP and CFO: Joseph G. Meehan, age 59, $348,881 pay
SVP Human Resources: Thomas W. Ward, age 56
Auditors: KPMG Peat Marwick
Employees: 9,304

WHERE

HQ: 1147 Akron Rd., Wooster, OH 44691-2596
Phone: 216-264-6464
Fax: 216-287-2739 (Administrative Office)

The company operates 43 major manufacturing and/or warehousing facilities in 14 US states and 5 foreign countries. Rubbermaid products are distributed in 116 nations.

	1990 Sales		1990 Operating Income	
	$ mil.	% of total	$ mil.	% of total
US	1,371	89	219	94
Other countries	163	11	14	6
Total	**1,534**	**100**	**233**	**100**

WHAT

	1990 Sales
	% of total
Consumer	73
Institutional	27
Total	**100**

Products

Housewares
Bathware
Casual dinnerware
Decorative coverings
Food utensils
Laundry baskets
Microwave cookware
Recycling bins
Rubber gloves
Tool boxes
Trash containers
Vacuum cleaner bags
Workshop organizers

Specialty Products
Bird feeders
Blue Ice refreezable ice substitute
Horticulture products
Insulated chests
Lawn carts

Outdoor resin furniture
Picnic baskets
Planters

Toys
Little Tikes

Commercial Products
Ash/trash receptacles
Cleaning products
Floor care supplies
Recycling containers
Serving trays
Water troughs

Office Products
Accessories
Building directories
Floormats
Furniture

HOW MUCH

	9-Year Growth	1981	1982	1983	1984	1985	1986	1987	1988	1989	1990
Sales ($ mil.)	17.6%	357	376	436	566	671	795	1,015	1,194	1,344	1,534
Net income ($ mil.)	21.1%	26	28	36	47	57	70	85	99	116	144
Income as % of sales	—	7.2%	7.3%	8.2%	8.3%	8.5%	8.8%	8.3%	8.3%	8.7%	9.4%
Earnings per share ($)	17.7%	0.41	0.45	0.58	0.69	0.79	0.96	1.15	1.35	1.58	1.80
Stock price – high ($)	—	5.06	8.00	12.50	11.31	17.44	28.50	35.00	27.00	37.75	45.00
Stock price – low ($)	—	2.92	4.36	7.31	8.16	10.94	16.63	19.00	21.00	25.00	31.00
Stock price – close ($)	27.8%	4.61	7.50	9.78	11.13	17.25	24.25	24.88	25.13	36.75	42.00
P/E – high	—	12	18	22	16	22	30	30	20	24	25
P/E – low	—	7	10	13	12	14	17	17	16	16	17
Dividends per share ($)	16.7%	0.14	0.16	0.18	0.20	0.23	0.26	0.32	0.38	0.46	0.54
Book value per share ($)	16.1%	2.51	2.77	3.18	3.53	4.16	4.91	5.94	6.95	8.12	9.60

1990 Year-end:
Debt ratio: 4.9%
Return on equity: 20.3%
Cash (mil.): $78
Current ratio: 2.56
Long-term debt (mil.): $39
No. of shares (mil.): 80
Dividends:
  1990 average yield: 1.3%
  1990 payout: 30.0%
Market value (mil.): $3,360

Stock Price History High/Low 1981–90

RANKINGS

259th in *Fortune* 500 Industrial Cos.
184th in *Business Week* 1000

KEY COMPETITORS

Amway
Avon
Gerber
Hanson
Hasbro
MacAndrews & Forbes
Mattel
Mobil
Premark

RYDER SYSTEM, INC.

OVERVIEW

Known best for its bright yellow One-Way rental trucks, Ryder is the world's foremost supplier of highway transportation services. It continues as the #1 provider of commercial truck rentals and offers full-service truck leasing, which supplies clients such as Borden and GM with everything from custom vehicles, fuel, and maintenance to safety training and insurance. Ryder is the leading North American transporter of new cars and light trucks (more than 6 million vehicles in 1990) and hauls materials under contract for corporations such as Xerox and Toyota. Every school day Ryder carries 400,000 students, with more than 6,940 buses operating in 16 states.

Through Aviall and Caledonian Airmotive, Ryder offers many of the world's commercial airlines jet engine maintenance and service. Aviall is also the world's #1 independent distributor of new aviation supplies and parts.

Persistent problems (some related to the slow economy) in Ryder's truck leasing division led to a shake-up in 1991, when CEO Burns ousted president David Parker (who was widely considered Burns's heir apparent) and took over the division's management himself. The division, Ryder's largest, had been losing market share (down to 32%, compared to U-Haul's 50%) and posted losses for the first half of 1991.

WHEN

Ryder Truck Rental, founded in Miami by Jim Ryder in 1933, was America's first truck leasing firm. The company offered truck rentals in 4 southern states until 1952 when it bought a southeastern freight hauler, Great Southern Trucking (renamed Ryder Truck Lines), which effectively doubled Ryder's size. Renamed Ryder System, the company went public in 1955.

That year the company bought Carolina Fleets (a South Carolina trucking company) and Yellow Rental (a northeastern leasing service). More purchases over the next decade extended rental services (called Ryder Truck Rentals) across the US and into Canada. Ryder Truck Lines, which had expanded service throughout the South, East, and Midwest, was sold to International Utilities in 1965.

After establishing One-Way truck rental services for self-movers in 1968, Ryder entered several new markets, including new automobile transport (1968), truck driver and heavy equipment training (1969), temporary services (1969), insurance (1970), truck stops (1971), and oil refining (1974). Profits reached $20 million in 1973, but the company's debt ($500 million), mostly in high-interest loans, cost Ryder $20 million in losses when interest rates soared in 1974.

In 1975 former Allegheny Airlines (USAir) president Leslie Barnes replaced Jim Ryder as Ryder's CEO. By selling the oil refinery and other assets, Barnes had the company in the black by the end of the year. Jim Ryder (who had moved into the chairmanship) left Ryder in 1978 and founded Jartran that year.

Anthony Burns became Ryder's president in 1979 (and CEO in 1983 when Barnes retired). Burns sold Ryder's truck stops (1984) and, through 65 acquisitions, moved the company into aviation sales and service (1982), freight hauling (1983), aircraft leasing (1984), aircraft engine overhauling (1985), and school busing (1985). By 1987 Ryder had become America's leader in truck leasing and automobile hauling, the world's largest non-airline provider of aviation maintenance and parts, and 2nd only to Canada's Laidlaw in the management of school bus fleets. It also briefly surpassed U-Haul as America's leader in one-way moving services in 1987.

In 1989 Ryder sold Ryder Freight System (full truckload freight hauling) and most of its insurance interests. In response to the weak economy (and financial turmoil in the airline industry), the company moved to discontinue its aircraft leasing business (taking a related charge of $36 million) in 1990.

NYSE symbol: R
Fiscal year ends: December 31

Hoover's Rating C

WHO

Chairman, President, and CEO: M. Anthony Burns, age 48, $916,739 pay
SEVP Finance and CFO: Edwin A. Huston, age 52, $526,044 pay
EVP Human Resources and Administration: C. Robert Campbell, age 46
Auditors: KPMG Peat Marwick
Employees: 40,362

WHERE

HQ: 3600 N.W. 82nd Ave., Miami, FL 33166
Phone: 305-593-3726
Fax: 305-593-3336

Ryder offers truck rentals through 1,403 locations in the US, Canada, Germany, and the UK. The company operates 5 aircraft engine overhaul facilities in the US and the UK and sells aircraft parts on 4 continents. Ryder operates a fleet of 161,280 vehicles and 34 commercial aircraft.

	1990 Sales		1990 Operating Income	
	$ mil.	% of total	$ mil.	% of total
US	4,593	89	334	89
Other countries	569	11	41	11
Adjustments	—	—	(10)	—
Total	**5,162**	**100**	**365**	**100**

WHAT

	1990 Sales		1990 Operating Income	
	$ mil.	% of total	$ mil.	% of total
Vehicle leasing & services	3,286	63	289	77
Automotive carriers	689	13	20	5
Aviation services	1,212	24	66	18
Other	3	—	—	—
Adjustments	(28)	—	(10)	—
Total	**5,162**	**100**	**365**	**100**

Highway Transportation Services
Automotive carriers
Commercial truck rental
Consumer truck rental
Dedicated contract carriage
Full-service truck leasing
Student transportation

Aviation Services
Aircraft engine repair and maintenance
Aircraft parts
Aviation and marine parts inventory database
Jet engine repair and maintenance

RANKINGS

21st in *Fortune* 100 Diversified Service Cos.
423rd in *Business Week* 1000

KEY COMPETITORS

Canadian Pacific
Consolidated Freightways
Consolidated Rail
CSX
Federal Express
General Electric
Mayflower
Norfolk Southern
Rolls-Royce
Ryder
Southland
TRW
UPS
United Technologies
Other trucking companies

HOW MUCH

	9-Year Growth	1981	1982	1983	1984	1985	1986	1987	1988	1989	1990
Sales ($ mil.)	11.4%	1,946	2,076	2,384	2,486	2,905	3,768	4,609	5,030	5,073	5,162
Net income ($ mil.)	1.2%	74	83	101	118	125	161	187	135	52	82
Income as % of sales	—	3.8%	4.0%	4.2%	4.7%	4.3%	4.3%	4.1%	2.7%	1.0%	1.6%
Earnings per share ($)	(2.2%)	1.17	1.21	1.43	1.65	1.73	2.09	2.29	1.61	0.58	0.96
Stock price – high ($)	—	12.35	16.65	19.86	19.05	24.67	35.50	43.00	32.50	31.13	23.38
Stock price – low ($)	—	7.96	7.09	14.26	12.71	14.67	21.50	15.00	22.63	19.75	12.25
Stock price – close ($)	5.9%	8.96	15.79	18.85	16.21	22.25	33.38	26.50	26.00	20.38	15.00
P/E – high	—	11	14	14	12	14	17	19	20	54	24
P/E – low	—	7	6	10	8	8	10	7	14	34	13
Dividends per share ($)	7.1%	0.32	0.34	0.34	0.35	0.40	0.44	0.52	0.56	0.60	0.60
Book value per share ($)	10.4%	7.42	8.19	9.32	10.84	12.20	14.72	16.75	18.71	18.24	18.06

1990 Year-end:
Debt ratio: 57.4%
Return on equity: 5.3%
Cash (mil.): $101
Current ratio: 0.89
Long-term debt (mil.): $1,923
No. of shares (mil.): 74
Dividends:
1990 average yield: 4.0%
1990 payout: 62.5%
Market value (mil.): $1,105

Stock Price History High/Low 1981–90

SAFEWAY INC.

NYSE symbol: SWY
Fiscal year ends: Saturday closest to December 31

Hoover's Rating: **D**

OVERVIEW

Oakland-based Safeway underwent a radical transformation in the late 1980s. Formerly the world's largest grocer and long known for job security, Safeway emerged from a 1986 buyout, orchestrated by KKR, 1,130 stores and 63,000 employees lighter. Operations sold in the restructuring included those in Texas, Oklahoma, and Southern California, areas where the company's labor costs were high. Safeway's prized 132-store UK holdings were also sold to reduce acquisition debt.

The disposals and recent openings have increased average store size; 46% of Safeway's 1,121 US and Canadian locations are superstores averaging 43,700 square feet, compared to 31% before the buyout. Openings and modernizations focus on the company's

"marketplace" format, emphasizing specialty departments in a boutique atmosphere. To encourage one-stop shopping, stores are providing a broader selection of food and other items. The company is also offering more packaging sizes catering to single persons and large families and is adding more kitchen-ready and easy-to-prepare foods. A number of stores with delis have added Chinese takeout kitchens.

Safeway went public again in 1990, but KKR still controls about 69% of the stock. The company's earnings before interest in 1989 were almost as much as in 1985, despite $5.3 billion lower sales. Earnings before interest for 1990 were up $72.9 million.

WHEN

Marion Skaggs bought a grocery from his father in American Falls, Idaho, in 1915 and started Skaggs United Stores. Unlike other stores of the day, where merchandise was kept in barrels or stacked on tables, Skaggs installed shelves and made goods easy to reach. In 1926 Safeway, a 338-unit California and Hawaii grocer, merged with the 428 Skaggs stores to form Safeway Stores. M. B. Skaggs, son of the founder, became president and his brother L. S. Skaggs (founder of what is now American Stores) became VP.

Safeway bought Arizona Grocery, Piggly Wiggly Pacific, and Eastern Stores in 1928 and Piggly Wiggly Western States, a grocer operating in California, Texas, and Nevada, in 1929. Since that time the company has made numerous acquisitions, expanding nationwide. In 1931 the company had its greatest number of stores (3,527); this number was reduced as Safeway eliminated smaller stores and adopted the supermarket format. In addition the company expanded internationally, into western Canada, the UK, and Australia. The company sold both its Australian and German operations in 1985.

The Magowan family has been important to Safeway. Robert Magowan, a former Macy's executive, was chairman of Safeway in the 1950s, retiring in 1970. Robert's son Peter (the current chairman and CEO) has been a key executive in the company since 1979.

In 1986 Safeway received an unsolicited buyout bid from the Dart Group. In response, Peter Magowan and takeover specialists KKR took Safeway private in a leveraged deal, paying Dart $159 million profit on its shares. The company sold some 1,200 locations in Utah, Oklahoma, Kansas, Arkansas, and the UK in 1987 and in Texas in 1988. Safeway sold stores in Southern California to the Vons Companies for 35% of Vons's stock.

In 1990 Safeway reemerged as a public company by selling 10% of its stock. The proceeds are earmarked for store expansion and remodeling. In April 1991 the company made a public offering of 17.5 million shares of stock. Safeway received about $341 million in net proceeds from the offering. Due to the proceeds the company's bank credit was removed from highly leveraged status, and in July 1991 Moody's upgraded the company's long-term debt rating.

WHO

Chairman, President, and CEO: Peter A. Magowan, age 48, $1,405,652 pay
VC: Harry D. Sunderland, age 55, $707,206 pay
EVP; Chairman, President, and CEO, Canada Safeway Limited: Robert H. Kinnie, age 51, $593,869 pay
EVP, CAO, and CFO: Michael M. Pharr, age 50, $582,386 pay
SVP Human Resources: Ronald F. Zachary, age 52
Auditors: Deloitte & Touche
Employees: 114,000

WHERE

HQ: 4th and Jackson Sts., Oakland, CA 94660
Phone: 415-891-3000
Fax: 415-444-5135

Safeway operates 1,121 stores in the western and mid-Atlantic US and in Canada. The company currently owns 31% of Vons, which operates in Southern California, and 49% of Casa Ley, a company in western Mexico.

	1990 Sales		1990 Operating Income	
	$ mil.	% of total	$ mil.	% of total
US	11,173	75	408	76
Canada	3,701	25	128	24
Total	**14,874**	**100**	**536**	**100**

	1990 Store Locations	
	No. of stores	% of total
Northern California, Nevada & Hawaii	249	22
Western Canada	238	21
Washington state & parts of Idaho, Montana & Wyoming	176	16
Maryland, Virginia & Washington, DC	147	13
Colorado & parts of New Mexico, Wyoming, Kansas, Nebraska & South Dakota	123	11
Oregon	102	9
Arizona	86	8
Total	**1,121**	**100**

HOW MUCH

	9-Year Growth	1981	1982	1983	1984	1985	1986	1987	1988	1989	1990
Sales ($ mil.)	(1.2%)	16,580	17,633	18,585	19,642	19,651	20,311	18,301	13,612	14,325	14,874
Net income ($ mil.)	(3.0%)	115	160	183	185	231	(14)	(112)	(17)	3	87
Income as % of sales	—	0.7%	0.9%	1.0%	0.9%	1.2%	(0.1%)	(0.6%)	(0.1%)	0.0%	0.6%
Earnings per share ($)	(9.3%)	2.20	3.06	3.26	3.12	3.83	(0.24)	(1.78)	(0.31)	0.03	0.91
Stock price – high ($)	—	18.88	25.13	30.00	29.25	37.63	67.13	—	—	—	16.88
Stock price – low ($)	—	12.13	13.13	21.31	21.25	26.88	34.25	—	—	—	10.25
Stock price – close ($)	(0.9%)	13.25	22.88	25.75	27.13	36.88	61.38	—	—	—	12.25
P/E – high	—	9	8	9	9	10	—	—	—	—	19
P/E – low	—	6	4	7	7	7	—	—	—	—	11
Dividends per share ($)	—	1.30	1.33	1.43	1.53	1.63	1.28	0.00	0.00	0.00	0.00
Book value per share ($)	—	21.27	21.75	23.66	24.54	26.67	0.04	(6.83)	(5.44)	(5.74)	(2.31)

1990 Year-end:
Debt ratio: —
Return on equity: —
Cash (mil.): $151
Current ratio: 1.15
Long-term debt (mil.): $3,005
No. of shares (mil.): 79
Dividends:
  1990 average yield: 0.0%
  1990 payout: 0.0%
Market value (mil.): $971

Stock Price History High/Low 1981–90

WHAT

	1990 Store Formats		
	No. of stores	% of total	Average sq. ft.
Conventional format	603	54	25,800
Superstore format	518	46	43,700
Total	**1,121**	**100**	

Safeway also produces about 3,000 private-label items through a number of plants that supply its stores with dairy products (Lucerne), soft drinks (Cragmont), baked goods, and other items.

RANKINGS

7th in *Fortune* 50 Retailing Cos.
407th in *Business Week* 1000

KEY COMPETITORS

Albertson's
American Stores
Food Lion
Fred Meyer

Giant Food
Great A&P
Kroger
Winn-Dixie

SALOMON INC

NYSE symbol: SB
Fiscal year ends: December 31

Hoover's Rating: **D**

OVERVIEW

Salomon is an international investment banking and securities trading firm as well as an oil and commodities leader. New York–based Salomon is the 3rd largest diversified financial company in the US after American Express and Fannie Mae, with 1990 year-end assets of $110 billion.

Salomon is also the largest foreign securities firm in Japan and the 5th largest of all security firms in that country. Salomon's Phibro Energy, which made $492 million in pretax earnings, is a leading global trader of crude oil and is the 4th largest independent oil refiner in the US.

In the first half of 1991, earnings declined 74% as oil prices fell after the Gulf War. Things got worse later in 1991 when revelations of illegal trading in T-bills became public.

In 1991 Salomon downsized its Philipp Bros. commodities trading arm, shifting most commodity trading to Salomon and Phibro. Salomon and Phibro entered into joint ventures with the USSR for production and marketing of precious metals and oil.

WHEN

Arthur, Herbert, and Percy Salomon founded Salomon Brothers as a money brokerage firm in 1910. In 1917 the company became an authorized US government securities dealer, specializing in buying and selling large blocks of securities. Growth until the 1960s came from corporate and government bond trading.

In the 1950s and 1960s, Salomon expanded its research and trading departments and entered stock underwriting. Salomon added a corporate finance department in the late 1960s. In 1970 Salomon opened branches in London and Tokyo.

In 1978 John Gutfreund, head of corporate finance, became managing partner. In the early 1980s mergers increased competition in the industry. Gutfreund sought more capital by merging with Phibro Corporation, an international oil and commodities trader. Salomon Brothers remained autonomous and Gutfreund and Phibro's John Tendler became co-CEOs.

Gutfreund became sole CEO in 1984. As the economy boomed in the 1980s, Salomon increased its staff by 40% in 1986 alone, trying to keep pace.

In 1987 the company suffered losses in its mortgage-backed securities business (40% of earnings) and in the 1987 stock market crash. The company withdrew from the municipal bond and commercial paper business and got on the LBO bandwagon. Two of its LBOs,

Revco and Southland, ended in Chapter 11 while a 3rd, Grand Union, is a financial drain.

In 1991 there were rumors that Salomon was manipulating US treasury securities auctions. The company was allowed to buy up to 35% of an issue at each auction. In April, Gutfreund and other managers became aware that the 35% limit had been violated in February through unauthorized bids on a client's behalf. Complaints prompted an SEC investigation of the May auction, at which Salomon bought 94% of the issue, on its own behalf or for clients (knowingly or unknowingly), and then bought back the excess.

When this became public, Gutfreund and President Strauss resigned and investor Warren Buffett (16% owner) became chairman. He made a full revelation of Salomon's actions and took steps to prevent their recurrence. Since the scandal broke, however, the price of the company's stock has declined, and Salomon has been forced to sell off assets to continue operating as credit became more difficult to obtain, and employee morale has plunged (because of the clash of Buffett's public probity with the anything-goes corporate culture fostered by Gutfreund). Salomon has lost clients (including the California state pension system), has been refused issues (British Telecom's US offering), and was suspended from dealing with the World Bank. But it remains a primary dealer of US treasury instruments.

WHO

Chairman and CEO: Warren E. Buffett, age 61
COO: Deryk C. Maughn, age 43
EVP: James L. Massey, age 48, $2,009,290 pay
Managing Director, Human Resources:
 Ed Weihenmayer
EVP and CFO: Donald S. Howard, age 62
Treasurer: John G. MacFarlane, age 37
Auditors: Arthur Andersen & Co.
Employees: 8,883

WHERE

HQ: One New York Plaza, New York, NY 10004
Phone: 212-747-7000
Fax: 212-422-3417

Salomon has offices worldwide.

	1990 Pretax Income	
	$ mil.	% of total
North America	(27)	(5)
Europe	392	77
Asia & other regions	141	28
Total	**506**	**100**

WHAT

	1990 Net Revenue		1990 Pretax Income	
	$ mil.	% of total	$ mil.	% of total
Securities	8,193	92	416	71
Energy	762	8	492	84
Commodities	(10)	—	(323)	(55)
Adjustments	1	—	(79)	—
Total	**8,946**	**100**	**506**	**100**

Financial Services (Salomon Brothers)
Institutional money management
Investment banking
Merchant banking
Research and advisory services
Securities and foreign currency trading
Securities underwriting

Energy (Phibro Energy)
Crude oil trading
Energy-related commodities trading
Oil refining (Phibro Refining and Hill Petroleum)

Commodities (Philipp Brothers)
Agricultural products trading
Metals trading
Non-energy-related commodities trading

RANKINGS

3rd in *Fortune* 50 Diversified Financial Cos.
211th in *Business Week* 1000

KEY COMPETITORS

American Express	Goldman Sachs
ADM	Kemper
Bear Stearns	Merrill Lynch
Cargill	Morgan Stanley
ConAgra	Paine Webber
Continental Grain	Prudential
CS Holding	Sears
Equitable	Travelers
General Electric	Oil refiners

HOW MUCH

	9-Year Growth	1981	1982	1983	1984	1985	1986	1987	1988	1989	1990
Sales ($ mil.)	4.1%	25,098	26,703	29,757	28,911	27,896	22,789	25,103	28,808	38,608	35,946
Net income ($ mil.)	0.5%	289	337	470	212	557	516	142	280	470	303
Income as % of sales	—	1.2%	1.3%	1.6%	0.7%	2.0%	2.3%	0.6%	1.0%	1.2%	0.8%
Earnings per share ($)	0.0%	2.06	2.27	3.10	1.41	3.60	3.32	0.86	1.63	3.20	2.05
Stock price – high ($)	—	27.88	30.44	40.63	34.75	46.75	59.38	44.50	28.38	29.38	27.00
Stock price – low ($)	—	11.25	10.06	23.69	20.75	30.00	37.38	16.63	19.38	20.50	20.00
Stock price – close ($)	7.2%	13.00	24.75	31.88	32.00	43.50	38.38	19.63	24.13	23.38	24.38
P/E – high	—	14	13	13	25	13	18	52	17	9	13
P/E – low	—	5	4	8	15	8	11	19	12	6	10
Dividends per share ($)	2.8%	0.50	0.47	0.52	0.54	0.54	0.64	0.64	0.64	0.64	0.64
Book value per share ($)	10.0%	10.85	12.84	15.73	16.62	19.93	22.72	21.15	21.82	24.08	25.68

1990 Year-end:
Debt ratio: 79.5%
Return on equity: 8.2%
Cash (mil.): $1,252
Assets (mil.): $109,877
Long-term debt (mil.): $10,956
No. of shares (mil.): 110
Dividends:
  1990 average yield: 2.6%
  1990 payout: 31.2%
Market value (mil.): $2,680

Stock Price History
High/Low 1981–90

SANTA FE PACIFIC CORPORATION

NYSE symbol: SFX
Fiscal year ends: December 31

 Hoover's Rating **D**

OVERVIEW

Santa Fe Pacific (SFP) is known best for its 132-year-old railroad, the Atchison, Topeka & Santa Fe. In 1990 the Santa Fe hauled nearly 78 billion tons of freight, primarily of intermodal (truck-to-train) merchandise and coal, over 10,770 route-miles of railway linking Chicago with the West Coast and the Gulf of Mexico. The Santa Fe helped pioneer the development of intermodal rail service and in 1990 introduced Quantum, a service alliance with J. B. Hunt Transport (trucking company), offering customized door-to-door delivery.

Santa Fe Pipelines, SFP's petroleum transmission subsidiary, owns 44% of publicly traded Santa Fe Pacific Pipeline Partners LP, which operates the largest refined petroleum products pipeline system in the western US. Another SFP subsidiary, Santa Fe Coal, supplies coal from the Lee Ranch Mine in New Mexico to 2 major southwestern electric utilities (Texas Utilities and Tucson Electric Power Company). Overall, SFP owns or controls mineral rights over 7.3 million acres in 8 states, including 3 gold mines in Nevada.

As a part of a restructuring plan, SFP spun off its real estate and energy subsidiaries in 1990 and is now focusing on improving its core mineral, pipeline, and railway businesses.

WHO

Chairman, President, and CEO: Robert D. Krebs, age 48, $550,000 pay
VP, Treasurer, and CFO: Denis E. Springer, age 45
VP Human Resources: Russell E. Hagberg, age 40
Auditors: Price Waterhouse
Employees: 16,050

WHERE

HQ: 1700 E. Golf Rd., Schaumburg, IL 60173-5860
Phone: 708-995-6000
Fax: 708-995-6219

Principal Cities Served

Albuquerque, NM	Kansas City, MO
Chicago, IL	Los Angeles, CA
Dallas, TX	Phoenix, AZ
Denver, CO	San Francisco, CA
Houston, TX	

WHEN

Cyrus Kurtz Holliday founded the Atchison and Topeka Railroad Company in 1859 to build a line from Atchison to Topeka, Kansas. Corporate offices were established in Topeka, and in 1863 the company was renamed the Atchison, Topeka & Santa Fe Railroad.

The Civil War and cash shortages delayed construction until 1868. Then, instead of Atchison, construction commenced from Topeka, both to the east (toward Atchison) and to the west. The railroad reached Albuquerque in 1880 and Los Angeles in 1887. The company also bought several other railroads, including the Gulf, Colorado & Santa Fe (Galveston to Fort Worth, 1886).

By 1890 the railroad had grown into a 9,000-mile giant under the guidance of President William B. Strong. But the depression of 1893 left the Atchison (as it was called), like many other railroads, in bankruptcy. When the company reorganized in 1895, it did so minus much of its mileage. In 1904 the new Atchison, Topeka & Santa Fe Railway Company moved its headquarters to Chicago and by 1929 had built or acquired over 13,000 miles of track throughout the Southwest. Guided by a succession of strong leaders and a conservative financial policy, the Santa Fe prospered into the 1960s. Santa Fe Industries was created in 1968 as a holding company for the Santa Fe Railway and its subsidiaries.

In 1983 Santa Fe Industries agreed to merge with competitor Southern Pacific to create Santa Fe Southern Pacific Corporation. The combined company, with more than 38,000 miles of track stretching from the West Coast to the Gulf Coast and Midwest, would have been the 2nd largest railroad in America (after Burlington Northern). However, in 1988 the ICC ruled that the merger was anticompetitive and ordered the company to sell one of its railway holdings. The company sold Southern Pacific to Rio Grande Industries in 1988 and adopted its present name in 1989.

In the meantime, the company fought off a 1987 takeover attempt by The Henley Group, a La Jolla, California–based conglomerate spun off from Allied-Signal in 1986. The target of the takeover appears to have been Santa Fe's real estate subsidiary Catellus Development, which owned 3 million acres in 14 states. In 1990 Santa Fe spun off Catellus and Santa Fe Energy Resources (oil and gas subsidiary) to its stockholders.

Also in 1990 the company moved its headquarters from Chicago to the western suburb of Schaumburg as part of a cost-cutting program that includes a planned 5% work force reduction by the end of 1992.

WHAT

	1990 Sales		1990 Operating Income	
	$ mil.	% of total	$ mil.	% of total
Rail	2,112	92	189	65
Hard minerals	157	7	74	25
Pipeline	28	1	28	10
Total	**2,297**	**100**	**291**	**100**

	1990 Carloads	
Items transported	No. thou.	% of total
Grain	119	8
Food & farm products	107	7
Chemicals	103	7
Coal	292	19
Metal products	31	2
Petroleum products	52	3
Nonmetallic minerals	78	5
Paper products	34	2
Lumber, plywood & logs	15	1
Vehicles & parts	76	5
Merchandise	32	2
Intermodal	486	31
Other	117	8
Total	**1,542**	**100**

Rail
The Atchison, Topeka and Santa Fe Railway Co.

Hard Minerals
Lee Ranch Mine (New Mexico coal mine)
The Lone Tree Mine (Nevada gold-mining venture)
Marigold Joint Venture (30%, Nevada gold-mining venture)
Rabbit Creek Mine (Nevada gold-mining venture)
Santa Fe Pacific Coal Corporation

Pipeline
Santa Fe Pacific Pipelines, Inc. (refined petroleum products pipelines in 6 western and southwestern states)
Santa Fe Pacific Pipeline Partners, LP (44%-owned limited partnership)

RANKINGS

18th in *Fortune* 50 Transportation Cos.
439th in *Business Week* 1000

KEY COMPETITORS

American President	Rio Grande Industries
Burlington Northern	Roadway
Consolidated Freightways	Union Pacific
CSX	Yellow Freight

HOW MUCH

	9-Year Growth	1981	1982	1983	1984	1985	1986	1987	1988	1989	1990
Sales ($ mil.)	(3.9%)	3,272	3,104	5,976	6,662	6,438	5,631	5,448	3,144	2,978	2,297
Net income ($ mil.)	—	168	125	333	491	470	(269)	346	147	(195)	(101)
Income as % of sales	—	5.1%	4.0%	5.6%	7.4%	7.3%	(4.8%)	6.3%	4.7%	(6.6%)	(4.4%)
Earnings per share ($)	—	2.00	1.46	1.77	2.61	2.67	(1.63)	2.19	0.93	(1.23)	(0.62)
Stock price – high ($)	—	17.82	13.69	29.00	26.63	37.13	39.63	65.00	47.88	25.75	23.13
Stock price – low ($)	—	10.94	8.02	11.67	20.25	24.50	26.25	29.63	14.25	16.75	6.00
Stock price – close ($)	(7.6%)	13.20	11.75	26.25	25.75	34.88	29.63	46.00	17.25	18.50	6.50
P/E – high	—	9	9	16	10	14	—	30	51	—	—
P/E – low	—	5	6	7	8	9	—	14	15	—	—
Dividends per share ($)	(21.1%)	0.84	0.84	0.94	1.00	1.00	1.00	1.00	25.00	0.10	0.10
Book value per share ($)	(16.5%)	26.84	27.13	30.21	32.20	33.97	32.11	33.39	3.07	5.39	5.27

1990 Year-end:
Debt ratio: 66.4%
Return on equity: —
Cash (mil.): $100
Current ratio: 0.51
Long-term debt (mil.): $1,801
No. of shares (mil.): 173
Dividends:
  1990 average yield: 1.5%
  1990 payout: —
Market value (mil.): $1,124

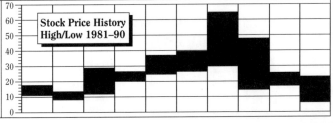
Stock Price History High/Low 1981–90

SARA LEE CORPORATION

OVERVIEW

Chicago-based Sara Lee is an international food and consumer goods company, with 1990 sales of $11.6 billion. In addition to its well-known frozen baked goods brand (which leads the US market with a 27% share), Sara Lee sells other brand names, including Hanes and L'eggs hosiery (53% market share), Kiwi shoe products (90% market share), Jimmy Dean breakfast sausage, Hillshire Farm smoked sausage, Ball Park hotdogs, Champion knitwear, and Douwe Egberts coffee. It also manufactures and markets underwear and household and personal care items and provides food service to restaurants.

The company has operations in more than 30 countries, with 28% of its sales from international markets, primarily Europe. Since the mid-1980s Sara Lee has spent over $1.5 billion to buy and consolidate European brands in preparation for the unification of European markets in 1992. Recent European purchases include Pretty Polly (hosiery, UK) and 51% of Compack, the #3 coffee company in Hungary.

NYSE symbol: SLE
Fiscal year ends: Saturday nearest June 30

Hoover's Rating **B+**

WHO

Chairman and CEO: John H. Bryan, age 53, $2,076,802 pay
President: Paul Fulton, age 55, $1,338,997 pay
EVP and CFO: Michael E. Murphy, age 53, $1,058,942 pay
VP Human Resources: Phillip A. Temple, age 50
Auditors: Arthur Andersen & Co.
Employees: 107,800

WHEN

Sara Lee Corporation began in 1939 when Nathan Cummings, a Canadian-born Chicago businessman, bought the C. D. Kenny Company, a small Baltimore wholesaler of coffee, tea, and sugar. Cummings soon purchased several grocery firms and subsequently changed the company's name to Consolidated Grocers (1945). In 1946 the company's stock was first listed on the New York Stock Exchange. In 1954 stockholders voted to rename the company Consolidated Foods Corporation (CFC).

Cummings served as company president until 1970. Focusing primarily on food and grocery concerns, he broadened his initial investments by buying and selling a diverse collection of food companies, grocery stores, and producers of personal care and consumer products. These included Piggly Wiggly Midwest supermarkets (1956) and Eagle Food Centers (1961). The company's Eagle Food Complex, which included Piggly Wiggly and Eagle stores, drug stores, and photo supply stores, was sold in 1968. The company also bought Shasta Water Company in 1960 (sold in 1985), Chicken Delight food franchises (bought in 1965, sold in 1979), and Electrolux Corporation (bought in 1968, sold in 1987).

In 1956 CFC purchased the Kitchens of Sara Lee, a Chicago bakery founded by Charles Lubin in 1951. Lubin had introduced Sara Lee cheesecake (named after his daughter) in 1949, and it became his most popular product. He remained with Consolidated Foods, successfully building the frozen desserts market under the Sara Lee brand name.

The company has continued to buy and sell a long list of businesses in the US and Europe — over 150 separate acquisitions since 1960. Its operations have included foods, beverages, grocery stores, apparel, appliances, food services, and chemicals. In 1962 Consolidated Foods made its first European acquisition and began to build its international markets. Some of its major purchases included Douwe Egberts (coffee, tea, and tobacco; Holland; 1978), Nicholas Kiwi (shoe polish and pharmaceuticals, Australia, 1984), Akzo Consumenten Produkten (food, household, and personal care products; Holland; 1987), and Dim (hosiery and underwear, France, 1989).

Some major US company purchases were Hanes Corporation (1979), Jimmy Dean Meat Company (1984), and Champion Products (athletic knitwear, 1989). Sales topped $5 billion in 1980 and $10 billion in 1988.

Consolidated Foods changed its name to Sara Lee Corporation in 1985, using one of its most respected brand names to enhance the public's awareness of the company.

In 1991 Sara Lee bought Playtex Apparel and sold its European drug business to Roche, creating speculation that it was raising money to buy a stake in Bic (pens and razors, France).

WHERE

HQ: Three First National Plaza, Chicago, IL 60602-4260
Phone: 312-726-2600
Fax: 312-726-3712

Sara Lee conducts operations in more than 30 countries and sells its products worldwide.

	1990 Sales		1990 Operating Income	
	$ mil.	% of total	$ mil.	% of total
US	8,302	71	561	60
Canada	163	1	17	2
Europe	2,766	24	306	32
Other countries	394	4	54	6
Adjustments	(19)	—	(79)	—
Total	**11,606**	**100**	**859**	**100**

WHAT

	1990 Sales		1990 Operating Income	
	$ mil.	% of total	$ mil.	% of total
Packaged meats & bakery	4,959	43	208	22
Coffee & grocery	1,834	16	199	21
Personal products	3,757	32	424	45
Household & personal care	1,060	9	107	12
Adjustments	(4)	—	(79)	—
Total	**11,606**	**100**	**859**	**100**

Brand Names

Foods	Sara Lee	**Shoe Care**
Ball Park	State Fair	Kiwi
Bryan	Sweet Sue	Tana
Chef Pierre		
Douwe Egberts	**Clothing**	**Home Care**
Droste	Aris	Biotex
Hillshire Farm	Bali	Bloo
Hygrade	Champion	Fuller Brush
Jimmy Dean	Dim	Ty-D-bol
Kahn's	Hanes	
Mr. Turkey	Isotoner	**Leather Goods**
Rudy's Farm	L'eggs	Coach

RANKINGS

38th in *Fortune* 500 Industrial Cos.
63rd in *Business Week* 1000

KEY COMPETITORS

Allied-Lyons	Philip Morris
Brown-Forman	Procter & Gamble
Campbell Soup	Riklis Family
Chiquita Brands	Sysco
ConAgra	TLC Beatrice
CPC	Tyson Foods
Grand Metropolitan	Unilever
Kellogg	V. F.
Nestlé	

HOW MUCH

	9-Year Growth	1981	1982	1983	1984	1985	1986	1987	1988	1989	1990
Sales ($ mil.)	8.4%	5,614	6,039	6,572	7,000	8,117	7,938	9,155	10,424	11,718	11,606
Net income ($ mil.)	14.4%	140	157	171	188	206	223	267	325	411	470
Income as % of sales	—	2.5%	2.6%	2.6%	2.7%	2.5%	2.8%	2.9%	3.1%	3.5%	4.1%
Earnings per share ($)	14.5%	0.55	0.65	0.71	0.81	0.90	1.01	1.18	1.42	1.75	1.87
Stock price – high ($)	—	4.31	5.94	6.81	8.72	13.00	18.41	24.56	25.75	33.75	33.38
Stock price – low ($)	—	2.92	3.72	4.77	6.25	7.78	11.78	13.25	16.44	21.44	24.13
Stock price – close ($)	26.1%	3.94	5.64	6.50	7.94	12.72	16.94	17.63	21.00	33.50	31.75
P/E – high	—	8	9	10	11	14	18	21	18	19	18
P/E – low	—	5	6	7	8	9	12	11	12	12	13
Dividends per share ($)	14.8%	0.23	0.26	0.28	0.32	0.35	0.39	0.48	0.58	0.69	0.81
Book value per share ($)	10.9%	3.92	3.97	4.05	4.33	4.63	5.41	6.39	7.12	8.42	9.95

1990 Year-end:
Debt ratio: 39.9%
Return on equity: 20.4%
Cash (mil.): $169
Current ratio: 1.16
Long-term debt (mil.): $1,524
No. of shares (mil.): 230
Dividends:
  1990 average yield: 2.6%
  1990 payout: 43.3%
Market value (mil.): $7,313

Stock Price History High/Low 1981–90

SCECORP

NYSE symbol: SCE
Fiscal year ends: December 31

Hoover's Rating **C+**

OVERVIEW

SCEcorp is the parent company of Southern California Edison, the 3rd largest electric utility in the US in terms of 1990 sales (after Pacific Gas and Electric and the Southern Company). Edison provides electricity to more than 4 million customers in a 50,000-square-mile area of central and southern California (excluding Los Angeles).

Edison, long an industry leader in the development of alternative and renewable fuel sources, currently uses 9 different resources to obtain electricity — more than any other utility in the world. These include coal, oil, natural gas, nuclear fuels, and several less frequently used resources such as the sun, wind, and geothermal energy. The company recently joined Texas Instruments to market a new solar cell that could cut the cost of solar energy by 80%. It is also working to develop and market electric vehicles.

Through the Mission Group, SCEcorp is also involved in other, nonutility businesses related to its expertise in the energy field, including the engineering and construction of generating plants and transmission systems, and real estate development.

WHEN

In 1896 Elmer Peck, Walter Wright, William Staats, and George Barker organized the West Side Lighting Company to provide electricity to the growing number of Los Angeles residents. Barker (of Barker Brothers furniture stores) became the company's first president.

In 1897 West Side Lighting agreed to merge with the Edison Electric Company of Los Angeles, which owned the rights to use Thomas Edison's name and patents in Los Angeles and the surrounding area. Barker continued as president of the resulting company (which kept the Edison company's name), overseeing the installation of the first underground electrical conduits in the Southwest.

John Barnes Miller became president in 1901. Known as the "Great Amalgamator," Miller bought numerous utilities throughout Southern California and constructed several generating facilities, including 3 hydroelectric plants on the Kern River. By 1909, when the company adopted the name Southern California Edison, it served 5 counties from Santa Barbara to Redlands.

In 1917 Henry Huntington (founder of Pacific Light & Power) sold his Southern California electrical interests, including 2 utilities in the San Joaquin Valley and the Big Creek generating complex, to Edison, doubling the company's assets. However, in 1912 the city of Los Angeles decided to develop its own power

distribution system, and by 1922 Edison's authority inside the city had ended.

A 1925 earthquake destroyed the company's Santa Barbara station, and the 1928 collapse of the St. Francis Dam washed out substations in the Santa Clara River valley and caused extensive damage throughout the Los Angeles area.

Edison's merger with California Electric Power in 1964 consolidated its service area throughout Southern California.

Although the company built 11 oil- and gas-fueled power stations (1948–73), it also diversified beyond the burning of fossil fuels. In 1963 Edison started construction of the San Onofre nuclear plant with San Diego Gas & Electric Company. In the late 1970s Edison began to build less conventional power plants, including solar, geothermal, and wind generators. In 1987 SCEcorp was formed as a holding company for Edison and a group of nonutility subsidiaries collectively named The Mission Group.

In 1988 Edison agreed to buy San Diego Gas & Electric, a purchase which, if approved by California regulators, would have added about 1 million customers and 4,100 square miles of service territory to Edison's system, creating America's largest investor-owned electric utility. However, in 1991 regulators shot down the proposal as anticompetitive.

WHO

Chairman and CEO: John E. Bryson, age 47, $505,700 pay (prior to promotion)
President: Michael R. Peevey, age 52, $479,750 pay (prior to promotion)
EVP, Treasurer, and CFO: Michael L. Noel, age 49
Manager, Employee Services of Edison: Diana L. Peterson-More
Auditors: Arthur Andersen & Co.
Employees: 16,925

WHERE

HQ: 2244 Walnut Grove Ave., Rosemead, CA 91770
Phone: 818-302-2222
Fax: 818-302-4815

Generating Facilities

Coal	San Onofre Units 2
Four Corners Units 4	and 3 (75.05%, CA)
and 5 (48.0%, NM)	**Oil and Gas**
Mohave (56.0%, NV)	Alamitos (CA)
Hydroelectric	Axis (CA)
Bishop hydro	Cool Water (CA)
division (CA)	El Segundo (CA)
Northern hydro	Etiwanda (CA)
division (CA)	Highgrove (CA)
Southern hydro	Huntington Beach (CA)
division (CA)	Long Beach (CA)
Nuclear	Mandalay (CA)
Palo Verde (15.8%, AZ)	Ormond Beach (CA)
San Onofre Unit 1	Pebbly Beach (CA)
(80.0%, CA)	Redondo (CA)
	San Bernardino (CA)

WHAT

	1990 Sales	
	$ mil.	% of total
Electricity		
Residential	2,393	33
Commercial	2,537	35
Industrial	1,137	16
Public authorities	584	8
Resale & other	335	5
Investment & other	213	3
Total	**7,199**	**100**

	1990 Fuel Source
	% of total
Oil	2
Natural gas	17
Coal	13
Nuclear	20
Hydro	3
Purchased & interchanged power	45
Total	**100**

Southern California Edison Co.

The Mission Group
Mission Energy Co. (cogeneration, geothermal, and other energy-related projects)
Mission First Financial (project financing, cash management, and venture capital)
Mission Land Co. (real estate development in California, Arizona, Indiana, and Illinois)
Mission Power Engineering Co. (energy-related engineering and construction for 3rd parties)

HOW MUCH

	9-Year Growth	1981	1982	1983	1984	1985	1986	1987	1988	1989	1990
Sales ($ mil.)	6.6%	4,055	4,304	4,466	4,901	5,171	5,313	5,494	6,253	6,904	7,199
Net income ($ mil.)	6.0%	490	556	691	732	774	769	721	809	823	830
Income as % of sales	—	12.1%	12.9%	15.5%	14.9%	15.0%	14.5%	13.1%	12.9%	11.9%	11.5%
Earnings per share ($)	4.3%	2.46	2.55	3.08	3.15	3.22	3.27	3.08	3.49	3.56	3.60
Stock price – high ($)	—	15.31	18.56	21.38	24.38	28.50	38.75	37.00	37.25	41.00	40.25
Stock price – low ($)	—	11.44	14.00	17.19	17.13	22.13	24.75	27.63	29.13	31.25	33.50
Stock price – close ($)	11.4%	14.38	17.56	19.88	22.75	26.63	33.88	30.50	32.38	39.38	37.88
P/E – high	—	6	7	7	8	9	12	12	11	12	11
P/E – low	—	5	6	6	5	7	8	9	8	9	9
Dividends per share ($)	6.0%	1.55	1.69	1.83	2.01	2.13	2.25	2.36	2.46	2.54	2.62
Book value per share ($)	4.5%	16.94	17.54	18.83	19.96	21.12	22.10	23.13	23.18	24.21	25.19

1990 Year-end:
Debt ratio: 47.4%
Return on equity: 14.6%
Cash (mil.): $479
Current ratio: 0.60
Long-term debt (mil.): $5,291
No. of shares (mil.): 218
Dividends:
  1990 average yield: 6.9%
  1990 payout: 72.8%
Market value (mil.): $8,275

Stock Price History High/Low 1981–90

RANKINGS

13th in *Fortune* 50 Utilities
72nd in *Business Week* 1000

SCHERING-PLOUGH CORPORATION

OVERVIEW

New Jersey–based Schering-Plough is a major producer of pharmaceuticals and consumer health products. The company makes such top-selling drugs as Proventil (antiasthmatic) and Intron A (cancer and hepatitis treatment) and through its DNAX subsidiary conducts research in biotechnology. In addition to such recognized OTC medicines as Coricidin and Afrin, Schering-Plough holds the #1 spots in foot products (Dr. Scholl's) and sun care (Coppertone).

Although the company's healthy R&D spending (11.4% of sales in 1990) provided it

with a lucrative pipeline in the 1980s, Schering-Plough has recently experienced troubles in bringing new products to the market. The FDA has delayed approval of its Claritin (allergy treatment) and Leucomax (white blood cell producer), while the company has had to scrap its new drugs Unicard (antihypertensive) and Geniconazole (antifungal) because of toxicity problems. The imminent introduction of generic versions of Proventil presents a challenge. However, the company's diverse product base and high profitability should offset these problems.

NYSE symbol: SGP
Fiscal year ends: December 31

Hoover's Rating **A**

WHO

Chairman and CEO: Robert P. Luciano, age 57, $1,694,498 pay
President and COO: Richard J. Kogan, age 49, $1,082,251 pay
EVP Finance: Harold R. Hiser, Jr., age 59
SVP Human Resources: Gordon C. O'Brien, age 50
Auditors: Deloitte & Touche
Employees: 19,700

WHERE

HQ: One Giralda Farms, Madison, NJ 07940
Phone: 201-822-7000
Fax: 201-822-7447

	1990 Sales		1990 Operating Income	
	$ mil.	% of total	$ mil.	% of total
US	1,890	59	572	70
Europe, Middle East & Africa	774	24	143	18
Latin America	190	6	37	4
Canada, Pacific	351	11	63	8
Adjustments	118	—	(92)	—
Total	**3,323**	**100**	**723**	**100**

WHAT

	1990 Sales		1990 Operating Income	
	$ mil.	% of total	$ mil.	% of total
Pharmaceuticals	2,586	78	672	83
Consumer products	618	19	142	17
Divested businesses	119	3	1	—
Adjustments	—	—	(92)	—
Total	**3,323**	**100**	**723**	**100**

Pharmaceuticals
Celestone (anti-inflammatory)
Diprospan (anti-inflammatory)
Elocon (topical anti-inflammatory)
Eulexin (for prostate cancer)
Garamycin (antibiotic)
Intron A (for cancer, hepatitis)
K-Dur (potassium)
Netromycin (antibiotic)
Nitro-Dur (antianginal)
Normodyne (antihypertensive)
Proventil (antiasthmatic)
Theo-Dur (antiasthmatic)
Trilafon (psychotherapeutic)
Vancenase AQ (antiallergy)
Vanceril (antiasthmatic)

Consumer Health Care
Afrin (decongestant)
Aftate (antifungal)
Aquaflex (contact lens)
Chlor-Trimeton (antihistamine)
Coppertone (sunscreen)
Coricidin (cold medicine)
Correctol (laxative)
Di-Gel (antacid)
Dr. Scholl's (foot care)
Drixoral (cold medicine)
Durasoft (contact lenses)
Feen-a-mint (laxative)
Gyne-Lotrimin (antifungal)
Lotrimin AF (antifungal)
Paas (holiday products)
Saint Joseph (aspirin)
Solarcaine (sunburn pain)
Tinactin (antifungal)

WHEN

Schering takes its name from Ernst Schering, a Berlin chemist who formed the company in 1864 to sell chemicals to local apothecary shops. By 1880 the German company was exporting pharmaceuticals to the US. An American subsidiary was established in 1928 and during the 1930s developed processes for the mass production of sex hormones. At the outbreak of WWII the US government seized the US subsidiary and appointed government attorney Francis Brown director. Brown put together a research team whose efforts led to new postwar drugs, including Chlor-Trimeton, one of the first antihistamines, and the cold medicine Coricidin in 1949.

In 1952 the government sold Schering to Merrill Lynch, which took it public with Brown as its president. Its most profitable products in the 1950s were new steroids. In 1957 Schering bought White Labs. In the 1960s the company introduced Tinactin (antifungal, 1965), Garamycin (antibiotic, 1964), and Afrin (decongestant, 1967).

The 1971 merger with Plough, Inc., expanded the product line to include cosmetics and consumer items such as Coppertone and Di-Gel. Plough had originated in Memphis, Tennessee, in 1908. Abe Plough, its founder, borrowed $125 from his father to create an "antiseptic healing oil" consisting of cottonseed oil, carbolic acid, and camphor. Plough

sold his concoction door-to-door and went on to acquire 28 companies. After the merger he served as chairman of the board until 1976. Known for his philanthropy in Memphis, Plough died in 1984 at the age of 92.

Schering-Plough has introduced various new products since the merger, including Lotrimin AF (antifungal, 1975), Drixoral (cold remedy, made nonprescription in 1982), and the antiasthmatics Vanceril (1976) and Proventil (1981). When Garamycin's patent expired in 1980, the company introduced a similar antibiotic, Netromycin.

Schering-Plough was one of the first of the drug giants to make significant investments in biotechnology: it owns a portion of Biogen of Cambridge, Massachusetts, and acquired DNAX Research Institute of Palo Alto, California, in 1982. From Biogen it licenses Intron A (alpha interferon), the first biotech medicine for treating cancer (approved in 1990 as a hepatitis treatment).

The company has made several acquisitions since the late 1970s, including Scholl (footcare products, 1979), Key Pharmaceuticals (cardiovascular drugs, 1986), and Cooper Companies (eye care, 1988).

In 1990 Schering-Plough sold its Maybelline division and received FDA approval to sell Gyne-Lotrimin (a treatment for yeast infections) as an OTC product.

RANKINGS

144th in *Fortune* 500 Industrial Cos.
46th in *Business Week* 1000

KEY COMPETITORS

Abbott Labs
American Home Products
Amgen
Bayer
Bristol-Myers Squibb
Ciba-Geigy
Eastman Kodak
Eli Lilly
Glaxo
Hoechst
Johnson & Johnson
Merck
Pfizer
Procter & Gamble
Rhône-Poulenc
Roche
Sandoz
SmithKline Beecham
Syntex
Upjohn
Warner-Lambert

HOW MUCH

	9-Year Growth	1981	1982	1983	1984	1985	1986	1987	1988	1989	1990
Sales ($ mil.)	7.0%	1,809	1,818	1,809	1,874	1,927	2,399	2,699	2,969	3,158	3,323
Net income ($ mil.)	13.6%	179	184	179	177	193	266	316	390	471	565
Income as % of sales	—	9.9%	10.1%	9.9%	9.5%	10.0%	11.1%	11.7%	13.1%	14.9%	17.0%
Earnings per share ($)	13.1%	0.83	0.85	0.84	0.87	0.92	1.07	1.35	1.72	2.06	2.50
Stock price – high ($)	—	10.63	10.94	12.03	10.00	16.63	22.00	27.63	29.69	43.00	50.75
Stock price – low ($)	—	6.22	6.56	9.19	8.25	8.81	14.00	15.63	22.63	27.69	36.94
Stock price – close ($)	22.8%	7.00	9.84	9.31	9.00	14.53	19.75	23.50	28.38	42.75	44.38
P/E – high	—	13	13	14	12	18	21	21	17	21	20
P/E – low	—	8	8	11	10	10	13	12	13	13	15
Dividends per share ($)	11.0%	0.42	0.42	0.42	0.42	0.42	0.45	0.51	0.70	0.89	1.07
Book value per share ($)	5.0%	6.05	6.23	6.28	6.49	7.15	6.24	6.45	7.46	8.64	9.37

1990 Year-end:
Debt ratio: 8.1%
Return on equity: 27.8%
Cash (mil.): $920
Current ratio: 1.31
Long-term debt (mil.): $183
No. of shares (mil.): 222
Dividends:
  1990 average yield: 2.4%
  1990 payout: 42.6%
Market value (mil.): $9,852

Stock Price History High/Low 1981–90

SCHLUMBERGER NV

OVERVIEW

New York–based Schlumberger is the worldwide leader in wireline logging (a process used to chart where oil and gas lie in a well) and petroleum exploration services. Schlumberger services run the gamut of oil production tasks, from exploration (subsidiary GECO-Prakla provides seismic surveys) to drilling (Schlumberger's Sedco Forex division operated 71 drilling rigs, 37 offshore and 34 on land, in 1990) to well productivity (the Dowell Schlumberger affiliate operates 180 service centers worldwide and 100 field labs).

Through its Schlumberger Industries division, the company manufactures 5.2 million electric meters, 4.8 million water meters, and more than 2.8 million gas meters each year.

Schlumberger's Technologies group manufactures automatic testing equipment and computer-aided design and manufacturing equipment. The company is a leading producer of smart cards (credit cards that contain microchips for conducting financial transactions) as part of its manufacturing of electronic transaction systems.

NYSE symbol: SLB
Fiscal year ends: December 31

Hoover's Rating **A-**

WHO

Chairman, President, and CEO: D. Euan Baird, age 53, $1,500,000 pay
VC: Roland Génin, age 63, $1,000,000 pay
EVP Finance and CFO: Arthur Lindenauer, age 53, $581,000 pay
VP Personnel: Jean-Dominique Percevault, age 45
Auditors: Price Waterhouse
Employees: 50,000

WHERE

HQ: 277 Park Ave., New York, NY 10172-0266
Phone: 212-350-9400
Fax: 212-350-9564

Schlumberger conducts business in more than 100 countries.

	1990 Sales		1990 Operating Income	
	$ mil.	% of total	$ mil.	% of total
US	1,278	24	66	9
Other Western Hemisphere	482	9	79	11
France	672	13	68	10
Other European	1,466	28	161	22
Other Eastern Hemisphere	1,408	26	340	48
Adjustments	—	—	(56)	—
Total	**5,306**	**100**	**658**	**100**

WHAT

	1990 Sales		1990 Operating Income	
	$ mil.	% of total	$ mil.	% of total
Oil field services	3,240	61	542	78
Measurement & systems	2,066	39	153	22
Adjustments	—	—	(37)	—
Total	**5,306**	**100**	**658**	**100**

Oil Field Services
Data services
Drilling services (onshore, offshore drilling; Sedco Forex)
Evaluation services
Measurement while drilling/directional drilling (Anadrill)
Pumping services (50%, Dowell Schlumberger)
Seismic services (GECO-Prakla)
Testing and production services

Measurement and Systems
Automatic test equipment (Schlumberger Technologies)
Automatic test equipment systems for circuitry
Computer-aided design (CAD)
Computer-aided manufacturing (CAM)
Electronic transaction systems
Transducers (pressure, temperature, flow rate, mass measurement)
Utility meters (Schlumberger Industries)

WHEN

Conrad and Marcel Schlumberger were Alsatian scientists who believed that electrical resistance could be used to measure the earth's subsurface. Paul Schlumberger, their father and fellow scientist, thought a business would follow and offered capital for the venture (1919); the brothers' Paris home became the site of Schlumberger.

Their theories were proven by the mid-1920s, but no application developed until 1927, when Pechelbronn Oil became interested in using their technique to search for oil. Conrad asked his son-in-law, Henri Doll, to design a tool for the purpose, and the process of wireline logging, akin to an X-ray for charting where oil and gas lie in a well, was born. Doll turned out to be a tremendous asset — upon his 1967 retirement, one analyst estimated that 40% of Schlumberger revenues stemmed from his inventions. By 1938 Schlumberger was operating worldwide.

Conrad died in 1936, leaving Marcel in charge until 1953; Marcel's death resulted in factionalism. Different family members controlled the 4 divisions (North American, South American/Middle Eastern, European, and Doll's US technical development), creating disorganization. Marcel's son Pierre took the company public, merged foreign operations with North American headquarters in Houston, and restructured the company in 1956 as Schlumberger Ltd, incorporated in the Netherlands Antilles. In 1965 Pierre ended nepotism, giving leadership of Schlumberger to another Frenchman, Jean Riboud. That year Riboud moved headquarters to New York, where it remains today.

Riboud began a series of acquisitions, including the Compagnie des Compteurs, a French electric-meter manufacturer (1970). He saw Schlumberger as an information vendor rather than an oil-services company and purchased Fairchild Camera & Instrument in 1979, believing that semiconductors would play an important future role. Today 39% of revenues are derived from non-oil-field products and services. Riboud bought Applicon, a producer of computer-aided design and manufacturing software, in 1982.

Schlumberger has invested through a series of acquisitions in artificial intelligence technology, which it introduced in oil fields in 1982. Known for providing state-of-the-art equipment to the oil industry, Schlumberger bought GECO (1986), a Norwegian geophysical company noted for marine seismic analysis.

In 1991 Schlumberger acquired 51% of Prakla Seismos, with strong onshore seismic operations, from the German government and folded it into its GECO unit. Schlumberger is to acquire the remaining 49% by 1993.

RANKINGS

260th in *Fortune* Global 500 Industrial Cos.
36th in *Business Week* 1000

KEY COMPETITORS

Ashland	Halliburton	LTV
Baker Hughes	Intergraph	McDermott
Dresser	Litton Industries	Prime
Fluor		

HOW MUCH

	9-Year Growth	1981	1982	1983	1984	1985	1986	1987	1988	1989	1990
Sales ($ mil.)	(1.0%)	5,783	6,025	5,513	5,979	6,119	4,568	4,402	4,925	4,686	5,306
Net income ($ mil.)	(8.5%)	1,266	1,348	1,084	1,182	351	(1,655)	503	454	420	570
Income as % of sales	—	21.9%	22.4%	19.7%	19.8%	5.7%	(36.2%)	11.4%	9.2%	9.0%	10.7%
Earnings per share ($)	(6.4%)	4.37	4.60	3.73	4.10	1.17	(5.76)	1.81	1.72	1.77	2.40
Stock price – high ($)	—	78.50	55.88	62.63	55.00	43.88	37.75	51.00	38.75	50.50	69.88
Stock price – low ($)	—	49.13	30.00	38.25	35.88	32.38	27.25	26.00	28.50	32.00	43.50
Stock price – close ($)	0.4%	55.88	46.63	50.00	38.13	36.50	31.75	28.75	32.63	49.13	57.88
P/E – high	—	18	12	17	13	38	—	28	23	29	29
P/E – low	—	11	7	10	9	28	—	14	17	18	18
Dividends per share ($)	5.1%	0.77	0.92	1.00	1.12	1.20	1.20	1.20	1.20	1.20	1.20
Book value per share ($)	(0.8%)	14.64	17.89	20.09	23.25	23.24	14.67	14.09	11.59	12.19	13.67

1990 Year-end:
Debt ratio: 9.3%
Return on equity: 18.6%
Cash (mil.): $1,324
Current ratio: 1.33
Long-term debt (mil.): $332
No. of shares (mil.): 238
Dividends:
 1990 average yield: 2.1%
 1990 payout: 50.0%
Market value (mil.): $13,781

Stock Price History
High/Low 1981–90

SCI SYSTEMS, INC.

OVERVIEW

Printed circuit-board assembler SCI Systems, based in Huntsville, Alabama, is the leading subcontractor to the computer and electronics industries. The $1.2 billion company is also a major supplier of instrumentation, computers, and communications systems for government aerospace and defense programs.

With 74 surface-mount technology (SMT) production lines, SCI is one of the largest SMT producers in the world. SMT involves gluing components to circuit boards instead of attaching them with wires (pin-in-hole method). The technology enables the same number of components to fit on a smaller board and in-creases reliability. In the first half of 1990, SCI added new circuit-board production capacity at the rate of one assembly line per week. The expense of this capital investment helped keep 1990 earnings down below 1989 levels.

During the 1980s IBM was by far SCI's biggest customer (63% of net sales in 1987). However, when IBM cut its orders, the company made considerable progress in its diversification efforts, expanding both its customer and product bases. In 1990 IBM represented only 32% of sales. Other major customers of SCI include Seagate Technology and Apple Computer.

WHEN

Olin King, a former employee of Wernher von Braun's army rocket center, and 2 friends started SCI Systems in 1961 in Huntsville, Alabama. The 3 men combined their $21,000 in savings with $300,000 in venture capital and started SCI as a contract engineering firm to NASA.

SCI specialized initially in building electronics systems for the Saturn rocket and later for other NASA and military missile and satellite programs. Its product line expanded to include subsystems for military aircraft (e.g., cockpit controls for the F-15 fighter plane) and military surface systems.

SCI's major breakthrough came in 1976 with a contract from IBM to produce subassemblies for IBM terminals. Subsequently, when IBM went to work on its personal computer (PC), introduced in 1981, it turned to SCI with a $30 million contract for the PC's first batch of circuit boards. IBM shipped 100,000 PCs in 1981. In 1984 that number had grown to 2.3 million — all outfitted with SCI boards. SCI's contracts with IBM, which extended to other parts and subassemblies for the PC, accelerated SCI's sales. The company was ranked as the 8th fastest-growing electronics company in the US in 1985, based on its sales growth between 1981 and 1985. SCI's 1985 sales totaled $538 million.

In an attempt to reduce its reliance on IBM contracts, which accounted for 60% of sales (1982–83), SCI expanded into making entire microcomputers (1984) and selling them to companies like Kodak, which resold them under its label. However, microcomputer sales could not compensate for SCI's loss when IBM cut its orders for circuit boards in 1985. SCI's sales dropped 12% in 1986.

The company's sales bounced back in 1987 after SCI negotiated a new contract with IBM for circuit boards for IBM's PS/2 computers, but the experience of losing IBM's business sent SCI looking for new customers.

SCI built additional facilities in the US and overseas and moved quickly into surface-mount technology. Because of the high cost of surface-mount production, companies rely on subcontractors like SCI to supply surface-mount boards. Since 1987 SCI has become a leader in surface-mount technology. Consequently, its sales have gone from $553 million (1987) to $1.17 billion (1990).

The company has organized into 3 US and 2 international divisions, consolidating plants and planning new ones to be easily accessible to SCI's customers. Even with significantly increased capital expenditures, the company brought its debt down over $70 million in 1990.

NASDAQ symbol: SCIS
Fiscal year ends: June 30

 Hoover's Rating C

WHO

Chairman and CEO: Olin B. King, age 56, $500,542 pay
President and COO: A. Eugene Sapp, Jr., age 54, $376,206 pay
Treasurer and CFO: Robert DeLaurentis
VP Personnel: Francis X. Henry
Auditors: Ernst & Young
Employees: 10,694

WHERE

HQ: 2101 W. Clinton Ave., Huntsville, AL 35805
Phone: 205-882-4800
Fax: 205-882-4804

The company has 18 plants throughout the US and in Scotland, Singapore, Thailand, Ireland, Canada, and Mexico.

	1990 Sales		1990 Operating Income	
	$ mil.	% of total	$ mil.	% of total
US	776	66	9	35
Foreign	403	34	17	65
Total	**1,179**	**100**	**26**	**100**

WHAT

	1990 Sales	
Customers	$ mil.	% of total
IBM	376	32
Seagate	162	14
All other	641	54
Total	**1,179**	**100**

Divisions

Manufacturing
Circuit boards
Electronic and mechanical components and products
Full-service contract manufacturing to the electronic equipment industry

Government Aerospace and Defense Programs
Aircraft flight test instrumentation systems (for A-12 fighter)
Cockpit controls
Core Avionics Processor (for F-16)
Data management systems (for Strategic Defense Initiative, MX missile)
Voice warning systems

Computers
OEM system blocks based on:
80286 microprocessor
80386 microprocessor
80386SX microprocessor
Banking automation systems
Airline ticket printers
Other peripherals

HOW MUCH

	9-Year Growth	1981	1982	1983	1984	1985	1986	1987	1988	1989	1990
Sales ($ mil.)	39.4%	59	90	183	437	538	470	553	774	987	1,179
Net income ($ mil.)	(3.2%)	3	4	7	12	14	14	16	19	21	2
Income as % of sales	—	5.2%	4.6%	3.6%	2.6%	2.6%	2.9%	2.9%	2.5%	2.1%	0.2%
Earnings per share ($)	(6.9%)	0.21	0.25	0.38	0.61	0.67	0.67	0.77	0.91	1.00	0.11
Stock price – high ($)	—	5.89	10.17	20.33	17.00	10.50	14.25	23.13	15.25	16.00	13.13
Stock price – low ($)	—	2.78	3.50	9.50	7.17	6.92	9.00	11.13	10.63	7.63	5.25
Stock price – close ($)	6.4%	4.72	9.92	15.00	9.33	10.08	11.75	13.25	15.00	8.63	8.25
P/E – high	—	28	40	54	28	16	21	30	17	16	119
P/E – low	—	13	14	25	12	10	14	14	12	8	48
Dividends per share ($)	0.0%	0.00	0.00	0.00	0.00	0.00	0.00	0.00	0.00	0.00	0.00
Book value per share ($)	21.8%	1.43	1.98	2.50	3.97	4.78	5.53	6.39	7.27	8.11	8.42

1990 Year-end:
Debt ratio: 64.3%
Return on equity: 1.3%
Cash (mil.): $28
Current ratio: 3.34
Long-term debt (mil.): $318
No. of shares (mil.): 21
Dividends:
1990 average yield: 0.0%
1990 payout: 0.0%
Market value (mil.): $173

Stock Price History
High/Low 1981–90

RANKINGS

308th in *Fortune* 500 Industrial Cos.

KEY COMPETITORS

AT&T	Dell	Intel
AMP	Deluxe	IBM
AST	Harris	Raytheon

SCOTT PAPER COMPANY

OVERVIEW

Scott Paper Company is the world's leading manufacturer of tissue products, such as toilet paper and paper towels, and one of America's leading producers of coated printing and publishing papers, made by the company's S. D. Warren division.

Best known for its tissue products for personal care, Scott was the first US company to market toilet paper. However, it also has substantial sales in the commercial sector, with items such as cloth replacement wipes and cleaners. Scott's health-care products include ProCare and Sani-Fresh soap-dispensing systems. The company sells its paper and nonwoven fiber products in over 60 countries, and most of its foreign operations are at least 50% locally owned.

Although Scott achieved record sales for the 8th consecutive year in 1990, earnings dropped by 61%. A poor performance at S. D. Warren was the most significant factor in the decline. Scott has responded by adopting a business improvement plan that includes a reduction in capital spending and the sale of certain nonstrategic assets, including its specialty papers, nonwovens, and food service businesses. The company took a $100 million charge in 1990 related to this plan.

WHEN

The Scott Paper Company, founded in Pennsylvania in 1879 by brothers Irvin and Clarence Scott, was first to market rolls of tissue specifically for use as toilet paper. Irvin's son, Arthur (president until 1927), came up with the advertising slogan "Soft as old linen." The company began making paper towels in 1907 and went public in 1915.

Before WWII Scott expanded overseas and now credits its international success to its 50-50 formula; Scott would own up to 50% of a foreign venture, and a local company would own 50% or more. Sanyo Scott produced Japan's top paper towel brand. Other joint ventures included Spain's Gureola-Scott, Australia's Bowater-Scott, and Italy's Burgo-Scott.

Until the 1960s Scott was the leader in the "Great Toilet Paper War," as the industry called it. But in 1957 Procter & Gamble introduced Charmin toilet tissue, which was soon outselling Scott's brand. Between 1960 and 1971 Scott's market share of consumer paper products dropped from 45% to 33%. The company diversified in 1967 by buying S. D. Warren (printing and publishing papers) and Plastic Coating Corporation. At the same time, Scott introduced babyScott disposable diapers to compete with Procter & Gamble's Pampers, but babyScott sold poorly.

Under CEO Charles Dickey, Jr. (1971–79), the company made major changes, reducing administrative expenses by about 20%, restructuring marketing and research efforts, and withdrawing unsuccessful items from the consumer market in order to concentrate on household and industrial paper products such as towels, napkins, cups, and plates. In 1976 Scott introduced Cottonelle to compete with Charmin. Cottonelle captured approximately 35% of the 4-roll-pack market within several months of its introduction.

Scott began a 5-year, $1.6 billion US plant upgrade (1981), a 3-year $250 million European plant upgrade (1988), and a $475 million upgrade to 3 S. D. Warren plants (1988). In 1989 the company began operating a rebuilt paper machine in Taiwan and paper-converting plants in France and Italy, and bought the White Swan Tissue Division (sanitary products) of E. B. Eddy Forest Products (Canada). It also sold 194,000 acres of timberland in the Pacific Northwest for a gain of $209 million.

The company bought a 51% stake in the sanitary tissue businesses of Feldmühle in Germany and the Netherlands (1990), planning to use the acquisitions to expand into the German, Dutch, and Eastern European markets.

NYSE symbol: SPP
Fiscal year ends: Last Saturday in December

Hoover's Rating C+

WHO

Chairman and CEO: Philip E. Lippincott, age 55, $603,462 pay
VC Human Resource Services, Public Affairs, and Communications: J. Lawrence Shane, age 56, $306,616 pay
SVP and CFO: Ashok N. Bakhru, age 48
Auditors: Price Waterhouse
Employees: 30,800

WHERE

HQ: Scott Plaza, Philadelphia, PA 19113
Phone: 215-522-5000
Fax: 215-522-5129

Owned Timberland	Acres (Thou.)
Alabama & Mississippi	608
Maine	944
Washington	5
Canada	1,229
Total	**2,786**

	1990 Sales		1990 Operating Income	
	$ mil.	% of total	$ mil.	% of total
US	3,837	72	394	84
Europe	1,290	24	54	11
Pacific	198	4	21	5
Latin America	31	—	1	—
Adjustments	—	—	(18)	—
Total	**5,356**	**100**	**452**	**100**

WHAT

	1990 Sales		1990 Operating Income	
	$ mil.	% of total	$ mil.	% of total
Personal care & cleaning	4,090	76	322	69
Printing & publishing papers	1,266	24	148	31
Adjustments	—	—	(18)	—
Total	**5,356**	**100**	**452**	**100**

Major Products

- Baby wipes (Baby Fresh, Wash a-bye Baby)
- Bathroom tissue (Cottonelle, Family Scott, JRT, ScotTissue, Soft Blend, Waldorf)
- Bladder control pads, pants, and briefs (Promise, Skin-Caring)
- Cleaning and wiping products (Dri-Tone, Dura-Weve, Sani-Prep, Sani-Qwik, Scottcloth, WypAll)
- Facial tissue (Scotties)
- Folded and industrial roll towels (Sequel)
- Napkins (Scott, Viva, Viva Accents)
- Paper towels (Job Squad, ScotTowels, Viva)
- Premoistened cleaning cloths (Sofkins)
- Soap dispensers (Euro-Bath, ProCare, Sani-Fresh, Sani-Tuff)
- Tabletop ensembles (Viva, Expressions)
- Toilet seat covers (P.S. Personal Seats)

RANKINGS

98th in *Fortune* 500 Industrial Cos.
206th in *Business Week* 1000

KEY COMPETITORS

Boise Cascade	International Paper
Champion International	James River
Fletcher Challenge	Kimberly-Clark
Georgia-Pacific	Mead
Gerber	Procter & Gamble
	Weyerhaeuser

HOW MUCH

	9-Year Growth	1981	1982	1983	1984	1985	1986	1987	1988	1989	1990
Sales ($ mil.)	9.8%	2,309	2,293	2,465	2,847	3,050	3,437	4,122	4,726	5,066	5,356
Net income ($ mil.)	1.2%	133	74	124	187	201	187	234	401	376	148
Income as % of sales	—	5.8%	3.2%	5.0%	6.6%	6.6%	5.4%	5.7%	8.5%	7.4%	2.8%
Earnings per share ($)	2.5%	1.61	0.81	1.29	1.92	2.26	2.47	3.06	5.21	5.11	2.01
Stock price – high ($)	—	14.25	10.56	16.13	17.44	26.13	33.31	43.50	42.75	52.50	51.38
Stock price – low ($)	—	7.50	6.81	9.31	12.63	16.69	24.00	27.50	32.38	38.38	30.00
Stock price – close ($)	18.9%	8.00	10.13	15.81	17.31	25.31	31.38	35.25	39.25	48.13	37.88
P/E – high	—	9	13	13	9	12	14	14	8	10	26
P/E – low	—	5	8	7	7	7	10	9	6	8	15
Dividends per share ($)	5.4%	0.50	0.50	0.50	0.56	0.61	0.64	0.68	0.76	0.80	0.80
Book value per share ($)	7.8%	15.01	15.04	15.03	16.23	16.30	18.57	21.44	26.54	28.02	29.54

1990 Year-end:
Debt ratio: 52.9%
Return on equity: 7.0%
Cash (mil.): $114
Current ratio: 1.09
Long-term debt (mil.): $2,455
No. of shares (mil.): 74
Dividends:
 1990 average yield: 2.1%
 1990 payout: 39.8%
Market value (mil.): $2,789

Stock Price History High/Low 1981–90

THE E.W. SCRIPPS COMPANY

OVERVIEW

E.W. Scripps is the 8th largest US newspaper publisher, with 19 metropolitan and suburban newspapers, 7 of which publish under joint operating agreements with competitors. The company's largest daily is the *Rocky Mountain News* (Denver). A Scripps family trust, the Edward W. Scripps Trust, owns 75.1% of the company's class A stock and 79.5% of its voting common stock.

United Media is a major syndicator, providing comic strips, features, and news columns to newspapers under trade names including United Feature Syndicate. The company distributes "Peanuts" and "Garfield" comics to 2,300 newspapers and owns licensing rights to the characters. In 1991 the Pharos book division published 73 titles, including *The World Almanac*.

Scripps Howard Broadcasting (80.4% owned) owns 10 TV stations and 5 radio stations. Combined, Scripps Howard and E. W. Scripps operate cable TV systems for more than 600,000 customers.

The national slowdown in advertising spending has hurt the profitability of the newspaper and broadcast operations. Cable keeps growing, partly because of continuing acquisitions of cable properties.

WHEN

With the launch of the *Cleveland Press* (1878) and the *Cincinnati Post* (1883), Edward Wyllis Scripps started the US's first newspaper chain. In 1889 Scripps and business manager Milton McRae formed the Scripps-McRae League which, by WWI, had 30 papers in 15 states.

Scripps conducted business from his California ranch, Miramar, where he moved in 1890 at the age of 36. At his death in 1926 he was worth $50 million. Scripps was one of the pioneers of the "people's papers," which he described as "schoolrooms" for the barely educated working classes of the day.

In 1907 the company combined 3 of its small wire services to form United Press, later headed by Roy Howard, a Scripps newspaper executive. Howard took over business management of the newspaper chain in 1922, operating the papers under the Scripps Howard trade name. The United Feature Service, an offshoot of United Press, was incorporated in 1923 to provide feature material to newspapers.

When E. W. Scripps died in 1926, most of the company's stock was assembled into a trust for his heirs. His son Robert gradually ceded editorial control of the company to Howard and his conservative bent.

In 1931 the company bought the *New York World* and merged it to create the *New York World-Telegram*. The paper later became the *World-Telegram and Sun* and then the *World Journal Tribune* before it fell prey to competition and closed in 1967.

Reporter Ernie Pyle, who died on the battlefield in WWII, was a Scripps Howard reporter. United Press employed Walter Cronkite, assigned to London during the war, and Merriman Smith, dean of White House correspondents for 30 years, whose "Thank you, Mr. President" close became a tradition.

In 1958 Scripps absorbed Hearst's International News Service into UP to form United Press International. It sold the wire service in 1982 to Media News Corporation.

Scripps folded the *Cleveland Press* in 1982 and the Memphis *Press-Scimitar* in 1983. In 1986 and 1987 Scripps bought television stations and cable systems and sold nondaily papers, business journals, and magazines. Cable's growth has fueled increases in cash flow and operating income.

In 1986 Scripps bought 7 newspapers developed independently by John P. Scripps, grandson of the founder. It went public in 1988, issuing class A nonvoting shares.

After terminating an earlier deal to buy Baltimore TV station WMAR for $154.7 million, Scripps Howard bought it in 1991 for $125 million from bankrupt Gillett Group.

NYSE symbol: SSP
Fiscal year ends: December 31

Hoover's Rating C+

WHO

Chairman: Charles E. Scripps, age 71, $385,000 pay
President and CEO: Lawrence A. Leser, age 55, $851,462 pay
EVP: William R. Burleigh, age 55, $447,961 pay
SVP Finance and Administration: Daniel J. Castellini, age 51, $403,099 pay
VP Human Resources: Robert E. Brophy, age 62
Auditors: Deloitte & Touche
Employees: 10,000

WHERE

HQ: 1105 N. Market St., Wilmington, DE 19801
Phone: 302-478-4141
Fax: 302-427-7663

Scripps operates in 18 states and Puerto Rico. Its comics and other features are syndicated and licensed worldwide.

WHAT

	1990 Sales		1990 Operating Income	
	$ mil.	% of total	$ mil.	% of total
Publishing	848	66	80	45
Broadcasting	236	18	69	39
Cable television	199	15	27	15
Other	14	1	1	1
Adjustments	—	—	22	—
Total	**1,297**	**100**	**199**	**100**

Major Newspapers
The Cincinnati Post
The Commercial Appeal (Memphis)
The Pittsburgh Press
The Rocky Mountain News (Denver)

Other Publishing Operations
Pharos Books
United Media (syndication and licensing)
  Newspaper Enterprise Association
  Scripps Howard News Service
  TV Data
  United Feature Syndicate

Cable Television Systems (E.W. Scripps)
Chattanooga, TN
Kentucky/Tennessee
Knoxville, TN
North Dekalb, GA
Rome, GA

Scripps Howard Broadcasting Company (80.4%)

Major TV stations	Major radio stations
WCPO, Cincinnati	KUPL (AM/FM),
WEWS, Cleveland	Portland, OR
WMAR, Baltimore	WBSB (FM), Baltimore
WXYZ, Detroit	WMC (AM/FM), Memphis

Cable television systems
  Colorado
  Lake County, FL
  Sacramento, CA (76.4%)

RANKINGS

296th in *Fortune* 500 Industrial Cos.
406th in *Business Week* 1000

KEY COMPETITORS

Advance	Gannett	TCI
Publications	Hearst	Times Mirror
Blockbuster	Knight-Ridder	Viacom
Cox	New York Times	Washington Post
Dow Jones		

HOW MUCH

	3-Year Growth	1981	1982	1983	1984	1985	1986	1987	1988	1989	1990
Sales ($ mil.)	4.2%	—	—	—	—	—	—	1,147	1,214	1,266	1,297
Net income ($ mil.)	2.2%	—	—	—	—	—	—	45	70	89	48
Income as % of sales	—	—	—	—	—	—	—	3.9%	5.8%	7.1%	3.7%
Earnings per share ($)	0.5%	—	—	—	—	—	—	0.62	0.93	1.14	0.63
Stock price – high ($)	—	—	—	—	—	—	—	—	18.13	27.00	24.00
Stock price – low ($)	—	—	—	—	—	—	—	—	14.50	16.88	13.00
Stock price – close ($)	—	—	—	—	—	—	—	—	17.13	24.00	17.00
P/E – high	—	—	—	—	—	—	—	—	19	24	38
P/E – low	—	—	—	—	—	—	—	—	16	15	21
Dividends per share ($)	—	—	—	—	—	—	—	0.00	0.15	0.35	0.40
Book value per share ($)	8.4%	—	—	—	—	—	—	6.72	7.98	8.43	8.57

1990 Year-end:
Debt ratio: 36.5%
Return on equity: 7.4%
Cash (mil.): $12
Current ratio: 1.50
Long-term debt (mil.): $368
No. of shares (mil.): 75
Dividends:
  1990 average yield: 2.4%
  1990 payout: 63.5%
Market value (mil.): $1,267

Stock Price History High/Low 1988–90

SEAGATE TECHNOLOGY, INC.

NASDAQ symbol: SGAT
Fiscal year ends: June 30

Hoover's Rating **B**

OVERVIEW

Seagate Technology, based in Scotts Valley, California, is the world's leading independent supplier of rigid magnetic disk drives (known popularly as "hard drives") for computers from notebook size to super computers. With close to 200 models, Seagate's drives range in capacity from 20 megabytes to 2.5 gigabytes.

Unlike primary competitors Quantum and Conner Peripherals, Seagate manufactures most of its components, assuring it of a reliable supply. Seagate controls approximately 30% of the disk drive market in the 2-1/2", 3-1/2", and 5-1/4" drives. Foreign sales make up 35% of Seagate's sales.

In 1989 Seagate purchased Imprimis Technology (the disk drive subsidiary of Control Data) for cash and stock. The acquisition nearly doubled Seagate's size, giving it an expertise in component manufacturing for further vertical integration and making it a leader in high-capacity (greater than one gigabyte) drives.

The recession and competitive pricing pressures have hurt 1991 earnings, causing Seagate to reduce its work force by 3%. Though it now accounts for under 10% of sales, IBM is still one of Seagate's primary customers.

WHO

Chairman: Gary B. Filler, age 49
President, CEO, and COO: Alan F. Shugart, age 60, $1,406,273 pay
SVP and CFO: Donald L. Waite, age 58, $792,110 pay
VP Administration: Robb Kundtz
Auditors: Ernst & Young
Employees: 38,000

WHERE

HQ: 920 Disc Drive, Scotts Valley, CA 95066
Phone: 408-438-6550
Fax: 408-438-6172

Seagate has sales offices in the US and 14 other countries around the world; primary manufacturing facilities are located in the US, Portugal, Scotland, Singapore, and Thailand.

	1990 Facilities	
	Sq. ft. thou.	% of total
California	1,135	22
Germany	101	2
Malaysia	101	2
Minnesota	918	17
Nebraska	279	5
Oklahoma	569	11
Portugal	109	2
Scotland	102	2
Singapore	1,083	21
Thailand	598	11
Other	286	5
Total	**5,281**	**100**

	1990 Sales		1990 Operating Income	
	$ mil.	% of total	$ mil.	% of total
US	1,560	65	39	24
Far East	853	35	124	76
Adjustments	—	—	23	—
Total	**2,413**	**100**	**186**	**100**

WHEN

In 1979 Seagate Technology was founded in Scotts Valley, California, by Alan Shugart, an 18-year IBMer who had made floppy disks standard on microcomputers at Shugart Associates; manufacturing expert Tom Mitchell, formerly of Commodore and Memorex; and design engineer Douglas Mahon. Seagate pioneered the downsizing of mainframe hard disk drives for PCs; the resulting drive had 30 times more storage than floppy disks, faster access times, and much higher long-term reliability.

Seagate's first product, the ST506 (a 5-1/4" hard disk, 1980), sold briskly. As IBM's memory choice for its new PCs, Seagate rose to $40 million in sales by 1982, with 1/2 of the market for small disk drives; by 1984 sales had reached $344 million. Soon, though, Seagate's heavy dependence on IBM showed its double edge, as eroding IBM PC demand prompted it to cut orders. Sales in 1985 dropped to $215 million and profits to $1 million (from $42 million the year before).

Having distinguished itself through high-volume, low-cost, reliable manufacturing, Seagate now hastened the transfer of manufacturing to Singapore (and later Thailand); the California work force was halved.

The company also accelerated its vertical integration to ensure availability of critical components and reduce time to market.

Seagate purchased Grenex (thin-film magnetic media, 1984), Aeon (aluminum substrates, 1987), and Integrated Power Systems (custom semiconductors, 1987). Seagate also lured back IBM, which had turned to an alternate supplier in the interim.

With revenues more than doubling in 1986 and again in 1987 (to $958 million), Seagate spent $290 million and doubled the work force to 30,000 to increase 5-1/4" production, ignoring signs of a coming 3-1/2" standard for hard disk drives. The strong market in 1988 for 3-1/2" drives, coupled with IBM's decision to produce more drives in-house, prompted Seagate to reduce its work force by almost 4,000 and shift quickly to 3-1/2" production.

Seagate purchased Imprimis from Control Data (October 1989), thus creating the world's premier independent drive maker. Imprimis's strengths in R&D and high-capacity drives for large computers (sold to OEMs), combined with Seagate's manufacturing talent, has resulted in a formidable competitor to both Asian and domestic drive producers. Nevertheless, Seagate was late in introducing a smaller 2-1/2" drive (1990) for the growing notebook computer market. That, along with slow PC sales and eroding drive prices, is to blame for the company's drop in earnings for fiscal year 1991 (down 42% from 1990).

WHAT

	1990 Sales
	% of total
Distributors	56
OEMs	44
Total	**100**

Rigid Disk Drives
2-1/2"
  40 megabytes (MB) of memory
3-1/2"
  20 to 480 MB
5-1/4"
  20 MB to 1.6 gigabyte (GB)
8" (Sabre series)
  386 MB to 2.5 GB
9" (fixed and removable)

Magnetic Recording Heads

RANKINGS

187th in *Fortune* 500 Industrial Cos.
558th in *Business Week* 1000

KEY COMPETITORS

Conner Peripherals	IBM	NEC
Fujitsu	Matsushita	Sony
Hitachi	Mitsubishi	Toshiba

HOW MUCH

	9-Year Growth	1981	1982	1983	1984	1985	1986	1987	1988	1989	1990
Sales ($ mil.)	84.4%	10	40	110	344	215	460	958	1,266	1,372	2,413
Net income ($ mil.)	60.2%	2	7	13	42	1	35	140	77	0	117
Income as % of sales	—	17.2%	17.2%	11.9%	12.2%	0.5%	7.5%	14.6%	6.1%	0.0%	4.9%
Earnings per share ($)	48.2%	0.06	0.20	0.33	0.95	0.02	0.72	2.81	1.57	0.22	1.90
Stock price – high ($)	—	8.88	12.44	22.13	17.00	8.75	21.00	45.75	23.38	16.13	19.75
Stock price – low ($)	—	5.38	4.31	8.25	4.00	4.75	7.13	9.75	6.50	8.50	5.63
Stock price – close ($)	5.5%	7.25	10.50	13.88	5.00	7.25	19.13	14.88	8.63	15.00	11.75
P/E – high	—	161	64	67	18	438	29	16	15	73	10
P/E – low	—	98	22	25	4	238	10	3	4	39	3
Dividends per share ($)	0.0%	0.00	0.00	0.00	0.00	0.00	0.00	0.00	0.00	0.00	0.00
Book value per share ($)	70.1%	0.09	0.96	2.77	3.74	3.66	4.41	7.36	8.89	8.85	10.64

1990 Year-end:
Debt ratio: 43.0%
Return on equity: 19.5%
Cash (mil.): $263
Current ratio: 2.07
Long-term debt (mil.): $510
No. of shares (mil.): 63
Dividends:
  1990 average yield: 0.0%
  1990 payout: 0.0%
Market value (mil.): $746

Stock Price History High/Low 1981–90

SEARS, ROEBUCK & CO.

OVERVIEW

NYSE symbol: S
Fiscal year ends: December 31

Hoover's Rating **C**

Sears, based in the Sears Tower in Chicago, has slipped from #1 retailer in the world to #3 in the US (after Wal-Mart and Kmart) but is the 2nd largest property-liability insurer in the US and a major force in financial services and real estate. Sears does business with 70% of US households and builds sales by using its marketing machinery to shuttle customers between its subsidiaries.

Sears's retail operations (863 department stores and 902 specialty stores) have declined in recent years as discounters and malls have drawn customers away. Sears has responded by adopting a strategy of developing "power formats" such as Brand Central. However,

positive results remain elusive; US retail operations (not counting SearsCharge credit cards) in 1990 realized only $77 million in pretax income on sales of over $25 billion.

Meanwhile, Sears's other businesses continue to improve. Coldwell Banker has increased its share of the residential real estate market from 2% to 11% since 1982; Dean Witter Reynolds is the most profitable of the 5 large retail brokerages and posted its best year ever in 1990; and Discover Card now has 37.8 million card members and 1.24 million merchant outlets.

Chairman Edward Brennan has personally taken charge of retail operations.

WHO

Chairman, President, and CEO: Edward A. Brennan, age 57, $978,854 pay
Chairman and CEO, Allstate: Wayne E. Hedien, age 57, $813,982 pay
Chairman and CEO, Coldwell Banker: Arthur J. Hill, age 51, $720,128 pay
Chairman and CEO, Dean Witter: Philip J. Purcell, age 47, $1,365,000 pay
SVP and CFO: James M. Denny, age 58, $425,004 pay
VP Human Resources: Warren F. Cooper, age 46
Auditors: Deloitte & Touche
Employees: 476,600

WHEN

In 1886 Richard W. Sears, a railway agent in Minnesota, purchased a shipment of watches being returned to the maker. He started the R. W. Sears Watch Company 6 months later, relocated to Chicago, and in 1887 hired watchmaker Alvah C. Roebuck. Sears sold the watch business in 1889, and 2 years later formed another mail-order business that adopted the name Sears, Roebuck, and Company in 1893. The company published its first general catalog in 1896, offering low prices and money-back guarantees to the farmers who were Sears's principal customers.

Roebuck left the young company in 1895 and Sears found 2 new partners: Aaron Nussbaum, who left in 1901, and Julius Rosenwald. In 1906 Sears went public to raise money for expansion. Differences soon arose between Sears and Rosenwald; Sears departed in 1908 and Rosenwald became president.

Anticipating the changes the automobile would bring to rural life, Sears opened its first retail store in 1924 so that farmers could drive to town to buy merchandise and in 1925 brought out a line of tires under the name Allstate. Sears eventually expanded Allstate into auto insurance (1931), life insurance (1957), and an auto club (1961).

The company bought Homart Development (shopping centers, 1959) and several savings and loans. The Sears Tower — the world's tallest building — opened in 1973. In 1981 Sears acquired Coldwell Banker (real estate sales and development) and Dean Witter Reynolds (stock brokerage). Under the Dean Witter umbrella, Sears in 1985 launched the Discover Card. In 1989 Coldwell Banker and Allstate ceased their commercial operations.

In reaction to steeply declining market share in the 1980s, Sears initiated a restructuring of its merchandising division, acquiring the 405-store Western Auto chain (1988) and introducing an "everyday low pricing" policy and adding non-Sears brands in early 1989. Sears also announced its relocation from the Sears Tower to a northwestern suburb starting in 1992.

Sears purchased an S&L in 1990 in order to begin issuing VISA cards; Visa USA has challenged the move in court, and the case is pending. The success of Sears's non-retail businesses, which in 1990 contributed 42% of sales and 51% of pretax profits, led investor Robert Monks to wage a proxy fight for a seat on the Sears board in 1991. Monks said he intended to investigate breaking up Sears if he was elected, which he was not.

WHERE

HQ: Sears Tower, Chicago, IL 60684
Phone: 312-875-2500
Fax: 312-875-8351

Sears operates throughout the US and in Mexico, Canada, Japan, Korea, and the UK.

	1990 Sales		1990 Pretax Income	
	$ mil.	% of total	$ mil.	% of total
US	51,751	92	1,360	93
Other countries	4,221	8	101	7
Adjustments	—	—	(790)	
Total	**55,972**	**100**	**671**	**100**

WHAT

	1990 Sales		1990 Pretax Income	
	$ mil.	% of total	$ mil.	% of total
Merchandising	31,986	58	710	49
Allstate	18,199	32	303	21
Dean Witter	4,607	8	404	27
Coldwell Banker	1,377	2	44	3
Adjustments	(197)	—	(790)	—
Total	**55,972**	**100**	**671**	**100**

Merchandising Group
Business Systems Centers
Eye Care Centers
Pinstripes Petites
Sears catalogs
Sears Logistics Services
Sears/Sears Canada/Sears Mexico
Sears Vacation Travel
SearsCharge (store credit)
Western Auto

Brand Names
Craftsman (tools)
Kenmore (appliances)

Allstate Insurance Group
Life
Property/liability
Reinsurance

Dean Witter Financial Services Group
Dean Witter Reynolds, Inc.
Asset management
Brokerage
Investment banking
Securities trading
Sears Consumer Financial Corp.
Greenwood Trust Co./ Discover Card Services
Hurley State Bank
MountainWest Financial
SCFC Lending Services

Coldwell Banker Real Estate Group
Coldwell Banker
Homart Development Corp.
Sears Mortgage Corp.
Sears Savings Bank

HOW MUCH

	9-Year Growth	1981	1982	1983	1984	1985	1986	1987	1988	1989	1990
Sales ($ mil.)	8.3%	27,357	30,020	35,883	38,828	40,715	44,282	48,440	50,251	53,794	55,972
Net income ($ mil.)	3.6%	650	861	1,342	1,455	1,303	1,351	1,649	1,032	1,446	892
Income as % of sales	—	2.4%	2.9%	3.7%	3.7%	3.2%	3.1%	3.4%	2.1%	2.7%	1.6%
Earnings per share ($)	2.6%	2.06	2.43	3.75	3.98	3.51	3.60	4.32	2.71	4.10	2.60
Stock price – high ($)	—	20.88	32.00	45.13	40.38	41.13	50.38	59.50	46.25	48.13	41.88
Stock price – low ($)	—	14.88	15.75	27.00	29.50	30.88	35.88	44.00	26.00	36.50	22.00
Stock price – close ($)	5.2%	16.13	30.13	37.13	31.75	39.00	39.75	33.50	40.88	38.13	25.38
P/E – high	—	10	13	12	10	12	14	14	17	12	16
P/E – low	—	7	6	7	7	9	10	6	12	9	8
Dividends per share ($)	4.4%	1.36	1.36	1.52	1.76	1.76	1.76	2.00	2.00	2.00	2.00
Book value per share ($)	5.2%	23.77	25.08	27.60	29.48	31.70	33.98	35.89	37.75	39.77	37.38

1990 Year-end:
Debt ratio: 49.3%
Return on equity: 6.7%
Cash (mil.): $5,217
Current ratio: —
Long-term debt (mil.): $12,493
No. of shares (mil.): 343
Dividends:
 1990 average yield: 7.9%
 1990 payout: 76.9%
Market value (mil.): $8,706

Stock Price History High/Low 1981–90

RANKINGS

1st in *Fortune* 50 Retailing Cos.
47th in *Business Week* 1000

KEY COMPETITORS

Department stores
Discount and specialty retailers
Diversified financial services companies
Insurance companies
Real estate companies

SECURITY PACIFIC CORPORATION

NYSE symbol: SPC
Fiscal year ends: December 31

Hoover's Rating **D**

OVERVIEW

Los Angeles–based Security Pacific has agreed to be acquired by San Francisco–based BankAmerica in the largest bank merger in US history. If the deal is completed, the new BankAmerica will dominate the West Coast and, in the US, trail only Citibank in total assets. The new bank will have the nation's largest branch network.

Before the recent spate of bank mergers, Security Pacific was the 5th largest US bank, with primary operations in California and an interstate banking network extending to Alaska, Arizona, Idaho, Nevada, Oregon, and Washington. The bank has a strong presence in the Pacific Rim and engages in many nonbanking financial activities.

Since 1990, earnings have been hammered by problem real estate loans in the UK, Australia, and Arizona. Mounting losses on bad loans resulted in Wells Fargo backing out of a tentative deal to buy Security Pacific in early 1991. The bank had cut its dividend prior to the BankAmerica merger announcement. BankAmerica is expected to slash expenses at Security Pacific, possibly reducing its old rival's payroll by 10,000.

WHO

Chairman: Richard J. Flamson III, age 61, $1,045,300 pay
President and CEO: Robert H. Smith, age 55, $789,600 pay
Chairman of the Executive Committee: George F. Moody, age 60
VC and CFO: John F. Kooken, age 39
EVP Administrative Services and Director, Personnel: Kathleen J. Burke
Auditors: KPMG Peat Marwick
Employees: 39,000

WHEN

Security Pacific had its origin with the founding of several banks that later merged. Isaias Hellman and John Downey founded the first, Farmers & Merchants, in 1871. In 1875 Los Angeles entrepreneur Hiram Mabury founded First National Bank of Los Angeles.

In 1889 attorney Joseph Sartori founded Security Savings Bank and Trust Company, which expanded rapidly within the growing Los Angeles area. Two more banks that would later join the Security Pacific system were Security Trust and Savings Bank of San Diego (founded in 1893 as Blochman Banking Company) and Citizens National Trust and Savings Bank of Riverside (1903).

In 1929 Sartori merged Security Trust with Los Angeles–First National to form Security–First National, one of the nation's 10 largest banks, with 142 branches and more than $600 million in assets.

Security merged with Farmers and Merchants (1956), Security Trust and Savings of San Diego (1957), and Citizens Bank of Riverside (1957) to establish the Security First National banking system, extending throughout Southern California and the southern San Joaquin Valley.

In 1968 Security made 3 significant strategic decisions: (1) to offer corporate banking to the Midwest and eastern US; (2) to expand internationally to assist its multinational customers; and (3) to become a statewide bank with expansion in Northern California. That same year the bank merged with Pacific National Bank of San Francisco, the largest one-office bank in the West, to form Security Pacific National Bank, the name in use today. Security Pacific Corporation, a holding company, was formed in 1971. Other banks in Northern California were acquired in the 1970s.

The holding company continued to make significant acquisitions in the 1980s, including Arizona Bancwest (1986), Seattle-based Rainier Bancorporation (1987), Oregon BanCorp (1987), San Francisco–based Hibernia (1988), Nevada National (1989), and Southwest of San Diego (1989).

The company's 1987 earnings dropped to $16 million after it reserved $1.3 billion for potential loan losses. Robert Smith, CEO since 1987, dramatically improved the bank's competitiveness by reducing staff by 30%, closing branch offices, centralizing operations, and setting a goal of establishing a sales mentality among branch office personnel.

In 1990 Security Pacific bought 6 financial institutions in California, Alaska, and Idaho, including Gibraltar Savings from the RTC, and announced it would close its international merchant bank unit.

WHERE

HQ: 333 S. Hope St., Los Angeles, CA 90071
Phone: 213-345-4540
Fax: 213-345-5598 (Public Affairs)

Security Pacific operates through 982 branches in 7 western states and offices in Hong Kong and London.

WHAT

	1990 Assets	
	$ mil.	% of total
Cash & due from banks	6,674	8
Investment securities	3,072	3
Trading account assets	1,402	2
Securities under resale agreements & federal funds sold	535	1
Loans	66,734	79
Reserve for credit losses	(1,448)	(2)
Customers' acceptance liability	877	1
Other	6,885	8
Total	**84,731**	**100**

Consumer and Commercial Banking
Security Pacific Bank
Interstate Banking Network
  SPB Northwest (Alaska, Idaho, Oregon, Washington)
  SPB Southwest (Arizona, Nevada)
Security Pacific Bankcard

Diversified Financing and Services
Financial Services System (finance, insurance, leasing, venture capital)
Sequor (securities clearing and lending, cash management)

Related Services
Asian Banking
Investment Management
Risk Management

RANKINGS

5th in *Fortune* 100 Commercial Banking Cos.
190th in *Business Week* 1000

KEY COMPETITORS

Security Pacific competes with all the Key Competitors of BankAmerica.

HOW MUCH

	9-Year Growth	1981	1982	1983	1984	1985	1986	1987	1988	1989	1990
Assets ($ mil.)	11.0%	32,999	36,991	40,382	46,117	53,503	62,606	72,838	77,870	83,943	84,731
Net income ($ mil.)	(2.7%)	206	234	264	291	323	386	16	639	741	161
Income as % of assets	—	0.6%	0.6%	0.7%	0.6%	0.6%	0.6%	0.0%	0.8%	0.9%	0.2%
Earnings per share ($)	(11.0%)	2.94	3.27	3.62	3.96	4.35	4.86	0.01	5.56	6.21	*1.03*
Stock price – high ($)	—	18.13	18.75	27.69	26.88	32.00	40.25	43.88	41.50	54.88	44.00
Stock price – low ($)	—	14.22	10.21	14.90	19.00	24.88	27.13	20.50	25.38	35.50	17.00
Stock price – close ($)	2.2%	16.98	15.42	25.50	25.75	31.88	34.63	25.38	36.13	40.63	20.63
P/E – high	—	6	6	8	7	7	8	4,388	7	9	43
P/E – low	—	5	3	4	5	6	6	2,050	5	6	17
Dividends per share ($)	11.9%	0.90	0.98	1.09	1.20	1.31	1.45	1.72	1.92	2.20	2.46
Book value per share ($)	5.8%	19.78	22.12	24.19	26.87	29.90	33.25	28.00	31.52	35.50	32.75

1990 Year-end:
Return on equity: 3.0%
Equity as % of assets: 5.4%
Cash (mil.): $6,674
Long-term debt (mil.): $8,645
No. of shares (mil.): 125
Dividends:
  1990 average yield: 11.9%
  1990 payout: 238.8%
Market value (mil.): $2,572
Sales (mil.): $10,327

Stock Price History High/Low 1981–90

SERVICE MERCHANDISE COMPANY, INC.

OVERVIEW

Service Merchandise, based near Nashville, is the largest retail catalog store in the US. The company primarily sells hard goods, such as jewelry, cameras, and toys, through a chain of catalog showrooms where customers select merchandise by viewing samples.

Customers can preshop with the 9,000+ item catalog — which lists products and prices, along with the suggested retail price — or order by mail; however, in recent years Wal-Mart, Target, and discount warehouses have raided the cataloger's market, and customers sometimes use the catalog merely to compare prices between retailers. A sophisticated on-line system permits round-the-clock ordering by fax or phone.

Service Merchandise calls itself "America's Leading Jeweler," offering jewelry repair and maintenance services as well as gold and gems. The company imported $223 million worth of gems and other goods in 1990.

Following the 1988 LBO of competitor Best Products, Service Merchandise leveraged itself in order to pay a special dividend and concentrated on expanding its catalog showrooms. Still, the company is dependent on jewelry sales and Christmas buying, and some analysts believe that the catalog showroom form of retailing has lost its competitive advantage, although Service Merchandise did manage to increase sales in 1990 despite a troubled retail climate.

WHEN

Harry and Mary K. Zimmerman and their son Raymond started Service Merchandise in 1960. Until 1967 they operated one Service Merchandise catalog showroom, located in Nashville, Tennessee. The idea was simple: the Zimmermans displayed samples of merchandise such as jewelry, toys, and appliances (almost no soft goods) on the showroom floor, from which customers made their selection and then ordered, paid, and waited while their merchandise was brought in from the adjoining warehouse. Service Merchandise went public in 1971, operating 5 showrooms in Tennessee by 1972. Raymond Zimmerman became president in 1973.

In 1974 the company acquired the catalog showroom operations of Malone & Hyde, which operated stores in Arkansas, Missouri, and Tennessee. By the end of the 1970s, Service Merchandise was a leader in the increasingly popular catalog showroom shopping business. Harry and Mary K. Zimmerman retired as chairman and secretary in 1980, leaving the operation of the company to Raymond, who began expanding into other formats to complement Service Merchandise's main business. The company opened Toy Store units — large discount stores stocking children's games, toys, and furniture — in Nashville and Louisville (1980) but abandoned the concept within a few years.

Service Merchandise bought Sam Solomon Company, a catalog showroom operator based in Charleston, South Carolina (1982); the Computer Shoppe, a computer retailer (1983); and Florida-based Home Owners Warehouse (1983). The company renamed Home Owners Warehouse Mr. HOW and tried to market it as a do-it-yourself discount home improvement center. The company disposed of the 22 Mr. HOW stores in 1986 after 3 years of poor sales.

Service Merchandise expanded its catalog merchandising business in 1985 with the purchase of Ellman's (Atlanta) and H. J. Wilson (Baton Rouge), catalog retailers that together added 87 stores to the chain. The absorption of these units depressed earnings through 1987. In 1988 the company's largest catalog competitor, Best Products, was bought by New York investment firm Adler and Shaykin. In order to discourage any potential takeovers, Service Merchandise took on close to $1 billion of debt in 1989, using part of the borrowed funds to pay stockholders a special dividend of $10 per share. Twelve new stores were added in 1990.

NYSE symbol: SME
Fiscal year ends: Saturday nearest December 31

Hoover's Rating **D**

WHO

Chairman, President, and CEO: Raymond Zimmerman, age 58, $844,392 pay
VP and CFO: S. P. Braud III, age 60, $330,183 pay
VP and General Counsel: Glen A. Bodzy, age 38, $315,052 pay
VP Personnel: Brian Rettaliata
Auditors: Deloitte & Touche
Employees: 22,675

WHERE

HQ: 7100 Service Merchandise Dr., Brentwood, TN 37027
Phone: 615-660-6000
Fax: 615-660-7912

Service Merchandise operates 346 catalog stores in 37 states.

	1990 Store Locations	
	No. of locations	% of total
Alabama	8	2
Arkansas	4	1
California	14	4
Colorado	8	2
Connecticut	4	1
Florida	42	12
Georgia	16	5
Illinois	24	7
Indiana	16	5
Kansas	4	1
Kentucky	7	2
Louisiana	14	4
Maine	6	2
Maryland	4	1
Massachusetts	10	3
Michigan	10	3
Mississippi	6	2
Missouri	7	2
New Hampshire	5	1
New Jersey	4	1
New York	20	6
North Carolina	5	1
Ohio	13	4
Oklahoma	8	2
Pennsylvania	9	3
South Carolina	6	2
Tennessee	18	5
Texas	35	10
Virginia	6	2
Other states	13	4
Total	**346**	**100**

WHAT

Retail catalog showrooms
Service Jewelry (Nashville)

RANKINGS

34th in *Fortune* 50 Retailing Cos.
865th in *Business Week* 1000

KEY COMPETITORS

Ames	Riklis Family
Circuit City	Sears
Costco	Stop & Shop
Dayton Hudson	Tandy
Kmart	Wal-Mart
Montgomery Ward	Department & specialty
J. C. Penney	stores
Price Co.	

HOW MUCH

	9-Year Growth	1981	1982	1983	1984	1985	1986	1987	1988	1989	1990
Sales ($ mil.)	14.4%	1,027	1,195	1,458	1,657	2,526	2,527	2,719	3,093	3,307	3,435
Net income ($ mil.)	11.4%	23	32	45	45	11	(17)	25	76	72	61
Income as % of sales	—	2.2%	2.6%	3.1%	2.7%	0.4%	(0.7%)	0.9%	2.5%	2.2%	1.8%
Earnings per share ($)	7.5%	0.61	0.77	0.92	0.91	0.21	(0.34)	0.50	1.50	1.38	1.16
Stock price – high ($)	—	4.88	9.42	18.00	11.08	10.92	10.08	6.33	12.50	22.38	9.88
Stock price – low ($)	—	3.46	3.17	8.75	7.08	7.33	4.92	2.00	2.33	7.63	3.75
Stock price – close ($)	5.1%	3.92	9.33	10.75	7.92	8.25	5.17	2.33	11.92	9.38	6.13
P/E – high	—	8	12	20	12	51	—	13	8	16	9
P/E – low	—	6	4	10	8	34	—	4	2	6	3
Dividends per share ($)	(100.0%)	0.05	0.05	0.05	0.05	0.05	0.05	0.05	0.05	10.03	0.00
Book value per share ($)	(20.3%)	3.74	4.72	5.58	6.42	6.57	5.57	6.14	7.62	(0.80)	0.49

1990 Year-end:
Debt ratio: 97.0%
Return on equity: —
Cash (mil.): $208
Current ratio: 1.32
Long-term debt (mil.): $827
No. of shares (mil.): 52
Dividends:
  1990 average yield: 0.0%
  1990 payout: 0.0%
Market value (mil.): $320

Stock Price History High/Low 1981–90

SHARPER IMAGE CORPORATION

NASDAQ symbol: SHRP
Fiscal year ends: January 31

Hoover's Rating **C-**

OVERVIEW

San Francisco–based Sharper Image is a purveyor of unique, intriguing, and often eccentric gadgets that are intended to appeal to style-conscious customers. Through the company's award-winning monthly catalog or at one of its 75 US stores, the discriminating consumer can find high-tech fitness equipment, ultramodern electronic gadgetry, and captivating entertainment objects. The typical Sharper Image customer is a middle- to upper-class, college-educated professional.

Sharper Image is the brainchild of founder Richard Thalheimer, a yuppiesque multimillionaire who serves as the company's chairman, president, CEO, and primary stockholder (he owns 73% of the company).

In response to declining sales and its first loss in 1990, Sharper Image is trying to redefine its own image. Once known for selling expensive and frivolous items that were well-received in the high-flying 1980s, the company is now moving to selling timely, lower-cost, and more practical items (such as sportswear and environmentally sound products like its Victorian parkbench constructed from 100% recycled materials) while it halts new store expansion in favor of its reliable mail-order operations.

WHO

Chairman, President, and CEO: Richard Thalheimer, age 43, $437,650 pay
EVP and COO: Craig Womack, age 40, $221,231 pay
SVP and CFO: Robert Stoffregen
VP Human Resources: Barbara Demosthenes, age 38
Auditors: Deloitte & Touche
Employees: 950

WHEN

Richard Thalheimer worked his way through law school in California in the early 1970s by selling office supplies. A dedicated jogger, Thalheimer observed the growing number of runners and predicted that a good jogger's watch would sell. After locating a supplier, Thalheimer used $1,000 of his own money to run a magazine ad for a runner's stopwatch in 1978. The product sold well and Thalheimer decided to use the profits to form a catalog business that catered to upwardly mobile people like himself. He released the Sharper Image catalog that same year.

Throughout the late 1970s and early 1980s, Thalheimer's operation grew as he added items to his catalogs. Using himself as a model for the trendy consumer, Thalheimer actively sought out unique items for the catalog. If he liked them personally, he would purchase the items on credit, paying them off once he had sold them.

During the 1980s Thalheimer clashed frequently with his corporate staff over the running of the company. The disagreements (often personality conflicts with Thalheimer) were so severe that between 1984 and 1986 over half his staff resigned.

In 1985 the company decided to expand its catalog operations into retail outlets and opened 12 stores from Honolulu to New York.

Despite the higher costs involved in maintaining stores, Sharper Image continued to expand rapidly. By 1988 the company had 60 stores.

By 1990 the company had expanded to 75 stores in the US with several licensees overseas; however, by then, trouble had already set in. Department stores (as well as competitors such as Brookstone) sensed the popularity of Thalheimer's merchandise and began selling it as well, cutting into Sharper Image's market. Also, sales increases were coming only from the opening of new stores and not from existing outlets. Subsequently the company experienced its first loss in 1990, while sales dropped below the 1988 level and stock plummeted from $8.00 to under $1.00.

The 1990 loss prompted Thalheimer to reevaluate the company's direction, lay off 300 workers, and move the distribution center from pricey San Francisco to more moderately priced Little Rock, Arkansas. Sharper Image also revamped its product line for the 1990s and shifted to a consumer appeal to live better for less money. No new stores are planned for 1991, as the company is striving to reemphasize its mail-order operations.

The first half of 1991 has been a poor one for the company. It lost $6 million and saw sales drop by 26% over the previous year's same period.

WHERE

HQ: 650 Davis St., San Francisco, CA 94111
Phone: 415-445-6000
Fax: 415-781-5251

Sharper Image has 75 stores in the US and licensees in Japan, Switzerland, Germany, Liechtenstein, Mexico, and Argentina.

Location	No. of Stores
Arizona	1
California	19
Colorado	1
Connecticut	2
Florida	7
Georgia	1
Hawaii	2
Illinois	4
Indiana	1
Louisiana	1
Maryland	2
Massachusetts	3
Michigan	2
Minnesota	1
Missouri	2
Nevada	1
New Jersey	4
New York	4
Ohio	3
Oklahoma	1
Oregon	1
Pennsylvania	2
Tennessee	1
Texas	5
Virginia	1
Washington	1
Washington, DC	2
Total	**75**

HOW MUCH

	4-Year Growth	1981	1982	1983	1984	1985	1986	1987	1988	1989	1990
Sales ($ mil.)	16.6%	—	—	—	—	—	98	161	191	209	181
Net income ($ mil.)	—	—	—	—	—	—	4	6	5	4	(2)
Income as % of sales	—	—	—	—	—	—	3.7%	3.5%	2.5%	2.0%	(1.3%)
Earnings per share ($)	—	—	—	—	—	—	0.51	0.70	0.58	0.51	(0.28)
Stock price – high ($)	—	—	—	—	—	—	—	10.75	7.13	9.75	8.00
Stock price – low ($)	—	—	—	—	—	—	—	4.00	4.75	4.88	0.94
Stock price – close ($)	—	—	—	—	—	—	—	6.00	5.63	7.75	1.16
P/E – high	—	—	—	—	—	—	—	15	12	19	—
P/E – low	—	—	—	—	—	—	—	6	8	10	—
Dividends per share ($)	—	—	—	—	—	—	0.00	0.00	0.00	0.00	0.00
Book value per share ($)	34.6%	—	—	—	—	—	1.15	2.96	3.54	4.05	3.77

1990 Year-end:
Debt ratio: 25.1%
Return on equity: —
Cash (mil.): $12
Current ratio: 1.91
Long-term debt (mil.): $10
No. of shares (mil.): 8
Dividends:
  1990 average yield: 0.0%
  1990 payout: 0.0%
Market value (mil.): $10

Stock Price History High/Low 1987–90

WHAT

	1990 Sales	
	$ mil.	% of total
Store sales	147	81
Catalog sales	32	18
List rentals	2	1
Total	**181**	**100**

1990 Products by Category	% of Total
Electronics	39
Personal care & household	26
Games, luggage & gifts	19
Health & fitness	11
Gemstones, jewelry & art	5
Total	**100**

KEY COMPETITORS

Circuit City
Dillard
Montgomery Ward
Sears
Service Merchandise
Tandy
Wal-Mart
Other department stores

THE SHERWIN-WILLIAMS COMPANY

OVERVIEW

Sherwin-Williams, a leading manufacturer and distributor of paints, makes a wide variety of coatings for consumer, automotive, industrial, and architectural markets under a number of brand names, including Dutch Boy, Kem-Tone, Krylon, and Sherwin-Williams. The company also manufactures traffic paint and coatings for equipment manufacturers and industrial maintenance.

The company markets its brand products through more than 1,900 Sherwin-Williams stores, which also offer other home decorating materials, such as wallpaper.

Sherwin-Williams distributes its other brands through various dealers, including Sears, Wal-Mart, and many regionally based retailers and also manufactures paint for sale under private labels.

Sherwin-Williams has resumed sales of certain products in Canada now that a non-competition agreement with BAPCO has expired. Other plans include software enhancements to further improve the company's new point-of-sale system, now installed at all Sherwin-Williams stores.

WHEN

In 1870 Henry Sherwin bought out paint materials distributor Truman Dunham and joined with Edward Williams and A. T. Osborn to form Sherwin-Williams & Company, located in Cleveland, to make and sell paint. Sherwin improved the paint-grinding mill and initiated a line of paints in 1876. In 1877 Sherwin patented a reclosable can, and in 1880 he introduced an improved liquid paint, making Sherwin-Williams the industry leader.

In 1874 Sherwin-Williams introduced a special paint for carriages, beginning the concept of specific-purpose paint. By 1900 the company had paints for floors, roofs, barns, metal bridges, railroad cars, and automobiles. In 1891 the company established a dealership in Massachusetts, forerunner of the company-operated retail stores. In 1895 the company obtained its "Cover the Earth" trademark.

Before the Great Depression, Sherwin-Williams acquired a number of smaller paint manufacturers: Detroit White Lead (1910), Martin-Senour (1917), Acme White Lead & Color (1920), and The Lowe Brothers (1929). Responding to wartime government restrictions, Sherwin-Williams developed a new type of paint, fast drying and water reducible, called Kem-Tone, and a new paint applicator, the Roller-Koater, forerunner of the paint roller.

Company sales doubled during the 1960s as the company made several acquisitions,

including a chemical company and Sprayon (aerosol paint, 1966), but earnings remained flat due to rising expenses. In 1972 the company expanded its stores to include carpeting, draperies, wallpaper, and other interior decorating items. But long-term debt ballooned from $80 million in 1974 to $196 million by 1977, when the company lost $8.2 million, causing a suspension of dividends for the first time since 1885.

Present CEO John Breen joined Sherwin-Williams in 1979, reinstated the dividend, purged over 1/2 of the top 100 management positions, and closed inefficient plants. Breen concentrated company stores' products on paint and wallpaper and purchased Dutch Boy (1980). Company stores' sales have increased from 46% of 1980 sales to 63% of 1990 sales.

Sherwin-Williams sold its container business to private investors in 1983 and in 1985 sold most of the chemical business to PMC Specialties Group. Earnings have improved since Breen took over, rising fourfold on a sales increase of only 50% in the last decade.

During 1990 Sherwin-Williams began selling Dutch Boy in all Sears stores and Kem-Tone in 400 Wal-Mart stores. Acquisitions in 1990 included parts of the Krylon and Illinois Bronze aerosol business, DeSoto's consumer paint business, and Custom Colour Paints Limited, a Canadian company.

HOW MUCH

	9-Year Growth	1981	1982	1983	1984	1985	1986	1987	1988	1989	1990
Sales ($ mil.)	4.4%	1,537	1,852	1,973	2,075	2,195	1,553	1,793	1,950	2,123	2,267
Net income ($ mil.)	16.4%	31	43	55	65	75	96	94	101	109	123
Income as % of sales	—	2.0%	2.3%	2.8%	3.1%	3.4%	6.2%	5.2%	5.2%	5.1%	5.4%
Earnings per share ($)	17.1%	0.34	0.44	0.56	0.70	0.80	1.05	1.05	1.15	1.26	1.41
Stock price – high ($)	—	2.97	6.23	7.94	8.09	11.75	16.13	19.25	15.81	17.88	21.06
Stock price – low ($)	—	2.02	2.27	4.56	5.56	6.97	10.66	10.06	12.00	12.50	15.06
Stock price – close ($)	23.7%	2.75	5.50	6.56	7.00	11.06	13.81	12.19	12.69	17.19	18.69
P/E – high	—	9	14	14	12	15	15	18	14	14	15
P/E – low	—	6	5	8	8	9	10	10	10	10	11
Dividends per share ($)	16.0%	0.10	0.13	0.15	0.19	0.23	0.25	0.28	0.32	0.35	0.38
Book value per share ($)	9.9%	3.76	3.91	4.07	4.49	5.05	5.58	6.29	6.98	7.74	8.80

1990 Year-end:
Debt ratio: 15.3%
Return on equity: 17.0%
Cash (mil.): $99
Current ratio: 1.91
Long-term debt (mil.): $138
No. of shares (mil.): 87
Dividends:
  1990 average yield: 2.0%
  1990 payout: 27.0%
Market value (mil.): $1,621

Stock Price History High/Low 1981–90

NYSE symbol: SHW
Fiscal year ends: December 31

Hoover's Rating **A-**

WHO

Chairman and CEO: John G. Breen, age 56, $1,077,991 pay
President and COO: Thomas A. Commes, age 48, $637,745 pay
SVP Finance and CFO: Thomas R. Miklich, age 43, $375,604 pay
VP Human Resources: Thomas Kroeger, age 42
Auditors: Ernst & Young
Employees: 16,397

WHERE

HQ: 101 Prospect Ave. NW, Cleveland, OH 44115-1075
Phone: 216-566-2000
Fax: 216-566-3310

Sherwin-Williams operates plants in 16 states and has licensees in 30 countries. The company operates 1,934 Sherwin-Williams paint stores in 48 states and Canada.

	1990 Stores	
	No.	% of total
Mid-central	517	27
Southeast	472	24
East	375	19
South-central	379	20
West	190	10
Canada	1	—
Total	**1,934**	**100**

	1990 Pretax Income	
	$ mil.	% of total
US	178	95
Foreign	9	5
Total	**187**	**100**

WHAT

	1990 Sales		1990 Operating Income	
	$ mil.	% of total	$ mil.	% of total
Paint stores	1,434	63	86	39
Coatings	819	36	129	59
Other	14	1	4	2
Adjustments	—	—	(36)	—
Total	**2,267**	**100**	**183**	**100**

Brand Names

Paints and Coatings	
Acme	Rogers
Color Works	Sherwin-Williams
Dupli-Color	Sprayon
Dutch Boy	Stone Craft
Glas-Clad	SuperPaint
Illinois Bronze	Western Automotive Paint
Kem-Tone	**Paint Brushes and**
Krylon	**Applicators**
Martin-Senour	Rubberset
Perma-Clad	Sherwin-Williams

RANKINGS

196th in *Fortune* 500 Industrial Cos.
330th in *Business Week* 1000

KEY COMPETITORS

BASF	Imperial Chemical
Du Pont	Lowe's
Hoechst	PPG
Home Depot	USG

SKIDMORE, OWINGS & MERRILL

Private company
Fiscal year ends: September 30

OVERVIEW

Throughout the 1970s and 1980s, Skidmore, Owings & Merrill (SOM) was the world's largest architectural/engineering firm. Its early development of a coherent body of work, emphasizing a functional, modernistic look, has made it one of the most pervasive influences on US commercial and public architecture in the latter 1/2 of the 20th century.

The firm has designed buildings in more than 40 countries and has won more than 500 awards for excellence. In addition to the office buildings and other corporate structures for which it is so well known, SOM has designed campuses, museums, airports, hospitals, religious structures, railway stations, hotels, retail centers, residential facilities, and even cities.

But in 1990 and 1991, SOM was forced to cut back radically, reducing its total staff by 46% in a series of layoffs that have affected increasingly higher level senior personnel. Billings fell by about 25%, largely because of the depressed real estate climate of the 1990s after the boom of the 1980s.

WHEN

While studying and working in Paris in 1929, Louis Skidmore had become acquainted with 2 architects involved in planning the 1933–34 Century of Progress Exposition in Chicago. He arranged to be appointed chief designer for it and asked his brother-in-law Nathaniel Owings to assist him, thus beginning their professional association.

After the Exposition, Skidmore and Owings separated, only to come together again in 1936 to found a small design firm in Chicago bearing their names. Trading on corporate relationships developed at the Exposition, the firm soon had enough work for 3 draftsmen.

The next year Skidmore opened a New York office to serve one of its corporate clients, American Radiator Company. The New York presence and their experience at the Exposition made Skidmore & Owings a logical choice to participate in the design of the New York World's Fair of 1939–40. Gordon Bunshaft, who was to stay with the firm for 42 years and become its most famous and influential architect, joined the company in 1937. By 1939, when architectural engineer John Merrill joined the firm, it had already developed a reputation for clean, functional design for large corporate and institutional clients.

In 1940 the firm won the contract that brought it to national prominence: to design the defense community of Oak Ridge, Tennessee, home of part of the Manhattan (atomic bomb) Project.

After WWII the firm grew rapidly, as it was selected to design large institutional and corporate facilities, including Mount Zion Hospital in San Francisco, Fort Hamilton VA Hospital in Brooklyn, Lever House in New York City, and the H. J. Heinz vinegar plant in Pittsburgh. By 1950 the SOM modernistic look had become so distinctive that SOM was the first architectural firm to be granted an exhibition at the New York Museum of Modern Art.

By 1958 SOM had 14 partners and 1,000 employees at 4 offices (San Francisco opened in 1946 and Portland, Oregon, in 1952). The 1960s saw more corporate (e.g., IBM headquarters in Armonk, New York) and institutional (e.g., University of Illinois at Chicago) commissions, and in 1962 SOM received the American Institute of Architects' first firm award for architectural excellence.

In the 1970s the firm's influence was most profound in Chicago, where it designed the John Hancock building, the Sears Tower (the world's tallest building), Northwestern University's library, and Baxter Travenol's headquarters.

In the 1970s and 1980s, the firm obtained more commissions outside the US. By the mid-1980s it had 47 partners and 1,400 other employees in 9 offices. In 1986 it opened its first foreign office in London.

During the 1980s, however, the firm's commitment to modernism kept it from designing in the increasingly popular post modern style. By the time the firm had adapted, the 1980s building boom had turned into a glut of unused space. As real estate markets slowed, project volume fell 25%. In 1990 nearly 50% of the firm's staff was laid off. In response to difficult times, the firm appointed its first chairman, David Childs, of the New York office, which was not hit as hard by layoffs. It also began to enter the small institutional market (schools, churches), which is heavily competitive, and prepared for a decade of redesign and modernization work.

WHO

Partner Contact: David M. Childs, age 50
CFO: Dan A. DeCanniere
Auditors: Arthur Andersen & Co.
Employees: 863

WHERE

HQ: 33 W. Monroe, Chicago, IL 60603-5373
Phone: 312-641-5959
Fax: 312-332-5632

SOM has handled projects in the US and in more than 40 other countries.

	1990 Employees	
Office locations	**No.**	**% of total**
Chicago	224	26
London	160	19
Los Angeles	55	6
New York	228	26
San Francisco	132	15
Washington, DC	48	6
Other cities	16	2
Total	**863**	**100**

	1990 Sources of Revenue
	% of total
Illinois	20
Other US	45
Foreign	35
Total	**100**

WHAT

	1990 Types of Projects
	% of total
Commercial	40
Engineering	20
Planning	11
Interior design	10
All others	19
Total	**100**

Functional Disciplines

Architecture	Landscape architecture
Building services engineering	Site planning
Civil engineering	Space planning
Environmental analysis	Structural engineering
Equipment planning	Urban estimating

Notable Projects
Bank of America (San Francisco, 1971)
Chase Manhattan Bank (New York, 1961)
Exchange House (London, 1990)
Haj Terminal at international airport (Jiddah, Saudi Arabia; 1982)
Hirshhorn Museum and Sculpture Garden (Washington, DC; 1974)
John Hancock Center (Chicago, 1970)
LBJ Library (University of Texas, Austin)
Lever House (New York, 1952)
Library at Northwestern University (Evanston, IL; 1971)
Lincoln Center for the Performing Arts — Library-Museum (New York)
McCormick Place addition (Chicago)
New York City Building — 1939 World's Fair
Oak Ridge, TN (1942–46)
Sears Roebuck Tower (Chicago, 1974)
University of Illinois at Chicago Circle (1965)
US Air Force Academy (Colorado Springs, CO; 1962)
USG Building (Chicago)
Weyerhaeuser Headquarters (Tacoma, WA; 1971)

HOW MUCH

	9-Year Growth	1981	1982	1983	1984	1985	1986	1987	1988	1989	1990
Sales ($ mil.)	(7.3%)	105	90	99	98	99	76	75	78	71	53[1]
Employees	—	—	—	—	—	—	—	—	—	1,600	863

Sales ($ mil.) 1981–90

[Bar chart showing Sales in $ mil. from 1981 to 1990, with a y-axis scale from 0 to 120. Values approximately: 1981 ~105, 1982 ~90, 1983 ~99, 1984 ~98, 1985 ~99, 1986 ~76, 1987 ~75, 1988 ~78, 1989 ~71, 1990 ~53]

[1] Estimated

SNAP-ON TOOLS CORPORATION

OVERVIEW

Based in Kenosha, Wisconsin, Snap-on Tools makes and distributes over 13,000 tools and products to 5,242 independent dealers in the US and abroad. Dealers, who are given territories, sell the company's products out of van-type vehicles directly to mechanics at their shops. The dealers are given financial assistance and are supported by a network of branch offices, repair facilities, and distribution centers. Snap-on has over a 50% market share for professional tools.

Snap-on's products are divided into 2 groups: hand tools and other equipment.

Hand tools (which accounted for 78% of sales in 1990) include sockets, wrenches, screwdrivers, and drills. Other equipment (22% of sales) includes tool chests, roll cabinets, and automotive diagnostic equipment. Snap-on's tools are used primarily for automotive service, manufacturing, repair, and maintenance.

Starting in 1991, Snap-on signed new dealers on as franchisees and offered existing dealers the option to convert. The changeover was prompted by 35 lawsuits against Snap-on from dealers claiming the company misrepresented their earnings potential.

NYSE symbol: SNA
Fiscal year ends: Saturday nearest December 31

Hoover's Rating **A-**

WHO

Chairman, President, and CEO: Robert A. Cornog, age 51
SVP Administration: Jay H. Schnabel, age 48, $204,932 pay
SVP Sales: Daniel J. Riordan, age 47, $267,875 pay
SVP Manufacturing and R&E: James L. Somers, age 47, $184,251 pay
SVP Finance: Michael F. Montemurro, age 42
VP Human Resources: Donald E. Lyons, age 58
Auditors: Arthur Andersen & Co.
Employees: 7,600

WHEN

Joe Johnson's boss at American Grinder Manufacturing rejected Joe's idea of interchangeable wrench handles and sockets in 1919, and Snap-on Tools was born. Joe and coworker William Seidemann did not have the money to support his idea, but they made a sample set of 5 handles and 10 sockets, and 2 Wisconsin salesmen sold over 500 orders. Snap-on Wrench Company was incorporated in 1920.

Stanton Palmer and Newton Tarble, both salesmen, developed a distribution business demonstrating tool sets at customer sites, forming Motor Tool Specialty Company in 1920. The next year Palmer and Tarble bought out Johnson's original financial supporters, became partners, and elected Palmer president.

Snap-on's first catalog was published in 1923 with almost 50 items. In 1925 Snap-on had salesmen working out of 17 branches; by 1929 it had about 300 salesmen and 26 branches.

In 1930 the company reincorporated as Snap-on Tools, Inc., adopting its present name in 1937. In 1931 Palmer died, and Snap-on opened its first foreign subsidiary in Canada. Strapped from impending expansion and the Great Depression, Snap-on went to Forged Steel Products for help. Forged Steel rescued Snap-on, and William Myers, its owner, became the new president of the company.

Sales grew as Snap-on extended credit to Depression-battered mechanics. Myers died in 1939, leaving Johnson as president.

By 1940 Snap-on had 556 salesmen and was making hand tools for military use. Due to tool shortages in the civilian arena during WWII, salesmen began carrying excess stock in their trucks and station wagons, and by 1945 walk-in vans loaded with tools were commonplace. Salesmen retailing to mechanics became independent dealers with their own regions.

In 1952 Snap-on opened a Mexican subsidiary. Seidemann retired in 1954 and 5 years later Johnson became chairman. In the 1960s Snap-on began buying branch outlets to give the company complete command over distribution and marketing. In 1965 Snap-on opened a branch in the UK and patented its Flank Drive wrench (which had superior gripping ability over its predecessors).

R&D during the 1960s produced pneumatic, hydraulic, and electric tools. The company was listed on the NYSE in 1978. During the 1980s, Snap-on became the sole supplier of tools to NASA for the space shuttles. In 1985 Snap-on had 4,000 dealers, which by 1990 had expanded to over 5,000. Snap-on's unit sales and earnings were down in 1990 for the 2nd year in a row, due largely to the recession and the slowdown in the auto industry.

WHERE

HQ: 2801 80th St., Kenosha, WI 53141
Phone: 414-656-5200
Fax: 414-656-5123

Snap-on has 11 manufacturing locations in the US and 2 in Canada, as well as 5 distribution centers in the US and one in Canada. The company sells in Australia, Belgium, Canada, France, Germany, Japan, Mexico, the Netherlands, the UK, and the US.

	1990 Sales		1990 Operating Income	
	$ mil.	% of total	$ mil.	% of total
US	768	82	149	89
Foreign	163	18	19	11
Adjustments	54	—	(5)	—
Total	**985**	**100**	**163**	**100**

WHAT

1990 Sales by Source	% of Total
Dealers & distributors	78
Specialized industrial representatives	18
Foreign sales corporation	4
Total	**100**

1990 Sales of Products by Type	% of Total
Hand tools	78
Equipment, cabinets & chests	22
Total	**100**

Hand Tools

Aircraft tools
Auto body tools
Chisels
Hammers
Pliers
Pneumatic impact wrenches

Power-assisted drills
Punches
Screwdrivers
Sockets
Wheel balancing and aligning equipment
Wrenches

Other Products
Electronic automotive diagnostic equipment
Roll cabinets
Tool chests

US Subsidiaries
ATI Industries, Inc.
Balco, Inc.

HOW MUCH

	9-Year Growth	1981	1982	1983	1984	1985	1986	1987	1988	1989	1990
Sales ($ mil.)	8.9%	457	450	477	566	623	696	785	893	938	985
Net income ($ mil.)	10.8%	40	37	43	60	60	66	89	113	105	101
Income as % of sales	—	8.8%	8.3%	9.0%	10.5%	9.6%	9.4%	11.3%	12.7%	11.2%	10.2%
Earnings per share ($)	10.6%	0.99	0.92	1.06	1.47	1.46	1.59	2.13	2.72	2.55	2.45
Stock price – high ($)	—	15.13	14.75	17.13	18.75	21.19	32.13	46.50	44.88	41.88	38.00
Stock price – low ($)	—	9.00	8.25	12.25	13.50	16.00	20.38	24.25	32.63	28.88	26.25
Stock price – close ($)	13.0%	10.56	13.50	15.38	17.38	20.94	25.63	34.75	35.00	32.50	31.75
P/E – high	—	15	16	16	13	15	20	22	17	16	16
P/E – low	—	9	9	12	9	11	13	11	12	11	11
Dividends per share ($)	11.1%	0.42	0.42	0.43	0.47	0.58	0.61	0.70	0.88	1.04	1.08
Book value per share ($)	12.6%	5.28	5.75	6.38	7.33	8.24	9.28	10.97	12.35	13.93	15.42

1990 Year-end:
Debt ratio: 1.1%
Return on equity: 16.7%
Cash (mil.): $7
Current ratio: 2.85
Long-term debt (mil.): $7
No. of shares (mil.): 41
Dividends:
  1990 average yield: 3.4%
  1990 payout: 44.1%
Market value (mil.): $1,311

Stock Price History
High/Low 1981–90

RANKINGS

354th in *Fortune* 500 Industrial Cos.
460th in *Business Week* 1000

KEY COMPETITORS

Black & Decker
Cooper Industries
Emerson
Stanley Works
Textron

THE SOUTHERN COMPANY

NYSE symbol: SO
Fiscal year ends: December 31

Hoover's Rating C-

OVERVIEW

The Southern Company is America's 2nd largest electric utility, after Pacific Gas and Electric, with 1990 sales nearing $8 billion. The company provides electricity to more than 3 million customers in 4 southern and southeastern states through 5 utilities: Alabama Power Company, Georgia Power Company, Gulf Power Company, Mississippi Power Company, and Savannah Electric and Power Company. SEGCO (Southern Electric Generating Company) operates electric generating plants on Alabama's Coosa River, with Alabama and Georgia Power each entitled to 50% of the power SEGCO generates. Southern's stock is among the 20 most widely held in America.

Southern has weathered a history of anti-utility sentiment, especially in Georgia (its largest service territory). Its public image continues to suffer as a federal grand jury proceeds with an investigation of Southern's alleged illegal political contributions. The company was recently cleared by the IRS and the SEC for alleged accounting and filings violations.

WHO

President and CEO: Edward L. Addison, age 60, $883,775 pay
Financial VP: W. L. Westbrook, age 51
Auditors: Arthur Andersen & Co.
Employees: 30,263

WHERE

HQ: 64 Perimeter Center East, Atlanta, GA 30346
Phone: 404-393-0650
Fax: 404-668-3559

The Southern Company operates in Alabama, Georgia, northwestern Florida, and southeastern Mississippi.

Generating Facilities

Fossil Fueled	Hydroelectric
Barry (APC)	Bartletts Ferry (GPC)
Bowen (GPC)	H. Neely Henry Dam (APC)
Crist (Gulf)	Harris Dam (APC)
Daniel (50% Gulf, 50% MPC)	Jordan Dam (APC)
Eaton (MPC)	L. Smith Dam (APC)
Gaston (SEGCO)	Lay Dam (APC)
Gaston #5 (APC)	Logan Martin Dam (APC)
Gorgas (APC)	Martin Dam (APC)
Hammond (GPC)	Tallulah Falls (GPC)
Harlee Branch (GPC)	Wallace Dam (GPC)
Miller (APC)	Walter Bouldin Dam (APC)
Standard Oil Generating Station (MPC)	Weiss Dam (APC)
Sweatt (MPC)	**Nuclear**
Wansley (GPC)	Farley (APC)
Watson (MPC)	Hatch (50.1%, GPC)
Yates (GPC)	Vogtle (45.7%, GPC)

WHEN

Steamboat captain W. P. Lay founded the Alabama Power Company in 1906 to develop electric power on the Coosa River. James Mitchell took over the company in 1912, moving its headquarters from Montgomery to Birmingham. From 1912 until his death in 1920, he bought a number of Alabama's utilities, consolidating them with Alabama Power under his Canadian holding company Alabama Traction Light & Power (ATL&P).

Tom Martin, Alabama Power's legal counsel, became president in 1920 and reorganized ATL&P into Southeastern Power & Light. Southeastern formed Mississippi Power Company to take over electric utilities in Mississippi (1924) and Gulf Power Company to do the same in northern Florida (1925). In 1926 Southeastern bought several Georgia utilities, which were consolidated as Georgia Power Company in 1927.

In 1929 B. C. Cobb acquired Southeastern, combining its assets with those of Penn-Ohio Edison to form Commonwealth & Southern Corporation, a New York holding company that owned about 165 utilities. Martin served as president of Commonwealth & Southern until 1933 and was replaced by Wendell Willkie (Republican nominee for president in 1940).

In 1942 Commonwealth & Southern was dissolved by the SEC. Four of its southern holdings (Alabama Power, Georgia Power, Gulf Power, and Mississippi Power) were placed under the authority of the Southern Company (a new holding company) in 1949.

During the energy shortages of the 1970s, both Alabama and Georgia Power faced an anti-utility political environment, spearheaded by Alabama's governor, George Wallace. In late 1974 and early 1975 Georgia Power approached bankruptcy. Alabama Power suspended its $700 million construction program and laid off 4,000 employees in 1978. Wallace left office that year, and state regulators allowed much-needed rate relief, ushering in a period of moderate growth for the Southern Company as a whole. In 1988 Southern added Savannah, Georgia–based Savannah Electric & Power to its electric power system.

In 1990 Georgia Power took a $218 million charge, which contributed to Southern's 25.8% drop in earnings for that year. This charge related to a Georgia Supreme Court decision preventing the company from passing on to its customers certain costs related to the construction of the nuclear plant Vogtle (which went on-line in 1989). Georgia Power also agreed to sell unit 4 of its Scherer plant to 2 Florida utilities (including Florida Power and Light) for $810 million in 1990. The sale is pending regulatory approval.

WHAT

	1990 Sales	
	$ mil.	% of total
Electricity		
Residential	2,342	30
Commercial	2,062	26
Industrial	2,085	26
Sales for resale	412	5
Nonterritorial & other	963	12
Other	111	1
Total	**7,975**	**100**

	1990 Fuel Sources
	% of total
Coal	79
Nuclear	13
Hydroelectric	3
Oil & gas	1
Purchased power	4
Total	**100**

System Companies
Alabama Power Co.
Georgia Power Co.
Gulf Power Co.
Mississippi Power Co.
Savannah Electric and Power Co.
Southern Electric Generating Co.

Engineering and Technical Services
Southern Company Services, Inc.
Southern Electric International, Inc.
Southern Nuclear Operating Co., Inc.

Financial Services
The Southern Investment Group, Inc.

HOW MUCH

	9-Year Growth	1981	1982	1983	1984	1985	1986	1987	1988	1989	1990
Sales ($ mil.)	7.2%	4,256	4,927	5,418	6,124	6,814	6,847	7,010	7,235	7,492	7,975
Net income ($ mil.)	6.3%	413	545	699	828	947	1,003	678	966	969	719
Income as % of sales	—	9.7%	11.1%	12.9%	13.5%	13.9%	14.6%	9.7%	13.4%	12.9%	9.0%
Earnings per share ($)	0.6%	1.81	2.26	2.72	3.00	3.20	3.17	1.92	2.72	2.68	1.91
Stock price – high ($)	—	12.88	15.88	17.75	18.88	23.75	27.25	29.00	24.25	29.75	29.38
Stock price – low ($)	—	10.88	11.00	14.50	14.38	17.88	20.38	17.88	20.38	22.00	23.00
Stock price – close ($)	9.8%	12.00	15.63	16.38	18.88	22.25	25.38	22.38	22.38	29.13	27.88
P/E – high	—	7	7	7	6	7	9	15	9	11	15
P/E – low	—	6	5	5	5	6	6	9	8	8	12
Dividends per share ($)	3.1%	1.62	1.66	1.73	1.83	1.95	2.07	2.14	2.14	2.14	2.14
Book value per share ($)	3.1%	16.35	16.78	17.60	18.55	19.83	21.09	20.89	21.20	21.74	21.47

1990 Year-end:
Debt ratio: 51.4%
Return on equity: 8.8%
Cash (mil.): $186
Current ratio: 1.25
Long-term debt (mil.): $8,458
No. of shares (mil.): 316
Dividends:
  1990 average yield: 7.7%
  1990 payout: 112.0%
Market value (mil.): $8,809

Stock Price History
High/Low 1981–90

RANKINGS

10th in *Fortune* 50 Utilities
65th in *Business Week* 1000

THE SOUTHLAND CORPORATION

OVERVIEW

The Dallas-based Southland Corporation, under the 7-Eleven banner, is the world's largest operator of convenience stores. The company has 6,455 7-Eleven stores in the US and Canada, with about 13,000 operated by the company, franchised, or operated under license worldwide, including 250 High's, Quik Marts, and Super-7s. The stores are extended-hour retail stores emphasizing customer convenience and are supported by 5 distribution centers and 6 food-making centers. The average store size is about 2,600 square feet; newer stores average 3,000 square feet. Southland estimates that 7 million customers shop at 7-Eleven stores in the US and Canada daily.

The company's stores sell consumer items, including take-out food and beverages, dairy products, nonfood merchandise, and gasoline (at certain locations). Since much of the stores' merchandise is consumed during periods of increased leisure-time activities, operations are influenced favorably by warm weather.

After trying to avoid Chapter 11 bankruptcy for most of 1990, the company was forced to file in October 1990. It emerged reorganized in March 1991 with its longtime Japanese partner controlling 70% of the company. Although the company has successfully reorganized, its entire industry has troubles. Southland stores have increased competition from gasoline chains, supermarkets, and drugstores. Some analysts believe this competition may be exacerbated by a shrinking customer base for convenience stores primarily due to aging of the baby-boomers.

WHEN

Backed by Chicago utility magnate Martin Insull, Claude Dawley formed the Southland Ice Company in Dallas in 1927 to buy 4 other Texas ice plants. Ice was a rare commodity and a basic necessity during Texas summers for storing and transporting food.

One of Dawley's plants was Consumers Ice, where an employee, Joe C. Thompson, Jr., had begun selling chilled watermelons off the truck docks. Later, a Southland Ice dock manager in Dallas, John Green, began stocking a few food items for customers. He told Thompson, who ran the ice operations, and soon all company locations adopted the idea. Thompson called the grocery operations Tote'm Stores and erected Alaska-made totem poles by the docks. In 1928 he arranged for the construction of gas stations at some stores.

Insull bought out Dawley in 1930, and Thompson became president. Southland expanded even as the Depression-hurt company operated briefly under the direction of the bankruptcy court (1932–34). When the company became the largest dairy retailer in the Dallas–Fort Worth area, it started a dairy, Oak Farms (1936). By 1946 the company had bought other ice-retail operations in Texas, changed its name to Southland Corporation, and adopted the name 7-Eleven, a reference to the store hours, for its stores.

When Thompson died in 1961, his eldest son, John, became president. New stores were opened in Colorado, New Jersey, and Arizona in 1962 and in Utah, California, and Missouri in 1963. The company made other acquisitions in the 1960s and '70s. Southland franchised the 7-Eleven format in the UK (1971) and in Japan (1973, through Ito-Yokado). In 1983 Southland bought Citgo, a gasoline refining and marketing business, but sold 50% of it to PDVSA, the Venezuelan oil company, in 1986.

In 1987 John Thompson borrowed heavily to buy Southland's stock in a $4.9 billion LBO. The company sold 1,000 stores and its remaining interest in Citgo but still defaulted on $1.8 billion in publicly traded debt in mid-1990. Southland hoped to persuade bondholders to swap debt for stock and clear the way for the purchase of 70% of Southland by its Japanese partner, Ito-Yokado. Time ran out; the company filed for bankruptcy protection in October 1990. Its bankruptcy papers included the reorganization to which it had been trying to get bondholders to agree; eventually they did. In March 1991 the company emerged from bankruptcy following its stock purchase agreement with Ito-Yokado. The agreement gave 70% control of Southland to Ito-Yokado for $430 million (which reduced debt service and reestablished long-term liquidity); bondholders got 25%, and the Thompson family retained 5% of Southland's once again publicly traded stock.

In 1991 New England–based Christy's bought 53 Southland stores and agreed to convert all its own stores to 7-Elevens.

OTC symbol: SLCC
Fiscal year ends: December 31

WHO

Chairman: Masatoshi Ito, age 66
President and CEO: Clark J. Matthews II, age 54, $553,800 pay (prior to promotion)
SVP Finance: Frank J. Gangi, age 50
VP Human Resources: David M. Finley, age 50
Auditors: Coopers & Lybrand
Employees: 45,665

WHERE

HQ: 2711 N. Haskell Ave., Dallas, TX 75204-2906
Phone: 214-828-7011
Fax: 214-828-7848

Southland operates 7-Eleven stores in 43 states, the District of Columbia, Canada, Mexico, and Sweden. Stores operated by others under license are located in 20 additional foreign countries.

	No. of Stores	% of Total
California	1,283	20
Virginia	661	10
Florida	579	9
Texas	584	9
Maryland	315	5
Other states	2,521	39
Canada	512	8
Total	**6,455**	**100**

WHAT

	1990 Sales	
	$ mil.	% of total
Convenience stores	7,700	97
Other operations	213	2
Royalties & capital gains	62	1
Total	**7,975**	**100**

Convenience Stores
7-Eleven
High's Dairy Stores
Quik Mart
Super-7
Super Siete (Mexico)
7-Eleven/Naroppet (Sweden)

Other Holdings
Citijet (aviation services)
Cityplace (Dallas real estate)
Rainbow Ticketmaster
Southland Foods (food supplier)

Brand Names
Aunt Bea's
Big Bite
Big Gulp
Casa Buena
Deli Shoppe
Hot-to-Go
Italini
Slurpee
Smileys
Sonritos
Super-7

RANKINGS

15th in *Fortune* 50 Retailing Cos.
6th in *Forbes* 400 US Private Cos.

KEY COMPETITORS

Amoco
Atlantic Richfield
Chevron
Circle K
Coastal
Exxon
Federal Express
Kroger
Mobil
Phillips Petroleum
Royal Dutch/Shell
Ryder
Texaco
Grocery retailers

HOW MUCH

	9-Year Growth	1981	1982	1983	1984	1985	1986	1987	1988	1989	1990
Sales ($ mil.)	4.1%	5,575	6,612	8,512	11,661	12,377	8,187	7,629	7,602	7,916	7,975
Net income ($ mil.)	—	94	108	132	160	213	200	(75)	(216)	(1,320)	(302)
Income as % of sales	—	1.7%	1.6%	1.5%	1.4%	1.7%	2.4%	(1.0%)	(2.8%)	(16.7%)	(3.8%)
Employees	(0.9%)	49,600	49,900	60,834	61,800	63,548	67,174	65,800	50,724	48,114	45,665

1990 Year-end:
Debt ratio: —
Return on equity: —
Cash (mil.): $108
Current ratio: 0.15
Long-term debt (mil.): $183

Net Income ($ mil.)
1981–90

SOUTHWEST AIRLINES CO.

NYSE symbol: LUV
Fiscal year ends: December 31

Hoover's Rating **C+**

OVERVIEW

Southwest Airlines made a profit in 1990. Few other US airlines can make that claim. The company kept nonfuel costs down (it has the industry's lowest labor costs), and 1990 would have been a record year if fuel prices had not escalated when Iraq invaded Kuwait. As it turned out, Southwest's employees set up a voluntary program to buy fuel for the company with money out of their own paychecks.

That sort of company spirit characterizes Southwest, which is known for its offbeat corporate culture and its fun-loving, Elvis-impersonating CEO, Herb Kelleher. The airline specializes in single-class, frequent, low-fare flights, which average an hour or less in duration. Schedules are geared toward city-to-city (as opposed to hub-and-spoke) flights. No meals are served (although complimentary peanuts and drinks abound), and between flights Southwest's planes spend less than 15 minutes on the ground — one of the fastest turnaround times in the industry. The company emphasizes customer service, now running a close 2nd to Delta for the lowest number of customer complaints.

WHO

Chairman, President, and CEO: Herbert D. Kelleher, age 59, $466,608 pay
EVP and COO: Gary A. Barron, age 46, $209,723 pay
VP Finance and CFO: Gary C. Kelly, age 35
VP People: Margaret Ann Rhoades
Auditors: Ernst & Young
Employees: 8,620

WHERE

HQ: PO Box 36611, Love Field, Dallas, TX 75235-1611
Phone: 214-904-4000
Fax: 214-904-4200
Reservations: 800-531-5601

Southwest flies to 32 cities in 14 states.

Cities Served

Albuquerque, NM	Los Angeles, CA
Amarillo, TX	Lubbock, TX
Austin, TX	Midland, TX
Birmingham, AL	Nashville, TN
Burbank, CA	New Orleans, LA
Chicago, IL	Oakland, CA
Corpus Christi, TX	Oklahoma City, OK
Dallas, TX	Ontario, CA
Detroit, MI	Phoenix, AZ
El Paso, TX	Reno, NV
Harlingen, TX	Sacramento, CA
Houston, TX	San Antonio, TX
Indianapolis, IN	San Diego, CA
Kansas City, MO	San Francisco, CA
Las Vegas, NV	St. Louis, MO
Little Rock, AR	Tulsa, OK

WHEN

Texas businessman Rollin King and lawyer Herb Kelleher founded Air Southwest Company in 1967 as an intrastate airline, linking Dallas, Houston, and San Antonio. Braniff and Texas International immediately sued the company, questioning whether the region needed another airline, but the Texas Supreme Court ruled in Southwest's favor. In 1971 the company (renamed Southwest Airlines) made its first scheduled flight from Dallas Love Field to San Antonio.

Capitalizing on its home base at Love Field, Southwest adopted love as the theme of its early ad campaigns, complete with stewardesses wearing hot pants and serving love potions (drinks) and love bites (peanuts). When other airlines moved to the Dallas–Fort Worth (D-FW) airport in 1974, Southwest stayed at Love Field, contributing to its virtual monopoly at the airfield. This monopoly proved to be limiting, however, when the Wright Amendment became law in 1979, preventing companies operating out of Love Field from providing direct service to states except those neighboring Texas. Southwest's customers could fly from Love Field to New Mexico, Oklahoma, Arkansas, and Louisiana but had to buy new tickets and board different Southwest flights to points beyond.

When Lamar Muse, Southwest's president, resigned in 1978 because of differences with King, Kelleher became president. Muse later took over his son Michael's nearly bankrupt airline, Muse Air Corporation, and in 1985 sold it to Southwest. Kelleher operated the Houston-based airline as TranStar but liquidated it in 1987 when competition from another Houston-based airline, Continental, caused Southwest's profits to fall.

Kelleher then devoted his full attention to making Southwest the industry low-fare leader. He introduced advance purchase "Fun Fares" in 1986 and a frequent-flyer program based on the number of flights rather than mileage in 1987. As an airline executive, Kelleher is regarded as something of a maverick. He has often starred in Southwest's unconventional TV commercials, and when Southwest became the official airline of Sea World (Texas) in 1988, Kelleher painted a 737 to resemble Shamu, the park's killer whale.

Southwest established an operating base at Phoenix Sky Harbor Airport in 1990, sparking direct competition with rival America West. That year Southwest's flagship, the Lone Star One (a 737 painted to look like the Texas flag), took to the air as part of the company's 20th anniversary celebration. Southwest continues to develop its route structure, especially on the West Coast, adding Oakland and Indianapolis (1989), Burbank and Reno (1990), and Sacramento (1991) to its route map.

WHAT

	1990 Sales	
	$ mil.	% of total
Passengers	1,145	96
Freight	22	2
Other	20	2
Total	**1,187**	**100**

Services
The Company Club (frequent-flyer program based on trips rather than mileage)
In-flight beverage services
Quick ticketing and boarding procedures

Flight Equipment	No.	Average Age in Years
Boeing 737	106	6.1
Total	**106**	**6.1**

RANKINGS

24th in *Fortune* 50 Transportation Cos.
512th in *Business Week* 1000

KEY COMPETITORS

America West
AMR
Continental Airlines
Delta
Midway
NWA
TWA
UAL
USAir

HOW MUCH

	9-Year Growth	1981	1982	1983	1984	1985	1986	1987	1988	1989	1990
Sales ($ mil.)	17.9%	270	331	448	536	680	769	778	860	1,015	1,187
Net income ($ mil.)	3.6%	34	34	41	50	47	50	20	58	72	47
Income as % of sales	—	12.6%	10.3%	9.1%	9.3%	7.0%	6.5%	2.6%	6.7%	7.1%	4.0%
Earnings per share ($)	2.3%	0.90	0.84	0.92	1.09	1.01	1.03	0.42	1.23	1.57	1.10
Stock price – high ($)	—	12.91	17.00	23.47	19.60	20.67	18.33	16.83	13.92	20.50	20.00
Stock price – low ($)	—	6.29	7.33	13.33	9.83	14.17	12.17	7.83	8.75	13.08	12.75
Stock price – close ($)	9.6%	7.70	14.20	18.13	14.67	17.92	13.75	8.92	13.50	16.00	17.50
P/E – high	—	14	20	25	18	21	18	40	11	13	18
P/E – low	—	7	9	14	9	14	12	19	7	8	12
Dividends per share ($)	4.0%	0.07	0.09	0.09	0.09	0.09	0.09	0.09	0.09	0.09	0.10
Book value per share ($)	13.7%	4.52	5.74	7.12	8.17	9.63	10.58	10.95	12.10	13.40	14.35

1990 Year-end:
Debt ratio: 35.1%
Return on equity: 7.9%
Cash (mil.): $88
Current ratio: 0.70
Long-term debt (mil.): $327
No. of shares (mil.): 42
Dividends:
  1990 average yield: 0.6%
  1990 payout: 8.8%
Market value (mil.): $738

Stock Price History High/Low 1981–90

SOUTHWESTERN BELL CORPORATION

OVERVIEW

St. Louis–based Southwestern Bell Corporation, a spinoff of the Bell system, provides telephone service, cellular telephone service, paging, directory advertising, publishing, and cable television. The company has also bought a large stake in the recently privatized Telmex, Mexico's national telephone system.

Southwestern Bell Telephone provides telephone exchange services to more than 9 million subscribers in 5 central and southwestern states. During 1990 the company provided almost 37 billion minutes of network usage and connected more than one billion long-distance calls.

Southwestern Bell Mobile Systems provides service to more than 731,000 cellular subscribers in 28 markets (including 6 of the largest 15). Subsidiary Metromedia Paging, based in Secaucus, New Jersey, provides paging services to 884,000 paging subscribers in 31 markets (including 9 of the 10 largest US markets). Southwestern Bell Telecom markets communications equipment.

Southwestern Bell Yellow Pages publishes more than 420 phone directories in its region. Mast Advertising & Publishing produces maps, guides, and other specialized publications and markets 6,000 directories worldwide.

WHEN

Southwestern Bell was once an arm of AT&T, providing local communications services in its present region. Telephone service first arrived in Southwestern Bell territory in 1878, just 2 years after the telephone was invented. One man responsible for early growth of telephony in this region was George Durant, who located 12 customers for St. Louis's first telephone exchange. This grew into Bell Telephone Company of Missouri.

Meanwhile, the Missouri and Kansas Telephone Company had also been established. The first president of Southwestern Bell, Eugene Nims, negotiated the merger of Missouri and Kansas and Southwestern Bell into the Southwestern Telephone System around 1912. Southwestern Bell became part of AT&T in 1917; Nims served as president from 1919 to 1929. After WWII, demand for new telephone lines grew rapidly. By 1945 Southwestern Bell was providing service to one million telephones; by the 1980s this number had grown nearly tenfold.

In 1983 AT&T was split from the Bell Operating Companies, and Southwestern Bell became a separate legal entity; it began operations in 1984. At the time of the breakup, Southwestern Bell received local phone service rights in 5 states; Southwestern Bell

Mobile Systems (cellular service provider); the directory advertising business; and a 1/7 share in Bell Communications Research (Bellcore), the R&D arm shared by the Bell companies. The company set up its telecommunications and publishing groups later.

Southwestern Bell has concentrated much of its diversification effort in mobile communications. The company purchased operations from Metromedia (1987), which included paging in 19 cities and 6 major cellular franchises. Southwestern Bell also bought paging assets from Omni Communications (1988).

By 1988 Southwestern Bell had deployed more lines than any other company for an integrated voice and data phone service known as ISDN. That year the company began testing residential fiber-optic service in Kansas.

In 1990 Southwestern Bell joined with France Télécom and Grupo Carso (mining, manufacturing, and tobacco) to purchase 20.4% of Teléfonos de México, the previously state-owned telephone monopoly, for a total of $1.76 billion.

Telmex ADRs had long been a favorite of Wall Street because of Telmex's growth potential as the Mexican economy cast off its government hobbles. In 1991 Southwestern Bell exercised its option to double its Telmex stake.

NYSE symbol: SBC
Fiscal year ends: December 31

Hoover's Rating **B-**

WHO

Chairman and CEO: Edward E. Whitacre, Jr., age 49, $1,374,300 pay
VC and CFO: Robert G. Pope, age 55, $946,400 pay
VC: Gerald D. Blatherwick, age 55, $892,800 pay
SEVP and General Counsel: James D. Ellis, age 48, $493,400 pay
SVP Strategic Planning: J. Cliff Eason, age 43
President and CEO, Southwestern Bell Telephone Co.: James R. Adams, age 52, $846,600 pay
Group President: Royce S. Caldwell, age 52
Group President: Charles E. Foster, age 54
SEVP Human Resources: Richard A. Harris, age 50
Auditors: Ernst & Young
Employees: 66,900

WHERE

HQ: One Bell Center, St. Louis, MO 63101-3099
Phone: 314-235-9800
Fax: 314-235-2627 (Investor Relations)

Southwestern Bell Telephone provides telephone services in Texas, Kansas, Oklahoma, Arkansas, and Missouri. Other divisions operate nationally or internationally.

WHAT

| | 1990 Sales | |
	$ mil.	% of total
Local telephone service	3,396	37
Network access	2,631	29
Long-distance service	1,065	12
Directory advertising	794	9
Other	1,227	13
Total	**9,113**	**100**

Subsidiaries and Affiliates
Bell Communications Research (14%)
Gulf Printing Co.
Mast Advertising & Publishing
Metromedia Paging Services
Southwestern Bell International Holdings
Southwestern Bell Mobile Systems
Southwestern Bell Telecom
Southwestern Bell Telephone Co.
Southwestern Bell Yellow Pages

RANKINGS

6th in *Fortune* 50 Utilities
34th in *Business Week* 1000

KEY COMPETITORS

Ameritech	Dun & Bradstreet
Bell Atlantic	Ericsson
BellSouth	GTE
British Telecom	McCaw
Cable & Wireless	NYNEX
Centel	Pacific Telesis
R. R. Donnelley	U S West

HOW MUCH

	6-Year Growth	1981	1982	1983	1984	1985	1986	1987	1988	1989	1990
Sales ($ mil.)	4.0%	—	—	—	7,191	7,925	7,902	8,003	8,453	8,730	9,113
Net income ($ mil.)	3.8%	—	—	—	883	996	1,023	1,047	1,060	1,093	1,101
Income as % of sales	—	—	—	—	12.3%	12.6%	12.9%	13.1%	12.5%	12.5%	12.1%
Earnings per share ($)	3.4%	—	—	—	3.01	3.33	3.42	3.48	3.53	3.64	3.67
Stock price – high ($)	—	—	—	—	23.83	29.50	38.79	45.50	42.63	64.38	64.75
Stock price – low ($)	—	—	—	—	18.33	22.79	26.33	28.25	33.00	38.88	47.25
Stock price – close ($)	15.5%	—	—	—	23.58	28.50	37.42	34.38	40.38	63.88	56.00
P/E – high	—	—	—	—	8	9	11	13	12	18	18
P/E – low	—	—	—	—	6	7	8	8	9	11	13
Dividends per share ($)	11.7%	—	—	—	1.40	1.97	2.10	2.27	2.44	2.57	2.72
Book value per share ($)	3.4%	—	—	—	23.43	24.75	26.07	27.26	28.31	27.83	28.62

1990 Year-end:
Debt ratio: 39.0%
Return on equity: 13.0%
Cash (mil.): $250
Current ratio: 0.75
Long-term debt (mil.): $5,483
No. of shares (mil.): 300
Dividends:
  1990 average yield: 4.9%
  1990 payout: 74.1%
Market value (mil.): $16,793

Stock Price History High/Low 1984–90

SPRINGS INDUSTRIES, INC.

NYSE symbol: SMI
Fiscal year ends: Saturday nearest December 31

Hoover's Rating **C**

OVERVIEW

Springs Industries is the largest manufacturer of sheets and bedding in the US and the 2nd largest public textile company, after Wickes. Headquartered for over a century in Fort Mill, South Carolina, the $1.9 billion company operates 44 plants in 10 states in the US (23 in South Carolina), Belgium, and England, and has a minority interest in a Japanese textile plant.

The company, the largest industrial employer in South Carolina, operates in 3 industry segments — home furnishings, finished fabrics, and industrial fabrics. Home furnishing products include sheets and bedding accessories, bathroom furnishings, window shades, and blinds. Springs's recently downsized finished-fabrics segment includes textiles for the home sewing market and for other manufacturers. Springs is the world's largest producer of woven fiberglass fabrics for industrial use, and the company weaves protective fabrics used by firefighters, race car drivers, and soldiers during Operation Desert Storm.

The Close family, descendants of the founders, retains voting control of the company, and 2 family members sit on the board.

WHO

Chairman, CEO, and President: Walter Y. Elisha, age 58, $470,000 pay
EVP; President, Home Furnishings Group: Julius Lasnick, age 61, $320,586 pay
EVP New Technology: John V. Cauthen, age 62, $269,340 pay
EVP; President, Finished Fabrics Group: Robert W. Moser, age 52, $223,334 pay
EVP and CFO: A. Ward Peacock, age 61, $218,340 pay
VP Human Resources: Richard D. Foster, age 51
Auditors: Deloitte & Touche
Employees: 22,770

WHEN

Springs Industries began in 1887 as Fort Mill Manufacturing Company, organized by Samuel Elliott White and 15 others, including Leroy Springs, his future son-in-law. Springs, a self-made millionaire, obtained control of Fort Mill Manufacturing in the late 1890s.

In 1931 Elliott Springs, Leroy's only son, became president when his father died, leaving massive debts and decaying plants. Elliott saved the company by modernizing mill equipment and consolidating the plants into The Springs Cotton Mills (1933). During WWII the company's 7 mills made fabric for military use (up to 6 million yards a week).

In 1945 Springs started the Springmaid line of bedding and fabrics. Elliott Springs's satiric, risqué, but effective ads (beginning in 1948) helped the company become the world's biggest producer of sheets.

In 1959 Elliott died and his son-in-law H. William Close became president. Close oversaw construction of the Springs Building, current New York sales headquarters (1962), and a $200 million program to expand product lines and modernize plants. With profits sharply declining, the company went public as Springs Mills, Inc. (1966).

In 1969 the first nonfamily member, Peter G. Scotese from Federated Department Stores, was hired as president. Springs diversified into synthetic fabrics, buying a minority interest in a Japanese textile plant to produce Ultrasuede (apparel fabric and car upholstery, 1971), and into frozen foods, buying Seabrook Foods (1973, sold 1981).

Along with a name change to Springs Industries in 1982, recent acquisitions and mergers reflect the company's focus on home furnishings and industrial textiles — Lawtex Industries (bedspreads, draperies, 1979), Graber Industries (window decorating products, 1979), M. Lowenstein (Wamsutta home furnishings and industrial textiles, 1985), Clark-Schwebel Fiber Glass (industrial fabrics, 1985), Carey-McFall (Bali blinds, 1989), and C.S. Brooks (bathroom furnishings, 1991).

Declining economic conditions throughout the textile industry forced Springs to implement an $18 million restructuring in 1988 and a further $70 million charge in 1990, with the company closing plants, offering early retirements and trimming its weakened finished-fabrics segment. The 1990 charge led to Springs reporting a $7 million loss, its first in 25 years as a public company. With first-quarter 1991 earnings down 81%, Springs further reduced its finished-fabrics lines by selling its Doblin division, a maker of upholstery fabrics, to Collins and Aikman.

WHERE

HQ: PO Box 70, 205 N. White St., Fort Mill, SC 29715
Phone: 803-547-1500
Fax: 803-547-1636

Springs operates 44 manufacturing plants (including 30 textile plants) located primarily in the Southeast, with others in the Midwest, West, Belgium, and England.

	1990 Sales	
	$ mil.	% of total
US	1,762	94
Foreign	116	6
	1,878	100

WHAT

	1990 Sales		1990 Operating Income	
	$ mil.	% of total	$ mil.	% of total
Finished fabrics	480	26	(6)	(7)
Home furnishings	1,000	53	80	87
Industrial fabrics	398	21	19	20
Total	**1,878**	**100**	**93**	**100**

Home Furnishings
Bed and bath products
  Andre Richard
  Custom Designs
  Pacific
  Performance
  Springmaid
  Supercale
  Wamsutta
  Wondercale
Window furnishings
  Bali
  CrystalPleat
  FashionPleat
  Graber
Specialty products
  Pacific Silvercloth
  (antitarnish fabric)

Finished Fabrics
(for apparel, upholstery, home sewing market)
  Skinner
  Springmaid
  Ultraleather
  Ultrasuede
  Wamsutta

Industrial Fabrics
  Clark-Schwebel Fiber Glass
  Firegard/Synergy/Ultima
  (flame-retardant Kevlar fabrics)

RANKINGS

222nd in *Fortune* 500 Industrial Cos.
841st in *Business Week* 1000

KEY COMPETITORS

Burlington Holdings
Du Pont
Farley
Fieldcrest Cannon
W. R. Grace
Milliken

HOW MUCH

	9-Year Growth	1981	1982	1983	1984	1985	1986	1987	1988	1989	1990
Sales ($ mil.)	8.3%	917	875	894	945	1,014	1,505	1,661	1,825	1,909	1,878
Net income ($ mil.)	—	40	37	37	36	13	33	56	53	65	(7)
Income as % of sales	—	4.4%	4.3%	4.1%	3.8%	1.3%	2.2%	3.4%	2.9%	3.4%	(0.4%)
Earnings per share ($)	—	2.25	2.11	2.08	2.03	0.75	1.83	3.13	2.98	3.64	(0.39)
Stock price – high ($)	—	13.38	20.13	22.50	20.13	23.00	28.44	38.25	38.75	45.25	39.50
Stock price – low ($)	—	8.13	10.00	17.06	15.25	15.63	20.50	20.75	27.00	30.50	16.88
Stock price – close ($)	7.6%	11.75	19.63	19.88	16.88	22.00	24.94	30.25	31.50	38.25	22.63
P/E – high	—	6	10	11	10	31	16	12	13	12	—
P/E – low	—	4	5	8	8	21	11	7	9	8	—
Dividends per share ($)	6.5%	0.68	0.72	0.76	0.76	0.76	0.76	0.82	1.01	1.20	1.20
Book value per share ($)	4.9%	20.76	22.47	23.74	25.04	25.03	26.24	28.64	30.67	33.08	32.05

1990 Year-end:
Debt ratio: 31.7%
Return on equity: —
Cash (mil.): $5
Current ratio: 2.54
Long-term debt (mil.): $260
No. of shares (mil.): 18
Dividends:
  1990 average yield: 5.3%
  1990 payout: —
Market value (mil.): $396

Stock Price History High/Low 1981–90

SQUARE D COMPANY

OVERVIEW

Formerly one of America's more stable companies, with only 2 annual losses in its 90-year history, Square D succumbed in 1991 to takeover by Paris-based Groupe Schneider, creating one of the world's largest manufacturers of electrical products.

Both Square D and Schneider produced electrical distribution equipment (such as transformers, connectors, and Square D's trademark safety switch) and industrial controls (including automation products, surge protectors, and process controls). The much larger Schneider (80,000 employees, FFr. 50 billion sales in 1989) shared (with Siemens and ABB Asea Brown Boveri) European dominance in these markets, while Square D held a solid position in the US marketplace. Neither had been able to expand beyond its base.

In 1988 Square D and Schneider began joint venture talks, which failed according to Square D, because Schneider insisted on an equity swap. In February 1991, Schneider offered $78 a share for Square D. Square D vigorously resisted, leading to suits and counter-suits, antitrust claims against Schneider, and preparations for a proxy fight to remove the Square D directors. After receiving tender offers for 69% of Square D's shares, Schneider sweetened its bid to $88 a share, which Square D accepted after learning that the US Justice Department would not intervene.

Schneider has promised not to disturb Square D in any way; yet, shortly after the takeover, Square D Chairman/President/CEO Jerre L. Stead resigned and Didier Pineau-Valencienne stepped in.

Private company
Fiscal year ends: December 31

Hoover's Rating **B-**

WHO

Chairman and CEO: Didier Pineau-Valencienne, age 59
EVP and COO: Charles W. Denny, age 55, $380,962 pay (prior to promotion)
EVP and CFO: Thomas L. Bindley, age 47, $320,885 pay
EVP, Industrial Control Sector: John C. Garrett, age 48, $269,037 pay
EVP, International Sector: Donald E. Marquart, age 53
VP Human Resources: Charles L. Hite, age 54
Auditors: Deloitte & Touche
Employees: 18,500

WHERE

HQ: 1415 S. Roselle, Palatine, IL 60067
Phone: 708-397-2600
Fax: 708-397-8814

Square D operates 33 plants in 31 US cities and 18 plants in 11 foreign countries.

	1990 Sales		1990 Operating Income	
	$ mil.	% of total	$ mil.	% of total
US	1,332	81	164	92
Europe	139	8	3	2
Latin America	79	5	10	6
Other countries	103	6	1	0
Total	**1,653**	**100**	**178**	**100**

WHAT

	1990 Sales		1990 Operating Income	
	$ mil.	% of total	$ mil.	% of total
Electrical distrib.	1,170	71	152	85
Industrial controls	483	29	26	15
Total	**1,653**	**100**	**178**	**100**

Electrical Distribution Sector
Connectors
Distribution equipment
Power equipment
Power protection systems
Transformers

Industrial Control Sector
Automation products
Control products
Engineered systems
Infrared measurement devices
Technical services

WHEN

In 1902 Bryson Horton and James McCarthy founded the McBride Manufacturing Company in Detroit to manufacture electrical fuses. In 1908 the company changed its name to Detroit Fuse and Manufacturing and bought the rights to an English invention, the Berry enclosed safety switch.

In 1915 Detroit Fuse marketed a new version of the switch with its logo — a "D" in a square — embossed on the cover. It was very successful, becoming known as the "square D" switch. The company sold its fuse business and changed its name to Square D in 1917. Sales topped $1 million in 1919. The Great Depression led to Square D's most recent annual loss, in 1932, but by 1937 the company had over $1 million in profits. Square D entered the aircraft instrumentation field in 1939, and by 1941 defense work accounted for 90% of the company's production.

The postwar construction boom made Square D's products fixtures in many new American homes, and the company's sales doubled by 1951. Throughout the 1950s and 1960s the company continued to broaden its line of products. Square D moved its headquarters to suburban Chicago in 1960.

During the 1970s the company added millions of square feet to its existing operations while also growing through acquisitions in the US and Europe.

In 1984 the company initiated programs to cut costs and boost productivity in response to intensifying global competition. By 1988 the work force had been reduced by 14% and 80 of the top 120 managers had been replaced.

Square D's management wrote in 1990 that "the company's future had never been brighter"; this optimism led to their being caught off guard by Schneider's unsolicited offer. Schneider CEO Didier Pineau-Valencienne (also known as "DPV" and "Doctor Attila"), a Dartmouth-trained former executive at Rhône-Poulenc, had restored Schneider's decaying fortunes and led France's first hostile takeover. With the aid of a weak dollar, he persuaded Square D shareholders (many of whom were Wall Street arbitrageurs) that the company, despite its bravado, could not effectively compete in a global economy.

RANKINGS

245th in *Fortune* 500 Industrial Cos.
356th in *Business Week* 1000

KEY COMPETITORS

ABB	Mitsubishi
AMP	Reliance Electric
Borg-Warner	Rockwell
Cooper Industries	Rolls-Royce
Daimler-Benz	Siemens
Eaton	Teledyne
Emerson	Texas Instruments
GEC	Thomson SA
General Electric	Westinghouse
General Signal	

HOW MUCH

	9-Year Growth	1981	1982	1983	1984	1985	1986	1987	1988	1989	1990
Sales ($ mil.)	4.2%	1,144	1,057	1,144	1,366	1,348	1,403	1,484	1,657	1,631	1,653
Net income ($ mil.)	1.4%	103	72	63	106	102	99	110	119	104	117
Income as % of sales	—	9.0%	6.8%	5.5%	7.8%	7.6%	7.0%	7.4%	7.2%	6.4%	7.1%
Earnings per share ($)	2.0%	3.82	2.61	2.22	3.71	3.52	3.40	3.79	4.42	3.99	4.57
Stock price – high ($)	—	37.38	34.75	41.25	41.50	43.63	50.00	65.50	55.75	62.75	60.25
Stock price – low ($)	—	24.38	21.75	30.38	31.13	35.13	39.25	43.00	45.38	47.50	33.88
Stock price – close ($)	6.2%	28.88	34.25	40.00	39.38	42.75	46.38	52.25	48.00	53.38	49.75
P/E – high	—	10	13	19	11	12	15	17	13	16	13
P/E – low	—	6	8	14	8	10	12	11	10	12	7
Dividends per share ($)	2.7%	1.74	1.84	1.84	1.84	1.84	1.84	1.86	2.04	2.00	2.20
Book value per share ($)	4.7%	17.50	17.32	17.70	19.17	21.00	23.16	24.57	24.76	23.68	26.37

1990 Year-end:
Debt ratio: 28.9%
Return on equity: 18.3%
Cash (mil.): $245
Current ratio: 2.05
Long-term debt (mil.): $245
No. of shares (mil.): 23
Dividends:
 1990 average yield: 4.4%
 1990 payout: 48.1%
Market value (mil.): $1,139

Stock Price History High/Low 1981–90

STANFORD UNIVERSITY

OVERVIEW

Stanford University, a private, coed institution located 30 miles south of San Francisco near Palo Alto, is widely regarded as one of the nation's finest schools. Enrollment at Stanford totals 13,445 students with a full-time faculty of 1,288 (97% have doctoral degrees).

Stanford is a member of the NCAA (Division 1) and, unlike its Ivy League colleagues, is nationally competitive.

Admission to Stanford is competitive as well: 81% of undergraduate applications for the 1989–90 school year were rejected. Approximately 40% of the students participate in overseas studies.

The school library system holdings consist of 5.5 million bound volumes, 3.1 million microforms, 5,000 periodical subscriptions, and 200,000 records and tapes. The Green Library (the main campus library) holds original works of such famous names as Martin Luther, Sir Isaac Newton, John Steinbeck, and William Butler Yeats.

Notable Stanford alumni include Herbert Hoover, William Rehnquist, Anthony Kennedy, Sandra Day O'Connor, John Elway, Ted Koppel, and Derek Bok (Harvard's former president). In 1991 financier alumnus Robert Bass gave the school $25 million.

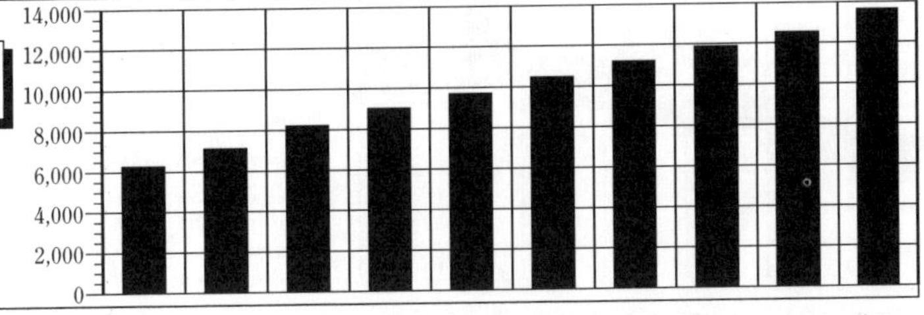

Private university
Fiscal year ends: August 31

Hoover's Rating **A**

WHO

President: Donald Kennedy
VP and Provost: James N. Rosse
Director of Admissions: Jean H. Fetter
Director of Financial Aid: Robert P. Huff
VP Finance: William F. Massy
Employees: 9,038

WHERE

HQ: Office of Admissions, Old Union, Leland Stanford, Jr., University, Stanford, CA 94305
Phone: 415-723-2300
Fax: 415-725-0247 (News Service)

Stanford University's 8,800-acre campus is adjacent to the suburban communities of Palo Alto and Menlo Park. The school operates study centers in France, Germany, Italy, Poland, and the UK.

Geographic Distribution of Freshman Class	% of Total
California	37
Other US	60
Foreign	3
Total	**100**

WHEN

In 1885 Senator Leland Stanford, a wealthy California railroad magnate (he built the Central Pacific Railroad) and former governor, and his wife Jane established Leland Stanford Junior University in Palo Alto in memory of their recently deceased son. The Stanfords provided land from their own estate and established an endowment of more than $20 million for the new school.

Although the buildings were still under construction, the university opened its doors in 1891 to a freshman class of 559 students, one of whom was future president Herbert Hoover. David Starr Jordan, the former president of Indiana University, became Stanford's first president.

Leland Stanford died in 1893, but the Stanford family continued to oversee the school's development until 1903, when Jane Stanford turned the university over to the board of trustees. In 1906 an earthquake centered in nearby San Francisco killed 2 people on the Stanford campus and destroyed the library and gymnasium. The university rebuilt and in 1909 affiliated itself with the Cooper School of Medicine (changed to Stanford College of Medicine in 1912). In 1912 Herbert Hoover was elected to the board of trustees, where he would sit for almost 50 years.

During WWI the university mobilized 1/2 of its students into the Students' Army Training Corps. In 1917 the School of Education was founded, and the Hoover War Collection (which would become the Hoover Institution on War, Revolution, and Peace) was established in 1919. In 1921 Stanford established its Food Research Institute and in 1925 opened its School of Engineering and its Graduate School of Business.

After WWII J. E. Wallace Sterling became president of the university and started the transformation of Stanford from an average California school to a world-class institution. Sterling worked to develop Stanford's reputation for teaching and research. In 1947 the School of Mineral Sciences was opened. Under Sterling, the university started leasing some of its nearby land holdings to electronics companies. This policy augmented Stanford's revenues and resulted in the formation of Silicon Valley, the nation's preeminent high-tech center, which is still closely associated with the school. William Hewlett and David Packard, 2 students at this time, formed their electronics company (Hewlett-Packard) with a $538 Stanford grant and have since become major contributors to the university.

In 1958 Stanford opened its first overseas campus (near Stuttgart, Germany) and in 1959 completed the Stanford Medical Center.

In 1980 Donald Kennedy became president, and subsequently launched a fund-raiser that brought in over $1 billion. Scandal struck in 1991, when it was revealed that Stanford had overcharged the US government as much as $200 million for overhead on research (some was spent on refurbishing Kennedy's mansion). The revelations prompted Kennedy to announce his resignation effective at the end of the 1991–92 academic year.

WHAT

	1990 Consolidated Budget	
	$ mil.	% of total
Linear Accelerator Center	131	14
Government research	196	20
Student aid expense	53	5
Endowment	76	8
Expendable gifts & grants	96	10
Tuition & fees	169	17
Other	254	26
Total	**975**	**100**

Academic Unit	1990 Enrollment	% of Total
Graduate School of Business	789	6
School of Earth Sciences	315	2
Graduate School of Education	315	2
School of Engineering	3,078	23
School of Humanities and Sciences	4,232	32
School of Law	532	4
School of Medicine	629	5
Undeclared	3,555	26
Total	**13,445**	**100**

Affiliated Institutions
Environmental and Water Quality Laboratory
Frederick E. Terman Engineering Center
Hoover Institution on War, Revolution, and Peace
Hopkin's Marine Station
Institute for Electronics in Medicine
Institute for Energy Studies
Institute for Plasma Research
Jasper Ridge Biological Preserve
John C. Blume Earthquake Engineering Center
Joint Institute for Aeronautics and Acoustics
Leland Stanford, Jr. Museum
Radio Astronomy Institute
Remote Sensing Laboratory
Stanford Linear Accelerator Center
Stanford Medical Center
Thomas Welton Stanford Art Gallery

KEY COMPETITORS

Harvard
Ohio State
University of Chicago
University of Texas

HOW MUCH

	9-Year Growth	1981	1982	1983	1984	1985	1986	1987	1988	1989	1990
Enrollment	0.5%	12,866	12,870	13,075	13,217	13,261	13,079	13,272	13,292	13,224	13,445
Faculty	0.5%	1,230	1,260	1,266	1,292	1,292	1,295	1,315	1,335	1,325	1,288
Student/faculty ratio	—	10.5	10.2	10.3	10.2	10.3	10.1	10.1	10.0	10.0	10.4
Tuition ($)	8.9%	6,285	7,140	8,220	9,027	9,705	10,476	11,208	11,880	12,564	13,569
Endowment market value ($ mil.)	13.2%	673	738	935	1,038	1,199	1,503	1,741	1,637	2,088	2,060

Annual Tuition ($) 1981–90

(bar chart, values ranging from 14,000 at top down to 0)

THE STANLEY WORKS

OVERVIEW

Stanley Works, a hardware manufacturer based in New Britain, Connecticut, is the world's leading producer of hand tools. The company's operations are divided into 2 industry segments: home improvement and consumer products (hand tools, hardware, and residential door systems), which accounts for 51% of sales and profits; and industrial and professional products (industrial and hydraulic tools, power-operated doors and gates, and high-density industrial storage and retrieval systems). The company hopes to rebound after recession hammered its sales flat in 1990.

The company has remained devoted to its core tool business and its reputation for quality. Aside from hand tools, Stanley claims a leadership position in hinges, pedestrian-powered doors, air-powered tools, fasteners, industrial storage and retrieval systems, and mounted and portable hydraulic tools.

Stanley has consolidated its market position through an aggressive acquisition policy begun in the 1980s, when Stanley bought 20 businesses. The company is bolstering its foreign operations with the 1991 acquisition of Nirva, a French fabricator of closet systems; Mosley-Stone, a UK maker of paintbrushes and decorator tools; and a joint venture with Poland's largest hand-tool manufacturer, Fabryka Narzedzi Kuznia.

NYSE symbol: SWK
Fiscal year ends: December 29

Hoover's Rating **B**

WHO

Chairman, President, and CEO: Richard H. Ayers, age 48, $782,410 pay
Group VP: David M. Hadlow, age 62, $415,100 pay
Group VP: Robert G. Widham, age 55, $406,309 pay
VP Finance and CFO: R. Alan Hunter, age 44, $343,131 pay
VP Human Resources: Paul A. Marier, age 62
Auditors: Ernst & Young
Employees: 17,784

WHEN

In 1843 Frederick T. Stanley opened a bolt shop in a converted War of 1812–era armory in New Britain, Connecticut. With the first steam engine used in New Britain industry, he produced bolts and house trimmings. In 1852 he teamed with his brother and 5 friends to form The Stanley Works to cast, form, and manufacture various types of metal.

The business prospered during the 1860s when the Civil War and westward migration created a need for hardware and tools. When Stanley started to devote less time to the business to concentrate on political and civic affairs, management of the company fell to William H. Hart.

Hart quickly demonstrated his competitive business ability. He expanded the company, engaging in a "knuckles-bared" fight with Stanley's 4 leading (and larger) competitors. Through a combination of innovation, efficiency, quality, and marketing, Hart emerged as the sole survivor. He led the company into steel strapping production, which would become a major element in Stanley's operations. He was named president in 1884.

Stanley entered a period of rapid expansion in the early 20th century. During WWI the company produced belt buckles and rifle and gas mask parts. In addition to numerous domestic acquisitions, the company established operations in Canada (1914) and Germany (1926). In 1920 the company merged with Stanley Rule and Level (a local tool company formed in 1857 by a cousin of Frederick Stanley) and in 1925 opened a new hydroelectric plant near Windsor to provide power for all its operations. In 1929 Stanley organized its electric tool division.

After a difficult decade caused by the Great Depression, Stanley geared up production in the early 1940s. Following WWII the company embarked on a massive period of expansion which lasted 4 decades. Staying within its traditional product line, Stanley acquired a myriad of companies, including Berry Industries (garage doors, 1965), Ackley Manufacturing and Sales (hydraulic tools, 1972), Mac Tools (1980), and National Hand Tool Corporation (1986). In the late 1980s the company grew globally by establishing high-tech plants in Europe and the Far East.

Newell Company made a brief bid in 1991 to buy as much as 25% of Stanley. To fend off a takeover, Stanley sued Newell on antitrust grounds and stoked the employee stock plan with about 25% of the outstanding stock. Newell backed off and turned its gaze on Black & Decker, buying 10% of the toolmaker.

WHERE

HQ: 1000 Stanley Dr., PO Box 7000, New Britain, CT 06050
Phone: 203-225-5111
Fax: 203-827-3901

The company operates manufacturing facilities in 19 states and 11 foreign countries.

	1990 Sales		1990 Operating Income	
	$ mil.	% of total	$ mil.	% of total
US	1,405	71	156	68
Europe	307	16	44	19
Other countries	265	13	29	13
Adjustments	—	—	(15)	—
Total	**1,977**	**100**	**214**	**100**

WHAT

	1990 Sales		1990 Operating Income	
	$ mil.	% of total	$ mil.	% of total
Home improvement & consumer products	999	51	112	49
Industrial & professional products	978	49	116	51
Adjustments	—	—	(14)	—
Total	**1,977**	**100**	**214**	**100**

Products	Rules
Air tools	Saws
Automatic parking gates	Screwdrivers
Bolts and brackets	Shelving
Chisels	Sockets
Closet organizers	Squares
Door hardware	Wrenches
Electronic controls	
Fasteners	**Brand Names**
Garage doors and openers	Lightmaker
Hammers	MAC mechanic's tools
Hasps	Powerlock
Hinges	Stanley
Hydraulic tools	Stanley-Bostitch
Industrial storage systems	Stanley-Proto
Knives	Stanley-Vidmar
Levels	Taylor Rental
Planes	U-install
Power-operated doors	

HOW MUCH

	9-Year Growth	1981	1982	1983	1984	1985	1986	1987	1988	1989	1990
Sales ($ mil.)	7.8%	1,009	963	984	1,158	1,208	1,371	1,763	1,909	1,972	1,977
Net income ($ mil.)	7.6%	55	38	53	72	78	78	96	103	118	107
Income as % of sales	—	5.5%	3.9%	5.4%	6.2%	6.5%	5.7%	5.5%	5.4%	6.0%	5.4%
Earnings per share ($)	6.9%	1.39	0.93	1.27	1.73	1.89	1.84	2.22	2.39	2.70	2.53
Stock price – high ($)	—	14.42	18.00	19.00	19.67	22.50	30.83	36.63	31.75	39.25	40.00
Stock price – low ($)	—	10.42	8.50	13.50	13.00	16.33	20.50	21.25	23.63	27.50	26.38
Stock price – close ($)	10.6%	11.67	16.33	18.17	17.25	21.33	25.50	25.88	28.50	39.00	29.00
P/E – high	—	10	19	15	11	12	17	17	13	15	16
P/E – low	—	7	9	11	8	9	11	10	10	10	10
Dividends per share ($)	10.1%	0.48	0.51	0.52	0.60	0.67	0.73	0.82	0.92	1.02	1.14
Book value per share ($)	6.4%	9.66	9.66	10.35	11.00	12.03	13.05	14.59	16.31	15.67	16.92

1990 Year-end:
Debt ratio: 36.4%
Return on equity: 15.5%
Cash (mil.): $95
Current ratio: 2.64
Long-term debt (mil.): $398
No. of shares (mil.): 41
Dividends:
  1990 average yield: 3.9%
  1990 payout: 45.1%
Market value (mil.): $1,194

Stock Price History High/Low 1981–90

RANKINGS

215th in *Fortune* 500 Industrial Cos.
415th in *Business Week* 1000

KEY COMPETITORS

Black & Decker	Masco
Cooper Industries	Robert Bosch
Emerson	Snap-on Tools
Ingersoll-Rand	Textron

STATE FARM

Mutual company
Fiscal year ends: December 31

 Hoover's Rating **A-**

OVERVIEW

State Farm Mutual Automobile Insurance, owned by policyholders but run for 70 years by 2 families, the Mercherles (1922–54) and the Rusts (1954–present), is the US's largest auto and homeowners' insurance underwriter, with 21% and 18% market share, respectively. Subsidiaries provide property and life insurance.

The company has over 58 million policies in force and over 18,500 agents who follow the company's small-town approach of being "Like a Good Neighbor," as advertised. Agents, who sell State Farm Products exclusively, target consumers who typically live near their neighborhood offices. The company has an unusually high agent retention rate (near 80% after 4 years).

State Farm Mutual maintains almost 1,000 offices in the US and Canada. The company has been able to maintain steady, profitable growth and low-cost insurance to policyholders by keeping risks and expenses low.

In 1990 the company experienced its worst single payment ever — $61 million — after a Colorado hailstorm. The effect of the new regulatory limits in California and other states remains unknown.

WHO

Chairman, President, and CEO: Edward B. Rust, Jr., age 41, $599,000 pay
VC, Financial VP, and Chief Investment Officer: Rex J. Bates, age 68
EVP and COO: Vincent J. Trosino, age 51
SVP and Treasurer: Roger S. Joslin, age 55
VP (Personnel): James E. Rutrough
Auditors: Coopers & Lybrand
Employees: 55,133

WHEN

Retired farmer George Mecherle founded State Farm Mutual Automobile Insurance Company in Bloomington, Illinois, in 1922.

Endorsed by the Illinois State Association of Mutual Insurance Companies, State Farm trained secretaries of the association's member organizations to sell its policies. State Farm restricted membership, primarily to members of farm bureaus and farm mutual insurance companies, and charged a one-time membership fee and a premium to protect an automobile against loss or damage.

From the beginning State Farm, unlike most of its competitors, offered semiannual premium payments, which were easier to sell because customers had to pay only 6 months instead of a year in advance. State Farm also billed and collected renewal premiums from its home office, relieving the agent of the task. Another State Farm feature was a simplified system of classifying all automobiles into 7 classes, A to G, instead of charging separate rates for each auto model, as most stock (nonmutual) companies did.

Before the end of its first year, State Farm had placed policies in 46 rural Illinois counties. In order to insure autos of nonfarmers, the company in 1926 started City and Village Mutual Automobile Insurance Company, which became part of State Farm the following year. Between 1927 and 1931 State Farm introduced wind coverage, borrowed-car protection, and insurance for buses or cars used in transporting children to school.

State Farm opened a branch office in Berkeley, California, in 1928 and started State Farm Life Insurance Company, a wholly owned subsidiary, in 1929. In 1935 the company established State Farm Fire Insurance Company. President George Mecherle became chairman in 1937, and his son Ramond assumed the presidency. George Mecherle remained active in the company, challenging company agents in 1939 to write "A Million or More (auto policies) by '44." State Farm passed the one million mark in 5-1/2 years, with a 110% increase in policies.

In the 1940s State Farm began to concentrate more on metropolitan areas after most of the farm bureaus canceled their contracts with State Farm to form their own companies. By 1941 State Farm was the largest insurance company in total automobile premiums written. In the late 1940s and 1950s, the company moved to a full-time agency force.

In the late 1970s the company was hit by several sex discrimination suits (some still pending). Since then the company has tried to hire more women and minorities.

A series of disasters in 1989 brought State Farm the highest claims payments in its history, resulting in a 42% decline in earnings. Losses continued in 1990.

In the face of increasing state regulation (which State Farm adamantly opposed), the company has instructed its Pennsylvania agents to stop writing new auto business. Following the passage of California's Proposition 103, which prompted other insurers to start pulling out of the state, State Farm faced the dilemma of using the exodus to pick up market share or guarding against taking on risky new clients.

WHERE

HQ: State Farm Mutual Automobile Insurance Company, One State Farm Plaza, Bloomington, IL 61710
Phone: 309-766-2311
Fax: 309-766-6169

State Farm has operations in all 50 states, the District of Columbia, and Canada.

WHAT

	1990 Assets	
	$ mil.	% of total
Bonds	20,095	54
Cash	399	1
Stocks	7,478	20
Equity in subsidiaries	5,376	14
Other	4,160	11
Total	**37,508**	**100**

Financial Services
Automobile insurance
Fire insurance
Homeowners insurance
Life insurance
Inland marine insurance

Subsidiaries
State Farm Fire and Casualty Co.
State Farm General Insurance Co.
State Farm Life Insurance Co.
State Farm County Mutual Insurance Co. of Texas
State Farm Lloyds

RANKINGS

21st in *Fortune* 50 Life Insurance Cos.

KEY COMPETITORS

Aetna	MassMutual
American Financial	MetLife
AIG	New York Life
Berkshire Hathaway	Northwestern Mutual
CIGNA	Primerica
Equitable	Prudential
First Executive	Sears
GEICO	Teachers Insurance
General Re	Transamerica
ITT	Travelers
John Hancock	USF&G
Kemper	Other insurance
Loews	companies

HOW MUCH

	9-Year Growth	1981	1982	1983	1984	1985	1986	1987	1988	1989	1990
Assets ($ mil.)	14.0%	11,537	13,197	15,375	16,671	19,695	23,679	27,101	30,922	35,493	37,508
Income ($ mil.)	(2.1%)	450	491	691	808	666	1,033	1,041	721	419	372
Income as % of assets	—	3.9%	3.7%	4.5%	4.8%	3.4%	4.4%	3.8%	2.3%	1.2%	1.0%
Employees[1]	—	31,955	32,447	32,450	34,160	37,543	40,748	44,086	48,082	52,236	55,133

1990 Year-end:
Equity as % of assets: 25.9%
Return on equity: 1.9%
Cash (mil.): $399
Sales (mil.): $18,208

Assets (mil.) 1981–90

[1] Employees of State Farm Insurance Companies only

THE STOP & SHOP COMPANIES, INC.

OVERVIEW

Stop & Shop, based near Boston, is one of the largest private companies in New England. It operates 117 Stop & Shop supermarkets and 130 Bradlees discount department stores in the eastern US.

Stop & Shop is getting its house in order after the 1988 LBO that, with the assistance of takeover maven Kohlberg Kravis Roberts, took the company private. Chairman Avram Goldberg and his wife, President Carol Goldberg, daughter of the founding Rabb family, quit abruptly in 1989 over differences with KKR, and Lewis Schaeneman succeeded Avram Goldberg as CEO.

Stop & Shop is highly leveraged. Some Bradlees stores have been sold to reduce debt. In 1991 the company extended the maturity date and reset the interest rate on $371 million of its debt. To get out from under some of its debt and to increase the paper value of its holdings, KKR announced in late 1991 that it would take the company public, selling 33% to the public for about $250 million.

Private company
Fiscal year ends: Saturday nearest January 31

Hoover's Rating **D**

WHO

Chairman and CEO: Lewis G. Schaeneman, Jr.
SVP, General Counsel, Clerk, and Secretary: Samuel W. W. Mandell
SVP Administration (Personnel): Donald J. Comeau
SVP, Treasurer, and CFO: Joseph D. McGlinchey
President and COO, Stop & Shop Co.: Robert G. Tobin
President and COO, Bradlees Discount Department Store: Barry Berman
Auditors: KPMG Peat Marwick
Employees: 42,100

WHERE

HQ: PO Box 369, Boston, MA 02101
Phone: 617-380-8000
Fax: 617-380-5915 (Public Affairs)

Stop & Shop operates 117 supermarkets in the Northeast. The Bradlees Discount Department Store Company has 130 locations in the Northeast and Virginia.

	No. of Stores	
States	**Stop & Shop stores**	**Bradlees stores**
Pennsylvania	—	10
New Jersey	—	32
Connecticut	47	26
Massachusetts	58	38
New York	1	10
Maine	—	4
New Hampshire	—	8
Rhode Island	11	—
Virginia	—	2
Total	**117**	**130**

WHAT

	Approximate Sales
	% of total
Stop & Shop Supermarket	62
Bradlees	38
Total	**100**

Stop & Shop Supermarkets

Stop & Shop Manufacturing
Bakery operations
Carbonated beverage processing
Commissaries
Cooked meat processing
Dairy operations
Household chemical manufacturing
Photo processing
Recycling operations
Salad processing
Seafood processing

Bradlees Discount Stores
General merchandise

WHEN

Stop & Shop was originally formed as the Economy Grocery Stores chain by the Rabinovitz family in Boston in 1914. By 1925, the year that guiding force Sidney Rabinovitz (later shortened to Rabb) became chairman, the company had 262 stores in the Boston area. Through the purchase of additional locations from Rood & Woodbury (1929) and United-Gray Stores (1932), the company grew to more than 400 stores. During the Great Depression, Economy Grocery Stores opened a massive store at the site of a former Ford assembly plant, which was to be one of the earliest supermarkets in the US. The larger stores were dubbed Stop & Shop Supermarkets.

By 1945 the company operated 120 stores in Massachusetts and Vermont, 79 of which were operating under the Stop & Shop name. Stop & Shop was adopted as the corporate name in 1946.

The company expanded into discount department stores in 1961 with the purchase of the 7-store Bradlees chain and entered the discount drugstore market by launching Medi Mart (1968). Stop & Shop acquired Charles B. Perkins Tobacco Shops, an eastern New England chain, which it proceeded to develop as Hallmark Cards gift shops (1969).

A 1969 fire at the Readville, Massachuestts, food distribution center hobbled supermarket operations for a time, and Rabb pushed to diversify by adding new Bradlees, Medi Mart, and Perkins locations.

In 1978 the company started Raxton Corporation, which operated women's clothing stores under the names Off the Rax and Raxton, Ltd., but Stop & Shop sold the company to Dress Barn in 1984. It continued to add stores, expanding its grocery and discount drug chains along the Eastern Seaboard. In the mid-1980s the department store segment grew through the purchase of 19 Almy Stores (New York and New England) and 18 Jefferson Ward stores, acquired from Montgomery Ward (Philadelphia and Delaware), reaching 171 locations by the end of 1987. But the expanded Bradlees operations struggled against such strong competitors as Caldor. Bradlees, which accounted for almost 1/2 of Stop & Shop's revenues, had positioned itself at the upscale end of the discount store market, which was hurt when customers sought lower prices.

In 1985 Rabb died, and son-in-law Avram Goldberg, who had been CEO since 1979, was named chairman. His wife, Carol Goldberg (Rabb's daughter), was named president.

In 1986 Stop & Shop sold its Medi Mart and Perkins chains in order to focus on its grocery and department stores. Walgreen bought the 67 Medi Mart stores, and the Perkins chain was divided among 3 purchasers. In 1988 the Haft family's Dart Group made a hostile takeover bid. The Goldbergs turned to Kohlberg Kravis Roberts, which staged a $1.3 billion LBO and took the company private. To reduce Stop & Shop's debt, the company sold 70 locations of the Bradlees chain and trimmed 450 employees from the headquarters payroll.

The Goldbergs, who reportedly made $22 million from the LBO, resigned unexpectedly after 30 years of service in 1989, and Lewis Schaeneman, Jr., was named chairman and CEO. In 1991 black widow spiders were found in grapes in company stores. The company quickly responded by allowing customers to bring back any grapes about which there was a concern.

RANKINGS

26th in *Fortune* 50 Retailing Cos.
23rd in *Forbes* 400 US Private Cos.

KEY COMPETITORS

American Stores	Great A&P	Riklis Family
Ames	Kmart	Supermarkets
Dayton Hudson	Price Co.	General

HOW MUCH

	9-Year Growth	1981	1982	1983	1984	1985	1986	1987	1988	1989	1990
Sales ($ mil.)	9.7%	2,168	2,342	2,791	3,247	3,689	3,872	4,343	4,624	4,636	4,990
Net income ($ mil.)	(23.5%)	25	35	51	55	30	44	56	(22)	(23)	2
Income as % of sales	—	1.1%	1.5%	1.8%	1.7%	0.8%	1.1%	1.3%	(0.5%)	(0.5%)	0.0%
Employees	5.5%	26,000	29,000	35,000	39,000	48,000	46,000	44,000	44,000	42,000	42,100

1990 Year-end:
Debt ratio: 93.1%
Return on equity: 2.3%
Cash (mil.): $15
Current ratio: 0.95
Long-term debt (mil.): $1,276
No. of shares (mil.): 21

Net Income ($ mil.) 1981–90

STORAGE TECHNOLOGY CORPORATION

NYSE symbol: STK
Fiscal year ends: Last Friday in December

Hoover's Rating **B-**

OVERVIEW

Storage Technology, based in Louisville, Colorado, is a world leader in computer data storage and retrieval systems, ranking first in tape drives and 4th in disk drives.

StorageTek's products are designed for IBM mainframe and other high-performance computers. Besting its prime competitor, IBM, StorageTek introduced the first solid-state disk drives (fast, high-density) and the first automated mass tape storage system (the Automated Cartridge System, or ACS), an automated robotic cartridge handling system.

StorageTek's tape products, which account for 73% of the firm's revenues, have the highest reliability statistics in the industry. Other products include printers and specialized data storage management software. StorageTek's Consulting Group expanded its service offerings by teaming with insurer American International Group in 1991 to provide customer automation planning and implementation.

The company's 1987 emergence from bankruptcy was fueled by booming demand for the ACS. While revenues from sales of its disk system products declined 18% in 1990, StorageTek's tape system products—led by ACS sales—increased 33%, driven by the needs of PC networks for a central storage system.

WHEN

A group of 4 former IBM engineers founded Storage Technology in Colorado in 1969 to fill a niche in tape drives for IBM-compatible mainframe computers. One of the founders, a Palestinian refugee named Jesse Aweida, led the company (dubbed StorageTek) to the top of its industry.

Heady growth inspired StorageTek to become a full-line supplier of peripherals. Acquisitions included Promodata (1973), Disk Systems (1974), Microtechnology (1979), and Documation (1980). The company also began developing an IBM-compatible mainframe computer and an optical laser disk.

The Aweida whirlwind swept StorageTek's sales from $4 million to $922 million between 1971 and 1981, creating the world's leading supplier of tape drives (55% market share for IBM-compatible tape drives) and disk drives (35%) and the 9th largest company in the computer industry.

In 1982, however, delayed expansion projects ate capital while providing no return. In addition, malfunctions on disk drives installed earlier caused costly replacements and damage to the company's reputation. Aweida's termination of several product lines could not prevent a cash-flow crisis, and in late 1984 StorageTek filed for bankruptcy.

Aweida stepped down, and turnaround artist Ryal Poppa (CEO in 1985) sliced $85 million in expenses by eliminating 2 layers of management, 5,000 workers (down to 9,000), and the mainframe and optical disk projects.

Although awash in red ink, Poppa was able to convince creditors to fund his vision of automated tape storage at a fraction of disk drive prices. The resulting 4400 ACS (1987) was instrumental to the company's success after its emergence from bankruptcy in 1987. The company's Library Server software has allowed StorageTek to adapt the ACS for most vendors' high-performance computers, reducing StorageTek's dependence on IBM machines.

In 1989 the company purchased Aspen Peripherals to enter the mid-range tape market. Aspen president Jesse Aweida did not rejoin the company he helped found.

In 1991 StorageTek established a joint venture with Siemens Nixdorf, merging its high-performance nonimpact printer operations into a limited partnership, and also agreed to purchase troubled computer distributor XL/Datacomp for $150 million.

An advanced, fault-tolerant disk drive line using the inexpensive disks of personal computers (disk array architecture) is scheduled for 1992.

WHO

Chairman, CEO, and President: Ryal R. Poppa, age 57, $1,207,574 pay
EVP Europe, Africa, and Middle East Operations: Harris Ravine, age 48, $442,843 pay (prior to promotion)
EVP Worldwide Field Operations: Derek Thompson
EVP Operations: Lowell Thomas Gooch, age 46, $288,347 pay
EVP: Geoffroy de Belloy, age 54
SVP and CFO: Gregory A. Tymn, age 41, $282,056 pay (prior to promotion)
VP Human Resources: Sewell I. Sleek, age 54
Auditors: Price Waterhouse
Employees: 9,100

WHERE

HQ: 2270 S. 88th St., Louisville, CO 80028-0001
Phone: 303-673-5151
Fax: 303-673-5019

StorageTek has operations in the US, Canada, Europe, Japan, and Australia. Manufacturing facilities are located in the US and the UK.

	1990 Sales		1990 Operating Income	
	$ mil.	% of total	$ mil.	% of total
US	728	64	89	94
Europe	305	27	7	8
Other countries	108	9	(2)	(2)
Adjustments	—	—	(13)	—
Total	**1,141**	**100**	**81**	**100**

WHAT

	1990 Sales	
	$ mil.	% of total
Sales	815	71
Rental & service	326	29
Total	**1,141**	**100**

	1990 Sales	
	$ mil.	% of total
Tape systems	833	73
Disk systems	183	16
Printer subsystems	125	11
Total	**1,141**	**100**

Disk Systems	6100 series nonimpact
Disk controllers	
Rotating magnetic	**Tape Systems**
8380 family	4400 ACS library
Solid state	4480 18-track
4080	4980 18-track
4305	9914/13 9-track
	Summit 4180 18-track
Printers	Summit 4280 18-track
5000 series impact	
	Software
Siemens Nixdorf Printing	Expert Library Manager
(49%)	Library Server (for ACS) for
6024 nonimpact	Bull HNSA, Cray, Unisys,
6060 nonimpact	Control Data

RANKINGS

311th in *Fortune* 500 Industrial Cos.
539th in *Business Week* 1000

KEY COMPETITORS

Amdahl	Hitachi	NEC
Control Data	IBM	Siemens
Fujitsu	Machines Bull	Tandem

HOW MUCH

	9-Year Growth	1981	1982	1983	1984	1985	1986	1987	1988	1989	1990
Sales ($ mil.)	2.4%	922	1,079	887	809	673	696	750	874	983	1,141
Net income ($ mil.)	(1.7%)	82	63	(9)	(505)	(44)	17	19	44	36	71
Income as % of sales	—	8.9%	5.9%	(1.1%)	(62.5%)	(6.5%)	2.4%	2.5%	5.1%	3.7%	6.2%
Earnings per share ($)	(23.4%)	25.00	18.40	(2.80)	(146.20)	(12.60)	4.80	0.80	1.90	1.40	2.26
Stock price – high ($)	—	403.75	361.25	250.00	146.25	38.75	73.75	50.00	36.25	22.50	35.25
Stock price – low ($)	—	177.50	162.50	135.00	20.00	10.00	17.50	11.25	12.50	9.25	11.00
Stock price – close ($)	(26.7%)	350.00	212.50	136.25	22.50	17.50	35.00	18.75	17.50	11.75	21.50
P/E – high	—	16	20	—	—	—	15	63	19	16	16
P/E – low	—	7	9	—	—	—	4	14	7	7	5
Dividends per share ($)	—	0.00	0.00	0.00	0.00	0.00	0.00	0.00	0.00	0.00	0.00
Book value per share ($)	(21.3%)	139.70	159.21	147.03	0.81	(15.69)	(5.20)	10.23	12.46	13.12	16.15

1990 Year-end:
Debt ratio: 29.0%
Return on equity: 15.4%
Cash (mil.): $64
Current ratio: 1.72
Long-term debt (mil.): $216
No. of shares (mil.): 33
Dividends:
  1990 average yield: 0.0%
  1990 payout: 0.0%
Market value (mil.): $706

Stock Price History High/Low 1981–90

STROH COMPANIES INC.

OVERVIEW

Headquartered in Detroit, privately owned Stroh is the 4th largest US brewer (1990 sales about $1.3 billion), producing such beers as Stroh's, Schlitz, Schaefer, and Old Milwaukee. Since its founding in 1850, the brewery has rested firmly in the hands of the Stroh family, descendants of founder Bernhard Stroh, who own 100% of the company.

Once a regional operation, Stroh rose to prominence during the 1980s through aggressive marketing and acquisition of brewers F&M Schaefer and Schlitz. Until recently, Stroh held the #3 spot in the country but was passed in 1990 by Adolph Coors, who almost bought Stroh in 1989. Today the company's position continues to slip, with beer shipments dropping 12% in 1990.

The company brews its flagship brand, Stroh's beer, by its noted fire-brewing process, in which copper brewing kettles are heated over an open flame rather than by steam, the method used by other US brewers. Aside from adding to the mystique of the product, fire-brewing, according to the company, produces a better-tasting beer.

Although beer is the central focus of the company, Stroh's nonbrewing subsidiaries have operations in alcoholic coolers (made with malt rather than the usual wine) and real estate.

WHEN

Bernhard Stroh fled Germany in 1848 to escape the German Revolution. In 1850 he settled in Detroit, establishing a brewery to make Bohemian-style beer. Stroh expanded his operation and named it the Lion's Head Brewery, adopting a logo from the Kyrburg Castle in his native town of Kirn.

When Stroh died in 1882, his son Bernhard Stroh, Jr., took charge. Bernhard operated the company until 1908, when management passed to his brother Julius, who renamed the brewery the Stroh Brewing Company.

Julius Stroh embarked on a tour of European breweries and brought back the fire-brewing process that is still a hallmark of the company. To survive Prohibition, Stroh shifted production to alcohol-free beer, malt products, soft drinks, and ice cream.

Following Julius's death in 1939, the company's management passed from one family member to the next, with little change excepting the 1964 purchase of the Goebel Brewery (which was across the street from Stroh in Detroit). Peter Stroh, great-grandson of the company's founder, became president in 1968 and shifted away from the company's previously conservative pattern.

During the early 1970s the local market was ailing alongside the auto industry, and Anheuser-Busch and Miller were making life miserable for many regional brewers; subsequently, Peter Stroh made the decision to go national. He hired a team of savvy marketers and in 1978 launched Stroh's Light, the company's first new product in 128 years. By 1979 Stroh's was sold in 17 states.

In 1981 Stroh acquired the F&M Schaefer Brewing Corporation in New York and became the 7th largest brewer in the US. The company jumped into the 3rd largest spot the following year by acquiring the Schlitz brewing company, which was founded in Milwaukee in 1849 by August Krug. Joseph Schlitz, formerly Krug's bookkeeper, named the brewery for himself after Krug died. After Schlitz's death, the company was managed by Krug's descendants (the wealthy Uihlein family) and became the nation's leading brewery for a short time during the 1950s, although it had sunk to the #3 spot at the time Stroh bought it.

In the 1980s Stroh's advertising became more upscale as it tried to play down its blue-collar image. Notable during this time was the "From One Beer Lover to Another" campaign. Finding itself unable to effectively compete against Miller and Anheuser-Busch for prime time sports advertising spots, the company began its Stroh Circle of Sports, a program that featured live sporting events with professional commentary, in the mid-1980s. Stroh also began its "Schlitz Rocks America" concert series.

In 1985 the company introduced White Mountain Cooler and Sundance (a sparkling-water fruit drink; sold to a partnership that included Guinness, Stroh, and a management group in 1989). In 1989 Adolph Coors proposed to buy Stroh, but the 2 companies could not reach an agreement. Stroh then made an unsuccessful pass at Heileman (which has recently filed for bankruptcy). In 1990 the company sold its Memphis brewery to Coors.

Private company
Fiscal year ends: March 31

WHO

Chairman: Peter W. Stroh, age 64
First VC: John W. Stroh, Jr., age 56
Second VC: Harold A. Ruemenapp, age 62
President: William L. Henry, age 43
SVP Operations: James R. Avery
SVP and CFO: Christopher T. Sortwell
Director of Human Resources: Bob Inskeep
Auditors: Deloitte & Touche
Employees: 3,732

WHERE

HQ: 100 River Place, Detroit, MI 48207-4225
Phone: 313-446-2000
Fax: 313-446-2206

The company operates breweries in Allentown, PA; Longview, TX; St. Paul, MN; Tampa, FL; and Winston-Salem, NC.

WHAT

Brands
Erlanger
Goebel
Old Milwaukee
Old Milwaukee Light
Piels Draft Style
Piels Lights
Primo
Schaefer
Schaefer Light
Schlitz
Schlitz Light
Schlitz Malt Liquor
Schlitz Red Bull
Signature
Silver Thunder
Stroh's
Stroh's Light

Subsidiaries
Stroh Brewery Company
Stroh Cooler Company
Stroh Properties Inc.
Strohtech Inc. (R&D)

RANKINGS

112th in *Forbes* 400 US Private Cos.

KEY COMPETITORS

Adolph Coors
Allied-Lyons
Anheuser-Busch
Bass
Bond
BSN
Carlsberg
Foster's Brewing
Gallo
Guinness
Heineken
John Labatt
Kirin
Philip Morris
San Miguel
Seagram

HOW MUCH

Fiscal year ends March of following year	9-Year Growth	1981	1982	1983	1984	1985	1986	1987	1988	1989	1990
Estimated sales ($ mil.)	—	—	—	—	—	1,600	1,500	1,500	1,450	1,300	1,293
US sales (thou. of barrels)	6.5%	9,133	22,900	24,300	23,900	23,400	22,400	21,600	20,520	18,250	16,100
US market share (%)	—	5.2	13.0	13.7	13.4	13.1	12.6	11.9	11.3	9.9	8.3
Employees	—	—	—	—	—	6,000	6,000	5,000	5,000	3,500	3,732

US Sales (thou. of barrels) 1981–90

SUN COMPANY, INC.

OVERVIEW

Sun is the 11th largest petroleum refiner in the US. The company spun off its domestic production as independent Oryx Energy in 1988 but continues to drill for and produce oil and natural gas internationally, mostly in the UK sector of the North Sea.

Still, more than 90% of Sun's 1990 sales came from refining and marketing. Sun's refining and marketing group operates 5 US refineries that can process 600,000 barrels of crude oil a day. Sun owns 4 ocean tankers,

pipeline interests, and petroleum terminals. In 23 eastern states, the company sells gasoline in 6,054 Sunoco and Atlantic service stations. The company is focusing on high-volume gas and food sales, converting promising gasoline outlets to convenience stores with pumps.

Sun owns 75% of Suncor, an integrated petroleum company (from drilling to refining to marketing) in Canada. Subsidiary Sun Coal boasts 806 million tons of reserves in its mines in 5 states.

WHEN

Joseph Newton Pew began his energy career in 1876 in a Pennsylvania natural gas pipeline partnership. One arm of his enterprise supplied Pittsburgh with the first-ever natural gas system for a major city's home and industrial use.

When oil discoveries in northwest Ohio sparked an 1886 boom, Pew organized Sun Oil Line, consolidated in 1890 as Sun Oil (Ohio). In an 1894 transaction, Sun created Diamond Oil to purchase a Toledo refinery; Sun traces its trademark diamond pierced by an arrow to that short-lived Diamond subsidiary.

With the 1901 Spindletop gusher, Pew dispatched nephew J. Edgar Pew to Texas, where he bought land for a storage terminal and in 1902 won an auction for oil-rich properties of a bankrupt firm. Back East, the elder Pew bought Delaware River acreage in Pennsylvania for a shipping terminal and refinery to process Texas crude into Red Stock. The lubricating oil carved Sun a place in the Standard Oil–dominated petroleum industry.

Joseph Newton Pew died in 1912 and was succeeded by sons J. Howard, 30, and Joseph Newton, Jr., 26. The young Pews launched the company into shipbuilding (1916) and gasoline stations (1920). Sun's gasoline was dyed blue (legend says it matched a Chinese tile chip Joe Pew and his wife had received on their honeymoon) and sold as Blue Sunoco.

When Howard Pew retired in 1947, brother Joe became chairman and Robert Dunlop

became the first non-Pew president of Sun. Dunlop led the company to the first major foreign oil strike, in Venezuela's Lake Maracaibo in 1957.

In 1967, Dunlop's chance meeting with a Sunray DX executive in Midland, Texas, led Sun to acquire Sunray DX the next year. The addition of Sunray DX diluted the Pew family's stake in the company. In the 1970s President Robert Sharbaugh diversified the company away from its energy roots. The company dropped "oil" from its name in 1976. Sharbaugh left in 1978 after Sun's foray into the medical supply business.

To refocus on the oil business, the company purchased Seagram's Texas Pacific Oil for $2.3 billion in 1980, sold its venerable shipbuilding arm in 1982, and sold the medical supply business in 1985. In 1988 Sun acquired Atlantic Petroleum and its more than 1,000 service stations. Sun decided to forsake drilling in the US when, in 1988, it spun off its domestic oil and gas properties into the company renamed Oryx Energy in 1989. Sun retained its international exploration and production business. Sun curtailed its leasing activities in 1990 and said it would halve its real estate portfolio in 1991.

Sun began another transition in 1991 when it named Robert Campbell president and COO. Seven months later, Chairman Robert McClements relinquished the CEO title to Campbell.

WHO

Chairman: Robert McClements, Jr., age 62, $972,192 pay
President and CEO: Robert H. Campbell, age 53, $485,664 pay (prior to promotions)
SVP Finance: Robert M. Aiken, Jr., age 48
SVP Human Resources and Administration: Bill N. Rutherford, age 58, $347,319 pay
Auditors: Coopers & Lybrand
Employees: 20,926

WHERE

HQ: 100 Matsonford Rd., Radnor, PA 19087-4597
Phone: 215-293-6000
Fax: 215-293-6204

Sun operates in the US, Canada, and 12 other foreign countries.

	1990 Sales		1990 Net Income	
	$ mil.	% of total	$ mil.	% of total
US	10,055	76	177	67
Canada	1,587	12	86	32
Other countries	1,628	12	2	1
Adjustments	(1,458)	—	(66)	—
Total	**11,812**	**100**	**199**	**100**

WHAT

	1990 Sales		1990 Operating Income	
	$ mil.	% of total	$ mil.	% of total
Exploration & production	463	3	141	28
Refining & mktg.	12,078	91	264	53
Mining	433	3	118	23
Real estate & leasing	296	2	(20)	(4)
Adjustments	(1,458)	—	(53)	—
Total	**11,812**	**100**	**450**	**100**

Subsidiaries
Sun International E&P (exploration and production outside the US)
Sun Refining and Marketing Co.
Sun Coal Co. (coal mining in Kentucky, Utah, Virginia, West Virginia, Wyoming)
Suncor Inc. (75%, Canadian petroleum exploration, production, marketing; mining; synthetic crude oil production)
Radnor Corp. (real estate development)
Helios Capital Corp. (equipment leasing, secured lending)
Sunoco Credit Corp. (commercial paper)

HOW MUCH

	9-Year Growth	1981	1982	1983	1984	1985	1986	1987	1988	1989	1990
Sales ($ mil.)	(2.6%)	15,012	15,519	14,730	14,466	13,769	9,376	8,691	8,612	9,805	11,812
Net income ($ mil.)	(17.1%)	1,076	537	453	538	527	385	348	7	98	199
Income as % of sales	—	7.2%	3.5%	3.1%	3.7%	3.8%	4.1%	4.0%	0.1%	1.0%	1.7%
Earnings per share ($)	(15.6%)	8.59	4.40	3.78	4.59	4.65	3.51	3.18	0.06	0.92	1.86
Stock price – high ($)	—	49.38	45.75	46.50	59.50	56.25	59.50	73.13	61.75	43.25	41.88
Stock price – low ($)	—	29.00	26.75	30.25	43.38	43.63	42.25	36.00	28.00	31.38	25.75
Stock price – close ($)	(5.3%)	45.50	31.38	43.75	46.13	51.75	54.25	51.38	32.13	40.88	27.88
P/E – high	—	6	10	12	13	12	17	23	1,029	47	23
P/E – low	—	3	6	8	9	9	12	11	467	34	14
Dividends per share ($)	(1.3%)	2.03	2.25	2.30	2.30	2.30	3.00	3.00	2.70	1.80	1.80
Book value per share ($)	(3.3%)	41.87	43.95	45.08	46.80	48.71	49.03	49.36	31.24	30.50	30.83

1990 Year-end:
Debt ratio: 30.8%
Return on equity: 6.1%
Cash (mil.): $298
Current ratio: 0.96
Long-term debt (mil.): $1,459
No. of shares (mil.): 106
Dividends:
  1990 average yield: 6.5%
  1990 payout: 96.8%
Market value (mil.): $2,960

**Stock Price History
High/Low 1981–90**

RANKINGS

37th in *Fortune* 500 Industrial Cos.
186th in *Business Week* 1000

KEY COMPETITORS

Amoco	Occidental
Ashland	Oryx
Atlantic Richfield	Pennzoil
British Petroleum	Petrofina
Chevron	PDVSA
Coastal	Pemex
Du Pont	Phillips Petroleum
Elf Aquitaine	Royal Dutch/Shell
Exxon	Texaco
Imperial Oil	Unocal
Koch	USX
Mobil	Convenience store
Norsk Hydro	operators

SUN MICROSYSTEMS, INC.

OVERVIEW

Sun Microsystems is the world's leading supplier of workstations (powerful, high-resolution color graphics computers), with almost 38% of the market. Workstations are the computer industry's fastest-growing segment, with 30% yearly growth expected over the next 5 years. *Wünderkind* Sun has shipped over 400,000 computers since its birth in 1982 and had entered the *Fortune* 500 and exceeded $1 billion in sales by its 6th year. While growth of other computer makers has slowed, Sun continues to report record increases (revenues up 40% in 1990).

Sun has hitched its star to client/server computing — distributing processing across networks of desktop (client) and larger (server) machines. For this to work in practice Sun promotes open systems (where computers of different vendors communicate freely). The company was a pioneer in supporting the UNIX operating system and the widespread licensing of its SPARC microprocessors and workstation connectivity software.

Engineering clients (design, manufacturing) still predominate; however, sales to commercial users (electronic publishing, financial services, etc.) are taking off. It is estimated that 30% of Sun's revenues are from commercial sales in 1991 compared to 8% in 1990.

WHEN

The 4 27-year-olds who founded Sun Microsystems in 1982 saw great market potential for workstations able to share data using the UNIX operating system so popular with scientists and engineers.

German-born Andreas Bechtolsheim, a Stanford engineering graduate student, had built a workstation from spare parts for his numerical problems. Two Stanford MBA graduates, Scott McNealy and India-born Vinod Khosla, liked Bechtolsheim's creation, and they tapped Berkeley's UNIX guru William Joy to supply the software.

By adopting AT&T's UNIX operating system, Sun's workstations, unlike those of industry pioneer Apollo, from the outset networked easily with the hardware and software of other vendors. Sun, with lower prices afforded by existing technologies, zoomed to $500 million in sales in just 5 years, with only one major ad campaign.

The engineering market devoured such Sun offerings as the Sun-3 family (1985) and the 386i (1987). Sun hooked its workstations into networks with its NFS (a file access system widely adopted by others), SunNet, and SunLINK.

In 1987 Sun signed with AT&T to develop an enhanced UNIX operating system; AT&T took a 19% equity investment in Sun the following year (sold in 1991). The product that emerged in late 1989 established a de facto high-end UNIX standard (System V, Release 4.0). Sun's development of the fast and highly adaptable SPARC microprocessor (which uses a simplified RISC design) gave its SPARCstation 2 (1990) minicomputer power.

Sun licensed SPARC to stimulate low-cost, high-volume production of SPARC systems and thus increase the number of 3rd-party applications available. Its open software strategy has paid off with over 2,800 software packages available for its machines—more than for any other workstation. PC programs such as Lotus 1-2-3, WordPerfect, and Ashton-Tate's dBASE IV for Sun systems have broadened Sun's commercial market.

With workstations now so clonable, Sun maintains short product life cycles (average 12 months) and high R&D (12% of revenues). The company has also restricted Sun dealers from selling Sun clones.

Sun continued its record pace in the first 9 months of fiscal 1991, doubling its profits on a 29% sales increase over the same period in 1990.

OTC symbol: SUNW
Fiscal year ends: June 30

Hoover's Rating **A**

WHO

Chairman, President, and CEO: Scott G. McNealy, age 36, $1,406,600 pay
VP Worldwide Field Operations: Carol A. Bartz, age 42
VP Finance and CFO: William J. Raduchel, age 45, $509,520 pay
VP Corporate Resources: Crawford W. Beveridge, age 45, $488,400 pay
Auditors: Ernst & Young
Employees: 12,223

WHERE

HQ: 2550 Garcia Ave., Mountain View, CA 94043
Phone: 415-960-1300
Fax: 415-969-9131

Sun has manufacturing facilities in the US and Scotland and distributes its products through 94 domestic and 65 foreign sales and service offices.

	1990 Sales		1990 Operating Income	
	$ mil.	% of total	$ mil.	% of total
US	1,280	52	103	90
Europe	676	27	(1)	(1)
Pacific Rim	510	21	12	11
Adjustments	—	—	(3)	—
Total	**2,466**	**100**	**111**	**100**

WHAT

SPARC-Based Family
SPARC server 490
SPARC server 470
SPARCstation IPC (graphics system)
SPARCstation 1+
SPARCstation SLC
SPARCstation 2

Software
Development tools for computer-aided design, manufacturing, and engineering
Network File System
Open Network Computing
SunOS-System V Release 4 (UNIX)
OpenWindows
  OPEN LOOK (graphical interface)
  OpenWindows DeskSet (personal productivity tools)
  Xtoolkit
SunLink (wide-area networking)

Other Products
Board-level central processing units
Specialized processors and peripherals (laser printers, mass storage devices)
Sun-3/80 and 3/400 (workstations and servers based on Motorola chips)
Sun 386i – Intel 80386-based workstations

RANKINGS

181st in *Fortune* 500 Industrial Cos.
205th in *Business Week* 1000

KEY COMPETITORS

Adobe	Harris	Prime
AT&T	Hewlett-Packard	Schlumberger
Apple	Hitachi	Siemens
Compaq	Intel	Sony
Control Data	Intergraph	Tandem
Data General	IBM	Toshiba
DEC	Machines Bull	Unisys
Fujitsu	NEC	Wang

Other personal computer manufacturers

HOW MUCH

	5-Year Growth	1981	1982	1983	1984	1985	1986	1987	1988	1989	1990
Sales ($ mil.)	84.6%	—	—	—	—	115	210	538	1,052	1,765	2,466
Net income ($ mil.)	65.3%	—	—	—	—	9	12	36	66	61	111
Income as % of sales	—	—	—	—	—	7.4%	5.7%	6.8%	6.3%	3.4%	4.5%
Earnings per share ($)	46.4%	—	—	—	—	0.18	0.23	0.55	0.90	0.76	1.21
Stock price – high ($)	—	—	—	—	—	—	12.19	22.88	20.38	23.00	37.25
Stock price – low ($)	—	—	—	—	—	—	5.63	11.00	13.00	13.38	15.00
Stock price – close ($)	—	—	—	—	—	—	12.00	16.75	16.63	17.25	21.38
P/E – high	—	—	—	—	—	—	53	42	23	30	31
P/E – low	—	—	—	—	—	—	24	20	15	18	12
Dividends per share ($)	—	—	—	—	—	0.00	0.00	0.00	0.00	0.00	0.00
Book value per share ($)	69.3%	—	—	—	—	0.72	2.00	3.58	5.11	7.88	10.01

1990 Year-end:
Debt ratio: 27.9%
Return on equity: 13.5%
Cash (mil.): $394
Current ratio: 2.63
Long-term debt (mil.): $359
No. of shares (mil.): 93
Dividends:
  1990 average yield: 0.0%
  1990 payout: 0.0%
Market value (mil.): $1,980

Stock Price History High/Low 1986–90

SUNTRUST BANKS, INC.

NYSE symbol: STI
Fiscal year ends: December 31

Hoover's Rating **A-**

OVERVIEW

Atlanta-based SunTrust is the 17th largest publicly traded banking concern in the US. It oversees state holding companies in Georgia, Florida, and Tennessee.

SunTrust's book value per share would be 24% higher if it figured the appreciation of its 12 million shares of Coca-Cola stock. The stock has been held since the old Trust Company of Georgia received stock for helping with the initial underwriting of Coca-Cola in 1919. Ever since, SunTrust has carried the stock on its books at $110,000. At the end of 1990, the Coke stock would have sold for $561 million.

SunTrust operates one of the largest trust and investment management businesses in its 3 states, and trust and investment management fee income has increased more than 18% a year since 1985. The bank expects continued increases as the population grows and, in the retirement haven of the Southeast, ages.

Having once basked in the boom of the Sunbelt, SunTrust has been burned a bit by bad real estate loans in Tennessee, but the bank's conservative lending habits have kept its percentage of nonperforming loans relatively modest.

WHEN

SunTrust was formed by the union of old-money Georgia and new-money Florida. Founded in 1891 as the Commercial Traveler's Savings Bank, the Trust Company of Georgia served Atlanta's oldest and richest institutions. It helped underwrite Coca-Cola's first public stock sale in 1919, and the only written copy of the Coke formula rests in a Trust vault.

Beginning in 1933 Trust acquired controlling interests in 5 other Georgia banks. As regulation of multibank ownership relaxed in the 1970s, Trust acquired the remaining interests in its original banks and bought 25 more. At the height of the Sunbelt boom in 1984, Trust was the most profitable bank in the nation, with a low ratio of nonperforming assets — 0.9% of total loans.

Sun Banks began in 1934 as the First National Bank at Orlando. It grew into a holding company in 1967, and the Sun name was adopted in 1973. In the early 1970s the bank helped assemble the land for Orlando's Walt Disney World. It is the official bank of the Magic Kingdom.

Under Joel Wells, then president and CEO, Sun Banks acquired Florida's Century Banks ($1.2 billion in assets, 1982) and the Flagship Banks group ($3.3 billion in assets, 1984). Sun Banks grew from $1.9 billion to $9 billion in assets in only 8 years (1976–84) and increased the number of its branches more than fivefold (51 to 274).

After a lingering courtship, Sun and Trust executives agreed in 1984 to wed the 2 companies, forming a super-holding company over the 2 organizations. The union followed state legislation in Georgia and Florida that permitted multistate bank holding companies, and, when the marriage was consummated in 1985, Sun brought a dowry of $9.4 billion in assets and Trust contributed $6.2 billion. Bob Strickland, Trust's chairman, became chairman and CEO for the new Atlanta-based SunTrust, and Wells became president.

In 1986 SunTrust bought Nashville-based Third National Bank, the 2nd largest bank holding company in Tennessee, with assets of $5 billion. But problems with Tennessee real estate loans increasingly plagued SunTrust. In 1990 it increased the amount of loans it wrote off, and a credit-rating service lowered SunTrust's ratings in light of nonperforming loans for properties in overbuilt Florida.

Strickland stepped down as chairman and CEO in 1990 but remained as chairman of the board's executive committee. Wells died in 1991, and James Williams, a conservative banker who instilled strict fiscal management in Trust's Georgia banks, assumed both the chairman and CEO roles.

WHO

Chairman and CEO: James B. Williams, age 57, $440,667 pay (prior to promotion)
President: L. Phillip Humann, age 45, $247,667 pay (prior to promotion)
EVP and CFO: John W. Spiegel, age 49, $190,000 pay
SVP Human Resources: Robert H. Bowen
Auditors: Arthur Andersen & Co.
Employees: 19,739

WHERE

HQ: 25 Park Place, NE, Atlanta, GA 30303
Phone: 404-588-7711
Fax: 404-827-6001

SunTrust operates 322 offices in Florida, 189 in Georgia, and 113 in Tennessee.

	1990 Net Income	
	$ mil.	% of total
Banking subsidiaries		
Florida	173	50
Georgia	171	49
Tennessee	23	6
Nonbanking net income	(17)	(5)
Total	**350**	**100**

WHAT

	1990 Assets	
	$ mil.	% of total
Cash & due from banks	2,736	8
Interest-bearing deposits	591	2
Trading account	116	—
Investment securities	6,012	18
Funds sold	458	1
Loans	22,111	67
Reserve for loan losses	(360)	(1)
Premises & equipment	664	2
Other	1,083	3
Total	**33,411**	**100**

Services

Corporate Banking	Trust and Investment
Cash management	Management
Corporate finance	Equity funds
Credit products	Trust services
Investment services	
Trust services	**Mortgage Banking**
Community Banking	**Insurance**
Commercial loans	Customer reinsurance
Deposit accounts	
Individual loans	**Data Systems**
Small business loans	Processing for correspondent banks in 6 states

HOW MUCH

	9-Year Growth	1981	1982	1983	1984	1985	1986	1987	1988	1989	1990
Assets ($ mil.)	27.7%	3,711	5,004	8,901	9,402	19,406	26,166	27,188	29,177	31,044	33,411
Net income ($ mil.)	33.0%	27	34	46	65	167	245	283	309	337	350
Income as % of assets	—	0.7%	0.7%	0.5%	0.7%	0.9%	0.9%	1.0%	1.1%	1.1%	1.0%
Earnings per share ($)	9.9%	1.18	1.28	1.53	1.47	1.65	1.85	2.17	2.38	2.61	2.75
Stock price – high ($)	—	12.44	12.19	14.75	15.19	20.31	27.25	27.75	24.50	26.88	24.25
Stock price – low ($)	—	8.38	7.50	10.00	10.88	13.63	17.31	17.00	18.50	19.75	16.50
Stock price – close ($)	10.5%	9.25	11.06	13.25	15.19	19.13	20.00	18.25	19.88	22.88	22.75
P/E – high	—	11	10	10	10	12	15	13	10	10	9
P/E – low	—	7	6	7	7	8	9	8	8	8	6
Dividends per share ($)	7.3%	0.46	0.51	0.56	0.60	0.60	0.61	0.65	0.70	0.78	0.86
Book value per share ($)	7.3%	9.65	10.00	11.68	12.60	10.72	11.59	12.92	14.57	16.32	18.18

1990 Year-end:
Return on equity: 15.9%
Equity as % of assets: 7.1%
Cash (mil.): $3,327
Long-term debt (mil.): $480
No. of shares (mil.): 127
Dividends:
  1990 average yield: 3.8%
  1990 payout: 31.3%
Market value (mil.): $2,884
Sales (mil.): $3,408

Stock Price History High/Low 1981–90

RANKINGS

17th in *Fortune* 100 Commercial Banking Cos.
204th in *Business Week* 1000

KEY COMPETITORS

H. F. Ahmanson
Barnett Banks
Chase Manhattan
Citicorp
Great Western
NCNB
Other multistate bank holding companies

SUPER VALU STORES, INC.

OVERVIEW

Super Valu is the leading US food distributor to independent retailers. Super Valu distinguishes itself from other food wholesalers by calling itself "The Retail Support Company." This support stretches across the nation to about 2,723 independent grocers, most of whom own fewer than 4 locations.

The company helps independent grocers compete against large supermarket chains by providing services in all phases of store operations, including store location, management and employee training, accounting, marketing, modernization, and insurance. Super Valu wholesales goods to the grocers at razor-thin margins, allowing them to buy as cheaply as the chain stores. Occasionally, Super Valu develops new store formats (Cub, Twin Valu). It currently operates 94 of its own grocery stores and the 104-store ShopKo general merchandise chain.

With revenues of $11.6 billion in 1990, Super Valu ranks as the 5th largest diversified service company in the US, behind AT&T, Enron, rival distributor Fleming, and Time Warner. The company is held in high regard throughout the industry for its level of service and attention to customer needs.

NYSE symbol: SVU
Fiscal year ends: Last Saturday in February

Hoover's Rating **B**

WHO

Chairman, President, and CEO: Michael W. Wright, age 52, $649,141 pay
SVP and Chairman, ShopKo Stores: William J. Tyrrell, age 61, $330,200 pay
President and CEO, ShopKo Stores: Dale P. Kramer
SVP: Laurence L. Anderson, age 49, $309,940 pay
SVP: Phillip A. Dabill, age 48, $334,940 pay
SVP Human Resources: Ronald C. Tortelli, age 44
Treasurer: David Cairns, age 44
Auditors: Deloitte & Touche
Employees: 42,900

WHEN

Super Valu was formed as Winston & Newell of Minneapolis in 1926, through the combination of the 2 largest grocery distributors in the Midwest: Winston, Harper, Fisher and George R. Newell, both of Minneapolis and both founded in the 1870s. The public company's purpose was to help independent grocers compete with the new chain stores then becoming prevalent.

The company adopted its name in 1954 and began expanding, acquiring Joannes Brothers of Green Bay (1955) and Piggly-Wiggly Midland of La Crosse, Wisconsin (1958). Super Valu continued making acquisitions and expanding its territory through the 1960s.

In 1971 Super Valu entered nonfood retailing by acquiring ShopKo, a discount department store chain in Minnesota, Michigan, and Wisconsin. ShopKo has 104 stores and distribution centers in Green Bay, Omaha, and Boise. Super Valu added a new format to its food operations by purchasing Cub Stores warehouse-style groceries in 1980. In 1989 and 1990 Super Valu combined its Cub Stores and ShopKo formats and opened 2 supercenters in the Cleveland area called Twin Valu.

The company also has continued building its wholesale distribution and services businesses. It formed SUVACO, a Bermuda-based reinsurance company, in 1979 to provide insurance to hundreds of independent grocers. Super Valu acquired West Coast Grocery Company, a large distributor in Oregon and Washington (1985), and West Coast Fruit & Produce (1986). In 1986 the company bought assets of Southern Supermarket Services of Louisiana and acquired Food Giant, a large Atlanta grocery chain, from Delhaize Frères, the Belgian owner of Food Lion. Super Valu either closed all its Food Giant stores, reopened them as new businesses, or sold them to independents by the end of 1989.

Super Valu's acquisitions and internal growth almost tripled sales levels from $4.2 billion in 1980 to $11.6 billion in 1990. The company has kept long-term debt low and plans to continue looking for acquisitions.

The decentralized management style of Super Valu's subsidiary ShopKo allows managers to customize merchandise to suit a particular market. In June 1991 Super Valu announced ShopKo's intention to go public. ShopKo is expected to offer 16.5 million shares at between $14 and $17. Super Valu's Chairman Michael Wright stated that the ShopKo offering reflects the company's belief that the marketplace will more accurately value the businesses as 2 distinctly capitalized entities. Super Valu will retain less than 50% of ShopKo.

WHERE

HQ: PO Box 990, Minneapolis, MN 55440; 11840 Valley View Rd., Eden Prairie, MN 55344
Phone: 612-828-4000
Fax: 612-828-8998

The 17 retail support divisions serve 2,723 stores in 33 states. ShopKo stores (104) are located in 13 states, primarily in the Midwest and Northwest. The company also exports fresh produce and meats to 35 countries.

WHAT

	1990 Sales		1990 Operating Income	
	$ mil.	% of total	$ mil.	% of total
Retail general merchandise	1,737	15	92	29
Retail support	9,460	82	223	69
Retail food	1,781	15	7	2
Adjustments	1,366	(12)	—	—
Total	**11,612**	**100**	**322**	**100**

Services Offered	Stores Served
Advertising and sales promotion	bigg's
	Byerly's
Commercial and group insurance	County Market
	Cub Foods (some company-owned)
Consumer research	Dierberg's
Labor management	Great Scot
Merchandising consulting	Hornbachers
	IGA
New store development and design	Niemann's
Retail accounting and tax services	QFC
	Shop 'n Save
Retail data systems	Sunflower
Super Valu University	Super Valu
Wholesaling	Twin Valu (company-owned)

RANKINGS

5th in *Fortune* 100 Diversified Service Cos.
326th in *Business Week* 1000

KEY COMPETITORS

Fleming
Kmart
McKesson

HOW MUCH

Fiscal year ends February of following year	9-Year Growth	1981	1982	1983	1984	1985	1986	1987	1988	1989	1990
Sales ($ mil.)	10.8%	4,622	5,197	5,923	6,548	7,905	9,066	9,372	10,296	11,136	11,612
Net income ($ mil.)	10.2%	65	68	77	83	91	89	112	135	148	155
Income as % of sales	—	1.4%	1.3%	1.3%	1.3%	1.2%	1.0%	1.2%	1.3%	1.3%	1.3%
Earnings per share ($)	9.8%	0.89	0.93	1.04	1.13	1.23	1.20	1.50	1.81	1.97	2.06
Stock price – high ($)	—	10.06	14.06	18.50	16.88	23.88	27.88	30.38	26.38	30.13	29.00
Stock price – low ($)	—	7.13	7.75	12.75	11.75	15.13	19.75	16.00	17.00	22.63	21.75
Stock price – close ($)	10.3%	9.81	12.94	14.63	15.81	22.38	24.50	17.88	24.50	29.00	23.75
P/E – high	—	11	15	18	15	19	23	20	15	15	14
P/E – low	—	8	8	12	10	12	16	11	9	11	11
Dividends per share ($)	12.1%	0.23	0.27	0.30	0.33	0.37	0.41	0.44	0.49	0.59	0.65
Book value per share ($)	14.7%	3.79	4.45	5.21	6.33	7.20	8.00	9.07	10.39	11.59	13.01

1990 Year-end:
Debt ratio: 37.1%
Return on equity: 16.8%
Cash (mil.): $3
Current ratio: 1.15
Long-term debt (mil.): $577
No. of shares (mil.): 75
Dividends:
  1990 average yield: 2.7%
  1990 payout: 31.3%
Market value (mil.): $1,787

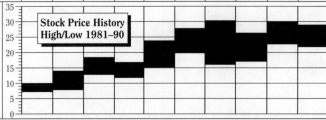

Stock Price History High/Low 1981–90

SUPERMARKETS GENERAL HOLDINGS CORP.

OVERVIEW

Supermarkets General is one of the 10 largest supermarket retailers in the US. Its stores are principally located in densely populated suburban and urban residential areas in the middle Atlantic and New England regions. The Woodbridge, New Jersey–based company, while still deeply in debt, shows some signs of improvement.

During the first half of the 1980s, Supermarkets General, with stores under its Pathmark banner, was a high flier in the food retailing industry. The company had an aver-age 33.6% return on equity during the 10 years leading up to 1987. It was the first to build mammoth (over 45,000 square feet) supermarkets on the East Coast, and it extended its reach into New England through acquisitions in the mid-1980s.

Dodging a Dart Group takeover, Supermarkets General went private and into debt with a 1987 buyout of $1.8 billion. Recent recapitalization efforts have reduced its debt by about $95 million, and earnings are up during a period with weak economic signs.

WHEN

After WWII, supermarket operators in New York and New Jersey banded together to form a cooperative to combat chain grocers, and the Wakefern Cooperative was born. Members enjoyed enhanced buying power and, with some stores sharing the name Shop-Rite, extended advertising reach.

Three participants in the cooperative — Alex Aidekman, Herbert Brody, and Milton Perlmutter — combined in a smaller group to form Supermarkets Operating Company in 1956. Supermarkets Operating's stores continued to use the Shop-Rite name and the Wakefern Cooperative's services.

In 1966 Supermarkets Operating merged with General Super Markets to become Supermarkets General Corporation. Supermarkets General was the largest member of the Wakefern organization.

Supermarkets General broke from Wakefern in 1968 and gave its stores the Pathmark name. The company branched into small-town department stores with the purchase of Genung's, which operated chains under the names Steinbach (New Jersey) and Howland (New York and New England). In 1969 the company added to its department store holdings with the purchase of Baltimore retailer Hochschild, Kohn & Co., and entered the home improvement market by purchasing the 6-store Rickel chain. The company grew steadily through the 1970s, pioneering the large supermarket and grocery/drug combinations in densely populated areas of New York, New Jersey, and Connecticut. Supermarkets General's aggressive discounting and experimentation made it profitable, and it gained a reputation as one of the best-run supermarket chains in the US.

Value House, a catalog showroom outgrowth of the company's department store business, grew to 20 locations and was sold in 1978. Leonard Lieberman became CEO in 1983. Supermarkets General acquired Boston's Purity Supreme, operator of Purity Supreme and Heartland grocery stores and Li'l Peach convenience stores, for $80 million (1984). In 1985 the company opened Super Stores, under both the Pathmark and Purity Supreme names, that offered a great variety of merchandise. Supermarkets General boosted its New England market share with the purchase of Angelo's Supermarkets in 1986. The company sold its department store operations in 1986, and Aidekman stepped down as chairman the same year.

Supermarkets General's expansion plans slowed when the Haft family's Dart Group made a $1.62 billion raid on the company in 1987. Merrill Lynch Capital Partners stepped in with an LBO, retaining control of Supermarkets General after the company was taken private. CEO Kenneth Peskin, who replaced Lieberman, resigned and was replaced in 1989 by Jack Futterman. Faced with high interest payments on junk bonds, management has been unable to build on its market base, and market share has eroded.

In July 1991 the company announced a definitive agreement to sell its Purity Supreme operation for about $300 million, including the assumption of Purity's debt, to Freeman Spogli & Co. The sale's cash proceeds will be used to retire debt. The sale will allow the company to devote all resources to the remaining Pathmark chain and to pursue a 3-year, $385 million expansion.

Private company — Hoover's Rating **D**
Fiscal year ends: Saturday closest to January 31

WHO

Chairman, President, and CEO: Jack Futterman, age 57, $600,088 pay
EVP: Isadore Lemmerman, age 66, $362,695 pay
EVP Finance and CFO: Anthony J. Cuti, age 45, $199,038 pay
EVP; President, Purity Supreme: Frank Giacomazzi, age 59, $304,113 pay
EVP; President, Rickel Home Centers: Jules Borshadel, age 51, $306,670 pay
VP Human Resources: Maureen McGurl, age 43
Auditors: Deloitte & Touche
Employees: 46,000

WHERE

HQ: 301 Blair Rd., Woodbridge, NJ 07095
Phone: 908-499-3000
Fax: 908-499-3072

The company operates 146 Pathmark supermarkets, 32 drugstores, and 45 Rickel home centers (New Jersey, New York, Pennsylvania, Connecticut, and Delaware). The company also operates 65 Purity Supreme, Heartland, and Angelo's supermarkets (Massachusetts, New Hampshire, and Connecticut). The 63 Li'l Peach convenience stores operate exclusively in Massachusetts.

WHAT

	1990 Sales		1990 Operating Income	
	$ mil.	% of total	$ mil.	% of total
Supermarkets & drugstores	5,705	93	209	100
Home centers	421	7	(1)	—
Adjustments	—	—	(14)	—
Total	**6,126**	**100**	**194**	**100**

Supermarkets and Drugstores
Pathmark
  Drugstores (32)
  Supermarkets (146)
Purity Supreme
  Super Stores (26)
  Supermarkets (39)
    Angelo's
    Heartland
    Purity Supreme

Convenience Stores
Li'l Peach (63)

Home Centers
Rickel (45)

RANKINGS

18th in *Fortune* 50 Retailing Cos.
10th in *Forbes* 400 US Private Cos.

KEY COMPETITORS

American Stores	Rite Aid
Great A&P	Sears
Home Depot	Southland
Kmart	Stop & Shop
Melville	

HOW MUCH

	9-Year Growth	1981	1982	1983	1984	1985	1986	1987	1988	1989	1990
Sales ($ mil.)	8.3%	2,999	3,247	3,518	4,347	5,123	5,508	5,767	5,962	6,299	6,126
Net income ($ mil.)	—	30	38	41	52	64	63	(66)	(59)	(77)	(41)
Income as % of sales	—	1.0%	1.2%	1.2%	1.2%	1.2%	1.1%	(1.1%)	(1.0%)	(1.2%)	(0.7%)
Employees	—	30,000	31,000	33,000	45,000	52,000	53,000	53,000	52,000	51,000	46,000

1990 Year-end:
Debt ratio: —
Return on equity: —
Cash (mil.): $5
Current ratio: 0.78
Long-term debt (mil.): $1,629

Net Income ($ mil.) 1981–90

SYNTEX CORPORATION

OVERVIEW

Although now best known for its arthritis drugs Naprosyn and Anaprox, pharmaceutical producer Syntex owes its success to the birth control pill, which it helped to pioneer through its early work in the synthesis of sex hormones. For tax reasons (to get an effective tax rate of 10%), the company is incorporated in Panama, although its main office is in Palo Alto, California.

Once guilty of relying too heavily on a single product, Syntex has created a lucrative pipeline of drugs through stepped-up R&D spending (now running at about 18% of sales). Areas targeted for research during the 1990s

include cancer, cardiology, endocrinology, immunology, gastroenterology, neurology, and pain control. Among the promising new drugs on the company's horizon are Ticlid (an antistroke agent with the potential for annual sales of $300 million), and Toradol (a painkiller with potential first-year sales of $80 million).

Syntex has also garnered a reputation as a great place to work. Located a mile from Stanford, the company has a casual corporate culture that emulates a college environment. Syntex also offers superb childcare facilities and maintains a professional staff that is almost 50% female.

NYSE symbol: SYN
Fiscal year ends: July 31

Hoover's Rating **A**

WHO

Chairman and CEO: Paul E. Freiman, age 56, $814,583 pay
President and COO: James N. Wilson
SVP and CFO: Richard P. Powers, age 49
SVP Human Resources: Andrew Oravets, age 49
Auditors: Deloitte & Touche
Employees: 10,300

WHERE

HQ: 3401 Hillview Ave., Palo Alto, CA 94304
Phone: 415-855-5050
Fax: 415-855-5103

The company has operations in 24 countries.

	1990 Sales		1990 Operating Income	
	$ mil.	% of total	$ mil.	% of total
US	1,046	69	186	38
Europe	215	14	(23)	(5)
Canada/Latin America	139	9	12	2
Other	121	8	320	65
Adjustments	—	—	(56)	—
Total	**1,521**	**100**	**439**	**100**

WHAT

	1990 Sales		1990 Operating Income	
	$ mil.	% of total	$ mil.	% of total
Drugs	1,342	88	405	92
Diagnostics	179	12	34	8
Total	**1,521**	**100**	**439**	**100**

Pharmaceuticals
Allergies
  Nasalide
Anti-inflammatory/
  analgesic
  Anaprox
  Naprosyn
  Toradol
Antiviral
  Cytovene
Cardiovascular
  Cardene
Dermatologic
  Exelderm
  Lidex
  Neo-Synalar
  Synacort
  Synalar

Reproductive/gynecologic
  Brevicon
  Femstat
  Norinyl
  Synarel
  Tri-Norinyl

Diagnostics
  AccuLevel
  Emit
  ETS
  MicroTrak

Animal Health
  Synanthic
  Synovex

RANKINGS

64th in *Business Week* 1000

KEY COMPETITORS

Abbott Labs
American Home Products
Amgen
C. R. Bard
Baxter
Bayer
Becton, Dickinson
Bristol-Myers Squibb
Ciba-Geigy
Eli Lilly
Genentech

Glaxo
Johnson & Johnson
Merck
Pfizer
Rhône-Poulenc
Roche
Sandoz
Schering-Plough
SmithKline Beecham
Upjohn
Warner-Lambert

WHEN

Working out of a Mexico City laboratory in 1944, Penn State chemist Russell Marker discovered that he could inexpensively synthesize the sex hormone progesterone from the roots of the barbasco plant, which grows in the jungles of southwestern Mexico. With the assistance of 2 European scientists, Marker formed Syntex (an abbreviation for Synthesis-Mexico) that same year to mass-produce progesterone and other hormones.

By applying its research in sex hormones, Syntex became a pioneer in the development of oral contraceptives. Although not the first to release birth control pills to the US market (G. D. Searle launched its Enovid in 1960), Syntex supplied the active ingredients for 3 of the first 4 pills on the market. After licensing its technology for Johnson & Johnson's Ortho-Novum pill, Syntex released its own Norinyl pill in 1964. That same year the company established its administrative and research headquarters in Palo Alto, California. In 1966 Syntex released the Syva drug-monitoring test, its first diagnostics product.

Because of its birth control pill technology, Syntex became one of the hottest stocks of the 1960s, trading as high as 100 times earnings by 1969. The bottom fell out in 1970 when government investigation of the side effects of

birth control pills sent sales and company stocks plummeting. Syntex found itself in the unenviable position of a one-hit pharmaceutical company whose product's time had momentarily passed.

Finding its second wind, Syntex launched its next smash product, Naprosyn, an anti-inflammatory, in 1972. Also during the 1970s the company attempted a diversification into dental products, ophthalmics, and cosmetics, all of which were divested in the 1980s.

Realizing that the patent for Naprosyn would expire in 1993, Syntex launched a major R&D drive during the 1980s to assure a pipeline of future drugs. By 1987 company sales had passed the $1 billion mark. In 1988 Syntex announced a joint venture with Procter & Gamble to develop an over-the-counter version of Naprosyn (still waiting for FDA approval).

The company's R&D efforts began paying off in the late 1980s and early 1990s when it released Cardene (a calcium-channel blocker, 1989), Cytovene (an antiviral drug, 1989), Synarel (for the treatment of endometriosis, 1990), and Toradol (an anti-inflammatory drug, 1990). Syntex had a record year in 1991, posting a 19.5% increase in sales (to over $1.8 billion) and a 24% increase in profits (to $424 million).

HOW MUCH

	9-Year Growth	1981	1982	1983	1984	1985	1986	1987	1988	1989	1990
Sales ($ mil.)	8.8%	711	813	870	916	949	980	1,129	1,272	1,349	1,521
Net income ($ mil.)	14.8%	99	134	149	135	150	208	249	297	303	342
Income as % of sales	—	13.9%	16.5%	17.2%	14.7%	15.8%	21.2%	22.0%	23.3%	22.5%	22.5%
Earnings per share ($)	17.7%	0.70	0.96	1.08	1.02	1.16	1.61	2.03	2.47	2.64	3.02
Stock price – high ($)	—	9.25	15.25	15.63	14.06	23.38	37.38	48.75	44.13	54.50	63.75
Stock price – low ($)	—	6.03	7.16	11.03	9.44	11.88	20.25	23.00	32.13	36.50	46.75
Stock price – close ($)	25.5%	7.70	12.00	13.31	12.16	23.38	28.81	32.00	40.63	50.00	59.38
P/E – high	—	13	16	15	14	20	23	24	18	21	21
P/E – low	—	9	7	10	9	10	13	11	13	14	15
Dividends per share ($)	27.5%	0.17	0.25	0.33	0.38	0.44	0.57	0.85	1.08	1.35	1.53
Book value per share ($)	7.6%	3.54	4.26	4.53	4.70	5.42	5.77	5.11	6.38	5.26	6.88

1990 Year-end:
Debt ratio: 22.6%
Return on equity: 49.7%
Cash (mil.): $558
Current ratio: 1.47
Long-term debt (mil.): $225
No. of shares (mil.): 112
Dividends:
  1990 average yield: 2.6%
  1990 payout: 50.5%
Market value (mil.): $6,656

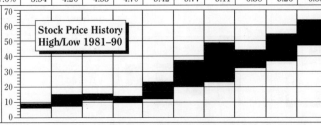
Stock Price History High/Low 1981–90

SYSCO CORPORATION

OVERVIEW

Houston-based SYSCO is the nation's largest distributor of food products to the food service industry. SYSCO celebrated its 20th year in 1990. The company serves a variety of away-from-home eating establishments including restaurants, hotels, schools, hospitals, and fast-food outlets. SYSCO has operations in more than 150 US cities and the Pacific Coast region of Canada and has approximately 230,000 customers.

SYSCO buys goods from more than 2,700 sources in a number of countries. The company sells about 150,000 products including fully prepared frozen entrees; frozen fruits, vegetables and desserts; and a full line of canned and dry goods. Other SYSCO products include fresh meat, imported specialties, and

fresh produce. They also sell disposable napkins, plates, and cups; china and silverware; restaurant and kitchen equipment and supplies; and cleaning supplies. Two recently added items, reflecting increased health consciousness, are prewashed and preprepared fresh vegetables and SYSCO's Imperial Frozen Yogurt.

Although it serves less than 8% of the market, SYSCO is the giant in the food service industry, which is composed of more than 3,500 regional and local distributors. With its 1988 acquisition of CFS Continental, SYSCO extended into all parts of the US, building its market position in West Coast states and British Columbia.

WHEN

SYSCO was founded in 1969 when John Baugh, a Houston wholesale foods distributor, convinced the owners of 8 other US wholesalers that they should combine and form a national distribution company. Joining Baugh's Zero Foods of Houston to form SYSCO were Frost-Pack Distributing (Grand Rapids, Michigan), Louisville Grocery (Louisville, Kentucky), Plantation Foods (Miami), Thomas Foods and its Justrite subsidiary (Cincinnati), Wicker (Dallas), Houston's Food Service Company (Houston), Global Frozen Foods (New York), and Texas Wholesale Grocery (Dallas). SYSCO, which derives its name from Systems and Services Company, benefited from Baugh's recognition of the trend toward dining out in American society. Until SYSCO was formed, food distribution to restaurants, hotels, and other nongrocers was provided by thousands of small, independent, regional operators.

During the 2 decades since its inception, SYSCO has grown to 25 times its original size, mostly through the acquisition of strong local distributors. The company has ensured the success of its acquisitions through buyout

agreements requiring the seller to continue managing the company and earn a portion of the sale price with future profits. From its inception to the end of June 1988 SYSCO acquired 44 companies.

In 1988, when SYSCO was already the largest food service distributor, it purchased Olewine's, a Harrisburg, Pennsylvania, distributor. It also acquired, for $800 million, CFS Continental, the food distribution unit of Staley Continental and the 3rd largest food distributor at the time. The CFS acquisition added several warehouses and a large truck fleet and increased the company's penetration along the West Coast of the US and Canada. In 1990 SYSCO acquired the Oklahoma City–based foodservice distribution business of Scrivner (renamed SYSCO Food Services of Oklahoma). SYSCO plans to continue expanding by buying smaller competitors. In July 1991 SYSCO pleaded guilty to one count of conspiring to rig contract bids for wholesale groceries to public schools in southeastern Texas. The company has reorganized its school-bid department and has added controls to prevent any recurrences.

HOW MUCH

	9-Year Growth	1981	1982	1983	1984	1985	1986	1987	1988	1989	1990
Sales ($ mil.)	20.9%	1,376	1,700	1,950	2,312	2,628	3,172	3,656	4,385	6,851	7,591
Net income ($ mil.)	19.4%	27	34	40	45	50	58	62	80	108	132
Income as % of sales	—	1.9%	2.0%	2.1%	2.0%	1.9%	1.8%	1.7%	1.8%	1.6%	1.7%
Earnings per share ($)	17.0%	0.35	0.43	0.49	0.54	0.59	0.67	0.70	0.90	1.19	1.45
Stock price – high ($)	—	5.28	10.47	11.13	9.59	11.63	16.94	20.75	19.44	32.00	38.38
Stock price – low ($)	—	3.34	4.64	7.81	6.44	7.94	11.19	11.25	13.00	18.31	25.63
Stock price – close ($)	23.8%	4.94	9.81	9.13	8.44	11.19	15.00	13.56	19.25	31.63	33.63
P/E – high	—	15	24	23	18	20	25	30	22	27	26
P/E – low	—	9	11	16	12	14	17	16	15	15	18
Dividends per share ($)	17.2%	0.05	0.06	0.08	0.09	0.10	0.11	0.13	0.15	0.17	0.20
Book value per share ($)	17.4%	1.99	2.50	2.89	3.42	3.93	4.50	5.10	6.02	7.07	8.40

1990 Year-end:
Debt ratio: 43.1%
Return on equity: 18.7%
Cash (mil.): $56
Current ratio: 1.83
Long-term debt (mil.): $584
No. of shares (mil.): 92
Dividends:
  1990 average yield: 0.6%
  1990 payout: 13.4%
Market value (mil.): $3,085

Stock Price History High/Low 1981–90

NYSE symbol: SYY
Fiscal year ends: Saturday closest to June 30

Hoover's Rating **B+**

WHO

Senior Chairman of the Board: John E. Baugh, age 74
Chairman and CEO: John F. Woodhouse, age 59, $871,953 pay
President and COO: Bill M. Lindig, age 53, $738,816 pay
VC: Herbert Irving, age 72
EVP Finance and Administration: E. James Lowrey, age 62, $551,802 pay
VP Management Development and Training: Lawrence H. Pete
Auditors: Arthur Andersen & Co.
Employees: 20,000

WHERE

HQ: 1390 Enclave Pkwy., Houston, TX 77077
Phone: 713-584-1390
Fax: 713-584-1188

SYSCO has facilities in 35 states and western Canada.

	No. of Facilities
California	12
Texas	10
New York	9
Other states and Canada	74
Total	**105**

WHAT

	1990 Sales	
	$ mil.	% of total
Food service — traditional	6,721	89
Food service — quick service	615	8
Consumer-sized products	255	3
Total	**7,591**	**100**

	1990 Sales
Customers	% of total
Hospitals & nursing homes	14
Hotels & motels	7
Restaurants	57
Schools & colleges	9
Other	13
Total	**100**

	1990 Sales
Products	% of total
Beverage products	3
Canned & dry products	27
Consumer-sized frozen products	3
Dairy products	7
Equipment & smallwares	3
Fresh & frozen meats	16
Fresh produce	5
Janitorial products	2
Other frozen products	15
Paper & disposable products	8
Poultry	6
Seafoods	5
Total	**100**

RANKINGS

12th in *Fortune* 100 Diversified Service Cos.
183rd in *Business Week* 1000

KEY COMPETITORS

Sara Lee

TANDEM COMPUTERS INC.

NYSE symbol: TDM
Fiscal year ends: September 30

Hoover's Rating **B+**

OVERVIEW

Cupertino, California–based Tandem Computers is a leading manufacturer of fault-tolerant computers. Used around the world for varied applications, the computers process thousands of transactions a second without interruption.

The finance industry — banks, stock exchanges, and brokerage firms — is Tandem's largest market (37%), followed by communications (15%). Tandem computers are used in banks' ATM networks. Its largest installation — the Securities Industry Automation Corporation — is responsible for the automation of the American and New York stock exchanges.

The $1.8 billion company is the 8th largest midrange computer manufacturer in the world according to the 1990 Datamation 100. International sales account for 53% of Tandem's revenues.

The core of Tandem's product line is the NonStop system family — computers ranging in size from the CLX minicomputer to the newer NonStop Cyclone (Tandem's first mainframe model). In 1990 Tandem introduced the Integrity S2, a UNIX-based fault-tolerant computer based on RISC (Reduced Instruction Set Computing) technology. If a processor in the S2 fails, the computer takes it off-line, notifies the system operator, and reports the failure to a Tandem support center — all without interruption to the tasks in process.

WHO

Chairman: Thomas J. Perkins, age 58
President and CEO: James G. Treybig, age 50, $543,366 pay
SVP and COO: Robert C. Marshall, age 59, $359,538 pay
SVP and CFO: David J. Rynne, age 49, $328,409 pay
VP Human Resources: Susan J. Cook
Auditors: Ernst & Young
Employees: 10,936

WHEN

Tandem Computers was started in Cupertino, California, in 1974 by James Treybig, a former marketing manager at Hewlett-Packard and limited partner in venture capital firm Kleiner, Perkins, Caufield & Byers (KPC&B). Along with 2 computer engineers, and with initial funding from KPC&B, Treybig pioneered a way to link computers to work in tandem so that if one failed, another would take over without interruption. Tandem introduced its first fail-safe minicomputer, the NonStop16, in 1976.

Tandem's computers quickly became a success. Revenues doubled every year from 1976 to 1981. Designed to process on-line transactions quickly, the computers were popular with banks, brokerage firms, manufacturers, and hospitals. By 1987 Tandem was a $1 billion company with 130 offices worldwide.

Although Tandem dominated the fail-safe computer market in the 1970s, it faced stiff competition in the early 1980s from companies like Stratus Computer. From 1982 to 1985 Tandem's earnings were flat. Tandem, long noted for its unorthodox, people-oriented management, was forced to reassess both its product line and its business methods. By 1987 the company had tightened its management

control and substantially revamped and expanded its product line. That year revenues grew 35%. Contributing to the rise in sales were Tandem's 1987 introduction of a smaller CLX minicomputer and announcement of a new database software product (NonStop SQL) that offered greater versatility.

In developing a more diversified product line, Tandem expanded into complementary specialty areas through acquisition of Atalla (1987, data security products), Integrated Technology (1988, telecommunications software), Ungermann-Bass (1988, network specialists), and Array Technology (1990, disk storage systems). The 1989 introduction of the NonStop Cyclone moved Tandem into the mainframe market, competing head-on with IBM's comparable machine at 1/3 the cost.

Because of a depressed finance industry — Tandem's largest market — the company's revenue growth slowed to 14% in 1990, compared to 24% in 1989. Revenue growth for the first half of fiscal 1991 was relatively flat (5%). Tandem's strongest sales gains came from its Ungermann-Bass subsidiary (network products), which reported a 25% increase in sales for the first 2 quarters of fiscal 1991.

WHERE

HQ: 19333 Vallco Pkwy., Cupertino, CA 95014
Phone: 408-285-6000
Fax: 408-865-4545

The company makes products in the US, Germany, and Mexico, and has 180 locations around the world.

	1990 Sales		1990 Pretax Income	
	$ mil.	% of total	$ mil.	% of total
US	882	47	132	67
Europe	620	33	51	26
Other countries	364	20	14	7
Adjustments	—	—	(10)	—
Total	**1,866**	**100**	**187**	**100**

WHAT

1990 Product Sales	% of Total
Banking	23
Communications	15
Manufacturing	14
Services	12
Distribution	9
Other financial	8
Brokerage & securities	6
Government	5
Health care	4
Transportation	4
Total	**100**

Computer Systems	System Software
Integrity S2	Guardian Operating System
NonStop CLX	NonStop SQL Software
NonStop Cyclone	NonStop-UX Operating
NonStop VLX	System

Networking
Distributed Systems Management
Network security products offered through Tandem's subsidiary Atalla Corporation
Various networking products offered through Tandem's subsidiary Ungermann-Bass, Inc. (Net/One)

Storage Products
4210/4220 disk subsystem
5200 optical storage facility
V80 disk storage
V90 disk subsystem
XL80 disk storage

RANKINGS

220th in *Fortune* 500 Industrial Cos.
386th in *Business Week* 1000

KEY COMPETITORS

Amdahl	Hewlett-Packard	Prime
Apple	Hitachi	Siemens
Control Data	IBM	Storage Technology
Data General	Machines Bull	Sun Microsystems
DEC	NEC	Unisys
Fujitsu	Novell	Wang

HOW MUCH

	9-Year Growth	1981	1982	1983	1984	1985	1986	1987	1988	1989	1990
Sales ($ mil.)	27.6%	208	312	418	533	624	768	1,036	1,315	1,633	1,866
Net income ($ mil.)	18.4%	27	30	31	43	34	64	106	94	118	122
Income as % of sales	—	12.7%	9.6%	7.4%	8.1%	5.5%	8.3%	10.2%	7.2%	7.2%	6.5%
Earnings per share ($)	13.6%	0.36	0.38	0.38	0.52	0.41	0.72	1.08	0.96	1.17	1.13
Stock price – high ($)	—	17.29	16.38	19.75	20.13	14.31	19.75	37.63	29.50	26.38	30.13
Stock price – low ($)	—	10.21	7.25	11.81	6.50	6.44	9.75	17.19	12.38	14.75	8.88
Stock price – close ($)	(1.9%)	13.88	12.69	17.56	9.75	11.13	17.13	27.50	16.88	23.00	11.63
P/E – high	—	48	43	52	39	35	27	35	31	23	27
P/E – low	—	28	19	31	13	16	14	16	13	13	8
Dividends per share ($)	—	0.00	0.00	0.00	0.00	0.00	0.00	0.00	0.00	0.00	0.00
Book value per share ($)	16.9%	2.81	3.33	3.93	4.62	5.08	6.09	7.74	8.92	9.82	11.46

1990 Year-end:
Debt ratio: 7.4%
Return on equity: 10.6%
Cash (mil.): $91
Current ratio: 1.74
Long-term debt (mil.): $96
No. of shares (mil.): 105
Dividends:
1990 average yield: 0.0%
1990 payout: 0.0%
Market value (mil.): $1,221

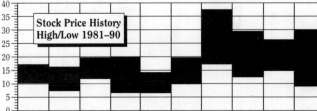

Stock Price History
High/Low 1981–90

TANDY CORPORATION

OVERVIEW

Tandy Corporation is the largest retailer of consumer electronics in the world, with sales of over $4.5 billion in 1990. In mid-1990 Tandy owned 4,830 Radio Shack stores and had 2,204 Radio Shack franchisees; the company also operated 263 Radio Shack Computer Centers, 50 GRiD Systems Centers, and 322 McDuff and VideoConcepts name-brand retail stores, opening 48 more by the end of 1990. In 1991 the company debuted its Computer City discount-warehouse format.

Tandy's Marketing Companies division includes GRiD Systems (large-business and government computer systems), Memtek Products (Memorex tapes), O'Sullivan Industries (office furniture), and Lika Corporation (circuit boards), as well as Sweden-based acquisition Victor Technologies, which markets both its own and GRiD's products throughout Europe. The company's products are also sold through InterTAN — Tandy's spun-off foreign Radio Shack stores — and via direct mail, in university bookstores, and through US military base exchanges

Tandy Electronics, the company's $1.1 billion manufacturing operation, produces over 50% of the products sold at Radio Shack and employs nearly 1/5 of Tandy's 40,000 workers. The company's products are sold under its own brand names, under OEM agreements with Digital Equipment and Matsushita, and as private-label brands.

WHEN

During the 1950s Charles Tandy expanded his family's small Fort Worth leather business, dating back to 1919, into a nationwide chain of leathercraft and hobby stores. By 1960 Tandy Corporation stock was being traded on the NYSE. In the early 1960s Tandy began to expand into other retail areas, buying a Fort Worth department store, Leonard's.

In 1963 Tandy purchased Radio Shack, a nearly bankrupt electronic parts supplier with a mail-order business and 9 retail stores in the Boston area. Tandy collected part of the $800,000 owed the company and began expansion, stocking the stores with quick turnover items and putting 8–9% of sales revenue into advertising. Between 1961 and 1969 Tandy sales grew from $16 million to $180 million, and earnings rose from $720,000 to $7.7 million, with the bulk of the growth due to the expansion of Radio Shack. Between 1968 and 1973 Tandy expanded from 172 to 2,294 stores, with Radio Shack providing over 50% of Tandy's sales and 80% of earnings in 1973.

In 1974 the company sold its department store operations to Dillard. In 1975 Tandy spun off to shareholders its leather products business as Tandy Brands and its hobby and handicraft business as Tandycrafts, focusing Tandy Corporation on the consumer electronics business. During 1976 the boom in CB radio sales pushed income up 125% as Tandy opened 1,200 stores. In 1977 Tandy introduced the first mass-marketed personal computer, the TRS-80, which became the #1 PC on the market. In 1979, the year after Charles Tandy died, there were 5,530 McDonald's, 6,805 7-Elevens, and 7,353 Radio Shacks.

In 1984 the company introduced the Tandy 1000, the first IBM-compatible PC priced under $1,000. Since 1984 Tandy has expanded through acquisitions — Scott/McDuff and VideoConcepts in 1985, GRiD Systems in 1988, and Victor Technologies in 1990.

In 1987 Tandy spun off its foreign retail operations as InterTAN. Realizing that Radio Shack had nearly exhausted its expansion possibilities, the company focused on alternate retail formats such as GRiD Systems Centers, the name-brand retailers, and its new Computer City warehouses. In 1991 Tandy announced the introduction of name-brand products into Radio Shack stores. The company has also increased its manufacturing and R&D capacity, intending to focus on emerging technologies such as digital audio recording and multimedia computing.

HOW MUCH

	9-Year Growth	1981	1982	1983	1984	1985	1986	1987	1988	1989	1990
Sales ($ mil.)	11.5%	1,691	2,033	2,475	2,737	2,841	3,036	3,452	3,794	4,181	4,500
Net income ($ mil.)	6.2%	170	224	279	282	189	198	242	316	324	290
Income as % of sales	—	10.0%	11.0%	11.3%	10.3%	6.7%	6.5%	7.0%	8.3%	7.7%	6.5%
Earnings per share ($)	8.9%	1.65	2.17	2.67	2.75	2.11	2.22	2.70	3.54	3.64	3.54
Stock price – high ($)	—	39.13	60.75	64.50	43.38	42.13	45.00	56.50	48.63	48.75	41.13
Stock price – low ($)	—	20.06	22.75	33.25	23.25	24.00	30.50	28.00	31.50	37.00	23.50
Stock price – close ($)	(1.6%)	33.75	50.75	43.38	24.25	40.75	42.50	33.00	41.00	39.13	29.25
P/E – high	—	24	28	24	16	20	20	21	14	13	12
P/E – low	—	12	10	12	8	11	14	10	9	10	7
Dividends per share ($)	—	0.00	0.00	0.00	0.00	0.00	0.00	0.38	0.58	0.60	0.60
Book value per share ($)	16.4%	5.56	7.83	10.71	10.64	12.00	14.57	15.38	18.10	20.65	21.78

1990 Year-end:
Debt ratio: 12.8%
Return on equity: 16.7%
Cash (mil.): $135
Current ratio: 2.12
Long-term debt (mil.): $253
No. of shares (mil.): 79
Dividends:
  1990 average yield: 2.1%
  1990 payout: 17.0%
Market value (mil.): $2,315

Stock Price History
High/Low 1981–90

NYSE symbol: TAN
Fiscal year ends: June 30

Hoover's Rating **A-**

WHO

Chairman, CEO, and President: John V. Roach, age 51, $873,749 pay
President, Radio Shack Division: Bernard S. Appel, age 58, $552,981 pay
President, Tandy Electronics Division: Robert M. McClure, age 54, $320,177 pay
VP and Controller: Richard L. Ramsey, age 44
VP Human Resources: George Berger
Auditors: Price Waterhouse
Employees: 40,000

WHERE

HQ: 1800 One Tandy Center, Fort Worth, TX 76102
Phone: 817-390-3700
Fax: 817-390-2774

Tandy has Radio Shacks throughout the US and name-brand stores in 23 states. Its 29 plants are in the US, Mexico, the UK, Taiwan, Korea, and China. Victor operates in 11 European nations, and Tandy products are marketed worldwide.

	1990 Sales		1990 Operating Income	
	$ mil.	% of total	$ mil.	% of total
US	4,195	93	500	101
Other countries	305	7	(4)	(1)
Adjustments	—	—	(16)	—
Total	**4,500**	**100**	**480**	**100**

WHAT

	1990 Sales	
	$ mil.	% of total
Radio Shack–US	2,938	66
Tandy Name Brand Retail	470	10
Tandy Marketing	724	16
Outside sales	368	8
Total	**4,500**	**100**

Divisions
Radio Shack/Radio Shack Computer Centers (sells under Archer, DUoFONE, Optimus, and Realistic brands)
Tandy Name Brand Retail
  McDuff
  VideoConcepts
Tandy Marketing Cos.
  GRiD Systems/GRiD Systems Centers (business systems)
  Victor Technologies/Micronic (Europe)
  Memtek Products (Memorex audio and video tape)
  O'Sullivan Industries (office furniture)
  Lika Corporation (printed circuit boards)
Tandy Electronics (manufacturing)

RANKINGS

28th in *Fortune* 50 Retailing Cos.
254th in *Business Week* 1000

KEY COMPETITORS

AT&T	Fuji Photo	Office Depot
Apple	Harris	Oki
AST	Hitachi	Olivetti
Atari	IBM	Philips
BASF	JWP	Pioneer
Canon	Machines Bull	SCI Systems
Circuit City	Matsushita	Sears
Commodore	3M	Sharp
Compaq	Montgomery Ward	Siemens
Costco	Motorola	Sony
Dell	NEC	Toshiba

TEACHERS INSURANCE

OVERVIEW

Teachers Insurance and Annuity Association (TIAA) and College Retirement Equities Fund (CREF) provide educational institutions in North America with an employee pension and insurance program that is fully funded, immediately vested, and portable.

TIAA offers life and health insurance programs to more than 1.4 million members in over 4,400 institutions. TIAA has no agents, gaining new clients through direct mail and phone service. Trustees are educators and administrators from member organizations. TIAA's stable and conservative investment program has the A. M. Best Superior rating.

Only about 1.5% of its more than $9 billion in income is used for operating expenses.

CREF, a separate comanaged organization, provides investment vehicles intended to protect members from the impact of inflation on their retirement benefits. With about $37 billion invested (down from $38 billion in 1989), members have a variety of investment alternatives ranging from money-market accounts, stocks and bonds, and annuities to its innovative Social Choice account. Though return rates for both funds have declined in 1990 and 1991, they remain competitive with industry averages, with the exception of the Social Choice fund, with returns of under 5%.

WHEN

The Carnegie Foundation for the Advancement of Teaching established New York City–based TIAA in 1905 with an endowment of $15 million to provide retirement benefits and other forms of financial security to employees of educational and research organizations. The original endowment was insufficient, and in 1918 the fund was reorganized into a defined contribution plan with another $1 million from Carnegie. TIAA, now the major pension system of higher education in the US, was the first portable pension plan, allowing participants to move between institutions without losing retirement benefits and offering a fixed annuity. But the fund kept requiring cash from the foundation until 1947.

In 1952 CEO William Greenough established the College Retirement Equities Fund (CREF) to augment the TIAA funds with stock earnings. Designed to supplement TIAA's fixed-dollar annuity, CREF invested part of the premiums paid to TIAA in common stocks for retirement purposes. CREF, like sister TIAA, was subject to New York insurance regulation but not SEC regulation.

In the 1950s TIAA led the fight for Social Security benefits for university employees and began offering group disability (1957) and group life insurance (1958).

In the 1970s TIAA established The Common Fund to help colleges boost investment returns from their endowments; TIAA went on to help manage endowments.

For 70 years TIAA/CREF members had no way to exit the system other than retirement. In addition, members had only 2 investment choices, stocks through CREF or a transfer into TIAA's long-term bond, real estate, and mortgage fund. In the 1980s CREF indexed its funds to the S&P average. By the 1987 stock crash, the organization had 3,800 participant institutions and more than $63 billion in assets. It also had one million members, many of whom were dismayed by CREF's reliance on the stock market and by the fact that the only place they could move their CREF funds was to TIAA, from which they could never be withdrawn. CREF proposed adding a money market fund, but this required SEC oversight, and the SEC required complete transferability, even outside of TIAA-CREF. In 1988 TIAA-CREF introduced a money market fund and 6 mutual funds.

Since transferability made TIAA-CREF vulnerable to competition, it began to add more investment options: in 1989 it introduced the TIAA Interest Payment Retirement Option and announced new CREF accounts for 1990. Many states are now setting up optional retirement programs (ORPs) as alternatives or supplements to their regular public employee retirement plans. TIAA-CREF is now a carrier in 41 states (and Washington, DC) to provide ORPs. It has also begun offering long-term care plans and increased its informational outreach to clients through money management seminars.

Nonprofit organization
Fiscal year ends: December 31

Hoover's Rating B+

WHO

Chairman and CEO: Clifton R. Wharton, Jr.
President and COO: John H. Biggs
EVP Finance and Planning: Thomas W. Jones
EVP and General Counsel: Charles H. Stamm
EVP Human Resources: Martina S. Horner
Auditors: Deloitte & Touche
Employees: 3,800

WHERE

HQ: Teachers Insurance and Annuity Association and College Retirement Equities Fund, 730 Third Ave., New York, NY 10017
Phone: 212-490-9000
Fax: 212-775-8424

TIAA/CREF is licensed in 41 states; Washington, DC; 9 Canadian provinces; and other states by correspondence.

WHAT

TIAA Insurance Assets	1990
	% of total
Commercial mortgage loans	43
Bonds	24
Direct loans	23
Real estate	10
Total	**100**

CREF Investments		1990
	$ mil.	% of total
Stocks	33,634	92
Money markets	2,926	8
Bonds	120	—
Social Choice	60	—
Total	**36,740**	**100**

TIAA Insurance Assets
Cost-of-living life insurance
Group life insurance
Health insurance
Individual life insurance
Interest Payment Retirement Option
Retirement and Group Retirement Annuities

CREF Investment Vehicles
Bond Market Account
Money Market Account
Social Choice Account
Stock Account
Variable annuity

RANKINGS

5th in *Fortune* 50 Life Insurance Cos.

KEY COMPETITORS

Aetna	Primerica
American Express	Prudential
CIGNA	Sears
Equitable	State Farm
John Hancock	Transamerica
Kemper	Travelers
MassMutual	USF&G
MetLife	Major banks
New York Life	Investment managers
Northwestern Mutual	

HOW MUCH

	9-Year Growth	1981	1982	1983	1984	1985	1986	1987	1988	1989	1990
Insurance assets ($ mil.)	17.8%	11,439	13,520	16,144	19,205	21,825	26,446	27,510	30,768	44,374	49,894
Change in contingency reserves ($ mil.)	—	(4)	(11)	12	106	58	138	178	191	125	228
Change as % of assets	—	0.0%	(0.1%)	0.1%	0.6%	0.3%	0.5%	0.6%	0.6%	0.3%	0.5%
CREF (stock) unit price ($)	16.2%	11.54	14.06	17.58	18.41	24.42	29.75	31.28	36.74	47.02	44.41
Employees	—	—	—	—	—	—	—	—	—	3,500	3,800

1990 Year-end:
Insurance only
Equity as % of assets: 4.2%
Sales (mil.): $9,360

Insurance Assets ($ mil.) 1981–90

TEAMSTERS

OVERVIEW

Headquartered in Washington, DC, the International Brotherhood of Teamsters is the US's largest and most diverse union. Its more than 1.7 million members include truckers, United Parcel Service drivers (UPS is the union's largest employer), warehouse workers, cab drivers, airline employees, and factory and sanitation workers. The Teamsters are also a force in politics; their political action committee (DRIVE) is the nation's richest.

The union consists of 620 local chapters across the US and Canada. The locals elect their own officers, employ their own full-time staff, and vote on their own contracts. Representatives of the locals elect the national leadership at the Teamsters convention.

Historically, some members of the Teamsters' leadership have been alleged to have connections with organized crime. Several have been convicted of crimes themselves, including Jimmy Hoffa (jury tampering) and Roy Lee Williams (conspiracy to bribe a US senator). Over 100 local Teamsters leaders have been prosecuted, while several local unions have been taken over by court-appointed trustees.

As the result of a civil RICO (racketeering) suit brought by the federal government and settled by the Teamsters in 1989, the union will conduct its first government-supervised, direct, secret-ballot election of executive officers in 1991.

Labor union
Fiscal year ends: December 31

Hoover's Rating **B-**

WHO

General President: William J. McCarthy
General Secretary-Treasurer: Weldon L. Mathis
General Counsel: James T. Grady
Auditors: Watchmaker & Company

WHERE

HQ: International Brotherhood of Teamsters, Chauffeurs, Warehousemen, and Helpers of America, 25 Louisiana Ave. NW, Washington, DC 20001
Phone: 202-624-6800
Fax: 202-624-6918

The Teamsters have 620 local unions in the US and Canada. The union also maintains 43 joint councils and 10 state conferences to provide an additional level of administrative support.

State Conferences
Arkansas-Oklahoma Conference
Georgia-Florida Conference
Illinois Conference
Indiana Conference
Iowa Conference
Kentucky–West Virginia Conference
Missouri-Kansas Conference
Ohio Conference
Pennsylvania Conference
Texas Conference

WHEN

In 1903, 2 rival team-driver unions, the Drivers International Union and the Teamsters National Union, merged to form the International Brotherhood of Teamsters. Led by Cornelius Shea, the Teamsters established headquarters in Indianapolis.

Daniel Tobin (president for 45 years from 1907) demanded that union locals obtain executive approval before striking. Membership expanded from the team-driver base, prompting the union to add Chauffeurs, Stablemen, and Helpers to its name (1909).

Following the first transcontinental delivery by motor truck (1912), the Teamster deliverymen abandoned their horses for trucks. The union then began recruiting food processing, brewery, farm, and other workers to augment Teamster effectiveness during strikes; jurisdictional disputes with other unions soon became a Teamster trademark. In 1920 the Teamsters joined the AF of L.

Until the Depression era, the Teamsters were still a relatively small union (about 100,000 members) of predominantly in-city deliverymen. Then a Teamster Trotskyite from Minneapolis (Farrell Dobbs) organized the famous Minneapolis strikes in 1934 to protest local management's refusal to allow the workers to unionize. Militant workers clashed with police and National Guard units for 11 days before management conceded to the workers' demands. The strikes demonstrated the potential strength of unions, and Teamsters membership swelled.

Union power was greatly curtailed during WWII when union officials were assigned positions on production committees. Nevertheless, the Teamsters continued to grow and in 1953 moved headquarters to Washington, DC.

The AFL-CIO expelled the Teamsters in 1957 when its ties to "the mob" became public during a US Senate investigation. New Teamsters boss Jimmy Hoffa eluded indictment and took advantage of America's growing dependence on trucking to negotiate the powerful National Master Freight Agreement (1964). Hoffa also organized industrial workers and added enticements such as medical programs and a strong political voice (DRIVE, 1963).

Hoffa also used the Teamsters' Central States Pension Fund to make mob-connected loans. Hoffa was later convicted of jury tampering and sent to prison. In 1975, after his release, Hoffa disappeared.

In 1987 the Teamsters rejoined the AFL-CIO. In 1988 the government sued the Teamsters, who settled the suit in 1989 by agreeing to allow government-appointed officials to discipline corrupt union leaders, help run the union, and supervise its elections.

Prior to the 1991 election, allegations were made that President William McCarthy had fired several underlings for refusing to support presidential frontrunner R. V. Durham. Also in 1991 the Teamsters signed a new 3-year contract with the trucking industry, and James Hoffa (son of Jimmy Hoffa) was ruled ineligible to run for president.

WHAT

	1990 Income	
	$ mil.	% of total
Per capita fees	364	83
Initiation fees	3	1
Investment income	67	15
Other sources	5	1
Total	**439**	**100**

	1990 Expenses	
	$ mil.	% of total
Out-of-work benefits	30	7
Teamster Affiliates Pension	54	12
Officers & employees retirement	2	1
Affiliation fees	19	4
Organizing campaign expenses	31	7
Administrative, office & general	113	26
Convention	5	1
Magazine	31	7
Legislative & political education	11	2
Communications	11	2
Legal fees, expenses & related costs	11	2
Civil RICO	17	4
Judgments, suits & settlements	1	–
Divisional & departmental	82	19
National headquarters building	20	5
Other	3	1
Total	**441**	**100**

Trade Divisions
Airline Division
Automotive, Petroleum, and Allied Trades Division
Building Material and Construction Division
Freight Division
Household Goods, Moving and Storage Trade Division
Industrial Trade Division
Laundry Division
Newspaper Drivers Division
Public Employees' Trade Division
Trade-Show and Movie-Making Trade Division
Warehouse Division

HOW MUCH

	9-Year Growth	1981	1982	1983	1984	1985	1986	1987	1988	1989	1990
Assets ($ mil.)	2.9%	149.7	155.3	176.0	193.7	198.6	198.6	198.0	193.8	191.6	207
Total receipts ($ mil.)	—	137.4	242.9	255.5	215.2	445.0	831.7	1,716.2	1,939.7	1,544.7	—
Total disbursements ($ mil.)	—	130.8	263.6	251.7	206.2	438.9	842.9	1,720.7	1,928.4	1,540.4	—

Assets ($ mil.) 1981–90

[Bar chart showing assets from 1981 to 1990, ranging from 0 to 250, with values approximately: 1981 ≈150, 1982 ≈155, 1983 ≈176, 1984 ≈194, 1985 ≈199, 1986 ≈199, 1987 ≈198, 1988 ≈194, 1989 ≈192, 1990 ≈207]

TELE-COMMUNICATIONS, INC.

OVERVIEW

Denver-based Tele-Communications, Inc. (TCI) is the nation's largest cable systems operator, serving approximately 8.5 million subscribers directly and through subsidiaries. TCI owns a 42.5% indirect interest in SCI Holdings, a major cable operator. The company also owns 49% of the Discovery Channel and a 10.5% voting interest in Turner Broadcasting.

CEO John Malone continues his rapid-fire wheeling and dealing. In an effort to ward off government actions that could force divestitures or limit growth, in 1991 TCI spun off many of its investments in cable programmers into a new company, Liberty Media, in which TCI retains a 5% interest.

Having agreed to purchase the shares of United Artists Entertainment it does not already own, TCI will become the nation's largest motion picture theater operator, with 2,506 screens. The acquisition will also give TCI full control of UAE's cable subscription base of 2.6 million households.

TCI announced plans to purchase 50% of Showtime Networks from Viacom in 1989, but by the conclusion of a lengthy FTC review of the transaction, both parties appeared to have lost interest in completing the deal.

WHEN

Tele-Communications began in 1956 when rancher Bob Magness sold some cattle to raise money to build his first cable system in the Texas Panhandle hamlet of Memphis. In 1965 Magness moved the company to Denver to serve small Rocky Mountain towns.

TCI went public in 1970 just as the capital-intensive cable TV industry was taking its first steps. Magness hired 32-year-old John Malone from General Instrument Corporation in 1973. The deal-making Malone became known as the "godfather" of cable because he stabilized the company and extended its reach.

Malone's first battle was with the city of Vail, Colorado, over cable services and rates. At the height of the argument, Malone showed nothing on the cable system for a weekend but the names and phone numbers of city officials. The city backed down.

In 1977 Malone restructured TCI's debt. He sat out the bidding for big-city franchises, buying them instead at hefty discounts after bigger competitors stumbled.

Congress deregulated the cable industry in 1984, and TCI aggressively bought new systems. In 1986 it won control of United Artists Communications, the largest operator of movie theaters as well as the 11th largest cable operator. TCI purchased Heritage Communications, including its Dallas system, in 1987

for $1.3 billion. In the late 1980s TCI spent nearly $3 billion for more than 150 cable companies, often in joint ventures with other multisystem operators. The debt TCI ran up led to losses in 1989 and early 1990.

TCI's size gave it clout with cable programmers, who kept their prices low to curry favor. Malone, recognizing that his systems would need a variety of programming to attract viewers, financed nascent channels in exchange for stock. Malone led a group of cable operators who chipped in to save Ted Turner's debt-plagued TBS in 1987; TCI came away with a substantial interest in TBS stock and spearheaded the launch of TBS's TNT channel. TCI also has investments in Black Entertainment Television (1979), Discovery Channel (1986), Think Entertainment (1987), and American Movie Classics (1987).

TCI bought more cable systems in 1990 and, in an unusually complex transaction, spun off cable programming interests including regional sports networks, The Family Channel, QVC Network (shopping), Black Entertainment Television, and American Movie Classics, as well as various cable systems, to shareholders as Liberty Media in 1991. Liberty announced it would launch Encore, a low-cost movie channel, and join a partnership to start a sports news channel.

NYSE symbol: TCOMA, TCOMB
Fiscal year ends: December 31

Hoover's Rating **C-**

WHO

Chairman: Bob Magness, age 67, $454,136 pay
President and CEO: John C. Malone, age 50, $404,629 pay
EVP and COO: J. C. Sparkman, age 59, $329,128 pay
SVP and Treasurer: Donne F. Fisher, age 53, $329,133 pay
VP (Personnel): Madonna B. Guenthner
Auditors: KPMG Peat Marwick
Employees: 33,000

WHERE

HQ: 4643 S. Ulster St., Denver, CO 80237
Phone: 303-721-5500
Fax: 303-779-1228

TCI and its affiliates operate cable television systems in all 50 states and 540 multi-screen theaters in 37 states, Hong Kong, and Puerto Rico.

	Movie Theater Locations	
	No. of screens	% of total
California	321	13
Florida	255	10
Texas	215	9
New York	205	8
Georgia	161	6
Other	1,349	54
Total	**2,506**	**100**

WHAT

	1990 Sales	
	$ mil.	% of total
Cable TV	2,932	81
Movie theaters	693	19
Total	**3,625**	**100**

Cable Television Systems
Communication Services, Inc.
Heritage Communications, Inc.
SCI Holdings, Inc. (42.5%)
Tele-Communications, Inc.
United Artists Entertainment Company
WestMarc

Cable Programming Services
Cable Educational Network, Inc. (49%, Discovery Channel)
Liberty Media, Inc. (5%)
Turner Broadcasting System, Inc. (10.5% voting interest)

Motion Picture Theater Exhibition
United Artists Entertainment Company

Publications
Cabletime (cable guide)

RANKINGS

20th in *Fortune* 50 Utilities
115th in *Business Week* 1000

KEY COMPETITORS

Advance Publications	Knight-Ridder
Blockbuster	Matsushita
Capital Cities/ABC	Paramount
CBS	Sony
Cox	Time Warner
General Cinema	Times Mirror
General Electric	Viacom
Hallmark	Washington Post
Hearst	

HOW MUCH

	9-Year Growth	1981	1982	1983	1984	1985	1986	1987	1988	1989	1990
Sales ($ mil.)	39.5%	181	283	347	449	577	646	1,709	2,282	3,026	3,625
Net income ($ mil.)	—	13	10	16	17	10	72	6	56	(257)	(287)
Income as % of sales	—	7.1%	3.7%	4.6%	3.8%	1.8%	11.2%	0.3%	2.5%	(8.5%)	(7.9%)
Earnings per share ($)	—	0.04	0.04	0.06	0.06	0.04	0.24	0.02	0.16	(0.73)	(0.81)
Stock price – high ($)	—	2.65	2.39	3.71	4.13	6.50	9.71	15.13	14.00	21.63	18.50
Stock price – low ($)	—	1.39	1.06	1.98	2.58	3.75	5.85	7.63	10.19	12.63	8.38
Stock price – close ($)	27.1%	1.53	2.31	3.38	3.88	6.10	7.63	11.81	13.06	17.88	13.25
P/E – high	—	66	62	62	65	177	40	756	90	—	—
P/E – low	—	35	28	33	41	102	24	381	66	—	—
Dividends per share ($)	0.0%	0.00	0.00	0.00	0.00	0.00	0.00	0.00	0.00	0.00	0.00
Book value per share ($)	9.8%	0.75	0.86	0.93	0.91	1.31	2.44	2.60	3.41	2.57	1.74

1990 Year-end:
Debt ratio: 93.7%
Return on equity: —
Cash (mil.): $31
Current ratio: —
Long-term debt (mil.): $9,300
No. of shares (mil.): 358
Dividends:
 1990 average yield: 0.0%
 1990 payout: 0.0%
Market value (mil.): $4,743

Stock Price History High/Low 1981–90

TELEDYNE, INC.

NYSE symbol: TDY
Fiscal year ends: December 31

Hoover's Rating **C-**

OVERVIEW

Teledyne is a technology-oriented conglomerate of 100 different businesses. US government business, mostly related to aviation electronics, accounts for 35% of Teledyne's sales. The company's defense electronics products include electronic components and radar, navigation, and electronic warfare systems.

Teledyne's most profitable segment processes specialty metals like zirconium and titanium into alloys and end products. The company's best-known consumer brand is Water-Pik. Teledyne's industrial products include engines, machine tools, factory automation equipment and analytical instruments.

Henry Singleton, who owns 13.1% of Teledyne stock, stepped down from the post of chairman in 1991. In its 30 years under Singleton, Teledyne never lost money. Under new chairman George Roberts and CEO William Rutledge, Teledyne is considering the sale or closure of many of the broadly diversified company's operations. Teledyne's earnings have been hurt by the recession, losses on fixed-rate government contracts, and the US government's suspension of purchases from a Teledyne unit over product performance failures.

WHO

Chairman: George A. Roberts, age 72, $819,700 pay (prior to promotion)
President and CEO: William P. Rutledge, age 49, $583,500 pay (prior to promotion)
Treasurer and Principal Financial and Accounting Officer: Douglas Grant, age 40
Director Human Resources: Dan Lucasik
Auditors: Arthur Andersen & Co.; KPMG Peat Marwick
Employees: 33,200

WHERE

HQ: 1901 Ave. of the Stars, Los Angeles, CA 90067
Phone: 213-277-3311
Fax: 213-551-4365

Teledyne operates in the US and 13 foreign countries.

WHEN

Teledyne is the creation of Henry Singleton. The son of a well-to-do Texas rancher, Singleton earned a PhD in electrical engineering from MIT and learned business management while working for Hughes Aircraft, North American Aviation, and Litton Industries in the 1950s.

Singleton and another Litton executive, George Kozmetsky, invested $225,000 each and founded Teledyne in 1960 to make electronic components for aircraft manufacturers. The company grew from $4.5 million in sales its first year to nearly $90 million in 4 years. It beat out IBM and Texas Instruments to win the contract for an avionics system for a navy helicopter in 1965, and sales jumped to $250 million in 1966. Kozmetsky, laden with Teledyne stock, left in 1966 to become dean of the University of Texas Business School and, later, to found a think tank, the Institute for Constructive Capitalism, at UT.

Teledyne grew into a conglomerate, buying over 100 companies in a variety of mostly high-tech, defense-related businesses, including engines, unmanned aircraft, specialty metals, computers, and semiconductors. The company also moved into offshore oil drilling equipment, insurance and finance, and the Water-Pik line of bathroom hardware.

By 1969, as sales passed $1 billion, Singleton had realized a boyhood goal of creating a giant corporation. But in 1970 Singleton stopped buying companies, and Teledyne lost favor with investors. Earnings flattened, then dropped in 1974, when one of its insurance divisions lost money writing malpractice insurance for physicians.

In an unusual and now widely admired masterstroke, Singleton bought Teledyne shares back from stockholders between 1972 and 1976, when they sold as low as 7-7/8 a share. Yet the company continued to grow from within. Sales of $1.2 billion in 1970 reached $2.7 billion in 1979, and profits increased 315% from 1969 to 1978. Earnings per share skyrocketed 1,226%. When Wall Street rediscovered the company, happy shareholders enjoyed the appreciation. By 1979 Teledyne stock sold for well over $100 a share.

In 1986 Teledyne spun off its Argonaut Insurance unit and left the insurance business entirely with its 1990 spinoff of Unitrin, which owned 25% of the company stock of Litton Industries and 44% of Curtiss-Wright Corporation. Teledyne's defense businesses suffered a setback in 1989 when caught in an FBI investigation of fraud by defense contractors (Operation Ill Wind). The company paid $4.4 million in restitution.

WHAT

	1990 Sales		1990 Operating Income	
	$ mil.	% of total	$ mil.	% of total
Aviation & electronics	1,471	43	45	20
Specialty metals	854	25	92	41
Industrial products	796	23	48	22
Consumer products	325	9	39	17
Adjustments	—	—	(77)	—
Total	**3,446**	**100**	**147**	**100**

Aviation and Electronics
Aviation piston engines
Avionics
Electromechanical relays
Electronic navigation systems
Microcircuitry and components
Remotely piloted aircraft
Systems engineering for military, space shuttle

Specialty Metals

Molybdenum	Tantalum	Tungsten
Niobium	Titanium	Zirconium

Industrial
Analytical instruments
Electrical equipment
Engines
Factory automation equipment
Machine tools and dies
Seismic surveying
Valves

Commercial and Consumer Products
Instapure water and air filters
Laars swimming pool and spa heaters
Water-Pik oral hygiene products
Water-Pik Shower Massage

HOW MUCH

	9-Year Growth	1981	1982	1983	1984	1985	1986	1987	1988	1989	1990
Sales ($ mil.)	0.7%	3,238	2,864	2,979	3,494	3,256	3,241	3,217	4,523	3,531	3,446
Net income ($ mil.)	(18.0%)	412	261	305	574	546	238	377	392	150	69
Income as % of sales	—	12.7%	9.1%	10.2%	16.4%	16.8%	7.4%	11.7%	8.7%	4.3%	2.0%
Earnings per share ($)	(12.1%)	3.99	2.52	2.97	7.54	9.33	4.07	6.45	6.81	2.71	1.25
Stock price – high ($)	—	34.95	28.75	34.70	60.48	67.60	73.55	78.00	69.70	76.15	72.78
Stock price – low ($)	—	23.60	13.90	24.60	29.45	45.40	58.20	48.40	58.05	63.50	12.00
Stock price – close ($)	(6.8%)	27.70	25.88	33.45	49.20	66.08	60.30	60.80	66.45	68.65	14.75
P/E – high	—	9	11	12	8	7	18	12	10	28	58
P/E – low	—	6	6	8	4	5	14	8	9	23	10
Dividends per share ($)	—	0.00	0.00	0.00	0.00	0.00	0.00	0.80	0.80	0.80	0.80
Book value per share ($)	(6.0%)	16.52	20.20	25.93	19.80	26.94	27.95	33.87	38.22	41.99	9.45

1990 Year-end:
Debt ratio: 49.4%
Return on equity: 4.9%
Cash (mil.): $186
Current ratio: 2.07
Long-term debt (mil.): $511
No. of shares (mil.): 55
Dividends:
  1990 average yield: 5.4%
  1990 payout: 64.0%
Market value (mil.): $817

Stock Price History
High/Low 1981–90

RANKINGS

130th in *Fortune* 500 Industrial Cos.
468th in *Business Week* 1000

KEY COMPETITORS

Amway	Ingersoll-Rand	TRW
Clorox	Litton Industries	Other defense
Emerson	Raytheon	electronics
General Electric	Texas Instruments	companies
Henley	Textron	
Honeywell	Thomson SA	

TENNECO, INC.

NYSE symbol: TGT
Fiscal year ends: December 31

Hoover's Rating **C**

OVERVIEW

Although Houston-based Tenneco generates more revenues from its J. I. Case farm and construction equipment division than any other, it is most noted for its profit-leading natural gas operations. Running from Texas to Massachusetts, 18,000 miles of pipeline delivered 2.6 trillion cubic feet of natural gas (or 13% of US consumption) and generated revenues of $2.5 billion in 1990.

J. I. Case, the world's 2nd largest agricultural equipment maker after Deere, provides farm and construction equipment through a worldwide dealer network ($5.4 billion).

Newport News Shipbuilding and Dry Dock Company is the US's largest shipbuilder, selling nuclear-powered submarines and aircraft carriers to the navy ($2.1 billion in 1990 sales).

Auto parts (brakes, exhaust systems, and shock absorbers) brought in $1.7 billion in 1990.

Packaging Corporation of America supplies paperboard, shipping, and disposable plastic and aluminum containers ($1.5 billion). Tenneco sells phosphorus chemicals, bleaches, and surfactants ($1.3 billion) through Albright & Wilson, the 2nd largest specialty chemical producer headquartered in the UK.

Operating income was down for all of Tenneco's divisions in the first half of 1991 due to the recession. Farm and construction equipment was particularly hurt, reporting a 2nd-quarter loss of $123 million versus a $57 million profit for the year ago period.

New president Michael Walsh is scheduled to become CEO in January 1992 and chairman in May 1992.

WHO

Chairman and CEO: James L. Ketelsen, age 60, $1,644,321 pay
President: Michael H. Walsh, age 49
EVP: Allen T. McInnes, age 54, $760,418 pay
SVP and CFO: Robert T. Blakely, age 49, $512,246 pay
Director of Human Resources: Gloria Garza
Auditors: Arthur Andersen & Co.
Employees: 92,000

WHERE

HQ: Tenneco Bldg., PO Box 2511, Houston, TX 77252-2511
Phone: 713-757-2131
Fax: 713-757-1410

The company operates worldwide.

	1990 Sales		1990 Operating Income	
	$ mil.	% of total	$ mil.	% of total
US	9,985	69	1,129	78
Canada	798	6	89	6
Europe	3,105	21	155	11
Other countries	623	4	79	5
Adjustments	—	—	(212)	—
Total	**14,511**	**100**	**1,240**	**100**

WHAT

	1990 Sales		1990 Operating Income	
	$ mil.	% of total	$ mil.	% of total
Nat. gas pipelines	2,459	17	357	25
Shipbuilding	2,113	15	238	16
Automotive parts	1,731	12	222	15
Packaging	1,469	10	197	14
Chem. & minerals	1,298	9	167	12
Farm & const. equip.	5,390	37	208	14
Other	51	—	63	4
Adjustments	—	—	(212)	—
Total	**14,511**	**100**	**1,240**	**100**

Pipeline Operations
Altamont Gas Transmission Co. (40%)
Channel Industries Gas
Creole Gas Pipeline
East Tennessee Natural Gas
Iroquois Gas Transmission System (13.2%)
Kern River Gas Transmission Co. (50%)
Midwestern Gas Transmission
State Gas Pipeline
Tennessee Gas Pipeline
THC Pipeline
Viking Gas Transmission

Major Manufacturing Companies
Albright & Wilson Ltd. (chemicals)
J. I. Case Co. (farm and construction equipment)
Monroe Auto Equipment Co. (automotive parts)
Newport News Shipbuilding and Dry Dock Co.
Packaging Corp. of America
Tenneco Minerals Co.
Walker Manufacturing Co. (automotive parts)

WHEN

Tennessee Gas and Transmission began in 1943 as a division of The Chicago Corporation, headed by Gardiner Symonds and authorized to construct a 1,265-mile pipeline between the Gulf of Mexico and West Virginia. As the nation faced WWII fuel shortages, the fledgling group completed the project in a record 11 months, obtaining right-of-way from thousands of landowners and crossing 67 rivers.

Just after WWII, Tennessee Gas went public; Symonds became president. While expanding the pipeline, the company merged its oil and gas exploration interests into Tennessee Production Company (1954), which, with Bay Petroleum (bought 1955), formed subsidiary Tenneco Oil (1961). Symonds entered the chemical industry by acquiring 50% of Petro-Tex Chemical (1955), now Tenneco Chemicals.

In 1963 Tennessee Gas moved to its present Houston headquarters and in 1966 adopted the Tenneco name. In 1967 Tenneco purchased Kern County Land Company, which owned 2.5 million acres of California farmland and mineral rights. The purchase thrust Tenneco into the farming business; by 1984 Tenneco was the US's largest grower/shipper of table grapes and 2nd largest almond processor. The Kern purchase also included 2 Racine, Wisconsin–based manufacturers: J. I. Case is known for tractors and construction digging equipment; Walker Manufacturing entered the automotive field in 1912 producing jacks.

Symonds purchased Evanston, Illinois–based Packaging Corporation of America in 1965, maker of shipping containers, pulp, and paperboard products. In 1968 he acquired Newport News Shipbuilding, founded by Collis Huntington in 1886. Newport News began building submarines and nuclear-powered aircraft carriers in the 1960s.

Following Symonds's death in 1971, Tenneco bought shock absorber manufacturer Monroe of Monroe, Michigan (1977) and Philadelphia Life Insurance Company (1977); Philadelphia Life was sold to ICH Corporation in 1986. In 1985 Case bought major competitor International Harvester's agricultural equipment operations. Tenneco sold its agricultural operations (1987) and its oil operations (1988).

In 1990 Case was late in responding to the recession and reacted by reducing prices to lower inventory and by slashing 4,000 jobs.

RANKINGS

26th in *Fortune* 500 Industrial Cos.
102nd in *Business Week* 1000

KEY COMPETITORS

American Standard
Borg-Warner
Caterpillar
Coastal
Columbia Gas
Daewoo
Deere
Eaton
Fiat
General Dynamics
Johnson Controls
Litton Industries
Peter Kiewit Sons'
Occidental
Owens-Illinois
Automotive parts manufacturers
Chemical companies
Other natural gas pipeline companies
Packaging companies
Shipbuilders

HOW MUCH

	9-Year Growth	1981	1982	1983	1984	1985	1986	1987	1988	1989	1990
Sales ($ mil.)	(0.7%)	15,462	14,979	14,449	14,890	15,270	14,529	14,790	13,234	14,083	14,511
Net income ($ mil.)	(4.0%)	813	840	716	631	431	139	(132)	(1)	584	561
Income as % of sales	—	5.3%	5.6%	5.0%	4.2%	2.8%	1.0%	(0.9%)	0.0%	4.1%	3.9%
Earnings per share ($)	(3.5%)	5.99	5.89	4.74	4.00	2.52	0.50	(1.22)	(0.18)	4.45	4.36
Stock price – high ($)	—	51.88	36.50	42.38	44.75	45.25	43.13	62.50	51.00	64.25	71.00
Stock price – low ($)	—	29.88	22.88	31.88	32.38	36.50	34.50	36.13	38.25	46.88	40.00
Stock price – close ($)	4.0%	33.50	32.38	41.00	37.88	39.75	38.25	39.75	48.88	62.25	47.50
P/E – high	—	9	6	9	11	18	86	—	—	14	16
P/E – low	—	5	4	7	8	14	69	—	—	11	9
Dividends per share ($)	2.0%	2.60	2.63	2.74	2.83	2.95	3.04	3.04	3.04	3.04	3.12
Book value per share ($)	(3.8%)	39.05	40.14	41.75	42.24	40.20	30.02	25.66	24.93	26.02	27.60

1990 Year-end:
Debt ratio: 64.0%
Return on equity: 16.3%
Cash (mil.): $147
Current ratio: 1.1
Long-term debt (mil.): $5,976
No. of shares (mil.): 122
Dividends:
　1990 average yield: 6.6%
　1990 payout: 71.6%
Market value (mil.): $5,794

Stock Price History High/Low 1981–90

TEXACO INC.

NYSE symbol: TX
Fiscal year ends: December 31

OVERVIEW

Texaco is the 3rd largest integrated oil company in the US, behind Exxon and Mobil. With its famous and costly legal battle with Pennzoil concluded, it has scaled down into one of the most productive (in sales per employee) companies.

In "upstream" (exploration and production) activities, Texaco has focused on finding oil in existing fields where the risk is low. It has also used its financial muscle to buy new properties. In "downstream" (refining and marketing) operations, it has squeezed more bucks for the barrel at the refinery. It has added convenience food marts/gas stations, known as Star Marts (harking back to Texaco's well-known logo), to the landscape.

Overseas, its 50% stake in Caltex (along with Chevron) places Texaco in 58 nations in Asia and the Pacific Rim. Caltex sells nearly 18% of the fuels and lubricants used there.

WHEN

"Buckskin Joe" Cullinan came to Texas in 1897 and, relying on sales to old friends from his days as a Standard Oil worker in Pennsylvania, began his own oil company.

When the Spindletop gusher hit in 1901, some 200 "oil companies" swarmed onto the scene. Cullinan surveyed the chaos around Beaumont and decided the way to make money was to sell oil other people had found. He enlisted the support of Arnold Schlaet, who managed investments for 2 New York leather merchants. Cullinan and the Schlaet interests formed Texas Fuel in 1902. In a few months, they changed the name to The Texas Company, selling under the Texaco brand.

The colorful Cullinan was deposed in a 1916 fight with New York executives. From its New York base The Texas Company quickly expanded across the globe. When Standard of California's discoveries in Saudi Arabia proved more than it could handle, it summoned Texaco, and the 2 companies spawned Caltex for overseas marketing in 1936. Again, Texaco was selling oil someone else had found.

Also in the 1930s, Texaco, partly through a company controlled by political boss Huey Long's family, leased a million acres of state-owned, oil-rich marshland in Louisiana. With such resources Texaco became the only oil company with service stations in all states. In the 1940s it began sponsoring radio opera (the program marked its 50th anniversary in 1990) and Milton Berle's TV show. Its ads urged that "You can trust your car to the man who wears the star," a reference to the company logo.

But Texaco, which took its trade name as its corporate name in 1959, fell from atop the oil industry in the 1960s and 1970s. US wells dried up. Texaco passed up drilling in Alaska's Prudhoe Bay and lost crude supplies when Third World governments nationalized them.

Texaco thought it had found a source of oil in the $8.6 billion purchase of Getty Oil in 1983. But Getty had already agreed to be acquired by Pennzoil. A Texas court ordered Texaco to pay Pennzoil $10.53 billion in damages, and Texaco sought bankruptcy protection in 1987. After a $3 billion settlement with Pennzoil later that year, Texaco emerged from bankruptcy — just in time to fend off raider Carl Icahn.

After the Pennzoil and Icahn battles, Texaco raised about $7 billion, partly by selling its West German subsidiary and Texaco Canada (1988). Texaco shucked 2,500 unprofitable gas stations, pulling out of 11 states.

In 1989 Texaco launched a joint venture, Star Enterprise, with Saudi Arabia. Texaco put in 60% of its US refining and marketing operations, and the Saudis chipped in $812 million cash and a steady flow of crude. The Gulf War, though, pointed up the weakness in that arrangement: 60% of Texaco's refinery output relied on Saudi crude. In 1990 the company nearly doubled its capital spending (to $3.1 billion) to find new sources of oil.

WHO

President and CEO: James W. Kinnear, age 63, $1,928,282 pay
Chairman: Alfred C. DeCrane, Jr., age 59, $1,504,868 pay
SVP and CFO: Allen J. Krowe, age 58, $996,306 pay
SVP; President, Texaco USA: James L. Dunlap, age 53, $564,092 pay
SVP and General Counsel: Stephen M. Turner, age 51
VP Human Resources: John D. Ambler, age 56
Auditor: Arthur Andersen & Co.
Employees: 39,199

WHERE

HQ: 2000 Westchester Ave., White Plains, NY 10650
Phone: 914-253-4000
Fax: 914-253-7753

Texaco operates worldwide.

	1990 Sales		1990 Operating Income	
	$ mil.	% of total	$ mil.	% of total
US	23,379	57	860	58
Other Americas	4,411	11	49	3
Eastern Hemisphere	13,109	32	575	39
Adjustments	—	—	348	—
Total	**40,899**	**100**	**1,832**	**100**

WHAT

	1990 Sales		1990 Operating Income	
	$ mil.	% of total	$ mil.	% of total
Petroleum, natural gas & other	39,431	96	2,366	98
Petrochemical	1,468	4	60	2
Adjustments	—	—	(594)	—
Total	**40,899**	**100**	**1,832**	**100**

Brand Names
Havoline (motor oils)
Star Enterprise (60%, refining and marketing venture with Saudi Aramco, 26 US states)
Star Mart (convenience/gas stores)
System[3] (gasolines, successor to Texaco Fire Chief and Sky Chief gasolines)

RANKINGS

8th in *Fortune* 500 Industrial Cos.
32nd in *Business Week* 1000

KEY COMPETITORS

Amoco	Mobil
Ashland	Norsk Hydro
Atlantic Richfield	Occidental
British Petroleum	Pennzoil
Broken Hill	Petrofina
Chevron	Petrobrás
Circle K	PDVSA
Coastal	Pemex
Du Pont	Phillips Petroleum
Elf Aquitaine	Royal Dutch/Shell
Exxon	Southland
Imperial Oil	Sun
Koch	Unocal
Kroger	USX

HOW MUCH

	9-Year Growth	1981	1982	1983	1984	1985	1986	1987	1988	1989	1990
Sales ($ mil.)	(3.7%)	57,628	46,986	40,068	47,334	46,297	31,613	34,372	33,544	32,416	40,899
Net income ($ mil.)	(5.0%)	2,310	1,281	1,233	306	1,233	725	(4,407)	1,304	2,413	1,450
Income as % of sales	—	4.0%	2.7%	3.1%	0.6%	2.7%	2.3%	(12.8%)	3.9%	7.4%	3.5%
Earnings per share ($)	(5.9%)	8.75	4.92	4.80	1.03	4.84	3.00	(18.15)	5.19	8.74	5.08
Stock price – high ($)	—	49.13	34.88	39.13	48.38	40.88	37.13	47.50	52.50	59.00	68.50
Stock price – low ($)	—	31.50	26.00	30.50	31.50	27.00	26.00	23.50	35.63	48.50	55.00
Stock price – close ($)	7.0%	33.00	31.13	35.88	34.13	30.00	35.88	37.25	51.13	58.88	60.50
P/E – high	—	6	7	8	47	8	12	—	10	7	13
P/E – low	—	4	5	6	31	6	9	—	7	6	11
Dividends per share ($)	1.0%	2.80	3.00	3.00	3.00	3.00	3.00	0.75	2.25	10.10	3.05
Book value per share ($)	(5.6%)	53.11	55.12	56.86	55.15	57.04	56.71	37.76	31.13	30.31	31.72

1990 Year-end:
Debt ratio: 32.3%
Return on equity: 16.4%
Cash (mil.): $829
Current ratio: 1.04
Long-term debt (mil.): $4,485
No. of shares (mil.): 258
Dividends:
1990 average yield: 5.0%
1990 payout: 60.0%
Market value (mil.): $15,619

Stock Price History High/Low 1981–90

TEXAS INSTRUMENTS INC.

OVERVIEW

NYSE symbol: TXN
Fiscal year ends: December 31

Hoover's Rating **C+**

Electronics pioneer Texas Instruments, the company that invented the integrated circuit, the single-chip microcomputer, liquid-crystal display technology, and the pocket calculator, entered the 1990s with a $39 million loss (its first since 1985 and 3rd ever) and annual sales growth of just 5.1% over the previous decade.

TI's results would have been much worse but for the company's success in obtaining royalties on its patents for basic electronic designs, such as the "Kilby patent" for the integrated circuit (named after the TI engineer who co-invented the IC). TI has collected over $700 million in royalties since 1986, including $172 million in 1990. In 1989 the Kilby patent was upheld in Japan, and all major Japanese electronics firms save Fujitsu now pay royalties to TI.

After an abortive attempt in the 1970s to dominate consumer markets, TI has been aided in recent years by defense electronics, the company's only profitable major industry segment in 1990. TI makes 21% of its sales to the US government; the HARM missile alone accounts for 9%.

TI's flagship business, semiconductors, still produces the largest share of the company's revenues. Like other troubled chip makers, TI has announced a shift toward more profitable application-specific integrated circuits (ASICs) and microcontrollers.

WHO

Chairman, President, and CEO: Jerry R. Junkins, age 53, $599,470 pay
EVP: William P. Weber, age 50, $346,730 pay
EVP: William B. Mitchell, age 55, $306,730 pay
EVP: William I. George, age 59, $266,432 pay
SVP, Treasurer, and CFO: William A. Aylesworth, age 48, $265,550 pay
Auditors: Ernst & Young
Employees: 70,138

WHEN

"Doc" Karcher and Eugene McDermott founded Geophysical Service Inc. (GSI) in Newark, New Jersey, in 1930. The company specialized in reflective seismology, a new technology used to explore for oil and gas deposits. In 1934 GSI moved its headquarters to Dallas.

GSI started making defense electronics during WWII, when it made submarine detectors for the US Navy, and established a defense division in 1946. The company changed its name to Texas Instruments in 1951 and was listed on the NYSE in 1953.

TI started manufacturing transistors in 1952 after buying a license from Western Electric. Former Bell Laboratories scientist Dr. Gordon Teal handled research for TI, and in an effort to reduce the price of the germanium transistor, the company invested about $2 million, which expanded the market for its uses and made possible the pocket transistor radio (1954). TI produced the first commercial silicon transistor in 1954, and TI engineer Jack Kilby (with Intel founder Bob Noyce) invented the integrated circuit in 1958. By 1959 TI's semiconductor manufacturing division accounted for 1/2 of the company's total sales.

TI's technological know-how led to other firsts in microelectronics, including terrain-following airborne radar (1958), forward-looking infrared (FLIR) systems (1964), hand-held calculators (1967), single-chip microcomputers (1971), and the LISP chip, a 32-bit microcomputer for artificial intelligence applications (1987). GSI, now TI's oil-exploration subsidiary, introduced equipment capable of digitally recording seismic data in 1961.

TI moved from defense and semiconductors into consumer products in the 1970s with hand-held calculators, digital watches, and home computers. Although TI had developed the basic technologies for these products, its inability to follow through in the face of low-cost foreign competition led it to lose money and then abandon both its digital watch and PC businesses. Attempts to meet competitors' prices, as well as plunging semiconductor prices, led TI to its first-ever annual loss in 1983.

In 1988 TI sold 60% of GSI to Halliburton, the balance in 1991. The company remains vulnerable to cuts in the defense budget and declines in chip prices. The company took a $130-million charge and announced the elimination of 3,200 jobs in the 2nd quarter of 1991; it also announced its intention to sell its industrial controls business to Siemens.

WHERE

HQ: 13500 N. Central Expressway, PO Box 655474, Dallas, TX 75265
Phone: 214-995-2551
Fax: 214-995-4360

TI has manufacturing facilities in 18 countries and subsidiaries in 27 countries.

	1990 Sales		1990 Operating Income	
	$ mil.	% of total	$ mil.	% of total
US	4,387	67	149	—
Europe	1,063	16	(21)	—
East Asia	1,027	16	(8)	—
Other regions	90	1	(24)	—
Adjustments	—	—	(122)	—
Total	**6,567**	**100**	**(26)**	**—**

WHAT

	1990 Sales		1990 Operating Income	
	$ mil.	% of total	$ mil.	% of total
Components	3,103	47	(76)	—
Digital products	1,210	19	(13)	—
Defense electronics	2,111	32	170	—
Metallurgical matls.	138	2	6	—
Adjustments	5	—	(113)	—
Total	**6,567**	**100**	**(26)**	**—**

Products
Calculators and learning aids
Clad metals
Data terminals and printers
Electrical and electronic control devices
Electronic connectors
Electronic warfare systems
HARM defensive missiles
Industrial automation systems
Missile guidance and control systems
Multiuser minicomputers
Personal computers and workstations
Radar and infrared surveillance systems
Semiconductors
Software-development tools

RANKINGS

74th in *Fortune* 500 Industrial Cos.
187th in *Business Week* 1000

KEY COMPETITORS

Apple	Hitachi	Raytheon
Canon	Honeywell	Rockwell
Casio	Hyundai	Samsung
Compaq	Ingersoll-Rand	Sharp
EG&G	Intel	Siemens
Emerson	IBM	Sun Microsystems
Fujitsu	Lucky-Goldstar	Teledyne
General	Motorola	Thomson SA
Dynamics	National	Thorn EMI
General Electric	Semiconductor	Toshiba
Harris	NEC	Other electronics
Hewlett-Packard	Oki	companies

HOW MUCH

	9-Year Growth	1981	1982	1983	1984	1985	1986	1987	1988	1989	1990
Sales ($ mil.)	5.1%	4,206	4,327	4,580	5,742	4,925	4,974	5,595	6,295	6,522	6,567
Net income ($ mil.)	—	109	144	(145)	316	(119)	40	257	366	292	(39)
Income as % of sales	—	2.6%	3.3%	(3.2%)	5.5%	(2.4%)	0.8%	4.6%	5.8%	4.5%	(0.6%)
Earnings per share ($)	—	1.54	2.01	(2.01)	4.32	(1.58)	0.38	2.95	4.05	3.04	(0.92)
Stock price – high ($)	—	42.08	50.83	58.67	49.83	43.92	49.42	80.25	60.00	46.75	44.00
Stock price – low ($)	—	25.00	23.50	37.25	37.25	28.75	34.25	36.25	34.50	28.13	22.50
Stock price – close ($)	3.9%	26.83	44.88	46.21	39.83	35.17	39.38	55.75	41.00	35.88	38.00
P/E – high	—	27	25	—	12	—	130	27	15	15	—
P/E – low	—	16	12	—	9	—	90	12	9	9	—
Dividends per share ($)	0.9%	0.67	0.67	0.67	0.67	0.67	0.67	0.71	0.72	0.72	0.72
Book value per share ($)	2.6%	17.81	19.18	16.69	20.86	18.91	22.51	21.95	21.36	24.10	22.46

1990 Year-end:
Debt ratio: 23.3%
Return on equity: —
Cash (mil.): $412
Current ratio: 1.56
Long-term debt (mil.): $715
No. of shares (mil.): 82
Dividends:
  1990 average yield: 1.9%
  1990 payout: —
Market value (mil.): $3,108

**Stock Price History
High/Low 1981–90**

TEXAS UTILITIES COMPANY

OVERVIEW

Texas Utilities (TU) is America's 9th largest electric utility, with $4.5 billion in 1990 sales. The company provides electric service to nearly 2.2 million customers in 370 Texas cities and towns (including the Dallas–Fort Worth Metroplex) through its principal subsidiary, Texas Utilities Electric Company (TU Electric). An especially hot summer helped TU Electric sell a record 83.7 billion kilowatt-hours of electricity in 1990.

Other TU subsidiaries support TU Electric by providing the lignite coal (Texas Utilities Mining Company) and natural gas and oil (Texas Utilities Fuel Company) necessary to fuel the company's generating plants. In addition, TU Fuel Company owns 50% of a 395-mile natural gas pipeline, linking the Dallas–Fort Worth area to West Texas producing fields. Chaco Energy owns coal reserves totaling some 120 million recoverable tons. Another subsidiary, Texas Utilities Services, furnishes administrative services to the other system companies.

TU has paid dividends every year since its incorporation in 1945 and has increased its dividend every year since 1948.

WHO

Chairman and CEO: Jerry S. Farrington, age 56, $658,333 pay
President: Erle Nye, age 53, $518,750 pay
VP and Principal Financial Officer: T. L. Baker, age 45, $202,500 pay
Auditors: Deloitte & Touche
Employees: 15,216

WHERE

HQ: 2001 Bryan Tower, Dallas, TX 75201
Phone: 214-812-4600
Fax: 214-812-4079

Texas Utilities serves 370 communities in 87 North-Central, East, and West Texas counties.

Principal Cities Served

Arlington	Mesquite	Richardson
Dallas	Midland	Tyler
Fort Worth	Odessa	Waco
Irving	Plano	Wichita Falls
Killeen		

Generating Facilities

Oil and Gas	Permian Basin
Collin	River Crest
Dallas	Stryker Creek
Decordova	Tradinghouse Creek
Eagle Mountain	Trinidad
Forest Grove	Twin Oak
Graham	Valley
Handley	
Lake Creek	**Lignite**
Lake Hubbard	Big Brown
Morgan Creek	Martin Lake
Mountain Creek	Monticello
North Lake	Sandow
North Main	
Parkdale	**Nuclear**
	Comanche Peak

WHEN

The first electric power company in North Texas was founded in Dallas in 1883. Another was built in 1885 in Fort Worth. From these and other small power plants grew 3 companies that developed to serve the north-central, western, and eastern regions of the state: Texas Power and Light (1912), Dallas Power and Light (1917), and Texas Electric Service Company (1929). By 1932 a network of transmission lines connecting these 3 utilities was virtually complete. Texas Utilities Company was formed in 1945 as a holding company to enable the 3 utilities to raise capital and obtain construction financing at lower cost.

Beginning in the 1940s TU moved away from strict dependence on natural gas, which was cheap and abundant at that time, and began to lease large lignite coal reserves. In 1952 the company formed Industrial Generating Company to mine lignite and operate an early coal-fired generating plant. The utility pioneered new lignite coal–burning technology during the 1960s, building larger boilers than had ever been used in the US. The first of 9 large lignite plants went in use in 1971, and TU began construction of the Comanche Peak nuclear plant, 45 miles southwest of Fort Worth, in 1974.

In 1984 Dallas Power and Light, Texas Electric Service, Texas Power and Light, and Texas Utilities Generating Company were combined as Texas Utilities Electric. The mining company was renamed Texas Utilities Mining.

In 1985 the Nuclear Regulatory Commission suspended licensing of the Comanche Peak nuclear plant, citing both design and construction faults. Further negotiations with the NRC resulted in the granting of a license to operate the plant at 5% of capacity in 1990, followed by a full-power license in the spring of that year. In the interim TU lost its 3 construction partners over the issue of multibillion dollar cost overruns and bought their interests for $984.5 million.

In 1990 Santa Fe Pacific Corporation agreed to settle an antitrust suit brought by TU in 1981 over a 1977 lease agreement granting TU the right to mine about 228 million tons of coal owned by Santa Fe. TU, the 4th largest coal producer in the US in 1988, won substantial royalty and lease agreement concessions from Santa Fe in a new agreement, running from 1990 through 2017.

An attempt by the company to pass to its customers costs related to Comanche Peak's construction was rejected by regulators in 1991, resulting in a $1 billion third-quarter charge. At the same time, regulators recommended an 8.2% rate increase that should generate $354 million in new revenues for the company, if approved.

WHAT

	1990 Sales	
	$ mil.	% of total
Residential	1,852	41
Commercial	1,337	29
Industrial	841	19
Government & municipal	171	4
Other utilities	233	5
Other	109	2
Total	**4,543**	**100**

	1990 Fuel Sources
	% of total
Lignite	44
Oil & gas	38
Purchased power	14
Nuclear	4
Total	**100**

Subsidiaries
Basic Resources (resource development)
Chaco Energy Company (coal)
Texas Utilities Electric Co.
Texas Utilities Fuel Co. (pipeline, storage)
Texas Utilities Mining Co.
Texas Utilities Services Inc. (accounting and administrative services)

RANKINGS

11th in *Fortune* 50 Utilities
84th in *Business Week* 1000

HOW MUCH

	9-Year Growth	1981	1982	1983	1984	1985	1986	1987	1988	1989	1990
Sales ($ mil.)	5.8%	2,738	3,238	3,488	3,932	4,170	3,932	4,083	4,154	4,321	4,543
Net income ($ mil.)	10.2%	406	475	513	587	654	705	769	738	888	969
Income as % of sales	—	14.8%	14.7%	14.7%	14.9%	15.7%	17.9%	18.8%	17.8%	20.5%	21.3%
Earnings per share ($)	2.5%	3.51	3.85	3.90	4.15	4.35	4.45	4.55	4.00	4.44	4.40
Stock price – high ($)	—	22.13	25.75	27.38	28.13	31.88	37.50	36.63	30.63	37.50	39.00
Stock price – low ($)	—	16.25	19.13	22.25	20.75	25.13	29.50	25.50	24.63	27.75	32.00
Stock price – close ($)	7.2%	19.63	23.50	23.25	26.38	29.88	31.50	27.00	28.13	35.13	36.63
P/E – high	—	6	7	7	7	7	8	8	8	8	9
P/E – low	—	5	5	6	5	6	7	6	6	6	7
Dividends per share ($)	5.2%	1.88	2.04	2.20	2.36	2.52	2.68	2.80	2.88	2.92	2.96
Book value per share ($)	4.7%	23.01	24.61	26.16	27.79	29.46	31.24	33.02	33.38	34.56	34.66

1990 Year-end:
Debt ratio: 48.5%
Return on equity: 12.7%
Cash (mil.): $45
Current ratio: 0.47
Long-term debt (mil.): $7,381
No. of shares (mil.): 197
Dividends:
  1990 average yield: 8.1%
  1990 payout: 67.3%
Market value (mil.): $7,214

Stock Price History High/Low 1981–90

TEXTRON INC.

OVERVIEW

Providence, Rhode Island–based Textron is one of the oldest US conglomerates. The company's 3 business units are: aerospace technology, commercial products, and financial services. Employees own 21.2% of the company.

Textron's aerospace unit produces aircraft wings; engines for military aircraft, tanks, and business jets; commercial and military helicopters (including the V-22 Osprey TiltRotor); and aerospace systems and components. US military contracts have declined from approximately 50% of Textron's revenues in 1987 to 24% in 1990, reflecting lowered defense spending and Textron's efforts to capture more of the commercial aviation market.

Textron's commercial products sector manufactures products ranging from specialty fasteners to fashion jewelry to golf carts. Sales to the automotive industry totaled $790 million in 1990, or $68 for every North American–built car and light truck.

Textron's financial service segment provides business and consumer loans and credit-related insurance. A full line of insurance products—life, health, and disability—is offered through the division's Paul Revere Insurance Group.

WHEN

Pioneer conglomerate builder Royal Little founded Special Yarns Corporation, a Boston textile business, in 1923. To save the company from bankruptcy, he merged it with the Franklin Rayon Dyeing Company in 1928. The resulting company, Franklin Rayon Corporation, moved its headquarters to Providence, Rhode Island, in 1930 and changed its name to Atlantic Rayon in 1938.

The company expanded during WWII to keep up with government orders for parachutes and in 1944 adopted the name Textron (connoting "textile products made from synthetics"). But Textron failed in its postwar efforts to distribute Textron-brand consumer products. In 1952 Little convinced Textron's shareholders to allow the company to diversify beyond the textile industry, and between 1953 and 1960 bought more than 40 different companies, including Randall (auto parts, 1959) and E-Z-Go (golf carts, 1960). Before turning over the company to banker Rupert ("Rupe") Thompson in 1960, Little bought Bell Helicopter. Within 6 years, defense-related sales accounted for 41% of Textron's revenues.

Under Thompson, businesses deemed incapable of earning a 20% ROE were sold, including Amerotron, Textron's last textile business (1963). Known on Wall Street as "Miscellaneous, Inc.," Textron bought 20 companies between 1960 and 1965, mostly to enhance its existing business divisions. By 1968, when former Wall Street attorney G. William Miller stepped up to replace Thompson as CEO, Textron made products ranging from Homelite chain saws (acquired 1955) to Speidel watchbands (acquired 1964).

Miller tried unsuccessfully to make several large acquisitions, including Lockheed (1974). He sold several companies and bought Jacobsen Manufacturers (lawn care equipment, 1978). Miller left Textron in 1978 to head the Federal Reserve Board and became treasury secretary under President Carter. B. F. Dolan, who became president in 1980, sold Textron's least-profitable businesses, including its zipper and snowmobile makers (1980) and machine tool manufacturer Jones & Lamson (1985).

Textron bought Avco Corporation (aerospace and financial services, 1985) and Ex-Cell-O (defense and auto parts, 1986), financing these acquisitions by selling nondefense companies and increasing debt.

Textron's $250 million purchase in 1989 of British-based Avdel (metal fastening systems) remained held up in 1991 awaiting a decision on FTC's challenge that the acquisition will restrict competition. Textron reported flat earnings for the first half of 1991.

NYSE symbol: TXT
Fiscal year ends: December 30

Hoover's Rating C-

WHO

Chairman: B. F. Dolan, age 63, $2,599,075 pay
President and CEO: James F. Hardymon, age 56, $1,472,917 pay (prior to promotion)
EVP and COO: John S. Kleban, age 52
EVP and CFO: Dennis G. Little, age 55, $858,717 pay
EVP Human Resources: William F. Wayland, age 55, $616,750 pay
Auditors: Ernst & Young
Employees: 54,000

WHERE

HQ: 40 Westminster St., Providence, RI 02903
Phone: 401-421-2800
Fax: 401-421-2878

Textron operates worldwide.

	1990 Sales		1990 Operating Income	
	$ mil.	% of total	$ mil.	% of total
US	6,836	86	666	84
Canada	692	9	68	9
Europe	171	2	24	3
Other countries	216	3	31	4
Adjustments	—	—	442	—
Total	**7,915**	**100**	**1,231**	**100**

WHAT

	1990 Sales		1990 Operating Income	
	$ mil.	% of total	$ mil.	% of total
Helicopters	1,195	15	90	11
Systems	1,115	14	102	13
Propulsion	1,328	17	139	18
Commercial prods.	1,832	23	166	21
Finance & related insurance	1,307	17	189	24
Other insurance	1,138	14	103	13
Adjustments	—	—	442	—
Total	**7,915**	**100**	**1,231**	**100**

Aerospace
Airfoil (blades and vanes)
Bell Aerospace (aircraft wings and systems)
Bell Helicopter
Cadillac Gage (armored vehicles)
Textron Lycoming (aircraft engines)

Commercial Products
Automotive trim and electromechanical parts
Chain saws (Homelite)
Fasteners and fastener systems
Golf carts (E-Z-Go)
Hand tools, power tools, machine tools
Lawn care equipment (Jacobsen)
Watches and fashion jewelry (Speidel)

Financial Services
Consumer loans (Avco)
Credit-related insurance
Life, medical, and disability insurance (Paul Revere)

RANKINGS

61st in *Fortune* 500 Industrial Cos.
253rd in *Business Week* 1000

KEY COMPETITORS

Aerospace, finance, and insurance companies
Automotive trim makers
Lawn care equipment makers
Power and machine tool makers

HOW MUCH

	9-Year Growth	1981	1982	1983	1984	1985	1986	1987	1988	1989	1990
Sales ($ mil.)	10.1%	3,328	2,936	2,980	3,221	4,039	5,023	5,388	7,279	7,431	7,915
Net income ($ mil.)	7.6%	146	84	89	114	180	242	261	272	269	283
Income as % of sales	—	4.4%	2.9%	3.0%	3.5%	4.5%	4.8%	4.8%	3.7%	3.6%	3.6%
Earnings per share ($)	5.6%	1.95	1.15	1.20	1.56	2.42	2.93	2.97	3.10	3.02	3.18
Stock price – high ($)	—	19.25	14.06	18.44	21.75	29.88	35.00	39.75	30.00	29.38	27.63
Stock price – low ($)	—	12.25	8.63	11.75	12.94	16.19	24.31	17.25	20.63	22.63	18.75
Stock price – close ($)	8.3%	13.31	11.88	16.31	16.94	24.50	31.50	22.63	23.75	24.63	27.38
P/E – high	—	10	12	15	14	12	12	13	10	10	9
P/E – low	—	6	8	10	8	7	8	6	7	8	6
Dividends per share ($)	1.2%	0.90	0.90	0.90	0.90	0.90	0.90	0.98	1.00	1.00	1.00
Book value per share ($)	6.8%	17.19	—	—	—	—	22.38	25.39	27.60	28.24	31.00

1990 Year-end:
Debt ratio: 70.8%
Return on equity: 10.9%
Cash (mil.): $66
Current ratio: —
Long-term debt (mil.): $6,449
No. of shares (mil.): 85
Dividends:
1990 average yield: 3.7%
1990 payout: 31.4%
Market value (mil.): $2,321

Stock Price History High/Low 1981–90

THIOKOL CORPORATION

NYSE symbol: TKC
Fiscal year ends: June 30

Hoover's Rating **B-**

OVERVIEW

Utah-based Thiokol, the largest US producer of solid fuel systems for rockets, has successfully redesigned the solid rocket motor for NASA's space shuttles and is benefiting from the space shuttle program's recovery from the 1986 *Challenger* disaster (caused by failure of the Thiokol-manufactured O-rings for the solid-fuel booster rockets). Thiokol also provides solid motor propulsion systems for the Delta, Scout, and other launch vehicles and communications satellite placement motors.

Thiokol works on various military missile programs (surface-to-air, air-to-surface, and air-to-air) and manufactures systems for Peacekeeper, Trident II, and Midgetman ICBM missiles. The company manages 2 US Army ammunition plants in Louisiana and Texas that have been targeted for possible closure by the Secretary of Defense.

Thiokol currently derives 91% (down from 98% in 1989) of its sales from US government contracts. The former astronaut and first man on the moon Neil Armstrong is a board member. To cushion itself against lower defense spending and program cancellations in the 1990s, the company plans to diversify into the commercial sector and is actively seeking possible acquisition targets.

WHEN

Joseph Patrick, a chemist conducting a experiment in Kansas City to develop a cheap antifreeze, instead discovered synthetic rubber. As a result Thiokol (Greek for sulfur glue) Chemical Company started in 1929.

In 1943 the company developed a liquid polysulfide polymer, a nearly indestructible sealant for airplane fuel tanks, gun turrets, and seams for aircraft carriers. Scientists at the Jet Propulsion Laboratory of the California Institute of Technology discovered in the late 1940s that liquid polymer was the best solid propellant fuel binder. Thiokol immediately started rocket operations in Elkton, Maryland, with a US Army contract.

In 1958 Thiokol got a US Air Force contract to build the first stage of the Minuteman missile, the largest solid rocket motor built at that time. Thiokol joined an air force research program for giant solid rocket motors in 1963. The Peacekeeper missile and space shuttle boosters were ultimate products of this research. The company at the same time entered into a joint venture with Hercules to develop a propulsion system for the navy's Poseidon submarine–launched missile. The joint venture also developed the Trident I and Trident II programs.

Thiokol diversified into specialty chemicals in 1974 by purchasing Dynachem, a leading world supplier of photopolymers and finishing compounds for printed circuits. In 1976 Thiokol bought Ventron Corporation, a producer of sodium borohydride for pharmaceuticals and fine chemicals.

In 1982 the company merged with Morton International to become Morton Thiokol, a specialty chemicals, solid propulsion, and salt company. Only 4 years later, Morton Thiokol came under intense scrutiny after the explosion of the *Challenger* Space Shuttle, caused by failure inside the company's booster rockets.

To recover from the nationally televised disaster, the company bought 3 chemical companies and developed its automobile air bag business (using the same technology Thiokol developed to propel torpedoes from navy submarines). The bags are hidden inside a car until an accident occurs, when they inflate automatically to cushion passengers.

In 1989 the limited growth in aerospace prompted Morton Thiokol to spin off to the public its specialty chemicals, salt, and automobile air bags businesses into the newly formed Morton International. The remaining aerospace operations were renamed Thiokol Corporation.

In 1991 it bought Huck Manufacturing, a maker of aircraft fastening systems.

WHO

Chairman, President, and CEO: U. Edwin Garrison, age 62, $738,500 pay (prior to promotion)
VP and CFO: James R. Wilson, age 49, $364,109 pay
VP Human Resources: James F. McNulty, age 46
Auditors: Ernst & Young
Employees: 11,500

WHERE

HQ: 2475 Washington Blvd., Ogden, UT 84401
Phone: 801-629-2000
Fax: 801-629-2420

Thiokol has operations in Alabama, Florida, Louisiana, Maryland, Nevada, Texas, Utah, and Virginia.

WHAT

	1990 Sales		1990 Operating Income	
	$ mil.	% of total	$ mil.	% of total
Space	568	48	45	51
Strategic	224	19	17	19
Tactical	201	17	19	21
Ordnance	188	16	7	9
Total	**1,181**	**100**	**88**	**100**

Products
Explosive devices
Flares
Infrared decoys
Missile launching systems
Mortar rounds
Munitions
Rocket propellant
Satellite positioning motors
Space shuttle booster motors

Subsidiary
Omneco, Inc.
Huck Manufacturing

RANKINGS

306th in *Fortune* 500 Industrial Cos.

KEY COMPETITORS

Allied-Signal
Daimler-Benz
EG&G
General Dynamics
Grumman
Harley-Davidson
Hercules
Martin Marietta
McDonnell Douglas
Nissan
Nobel
Northrop
Raytheon
Siemens
Rockwell
Textron
Thomson SA
Thorn EMI
United Technologies

HOW MUCH

	9-Year Growth	1981	1982	1983	1984	1985	1986	1987	1988	1989	1990
Sales ($ mil.)	2.4%	958	787	1,509	2,002	1,832	1,950	1,987	2,316	1,168	1,181
Net income ($ mil.)	(2.7%)	53	49	78	110	120	133	138	159	18	41
Income as % of sales	—	5.5%	6.2%	5.2%	5.5%	6.5%	6.8%	6.9%	6.9%	1.5%	3.5%
Earnings per share ($)	(4.5%)	3.24	3.00	4.29	5.42	6.10	7.00	7.25	8.33	0.93	2.15
Stock price – high ($)	—	32.19	46.67	67.08	78.54	101.25	106.25	136.88	115.00	120.94	14.50
Stock price – low ($)	—	21.77	23.13	41.15	50.00	65.00	75.00	77.50	89.06	12.13	9.13
Stock price – close ($)	(7.2%)	28.44	41.46	63.96	68.44	91.88	92.81	99.38	92.19	13.13	14.50
P/E – high	—	10	16	16	15	17	15	19	14	131	7
P/E – low	—	7	8	10	9	11	11	11	11	13	4
Dividends per share ($)	(14.6%)	1.24	1.27	1.32	1.43	1.57	1.71	1.86	2.05	2.25	0.30
Book value per share ($)	(5.4%)	23.50	29.48	27.32	31.29	37.49	43.63	49.68	55.95	12.39	14.20

1990 Year-end:
Debt ratio: 44.5%
Return on equity: 16.2%
Cash (mil.): $113
Current ratio: 3.11
Long-term debt (mil.): $220
No. of shares (mil.): 19
Dividends:
  1990 average yield: 2.1%
  1990 payout: 14.0%
Market value (mil.): $280

Stock Price History High/Low 1981–90

TIME WARNER INC.

OVERVIEW

NYSE symbol: TWX
Fiscal year ends: December 31

Time Warner is the largest media and entertainment company in the world. With titles including *Time*, *People*, and *Sports Illustrated*, the company is #1 in the US in magazine revenues and profits. Book-of-the-Month Club is an industry leader. Time Warner is the world leader in music, featuring such artists as Madonna and R.E.M.

In the US, Time Warner is an integrated video entertainment giant. The company is the leader in TV programming and a major player in film production, dominates pay-cable services with HBO and Cinemax, and is #2, after TCI, in cable TV systems. The company controls 100% of the distribution of its filmed

entertainment, operates movie theaters, and is the world's largest home video distributor.

CEO Steve Ross had hoped to realize his vision of a fully integrated, global media powerhouse and to alleviate a large, merger-related debt problem by swinging a big deal with a foreign partner. When no one stepped forward, he pushed through a $2.8 billion rights offering in 1991. Prior to a major revision, the plan had been criticized as coercive and arrogant in light of the company's continued ownership of 7 aircraft and lavish homes in Acapulco and Aspen. After the offering Toshiba and C. Itoh expressed interest in buying 12% of Time Warner for $1 billion.

WHO

Chairman and Co-CEO: Steven J. Ross, age 63, $3,263,492 pay
President and Co-CEO: N. J. Nicholas, Jr., age 51, $2,362,306 pay
VC and COO: Gerald M. Levin, age 52, $1,980,287 pay (prior to promotion)
EVP and CFO: Bert W. Wasserman, age 58, $1,298,236 pay
VP Human Resources: Carolyn McCandless
Auditors: Ernst & Young
Employees: 41,000

WHEN

Time Warner Inc. was created in 1990 when Time Inc. merged with Warner Communications Inc.

Time Inc. was founded by Henry R. Luce, the son of missionaries, in 1922 when he and friend Briton Hadden created a news magazine, *Time*, that summarized a week's worth of news. They added other magazines in the next decade, including *Fortune* (1930) and *Life* (1936). Luce, a controversial business manager and political philosopher, stepped down as editor-in-chief in 1964 and died in 1967. Luce's influence on the company, after 4 decades of his powerful presence, survived his death.

During the 1970s and 1980s Time Inc. explored new ventures. *People* was enormously successful; *Money* was a moderate success; *Discover*, its science magazine, was struggling; and *TV-Cable Weekly* was a disaster. The company established Home Box Office in 1972, entering the cable television market.

Warner Brothers, founded by brothers Harry, Albert, Jack, and Sam Warner, was one of Hollywood's Big 5 movie studios (with Loew's, Paramount, Fox, and RKO). Although known best for its genre movies (westerns, musicals, crime stories) of the 1930s, Warner Brothers did poorly at the box office but owned a large number of movie theaters until they

were sold for antitrust reasons. The studio advanced to 2nd place in the late 1940s and to first place in the early 1950s. From the 1930s to the early 1950s, the studio made such classics as *Little Caesar*, *Casablanca*, and *Rebel Without a Cause*. Brothers Harry and Albert retired in 1951; Jack remained until 1967 when Seven Arts Ltd. bought the studio. Warner Brothers–Seven Arts was bought in 1969 by Kinney National Services, owner of Famous Agency talent agency and National Periodical Publications (*Superman* and *Batman* comic books and *Mad Magazine)*.

After acquiring the company, Kinney sold the pre-1948 movies to United Artists and shared the studios with Columbia. The company changed its name to Warner Communications Inc. (WCI) in February 1972. During the 1970s and early 1980s WCI made most of its money with its game subsidiary, Atari (1976), but waning public enthusiasm and a flood of game companies brought great losses by 1983 and in 1984 Warner sold Atari.

In 1989 after an unsuccessful bid by Paramount to buy Time, Time agreed to merge with Warner. The company bought Lorimar (TV programming) and sold Scott, Foresman (textbooks) and in 1990 bought *Sunset* magazine and launched *Entertainment Weekly*.

WHERE

HQ: 75 Rockefeller Plaza, New York, NY 10019
Phone: 212-484-8000
Fax: 212-484-8734 (Corporate Communications)

	1990 Sales		1990 Operating Income	
	$ mil.	% of total	$ mil.	% of total
US	9,628	83	1,035	93
Europe	1,229	11	66	6
Other countries	660	6	13	1
Adjustments	—	—	(126)	—
Total	**11,517**	**100**	**988**	**100**

WHAT

	1990 Sales		1990 Operating Income	
	$ mil.	% of total	$ mil.	% of total
Programming	1,266	11	170	15
Cable	1,751	15	249	23
Film	2,904	24	134	12
Music	2,931	25	260	23
Publishing	2,926	25	301	27
Adjustments	(261)	—	(126)	—
Total	**11,517**	**100**	**988**	**100**

Magazines
Entertainment Weekly
Fortune
Life
Money
People
Sports Illustrated
Time

Filmed Entertainment
DC Comics Inc.
Lorimar Telepictures
Warner Bros. Inc.
Warner Bros. Int. Theatres
Warner Home Video Inc.

Music
Atlantic Recording Corp.
Columbia House Co. (50%)
Warner Bros. Records
Warner Elektra Atlantic
WEA Manufacturing

Cable Systems
American Television and Communications (82%)
Warner Cable Communications

Books
Book-of-the Month Club
Little, Brown & Company
Time-Life Books
Warner Books

Programming-HBO
Home Box Office, Inc. (includes Cinemax)
CTV (50%, cable comedy network)

Other Interests
Atari Corp. (25%)
Six Flags Corp. (19.5%)
Turner Broadcasting (19.1%)

HOW MUCH

	9-Year Growth	1981	1982	1983	1984	1985	1986	1987	1988	1989	1990
Sales ($ mil.)	14.9%	3,296	3,564	2,717	3,067	3,404	3,762	4,193	4,507	7,642	11,517
Net income ($ mil.)	—	185	156	143	216	200	376	250	289	(256)	(227)
Income as % of sales	—	5.6%	4.4%	5.3%	7.1%	5.9%	10.0%	6.0%	6.4%	(3.4%)	(2.0%)
Earnings per share ($)	—	3.02	2.50	2.25	3.37	3.15	5.95	4.18	5.01	(4.34)	(13.67)
Stock price – high ($)	—	41.38	52.38	78.38	62.75	65.25	91.38	116.88	122.50	182.75	124.63
Stock price – low ($)	—	26.63	25.50	44.50	33.75	42.50	57.50	65.75	78.75	103.63	66.13
Stock price – close ($)	9.4%	38.25	52.13	62.88	42.75	62.13	70.00	82.25	107.00	120.63	85.75
P/E – high	—	14	21	35	19	21	15	28	24	—	—
P/E – low	—	9	10	20	10	14	10	16	16	—	—
Dividends per share ($)	0.6%	0.95	1.00	1.00	0.82	1.00	1.00	1.00	1.00	1.00	1.00
Book value per share ($)	—	21.64	23.96	14.81	16.99	19.28	21.60	21.60	23.97	117.60	

1990 Year-end:
Debt ratio: 63.9%
Return on equity: —
Cash (mil.): $172
Current ratio: 1.08
Long-term debt (mil.): $11,184
No. of shares (mil.): 58
Dividends:
  1990 average yield: 1.2%
  1990 payout: —
Market value (mil.): $4,931

Stock Price History High/Low 1981–90

RANKINGS

4th in *Fortune* 100 Diversified Service Cos.
99th in *Business Week* 1000

KEY COMPETITORS

Bertelsmann
Blockbuster
Capital Cities/ABC
CBS
Cox
Dow Jones
General Cinema
General Electric
Hearst
McGraw-Hill
MacAndrews & Forbes
Matsushita
Maxwell
Metromedia
Paramount
Rank
Sony
Viacom
Walt Disney
Washington Post

THE TIMES MIRROR COMPANY

NYSE symbol: TMC
Fiscal year ends: December 31

Hoover's Rating **C+**

OVERVIEW

Times Mirror is a 107-year-old multimedia conglomerate. The company's flagship newspaper, the *Los Angeles Times*, is the nation's largest metropolitan daily paper and 2nd after the *New York Times* in Sunday circulation. Other Times Mirror newspapers include New York City and Long Island editions of *Newsday* and the Baltimore Sun newspapers. Newspaper circulation has benefited from the 1989 shutdown of the *Los Angeles Herald Examiner* and from a lengthy strike at the *New York Daily News* in 1990. Times Mirror's magazines, including *Field & Stream, Popular Science,* the *Sporting News,* and *Golf Magazine* are largely targeted to male audiences. The company's print media properties are suffering from recession-related weakness in advertising revenue.

Times Mirror also owns 4 TV stations and is the 12th largest US multiple-system cable operator, with over one million cable subscribers in 13 states. The company publishes law, medical, science, and technical books under imprints including Matthew Bender and Richard D. Irwin.

Times Mirror president David Laventhol is shaking up the company, as he oversees the revamping of its newspapers. Times Mirror has become less of a family-run business, although the Chandler family still owns a 51% voting interest in the company.

WHO

Chairman and CEO: Robert F. Erburu, age 60, $881,971 pay
President and Publisher, *Los Angeles Times*: David A. Laventhol, age 57, $584,462 pay
EVP (Principal Financial Officer): Charles R. Redmond, age 64, $444,634 pay
VP Human Resources: James R. Simpson, age 50
Auditors: Ernst & Young
Employees: 22,191

WHERE

HQ: Times Mirror Sq., Los Angeles, CA 90053
Phone: 213-237-3700
Fax: 213-237-3800

Times Mirror operates throughout the US.

WHEN

Union Army general Gray Otis moved to California after the Civil War and became rich buying land during the boom of the 1880s. Among his acquisitions was the *Los Angeles Times* (started 1881). Son-in-law Harry Chandler destroyed rival papers by controlling circulation routes. Otis and Chandler formed Times Mirror in 1884 to own the *LA Times*. Chandler took over in 1917 and by the 1930s had amassed a fortune in shipping, road construction, oil, and California land (over 2 million acres).

The *LA Times* had a reputation for serving Chandler's political and economic interests in Southern California. The paper successfully prevented unionization long after unions had become strong in the East. Editors allegedly faked photos as part of the paper's campaign against a 1934 gubernatorial candidate. For years the paper was known for its right-wing slant, including support of Richard Nixon.

In 1960 the paper took on a more balanced character after Otis Chandler, grandson of Harry, took over. He hired the best journalists and transformed the paper into one of the nation's finest. During his tenure the paper was awarded 7 Pulitzer Prizes.

The 1960s also marked the beginning of Times Mirror diversification. The company acquired Jeppesen Sanderson (publisher of pilot information, 1961); Matthew Bender (legal publisher, 1963); C.V. Mosby (medical publisher, 1967); Long Island Cablevision (1970); KDFW-TV, Dallas–Ft. Worth (1970); and *Newsday* (1970). Times Mirror entered the magazine field by purchasing *Popular Science* and *Outdoor Life* (1967) and *Ski* and *Golf* magazines (1972). The *LA Times* also improved; it was ranked 4th best in the US in a 1982 poll of publishers, editors, and journalism professors.

Gateway, an on-line videotex service experimented with in the mid-1980s, failed to generate much consumer interest. Times Mirror also sold businesses in the 1980s, including the New American Library (1984) and the *Denver Post* and the *Dallas Times Herald* (1987).

In the late 1980s Times Mirror spent $1.5 billion on acquisitions of TV stations, cable TV systems, newspapers (Baltimore Sun, 1986), magazines (*Yachting, Skiing, Field & Stream, Home Mechanix,* 1987), and publishers (CRC Press, 1986; Richard D. Irwin, 1988). New divisions included training systems Zenger-Miller and Kaset (1989). In 1990 the company bought 50% of *La Opinion,* the #1 US Spanish-language newspaper, and in 1991 sold *Broadcasting* magazine to Reed.

WHAT

	1990 Sales		1990 Operating Income	
	$ mil.	% of total	$ mil.	% of total
Newspaper publishing	2,066	57	170	44
Book, magazine & other publishing	1,071	29	158	41
Broadcast television	105	3	33	9
Cable television	371	10	71	19
Corporate & other	22	1	(49)	(13)
Adjustments	(14)	—	(12)	—
Total	**3,621**	**100**	**371**	**100**

Newspapers
The Advocate (Stamford, CT)
Baltimore Sun newspapers
Greenwich Time
The Hartford Courant
LA Times Syndicate
LA Times–Washington Post News Service
Los Angeles Times
The Morning Call (Allentown, PA)
New York Newsday
Newsday
La Opinion (50%)

Magazines
Field & Stream
Golf Magazine
Home Mechanix
Outdoor Life
Popular Science
Salt Water Sportsman
Ski Magazine
Skiing Magazine
The Sporting News
Yachting

Book Publishing
CRC Press (science)
Harry N. Abrams (art)
Jeppesen Sanderson (aeronautical)
Matthew Bender & Co. (legal, accounting, and other professional)
Mosby-Year Book (medical)
Richard D. Irwin (business)

TV and Cable
Dimension Cable Services
KDFW-TV, Dallas–Ft. Worth
KTBC-TV, Austin
KTVI-TV, St. Louis
WVTM-TV, Birmingham

Professional Training
Kaset, Inc.
Learning International, Inc.
Zenger-Miller, Inc.

HOW MUCH

	9-Year Growth	1981	1982	1983	1984	1985	1986	1987	1988	1989	1990
Sales ($ mil.)	6.1%	2,131	2,200	2,479	2,771	2,947	2,920	3,080	3,259	3,475	3,621
Net income ($ mil.)	2.1%	150	140	200	233	237	408	267	332	298	180
Income as % of sales	—	7.1%	6.4%	8.1%	8.4%	8.0%	14.0%	8.7%	10.2%	8.6%	5.0%
Earnings per share ($)	2.7%	1.10	1.02	1.45	1.69	1.75	3.16	2.06	2.58	2.30	1.40
Stock price – high ($)	—	14.63	17.13	22.00	22.81	29.50	36.94	52.94	40.25	45.00	39.38
Stock price – low ($)	—	9.94	8.88	14.75	14.13	19.00	25.06	30.19	29.00	32.38	21.25
Stock price – close ($)	9.9%	11.44	15.59	18.75	20.19	28.81	31.75	35.88	32.88	35.75	26.75
P/E – high	—	13	17	15	14	17	12	26	16	20	28
P/E – low	—	9	9	10	8	11	8	15	11	14	15
Dividends per share ($)	10.8%	0.43	0.50	0.50	0.60	0.68	0.75	0.82	0.92	1.00	1.08
Book value per share ($)	9.3%	6.70	7.23	8.16	9.25	7.56	10.09	11.31	13.12	14.54	14.92

1990 Year-end:
Debt ratio: 35.8%
Return on equity: 9.5%
Cash (mil.): $37
Current ratio: 1.24
Long-term debt (mil.): $1,068
No. of shares (mil.): 128
Dividends:
 1990 average yield: 4.0%
 1990 payout: 77.1%
Market value (mil.): $3,437

Stock Price History High/Low 1981–90

RANKINGS

135th in *Fortune* 500 Industrial Cos.
175th in *Business Week* 1000

KEY COMPETITORS

Advance Publications
Blockbuster
Commerce Clearing House
Cox
Dow Jones
Gannett
Hearst
Knight-Ridder
Maxwell
New York Times
Reed
E.W. Scripps
Thomson Corp.
Time Warner
Tribune
Other publishers

TLC BEATRICE INTERNATIONAL HOLDINGS, INC.

OVERVIEW

TLC Beatrice International Holdings is a privately owned food company created by the 1987 spinoff of Beatrice's foreign operations. The company is engaged in 2 primary business segments: wholesale and retail food distribution, and the manufacturing and marketing of grocery products. Although the company is based in New York and is the nation's largest black-owned enterprise, it sells no products in the US but rather is focused on the EC.

Food distribution includes wholesale distribution of grocery products to more than 470 independent grocers operating in the Paris area under the name Franprix. The company also provides marketing and other services to these grocers. In addition, TLC

Beatrice owns and operates 44 Franprix and Leader Price stores in France through Minimarché.

The grocery products division makes and sells ice cream, dairy, and dessert products under the names La Menorquina (Spain), Interglas (Canary Islands), Sanson (Italy), Artic (Belgium and France), and Premier Is (Denmark). The Tayto subsidiary is the leader in the Irish potato chip market, and TLC Beatrice bottles soft drinks under several names.

Reginald Lewis, who completed the buyout of TLC Beatrice, remains as chairman, CEO, and principal stockholder.

Private company
Fiscal year ends: December 31

Hoover's Rating C+

WHO

Chairman and CEO: Reginald F. Lewis, age 48
President and COO: Dumas M. Siméus, age 51, $111,333 pay
President, European Grocery Products Division: John F. Sipple-Asher, age 67, $288,485 pay
VP Finance and CFO: Mark J. Thorne, age 34, $154,500 pay
Director of Administration: Bimal Amin
Auditors: Deloitte & Touche
Employees: 4,500

WHERE

HQ: 9 West 57th St., New York, NY 10019
Phone: 212-756-8900
Fax: 212-888-3093

The company sells its products in 30 countries and has manufacturing facilities in 11.

	1990 Sales		1990 Operating Income	
	$ mil.	% of total	$ mil.	% of total
France	1,025	69	46	44
Other EC countries	471	31	58	56
Adjustments	—	—	(10)	—
Total	**1,496**	**100**	**94**	**100**

WHAT

	1990 Sales		1990 Operating Income	
	$ mil.	% of total	$ mil.	% of total
Food distribution	996	67	46	44
Grocery products	500	33	58	56
Adjustments	—	—	(10)	—
Total	**1,496**	**100**	**94**	**100**

Food Distribution Operations
Beatrice Foods (20%, Canada)
Bireley's (88%, beverages, Thailand)
Choky and Sodialim (distributes food and beverage mixes, France)
Dairyworld SA (dairy products, Switzerland)
Etablissements Baud SA (97%, supplies 470 Franprix grocery stores, France)
Mantecados Payco (ice cream, Puerto Rico)
Maxime Delrue (distributes Tropicana juice in France)
Minimarché Group (74%, operates 44 Franprix and Leader Price grocery stores, France)

Grocery Products Operations
Artic and Artigel (ice cream and desserts, Europe)
Gelati Sanson (ice cream and desserts, Italy)
Interglas (60%, ice cream, Canary Islands)
La Menorquina (77%, ice cream and desserts, Spain)
Premier Is (75%, ice cream, Denmark)
Sunco (80%, beverages, Belgium)
Tayto (97%, potato chips, Ireland)
Winters (beverages, Netherlands)

Affiliates
Onex Food Holdings, Inc. (20%, Canada)

WHEN

Reginald F. Lewis played quarterback for Virginia State in the mid-1960s and hoped for a pro career. After a shoulder injury ended his future in sports, Lewis concentrated on his studies and graduated from Harvard Law School in 1968. He worked briefly for the New York law firm of Paul, Weiss, Rifkind, Wharton & Garrison but left in 1970 to form Lewis and Clarkson, a firm specializing in providing venture capital to growing companies. Lewis then decided to move into the world of high finance. In 1983 he started TLC Group as a holding company. Lewis keeps the source of the name a secret.

The first move by TLC Group was the purchase of McCall Pattern Company for $24.5 million (only $1 million of which was Lewis's money; the rest was borrowed) in 1984. McCall, a Manhattan, Kansas–based sewing-pattern company founded in 1871, had stagnated, but under TLC sales increased from $6.5 million in 1984 to $14 million in 1986 (the 2 most profitable years of the company's history despite a declining market for home sewing products). Lewis raised the company's net worth by shuffling assets (he bought McCall's Manhattan factory through an affiliate and leased it back to the company) and was able to raise an additional $22 million through the bond market. At the end of 1986, TLC sold McCall to Britain's John Crowther Group for $95 million ($63 million cash and $32 million of assumed debt) — a return of 9,000%.

In 1987 the breakup of Beatrice by Donald Kelly and the buyout firm of Kohlberg Kravis

Roberts & Company provided Lewis with another opportunity. Since first going overseas in 1961, Beatrice Foods had increased its international holdings to 64 food and consumer products companies in 31 countries, with a combined $2.5 billion in sales by 1987. Lewis arranged for a $495 million junk bond financing through Drexel Burnham Lambert's Michael Milken and purchased the international holdings of Beatrice (Beatrice International Companies) for $985 million. Lewis assumed the positions of chairman and CEO of Beatrice International. The acquisition increased TLC's sales from $63 million in 1986 to almost $1.5 billion in 1987.

Soon after the Beatrice purchase, TLC changed its name to TLC Beatrice International Holdings. Lewis retained his position as head of the company and began selling off numerous operations in Australia and Latin America to pay down the acquisition debt. He sold 80% of the company's Canadian interests to Toronto-based Onex Corporation.

In 1989, with the company's debt brought down, TLC Beatrice International Holdings attempted a public stock offering in order to raise $180 million to buy privately owned shares from insiders and creditors. TLC Beatrice offered 18.5 million new shares at $9 to $10.50 apiece. Potential buyers were unhappy with the terms, and the company rescinded the offer.

In 1990 TLC Beatrice sold Boizet (specialty meats, France) and its French hypermarkets.

KEY COMPETITORS

Allied-Lyons
American Brands
Borden
BSN
Cadbury Schweppes
Chiquita Brands
Coca-Cola
Dole

Grand Metropolitan
John Labatt
Nestlé
PepsiCo
Philip Morris
Sara Lee
Source Perrier
Unilever

HOW MUCH

	3-Year Growth	1981	1982	1983	1984	1985	1986	1987	1988	1989	1990
Sales ($ mil.)	1.1%	—	—	—	—	—	—	1,446	1,639	1,141	1,496
Net income ($ mil.)	5.7%	—	—	—	—	—	—	39	(8)	16	46
Income as % of sales	—	—	—	—	—	—	—	2.7%	(0.5%)	1.4%	3.0%
Employees	13.7%	—	—	—	—	—	—	7,000	7,300	4,500	4,500

1990 Year-end:
Debt ratio: 61.3%
Return on equity: 38.4%
Cash (mil.): $168
Current ratio: 1.49
Long-term debt (mil.): $189

Net Income ($ mil.) 1987–90

TOYS "R" US, INC.

OVERVIEW

New Jersey–based Toys "R" Us is a $5.5-billion chain of toy and children's clothing stores. The company, still run by its founder Charles Lazarus, is the largest and fastest-growing children's specialty retail chain in the world. In 1990 the company opened 47 toy stores in the US and 23 abroad, for a total of 548 stores.

Toys "R" Us owes its success to rigorous adherence to a formula that combines meticulous attention to operational detail, tough site-selection requirements, wide selection, high volume, and relentless cost cutting. Many credit the company with inventing the "category killer" superstore on which such imitators as Blockbuster and Home Depot have built empires.

The company has captured 22% of the US toy market. As a result toymakers listen closely to Toys "R" Us buyers when the buyers preview new offerings.

Toys "R" Us has also successfully applied its discount warehousing formula to the children's clothing market with its Kids "R" Us stores. The company plans to add 25 to 30 new Kids "R" Us clothing stores in 1991.

While most retailers experienced difficult times in 1990, Toys "R" Us reported a 15.1% increase in revenues and a 1.5% rise in earnings. Much of the growth of Toys "R" Us will come from its continued and highly successful expansion overseas. Of the 75 to 85 toy stores planned for 1991, 30 to 35 will be in foreign countries.

NYSE symbol: TOY
Fiscal year ends: Sunday nearest January 31

WHO

Chairman and CEO: Charles Lazarus, age 67, $5,371,920 pay
VC and President, World Wide Toy Stores: Robert C. Nakasone, age 43, $684,332 pay
VC, CFO, and Chief Administrative Officer: Michael Goldstein, age 49, $648,971 pay
EVP and General Merchandise Manager, US Toys: Roger V. Goddu, age 40, $470,926 pay
VP Employee and Labor Relations: Richard N. Cudrin
Auditors: Deloitte & Touche
Employees: 41,000

WHERE

HQ: 461 From Rd., Paramus, NJ 07652
Phone: 201-262-7800
Fax: 201-262-7606

	No. of Stores	
	Toys "R" Us	Kids "R" Us
California	57	24
Texas	34	1
New York	31	12
Florida	31	5
Illinois	27	18
Ohio	25	18
Pennsylvania	23	11
Michigan	19	16
New Jersey	18	13
Maryland	13	6
Virginia	12	6
Georgia	11	2
Indiana	11	7
Other US	139	25
Total US	**451**	**164**

	No. of Stores
	Toys "R" Us
Canada	32
United Kingdom	28
Germany	18
France	10
Hong Kong	3
Malaysia	2
Taiwan	2
Singapore	2
Total Foreign	**97**

WHEN

Charles Lazarus entered retailing in 1948, adding his $2,000 savings to a $2,000 bank loan to convert his father's Washington, DC, bicycle-repair shop into a children's furniture store. Customers persuaded him to add toys. He renamed the store Children's Supermart. Lazarus added a 2nd store, which he later converted to a cash-and-carry self-service, but it was with his 3rd store that he established the pattern for his success. Opened in 1958, this 25,000-square-foot discount toy store offered a wider variety of toys than other retailers at 20% to 50% lower prices.

By 1966 sales had reached $12 million, but Lazarus had managed to add only one store and needed cash to expand, so he sold his company to discount-store operator Interstate Stores for $7.5 million with the condition that he would retain control of the toys operation. Initially, the arrangement worked, but after a 1969 high of $11 million profit on $589 million in sales, Interstate began to feel the competition from stronger chains such as Kmart. By 1974, although Lazarus had expanded to 47 stores and $130 million yearly sales, the parent showed a loss of $92 million and filed for bankruptcy.

Lazarus kept increasing sales in the toy division. His approach of selling toys year-round (not just during the Christmas season) was encouraged by toy manufacturers in the form of generous credit terms. By 1978 he had generated enough profit to pull Interstate Stores out of bankruptcy. Now under his control, the company adopted a new name: Toys "R" Us, with the R backwards to grab attention. With 72 toy stores (and 10 department stores remaining from Interstate) and a 5% share of the toy market, Toys "R" Us posted a $36 million pretax profit on $349 million in sales that year.

From 1978 to 1983 net earnings grew at an annual rate of 40%, market share climbed to 12.5%, and the number of toy stores grew to 169. The company diversified by opening 2 Kids "R" Us children's clothing stores in 1983, copying the toy stores' success formula of huge discount stores.

By 1990 Toys "R" Us had opened a total of 548 toy stores in North America and abroad. The company has become particularly successful in the European and Asian markets where there is no dominant toy retailer. Stores are planned for Japan and Spain in 1991.

	1990 Sales		1990 Operating Income	
	$ mil.	% of total	$ mil.	% of total
US	4,737	86	513	87
Foreign	773	14	77	13
Adjustments	—	—	(5)	—
Total	**5,510**	**100**	**585**	**100**

WHAT

Toys "R" Us (toy stores)
Kids "R" Us (children's apparel stores)

RANKINGS

22nd in *Fortune* 50 Retailing Cos.
75th in *Business Week* 1000

HOW MUCH

	9-Year Growth	1981	1982	1983	1984	1985	1986	1987	1988	1989	1990
Sales ($ mil.)	24.2%	783	1,042	1,320	1,702	1,976	2,445	3,137	4,000	4,788	5,510
Net income ($ mil.)	23.5%	49	64	92	111	120	152	204	268	321	326
Income as % of sales	—	6.2%	6.2%	7.0%	6.5%	6.1%	6.2%	6.5%	6.7%	6.7%	5.9%
Earnings per share ($)	22.1%	0.18	0.23	0.32	0.39	0.41	0.52	0.69	0.91	1.09	1.11
Stock price – high ($)	—	2.95	7.36	9.61	10.44	12.22	15.3	19	18	26.83	35
Stock price – low ($)	—	1.39	2.52	5.14	6.27	7.48	9.74	9.78	13.33	16	19.88
Stock price – close ($)	27.1%	2.60	5.37	7.11	7.63	10.41	12.78	14.00	16.50	23.92	22.50
P/E – high	—	16	32	30	27	30	29	27	20	25	32
P/E – low	—	8	11	16	16	18	19	14	15	15	18
Dividends per share ($)	0.0%	0.00	0.00	0.00	0.00	0.00	0.00	0.00	0.00	0.00	0.00
Book value per share ($)	26.2%	0.88	1.21	1.72	2.11	2.58	3.22	3.94	4.94	5.95	7.11

1990 Year-end:
Debt ratio: 8.7%
Return on equity: 17.0%
Cash (mil.): $35
Current ratio: 1.14
Long-term debt (mil.): $195
No. of shares (mil.): 288
Dividends:
  1990 average yield: 0.0%
  1990 payout: 0.0%
Market value (mil.): $6,472

Stock Price History High/Low 1981–90

KEY COMPETITORS

Ames
Avon
Kmart
Melville
Pacific Enterprises
Riklis Family
Service Merchandise
Stop & Shop
Wal-Mart

TRAMMELL CROW COMPANY

OVERVIEW

Trammell Crow Company is the nation's largest real estate developer. While the numbers that spring from its $14 billion portfolio of owned and managed properties are staggering — 350 office buildings in 50 cities, 160 shopping centers, 90,000 residential units, 35 hotels — the company has historically been an incubator for developers.

Other operations include Trammell Crow Ventures (in-house investment banking), Trammell Crow Realty Advisers (3rd-party property management), and Trammell Crow Real Estate Investors (a publicly traded real estate investment trust). Trammell Crow Residential is the nation's largest residential developer. Holdings of the Crow family and its partners — organized under Trammell Crow Interests — include Wyndham Hotels, Trammell Crow Distribution public warehousing, and farmland.

In 1991, as the real estate recession spread across the country, Trammell Crow abandoned its partnership structure for a corporate one, closed 9 of 15 regional units, and aimed to increase its fee income from property management and sales.

WHEN

Trammell Crow returned to his native Dallas after WWII. An accountant who earned his degree in night school, he tried the moving business, then went to work for the grain wholesaling firm of his wife's family. When Crow found tenants for vacant warehouse space in the firm's building, he took his first steps to becoming the US's largest landlord.

When Ray-O-Vac, a tenant, outgrew the grain firm's space in 1948, Crow bought land and built a warehouse for the battery firm. Spurred by a booming postwar economy and the emergence of Dallas as a regional business center, Crow and his partners, the Stemmons brothers, would build more than 50 warehouses in one section of Dallas alone. Much of Crow's success sprang from his knack of anticipating the needs of his tenants and adding amenities to the workplace.

Crow's methods revolutionized real estate. Ebullient with sunny optimism, he broke with Depression-spawned conventional wisdom and built even when no tenants were signed. He avoided long leases so he could raise rents in an expanding economy. He formed partnerships, often with little more than a handshake and a smile, that shared incentives and rewards with those who would otherwise be employees. Crow partners started at a low salary but earned sales commissions and equity participation in their projects.

Crow developed the Dallas Decorative Center in 1955. Emboldened by success, Crow began to change the face of Dallas with his masterpiece, the Dallas Market Center, a complex of buildings along the Trinity River. He first built the Dallas Homefurnishing Mart

(1957), then the Trade Mart (1960), whose atrium became a Trammell Crow signature feature. Crow next added Market Hall, the largest privately owned exhibition hall in the US, and combined the buildings' operations in 1963.

In 1972 Crow planned to add the 1.5-million-square-foot World Trade Center to the Market Center, but longtime partner John Stemmons balked and Crow offered to buy him out. Crow valued Stemmons's interests at $8 million, but his friend wouldn't take a penny more than $7 million. Finally Crow "lost" the argument and paid the lower figure.

In the 1960s and 1970s Crow helped develop Atlanta's Peachtree Center and San Francisco's Embarcadero Center and entered residential real estate development.

Struggling with high interest rates and heavy debts, Crow's enterprises faltered in 1975. Crow and his partners sold off $100 million in properties to raise money and reorganized the company in 1977. The founder's wheeler-dealer instincts were curbed.

In the mid-1980s some longtime Crow partners defected as control became centralized in Dallas. Crow's company formally diversified into investment banking and properties management and put 13 properties into Trammell Crow Real Estate Investors.

Trammell Crow continued to lose partners. Southwestern real estate problems forced the company to refinance 150 properties in 1990. Planned new construction totalled only $500 million in 1991, down from $2.2 billion in 1985.

Private company
Fiscal year ends: December 31

Hoover's Rating **B**

WHO

Chairman: Trammell Crow, age 77
CEO, Trammell Crow Co.: J. McDonald "Don" Williams, age 49
CEO, Trammell Crow Ventures, Inc.; President, Trammell Crow Real Estate Investors: Robert A. Whitman, age 37
Chief Administrative Officer (Personnel): Steve Laver
Auditors: Kenneth Leventhal and Co.
Employees: 3,000

WHERE

HQ: 3500 Trammell Crow Center, 2001 Ross Ave., Dallas, TX 75201
Phone: 214-979-5100
Fax: 214-979-6058

Trammell Crow Co. includes 6 regional companies: Pacific Northwest, Southern California, the Midwest, the Southwest, the Northeast and Texas.

Top Markets

Atlanta	Houston	San Francisco
Chicago	Los Angeles	Seattle
Dallas	Memphis	Washington, DC

WHAT

Major Projects
Allen Center, Houston
Chicago Trade Mart, Chicago
Dallas Market Center, Dallas
Embarcadero Center, San Francisco
Hamilton Lakes, suburban Chicago
InfoMart, Dallas
Lincoln Tower, Portland
Loew's Anatole Hotel, Dallas
LTV Center, Dallas
Market Square, Washington, DC
Milwaukee Center, Milwaukee
999 Peachtree, Atlanta
One Dallas Center, Dallas
One Renaissance Center, Phoenix
Peachtree Center, Atlanta
Tamarac Square Mall, Denver
Times Square redevelopment, New York

Subsidiaries/Affiliates
Trammell Crow Capital (asset management)
Trammell Crow Interests
  Trammell Crow Agriculture
  Trammell Crow Distribution Corp. (public warehousing)
  Trammell Crow International
  Trammell Crow Medical
  Wyndham Hotels
Trammell Crow Real Estate Investors (investment trust)
Trammell Crow Realty Advisers (portfolio management services)
Trammell Crow Residential (develops rental apartments)
Trammell Crow Ventures (investment banking)

RANKINGS

115th in *Forbes* 400 US Private Cos.

KEY COMPETITORS

Bass	Helmsley	Prudential
Campeau	Enterprises	Rank
Canadian Pacific	Hilton	Sears
Carlson	Hyatt	Other real estate
Edward J.	ITT	developers
DeBartolo	Loews	Other hotel companies

HOW MUCH

	4-Year Growth	1981	1982	1983	1984	1985	1986	1987	1988	1989	1990
Estimated sales ($ mil.)	6.3%	—	—	—	—	—	1,000	1,074	1,400	1,628	1,275
No. of employees	10.7%	—	—	—	—	—	2,000	5,000	7,500	12,324	3,000
Total sq. ft. under construction (thou.)	—	—	—	—	—	—	—	—	61,383	43,537	26,635

Sales ($ mil.) 1986–90

1,800	
1,600	
1,400	
1,200	
1,000	
800	
600	
400	
200	
0	

TRANS WORLD AIRLINES, INC.

OVERVIEW

TWA, once the leading US airline to Europe, is teetering on the edge of bankruptcy. Unprofitable for 4 of the 6 years since corporate raider Carl Icahn took control, the company has the added burden of long-term debt and capital leases exceeding $2.6 billion (most of which is related to Icahn taking it private in 1988). Employee morale is extremely low (TWA has furloughed about 3,800 workers since October 1990), and the company ranks as one of the worst among US airlines for quality of service. Icahn has been at the bargaining table with TWA's machinists since 1988, but no contract seems forthcoming.

Icahn has managed to satisfy TWA's bondholders, though, who went to court after the airline defaulted on $75.5 million in loan and interest payments in January 1991. In mid-1991 Icahn agreed to take TWA into Chapter 11 in the first part of 1992, at which time he will trade his 90% stake in the airline (as well as TWA employees' 10% stake) for $1 billion of TWA's debt. Afterward, Icahn will be allowed to buy a 3.3% equity stake in the airline for $5 million and will receive warrants allowing him to buy up to 45% of the company's stock.

Private company
Fiscal year ends: December 31

Hoover's Rating **F**

WHO

Chairman and CEO: Carl C. Icahn, age 55
VC: Lester L. Cox, age 68
VC: Alfred D. Kingsley, age 48
EVP Operations and COO: J. William Hoar, age 52, $275,000 pay
SVP Finance, Principal Financial Officer, and Principal Accounting Officer: Glenn R. Zander, age 44
VP Employee Relations: Charles J. Thibaudeau, age 44
Auditors: KPMG Peat Marwick
Employees: 33,725

WHEN

Western Air Express, founded in 1925 by Los Angeles businessmen Harry Chandler and James Talbot, started flying from Los Angeles to Salt Lake City in 1926. It merged with Transcontinental Air Transport (TAT) in 1930 to form Transcontinental and Western Air (TWA), America's first coast-to-coast airline.

Airline magnate Clement Keys had formed TAT in 1928, coordinating operations with the Pennsylvania and Santa Fe Railroads to establish air-rail service from New York to the West Coast. The service lost money (fares were too high at $350 per seat) and was terminated after the WAE-TAT merger.

Howard Hughes bought TWA in 1939. The company (then based in Kansas City) introduced transatlantic service (New York–Paris) in 1946, moved its headquarters to New York in 1947, and changed its name to Trans World Airlines in 1950, reflecting its expansion to over 21,000 international route miles. TWA offered America's first nonstop flight from Los Angeles to New York in 1953.

In 1956 Hughes ordered 63 jets, with long-term financing through a New York investment banker. When he was unable to meet the terms of the loan in 1960, the bank placed Hughes's TWA stock in a voting trust. Hughes sold his interest to the public in 1966.

TWA tried to stabilize earnings through acquisitions (consolidated under Trans World Corporation in 1979). These included Hilton International (hotels, 1967), the Canteen

Corporation (food services and vending machines, 1973), Spartan Food Systems (Hardee's restaurants, 1979), and Century 21 (real estate, 1979). However, in 1984 TWA's losses ($128 million between 1973 and 1980) led to a split from Trans World Corporation, which became TW Services in 1986 after selling its hotels to United Air Lines.

In 1986 Carl Icahn took over TWA after winning a takeover battle with airline raider Frank Lorenzo. Icahn, as CEO, bought Ozark Air Lines (TWA's main competitor at its St. Louis hub) in 1987. By 1988 when he took TWA private (recouping his $356 million investment), Icahn owned 90% of TWA, with the other 10% owned by its employees. TWA, Delta, and NWA formed the computer reservation system WORLDSPAN in 1990.

Late in 1990 Icahn proposed merging TWA with financially beleaguered Pan Am. Talks failed when Pan Am agreed to sell its London routes to United. Fearing transatlantic competition from United, TWA agreed to sell its own London routes to American Airlines, planning to use the proceeds to buy Pan Am, which then entered bankruptcy. Early in 1991 Icahn used threats of bankruptcy to stave off a union-backed takeover of TWA by billionaire Kirk Kerkorian. Icahn then tried to buy Pan Am again, this time planning to sell chunks of it to American to raise cash he needed to pay off angry bondholders, but he was outbid by Delta.

WHERE

HQ: 100 S. Bedford Rd., Mt. Kisco, NY 10549
Phone: 914-242-3000
Fax: 914-242-3109 (Customer Relations)

TWA flies to cities in the US, Europe, and the Middle East.

Hub Locations
New York
St. Louis
Paris

	1990 Sales		1990 Operating Income	
	$ mil.	% of total	$ mil.	% of total
US	2,878	62	(134)	—
Other countries	1,728	38	(28)	—
Adjustments	(5)	—	(5)	—
Total	**4,601**	**100**	**(167)**	**—**

WHAT

	1990 Sales	
	$ mil.	% of total
Passengers	3,849	83
Freight & mail	223	5
Other	534	12
Adjustments	(5)	—
Total	**4,601**	**100**

Major Subsidiaries and Affiliates
The Travel Channel (96.7%, cable TV travel programming)
TWA Investment Plan, Inc. (part of partnership owning 9.3% of USX Corporation)

Computer Reservation System
WORLDSPAN (25%, joint venture with Delta, NWA, and Abacus)

Flight Equipment	No.	Average Age in Years
Boeing 727	66	19.5
Boeing 747	17	19.8
Boeing 767	11	7.6
DC-9	48	20.7
L-1011	32	15.6
MD-80	33	5.6
Total	**207**	**16.4**

RANKINGS

13th in *Fortune* 50 Transportation Cos.
20th in *Forbes* 400 US Private Cos.

KEY COMPETITORS

America West	HAL	SAS
AMR	KLM	Southwest
British Airways	Lufthansa	UAL
Continental Airlines	Midway	USAir
Delta	NWA	

HOW MUCH

	9-Year Growth	1981	1982	1983	1984	1985	1986	1987	1988	1989	1990
Sales ($ mil.)	3.1%	3,509	3,320	3,354	3,657	3,725	3,145	4,056	4,361	4,507	4,601
Net income ($ mil.)	—	(7)	(31)	(36)	30	(208)	(106)	45	250	(287)	(274)
Income as % of sales	—	(0.2%)	(0.9%)	(1.1%)	0.8%	(5.6%)	(3.4%)	1.1%	5.7%	(6.4%)	(5.9%)
Available seat miles (mil.)	3.2%	41,252	40,426	42,501	45,510	49,178	46,880	51,811	56,102	57,230	54,958
Rev. passenger mi. (mil.)	3.2%	25,727	25,531	27,261	28,297	32,047	27,334	32,861	34,700	35,046	34,236
Passenger load factor	—	62.4%	63.2%	64.1%	62.2%	65.2%	58.3%	63.4%	61.9%	61.2%	62.3%
Size of fleet	(0.7%)	221	184	175	159	167	207	213	214	213	207
Employees	—	—	27,100	26,200	27,320	29,080	27,442	29,919	30,817	32,895	33,725

1990 Year-end:
Debt ratio: —
Return on equity: —
Cash (mil.): $216
Current ratio: 0.74
Long-term debt (mil.): $2,465

Net Income ($ mil.) 1981–90

TRANSAMERICA CORPORATION

OVERVIEW

One of America's largest financial services companies, Transamerica controls assets of over $30 billion.

Transamerica Finance Group, encompassing consumer and commercial lending, leasing, and real estate services, provides about 40% of the parent's total income. The commercial lending segment, which includes financing inventories and consumer goods, lost money in 1990 and was responsible for Transamerica's overall lackluster performance. The group also leases (and lease-finances) the world's largest fleet of intermodal transportation equipment (e.g., rail and over-the-road trailers).

The company's insurance operations include life insurance, annuities, and related financial planning products; property and casualty insurance (but not health or auto); entertainment lines; and reinsurance.

The company has shed noncore businesses to focus on financial services. Transamerica emphasizes balance among its segments and conservative management of assets.

NYSE symbol: TA
Fiscal year ends: December 31

WHO

Chairman: James R. Harvey, age 56, $1,410,856 pay
President and CEO: Frank C. Herringer, age 48, $1,108,685 pay
VP and Treasurer (Principal Financial Officer): Robert L. Lindberg, age 50
VP Human Resources: Rona I. King, age 43
Auditors: Ernst & Young
Employees: 15,280

WHEN

A. P. Giannini's Bank of Italy (founded 1904) rose from the rubble of the San Francisco earthquake to become one of California's largest bank companies.

In 1918 Giannini formed Bancitaly Corp., hoping to create a national branch banking system. By 1928 Bancitaly had bought 5 banks including the Bank of America (BOA). Giannini formed Transamerica Corp. in 1928 as a holding company for Bancitaly, BOA, and new nonbanking businesses.

Despite the Depression, management infighting, and regulatory investigations, Transamerica kept buying banks; by 1936 it had 475 offices in 294 cities and had diversified into insurance (Occidental Life) and real estate foreclosures (subsidiaries Capital Company and California Lands).

In 1937 regulators forced Transamerica to sell 58% of BOA, but the company kept 54 banks. This situation existed until after WWII.

By 1953 SEC antitrust action had resulted in divestiture of all BOA stock. After a period of banking expansion was ended by the 1956 Bank Holding Company Act, Transamerica turned to insurance, with Occidental, Paramount Fire, Pacific National, and Manufacturers Casualty, acquired in the 1920s, 1930s, and 1940s.

In the 1960s Transamerica diversified into financial services (Pacific Financial, 1961), title insurance (City Title, 1962), manufacturing (Delaval Turbine, 1962; spun off to shareholders, 1986), entertainment (United Artists, 1967; sold to MGM, 1981), transportation (Budget Rent-a-Car, 1968, sold 1986; TransInternational Airlines, 1968, closed 1986), and leasing (Interway, 1979).

James Harvey (CEO 1981–present) made strategic additions, including insurance brokers (Fred S. James, 1982; exchanged for 39% of Sedgwick Group, 1985; reduced to 25%, 1991), consumer financing (The Money Stores, 1983), commercial financing (BWAC, 1987; TIFCO, 1988), worker's compensation insurance (Fairmont Financial, 1987), and investment management (Criterion Group, 1989).

Harvey exchanged $1.5 billion worth of old businesses for $1.7 billion of new, to great effect: between 1985 and 1987 alone, net income tripled. In 1989 the company reduced costs by merging lending and leasing operations into the financial division.

In 1990 and 1991 Transamerica sold its title insurance, car leasing, and UK and Australian life insurance operations and bought NOVA Financial Services, a consumer lender. The company looks to 1992 EC unification to improve its European transport leasing business.

WHERE

HQ: 600 Montgomery St., San Francisco, CA 94111
Phone: 415-983-4000
Fax: 415-983-4234

Transamerica operates in all 50 states and in 45 other countries.

	1990 Pretax Income	
	$ mil.	% of total
US	327	89
Other countries	42	11
Total	**369**	**100**

WHAT

	1990 Assets		1990 Operating Income	
	$ mil.	% of total	$ mil.	% of total
Consumer lending	3,367	10	156	27
Commercial lending	3,982	12	(36)	(6)
Leasing	1,144	4	65	11
Real estate services	286	1	57	10
Life insurance	18,330	58	235	41
Property & casualty insurance	4,398	14	47	8
Insurance brokerage	537	2	49	9
Other & adjustments	(260)	(1)	554	—
Total	**31,784**	**100**	**1,127**	**100**

Major Subsidiaries and Affiliates
Sedgwick Group plc (25%, UK)
Transamerica Criterion Group (mutual funds and investment management)
Transamerica Finance Group (consumer and commercial lending, leasing of freight containers and trailers)
Transamerica Insurance Group (homeowners' insurance, commercial insurance, and specialty insurance)
Transamerica Life Companies, including Transamerica Occidental Life (life insurance and related products)
Transamerica Real Estate Services (tax service, TRANSTAX on-line service; investment properties)

RANKINGS

15th in *Fortune* 50 Diversified Financial Cos.
236th in *Business Week* 1000

KEY COMPETITORS

AIG
General Re
Household International
Primerica
Other insurance companies
Other consumer lending companies

HOW MUCH

	9-Year Growth	1981	1982	1983	1984	1985	1986	1987	1988	1989	1990
Assets ($ mil.)	15.5%	8,658	10,006	10,426	12,027	13,998	16,562	23,488	26,946	29,840	31,784
Net income ($ mil.)	2.0%	223	186	198	172	111	252	354	346	332	266
Income as % of assets	—	2.6%	1.9%	1.9%	1.4%	0.8%	1.5%	1.5%	1.5%	1.1%	0.8%
Earnings per share ($)	(0.5%)	3.45	2.95	3.12	2.64	1.62	3.36	4.51	4.42	4.18	3.29
Stock price – high ($)	—	26.25	24.38	33.00	30.75	36.25	40.13	51.50	36.75	48.00	44.63
Stock price – low ($)	—	17.50	16.50	21.13	20.88	26.00	31.75	22.63	29.75	32.75	23.25
Stock price – close ($)	3.8%	23.38	23.38	31.13	26.13	33.75	32.63	29.88	33.88	44.25	32.63
P/E – high	—	8	8	11	12	22	12	11	8	11	14
P/E – low	—	5	6	7	8	16	9	5	7	8	7
Dividends per share ($)	4.2%	1.34	1.45	1.53	1.60	1.66	1.28	2.24	1.86	1.90	1.94
Book value per share ($)	4.3%	24.93	26.71	28.21	28.57	29.12	28.61	31.84	34.63	35.63	36.56

1990 Year-end:
Return on equity: 9.1%
Equity as % of assets: 9.5%
Cash (mil.): $679
Long-term debt (mil.): $6,641
No. of shares (mil.): 76
Dividends:
  1990 average yield: 5.9%
  1990 payout: 59.0%
Market value (mil.): $2,491
Sales (mil.): $6,703

Stock Price History High/Low 1981–90

THE TRAVELERS CORPORATION

NYSE symbol: TIC
Fiscal year ends: December 31

OVERVIEW

Travelers is the 9th largest US insurance company based on total assets, providing property and casualty, life, and health insurance. Only Aetna is a larger stock (publicly owned) life insurer. Hartford-based Travelers also offers managed health care and investment services.

Travelers's managed health care and employee benefits provide coverage through group health and life programs. Travelers also has one of the largest managed health care networks in the US, serving 130 metropolitan areas.

Traveler's noninsurance operations include investment banking (Dillon, Read), banking (The Massachusetts Company), and real estate. After diversification in the 1980s led to overinvestment in risky real estate ventures, Travelers decided to extricate itself from real estate (currently a drag on earnings), restructure along product lines, and concentrate on its most successful geographical areas.

WHEN

In 1864 James Batterson and 9 other Hartford businessmen founded Travelers as the first accident insurance company in the US. The company's red umbrella logo, used as a symbol of protection in ads as early as 1870, became a trademark in 1960.

Diversification was a principal reason the company, unlike other travel accident companies, survived. Travelers introduced life insurance (1865), annuities (1884), and liability insurance (1889). In 1897 the company issued the first automobile policy and in 1919 sold President Woodrow Wilson the industry's first air travel accident policy.

In 1903 Travelers opened the industry's first training school and in 1904 started an advisory group on safety. In 1907 the school provided training in new services such as workers' compensation, 4 years before this coverage was declared constitutional. The company added group life insurance coverage in 1913, with the Victor Company (later part of RCA) as one of its first clients.

L. Edmund Zacher managed the company's investments in the 1920s and is credited with selling gold stocks and buying US government bonds before the 1929 stock market crash. Two days after the crash, he was named president.

In 1940 the company agreed to insure all risks on projects (highways, roads, railroads) done by civilian defense contractors (including the army and navy) during WWII.

The post-WWII boom meant growth to Travelers in insuring people and property. In 1964 the company developed a standard homeowner's policy that became the industry model. Travelers issued the first space travel accident insurance, covering the Apollo 11 astronauts in their historic lunar landing.

The company bought Keystone (mutual funds, 1979; sold 1989) and Dillon, Read (investment banking, 1986). In 1990 Travelers sold Travelers Mortgage Services (home mortgage and relocation business) as part of a strategy to use capital for its core investment and insurance business.

In 1990 and 1991 the company withdrew from personal lines business (auto and homeowners) in 9 states in which they were not competitive (each less than 2% of Traveler's total segment business) to concentrate on more profitable regions. In the current regulatory climate, auto insurance is becoming less profitable, and the company announced its withdrawal from California auto insurance business after the passage of Proposition 103.

The company has also terminated contracts for 1,400 underperforming agents. In the future the company will focus on core commercial and personal lines, asset management (particularly pensions), and health care benefit management. In 1991 American General bought a stake of under 5% in Travelers.

WHO

Chairman and CEO: Edward H. Budd, age 57, $700,000 pay
President and COO: Richard H. Booth, age 43, $488,458 pay (prior to promotion)
VC and CFO: Thomas O. Thorsen, age 59, $600,000 pay
VC and Chief Investment Officer: Robert W. Crispin
SVP Corporate Human Resources: Thomas E. Hilfrich, age 40
General Counsel: George A. McKeon, age 53, $479,231 pay
Auditors: Coopers & Lybrand
Employees: 34,000

WHERE

HQ: One Tower Sq., Hartford, CT 06183
Phone: 203-277-0111
Fax: 203-277-7979

Travelers operates throughout the US and insures US businesses in more than 100 countries.

WHAT

	1990 Assets		1990 Net Income	
	$ mil.	% of total	$ mil.	% of total
Life insurance	36,724	69	(327)	—
Property/casualty insurance	16,531	31	147	—
Adjustments	2,101	—	2	—
Total	**55,356**	**100**	**(178)**	**100**

Product Lines
Annuities
Consumer banking services
Investment banking
Life, health, and disability insurance
Managed health care
Pension and investment management services
Private placement loans
Property-casualty insurance

Subsidiaries
Dillon, Read Inc. (investment banking)
Prospect Company (real estate)
The Massachusetts Co. (bank)
The Travelers Asset Management International Co.
The Travelers Investment Management Co.
The Travelers Realty Investment Co.

RANKINGS

9th in *Fortune* 50 Life Insurance Cos.
283rd in *Business Week* 1000

KEY COMPETITORS

Aetna	Loews
American Express	MassMutual
American Financial	Merrill Lynch
AIG	MetLife
Bear Stearns	Morgan Stanley
Berkshire Hathaway	New York Life
Blue Cross	Nomura
CIGNA	Northwestern Mutual
CS Holding	Primerica
Equitable	Prudential
GEICO	Sears
Goldman Sachs	State Farm
ITT	Teachers Insurance
John Hancock	Transamerica
Kemper	USF&G
Lloyd's of London	

HOW MUCH

	9-Year Growth	1981	1982	1983	1984	1985	1986	1987	1988	1989	1990
Assets ($ mil.)	9.7%	23,982	27,989	32,876	36,435	41,642	46,300	50,165	53,332	56,563	55,356
Net income ($ mil.)	—	359	310	343	346	360	444	429	430	424	(178)
Income as % of sales	—	1.5%	1.1%	1.0%	1.0%	0.9%	1.0%	0.9%	0.8%	0.8%	(0.3%)
Earnings per share ($)	—	4.23	3.67	4.08	4.11	4.00	4.45	4.10	4.14	3.99	(1.85)
Stock price – high ($)	—	27.00	28.88	34.25	38.25	49.25	59.50	52.63	40.00	45.00	37.75
Stock price – low ($)	—	18.81	16.50	22.38	25.50	36.88	42.50	30.75	33.00	34.50	11.50
Stock price – close ($)	(3.0%)	21.94	24.13	31.75	37.25	48.00	44.63	35.13	34.75	36.88	16.63
P/E – high	—	6	8	8	9	12	13	13	10	11	—
P/E – low	—	4	5	5	6	10	10	8	8	9	—
Dividends per share ($)	4.8%	1.44	1.64	1.80	1.92	2.04	2.16	2.28	2.40	2.40	2.20
Book value per share ($)	2.5%	33.12	35.37	36.53	38.89	41.16	45.17	45.28	44.85	47.02	41.47

1990 Year-end:
Return on equity: —
Equity as % of assets: 8.5%
Cash (mil.): $2,818
Long-term debt (mil.): $957
No. of shares (mil.): 102
Dividends:
  1990 average yield: 13.2%
  1990 payout: —
Market value (mil.): $1,699
Sales (mil.): $11,313

Stock Price History
High/Low 1981–90

TRIBUNE COMPANY

OVERVIEW

Conservatively managed, Chicago-based Tribune Company is a diversified media giant. In 1990, prior to the company's sale of the *New York Daily News*, Tribune Company's newspapers ranked 5th in combined nationwide daily circulation and 4th in Sunday sales. Important newspaper properties include the *Chicago Tribune* and the *Orlando Sentinel*, both leaders in their markets.

Tribune Company's leading television stations, WPIX (New York), KTLA (Los Angeles), and WGN (Chicago), have benefited from cable to become the nation's top 3 stations, and, with the company's other 3 TV stations, reach more households than the Fox Network. The Tribune also manages 4 radio stations.

Tribune Entertainment Company distributes "The Joan Rivers Show" and "Geraldo," which in 1991 became the first US TV program to be shown in the Soviet Union on a daily basis. Other businesses include Canadian newsprint manufacturing and Chicago Cubs baseball.

Tribune Company has suffered from a recession-induced advertising slowdown and strikes at its paper mills and at the *Daily News*, but the company's broadcast and entertainment units continue to thrive.

WHEN

Tribune Company had its beginnings as the *Chicago Tribune*, which produced just 400 newspapers on its first day in 1847. Joseph Medill, a major promoter of Lincoln for president, and who, some say, gave the Republican party its name, became part owner and editor in 1855 and spent the next 44 years building the *Chicago Tribune* into a conservative, Republican newspaper. One of the great legends about Medill involves his prophetic warning that Chicago was a fire hazard just a month before the great fire of 1871. He was able to rally his employees to publish the paper despite being burned out of their building and wrote his famous "Cheer Up" editorial to renew the spirit of the people. Joseph Medill died in 1899. In 1912 his grandsons Robert McCormick and Joseph Patterson took over the newspaper.

Patterson went to New York in 1919 to found the *Daily News*. McCormick, the great-nephew of the inventor of the harvest machine, carried on the Medill legacy, building the *Chicago Tribune* into the "World's Greatest Newspaper," a slogan that, though self-claimed, survives to this day.

During WWI the *Tribune* doubled in advertising and circulation. In 1924 the company began radio station WGN. The station was the first to broadcast the World Series, the Indianapolis 500, and the Kentucky Derby. WGN began TV broadcasts in 1948.

After Patterson's death in 1946, McCormick became head of both newspapers, preferring to run the *Daily News* from headquarters in Chicago. He remained at that post until his death in 1955.

Tribune Company has expanded into other media since the 1950s. The company founded WPIX-TV in New York (1948) and bought stations in Denver (1965), New Orleans (1983), Atlanta (1984), and Los Angeles (1985). The company has also purchased other newspapers across the nation: Fort Lauderdale (1963), Orlando (1965), Los Angeles (1973), Escondido, California (1977), Northern California (1978), and Newport News, Virginia (1986).

Tribune Company has also moved into news and entertainment programming, beginning the Independent Network News (INN) in 1980 (shut down in 1990) and the Tribune Broadcasting Company in 1981. Also that year the company acquired the Chicago Cubs baseball team from chewing-gum manufacturer William Wrigley. The company went public in 1983.

A protracted strike at the unprofitable *Daily News* led to its acquisition by Robert Maxwell's Mirror Group in 1991. Tribune Company paid Mirror $60 million to take over the newspaper.

NYSE symbol: TRB
Fiscal year ends: Last Sunday in December

Hoover's Rating C-

WHO

Chairman: Stanton R. Cook, age 65, $1,116,418 pay (prior to promotion)
President and CEO: Charles T. Brumback, age 62, $860,657 pay (prior to promotion)
President and CEO, Chicago Tribune Company; Publisher, *Chicago Tribune*: John W. Madigan, age 53, $793,902 pay (prior to promotion)
President and CEO, Tribune Broadcasting Company: James C. Dowdle, age 57, $602,502 pay
SVP and CFO: Scott C. Smith, age 40
VP Human Resources: Robert D. Bosau, age 44
Auditors: Price Waterhouse
Employees: 16,100

WHERE

HQ: 435 N. Michigan Ave., Chicago, IL 60611
Phone: 312-222-9100
Fax: 312-222-0449

	1990 Sales		1990 Operating Income	
	$ mil.	% of total	$ mil.	% of total
US	2,143	91	272	104
Canada	210	9	(11)	(4)
Adjustments	—	—	(23)	—
Total	**2,353**	**100**	**238**	**100**

WHAT

	1990 Sales		1990 Operating Income	
	$ mil.	% of total	$ mil.	% of total
Newspapers	1,519	65	164	63
Broadcasting & entertainment	624	26	108	41
Newsprint operations	210	9	(11)	(4)
Adjustments	—	—	(23)	—
Total	**2,353**	**100**	**238**	**100**

Newspapers
Chicago Tribune
Daily Press and *The Times-Herald* (Newport News, VA)
The Orlando Sentinel
Peninsula Times Tribune (Palo Alto, CA)
Sun-Sentinel (Ft. Lauderdale)
Times Advocate (Escondido, CA)

Broadcasting and Entertainment
Television stations:
WPIX (New York)
KTLA (Los Angeles)
WGN (Chicago)
WGNX (Atlanta)
KWGN (Denver)
WGNO (New Orleans)

Radio stations:
WQCD (New York)
WGN (Chicago)
KYMX (Sacramento)
KCTC (Sacramento)

Tribune Entertainment Co. (TV program distribution)
Chicago Cubs baseball team

Newsprint Operations
Quebec and Ontario Paper Company Ltd.

RANKINGS

192nd in *Fortune* 500 Industrial Cos.
235th in *Business Week* 1000

KEY COMPETITORS

Advance Publications
Anheuser-Busch
Capital Cities/ABC
CBS
Cox
Gannett
General Electric
Hearst
Knight-Ridder
New York Times
News Corp.
Times Mirror
Turner Broadcasting
Washington Post

HOW MUCH

	7-Year Growth	1981	1982	1983	1984	1985	1986	1987	1988	1989	1990
Sales ($ mil.)	5.8%	—	—	1,587	1,794	1,938	2,030	2,160	2,335	2,455	2,353
Net income ($ mil.)	—	—	—	69	103	124	293	142	210	242	(64)
Income as % of sales	—	—	—	4.4%	5.7%	6.4%	14.4%	6.6%	9.0%	9.9%	(2.7%)
Earnings per share ($)	—	—	—	0.95	1.28	1.53	3.63	1.80	2.78	3.00	(1.22)
Stock price – high ($)	—	—	—	16.50	17.44	28.94	39.00	49.75	43.00	63.13	48.25
Stock price – low ($)	—	—	—	13.38	12.00	16.00	24.75	28.63	33.75	36.38	31.25
Stock price – close ($)	12.7%	—	—	15.31	17.25	27.88	28.50	41.00	38.88	47.38	35.25
P/E – high	—	—	—	17	14	19	11	28	15	21	—
P/E – low	—	—	—	14	9	10	7	16	12	12	—
Dividends per share ($)	40.2%	—	—	0.09	0.38	0.44	0.53	0.69	0.76	0.88	0.96
Book value per share ($)	(5.2%)	—	—	9.55	10.23	11.19	13.91	14.35	15.88	10.63	6.49

1990 Year-end:
Debt ratio: 56.6%
Return on equity: —
Cash (mil.): $14
Current ratio: 1.00
Long-term debt (mil.): $999
No. of shares (mil.): 64
Dividends:
1990 average yield: 2.7%
1990 payout: —
Market value (mil.): $2,262

Stock Price History High/Low 1983–90

TRW INC.

NYSE symbol: TRW
Fiscal year ends: December 31

Hoover's Rating: C+

OVERVIEW

Cleveland-based TRW is a large automotive, space and defense, and information systems company. TRW's automotive products, which accounted for 54% of its revenues in 1990, range from engine valves, pistons, and steering systems to seat belts and airbag systems. In 1989 Ford designated TRW as its sole airbag supplier (a contract worth $1 billion), but TRW's image was blemished when Ford recalled 55,000 defective airbag systems in 1990. TRW's space and defense segment produces satellites, surveillance, and communications equipment for the US government, TRW's largest customer, accounting for 40% of sales

in 1990. In 1990 the company won a $139 million contract to modernize the US national air traffic control system.

With the acquisition of Chilton in 1989, TRW's information systems and services segment has one of the largest credit reporting services in the world.

The company's 43 divisions supply over 100 categories of products and services. TRW is a high-technology company and has made significant contributions to the development of microprocessors, computer-aided design and manufacturing, advanced composite materials, fiber optics, lasers, and satellites.

WHEN

TRW began as Cleveland Cap Screw Company, founded in 1901. In 1904 company welder Charles Thompson devised an improved method for assembling automobile valves, similar to the methods used to make cap screws. Within 3 years the firm was making most of the engine valves for the mushrooming automobile industry. Renamed the Steel Products Company in 1915, the company also made valves for American and French aircraft used in WWI. In 1921 the company produced the Silcrome metal valve that allowed aircraft to fly longer distances. A similar Thompson valve was used in Lindbergh's plane on the first transatlantic flight. Charles Thompson became president in 1915, and in 1926 the company name became Thompson Products.

Thompson suffered losses in the Great Depression years, but under the leadership of new president Frederick Crawford it avoided major plant closings and layoffs. Diversification began in the 1930s under Crawford, especially into products for the aviation industry (the company developed an improved fuel pump that prevented vapor lock at high altitudes). At the government-built Tapco plant (Thompson Aircraft Products Company) in

Cleveland, the company hired up to 16,000 workers during WWII. By 1945 sales were 7 times those in 1939.

In 1953 the company provided financial support for the Ramo-Wooldridge Corporation, founded by former Hughes Aircraft engineers Simon Ramo and Dean Wooldridge to build the intercontinental ballistic missile. In one of the first uses of "systems engineering" to coordinate the work of 220 prime contractors, the Atlas ICBM was launched 5 years later. In 1958 the companies merged to form Thompson Ramo Wooldridge (name officially shortened to TRW in 1965).

In the 1960s TRW diversified, and its current structure began to take shape. Internal development and acquisitions created the space and defense, automotive, and information systems segments. The company built rocket engines for the Apollo program, satellites, and missiles, and participated in numerous space and defense projects.

In the 1980s, TRW sold its marginal businesses and focused on automotive, space and defense, and information services. In 1990 TRW sold off its once-profitable computer repair business.

WHO

Chairman and CEO: Joseph T. Gorman, age 53, $1,023,750 pay
President and COO: Edsel D. Dunford, age 55, $580,000 pay
EVP and CFO: Peter S. Hellman, age 41
EVP Human Resources: Howard V. Knicely, age 55
Auditors: Ernst & Young
Employees: 75,600

WHERE

HQ: 1900 Richmond Rd., Cleveland, OH 44124
Phone: 216-291-7000
Fax: 216-291-7629

TRW conducts operations at 114 facilities in 24 states and 95 facilities in 15 other countries.

	1990 Sales		1990 Operating Income	
	$ mil.	% of total	$ mil.	% of total
US	5,617	69	306	53
Europe	1,770	21	165	29
Other countries	782	10	102	18
Total	**8,169**	**100**	**573**	**100**

WHAT

	1990 Sales		1990 Operating Income	
	$ mil.	% of total	$ mil.	% of total
Automotive	4,079	50	268	47
Space & defense	3,311	41	254	44
Information systems	760	9	49	9
Other	19	—	2	—
Total	**8,169**	**100**	**573**	**100**

Automotive
Engine valves, pistons, rings
Passenger restraint systems (seat belts and airbags)
Steering systems
Suspension systems

Space and Defense
Spacecraft
High-energy lasers
Software and systems engineering support services
High-tech space and defense mission support systems
Electronic systems

Information Systems and Services
Credit reporting
Real estate information and services
Imaging systems

Other
Coal combustion systems
Environmental waste reduction and cleanup services

RANKINGS

58th in *Fortune* 500 Industrial Cos.
265th in *Business Week* 1000

KEY COMPETITORS

Allied-Signal	Harris
Browning-Ferris	ITT
Consolidated Rail	Martin Marietta
Dun & Bradstreet	Morton
Electrolux	Ogden
General Electric	Teledyne
Halliburton	Waste Management

HOW MUCH

	9-Year Growth	1981	1982	1983	1984	1985	1986	1987	1988	1989	1990
Sales ($ mil.)	5.0%	5,285	5,132	5,493	6,062	5,917	6,036	6,821	6,982	7,340	8,169
Net income ($ mil.)	(1.1%)	229	196	205	267	134	218	243	261	263	208
Income as % of sales	—	4.3%	3.8%	3.7%	4.4%	2.3%	3.6%	3.6%	3.7%	3.6%	2.5%
Earnings per share ($)	1.0%	3.07	2.60	2.68	3.48	1.90	3.56	3.95	4.23	4.25	3.36
Stock price – high ($)	—	32.75	37.00	41.00	41.00	48.50	55.00	70.00	54.00	49.88	51.75
Stock price – low ($)	—	24.50	22.81	30.25	29.19	34.50	41.13	37.00	40.63	41.25	31.38
Stock price – close ($)	3.7%	27.38	33.81	39.81	36.25	44.00	42.25	47.63	41.63	49.38	37.88
P/E – high	—	11	14	15	12	26	15	18	13	12	15
P/E – low	—	8	9	11	8	18	12	9	10	10	9
Dividends per share ($)	4.5%	1.18	1.28	1.33	1.43	1.50	1.53	1.60	1.68	1.72	1.74
Book value per share ($)	4.6%	21.24	21.46	22.19	23.86	18.03	21.03	24.54	26.89	29.33	31.87

1990 Year-end:
Debt ratio: 35.3%
Return on equity: 11.0%
Cash (mil.): $72
Current ratio: 1.15
Long-term debt (mil.): $1,042
No. of shares (mil.): 60
Dividends:
1990 average yield: 4.6%
1990 payout: 51.8%
Market value (mil.): $2,265

Stock Price History
High/Low 1981–90

TURNER BROADCASTING SYSTEM, INC.

OVERVIEW

Turner Broadcasting is the #1 supplier of basic cable television programming. The company's 4 basic cable channels, Cable News Network (CNN), Headline News, WTBS (TBS SuperStation), and Turner Network Television (TNT), garnered an impressive 40% share of cable advertising revenue in 1990.

Turner's film library, containing 3,700 feature-length films, 1,150 cartoons, 1,150 short subjects, and many television programs, provides TBS and TNT with programming and generates syndication and licensing revenue. The company is negotiating the purchase of the Hanna-Barbera cartoon library (Yogi Bear, Flintstones) from an American Financial subsidiary. Turner owns the Atlanta Braves and 96% of the Atlanta Hawks and broadcasts many of their games over TBS.

CNN enjoyed a surge in viewership during the Gulf War. Although postwar ratings subsided to prewar levels, Turner had already capitalized on CNN's crisis-related notoriety by expanding internationally, initiating customized broadcasts to Latin America and Asia in 1991. CNN is also beginning special broadcasts to airports and supermarket checkout areas.

A budding romance with actress Jane Fonda and a board dominated by cable executives who bailed out a cash-strapped Turner Broadcasting in 1987 have combined to slow the deal-making pace of founder and president Ted Turner. Ted Turner owns 39.3% of the company; Tele-Communications, Inc. (TCI), 23.4%; and Time Warner, 19.1%.

WHEN

In 1970 Ted Turner bought Rice Broadcasting, a small Atlanta UHF TV station, with profits from his billboard advertising business and formed Turner Communications Corporation. In its first year Channel 17 lost $689,000, but its prospects were considered good enough to justify keeping it on the air. The following year, WTSG-TV (which stood for "watch this station grow" according to staffers) was the leading independent TV station in the South. Turner spun the billboard business off in 1975.

Discovering he could reach cable systems around the country by satellite, Turner created "superstation" WTBS, which broadcast older TV shows, movies, and Atlanta Braves and Hawks games (teams bought by Turner in 1976 and 1977, respectively). The station grew, reaching 5.8 million homes by 1979.

The first serious challenge to the major TV news networks, Turner's CNN (Cable News Network), launched in 1980, provided 24-hour, usually live news coverage and reached 1.7 million households its first year. Although criticized initially for its quality, CNN frequently "scooped" the major networks with its around-the-clock coverage, reporting first on

the attempted assassination of President Reagan in 1981 and broadcasting live the explosion of the space shuttle in 1986. CNN2 (later Headline News) was introduced in 1982 in response to ABC-Westinghouse's Satellite News Channel, which offered news on an 18-minute cycle. Turner bought out SNC in 1983.

In 1986, after failing in an attempt to take over CBS, Turner bought a large film library from MGM/UA for $1.4 billion. The purchase nearly caused Turner to founder, but the company was bailed out by cable operators who recognized Turner's importance to their operations. In 1988 Turner formed Turner Network Television (TNT), which broadcasts the film classics acquired in the MGM/UA purchase, many in a colorized version that has been criticized by purists.

Since beginning European distribution in 1985, CNN has expanded its geographic reach. A Spanish-language version of Headline News appeared in 1988. In 1990 Turner licensed TV rights to hundreds of films and cartoons from MGM/Pathe and launched the SportSouth sports network. TNT started operating in Latin America in 1991.

NYSE symbol: TBS
Fiscal year ends: December 31

 Hoover's Rating C+

WHO

Chairman and President: R. E. "Ted" Turner, age 52, $879,603 pay
EVP: Terence F. McGuirk, age 39, $584,777 pay
VP; President, CNN: W. Thomas Johnson, Jr., age 49
VP Finance and CFO: Randolph L. Booth, age 38
VP Human Resources: Allan DeNiro
Auditors: Price Waterhouse
Employees: 3,802

WHERE

HQ: One CNN Center, 100 International Blvd., Atlanta, GA 30303
Phone: 404-827-1700
Fax: 404-827-1066

Although Turner Broadcasting operates worldwide, its activities are centered in Atlanta, where it owns CNN Center and Omni Coliseum and maintains offices and studios.

WHAT

	1990 Sales		1990 Operating Income	
	$ mil.	% of total	$ mil.	% of total
Entertainment	663	48	75	37
News	405	29	134	66
Syndication & licensing	249	18	29	14
Professional sports	31	2	(16)	(8)
Real estate	43	3	3	2
Other	3	—	(24)	(11)
Adjustments	—	—	—	—
Total	**1,394**	**100**	**201**	**100**

Entertainment Segment
Goodwill Games (international multi-sport event)
TBS SuperStation
TNT
TNT Latin America

News Segment
Cable News Network
Headline News

Syndication and Licensing Segment
Home video (MGM and pre-1950 Warner Bros. films)
Licensing to commercial television

Pay television (HBO and Showtime) licensing
Turner Entertainment Co. Film Library
World Championship Wrestling, Inc. (80%)

Sports Segment
Atlanta Braves (baseball)
Atlanta Hawks (96%, basketball)
SportSouth Network (44%)

Real Estate
CNN Center, Atlanta
Omni Coliseum, Atlanta

RANKINGS

73rd in *Fortune* 100 Diversified Service Cos.
308th in *Business Week* 1000

KEY COMPETITORS

Anheuser-Busch
Blockbuster
Boston Celtics
Capital Cities/ABC
CBS
Cox
General Electric
Matsushita
News Corp.

Paramount
Sony
TCI
Time Warner
Tribune
Viacom
Walt Disney
Westinghouse

HOW MUCH

	9-Year Growth	1981	1982	1983	1984	1985	1986	1987	1988	1989	1990
Sales ($ mil.)	34.8%	95	165	224	282	352	557	652	807	1,065	1,394
Net income ($ mil.)	—	(13)	(3)	3	5	17	(187)	(131)	(95)	28	(16)
Income as % of sales	—	(14.2%)	(2.0%)	1.5%	1.8%	4.9%	(33.6%)	(20.1%)	(11.7%)	2.6%	(1.1%)
Earnings per share ($)	—	(0.11)	(0.03)	0.03	0.04	0.13	(1.83)	(1.47)	(1.06)	(0.13)	(0.42)
Stock price – high ($)	—	3.33	3.25	5.21	4.50	4.21	4.88	4.50	5.63	21.33	17.92
Stock price – low ($)	—	1.19	1.42	2.54	2.50	1.79	1.92	2.29	3.50	5.67	8.25
Stock price – close ($)	22.5%	1.83	3.17	3.96	2.92	2.35	2.31	3.63	5.63	17.00	11.38
P/E – high	—	—	—	195	108	32	—	—	—	—	—
P/E – low	—	—	—	95	60	14	—	—	—	—	—
Dividends per share ($)	0.0%	0.00	0.00	0.00	0.00	0.00	0.00	0.00	0.00	0.00	0.00
Book value per share ($)	—	(0.12)	(0.14)	(0.09)	0.22	0.23	(1.60)	(4.06)	(4.61)	(4.65)	(4.92)

1990 Year-end:
Debt ratio: —
Return on equity: —
Cash (mil.): $44
Current ratio: 1.76
Long-term debt (mil.): $1,856
No. of shares (mil.): 149
Dividends:
 1990 average yield: 0.0%
 1990 payout: 0.0%
Market value (mil.): $1,697

Stock Price History High/Low 1981–90

TW HOLDINGS, INC.

NASDAQ symbol: TWFS
Fiscal year ends: December 31

Hoover's Rating **D**

OVERVIEW

TW Holdings (through its TW Services subsidiary) is America's 4th largest food service company. Besides owning and operating Denny's (America's largest full-service family restaurant chain based on number of restaurants), Quincy's Family Steak Houses, and El Pollo Loco fast-food broiled chicken restaurants, TW Holdings was the first and remains the largest franchisee of Hardee's fast-food hamburger restaurants.

The company's Canteen subsidiary is one of America's 3 largest contract food service companies. Canteen has 8,500 vending accounts (owning 118,000 vending machines) and more than 1,600 commercial food service accounts, which include factories, hospitals, offices, and other facilities. Canteen also provides food and lodging at Yellowstone and the North Rim of the Grand Canyon.

With 52.12% of its stock owned by Keith Gollust, Paul Tierney, and Augustus Oliver (Coniston Partners), TW Holdings is the result of the last LBO to close in the 1980s. Its balance sheet is burdened with debt (more than half related to the buyout); interest payments cost it at least $225 million annually.

WHEN

In the late 1960s, in an effort to stabilize earnings, Trans World Airlines diversified by acquiring businesses outside the volatile airline industry. Starting with Hilton International Hotels (hotels outside the US) in 1967, TWA also bought Canteen (food services, 1973), Spartan Food Systems (Hardee's and Quincy's restaurants, 1979), and Century 21 (real estate, 1979). These companies were consolidated with the airline under the holding company Trans World Corporation in 1979.

Ironically, the unstable earnings of the airline, which lost $128 million between 1973 and 1980, led Trans World to spin off TWA to its shareholders in 1984. The company then sold Century 21 to Metropolitan Life for $251 million in 1985.

Of the 3 businesses remaining at the end of 1985, Canteen was the largest, generating 46% of sales through food service contracts and vending machines in businesses, recreation areas, schools, and health care facilities. Hilton International, with 90 hotels in the US (under the Vista International name), Guam, Puerto Rico, and 43 foreign countries, generated 32% of sales, and Spartan, which operated 332 Hardee's restaurant franchises and 216 Quincy's Family Steak Houses in the southeastern US, generated 22% of sales. Trans World sold Hilton, which had an inconsistent earnings record, to UAL (parent of United Air Lines) in 1986 for $835 million and 2.5 million shares of UAL common stock.

That year Trans World bought nursing home operator American Medical Services and adopted its present name. The company outbid Marriott for Denny's (paying $843 million) in 1987. With the purchase came El Pollo Loco, a Denny's subsidiary purchased in 1983. TW Holdings formed a joint venture (EPL Japan) with Japan's Mitsui in 1987, allowing the operation of El Pollo Loco restaurants in Japan through 1998. By 1988 TW Services was the 4th largest US restaurant company, with food sales of nearly $3.6 billion.

After a 9-month takeover fight, Coniston Partners paid $1.7 billion to increase its ownership of TW Services stock from 19% to 80% in 1989; TW Services agreed to a merger and became a wholly owned subsidiary of TW Holdings, the name of Coniston's acquisition company. The company is now about 30% publicly owned.

The buyout left TW Holdings with considerable debt ($1.9 billion at the end of 1989). Buyout-related costs contributed to losses in 1989 and 1990. In an effort to raise cash (to pay off its $2.8 billion debt) the company sold several noncore assets in 1990, including American Medical Services. In 1991 the company plans to invest $162 million in existing businesses and open 45 restaurants.

WHO

Chairman: Paul E. Tierney, Jr., age 48
President and CEO: Jerome J. Richardson, age 54, $1,126,123 pay
VP, CFO, and Assistant Secretary; SVP and CFO, TW Services, Inc.: Walter M. Brice, III, age 57, $363,514 pay
SVP and COO, TW Services, Inc.: Theodorus H. Arts, age 62
SVP Human Resources, TW Services, Inc.: Donald H. Turner, age 55
Auditors: Deloitte & Touche
Employees: 100,000

WHERE

HQ: PO Box 3800, 203 E. Main St., Spartanburg, SC 29304-3800
Phone: 803-597-8700
Fax: 803-597-8780 (Public Relations)

TW Holdings has operations in the US, in Canada, and overseas.

	Restaurants by Geographic Area	
	No.	% of total
US	2,211	96
Canada	14	1
Other countries	78	3
Total	**2,303**	**100**

WHAT

	1990 Sales		1990 Operating Income	
	$ mil.	% of total	$ mil.	% of total
Restaurants	2,311	63	196	80
Contract food service	1,371	37	50	20
Adjustments	—	—	(10)	—
Total	**3,682**	**100**	**236**	**100**

Chain	No. of Restaurants
Hardee's	483
Quincy's	212
Denny's (owned)	992
Denny's (franchised/licensed)	366
El Pollo Loco (owned)	119
El Pollo Loco (franchised/licensed)	131
Total	**2,303**

Major Subsidiaries and Affiliates
Canteen Corporation
EPL Japan, Inc. (15%, joint venture with Mitsui and other Japanese interests)
TW Services, Inc.
 Denny's Inc.
 Spartan Food Systems, Inc.

RANKINGS

33rd in *Fortune* 50 Retailing Cos.
849th in *Business Week* 1000

KEY COMPETITORS

ARA	Metromedia
Carlson	McDonald's
General Mills	Ogden
Grand Metropolitan	PepsiCo
Marriott	Wendy's
Matsushita	

HOW MUCH

	9-Year Growth	1981	1982	1983	1984	1985	1986	1987	1988	1989	1990
Sales ($ mil.)	(4.0%)	5,265	5,108	1,889	2,002	2,152	1,918	2,492	3,574	3,485	3,682
Net income ($ mil.)	—	42	30	60	115	105	16	56	54	(56)	(68)
Income as % of sales	—	0.8%	0.6%	3.2%	5.7%	4.9%	0.8%	2.3%	1.5%	(1.6%)	(1.8%)
Earnings per share ($)	—	—	—	—	—	—	—	—	—	(1.74)	(0.61)
Stock price – high ($)	—	—	—	—	—	—	—	—	—	4.50	5.94
Stock price – low ($)	—	—	—	—	—	—	—	—	—	3.50	2.44
Stock price – close ($)	—	—	—	—	—	—	—	—	—	4.50	2.88
P/E – high	—	—	—	—	—	—	—	—	—	—	—
P/E – low	—	—	—	—	—	—	—	—	—	—	—
Dividends per share ($)	—	—	—	—	—	—	—	—	—	0.00	0.00
Book value per share ($)	—	—	—	—	—	—	—	—	—	1.88	1.27

1990 Year-end:
Debt ratio: 94.3%
Return on equity: —
Cash (mil.): $23
Current ratio: 0.39
Long-term debt (mil.): $2,306
Number of shares (mil.): 110
Dividends:
 1990 average yield: 0.0%
 1990 payout: 0.0%
Market value (mil.): $316

Stock Price History High/Low 1989–90

TYSON FOODS, INC.

OVERVIEW

Headquartered in Springdale, Arkansas, Tyson Foods is the world's largest producer, processor, and marketer of poultry-based food products. Value-enhanced poultry products (including chicken patties, precooked and prepackaged chicken, and Rock Cornish game hens) account for about 69% of revenues. The company is the leader in both the food service (with over 500 value-enhanced products available to restaurants and fast-food operations) and retail poultry markets.

Tyson's vertically integrated poultry operations control every aspect of poultry production including genetic research, breeding, hatching, rearing, feed milling, veterinary and technical services, transportation, and delivery.

The company's 1989 acquisition of Holly Farms strengthened its lead in poultry and made the company a major supplier of beef and pork products. Other Tyson products include Mexican food (tortillas and chips) and protein by-products for pet food.

Tyson continues to export its chicken to new markets overseas. During 1990 the company penetrated the Eastern European market. The Soviet Union is now Tyson's #1 foreign customer by volume, and all foreign sales represent nearly 5% of total sales.

WHEN

During the Great Depression, Arkansas poultry farmer John Tyson supported his family by buying, transporting, and selling vegetables and poultry. In 1935 he developed a method for transporting live poultry (he installed a food-and-water trough and nailed small feed cups on a trailer) and bought 500 Arkansas chickens (springers) that he sold for a profit of $235 in Chicago.

For the next decade Tyson bought, sold, and transported chickens exclusively. By 1947, the year Tyson incorporated his company as Tyson Feed & Hatchery, he was raising the chickens himself.

Tyson emphasized chicken production significantly more during the early 1950s by expanding the company's facilities and capabilities. In 1958 Tyson opened his first processing plant in Springdale, Arkansas, at which he implemented an ice-packing system that allowed the company to send its chicken products greater distances.

In 1960 Tyson's son Don took over as manager of the company. In 1962 the company began processing Rock Cornish game hens, and the following year went public and assumed the name Tyson Foods. The company introduced Tyson Country Fresh Chicken (packaged chicken that would become the company's mainstay) in 1967. In 1969 Tyson underwent an expansion and modification program that included the acquisition of Prospect Farms (precooked chicken for the food service industry).

During the early 1970s Tyson experienced rapid expansion that included a new egg building (1970), a new plant and computerized feed mill (1971), and the acquisition of Consolidated Foods's (now Sara Lee) Ocoma Foods Division (poultry, 1972). This period of growth concluded with the acquisition of the Creswell, North Carolina, hog operation and Wilson Foods's Poultry Division.

During the 1980s health-conscious consumers increasingly turned away from red meats to poultry, causing phenomenal growth in the industry and at Tyson. In 1985 the company reached $1 billion in annual sales. Tyson became the industry leader with several key poultry operation acquisitions that included the Tastybird division of Valmac (1985), Lane Processing (1986), and Heritage Valley (1986).

In 1989 after a lengthy bidding struggle with ConAgra, Tyson purchased Holly Farms for $1.5 billion. The acquisition contributed to Tyson's 51% sales increase in 1990 and greatly strengthened its lead in the poultry industry.

In 1990 the company rolled out its Looney Tunes line of children's meals.

OTC symbol: TYSNA
Fiscal year ends: Saturday nearest September 30th

Hoover's Rating **B+**

WHO

Chairman and CEO: Don Tyson, age 60, $3,074,351 pay
President and COO: Leland Tollett, age 53, $1,272,940 pay
EVP Finance: Gerald Johnston, age 48, $392,059 pay
VP Human Resources: William P. Jaycox, age 44
Auditors: Ernst & Young
Employees: 44,000

WHERE

HQ: 2210 W. Oaklawn, Springdale, AR 72764
Phone: 501-756-4000
Fax: 501-756-4061 (Public Relations)

The company owns processing plants in 13 states. Foreign sales are primarily to the Soviet Union, the Far East, the Middle East, Canada, and the Caribbean.

WHAT

	1990 Sales
	% of total
Value-enhanced poultry	69
Basic poultry	12
Red meat	13
Pork	2
Mexican food	1
Other	3
Total	**100**

Brand Names
Canadian Gourmet Selection (frozen dinners for the Canadian market)
Harker's (beef)
Henry House (pork)
Holly Farms (processed chicken)
Holly Oven Roasted (microwaveable chicken)
Holly Pak (fresh chicken)
Mexican Original Products (tortillas)
Quik-to-Fix (beef)
Tastybird (military/commissary chicken)
Tyson (fresh, frozen, and processed chicken products)
Tyson Cornish Game Hens
Tyson Gourmet Selection (frozen dinners)
Tyson Looney Tunes Meals (frozen children's dinners)
Weaver (processed chicken)

RANKINGS

127th in *Fortune* 500 Industrial Cos.
257th in *Business Week* 1000

KEY COMPETITORS

Campbell Soup
Cargill
Chiquita Brands
ConAgra
Continental Grain
Metromedia
Sara Lee

HOW MUCH

	9-Year Growth	1981	1982	1983	1984	1985	1986	1987	1988	1989	1990
Sales ($ mil.)	25.3%	502	559	604	750	1,136	1,504	1,786	1,936	2,538	3,825
Net income ($ mil.)	56.7%	2	9	11	18	35	50	68	81	101	120
Income as % of sales	—	0.4%	1.7%	1.8%	2.4%	3.1%	3.3%	3.8%	4.2%	4.0%	3.1%
Earnings per share ($)	54.2%	0.04	0.16	0.19	0.31	0.59	0.79	1.06	1.27	1.55	1.81
Stock price – high ($)	—	1.18	1.57	2.33	4.80	9.50	25.50	24.00	20.38	26.25	35.38
Stock price – low ($)	—	0.75	0.82	1.40	1.97	3.67	8.42	10.88	11.00	14.75	22.75
Stock price – close ($)	48.8%	0.87	1.57	2.20	4.80	9.17	18.17	12.88	17.25	24.88	31.00
P/E – high	—	32	10	12	15	16	32	23	16	17	20
P/E – low	—	20	5	7	6	6	11	10	9	10	13
Dividends per share ($)	15.8%	0.01	0.01	0.01	0.01	0.02	0.02	0.04	0.04	0.04	0.04
Book value per share ($)	31.8%	0.81	0.96	1.14	1.44	2.43	3.19	4.20	5.35	6.92	9.71

1990 Year-end:
Debt ratio: 58.9%
Return on equity: 21.8%
Cash (mil.): $17
Current ratio: 1.21
Long-term debt (mil.): $950
No. of shares (mil.): 68
Dividends:
1990 average yield: 0.1%
1990 payout: 2.2%
Market value (mil.): $2,118

Stock Price History High/Low 1981–90

UAL CORPORATION

NYSE symbol: UAL
Fiscal year ends: December 31

Hoover's Rating **C+**

OVERVIEW

Despite a difficult year in 1990 that included high fuel prices and a soft travel market as a prelude to the Gulf War, UAL (the parent company of United Air Lines) remains on track. After years of labor strife and repeated union buy-out efforts, the company has ironed out a labor agreement with its pilots and is in a pitched battle with American and Delta to dominate the air lanes of the world.

With a well-established position in the US air travel market, United is building itself into an airline of worldwide stature. Already a leading force in the Pacific, United became a major player in the lucrative European market in 1991 after US and UK authorities approved its purchase of Pan Am's London routes. United also hopes to inaugurate flights to Brazil in 1992 — its first to South America.

But Delta has thrown a monkey wrench into the works. In August 1991, after winning bankruptcy court approval to buy Pan Am's European routes, the Atlanta-based carrier (traditionally #3, after American and United) outstripped its competitors, becoming, by many standards, the world's largest airline.

WHEN

In 1929 aircraft designer Bill Boeing (Boeing Airplane and Transport) and engine designer Fred Rentschler (Pratt & Whitney) merged their companies to form United Aircraft and Transport. Renamed United Air Lines in 1931, this New York–based combination offered one of America's first coast-to-coast airline services, with flights from New York to San Francisco. When United's manufacturing and transportation divisions split up in 1934, ex-banker Bill Patterson became president of the transportation company (United Airlines) and moved its headquarters to Chicago.

In the years of Patterson's stewardship (1934–63), United was slow to utilize new technology, offering jet service 8 months later than American, its leading competitor (1959). Still, in 1961 the company became America's #1 airline after buying Capital Airlines, which added Washington, DC, and points along the Great Lakes and in Florida to its route network, which totaled 116 cities at the time of the acquisition.

The company bought the Westin Hotel Company in 1970 and named Westin president Eddie Carlson as United's CEO in 1971. Another hotelier, Richard Ferris, became CEO in 1979. Hoping to build United into a major travel conglomerate, Ferris spent $2.3 billion buying Hertz Corporation (1985), Pan Am's

routes to Australia and the Orient (1986), and Transworld Corporation's Hilton International Company (1987). In 1987, after spending an additional $7.3 million to change United's name to Allegis Corporation, Ferris resigned when Coniston Partners, the company's largest shareholder, threatened to oust the board and liquidate the company in a proxy fight. Assuming its old name under the leadership of Stephen Wolf (former Flying Tigers chief), United sold its hotels and car rental business, as well as 50% of its computer reservation partnership (Covia) to 5 other airlines.

Another takeover bid in 1989 by Los Angeles billionaire Marvin Davis led to a proposed $6.6 billion management and union buyout plan, which collapsed in October. A new $4.4 billion union buyout offer, supported by Coniston, was approved by the UAL board in April 1990 but collapsed in October when financing fell through. The company then reached an accord with Coniston, which sold most of its stake in UAL in exchange for 2 seats on the board.

In 1990 United won authority from the DOT to fly from Chicago to Tokyo and agreed to buy Pan Am's routes to London and Paris, including gate facilities at London's Heathrow Airport and other assets, for $400 million.

WHO

Chairman, President, and CEO: Stephen M. Wolf, age 49, $1,150,000 pay
VC, CFO, and Treasurer: John C. Pope, age 41, $655,000 pay
SVP Human Resources, United Air Lines, Inc.: Paul G. George
Auditors: Arthur Andersen & Co.
Employees: 76,000

WHERE

HQ: 1200 Algonquin Rd., Elk Grove Township, IL 60007; PO Box 66919, Chicago, IL 60666
Phone: 708-952-4000
Fax: 708-952-7680
Reservations: 800-241-6522

United flies to 156 cities in the US and 14 other countries.

Hub Locations

Chicago, IL	San Francisco, CA
Denver, CO	Tokyo, Japan
London, UK	Washington, DC

	1990 Sales	
	$ mil.	% of total
US	8,027	73
Other countries	3,010	27
Total	**11,037**	**100**

WHAT

	1990 Sales	
	$ mil.	% of total
Passengers	9,633	87
Cargo	593	6
Contract services & other	811	7
Total	**11,037**	**100**

Major Subsidiaries and Affiliates
Mileage Plus, Inc. (administers frequent flyer programs)
United Express (commuter services)

Air Wisconsin	Atlantic Coast
Aspen	WestAir

United Air Lines, Inc.

Computer Reservation System
The Covia Partnership (50%, owns and operates Apollo reservation system)

Flight Equipment	No.	Average Age in Years
Boeing 727	128	16.8
Boeing 737	179	8.7
Boeing 747	39	12.8
Boeing 757	24	1.0
Boeing 767	19	8.0
DC-8	19	23.0
DC-10	54	15.3
Total	**462**	**12.2**

RANKINGS

3rd in *Fortune* 50 Transportation Cos.
213th in *Business Week* 1000

HOW MUCH

	9-Year Growth	1981	1982	1983	1984	1985	1986	1987	1988	1989	1990
Sales ($ mil.)	8.9%	5,141	5,320	6,022	6,968	6,383	9,196	8,293	8,982	9,794	11,037
Net income ($ mil.)	—	(71)	11	142	261	(49)	12	(4)	600	324	94
Income as % of sales	—	(1.4%)	0.2%	2.4%	3.7%	(0.8%)	0.1%	(0.1%)	6.7%	3.3%	0.9%
Earnings per share ($)	—	(2.40)	0.36	3.91	6.40	(1.20)	0.25	0.25	19.95	14.65	4.33
Stock price – high ($)	—	31.38	36.50	41.63	46.75	59.50	64.75	105.88	110.00	294.00	171.00
Stock price – low ($)	—	16.50	15.13	27.88	28.00	39.75	46.25	52.25	68.50	105.25	84.25
Stock price – close ($)	23.5%	16.50	33.25	36.75	44.00	49.75	52.25	71.50	109.50	171.25	110.13
P/E – high	—	—	101	11	7	—	259	424	6	20	40
P/E – low	—	—	42	7	4	—	185	209	3	7	19
Dividends per share ($)	0.0%	0.00	0.00	0.00	0.50	1.00	1.00	0.75	0.00	0.00	0.00
Book value per share ($)	8.4%	36.99	37.66	40.56	47.29	44.21	45.70	51.50	56.75	71.64	76.34

1990 Year-end:
Debt ratio: 42.8%
Return on equity: 5.9%
Cash (mil.): $1,195
Current ratio: 0.70
Long-term debt (mil.): $1,249
No. of shares (mil.): 22
Dividends:
  1990 average yield: 0.0%
  1990 payout: 0.0%
Market value (mil.): $2,410

Stock Price History High/Low 1981–90

KEY COMPETITORS

Alaska Air	HAL	SAS
America West	JAL	Singapore Airlines
AMR	KLM	Southwest
British Airways	Lufthansa	Swire Pacific
Continental Airlines	NWA	TWA
Delta	Pan Am	USAir
	Qantas	

UNION CARBIDE CORPORATION

OVERVIEW

Danbury, Connecticut–based Union Carbide is the 4th largest US chemical company (after Du Pont, Dow, and Monsanto).

After selling 1/2 its carbon products business to Mitsubishi in 1990, it remains the holding company for Union Carbide Chemicals and Plastics Company (UCC&P) and for Union Carbide Industrial Gases (UCIG). UCC&P leads the world in production of ethylene glycol (for antifreeze and polyester). It leads North America in the production of industrial gases (air separated into its component gases for industrial and medicinal use).

Union Carbide continues to feel the effects of the Bhopal, India, industrial accident. A 1991 explosion at its Seadrift plant in Port Lavaca, Texas, caused the death of one person and injured 26 others. Activities at the plant were suspended — lopping off 2/3 of the company's polyethylene production, 1/4 of its ethylene capacity, and 1/3 of its ethylene oxide capacity in North America.

NYSE symbol: UK
Fiscal year ends: December 31

 Hoover's Rating C-

WHO

Chairman and CEO: Robert D. Kennedy, age 58, $1,415,417 pay
President and COO; President, Union Carbide Chemicals and Plastics Company, Inc.: H. William Lichtenberger, age 55, $900,577 pay
VP; President, Union Carbide Industrial Gases, Inc.: Edgar G. Hotard, age 47, $442,905 pay
VP, Treasurer, and CFO: John A. Clerico, age 49, $463,333 pay
VP Human Resources: Malcolm A. Kessinger, age 47
Auditors: KPMG Peat Marwick
Employees: 37,756

WHEN

The beginnings of Union Carbide Corporation trace back to an 1886 company (National Carbon Company), which manufactured carbons for street lights and began the Eveready trademark, and an 1898 company (Union Carbide), which manufactured calcium carbide. In 1917 the 2 companies — along with Linde Air Products (oxygen), Prest-O-Lite (calcium carbide), and Electro Metallurgical (metals) — joined to form Union Carbide & Carbon Corporation (UCC).

In 1919 the company began forming subsidiaries in Canada and in 1925 expanded overseas with the purchase of a Norwegian hydroelectric power plant. UCC expanded into chemical manufacturing and in 1920 established its own chemicals division, which developed ethylene glycol (antifreeze), eventually marketed as Prestone. The company bought vanadium interests in Colorado from U.S. Vanadium in 1926. UCC continued to grow with purchases including Acheson Graphite (1928) and Bakelite (an early developer of plastics, 1939). In the 1940s the company entered the atomic field and ran the US government's nuclear laboratories in Oak Ridge, Tennessee, and in Paducah, Kentucky, until 1984.

UCC bought Visking (food casings) in 1956. The company changed its name to Union Carbide Corporation in 1957. In the early 1960s the company introduced its Glad plastic household products (sold in 1985).

In 1975 the company built a pesticide plant in Bhopal, India, and kept 51% ownership (giving 49% to Indian companies). In 1984 a tank at the Bhopal plant leaked 5 tons of poisonous methyl isocyanate gas, killing more than 3,000 people and permanently injuring 50,000, the worst recorded industrial accident. Legal action against Union Carbide stemming from the Bhopal disaster led to a $470 million settlement in India's Supreme Court in 1989. However, in 1990 the new Indian government indicated that it wished to change the settlement.

In 1985 GAF (chemicals and roofing materials) tried to take over Union Carbide, costing the company $3 billion in debt, which it used to buy back 55% of its stock to defeat the attempt. In 1986 Union Carbide sold its battery division (including Eveready) to Ralston Purina, its agricultural products business to Rhône-Poulenc, and its home and auto products business to First Brands in order to concentrate on its 3 core businesses: chemicals and plastics, industrial gases, and carbon products. In 1989 Union Carbide agreed to sell its urethane polyols (urethane foams) and propylene glycols (personal care products) businesses to Arco Chemical; the deal cleared FTC and Department of Justice hurdles in 1990. Union Carbide later sold 50% of its carbon business to Mitsubishi, and some analysts speculated the deal was the forerunner of a Union Carbide sell-off.

WHERE

HQ: 39 Old Ridgebury Rd., Danbury, CT 06817-0001
Phone: 203-794-2000
Fax: 203-794-4336

Union Carbide has 430 manufacturing facilities and laboratories operating worldwide.

	1990 Sales		1990 Operating Income	
	$ mil.	% of total	$ mil.	% of total
US & Puerto Rico	4,846	64	687	67
Europe	799	10	46	5
Latin America	1,087	14	220	21
Canada	393	5	44	4
Far East & other countries	496	7	35	3
Adjustments	—	—	1	—
Total	**7,621**	**100**	**1,033**	**100**

WHAT

	1990 Sales		1990 Operating Income	
	$ mil.	% of total	$ mil.	% of total
Chemicals & Plastics	5,238	69	624	60
Industrial Gases	2,383	31	409	40
Total	**7,621**	**100**	**1,033**	**100**

Chemicals and Plastics
Alkanolamines
Brake fluids
Glycol ethers
Latexes
Olefins
Photoresists
Polyethylene
Polypropylene

Silicones
Vinyl acetate

Industrial Gases
Coatings service
Helium
Hydrogen
Specialty gases

RANKINGS

65th in *Fortune* 500 Industrial Cos.
264th in *Business Week* 1000

KEY COMPETITORS

Atlantic Richfield
BASF
Bayer
British Petroleum
Chevron
Dow Chemical
Du Pont
Eastman Kodak
Exxon
Formosa Plastics
Hercules

Hoechst
Imperial Chemical
Mobil
Monsanto
Occidental
Phillips Petroleum
Rhône-Poulenc
Royal Dutch/Shell
Texaco
Other chemical
   companies

HOW MUCH

	9-Year Growth	1981	1982	1983	1984	1985	1986	1987	1988	1989	1990
Sales ($ mil.)	(3.2%)	10,168	9,061	9,001	9,508	9,003	6,343	6,914	8,324	8,744	7,621
Net income ($ mil.)	(7.9%)	649	310	79	341	(599)	130	232	662	573	308
Income as % of sales	—	6.4%	3.4%	0.9%	3.6%	(6.7%)	2.1%	3.4%	8.0%	6.6%	4.0%
Earnings per share ($)	(4.4%)	3.19	1.49	0.38	1.61	(2.86)	1.24	1.75	4.66	3.92	2.13
Stock price – high ($)	—	20.71	20.33	24.63	21.75	24.75	33.17	32.50	28.38	33.25	24.88
Stock price – low ($)	—	15.08	13.38	17.00	10.92	12.00	18.75	15.50	17.00	22.75	14.13
Stock price – close ($)	(0.5%)	17.13	17.63	20.92	12.25	23.63	22.50	21.75	25.63	23.25	16.38
P/E – high	—	7	14	65	13	—	27	19	6	8	12
P/E – low	—	5	9	45	7	—	15	9	4	6	7
Dividends per share ($)	(1.1%)	1.10	1.13	1.13	1.13	1.13	1.50	1.50	1.15	1.00	1.00
Book value per share ($)	(3.3%)	25.58	24.51	23.32	23.30	19.82	7.87	9.43	13.34	16.83	18.88

1990 Year-end:
Debt ratio: 49.7%
Return on equity: 11.9%
Cash (mil.): $127
Current ratio: 1.15
Long-term debt (mil.): $2,340
No. of shares (mil.): 126
Dividends:
   1990 average yield: 6.1%
   1990 payout: 46.9%
Market value (mil.): $2,058

Stock Price History High/Low 1981–90

UNION PACIFIC CORPORATION

NYSE symbol: UNP
Fiscal year ends: December 31

Hoover's Rating **C+**

OVERVIEW

Union Pacific Corporation controls a 21,130-mile rail network spanning the West, Midwest, and Gulf Coast regions. The familiar yellow locomotives of the nation's 2nd largest railroad system (after Burlington Northern) hauled nearly 4 million carloads in 1990, principally of chemicals, coal, grain, automotive products, machinery, forest products, and intermodal (truck-to-train) merchandise.

Overnite Transportation, UP's trucking subsidiary, focuses on the fast growing and most profitable less-than-truckload (LTL) business with 143 terminals across the US and Canada. Other UP subsidiaries explore for oil and gas (Union Pacific Resources), manage and transport hazardous waste (USPCI), and provide computer systems and services to UP and other shippers (Union Pacific Technologies).

In recent years UP has begun to focus on its core transportation and resource businesses. The company decided to sell its real estate business in 1989 and had sold about 50% of its assets by 1991. Rail earnings remain strong despite high fuel prices and a sluggish US economy. UP views intermodal shipping and the transportation of municipal waste as potential opportunities for growth.

WHEN

In 1862 Congress chartered the Union Pacific Railroad to build a key part of the first transcontinental railway. Construction began at Omaha in 1865 and proceeded west under the direction of Major General Grenville Dodge. The driving of the Golden Spike at Promontory, Utah, in 1869 marked the linking of the East and West Coasts as the UP's rails met those of the Central Pacific (which had been built east from Sacramento).

In 1872 the New York *Sun* revealed UP's role in the Credit Mobilier scandal. The chief promoters had cheated other stockholders and the government by taking excess profits from the railroad's construction. UP continued to expand, but the lingering effects of the scandal, further mismanagement, and deepening debt forced it into bankruptcy in 1893.

A syndicate headed by E. H. Harriman bought UP in 1897. Harriman instituted a program of physical and financial improvements that tripled UP's earnings within 3 years. After reacquiring branches lost in the bankruptcy (Oregon Railway & Navigation Company and Oregon Short Line, 1899), UP gained control of the Southern Pacific (1901) and the Chicago & Alton (1904). Harriman died in 1909; the Supreme Court ordered UP to sell its Southern Pacific holdings in 1913 on antitrust grounds.

In the 1930s UP used acquisitions to diversify into trucking. It continued to expand its rail holdings (buying Spokane International Railway in 1958) and moved into energy in 1970, when it bought Champlin Petroleum and Pontiac Refining. UP bought the 11,547-mile Missouri Pacific railroad in 1982. Other major acquisitions in the 1980s included Overnite Transportation (trucking company, 1986), the 2,175-mile Missouri-Kansas-Texas Railroad (1988), and USPCI (hazardous waste disposal, 1988). To remain competitive in the 1980s, UP cut about 40% of its work force (particularly layers of middle management), improved customer service, and invested heavily in new equipment.

After Drew Lewis (former transportation secretary under President Reagan) became CEO in 1987, UP started to focus on its core businesses. The company sold its refineries in 1988 and decided to sell its real estate interests in 1989. UP joined certain Chicago and North Western (CNW) managers to form Blackstone Capital Partners, a limited partnership that bought CNW in 1989. UP now owns $100 million of CNW's preferred stock, which may be converted to a 25% interest in 1994. Its investment in CNW assured UP continued access to the rail yards of Chicago.

WHO

Chairman, President, and CEO: Drew Lewis, age 59, $1,910,000 pay
SVP Human Resources: Ursula F. Fairbairn, age 48
SVP Finance: L. White Matthews III, age 45
Auditors: Deloitte & Touche
Employees: 48,300

WHERE

HQ: Martin Tower, Eighth and Eaton Aves., Bethlehem, PA 18018
Phone: 215-861-3200
Fax: 215-861-3220

Besides its rail activities, UP conducts trucking operations in 41 states and part of Canada; oil, gas, and mining operations primarily in the US, the Gulf of Mexico, and offshore California and Canada; and hazardous-waste management services in 21 states.

WHAT

	1990 Sales		1990 Operating Income	
	$ mil.	% of total	$ mil.	% of total
Railroad	4,700	68	900	68
Natural resources	996	14	316	24
Trucking	804	12	56	4
Land	235	3	37	3
Hazardous-waste management	229	3	15	1
Adjustments	—	—	(87)	—
Total	**6,964**	**100**	**1,237**	**100**

Freight Transportation
Missouri Pacific Railroad Co.
Overnite Transportation Co. (trucking company)
Union Pacific Railroad Co.

Natural Resources
Union Pacific Resources Co.
 Black Butte Coal Co. (50%, coal mining joint venture with Peter Kiewit Sons')
 Rhône-Poulenc Chemical Company of Wyoming (49%, trona mining and soda ash production joint venture with Rhône-Poulenc)

Real Estate
Union Pacific Realty (real estate sales)

Hazardous Waste Management
USPCI (United States Pollution Control, Inc.)

Other Subsidiaries
Union Pacific Technologies (technological support)

RANKINGS

7th in *Fortune* 50 Transportation Cos.
81st in *Business Week* 1000

HOW MUCH

	9-Year Growth	1981	1982	1983	1984	1985	1986	1987	1988	1989	1990
Sales ($ mil.)	1.0%	6,375	5,818	8,353	7,789	7,798	6,574	5,943	6,068	6,492	6,964
Net income ($ mil.)	4.6%	411	327	441	494	501	(414)	560	559	595	618
Income as % of sales	—	6.4%	5.6%	5.3%	6.3%	6.4%	(6.3%)	9.4%	9.2%	9.2%	8.9%
Earnings per share ($)	4.2%	4.27	3.38	3.57	4.01	4.18	(4.13)	4.90	4.90	5.62	6.17
Stock price – high ($)	—	79.25	51.75	61.88	52.75	55.25	67.38	86.63	70.13	81.00	79.75
Stock price – low ($)	—	42.50	29.25	44.00	34.25	39.75	45.50	45.13	51.00	63.25	61.38
Stock price – close ($)	3.5%	52.00	47.00	50.75	40.88	53.88	62.25	54.00	64.25	76.63	70.63
P/E – high	—	19	15	17	13	13	—	18	14	14	13
P/E – low	—	10	9	12	9	10	—	9	10	11	10
Dividends per share ($)	4.1%	1.65	1.80	1.80	1.80	1.80	1.85	2.00	2.10	2.23	2.37
Book value per share ($)	3.2%	32.14	34.01	35.34	37.52	39.67	32.47	35.79	39.69	39.00	42.71

1990 Year-end:
Debt ratio: 47.6%
Return on equity: 15.1%
Cash (mil.): $169
Current ratio: 0.69
Long-term debt (mil.): $3,883
No. of shares (mil.): 100
Dividends:
 1990 average yield: 3.3%
 1990 payout: 38.3%
Market value (mil.): $7,072

Stock Price History
High/Low 1981–90

KEY COMPETITORS

American President
Amoco
Ashland
Atlantic Richfield
Bechtel
Browning-Ferris
Burlington Northern
Canadian Pacific
Chevron
Chicago and North Western
Coastal
Consolidated Freightways
Consolidated Rail
CSX
Exxon
Halliburton
Mobil
Norfolk Southern
Occidental
Ogden
Phillips Petroleum
Rio Grande Industries
Roadway
Santa Fe Pacific
Sun
Tenneco
Texaco
TRW
Unocal
Waste Management
Yellow Freight

UNISYS CORPORATION

OVERVIEW

Blue Bell, Pennsylvania–based Unisys is the 3rd largest computer maker in the US (after IBM and DEC) and the 6th largest in the world (after Fujitsu, NEC and Hitachi). Unisys is a leading systems integrator and manufacturer of on-line transaction-processing systems.

Unisys markets its mainframes, workstations, servers, software, communication network products, imaging systems, and information-system services to transaction-intensive businesses such as banks, insurance companies, airlines, telephone companies, and government agencies. Sales to the US government and related defense contractors account for 24% of Unisys revenues.

The company's strategic move into building open (nonproprietary) systems and systems integration was not enough to stave off heavy losses in 1989 and 1990. The weakened mainframe market (29% of Unisys's sales) and the economic recession resulted in further losses in 1991 ($1.3 billion alone in the 2nd quarter, due mainly to further consolidation) and catalyzed a new round of layoffs (10,000 announced in 1991) and corporate restructuring. Unisys is spinning off its defense-electronics unit.

WHEN

Unisys was formed in 1986 when struggling mainframe computer giant Burroughs swallowed fellow mainframe manufacturer Sperry Corporation. Burroughs traces its roots back to American Arithmometer (St. Louis, 1886), later Burroughs Adding Machine (Detroit, 1905) and Burroughs Corporation (1953). Burroughs entered data processing by purchasing Electrodata (1956) and many others, including Memorex (1982).

Sperry was the product of a 1955 merger of Sperry Gyroscope (an electronics company founded in 1910 by Elmer Sperry) and Remington Rand, an old-line typewriter manufacturer and maker of the first commercially viable computer, the UNIVAC. Sperry bought RCA's faltering computer business in 1971.

In 1986 Burroughs president Michael Blumenthal, a former treasury secretary to Carter, sought to achieve efficiencies in parts and development by merging Burroughs's small database managers with Sperry's defense-related number crunchers.

As Unisys's president, Blumenthal quickly disposed of $1.8 billion in assets (Sperry Aerospace and Marine divisions, Memorex), closed plants and cut the combined workforce of 120,000 by 24,000. He also promised continued support for Sperry's flagship 1100 line of mainframes and nourished Burroughs's prized A series of computers. The initial results were positive, with 1986's $43 million loss followed by 1987's $578 million profit.

Amidst an industry trend to stronger, smaller systems (where PCs could access mainframe power), Unisys in 1988 equipped its U line of servers with the open UNIX operating system, sponsored 4th-generation languages (4GLs) to connect its new 2200 and A mainframe series, and moved to networked smaller systems, spending $650 million to buy Timeplex (voice/data networks) and Convergent (UNIX-based workstations).

Plummeting mainframe demand in 1989 and 1990 caught Unisys in mid-transition; company losses in 1990 totaled $437 million. Blumenthal left Unisys in 1990. Heavy losses continued into 1991, triggering a new round of layoffs and asset sales aimed at reducing the company's nearly $3 billion in debt. Recent efforts are aimed at paring its product line, focusing its markets, and shedding noncore assets. The company sold its network subsidiary, Timeplex, in 1991.

1991 introductions included a UNIX-based fault-tolerant mainframe (Gladiator Series) and a line of self-service workstations (SuperGen Series) that use plug-in components for easy repair and upgrades.

NYSE symbol: UIS
Fiscal year ends: December 31

WHO

Chairman and CEO: James A. Unruh, age 49, $581,253 pay
President and COO: Reto Braun, age 49, $329,167 pay (prior to promotion)
VP and CFO: George T. Robson, age 43
VP Human Resources: Thomas E. McKinnon, age 46
Auditors: Ernst & Young
Employees: 70,000

WHERE

HQ: Township Line and Union Meeting Rds., Blue Bell, PA 19424-0001
Phone: 215-986-4011
Fax: 215-986-6850

Unisys has operations in approximately 100 countries.

	1990 Sales		1990 Operating Income	
	$ mil.	% of total	$ mil.	% of total
US	4,871	48	(61)	—
Europe	3,088	31	(196)	—
Americas/Pacific	2,152	21	556	—
Adjustments	—	—	(256)	—
Total	**10,111**	**100**	**43**	**—**

WHAT

	1990 Sales	
	$ mil.	% of total
Mainframes & peripherals	2,919	29
Departmental servers & workstations	1,407	14
Software & related services	2,004	20
Equipment maintenance	1,990	20
Custom products & services	1,606	16
Other	185	1
Total	**10,111**	**100**

Computer Systems
Mainframes
  2200 Series
  Gladiator Series
  A Series
  Micro A (desktop)
Servers
  U Series
Workstations
  SuperGen Series
Personal computers
  Personal Workstation[2]
Disk subsystems
  M Series
Peripherals
  Printers, storage devices

Communication processors
  CP Series
  DCP Series

Software Systems
4th-generation languages
  LINC
  MAPPER
  Ally
Computer-aided software engineering (CASE)
InfoImage (imaging technology)
Operating systems
  BTOS/CTOS
  MCP/AS
  Open/OLTP

RANKINGS

49th in *Fortune* 500 Industrial Cos.
549th in *Business Week* 1000

KEY COMPETITORS

Amdahl	DEC	Prime
AT&T	Dun & Bradstreet	Siemens
Apple	Fujitsu	Sony
Compaq	Hewlett-Packard	Storage
Computer	Hitachi	Technology
Associates	IBM	Sun
Control Data	Machines Bull	Microsystems
Data General	NEC	Tandem
Dell	Oracle	Wang

HOW MUCH

	9-Year Growth	1981	1982	1983	1984	1985	1986	1987	1988	1989	1990
Sales ($ mil.)	13.2%	3,319	4,095	4,297	4,808	5,038	7,432	9,713	9,902	10,097	10,111
Net income ($ mil.)	—	130	110	197	245	248	(43)	578	681	(639)	(437)
Income as % of sales	—	3.9%	2.7%	4.6%	5.1%	4.9%	(0.6%)	6.0%	6.9%	(6.3%)	(4.3%)
Earnings per share ($)	—	1.04	0.87	1.53	1.80	1.82	(0.54)	2.93	3.27	(4.71)	(3.45)
Stock price – high ($)	—	18.46	16.38	19.21	19.96	22.67	28.83	48.38	39.00	30.50	17.13
Stock price – low ($)	—	9.04	9.88	13.42	14.79	17.33	19.17	24.00	25.00	12.38	1.75
Stock price – close ($)	(15.5%)	11.33	13.92	16.79	18.92	21.13	26.67	33.63	28.13	14.75	2.50
P/E – high	—	18	19	13	11	12	—	17	12	—	—
P/E – low	—	9	11	9	8	10	—	8	8	—	—
Dividends per share ($)	(5.9%)	0.87	0.87	0.87	0.87	0.87	0.87	0.91	0.98	1.00	0.50
Book value per share ($)	(4.1%)	17.14	16.12	16.37	16.88	18.24	17.31	20.90	22.24	15.49	11.79

1990 Year-end:
Debt ratio: 41.7%
Return on equity: —
Cash (mil.): $403
Current ratio: 1.16
Long-term debt (mil.): $2,495
No. of shares (mil.): 162
Dividends:
  1990 average yield: 20.0%
  1990 payout: —
Market value (mil.): $404

Stock Price History High/Low 1981–90

UNITED PARCEL SERVICE OF AMERICA, INC.

OVERVIEW

UPS is the world's largest package delivery service, with sales exceeding $13.6 billion in 1990. Nicknamed "Big Brown" after the color of its trucks, it is ranked #1 in the *Fortune* 50 Transportation Companies for the 3rd consecutive year. UPS delivered about 2.9 billion packages in 1990, while offering reliable service to more than a million customers every day. It has become a key player in the air-express market (with a 26% market share), taking on the expert, Federal Express, by matching Saturday and 10:30 a.m. next-day deliveries.

In 1990 UPS Air Cargo filled 30,000 container positions on what would have been empty space on regularly scheduled UPS flights. Other UPS subsidiaries lease trucks (UPS Truck Leasing), deliver food and other perishables in refrigerated rail containers (Martrac), and develop and lease company-owned real estate (UPS Properties).

The company has expanded its international service since the mid-1980s. International Air service, to 41 countries in 1988, is now available in more than 180 countries. Earnings have declined in the same period, primarily due to expansion-related costs; 1990 earnings were impacted further by higher fuel prices and a softening economy.

UPS's stock is owned primarily by its employees and their families and heirs. In 1990 the UPS Foundation approved $9.2 million in grants to 277 causes, including efforts to improve adult literacy and to feed the poor.

WHEN

Seattle teenagers Jim Casey and Claude Ryan started American Messenger Company, a telephone-message service, in 1907. They were soon making small-parcel deliveries for local department stores and in 1913 changed the company's name to Merchants Parcel Delivery. By 1915 the company had a staff of 20 messengers, and 2 important events had already occurred — Casey, who led the company for the next 47 years, had established a policy of manager-ownership, and Charlie Soderstrom (one of the company's 4 stockholders) had chosen the brown paint still used on the company's delivery vehicles.

Service expanded outside Seattle in 1919 when Merchants Parcel bought Oakland-based Motor Parcel Delivery. Renamed United Parcel Service (UPS), the company by 1930 served residents in New York City (its headquarters from 1930 to 1975); Newark, New Jersey; and Greenwich, Connecticut.

UPS expanded small-package delivery to include addresses within a 150-mile radius of certain metropolitan areas, starting with Los Angeles in 1952. Expanding westward from the East Coast and eastward from the West, the company had slowly blanketed the US mainland by 1975.

The company had already gained heightened public awareness when in 1972 the US Postal Service, in an effort to improve its own public image, cited UPS as a competitor. Up to this time UPS had developed in relative obscurity, with most of its stock owned by managers, their families, heirs, or estates.

After moving its headquarters to Greenwich, Connecticut, in 1975, UPS expanded to Europe in 1976, with service to West Germany, and in the late 1970s established a base at Standiford Airfield in Louisville, Kentucky, to start an air express delivery service. By 1982 UPS Blue Label Air Service (now UPS 2nd Day Air) guaranteed delivery anywhere on the mainland US and Oahu, Hawaii, within 48 hours. Overnight service (UPS Next Day Air) began in 1982, expanding nationwide and to Puerto Rico by 1985. In the late 1980s, when UPS adopted the slogan "We run the tightest ship in the shipping business" for its first TV advertising campaign, it was already one of America's most profitable transportation companies.

In 1990 UPS spent $11.3 million to buy a 9.5% stake in Mail Boxes Etc., America's leading neighborhood mailing and business service center franchise. UPS expanded service in Eastern Europe that year to include cities in Poland, Czechoslovakia, Hungary, Yugoslavia, Rumania, and the USSR. A joint venture (UniStar Air Cargo), formed with Japanese partner Yamato Transport in 1990, has given UPS a foothold in the Japanese package delivery and air freight markets.

Because of the high cost of living in Connecticut, UPS plans to start moving its headquarters to Atlanta late in 1991.

HOW MUCH

	9-Year Growth	1981	1982	1983	1984	1985	1986	1987	1988	1989	1990
Sales ($ mil.)	12.0%	4,911	5,213	6,015	6,833	7,687	8,620	9,682	11,032	12,358	13,606
Net income ($ mil.)	6.9%	328	332	490	477	568	669	784	759	693	597
Income as % of sales	—	6.7%	6.4%	8.1%	7.0%	7.4%	7.8%	8.1%	6.9%	5.6%	4.4%
Employees	8.9%	114,300	117,800	124,200	141,000	152,400	168,200	191,600	219,400	237,700	246,800

1990 Year-end:
Debt ratio: 19.2%
Return on equity: 16.6%
Cash (mil.): $147
Long-term debt (mil.): $855

Net Income (mil.) 1981–90

WHO

Private company
Fiscal year ends: December 31

Hoover's Rating **A**

Chairman and CEO: Kent C. (Oz) Nelson, age 53, $519,633 pay
SVP and COO: Frank J. Middendorf, age 62, $361,750 pay
SVP, Treasurer, and CFO: Edwin A. Jacoby, age 58, $283,800 pay
SVP and Human Resources Manager: John J. Kelley, age 55
Auditors: Deloitte & Touche
Employees: 246,800

WHERE

HQ: Greenwich Office Park 5, Greenwich, CT 06831
Phone: 203-862-6000
Fax: 203-862-6593

UPS operates in more than 180 countries worldwide. The company owns and operates about 122,000 automotive delivery vehicles and rents trucks and tractors to commercial users in 28 southeastern and southwestern states.

Hub Locations
Cologne/Bonn, Germany	Miami, FL
Dallas, TX	Ontario, CA
Hong Kong	Philadelphia, PA
Louisville, KY	Singapore

WHAT

Ground Delivery Services
Hundredweight Service
UPS Ground
UPS GroundSaver
UPS Next Day Ground

Air Delivery Services
Call Air Pickup
Domestic Air
International Air
Priority Air Pickup
UPS Air Cargo Service
UPS Next Day Air
UPS 2nd Day Air
Worldwide Expedited Package Service

Major Subsidiaries and Affiliates
Mail Boxes Etc. (9.5%)
Martrac
Roadnet Technologies (technological support)
II Morrow (technological support)
UniStar Air Cargo, Inc.
UPS Properties, Inc.
UPS Truck Leasing, Inc.

Flight Equipment	No.	Orders
Boeing 727	47	—
Boeing 747	8	—
Boeing 757	20	35
DC 8	49	—
Other	291	—
Total	**415**	**35**

RANKINGS

1st in *Fortune* 50 Transportation Cos.
5th in *Forbes* 400 US Private Cos.

KEY COMPETITORS

American President	NWA
AMR	Qantas
British Airways	Rio Grande
Burlington Northern	Industries
Chicago and North Western	Roadway
Consolidated Freightways	Ryder
Continental Airlines	Santa Fe Pacific
CSX	SAS
Delta	Singapore Airlines
Federal Express	TWA
JAL	UAL
KLM	Union Pacific
Lufthansa	USAir
Norfolk Southern	Yellow Freight

UNITED STATES

OVERVIEW

The US is the most economically and militarily powerful nation on earth. Its role as a leader in ensuring world peace and economic prosperity has led commentators to call the current era a "Pax Americana."

Endowed with rich farmland capable of feeding the nation several times over, minerals of almost every kind in abundance, vast forests and fisheries, and a commercial infrastructure unrivaled in the world, the US dominates the world economy. Most currencies are measured by their exchange rate with the US dollar, many international commodities (e.g., oil) are priced only in US dollars, and the US remains the world's single largest truly unified market.

Its adherence to principles of free trade, its democratic political institutions, and its minimal regulation of industry make the US an archetypal capitalist nation. While the US has

fallen behind Japan and Europe in some industries (notably steel and consumer electronics), its knowledge-based economy makes it a leader in computers, software design, financial services, medicine/biotechnology, and innovations in retailing. Its higher education system is the envy of the world.

Despite its prosperity, it faces numerous challenges, including dependence on foreign oil (45% imported), government overspending, a faltering primary and secondary education system, a large underclass in danger of permanent exclusion from the country's affluence, and a health care system with costs that are spiraling out of control.

The US is a nation of immigrants, and ongoing immigration (particularly from Latin America and Asia) is continually renewing the nation's economic and cultural vigor.

WHEN

In 1617 Jamestown (founded 1607) began shipping tobacco to England. Tobacco required intensive cultivation, so African slaves were imported starting in 1620. In 1621 religious dissidents landed at Cape Cod and established a society of farmers, merchants, and small manufacturers. In the 17th and 18th centuries, the colonies exported raw materials and developed manufacturing and trade. After the American Revolution (1775–81), in which the US won independence from Britain, settlement expanded westward. This coincided with the development of new technologies (canal excavation and steam power) that facilitated agricultural and mining products transport.

Disagreement over slavery led to the Civil War (1861–65), which cost 620,000 lives and over $25 billion; war ruined the South's economy and strengthened the North's.

Western settlement was aided by railroads, which received grants of land that they gave or sold to settlers. Immigration exploded. Besides farmers, new immigrants included urbanites seeking industrial work.

By 1880 the US led the world in food exports (thanks to innovations in farm machinery) and in railroad and telegraph mileage. More people worked in industry than in farming. Over 10% of the population was foreign born. In the 1890s the US expanded, annexing Hawaii and taking the Philippines, Cuba, and Puerto Rico from Spain.

After WWI the US became the world's greatest industrial power because of the

modernity of its industrial plant and its lack of war damage. In the 1920s US prosperity seemed unbounded. However, the 1929 stock market crash, caused by inflated stock values and unrestrained margin trading, tripped the US into depression and brought protectionist legislation. Bank failures, industrial contraction, and bankrupt farms threw 16 million out of work. Despite public works and welfare projects, the US did not recover until WWII.

After WWII the US became the major economic force in the world. In the late 1960s attempts to fund the Vietnam War without new taxes brought inflation. In the 1970s Europe and Japan boasted newer industrial plants than the US and proved very competitive. The oil shocks of the 1970s upset the oil, auto, and housing industries. Stagflation set in. Unemployment reached 11% in 1982.

In the 1980s conservation and more efficient energy use slowed the growth of the demand for oil. Starting in 1983, the US enjoyed its longest postwar economic boom. However, the number of poor increased, and S&L deregulation brought abuses.

In 1990, as the US faced staggering costs for resolution of the S&L crisis, recession slowed the economy. By 1991 some banks and insurance companies seemed likely to follow S&Ls into failure, but the economy appeared to recover as consumer confidence rose and the housing market improved, and the US enjoyed renewed world prestige following its military success in the Gulf War.

Official name:
United States of America
Official language: English
Currency: 1 dollar ($) = 100 cents
Fiscal year ends: September 30

Hoover's Rating A

WHO

President: George Herbert Walker Bush, age 67, $200,000 pay
Vice President: J. Danforth Quayle, age 44, $115,000 pay
Secretary of State: James Addison Baker III, age 61, $99,500 pay
Secretary of the Treasury: Nicholas F. Brady, age 61, $99,500 pay

WHERE

Executive HQ: President, 1600 Pennsylvania Ave. NW, Washington, DC 20510
Phone: 202-456-1414
Fax: 202-456-2883
Chamber of Commerce: Chamber of Commerce of the United States, 1615 H St. NW, Washington, DC 20062-4902
Phone: 202-659-6000
Fax: 202-463-5836

The US has 50 states, one federal district, 2 commonwealths, and 15 other dependent areas and has diplomatic representatives in 157 countries.

Capital city: Washington, DC
Time change from EST: 0 hours
Avg. high/low temp: Jan. 42°F (6°C)/27°F (-3°C)
July 87°F (31°C)/68°F (20°C)
Urbanization: 74%
Population density: 69/sq. mi. (27/sq. km)

Exports as % of Total		Imports as % of Total	
Canada	22	Japan	20
Japan	12	Canada	19
Mexico	7	Mexico	6
UK	6	Germany	5
Germany	5	Taiwan	5
South Korea	4	South Korea	4
Other countries	44	Other countries	41
Total	**100**	**Total**	**100**

WHAT

Origins of GNP	% of Total
Manufacturing	22
Services	16
Finance, insurance & real estate	14
Government & its enterprises	11
Retail trade	9
Transport & utilities	9
Wholesale trade	7
Construction	4
Mining	3
Communications	3
Agriculture, forestry & fishing	2
Total	**100**

1990 GNP per capita: $21,773
1990 year-end external debt: $393 billion
Literacy rate: 99%
UN Human Development Index: 98%
Human Freedom Index (0-40 scale): 33
Defense as % of GNP: 6%
Education as % of GNP: 7%
Principal exchange: New York Stock Exchange

HOW MUCH

	4-Year Growth	1986	1987	1988	1989	1990
Population (mil.)	1.0%	241.6	243.9	246.3	248.8	251.0
GNP ($ bil.)	6.6%	4,238	4,516	4,881	5,201	5,465
Real GNP growth rate	—	2.7%	3.5%	4.5%	2.5%	1.0%
Exports ($ mil.)	14.8%	227,200	254,100	322,400	363,900	394,100
Imports ($ mil.)	7.8%	382,300	424,400	459,500	492,900	516,700
Trade balance ($ mil.)	—	(155,100)	(170,300)	(137,100)	(129,000)	(122,600)
Current account ($ mil.)	—	(145,400)	(162,200)	(128,900)	(110,000)	(99,300)
Govt. budget bal. ($ mil.)	—	(221,200)	(149,700)	(155,200)	(152,000)	(123,800)
Consumer inflation	—	1.9%	3.7%	4.1%	4.9%	5.4%
Unemployment rate	—	6.9%	6.1%	5.4%	5.2%	5.5%

THE UNITED STATES SHOE CORPORATION

OVERVIEW

Despite the name, shoes account for only 30% of U.S. Shoe's $2.7 million in sales; the company operates the 2nd largest group of women's apparel stores in the US (after The Limited) and the largest optical group, LensCrafters.

U.S. Shoe's apparel operations include such chains as Casual Corner (the 3rd largest women's apparel chain), Petite Sophisticate, Ups 'N Downs, Caren Charles, August Max Woman, Career Image, and T. H. Mandy. The optical group includes LensCrafters throughout North America and a new low-price venture, Sight & Save. The group also employs optometrists in its Eyexam 2000 labs.

The footwear division manufactures, imports, and sells footwear both wholesale and retail. Stores include Hahn, Cincinnati Shoe, Banister factory outlet stores, and the Concept Stores division, which includes single-brand stores such as Shop for Pappagallo.

U.S. Shoe has been restructuring of late, closing 3 shoe plants and 10 LensCrafters stores, merging its David Evins and Amalfi footwear branches, selling its Cabaret accessories stores and many of its Ups 'N Downs fashion outlets and terminating its footwear licensing agreements with Leslie Fay and Liz Claiborne. Analysts who follow the company think more stores may go on the block, including the T. H. Mandy chain.

NYSE symbol: USR
Fiscal year ends: Saturday nearest January 31

Hoover's Rating **C-**

WHO

Chairman: Philip G. Barach, age 60, $568,750 pay
President and CEO: Bannus B. Hudson, age 45, $550,000 pay
SVP; CEO, Retail Development and Services Division: Martin Sherman, age 61, $353,750 pay
VP Finance: K. Brent Somers, age 42, $242,500 pay
Corporate Director Human Resources: Renee Whitehead
Auditors: Arthur Andersen & Co.
Employees: 49,000

WHERE

HQ: 1 Eastwood Dr., Cincinnati, OH 45227
Phone: 513-527-7000
Fax: 513-561-2007

U.S. Shoe operates in the US, Canada, and the UK.

WHEN

U.S. Shoe was incorporated in Ohio in 1923 to consolidate the business of 5 smaller shoe manufacturers. The company's Red Cross brand women's shoes have been advertised nationally since 1892. In 1928 the company's sales were almost $8 million. In 1955 U.S. Shoe bought Joyce, a maker of women's casual shoes. A series of acquisitions followed, including women's shoemaker Selby (1957), the maker of Jumping Jacks children's shoes (1961), importer of Italian women's shoes Marx and Newman (1962), and the Wm. Hahn chain of 21 family shoe stores (1963). By 1964 the company was the 5th largest US shoemaker, with sales of $108 million.

In 1966 the company merged with privately owned Freeman-Toor, maker of Freeman and Botany men's shoes. New chairman and CEO Harold O. Toor, whose family owned 16% of company stock after the merger, favored branching out into men's apparel. U.S. Shoe company officials disagreed, and the merger was dissolved by both parties in 1967. Philip Barach was reinstated as CEO, a position he held until resigning in 1990. (He remains as chairman until 1993. Toor also remained a director until his retirement in 1990.)

The company bought Texas Boot (1966), Pappagallo shoe manufacturers and H. Scheft retail shoe stores (1968), the Casual Corner chain of 20 clothing stores (1970), the Capezio trademark (1974), and 171 Ups 'N Downs stores (1982). U.S. Shoe led Casual Corner into an aggressive expansion program and merchandising shift beginning in 1977. By 1980 the company operated 419 Casual Corner locations; by 1990 U.S. Shoe operated over 2,000 shopping mall locations, including 767 Casual Corner stores. The figure also includes 443 LensCrafters stores; U.S. Shoe bought the chain in 1984 and has added 156 stores since January 1989, including 5 in the UK.

After net profit decreased from $65 million in 1985 to $36 million in 1987, Barach put the company up for sale in 1988. In 1989, however, the company announced that it would sell only the shoe manufacturing division to an investment group led by Merrill Lynch, but the deal soured later that year.

As profits continued to erode, the company announced a $90 million restructuring in 1990, to include the sale of 155 retail outlets and the closure of 3 shoe plants. The charge led to U.S. Shoe's first annual loss in over a decade.

WHAT

	1990 Sales		1990 Operating Income	
	$ mil.	% of total	$ mil.	% of total
Footwear	803	30	(14)	—
Apparel	1,336	49	(5)	—
Optical	580	21	13	—
Adjustments	—	—	74	—
Total	**2,719**	**100**	**68**	**—**

Women's Apparel Chains	No. of Stores
August Max Woman	92
Career Image	8
Caren Charles	195
Casual Corner	767
Petite Sophisticate	297
T. H. Mandy	26
Ups 'N Downs	223
Total	**1,608**

Optical Retailing	No. of Stores
LensCrafters	443
Optometric practices	77
Sight & Save	3
Total	**523**

Footwear Retailing	No. of Stores
Shoe stores	370
Leased departments	159
Total	**529**

Footwear — Brand Names

Amalfi	Imperial boots	Red Cross
Bandolino	J. Chisholm boots	Selby
Capezio	Joyce	Vittorio Ricci Studio
Cobbie	Kenny Rogers	Wrangler boots
Easy Spirit	boots (license)	(license)
Evan-Picone	Pappagallo	
(license)		

RANKINGS

44th in *Fortune* 50 Retailing Cos.
768th in *Business Week* 1000

KEY COMPETITORS

American Brands	Jack Eckerd	NIKE
Brown Group	L.A. Gear	Nordstrom
Costco	The Limited	J. C. Penney
Edison Brothers	Macy	Price Co.
The Gap	May	Reebok
General Cinema	Melville	Woolworth
Grand Metropolitan		

HOW MUCH

	9-Year Growth	1981	1982	1983	1984	1985	1986	1987	1988	1989	1990
Sales ($ mil.)	10.7%	1,088	1,254	1,508	1,717	1,920	2,003	2,168	2,343	2,557	2,719
Net income ($ mil.)	—	59	60	75	53	65	25	36	13	49	(28)
Income as % of sales	—	5.4%	4.8%	5.0%	3.1%	3.4%	1.3%	1.7%	0.6%	1.9%	(1.0%)
Earnings per share ($)	—	1.33	1.35	1.71	1.21	1.46	0.57	0.80	0.29	1.10	(0.61)
Stock price – high ($)	—	9.09	14.19	24.50	18.88	23.00	27.31	34.75	29.00	27.50	26.25
Stock price – low ($)	—	4.92	5.66	12.44	11.50	12.13	19.50	12.75	14.00	16.38	7.00
Stock price – close ($)	1.5%	8.34	13.72	18.81	13.31	21.38	20.75	13.88	24.75	20.13	9.50
P/E – high	—	7	11	14	16	16	48	43	100	25	—
P/E – low	—	4	4	7	10	8	34	16	48	15	—
Dividends per share ($)	5.6%	0.31	0.33	0.37	0.42	0.45	0.46	0.46	0.46	0.46	0.51
Book value per share ($)	5.7%	6.69	7.71	9.08	9.82	10.86	11.02	11.74	11.60	12.22	11.03

1990 Year-end:
Debt ratio: 33.0%
Return on equity: —
Cash (mil.): $60
Current ratio: 1.60
Long-term debt (mil.): $245
No. of shares (mil.): 45
Dividends:
1990 average yield: 5.3%
1990 payout: —
Market value (mil.): $429

Stock Price History High/Low 1981–90

UNITED TECHNOLOGIES CORPORATION

OVERVIEW

Hartford, Connecticut–based United Technologies is a world leader in jet engines (Pratt & Whitney), helicopters (Sikorsky), heating and air-conditioning (Carrier), and elevators/escalators (Otis). In addition to these well-known businesses, UTC manufactures automotive components, rocket engines, space suits, and a host of other products.

UTC's fast-growing international business provides 34% of sales, with another 22% (approximately) coming from the US miltary and space-related work.

Pratt & Whitney (P&W) is the world's largest manufacturer of small gas turbine engines.

It is also the 2nd largest jet engine manufacturer, after General Electric, with P&W power plants on all types of wide-body jetliners now in service. P&W, crown jewel of UTC, had lost market share in the mid-1980s, but in 1990 it received a $4 billion order — its largest ever — from United Airlines for its commercial PW4000 jet engine. P&W's F119 engine was picked by the US Air Force to power its new Advanced Tactical Fighter aircraft.

Sikorsky, builder of the Seahawk and Black Hawk, was recently chosen to co-develop the next generation of Army light helicopters.

NYSE symbol: UTX
Fiscal year ends: December 31

Hoover's Rating **B-**

WHO

Chairman, President, CEO, and COO: Robert F. Daniell, age 57, $1,368,330 pay
EVP and CFO: John A. Rolls, age 49, $640,830 pay
SVP Human Resources and Organization: Franklyn A. Caine, age 40
Auditors: Price Waterhouse
Employees: 192,600

WHERE

HQ: United Technologies Bldg., Hartford, CT 06101
Phone: 203-728-7000
Fax: 203-728-7979

UTC operates plants throughout the world.

	1990 Sales		1990 Operating Income	
	$ mil.	% of total	$ mil.	% of total
US	15,015	66	909	51
Europe	3,987	17	524	29
Other countries	3,854	17	349	20
Adjustments	(1,306)	—	(363)	—
Total	**21,550**	**100**	**1,419**	**100**

WHAT

	1990 Sales		1990 Operating Income	
	$ mil.	% of total	$ mil.	% of total
Jet engines	7,292	33	1,010	61
Flight systems	4,034	18	90	5
Building systems	7,988	37	425	26
Other industrial products	2,621	12	150	9
Other	33		(13)	(1)
Adjustments	(418)	—	(243)	—
Total	**21,550**	**100**	**1,419**	**100**

Brand Names
Carrier (heating, air-conditioning)
Hamilton Standard (engine controls, flight systems)
Missile and Space Systems (rocket boosters)
Norden (radar and displays)
Otis (elevators, escalators)
Pratt & Whitney (engines and parts)
Sikorsky (helicopters and parts)

Jet Engines	Helicopters
F100	Black Hawk
F117	CH-53E Super Stallion
F404	Jayhawk/Seahawk
IAE V2500	MH-53E Sea Dragon
J52	S-76
JT8D-200	
JT9D	
JT15D	
PW305	
PW2000	
PW4000	

WHEN

In 1925 Frederick Rentschler and engine designer George Mead founded Pratt & Whitney Aircraft, precursor of United Technologies, in Hartford, Connecticut, to develop aircraft engines. Rentschler merged P&W with William Boeing's Seattle-based Boeing Airplane Company and with Chance Vought Corporation in 1929 to form United Aircraft & Transport. United Aircraft soon acquired other aviation manufacturers, including Hamilton Aero, Standard Steel Propeller, and Sikorsky.

In 1934, after congressional investigations led to new antitrust laws, United Aircraft's management split the corporation into 3 independent companies: United Airlines in Chicago, Boeing Airplane Company in Seattle, and United Aircraft in Hartford. United Aircraft retained P&W and several of Rentschler's other manufacturing interests.

During WWII United Aircraft produced half the engines used by US warplanes. Igor Sikorsky developed helicopters, and Vought produced the Corsair and Cutlass airplanes. After an initial postwar decline in sales, the company retooled for production of jet engines. United Aircraft spun off Chance Vought in 1954 and in 1958 bought Norden-Ketay, a manufacturer of aeronautical electronics.

In the late 1960s engines produced for the Boeing 747 proved costly for P&W when a

design flaw sparked an expensive return to the drawing boards. A concerned board of directors appointed Harry Gray, a 17-year Litton Industries executive, as president in 1971. Taking a page from the Litton script, Gray turned the company into a conglomerate, renaming it United Technologies Corporation (UTC) in 1975. To decrease UTC's dependence on government business, Gray diversified the company with numerous purchases, including Otis Elevator Company (1975) and Carrier Corporation, a large heating and air-conditioning company (1979). By 1986 Gray's acquisitions had expanded the company's sales to $15.7 billion. Gray, under pressure from his board to name a successor, tapped Bob Daniell in 1986. Gray retired a year later.

Daniell, a 25-year Sikorsky veteran, emphasized profitability rather than growth, selling many businesses (such as Mostek, a semiconductor firm) and implementing layoffs and management changes. After a year of record earnings in 1990 — $751 million on sales of $21.6 billion — UTC initiated a series of cost-cutting measures in 1991 in response to reduced military orders, a slump in the auto and building industries, and slack demand for commercial airline parts.

HOW MUCH

	9-Year Growth	1981	1982	1983	1984	1985	1986	1987	1988	1989	1990
Sales ($ mil.)	5.2%	13,668	13,577	14,669	16,332	14,992	15,669	17,170	18,088	19,614	21,550
Net income ($ mil.)	5.7%	458	427	509	645	636	48	592	659	702	751
Income as % of sales	—	3.3%	3.1%	3.5%	4.0%	4.2%	0.3%	3.4%	3.6%	3.6%	3.5%
Earnings per share ($)	5.1%	3.53	3.21	3.74	4.70	4.58	0.36	4.52	5.05	5.20	5.53
Stock price – high ($)	—	32.88	29.44	38.38	41.63	46.50	56.25	60.50	42.63	57.38	62.50
Stock price – low ($)	—	20.00	15.63	26.94	28.50	34.50	39.25	30.00	33.00	39.88	40.13
Stock price – close ($)	9.7%	20.88	28.31	36.25	36.25	43.75	46.00	33.88	41.13	54.25	47.88
P/E – high	—	9	9	10	9	10	156	13	8	11	11
P/E – low	—	6	5	7	6	8	109	7	7	8	7
Dividends per share ($)	4.6%	1.20	1.20	1.28	1.38	1.40	1.40	1.40	1.55	1.60	1.80
Book value per share ($)	7.1%	23.72	25.64	27.19	30.01	31.29	29.14	32.90	36.88	39.14	44.10

1990 Year-end:
Debt ratio: 35.2%
Return on equity: 13.3%
Cash (mil.): $201
Current ratio: 1.51
Long-term debt (mil.): $2,902
No. of shares (mil.): 121
Dividends:
 1990 average yield: 3.8%
 1990 payout: 32.6%
Market value (mil.): $5,800

Stock Price History High/Low 1981–90

RANKINGS

17th in *Fortune* 500 Industrial Cos.
101st in *Business Week* 1000

KEY COMPETITORS

Allied-Signal	Johnson Controls	Raytheon
American Standard	Lockheed	Rockwell
Boeing	Martin Marietta	Rolls-Royce
General Dynamics	McDonnell	Textron
General Electric	Douglas	Thiokol
Grumman	Nissan	Westinghouse
Henley	Northrop	Whitman

UNITED TELECOMMUNICATIONS, INC.

NYSE symbol: UT
Fiscal year ends: December 31

Hoover's Rating **C**

OVERVIEW

United Telecommunications is the nation's 9th largest telephone company, providing local phone services in 17 states to nearly 4 million lines. United is the 2nd largest non-Bell telephone company (after GTE).

United owns 80.1% of US Sprint, the nation's 3rd largest long-distance provider, with 10% of the market, and has announced plans to purchase the remainder. When United completes the transaction, it will change its name to Sprint Corporation. The company owns Sprint International, the largest data communications network in the world. Sprint provides service throughout the US and

internationally and, through subsidiary Private Transatlantic Telecommunications Systems, owns 50% of a transatlantic fiber-optic cable. In a contract worth $3–5 billion over the next 10 years, Sprint provides phone services to the US government.

United points out that, since the breakup of AT&T, it is the only major telecommunications company that controls a long-distance service and, at the same time, local telephone operations. United publishes telephone directories through DirectoriesAmerica and distributes telecommunications equipment through its North Supply subsidiary.

WHO

Chairman and CEO: William T. Esrey, age 51, $1,142,520 pay
President, Local Telecommunications Division: Curtis G. Fields, age 57, $497,154 pay
President, Long-Distance Division: Ronald T. LeMay, age 45, $467,564 pay
EVP and Chief Financial and Information Officer: Arthur B. Krause, age 49, $353,064 pay
EVP and Chief Human Resources, Technology, and Planning Officer: David D. King, age 55, $322,517 pay
Auditors: Ernst & Young
Employees: 43,100

WHEN

In 1899 Jacob and son Cleyson Brown received a franchise from the city of Abilene, Kansas, for one of the first non-Bell telephone companies in the West. Using poles from their electric utility, the men had their telephone company operational within 3 months. By 1903 they had 1,400 subscribers.

Cleyson formed Union Electric Company to sell telephone equipment (1905), and a long-distance company, Home Telephone and Telegraph (1910). In 1911 he consolidated with other Kansas independents as United Telephone Company. That year he obtained capital from his fiercest competitor, Missouri and Kansas Telephone (later renamed Southwestern Bell), which bought 60% of United's stock. Missouri and Kansas could have seized control but feared antitrust regulation, and United continued to thrive.

WWI brought labor and materials shortages that curtailed growth until its end, when Cleyson resumed acquisitions in Kansas. His electric utility was sold (1925) to finance telephony. Cleyson incorporated (1925) United Telephone and Electric and acquired more exchanges, even during the Great Depression while he was losing subscribers. He retired in 1934. WWII shortages curtailed growth and created several years of order backlog, so acquisitions ceased until 1952, when United

bought control of Investors Telephone, with operations in 8 states; further purchases followed.

In 1959 Carl Scupin took over the company and updated equipment and services. After Scupin's retirement (1964), president Paul Henson focused on satellite communications, nuclear power plants, and cable TV. He bought North Electric (1965), the oldest independent telephone equipment manufacturer in the US; Automated Data Service (1967) to offer batch processing and time-sharing; and United Business Communications (1970) to sell telephone and data hardware (sold to Stromberg-Carlson in 1974). He renamed the company United Telecommunications (1971) and purchased Florida Telephone (1974).

United prospered through industry deregulation in the 1970s and the 1983 AT&T breakup. In 1985 United bought 50% of GTE's long-distance provider, GTE Sprint, started in 1970 by Southern Pacific and acquired by GTE in 1983. United bought another 30.1% in 1989 and may buy out GTE by 1995.

In 1990 competition among long-distance services heated up and ate into United's profits. Sprint countered with a new marketing focus on the residential and small-business markets and with TV's Candice Bergen as spokeswoman.

WHERE

HQ: 2330 Shawnee Mission Pkwy., Westwood, KS 66205
Phone: 913-624-3000
Fax: 913-624-3281

United Telecom has nearly 4 million local customers in 17 states. US Sprint and North Supply operate throughout the US.

WHAT

	1990 Sales		1990 Operating Income	
	$ mil.	% of total	$ mil.	% of total
Local services	2,710	32	650	76
Long-distance svcs.	5,065	59	148	17
Other	807	9	56	7
Adjustments	(237)	—	—	—
Total	**8,345**	**100**	**854**	**100**

Telephone Companies
Carolina Telephone and Telegraph Co.
Florida Telephone Corp.
Private Transatlantic Telecommunications Systems Inc.
United Inter-Mountain Telephone Co.
United Telephone Co. of Arkansas
United Telephone Co. of the Carolinas
United Telephone Co. of Florida
United Telephone Co. of Indiana
United Telephone Co. of Iowa
United Telephone Co. of Kansas
United Telephone Co. of Minnesota
United Telephone Co. of Missouri
United Telephone Co. of New Jersey
United Telephone Co. of the Northwest
United Telephone Co. of Ohio
United Telephone Co. of Pennsylvania
United Telephone Co. of Texas
United Telephone Co. of the West
US Sprint (80.1%)

Other Companies
DirectoriesAmerica, Inc.
North Supply Co.

HOW MUCH

	9-Year Growth	1981	1982	1983	1984	1985	1986	1987	1988	1989	1990
Sales ($ mil.)	15.6%	2,255	2,429	2,474	2,858	3,219	2,857	3,064	6,493	7,549	8,345
Net income ($ mil.)	4.6%	206	202	233	216	21	187	(52)	142	363	309
Income as % of sales	—	9.1%	8.3%	9.4%	7.6%	0.6%	6.6%	(1.7%)	2.2%	4.8%	3.7%
Earnings per share ($)	1.0%	1.31	1.22	1.33	1.16	0.09	0.93	(0.28)	0.68	1.71	1.43
Stock price – high ($)	—	12.00	11.75	12.50	11.38	12.50	15.63	16.69	23.94	43.75	46.38
Stock price – low ($)	—	7.19	7.88	10.06	8.69	10.06	11.63	11.75	12.13	22.00	20.63
Stock price – close ($)	8.8%	10.88	10.44	10.56	11.13	11.88	12.75	12.31	23.19	38.00	23.25
P/E – high	—	9	10	9	10	139	17	—	35	26	32
P/E – low	—	5	6	8	7	112	13	—	18	13	14
Dividends per share ($)	2.2%	0.82	0.86	0.90	0.94	0.96	0.96	0.96	0.96	1.00	1.00
Book value per share ($)	1.8%	9.14	9.21	9.69	9.48	8.81	8.75	7.58	9.13	10.01	10.68

1990 Year-end:
Debt ratio: 63.3%
Return on equity: 13.8%
Cash (mil.): $119
Current ratio: 0.73
Long-term debt (mil.): $3,974
No. of shares (mil.): 215
Dividends:
 1990 average yield: 4.3%
 1990 payout: 69.9%
Market value (mil.): $4,997

Stock Price History High/Low 1981–90

RANKINGS

6th in *Fortune* 100 Diversified Service Cos.
116th in *Business Week* 1000

KEY COMPETITORS

AT&T
Ameritech
BCE
Bell Atlantic
BellSouth
British Telecom

Cable & Wireless
Centel
R. R. Donnelley
Dun & Bradstreet
MCI
Metromedia

NYNEX
Pacific Telesis
Southwestern Bell
U S West

UNITED WAY OF AMERICA

OVERVIEW

United Way of America is a nonprofit service agency that provides assistance to local United Way chapters across the country. There are about 2,300 local United Way chapters, each of which is an independent, autonomous organization that coordinates its own fund-raising campaigns to support numerous agencies and causes (such as the American Red Cross, Easter Seals, and YMCA). In addition to its headquarters in Alexandria, Virginia, United Way maintains 5 regional offices.

The national organization is directed by a voluntary board of governors and an executive committee. Funding comes primarily from member chapters, which pay 1% of total money raised to the United Way. Other sources of income include program services fees, conferences, sales of supplies, and private sources, such as NFL Charities, which, aside from raising money, donated over $45 million in TV advertising time to the United Way in 1990.

As part of its Second Century Initiative, the United Way is committing its prodigious resources to combating such problems as drug abuse, homelessness, and illiteracy. In 1990 United Way chapters raised over $3 billion.

WHEN

United Way traces its origins to the Charity Organizations Society, which was founded in Denver in 1887 to help coordinate the services of 22 local charitable agencies. The society raised $21,700 at its first fund-raiser in 1888.

The Denver Society was followed by the first independent Jewish federation of agencies in Boston (1895) and Associated Charities in Pittsburgh (1908), which was organized to coordinate services for the urban poor. In 1910 a council was established in Columbus, Ohio, to better coordinate charitable services, and the following year the National Association of Societies for Organizing Charity was formed to provide a channel of communication among social agencies. In 1913 the Federation for Charity and Philanthropy was created in Cleveland; its practice of raising funds from all social classes and allocating them according to need would serve as a model for the present-day United Way.

In 1918 representatives from 12 fund-raising organizations met in Chicago and established the American Association for Community Organizations (AACO), which changed its name to the Association of Community Chests and Councils (ACCC) in 1927 (shortened to CCC in 1933). By 1929 there were 353 Community Chest organizations in the US.

In 1943 the government introduced payroll deductions for charitable contributions, which allowed every worker to become a philanthropist. By 1948 there were more than 1,000 Community Chests, raising almost $182 million. Community Chests formed a cooperative relationship with the AFL and CIO in 1946, and in 1955 the AFL-CIO Services Committee was created. In 1949 the Detroit organization adopted the name United Fund.

In 1963 Los Angeles became the first city to adopt the United Way name, when over 30 local Community Chests and United Funds merged. By 1967, 31,300 agencies serving 27.5 million families were affiliated with United Way. The CCC reorganized as United Way of America in 1970; established its headquarters in Alexandria, Virginia, in 1971; and in the early 1970s introduced the person/hand/rainbow logo.

United Way established a set of operating standards for community service agencies in 1973. The next year the organization launched the largest public service campaign in US history (which included its first public service announcements in conjunction with the National Football League) and established United Way International to facilitate the formation of United Way organizations worldwide. That same year United Way became the first single organization to raise over $1 billion in an annual fund-raising campaign.

When Congress made its first emergency food and shelter grant to the private sector in 1983 ($50 million), United Way was selected as the fiscal agent. As a result of the grant, over 51 million meals and almost 7 million nights' shelter were provided to the needy. The US Postal Service recognized the organization's centennial by issuing a United Way postage stamp in 1987. In 1990 the organization published its 6 Principles for the 1990s, which it listed as: providing leadership on urgent needs, supporting self-sufficiency, building coalitions, exploring new forms of access, empowering people with knowledge, and providing choice.

HOW MUCH

	9-Year Growth	1981	1982	1983	1984	1985	1986	1987	1988	1989	1990
National amount raised ($ mil.)	7.1%	1,680	1,780	1,950	2,145	2,330	2,440	2,600	2,780	2,980	3,110
Increase over prev. yr.	—	10.1%	6.0%	9.5%	10.0%	9.0%	5.7%	6.4%	6.9%	7.2%	4.4%

1990 Year-end:
Revenues (mil.): $33
Assets (mil.): $38

Natl. Amt. Raised ($ mil.) 1981–90

Nonprofit organization
Fiscal year ends: December 31

Hoover's Rating **A**

WHO

Chairman: John F. Akers (Chairman, IBM Corporation)
VC: Edward A. Brennan (Chairman and CEO, Sears, Roebuck & Co.)
VC: James D. Robinson III (Chairman, President, and CEO, American Express Co.)
VC: Morton Bahr (President, Communications Workers of America, AFL-CIO)
Chair-Elect (1992–94): W. R. Howell (Chairman and CEO, J. C. Penney Co., Inc.)
President: William Aramony
Treasurer: Edward E. Phillips
Auditors: Arthur Andersen & Co.
Employees: 290

WHERE

HQ: 701 N. Fairfax St., Alexandria,VA 22314-2045
Phone: 703-836-7100
Fax: 703-683-7840 (Public Relations)

UWA operates from its headquarters and 5 regional offices in the US. There are approximately 2,300 local chapters coast to coast.

WHAT

	1990 Sources of Income
	% of total
Corporation and small-business employees	51
Corporations	23
Nonprofit and government employees	14
Small businesses	2
Professionals	3
Noncorporate foundations	1
Other	6
Total	**100**

	1990 Distribution of Funds
Recipient	% of total
Family service	22
Health	21
Youth and social development	17
Food/clothing/housing	9
Day care	8
Public safety	6
Community development	5
Income and jobs	5
Education	3
Other	4
Total	**100**

Representative recipients of United Way funds

Agencies for the Aged	Goodwill Industries
American Red Cross	Jewish Federations
Association for Retarded Citizens	Mental Health Associations
Big Brothers/Big Sisters	National Council on Alcoholism
Boy Scouts	National Recreation and Park Association
Boys Clubs	
Camp Fire	
Catholic Charities	Salvation Army
Cerebral Palsy Associations	Urban League
Child Welfare League	Visiting Nurse Associations
Easter Seal Societies	
Girl Scouts	YMCA
Girls Clubs	YWCA

UNIVERSAL CORPORATION

NYSE symbol: UVV
Fiscal year ends: June 30

Hoover's Rating **B-**

OVERVIEW

Richmond, Virginia–based Universal, the world's largest tobacco dealer, purchases and processes leaf tobacco for sale to cigarette and other tobacco product companies. Additional operations include other agricultural products and title insurance. The company maintains a strategy of adding value to agriproducts as opposed to just trading.

Universal Leaf (the company's tobacco division) does not manufacture any tobacco products. Rather, it selects, buys, processes, packs, stores, and finances leaf tobacco on the account of, or for resale to, tobacco products manufacturers. The company has buyers in every domestic tobacco market and numerous foreign markets. Universal also maintains a global sales force to serve foreign customers

(mainly large firms or government monopolies). Philip Morris is the company's largest customer. In recent years the decline in US tobacco consumption has been offset by increases in developing nations.

Universal's agriproducts division (Deli) buys, ships, packs, stores, finances, and sells various agricultural products, including coffee, tea, rubber, and vegetable oil. The division also distributes and sells timber and other building products in the Netherlands and Belgium. The company's Blakely Peanut subsidiary buys and processes peanuts.

Universal's Lawyers Title Insurance issues both owner's and lender's title policies to protect customers against title defects on real property.

WHO

Chairman: Gordon L. Crenshaw, age 69
President and CEO: Henry H. Harrell, age 51, $534,975 pay
EVP: Allen B. King, age 44, $370,615 pay
VP and Treasurer: O. Kemp Dozier, age 61
VP: William L. Taylor, $301,999 pay
VP: Houtwell H. Roper, age 42, $220,266 pay
Director Human Resources: Mike Oberschmidt, Jr.
Auditors: Ernst & Young
Employees: 20,000

WHERE

HQ: PO Box 25099, Hamilton St. at Broad, Richmond, VA 23260
Phone: 804-359-9311
Fax: 804-254-3584

The company is engaged in selecting, buying, shipping, processing, storing, financing, and selling tobacco in 26 countries. Its title insurance business is licensed in 49 states and in several Canadian provinces and Caribbean islands.

	1990 Sales		1990 Operating Income	
	$ mil.	% of total	$ mil.	% of total
US	1,842	66	41	46
South/Central America	118	4	10	11
Western Europe	712	25	32	36
Other	143	5	6	7
Adjustments	—	—	(9)	—
Total	**2,815**	**100**	**80**	**100**

WHEN

In 1918 the American tobacco industry was booming because of increased cigarette demand and the recent invention of a cigar-making machine. Universal Leaf was formed that year to consolidate and expand the J.P. Taylor Company (tobacco buyer, incorporated in North Carolina in 1904). Universal quickly acquired interests in a number of other competitors.

During the 1930s Philip Morris became a customer. Universal financed the tobacco for Philip Morris, which was trying to increase its market share. For 1990 Philip Morris provided over 10% of Universal's consolidated revenue.

By 1940 the company was purchasing as much leaf tobacco as any other domestic company. That year the US government filed antitrust charges against Universal and 7 other tobacco companies. American, Liggett & Myers, and Reynolds stood trial for the whole group, and, 4 years later, each of the 8 was fined $15,000.

Universal grew during the next several decades by concentrating on buying and selling tobacco. It diversified in 1968, buying Inta-Roto Machine (packaging machinery and steel cylinders for printing fabrics) and

Overton Container (tobacco containers). Universal also acquired a division of Usry Inc. (modular buildings).

The company diversified further in 1980 by purchasing Royster (fertilizer, sold in 1984 after poor returns). In 1984 Universal bought Lawyers Title and Continental Land Title together for $115 million. In 1986 the company acquired Netherlands-based Deli (timber and building products) for $48 million. Universal bought Thorpe and Ricks (tobacco processor) in 1988 and in August 1990 bought Gebreder Kulenkampffag, a German tobacco company, to give Universal a greater presence in the opening East European market.

In 1991 the company acquired Kliemann SA, a Brazilian tobacco supplier, which ensures access to Brazilian flue-cured tobacco. In October 1991 the corporation's title insurance company, Lawyers Title, is scheduled to separate from Universal. The corporation believes the separation will signficantly improve Lawyers Title's long-run competitiveness.

WHAT

	1990 Sales		1990 Operating Income	
	$ mil.	% of total	$ mil.	% of total
Tobacco	1,557	55	81	91
Title insurance	426	15	(19)	(21)
Agriproducts	520	19	9	10
Lumber	312	11	18	20
Adjustments	—	—	(9)	—
Total	**2,815**	**100**	**80**	**100**

Tobacco Products
Air-cured
Burley
Chewing
Cigar
Dark air-cured
Dark fired
Flue-cured
Maryland

Title Insurance
Lawyers Title

Agricultural Products
Cocoa
Coffee
Oilseeds
Peanuts
Rubber
Sunflower seeds
Tea
Timber
Vegetable oils

RANKINGS

162th in *Fortune* 500 Industrial Cos.
857th in *Business Week* 1000

KEY COMPETITORS

ADM
Cargill
ConAgra
Continental Grain
W. R. Grace
Other agribusinesses

HOW MUCH

	9-Year Growth	1981	1982	1983	1984	1985	1986	1987	1988	1989	1990
Sales ($ mil.)	11.7%	1,040	1,253	1,082	1,019	1,079	1,145	2,116	2,420	2,920	2,815
Net income ($ mil.)	1.9%	31	34	37	38	46	47	56	61	54	37
Income as % of sales	—	3.0%	2.7%	3.4%	3.8%	4.3%	4.1%	2.6%	2.5%	1.9%	1.3%
Earnings per share ($)	2.5%	1.78	1.97	2.11	2.21	2.66	2.74	3.56	3.19	3.19	2.22
Stock price – high ($)	—	17.44	17.00	21.13	22.00	24.50	31.00	36.75	33.75	39.00	36.13
Stock price – low ($)	—	10.88	11.25	13.25	15.25	18.75	23.25	25.63	27.88	33.00	22.00
Stock price – close ($)	7.8%	12.13	13.31	17.19	19.88	24.25	26.88	30.88	33.00	35.50	23.75
P/E – high	—	10	9	10	10	9	11	11	9	12	16
P/E – low	—	6	6	6	7	7	8	8	8	10	10
Dividends per share ($)	8.3%	0.71	0.79	0.85	0.90	0.96	1.04	1.12	1.25	1.37	1.46
Book value per share ($)	10.1%	10.16	11.32	12.35	13.48	15.17	17.08	18.94	21.04	22.82	24.15

1990 Year-end:
Debt ratio: 26.7%
Return on equity: 9.5%
Cash (mil.): $51
Current ratio: 1.58
Long-term debt (mil.): $144
No. of shares (mil.): 16
Dividends:
1990 average yield: 6.1%
1990 payout: 65.8%
Market value (mil.): $390

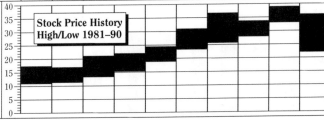

Stock Price History High/Low 1981–90

THE UNIVERSITY OF CHICAGO

OVERVIEW

Founded in 1891, the University of Chicago is among the youngest of America's major universities. It is a private, nonsectarian institution devoted to research and teaching. Unlike many of America's colleges that in the 1960s and 1970s allowed students to select and even create their own courses, the university has been unwavering in its approach to undergraduate education. Its "common core" of courses ensures that every student receives exposure to the social, physical, and biological sciences and the humanities.

The university is known as the "teacher of teachers"; more than 81% of its undergraduate class of 1988 planned to go on to graduate studies. Many distinguished scholars have been associated with the university, including 62 Nobel laureates (among them, Milton Friedman, James Watson, and Saul Bellow), and more than 70 alumni serve as leaders of other colleges and universities. Among its strongest disciplines are sociology (in which it was a pioneer), archeology, economics, and the sciences. It operates the largest and most active university press in the country.

Despite the university's early reputation as a hotbed of radicalism, the "Chicago school" of thought is characterized by a free-market, conservative philosophy. Director Mike Nichols said of the school, "Everybody was strange at the University of Chicago. It was paradise."

WHEN

The first University of Chicago was a small Baptist school (1858–86). The name was appropriated later, when a $600,000 gift from John D. Rockefeller, $400,000 in contributions from members of the American Baptist Education Society, and land donated by department store owner Marshall Field made possible the creation of the University of Chicago in 1891.

William Rainey Harper, a noted Bible scholar, was the university's first president. On October 1, 1892, the university opened with a faculty of 103, including 8 former college presidents and 594 students.

While intellectual in outlook, the university organized its first football team, under famed coach Amos Alonzo Stagg, the day it opened. Its first games were against high school and YMCA teams, and at times the coach had to play in order to field enough men. The team won one game its first season. Improving in later seasons and earning the nickname "Monsters of the Midway," the team became a member of the Big 10. It later relapsed to its losing ways and withdrew from intercollegiate play in 1939.

So enthusiastic was the response to the new university that, 4 years after its founding, its enrollment of 1,815 exceeded Harvard's. By 1907 enrollment was 5,038, of which 43% were women. Rockefeller continued to contribute to the university (calling his $36 million of contributions the best investment he ever made), enabling the university to expand in size and intellectual influence under Harper and his successor, Harry Pratt Judson.

The university's greatest intellectual flowering came with Robert Maynard Hutchins's presidency (1929–51), during which he revolutionized the university and American higher education by insisting on the study of original sources (the Great Books) and competency testing through comprehensive exams.

He organized the college and graduate divisions into their present structure, reaffirming the role of the university as a place for intellectual exploration rather than vocational training. It was during his tenure, in 1942, that the nuclear age began when Enrico Fermi created the first self-sustaining nuclear chain reaction in the abandoned football stadium.

From the 1950s through the 1970s, the university consolidated its position as one of the world's great centers of learning and successfully stemmed the tide of urban decay encroaching on its South Side Chicago campus. During this time it purchased and restored Frank Lloyd Wright's famed Robie House (now used by the Alumni Association), built the Joseph Regenstein Library (1970), and reinstated intercollegiate football (1969). Since 1978 the university has been led by Hanna Gray, until recently the only woman president of a major university. The university is currently celebrating its centennial with a series of academic and cultural events.

Private university
Fiscal year ends: June 30
Motto: Crescat Scientia Vita Excolatur

Hoover's Rating **A-**

WHO

President: Hanna H. Gray, age 59
Provost: Gerhard Casper
VP Business and Finance: Alexander E. Sharp
General Counsel and VP Administration: Arthur M. Sussman
Auditors: KPMG Peat Marwick
Employees: 3,594

WHERE

HQ: 5801 S. Ellis Ave., Chicago, IL 60637
Phone: 312-702-1234
Fax: 312-702-8324

The university has a 175-acre campus in Hyde Park on Chicago's South Side, maintains a downtown Chicago campus, and owns Yerkes Observatory in Williams Bay, Wisconsin.

Geographic Distribution, Class of 1993	% of Total
Midwest	46
Mid-Atlantic	21
West	11
New England	9
South & Southwest	11
Foreign	2
Total	**100**

WHAT

	1990 Revenues	
	$ mil.	% of total
Tuition & fees	142	25
Government grants	122	21
Private gifts	54	9
Endowment income	47	8
Professional fees	88	15
Auxiliary activities	102	18
Other	24	4
Total	**579**	**100**

Academic Unit	1990 Enrollment	% of Total
The College	3,433	30
Graduate Divisions		
Biological Sciences	288	3
Physical Sciences	522	5
Humanities	726	7
Social Sciences	1,329	12
Professional Schools		
Business	2,582	24
Divinity	303	3
Law	571	5
Library Science	10	—
Medicine	429	4
Public Policy	88	1
Social Service	291	3
Nondegree	378	3
Total	**10,950**	**100**

Affiliated Institutions
Argonne National Laboratory
Bergmann Gallery
Court Theatre
Enrico Fermi Institute
James Franck Institute
Laboratory School
Midway Studios
National Opinion Research Center
Office of Continuing Education
Oriental Institute
Smart Museum
The University of Chicago Medical Center
The University of Chicago Press
Yerkes Observatory

KEY COMPETITORS

Harvard
Stanford
Ohio State
University of Texas

HOW MUCH

	9-Year Growth	1981	1982	1983	1984	1985	1986	1987	1988	1989	1990
Enrollment	2.0%	9,182	9,336	9,096	9,087	9,465	9,783	10,217	10,431	10,625	10,950
Faculty	0.5%	1,138	1,144	1,129	1,123	1,129	1,156	1,166	1,178	1,200	1,193
Student/faculty ratio	—	8.1	8.2	8.1	8.1	8.4	8.5	8.8	8.9	8.9	9.2
First-year tuition ($)	12.6%	5,100	6,000	7,050	7,920	8,670	9,600	11,352	12,120	12,930	14,895
Endowment market value ($ mil.)	11.9%	397	394	541	517	641	801	914	898	974	1,093

First-Year Tuition ($) 1981–90

THE UNIVERSITY OF TEXAS AT AUSTIN

OVERVIEW

The University of Texas at Austin is the 2nd largest school by enrollment in the US (after Ohio State). The school trails only Harvard in the size of its endowment and maintains its wealth through royalties on West Texas oil.

UT's internationally recognized research facilities include the McDonald Observatory, the Institute for Geophysics (Galveston), and the Marine Science Institute (Port Aransas). The school boasts the 6th largest academic library in the nation and was named in *Great Libraries* as one of the 32 best in the world. UT's affiliated institutions include the LBJ Library and School of Public Affairs, and the Harry Ransom Humanities Research Center, which houses a renowned collection of rare books (including a Gutenberg Bible).

In 1990 UT's privately funded faculty endowments numbered 1,051. The school's current staff includes 2 Nobel and 2 Pulitzer Prize winners.

UT's alumni list includes Walter Cronkite, Lady Bird Johnson, Bill Moyers, Earl Campbell (who won a Heisman Trophy as a Longhorn), Nobel laureate E. Donnall Thomas, and Secretary of State James Baker.

Public university
Fiscal year ends: August 31

Hoover's Rating **A-**

WHO

Chairman Board of Regents: Louis A. Beecherl, Jr.
President: William H. Cunningham
EVP and Provost: Gerhard J. Fonken
VP Business Affairs: G. Charles Franklin
Auditors: Texas State Auditor
Employees: 20,014

WHERE

HQ: UT Station, Austin, TX 78713
Phone: 512-471-3434
Fax: 512-471-8102

The University of Texas at Austin has a main campus with 119 buildings on 357 acres in central Austin. Other facilities include the 475-acre Balcones Research Center, the 94-acre Montopolis Research Center, and a biological field lab and married student housing complex on a 445-acre tract.

Geographic Distribution of Students		
	1990 enrollment	% of total
Texas	40,413	81
Other states	5,344	11
Foreign	3,860	8
Total	**49,617**	**100**

WHEN

In 1836 the Texas Declaration of Independence admonished Mexico for having failed to establish a public education system in Texas territory, yet over 40 more years passed before Texas had a university. In 1880 the statute creating the university was adopted, and in 1881 Texans voted to locate the main university in Austin. The first 2 departments, law and academic, were organized in 1882, and the first classes met in partitioned rooms of the capitol in 1883, with 8 professors teaching 218 students.

The school's first building, Old Main, opened in 1884, and in 1891 the school's medical branch opened. By 1894 UT had enrolled 534 students and hired its first football coach. The *Ranger*, a student newspaper first published in 1900, became the *Daily Texan* in 1916. In 1905 the College of Education opened, followed by the Graduate School (1910) and the College of Business Administration (1924).

UT's financial needs were met in 1923 when the Santa Rita, a well in the West Texas desert given to UT by the legislature, hit oil. The income from oil production became the Permanent University Fund (PUF), from which only interest on the revenues could be used, 2/3 by UT and 1/3 by Texas A&M University. By 1926 UT's oil royalties were over $4 million, twice as much as UT's state funding ($1.8 million). In 1928 Herman Joseph Muller won a Nobel Prize for genetic research he had done at UT. In 1933, 9 new buildings were dedicated. The Tower was built in 1937 to replace Old Main, and in 1938 the College of Fine Arts opened. By 1940 the PUF was over $100 million. In the 1940s and 1950s, the Graduate Schools of Library Science and Social Work opened, as did the School of Architecture.

In 1946 Heman Sweatt was denied admission to the law school because he was black, beginning a fight that ended with a Supreme Court order that UT admit him in 1950. UT hired its first black professor in 1964.

The College of Communication opened in 1965. Tragedy struck the school in 1966 when Charles Whitman shot 47 people from the Tower, killing 16, before he was killed by a policeman. The late 1960s and early 1970s brought to UT student unrest related to the Vietnam War, environmental and race issues, and even the quality of food on campus. In 1969 the Longhorn football team became the national champions, and UT alumnus Alan Bean became the 4th man on the moon.

In 1970 and 1971 the Lyndon Baines Johnson School of Public Affairs and the LBJ Library opened. In 1978 UT bought one of only 5 Gutenberg Bibles in the US for $2.4 million.

UT celebrated its centennial in 1983, creating many new faculty endowments. In 1990 UT was chosen by the federal government as the site for a $13 million defense research facility. More than 51% of enrolled students in 1991 were receiving some form of financial assistance.

WHAT

	1990 Revenues
	% of total
General appropriations (taxes)	32
Federal, state & private grants	22
Auxiliary enterprises (dormitories, athletics, student union)	16
Available University Fund	12
Private gifts & endowments	6
Fees & revolving fund	6
Tuition	5
Other	1
Total	**100**

Academic Unit	1990 Enrollment
Architecture	567
Business	9,847
Communication	4,166
Education	3,003
Engineering	6,670
Fine Arts	2,019
Law	1,598
Liberal Arts	12,074
Library/Info Science	303
Natural Sciences	7,334
Nursing	721
Pharmacy	584
Public Affairs	214
Social Work	517
Total	**49,617**

Affiliated Institutions

Archer M. Huntington Art Gallery	Marine Science Institute
Balcones Research Center	McDonald Observatory
Harry Ransom Humanities Research Center	Montopolis Research Center
Institute for Geophysics	Paisano Ranch
LBJ Library and Museum	Sam Rayburn Library
LBJ School of Public Affairs	Texas Center for Writers
	Texas Memorial Museum
	Winedale Historical Center

HOW MUCH

	9-Year Growth	1981	1982	1983	1984	1985	1986	1987	1988	1989	1990
Enrollment	0.3%	48,145	48,039	47,631	47,973	47,838	46,140	47,743	50,107	50,245	49,617
Faculty	1.4%	2,105	2,188	2,191	2,278	2,189	2,215	2,215	2,245	2,273	2,395
Student/faculty ratio	—	22.2	22.2	21.5	21.4	21.1	20.5	21.7	22.3	21.9	20.7
Tuition & fees ($)	9.2%	396	396	406	419	621	731	739	742	811	877
% receiving financial aid	—	—	—	—	44.8%	46.7%	48.0%	47.7%	49.2%	—	51.1%
Endowment market value ($ mil.)[1]	11.7%	862	1,077	1,341	1,434	1,704	2,075	2,263	2,152	2,494	2,337

Tuition & Fees ($) 1981–90

[1] Represents market value of endowment for entire University of Texas system

KEY COMPETITORS

Harvard	Stanford
Ohio State	University of Chicago

UNOCAL CORPORATION

NYSE symbol: UCL
Fiscal year ends: December 31

Hoover's Rating C

OVERVIEW

Unocal, the 11th largest US petroleum company, is also the world's largest producer of geothermal energy. It owns 2 geothermal electricity plants in Southern California and is the major producer at a Northern California field.

Unocal is one of those companies struggling to cope with the takeover hangover left from the 1980s. To deal with the debt it raised to defend itself from a hostile 1985 bid, Unocal has butchered once-sacred cows. It has shuttered its shale oil project, the pet of former chairman Fred Hartley, and closed its refinery R&D operation, long at the core of Unocal's corporate culture.

Unocal has been adding hydrocarbon reserves through acquisitions. Replacement of proven reserves has outpaced production for 4 years (at a low $3.77 per barrel cost in 1990).

The company has converted its drilling partnership to a publicly traded, 96%-owned corporation, Unocal Exploration. Unocal is also exploring overseas, notably Southeast Asia, for "elephants" — industry jargon for huge oil fields.

WHEN

Not far from the 1859 Pennsylvania well that ushered in the modern oil industry, Lyman Stewart, just 19, hoped to finance Presbyterian evangelism by joining the boom. He plunked down $124 for a 1/8 interest in a Pennsylvania oil lease.

By the 1880s Stewart had put aside a religious career in favor of the oil business. He and partner Wallace Hardison headed for Southern California. When they united 3 oil companies in 1890, the result was Union Oil of California.

The fledgling company boasted a petroleum laboratory — the West's first — at its Santa Paula refinery. In 1901 one of its geologists discovered a trove of prehistoric bones in the La Brea tar pits. In 1903 Union Oil built the world's first oil tanker, a wooden ship outfitted with steel tanks.

As Union service stations multiplied in the 1930s, the company cast about for a new name for its gasoline. Lead in the gas added a reddish tinge and made the old brand name, White Magic, obsolete. An executive suggested 76 to conjure the spirit of America.

In 1965 Union Oil of California acquired Pure Oil, formed in New Jersey in 1895 when independent refiners bristled at the dictates of the Standard Oil colossus. Pure Oil became the largest independent to challenge Standard. The merger with Pure Oil doubled Union's size.

Union operated the offshore well that produced the infamous 1969 Santa Barbara oil spill. The damage became a rallying point for the fledgling US environmental movement. During the 1970s Fred Hartley, named CEO in 1964, steered the company to develop alternative energy sources. Geothermal development proved profitable, but extracting oil from Colorado shale, underwritten by federal subsidies, has not lived up to company expectations.

The company adopted its Unocal nickname as the name for its corporate umbrella in 1983. In 1985 takeover artist T. Boone Pickens targeted Unocal, and the tenacious Hartley ran debt to more than $5.5 billion to repurchase almost 1/3 of Unocal's outstanding stock.

Unocal spent the rest of the 1980s coping with the debt. Hartley's successor, Richard Stegemeier, sold the Los Angeles headquarters complex (1988). In 1989 Unocal raised cash by transferring midwestern refining and marketing operations to UNO-VEN, a joint venture with a Petróleos de Venezuela subsidiary.

In 1990 the company sold its Norwegian subsidiary for $322 million but bought Prairie Holdings (20,000 acres, 115 billion cubic feet of natural gas reserves and 9 million barrels of crude oil reserves) in the US. The company resumed its sell-off in 1991, seeking buyers for its truck stops nationwide, for marketing assets in the Southeast, and for assorted chemical operations.

WHO

Chairman, President, and CEO: Richard J. Stegemeier, age 62, $1,191,557 pay

VC and EVP: Claude S. Brinegar, age 64, $729,080 pay (prior to reassignment)

SVP and CFO: Thomas B. Sleeman, age 58, $420,824 pay (prior to promotion)

VP Corporate Human Resources: Wellman E. Branstrom, age 55

Auditors: Coopers & Lybrand

Employees: 17,518

WHERE

HQ: 1201 W. Fifth St., Los Angeles, CA 90017
Phone: 213-977-7600
Fax: 213-977-5362 (Personnel)

Most of Unocal's oil and gas is produced in Alaska, California, Louisiana, New Mexico, Oklahoma, and Texas and in 6 foreign countries.

	1990 Sales		1990 Pretax Income	
	$ mil.	% of total	$ mil.	% of total
US	10,515	87	650	56
Foreign	1,607	13	518	44
Adjustments	(1,477)	—	(416)	—
Total	**10,645**	**100**	**752**	**100**

WHAT

	1990 Sales		1990 Pretax Income	
	$ mil.	% of total	$ mil.	% of total
Chemicals	1,236	9	62	5
Exploration & production	3,256	24	970	82
Refining & marketing	8,704	64	115	10
Metals	103	1	(1)	—
Geothermal	210	1	62	5
Other	77	1	(25)	(2)
Adjustments	(2,941)	—	(431)	—
Total	**10,645**	**100**	**752**	**100**

Subsidiaries and Affiliates
Union Oil Co. of California (integrated petroleum)
Unocal Exploration Corp. (96%, exploration and production, Gulf Coast)
Unocal Indonesia, Ltd.
Unocal Land & Development Co.
Unocal Netherlands BV
Unocal UK Ltd.
Unocal Pipeline (Alaska)
Unocal Thailand, Ltd.
UNO-VEN (50%, refining and marketing, Midwest)

RANKINGS

45th in *Fortune* 500 Industrial Cos.
92nd in *Business Week* 1000

KEY COMPETITORS

Amoco	Koch	Royal Dutch/
Ashland	Mobil	Shell
Atlantic	Norsk Hydro	Sun
Richfield	Occidental	Texaco
British	Oryx	USX
Petroleum	Pennzoil	Other oil,
Chevron	Petrofina	chemical,
Coastal	Petrobrás	and mining
Du Pont	Pemex	companies
Exxon	Phillips	
Imperial Oil	Petroleum	

HOW MUCH

	9-Year Growth	1981	1982	1983	1984	1985	1986	1987	1988	1989	1990
Sales ($ mil.)	(0.1%)	10,746	10,390	10,066	10,838	10,738	7,482	8,466	8,853	10,056	10,645
Net income ($ mil.)	(7.3%)	791	804	626	700	325	176	181	24	358	401
Income as % of sales	—	7.4%	7.7%	6.2%	6.5%	3.0%	2.4%	2.1%	0.3%	3.6%	3.8%
Earnings per share ($)	(3.1%)	2.28	2.32	1.80	2.02	1.18	0.76	0.78	0.11	1.53	1.71
Stock price – high ($)	—	23.00	18.94	18.81	21.63	25.50	14.13	22.50	20.19	31.25	34.50
Stock price – low ($)	—	14.13	10.63	13.50	15.00	12.81	7.81	10.50	14.25	18.69	24.63
Stock price – close ($)	3.8%	18.81	13.31	15.81	18.50	13.44	13.31	14.13	18.94	29.75	26.25
P/E – high	—	10	8	10	11	22	19	29	192	20	20
P/E – low	—	6	5	8	7	11	10	13	136	12	14
Dividends per share ($)	5.7%	0.43	0.50	0.50	0.50	0.58	0.55	0.50	0.50	0.55	0.70
Book value per share ($)	(0.9%)	11.85	13.66	14.91	16.39	7.01	7.23	7.58	9.26	9.83	10.87

1990 Year-end:
Debt ratio: 61.3%
Return on equity: 16.5%
Cash (mil.): $130
Current ratio: 1.12
Long-term debt (mil.): $4,047
No. of shares (mil.): 235
Dividends:
 1990 average yield: 2.7%
 1990 payout: 40.9%
Market value (mil.): $6,156

Stock Price History High/Low 1981–90

THE UPJOHN COMPANY

NYSE symbol: UPJ
Fiscal year ends: December 31

Hoover's Rating A-

OVERVIEW

Upjohn of Kalamazoo, Michigan, is the maker of several well-known pharmaceuticals, including the pain-reliever Motrin (now sold nonprescription) and Rogaine (baldness treatment), one of the few prescription drugs advertised directly to the consumer. Besides pharmaceuticals, Upjohn produces animal health products, seeds, and chemicals.

Like other companies, Upjohn markets foreign drug company products in the US and licenses its products to be sold overseas. Major alliances include an agreement with SmithKline Beecham to sell Eminase (for heart attacks) and a joint venture with Solvay to market fluvoxamine (for depression).

Four relatives of founder William Upjohn (the Parfets and Preston Parish) serve as board members or officers. Family members own about 10% of the stock.

R&D expenditures run at 14% of sales. Promising drugs in the company's pipeline include treatments for irregular heartbeat, cancer, diabetes, and AIDS. New products are crucial for Upjohn's success as patents for its 4 leading drugs (Ansaid, Halcion, Micronase, and Xanax) all expire in 1993–94.

WHO

Chairman and CEO: Theodore Cooper, age 62, $1,343,727 pay
President: William U. Parfet, age 44, $386,087 pay (prior to promotion)
SVP Finance and CFO: Robert C. Salisbury, age 47
VP Human Resources: Richard G. Tomlinson
Auditors: Coopers & Lybrand
Employees: 18,500

WHERE

HQ: 7000 Portage Rd., Kalamazoo, MI 49001
Phone: 616-323-4000
Fax: 616-323-7034

Upjohn has research facilities in more than 200 locations worldwide.

	1990 Sales		1990 Operating Income	
	$ mil.	% of total	$ mil.	% of total
US	1,821	60	606	86
Europe	676	23	33	5
Japan & Pacific	311	10	29	4
Other regions	213	7	38	5
Adjustments	12	—	(82)	—
Total	**3,033**	**100**	**624**	**100**

WHEN

Dr. William Upjohn formed the Upjohn Pill and Granule Company in partnership with his brothers in Kalamazoo, Michigan, in 1886. William's patented "friable" pill (which disintegrated readily after swallowing) was the basis for the company's success over early competitors. (Some pills of the day would not disintegrate when struck with a hammer.) Upjohn took its current name in 1902. The company's most successful products at the turn of the century were the antimalarial quinine and the Phenolax wafer, a candy-type laxative.

By 1912 annual sales had passed $1 million. Research initiated the following year led to the development of several new products, including Citrocarbonate, an effervescent antacid, which had sales of over $1 million in 1926. Other products included Cheracol cough syrup (1924), Kaopectate antidiarrheal (1936), and Unicap multivitamins (1940).

During WWII the company produced large amounts of penicillin and sulfanilamide. Research on steroids after the war eventually yielded important medicines for treating a variety of inflammatory conditions, including Medrol (methylprednisolone, 1956), which had fewer side effects than others.

Completion of a new manufacturing plant near Kalamazoo in 1951 at a cost of $33 million increased production by 1/3 and consolidated operations in one location. Increasing demand for the company's products overseas led to the formation of the Upjohn International Division in 1952. By 1955 annual sales had reached $100 million.

In 1957 Upjohn introduced Orinase, the first oral agent for diabetes. The company went public the following year, and in 1959 introduced Depo-Provera, a long-acting contraceptive sold throughout the world but not yet approved in the US. In the 1960s Upjohn combined its plant and animal health operations and acquired companies involved in agricultural products, home health care, and medical testing labs.

Motrin (generic name ibuprofen), an analgesic introduced in 1974, achieved greater first-year sales than any other drug and continued to be a top seller into the 1980s. The antidiabetes agent Micronase (1984) and the tranquilizers Xanax (1982) and Halcion (1983) have also sold well in the 1980s. In 1988 Upjohn marketed Rogaine, the first FDA-approved treatment for baldness.

In 1990 the company sold its health care services business and was dealt a blow in 1991 when an appeals court ruled that Genetics Institute's version of the drug EPO (marketed in the US by Upjohn under the name Marogen) violated Amgen's patent. That same year the company temporarily suspended testing of its blood substitute Hemopure.

WHAT

	1990 Sales		1990 Operating Income	
	$ mil.	% of total	$ mil.	% of total
Agriculture	615	20	74	10
Human health care	2,406	80	632	90
Adjustments	12	—	(82)	—
Total	**3,033**	**100**	**624**	**100**

Brand Names

Major Prescription Drugs
Ansaid (arthritis drug)
Colestid (cholesterol-lowering drug)
Eminase (blood clot dissolver)
Fluvoxamine (antidepressant)
Halcion (tranquilizer)
Lincocin (antibiotic)
Medrol (hormone)
Micronase (diabetic drug)
Motrin (painkiller)
Provera (hormonal drug)
Rogaine (baldness treatment)
Xanax (tranquilizer)
Zefazone (antibiotic)

Animal Drugs
Bovine somatotropin (BST, a lactation stimulant for cattle)
Lincomix (feed additive)
Naxcel (antibiotic)

Consumer Products
Cortaid (ointment)
Doxidan (laxative)
Kaopectate (antidiarrheal drug)
Motrin IB (painkiller)
Mycitracin (antibiotic)
Surfak (laxative)
Unicap (vitamins)

RANKINGS

153rd in *Fortune* 500 Industrial Cos.
79th in *Business Week* 1000

KEY COMPETITORS

Abbott Labs
American Cyanamid
American Home Products
Amgen
Baxter
Bayer
Bristol-Myers Squibb
Ciba-Geigy
Du Pont
Eastman Kodak
Elf Aquitaine
Eli Lilly
Genentech
Glaxo

Hoechst
Johnson & Johnson
L'Oréal
Merck
Monsanto
Pfizer
Procter & Gamble
Rhône-Poulenc
Roche
Sandoz
Schering-Plough
SmithKline Beecham
Syntex
Warner-Lambert

HOW MUCH

	9-Year Growth	1981	1982	1983	1984	1985	1986	1987	1988	1989	1990
Sales ($ mil.)	5.3%	1,903	1,836	1,993	2,188	2,017	2,291	2,530	2,754	2,916	3,033
Net income ($ mil.)	10.8%	182	126	160	173	203	253	305	353	311	458
Income as % of sales	—	9.6%	6.9%	8.0%	7.9%	10.1%	11.0%	12.1%	12.8%	10.7%	15.1%
Earnings per share ($)	10.2%	1.01	0.70	0.88	0.95	1.10	1.35	1.63	1.90	1.67	2.41
Stock price – high ($)	—	11.50	9.90	11.46	12.02	23.58	35.42	53.75	35.25	42.13	44.63
Stock price – low ($)	—	7.60	6.33	7.71	7.50	11.13	20.58	22.63	26.88	27.63	33.00
Stock price – close ($)	17.4%	8.96	7.73	9.88	11.69	22.25	31.08	30.00	28.75	38.50	38.00
P/E – high	—	11	14	13	13	22	26	33	19	25	19
P/E – low	—	8	9	9	8	10	15	14	14	17	14
Dividends per share ($)	13.0%	0.33	0.38	0.38	0.43	0.44	0.50	0.58	0.76	0.91	1.00
Book value per share ($)	5.4%	5.34	5.37	5.79	6.17	6.96	7.85	8.95	9.83	9.44	8.54

1990 Year-end:
Debt ratio: 23.6%
Return on equity: 26.8%
Cash (mil.): $216
Current ratio: 1.94
Long-term debt (mil.): $550
No. of shares (mil.): 176
Dividends:
1990 average yield: 2.6%
1990 payout: 41.5%
Market value (mil.): $6,704

Stock Price History High/Low 1981–90

USAIR GROUP, INC.

OVERVIEW

USAir, the world's 8th largest airline in terms of revenue passenger miles, carried more than 60 million passengers in 1990. It is supported by USAir Express, a group of commuter airlines serving 156 airports in the US, Canada, and the Bahamas. USAir also has subsidiaries that specialize in aviation-related activities.

The company's earnings (like those of many other airlines) have been in a downward spiral since 1989. USAir has responded by cutting 142 flights, reducing staff, and phasing out older, less fuel-efficient airliners.

In light of industry-wide hardships, the company is faring better than some; it has created a stronger market position at its Philadelphia hub since Midway Airlines phased out operations there (late in 1990), and it has bought routes from Midway and Eastern (now defunct) to 3 Canadian cities. But USAir lost out to American and Delta on a bid to open service to Manchester (England), and since it primarily serves the northeast (an area especially hit by the recession), its recovery could take some time.

WHEN

Pilot Richard C. du Pont (of the du Pont chemical dynasty) founded All American Aviation, a Washington, DC–based air mail service, in 1937. Serving small northeastern communities, All American picked up and delivered mail "on the fly," using a system of hooks and ropes. The service continued until 1949, the year passenger service commenced.

The company (renamed Allegheny Airlines in 1953) developed as a federally subsidized regional airline by serving communities too remote for major airline service in an area bounded by Boston, Washington, Cleveland, and Detroit. Allegheny Commuters (now USAir Express) began offering commuter links with Allegheny's route system in 1967.

The airline gained routes in the Great Lakes area and in New York and along the East Coast by buying Lake Central Airlines (1968) and Mohawk Airlines (1972). The company was listed on the NYSE in 1978.

Edwin Colodny, the airline's legal counsel and president, became chairman in 1978, replacing Henry Satterwhite, who had retired after 25 years with the airline. Colodny decided the best way to assure the airline's growth was to reemphasize its original purpose: shorter flights to smaller cities. He extended service to the South and in 1979 renamed the company USAir.

USAir augmented its commuter service by purchasing Pennsylvania Commuter Airlines

(1985) and Suburban Airlines (1986). After rebuffing a takeover bid by TWA in 1987, the company became America's 7th largest airline (in terms of passenger miles) by acquiring Piedmont Aviation (a major airline operating primarily in the Southeast) and Los Angeles–based PSA (Pacific Southwest Airlines). Piedmont's 2 commuters, Henson Aviation and Jetstream International Airlines, joined USAir Express in 1988.

In 1988 Colodny piloted USAir through its 12th consecutive year of profitability and bought 11% of Covia Partnership, a joint venture established to operate United Airlines' Apollo computerized reservations system, for $113 million. USAir offered its first transatlantic flight (Charlotte to London) in 1989.

But that year difficulties related to the integration of USAir and Piedmont (one of the largest airline mergers in history) combined with the rising cost of jet fuel to result in USAir's only loss during the 1980s ($63 million). As losses continued in 1990 (due in part to a weak economy and high fuel prices), the company laid off 3,600 workers. More layoffs (3,500 workers) followed in 1991. Also in 1991 USAir began disposing of its engine maintenance and general aviation units. Colodny, who reached age 65 in June 1991, retired as CEO, leaving Seth Schofield in charge.

NYSE symbol: U
Fiscal year ends: December 31

Hoover's Rating **D**

WHO

Chairman: Edwin I. Colodny, age 64, $625,000 pay
President and CEO: Seth E. Schofield, age 51, $381,154 pay (prior to promotion)
VC and EVP: Randall Malin, age 53, $353,077 pay
EVP Finance: Frank L. Salizzoni, age 52
SVP Human Resources, USAir, Inc.: John P. Frestel, Jr., age 51, $210,000 pay
Auditors: KPMG Peat Marwick
Employees: 53,000

WHERE

HQ: 2345 Crystal Dr., Arlington, VA 22227
Phone: 703-418-5306
Fax: 703-418-5307 (Investor Relations)
Reservations: 800-428-4322

USAir serves more than 170 cities in 48 states, Canada, the Bahamas, Bermuda, Puerto Rico, Germany, and the UK.

Hub Locations

Baltimore, MD/	Dayton, OH
Washington, DC	Philadelphia, PA
Charlotte, NC/Douglas, NC	Pittsburgh, PA

WHAT

	1990 Sales	
	$ mil.	% of total
Passenger transportation	6,073	93
Cargo & freight	160	2
Other	326	5
Total	**6,559**	**100**

Major Subsidiaries and Affiliates
Air Service, Inc.
Aviation Supply Corp.
Piedmont Aviation Services, Inc.
USAir Express (commuter airlines)
   Allegheny Commuter Airlines, Inc.
   Henson Aviation, Inc.
   Jetstream International Airlines, Inc.
   Pennsylvania Commuter Airlines, Inc.
USAir, Inc. (airline)
USAir Leasing and Services, Inc.
USAM Corp. (owns 11% of Covia Partnership, owner and operator of Apollo computer reservation system)

Flight Equipment	No.	Average Age in Years
Boeing 727	29	15.1
Boeing 737	228	6.0
Boeing 767	9	2.3
DC-9	74	17.8
MD-80	31	8.3
Other	199	6.0
Total	**570**	**8.1**

HOW MUCH

	9-Year Growth	1981	1982	1983	1984	1985	1986	1987	1988	1989	1990
Sales ($ mil.)	21.8%	1,110	1,273	1,432	1,630	1,765	1,835	3,001	5,707	6,252	6,559
Net income ($ mil.)	—	51	59	81	122	117	98	195	165	(63)	(454)
Income as % of sales	—	4.6%	4.6%	5.6%	7.5%	6.6%	5.4%	6.5%	2.9%	(1.0%)	(6.9%)
Earnings per share ($)	—	2.66	2.88	3.22	4.46	3.98	3.33	5.27	3.81	(1.36)	(10.89)
Stock price – high ($)	—	26.13	36.50	39.88	35.00	38.50	41.00	53.50	40.13	54.75	33.75
Stock price – low ($)	—	11.00	10.00	25.88	22.00	27.25	30.13	26.00	28.00	30.63	12.63
Stock price – close ($)	3.2%	11.88	33.25	31.75	33.25	34.38	36.25	33.75	34.50	33.38	15.75
P/E – high	—	10	13	12	8	10	12	10	11	—	—
P/E – low	—	4	3	8	5	7	9	5	7	—	—
Dividends per share ($)	(3.1%)	0.12	0.12	0.12	0.12	0.12	0.12	0.12	0.12	0.12	0.09
Book value per share ($)	4.9%	20.45	22.97	26.82	31.92	35.47	38.78	43.90	47.28	42.86	31.50

1990 Year-end:
Debt ratio: 61.2%
Return on equity: —
Cash (mil.): $408
Current ratio: 0.66
Long-term debt (mil.): $2,263
No. of shares (mil.): 46
Dividends:
  1990 average yield: 0.6%
  1990 payout: —
Market value (mil.): $717

Stock Price History High/Low 1981–90

RANKINGS

9th in *Fortune* 50 Transportation Cos.
544th in *Business Week* 1000

KEY COMPETITORS

Alaska Air	Continental	NWA
America West	Airlines	Southwest
AMR	Delta	TWA
British	Lufthansa	UAL
Airways	Midway	

USF&G CORPORATION

NYSE symbol: FG
Fiscal year ends: December 31

Hoover's Rating C-

OVERVIEW

USF&G provides property/casualty insurance, life insurance, and investment management services. The company's largest subsidiary, United States Fidelity and Guaranty, is the 13th largest US property/casualty insurer based on premiums written. Property/casualty insurance operations include underwriting, marketing, and claims services, and represented 86% of USF&G's revenues in 1990.

Life insurance operations are carried on through Fidelity and Guaranty Life and Thomas Jefferson Life. USF&G's Investment Management Group provides investment management, real estate and leasing, and consulting services.

Norman P. Blake, Jr., named CEO in 1990, is trying to rebuild the company around its core businesses after declines in profits that caused the company's stock price to plummet from a high of $30 to a 1990 year-end close of $7. Reasons include the extreme competitiveness of the market, which has kept premiums low; regulatory pressures, particularly in auto insurance and workers compensation, which have made these segments so unprofitable that USF&G has ceased writing property and casualty insurance in Texas and Louisiana; and former management's decision in the 1980s to diversify into high yield financial investments to pay dividends in excess of earnings.

WHEN

In 1896 Baltimore businessman John Bland had the idea of selling businesses a list of attorneys bonded by a surety company. He formed United States Fidelity and Guaranty Company to write surety bonds guaranteeing prompt remittance of money collected by attorneys for mercantile houses.

In 1900 the company added burglary insurance to operations that already had expanded to include the entire country. The company grew through a network of independent agents, many of whom were personally selected by Bland. By 1903 USF&G was also doing business in Alaska, Hawaii, and Canada. In 1906 the company moved to a larger facility.

Following the introduction of the automobile and enactment of workman's compensation laws, the company added casualty insurance in 1910. Within 5 years casualty insurance premiums equaled the combined total premiums of fidelity (bonds covering employee dishonesty), surety, and burglary insurance. In 1920 the company first offered fire and inland marine insurance.

In 1952, following the purchase of Fidelity and Guaranty Fire Insurance, the company was able to write all lines of property insurance. During the 1950s the company established new branches and further developed its agency force. In 1960 it formed F&G Life, and in 1962 bought Merchants Fire Assurance and Merchants Indemnity. In 1969 USF&G purchased Thomas Jefferson Life Insurance from First Executive Corporation.

In the early 1970s the company centralized operations in Baltimore. In 1975 the company experienced record losses of about $1 million per month but in 1978 was back on track with the highest underwriting profits of any stock insurance company.

In 1981 the life insurance business and property/casualty operation became part of holding company USF&G. In 1985 USF&G created USF&G Financial Services Corporation to provide investment management services to corporate and institutional clients worldwide. In 1988 the company purchased Citicorp Investment Management (renamed Chancellor Capital Management).

In 1990 the entire management team was replaced by a new group led by Norman Blake. He cut expenses, firing over 2,700 by mid-1991, divested non-performing sectors and investments, suspended dividends, and established loss reserves for junk bonds and real estate. In 1991 USF&G raised more money through a new private stock offering and sold 51% of Chancellor to its employees.

WHO

Chairman, President, and CEO: Norman P. Blake, Jr., age 49, $957,708 pay
EVP and CFO: Edwin G. Pickett, age 44
EVP and Chief Investment Officer: J. Michael Gaffney, age 49
EVP, Diversified Investment Group: Dan L. Hale, age 47
SVP Human Resources: John M. Hart, age 43
Auditors: Ernst & Young
Employees: 10,600

WHERE

HQ: 100 Light St., Baltimore, MD 21202
Phone: 301-547-3000
Fax: 301-625-2829

USF&G property/casualty insurance is sold nationwide by 5,300 independent agencies; life insurance is sold by 6,500 independent agencies. USF&G Financial Services Corporation also has operations in 43 foreign countries.

WHAT

	1990 Assets		1990 Pretax Income	
	$ mil.	% of total	$ mil.	% of total
Property/casualty	8,925	64	(207)	—
Life insurance	4,721	34	(19)	—
Investment mgmt.	170	2	(12)	—
Adjustments	94	—	(220)	—
Total	**13,910**	**100**	**(458)**	**—**

Property/Casualty Insurance	Life Insurance
Auto	Annuities
Business	Individuals
Home	Universal life
Reinsurance	

Investment Management
Advisory services
Management consulting
Mutual funds
Real estate

Major Subsidiaries
Axe-Houghton Mgt. (investment management)
Chancellor Capital Mgt. (49%, investment management)
F&G Re, Inc.
Fidelity and Guaranty Life Insurance Co.
Thomas Jefferson Life
United States Fidelity and Guaranty

RANKINGS

23rd in *Fortune* 50 Diversified Financial Cos.
211th in *Business Week* 1000

KEY COMPETITORS

Aetna	Loews
AIG	Merrill Lynch
Allianz	MetLife
American Express	Morgan Stanley
American Financial	New York Life
BankAmerica	Nomura
Charles Schwab	Northwestern Mututal
CIGNA	Primerica
GEICO	Prudential
General Electric	Sears
General Re	State Farm
ITT	Tokio Marine and Fire
John Hancock	Transamerica
Kemper	Travelers
Lloyd's of London	Xerox

HOW MUCH

	9-Year Growth	1981	1982	1983	1984	1985	1986	1987	1988	1989	1990
Assets ($ mil.)	12.7%	4,749	5,079	5,279	6,158	7,674	8,936	10,141	12,361	13,604	13,910
Net income ($ mil.)	—	169	114	172	93	(258)	243	373	306	117	(461)
Income as % of assets	—	3.6%	2.2%	3.3%	1.5%	(3.4%)	2.7%	3.7%	2.5%	0.9%	(3.3%)
Earnings per share ($)	—	2.99	1.99	3.02	1.72	(4.30)	3.60	4.92	3.58	1.33	(5.71)
Stock price – high ($)	—	26.00	23.25	30.00	30.94	41.50	46.75	48.75	34.38	34.00	30.38
Stock price – low ($)	—	18.69	15.63	19.69	17.63	25.50	36.25	26.25	28.50	28.25	7.00
Stock price – close ($)	(10.7%)	20.69	22.69	27.69	27.50	39.00	39.75	28.38	28.50	29.00	7.50
P/E – high	—	9	12	10	18	—	13	10	10	26	—
P/E – low	—	6	8	7	10	—	10	5	8	21	—
Dividends per share ($)	4.8%	1.60	1.80	1.92	2.08	2.20	2.32	2.48	2.64	2.80	2.44
Book value per share ($)	(7.3%)	23.63	24.29	22.61	20.14	18.91	20.19	19.53	22.57	21.60	11.97

1990 Year-end:
Debt ratio: 21.7%
Return on equity: —
Cash (mil.): $51
Long-term debt (mil.): $333
No. of shares (mil.): 84
Dividends:
　1990 average yield: 32.5%
　1990 payout: —
Market value (mil.): $630
Sales (mil.): $4,181

Stock Price History High/Low 1981–90

USG CORPORATION

OVERVIEW

Chicago-based USG is the largest manufacturer of gypsum in North America and also leads the US in the production of plaster, joint compounds, cement board systems, and ceiling tile and suspension systems. USG unit L&W Supply is the #1 gypsum distributor in the US. Company-owned gypsum mines hold in excess of 30 years' supply. Settsu, a large Japanese construction company, owns 8.9% of USG.

Despite a 40% drop in gypsum prices since 1985, gypsum operations remain profitable and the company is growing overseas. However, a crushing debt load left over from a 1988 antitakeover defense has pushed USG to the brink of bankruptcy. A sizeable potential liability related to asbestos ceilings USG installed in the 1960s, some in schools, also looms over the company.

USG CEO Eugene Connolly is cutting costs and laying off workers while pushing creditors to accept his financial restructuring plan. The plan calls for issuance of equity in place of debt, an easing of terms with banks, and the discontinuance of DAP, the company's caulking and sealant subsidiary. Junk bondholders would assume 81% of USG's common stock under the plan.

WHEN

In 1901, 35 companies joined to form the largest gypsum-producing and -processing company in the industry, headquartered in Chicago. Sewell Avery became CEO in 1905 and led the company until 1951.

U.S. Gypsum started lime production in 1915 and paint manufacturing in 1924. By 1931 the company had diversified into the metal lath business and insulating board production, and added 2 more lime companies and 2 gypsum concerns.

In 1931 Avery became chairman of Montgomery Ward, managing both companies simultaneously. USG continued making profits and paying dividends throughout the Great Depression. The company entered the asphalt roofing and mineral wool business in 1933, began making hardboard from highly compressed wood fibers in 1934, and entered the asbestos-cement siding field in 1937.

Beginning in the late 1960s USG diversified into the building materials and remodeling businesses, acquiring A.P. Green Refractories (1967; refractory brick, tile, and accessories), Wallace Manufacturing (1970; prefinished wood panels), Chicago Mastic (1971; mastics, cements, and adhesives), Kinkead Industries (1972; steel doors and frames), and various smaller businesses.

In 1971 USG initiated the operations of L&W Supply, now the largest distributor of gypsum in the US.

Following the 1984 purchase of the Masonite Corporation for $380 million, the company adopted its present name (1985). USG acquired Donn (remodeling materials) in 1986 and DAP (caulk and sealants) in 1987 for a total of $260 million.

In 1987 USG engineered a $776 million buyback of 20% of its stock to ward off a takeover attempt. The following year Desert Partners of Midland, Texas, attempted another takeover, resolved 9 months later when shareholders approved a management plan to keep control of the company. The plan included taking on $2.5 billion of new debt, a $37-per-share payout, and a $5-per-share payment-in-kind debenture. Employees are now the largest stockholders, with 26% of the total.

After completing virtually all asset sales envisioned in the reorganization plan by the end of 1989, USG became about 25% smaller. Proceeds from the sale of Masonite (to International Paper), Kinkead, and Marlite netted a total of $560 million, used to repay debt.

In 1991 USG defaulted on scheduled payments to bondholders and banks.

NYSE symbol: USG
Fiscal year ends: December 31

Hoover's Rating **D**

WHO

Chairman and CEO: Eugene B. Connolly, age 59, $404,166 pay
President and COO: Anthony J. Falvo, Jr., age 60, $320,000 pay
VP and CFO: J. Bradford James, age 44
SVP and Chief Administration Officer: Harold E. Pendexter, Jr., age 56
Director Human Resources: Gary Snodgrass
Auditors: Arthur Andersen & Co.
Employees: 12,000

WHERE

HQ: 101 S. Wacker Dr., Chicago, IL 60606
Phone: 312-606-4000
Fax: 312-606-4093

USG operates plants in the US, Canada, Mexico, and 7 other countries.

	1990 Sales		1990 Operating Income	
	$ mil.	% of total	$ mil.	% of total
US	1,558	81	164	71
Canada	173	9	31	14
Other foreign	184	10	35	15
Adjustments	—	—	(17)	—
Total	**1,915**	**100**	**213**	**100**

WHAT

	1990 Sales		1990 Operating Income	
	$ mil.	% of total	$ mil.	% of total
Gypsum products	833	43	149	65
Building products distribution	478	25	4	2
Interior systems	604	32	77	33
Adjustments	—	—	(17)	—
Total	**1,915**	**100**	**213**	**100**

Principal Subsidiaries
CGC Inc. (76%, gypsum and building products, Canada)
DAP Inc. (adhesives, caulks, paints, and sealants)
L&W Supply Corp. (gypsum board and building materials distribution)
United States Gypsum Co. (gypsum products for construction and industrial markets)
USG Interiors, Inc. (ceiling, wall, and floor systems)

Brand Names

Acoustone	Intersections
Alex Plus	Kwik-Seal
Auratone	Linear Expressions
DAP	Orion
Donn	Plus 3
Durabond	Sheetrock
Durock	Textone
DX	Tuf-Tex
Eclipse	USG
Fineline	Woodlife

RANKINGS

206th in *Fortune* 500 Industrial Cos.

KEY COMPETITORS

Armstrong World	Hanson
Borden	Imperial Chemical
Fletcher Challenge	3M
General Electric	PPG
Georgia-Pacific	Sherwin-Williams

HOW MUCH

	9-Year Growth	1981	1982	1983	1984	1985	1986	1987	1988	1989	1990
Sales ($ mil.)	2.8%	1,491	1,325	1,611	2,319	2,526	2,724	2,898	2,248	2,191	1,915
Net income ($ mil.)	—	74	44	80	187	224	255	204	73	26	(54)
Income as % of sales	—	5.0%	3.3%	5.0%	8.0%	8.9%	9.4%	7.1%	3.2%	1.2%	(2.8%)
Earnings per share ($)	—	1.11	0.65	1.18	2.78	3.32	3.98	3.93	1.38	0.48	(0.99)
Stock price – high ($)	—	9.69	13.50	14.94	16.31	25.31	46.50	55.88	49.50	7.38	4.88
Stock price – low ($)	—	7.56	6.50	10.00	11.25	14.69	22.25	23.50	4.75	2.88	0.75
Stock price – close ($)	(22.8%)	8.38	12.63	14.81	14.84	25.31	37.75	29.13	5.63	4.50	0.81
P/E – high	—	9	21	13	6	8	12	14	36	15	—
P/E – low	—	7	10	9	4	4	6	6	3	6	—
Dividends per share ($)	—	0.60	0.60	0.61	0.70	0.84	1.04	1.12	37.56	0.00	0.00
Book value per share ($)	—	10.75	10.61	11.13	13.01	15.18	11.15	11.81	(27.26)	(26.55)	(27.55)

1990 Year-end:
Debt ratio: —
Return on equity: —
Cash (mil.): $175
Current ratio: 0.24
Long-term debt (mil.): $2,176
No. of shares (mil.): 55
Dividends:
 1990 average yield: 0.0%
 1990 payout: 0.0%
Market value (mil.): $45

Stock Price History High/Low 1981–90

U S WEST, INC.

NYSE symbol: USW
Fiscal year ends: December 31

Hoover's Rating **B-**

OVERVIEW

Denver-based U S WEST provides local telephone services to more than 12 million customers in 14 states. To support U S WEST Communications, the company's telephone subsidiary, the company plans to spend $2 billion annually on network improvements.

U S WEST's NewVector Group has approximately 209,700 mobile telephone and 161,600 paging customers. U S WEST is a partner in cable TV franchises in the UK, Norway, Sweden, and France, but it and its Hong Kong partners pulled the plug on a cable project there. In Eastern Europe, it has launched the first cellular system, in Hungary.

It is involved in partnerships to offer cellular service in Moscow and St. Petersburg, scheduled to begin in late 1991. In the UK, U S WEST is a partner in developing the next generation of mobile communications, known as personal communications networks (PCNs). The company plans to devote $600 million to international ventures through 1995.

The company also publishes 400 directories and provides financial services, including equipment leasing, asset-based lending, and financial guaranty insurance. The company is extricating itself from its real estate business.

WHO

Chairman: Jack A. MacAllister, age 63, $1,240,138 pay
President and CEO: Richard D. McCormick, age 50, $851,800 pay (prior to promotion)
EVP and CFO: Howard P. Doerr, age 61, $517,829 pay
EVP, General Counsel, and Secretary: Laurence W. DeMuth, Jr., age 62
SVP and Chief Human Resource Officer: J. Thomas Bouchard, age 50
Auditors: Coopers & Lybrand
Employees: 65,469

WHEN

U S WEST, incorporated in 1983 as one of 7 regional operating companies formed when AT&T was split, is rooted in AT&T's Mountain Bell, Northwestern Bell, and Pacific Northwest Bell companies. Before the Bell breakup, Chairman Jack MacAllister had earned a reputation as a maverick while CEO of Northwestern Bell. He built on that reputation as CEO of U S WEST, moving the company into risky fields such as cable TV and equipment financing.

At divestiture U S WEST was composed of phone operations in 14 states; 1/7 interest in Bell Communications Research (Bellcore, the R&D arm shared by the regional Bell companies); and NewVector, a cellular service provider eventually traded publicly. The company's primary business, local phone service, was growing only 3% to 5% annually. U S WEST, hoping to expand its ability to enter unregulated markets, sought changes in the divestiture agreement under which it was established in 1984 — the first Bell company to do so.

Within a few days of independence, MacAllister removed Yellow Pages operations to a new subsidiary, Landmark Communication (now part of U S WEST Marketing Resources), which has added approximately 20 smaller directory publishers. In 1984

U S WEST established U S WEST Financial Services to provide diversified financial services and leasing. Other new subsidiaries included BetaWest Properties (1986), a developer of commercial real estate, and Applied Communications (1987), which provides software to the banking industry.

MacAllister stunned the industry in 1988 when he removed Bell's name, synonymous with telecommunications since the phone was invented, from local operations, consolidating operations as U S WEST Communications, a process completed in 1991. Also in 1988 U S WEST announced investment in a French cable TV company, made plans to offer cable billing and maintenance services domestically, and broke ground on a $45 million R&D facility in Boulder after expressing dissatisfaction with Bellcore. The company is expanding internationally with projects in the UK, France, Czechoslovakia, Hungary, and the USSR.

In 1990 U S WEST announced a stock swap to buy the 19% of NewVector that it didn't own. MacAllister retired as CEO at the beginning of 1991, turning the reins over to Richard McCormick. U S WEST joined forces with AT&T and cable TV giant Tele-Communications Inc. in 1991 to announce a test of a fiber-optic-coaxial hybrid system offering video on demand to consumers' homes.

WHERE

HQ: 7800 E. Orchard Rd., Englewood, CO 80111
Phone: 303-793-6500
Fax: 303-793-6654

U S WEST provides telephone exchange service in 14 states (Arizona, Colorado, Idaho, Iowa, Minnesota, Montana, Nebraska, New Mexico, North Dakota, Oregon, South Dakota, Utah, Washington, and Wyoming) and has international ventures in Czechoslovakia, France, Hungary, Norway, USSR, Sweden, and the UK.

WHAT

	1990 Sales		1990 Operating Income	
	$ mil.	% of total	$ mil.	% of total
Communications & related services	9,369	94	2,091	96
Capital assets	643	6	81	4
Adjustments	(55)	—	261	—
Total	**9,957**	**100**	**2,433**	**100**

Operations
Bell Communications Research (14.3%)
Financial Security Assurance Holdings Ltd. (90%, debt guarantees)
U S WEST Capital Corporation
U S WEST Communications, Inc. (telephone services)
U S WEST Financial Services, Inc. (manages $3 billion portfolio)
U S WEST Marketing Resources Group, Inc. (Yellow Pages and specialty directory publishing)
U S WEST NewVector Group, Inc. (cellular and paging services)
U S WEST Real Estate, Inc.

RANKINGS

4th in *Fortune* 50 Utilities
38th in *Business Week* 1000

KEY COMPETITORS

AT&T	Ericsson
Ameritech	GTE
Bell Atlantic	McCaw
BellSouth	MCI
British Telecom	NYNEX
Cable & Wireless	Pacific Telesis
R. R. Donnelley	Southwestern Bell
Dun & Bradstreet	United Telecom

HOW MUCH

	6-Year Growth	1981	1982	1983	1984	1985	1986	1987	1988	1989	1990
Sales ($ mil.)	5.4%	—	—	—	7,280	7,813	8,308	8,445	9,221	9,691	9,957
Net income ($ mil.)	5.2%	—	—	—	887	926	924	1,006	1,132	1,111	1,199
Income as % of sales	—	—	—	—	12.2%	11.8%	11.1%	11.9%	12.3%	11.5%	12.0%
Earnings per share ($)	5.1%	—	—	—	2.31	2.42	2.43	2.66	3.09	3.01	3.11
Stock price – high ($)	—	—	—	—	17.72	22.25	31.00	30.13	29.81	40.31	40.50
Stock price – low ($)	—	—	—	—	13.91	17.13	20.81	21.25	24.38	28.38	32.38
Stock price – close ($)	14.1%	—	—	—	17.63	22.25	27.00	25.56	28.88	40.06	38.88
P/E – high	—	—	—	—	8	9	13	11	10	13	13
P/E – low	—	—	—	—	6	7	9	8	8	9	10
Dividends per share ($)	6.5%	—	—	—	1.35	1.07	1.50	1.61	1.73	1.85	1.97
Book value per share ($)	5.3%	—	—	—	17.25	18.24	19.16	20.09	21.31	21.58	23.48

1990 Year-end:
Debt ratio: 43.7%
Return on equity: 13.8%
Cash (mil.): $338
Current ratio: 0.65
Long-term debt (mil.): $7,175
No. of shares (mil.): 394
Dividends:
  1990 average yield: 5.1%
  1990 payout: 63.3%
Market value (mil.): $15,297

Stock Price History High/Low 1984–90

USX CORPORATION

OVERVIEW

USX is the nation's largest steelmaker, but it's an oil company. That diversity was reflected when the company's shareholders in 1991 approved splitting USX stock into 2 classes — USX–Marathon Group and USX–U.S. Steel Group.

Energy activities supplied 69% of revenues, making USX the 7th largest integrated petroleum company in the US. Marathon Oil, USX's largest holding, conducts exploration and production worldwide. It owns 5 US refineries and wholesales 64% of its output to private-brand marketers. Marathon absorbed USX's Texas Oil & Gas unit in 1990.

USX's U.S. Steel Group manufactures at its own mills and participates in joint steelmaking ventures, sometimes with foreign competitors such as Pohang of South Korea (in Pittsburg, California) and Kobe of Japan (in Lorain, Ohio). Steel operations are being scaled back in the face of lower demand. The U.S. Steel Group also includes USX's Diversified Businesses segment, ranging from engineering consulting to Cyclone fences.

WHEN

USX was born a billion-dollar baby in 1901. Its birthname was United States Steel, and its daddy was financier J. P. Morgan.

Morgan forged U.S. Steel from the Federal Steel he controlled and from the steel holdings of Andrew Carnegie. Carnegie, a Scot who began as a Pennsylvania telegraph messenger, built a far-flung empire after the Civil War.

At the beginning of the 20th century, Carnegie's president, Charles Schwab, spoke at a New York dinner about the future of steel. An impressed Morgan told Schwab to get Carnegie to name a price for his mills. Carnegie did, and Morgan didn't haggle.

Carnegie received almost half a billion dollars for his interest in U.S. Steel. He retired to pursue philanthropy, giving away 90% of his wealth. He poured $60 million into 2,811 free public libraries worldwide.

The Carnegie-Morgan combination created an enterprise with capitalization of $1.4 billion, the world's first billion-dollar company. In its first year it produced 67% of the US's steel output. But its weight also kept the company from changing its direction as foreign competition and aging plants ate into profits. When the 1980s began, U.S. Steel began to change.

In 1982 U.S. Steel purchased Marathon Oil, then the 17th largest US petroleum producer, and doubled its revenues.

Findlay, Ohio–based Marathon had begun in 1887 as Ohio Oil. Founded by 14 independents, Ohio Oil attracted the attention of Standard Oil, which purchased it in 1889. After the 1911 Standard Oil breakup, Ohio Oil drilled in the Rocky Mountains of Wyoming and in Kansas, Louisiana, and Texas. A major discovery came almost by accident. In 1924 Ohio Oil agreed to drill 3 wells on leases west of the Pecos River in Texas. By mistake, Ohio Oil drilled 3 dry holes on leases east of the river. Ohio Oil planned to abandon the properties when a frantic geologist reported the error. Drilled in the right place, the well flowed voluminously. Ohio Oil became Marathon in 1962.

In 1986 U.S. Steel paid $3 billion in stock for Texas Oil & Gas, and U.S. Steel became USX to reflect the decreasing role of steel. Investor Carl Icahn, USX's largest single shareholder with 13.3%, wanted the company to sell its steel operations but was rebuffed in a 1990 shareholder referendum.

After hammering out a 3-year contract with the United Steelworkers in 1991, CEO Charles Corry scored a 2nd coup by resolving the Icahn dispute. Icahn, facing financial problems elsewhere, sold his USX shares for $1.02 billion after USX stockholders approved creation of 2 classes of stock — one for steel and one for energy. J. P. Morgan's baby had become twins.

NYSE symbols:
MRO (USX–Marathon Group);
X (USX–U.S. Steel Group)
Fiscal year ends: December 31

Hoover's Rating C

WHO

Chairman and CEO: Charles A. Corry, age 59, $1,593,106 pay
VC Administration and CFO: W. Bruce Thomas, age 64, $1,032,488 pay
SVP Employee Relations: Louis A. Valli, age 58
Auditors: Price Waterhouse
Employees: 51,523

WHERE

HQ: 600 Grant St., Pittsburgh, PA 15219-4776
Phone: 412-433-1121
Fax: 412-433-5733

USX produces steel and oil and sells gas in 16 states. It also produces oil and gas in Abu Dhabi, Australia, Indonesia, Ireland, Norway, Tunisia, the UK, and the US.

	1990 Sales		1990 Operating Income	
	$ mil.	% of total	$ mil.	% of total
US	19,670	95	1,297	83
Other North America	65	—	1	—
Europe	837	4	274	18
Middle East & Africa	—	—	(41)	(3)
Other regions	87	1	25	2
Adjustments	(1,333)	—	—	—
Total	**19,326**	**100**	**1,556**	**100**

WHAT

	1990 Sales		1990 Operating Income	
	$ mil.	% of total	$ mil.	% of total
Energy	13,253	69	1,138	79
Steel	5,465	28	255	18
Diversified Businesses	608	3	46	3
Adjustments	—	—	117	—
Total	**19,326**	**100**	**1,556**	**100**

Principal Products and Activities
Auto parts and precision fasteners
Coal mining
Crude oil and natural gas production
Engineering services
Fencing products (Cyclone)
Financial services
Land management
Petroleum pipelining, refining, and marketing
Real estate development
Steel production

Brand Names

Bonded	Marathon
Cheker	Port
Ecol	Speedway
Emro	Starvin' Marvin
Gastown	United

RANKINGS

19th in *Fortune* 500 Industrial Cos.
76th in *Business Week* 1000

KEY COMPETITORS

Amoco	Exxon	Phillips Petroleum
Ashland	Friedrich Krupp	Royal Dutch/Shell
British Petroleum	IRI	Sun
	Koch	Texaco
Cargill	Mobil	Thyssen
Chevron	Nippon Steel	Other oil, chemical,
Coastal	Occidental	and mining
Du Pont	Pennzoil	companies

HOW MUCH

	9-Year Growth	1981	1982	1983	1984	1985	1986	1987	1988	1989	1990
Sales ($ mil.)	3.7%	13,941	18,375	16,869	18,274	18,429	14,000	13,898	15,792	17,533	19,326
Net income ($ mil.)	(3.0%)	1,077	(361)	(1,161)	414	313	(1,593)	206	756	965	818
Income as % of sales	—	7.7%	(2.0%)	(6.9%)	2.3%	1.7%	(11.4%)	1.5%	4.8%	5.5%	4.2%
Earnings per share ($)	(13.6%)	11.47	(3.99)	(12.07)	2.79	1.81	(6.53)	0.52	2.62	3.49	3.08
Stock price – high ($)	—	35.25	30.13	31.00	33.25	33.00	28.75	39.38	34.38	39.50	37.50
Stock price – low ($)	—	23.38	16.00	19.63	22.00	24.38	14.50	21.00	26.00	28.88	29.63
Stock price – close ($)	0.2%	29.88	21.00	30.38	26.13	26.63	21.50	29.75	29.25	35.75	30.50
P/E – high	—	3	—	—	12	18	—	76	13	11	12
P/E – low	—	2	—	—	8	13	—	40	10	8	10
Dividends per share ($)	(3.9%)	2.00	1.75	1.00	1.00	1.10	1.20	1.20	1.25	1.40	1.40
Book value per share ($)	(11.7%)	69.11	58.11	43.67	45.36	43.80	18.26	17.77	18.91	20.95	22.64

1990 Year-end:
Debt ratio: 47.9%
Return on equity: 14.1%
Cash (mil.): $263
Current ratio: 1.11
Long-term debt (mil.): $5,390
No. of shares (mil.): 255
Dividends:
  1990 average yield: 4.6%
  1990 payout: 45.5%
Market value (mil.): $7,763

Stock Price History High/Low 1981–90

V. F. CORPORATION

OVERVIEW

V. F. Corporation is the world's 2nd largest clothing company, after Levi Strauss. Its subsidiaries produce such well-known brands as Lee, Rustler, and Wrangler jeans (the #2, #3, and #4 brands in the US), Jantzen swimsuits, Vanity Fair lingerie, and Red Kap work clothes. Most of V. F.'s products are sold in department stores or specialty shops, including upscale discount stores (Lee), western specialty stores (Wrangler), national discount chains (Rustler), and sporting goods stores (JanSport). V.F. also operates factory outlets and warehouses that cover over 1.7 million square feet of space.

Although V. F. commands 25% of the US jeanswear market, sales have been disappointing, largely because of problems within the Lee division (further exacerbated by a sluggish denim market). The company has responded by streamlining Lee's management and refocusing the division on basic jeanswear (rather than high fashion garments). The Jantzen sportswear line also experienced a drop in sales in 1990. V. F.'s 1990 earnings were negatively affected by $57.3 million in charges, largely related to the company's restructuring program.

WHO

Chairman, President, and CEO: Lawrence R. Pugh, age 58, $890,000 pay
VP Finance and CFO: Gerard G. Johnson, age 50, $375,000 pay
VP Human Resources and Administration: Harold E. Addis, age 60
Auditors: Ernst & Young
Employees: 40,300

WHERE

HQ: 1047 North Park Rd., Wyomissing, PA 19610
Phone: 215-378-1151
Fax: 215-375-9371

	1990 Pretax Income	
	$ mil.	% of total
US	117	82
Other countries	26	18
Total	**143**	**100**

WHEN

In 1899, 6 partners, including banker John Barbey, started the Reading Glove and Mitten Manufacturing Company. Barbey bought out his 5 partners in 1911 and changed the name of the Reading, Pennsylvania, company to Schuylkill Silk Mills in 1913.

Barbey expanded the mills' production to underwear and, in the 1920s, discontinued glove manufacturing. A company contest with a $25 prize produced the brand name Vanity Fair in 1917. Barbey changed the mills' name to Vanity Fair Silk Mills in 1919.

Barbey and his son J. E. Barbey led their lingerie company (Barbey banned the word *underwear*) to national prominence. The mills produced only silk garments until the development of synthetics such as rayon and acetate in the 1920s. In response to the national embargo on silk in 1941, Vanity Fair converted to rayon, finally converting all production to the new wonder fabric, nylon tricot, in 1948.

Vanity Fair opened its first Alabama production plant in 1937, with 5 more opening between 1939 and 1962. Its Pennsylvania mill closed in 1948, but the company maintains its offices there. By 1948 Vanity Fair manufactured all stages of its nylon products, from filament to finished garment. It expanded its color offerings and introduced permanent pleating and printed lingerie, including leopard and mermaid prints. Vanity Fair won the *American*

Fabrics Magazine award for textile achievement in 1948 and the Coty award for design in 1950. Innovative advertising, considered daring at the time, brought awards for photographs of live models in Vanity Fair lingerie.

J. E. Barbey still owned all of Vanity Fair's stock in 1951, when he sold 1/3 of his holdings to the public. In 1966 the stock, previously traded OTC, was listed on the NYSE.

After changing its name to V. F. Corporation in 1969, the company used acquisitions to expand its lingerie business and to begin producing sportswear and bluejeans. It bought Berkshire International (hosiery, 1969), H.D. Lee (jeans, 1969), and Kay Windsor (lingerie, 1971). V. F. sold Berkshire International's US operations in 1976, but the site of the division's Reading, Pennsylvania, hosiery mill (once the world's largest) now houses the original VF Factory Outlet.

More acquisitions followed, including Modern Globe (lingerie, 1984) and Bassett-Walker (fleecewear, 1984). In 1986 V. F. bought Blue Bell, a North Carolina maker of bluejeans (Wrangler and Rustler), sportswear (Jantzen and JanSport), and occupational clothing (Red Kap and Big Ben). V. F. bought the Vassarette brand name (lingerie) from Munsingwear in 1990 and followed with Health-tex, a maker of infant's and children's apparel, in 1991.

WHAT

	1990 Sales		1990 Operating Income	
	$ mil.	% of total	$ mil.	% of total
Jeanswear	1,437	55	122	53
Sportswear/ activewear	488	19	15	6
Intimate apparel	360	14	52	22
Occupational apparel & other	328	12	43	19
Adjustments	—	—	18	—
Total	**2,613**	**100**	**250**	**100**

Brand Names
Jeanswear
  Girbaud
  Lee
  Rustler
  Wrangler
Sportswear/activewear
  Bassett-Walker
  JanSport
  Jantzen
  Lee
  Sturdy Sweats by Lee
Intimate apparel
  Lee
  Lollipop
  Modern Globe
  Vanity Fair
  Vassarette
Occupational apparel
  Big Ben
  Red Kap
Children's apparel
  Health-tex

RANKINGS

171st in *Fortune* 500 Industrial Cos.
409th in *Business Week* 1000

KEY COMPETITORS

Berkshire Hathaway	Liz Claiborne
The Gap	Marks and Spencer
Gerber	Melville
Hartmarx	NIKE
Levi Strauss	Reebok
The Limited	Riklis Family

HOW MUCH

	9-Year Growth	1981	1982	1983	1984	1985	1986	1987	1988	1989	1990
Sales ($ mil.)	14.9%	746	880	1,101	1,167	1,481	1,545	2,574	2,516	2,533	2,613
Net income ($ mil.)	5.0%	52	92	119	125	139	129	180	174	176	81
Income as % of sales	—	7.0%	10.4%	10.8%	10.7%	9.4%	8.4%	7.0%	6.9%	7.0%	3.1%
Earnings per share ($)	5.7%	0.81	1.41	1.82	1.96	2.25	2.05	2.62	2.54	2.70	1.33
Stock price – high ($)	—	5.66	10.72	20.69	16.25	27.00	36.00	48.25	33.88	38.38	34.25
Stock price – low ($)	—	3.33	3.78	9.13	10.88	12.94	24.00	22.00	24.75	27.75	11.63
Stock price – close ($)	15.3%	5.09	9.91	15.06	13.31	25.94	30.88	24.50	28.75	31.88	18.38
P/E – high	—	7	8	11	8	12	18	18	13	14	26
P/E – low	—	4	3	5	6	6	12	8	10	10	9
Dividends per share ($)	16.0%	0.26	0.33	0.43	0.52	0.58	0.66	0.75	0.85	0.91	1.00
Book value per share ($)	16.1%	3.75	4.73	6.09	7.14	8.91	12.20	14.43	16.05	14.14	14.44

1990 Year-end:
Debt ratio: 41.6%
Return on equity: 9.3%
Cash (mil.): $62
Current ratio: 2.35
Long-term debt (mil.): $585
No. of shares (mil.): 57
Dividends:
  1990 average yield: 5.4%
  1990 payout: 75.2%
Market value (mil.): $1,048

Stock Price History High/Low 1981–90

VIACOM INC.

OVERVIEW

Sumner Redstone's National Amusements owns 84% of Viacom, a major video-oriented media company. Viacom operates MTV, VH-1, and Nickelodeon basic cable TV channels, all of which appeal to demographic segments popular with advertisers. The company also owns interests in Lifetime and CTV (comedy) cable channels. Viacom's Showtime, The Movie Channel, and SET Pay Per View pay-cable services rank 2nd to Time Warner's. A 1989 deal to sell 50% of Viacom's pay-cable business to Tele-Communications appears to have failed.

The company's cable systems serve more than one million subscribers in California, the Midwest, and the Pacific Northwest. Viacom Broadcasting owns 5 network affiliate TV stations and 14 radio stations.

Viacom Entertainment syndicates TV programming ("Roseanne," "The Cosby Show") and produces TV series and programs for prime time ("Matlock"). Viacom controls a large library of television programming. In 1990 the company began production of movies for theatrical distribution abroad and broadcast over its cable networks.

NYSE symbol: VIA
Fiscal year ends: December 31

Hoover's Rating **C-**

WHO

Chairman: Sumner M. Redstone, age 67
President and CEO: Frank J. Biondi, Jr., age 46, $1,459,229 pay
SVP; President and CEO, Viacom Cable Television: John W. Goddard, age 49, $1,103,795 pay
SVP; Chairman and CEO, Viacom Broadcasting and Entertainment: Henry S. Schleiff, age 42, $1,051,923 pay
SVP and CFO: George S. Smith, Jr., age 42
VP Human Resources and Administration: William A. Roskin, age 48
Auditors: Price Waterhouse
Employees: 5,000

WHEN

Viacom International was formed by CBS in 1970. When the FCC ruled that TV networks could not own cable systems and TV stations in the same market, Viacom stock was issued to CBS shareholders, and the new company also took over CBS's program syndication division, selling programs for reruns after network airing.

In the early 1970s Viacom bought cable systems in California, Washington, Ohio, New York, and Indiana. In 1978 Viacom and Teleprompter formed Showtime, one of the first subscription TV services. Viacom bought out Teleprompter's interest in 1982.

Also in 1978 Viacom purchased WVIT-TV (Hartford) from Connecticut Television. From 1980 to 1983 the company bought TV and radio stations in Louisiana, Chicago, New York, and Houston. Viacom and Warner/Amex (a joint cable venture between Warner and American Express) combined Showtime with The Movie Channel to form Showtime Networks in 1983. As American Express bowed out of the scene in 1986, Viacom purchased the Warner Communications share of Showtime Networks and 2/3 of MTV Networks, including cable's first all-music video channel, started in 1981. Viacom also began producing series for network television and bought the remainder of MTV and a St. Louis TV station.

Carl Icahn attempted a hostile takeover of Viacom in 1986. A management group led by CEO Terrence Elkes in 1986 attempted an LBO and became enmeshed in a 6-month bidding war with Sumner Redstone's National Amusements, a movie theater chain. Viacom Inc. was formed as a merger vehicle to acquire Viacom International. When the cable untangled in 1987, Redstone bought 83% of Viacom for $3.4 billion. Redstone replaced Elkes with former HBO executive Frank Biondi. Also in 1987 MTV Europe began broadcasting, and MTV Networks licensed Australian, Latin American, and Japanese broadcasting companies to air MTV programming.

In 1988 Viacom sold the rerun syndication rights of "The Cosby Show" for more than $515 million, the highest gross in TV syndication history. The company also produced 5 network television shows in 1988 and, after a short-lived run at acquiring Orion Pictures, sold its Orion stock for an $18 million profit. Viacom sold its Long Island and Cleveland cable TV systems in 1989 for $545 million.

In 1990 Viacom bought 4 FM radio stations and British Telecom's stake in MTV Europe, raising its holdings to 49.9%. The company merged its Ha! cable comedy network with Time Warner's Comedy Channel to form CTV: The Comedy Network in 1991.

WHERE

HQ: 1515 Broadway, New York, NY 10036
Phone: 212-258-6000
Fax: 212-258-6354

	1990 Sales	
	$ mil.	% of total
US	1,587	99
Foreign	13	1
Total	**1,600**	**100**

WHAT

	1990 Sales		1990 Operating Income	
	$ mil.	% of total	$ mil.	% of total
Cable television	330	21	76	27
Entertainment	282	17	76	27
Networks	843	52	90	32
Broadcasting	164	10	38	14
Adjustments	(19)	—	(56)	—
Total	**1,600**	**100**	**224**	**100**

Viacom Networks
Lifetime (33.3%)
MTV Networks
  CTV: The Comedy Network (50%)
  MTV
  MTV Europe (49.9%)
  Nickelodeon/Nick at Nite
  VH-1
Showtime Networks Inc.
  The Movie Channel
  SET Pay Per View
  Showtime
Showtime Satellite
  Networks
  Viewer's Choice (10%)

Radio Stations
KBSG (AM/FM), Tacoma
KDBK-FM, San Francisco
KDBQ-FM, Santa Cruz/San Jose
KHOW (AM)/KSYY(FM), Denver

KIKK (AM/FM), Houston
KXEZ (FM), Los Angeles
WLIT (FM), Chicago
WLTI (FM), Detroit
WLTW (FM), New York
WMZQ (AM/FM), Washington, DC

Television Stations
KMOV, St. Louis
KSLA, Shreveport
WHEC, Rochester
WNYT, Albany
WVIT, Hartford

Viacom Entertainment
Viacom Enterprises (film and TV program distrib.)
Viacom MGS Services (distrib. of commercials)
Viacom Productions (TV programming)
Viacom World Wide (international business)

HOW MUCH

	9-Year Growth	1981	1982	1983	1984	1985	1986	1987	1988	1989	1990
Sales ($ mil.)	25.3%	210	275	316	320	444	919	1,011	1,259	1,436	1,600
Net income ($ mil.)	—	17	25	28	31	37	(10)	(123)	(123)	131	(90)
Income as % of sales	—	8.1%	8.9%	8.9%	9.6%	8.3%	(1.1%)	(12.2%)	(9.8%)	9.1%	(5.6%)
Earnings per share ($)	—	1.69	2.44	2.56	2.78	2.71	(0.65)	(1.69)	(1.77)	1.07	(0.84)
Stock price – high ($)	—	42.19	43.91	51.09	43.44	82.81	112.19	138.75	15.69	32.63	29.56
Stock price – low ($)	—	27.50	21.56	33.44	29.69	40.47	63.13	5.00	8.88	15.25	15.63
Stock price – close ($)	(1.5%)	30.00	37.81	40.94	40.63	68.13	98.75	9.06	15.56	28.75	26.25
P/E – high	—	25	18	20	16	31	—	—	—	31	—
P/E – low	—	16	9	13	11	15	—	—	—	14	—
Dividends per share ($)	—	0.28	0.34	0.52	0.50	0.58	0.68	21.78	0.00	0.00	0.00
Book value per share ($)	(16.2%)	16.85	18.98	19.91	22.47	36.55	29.61	4.98	3.21	4.27	3.43

1990 Year-end:
Debt ratio: 87.4%
Return on equity: —
Cash (mil.): $43
Current ratio: 0.82
Long-term debt (mil.):$2,537
No. of shares (mil.): 107
Dividends:
  1990 average yield: 0.0%
  1990 payout: 0.0%
Market value (mil.): $2,802

**Stock Price History
High/Low 1981–90**

RANKINGS

65th in *Fortune* 100 Diversified Service Cos.
258th in *Business Week* 1000

KEY COMPETITORS

Blockbuster	Matsushita	Turner
Capital Cities/ABC	Paramount	Broadcasting
CBS	E.W. Scripps	Walt Disney
Cox	Sony	Washington Post
General Electric	TCI	Other media
Hearst	Time Warner	companies

THE VONS COMPANIES, INC.

NYSE symbol: VON
Fiscal year ends: Sunday closest to December 31

Hoover's Rating **B-**

OVERVIEW

Vons is the 10th largest US supermarket chain and the largest in Southern California, with a 27% market share. Vons, recognized as a customer-oriented grocer, has a "three's a crowd" policy that another register is opened whenever lines exceed 3 people. Vons Express, a glass-enclosed convenience store within a Vons grocery store, has convenience store items at grocery store prices. Vons also is testing in-store branch banks to be open 7 days a week.

The company's unique store formats address Southern California's diverse cultures and lifestyles. Its upscale Pavilions stores have 3 times the normal produce selection, 1,500 wines, a coffee corner, a lobster tank, and a bakery. Its Tianguis (pronounced Tee-ON-geese, Aztec for "marketplace") stores offer fresh tortillas, many Latin American brands, a catfish tank, chorizo, carnitas, and Mexican baked goods.

Toward the end of delivering competitively priced merchandise, Vons struck an unusual yearlong deal with Chiquita to carry only Chiquita fruit beginning in December 1990. During April 1991 Vons sold bananas for less than half of what other retailers needed to charge due to wholesale price increases. Vons is controlling costs by using higher shelving to display more products in the same space ("densing up"). The company is a leader in high-tech retailing through its increased bar code ringing speed, electronic couponing, and a computer disaster recovery center.

WHEN

Charles Von der Ahe opened a small grocery market in Los Angeles in 1906 with $1,200. Prior to the 1929 stock market crash, Von der Ahe sold his 87 stores to McMarr Stores (eventually bought by Safeway) and soon retired. His 2 sons, Ted and Wil, restarted Vons stores with their father's financing.

In 1948 Vons opened a 50,300-square-foot store (Los Angeles) that was the first US grocery to feature self-service produce, meat, and delicatessen sections. In 1960 Vons bought Shopping Bag Food Stores but, 7 years later, was forced by the US Supreme Court to divest. The company opened 10 stores in 1968, bringing the total to 80 locations. In 1969 Household Finance (now Household International) bought Vons. During the 1970s Vons added stores in the San Diego area and sold products wholesale to retailers and fast-food restaurants.

The company was the official supermarket for the 1984 Olympics in Los Angeles, providing meat and produce for a million meals a day. A management team led by Roger Stangeland, the current CEO, bought Vons supermarkets and other retail units from Household International in a 1986 LBO. That year Vons opened its first Vons Pavilions, a huge store featuring a wide merchandise selection and specialty items, and bought the 10-store Pantry Food Markets of California. In 1987 Vons built its first Tianguis, a superstore targeted toward Hispanics.

During 1987 Vons completed a complicated merger and divestiture with publicly owned Allied Supermarkets, which operated Great Scott! Supermarkets in Detroit. Under the merger Allied bought Vons's Michigan operations. Vons emerged as a public company with its Southern California locations intact and $100 million in cash.

Vons bought Safeway's 162 Southern California locations in 1988, doubling its size. In addition to incurring much new debt, the acquisition gave a large interest (31.3%) in Vons to Kohlberg Kravis Roberts. The company's improved operating performance and offering of 4.5 million shares significantly decreased debt, leading to better Moody's ratings and to Security Pacific's removing Vons from its highly leveraged transaction status in August 1991.

WHO

Chairman and CEO: Roger E. Stangeland, age 61, $884,440 pay
VC and COO: Dennis K. Eck, age 47, $783,047 pay
President: William S. Davila, age 59, $555,358 pay
EVP: Garrett R. Nelson, age 51, $467,680 pay
EVP and CFO: Michael F. Henn, age 42, $479,387 pay
SVP Human Resources: Kenneth F. Sekella, age 48
Auditors: KPMG Peat Marwick
Employees: 33,900

WHERE

HQ: 618 Michillinda Ave., Arcadia, CA 91007
Phone: 818-821-7000
Fax: 818-821-7933 (Corporate Communications)

Vons's stores are located in Los Angeles, Orange, Ventura, Riverside, San Bernardino, San Diego, Kern, and Santa Barbara counties of Southern California, and the city of Fresno. The company also operates stores in the Las Vegas, Nevada, area.

WHAT

	1990 Store Formats	
	No. of stores	% of total
Vons Supermarkets	209	65
Vons Food and Drug	77	24
Pavilions	14	4
Pavilions Place	12	4
Tianguis	8	3
Total	**320**	**100**

Store Formats
Vons Supermarkets
　Traditional grocery stores, some featuring in-store bakeries and delis
Vons Food and Drug
　Combination stores generally including housewares and specialty departments
Pavilions
　50,000- to 75,000-square-foot superstores featuring various specialty "shopping pavilions"
Pavilions Place
　Scaled-down versions of Pavilions with less general merchandise
Tianguis
　Stores designed to resemble a Mexican market, with a colorful atmosphere, bilingual employees, Spanish signs, and mariachis

HOW MUCH

	2-Year Growth	1981	1982	1983	1984	1985	1986	1987	1988	1989	1990
Sales ($ mil.)	16.7%	—	—	—	—	—	—	—	3,917	5,221	5,334
Net income ($ mil.)	—	—	—	—	—	—	—	—	(24)	(25)	50
Income as % of sales	—	—	—	—	—	—	—	—	(0.6%)	(0.5%)	0.9%
Earnings per share ($)	—	—	—	—	—	—	—	—	(0.77)	(0.65)	1.28
Stock price – high ($)	—	—	—	—	—	—	—	13.75	13.50	23.75	23.88
Stock price – low ($)	—	—	—	—	—	—	—	6.00	6.75	11.38	14.75
Stock price – close ($)	—	—	—	—	—	—	—	7.38	11.50	19.50	22.50
P/E – high	—	—	—	—	—	—	—	—	—	—	19
P/E – low	—	—	—	—	—	—	—	—	—	—	12
Dividends per share ($)	—	—	—	—	—	—	—	0.00	0.00	0.00	0.00
Book value per share ($)	—	—	—	—	—	—	—	5.69	5.53	4.91	7.04

1990 Year-end:
Debt ratio: 74.0%
Return on equity: 21.4%
Cash (mil.): $6
Current ratio: 0.78
Long-term debt (mil.): $775
No. of shares (mil.): 39
Dividends:
　1990 average yield: 0.0%
　1990 payout: 0.0%
Market value (mil.): $872

Stock Price History
High/Low 1987–90

RANKINGS

24th in *Fortune* 50 Retailing Cos.
496th in *Business Week* 1000

KEY COMPETITORS

Albertson's
American Stores
Edward J. DeBartolo

VULCAN MATERIALS COMPANY

NYSE symbol: VMC
Fiscal year ends: December 31

Hoover's Rating **B+**

OVERVIEW

Vulcan Materials Company is a leading US producer of construction aggregates (e.g., gravel, sand, rock, and slag) as well as a major manufacturer of industrial chemicals (e.g., chlorine, muriatic acid, sodium hydroxide, potassium hydroxide, and chlorinated hydrocarbons). Crushed stone accounts for almost 80% of sales revenue in the construction segment and 50% overall. Vulcan's total production of construction aggregates was 121 million tons in 1990.

Vulcan's Chemicals division (1990 sales of $409 million) produces a wide range of industrial chemicals, and the company's chemical trucking fleet is one of the largest in the nation.

To overcome the tremendous cost of transporting its construction materials (a trip of 30 miles can more than double the cost of the materials), Vulcan maintains a strategic distribution network, with facilities close to key marketing areas, and also operates 2 portable stone-crushing plants.

In 1990 Vulcan made the largest acquisition in its history with the purchase of the Reed companies (Reed Crushed Stone, Reed Terminal, and BRT Transfer Terminal). The acquisition included the nation's largest crushed rock quarry (in Paducah, Kentucky) and increased Vulcan's estimated stone reserves by 500 million tons. Vulcan spent almost 3 times as much ($99 million) on acquisitions in 1990 as it did in 1989 ($34 million).

WHEN

In 1916 the Ireland family purchased a 75% interest in Birmingham Slag, a small Alabama company established in 1909 to process slag from a Birmingham steel plant. For the next several decades, under the leadership of brothers Glenn, Gene, and Barney Ireland, the small company prospered by selling its processed slag for construction use.

Third-generation family member Charles Ireland became president in 1951 and transformed Birmingham Slag from a regional to a national operation. In 1956 the company bought Vulcan Detinning, renamed itself Vulcan Materials, and went public. By 1959 Vulcan had acquired a variety of companies and was the largest producer of aggregates in the US, with sales of over $100 million.

By 1981 Vulcan owned 90 quarries and claimed sales of $783 million. The company added about 50 operations and plants in the 1980s. In 1987 the company entered a joint venture with a Mexican partner (Grupo ICA), largely to supply aggregates for Gulf Coast markets.

Purchase of the Reed companies in 1990 pushed stone reserves to 6.8 billion tons, compared to 3.3 billion tons a decade before.

Overall property additions amounted to $222 million in 1990 ($147 million in 1989).

Grupo ICA began shipments in 1990, although they were below expected levels because of delayed completion (January 1991) of the jointly owned permanent plant in Mexico.

Vulcan expects to substantially reduce shipment costs through the purchase of 2 ships. In 1990 the company completed construction of a Houston sales yard and in 1991 finished yards in Galveston and Tampa.

Vulcan's chemicals segment completed its new plant (methyl chloride production) at Geismar, Louisiana, while continuing to look for ways to cope with declining demand for chlorine. Vulcan is capable of shipping 1,640 tons of chlorine and sodium hydroxide throughout the world each day. The company expects increasing demand for chloroform, which is required to produce compounds to replace chlorofluorocarbons.

Vulcan has faced criticism for noise, dust, and chemical pollution and has undertaken an ambitious program to reduce emissions by 90% between 1988 and 1995. Between 1988 and 1990 the company was able to cut air emissions by more than a third.

WHO

President and CEO: Herbert A. Sklenar, age 60, $726,253 pay
EVP Construction Materials: William J. Grayson, Jr., age 61, $386,501 pay
SVP Finance: Peter J. Clemens III, age 48, $300,982 pay
SVP Human Resources: R. Morrieson Lord, age 61
SVP and General Counsel: Robert A. Wason IV, age 40
Auditors: Deloitte & Touche
Employees: 6,600

WHERE

HQ: One Metroplex Dr., Birmingham, AL 35209
Phone: 205-877-3000
Fax: 205-877-3094

The company operates 119 stone quarries, 3 chemical plants, 6 ready-mixed concrete plants, and over 100 production and distribution facilities. The company has plants in 16 states.

WHAT

	1990 Sales		1990 Operating Income	
	$ mil.	% of total	$ mil.	% of total
Construction matls.	696	63	112	61
Chemicals	409	37	72	39
Total	**1,105**	**100**	**184**	**100**

Construction Materials
Crushed limestone
Crushed slag
Crushed stone
Expanded shale
Gravel
Ready-mixed concrete
Rock asphalt
Sand
Other aggregates

Chemicals
Anhydrous hydrogen chloride
Chlorinated hydrocarbons
Chlorine
Hydrogen
Methyl chloride
Muriatic acid
Potassium hydroxide
Sodium hydroxide

RANKINGS

326th in *Fortune* 500 Industrial Cos.
437th in *Business Week* 1000

KEY COMPETITORS

American Cyanamid
ASARCO
Dow Chemical
Du Pont
FMC
W. R. Grace
General Dynamics
Hercules
Inco
Martin Marietta
Monsanto
Morton
Union Carbide

HOW MUCH

	9-Year Growth	1981	1982	1983	1984	1985	1986	1987	1988	1989	1990
Sales ($ mil.)	3.9%	783	719	821	983	972	958	923	1,053	1,076	1,105
Net income ($ mil.)	4.9%	78	55	54	78	80	93	114	136	133	120
Income as % of sales	—	10.0%	7.6%	6.6%	8.0%	8.2%	9.7%	12.4%	12.9%	12.4%	10.9%
Earnings per share ($)	7.0%	1.69	1.18	1.17	1.69	1.72	2.10	2.69	3.30	3.30	3.10
Stock price – high ($)	—	14.00	14.00	17.50	18.44	22.75	31.38	41.00	41.50	48.50	46.75
Stock price – low ($)	—	10.03	9.69	13.38	14.50	16.63	22.06	23.75	31.00	40.50	29.38
Stock price – close ($)	10.8%	13.50	13.50	16.97	17.34	22.75	31.13	32.75	41.50	44.50	34.00
P/E – high	—	8	12	15	11	13	15	15	13	15	15
P/E – low	—	6	8	11	9	10	11	9	9	12	9
Dividends per share ($)	9.1%	0.55	0.61	0.61	0.61	0.70	0.74	0.85	0.98	1.12	1.20
Book value per share ($)	8.1%	8.82	9.39	9.97	11.05	11.67	13.70	15.56	16.80	17.85	

1990 Year-end:
Debt ratio: 6.2%
Return on equity: 17.9%
Cash (mil.): $19
Current ratio: 1.26
Long-term debt (mil.): $45
No. of shares (mil.): 38
Dividends:
  1990 average yield: 3.5%
  1990 payout: 38.7%
Market value (mil.): $1,296

Stock Price History High/Low 1981–90

WALGREEN CO.

NYSE symbol: WAG
Fiscal year ends: August 31

Hoover's Rating **A**

OVERVIEW

Walgreen's is the largest drugstore chain in the US, claiming roughly twice the sales and profits of its closest publicly owned competition, Rite Aid. Walgreen's also manages 5 regional photofinishing labs. In 1990 alone Walgreen's sold more than $6 billion in merchandise through its 1,564 stores, located in 28 states and Puerto Rico, and continued the aggressive-growth strategies that have yielded record sales and earnings for 16 years in a row.

By acquiring new stores, remodeling older ones, and streamlining operations, Walgreen's leadership hopes to continue the company's tradition of adaptation to new market demands. About 600 stores are scheduled to open in the next 5 years, and remodeling of 225 stores was set for 1991 (compared to 165 in 1990). Approximately 80% of Walgreen's stores were opened or remodeled in the past 5 years.

Walgreen's is first or 2nd in about 80% of the markets it serves. The company's pharmacies account for 1/3 of all sales; the company projects that pharmacy sales will account for 1/2 of its overall sales by the year 2000.

WHO

Chairman and CEO: Charles R. Walgreen III, age 55, $1,008,564 pay
President and COO: L. Daniel Jorndt, age 49, $471,186 pay
VC and CFO: Charles D. Hunter, age 61, $574,081 pay
EVP: Glenn S. Kraiss, age 57, $438,199 pay
EVP: Vernon A. Brunner, age 50, $438,109 pay
SVP: John R. Brown, age 54
VP Human Resources: John A. Rubino
Auditors: Arthur Andersen & Co.
Employees: 48,500

WHEN

In 1901 Chicago pharmacist Charles Walgreen borrowed $2,000 from his father for a down payment on his first drugstore. In 1909 Walgreen sold 1/2 interest in his first store and bought a 2nd, where he installed a large soda fountain and began serving lunches. In 1916, 9 stores consolidated under the corporate name Walgreen Co. By 1920 there were 20 stores in Chicago, with sales of $1.55 million. The firm was first listed on the NYSE in 1927. In 1929 the chain's 397 stores in 87 cities had sales of $47 million.

During the Great Depression Walgreen's did comparatively well. Although average sales per store dropped between 1931 and 1935, per-store earnings went up, thanks to a chain-wide emphasis on efficiency. In 1940 there were 489 Walgreen stores, but the chain shrank during WWII when unprofitable stores were closed.

The 1950s saw a major change in the way retailers did business. Walgreen's was an early leader in self-service merchandising. The company opened its first self-serve store in 1952 and had 22 by the end of 1953, leading the industry. Between 1950 and 1960, as small, older stores were replaced with larger, more efficient, self-service units, the total number of stores in the chain increased only about 10%, but sales grew by over 90%.

In 1960 there were 451 Walgreen's stores, 1/2 of which were self-service. In 1962 the company bought 3 huge Globe discount department stores in Houston. By 1966 there were 13 Globes in the Southwest, doing over $120 million in annual sales, but these survived only 11 years. During the 1960s Walgreen's soda fountains proved unprofitable and were phased out.

The 1970s and 1980s saw rapid growth and modernization in the chain. In 1973 company management organized a planning committee to boost Walgreen's sagging return on investment. After a customer survey characterized the stores as "junky, disorganized, and hard-to-shop," Walgreen's modernized them and emphasized health aid and pharmacy business. In 1986 the company purchased Medi Mart.

Adapting to the public's demand for convenient shopping and its own desire for greater efficiency, Walgreen's since 1989 has installed point-of-sale scanning equipment, linked its stores through a satellite network, and completed its 8th regional distribution center. Steady growth continued in 1990 with the opening of 104 stores, and overall sales increased by 12.4% over 1989 sales. Prescription drug sales increased by 21.3% (to almost $2 billion) in 1990, the 9th consecutive year that such sales grew by more than 20%. By 1990 Walgreen's was selling 6% of the nation's retail prescriptions, twice the company's share just 5 years before.

WHERE

HQ: 200 Wilmot Rd., Deerfield, IL 60015
Phone: 708-940-2500
Fax: 708-940-2804

Walgreen's operates drugstores in over 650 communities in 28 states and Puerto Rico.

	1990 Stores	
	No.	% of total
Illinois	273	18
Florida	270	17
Texas	177	11
Wisconsin	95	6
Arizona	88	6
Indiana	65	4
California	65	4
Tennessee	62	4
Missouri	52	3
Minnesota	44	3
Colorado	42	3
Other states & Puerto Rico	331	21
Total	**1,564**	**100**

1990 Sales by Geographic Area	% of Total
Chicago & suburbs	16
Other Midwest locations	21
Southwest	18
South & Southeast	27
West	10
East	8
Total	**100**

WHAT

Estimated Sales by Product Class	% of Total
Prescription drugs	33
General merchandise	26
Proprietary drugs	14
Liquor, beverages	12
Cosmetics, toiletries	10
Tobacco products	5
Total	**100**

HOW MUCH

	9-Year Growth	1981	1982	1983	1984	1985	1986	1987	1988	1989	1990
Sales ($ mil.)	14.8%	1,743	2,040	2,361	2,745	3,162	3,661	4,282	4,884	5,380	6,048
Net income ($ mil.)	17.1%	42	56	70	85	94	103	104	129	154	175
Income as % of sales	—	2.4%	2.7%	3.0%	3.1%	3.0%	2.8%	2.4%	2.6%	2.9%	2.9%
Earnings per share ($)	17.0%	0.35	0.46	0.57	0.70	0.77	0.84	0.84	1.05	1.25	1.42
Stock price – high ($)	—	3.42	7.30	10.09	11.31	15.13	19.75	22.44	18.69	25.13	26.63
Stock price – low ($)	—	2.40	2.78	6.50	7.16	10.75	12.13	12.38	13.56	15.00	19.94
Stock price – close ($)	26.8%	3.04	7.02	9.56	11.25	14.06	16.19	15.38	15.13	23.38	25.69
P/E – high	—	10	16	18	16	20	24	27	18	20	19
P/E – low	—	7	6	11	10	14	15	15	13	12	14
Dividends per share ($)	15.4%	0.11	0.13	0.15	0.18	0.22	0.25	0.27	0.30	0.34	0.40
Book value per share ($)	15.4%	2.12	2.45	2.87	3.38	3.92	4.50	5.06	5.79	6.69	7.70

1990 Year-end:
Debt ratio: 14.7%
Return on equity: 19.7%
Cash (mil.): $214
Current ratio: 1.88
Long-term debt (mil.): $163
No. of shares (mil.): 123
Dividends:
　1990 average yield: 1.6%
　1990 payout: 28.3%
Market value (mil.): $3,161

Stock Price History
High/Low 1981–90

RANKINGS

19th in *Fortune* 50 Retailing Cos.
171st in *Business Week* 1000

KEY COMPETITORS

American Stores
Costco
Fred Meyer
Jack Eckerd
Kmart

Longs
Melville
J. C. Penney
Rite Aid

WAL-MART STORES, INC.

OVERVIEW

Wal-Mart, based in Bentonville, Arkansas, is the largest, fastest-growing, and most profitable retailer in the US. Founder Sam Walton and his family still own nearly 40% of Wal-Mart's common stock, making the family the wealthiest in the US.

Wal-Mart's large general-merchandise discount stores, with their extensive product selection and ultra-low prices, have earned a reputation for annihilating small competitors in rural towns throughout the South and Midwest. The company's SuperCenters (which include grocery sections), Sam's Clubs (ware-

house stores that generated 20% of Wal-Mart's 1990 sales), and Hypermart*USAs (combination supermarkets and discount stores with retail service outlets) have enjoyed similar success in their market niches.

Wal-Mart has begun using its strengths — virtuoso cost control, hands-on management, integrated distribution systems, state-of-the-art computers, and down-home friendly customer service—to challenge archrivals Dayton Hudson (Target stores) and Kmart in larger metropolitan areas, and expanded abroad in a 1991 joint venture with a Mexican retailer.

WHEN

Sam Walton began his retail career as a J. C. Penney management trainee and later leased a Ben Franklin franchised dimestore in Newport, Arkansas (1945). In 1950 he relocated to Bentonville, Arkansas, and opened a Walton 5&10. By 1962, Walton owned 15 Ben Franklin stores under the Walton 5&10 name.

After Ben Franklin management rejected his suggestion to open discount stores in small towns, Walton, with his brother James (Bud) Walton, opened the first Wal-Mart Discount City in Rogers, Arkansas (1962). Growth was slow at first. Wal-Mart Stores, Inc., went public (1970) with only 18 stores and sales of $44 million.

During the 1970s growth accelerated due to 2 key developments in distribution and computerization. Each of the 17 highly automated distribution centers serves approximately 150 nearby stores, cutting shipping costs and time. Computerization tracks inventory and speeds checkout and reordering. By 1980 the 276 stores had sales of $1.2 billion.

Acquisitions included Mohr Value (1977), Hutchinson Wholesale Shoe (1978), Kuhn's Big-K Stores (1981), and Super Saver Warehouse Club (1987). Wal-Mart phased out Ben Franklin stores (1976) and sold the 15 dot Discount Drugstores (1989, opened 1983).

In 1983 Wal-Mart opened Sam's Wholesale Club, modeled on the successful format of

cash-and-carry, membership-only warehouse retailing pioneered by the Price Company of California. Sam's lures small-business owners in metropolitan areas with extremely slim profit margins on large merchandise quantities. An estimated 38% of Sam's shoppers, however, are ordinary consumers who pay annual membership fees.

In 1987 Wal-Mart started Hypermart*USA, originally a joint venture with Cullum Companies, a Dallas-based supermarket chain (Wal-Mart bought out Cullum's interest in 1989). The hypermarket, a huge European hybrid of the discount store and supermarket, features over 200,000 square feet of shopping in a mall-like setting, including ancillary businesses and services (branch bank, fast food outlets, express photo developer, hair salon, supervised playroom for shoppers' children).

Wal-Mart is also experimenting with other formats. SuperCenters (90,000 to 120,000 square feet) are large Wal-Mart Discount Cities with supermarkets. Sam's has added meat and produce sections and bakeries. In 1989 and 1990 the company tested convenience stores next to existing company units. Wal-Mart continues to expand at its usual breakneck pace, buying complementary businesses (McLane Company, distribution services, 1990; The Wholesale Club, warehouse stores, 1991) and opening over 100 new stores annually.

HOW MUCH

	9-Year Growth	1981	1982	1983	1984	1985	1986	1987	1988	1989	1990
Sales ($ mil.)	33.4%	2,445	3,376	4,667	6,401	8,451	11,909	15,959	20,649	25,811	32,602
Net income ($ mil.)	35.7%	83	124	196	271	327	450	628	837	1,076	1,291
Income as % of sales	—	3.4%	3.7%	4.2%	4.2%	3.9%	3.8%	3.9%	4.1%	4.2%	4.0%
Earnings per share ($)	34.7%	0.08	0.11	0.18	0.24	0.29	0.40	0.56	0.74	0.95	1.14
Stock price – high ($)	—	1.37	3.38	5.83	5.88	8.63	13.47	21.44	16.94	22.44	36.75
Stock price – low ($)	—	0.84	1.20	2.73	3.78	4.73	7.28	10.00	12.13	15.00	20.19
Stock price – close ($)	41.5%	1.33	3.12	4.88	4.73	7.97	11.63	13.00	15.69	22.44	30.25
P/E – high	—	18	30	33	25	30	34	39	23	24	32
P/E – low	—	11	11	16	16	16	18	18	16	16	18
Dividends per share ($)	37.2%	0.01	0.01	0.02	0.03	0.04	0.04	0.06	0.08	0.11	0.14
Book value per share ($)	35.1%	0.31	0.45	0.66	0.88	1.14	1.50	2.00	2.66	3.50	4.70

1990 Year-end:
Debt ratio: 26.1%
Return on equity: 27.8%
Cash (mil.): $13
Current ratio: 1.61
Long-term debt (mil.): $1,899
No. of shares (mil.): 1,142
Dividends:
　1990 average yield: 0.5%
　1990 payout: 12.3%
Market value (mil.): $34,554

Stock Price History High/Low 1981–90

Hoover's Rating **A+**

WHO

Chairman: Sam M. Walton, age 73
President and CEO: David D. Glass, age 55, $710,000 pay
VC and COO: Donald G. Soderquist, age 57, $600,000 pay
VC; CEO, Sam's Clubs: A. L. Johnson, age 56, $525,000 pay
EVP and CFO: Paul R. Carter, age 50, $375,000 pay
VC: S. Robson Walton, age 46
VP, People Division: Suzanne Allford
Auditors: Ernst & Young
Employees: 328,000

WHERE

HQ: 702 SW 8th St., Bentonville, AR 72716
Phone: 501-273-4000
Fax: 501-273-8650

Wal-Mart operates 1,573 Wal-Mart Stores (including Discount Cities and SuperCenters), 148 Sam's Clubs, and 4 Hypermart*USAs in 35 states.

State	Wal-Mart Stores	Sam's Clubs	Hypermarts
Alabama	73	5	—
Arkansas	77	4	—
Florida	113	15	—
Georgia	79	8	—
Illinois	80	8	—
Indiana	49	6	—
Iowa	37	2	—
Kansas	41	2	1
Kentucky	64	3	—
Louisiana	74	9	—
Mississippi	56	2	—
Missouri	105	8	1
North Carolina	58	5	—
Ohio	28	4	—
Oklahoma	80	5	—
South Carolina	47	4	—
Tennessee	85	7	—
Texas	230	34	2
Wisconsin	33	4	—
Other states	164	13	—
Total	**1,573**	**148**	**4**

WHAT

	1990 Sales
Category	% of total
Hard goods	27
Soft goods	27
Stationery & candy	11
Sporting goods & toys	9
Health & beauty aids	9
Gifts, records & electronics	6
Pharmaceuticals	6
Shoes	3
Jewelry	2
Total	**100**

RANKINGS

2nd in *Fortune* 50 Retailing Cos.
6th in *Business Week* 1000

KEY COMPETITORS

Ames	Home Depot	Price Co.
Circuit City	Kmart	Riklis Family
Costco	Montgomery Ward	Sears
Dayton Hudson	Pacific Enterprises	Service
Fred Meyer	J. C. Penney	Merchandise

THE WALT DISNEY COMPANY

NYSE symbol: DIS
Fiscal year ends: September 30

Hoover's Rating **A**

OVERVIEW

CEO Michael Eisner, credited with Disney's resurgence in the 1980s, rules a Magic Kingdom built on the enduring international popularity of Mickey Mouse, Donald Duck, et al. Disney characters have spearheaded the company's entry into movies; theme parks and hotels; TV production and syndication; audio recordings; a cable TV network; and the licensing, production, and retailing of Disney merchandise. Animation, Disney's original product, still creates fans today. The company re-releases its classic films every 7 years.

Recession-related declines in park attendance and the lack of mega-hit movies have

not slowed Disney's expansion. Coming attractions include Euro Disneyland, scheduled to open near Paris in 1992, European TV programming, and full-scale book and magazine publishing. Facing capacity limitations at Disneyland, the company will build either "Westcot" center, a Disney-style world's fair, in Anaheim, or DisneySea, a maritime theme park alongside the company's Queen Mary and Spruce Goose in Long Beach. Also in the works are more hotels and a planned community in Walt Disney World in Orlando, another Tokyo theme park, and timeshare resorts near Disney parks.

WHEN

After his first animated film business failed, artist Walt Disney and his brother Roy started a film studio in 1923 in Hollywood. Walt directed the first Mickey Mouse cartoon, *Plane Crazy*, in 1928. Disney's studio created short animated cartoons like *The Three Little Pigs*.

The studio produced its first animated feature film, *Snow White*, in 1937 and *Fantasia* and *Pinocchio* in the 1940s. Disney produced "The Mickey Mouse Club" (1955–59, restarted 1989) and "Disney's Wonderful World," the longest-running network series in television history, today in its 34th season. Disneyland opened in 1955 in Anaheim, California, with over a million visitors in its first 6 months.

Walt Disney died in 1966 of lung cancer, and his brother Roy became chairman. Disney World opened in Florida in 1971, and Roy died the same year, leaving E. Cardon Walker as president. Roy's son Roy E. Disney, VP of Disney's animation division, became the company's principal individual shareholder upon his father's death. Without Walt's and Roy's leadership and creativity, Disney films went from producing over 50% of the company's revenues in 1971 to only 20% in 1979.

In 1980 Walker became CEO and appointed Walt's son-in-law Ron Miller president and COO. Epcot Center opened in Florida in 1982, and in 1983 Miller became CEO. Miller started

Touchstone Pictures in order to produce films like *Splash* (1984), Disney's first hit since *The Love Bug* (1969).

In 1984 Texas's wealthy Bass family, in alliance with Roy E. Disney, bought a controlling interest in Disney. Management was replaced by new CEO Michael Eisner (from Paramount) and president Frank Wells (from Warner Bros.), bringing a new era of innovation, prosperity, and high executive salaries.

The company started The Disney Channel and opened Disney retail stores in the 1980s. Tokyo Disneyland opened in 1984. As the 1980s ended, the company expanded its production of mainstream movies with hits such as *Dead Poets Society*, *Dick Tracy*, and *Who Framed Roger Rabbit?*; and opened the Disney-MGM Studios Theme Park in Florida.

In 1988 Disney bought the Disneyland Hotel, the Queen Mary and Spruce Goose in Long Beach, and KCAL-TV in Los Angeles. In 1989 Disney started a record division. Disney's 1989 agreement to purchase Henson Associates (the Muppets) fell apart following founder Jim Henson's sudden death in 1990. Also in 1990 Disney opened Mickey's Kitchen, its first mall restaurant, and established Hollywood Records, a mainstream label. The company bought *Discover* magazine and finally settled its legal feud with Henson's heirs in 1991.

WHO

Chairman and CEO: Michael D. Eisner, age 48, $11,233,229 pay
President and COO: Frank G. Wells, age 58, $5,641,615 pay
SVP and CFO: Richard D. Nanula, age 31
VP Human Resources: Mike Buckhoff
Auditors: Price Waterhouse
Employees: 52,000

WHERE

HQ: 500 S. Buena Vista St., Burbank, CA 91521
Phone: 818-560-1000
Fax: 818-560-1930

Disney-owned theme parks are located in California and Florida. Other major facilities are located in southern California.

	1990 Pretax Income	
	$ mil.	% of total
US (including US exports)	1,270	96
Other countries	55	4
Total	**1,325**	**100**

WHAT

	1990 Sales		1990 Operating Income	
	$ mil.	% of total	$ mil.	% of total
Theme parks & resorts	3,020	52	889	62
Filmed entertainment	2,250	38	313	22
Consumer products	574	10	223	16
Adjustments	—	—	(138)	—
Total	**5,844**	**100**	**1,287**	**100**

Theme Parks and Resorts
Disney Development Company (real estate)
Disneyland
Euro Disney (49%, scheduled to open in 1992)
Hotel Queen Mary
Spruce Goose
Tokyo Disneyland (royalty interest only)
Walt Disney Imagineering (attraction design)
Walt Disney World
Disney-MGM Studios Theme Park
Epcot Center
Magic Kingdom
Resorts, hotels, and Disney Village Marketplace

Filmed Entertainment
Buena Vista Television (syndication)
The Disney Channel
Hollywood Pictures
KCAL-TV, Los Angeles
Touchstone Pictures
Touchstone Television
Walt Disney Pictures
Walt Disney Televison

Consumer Products
Childcraft catalog
Disney Stores
Hollywood Records
Mickey's Kitchen
Walt Disney Records

Other
Discover magazine

HOW MUCH

	9-Year Growth	1981	1982	1983	1984	1985	1986	1987	1988	1989	1990
Sales ($ mil.)	21.6%	1,005	1,030	1,307	1,656	2,015	2,471	2,877	3,438	4,594	5,844
Net income ($ mil.)	23.7%	121	100	93	22	174	247	392	522	703	824
Income as % of sales	—	12.1%	9.7%	7.1%	1.3%	8.6%	10.0%	13.6%	15.2%	15.3%	14.1%
Earnings per share ($)	23.0%	0.93	0.75	0.68	0.15	1.29	1.82	2.85	3.80	5.10	6.00
Stock price – high ($)	—	16.78	17.88	21.19	17.13	29.38	54.88	82.50	68.38	136.25	136.50
Stock price – low ($)	—	10.84	11.75	11.81	11.31	14.81	28.06	41.25	54.00	64.88	86.00
Stock price – close ($)	25.6%	13.06	15.81	13.16	14.97	28.22	43.13	59.25	65.75	112.00	101.50
P/E – high	—	18	24	31	112	23	30	29	18	27	23
P/E – low	—	12	16	18	74	12	15	14	14	13	14
Dividends per share ($)	8.7%	0.25	0.30	0.23	0.38	0.30	0.32	0.32	0.28	0.44	0.53
Book value per share ($)	12.7%	9.00	9.56	10.15	8.56	9.16	10.85	14.01	17.71	22.50	26.47

1990 Year-end:
Debt ratio: 31.2%
Return on equity: 24.5%
Cash (mil.): $820
Current ratio: —
Long-term debt (mil.): $1,585
No. of shares (mil.): 132
Dividends:
 1990 average yield: 0.5%
 1990 payout: 8.8%
Market value (mil.): $13,378

Stock Price History High/Low 1981–90

RANKINGS

18th in *Fortune* 100 Diversified Service Cos.
33rd in *Business Week* 1000

KEY COMPETITORS

Accor
American Financial
American Greetings
Anheuser-Busch
Blockbuster
Capital Cities/ABC
CBS
General Electric
MacAndrews & Forbes
Matsushita

Metromedia
National Geographic
Paramount
Sony
TCI
Time Warner
Turner Broadcasting
Viacom
Other entertainment companies

WANG LABORATORIES, INC.

OVERVIEW

Forty-year-old Wang Laboratories, based in Lowell, Massachusetts, manufactures computers, networking devices, and imaging products. Its VS minicomputer line ranges from the VS 5000 (10 to 128 users) to the super-minicomputer VS 10000 (up to 511 users).

Once a leader in proprietary word processors, Wang has been trounced in recent years by more flexible and less expensive PCs. Struggling to staunch huge losses, Wang is concentrating its resources on office automation systems that store, sort, and retrieve electronic images, including drawings, photos, and written documents input by scanner or fax.

In shifting its focus from hardware manufacturing to software development, systems integration, and reselling (for IBM's RS/6000, P/S2, and AS/400 products), Wang has slashed jobs from 31,500 (1988) to 13,500 (1991).

WHEN

In 1951, with $600 in savings, An Wang started Wang Laboratories in Boston. An Wang had come to the US from China in 1945 to earn a PhD at Harvard. While working for Harvard's Computation Laboratory, he patented a magnetic pulse device that led to the development of memory cores. The small rings of iron were the central components of computer memory until replaced by microchips in the late 1960s. IBM bought Wang's patent in 1956 for $500,000.

Wang's next success came from engineering custom digital devices (e.g., the first digitally programmed scoreboard in New York's Shea Stadium). Another was the successful semiautomatic typesetter (Linasec) Wang developed in 1963 under contract, which increased sales to over $1 million in 1964.

Adhering to An Wang's philosophy of "find a need and fill it," Wang entered the calculator business, introducing an innovative desktop calculator, the LOCI, in 1965. The subsequent demand for Wang calculators caused the company to go public in 1967 to finance its expansion.

In the mid-1970s Wang relinquished the calculator business to its competitors and entered the word-processor market. Wang introduced the first screen-based (TV-like display) word processor in 1976, and by 1978 it had become the largest supplier of screen-based systems. In 1977 Wang introduced its VS minicomputer series — a product line built on compatibility among existing and future VS computers. The success of the VS series combined with strong sales of word processors caused Wang's revenues to rise from $543 million in 1980 to $2.4 billion in 1985.

In 1985 Wang's earnings declined 92% from the previous year, forcing layoffs and causing An Wang to return to active management of the company. The company has still not fully recovered. In 1986 Wang made his son Fred president, but his efforts to revitalize the company failed. Massive losses in 1989 caused Fred Wang to resign as president that year. In 1990 An Wang died from cancer of the esophagus. His heirs and other Wang family members own almost 40% of the company.

Wang's sales have been hurt by the decreasing demand for minicomputers with proprietary architectures and by Wang's slowness in entering the desktop-computer and local area network arenas.

In 1991 Wang reported a net loss of $715 million on revenues of $2.5 billion. Even after taking a 1990 restructuring charge of $338 million, Wang suffered its 3rd straight year of losses in 1991, with annualized revenue sliding to around $2 billion. Shortly after forming an alliance to remarket selected IBM systems (in turn receiving from IBM fresh capital up to $100 million), Wang announced yet another "significant restructuring" including the layoff of 3-4,000 workers.

ASE symbol: WANB
Fiscal year ends: June 30

Hoover's Rating **D**

WHO

Chairman and CEO: Richard W. Miller, age 50, $875,487 pay
EVP and Chief Development Officer: Horace Tsiang, age 49, $273,854 pay
EVP Operations: Joseph M. Tucci, age 44
EVP and CFO: Michael F. Mee, age 49, $330,835 pay
SVP Human Resources: Edward J. Devin, age 54
Auditors: Ernst & Young
Employees: 13,500

WHERE

HQ: One Industrial Ave., Lowell, MA 01851
Phone: 508-459-5000
Fax: 508-458-8969

Wang has sales offices in 23 countries and manufacturing operations in the US, Ireland, and Taiwan.

	1990 Sales		1990 Pretax Income	
	$ mil.	% of total	$ mil.	% of total
US	1,230	49	(525)	—
Europe	799	32	(66)	—
Asia/Pacific	361	15	50	—
Other Americas	107	4	(1)	—
Adjustments	—	—	(37)	—
Total	**2,497**	**100**	**(579)**	**—**

WHAT

	1990 Sales	
	$ mil.	% of total
Product sales	1,558	62
Service & rental income	939	38
Total	**2,497**	**100**

Computers
VS 5000 series
VS 8000 series
VS 10000 series

Workstations
Wang PC 200/300

Communications
Wang PC LAN
Wang Open Systems Networking (OSN)
WangNet

Software
Wang Integrated Image System (WIIS)
Wang Freestyle Personal Computing System
WP Plus (word processor)
Wang OFFICE (office automation)
Professional Application Creation Environment (PACE)
Speech and Telephony Environment for Programmers (STEP)

RANKINGS

169th in *Fortune* 500 Industrial Cos.
802nd in *Business Week* 1000

KEY COMPETITORS

Apple	GEC	Novell
Borland	Harris	Oracle
Compaq	Hewlett-Packard	Prime
Computer	Lotus	Siemens
Associates	Machines Bull	Tandem
Control Data	Microsoft	Unisys
Data General	NCR	Xerox
DEC		

HOW MUCH

	9-Year Growth	1981	1982	1983	1984	1985	1986	1987	1988	1989	1990
Sales ($ mil.)	12.6%	856	1,159	1,538	2,185	2,352	2,643	2,837	3,068	2,869	2,497
Net income ($ mil.)	—	78	107	152	210	16	51	(71)	93	(321)	(629)
Income as % of sales	—	9.1%	9.2%	9.9%	9.6%	0.7%	1.9%	(2.5%)	3.0%	(11.2%)	(25.2%)
Earnings per share ($)	—	0.67	0.88	1.16	1.52	0.11	0.35	(0.44)	0.56	(1.96)	(3.82)
Stock price – high ($)	—	22.81	31.69	42.50	37.63	29.25	21.75	19.13	16.50	10.88	6.25
Stock price – low ($)	—	12.00	12.31	28.00	23.00	15.00	10.50	9.63	7.50	4.63	2.00
Stock price – close ($)	(18.5%)	16.63	29.50	35.63	25.88	19.63	11.63	11.50	8.75	5.13	2.63
P/E – high	—	34	36	37	25	266	62	—	29	—	—
P/E – low	—	18	14	24	15	136	30	—	13	—	—
Dividends per share ($)	—	0.06	0.06	0.09	0.12	0.16	0.16	0.16	0.16	0.16	0.00
Book value per share ($)	(4.8%)	3.91	4.81	7.09	9.01	8.93	9.59	9.15	9.67	6.90	2.51

1990 Year-end:
Debt ratio: 57.3%
Return on equity: —
Cash (mil.): $169
Current ratio: 1.24
Long-term debt (mil.): $556
No. of shares (mil.): 165
Dividends:
　1990 average yield: 0.0%
　1990 payout: 0.0%
Market value (mil.): $434

Stock Price History High/Low 1981–90

WARNER-LAMBERT COMPANY

NYSE symbol: WLA
Fiscal year ends: December 31

Hoover's Rating: A

OVERVIEW

While better known for its OTC health care products (Listerine, Rolaids, Halls) and confections (Trident, Dentyne, Certs), New Jersey–based Warner-Lambert is also a major international drug maker, with such pharmaceutical brands as Accupril, Dilantin, and Lopid, most of which are marketed under the Parke-Davis name. The company has leading nonprescription products for health and oral hygiene and sells more breath-mint and gum brands than anyone else in the world.

Warner-Lambert invested $379 million (8% of sales) in R&D in 1990 and plans to spend over $2 billion on pharmaceutical research in the next 5 years. Promising drugs in the company's pipeline include Cognex (a treatment for Alzheimer's disease) and Neurontin (an anticonvulsant).

Warner-Lambert also produces the Schick line of razors and holds the #1 position in both aquarium products (Tetra) and gelatin capsules for the pharmaceutical industry (Capsugel). By 1992 the company hopes to begin shipments of Novon, its new starch-based, biodegradable polymer material.

WHO

Chairman and CEO: Joseph D. Williams, age 64, $1,585,000 pay
President and COO: Melvin R. Goodes, age 55, $1,040,833 pay
EVP and CFO: Robert J. Dircks, age 63, $545,917 pay
VP Human Resources: Raymond M. Fino, age 48
Auditors: Price Waterhouse
Employees: 34,000

WHERE

HQ: 201 Tabor Rd., Morris Plains, NJ 07950
Phone: 201-540-2000
Fax: 201-540-3761

The company has 75 plants in over 39 countries.

	1990 Sales		1990 Operating Income	
	$ mil.	% of total	$ mil.	% of total
US	2,445	52	740	59
Americas & Asia	1,148	25	275	22
Other regions	1,094	23	239	19
Adjustments	—	—	(573)	—
Total	**4,687**	**100**	**681**	**100**

WHEN

In 1856 pharmacist William Warner opened a drugstore in Philadelphia and soon made his mark on the industry by developing a method for sugar-coating pills and tablets (the copper pan that he used now resides at the Smithsonian Institution). In 1886 he moved into drug production by opening William R. Warner & Co. St. Louis–based Pfeiffer Chemical bought the company in 1908, adopted the Warner name, and moved it to New York in 1916. By 1945 the company had established several overseas operations and had acquired over 50 businesses including Sloan's (liniment), Corn Husker's (lotion), and Hudnut (cosmetics).

In 1950 the company, under the leadership of Elmer Bobst, changed its name to Warner-Hudnut (cosmetics then accounted for most of its sales) and went public. Two years later Warner purchased Chilcott Labs (founded in 1874 as the Maltine Company). In 1955 the company assumed its present name following the purchase of Lambert Pharmacal (founded in 1884 by Jordan Lambert after he acquired the formula for Listerine antiseptic).

Acquisition continued throughout the next 2 decades including Emerson Drugs (Bromo-Seltzer, 1956), Nepera Chemical (antihistamines, 1956), American Chicle (chewing gum, 1962), and Schick (razors, 1970). The purchase of Parke-Davis in 1970 resulted in an antitrust investigation and the selling of certain product lines in 1976 (thyroid preparations, blood products, vaccines, and others). Founded in Detroit in 1866, Parke-Davis was the first company to make "biologicals" (vaccines). It later introduced Dilantin (anticonvulsant, 1938), Benadryl (antihistamine, 1946), and Chloromycetin (antibiotic, 1949), all still sold today.

Slipping profits in the 1970s motivated the selling of unprofitable divisions and consolidation of others in the early 1980s. In 1985 the company's divestment of its ailing health technologies businesses, along with the costs associated with its restructuring and streamlining program, caused it to take a $553 million write-down. The restructuring, however, along with new robotic manufacturing methods for increased efficiency, resulted in annual savings of over $300 million and led to generally profitable results throughout the rest of the 1980s.

Warner-Lambert's biggest drug product success has been Lopid (introduced in 1981), a cholesterol-lowering drug. Facing the expiration of Lopid's patent in 1993, the company is pushing for FDA approval of its next potential blockbuster, Cognex, the first drug to treat Alzheimer's disease.

The company launched its new Tracer shaving system in 1991 in response to archrival Gillette's Sensor System.

WHAT

	1990 Sales		1990 Operating Income	
	$ mil.	% of total	$ mil.	% of total
Nonprescription	1,526	33	367	29
Gum & mints	1,054	22	208	17
Ethical products	1,555	33	560	45
Other products	552	12	119	9
Adjustments	—	—	(573)	—
Total	**4,687**	**100**	**681**	**100**

Ethical Products
Accupril (hypertensive)
Chloromycetin (antibiotic)
Comprecin (anti-infective)
Dilantin (anticonvulsant)
Doryx (anti-infective)
ERYC (erythromycin)
Loestrin (contraceptive)
Lopid (lipid regulator)
Procan SR (cardiovascular)

Nonprescription Products
Anusol (hemorrhoidal preparation)
Benadryl (antihistamine)
Benylin (cough syrup)
Caladryl (anti-itch lotion)
E.P.T. (pregnancy test)
Efferdent (denture cleanser)
Gelusil (antacid)
Halls (cough tablets)
Listerine (mouthwash)
Lubriderm (skin lotion)
Myadec (vitamins)

Rolaids (antacid)
Sinutab
Tucks (medicated pads)

Confections
Beeman's
Bubblicious
Certs
Chiclets
Choclairs
Clorets
Dentyne
Freshmint
Junior Mints
mentos
Sugar Babies
Sugar Daddy
Trident

Other
Capsugel (empty gelatin capsules)
Schick (razors)
Tetra (aquarium supplies)

RANKINGS

110th in *Fortune* 500 US Industrial Cos.
50th in *Business Week* 1000

KEY COMPETITORS

American Home Products
Amway
Bristol-Myers Squibb
Cadbury Schweppes
Colgate-Palmolive
Dow Chemical
Eastman Kodak
Gillette
Hershey
Nestlé
Procter & Gamble
RJR Nabisco
Schering-Plough
Unilever
Wrigley
Other drug companies

HOW MUCH

	9-Year Growth	1981	1982	1983	1984	1985	1986	1987	1988	1989	1990
Sales ($ mil.)	3.7%	3,380	3,246	3,108	3,167	3,200	3,103	3,485	3,908	4,196	4,687
Net income ($ mil.)	55.3%	9	175	201	224	(316)	309	296	340	413	485
Income as % of sales	—	0.3%	5.4%	6.5%	7.1%	(9.9%)	10.0%	8.5%	8.7%	9.8%	10.3%
Earnings per share ($)	57.7%	0.06	1.10	1.26	1.41	(2.03)	2.09	2.08	2.50	3.05	3.61
Stock price – high ($)	—	12.50	15.06	17.50	18.06	24.69	31.56	43.75	39.75	59.38	70.38
Stock price – low ($)	—	8.50	9.81	12.88	14.38	16.69	21.69	24.13	29.94	37.25	49.63
Stock price – close ($)	22.2%	11.13	14.13	14.81	17.38	23.75	29.31	33.75	39.19	57.75	67.50
P/E – high	—	208	14	14	13	—	15	21	16	19	20
P/E – low	—	142	9	10	10	—	10	12	12	12	14
Dividends per share ($)	9.5%	0.67	0.70	0.71	0.74	0.75	0.80	0.89	1.08	1.28	1.52
Book value per share ($)	2.1%	8.69	8.64	8.88	9.09	5.89	6.32	6.37	7.36	8.38	10.44

1990 Year-end:
Debt ratio: 18.0%
Return on equity: 38.4%
Cash (mil.): $306
Current ratio: 1.42
Long-term debt (mil.): $307
No. of shares (mil.): 134
Dividends:
　1990 average yield: 2.3%
　1990 payout: 42.1%
Market value (mil.): $9,068

Stock Price History High/Low 1981–90

THE WASHINGTON POST COMPANY

OVERVIEW

The Washington Post Company publishes the *Washington Post*, the District of Columbia's dominant newspaper. The company also publishes the *Herald* (Everette, WA); *Newsweek* magazine (3.1 million average weekly circulation); English language *Newsweek International* in Atlantic, Pacific, and Latin American editions; and *Newsweek Nihon Ban* in Japanese. US print operations have been adversely affected by the recession.

The Washington Post owns 4 network-affiliated TV stations and 52 cable systems with over 400,000 US subscribers. The company also controls 2 firms holding unbuilt UK cable franchises.

The company's 146 Stanley H. Kaplan Educational Centers prepare students for licensing exams and admission tests. Legi-Slate is an online government information service subsidiary. The company also owns interests in paper companies and timberland. It is a 50% owner of the *International Herald Tribune*, published in Europe and Asia, and owns 28% of Cowles Media Company, owners of the *Minneapolis Star* and *Tribune* and other publications.

WHEN

Stilson Hutchins, journalist and politician, published the first edition of the *Washington Post* in 1877. Strong reporting made the *Post* successful, and Hutchins retired in 1889, selling the *Post* to Beriah Wilkins, a banker and politician, and Frank Hatton, a journalist. Hatton died in 1894, and the *Post* took on the conservative leanings of Wilkins and the Victorian perspective of the times. Wilkins died in 1905, and his heirs sold the *Post* to John R. McLean, an Ohio Democratic politician and inheritor of the Cincinnati *Enquirer*.

McLean changed the *Post*, focusing on society columns and features, adding color comics and the big headline style found in sensationalist papers. Hard news coverage suffered, while crime and scandal were emphasized. By the time McLean died in 1916, the *Post* had resorted to yellow journalism.

McLean's son Ned took over the *Post* and the *Enquirer*. Ned ruined the *Post*'s integrity by lying to a Senate committee (1924) about his involvement in the Teapot Dome oil scandal. He yielded the *Post*'s management in 1932 and died from alcoholism in 1941.

Wealthy, conservative banker Eugene Meyer bought the bankrupt *Post* for $825,000 in 1933. Meyer's credo of hard work, honesty, hands-on management, and personal funding saved the *Post*. Meyer spent the next 12 years building a first-class news staff. By 1946, when Meyer's son-in-law Philip Graham took over as publisher, the *Post* was in the black again. In 1948 Meyer transferred his stock to his daughter Katharine and Philip. In 1954 the *Post* bought the Washington *Times-Herald*, eliminating its morning competition.

Philip Graham bought radio and TV stations and established overseas bureaus. In 1961 he started a news service with the Los Angeles *Times* and bought *Newsweek* magazine. In 1963 Philip Graham lost a struggle with manic depression and killed himself.

Katharine Graham became publisher of the *Post*, where she had been an editor since 1939. In 1971 the *Post* went public. In 1972 reporters Bob Woodward and Carl Bernstein broke the Watergate story, which won a Pulitzer Prize in 1973 and led to Richard Nixon's resignation. In the 1970s and 1980s, Katharine Graham bought TV and radio stations, databases, cable companies, newspapers, newsprint mills, and the Stanley H. Kaplan Educational Centers. In 1979 her son Donald Graham, an 8-year *Post* veteran, became publisher. In 1991 Katharine Graham, age 73, relinquished her CEO position to Donald. In the same year, the *Washington Post* and the *New York Times* bought out Whitcom's 1/3 interest in the *International Herald Tribune*.

NYSE symbol: WPO
Fiscal year ends: December 31

Hoover's Rating **A-**

WHO

Chairman: Katharine Graham, age 73, $554,986 pay
President, CEO, and Publisher, *The Washington Post*: Donald E. Graham, age 45, $324,996 pay (prior to promotion)
VP and COO: Alan G. Spoon, age 39, $405,000 pay (prior to promotion)
VP Finance: John B. Morse, age 44
VP Human Resources: Beverly R. Keil, age 44
Auditors: Price Waterhouse
Employees: 6,200

WHERE

HQ: 1150 15th St. NW, Washington DC 20071
Phone: 202-334-6000
Fax: 202-334-4613

The company owns newspapers in Washington, DC, and Everett, WA; 4 TV stations in 3 states; and 52 cable TV systems in 15 states.

WHAT

	1990 Sales		1990 Operating Income	
	$ mil.	% of total	$ mil.	% of total
Newspaper publishing	691	48	144	51
Magazine publishing	340	24	27	10
Broadcasting	179	12	69	24
Cable television	146	10	29	10
Other	83	6	13	5
Total	**1,439**	**100**	**282**	**100**

Newspapers
The Herald (Everett, WA)
The Washington Post

Magazines
Newsweek
Newsweek International
Newsweek Nihon Ban (Japan)

TV Stations
WDIV-4, Detroit
WFSB-3, Hartford
WJXT-4, Jacksonville
WPLG-10, Miami

Other Businesses and Holdings
Bear Island Paper (33 1/3%, newsprint)
Bear Island Timberlands (33 1/3%)
Bowater Mersey Paper (49%, newsprint)
Cowles Media Company (28%)
International Herald Tribune, SA (50%)
Legi-Slate, Inc. (on-line database)
Los Angeles Times–Washington Post News Service, Inc. (50%)
Post-Newsweek Cable
Stanley H. Kaplan Educational Centers

RANKINGS

271st in *Fortune* 500 Industrial Cos.
226th in *Business Week* 1000

HOW MUCH

	9-Year Growth	1981	1982	1983	1984	1985	1986	1987	1988	1989	1990
Sales ($ mil.)	7.5%	753	801	878	984	1,079	1,215	1,315	1,368	1,444	1,439
Net income ($ mil.)	20.5%	33	52	68	86	114	100	187	269	198	175
Income as % of sales	—	4.3%	6.5%	7.8%	8.7%	10.6%	8.2%	14.2%	19.7%	13.7%	12.1%
Earnings per share ($)	22.5%	2.32	3.70	4.82	6.11	8.66	7.80	14.52	20.91	15.50	14.45
Stock price – high ($)	—	33.00	60.88	73.25	85.00	130.00	184.50	269.00	229.00	311.00	295.50
Stock price – low ($)	—	19.38	27.38	54.50	60.75	77.75	115.00	150.00	186.50	204.00	167.00
Stock price – close ($)	22.7%	31.38	55.25	73.25	80.25	118.75	156.00	187.00	210.75	281.50	198.00
P/E – high	—	14	16	15	14	15	24	19	11	20	20
P/E – low	—	8	7	11	10	9	15	10	9	13	12
Dividends per share ($)	26.0%	0.50	0.56	0.66	0.80	0.96	1.12	1.28	1.56	1.84	4.00
Book value per share ($)	19.6%	15.17	18.32	22.50	27.17	27.26	34.04	47.80	67.50	75.40	76.31

1990 Year-end:
Debt ratio: 12.3%
Return on equity: 19.1%
Cash (mil.): $277
Current ratio: 1.59
Long-term debt (mil.): $127
No. of shares (mil.): 12
Dividends:
  1990 average yield: 2.0%
  1990 payout: 27.7%
Market value (mil.): $2,348

Stock Price History High/Low 1981–90

KEY COMPETITORS

Advance Publications	Maxwell
Blockbuster	New York Times
CBS	Pearson
Cox	E. W. Scripps
Dow Jones	TCI
Gannett	Thomson Corp.
H&R Block	Time Warner
Hearst	Tribune
Knight-Ridder	Viacom

WASTE MANAGEMENT, INC.

OVERVIEW

Waste Management is the largest waste collection, disposal, and recycling company in the world, with revenues of $6 billion in 1990. It offers municipal, industrial, medical, and commercial waste pickup, transport, and disposal; owns and operates landfills; and generates electricity from landfill-produced methane gas or sells the gas directly to industrial end users. It also offers waste-stream consulting services to industry and site-cleanup services for toxic wastes.

Repeated actions by environmental groups against disposal companies have helped, rather than hindered, Waste Management's growth by driving smaller rivals out of the field and discouraging the formation of new companies. Waste is a growth industry. Though the recession of 1990 and 1991 has reduced the waste stream, the company expects to add or expand many sites. In late 1990 the company won a contract for a chemical waste facility in Hong Kong; in 1991 it contracted with Kuwait to clean up war damage and began to examine the opportunities posed by Eastern Europe's massive environmental degradation.

WHEN

In 1956 Dean L. Buntrock joined Ace Scavenger Service in Illinois, which had 12 collection trucks and $750,000 per year in revenues. Under Buntrock's leadership, the company expanded into Wisconsin.

In 1971 Waste Management, Inc., was formed when Buntrock joined forces with H. Wayne Huizenga, who had bought 2 waste routes in Broward County, Florida, in 1962. (Huizenga retired in 1983 and went on to control Blockbuster Video, the #1 video rental chain in the country.) Both companies had grown rapidly during the 1960s, as concern with air quality prompted bans on residential and industrial on-site waste burning. During 1969 and 1970 some of the company's future competitors began to form through acquisition. Waste Management reported earnings of $1.2 million on revenues of $16.8 million its first year, with customers in Florida, Illinois, Indiana, Minnesota, Ohio, and Wisconsin. In the 1970s it made acquisitions in Michigan, New York, Ohio, Pennsylvania, and Canada.

In 1975 the company bid on and won a contract in Riyadh, Saudi Arabia (service started in 1978), and formed its international subsidiary. Other foreign contracts followed, and the company now operates in 17 foreign countries including Argentina, Venezuela, Australia, New Zealand, Germany, Italy, and the Netherlands.

The company went into specialty areas, forming Chemical Waste Management (76% owned, 1975), which now offers site cleanup services (ENRAC, 1980) and low-level nuclear waste disposal (Chem-Nuclear Systems, 1982). Expansion in this period included companies in the Pacific Northwest and California and new contracts in Louisiana, Mississippi, and Texas. A great coup was acquisition of 60% of competitor SCA of Boston (1984).

Recent projects include joint ventures for sale of recyclable materials with Du Pont, Stone Container Corporation, and American National Can, and a partnership with Henley Group that created Wheelabrator Technologies (22% owned in 1988; now 55%).

For many years Waste Management has been the target of accusations, and in some cases has been fined, for violation of antitrust ($2 million in fines) and pollution ($12.5 million for the Vickery, Ohio, hazardous-waste facility, 1985) laws. But the company is frequently successful in legal actions because of its massive wealth and large legal staff. Most recently it won an appeal against the State of Alabama, which attempted to impose a $112-per-ton tax on out-of-state waste brought into the company's Emelle site (the largest toxic dump in the US). The tax had already begun to depress profitability. The company is fighting similar laws in New York and Louisiana.

NYSE symbol: WMX
Fiscal year ends: December 31

Hoover's Rating A

WHO

Chairman and CEO: Dean L. Buntrock, age 59, $1,581,750 pay
President and COO: Phillip B. Rooney, age 46, $1,165,500 pay
SVP: Donald F. Flynn, age 51, $582,750 pay
SVP: Jerry E. Dempsey, age 58, $659,180 pay
VP Human Resources: David C. Coleman, age 52
VP, Treasurer, and CFO: James E. Koenig, age 43
Auditors: Arthur Andersen & Co.
Employees: 62,050

WHERE

HQ: 3003 Butterfield Rd., Oak Brook, IL 60521
Phone: 708-572-8800
Fax: 708-572-3094

The company has customers in 48 states, Canada, and 17 other countries.

	1990 Sales		1990 Operating Income	
	$ mil.	% of total	$ mil.	% of total
US	5,078	84	1,089	90
Foreign	956	16	126	10
Total	**6,034**	**100**	**1,215**	**100**

WHAT

	1990 Sales		1990 Operating Income	
	$ mil.	% of total	$ mil.	% of total
Waste Management of North America	3,643	60	779	64
Chemical Waste Management	1,147	19	278	23
Waste Management International	827	14	113	9
Wheelabrator Technologies, Inc.	417	7	45	4
Total	**6,034**	**100**	**1,215**	**100**

Waste Management of North America
Modulaire (mobile offices)
Port-O-Let (portable sanitation)
WMI Medical Services (medical refuse disposal)

Chemical Waste Management (76%)
Chem-Nuclear Systems (low-level radioactive material disposal)
ENRAC (site remediation)
The Brand Companies (56%, asbestos abatement)

Waste Management International (cleaning/waste services)

Wheelabrator Technologies (55%, waste to energy)

RANKINGS

17th in *Fortune* 100 Diversified Service Cos.
22nd in *Business Week* 1000

KEY COMPETITORS

Bechtel
Browning-Ferris
Consolidated Rail
CSX
Halliburton
JWP
Ogden
TRW
Union Pacific

HOW MUCH

	9-Year Growth	1981	1982	1983	1984	1985	1986	1987	1988	1989	1990
Sales ($ mil.)	25.7%	773	967	1,040	1,315	1,625	2,018	2,758	3,566	4,459	6,034
Net income ($ mil.)	26.7%	84	107	120	143	172	371	327	464	562	709
Income as % of sales	—	10.9%	11.0%	11.6%	10.8%	10.6%	18.4%	11.9%	13.0%	12.6%	11.8%
Earnings per share ($)	22.3%	0.24	0.30	0.31	0.37	0.43	0.88	0.73	1.03	1.22	1.49
Stock price – high ($)	—	5.14	6.97	7.73	5.98	9.50	14.94	24.25	21.38	35.88	45.50
Stock price – low ($)	—	3.24	3.19	4.69	3.41	5.42	8.63	13.88	15.75	20.38	28.63
Stock price – close ($)	26.5%	4.23	6.69	5.80	5.48	8.88	13.91	18.81	20.69	35.00	35.00
P/E – high	—	21	23	25	16	22	17	33	21	29	31
P/E – low	—	13	11	15	9	13	10	19	15	17	19
Dividends per share ($)	26.0%	0.04	0.06	0.08	0.10	0.11	0.14	0.18	0.23	0.29	0.35
Book value per share ($)	22.4%	1.22	1.76	2.00	2.27	2.79	3.67	4.19	4.82	5.88	7.52

1990 Year-end:
Debt ratio: 46.1%
Return on equity: 22.2%
Cash (mil.): $233
Current ratio: 0.99
Long-term debt (mil.): $3,140
No. of shares (mil.): 489
Dividends:
   1990 average yield: 1.0%
   1990 payout: 23.5%
Market value (mil.): $17,103

Stock Price History High/Low 1981–90

WELLS FARGO & COMPANY

OVERVIEW

San Francisco–based Wells Fargo had structured a secret deal in late 1990 to buy Security Pacific but backed away when its prospective partner reported worse-than-expected loan problems. BankAmerica and Security Pacific subsequently announced plans to merge and create a western US banking colossus, leading to rumors that Wells would buy First Interstate instead. So far Wells has resisted peer pressure to merge.

Before the urge to merge engulfed the banking industry, Wells was the nation's 10th largest bank holding company. Business is concentrated in California. Wells holds nearly no international loans and provides

international services through an agreement with Hongkong & Shanghai Bank. Wells Fargo Nikko Investment Advisors, 50%-owned, is the largest index fund manager. Wells's management is highly regarded by Warren Buffett, whose Berkshire Hathaway company owns 9.7% of Wells and has received Federal Reserve approval to up its stake to 22%.

A sluggish California economy and critical bank regulators are forcing Wells to make big additions to its bad loan reserves. Wells is relatively highly exposed in commercial and highly leveraged transaction loans, which represents 30% and 7% of the bank's loan portfolio, respectively.

NYSE symbol: WFC
Fiscal year ends: December 31

Hoover's Rating B-

WHO

Chairman and CEO: Carl E. Reichardt, age 59, $1,468,333 pay
President and COO: Paul Hazen, age 49, $1,081,667 pay
VC: William F. Zuendt, age 44, $753,333 pay
VC: Robert L. Joss, age 49, $750,000 pay
VC: David M. Petrone, age 46, $703,333 pay
VC: Clyde W. Ostler, age 44
VC and CFO: Rodney L. Jacobs, age 50
Director Personnel: Stephen A. Enna
Auditors: KPMG Peat Marwick
Employees: 21,800

WHEN

Henry Wells and William G. Fargo started Wells Fargo & Company as an express delivery service and banking operation in San Francisco in 1852, 2 years after they had started American Express. The company separated its banking business from the express business in 1905.

That same year Wells Fargo & Company Bank merged with Nevada National Bank. The new institution, Wells Fargo Nevada National Bank, grew under the leadership of President Isaias W. Hellman, a pioneer in California banking. The express business later ran the western leg of the Pony Express and stagecoach lines in the western US. It became part of American Railway Express in 1918 when the US nationalized the express industry.

In 1923 Wells Fargo Nevada National Bank merged with Union Trust Company to form Wells Fargo Bank & Union Trust Company. The bank maintained this form until it merged with American Trust Company, one of the oldest western banks, in 1960. The present name was adopted in 1962.

The bank added branch operations in the 1960s. Much of its growth was from acquisitions of smaller banks in California. When it formed a bank holding company in 1969,

Wells Fargo had more than 250 branches in the state, a total that would almost double to 452 by the end of 1988.

In 1970 Carl Reichardt and Paul Hazen joined the bank's real estate investment trust and in 1983 took over management of the bank. As CEO, Reichardt sold underperforming operations, cut costs, and made important acquisitions. He transformed the bank into a regional institution focused on basic banking and the middle market. The bank reorganized small loan operations to reduce costs and improve service at its branches.

The first major acquisition by Reichardt was Crocker National Bank (San Francisco, 1986), whose assets made Wells Fargo the 11th largest bank holding company in the US. Then Wells Fargo bought Bank of America's personal trust business (1987) and Barclays Bank of California (1988). By 1989 the bank was 2nd only to Citicorp in leveraged buyout loans and had eliminated loans to developing countries.

In 1990 Wells Fargo merged its investment advisory business with a unit of Japan's Nikko Securities and bought 4 small California banks and 92 branches of California's Great American Bank. The remaining branches were purchased in 1991.

WHERE

HQ: 420 Montgomery St., San Francisco, CA 94163
Phone: 415-477-1000
Fax: 415-362-6958

Wells Fargo operates in California.

	1990 Assets	
	$ mil.	% of total
US	56,156	100
Latin America	2	—
Other	41	—
Total	**56,199**	**100**

WHAT

	1990 Assets	
	$ mil.	% of total
Cash & due from banks	2,508	5
Investment securities	1,387	3
Loans	48,977	87
Loan loss allowance	(885)	(2)
Other	4,212	7
Total	**56,199**	**100**

Banking Groups
Branch Banking (consumer and small business)
Commercial Banking (middle market)
Corporate Banking (large corporations)
International Trade Services
Private Banking
Real Estate
Wells Fargo Nikko Investment Advisors (50%)
Wholesale Services (integrated cash management and other noncredit-related services)

RANKINGS

10th in *Fortune* 100 Commercial Banking Cos.
159th in *Business Week* 1000

KEY COMPETITORS

H. F. Ahmanson
BankAmerica
Citicorp
First Interstate
Great Western
Sumitomo
Other investment managers
Other major US banks

HOW MUCH

	9-Year Growth	1981	1982	1983	1984	1985	1986	1987	1988	1989	1990
Assets ($ mil.)	10.3%	23,219	24,814	27,018	28,184	29,429	44,577	44,183	46,617	48,737	56,199
Net income ($ mil.)	21.4%	124	139	155	169	190	274	51	513	601	712
Income as % of assets	—	0.5%	0.6%	0.6%	0.6%	0.6%	0.6%	0.1%	1.1%	1.2%	1.3%
Earnings per share ($)	19.6%	2.67	2.91	3.02	3.43	4.15	4.93	0.51	9.06	10.84	*13.39*
Stock price – high ($)	—	18.06	17.13	20.88	24.88	32.50	57.50	60.13	71.25	87.50	86.00
Stock price – low ($)	—	12.44	9.13	13.00	15.44	22.75	30.50	37.50	43.13	59.00	41.25
Stock price – close ($)	18.3%	12.75	13.44	19.81	23.56	31.69	50.75	43.00	60.38	74.13	57.88
P/E – high	—	7	6	7	7	8	12	118	8	8	6
P/E – low	—	5	3	4	5	5	6	74	5	5	3
Dividends per share ($)	16.9%	0.96	0.96	0.99	1.08	1.24	1.41	1.67	2.45	3.30	3.90
Book value per share ($)	11.7%	21.19	23.31	25.08	28.11	30.94	36.11	34.93	41.38	48.08	57.44

1990 Year-end:
Return on equity: 25.4%
Equity as % of assets: 6.0%
Cash (mil.): $2,508
Long-term debt (mil.): $2,417
No. of shares (mil.): 51
Dividends:
  1990 average yield: 6.7%
  1990 payout: 29.1%
Market value (mil.): $2,977
Sales (mil.): $5,960

Stock Price History High/Low 1981–90

WENDY'S INTERNATIONAL, INC.

NYSE symbol: WEN
Fiscal year ends: December 31

Hoover's Rating **C+**

OVERVIEW

Wendy's is the world's 3rd largest chain of quick-service hamburger restaurants (after McDonald's and Grand Metropolitan's Burger King), with 3,727 locations worldwide. The company's advertising stresses the quality of its food, including the facts that its hamburgers are cooked to order and are made from fresh, not frozen, meat. About 71% of all Wendy's restaurants are franchises; the remaining 29% are company owned.

Under Wendy's franchising system, owners locate, purchase, and build on company-approved property. Franchisees pay a $25,000 technical assistance fee, which covers the cost of training in Wendy's operational techniques, and royalties equal to 4% of gross sales. Franchisees also contribute 2% to national and 2% to local advertising. Wendy's does not sell fixtures, supplies, or food (with the exception of buns sold by its New Bakery of Ohio subsidiary to 1,521 restaurants) to its franchisees.

The company is 7.6% owned by founder R. David Thomas, who continues to star in a series of national TV advertisements.

WHO

Senior Chairman and Founder: R. David Thomas, age 58, $784,650 pay
Chairman and CEO: James W. Near, age 52, $727,402 pay (prior to promotion)
President and COO: Gordon F. Teter, age 47, $383,055 (prior to promotion)
VC and CFO: John K. Casey, age 58, $373,969 pay (prior to promotion)
SVP Human Resources: Kathleen McGinnis
Auditors: Coopers & Lybrand
Employees: 35,000

WHEN

R. David Thomas began his fast-food career in 1956 in a Knoxville, Tennessee, restaurant. According to a Harvard Business School study, it was Thomas who persuaded Colonel Harland Sanders to open a restaurant that sold only chicken. In 1962 Thomas moved to Columbus, Ohio, to revive 4 failing Kentucky Fried Chicken (KFC) restaurants owned by Sanders. His success was rewarded with a 45% interest in the 4 restaurants, which he sold back to KFC for $1.5 million in 1968.

Thomas traveled with and learned from Sanders while working as regional operations director for KFC. Thomas left the chicken business and, after helping found the Arthur Treacher's Fish & Chips chain, opened his first Wendy's restaurant in 1969, naming it after his 8-year-old daughter. Thomas limited the menu to cooked-to-order hamburgers, chili, and shakes, at prices slightly higher than rivals Burger King and McDonald's. The restaurants were decorated with carpeting, wood paneling, and tiffany-style lamps to reinforce the upscale theme.

In 1972 the company began franchising to accelerate national expansion and founded its Management Institute to train owners and managers in Wendy's operational techniques.

In 1977, with 520 units across the US and in Canada, Wendy's started advertising on national TV. The number of Wendy's outlets had risen to 1,407 by the end of 1978. That year's $800 million in sales ranked Wendy's 3rd, behind McDonald's and Burger King. In 1979 Wendy's expanded its menu to include a salad bar and opened its first restaurants in Puerto Rico, Switzerland, and West Germany. The company granted J. C. Penney the franchise rights to France, Belgium, and Holland, and in 1980 the first Wendy's in Belgium opened.

Thomas began competing with his old mentor Colonel Sanders with Sisters Chicken and Biscuit restaurants in 1981 but sold this subsidiary in 1987. Thomas retired as CEO in 1982. Wendy's launched an $8 million TV ad campaign featuring Clara Peller asking "Where's the beef?" in 1984, increasing market share to 12% in 1985. McDonald's and Burger King responded with aggressive advertising of their Big Mac and Whopper hamburgers. Wendy's introduced a breakfast menu (1985), but it was not well received; and the introduction of the Big Classic burger (1986) and SuperBar buffet (1987) did not reverse the erosion of Wendy's market share to 9% by 1987. A foundering 1987 ad campaign was canceled after only 7 weeks, and profits fell from a 1985 peak of $76 million to $24 million in 1989. Dave Thomas became Wendy's TV spokesman in a new series of ads in 1989.

Wendy's responded to growing concern about nutrition and health by introducing a grilled chicken sandwich in 1990. Its new Super Value Menu offers 7 products for $.99 each.

WHERE

HQ: PO Box 256, 4288 W. Dublin-Granville Rd., Dublin, OH 43017-0256
Phone: 614-764-3100
Fax: 614-764-3459

Wendy's and its franchisees operate restaurants in 49 states (Hawaii is the exception) and 23 foreign countries and territories.

	No. of Restaurants
California	206
Florida	254
Illinois	175
Michigan	169
Ohio	287
Texas	215
Other states	2,130
Canada	141
Other countries	150
Total	**3,727**

WHAT

	Restaurants	
	No.	% of total
Operated by the company	1,070	29
Operated by franchisees	2,657	71
Total	**3,727**	**100**

	1990 Sales	
	$ mil.	% of total
Company restaurants	922	92
Fees from franchised restaurants	80	8
Total	**1,002**	**100**

Products
Big Classic Burger
Biggie Drink and Fry Super Value items
Chicken Club sandwich
Chicken Cordon Bleu sandwich
Chicken Parmesan sandwich
Chili
Dave's Deluxe gourmet bacon cheeseburger
French fries
Frosty chocolate milkshake
Grilled Chicken sandwich
Kids' Meal
Stuffed baked potatoes
SuperBar hot-and-cold buffet
Wendy's Single and Double hamburgers

RANKINGS

580th in *Business Week* 1000

KEY COMPETITORS

Accor	Grand Metropolitan	Metromedia
Carlson	Imasco	PepsiCo
General Mills	McDonald's	TW Holdings

HOW MUCH

	9-Year Growth	1981	1982	1983	1984	1985	1986	1987	1988	1989	1990
Sales ($ mil.)	8.4%	487	604	715	939	1,100	1,103	1,051	1,046	1,051	1,002
Net income ($ mil.)	0.5%	37	44	55	69	76	(5)	3	29	24	39
Income as % of sales	—	7.6%	7.3%	7.7%	7.3%	6.9%	(0.4%)	0.3%	2.7%	2.3%	3.9%
Earnings per share ($)	(1.4%)	0.46	0.51	0.61	0.75	0.82	(0.03)	0.31	0.26	0.26	0.40
Stock price – high ($)	—	5.81	7.54	9.90	12.30	15.30	17.80	13.25	8.00	7.00	7.50
Stock price – low ($)	—	3.10	3.68	5.85	7.88	9.98	10.00	4.13	5.13	4.50	3.88
Stock price – close ($)	4.4%	4.24	6.58	9.39	9.98	13.40	10.25	5.63	5.75	4.63	6.25
P/E – high	—	13	15	16	16	19	—	265	26	27	19
P/E – low	—	7	7	10	11	12	—	83	17	17	10
Dividends per share ($)	12.4%	0.08	0.09	0.12	0.15	0.17	0.21	0.24	0.24	0.24	0.24
Book value per share ($)	7.7%	2.37	2.92	3.40	3.98	4.65	4.45	4.29	4.36	4.45	4.61

1990 Year-end:
Debt ratio: 27.3%
Return on equity: 8.8%
Cash (mil.): $55
Current ratio: 0.90
Long-term debt (mil.): $168
No. of shares (mil.): 97
Dividends:
  1990 average yield: 3.8%
  1990 payout: 60.0%
Market value (mil.): $605

Stock Price History High/Low 1981–90

WESTINGHOUSE ELECTRIC CORPORATION

NYSE symbol: WX
Fiscal year ends: December 31

Hoover's Rating: C-

OVERVIEW

Westinghouse Electric is a diversified international company with 7 major operating groups: Broadcasting, Electronic Systems, Environmental Systems, Financial Services, Industries, The Knoll Group, and Power Systems.

Westinghouse Broadcasting (Group W) owns and operates 5 TV stations and 20 radio stations. Westinghouse Electronics Systems is a world leader in the production of advanced electronic systems for the DOD, FAA, and NASA.

The company's Environmental Systems includes operations involved in the treatment and disposal of radioactive, hazardous and toxic, and municipal waste. Under contract with DOE the company operates 6 government-owned facilities, including nuclear weapons plants.

Westinghouse Financial Services provides a wide range of financial services, including real estate and commercial lending.

The Industries group includes 4 business units: Thermo King, Distribution and Control, Electric Supply, and Communities (land development). In 1990 Westinghouse acquired Knoll International, an office furniture maker, combined it with its furniture business, and established The Knoll Group.

The company's Power Systems segment builds power-generation equipment (combustion turbine and nuclear). Westinghouse shares a $200-million contract with General Dynamics for work on superconducting magnets for the Super Collider.

WHO

Chairman and CEO: Paul E. Lego, age 60, $1,681,252 pay
EVP Finance: Warren H. Hollinshead, age 55
EVP Human Resources: George C. Dorman, age 61
EVP: Theodore Stern, age 61, $820,826 pay
Auditors: Price Waterhouse
Employees: 116,000

WHERE

HQ: Westinghouse Bldg., Gateway Center, Pittsburgh, PA 15222
Phone: 412-244-2000
Fax: 412-642-3404

Westinghouse has operations all over the world.

	1990 Sales		1990 Operating Income	
	$ mil.	% of total	$ mil.	% of total
US	11,359	88	389	78
Foreign	1,556	12	113	22
Adjustments	—	—	778	—
Total	**12,915**	**100**	**1,280**	**100**

WHEN

George Westinghouse, inventor of the train air brake, founded Westinghouse Electric in Pittsburgh in 1886. He entered the newly developing electric industry after having devised a method for transmitting electric current over long distances. The success of his system was due to his choice of using alternating current (AC) as opposed to the direct current (DC) favored by Thomas Edison. He paid Nikola Tesla, an eccentric Croatian inventor, $1 million for his AC patents and installed the first AC power system in Telluride, Colorado, in 1891. One of the company's early successes was powering the 1893 Chicago World's Fair. In 1896 Westinghouse and rival General Electric formed a patent pool that allowed the 2 companies to continue further development of electrical generation and distribution technology without the threat of being sued by the other for patent infringement.

Westinghouse expanded into manufacturing electrical products — from light bulbs (1890s) to radios (1920) to major appliances — as well as into building nuclear reactors for ship propulsion. In 1920 the company set up KDKA, the nation's first radio broadcasting station, in East Pittsburgh.

Westinghouse, which concentrated on the market for huge turbines and generators, got a late start in the post-WWII home appliances market — and consequently was 2nd to GE.

In the mid-1970s, Westinghouse lost a large part of its main business (utility generators) to GE when its turbine generators were found defective. And after years as an also-ran, Westinghouse sold its appliance business to White Consolidated in 1975.

The 1980s was a period of restructuring for Westinghouse. It dropped its unprofitable businesses (sold 70 businesses between 1985 and 1987), acquired complementary ones, and entered into a series of joint ventures with foreign companies (Mitsubishi Electric, Siemens, Asea Brown Boveri, and AEG).

Following a 1990 4th-quarter write-off of $975 million for bad real-estate and commercial loans made through its credit corporation, Westinghouse placed $3.2 billion of its problem loans and properties up for sale and froze much of its new lending.

WHAT

	1990 Sales		1990 Operating Income	
	$ mil.	% of total	$ mil.	% of total
Broadcasting	858	7	186	—
Electronic Systems	3,196	24	329	—
Environmental Systems	1,347	10	154	—
Financial Services	1,209	9	(844)	—
Industries	3,442	26	342	—
The Knoll Group	422	3	28	—
Power Systems	2,442	19	323	—
Divested & other	310	2	(16)	—
Adjustments	(311)	—	778	—
Total	**12,915**	**100**	**1,280**	**—**

Major Subsidiaries
The Knoll Group (office furniture)
Longines-Wittnauer Watch Co.
Thermo King Corp. (refrigeration transport systems)
Westinghouse Broadcasting Co. (Group W)
Westinghouse Communications Resources, Inc., (telecommunications)
Westinghouse Electric Supply Co. (WESCO)
Westinghouse Environmental and Geotechnical Services, Inc.

Westinghouse Financial Services

Other Activities
Electricity generation plants
Electronic systems for military, commercial, and space applications
Nuclear and fossil steam turbines and generators
Nuclear-waste management
Hazardous- and industrial-waste management
Waste-to-energy projects

RANKINGS

33rd in *Fortune* 500 Industrial Cos.
67th in *Business Week* 1000

KEY COMPETITORS

Broadcasting companies
Defense-electronics contractors
Financial-service companies
Office-furniture manufacturers
Power-equipment companies
Waste-management companies

HOW MUCH

	9-Year Growth	1981	1982	1983	1984	1985	1986	1987	1988	1989	1990
Sales ($ mil.)	3.6%	9,368	9,745	9,533	10,265	10,700	10,731	10,679	12,500	12,844	12,915
Net income ($ mil.)	(5.3%)	438	449	449	536	605	671	739	823	922	268
Income as % of sales	—	4.7%	4.6%	4.7%	5.2%	5.7%	6.3%	6.9%	6.6%	7.2%	2.1%
Earnings per share ($)	(3.7%)	1.28	1.29	1.27	1.51	1.73	2.16	2.52	2.78	3.11	0.91
Stock price – high ($)	—	8.63	10.13	14.09	14.19	23.38	31.25	37.50	28.69	38.13	39.38
Stock price – low ($)	—	5.75	5.47	9.31	9.88	12.69	21.00	20.00	22.81	25.63	24.25
Stock price – close ($)	18.1%	6.38	9.72	13.69	13.06	22.25	27.88	24.88	26.31	37.00	28.50
P/E – high	—	7	8	11	9	14	15	15	10	12	43
P/E – low	—	5	4	7	7	7	10	8	8	8	27
Dividends per share ($)	13.0%	0.45	0.45	0.45	0.49	0.58	0.68	0.82	0.97	1.15	1.35
Book value per share ($)	5.5%	8.27	9.08	9.74	10.70	10.52	10.56	12.46	13.18	15.10	13.43

1990 Year-end:
Debt ratio: 61.0%
Return on equity: 6.4%
Cash (mil.): $1,523
Current ratio: —
Long-term debt (mil.): $6,091
No. of shares (mil.): 290
Dividends:
  1990 average yield: 4.7%
  1990 payout: 148.4%
Market value (mil.): $8,268

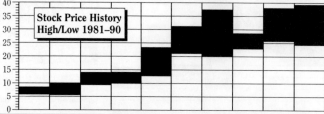

Stock Price History High/Low 1981–90

WEYERHAEUSER COMPANY

NYSE symbol: WY
Fiscal year ends: December 30

Hoover's Rating **C**

OVERVIEW

The world's 4th largest forest products company, Weyerhaeuser is the world leader in softwood lumber production, the world's #3 producer of containerboard, and a major exporter of newsprint to the Pacific Rim. Other wood-based products produced by the company include plywood, pulp, and fine papers. Weyerhaeuser (through Weyerhaeuser Real Estate) builds homes, apartments, and commercial buildings for resale. Its GNA Corporation is licensed to offer financial services in 47 states and the District of Columbia.

Weyerhaeuser is considered one of the most environmentally responsible of the major forest products companies. It is a pioneer in the reforestation of harvested timberlands. In 1991 the company plans to increase its paper recycling capacity by 42% to 3.4 billion pounds of paper a year. Weyerhaeuser has long been considered a paternalistic employer and recently stopped shipping raw timber to mills in Japan to relieve unemployment at its own Oregon sawmills.

WHO

Chairman: George H. Weyerhaeuser, age 65, $1,106,860 pay
President and COO: John W. Creighton, Jr., age 58, $652,910 pay
SVP and CFO: William C. Stivers, age 52
SVP Human Resources: Steven R. Hill, age 43
Auditors: Arthur Andersen & Co.
Employees: 40,621

WHEN

Frederick Weyerhaeuser, a 24-year-old German immigrant, bought his first lumberyard (in Illinois) in 1858. He went on to participate in several joint logging ventures, particularly in Illinois, Wisconsin, and Minnesota. In 1900 he and 15 partners bought 900,000 timbered acres near Tacoma, Washington, from the Northern Pacific Railway. The venture was named Weyerhaeuser Timber Company.

During the Great Depression the company recouped losses in the deflated lumber market through the sale of wood pulp. Frederick's grandson J. P. "Phil" Weyerhaeuser, Jr. took over as CEO in 1933. Phil championed the reforestation of harvested timberlands, proposing a visionary program to replant and manage cutover timberlands in Grays Harbor County, Washington, dubbed Clemons Tree Farm (America's first tree farm) and dedicated in 1941.

Diversification into the production of containerboard (1949), particleboard (1955), paper (1956), and other products led the company to drop the word "timber" from its name in 1959. In 1963, under Norton Clapp (president 1960–66), grandson of one of the company's original investors, Weyerhaeuser went public and opened its first overseas office, in Tokyo.

In the 1970s, under George Weyerhaeuser (Phil's son), the company again diversified,

this time to insulate itself from the cyclical nature of the forest products industry, and ended up with a mishmash of businesses and products, from private-label disposable diapers to pet supplies. The company got into the garden supply business in 1976 by buying Hines Wholesale Nurseries.

The eruption of Mount St. Helens in 1980 killed 68,000 acres of Weyerhaeuser timber. The costs of this disaster and the soft US lumber market combined to depress the company's earnings through 1982. To cut costs Weyerhaeuser reduced its salaried work force by 25% during this period. In 1983 the company bought GNA Corporation, which sells annuities through financial institutions. The following year Weyerhaeuser opened an office in Beijing to take advantage of the growing Chinese wood and paper products market.

Under John Creighton, president since 1988, Weyerhaeuser developed a new business strategy. Creighton has refocused the company on forest products while putting less successful ventures up for sale, including its milk carton plant (1989), a hardwood plant (1989) and a gypsum board plant (1989). As part of its restructuring, the company took a $497 million pretax charge against 1989 earnings. Earnings dropped again in 1990, when Weyerhaeuser's wood products businesses starting feeling the effects of the US economic downturn.

WHERE

HQ: Tacoma, WA 98477
Phone: 206-924-2345
Fax: 206-924-7407

Owned or Leased Timberland	Acres (thou.)
Washington	1,544
Oregon	1,259
Alabama, Arkansas, Mississippi, North Carolina & Oklahoma	2,924
Canada	13,520
Total	**19,247**

	1990 Sales	
	$ mil.	% of total
US	8,126	90
Other countries	898	10
Total	**9,024**	**100**

WHAT

	1990 Sales		1990 Operating Income	
	$ mil.	% of total	$ mil.	% of total
Forest products	3,152	35	312	42
Pulp & paper	3,931	43	468	62
Diversified business	232	3	—	—
Real estate	811	9	35	5
Financial services	808	9	47	6
Corporate & other	90	1	(112)	(15)
Adjustments	—	—	253	—
Total	**9,024**	**100**	**1,003**	**100**

Forest Products
Doors
Fiber-based specialty products
Hardwood and softwood lumber and logs
Particleboard
Plywood and veneer

Pulp and Paper Products and Services
Coated and uncoated papers
Containerboard packaging
Disposable diapers
Newsprint
Pulp
Waste-paper recycling

Diversified Businesses
Nursery and garden supplies

Real Estate
Builds and develops commercial and residential properties in 15 states

Financial Services
GNA Corporation
Republic Federal Savings and Loan Association (California)
Weyerhaeuser Mortgage

RANKINGS

54th in *Fortune* 500 Industrial Cos.
141st in *Business Week* 1000

KEY COMPETITORS

Boise Cascade
Champion International
Fletcher Challenge
Georgia-Pacific
Gerber
International Paper
James River
Kimberly-Clark
Manville
Mead
Procter & Gamble
Scott

HOW MUCH

	9-Year Growth	1981	1982	1983	1984	1985	1986	1987	1988	1989	1990
Sales ($ mil.)	8.0%	4,502	4,186	4,883	5,550	5,206	5,652	6,990	10,004	10,106	9,024
Net income ($ mil.)	5.9%	234	140	205	226	200	277	447	564	341	394
Income as % of sales	—	5.2%	3.3%	4.2%	4.1%	3.8%	4.9%	6.4%	5.6%	3.4%	4.4%
Earnings per share ($)	5.9%	1.11	0.60	0.91	1.01	0.88	1.27	2.12	2.68	1.62	1.87
Stock price – high ($)	—	27.17	26.17	27.83	23.67	22.67	27.50	40.00	29.50	32.75	28.38
Stock price – low ($)	—	16.08	15.00	20.75	16.67	16.50	19.75	19.92	23.17	24.50	17.38
Stock price – close ($)	1.4%	19.33	24.00	22.50	19.42	20.50	25.17	25.83	25.13	27.63	21.88
P/E – high	—	24	44	31	23	26	22	19	11	21	15
P/E – low	—	14	25	23	16	19	16	9	9	16	9
Dividends per share ($)	3.7%	0.87	0.87	0.87	0.87	0.87	0.87	0.90	1.15	1.20	1.20
Book value per share ($)	1.9%	16.20	16.08	16.28	16.33	17.02	16.59	18.24	19.84	20.24	19.21

1990 Year-end:
Debt ratio: 57.4%
Return on equity: 9.5%
Cash (mil.): $215
Current ratio: 1.8
Long-term debt (mil.): $5,209
No. of shares (mil.): 201
Dividends:
1990 average yield: 5.5%
1990 payout: 64.2%
Market value (mil.): $4,400

Stock Price History
High/Low 1981–90

WHIRLPOOL CORPORATION

NYSE symbol: WHR
Fiscal year ends: December 31

Hoover's Rating **C+**

OVERVIEW

Whirlpool claims to be the largest white-goods manufacturer and marketer in the world and sells major home appliances under the Whirlpool, KitchenAid, Roper, and Estate names in the US. The company also supplies Sears with appliances sold under the Kenmore and Capri brand names; Sears accounted for 20% of sales in 1990. Whirlpool is consolidating its refrigerator business, and US sales remain soft.

Whirlpool has aggressively globalized in recent years. Wholly owned Whirlpool International, formerly the appliance business of Dutch electronics giant Philips, has a strong market position in Europe. The dual-branding of some of the company's products as Philips-Whirlpool is intended to increase recognition of the Whirlpool name in new markets. The Philips name will be phased out in the future. The company is restructuring the inefficient unit.

Whirlpool's affiliates in Brazil, India, and Mexico have begun producing a "world washer" for developing countries. The washer was designed to accommodate variations in component availability and local tastes.

Profits were hit in 1990 by the US recession, hyperinflation in Brazil, and a restructuring charge.

WHO

Chairman, President, and CEO: David R. Whitwam, age 48, $996,250 pay
EVP and CFO: James R. Samartini, age 55, $411,733 pay
EVP: William D. Marohn, age 50, $426,000 pay
VP Human Resources and Asst. Secretary: E. R. (Ed) Dunn
Auditors: Ernst & Young
Employees: 36,157

WHERE

HQ: 2000 M-63, Benton Harbor, MI 49022-2692
Phone: 616-926-5000
Fax: 616-926-3568

Whirlpool sells products in over 45 countries.

	1990 Sales		1990 Operating Income	
	$ mil.	% of total	$ mil.	% of total
North America	4,175	63	271	78
Europe	2,456	37	75	22
Adjustments	(8)	—	103	—
Total	**6,623**	**100**	**449**	**100**

WHEN

The Upton Machine Company was founded in St. Joseph, Michigan, in 1911 by brothers Fred and Lou Upton and their uncle, Emory Upton. The company made hand-operated washing machines. In 1916 Sears, Roebuck began buying washing machines from the Uptons, and by 1925 the company was supplying all of Sears's washers. The Uptons combined their company with the Nineteen Hundred Washer Company in 1929 to form the Nineteen Hundred Corporation, the world's largest washing machine company. Sears and Nineteen Hundred continued to prosper through the Great Depression. During the WWII years Nineteen Hundred's factories produced products for the war effort. Sears was still Nineteen Hundred's principal customer in 1947 when the company decided to market a washing machine under the brand name Whirlpool. The new machine was a success, and the company adopted its current name in 1950.

During the 1950s and 1960s Whirlpool became a full-line appliance manufacturer while continuing as Sears's principal Kenmore appliance supplier. The company bought Seeger Refrigerator Company and the stove and air conditioning interests of RCA (1955); the gas refrigeration and ice-maker manufacturing facilities of Servel (1958); a majority interest in Heil-Quaker, makers of central heaters and space heaters (1964); Sears's major television set supplier, Warwick Electronics (1966); and 33% of Canadian appliance manufacturer/distributor John Inglis Company (1969). The company entered into an agreement with Sony in 1973 to distribute Whirlpool brand products in Japan. Whirlpool sold its television manufacturing business to Sanyo of Japan in 1976.

Between 1981 and 1990, in a static US market, Whirlpool net sales nearly tripled from $2.4 billion to $6.6 billion. In 1986 Whirlpool bought top-end appliance manufacturer KitchenAid from Dart and Kraft, kitchen cabinet maker St. Charles Manufacturing, and 65% of Italian cooling compressor manufacturer Aspera. Also in 1986 it sold its Heil-Quaker central heating business for $156 million to Inter City Gas and closed much of its original St. Joseph, Michigan, manufacturing facility. The company increased its ownership of Inglis to 70% in 1987 and to 100% in 1990. In 1989 Whirlpool sold its kitchen cabinet interests and formed Whirlpool International with Philips.

In 1990 Whirlpool bought the rest of its Aspera subsidiaries and formed a US vacuum cleaner joint venture with Matsushita. In 1991 Whirlpool bought Philips's share of Whirlpool International.

WHAT

	1990 Sales		1990 Operating Income	
	$ mil.	% of total	$ mil.	% of total
Major home apps.	6,434	97	286	87
Financial services	189	3	43	13
Adjustments	—	—	120	—
Total	**6,623**	**100**	**449**	**100**

	1990 Sales	
	$ mil.	% of total
Home laundry appliances	2,223	34
Home refrigeration equipment	2,212	33
Other home appliances	1,999	30
Financial services	189	3
Total	**6,623**	**100**

	1990 Sales	
	$ mil.	% of total
Whirlpool International	2,156	33
Whirlpool Appliance	1,834	28
Kenmore Appliance	1,078	16
KitchenAid Appliance	420	6
Inglis	335	5
Whirlpool Overseas	220	3
Whirlpool Financial	218	3
Other	362	6
Total	**6,623**	**100**

Appliance Brands

US	Canada	Other countries
Estate	Admiral	Bauknecht
KitchenAid	Inglis	Ignis
Roper	KitchenAid	Laden
Whirlpool	Whirlpool	Philips-Whirlpool
	Speed Queen	

RANKINGS

72nd in *Fortune* 500 Industrial Cos.
340th in *Business Week* 1000

KEY COMPETITORS

Amway	General Electric	Raytheon
Berkshire Hathaway	Hitachi	Robert Bosch
Black & Decker	Masco	Siemens
Electrolux	Maytag	Toshiba
GEC		

HOW MUCH

	9-Year Growth	1981	1982	1983	1984	1985	1986	1987	1988	1989	1990
Sales ($ mil.)	11.7%	2,437	2,271	2,668	3,137	3,474	4,009	4,179	4,421	6,289	6,623
Net income ($ mil.)	(6.8%)	135	136	163	190	182	200	181	161	187	72
Income as % of sales	—	5.6%	6.0%	6.1%	6.0%	5.2%	5.0%	4.3%	3.6%	3.0%	1.1%
Earnings per share ($)	(6.3%)	1.87	1.88	2.24	2.59	2.49	2.70	2.53	2.33	2.70	1.04
Stock price – high ($)	—	15.25	23.75	28.50	25.00	25.38	41.50	40.88	29.88	33.25	33.50
Stock price – low ($)	—	9.44	11.50	20.13	18.25	20.25	24.25	20.25	23.50	24.25	17.50
Stock price – close ($)	7.1%	12.69	21.88	24.25	23.25	24.69	33.88	24.38	24.75	33.00	23.50
P/E – high	—	8	13	13	10	10	15	16	13	12	32
P/E – low	—	5	6	9	7	8	9	8	10	9	17
Dividends per share ($)	3.6%	0.80	0.83	0.93	1.00	1.00	1.03	1.10	1.10	1.10	1.10
Book value per share ($)	7.2%	10.92	12.01	13.38	14.97	16.46	18.21	18.83	19.06	20.49	20.50

1990 Year-end:
Debt ratio: 38.0%
Return on equity: 5.1%
Cash (mil.): $80
Current ratio: 1.09
Long-term debt (mil.): $874
No. of shares (mil.): 69
Dividends:
 1990 average yield: 4.7%
 1990 payout: 105.8%
Market value (mil.): $1,632

Stock Price History High/Low 1981–90

WHITMAN CORPORATION

NYSE symbol: WH
Fiscal year ends: December 31

Hoover's Rating **D**

OVERVIEW

Chicago-based Whitman is a diversified consumer products and services company with operations in 3 primary areas: Pepsi-Cola bottling (Pepsi-Cola General), auto service shops (Midas), and refrigeration equipment (Hussmann). Until recently Whitman was a major food concern as well. In 1991 the company spun off its food segment (Pet) to shareholders, losing such brands as Old El Paso (Mexican foods), Progresso (Italian foods), and the familiar chocolate for which Whitman was named.

Pepsi-Cola General bottles Pepsi in 12 midwestern and southeastern states, and accounts for 12% of Pepsi sales in the US.

Midas International operates a chain of 2,410 auto shops worldwide, making it the global leader in automotive service franchises. Midas recently increased its presence in Europe through the purchase of 39 shops from the Carex muffler chain.

Hussmann is the market leader in refrigeration and display systems for food stores in the US and several foreign countries.

WHO

Chairman and CEO: James W. Cozad, age 64, $975,000 pay
EVP: Bruce S. Chelberg, age 56, $577,500 pay
EVP Finance: John P. Fagan, age 60, $456,666 pay
SVP Human Resources and Administration: Ronald A. Wright
Auditors: KPMG Peat Marwick
Employees: 15,129

WHEN

Whitman Corporation is a very different business from its grandparent company, the Illinois Central Railroad. Started in 1851 with a 3.6 million-acre land grant, Illinois Central became one of the nation's 10 largest rail systems. In 1901, its 50th year, it boasted 4,200 rail miles, a $32 million income, and freight and passenger service in 13 states. Its famous passenger trains included the Green Diamond (Chicago to St. Louis) and the Diamond Special and City of New Orleans (Chicago to New Orleans). Passenger service, no longer profitable, was sold to Amtrak in 1971. In 1972 the company (renamed Illinois Central Industries in 1962) acquired the Gulf, Mobile and Ohio Railroad (Chicago to Mobile), and the railroad was renamed Illinois Central Gulf (ICG).

The company maintained its focus on railroads until William Johnson, former president of Railway Express Agency, became president in 1966. Johnson served as president for 21 years and guided its transformation to a multinational conglomerate that was renamed IC Industries in 1975. IC bought numerous companies, including: Pepsi-Cola General Bottlers (1970); Midas International auto muffler shops (1972); and the venerable St. Louis company, Pet Inc. (for $406 million in 1978). Pet began in 1885 as an evaporated milk company and had made substantial diverse purchases of its own, including Hussmann Refrigeration, a leading producer of refrigera-

tion systems for grocery stores; Downyflake Foods; Stuckey roadside candy stores; and the Philadelphia chocolate company, Stuart F. Whitman and Son.

By the late 1970s the ICG railroad provided only 1% of the company's pretax profits. IC was determined to sell it, but it wasn't until 1989 that IC spun off ICG to its stockholders. In the interim, IC sold many of its real estate holdings and ICG's trackage shrank by 2/3. A private concern, Prospect Group, bought the railroad within a month of the spin-off.

The company changed its name in 1988 to Whitman Corporation (after Pet's well-known chocolate brand) to reflect its concentration on consumer goods and services. Since 1979 Whitman has sold 65 companies, including its Pneumo Abex aerospace operations (for $1.2 billion, 1988). In the same time period, Whitman has bought 98 companies, including Orval Kent refrigerated salad products (1988) and Van de Kamp's Frozen Seafoods (1989), which were marketed by Pet. In 1989 Whitman announced plans to sell Hussmann but, lacking an acceptable offer, decided in 1990 to keep the unit.

In an attempt to restructure, the company spun off its Pet food unit to shareholders, and pared jobs to reduce debt. The newly focused company expanded its operations in the early 1990s with the purchase of 39 European muffler shops and 3 Pepsi franchises.

WHERE

HQ: III Crossroads of Commerce, 3501 Algonquin Rd., Rolling Meadows, IL 60006
Phone: 708-818-5000
Fax: 708-818-5045 (Corporate Affairs)

Whitman's Pepsi bottling operations are located in 12 midwestern and southeastern states. Midas has 1,763 shops in the US and 647 overseas. Hussmann operates 21 facilities in 5 countries.

	Midas Shops
US	1,763
Canada	242
Europe	266
Australia	129
Other	10
Total	**2,410**

	1990 Sales		1990 Operating Income	
	$ mil.	% of total	$ mil.	% of total
US	1,908	82	222	94
Foreign	408	18	15	6
Adjustments	(11)	—	(5)	—
Total	**2,305**	**100**	**232**	**100**

WHAT

	1990 Sales		1990 Operating Income	
	$ mil.	% of total	$ mil.	% of total
Automotive services	477	21	70	30
Soft drinks	1,041	45	131	55
Refrigeration prods.	787	34	37	15
Adjustments	—	—	(6)	—
Total	**2,305**	**100**	**232**	**100**

Pepsi-Cola General Bottlers, Inc. (soft drink bottling in the midwestern US)
Canada Dry
Dad's Root Beer
Dr Pepper
Hawaiian Punch
Pepsi-Cola
7-Up

Midas International Corp.
Auto service shops

Hussmann Corp.
Condensers
Custom wood products
Customized air conditioning and ventilating equipment
Energy management devices
Evaporators
Refrigerated display cases
Refrigeration systems
Storage coolers

RANKINGS

117th in *Fortune* 500 Industrial Cos.
272nd in *Business Week* 1000

KEY COMPETITORS

American Standard
Bridgestone
Coca-Cola
Dr Pepper/Seven-Up
Electrolux
Goodyear
United Technologies

HOW MUCH

	9-Year Growth	1981	1982	1983	1984	1985	1986	1987	1988	1989	1990
Sales ($ mil.)	(6.4%)	4,195	3,868	3,734	4,234	4,405	4,222	4,027	3,583	3,986	2,305
Net income ($ mil.)	—	134	68	95	133	154	(56)	249	177	228	(31)
Income as % of sales	—	3.2%	1.8%	2.5%	3.1%	3.5%	(1.3%)	6.2%	4.9%	5.7%	(1.4%)
Earnings per share ($)	—	1.38	0.80	1.10	1.46	1.42	(0.51)	2.20	1.66	1.87	(0.68)
Stock price – high ($)	—	10.28	9.06	12.25	14.38	20.31	30.38	41.25	37.25	38.25	29.75
Stock price – low ($)	—	7.13	6.16	8.75	10.50	13.44	17.81	22.38	29.63	27.50	17.00
Stock price – close ($)	8.3%	8.75	8.75	11.94	14.38	19.19	23.00	32.88	35.75	28.75	18.00
P/E – high	—	7	11	11	10	14	—	19	22	20	—
P/E – low	—	5	8	8	7	9	—	10	18	15	—
Dividends per share ($)	7.7%	0.54	0.57	0.59	0.64	0.70	0.78	0.86	0.94	1.01	1.05
Book value per share ($)	(17.4%)	19.52	19.72	17.59	16.13	15.99	13.61	14.67	8.44	3.85	3.47

1990 Year-end:
Debt ratio: 65.8%
Return on equity: —
Cash (mil.): $80
Current ratio: 1.96
Long-term debt (mil.): $1,643
No. of shares (mil.): 103
Dividends:
  1990 average yield: 5.8%
  1990 payout: —
Market value (mil.): $1,854

Stock Price History
High/Low 1981–90

WINN-DIXIE STORES, INC.

OVERVIEW

Winn-Dixie operates over 1,200 supermarkets in 13 states in the southern US and in the Bahama Islands, making it the 5th largest supermarket operator in the US and the largest food retailer in the Sunbelt in 1990. The company has 16 food distribution centers and 22 plants for producing and processing dairy products, coffee, tea, spices, and detergents.

Winn-Dixie has successfully resisted unionization. About half of the company's full-time employees participate in its employee stock-option plan, through which they had purchased about $35 million worth of stock at a discount by the end of 1990.

Winn-Dixie has increased its stock dividend for 47 consecutive years — an NYSE record. With no long-term debt other than leases, the company is in good financial health. Two sons and 3 grandsons of founder William Davis sit on the company's board of directors, and the Davis family still controls about 39% of the company's outstanding stock.

WHEN

In 1925 William Davis borrowed $10,000 to open a cash-and-carry grocery in Lemon City near Miami. After a slow start Davis expanded his chain of Table Supply Stores to 34 by the time of his death in 1934, when his 4 sons took control. In 1939 they purchased control of Winn & Lovett Grocery Company, which operated 78 stores in Florida and Georgia. Winn & Lovett, incorporated in 1928, was a leader in the 1930s in building new "supermarket" type stores. In 1944 the company headquartered in Jacksonville and became Winn & Lovett.

After WWII the company, still controlled by the Davis family, acquired grocery chains throughout the South, including the Steiden Stores in Kentucky, Margaret Ann Stores in Florida, Wylie Company Stores in Alabama, Penney Stores in Mississippi, King Stores in Georgia, and the Eden and Ballentine Stores in South Carolina. In 1955 the company consolidated with Dixie Home Stores of the Carolinas and changed its name to Winn-Dixie Stores, Inc. During the 1950s and early 1960s, Winn-Dixie continued to expand by acquisitions, adding the Ketner and Milner Stores in the Carolinas and the Hill Stores of Louisiana and Alabama.

By 1966 the company controlled so much of the grocery business in the South that, for antitrust reasons, the FTC imposed a 10-year moratorium on its buying stores. The company responded by buying 9 stores outside the US, in Nassau and Freeport in the Bahama Islands. At the end of the moratorium in 1976, the company bought Kimbell of Texas, adding stores and extensive support facilities in Texas, Oklahoma, and New Mexico. Winn-Dixie refused to deal with the workers' union in New Mexico. When a pro-union boycott was organized in 1979, the company sold its 23 stores there. The company had expanded to 1,271 stores by 1987; however, by 1990 it had closed smaller, less productive stores, decreasing the total number of stores to 1,217.

Winn-Dixie is moving toward the one-stop-shopping concept by expanding store size, products, and services. The total square footage for all stores increased by 500,000 square feet to 37 million. The company's 1990 sales and profits increased 6.5% and 13.4%, respectively. Winn-Dixie continues expanding its everyday-low-price marketing. This approach lowers gross margins but raises sales per store and spreads corporate overhead across a larger sales base. At the end of 1990, 9 of its 12 geographic divisions were using this marketing tool; by 1993 all are expected to be. The company attributes to this approach its 5.2% improvement in 1990 (over the previous year) in same-store sales growth.

Continued emphasis in 1991 on expanding the retail automation program is designed to reduce costs and improve efficiency, resulting in lower food prices to customers.

NYSE symbol: WIN
Fiscal year ends: Last Wednesday in June

Hoover's Rating **A-**

WHO

Chairman and Principal Executive Officer:
A. Dano Davis, age 46, $600,866 pay
VC: Robert D. Davis, age 59, $292,000 pay
President: James Kufeldt, age 53, $598,701 pay
EVP: Charles H. McKellar, age 53, $494,023 pay
Human Resources: Larry H. May, age 46
Auditors: KPMG Peat Marwick
Employees: 101,000

WHERE

HQ: PO Box B, 5050 Edgewood Ct., Jacksonville, FL 32203
Phone: 904-783-5000
Fax: 904-783-5294

Winn-Dixie operates primarily in the southern US.

	No. of Stores
Alabama	89
Florida	474
Georgia	125
Indiana	4
Kentucky	46
Louisiana	86
Mississippi	19
North Carolina	144
Oklahoma	7
South Carolina	88
Tennessee	22
Texas	78
Virginia	35
Total	**1,217**

WHAT

Subsidiaries	
Astor Products	Winn-Dixie Louisville
Crackin' Good Bakers	Winn-Dixie Montgomery
Deep South Products	Winn-Dixie Raleigh
Dixie Packers	Winn-Dixie Texas
Fairway Food Stores Co.	
First Northern Supply	**Winn-Dixie produces or**
Monterey Canning	**processes its own:**
Save Rite Foods	Carbonated beverages
Second Northern Supply	Cheese
Sunbelt Products	Coffee and tea
Superbrand Dairy Products	Eggs
Superior Food	Frozen pizza
Third Northern Supply	Ice cream
W-D (Bahamas)	Jams and jellies
Bahamas Supermarkets	Margarine
The City Meat Markets	Mayonnaise
Winn-Dixie Atlanta	Meats
Winn-Dixie Charlotte	Milk
Winn-Dixie Greenville	Paper bags and boxes
Winn-Dixie Louisiana	Peanut butter
	Salad dressing

RANKINGS

12th in *Fortune* 50 Retailing Cos.
229th in *Business Week* 1000

KEY COMPETITORS

Albertson's
American Stores
Bruno's
Food Lion
Great A&P
Kroger
Publix
Safeway

HOW MUCH

	9-Year Growth	1981	1982	1983	1984	1985	1986	1987	1988	1989	1990
Sales ($ mil.)	5.2%	6,200	6,764	7,019	7,302	7,774	8,225	8,804	9,008	9,151	9,745
Net income ($ mil.)	5.4%	95	104	113	116	108	116	112	117	135	153
Income as % of sales	—	1.5%	1.5%	1.6%	1.6%	1.4%	1.4%	1.3%	1.3%	1.5%	1.6%
Earnings per share ($)	6.5%	1.10	1.25	1.36	1.42	1.32	1.42	1.36	1.44	1.68	1.93
Stock price – high ($)	—	11.18	15.11	18.71	17.00	19.44	29.50	26.00	23.50	32.50	38.63
Stock price – low ($)	—	7.99	8.48	12.53	12.88	15.75	17.44	18.75	18.75	21.44	28.38
Stock price – close ($)	15.0%	9.19	13.43	14.44	15.94	19.19	22.94	22.13	22.00	32.50	32.38
P/E – high	—	10	12	14	12	15	21	19	16	19	20
P/E – low	—	7	7	9	9	12	12	14	13	13	15
Dividends per share ($)	6.2%	0.58	0.65	0.72	0.78	0.84	0.87	0.90	0.93	0.96	0.99
Book value per share ($)	7.0%	5.65	6.24	6.96	7.43	7.90	8.53	8.97	9.10	9.81	10.38

1990 Year-end:
Debt ratio: 9.3%
Return on equity: 19.1%
Cash (mil.): $198
Current ratio: 1.57
Long-term debt (mil.): $83
No. of shares (mil.): 78
Dividends:
  1990 average yield: 3.1%
  1990 payout: 51.3%
Market value (mil.): $2,535

Stock Price History High/Low 1981–90

WM. WRIGLEY JR. COMPANY

NYSE symbol: WWY
Fiscal year ends: December 31

Hoover's Rating **A+**

OVERVIEW

Headquartered in Chicago's historic Wrigley Building, the Wm. Wrigley Jr. Company is the largest producer of chewing gum and gum base in the world and makes 47% of the gum chewed in the US. Popular for generations, the company's chewing gum brands (including Doublemint, Spearmint, and Juicy Fruit) account for more than 90% of revenues. Wrigley's Extra brand is the #1 sugar-free gum in the US. Company sales and profits rose in 1990 due, in part, to its increasing brand name recognition overseas, particularly in former East Germany.

Wrigley's operations cover numerous facets of chewing gum production: its L.A. Dreyfus subsidiary produces gum base; its Northwest Flavors unit processes mint and flavorings; and its Wrico division makes the packaging for its gum. Wrigley also owns Amurol Products, best known for its Hubba Bubba brand, which makes bubble gum, suckers, baseball cards, and other youth products.

Wrigley is noted as a fiscally conservative company, one responding to market changes cautiously, understating assets, and holding no long-term debt.

WHO

President and CEO: William Wrigley III, age 57, $731,292 pay
EVP: R. Darrell Ewers, age 57, $478,556 pay
SVP: Paul W. Rogers, age 64, $264,436 pay
SVP: John F. Bard
VP Finance: Edmund R. Meyer, age 61
VP Personnel & Assistant to the President: Edgar L. Swanson, Jr., age 64
Assistant to the President: William Wrigley, Jr., age 27
Auditors: Ernst & Young
Employees: 5,463

WHEN

William Wrigley, Jr., a rebellious Philadelphia youth, got a start in sales at the age of 13. After being expelled from school, he was put to work by his father selling door-to-door. In 1891 he moved to Chicago to sell soap and baking powder. Wrigley began offering customers free chewing gum made of spruce gum and paraffin by Zeno Manufacturing (1892) and received numerous requests to buy the gum. Simultaneously, chicle (a naturally sweet gum base from Central America) was being imported for the rubber industry. Wrigley successfully gambled on the idea that chicle would work as a main ingredient for chewing gum.

By 1893 Wrigley had introduced Spearmint and Juicy Fruit and was selling only gum. He continued to use sales incentives, offering dealers counter scales, cash registers, and display cases for volume purchases. In 1898 he merged with Zeno to form Wm. Wrigley, Jr. & Co. By 1910 Spearmint gum was the leading US brand, and Wrigley began to expand into Canada (1910), Australia (1915), and Great Britain (1927).

The Wrigley family bought real estate, including Catalina Island (1919) and the Arizona Biltmore Hotel (1931), built the Wrigley building (1924), and purchased the Chicago Cubs (1924, sold in 1981). Wrigley was keen on advertising; by the time of his death (1932),

the company was the largest single-product advertiser. At that time son Philip took over.

For over 75 years the company made only 3 gums: Doublemint (introduced in 1914), Spearmint, and Juicy Fruit. During WWII Wrigley could not obtain the desired ingredients for his products; instead, the company produced inferior gum under a different label but kept the Wrigley brand alive with a picture of his former gum and the ad slogan "Remember this Wrapper." It worked; after the war Wrigley's popularity increased. The company did not raise its original 5¢ price until 1971, when management grudgingly went to 7¢.

By 1974 Wrigley faced severe competition from sugar-free gums. In spite of declining market share, management refused to bring out a sugar-free gum, instead introducing Freedent for denture wearers. Later the company introduced Big Red (1975); Orbit, a sugar-free gum that flopped because its sweetener was labeled a possible carcinogen (1977); and Hubba Bubba (1978). Philip died in 1977, and a 3rd-generation Wrigley (William III) took over. In 1984 Wrigley finally introduced a successful sugar-free gum, Extra.

In 1991 Amurol launched Michael Jordan Hang Time shredded bubble gum, a companion brand to its Big League Chew. Wrigley also unleashed a sugar-free version of Freedent and a bubble gum version of Extra.

WHERE

HQ: 410 N. Michigan Ave., Chicago, IL 60611
Phone: 312-644-2121
Fax: 312-644-2135 (Marketing)

Wrigley gum is produced in 13 company-owned factories worldwide and is sold in 103 countries and territories. The company's largest markets outside the US in 1990 were Australia, Canada, Germany, the Philippines, Taiwan, and the UK.

	1990 Sales		1990 Operating Income	
	$ mil.	% of total	$ mil.	% of total
US	715	61	112	59
Europe	277	24	50	27
Other	173	15	27	14
Adjustments	(54)	—	(12)	—
Total	**1,111**	**100**	**177**	**100**

WHAT

US Brands (Gum)	Foreign Brands (Gum)
Big Red	Arrowmint
Doublemint	Big Boy
Extra	Big G
Freedent	Cool Crunch
Juicy Fruit	Dulce 16
Spearmint	Freedent
Winter Fresh	Juicy Fruit
	Orbit
Amurol Products Co. Brands	P.K.
Big League Chew	
Bubble Tape	
Hang Time	
Hubba Bubba	
Reed's Candy	

Real Estate
Wrigley Building, Chicago

US Subsidiaries and Divisions
Four-Ten Corporation
L.A. Dreyfus Co. (gum factories)
Northwestern Flavors, Inc. (flavorings)
Wrico Packaging (wrapping supplies)

RANKINGS

319th in *Fortune* 500 Industrial Cos.
281st in *Business Week* 1000

KEY COMPETITORS

Bayer	RJR Nabisco
Hercules	Roche
IFF	Warner-Lambert
MacAndrews & Forbes	

HOW MUCH

	9-Year Growth	1981	1982	1983	1984	1985	1986	1987	1988	1989	1990
Sales ($ mil.)	6.9%	608	581	582	591	620	699	781	891	993	1,111
Net income ($ mil.)	17.1%	28	36	39	40	44	54	70	87	106	117
Income as % of sales	—	4.7%	6.2%	6.7%	6.7%	7.0%	7.7%	9.0%	9.8%	10.7%	10.6%
Earnings per share ($)	19.5%	0.60	0.76	0.85	0.93	1.03	1.28	1.69	2.18	2.70	2.99
Stock price – high ($)		7.21	7.67	9.38	10.00	15.83	26.00	35.50	41.00	53.75	59.25
Stock price – low ($)		5.29	4.85	6.54	7.50	9.58	13.75	19.50	32.00	35.50	43.75
Stock price – close ($)	27.3%	5.83	6.71	8.77	9.96	15.50	22.88	34.56	36.13	53.63	51.25
P/E – high	—	12	10	11	11	15	20	21	19	20	20
P/E – low	—	9	6	8	8	9	11	12	15	13	15
Dividends per share ($)	16.5%	0.37	0.39	0.42	0.47	0.52	0.62	0.85	1.09	1.36	1.48
Book value per share ($)	7.9%	5.18	5.27	5.38	5.43	6.13	6.93	7.18	7.77	8.73	10.25

1990 Year-end:
Debt ratio: 0.0%
Return on equity: 31.5%
Cash (mil.): $114
Current ratio: 2.80
Long-term debt (mil.): $0
No. of shares (mil.): 39
Dividends:
　1990 average yield: 2.9%
　1990 payout: 49.5%
Market value (mil.): $2,007

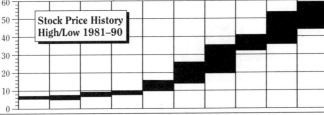

Stock Price History High/Low 1981–90

WOOLWORTH CORPORATION

OVERVIEW

Once the king of downtown dime stores, the Woolworth Corporation is now a worldwide leader in specialty retailing, generating $9.8 billion in sales in 1990. The 8,619 stores in the US, Canada, Mexico, Australia, and Europe sell general merchandise, clothing, shoes, sporting goods, and accessories in more than 40 different store formats. This diversity allows Woolworth to operate 14 different stores in one California shopping mall alone.

Although nearly 1,400 Woolworth variety stores are still in business worldwide, recent expansion has been focused on nearly 7,000 specialty stores, such as Afterthoughts/Carimar (boutique) and the Foot Locker stores (athletic shoes). In 1990 the company opened a net of 565 new specialty stores, with 760 more planned for 1991. The company plans to open nearly 3,000 additional Foot Locker and Lady Foot Locker stores by the year 2000.

Perhaps more than any other US retailer, Woolworth has realized the potential of foreign markets, which in 1990 accounted for 44% of sales and 30% of its store count.

NYSE symbol: Z
Fiscal year ends: Last Saturday in January

 Hoover's Rating **A-**

WHO

Chairman and CEO: Harold E. Sells, age 62, $2,045,506 pay
President and COO: Frederick E. Hennig, age 58, $1,366,794 pay
EVP Finance and CFO: William K. Lavin, age 46, $1,042,017 pay
VP Human Resources: William R. Forcht, age 61
Auditors: Price Waterhouse
Employees: 73,000 full-time and 69,000 part-time

WHEN

With the idea of selling merchandise priced at no more than 5 cents (and later 10 cents), Frank Winfield Woolworth opened The Great Five Cent Store in Utica, New York, in 1879. It failed. That same year he moved to Lancaster, Pennsylvania, and created the first five-and-dime.

Woolworth moved his headquarters to New York City (1886) and spent the rest of the century acquiring other dime-store chains. The company also expanded into Canada (1897) and later England (1909), France (1922), and Germany (1927).

With $10 million in sales, the 120-store chain incorporated as F.W. Woolworth & Company, with Frank Woolworth as president (1905). In 1912 the company merged with 5 rival chains and went public with 596 stores, producing $52 million in sales the first year.

Frugal with his business, Frank Woolworth built lavish homes and corporate headquarters. In 1913, paying $13.5 million in cash, he completed construction of the Woolworth Building, then the world's tallest skyscraper (792 feet). When Woolworth died in 1919, the chain had 1,081 stores with sales of $119 million.

Woolworth became more competitive after WWII by advertising, establishing revolving credit and self-service, moving stores to the suburbs, and expanding merchandise selections. In 1962 Woolworth opened Woolco, a US and Canadian discount chain. The US stores were closed in 1982, but the Canadian Woolco stores remain.

Since the 1960s the company has become a specialty retailer, growing by acquiring and expanding US, Canadian, Australian, and European footwear, apparel, and sporting goods chains. Acquisitions included G.R. Kinney (shoes, 1963), Richman Brothers (men's clothing, 1969), Holtzman's Little Folk Shop (1983), Champs (sporting goods, 1987), Moderna Shuh Center (shoes, Germany, 1988), Mathers (shoes, Australia, 1988), and Profoot (Netherlands and Belgium, 1990).

In 1974 the company introduced Foot Locker, the athletic-shoe chain, later developing Lady Foot Locker (1982) and Kids Foot Locker (1987). Woolworth Express (1987) is a smaller version of the original dime store.

Since 1980 specialty stores have increased from 2,936 to 6,966, while general merchandise stores have decreased from 1,851 to 1,653. The company reacquired its Mexican Woolworth's locations in 1990 and anticipates opening more dime stores in Germany, but 92% of 1991 openings will be in specialty formats, with Foot Lockers opening in Turin, Italy, and Mexico City. In December 1990, Woolworth "re-opened" a store in Halle, the first opened by any US retailer in eastern Germany. The company had occupied the very same location before WWII.

WHERE

HQ: 233 Broadway, New York, NY 10279-0001
Phone: 212-553-2000
Fax: 212-553-2042 (Public Affairs)

Woolworth operates 8,619 stores in all 50 states and 17 countries on 4 continents.

	1990 Sales		1990 Operating Income	
	$ mil.	% of total	$ mil.	% of total
US	5,522	56	333	52
Canada	2,396	25	142	22
Europe	1,678	17	154	24
Australia	193	2	10	2
Adjustments	—	—	(51)	—
Total	**9,789**	**100**	**588**	**100**

WHAT

	1990 Sales		1990 Operating Income	
	$ mil.	% of total	$ mil.	% of total
General merchandise	5,641	57	333	52
Specialty stores	4,276	43	306	48
Adjustments	(128)	—	(51)	—
Total	**9,789**	**100**	**588**	**100**

Specialty Stores	No. of Stores 1/26/91
Kinney (shoes)	1,659
Foot Locker (athletic footwear)	1,503
Lady Foot Locker (athletic footwear)	403
Kids Foot Locker (athletic footwear)	42
Kids Mart (children's apparel)	424
Afterthoughts/Carimar (boutique)	497
Susie's (women's apparel)	216
Champs Sports (sporting goods)	251
Athletic X-Press (sporting goods)	186
Williams the Shoemen (Australia)	177
Mathers (shoes, Australia)	153
Richman (men's and women's apparel)	147
Other formats	1,308
Total	**6,966**

General Merchandise Stores	No. of Stores 1/26/91
Woolworth	1,388
Woolco (Canada)	147
Woolworth Express	118
Total	**1,653**

HOW MUCH

	9-Year Growth	1981	1982	1983	1984	1985	1986	1987	1988	1989	1990
Sales ($ mil.)	3.4%	7,223	5,124	5,456	5,737	5,958	6,501	7,134	8,088	8,820	9,789
Net income ($ mil.)	16.2%	82	82	118	141	177	214	251	288	329	317
Income as % of sales	—	1.1%	1.6%	2.2%	2.5%	3.0%	3.3%	3.5%	3.6%	3.7%	3.2%
Earnings per share ($)	15.9%	0.65	0.65	0.92	1.10	1.36	1.61	1.89	2.22	2.53	2.45
Stock price – high ($)	—	6.91	7.28	9.84	9.72	15.63	24.50	29.81	30.38	36.13	36.63
Stock price – low ($)	—	4.25	3.97	5.66	7.47	9.16	14.53	14.75	17.06	24.19	22.88
Stock price – close ($)	23.6%	4.50	6.47	8.78	9.25	15.00	19.31	17.25	25.88	31.94	30.25
P/E – high	—	11	11	11	9	11	15	16	14	14	15
P/E – low	—	7	6	6	7	7	9	8	8	10	9
Dividends per share ($)	9.8%	0.45	0.45	0.45	0.45	0.50	0.56	0.66	0.82	0.94	1.04
Book value per share ($)	5.4%	11.28	8.13	8.16	8.33	9.53	11.32	13.33	14.40	16.08	18.04

1990 Year-end:
Debt ratio: 10.3%
Return on equity: 14.4%
Cash (mil.): $50
Current ratio: 1.67
Long-term debt (mil.): $269
No. of shares (mil.): 130
Dividends:
  1990 average yield: 3.4%
  1990 payout: 42.4%
Market value (mil.): $3,922

Stock Price History High/Low 1981–90

RANKINGS

11th in *Fortune* 50 Retailing Cos.
153rd in *Business Week* 1000

KEY COMPETITORS

General merchandise and specialty retail companies

XEROX CORPORATION

NYSE symbol: XRX
Fiscal year ends: December 31

Hoover's Rating **C**

OVERVIEW

Xerox is the world's leading manufacturer of high-end copiers. Its name is synonymous with photocopying. The company also makes scanners, printers, and document processing software. Now calling itself The Document Company, Xerox hopes to redefine the way information, whether in paper or electronic form, moves through corporate offices.

With a distracting foray into finance and insurance now largely behind it, Xerox is again emerging as a leader in office automation. With its new DocuTech Production Publisher, which combines copying, printing, and scanning technology, Xerox hopes its products will become the nerve center of the office of the future. By tying the DocuTech system into customers' computing systems through its alliances with Adobe, Aldus, Andersen Consulting, DEC, Novell, Sun Microsystems, and others, the company hopes to gain an edge on its competitors.

Xerox is obsessed with quality (it was a 1989 Malcolm Baldridge Award winner) and is finally beginning to apply the research of its world-renowned Palo Alto Research Center (where the personal computer, computer networking, and graphical user interface were all invented but never commercially exploited) to its business.

WHO

Chairman and CEO: Paul A. Allaire, age 52, $1,197,294 pay (prior to promotion)
VP Finance: Alan Z. Senter, age 49
SVP Human Resources: William F. Buehler, age 51
Auditors: KPMG Peat Marwick
Employees: 110,000

WHERE

HQ: PO Box 1600, 800 Long Ridge Rd., Stamford, CT 06904
Phone: 203-968-3000
Fax: 203-968-4312 (Public Relations)

Xerox sells business products in over 130 countries.

	1990 Sales		1990 Net Income	
	$ mil.	% of total	$ mil.	% of total
US	11,083	62	322	52
Europe	4,734	26	143	24
Other countries	2,156	12	149	24
Adjustments	(1,022)	—	(9)	—
Total	**16,951**	**100**	**605**	**100**

WHAT

	1990 Sales		1990 Operating Income	
	$ mil.	% of total	$ mil.	% of total
Business equip.	12,692	71	1,045	70
Equip. financing	891	5	307	20
Insurance	4,184	23	129	9
Other financial services	206	1	16	1
Adjustments	(1,022)	—	(721)	—
Total	**16,951**	**100**	**776**	**100**

Business Products and Systems
Copiers (50 Series)
Duplicators
Electronic publishing (DocuTech)
Networks (Ethernet)
Printers
Scanners
Software and supplies
Typewriters
Workstations

Financial Services
Crum and Forster, Inc. (insurance)

Furman Selz (investment advice and services)
Van Kampen Merrit Inc. (trusts and funds)
Xerox Credit Corp. (purchase financing)
Xerox Life (insurance)

Other
Computer services
Medical systems
Realty
Technology ventures
Venture capital
Voice systems

Selected Major Subsidiaries and Affiliates
Xerox Canada Inc. (84%)
Fuji Xerox Co., Ltd. (25.7%, Japan)
Modi Xerox Ltd. (35.9%, India)
Rank Xerox Ltd. (51.2%, UK)

WHEN

The Haloid Company was incorporated in 1906 to make and sell photographic paper. In 1935 it bought the Rectigraph Company (photocopiers), which led Haloid to take a license for a new process of electrophotography (later renamed xerography from the ancient Greek words for dry and writing) from the Battelle Memorial Institute in 1947. Battelle had backed inventor Chester Carlson, who had labored since 1937 to perfect a process of transferring electrostatic images from a photoconductive surface to paper.

Haloid commercialized the process, introducing the Model A copier in 1949 and the Xerox Copyflo in 1955. By 1956 xerographic products represented 40% of the company's sales. The company became Haloid Xerox in 1958 and in 1959 introduced the Xerox 914, the first simplified office copier. The 914 took the world by storm, beating out competing mimeograph (A.B. Dick), thermal paper (3M), and damp copy (Kodak) technologies. Xerox's revenues soared from $37 million in 1960 to $268 million in 1965. The company dropped Haloid from its name in 1961.

The company began to diversify in the 1960s. It bought into publishing (Wesleyan University Press, 1965; Learning Materials, 1966; R.R. Bowker, 1967) and computers (Scientific Data Systems, 1969), all subsequently sold or discontinued.

In the 1970s Xerox bought companies that made printers (Diablo, 1972), plotters (Versatec, 1975), and disk drives (Shugart, 1977; sold 1984); it also bought international record carrier Western Union International (1979, sold 1982). In 1974 the FTC, believing Xerox was too dominant in the market, forced the company to license other manufacturers to use its xerographic technology.

In the 1980s the company bought companies in optical character recognition (Kurzweil, 1980), scanning and fax (Datacopy, 1988), and desktop publishing (Ventura, 1990); it also entered financial services, buying insurance companies (Crum and Forster, 1983) and investment banking companies (Van Kampen Merritt, 1984), among others.

Financial services became an albatross for Xerox and it has committed to disposing of its 3rd-party financing and leasing services. After a $375 million 1990 write-down of its 25% investment in failed Chicago-based VMS Realty Xerox decided to quit real estate, too. Xerox is also paring its insurance operations, selling its NAVCO auto insurance unit in 1990 and cutting 400 jobs from its Crum and Forster insurance operation in 1991.

RANKINGS

22nd in *Fortune* 500 Industrial Cos.
125th in *Business Week* 1000

KEY COMPETITORS

Canon	IBM	NEC
Eastman Kodak	Machines Bull	Olivetti
Fuji Photo	Matsushita	Pitney Bowes
GEC	3M	Polaroid
Harris	Matsushita	Sharp
Hewlett-Packard	Minolta	Siemens
Hitachi	Mitsubishi	Toshiba

Insurance and financial services companies

HOW MUCH

	9-Year Growth	1981	1982	1983	1984	1985	1986	1987	1988	1989	1990
Sales ($ mil.)	7.7%	8,691	8,456	8,464	8,792	8,732	9,355	10,320	15,994	16,806	16,951
Net income ($ mil.)	0.1%	598	368	466	376	381	488	578	388	704	605
Income as % of sales	—	6.9%	4.3%	5.5%	4.3%	4.4%	5.2%	5.6%	2.4%	4.2%	3.6%
Earnings per share ($)	(3.0%)	6.94	4.29	4.36	3.38	3.40	4.44	5.25	3.49	6.41	5.26
Stock price – high ($)	—	64.00	41.75	52.13	51.13	60.50	72.25	85.00	63.00	69.00	58.88
Stock price – low ($)	—	37.38	27.13	35.00	33.25	37.25	48.63	50.00	50.25	54.38	29.00
Stock price – close ($)	(1.5%)	40.50	37.38	49.50	37.88	59.75	60.00	56.63	58.38	57.25	35.50
P/E – high	—	9	10	12	15	18	16	16	18	11	11
P/E – low	—	5	6	8	10	11	11	10	14	8	6
Dividends per share ($)	0.0%	3.00	3.00	3.00	3.00	3.00	3.00	3.00	3.00	3.00	3.00
Book value per share ($)	2.4%	44.11	43.96	44.40	42.77	45.47	48.00	51.00	52.22	53.61	54.76

1990 Year-end:
Debt ratio: 54.9%
Return on equity: 9.6%
Cash (mil.): $1,407
Assets (mil.): $31,495
Long-term debt (mil.): $7,108
No. of shares (mil.): 92
Dividends:
  1990 average yield: 8.5%
  1990 payout: 57.0%
Market value (mil.): $3,274

Stock Price History High/Low 1981–90

YELLOW FREIGHT SYSTEM

OVERVIEW

Unlike its main trucking competitors (Consolidated Freightways and Roadway), Yellow Freight focuses almost exclusively on long-haul freight transportation. In 1990 Yellow's orange trucks traveled over 670 million route miles to transport 8.4 million tons of freight to more than 35,000 North American destinations. Less-than-truckload (LTL) shipments (those weighing less than 10,000 pounds) accounted for most of the freight carried.

As the LTL market matures, Yellow hopes to start up regional trucking operations. In the interim it will expand long-haul service to Mexico in 1991 and possibly to Europe in the near future.

After experiencing a precipitous drop in earnings in 1989, the company worked to improve profitability in 1990 by limiting price discounting and implementing cost control measures, including improved utilization of vehicle freight capacity. But with traffic soft (due to the recession) and wage and employee benefits up by 4%, sales and earnings dipped early in 1991; Yellow has responded with a 3.5% rate increase.

Since 1952, 3 generations of the Powell family have managed Yellow's daily affairs. The company's stock is 11.8% manager-owned; another 17% is controlled by the Powells and the Powell Family Foundation.

WHEN

In 1924 A. J. Harrell established a trucking company in conjunction with his Oklahoma City busline and Yellow Cab franchise. Operating as Yellow Transit, Harrell's trucking company hauled LTL shipments between Oklahoma City and Tulsa. By 1944 Yellow was operating in Texas, Kansas, Missouri, Illinois, Indiana, and Kentucky, through 51 independent subsidiaries. However, its policy of high dividends stunted growth, and by 1951 Yellow faced bankruptcy.

The company was losing about $75,000 a month in 1952 when George Powell, formerly of Riss & Company (a leading trucking company of the time), took over. Within 5 months he had turned Yellow around.

Powell focused the company on long-haul interstate shipments (i.e., from Chicago to Los Angeles) rather than shorter hauls of a few hundred miles. To accomplish this Yellow needed a more extensive route network, so Powell established a central dispatch office in Kansas City and started to buy other trucking companies to extend Yellow's operations.

In 1965 the company expanded to the West Coast and to the Southeast by purchasing Watson-Wilson Transportation System. After changing its name to Yellow Freight System (1968), the company acquired part of Norwalk Truck Lines, gaining routes in the Northeast (1970). Other purchases, including Adley Express (1973), connected Yellow's eastern US routes.

The company then extended routes into the Pacific Northwest by purchasing Republic Freight Systems in 1975. It bought Braswell Motor Freight, consolidating its routes in Texas, California, and the Southeast in 1977. Yellow's only deviation from route acquisitions was its $4 million investment in Overland Energy (oil and gas exploration) in 1976.

Yellow was unprepared, however, when Congress passed the Motor Carrier Act of 1980, deregulating operating routes and shipping rates. Yellow started a belated effort to upgrade its aging depots and terminals, but still experienced a decline in profits between 1980 and 1983. The company extended service to all 50 states in 1987 after opening a terminal in Alaska. Sales exceeded $2 billion in 1988 and continued to grow, to $2.2 billion in 1989. But discounting and rising fuel and labor costs caused profits to drop that year.

In 1990 the company introduced EDIPartners, software that will allow customers to use their PCs to access information in Yellow's computer regarding their shipments.

NASDAQ symbol: YELL
Fiscal year ends: December 31

Hoover's Rating B-

WHO

Chairman: George E. Powell, Jr., age 64, $781,829 pay
President and CEO: George E. Powell III, age 42, $534,065 pay
SVP Finance and Administration: David E. Loeffler, age 44, $339,190 pay
SVP Marketing: Robert W. Burdick, age 48, $330,190 pay
SVP Operations: M. Reid Armstrong, age 53, $326,190 pay
SVP and Secretary: Stephen P. Murphy, age 64
VP Human Resources: Philip D. Parkey
Auditors: Arthur Andersen & Co.
Employees: 28,900

WHERE

HQ: Yellow Freight System, Inc. of Delaware, 10990 Roe Ave., PO Box 7563, Overland Park, KS 66207
Phone: 913-345-1020
Fax: 913-344-3433

Yellow Freight operates 26 hubs and 631 freight terminals (261 owned, 370 leased) throughout the US, Puerto Rico, and the Canadian provinces of Alberta, British Columbia, Manitoba, Ontario, Quebec, and Saskatchewan. The company owns 44,734 trucks, tractors, and trailers.

WHAT

	1990 Sales*	
	$ mil.	% of total
Less-than-truckload	2,071	91
Truckload	208	9
Total	**2,279**	**100**

*Sales do not include Yellow Freight's Canadian subsidiaries.

Major Subsidiaries
Overland Energy, Inc. (oil and gas exploration in Kansas, Louisiana, Mississippi, Oklahoma, and Texas)
Yellow Freight System, Inc. (motor freight transport in the US, Puerto Rico, Alberta, Manitoba, Quebec, and Saskatchewan)
Yellow Freight System of British Columbia, Inc. (motor freight transport between British Columbia and the US)
Yellow Freight System of Ontario, Inc. (motor freight transport between Ontario and the US)

RANKINGS

20th in *Fortune* 50 Transportation Cos.
601st in *Business Week* 1000

KEY COMPETITORS

American President
Burlington Northern
Canadian Pacific
Chicago and North Western
Consolidated Freightways
Consolidated Rail
CSX
Norfolk Southern
Rio Grande Industries
Roadway
Santa Fe Pacific
Union Pacific

HOW MUCH

	9-Year Growth	1981	1982	1983	1984	1985	1986	1987	1988	1989	1990
Sales ($ mil.)	10.5%	936	936	1,089	1,380	1,530	1,714	1,760	2,016	2,220	2,302
Net income ($ mil.)	16.5%	16	11	49	44	56	67	41	69	19	65
Income as % of sales	—	1.8%	1.1%	4.5%	3.2%	3.6%	3.9%	2.3%	3.4%	0.8%	2.8%
Earnings per share ($)	16.6%	0.58	0.38	1.73	1.55	1.95	2.35	1.44	2.40	0.65	2.31
Stock price – high ($)	—	10.63	10.75	24.25	22.81	29.88	41.50	42.50	34.00	32.88	31.25
Stock price – low ($)	—	7.38	5.44	9.25	11.63	15.81	27.50	20.88	23.88	23.88	18.75
Stock price – close ($)	14.4%	7.88	9.50	21.50	16.00	29.00	36.88	27.88	31.63	26.75	26.50
P/E – high	—	18	29	14	15	15	18	30	14	51	14
P/E – low	—	13	15	5	8	8	12	15	10	37	8
Dividends per share ($)	8.3%	0.40	0.42	0.44	0.48	0.52	0.58	0.62	0.66	0.73	0.82
Book value per share ($)	9.2%	7.53	7.48	8.77	9.84	11.27	13.14	13.82	14.21	15.24	16.70

1990 Year-end:
Debt ratio: 25.9%
Return on equity: 14.5%
Cash (mil.): $8
Current ratio: 0.93
Long-term debt (mil.): $164
No. of shares (mil.): 28
Dividends:
1990 average yield: 3.1%
1990 payout: 35.5%
Market value (mil.): $744

Stock Price History
High/Low 1981–90

YOUNG & RUBICAM INC.

OVERVIEW

Young & Rubicam (Y&R) is the largest independent advertising agency (measured by billings) in the US and the 6th largest in the world.

Of the largest agencies in the US, it is one of only a few that are privately held. This has worked to its advantage with clients who are concerned about privacy and conflicts of interest and has allowed Y&R to take a long-term view. Prior to a tumultuous 1990, Y&R had typically promoted from within and had enjoyed a degree of stability unusual in the advertising industry.

Newly installed management teams throughout Y&R are facing a dismal advertising market and must figure out how to deliver to clients the long-promised integration of the organization's products and services. Y&R's 5 divisions provide advertising, public relations, sales promotion, corporate identity consulting, and direct marketing services.

WHEN

Raymond Rubicam and John Orr Young founded the advertising agency that bears their names in Philadelphia in 1923 quite literally on a shoestring — their first client was Presto Quick Tip Shoelaces. Y&R got its first major client, General Foods, when it asked for and received the account for the company's least successful product, a beverage. Its success in increasing sales of that product, Postum, led to more business with General Foods and to a move to New York in 1926 at that client's request. With its informal atmosphere and tolerance for eccentric behavior, the agency soon became a haven for the leading creative people in the industry.

In 1931 the firm opened its second office — in Chicago. In the early 1930s Rubicam, who by then dominated the firm, recruited George Gallup to create the first research department in the industry. In 1934 Young (who had a relaxed approach to business) was forced out of the agency, which despite its unconventional working environment had become an intensely hard-driving place.

Although the Great Depression put many agencies out of business, Y&R prospered. Billings grew from $6 million in 1927 to $22 million in 1937, making Y&R the 2nd largest agency (behind J. Walter Thompson).

WWII brought surprising prosperity to the advertising industry. By 1945 Y&R's billings had reached $53 million. Rubicam, suffering from professional ennui and indulging a desire to lead a less hectic life, retired to Arizona in 1944 at age 52.

During the 1950s the agency prospered; billings reached $212 million in 1960. During the 1960s, Y&R was a leading creative force in the field, producing the first color television commercials and fielding a series of notable advertising campaigns. The emphasis on creativity, teamwork, and group management instilled in the firm by Rubicam worked. However, it was also during this period that growth slowed, and expenses and staff grew.

In 1970 Edward Ney took over as CEO, cutting staff and installing Alex Kroll as creative director. Kroll required that creativity be controlled, disciplined, and quantifiable by sales results. Ney expanded the agency through acquisitions paid for with internally generated cash. Acquisitions included Wunderman Worldwide (direct marketing, 1973), Cato Johnson (sales promotion, 1976), and Burson-Marsteller (one of the largest public-relations firms in the US, 1979).

In 1975, when Kroll became president of US operations, Y&R's billings of $477 million had made it the #1 agency in America. Since 1979 it has been the largest independent agency in the US. The 1980s saw challenges to Y&R's dominance from the growth of such huge holding company agencies as Saatchi & Saatchi and other large agencies. Y&R's size and concomitant bureaucracy also threatened its reputation for creativity. Kroll became CEO in 1985.

Y&R had a tough year in 1990. The agency pleaded guilty to bribery charges in connection with the Jamaican tourism account. The stodgy reputation of its New York office's creative department forced a reorganization. HDM Worldwide, a partnership with Dentsu (Japan) and Eurocom (France), fell apart as Eurocom withdrew. Y&R and Dentsu, partners for 30 years, regrouped as Dentsu, Young & Rubicam Partnerships.

Private company
Fiscal year ends: December 31

Hoover's Rating **B**

WHO

Chairman and CEO: Alexander S. Kroll
President: Peter A. Georgescu, age 52
EVP and CFO: Roger Craton
Director Human Resources: Alan Gaynor
Auditors: Price Waterhouse
Employees: 11,133

WHERE

HQ: 285 Madison Ave., New York, NY 10017-6486
Phone: 212-210-3000
Fax: 212-490-6397

Y&R has 299 offices in 52 countries.

	1990 Billings		1990 Sales	
	$ mil.	% of total	$ mil.	% of total
US	3,937	49	487	45
Foreign	4,064	51	587	55
Total	**8,001**	**100**	**1,074**	**100**

WHAT

	1990 Billings	
	$ mil.	% of total
Advertising & other	5,885	74
Public Relations	764	10
Sales Promotion	418	5
Direct marketing	667	8
Other	267	3
Total	**8,001**	**100**

Divisions
Young & Rubicam Advertising
Burson-Marsteller (public relations)
Cato Johnson (sales promotion)
   Arthur E. Wilk Communications Professional Services (consumer healthcare products promotion)
   Cato Johnson Entertainment (studio/film promotions)
   Cato Johnson Promotion Marketing (sales promotion)
   Cato Johnson Sports Marketing
   HH&B Promotion Resources (point-of-purchase displays, sweepstakes, telemarketing)
   Hutchins/Y&R (Yellow Page placement, promotion, advertising)
Landor Associates (corporate identity management)
Wunderman Worldwide (direct marketing)

Joint Ventures
Dentsu/Burson-Marsteller (public relations)
Dentsu Wunderman Direct (Japanese direct marketing)
Dentsu, Young & Rubicam Partnerships (advertising)
Y&R/Sovero (marketing, with Sovero of Moscow)

Representative Clients

American Home Products	Metropolitan Life
AT&T	Monsanto
BSN	News Corp.
Chevron	Pepsico
Clorox	Perrier (US)
Colgate-Palmolive	Philip Morris
Dr Pepper/Seven-Up	RJR
Du Pont	Time Warner
Eastman Kodak	Unisys
Ford	United States Army
H. J. Heinz	Warner-Lambert
Johnson & Johnson	Xerox

RANKINGS

196th in *Forbes* 400 US Private Cos.

KEY COMPETITORS

Carlson   Dentsu   Saatchi & Saatchi

HOW MUCH

	9-Year Growth	1981	1982	1983	1984	1985	1986	1987	1988	1989	1990
Total billings ($ mil.)	14.7%	2,334	2,512	2,761	3,202	3,575	4,191	4,905	5,390	6,251	8,001
Total sales ($ mil.)	13.3%	350	377	414	480	536	628	736	758	865	1,074
US billings ($ mil.)	11.4%	1,490	1,645	1,828	2,155	2,272	2,389	2,577	2,792	3,115	3,937
US sales ($ mil.)	9.1%	223	247	274	323	341	358	386	373	410	487
Employees	5.5%	6,861	7,025	7,745	8,418	9,030	10,844	11,634	12,311	10,473	11,133

Total Sales ($ mil.) 1981–90

ZENITH ELECTRONICS CORPORATION

NYSE symbol: ZE
Fiscal year ends: December 31

Hoover's Rating C-

OVERVIEW

Zenith has been responsible for much of the innovation in radio and TV technology in the last 70 years. Retaining a 12% market share, Zenith is the last remaining independent color television and picture tube manufacturer in the US. The company's consumer products also include videocassette recorders, computer monitors, cable TV products, and electronics parts and accessories. Recession and price-cutting have led to continuing losses.

Zenith's survival may ride on high-definition television (HDTV) technology. The company has teamed with AT&T to enter the Federal Communications Commission's (FCC) HDTV transmission technology competition. The FCC is expected to select an HDTV broadcast technology and establish it as a US standard in 1993. Zenith is also developing new manufacturing technology for its patented flat-tension-mask (FTM), high-resolution picture tube, which has applications in the HDTV and computer-monitor fields. The company plans to introduce its first TVs with FTM tubes in 1992.

WHEN

In 1915 Karl Hassel and R. H. G. Mathews, 2 ham radio operators, formed Chicago Radio Laboratory. In 1918 they began manufacturing radio equipment. In 1921 they were joined by Eugene F. McDonald, Jr., a wealthy investor who formed Zenith Radio Corporation in 1923 to act as the sales agent for Chicago Radio Laboratory. Zenith was an early innovator in radio, developing the first portable (1924), the first home receiver to run on alternating current (1926), and the first push-button radio (1927). The Great Depression caused sales to drop 80%, but the company survived. It started a radio station and a television station and began making hearing aids prior to WWII. During the war the company produced radar and communications equipment.

In 1948 Zenith bought the Rauland Corporation, which manufactured picture tubes, and produced its first black-and-white television sets. In 1956 Zenith's Robert Adler invented the first practical television remote control device. By 1959 the company was black-and-white sales leader. In 1961 Zenith introduced its first line of color televisions. In the same year the FCC adopted Zenith's system for broadcasting FM radio in stereo.

During the 1970s and 1980s Zenith had to face the challenge of low-priced Japanese imports. The company led the market in color television sales from 1972 to 1978, but prices were held down by the Japanese "dumping" of television sets in the US market (selling sets in America for less than their cost or home market price). Under the pressure of falling prices, the company moved some of its manufacturing operations to Mexico and Taiwan. Zenith chairman John Nevin lobbied Congress and filed suits against the Japanese TV manufacturers, eventually winning the battle but losing market share.

In 1979, in its first significant move away from the radio and television industry, Zenith acquired The Heath Company, manufacturers of microcomputers and do-it-yourself electronics kits. The company's Zenith Data Systems subsidiary grew from sales of around $10 million in 1980 to over $1 billion in 1989, largely on the strength of government and university contracts for its IBM-compatible personal computers. In 1989 Zenith sold all computer operations, including the industry-leading laptop computer business, to Groupe Bull of France. Zenith used the proceeds to retire much of its debt. In 1989 Zenith entered a joint venture with AT&T to develop an HDTV broadcast system, which, if adopted, could provide Zenith with substantial royalties in the future.

Korea's GoldStar bought 5% of Zenith in 1991. The same year Zenith management won a proxy fight with Nycor, an investment company critical of Zenith management that sought 3 board seats.

WHO

Chairman, President, and CEO: Jerry K. Pearlman, age 51, $450,000 pay
VP and General Counsel: John Borst, Jr., age 63, $139,750 pay
VP Finance and CFO: Kell B. Benson, age 43, $134,167 pay
VP Human Resources and Public Affairs: Michael J. Kaplan, age 51
Auditors: Arthur Andersen & Co.
Employees: 27,000

WHERE

HQ: 1000 Milwaukee Ave., Glenview, IL 60025
Phone: 708-391-7000
Fax: 708-391-7253

	Factories and Warehouses
Arizona	1
Canada	4
Illinois	5
Mexico	14
Missouri	1
Taiwan	1
Texas	3
Other locations	8
Total	**37**

	1990 Sales		1990 Pretax Income	
	$ mil.	% of total	$ mil.	% of total
US	1,325	94	(55)	—
Foreign	85	6	4	—
Total	**1,410**	**100**	**(51)**	**—**

WHAT

	1990 Sales		1990 Operating Income	
	$ mil.	% of total	$ mil.	% of total
Consumer electronics	1,229	87	(25)	—
Components	181	13	(2)	—
Adjustments	—	—	(20)	—
Total	**1,410**	**100**	**(47)**	**—**

Products
Cable TV management software
Camcorders
Color televisions
Computer display tubes
Computer monitors
Electronic parts and accessories
Hybrid circuits
Pay TV decoders
Power supplies
Television picture tubes
Videocassette recorders

RANKINGS

275th in *Fortune* 500 Industrial Cos.

KEY COMPETITORS

Daewoo	Philips
General Electric	Samsung
Hitachi	Sharp
Lucky-Goldstar	Sony
Matsushita	Tandy
Mitsubishi	Thomson SA
NEC	Toshiba

HOW MUCH

	9-Year Growth	1981	1982	1983	1984	1985	1986	1987	1988	1989	1990
Sales ($ mil.)	1.1%	1,275	1,239	1,361	1,716	1,624	1,892	2,363	2,686	1,549	1,410
Net income ($ mil.)	—	16	(22)	46	64	(8)	(10)	(19)	5	(17)	(52)
Income as % of sales	—	1.2%	(1.8%)	3.4%	3.7%	(0.5%)	(0.5%)	(0.8%)	(0.2%)	(1.1%)	(3.7%)
Earnings per share ($)	—	0.82	(1.15)	2.11	2.88	(0.33)	(0.43)	(0.78)	(0.20)	(0.64)	(1.95)
Stock price – high ($)	—	21.50	16.63	36.00	38.63	25.00	29.88	33.63	30.00	21.50	13.63
Stock price – low ($)	—	10.25	9.75	13.38	19.50	16.25	17.88	10.00	13.50	11.50	4.00
Stock price – close ($)	(5.6%)	11.13	14.38	35.50	19.75	20.50	21.88	14.75	19.00	12.75	6.63
P/E – high	—	26	—	17	13	—	—	—	150	—	—
P/E – low	—	13	—	6	7	—	—	—	68	—	—
Dividends per share ($)	—	0.53	0.15	0.00	0.00	0.00	0.00	0.00	0.00	0.00	0.00
Book value per share ($)	(2.7%)	15.73	14.42	17.08	20.00	18.90	18.49	18.45	18.84	14.90	12.32

1990 Year-end:
Debt ratio: 30.7%
Return on equity: —
Cash (mil.): $56
Current ratio: 2.21
Long-term debt (mil.): $151
No. of shares (mil.): 28
Dividends:
  1990 average yield: 0.0%
  1990 payout: 0.0%
Market value (mil.): $184

**Stock Price History
High/Low 1981–90**

The Indexes

INDEX OF PROFILES BY INDUSTRY

INDEX OF PROFILES BY HEADQUARTERS LOCATION

Eidenberg, Eugene 371
883cc Sportster 293
Einbender, Alvin H. 138
EISA. *See* Extended Industry Standard Architecture
Eisenhower, Dwight D. 458, 468
Eisenstat, Albert A. 113
Eisner, Michael D. 559
Ekco 99
Ektachrome 234
El Charrito 112
El Dorado Investment Co. 438
El Pollo Loco 531
El Torito–La Fiesta Restaurants 283
Elafros, Bernard 189
Elanco Products Co. 239
Elco Diagnostics Co. 239
Eldon Industries 469
Electec, Inc. 242
Electra transport 345
Electric Avenue 388
Electric Boat Company 271
Electric Bond & Share 149
Electric Company of America 95
Electro Dynamics 343
Electro Metallurgical 534
Electro-Alkaline Company 184
Electro-Motive Division 274
Electrodata 536
Electrolux Corporation 365, 419, 474
Electronic Data Systems Corporation 199, 217, 274
Electronic News 164
Electronic Transaction Corp. 220
Electrospace Systems, Inc. 179
Elephant Malt Liquor 112
Elf Aquitaine 108, 234, 413
Eli Lilly and Company 227, **239**, 269
Eliot, Charles W. 296
Eliot, T. S. 296
Elisabeth 344
Elisha, Walter Y. 493
Elite 405
Elizabeth Arden 239, 245, 460
Eljer Industries 310
Elkes, Terrence 554
Elkin, Irvin J. 120
Elle 245
Eller, Karl 97, 181
Ellesse 456
Ellig, Bruce R. 434
Elliott, Charles W. 330
Elliott, Steven G. 375
Ellis, Carlene M. 315
Ellis, Harry 327
Ellis, James D. 492
Ellison, Lawrence J. 417
Ellman's 484
Elmer's 150
Elmira Gazette 266
Elocon 476
ELS NetWare Levels 1 and 2 410
Elsesser, James R. 453
Elsie the Cow 150
ELTO Outboard Motor Company 419
Eltra Corporation 86
Elway, John 495
EM (Ebony Man) 328
Embarcadero Center, San Francisco 524
EMCON 197
Emerald City Software 78
Emerine, Wendell R. 349
Emerson Drugs 561
Emerson Electric Co. **240**
Emerson, John 240
Emerson Motors 240

Emerson, Ralph Waldo 296
Emery, John 197
Emery Worldwide 197, 363
Emhart Corporation 145
Eminase 547
Emit 506
Emory University 186
Empire Hotel 380
Empire National Bank 132
Empire Pencil Corporation 297
Empire State Building 300
Empire Trust Company 132
Employee Benefits Update 127
Employers Reinsurance 272
Emporium 167
Empresas Gamesa 432
Empros Systems International 202
Emro 552
Encee, Inc. 250
Encore (TV channel) 512
Encore Books 462
Encore Service Systems 114
Encycle, Inc. 118
Encyclopædia Britannica 226
Encyclopedia Americana 111
Endeavour space shuttle 466
Enders, Thomas 81
Endust 154
Energaire 456
Energizer 453
Energy Department. *See* Department of Energy
Energy Development Corp. 450
Energy Foundation 465
EnergyWave 316
Enfamil 154
Engineered Equipment 313
England, Joseph W. 216
English, John W. 261
English Ovals 436
Enna, Stephen A. 564
Enouen, William A. 374
Enovid 506
ENRAC 563
Enrico Fermi Institute 544
Enrico, Roger A. 432
Enron Corp. 210, **241,** 504
Enseco Inc. 205
Ensure 77
Entenmann's 436
Entergy Corporation **242**
Enterprise Capital Funding Corp. 450
Enterprise Group Development Corp. 450
Enterprise System/3090 318
Entertainment Weekly 520
Entex 241
Enthone 118
Enthone–OMI, Inc. 118
Environmental and Water Quality Laboratory 495
Environmental Defense Fund 465
Environmental Protection Agency 157, 259
EOL. *See* Extra Ordinary Life
EPA. *See* Environmental Protection Agency
Epcot Center 559
Epic (plumbing products) 359
Epic Waves 280
EPL Japan, Inc. 531
Epogen 107
Eprex 325
EPROM 315
Equal 387
Equal Rights Amendment 395
Equalizer 172

Equico Securities, Inc. 243
Equicor 309
EQUICOR-Equitable HCA Corporation 180
Equitable **243,** 309, 355
Equitable building 300
Equitable Securities 96
Equitable Trust 173
ERA. *See* Equal Rights Amendment
Eraser Mate 280
Erburu, Robert F. 521
ERC International 415
Ergamisol 325
Erhart, Charles 434
ERIC Information Analysis Center 416
Erickson, Richard T. 430
Ericson, James D. 409
Ericsson 366
Erie Lackawanna 198
Erlanger 500
Ermer, James 210
Ernest & Julio Gallo 265
Ernst & Whinney 218, 244
Ernst & Young 218, **244**
Ernst, Alwin 244
Ernst, Theodore 244
Erol's 146
ERS 456
ERYC 561
Erythrocin 77
Erythromycin 77
ES 9000 318
Escadrille 295
Escondido (CA) *Times Advocate* 528
Escort 159, 262
ESI Energy, Inc. 263
ESI Meats, Inc. 380
Eskimo Pies 459
Eskridge, James A. 361
Esmark 125, 194
ESPN 164, 298
Esposito, Michael P. 173
Esquire 298
Esrey, William T. 541
ESS 141
Essilor International 442
Esso 246
Estate 568
Estée Lauder Inc. **245,** 319
ETA Systems 202
Etablissements Baud SA 522
Etablissements Delhaize Freres et Cie, "Le Lion" 260
Eternity 319
Ethan Allen 316
Ethel M Chocolates 356
Ethel Percy Andrus Gerontology Center 91
Ethernet 109, 317, 397, 446, 573
Ethyl Corporation 323
Etling, John C. 275
ETS 506
Eu, March Fong 162
Eulexin 476
Eureka X-Ray Tube 343
Eurexpansion 228
Euro Disney 559
Euro-Bath 479
Eurocom 575
European Benefits Update 127
European Common Market 189
European Community 357, 526
European Legal Developments Bulletin 127
Europolis 243
Eurotunnel 139
Evan-Picone 539

Evans, Jim 312
Evans, John D. 235
Evans, John R. 465
Evans, Michael B. 214
Evening News Association 266
Eveready 453, 454, 534
Everest, Hiram Bond 386
Everett, Edward 296
Everett (WA) *Herald* 562
Everflex 213
Everglades National Park 396
Everingham, Lyle 339
Evinrude 419
Evinrude, Ole 419
EVOLO 316
Ewalt, Alan R. 394
Ewers, R. Darrell 571
Ewing, Matthew 386
EWU AG 469
Ex-Cell-O 518
Excedrin 154
Excel 348
Excelan 410
Exchange House 487
Exchange Oil and Gas 277
Execunet 371
Executive Airlines, Inc. 110
Executive Life Insurance Co. 252, 381
Exelderm 154, 506
EXL 7000 446
Exley, Charles E., Jr 400
Expert Library Manager 499
Explorer 262
Express (stores) 342
Express Photo 322
Expressions 479
ExpressTalk 439
Extel Corporation 329
Extended Industry Standard Architecture 192
Extendicare 311
Extra (gum) 571
Extra Ordinary Life 409
Exxon Corporation 86, 123, 175, 241, **246,** 333, 386, 457, 515
Exxon Valdez 108, 246
Eyexam 2000 539
Eynard (J) 135

F

F&G Re, Inc. 549
F&M Schaefer Brewing Corporation 500
F-4 Phantom II 369
F-14 Tomcat fighter 287
F-15 fighter 369, 478
F-16 271, 408, 478
F-18 Hornet 408
F-20 fighter 408
F-22 Advanced Tactical Fighter 345
F-23 Advanced Tactical Fighter 408
F-86 jet fighter 466
F-100 supersonic aircraft 466
F-111 fighter 271
F-117A 345
F-Series 262
F.W. Dodge Group. *See* Dodge (F.W.) Group
F/A-18 Hornet 408
F119 540
Fab 187
Fabergé 460
Fabryka Narzedzi Kuznia 496
Facts on File, Inc. 189
Fafnir Bearings 313
Fagan, John P. 569

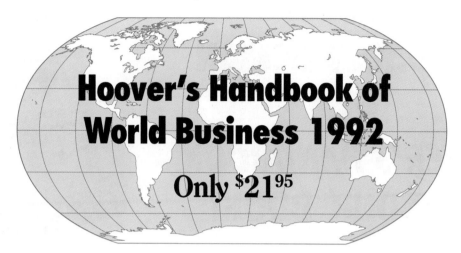

I want to order the indicated quantities of:

Books

___ *Hoover's Handbook of American Business 1992* — $24.95 plus $3.00 shipping/handling
___ *Hoover's Handbook of World Business 1992* — $21.95 plus $3.00 shipping/handling
___ *Hoover's Handbook 1991: Profiles of Over 500 Major Corporations* — $19.95 plus $3.00 shipping/handling
___ *The complete set of 3 Hoover's Handbooks* (a $66.85 value) — $49.95 plus $6.00 shipping/handling

Future Editions

Please enter my standing order for future copies of:

___ *Hoover's Handbook of American Business*
___ *Hoover's Handbook of World Business*

I understand that I am entitled to a 5% discount on all standing orders and will receive the books as soon as they are published. Bill my credit card on shipment. If I am not satisfied, I may return any book received on standing order for a full refund.

Mailing Labels

___ Names and headquarters addresses (includes US headquarters of foreign companies) of companies listed in both 1992 *Hoover's Handbooks* (800 total) — $35.00 per set plus $3.00 shipping/handling

Electronic Book

___ Sony Data Discman Electronic Book disc version of *Hoover's Handbook*— $39.95 plus $3.00 shipping/handling
___ Sony Data Discman Electronic Book Player — $499.00 plus $7.00 shipping/handling
Surface mail outside the US is $6.00 per item. Texas residents will be charged 8% sales tax.   AM92

Fold along dashed line.

☐ Send me information about future *Hoover's Handbook*s.
☐ I have the following suggestions for future editions:

_____
_____
_____

☐ I use *Hoover's Handbook*s primarily for (e.g., investing, selling) _____

Name _____ Telephone No. (___) _____
Affiliation _____ Title _____
Street Address _____
City _____ State _____ Zip _____
☐ MasterCard ☐ Visa ☐ American Express Account No. _____
Signature _____ Expiration Date _____

Visa/MC/Amex or prepaid orders only.

To order call 800-486-8666 or fax us at 512-454-9401

The Reference Press, Inc. • 6448 Hwy. 290 East, Suite E-104, Austin, Texas 78723 • 512-454-7778

I want to order the indicated quantities of:

Books

___ *Hoover's Handbook of American Business 1992* — $24.95 plus $3.00 shipping/handling
___ *Hoover's Handbook of World Business 1992* — $21.95 plus $3.00 shipping/handling
___ *Hoover's Handbook 1991: Profiles of Over 500 Major Corporations* — $19.95 plus $3.00 shipping/handling
___ *The complete set of 3 Hoover's Handbooks* (a $66.85 value) — $49.95 plus $6.00 shipping/handling

Future Editions

Please enter my standing order for future copies of:

___ *Hoover's Handbook of American Business*
___ *Hoover's Handbook of World Business*

I understand that I am entitled to a 5% discount on all standing orders and will receive the books as soon as they are published. Bill my credit card on shipment. If I am not satisfied, I may return any book received on standing order for a full refund.

Mailing Labels

___ Names and headquarters addresses (includes US headquarters of foreign companies) of companies listed in both 1992 *Hoover's Handbooks* (800 total) — $35.00 per set plus $3.00 shipping/handling

Electronic Book

___ Sony Data Discman Electronic Book disc version of *Hoover's Handbook*— $39.95 plus $3.00 shipping/handling
___ Sony Data Discman Electronic Book Player — $499.00 plus $7.00 shipping/handling
Surface mail outside the US is $6.00 per item. Texas residents will be charged 8% sales tax.   AM92

Fold along dashed line.

☐ Send me information about future *Hoover's Handbook*s.
☐ I have the following suggestions for future editions:

_____
_____
_____

☐ I use *Hoover's Handbook*s primarily for (e.g., investing, selling) _____

Name _____ Telephone No. (___) _____
Affiliation _____ Title _____
Street Address _____
City _____ State _____ Zip _____
☐ MasterCard ☐ Visa ☐ American Express Account No. _____
Signature _____ Expiration Date _____

Visa/MC/Amex or prepaid orders only.

To order call 800-486-8666 or fax us at 512-454-9401

The Reference Press, Inc. • 6448 Hwy. 290 East, Suite E-104, Austin, Texas 78723 • 512-454-7778

Please tape this edge before mailing.

BUSINESS REPLY MAIL
FIRST-CLASS MAIL   PERMIT NO. 7641   AUSTIN, TEXAS

POSTAGE WILL BE PAID BY ADDRESSEE

THE REFERENCE PRESS INC
6448 HWY 290 E STE E 104
AUSTIN TX 78723-9828

NO POSTAGE
NECESSARY
IF MAILED
IN THE
UNITED STATES

Please tape this edge before mailing.

BUSINESS REPLY MAIL
FIRST-CLASS MAIL   PERMIT NO. 7641   AUSTIN, TEXAS

POSTAGE WILL BE PAID BY ADDRESSEE

THE REFERENCE PRESS INC
6448 HWY 290 E STE E 104
AUSTIN TX 78723-9828

NO POSTAGE
NECESSARY
IF MAILED
IN THE
UNITED STATES

OFFICIAL SWEEPSTAKES ENTRY

We want your help in making *Hoover's Handbooks* better. Please answer the following questions and your name will be entered in a drawing to win the Grand Prize — a Sony Data Discman Player complete with *Hoover's Handbook* disc. All questionnaires postmarked before March 31, 1992, will be eligible. Twenty first-prize winners will receive a free copy of next year's *Hoover's Handbook of American Business.* Winners will be notified by mail.

1. Did you buy this book primarily for
   - ❏ Investment information   ❏ Selling to the companies in it   ❏ Academic use
   - ❏ General reference   ❏ Job hunting   ❏ Other _____

2. Where did you first hear about/see *Hoover's Handbook?*
   - ❏ Advertisement in _____   ❏ Book review in _____
   - ❏ Other media mention in _____   ❏ Received as gift
   - ❏ Direct mail   ❏ Library   ❏ Friend   ❏ Co-worker   ❏ Teacher
   - ❏ Book store: name _____ city _____ state _____
   - ❏ Other retail outlet: name _____ city _____ state _____
   - ❏ Other _____

3. What is your primary job description? (e.g., executive, salesperson, student, librarian, etc.)
   _____

4. Do you presently invest in   ❏ Stocks   ❏ Corporate bonds   ❏ Mutual funds
5. Do you read   ❏ Wall Street Journal   ❏ Business Week   ❏ Forbes   ❏ Fortune
   ❏ Economist   ❏ Financial Times   ❏ New York Times
   Do you watch   ❏ CNBC/FNN   ❏ CNN

Fold along dashed line.

6. Would you buy this book again?   ❏ Yes   ❏ No
   If not, why not? _____
7. What features in it did you find the most helpful? _____

What features did you find least helpful? _____

8. How could we improve the book? _____

9. What companies would you like to see added next year? _____

10. What other books would you like to see us publish? _____

11. Would you buy this book on a CD-ROM?   ❏ Yes   ❏ No

Please complete the reverse side.

The Reference Press, Inc.
6448 Hwy. 290 East, Suite E-104, Austin, Texas 78723 • 512-454-7778 • Fax 512-454-9401

OFFICIAL SWEEPSTAKES ENTRY

We want your help in making *Hoover's Handbooks* better. Please answer the following questions and your name will be entered in a drawing to win the Grand Prize — a Sony Data Discman Player complete with *Hoover's Handbook* disc. All questionnaires postmarked before March 31, 1992, will be eligible. Twenty first-prize winners will receive a free copy of next year's *Hoover's Handbook of American Business.* Winners will be notified by mail.

1. Did you buy this book primarily for
   - ❏ Investment information   ❏ Selling to the companies in it   ❏ Academic use
   - ❏ General reference   ❏ Job hunting   ❏ Other _____

2. Where did you first hear about/see *Hoover's Handbook?*
   - ❏ Advertisement in _____   ❏ Book review in _____
   - ❏ Other media mention in _____   ❏ Received as gift
   - ❏ Direct mail   ❏ Library   ❏ Friend   ❏ Co-worker   ❏ Teacher
   - ❏ Book store: name _____ city _____ state _____
   - ❏ Other retail outlet: name _____ city _____ state _____
   - ❏ Other _____

3. What is your primary job description? (e.g., executive, salesperson, student, librarian, etc.)
   _____

4. Do you presently invest in   ❏ Stocks   ❏ Corporate bonds   ❏ Mutual funds
5. Do you read   ❏ Wall Street Journal   ❏ Business Week   ❏ Forbes   ❏ Fortune
   ❏ Economist   ❏ Financial Times   ❏ New York Times
   Do you watch   ❏ CNBC/FNN   ❏ CNN

Fold along dashed line.

6. Would you buy this book again?   ❏ Yes   ❏ No
   If not, why not? _____
7. What features in it did you find the most helpful? _____

What features did you find least helpful? _____

8. How could we improve the book? _____

9. What companies would you like to see added next year? _____

10. What other books would you like to see us publish? _____

11. Would you buy this book on a CD-ROM?   ❏ Yes   ❏ No

Please complete the reverse side.

The Reference Press, Inc.
6448 Hwy. 290 East, Suite E-104, Austin, Texas 78723 • 512-454-7778 • Fax 512-454-9401

OFFICIAL SWEEPSTAKES ENTRY

Name _____ Telephone No. (_____) _____

Affiliation _____ Title _____

Street Address _____

City _____ State _____ Zip _____

Please tape this edge before mailing. Do not staple.

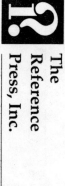

The Reference Press, Inc.

6448 Highway 290 East, Suite E-104
Austin, Texas 78723-9828

PLACE STAMP HERE
The Post Office will not deliver mail without postage.

OFFICIAL SWEEPSTAKES ENTRY

Name _____ Telephone No. (_____) _____

Affiliation _____ Title _____

Street Address _____

City _____ State _____ Zip _____

Please tape this edge before mailing. Do not staple.

The Reference Press, Inc.

6448 Highway 290 East, Suite E-104
Austin, Texas 78723-9828

PLACE STAMP HERE
The Post Office will not deliver mail without postage.